August 13-17, 2016
San Francisco, CA, USA

Association for
Computing Machinery

Advancing Computing as a Science & Profession

San Francisco, CA, USA
KDD 2016

KDD'16

Proceedings of the 22nd ACM SIGKDD International Conference on Knowledge Discovery and Data Mining

Sponsored by:

ACM SIGKDD and ACM SIGMOD

Association for
Computing Machinery

Advancing Computing as a Science & Profession

The Association for Computing Machinery
2 Penn Plaza, Suite 701
New York, New York 10121-0701

ISBN: 978-1-4503-4232-2 (Digital)

ISBN: 978-1-4503-4623-8 (Print)

Additional copies may be ordered prepaid from:

ACM Order Department
PO Box 30777
New York, NY 10087-0777, USA

Phone: 1-800-342-6626 (USA and Canada)
+1-212-626-0500 (Global)
Fax: +1-212-944-1318
E-mail: acmhelp@acm.org
Hours of Operation: 8:30 am – 4:30 pm ET

Printed in the USA

KDD 2016 Chairs' Welcome Message

It is our great pleasure to welcome you to the 2016 ACM Conference on Knowledge Discovery and Data Mining – KDD'16. We hope that the content and the professional network at KDD'16 will help you succeed professionally by enabling you to: identify technology trends early; make new/creative contributions; increase your productivity by using newer/better tools, processes or ways of organizing teams; identify new job opportunities; and hire new team members.

We are living in an exciting time for our profession. On the one hand, we are witnessing the *industrialization of data science*, and the emergence of the *industrial assembly line* processes characterized by the division of labor, integrated processes/pipelines of work, standards, automation, and repeatability. Data science practitioners are organizing themselves in more sophisticated ways, embedding themselves in larger teams in many industry verticals, improving their productivity substantially, and achieving a much larger scale of social impact. On the other hand we are also witnessing astonishing progress from research in algorithms and systems — for example the field of deep neural networks has revolutionized speech recognition, NLP, computer vision, image recognition, etc. By facilitating interaction between practitioners at large companies & startups on the one hand, and the algorithm development researchers including leading academics on the other, KDD'16 fosters technological and entrepreneurial innovation in the area of data science.

This year's conference continues its tradition of being the premier forum for presentation of results in the field of data mining, both in the form of cutting edge research, and in the form of insights from the development and deployment of real world applications. Further, the conference continues with its tradition of a strong tutorial and workshop program on leading edge issues of data mining. The mission of this conference has broadened in recent years even as we placed a significant amount of focus on both the research and applied aspects of data mining. As an example of this broadened focus, this year we have introduced a strong hands-on tutorial program during the conference in which participants will learn how to use practical tools for data mining. KDD'16 also gives researchers and practitioners a unique opportunity to form professional networks, and to share their perspectives with others interested in the various aspects of data mining. For example, we have introduced office hours for budding entrepreneurs from our community to meet leading Venture Capitalists investing in this area. We hope that KDD 2016 conference will serve as a meeting ground for researchers, practitioners, funding agencies, and investors to help create new algorithms and commercial products.

The call for papers attracted a significant number of submissions from countries all over the world. In particular, the research track attracted 784 submissions and the applied data science track attracted 331 submissions. Papers were accepted either as full papers or as posters. The overall acceptance rate either as full papers or posters was less than 20%. For full papers in the research track, the acceptance rate was lower than 10%. This is consistent with the fact that the KDD Conference is a premier conference in data mining and the acceptance rates historically tend to be low. It is noteworthy that the applied data science track received a larger number of submissions compared to previous years. We view this as an encouraging sign that research in data mining is increasingly becoming relevant to industrial applications. All papers were reviewed by at least three program committee members and then discussed by the PC members in a discussion moderated by a meta-reviewer. Borderline papers were thoroughly reviewed by the program chairs before final decisions were made.

In addition, KDD'16 continues to have a strong tutorial and workshop program, as is its tradition since its inception. The program committee reviewed and accepted the following:

Venue or Track	*Reviewed*	*Accepted*	*Acceptance Rate*
Research Track Papers	784	70+72	8.9%+9.2%
Applied Data Science Track Papers	331	40+26	12%+7.9%
Workshops	47	17	36.2%
Tutorials	37	11	29.7%
Applied Data Science Talks	Invited	12	Invited
Hands-on Tutorials	Invited	8	Invited
Regular Keynotes	Invited	4	Invited
Turing Award Winner Talk	Special	1	Special

In the table above the research track papers and applied data science track papers are broken up into the full presentations and poster presentations. We have four excellent keynote presentations from Jennifer Chayes, Joe Hellerstein, Greg Papadopoulous, and Nando de Freitas. In addition, we are honored to have a Turing Award winner, Whitfield Diffie, as one of the keynote speakers. We also encourage attendees to attend the keynote and invited talk presentations.

Putting together *KDD'16* was a team effort. We first thank the authors for providing the content of the program. We are grateful to the program committee and the senior program committee, who worked very hard in reviewing papers and providing feedback for authors. Finally, we thank the numerous sponsors and ACM SIGKDD for their support in hosting the conference.

We hope that you will find this program interesting and thought-provoking and that the conference will provide you with a valuable opportunity to share ideas with other researchers and practitioners from institutions around the world.

Charu Aggarwal
Alex Smola
KDD'16 Research Track Chairs

Rajeev Rastogi
Dou Shen
KDD'16 Applied Data Science Track Chairs

Balaji Krishnapuram
Mohak Shah
KDD'16 General Chairs

Table of Contents

Applied Data Science Track Invited Talks

Applied Data Science Track Posters

Research Track Oral Papers

Research Track Posters

Tutorials

KDD 2016 Conference Organization

General Chairs:	Balaji Krishnapuram *(IBM)* Mohak Shah *(Bosch)*
Research Track Program Chairs:	Alex Smola *(Amazon)* Charu Aggarwal *(IBM)*
Applied Data Science Track Program Chairs:	Dou Shen *(Baidu)* Rajeev Rastogi *(Amazon)*
Associate General Chair	Shipeng Yu (LinkedIn)
Workshop Chairs:	Quoc Le *(Google)* Zhi-Hua Zhou *(Nanjing University)*
Tutorial Chairs:	Hanghang Tong *(Arizona State University)* S V N Vishwanathan *(UCSC)*
KDD Cup Chairs:	Markus Weimer *(Microsoft)* Shou-De Lin *(National Taiwan University)* Vijay Narayanan *(Microsoft)*
Panel Chair:	Andrei Broder *(Google)*
Applied Data Science Invited Talks Chairs:	Evangelos Simoudis *(Synapse Partners)* Usama Fayyad *(Barclays Bank and Oasis500)* Rajesh Parekh *(Facebook)*
Poster Chair:	Jiliang Tang *(Yahoo Labs)*
Best Paper Chairs:	Jiliang Tang *(Yahoo Labs)*
Doctoral Dissertation Award Chair:	Haixun Wang *(Facebook)*
Innovation and Service Award Chair:	Jian Pei *(Simon Fraser University)*
Test-of-Time Award Chair:	Wei Wang *(UCLA)*
Local Arrangements Chairs:	Joaquin Quiñonero Candela *(Facebook)* Olivier Chapelle *(Google)*
Student Travel Award Chairs:	Jure Leskovec *(Stanford University)* Leman Akoglu *(Stony Brook University)*
Media and Publicity Chairs:	Ankur Teredesai *(University of Washington)* Gabor Melli *(Opengov)*
Proceedings Chairs:	Rómer Rosales *(LinkedIn)* Stefanie Jegelka *(MIT)*

Social Networking Chairs: Faisal Farooq *(IBM)*
Ron Bekkerman *(University of Haifa)*

Sponsorship Chair: Claudia Perlich *(Dstillery)*
Yu Zheng *(Microsoft Research)*

Treasurer: Ying Li *(EV Analysis)*

Video and Streaming Chairs: Jie Tang *(Tsinghua University)*
Marko Grobelnik *(Jozef Stefan Institute)*

Web Chairs: David Hazel *(University of Washington)*
Derek Young *(Seasonal View)*

Job Match Chair: Unmesh Kurup *(Bosch)*

Social Impact Chair: Rayid Ghani *(University of Chicago)*

Research Track Senior Program Committee:
Alice Oh *(KAIST)*
Ambuj Singh *(UCSB)*
Amr Ahmed *(Google)*
Andrew Tomkins *(Google Research)*
Anil Vullikanti *(Virginia Tech)*
Aristides Gionis *(Aalto University)*
Arno Siebes
Bart Goethals *(University of Antwerp)*
Chih-Jen Lin *(National Taiwan University)*
Christos Faloutsos *(Carnegie Mellon University)*
Corinna Cortes *(Google)*
Dacheng Tao *(The University of Technology, Sydney)*
Deepak Agarwal *(LinkedIn)*
Diane Cook *(Washington State University)*
Dimitrios Gunopulos
Eamonn Keogh *(UC Riverside)*
Edo Liberty *(Yahoo Labs)*
Evgeniy Gabrilovich *(Google)*
Evimaria Terzi *(Boston University)*
Fei Wang *(University of Connecticut)*
Francesco Bonchi *(Yahoo Barcelona)*
George Karypis
Graham Cormode *(Warwick)*
Guojun Qi *(University of Central Florida)*
Hong Cheng *(Chinese University of Hong Kong)*
Huan Liu *(ASU)*
Hui Xiong *(Rutgers)*
Ian Davidson *(University of California-Davis)*
James Bailey

Research Track Senior Program Committee (continued):

Jeffrey Yu *(Chinese University of Hong Kong)*
Jennifer Neville *(Purdue)*
Jennifer Dy *(Northeastern University)*
Jian Pei *(Simon Fraser University)*
Jiawei Han *(University of Illinois at Urbana-Champaign)*
Jie Tang *(Tsinghua University)*
Jieping Ye *(University of Michigan at Ann Arbor)*
Jimeng Sun *(Georgia Tech)*
Jing Gao
Johannes Fuernkranz *(TU Darmstadt)*
Johannes Gehrke *(Microsoft Research)*
Jure Leskovec *(Stanford University)*
Karsten Borgwardt *(ETH Zurich)*
Katharina Morik *(TU Dortmund)*
Kristian Kersting *(TU Dortmund)*
Martin Ester *(Simon Fraser University)*
Mohammed Zaki *(RPI)*
Naoki Abe *(IBM T J Watson Research Center)*
Osmar Zaiane *(University of Alberta)*
Paul Bradley *(MethodCare)*
Paul Bennett *(Microsoft Research)*
Peter Flach *(University of Bristol)*
Philip S. Yu *(UI Chicago)*
Qiang Yang *(HKUST)*
Ravi Kumar *(Google)*
Saharon Rosset *(Tel Aviv University)*
Sanjay Chawla
Siegfried Nijssen *(Universiteit Leiden)*
Stefan Wrobel *(Universitaet Bonn)*
Suchi Saria *(Johns Hopkins University)*
Tanya Berger-Wolf *(University of Illinois)*
Thomas Seidl *(LMU Munich)*
Thomas Gaertner *(University of Nottingham)*
Thorsten Joachims *(Cornell University)*
Tie-Yan Liu *(Microsoft Research)*
Tijl De Bie *(Ghen University)*
Vanja Josifovski *(Pinterest)*
Wei Wang *(UC Los Angeles)*
Wray Buntine *(Monash University)*
Xavier Amatriain *(Quora)*
Yan Liu
Yehuda Koren *(Google)*
Yisong Yue *(Caltech)*
Yizhou Sun *(Northeastern University)*
Zhi-Hua Zhou

Applied Data Science Track Senior Program Committee:

Anitha Kannan *(Facebook)*
Balaraman Ravindran *(Indian Institute of Technology Madras)*
Brian D'Alessandro *(Facebook)*
Chao Liu *(Jindi Data Technology Ltd Co.)*
Chiranjib Bhattacharya *(Indian Institute of Science Bangalore)*
Divesh Srivastava *(AT&T Research)*
Gautam Das *(University of Texas Arlington)*
Gautam Shroff *(Tata Consultancy Services Research)*
Graham Williams *(Australian Taxation Office)*
Haixun Wang *(Google)*
Hang Li *(Huawei Technologies)*
Hema Raghavan *(LinkedIn)*
Hui Xiong *(Rutgers University)*
Jan Pedersen *(Microsoft)*
Jeffrey Pan *(Facebook)*
Jun Yan *(Microsoft Research Asia)*
Minos Garofalakis *(University of Chania)*
Ping Luo *(Chinese Academy of Sciences)*
Ralf Herbrich *(Amazon)*
Rayid Ghani *(University of Chicago)*
Roberto Bayardo *(Google)*
S. Muthukrishnan *(Rutgers Univ)*
Sinno Pan *(Nanyang Technological University)*
Tina Eliassi-Rad *(Rutgers Univ)*
Vincent Tseng *(National Chiao Tung University)*
Vipin Kumar *(University of Minnesota)*
Wayne Thompson *(SAS)*
Wei Fan *(Baidu)*
Xiaoming Jin *(Tsinghua University)*
Ying Li *(EV Analysis Corp)*
Yoelle Maarek *(Yahoo! Labs)*
Yu Zheng *(Microsoft Research)*

KDD 2016 Sponsors & Supporters

Sponsor: ACM SIGKDD

Supporters: Diamond

Supporters: Platinum

Supporters: Gold

\Orchestrating a brighter world

NEC

Supporters: Silver

ebay

Tencent 腾讯

SIEMENS

Ingenuity for life

UBER

sas

Supporters: Bronze

Supporters: Lanyard Sponsor

Supporters: KDD CUP Sponsor

Supporters: Student Travel Awards

Supporters: Program Ad Sponsor

Supporters: Media Sponsor

BIG DATA

Mary Ann Liebert, Inc. publishers

Exhibitors:

INDIANA UNIVERSITY
DATA SCIENCE PROGRAM

MORGAN & CLAYPOOL PUBLISHERS

NON SOLUS

ELSEVIER

Springer

MathWorks®

FRONTLINE
solvers
Solver.com • XLMiner.com

spare 5

SALFORD
SYSTEMS

Georgia Institute of Technology

TELLIGENT
DATA

Compact and Scalable Graph Neighborhood Sketching

Takuya Akiba
National Institute of Informatics
JST PRESTO & CIT STAIR Lab
takiba@nii.ac.jp

Yosuke Yano*
National Institute of Informatics
JST PRESTO
yyano@nii.ac.jp

ABSTRACT

The *all-distances sketch (ADS)* has recently emerged as a promising paradigm of graph neighborhood sketching. An ADS is a probabilistic data structure that is defined for each vertex of a graph. ADSs facilitate accurate estimation of many useful indicators for network analysis with the guarantee of accuracy, and the ADSs for all the vertices in a graph can be computed in near-linear time. Because of these useful properties, ADS has attracted considerable attention. However, a critical drawback of ADS is its space requirement, which tends to be much larger than that of the graph itself. In the present study, we address this issue by designing a new graph sketching scheme, namely, *sketch retrieval shortcuts (SRS)*. Although SRSs are more space-efficient than ADSs by an order of magnitude, an ADS of any vertex can be quickly retrieved from the SRSs. The retrieved ADSs can be used to estimate the aforementioned indicators in exactly the same manner as with plain ADSs, inheriting the same accuracy guarantee. Our experiments on real-world networks demonstrate the usefulness of SRSs as a practical back-end of large-scale graph data mining.

Keywords

Graphs; Min-hash sketches; All-distances sketches

1. INTRODUCTION

Many types of indicators and measures play key roles as building blocks for graph analysis and mining. *Vertex centralities* constitute one of the the most fundamental classes of indicators. They are defined for a vertex to measure the relative importance of every other vertex [9, 8, 12]. Other common classes include *vertex similarities*, which are defined for a pair of vertices to estimate their similarity or strength of relevance [23, 13]. Graph properties, which are defined for a whole graph, have also attracted considerable attention for understanding the underlying mechanisms and developing realistic models [21, 4, 6].

Computing these measures in an ad-hoc manner is almost always unrealistic for large-scale graphs. Let us take vertex centralities as an example. Most types of centralities require time at least proportional to the graph size. Moreover, centralities are usually employed to compare vertices in a graph; thus, centrality values are necessary for a subset of vertices, or sometimes, even for all vertices.

Therefore, algorithmic frameworks called *sketching* or *indexing* are employed to compute these indicators and properties [2, 28, 6, 25, 12, 19, 11, 1, 3]. In such frameworks, we first compute a data structure called a *sketch* or an *index* from a graph, which can substantially accelerate the computation of these useful indicators. This not only results in better scalability of graph analysis but also makes it possible to use such indicators in applications that require quick interactive response, such as drill-down analytics and network-aware search systems [27, 24].

The *all-distances sketch (ADS)* [11, 12] has recently emerged as a paradigm of graph neighborhood sampling. An ADS is defined for a vertex, and is an extension of the min-hash sketch [18, 11] (see Section 3.1 for the definition). The ADSs for all the vertices in a graph can be computed efficiently, and once they are obtained, the values of the many useful indicators can be efficiently and accurately estimated. To the best of our knowledge, ADS is the only sketching paradigm that combines the following three properties.

- **Multi-Functionality**: Using ADSs, we can estimate many types of useful indicators such as shortest-path distance, closeness centrality, closeness similarity, and reverse ranking (see Section 3.2).
- **Guaranteed Accuracy**: Estimation using ADSs is quite accurate and has tight theoretical error bounds.
- **Scalability** (in theory): The ADSs for all the vertices in a graph can be computed in near-linear time, and their total size is also near-linear to the number of vertices.

Because of these useful properties, ADS has attracted considerable attraction. However, in practice, ADS has turned out to be not as scalable as expected theoretically. The main drawback is its space requirement. An ADS is an array of length approximately $k \ln n$, where n is the number of vertices and k is an accuracy-space trade-off parameter. In order to achieve accurate estimation, k is set to a value of the order of tens or hundreds. Thus, the length of an ADS is of the order of hundreds or thousands. Therefore,

*Y. Yano's current affiliation: Recruit Holdings Co., Ltd.

KDD '16, August 13 - 17, 2016, San Francisco, CA, USA

ISBN 978-1-4503-4232-2/16/08...$15.00
DOI: http://dx.doi.org/10.1145/2939672.2939762

ADSs require more space than the graph itself, which is unreasonable for large graphs. Moreover, because there are few repetitions in an ADS, standard compression methods, such as the LZ family, do not work well, as discussed in Section 8.2. Thus, substantial space reduction techniques are required to make ADS practical.

1.1 Contributions

To address the above-mentioned issue, we propose a new graph sketching data structure, namely, *sketch retrieval shortcuts (SRS)*. Instead of ADSs, we propose that SRSs be computed for the all vertices in a graph. Then, using the SRSs, an ADS of a vertex can be quickly retrieved. SRSs can be computed with acceptable additional computation cost in comparison to ADSs. Although SRSs are an order of magnitude smaller than ADSs, once we obtain them, an ADS of a vertex can be quickly retrieved from the SRSs; thus, the various aforementioned measures and indicators can be estimated in exactly the same manner as with ADSs, inheriting the same accuracy guarantee.

The idea underlying the definition of SRSs is to consider the ADSs of a graph as another weighted graph, and sparsify it such that an ADS of a vertex can still be quickly retrieved by a *restricted* search on it. The retrieval algorithm is designed such that it visits only vertices in an ADS; thus, an ADS is efficiently retrieved in time that is almost linear to the ADS size. SRSs are carefully defined to ensure that an ADS of any vertex can be correctly retrieved using this procedure.

We propose two types of construction algorithms: the first constructs SRSs from ADSs, whereas the second constructs SRSs directly from graphs. The former is faster, whereas the latter requires less working memory and provides a flexible trade-off between time and space consumption.

Our experiments on real-world networks demonstrate the usefulness of SRSs as a practical back-end of large-scale graph data mining. Specifically, we can confirm that *(1)* SRSs can be constructed for very large graphs with millions of vertices and hundreds of millions of edges, *(2)* SRSs are an order of magnitude smaller than ADSs, and *(3)* ADS retrieval is sufficiently quick, i.e., the retrieval time is of the order of milliseconds.

Organization. The remainder of this paper is organized as follows. Section 2 provides the relevant definitions and notations. Section 3 reviews the definition and usage of ADSs. Section 4 presents the definition and crucial properties of our SRSs. Sections 5 and 6 propose efficient SRS construction algorithms with different performance characteristics. Section 7 proposes techniques to further improve the practicality of SRSs. Section 8 presents our experimental results. Section 9 concludes the paper.

2. PRELIMINARIES

2.1 Notations

Table 1 lists the frequently used notations in the paper. Let $G = (V, E)$ be a graph where V and E are a vertex set and an edge set, respectively. We denote $|V|$ and $|E|$ by n and m, respectively. For generality, we assume that G is a weighted and directed graph. We denote the length of an edge e by $\ell(e)$. Further, we assume that $\ell(e) > 0$ for any $e \in E$. Our discussions can be applied to unweighted graphs by introducing a constant length function, e.g., $\ell(e) = 1$ for any $e \in E$. Let $d(u, v)$ denote the distance from u to v. Let $P(u, v)$ denote the vertices on the shortest paths from u to v, i.e., $P(u, v) = \{w \in V \mid d(u, w) + d(w, v) = d(u, v)\}$.

Table 1: Frequently used notations.

Notation	Description
$G = (V, E)$	A graph.
n, m	Numbers of vertices and edges in G.
$\ell(u, v)$	Length of an edge $(u, v) \in E$.
$d(u, v)$	Distance from u to v.
$P(u, v)$	Vertices on the shortest paths from u to v.
k	Accuracy-space trade-off parameter.
$r(u)$	Rank of vertex u.
$k_r^{\text{th}}(S)$	k-th smallest rank in vertex set S.
$\pi(u, v)$	Threshold rank of vertex v against vertex u.
$\mathcal{A}(u)$	All-distances sketch (ADS) of vertex u.
$\mathcal{B}(u)$	Sketch retrieval shortcuts (SRS) of vertex u.

We always compare tuples by lexicographic order. For example, $(a, b) < (c, d)$ if and only if *(1)* $a < c$ or *(2)* $a = c$ and $b < d$. We also use this lexicographic comparison in sorting and priority queues, unless otherwise stated.

2.2 Distance Tie-Breaking

The strict definition of ADSs assumes that distances are unique [12]. In theory, an arbitrary tie-breaking rule can be employed. However, when closely looking at algorithms and implementation, the selection of the tie-breaking rule is highly important for simplicity and performance.

In this paper, we propose that the following tie-breaking rule be used. We conduct lexicographic comparison using the pair of *(1)* the original distance and *(2)* the destination vertex ID. In other words, v is *closer* to u than w if and only if $(d(u, v), v) < (d(u, w), w)$. For the definition of ADSs, we do not need to break all the ties among any pairs of vertices; instead, we just need to break the ties among the distances from a single vertex to other vertices. Therefore, this simple tie-breaking rule works, and we find that this rule can be effectively accommodated in our algorithms.

In this paper, this tie-breaking rule is explicit: the definition of "distance" $d(u, v)$ remains unchanged, and we explicitly conduct this tie-breaking as part of our algorithm. On the other hand, our algorithms and data structures are essentially compatible with any other tie-breaking rule.

3. ALL-DISTANCES SKETCHES

In this section, we review the all-distances sketch (ADS). We first explain the definition and basic properties, and then introduce the examples of the useful indicators that can be accurately estimated by ADSs.

3.1 Definition and Construction

All-distances sketches (ADSs) are defined with respect to an integer parameter k and a random rank assignment to vertices. The parameter k gives the trade-off between sketch size and estimation precision. Throughout this paper, we use a random function $r : V \to [0, 1]$ as the rank function, where $r(v) \sim U[0, 1]$ for any vertex v. In other words, $r(v)$ is independently drawn from the uniform distribution on $[0, 1]$.

For $u, v \in V$, we define $N(u, v)$ as the set of vertices that are closer to u than v, i.e., $N(u, v) = \{w \in V \mid (d(u, w), w) < (d(u, v), v)\}$. For a vertex subset $X \subseteq V$, we define the function $k_r^{\text{th}}(X)$ as the k-th smallest value of ranks for vertices in X. If $|X| < k$, we define $k_r^{\text{th}}(X) = 1$. For vertices u and v, we define *threshold rank* $\pi(u, v)$ as $\pi(u, v) = k_r^{\text{th}}(N(u, v))$, which denotes the k-th smallest value of ranks for vertices that are closer to u than v. Using $\pi(u, v)$, ADSs are defined as follows[1].

Definition 3.1 (ADS [12]): *The* all-distances sketch (ADS) *of a vertex u is defined as* $\mathcal{A}(u) = \{(v, \delta_{uv}) \mid v \in V, r(v) < \pi(u, v)\}$, *where* $\delta_{uv} = d(u, v)$.

In this paper, we use the singular form, i.e., "an ADS," to indicate the sketch of a single vertex (i.e., $\mathcal{A}(v)$ for a vertex v), and the plural form, i.e., "ADSs," sometimes indicates the whole set of sketches for all the vertices in a graph (i.e., $\{\mathcal{A}(v)\}_{v \in V}$). For directed graphs, we distinguish between the *forward ADS* $\overrightarrow{\mathcal{A}}(u)$ and the *backward ADS* $\overleftarrow{\mathcal{A}}(u)$. For the forward ADS $\overrightarrow{\mathcal{A}}(u)$, we use the distances *from* u (as in the above definition), and, for the backward ADS $\overleftarrow{\mathcal{A}}(u)$, we use the distances *to* u. Note that, on an undirected graph, the forward and backward ADSs are exactly the same.

3.1.1 *Size*

The size of an ADS can be calculated as follows.

Lemma 3.2 (ADS Size [12]): *For a vertex u, let n_u be the number of reachable vertices from u, and $H(i)$ be the i-th harmonic number. The expected size of $\mathcal{A}(u)$ is $k(1 + H(n_u) - H(k))$.*

As $n_u \le n$ and $H(n) = O(\log n)$, the expected size of $\mathcal{A}(u)$ is $O(k \log n)$. Therefore, the expected total storage usage of the ADSs for all vertices is $O(nk \log n)$.

3.1.2 *Construction*

There are two efficient approaches for computing ADSs from a graph. The first is the *pruned-search approach* [11], which conducts a pruned version of shortest-path searches from all vertices in ascending order of their ranks. The other approach is the *scan-and-merge approach* [25, 6], which repeats iterations until convergence. In each iteration, the ADS of each vertex is grown by scanning all outgoing edges and merging the ADSs of the neighbors into it.

3.2 Estimation Using ADSs

Once we obtain ADSs, many types of graph properties and features can be efficiently estimated with the guarantee of accuracy, as follows.

Neighborhood Function [11, 16, 12]. The neighborhood function $n_\delta(v)$ is the number of vertices that can be reached from v within distance δ. The value of $n_\delta(v)$ can be estimated from ADS $\mathcal{A}(v)$, and its coefficient of variation is bounded by $1/\sqrt{2(k-1)}$.

Shortest-Path Distance [13, 26]. For $u, v \in V$, distance $d(u, v)$ can be estimated by ADSs $\mathcal{A}(u)$ and $\mathcal{A}(v)$. It is $O(\log n)$-approximation for constant k, and $(2a-1)$-approximation when $k = n^{1/a}$ (for some $a \ge 1$).

Closeness Centrality [12]. Closeness centrality is one of the most fundamental measures of vertex importance. it is defined for a vertex u, *distance decay function* α, and vertex weight function β, as $C_{\alpha,\beta}(u) = \frac{1}{n} \sum_{v \in V} \alpha(d(u, v))\beta(v)$. Using ADS $\mathcal{A}(u)$, the estimation of $C_{\alpha,\beta}(u)$ can be obtained with coefficient of variation bounded by $1/\sqrt{2(k-1)}$.

Closeness Similarity [13]. Closeness similarity is a proximity measure that is used to estimate the strength of relevance of a pair of vertices. It is based on the similarity of their distances to all other nodes. For two vertices $u, v \in V$, the closeness similarity between u and v can be estimated using ADSs $\mathcal{A}(u)$ and $\mathcal{A}(v)$, and the root of its expected square error is guaranteed as $O(1/\sqrt{k})$.

Average Distance and Effective Diameter [6]. Average distance and effective diameter are fundamental properties of a graph, and of considerable interest because of their relation to so-called *small world phenomenon.* They can be accurately estimated with confidence intervals.

Reverse Raking and Nearest Neighbors [10]. Reverse ranking measures the relevance of vertex u to vertex v by the number of vertices that are closer to v than u. Based on the neighborhood function estimation, approximated reverse nearest neighbors (rNNs) of arbitrary size can be efficiently obtained.

Continuous-Time Influence [17, 15, 14]. The continuous-time influence model is an influence propagation model with the time decay property. The expected influence of vertex set S can be estimated using a *combined ADS* $\mathcal{A}(S)$, which can be computed from ADSs $\mathcal{A}(v)$ for all $v \in S$. Its coefficient of variation is bounded by $1/\sqrt{2(k-1)}$. ADSs can also facilitate efficient influence maximization for such a model.

4. SKETCH RETRIEVAL SHORTCUTS

In this section, we present our new graph sketching scheme, namely, *sketch retrieval shortcuts (SRS).* First, we explain the underlying idea. Then, we mathematically define SRSs. Finally, we present the retrieval algorithm that quickly instantiates an ADS from SRSs.

4.1 Underlying Idea

Before explaining the idea underlying SRSs, we discuss the difficulty in ad-hoc ADS retrieval, i.e., we cannot obtain an ADS quickly from a graph without any preprocessing. Figure 1a shows a graph. Each vertex is drawn as a box, where its ID and rank are denoted in the upper and lower parts, respectively. In, Figure 1b the vertices in the ADS $\mathcal{A}(1)$ are highlighted ($k = 2$). We observe that in this example, vertex 6 is *isolated* from the other vertices in $\mathcal{A}(1)$, in the sense that we cannot reach vertex 6 from vertex 1 without passing vertices that are not in the ADS. This suggests that without any preprocessing, we cannot avoid a full search on the graph to collect all the vertices that are contained in an ADS. A full search requires time at least linear to the graph size, and is thus too time-consuming for large-scale network analysis. On the other hand, full precomputation of ADSs for all vertices requires too much storage. Therefore, we aim to achieve a good trade-off such that an ADS can be quickly retrieved with less precomputed data.

The general idea underlying SRSs is to overcome the need for a full search on a graph and realize the retrieval of an ADS by a smaller search on another graph. Toward this end, we consider a search that starts from a specified vertex u and is allowed to visit only vertices in the ADS $\mathcal{A}(u)$. As

[1] The definition of an ADS has some variations, though, in this paper, we focus on the *bottom-k ADS* [12]. Cohen proved that they have similar estimation ability, but, among them, the bottom-k ADSs are slightly better [12].

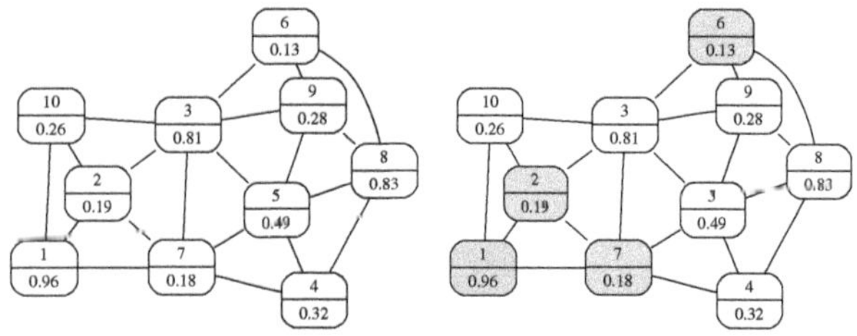

(a) A graph. (b) The vertices in $\mathcal{A}(1)$.

Figure 1: Examples of a graph and an ADS ($k = 2$).

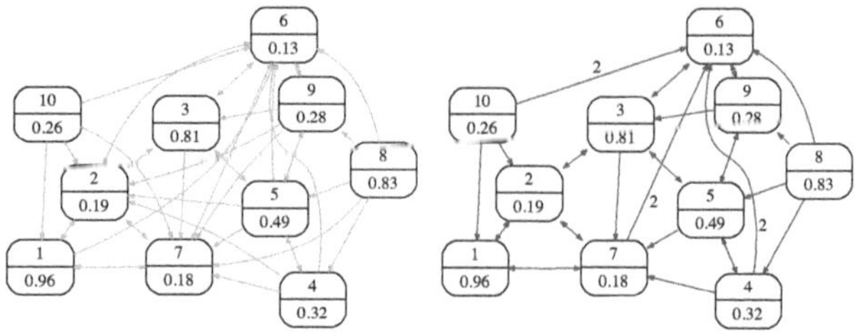

(a) ADSs as a graph. (b) SRSs as a graph.

Figure 2: ADSs and SRSs as graphs.

the number of vertices in an ADS is $O(k \log n)$ and usually $k \log n$ is much smaller than n, we expect that this search is much more efficient than a full search.

To realize such searches for ADS retrieval, we first take a different view of ADSs. We consider the ADSs of the graph as another weighted graph, where each entry $(v, \delta_{uv}) \in \mathcal{A}(u)$ corresponds to an edge from u to v with weight δ_{uv} (Figure 2a). In this "graph", obviously, the vertices in an ADS $\mathcal{A}(u)$ are directly connected from vertex u; thus, the above-mentioned search from u can successfully visit all these vertices (with only 1 hop).

Intuitively, for this purpose, this ADS graph has a considerable number of redundant edges, and herein lies the concept of our SRSs. In general, SRSs are yet another weighted graph whose edges are selected from the ADS graph such that the above-mentioned search can always succeed from any vertex (Figure 2b). In other words, SRSs are defined such that, when considering a subgraph induced by the vertex set of $\mathcal{A}(u)$, the subgraph is connected, and the distances from u to all these vertices remain unchanged (Figure 3). We call this the *reachability property*.

This might seem like an intuitive and simple idea. However, to guarantee the above property, the definitions and algorithms need to be designed carefully. Indeed, there is a common misunderstanding about the definition of SRSs, which is explained with a counterexample in Appendix A.

4.2 Definition and Properties

4.2.1 Definition

Now, we mathematically define SRSs. As with ADSs, SRSs are defined for a graph $G = (V, E)$, a trade-off parameter k, and a random rank function $r : V \to [0, 1]$.

Let Δ be the set of distances between any pair of vertices, i.e. $\Delta = \{d(u, v) \mid u, v \in V\}$. We assume that $\Delta = \{d_0, d_1, \ldots, d_h\}$, where $d_0 < d_1 < \cdots < d_h$. Note that $d_0 = 0$ and d_h corresponds to the diameter of the graph. We define $\mathcal{B}_i$ ($i = 0, 1, \ldots, h$) and $\mathcal{C}_i, \mathcal{D}_i$ ($i = 1, 2, \ldots, h$) recursively as follows.

- $\mathcal{B}_0(u) = \emptyset$ and $\mathcal{B}_i(u) = \mathcal{B}_{i-1}(u) \cup \mathcal{D}_i(u)$ for $i > 0$.
- $\mathcal{C}_i(u, v) = \{w \in P(u, v) \mid w \in \mathcal{A}(u), v \in \mathcal{B}_{i-1}(w)\}$.
- $\mathcal{D}_i(u) = \{(v, \delta_{uv}) \in \mathcal{A}(u) \mid \delta_{uv} = d_i, \mathcal{C}_i(u, v) = \emptyset\}$.

Intuitively, $\mathcal{C}_i(u, v)$ corresponds to possible transit vertices from u to v for the reachability property, and $\mathcal{B}_i(u)$ contains ADS entries with distance at most d_i that have no such transit vertices. The SRSs are defined as follows.

Definition 4.1 (SRS)**:** *The* sketch retrieval shortcuts (SRS) *of vertex u is $\mathcal{B}_h(u)$.*

Hereafter, for simplicity, we simply denote $\mathcal{B}_h(u)$ by $\mathcal{B}(u)$. Similarly to ADSs, we use the singular form to indicate the sketch of a single vertex, and the plural form to indicate the whole set of sketches for all vertices in a graph. For directed graphs, as with ADSs, we distinguish between the *forward SRS* $\overrightarrow{\mathcal{B}}(v)$ and the *backward SRS* $\overleftarrow{\mathcal{B}}(v)$. For the forward SRS, we use the forward ADS $\overrightarrow{\mathcal{A}}(u)$ for defining $\mathcal{C}_i$. The backward SRS is similarly defined on backward ADSs.

4.2.2 Reachability Property

The following lemma mathematically states the property discussed in Section 4.1.

Lemma 4.2: *If $v \in \mathcal{A}(u)$, there exists a sequence of vertices $\mathcal{W}(u, v) = (w_1, w_2, \ldots, w_p)$ such that, (1) $w_1 = u$, $w_p = v$, (2) $w_i \in \mathcal{A}(u)$ for all $1 \le i \le p$, (3) $w_{i+1} \in \mathcal{B}(w_i)$ for all $1 \le i \le p - 1$, and (4) $\sum_{i=1}^{p-1} d(w_i, w_{i+1}) = d(u, v)$.*

Proof. We prove the lemma by mathematical induction on the distance $d(u, v)$. Since $\mathcal{W}(u, u) = (u)$ satisfies the above conditions, it is true for distance zero. Now, we assume that it holds for pairs within distance d_{i-1} and prove it also holds for pairs with distance d_i. Let u, v be a pair of vertices such that $v \in \mathcal{A}(u)$ and $d(u, v) = d_i$. If $v \in \mathcal{B}(u)$, then $\mathcal{W}(u, v) = (u, v)$ satisfies the conditions. Otherwise, $v \notin \mathcal{D}_i(u)$, and thus, $\mathcal{C}_i(u, v) \neq \emptyset$. Let $w \in \mathcal{C}_i(u, v)$. Then, $\mathcal{W}(u, v)$ can be obtained by appending v to $\mathcal{W}(u, w)$. □

4.2.3 Theoretical Size Upper Bound

By definition, $\mathcal{B}(u)$ is a subset of $\mathcal{A}(u)$ for any vertex u. Therefore, the upper bound of the expected size is as below.

Lemma 4.3: *The expected size of $\mathcal{B}(u)$ is $O(k \log n)$.*

In total, the theoretical upper bound of the expected space usage of the all SRSs is $O(nk \log n)$. This bound is tight, as it is $\Theta(k \log n)$ on some pathological cases such as a clique. In practice, SRSs are much smaller than ADSs, as seen in our experiments.

4.3 Retrieving an ADS from SRSs

The main feature of SRSs is to enable quick retrieval of an ADS of any vertex. By obtaining an ADS, the various graph properties can be estimated in exactly the same manner as with a plain ADS as mentioned in Section 3.2. The retrieval algorithm Retrieve-ADS is explained as Algorithm 1. Note that, unless otherwise stated, sorting and priority queues on tuples use the ascending order in lexicographic comparison.

To retrieve the ADS of vertex u, in general, the retrieval algorithm conducts a pruned version of Dijkstra's algorithm

Algorithm 1: Retrieving the ADS of vertex u

```
  Procedure Retrieve-ADS(B, u, k)
1   A ← an empty all-distances sketch;
2   Q ← a priority queue with only one element (0, u);
3   while Q is not empty do
4     (δ_uv, v) ← Q.Pop;
5     if v ∉ A and r(v) < π(u, v) then
6       Add (v, δ_uv) to A;
7       for all (δ_vw, w) ∈ B(v) do
8         Q.Push(δ_uv + δ_vw, w);
9   return A;
```

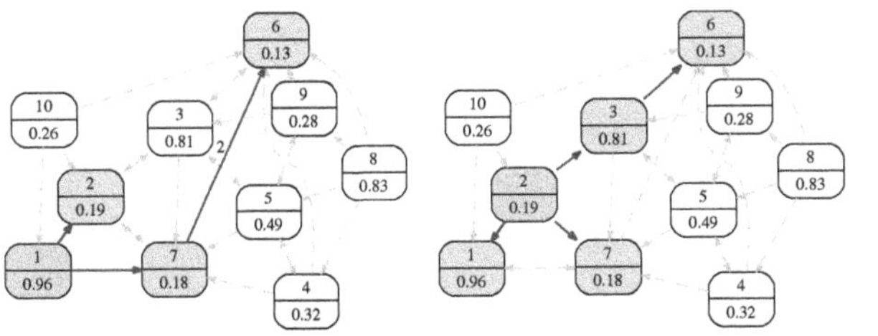

(a) Retrieving $\mathcal{A}(1)$. (b) Retrieving $\mathcal{A}(2)$.

Figure 3: Retrieval of ADSs from SRSs.

from u on the SRSs such that it only visits vertices in $\mathcal{A}(u)$ (Figure 3). We start with an empty sketch A, and entries are added in increasing order of distances to build A. For each visited vertex v with distance δ_{uv}, we check whether (v, δ_{uv}) is *necessary* for A, i.e., whether (v, δ_{vu}) should be included in $\mathcal{A}(u)$ (Line 5). As A contains all the entries in $\mathcal{A}(v)$ with smaller distances at this point, $\pi(u, v)$ can be computed from A. We can use a priority queue that manages the top-k ranks in A to obtain $\pi(u, v)$ quickly. If v is unnecessary for A, we prune the search and do nothing. Otherwise, we add v to A and expand the search by entries in $\mathcal{B}(v)$. Note that the lexicographic comparison in the priority queue substantiates the distance tie-breaking rule discussed in Section 2.2. Lemmas 4.4 and 4.5 state the correctness and complexities of the algorithm.

Lemma 4.4: *Retrieve-ADS returns $\mathcal{A}(u)$.*

Proof Sketch. This is almost immediate from Lemma 4.2. From the lemma, any vertex in $\mathcal{A}(u)$ can be reached with correct distance on SRSs through other vertices in $\mathcal{A}(u)$. □

Lemma 4.5: *Retrieve-ADS runs in $O(k^2 \log^2 n \log(k \log n))$ expected time and $O(k^2 \log^2 n)$ expected space.*

Proof Sketch. Line 8 is executed for $|\mathcal{B}(v)|$ time for each vertex $v \in \mathcal{A}(u)$, and the expected size of $\mathcal{B}(u)$ and $\mathcal{A}(v)$ is $O(k \log n)$. The priority queue takes $O(\log(k \log n))$ time to push an element. □

We stress that the retrieval time only has a logarithmic dependence on the graph size. Therefore, ADSs can be efficiently retrieved even on very large graphs.

5. CONSTRUCTION VIA ADS

Then, we study construction algorithms for SRSs. In this section, we design algorithms that construct SRSs from ADSs. First, we explain the basic algorithm with our *retrieve-and-verify* principle, which is common to all of our construction algorithms. Second, we speed up the algorithm by introducing *eager entry generation.*

Algorithm 2: Constructing SRSs from ADSs (naive).

```
  Procedure Construct-SRS-Naive(G = (V, E), A, k)
1   B[u] ← ∅ for all u ∈ V;
2   T ← {(δ_uv, v, u) | (v, δ_uv) ∈ A(u)};
3   Sort T;
4   for (δ_uv, v, u) ∈ T do
5     A ← Retrieve-ADS(B, u, k);
6     if (v, δ_uv) ∉ A then Add (v, δ_uv) to B[u];
7   return B;
```

5.1 Basic Algorithm

We know that SRSs are recursively defined, and the inclusion of pairs with longer distances depends on pairs with shorter distances. Therefore, in general, we need to construct SRSs in ascending order of distances. Algorithm 2 outlines algorithm Construct-SRS-Naive, our first construction algorithm. It examines the entries of all the ADSs in ascending order of distances. We check each ADS entry to determine whether it is necessary for the SRSs, and if so, we add it.

The tricky part of this algorithm is that, even for construction, we use the retrieval algorithm Retrieve-ADS. At Line 5, algorithm Retrieve-ADS retrieves an "ADS" A from the current incomplete SRSs B. As the current SRSs are incomplete, A does not always match the correct ADS $\mathcal{A}(u)$. However, interestingly, we can use A to check whether entry (v, δ_{uv}) is necessary for the SRS of u as follows.

Lemma 5.1: *At Line 5 in Algorithm 2, assuming $B[w]$ contains SRS entries with distances less than δ_{uv} for any $w \in V$, $(v, \delta_{uv}) \notin A$ if and only if $(v, \delta_{uv}) \in \mathcal{B}(u)$.*

Proof Sketch. Let $\delta_{uv} = d_i$. If $(v, \delta_{uv}) \in A$, then $\mathcal{C}_i(u, v) \neq \emptyset$, and thus $(v, \delta_{uv}) \notin \mathcal{B}(u)$. Otherwise, from Lemma 4.2, (v, δ_{uv}) must be in $\mathcal{B}(u)$. □

As a corollary of this lemma, we obtain the correctness of the algorithm with mathematical induction on the distance.

Corollary 5.2: *Construct-SRS-Naive returns $\{\mathcal{B}(u)\}_{u \in V}$.*

The time and space complexities of this algorithm can be bounded as follows.

Lemma 5.3: *Construct-SRS-Naive runs in $O(nk^3 \log^3 n \log(k \log n))$ expected time and $O(nk \log n)$ expected space.*

Proof Sketch. The ADSs contain $O(nk \log n)$ entries, and Retrieve-ADS is called for each entry. □

5.2 Eager Entry Generation

Algorithm 3 describes another SRS construction algorithm called Construct-SRS-Fast that shares the general idea, but is faster than the previous algorithm. In the previous algorithm, repeated call of Retrieve-ADS was the bottleneck. The high-level difference from the previous algorithm is that, instead of calling Retrieve-ADS, we eagerly generate what can be retrieved from the current incomplete SRSs, immediately after adding an entry to a SRS.

Algorithm 3: Constructing SRSs from ADSs (fast).

```
  Procedure Construct-SRS-Fast(G = (V, E), 𝒜, k)
1   B[u] ← 𝒜(u) for all u ∈ V;
2   T ← {(δ_uv, v, u) | (v, δ_uv) ∈ 𝒜(u)};
3   Sort T;
4   for (δ_uv, v, u) ∈ T do
5       if (v, δ_uv) ∉ B[u] then continue;
6       for x ∈ V s.t. (u, δ_xu) ∈ 𝒜[x] do
7           Remove (v, δ_xu + δ_uv) from B[x] if it exists;
8   return B;
```

The eager generation corresponds to Lines 6–7. As the inclusion of entry (v, δ_{uv}) in SRS $\mathcal{B}(u)$ has been determined, we generate the ADS entries that can be retrieved through that SRS entry. Compared to the previous algorithm, the time complexity is improved as follows.

Lemma 5.4: *Construct-SRS-Fast runs in $O(nk \log n \log(nk \log n) + |\mathcal{B}|\, k \log n)$ expected time and $O(nk \log n)$ expected space, where $|\mathcal{B}|$ is the total size of whole SRSs.*

Proof Sketch. We first sort the whole $O(nk \log n)$ ADS entries, and then, for each SRS entry, we traverse $O(k \log n)$ ADS entries. □

6. DIRECT CONSTRUCTION

Finally, we present a direct construction algorithm for SRSs. Previous algorithms explicitly instantiate ADSs in memory once, the required working space for which may be too large. The following direct algorithm achieves a trades-off between the time consumption and the space efficiency by building SRSs and *virtually* constructing ADSs simultaneously. We start by explaining the basic form, and then make the trade-off more flexible by introducing the *partial ADS caching technique*.

6.1 Basic Algorithm

For simplicity, we first assume that G is an unweighted graph. Our direct algorithm Construct-SRS-Direct is described as Algorithm 4. At a high level, this algorithm combines the retrieve-and-verify principal of the previous indirect SRS construction algorithms with scan-and-merge ADS construction algorithms.

We generally repeat iterations until convergence, where each iteration merges ADSs of neighbors into the SRS of each vertex. Specifically, in the i-th iteration, the SRSs are grown so that the retrieved ADS of any vertex is correct with regard to entries with distances less than or equal to i. In i-th iteration, for each vertex u, we first retrieve the incomplete "ADSs" of its neighbors by Retrieve-ADS, and extract the entries with distance $i-1$ as possible entries for u with distance i (Lines 5–9). Then, we again use Retrieve-ADS to retrieve an incomplete "ADS" A of vertex u to judge whether *(1)* the entry is an actual ADS entry (Line 13), and *(2)* the entry is necessary as an SRS entry (Line 14).

The correctness and complexities of the algorithm are as follows. This space consumption is almost just for the graph and SRSs themselves and essentially minimal.

Lemma 6.1: *Construct-SRS-Direct returns $\{\mathcal{B}(u)\}_{u \in V}$.*

Proof Sketch. By mathematical induction on the distance δ, we can prove that B always matches the SRSs for entries

Algorithm 4: Constructing SRSs directly.

```
   Procedure Construct-SRS-Direct(G = (V, E), k)
1    B[u] ← ∅ for all u ∈ V;
2    for i = 1, 2, ... do
3        f ← FALSE;
4        for u ∈ V do
5            T ← ∅;
6            for v ∈ V such that (u, v) ∈ E do
7                A ← Retrieve-ADS(B, v, k);
8                for (w, δ_vw) ∈ A do
9                    if δ_vw = i − 1 then Add w to T;
10           Sort T;
11           A ← Retrieve-ADS(B, u, k);
12           for w ∈ T do
13               if r(w) ≥ π(u, w) then continue;
14               if w ∉ A then Add (w, i) to B[u];
15               f ← TRUE;
16       if f = FALSE then break;
17   return B;
```

with distances at most δ. From the initial condition, it holds for $\delta = 0$. Assuming it holds for distances less than δ, retrieved ADSs are also correct for entries with distances less than δ; thus, all ADS entries with distance δ are obtained from them. Then, similarly to Lemma 5.1, we can prove that B is also updated for distance δ. □

Lemma 6.2: *Construct-SRS-Direct runs in $O(D(n+m)k^2 \log^2 n \log(k \log n))$ expected time and $O(n+m+|\mathcal{B}|+k \log n)$ expected space, where D is the diameter of G.*

Proof Sketch. The number of iterations is at most D. In each iteration, Retrieve-ADS is called for each edge. With regard to space consumption, we just need additional space for an ADS and extracted possible entries. □

6.2 Partial ADS Caching

To improve the running time of the above algorithm, we here introduce a caching technique that can flexibly adjust the trade-off between space and time consumption. The most time-consuming part is retrieving the current ADS of each neighbor (Line 7 in Algorithm 4). We cache these retrieval results to reuse them.

We propose to use the following strategy, which is simple but sufficiently effective in practice. Let us first assume that we receive a parameter α ($0 \le \alpha \le 1$). Before each iteration, we retrieve and cache the current ADSs for the top-αn vertices with the highest degrees. As each cached ADS takes $O(k \log n)$ expected space, the expected space consumption increases to $O(n + m + |\mathcal{B}| + \alpha nk \log n)$. On the other hand, as the ADSs of the ends of at least αm edges are cached, the expected running time improves to $O(D(n + (1-\alpha)m)k^2 \log^2 n \log(k \log n) + \alpha mk \log n)$. The latter term is the total time consumption for reading cached entries, as the total number of entries that pass through each edge in total corresponds to the size of an ADS.

The space consumption can be further improved as follows. During the i-th iteration, the entries of our interest in cached ADSs are only those with distance $i-1$, and thus other entries are unnecessary to store in the cache. Therefore, interestingly, even with the full cache setting (i.e.,

$\alpha = 1$), this algorithm may work with less space than the size of a full ADS.

In practice, if necessary, we can adjust the space consumption more precisely as below. Given the cache size limit, we retrieve and cache ADSs of vertices in the decreasing order of their degrees, until the total cache size exceeds the limit.

Weighted Graphs. Although the indirect algorithms such as Construct-SRS-Fast perfectly work with weighted graphs, the direct approach has some difficulty with them. If weight values are small integers, the above direct algorithm still works fine. Otherwise, one way is to consider a little relaxed version of ADSs called the $(1+\epsilon)$-*ADSs* [12], which is designed to be efficiently built with scan-and-merge-based algorithms.

7. PRACTICAL IMPROVEMENT

7.1 Implicit Neighborhood

To further reduce the storage requirement of SRSs, we propose the *implicit neighborhood technique.* The idea underlying this technique is that, when we use SRSs for analyzing a graph, the original graph itself is often also available for access. Therefore, under such circumstances, we do not need to store what we can immediately obtain from the original graph, i.e., the neighbors in the original graph.

The implicit neighborhood technique redefines the SRS of vertex u as

$$\mathcal{B}'(u) = \{(v, \delta_{uv}) \in \mathcal{B}(u) \mid (u,v) \notin E \text{ or } \ell(u,v) > \delta_{uv}\}.$$

That is, we basically remove v in $\mathcal{B}(u)$ if (u,v) is in E. However, if $\delta_{uv} < \ell(u,v)$, then it cannot be removed, since otherwise the correct distance from u to v cannot be obtained. We modify the retrieval algorithm Retrieve-ADS as follow. When we expand the search from v (Line 7 in Algorithm 1), in addition to entries in $\mathcal{B}'(v)$, we also use $(w, \ell(v,w))$ for all $(v,w) \in E$. The time complexity becomes $O((\deg_{\max} + k \log n) k \log n \log(k \log n))$, where $\deg_{\max}$ is the maximum degree in the original graph. To construct $\{\mathcal{B}'(u)\}_{u \in V}$, we once construct $\{\mathcal{B}(u)\}_{u \in V}$ and then remove entries that correspond to original edges.

As seen in Section 8, this technique reduces the storage requirement of SRSs drastically. On the other hand, the retrieval time does not degrade significantly.

7.2 Parallelization

The construction algorithms described above can be easily parallelized to exploit the thread-level parallelism of modern computer systems. As confirmed in our experiments, their performance well scales with the number of threads.

Specifically, in Construct-SRS-Fast, different tuples in the list can be processed in parallel. To guarantee the same result, we need to restrict the tuples processed in parallel to those with the same distance. Similarly, in Construct-SRS-Direct, different vertices can be processed in parallel.

8. EXPERIMENTS

8.1 Setup

Environment. All the experiments were conducted on a Linux server with two Intel Xeon X5650 processors (2.67 GHz, 6 cores, 12 threads) and 96 GB of main memory. All the algorithms were implemented in C++ and compiled using gcc 4.8.4. We used Google Snappy as a general-purpose LZ-family compression algorithm. Each entry of ADSs and SRSs was represented by 32 bits, where 26 bits are for the vertex ID and 6 bits are for the distance.

Table 2: Datasets used in our experiments.

Name	Type	$\lvert V\rvert$	$\lvert E\rvert$
wiki-Vote	Social (d)	7,115	103,689
email-Enron	Social (u)	36,692	367,662
web-NotreDame	Web (d)	325,729	1,497,134
com-dblp	Social (u)	317,080	2,099,732
web-Google	Web (d)	875,713	5,105,039
com-youtube	Social (u)	1,134,891	5,975,248
in-2004	Web (d)	1,382,870	16,917,053
flickr-links	Social (u)	1,715,256	31,101,563
soc-LiveJournal1	Social (d)	4,847,571	68,993,773
hollywood-2009	Social (u)	1,139,905	113,891,327
indochina-2004	Web (d)	7,414,768	194,109,311
com-orkut	Social (u)	3,072,441	234,370,166

Methods. We compared five sketch construction methods in our experiments. *(1)* ADS denotes the all-distances sketches construction method. *(2)* ADS-c denotes an ADS construction method with compression, which simply compresses sketches using an LZ-family compressor for each vertex. *(3)* SRS denotes the SRS construction algorithm using ADSs (Algorithm 3). *(4)* SRS-d denotes the direct SRS construction algorithm (Algorithm 4). *(5)* SRS-i denotes the SRS construction algorithm with the implicit neighborhood technique described in Section 7.1. Note that the algorithm of SRS and SRS-i are the same, and the constructed indexes of SRS and SRS-d are also the same. The SRS construction algorithms are parallelized, and run for 24 threads unless otherwise specified. For SRS-d, we set $\alpha = 1$ unless otherwise specified.

Datasets. We used publicly available real-world networks from the Stanford Large Network Dataset Collection [22], the Koblenz Network Collection [20] and Laboratory for Web Algorithms [5, 7], which include social networks and web graphs of various sizes. Table 2 summarizes the details of the real-world networks used in the experiments, where (d) and (u) stand for directed and undirected networks, respectively. It shows the number of directed edges, i.e., an undirected edge corresponds to two directed edges. For directed graphs, we constructed forward ADSs and SRSs.

8.2 Sketch Size

Table 3 summarizes the performances of each method for $k = 16$. The sketch size for each method and dataset is shown in the upper-left part of the table. ADS-c performed slightly worse than ADS, which suggests that simple compression does not work for ADSs. This is because an ADS for each vertex is too small to compress, although the ADSs for all the vertices can be large. SRS consistently generated smaller sketches than ADS, which ranged in 7% to 34% of the sizes of the original ADSs. The SRSs become even smaller with the implicit neighborhood technique, i.e., less than half of the size of the original SRSs in some datasets.

Effect of k. Figures 4a and 4b show the sketch size for different k values in web-Google and com-DBLP, respectively. It is should be emphasized that the relative size of SRSs as

Table 3: **The columns on the left show the sizes of the sketches and the average ADS retrieval time, and the columns on the right show the time and memory consumption for construction ($k = 16$).**

Dataset	Sketch size (MB)				Construction space (MB)			
	ADS	ADS-c	SRS	SRS-i	ADS	ADS-c	SRS	SRS-d
wiki-Vote	1.96	1.98	0.29	0.06	8.93	8.93	20.65	7.08
email-Enron	19.46	19.63	1.53	0.56	59.11	59.40	182.85	40.57
web-NotreDame	59.90	60.89	8.75	4.48	201.12	201.12	579.60	234.02
com-dblp	222.15	223.73	22.30	14.66	529.67	532.26	1929.51	303.22
web-Google	451.38	455.01	78.42	58.45	1055.01	1052.66	3956.93	734.14
com-youtube	873.19	878.85	30.37	13.79	1869.00	1863.96	7512.91	1103.72
in-2004	597.66	603.18	138.63	92.68	1468.30	1489.94	5049.08	1272.42
flickr-links	1277.11	1285.42	59.56	16.84	2866.05	2893.68	11344.86	2045.52
soc-LiveJournal1	3552.90	3575.24	552.34	367.78	7479.33	7480.42	30822.70	5341.82
hollywood-2009	843.54	849.01	289.21	165.82	5189.92	5190.38	7997.62	5189.80
indochina-2004	4255.40	4286.35	1443.24	1048.27	9440.30	9556.09	35403.26	9629.31
com-orkut	2534.30	2549.65	813.91	431.16	7801.51	7803.18	23531.55	7802.66
	Retrieval time (μs)				**Construction time (s)**			
	ADS	ADS-c	SRS	SRS-i	ADS	ADS-c	SRS	SRS-d
wiki-Vote	—	0.40	73.68	119.92	0.26	0.27	0.56	0.81
email-Enron	—	0.84	182.71	538.69	2.26	2.40	5.32	11.46
web-NotreDame	—	0.54	36.26	53.47	5.86	6.14	13.70	142.44
com-dblp	—	1.33	413.76	494.32	45.83	46.12	84.60	324.12
web-Google	—	1.16	271.13	260.74	82.57	81.32	173.13	952.80
com-youtube	—	2.33	391.58	4522.63	145.57	146.67	301.00	977.78
in-2004	—	0.91	160.90	189.82	64.67	66.12	171.73	3473.29
flickr-links	—	1.85	517.60	8163.60	341.40	319.07	599.38	1954.50
soc-LiveJournal1	—	1.54	1008.34	2273.50	1584.42	1627.21	2685.72	9142.96
hollywood-2009	—	2.70	1073.94	4270.85	845.68	802.59	1082.13	2709.84
indochina-2004	—	1.36	357.28	412.61	597.31	602.28	1685.47	34237.70
com-orkut	—	1.40	1629.66	11186.20	3798.51	3772.43	4557.96	5093.08

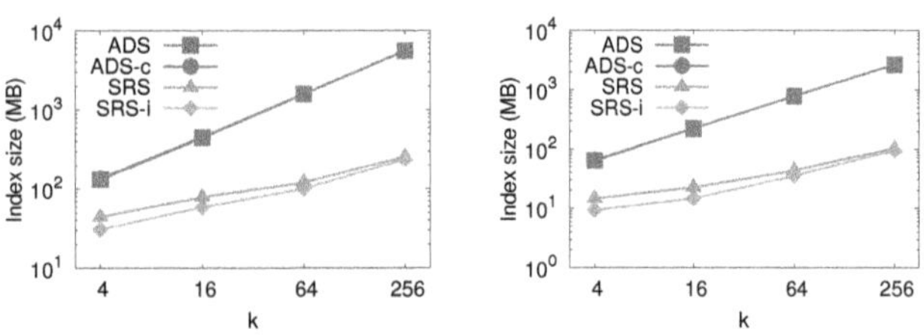

(a) web-Google (b) com-DBLP

Figure 4: Sketch sizes for varying k.

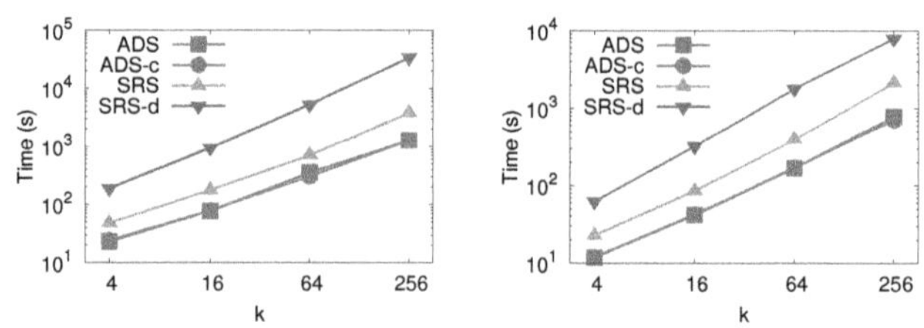

(a) web-Google (b) com-DBLP

Figure 5: Construction time for varying k.

compared to ADSs further decreases as the value of k increases in both datasets, which suggests that SRS is more efficient when k is large. In contrast, the implicit neighborhood technique is more effective when k is small because the ratio of entries of neighboring vertices in an SRS will also be small when the size of the SRS increases.

8.3 Construction Time and Space

The right-hand side of Table 3 compares the construction time and space for $k = 16$. The construction time for SRS includes the ADS construction time. In all datasets, ADS and ADS-c perform the best in terms of construction time. SRS constructed sketches for the com-Orkut dataset with 234 million edges in around 75 minutes. SRS-d took more time for SRS construction, i.e., up to 21 times longer than SRS, and it processed the indochina-2004 dataset in around 10 hours, which was the toughest instance for SRS-d in the experiments. In social networks, however, SRS-d took up to four times longer than SRS. This is attributed to the difference of diameters between web graphs and social networks.

As for the construction space, SRS-d performs the best in most of the datasets, and shows quite similar performance to ADS in the other datasets. The construction space of SRS-d tends to be small when the SRSs themselves are also small, since it does not keep the whole ADSs during the construction. SRS basically required two to four times more space than ADS because it internally keeps ADSs and other data structures linear to the size of the ADSs.

Effect of k. Figures 5a and 5b show the construction time for different values of k in web-Google and com-DBLP, respectively. Although the construction time of SRS-d grows slightly faster than that of the other methods, all the methods constructed sketches for $k = 256$ within several hours in web-Google.

Effect of Partial ADS Caching. Figure 6 shows the trade-off between time and space consumption of our direct construction algorithm for varying α, which is the ratio of cached ADSs ($k = 16$). Partial ADS caching significantly improves the construction time even when $\alpha = 0.2$. This is because a small fraction of vertices cover a large number of

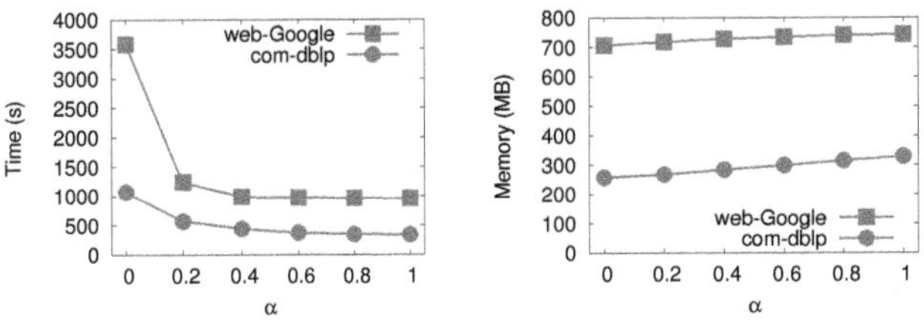

(a) Construction time (b) Construction space

Figure 6: The effect of partial ADS caching.

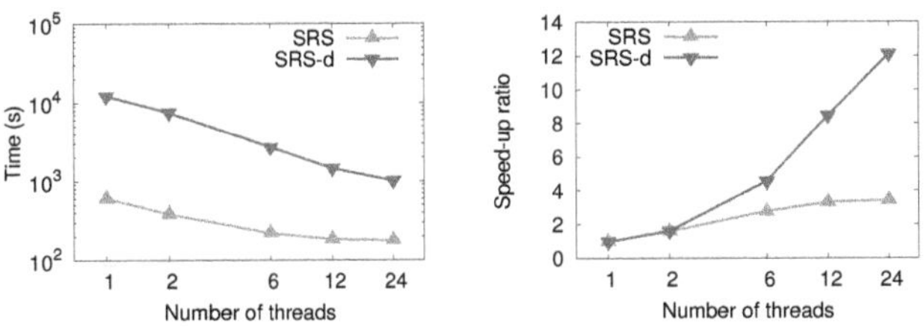

(a) Construction time (b) Speed-up ratio

Figure 7: The effect of parallelization for varying numbers of threads in web-Google.

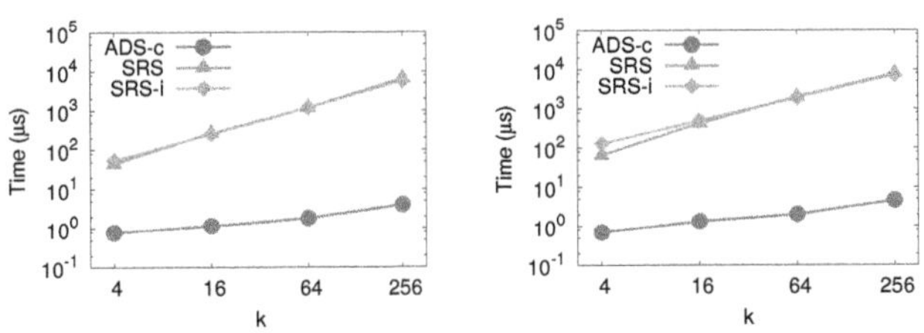

(a) web-Google (b) com-DBLP

Figure 8: Retrieval time for varying values of k.

number of edges in real-world networks owing to their power law degree distributions. In contrast, the construction space does not seem to increase fast and it is not very large even when $\alpha = 1$.

Effect of Parallelization. Figure 7 shows the effect of parallelization of SRS construction algorithms ($k = 16$). These methods, especially SRS-d, have quite high parallelizability. SRS-d constructed SRSs around 12 times faster for 24 threads than for a single thread, which makes the algorithm more practical.

8.4 Retrieval Time

The lower-left part of Table 3 shows the average time of retrieval of an ADS for $k = 16$. For each method and dataset, we conducted retrievals from 10,000 randomly chosen vertices and took their average. The retrieval times of SRS are within around 1 ms in those datasets. SRS-i showed similar performance to SRS in some datasets, whereas it took up to seven times longer in other datasets. The retrieval times of these methods seem to depend not only on the size of ADSs or SRSs. We can observe that the retrieval tends to takes a long time when the sketch size is small compared with the original ADS.

Effect of k. Figures 8a and 8b show the retrieval time for different k values in web-Google and com-DBLP. The retrieval times of SRS and SRS-i grow almost linearly to k.

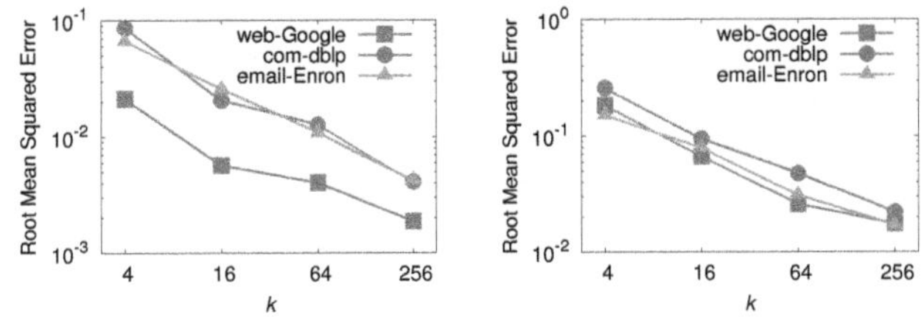

(a) Closeness centrality (b) Closeness similarity

Figure 9: Accuracy of estimated values.

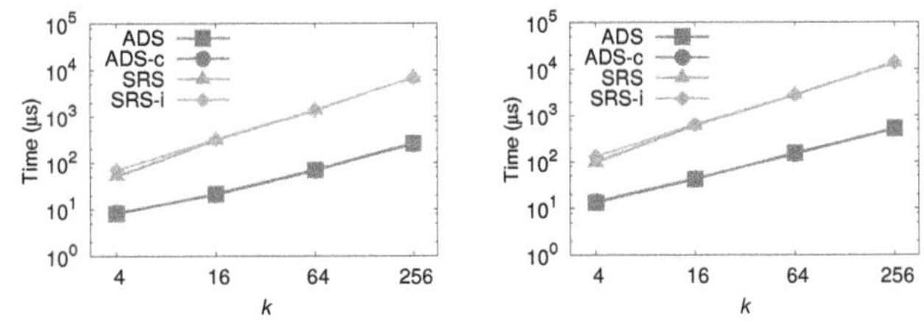

(a) Closeness centrality (b) Closeness similarity

Figure 10: Estimation time in web-Google.

The difference between SRS and SRS-i becomes less significant as k increases.

8.5 Estimation

Further, we conducted experiments for estimating graph properties to examine the practical applicability of SRS. It has been shown that several indicators of graphs can be estimated using ADS, as discussed in Section 3.2. We estimated the closeness centrality [12] and closeness similarity [13] of 1,000 uniformly chosen vertices or pairs of vertices for each dataset using the constructed ADSs and SRSs, and evaluated the approximation error and estimation time for varying values of k. Note that the accuracy results of SRSs and ADSs are exactly the same.

Accuracy. Figures 9a and 9b show the root-mean-square error (RMSE) of estimated centrality and similarity values compared with the exact values. For the three datasets shown in the figures, the RMSEs of both centrality and similarity basically decrease as the value of k increases. The other datasets also showed similar results, as suggested theoretically.

Estimation Time. Figures 10a and 10b show the average estimation time of closeness centrality and closeness similarity values in web-Google. The bottleneck of the estimation is ADS retrieval because a vertex centrality or similarity is estimated in linear time to the size of the ADSs. Thus, these figures show a similar trend to retrieval time. The values can be estimated within 20 ms even for $k = 256$, which should be acceptable in typical situations.

9. CONCLUSIONS

In this paper, we proposed a new scheme for graph neighborhood sketching, called the *sketch retrieval shortcuts* (SRS). The SRS complements the recently-emerging powerful sketching method *all-distances sketches (ADS)* [11, 12]. The ADS combines preferable properties: multi-functional, accuracy guaranteed, and scalable (in theory). However, in practice, it is not as scalable as expected, due to its large storage consumption. The SRS is designed so that, while it is much smaller than the ADS, from SRSs, an ADS of any vertex can be quickly retrieved. Therefore, once we have obtained SRSs, various graph properties can be estimated on massive graphs with the exactly same procedure as that of plain ADSs. In our experiments, we observed that SRSs are orders of magnitude smaller than ADSs, we can construct SRSs for million-scale graphs, and the retrieval time is in milliseconds and sufficiently quick. These results show the high practicality of SRSs as a back-end for large-scale graph analysis.

Acknowledgement. This work was supported by JSPS Grant-in-Aid for Research Activity Startup (No. 15H06828) and JST, PRESTO. The authors thank E. Cohen, D. Delling, A. V. Goldberg, T. Pajor, and R. F. Werneck for fruitful discussion.

10. REFERENCES

[1] T. Akiba, T. Hayashi, N. Nori, Y. Iwata, and Y. Yoshida. Efficient top-k shortest-path distance queries on large networks by pruned landmark labeling. In *AAAI*, pages 56–67, 2015.

[2] T. Akiba, Y. Iwata, and Y. Yoshida. Fast exact shortest-path distance queries on large networks by pruned landmark labeling. In *SIGMOD*, pages 349–360, 2013.

[3] T. Akiba, C. Sommer, and K. Kawarabayashi. Shortest-path queries for complex networks: exploiting low tree-width outside the core. In *EDBT*, pages 144–155, 2012.

[4] L. Backstrom, P. Boldi, M. Rosa, J. Ugander, and S. Vigna. Four degrees of separation. In *WebSci*, pages 33–42, 2012.

[5] P. Boldi, M. Rosa, M. Santini, and S. Vigna. Layered label propagation: A multiresolution coordinate-free ordering for compressing social networks. In *WWW*, pages 587–596, 2011.

[6] P. Boldi, M. Rosa, and S. Vigna. HyperANF: Approximating the neighbourhood function of very large graphs on a budget. In *WWW*, pages 625–634, 2011.

[7] P. Boldi and S. Vigna. The WebGraph framework I: Compression techniques. In *WWW*, pages 595–601, 2004.

[8] P. Boldi and S. Vigna. Axioms for centrality. *Internet Mathematics*, 10(3-4):222–262, 2014.

[9] S. Brin and L. Page. The anatomy of a large-scale hypertextual web search engine. In *WWW*, pages 107–117, 1998.

[10] E. Buchnik and E. Cohen. Reverse ranking by graph structure: Model and scalable algorithms. *CoRR*, abs/1506.02386, 2015.

[11] E. Cohen. Size-estimation framework with applications to transitive closure and reachability. *J. Comput. Syst. Sci.*, 55(3):441–453, 1997.

[12] E. Cohen. All-distances sketches, revisited: HIP estimators for massive graphs analysis. *TKDE*, 27(9):2320–2334, 2015.

[13] E. Cohen, D. Delling, F. Fuchs, A. V. Goldberg, M. Goldszmidt, and R. F. Werneck. Scalable similarity estimation in social networks: closeness, node labels, and random edge lengths. In *COSN*, pages 131–142, 2013.

[14] E. Cohen, D. Delling, T. Pajor, and R. F. Werneck. Sketch-based influence maximization and computation: Scaling up with guarantees. In *CIKM*, pages 629–638, 2014.

[15] E. Cohen, D. Delling, T. Pajor, and R. F. Werneck. Timed influence: Computation and maximization. *CoRR*, abs/1410.6976, 2014.

[16] E. Cohen and H. Kaplan. Summarizing data using bottom-k sketches. In *PODC*, pages 225–234, 2007.

[17] N. Du, L. Song, M. Gomez-Rodriguez, and H. Zha. Scalable influence estimation in continuous-time diffusion networks. In *NIPS*, pages 3147–3155, 2013.

[18] P. Flajolet and G. N. Martin. Probabilistic counting algorithms for data base applications. *J. Comput. Syst. Sci.*, 31(2):182–209, Sept. 1985.

[19] Y. Fujiwara, M. Nakatsuji, T. Yamamuro, H. Shiokawa, and M. Onizuka. Efficient personalized pagerank with accuracy assurance. In *KDD*, pages 15–23, 2012.

[20] J. Kunegis. Konect: The koblenz network collection. In *WWW Companion*, pages 1343–1350, 2013.

[21] J. Leskovec, J. Kleinberg, and C. Faloutsos. Graph evolution: Densification and shrinking diameters. *TKDD*, 1(1), 2007.

[22] J. Leskovec and A. Krevl. SNAP Datasets: Stanford large network dataset collection, 2014.

[23] D. Liben-Nowell and J. Kleinberg. The link prediction problem for social networks. In *CIKM*, pages 556–559, 2003.

[24] S. Maniu and B. Cautis. Network-aware search in social tagging applications: Instance optimality versus efficiency. In *CIKM*, pages 939–948, 2013.

[25] C. R. Palmer, P. B. Gibbons, and C. Faloutsos. ANF: A fast and scalable tool for data mining in massive graphs. In *KDD*, pages 81–90, 2002.

[26] M. Thorup and U. Zwick. Approximate distance oracles. *J. ACM*, 52(1):1–24, 2005.

[27] S. A. Yahia, M. Benedikt, L. V. S. Lakshmanan, and J. Stoyanovich. Efficient network aware search in collaborative tagging sites. *PVLDB*, 1(1):710–721, 2008.

[28] A. D. Zhu, X. Xiao, S. Wang, and W. Lin. Efficient single-source shortest path and distance queries on large graphs. In *KDD*, pages 998–1006, 2013.

APPENDIX

A. COMMON MISUNDERSTANDING

A common misunderstanding about the definition of SRSs is that $\mathcal{B}(u)$ is equivalent to

$$\mathcal{E}(u) = \{(v, \delta_{uv}) \in \mathcal{A}(u) \mid P(u, v) \cup \mathcal{A}(u) = \emptyset\}.$$

Intuitively this may seem true, but it is false. Figure 11 shows a counterexample ($k = 1$). As vertex $4 \in \mathcal{A}(1)$ and $4 \in P(1, 6)$, $6 \notin \mathcal{E}(1)$. However, $6 \in \mathcal{B}(1)$, and indeed, the SRS entry from vertex 1 to vertex 6 is necessary for retrieval; otherwise, vertex 6 would be isolated.

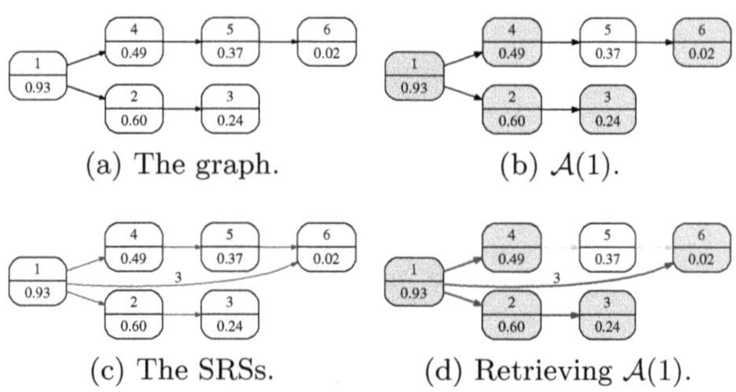

(a) The graph. (b) $\mathcal{A}(1)$.

(c) The SRSs. (d) Retrieving $\mathcal{A}(1)$.

Figure 11: A counterexample where $\mathcal{B}(1) \neq \mathcal{E}(1)$.

B. RETRIEVING A COMBINED ADS

To estimate the expected influence of a vertex set under the continuous-time influence model, we need its *combined ADS* [17, 18]. The combined ADS can also be quickly retrieved from SRSs by slightly modifying the retrieval algorithm. At Line 2 in Algorithm 1, we push all all vertices in S. It works in $O(|S| \log |S| + k^2 \log^2 n \log(k \log n))$ time and $O(|S| + k^2 \log^2 n)$ space.

Streaming-LDA: A Copula-based Approach to Modeling Topic Dependencies in Document Streams

Hesam Amoualian
University of Grenoble Alps - CNRS / LIG
hesam.amoualian@imag.fr

Marianne Clausel
University of Grenoble Alps - CNRS / LJK
marianne.clausel@imag.fr

Eric Gaussier
University of Grenoble Alps - CNRS / LIG
eric.gaussier@imag.fr

Massih-Reza Amini
University of Grenoble Alps - CNRS / LIG
massih-reza.amini@imag.fr

ABSTRACT

We propose in this paper two new models for modeling topic and word-topic dependencies between consecutive documents in document streams. The first model is a direct extension of Latent Dirichlet Allocation model (LDA) and makes use of a Dirichlet distribution to balance the influence of the LDA prior parameters wrt to topic and word-topic distribution of the previous document. The second extension makes use of copulas, which constitute a generic tools to model dependencies between random variables. We rely here on Archimedean copulas, and more precisely on Franck copulas, as they are symmetric and associative and are thus appropriate for exchangeable random variables. Our experiments, conducted on three standard collections that have been used in several studies on topic modeling, show that our proposals outperform previous ones (as dynamic topic models and temporal LDA), both in terms of perplexity and for tracking similar topics in a document stream.

CCS Concepts

•**Computing methodologies** → *Latent Dirichlet allocation;* •**Mathematics of computing** → *Bayesian computation; Gibbs sampling; Metropolis-Hastings algorithm;*

Keywords

Latent Dirichlet allocation, Copulas, Document Streams, Topic Dependencies

1. INTRODUCTION

The recent proliferation of temporal textual data on the Internet such as Tweets or comments on Youtube has brought new challenges for learning with interdependent data. Though important progress has been made in some directions [8], popular approaches for most of these tasks are designed to deal with static collections of documents. This is specially the case for latent topic modeling, albeit analyzes of social content have gained much attention in recent years for different aspects of daily life, such as latent health-related topic analysis [19] or buzz detection [20].

Although the main goal of probabilistic modeling is to find word topics, an equally interesting objective is to examine topic evolutions and transitions. The seminal work of [4] proposed to model the dynamic evolution of topics by first grouping documents into time slices and then to chain the evolution of both the word-topic and topic mixture distributions via a Gaussian process. In some cases, the Gaussian distribution was not found to be the appropriate distribution in modeling the topic shifts and some studies considered other probability distributions for capturing the evolution of topics over time [22]. However, the idea of grouping documents into epochs for modeling topic evolution was echoed in a number of studies. For example, [24] estimated a transition matrix over topic vectors between two predefined epochs and they showed that the LDA model [5] can be enhanced by considering directly the evolution of the topics over time.

In this paper we propose two extensions of LDA for modeling the dependency between two consecutive documents in a stream. In our first model, we suppose that the dependency between topic distributions of two consecutive documents follows a Dirichlet distribution controlled by an hyperparameter. This model is similar to the one of [4] with time slices equal to 1, but it offers a more precise mechanism for controlling the dependencies and is based on a framework encompassing all the situations (from complete independence to plain equality). This first study paves the way for a more general topic model in which the dependencies between the topics of two consecutive documents are captured by copulas which constitute generic tools to model dependencies between random variables [6]. Among the several families of copulas that have been defined in the literature, our choice fell on Archimedean copulas [13, 14] as they are symmetric and associative, necessary conditions when dealing with exchangeable random variables [18]. More particularly, we use Franck copulas, a special case of Archimedean copulas that rely on a single parameter, easier to estimate and more robust to sparse data. Using three collections with different characteristics, we show that our approaches are faster and improve over state-of-the-art topic models. We also analyze

KDD '16, August 13-17, 2016, San Francisco, CA, USA

DOI: http://dx.doi.org/10.1145/2939672.2939781

the precision of our models to track the topics on a labeled dataset.

The outline of this paper is as follows. In the next section, we present our models. In Section 3, we introduce an efficient procedure to estimate the most important, in terms of size, parameters. We then describe in Section 4 the experimental results obtained with our approaches on three distinct datasets. In Section 5, we position our work with respect to the state of the art. Finally, Section 6 concludes our study by summarizing its main results and by giving some pointers to future research.

2. STREAMING LDA

Latent Dirichlet Allocation (LDA, [5]) is a probabilistic Bayesian model used to describe a corpus of D documents, associated with a vocabulary of size V. In this model, latent variables, indexed in $\{1, \cdots, K\}$, are used to represent the *hidden* (in the sense non-observed) topics underlying each document. LDA is associated to the following generative model[1]:

- Generate, for each topic $k, 1 \leq k \leq K$, a distribution over the words: $\phi_k \sim Dir(\beta)$, where ϕ_k and β are V dimensional vectors;
- For each document d:
  - Choose a distribution over the topics: $\theta^d \sim Dir(\alpha)$, where θ^d and α are K dimensional vectors;
  - For each position (indexed by n, $1 \leq n \leq N$) in d: (a) Choose a topic assignment: $z_n^d \sim mult(1, \theta^d)$; (b) Choose the word w_n^d from the topic z_n^d with probability $P(w_n^d = v | z_n^d = k) = \phi_{k,v}$;

where N is the length of each document and $\phi_{k,v}$ is the vth coordinate of ϕ_k. α and β correspond to the priors of the model. They are usually fixed, following [5]. Furthermore, in almost all previous studies on LDA, the priors are considered to be symmetric, each coordinate of the vector being equal: $\alpha_1 = \cdots = \alpha_K$. If one assumes a broad Gamma prior for both α and β, then their value can be easily learned from data by *maximum a posteriori* [1] or *Markov Chain Monte Carlo* [15] methods. One can also envisage learning asymmetric Dirichlet priors [21], which raises no particular difficulties for the models we are considering. For clarity sake, we however assume here fixed, symmetric priors; the extension to their learning through Gamma priors or through asymmetric priors is purely technical. In the remainder, we will denote by α and β the priors for the Dirichlet distributions as well the constant value taken by each coordinate of these priors, the context being sufficient to determine which element is referred to.

An important characteristic of LDA is that each document is generated independently from the previous ones. This is not a realistic assumption in different settings, as document streams, and we introduce below two extensions of LDA that model such dependencies.

2.1 Dirichlet-based dependencies

We introduce here a first extension of LDA, that we refer to as ST-LDA-D.

[1]For simplification and following standard practice, we do not model here the length of each document, assumed to be fixed and equal to N.

2.1.1 Presentation of the model

In this first model, we rely on a direct extension of the LDA model to take into account dependencies between the document-specific topic distributions of two sequential documents, denoted $(d-1)$ and d $(2 \leq d \leq D)$. This extension uses, as the standard LDA model, Dirichlet distributions for the document-specific topic distributions, the parameters of which are linear combination of the standard prior α and the topic distribution estimated in the previous document:

$$\theta^d | \theta^{d-1} \sim Dir(\alpha + \lambda_d \theta^{d-1}) \quad (1)$$

where λ_d is a uniformly distributed parameter that controls the influence of the topics of document $(d-1)$ on the topics of document d (see Figure 1). The expectation of each component of θ^d is given by:

$$\mathbb{E}[\theta_i^d | \theta_i^{d-1}] = \frac{\alpha + \lambda_d \theta_i^{d-1}}{K\alpha + \lambda_d} \quad (2)$$

Hence, if λ_d is high, i.e. if document d covers the same topics as document $(d-1)$, then $\mathbb{E}[\theta_i^d | \theta_i^{d-1}] \approx \theta_i^{d-1}$.

We furthermore assume that the previous document, $(d-1)$, can influence the word-topic distributions of the current document d. This assumption, also made in dynamic topic models [4] and topic tracking models [11], is motivated by the fact that, within a given topic, if word distributions evolve over time, they tend to do so in a smooth way. As before, one can use a direct extension of the LDA model to account for dependencies between word-topic distributions in sequential documents:

$$\forall k, 1 \leq k \leq K, \phi_k^d | \phi^{d-1} \sim Dir(\beta + \mu_d \phi_k^{d-1}) \quad (3)$$

Here μ_d is again a uniformly distributed parameter that controls the tradeoff between the prior β and the learned topic-word distributions ϕ^{d-1}. As usual ϕ_k^{d-1} is the word distribution of topic k. The conditional mean of each component of ϕ_k^d is given by:

$$\mathbb{E}[\phi_k^d | \phi^{d-1}] = \frac{\beta + \mu_d \phi_k^{d-1}}{V\beta + \mu_d} \quad (4)$$

and is approximately the value of the same component of document $(d-1)$ when the two documents are strongly dependent.

Lastly, as one can note, by setting $\lambda_d = \mu_d = 0, \forall d, 2 \leq d \leq D$, one "forgets" the dependencies between consecutive documents. The streaming model is in this case identical to the standard LDA model.

2.1.2 Inference with Gibbs sampling

As mentioned before, the parameters α and β are considered fixed. The other parameters can be estimated through Gibbs sampling, with Metropolis-Hasting updates for the parameters λ_d and β_d. We give here the update formulas of each parameter.

For θ, one has:

$$\begin{aligned} \theta^d &\sim P(\theta | \theta^{d-1}, z^d, w^d, \alpha, \beta, \lambda_d, \phi^{d-1}, \phi^d, \mu_d) \\ &= \frac{B(\alpha) B(\alpha + \lambda_d \theta^{d-1} + \Omega_d)}{B(\alpha + \Omega_d) B(\alpha + \lambda_d \theta^{d-1})} \times \\ & \quad Dir(\Omega_d + \alpha + \lambda_d \theta^{d-1}) \end{aligned} \quad (5)$$

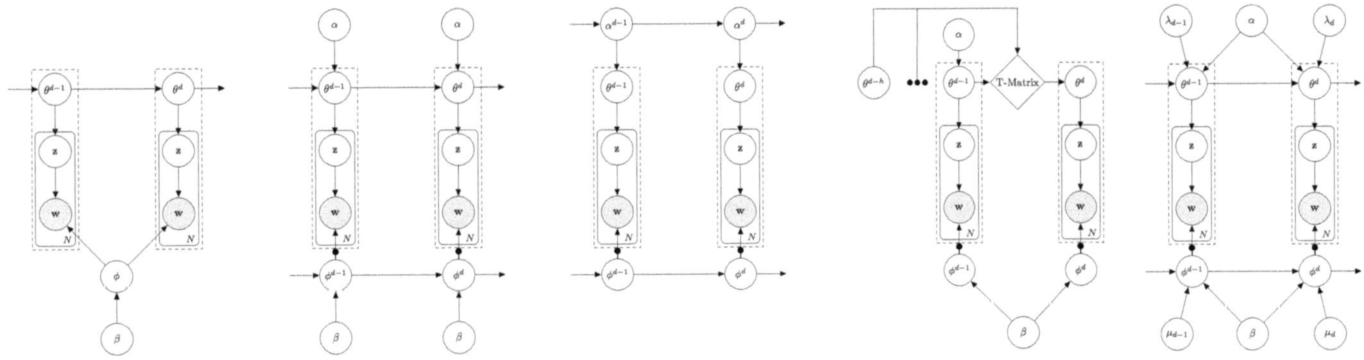

(a) DMM (b) TTM (c) DTM (d) TM-LDA (e) ST-LDA-[D|C]

Figure 1: Graphical models for Dynamic Mixture Models (DMM, [25]), Topic Tracking Models (TTM, [11]), Dynamic Topic Models (DTM, [4]), Temporal LDA (TM-LDA, [24]) and Streaming-LDA (ST-LDA-[D|C])

where Ω_d is defined as in [23] and represents the dth row of the $D \times K$ count matrix Ω, with $\Omega_{d,k}$ being the number of times that topic k is assigned to words in document d.

The update for ϕ_k^d, $1 \le k \le K$ is similar:

$$\begin{aligned} \phi_k^d &\sim P(\phi_k|\theta^{d-1}, \theta^d, z^d, w^d, \alpha, \beta, \lambda_d, \phi^{d-1}, \mu_d) \\ &= \frac{B(\beta)B(\beta + \mu_d\phi_k^{d-1} + \Psi_k)}{B(\beta + \Psi_k)B(\beta + \mu_d\phi_k^{d-1})} \times \\ &\quad Dir(\Psi_k + \beta + \mu_d\phi_k^{d-1}) \end{aligned} \quad (6)$$

where Ψ_k is again defined as in [23] and represents the kth row of a $K \times V$ count matrix, $\Psi_{k,v}$ being the number of times that topic k is assigned to word v in the documents seen so far.

The Gibbs update for z is the same as the one for the standard LDA model:

$$\forall k, 1 \le k \le K, P(z_v^d = k|\theta^d, \phi^d) = \frac{\theta_k^d \times \phi_{k,v}^d}{\sum_j \theta_j^d \times \phi_{j,v}^d} \quad (7)$$

Finally, for λ_d and μ_d, one can not directly compute Gibbs updates as the normalizing factor for the distribution of λ given all the other parameters can not be computed exactly. One can nevertheless rely on a Metropolis-Hasting procedure, detailed in Appendix A.

2.2 Copula-based dependencies

Model ST-LDA-D captures topic and word-topic dependencies through Dirichlet distributions, which allow one to balance the influence of the priors (α and β) and of the topic and topic-word distributions of the previous document. We introduce now another extension of LDA in which the dependencies between the topics of consecutive documents are modeled through copulas, which constitute a generic tool to model dependencies and do not rely on a specific distribution. We first provide a brief overview of copulas, prior to describe our model.

2.2.1 Basics on copulas

For every $p \ge 2$, a p–dimensional copula is a p–variate density function on $[0,1]^p$, whose univariate marginals are uniformly distributed on $[0,1]$. Copulas are particularly useful when modeling dependencies between random variables. Indeed, the joint cumulative distribution function (CDF) $F_{X_1,\cdots,X_p}$ of any random vector $\mathbf{X} = (X_1, \cdots, X_p)$ can be written as a function of its marginals, as follows:

Theorem 1 (Sklar's theorem Theorem 2.3.3 of [16]) *Let $F_{X_1,\cdots,X_p}$ be a p-dimensional distribution function with marginals $F_{X_1}, \cdots, F_{X_p}$. Then there exists a copula C with uniform marginals such that:*

$$F_{X_1,\cdots,X_p}(x_1, \cdots, x_p) = C(F_{X_1}(x_1), \cdots, F_{X_p}(x_p))$$

Furthermore, when the CDF $F_{X_1,\cdots,X_p}$ is continuous, the copula is unique.

Copulas represent a general way of modeling the dependencies between random variables, from complete independence to equality. If the random variables $X_1, \cdots, X_p$ are pairwise independent, their copula is the so–called *independency copula*:

$$F_{X_1,\cdots,X_p}(x_1, \cdots, x_p) = F_{X_1}(x_1) \cdots F_{X_p}(x_p)$$

whereas in the case $X_1 = \cdots = X_d$, one gets the *comonotonicity copula*:

$$F_{X_1,\cdots,X_p}(x_1, \cdots, x_p) = \min_{i \in \{1,\cdots,p\}} F_{X_i}(x_i)$$

Several copula families have been defined in the literature, among which the Archimedean copulas ([16, Ch. 4]), particularly interesting in our case. A p–dimensional Archimedean copula C with generator ψ is defined as:

$$C_p(u;\psi) := \psi(\psi^{-1}(u_1) + \cdots + \psi^{-1}(u_p)), u \in [0,1]^p$$

where ψ is a continuous, decreasing function, from $[0,\infty]$ to $(0,1)$, strictly decreasing on $[0, \inf\{t : \psi(t) = 0\}]$, and satisfying:

$$\psi(0) = 1, \psi(\infty) = \lim_{t\to\infty} \psi(t) = 0$$

Archimedean copulas have the following interesting properties:

- They are symmetric, that is invariant by any permutation of their coordinates, which is important when dealing with exchangeable random variables, as is the case here[2];

[2]The LDA model is based on the assumption that topics are infinitely exchangeable within a document.

- They are associative: for any $(u_1, \cdots, u_p) \in [0,1]^p$, one has:

$$C_{p-1}(C_2(u_1, u_2; \psi), u_3, \cdots, u_p; \psi) = C_{p-1}(u, \cdots, u_{p-2}, C_2(u_{p-1}, u_p; \psi); \psi)$$

This means that the dependency properties are the same whatever the way we group the random variables.

In this study, we further consider a particular case of the Archimedean copulas, namely the one-parameter family of Franck copula, defined, for any $\lambda \in \mathbb{R} \setminus \{0\}$, as:

$$C_\lambda(u, v) = -(1/\lambda)\ln(1 + \frac{(e^{-\lambda u} - 1)(e^{-\lambda v} - 1)}{e^{-\lambda} - 1}) \quad (8)$$

When $\lambda \to 0$, one approaches the independency copula, whereas $\lambda = \infty$ yields the comonotonicity copula. Lastly, for any $\lambda \in \mathbb{R} \setminus \{0\}$, C_λ is twice differentiable on $[0,1]^2$ so that the copula function admits a density, denoted in the sequel c_λ. By varying λ from 0 to ∞, Franck copula allows one to model all the possible dependencies between two random variables, from complete independency to equality. Dependency/independency is furthermore controlled by a single parameter, λ, which makes parameter estimation both easier and more robust.

2.2.2 Generative process

Instead of generating the topic distribution of each document θ^d independently, as is done in standard LDA we bind, as for our first model, ST-LDA-D, the topic distributions θ^{d-1} and θ^d of consecutive documents, this time by using copulas, and more precisely Franck copula.

One can not however directly use Sklar's theorem as it does not extend to joint distributions over random vectors. This means that if we are given two random vectors $\mathbf{X}_1, \mathbf{X}_2$, one can not claim that there exists a copula C such that, for any $(\mathbf{x_1}, \mathbf{x_2}) \in [0,1]^{p_1} \times [0,1]^{p_2}$:

$$F_{\mathbf{X}_1,\mathbf{X}_2}(\mathbf{x_1}, \mathbf{x_2}) = C(F_{\mathbf{X}_1}(\mathbf{x_1}), F_{\mathbf{X}_2}(\mathbf{x_2}))$$

except in very specific situation as when $\mathbf{X_1}$ and $\mathbf{X_2}$ are independent for example. One can nevertheless relate latent topics θ^{d-1} and θ_d through their components. Indeed, the topic Dirichlet distribution can be decomposed into univariate Gamma distributions with parameters $(\alpha, 1)$, denoted $Ga(\alpha)$:

Theorem 2 (from Theorem 2.1 of [17]) A random vector θ follows a Dirichlet distribution $Dir(\alpha)$ iff there exists a random vector $\mathcal{T} \sim Ga(\alpha) \otimes \cdots \otimes Ga(\alpha)$ such that:

$$\theta \overset{(\mathcal{L})}{=} \frac{\mathcal{T}}{\|\mathcal{T}\|_{\ell_1}} \quad (9)$$

where $\overset{(\mathcal{L})}{=}$ means "equality in distribution". In addition, if we are given $\theta \sim Dir(\alpha)$ and $R \sim Ga(K\alpha)$ independent, then $\mathcal{T} = R\theta \sim Ga(\alpha) \otimes \cdots \otimes Ga(\alpha)$.

To bind the topic distributions θ^{d-1} and θ^d of two consecutive documents, we thus consider the associated vectors $\mathcal{T}^{d-1}$ and $\mathcal{T}^d$, and bind them coordinate per coordinate using Franck copula. For the word-topic distributions, we use the same coupling between consecutive documents as the one used in model ST-LDA-D, as a tighter coupling through copulas would be too costly. We will come back to this issue in Section 3.

In the sequel for any $\gamma > 0$, f_γ (resp. F_γ) denotes the pdf (resp. cdf) of the Gamma distribution with parameters $(\gamma, 1)$. The global generative model is thus as follows:

1. Generate the first document according to the standard LDA model
2. For each document d, $2 \le d \le D$:
   (a) Generate $\lambda_d \sim U[0, \tau_\lambda]$
   (b) Generate $\mu_d \sim U[0, \tau_\mu]$
   (c) For each topic k, $1 \le k \le K$:
      - Generate $\mathcal{T}_k^d$ whose conditional density w.r.t. $\mathcal{T}_k^{d-1}$ is:
      $$P(\mathcal{T}_k^d|\mathcal{T}_k^{d-1}) = f_\alpha(\mathcal{T}_k^d)\, c_{\lambda_d}(F_\alpha(\mathcal{T}_k^{d-1}), F_{\alpha_k}(\mathcal{T}_k^d))$$
      - Generate $\phi_k^d|\phi^{d-1} \sim Dir(\beta + \mu_d\phi_k^{d-1})$
   (d) Set $\theta^d = \mathcal{T}^d / \|\mathcal{T}^d\|_{\ell_1}$
   (e) For each word n, $1 \le n \le N$ in d:
      - Choose a topic assignment: $z_n^d \sim mult(1, \theta^d)$
      - Choose the word w_n^d from the topic z_n^d with probability $P(w_n^d|z_n^d) = \phi^d_{z_n^d, w_n^d}$

where $\mathcal{T}_k^d$ represents the kth coordinate of the vector $\mathcal{T}^d$, and follows a distribution $Ga(\alpha)$ according to Theorem 9. We refer to the corresponding model as ST-LDA-C. Figure 1 provides a graphical representation of this model, together with the ones of previous models.

2.2.3 Inference with Gibbs sampling

The updates for z^d, ϕ^d and μ_d are identical to the ones for model ST-LDA-D. For λ_d, one gets:

$$P(\lambda_d|\mathcal{T}^{d-1}, \mathcal{T}^d, z^d, w^d, \alpha, \beta, \phi^{d-1}, \phi^d, \mu_d) \propto$$

$$P(\lambda_d)\prod_{k=1}^{K} f_\alpha(\mathcal{T}_k^{d-1}) f_\alpha(\mathcal{T}_k^d) c_\lambda(F_\alpha(\mathcal{T}_k^{d-1}), F_\alpha(\mathcal{T}_k^d))$$

The same Metropolis-Hasting procedure as the one used for model ST-LDA-D and detailed in Appendix A can then be used.

For θ^d, one needs first to estimate the conditional probability of the random vector $\mathcal{T}^d$ with respect to the other parameters. This expression can be factored as follows:

$$P(\mathcal{T}^d|\mathcal{T}^{d-1}, z^d, w^d, \alpha, \beta, \lambda_d, \phi^{d-1}, \phi^d, \mu_d) = \frac{P(\mathcal{T}^d|\mathcal{T}^{d-1}, \alpha, \lambda_d) P(z^d|\mathcal{T}^d)}{P(z^d|\alpha)}$$

As in the classical context of LDA, one has $P(z^d|\alpha) = B(\Omega_d + \alpha)/B(\Omega_d)$ where Ω_d is defined as before. By assumption on the distribution of the random vectors $(\mathcal{T}^{d-1}, \mathcal{T}^d)$:

$$P(\mathcal{T}^d|\mathcal{T}^{d-1}, \alpha, \lambda_d) = \prod_{k=1}^{K} f_\alpha(\mathcal{T}_k^d) c_\lambda(F_\alpha(\mathcal{T}_k^{d-1}), F_\alpha(\mathcal{T}_k^d))$$

Developing $P(z^d|\mathcal{T}^d)$ as detailed in Appendix B, finally leads to:

$$P(\mathcal{T}^d|\mathcal{T}^{d-1}, z_d, w_d, \alpha, \beta, \lambda_d, \phi^{d-1}, \phi^d, \mu_d) \propto (\sum_{k=1}^{K} \mathcal{T}_k^d)^{-N}$$

$$\times \prod_{k=1}^{K} f_{(\Omega_{d,k}+\alpha-1)}(\mathcal{T}_k^d) \times c_\lambda(F_\alpha(\mathcal{T}_k^{d-1}), F_\alpha(\mathcal{T}_k^d)) \quad (10)$$

Each $\mathcal{T}_k^d$ can then be estimated through the Metropolis-Hasting procedure presented in Appendix A; θ^d is finally obtained from $\mathcal{T}^d$ through Eq. 9.

3. COMPUTATIONAL CONSIDERATIONS

For model ST-LDA-C, the word-topic distributions ϕ_k^d $(1 \leq k \leq K)$ could be estimated in the same way as θ^d is estimated, as mentioned in Section 2.2. However, this would entail running $K \times V$ Metropolis-Hasting procedures, which is problematic as soon as the collections considered are relatively large. We thus proposed in Section 2.2 to estimate it through Eq. 6, as done for ST-LDA-D. This time, $K \times V$ Gibbs sampling updates are required. If this estimation procedure is faster, it may still be too slow for really large collections. Theorem 2 nevertheless suggests a way to approximate ϕ_k^d $(1 \leq k \leq K,\ 2 \leq d \leq D)$ through Gamma updates, as follows:

1. For each word v in d, generate $t_{k,v} \sim Ga(\beta + \phi_{k,v}^{d-1})$
2. For each word v in the vocabulary $\mathcal{V}$, $\phi_{k,v}^d \leftarrow \frac{t_{k,v}}{\sum_{v \in \mathcal{V}} t_{k,v}}$

where β corresponds to the real parameter (*i.e.*, the constant value that makes up the V dimensional vector of priors). The quantities $t_{k,v}$ are first initialized through $t_{k,v} \sim Ga(\beta)$, and updated each time a new document is encountered. As one can note, this update primarily concerns the words present in the current document (step 1), the components for the other words being just renormalized (step 2). This contrasts with Eq. 6 in which the contribution of all words is resampled for each document via a multivariate Dirichlet distribution. The above procedure simplifies this by relying on the univariate equivalent of the Dirichlet distribution, namely the Gamma distribution, and by binding the variables through the renormalization step. It is faster as it involves only $K \times N$ samplings from a Gamma distribution instead of K samplings from a multivariate, $V (V >> N)$ dimensional Dirichlet distribution (the $K \times V$ renormalizations in step 2 do not really harm the procedure and are negligible compared to the Dirichlet samplings). We have observed in practice no difference, in terms of performance measures we consider (see Section 4), between this procedure and the more complex ones mentioned before, and make use of it in the remainder of the paper. In terms of speed, this procedure performed 1.5 times faster on the NIPS collection, which contains long documents and a relatively small vocabulary (*ca.* 12,000 words), and 2 times faster for the TDT4 and Tweets collections, which contain shorter documents with a larger vocabulary (up to 42,000 words).

Algorithm 1 summarizes the inference process we rely on. It makes use of the above procedure to estimate ϕ, referred to as ϕ-procedure.

Algorithm 1: Inference process for ST-LDA-[D|C]

```
Input: Stream of D documents of length N; number of
       topics K
Output: For each document d, topic distribution θ^d,
        word-topic distributions φ_k^d (1 ≤ k ≤ K); for
        each word v in d, topic assignment z_v^d
// Initialization
for k = 1 to K, v ∈ V do
    t_{k,v} ~ Ga(β)
for d = 1 to D do
    Random initialization of λ_d, μ_d and z_n^d, 1 ≤ n ≤ N
λ_1 = μ_1 = 0
// Document processing
for d = 1 to D do
    repeat
        For ST-LDA-D: update θ^d acc. to Eq. 5
        For ST-LDA-C:
            (a) update T^d (Metropolis-Hasting)
            (b) obtain θ^d from T^d through Eq. 9
        Update φ_k^d acc. φ-procedure
        Update λ_d and μ_d (Metropolis-Hasting), d > 2
        Update z_n^d acc. to Eq. 7, 1 ≤ k ≤ K, 1 ≤ n ≤ N
    until estimates are stable
```

4. EXPERIMENTAL STUDY

We conducted a number of experiments aimed at evaluating how the proposed models behave on different collections by analyzing their stability, convergence time and performance.

Datasets. We performed experiments on three datasets with different characteristics. The NIPS dataset contains 1,500 scientific papers with no time dependency between them. The size of the vocabulary is 12,375 and documents contain 500 unique words in average. The collection was collected from the NIPS proceedings and is relatively homogeneous in terms of the topics covered. It allows us to assess whether topic dependencies are still useful in a "loose" context in which there is no more temporal dependency. It is available at the UCI ML Repository [12].

The Multilingual Text and Annotations data set (TDT4)[3] proposed for topic detection and tracking, has 3,190 original documents in English and a vocabulary size of 22,965. Documents here are newswires extracted from different broadcasts and the number of unique words per document is 100 in average. Even though newswires are not extracted from the same source, they are ranked by the time.

The Tweets dataset is collected using Twitter's streaming API during 20 days from 8/10/2014 to 27/10/2014. The collection contains 72,592 tweets and a vocabulary of size 42,336. Tweets have been sequenced by time and are filtered over health issues using an SVM classifier trained over MeSH categories[4].

Each dataset was separated into training and test sets. The NIPS collection was randomly splitted into training (90% of the collection) and test (10% of the collection) sets. For TDT4, we used the first 2800 newswires released in time for training, and the last 390 ones for testing. For the Tweets dataset, we used the tweets issued in the first 17 days for training (60,000 documents) and those of the last 3 days (12,000 documents) for testing. Table 1 summarizes the characteristics of these collections.

Evaluation. Results are evaluated over the test set using the widely used perplexity measure that can be approximated by [5].

$$perplexity(C^{test}) = \exp\left(\frac{-\sum_{d}\sum_{n}\log\sum_{k}\theta_k^d \times \phi_{k,v_n^d}^d}{D^{test} \times N}\right) \tag{11}$$

[3]Linguistic Data Consortium, The Trustees of the University of Pennsylvania https://catalog.ldc.upenn.edu/LDC2005T16.

[4]https://www.nlm.nih.gov/mesh/

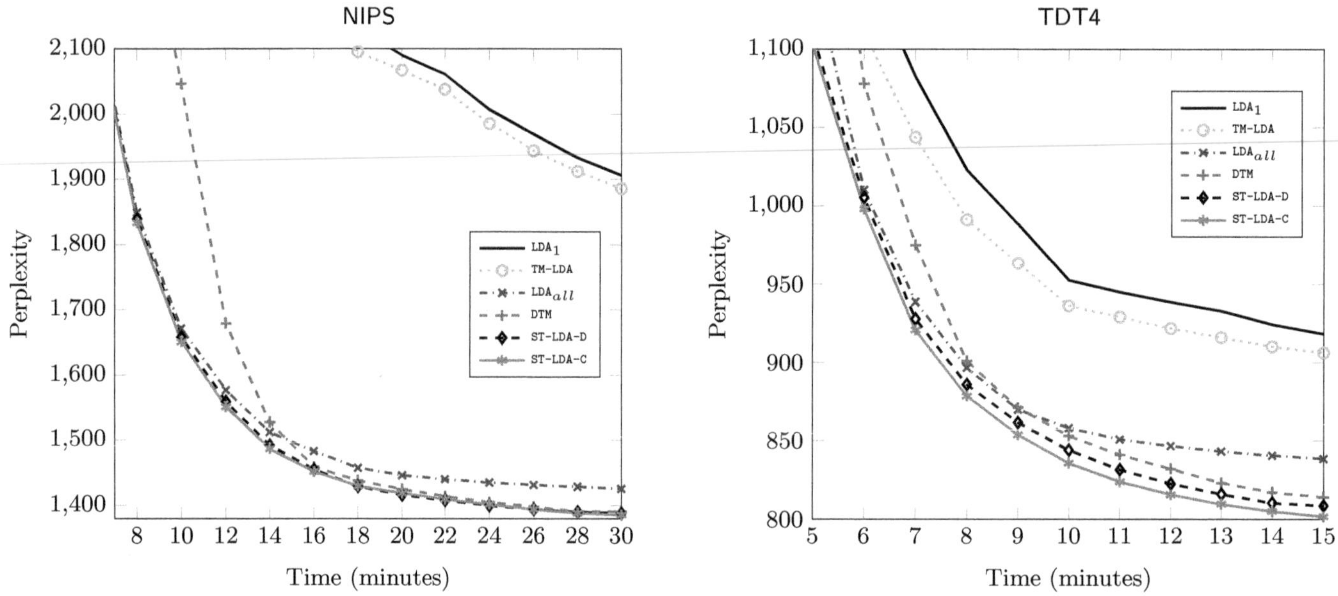

Figure 2: Perplexity curves with respect to time for all methods on NIPS and TDT4 collections (80 topics).

Table 1: Datasets used in our experiments along with their properties.

	NIPS	TDT4	Tweets
Documents in Train set	1,350	2,800	60,000
Documents in Test set	150	390	12,000
Vocabulary size	12,375	22,965	42,336
# of unique words per doc.	500	100	15
Words in total	1,900,000	779,000	904,262

where C^{test} denotes the test collection, D^{test} is its size and v_n^d represents the word at position n in document d. The parameters θ_k^d and ϕ_k^d are estimated on the training set. Furthermore, for the TDT4 collection we use the available semantic labels of newswires in the test set in order to evaluate the ability of the models to find documents of the same semantic labels using only their predicted topic distributions (Section 4.2). To this aim, we measure ROC curves and AUC of different topic models on TDT4.

Settings and comparisons. For all models, both hyperparameters α and β were fixed to 0.5. Documents of the NIPS dataset are initially stoplisted, we did not perform further preprocessing of the data nor removed stop words from the TDT4 and Tweets documents as for all methods best results are obtained when collections are not filtered.

To validate the streaming LDA models described in the previous section, we test the following six methods. The first two are LDA models [5]: (a) $\texttt{LDA}_1$, which consists in training an LDA model on the whole training data, then fixing ϕ and updating θ for each document in the test set, (b) $\texttt{LDA}_{all}$, which consists in training an LDA model on the whole on training data and updating both ϕ and θ for each document in the test set. In addition, we consider two state-of-the-art latent models that take into account dependencies between topics: Dynamic Topic Model (DTM) [4] and Temporal LDA (TM-LDA) [24]. DTM is certainly the most popular model to take into account topic dependencies. It is furthermore complete in the sense that it integrates both topic and word-topic distributions. TM-LDA is a very recent proposal with nice features. Lastly, we also consider the two streaming LDA models we have introduced (ST-LDA-D and ST-LDA-C). For these last two models, τ_λ (see Appendix A) is set to 30,000[5]. All the algorithms were implemented in Python with Numpy and Scipy[6] except DTM that is a C++ implementation tool from [3]. For both training and test, DTM is used considering that each document corresponds to a time slice.

4.1 The effect of streams of documents

We start our evaluation by analyzing the gains provided by modeling dependencies between topics by streaming (as with ST-LDA-D and ST-LDA-C) compared to other approaches on the different datasets. Figure 2 shows the evolution of perplexities of different models over the test set with respect to the training time of each model on NIPS and TDT4 datasets. The code program of DTM (in C++) generally executes faster than the other code programs (written in pyhton), nevertheless we ignore this detail and consider all the curves identically.

To measure the perplexity for each model, we estimate θ and ϕ over respectively all documents and all words of the training set. These estimates are then used to evaluate iteratively new ϕ and θ distributions for each document in the test set. This iterative update of ϕ and θ is done for all of the methods except $\texttt{LDA}_1$ which updates the distributions θ and ϕ over the whole documents in the test set with the last parameters that were obtained from the training set.

As expected, all perplexity curves decrease monotonically with respect to time. On both datasets, perplexity curves

[5]This value, upper bounding λ_d, corresponds to a regime of the Franck copula close to comonotonicity.

[6]We are working to release all the programs developed in this study publicly available for research purpose.

Table 2: Perplexity with respect to different number of topics in {20, 40, 60}.

Models	NIPS			TDT4			Tweets		
	20	40	60	20	40	60	20	40	60
LDA_1	2068.4	2034.5	1986.4	900.8	930.2	960.4	470.8	580.3	615.5
LDA_{all}	1625.4	1534.7	1458.1	723.1	768.4	792.7	431.8	508.6	577.1
TM-LDA	2038.7	2025.4	1985.3	876.7	900.3	916.3	455.1	520.1	585.2
DTM	1737.5	1551.2	1450.7	869.1	836.7	820.9	559.45	578.25	607.41
ST-LDA-D	1620.4	1520.9	1450.2	724.4	758.1	784.4	393.9	480.1	552.7
ST-LDA-C	**1612.8**	**1497.6**	**1434.5**	**720.6**	**752.5**	**780.8**	**388.2**	**474.1**	**546.8**

ST-LDA-D and ST-LDA-C lower-bound the other curves on all iterations. On the NIPS dataset, DTM becomes competitive with the two others, at the end of the iterations, while on TDT4, where test documents come in a stream, ST-LDA-C stands clearly as the best model. These results show the ability of ST-LDA-C to capture dependencies between topics in document streams. Further, we note that at the beginning of iterations where dependencies are not yet apparent, the perplexity curves of both models are very similar to the one of LDA_{all}. This is in line with our assertion of the previous section supporting that both models reduce to LDA in the case where topics are independent. TM-LDA is not competitive in this setting as it does really not make advantage of the fact that the words in the new, arriving documents are known. Its ability to predict future topics is not exploited in this setting.

The evolution of perplexity on Tweets from the three last consecutive days considered in our experiments is shown in Figure 3. The behavior of perplexity curves here are accentuated with the total stream characteristics of Tweets; the curve of LDA_{all} gets away from those of ST-LDA-C and ST-LDA-D, while DTM comes close. In order to see if the number of topics, that we fixed for all models to 80, have an impact on these results or not, we repeated the experiments by varying the number of topics in the set {20, 40, 60}.

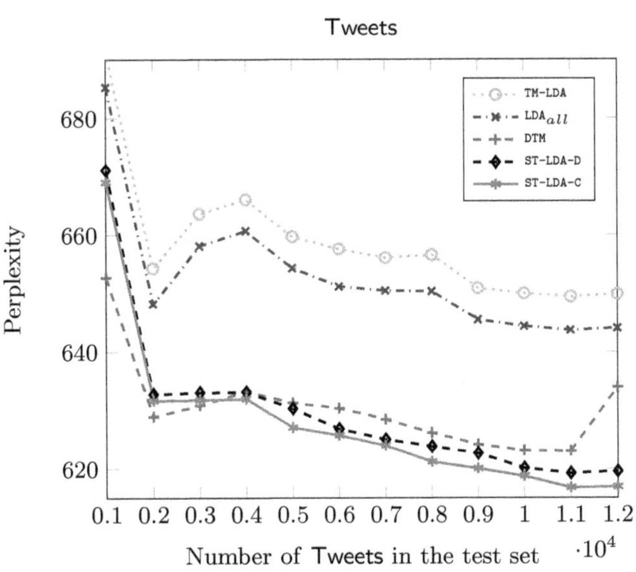

Figure 3: Perplexity of each method by number of tweets that are added to the test set (80 topics).

Table 2 depicts the perplexities of all models on the three collections at the end when the parameters ϕ and θ have been estimated over all the test documents. In all experiments, best results are obtained with ST-LDA-C and ST-LDA-D, followed by DTM on NIPS and TDT4 and by LDA_{all} on Tweets. These results are consistent with those of the figures 2 and 3. Again, TM-LDA does not perform well (as explained before); LDA_{all} which is a standard LDA model, performs relatively well; however, both DTM and the ST-LDA-[D|C] models outperform it by taking into account dependencies between topics. We see here that the extra flexibility of the ST-LDA-[D|C] models allow them to outperform DTM.

4.2 Ability to detect semantic correlations

We further investigate on the ability of models to find topics that can detect documents of the same semantic class. For doing so, we used the TDT4 collection for which some documents are assigned semantic classes by experts. We hence use the cosine measure or the λ_d parameter of ST-LDA-C, to detect consecutive documents in the test set of this collection that are found similar on the basis of their topic distributions; two consecutive documents are considered as similar if the cosine measure of their topic distributions (resp. estimated λ_d - line 13 Algorithm 1) is higher than a given threshold. If two consecutive and similar documents share the same semantic label, we count them as a true positive; if they do not share the same semantic label, we count them as false positive. By changing the threshold, we can plot the ROC curves for the corresponding method.

Figure 4 depicts ROC curves of DTM, TM-LDA and ST-LDA-C defined over 8 different thresholds taken in the set [0.2 0.5 0.7 0.86 0.89 0.92 0.95 0.98] for the cosine measure and [0.5 1 2 5 10 15 20 50] for λ_d when the number of topics is fixed to 20 and to 80.

In order to compare between the different ROC curves, we estimated the area under them, shown in Table 3. From these results it comes clear, that topic distributions found by ST-LDA-C are more able to detect these semantic classes than topic distributions of DTM and TM-LDA.

Table 3: Areas under the ROC curves of figure 4.

Methods	20 (Fig. 4, left)	80 (Fig. 4, right)
ST-LDA-C with λ_d	0.7982	**0.8306**
ST-LDA-C with cosine	**0.8004**	0.7755
TM-LDA with cosine	0.7652	0.7349
DTM with cosine	0.7357	0.6301

Finally, to further illustrate the role of λ_d, we pictorially illustrate the correlation between the estimated λ_d and the topic distributions of three consecutive documents (Figure 5) with identical labels in the TDT4 collection. As one can

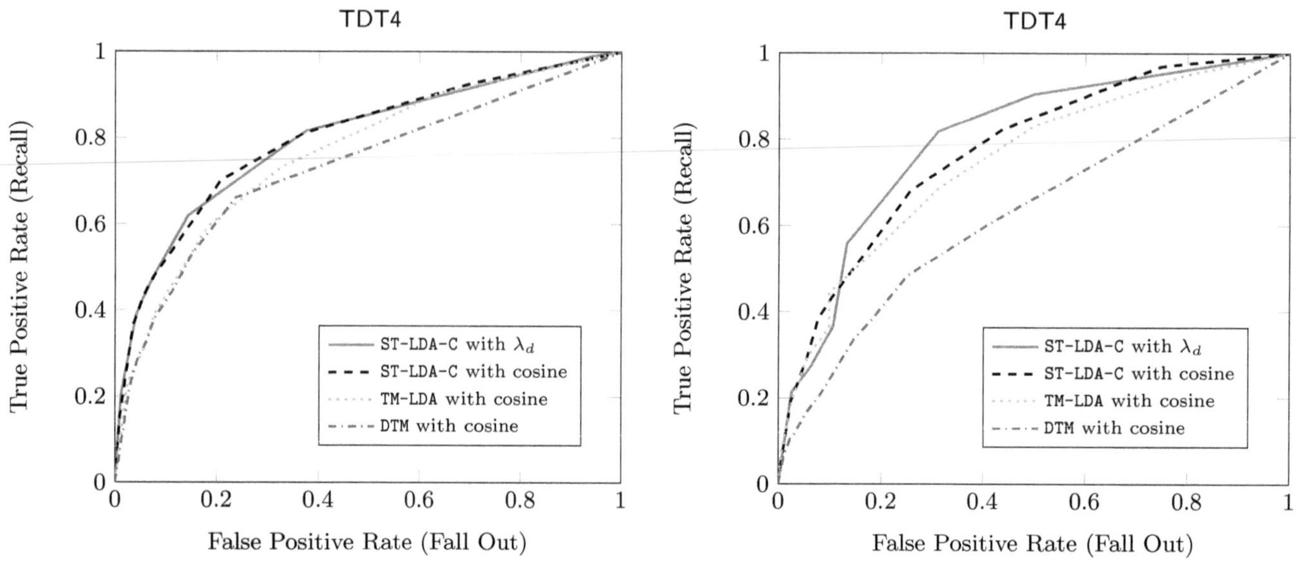

Figure 4: ROC curves of "semantic class matching" methods working over the topic distributions found by DTM, TM-LDA and ST-LDA-C, for the number of topics fixed to 20 (left) and 80 (right).

see, the distributions of topics in the three pairs of consecutive documents with high λ_d are similar. In addition, the two most probable topics of the document pairs retained in Figure 6, also taken from TDT4, do not share any word when λ_d is small and are almost identical when λ_d is high. These examples illustrate the fact that λ_d is a good indicator of the topic dependencies between documents.

5. RELATED WORK

Some studies have considered the possibility to model different streams of documents, as in [10], trying to leverage standard models (as LDA) by considering topics common to the different streams. In such studies the evolution of topics over time is not considered. The study presented in [22] aims at modeling, through an extension of LDA, the timestamp associated with each token in a document. If dependencies between topics are not explicitly modeled, topics tend to specialize over different time periods through the joint dependence of each word and timestamp on the topic variable (z in LDA). Other studies have addressed the problem of topic evolution and dependencies within a single document, as the recent *sequential* LDA model described in [7]. We rather focus in this study on explicitly modeling topic dependencies across documents, for both topic and word-topic distributions. Several studies have addressed a similar problem. One of the first proposals corresponds to the Dynamic Topic Model (DTM), introduced in [4] and illustrated in Figure 1. An interesting feature of DTM is its use of time slices; we have not considered time slices in this study, but our models (as most dynamic models) can be extended to deal with them. DTM captures dependencies for both topic and word-topic distributions. These dependencies are however captured through Gaussian distributions, the expectation of which corresponds to the previous parameters. This entails that new parameter values are constrained to be distributed around the values observed previously. In contrast, even in model ST-LDA-D, the expectations of the new topic and word-topic distributions (Eqs. 2 and 4) can be uncorrelated to the previous distributions in the absence of dependencies. Our models thus offer additional flexibility over the presence or absence of dependencies between consecutive documents in a stream. The Dynamic Mixture Model (DMM, see Fig.1) introduced in [25] is similar to DTM except that topic dependencies are directly considered at the topic level (as is the case for ST-LDA-D and ST-LDA-C but not for DTM which operates at the prior level) and that word-topic dependencies are dropped. As for DTM, the expectation of a new topic distribution is given by the values obtained in the previous document. This again contrasts with our proposal that introduces additional flexibility, as mentioned before. The Topic Tracking Model (TTM, see Fig.1) introduced in [11] is similar to our models in the sense that both topic and word-topic (more precisely interest-topic) dependencies are considered. However, as for DTM and DMM, the mean of the current topics and interests are the same as the ones of the previous topics and interests. The model is thus again limited in its ability to model the presence or absence of dependencies between consecutive documents. A more recent proposal, called Temporal LDA (TM-LDA, see Fig.1), was introduced in [24]. TM-LDA differs from the previous models as it also aims at predicting future topics even in the situation where future documents are not seen. It thus assumes a strong dependency between consecutive documents, which is not always realistic, even on such collections as Tweets. Furthermore, TM-LDA does not consider dependencies for the word-topic distributions.

6. CONCLUSION

We have proposed in this paper two new models for modeling topic and word-topic dependencies between consecutive documents in document streams. The first model is a direct extension of Latent Dirichlet Allocation model (LDA) and makes use of a Dirichlet distribution to balance the influence of the LDA prior parameters wrt to topic and word-topic distribution of the previous document. The second extension makes use of copulas, which constitute a generic

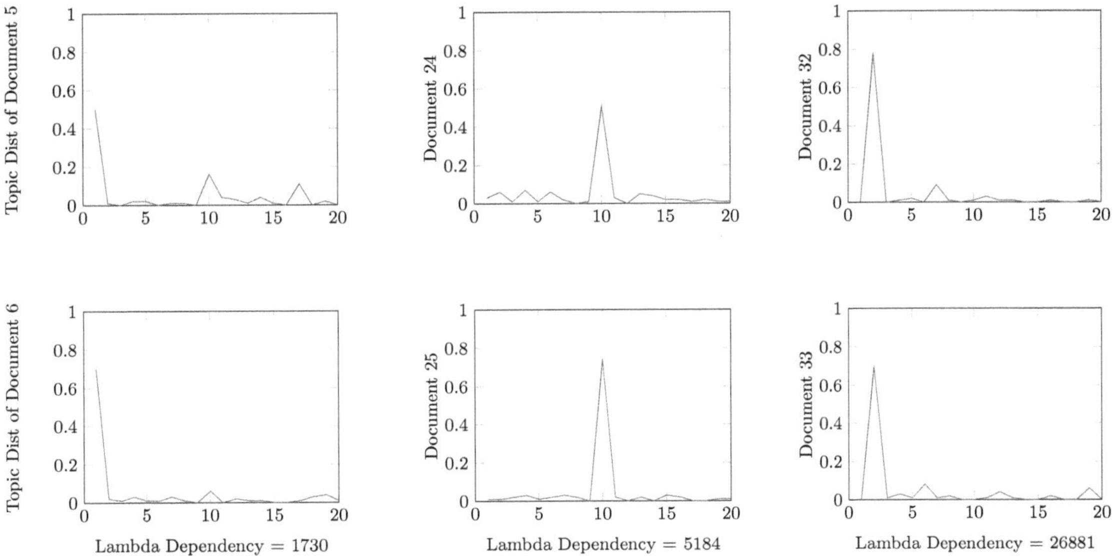

Figure 5: Topic distribution of three pairs consecutive documents that have the same topic (*Olympic* - left, *Election* - middle, *Sport* - right) and subject labels in TDT4 dataset (20 topics).

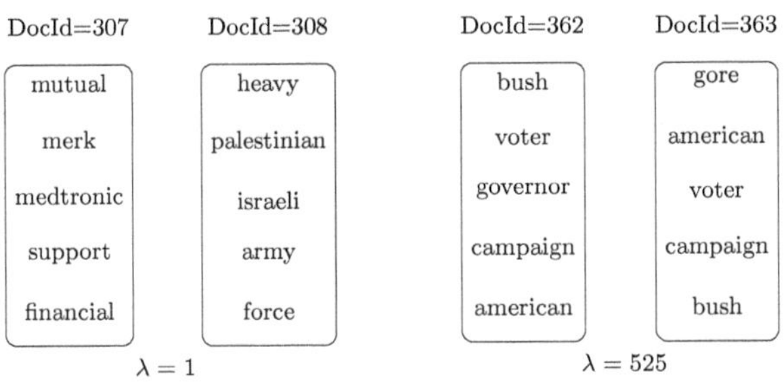

Figure 6: 5 most frequent words of the most probable topic (20 topics).

tool to model dependencies between random variables. Our experiments, conducted on three standard collections that have been used in several studies on topic modeling, show that our proposals outperform previous ones (as dynamic topic models and temporal **LDA**), both in terms of perplexity and for tracking similar topics in a document streams. Compared to previous proposals, our models have extra flexibility and can adapt to situations where there is in fact no dependencies between the documents.

In the future, we plan to develop non-parametric extensions as well as versions of these models that scale well, following the improvements on the inference methods for **LDA**, proposed in streams [26] or in online settings [9, 2].

7. ACKNOWLEDGMENTS

We thank the anonymous reviewers for their useful comments. This work was partly supported by the LabEx PERSYVAL-Lab ANR-11-LABX-0025.

8. REFERENCES

[1] A. Asuncion, M. Welling, P. Smyth, and Y. W. Teh. On smoothing and inference for topic models. In *Proceedings of the 25th Conference on Uncertainty in Artificial Intelligence, UAI*, 2009.

[2] A. Banerjee and S. Basu. Topic models over text streams: A study of batch and online unsupervised learning. In *Proceedings of the 7th SIAM conference on Data Mining, SDM*, 2007.

[3] D. M. Blei. Free C++ implementation for dtm. https://www.cs.princeton.edu/~blei/topicmodeling.html.

[4] D. M. Blei and J. D. Lafferty. Dynamic topic models. In *ACM International Conference Proceeding Series, ICML*, 2006.

[5] D. M. Blei, A. Y. Ng, and M. I. Jordan. Latent dirichlet allocation. *J. Mach. Learn. Res.*, 2003.

[6] S. Derrode and W. Pieczynski. Unsupervised data classification using pairwise markov chains with automatic copulas selection. *Computational Statistics & Data Analysis*, 2013.

[7] L. Du, W. L. Buntine, and H. Jin. Sequential latent dirichlet allocation: Discover underlying topic structures within a document. In *IEEE Computer Society, ICDM*, 2010.

[8] M. M. Gaber, A. Zaslavsky, and S. Krishnaswamy. Mining data streams: A review. *ACM SIGMOD Record*, 2005.

[9] M. D. Hoffman, D. M. Blei, and F. Bach. Online learning for latent dirichlet allocation. In *NIPS*, 2010.

[10] L. Hong, B. Dom, S. Gurumurthy, and K. Tsioutsiouliklis. A time-dependent topic model for multiple text streams. In *Proceedings of the 17th ACM SIGKDD International Conference on Knowledge Discovery and Data Mining, KDD*, 2011.

[11] T. Iwata, S. Watanabe, T. Yamada, and N. Ueda. Topic tracking model for analyzing consumer purchase behavior. In *Proceedings of the 21st International Jont Conference on Artifical Intelligence, IJCAI*, 2009.

[12] M. Lichman. UCI machine learning repository, 2013.

[13] A. J. McNeil. Sampling nested Archimedean copulas. *Journal of Statistical Computation and Simulation*, 2008.

[14] A. J. McNeil and J. Nešlehovà. Multivariate Archimedean copulas, D-monotone functions and ℓ_1-norm symmetric distributions. *Annals of Statistics*, 2009.
[15] R. Neal. Slice sampling. *Annals of Statistics*, 2000.
[16] R. B. Nelsen. *An introduction to copulas.* Springer Science & Business Media, 2007.
[17] K. W. Ng, G.-L. Tian, and M.-L. Tang. *Dirichlet and related distributions: Theory, methods and applications.* John Wiley & Sons, 2011.
[18] O. Ostap, O. Yarema, and S. Wolfgang. Properties of hierarchical Archimedean copulas. *Statistics & Risk Modeling*, 2013.
[19] M. J. Paul and M. Dredze. You are what you tweet: Analyzing twitter for public health. In *International Conference on Weblogs and Social Media*, 2011.
[20] T. Sakaki, M. Okazaki, and Y. Matsuo. Earthquake shakes twitter users: Real-time event detection by social sensors. In *International Conference on World Wide Web*, 2010.
[21] H. M. Wallach, D. M. Mimno, and A. McCallum. Rethinking LDA: why priors matter. In *Advances in Neural Information Processing Systems Conference*, 2009.
[22] X. Wang and A. McCallum. Topics over time: A non-markov continuous-time model of topical trends. In *Proceedings of the 12th ACM SIGKDD International Conference on Knowledge Discovery and Data Mining, KDD*, 2006.
[23] Y. Wang. Distributed gibbs sampling of latent topic models: The gritty details. Technical report, 2008.
[24] Y. Wang, E. Agichtein, and M. Benzi. TM-LDA: Efficient online modeling of latent topic transitions in social media. In *Proceedings of the 18th ACM SIGKDD International Conference on Knowledge Discovery and Data Mining, KDD*, 2012.
[25] X. Wei, J. Sun, and X. Wang. Dynamic mixture models for multiple time series. In *Proceedings of the 20th International Joint Conference on Artificial Intelligence, IJCAI*, 2007.
[26] L. Yao, D. Mimno, and A. McCallum. Efficient methods for topic model inference on streaming document collections. In *Proceedings of the 15th ACM SIGKDD International Conference on Knowledge Discovery and Data Mining, KDD*, 2009.

APPENDIX

A. METROPOLIS-HASTING PROCEDURE

The Metropolis-Hasting procedure is based on the following steps:

1. Generate an initial value of x: draw $x^1 \sim P_{\text{prior}}(x)$
2. Initialize $j = 1$
3. Repeat till sequence is stable
   (a) Draw $x \sim q$, where q represents the "jump" function
   (b) Draw $u \sim U[0,1]$
   (c)
$$\alpha = \begin{cases} \frac{\Pi(x^j)q(x)}{\Pi(x)q(x^j)} & \text{if } \Pi(x^j)q(x) < \Pi(x)q(x^j) \\ \frac{\Pi(x)q(x^j)}{\Pi(x^j)q(x)} & \text{otherwise} \end{cases}$$
   (d) If $u \leq \alpha$, then $x^{j+1} = x$; $x^{j+1} = x^j$ otherwise

For $x = \lambda_d$, one has:

$$\begin{aligned} & P(\lambda_d|\theta^{d-1}, \theta^d, z^d, w^d, \alpha, \beta, \phi^{d-1}, \phi^d, \mu_d) \\ \propto \; & P_{\text{prior}}(\lambda_d)P(\theta^d|\theta^{d-1}, \alpha, \lambda_d) := \Pi(\lambda_d) \end{aligned}$$

where $P_{\text{prior}}(\lambda_d) \sim U[0, \tau_\lambda]$. As λ_d should be higher when θ^{d-1} and θ^d are more similar (as in such a case the influence of θ^{d-1} on θ^d is more important), we make use of the following jump function, based on the exponential distribution:

$$q(\lambda_d) = (1 - cos(\theta^{d-1}, \theta^d)) \times e^{-(1-cos(\theta^{d-1},\theta^d))\times\lambda_d}$$

For $x = \mu_d$, the same distribution is used for the jump function, the cosine being taken between the vectors that correspond to the column-wise concatenation of the columns of each matrix ϕ^{d-1} and ϕ^d. The prior this time is $P(\mu_d) \sim U[0, \tau_\mu]$. Lastly, for $x = \mathcal{T}_k^d$, $P_{\text{prior}}(\mathcal{T}_k^d) \sim Ga(\alpha)$, the jump function corresponds to Franck copula, and $\Pi(\mathcal{T}_k^d)$ corresponds to the kth contribution in Eq. 10.

B. GIBBS SAMPLING UPDATES (*ST-LDA-C*)

We provide here the complete derivation of Eq. 10. For any $d \geq 2$, one has:

$$\begin{aligned} \mathcal{T}^d & \sim P(\mathcal{T}^d|\mathcal{T}^{d-1}, z^d, w^d, \alpha, \beta, \lambda_d, \phi^{d-1}, \phi^d, \mu_d) \\ & = \frac{P(\mathcal{T}^{d-1}|\alpha)P(\mathcal{T}^d|\mathcal{T}^{d-1}, \alpha, \lambda_d)P(z^d|\mathcal{T}^d)P(w^d|z^d)}{P(\mathcal{T}^{d-1}|\alpha)p(z^d|\alpha)P(w^d|z^d)} \\ & = \frac{P(\mathcal{T}^d|\mathcal{T}^{d-1}, \alpha, \lambda_d)P(z^d|\mathcal{T}^d)}{P(z^d|\alpha)} \end{aligned}$$

Let F_α (resp f_α) denote the cdf (resp pdf) of the Gamma distribution with parameters $(\alpha, 1)$. By assumption:

$$P(\mathcal{T}^d|\mathcal{T}^{d-1}, \alpha, \lambda_d) = \prod_{k=1}^{K} f_\alpha(\mathcal{T}_k^d)c_\lambda(F_\alpha(\mathcal{T}_k^{d-1}), F_\alpha(\mathcal{T}_k^d))$$

and, since $\theta^d = \mathcal{T}^d / \left(\sum_{k=1}^K \mathcal{T}_k^d\right)$,:

$$P(z^d|\mathcal{T}^d) = \prod_{n=1}^{N} \theta_{z_n^d}^d = \left(\sum_{k=1}^{K} \mathcal{T}_k^d\right)^{-N} \prod_{n=1}^{N} \mathcal{T}_{z_n^d}^d$$

Further, as usual [23]:

$$P(z^d|\alpha) = \int P(z^d|\theta^d)P(\theta^d|\alpha)d\theta^d = \frac{B(\Omega_d + \alpha)}{B(\Omega_d)}$$

Hence:

$$\begin{aligned} p(\mathcal{T}^d|\mathcal{T}^{d-1}, z^d, \cdots) & = \frac{\left(\sum_{k=1}^K \mathcal{T}_k^d\right)^{-N} \prod_{n=1}^N \mathcal{T}_{z_n^d}^d}{\left[\prod_{k=1}^K \Gamma(\alpha)\right] B(\Omega_d + \alpha)/B(\Omega_d)} \times \\ & \left[\prod_{k=1}^{K} \mathcal{T}_k^{d\,\alpha-1} \exp^{-\mathcal{T}_k^d} c_\lambda(F_\alpha(\mathcal{T}_k^{d-1}), F_\alpha(\mathcal{T}_k^d))\right] \\ & = \frac{\left(\sum_{k=1}^K \mathcal{T}_k^d\right)^{-N} \prod_{k=1}^K \mathcal{T}_k^{d\,\Omega_{d,k}+\alpha-1}}{\left[\prod_{k=1}^K \Gamma(\alpha)\right] B(\Omega_d + \alpha)/B(\Omega_d)} \times \\ & \exp^{-\sum_{k=1}^K \mathcal{T}_k^d} \prod_{k=1}^{K} c_\lambda(F_\alpha(\mathcal{T}_k^{d-1}), F_\alpha(\mathcal{T}_k^d)) \end{aligned}$$

leading to the desired result.

Assessing Human Error Against a Benchmark of Perfection

Ashton Anderson
Microsoft Research

Jon Kleinberg
Cornell University

Sendhil Mullainathan
Harvard University

ABSTRACT

An increasing number of domains are providing us with detailed trace data on human decisions in settings where we can evaluate the quality of these decisions via an algorithm. Motivated by this development, an emerging line of work has begun to consider whether we can characterize and predict the kinds of decisions where people are likely to make errors.

To investigate what a general framework for human error prediction might look like, we focus on a model system with a rich history in the behavioral sciences: the decisions made by chess players as they select moves in a game. We carry out our analysis at a large scale, employing datasets with several million recorded games, and using *chess tablebases* to acquire a form of ground truth for a subset of chess positions that have been completely solved by computers but remain challenging even for the best players in the world.

We organize our analysis around three categories of features that we argue are present in most settings where the analysis of human error is applicable: the skill of the decision-maker, the time available to make the decision, and the inherent difficulty of the decision. We identify rich structure in all three of these categories of features, and find strong evidence that in our domain, features describing the inherent difficulty of an instance are significantly more powerful than features based on skill or time.

1. INTRODUCTION

Several rich strands of work in the behavioral sciences have been concerned with characterizing the nature and sources of human error. These include the broad of notion of *bounded rationality* [25] and the subsequent research beginning with Kahneman and Tversky on heuristics and biases [26]. With the growing availability of large datasets containing millions of human decisions on fixed, well-defined, real-world tasks, there is an interesting opportunity to add a new style of inquiry to this research — given a large stream of decisions, with rich information about the context of each decision, can we algorithmically characterize and predict the instances on which people are likely to make errors?

This genre of question — analyzing human errors from large traces of decisions on a fixed task — also has an interesting relation to the canonical set-up in machine learning applications. Typically, using instances of decision problems together with "ground truth" showing the correct decision, an algorithm is trained to produce the correct decisions in a large fraction of instances. The analysis of human error, on the other hand, represents a twist on this formulation: given instances of a task in which we have both the correct decision *and* a human's decision, the algorithm is trained to recognize future instances on which the human is likely to make a mistake. Predicting human error from this type of trace data has a history in human factors research [14, 24], and a nascent line of work has begun to apply current machine-learning methods to the question [16, 17].

KDD '16, August 13 - 17, 2016, San Francisco, CA, USA

ISBN 978-1-4503-4232-2/16/08...$0.00

DOI: http://dx.doi.org/10.1145/2939672.2939803

Model systems for studying human error. As the investigation of human error using large datasets grows increasingly feasible, it becomes useful to understand which styles of analysis will be most effective. For this purpose, as in other settings, there is enormous value in focusing on model systems where one has exactly the data necessary to ask the basic questions in their most natural formulations.

What might we want from such a model system?

(i) It should consist of a task for which the context of the human decisions has been measured as thoroughly as possible, and in a very large number of instances, to provide the training data for an algorithm to analyze errors.

(ii) So that the task is non-trivial, it should be challenging even for highly skilled human decision-makers.

(iii) Notwithstanding the previous point (ii), the "ground truth" — the correctness of each candidate decision — should be feasibly computable by an algorithm.

Guided by these desiderata, we focus in this paper on chess as a model system for our analysis. In doing so, we are proceeding by analogy with a long line of work in behavioral science using chess as a model for human decision-making [4, 5, 6]. Chess is a natural domain for such investigations, since it presents a human player with a sequence of concrete decisions — which move to play next — with the property that some choices are better than others. Indeed, because chess provides data on hard decision problems in such a pure fashion, it has been described as the "drosophila of psychology" [7, 10]. (It is worth noting our focus here on *human* decisions in chess, rather than on designing algorithms to play chess [22]. This latter problem has also, of course, generated a rich literature, along with a closely related tag-line as the "drosophila of artificial intelligence" [19].)

Chess as a model system for human error. Despite the clean formulation of the decisions made by human chess players, we still must resolve a set of conceptual challenges if our goal is to assemble a large corpus of chess moves with ground-truth labels that classify certain moves as errors. Let us consider three initial ideas for how we might go about this, each of which is lacking in some crucial respect for our purposes.

First, for most of the history of human decision-making research on chess, the emphasis has been on focused laboratory studies at small scales in which the correct decision could be controlled by design [4]. In our list of desiderata, this means that point (iii), the availability of ground truth, is well under control, but a significant aspect of point (i) — the availability of a vast number of instances — is problematic due to the necessarily small scales of the studies.

A second alternative would be to make use of two important computational developments in chess — the availability of databases with millions of recorded chess games by strong players; and the fact that the strongest chess programs — generally referred to as *chess engines* — now greatly outperform even the best human players in the world. This makes it possible to analyze the moves of strong human players, in a large-scale fashion, comparing their choices to those of an engine. This has been pursued very effectively in the last several years by Biswas and Regan [2, 3, 23]; they have used the approach to derive interesting insights including proposals for how to estimate the depth at which human players are analyzing a position.

For the current purpose of assembling a corpus with ground-truth error labels, however, engines present a set of challenges. The basic difficulty is that even current chess engines are far from being able to provide guarantees regarding the best move(s) in a given position. In particular, an engine may prefer move m to m' in a given position, supplementing this preference with a heuristic numerical evaluation, but m' may ultimately lead to the same result in the game, both under best play and under typical play. In these cases, it is hard to say that choosing m' should be labeled an error. More broadly, it is difficult to find a clear-cut rule mapping an engine's evaluations to a determination of human error, and efforts to label errors this way would represent a complex mixture of the human player's mistakes and the nature of the engine's evaluations.

Finally, a third possibility is to go back to the definition of chess as a deterministic game with two players (White and Black) who engage in alternating moves, and with a game outcome that is either (a) a win for White, (b) a win for Black, or (c) a draw. This means that from any position, there is a well-defined notion of the outcome with respect to optimal play by both sides — in game-theoretic terms, this is the *minimax value* of the position. In each position, it is the case that White wins with best play, or Black wins with best play, or it is a draw with best play, and these are the three possible minimax values for the position.

This perspective provide us with a clean option for formulating the notion of an error, namely the direct game-theoretic definition: a player has committed an error if their move worsens the minimax value from their perspective. That is, the player had a forced win before making their move but now they don't; or the player had a forced draw before making their move but now they don't. But there's an obvious difficulty with this route, and it's a computational one: for most chess positions, determining the minimax value is hopelessly beyond the power of both human players and chess engines alike.

We now discuss the approach we take here.

Assessing errors using tablebases. In our work, we use minimax values by leveraging a further development in computer chess — the fact that chess has been solved for all positions with at most k pieces on the board, for small values of k [18, 21, 15]. (We will refer to such positions as *$\leq k$-piece positions*.) Solving these positions has been accomplished not by forward construction of the chess game tree, but instead by simply working backward from terminal positions with a concrete outcome present on the board and filling in all other minimax values by dynamic programming until all possible $\leq k$-piece positions have been enumerated. The resulting solution for all $\leq k$-piece positions is compiled into an object called a *k-piece tablebase*, which lists the game outcome with best play for each of these positions. The construction of tablebases has been a topic of interest since the early days of computer chess [15], but only with recent developments in computing and storage have truly large tablebases been feasible. Proprietary tablebases with $k = 7$ have been built, requiring in excess of a hundred terabytes of storage [18]; tablebases for $k = 6$ are much more manageable, though still very large [21], and we focus on the case of $k = 6$ in what follows.[1]

Tablebases and traditional chess engines are thus very different objects. Chess engines produce strong moves for arbitrary positions, but with no absolute guarantees on move quality in most cases; tablebases, on the other hand, play perfectly with respect to the game tree — indeed, effortlessly, via table lookup — for the subset of chess containing at most k pieces on the board.

Thus, for arbitrary $\leq k$-piece positions, we can determine minimax values, and so we can obtain a large corpus of chess moves with ground-truth error labels: Starting with a large database of recorded chess games, we first restrict to the subset of $\leq k$-piece positions, and then we label a move as an error if and only it worsens the minimax value from the perspective of the player making the move. Adapting chess terminology to the current setting, we will refer to such an instance as a *blunder*.

This is our model system for analyzing human error; let us now check how it lines up with desiderata (i)-(iii) for a model system listed above. Chess positions with at most $k = 6$ pieces arise relatively frequently in real games, so we are left with many instances even after filtering a database of games to restrict to only these positions (point (i)). Crucially, despite their simple structure, they can induce high error rates by amateurs and non-trivial error rates even by the best players in the world; in recognition of the inherent challenge they contain, textbook-level treatments of chess devote a significant fraction of their attention to these positions [9] (point (ii)). And they can be evaluated perfectly by tablebases (point (iii)).

Focusing on $\leq k$-piece positions has an additional benefit, made possible by a combination of tablebases and the recent availability of databases with millions of recorded chess games. The most frequently-occurring of these positions arise in our data thousands of times. As we will see, this means that for some of our analyses, we can control for the exact position on the board and still have enough instances to observe meaningful variation. Controlling for the exact position is not generally feasible with arbitrary positions arising in the middle of a chess game, but it becomes possible with the scale of data we now have, and we will see that in this case it yields interesting and in some cases surprising insights.

Finally, we note that our definition of blunders, while concrete and precisely aligned with the minimax value of the game tree, is not the only definition that could be considered even using tablebase evaluations. In particular, it would also be possible to consider "softer" notions of blunders. Suppose for example that a player is choosing between moves m and m', each leading to a position

[1] There are some intricacies in how tablebases interact with certain rules for draws in chess, particularly *threefold-repetition* and *the 50-move rule*, but since these have essentially negligible impact on our use of tablebases in the present work, we do not go into further details here.

whose minimax value is a draw, but suppose that the position arising after m is more difficult for the opponent, and produces a much higher empirical probability that the opponent will make a mistake at some future point and lose. Then it can be viewed as a kind of blunder, given these empirical probabilities, to play m' rather than the more challenging m. This is sometimes termed *speculative play* [12], and it can be thought of primarily as a refinement of the coarser minimax value. This is an interesting extension, but for our work here we focus on the purer notion of blunders based on the minimax value.

2. SETTING UP THE ANALYSIS

In formulating our analysis, we begin from the premise that for analyzing error in human decisions, three crucial types of features are the following:

(a) the skill of the decision-maker;

(b) the time available to make the decision; and

(c) the inherent difficulty of the decision.

Any instance of the problem will implicitly or explicitly contain features of all three types: an individual of a particular level of skill is confronting a decision of a particular difficulty, with a given amount of time available to make the decision.

In our current domain, as in any other setting where the question of human error is relevant, there are a number of basic genres of question that we would like to ask. These include the following.

- For predicting whether an error will be committed in a given instance, which types of features (skill, time, or difficulty) yield the most predictive power?
- In which kinds of instances does greater skill confer the largest relative benefit? Is it for more difficult decisions (where skill is perhaps most essential) or for easier ones (where there is the greatest room to realize the benefit)? Are there particular kinds of instances where skill does not in fact confer an appreciable benefit?
- An analogous set of questions for time in place of skill: In which kinds of instances does greater time for the decision confer the largest benefit? Is additional time more beneficial for hard decisions or easy ones? And are there instances where additional time does not reduce the error rate?
- Finally, there are natural questions about the interaction of skill and time: is it higher-skill or lower-skill decision-makers who benefit more from additional time?

These questions motivate our analyses in the subsequent sections. We begin by discussing how features of all three types (skill, time, and difficulty) are well-represented in our domain.

Our data comes from two large databases of recorded chess games. The first is a corpus of approximately 200 million games from the Free Internet Chess Server (FICS), where amateurs play each other on-line[2]. The second is a corpus of approximately 1 million games played in international tournaments by the strongest players in the world. We will refer to the first of these as the FICS dataset, and the second as the GM dataset. (GM for "grandmaster," the highest title a chess player can hold.) For each corpus, we extract all occurrences of $\leq$6-piece positions from all of the games; we record the move made in the game from each occurrence of each position, and use a tablebase to evaluate all possible moves from the position (including the move that was made). This forms a single instance for our analysis. Since we are interested in studying errors, we exclude all instances in which the player to move is in a theoretically losing position — where the opponent has a direct path to checkmate — because there are no blunders in losing positions (the minimax value of the position is already as bad as possible for the player to move). There are 24.6 million (non-losing) instances in the FICS dataset, and 880,000 in the GM dataset.

We now consider how feature types (a), (b), and (c) are associated with each instance. First, for skill, each chess player in the data has a numerical rating, termed the *Elo rating*, based on their performance in the games they've played [8, 11]. Higher numbers indicate stronger players, and to get a rough sense of the range: most amateurs have ratings in the range 1000-2000, with extremely strong amateurs getting up to 2200-2400; players above 2500-2600 belong to a rarefied group of the world's best; and at any time there are generally about fewer than five people in the world above 2800. If we think of a game outcome in terms of points, with 1 point for a win and 0.5 points for a draw, then the Elo rating system has the property that when a player is paired with someone 400 Elo points lower, their expected game outcome is approximately 0.91 points — an enormous advantage.[3]

For our purposes, an important feature of Elo ratings is the fact that a single number has empirically proven so powerful at predicting performance in chess games. While ratings clearly cannot contain all the information about players' strengths and weaknesses, their effectiveness in practice argues that we can reasonably use a player's rating as a single numerical feature that approximately represents their skill.

With respect to temporal information, chess games are generally played under time limits of the form, "play x moves in y minutes" or "play the whole game in y minutes." Players can choose how they use this time, so on each move they face a genuine decision about how much of their remaining allotted time to spend. The FICS dataset contains the amount of time remaining in the game when each move was played (and hence the amount of time spent on each move as well); most of the games in the FICS dataset are played under extremely rapid time limits, with a large fraction of them requiring that the whole game be played in 3 minutes for each player. To avoid variation arising from the game duration, we focus on this large subset of the FICS data consisting exclusively of games with 3 minutes allocated to each side.

Our final set of features will be designed to quantify the difficulty of the position on the board — i.e. the extent to which it is hard to avoid selecting a move that constitutes a blunder. There are many ways in which one could do this, and we are guided in part by the goal of developing features that are less domain-specific and more applicable to decision tasks in general. We begin with perhaps the two most basic parameters, analogues of which would be present in any setting with discrete choices and a discrete notion of error — these are the number of legal moves in the position, and the number of these moves that constitute blunders. Later, we will also consider a general family of parameters that involve looking more deeply into the search tree, at moves beyond the immediate move the player is facing.

To summarize, in a single instance in our data, a player of a given rating, with a given amount of time remaining in the game, faces a specific position on the board, and we ask whether the move they select is a blunder. We now explore how our different types of

[2]This data is publicly available at ficsgames.org.

[3]In general, the system is designed so that when the rating difference is $400d$, the expected score for the higher-ranked player under the Elo system is $1/(1+10^{-d})$.

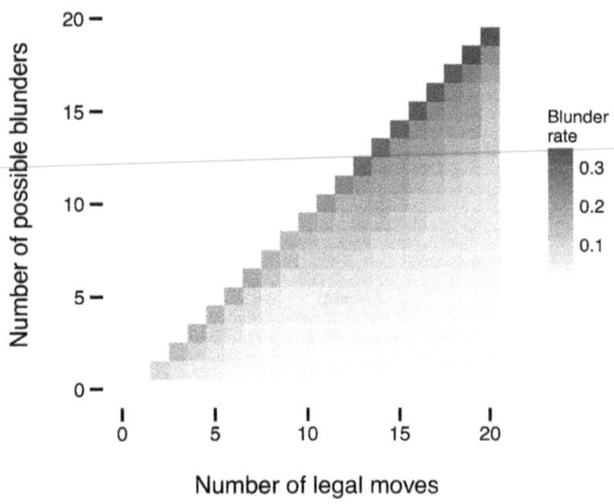

Figure 1: A heat map showing the empirical blunder rate as a function of the two variables $(n(P), b(P))$, for the FICS dataset.

features provide information about this question, before turning to the general problem of prediction.

3. FUNDAMENTAL DIMENSIONS

3.1 Difficulty

We begin by considering a set of basic features that help quantify the difficulty inherent in a position. There are many features we could imagine employing that are highly domain-specific to chess, but our primary interest is in whether a set of relatively generic features can provide non-trivial predictive value.

Above we noted that in any setting with discrete choices, one can always consider the total number of available choices, and partition these into the number that constitute blunders and the number that do not constitute blunders. In particular, let's say that in a given chess position P, there are $n(P)$ legal moves available — these are the possible choices — and of these, $b(P)$ are blunders, in that they lead to a position with a strictly worse minimax value. Note that it is possible to have $b(P) = 0$, but we exclude these positions because it is impossible to blunder. Also, by the definition of the minimax value, we must have $b(P) \leq n(P) - 1$; that is, there is always at least one move that preserves the minimax value.

A global check of the data reveals an interesting bimodality in both the FICS and GM datasets: positions with $b(P) = 1$ and positions with $b(P) = n(P) - 1$ are both heavily represented. The former correspond to positions in which there is a unique blunder, and the latter correspond to positions in which there is a unique correct move to preserve the minimax value. Our results will cover the full range of $(n(P), b(P))$ values, but it is useful to know that both of these extremes are well-represented.

Now, let us ask what the empirical blunder rate looks like as a bivariate function of this pair of variables $(n(P), b(P))$. Over all instances in which the underlying position P satisfies $n(P) = n$ and $b(P) = b$, we define $r(n, b)$ to be the fraction of those instances in which the player blunders. How does the empirical blunder rate vary in $n(P)$ and $b(P)$? It seems natural to suppose that for fixed $n(P)$, it should generally increase in $b(P)$, since there are more possible blunders to make. On the other hand, instances with $b(P) = n(P) - 1$ often correspond to chess positions in which the only non-blunder is "obvious" (for example, if there is only one way to recapture a piece), and so one might conjecture that the empirical blunder rate will be lower for this case.

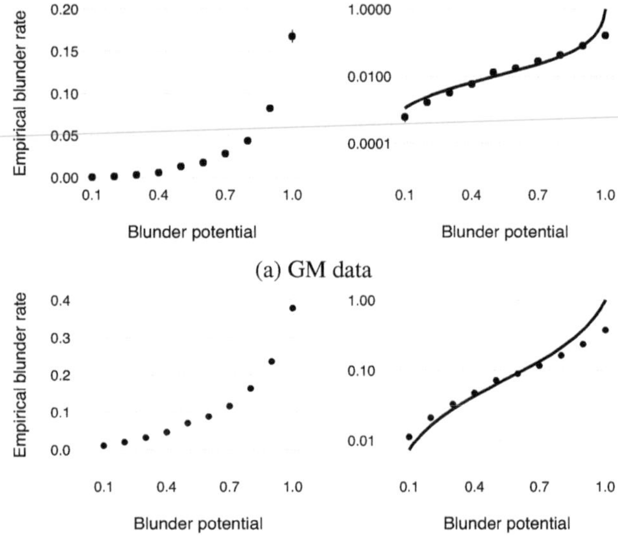

(a) GM data

(b) FICS data

Figure 2: The empirical blunder rate as a function of the blunder potential, shown for both the GM and the FICS data. On the left are standard axes, on the right are logarithmic y-axes. The plots on the right also show an approximate fit to the γ-value defined in Section 3.1.

In fact, the empirical blunder rate is generally monotone in $b(P)$, as shown by the heatmap representation of $r(n, b)$ in Figure 1. (We show the function for the FICS data; the function for the GM data is similar.) Moreover, if we look at the heavily-populated line $b(P) = n(P) - 1$, the blunder rate is increasing in $n(P)$; as there are more blunders to compete with the unique non-blunder, it becomes correspondingly harder to make the right choice.

Blunder Potential. Given the monotonicity we observe, there is an informative way to combine $n(P)$ and $b(P)$: by simply taking their ratio $b(P)/n(P)$. This quantity, which we term the *blunder potential* of a position P and denote $\beta(P)$, is the answer to the question, "If the player selects a move uniformly at random, what is the probability that they will blunder?". This definition will prove useful in many of the analyses to follow. Intuitively, we can think of it as a direct measure of the *danger* inherent in a position, since it captures the relative abundance of ways to go wrong.

In Figure 2 we plot the function $y = r(x)$, the proportion of blunders in instances with $\beta(P) = x$, for both our GM and FICS datasets on linear as well as logarithmic y-axes. The striking regularity of the $r(x)$ curves shows how strongly the availability of potential mistakes translates into actual errors. One natural starting point for interpreting this relationship is to note that if players were truly selecting their moves uniformly at random, then these curves would lie along the line $y = x$. The fact that they lie below this line indicates that in aggregate players are preferentially selecting non-blunders, as one would expect. And the fact that the curve for the GM data lies much further below $y = x$ is a reflection of the much greater skill of the players in this dataset, a point that we will return to shortly.

The γ-value. We find that a surprisingly simple model qualitatively captures the shapes of the curves in Figure 2 quite well. Suppose that instead of selecting a move uniformly at random, a player selected from a biased distribution in which they were preferen-

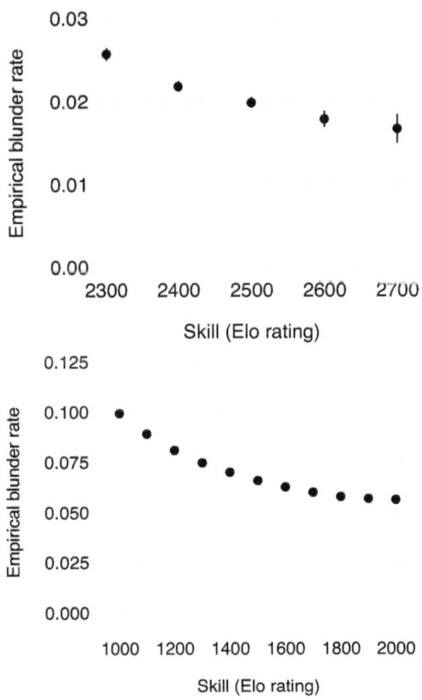

Figure 3: The empirical blunder rate as a function of player rating, shown for both the (top) GM and (bottom) FICS data.

tially c times more likely to select a non-blunder than a blunder, for a parameter $c > 1$.

If this were the true process for move selection, then the empirical blunder rate of a position P would be

$$\gamma_c(P) = \frac{b(P)}{c(n(P) - b(P)) + b(P)}.$$

We will refer to this as the *γ-value* of the position P, with parameter c. Using the definition of the blunder potential $\beta(P)$ to write $b(P) = \beta(P)n(P)$, we can express the γ-value directly as a function of the blunder potential:

$$\gamma_c(P) = \frac{\beta(P)n(P)}{c(n(P) - \beta(P)n(P)) + \beta(P)n(P)} = \frac{\beta(P)}{c - (c-1)\beta(P)}.$$

We can now find the value of c for which $\gamma_c(P)$ best approximates the empirical curves in Figure 2. The best-fit values of c are $c \approx 15$ for the FICS data and $c \approx 100$ for the GM data, again reflecting the skill difference between the two domains. These curves are shown superimposed on the empirical plot in the figure (on the right, with logarithmic y-axes).

We note that in game-theoretic terms the γ-value can be viewed as a kind of *quantal response* [20], in which players in a game select among alternatives with a probability that decreases according to a particular function of the alternative's payoff. Since the minimax value of the position corresponds to the game-theoretic payoff of the game in our case, a selection rule that probabilistically favors non-blunders over blunders can be viewed as following this principle. (We note that our functional form cannot be directly mapped onto standard quantal response formulations. The standard formulations are strictly monotonically decreasing in payoff, whereas we have cases where two different blunders can move the minimax value by different amounts — in particular, when a win changes to a draw versus a win changes to a loss — and we treat these the same in our simple formulation of the γ-value.)

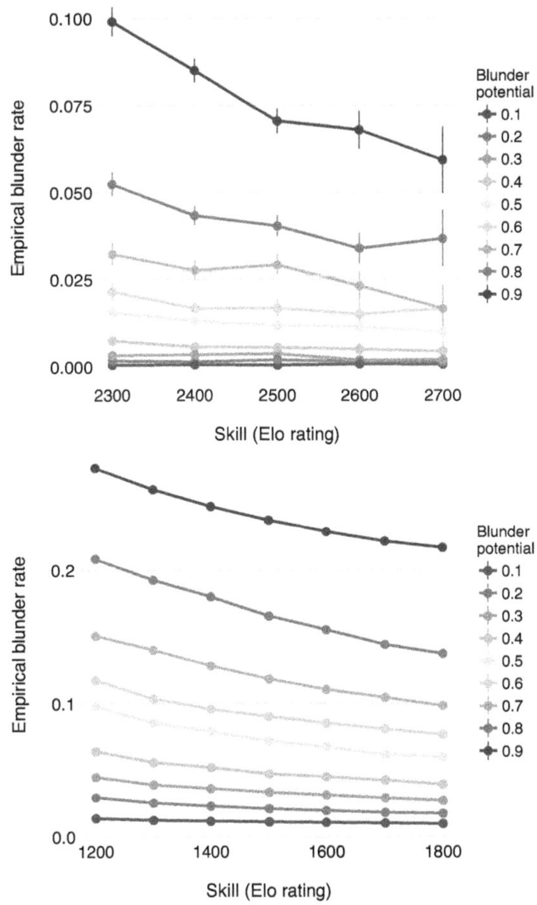

Figure 4: The empirical blunder rate as a function of Elo rating in the (top) GM and (bottom) FICS data, for positions with fixed values of the blunder potential.

3.2 Skill

A key focus in the previous subsection was to understand how the empirical blunder rate varies as a function of parameters of the instance. Here we continue this line of inquiry, with respect to the skill of the player in addition to the difficulty of the position.

Recall that a player's *Elo rating* is a function of the outcomes of the games they've played, and is effective in practice for predicting the outcomes of a game between two rated players [8]. It is for this reason that we use a player's rating as a proxy for their skill. However, given that ratings are determined by which games a player wins, draws, or loses, rather than by the extent to which they blunder in $\leq$6-piece positions, a first question is whether the empirical blunder rate in our data shows a clean dependence on rating.

In fact it does. Figure 3 shows the empirical blunder rate $f(x)$ averaged over all instances in which the player has rating x. The blunder rate declines smoothly with rating for both the GM and FICS data, with a flattening of the curve at higher ratings.

The Skill Gradient. We can think of the downward slope in Figure 3 as a kind of *skill gradient*, showing the reduction in blunder rate as skill increases. The steeper this reduction is in a given setting, the higher the empirical benefit of skill in reducing error.

It is therefore natural to ask how the skill gradient varies across different conditions in our data. As a first way to address this, we take each possible value of the blunder potential β (rounded to the

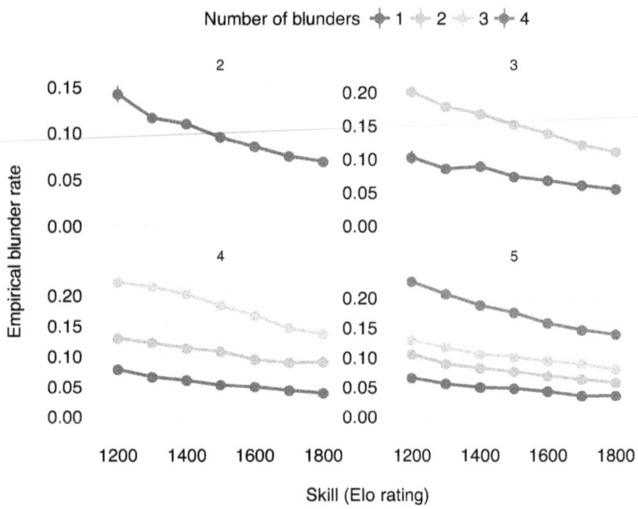

Figure 5: The empirical blunder rate as a function of Elo rating in the FICS data, for positions with fixed values of $(n(P), b(P))$.

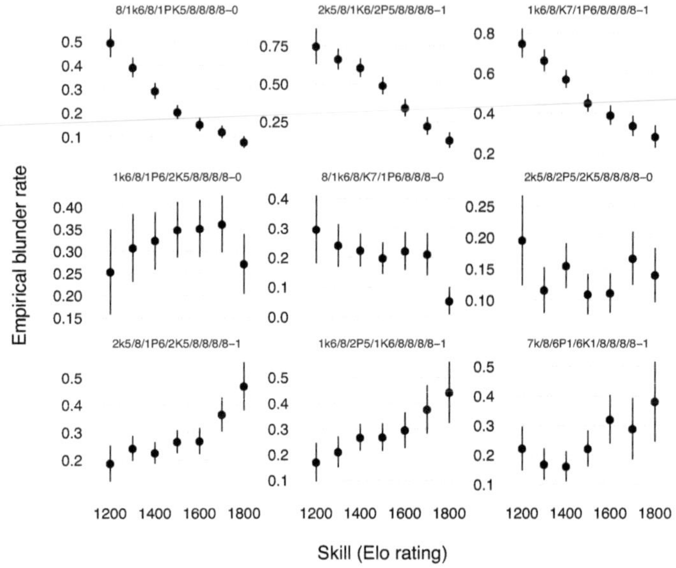

Figure 6: The empirical blunder rate as a function of Elo rating, for a set of frequently-occurring positions.

nearest multiple of 0.1), and define the function $f_\beta(x)$ to be the empirical error rate of players of rating x in positions of blunder potential β. Figure 4 shows plots of these curves for β equal to each multiple of 0.1, for both the GM and FICS datasets.

We observe two properties of these curves. First, there is remarkably little variation among the curves. When viewed on a logarithmic y-axis the curves are almost completely parallel, indicating the same rate of proportional decrease across all blunder potentials.

A second, arguably more striking, property is how little the curves overlap in their ranges of y-values. In effect, the curves form a kind of "ladder" based on blunder potential: for every value of the discretized blunder potential, every rating in 1200-1800 range on FICS has a lower empirical blunder rate at blunder potential β than the best of these ratings at blunder potential $\beta + 0.2$. In effect, each additional 0.2 increment in blunder potential contributes more, averaging over all instances, to the aggregate empirical blunder rate than an additional 600 rating points, despite the fact that 600 rating points represent a vast difference in chess performance. We see a similar effect for the GM data, where small increases in blunder potential have a greater effect on blunder rate than the enormous difference between a rating of 2300 and a rating of 2700. (Indeed, players rated 2700 are making errors at a greater rate in positions of blunder potential 0.9 than players rated 1200 are making in positions of blunder potential 0.3.) And we see the same effects when we separately fix the numerator and denominator that constitute the blunder potential, $b(P)$ and $n(P)$, as shown in Figure 5.

To the extent that this finding runs counter to our intuition, it bears an interesting relation to the *fundamental attribution error* — the tendency to attribute differences in people's performance to differences in their individual attributes, rather than to differences in the situations they face [13]. What we are uncovering here is that a basic measure of the situation — the blunder potential, which as we noted above corresponds to a measure of the *danger* inherent in the underlying chess position — is arguably playing a larger role than the players' skill. This finding also relates to work of Abelson on quantitative measures in a different competitive domain, baseball, where he found that a player's batting average accounts for very little of the variance in their performance in any single at-bat [1].

We should emphasize, however, that despite the strong effect of blunder potential, skill does play a fundamental role role in our domain, as the analysis of this section has shown. And in general it is important to take multiple types of features into account in any analysis of decision-making, since only certain features may be under our control in any given application. For example, we may be able to control the quality of the people we recruit to a decision, even if we can't control the difficulty of the decision itself.

The Skill Gradient for Fixed Positions. Grouping positions together by common $(n(P), b(P))$ values gives us a rough sense for how the skill gradient behaves in positions of varying difficulty. But this analysis still aggregates together a large number of different positions, each with their own particular properties, and so it becomes interesting to ask — how does the empirical blunder rate vary with Elo rating *when we fix the exact position on the board?*

The fact that we are able to meaningfully ask this question is based on a fact noted in Section 1, that many non-trivial $\leq$6-piece positions recur in the FICS data, exactly, several thousand times.[4] For each such position P, we have enough instances to plot the function $f_P(x)$, the rate of blunders committed by players of rating x in position P.

Let us say that the function $f_P(x)$ is *skill-monotone* if it is decreasing in x — that is, if players of higher rating have a lower blunder rate in position P. A natural conjecture would be that every position P is skill-monotone, but in fact this is not the case. Among the most frequent positions, we find several that we term *skill-neutral*, with $f_P(x)$ remaining approximately constant in x, as well as several that we term *skill-anomalous*, with $f_P(x)$ increasing in x. Figure 6 shows a subset of the most frequently occurring

[4]To increase the amount of data we have on each position, we cluster together positions that are equivalent by symmetry: we can apply a left-to-right reflection of the board, or we can apply a top-bottom reflection of the board (also reversing the colors of the pieces and the side to move), or we can do both. Each of the four resulting positions is equivalent under the rules of chess.

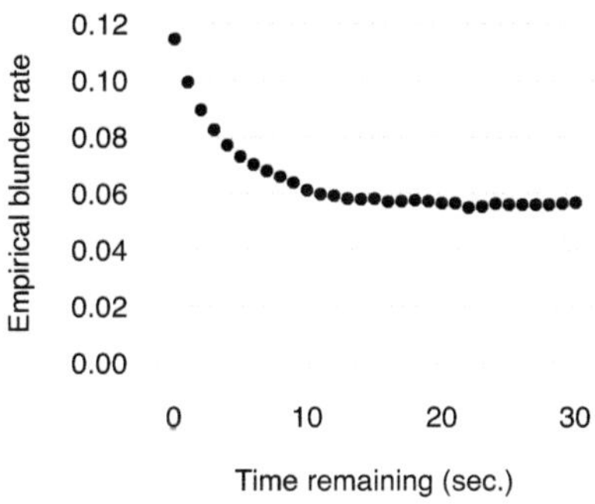

Figure 7: The empirical blunder rate as a function of time remaining.

positions in the FICS data that contains examples of each of these three types: skill-monotone, skill-neutral, and skill-anomalous.[5]

The existence of skill-anomalous positions is surprising, since there is a no *a priori* reason to believe that chess as a domain should contain common situations in which stronger players make more errors than weaker players. Moreover, the behavior of players in these particular positions does not seem explainable by a strategy in which they are deliberately making a one-move blunder for the sake of the overall game outcome. In each of the skill-anomalous examples in Figure 6, the player to move has a forced win, and the position is reduced enough that the worst possible game outcome for them is a draw under any sequence of moves, so there is no long-term value in blundering away the win on their present move.

3.3 Time

Finally, we consider our third category of features, the time that players have available to make their moves. Recall that players have to make their own decisions about how to allocate a fixed budget of time across a given number of moves or the rest of the game. The FICS data has information about the time remaining associated with each move in each game, so we focus our analysis on FICS in this subsection. Specifically, as noted in Section 2, FICS games are generally played under extremely rapid conditions, and for uniformity in the analysis we focus on the most commonly-occurring FICS time constraint — the large subset of games in which each player is allocated 3 minutes for the whole game.

As a first object of study, let's define the function $g(t)$ to be the empirical blunder rate in positions where the player begins considering their move with t seconds left in the game. Figure 7 shows a plot of $g(t)$; it is natural that the blunder rate increases sharply as t approaches 0, though it is notable how flat the value of $g(t)$ becomes once t exceeds roughly 10 seconds.

The Time Gradient. This plot in Figure 7 can be viewed as a basic kind of *time gradient*, analogous to the skill gradient, showing the overall improvement in empirical blunder rate that arises from having extra time available. Here too we can look at how the time gradient restricted to positions with fixed blunder potential, or fixed blunder potential and player rating.

We start with Figure 8, which shows $g_\beta(t)$, the blunder rate for players within a narrow skill range (1500-1599 Elo) with t seconds remaining in positions with blunder potential β. In this sense, it is a close analogue of Figure 4, which plotted $f_\beta(x)$, and for values of t above 8 seconds, it shows a very similar "ladder" structure in which the role of blunder potential is dominant. Specifically, for every β, players are blundering at a lower rate with 8 to 12 seconds remaining at blunder potential β than they are with over a minute remaining at blunder potential $\beta+0.2$. A small increase in blunder potential has a more extensive effect on blunder rate than a large increase in available time.

[5]For readers interested in looking at the exact positions in question, each position in Figure 6 is described in Forsyth-Edwards notation (FEN) above the panel in which its plot appears.

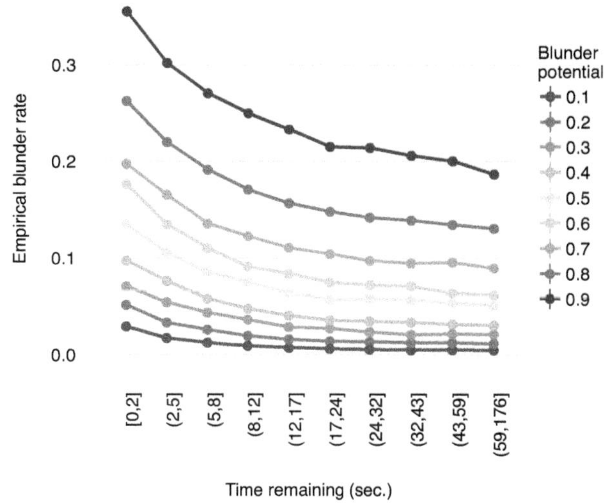

Figure 8: The empirical blunder rate as a function of the time remaining, for positions with fixed blunder potential values.

We can separate the instances further both by blunder potential and by the rating of the player, via the function $g_{\beta,x}(t)$ which gives the empirical blunder rate with t seconds remaining when restricted to players of rating x in positions of blunder potential β. Figure 9 plots these functions, with a fixed value of β in each panel. We can compare curves for players of different rating, observing that for higher ratings the curves are steeper: extra time confers a greater relative empirical benefit on higher-rated players. Across panels, we see that for higher blunder potential the curves become somewhat shallower: more time provides less relative improvement as the density of possible blunders proliferates. But equally or more striking is the fact that all curves retain a roughly constant shape, even as the empirical blunder rate climbs by an order of magnitude from the low ranges of blunder potential to the highest.

Comparing across points in different panels helps drive home the role of blunder potential even when considering skill and time simultaneously. Consider for example (a) instances in which players rated 1200 (at the low end of the FICS data) with 5-8 seconds remaining face a position of blunder potential 0.4, contrasted with (b) instances in which players rated 1800 (at the high end of the FICS data) with 42-58 seconds remaining face a position of blunder potential 0.8. As the figure shows, the empirical blunder rate is lower in instances of type (a) — a weak player in extreme time pressure is making blunders at a lower rate because they're dealing with positions that contain less danger.

Time Spent on a Move. Thus far we've looked at how the empirical blunder rate depends on the amount of time remaining in the game. However, we can also ask how the probability of a blunder varies with the amount of time the player actually spends considering their move before playing it. When a player spends more time on a move, should we predict they're less likely to blunder (because they gave the move more consideration) or more likely to blunder (because the extra time suggests they didn't know what do)?

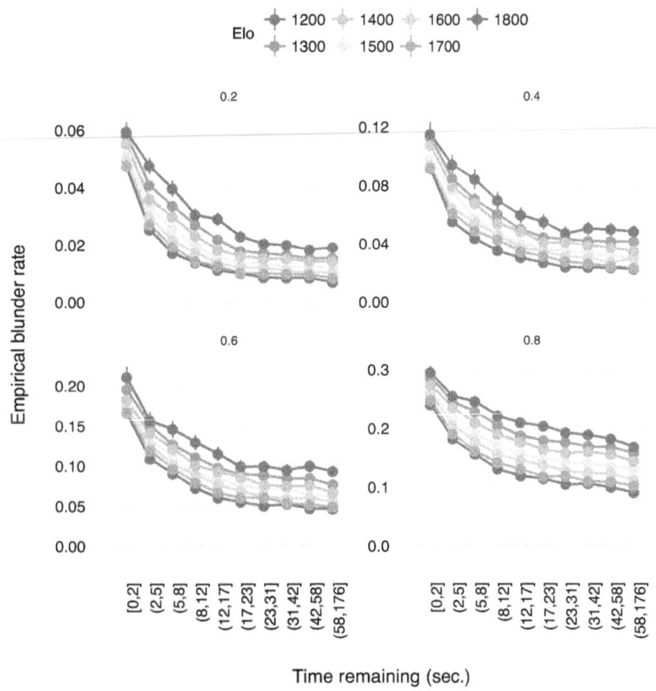

Figure 9: The empirical blunder rate as a function of time remaining, fixing the blunder potential and player rating.

The data turns out to be strongly consistent with the latter view: the empirical blunder rate is higher in aggregate for players who spend more time playing a move. We find that this property holds across the range of possible values for the time remaining and the blunder potential, as well as when we fix the specific position.

4. PREDICTION

We've now seen how the empirical blunder rate depends on our three fundamental dimensions: difficulty, the skill of the player, and the time available to them. We now turn to a set of tasks that allow us to further study the predictive power of these dimensions.

4.1 Greater Tree Depth

In order to formulate our prediction methods for blunders, we first extend the set of features available for studying the difficulty of a position. Once we have these additional features, we will be prepared to develop the predictions themselves.

Thus far, when we've considered a position's difficulty, we've used information about the player's immediate moves, and then invoked a tablebase to determine the outcome after these immediate moves. We now ask whether it is useful for our task to consider longer sequences of moves beginning at the current position. Specifically, if we consider all d-move sequences beginning at the current position, we can organize these into a *game tree* of depth d with the current position P as the root, and nodes representing the states of the game after each possible sequence of $j \leq d$ moves. Chess engines use this type of tree as their central structure in determining which moves to make; it is less obvious, however, how to make use of these trees in analyzing blunders by human players, given players' imperfect selection of moves even at depth 1.

Let us introduce some notation to describe how we use this information. Suppose our instance consists of position P, with n legal moves, of which b are blunders. We will denote the moves by $m_1, m_2, ..., m_n$, leading to positions $P_1, P_2, \ldots, P_n$ respectively, and we'll suppose they are indexed so that $m_1, m_2, \ldots, m_{n-b}$ are the non-blunders, and $m_{n-b+1}, \ldots, m_n$ are the blunders. We write T_0 for the indices of the non-blunders $\{1, 2, \ldots, n-b\}$ and T_1 for the indices of the blunders $\{n-b+1, \ldots, n\}$. Finally, from each position P_i, there are n_i legal moves, of which b_i are blunders.

The set of all pairs (n_i, b_i) for $i = 1, 2, \ldots, n$ constitutes a potentially useful source of information in the depth-2 game tree from the current position. What might it tell us?

First, suppose that position P_i, for $i \in T_1$, is a position reachable via a blunder m_i. Then if the blunder potential $\beta(P_i) = b_i/n_i$ is large, this means that it may be challenging for the opposing player to select a move that capitalizes on the blunder m_i made at the root position P; there is a reasonable chance that the opposing will instead blunder, restoring the minimax value to something larger. This, in turn, means that it may be harder for the player in the root position of our instance to see that move m_i, leading to position P_i, is in fact a blunder. The conclusion from this reasoning is that when the blunder potentials of positions P_i for $i \in T_1$ are large, it suggests a larger empirical blunder rate at P.

It is less clear what to conclude when there are large blunder potentials at positions P_i for $i \in T_0$ — positions reachable by non-blunders. Again, it suggests that player at the root may have a harder time correctly evaluating the positions P_i for $i \in T_0$; if they appear better than they are, it could lead the player to favor these non-blunders. On the other hand, the fact that these positions are hard to evaluate could also suggest a general level of difficulty in evaluating P, which could elevate the empirical blunder rate.

There is also a useful aggregation of this information, as follows. If we define $b(T_1) = \sum_{i \in T_1} b_i$ and $n(T_1) = \sum_{i \in T_1} n_i$, and analogously for $b(T_0)$ and $n(T_0)$, then the ratio $\beta_1 = b(T_1)/n(T_1)$ is a kind of aggregate blunder potential for all positions reachable by blunders, and analogously for $\beta_0 = b(T_0)/n(T_0)$ with respect to positions reachable by non-blunders.

In the next subsection, we will see that the four quantities $b(T_1)$, $n(T_1)$, $b(T_0)$, $n(T_0)$ indeed contain useful information for prediction, particularly when looking at families of instances that have the same blunder potential at the root position P. We note that one can construct analogous information at greater depths in the game tree, by similar means, but we find in the next subsection that these do not currently provide improvements in prediction performance, so we do not discuss greater depths further here.

4.2 Prediction Results

We develop three nested prediction tasks: in the first task we make predictions about an unconstrained set of instances; in the second we fix the blunder potential at the root position; and in the third we control for the exact position.

Task 1. In our first task we formulate the basic error-prediction problem: we have a large collection of human decisions for which we know the correct answer, and we want to predict whether the decision-maker will err or not. In our context, we predict whether the player to move will blunder, given the position they face and the various features of it we have derived, how much time they have to think, and their skill level. In the process, we seek to understand the relative value of these features for prediction in our domain.

We restrict our attention to the 6.6 million instances that occurred in the 320,000 empirically most frequent positions in the FICS dataset. Since the rate of blundering is low in general, we down-sample the non-blunders so that half of our remaining instances are blunders and the other half are non-blunders. This results in a balanced dataset with 600,000 instances, and we evaluate

Feature	Description
$\beta(P)$	Blunder potential ($b(P)/n(P)$)
$a(P), b(P)$	# of non-blunders, # of blunders
$a(T_0), b(T_0)$	# of non-blunders and blunders available to opponent following a non-blunder
$a(T_1), b(T_1)$	# of non-blunders and blunders available to opponent following a blunder
$\beta_0(P)$	Opponent's aggregate β after a non-blunder
$\beta_1(P)$	Opponent's aggregate β after a blunder
Elo, Opp-elo	Player ratings (skill level)
t	Amount of time player has left in game

Table 1: Features for blunder prediction.

Model	Accuracy
Random guessing	0.50
$\beta(P)$	0.73
D_1	0.73
D_2	0.72
$D_1 \cup D_2$	**0.75**
S	0.55
$S \cup D_1 \cup D_2$	**0.75**
$\{t\}$	0.53
$\{t\} \cup D_1 \cup D_2$	**0.75**
$S \cup \{t\} \cup D_1 \cup D_2$	**0.75**

Table 2: Accuracy results on Task 1.

model performance with accuracy. For ease of interpretation, we use both logistic regression and decision trees. Since the relative performance of these two classifiers is virtually identical, but decision trees perform slightly better, we only report the results using decision trees here.

Table 1 defines the features we use for prediction. In addition the notation defined thus far, we define: $S = \{\text{Elo}, \text{Opp-elo}\}$ to be the skill features consisting of the rating of the player and the opponent; $a(P) = n(P) - b(P)$ for the number of non-blunders in position P; $D_1 = \{a(P), b(P), \beta(P)\}$ to be the difficulty features at depth 1; $D_2 = \{a(T_0), b(T_0), a(T_1), b(T_1), \beta_0(P), \beta_1(P)\}$ as the difficulty features at depth 2 defined in the previous subsection; and t as the time remaining.

In Table 2, we show the performance of various combinations of our features. The most striking result is how dominant the difficulty features are. Using all of them together gives 0.75 accuracy on this balanced dataset, halfway between random guessing and perfect performance. In comparison, skill and time are much less informative on this task. The skill features S only give 55% accuracy, time left t yields 53% correct predictions, and neither adds predictive value once position difficulty features are in the model.

The weakness of the skill and time features is consistent with our findings in Section 3, but still striking given the large ranges over which the Elo ratings and time remaining can extend. In particular, a player rated 1800 will almost always defeat a player rated 1200, yet knowledge of rating is not providing much predictive power in determining blunders on any individual move. Similarly, a player with 10 seconds remaining in the entire game is at an enormous disadvantage compared to a player with two minutes remaining, but this too is not providing much leverage for blunder prediction at the move level. While these results only apply to our particular domain, it suggests a genre of question that can be asked by analogy in many domains. (To take one of many possible examples, one could similarly ask about the error rate of highly skilled drivers in difficult conditions versus bad drivers in safe conditions.)

Another important result is that most of the predictive power comes from depth 1 features of the tree. This tells us the immediate situation facing the player is by far the most informative feature.

Finally, we note that the prediction results for the GM data (where we do not have time information available) are closely analogous; we get a slightly higher accuracy of 0.77, and again it comes entirely from our basic set of difficulty features for the position.

Human Performance on a Version of Task 1. Given the accuracy of algorithms for Task 1, it is natural to consider how this compares to the performance of human chess players on such a task.

To investigate this question, we developed a version of Task 1 as a web app quiz and promoted it on two popular Internet chess forums. Each quiz question provided a pair of ≤6-piece instances with White to move, each showing the exact position on the board, the ratings of the two players, and the time remaining for each. The two instances were chosen from the FICS data with the property that White blundered in one of them and not the other, and the quiz question was to determine in which instance White blundered.

In this sense, the quiz is a different type of chess problem from the typical style, reflecting the focus of our work here: rather than "White to play and win," it asked "Did White blunder in this position?". Averaging over approximately 6000 responses to the quiz from 720 participants, we find an accuracy of 0.69, non-trivially better than random guessing but also non-trivially below our model's performance of 0.79.[6]

The relative performance of the prediction algorithm and the human forum participants forms an interesting contrast, given that the human participants were able to use domain knowledge about properties of the exact chess position while the algorithm is achieving almost its full performance from a single number – the blunder potential — that draws on a tablebase for its computation. We also investigated the extent to which the guesses made by human participants could be predicted by an algorithm; our accuracy on this was in fact lower than for the blunder-prediction task itself, with the blunder potential again serving as the most important feature for predicting human guesses on the task.

Task 2. Given how powerful the depth 1 features are, we now control for $b(P)$ and $n(P)$ and investigate the predictive performance of our features once blunder potential has been fixed. Our strategy on this task is very similar to before: we compare different groups of features on a binary classification task and use accuracy as our measure. These groups of features are: D_2, S, $S \cup D_2$, $\{t\}$, $\{t\} \cup D_2$, and the full set $S \cup \{t\} \cup D_2$. For each of these models, we have an accuracy score for every $(b(P), n(P))$ pair. The relative performances of the models are qualitatively similar across all $(b(P), n(P))$ pairs: again, position difficulty dominates time and rating, this time at depth 2 instead of depth 1. In all cases, the performance of the full feature set is best (the mean accuracy is 0.71), but D_2 alone achieves 0.70 accuracy on average. This further underscores the importance of position difficulty.

Additionally, inspecting the decision tree models reveals a very interesting dependence of the blunder rate on the depth 1 structure of the game tree. First, recall that the most frequently occurring positions in our datasets have either $b(P) = 1$ or $b(P) = n(P) - 1$. In so-called "only-move" situations, where there is only one move

[6]Note that the model performs slightly better here than in our basic formulation of Task 1, since there instances were not presented in pairs but simply as single instances drawn from a balanced distribution of positive and negative cases.

that is not a blunder, the dependence of blunder rate on D_2 is as one would expect: the higher the $b(T_1)$ ratio, the more likely the player is to blunder. But for positions with only one blunder, the dependence reverses: blunders are *less* likely with higher $b(T_1)$ ratios. Understanding this latter effect is an interesting open question.

Task 3. Our final prediction question is about the degree to which time and skill are informative once the position has been fully controlled for. In other words, once we understand everything we can about a position's difficulty, what can we learn from the other dimensions? To answer this question, we set up a final task where we fix the position completely, create a balanced dataset of blunders and non-blunders, and consider how well time and skill predict whether a player will blunder in the position or not. We do this for all 25 instances of positions for which there are over 500 blunders in our data. On average, knowing the rating of the player alone results in an accuracy of 0.62, knowing the times available to the player and his opponent yields 0.54, and together they give 0.63. Thus once difficulty has been completely controlled for, there is still substantive predictive power in skill and time, consistent with the notion that all three dimensions are important.

5. DISCUSSION

We have used chess as a model system to investigate the types of features that help in analyzing and predicting error in human decision-making. Chess provides us with a highly instrumented domain in which the time available to and skill of a decision-maker are often recorded, and, for positions with few pieces, the set of optimal decisions can be determined computationally.

Through our analysis we have seen that the inherent difficulty of the decision, even approximated simply by the proportion of available blunders in the underlying position, can be a more powerful source of information than the skill or time available. We have also identified a number of other phenomena, including the ways in which players of different skill levels benefit differently, in aggregate, from easier instances or more time. And we have found, surprisingly, that there exist *skill-anomalous* positions in which weaker players commit fewer errors than stronger players.

We believe there are natural opportunities to apply the paper's framework of skill, time, and difficulty to a range of settings in which human experts make a sequence of decisions, some of which turn out to be in error. In doing so, we may be able to differentiate between domains in which skill, time, or difficulty emerge as the dominant source of predictive information. Many questions in this style can be asked. For a setting such as medicine, is the experience of the physician or the difficulty of the case a more important feature for predicting errors in diagnosis? Or to recall an analogy raised in the previous section, for micro-level mistakes in a human task such as driving, we think of inexperienced and distracted drivers as a major source of risk, but how do these effects compare to the presence of dangerous road conditions?

Finally, there are a number of interesting further avenues for exploring our current model domain of chess positions via tablebases. One is to more fully treat the domain as a competitive activity between two parties. For example, is there evidence in the kinds of positions we study that stronger players are not only avoiding blunders, but also steering the game toward positions that have higher blunder potential for their opponent? More generally, the interaction of competitive effects with principles of error-prone decision-making can lead to a rich collection of further questions.

Acknowledgments. We thank Tommy Ashmore for valuable discussions on chess engines and human chess performance, the ficsgames.org team for providing the FICS data, Bob West for help with web development, and Ken Rogoff, Dan Goldstein, and Sébastien Lahaie for their very helpful feedback. This work has been supported in part by a Simons Investigator Award, an ARO MURI grant, a Google Research Grant, and a Facebook Faculty Research Grant.

6. REFERENCES

[1] R. Abelson. A variance explanation paradox: When a little is a lot. *Psych. Bulletin*, 97(1985).

[2] T. T. Biswas and K. W. Regan. Measuring level-k reasoning, satisficing, and human error in game-play data. In *IEEE Intl. Conf. on Machine Learning and Applications*, 2015.

[3] T. T. Biswas and K. W. Regan. Quantifying depth and complexity of thinking and knowledge. In *ICAART 2015*.

[4] N. Charness. The impact of chess research on cognitive science. *Psychological Research*, 54(1):4–9, 1992.

[5] W. G. Chase and H. A. Simon. Perception in chess. *Cognitive Science*, 4(1):55–81, Jan. 1973.

[6] A. de Groot. *Thought and Choice in Chess*. Mouton, 1965.

[7] A. Didierjean, V. Ferrari, and E. Marmèche. L'expertise cognitive au jeu d'echecs: Quoi de neuf depuis de groot (1946)? *L'annee Psychologique*, 104:771–793, 2004.

[8] A. Elo. *The Rating of Chess Players, Past and Present*. Ishi Press, 1978.

[9] R. Fine. *Basic Chess Endings*. McKay, 1941.

[10] D. F. Halpern and J. Wai. The world of competitive scrabble: Novice and expert differences in visuospatial and verbal abilities. *J. Expmtl. Psych: Appl*, 13(2007).

[11] R. Herbrich, T. Minka, and T. Graepel. Trueskill^{tm}: A Bayesian skill rating system. In *Proc. NIPS*, 2006.

[12] P. Jansen. Problematic positions and speculative play. In *Computers, Chess, and Cognition*, Springer, 1990.

[13] E. Jones, V. Harris. The attribution of attitudes. *J. Experimental Social Psych.*, 3(1967).

[14] B. Kirwan. Human reliability assessment. In *Encyclopedia of Quantitative Risk Analysis and Assessment*. Wiley, 2008.

[15] D. Kopec. Advances in man-machine play. In *Computers, Chess, and Cognition*, Springer, 1990.

[16] H. Lakkaraju, J. Kleinberg, J. Leskovec, J. Ludwig, and S. Mullainathan. Human decisions and machine predictions, 2016. Working paper.

[17] H. Lakkaraju, J. Leskovec, J. M. Kleinberg, and S. Mullainathan. A Bayesian framework for modeling human evaluations. In *Proc. SIAM Intl. Conf. on Data Mining*, 2015.

[18] Lomonosov tablebases. http://tb7.chessok.com.

[19] J. McCarthy. Chess as the drosophila of AI. In *Computers, Chess, and Cognition*, Springer, 1990.

[20] R. McKelvey and T. Palfrey. Quantal response equilibria for extensive form games. *Expmtl. Econ.*, 1:9–41, 1998.

[21] Nalimov tablebases. www.k4it.de/?topic=egtb&lang=en.

[22] M. Newborn. *Kasparov versus Deep Blue: Computer chess comes of age*. Springer, 1997.

[23] K. W. Regan and T. Biswas. Psychometric modeling of decision making via game play. In *IEEE Conference on Computational Inteligence in Games (CIG)*, 2013.

[24] G. Salvendy and J. Sharit. Human error. In *Handbook of Human Factors and Ergonomics*. John Wiley & Sons, 2006.

[25] H. A. Simon, editor. *Models of man, social and rational*. John Wiley & Sons, 1957.

[26] A. Tversky and D. Kahneman. Judgement under uncertainty: Heuristics and biases. *Science*, 185(4157):1124–1131, 1974.

Inferring Network Effects from Observational Data

David Arbour* darbour@cs.umass.edu
Dan Garant* dgarant@cs.umass.edu
David Jensen jensen@cs.umass.edu

College of Information and Computer Sciences
University of Massachusetts, Amherst

ABSTRACT

We present Relational Covariate Adjustment (RCA), a general method for estimating causal effects in relational data. Relational Covariate Adjustment is implemented through two high-level operations: identification of an adjustment set and relational regression adjustment. The former is achieved through an extension of Pearl's back-door criterion to relational domains. We demonstrate how this extended definition can be used to estimate causal effects in the presence of network interference and confounding. RCA is agnostic to functional form, and it can easily model both discrete and continuous treatments as well as estimate the effects of a wider array of network interventions than existing experimental approaches. We show that RCA can yield robust estimates of causal effects using common regression models without extensive parameter tuning. Through a series of simulation experiments on a variety of synthetic and real-world network structures, we show that causal effects estimated on observational data with RCA are nearly as accurate as those estimated from well-designed network experiments.

1. INTRODUCTION

Causal inference—estimating the effect of interventions—is central to data-driven decision making. Increased attention has been paid to randomized experimentation (A/B testing) as a method for causal inference [11, 3, 5, 6]. Recent work has extended randomized experimentation to the case of network interventions [27]. However, there are numerous circumstances where performing an experiment may be infeasible, expensive, or time-consuming.

Fortunately, a variety of methods have been devised for inferring causal effects from *observational* data. Classical methods for causal inference from observational data consist of two steps. First, an *adjustment set* [22] is identified, which consists of variables that are causally related to both the prospective cause variable (termed a *treatment*) and the potential effect variable (termed an *outcome*). Second, a procedure such as regression [21] or matching [24] is used to estimate the direct effect of treatment on outcome, correcting for the effects of the adjustment set. Extending this classical framework of estimation to relational data requires: (1) identifying adjustment sets in relational data, and (2) adjusting for the full range of the effects of those variables. Item 1 is primarily a structural question, and item 2 concerns estimation.

As a motivating example, consider the problem of estimating how a user-selected privacy setting influences the time that users spend interacting with an online social network. The privacy setting either requires users to explicitly approve others' posts to their page or it allows posting without such an approval process. Site administrators may be interested in changing the default privacy setting but want to ensure that such a change would not adversely affect site usage. Randomized experimentation on privacy settings may be controversial. Further, the propensity of users to share their posts with their friends could be influenced by characteristics of those friends. Figure 1 illustrates this example by indicating an implied correlation between social disposition and use of the privacy setting as well as a correlation between social disposition and time spent on site.

The task of adjusting for this confounding is particularly challenging because some confounding variables can be properties of neighbors in the friendship network. In Figure 1, the social disposition and privacy settings of Lucy, Sue, John, and Fred could affect both the privacy settings of Carl and the amount of time he spends on the site. The task of deciding how to set privacy policy is an intrinsically causal question because it requires reasoning about the effect that intervening on the privacy setting would have on site usage. Additionally, modeling *network effects* is of central importance—time on site is a function of the privacy settings of an entire sub-network of friends rather than the privacy setting of an individual.

In this paper, we present Relational Covariate Adjustment (RCA), the first reliable method for inferring arbitrary causal effects in networks from observational data. RCA uses a two-stage procedure. The first stage automatically identifies the set of variables that must be adjusted for. This stage uses relational d-separation [17], an extension of d-separation [22] to relational data. The second stage performs regression adjustment using relational non-parametric estimators. This adjustment procedure makes limited assumptions about the nature of the causal relationship between treatment and outcome. We provide theoretical guar-

*Equal contribution.

KDD '16, August 13-17, 2016, San Francisco, CA, USA

DOI: http://dx.doi.org/10.1145/2939672.2939791

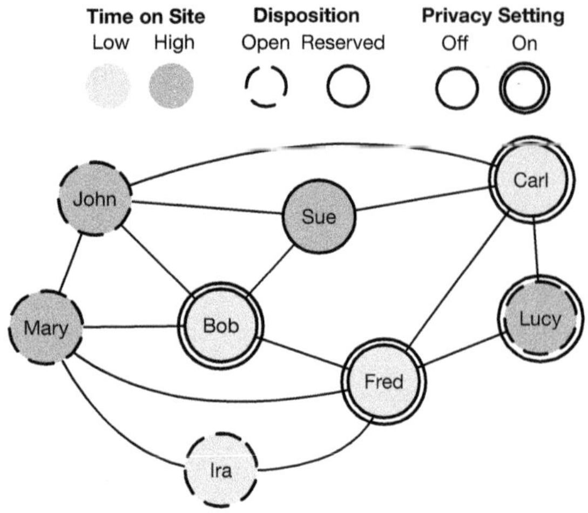

Figure 1: Social Network Privacy Example

antees showing that RCA produces a consistent estimate of causal effect.

The rest of the paper is structured as follows. Section 2 provides background for causal effect estimation and relational d-separation. Sections 3 and 4 introduce Relational Covariate Adjustment and discuss practical issues of implementation. Section 5 compares the estimates of RCA to estimates obtained via experimentation using multiple graph structures with data simulated under multiple functional forms, and shows that the performance of RCA can be competitive with experimental results.

2. PROBLEM SETUP

We assume that we are given an undirected graph $G = \langle V, E\rangle$. Let $N = |V|$, the number of vertices in the graph. Let T be a random variable composed of the treatment variables t_i of each node i in the network, so that $T = \langle t_1, t_2, \ldots, t_N\rangle$. Let $\boldsymbol{\pi}$ be an assignment to T, that is, $\boldsymbol{\pi} = \langle \pi_1, \pi_2, \ldots, \pi_N\rangle$, where π_i is an assignment to t_i. The *average causal effect* (ACE) is defined as the expected difference in outcome Y under treatment $\boldsymbol{\pi}$, contrasted with an alternate treatment $\boldsymbol{\pi}'$:

$$\text{ACE}(\boldsymbol{\pi}, \boldsymbol{\pi}') = E[Y|do(T = \boldsymbol{\pi})] - E[Y|do(T = \boldsymbol{\pi}')]. \quad (1)$$

Throughout the paper, we use the *do* operator [22] to refer to the interventional distribution, that is, the distribution that would arise due to manipulation of T rather than passive observation. Equation 1 may also be expressed in the potential outcomes framework [25] by regarding Y as a node-specific function of treatment. Ugander et al. [27] consider a special case of equation 1 where $\boldsymbol{\pi} = \vec{1}$ and $\boldsymbol{\pi}' = \vec{0}$. Hudgens and Halloran [9] refer to the above quantity as the *population average overall causal effect.*

Expressed directly in equation 1 is the notion that the outcome of subject i is a function of the entire treatment assignment vector, not only π_i. This distinction is critical for estimating network effects, as we now have a language to express interventions on multiple subjects. When dealing with causal quantities as in equation 1, it is common to assume that $E[Y|do(T = \boldsymbol{\pi})]$ is invariant with respect to treatment assignments to nodes which do not neighbor i. Let T_{nbr_i} denote the treatment variables of i's neighbors, and let $\boldsymbol{\pi}_{nbr_i} = \{\pi_j|\{i,j\} \in E\}$ and $\boldsymbol{\pi}'_{nbr_i}$ be multisets representing assignments to T_{nbr_i}. The neighborhood invariance assumption leads to the following reformulation of the average causal effect:

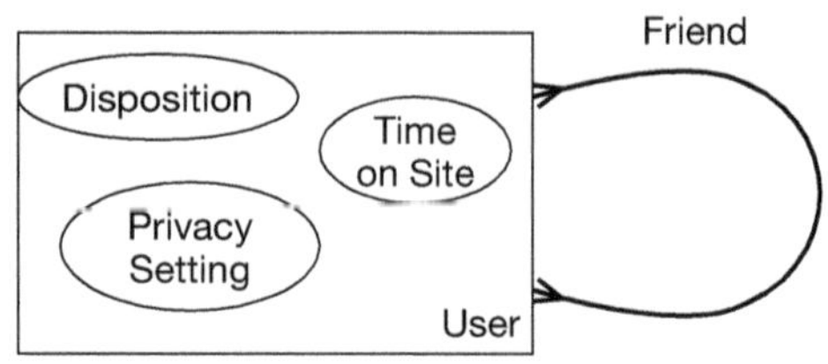

Figure 2: ER Diagram for Social Network Example

$$\text{ACE}(\boldsymbol{\pi}, \boldsymbol{\pi}') = \frac{1}{N}\sum_{i=1}^{N} E[Y|do(t_i = \pi_i, T_{nbr_i} = \boldsymbol{\pi}'_{nbr_i})]$$
$$-E[Y|do(t_i = \pi'_i, T_{nbr_i} = \boldsymbol{\pi}'_{nbr_i})]. \quad (2)$$

Equation 2 is consistent with the peer exposure models considered by Aronow et al. [2], Toulis and Kao [26], and the notion of effective treatments considered by Manski [18]. These causal quantities facilitate answering questions about interventional strategies including:

1. $E[Y|do(t_i = 1, T_{nbr_i} = \vec{1})] - E[Y|do(t_i = 0, T_{nbr_i} = \vec{0})]$: How would individual i's outcome change if i and its neighborhood were to be treated, as opposed to untreated? This quantity is the basis of $\text{ACE}(\vec{1}, \vec{0})$, the quantity considered by Ugander et al. [27] and Gui et al. [8].

2. $E[Y|do(t_i = 1, T_{nbr_i} = \vec{0})] - E[Y|do(t_i = 0, T_{nbr_i} = \vec{0})]$: How does subject i's expected outcome change if i is treated but no neighbors are treated? We might think of this effect as an "insulated" individual effect.

3. $E[Y|do(t_i = 0, T_{nbr_i} = \vec{1})] - E[Y|do(t_i = 0, T_{nbr_i} = \vec{0})]$: How does subject i's expected outcome change if i is left untreated but all neighbors are treated?

By considering different settings of $\boldsymbol{\pi}$ and $\boldsymbol{\pi}'$, we can examine a large number of possible intervention strategies, without being restricted to applying the same "type" of intervention to each node in the network. In practice, no single value of $\boldsymbol{\pi}$ could be used to apply interventions (2) and (3) in the list above to all nodes in the network. However, we can consider targeted interventions on specific individuals in the network, so it is useful to consider these effects.

3. RELATIONAL ADJUSTMENT SETS

We now briefly introduce the relational concepts necessary to describe Relational Covariate Adjustment, following the notation and terminology of Maier et al. [17, 16].

3.1 Relational Causal Graphical Models

Let a *relational schema* $\mathcal{S} = (\mathcal{E}, \mathcal{R}, \mathcal{A}, card)$ be the set of entity, relationship, and attribute classes of a domain. It includes a cardinality function that imposes constraints on the number of times an entity instance can participate in a relationship. Without loss of generality, we will focus our presentation on the case of a simple network, where there is a single entity, and a single many-to-many relationship, e.g. a social network. Continuing the example of Figure 1:

$$\mathcal{E} = \{\text{Users}\},$$
$$\mathcal{R} = \{\text{Friend}\},$$
$$\mathcal{A} = \{\text{time on site, disposition, privacy setting}\},$$
$$card(\text{Connected}) = \text{Many}.$$

Users are connected to potentially many other users, each of which has a time on site, disposition, and privacy setting attribute. Relational schemas are often visualized with entity-relationship diagrams as in Figure 2.

A *relational skeleton* is a partial instantiation of a relational schema that specifies the set of entity and relationship instances that exist in the domain. Using our online social network example, this corresponds to specific users and the friends that they connect to through the site. With a given schema, a *relational path* can be defined, which is a predicate that defines a path with respect to a schema. In our example, relational paths correspond to friendship paths, defined through the connectivity properties of the online social network. We will refer to variables with a trivial relational path (e.g., the immediate attributes of individuals), as *propositional variables*. *Relational variables* consist of a relational path and an attribute that can be reached through that path. For instance, the multiset of privacy settings for friends adjacent to user i is a relational variable. Relational variables can have causal dependencies defined between them, specified by a *relational model* $\mathcal{M} = (\mathcal{S}, \mathcal{D})$. This model consists of a collection of relational dependencies ($\mathcal{D}$) defined over a relational schema ($\mathcal{S}$). The relational model represents, as one example, the property that a user's time on site is affected by the privacy settings of adjacent users. $\mathcal{M}$ also specifies a parametrized conditional distribution of each relational variable given its parents. In the context of this work, we do not have access to these distributions and must estimate them from data.

To evaluate conditional independence queries on a model $\mathcal{M}$, we first construct an abstract ground graph (AGG) [17], a lifted representation that admits the computation of d-separation queries on multi-relational domains. Abstract ground graphs are defined from a given perspective, specifying a *base item* of the analysis, and include nodes that correspond to relational variables. In general, the construction of an AGG can involve creating auxiliary "intersection" variables. However, for the case of single-entity, single-relationship networks (e.g. social networks or simple communication networks) there exists a single AGG that can be represented without the use of auxiliary variables. That is:

PROPOSITION 1. *Given a model with a single entity single, relationship schema, the complete set of d-separation facts can be determined by considering only propositional variables and relational variables.*

The proof stems from a direct application of relational d-separation and is presented in the Appendix. The consequence of Proposition 1 is a relatively simple representation[1]. Within our running example there is a single perspective (person) and relational variables are defined with

[1]Relative to those required for multi-relational domains.

Notation	Meaning
$U_i^0.ToS$	The value of variable ToS for instance i of entity U. For instance, this could represent the time on site of user i.
$U_i^1.\mathbf{ToS}$	A multiset representing the value of variable ToS on instances related to instance i of entity U through a path of length 1. For instance, this could represent the time that friends of user i spend on the site. We can represent users that are friends with i's friends with the notation U_i^2, and so on.

Table 1: Relational Notation

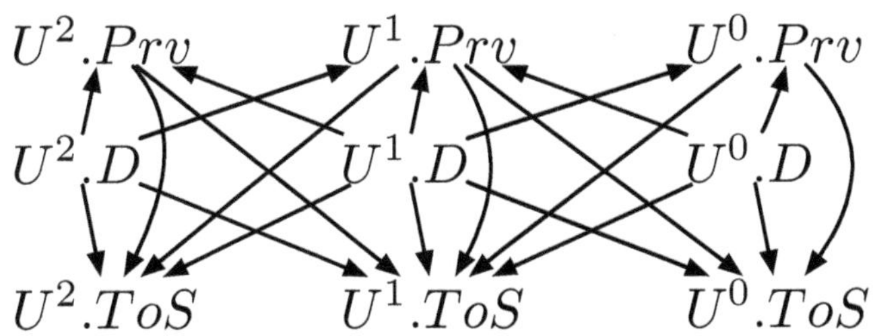

Figure 3: Abstract Ground Graph for the Social Network Example. In this example, each user's disposition ($U^0.D$) affects that user's privacy settings ($U^0.Prv$) and time on site ($U^0.ToS$). Further, the dispositions and privacy settings of a user's immediate peers ($U^1.D$ and $U^1.D$, respectively) affect that user's time on site. A user's privacy settings are also influenced by their peers' privacy settings. This structure repeats for U^2, representing friends of friends. Higher orders of U^p can be considered, but are not shown here.

respect to the relative distance to an individual (e.g. friends and friends of friends). One plausible abstract ground graph for this example is shown in Figure 3, in which the disposition and privacy settings of a person and her friends affect her time spent on site. Note that in Figure 3 there are two different types of variables present. Propositional variables are those preceded by U^0, and are measured on a single instance. Relational variables are named as U^i, for $i > 0$. These variables representing the values of a person's friends and the friends of her friends, respectively. Given the AGG, conditional independence facts can be computed directly using the same rules of d-separation used for Bayesian networks. For instance, from Figure 3, we can see that $U^2.Prv \perp\!\!\!\perp U^0.Prv | U^1.Prv$, because $U^1.Prv$ blocks all d-connecting pathways between the privacy settings of *friends of friends* and a user's time spent on site. These d-separation properties are essential to identifying a sufficient set of conditioning variables for a given causal query, discussed in more detail in the following section.

3.2 Relational Backdoor Criterion

With a suitable representation in hand, we now turn to the core aim of this work: identifying interventional distributions. The approach taken here is to use an extension of the *back-door criterion* [22] to relational domains:

DEFINITION 1. *(Relational Back-Door Criterion) A set of variables* $\mathbf{C}$ *satisfies the* relational back-door criterion *with respect to variable sets* (X_1, X_2) *in an AGG G if:*

1. *No node in* $\mathbf{C}$ *is a descendant of any node in* X_1 *in the AGG (equivalently, no node in* $\mathbf{C}$ *is a post-treatment variable); and*

2. $\mathbf{C}$ *blocks every back-door path between* X_1 *and* X_2 *in the AGG*

Note that here a *back-door path* refers to a path with an arrow into a member of X_1. Definition 1 is a direct extension to relational data of the back-door criterion presented by Pearl [22]. In the case of a single entity with no relationships, the definition reduces to the propositional case.

When such a set $\mathbf{C}$ can be identified, an estimate of the interventional distribution can be obtained through a simple application of the adjustment formula:

$$P(X_2|do(X_1{=}x)) = \int_c P(Y|X_1{=}x, \mathbf{C}{=}c)\mathrm{d}P(\mathbf{C}{=}c) \quad (3)$$

Then, average causal effects can be computed as follows:

$$\begin{aligned} ACE &= E[X_2|do(X_1 = x)] - E[X_2|do(X_1 = x')] \quad (4)\\ &= \int_c yP(X_2|X_1 = x, \mathbf{C} = c)\mathrm{d}P(\mathbf{C} = c)\\ &- \int_c yP(X_2|X_1 = x', \mathbf{C} = c)\mathrm{d}P(\mathbf{C} = c), \quad (5)\end{aligned}$$

where P represent either a probability density or probability mass function. Semantically, because relational variables take on values that may be multisets, there is a notion of *exhangeability* encoded in this estimation framework. Consider once again the example of Figure 1. In this case, Sue has three neighbors, John, Bob and Carl. Let $U^1_{\text{Sue}}.\mathbf{Prv}$ represent the multiset of time on site values of these neighbors (see Table 1). As presented, $U^1_{\text{Sue}}.\mathbf{Prv}$ takes on the value {On, On, Off}. Intervention on Carl or Bob's privacy setting would yield the interventional regime $do(U^1_{\text{Sue}}.\mathbf{Prv} =$ {On, Off, Off}). As such, our interventional language is invariant with respect to the *identities* of the instances under intervention, and focuses strictly on the variables measurable on those entities.

3.2.1 Connection to Network Experimentation

There is a close relationship between Relational Covariate Adjustment and the adjustments performed for peer-effects in the network experimentation literature (c.f., [2, 27, 8]). Given this connection, we discuss this relationship for readers familiar with network experimentation. Current work in network experimentation are described within the potential-outcomes framework and assume *strong ignorability*, i.e., that (1) the outcome is rendered independent of treatment given treatment status and (2) that all instances have a treatment probability, $p \in (0, 1)$. Within non-network experiments condition (1) is trivially satisfied via randomization. However, even in the simple network setting there is dependence between other treatments and an individual's outcome. Further, by virtue of network randomization designs (i.e., [27, 8]), dependence is induced between the treatment status of instances. This dependence is depicted in Figure 4. The graphical view shows that simple use of Relational Covariate Adjustment can be applied to adjust for network bias, with $U^1.Prv$ constituting the adjustment set. Thus, the estimator of Gui et al. [8] can be seen as a special case of Relational Covariate Adjustment, with an assumed dependence structure of Figure 4 and adjustment performed with a linear model. However, in contrast to current network experimentation estimation methods, Relational Covariate Adjustment can be applied easily to observational data with multi-valued and continuous treatments and an arbitrary number of confounders without modification.

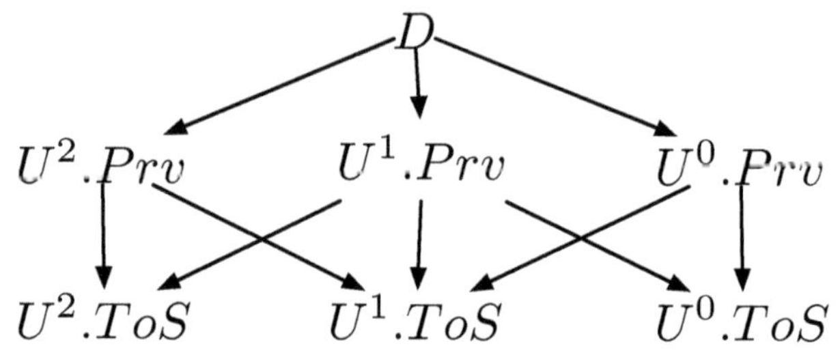

Figure 4: An abstract ground graph representing the dependence structure under network experiment. This structure is similar to 3, except that disposition no longer influences privacy settings, and is excluded from the diagram. A variable D representing the experimental design may induce marginal dependence between treatments. It is possible that the outcome of peers ($U^1.ToS$) affects $U^0.ToS$, but including $U^1.Prv$ in a conditioning set is sufficient to satisfy the back-door criterion for treatment $U^0.Prv$.

4. EMPIRICAL ESTIMATION

We now discuss how to practically estimate the effects of interventions in relational domains. In contrast to the non-relational setting, computing the adjustment formula in equation 5 is not straightforward because the hypothetical values of X_1 could be multisets. We present a strategy for conditioning on multisets that does not make strong assumptions about functional form. Algorithm 1 presents the procedure. Step 1 identifies the adjustment set by using relational *d*-seperation to find the necessary set of variables $\mathbf{C}$ to block all back-door paths between T and Y.

The causal effect is then estimated as

$$\mathbb{E}[Y|do(T = t)] = \int_C yP(Y = y|T = t, \mathbf{C} = c)\mathrm{d}P(\mathbf{C} = c) \quad (6)$$

$$\approx \frac{1}{N}\sum_{i=1}^{N} y_i P(Y = y_i|T = t, \mathbf{C} = c_i) \quad (7)$$

$$= \frac{1}{N}\sum_{i=1}^{N} E[Y|T = t, \mathbf{C} = c_i], \quad (8)$$

where equation 7 is a Monte-Carlo approximation to the integral. $E[Y|T = t, \mathbf{C} = c_i]$ can be estimated from a regression of y on features T and $\mathbf{C}$.

4.1 Calculating Network Effects

Algorithm 1 can be applied to estimate a variety of causal effects derived from the definition presented in equation 2. In what follows, $U^0.T$ refers to a subject's treatment and $U^1.T$ refers to the treatments of immediate neighbors.

Algorithm 1: `RelationalAdjustment`

Input: Relational model $\mathcal{M}$, outcome Y, treatment(s) X

Output: $h(x) = \sum_{i=1}^{N} E[Y|do(X=x)]$

1 Use relational d-separation to identify adjustment set $\mathbf{C}$ for causal effect of X on Y

2 Estimate $E[Y|X, \mathbf{C}]$ via regression or classification

3 $h(x) = \sum_{i=1}^{N} E[Y|X=x, \mathbf{C}=\mathbf{c}_i]$

4 **return** $h(x)$

Marginal Individual Effect

$$h = \texttt{RelationalAdjustment}(\mathcal{M}, U^0.Y, U^0.T)$$
$$h(1)-h(0) = E[U^0.Y|do(U^0.T=1)] - E[U^0.Y|do(U^0.T=0)] \quad (9)$$

This effect represents the expected change in an arbitrary subject's outcome, $U^0.Y$, when considering two alternate settings of that subject's treatment, $U^0.T$ (1 and 0). The function h represents the expected outcome when applying a hypothetical intervention to $U^0.T$, conditioning on $\mathbf{C}$. Additionally, the treatment assignment of peers, $U^1.T$, can influence both $U^0.T$ and $U^0.Y$, which requires including peer treatment values in the set of confounders, i.e, $U^1.T \in \mathbf{C}$.

Marginal Peer Effect

$$h = \texttt{RelationalAdjustment}(\mathcal{M}, Y, U^1.T)$$
$$h(\theta)-h(\theta') = E[U^0.Y|do(U^1.T=\theta)] - E[U^0.Y|do(U^0.T=\theta')] \quad (10)$$

The above case concerns the causal effect of settings of the treatment assignments of peers, $U^1.T$. θ and θ' are multisets consisting of the treatment values of neighbors. For instance, in the context of Figure 1, $\theta_{\text{Sue}} = \{\text{On}, \text{On}, \text{Off}\}$. We could consider altering the treatment of Sue's neighborhood to $\theta'_{\text{Sue}} = \{\text{Off}, \text{Off}, \text{On}\}$. The effect of the intervention is given by $h(\theta_{\text{Sue}}) - h(\theta'_{\text{Sue}})$. This formulation facilitates the estimation of arbitrary treatment settings of a node's neighborhood.

Total Effect

$$h = \texttt{RelationalAdjustment}\big(\mathcal{M}, Y, (U^0.T, U^1.T)\big)$$
$$h(1, \vec{1}) - h(0, \vec{0}) = E[U^0.Y|do(U^0.T=1, U^1.T=\vec{1})] - E[U^0.Y|do(U^0.T=0, U^1.T=\vec{0})] \quad (11)$$

This effect represents an intervention on both $U^0.T$ and $U^1.T$. The adjustment procedure is valid for simultaneous interventions on these variables because the back-door criterion (Definition 1) applies to *sets* of variables. Now, h is a function of two variables, the hypothetical intervention to $U^0.T$ and the hypothetical intervention to $U^1.T$. The first argument to h is, in the case of binary treatments, 0 or 1. The second argument to h is a multiset. This class of effects is most applicable to estimation of applying an intervention to all individuals on a network, e.g., a site-wide feature rollout.

4.2 Summarizing Relational Features

When any term in the adjustment equation is a relational variable, $E[Y|T, \mathbf{C}]$ cannot be directly estimated using regression or classification estimators designed for independent and identically distributed data because relational variables' instances consist of multisets rather than single observations. A common approach to address this is to create aggregations to succinctly represent the sets with a small number of real-valued features. There is a long history in statistical relational learning of using user-specified aggregation functions to model the distribution of a relational variable [12, 23]. While these approaches have yielded impressive results for the task of prediction, causal inference requires stronger guarantees about what is being captured by the aggregation functions. The aggregation function should be a sufficient statistic of the underlying distribution of the variable, rendering model parameters independent of the data. For instance, specifying the `mean` aggregation would be sufficient if the values of a relational variable are Poisson distributed, and in the case of a normal distribution, the `variance` aggregation must also be present. When sufficient statistics are employed, then we can be confident that *all relevant aspects* of the distribution of a set have been accounted for when marginalizing to compute the interventional distribution. When assumptions can be made about the marginal distribution of relational variables, a set of features can be constructed for regression by taking the sufficient statistics for each instance of a relational variable. Once this set is constructed, any consistent regression or classification model can be used to estimate $E[Y|T, \mathbf{C}]$. In the absence of known sufficient statistics, estimates of a number of the moments of a distribution can be used as an approximate solution. We assume that the sufficient statistics S_x of the true distribution can be described as a function of its k-th order moments:

$$S_x = f(M_1(X), \ldots, M_k(X))$$

where $M_k(X) = \frac{\sum_i^N X_i^k}{N} \approx \int x^k \hat{p}(x)dx$ is the empirical estimate of the k-th moment of X. This implies the following procedure: (1) for each relational variable generate a set of k aggregates of the $1, \ldots, k$ moments of the set, (2) use this new data set as the features to a non-linear regression or classification model to estimate $E[Y|T, \mathbf{C}]$.

5. EXPERIMENTS

In this section we evaluate whether, and under which circumstances, Relational Covariate Adjustment can serve as a feasible alternative to experimentation for causal inference. To that end, we constructed an evaluation suite to compare RCA to state-of-the-art techniques for estimating causal effects from experiments. We provided experimental techniques with *experimental* data, and we provided RCA-data with more challenging data sets in which relational confounding variables are present. We examined a variety of real and synthetic networks, using simulated data with multiple functional relationships between treatment and outcome.

5.1 Synthetic Data Generation

Data generation process was performed as follows:

1. Generate a random network

2. Sample treatment using one of two regimes:
   (a) Exp: Sample treatment from an experimental context, in which treatment is assigned using a graph clustering technique
   (b) Obs: Sample treatment as a function of confounding variables and possibly treatments of neighbors in the network
3. Sample outcome according to the treatment assigned in step (2). In the Obs regime, outcome is a function of confounding variables and treatment. In the Exp regime, outcome is a function of treatment assignments.

In both the Obs regime and the Exp regime, the task is identical: estimate the relationship between treatments (individual and those of peers) and outcomes. We compared the performance of models learned from the observational data to estimates obtained by experimentation[2].

5.1.1 Synthetic networks

We considered two network structures in our synthetic experiments: small-world networks and preferential attachment networks. For small-world networks, each node has degree (in+out) of 10 in the initial lattice. We varied the rewiring probability in $\{0, 0.01, 0.1, 0.15\}$. A rewiring probability of 0 results in a regular lattice, and a rewiring probability of 1 results in a random (Erdős-Rényi) network. For preferential attachment networks, we varied the power of the attachment in $\{0.1, 0.5, 1\}$. In all cases, the synthetic networks we consider have 1024 nodes.

Each network has a simple relational model consisting of a single entity (U) and relationship (adjacency). Each instance of U (i.e., a node in the network) has four attributes, C_1, C_2, T, and Y. We are interested in estimating the effects of $U^0.T$ (intrinsic treatment) and $U^1.T$ (treatment of peers) on $U^0.Y$ (intrinsic outcome).

5.1.2 Treatment Models

In the Obs regime, propensity for treatment can be caused by intrinsic covariates, covariates of peers, and treatments of peers. To simulate data from that regime, we first constructed a confounding term L_i which is a linear combination of:

- $U^0.C_1$
- $U^0.C_2$
- $\mathtt{mean}(U^1.C_1)$
- $\mathtt{mean}(U^1.C_2)$
- $\mathtt{var}(U^1.C_1)$
- $\mathtt{var}(U^1.C_2)$
- $\mathtt{mean}(U^1.C_1) * \mathtt{var}(U^1.C_1)$
- $\mathtt{mean}(U^1.C_2) * \mathtt{var}(U^1.C_2)$

Then, treatment is sampled as a binomial random variable with success probability that is a logistic function of L_i. To simulate influence between the treatments of subject i and its neighbors, we use a Gibbs sampling technique inspired by Manski [18]. After initially assigning treatment, we resample treatment with an additional parameter $\theta_{nbr_i,s-1}$, the proportion of i's neighbors that are treated at the previous iteration. This process is repeated until $s = 3$.

$$T_{i,0} \sim \mathit{Binom}\left(\mathit{logistic}\left(\beta_L L_i + \epsilon\right)\right) \quad (12)$$

$$T_{i,s} \sim \mathit{Binom}\left(\mathit{logistic}\left(\beta_L L_i + \beta_T \theta_{nbr_i,s-1} + \epsilon\right)\right) \quad (13)$$

Here, $\epsilon \sim \mathcal{N}(0, 1)$. We vary the strength of the confounding coefficient, β_L, from 0 to 3. We vary the strength of dependence on peers' treatments, β_T, from 0 to 10. When $\beta_T = 2$, we find that the distribution of peer treatment proportions, θ_{nbr_i}, is roughly uniform. When $\beta_T = 10$, this distribution is bi-modal with peaks at 0 and 1.

In the Exp regime, treatment was assigned randomly (with probability 0.5) at the level of *graph clusters* rather than individuals using a technique outlined by Ugander *et al.* [27]. This clustering technique assigns treatment in such a way that nodes are more likely to have completely treated or completely untreated neighborhoods. In other words, graph cluster randomization leads to bi-modal distributions of θ_{nbr_i} with peaks at 0 and 1. This randomization technique is employed by experimental estimators to estimate the total effect of equation 11.

5.1.3 Outcome Models

We explored the use of three distinct outcome forms. In the first case, outcome is a linear function of individual treatment, the proportion of treated peers, θ_{adj_i}, confounding variables L_i, with noise that is distributed as a standard normal. The general form of this function is shown below in equation 14. The relationship between the θ_{adj_i} and outcome is shown in Figure 5b for a specific parameter setting.

$$Y_i \sim \beta_I T_i + \beta_P \theta_{nbr_i} + \beta_L L_i + \epsilon \quad (14)$$

We also considered non-linear functions of treatment and covariates. The first of these is shown in equation 15, and is a sigmoid function of T_i, θ_{nbr_i}, and L_i. Figure 5a shows one instance of this function class. This function is bounded in the range $(0, 1)$. As β_I and β_P grow, the outcome approaches 1 more sharply.

$$Y_i \sim (1 + \exp\left(-\left(2\beta_I T_i + 2\beta_P \theta_{nbr_i} + \beta_L L_i + \epsilon\right)\right))^{-1} \quad (15)$$

The final outcome model we use is linear in T_i and L_i, but depends on θ_{nbr_i} through a radial basis function about 0.5. An instance of this function can be seen in Figure 5c. In this case, the outcome peaks when $\theta_{nbr_i} = 0.5$.

$$Y_i \sim \beta_I T_i + \exp\left(-\left(\beta_P \theta_{nbr_i} - 0.5\right)^2\right) + \beta_L L_i + \epsilon \quad (16)$$

In what follows, we refer to the functions outlined in equations 14, 15, and 16 as *linear*, *sigmoid*, and *RBF*, respectively.

5.2 Estimators

In practice, any consistent conditional estimator of $E[Y|T, \theta_{nbr_i}, \mathbf{C}]$ will satisfy the requirements of the relational adjustment technique, provided $\mathbf{C}$ satisfies the relational back-door criterion. For our experiments, we used gradient boosted trees (GBMs) to model this expectation, where $\mathbf{C}$ consists of the means and variances of $U^1.C_1$ and $U^1.C_2$.

Gradient boosted trees [7] are a nonparametric ensemble where each base learner is a low-depth decision tree. At each iteration training samples are reweighted according to their predictive error on the previous iteration. The boosting procedure has been shown to be consistent [7], and provides near state-of-the-art results on a variety of tasks.

We employed two experimental effect estimators within the Exp regime, Horvitz-Thompson estimation [27] and a linear additive model [8]. The Horvitz-Thompson estimator can be written as a weighted sum of outcomes of nodes which fall into two distinct exposure categories. We defined a node i as "exposed" if $T_i = 1$ and $\theta_{nbr_i} > 0.75$. We defined a node

[2]Code used to reproduce these experiments is available at https://github.com/darbour/RelationalAdjustment

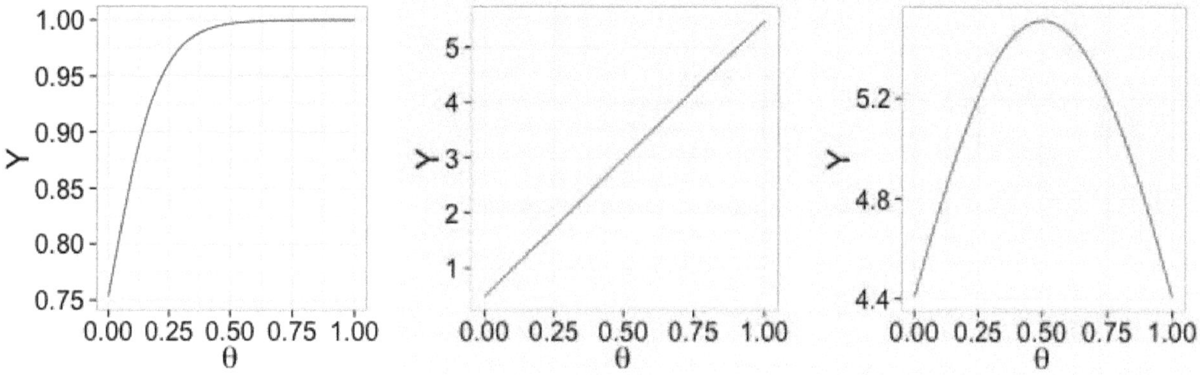

(a) Sigmoid, $\beta_P = 10$ (b) Linear, $\beta_P = 5$ (c) RBF, $\beta_P = 5$

Figure 5: Examples of outcome models considered in this work, shown here as a function of the proportion of treated friends.

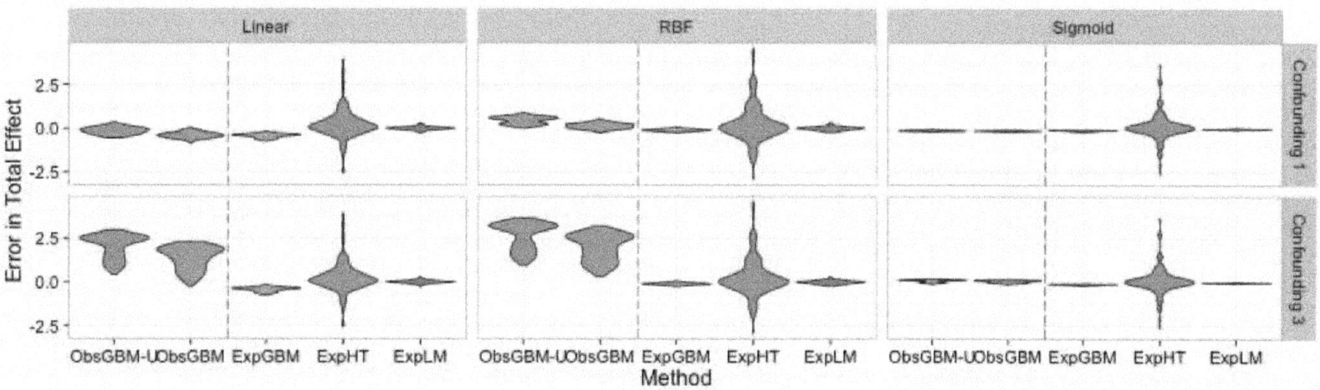

Figure 6: Accuracy of experimental and observational effect estimates across various outcome models as confounding strength is varied.

as "non-exposed" if $T_i = 0$ and $\theta_{nbr_i} < 0.25$. Nodes which do not fall into one of these categories are not used in the estimation process.

$$\frac{1}{N}\sum_{i=1}^{N}\frac{Y_i\mathbb{I}(\theta_{nbr_i} > 0.75, T_i = 1)}{P(\theta_{nbr_i} > 0.75, T_i = 1)} - \frac{Y_i\mathbb{I}(\theta_{nbr_i} < 0.25, T_i = 0)}{P(\theta_{nbr_i} < 0.25, T_i = 0)}.$$

The probabilities in the denominator are estimated using the dynamic programming algorithm introduced by Ugander et al. [27]. This method is useful primarily when the effect of interest is the total effect and the distribution of θ_{nbr_i} is bimodal with peaks at 0 and 1. We refer to this estimation strategy as `ExpHT`.

The linear additive model introduced by Gui et al. [8] fits the conditional expectation $E[Y|T, \theta_{nbr_i}]$, which is appropriate when treatment is assigned experimentally and outcome is a linear model. We refer to this model as `ExpLM`.

It is important to note that, for both `ExpHT` and `ExpLM`, the results reported are with respect to a performed experiment. This is contrast to the setting of Relational Covariate Adjustment, which is given access *only* to observational data, without the benefit of randomization.

5.3 Findings

For each combination of parameter settings, spanning rewiring probability, β_I (individual effect), β_P (peer effect), β_L (confounding strength), and β_T (treatment auto-correlation), we performed 25 trials to assess variance. This resulted in $2269 \times 25 = 56{,}725$ datasets, some belonging to the experimental regime (`Exp`) and some belonging to the observational regime (`Obs`). Within the experimental regime, we estimated total effect using `ExpHT` and `ExpLM`, the current state-of-the-art techniques for effect estimation on networks. Within the observational regime, we used the Relational Covariate Adjustment procedure with gradient boosted trees. This is referred to as `ObsGBM` in what follows. We also include results for an unadjusted GBM which does not include any relational covariates. We refer to this model as `ObsGBM-U`.

Accuracy of the total causal effect estimates for the linear outcome model are shown in Figure 7. Each box in this figure represents the distribution of performance values across all network settings and model parameterizations. These results indicate that the `ExpLM` model performs best in this context, with `ExpHT` yielding slightly more bias and significantly more variance. However, in the observational case, which is a more complex estimation task, the Relational Covariate Adjustment implementation, `ObsGBM` is competitive with the linear model in terms of bias, and yields only slightly more variance than the HT estimator.

We also examined the performance of these models across a variety of outcome functions. The error in total causal ef-

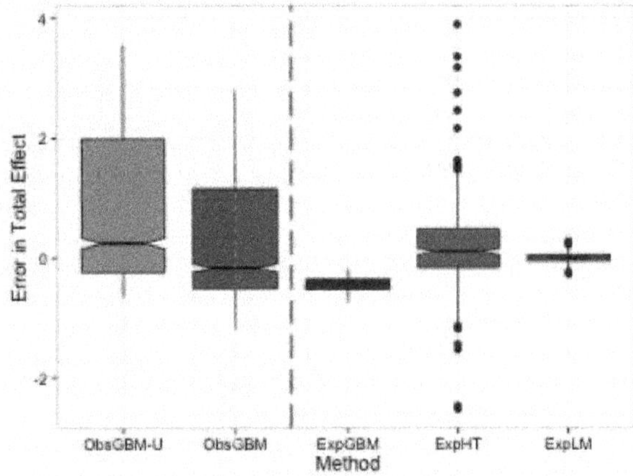

Figure 7: Comparison of estimates obtained from retrospective, confounded, observational data (left) and those from experimentation (right). An *overestimated* effect results in positive error, and an *underestimated* effect results in negative error. These methods almost always overestimate the true global effect.

	Exp. LM	Obs. GLM
Linear	**0.0869 (0.0752)**	0.6527 (0.5936)
RBF	**0.102 (0.0877)**	0.2342 (0.1687)
Sigmoid	**0.0178 (0.0158)**	0.0269 (0.0157)

Table 2: Root mean squared error for marginal individual effects. One standard error is shown in parentheses.

fect estimates are shown in Figure 6. This demonstrates two dimensions of variability in our simulations. First, different functional forms lead to more or less challenging estimation tasks. Most significantly, as the strength of confounding (β_L) is increased from 1 to 3, the observational regime becomes more challenging. This matches intuition—in the extreme, where $\beta_L = 0$, any confounding between treatment and outcome disappears.

While the **ExpHT** model is specifically designed to estimate only total effects, **ExpLM** and **ObsGBM** can also compute marginal individual effects and marginal peer effects. We computed the root mean squared error between estimated individual effects and actual individual effects—this error is shown in Table 2. **ObsGBM** is competitive with **ExpLM** primarily for non-linear functional forms.

Finally, we examined the ability of the **ExpLM** and **ObsGBM** to model marginal peer effects. Unlike the total effect and the marginal individual effect, there is a *spectrum* of peer effects induced by varying θ_{nbr_i}. The possible functional relationships between θ_{nbr_i} and Y_i are shown in Figure 5. Figure 8 provides another concrete example of such a function along with the models estimated by **ExpLM** and **ObsGBM**.

	Exp. LM	Obs. GBM
Linear	**0.0535 (0.021)**	0.6241 (0.485)
RBF	0.4476 (0.248)	**0.403 (0.264)**
Sigmoid	0.0661 (0.015)	**0.0391 (0.027)**

Table 3: Root mean squared error for marginal peer effects. One standard error is shown in parentheses.

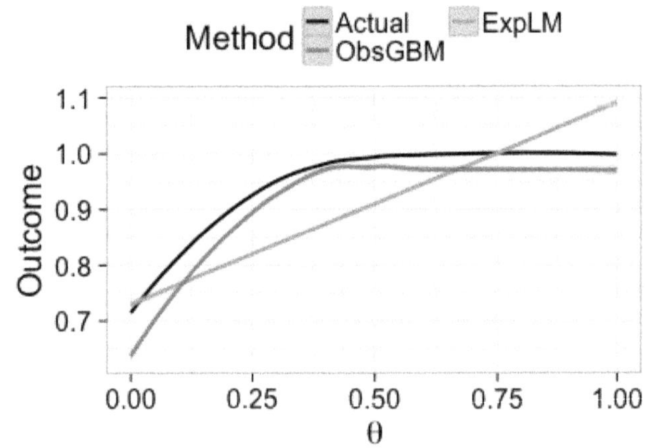

Figure 8: An example of the sigmoid outcome model. In this case, a model of the marginal peer effect is estimated from observational data using a boosted model and from experimental data with a linear model, with $\beta_I = \beta_P = 5$ and $\beta_L = 1$.

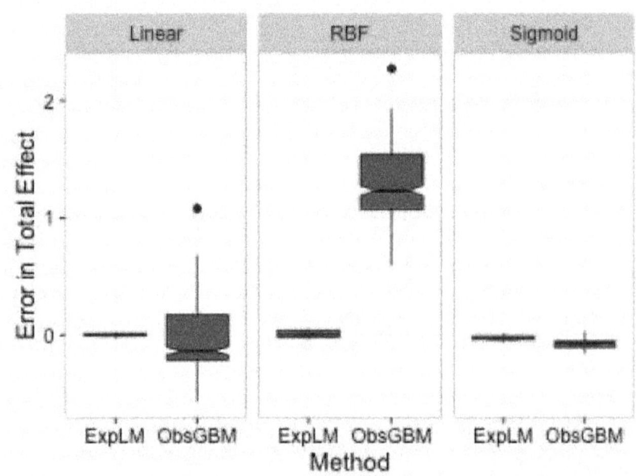

Figure 9: Estimated Total Effects in the Enron Data

Table 3 shows the root mean squared error for peer effects $\theta_{nbr_i} \in \{0, 0.1, \ldots, 0.9, 1\}$. In the linear case, the **ExpLM** model has an advantage over **ObsGBM**. However, the importance of modeling non-linearity becomes clear in the RBF and sigmoid examples, for which the observational estimator is superior to the experimental estimator.

5.4 Real Networks

To demonstrate the applicability of RCA to large networks for which the edge generation process is unknown, we also compared the performance of **ObsGBM** and **ExpLM** on the Enron graph [14]. The nodes of the Enron network are individuals, with an edge between them if either of them have sent an email to the other. The network is contains 36,692 nodes and 183,831 edges in total, with a clustering coefficient of approximately 0.5 and diameter of 11. In the absence of ground truth measures, we generated synthetic random variables following the procedure of Section 5.1, and use the real

	ExpLM	ObsGBM
Linear	**0.0399 (0.0279)**	1.4038 (0.3772)
RBF	**0.6242 (0.2571)**	1.2883 (0.3778)
Sigmoid	0.3439 (0.2113)	**0.0561 (0.0101)**

Table 4: Root mean squared error for marginal individual effects in Enron data.

	ExpLM	ObsGBM
Linear	**0.0213 (0.007)**	0.4855 (0.195)
RBF	0.5255 (0.148)	**0.2278 (0.112)**
Sigmoid	0.2703 (0.14)	**0.0266 (0.025)**

Table 5: Root mean squared error for marginal peer effects in Enron data.

graph topology to test scalability and efficacy. The form of the generative functions were identical to those used in the observational setting. We then measured the estimates of the total effect, marginal peer effects, marginal individual effects for each method.

Figure 9 shows the quality of estimated total effects across each outcome model. While the results from a synthesized network experiment are superior to the estimates from ObsGBM, the results are on comparable scales. Table 4 and Table 5 show the error in estimated individual and peer effects, respectively. Again, the results from ObsGBM are similar to ExpLM. ExpLM performs exceptionally well at experimental data with a linear outcome. However, ObsGBM has a clear advantage in estimating marginal peer effects under the RBF and Sigmoid models. We conjecture that the scale-free nature of the Enron network leads to particularly favorable circumstances for experimental approaches such as ExpLM. Scale-free networks have many nodes with only one or two neighbors, thus the probability that an entire neighborhood will be completely treated or completely untreated is relatively high.

6. RELATED WORK

Ugander et al. [27] and Gui et al. [8] present methods which aim to measure the effect of placing the entire network under treatment versus control. In both cases, this is achieved by partitioning the graph into clusters, treating each cluster randomly and estimating the the average causal effect after adjustment for peer confounding. Toulis and Kao [26] consider experimental design and estimation to measure average peer effect as a quantity of interest. In both cases, the methods discussed within this paper can be seen as complimentary work, providing interpretation within the causal graphical models framework. This interpretation aids the identification of threats to validity and provides a unified framework for estimation of a variety of causal effects. Importantly, the causal graphical model view of this work also admits inference in the non-experimental setting.

There have been numerous applications in recent year that seek to measure causal effects in real relational domains. Bakshy et al. [4] performed large scale experiments to understand the effect of social cues on consumers' receptiveness to advertisements. Aral and Walker [1] used experimentation to understand the process of social diffusion, or "virality" in large-scale social systems.

Within the observational setting, researchers have applied quasi-experimental designs (QEDs) to perform causal inference in relational data. QEDs exploit fortuitous circumstances in data that allow for the approximation of an experimental design post-hoc. For example, Oktay et al. [20] apply QEDs to Stack Overflow, an online question and answer site for programming, to understand the dynamics of users' behavior on the site. Krishnan and Sitaraman [13] consider a quasi-experimental design to determine the relationship between network quality and user engagement with online content. Kearns et al. [10] study patterns of network formation by performing an experiment where subjects were anonymously paired, and subsequently were asked to interactively complete a graph-coloring video game.

Manski [18] considers the problem of identifiability in the potential-outcomes framework in the presence of peer influence. Ogburn and VanderWheele [19] enumerate configurations of causal graphs that result in bias from social effects on single entity, single relationship networks. Maier et al. [17] considers the more general case of d-separation for multi-relational domains. Maier et al. [15] apply the rules implied by Maier et al. [17] to learn the causal structure of relational domains, but explicitly do not consider inference of individual causal effects.

7. CONCLUSION AND FUTURE WORK

We have described and evaluated Relational Covariate Adjustment, an extension of nonparametric adjustment to relational data. Through the use of nonparametric regression estimators, RCA allows for estimation of a wide range of functional dependencies without modification. We showed the efficacy of this approach to causal inference with a set of experiments that examine Relational Covariate Adjustment and other experimental adjustment methods over a range of graph topologies.

This work represents one step toward a much larger goal of general causal inference in relational domains. Toward that end, we plan to extend RCA to the case of multiple entities and relationships and to extend the calculus of interventions by developing techniques that can estimate the effects of interventions that add or remove nodes or edges from the network.

References

[1] S. Aral and D. Walker. Creating social contagion through viral product design: A randomized trial of peer influence in networks. *Management Science*, 57(9):1623–1639, 2011.

[2] P. M. Aronow and C. Samii. Estimating average causal effects under general interference. In *Summer Meeting of the Society for Political Methodology, University of North Carolina, Chapel Hill, July*, pages 19–21, 2012.

[3] E. Bakshy, D. Eckles, and M. S. Bernstein. Designing and deploying online field experiments. In *Proceedings of the 23rd international conference on World wide web*, pages 283–292. ACM, 2014.

[4] E. Bakshy, D. Eckles, R. Yan, and I. Rosenn. Social influence in social advertising: Evidence from field experiments. In *Proceedings of the 13th ACM Conference on Electronic Commerce*, pages 146–161. ACM, 2012.

[5] J. Bosch. Building products as innovation experiment systems. In *Software Business*, pages 27–39. Springer, 2012.

[6] D. S. Choi. Estimation of monotone treatment effects in network experiments. *arXiv preprint arXiv:1408.4102*, 2014.

[7] J. H. Friedman. Greedy function approximation: A gradient boosting machine. *Annals of Statistics*, pages 1189–1232, 2001.

[8] H. Gui, Y. Xu, A. Bhasin, and J. Han. Network a/b testing: From sampling to estimation. In *Proceedings of the 24th International Conference on World Wide Web*, pages 399–409. International World Wide Web Conferences Steering Committee, 2015.

[9] M. G. Hudgens and M. E. Halloran. Toward causal inference with interference. *Journal of the American Statistical Association*, 2012.

[10] M. Kearns, S. Judd, and Y. Vorobeychik. Behavioral experiments on a network formation game. In *Proceedings of the 13th ACM Conference on Electronic Commerce*, pages 690–704. ACM, 2012.

[11] R. Kohavi, A. Deng, B. Frasca, T. Walker, Y. Xu, and N. Pohlmann. Online controlled experiments at large scale. In *Proceedings of the 19th ACM SIGKDD international conference on Knowledge discovery and data mining*, pages 1168–1176. ACM, 2013.

[12] D. Koller. Probabilistic relational models. In *Inductive logic programming*, pages 3–13. Springer, 1999.

[13] S. S. Krishnan and R. K. Sitaraman. Video stream quality impacts viewer behavior: Inferring causality using quasi-experimental designs. *Networking, IEEE/ACM Transactions on*, 21(6):2001–2014, 2013.

[14] J. Leskovec and A. Krevl. SNAP Datasets: Stanford large network dataset collection. http://snap.stanford.edu/data, June 2014.

[15] M. Maier, K. Marazopoulou, D. Arbour, and D. Jensen. A sound and complete algorithm for learning causal models from relational data. In *Uncertainty in Artificial Intelligence*, page 371. Citeseer, 2013.

[16] M. E. Maier. *Causal Discovery for Relational Domains: Representation, Reasoning, and Learning.* PhD thesis, University of Massachusetts Amherst, 2014.

[17] M. E. Maier, K. Marazopoulou, and D. D. Jensen. Reasoning about independence in probabilistic models of relational data. arXiv preprint arXiv:1302.4381, 2014.

[18] C. F. Manski. Identification of treatment response with social interactions. *The Econometrics Journal*, 16(1):S1–S23, 2013.

[19] E. L. Ogburn and T. J. VanderWeele. Causal diagrams for interference. *Statist. Sci.*, 29(4):559–578, 11 2014.

[20] H. Oktay, B. J. Taylor, and D. Jensen. Causal discovery in social media using quasi-experimental designs. In *Proceedings of the SIGKDD/ACM Workshop on Social Media Analytics*, 2010.

[21] J. Pearl. Graphs, causality, and structural equation models. *Sociological Methods & Research*, 27(2):226–284, 1998.

[22] J. Pearl. *Causality.* Cambridge university press, 2009.

[23] C. Perlich and F. Provost. Distribution-based aggregation for relational learning with identifier attributes. *Machine Learning*, 62(1-2):65–105, 2006.

[24] D. B. Rubin. Matching to remove bias in observational studies. *Biometrics*, pages 159–183, 1973.

[25] D. B. Rubin. Causal inference using potential outcomes. *Journal of the American Statistical Association*, 2011.

[26] P. Toulis and E. Kao. Estimation of causal peer influence effects. In *Proceedings of The 30th International Conference on Machine Learning*, pages 1489–1497, 2013.

[27] J. Ugander, B. Karrer, L. Backstrom, and J. Kleinberg. Graph cluster randomization: Network exposure to multiple universes. In *Proceedings of the 19th ACM SIGKDD international conference on Knowledge discovery and data mining*, pages 329–337. ACM, 2013.

8. APPENDIX

8.1 Proof of Proposition 1

PROOF. In constructing a conditional independence query with relational d-separation [15], paths composed of propositional variables, relational variables, and *intersection variables* must be considered. The set of propositional and relational variables to be considered for a perspective is directly identifiable from the relational model. Intersection variables, as defined by Maier et al. [15], are required for sound and complete reasoning of d-separation in relational domains whenever there exists two paths, $P_1 = [A, \ldots, B], P_2 = [A', \ldots, B']$ that are not subsets of each other and whose beginning and ending entity are the same, i.e., $A = A'$ and $B = B'$. We consider the case of the single entity, single relationship graph. Denote E to be the entity and R to be the relationship. Without loss of generality, we consider paths that begin at the entity. All possible path specifications then must be of the form $[A(BA)^*]$, where $*$ is the Kleene star. It follows directly that any two path specifications are either identical, or the shorter path is a sub-path of the other. This implies that for single entity, single relationship networks, intersection variables do not exist. □

Communication Efficient Distributed Kernel Principal Component Analysis

Maria-Florina Balcan*
School of Computer Science
Carnegie Mellon University
ninamf@cs.cmu.edu

Yingyu Liang
Computer Science
Princeton University
yingyul@cs.princeton.edu

Le Song
College of Computing
Georgia Institute of Technology
lsong@cc.gatech.edu

David Woodruff
Almaden Research Center
IBM Research
dpwoodru@us.ibm.com

Bo Xie
College of Computing
Georgia Institute of Technology
bo.xie@gatech.edu

ABSTRACT

Kernel Principal Component Analysis (KPCA) is a key machine learning algorithm for extracting nonlinear features from data. In the presence of a large volume of high dimensional data collected in a distributed fashion, it becomes very costly to communicate all of this data to a single data center and then perform kernel PCA. Can we perform kernel PCA on the entire dataset in a distributed and communication efficient fashion while maintaining provable and strong guarantees in solution quality?

In this paper, we give an affirmative answer to the question by developing a communication efficient algorithm to perform kernel PCA in the distributed setting. The algorithm is a clever combination of subspace embedding and adaptive sampling techniques, and we show that the algorithm can take as input an arbitrary configuration of distributed datasets, and compute a set of global kernel principal components with relative error guarantees independent of the dimension of the feature space or the total number of data points. In particular, computing k principal components with relative error ϵ over s workers has communication cost $\tilde{O}(s\rho k/\epsilon + sk^2/\epsilon^3)$ words, where ρ is the average number of nonzero entries in each data point. Furthermore, we experimented the algorithm with large-scale real world datasets. The experimental results showed that the algorithm produces a high quality kernel PCA solution while using significantly less communication than alternative approaches.

Keywords

Kernel method; Principal Component Analysis; distributed computing

*The authors are listed in alphabetical order.

KDD '16, August 13-17, 2016, San Francisco, CA, USA

DOI: http://dx.doi.org/10.1145/2939672.2939796

1. INTRODUCTION

Kernel Principal Component Analysis (KPCA) is a key machine learning algorithm for extracting nonlinear features from complex datasets, such as image, text, healthcare and biological data [27, 26, 28]. The original kernel PCA algorithm is designed for a batch setting, where all data points need to fit into a single machine. However, nowadays large volumes of data are being collected increasingly in a distributed fashion, which poses new challenges for running kernel PCA. For instance, a large network of distributed sensors can collect temperature readings from geographically distant locations; a system of distributed data centers in an Internet company can process user queries from different countries; a fraud detection system in a bank needs to perform credit checks on people opening accounts from different branches; and a network of electronic healthcare systems can store patient records from different hospitals. It is very costly in terms of network bandwidth and transmission delays to communicate all of the data collected in a distributed fashion to a single data center, and then run kernel PCA on the central node. In other words, communication now becomes the bottleneck to the nonlinear feature extraction pipeline. How can we leverage the aggregated computing power in a large distributed system? Can we perform kernel PCA on the entire dataset in a distributed and communication efficient fashion while maintaining provable and strong guarantees in solution quality?

While recent work shows how to do linear PCA in a communication efficient and distributed fashion [8], the kernel setting is significantly more challenging. The main problem with previous work is that it achieves communication proportional to the dimension of the data points, which if implemented straightforwardly in the kernel setting would give communication proportional to the dimension of the feature space which can be very large or even infinite. Kernel PCA uses the kernel trick to avoid going to the potentially infinite dimensional kernel feature space explicitly, so intermediate results are often represented by a function (*e.g.*, a weighted combination) of the feature mapping of some data points. Communicating such intermediate results requires communicating all the data points they depend on. To lower the communication, the intermediate results should only depend on a small number of data points. A distributed algorithm then needs to be carefully designed to meet this constraint.

In this paper, we propose a communication efficient algorithm for distributed KPCA in a master-worker setting where the dataset is arbitrarily partitioned and each portion sits in one worker, and the workers can communicate only through the master. Our key idea is to design a communication efficient way of generating a small representative subset of the data, and then performing kernel PCA based on this subset. We show that the algorithm can compute a rank-k subspace in the kernel feature space using just a representative subset of size $O(k/\epsilon)$ built in a distributed fashion. For polynomial kernels, it achieves a $(1+\epsilon)$ relative-error approximation to the best rank-k subspace, and for shift-invariant kernels (such as the Gaussian kernel), it achieves $(1+\epsilon)$-approximation with an additive error term that can be made arbitrarily small. In both cases, the total communication for a system of s workers is $\tilde{O}(s\rho k/\epsilon + sk^2/\epsilon^3)$ words, where ρ is the average number of nonzero entries in each data point, and is always bounded by the dimension of the data d and independent of the dimension of the kernel feature space. This for constant ϵ nearly matches the lower bound $\Omega(sdk)$ for linear PCA [8]. As far as we know, this is the first algorithm that can achieve provable approximation with such communication bounds.

As a subroutine of our algorithm, we have also developed an algorithm for the distributed Column Subset Selection (CSS) problem, which can select a set of $O(k/\epsilon)$ points whose span contains $(1+\epsilon)$-approximation, with communication $O(s\rho k/\epsilon + sk^2)$. This is the first algorithm that addresses the problem for kernels, and it nearly matches the communication lower bound $\Omega(s\rho k/\epsilon)$ for this problem in the linear case [10]. The column subset selection problem has various applications in big data scenarios, so this result could be of independent interest.

Furthermore, our algorithm also leads to some other distributed kernel algorithms: the data can then be projected onto the subspace found and processed by downstream applications. For example, an immediate application is for distributed spectral clustering, that first computes KPCA to rank-k/ϵ and then does k-means on the data projected on the subspace found by KPCA (*e.g.*, [17]). This can be done by combining our algorithm with any efficient distributed k-means algorithms (*e.g.*, [6]).

We evaluate our algorithm on datasets with millions of data points and hundreds of thousands of dimensions where non-distributed algorithms such as batch KPCA are impractical to run. Furthermore, comparing to other distributed algorithms, our algorithm requires less communication and fewer representation data points to achieve the same approximation error.

2. RELATED WORK

There has been a surge of recent work on distributed machine learning, *e.g.*, [5, 30, 20, 6]. In this setting, the data sets are typically large, and small error rate is required. This is because if only a coarse error is needed then there is no need to use large-scale data sets; a small subset of the data will be sufficient. Furthermore, one prefers relative error rates instead of additive error rates, since the latter is worse and harder to interpret without knowing the optimum. Our algorithm can achieve small relative error with limited communication.

Since there exist communication efficient distributed linear PCA algorithms [6, 20], it is tempting to adopt the random feature approach for distributed kernel PCA: first construct m random features and then solve PCA in the primal form, *i.e.*, apply distributed linear PCA on the random features. However, the communication of this method is too high. One needs $m = \tilde{O}(d/\epsilon^2)$ random features to preserve the kernel values up to additive error ϵ, leading to a communication of $O(skm/\epsilon) = O(skd/\epsilon^3)$. Another drawback of using random features is that it only produces a solution in the space spanned by the random features, but not a solution in the feature space of the kernel.

The Nyström method is another popular tool for large-scale kernel methods: sample a subset of data points uniformly at random, and use them to construct an approximation of the original kernel matrix. However, it also suffers from high communication cost, since one needs $O(1/\epsilon^4)$ sampled points to achieve additive ϵ error in the Frobenius norm of the kernel matrix [21]. A closely related method is incomplete Cholesky decomposition [3], where a few pivots are greedily chosen to approximate the kernel matrix. It is unclear how to design a communication efficient distributed version since it requires as many rounds of communication as the number of pivots, which is costly.

Leverage score sampling is a related technique for low-rank approximation [29]. A prior work of Boutsidis et al. [8] gives the first distributed protocol for column subset selection. [11] gives a distributed PCA algorithm with optimal communication cost, but only for linear PCA. In comparison, our work is the first communication efficient distributed algorithm for low rank approximation in the kernel space.

3. BACKGROUNDS

For any vector v, let $\|v\|$ denote its Euclidean norm. For any matrix $M \in \mathbb{R}^{d\times n}$, let $M_{i:}$ denote its i-th row and $M_{:j}$ its j-th column. Let $\|M\|_F$ denote its Frobenius norm, and $\|M\|_2$ denote its spectral norm. Let its rank be $r \le \min\{n, d\}$, and denote its SVD as $M = U\Sigma V^\top$ where $U \in \mathbb{R}^{d\times r}, \Sigma \in \mathbb{R}^{r\times r}$, and $V \in \mathbb{R}^{n\times r}$. Let $[M]_k$ denote its best rank-k approximation. Finally, denote its number of non-zero entries as $\mathrm{nnz}(M)$.

In the distributed setting, there are s workers that are connected to a master processor. Worker i has a local data set $A^i \in \mathbb{R}^{d\times n_i}$, and the global data set $A \in \mathbb{R}^{d\times n}$ is the concatenation of the local data ($n = \sum_{i=1}^s n_i$).

Kernels and Random Features. For a kernel $\kappa(x, x')$, let $\mathcal{H}$ denote its feature space, i.e., there exists a feature mapping $\phi(\cdot) \in \mathcal{H}$ such that $\kappa(x, x') = \langle\phi(x), \phi(x')\rangle_{\mathcal{H}}$. Let $\phi(A) \in \mathcal{H}^n$ denote the matrix obtained by applying ϕ on each column of A and concatenating the results. Throughout the paper, we regard any $M \in \mathcal{H}^n$ as a matrix whose columns are elements in $\mathcal{H}$ and define matrix operations accordingly. For example, for any $M \in \mathcal{H}^n$ and $N \in \mathcal{H}^m$, let $B = M^\top N \in \mathbb{R}^{n\times m}$ where $B_{ij} = \langle M_{:i}, N_{:j}\rangle_{\mathcal{H}}$, and let $\|M\|_{\mathcal{H}}^2 = \mathrm{tr}\left(M^\top M\right)$. When there is no ambiguity, we omit the subscript $\mathcal{H}$.

The random feature approach is a recent technique to scale up kernel methods. Many kernels can be approximated by $\frac{1}{m}\sum_{i=1}^m \xi_{\omega_i}(x)\xi_{\omega_i}(y)$ where ω_i's are randomly sampled. These include Gaussian RBF kernels and other shift-invariant kernels, inner product kernels, etc ([24, 15]). For example, Gaussian RBF kernels, $\kappa(x, y) = \exp(-\|x - y\|^2/2\sigma^2)$, can be approximated by $\frac{1}{m}\sum_{i=1}^m z_{\omega_i,b_i}(x)z_{\omega_i,b_i}(y)$ where $z_{\omega,b}(x) = \sqrt{2}\cos(\omega^\top x + b)$ and ω_i is from a Gaussian distribution with density proportional to $\exp(-\sigma^2 \|\omega\|^2 / 2)$ and b_i is uniform over $[0, 2\pi]$.

In this paper, we provide guarantees for shift-invariant kernels using Fourier random features (the extension to other kernels/random features is straightforward). We assume the kernel satisfies some regularization conditions: it is defined over bounded compact domain in $\mathbb{R}^d$, with $\kappa(0) \leq 1$ and bounded $\nabla^2 k(0)$ [24]. Such conditions are standard in practice, and thus we assume them throughout the paper.

Kernel PCA. An element $u \in \mathcal{H}$ is an eigenfunction of $\phi(A)\phi(A)^\top$ with the corresponding eigenvalue λ if $\|u\| = 1$ and $\phi(A)\phi(A)^\top u = \lambda u$. Given eigenfunctions $\{u_i\}$ of $\phi(A)\phi(A)^\top$ and eigenvectors $\{v_i\}$ of $\phi(A)^\top \phi(A)$, $\phi(A)$ has the singular decomposition $U\Sigma_k V^\top + U_\perp \Sigma_\perp V_\perp^\top$, where U, V are the lists of top k eigenfunctions/vectors, Σ_k is a diagonal matrix with the corresponding singular values, $U_\perp$, $V_\perp$ are the lists of the rest of the eigenfunctions/vectors, and $\Sigma_\perp$ is a diagonal matrix with the rest of the singular values. Kernel PCA aims to identify the top k subspace U, since the best rank-k approximation $[\phi(A)]_k = U\Sigma_k V^\top = UU^\top \phi(A)$. Typically, the goal is to find a good approximation to this subspace. Formally,

Definition 1. *A subspace $L \in \mathcal{H}^k$ is a rank-k $(1+\epsilon, \Delta)$-approximation for kernel PCA on A if $L^\top L = I_k$ and*

$$\left\|\phi(A) - LL^\top \phi(A)\right\|^2 \leq (1+\epsilon) \left\|\phi(A) - [\phi(A)]_k\right\|^2 + \Delta.$$

Kernel PCA leads to immediate solutions for some other nonlinear component analysis (e.g., kernel CCA), and provides needed subroutines for tasks like spectral clustering.

Subspace Embeddings. Subspace embeddings are a useful technique that can improve the computational and space costs by embedding data into lower dimension while preserving interesting properties. They have been extensively studied in recent years [25, 1, 13]. The recent fast sparse subspace embeddings [13] and its optimizations [22, 23] are particularly suitable for large-scale sparse datasets, since their running time is linear in the number of non-zero entries in the data matrix. They also preserve the sparsity of the input data. Formally,

Definition 2. *An ϵ-subspace embedding of $M \in \mathbb{R}^{m\times n}$ is a matrix $S \in \mathbb{R}^{t\times m}$ such that for any x,*

$$\|SMx\| = (1 \pm \epsilon) \|Mx\|.$$

Subspace embeddings can also be done on the right hand side, i.e., *$S \in \mathbb{R}^{n\times t}$ and $\|x^\top MS\| = (1 \pm \epsilon) \|x^\top M\|$.*

Mx is in the column space of M and SMx is its embedding, so the definition means that the norm of any vector in the column space of M is approximately preserved. This then provides a way to do dimensional reduction for problems depending on inner products of vectors. Our algorithm repeatedly makes use of subspace embeddings. In particular, the embedding we use is the concatenation of the following known sketching matrices: CountSketch and i.i.d. Gaussians (or the concatenation of CountSketch, fast Hadamard and i.i.d. Gaussians). The details can be found in [29]; we only need the following fact.

Lemma 1. *For $M \in \mathbb{R}^{d\times n}$, there exist sketching matrices $S \in \mathbb{R}^{t\times d}$ with $t = O(n/\epsilon^2)$ that are ϵ-subspace embeddings. Furthermore, SM can be successfully computed in time $\tilde{O}(\mathrm{nnz}(M))$ with probability at least $1 - \delta$.*

The work of [2] shows that a fast computational approach, TensorSketch, is indeed a subspace embedding for the polynomial kernel. However, there are no previously known subspace embeddings for other kernels. We develop efficient and provable embeddings for a large family of kernels including Gaussian kernel and other shift invariant kernels. These embeddings will be a key tool used by our algorithm.

4. OVERVIEW

In view of the limitations of the related work, we instead take a different approach, which first selects a small subset of points whose span contains an approximation with relative error rate ϵ, and then find a low rank approximation in their span. It is important to keep the size of the subset small and also guarantee that their span contains a good approximation (this is also called kernel column subset selection). A well known technique is to sample according to the statistical leverage scores.

Challenges. However, this immediately raises the following technical challenges.

I. Computing the statistical leverage scores is prohibitively expensive. Naïvely computing them requires communicating all data points. There exist non-trivial fast algorithms [18], but they are designed for the non-distributed setting. Using them in the distributed setting leads to communication linear in the number of data points, or linear in the number of random features if one uses random features and computes the leverage scores for them.
Our key idea is that it is sufficient to compute the (generalized) leverage scores of the data points, i.e., the leverage scores of another matrix whose row space approximates that of the original data matrix. So the problem is reduced to designing kernel subspace embeddings that can approximate the row space of the data.

II. Even given the embedded data, it is unclear how to compute its leverage scores in a communication efficient way. Although the dimension of the embedded data is small, existing algorithms will lead to communication linear in the number of data points, which is impractical.

III. Simply sampling according to the generalized leverage scores does not give the desired results: a good approximation can only be obtained using a much larger rank, specifically, $O(k/\epsilon)$.

IV. After selecting the small subset of points, we need to design a distributed algorithm to compute a good low rank approximation in their span.

Algorithm. We have designed a distributed kernel PCA algorithm that computes an approximated solution with relative error rate ϵ using low communication. The algorithm operates in following key steps, each of which addresses one of the challenges mentioned above (See Figure 1):

I. Kernel Subspace Embeddings. To approximate the subspace of the original data matrix, we propose subspace embeddings for a large family of kernels. For polynomial kernels we improve the prior work by reducing the embedding dimension and thus lowering the communication. Furthermore, we propose new subspace embeddings for kernels with random feature expansions, allowing PCA for these kernels to be computed in a communication efficient manner. See Section 5.1 for the details.

II. Distributed Leverage Scores. To compute the leverage scores, sampling with constant approximations is sufficient. We can thus drastically reduce the number of data points:

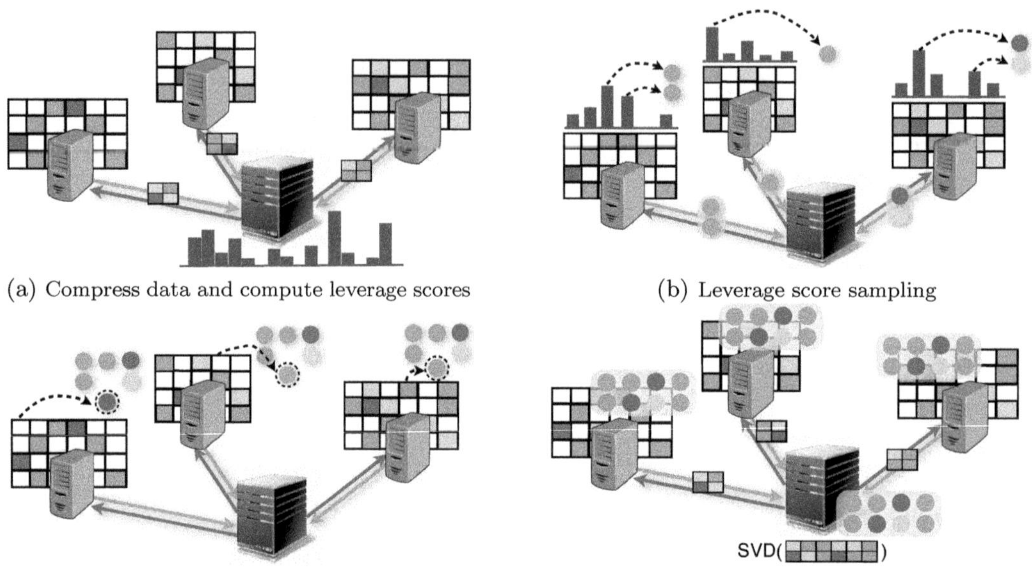

(a) Compress data and compute leverage scores (b) Leverage score sampling

(c) Adaptive sampling (d) Project data and compute KPCA

Figure 1: Algorithm overview. The black machine at the center is the master and the gray machines are the workers. Each worker stores its portion of the dataset, and the algorithm computes the top k principle components on the whole dataset. The arrows between the machines denote the direction of communications. In each round, the communication always starts from the workers to the master (lighter arrows) and then from the master to the workers (darker arrows). (a) Each worker compresses its data by using (kernel) subspace embeddings and sends it to the master. The master aggregates the data and computes intermediate results for leverage scores and sends back to the workers. (b) Each worker computes the leverage scores, samples data points (denoted by circles) and then sends them to the master. The master distributes back the union of the sampled data points. (c) Each worker conducts adaptive sampling and sends newly sampled points to the master. The master distributes back the union of all sampled points. (d) Each worker projects its data onto the subspace spanned by the sampled data points and sends the compressed projections to the master. The master computes coefficients for the top k principle components by running SVD, and then sends them back to the workers. (best viewed in color)

first do another (non-kernel) subspace embeddings on the embedded data, and then send the result to the master for computing the scores. See Figure 1(a) for an illustration and Section 5.2 for the details.

III. Sampling Representative Points. We take a two-step approach as leverage scores alone is not good enough : first sample according to generalized leverage scores, and then sample additional points according to their distances to the span of the points sampled in the first step. The first step gains some coarse information about the data, and the second step use it to get the desired samples. The two steps are illustrated in Figure 1(b) and 1(c), respectively, while the details are in Section 5.3.

IV. Computing an Approximation. After projecting the data to the span of the representative points, we sketch the projections by (non-kernel) subspace embeddings. We then send the compressed projections to the master and compute the solution there. See Figure 1(d) for an illustration and Section 5.4 for the details.

Main Theoretical Results. Given as input the local datasets, the rank k and error parameters ϵ, Δ, our algorithm outputs a $(1+\epsilon, \Delta)$-approximation to the optimum with large probability. Formally, we have the following theorem.

THEOREM 1. *Algorithm 4 produces a subspace L for kernel PCA on A that with probability ≥ 0.99 satisfies:*

1. *L is a rank-k $(1+\epsilon, 0)$-approximation when applied to polynomial kernels.*
2. *L is a rank-k $(1+\epsilon, \Delta)$-approximation when applied to shift-invariant kernels with regularization.*

The total communication is $\tilde{O}(\frac{s\rho k}{\epsilon} + \frac{sk^2}{\epsilon^3})$ words, where ρ is the average number of nonzero entries in one data point.

The constant success probability can be boosted up to any high probability $1-\delta$ by repetition, which adds only an extra $O(\log \frac{1}{\delta})$ term to communication and computation.

The output subspace L is represented by $\tilde{O}(k/\epsilon)$ sampled points Y from A (*i.e.*, $L = \phi(Y)C$ for some coefficient matrix C), so L can be easily communicated and the projection of any point on L can be easily computed by the kernel trick. The communication has linear dependence on the dimension and the number of workers, and has no dependence on the number of data points, which is crucial for big data scenarios. Moreover, it does not depend on Δ (but the computation does), so the additive error can be made arbitrarily small with more computation.

The theorem also holds for other properly regularized kernels with random feature expansions (see [24, 15] for more such kernels); the extension of our proof is straightforward.

We also make the following contributions: (*i*) Subspace embedding techniques for many kernels. (*ii*) Distributed algorithm for computing generalized leverage scores with low communication. (*iii*) Distributed algorithm for kernel column subset selection.

5. DISTRIBUTED KERNEL PRINCIPAL COMPONENT ANALYSIS

Our algorithm first computes the (generalized) leverage scores that measure the non-uniform structure, then samples a subset of points whose span contains a good approximated solution, and finally finds such a solution in the span.

Leverage scores are critical for importance sampling in many fast randomized algorithms. The leverage scores are defined as follows.

Definition 3. *For $E \in \mathbb{R}^{t \times n}$ with SVD $E = U\Sigma V^\top$, the leverage score ℓ_j for its j-th column is $\ell_j = \|V_{j:}\|^2$.*

Their importance is reflected in the following fact: suppose E has rank at most k, and suppose P is a subset of $O(\frac{k \log k}{\epsilon^2})$ columns obtained by repeatedly sampled from the columns of E according to their leverage scores, then the span of P contains an $(1+\epsilon, 0)$-approximation subspace for E with probability ≥ 0.99 (see,*e.g.*, [19]). Here, sampling one column according to the leverage scores ℓ_j means to define sampling probabilities p_j such that $p_j \geq \frac{\ell_j}{4\sum_j \ell_j}$ for all j, and then pick one column where the j-th column is picked with probability p_j. Note that setting $p_j = \frac{\ell_j}{\sum_j \ell_j}$ is clearly sufficient, but a constant variance of p_j is allowed at the expense of an extra constant factor in the sample size. This means that it is sufficient to compute constant approximations $\tilde{\ell}_j$ for ℓ_j, and then sample according to $p_j = \frac{\tilde{\ell}_j}{\sum_j \tilde{\ell}_j}$.

However, even computing constant approximations of the leverage scores are non-trivial: naïve approaches require SVD, which is expensive. Actually, SVD is more expensive than the task of PCA itself. Even ignoring computation cost, naïve SVD is prohibitive in the distributed setting due to its high communication cost. Fortunately, it turns out that the leverage scores are an over kill for our purpose; it suffices to compute the generalized leverage scores, i.e., the leverage scores of a proxy matrix.

Definition 4. *If E has rank q and can approximate the row space of M up to $(1+\epsilon, \Delta)$,* i.e., *there exists X with*

$$\|XE - M\|_F \leq (1+\epsilon)\|M - [M]_k\|_F + \Delta,$$

then the leverage scores of E are called the generalized leverage scores of M with respect to rank q.

This generalizes the definition in [18] by allowing the rank of E to be larger than k and allowing additive error Δ, which are important for our application. The generalized leverage scores can act as the leverage scores for our purpose in the following sense.

Lemma 2. *Let P be $O(\frac{q \log q}{\epsilon^2})$ columns sampled from M according to their generalized leverage scores w.r.t. rank q. Then with probability ≥ 0.99, the span of P has a rank-s $(1+2\epsilon, 2\Delta)$-approximation subspace for M.*

Proof. It follows from combining Theorem 5 in [19] and the definition of the generalized leverage scores. □

Computing the generalized scores with respect to rank q could be much more efficient, since the intrinsic dimension now becomes q, which can be much smaller than the ambient dimension (the number of points or the dimension of the feature space). However, as noted in the overview, there are still a few technical challenges.

- Efficiently find a smaller matrix E that can approximate the row space of the original data.
- Compute the leverage scores of E in a communication efficient way.
- The approximation solution in the span of P has the same rank as E, which is $O(k/\epsilon)$ when we use kernel subspace embedding to obtain E. This is not satisfying since our final goal is to compute a rank-k solution.
- Find a good approximation in the span of $\phi(Y)$ with low communication.

Our final algorithm consists of four key steps, each of which addresses one of the above challenges. They are elaborated in the following four subsections respectively, and the final subsection presents the overall algorithm.

5.1 Kernel Subspace Embeddings

Recall that a subspace embedding S for a matrix M is such that $\|SMx\| \approx \|Mx\|$, *i.e.*, the norm of any vector in the column space of M is approximately preserved. Subspace embeddings can also be generalized for the feature mapping of kernels, simply by setting $M = \phi(A)$, S a linear mapping from $\mathcal{H} \mapsto \mathbb{R}^t$ and using the corresponding inner product. If the data after the kernel subspace embedding is sufficient for solving the problem under consideration, then only $S\phi(A)$ in much lower dimension is needed. This is especially interesting for distributed kernel methods, since directly using the feature mapping or the kernel trick in this setting will lead to high communication cost, while the data after embedding can be smaller and lead to lower communication cost.

A sufficient condition for solving many problems (in particular, kernel PCA) is to preserve the low rank structure of the data. More precisely, the row space of $S\phi(A)$ is a good approximation to that of $\phi(A)$, where the error is comparably to the best rank k approximation error. Then $S\phi(A)$ can be used to compute the generalized leverage scores for $\phi(A)$, which can then be utilized to compute kernel PCA as mentioned above.

More precisely, we would like $S\phi(A)$ to approximate the row space of $\phi(A)$ up to $(1+\epsilon, \Delta)$, as required in the definition of the generalized leverage scores. We give such embeddings a particular name.

Definition 5. *S is called a $(1+\epsilon, \Delta)$-good subspace embedding for $\phi(A) \in \mathcal{H}^n$, if there exists X such that*

$$\|X(S\phi(A)) - \phi(A)\|^2 \leq (1+\epsilon)\|\phi(A) - [\phi(A)]_k\|^2 + \Delta.$$

We now identify the sufficient conditions for $(1+\epsilon, \Delta)$-good subspace embeddings, which can then be used in constructing such embeddings for various kernels.

Lemma 3. *S is a $(1+\epsilon, \Delta)$-good subspace embedding for $\phi(A) \in \mathcal{H}^n$ if it satisfies the following.*

P1 *(Subspace Embedding): For any orthonormal $V \in \mathcal{H}^k$* (i.e., *$V^\top V$ is the identity), for all $x \in \mathbb{R}^k$,*

$$\|SVx\| = (1 \pm c)\|Vx\|$$

where c is a sufficiently small constant.

P2 *(Approximate Product): for any $M \in \mathcal{H}^n, N \in \mathcal{H}^k$,*

$$\left\|(SN)^\top (SM) - N^\top M\right\|_F^2 \leq \frac{\epsilon}{k}\|N\|^2\|M\|^2 + \Delta.$$

Polynomial Kernels. For polynomial kernels, there exists an efficient algorithm TensorSketch to compute the embedding [2]. However, the embedding dimension has a

Algorithm 1 Distributed Leverage Scores: $\{\tilde{\ell}_j^i\} = \textbf{disLS}(\{E^i\}_{i=1}^s, k)$

1: Each worker i: do $\frac{1}{4}$-subspace embedding $E^iT^i \in \mathbb{R}^{t\times p}$ with $p = O(t)$; send E^iT^i to Master.
2: Master: QR-factorize $\left[E^1T^1, \ldots, E^sT^s\right]^\top = UZ$; send Z to all workers.
3: Each worker i: compute $\tilde{\ell}_j^i = \left\| ((Z^\top)^{-1}E^i)_{:j} \right\|_2^2$.

quadratic dependence on the rank k, which will increase the communication. Fortunately, subspace embedding can be concatenated, so we can further apply another known subspace embedding such as one of those in Lemma 1 which, though not fast for feature mapping, is fast for the already embedded data and has lower dimension. In this way, we can enjoy the benefits of both approaches.

The guarantee of TensorSketch in [2] and the property of the subspace embeddings in Lemma 1 can be combined to verify **P1** and **P2**. So we have

Lemma 4. *For polynomial kernels $\kappa(x, y) = (\langle x, y\rangle)^q$, there exists a $(1+\epsilon, 0)$-good subspace embedding matrix $S : \mathbb{R}^{d^q} \mapsto \mathbb{R}^t$ with $t = O(k/\epsilon)$.*

Kernels with Random Feature Expansions. Polynomial kernels have finite dimensional feature mappings, for which the sketching seems natural. It turns out that it is possible to extend subspace embeddings to kernels with infinite dimensional feature mappings. More precisely, we propose subspace embeddings for kernels with random feature expansions, *i.e.*, $\kappa(x, y) = \mathbb{E}_\omega\left[\xi_\omega(x)\xi_\omega(y)\right]$ for some function $\xi(\cdot)$. Therefore, one can approximate the kernel by using m features $z_\omega(x)$ on randomly sampled ω. Such random feature expansion can be exploited for subspace embeddings: view the expansion as the "new" data points and apply a sketching matrix on top of it. Compared to polynomial kernels, the finite random feature expansion leads to an additional additive error term. Our analysis shows that bounding the additive error term only requires sufficiently large sampled size m, which affects the computation but does not affect the final embedding dimension and thus the communication.

In summary, the embedding is $S\phi(x) = TR(\phi(x))$, where $R(\phi(x)) \in \mathbb{R}^m$ is m random features for x and $T \in \mathbb{R}^{t\times m}$ is an embedding as in Lemma 1. The properties **P1** and **P2** can be verified by combining Lemma 1 and the guarantees of random features.

Lemma 5. *For a continuous shift-invariant kernels $\kappa(x, y) = \kappa(x - y)$ with regularization, there exists a $(1 + \epsilon, \Delta)$-good subspace embedding $S : \mathcal{H} \mapsto \mathbb{R}^t$ with $t = O(k/\epsilon)$.*

5.2 Computing Leverage Scores

Given the matrix E obtained from kernel subspace embedding, we would like to compute the leverage scores of E. First note that this cannot be done simply in a local manner: the leverage score of a column in E^i is different from the leverage score of the same column in E. Furthermore, though data in E have low dimension, communicating all points in E to the master is still impractical, since it leads to communication linear in the total number of points.

Fortunately, we only need to compute constant approximations of the scores, which allows us to use subspace embedding on E to greatly reduce the number of data points.

Algorithm 2 Sampling Representative Points: $Y = \textbf{RepSample}(\{A^i\}_{i=1}^s, \{\tilde{\ell}_j^i\}, k, \epsilon)$

1: Workers: sample $O(k \log k)$ points according to $\{\tilde{\ell}_j^i\}$; send to Master;
2: Master: send all the sampled points P to the workers;
3: Workers: sample $O(k/\epsilon)$ points $\tilde{Y}$ according to the square distances to P in the feature space; send to Master;
4: Master: send $Y = \tilde{Y} \cup P$ to all the workers.

In particular, we apply a $\frac{1}{4}$-subspace embedding T^i (*e.g.*, one of those in Lemma 1) on each local data set E^i, and then send them to the master. Let ET denote all the embedded data, and do QR factorization $(ET)^\top = UZ$. Now, the rows of $U^\top = \left(Z^\top\right)^{-1}ET$ are a set of basis for ET. Then, think of $U^\top T^\dagger = \left(Z^\top\right)^{-1}E$ as the basis for E, so it suffices to compute the norms of the columns in $\left(Z^\top\right)^{-1}E$.

The details are described in Algorithm 1 and Figure 1(a) shows an illustration. The algorithm is guaranteed to output constant approximations of the leverage scores of E.

Lemma 6. *Let ℓ_j^i be the true leverage scores of E. Then Algorithm 1 outputs $\tilde{\ell}_j^i = (1 \pm 1/2)\ell_j^i$.*

Proof. The algorithm can be viewed as applying an embedding $T = \text{diag}\left(T^1, \ldots, T^s\right)$ on E to approximate the scores while saving the costs. Each T^i is an $\frac{1}{4}$-subspace embedding matrix, then for any x,

$$\begin{aligned}\left\|x^\top ET\right\|^2 &= \left\|[x^\top E^1T^1, x^\top E^2T^2, \ldots, x^\top E^sT^s]\right\|^2 \\ &= \sum_{i=1}^s \left\|x^\top E^iT^i\right\|^2 = \sum_{i=1}^s (1 \pm 1/4)^2 \left\|x^\top E^i\right\|^2 \\ &= (1 \pm 1/4)^2 \left\|x^\top E\right\|^2.\end{aligned}$$

So T is also $\frac{1}{4}$-subspace embedding. Such a scheme of using embedding for approximating the scores has been analyzed (Lemma 6 in [18]), and the lemma follows. □

We note that though a constant approximation is sufficient for our purpose, but the algorithm can output $\tilde{\ell}_j^i = (1 \pm \epsilon)\ell_j^i$ by doing an $\frac{\epsilon}{2}$-subspace embedding (instead of $\frac{1}{4}$), which can be useful for other applications.

5.3 Sampling Representative Points

Sampling directly to the leverage scores can produce a set of points P such that the span of $\phi(P)$ contains a $(1+\epsilon, \Delta)$-approximation to $\phi(A)$. However, the rank of that approximation can be as high as $O(k/\epsilon)$, since its rank is the same as that of the embedded data (see Lemma 2), which will be $O(k/\epsilon)$ to achieve ϵ error. To get a rank-k approximation and also enjoy the advantage of leverage scores, we propose to combine leverage score sampling and the adaptive sampling algorithm in [16, 9].

The details are presented in Algorithm 2. We first sample a set P of $O(k \log k)$ points according to the leverage scores, so that the span of $\phi(P)$ contains a $(2, \Delta)$-approximation. Then we use the adaptive sampling method: sample $O(k/\epsilon)$ points according to the square distances from the points to their projections on P and then add them to P to get the

Algorithm 3 Computing an Approximation:
$L = \textbf{disLR}(\{A^i\}_{i=1}^s, Y, k, \epsilon, \Delta)$

1: Each worker i: compute the basis Q for $\phi(Y)$ and $\Pi^i = Q^\top \phi(A^i)$; do an ϵ-subspace embedding $\Pi^i T^i \in \mathbb{R}^{|Y| \times w}$ with $w = O(|Y|/\epsilon^2)$, and send $\Pi^i T^i$ to Master;
2: Master: concatenate $\Pi T = [\Pi^1 T^1, \ldots, \Pi^s T^s]$ and send the top k singular vectors W of ΠT to the workers.
3: Each worker i: set $L = QW$.

desire set Y of representative points. Figure 1(b) and 1(c) demonstrate the two steps of the algorithm.

Adaptive sampling has the following guarantee:

LEMMA 7. *Suppose there is a $(2, \Delta)$-approximation for $\phi(A)$ in the span of $\phi(P)$. Then with probability ≥ 0.99, the span of $\phi(Y)$ has a rank-k $(1+\epsilon, \Delta)$-approximation.*

Therefore, we solves the column subset selection problem for kernels in the distributed setting, with $O(k \log k + k/\epsilon)$ selected columns and with a communication of only $O(s\rho k/\epsilon + sk^2)$. This also provides the foundation for kernel PCA task.

5.4 Computing an Approximation

To compute a good approximation in the span of $\phi(Y)$, the naïve approach is to project the data to the span and compute SVD there. However, the communication will be linear in the number of data points. Subspace embedding can be used to sketch the projected data, so that the number of data points is greatly reduced.

Algorithm 4 describes the details and Figure 1(d) shows an illustration. To compute the best rank-k approximation for the projected data Π, we do a subspace embedding on the right hand side, *i.e.*, compute $\Pi T = [\Pi^1 T^1, \ldots, \Pi^s T^s]$. Then the algorithm computes the best rank-k approximation W for ΠT, which is then a good approximation for Π and thus $\phi(A)$. It then returns L, the representation of W in the coordinate system of $\phi(A)$. The output L is guaranteed to be a good approximation.

LEMMA 8. *If there is a rank-k $(1+\epsilon, \Delta)$-approximation subspace in the span of $\phi(Y)$, then*

$$\left\| LL^\top \phi(A) - \phi(A) \right\|^2 \leq (1+\epsilon)^2 \left\| \phi(A) - [\phi(A)]_k \right\|^2 + (1+\epsilon)\Delta.$$

Proof Sketch. For our choice of w, T^i is an ϵ-subspace embedding matrix for Π^i. Then their concatenation B is an ϵ-subspace embedding for Π, the concatenation of Π^i. Then we can apply the idea implicit in [20].

By Pythagorean Theorem, the error can be factorized into

$$\underbrace{\left\| LL^\top \phi(A) - QQ^\top \phi(A) \right\|^2}_{T1} + \underbrace{\left\| \phi(A) - QQ^\top \phi(A) \right\|^2}_{T2}.$$

Since $LL^\top = QWW^\top Q^\top$,

$$T1 = \left\| WW^\top Q^\top \phi(A) - Q^\top \phi(A) \right\|^2.$$

Note that $\Pi = Q^\top \phi(A)$, and W is the best rank-k subspace for its embedding ΠT. By property of T (Theorem 7 in [20]), it is also a good approximation for Π. So

$$T1 \approx \left\| [Q^\top \phi(A)]_k - Q^\top \phi(A) \right\|^2 = \left\| Q[Q^\top \phi(A)]_k - QQ^\top \phi(A) \right\|^2.$$

Algorithm 4 Distributed Kernel PCA:
$L = \textbf{disKPCA}(\{A^i\}_{i=1}^s, k, \epsilon, \Delta)$

1: Each worker i: do a $(1/4, \Delta)$-good subspace embedding $E^i = S(\phi(A^i)) \in \mathbb{R}^{t \times n_i}, t = O(k)$;
2: Compute the leverage scores: $\{\tilde{\ell}_j^i\} = \textbf{disLS}(\{E^i\}_{i=1}^s, k)$;
3: Sample points: $Y = \textbf{RepSample}(\{A^i\}_{i=1}^s, \{\tilde{\ell}_j^i\}, k, \epsilon)$;
4: Output $L = \textbf{disLR}(\{A^i\}_{i=1}^s, Y, k, \epsilon, \Delta)$.

Table 1: Dataset specification: d is the original feature dimension, n is the number of data points, and s is the total number of workers storing the dataset distributedly. Among them, bow and 20news are sparse datasets. All datasets except mnist8m are taken from UCI repository [4] and [7].

Dataset	d	n	s
bow	100,000	8,000,000	200
higgs	28	11,000,000	200
mnist8m	784	8,000,000	100
susy	18	5,000,000	100
yearpredmsd	90	463,715	10
ctslice	384	53,500	10
20news	61,118	11,269	5
protein	9	41,157	5
har	561	10,299	5
insurance	85	9,822	5

Combining this with $T2$, and applying Pythagorean Theorem again, we know that the error is roughly

$$\left\| Q[Q^\top \phi(A)]_k - \phi(A) \right\|^2.$$

Now, by assumption, there is a rank-k $(1+\epsilon, \Delta)$-approximation subspace X in the span of $\phi(Y)$. Since $[Q^\top \phi(A)]_k$ is the best rank-k approximation to $Q^\top \phi(A)$,

$$\begin{aligned} & \left\| Q[Q^\top \phi(A)]_k - \phi(A) \right\|^2 \\ = & \left\| Q[Q^\top \phi(A)]_k - QQ^\top \phi(A) \right\|^2 + \left\| QQ^\top \phi(A) - \phi(A) \right\|^2 \\ \leq & \left\| X - QQ^\top \phi(A) \right\|^2 + \left\| QQ^\top \phi(A) - \phi(A) \right\|^2 \\ = & \left\| X - \phi(A) \right\|^2. \end{aligned}$$

The lemma then follows.

5.5 Overall Algorithm

Now, putting things together, we obtain our final algorithm for distributed kernel PCA (Algorithm 4). Our main result, Theorem 1, follows by combining all the lemmas in the previous subsections (with properly adjusted ϵ and Δ).

6. EXPERIMENTS

6.1 Datasets

We use ten datasets to evaluate our algorithm. They contain both sparse and dense data and come from a variety of different domains, such as text, images, high energy physics and biology. We use two smaller ones to benchmark against the single-machine batch KPCA algorithm while the rest are large-scale datasets with up to tens of millions of data points and hundreds of thousands dimensions. Refer to Table 1 for detailed specifications.

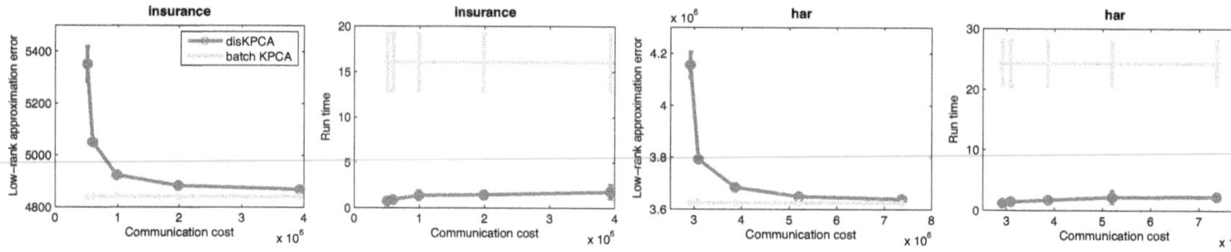

(a) error on insurance (b) runtime on insurance (c) error on har (d) runtime on har

Figure 2: KPCA for polynomial kernels on small datasets: low-rank approximation error and runtime

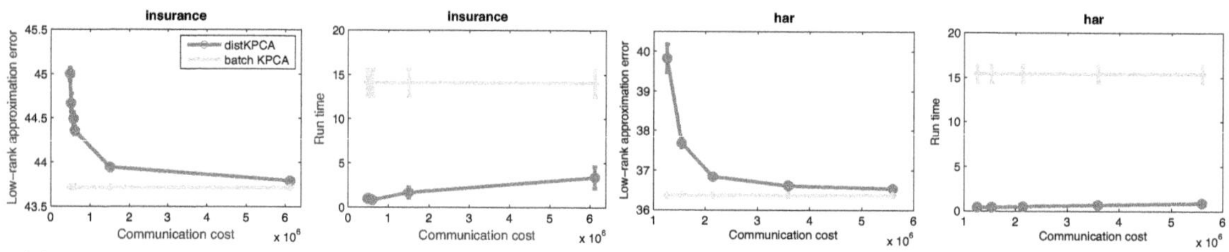

(a) error on insurance (b) runtime on insurance (c) error on har (d) runtime on har

Figure 3: KPCA for Gaussian kernels on small datasets: low-rank approximation error and runtime

Each dataset is partitioned on different workers according to the power law distribution with exponent 2 to simulate the distribution of the data over large networks [14]. Depending on the size of the dataset, the number of workers used ranges from 5 to 200 (see Table 1 for details).

6.2 Experiment Settings

Since our key contribution is sampling a small set of data points intelligently, the natural alternative is uniformly sampling. We compare with two variants of uniform sampling algorithms: 1) uniformly sampling representative points and use Algorithm 3 to get KPCA solution (denoted as uniform+disLR); 2) uniformly sampling data points and apply batch KPCA (denoted as uniform+batch KPCA).

For both algorithms, we compare the tradeoff of low rank approximation error and communication cost. Particularly, we compare the communication needed to achieve the same error. Each method is run 5 times and the mean and the standard deviation are reported.

For polynomial kernel, the degree is $q = 4$ and for Gaussian RBF kernel, the kernel bandwidth σ is set to 0.2 of the median pairwise distance among a subset of 20000 randomly chosen data points (a.k.a, the "median trick"). For Gaussian random feature expansion, we use 2000 random features.

In all experiments, we set the number of principle components $k = 10$, which is the same number for k-means. The algorithm specific parameters are set as follows: 1) The subspace embedding dimension for the feature expansion t is 50; 2) The subspace embedding dimension for the data points p is 250; 3) We vary the number of adaptively sampled points $|\tilde{Y}|$ from 50 to 400 to simulate different communication cost; 4) The subspace embedding dimension w is set to equal $|Y|$.

6.3 Comparison with Batch Algorithm

We compare to the "ground-truth" solutions produced by batch KPCA on two small datasets where it is feasible. The experiment results for the polynomial kernel and the Gaussian RBF kernel are presented in Figures 2 and 3, respectively. In both cases, the approximation error of disKPCA decreases as more communication is allowed. It can nearly match the optimum low-rank approximation error with much fewer data points. In addition, it is much faster: we gain a speed up of 10× by using five workers.

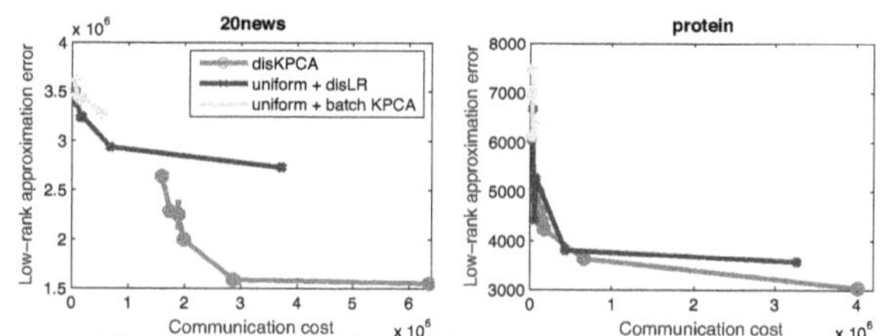

Figure 6: KPCA results for arc-cos kernels

6.4 Communication Efficiency

In these experiments, we compare the tradeoff between communication cost and approximation accuracy on large-scale datasets. The alternative, uniform + batch KPCA, is stopped short in many experiments due to its excessive computation cost for larger number of sampled data points.

Figure 4 demonstrates the performance on polynomial kernels on four large datasets. On all four datasets, our algorithm outperforms the alternatives by significant margins. Especially on bow, which is a sparse dataset, the usage of kernel embeddings takes advantage of the sparsity structure and leads to much smaller error. On other datasets, uniform + disLR cannot match the error achieved by our algorithm even when using much more communication.

Figure 5 shows the performance on Gaussian kernels. On mnist8m, the error for uniform + batch KPCA is so large (almost twice of the errors in the figure) that it is not shown. On other datasets, disKPCA achieves significant smaller error. For example, on higgs dataset, to achieve the same error, uniform + disLR requires more than 5 times communication. Since it does not have the communication of computing leverage scores, this means that it needs to sample much more points to get similar performance. Therefore, our algorithm is very efficient in communication.

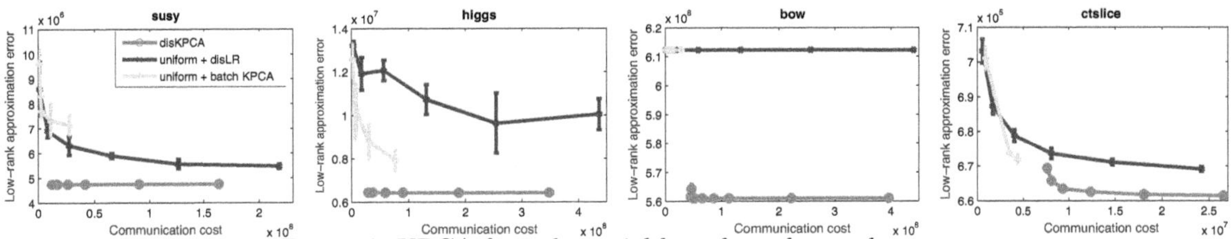

Figure 4: KPCA for polynomial kernels on larger datasets

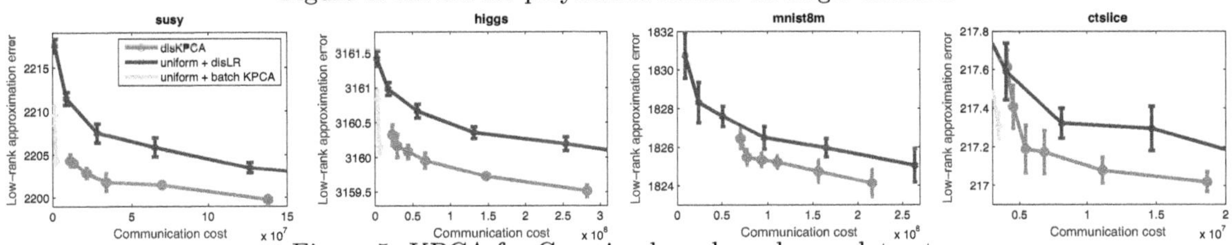

Figure 5: KPCA for Gaussian kernels on larger datasets

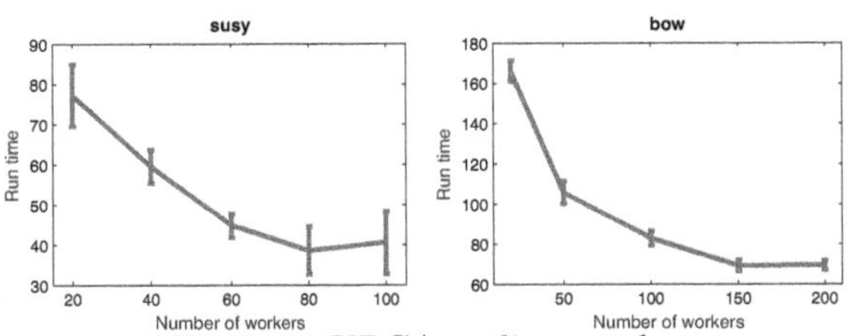

Figure 7: KPCA scaling results

Besides polynomial and Gaussian kernels, we have also conducted experiments using arc-cos kernel [12]. The arc-cosine kernels have random feature bases similar to the Rectified Linear Units (ReLU) used in deep learning. We use degree $n = 2$ and Figure 6 shows the results. Our algorithm consistently achieves better tradeoff between communication and approximation and the benefit is especially more pronounced on sparser dataset such as 20news.

6.5 Scaling Results

In Figure 7, we present the scaling results for disKPCA. In these experiments, we vary the number of workers and record the corresponding computation time (communication time excluded). On both datasets, the runtime decreases as we use more workers, and it eventually plateaus. Our algorithm gains about 2× speedup by using 4× more workers. Note that our algorithm is designed to strike a good balance between communication and approximation. Even though computation complexity is not our first priority, the experiments show disKPCA still enjoys favorable scaling property.

6.6 Distributed Spectral Clustering

We have also experimented a form of spectral clustering (KPCA followed by k-means clustering). We project the data onto the top k principle components and then apply a distributed k-means clustering algorithm [6]. The evaluation criterion is the k-means objective, *i.e.*, average distances to the corresponding centers, in the feature space.

Figure 8(a) presents results for polynomial kernels on the 20news and susy and Figure 8(b) presents results for Gaussian kernels on ctslice and yearpredmsd. Our algorithm compares favorably with the other methods and achieves a better tradeoff of communication and error. This means that although the other methods require similar communication, they need to sample more data points to achieve the same loss, demonstrating the effectiveness of our algorithm.

7. CONCLUSION

This paper proposes a communication efficient distributed algorithm for kernel Principal Component Analysis with theoretical guarantees. It computes a relative-error approximation compared to the best rank-k subspace, using communication that nearly matches that of the state-of-the-art algorithms for distributed linear PCA. This is the first distributed algorithm that can achieve such provable approximation and communication bounds. The experimental results show that it can achieve better performance than the baseline using the same communication budget.

8. ACKNOWLEDGMENTS

M.-F. B. and Y. L. were supported in part by NSF grants CCF-0953192 and CCF-1101283, ONR N00014-09-1-0751, AFOSR grant FA9550-09-1-0538, a Microsoft Faculty Fellowship, and a Google Research Award. Y. L. was also supported in part by NSF grants CCF-1527371, DMS-1317308, Simons Investigator Award, Simons Collaboration Grant, and ONR-N00014-16-1-2329. L. S. and B. X. were supported in part by NSF/NIH BIGDATA 1R01GM108341, ONR N00014-15-1-2340, NSF IIS-1218749, and NSF CAREER IIS-1350983. D.W. acknowledges the support from XDATA program of the Defense Advanced Research Projects Agency (DARPA), administered through Air Force Research Laboratory contract FA8750-12-C-0323.

9. REFERENCES

[1] N. Ailon and B. Chazelle. The fast johnson-lindenstrauss transform and approximate nearest neighbors. *SIAM Journal on Computing*, 39(1):302–322, 2009.

[2] H. Avron, H. Nguyen, and D. Woodruff. Subspace embeddings for the polynomial kernel. In *Advances in Neural Information Processing Systems*, pages 2258–2266, 2014.

[3] F. Bach and M. Jordan. Predictive low-rank decomposition for kernel methods. In *Proceedings of the International Conference on Machine Learning*, 2005.

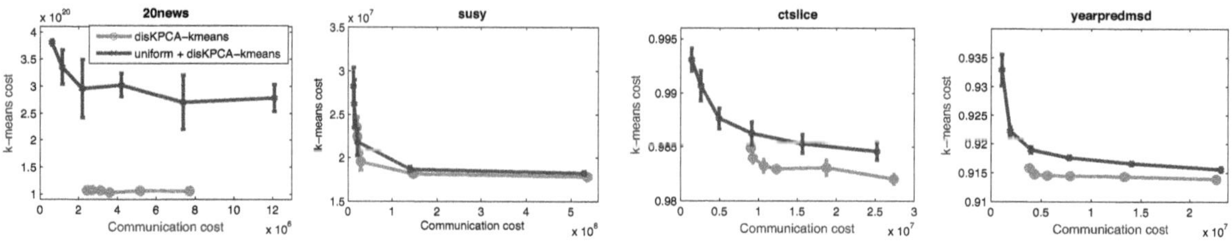

(a) Polynomial kernels (b) Gaussian kernels

Figure 8: KPCA + k-means clustering

[4] K. Bache and M. Lichman. UCI machine learning repository, 2013.

[5] M.-F. Balcan, A. Blum, S. Fine, and Y. Mansour. Distributed learning, communication complexity and privacy. *COLT*, 2012.

[6] M.-F. Balcan, V. Kanchanapally, Y. Liang, and D. Woodruff. Improved distributed principal component analysis. In *Advances in Neural Information Processing Systems 27*, pages 3113–3121. Curran Associates, Inc., 2014.

[7] P. Baldi, P. Sadowski, and D. Whiteson. Searching for exotic particles in high-energy physics with deep learning. *Nature Communications*, 2014.

[8] C. Boutsidis, M. Sviridenko, and D. P. Woodruff. Optimal distributed principal component analysis. In *manuscript*, 2015.

[9] C. Boutsidis and D. P. Woodruff. Optimal cur matrix decompositions. *arXiv preprint arXiv:1405.7910*, 2014.

[10] C. Boutsidis and D. P. Woodruff. Communication-optimal distributed principal component analysis in the column-partition model. *CoRR*, abs/1504.06729, 2015.

[11] C. Boutsidis, D. P. Woodruff, and P. Zhong. Communication-optimal distributed principal component analysis in the column-partition model. In *ACM Symposium on Theory of Computing*, 2015.

[12] Y. Cho and L. K. Saul. Kernel methods for deep learning. In *NIPS*, pages 342–350, 2009.

[13] K. L. Clarkson and D. P. Woodruff. Low rank approximation and regression in input sparsity time. In *Proceedings of the Annual ACM Symposium on Theory of Computing*, 2013.

[14] A. Clauset, C. R. Shalizi, and M. E. Newman. Power-law distributions in empirical data. *SIAM review*, 51(4):661–703, 2009.

[15] B. Dai, B. Xie, N. He, Y. Liang, A. Raj, M.-F. F. Balcan, and L. Song. Scalable kernel methods via doubly stochastic gradients. In *Advances in Neural Information Processing Systems*, pages 3041–3049, 2014.

[16] A. Deshpande and S. Vempala. Adaptive sampling and fast low-rank matrix approximation. *Algorithms and Techniques in Approximation, Randomization, and Combinatorial Optimization*, pages 292–303, 2006.

[17] I. S. Dhillon, Y. Guan, and B. Kulis. Kernel kmeans, spectral clustering and normalized cuts. In *Conference on Knowledge Discovery and Data Mining*, 2004.

[18] P. Drineas, M. Magdon-Ismail, M. Mahoney, and D. Woodruff. Fast approximation of matrix coherence and statistical leverage. *The Journal of Machine Learning Research*, 13(1):3475–3506, 2012.

[19] P. Drineas, M. W. Mahoney, and S. Muthukrishnan. Relative-error cur matrix decompositions. *SIAM Journal on Matrix Analysis and Applications*, 30(2):844–881, 2008.

[20] R. Kannan, S. Vempala, and D. Woodruff. Principal component analysis and higher correlations for distributed data. In *Proceedings of The 27th Conference on Learning Theory*, pages 1040–1057, 2014.

[21] S. Kumar, M. Mohri, and A. Talwalkar. Sampling methods for the nyström method. *Journal of Machine Learning Research*, 13:981–1006, 2012.

[22] X. Meng and M. W. Mahoney. Low-distortion subspace embeddings in input-sparsity time and applications to robust linear regression. In *Proceedings of the Annual ACM symposium on Symposium on Theory of Computing*, 2013.

[23] J. Nelson and H. L. Nguyên. Osnap: Faster numerical linear algebra algorithms via sparser subspace embeddings. In *IEEE Annual Symposium on Foundations of Computer Science*, 2013.

[24] A. Rahimi and B. Recht. Random features for large-scale kernel machines. In J. Platt, D. Koller, Y. Singer, and S. Roweis, editors, *Advances in Neural Information Processing Systems 20*. MIT Press, Cambridge, MA, 2008.

[25] T. Sarlós. Improved approximation algorithms for large matrices via random projections. In *IEEE Symposium on Foundations of Computer Science*, 2006.

[26] B. Schölkopf and A. J. Smola. *Learning with Kernels*. MIT Press, Cambridge, MA, 2002.

[27] B. Schölkopf, A. J. Smola, and K.-R. Müller. Kernel principal component analysis. In *Artificial Neural Networks ICANN'97*, volume 1327, pages 583–588, Berlin, 1997.

[28] B. Schölkopf, K. Tsuda, and J.-P. Vert. *Kernel Methods in Computational Biology*. MIT Press, Cambridge, MA, 2004.

[29] D. P. Woodruff. Sketching as a tool for numerical linear algebra. *Theoretical Computer Science*, 10(1-2):1–157, 2014.

[30] Y. Zhang, M. J. Wainwright, and J. C. Duchi. Communication-efficient algorithms for statistical optimization. In *Advance in Neural Information Processing Systems*, 2012.

Keeping it Short and Simple: Summarising Complex Event Sequences with Multivariate Patterns

Roel Bertens
Department of Information and Computing Sciences
Utrecht University
Utrecht, The Netherlands
R.Bertens@uu.nl

Jilles Vreeken
Max Planck Institute for Informatics and Saarland University
Saarbrücken, Germany
jilles@mpi-inf.mpg.de

Arno Siebes
Department of Information and Computing Sciences
Utrecht University
Utrecht, The Netherlands
A.P.J.M.Siebes@uu.nl

ABSTRACT

We study how to obtain concise descriptions of discrete multivariate sequential data. In particular, how to do so in terms of rich multivariate sequential patterns that can capture potentially highly interesting (cor)relations between sequences. To this end we allow our pattern language to span over the domains (alphabets) of all sequences, allow patterns to overlap temporally, as well as allow for gaps in their occurrences.

We formalise our goal by the Minimum Description Length principle, by which our objective is to discover the set of patterns that provides the most succinct description of the data. To discover high-quality pattern sets directly from data, we introduce DITTO, a highly efficient algorithm that approximates the ideal result very well.

Experiments show that DITTO correctly discovers the patterns planted in synthetic data. Moreover, it scales favourably with the length of the data, the number of attributes, the alphabet sizes. On real data, ranging from sensor networks to annotated text, DITTO discovers easily interpretable summaries that provide clear insight in both the univariate and multivariate structure.

Keywords

summarisation; multivariate sequences; multivariate patterns; MDL

1. INTRODUCTION

Most real sequential data is multivariate, as when we measure data over time, we typically do so over multiple attributes. Examples include sensors in a network, frequency bands in seismic or ECG data, transaction records, and annotated text. In this paper we investigate how to succinctly summarise such data in terms of those patterns that are most characteristic for the data.

To capture these characteristics, our pattern language needs to be rich, i.e., patterns may span multiple aligned sequences (attributes) in which no order between these attributes is assumed and occurrences may contain gaps. For example, if we consider a sensor network, a pattern could be a characteristic set of values for multiple attributes at one point in time, or, more complex, a specific value for one sensor, temporally followed by certain readings of one or more other sensors. That is, patterns that are able to identify associations and correlations between one or multiple attributes.

Having such a rich pattern language has as immediate consequence that the well-known frequent pattern explosion hits particularly hard. Even for trivial data sets one easily finds enormous numbers of frequent patterns, even at modest minimal frequency thresholds [27]; the simplest synthetic dataset we consider contains only five true patterns, yet the *lower bound* on the number of frequent patterns is more than a billion.

Clearly, returning collections of such magnitude is useless, as they cannot be inspected in any meaningful way. Rather, we want a small set of such patterns that collectively describe the data well. To find such sets, we employ the Minimum Description Length (MDL) principle [8]. This approach has a proven track record in the domain of transaction data mining [32, 24] and has also been successfully applied to, e.g. sequential data [28, 10]. Because complex multivariate sequential data is ubiquitous and correlation between multiple sequences can give much insight to domain experts, here we take this research further by defining a framework to summarise this data, while able to efficiently deal with the enormous space of frequent patterns. Note that, all real-valued time series can easily be discretised to fit our framework, for example using SAX [13].

The humongous number of frequent patterns makes it intractable to discover a small set of characteristic patterns by post-processing the set of all frequent patterns; all the more because the MDL objective function on pattern sets is neither monotone nor sub-modular. Hence we introduce a heuristic algorithm, called DITTO,[1] that mines characteristic sets of patterns directly from the data. In a nutshell, DITTO mines good models by iteratively adding those patterns to the model that maximally reduce redundancy. That is, it iteratively considers the current description of the data and searches for patterns that most frequently occur one after the other, and considers the union of such pairs as candidates to add to the model. As such, DITTO focusses on exactly those patterns that are likely to improve our score, pruning large parts of the search space, and hence only needs seconds to mine high-quality summaries.

Our extensive empirical evaluation of DITTO shows it ably discovers succinct summaries that contain the key patterns of the data at hand, and, importantly, that it does not pick up on noise. An example of what we discover includes the following. When applied to the novel Moby Dick by Herman Melville (one attribute) aligned

[1]The ditto mark (") is used in lists to indicate that an item is repeated, i.e., a multivariate pattern.

KDD '16, August 13 - 17, 2016, San Francisco, CA, USA

ISBN 978-1-4503-4232-2/16/08...$15.00

DOI: http://dx.doi.org/10.1145/2939672.2939761

with the corresponding part-of-speech tags (another attribute), the summary DITTO discovers consists of meaningful non-trivial linguistic patterns including "⟨noun⟩ of the ⟨noun⟩", e.g. "Man of the World", and "the ⟨noun⟩ of", as used in "the ship of (somebody)". These summaries hence give clear insight in the writing style of the author(s). Besides giving direct insight, the summaries we discover have high downstream potential. One could, for example, use them for comparative analysis [4]. For example, for text identifying similarities and differences between authors, for sensor networks detecting and describing concept drift over time, and characterising differences between patients. Such analysis is left for future work, as we first have to be able to efficiently discover high quality pattern-based summaries from multivariate sequential data. That is what we focus on in this paper.

The remainder of this paper is organised as follows. We first cover preliminaries and introduce notation in Section 2. In Section 3 we formally introduce the problem. Section 4 gives the details of the DITTO algorithm. We discuss related work in Section 5, and empirically evaluate our score in Section 6. We round up with discussion and conclusions in Sections 7 and 8, respectively.

2. PRELIMINARIES AND NOTATION

As data type we consider databases D of $|D|$ multivariate event sequences $S \in D$, all over attributes A. We assume that the set of attributes is indexed, such that A_i refers to the ith attribute of D.

A multivariate, or *complex*, event sequence S is a bag of $|A|$ univariate event sequences, $S = \{S^1, \ldots, S^{|A|}\}$. An event sequence $S^i \in \Omega_i^n$ is simply a sequence of n events drawn from discrete domain Ω_i, which we will refer to as its *alphabet*. An event is hence simply an attribute–value pair. That is, the jth event of S^i corresponds to the value of attribute A_i at time j. We will write Ω for the union over these attribute alphabets, i.e. $\Omega = \cup_{i \in |A|} \Omega_i$.

By $||S||$ we indicate the number of events in a multivariate sequence S, and by $t(S)$ the length of the sequence, i.e. the number of time steps. We will refer to the set of events at a single time step j as a *multi-event*, writing $S[j]$ for the jth multi-event of S. To project a multivariate event sequence S onto an individual attribute, we write S^i for the univariate event sequence on the ith attribute, and analogously define D^i. For completeness, we define $||D|| = \sum_{S \in D} ||S||$ for the total number of events, and $t(D) = \sum_S t(S)$ for the total number of time steps in D.

Our framework fits both categorical and transaction (item set) data. With categorical data the number of events at each time step is equal to the number of attributes. For simplicity, w.l.o.g., we consider categorical data in the remainder.

As patterns we consider partial orders of multi-events, i.e. sequences of multi-events, allowing for gaps between time steps in their occurrences. By $t(X)$ we denote the *length* of a pattern X, i.e. the number of time steps for which a pattern X defines a value. In addition, we write $||X||$ to denote the *size* of a pattern X, the total number of values it defines, i.e. $\sum_{X[i] \in X} \sum_{x \in X[i]} 1$. For example, in Figure 1 it holds that $||X|| = 4$ and $t(X) = 3$.

We say a pattern X is *present* in a sequence $S \in D$ of the data when there exists an interval $[t_{start}, \cdots, t_{end}]$ in which all multi-events $X[i] \in X$ are contained in the order specified by X, allowing for gaps in time. That is, $\forall_{X[i] \in X} \exists_{j \in [start,end]} X[i] \subseteq S[j]$, and $k \geq j + 1$ for $X[i] \subseteq S[j]$ and $X[i+1] \subseteq S[k]$. A singleton pattern is a single event $e \in \Omega$ and $\mathcal{P}$ is the set of all non-singleton patterns. A minimal window for a pattern is an interval in the data in which a pattern occurs which can not be shortened while still containing the whole pattern [26]. In the remainder of this paper when we use the term pattern occurrence we always expect it to be a minimal window. Further, we use $occs(X, S)$ for the disjoint set of all occurrences of X in S. Figure 1 shows examples of two categorical patterns occurring both with and without gaps.

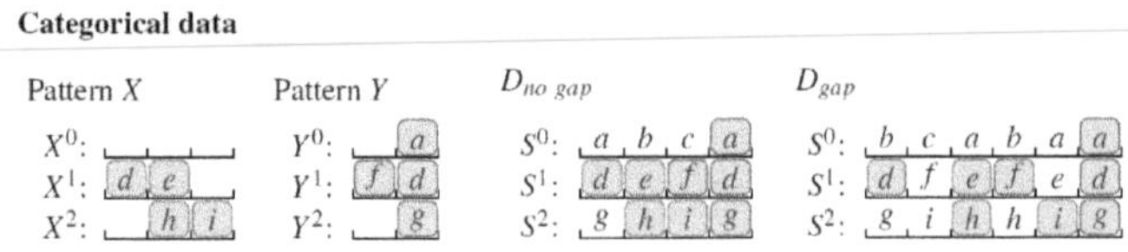

Figure 1: Patterns X and Y occurring with (D_{gap}) and without ($D_{no\ gap}$) gaps in the data.

Our method operates on categorical data. To find patterns in continuous real-valued time series we first have to discretise it. SAX [13] is a celebrated approach for doing so, and we will use it in our experiments – though we note that any discretisation scheme can be employed. This ordinal data can either be represented by absolute values per time step, or by relative values that represent the difference between each pair of subsequent values. These relative values describe the changes in the data rather than the exact values – by which different types of patterns can be discovered.

3. THEORY

In this section we give a brief introduction to the MDL principle, we define our objective function, and analyse the complexity of the optimization problem.

3.1 MDL Introduction

The Minimum Description Length principle (MDL) [8] is a method for inductive inference that aims to find the best model for the data. It is based on the insight that any regularity in the data can be used to compress the data: the more we can compress, the more regularity we have found. More formally, given a set of models $\mathcal{M}$, the best model $M \in \mathcal{M}$ is the one that minimises

$$L(M) + L(D \mid M)$$

where $L(M)$ is the length of the description of M, and $L(D \mid M)$ is the length of the description of the data.

To use MDL, we have to define how our model looks and how we can use it to describe the data. That is, we need to be able to encode and decode the data using our model.

3.2 MDL for Multivariate Sequential Data

As models for our data we consider code tables (CT) [32, 28]; these are simple four-column look-up tables (or, dictionaries) between patterns on the left hand side, and associated codes on the right hand side. In this paper we consider three types of codes, i.e. pattern codes, gap codes and fill codes. We will explain the use of these below, in Section 3.2.2 and Example 2.

Loosely speaking, whenever we read a pattern code $code_p(X \mid CT)$ we know we can start to decode the events of pattern X. A fill code $code_f(X \mid CT)$ tells us we can decode the next time step of pattern X, whereas a gap code $code_g(X \mid CT)$ tells us there is a gap in this occurrence of pattern X. To fill such a gap we read the next pattern code. Note that, our approach thus allows for patterns to interleave. For readability, we do not write CT wherever clear from context. To make sure we can encode any multivariate event sequence over Ω, we require that a code table at least contains all singleton events. Next, we will describe how to use these code tables to cover and encode a dataset. Further, we define how to compute

$L(CT)$ and $L(D \mid CT)$ and we conclude with our formal problem definition.

3.2.1 *Covering*

A cover determines where we use each pattern when encoding a dataset and also where gaps in patterns occur. More formally, a cover $\mathcal{C}$ defines the set of all pattern occurrences that are used to cover the complete dataset. Therefore, if one of the events from pattern occurrence o is already covered by another pattern occurrence $o' \in \mathcal{C}$ we say that the occurrence o *overlaps* with the current cover $\mathcal{C}$, i.e. $\mathcal{C} \cap o \neq \emptyset$, which we do not allow.

As we are after the minimal description, we want to use optimal codes. Clearly, the more often a code is used, the shorter it should be. This, however, creates a non-trivial connection between how often a pattern is used to describe part of the data, and its code length. This, in turn, makes the complete optimisation process, and in particular that of finding a good cover of the data given a set of patterns non-trivial. For the univariate case, we showed [28] that when we know the optimal code lengths we can determine the optimal cover by dynamic programming, and that we can approximate the optimal cover by iteratively optimising the code lengths and the cover. Although computationally expensive, for univariate data this strategy works well. For multivariate data, naively seen the search space grows enormously. More importantly, it is not clear how this strategy can be generalised, as now the usages of two patterns are allowed to temporally overlap as long as they do not cover the same events. We therefore take a more general and faster greedy strategy.

To cover a dataset we need the set of patterns from the first column of a code table CT, which we will refer to as PS (Patterns and Singletons). In Algorithm 1 we specify our COVER algorithm, which iterates through PS in a pre-specified order that we will detail later. For each pattern X the algorithm greedily covers all occurrences that do not overlap with already covered data, and have fewer than $t(X)$ gaps. To bound the number and size of gaps we only allow occurrences where the number of gap positions is smaller than the length of the pattern itself. This avoids gap codes becoming cheaper than fill codes, by which occurrences with more gaps would be preferred over compact occurrences. This process continues until all data is covered. In Figure 2 we show in 3 steps how a PS is used to cover the example dataset.

Example 1. In Algorithm 1, we start with an empty cover, corresponding to an uncovered dataset as in the top left of Fig 2. Next, we cover the data using the first pattern from the PS (line 1). For each occurrence of the pattern $\{ {a \atop d} \}$ (line 2), we add it to our cover (line 4) when it does not overlap previously added elements and has a limited number of gaps (line 3). In Step 1 of Fig 2 we show the result of covering the data with the pattern $\{ {a \atop d} \}$. We continue to do the same for the next pattern $\{h, e\}$ in CT. This gives us the cover as shown in Step 2. With only the singleton patterns left to consider in CT there is only one way to complete our cover by using them for all so far uncovered events. Now all events in the dataset are covered, thus we can break out of our loop (line 6) and return the final cover of Step 3 in Fig. 2 (line 7).

3.2.2 *Encoding*

A cover $\mathcal{C}$ specifies how the data will be encoded. Conceptually, we can decompose it into a pattern code stream and a gap code stream. The pattern stream C_p contains a sequence of pattern codes, $code_p(X)$ for pattern $X \in CT$, used to describe the data, whereas the gap code stream C_g consists of codes $code_g(X)$ and $code_f(X)$ indicating whether and where a pattern instance contains gaps or not.

To encode a dataset we traverse our dataset from left-to-right and top-to-bottom and each time we encounter a new pattern in our cover we add the code for this pattern to C_p. When moving to the next multi-event in the dataset we add for each pattern, that we already encountered but not yet completely passed by, a gap or fill code to C_g. We choose a gap code for a pattern if the current multi-event does not contain any event from the pattern or a fill code if it does. We are finished when we have encoded all multi-events in the data.

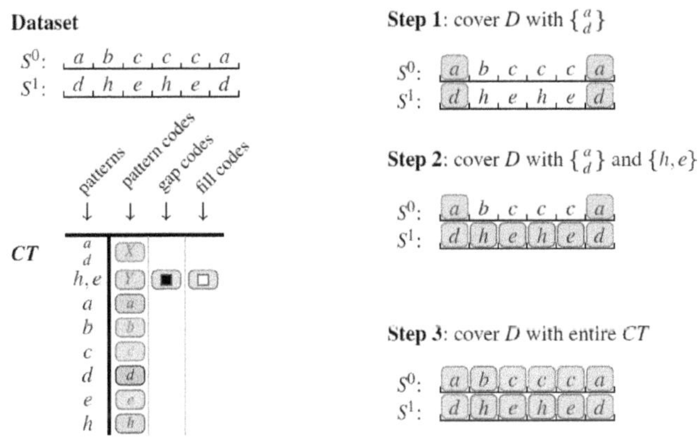

Figure 2: Sample data D, code table CT, and cover $\mathcal{C}$.

Algorithm 1 The COVER Algorithm

Input: A sequence S, a set of patterns PS, and $\mathcal{C} = \emptyset$
Output: A cover $\mathcal{C}$ of $S \in D$ using PS

```
1: for each X ∈ PS in order do                    // see Sec. 4 for order
2:     for all o ∈ occs(X, S) do                  // all occurrences of X
3:         if C ∩ o = ∅ and t(o) < 2t(X) then
4:             C ← C ∪ o
5:     if C completely covers S then
6:         break
7: return C
```

Example 2. In Figure 3 we show how a cover is translated to an encoding. To encode the first multi-event we first add $code_p(a)$ and then $code_p(Y)$ to C_p. For the second multi-event we add $code_p(X)$ to C_p and $code_g(Y)$ to C_g, because event e from pattern Y does not yet occur in this multi-event. For the third multi-event we add $code_p(a)$ to C_p, and $code_g(X)$ and $code_f(Y)$ to C_g. Code $code_g(X)$ marks the gap for pattern X and $code_f(Y)$ indicates that event e from pattern Y does occur in this multi-event. The fourth multi-event results in the addition of $code_p(Y)$ to C_p and $code_f(X)$ to C_g, where the latter marks the presence of event b from pattern X in this multi-event. For the last multi-event we add $code_p(a)$ to C_p and $code_f(Y)$ to C_g, which completes the encoding.

Using C_p and C_g we can compute the actual codes to construct the code table CT corresponding to PS used to cover the data. We will encode the data using optimal prefix codes [7], the length of which we can compute by Shannon entropy. In our case this means that the length of an optimal pattern code for pattern X is the negative log-likelihood of a pattern in the cover [8], that is

$$L(code_p(X \mid CT)) = -\log\left(\frac{usage(X)}{\sum_{Y \in CT} usage(Y)}\right) ,$$

where $usage(X)$ is the number of times a pattern X is used to describe the data, i.e. $usage(X) = |\{Y \in C_p | Y = code_p(X)\}|$.

Gap and fill code lengths are computed similarly, corresponding to the negative log-likelihood of these codes within the usages of

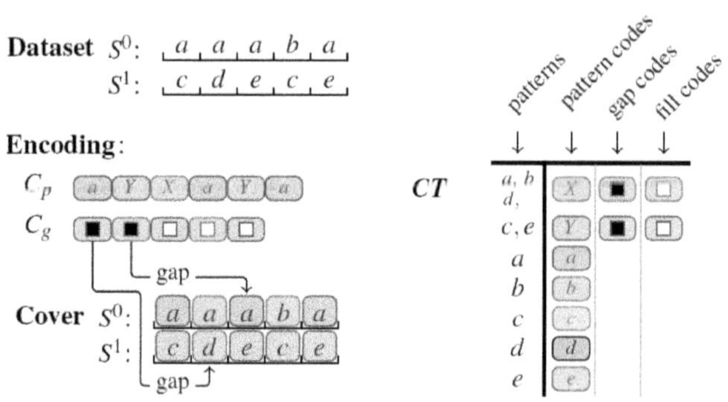

Figure 3: The encoding of the dataset given a cover and CT. See Example 2 for more details.

the corresponding pattern. That is, we have

$$L(code_g(X \mid CT)) = -\log\left(\frac{gaps(X)}{gaps(X) + fills(X)}\right) \quad ,$$

$$L(code_f(X \mid CT)) = -\log\left(\frac{fills(X)}{gaps(X) + fills(X)}\right) \quad .$$

where $gaps(X)$ and $fills(X)$ are the number of times a gap, resp. fill-code of pattern X is used in the cover of the data, i.e. $gaps(X) = |\{Y \in C_g \mid Y = code_g(X)\}|$ and analogue for $fills(X)$.

3.2.3 Encoded Length of Data Given Code Table

Now that we have determined the cover and encoding scheme, we can formalise the calculation of the encoded length of the data given the CT. This encoded length is the sum of the encoded length of following terms: the pattern stream, the gap stream, the number of attributes, the number of sequences and the length of each sequence. Formally, we have

$$L(D \mid CT) = L(C_p \mid CT) + L(C_g \mid CT) + L_{\mathbb{N}}(|A|) + L_{\mathbb{N}}(|D|) + \sum_{S \in D} L_{\mathbb{N}}(|S|) \quad ,$$

where $L_{\mathbb{N}}$ is the MDL optimal Universal code for integers [8] and the encoded length of the pattern and gap stream are simply the code lengths of all codes in the streams,

$$L(C_p \mid CT) = \sum_{X \in CT} usage(X) L(code_p(X))$$

$$L(C_g \mid CT) = \sum_{\substack{X \in CT \\ t(X)>1}} \left[gaps(X) L(code_g(X)) + fills(X) L(code_f(X))\right] \quad .$$

3.2.4 Encoded Length of Code Table

The encoded length of the code table consists of the following parts. For each attribute A_j we encode the number of singletons and their support in D^j. Then we encode the number of non-singleton patterns in the code table, the sum of their usages, and then using a strong number composition their individual usages. Last, we encode the patterns themselves using $L(X \in CT)$. We hence have

$$L(CT \mid \mathcal{C}) = \sum_{j \in |A|} \left(L_{\mathbb{N}}(|\Omega_j|) + \log\binom{|D^j|}{|\Omega_j|}\right) + L_{\mathbb{N}}(|\mathcal{P}| + 1) + L_{\mathbb{N}}(usage(\mathcal{P}) + 1) + \log\binom{usage(\mathcal{P})}{|\mathcal{P}|} + \sum_{X \in \mathcal{P}} L(X \in CT) \quad .$$

For the encoded length of a non-singleton pattern $X \in CT$ we have

$$L(X \in CT) = L_{\mathbb{N}}(t(X)) + L_{\mathbb{N}}(gaps(X) + 1) + \sum_{t(X)} \log(|A|) + \sum_{x \in X} L(code_p(x \mid ST)) \quad ,$$

where we first encode its length, and its total number of gaps – note that we can derive the total number of fills for this pattern from these two values. As $L_{\mathbb{N}}$ is defined for integers $z \geq 1$, we apply a $+1$ shift wherever z can be zero [8]. Then, per time step, we encode for how many attributes the pattern defines a value, and what these values are using the singleton-only, or Standard Code Table (ST). For the encoded length of an event given the ST we have

$$L(code_p(x \mid ST)) = -\log\left(\frac{support(x \mid D)}{||D||}\right) \quad ,$$

which is simply the negative log-likelihood of the event under an independence assumption.

3.3 Formal Problem Definition

Loosely speaking, our goal is to find the most succinct description of the data. By MDL, we define the optimal set of patterns for the given data as the set for which the optimal cover and associated optimal code table minimise the total encoded length. As such we have the following problem definition.

Minimal Pattern Set Problem *Let Ω be a set of events and let D be a multivariate sequential dataset over Ω, find the minimal set of multivariate sequential patterns $\mathcal{P}$ and cover $\mathcal{C}$ of D using $\mathcal{P}$ and Ω, such that the encoded length $L(CT, D) = L(CT \mid \mathcal{C}) + L(D \mid CT)$ is minimal, where CT is the code-optimal code table for $\mathcal{C}$.*

Let us consider how complex this problem is. Firstly, the number of possible pattern sets (with a maximum pattern length of n) is

$$\sum_{k=1}^{2^{|\Omega|^n} - |\Omega| - 1} \binom{2^{|\Omega|^n} - |\Omega| - 1}{k} \quad .$$

Secondly, to use a pattern set to cover the data we also need to specify the order of the patterns in the set. That is, we need to find the optimal order for the elements in the pattern set to find the one that minimises the total encoded length. The total number of ways to cover the dataset using one of the possible ordered pattern sets is

$$\sum_{k=1}^{2^{|\Omega|^n} - |\Omega| - 1} \binom{2^{|\Omega|^n} - |\Omega| - 1}{k} \times (k + |\Omega|)! \quad .$$

Moreover, unfortunately, it does not show submodular structure nor (weak) (anti-)monotonicity properties by which we would be able to prune large parts of it. Hence, we resort to heuristics.

4. THE DITTO ALGORITHM

In this section we present DITTO, an efficient algorithm to heuristically approximate the MDL optimal summary of the data. In

Algorithm 2 The DITTO Algorithm

Input: The dataset D and singleton code table ST
Output: An approximation to the **Minimal Pattern Set Problem**

1: $CT \leftarrow ST$
2: $Cand \leftarrow CT \times CT$
3: **for** $X \in Cand$ in **Candidate Order do**
4:     **if** $L(D, CT \oplus X) < L(D, CT)$ **then**
5:         $CT \leftarrow$ PRUNE$(D, CT \oplus X)$
6:         $CT \leftarrow$ VARIATIONS(D, X, CT)
7:         $Cand \leftarrow CT \times CT$
8: **return** CT

particular, it avoids enumerating all multivariate patterns, let alone all possible subsets of those. Instead, it considers a small but highly promising part of this search space by iterative bottom-up search for those patterns that maximally improve the description. More specifically, we build on the idea of SLIM [24] and SQS [28]. That is, as candidates to add to our model, we only consider the most promising combinations of already chosen patterns – as identified by their estimated gain in compression.

We give the pseudo code of DITTO as Algorithm 2. We start with singleton code table ST (line 1) and a set of candidate patterns of all pairwise combinations of singletons (line 2). We then iteratively add patterns from the candidate set to code table CT in **Candidate Order**: $\downarrow$ $estimated\ gain(X)$, $\downarrow$ $support(X \mid D)$, $\downarrow$ $||X||$, $\downarrow$ $L(X \mid ST)$ and $\uparrow$ lexicographically (line 3). This order prefers the most promising candidates in terms of compression gain. When a new pattern improves the total encoded length $L(D, CT)$ we keep it, otherwise we discard it (line 4). After acceptance of a new pattern we prune (line 5) CT and recursively test whether to add variations (line 6) of the accepted pattern in combination with its gap events. When all variations are tested recursively, we update the candidate set by combining $CT \times CT$ (line 7).

We give the details of each of these steps below, as well as explain how to gain efficiency through smart caching, and discuss the computational complexity of DITTO.

4.1 Covering

As detailed in the previous sections, to compute $L(D, CT)$, we first need to cover the data with CT. The COVER algorithm covers the data using the patterns as they are ordered in CT. To find the optimal cover we need to identify the cover order that leads to the smallest encoded length of the data. We do so greedily, by considering the pattern set in a fixed order. As our goal is to compress the data, we prefer patterns that cover many events with just a short code length. We hence define the **Cover Order** as follows: $\downarrow$ $||X||$, $\downarrow$ $support(X \mid D)$, $\downarrow$ $L(X \mid ST)$ and $\uparrow$ lexicographically. It follows the intuition that we give preference to larger and more frequent patterns, for which we expect a higher compression gain, to cover the data first, as these maximise the likelihood of the cover.

4.2 Candidates and Estimation

Conceptually, at every iteration the set of candidates from which we can choose, consists of the Cartesian product of the code table with itself. Two patterns X and Y can be combined to form new candidate patterns. Each alignment of X and Y without gaps in either X, Y and the resulting pattern, forms a new candidate, with the exception of alignments in which X and Y overlap. See Figure 4 for an example.

Selecting the candidate with the highest gain is very expensive – we would need to cover the whole data for every candidate. Instead,

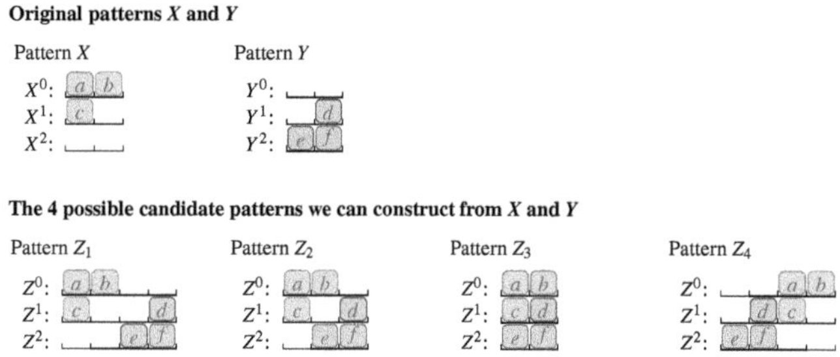

Figure 4: The 4 possible candidate patterns constructed from different alignments of X and Y.

we select the candidate with the highest *estimated* gain – which can be done much more efficiently. Intuitively, based on the estimated gain ($\Delta L'$) we only consider candidate patterns in a lazy fashion based on their usage and do not consider patterns with a lower usage than the current best candidate. For notational brevity, for a pattern $X \in CT$ we use $x = usage(X)$. Further, let s be the total usage count of all patterns in CT, i.e. $s = \sum_{X \in CT} x$. For $CT' = CT \oplus Z$, we use x' and s' similarly. We estimate z, the usage of Z, optimistically as the minimum of the usages of X and Y – and as $x/2$ when $X = Y$ (because the usage of XX can not be higher). Formally, our gain estimate $\Delta L'(CT \oplus Z, D)$ of the true gain $\Delta L(CT \oplus Z, D)$ for adding pattern $Z = X \cup Y$ to CT is as follows,

$$\begin{aligned}
\Delta L'(CT', D) &= \Delta L'(CT' \mid D) + \Delta L'(D \mid CT') \quad , \\
\Delta L'(CT' \mid D) &= - L_{\mathbb{N}}(|Z|) - \sum_{l(Z)} \log(|A|) \\
&\quad - \sum_{Z[i] \in Z} \sum_{z \in Z[i]} L(code_p(z \mid ST)) \quad , \\
\Delta L'(D \mid CT') &= s \log s - s' \log s' + z \log z - x \log x \\
&\quad + x' \log x' - y \log y + y' \log y' \quad .
\end{aligned}$$

That is, the estimated gain of adding pattern Z to CT thus consists of the estimated gain in the size of the data, minus the increase in the size of CT. Note that, $\Delta L'$ is an estimate and for simplicity we ignore the effects of adding pattern Z to code table CT on the pattern and (no-)gap usages of patterns other than X and Y.

4.3 Pruning

After the acceptance of a new pattern in our code table other patterns may have become redundant as their role may have been overtaken by the newer pattern. Therefore, each time a pattern X is successfully added to the code table, we consider removing those $Y \in CT$ for which the usage decreased and hence the pattern code length increased. Algorithm 3 describes how a code table is pruned.

4.4 Generating Pattern Variations

To efficiently discover a large and diverse set of promising patterns – without breadth-first-search, which takes long to find large patterns, and without depth-first-search, which would be prohibitively costly – we consider *variations* of each accepted pattern to the code table. That is, when a pattern leads to a gain in compression, we consider all ways by which we can extend it using events that occur in the gaps of its usages. This way we consider a rich set of candidates, plus speed up the search as we are automatically directed to patterns that actually exist in the data. Algorithm 4 outputs a code table possibly containing variations of the lastly added pattern Y.

Algorithm 3 The PRUNE Algorithm

Input: The dataset D and a code table CT
Output: A pruned code table

$Cand \leftarrow X \in CT$ with decreased usage
for $X \in Cand$ in **Prune Order do**
  if $L(D, CT \setminus X) < L(D, CT)$ **then**
    $CT \leftarrow CT \setminus X$
    $Cand \leftarrow Cand \cup \{Y \in CT \mid \text{usage decreased}\}$
  $Cand \leftarrow Cand \setminus X$
return CT

Algorithm 4 The VARIATIONS Algorithm

Input: The dataset D, a pattern Y and a code table CT
Output: A code table possibly containing variations of Y

$Cand \leftarrow Y \times gap\ events(Y)$
for $X \in Cand$ **do**
  if $L(D, CT \oplus X) < L(D, CT)$ **then**
    $CT \leftarrow$ PRUNE$(D, CT \oplus X)$
    $CT \leftarrow$ VARIATIONS(D, X, CT)
  $Cand \leftarrow Cand \setminus X$
return CT

For example, consider the dataset $\{a, b, a, b, c, a, c, a\}$ where pattern $\{a, a\}$ occurs twice with a gap of length one. After adding pattern $\{a, a\}$ to CT we consider the patterns $\{a, b, a\}$ and $\{a, c, a\}$ for addition to CT.

4.5 Faster Search through Caching

The space of all possible multivariate patterns is extremely rich. Moreover, in practice many candidate patterns will not lead to any gain in compression. In particular, those that occur only very infrequently in the data are unlikely to provide us any (or much) gain in compression. We thus can increase the efficiency of DITTO by allowing the user to impose a minimum support threshold for candidates. That is, only patterns X will be evaluated if they occur at least σ times in the data. To avoid time and again re-evaluating candidates of which we already know that they are infrequent, we cache these in a tree-based data structure. Only *materialised* infrequent pattern are added to the tree. Future candidates are only materialised when none of its subsets are present in the tree, as by the a priori principle we know it can not be frequent [15].

Even though this tree can theoretically grow very large, in practice it stays relatively small because we only consider a small part of the candidate space. That is, we only combine patterns we know to be frequent to form new candidate patterns. In practice, we found that DITTO only has to cache up to a few thousand candidates. Using this tree we see speed ups in computation of 2 to 4 times, while also memory consumption is strongly reduced. For some datasets the difference is even bigger, up to an order of magnitude.

In this work we only consider keeping track of infrequent candidates. Note, however, that at the expense of some optimality in the search additional efficiency can be gained by also storing *rejected* candidates in the tree. In both theory and practice, however, candidates rejected in one iteration may lead to compression gain later in the process [24].

4.6 Complexity

The time complexity of DITTO has a simple upper bound as follows. In the worst-case we cover the data for each frequent pattern from the set of all frequent patterns $\mathcal{F}$ in each iteration. Covering takes $O(|CT| \times ||D||)$ and the number of iterations is worst-case $O(|\mathcal{F}|)$. Together, the worst-case time complexity is

$$O(|\mathcal{F}|^2 \times |CT| \times ||D||) \quad .$$

From the experiments in Section 6, however, we will learn that this estimate is rather pessimistic. In practice the code table stays small ($|CT| \ll |\mathcal{F}|$), we only consider a subset of all frequent patterns and we do this greedily. In practice the runtime of DITTO therefore stays in the order of seconds to minutes.

5. RELATED WORK

The first to use MDL to summarise transaction data were Siebes et al. [22], resulting in KRIMP [32]. It shifted focus from the long-standing goal of mining collections of patterns that describe the set of all frequent patterns, e.g. closed [20] frequent patterns, to a *pattern set* that describes the data.

Similar to the transaction data domain, summarisation of sequential data also developed from frequent pattern mining. For sequential data, the key types of patterns studied are frequent subsequences [21], and frequent episodes [1, 16]. As with all traditional pattern mining approaches, redundancy is also a key problem when mining sequential patterns [33, 9]. To this end, Tatti and Vreeken [28] proposed to instead approximate the MDL-optimal summarisation of event sequence data using serial episodes. Their method SQS deals with many challenges inherent to this type of data, such as the importance of the order of events and the possibility for patterns to allow gaps in their occurrences – aspects we build upon and extend. Other methods exist, but either do not consider [2, 14] or do not punish gaps [10, 11] with optimal codes. None of these methods consider, or are easily extended to multivariate sequential data.

One of the first to consider multivariate sequential patterns, by searching for multi-stream dependencies, were Oates et al. [19]. Tatti and Cule [27] formalised how to mine the set of closed frequent patterns from multivariate sequential data, where patterns allow simultaneous events. In [35] the mining of high utility sequential patterns is studied, where they allow simultaneous events. Chen et al. [5] and Moerchen et al. [18] study mining interval-based patterns, where frequency is determined by how often univariate patterns co-occur within a given interval. All these methods are traditional pattern mining techniques in the sense that they return all patterns that pass an interestingness threshold.

Whereas traditional pattern mining techniques often only consider discrete data, there does exist extensive literature on mining patterns in continuous valued time series. These patterns are often called 'motifs' [12, 6]. For computational reasons, many of these methods first discretise the data [13]. Most motif discovery algorithms consider only univariate data. Example proposals for motif discovery in a multivariate setting include that by Tanaka et al. [25], who first transform the data into one dimension before the pattern discovery process and do not consider gaps, and by [17], who do not allow patterns to temporally overlap even if they span different dimensions and do not consider variable-length motifs. More recently Vespier et al. [30], mine characteristic multi-scale motifs in sensor-based time series but aim at mining all motifs, not a succinct summary.

To the best of our knowledge there are no methods yet to summarise *multivariate* sequential data, other than regarding each attribute separately or with restrictions on the pattern language [3]. In this work we introduce DITTO to discover important sequential associations between attributes by mining succinct summaries using rich multivariate patterns.

6. EXPERIMENTS

We implemented DITTO in C++ and generated our synthetic data and patterns using Python. We make our code available for research purposes.[2] All experiments were conducted on a 2.6 GHz system with 64 GB of memory. For our experiments on real data we always set the minimum support threshold as low as feasible, unless domain knowledge suggests otherwise.

We evaluate DITTO on a wide range of synthetic and real world data. As discussed in Sec. 5, there exist no direct competitors to DITTO. Traditional pattern mining and motif discovery methods 'simply' mine all patterns satisfying some constraints. For summarising sequential data, most existing methods consider univariate data [28, 10]. The only summarisation approach for multivariate sequential data considers the special case where attributes are ordered (e.g. frequency bands) [3], whereas we consider multivariate sequential data in general. We empirically compare DITTO to SQS [28]. We do so by applying SQS to each univariate sequence $S^i \in D$, combining these results into one pattern set.

6.1 Synthetic Data

To validate whether DITTO correctly identifies true multivariate sequential patterns from a dataset, we first consider synthetic data. In particular, we generate random data in which we plant a number of randomly generated patterns of different characteristics. Clearly, ideally the true patterns are recovered. Moreover, ideally no other, spurious patterns that are only due to noise are returned. To this end we perform an extensive set of experiments varying the number of events, the number of attributes and the alphabet size of the dataset, and the number, frequency and size of the planted patterns.

Data Generation

As noted in Table 1, for each experiment we generated $t(D)$ random multi-events on $|A|$ attributes (i.e. a total of $||D||$ events) with an alphabet size per attribute of $|\Omega_i|$. Further, after the data generation $|\mathcal{P}|$ patterns are planted, where each pattern X has a size $||X||$, a 5% chance on a gap between subsequent multi-events, and a support such that each pattern spans $support\%$ of all events in the dataset. An example of an insertion of a pattern in a random dataset that does not lead to an actual occurrence of that pattern is when due to the gap chance the minimal window of the pattern contains too many gaps. We do not allow patterns to overwrite each other during generation, as this makes evaluation much more complicated – i.e. it becomes unclear whether not recovering a pattern is an artefact of the search or of the data generation process. Further, only for experiments with 50 attributes, we prevented that pattern occurrences interleave and did not allow an event to be used in more than one pattern to assure that the planted patterns are actually present in the data. This restriction is justified because we are merely testing whether our algorithm is able to find multivariate patterns in multivariate data and without it patterns will easily crowd each other because of the high number of attributes.

Evaluation

We evaluate the quality of the pattern set discovered by considering how close they represent the planted patterns. In particular, following [34] we consider both exact (=) and subset ($\subset$) matches. Exact indicates that the pattern exactly corresponds with a planted pattern, whereas subset implies that it is only part of a planted pattern. In addition, we consider how well the planted patterns are recovered; we report how many of the events of the ground truth pattern set $\mathcal{P}$ we can cover with the discovered patterns. The higher this ratio, the better this result. Last, we consider the gain in compression of the discovered model over the initial, Standard Code Table. The higher this number, the better – the best score is attained when we recover all patterns exactly, and no further noise.

Results

We first consider the traditional approach of mining all (closed) frequent multivariate patterns. We do so using the implementation of Tatti and Cule [27]. We use a minimal support of 90% of the lower-support planted pattern. This choice is made to ensure that even when not all insertions of a pattern result in an actual occurrences, it can still be discovered. For the most simple synthetic dataset we consider, corresponding to the first row of Table 1, this takes a few days, finally reporting a *lower bound* of 14 092 944 394 frequent patterns, and returning 6 865 closed frequent patterns – hardly a summary, knowing there are only 5 true patterns. In the remainder we therefore do not consider traditional pattern mining.

Next, we consider DITTO and SQS. We report the results in Table 1. On the right hand side of the table we see that DITTO recovers all planted patterns, and does not report a single spurious pattern (!). In all cases it recovers the ground truth model, and obtains the best possible gain in compression. Next to the exactly identified planted pattern sometimes it also identifies some subsets of the planted patterns. This is a result of the data generation, i.e. subsets are sometimes included in the code table when planted occurrences contain too many gaps to be covered with the exact pattern. The patterns SQS discovers, on the other hand, are only small univariate fragments of the ground truth, recovering roughly only 10% to 30% of the ground truth. The near-zero gains in compression corroborate it is not able to detect much structure.

Regarding runtime and scalability, DITTO scales very favourably. Although SQS is faster it considers only the much simpler case of univariate data and patterns. DITTO requires seconds, up to a few minutes for the largest data, even for very low minimal support thresholds. Analysing the runtime of DITTO in more detail show how well its heuristics work; most time is spent on computing the minimal windows for candidates, of which up to ten thousand are materialised. Only for a few hundred of these a full cover of the data is required to evaluate their contribution to the model. Smart implementation for computing the minimal windows of all candidates in one pass will hence likely speed up DITTO tremendously.

6.2 Real World Data

As case studies we consider 4 datasets. An ECG sensor dataset, a structural integrity sensor dataset of a Dutch bridge, the text of the novel Moby Dick tagged with part-of-speech tags, and a multilingual text of an European Parliament resolution. See Table 2 for their characteristics.

ECG.

To investigate whether DITTO can find meaningful patterns on real-valued time series we consider a well-known ECG dataset.[3] For ease of presentation, and as our main goal is to show that DITTO can discover multivariate patterns, we consider only two sensors. As preprocessing steps we applied 3 transformations: we subsampled the data, we transformed it from absolute to relative, and we discretised it using SAX [13]. For the subsampling we replaced each 5 subsequent values with their average, thus creating a sequence 5 times shorter. Thereafter, we transformed the absolute data into relative data by replacing each value by the difference of its successor and its own value. Lastly, we discretised each

[2]http://eda.mmci.uni-saarland.de/ditto/

[3]ECG – physionet.org/physiobank/database/stdb

Table 1: DITTO discovers all planted patterns on all synthetic datasets, without picking up on noise. Given are the base statistics of the synthetic datasets, and the results of SQS and DITTO. For SQS and DITTO we give the number of exactly recovered patterns (=) and the number of discovered patterns that are subsets of planted patterns (⊂). Further, we report how much of the ground truth is recovered ($R\%$), as well as the gain in compression over the singleton-only model ($L\%$), for both higher is better. Last, we give the runtime in seconds.

Data				**Planted Patterns**			**SQS**					**DITTO**				
$\|\|D\|\|$	$t(D)$	$\|A\|$	$\|\Omega_i\|$	$\|\mathcal{P}\|$	$\|\|X\|\|$	*support*	$=$	$\subset$	$R\%$	$\Delta L\%$	time	$=$	$\subset$	$R\%$	$\Delta L\%$	time
100 000	10 000	10	100	5	3–7	1%	0	1	9.5	0.1	3	5	0	100.0	3.0	2
100 000	10 000	10	100	5	**5**	**10%**	0	0	0	0	3	5	5	100.0	31.6	31
100 000	10 000	10	**1 000**	5	3–7	1%	0	1	8.0	0	12	5	0	100.0	2.9	4
100 000	10 000	10	100	**20**	3–7	1%	0	9	19.5	0.9	4	20	0	100.0	12.9	15
500 000	10 000	**50**	100	5	3–7	1%	0	0	0	0	15	5	1	100.0	3.1	41
500 000	**50 000**	10	100	5	3–7	1%	0	1	10.0	0.2	4	5	0	100.0	3.1	28
1 000 000	**100 000**	10	100	5	3–7	1%	0	4	31.8	0.3	4	5	14	100.0	3.3	374

Table 2: Results on 4 real datasets. We give the basic statistics, as well as the number of patterns and relative gain in compression for both SQS and DITTO. The high compression gains show that DITTO discovers much more relevant structure than SQS.

Data						**SQS**			**DITTO**		
Dataset	$t(D)$	$\|D\|$	$\|A\|$	$\|\Omega\|$	*support*	$\|\mathcal{P}\|$	$\Delta L\%$	time (s)	$\|\mathcal{P}\|$	$\Delta L\%$	time (s)
ECG	2 999	1	2	6	10	57	38.8	1	11	**75.3**	360
Bridge	5 000	1	2	10	100	21	58.8	1	22	**76.3**	325
Moby Dick	2 248	103	2	887	5	20	1.7	3	79	**14.3**	102
Text	5 960	115	3	4 250	10	35	1.6	12	51	**2.2**	136

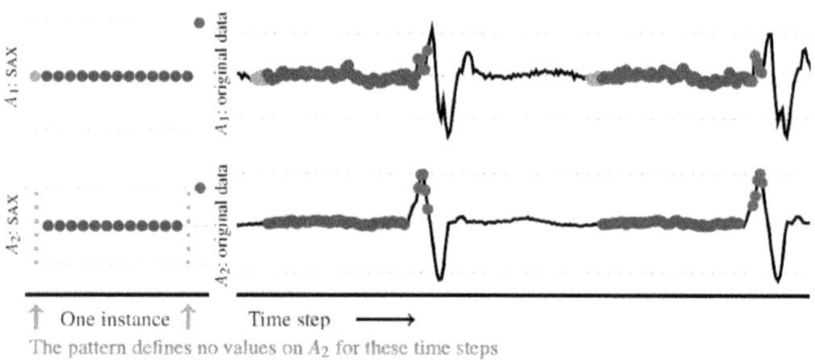

Figure 5: The top ordered pattern for the ECG data in the code table (left) and its first 2 occurrences in the data (right). The first time step of an occurrence is marked in green, subsequent ones in blue, and the last in red.

attribute into 3 intervals using SAX. Using a minimum support of 10, within 360 seconds DITTO discovers a code table containing 11 non-singleton patterns that capture the main structure of the data. In Figure 5 we plotted 2 occurrences of the top ordered pattern of this code table. This is a multivariate pattern which shows a very characteristic repeating structure in the data comprising a longer flat line ending with a peak on both attributes simultaneously. Showing the power of our pattern language, note that the pattern does not define any values on the second attribute for the first and second-last time steps (indicated with arrows in Figure 5), while it does on the first attribute. This flexibility allows us to use this multivariate pattern to describe a larger part of the data.

Like for the synthetic data, we also ran SQS. Again we see that as it cannot reward multivariate structure it does not obtain competitive gains in compression. Close inspection shows it returns many small patterns, identifying consecutive values.

Bridge.

Next we consider the setting of monitoring the structural integrity of a bridge in the Netherlands.[4] Amongst the collected sensor data are the strain, vibration and temperature. We selected 2 strain sensors (1 Hz) on consecutive pillars of the bridge and decomposed the signals into low, medium and high frequency components using techniques from [29]. We used the medium frequency components, after preprocessing, as our dataset. As preprocessing, we transformed the absolute values into relative values by replacing each value by the difference of its successor and its own value. We then discretised each z-normalised attribute into 5 intervals using SAX [13].

For a support threshold of 100, it takes DITTO 325 seconds to discover a code table with 22 non-singleton patterns. Although only one more than SQS at the same threshold, the patterns DITTO discovers are more descriptive. That is, they are multivariate and larger, leading to a much higher gain in compression. Moreover, the patterns it discovers correctly show the correlation between the attributes, whereas the patterns SQS discovers only identify univariate patterns.

Moby Dick.

For more interpretable results, we next evaluate on text data. In particular we considered the first chapter of the book Moby Dick, written by Herman Melville,[5] aligning the text with part-of-speech tags.[6,7] That is, one attribute comprises a stream of the words used in the book; each sentence is regarded as a sequence. The other attribute contains the tags that identify the type and function of each of these words. For example,

[4]Bridge – infrawatch.liacs.nl
[5]www.gutenberg.org
[6]http://nlp.stanford.edu/software/tagger.shtml
[7]https://gate.ac.uk/wiki/twitter-postagger.html

attribute 1:	VB	PRP	NNP
attribute 2:	Call	me	Ishmael

for which we will further use the following notation, where each time step is enclosed by curly brackets and the symbols for different attributes within a time step are divided by a comma: {VB, Call}{PRP, me}{NNP, Ishmael}. A short description for the part-of-speech tags in this example can be found in Table 4.

With a support threshold of 5, it takes DITTO 102 seconds to discover 79 non-singleton patterns. After studying the resulting pattern set we found that the identified patterns show highly intuitive multivariate structure. The highest ordered patterns together with examples of text fragments that match these patterns are shown in Table 3.

Table 3: The highest ordered patterns in the code table for the Moby Dick dataset, together with example fragments of from the text which correspond to the patterns.

Pattern	**Example text fragments**
{TO, to}{VB}{DT, a}{NN}	to get a broom, to buy (him) a coat
{DT, the}{JJ}{NN}	the green fields, the poor poet
{DT, a}{JJ}{NN}	a mazy way, a hollow trunk
{DT, the}{JJ}{NNS}	the wild conceits, the old (sea-)captains
{PRP, i}{RB}{VB}	I quietly take, I always go
{EX, there}{VBZ, is}	there is

Table 4: A short description of the part-of-speech tags used in the examples in this paper for the Moby Dick experiment.

Tag	**Explanation**
DT	Determiner
EX	Existential *there*
JJ	Adjective
NN	Noun, singular or mass
NNP	Proper noun, singular
NNS	Noun, plural
PRP	Personal pronoun
RB	Adverb
TO	*to*
VB	Verb, base form
VBZ	Verb, 3rd person singular present

Given the modest compression gain that SQS obtains, see Table 2, it is clear there is not much structure in each of the attributes separately; DITTO, however, is able to find a significant amount of multivariate structure.

Multilingual Text.

As a final experiment, to further corroborate whether DITTO discovers meaningful and interpretable multivariate patterns, we consider mining patterns between the same text in different languages. To this end we collected a text in English, French and German from the European Parliament register of documents.[8] In this data we expect frequent combinations of words within one (or more) language(s), as well as (and of more interest), multivariate patterns in the form of translations between the languages. As a preprocessing step all text data was stemmed and stop words were removed. To keep the different languages aligned we regarded every paragraph as a subsequence and padded shorter aligned subsequences with sentinel events which are ignored by DITTO. This ensures that the difference in length of the sentences in different languages will not lead to very big misalignments.

For a support threshold of 10, DITTO takes 136 seconds to discover 51 non-singleton patterns. The highest ordered pattern, i.e. the one that aids compression most, is a translation pattern; it identifies the correct relation between the French word *relève*, the German phrase *stellt fest dass* and the English word *note*. Other high ordered patterns are the English *EUR* (x) *million* and the German (x) *Millionen EUR*, and the words *parliament*, *Parlament* and *parlement* in English, German and French, respectively.

The modest compression gain of DITTO over SQS, see Table 2, indicates this data is not very structured, neither univariately, nor multivariately. One of the reasons being the different order of words between different languages which results in very large gaps between translation patterns.

7. DISCUSSION

Overall, the experiments show that DITTO works well in practice. In particular, the experiments on synthetic data show that DITTO accurately discovers planted patterns in random data for a wide variety of data and patterns dimensions. That is, DITTO discovers the planted patterns regardless of their support, their size, and the number of planted patterns – without discovering any spurious patterns. DITTO also performed well on real data – efficiently discovering characteristic multivariate patterns.

The results on the annotated text are particularly interesting; they give clear insight in non-trivial linguistic constructs, characterising the style of writing. Besides giving direct insight, these summaries have high downstream potential. One could, for example, use them for comparative analysis [4]. For example, for text identifying similarities and differences between authors, for sensor networks detecting and describing concept drift over time, and characterising differences between patients.

Although DITTO performs very well in practice, we see ways to improve over it. Firstly, MDL is not a magic wand. That is, while our score performs rather well in practice, we carefully constructed it to reward structure in the form of multivariate patterns. It will be interesting to see how our score and algorithms can be adapted to work directly on real-valued data. Secondly, it is worth investigating whether our current encoding can be refined, e.g. using prequential codes [4]. A strong point of our approach is that we allow for noise in the form of gaps in patterns. We postulate that we can further reduce the amount of redundancy in the discovered pattern sets by allowing noise *in the occurrences* of a pattern, as well as when we allow *overlap* between the occurrences of patterns in a cover. For both cases, however, it is not immediately clear how to adapt the score accordingly, and even more so, how to maintain the efficiency of the cover and search algorithms.

Last, but not least, we are interested in applying DITTO on vast time series. To accomodate, the first step would be to investigate parallelisation; the search algorithm is trivially parallelisable, as candidates can be generated and estimated in parallel, as is the covering of the data. More interesting is to investigate more efficient candidate generation schemes, in particular top-k mining, or lazy materialization of candidates.

Previous work has shown that MDL-based methods work particularly well for a wide range of data mining problems, including classification [32, 11] and outlier detection [23]. It will make for interesting future work to investigate how well DITTO solves such problems for multivariate event sequences. Perhaps the most promising direction of further study is that of causal inference [31].

[8] Text – www.europarl.europa.eu/RegistreWeb

8. CONCLUSION

We studied the problem of mining interesting patterns from multivariate sequential data. We approached the problem from a pattern set mining perspective, by MDL identifying the optimal set of patterns as those that together describe the data most succinctly. We proposed the DITTO algorithm for efficiently discovering high-quality patterns sets from data.

Experiments show that DITTO discovers patterns planted in synthetic data with high accuracy. Moreover, it scales favourably with the length of the data, the number of attributes, and alphabet sizes. For real data, it discovers easily interpretable summaries that provide clear insight in the associations of the data.

As future work, building upon our results on the part-of-speech tagged text data, we are collaborating with colleagues from the linguistics department to apply DITTO for analysis of semantically annotated text and for inferring patterns in morphologically rich languages.

Acknowledgments

The authors wish to thank Kathrin Grosse for her help with and analysis of the part-of-speech tagged text experiments. Roel Bertens and Arno Siebes are supported by the Dutch national program COMMIT. Jilles Vreeken is supported by the Cluster of Excellence "Multimodal Computing and Interaction" within the Excellence Initiative of the German Federal Government.

9. REFERENCES

[1] R. Agrawal and R. Srikant. Mining sequential patterns. In *ICDE*, pages 3–14, Los Alamitos, CA, USA, 1995. IEEE Computer Society.

[2] R. Bathoorn, A. Koopman, and A. Siebes. Reducing the frequent pattern set. In *ICDM-Workshop*, pages 1–5, 2006.

[3] R. Bertens and A. Siebes. Characterising seismic data. In *SDM*, pages 884–892. SIAM, 2014.

[4] K. Budhathoki and J. Vreeken. The difference and the norm – characterising similarities and differences between databases. In *ECML PKDD*. Springer, 2015.

[5] Y.-C. Chen, J.-C. Jiang, W.-C. Peng, and S.-Y. Lee. An efficient algorithm for mining time interval-based patterns in large database. In *CIKM*, pages 49–58. ACM, 2010.

[6] B. Chiu, E. Keogh, and S. Lonardi. Probabilistic discovery of time series motifs. In *KDD*, pages 493–498. ACM, 2003.

[7] T. M. Cover and J. A. Thomas. *Elements of Information Theory*. Wiley-Interscience New York, 2006.

[8] P. Grünwald. *The Minimum Description Length Principle*. MIT Press, 2007.

[9] Y. He, J. Wang, and L. Zhou. Efficient incremental mining of frequent sequence generators. In *DASFAA*, pages 168–182, 2011.

[10] H. T. Lam, F. Mörchen, D. Fradkin, and T. Calders. Mining compressing sequential patterns. In *SDM*, 2012.

[11] H. T. Lam, F. Mörchen, D. Fradkin, and T. Calders. Mining compressing sequential patterns. *Statistical Analysis and Data Mining*, 7(1):34–52, 2014.

[12] J. Lin, E. Keogh, P. Patel, and S. Lonardi. Finding motifs in time series. In *KDD-TDM*, pages 53–68, 2002.

[13] J. Lin, E. Keogh, L. Wei, and S. Lonardi. Experiencing sax: A novel symbolic representation of time series. *Data Min. Knowl. Disc.*, 15(2):107–144, Oct. 2007.

[14] H. Mannila and C. Meek. Global partial orders from sequential data. In *KDD*, pages 161–168, 2000.

[15] H. Mannila, H. Toivonen, and A. I. Verkamo. Efficient algorithms for discovering association rules. In *KDD*, pages 181–192, 1994.

[16] H. Mannila, H. Toivonen, and A. I. Verkamo. Discovery of frequent episodes in event sequences. *Data Min. Knowl. Disc.*, 1(3):259–289, 1997.

[17] D. Minnen, C. Isbell, I. Essa, and T. Starner. Detecting subdimensional motifs: An efficient algorithm for generalized multivariate pattern discovery. In *ICDM*, pages 601–606. IEEE, 2007.

[18] F. Mörchen and A. Ultsch. Efficient mining of understandable patterns from multivariate interval time series. *Data Min. Knowl. Disc.*, 15(2):181–215, 2007.

[19] T. Oates and P. R. Cohen. Searching for structure in multiple streams of data. In *ICML*, pages 346–354, 1996.

[20] N. Pasquier, Y. Bastide, R. Taouil, and L. Lakhal. Discovering frequent closed itemsets for association rules. In *ICDT*, pages 398–416. ACM, 1999.

[21] J. Pei, J. Han, B. Mortazaviasl, J. Wang, H. Pinto, Q. Chen, U. Dayal, and M. Hsu. Mining sequential patterns by pattern-growth: The prefixspan approach. *IEEE TKDE*, 16(11):1424–1440, 2004.

[22] A. Siebes, J. Vreeken, and M. van Leeuwen. Item sets that compress. In *SDM*, pages 393–404. SIAM, 2006.

[23] K. Smets and J. Vreeken. The odd one out: Identifying and characterising anomalies. In *SDM*, pages 804–815. SIAM, 2011.

[24] K. Smets and J. Vreeken. SLIM: Directly mining descriptive patterns. In *SDM*, pages 236–247. SIAM, 2012.

[25] Y. Tanaka, K. Iwamoto, and K. Uehara. Discovery of time-series motif from multi-dimensional data based on mdl principle. *Mach. Learn.*, 58(2–3):269–300, 2005.

[26] N. Tatti. Significance of episodes based on minimal windows. In *ICDM*, pages 513–522, 2009.

[27] N. Tatti and B. Cule. Mining closed episodes with simultaneous events. In *KDD*, pages 1172–1180, 2011.

[28] N. Tatti and J. Vreeken. The long and the short of it: Summarizing event sequences with serial episodes. In *KDD*, pages 462–470. ACM, 2012.

[29] U. Vespier, A. J. Knobbe, S. Nijssen, and J. Vanschoren. MDL-based analysis of time series at multiple time-scales. In *ECML PKDD*, pages 371–386. Springer, 2012.

[30] U. Vespier, S. Nijssen, and A. Knobbe. Mining characteristic multi-scale motifs in sensor-based time series. In *CIKM*, pages 2393–2398. ACM, 2013.

[31] J. Vreeken. Causal inference by direction of information. In *SDM*. SIAM, 2015.

[32] J. Vreeken, M. van Leeuwen, and A. Siebes. KRIMP: Mining itemsets that compress. *Data Min. Knowl. Disc.*, 23(1):169–214, 2011.

[33] J. Wang and J. Han. Bide: Efficient mining of frequent closed sequences. In *ICDE*, page 79, 2004.

[34] G. Webb and J. Vreeken. Efficient discovery of the most interesting associations. *ACM TKDD*, 8(3):1–31, 2014.

[35] C.-W. Wu, Y.-F. Lin, P. S. Yu, and V. S. Tseng. Mining high utility episodes in complex event sequences. In *KDD*, pages 536–544. ACM, 2013.

The Limits of Popularity-Based Recommendations, and the Role of Social Ties

Marco Bressan*†
Sapienza University of Rome
Rome, Italy

Stefano Leucci*
Sapienza University of Rome
Rome, Italy

Alessandro Panconesi*
Sapienza University of Rome
Rome, Italy

Prabhakar Raghavan
Google
Mountain View, CA

Erisa Terolli*
Sapienza University of Rome
Rome, Italy

ABSTRACT

In this paper we introduce a mathematical model that captures some of the salient features of recommender systems that are based on popularity and that try to exploit social ties among the users. We show that, under very general conditions, the market always converges to a steady state, for which we are able to give an explicit form. Thanks to this we can tell rather precisely how much a market is altered by a recommendation system, and determine the power of users to influence others. Our theoretical results are complemented by experiments with real world social networks showing that social graphs prevent large market distortions in spite of the presence of highly influential users.

1. INTRODUCTION

Recommender systems (RS's) are a paradigmatic example of the interaction between humans and algorithms in the cultural arena. From YouTube videos to books on Amazon and movies on iTunes or Netflix, online choices are increasingly mediated by such algorithms. RS's are popular for their ability to conjure up non-trivial relationships between products or news stories, and as such they are becoming powerful economic actors. It is this economic dimension of RS's that we intend to explore in this paper.

A fundamental question in this context, and the one we intend to tackle in this paper, is the following: to what extent can a market be altered by a RS? For instance, assume that an online bookstore starts adopting a RS. Will unknown books become hits and vice-versa? How and how much will the habit of the typical reader change? A large body of work has investigated questions of this kind at the individual, user level [8, 25, 26, 35]. For instance, a nice experiment described in [25] suggests that even a simple type of feedback, such as providing the ranking based on the number of downloads, may significantly boost market shares. Studies such as these provide precious insights but it is difficult to derive from them quantitatively accurate predictions about markets in the long-run. Also, it is entirely conceivable that the amplification effects observed be temporary, or not transferable to markets whose sheer size and complexity dwarfs that of artificial settings. Other studies have tried to draw conclusions from behavioural data of real markets [11, ?, 10, 23], but the paucity of available data makes them tentative.

In this paper we try a different approach by introducing a natural model for markets that are governed by a RS. Our model is simple enough to allow for a precise mathematical analysis of long-term behaviours, while at the same time it captures some of the relevant features of RS's. Specifically, there are two ingredients that are known to play an important role in RS's and that we want our model to represent. The first is popularity, *i.e.* the degree of success of an item in its market. Several studies indicate that popularity feedback (*e.g.* number of downloads, user ratings, number of views, etc) can be a powerful determinant of online behaviour [25, 5, 35]. The second ingredient is, for lack of a better terminology, the "web of kinship" among users. Social ties are the paradigmatic example here. They are recognized to be an important factor that shape user choices, and recommenders try to leverage them in a variety of ways [22, 31, 33, 6]. More generally RS's try to exploit different types of similarities between users, such as explicit links in an online social network, similarity between patterns of consumer choice, or even the result of complex computations like matrix factorization. All these diverse situations can be simply and usefully represented, as we show in this paper, by assuming the existence of a (weighted) network connecting the users.

In simplified form, our mathematical model of market evolution is as follows. In the market we have users (or buyers), connected via a network, and products. When a user buys a product, it either follows its personal inclinations (mode led by a private probability distribution over the products) or it follows a recommendation with a certain probability. When it does, it consults a random neighbour in the network, the *recommender node*. The recommender node picks a random product from its own list of products purchased so far, with a probability that is proportional to the popularity of the product in that moment, and the item so selected is bought by the current buyer.

---

*Supported in part by a Google Focused Research Award, by the Sapienza Grant C26M15ALKP, by the SIR Grant RBSI14Q743, and by the ERC Starting Grant DMAP 680153.

†Corresponding author. Address: bressan@di.uniroma1.it

KDD '16, August 13 - 17, 2016, San Francisco, CA, USA

ISBN 978-1-4503-4232-2/16/08...$15.00

DOI: http://dx.doi.org/10.1145/2939672.2939797

The main theoretical result in this paper is that this type of system, encompassing a large class of recommenders, always converges to a unique, stationary limit. The result holds under very general conditions. First, users can buy products at different rates. User u, say, can be ten times faster than user v and one thousand times slower than user w etc. Second, the probability of following the recommendation may change from person to person – each buyer can have his/her own personal level of trust in recommendations, and also trust his/her friends to differing degrees. Third, the probability with which a product is recommended does not need to be uniform, but it can depend on time. For instance, we could recommend only the last ten items bought, or skew the probability with which an item is recommended in many other ways. Finally, the graph can be any directed graph (so u could follow v's recommendations but not vice versa) and users can have their own personal history of purchases before the recommendation mechanism starts operating. None of these affects the result– the market always converges to a unique limit.

It is natural to think of the network connecting the users as a social network, but it can in fact be used to model many more scenarios. For instance, we can make the popularity of an item directly proportional to its number of sales in the whole market by assuming the network to be a clique, or we can represent a powerful super-user that influences the entire network without being affected by it by assuming the network to be an oriented star.

A nice feature of our result is that the limit is given explicitly, in closed form. This makes it possible to explore important properties of the steady state both analytically and computationally. For instance, we can answer easily our motivating question– can the recommendation mechanism alter the market in a significant way? We can easily tell the distance, in whatever norm, between the initial market shares of every product and those at steady state. We can gain insight into what type of topologies amplify or dampen distorting effects, and we can also carry out a fine grained analysis that tells, for each user, how much it affects the final outcome. A by-product of our analysis is a quantitative notion of user influence that pinpoints exactly how much each user affects the market at the limit. Interestingly, this notion turns out to be a generalization of Personalized PageRank (PPR) and it is related to the Shapley values of a coalition game that can be defined in our model.

Our limit theorems provide a rich landscape for computational explorations with real-world social networks. We explore the distorting effects of various graph topologies and the extent to which a user can influence the market. What emerges is a rather nuanced landscape that is spelled out in full in the rest of the paper. Perhaps the most interesting outcome is that real social networks prove themselves to be a bulwark against market distortion, in spite of the presence of celebrities in their midst.

To summarize, this paper is a step in the direction of a systematic investigation of the long-term effects of recommender systems on the markets in which they are operating. This is an important and fascinating topic that deserves more attention that it has gotten so far. We hope that this paper provides some actionable insight into this important problem.

The paper is organized as follows. In § 2 we discuss the relevant literature, in § 3 we define our model and analyse its properties mathematically. We conclude with experiments in § 4.

2. RELATED WORK

Product popularity is known to have powerful feedback effects on user behaviour and choices, and is leveraged by many existing RS's. In one of the most eloquent demonstrations, [25] shows that, in a digital cultural market, just reporting the ranking based on the number of downloads significantly affects user choices and increases the market's inequality and unpredictability. Another telling illustration, [35], proves that users are likely to change their mind and reverse their previous choices when given information about the popularity of items. A study of friend recommendation in Twitter, [28], shows that recommendations of popular users are much more likely to be accepted than recommendations of "average" users. Several existing online marketplaces make use of popularity-based recommendations – for instance Amazon[1], Yelp[2], TripAdvisor[3], SoundCloud[4] and Last.fm[5] all suggest items that are currently trending.

Social ties are also understood to play a key role in the recommendation and purchase processes, and are increasingly exploited by modern RS's. A study on the Epinions[6] network [7] finds that a large part of the items adopted by a user are also adopted by his/her friends. Similarly, a study on the Yahoo! Pulse network [30] shows that a user's interests are highly correlated with, and can be predicted by, the interests of his/her social ties – and vice versa. An emblematic example of RS based on social ties is [31], which uses a generative influence model where users probabilistically pick items according to both their and their friends' preferences. Another study, [6], builds a recommendation algorithm assuming that the two forces driving a user's actions are latent preferences and the influence of friends. Several other works show or propose that recommendations take place over some social network structure [16, 17, 33, 15, 34].

On the other hand, investigations on the long-term market effects of RS's are scarce; as long as mathematical models are concerned, existing work seems confined to the economic literature. To the best of our knowledge, the only theoretical investigation on the market effects of RS's is [12]. In their work, a single user repeatedly buys one of two products according to either his/her personal taste or to a recommendation consisting in the most-bought product so far; depending on the choice of parameters, the process can lead to a concentration of sales. There are many differences between their model and ours – in particular, our model allows users to influence each other. Two earlier studies, [9] on consensus reaching and [13] on opinion formation, investigated the convergence of personal beliefs of users interacting in a social group, similarly to how we investigate convergence in a market with social ties. Their models are however far from ours in many aspects; for instance, ours is stochastic and allows for complex dependences on past events. Another paper, [14], studies the effects of word-of-mouth on product sales, but focusing on equilibrium strategies for maximizing

[1]http://www.amazon.com
[2]http://www.yelp.com
[3]http://www.tripadvisor.com
[4]http://www.soundcloud.com
[5]http://www.last.fm
[6]http://www.epinions.com

user satisfaction. Finally, a few other works have analysed the interactions between RS's and markets, but either with different aims [18, 24] or by simulation instead of analysis [32].

3. A MODEL FOR RECOMMENDER SYSTEMS

Let us begin with the formal definition of our model.

Products.

We have a set $\mathcal{P}$ of m products; each product can be bought multiple times during the purchasing process. Products are bought one at a time in an infinite sequence of time steps $t = 1, 2, \ldots$. The purchasing process is specified below.

Users (or Buyers).

We have a set $\mathcal{U} := \{1, \ldots, n\}$ of n users. To each user u is associated:

- a fixed purchasing rate $f_u \in (0, 1)$ representing the rate at which u buys products. The f_u's form a probability distribution, i.e. $\sum_{u \in \mathcal{U}} f_u = 1$. The precise role of f_u is clarified below when the purchasing process is defined
- a probability distribution B_u over the set of products $\mathcal{P}$ reflecting its *personal preferences*. The probability $B_u(p), p \in \mathcal{P}$ is u's *personal preference* for p.
- a fixed probability $\alpha_u \in [0, 1)$; when u buys a product it follows a recommendation with probability α_u (see the definition of the purchasing process below)
- a list of products purchased in the past (before time 0), initially containing $k_u > 0$ items. This list can be arbitrary

The graph.

Users are connected via a directed, weighted graph $G = (\mathcal{U}, E)$, possibly with self-loops. Intuitively, an edge vu denotes the fact that v can influence u when u decides to follow a recommendation, or alternatively, that u "trusts" v. The arc has weight w_{vu} which gives the strength of this trust relationship. The weights are normalised: the weights of the arcs entering each vertex u (if any) sum up to one.

It is natural to think of this graph as a social network among the users, but it is in fact a very versatile tool with which we can model several different situations. For instance, when the graph is a clique and the weights are uniform we have the traditional popularity feedback – an item is recommended with a probability that is proportional to the number of sales in the whole market. Or, the graph could embed similarities between users, with the weights reflecting the degree of similarity, and so on so forth. The graph is a flexible tool thanks to which several situation can be cast in our framework and network effects be explored.

The purchasing process.

At each time step $t = 1, 2, \ldots$, a user u is chosen with probability f_u and buys a product in one of two ways:

- With probability $1 - \alpha_u$, it chooses a product at random according to its own distribution B_u of personal preferences.
- Alternatively, with probability α_u, it follows the recommendation:
  - First, u picks a *recommender node* v at random among those pointing to him (if u has no entering arcs then $\alpha_u = 0$). The recommender node v is picked with probability w_{vu}, the weight of the arc vu.
  - Once the recommender node v is chosen, a product p is selected at random from the multiset of products acquired by v up to that moment. Let us denote for now this probability simply as $x_v^t(p)$ and postpone to later its precise definition.
  - The product p so selected is bought, i.e. it is added to the multiset of products purchased by the current buyer u.

Note that even if we say for convenience that the i-th purchase takes place at "time" i, we make no assumptions about time itself (i.e. the wall clock time between any one purchase and the next can be arbitrary). The process simply stipulates that items are bought one after the other, in an infinite sequence.

The weight of history.

To conclude the description of the model we need to define the probability distribution, that we denoted as $\{x_v^t(p)\}_{p \in \mathcal{P}}$, with which the products of the recommender node are picked. A reasonable choice to model popularity-based recommendations would be simply to select a product uniformly at random from v's multiset of past purchases. In this way popular items have a higher probability of being recommended. But we want to take a more general approach by allowing time-dependent weights. For instance, we would like to be able to deal with a situation in which, say, only the ten most recent purchases matter, or where the influence of purchases fades away with time in a specific way, and so on so forth. To this end, focus on a vertex u and recall that we allow users to have made k_u purchases before starting the system. Suppose now that we are at time $t > 0$, and let $I_u^t \subseteq [t-1]$ denote the set of times when u previously made a purchase. We denote the weight of a purchase made by u at time $i < t$ as $h_u^{t,i}$. First, we assume these weights to be normalised, that is, for all $t > 0$,

$$\sum_{i=1}^{k_u} h_u^{t,-i} + \sum_{i \in I_u^t} h_u^{t,i} = 1,$$

For a given product p, let $J_{u,p}^t \subseteq \{-k_u, \ldots, -1\} \cup I_u^t$ be the set of times when u bought p. Then, given that u is the recommender node at time t, product p will be recommended by u and purchased by the buyer with probability

$$x_u^t(p) := \sum_{i \in J_{u,p}^t} h_u^{t,i}.$$

This formalization captures a large spectrum of natural scenarios. For example, if the recommendation consists in picking from u's past purchases uniformly at random, this amounts to setting $h_u^{t,-i} = h_u^{t,i} = 1/k_u+|I_u^t|$ for all i. Picking one at random among the 10 most recent purchases corresponds instead to setting $h_u^{t,i} = 1/10$ for all i such that $|I_u^i| \geq |I_u^t| - 10$ and $h_u^{t,i} = 0$ otherwise. Note that the values of the weights $h_u^{t,i}$ depend on the outcome of the process, thus the $h_u^{t,i}$ are random variables themselves.

While our theorems will be given for the full model, it may help the intuition to consider the following simplified version, to which we will sometime refer in the remainder of the paper.

DEFINITION 1. [THE BASIC SCENARIO] *The special case where users buy at the same rate (i.e.* $f_u = 1/n, u \in \mathcal{U}$*), follow recommendations with the same probability (i.e.* $\alpha_u = \alpha, u \in \mathcal{U}$*), pick the recommender with uniform probability (i.e.* $w_{vu} = 1/\mathrm{indeg}(u), u \in \mathcal{U}$*), and recommend items by picking a random product from their list with uniform probability (i.e.* $h_u^{t,-i} = h_u^{t,i} = 1/k_u+|I_u^t|, u \in \mathcal{U}$*), is called the* basic scenario.

Remarks. Our model only considers products that can be bought multiple times. Food items are a natural example, but there are very many cultural products that fall into this category: going out to a specific club, attending sport events, or participating to concerts at specific venues are just a few examples. The case of items for which multiple purchases make little sense, such as books or movies, is also of great interest but is left for future work. It is worth noting that our model can capture to a certain extent *repeat consumption*, the empirical principle that people tend to re-purchase a product they recently bought [1, 2]. More precisely, our model can mimic the one in [1], where a user buys a product that is either new or drawn from a distribution over his/her purchasing history. We can mimic this model by allowing self-loops in the graph: a user can then pick itself as the recommender node and, with properly defined weights, re-purchase a product he bought in the near past.

3.1 Analysis of the model

To analyse the evolution of the process we focus, from now on, on a particular product $p^* \in \mathcal{P}$, and look at all the others as aggregated into a second product.

Let us begin with some necessary notation. Recall that $x_u^t(p)$ is the probability with which p is recommended and bought given that u is the recommender node at time t. To simplify notation, let $x_u^t(p^*)$ be denoted simply as x_u^t. Similarly, let b_u be u's personal preference for p^*, and let $\boldsymbol{b} = (b_1, \ldots, b_n)$. We want to study the evolution of $\boldsymbol{x}^t := (x_1^t, \ldots, x_n^t)$ as t grows. We define $\boldsymbol{A} = \mathrm{diag}(\alpha_1, \ldots, \alpha_n)$ and denote by $\boldsymbol{M}$ the weighted transposed adjacency matrix of G, i.e. $M_{uv} = w_{vu}$ (which is 0 if $vu \notin G$). For any random vector $\boldsymbol{y} = (y_1, y_2, \ldots)$ we denote by $\mathbf{E}[\boldsymbol{y}]$ the vector $(\mathbf{E}[y_1], \mathbf{E}[y_2], \ldots)$ of the expectations of its components.

With the notation pinned down, we can now address our main question: does the market share of p^* converge? The theorem below states that this happens if the weights $h_u^{t,i}$ satisfy the following condition.

The past fades away, i.e. $\lim_{t\to\infty} \mathbf{E}[h_u^{t,i}] = 0$.

This condition is very natural. It states that past purchases will eventually be forgotten. For instance it is satisfied when the recommended product is chosen uniformly at random or when only the last few purchases have non-zero weight. We can now give our main result, which is proven in the appendix.

THEOREM 1. *If the past fades away, then*

$$\lim_{t\to\infty} \mathbf{E}[\boldsymbol{x}^t] = \boldsymbol{x}^\infty \tag{1}$$

where $\boldsymbol{x}^\infty = (\boldsymbol{I} - \boldsymbol{AM})^{-1}(\boldsymbol{I} - \boldsymbol{A})\boldsymbol{b}$*. Otherwise* $\mathbf{E}[\boldsymbol{x}^t]$ *might not converge, or converge but not to* $\boldsymbol{x}^\infty$*.*

Let us discuss a few interesting consequences of this result.

First, notice that since the network and the values $\boldsymbol{\alpha} = (\alpha_1, \ldots, \alpha_n)$, $\boldsymbol{f} = (f_1, \ldots, f_n)$, and $\boldsymbol{b}$, stay put and only $\boldsymbol{x}^t$ changes, the theorem gives a complete characterization of the market at the limit. The limit vector $\boldsymbol{x}^\infty$ has a natural and quite useful interpretation, given in the next corollary.

DEFINITION 2. *The fraction of times that a user u has bought p^* at time $t \in \mathbb{N}^+ \cup \{\infty\}$ is called the* local market share (LMS) *of p^* w.r.t. u at time t.*

COROLLARY 1. *For every user u, x_u^∞ is the local market share of p^* w.r.t. u at the limit.*

The proof of this corollary in the general case is slightly technical but in the basic scenario (see Definition 1) follows immediately from Theorem 1. In this scenario, by definition of the model, x_u^t is the fraction of times that u has bought p^* up to time t, *i.e.* it is p^*'s LMS w.r.t. u, and Theorem 1 states that this value converges to x_u^∞.

Consider now the matrix

$$\boldsymbol{L} := (\boldsymbol{I} - \boldsymbol{AM})^{-1}(\boldsymbol{I} - \boldsymbol{A}) \tag{2}$$

This matrix contains a lot of information about the steady state. Now, since $\boldsymbol{x}^\infty = \boldsymbol{Lb}$ we have that $x_u^\infty = \sum_v L_{uv} b_v$. We can think of x_u^∞ as consisting of a set of "slices", each of size $L_{uv} b_v$, $v \in \mathcal{U}$. Each slice is the contribution of v to x_u^∞ which is, as we have seen, p^*'s LMS w.r.t u at the limit. We thus have a measure of how much each user can influence every other user.

If L_{vu} is how much u influences v then $\sum_v L_{vu}$ quantifies u's influence on the entire market. We can collect these individual market influences in an *influence vector*:

$$\boldsymbol{\gamma}^T := \boldsymbol{f}^T \boldsymbol{L} \tag{3}$$

where $\boldsymbol{f} = [f_1, \ldots, f_n]$. The vector $\boldsymbol{\gamma}$ is stochastic (its entries sum up to one), and its element γ_u is the relative weight of u's personal distribution in the overall sales distribution at equilibrium. The larger the value of γ_u the greater the influence of u on the final market share of p^*. We thus define the *maximum influence* of any user as,

$$\gamma(G) := \max_{u\in G} \gamma_u = \|\boldsymbol{\gamma}\|_\infty \tag{4}$$

For instance, in the basic scenario, when G is a star $\gamma_u = \Theta(1)$ if u is the centre and $\gamma_u = \Theta(1/n)$ otherwise, so that $\gamma(G) = \Theta(1)$, while when G is a clique $\gamma(G) = \gamma_u = 1/n$ for every u.

Thanks to Theorem 1 we can now easily answer our motivating question– how much can the market be distorted? By combining $\boldsymbol{\gamma}$ and the vector $\boldsymbol{b}$ of personal preferences we can quantify how much the recommender system distorts (i.e. increases or decreases) the overall market share of p^*.

We define the *market distortion* as:

$$\Delta := \frac{\boldsymbol{f} \cdot \boldsymbol{x}^\infty}{\boldsymbol{f} \cdot \boldsymbol{b}} = \frac{\boldsymbol{\gamma} \cdot \boldsymbol{b}}{\boldsymbol{f} \cdot \boldsymbol{b}}, \tag{5}$$

where $\cdot$ denotes the dot product. This is the ratio between the market share of p^* at the limit and that without the recommender.

Influence, PageRank and Shapley Values.

The influence vector $\boldsymbol{\gamma}$ has a natural interpretation in terms of personalized PageRank. Consider the graph G^T

obtained by transposing G, the graph among the users, and suppose it has no dangling nodes (i.e. no node with outdegree zero). Let $\boldsymbol{W}$ be the normalised adjacency matrix of G^T, i.e. $W_{uv} = 1/\mathtt{outdeg}(u)$ with the outdegree measured in G^T. Finally, pick any $\alpha \in [0, 1)$ and any n-entry stochastic vector $\boldsymbol{r}$. The personalized PageRank vector $\boldsymbol{p}$ with respect to $\boldsymbol{r}$ with damping factor α on G^T is defined as (see e.g. [19]):

$$\boldsymbol{p}^T = \boldsymbol{r}^T(\boldsymbol{I} - \alpha \boldsymbol{W})^{-1}(1 - \alpha) \quad (6)$$

Compare the above expression with that of $\boldsymbol{\gamma}^T$ given by Equation 3 and the definition of $\boldsymbol{L}$:

$$\boldsymbol{\gamma}^T = \boldsymbol{f}^T(\boldsymbol{I} - \boldsymbol{AM})^{-1}(\boldsymbol{I} - \boldsymbol{A}) \quad (7)$$

The vector $\boldsymbol{\gamma}^T$ is the perfect analogue of $\boldsymbol{p}^T$. Indeed, the two coincide by choosing $\boldsymbol{r} = \boldsymbol{f}$ if each node u in G has $\alpha_u = \alpha$ and has a nonempty set of incoming arcs all with the same weight. Our notion of influence is thus a generalization of the standard personalized PageRank, allowing for personalized values of α, graphs with dangling nodes, and arbitrary arc weights. In fact, our model offers an intuitive interpretation similar to that of PageRank: the influence of nodes can be seen as the stationary distribution of a "reverse" random walk on G which at each step, from the current node u, either moves to an incoming neighbour v with probability $\alpha_u w_{vu}$ or, with probability $1-\alpha_u$, moves to a random node in G chosen according to the distribution $\{f_v\}_{v \in G}$. This walk can be seen as propagating the "credit" for the choice of a purchased product back to the incoming neighbours, the neighbours of the incoming neighbours and so on, recursively. The purchasing rates play the intuitive role of the personalization vector: the more a user buys, the more the users who influence him are influential overall (and they are indeed reached more often by the random walk).

The influence vector $\boldsymbol{\gamma}$ also has an interpretation in terms of the classical notion of Shapley value, which is a mechanism to determine payoffs in coalition games. Shapley values have been proposed as a mechanism to determine fair compensation for user's participation to recommendation systems [18]. Let b_u denote, as usual, u's personal preference for p^*. Consider now the following game: each user can either participate to the market with b_u or set its preference to 0; the value assigned to the coalition is the total market share of p^*. Then, the following holds.

FACT 1. *The Shapley value of each user u in the above game is exactly $\gamma_u b_u$.*

It is worth pointing out that, uncharacteristically, this Shapley value can be computed in polynomial-time.

Speed of convergence.

Theorem 1 does not tell how much time it takes for the market to reach the steady-state; in fact, this depends on how fast the weights decay with t. In the case of the simple uniform random recommendation, one can prove that the system converges to the steady state reasonably fast:

THEOREM 2. *If the recommender node recommends an item picked at random from its purchasing history, then*

$$\|\mathbf{E}[\mathbf{x}^t] - \boldsymbol{x}^\infty\| = O(t^{\alpha-1}) \quad (8)$$

where α is the maximum α_u over all users.

The proof is omitted from this extended abstract.

Computing $\boldsymbol{\gamma}$.

Clearly, computing $\boldsymbol{\gamma}$ efficiently is a crucial task to the aims of the present paper. Doing this directly through Equations 2 and 3 requires to explicitly invert the matrix $(\boldsymbol{I}-\boldsymbol{AM})$, which can be prohibitively expensive is the inverse is dense (which is the case if G is well-connected). We instead follow a standard alternative approach. Rewrite $(\boldsymbol{I} - \boldsymbol{AM})$ as $\sum_{i=0}^{+\infty}(\boldsymbol{AM})^i$, plug it into Equation 3 and obtain:

$$\boldsymbol{\gamma}^T = \boldsymbol{f}^T \sum_{i=0}^{+\infty}(\boldsymbol{AM})^i(\boldsymbol{I} - \boldsymbol{A}) \quad (9)$$

Now, if G is sparse, so is $\boldsymbol{M}$ and thus all the terms of the summation in Equation 9. We can then approximate $\boldsymbol{\gamma}$ efficiently by truncating the series, which only requires to keep trace of a sparse matrix and vectors. To be more precise, computing all entries of $\boldsymbol{\gamma}$ up to an additive error $O(\epsilon)$ requires time $O\big((|V| + |E|)\log(\frac{1}{\epsilon})/\log(\frac{1}{\alpha})\big)$ and space $O(|V| + |E|)$, where $\alpha = \max_{u \in G} \alpha_u$. We use this technique throughout our experiments.

4. EXPERIMENTAL RESULTS

In this section we discuss a series of experiments where the underlying graph of our model is a real world social network.

Theorem 1 says that $\boldsymbol{x}^t$ converges to $\boldsymbol{x}^\infty$ in expectation. A first set of experiments shows that the expectation does captures what happens at the limit, *i.e.* the variance is small. We then investigate the question of market distortion – for a given product p^*, how much does its market share change at the limit? A related question concerns so-called influencers. What is their influence and how much can they change the market? We show that when the underlying network is a real world social network market distortion is negligible and even "celebrities" cannot have significant impact. Vice versa, there are other realistic situations, such as the presence of a super-node acting as a "media tycoon", where certain nodes can conquer a significant share of the market thanks to the recommendation mechanism. We also give a rule of thumb to identify top influencers on the basis of their 2-hop neighbourhood. Finally, we explore recommenders not covered by our theoretical results, in which products are recommended with super-linear probabilities. We find that the results vary widely from graph to graph, and depend also heavily on the starting share of products.

Let us now describe the experimental setup.

4.1 Experimental setup

We run our experiments on six following real-world graphs.

`Google+` The ego-Gplus graph from SNAP Datasets [21]. It contains 107,614 nodes (users) and 13,673,453 arcs representing a follower-to-followed relationship in the Google+ social network.

`Twitter SNAP` The ego-Twitter graph from SNAP Datasets. It contains 81,306 nodes and 2,420,766 follower-to-followed arcs crawled from Twitter.

`Twitter LAW` The twitter-2010 graph by the Laboratory for Web Algorithmics, Univ. Milan [4, 3]. It contains 41,652,230 nodes and 1,468,365,182 follower-to-followed arcs from Twitter.

`Slashdot` The soc-sign-Slashdot090221 graph from SNAP Datasets. It contains 82,144 users and 549,202 signed (i.e. "friends" or "foes") arcs between users. We kept only the 425,072 "friend" arcs.

`Yelp` A social graph extracted from friendships in the Yelp Dataset Challenge dataset.[7] The graph is undirected and contains 365,759 users and 1,288,031 edges.[8]

`Facebook` The graph from the "List of links" Facebook dataset by MPI-SWS [29].[9] The graph is undirected and contains 63,731 users and 817,090 edges.

When the graphs are directed we reverse the edges (except for `Twitter LAW` that was already oriented correctly). This is because in social graphs an edge uv denotes the fact that u "trusts" or "follows" v, while in our model the meaning is that u influences v.

Two kinds of experiments are carried out in the following: simulations and computations. In the first, we simulate the purchasing process for $10,000n$ steps and in the basic scenario (see Definition 1), unless otherwise specified. The probability with which users follow a recommendation is set to $\alpha = 0.2$ for every user. Note that this is a conservative estimate, since the available evidence suggests both the relative influence of friends' recommendations (see e.g. [20, 31]) and the fraction of sales causally imputable to recommender systems (see [27]) to be significantly smaller. We are thus intentionally putting the RS in favourable conditions to distort the market.

In computations, we use the adjacency matrix of the underlying graph and the other parameters of the model to compute explicitly the influence vector $\boldsymbol{\gamma}$ (and related quantities), using the techniques described at the end of Section 3.

Our code was partly written in C++ using Eigen[10] and the GNU Scientific Library[11], and partly in Java using the WebGraph framework[12]. We ran it on a distributed-memory 50-node cluster provided by CINECA[13], where each node is equipped with two ten-core Intel Xeon CPUs and 128GiB of main memory. The source code can be downloaded from `https://github.com/Steven--/recommender`.

4.2 Convergence to the equilibrium

The first experiment checks that the purchasing process unrolls as predicted by our theoretical results. As in § 3.1, we focus on a single product p^*, with the remaining products coalesced into one. Figure 1 shows that $\boldsymbol{x}^t$ quickly converges to $\boldsymbol{x}^\infty$ as t grows (the plot follows a power-law).

Figure 2 shows what happens in the short-term setting. Initially, $\|\boldsymbol{x}_t - \boldsymbol{x}\|_\infty$ decreases rapidly, as expected, but then it starts oscillating around the value 0.22. This behaviour might seem counter-intuitive at first, but it is a natural consequence of the short-memory of the users. As the users only consider the last 100 purchases when making a recommendation, small differences in the number of times p^* is purchased may considerably change the probability with which p^* is recommended. This is a setting where $\mathbf{E}[\boldsymbol{x}^t]$ converges to $\boldsymbol{x}^\infty$ but $\boldsymbol{x}^t$ does not. Note however the following. If we consider the vector $\boldsymbol{z}^t$ containing the local market shares of p^* w.r.t. every user u (Definition 2) then, as predicted by Corollary 1, $\|\boldsymbol{z}^t - \boldsymbol{x}^\infty\|_\infty$ goes to 0 as t increases (see Figure 3). In conclusion, these experiments suggest that the LMS converges not only in expectation but in high probability. We leave this as an open problem.

[7] `https://www.yelp.com/dataset_challenge/`

[8] Actually, the original Yelp dataset contains 117 spurious directed edges that are not reciprocated.

[9] `http://socialnetworks.mpi-sws.org/data-wosn2009.html`

[10] `http://eigen.tuxfamily.org`

[11] `http://www.gnu.org/software/gsl/`

[12] `http://webgraph.di.unimi.it/`

[13] `http://www.cineca.it/en`

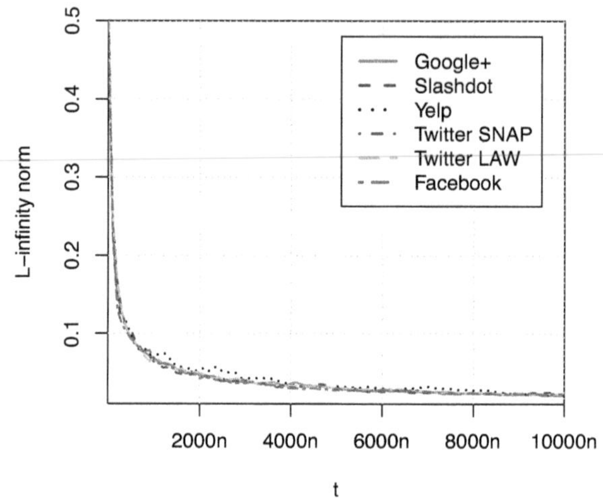

Figure 1: $\|\boldsymbol{x}^t - \boldsymbol{x}^\infty\|_\infty$ goes to 0 as t grows (long-memory scenario).

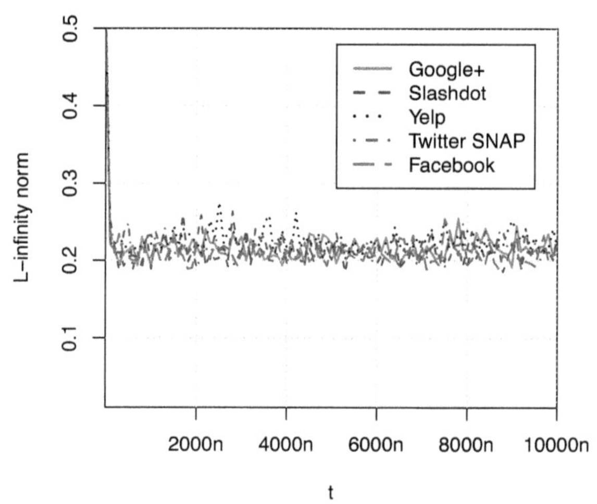

Figure 2: Plot of $\|\boldsymbol{x}^t - \boldsymbol{x}^\infty\|_\infty$ in the short-memory scenario.

4.3 Market distortion

In this section we try to understand how much the market can be distorted by the recommendation system. To this end we consider the quantity Δ defined by Equation 5 In the experiments $\boldsymbol{b}$ was instantiated with different types of distributions: uniform in $[0, 1]$, exponential of mean $1/2$, a power-law of exponent -0.01 (i.e., $p(x) \propto x^{-0.01}$), and normal of mean $1/2$ and standard deviation $1/6$ (for distributions having support wider than $[0, 1]$, the truncated version was used).

In all cases the value of Δ was always in the range 1 ± 0.002, which means that market distortion was negligible for all networks considered. This is an indication that social graphs prevent the recommender from distorting the market.

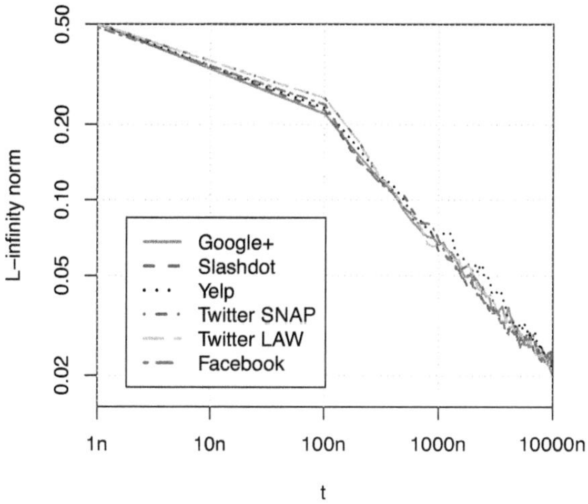

Figure 3: Log-log plot of $\|z^t - x^\infty\|_\infty$ in the short-memory scenario. The vector z^t keeps track, for each user, of the fraction of products p^* bought since the beginning of the process.

The next experiment determines how much (of the overall market share of p^*) can be ascribed to the most influential users. Recall from § 3.1 that $\gamma(G) = \max_u \gamma_u$ is the maximum influence of any user. While $\gamma(G)$ can be seen as a *relative* measure of the importance of the most influential user, i.e., as the fraction of the network that a single user can influence, $n \cdot \gamma(G)$ is an *absolute* measure: the most influential user u can be seen as controlling a group of $n \cdot \gamma(G)$ users that buy p^* with probability b_u at rate $1/n$. Figure 4 shows the values of $n \cdot \gamma(G)$ and of $\gamma(G)$ for the networks we tested. Even if there are users whose purchasing power corresponds to that of more than 80 "average users", none of them can influence a significant portion of the network.

In order to understand if the fairness of these social graphs is an artefact of our model or one of their intrinsic properties, we investigated a modified version of our model not covered by Theorem 1. In the modified model, the probability with which u recommends p^* becomes super-linear and is proportional to x_u^2. Intuitively, this should boost the final market share of p^* as soon as p^* has a small advantage in the user's preference distributions. Therefore, we draw the personal preferences of the users so that the mean of p^* is k times larger than the mean of any other product, where the *imbalance* k ranges from 1 to 5. We considered markets having both two and ten different products: the corresponding results can be seen in Figures 6 and 7. The purchasing process was simulated until the change in the market share of the products dropped below 0.001, and the experiment was repeated 10 times in order to compute the standard deviation of Δ, which was always smaller than 0.007. Even with this favourable setting we saw a market distortion effect on social networks that was always less than the one observed on a Clique. We conclude that, although the market share of the leading product p^* can increase significantly when there are many competing products, social graphs do not promote, and often damps, this growth phenomena.

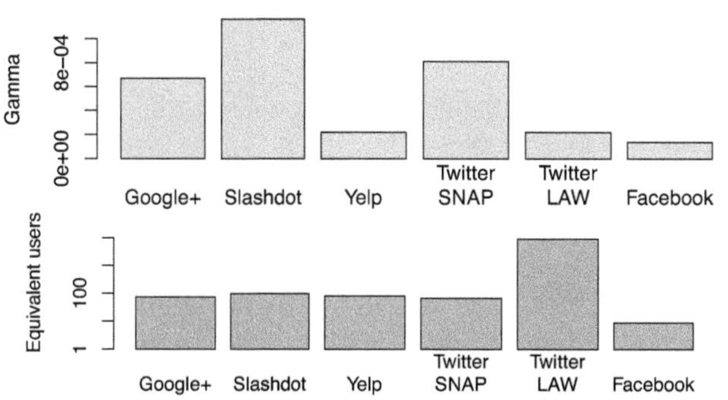

Figure 4: Fairness of social ties: values of $\gamma(G)$ (light grey) and $n \cdot \gamma(G)$ (dark grey) on different social graphs.

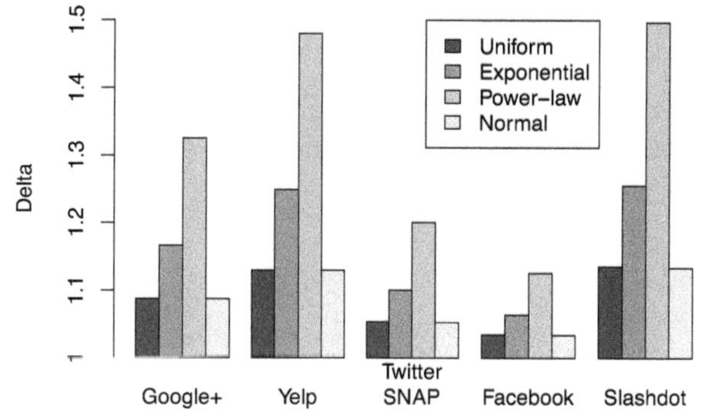

Figure 5: The effect of media tycoons: variation of the market share of p^* (i.e., Δ) for different graphs and starting distributions when a super-node is inserted.

In the last experiment of this section we modify the topology of the networks by inserting a super-node that points to every user and always recommends p^*. This models the effects of mass media such as television, radio, mass advertising, etc. Perhaps unsurprisingly, we observe that such "media tycoons" can influence a relevant portion of the market. Depending on the graph, $\gamma(G)$ ranges from 3.4% to 13.4%. Market distortion can be significant, with values of Δ ranging from 105.3% to 149.7%, as Figure 5 shows.

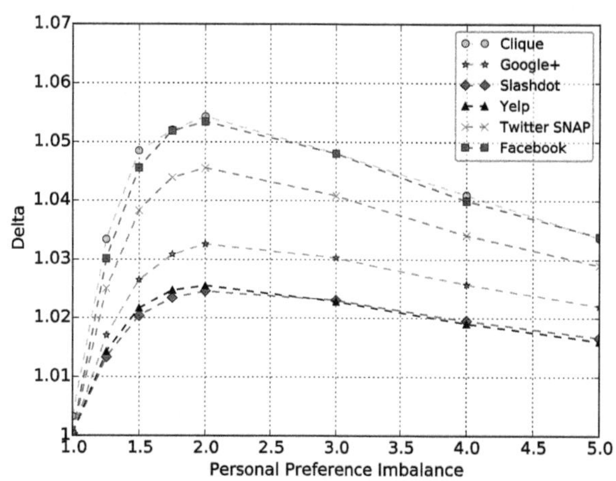

Figure 6: Δ for a market with 2 products as a function of the initial imbalance for product p^*.

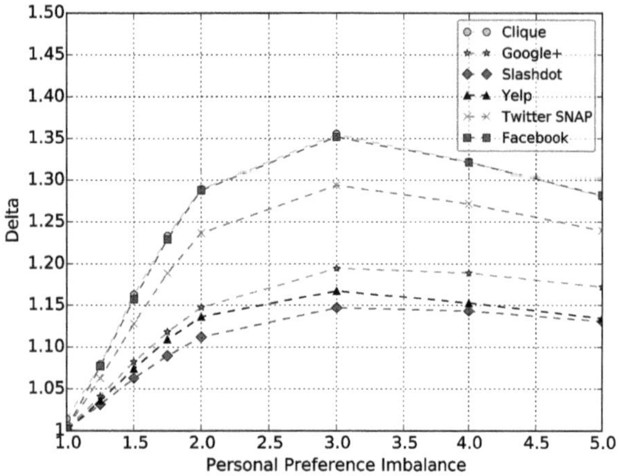

Figure 7: Δ for a market with 10 products as a function of the initial imbalance for product p^*.

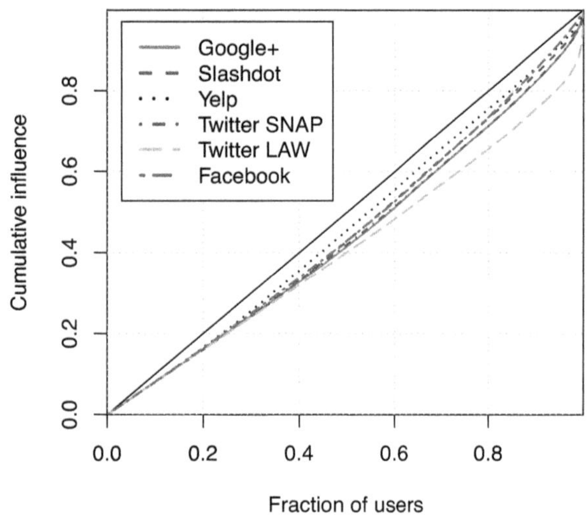

Figure 8: Lorenz curve of the vector γ for the different graphs. The corresponding Gini indices are 0.128, 0.109, 0.076, 0.125, 0.180, 0.101, **in order.**

4.4 Looking for the influencers

In this section we look at the distribution of influence in social networks and give a rule of thumb to identify the most influential users.

In a clique every vertex has the same influence ($\gamma_u = 1/n$ for each user u). We want to know how far real social networks are from this perfectly "egalitarian" situation. Figure 8 shows that real social networks are quite fair in the sense that most of the users have an influence that is slightly smaller than $1/n$, while only a small elite of users has a very large influence. The graph where this "oligarchy" is most prominent is `Twitter LAW`, where 10% of the overall influence on the market is due to 0.6% of the users. In all the other networks, at least 4% of all the users are needed to reach the same combined influence.

Next, we try to give a simple rule of thumb to identify the most influential users in a network. The bottom of Figure 9 shows the first one hundred nodes ranked by out-degree from left to right on the x-axis. The y-axis reports their γ-rank (the shorter the bar the higher the rank). The figure shows that if a node has high out-degree than it will be influential. The top of Figure 9 shows that the converse is not true. Among the one hundred most influential users there are nodes with moderate to low out-degree. Who are these nodes? To illustrate, consider the case of the user whose

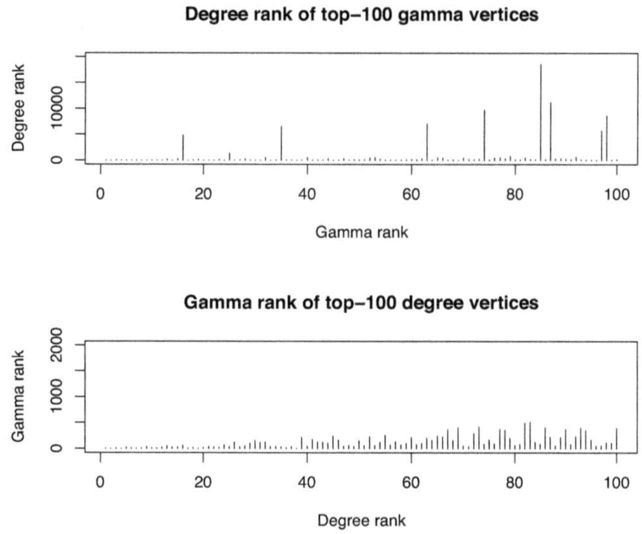

Figure 9: Top: Outdegree rank for the top-100 ranked users w.r.t. γ. Bottom: γ rank for the top-100 ranked users w.r.t. their outdegree. The data refer to `Google+`.

γ-rank in `Google+` is 88. This user lies within the top 1% of the influential users, but his/her 243 followers place him/her in position 11,155 of the out-degree ranking, outside of the top 10%. This user however has 48 followers each of which follows 3 users or less and, among these, 34 happen to follow only him. In other words, this user is highly "trusted" in a small community. When this happens, the node will have a high γ-rank.

Finally, consider a user u who is trusted by a user v having high degree. We know already that v will be influential. Suppose now that v follows a small number of people that is, u is among the few "confidants" of an influential user. Then, u too will be influential.

To summarize, we can characterize influential users as users who have at least one of the following properties:

- A large number of followers.
- A non-negligible group of followers which, in turn, follow few other users.
- Are among the few friends of an influential user.

This rule of thumb gives a heuristic characterization of all influential users.

Acknowledgments. The authors are grateful to Tiziana Castrignanò at CINECA for her precious help with the technical setup of the experiments, and to Flavio Chierichetti for the stimulating and insightful discussions throughout the development of this work.

5. REFERENCES

[1] A. Anderson, R. Kumar, A. Tomkins, and S. Vassilvitskii. The dynamics of repeat consumption. In *Proc. of WWW*, pages 419–430. 2014.

[2] A. R. Benson, R. Kumar, and A. Tomkins. Modeling User Consumption Sequences. In *Proc. of WWW*, pages 519–529. 2016.

[3] P. Boldi, M. Rosa, M. Santini, and S. Vigna. Layered label propagation: A multiresolution coordinate-free ordering for compressing social networks. In *Proc. of WWW*, pages 587–596. 2011.

[4] P. Boldi and S. Vigna. The WebGraph framework I: Compression techniques. In *Proc. WWW*, pages 595–601. 2004.

[5] O. Celma and P. Cano. From hits to niches?: Or how popular artists can bias music recommendation and discovery. In *Proc. NETFLIX Competition*, pages 5:1–5:8. ACM.

[6] A. J. Chaney, D. M. Blei, and T. Eliassi-Rad. A probabilistic model for using social networks in personalized item recommendation. In *Proc. of ACM RecSys*, pages 43–50. 2015.

[7] F. C. T. Chua, H. W. Lauw, and E.-P. Lim. Predicting Item Adoption Using Social Correlation. In *Proc. of SIAM ICDM*, pages 367–378. 2011.

[8] D. Cosley, S. K. Lam, I. Albert, J. A. Konstan, and J. Riedl. Is seeing believing?: How recommender system interfaces affect users' opinions. In *Proc. of CHI*, pages 585–592. 2003.

[9] M. H. DeGroot. Reaching a consensus. *Journal of the American Statistical Association* 69(345):118 – 121, 1974.

[10] W. Duan, B. Gu, and A. B. Whinston. The dynamics of online word-of-mouth and product sales – an empirical investigation of the movie industry. *Journal of Retailing*, 84(2):233 – 242, 2008.

[11] T. Ehrmann and H. Schmale. The hitchhiker's guide to the long tail: The influence of online-reviews and product recommendations on book sales – evidence from german online retailing. In *Proc. ICIS*, 2008.

[12] D. Fleder and K. Hosanagar. Blockbuster culture's next rise or fall: The impact of recommender systems on sales diversity. *Management science*, 55(5):697–712, 2009.

[13] N. E. Friedkin and E. C. Johnson. Social influence and opinions. *Journal of Mathematical Sociology*, 15(3-4):193–206, 1990.

[14] A. Hervas-Drane. Recommended for you: The effect of word of mouth on sales concentration. *International Journal of Research in Marketing*, 32(2):207–218, 2015.

[15] J. Huang and X. Hu. Information passing in online recommendation. In *Proc. of UEO*, pages 3–6. 2013.

[16] M. Jamali and M. Ester. Trustwalker: A random walk model for combining trust-based and item-based recommendation. In *Proc. of KDD*, pages 397–406. 2009.

[17] M. Jamali and M. Ester. A matrix factorization technique with trust propagation for recommendation in social networks. In *Proc. of ACM RecSys*, pages 135–142. 2010.

[18] J. Kleinberg, P. Raghavan, and C. Papadimitriou. On the value of private information. In *Proc. TARK*, 2001.

[19] A. N. Langville and C. D. Meyer. Deeper inside PageRank. *Internet Mathematics*, 1(3):335–380, 2004.

[20] J. Leskovec, L. A. Adamic, and B. A. Huberman. The dynamics of viral marketing. *ACM Trans. Web*, 1(1), May 2007.

[21] J. Leskovec and A. Krevl. SNAP Datasets: Stanford large network dataset collection. `http://snap.stanford.edu/data`.

[22] H. Ma, I. King, and M. R. Lyu. Learning to recommend with social trust ensemble. In *Proc. of ACM SIGIR*, pages 203–210. 2009.

[23] T. T. Nguyen, P.-M. Hui, F. M. Harper, L. Terveen, and J. A. Konstan. Exploring the filter bubble: The effect of using recommender systems on content diversity. In *Proc. WWW*, pages 677–686. 2014.

[24] S. Prawesh and B. Padmanabhan. The "Top N" news recommender: Count distortion and manipulation resistance. In *Proc. of ACM RecSys*, pages 237–244. 2011.

[25] M. J. Salganik, P. S. Dodds, and D. J. Watts. Experimental study of inequality and unpredictability in an artificial cultural market. *Science*, 311(5762):854–856, 2006.

[26] A. Sharma and D. Cosley. Do social explanations work?: Studying and modeling the effects of social explanations in recommender systems. In *Proc. of WWW*, pages 1133–1144. 2013.

[27] A. Sharma, J. M. Hofman, and D. J. Watts. Estimating the Causal Impact of Recommendation Systems from Observational Data. In *Proc. of ACM EC*, pages 453–470. 2015.

[28] J. Su, A. Sharma, and S. Goel. The effect of recommendations on network structure. In *Proc. of WWW*. 2016 (to appear).

[29] B. Viswanath, A. Mislove, M. Cha, and K. P. Gummadi. On the evolution of user interaction in Facebook. In *Proc. of ACM WOSN*, pages 37–42. 2009.

[30] S.-H. Yang, B. Long, A. Smola, N. Sadagopan, Z. Zheng, and H. Zha. Like like alike: Joint friendship and interest propagation in social networks. In *Proc. of WWW*, pages 537–546. 2011.

[31] M. Ye, X. Liu, and W.-C. Lee. Exploring social influence for recommendation: A generative model approach. In *Proc. of ACM SIGIR*, pages 671–680. 2012.

[32] A. Zeng, C. H. Yeung, M. Medo, and Y.-C. Zhang. Modeling mutual feedback between users and recommender systems. *Journal of Statistical Mechanics: Theory and Experiment*, 2015(7):P07020, 2015.

[33] T. Zhao, C. Li, M. Li, Q. Ding, and L. Li. Social recommendation incorporating topic mining and social trust analysis. In *Proc. of ACM CIKM*, pages 1643–1648, 2013.

[34] T. Zhao, J. McAuley, and I. King. Leveraging social connections to improve personalized ranking for collaborative filtering. In *Proc. of ACM CIKM*, pages 261–270. 2014.

[35] H. Zhu and B. A. Huberman. To switch or not to switch. Understanding social influence in online choices. *American Behavioral Scientist*, 58(10):1329–1344, 2014.

APPENDIX

Proof of Theorem 1.

We make use of the following lemma:

LEMMA 1. *The matrix* $(\boldsymbol{I}-\boldsymbol{AM})$ *is nonsingular, and the matrix* $(\boldsymbol{I}-\boldsymbol{AM})^{-1}(\boldsymbol{I}-\boldsymbol{A})$ *is row stochastic (i.e. is real, non-negative, and each row sums to 1).*

PROOF. Since $\alpha_u < 1$ for all u and $\boldsymbol{M}$ is row-stochastic, then $(\boldsymbol{I}-\boldsymbol{AM})$ is strictly diagonally dominant; hence it is invertible by the Levy-Desplanques theorem. Now $(\boldsymbol{I}-\boldsymbol{AM})^{-1}=\sum_{i\geq 0}(\boldsymbol{AM})^i$ is real and nonnegative, as well as $(\boldsymbol{I}-\boldsymbol{A})$, hence so is their product $(\boldsymbol{I}-\boldsymbol{AM})^{-1}(\boldsymbol{I}-\boldsymbol{A})$. Finally, since $\boldsymbol{M}\cdot\mathbf{1}=\mathbf{1}$, then also $(\boldsymbol{I}-\boldsymbol{A})\cdot\mathbf{1}=(\boldsymbol{I}-\boldsymbol{AM})\cdot\mathbf{1}$, and thus $(\boldsymbol{I}-\boldsymbol{AM})^{-1}(\boldsymbol{I}-\boldsymbol{A})\cdot\mathbf{1}=(\boldsymbol{I}-\boldsymbol{AM})^{-1}(\boldsymbol{I}-\boldsymbol{AM})\cdot\mathbf{1}=\mathbf{1}$. □

Lemma 1 implies that the vector $\boldsymbol{x}^\infty$ exists and has components in $[0,1]$. Let us now turn to prove the main statement.

"IF" SIDE. This part is divided in three steps: writing a recurrence equation for $\mathbf{E}[x_u^t]$, converting it into a matricial recurrence equation for $\mathbf{E}[\mathbf{x}^t]-\boldsymbol{x}^\infty$, and showing that $|\mathbf{E}[\mathbf{x}^t]-\boldsymbol{x}^\infty|$ tends to the null vector $\mathbf{0}$.

A recurrence equation for $\mathbf{E}[x_u^t]$. The proof makes use of two additional random variables: ψ_u^t, which indicates the event that u buys at step t, and χ_u^t, which indicates the event that u buys p^* at step t. Then x_u^t can be written as:

$$x_u^t = \sum_{i=1}^{k_u} h_u^{t,-i}\chi_u^{-i} + \sum_{i=1}^{t-1} h_u^{t,i}\chi_u^i \qquad (10)$$

where the χ_u^{-i} are actually constants since the initial history is fixed. Gather the first summation in a single random variable $h_u^{t,0}$, and take the expectation of both sides:

$$\mathbf{E}[x_u^t] = \mathbf{E}[h_u^{t,0}] + \sum_{i=1}^{t-1} \mathbf{E}[h_u^{t,i}\chi_u^i] \qquad (11)$$

Note that $\mathbf{E}[\cdot\, z] = \mathbf{E}[\cdot\,|z=1]\mathbf{E}[z]$ if z is a binary random variable. Also, the weights do not depend on the specific products bought, so $\mathbf{E}[h_u^{t,i}|\chi_u^i=1] = \mathbf{E}[h_u^{t,i}|\psi_u^i=1]$. Using these facts, one can easily rewrite $\mathbf{E}[h_u^{t,i}\chi_u^i]$ as $\mathbf{E}[h_u^{t,i}\psi_u^i]\mathbf{E}[\chi_u^i|\psi_u^i=1]$. We can then restate Equation 11 in the following way:

$$\mathbf{E}[x_u^t] = \mathbf{E}[h_u^{t,0}] + \sum_{i=1}^{t-1} \mathbf{E}[h_u^{t,i}\psi_u^i]\mathbf{E}[\chi_u^i|\psi_u^i=1] \qquad (12)$$

Let us now focus on $\mathbf{E}[\chi_u^i|\psi_u^i=1]$, the probability that u buys p^* at step i given that he buys. By definition of the purchasing process, we have:

$$\mathbf{E}[\chi_u^i|\psi_u^i\!=\!1] = (1-\alpha_u)b_u + \alpha_u \sum_{(v,u)\in G} w_{vu}\, \mathbf{E}[x_v^i|\psi_u^i=1] \quad (13)$$

However, we can replace $\mathbf{E}[x_v^i|\psi_u^i=1]$ by $\mathbf{E}[x_v^i]$ as x_v^i only depends on v's past purchases. Plugging the resulting expression for $\mathbf{E}[\chi_u^i|\psi_u^i=1]$ into Equation 12, we obtain the following recurrence relation:

$$\mathbf{E}[x_u^t] = \mathbf{E}[h_u^{t,0}] + \sum_{i=1}^{t-1} \mathbf{E}[h_u^{t,i}\psi_u^i]((1-\alpha_u)b_u + \alpha_u \sum_{(v,u)\in G} w_{vu}\, \mathbf{E}[x_v^i]) \qquad (14)$$

A recurrence equation for $\mathbf{E}[\mathbf{x}^t] - \boldsymbol{x}^\infty$. We next turn Equation 14 into an expression for $\mathbf{E}[\mathbf{x}^t]$. For all $t > 0$ let $\mathbf{h}_{t,0}$ be the vector $[\mathbf{E}[h_1^{t,0}], \ldots, \mathbf{E}[h_n^{t,0}]]$; similarly, for all $t > i > 0$ let $\mathbf{H}_{t,i}$ be the matrix $\mathrm{diag}(\mathbf{E}[h_1^{t,i}\psi_1^i], \ldots, \mathbf{E}[h_n^{t,i}\psi_n^i])$. Finally, recall the definitions of $\boldsymbol{A}, \boldsymbol{M}, \boldsymbol{b}, \mathbf{x}^i$. The following matricial counterpart to Equation 14 holds:

$$\mathbf{E}[\mathbf{x}^t] = \mathbf{h}_{t,0} + \sum_{i=1}^{t-1} \mathbf{H}_{t,i}((\boldsymbol{I}-\boldsymbol{A})\boldsymbol{b} + \boldsymbol{A}\boldsymbol{M}\mathbf{E}[\mathbf{x}^i]) \qquad (15)$$

We now subtract $\boldsymbol{x}^\infty$ from both sides – but putting the right-hand side in a convenient form. Indeed, by definition of $\mathbf{h}_{t,0}$ and $\mathbf{H}_{t,i}$ and by the fact that $\sum_{i=1}^{k_u} h_u^{t,-i} + \sum_{i=1}^{t-1} h_u^{t,i}\psi_u^i = 1$, if we define $\mathbf{h}'_{t,0}$ as the vector whose u-th component is $\mathbf{E}[h_u^{t,0}] - \mathbf{E}[\sum_{i=1}^{k_u} h_u^{t,-i}]x_u^\infty$, one can write:

$$\mathbf{E}[\mathbf{x}^t] - \boldsymbol{x}^\infty = \mathbf{h}'_{t,0} + \sum_{i=1}^{t-1} \mathbf{H}_{t,i}((\boldsymbol{I}-\boldsymbol{A})\boldsymbol{b} + \boldsymbol{A}\boldsymbol{M}\mathbf{E}[\mathbf{x}^i] - \boldsymbol{x}^\infty) \qquad (16)$$

But by definition of $\boldsymbol{x}^\infty$ we have $(\boldsymbol{I}-\boldsymbol{A})\boldsymbol{b} = (\boldsymbol{I}-\boldsymbol{A}\boldsymbol{M})\boldsymbol{x}^\infty$; thus $(\boldsymbol{I}-\boldsymbol{A})\boldsymbol{b} - \boldsymbol{x}^\infty = -\boldsymbol{A}\boldsymbol{M}\boldsymbol{x}^\infty$ and Equation 16 becomes:

$$\mathbf{E}[\mathbf{x}^t] - \boldsymbol{x}^\infty = \mathbf{h}'_{t,0} + \sum_{i=1}^{t-1} \mathbf{H}_{t,i}\boldsymbol{A}\boldsymbol{M}(\mathbf{E}[\mathbf{x}^i] - \boldsymbol{x}^\infty) \qquad (17)$$

$|\mathbf{E}[\mathbf{x}^t] - \boldsymbol{x}^\infty|$ goes to zero. We finally show that $|\mathbf{E}[\mathbf{x}^t] - \boldsymbol{x}^\infty|$, the vector of the absolute values of $\mathbf{E}[\mathbf{x}^t] - \boldsymbol{x}^\infty$, vanishes with t. The intuition is that $\mathbf{h}'_{t,0}$ and some of the first terms of the summation in Equation 17 go to zero with t by hypothesis, and the rest is damped by the norm of $\boldsymbol{A}$ which is strictly smaller than 1; this gives a bound on $|\mathbf{E}[\mathbf{x}^t] - \boldsymbol{x}^\infty|$ which can be plugged in again, proving the thesis by induction.

Hereafter, inequalities are meant component-wise. First, since $\mathbf{H}_{t,i}$, $\boldsymbol{A}$, $\boldsymbol{M}$ are non-negative, Equation 17 implies:

$$|\mathbf{E}[\mathbf{x}^t] - \boldsymbol{x}^\infty| \le |\mathbf{h}'_{t,0}| + \sum_{i=1}^{t-1} \mathbf{H}_{t,i}\boldsymbol{A}\boldsymbol{M}|\mathbf{E}[\mathbf{x}^i] - \boldsymbol{x}^\infty| \qquad (18)$$

Suppose now $|\mathbf{E}[\mathbf{x}^t] - \boldsymbol{x}^\infty| \le c\mathbf{1}$ for all $t > \tau$, for some constants $\tau, c \ge 0$; this trivially holds for $\tau = 0$ and $c = 1$. One can check that, by hypothesis of forgetfulness, each element of $\mathbf{h}'_{t,0}$ goes to zero with t, and the same does each element of $\mathbf{H}_{t,i}$ for any fixed i. Thus for any given $\epsilon > 0$ there exists a $t' \ge \tau$ such that for all $t > t'$:

$$|\mathbf{h}'_{t,0}| + \sum_{i=1}^{\tau} \mathbf{H}_{t,i}\boldsymbol{A}\boldsymbol{M}|\mathbf{E}[\mathbf{x}^i] - \boldsymbol{x}^\infty| \le \epsilon \qquad (19)$$

and then Equation 18 gives, for all $t > t'$:

$$|\mathbf{E}[\mathbf{x}^t] - \boldsymbol{x}^\infty| \le \epsilon\mathbf{1} + \sum_{i=\tau+1}^{t-1} \mathbf{H}_{t,i}\boldsymbol{A}\boldsymbol{M}|\mathbf{E}[\mathbf{x}^i] - \boldsymbol{x}^\infty| \qquad (20)$$

$$\le \epsilon\mathbf{1} + \sum_{i=\tau+1}^{t-1} \mathbf{H}_{t,i}\boldsymbol{A}\boldsymbol{M}\cdot c\mathbf{1} \qquad (21)$$

Each row of $\boldsymbol{A}\boldsymbol{M}$ sums to at most α where $\alpha = \max_{v\in G}\alpha_v$; while, since $\sum_{i=1}^{t-1} h_u^{t,i}\psi_u^i \le 1$, each row of $(\sum_{i=\tau+1}^{t-1} \mathbf{H}_{t,i})$ sums to at most 1. Each row of $\sum_{i=\tau+1}^{t-1} \mathbf{H}_{t,i}\boldsymbol{A}\boldsymbol{M}$ thus sums to at most α. And then for all $t > t'$:

$$|\mathbf{E}[\mathbf{x}^t] - \boldsymbol{x}^\infty| \le \epsilon\mathbf{1} + \alpha c\mathbf{1} \qquad (22)$$

which for e.g. $\epsilon = \frac{1-\alpha}{2}c$ gives $|\mathbf{E}[\mathbf{x}^t] - \boldsymbol{x}^\infty| \le \frac{1+\alpha}{2}c\mathbf{1}$. But we can then repeat the whole argument multiple times, each time replacing τ by t' and c by $\frac{1+\alpha}{2}c$ and tightening the bound on $|\mathbf{E}[\mathbf{x}^t] - \boldsymbol{x}^\infty|$ by a factor $\frac{1+\alpha}{2}$ for all sufficiently large t. Since $\alpha < 1$ and thus $\frac{1+\alpha}{2} < 1$, this implies

$$\lim_{t\to+\infty} |\mathbf{E}[\mathbf{x}^t] - \boldsymbol{x}^\infty| = \mathbf{0} \qquad (23)$$

which concludes this part of the proof.

"ONLY IF" SIDE. We show a simple counterexample. Pick a G where all u have incoming arcs and let all $\alpha_u > 0$. Also, let all u buy the same product a at time -1 and set $h_u^{t,-1} = 1$ for every t. All nodes thus always recommend a, so if $\lim_{t\to\infty}\mathbf{E}[\mathbf{x}^t]$ exists it must depend on whether or not $p^* = a$; thus it cannot be $\boldsymbol{x}^\infty$. Moreover, one can make the system never converge by putting two different products a and b in the initial purchasing history of all users and making them periodically recommend only a or only b.

Positive-Unlabeled Learning in Streaming Networks

Shiyu Chang[1]*, Yang Zhang[1]*, Jiliang Tang[2],
Dawei Yin[3], Yi Chang[3], Mark A. Hasegawa-Johnson[1], Thomas S. Huang[1]
[1] Beckman Institute, University of Illinois at Urbana-Champaign, IL 61801.
[2] Computer Science and Engineering, Michigan State University. East Lansing, MI 48824.
[3] Yahoo! Labs, Yahoo! Inc. Sunnyvale, CA 94089.
{chang87, yzhan143, jhasegaw, t-huang1}@illinois.edu,
jiliang.tang@cse.msu.edu, {daweiy,yichang}@yahoo-inc.com

ABSTRACT

Data of many problems in real-world systems such as link prediction and one-class recommendation share common characteristics. First, data are in the form of positive-unlabeled (PU) measurements (*e.g.* Twitter "following", Facebook "like", *etc.*) that do not provide negative information, which can be naturally represented as networks. Second, in the era of big data, such data are generated temporally-ordered, continuously and rapidly, which determines its streaming nature. These common characteristics allow us to unify many problems into a novel framework – PU learning in streaming networks. In this paper, a principled probabilistic approach SPU is proposed to leverage the characteristics of the streaming PU inputs. In particular, SPU captures temporal dynamics and provides real-time adaptations and predictions by identifying the potential negative signals concealed in unlabeled data. Our empirical results on various real-world datasets demonstrate the effectiveness of the proposed framework over other state-of-the-art methods in both link prediction and recommendation.

Keywords

PU learning, dynamic network, online learning, continuous time, streaming link prediction, streaming recommendation.

1. INTRODUCTION

Networks have been widely adopted to represent relations among entities in many real-world systems. For example, in link prediction, a network can indicate friendships among users; in one-class recommendation, a bipartite network can capture purchase relations between users and items; while in relevance ranking for modern search engines, a bipartite network can represent the clicking behaviors from users to documents. One common characteristic of these networks is that they only provide positive information, *i.e.* a connection between a pair of nodes; while negative information is hidden in unlabeled data, *i.e.* no connection between a pair of nodes. Therefore, these problems can be unified as the positive-unlabeled (PU) learning in networks.

Although learning from only PU examples has been studied in the context of binary classification [8, 20, 35], vectorized content representations are required. However, in many cases, the aforementioned applications only assume the availability of networks. Furthermore, in the era of big data, data are generated at an unprecedented rate. For example, Facebook users exceeded one billion in 2012, which doubled from the previous year[1]. Such data present distinct properties such as temporally ordered, continuous and at high-velocity, and thus link creations should be considered as data streams. Therefore we need to incorporate the streaming nature of networks, which motivates a novel problem – PU learning in streaming networks. The following three challenges have to be tackled simultaneously.

- **Streaming nature**: Data streams are massive and generated at high velocity. Therefore the learning algorithm needs to be implemented very efficiently and is able to work with one pass of the data. Specifically, the algorithm has to perform an incremental update in order to process massive volume of data in an online fashion. Furthermore, the input streams consist of not only new relations, but also new registered entities which can be introduced to the system for any given time. Therefore, it requires the algorithm to provide instant responses to any unseen candidates without assuming a fixed number of nodes in the network.
- **Unlabeled negativity**: One key problem of PU Learning in networks is to discover users' hidden preferences from data. These preferences should include not only what they like, but also what they dislike. It is evident from recent work [29] that the negative information has significant added value in various analytical tasks. Due to the one-side characteristic of PU inputs, we need to identify the potential "negative" signals from unlabeled ones to yield a more accurate performance.
- **Concept shift**: The underlying user preferences (or item characteristics) continuously evolve over time, which can have significant effects on predictions. For instance, in the context of co-authorship prediction, one may change the research interest from one field to another, which decreases the likelihood of connecting to people from the original field.

*Authors contributed equally to this work.

[1] http://www.businessinsider.com/facebook-350-million-photos-each-day-2013-9

KDD '16, August 13-17, 2016, San Francisco, CA, USA
© 2016 ACM. ISBN 978-1-4503-4232-2/16/08...$15.00
DOI: http://dx.doi.org/10.1145/2939672.2939744

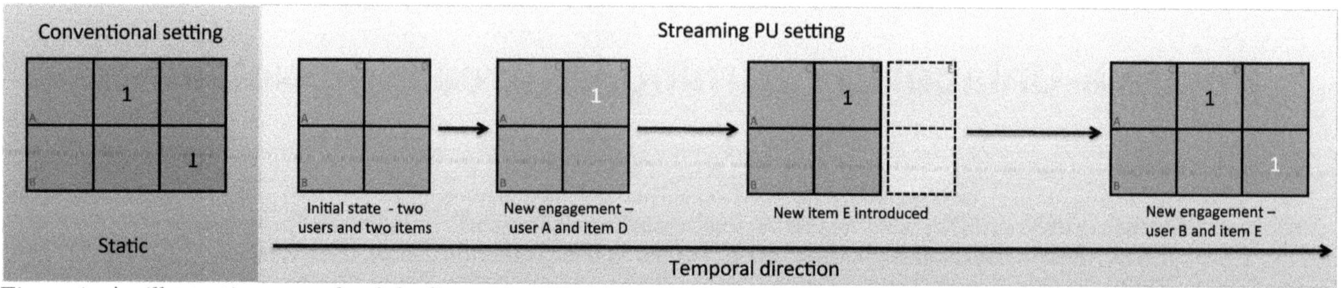

Figure 1: An illustrative example of the Streaming PU relational learning. Compared to the conventional setting that assumes aggregated feedbacks, the streaming PU setting unfolds events along the temporal direction. The "*yellow 1*"s indicate new appeared relationship at that time, while the dashed rectangle represents a new item introduced. The length of the arrows between each block figure under the streaming PU settings represents the time difference between two consecutive events.

In this paper, we explicitly consider the problem of PU learning in networks under streaming scenarios. An illustrative example of the proposed streaming PU learning framework is shown in figure 1. The input streams are modeled as two types of events: new relation engagements and new node introductions. Events are temporally ordered and received by online systems continuously. The time difference between two consecutive events can be nonuniform and arbitrarily small. In particular, we tackle all three aforementioned challenges by a unified framework termed streaming positive-unlabeled learning (SPU). The major contributions of this paper are three.

- We unify a number of real-world applications to the problem of PU learning in streaming networks.
- The novel framework SPU discovers the negative information from unlabeled samples through time to power predictions. Its self-adaptive mechanism can efficiently work with one pass of the data and capture temporal drifts of latent characteristics.
- Extensive empirical studies reveal the successful use of the proposed framework in the application of link prediction and recommendation.

2. PROBLEM DEFINITION AND NOTATION

Here we first define some notation:

- Upper-cased letters, A, denote random variables/vectors. Lower-cased letters, a, denote deterministic values. Script letters, $\mathcal{A}$, denote sets.
- $p(\cdot)$ or $q(\cdot)$ denote probability density function or probability mass function, depending on whether the random variable is continuous or discrete.
- $\mathbb{E}_p(A)$ and $\mathrm{Cov}_p(A)$ denote expectation and covariance of A respectively, under the probability measure p.
- $\mathcal{N}(\mu, \Sigma)$ denotes normal distribution with mean μ and covariance Σ.
- $\{A_i\}_i$ is a set of random variables A_i with subscript i running through the index set, *i.e.* $\cup_i\{A_i\}$.

2.1 The Network Representation

We assume there are two types of nodes: type-1 node and type-2 node. Note that type-1 can be identical to type-2 in some problems such as link prediction. The number of these two types of nodes at time t are m^t and n^t respectively. The reason why they depend on t is that the proposed model accommodates the introduction of new nodes. For each type-1-type-2 node pair (i, j), L^t_{ij} is an indicator variable of whether they connect, *i.e.* it is 1 if there is an edge connecting them at time t and 0 otherwise.

This network representation is applicable to a number of real-world applications. For example, in social networks, the two types of nodes are homogeneous and represent the users, and $L^t_{ij} = 1$ represents that users i and j connect at time t. While in one-class recommendations, the two types of nodes are heterogeneous, with one representing the users and the other denoting the items, such as movies or social media posts. The two types of nodes form a bipartite graph, where $L^t_{ij} = 1$ denotes that user i interacts with (*e.g.* downloads, or gives "like" to) item j. Without the loss of generality, we assume the two types of nodes are heterogeneous. Homogeneity is merely a special case by imposing symmetry on the connections.

2.2 The Streaming PU Setting

It is now important to emphasize the streaming nature of our setting. First, rather than presetting a fixed number of nodes, our setting allows the size of the network to be constantly and continuously changing. Second, rather than regarding the connection status between nodes as stationary, our setting regards each link status as dynamic and instantaneous. In other words, $L^t_{ij} = 1$ only reflects the connection status at that particular time t when the edge is established. It does not imply the node pair (i, j) keep connecting at any future times.

The instantaneity of connection status is a natural assumption for applications where the connection represents a click, a message sent *etc.*, because these interactions are themselves instantaneous. Even for applications where the connection represents some durable relation such as a "like", a Twitter "follow" *etc.*, this assumption is still reasonable, because in most real-world scenarios canceling an edge may be reluctant or impossible, even though their actual connection status may have changed. For example, suppose a user gives a "like" to a Facebook post, expressing his/her interest in the post. This "like" is likely to sustain even if the user's interest in the post diminishes over time. Therefore, the "like" merely reflects the user's interest at that particular moment, but hardly any time afterwards.

2.3 The Prediction Task

Our goal is to predict the node pairs that would connect in the near future, given any time t. Formally, $\forall (i, j) : L^t_{ij} = 0$, provide the prediction $\hat{L}^{t+}_{ij}$ *s.t.* the probability of error

$$P(\hat{L}^{t+}_{ij} \neq L^{t+}_{ij}) = \mathbb{E}[(\hat{L}^{t+}_{ij} - L^{t+}_{ij})^2]$$

is minimized; where $t+$ denotes a sufficiently small amount of time after t. We adopt the standard Bayesian approach for the task, which consists of two steps: 1) model the probability distribution of L_{ij}^t; and 2) predict the connection status with a tractable inference scheme under the modeled distribution. These two steps will be detailed in the following two sections respectively.

3. THE PROBABILISTIC MODEL

This section proposes the probabilistic model, which involves the joint probability distribution of $\{L_{ij}^t\}_{i,j,t}$, and a set of auxiliary hidden variables.

3.1 Partially Observed Connection

To address the positive-unlabeled nature of our data, we assume L_{ij}^t depends on two factors: 1) The "mutual interest" of the node pair, and 2) whether their connection status is observed. In other words, the node pair (i,j) connects only when these two nodes are of interest to each other, and their connection status is observed. More concretely, in Facebook, for instance, there are two reasons that a user have not given a "thumb up" to a post: 1) this user does not like the post at all (no mutual interests), or 2) this user have not seen the post yet (connection status unobserved).

To model the above intuition, we adapt the popular Probit model. Denote X_{ij}^t as a real valued hidden variable modeling their mutual interests. And O_{ij}^t is the indicator variable of whether the connection status of node pair (i,j) is observed at time t. Then, the conditional distribution of L_{ij}^t is

$$L_{ij}^t = \begin{cases} 1 & \text{if } O_{ij}^t = 1 \wedge X_{ij}^t > \theta \\ 0 & \text{otherwise.} \end{cases} \tag{1}$$

The prior distributions of O_{ij}^t and X_{ij}^t are given in the following two subsections respectively.

3.2 Connection Observability

This section proposes the prior distribution of O_{ij}^t, which denotes the connection observability. Intuitively, the connection observability is affected by several factors. The first factor is the liveliness of the network. If the amount of activity is great, *i.e.* the nodes are actively seeking links with others, then the probability of not meeting a node is low. The second factor is the cost to connect. If the cost of connection is low, *i.e.* the nodes can easily find other nodes, and can easily connect to whichever nodes they want, then the probability of having an unobserved link is also low.

While these factors are hard to evaluate explicitly, we find that the network liveliness is intuitively correlated with the number of recently established links; and the connection difficulty is inversely correlated with the number of recently born pairs, *i.e.* pairs with at least one node that is recently born. This is because the faster new content is introduced, the harder for the nodes to traverse the new content and find the nodes of interests.

Based on these intuitions, we first define the new-link-to-new-node ratio:

$$\eta^t = \frac{\#\left\{(i,j) : \exists\tau \in (t-\Delta t, t), L_{ij}^\tau = 1\right\}}{\#\left\{(i,j) : a_i \in (t-\Delta t, t) \vee b_j \in (t-\Delta t, t)\right\}}, \tag{2}$$

where Δt is a time window; a_i and b_j denote the birth times for the type-1 node i and type-2 node j respectively. Then the prior distribution of O_{ij}^t is given by

$$p\left(O_{ij}^t = 1\right) = \max\left\{\lambda\eta^t, 1\right\}, \tag{3}$$

where λ is a model parameter. The appropriateness of equation (3) will be demonstrated in section 5.5.

3.3 Mutual Interests between Nodes

This section introduces the conditional prior of X_{ij}^t. For each type-1 node i at time t, we assume there exists a hidden topic random vector U_i^t of length r, whose elements represent type-1 node i's affinities to r hidden topics. Likewise, we use V_j^t to denote the length-r characteristic vector of type-2 node j at time t.

For each type-1-type-2 node pair (i,j), their mutual interests, X_{ij}^t, depends on the similarity between their hidden topic vectors. Intuitively, the more similar their affinity patterns are, the more mutual interests they have. Formally, the pdf of X_{ij}^t is given by

$$p\left(X_{ij}^t | U_i^t, V_j^t\right) = \mathcal{N}\left(\left(U_i^t\right)^T V_j^t, \sigma_E^2\right), \tag{4}$$

where σ_E^2 is a model parameter.

3.4 Temporal Dynamics

The hidden topic vectors of nodes tend to shift over time. To model their temporal dynamics, we assume Brownian motion:

$$\begin{aligned} p\left(U_i^t | U_i^{t-\tau}\right) &= \mathcal{N}\left(U_i^{t-\tau}, \sigma_U^2 \tau I\right) \\ p\left(V_j^t | V_j^{t-\tau}\right) &= \mathcal{N}\left(V_j^{t-\tau}, \sigma_V^2 \tau I\right). \end{aligned} \tag{5}$$

The initial distribution, namely the distribution at birth time, is defined differently for two distinct cases. For those nodes that are born at $t > 0$, recall that a_i and b_j denote the birth times for the type-1 node i and type-2 node j respectively. Also, for notation ease, the nodes are indexed by birth order. Then we have

$$\begin{aligned} p\left(U_i^{a_i} | \mathcal{L}^{a_i -}\right) &= \mathcal{N}\left(\frac{1}{i-1}\sum_{k=1}^{i-1}\mathbb{E}\left[U_k^{a_i} | \mathcal{L}^{a_i -}\right], \sigma_{U0}^2 I\right) \\ p\left(V_j^{b_j} | \mathcal{L}^{b_j -}\right) &= \mathcal{N}\left(\frac{1}{j-1}\sum_{k=1}^{j-1}\mathbb{E}\left[V_k^{b_j} | \mathcal{L}^{b_j -}\right], \sigma_{V0}^2 I\right), \end{aligned} \tag{6}$$

where $\mathcal{L}^{t-}$ is the set of observed $L_{ij}^{t'}, t' < t$, whose formal definition will be given in section 3.5. Equation (6) essentially assumes that the initial preference of a newly-born node follows the general taste of the current population, because $\mathbb{E}\left[U_k^{t-\tau} | \mathcal{L}^{t-}\right]$ and $\mathbb{E}\left[V_k^{t-\tau} | \mathcal{L}^{t-}\right]$ are MMSE estimates of the hidden topic vectors. Averaging across the whole population extracts the general topic vector.

For those nodes that exist at the beginning of the world, $t = 0$, we assume zero-mean Gaussian distribution:

$$p\left(U_i^0\right) = \mathcal{N}\left(0, \sigma_{U0}^2 I\right) \text{ and } p\left(V_j^0\right) = \mathcal{N}\left(0, \sigma_{V0}^2 I\right). \tag{7}$$

σ_U^2, σ_V^2, σ_{U0}^2 and σ_{V0}^2 are model parameters.

3.5 The Observation Set and Events

A link L_{ij}^t is defined as an observation if and only if the following two conditions are satisfied.

Condition 1: the value of L_{ij}^t first appears or changes at time t, which involves two scenarios: 1) all L_{ij}^ts whose corresponding type-1 node i and/or type-2 node j are born at time t; 2) all L_{ij}^ts whose values jump to 1 at time t (recall that all the 1's are instantaneous as discussed in section 3.1).

Condition 2: For an $L_{ij}^t = 0$ to be an observation, $O_{ij}^t = 1$.

Here we would like to reiterate that the L_{ij}^ts that meet the above conditions are considered as observations at that specific time t only. Based on these two conditions, the observation set $\mathcal{L}|\mathcal{O}$ is rigorously defined by

$$\mathcal{L}|\mathcal{O} = \{L_{ij}^t : ((a_i = t \vee b_j = t) \wedge O_{ij}^t = 1) \vee L_{ij}^t = 1\}, \quad (8)$$

where $\mathcal{O}$ denotes the set of all O_{ij}^ts. As implied by equation (8), the observation set is conditional on $\mathcal{O}$ which is hidden, and thus is impossible to evaluate. Following the common paradigm to marginalize over unobserved randomness, we define the unconditional observation set $\mathcal{L}$ as the set of L_{ij}^ts that satisfy condition 1:

$$\mathcal{L} = \bigcup_{\mathcal{O} \in \{0,1\}^{|\mathcal{O}|}} \mathcal{L}|\mathcal{O} = \{L_{ij}^t : a_i = t \vee b_j = t \vee L_{ij}^t = 1\}. \quad (9)$$

The definition of observation set introduces our important concept of events. An event is a time instance t at which new observations are introduced. As already discussed, this includes: 1) the world starts $t = 0$; 2) a new node is introduced ($t = a_i$ or b_j); and 3) a new edge is established.

Here we define some observation- and event-related notations. For any time t, we have the following definitions:

- $\mathcal{L}$ - the unconditional observation set as in equation (9);
- $\mathcal{L}^t$ - the subset of $\mathcal{L}$ with time up to and including time t;
- $\mathcal{L}^{t-}$ - the subset of $\mathcal{L}$ with time up to but not including time t;
- $\mathcal{T}$ - the set of all event times;
- $\tau(t)$ - the time elapsed after the most recent (excluding current) event;
- $\tau_U(i, t)$ - the time elapsed after the most recent (excluding current) event that is related to type-1 node i;
- $\tau_V(j, t)$ - the time elapsed after the most recent (excluding current) event that is related to type-2 node j.

3.6 Model Summary and Joint Distribution

To sum up, the probabilistic model involves observed variables $\mathcal{L}^t$ and hidden variables $\{O_{ij}^t, X_{ij}^t, U_i^t, V_j^t\}$. The prior distributions are given by equations (1)-(7). In particular, for an event time t, the joint posterior distributions of all the hidden variables is given recursively by

$$p\left(\{U_i^t, V_j^t, X_{ij}^t, O_{ij}^t\}_{i,j} | \mathcal{L}^t\right) \propto p\left(\{U_i^t, V_j^t\}_{i,j} | \mathcal{L}^{t-\tau(t)}\right) \cdot \prod_{i,j} p\left(X_{ij}^t | U_i^t, V_j^t\right) p\left(O_{ij}^t\right) \cdot \prod_{i,j: L_{ij}^t \in \mathcal{L}|\mathcal{O}} p\left(L_{ij}^t | X_{ij}^t, O_{ij}^t\right), \quad (10)$$

where

$$\prod_{i,j: L_{ij}^t \in \mathcal{L}|\mathcal{O}} p\left(L_{ij}^t | X_{ij}^t, O_{ij}^t\right) = \prod_{i,j: L_{ij}^t = 1, L_{ij}^t \in \mathcal{L}} p\left(L_{ij}^t | X_{ij}^t, O_{ij}^t\right) \cdot \prod_{i,j: L_{ij}^t = 0, L_{ij}^t \in \mathcal{L}} p\left(L_{ij}^t | X_{ij}^t, O_{ij}^t\right)^{O_{ij}^t}, \quad (11)$$

and

$$p(\{U_i^t, V_j^t\}_{i,j} | \mathcal{L}^{t-\tau(t)}) = p(\{U_i^{t-\tau(t)}, V_j^{t-\tau(t)}\}_{i,j} | \mathcal{L}^{t-\tau(t)}) \cdot \prod_i p(U_i^t | U_i^{t-\tau(t)}) \prod_j p(V_j^t | V_j^{t-\tau(t)}). \quad (12)$$

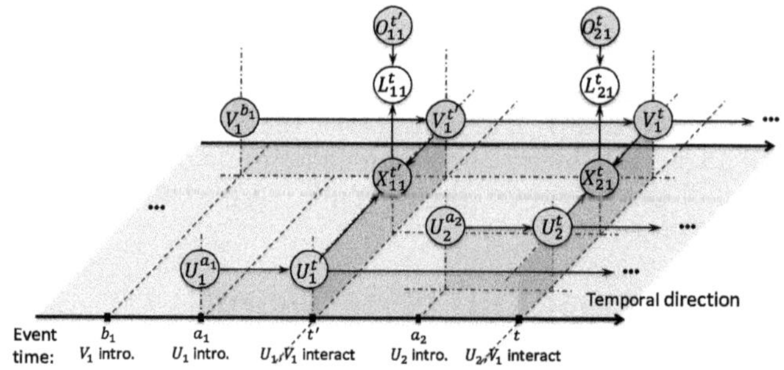

Figure 2: An illustrative framework of Streaming PU learning. White nodes denote observed variables, and shaded nodes denote hidden variables. The nodes are shown in a 3D coordinate with the time axis being the canonical x-axis as labeled. All the hidden nodes are a subset of the underlying continuous hidden process sampled at event times.

As can be seen, the last term of equation (11) is raised to the power of O_{ij}^t. This is merely a compact way of expressing only those L_{ij}^ts with $O_{ij}^t = 1$ (condition 2 of being an observation) are incorporated into the joint probability distribution. An illustration of the probabilistic model is shown in figure 2.

4. MODEL INFERENCE

With the model established, we formulate the prediction of future connection status as a standard inference problem based on the observed connection status up to current time.

4.1 The Prediction Task

Our goal is to identify connections that are about to establish, *i.e.*

$$L_{ij}^t = 0, \text{ but } L_{ij}^{t+} = 1. \quad (13)$$

According to equation (1), one of the necessary conditions is to identify

$$L_{ij}^t = 0, \text{ but } X_{ij}^t > \theta. \quad (14)$$

The posterior expectation, *a.k.a.* the MMSE estimate, $\mathbb{E}\left[X_{ij}^t | \mathcal{L}^t\right]$, is applied to infer the hidden X_{ij}^t. However, this involves evaluating the posterior distribution as in equation (10), which does not bear a closed-form solution due to the complex nonlinearity of the model. Therefore, we would apply a variant of variational approach to approximate the posterior distribution, as will be introduced in the remainder of the section.

4.2 Recursive Variational Inference

Approximating equation (10) involves two steps alternatively and recursively. First, it is approximated by the following distribution

$$p\left(\{U_i^t, V_j^t, X_{ij}^t, O_{ij}^t\}_{i,j} | \mathcal{L}^t\right) \approx p'\left(\{U_i^t, V_j^t, X_{ij}^t, O_{ij}^t\}_{i,j} | \mathcal{L}^t\right) \triangleq p'\left(\{U_i^t, V_j^t\}_{i,j} | \mathcal{L}^{t-\tau(t)}\right) p\left(X_{ij}^t | U_i^t, V_j^t\right) p\left(O_{ij}^t\right) \cdot \prod_{i,j: L_{ij}^t \in \mathcal{L}|\mathcal{O}} p\left(L_{ij}^t | X_{ij}^t, O_{ij}^t\right). \quad (15)$$

The only difference between equations (10) and (15) is that the first term is replaced with an approximate distribution $p'(\{U_i^t, V_j^t\}_{i,j} | \mathcal{L}^{t-\tau(t)})$, which will be defined soon.

Then, we apply the variational approximation approach to approximate $p'(\{U_i^t, V_j^t, X_{ij}^t, O_{ij}^t\}_{i,j} | \mathcal{L}^t)$ as in equation (15) to the distribution q with the following form (for notation ease, condition on observation is omitted without causing ambiguity):

$$p'\left(\{U_i^t, V_j^t, X_{ij}^t, O_{ij}^t\}_{i,j} | \mathcal{L}^t\right) \approx q\left(\{U_i^t, V_j^t, X_{ij}^t, O_{ij}^t\}_{i,j}\right) = \prod_i q(U_i^t) \prod_j q(V_j^t) \prod_{i,j} q(O_{ij}^t) q_0(X_{ij}^t | U_i^t, V_j^t)^{(1-O_{ij}^t)} q_1(X_{ij}^t)^{O_{ij}^t}. \tag{16}$$

The key idea behind this approximation form is that when L_{ij}^t is observed, *i.e.* $O_{ij}^t = 1$, we apply the simple mean-field approximation, where each hidden variable is independent; otherwise we add the dependency on U_i^t and V_j^t to X_{ij}^t. The advantages to choose this approximation form are twofold. First, this approximation yields a *smaller* error than the simple mean-field approximation, because the latter is merely a special case of equation (16) by constraining $q_0(X_{ij}^t | U_i^t, V_i^t) = q_1(X_{ij}^t)$. Second, though complicated with more dependencies, this approximation still has a tractable and concise closed-form solution.

We find the closest approximation by minimizing the KL divergence between p' and q:

$$\min_q D = \min_q \mathrm{KL}\left[q\left(\{U_i^t, V_j^t, X_{ij}^t, O_{ij}^t\}_{i,j}\right) \middle\| p'\left(\{U_i^t, V_j^t, X_{ij}^t, O_{ij}^t\}_{i,j} | \mathcal{L}^t\right)\right]. \tag{17}$$

Now we are ready to define p' as in equation (15), which depends on the q distribution at the preceding event in a similar way to equation (12):

$$p'\left(\{U_i^t, V_j^t\}_{i,j} | \mathcal{L}^{t-\tau(t)}\right) = \prod_i p'\left(U_i^t | \mathcal{L}^{t-\tau(t)}\right) \prod_j p'\left(V_j^t | \mathcal{L}^{t-\tau(t)}\right), \tag{18}$$

where

$$p'\left(U_i^t | \mathcal{L}^{t-\tau(t)}\right) = \int dU_i^{t-\tau(t)} q\left(U_i^{t-\tau(t)}\right) p\left(U_i^t | U_i^{t-\tau(t)}\right)$$
$$p'\left(V_j^t | \mathcal{L}^{t-\tau(t)}\right) = \int dV_j^{t-\tau(t)} q\left(V_j^{t-\tau(t)}\right) p\left(V_j^t | V_j^{t-\tau(t)}\right). \tag{19}$$

To sum up, our inference scheme can be described as:

$$\cdots \Rightarrow q \text{ at } t - \tau(t) \Rightarrow p' \text{ at } t \Rightarrow q \text{ at } t \Rightarrow \cdots,$$

at each **event times** t, first obtain the current p' from the q at the previous event according to equations (15), (18) and (19). Then, approximate the current p' with the current q according to equations (16) and (17), and so on. The q distributions are the distributions over which we perform the inference. Hence we name our inference scheme as the recursive variational inference.

4.3 The Streaming Inference Scheme

In this section, we briefly state the final solution to equation (17). The inference scheme consists of two parts:

- Update the posterior moments of hidden variables (under $q(\cdot|\mathcal{L}^t)$) at each event time t;
- Predict future connection based on the most recent updated posterior moments.

4.3.1 Updating Posterior Moments

Recall that the q distribution is the approximate distribution for the posterior distribution $p(\cdot|\mathcal{L}^t)$. Since at each event time t, the observation set $\mathcal{L}^t$ is augmented, the q distribution should be updated accordingly. Furthermore, the q distribution is characterized by its moments, and so it is suffice just to update the moments. The update process is iterative: posterior moments obtained in the previous iteration is applied to update the posterior moments in the current iteration until convergence. The update equations in each iteration are given as follows.

- **The update equations for U_i^t and V_j^t:**

For a given event time t, for any type-1 node i that is involved in the event, the update equation is given by

$$\mathrm{Cov}_q\left(U_i^t\right) = \left(\Sigma_{Ui}^{-1} + \sigma_E^{-2} \sum_{j:L_{ij}^t \in \mathcal{L}^t} q\left(O_{ij}^t = 1\right) \mathbb{E}_q\left(\left(V_j^t\right)^T V_j^t\right)\right)^{-1},$$
$$\mathbb{E}_q\left(U_i^t\right) = \mathrm{Cov}_q\left(U_i^t\right)\left(\Sigma_{Ui}^{-1}\mu_{Ui} + \sigma_E^{-2} \sum_{j:L_{ij}^t \in \mathcal{L}^t} q\left(O_{ij}^t = 1\right) \mathbb{E}_q\left(V_j^t\right) \mathbb{E}_{q_1}\left(X_{ij}^t\right)\right). \tag{20}$$

where, for type-1 nodes who were born *before* t,

$$\Sigma_{Ui} = \mathrm{Cov}_q(U_i^{t-\tau_U(i,t)}) + \sigma_U^2 \tau_U(i,t) I, \quad \mu_{Ui} = \mathbb{E}_q(U_i^{t-\tau_U(i,t)});$$

and for type-1 nodes who are born *at* t, μ_{Ui} and Σ_{Ui} are the corresponding mean and covariance in either equation (7) or (6) depending on whether t is zero or not. More importantly, for nodes that are not involved in the event, no update is needed. The update equations for V_j^t is symmetric to equation (20) except that U and V, and subscripts i and j are interchanged.

- **The update equations for X_{ij}^t:** For a given event time t, for any X_{ij}^t whose corresponding L_{ij}^t is in the observation set $\mathcal{L}^t$, the posterior expectation is given by

$$\mathbb{E}_{q_1}\left(X_{ij}^t\right) = \mu_{ij}^t + \left(\frac{\phi\left(e_{ij}^t\right) - \phi\left(f_{ij}^t\right)}{\Phi\left(e_{ij}^t\right) - \Phi\left(f_{ij}^t\right)}\right)\sigma_E, \tag{21}$$

where $\phi(\cdot)$ and $\Phi(\cdot)$ are pdf and cdf of standard Gaussian distribution respectively; and $\mu_{ij}^t = \mathbb{E}_q(U_i^t)^T \mathbb{E}_q(V_j^t)$,

$$e_{ij}^t = \begin{cases} \frac{\theta - \mu_{ij}^t}{\sigma_E} & \text{if } L_{ij}^t = 1 \\ -\infty & \text{otherwise} \end{cases}, \quad f_{ij}^t = \begin{cases} \infty & \text{if } L_{ij}^t = 1 \\ \frac{\theta - \mu_{ij}^t}{\sigma_E} & \text{otherwise.} \end{cases}$$

- **The update equations for O_{ij}^t:**

At an event time t, if either type-1 node i or type-2 node j are involved, the update equation for O_{ij}^t is given by

$$q(O_{ij}^t = 1) = \begin{cases} 1 & \text{if } L_{ij}^t = 1 \\ \frac{p\left(O_{ij}^t = 1\right)\exp\left(\kappa_{ij}^t\right)}{1 + p\left(O_{ij}^t = 1\right)\left[\exp\left(\kappa_{ij}^t\right) - 1\right]} & \text{otherwise,} \end{cases} \tag{22}$$

where

$$\kappa_{ij}^t = \ln \Phi(\theta - \mathbb{E}_q(U_i^t)^T \mathbb{E}_q(V_j^t)) - \frac{1}{2\sigma_E^2}\mathrm{tr}\Big[\mathrm{Cov}_q(U_i^t)\mathbb{E}_q(V_j^t)\mathbb{E}_q(V_j^t)^T + \mathbb{E}_q(U_i^t)\mathbb{E}_q(U_i^t)^T \mathrm{Cov}_q(V_j^t) + \mathrm{Cov}_q(U_i^t)\mathrm{Cov}_q(V_j^t)\Big]. \tag{23}$$

In practice, we find that the trace term in equation (23) is often dominated, and thus is omitted to reduce computational complexity.

Algorithm 1 Streaming Posterior Update Algorithm

Input: a set of $L_{ij}^t \in \mathcal{L}$ just arrived
Output: Updated posterior moments (under q) of the hidden variables

while Convergence not reached **do**
- $\forall i$ involved in the current events, update $\mathbb{E}_q(U_i^t)$ and $\text{Cov}_q(U_i^t)$ according to equation (20);
- $\forall j$ involved in the current events, update $\mathbb{E}_q(V_j^t)$ and $\text{Cov}_q(V_j^t)$ according to equation (20) with U and V, and subscripts i and j interchanged;
- $\forall i, j$ pair involved in the current events, update $\mathbb{E}_{q_1}(X_{ij}^t)$ according to equation (21);
- $\forall i, j$ pair involved in the current events, update $q(O_{ij}^t = 1)$ according to equation (22).

end

4.3.2 Predicting Future Connections

As discussed before, for any time t and $L_{ij}^t = 0$, the prediction is based on the approximated posterior expectation of X_{ij}^t. Formally, based on equation (14), we would like to find those

$$L_{ij}^t = 0, \text{but } \mathbb{E}_q\left(X_{ij}^t\right) > \theta,$$

according to

$$\begin{aligned} \mathbb{E}_q\left(X_{ij}^t\right) &\approx \mathbb{E}_q\left(X_{ij}^t | O_{ij}^t = 0\right) = \mathbb{E}_q\left(U_i^t\right)^T \mathbb{E}_q\left(V_j^t\right) \\ &= \mathbb{E}_q\left(U_i^{t-\tau_U(i,t)}\right)^T \mathbb{E}_q\left(V_j^{t-\tau_V(j,t)}\right). \end{aligned} \tag{24}$$

Here are some intuitions. The first equality is because when there is no observation $O_{ij}^t = 0$, the posterior expectation of X_{ij}^t is equal to its prior expectation. The last equality is because U_i^t and V_j^t follow Brownian motion, and their expectations remain the same when there are no observations.

4.4 The Algorithm Table and Complexity

The posterior moment updating scheme is summarized in algorithm 1. In terms of computational complexity, each $L_{ij}^t \in \mathcal{L}$ appears in equation (20) once for each iteration; its corresponding X_{ij}^t and O_{ij}^t appear once in equations (21) and (22) respectively. Hence the total complexity over all times is $O(|\mathcal{L}|I)$, where I is the number of iterations for each update. This is a very efficient algorithm.

5. EXPERIMENT

In this section, we demonstrate the practical usage of the purposed SPU framework by considering two important data mining applications: link predictions and recommendations. Our empirical studies on five real-world datasets provide strong evidence that SPU significantly improves over many state-of-the-art baselines.

5.1 Datasets

We utilize two link prediction and three recommendation datasets. It is worth mentioning that all five datasets are publicly available and the download links are provided. The detailed descriptions of each are listed below:

- **Link Predictions:**
  - ***DBLP***[2] [18]: This dataset is a undirected collaboration network of authors of scientific papers from DBLP computer science bibliography. An edge between two authors represents a common publication. Edges are annotated with the date of the publication. We randomly sample 49,945 nodes among top active authors.
  - ***Epinion***[3] [30]: Epinion is a popular product review site, where people can rate various products and add others members to their own trust networks or "circle of trust". Such trustworthy relationships among users are directional and represent who they may seek advice to make decisions. We collect a total of 11,752 registered users whose in-degree and out-degree are at least one.
- **Recommendations:**
  - ***Facebook-like Forum***[4] [24]: The Facebook-like forum dataset consists of the Internet "post" activities among 899 users and 522 topics from an online community. The goal is to recommend interesting topics to candidate users that they will comment on in the near future.
  - ***MovieTweeting***[5] [7]: This dataset contains the tweeting activities that consist of ratings on movies to IMDB from Twitter. Instead of predicting the specific movie ratings, we are focusing on tweeting activity itself by predicting what movie a user will rate.
  - ***Last.fm Music***[6] [3]: The dataset contains the full listening history for registered users at Last.fm[7]. We only use their user ID, track ID and time-stamp for the purpose of recommendations.

The statistics of the aforementioned datasets are summarized in Table 1.

5.2 Baseline Methods

We compare our proposed framework SPU with several representative baseline algorithms as follows:

- **JC / ItemKNN**: Jaccard's coefficient (JC) and item-based k-nearest neighbor (ItemKNN) are one of the most fundamental baselines for link prediction and recommendation respectively. We include either of them based on the task that we evaluate on.
- **PageRank**: PageRank is an iterative fixed-point algorithm over graphs, which can be applied to compute "importance" scores for each node. The prediction weight for each node pair is calculated as the product of their PageRank scores [32].
- **OCCF** [25]: One-class collaborative filtering assigns weights to unlabeled data to distinguish negative examples and unlabeled positive ones.
- **Time-SVD++ with weighted sampling** [17]: It is a variant of the Time-SVD++ algorithm, since the original one specifically takes inputs as explicitly scaled form. We utilize the same "user-oriented sampling scheme" that has been adopted by OCCF [25] to alleviate the problem under PU settings.
- **NTF** [16]: Nonnegative tensor factorization handles both temporal dynamics as well as the PU inputs. However, it differs from OCCF and Time-SVD++ with weighted sampling in that it considers all missing entries as negative.

[2] http://konect.uni-koblenz.de/networks/dblp_coauthor

[3] http://www.jiliang.xyz/trust.html

[4] http://toreopsahl.com/datasets/#online_forum_network

[5] https://github.com/sidooms/MovieTweetings

[6] http://www.dtic.upf.edu/~ocelma/MusicRecommendationDataset/lastfm-1K.html

[7] http://www.last.fm/

Table 1: Detailed statistics of the datasets. Type-1 and type-2 nodes represent users and items respectively under the recommendation setting.

	Link predictions		Recommendations		
Dataset	*DBLP*	*Epinion*	*Facebook-like*	*MovieTweeting*	*Last.fm*
Number of type-1 node	49,945	11,752	899	39,395	992
Number of type-2 node	uniform node type	uniform node type	522	22,637	107,397
Network property	undirected	directed	bipartite, heterogeneous node type		
Temporal range	12/1959-12/2013	01/2001-04/2011	05/2004-10/2004	02/2013-11/2015	02/2005-06/2009
Temporal resolution	month	second	second	second	second
Number of links	1,277,690	187,563	7,089	432,443	820,050
Sparsity	5.12×10^{-4}	1.36×10^{-3}	1.51×10^{-2}	4.85×10^{-4}	7.70×10^{-3}

- **PUMC** [13]: PU learning for matrix completion is a state-of-the-art one-bit factorization algorithm that targets to recover possible true negative samples by using different costs in the objective for observed and unobserved entries.

In summary, JC, ItemKNN and PageRank are three conventional methods that compute affinity scores among node pairs only based on the graph topologies. While all the other four baselines leverage the PU inputs in various ways. Among these four, Time-SVD++ and NTF also incorporate the temporal factor by confidence decay and temporal aggregation, respectively. We make use of the open-source C++ framework from GraphChi [19] for the implementation of OCCF and Time-SVD++. The graph based algorithms including JC and PageRank are publicly available from the package in [32]. Moreover, the implementations of NTF and PUMC are acquired from the original authors.

5.3 Experimental Settings

For the purpose of quantitative evaluations, we follow the standard online testing protocol. Given a set of time-ordered data, we divide them into two subsets along the temporal direction. We call the first one the "validation set", and the second one the "updating and testing set". An illustrative example is shown in figure 3, where t_O, t_V and t_E represent the starting time, the end time of validation set and the end time of the dataset, respectively. The size of validation set is chosen to be 30% of the entire dataset. In other words, t_V is the time when 30% of connections are presented.

The testing task is to predict the possible connections of the network in the next time base on the "historical" data. Specifically, we first align the reference time t_r, also considered as the "current" time, to t_V. The prediction is evaluated at time $t_r + \Delta t$, where Δt equals the smallest temporal granularity of the dataset. The only information that can be used for model update (refining/learning latent representations) is the list of connections appearing in the time interval $[t_V, t_r]$. After performance evaluation at this specific time, we then shift t_r by Δt. In other worlds, the "current" time is now $t_V + \Delta t$. Therefore, all the data generated from temporal horizon $[t_V, t_V + \Delta t]$ can be used for prediction at $t_V + 2\Delta t$. The same procedure is performed until t_r reaches end time of the dataset t_E.

It is worth mentioning that, our proposed algorithm is a fully online model, which means there is no need to retrain all latent representations from the sketch when the reference time t_r shifts by Δt. For the batch baselines, we retrain the entire model every time when t_r moves, which is much less efficient. Moreover, many baselines are insufficient to consider the case of "multiple connections" or handle the temporal resolution in a very fine grid. Although our SPU

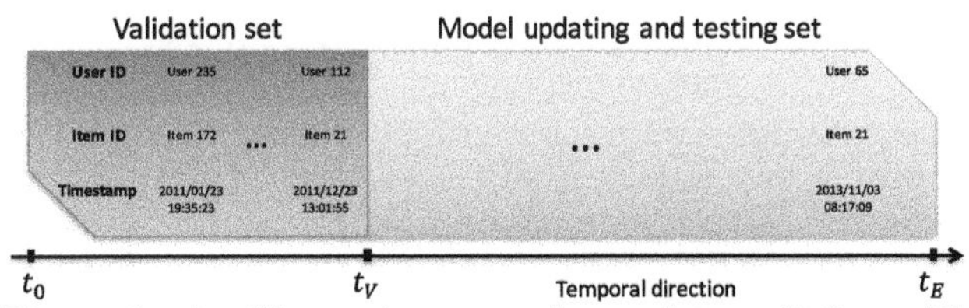

Figure 3: An Illustrative example on data splitting. The blue region indicates the validation set while data from the green region are used for testing and model updating. At each time, the data are in a triplet format as (user ID, item ID, time-stamp).

algorithm explicitly consider both aforementioned issues, for fair comparison all multiple edges are merged to the one that first appears; and temporal granularity (Δt) is set to be a year for the DBLP and as a week for the other four datasets.

The validation set is used to seek the best hyper parameters for each algorithm. For instance, the latent dimensionality is a model sensitive parameter that needs to be chosen independently. Therefore, all models follow the same protocol to obtain the best set of parameters on the validation set. Once these hyper parameters are chosen, they remain the same in the testing phase.

Two commonly used metrics are suitable for both link prediction and recommendation. They are the area under the ROC curve (AUC) as well as the equal error rate accuracy (ACC). These two metrics are considered as classification metrics which are extremely appropriate for tasks such as "finding good objects", especially when only PU inputs are available [21, 23]. Since the evaluation task is highly imbalanced, we randomly sample the same number of negative samples (zeros) as that of positive ones at each testing time. To ensure reliability, all experimental results are averaged over 10 runs using different negative samplings.

5.4 Experimental Results

In this subsection, we present the empirical results of our proposed SPU framework compared to the aforementioned state-of-the-arts in both link prediction and recommendation in table 2. We observe that the proposed algorithm consistently achieves the best performance on all five datasets. It is evident that explicitly modeling the streaming network under PU settings significantly improves the performance for both tasks. The demonstrative features of the proposed SPU algorithm will be detailed in the following subsections.

Time-SVD++ is considered as the second best algorithm, which outperforms other baselines in three datasets. We extended the original Time-SVD++ to utilize the unlabeled data through a weighted sampling approach proposed by OCCF. The reason why Time-SVD++ outperforms not only

Table 2: Performance comparison. The best performance is highlighted in bold.

	Link predictions				Recommendations					
Dataset	*DBLP*		*Epinion*		*Facebook-like*		*Twitter*		*Last.fm*	
Metric	AUC	ACC	AUC	ACC	AUC	ACC	AUC	ACC	AUC	ACC
JC / ItemKNN	0.6071	0.6162	0.8066	0.8062	0.6590	0.6240	0.6381	0.6756	0.5448	0.5671
PageRank	0.6328	0.5935	0.7806	0.7118	0.7116	0.6579	0.7960	0.7282	0.7707	0.7028
OCCF	0.7093	0.6584	0.9086	0.8736	0.6959	0.6470	0.8774	0.8360	0.8616	0.8038
Time-SVD++	0.7133	0.6635	0.9398	0.8826	0.7031	0.6454	0.9167	0.8515	0.8718	0.7985
NTF	0.6920	0.6475	0.9087	0.8476	0.6378	0.6065	0.9040	0.8381	0.8597	0.7927
PUMC	0.7259	0.6660	0.9234	0.8705	0.6835	0.6404	0.9174	0.8709	0.8686	**0.8094**
SPU	**0.7412**	**0.6756**	**0.9534**	**0.8995**	**0.7339**	**0.6812**	**0.9495**	**0.8878**	**0.8831**	0.8066

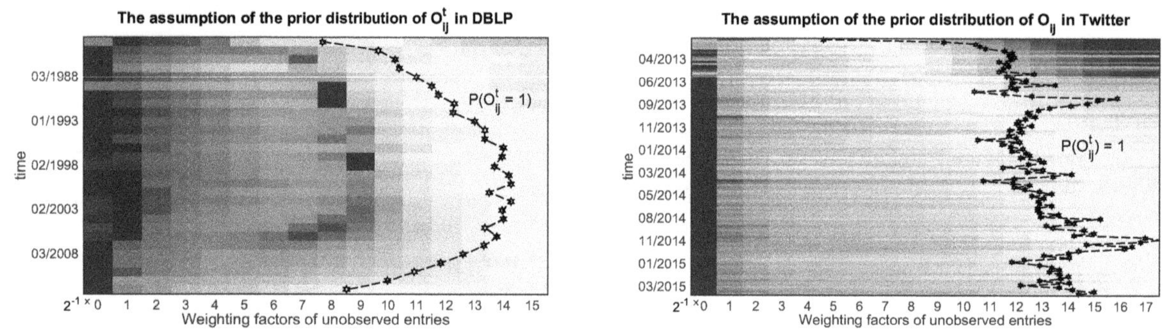

(a) DBLP

(b) Twitter

Figure 4: Verification of the proposed form of $q\left(O^t_{ij} = 1\right)$. The color in each cell denotes the accuracy if the prior is set to the candidate value. The proposed prior, denoted by dotted lines, roughly follows the high accuracy region.

OCCF but also other baselines is that it models the temporal information in a more suitable way. On the other hand, there is no explicit temporal consideration in OCCF. Similar to Time-SVD++, NTF also considers the temporal dynamics, but in a different way. However, its performance is even worse than OCCF for some datasets. It could be because treating all unlabeled data as negative samples hurts the performance of NTF. Another potential reason is that the algorithm considers temporal information in a retrospective way, which is inadequate to model the prospective aspect of the data streams. Moreover, PUMC obtains comparable results to Time-SVD++ across all five datasets without using any temporal information. PUMC models the PU setup in a principled way, which is able to identify the potential negative samples more accurately. At last, JC/ItemKNN and PageRank reveal the worst performance. They all belong to the standard similarity based algorithms without considering either temporal or PU characteristics of the inputs.

From the above observations, we can conclude that both temporal information and the unlabeled negativity play very important roles in the task of link prediction and recommendations. Inadequate modeling of either of these two characteristics will lead to a degradation in performance.

5.5 Prior Distribution Validation

In this subsection, we will examine the appropriateness of the prior of O^t_{ij} as given by equations (2) and (3). Recall that this prior is defined by our intuition that the probability of observing a connection is affected by the network liveliness and the cost of connections, which are correlated with the ratio of the number of recently established links over that of recently introduced nodes. We will apply a data-driven approach to validate this assumption.

The basic idea is that a good prior should maximize the accuracy of link prediction, and therefore we performed a greedy search to find a suboptimal path of priors across every time t that maximizes the overall prediction accuracy. Our proposed prior, as a function of event time t, will be validated if it agrees with this suboptimal path.

Specifically, the candidate values of the prior are quantized into discrete levels uniformly in the logarithmic scale from 2^0 to 2^{-17}. At each event time t, the accuracy of prediction is computed for every candidate value of the current prior, given that the priors at previous times are set to the optimal candidates in their respective greedy searches.

Figure 4 shows the results of this greedy search test. Each pixel of the images denotes the prediction accuracy as a function of prior candidates (horizontal axis) and event times (vertical axis). As can be seen, the yellow belt in each subplot corresponds to the prior values that yield high prediction accuracy, wherein the suboptimal path lies. The black dotted line denotes the proposed prior, which roughly follows the yellow belt of the suboptimal path. This validates our proposed prior.

5.6 True Negatives vs. Unlabeled

This subsection illustrates the mechanism through which O^t_{ij} deals with the positive-unlabeled data. Essentially, the key is to distinguish the true negatives from unlabeled data among all L^t_{ij}s that are 0, and place greater emphasis on the former during inference. According to the inference equation (20), each summation term, which corresponds to each observation at time t, is multiplied by $q(O^t_{ij} = 1)$ as weights. We will inspect if these weights are able to discriminate between true negatives and unlabeled data.

Figure 5 shows the weights $q(O^t_{ij} = 1)$ on 3-by-3 subsets of two datasets. At event time t, all the L^t_{ij}s in these subsets are 0, but a portion of them turn to 1 immediately

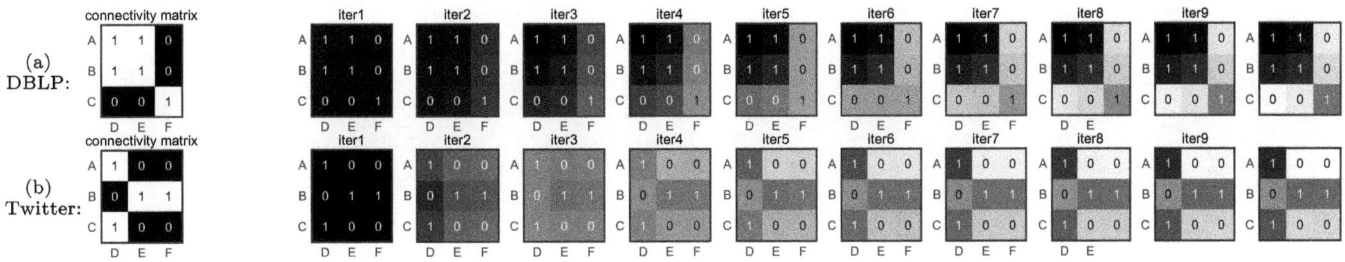

Figure 5: Evolution of weight matrix $q\left(O_{ij}^{t}=1\right)$. Vertical axis denotes user, and horizontal axis denotes item. The corresponding connection statuses L_{ij}^{t} are all 0 at time t when the inference is performed, but a subset of them, numbered 1, soon turn to 1, and hence are originally likely to be unlabeled data. The weights, denoted by the gray scale, managed to deemphasize these unlabeled data upon convergence.

afterwards, as shown by the cells marked 1 in the leftmost plots. Therefore the observed 0 in these cells are actually unlabeled data, whereas the rest of the data (marked 0) are more likely to be true negatives.

The right panel plots the evolution of the weight matrix as iteration proceeds. The gray scale in each cell denotes the weight, and the numbers are replicates of the left panel for clarity. At first, all the weights are uniform, where our proposed algorithm essentially reduces to many traditional link prediction algorithms that treat the all observed 0s indiscriminately as true negatives. However, upon convergence, the weights display a discriminative pattern: the weights of the unlabeled data (marked 1 as discussed) get smaller; the weights of those more probable true negatives (marked 0) become larger. In other words, during the inference iteration, the posterior distributions of the hidden topic vectors are reinforced by the data believed to be true negatives, and the interference from the unlabeled data is alleviated.

5.7 Temporal Drifting

Figure 6 shows the evolution of averaged hidden topic vectors, *i.e.* $\mathbb{E}_q\left(U_i^t\right)$ averaged across i, and $\mathbb{E}_q\left(V_j^t\right)$ averaged across j, through time. In each subplot, the left figure is for the type-1 node topic and the right for type-2. There are three observations. First, the proposed algorithm is able to capture the dynamic changes of topics, hence can produce different predictions at different times. Second, figure 6a plots the result for DBLP, which is a user-user network with the two types of nodes being identical. The inference algorithm naturally yields identical topic vectors. In figure 6b, where the two types of nodes are heterogeneous, the corresponding topic vectors are completely distinct. Third, in 6b, we can observe a more drastic evolution in user topics (left) than in item topics (right) - there are more fluctuations in the former whereas changes in the latter are all monotonic. This agrees with our intuition that users' tastes are more volatile and influenced by trend.

6. RELATED WORK

6.1 PU Learning

The problem of PU learning is first studied in binary classification, where training examples only consist of positive labels. Two general approaches have been previously proposed to handle such "one-side" measurements. The first approach involves iterating between two steps, which are 1) identifying possible negative samples (some approaches also include positive ones [9]) from unlabelled data, and 2) applying standard binary classification methods on negative samples identified the previous step [31, 33, 34]. The other approach assigns weights to each unlabeled datum, and then trains a classifier with the unlabeled data interpreted as weighted negative samples [8, 20, 35]. Although many algorithms have been well developed for classification with PU inputs, they assume data are in the form of vectorized representations, which is not applicable to problems where only network topology information is available.

Matrix completion [4, 15, 16] is one of the most popular approaches to link prediction or recommendation since it does not require any auxiliary content features. However, most of the existing approaches are not specifically designed for the PU inputs. An important variant of the matrix completion problem is to recover an underlying matrix from one-bit quantizations, which is an instance of PU learning. Davenport *et. al.* [6] first analyzes one-bit matrix completion under a uniform sampling model, where observed entries are assumed to be sampled uniformly at random. However, in data mining applications such as collaborative filtering, the uniform sampling model is over idealized. An improved method have been proposed in [2], which replaces the uniform sampling assumption with the max-norm as a convex relaxation for the rank. Recently, Hsieh *et. al.* [13] proposed a method termed PUMC, which contains well developed theories on performing one-bit matrix completion by on assigning different costs to observed and unobserved entries in the objective. Similar ideas [5, 14, 26, 28] have also been used in recommender systems, albeit heuristically. It is worth mentioning that all these methods are batch models without considering any temporal aspect of the data.

6.2 Learning from Data Streams

In the era of big data, the inputs for many online systems arrive in a streaming fashion. These data flow into a system in vast volumes, change dynamically and are possibly infinite [12, 36]. When the data are of large volume, they cannot be stored in traditional database systems. Moreover, most systems may only be able to access the stream once. This poses great computational and mining challenges. There have been many works on efficient methods for mining data streams, which specifically work with one pass of the data. On the other hand, the stream mining process is dynamic since user behaviors as well as item characteristics may evolve over time. Many stream mining algorithms focus on the evolution of the underlying data [1]. Most of applications in data mining such as clustering, classification, recommendation, frequent pattern mining, *etc.* have been studied under the streaming settings. Readers could refer to these books [1, 12] and surveys [10, 11, 22, 27] for details.

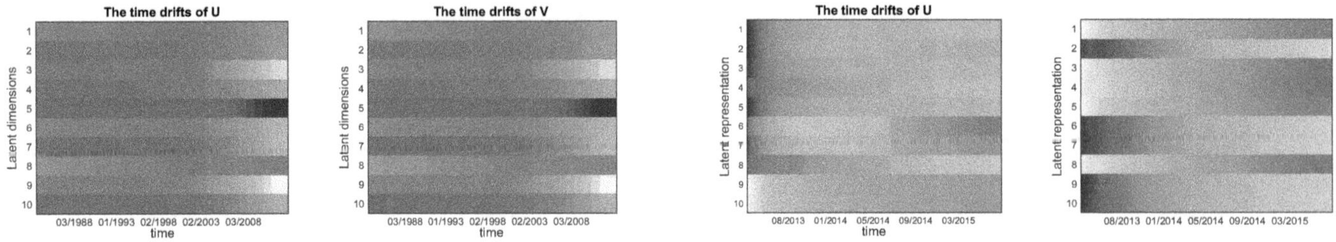

(a) DBLP (type-1 = type-2 = user)

(b) Twitter (type-1: user, type-2: item)

Figure 6: The evolution of the averaged latent topics over time. In each panel, left is type-1 node and right is type-2 node.

7. CONCLUSION

Data in many real-world problems in the era of big data such as link prediction and one-class recommendations present similar features – positive-unlabeled (PU) and streaming networks. The common features enable us to unify a number of such problems into the novel problem – PU learning in streaming networks. We delineate three challenges in the problem, *i.e.*, streaming nature, unlabeled negativity and concept shift, and then propose a PU learning framework SPU that provides a principled and efficient solution to address these challenges simultaneously. We conducted experiments on various real-world datasets and experimental results suggest that SPU can significantly advance the tasks of link prediction and recommendations.

8. ACKNOWLEDGMENT

This research was supported in part to Shiyu Chang and Thomas Huang by a research grant from Jump Labs. Yang Zhang and Mark Hasegawa-Johnson was in part supported by the AHRQ grant number 1-483711-392030-191100.

9. REFERENCES

[1] C. C. Aggarwal. *Data streams: models and algorithms*, volume 31. Springer, 2007.
[2] T. Cai and W.-X. Zhou. A max-norm constrained minimization approach to 1-bit matrix completion. *JMLR*, 2013.
[3] O. Celma. *Music Recommendation and Discovery in the Long Tail.* Springer, 2010.
[4] L. Charlin, R. Ranganath, J. McInerney, and D. M. Blei. Dynamic poisson factorization. In *Recsys*, 2015.
[5] P. Cui, H. Liu, C. Aggarwal, and F. Wang. Computational modeling of complex user behaviors: Challenges and opportunities. *Intelligent Systems*, 2016.
[6] M. A. Davenport, Y. Plan, E. van den Berg, and M. Wootters. 1-bit matrix completion. *Information and Inference*, 2014.
[7] S. Dooms, T. De Pessemier, and L. Martens. Movietweetings: a movie rating dataset collected from twitter. In *CrowdRec at RecSys*, 2013.
[8] C. Elkan and K. Noto. Learning classifiers from only positive and unlabeled data. In *KDD*, 2008.
[9] G. P. C. Fung, J. X. Yu, H. Lu, and P. S. Yu. Text classification without negative examples revisit. *TKDE*, 2006.
[10] L. Golab and M. T. Özsu. Issues in data stream management. *ACM Sigmod Record*, 2003.
[11] M. Gupta, J. Gao, C. Aggarwal, and J. Han. Outlier detection for temporal data. *DMKD*, 2014.
[12] J. Han, M. Kamber, and J. Pei. *Data mining: concepts and techniques.* Elsevier, 2011.
[13] C. Hsieh, N. Natarajan, and I. S. Dhillon. PU learning for matrix completion. In *ICML*, pages 2445–2453, 2015.
[14] Y. Hu, Y. Koren, and C. Volinsky. Collaborative filtering for implicit feedback datasets. In *ICDM*, 2008.
[15] M. Jiang, P. Cui, F. Wang, W. Zhu, and S. Yang. Scalable recommendation with social contextual information. *TKDE*, 2014.
[16] J. Kim and H. Park. Fast nonnegative tensor factorization with an active-set-like method. In *High-Performance Scientific Computing.* Springer, 2012.
[17] Y. Koren. Collaborative filtering with temporal dynamics. *Communications of the ACM*, 2010.
[18] J. Kunegis. KONECT – The Koblenz Network Collection. In *WWW Companion*, pages 1343–1350, 2013.
[19] A. Kyrola, G. E. Blelloch, and C. Guestrin. Graphchi: Large-scale graph computation on just a pc. In *OSDI*, 2012.
[20] B. Liu, W. S. Lee, P. S. Yu, and X. Li. Partially supervised classification of text documents. In *ICML*, 2002.
[21] L. Lü, M. Medo, C. H. Yeung, Y.-C. Zhang, Z.-K. Zhang, and T. Zhou. Recommender systems. *Physics Reports*, 2012.
[22] A. McGregor. Graph stream algorithms: a survey. *SIGMOD Record*, 2014.
[23] A. K. Menon and C. Elkan. Link prediction via matrix factorization. In *ECML PKDD.* 2011.
[24] T. Opsahl. Triadic closure in two-mode networks: Redefining the global and local clustering coefficients. *Social Networks*, 2013.
[25] R. Pan, Y. Zhou, B. Cao, N. N. Liu, R. Lukose, M. Scholz, and Q. Yang. One-class collaborative filtering. In *ICDM*, 2008.
[26] S. Rendle, C. Freudenthaler, Z. Gantner, and L. Schmidt-Thieme. Bpr: Bayesian personalized ranking from implicit feedback. In *UAI*, 2009.
[27] J. A. Silva, E. R. Faria, R. C. Barros, E. R. Hruschka, A. C. de Carvalho, and J. Gama. Data stream clustering: A survey. *ACM Computing Surveys*, 2013.
[28] V. Sindhwani, S. S. Bucak, J. Hu, and A. Mojsilovic. One-class matrix completion with low-density factorizations. In *ICDM*, 2010.
[29] J. Tang, S. Chang, C. Aggarwal, and H. Liu. Negative link prediction in social media. In *WSDM*, 2015.
[30] J. Tang, H. Gao, and H. Liu. mTrust: Discerning multi-faceted trust in a connected world. In *WSDM*, 2012.
[31] C. Wang, C. Ding, R. F. Meraz, and S. R. Holbrook. Psol: a positive sample only learning algorithm for finding non-coding rna genes. *Bioinformatics*, 2006.
[32] X. Wang and G. Sukthankar. Link prediction in multi-relational collaboration networks. In *ASONAM*, pages 1445–1447, 2013.
[33] F. Wu and D. S. Weld. Autonomously semantifying wikipedia. In *CIKM*, 2007.
[34] H. Yu, J. Han, and K. C.-C. Chang. Pebl: Web page classification without negative examples. *TKDE*, 2004.
[35] D. Zhang and W. S. Lee. A simple probabilistic approach to learning from positive and unlabeled examples. In *UKCI*, 2005.
[36] P. Zhao, C. Aggarwal, and G. He. Link prediction in graph streams. In *ICDE*, 2016.

FASCINATE: Fast Cross-Layer Dependency Inference on Multi-layered Networks

Chen Chen†, Hanghang Tong†, Lei Xie‡, Lei Ying†, and Qing He§
†Arizona State University, {chen_chen, hanghang.tong, lei.ying.2}@asu.edu
‡City University of New York, lei.xie@hunter.cuny.edu
§University at Buffalo, qinghe@buffalo.edu

ABSTRACT

Multi-layered networks have recently emerged as a new network model, which naturally finds itself in many high-impact application domains, ranging from critical inter-dependent infrastructure networks, biological systems, organization-level collaborations, to cross-platform e-commerce, etc. Cross-layer dependency, which describes the dependencies or the associations between nodes across different layers/networks, often plays a central role in many data mining tasks on such multi-layered networks. Yet, it remains a daunting task to accurately know the cross-layer dependency a prior. In this paper, we address the problem of inferring the missing cross-layer dependencies on multi-layered networks. The key idea behind our method is to view it as a collective collaborative filtering problem. By formulating the problem into a regularized optimization model, we propose an effective algorithm to find the local optima with linear complexity. Furthermore, we derive an online algorithm to accommodate newly arrived nodes, whose complexity is just linear wrt the size of the neighborhood of the new node. We perform extensive empirical evaluations to demonstrate the effectiveness and the efficiency of the proposed methods.

1. INTRODUCTION

In an increasingly connected world, networks from many high-impact areas are often collected from multiple *inter-dependent* domains, leading to the emergence of *multi-layered networks* [4, 9, 26, 29, 30]. A typical example of multi-layered networks is inter-dependent critical infrastructure network. As illustrated in Figure 1, the full functioning of the telecom network, the transportation network and the gas pipeline network is dependent on the power supply from the power grid. While for the gas-fired and coal-fired generators in the power grid, their functioning is fully dependent on the gas and coal supply from the transportation network and the gas pipeline network. Moreover, to keep the whole complex system working in order, extensive communications are needed across the networks, which are in turn supported by the telecom network. Another example is *biological system*, where the protein-protein interaction network (PPI/gene network) is naturally linked to the disease similarity network by the known disease-gene associations,

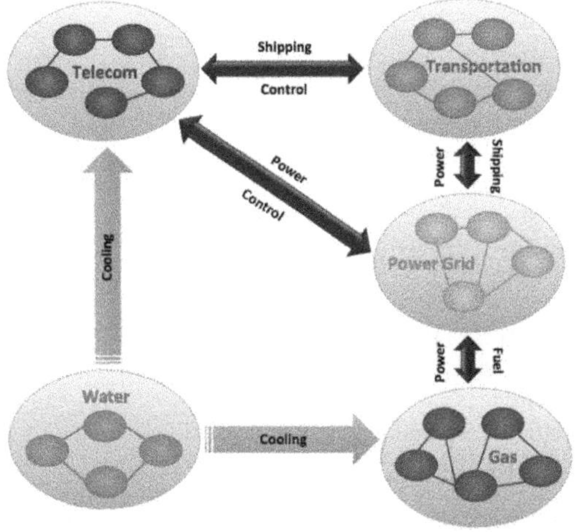

Figure 1: An illustrative example of multi-layered networks. Each gray ellipse is a critical infrastructure network (e.g., Telecom network, power grid, transportation network, etc). A thick arrow between two ellipses indicates a cross-layer dependency between the corresponding two networks (e.g., a router in the telecom network depends on one or more power plants in the power grid).

and the disease network is in turn coupled with the drug network by drug-disease associations. Multi-layered networks also appear in many other application domains, such as organization-level collaboration platform [5] and cross-platform e-commerce [6, 16, 21, 36].

Compared with single-layered networks, a unique topological characteristic of multi-layered networks lies in its *cross-layer dependency* structure. For example, in the critical infrastructure network, the full functioning of the telecom layer *depends* on the sufficient power supply from the power grid layer, which in turn relies on the functioning of the transportation layer (e.g., to deliver the sufficient fuel). While in the biological systems, the dependency is represented as the associations among diseases, genes and drugs. In practice, the cross-layer dependency often plays a central role in many multi-layered network mining tasks. For example, in the critical infrastructure network, the existence of the cross-layer dependency is in general considered as a major factor of the vulnerability of the entire system. This is because a small disturbance on one supporting layer/network (e.g., power grid) might cause a ripple effect to all the dependent layers, leading to a catastrophic/cascading failure of the entire system. On the other hand, the cross-layer dependency in the biological system is often the key to new discoveries, such as new treatment associations between existing drugs and new diseases (e.g., drug re-purposing).

Despite its key importance, it remains a daunting task to accurately know the cross-layer dependency in a multi-layered net-

KDD '16, August 13-17, 2016, San Francisco, CA, USA
© 2016 ACM. ISBN 978-1-4503-4232-2/16/08... $15.00
DOI: http://dx.doi.org/10.1145/2939672.2939784

work, due to a number of reasons, ranging from noise, incomplete data sources, limited accessibility to network dynamics. For example, an extreme weather event might significantly disrupt the power grid, the transportation network and the cross-layer dependencies in between at the epicenter. Yet, due to limited accessibility to the damage area during or soon after the disruption, the cross-layer dependency structure might only have a probabilistic and/or coarse-grained description. On the other hand, for a newly identified chemical in the biological system, its cross-layer dependencies wrt proteins and/or the diseases might be completely unknown due to clinical limitations.(i.e., the *zero-start* problem).

In this paper, we aim to tackle the above challenges and develop effective and efficient methods to infer cross-layer dependency on multi-layered networks. The main contributions of the paper can be summarized as

- *Problem Formulations.* We formally formulate the cross-layer dependency inference problem as a regularized optimization problem. The key idea of our formulation is to collectively leverage the within-layer topology as well as the observed cross-layer dependency to infer a latent, low-rank representation for each layer, based on which the missing cross-layer dependencies can be inferred.
- *Algorithms and Analysis.* We propose an effective algorithm (FASCINATE) for cross-layer dependency inference on multi-layered networks, and analyze its optimality, convergence and complexity. We further present its variants and generalizations, including an online algorithm to address the *zero-start* problem.
- *Evaluations.* We perform extensive experiments on real datasets to validate the effectiveness, efficiency and scalability of the proposed algorithms. Specially, our experimental evaluations show that the proposed algorithms outperform their best competitors by 8.2%-41.9% in terms of inference accuracy while enjoying linear complexity. Specifically, the proposed FASCINATE-ZERO algorithm can achieve up to $10^7\times$ speedup with barely no compromise on accuracy.

The rest of the paper is organized as follows. Section 2 gives the formal definitions of the cross-layer dependency inference problems. Section 3 proposes FASCINATE algorithm with its analysis. Section 4 introduces the *zero-start* algorithm FASCINATE-ZERO. Section 5 presents the experiment results. Section 6 reviews the related works. Section 7 summarizes the paper.

2. PROBLEM DEFINITION

In this section, we give the formal definitions of the cross-layer dependency inference problems. The main symbols used throughout the paper are listed in Table 1. Following the convention, we use bold upper-case for matrices (e.g., $\mathbf{A}$), bold lower-case for vectors (e.g., $\mathbf{a}$) and calligraphic for sets (e.g., $\mathcal{A}$). $\mathbf{A}'$ denotes the transpose of matrix $\mathbf{A}$. We use the ˆ sign to denote the notations after a new node is accommodated to the system (e.g., $\hat{\mathcal{J}}$, $\hat{\mathbf{A}}_1$), and the ones without the ˆ sign as the notations before the new node arrives.

While several multi-layered network models exist in the literature (See Section 6 for a review), we will focus on a recent model proposed in [5], due to its flexibility to model more complicated cross-layer dependency structure. We refer the readers to [5] for its full details. For the purpose of this paper, we mainly need the following notations to describe a multi-layered network with g layers. First, we need a $g \times g$ layer-layer dependency matrix $\mathbf{G}$, where $\mathbf{G}(i,j) = 1$ if layer-j depends on layer-i, and $\mathbf{G}(i,j) = 0$ otherwise. Second, we need a set of g within-layer connectivity matrices: $\mathcal{A} = \{\mathbf{A}_1, ..., \mathbf{A}_g\}$ to describe the connectivities/similarities between nodes within the same layer. Third, we need a set of cross-layer dependency matrices $\mathcal{D} = \{\mathbf{D}_{i,j}\ i,j = 1,...,g\}$, where $\mathbf{D}_{i,j}$ describes the dependencies between the nodes from layer-i and the nodes from layer-j if these two layers are directly dependent (i.e., $\mathbf{G}(i,j) = 1$). When there is no direct dependencies between the two layers (i.e., $\mathbf{G}(i,j) = 0$), the corresponding dependency matrix $\mathbf{D}_{i,j}$ is absent. Taking the multi-layered network in Figure 2 for an example, the abstract layer-layer dependency network $\mathbf{G}$ of this biological system can be viewed as a line graph. The four within-layer similarity matrices in $\mathcal{A}$ are the *chemical network* ($\mathbf{A}_1$), the *drug network* ($\mathbf{A}_2$), the *disease network* ($\mathbf{A}_3$) and the *protein-protein interaction (PPI) network* ($\mathbf{A}_4$). Across those layers, we have three non-empty dependency matrices, including the *chemical-drug* dependency matrix ($\mathbf{D}_{1,2}$), the *drug-disease* interaction matrix ($\mathbf{D}_{2,3}$) and the *disease-protein* dependency matrix ($\mathbf{D}_{3,4}$).

As mentioned earlier, it is often very hard to accurately know the cross-layer dependency matrices $\{\mathbf{D}_{i,j}\ i,j = 1,...,g\}$. In other words, such *observed* dependency matrices are often incomplete and noisy. Inferring the missing cross-layer dependencies is an essential prerequisite for many multi-layered network mining tasks. On the other hand, real-world networks are evolving over time. Probing the cross-layer dependencies is often a time-consuming process in large complex networks. Thus, a newly added node could have no observed cross-layer dependencies for a fairly long period of time since its arrival. Therefore, inferring the dependencies of such kind of *zero-start* nodes is an important problem that needs to be solved efficiently. Formally, we define the cross-layer dependency inference problem (CODE) and its corresponding *zero-start* variant (CODE-ZERO) as follows.

Table 1: Main Symbols.

Symbol	Definition and Description
$\mathbf{A}, \mathbf{B}$	the adjacency matrices (bold upper case)
$\mathbf{a}, \mathbf{b}$	column vectors (bold lower case)
$\mathcal{A}, \mathcal{B}$	sets (calligraphic)
$\mathbf{A}(i,j)$	the element at i^{th} row j^{th} column in matrix $\mathbf{A}$
$\mathbf{A}(i,:)$	the ith row of matrix $\mathbf{A}$
$\mathbf{A}(:,j)$	the jth column of matrix $\mathbf{A}$
$\mathbf{A}'$	transpose of matrix $\mathbf{A}$
$\hat{\mathbf{A}}$	the adjacency matrix of $\mathbf{A}$ with the newly added node
$\mathbf{G}$	the layer-layer dependency matrix
$\mathcal{A}$	within-layer connectivity matrices of the network $\mathcal{A} = \{\mathbf{A}_1, \ldots, \mathbf{A}_g\}$
$\mathcal{D}$	cross-layer dependency matrices $\mathcal{D} = \{\mathbf{D}_{i,j}\ i,j = 1,...,g\}$
$\mathbf{W}_{i,j}$	weight matrix for $\mathbf{D}_{i,j}$
$\mathbf{F}_i$	low-rank representation for layer-i ($i = 1,...,g$)
m_i, n_i	number of edges and nodes in graph $\mathbf{A}_i$
$m_{i,j}$	number of dependencies in $\mathbf{D}_{i,j}$
g	total number of layers
r	the rank for $\{\mathbf{F}_i\}_{i=1,\ldots,g}$
t	the maximal iteration number
ξ	the threshold to determine the iteration

PROBLEM 1. **(CODE) Cross-Layer Dependency Inference**

Given: *a multi-layered network with (1) layer-layer dependency matrix* $\mathbf{G}$*; (2) within-layer connectivity matrices* $\mathcal{A} = \{\mathbf{A}_1, ..., \mathbf{A}_g\}$*; and (3) observed cross-layer dependency matrices* $\mathcal{D} = \{\mathbf{D}_{i,j}\ i,j = 1,...,g\}$*;*

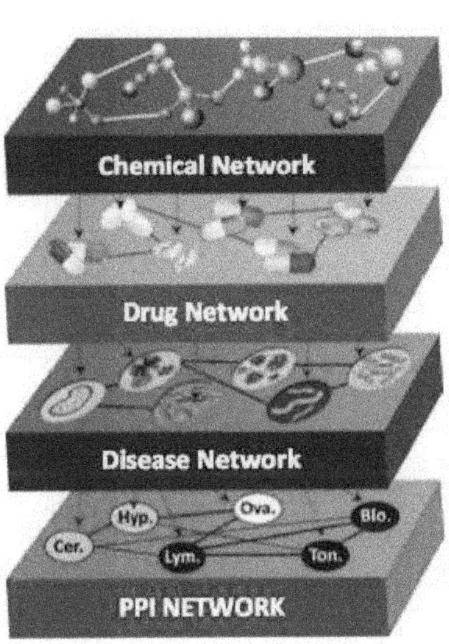

Figure 2: A simplified 4-layered network for biological systems.

Output: *the true cross-layer dependency matrices* $\{\tilde{\mathbf{D}}_{i,j}\ i,j = 1,...,g\}$.

PROBLEM 2. **(CODE-ZERO) Cross-Layer Dependency Inference for *zero-start* Nodes**

Given: *(1) a multi-layered network* $\{\mathbf{G}, \mathcal{A}, \mathcal{D}\}$*; (2) a newly added node p in the* l^{th} *layer; (3) a* $1 \times n_l$ *vector* $\mathbf{s}$ *that records the connections between p and the existing* n_l *nodes in layer l;*

Output: *the true dependencies between node p and nodes in dependent layers of layer-l, i.e.,* $\tilde{\mathbf{D}}_{l,j}(p,:)$ $(j = 1,...,g,\ \mathbf{G}(l,j) = 1)$.

3. FASCINATE FOR PROBLEM 1

In this section, we present our proposed solution for Problem 1 (CODE). We start with the proposed optimization formulation, and then present our algorithm (FASCINATE), followed by some effectiveness and efficiency analysis.

3.1 FASCINATE: Optimization Formulation

The key idea behind our formulation is to treat Problem 1 as a *collective collaborative filtering* problem. To be specific, if we view (1) nodes from a given layer (e.g., power plants) as objects from a given domain (e.g., users/items), (2) the within-layer connectivity (e.g., communication networks) as an object-object similarity measure, and (3) the cross-layer dependency (e.g., dependencies between computers in the communication layer and power plants in power grid layer) as the 'ratings' from objects of one domain to those of another domain; then inferring the missing cross-layer dependencies can be viewed as a task of inferring the missing ratings between the objects (e.g., users, items) across different domains. Having this analogy in mind, we propose to formulate Problem 1 as the following regularized optimization problem

$$\min_{\mathbf{F}_i \geq \mathbf{0}(i=1,...,g)} J = \underbrace{\sum_{i,j:\ \mathbf{G}(i,j)=1} \|\mathbf{W}_{i,j} \odot (\mathbf{D}_{i,j} - \mathbf{F}_i\mathbf{F}_j{}')\|_F^2}_{\text{C1: Matching Observed Cross-Layer Dependencies}} \quad (1)$$
$$+ \underbrace{\alpha \sum_{i=1}^{g} \text{tr}(\mathbf{F}_i{}'(\mathbf{T}_i - \mathbf{A}_i)\mathbf{F}_i)}_{\text{C2: Node Homophily}} + \underbrace{\beta \sum_{i=1}^{g} \|\mathbf{F}_i\|_F^2}_{\text{C3: Regularization}}$$

where $\mathbf{T}_i$ is the diagonal degree matrix of $\mathbf{A}_i$ with $\mathbf{T}_i(u,u) = \sum_{v=1}^{n_i} \mathbf{A}_i(u,v)$; $\mathbf{W}_{i,j}$ is an $n_i \times n_j$ weight matrix to assign different weights to different entries in the corresponding cross-layer dependency matrix $\mathbf{D}_{i,j}$; and $\mathbf{F}_i$ is the low-rank representation for layer i. For now, we set the weight matrices as follows: $\mathbf{W}_{i,j}(u,v) = 1$ if $\mathbf{D}_{i,j}(u,v)$ is observed, and $\mathbf{W}_{i,j}(u,v) \in [0,1]$ if $\mathbf{D}_{i,j}(u,v) = 0$ (i.e., unobserved). To simplify the computation, we set the weights of all unobserved entries to a global value w. We will discuss alternative choices for the weight matrices in Section 3.3.

In this formulation (Eq. (1)), we can think of $\mathbf{F}_i$ as the low-rank representations/features of the nodes in layer i in some latent space, which is shared among different layers. The cross-layer dependencies between the nodes from two dependent layers can be viewed as the inner product of their latent features. Therefore, the intuition of the first term (i.e. C1) is that we want to match all the cross-layer dependencies, calibrated by the weight matrix $\mathbf{W}_{i,j}$. The second term (i.e., C2) is used to achieve node homophily, which says that for a pair of nodes u and v from the same layer (say layer-*i*), their low-rank representations should be similar (i.e., small $\|\mathbf{F}_i(u,:) - \mathbf{F}_i(v,:)\|_2$) if the within-layer connectivity between these two nodes is strong (i.e., large $\mathbf{A}_i(u,v)$). The third term (i.e. C3) is to regularize the norm of the low-rank matrices $\{\mathbf{F}_i\}_{i=1,...,g}$ to prevent over-fitting.

Once we solve Eq. (1), for a given node u from layer-*i* and a node v from layer-*j*, the cross-layer dependency between them can be estimated as $\tilde{\mathbf{D}}_{i,j}(u,v) = \mathbf{F}_i(u,:)\mathbf{F}_j(v,:)'$.

3.2 FASCINATE: Optimization Algorithm

The optimization problem defined in Eq. (1) is non-convex. Thus, we seek to find a local optima by the block coordinate descent method, where each $\mathbf{F}_i$ naturally forms a 'block'. To be specific, if we fix all other $\mathbf{F}_j (j = 1, \ldots, g, j \neq i)$ and ignore the constant terms, Eq. (1) can be simplified as

$$\underset{\mathbf{F}_i \geq \mathbf{0}}{J_i} = \sum_{j:\ \mathbf{G}(i,j)=1} \|\mathbf{W}_{i,j} \odot (\mathbf{D}_{i,j} - \mathbf{F}_i\mathbf{F}_j{}')\|_F^2 + \alpha\text{tr}(\mathbf{F}_i{}'(\mathbf{T}_i - \mathbf{A}_i)\mathbf{F}_i) + \beta\|\mathbf{F}_i\|_F^2 \quad (2)$$

The derivative of J_i wrt $\mathbf{F}_i$ is

$$\frac{\partial J_i}{\partial \mathbf{F}_i} = 2\Big(\sum_{j:\ \mathbf{G}(i,j)=1} [-(\mathbf{W}_{i,j} \odot \mathbf{W}_{i,j} \odot \mathbf{D}_{i,j})\mathbf{F}_j + (\mathbf{W}_{i,j} \odot \mathbf{W}_{i,j} \odot (\mathbf{F}_i\mathbf{F}_j{}'))\mathbf{F}_j] + \alpha\mathbf{T}_i\mathbf{F}_i - \alpha\mathbf{A}_i\mathbf{F}_i + \beta\mathbf{F}_i\Big) \quad (3)$$

A fixed-point solution of Eq. (3) with non-negativity constraint on $\mathbf{F}_i$ leads to the following multiplicative updating rule for $\mathbf{F}_i$

$$\mathbf{F}_i(u,v) \leftarrow \mathbf{F}_i(u,v)\sqrt{\frac{\mathbf{X}(u,v)}{\mathbf{Y}(u,v)}} \quad (4)$$

where

$$\mathbf{X} = \sum_{j:\ \mathbf{G}(i,j)=1} (\mathbf{W}_{i,j} \odot \mathbf{W}_{i,j} \odot \mathbf{D}_{i,j})\mathbf{F}_j + \alpha\mathbf{A}_i\mathbf{F}_i \quad (5)$$
$$\mathbf{Y} = \sum_{j:\ \mathbf{G}(i,j)=1} (\mathbf{W}_{i,j} \odot \mathbf{W}_{i,j} \odot (\mathbf{F}_i\mathbf{F}_j{}'))\mathbf{F}_j + \alpha\mathbf{T}_i\mathbf{F}_i + \beta\mathbf{F}_i$$

Recall that we set $\mathbf{W}_{i,j}(u,v) = 1$ when $\mathbf{D}_{i,j}(u,v) > 0$, and $\mathbf{W}_{i,j}(u,v) = w$ when $\mathbf{D}_{i,j}(u,v) = 0$. Here, we define $\mathbf{I}_{i,j}^{O}$ as an indicator matrix for the observed entries in $\mathbf{D}_{i,j}$, that is, $\mathbf{I}_{i,j}^{O}(u,v) = 1$ if $\mathbf{D}_{i,j}(u,v) > 0$, and $\mathbf{I}_{i,j}^{O}(u,v) = 0$ if $\mathbf{D}_{i,j}(u,v) = 0$. Then, the estimated dependencies over the observed data can be represented as $\tilde{\mathbf{R}}_{i,j} = \mathbf{I}_{i,j}^{O} \odot (\mathbf{F}_i\mathbf{F}_j)$. With these notations, we can further simplify the update rule in Eq. (5) as follows

$$\mathbf{X} = \sum_{j:\ \mathbf{G}(i,j)=1} \mathbf{D}_{i,j}\mathbf{F}_j + \alpha \mathbf{A}_i \mathbf{F}_i \tag{6}$$

$$\mathbf{Y} = \sum_{j:\ \mathbf{G}(i,j)=1} ((1-w^2)\tilde{\mathbf{R}}_{i,j} + w^2 \mathbf{F}_i {\mathbf{F}_j}')\mathbf{F}_j + \alpha \mathbf{T}_i \mathbf{F}_i + \beta \mathbf{F}_i \tag{7}$$

The proposed FASCINATE algorithm is summarized in Alg. 1. First, it randomly initializes the low-rank matrices for each layer (line 1 - line 3). Then, it begins the iterative update procedure. In each iteration (line 4 - line 10), the algorithm alternatively updates $\{\mathbf{F}_i\}_{i=1,\dots,g}$ one by one. We use two criteria to terminate the iteration: (1) either the Frobenius norm between two successive iterations for all $\{\mathbf{F}_i\}_{i=1,\dots,g}$ is less than a threshold ξ, or (2) the maximum iteration number t is reached.

Algorithm 1 The FASCINATE Algorithm

Input: (1) a multi-layered network with (a) layer-layer dependency matrix $\mathbf{G}$, (b) within-layer connectivity matrices $\mathcal{A} = \{\mathbf{A}_1, \dots, \mathbf{A}_g\}$, and (c) observed cross-layer node dependency matrices $\mathcal{D} = \{\mathbf{D}_{i,j}\ i,j = 1, \dots, g\}$; (2) the rank size r; (3) weight w; (4) regularized parameters α and β;
Output: low-rank representations for each layer $\{\mathbf{F}_i\}_{i=1,\dots,g}$

```
1: for i = 1 to g do
2:    initialized F_i as n_i × r non-negative random matrix
3: end for
4: while not converge do
5:    for i = 1 to g do
6:       compute X as Eq. (6)
7:       compute Y as Eq. (7)
8:       update F_i as Eq. (4)
9:    end for
10: end while
11: return {F_i}_{i=1,...,g}
```

3.3 Proof and Analysis

Here, we analyze the proposed FASCINATE algorithm in terms of its effectiveness as well as its efficiency.

A - Effectiveness Analysis.

In terms of effectiveness, we show that the proposed FASCINATE algorithm indeed finds a local optimal solution to Eq. (1). To see this, we first give the following theorem, which says that the fixed point solution of Eq. (4) satisfies the *KKT* condition.

THEOREM 1. *The fixed point solution of Eq.* (4) *satisfies the KKT condition.*

PROOF. The Lagrangian function of Eq. (2) can be written as

$$L_i = \sum_{j:\ \mathbf{G}(i,j)=1} \|\mathbf{W}_{i,j} \odot (\mathbf{D}_{i,j} - \mathbf{F}_i {\mathbf{F}_j}')\|_F^2 + \alpha \mathrm{tr}({\mathbf{F}_i}'\mathbf{T}_i\mathbf{F}_i) - \alpha \mathrm{tr}({\mathbf{F}_i}'\mathbf{A}_i\mathbf{F}_i) + \beta\|\mathbf{F}_i\|_F^2 - \mathrm{tr}(\mathbf{\Lambda}'\mathbf{F}_i) \tag{8}$$

where $\mathbf{\Lambda}$ is the Lagrange multiplier. Setting the derivative of L_i wrt $\mathbf{F}_i$ to 0, we get

$$2(\sum_{j:\ \mathbf{G}(i,j)=1} [-(\mathbf{W}_{i,j} \odot \mathbf{W}_{i,j} \odot \mathbf{D}_{i,j})\mathbf{F}_j + (\mathbf{W}_{i,j} \odot \mathbf{W}_{i,j} \odot (\mathbf{F}_i {\mathbf{F}_j}'))\mathbf{F}_j] + \alpha \mathbf{T}_i \mathbf{F}_i - \alpha \mathbf{A}_i \mathbf{F}_i + \beta \mathbf{F}_i) = \mathbf{\Lambda} \tag{9}$$

By the KKT complementary slackness condition, we have

$$[\underbrace{\sum_{j:\ \mathbf{G}(i,j)=1} (\mathbf{W}_{i,j} \odot \mathbf{W}_{i,j} \odot (\mathbf{F}_i {\mathbf{F}_j}'))\mathbf{F}_j + \alpha \mathbf{T}_i \mathbf{F}_i + \beta \mathbf{F}_i}_{\mathbf{Y}} - (\underbrace{\sum_{j:\ \mathbf{G}(i,j)=1} (\mathbf{W}_{i,j} \odot \mathbf{W}_{i,j} \odot \mathbf{D}_{i,j})\mathbf{F}_j + \alpha \mathbf{A}_i \mathbf{F}_i}_{\mathbf{X}})](u,v)\mathbf{F}_i(u,v) = 0 \tag{10}$$

Therefore, we can see that the fixed point solution of Eq. (4) satisfies the above equation. □

The convergence of the proposed FASCINATE algorithm is given by the following lemma.

LEMMA 1. *Under the updating rule in Eq.* (4)*, the objective function in Eq.* (2) *decreases monotonically.*

PROOF. Omitted for brevity. □

According to Theorem 1 and Lemma 1, we conclude that Alg. 1 converges to a local minimum solution for Eq. 2 wrt each individual $\mathbf{F}_i$.

B - Efficiency Analysis.

In terms of efficiency, we analyze both the time complexity as well as the space complexity of the proposed FASCINATE algorithm, which are summarized in Lemma 2 and Lemma 3. We can see that FASCINATE scales linearly wrt the size of the entire multi-layered network.

LEMMA 2. *The time complexity of Alg. 1 is* $O([\sum_{i=1}^{g}(\sum_{j:\ \mathbf{G}(i,j)=1}(m_{i,j}r + (n_i + n_j)r^2) + m_i r)]t)$.

PROOF. In each iteration in Alg. 1 for updating $\mathbf{F}_i$, the complexity of calculating $\mathbf{X}$ by Eq. (6) is $O(\sum_{j:\ \mathbf{G}(i,j)=1} m_{i,j}r + m_i r)$ due to the sparsity of $\mathbf{D}_{i,j}$ and $\mathbf{A}_i$. The complexity of computing $\tilde{\mathbf{R}}_{i,j}$ in $\mathbf{Y}$ is $O(m_{i,j}r)$. Computing $\mathbf{F}_i(\mathbf{F}_j'\mathbf{F}_j)$ requires $O((n_i + n_j)r^2)$ operations and computing $\alpha \mathbf{T}_i \mathbf{F}_i + \beta \mathbf{F}_i$ requires $O(n_i r)$ operations. So, it is of $O(\sum_{j:\ \mathbf{G}(i,j)=1}(m_{i,j}r + (n_i + n_j)r^2))$ complexity to get $\mathbf{Y}$ in line 7. Therefore, it takes $O(\sum_{j:\ \mathbf{G}(i,j)=1}(m_{i,j}r + (n_i + n_j)r^2) + m_i r)$ to update $\mathbf{F}_i$. Putting all together, the complexity of updating all low-rank matrices in each iteration is $O(\sum_{i=1}^{g}(\sum_{j:\ \mathbf{G}(i,j)=1}(m_{i,j}r + (n_i + n_j)r^2) + m_i r))$. Thus, the overall complexity of Alg. 1 is $O([\sum_{i=1}^{g}(\sum_{\mathbf{G}(i,j)=1}(m_{i,j}r + (n_i + n_j)r^2) + m_i r)]t)$, where t is the maximum number of iterations in the algorithm. □

LEMMA 3. *The space complexity of Alg. 1 is* $O(\sum_{i=1}^{g}(n_i r + m_i) + \sum_{i,j:\ \mathbf{G}(i,j)=1} m_{i,j})$.

PROOF. It takes $O(\sum_{i=1}^{g} n_i r)$ to store all the low-rank matrices, and $O(\sum_{i=1}^{g} m_i + \sum_{i,j:\ \mathbf{G}(i,j)=1} m_{i,j})$ to store all the within-layer connectivity matrices and dependency matrices in the multi-layered network. To calculate $\mathbf{X}$ for $\mathbf{F}_i$, it costs $O(n_i r)$ to compute $\sum_{j:\ \mathbf{G}(i,j)=1} \mathbf{D}_{i,j}\mathbf{F}_j$ and $\alpha \mathbf{A}_i \mathbf{F}_i$. For $\mathbf{Y}$, the space cost of computing $\tilde{\mathbf{R}}_{i,j}$ and $\mathbf{F}_i(\mathbf{F}_j'\mathbf{F}_j)$ is $O(m_{i,j})$ and $O(n_i r)$ respectively.

Therefore, the space complexity of calculating $\sum_{j:\, \mathbf{G}(i,j)=1} ((1-w^2)\tilde{\mathbf{R}}_{i,j} + w^2\mathbf{F}_i\mathbf{F}_j{}')\mathbf{F}_j$ is $O(\max_{j:\, \mathbf{G}(i,j)=1} m_{i,j} + n_i r)$. On the other hand, the space required to compute $\alpha\mathbf{T}_i\mathbf{F}_i + \beta\mathbf{F}_i$ is $O(n_i r)$. Putting all together, the space cost of updating all low-rank matrices in each iteration is of $O(\max_{i,j:\, \mathbf{G}(i,j)=1} m_{i,j} + \max_i n_i r)$. Thus, the overall space complexity of Alg. 1 is $O(\sum_{i=1}^{g}(n_i r + m_i) + \sum_{i,j:\, \mathbf{G}(i,j)=1} m_{i,j})$. □

C - Variants.

Here, we discuss some variants of the proposed FASCINATE algorithm. First, by setting all the entries in the weight matrix $\mathbf{W}_{i,j}$ to 1, FASCINATE becomes a clustering algorithm (i.e., $\mathbf{F}_i$ can be viewed as the cluster membership matrix for nodes in layer-*i*). Furthermore, if we restrict ourselves to two-layered networks (i.e., $g = 2$), FASCINATE becomes a dual regularized co-clustering algorithm [20]. Second, by setting $w \in (0, 1)$, FASCINATE can be used to address one class collaborative filtering problem, where implicit dependencies extensively exist between nodes from different layers. Specifically, on two-layered networks, FASCINATE is reduced to a weighting-based, dual-regularized one class collaborative filtering algorithm [37]. Third, when the within-layer connectivity matrices $\mathcal{A} = \{\mathbf{A}_1, \ldots, \mathbf{A}_g\}$ are absent, the proposed FASCINATE can be viewed as a collective matrix factorization method [32].

While the proposed FASCINATE includes these existing methods as its special cases, its major advantage lies in its ability to collectively leverage all the available information (e.g., the within-layer connectivity, the observed cross-layer dependency) for dependency inference. As we will demonstrate in the experimental section, such a methodical strategy leads to a substantial and consistent inference performance boosting. Nevertheless, a largely unanswered question for these methods (including FASCINATE) is how to handle *zero-start* nodes. That is, when a new node arrives with no observed cross-layer dependencies, how can we effectively and efficiently infer its dependencies without rerunning the algorithm from scratch. In the next section, we present a *sub-linear* algorithm to solve this problem (i.e., Problem 2).

4. FASCINATE-ZERO FOR PROBLEM 2

A multi-layered network often exhibits high dynamics, e.g., the arrival of new nodes. For example, for a newly identified chemical in the biological system, we might know how it interacts with some existing chemicals (i.e., the within-layer connectivity). However, its cross-layer dependencies wrt proteins and/or diseases might be completely unknown . This section addresses such *zero-start* problems (i.e., Problem 2). Without loss of generality, we assume that the newly added node resides in layer-*1*, indexed as its $(n_1+1)^{\text{th}}$ node. The within-layer connectivity between the newly added node and the existing n_1 nodes is represented by a $1 \times n_1$ row vector $\mathbf{s}$, where $\mathbf{s}(u)$ $(u = 1, ..., n_1)$ denotes the (within-layer) connectivity between the newly added node and the uth existing node in layer-*1*.

We could just rerun our FASCINATE algorithm on the entire multi-layered network with the newly added node to get its low-rank representation (i.e., a $1 \times r$ row vector $\mathbf{f}$), based on which its cross-layer dependencies can be estimated. However, the running time of this strategy is linear wrt the size of the *entire* multi-layered network. For example, on a three-layered infrastructure network whose size is in the order of 14 million, it would take FASCINATE 2,500+ seconds to update the low-rank matrices $\{\mathbf{F}_i\}$ for a *zero-start* node with rank $r = 200$, which might be too costly in online settings. In contrast, our upcoming algorithm is *sub-linear*, and it only takes less than 0.001 seconds on the same network without jeopardizing the accuracy.

There are two key ideas behind our online algorithm. The first is to view the newly added node as a perturbation to the original network. In detail, the updated within-layer connectivity matrix $\hat{\mathbf{A}}_1$ for layer-*1* can be expressed as

$$\hat{\mathbf{A}}_1 = \begin{bmatrix} \mathbf{A}_1 & \mathbf{s}' \\ \mathbf{s} & 0 \end{bmatrix} \tag{11}$$

where $\mathbf{A}_1$ is the within-layer connectivity matrix for layer-*1* before the arrival of the new node.

Correspondingly, the updated low-rank representation matrix for layer-*1* can be expressed as $\hat{\mathbf{F}}_1 = [\hat{\mathbf{F}}'_{1(n_1\times r)}\ \mathbf{f}']'$, where $\hat{\mathbf{F}}_{1(n_1\times r)}$ is the updated low-rank representation for the existing n_1 nodes in layer-*1*. Then the new objective function $\hat{J}$ in Eq. (1) can be reformatted as

$$\begin{aligned}
\hat{J} = & \sum_{\substack{i,j:\, \mathbf{G}(i,j)=1 \\ i,j\neq 1}} \|\mathbf{W}_{i,j} \odot (\mathbf{D}_{i,j} - \hat{\mathbf{F}}_i\hat{\mathbf{F}}'_j)\|_F^2 \\
& + \sum_{j:\, \mathbf{G}(1,j)=1} \|\hat{\mathbf{W}}_{1,j} \odot (\hat{\mathbf{D}}_{1,j} - \hat{\mathbf{F}}_1\hat{\mathbf{F}}'_j)\|_F^2 \\
& + \sum_{i=2}^{g} \frac{\alpha}{2} \sum_{u=1}^{n_i}\sum_{v=1}^{n_i} \mathbf{A}_i(u,v)\|\hat{\mathbf{F}}_i(u,:) - \hat{\mathbf{F}}_i(v,:)\|_2^2 \\
& + \frac{\alpha}{2} \sum_{u=1}^{n_1}\sum_{v=1}^{n_1} \mathbf{A}_1(u,v)\|\hat{\mathbf{F}}_1(u,:) - \hat{\mathbf{F}}_1(v,:)\|_2^2 \\
& + \beta \sum_{i=2}^{g} \|\hat{\mathbf{F}}_i\|_F^2 + \beta\|\hat{\mathbf{F}}'_{1(n_1\times r)}\|_F^2 \\
& + \alpha \sum_{v=1}^{n_1} \mathbf{s}(v)\|\mathbf{f} - \hat{\mathbf{F}}_1(v,:)\|_2^2 + \beta\|\mathbf{f}\|_2^2
\end{aligned} \tag{12}$$

Since the newly added node has no dependencies, we can set

$$\hat{\mathbf{W}}_{1,j} = \begin{bmatrix} \mathbf{W}_{(1,j)} \\ \mathbf{0}_{(1\times n_j)} \end{bmatrix}, \quad \hat{\mathbf{D}}_{1,j} = \begin{bmatrix} \mathbf{D}_{(1,j)} \\ \mathbf{0}_{(1\times n_j)} \end{bmatrix}$$

Therefore, the second term in $\hat{J}$ can be simplified as

$$\sum_{j:\, \mathbf{G}(1,j)=1} \|\mathbf{W}_{1,j} \odot (\mathbf{D}_{1,j} - \hat{\mathbf{F}}_{1(n_1\times r)}\hat{\mathbf{F}}'_j)\|_F^2 \tag{13}$$

Combining Eq. (12), Eq. (13) and J in Eq. (1) together, $\hat{J}$ can be expressed as

$$\hat{J} = J + J^1 \tag{14}$$

where $J^1 = \alpha\sum_{v=1}^{n_1}\mathbf{s}(v)\|\mathbf{f} - \hat{\mathbf{F}}_1(v,:)\|_2^2 + \beta\|\mathbf{f}\|_2^2$, and J is the objective function without the newly arrived node.

The second key idea of our online algorithm is that in Eq. (14), J is often orders of magnitude larger than J^1. For example, in the **BIO** dataset used in Section 5.2.2, J is in the order of 10^3, while J^1 is in the order of 10^{-1}. This naturally leads to the following approximation strategy, that is, we (1) fix J with $\{\mathbf{F}_i^*\}_{i=1,\ldots,g}$ (i.e., the previous local optimal solution to Eq. (1) without the newly arrived node), and (2) optimize J^1 to find out the low-rank representation $\mathbf{f}$ for the newly arrived node. That is, we seek to solve the following optimization problem

$$\mathbf{f} = \arg\min_{\mathbf{f}\geq \mathbf{0}} J^1 \quad \text{subject to: } \hat{\mathbf{F}}_{1(n_1\times r)} = \mathbf{F}_1^* \tag{15}$$

with which, we can get an approximate solution $\{\hat{\mathbf{F}}_i\}_{i=1,\ldots,g}$ to $\hat{J}$.

To solve $\mathbf{f}$, we take the derivative of J^1 wrt $\mathbf{f}$ and get

$$\frac{1}{2}\frac{\partial J^1}{\partial \mathbf{f}} = \beta \mathbf{f} + \alpha \sum_{v=1}^{n_1} \mathbf{s}(v)(\mathbf{f} - \mathbf{F}_1^*(v,:)) \qquad (16)$$

$$= (\beta + \alpha \sum_{v=1}^{n_1} \mathbf{s}(v))\mathbf{f} - \alpha \mathbf{s}\mathbf{F}_1^*$$

Since α and β are positive, the Hessian matrix of J^1 is a positive diagonal matrix. Therefore, the global minimum of J^1 can be obtained by setting its derivative to zero. Then the optimal solution to J^1 can be expressed as

$$\mathbf{f} = \frac{\alpha \mathbf{s}\mathbf{F}_1^*}{\beta + \alpha \sum_{v=1}^{n_1} \mathbf{s}(v)} \qquad (17)$$

For the newly added node, $\mathbf{f}$ can be viewed as the weighted average of its neighbors' low-rank representations. Notice that in Eq. (17), the non-negativity constraint on $\mathbf{f}$ naturally holds. Therefore, we refer to this solution (i.e., Eq. (17)) as FASCINATE-ZERO. In this way, we can successfully decouple the cross-layer dependency inference problem for *zero-start* node from the entire multi-layered network and localize it only among its neighbors in layer-*1*. The localization significantly reduces the time complexity, as summarized in Lemma 4, which is linear wrt the number of neighbors of the new node (and therefore is *sub-linear* wrt the size of the entire network).

LEMMA 4. *Let nnz*($\mathbf{s}$) *denotes the total number of within-layer links between the newly added node and the original nodes in layer-1 (i.e., nnz*($\mathbf{s}$) *is the degree for the newly added node). Then the time complexity of* FASCINATE-ZERO *is* $O(nnz(\mathbf{s})r)$.

PROOF. Since the links between the newly added node and the original nodes in layer-*1* are often very sparse, the number of non-zero elements in $\mathbf{s}$ (nnz($\mathbf{s}$)) is much smaller than n_1. Therefore, the complexity of computing $\mathbf{s}\mathbf{F}_1^*$ can be reduced to $O(\text{nnz}(\mathbf{s})r)$. The multiplication between α and $\mathbf{s}\mathbf{F}_1^*$ takes $O(r)$. Computing $\sum_{v=1}^{n_1} \mathbf{s}(v)$ takes $O(\text{nnz}(\mathbf{s}))$. Thus, the overall complexity of computing $\mathbf{f}$ is $O(\text{nnz}(\mathbf{s})r)$. ☐

5. EVALUATIONS

In this section, we evaluate the proposed FASCINATE algorithms. All experiments are designed to answer the following questions:

- *Effectiveness.* How effective are the proposed FASCINATE algorithms in inferring the missing cross-layer dependencies?
- *Efficiency.* How fast and scalable are the proposed algorithms?

5.1 Experimental Setup

5.1.1 Datasets Description

We perform our evaluations on four different datasets, including (1) a three-layer Aminer academic network in the social collaboration domain (SOCIAL); (2) a three-layer CTD (Comparative Toxicogenomics Database) network in the biological domain (BIO); (3) a five-layer Italy network in the critical infrastructure domain (INFRA-5); and (4) a three-layer network in the critical infrastructure domain (INFRA-3). The statistics of these datasets are shown in Table 2, and the abstract layer-layer dependency graphs of these four datasets are summarized in Figure 3. In all these four datasets, the cross-layer dependencies are binary and undirected (i.e., $\mathbf{D}_{i,j}(u,v) = \mathbf{D}_{j,i}(v,u)$).

Table 2: Statistics of Datasets.

Dataset	# of Layers	# of Nodes	# of Links	# of CrossLinks
SOCIAL	3	125,344	214,181	188,844
BIO	3	35,631	253,827	75,456
INFRA-5	5	349	379	565
INFRA-3	3	15,126	29,861	28,023,500

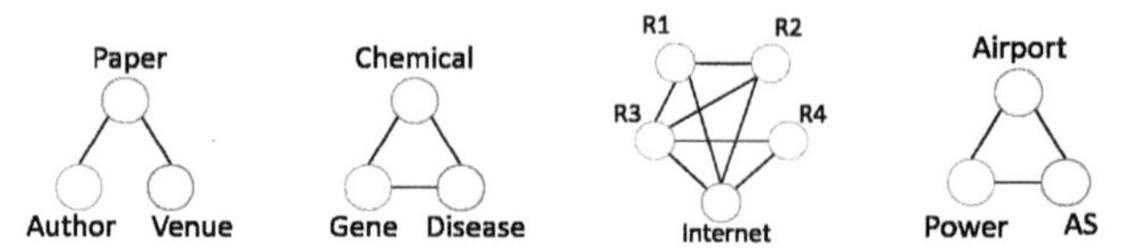

(a) SOCIAL (b) BIO (c) INFRA-5 (d) INFRA-3

Figure 3: The abstract dependency structure of each dataset.

SOCIAL. This dataset contains three layers, including a collaboration network among authors, a citation network between papers and a venue network [33]. The number of nodes in each layer ranges from 899 to $62,602$, and the number of within-layer links ranges from $2,407$ to $201,037$. The abstract layer-layer dependency graph of SOCIAL is shown in Figure 3(a). The collaboration layer is connected to the paper layer with the authorship dependency, while the venue layer is connected to the paper layer with publishing dependency. For the *Paper-Author* dependency, we have 126,242 links cross the two layers; for the *Paper-Venue* dependency, we have 62,602 links.

BIO. The construction of CTD network is based on the works in [7, 27, 34]. It contains three layers, which are chemical, disease and gene similarity networks. The number of nodes in these networks ranges from $4,256$ to $25,349$, and the number of within-layer links ranges from $30,551$ to $154,167$. The interactions between chemicals, genes, and diseases form the cross-layer dependency network as shown in Figure 3(b). For *Chemical-Gene* dependency, we have 53,735 links cross the two layers; for *Chemical-Disease* dependency, we have 19,771 links; and for *Gene-Disease* dependency, we have 1,950 links.

INFRA-5. The construction of this critical infrastructure network is based on the data implicated from an electrical blackout in Italy in Sept 2003 [28]. It contains five layers, including four layers of regional power grids and one Internet network [28]. The regional power grids are partitioned by macroregions[1]. To make the regional networks more balanced, we merge the Southern Italy power grid and the Island power grid together. The power transfer lines between the four regions are viewed as cross-layer dependencies. For the Italy Internet network, it is assumed that each Internet center is supported by the power stations within a radius of 70km. Its abstract dependency graph is shown in Figure 3(c). The smallest layer in the network has 39 nodes and 50 links; while the largest network contains 151 nodes and 158 links. The number of dependencies is up to 307.

INFRA-3. This dataset contains the following three critical infrastructure networks: an airport network[2], an autonomous system network[3] and a power grid [35]. We construct a three-layered network in the same way as [5]. The three infrastructure networks are functionally dependent on each other. Therefore, they form a triangle-shaped multi-layered network as shown in Figure 3(d). The construction of the cross-layer dependencies is based on geographic proximity. The number of nodes in each layer varies from

[1]https://en.wikipedia.org/wiki/First-level_NUTS_of_the_European_Union

[2]http://www.levmuchnik.net/Content/Networks/NetworkData.html

[3]http://snap.stanford.edu/data/

2,833 to 7,325, and the number of within-layer links ranges from 6,594 to 15,665. The number of cross-layer dependencies ranges from 4,434,116 to 14,921,765.

For all datasets, we randomly select 50% cross-layer dependencies as the training set and use the remaining 50% as the test set.

5.1.2 *Comparing Methods*

We compare FASCINATE with the following methods, including (1) FASCINATE-CLUST - a variant of the proposed method for the purpose of dependency clustering, (2) *MulCol* - a collective matrix factorization method [32], (3) *PairSid* - a pairwise one-class collaborative filtering method proposed in [37], (4) *PairCol* - a pairwise collective matrix factorization method degenerated from *MulCol* (5) *PairNMF* - a pairwise non-negative matrix factorization (*NMF*) based method [19], (6) *PairRec* - a pairwise matrix factorization based algorithm introduced in [15], (7) *FlatNMF* - an NMF based method that treats the input multi-layered network as a flat-structured single network (i.e., by putting the within-layer connectivity matrices in the diagonal blocks, and the cross-layer dependency matrices in the off-diagonal blocks), and (8) *FlatRec* - a matrix factorization based method using the same techniques as *PairRec* but treating the input multi-layered network as a single network as in *FlatNMF*.

For the experimental results reported in this paper, we set rank $r = 100$, maximum iteration $t = 100$, termination threshold $\xi = 10^{-8}$, weight $w^2 = 0.1$ and regularization parameters $\alpha = 0.1$, $\beta = 0.1$ unless otherwise stated.

5.1.3 *Evaluation Metrics*

We use the following metrics for the effectiveness evaluations.

- **MAP**. It measures the mean average precision over all entities in the cross-layer dependency matrices [18]. A larger *MAP* indicates better inference performance.
- **R-MPR**. It is a variant of Mean Percentage Ranking for one-class collaborative filtering [12]. *MPR* is originally used to measure the user's satisfaction of items in a ranked list. In our case, we can view the nodes from one layer as users, and the nodes of the dependent layer(s) as items. The ranked list therefore can be viewed as ordered dependencies by their importance. Smaller *MPR* indicates better inference performance. Specifically, for a randomly produced list, its *MPR* is expected to be 50%. Here, we define R-MPR = 0.5 − MPR, so that larger *R-MRP* indicates better inference performance.
- **HLU**. Half-Life Utility is also a metric from one-class collaborative filtering. By assuming that the user will view each consecutive items in the list with exponential decay of possibility, it estimates how likely a user will choose an item from a ranked list [25]. In our case, it measures how likely a node will establish dependencies with the nodes in the ranked list. A larger *HLU* indicates better inference performance.
- **AUC**. Area Under ROC Curve is a metric that measures the classification accuracy. A larger *AUC* indicates better inference performance.
- **Prec@K**. Precision at K is defined by the proportion of true dependencies among the top K inferred dependencies. A larger *Prec@K* indicates better inference performance.

5.1.4 *Machine and Repeatability*

All the experiments are performed on a machine with 2 processors Intel Xeon 3.5GHz with 256GB of RAM. The algorithms are programmed with MATLAB using single thread. We will release the code and the non-proprietary datasets after the paper is published.

5.2 Effectiveness

In this section, we aim to answer the following three questions, (1) how effective is FASCINATE for Problem 1 (i.e., CODE)? (2) how effective is FASCINATE-ZERO for Problem 2 (i.e., CODE-ZERO)? and (3) how sensitive are the proposed algorithms wrt the model parameters?

5.2.1 *Effectiveness of* FASCINATE

We compare the proposed algorithms and the existing methods on all the four datasets. The results are shown in Table 3 through Table 6. There are several interesting observations. First is that our proposed FASCINATE algorithm and its variant (FASCINATE-CLUST) consistently outperform all other methods in terms of all the five evaluation metrics. Second, by exploiting the structure of multi-layered network, FASCINATE, FASCINATE-CLUST and *MulCol* have significantly better performance than the pairwise methods. Third, among the pairwise baselines, *PairSid* and *PairCol* are better than *PairNMF* and *PairRec*. The main reason is that the first two algorithms utilize both within-layer connectivity matrices and cross-layer dependency matrix for matrix factorization, while the latter two only use the observed dependency matrix. Finally, the relatively poor performance of *FlatNMF* and *FlatRec* implies that simply flattening the multi-layered network into a single network is insufficient to capture the intrinsic correlations across different layers.

We also test the sensitivity of the proposed algorithms wrt the sparsity of the observed cross-layer dependency matrices (i.e., the ratio of the missing values) on INFRA-3. The results in Figure 4 demonstrate that both FASCINATE and FASCINATE-CLUST perform well even when 90%+ entries in the dependency matrices are missing.

5.2.2 *Effectiveness of* FASCINATE-ZERO

To evaluate the effectiveness of FASCINATE-ZERO, we randomly select one node from the *Chemical* layer in the BIO dataset as the newly arrived node and compare the inference performance between FASCINATE-ZERO and FASCINATE. The average results over multiple runs are presented in Figure 5. We can see that FASCINATE-ZERO bears a very similar inference power as FASCINATE, but it is orders of magnitude faster. We observe similar performance when the *zero-start* nodes are selected from the other two layers (i.e., *Gene* and *Disease*).

5.2.3 *Parameter Studies*

There are three parameters α, β and r in the proposed FASCINATE algorithm. α is used to control the impact of node homophily, β is used to avoid over-fitting, and r is the number of columns of the low-rank matrices $\{\mathbf{F}_i\}$. We fix one of these parameters, and study the impact of the remaining two on the inference results. From Figure 6, we can see that *MAP* is stable over a wide range of both α and β. Specifically, a relatively high *MAP* can be achieved when α is between 0.1 to 1 and β is less than 1. As for the third parameter r, the inference performance quickly increases wrt r until it hits 200, after which the *MAP* is almost flat. This suggests that a relatively small size of the low-rank matrices might be sufficient to achieve a satisfactory inference performance.

5.3 Efficiency

The scalability results of FASCINATE and FASCINATE-ZERO are presented in Figure 7. As we can see in Figure 7(a), FASCI-

Table 3: Cross-Layer Dependency Inference on SOCIAL

Methods	MAP	R-MPR	HLU	AUC	Prec@10
FASCINATE	0.0660	**0.2651**	**8.4556**	**0.7529**	**0.0118**
FASCINATE-CLUST	**0.0667**	0.2462	8.2160	0.7351	0.0108
MulCol	0.0465	0.2450	6.0024	0.7336	0.0087
PairSid	0.0308	0.1729	3.8950	0.6520	0.0062
PairCol	0.0303	0.1586	3.7857	0.6406	0.0056
PairNMF	0.0053	0.0290	0.5541	0.4998	0.0007
PairRec	0.0056	0.0435	0.5775	0.5179	0.0007
FlatNMF	0.0050	0.0125	0.4807	0.5007	0.0007
FlatRec	0.0063	0.1009	0.6276	0.5829	0.0009

Table 4: Cross-Layer Dependency Inference on BIO.

Methods	MAP	R-MPR	HLU	AUC	Prec@10
FASCINATE	**0.3979**	**0.4066**	**45.1001**	**0.9369**	**0.1039**
FASCINATE-CLUST	0.3189	0.3898	37.4089	0.9176	0.0857
MulCol	0.3676	0.3954	42.8687	0.9286	0.0986
PairSid	0.3623	0.3403	40.4048	0.8682	0.0941
PairCol	0.3493	0.3153	38.4364	0.8462	0.0889
PairNMF	0.1154	0.1963	15.8486	0.6865	0.0393
PairRec	0.0290	0.2330	3.6179	0.7105	0.0118
FlatNMF	0.2245	0.2900	26.1010	0.8475	0.0615
FlatRec	0.0613	0.3112	8.4858	0.8759	0.0254

Table 5: Cross-Layer Dependency Inference on INFRA-5.

Methods	MAP	R-MPR	HLU	AUC	Prec@10
FASCINATE	**0.5040**	**0.3777**	**67.2231**	**0.8916**	**0.2500**
FASCINATE-CLUST	0.4297	0.3220	56.8215	0.8159	0.2340
MulCol	0.4523	0.3239	59.8115	0.8329	0.2413
PairSid	0.3948	0.2392	49.5484	0.7413	0.2225
PairCol	0.3682	0.2489	48.5966	0.7406	0.2309
PairNMF	0.1315	0.0464	15.7148	0.5385	0.0711
PairRec	0.0970	0.0099	9.4853	0.5184	0.0399
FlatNMF	0.3212	0.2697	44.4654	0.7622	0.1999
FlatRec	0.1020	0.0778	11.5598	0.5740	0.0488

Table 6: Cross-Layer Dependency Inference on INFRA-3.

Methods	MAP	R-MPR	HLU	AUC	Prec@10
FASCINATE	0.4780	0.0788	**55.7289**	0.6970	**0.5560**
FASCINATE-CLUST	**0.5030**	**0.0850**	49.1223	**0.7122**	0.4917
MulCol	0.4606	0.0641	49.3585	0.6706	0.4930
PairSid	0.4253	0.0526	47.7284	0.5980	0.4773
PairCol	0.4279	0.0528	48.1314	0.5880	0.4816
PairNMF	0.4275	0.0511	48.8478	0.5579	0.4882
PairRec	0.3823	0.0191	38.9226	0.5756	0.3895
FlatNMF	0.4326	0.0594	45.0090	0.6333	0.4498
FlatRec	0.3804	0.0175	38.0550	0.5740	0.3805

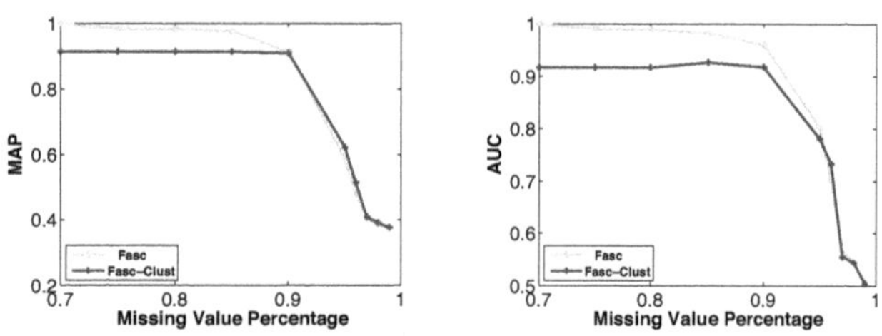

(a) MAP (b) AUC

Figure 4: Performance of FASCINATE and FASCINATE-CLUST on INFRA-3 dataset under different missing value percentages.

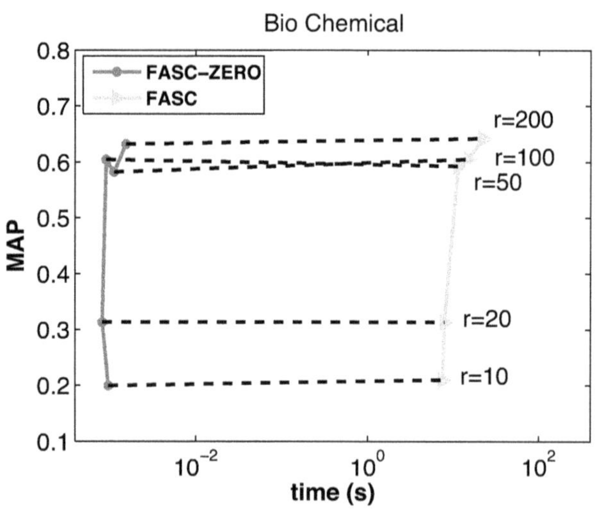

Figure 5: Effectiveness of FASCINATE-ZERO in BIO network wrt different rank r.

NATE scales linearly wrt the overall network size (i.e., $\sum_i(n_i + m_i) + \sum_{i,j} m_{i,j}$), which is consistent with our previous analysis in Lemma 2. As for FASCINATE-ZERO, it scales *sub-linearly* wrt the entire network size. This is because, by Lemma 4, the running time of FASCINATE-ZERO is only dependent on the neighborhood size of the newly added node, rather than that of the entire network. Finally, we can see that FASCINATE-ZERO is much more efficient than FASCINATE. To be specific, on the entire INFRA-3 dataset, FASCINATE-ZERO is $10,000,000+$ faster than FASCINATE (i.e., 1.878×10^{-4} seconds vs. 2.794×10^3 seconds)

6. RELATED WORK

In this section, we review the related literature, which can be classified into two categories: (1) multi-layered network, and (2) collaborative filtering.

Multi-layered Network. Multi-layered networks (also referred as Network of Networks in some scenarios), have attracted a lot research attentions in recent years. In [13], Kivela et al. provide a comprehensive survey about different types of multi-layered networks, including multi-modal networks [11], multi-dimensional networks [2], multiplex networks [1] and inter-dependent networks [4]. The network studied in our paper belongs to the category of inter-dependent networks. One of the mostly studied problems in inter-dependent networks is network robustness [8]. Most of the previous researches are based on *two-layered* networks [4, 9, 26, 31], with a few exceptions that focus on arbitrarily structured multi-layered networks [5]. Other remotely related studies in the context of multi-layered networks include cross-network ranking [23] and clustering [24]. Notice that all these existing works assume that the network structure (including both the within-layer connectivity and the cross-layer dependency) is *given* a prior. From this perspective, our proposed algorithms in this paper might benefit these works by providing a more accurate input network.

Collaborative Filtering. As mentioned earlier, the cross-layer dependency inference problem is conceptually related to collaborative filtering [10]. Commonly used collaborative filtering methods can be roughly classified into two basic models: neighborhood models [3] and latent factor models [15]. As the latent factor model is more effective in capturing the implicit dependencies between users and items, many variants have been proposed to address implicit feedback problems [12, 22], one class collaborative filtering (OCCF) problems [25], feature selection problems [17], etc. Instead of only using the user-item rating matrix for preference inference, Li et al. propose a method that can effectively incorporate

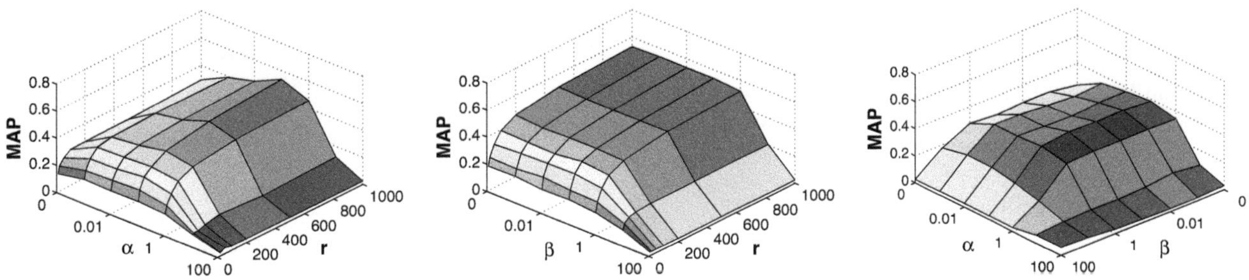

(a) Impact of α and r (fixing $\beta = 0.1$). (b) Impact of β and r (fixing $\alpha = 0.1$) (c) Impact of α and β (fixing $r = 100$).

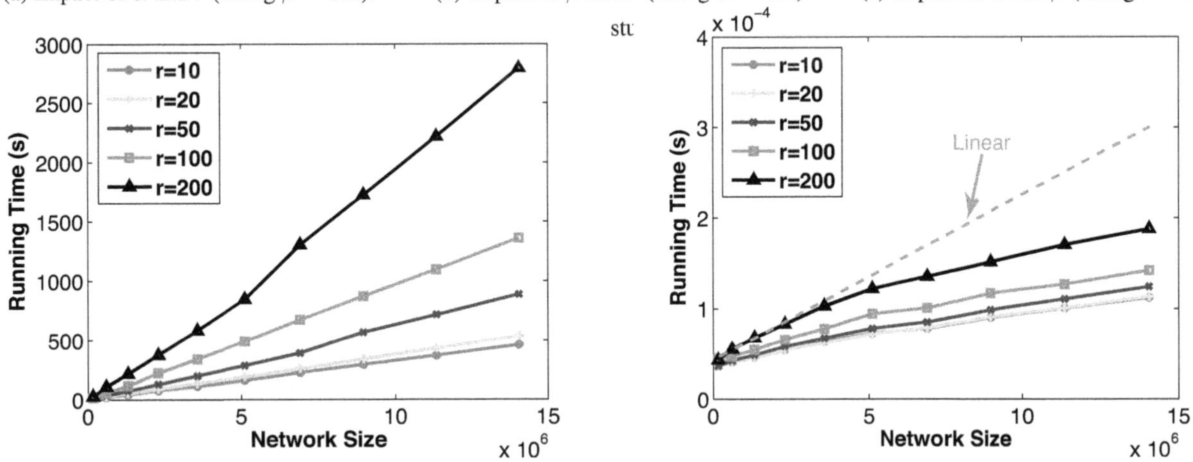

(a) FASCINATE (b)FASCINATE-ZERO

Figure 7: Wall-clock time vs. the size of the network.

user information into OCCF to improve the performance [18]. To further exploit more data resources for preference inference, Yao et al. propose *wiZAN-Dual* to take both user similarity network and item similarity network as side information for OCCF [37]. In [38], multiple similarity networks of users and items are integrated together for drug-target interaction prediction. In [16, 36], user and item features are incorporated into the traditional collaborative filtering algorithms for cross-domain recommendation. To deal with domains with multiple dependencies, Singh et al. propose a collective matrix factorization model to learn the dependencies across any two inter-dependent domains [32]. A less studied scenario in collaborative filtering is to handle user/item dynamics [14] (e.g., the arrival a new user or item, a new rating between an user and an item, etc).

7. CONCLUSIONS

In this paper, we address the cross-layer dependency inference problem (CODE) and the corresponding *zero-start* problem (CODE-ZERO) in multi-layered networks. By formulating CODE as a collective collaborative filtering problem, we propose an effective algorithm (FASCINATE), and prove its optimality, correctness and scalability. Moreover, by viewing the *zero-start* node as a perturbation to the multi-layered network system, we derive an effective and efficient algorithm (FASCINATE-ZERO) to approximate the dependencies of newly added nodes, whose complexity is *sub-linear* wrt the overall network size. We experiment on four real-world datasets from three different domains, which demonstrates the effectiveness and efficiency of FASCINATE and FASCINATE-ZERO.

Acknowledgements

We thank V. Rosato for providing the Italy 2003 blackout data. This work is partially supported by the National Science Foundation under Grant No. IIS1017415, by DTRA under the grant number HDTRA1-16-0017, by Army Research Office under the contract number W911NF-16-1-0168, by National Institutes of Health under the grant number R01LM011986, Region II University Transportation Center under the project number 49997-33 25 and a Baidu gift.

8. REFERENCES

[1] F. Battiston, V. Nicosia, and V. Latora. Structural measures for multiplex networks. *Physical Review E*, 89(3):032804, 2014.

[2] M. Berlingerio, M. Coscia, F. Giannotti, A. Monreale, and D. Pedreschi. Foundations of multidimensional network analysis. In *Advances in Social Networks Analysis and Mining (ASONAM), 2011 International Conference on*, pages 485–489. IEEE, 2011.

[3] J. S. Breese, D. Heckerman, and C. Kadie. Empirical analysis of predictive algorithms for collaborative filtering. In *Proceedings of the Fourteenth conference on Uncertainty in artificial intelligence*, pages 43–52. Morgan Kaufmann Publishers Inc., 1998.

[4] S. V. Buldyrev, R. Parshani, G. Paul, H. E. Stanley, and S. Havlin. Catastrophic cascade of failures in interdependent networks. *Nature*, 464(7291):1025–1028, 2010.

[5] C. Chen, J. He, N. Bliss, and H. Tong. On the connectivity of multi-layered networks: Models, measures and optimal control. In *Data Mining (ICDM), 2015 IEEE 15th International Conference on*, pages 715–720. IEEE, 2015.

[6] W. Chen, W. Hsu, and M. L. Lee. Making recommendations from multiple domains. In *Proceedings of the 19th ACM*

SIGKDD international conference on Knowledge discovery and data mining, pages 892–900. ACM, 2013.

[7] A. P. Davis, C. J. Grondin, K. Lennon-Hopkins, C. Saraceni-Richards, D. Sciaky, B. L. King, T. C. Wiegers, and C. J. Mattingly. The comparative toxicogenomics database's 10th year anniversary: update 2015. *Nucleic acids research*, page gku935, 2014.

[8] J. Gao, S. V. Buldyrev, S. Havlin, and H. E. Stanley. Robustness of a network of networks. *Physical Review Letters*, 107(19):195701, 2011.

[9] J. Gao, S. V. Buldyrev, H. E. Stanley, and S. Havlin. Networks formed from interdependent networks. *Nature physics*, 8(1):40–48, 2012.

[10] D. Goldberg, D. Nichols, B. M. Oki, and D. Terry. Using collaborative filtering to weave an information tapestry. *Communications of the ACM*, 35(12):61–70, 1992.

[11] L. S. Heath and A. A. Sioson. Multimodal networks: Structure and operations. *Computational Biology and Bioinformatics, IEEE/ACM Transactions on*, 6(2):321–332, 2009.

[12] Y. Hu, Y. Koren, and C. Volinsky. Collaborative filtering for implicit feedback datasets. In *Data Mining, 2008. ICDM'08. Eighth IEEE International Conference on*, pages 263–272. Ieee, 2008.

[13] M. Kivelä, A. Arenas, M. Barthelemy, J. P. Gleeson, Y. Moreno, and M. A. Porter. Multilayer networks. *Journal of Complex Networks*, 2(3):203–271, 2014.

[14] Y. Koren. Collaborative filtering with temporal dynamics. In *Proceedings of the 15th ACM SIGKDD international conference on Knowledge discovery and data mining*, pages 447–456. ACM, 2009.

[15] Y. Koren, R. Bell, and C. Volinsky. Matrix factorization techniques for recommender systems. *Computer*, (8):30–37, 2009.

[16] B. Li, Q. Yang, and X. Xue. Can movies and books collaborate? cross-domain collaborative filtering for sparsity reduction. In *IJCAI*, volume 9, pages 2052–2057, 2009.

[17] J. Li, X. Hu, L. Wu, and H. Liu. Robust unsupervised feature selection on networked data. In *Proceedings of SIAM International Conference on Data Mining*. SIAM, 2016.

[18] Y. Li, J. Hu, C. Zhai, and Y. Chen. Improving one-class collaborative filtering by incorporating rich user information. In *Proceedings of the 19th ACM international conference on Information and knowledge management*, pages 959–968. ACM, 2010.

[19] C.-b. Lin. Projected gradient methods for nonnegative matrix factorization. *Neural computation*, 19(10):2756–2779, 2007.

[20] J. Liu, C. Wang, J. Gao, Q. Gu, C. C. Aggarwal, L. M. Kaplan, and J. Han. Gin: A clustering model for capturing dual heterogeneity in networked data. In *SDM*, pages 388–396. SIAM, 2015.

[21] Z. Lu, W. Pan, E. W. Xiang, Q. Yang, L. Zhao, and E. Zhong. Selective transfer learning for cross domain recommendation. In *SDM*, pages 641–649. SIAM, 2013.

[22] H. Ma. An experimental study on implicit social recommendation. In *Proceedings of the 36th international ACM SIGIR conference on Research and development in information retrieval*, pages 73–82. ACM, 2013.

[23] J. Ni, H. Tong, W. Fan, and X. Zhang. Inside the atoms: ranking on a network of networks. In *Proceedings of the 20th ACM SIGKDD international conference on Knowledge discovery and data mining*, pages 1356–1365. ACM, 2014.

[24] J. Ni, H. Tong, W. Fan, and X. Zhang. Flexible and robust multi-network clustering. In *Proceedings of the 21th ACM SIGKDD International Conference on Knowledge Discovery and Data Mining*, pages 835–844. ACM, 2015.

[25] R. Pan, Y. Zhou, B. Cao, N. N. Liu, R. Lukose, M. Scholz, and Q. Yang. One-class collaborative filtering. In *Data Mining, 2008. ICDM'08. Eighth IEEE International Conference on*, pages 502–511. IEEE, 2008.

[26] R. Parshani, S. V. Buldyrev, and S. Havlin. Interdependent networks: reducing the coupling strength leads to a change from a first to second order percolation transition. *Physical review letters*, 105(4):048701, 2010.

[27] S. Razick, G. Magklaras, and I. M. Donaldson. irefindex: a consolidated protein interaction database with provenance. *BMC bioinformatics*, 9(1):1, 2008.

[28] V. Rosato, L. Issacharoff, F. Tiriticco, S. Meloni, S. Porcellinis, and R. Setola. Modelling interdependent infrastructures using interacting dynamical models. *International Journal of Critical Infrastructures*, 4(1-2):63–79, 2008.

[29] A. Sen, A. Mazumder, J. Banerjee, A. Das, and R. Compton. Multi-layered network using a new model of interdependency. *arXiv preprint arXiv:1401.1783*, 2014.

[30] J. Shao, S. V. Buldyrev, S. Havlin, and H. E. Stanley. Cascade of failures in coupled network systems with multiple support-dependent relations. *arXiv preprint arXiv:1011.0234*, 2010.

[31] J. Shao, S. V. Buldyrev, S. Havlin, and H. E. Stanley. Cascade of failures in coupled network systems with multiple support-dependence relations. *Physical Review E*, 83(3):036116, 2011.

[32] A. P. Singh and G. J. Gordon. Relational learning via collective matrix factorization. In *Proceedings of the 14th ACM SIGKDD international conference on Knowledge discovery and data mining*, pages 650–658. ACM, 2008.

[33] J. Tang, J. Zhang, L. Yao, J. Li, L. Zhang, and Z. Su. Arnetminer: extraction and mining of academic social networks. In *Proceedings of the 14th ACM SIGKDD international conference on Knowledge discovery and data mining*, pages 990–998. ACM, 2008.

[34] M. A. Van Driel, J. Bruggeman, G. Vriend, H. G. Brunner, and J. A. Leunissen. A text-mining analysis of the human phenome. *European journal of human genetics*, 14(5):535–542, 2006.

[35] D. J. Watts and S. H. Strogatz. Collective dynamics of small-world networks. *nature*, 393(6684):440–442, 1998.

[36] D. Yang, J. He, H. Qin, Y. Xiao, and W. Wang. A graph-based recommendation across heterogeneous domains. In *Proceedings of the 24rd ACM International Conference on Conference on Information and Knowledge Management*, pages 463–472. ACM, 2015.

[37] Y. Yao, H. Tong, G. Yan, F. Xu, X. Zhang, B. K. Szymanski, and J. Lu. Dual-regularized one-class collaborative filtering. In *Proceedings of the 23rd ACM International Conference on Conference on Information and Knowledge Management*, pages 759–768. ACM, 2014.

[38] X. Zheng, H. Ding, H. Mamitsuka, and S. Zhu. Collaborative matrix factorization with multiple similarities for predicting drug-target interactions. In *Proceedings of the 19th ACM SIGKDD international conference on Knowledge discovery and data mining*. ACM, 2013.

Predicting Matchups and Preferences in Context

Shuo Chen
Department of Computer Science
Cornell University
Ithaca, NY, USA
shuochen@cs.cornell.edu

Thorsten Joachims
Department of Computer Science
Cornell University
Ithaca, NY, USA
tj@cs.cornell.edu

ABSTRACT

We present a general probabilistic framework for predicting the outcome of pairwise matchups (e.g. two-player sport matches) and pairwise preferences (e.g. product preferences), both of which have widespread applications ranging from matchmaking in computer games to recommendation in e-commerce. Unlike existing models for these tasks, our model not only learns representations of the items in a more expressive latent vector space, but also models how context modifies matchup and preference outcomes. For example, the context "weather" may alter the winning probability in a tennis match, or the fact that the user is on a mobile device may alter his preferences among restaurants. More generally, the model is capable of handling any symmetric game/comparison problem that can be described by vectorized player/item and game/context features. We provide a comprehensive evaluation of its predictive performance with real datasets from both domains to show its ability to predict preference and game outcomes more accurately than existing models. Furthermore, we demonstrate on synthetic datasets the expressiveness of the model when compared against theoretical limits.

1. INTRODUCTION

A wide range of real-world prediction problems require modeling a pairwise relation between a potentially large set of objects. For example, when modeling competitive matchups in sports, the goal is to predict the outcome and the associated winning probability of a game between two players. By learning from historical game records among the players, traditional statistical models and their extensions [42, 7, 27] have been applied to both real-world sports prediction [29] and the matchmaking systems of online competitive video games [18]. Similarly, pairwise-relation models have been used for learning to predict human preferences and decision making. This ranges from purchasing choices people make between pairs of product, to aggregating pairwise preferences for learning the ranking of many items [12, 11]. In the context of search engines especially, it has been shown that treating clicks as revealing pairwise preferences is more reliable than treating clicks as absolute judgments [23].

KDD '16, August 13 - 17, 2016, San Francisco, CA, USA

ISBN 978-1-4503-4232-2/16/08...$15.00

DOI: http://dx.doi.org/10.1145/2939672.2939764

What motivates the work in this paper is that matchups and comparisons typically take place in varying contexts that can alter the outcome, and that both contexts and objects can be described by generalizing features. For example, in modeling sports matchups, characteristics of the game (i.e. the context) include weather, the time the game is played at, the importance of the game, the referee, antd the prize money. All these factors can affect the outcome of the game, and they are different from features describing the players (i.e. objects), like age, world ranking, recent game record, whether just returning from injury or not, and playing at home or away. Similarly in the preference domain, imagine the choices between restaurants. Each restaurant could have object features like food it serves, distance from current location, the environment, whether AC or Wi-Fi is installed. However, a customer's particular choice is also affected by context like whether he is hungry or not, lunch or dinner, weekday or weekend [3].

In this paper, we propose a general probabilistic framework for modeling pairwise relations that applies to any problem that can be modeled through object and context features. In particular, we show how the framework applies to accurately modeling and predicting the outcome of any type of game between two players, as well as to modeling human pairwise choices that are affected by context. This problem of learning from contextual pairwise comparisons has not been studied before, and we discuss how it is different from existing works in Section 4. In particular, unlike previous works on learning from pairwise preferences, our model naturally incorporates both features of objects (e.g., players, choices) and features of the context (e.g, game, framing). Furthermore, by building upon a recently introduced choice model that can represent intransitivity, our approach can model inherently intransitive relations that exist in sports matchups, and it can represent apparent intransitivities due to changing contexts in preference relations. The new model is evaluated in both the matchup and the preference domains, showing that it can produce results that surpass the fidelity of conventional models.

2. PRELIMINARIES

In this section, we first formally define the learning task. Then we discuss several conventional preference models, showing how they do not adequately address the task. They serve as baselines for empirical investigation later.

From now on, we are going to use the following concepts interchangeably for competitive matchup and pairwise preference modeling: matchup/pairwise preference, player/item, game/context, win/prefer. In this work we focus on modeling matchups between two players, and we assume the result for each individual match cannot be a draw. In the most general setting we are concerned about, a player a encounters player b in a game g. At the end of the game, there can be only one winner. We can assume it is a without loss of generality. In addition, we also have feature vectors that describe the players and the games: $\mathbf{x}_a, \mathbf{x}_b \in \mathbf{R}^{d_p}$ and $\mathbf{z}_g \in \mathbf{R}^{d_g}$. These feature vectors take very general form and can be used to encode any information we have regarding the players and game. Think about a professional tennis game for example. The feature vector of a player could contain: identity, age, nationality, world ranking, whether on a winning/losing streak, etc. These features are different for the two players. On the other hand, the feature vector of a game could contain: weather, surface of the ground, indoor or outdoor match, how deep into the tournament bracket, etc. They are the same for both players, but could affect them differently.

By learning from a training set D that contains multiple matches (triples of (a, b, g) and associated feature vectors), we want to predict the outcome of any future matchup as accurately as possible in terms of the probability $\Pr(a \text{ beats } b|g)$. In the following subsections, we discuss a few conventional methods from the existing literature that can be used for this learning task.

2.1 Rote learning

The most straightforward method for addressing the task is estimating each matchup probability $\Pr(a \text{ beats } b)$ individually while ignoring the context. The maximum likelihood estimator gives an intuitive formula

$$\Pr(a \text{ beats } b) = \frac{n_a}{n_a + n_b}, \tag{1}$$

where n_a and n_b are the numbers of times a and b wins respectively among the $n_a + n_b$ matches. The model contains $O(n^2)$ parameters, with n being the total number of players. One can imagine that, given enough data and assuming that context has no influence, it can model any matchup probability arbitrarily accurately. However, in reality not every possible matchup may be played enough times to get a good sample, or even played at all. For example, a comparatively lesser player who usually gets eliminated by a much better player in the first round of a tournament due to seeding, rarely gets a chance to play someone of similar competence. On the other hand, the duel between two big names takes place much more frequently in the later stages of the tournament. Some n_a and n_b could be zero, or even both of them, making it hard to model that matchup accurately. This also gives rise to a negative infinite log-likelihood, which is one of our evaluation measures. To avoid it, we do a simple add-one smoothing [24].

$$\Pr(a \text{ beats } b) = \frac{n_a + 1}{n_a + n_b + 2}, \tag{2}$$

We call this the rote learning method. Note that it cannot make use of any features of players or games except for the player's identity.

2.2 Bradley-Terry model

The seminal work of Bradley-Terry model [7, 27] is the basis of many research works in pairwise comparison, which naturally extends to matchup prediction. In the Bradley-Terry model, each player's strength is represented by a single real number γ, and there are $O(n)$ parameters. The probability of player a beating player b is modeled as

$$\begin{aligned}\Pr(a \text{ beats } b) &= \frac{\exp(\gamma_a)}{\exp(\gamma_a) + \exp(\gamma_b)} \\ &= \frac{1}{1 + \exp(-(\gamma_a - \gamma_b))} \\ &= S(M(a, b)).\end{aligned} \tag{3}$$

Here $S(x) = 1/(1 + \exp(-x))$ is the sigmoid or logistic function. $M(a, b)$ is what we call the matchup function of player a and player b, and it simply measures the edge given to player a when matched up against player b. In the Bradley-Terry model, it is modeled as $M(a, b) = \gamma_a - \gamma_b$, the difference of strengths between two players. Some properties of the Bradley-Terry model are:

1. The range of $M(a, b)$ is $\mathbb{R}$, with positive/negative meaning player a/b has more than 50% chance of winning, and 0 meaning it is an even matchup.
2. When $M(a, b) \to +\infty$, $\Pr(a \text{ beats } b) \to 1$. Similarly when $M(a, b) \to -\infty$, $\Pr(a \text{ beats } b) \to 0$.
3. $M(a, b) = -M(b, a)$. This makes sure that we always have $\Pr(a \text{ beats } b) = 1 - \Pr(b \text{ beats } a)$ satisfied.

Note that these three properties follow the properties of the sigmoid function. In fact, any real-valued function $M(a, b)$ that takes two players as arguments and satisfies property 3 can be plugged in and gives us a Bradley-Terry-like model.

The learning problem is to figure out the best strength parameter for each player from the training dataset, and is usually done via maximum likelihood estimation. Although the issue with $O(n^2)$ parameters is avoided, the Bradley-Terry model still only makes use of the identity of players, not additional features for players and games.

2.3 Pairwise logistic regression model

There is one way to extend the Bradley-Terry model to incorporate additional player information. One can model each player's strength as a weighted sum

$$\gamma_a = \mathbf{w}^T \mathbf{x}_a. \tag{4}$$

Then the matchup function becomes $M(a, b) = \mathbf{w}^T(\mathbf{x}_a - \mathbf{x}_b)$. The model can be interpreted as a logistic regression [6]: the input is the difference of the two player's feature vectors, and the output is 1/0 for the first player to win/lose. In fact, the Bradley-Terry model can be considered as a special case of this model, where the only feature used is the player's identity. Naturally, this model could and should be trained with regularization. We use an $L2$-norm regularizer in our experiments.

The inability to handle game features remains unfixed by the logistic model. One may think game features could be added to this model in two straightforward ways. For one, one could add an additional weight vector for the game feature $M(a, b) = \mathbf{w}^T(\mathbf{x}_a - \mathbf{x}_b) + \mathbf{w}'^T \mathbf{z}_g$. However, this is not a valid matchup function, because it does not satisfy property 3 introduced above. For the other, one could stack player and game feature vectors to form a new player feature vector, with the matchup function being

$$M(a, b) = \mathbf{w}^T \left(\begin{bmatrix} \mathbf{x}_a \\ \mathbf{z}_g \end{bmatrix} - \begin{bmatrix} \mathbf{x}_b \\ \mathbf{z}_g \end{bmatrix} \right). \tag{5}$$

However, the parts that are corresponding to the game features are the same for two players, and thus cancel out and have no effect on the output.

3. OUR FRAMEWORK

In this section, we detail our framework for general matchup modeling, which avoids the $O(n^2)$ paprameters, and can naturally incoporate all the player and game features. We first briefly review the *blade-chest* model from [10], which serves as the top layer of our framework. Then we introduce the bottom layers and explain how different features are added in.

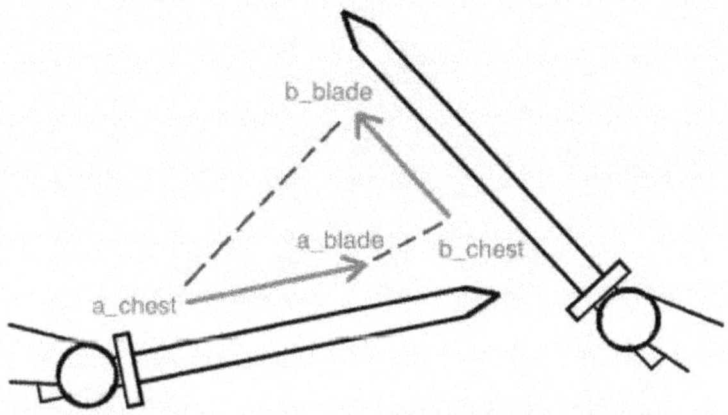

Figure 1: A metaphorical illustration of the *blade-chest* model for intransitivity. Player a and player b are in a sword duel. Player a's blade is closer to player b's chest than vice versa, as shown by the two blue dashed lines. This illustrates how player a has a better chance of winning than player b.

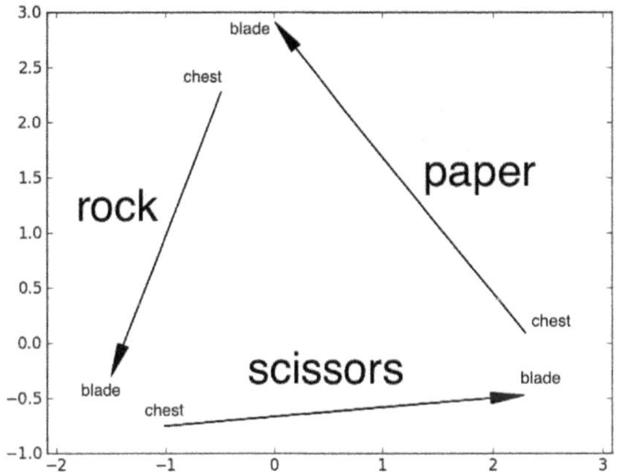

Figure 2: The visualization of the *blade-chest-dist* model trained on a synthetic rock-paper-scissors dataset with $1,000$ games for each matchup. d is set to 2. Each player is represented by an arrow, with the head being the blade vector and the tail being the chest vector.

3.1 The blade-chest model

Most of the previous works have the following in common: they use one single scalar to model the absolute strength of a player. Many of these works root from the Bradley-Terry model, and are surveyed in [8]. In some cases, a single scalar is an oversimplification, specifically since such models are not able to capture any intransitive rock-paper-scissors relation among three players if it exists in the data.

Our recent work of [10] models the intransitivity explicitly by using two d-dimensional vectors to represent a player. One is called the blade vector, and the other the chest vector. The winning and losing probabilities are decided based on the distance between one player's blade to his opponent's chest and vice versa. As depicted in Figure 1, player a has an edge over player b in this matchup.

Mathematically, one can write down the corresponding matchup function as

$$M(a,b) = ||\mathbf{b}_{\text{blade}} - \mathbf{a}_{\text{chest}}||_2^2 - ||\mathbf{a}_{\text{blade}} - \mathbf{b}_{\text{chest}}||_2^2, \quad (6)$$

which we call the *blade-chest-dist* model. The blade and chest vectors are the parameters of the model, and are learned from training data. Training this model on a synthetic rock-paper-scissors dataset gives us an interlocking visualization that correctly represents all three matchups as shown in Figure 2.

One variation of the *blade-chest-dist* model is to replace the Euclidean distance in the matchup function with the inner product, which gives

$$M(a,b) = \mathbf{a}_{\text{blade}} \cdot \mathbf{b}_{\text{chest}} - \mathbf{b}_{\text{blade}} \cdot \mathbf{a}_{\text{chest}}. \quad (7)$$

We call it the *blade-chest-inner* model. According to our empirical results in [10], modeling intransitivity this way is generally advantageous over the single-scalar methods. Between the two, the *blade-chest-inner* model usually performs better in terms of testing log-likelihood and accuracy, and is also more stable. Still these models cannot incorporate features other than the player's identity. In the later experimental section, we compare to this original *blade-chest-inner* model as a baseline, and call it the featureless model. In the rest of this section, we build upon the *blade-chest-inner* model for the general matchup modeling framework.

3.2 The blade-chest model as the top layer

Our framework has a two-layer structure. At the top layer, we use the *blade-chest-inner* model to output the winning probability,

$$\Pr(a \text{ beats } b|g) = S(M(a,b|g))$$
$$= S(\mathbf{a}_{\text{blade}}(\mathbf{x}_a,\mathbf{z}_g) \cdot \mathbf{b}_{\text{chest}}(\mathbf{x}_b,\mathbf{z}_g) - \mathbf{b}_{\text{blade}}(\mathbf{x}_b,\mathbf{z}_g) \cdot \mathbf{a}_{\text{chest}}(\mathbf{x}_a,\mathbf{z}_g)). \quad (8)$$

This top layer guarantees the needed symmetry, as $M(a,b|g) = -M(b,a|g)$ still holds. Instead of being d-dimensional vectors of free parameters for training, now the blade and chest vectors are functions of the player and game feature vectors. Our bottom layer serves as a feature mapper that bridges the blade/chest vectors and feature vectors, as detailed in the following subsections.

3.3 Bottom layer for player features only

For simplicity, we first discuss how the bottom layer works when we only use the player feature vectors. A natural way to link the space of blade/chest vectors and the space of feature vectors is by using a linear transformation. That is

$$\begin{aligned}\mathbf{a}_{\text{blade}}(\mathbf{x}_a) &= B\mathbf{x}_a \\ \mathbf{b}_{\text{blade}}(\mathbf{x}_b) &= B\mathbf{x}_b \\ \mathbf{a}_{\text{chest}}(\mathbf{x}_a) &= C\mathbf{x}_a \\ \mathbf{b}_{\text{chest}}(\mathbf{x}_b) &= C\mathbf{x}_b, \end{aligned} \quad (9)$$

where B and C are $d \times d_p$ parameter matrices that transform player feature vectors into blade or chest vectors respectively[1], and d is a tunable parameter. Alternatively, we can link the two spaces by using a fully-connected feedforward neural network layer:

$$\begin{aligned}\mathbf{a}_{\text{blade}}(\mathbf{x}_a) &= f(B\mathbf{x}_a) \\ \mathbf{b}_{\text{blade}}(\mathbf{x}_b) &= f(B\mathbf{x}_b) \\ \mathbf{a}_{\text{chest}}(\mathbf{x}_a) &= f(C\mathbf{x}_a) \\ \mathbf{b}_{\text{chest}}(\mathbf{x}_b) &= f(C\mathbf{x}_b), \end{aligned} \quad (10)$$

[1]Note that when $\mathbf{x}_a$ and $\mathbf{x}_b$ are 0-1 vectors that only encode the players' identities, this recovers the original *blade-chest-inner* model as a special case.

where f is the element-wise activation function. We choose hyperbolic tangent function $\tanh(\cdot)$ as f (over other popular choices including the sigmoid function and the rectified linear unit), as its range includes both positive and negative values, similar to the original blade/chest vectors with free parameters.

The linear transformation Eq. (9) can also be viewed as the special case of Eq. (10), with the identity function as activation function. We will refer to the two different options as NOACT and TANH in later discussions.

3.4 Adding game feature vectors

Next we add game feature vectors so that they affect the two players differently, and the effects do not cancel out. Unlike for the logistic model, the concatenation of player vector and game vector is now sensible

$$\begin{aligned}
\mathbf{a}_{\text{blade}}(\mathbf{x}_a, \mathbf{z}_g) &= f_{\text{blade}}\left(B\begin{bmatrix}\mathbf{x}_a\\ \mathbf{z}_g\end{bmatrix}\right)\\
\mathbf{b}_{\text{blade}}(\mathbf{x}_b, \mathbf{z}_g) &= f_{\text{blade}}\left(B\begin{bmatrix}\mathbf{x}_b\\ \mathbf{z}_g\end{bmatrix}\right)\\
\mathbf{a}_{\text{chest}}(\mathbf{x}_a, \mathbf{z}_g) &= f_{\text{chest}}\left(C\begin{bmatrix}\mathbf{x}_a\\ \mathbf{z}_g\end{bmatrix}\right)\\
\mathbf{b}_{\text{chest}}(\mathbf{x}_b, \mathbf{z}_g) &= f_{\text{chest}}\left(C\begin{bmatrix}\mathbf{x}_b\\ \mathbf{z}_g\end{bmatrix}\right). \qquad (11)
\end{aligned}$$

Passing through a NOACT layer, there will be nonzero cross terms $\mathbf{x}_a^T\mathbf{z}_g$ and $\mathbf{x}_b^T\mathbf{z}_g$ left to represent different influence of the game on each player. It applies to TANH similarly. We denote this choice of model as CONCAT. It is depicted in Figure 3.

An alternative model is to let the game feature vectors warp the blade and chest vectors directly. To do so, we first separately map the game feature vector into the same d-dimensional space as blade/chest vectors by applying a NOACT/TANH layer. Then we apply a Hadamard/entry-wise product for the warping,

$$\begin{aligned}
\mathbf{a}_{\text{blade}}(\mathbf{x}_a, \mathbf{z}_g) &= f(B'\mathbf{z}_g) \circ f(B\mathbf{x}_a)\\
\mathbf{b}_{\text{blade}}(\mathbf{x}_b, \mathbf{z}_g) &= f(B'\mathbf{z}_g) \circ f(B\mathbf{x}_b)\\
\mathbf{a}_{\text{chest}}(\mathbf{x}_a, \mathbf{z}_g) &= f(C'\mathbf{z}_g) \circ f(C\mathbf{x}_a)\\
\mathbf{b}_{\text{chest}}(\mathbf{x}_b, \mathbf{z}_g) &= f(C'\mathbf{z}_g) \circ f(C\mathbf{x}_b). \qquad (12)
\end{aligned}$$

We call this model choice SPLIT, as the mapping of the player and game features happens separately. The entire pipeline is shown in Figure 4.

3.5 Training

We train our model to maximize the log-likelihood on the training dataset, that is (assuming a is the winner)

$$\underset{\Theta}{\operatorname{argmax}} \sum_{(a,b,g)\in D} \log \Pr(a \text{ beats } b|\Theta, g). \qquad (13)$$

Θ denotes all the parameters, and it typically consists of B and C, with additional B' and C' for the SPLIT model. We use the Frobenius norms of these parameter matrices as regularization terms.

The training of our model is done via online backpropagation [38]. Until convergence, we iterate through the entire training dataset repeatedly, feed one game to the model at a time, update the parameters immediately based on the result of backpropagation. Our implementation in C that contains all the different training options and is available at http://www.cs.cornell.edu/~shuochen/.

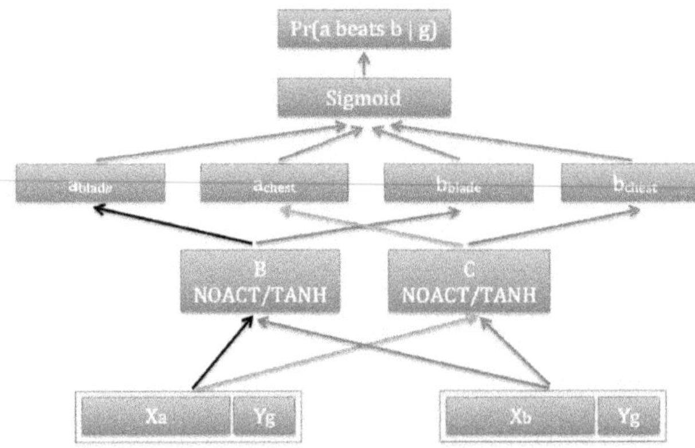

Figure 3: Pipeline of CONCAT model.

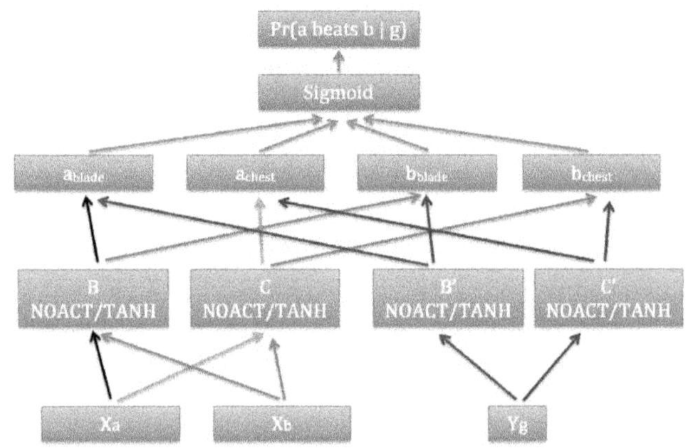

Figure 4: Pipeline of SPLIT model.

4. RELATED WORK

Pairwise comparison has been studied since the seminal work of [42], which later led to the well-known Bradley-Terry model [7, 27]. They paved the way for most of the research in the area, as surveyed in [8].

Learning to rank a player's strength in order to predict results or do matchmaking in sports or online video games has been a successful application of pairwise comparison modeling. The famous Elo rating system [17], a variation of Bradley-Terry model, started in rating chess players, and is now widely used in many sports prediction applications and matchmaking systems of online video games (a.k.a esports) [1]. Another example is the Trueskill™ ranking system [18] developed by Microsoft. It uses a univariate Gaussian distribution to model each player's skill and uncertainty, and its Bayesian inference is done via approximate message passing on a factor graph. Its follow-up works include [13, 32]. [45] proposes a factorization method to model players' ratings in different contexts[2]. There are also works that aim at inferring each player's strength through learning from group competition [19, 30]. The goal of these works and many others along the line is to learn a scalar parameter for each of the players from historical pairwise comparison data. These parameters usually represent the absolute strengths of the individuals, with larger values favored for the win over smaller values in future games.

[2]A context in their paper is represented by a set of discrete variables, e.g. a map one round of online video game is played on.

However, for many real-world settings, these types of models can be an oversimplification. For example, they are unable to capture effects like intransitivity (rock-paper-scissors relation) that exist in real data [10]. To remedy this, several works used more expressive ways of modeling players, and report improved performance. [9, 10] use one or more vectors to represent a player, and are able to explicitly model the intransitive behaviors. [21, 43] generalize the Bradley-Terry model with vectorized representations of a player's ranking. The previously discussed [19] could also fall into this category, as the player is represented by a vector of its ratings for different discrete contexts. [2] designs a matrix factorization algorithm to predict scores of professional basketball games.

It is worth noting that the intransitivity caused by multiple attributes has been studied in economics and decision theory [28, 16, 26]. Instead of taking a learning perspective, these works assume the features/attributes of items are given, and study what type of underlying thought process could cause intransitivity. Thus, it is an inverse process of what our work and the above works are about.

The BalanceNet model proposed in [14] is closely related to our work. It uses a multi-layer neural network to help matchmaking in *Ghost Recon Online*, a first-person shooter (FPS) online video game developed by Ubisoft. It can also account for player features such as number of matches played, average kill/death ratio, etc. The main differences that make it incomparable with our work are twofold. First, the game they addressed is asymmetric. The opposing players in one match are playing different roles, which means if you switch the input of them, you do not get one minus your previous probability. This comes with the nature of *Ghost Recon Online*, and makes it not applicable to general symmetric matchups unlike our framework[3]. Second, it is not designed to make use of any game features.

Most of the aforementioned works on player modeling and game prediction only take into account players' identities, with exceptions of [19] considering discrete context variables and [14] using additional player features. Different from them, our work in this paper is a general probabilistic matchup modeling framework for any two-player game with more expressive power than player-ranking. It can also utilize any vectorized player features and game features, no matter whether the features are discrete or continuous.

Another application of pairwise comparison is preference learning [15, 11, 44]. Instead of one player beating the other, here one observation in the dataset is one item being preferred (by a human) over the other. In a typical preference learning setting, the training data consists of pairwise preferences of instances, represented by a feature vector. The goal is to learn an underlying ranking function (with scalar output) that satisfies the training data as much as possible. A similar task arises in the context of search engines. It is studied as the "learning from implicit feedback problem" [12, 22, 34, 23], where user expresses his/her preference by clicking on retrieved items. The major difference between these work and our work is threefold. First, the items' identities are usually not part of the feature vectors in their empirical tests (although theoretically can be). Other auxiliary features are used instead. Second, similar to aforementioned player-ranking models, they try to learn a scalar ranking function for the instance, which has limited expressiveness in representing the relations between items. Lastly, there is no notion or no natural way of accounting for context information in which the choice is made.

[3]We would argue that a symmetric matchup is a more general form, as if the game is asymmetric, it could still be modeled as a symmetric one. One possible approach could be adding to the player feature vector to specify what asymmetric role he is playing in this game.

Learning with context has been studied in the recommendation community, and one line of research that is related to our work is context-aware recommender systems. While traditional recommender systems [37] consider only the ratings of users given to items[4], context-aware recommendation systems recognize that the context in which users rate items could be a crucial factor that impacts the evaluation [3]. There is also evidence from the research in decision-making domain that different contexts can change human decisions significantly [40, 20]. As a result, making use of the context information could significantly boost the performance of the recommender system, as reported in representative works like [5, 25, 39, 36]. Here, the task is learning from user ratings of items under different contexts to predicting any missing values, the unknown ratings for any triple of user, item and context. It is usually measured by mean average error (MAE) of the predicted ratings, or normalized discounted cumulative gain (NDCG) for retrieval tasks. This differs from our work, which concerns learning from user's pairwise preferences instead of cardinal ratings to predict the choice and its probability, not ratings for items, as accurately as possible.

5. EXPERIMENTS

We conducted an extensive empirical evaluation of the models on both competitive matchup data and pairwise preference data. In each domain, we report results on both real-world data to demonstrate applicability and practicality, and on synthesized data to demonstrate the expressiveness of our models.

5.1 Experiment setup

We first introduce the general setup of all the experiments. If not specified otherwise, the experiments are run as follows. We train various models (both ours and baselines) with different d's (where applicable) and regularization intensities[5] on the training dataset. The model that reports the best performance on the validation dataset in terms of log-likelihood is then tested on the test dataset.

For evaluation, we use two metrics: average test log-likelihood and test accuracy. The average test log-likelihood is defined similarly to the training log-likelihood. For the test partition D', assuming a is the winner,

$$L(D'|\Theta) = \frac{1}{|D'|} \sum_{(a,b,g)\in D'} \log(\Pr(a \text{ beats } b|\Theta, g)), \tag{14}$$

where $|D'|$ is the total number of games in the testing set. Log-likelihood is always a negative value. The higher the value is, the better the model performs. The test accuracy is defined as

$$A(D'|\Theta) = \frac{1}{|D'|} \sum_{(a,b,g)\in D'} \mathbb{1}^{\{\Pr(a \text{ beats } b|\Theta,g)\geq 0.5\}}. \tag{15}$$

$\mathbb{1}^{\{\cdot\}}$ is the indicator function. This metric is a real number in $[0, 1]$, representing the percentage of matches whose binary outcome can be correctly predicted by the model. The higher the value is, the better the model performs.

For the baselines, we compare our methods with Rote Learning, Bradley-Terry, the Pairwise Logistic Model and the Trueskill™

[4]Works that make use of the inherent features of users and items also exist [4, 41].

[5]The selection of these hyperparameters is through grid search, with d from 2 to 100, and the shared regularization hyperparameter λ across all parameter matrices from 1E-7 to 1E3.

ranking system[6]. For our methods, we also vary the information we input into the models, from featureless (Section 3.1) , player/item features only to both player/item features and game/context features. Note that methods from context-aware recommender system are not applicable to pairwise preference prediction as explained in the last paragraph of Section 4.

5.2 Experiments with synthetic datasets

We first explore the expressiveness of the models on three synthetic datasets that correspond to plausible real-world scenarios, but allow us to control the effect we aim to study.

5.2.1 Synthetic Datasets

For all datasets, we vary the amount of data, but always split to have roughly a $5:2:3$ training, validation and testing ratio.

Dataset "syn-rand". With this dataset, we explore how changes in context make the outcome of a game more random (e.g., bad weather making a tennis match more random). Furthermore, we simulate how the home-field advantage gives the home player an edge. Data is generated as follows. We create 50 players in total. In any game, there are also 2 game features: weather being normal or bad. Each happens 50% of the times. If the weather is bad, the outcome of the matchup is $50/50$ before considering the home-field's effect discussed below. Otherwise, we assign a $75/25$ chance for each player to win prior to considering home-field advantage. The favored player is selected via a coin toss. In addition to the game features, there are 3 players features (in addition to player's identity features): playing at home, playing away or playing in a neutral environment. In any game, one of the following two is true: one player is at home and the other is away, or both players are playing in neutral environments. The two scenarios are equally likely. If one player has the home-field advantage, the player's chances of winning increase by 10 percent (e.g. a $75/25$ matchup when the favored player is away becomes a $65/35$ matchup). Otherwise, the probability is not altered. To generate a game, we randomly sample two different players, the home-field and the weather features. We then sample the outcome according to the resulting matchup probability.

Dataset "syn-determ". This dataset is analogous to "*syn-rand*", but now context (i.e., weather) makes a game more deterministic. In particular, there are also 2 game features: weather being normal or good. Good weather alters the winning probability to $100/0$ while disregarding the home-field feature. Normal weather does not alter the winning probability.

Dataset "syn-attr". With this dataset we study a scenario where context can switch the polarity of a preference. For example, imagine a case when the user choose between two restaurant. If the user is already in town and logs on via a mobile device, the distance to the restaurants may be the most important factor in the decision. On the other hand, if we are still at home with a desktop, the quality of the restaurant may overweigh the distance, as we need to drive anyway. Using this scenario, the data contains 50 restaurants in total. Each restaurant is associated with two binary $0/1$ numbers that represent distance and quality. The chance for each number to be 0 or 1 is 50%. For each pairwise comparison, we uniformly select two restaurants and the mobile/desktop context, which is also equally likely. We compare the two $0/1$ numbers of the given context. If they are the same, we select the winner via a coin toss. Otherwise, the one with larger number (1 in this case) wins the comparison.

5.2.2 Empirical results

We test our models with different input information, and tune them across all training option combinations (NOACT, TANH, CONCAT, SPLIT) on the validation set. This ends up with "featureless" (no additional feature used other than identities), "player only" (best result by using only player features) and "player+game" (best result by using both player and game features)[7]. We compare the results against the aforementioned baselines. Note that "player only" and "logistic" do not apply to the preference data, as there are no player/item features other than identity. They are essentially the same as "featureless" and "Bradley-Terry".

We plot the performance metrics against the size of the dataset in Figure 5 and 6. In addition, we introduce two limits, denoted as "theoretical best" and "theoretical best rote"[8]. For the first, it is the limit we could get by being fully aware of how the data is generated and having an infinite amount of training and testing data. For the second, it is similar to "theoretical best", but the infinite amount of data only contains players' identities, not additional player and game features. This corresponds to the input information that featureless, Bradley-Terry, and Trueskill™ can make use of.

How do our models compare against the baselines? We observe that our models generally outperform all the baselines. With full information, our models are favored when compared with the rest in terms of log-likelihood, and are almost always better in terms of accuracy. The only exception is test accuracy for *syn-determ* data in the middle panel of Figure 6, where all methods perform well since there are so many 100/0 matchups generated.

How do different levels of input information affect our models? In general, we see that extra information helps improve the performance when comparing the curves of "player+game", "player only" and "featureless" in all plots, especially as the numbers of games grow. It is interesting to point out that including player feature does not help much when comparing against the featureless baselines on *syn-determ*, as the "player only" curve is barely above "featureless" in the middle panels of Figure 5 and Figure 6. This is due to the way in which the dataset is generated (when the weather is good, home-field advantage is ignored and the better player wins).

How do our models compare against the theoretical limits? On the *syn-rand* data where bad weather makes a game much more unpredictable, it seems that more games are needed for "featureless" to approach "theoretical best rote" (the two curves are still noticeably apart at the right end in the left panels of Figure 5 and Figure 6). Other than that we can see our context-sensitive methods "player+game" tend to converge to the corresponding theoretical limits as the numbers of games grow in all six plots. This provides evidence that our methods can indeed capture the underlying generation process, including the three distinct effects that context has in the three datasets.

5.3 Experiments with real-world datasets

We now turn to the real-world applications to verify the applicability and practicality of our methods. The datasets span the competitive matchup and preference domains: professional tennis and *Starcraft II* data for competitive matchups, and three datasets converted from context-aware recommender system research for pairwise preferences.

[6]The original Trueskill™ranking system runs in an online fashion: it sees a game, updates the parameters, and never sees that game again. However, to make it a fair comparison with other methods that run in batch mode, we also pass the training set through the Trueskill™ model multiple times until we have the best validation results.

[7]We only report the best results for each level of input information to keep the plots uncluttered.

[8]The derivations of the two limits are omitted due to limited space.

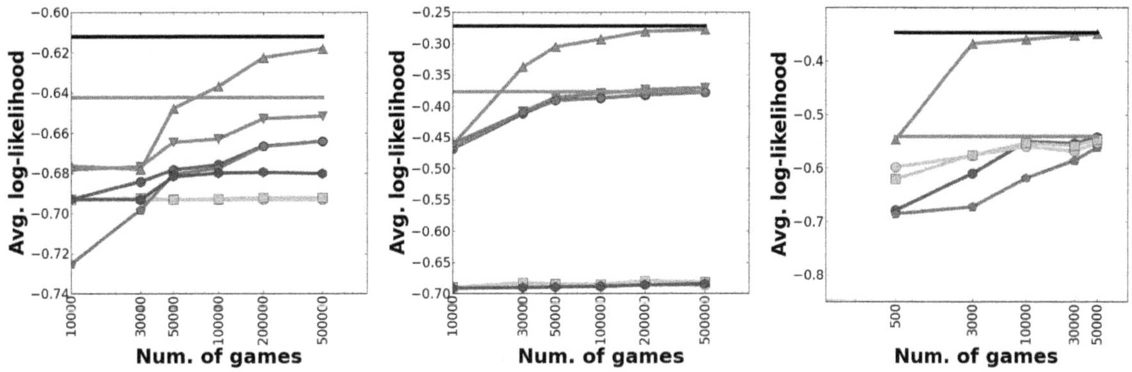

Figure 5: Average log-likelihood on *syn-rand* (left panel), *syn-determ* (middle panel) and *syn-attr* (right panel) datasets.

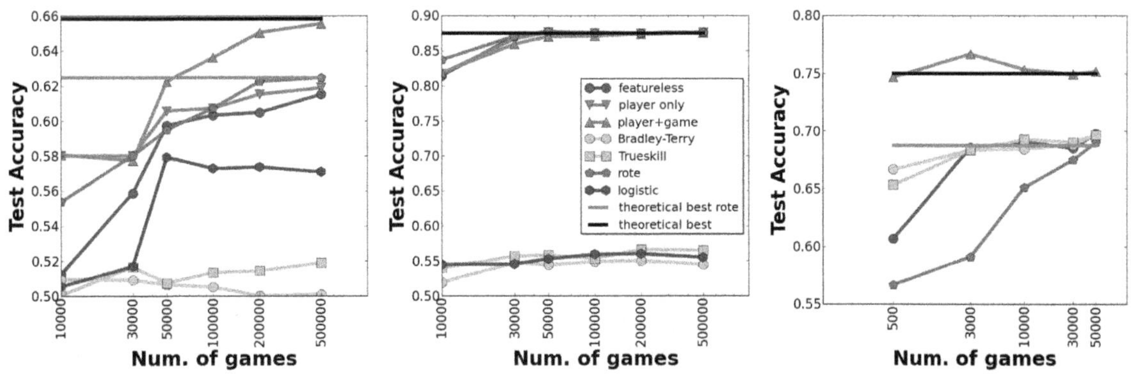

Figure 6: Average test accuracy on *syn-rand* (left panel), *syn-determ* (middle panel) and *syn-attr* (right panel) datasets. Note that the two limits overlap in the middle panel. Moreover, due to the fact that all the generated datasets are finite, it is possible for any method that learns from them to go above the limits that is assuming infinite data due to sampling error. It is the case here in the right panel.

5.3.1 Real-World Datasets

Tennis Datasets. We first look at the data of matches between top male tennis players in the world from year 2005-2015 and female players from year 2007-2015. These games are from all levels of tournaments organized by Association of Tennis Professionals (ATP) and Women's Tennis Association (WTA). The full collection of data can be found at http://tennis-data.co.uk/alldata.php. It contains match history of in total 914 players and 28,054 games for ATP, and 775 players and 21,488 games for WTA. For the experiments, we use the games before (including) the year 2012 for training and validation, and the later games for testing. The training/validation ratio is roughly 4: 1. We end up with 17,622 training games, 4,401 validation games and 6,031 testing games for ATP, and 11,725 training games, 2,928 validation games and 6,835 testing games for WTA.

The data source above also contains more detailed information about the players and games, which serves as feature vectors in our model. For players features we have player's identity, world ranking when the game was played, points for world ranking when the game was played, whether on a winning/losing streak and odds from several betting companies/websites (Bet365, Expekt, Ladbrokes, Pinnacles Sports and Stan James). The game features contain the location at which the game took place, the series the game belongs to (e.g. International Gold, Masters), indoor or outdoor court, surface of the court (e.g. Grass, Clay, Hard, Carpet), the stage the game was at (e.g. Group stage, Round of 16, Semifinal, Final) and the format of the game (usually best of 3 or best of 5). Overall, we extracted 927 player features for ATP and 788 for WTA, and also 119 games features. As one can see from above that most of the features are discrete, these feature vectors are very sparse.

Starcraft II Dataset. Starcraft II is an online military science fiction real-time strategy game developed and published by Blizzard Entertainment[9]. It is one of the most popular games in the esports scene. In the most common competitive setting, two players face off against each other. Each player as a war commander picks one from the three distinct in-game races: Terran, Protoss or Zerg as his army, each of which has different strengths, powers and abilities. The battle takes place on a battleground which is called a map. Both players collect resources on the map and build various of combat units to fight the opponents, until one player's force is completely wiped out and the other claims victory. The combat units all have different attributes such as building cost, building time, movement speed, attack range, toughness, etc. A set of *Starcraft II* strategies include managing different resources, building an army with right components at the right time, scouting and reacting to opponents' moves properly, etc.

We crawled *Starcraft II* competition data from a third-party website aligulac.com from the beginning of their database to April 8th, 2015. It contains 129,005 matches among 4,761 professional *Starcraft II* players from various online and offline tournaments. They are randomly divided into training, validation, testing sets according to a roughly 5: 2: 3 ratio, giving us 64,505 for training, 25,800 for validation, and 38,700 for testing. The reason we did not divide them according to some chronological order like the tennis

[9]http://us.battle.net/sc2/en/

data is because the game is evolving. There are at least two major phases of the game: the original release of the game with the subtitle Wings of Liberty (WoL), and an expansion three years later called Heart of the Swarm (HotS). Within each phase, there are many patches that modify the rules, the units or the maps to make the game more balanced and enjoyable. Some of these patches are more important than the others. By mixing up all games, we eliminate the possibility that the training and testing parts being based on very different phases of the game.

The website aligulac.com also contains rich information about these games, from which we select a few that we believe to be the most informative as player features. There are $4,851$ in total, including player's identity, in-game race, nationality[10], overall rating and standard deviation from aligulac.com and rating and standard deviation versus opponent's race from aligulac.com. We also use 40 game features, including the phase of the game (WoL or HotS), game being played online or offline, the quarter of the year in which the game was played and various keyword features contained in the event names that appear most often (e.g. Group, Qualifier, Invitational, Europe, ProLeague, Playoff, Dreamhack, etc.).

Context-Sensitive Preference Datasets. For our experiments, the ideal setting for collecting data would be presenting two choices to a human judge in various context and ask them to pick one over the other. However, there is no such a dataset that is publicly available as far as we know. Instead, we take the datasets from context-aware recommender systems and process them into the format we need. In these datasets, each entry is a user's rating for a given item under certain context. We group all the entries by user and context. Within each group, for any two items with different ratings, we can generate a pairwise comparison along with the context. The datasets we use are:

1. The Food dataset from [33]. It contains $4,036$ comparisons among 20 food menus from 212 users[11]. The user are in three different levels of hunger, each of which could either be real or supposed situation.
2. The Tijuana restaurant dataset from [35]. It is a dataset of 50 people taking questionnaire about their preference on nearby 40 restaurants. There are two different contexts: time (weekday or weekend) and location (at school, work or home) when the options are provided. We generate $4,041$ comparisons in total.
3. The DePaul movie dataset from [46]. 97 students of DePaul University participated in an online survey regarding 79 movies for different occasions. The context contains time (weekday, weekend or N/A), location (home, cinema or N/A) and companion (alone, partner, family or N/A). We create $26,264$ comparisons out of the original data.

Each dataset is randomly divided into training, validation and testing in a roughly $5:2:3$ ratio.

5.3.2 Empirical results

The results are in Table 1, 2, 3 and 4. In each table, we separate the baselines and our methods with a horizontal double line. In the lower section for our models, different training options are blocked and ordered according to increasing information for training: featureless for using only player/item's identity, NOACT and TANH for using all the player/item features, and the rest for using both player/item and game/context features. There are fewer rows in Table 3 and 4 than in Table 1 and 2. This is because we do not have additional item features there and therefore some methods are essentially the same.

How do our models compare against the baselines across different applications? Overall, our methods are favored against all the baselines. In all of the four tables, the best results appear in the sections of our models that use all information available. We also do paired t-tests between our best results and the best baselines[12], and all of them pass 0.05 significance level except for the accuracy on Food and WTA, for which we have a p-value of 0.76 and 0.18 against rote. When comparing our best results among "TANH" and "NOACT" with pairwise logistic regression, all of which only use player features, ours are also always better except for the accuracy on WTA (p-value of 0.07, while others are less than 0.05). On the other hand, our featureless model do not always beat its featureless counterparts in the baselines. This is similar to what we found in [10], where we need to include a Bradley-Terry-like bias term in our model in order to surpass the baselines on certain datasets. In terms of the extent of improvement over the best baselines, the results on *Starcraft II*, Tijuana and DePaul stand out.

How do additional player features affect the models? Comparing "featureless" with NOACT/TANH in Table 1 and 2, we can see the positive effect of adding additional player features, and all of the comparisons pass a $p < 0.05$ paired t-test. Moreover, the player features we use for tennis seem to be more influential than those used for *Starcraft II* (more than 5% boost versus about 1% in accuracy). Our conjecture is that the world ranking and points features, as well as the betting companies' odds features are the ones responsible. By using them, we are bootstrapping from other unknown prediction models. To test it, we run experiments while withholding some of these features. The results on ATP and WTA are quite similar: when the betting odds features are withheld, the performance dropped to around halfway in between TANH and "featureless". On the other hand, it is only slightly pushed down when the world ranking and points features are withheld. This suggests that the betting odds features are crucial in the improvement of performance on tennis data.

Does the contextual information have different effects in the two domains? Yes. Looking at the improvements between the best results with and without the game/context features, it seems the preference modeling, especially on Tijuana and DePaul, benefits more. In terms of accuracy, they both gain about 8%, while on matchup data it is around 1% (all pass $p < 0.05$ t-test except for WTA with p-value of 0.18). This suggests that in competition, the outcome depends more on the players' intrinsic properties than the environmental factors, while for human preference, the context in which the decision is made plays a much more important role.

Which training options are preferred? TANH appears to be better than NOACT for both log likelihood and accuracy and on all the datasets. When it comes to the choice between CONCAT and SPLIT, the choice is less clear. There are few occasions where SPLIT beats CONCAT as the bold numbers suggest, but usually not by a lot. On the other hand, SPLIT can be outperformed by the methods without using contextual features, on the tennis datasets for example. The significance tests suggest that TANH beats NOACT and CONCAT beats SPLIT in all scenarios ($p < 0.05$) except accuracy of TANH against NOACT on WTA and log-likelihood of CONCAT against SPLIT on Tijuana (both with p-values of 0.27).

[10] We think it is an important feature as the *Starcraft II* competitive scene is mostly dominated by Korean players.

[11] We directly use the data processed by [31], which can be found at https://github.com/trungngv/gpfm

[12] The t-tests here and hereafter are done on 10 random splits of the datasets, with hyperparameters fixed to the optimal values obtained from the main experiments. Bonferroni correction is used for multple comparisons.

Model	ATP	WTA	*Starcraft II*
rote	−0.6764	−0.6873	−0.5831
Bradley-Terry	−0.6092	−0.6721	−0.5778
Trueskill™	−0.6209	−0.6643	−0.6001
logistic	−0.5777	−0.6229	−0.5808
featureless	−0.6590	−0.6722	−0.5886
NOACT	−0.5974	−0.6174	−0.5299
TANH	−0.5633	−0.5874	−0.5232
NOACT CONCAT	−0.5970	−0.6166	−0.5229
TANH CONCAT	**−0.5616**	**−0.5865**	**−0.5177**
NOACT SPLIT	−0.6051	−0.6283	−0.5249
TANH SPLIT	−0.5981	−0.6228	−0.5178

Table 1: Test log-likelihood on competitive matchup datasets.

Model	ATP	WTA	*Starcraft II*
rote	55.63%	53.52%	68.77%
Bradley-Terry	66.66%	61.26%	69.21%
Trueskill™	66.97%	61.96%	69.82%
logistic	69.89%	68.02%	71.68%
featureless	63.70%	58.45%	73.08%
NOACT	69.72%	68.09%	73.75%
TANH	70.35%	68.46%	74.07%
NOACT CONCAT	69.86%	68.20%	74.22%
TANH CONCAT	**70.40%**	**68.62%**	74.66%
NOACT SPLIT	69.41%	67.18%	73.87%
TANH SPLIT	69.87%	68.11%	**75.10%**

Table 2: Test accuracy on competitive matchup datasets.

Model	Food	Tijuana	DePaul
rote	−0.6943	−0.7371	−0.6255
Bradley-Terry	−0.6927	−0.6929	−0.6082
Trueskill™	−0.6720	−0.7014	−0.5916
featureless	−0.6750	−0.6864	−0.6009
NOACT CONCAT	−0.6709	−0.4321	−0.6033
TANH CONCAT	−0.6709	**−0.4108**	**−0.5038**
NOACT SPLIT	−0.6741	−0.5597	−0.5927
TANH SPLIT	**−0.6701**	−0.4207	−0.5531

Table 3: Test log-likelihood on pairwise preference datasets with context.

Model	Food	Tijuana	DePaul
rote	59.08%	50.33%	65.60%
Bradley-Terry	58.33%	54.79%	66.69%
Trueskill™	57.59%	75.33%	67.67%
featureless	59.08%	58.00%	68.21%
NOACT CONCAT	57.34%	81.85%	68.29%
TANH CONCAT	57.26%	**82.10%**	**75.56%**
NOACT SPLIT	58.75%	80.53%	71.13%
TANH SPLIT	**60.81%**	80.36%	73.13%

Table 4: Test accuracy on pairwise preference datasets with context.

As a result, we would suggest TANH CONCAT to be the go-to option of our model.

6. CONCLUSIONS

We presented in this paper a general probabilistic framework for modeling competitive matchup and pairwise preference that can utilize any vectorized player/item and game/context features. We conducted experiments on synthetic datasets that simulate plausible real-world scenarios in both domains. The results demonstrate that our models, while outperforming the baselines, can also approach the theoretical best limit as the number of games/comparisons grows. Experimental results on the real-world datasets also clearly demonstrate the advantage of our models and the benefit of utilizing the additional features. It is interesting to see that the contextual features are more influential in the preference domain than in competitive matchups.

Acknowledgments

We thank Arzoo Katiyar and Yexiang Xue for their valuable suggestions and advice. This research was funded in part through NSF Awards IIS-1247637, IIS-1217686, and IIS-1513692.

7. REFERENCES

[1] Wikipedia page on elo rating system. https://en.wikipedia.org/wiki/Elo_rating_system.

[2] R. P. Adams, G. E. Dahl, and I. Murray. Incorporating side information in probabilistic matrix factorization with gaussian processes. *arXiv preprint arXiv:1003.4944*, 2010.

[3] G. Adomavicius, R. Sankaranarayanan, S. Sen, and A. Tuzhilin. Incorporating contextual information in recommender systems using a multidimensional approach. *ACM Transactions on Information Systems (TOIS)*, 23(1):103–145, 2005.

[4] D. Agarwal and B.-C. Chen. Regression-based latent factor models. In *Proceedings of the 15th ACM SIGKDD international conference on Knowledge discovery and data mining*, pages 19–28. ACM, 2009.

[5] L. Baltrunas and F. Ricci. Context-based splitting of item ratings in collaborative filtering. In *Proceedings of the third ACM conference on Recommender systems*, pages 245–248. ACM, 2009.

[6] C. M. Bishop. *Pattern recognition and machine learning*. springer, 2006.

[7] R. A. Bradley and M. E. Terry. Rank analysis of incomplete block designs: I. the method of paired comparisons. *Biometrika*, pages 324–345, 1952.

[8] M. Cattelan et al. Models for paired comparison data: A review with emphasis on dependent data. *Statistical Science*, 27(3):412–433, 2012.

[9] D. Causeur and F. Husson. A 2-dimensional extension of the bradley–terry model for paired comparisons. *Journal of statistical planning and inference*, 135(2):245–259, 2005.

[10] S. Chen and T. Joachims. Modeling intransitivity in matchup and comparison data. In *Proceedings of The 9th ACM International Conference on Web Search and Data Mining (WSDM)*. ACM, 2016.

[11] W. Chu and Z. Ghahramani. Preference learning with gaussian processes. In *Proceedings of the 22nd international conference on Machine learning*, pages 137–144. ACM, 2005.

[12] W. W. Cohen, R. E. Schapire, and Y. Singer. Learning to order things. In *Advances in Neural Information Processing Systems 10: Proceedings of the 1997 Conference*, volume 10, page 451. MIT Press, 1998.

[13] P. Dangauthier, R. Herbrich, T. Minka, T. Graepel, et al. Trueskill through time: Revisiting the history of chess. In *NIPS*, 2007.

[14] O. Delalleau, E. Contal, E. Thibodeau-Laufer, R. C. Ferrari, Y. Bengio, and F. Zhang. Beyond skill rating: Advanced matchmaking in ghost recon online. *Computational Intelligence and AI in Games, IEEE Transactions on*, 4(3):167–177, 2012.

[15] J. Fürnkranz and E. Hüllermeier. *Preference learning*. Springer, 2010.

[16] W. V. Gehrlein. The probability of intransitivity of pairwise comparisons in individual preference. *Mathematical social sciences*, 17(1):67–75, 1989.

[17] M. E. Glickman. A comprehensive guide to chess ratings. *American Chess Journal*, 3:59–102, 1995.

[18] R. Herbrich, T. Minka, and T. Graepel. Trueskill^{TM}: A bayesian skill rating system. In *Advances in Neural Information Processing Systems*, pages 569–576, 2006.

[19] T.-K. Huang, C.-J. Lin, and R. C. Weng. Ranking individuals by group comparisons. In *Proceedings of the 23rd international conference on Machine learning*, pages 425–432. ACM, 2006.

[20] J. Huber, J. W. Payne, and C. Puto. Adding asymmetrically dominated alternatives: Violations of regularity and the similarity hypothesis. *Journal of consumer research*, pages 90–98, 1982.

[21] D. R. Hunter. Mm algorithms for generalized bradley-terry models. *Annals of Statistics*, pages 384–406, 2004.

[22] T. Joachims et al. Evaluating retrieval performance using clickthrough data., 2003.

[23] T. Joachims, L. Granka, B. Pan, H. Hembrooke, and G. Gay. Accurately interpreting clickthrough data as implicit feedback. In *Proceedings of the 28th annual international ACM SIGIR conference on Research and development in information retrieval*, pages 154–161. ACM, 2005.

[24] D. Jurafsky and J. H. Martin. *Speech & language processing*. Pearson Education India, 2000.

[25] A. Karatzoglou, X. Amatriain, L. Baltrunas, and N. Oliver. Multiverse recommendation: n-dimensional tensor factorization for context-aware collaborative filtering. In *Proceedings of the fourth ACM conference on Recommender systems*, pages 79–86. ACM, 2010.

[26] P. Linares. Are inconsistent decisions better? an experiment with pairwise comparisons. *European Journal of Operational Research*, 193(2):492–498, 2009.

[27] R. D. Luce. *Individual Choice Behavior a Theoretical Analysis*. john Wiley and Sons, 1959.

[28] K. O. May. Intransitivity, utility, and the aggregation of preference patterns. *Econometrica: Journal of the Econometric Society*, pages 1–13, 1954.

[29] I. McHale and A. Morton. A bradley-terry type model for forecasting tennis match results. *International Journal of Forecasting*, 27(2):619–630, 2011.

[30] J. E. Menke and T. R. Martinez. A bradley–terry artificial neural network model for individual ratings in group competitions. *Neural computing and Applications*, 17(2):175–186, 2008.

[31] T. V. Nguyen, A. Karatzoglou, and L. Baltrunas. Gaussian process factorization machines for context-aware recommendations. In *Proceedings of the 37th international ACM SIGIR conference on Research & development in information retrieval*, pages 63–72. ACM, 2014.

[32] S. Nikolenko and A. Sirotkin. A new bayesian rating system for team competitions. In *Proceedings of the 28th International Conference on Machine Learning (ICML-11)*, pages 601–608, 2011.

[33] C. Ono, Y. Takishima, Y. Motomura, and H. Asoh. Context-aware preference model based on a study of difference between real and supposed situation data. *UMAP*, 9:102–113, 2009.

[34] F. Radlinski and T. Joachims. Query chains: learning to rank from implicit feedback. In *Proceedings of the eleventh ACM SIGKDD international conference on Knowledge discovery in data mining*, pages 239–248. ACM, 2005.

[35] X. Ramirez-Garcia and M. García-Valdez. Post-filtering for a restaurant context-aware recommender system. In O. Castillo, P. Melin, W. Pedrycz, and J. Kacprzyk, editors, *Recent Advances on Hybrid Approaches for Designing Intelligent Systems*, volume 547 of *Studies in Computational Intelligence*, pages 695–707. Springer International Publishing, 2014.

[36] S. Rendle, Z. Gantner, C. Freudenthaler, and L. Schmidt-Thieme. Fast context-aware recommendations with factorization machines. In *Proceedings of the 34th international ACM SIGIR conference on Research and development in Information Retrieval*, pages 635–644. ACM, 2011.

[37] P. Resnick and H. R. Varian. Recommender systems. *Communications of the ACM*, 40(3):56–58, 1997.

[38] D. E. Rumelhart, G. E. Hinton, and R. J. Williams. Learning representations by back-propagating errors. *Cognitive modeling*, 5:3, 1988.

[39] Y. Shi, A. Karatzoglou, L. Baltrunas, M. Larson, A. Hanjalic, and N. Oliver. Tfmap: Optimizing map for top-n context-aware recommendation. In *Proceedings of the 35th international ACM SIGIR conference on Research and development in information retrieval*, pages 155–164. ACM, 2012.

[40] I. Simonson and A. Tversky. Choice in context: Tradeoff contrast and extremeness aversion. *JMR, Journal of Marketing Research*, 29(3):281, 1992.

[41] D. H. Stern, R. Herbrich, and T. Graepel. Matchbox: large scale online bayesian recommendations. In *Proceedings of the 18th international conference on World wide web*, pages 111–120. ACM, 2009.

[42] L. L. Thurstone. A law of comparative judgment. *Psychological review*, 34(4):273, 1927.

[43] S. Usami. Individual differences multidimensional bradley-terry model using reversible jump markov chain monte carlo algorithm. *Behaviormetrika*, 37(2):135–155, 2010.

[44] G. N. Yannakakis, M. Maragoudakis, and J. Hallam. Preference learning for cognitive modeling: a case study on entertainment preferences. *Systems, Man and Cybernetics, Part A: Systems and Humans, IEEE Transactions on*, 39(6):1165–1175, 2009.

[45] L. Zhang, J. Wu, Z.-C. Wang, and C.-J. Wang. A factor-based model for context-sensitive skill rating systems. In *Tools with Artificial Intelligence (ICTAI), 2010 22nd IEEE International Conference on*, volume 2, pages 249–255. IEEE, 2010.

[46] Y. Zheng, B. Mobasher, and R. Burke. Carskit: A java-based context-aware recommendation engine. In *Proceedings of the 15th IEEE International Conference on Data Mining Workshops*. IEEE, 2015.

XGBoost: A Scalable Tree Boosting System

Tianqi Chen
University of Washington
tqchen@cs.washington.edu

Carlos Guestrin
University of Washington
guestrin@cs.washington.edu

ABSTRACT

Tree boosting is a highly effective and widely used machine learning method. In this paper, we describe a scalable end-to-end tree boosting system called XGBoost, which is used widely by data scientists to achieve state-of-the-art results on many machine learning challenges. We propose a novel sparsity-aware algorithm for sparse data and weighted quantile sketch for approximate tree learning. More importantly, we provide insights on cache access patterns, data compression and sharding to build a scalable tree boosting system. By combining these insights, XGBoost scales beyond billions of examples using far fewer resources than existing systems.

Keywords

Large-scale Machine Learning

1. INTRODUCTION

Machine learning and data-driven approaches are becoming very important in many areas. Smart spam classifiers protect our email by learning from massive amounts of spam data and user feedback; advertising systems learn to match the right ads with the right context; fraud detection systems protect banks from malicious attackers; anomaly event detection systems help experimental physicists to find events that lead to new physics. There are two important factors that drive these successful applications: usage of effective (statistical) models that capture the complex data dependencies and scalable learning systems that learn the model of interest from large datasets.

Among the machine learning methods used in practice, gradient tree boosting [10][1] is one technique that shines in many applications. Tree boosting has been shown to give state-of-the-art results on many standard classification benchmarks [16]. LambdaMART [5], a variant of tree boosting for ranking, achieves state-of-the-art result for ranking problems. Besides being used as a stand-alone predictor, it is also incorporated into real-world production pipelines for ad click through rate prediction [15]. Finally, it is the de-facto choice of ensemble method and is used in challenges such as the Netflix prize [3].

In this paper, we describe XGBoost, a scalable machine learning system for tree boosting. The system is available as an open source package[2]. The impact of the system has been widely recognized in a number of machine learning and data mining challenges. Take the challenges hosted by the machine learning competition site Kaggle for example. Among the 29 challenge winning solutions [3] published at Kaggle's blog during 2015, 17 solutions used XGBoost. Among these solutions, eight solely used XGBoost to train the model, while most others combined XGBoost with neural nets in ensembles. For comparison, the second most popular method, deep neural nets, was used in 11 solutions. The success of the system was also witnessed in KDDCup 2015, where XGBoost was used by every winning team in the top-10. Moreover, the winning teams reported that ensemble methods outperform a well-configured XGBoost by only a small amount [1].

These results demonstrate that our system gives state-of-the-art results on a wide range of problems. Examples of the problems in these winning solutions include: store sales prediction; high energy physics event classification; web text classification; customer behavior prediction; motion detection; ad click through rate prediction; malware classification; product categorization; hazard risk prediction; massive online course dropout rate prediction. While domain dependent data analysis and feature engineering play an important role in these solutions, the fact that XGBoost is the consensus choice of learner shows the impact and importance of our system and tree boosting.

The most important factor behind the success of XGBoost is its scalability in all scenarios. The system runs more than ten times faster than existing popular solutions on a single machine and scales to billions of examples in distributed or memory-limited settings. The scalability of XGBoost is due to several important systems and algorithmic optimizations. These innovations include: a novel tree learning algorithm is for handling *sparse data*; a theoretically justified weighted quantile sketch procedure enables handling instance weights in approximate tree learning. Parallel and distributed computing makes learning faster which enables quicker model exploration. More importantly, XGBoost exploits out-of-core

[1]Gradient tree boosting is also known as gradient boosting machine (GBM) or gradient boosted regression tree (GBRT)

[2]https://github.com/dmlc/xgboost

[3]Solutions come from of top-3 teams of each competitions.

KDD '16, August 13-17, 2016, San Francisco, CA, USA

DOI: http://dx.doi.org/10.1145/2939672.2939785

computation and enables data scientists to process hundred millions of examples on a desktop. Finally, it is even more exciting to combine these techniques to make an end-to-end system that scales to even larger data with the least amount of cluster resources. The major contributions of this paper is listed as follows:

- We design and build a highly scalable end-to-end tree boosting system.
- We propose a theoretically justified weighted quantile sketch for efficient proposal calculation.
- We introduce a novel sparsity-aware algorithm for parallel tree learning.
- We propose an effective cache-aware block structure for out-of-core tree learning.

While there are some existing works on parallel tree boosting [22, 23, 19], the directions such as out-of-core computation, cache-aware and sparsity-aware learning have not been explored. More importantly, an end-to-end system that combines all of these aspects gives a novel solution for real-world use-cases. This enables data scientists as well as researchers to build powerful variants of tree boosting algorithms [7, 8]. Besides these major contributions, we also make additional improvements in proposing a regularized learning objective, which we will include for completeness.

The remainder of the paper is organized as follows. We will first review tree boosting and introduce a regularized objective in Sec. 2. We then describe the split finding methods in Sec. 3 as well as the system design in Sec. 4, including experimental results when relevant to provide quantitative support for each optimization we describe. Related work is discussed in Sec. 5. Detailed end-to-end evaluations are included in Sec. 6. Finally we conclude the paper in Sec. 7.

2. TREE BOOSTING IN A NUTSHELL

We review gradient tree boosting algorithms in this section. The derivation follows from the same idea in existing literatures in gradient boosting. Specicially the second order method is originated from Friedman et al. [12]. We make minor improvements in the reguralized objective, which were found helpful in practice.

2.1 Regularized Learning Objective

For a given data set with n examples and m features $\mathcal{D} = \{(\mathbf{x}_i, y_i)\}$ ($|\mathcal{D}| = n, \mathbf{x}_i \in \mathbb{R}^m, y_i \in \mathbb{R}$), a tree ensemble model (shown in Fig. 1) uses K additive functions to predict the output.

$$\hat{y}_i = \phi(\mathbf{x}_i) = \sum_{k=1}^{K} f_k(\mathbf{x}_i), \quad f_k \in \mathcal{F}, \tag{1}$$

where $\mathcal{F} = \{f(\mathbf{x}) = w_{q(\mathbf{x})}\}(q : \mathbb{R}^m \to T, w \in \mathbb{R}^T)$ is the space of regression trees (also known as CART). Here q represents the structure of each tree that maps an example to the corresponding leaf index. T is the number of leaves in the tree. Each f_k corresponds to an independent tree structure q and leaf weights w. Unlike decision trees, each regression tree contains a continuous score on each of the leaf, we use w_i to represent score on i-th leaf. For a given example, we will use the decision rules in the trees (given by q) to classify

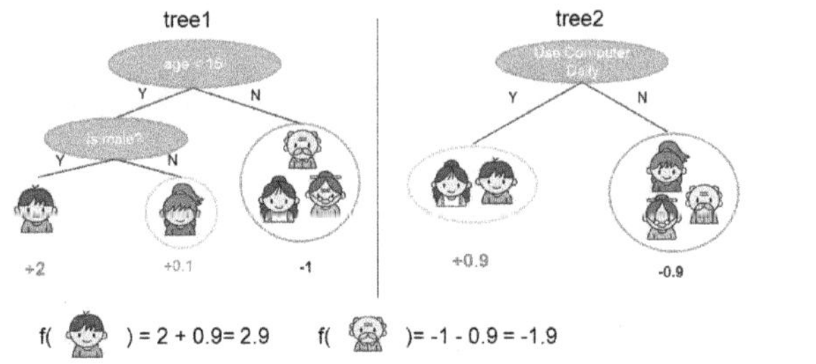

Figure 1: Tree Ensemble Model. The final prediction for a given example is the sum of predictions from each tree.

it into the leaves and calculate the final prediction by summing up the score in the corresponding leaves (given by w). To learn the set of functions used in the model, we minimize the following *regularized* objective.

$$\begin{split} \mathcal{L}(\phi) &= \sum_i l(\hat{y}_i, y_i) + \sum_k \Omega(f_k) \\ \text{where } \Omega(f) &= \gamma T + \frac{1}{2}\lambda \|w\|^2 \end{split} \tag{2}$$

Here l is a differentiable convex loss function that measures the difference between the prediction $\hat{y}_i$ and the target y_i. The second term Ω penalizes the complexity of the model (i.e., the regression tree functions). The additional regularization term helps to smooth the final learnt weights to avoid over-fitting. Intuitively, the regularized objective will tend to select a model employing simple and predictive functions. A similar regularization technique has been used in Regularized greedy forest (RGF) [25] model. Our objective and the corresponding learning algorithm is simpler than RGF and easier to parallelize. When the regularization parameter is set to zero, the objective falls back to the traditional gradient tree boosting.

2.2 Gradient Tree Boosting

The tree ensemble model in Eq. (2) includes functions as parameters and cannot be optimized using traditional optimization methods in Euclidean space. Instead, the model is trained in an additive manner. Formally, let $\hat{y}_i^{(t)}$ be the prediction of the i-th instance at the t-th iteration, we will need to add f_t to minimize the following objective.

$$\mathcal{L}^{(t)} = \sum_{i=1}^{n} l(y_i, \hat{y_i}^{(t-1)} + f_t(\mathbf{x}_i)) + \Omega(f_t)$$

This means we greedily add the f_t that most improves our model according to Eq. (2). Second-order approximation can be used to quickly optimize the objective in the general setting [12].

$$\mathcal{L}^{(t)} \simeq \sum_{i=1}^{n} [l(y_i, \hat{y}^{(t-1)}) + g_i f_t(\mathbf{x}_i) + \frac{1}{2} h_i f_t^2(\mathbf{x}_i)] + \Omega(f_t)$$

where $g_i = \partial_{\hat{y}^{(t-1)}} l(y_i, \hat{y}^{(t-1)})$ and $h_i = \partial^2_{\hat{y}^{(t-1)}} l(y_i, \hat{y}^{(t-1)})$ are first and second order gradient statistics on the loss function. We can remove the constant terms to obtain the following simplified objective at step t.

$$\tilde{\mathcal{L}}^{(t)} = \sum_{i=1}^{n} [g_i f_t(\mathbf{x}_i) + \frac{1}{2} h_i f_t^2(\mathbf{x}_i)] + \Omega(f_t) \tag{3}$$

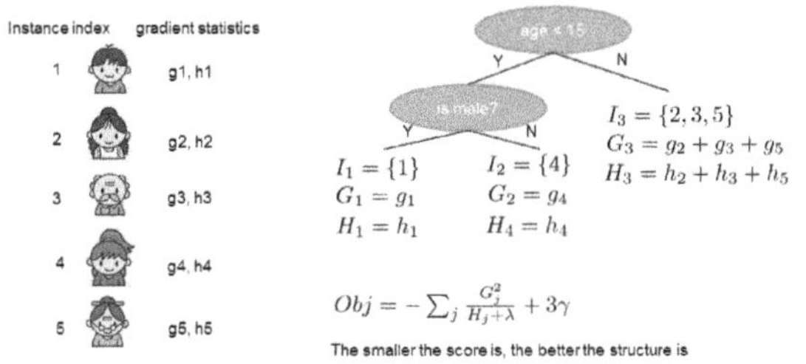

Figure 2: Structure Score Calculation. We only need to sum up the gradient and second order gradient statistics on each leaf, then apply the scoring formula to get the quality score.

Define $I_j = \{i|q(\mathbf{x}_i) = j\}$ as the instance set of leaf j. We can rewrite Eq (3) by expanding Ω as follows

$$\begin{aligned}\tilde{\mathcal{L}}^{(t)} &= \sum_{i=1}^{n}[g_i f_t(\mathbf{x}_i) + \frac{1}{2}h_i f_t^2(\mathbf{x}_i)] + \gamma T + \frac{1}{2}\lambda\sum_{j=1}^{T} w_j^2 \\ &= \sum_{j=1}^{T}[(\sum_{i\in I_j} g_i)w_j + \frac{1}{2}(\sum_{i\in I_j} h_i + \lambda)w_j^2] + \gamma T\end{aligned} \quad (4)$$

For a fixed structure $q(\mathbf{x})$, we can compute the optimal weight w_j^* of leaf j by

$$w_j^* = -\frac{\sum_{i\in I_j} g_i}{\sum_{i\in I_j} h_i + \lambda}, \quad (5)$$

and calculate the corresponding optimal value by

$$\tilde{\mathcal{L}}^{(t)}(q) = -\frac{1}{2}\sum_{j=1}^{T}\frac{(\sum_{i\in I_j} g_i)^2}{\sum_{i\in I_j} h_i + \lambda} + \gamma T. \quad (6)$$

Eq (6) can be used as a scoring function to measure the quality of a tree structure q. This score is like the impurity score for evaluating decision trees, except that it is derived for a wider range of objective functions. Fig. 2 illustrates how this score can be calculated.

Normally it is impossible to enumerate all the possible tree structures q. A greedy algorithm that starts from a single leaf and iteratively adds branches to the tree is used instead. Assume that I_L and I_R are the instance sets of left and right nodes after the split. Lettting $I = I_L \cup I_R$, then the loss reduction after the split is given by

$$\mathcal{L}_{split} = \frac{1}{2}\left[\frac{(\sum_{i\in I_L} g_i)^2}{\sum_{i\in I_L} h_i + \lambda} + \frac{(\sum_{i\in I_R} g_i)^2}{\sum_{i\in I_R} h_i + \lambda} - \frac{(\sum_{i\in I} g_i)^2}{\sum_{i\in I} h_i + \lambda}\right] - \gamma \quad (7)$$

This formula is usually used in practice for evaluating the split candidates.

2.3 Shrinkage and Column Subsampling

Besides the regularized objective mentioned in Sec. 2.1, two additional techniques are used to further prevent overfitting. The first technique is shrinkage introduced by Friedman [11]. Shrinkage scales newly added weights by a factor η after each step of tree boosting. Similar to a learning rate in tochastic optimization, shrinkage reduces the influence of each individual tree and leaves space for future trees to improve the model. The second technique is column (feature) subsampling. This technique is used in RandomForest [4, 13], It is implemented in a commercial software TreeNet [4] for gradient boosting, but is not implemented in existing opensource packages. According to user feedback, using column sub-sampling prevents over-fitting even more so than the traditional row sub-sampling (which is also supported). The usage of column sub-samples also speeds up computations of the parallel algorithm described later.

Algorithm 1: Exact Greedy Algorithm for Split Finding

Input: I, instance set of current node
Input: d, feature dimension
$gain \leftarrow 0$
$G \leftarrow \sum_{i\in I} g_i$, $H \leftarrow \sum_{i\in I} h_i$
for $k = 1$ *to* m **do**
  $G_L \leftarrow 0,\ H_L \leftarrow 0$
  for j *in sorted*$(I$, *by* $\mathbf{x}_{jk})$ **do**
    $G_L \leftarrow G_L + g_j,\ H_L \leftarrow H_L + h_j$
    $G_R \leftarrow G - G_L,\ H_R \leftarrow H - H_L$
    $score \leftarrow \max(score, \frac{G_L^2}{H_L+\lambda} + \frac{G_R^2}{H_R+\lambda} - \frac{G^2}{H+\lambda})$
  end
end
Output: Split with max score

Algorithm 2: Approximate Algorithm for Split Finding

for $k = 1$ *to* m **do**
  Propose $S_k = \{s_{k1}, s_{k2}, \cdots s_{kl}\}$ by percentiles on feature k.
  Proposal can be done per tree (global), or per split(local).
end
for $k = 1$ *to* m **do**
  $G_{kv} \leftarrow= \sum_{j\in\{j|s_{k,v}\geq \mathbf{x}_{jk}>s_{k,v-1}\}} g_j$
  $H_{kv} \leftarrow= \sum_{j\in\{j|s_{k,v}\geq \mathbf{x}_{jk}>s_{k,v-1}\}} h_j$
end
Follow same step as in previous section to find max score only among proposed splits.

3. SPLIT FINDING ALGORITHMS

3.1 Basic Exact Greedy Algorithm

One of the key problems in tree learning is to find the best split as indicated by Eq (7). In order to do so, a split finding algorithm enumerates over all the possible splits on all the features. We call this the *exact greedy algorithm*. Most existing single machine tree boosting implementations, such as scikit-learn [20], R's gbm [21] as well as the single machine version of XGBoost support the exact greedy algorithm. The exact greedy algorithm is shown in Alg. 1. It is computationally demanding to enumerate all the possible splits for continuous features. In order to do so efficiently, the algorithm must first sort the data according to feature values and visit the data in sorted order to accumulate the gradient statistics for the structure score in Eq (7).

3.2 Approximate Algorithm

The exact greedy algorithm is very powerful since it enumerates over all possible splitting points greedily. However, it is impossible to efficiently do so when the data does not fit entirely into memory. Same problem also arises in the dis-

[4]https://www.salford-systems.com/products/treenet

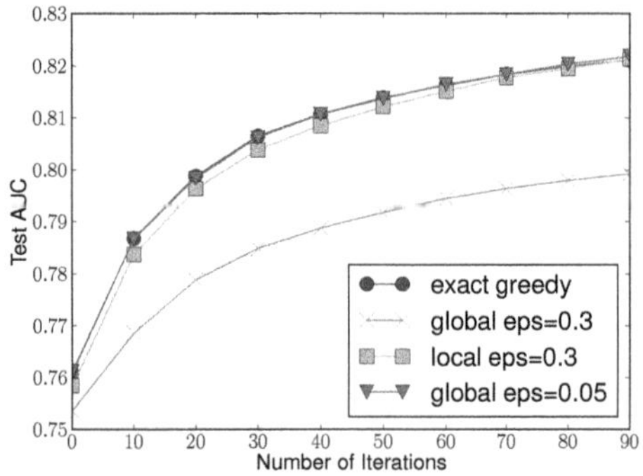

Figure 3: Comparison of test AUC convergence on Higgs 10M dataset. The eps parameter corresponds to the accuracy of the approximate sketch. This roughly translates to 1 / eps buckets in the proposal. We find that local proposals require fewer buckets, because it refine split candidates.

tributed setting. To support effective gradient tree boosting in these two settings, an approximate algorithm is needed.

We summarize an approximate framework, which resembles the ideas proposed in past literatures [17, 2, 22], in Alg. 2. To summarize, the algorithm first proposes candidate splitting points according to percentiles of feature distribution (a specific criteria will be given in Sec. 3.3). The algorithm then maps the continuous features into buckets split by these candidate points, aggregates the statistics and finds the best solution among proposals based on the aggregated statistics.

There are two variants of the algorithm, depending on when the proposal is given. The global variant proposes all the candidate splits during the initial phase of tree construction, and uses the same proposals for split finding at all levels. The local variant re-proposes after each split. The global method requires less proposal steps than the local method. However, usually more candidate points are needed for the global proposal because candidates are not refined after each split. The local proposal refines the candidates after splits, and can potentially be more appropriate for deeper trees. A comparison of different algorithms on a Higgs boson dataset is given by Fig. 3. We find that the local proposal indeed requires fewer candidates. The global proposal can be as accurate as the local one given enough candidates.

Most existing approximate algorithms for distributed tree learning also follow this framework. Notably, it is also possible to directly construct approximate histograms of gradient statistics [22]. It is also possible to use other variants of binning strategies instead of quantile [17]. Quantile strategy benefit from being distributable and recomputable, which we will detail in next subsection. From Fig. 3, we also find that the quantile strategy can get the same accuracy as exact greedy given reasonable approximation level.

Our system efficiently supports exact greedy for the single machine setting, as well as approximate algorithm with both local and global proposal methods for all settings. Users can freely choose between the methods according to their needs.

3.3 Weighted Quantile Sketch

One important step in the approximate algorithm is to propose candidate split points. Usually percentiles of a feature are used to make candidates distribute evenly on the da-

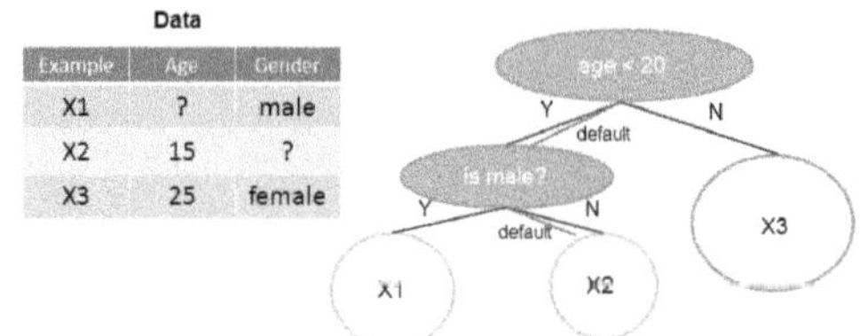

Figure 4: Tree structure with default directions. An example will be classified into the default direction when the feature needed for the split is missing.

ta. Formally, let multi-set $\mathcal{D}_k = \{(x_{1k}, h_1), (x_{2k}, h_2) \cdots (x_{nk}, h_n)\}$ represent the k-th feature values and second order gradient statistics of each training instances. We can define a rank functions $r_k : \mathbb{R} \to [0, +\infty)$ as

$$r_k(z) = \frac{1}{\sum_{(x,h)\in\mathcal{D}_k} h} \sum_{(x,h)\in\mathcal{D}_k, x<z} h, \tag{8}$$

which represents the proportion of instances whose feature value k is smaller than z. The goal is to find candidate split points $\{s_{k1}, s_{k2}, \cdots s_{kl}\}$, such that

$$|r_k(s_{k,j}) - r_k(s_{k,j+1})| < \epsilon, \quad s_{k1} = \min_i \mathbf{x}_{ik}, s_{kl} = \max_i \mathbf{x}_{ik}. \tag{9}$$

Here ϵ is an approximation factor. Intuitively, this means that there is roughly $1/\epsilon$ candidate points. Here each data point is weighted by h_i. To see why h_i represents the weight, we can rewrite Eq (3) as

$$\sum_{i=1}^{n} \frac{1}{2} h_i (f_t(\mathbf{x}_i) - g_i/h_i)^2 + \Omega(f_t) + constant,$$

which is exactly weighted squared loss with labels g_i/h_i and weights h_i. For large datasets, it is non-trivial to find candidate splits that satisfy the criteria. When every instance has equal weights, an existing algorithm called quantile sketch [14, 24] solves the problem. However, there is no existing quantile sketch for the weighted datasets. Therefore, most existing approximate algorithms either resorted to sorting on a random subset of data which have a chance of failure or heuristics that do not have theoretical guarantee.

To solve this problem, we introduced a novel distributed weighted quantile sketch algorithm that can handle weighted data with a *provable theoretical guarantee*. The general idea is to propose a data structure that supports *merge* and *prune* operations, with each operation proven to maintain a certain accuracy level. A detailed description of the algorithm as well as proofs are given in the supplementary material[5] (link in the footnote).

3.4 Sparsity-aware Split Finding

In many real-world problems, it is quite common for the input $\mathbf{x}$ to be sparse. There are multiple possible causes for sparsity: 1) presence of missing values in the data; 2) frequent zero entries in the statistics; and, 3) artifacts of feature engineering such as one-hot encoding. It is important to make the algorithm aware of the sparsity pattern in the data. In order to do so, we propose to add a default direction in each tree node, which is shown in Fig. 4. When a value is missing in the sparse matrix $\mathbf{x}$, the instance is

[5] Link to the supplementary material
http://homes.cs.washington.edu/~tqchen/pdf/xgboost-supp.pdf

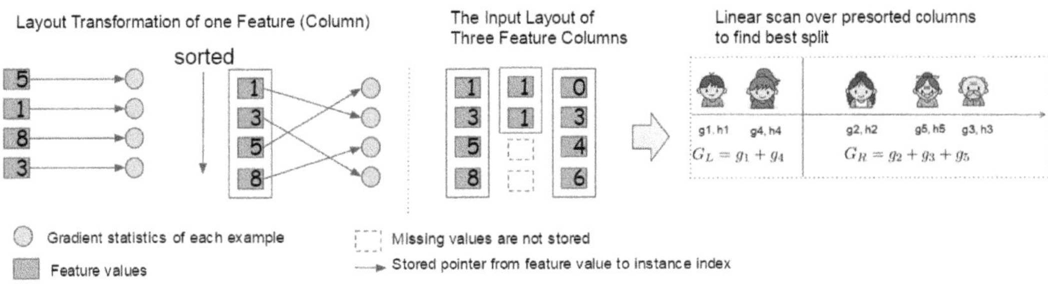

Figure 6: Block structure for parallel learning. Each column in a block is sorted by the corresponding feature value. A linear scan over one column in the block is sufficient to enumerate all the split points.

Algorithm 3: Sparsity-aware Split Finding

Input: I, instance set of current node
Input: $I_k = \{i \in I | x_{ik} \neq \text{missing}\}$
Input: d, feature dimension
Also applies to the approximate setting, only collect statistics of non-missing entries into buckets
$gain \leftarrow 0$
$G \leftarrow \sum_{i \in I} g_i, H \leftarrow \sum_{i \in I} h_i$
for $k = 1$ *to* m **do**
  // *enumerate missing value goto right*
  $G_L \leftarrow 0, \ H_L \leftarrow 0$
  for *j in sorted(I_k, ascent order by* $\mathbf{x}_{jk}$*)* **do**
    $G_L \leftarrow G_L + g_j, \ H_L \leftarrow H_L + h_j$
    $G_R \leftarrow G - G_L, \ H_R \leftarrow H - H_L$
    $score \leftarrow \max(score, \frac{G_L^2}{H_L+\lambda} + \frac{G_R^2}{H_R+\lambda} - \frac{G^2}{H+\lambda})$
  end
  // *enumerate missing value goto left*
  $G_R \leftarrow 0, \ H_R \leftarrow 0$
  for *j in sorted(I_k, descent order by* $\mathbf{x}_{jk}$*)* **do**
    $G_R \leftarrow G_R + g_j, \ H_R \leftarrow H_R + h_j$
    $G_L \leftarrow G - G_R, \ H_L \leftarrow H - H_R$
    $score \leftarrow \max(score, \frac{G_L^2}{H_L+\lambda} + \frac{G_R^2}{H_R+\lambda} - \frac{G^2}{H+\lambda})$
  end
end
Output: Split and default directions with max gain

---

classified into the default direction. There are two choices of default direction in each branch. The optimal default directions are learnt from the data. The algorithm is shown in Alg. 3. The key improvement is to only visit the non-missing entries I_k. The presented algorithm treats the non-presence as a missing value and learns the best direction to handle missing values. The same algorithm can also be applied when the non-presence corresponds to a user specified value by limiting the enumeration only to consistent solutions.

To the best of our knowledge, most existing tree learning algorithms are either only optimized for dense data, or need specific procedures to handle limited cases such as categorical encoding. XGBoost handles all sparsity patterns in a unified way. More importantly, our method exploits the sparsity to make computation complexity linear to number of non-missing entries in the input. Fig. 5 shows the comparison of sparsity aware and a naive implementation on an Allstate-10K dataset (description of dataset given in Sec. 6). We find that the sparsity aware algorithm runs 50 times faster than the naive version. This confirms the importance of the sparsity aware algorithm.

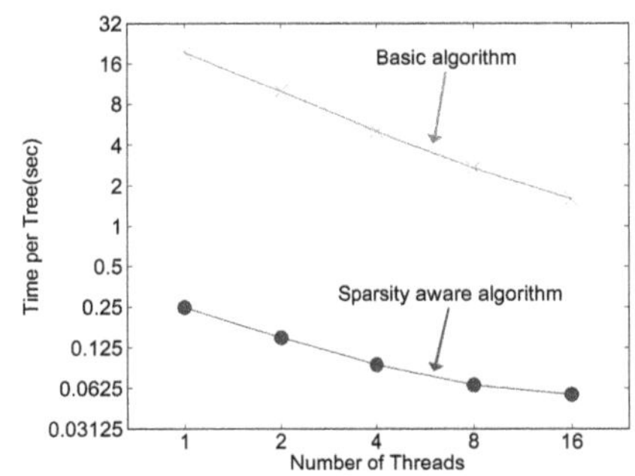

Figure 5: Impact of the sparsity aware algorithm on Allstate-10K. The dataset is sparse mainly due to one-hot encoding. The sparsity aware algorithm is more than 50 times faster than the naive version that does not take sparsity into consideration.

4. SYSTEM DESIGN

4.1 Column Block for Parallel Learning

The most time consuming part of tree learning is to get the data into sorted order. In order to reduce the cost of sorting, we propose to store the data in in-memory units, which we called *block*. Data in each block is stored in the compressed column (CSC) format, with each column sorted by the corresponding feature value. This input data layout only needs to be computed once before training, and can be reused in later iterations.

In the exact greedy algorithm, we store the entire dataset in a single block and run the split search algorithm by linearly scanning over the pre-sorted entries. We do the split finding of all leaves collectively, so one scan over the block will collect the statistics of the split candidates in all leaf branches. Fig. 6 shows how we transform a dataset into the format and find the optimal split using the block structure.

The block structure also helps when using the approximate algorithms. Multiple blocks can be used in this case, with each block corresponding to subset of rows in the dataset. Different blocks can be distributed across machines, or stored on disk in the out-of-core setting. Using the sorted structure, the quantile finding step becomes a *linear scan* over the sorted columns. This is especially valuable for local proposal algorithms, where candidates are generated frequently at each branch. The binary search in histogram aggregation also becomes a linear time merge style algorithm.

Collecting statistics for each column can be *parallelized*, giving us a parallel algorithm for split finding. Importantly, the column block structure also supports column subsampling, as it is easy to select a subset of columns in a block.

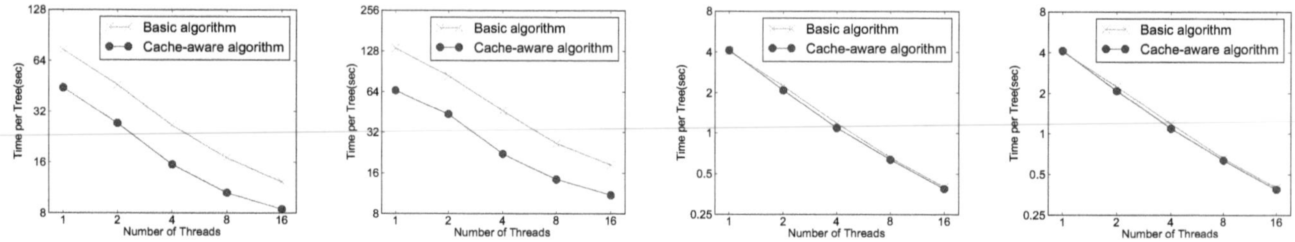

(a) Allstate 10M (b) Higgs 10M (c) Allstate 1M (d) Higgs 1M

Figure 7: Impact of cache-aware prefetching in exact greedy algorithm. We find that the cache-miss effect impacts the performance on the large datasets (10 million instances). Using cache aware prefetching improves the performance by factor of two when the dataset is large.

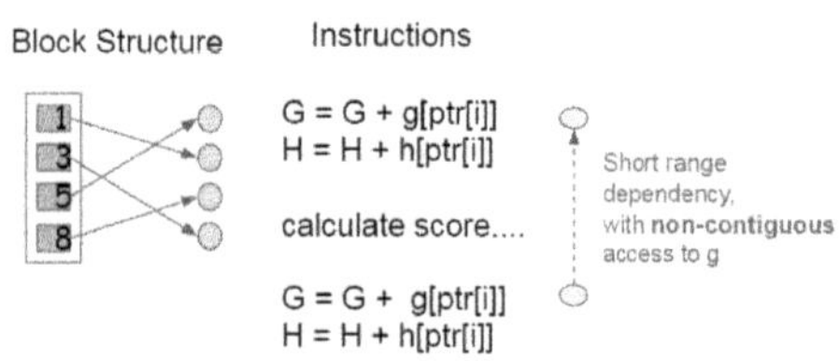

Figure 8: Short range data dependency pattern that can cause stall due to cache miss.

Time Complexity Analysis Let d be the maximum depth of the tree and K be total number of trees. For the exact greedy algorithm, the time complexity of original spase aware algorithm is $O(Kd\|\mathbf{x}\|_0 \log n)$. Here we use $\|\mathbf{x}\|_0$ to denote number of non-missing entries in the training data. On the other hand, tree boosting on the block structure only cost $O(Kd\|\mathbf{x}\|_0 + \|\mathbf{x}\|_0 \log n)$. Here $O(\|\mathbf{x}\|_0 \log n)$ is the one time preprocessing cost that can be amortized. This analysis shows that the block structure helps to save an additional $\log n$ factor, which is significant when n is large. For the approximate algorithm, the time complexity of original algorithm with binary search is $O(Kd\|\mathbf{x}\|_0 \log q)$. Here q is the number of proposal candidates in the dataset. While q is usually between 32 and 100, the log factor still introduces overhead. Using the block structure, we can reduce the time to $O(Kd\|\mathbf{x}\|_0 + \|\mathbf{x}\|_0 \log B)$, where B is the maximum number of rows in each block. Again we can save the additional $\log q$ factor in computation.

4.2 Cache-aware Access

While the proposed block structure helps optimize the computation complexity of split finding, the new algorithm requires indirect fetches of gradient statistics by row index, since these values are accessed in order of feature. This is a non-continuous memory access. A naive implementation of split enumeration introduces immediate read/write dependency between the accumulation and the non-continuous memory fetch operation (see Fig. 8). This slows down split finding when the gradient statistics do not fit into CPU cache and cache miss occur.

For the exact greedy algorithm, we can alleviate the problem by a cache-aware prefetching algorithm. Specifically, we allocate an internal buffer in each thread, fetch the gradient statistics into it, and then perform accumulation in a mini-batch manner. This prefetching changes the direct read/write dependency to a longer dependency and helps to reduce the runtime overhead when number of rows in the is large. Figure 7 gives the comparison of cache-aware vs. non cache-aware algorithm on the the Higgs and the Allstate dataset. We find that cache-aware implementation of the exact greedy algorithm runs twice as fast as the naive version when the dataset is large.

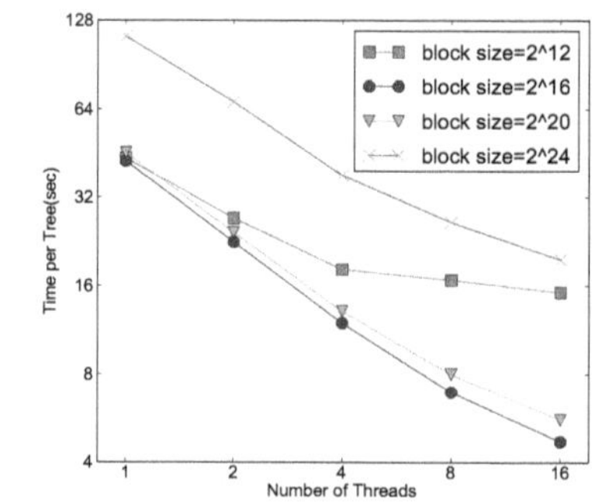

(a) Allstate 10M

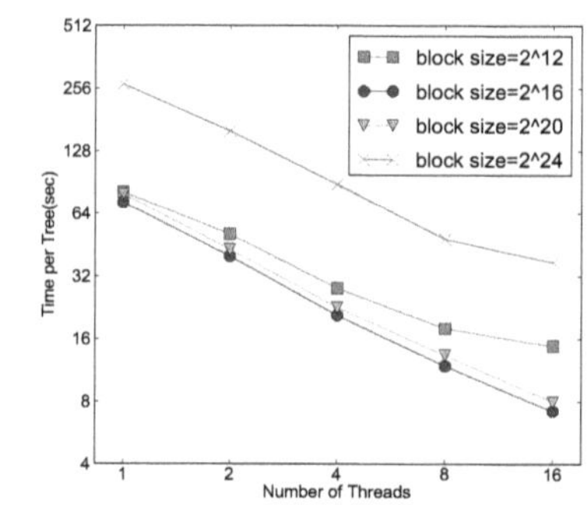

(b) Higgs 10M

Figure 9: The impact of block size in the approximate algorithm. We find that overly small blocks results in inefficient parallelization, while overly large blocks also slows down training due to cache misses.

For approximate algorithms, we solve the problem by choosing a correct block size. We define the block size to be maximum number of examples in contained in a block, as this reflects the cache storage cost of gradient statistics. Choosing an overly small block size results in small workload for each thread and leads to inefficient parallelization. On the other hand, overly large blocks result in cache misses, as the gradient statistics do not fit into the CPU cache. A good choice of block size balances these two factors. We compared various choices of block size on two data sets. The results are given in Fig. 9. This result validates our discussion and

Table 1: Comparison of major tree boosting systems.

System	exact greedy	approximate global	approximate local	out-of-core	sparsity aware	parallel
XGBoost	yes	yes	yes	yes	yes	yes
pGBRT	no	no	yes	no	no	yes
Spark MLLib	no	yes	no	no	partially	yes
H2O	no	yes	no	no	partially	yes
scikit-learn	yes	no	no	no	no	no
R GBM	yes	no	no	no	partially	no

shows that choosing 2^{16} examples per block balances the cache property and parallelization.

4.3 Blocks for Out-of-core Computation

One goal of our system is to fully utilize a machine's resources to achieve scalable learning. Besides processors and memory, it is important to utilize disk space to handle data that does not fit into main memory. To enable out-of-core computation, we divide the data into multiple blocks and store each block on disk. During computation, it is important to use an independent thread to pre-fetch the block into a main memory buffer, so computation can happen in concurrence with disk reading. However, this does not entirely solve the problem since the disk reading takes most of the computation time. It is important to reduce the overhead and increase the throughput of disk IO. We mainly use two techniques to improve the out-of-core computation.

Block Compression The first technique we use is block compression. The block is compressed by columns, and decompressed on the fly by an independent thread when loading into main memory. This helps to trade some of the computation in decompression with the disk reading cost. We use a general purpose compression algorithm for compressing the features values. For the row index, we substract the row index by the begining index of the block and use a 16bit integer to store each offset. This requires 2^{16} examples per block, which is confirmed to be a good setting. In most of the dataset we tested, we achieve roughly a 26% to 29% compression ratio.

Block Sharding The second technique is to shard the data onto multiple disks in an alternative manner. A pre-fetcher thread is assigned to each disk and fetches the data into an in-memory buffer. The training thread then alternatively reads the data from each buffer. This helps to increase the throughput of disk reading when multiple disks are available.

5. RELATED WORKS

Our system implements gradient boosting [10], which performs additive optimization in functional space. Gradient tree boosting has been successfully used in classification [12], learning to rank [5], structured prediction [8] as well as other fields. XGBoost incorporates a regularized model to prevent overfitting. This this resembles previous work on regularized greedy forest [25], but simplifies the objective and algorithm for parallelization. Column sampling is a simple but effective technique borrowed from RandomForest [4]. While sparsity-aware learning is essential in other types of models such as linear models [9], few works on tree learning have considered this topic in a principled way. The algorithm proposed in this paper is the first unified approach to handle all kinds of sparsity patterns.

There are several existing works on parallelizing tree learning [22, 19]. Most of these algorithms fall into the approximate framework described in this paper. Notably, it is also possible to partition data by columns [23] and apply the exact greedy algorithm. This is also supported in our framework, and the techniques such as cache-aware pre-fecthing can be used to benefit this type of algorithm. While most existing works focus on the algorithmic aspect of parallelization, our work improves in two unexplored system directions: out-of-core computation and cache-aware learning. This gives us insights on how the system and the algorithm can be jointly optimized and provides an end-to-end system that can handle large scale problems with very limited computing resources. We also summarize the comparison between our system and existing opensource implementations in Table 1.

Quantile summary (without weights) is a classical problem in the database community [14, 24]. However, the approximate tree boosting algorithm reveals a more general problem – finding quantiles on weighted data. To the best of our knowledge, the weighted quantile sketch proposed in this paper is the first method to solve this problem. The weighted quantile summary is also not specific to the tree learning and can benefit other applications in data science and machine learning in the future.

6. END TO END EVALUATIONS

6.1 System Implementation

We implemented XGBoost as an open source package[6]. The package is portable and reusable. It supports various weighted classification and rank objective functions, as well as user defined objective function. It is available in popular languages such as python, R, Julia and integrates naturally with language native data science pipelines such as scikit-learn. The distributed version is built on top of the rabit library[7] for allreduce. The portability of XGBoost makes it available in many ecosystems, instead of only being tied to a specific platform. The distributed XGBoost runs natively on Hadoop, MPI Sun Grid engine. Recently, we also enable distributed XGBoost on jvm bigdata stacks such as Flink and Spark. The distributed version has also been integrated into cloud platform Tianchi[8] of Alibaba. We believe that there will be more integrations in the future.

6.2 Dataset and Setup

We used four datasets in our experiments. A summary of these datasets is given in Table 2. In some of the experi-

[6]https://github.com/dmlc/xgboost
[7]https://github.com/dmlc/rabit
[8]https://tianchi.aliyun.com

Table 2: Dataset used in the Experiments.

Dataset	n	m	Task
Allstate	10 M	4227	Insurance claim classification
Higgs Boson	10 M	28	Event classification
Yahoo LTRC	473K	700	Learning to Rank
Criteo	1.7 B	67	Click through rate prediction

ments, we use a randomly selected subset of the data either due to slow baselines or to demonstrate the performance of the algorithm with varying dataset size. We use a suffix to denote the size in these cases. For example Allstate-10K means a subset of the Allstate dataset with 10K instances.

The first dataset we use is the Allstate insurance claim dataset[9]. The task is to predict the likelihood and cost of an insurance claim given different risk factors. In the experiment, we simplified the task to only predict the likelihood of an insurance claim. This dataset is used to evaluate the impact of sparsity-aware algorithm in Sec. 3.4. Most of the sparse features in this data come from one-hot encoding. We randomly select 10M instances as training set and use the rest as evaluation set.

The second dataset is the Higgs boson dataset[10] from high energy physics. The data was produced using Monte Carlo simulations of physics events. It contains 21 kinematic properties measured by the particle detectors in the accelerator. It also contains seven additional derived physics quantities of the particles. The task is to classify whether an event corresponds to the Higgs boson. We randomly select 10M instances as training set and use the rest as evaluation set.

The third dataset is the Yahoo! learning to rank challenge dataset [6], which is one of the most commonly used benchmarks in learning to rank algorithms. The dataset contains 20K web search queries, with each query corresponding to a list of around 22 documents. The task is to rank the documents according to relevance of the query. We use the official train test split in our experiment.

The last dataset is the criteo terabyte click log dataset[11]. We use this dataset to evaluate the scaling property of the system in the out-of-core and the distributed settings. The data contains 13 integer features and 26 ID features of user, item and advertiser information. Since a tree based model is better at handling continuous features, we preprocess the data by calculating the statistics of average CTR and count of ID features on the first ten days, replacing the ID features by the corresponding count statistics during the next ten days for training. The training set after preprocessing contains 1.7 billion instances with 67 features (13 integer, 26 average CTR statistics and 26 counts). The entire dataset is more than one terabyte in LibSVM format.

We use the first three datasets for the single machine parallel setting, and the last dataset for the distributed and out-of-core settings. All the single machine experiments are conducted on a Dell PowerEdge R420 with two eight-core Intel Xeon (E5-2470) (2.3GHz) and 64GB of memory. If not specified, all the experiments are run using all the available cores in the machine. The machine settings of the distributed and the out-of-core experiments will be described in the

[9]https://www.kaggle.com/c/ClaimPredictionChallenge
[10]https://archive.ics.uci.edu/ml/datasets/HIGGS
[11]http://labs.criteo.com/downloads/download-terabyte-click-logs/

Table 3: Comparison of Exact Greedy Methods with 500 trees on Higgs-1M data.

Method	Time per Tree (sec)	Test AUC
XGBoost	0.6841	0.8304
XGBoost (colsample=0.5)	0.6401	0.8245
scikit-learn	28.51	0.8302
R.gbm	1.032	0.6224

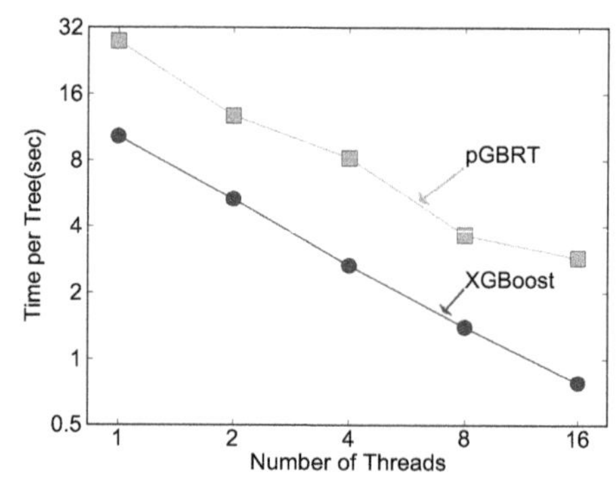

Figure 10: Comparison between XGBoost and pGBRT on Yahoo LTRC dataset.

Table 4: Comparison of Learning to Rank with 500 trees on Yahoo! LTRC Dataset

Method	Time per Tree (sec)	NDCG@10
XGBoost	0.826	0.7892
XGBoost (colsample=0.5)	0.506	0.7913
pGBRT [22]	2.576	0.7915

corresponding section. In all the experiments, we boost trees with a common setting of maximum depth equals 8, shrinkage equals 0.1 and no column subsampling unless explicitly specified. We can find similar results when we use other settings of maximum depth.

6.3 Classification

In this section, we evaluate the performance of XGBoost on a single machine using the exact greedy algorithm on Higgs-1M data, by comparing it against two other commonly used exact greedy tree boosting implementations. Since scikit-learn only handles non-sparse input, we choose the dense Higgs dataset for a fair comparison. We use the 1M subset to make scikit-learn finish running in reasonable time. Among the methods in comparison, R's GBM uses a greedy approach that only expands one branch of a tree, which makes it faster but can result in lower accuracy, while both scikit-learn and XGBoost learn a full tree. The results are shown in Table 3. Both XGBoost and scikit-learn give better performance than R's GBM, while XGBoost runs more than 10x faster than scikit-learn. In this experiment, we also find column subsamples gives slightly worse performance than using all the features. This could due to the fact that there are few important features in this dataset and we can benefit from greedily select from all the features.

6.4 Learning to Rank

We next evaluate the performance of XGBoost on the learning to rank problem. We compare against pGBRT [22], the best previously pubished system on this task. XGBoost

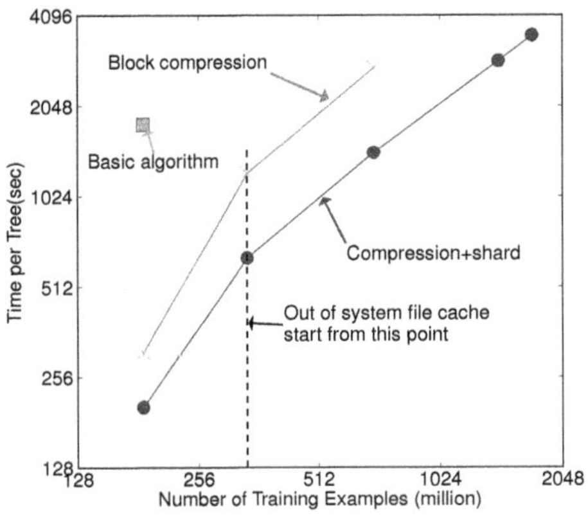

Figure 11: Comparison of out-of-core methods on different subsets of criteo data. The missing data points are due to out of disk space. We can find that basic algorithm can only handle 200M examples. Adding compression gives 3x speedup, and sharding into two disks gives another 2x speedup. The system runs out of file cache start from 400M examples. The algorithm really has to rely on disk after this point. The compression+shard method has a less dramatic slowdown when running out of file cache, and exhibits a linear trend afterwards.

runs exact greedy algorithm, while pGBRT only support an approximate algorithm. The results are shown in Table 4 and Fig. 10. We find that XGBoost runs faster. Interestingly, subsampling columns not only reduces running time, and but also gives a bit higher performance for this problem. This could due to the fact that the subsampling helps prevent overfitting, which is observed by many of the users.

6.5 Out-of-core Experiment

We also evaluate our system in the out-of-core setting on the criteo data. We conducted the experiment on one AWS c3.8xlarge machine (32 vcores, two 320 GB SSD, 60 GB RAM). The results are shown in Figure 11. We can find that compression helps to speed up computation by factor of three, and sharding into two disks further gives 2x speedup. For this type of experiment, it is important to use a very large dataset to drain the system file cache for a real out-of-core setting. This is indeed our setup. We can observe a transition point when the system runs out of file cache. Note that the transition in the final method is less dramatic. This is due to larger disk throughput and better utilization of computation resources. Our final method is able to process 1.7 billion examples on a single machine.

6.6 Distributed Experiment

Finally, we evaluate the system in the distributed setting. We set up a YARN cluster on EC2 with m3.2xlarge machines, which is a very common choice for clusters. Each machine contains 8 virtual cores, 30GB of RAM and two 80GB SSD local disks. The dataset is stored on AWS S3 instead of HDFS to avoid purchasing persistent storage.

We first compare our system against two production-level distributed systems: Spark MLLib [18] and H2O [12]. We use 32 m3.2xlarge machines and test the performance of the systems with various input size. Both of the baseline systems are in-memory analytics frameworks that need to store the data in RAM, while XGBoost can switch to out-of-core setting when it runs out of memory. The results are shown in Fig. 12. We can find that XGBoost runs faster than the baseline systems. More importantly, it is able to take advantage of out-of-core computing and smoothly scale to all 1.7 billion examples with the given limited computing resources. The baseline systems are only able to handle subset of the data with the given resources. This experiment shows the advantage to bring all the system improvement together and solve a real-world scale problem. We also evaluate the scaling property of XGBoost by varying the number of machines. The results are shown in Fig. 13. We can find XGBoost's performance scales linearly as we add more machines. Importantly, XGBoost is able to handle the entire 1.7 billion data with only four machines. This shows the system's potential to handle even larger data.

[12]www.h2o.ai

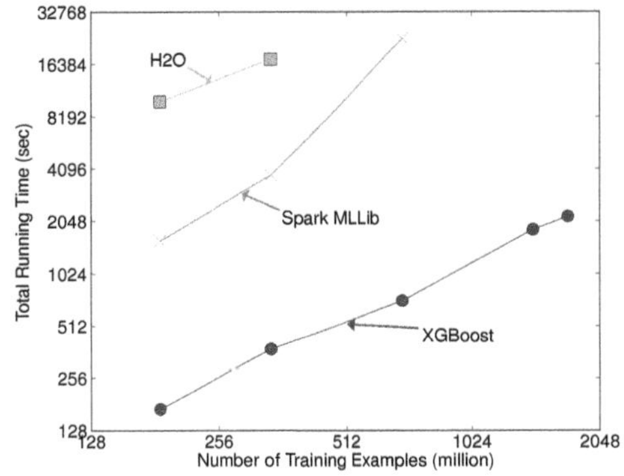

(a) End-to-end time cost include data loading

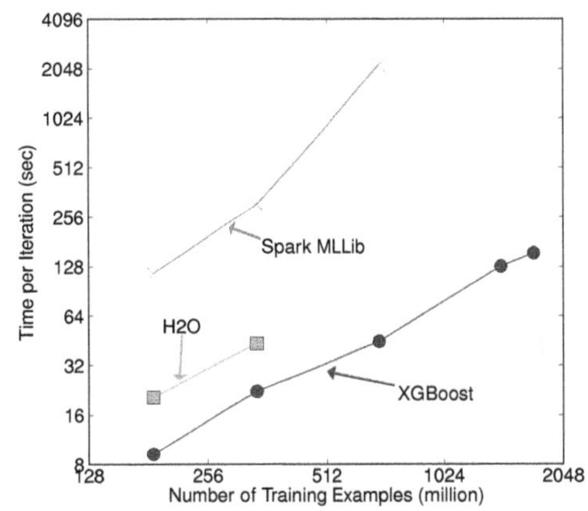

(b) Per iteration cost exclude data loading

Figure 12: Comparison of different distributed systems on 32 EC2 nodes for 10 iterations on different subset of criteo data. XGBoost runs more 10x than spark per iteration and 2.2x as H2O's optimized version (However, H2O is slow in loading the data, getting worse end-to-end time). Note that spark suffers from drastic slow down when running out of memory. XGBoost runs faster and scales smoothly to the full 1.7 billion examples with given resources by utilizing out-of-core computation.

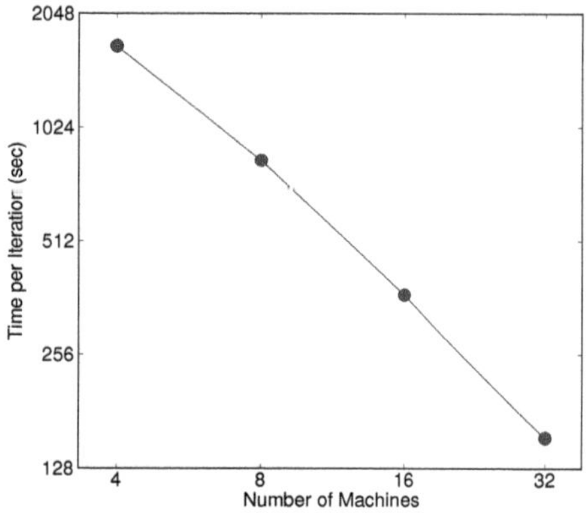

Figure 13: Scaling of XGBoost with different number of machines on criteo full 1.7 billion dataset. Using more machines results in more file cache and makes the system run faster, causing the trend to be slightly super linear. XGBoost can process the entire dataset using as little as four machines, and scales smoothly by utilizing more available resources.

7. CONCLUSION

In this paper, we described the lessons we learnt when building XGBoost, a scalable tree boosting system that is widely used by data scientists and provides state-of-the-art results on many problems. We proposed a novel sparsity aware algorithm for handling sparse data and a theoretically justified weighted quantile sketch for approximate learning. Our experience shows that cache access patterns, data compression and sharding are essential elements for building a scalable end-to-end system for tree boosting. These lessons can be applied to other machine learning systems as well. By combining these insights, XGBoost is able to solve real-world scale problems using a minimal amount of resources.

Acknowledgments

We would like to thank Tyler B. Johnson, Marco Tulio Ribeiro, Sameer Singh, Arvind Krishnamurthy for their valuable feedback. We also sincerely thank Tong He, Bing Xu, Michael Benesty, Yuan Tang, Hongliang Liu, Qiang Kou, Nan Zhu and all other contributors in the XGBoost community. This work was supported in part by ONR (PECASE) N000141010672, NSF IIS 1258741 and the TerraSwarm Research Center sponsored by MARCO and DARPA.

8. REFERENCES

[1] R. Bekkerman. The present and the future of the kdd cup competition: an outsider's perspective.

[2] R. Bekkerman, M. Bilenko, and J. Langford. *Scaling Up Machine Learning: Parallel and Distributed Approaches.* Cambridge University Press, New York, NY, USA, 2011.

[3] J. Bennett and S. Lanning. The netflix prize. In *Proceedings of the KDD Cup Workshop 2007*, pages 3–6, New York, Aug. 2007.

[4] L. Breiman. Random forests. *Maching Learning*, 45(1):5–32, Oct. 2001.

[5] C. Burges. From ranknet to lambdarank to lambdamart: An overview. *Learning*, 11:23–581, 2010.

[6] O. Chapelle and Y. Chang. Yahoo! Learning to Rank Challenge Overview. *Journal of Machine Learning Research - W & CP*, 14:1–24, 2011.

[7] T. Chen, H. Li, Q. Yang, and Y. Yu. General functional matrix factorization using gradient boosting. In *Proceeding of 30th International Conference on Machine Learning (ICML'13)*, volume 1, pages 436–444, 2013.

[8] T. Chen, S. Singh, B. Taskar, and C. Guestrin. Efficient second-order gradient boosting for conditional random fields. In *Proceeding of 18th Artificial Intelligence and Statistics Conference (AISTATS'15)*, volume 1, 2015.

[9] R.-E. Fan, K.-W. Chang, C.-J. Hsieh, X.-R. Wang, and C.-J. Lin. LIBLINEAR: A library for large linear classification. *Journal of Machine Learning Research*, 9:1871–1874, 2008.

[10] J. Friedman. Greedy function approximation: a gradient boosting machine. *Annals of Statistics*, 29(5):1189–1232, 2001.

[11] J. Friedman. Stochastic gradient boosting. *Computational Statistics & Data Analysis*, 38(4):367–378, 2002.

[12] J. Friedman, T. Hastie, and R. Tibshirani. Additive logistic regression: a statistical view of boosting. *Annals of Statistics*, 28(2):337–407, 2000.

[13] J. H. Friedman and B. E. Popescu. Importance sampled learning ensembles, 2003.

[14] M. Greenwald and S. Khanna. Space-efficient online computation of quantile summaries. In *Proceedings of the 2001 ACM SIGMOD International Conference on Management of Data*, pages 58–66, 2001.

[15] X. He, J. Pan, O. Jin, T. Xu, B. Liu, T. Xu, Y. Shi, A. Atallah, R. Herbrich, S. Bowers, and J. Q. n. Candela. Practical lessons from predicting clicks on ads at facebook. In *Proceedings of the Eighth International Workshop on Data Mining for Online Advertising*, ADKDD'14, 2014.

[16] P. Li. Robust Logitboost and adaptive base class (ABC) Logitboost. In *Proceedings of the Twenty-Sixth Conference Annual Conference on Uncertainty in Artificial Intelligence (UAI'10)*, pages 302–311, 2010.

[17] P. Li, Q. Wu, and C. J. Burges. Mcrank: Learning to rank using multiple classification and gradient boosting. In *Advances in Neural Information Processing Systems 20*, pages 897–904. 2008.

[18] X. Meng, J. Bradley, B. Yavuz, E. Sparks, S. Venkataraman, D. Liu, J. Freeman, D. Tsai, M. Amde, S. Owen, D. Xin, R. Xin, M. J. Franklin, R. Zadeh, M. Zaharia, and A. Talwalkar. MLlib: Machine learning in apache spark. *Journal of Machine Learning Research*, 17(34):1–7, 2016.

[19] B. Panda, J. S. Herbach, S. Basu, and R. J. Bayardo. Planet: Massively parallel learning of tree ensembles with mapreduce. *Proceeding of VLDB Endowment*, 2(2):1426–1437, Aug. 2009.

[20] F. Pedregosa, G. Varoquaux, A. Gramfort, V. Michel, B. Thirion, O. Grisel, M. Blondel, P. Prettenhofer, R. Weiss, V. Dubourg, J. Vanderplas, A. Passos, D. Cournapeau, M. Brucher, M. Perrot, and E. Duchesnay. Scikit-learn: Machine learning in Python. *Journal of Machine Learning Research*, 12:2825–2830, 2011.

[21] G. Ridgeway. *Generalized Boosted Models: A guide to the gbm package.*

[22] S. Tyree, K. Weinberger, K. Agrawal, and J. Paykin. Parallel boosted regression trees for web search ranking. In *Proceedings of the 20th international conference on World wide web*, pages 387–396. ACM, 2011.

[23] J. Ye, J.-H. Chow, J. Chen, and Z. Zheng. Stochastic gradient boosted distributed decision trees. In *Proceedings of the 18th ACM Conference on Information and Knowledge Management*, CIKM '09.

[24] Q. Zhang and W. Wang. A fast algorithm for approximate quantiles in high speed data streams. In *Proceedings of the 19th International Conference on Scientific and Statistical Database Management*, 2007.

[25] T. Zhang and R. Johnson. Learning nonlinear functions using regularized greedy forest. *IEEE Transactions on Pattern Analysis and Machine Intelligence*, 36(5), 2014.

Robust Influence Maximization

Wei Chen
Microsoft Research
weic@microsoft.com

Tian Lin
Tsinghua University
lint10@mails.tsinghua.edu.cn

Zihan Tan
IIIS, Tsinghua University
zihantan1993@gmail.com

Mingfei Zhao
IIIS, Tsinghua University
mingfeizhao@hotmail.com

Xuren Zhou
The Hong Kong University of Science and Technology
xzhouap@cse.ust.hk

ABSTRACT

In this paper, we address the important issue of uncertainty in the edge influence probability estimates for the well studied influence maximization problem — the task of finding k seed nodes in a social network to maximize the influence spread. We propose the problem of robust influence maximization, which maximizes the worst-case ratio between the influence spread of the chosen seed set and the optimal seed set, given the uncertainty of the parameter input. We design an algorithm that solves this problem with a solution-dependent bound. We further study uniform sampling and adaptive sampling methods to effectively reduce the uncertainty on parameters and improve the robustness of the influence maximization task. Our empirical results show that parameter uncertainty may greatly affect influence maximization performance and prior studies that learned influence probabilities could lead to poor performance in robust influence maximization due to relatively large uncertainty in parameter estimates, and information cascade based adaptive sampling method may be an effective way to improve the robustness of influence maximization.

Keywords

social networks, influence maximization, robust optimization, information diffusion

1. INTRODUCTION

In social and economic networks, *Influence Maximization* problem has been extensively studied over the past decade, due to its wide applications to viral marketing [13, 19], outbreak detection [22], rumor monitoring [6], etc. For example, a company may conduct a promotion campaign in social networks by sending free samples to the initial users (termed as seeds), and via the word-of-mouth (WoM) effect, more and more users are influenced by social links to join the campaign and propagate messages of the promotion. This problem is first introduced by Kempe et al. [19] under an algorithmic framework to find the most influential seeds, and they propose the *independent cascade* model and *linear threshold* model, which consider the social-psychological factors of information diffusion to simulate such a random process of adoptions.

Since Kempe et al.'s seminal work, extensive researches have been done on influence maximization, especially on improving the efficiency of influence maximization in the independent cascade model [11, 10, 16, 4, 28], all of which assume that the ground-truth influence probabilities on edges are exactly known. Separately, a number of studies [26, 27, 15, 25, 24] propose learning methods to extract edge influence probabilities. Due to inherent data limitation, no learning method could recover the exact values of the edge probabilities, and what can be achieved is the estimates on the true edge probabilities, with confidence intervals indicating that the true values are within the confidence intervals with high probability. The uncertainty in edge probability estimates, however, may adversely affect the performance of the influence maximization task, but this topic has left mostly unexplored. The only attempt addressing this question is a recent study in [18], but due to a technical issue as explained in [18], the results achieved by the study is rather limited.

In this paper, we utilize the concept of robust optimization [3] in operation research to address the issue of influence maximization with uncertainty. In particular, we consider that the input to the influence maximization task is no longer edge influence probability on every edge of a social graph, but instead an interval in which the true probability may lie. Thus the input is actually a parameter space Θ, which is the product of all intervals on all edges. For any seed set S, let $\sigma_\theta(S)$ denote the *influence spread* of S under parameter setting $\theta \in \Theta$. Then we define *robust ratio* of S as $g(\Theta, S) = \min_{\theta\in\Theta} \frac{\sigma_\theta(S)}{\sigma_\theta(S_\theta^*)}$, where S_θ^* is the optimal seed set achieving the maximum influence spread under parameter θ. Intuitively, robust ratio of S indicates the (multiplicative) gap between its influence spread and the optimal influence spread under the worse-case parameter $\theta \in \Theta$, since we are unsure which $\theta \in \Theta$ is the true probability setting. Then our optimization task is to find a seed set of size k that maximize the robust ratio under the known parameter space Θ — we call this task *Robust Influence Maximization (RIM)*.

It is clear that when there is no uncertainty on edge probabilities, which means Θ collapses to the single true parameter θ, RIM degenerates to the classical influence maximization problem. However, when uncertainty exists, solving RIM may be a more difficult task. In this paper, we first pro-

KDD '16, August 13 - 17, 2016, San Francisco, CA, USA

ISBN 978-1-4503-4232-2/16/08...$15.00

DOI: http://dx.doi.org/10.1145/2939672.2939745

pose an algorithm LUGreedy that solves the RIM task with a solution-dependent bound on its performance, which means that one can verify its performance after it selects the seed set (Section 3). We then show that if the input parameter space Θ is only given and cannot be improved, it is possible that even the best robust ratio in certain graph instances could be very small (e.g. $O(\log n/\sqrt{n})$ with n being the number of nodes in the graph). This motivates us to study sampling methods to further tighten parameter space Θ, and thus improving the robustness of our algorithm (Section 4). In particular, we study both uniform sampling and adaptive sampling for improving RIM performance. For uniform sampling, we provide theoretical results on the sample complexity for achieving a given robust ratio of the output seed set. For adaptive sampling, we propose an information cascade based sampling heuristic to adaptively bias our sampling effort to important edges often traversed by information cascades. Through extensive empirical evaluations (Section 5), we show that (a) robust ratio is sensitive to the width of the confidence interval, and it decreases rapidly when the width of the confidence interval increases; as a result prior studies that learned edge probabilities may result in poor robust ratio due to relative large confidence intervals (and thus high uncertainty); (b) information cascade based adaptive sampling method performs better than uniform sampling and other baseline sampling methods, and can significantly improve the robustness of the influence maximization task.

In summary, the contribution of our paper includes: (a) proposing the problem of robust influence maximization to address the important issue of uncertainty in parameter estimates adversely impacting the influence maximization task; (b) providing the LUGreedy algorithm that guarantees a solution-dependent bound; and (c) studying uniform and adaptive sampling methods to improve robust influence maximization.

Due to space constraint, the proofs of some technical results are omitted. The complete proofs of all results can be found in the full technical report [9].

1.1 Additional Related Work

Influence maximization has been extensively studied and we already point out a number of closely related studies to our work in the introduction. For a comprehensive survey, one can refer to the monograph [8]. We discuss a few most relevant work in more detail here.

To the best of our knowledge, the study by He and Kempe [18] is the only attempt prior to our work that also tries to address the issue of uncertainty of parameter estimates impacting the influence maximization tasks. However, besides the similarity in motivation, the technical treatments are quite different. First, their central problem, called influence difference maximization, is to find a seed set of size k that maximizes the additive difference between the two influence spreads of the *same* seed set using different parameter values. Their purpose is to see how large the influence gap could be due to the uncertainty in parameter space. However, our goal is still to find the best possible seed set for influence maximization purpose, while considering the adverse effect of the uncertainty, and thus we utilize the robust optimization concept and use the worse-case multiplicative ratio between the influence spread of the chosen seed set and the optimal seed set as our objective function. Second, their influence difference maximization turns out to be hard to approximate to any reasonable ratio, while we provide an actual algorithm for robust influence maximization that has both a theoretical solution-dependent bound and performs reasonably well in experiments. Third, we further consider using sampling methods to improve RIM, which is not discussed in [18].

In the context of robust optimization, Krause et al.'s work on robust submodular optimization [20] is possibly the closest to ours. Our RIM problem can be viewed as a specific instance of robust submodular optimization studied in [20]. However, due to the generality of problem scope studied in [20], they show strong hardness results and then they have to resolve to bi-criteria solutions. Instead, we are working on a particular instance of robust submodular optimization, and their bi-criteria solution may greatly enlarge the selected seed set size, which may not be allowed in our case. Furthermore, they work on finite set of submodular functions, but in our case our objective function is parametrized with θ from a continuous parameter space Θ, and it is unclear how their results work for the continuous case.

In a parallel work that will appear in the same proceeding, He and Kempe study the same subject of robust influence maximization [17], but they follow the bi-criteria approximation approach of [20], and thus in general their results are orthogonal to ours. In particular, they use essentially the same objective function, but they work on a finite set of influence spread functions Σ, and require to find $k \cdot \ln|\Sigma|$ seeds to achieve $1 - 1/e$ approximation ratio comparing to the optimal seed set of size k; when working on continuous parameter space Θ, they show that it is equivalent to a finite spread function space of size 2^n and thus requiring $\Theta(kn)$ seeds for a bi-criteria solution, which renders the bi-criteria solution useless. Thus their bi-criteria approach is suitable when the set of possible spread functions Σ is small.

Adaptive sampling for improving RIM bears some resemblance to pure exploration bandit research [5], especially to combinatorial pure exploration [7] recently studied. Both use adaptive sampling and achieve some optimization objective in the end. However, the optimization problem modeled in combinatorial pure exploration [7] does not have a robustness objective. Studying robust optimization together with combinatorial pure exploration could be a potentially interesting topic for future research. Another recent work [21] uses online algorithms to maximize the expected coverage of the union of influenced nodes in multiple rounds based on online feedbacks, and thus is different from our adaptive sampling objective: we use feedbacks to adjust adaptive sampling in order to find a seed set nearly maximizing the robust ratio after the sampling is done.

2. MODEL AND PROBLEM DEFINITION

As in [19], the *independent cascade (IC)* model can be equivalently modeled as a stochastic diffusion process from seed nodes or as reachability from seed nodes in random live-edge graphs. For brevity, we provide the live-edge graph description below. Consider a graph $G = (V, E)$ comprising a set V of nodes and a set E of directed edges, where every edge e is associated with probability $p_e \in [0, 1]$, and let $n = |V|$ and $m = |E|$. To generate a random live-edge graph, we declare each edge e as *live* if flipping a biased random coin with probability p_e returns success, declare e as *blocked* otherwise (with probability $1 - p_e$). The randomness on all edges are mutually independent. We define the subgraph L

Algorithm 1 Greedy(G, k, θ)

Input: Graph G, budget k, parameter vector θ

$S_0 \leftarrow \emptyset$
for $i = 1, 2, \ldots, k$ **do**
  $v \leftarrow \arg\max_{v \notin S_i} \{\sigma_\theta(S_{i-1} \cup \{v\}) - \sigma_\theta(S_{i-1})\}$
  $S_i \leftarrow S_{i-1} \cup \{v\}$
end for
return S_k

consisting of V and the set of live edges as the (random) *live-edge graph.* Given any set $S \subseteq V$ (referred as *seeds*), let $R_L(S) \subseteq V$ denote the *reachable set* of nodes from S in live-edge graph L, i.e., (1) $S \subseteq R_L(S)$, and (2) for a node $v \notin S$, $v \in R_L(S)$ iff there is a path in L directing from some node in S to v.

For convenience, we use *parameter vector* $\theta = (p_e)_{e \in E}$ to denote the probabilities on all edges. The *influence spread* function $\sigma_\theta(S)$ is defined as the expected size of the reachable set from S, that is

$$\sigma_\theta(S) := \sum_L \Pr_\theta[L] \cdot |R_L(S)|,$$

where $\Pr_\theta[L]$ is the probability of yielding live-edge graph L under vector θ. From [19], we know that the influence spread function is non-negative ($\forall S \subseteq V$, $\sigma_\theta(S) \geq 0$), monotone ($\forall S \subseteq T \subseteq V$, $\sigma_\theta(S) \leq \sigma_\theta(T)$), and submodular ($\forall S \subseteq T \subseteq V$, $\forall v \in V$ $\sigma_\theta(S \cup \{v\}) - \sigma_\theta(S) \geq \sigma_\theta(T \cup \{v\}) - \sigma_\theta(T)$).

The well-known problem of *Influence Maximization* raised in [19] is stated in the following.

PROBLEM 1 (INFLUENCE MAXIMIZATION [19]). *Given a graph $G = (V, E)$, parameter vector $\theta = (p_e)_{e \in E}$ and a fixed budget k, we are required to find a seed set $S \subseteq V$ of k vertices, such that the influence spread function $\sigma_\theta(S)$ is maximized, that is,*

$$S_\theta^* := \arg\max_{S \subseteq V, |S| = k} \sigma_\theta(S).$$

It has been shown that Influence Maximization problem is NP-hard [19]. Since the objective function $\sigma_\theta(S)$ is submodular, we have a $(1 - \frac{1}{e})$ approximation using standard greedy policy Greedy(G, k, θ) in Algorithm 1 (assuming a value oracle on function $\sigma_\theta(\cdot)$). Let S_θ^g be the solution of Greedy(G, k, θ). As a convention, we assume that both optimal seed set S_θ^* and greedy seed set S_θ^g in this paper are of fixed size k implicitly.

On the other hand, it is proved by Feige [14] that such an approximation ratio could not be improved for k-max cover problem, which is a special case of the influence maximization problem under the IC model.

However, the knowledge of the probability on edges is usually acquired by learning from the real-world data [26, 27, 15, 25, 24], and the obtained estimates always have some inaccuracy comparing to the true value. Therefore, it is natural to assume that, from observations of edge e, we can obtain the statistically significant neighborhood $[l_e, r_e]$, i.e., the *confidence interval* where the true probability p_e lies in with high probability. This confidence interval prescribes the uncertainty on the true probability p_e of the edge e, and such uncertainty on edges may adversely impact the influence maximization task. Motivated by this, we study the problem of *robust influence maximization* as specified below.

Suppose for every edge e, we are given an interval $[l_e, r_e]$ ($0 \leq l_e \leq r_e \leq 1$) indicating the range of the probability, and the ground-truth probability $p_e \in [l_e, r_e]$ of this edge is unknown. Denote $\Theta = \times_{e \in E}[l_e, r_e]$ as the *parameter space* of network G, and $\theta = (p_e)_{e \in E}$ as the latent parameter vector. Specifically, let $\theta^-(\Theta) = (l_e)_{e \in E}$ and $\theta^+(\Theta) = (r_e)_{e \in E}$ as the minimum and maximum parameter vectors, respectively, and when the context is clear, we would only use θ^- and θ^+. For a seed set $S \subseteq V$ and $|S| = k$, define its *robust ratio* under parameter space Θ as

$$g(\Theta, S) := \min_{\theta \in \Theta} \frac{\sigma_\theta(S)}{\sigma_\theta(S_\theta^*)}, \tag{1}$$

where S_θ^* is the optimal solution of size k when the probability on every edge is given by θ.

Given Θ and solution S, the robust ratio $g(\Theta, S)$ characterizes the *worst-case* ratio of influence spread of S and the underlying optimal one, when the true probability vector θ is unknown (except knowing that $\theta \in \Theta$). Then, the *Robust Influence Maximization* (RIM) problem is defined as follows.

PROBLEM 2 (ROBUST INFLUENCE MAXIMIZATION). *Given a graph $G = (V, E)$, parameter space $\Theta = \times_{e \in E}[l_e, r_e]$ and a fixed budget k, we are required to find a set $S \subseteq V$ of k vertices, such that robust ratio $g(\Theta, S)$ is maximized, i.e.,*

$$S_\Theta^* := \arg\max_{S \subseteq V, |S| = k} g(\Theta, S) = \arg\max_{S \subseteq V, |S| = k} \min_{\theta \in \Theta} \frac{\sigma_\theta(S)}{\sigma_\theta(S_\theta^*)}.$$

The objective of this problem is to find a seed set S_Θ^* that has the largest robust ratio, that is, S_Θ^* should maximize the worst-case ratio between its influence spread and the optimal influence spread, when the true probability vector θ is unknown. When there is no uncertainty, which means Θ collapses to the true probability θ, we can see that the RIM problem is reduced back to the original influence maximization problem.

In RIM, the knowledge of the confidence interval is assumed to be the input. Another interpretation is that, it can be viewed as given an estimate of probability vector $\hat{\theta} = (\hat{p}_e)_{e \in E}$ with a perturbation level δ_e on each edge e, such that the true probability $p_e \in [\hat{p}_e - \delta_e, \hat{p}_e + \delta_e] = [l_e, r_e]$, which constitutes parameter space $\Theta = \times_{e \in E}[l_e, r_e]$. Notice that, in reality, this probability could be obtained via edge samplings, i.e., we make samples on edges and compute the fraction of times that the edge is live. On the other hand, we can also observe information cascades on each edge when collecting the trace of diffusion in the real world, so that the corresponding probability can be learned.

However, when the amount of observed information cascade is small, the best robust ratio $\max_S g(\Theta, S)$ for the given Θ can be low so that the output for a RIM algorithm does not have a good enough guarantee of the performance in the worst case. Then a natural question is, given Θ, how to further make samples on edges (e.g., activating source node u of an edge (u, v) and see if the sink node v is activated through edge e) so that $\max_S g(\Theta, S)$ can be efficiently improved? To be specific, how to make samples on edges and output Θ' and S' according to the outcome so that (a) with high probability the true value θ lies in the output parameter space Θ', where the randomness is taken according to θ, and (b) $g(\Theta', S')$ is large. This sub-problem is called *Sampling for Improving Robust Influence Maximization*, and will be addressed in Section 4.

Algorithm 2 LUGreedy(G, k, Θ)

Input: Graph $G = (V, E)$, budget k, parameter space $\Theta = \times_{e \in E}[l_e, r_e]$

1: $S^g_{\theta^-} \leftarrow$ Greedy(G, k, θ^-)

2: $S^g_{\theta^+} \leftarrow$ Greedy(G, k, θ^+)

3: **return** $\arg\max_{S \in \{S^g_{\theta^-}, S^g_{\theta^+}\}} \{\sigma_{\theta^-}(S)\}$

3. ALGORITHM AND ANALYSIS FOR RIM

Consider the problem of RIM, parameter space $\Theta = \times_{e \in E}[l_e, r_e]$ is given, and we do not know the true probability $\theta \in \Theta$. Let $\theta^- = (l_e)_{e \in E}$ and $\theta^+ = (r_e)_{e \in E}$.

Our first observation is that, when Θ is a single vector ($l_e = r_e$, $\forall e \in E$), it is trivially reduced to the classical Influence Maximization problem. Therefore, we still have the following hardness result on RIM [19, 14]:

THEOREM 1. *RIM problem is* **NP**-*hard, and for any* $\varepsilon > 0$, *it is* **NP**-*hard to find a seed set* S *with robust ratio at least* $1 - \frac{1}{e} + \varepsilon$.

To circumvent the above hardness result, we develop algorithms that achieves reasonably large robust ratio. When we are not allowed to make new samples on the edges to improve the input interval, it is natural to utilize the greedy algorithm of submodular maximization in [19] (i.e., Algorithm 1) as the subroutine to calculate the solution. In light of this, we first propose Lower-Upper Greedy Algorithm and the solution-dependent bound for $g(\Theta, S)$, and then discuss $g(\Theta, S)$ in the worst-case scenario.

3.1 Lower-Upper Greedy Algorithm

Given parameter space $\Theta = \times_{e \in E}[l_e, r_e]$ with the minimum and maximum parameter vectors $\theta^- = (l_e)_{e \in E}$ and $\theta^+ = (r_e)_{e \in E}$, our *Lower-Upper Greedy algorithm* (LUGreedy(G, k, Θ)) is described in Algorithm 2 which outputs the best seed set S^{LU}_{Θ} for the minimum parameter vector θ^- such that

$$S^{\mathsf{LU}}_{\Theta} := \underset{S \in \{S^g_{\theta^-}, S^g_{\theta^+}\}}{\arg\max} \{\sigma_{\theta^-}(S)\}. \tag{2}$$

To evaluate the performance of this output, we first define the *gap ratio* $\alpha(\Theta) \in [0, 1]$ of the input parameter space to be

$$\alpha(\Theta) := \frac{\sigma_{\theta^-}(S^{\mathsf{LU}}_{\Theta})}{\sigma_{\theta^+}(S^g_{\theta^+})}. \tag{3}$$

Then, LUGreedy achieves the following result:

THEOREM 2 (SOLUTION-DEPENDENT BOUND). *Given a graph* G, *parameter space* Θ *and budget limit* k, LUGreedy *outputs a seed set* S^{LU}_{Θ} *of size* k *such that*

$$g(\Theta, S^{\mathsf{LU}}_{\Theta}) \geq \alpha(\Theta)\left(1 - \frac{1}{e}\right),$$

where $\alpha(\Theta) := \frac{\sigma_{\theta^-}(S^{\mathsf{LU}}_{\Theta})}{\sigma_{\theta^+}(S^g_{\theta^+})}$.

PROOF. For any seed set S, $g(\Theta, S) = \min_{\theta \in \Theta} \frac{\sigma_\theta(S)}{\sigma_\theta(S^*_\theta)}$ by definition. Obviously, it is a fact that $\sigma_\theta(S)$ is monotone on θ for any fixed S. From the definition of optimal solutions and the greedy algorithm, we can get $\sigma_\theta(S^*_\theta) \leq \sigma_{\theta^+}(S^*_\theta) \leq \sigma_{\theta^+}(S^*_{\theta^+}) \leq \frac{\sigma_{\theta^+}(S^g_{\theta^+})}{1-1/e}$. Moreover, it can be implied that

$$g(\Theta, S) \geq \min_{\theta \in \Theta} \frac{\sigma_\theta(S)}{\sigma_{\theta^+}(S^g_{\theta^+})}\left(1 - \frac{1}{e}\right) = \frac{\sigma_{\theta^-}(S)}{\sigma_{\theta^+}(S^g_{\theta^+})}\left(1 - \frac{1}{e}\right).$$

Use seed set S^{LU}_{Θ} from LUGreedy, and it follows immediately that $g(\Theta, S^{\mathsf{LU}}_{\Theta}) \geq \frac{\sigma_{\theta^-}(S^{\mathsf{LU}}_{\Theta})}{\sigma_{\theta^+}(S^g_{\theta^+})}\left(1 - \frac{1}{e}\right) = \alpha(\Theta)\left(1 - \frac{1}{e}\right)$. □

We refer $\alpha(\Theta)(1 - \frac{1}{e})$ as the *solution-dependent bound* of $g(\Theta, S^{\mathsf{LU}}_{\Theta})$ that LUGreedy achieves, because it depends on the solution S^{LU}_{Θ}. The good thing is that it can be evaluated once we have the solution, and then we know the robust ratio must be at least this lower bound. Note that the bound is good if $\alpha(\Theta)$ is not too small, and thus it in turn indicates that the influence spread $\sigma_\theta(S^{\mathsf{LU}}_{\Theta})$ we find has a good performance under any probability vector $\theta \in \Theta$.

It is worth remarking that the choice of using $\alpha(\Theta) = \sigma_{\theta^-}(S^{\mathsf{LU}}_{\Theta})/\sigma_{\theta^+}(S^g_{\theta^+})$ as a measurement is for the following reasons: (a) Intuitively, $S^g_{\theta^-}$ is expected to be the best possible seed set we can find that maximizes $\sigma_{\theta^-}(\cdot)$; (b) Meanwhile, we consider $S^g_{\theta^+}$ as a potential seed set for the later theoretical analysis (in the proof of Theorem 6), which requires the alignment of the same seed set for the numerator and denominator. Thus, $\alpha(\Theta) \geq \max\{\sigma_{\theta^-}(S^g_{\theta^-}), \sigma_{\theta^-}(S^g_{\theta^+})\}/\sigma_{\theta^+}(S^g_{\theta^+})$. In particular, when θ^+ and θ^- tend to the same value θ, RIM is tending towards the classical Influence Maximization, and thus the influence spread $\sigma_\theta(S^{\mathsf{LU}}_{\Theta})$ can be close to the best possible result $\sigma_\theta(S^g_\theta)$. The approach adopted by LUGreedy is similar to the sandwich approximation used in [23].

The following example shows that for certain problem instances, the gap ratio $\alpha(\Theta)$ of LUGreedy could match the robust ratio $g(\Theta, S^{\mathsf{LU}}_{\Theta})$, which also matches the best possible robust ratio $\max_{|S|=k} g(\Theta, S)$.

EXAMPLE 1. *Consider a graph* $G = (V, E)$ *where the set of nodes are equally partitioned into* $2k$ *subsets* $V = \cup_{i=1}^{2k} V_i$ *such that every* V_i *contains* $t + 1$ *nodes. Let* $V_i = \{v_i^j \mid 1 \leq j \leq t + 1\}$ *and set* $E = \cup_{i=1}^{2k} E_i$ *where* $E_i = \{(v_i^1, v_i^j) \mid 2 \leq j \leq t + 1\}$. *That is, every* (V_i, E_i) *forms a star with* v_i^1 *being the node at the center, all stars are disconnected from one another. For the parameter space we set the interval on every edge to be* $[l, r]$. *When* LUGreedy *selects* k *nodes, since all* v_i^1*'s have the same (marginal) influence spread, w.l.o.g., suppose that* LUGreedy *selects* $\{v_1^1, v_2^1, \ldots, v_k^1\}$. *Then if we set the true probability vector* $\theta \in \Theta$ *s.t.* $p_e = l$ *for every* $e \in \cup_{i=1}^k E_i$, *and* $p_e = r$ *for every* $e \in \cup_{i=k+1}^{2k} E_i$, *it is easy to check that* $\max_{|S|=k} g(\Theta, S) = g(\Theta, S^{\mathsf{LU}}_{\Theta}) = \alpha(\Theta) = \frac{1+tl}{1+tr}$.

The intuition from the above example is that, when there are many alternative choices for the best seed set, and these alternative seed sets do not have much overlap in their influence coverage, the gap ratio $\alpha(\Theta)$ is a good indicator of the best possible robust ratio one can achieve.

In the next subsection, we will show that the best robust ratio could be very bad for the worst possible graph G and parameter space Θ, which motivates us to do further sampling to improve Θ.

3.2 Discussion on the robust ratio

For the theoretical perspective, we show in this part that if we make no assumption or only add loose constraints to the input parameter space Θ, then no algorithm will guarantee good performance for some worst possible graph G.

THEOREM 3. *For RIM,*

1. *There exists a graph $G = (V, E)$ and parameter space $\Theta = \times_{e\in E}[l_e, r_e]$, such that*

$$\max_{|S|=k} g(\Theta, S) = \max_{|S|=k} \min_{\theta\in\Theta} \frac{\sigma_\theta(S)}{\sigma_\theta(S^*_\theta)} = O\left(\frac{k}{n}\right).$$

2. *There exists a graph $G = (V, E)$, constant $\delta = \Theta\left(\frac{1}{n}\right)$ and parameter space $\Theta = \times_{e\in E}[l_e, r_e]$ where $r_e - l_e \le \delta$ for every $e \in E$, such that*

$$\max_{|S|=k} g(\Theta, S) = O\left(\frac{\log n}{n}\right).$$

3. *Consider random seeds set $\tilde{S}$ of size k. There exists a graph $G = (V, E)$, constant $\delta = \Theta\left(\frac{1}{\sqrt{n}}\right)$ and parameter space $\Theta = \times_{e\in E}[l_e, r_e]$ where $r_e - l_e \le \delta$ for every $e \in E$, we have*

$$\max_{\Omega} \min_{\theta\in\Theta} \mathbb{E}_{\tilde{S}\in\Omega}\left[\frac{\sigma_\theta(\tilde{S})}{\sigma_\theta(S^*_\theta)}\right] = O\left(\frac{\log n}{\sqrt{n}}\right),$$

where Ω is any probability distribution over seed sets of size k, and $\mathbb{E}_{\tilde{S}\in\Omega}[\cdot]$ is the expectation of random set $\tilde{S}$ taken from the distribution Ω.

In the first case, we allow the input Θ to be an arbitrary parameter space. It is possible that $\Theta = \times_{e\in E}[0, 1]$ for some graph G, which means there is no knowledge at all for edge probabilities. Then any seed set may achieve $O\left(\frac{k}{n}\right)$-approximation of the optimal solution in the worst case. Intuitively, a selected seed set S may rarely activate other nodes (i.e., $O(k)$), while optimal solution (to the latent θ) may cover almost the whole graph (i.e., $\Omega(n)$).

In the second case, an additional constraint is assumed on the parameter space $\left\|\theta^+ - \theta^-\right\|_\infty \le \delta$, i.e., for every $e \in E$, $r_e - l_e \le \delta$, to see if we could obtain a better performance when δ is small. However, even though δ is in the order of $O(1/n)$, the robust ratio can be as small as $O(\log n/n)$. The proof is related to the phase transition in the Erdős-Rényi graph for the emergence of giant component. In particular, if we have a graph G consisting of two disconnected, equal-sized Erdős-Rényi random graphs with edge probabilities close to the critical value of generating a giant connected component, then whenever we select a seed in one component, that component could be just below the threshold resulting in $O(\log n)$ influence spread while the other component is just above the threshold leading to $\Theta(n)$ influence spread. Thus, the worst-case ratio for any one-node seed set is always $O(\log n/n)$. A similar discussion can be found in [18].

In the third case, we allow the algorithm to be randomized, namely the output seed set $\tilde{S}$ is a random set of size k. Even in this case, the robust ratio could be as bad as $O(\log n/\sqrt{n})$.

4. SAMPLING FOR IMPROVING RIM

From the previous section, we propose LUGreedy algorithm to check the solution-dependent bound of the robust ratio, and point out the worse-case bound could be small if Θ is not assumed to be tight enough.

Theorem 3 in the previous subsection points out that the best possible robust ratio $\max_S g(\Theta, S)$ can be too low so that the output for RIM could not provide us with a satisfying seed set in the worst case. Then a natural question is: given the input Θ, can we make efficient samples on edges so that Θ is narrowed into Θ' (this means the true $\theta \in \Theta'$ with high probability) and then output a seed set S' that makes $g(\Theta', S')$ large? This problem is called *Sampling for Improving RIM.*

In this section we study both uniform sampling and adaptive sampling for improving RIM. According to the Chernoff's bound, the more samples we make on an edge, the narrower the confidence interval we get that guarantees the true probability to be located within the confidence interval with a desired probability of confidence. After sampling to get a narrower parameter space, we could use LUGreedy algorithm to get the seed set.

4.1 Uniform Sampling

In Sampling for improving RIM, the goal is to design a sampling and maximization algorithm $\mathcal{A}$ that outputs Θ' and S' such that with high probability the robust ratio of S' in Θ' is large. After sampling edges, we can use Chernoff's bound to compute the confidence interval, and the confidence interval can be further narrowed down with more samples. However, the key issue is to connect the width of confidence interval with the stability of influence spread. We propose two ideas exploiting properties of additive and multiplicative confidence interval respectively to this issue, and incorporate into Uniform Sampling algorithm (in Algorithm 3) with theoretical justification (in Theorem 6).

Our first idea is inspired by the following lemma from [12] to build the connection in the additive form.

LEMMA 4 (LEMMA 7 IN [12]). *Given graph G and parameter space Θ such that $\forall\theta_1, \theta_2 \in \Theta$, $\|\theta_1 - \theta_2\|_\infty \le \delta$, then, $\forall S \subseteq V$,*

$$|\sigma_{\theta_1}(S) - \sigma_{\theta_2}(S)| \le mn\delta.$$

We use a tight example (in the order of $|V|$ and $|E|$) to illustrate the connection and give an insight of this lemma as follows. Consider graph $G = (V, E)$ with $|V| = n$ and $|E| = m$ ($m \gg n$). Let G be two disjoint cycles, each containing exactly $\frac{n}{2}$ nodes and $\frac{n}{2}$ edges. We arbitrarily assign the rest $m - n$ edges between two cycles. Then, for every edge e in the cycle, the interval is $l_e = r_e = 1$, and $l_e = 0$, $r_e = \delta$ for those between two cycles, which constitutes $\Theta = \times_{e\in E}[l_e, r_e]$. Suppose $\delta > 0$ is sufficiently small, and let budget $k = 1$. For any single-node set S, it is easy to check that for $\theta^- = (l_e)_{e\in E}$, $\sigma_{\theta^-}(S) = \frac{n}{2}$, and for $\theta^+ = (r_e)_{e\in E}$, $\sigma_{\theta^+}(S) \approx \frac{n}{2} + \frac{n}{2}(m-n)\delta$, thus $|\sigma_{\theta^+}(S) - \sigma_{\theta^-}(S)| \approx \frac{1}{2}n(m-n)\delta$ in this case. As a comparison, from Lemma 4, we know that $|\sigma_{\theta^+}(S) - \sigma_{\theta^-}(S)| \le mn\delta$.

Therefore, the above lemma establishes the guidance that we may sample every edge for sufficient times to shrink their confidence intervals in Θ, and feed LUGreedy with Θ as same as solving RIM, then the performance is guaranteed by Theorem 2, which matches our intuition that LUGreedy performs well with the satisfactory Θ.

On the other hand, our second idea is to use the multiplicative confidence interval to reduce the fluctuation of influence spread, then LUGreedy still applies. The next lemma is crucial to achieve this goal.

Algorithm 3 US-RIM

Input: Graph $G = (V, E)$, budget k, (ϵ, γ)
Output: Parameter space Θ_{out}, seed set S_{out}

```
for all e ∈ E do
    Sample e for t times, and observe x_e^1, ..., x_e^t
    p_e ← (1/t) Σ_{i=1}^t x_e^i, and set δ_e according to Theorem 6
    r_e ← min{1, p_e + δ_e}, l_e ← max{0, p_e − δ_e}
end for
Θ_out ← ×_{e∈E}[l_e, r_e]
S_out ← LUGreedy(G, k, Θ_out)
return (Θ_out, S_out)
```

LEMMA 5. *Given graph $G = (V, E)$ and parameter space Θ. If there exists $\lambda \geq 0$, for all edge $e \in E$, s.t., $r_e \leq (1+\lambda)l_e$, then for any nonempty set $S \subseteq V$,*

$$\frac{\sigma_{\theta^+}(S)}{\sigma_{\theta^-}(S)} \leq (1+\lambda)^n, \tag{4}$$

and

$$\max_{|S|=k} \min_{\theta \in \Theta} \frac{\sigma_\theta(S)}{\sigma_\theta(S_\theta^*)} \geq (1+\lambda)^{-n}. \tag{5}$$

In this lemma, the ratio of influence spread can be bounded based on the relation of l_e and r_e in the multiplicative form.

To unify both ideas mentioned above, we propose *Uniform Sampling for RIM* algorithm (US-RIM) in Algorithm 3, and the theoretical result is presented in Theorem 6. Basically, the algorithm samples every edge with the same number of times, and use LUGreedy to obtain the seed set. We set different t and δ_e for the two ideas. Henceforth, we explicitly refer the first setting as *Uniform Sampling with Additive form* (US-RIM-A), and the second one as *Uniform Sampling with Multiplicative form* (US-RIM-M).

THEOREM 6. *Given a graph $G = (V, E)$, budget k, and accuracy parameter $\epsilon, \gamma > 0$, let $n = |V|$ and $m = |E|$, then for any unknown ground-truth parameter vector $\theta = (p_e)_{e \in E}$, Algorithm* US-RIM *outputs (Θ_{out}, S_{out}) such that*

$$g(\Theta_{out}, S_{out}) \geq \left(1 - \frac{1}{e}\right)(1-\epsilon),$$

with $\Pr[\theta \in \Theta_{out}] \geq 1 - \gamma$, where the randomness is taken according to θ, if we follow either of the two settings:

1. *Set $t = \frac{2m^2n^2\ln(2m/\gamma)}{k^2\epsilon^2}$, and for all e, set $\delta_e = \frac{k\epsilon}{mn}$;*
2. *Assume we have p' such that $0 < p' \leq \min_{e \in E} p_e$, set $t = \frac{3\ln(2m/\gamma)}{p'}\left(\frac{2n}{\ln(1/1-\epsilon)} + 1\right)^2$, and for all edge, set $\delta_e = \frac{1}{n} p_e \log \frac{1}{\gamma}$.*

In general, the total number of samples summing up all edges is $O(\frac{m^3n^2\log(m/\gamma)}{k^2\epsilon^2})$ for US-RIM-A, and $O(\frac{mn^2\log(m/\gamma)}{p'\epsilon^2})$ for US-RIM-M with an additional constant p', the lower bound probability on all edge probabilities. The difference is that the former has a higher order of m, and the latter requires the knowledge of p' and has an extra dependency on $O(1/p')$. Since the sample complexity for both settings can be calculated in advance, one may compare the values and choose the smaller one when running the uniform sampling algorithm. An intuitive interpretation is that: (1) with high probability ($\geq 1 - \gamma$), the algorithm always outputs an $(1 - \frac{1}{e} - \epsilon)$-approximation solution guaranteed by US-RIM-A; (2) if $p' = \Omega(\frac{k^2}{m^2})$ (it is a loose assumption naturally satisfied in practice), we may choose US-RIM-M to achieve better sample complexity.

4.2 Non-uniform and Adaptive Sampling

In a real network, the importance of edges in an influence diffusion process varies significantly. Some edges may have larger influence probability than others or connect two important nodes in the network. Therefore, in sampling it is crucial to sample edges appropriately. Moreover, we can adapt our sampling strategy dynamically to put more sampling effort on critical edges when we learn the edge probabilities more accurately over time.

For convenience, given graph $G = (V, E)$, we define *observation set* $\mathcal{M} = \{M_e\}_{e \in E}$ as a collection of sets, where $M_e = \{x_e^1, x_e^2, \cdots, x_e^{t_e}\}$ denotes observed values of edge e via the first t_e samples on edge e. We allow that a parameter space $\Theta_0 \subseteq \times_{e \in E}[0, 1]$ is given, which can be obtained by some initial samples $\mathcal{M}_0$ (e.g., uniformly sample each edge of the graph for a fixed number of times).

The following lemma is used to calculate the confidence interval, which is a combination of additive and multiplicative Chernoff's Bound. We adopt this bound in the experiment since some edges in the graph have large influence probability while others have small ones, but using either additive or multiplicative bound may not be good enough to obtain a small confidence interval. The following bound is adapted from [1] and is crucial for us in the experiment.

LEMMA 7. *For each $e \in E$, let $M_e = \{x_e^1, x_e^2, \ldots, x_e^{t_e}\}$ be samples of e in $\mathcal{M} = \{M_e\}_{e \in E}$, and t_e be the sample number. Given any $\gamma > 0$, let confidence intervals for all edges be $\Theta = \times_{e \in E}[l_e, r_e]$, such that, for any $e \in E$,*

$$l_e = \min\left\{\hat{p}_e + \frac{c_e^2}{2} - c_e\sqrt{\frac{c_e^2}{4} + \hat{p}_e},\ 0\right\}$$

$$r_e = \max\left\{\hat{p}_e + \frac{c_e^2}{2} + c_e\sqrt{\frac{c_e^2}{4} + \hat{p}_e},\ 1\right\},$$

where $\hat{p}_e = \frac{\sum_{i=1}^{t_e} x_e^i}{t_e}$, $c_e = \sqrt{\frac{3}{t_e}\ln\frac{2m}{\gamma}}$. Then, with probability at least $1 - \gamma$, the true probability $\theta = (p_e)_{e \in E}$ satisfies that $\theta \in \Theta$.

Our intuition for non-uniform sampling is that the edges along the information cascade of important seeds determine the influence spread, and henceforth they should be estimated more accurately than other edges not along important information cascade paths. Thus, we use the following *Information Cascade Sampling* method to select edges. Starting from the seed set S, once node v is activated, v will try to activate its out-neighbors. In other words, for every out-edge e of v, denote t_e as the number of samples, then e will be sampled once to generate a new observation $x_e^{t_e}$ based on the latent Bernoulli distribution with success probability p_e, and t_e will be increased by 1. The process goes on until the end of the information cascade.

We propose *Information Cascade Sampling for RIM* (ICS-RIM) algorithm in Algorithm 4, which adopts information cascade sampling described above to select edges.

Algorithm 4 is an iterative procedure. In the i-th iteration, Lemma 7 is used to compute the confidence interval

Algorithm 4 ICS-RIM(τ): Information Cascade Sampling

Input: Graph $G = (V, E)$, budget k, initial sample $\mathcal{M}_0$, threshold κ, γ.
Output: Parameter space Θ_{out}, seed set S_{out}

```
i ← 0
repeat
    Get Θ_i based on M_i (see Lemma 7).
    S^LU_{Θ_i} = LUGreedy(G, k, Θ_i)
    M_{i+1} ← M_i
    for j = 1, 2, ..., τ do
        Do information cascade with the seed set S^LU_{Θ_i}
        During the cascade, once v ∈ V is activated, sample
        all out-edges of v and update M_{i+1}
    end for
    i ← i + 1
until α(Θ_i) > κ
S_out ← S^LU_{Θ_{i-1}}
Θ_out ← Θ_{i-1}
return (Θ_out, S_out)
```

Θ_i from observation set $\mathcal{M}_i$. Then according to Θ_i, we find the lower-upper greedy set $S^{\text{LU}}_{\Theta_i}$ and use information cascade to update observation set $\mathcal{M}_{i+1}$ by absorbing new samples.

Since the robust ratio $g(\Theta, S^{\text{LU}}_{\Theta_i})$ cannot be calculated efficiently, we will calculate $\alpha(\Theta)$ (defined in (3)) instead. In our algorithm, we use a pre-determined threshold κ ($\kappa \in (0, 1)$) as the stopping criteria. Therefore, for S_{out}, the robust ratio $g(\Theta, S_{\text{out}}) \geq \alpha(\Theta)\left(1 - \frac{1}{e}\right) > \kappa\left(1 - \frac{1}{e}\right)$ is guaranteed by Theorem 2, and the true probability $\theta \in \Theta_{\text{out}}$ holds with probability at least $1 - \gamma$ due to Lemma 7.

Compared with information cascade sampling method, calculating a greedy set is time-consuming. Therefore in Algorithm 4, we call LUGreedy once every τ rounds of information cascades to reduce the cost.

5. EMPIRICAL EVALUATION

We conduct experiments on two datasets, Flixster[1] and NetHEPT[2] to verify the robustness of influence maximization and our sampling methods.

5.1 Experiment Setup

5.1.1 Data Description

Flixster. The Flixster dataset is a network of American social movie discovery service (www.flixster.com). To transform the dataset into a weighted graph, each user is represented by a node, and a directed edge from node u to v is formed if v rates one movie shortly after u does so on the common movie. The dataset is analyzed in [2], and the influence probability are learned by the topic-aware model. We use the learning result of [2] in our experiment, which is a graph containing 29357 nodes and 212614 directed edges. There are 10 probabilities on each edge, and each probability represents the influence from the source user to the sink on a specific topic. Since most movies belong to at most two topics, we only consider 3 out of 10 topics in our experiment, and get two induced graphs whose number of edges are 23252 and 64934 respectively. For the first graph, probabilities of topic 8 are directly used as the ground truth parameter (termed as Flixster(Topic 8)). For the second graph, we mix the probabilities of Topic 1 and Topic 4 on each edge evenly to obtain the ground-truth probability (termed as as Flixster(Mixed)). After removing isolated nodes, the number of nodes in the two graphs are 14473 and 7118 respectively.

In [2], the probability for every edge (u, v) is learned by rating cascades that reach u and may or may not reach v, and in this cases we view that edge (u, v) are sampled. According to the data reported in [2], on average every edge is sampled 318 times for their learning process. We then use 318 samples on each edge as our initial sample $\mathcal{M}_0$.

NetHEPT. The NetHEPT dataset [11] is extensively used in many influence maximization studies. It is an academic collaboration network from the "High Energy Physics-Theory" section of arXiv form 1991 to 2003, where nodes represent the authors and each edge in the network represents one paper co-authored by two nodes. It contains 15233 nodes and 58891 undirected edges (including duplicated edges). We remove those duplicated edges and obtain a directed graph $G = (V, E), |V| = 15233, |E| = 62774$ (directed edges). Since the NetHEPT dataset does not contain the data of influence probability on edges, we set the probability on edges according to the *weighted cascade* model [19] as the ground truth parameter, i.e., $\forall e = (v, u) \in E$, let x_u be the in-degree of u in the edge-duplicated graph, y_e be the number of edges connecting node v and u, then the true probability is $p_e = 1 - (1 - \frac{1}{x_u})^{y_e}$. Following the same baseline of Flixster, we initially sample each edge for 318 times as $\mathcal{M}_0$.

5.1.2 Algorithms

We test both the uniform sampling algorithm US-RIM and the adaptive sampling algorithm ICS-RIM, as well as another adaptive algorithm OES-RIM (Out-Edge Sampling) as the baseline (to be described shortly). Each algorithm is given a graph G and initial observation set $\mathcal{M}_0$. Note that the method to estimate the parameter space based on sampling results in Algorithm 3 and Algorithm 4 are different. In order to make the comparison meaningful, in this section, for all three algorithms, a common method according to Lemma 7 is used to estimate the parameter space. In all tests, we set the size of the seed set $k = 50$. To reduce the running time, we use a faster approximation algorithm PMIA (proposed in [10]) to replace the well known greedy algorithm purposed in [19] in the whole experiment. The accuracy requirement $\gamma = o(1)$ is set to be $\gamma = m^{-0.5}$ where m is the number of edges.

US-RIM. The algorithm is slightly modified from Algorithm 3 for a better comparison of performance. The modified algorithm proceeds in an iterative fashion: In each iteration, the algorithm makes τ_1 samples on each edge, updates Θ according to Lemma 7 and computes $\alpha(\Theta)$. The algorithm stops when $\alpha(\Theta) \geq \kappa = 0.8$. τ_1 is set to 1000, 1000, 250 for NetHEPT, Flixster(Topic 8), Flixster(Mixed), respectively to achieve fine granularity and generate visually difference of $\alpha(\Theta)$ in our results.

[1] http://www.cs.sfu.ca/~sja25/personal/datasets/
[2] http://research.microsoft.com/en-us/people/weic/projects.aspx

ICS-RIM. As stated in Algorithm 4, in each iteration, the algorithm do $\tau_2 = 5000$ times information cascade sampling based on the seed set from the last iteration, and then it updates Θ according to Lemma 7, computes $\alpha(\Theta)$ and uses LUGreedy algorithm to compute the seed set for the next round. The algorithm stops when $\alpha(\Theta) \geq \kappa = 0.8$.

OES-RIM. This algorithm acts as a baseline, and it proceeds in the similar way to ICS-RIM. Instead of sampling information cascades starting from the current seed set as in ICS-RIM, OES-RIM only sample *out-edges* from the seed set. More specifically, in each iteration, the algorithm samples 5000 times of all out-edges of the seed set from last iteration, for the three graphs respectively, and then it updates Θ according to Lemma 7, computes $\alpha(\Theta)$ and uses LUGreedy algorithm to compute the seed set for the next round. Note that for OES-RIM, $\alpha(\Theta)$ remains small (with the increase of the number of samples) and cannot exceed the threshold κ even the iteration has been processed for a large number of times, therefore we will terminate it when $\alpha(\Theta)$ is stable.

5.1.3 $\bar{\alpha}$ as a Upper Bound

Theorem 2 shows that $\alpha(\Theta)\left(1-\frac{1}{e}\right)$ is a lower bound for the robust ratio $g(\Theta, S_\Theta^{\mathsf{LU}})$. We would also like to find some upper bound of $g(\Theta, S_\Theta^{\mathsf{LU}})$: If the upper bound is reasonably close to the lower bound or match in trend of changes, it indicates that $\alpha(\Theta)\left(1-\frac{1}{e}\right)$ is a reasonable indicator of the robust ratio achieved by the LUGreedy output S_Θ^{LU}. For any $\theta \in \Theta$, we define $\bar{\alpha}(\Theta, \theta) = \frac{\sigma_\theta(S_\Theta^{\mathsf{LU}})}{\sigma_\theta(S_\theta^g)}$. The following shows that $\bar{\alpha}(\Theta, \theta)$ is an upper bound for $g(\Theta, S_\Theta^{\mathsf{LU}})$:

$$\bar{\alpha}(\Theta, \theta) = \frac{\sigma_\theta(S_\Theta^{\mathsf{LU}})}{\sigma_\theta(S_\theta^g)} \geq \frac{\sigma_\theta(S_\Theta^{\mathsf{LU}})}{\sigma_\theta(S_\theta^*)} \geq \min_{\theta' \in \Theta} \frac{\sigma_{\theta'}(S_\Theta^{\mathsf{LU}})}{\sigma_{\theta'}(S_{\theta'}^*)} = g(\Theta, S_\Theta^{\mathsf{LU}}).$$

The next question is how to find a $\theta = (\theta_e)_{e \in E} \in \Theta$ to make the upper bound $\bar{\alpha}(\Theta, \theta)$ as small as possible. In our experiments, we use the following two heuristics and take their minimum.

The first heuristic borrows the intuition from Example 1, which says that the gap ratio $\alpha(\Theta)$ is close to the robust ratio $g(\Theta, S_\Theta^{\mathsf{LU}})$ when (a) there are two disjoint seed sets with similar influence spead, (b) their cascade overlap is small, and (c) the reachable edges from one seed set use lower end parameters values while the reachable edges from the other seed set use upper end parameters. Thus in our heuristic, we use PMIA algorithm to find another seed set S' of k nodes when we remove all nodes in S_Θ^{LU}. We then do information cascades from both S_Θ^{LU} and S' for an equal number of times. Finally, for every edge e, if it is sampled more in the information cascade with seed set S_Θ^{LU} than with S', we set $\theta_e = l_e$, otherwise we set $\theta_e = r_e$. The second heuristic is a variant of the first one, where we run a number of information cascades from S_Θ^{LU}, and for any edge e that is sampled in at least 10% of cascades, we set $\theta_e = l_e$, otherwise we set $\theta_e = r_e$.

Other more sophisticated heuristics are possible, but it could be a separate research topic to find tighter upper bound for the robust ratio, and thus we only use the simple combination of the above two in this paper, which is already indicative. We henceforth use $\bar{\alpha}(\Theta)$ to represent the upper bound found by the minimum of the above two heuristics.

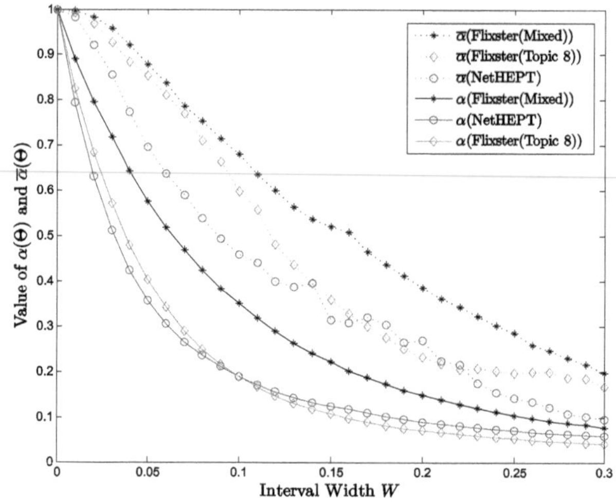

Figure 1: $\alpha(\Theta)$ and $\bar{\alpha}(\Theta)$ for different widths of confidence interval W.

5.2 Results

5.2.1 $\alpha(\Theta)$ and $\bar{\alpha}(\Theta)$ with Predetermined Intervals

In the first experiment we explore the relationship between the width of confidence interval $\Theta = \times_{e \in E}[l_e, r_e]$ and $\alpha(\Theta)$ together with $\bar{\alpha}(\Theta)$. For a given interval width W, we set $l_e = \min\{p_e - \frac{W}{2}, 0\}, r_e = \max\{p_e + \frac{W}{2}, 1\}$ $\forall e \in E$, where p_e is the ground-truth probability of e. Then we calculate $\alpha(\Theta)$ and $\bar{\alpha}(\Theta)$. We vary the width W to see the trend of changes of $\alpha(\Theta)$ and $\bar{\alpha}(\Theta)$. Figure 1 reports the result on the three graphs with seed set size $k = 50$.

First, we observe that as the parameter space Θ becomes wider, the value of both $\alpha(\Theta)$ and $\bar{\alpha}(\Theta)$ become smaller, which matches our intuition that larger uncertainty results in worse robustness. Second, there is a sharp decrease of $\alpha(\Theta)$ between $W \in [0, 0.1]$ and a much slower decrease afterwards for all three graphs. The decrease of $\bar{\alpha}(\Theta)$ is not as sharp as that of $\alpha(\Theta)$ but the decrease also slows down with larger W after 0.2. The overall trend of $\alpha(\Theta)$ and $\bar{\alpha}(\Theta)$ suggests that the robust ratio may be sensitive to the uncertainty of the parameter space, and only when the uncertainty of the parameter space reduces to a certain level that we can obtain reasonable guarantee on the robustness of our solution.

As a comparison, we know that the average number of samples on each edge is 318 for the learned probabilities in the Flixster dataset. This corresponds to an average interval width of 0.293 for topic 8 and 0.265 for the mixed topic. At these interval widths, $\alpha(\Theta)$ values are approximately 0.04 and 0.08 respectively for the two graphs, and $\bar{\alpha}(\Theta)$ are approximately 0.12 and 0.2 respectively. This means that, even considering the upper bound $\bar{\alpha}(\Theta)$, the robust ratio is pretty low, and thus the learned probabilities reported in [2] may result in quite poor performance for robust influence maximization.

Of course, our result of $\alpha(\Theta)$ and $\bar{\alpha}(\Theta)$ is only targeted at the robustness of our LUGreedy algorithm, and there could exist better algorithm having higher robustness performance at the same uncertainty level. Finding a better RIM algorithm seems to be a difficult task, and we hope that our study could motivate more research in searching for

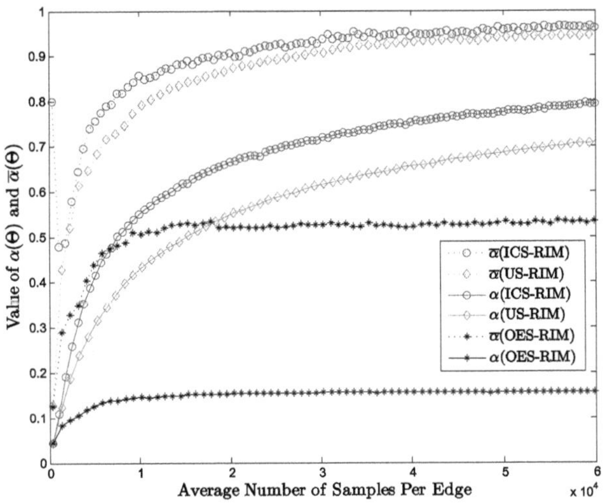

Figure 2: $\alpha(\Theta)$ and $\bar{\alpha}(\Theta)$ for different average number of samples per edge on graph NetHEPT.

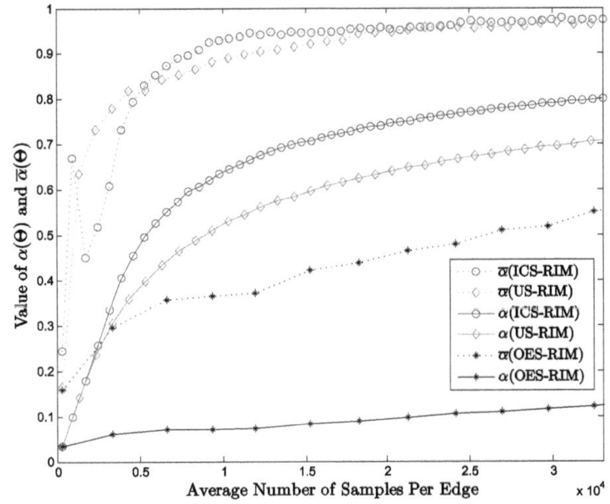

Figure 3: $\alpha(\Theta)$ and $\bar{\alpha}(\Theta)$ for different average number of samples per edge on graph Flixster(Topic 8).

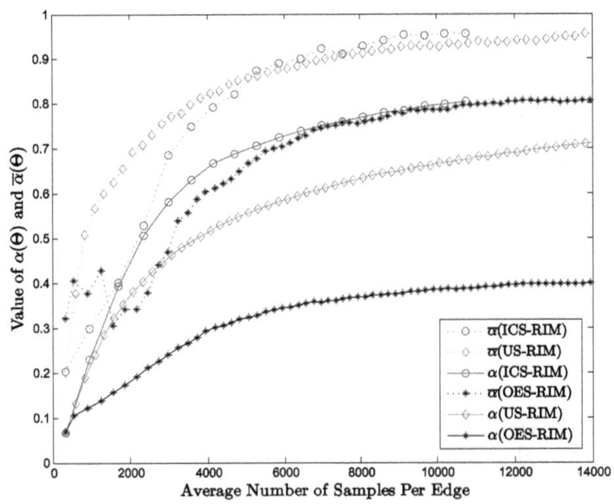

Figure 4: $\alpha(\Theta)$ and $\bar{\alpha}(\Theta)$ for different average number of samples per edge on graph Flixster(Mixed).

such better RIM algorithms. Besides S^{LU}_{Θ}, we also independently test the classical greedy seed set S^g_θ for $\theta = (p_e)_{e\in E}$ on the lower parameter vector θ^- (that is $\frac{\sigma_{\theta^-}(S^g_\theta)}{\sigma_{\theta^+}(S^g_{\theta^+})}$ versus $\alpha(\Theta)$), and the average performance on each data point is 2.45%, 1.05%, 6.11% worse than S^{LU}_{Θ} for Flixster(Mixed), Flixster(Topic 8) and NetHEPT, respectively. Therefore, it shows that S^{LU}_{Θ} outperforms σ^g_θ in the worse-case scenario, and henceforth we only use S^{LU}_{Θ} in the following experiments.

5.2.2 Results for Sampling algorithms

Figures 2, 3 and 4 reports the result of $\alpha = \alpha(\Theta)$ and $\bar{\alpha} = \bar{\alpha}(\Theta)$ for the three tested graphs respectively, when the average number of samples per edge increases. For better presentation, we trim all figures as long as α(US-RIM) = 0.7. (For example, in Flixster(Topic 8), US-RIM requires 77318 samples in average for α to reach 0.8, while ICS-RIM only needs 33033, and for OES-RIM α sticks to 0.118.)

For the sampling algorithms, after the i-th iteration, the observation set is updated from $\mathcal{M}_{i-1}$ to $\mathcal{M}_i$, and the average number of samples per edge in the network is calculated. Markers on each curve in these figures represent the result after one iteration of the corresponding sampling algorithm.

The results on all three graphs are consistent. First, for each pair of $\alpha(\Theta)$ and $\bar{\alpha}(\Theta)$, even though there is still some gap, indicating either the lower bound or the upper bound may not be tight yet, the trends on both $\alpha(\Theta)$ and $\bar{\alpha}(\Theta)$ are consistent: Both increase with the number of samples, even with similar slopes at each point; and among different algorithms, the ranking order and relative change are consistent with both $\alpha(\Theta)$ and $\bar{\alpha}(\Theta)$. All these consistency suggests that gap ratio $\alpha(\Theta)$ could be used as an indicator for the robustness of Algorithm LUGreedy, and it is reasonable to use $\alpha(\Theta)$ in comparing the performance of different algorithms.

Second, comparing the performance of three algorithms, we see that both US-RIM and ICS-RIM are helpful in improving the robust ratio of the selected seed set, and ICS-RIM is better than US-RIM, especially when the sample size increases. The baseline algorithm OES-RIM, however, performs significantly poorer than the other two, even though it is also an adaptive algorithm as ICS-RIM. The reason is that, the lower-upper greedy set S^{LU}_{Θ} changes little after a certain number of iterations in OES-RIM, and thus only a small number of edges (out edges of S^{LU}_{Θ}) are repeatedly sampled. The probabilities on these edges are already estimated very accurately while other edge probabilities are far from accurate. It is the inaccurate edges that make $\alpha(\Theta)$ and the best robust ratio small. In contrast, ICS-RIM uses information cascades to sample not only edges directly connecting to the seed set but also edges that can be potentially reached. This suggests that it is important for a sampling method to balance the sampling between critical edges and other potentially useful edges in order to achieve better robustness in influence maximization.

Overall, the results suggest that information cascade based sampling method stands out as a competitive choice when we can adaptively sample more edges to achieve better robustness. If adaptive sampling is not possible, predetermined uniform sampling may also perform reasonably well.

6. CONCLUSION

In this paper, we propose the study of robust influence maximization to address the impact of uncertainty in edge probability estimates that would inevitably occur in practice to the influence maximization task. We propose the LUGreedy algorithm with a proven solution-dependent bound, and further propose sampling methods, in particular information cascade based adaptive sample method to effectively reduce the uncertainty and increase the robustness of the LUGreedy algorithm. The experimental results validate the usefulness of the LUGreedy algorithm and the information cascade based sampling method ICS-RIM. Moreover, the results indicate that robustness may be sensitive to the uncertainty of parameter space, and learning algorithms may need more data to achieve accurate learning results for robust influence maximization.

Our work opens up a number of research directions. First, it is unclear what could be the upper bound of the best robust ratio given an actual network and learned parameter space. Answering this question would help us to understand whether robust influence maximization is intrinsically difficult for a particular network or it is just our algorithm that does not perform well. If it is the latter case, then an important direction is to design better robust influence maximization algorithms. Another direction is how to improve sampling methods and learning methods to achieve more accurate parameter learning, which seems to be crucial for robust influence maximization. In summary, our work indicates a big data challenge on social influence research — the data on social influence analysis is still not big enough, such that the uncertainty level in model learning may result in poor performance for influence maximization. We hope that our work could encourage further researches to meet this challenge from multiple aspects including data collection, data analysis, and algorithm design.

Acknowledgment

The research of Wei Chen is partially supported by the National Natural Science Foundation of China (Grant No. 61433014).

7. REFERENCES

[1] A. Badanidiyuru, R. Kleinberg, and A. Slivkins. Bandits with knapsacks. In *FOCS 2013*.

[2] N. Barbieri, F. Bonchi, and G. Manco. Topic-aware social influence propagation models. *Knowledge and information systems*, 37(3):555–584, 2013.

[3] A. Ben-Tal and A. Nemirovski. Robust optimization–methodology and applications. *Mathematical Programming*, 92(3):453–480, 2002.

[4] C. Borgs, M. Brautbar, J. T. Chayes, and B. Lucier. Maximizing social influence in nearly optimal time. In *SODA 2014*.

[5] S. Bubeck, R. Munos, and G. Stoltz. Pure exploration in finitely-armed and continuous-armed bandits. *Theoretical Computer Science*, 412:1832–1852, 2011.

[6] C. Budak, D. Agrawal, and A. El Abbadi. Limiting the spread of misinformation in social networks. In *WWW 2011*.

[7] S. Chen, T. Lin, I. King, M. R. Lyu, and W. Chen. Combinatorial pure exploration of multi-armed bandits. In *NIPS 2014*.

[8] W. Chen, L. V. Lakshmanan, and C. Castillo. Information and influence propagation in social networks. *Synthesis Lectures on Data Management*, 5(4):1–177, 2013.

[9] W. Chen, T. Lin, Z. Tan, M. Zhao, and X. Zhou. Robust influence maximization. *CoRR*, abs/1601.06551, 2016.

[10] W. Chen, C. Wang, and Y. Wang. Scalable influence maximization for prevalent viral marketing in large-scale social networks. In *KDD 2010*.

[11] W. Chen, Y. Wang, and S. Yang. Efficient influence maximization in social networks. In *KDD 2009*.

[12] W. Chen, Y. Wang, and Y. Yuan. Combinatorial multi-armed bandit and its extension to probabilistically triggered arms. *CoRR*, abs/1407.8339, 2014.

[13] P. Domingos and M. Richardson. Mining the network value of customers. In *KDD 2001*.

[14] U. Feige. A threshold of ln n for approximating set cover. *Journal of the ACM (JACM)*, 45(4):634–652, 1998.

[15] A. Goyal, F. Bonchi, and L. V. Lakshmanan. Learning influence probabilities in social networks. In *WSDM 2010*.

[16] A. Goyal, W. Lu, and L. V. Lakshmanan. Celf++: optimizing the greedy algorithm for influence maximization in social networks. In *WWW 2011*.

[17] X. He and D. Kempe. Robust influence maximization. In *KDD 2016*.

[18] X. He and D. Kempe. Stability of Influence Maximization. *ArXiv e-prints*, Jan. 2015.

[19] D. Kempe, J. Kleinberg, and É. Tardos. Maximizing the spread of influence through a social network. In *KDD 2003*.

[20] A. Krause, H. B. McMahon, C. Guestrin, and A. Gupta. Robust submodular observation selection. *JMLR*, 9:2761–2801, 2008.

[21] S. Lei, S. Maniu, L. Mo, R. Cheng, and P. Senellart. Online influence maximization. In *KDD 2015*.

[22] J. Leskovec, A. Krause, C. Guestrin, C. Faloutsos, J. VanBriesen, and N. Glance. Cost-effective outbreak detection in networks. In *KDD 2007*.

[23] W. Lu, W. Chen, and L. V. Lakshmanan. From competition to complementarity: comparative influence diffusion and maximization. In *VLDB 2015*.

[24] P. Netrapalli and S. Sanghavi. Learning the graph of epidemic cascades. In *SIGMETRICS 2012*.

[25] M. G. Rodriguez, D. Balduzzi, and B. Schölkopf. Uncovering the temporal dynamics of diffusion networks. In *ICML 2011*.

[26] K. Saito, R. Nakano, and M. Kimura. Prediction of information diffusion probabilities for independent cascade model. In *Knowledge-Based Intelligent Information and Engineering Systems*, pages 67–75. Springer, 2008.

[27] J. Tang, J. Sun, C. Wang, and Z. Yang. Social influence analysis in large-scale networks. In *KDD 2009*.

[28] Y. Tang, X. Xiao, and Y. Shi. Influence maximization: near-optimal time complexity meets practical efficiency. In *SIGMOD 2014*.

Ranking Causal Anomalies via Temporal and Dynamical Analysis on Vanishing Correlations

Wei Cheng[1], Kai Zhang[1], Haifeng Chen[1], Guofei Jiang[1], Zhengzhang Chen[1], Wei Wang[2]
[1]NEC Laboratories America
[2]Department of Computer Science, University of California, Los Angeles
[1]{weicheng, kzhang, haifeng, gfj, zchen}@nec-labs.com, [2]weiwang@cs.ucla.edu

ABSTRACT

Modern world has witnessed a dramatic increase in our ability to collect, transmit and distribute real-time monitoring and surveillance data from large-scale information systems and cyber-physical systems. Detecting system anomalies thus attracts significant amount of interest in many fields such as security, fault management, and industrial optimization. Recently, invariant network has shown to be a powerful way in characterizing complex system behaviours. In the invariant network, a node represents a system component and an edge indicates a stable, significant interaction between two components. Structures and evolutions of the invariance network, in particular the vanishing correlations, can shed important light on locating causal anomalies and performing diagnosis. However, existing approaches to detect causal anomalies with the invariant network often use the percentage of vanishing correlations to rank possible casual components, which have several limitations: 1) fault propagation in the network is ignored; 2) the root casual anomalies may not always be the nodes with a high-percentage of vanishing correlations; 3) temporal patterns of vanishing correlations are not exploited for robust detection. To address these limitations, in this paper we propose a network diffusion based framework to identify significant causal anomalies and rank them. Our approach can effectively model fault propagation over the entire invariant network, and can perform joint inference on both the structural, and the time-evolving broken invariance patterns. As a result, it can locate high-confidence anomalies that are truly responsible for the vanishing correlations, and can compensate for unstructured measurement noise in the system. Extensive experiments on synthetic datasets, bank information system datasets, and coal plant cyber-physical system datasets demonstrate the effectiveness of our approach.

Keywords

causal anomalies ranking, label propagation, nonnegative matrix factorization

KDD '16, August 13-17, 2016, San Francisco, CA, USA
© 2016 ACM. ISBN 978-1-4503-4232-2/16/08...$15.00
DOI: http://dx.doi.org/10.1145/2939672.2939765

1. INTRODUCTION

With the rapid advances in networking, computers, and hardware, we are facing an explosive growth of complexity in networked applications and information services. These large-scale, often distributed, information systems usually consist of a great variety of components that work together in a highly complex and coordinated manner. One example is the Cyber-Physical System (CPS) which is typically equipped with a large number of networked sensors that keep recording the running status of the local components; another example is the large scale Information Systems such as the cloud computing facilities in Google, Yahoo! and Amazon, whose composition includes thousands of components that vary from operating systems, application softwares, servers, to storage, networking devices, etc.

A central task in running these large scale distributed systems is to automatically monitor the system status, detect anomalies, and diagnose system fault, so as to guarantee stable and high-quality services or outputs. Significant research efforts have been devoted to this topic in the literatures. For instance, Gertler et al. [9] proposed to detect anomalies by examining monitoring data of individual component with a thresholding scheme. However, it can be quite difficult to learn a universal and reliable threshold in practice, due to the dynamic and complex nature of information systems. More effective and recent approaches typically start with building system profiles, and then detect anomalies via analyzing patterns in these profiles [5, 13]. The system profile is usually extracted from historical time series data collected by monitoring different system components, such as the flow intensity of software log files, the system audit events and the network traffic statistics, and sometimes sensory measurements in physical systems.

The invariant model is a successful example [13, 14] for large-scale system management. It focuses on discovering stable, significant dependencies between pairs of system components that are monitored through time series recordings, so as to profile the system status and perform subsequent reasoning. A strong dependency between a pair of components is called *invariant* (correlation) relationship. By combining the invariants learned from all monitoring components, a global system dependency profile can be obtained. The significant practical value of such an *invariant* profile is that it provides important clues on abnormal system behaviors and in particular the source of anomalies, by checking whether existing invariants are broken. Figure 1 illustrates one example of the invariant network and two snapshots of broken invariants at time t_1 and t_2, respectively. Each

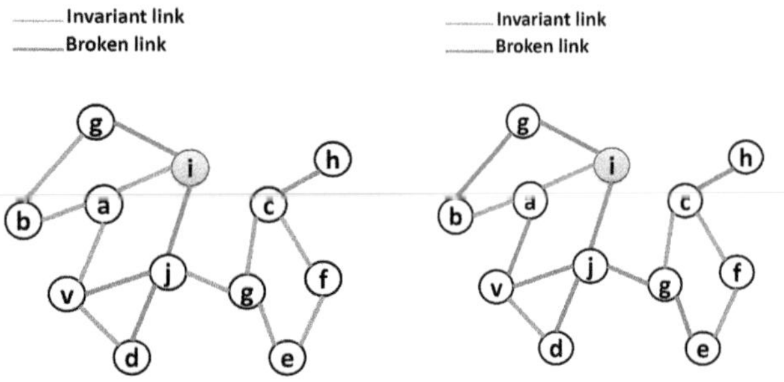

(a) t_1 (b) t_2

Figure 1: Invariant network and vanishing correlations(red edges).

node in the figure represents the observation from a monitoring component. The green line signifies an invariant link between two components, and a red line denotes broken invariant (i.e., vanishing correlation). The network including all the broken invariants at given time point is referred to as the *broken network.*

Although the broken invariants provide valuable information of the system status, how to locate true, causal anomalies can still be a challenging task due to the following reasons. First, system faults are seldom isolated. Instead, starting from the root location/component, anomalous behavior will propagate to neighboring components [13], and different types of system faults can trigger diverse propagation patterns. Second, monitoring data often contains a lot of noises due to the fluctuation of complex operation environments.

Recently, several ranking algorithms were developed to diagnose the system failure based on the percentage of broken invariant edges associated with the nodes, such as the egonet based method proposed by Ge et al. [8], and the loopy belief propagation (LBP) based method proposed by Tao et al. [22]. Despite the success in practical applications, existing methods still have certain limitations. First, they do not take into account the global structure of the invariant network, neither how the root anomaly/fault propagates in such a network. Second, the ranking strategies rely heavily on the percentage of broken edges connected to a node. For example, the mRank algorithm [8] calculated the anomaly score of a given node using the ratio of broken edges within the egonet [1] of the node. The LBP-based method [22] used the ratio of broken edges as the prior probability of abnormal state for each node. We argue that, the percentage of broken edges may not serve as a good evidence of the causal anomaly. This is because, although one broken edge can indicate that one (or both) of related nodes is abnormal, lack of a broken edge does not necessary indicate that related nodes are problem free. Instead, it is possible that the correlation is still there when two nodes become abnormal simultaneously [13]. Therefore the percentage of broken edges could give false evidences. For example, in Figure 1, the causal anomaly is node ⓘ. The percentage of broken edges for node ⓘ is 2/3, which is smaller than that of node ⓗ (which is equal to 1). Since there exists a clear evidence of fault propagation on node ⓘ, an ideal algorithm should rank ⓘ higher than ⓗ. Third, existing methods usually consider static broken network instead of multiple broken networks at successive time points together. While we believe that, jointly analyzing temporal broken networks can help resolve ambiguity and achieve a denoising effect. This is because, the root casual anomalies usually remain unchanged within a short time period, even though the fault may keep prorogating in the invariant network. As an example shown in Figure 1, it would be easier to detect the causal anomaly if we jointly consider the broken networks at two successive time points together.

[1]An egonet is the induced 1-step subgraph for each node.

To address the limitations of existing methods, we propose several network diffusion based algorithms for ranking causal anomalies. Our contributions are summarized as follows.

1. We employ the network diffusion process to model propagation of causal anomalies and use propagated anomaly scores to reconstruct the vanishing correlations. By minimizing the reconstruction error, the proposed methods simultaneously consider the whole invariant network structure and the potential fault propagation. We also provide rigid theoretical analysis on the properties of the proposed methods.
2. We further develop efficient algorithms which reduce the time complexity from $\mathcal{O}(n^3)$ to $\mathcal{O}(n^2)$, where n is the number of nodes in the invariant network. This makes it feasible to quickly localize root cause anomalies in large-scale systems.
3. We employ effective normalization strategy on the ranking scores, which can reduce the influence of extreme values or outliers without having to explicitly remove them from the data.
4. We develop a smoothing algorithm that enables users to jointly consider dynamic and time-evolving broken network, and thus obtain better ranking results.
5. We evaluate the proposed methods on both synthetic datasets and two real datasets, including the bank information system and the coal plant cyber-physical system datasets. Experimental results demonstrate the effectiveness of our methods.

2. BACKGROUND AND PROBLEM DEFINITION

In this section, we first introduce the technique of the invariant model [13] and then define our problem.

2.1 System Invariant and Vanishing Correlations

The *invariant* model is used to uncover significant pairwise relations among massive set of time series. It is based on the AutoRegressive eXogenous (ARX) model [10] with time delay. Let $x(t)$ and $y(t)$ be a pair of time series under consideration, where t is the time index, and let n and m be the degrees of the ARX model, with a delay factor k. Let $\widehat{y}(t;\boldsymbol{\theta})$ be the prediction of $y(t)$ using the ARX model parametarized by $\boldsymbol{\theta}$, which can then be written as

$$\widehat{y}(t;\boldsymbol{\theta}) = a_1 y(t-1) + \cdots + a_n y(t-n) \quad (1)$$
$$+ b_0 x(t-k) + \cdots + b_m x(t-k-m) + d$$
$$= \boldsymbol{\varphi}(t)^\top \boldsymbol{\theta}, \quad (2)$$

Table 1: Summary of notations

Symbol	Definition
n	the number of nodes in the invariant network
c, λ, τ	the parameters $0 < c < \ , \tau > 0, \lambda > 0$
$\sigma(\cdot)$	the softmax function
$\mathcal{G}_l$	the invariant network
$\mathcal{G}_b$	the broken network for $\mathcal{G}_l$
$\mathbf{A}\ (\tilde{\mathbf{A}}) \in \mathbb{R}^{n \times n}$	the (normalized) adjacency matrix of $\mathcal{G}_l$
$\mathbf{P}\ (\tilde{\mathbf{P}}) \in \mathbb{R}^{n \times n}$	the (normalized) adjacency matrix of $\mathcal{G}_b$
$\mathbf{M} \in \mathbb{R}^{n \times n}$	the logical matrix of $\mathcal{G}_l$
$d(i)$	the degree of the ith node in network $\mathcal{G}_l$
$\mathbf{D} \in \mathbb{R}^{n \times n}$	the degree matrix: $\mathbf{D} = diag(d(i), ..., d(n))$
$\mathbf{r} \in \mathbb{R}^{n \times 1}$	the prorogated anomaly score vector
$\mathbf{e} \in \mathbb{R}^{n \times 1}$	the ranking vector of causal anomalies
RCA	the basic ranking causal anomalies algorithm
R-RCA	the relaxed RCA algorithm
RCA-SOFT	the RCA with softmax normalization
R-RCA-SOFT	the relaxed RCA with softmax normalization
T-RCA	the RCA with temporal smoothing
T-R-RCA	the R-RCA with temporal smoothing
T-RCA-SOFT	the RCA-SOFT with temporal smoothing
T-R-RCA-SOFT	the R-RCA-SOFT with temporal smoothing

where $\boldsymbol{\theta} = [a_1, \ldots, a_n, b_0, \ldots, b_m, d]^\top \in \mathbb{R}^{n+m+2}$, $\varphi(t) = [y(t-1), \ldots, y(t-n), x(t-k), \ldots, x(t-k-m), 1]^\top \in \mathbb{R}^{n+m+2}$. For a given setting of (n, m, k), the parameter $\boldsymbol{\theta}$ can be estimated with observed time points $t = 1, \ldots, N$ in the training data, via least-square fitting. In real-world applications such as anomaly detection in physical systems, $0 \leq n, m, k \leq 2$ is a popular choice [6, 13]. We can define the "goodness of fit" (or *fitness score*) of an ARX model as

$$F(\boldsymbol{\theta}) = \quad - \sqrt{\frac{\sum_{t=1}^{N} |y(t) - \widehat{y}(t; \boldsymbol{\theta})|^2}{\sum_{t=1}^{N} |y(t) - \bar{y}|^2}}, \tag{3}$$

where $\bar{y}$ is the mean of the time series $y(t)$. A higher value of $F(\boldsymbol{\theta})$ indicates a better fitting of the model. An invariant (correlation) is declared on a pair of time series x and y if the fitness score of the ARX model is larger than a pre-defined threshold. A network including all the invariant links is referred to as the *invariant network*. Construction of the invariant network is referred to as the model training. The model $\boldsymbol{\theta}$ will then be applied on the time series x and y in the testing phase to track vanishing correlations.

To track vanishing correlations, we can use the techniques developed in [6, 15]. At each time point, we compute the (normalized) residual $R(t)$ between the measurement $y(t)$ and its estimate $\widehat{y}(t; \boldsymbol{\theta})$ by

$$R(t) = \frac{|y(t) - \widehat{y}(t; \boldsymbol{\theta})|}{\varepsilon_{\max}}, \tag{4}$$

where $\varepsilon_{\max}$ is the maximum training error $\varepsilon_{\max} = \max_{1 \leq t \leq N} |y(t) - \widehat{y}(t; \boldsymbol{\theta})|$. If the residual exceeds a prefixed threshold, then we declare the invariant as "broken", i.e., the correlation between the two time series vanishes. The network including all broken edges at given time point and all nodes in the invariant network is referred to as the *broken network*.

2.2 Problem Definition

Let $\mathcal{G}_l$ be the invariant network with n nodes. Let $\mathcal{G}_b$ be the broken network for $\mathcal{G}_l$. We use two symmetric matrices $\mathbf{A} \in \mathbb{R}^{n \times n}$, $\mathbf{P} \in \mathbb{R}^{n \times n}$ to denote the adjacency matrix of network $\mathcal{G}_l$ and $\mathcal{G}_b$, respectively. These two matrices can be obtained as discussed in Section 2.1. The two matrices can be binary or continuous. For binary case of $\mathbf{A}$, 1 is used to denote that the correlation exists between two time series, and 0 denotes the lack of correlation; while for $\mathbf{P}$, 1 is used to denote that the correlation is broken (vanishing), and 0 otherwise. For the continuous case, the fitness score $F(\boldsymbol{\theta})$ (3) and the residual $R(t)$ (4) can be used to fill the two matrices, respectively.

Our main goal is to detect the abnormal nodes in $\mathcal{G}_l$ that are most responsible for causing the broken edges in $\mathcal{G}_b$. In this sense, we call such nodes "causal anomalies". Accurate detection of causal anomalous nodes will be extremely useful for examination, debugging and repair of system failures.

3. RANKING CAUSAL ANOMALIES

In this section, we present the algorithm of Ranking Causal Anomalies (RCA), which takes into account both the fault propagation and fitting of broken invariants simultaneously.

3.1 Fault Propagation

We consider a very practical scenario of fault propagation, namely anomalous system status can always be traced back to a set of *root cause* anomaly nodes, or *causal anomalies*, as initial seeds. As the time passes, these root cause anomalies will then propagate along the invariant network, most probably towards their neighbors via paths identified by the invariant links in $\mathcal{G}_l$. To explicitly model this spreading process on the network, we have employed the label propagation technique [16, 24, 26]. Suppose that the (unknown) root cause anomalies are denoted by the indicator vector $\mathbf{e}$, whose entries $\mathbf{e}_i$'s ($1 \leq i \leq n$) indicate whether the ith node is the casual anomaly ($\mathbf{e}_i = 1$) or not ($\mathbf{e}_i = 0$). At the end of propagation, the system status is represented by the anomaly score vector $\mathbf{r}$, whose entries tell us how severe each node of the network has been impaired. The propagation from $\mathbf{e}$ to $\mathbf{r}$ can be modeled by the following optimization problem

$$\min_{\mathbf{r} \geq \mathbf{0}} c \sum_{i,j=1}^{n} \mathbf{A}_{ij} || \frac{1}{\sqrt{\mathbf{D}_{ii}}} \mathbf{r}_i - \frac{1}{\sqrt{\mathbf{D}_{jj}}} \mathbf{r}_j ||^2 + (1-c) \sum_{i=1}^{n} ||\mathbf{r}_i - \mathbf{e}_i||^2,$$

where $\mathbf{D} \in \mathbb{R}^{n \times n}$ is the degree matrix of $\mathbf{A}$, $c \in (0, 1)$ is the regularization parameter, $\mathbf{r}$ is the anomaly score vector after the propagation of the initial faults in $\mathbf{e}$. We can re-write the above problem as

$$\min_{\mathbf{r} \geq \mathbf{0}} c\mathbf{r}^\top (\mathbf{I}_n - \tilde{\mathbf{A}}) \mathbf{r} + (1-c) ||\mathbf{r} - \mathbf{e}||_F^2, \tag{5}$$

where $\mathbf{I}_n$ is the identity matrix, $\tilde{\mathbf{A}} = \mathbf{D}^{-1/2} \mathbf{A} \mathbf{D}^{-1/2}$ is the degree-normalized version of $\mathbf{A}$. Similarly we will use $\tilde{\mathbf{P}}$ as the degree-normalized $\mathbf{P}$ in the sequel. The first term in Eq. (5) is the *smoothness constraint* [26], meaning that a good ranking function should assign similar values to nearby nodes in the network. The second term is the *fitting constraint*, which means that the final status should be close to the initial configuration. The trade-off between these two competing constraints is controlled by a positive parameter c: a small c encourages a sufficient propagation, and a big c actually suppresses the propagation. The optimal solution of problem (5) is [26]

$$\mathbf{r} = (1-c)(\mathbf{I}_n - c\tilde{\mathbf{A}})^{-1} \mathbf{e}, \tag{6}$$

which establishes an explicit and closed-form solution between the initial configuration $\mathbf{e}$ and the final status $\mathbf{r}$ through fault propagation.

To encode the information of the broken network, we propose to use $\mathbf{r}$ to reconstruct the broken network $\mathcal{G}_b$. The intuition is illustrated in Figure 2. If there exists a broken

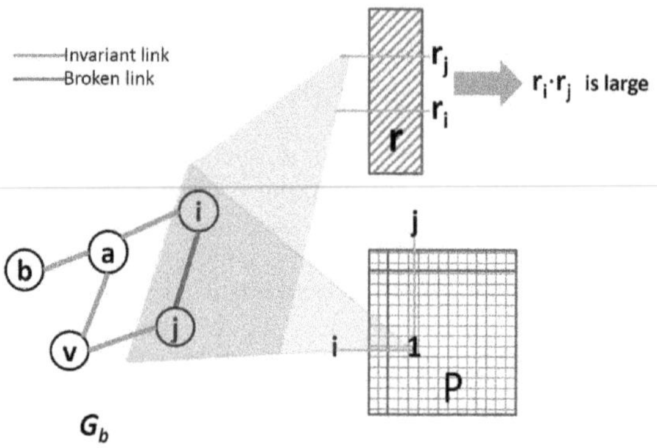

Figure 2: Reconstruction of the broken invariant network using anomaly score vector r.

link in $\mathcal{G}_b$, e.g., $\tilde{\mathbf{P}}_{ij}$ is large, then ideally at least one of the nodes i and j should be abnormal, or equivalently, either $\mathbf{r}_i$ or $\mathbf{r}_j$ should be large. Thus, we can use the product of $\mathbf{r}_i$ and $\mathbf{r}_j$ to reconstruct the value of $\tilde{\mathbf{P}}_{ij}$. In Section 5, we'll further discuss how to normalize them to avoid extreme values. Then, the loss of reconstructing the broken link $\tilde{\mathbf{P}}_{ij}$ can be calculated by $(\mathbf{r}_i \cdot \mathbf{r}_j - \tilde{\mathbf{P}}_{ij})^2$. The reconstruction error of the whole broken network is then $||(\mathbf{r}\mathbf{r}^\top) \circ \mathbf{M} - \tilde{\mathbf{P}}||_F^2$. Here, $\circ$ is element-wise operator, and $\mathbf{M}$ is the logical matrix of the invariant network $\mathcal{G}_l$ (1 with edge, 0 without edge). Let $\mathbf{B} = (1-c)(\mathbf{I}_n - c\tilde{\mathbf{A}})^{-1}$, by substituting $\mathbf{r}$ we obtain the following objective function.

$$\min_{\mathbf{e}_i \in \{0,1\}, 1 \le i \le n} ||(\mathbf{B}\mathbf{e}\mathbf{e}^\top\mathbf{B}^\top) \circ \mathbf{M} - \tilde{\mathbf{P}}||_F^2 \tag{7}$$

Considering that the integer programming in problem (7) is NP-hard, we relax it by using the ℓ_1 penalty on $\mathbf{e}$ with parameter τ to control the number of non-zero entries in $\mathbf{e}$ [23]. Then we reach the following objective function.

$$\min_{\mathbf{e} \ge \mathbf{0}} ||(\mathbf{B}\mathbf{e}\mathbf{e}^\top\mathbf{B}^\top) \circ \mathbf{M} - \tilde{\mathbf{P}}||_F^2 + \tau||\mathbf{e}||_1 \tag{8}$$

3.2 Learning Algorithm

In this section, we present an iterative multiplicative updating algorithm to optimize the objective function in (8). The objective function is invariant under these updates if and only if $\mathbf{e}$ are at a stationary point [17]. The solution is presented in the following theorem, which is derived from the Karush-Kuhn-Tucker (KKT) complementarity condition [3]. Detailed theoretical analysis of the optimization procedure will be presented in the next section.

THEOREM 1. *Updating* $\mathbf{e}$ *according to Eq.* (9) *will monotonically decrease the objective function in Eq.* (8) *until convergence.*

$$\mathbf{e} \leftarrow \mathbf{e} \circ \left\{ \frac{4\left[(\mathbf{B}^\top\tilde{\mathbf{P}}) \circ \mathbf{M}\right]\mathbf{B}\mathbf{e}}{4\left[(\mathbf{B}^\top\mathbf{B}\mathbf{e}\mathbf{e}^\top\mathbf{B}^\top) \circ \mathbf{M}\right]\mathbf{B}\mathbf{e} + \tau\mathbf{1}_n} \right\}^{\frac{1}{4}}, \tag{9}$$

where $\circ$, $\frac{[\cdot]}{[\cdot]}$ *and* $(\cdot)^{\frac{1}{4}}$ *are element-wise operators.*

Based on Theorem 1, we develop the iterative multiplicative updating algorithm for optimization and summarize it in Algorithm 1. We refer to this ranking algorithm as RCA.

Algorithm 1: Ranking Causal Anomalies (RCA)

Input: Network $\mathcal{G}_l$ denoting the invariant network with n nodes, and is represented by an adjacency matrix $\mathbf{A}$, c is the network propagation parameter, τ is the parameter to control the sparsity of $\mathbf{e}$, $\tilde{\mathbf{P}}$ is the normalized adjacency matrix of the broken network, $\mathbf{M}$ is the logical matrix of $\mathcal{G}_l$ (with edge, 0 without edge)
Output: Ranking vector $\mathbf{e}$

```
begin
    for i ← to n do
        D_ii ← Σ_{j=1}^n A_ij;
    end
    D ← diag(D_11, ..., D_ii);
    Ã ← D^{-1/2} A D^{-1/2};
    Initialize e with random values between (0, ];
    B ← ( − c)(I_n − cÃ)^{-1};
    repeat
        Update e by Eq. (9);
    until convergence;
end
```

3.3 Theoretical Analysis

3.3.1 Derivation

We derive the solution to problem (9) following the constrained optimization theory [3]. Since the objective function is not jointly convex, we adopt an effective multiplicative updating algorithm to find a local optimal solution. We prove Theorem 1 in the following.

We formulate the Lagrange function for optimization $L = ||(\mathbf{B}\mathbf{e}\mathbf{e}^\top\mathbf{B}^\top) \circ \mathbf{M} - \tilde{\mathbf{P}}||_F^2 + \tau\mathbf{1}_n^\top\mathbf{e}$. Obviously, $\mathbf{B}$, $\mathbf{M}$ and $\tilde{\mathbf{P}}$ are symmetric matrix. Let $\mathbf{F} = (\mathbf{B}\mathbf{e}\mathbf{e}^\top\mathbf{B}^\top) \circ \mathbf{M}$, then

$$\begin{aligned} \frac{\partial}{\partial \mathbf{e}_m}(\mathbf{F} - \tilde{\mathbf{P}})_{ij}^2 &= 2(\mathbf{F}_{ij} - \tilde{\mathbf{P}}_{ij})\frac{\partial \mathbf{F}_{ij}}{\mathbf{e}_m} \\ &= 4(\mathbf{F}_{ij} - \tilde{\mathbf{P}}_{ij})\mathbf{M}_{ij}(\mathbf{B}_{mi}^\top\mathbf{B}_{j:}\mathbf{e}) \text{ (by symmetry)} \\ &= 4\mathbf{B}_{mi}^\top(\mathbf{F}_{ij} - \tilde{\mathbf{P}}_{ij})\mathbf{M}_{ij}(\mathbf{B}\mathbf{e})_{j:} \end{aligned} \tag{10}$$

It follows that

$$\frac{\partial||\mathbf{F} - \tilde{\mathbf{P}}||_F^2}{\partial \mathbf{e}_m} = 4\mathbf{B}_{m:}^\top[(\mathbf{F} - \tilde{\mathbf{P}}) \circ \mathbf{M}](\mathbf{B}\mathbf{e}), \tag{11}$$

and thereby

$$\frac{\partial||\mathbf{F} - \tilde{\mathbf{P}}||_F^2}{\partial \mathbf{e}} = 4\mathbf{B}^\top[(\mathbf{F} - \tilde{\mathbf{P}}) \circ \mathbf{M}](\mathbf{B}\mathbf{e}). \tag{12}$$

Thus, the partial derivative of Lagrange function with respect to $\mathbf{e}$ is:

$$\nabla_{\mathbf{e}} L = 4\mathbf{B}^\top\left[(\mathbf{B}\mathbf{e}\mathbf{e}^\top\mathbf{B}^\top - \tilde{\mathbf{P}}) \circ \mathbf{M}\right]\mathbf{B}\mathbf{e} + \tau\mathbf{1}_n, \tag{13}$$

where $\mathbf{1}_n$ is the $n \times 1$ vector of all ones. Using the Karush-Kuhn-Tucker (KKT) complementarity condition [3] for the non-negative constraint on $\mathbf{e}$, we have

$$\nabla_{\mathbf{e}} L \circ \mathbf{e} = \mathbf{0} \tag{14}$$

The above formula leads to the updating rule for $\mathbf{e}$ that is shown in Eq. (9).

3.3.2 Convergence

We use the auxiliary function approach [17] to prove the convergence of Eq. (9) in Theorem 1. We first introduce the definition of auxiliary function as follows.

Definition 3.1. *$Z(h, \hat{h})$ is an auxiliary function for $L(h)$ if the conditions*

$$Z(h, \hat{h}) \geq L(h) \quad \text{and} \quad Z(h, h) = L(h), \tag{15}$$

are satisfied for any given $h, \hat{h}$ [17].

Lemma 3.1. *If Z is an auxiliary function for L, then L is non-increasing under the update [17].*

$$h^{(t+1)} = \underset{h}{\operatorname{argmin}}\, Z(h, h^{(t)}) \tag{16}$$

Theorem 2. *Let $L(\mathbf{e})$ denote the sum of all terms in L containing $\mathbf{e}$. The following function*

$$\begin{aligned} Z(\mathbf{e}, \hat{\mathbf{e}}) = & -2 \sum_{ij} \hat{\mathbf{e}}_i \left\{ \left[(\mathbf{B}^\top \tilde{\mathbf{P}}) \circ \mathbf{M} \right] \mathbf{B} \right\}_{ij} \hat{\mathbf{e}}_j \left(1 + \log \frac{\mathbf{e}_i \mathbf{e}_j}{\hat{\mathbf{e}}_i \hat{\mathbf{e}}_j} \right) \\ & + \sum_i \left\{ \left[(\mathbf{B}^\top \mathbf{B} \hat{\mathbf{e}} \hat{\mathbf{e}}^\top \mathbf{B}^\top) \circ \mathbf{M} \right] \mathbf{B} \hat{\mathbf{e}} \right\}_i \frac{\mathbf{e}_i^4}{\hat{\mathbf{e}}_i^3} \\ & + \frac{\tau}{4} \sum_i \frac{\mathbf{e}_i^4 + 3\hat{\mathbf{e}}_i^4}{\hat{\mathbf{e}}_i^3} \end{aligned} \tag{17}$$

is an auxiliary function for $L(\mathbf{e})$. Furthermore, it is a convex function in $\mathbf{e}$ and has a global minimum.

Theorem 2 can be proven in a similar way as in [7] by validating $Z(\mathbf{e}, \hat{\mathbf{e}}) \geq L(\mathbf{e})$, $Z(\mathbf{e}, \mathbf{e}) = L(\mathbf{e})$, and the Hessian matrix $\nabla\nabla_{\mathbf{e}} Z(\mathbf{e}, \hat{\mathbf{e}}) \succeq \mathbf{0}$. Due to space limitation, the detail of the proof is omitted.

Based on Theorem 2, we can minimize $Z(\mathbf{e}, \hat{\mathbf{e}})$ with respect to $\mathbf{e}$ with $\hat{\mathbf{e}}$ fixed. We set $\nabla_{\mathbf{e}} Z(\mathbf{e}, \hat{\mathbf{e}}) = \mathbf{0}$, and get the following updating formula

$$\mathbf{e} \leftarrow \hat{\mathbf{e}} \circ \left\{ \frac{4 \left[(\mathbf{B}^\top \tilde{\mathbf{P}}) \circ \mathbf{M} \right] \mathbf{B} \hat{\mathbf{e}}}{4 \left[(\mathbf{B}^\top \mathbf{B} \hat{\mathbf{e}} \hat{\mathbf{e}}^\top \mathbf{B}^\top) \circ \mathbf{M} \right] \mathbf{B} \hat{\mathbf{e}} + \tau \mathbf{1}_n} \right\}^{\frac{1}{4}}, \tag{18}$$

which is consistent with the updating formula derived from the KKT condition aforementioned.

From Lemma 3.1 and Theorem 2, for each subsequent iteration of updating $\mathbf{e}$, we have $L(\mathbf{e}^0) = Z(\mathbf{e}^0, \mathbf{e}^0) \geq Z(\mathbf{e}^1, \mathbf{e}^0) \geq Z(\mathbf{e}^1, \mathbf{e}^1) = L(\mathbf{e}^1) \geq ... \geq L(\mathbf{e}^{Iter})$. Thus $L(\mathbf{e})$ monotonically decreases. Since the objective function Eq. (8) is lower bounded by 0, the correctness of Theorem 1 is proven.

3.3.3 Complexity Analysis

In Algorithm 1, we need to calculate the inverse of an $n \times n$ matrix, which takes $\mathcal{O}(n^3)$ time. In each iteration, the multiplication between two $n \times n$ matrices is inevitable, thus the overall time complexity of Algorithm 1 is $\mathcal{O}(Iter \cdot n^3)$, where $Iter$ is the number of iterations needed for convergence. In the following section, we will propose an efficient algorithm that reduces the time complexity to $\mathcal{O}(Iter \cdot n^2)$.

4. COMPUTATIONAL SPEED UP

In this section, we will propose an efficient algorithm that avoids the matrix inverse calculations as well as the multiplication between two $n \times n$ matrices. The time complexity can be reduced to $\mathcal{O}(Iter \cdot n^2)$.

We achieve the computational speed up by relaxing the objective function in (8) to jointly optimize $\mathbf{r}$ and $\mathbf{e}$. The objective function is shown in the following.

$$\begin{aligned} \min_{\mathbf{e} \geq \mathbf{0}, \mathbf{r} \geq \mathbf{0}} & c\mathbf{r}^\top (\mathbf{I}_n - \tilde{\mathbf{A}})\mathbf{r} + (1-c)||\mathbf{r} - \mathbf{e}||_F^2 \\ & + \lambda ||(\mathbf{r}\mathbf{r}^\top) \circ \mathbf{M} - \tilde{\mathbf{P}}||_F^2 + \tau ||\mathbf{e}||_1 \end{aligned} \tag{19}$$

To optimize this objective function, we can use an alternating scheme. That is, we optimize the objective with respect to $\mathbf{r}$ while fixing $\mathbf{e}$, and vise versa. This procedure continues until convergence. The objective function is invariant under these updates if and only if $\mathbf{r}, \mathbf{e}$ are at a stationary point [17]. Specifically, the solution to the optimization problem in Eq. (19) is based on the following theorem, which is derived from the Karush-Kuhn-Tucker (KKT) complementarity condition [3]. The derivation of it and the proof of Theorem 3 is similar to that of Theorem 1.

Theorem 3. *Alternatively updating $\mathbf{e}$ and $\mathbf{r}$ according to Eq. (20) and Eq. (21) will monotonically decrease the objective function in Eq. (19) until convergence.*

$$\mathbf{r} \leftarrow \mathbf{r} \circ \left\{ \frac{\tilde{\mathbf{A}}\mathbf{r} + 2\lambda(\tilde{\mathbf{P}} \circ \mathbf{M})\mathbf{r} + (1-c)\mathbf{e}}{\mathbf{r} + 2\lambda \left[(\mathbf{r}\mathbf{r}^\top) \circ \mathbf{M} \right] \mathbf{r}} \right\}^{\frac{1}{4}} \tag{20}$$

$$\mathbf{e} \leftarrow \mathbf{e} \circ \left[\frac{2(1-c)\mathbf{r}}{\tau \mathbf{1}_n + 2(1-c)\mathbf{e}} \right]^{\frac{1}{2}} \tag{21}$$

Based on Theorem 3, we can develop the iterative multiplicative updating algorithm for optimization similar to Algorithm 1. Due to page limit we skip the details. We refer to this ranking algorithm as R-RCA. From Eq. (20) and Eq. (21), we observe that the calculation of the inverse of the $n \times n$ matrix and the multiplication between two $n \times n$ matrices in Algorithm 1 are not necessary. As we will see in Section 7.4, the relaxed versions of our algorithm can greatly improve the computational efficiency.

5. SOFTMAX NORMALIZATION

In Section 3, we use the product $\mathbf{r}_i \cdot \mathbf{r}_j$ as the strength of evidence that the correlation between node i and j is vanishing (broken). However, it suffers from the extreme values in the ranking values $\mathbf{r}$. To reduce the influence of the extreme values or outliers, we employ the softmax normalization on the ranking values $\mathbf{r}$. The ranking values are nonlinearly transformed using the sigmoidal function before the multiplication is performed. Thus, the reconstruction error is expressed by $||(\sigma(\mathbf{r})\sigma^\top(\mathbf{r})) \circ \mathbf{M} - \tilde{\mathbf{P}}||_F^2$, where $\sigma(\cdot)$ is the softmax function with:

$$\sigma(\mathbf{r})_i = \frac{e^{\mathbf{r}_i}}{\sum_{k=1}^n e^{\mathbf{r}_k}}, (i = 1, ..., n). \tag{22}$$

The corresponding objective function in Algorithm 1 is modified to the following

$$\min_{\mathbf{e} \geq \mathbf{0}} ||(\sigma(\mathbf{B}\mathbf{e})\sigma^\top(\mathbf{B}\mathbf{e})) \circ \mathbf{M} - \tilde{\mathbf{P}}||_F^2 + \tau ||\mathbf{e}||_1. \tag{23}$$

Similarly, the objective function for Eq. (19) is modified to the following

$$\begin{aligned} \min_{\mathbf{e} \geq \mathbf{0}, \mathbf{r} \geq \mathbf{0}} & c\mathbf{r}^\top (\mathbf{I}_n - \tilde{\mathbf{A}})\mathbf{r} + (1-c)||\mathbf{r} - \mathbf{e}||_F^2 \\ & + \lambda ||(\sigma(\mathbf{r})\sigma^\top(\mathbf{r})) \circ \mathbf{M} - \tilde{\mathbf{P}}||_F^2 + \tau ||\mathbf{e}||_1. \end{aligned} \tag{24}$$

The optimization of these two objective functions are based on the following two theorems.

THEOREM 4. *Updating* $\mathbf{e}$ *according to Eq. (25) will monotonically decrease the objective function in Eq. (23) until convergence.*

$$\mathbf{e} \leftarrow \mathbf{e} \circ \left\{ \frac{4\left[(\mathbf{B}^\top \mathbf{\Psi} \tilde{\mathbf{P}}) \circ \mathbf{M}\right] \sigma(\mathbf{Be})}{4\left[(\mathbf{B}^\top \mathbf{\Psi} \sigma(\mathbf{Be}) \sigma^\top(\mathbf{Be})) \circ \mathbf{M}\right] \sigma(\mathbf{Be}) + \tau \mathbf{1}_n} \right\}^{\frac{1}{4}}, \quad (25)$$

where $\mathbf{\Psi} = \{\mathrm{diag}\,[\sigma(\mathbf{Be})] - \sigma(\mathbf{Be})\sigma^\top(\mathbf{Be})\}$.

THEOREM 5. *Updating* $\mathbf{r}$ *according to Eq. (26) will monotonically decrease the objective function in Eq. (24) until convergence.*

$$\mathbf{r} \leftarrow \mathbf{r} \circ \left\{ \frac{\tilde{\mathbf{A}}\mathbf{r} \quad \lambda\left[\left((\sigma(\mathbf{r})\mathbf{1}_n^\top) \circ \tilde{\mathbf{P}} \quad \rho\mathbf{\Lambda}\right) \circ \mathbf{M}\right] \sigma(\mathbf{r}) \quad (\ - c)\mathbf{e}}{\mathbf{r} \quad \lambda\left[\left((\sigma(\mathbf{r}) \circ \sigma(\mathbf{r}))\sigma^\top(\mathbf{r}) \quad \sigma(\mathbf{r})(\sigma^\top(\mathbf{r})\tilde{\mathbf{P}})\right) \circ \mathbf{M}\right] \sigma(\mathbf{r})} \right\}^{\frac{1}{4}}, \quad (26)$$

where $\mathbf{\Lambda} = \sigma(\mathbf{r})\sigma^\top(\mathbf{r})$ *and* $\rho = \sigma^\top(\mathbf{r})\sigma(\mathbf{r})$.

Theorem 4 and Theorem 5 can be proven with a similar strategy to that of Theorem 1. We refer to the ranking algorithms with *softmax* normalization (Eq. (23) and Eq. (24)) as RCA-SOFT and R-RCA-SOFT respectively.

6. TEMPORAL SMOOTHING ON MULTIPLE BROKEN NETWORKS

As discussed in Section 1, although the number of anomaly nodes could increase due to fault propagation in the network, the root cause anomalies will be stable within a short time period T[14]. Based on this intuition, we further develop a smoothing strategy by jointly considering the temporal broken networks. Specifically, we add a smoothing term $||\mathbf{e}^{(t)} - \mathbf{e}^{(t-1)}||_2^2$ to the objective functions. Here, $\mathbf{e}^{(t-1)}$ and $\mathbf{e}^{(t)}$ are causal anomaly ranking vectors for two successive time points. For example, the objective function of algorithm RCA with temporal broken networks smoothing is shown in Eq. (27).

$$\min_{\mathbf{e}^{(t)} \geq \mathbf{0}, 1 \leq t \leq T} \sum_{t=1}^{T} \left[||(\mathbf{B}\mathbf{e}^{(t)}(\mathbf{e}^{(t)})^\top \mathbf{B}^\top) \circ \mathbf{M} - \tilde{\mathbf{P}}^{(t)}||_F^2 + \tau ||\mathbf{e}^{(t)}||_1 \right] + \alpha ||\mathbf{e}^{(t)} - \mathbf{e}^{(t-1)}||_2^2 \quad (27)$$

Here, $\tilde{\mathbf{P}}^{(t)}$ is the degree-normalized adjacency matrix of broken network at time point t. Similar to the discussion in Section 3.3, we can derive the updating formula of Eq. (27) in the following.

$$\mathbf{e}^{(t)} \leftarrow \mathbf{e}^{(t)} \circ \left\{ \frac{4\left[(\mathbf{B}^\top \tilde{\mathbf{P}}^{(t)}) \circ \mathbf{M}\right] \mathbf{B}\mathbf{e}^{(t)} \quad \alpha \mathbf{e}^{(t-1)}}{4\left[(\mathbf{B}^\top \mathbf{B}\mathbf{e}^{(t)}(\mathbf{e}^{(t)})^\top \mathbf{B}^\top) \circ \mathbf{M}\right] \mathbf{B}\mathbf{e}^{(t)} \quad \tau \mathbf{1}_n \quad \alpha \mathbf{e}^{(t)}} \right\}^{\frac{1}{4}} \quad (28)$$

The updating formula for R-RCA, RCA-SOFT, and R-RCA-SOFT with temporal broken networks smoothing is similar. Due to space limit, we skip the details. We refer to the algorithms with temporal smoothing as T-RCA, T-R-RCA, T-RCA-SOFT and T-R-RCA-SOFT respectively.

7. EMPIRICAL STUDY

In this section, we perform extensive experiments to evaluate the performance of the proposed methods (summarized in Table 1). We use both simulated data and real-world monitoring datasets for validation. For comparison, we select several state-of-the-art methods, including mRank and gRank in [8, 13], and LBP [22]. For all the methods, the tuning parameters were tuned using cross validation. We use several evaluation metrics including precision, recall, and nDCG [12] to measure the performance. The precision and recall are computed on the top-K ranking result, where K is typically chosen as twice the actual number of ground-truth causal anomalies [12, 22]. The nDCG of the top-p ranking result is defined as $nDCG_p = \frac{DCG_p}{IDCG_p}$, where $DCG_p = \sum_{i=1}^{p} \frac{2^{rel_i}-1}{\log_2(1+i)}$. Here, $IDCG_p$ is the DCG_p value on the ground-truth, and p is smaller than or equal to the actual number of ground-truth anomalies. The rel_i represents the anomaly score of the ith item in the ranking list of the ground-truth.

7.1 Simulation Study

We first evaluate the performance of the proposed methods using simulations. We have followed [8, 22] in generating the simulation data.

7.1.1 *Data Generation*

We first generate 5000 synthetic time series data to simulate the monitoring records[2]. Each time series contains 1,050 time points. Based on the invariant model introduced in Section 2.1, we build the invariant network by using the first 1,000 time points in the time series. This generates an invariant network containing 1,551 nodes and 157,371 edges. To generate invariant network of different sizes, we randomly sample 200, 500, and 1000 nodes from the whole invariant network and evaluate the algorithms on these sub-networks.

To generate the root cause anomaly, we randomly select 10 nodes from the network, and assign each of them an anomaly score between 1 and 10. The ranking of these scores is used as the ground-truth. To simulate the anomaly prorogation, we further use these scores as the vector $\mathbf{e}$ in Eq. (6) and calculate $\mathbf{r}$ ($c = 0.9$). The values of the top-30 time series with largest values in $\mathbf{r}$ are then modified by changing their amplitude value with the ratio $1+\mathbf{r}_i$. That is, if the observed values of one time series is y_1, after changing it from y_1 to y_2, the manually-injected degree of anomaly $\frac{|y_2-y_1|}{|y_1|}$ is equal to $1 + \mathbf{r}_i$. We denote this anomaly generation scheme as *amplitude-based* anomaly generation.

7.1.2 *Performance Evaluation*

Using the simulated data, we compare the performance of different algorithms. In this example, we only consider the training time series as one snapshot; multiple snapshot cases involving temporal smoothing will be examined in the real datasets. Due to the page limit, we report the precision, recall and nDCG for only the top-10 items considering that the ground-truth contains 10 anomalies. Similar results can be observed with other settings of K and p. For each algorithm, reported result is averaged over 100 randomly selected subsets of the training data.

From Figure 3, we have several key observations. First, the proposed algorithms significantly outperform other competing methods, which demonstrates the advantage of taking into account fault prorogation in ranking casual anomalies. We also notice that performance of all ranking algorithms will decline on larger invariant networks with more nodes, indicating that anomaly ranking becomes more challenging on

[2]http://cs.unc.edu/~weicheng/synthetics5000.csv

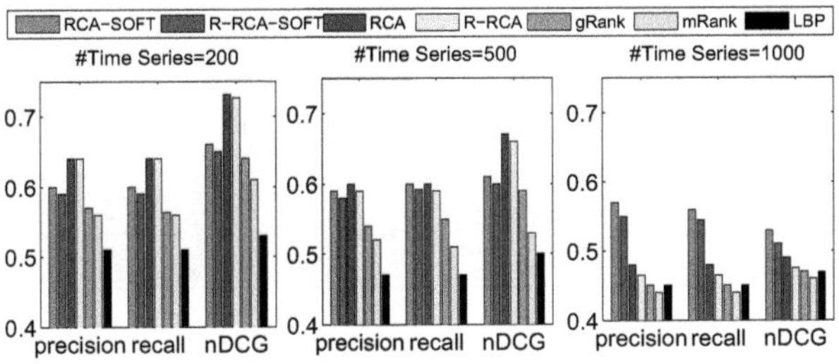

Figure 3: Comparison on synthetic data($K, p = 10$).

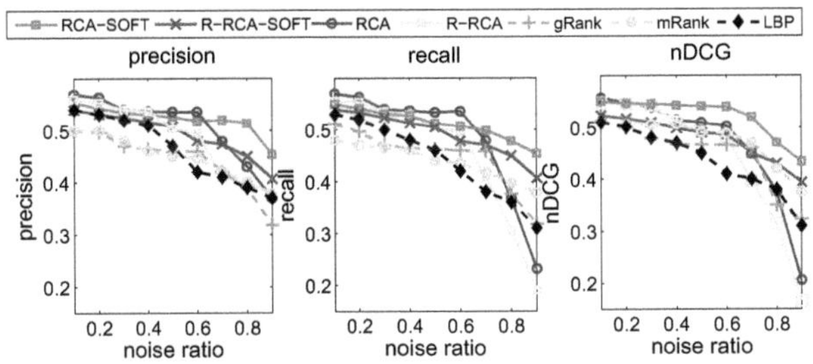

Figure 4: Performance with different noise ratio($K, p = 10$).

networks with more complex behaviour. However, the ranking result with *softmax* is less sensitive to the size of the invariant network, suggesting that the *softmax* normalization can effectively improve the robustness of the algorithm. This is quite beneficial in real-life applications, especially when data are noisy. Finally, we observe that RCA and RCA-SOFT outperform R-RCA and R-RCA-SOFT, respectively. This implies that the relaxed versions of the algorithms are less accurate. Nevertheless, their accuracies are still very comparable to those of the RCA and RCA-SOFT methods. In addition, the efficiency of the relaxed algorithms is greatly improved, as discussed in Section 4 and Section 7.4.

7.1.3 Robustness Evaluation

Practical invariant network and broken edges can be quite noisy. In this section, we further examine the performance of the proposed algorithms w.r.t. different noise levels. To do this, we randomly perturb a portion of non-broken edges in the invariant network. Results are shown in Figure 4. We observe that, even when the noise ratio approaches 50%, the precision, recall and nDCG of the proposed approaches still attain 0.5. This indicates the robustness of the proposed algorithms. We also observe that, when the noise ratio is very large, RCA-SOFT and R-RCA-SOFT work better than RCA and R-RCA, respectively. This is similar to those observations made in Section 7.1.2. As has been discussed in Section 5, the *softmax* normalization can greatly suppress the impact of extreme values and outliers in $\mathbf{r}$, thus improves the robustness.

7.2 Ranking Causal Anomalies on Bank Information System Data

In this section, we apply the proposed methods to detect causal abnormal components on a Bank Information System (BIS) data set [8, 22]. The monitoring data are collected from a real-world bank information system logs, which contain 11 categories. Each category has a varying number of time series, and Table 2 gives five categories as examples. The data set contains the flow intensities collected every 6 seconds. In total, we have 1,273 flow intensity time series. The training data is collected at normal system states, where each time series has 168 time points. The invariant network is then generated on the training data as described in Section 2.1. The testing data of the 1,273 flow intensity time series are collected during abnormal system states, where each time series contain 169 time points. We track the changes of the invariant network with the testing data using the method described in Section 2.1. Once we obtain the broken networks at different time points, we perform causal anomaly ranking in these temporal slots jointly. Properties of the networks constructed are summarized in Table 3.

Based on the knowledge from system experts, the root cause anomaly at $t = 120$ in the testing data is related to "DB16". An illustration of two "DB16" related monitoring data are shown in Figure 5. We highlight $t : 120$ with red square. Obviously, their behaviour looks anomalous from that time point on. Due to the complex dependency among different monitoring time series, it is impractical to obtain a full ranking of abnormal measurement. Fortunately, we have a unique semantic label associated with each measurement. For example, some semantic labels read "DB16:DISK hdx Request" and "WEB26 PAGEOUT RATE". Thus, we can extract all measurements whose titles have the prefix "DB16" as the ground-truth anomalies. The ranking score is

Categories	Samples of Measurements
CPU	utilization, user usage time, IO wait time
DISK	# of write operations, write time, weighted IO time
MEM	run queue, collision rate, UsageRate
NET	error rate, packet rate
SYS	UTIL, MODE UTIL

Table 2: Examples of categories and monitors.

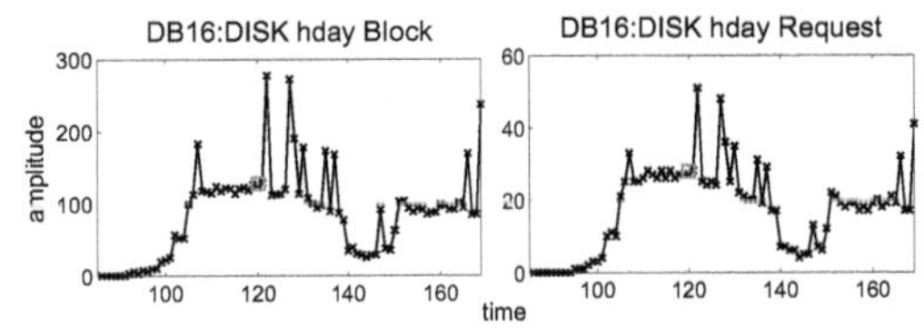

Figure 5: Two example monitoring data of BIS.

Data Set	#Monitors	#invariant links	#broken edges at given time point
BIS	1273	39116	18052
Coal Plant	1625	9451	56

Table 3: Data set description.

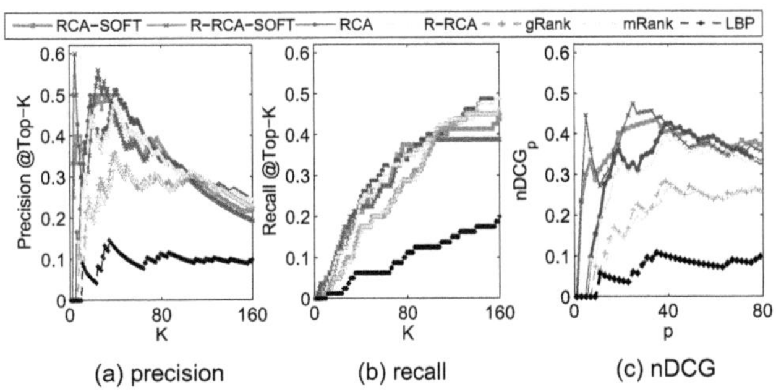

Figure 6: Comparison on BIS data.

mRank	gRank	LBP	RCA	RCA-SOFT	R-RCA	R-RCA-SOFT
WEB16:NET eth1 BYNETIF	HUB18:MEM UsageRate	WEB22:SYS MODE UTIL	HUB17:DISK hda Request	DB17:DISK hdm Block	HUB17:DISK hda Request	DB17:DISK hdm Block
HUB17:DISK hda Request	HUB17:DISK hda Request	DB15:DISK hdaz Block	DB17:DISK hday Block	DB17:DISK hdba Block	DB15:PACKET Output	DB17:DISK hdba Block
AP12:DISK hd45 Block	AP12:DISK hd45 Block	WEB12:NET eth1 BYNETIF	HUB17:DISK hda Busy	DB16:DISK hdm Block	HUB17:DISK hda Busy	DB16:DISK hdm Block
AP12:DISK hd1 Block	AP12:DISK hd1 Block	WEB17:DISK BYDSK	DB18:DISK hdba Block	DB18:DISK hdm Block	DB17:DISK hdm Block	DB16:DISK hdj Request
WEB19:DISK BYDSK	AP11:DISK hd45 Block	DB18:DISK hdt Busy	DB18:DISK hdm Block	DB16:DISK hdj Request	DB17:DISK hdba Block	DB16:DISK hdax Request
AP11:DISK hd45 Block	AP11:DISK hd1 Block	DB15:DISK hdl Request	DB16:DISK hdm Block	DB18:DISK hdba Block	DB18:DISK hdm Block	DB18:DISK hdag Request
AP11:DISK hd1 Block	DB17:DISK hday Block	WEB21:DISK BYDSK	DB17:DISK hdba Block	DB16:DISK hdax Request	DB16:DISK hdm Block	DB18:DISK hdm Block
DB16:DISK hdm Block	DB15:PACKET Input	WEB27:FREE UTIL	DB17:DISK hdm Block	DB18:DISK hdag Request	DB18:DISK hdba Block	DB18:DISK hdbu Request
DB17:DISK hdm Block	DB17:DISK hdm Block	WEB19:NET eth0	DB16:DISK hdba Block	DB18:DISK hdbu Request	DB17:DISK hday Block	DB18:DISK hdx Request
DB18:DISK hdm Block	DB16:DISK hdm Block	WEB25:PAGEOUT RATE	DB16:DISK hdj Request	DB16:DISK hdba Block	DB16:DISK hdba Block	DB18:DISK hdax Request
DB17:DISK hdba Block	DB17:DISK hdba Block	DB16:DISK hdy Block	DB18:DISK hdag Request	DB18:DISK hdx Request	DB16:DISK hdj Request	DB18:DISK hdba Block
DB18:DISK hdba Block	DB18:DISK hdm Block	AP13:DISK hd30 Block	DB16:DISK hdax Request	DB18:DISK hdax Request	DB18:DISK hdag Request	DB16:DISK hdx Request

Table 4: Top 12 anomalies detected by different methods on BIS data(t:120).

mRank	gRank	LBP	RCA	RCA-SOFT	R-RCA	R-RCA-SOFT
10	7	4	14	16	13	17

Table 5: Number of "DB16" related monitors in top 32 results on BIS data(t:120).

determined by the number of broken edges associated with each measurement. Here our goal is to demonstrate how the top-ranked measurements selected by our method are related to the "DB16" root cause. Altogether, there are 80 measurements related to "DB16" in the invariant network, so we report the precision, recall with K ranging from 1 to 160 and the nDCG with p ranging from 1 to 80, respectively.

The results are shown in Figure 6. The relative performance of different approaches is consistent with the observations in the simulation study. Again, the proposed algorithms outperform baseline methods by a large margin. To examine the top-ranked items more clearly, we list the top-12 results of different approaches in Table 4 and report the number of "DB16"-related monitors in Table 5. From Table 4, we observe that the three baseline methods only report one "DB16" related measurement in the top-12 results, and the actual rank of the "DB16"-related measurement appear lower (worse) than that of the proposed methods. We also notice that the ranking algorithms with *softmax* normalization outperform others. From Tables 4 and 5, we can see that top ranked items reported by RCA-SOFT and R-RCA-SOFT are more relevant than those reported by RCA and R-RCA, respectively. This clearly illustrates the effectiveness of the *softmax* normalization in reducing the influence of extreme values or outliers in the data.

As discussed in Section 1, the root anomalies could further propagate from one component to related ones over time, which may or may not necessarily relate to "DB16". Such anomaly propagation makes anomaly detection even harder. To study how the performance varies at different time points, we compare the performance at $t = 120$ and $t = 122$, respectively in Figure 7 (p,K=80). Clearly, the performance declines for all methods. However, the proposed methods are less sensitive to anomaly propagation than others, suggesting that our approaches can better handle the fault propagation problem. We believe this is attributed to the network diffusion model that explicitly captures the fault propagation processes. We also list the top-12 abnormal at $t = 122$ in Table 6. Due to page limit, we only show the results of mRank, gRank, RCA-SOFT and R-RCA-SOFT. By comparing the results in Tables 4 and 6, we can observe that RCA-SOFT and R-RCA-SOFT significantly outperform mRank and gRank, the latter two methods which are based on the percentage of broken edges are more sensitive to the anomaly prorogation.

mRank	gRank	RCA-SOFT	R-RCA-SOFT
WEB21:NET eth1 BYNETIF	WEB21:NET eth0 BYNETIF	DB17:DISK hdm Block	DB17:DISK hdm Block
WEB21:NET eth0 BYNETIF	WEB21:NET eth1 BYNETIF	DB17:DISK hdba Block	DB17:DISK hdba Block
WEB21:FREE UTIL	HUB18:MEM UsageRate	DB16:DISK hdm Block	DB16:DISK hdm Block
AP12:DISK hd45 Block	WEB21:FREE UTIL	DB18:DISK hdm Block	DB16:DISK hdj Request
AP12:DISK hd1 Block	WEB26:PAGEOUT RATE	DB16:DISK hdj Request	DB16:DISK hdax Request
DB18:DISK hday Block	AP12:DISK hd45 Block	DB18:DISK hdba Block	DB18:DISK hdm Block
DB18:DISK hdk Block	AP12:DISK hd1 Block	DB16:DISK hdax Request	DB18:DISK hdx Request
DB18:DISK hday Request	DB18:DISK hday Block	DB16:DISK hdba Block	DB18:DISK hdba Block
DB18:DISK hdk Request	DB18:DISK hdk Block	DB18:DISK hdx Request	DB16:DISK hdba Block
WEB26:PAGEOUT RATE	DB18:DISK hday Request	DB18:DISK hdbl Request	DB18:DISK hdax Request
DB17:DISK hdm Block	DB18:DISK hdk Request	DB16:DISK hdx Busy	DB16:PACKET Inputx
DB16:DISK hdm Block	AP11:DISK hd45 Block	DB16:DISK hdx Request	DB18:DISK hdbl Request

Table 6: Top 12 anomalies on BIS data(t:122).

T-RCA	T-RCA-SOFT	T-R-RCA	T-R-RCA-SOFT
WEB14:NET eth0 BYNETIF	DB17:DISK hdm Block	WEB14:NET eth0 BYNETIF	DB17:DISK hdm Block
WEB16:DISK BYDSK	DB17:DISK hdba Block	WEB21:NET eth0 BYNETIF	DB17:DISK hdba Block
DB18:DISK hdba Block	DB16:DISK hdm Block	WEB16:DISK BYDSK PHYS	DB16:DISK hdm Block
DB18:DISK hdm Block	DB18:DISK hdm Block	WEB21:FREE UTIL	DB18:DISK hdm Block
DB17:DISK hdba Block	DB16:DISK hdj Request	DB15:PACKET Output	DB16:DISK hdj Request
DB16:DISK hdm Block	DB18:DISK hdba Block	DB16:DISK hdj Request	DB18:DISK hdba Block
DB17:DISK hdm Block	DB16:DISK hdax Request	DB17:DISK hdm Block	DB16:DISK hdax Request
DB16:DISK hdba Block	DB16:DISK hdba Block	DB16:DISK hdba Block	DB18:DISK hdx Request
DB16:DISK hdj Request	DB18:DISK hdx Request	DB17:DISK hday Block	DB16:DISK hdba Block
DB16:DISK hdax Request	DB18:DISK hdbl Request	DB16:DISK hdm Block	DB18:DISK hdbl Request
DB16:DISK hdx Busy	DB16:DISK hdx Busy	DB16:DISK hdax Request	DB16:DISK hdx Request
DB16:DISK hdbl Busy	DB16:DISK hdx Request	DB18:DISK hdba Block	DB16:DISK hdx Busy

Table 7: Top 12 anomalies reported by methods with temporal smoothing on BIS data(t:120-121).

	RCA	RCA-SOFT	R-RCA	R-RCA-SOFT
Without temporal smoothing	4	4	3	4
With temporal smoothing	6	6	4	6

Table 8: Comparison on the number of "DB16" related anomalies in top-12 results on BIS data.

mRank	gRank	LBP	RCA	RCA-SOFT	R-RCA	R-RCA-SOFT
Y0039	Y0256	Y0256	X0146	X0146	X0146	X0146
X0128	Y0045	X0146	Y0045	Y0256	X0128	X0166
Y0256	Y0028	F0454	X0128	F0454	F0454	X0144
H0021	X0146	X0128	Y0030	J0079	Y0256	X0165
X0146	X0057	Y0039	X0057	Y0308	Y0039	X0142
X0149	X0061	X0166	X0158	X0166	Y0246	J0079
H0022	X0068	X0144	X0068	X0144	Y0045	X0164
F0454	X0143	X0149	X0061	X0128	Y0028	X0145
H0020	X0158	J0085	X0139	X0165	X0056	X0143
X0184	X0164	X0061	X0143	X0142	J0079	X0163
X0166	J0164	Y0030	H0021	H0022	X0149	J0164
J0164	H0021	J0079	F0454	X0143	X0145	X0149

Table 9: Top anomalies on coal plant data.

We further validate the effectiveness of proposed methods with temporal smoothing. We report the top-12 results of different methods with smoothing at two successive time points $t = 120$ and $t = 121$ in Table 7. The number of "DB16"-related monitors in the top-12 results is summarized in Table 8. From Tables 7 and 8, we observe a significant performance improvement of our methods with temporal broken networks smoothing compared with those without smoothing. As discussed in Section 6, since causal anomalies of a system usually do not change within a short period of time, utilizing such smoothness can effectively suppress noise and thus give better ranking accuracy.

7.3 Fault Diagnosis on Coal Plant Data

In this section, we test the proposed methods in the application of fault diagnosis on a coal plant cyber-physical

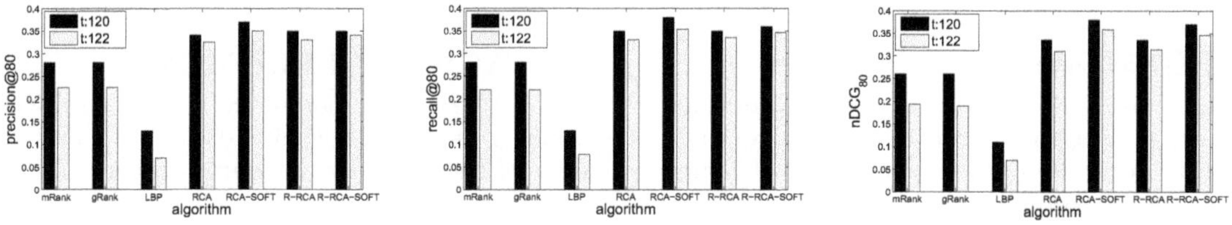

(a) precision (b) recall (c) nDCG

Figure 7: Performance at t:120 v.s. t:122 on BIS data(p,K=80).

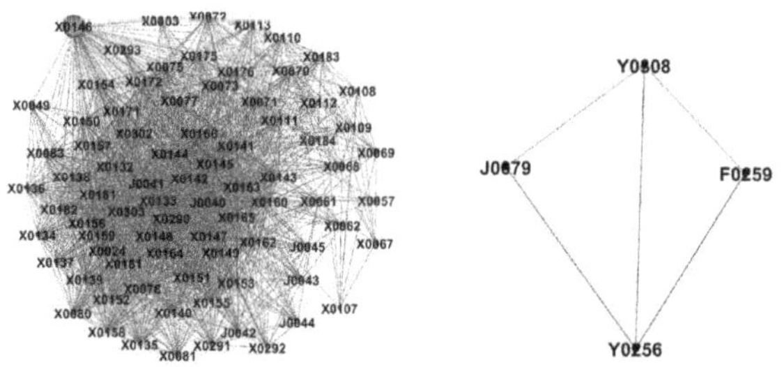

(a) Egonet of node "X0146" (b) Egonet of node "Y0256"

Figure 8: Egonet of node "X0146" and "Y0256" in invariant network and vanishing correlations(red edges) on coal plant data.

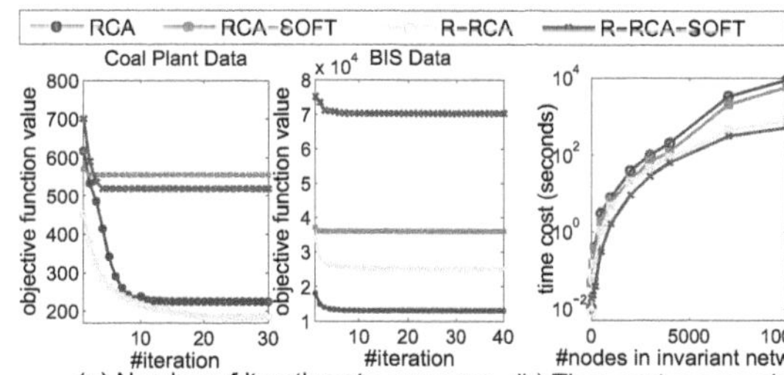

(a) Number of iterations to converge (b) Time costs comparison

Figure 9: Number of iterations to converge and time cost comparison.

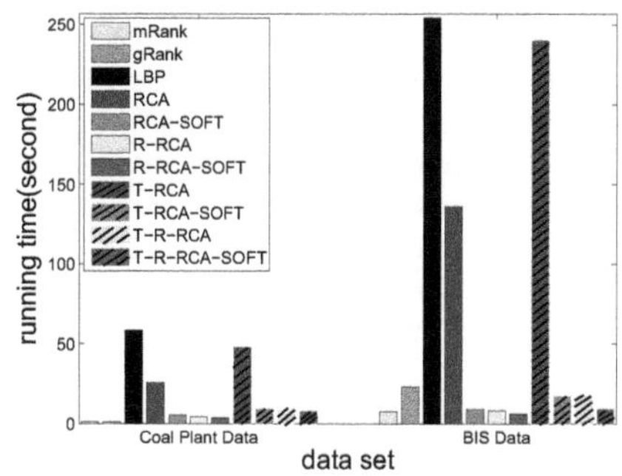

Figure 10: Running time on real data sets.

system data. The data set contains time series collected through 1625 electric sensors installed on different components of the coal plant system. Using the invariant model described in Section 2.1, we generate the invariant network that contains 9451 invariant links. For privacy reasons, we remove sensitive descriptions of the data.

Based on knowledge from domain experts, in the abnormal stage, the root cause is associated with component "X0146". We report the top-12 results of different ranking algorithms in Table 9. We observe that our algorithms all rank component "X0146" the highest, while the baseline methods could give higher ranks to other components. In Figure 8(a), we visualize the egonet of the node "X0146" in the invariant network, which is defined as the 1-step neighborhood around node "X0146", including the node itself, direct neighbors, and all connections among these nodes in the invariant network. Here, green lines denote the invariant link, and red lines denote vanishing correlations (broken links). Since the node "Y0256" is top-ranked by the baseline methods, we also visualize its egonet in Figure 8(b) for a comparison. There are 80 links related to "X0146" in the invariant network, and 14 of them are broken. Namely the percentage of broken edges is only 17.5% for a truly anomalous component. In contrast, the percentage of broken edges for the node "Y0256" is 100%, namely a false-positive node can have a very high percentage of broken edges in practice. This explains why baseline approaches using the percentage of broken edges could fail, because the percentage of broken edges does not serve as a reliable evidence of the degree of causal anomalies. In comparison, our approach takes into account the global structures of the invariant network via network propagation, thus the resultant ranking is more meaningful.

7.4 Time Performance Evaluation

In this section, we study the efficiency of proposed methods using the following metrics: 1) the number of iterations for convergence; 2) the running time (in seconds) ; and 3) the scalability of the proposed algorithms. Figure 9(a) shows the value of the objective function with respect to the number of iterations on different data sets. We can observe that, the objective value decreases steadily with the number of iterations. Typically less than 100 iterations are needed for convergence. We also observe that our method with *softmax* normalization takes fewer iterations to converge. This is because the normalization is able to reduce the influence of extreme values [21]. We also report the running time of each algorithm on the two real data sets in Figure 10. We can see that the proposed methods can detect causal anomalies very efficiently, even with the temporal smoothing module.

To evaluate the computational scalability, we randomly generate invariant networks with different number of nodes (with network density=10) and examine the computational cost. Here 10% edges are randomly selected as broken links. Using simulated data, we compare the running time of RCA, R-RCA, RCA-SOFT, and R-RCA-SOFT. Figure 9(b) plots the running time of different algorithms w.r.t. the number of nodes in the invariant network. We can see that the relaxed versions of our algorithm are computationally more efficient than the original RCA and RCA-SOFT. These results are consistent with the complexity analysis in Section 4.

8. RELATED WORK

In this section, we review the related work on anomaly detection and system diagnosis. In particular, we focus on the following two categories: 1) fault detection in distributed systems; and 2) graph-based methods.

For the first category, Yemini et al. [25] proposed to model event correlation and locate system faults using known dependency relationships between faults and symptoms. In real applications, however, it is usually hard to obtain such relationships precisely. To alleviate this limitation, Jiang et al. [13] developed several model-based approaches to detect the faults in complex distributed systems. They further proposed several Jaccard Coefficient based approaches to locate the faulty components [14, 15]. These approaches generally focus on locating the faulty components, they are not capable of spotting or ranking the causal anomalies.

Recently, graph-based methods have drawn a lot of interest in system anomaly detections [2, 5], either in static graphs or dynamic graphs [2]. In static graphs, the main task is to spot anomalous network entities given the graph structure [4, 11]. For example, Akoglu et al. [1] proposed OddBall to detect anomalous nodes in weighted graphs. Liu et al. [18] proposed to use frequent subgraph mining to detect non-crashing bugs in software flow graphs. However, these approaches only focus on a single graph; in comparison, we take into account both the invariant graph and the broken correlations, which provides a more dynamic and complete picture for anomaly ranking. In dynamic graphs, anomaly detection aims at detecting abnormal events [19]. Most approaches along this direction are designed to detect anomaly time-stamps in which suspicious events take place, but not to perform ranking on a large number of system components. Sun et al. proposed to use temporal graphs for anomaly detection [20]. In their approach, a set of initial suspects need to be provided; then internal relationship among these initial suspects is characterized for better understanding of the root cause of these anomalies.

In using the invariant graph and the broken invariance graph for anomaly detection, Jiang et al. [14] used the ratio of broken edges in the invariant network as the anomaly score for ranking; Ge et al. [8] proposed mRank and gRank to rank causal anomalies; Tao et al. [22] used the loopy belief propagation method to rank anomalies. As has been discussed, these algorithms rely heavily on the percentage of broken edges in egonet of a node. Such local approaches do not take into account the global network structures, neither the global fault propagation spreading on the network. Therefore the resultant rankings can be sub-optimal.

9. CONCLUSIONS

Detecting causal anomalies on monitoring data of distributed systems is an important problem in data mining research. Robust and scalable approaches that can model the potential fault propagation are highly desirable. We develop a network diffusion based framework, which simultaneously takes into account fault propagation on the network as well as reconstructing anomaly signatures using propagated anomalies. Our approach can locate causal anomalies more accurately than existing approaches; in the meantime, it is robust to noise and computationally efficient. Using both synthetic and real-life data sets, we show that the proposed methods outperform other competitors by a large margin.

10. ACKNOWLEDGMENTS

Wei Wang is supported by the National Science Foundation grants IIS-1313606, DBI-1565137, by National Institutes of Health under the grant number R01GM115833-01.

11. REFERENCES

[ ] L. Akoglu, M. McGlohon, and C. Faloutsos. Oddball: Spotting anomalies in weighted graphs. PAKDD, pages 4 0–4 .

[ ] L. Akoglu, H. Tong, and D. Koutra. Graph-based anomaly detection and description: A survey. *CoRR*, 0 4.

[3] S. Boyd and L. Vandenberghe. *Convex Optimization*. Cambridge University Press, 004.

[4] M. M. Breunig, H.-P. Kriegel, R. T. Ng, and J. Sander. Lof: Identifying density-based local outliers. SIGMOD, pages 93– 04, 000.

[5] V. Chandola, A. Banerjee, and V. Kumar. Anomaly detection: A survey. *ACM Computing Surveys*, 4 (3): –58, 009.

[6] H. Chen, H. Cheng, G. Jiang, and K. Yoshihira. Global invariants for the management of large scale information systems. In *ICDM*, 008.

[7] C. Ding, T. Li, W. Peng, and H. Park. Orthogonal nonnegative matrix t-factorizations for clustering. In *KDD*, pages 6– 35, 006.

[8] Y. Ge, G. Jiang, M. Ding, and H. Xiong. Ranking metric anomaly in invariant networks. *TKDD*, 8( ), Jun. 0 4.

[9] J. Gertler. *Fault Detection and Diagnosis in Engineering Systems*. Marcel Dekker, 998.

[0] Gertler: 998. *System Identification (2nd Ed.): Theory for the User*. 999.

[ ] K. Henderson, T. Eliassi-Rad, C. Faloutsos, L. Akoglu, L. Li, K. Maruhashi, B. A. Prakash, and H. Tong. Metric forensics: a multi-level approach for mining volatile graphs. In *KDD*, pages 63– 7 , 0 0.

[ ] Jarvelin, Kalervo and Kekalainen, Jaana. Cumulated gain-based evaluation of IR techniques. *TIS*, 0(4):4 –446, 00 .

[3] G. Jiang, H. Chen, and K. Yoshihira. Discovering likely invariants of distributed transaction systems for autonomic system management. *Cluster Computing*, 9(4):385–399, 006.

[4] G. Jiang, H. Chen, and K. Yoshihira. Modeling and tracking of transaction flow dynamics for fault detection in complex systems. *TDSC*, 3(4):3 –3 6, 006.

[5] G. Jiang, H. Chen, and K. Yoshihira. Efficient and scalable algorithms for inferring invariants in distributed systems. *TKDE*, 9( ): 508– 5 3, 007.

[6] T. H. Kim, K. M. Lee, and S. U. Lee. Generative image segmentation using random walks with restart. In *ECCV*, pages 64– 75, 008.

[7] D. D. Lee and H. S. Seung. Algorithms for non-negative matrix factorization. In *NIPS*, pages 556–56 , 000.

[8] C. Liu, X. Yan, H. Yu, J. Han, and P. S. Yu. Mining behavior graphs for "backtrace" of noncrashing bugs. In *SDM*, pages 86– 97, 005.

[9] R. A. Rossi, B. Gallagher, J. Neville, and K. Henderson. Modeling dynamic behavior in large evolving graphs. WSDM, pages 667–676, 0 3.

[0] J. Sun, D. Tao, and C. Faloutsos. Beyond streams and graphs: Dynamic tensor analysis. KDD '06, pages 374–383, 006.

[ ] R. S. Sutton and A. G. Barto. *Reinforcement Learning: An Introduction*. The MIT Press, Cambridge, MA, 998.

[ ] C. Tao, Y. Ge, Q. Song, Y. Ge, and F. Omitaomu. Metric ranking of invariant networks with belief propagation. In *ICDM*, 0 4.

[3] R. J. Tibshirani. Regression shrinkage and selection via the lasso. *Journal of the Royal Statistical Society, Series B*, 58( ): 67– 88, 996.

[4] H. Tong, C. Faloutsos, and J.-Y. Pan. Fast random walk with restart and its applications. In *ICDM*, pages 6 3–6 , 006.

[5] S. A. Yemini, S. Kliger, E. Mozes, Y. Yemini, and D. Ohsie. High speed and robust event correlation. *IEEE Communications Magazine*, 34:8 –90, 996.

[6] D. Zhou, O. Bousquet, T. N. Lal, J. Weston, and B. Schölkopf. Learning with local and global consistency. In *NIPS*, pages 3 –3 8, 003.

Towards Conversational Recommender Systems

Konstantina Christakopoulou*
University of Minnesota
United States
christa@cs.umn.edu

Filip Radlinski, Katja Hofmann
Microsoft
Cambridge, UK
{filiprad, katja.hofmann}@microsoft.com

ABSTRACT

People often ask others for restaurant recommendations as a way to discover new dining experiences. This makes restaurant recommendation an exciting scenario for recommender systems and has led to substantial research in this area. However, most such systems behave very differently from a human when asked for a recommendation. The goal of this paper is to begin to reduce this gap.

In particular, humans can quickly establish preferences when asked to make a recommendation for someone they do not know. We address this cold-start recommendation problem in an online learning setting. We develop a preference elicitation framework to identify which questions to ask a new user to quickly learn their preferences. Taking advantage of latent structure in the recommendation space using a probabilistic latent factor model, our experiments with both synthetic and real world data compare different types of feedback and question selection strategies. We find that our framework can make very effective use of online user feedback, improving personalized recommendations over a static model by 25% after asking only 2 questions. Our results demonstrate dramatic benefits of starting from offline embeddings, and highlight the benefit of bandit-based explore-exploit strategies in this setting.

Keywords

online learning; recommender systems; cold-start

1. INTRODUCTION

Recommendation is an everyday process that frequently touches people's lives. Hence, it has seen tremendous research interest (such as [9, 14]). Most work in recommendation falls into two broad classes: *Collaborative Filtering* starts with a set of user/item affinity scores and assumes that two users who agree about one item are more likely to agree about another item; *Content-Based Filtering* models users by the characteristics of the items they like or dislike. We note that neither model represents how real people make recommendations, particularly in a cold-start setting where the person making a recommendation does not know a lot about the person asking for one.

Consider what would happen if a conference attendee in your home town, whom you have never met before, asked for a recommendation on where to eat dinner today. Most likely, you would start with one or two clarifying questions, perhaps whether the person likes seafood, or whether they have a car. These questions would depend on the context; for instance if there are great restaurants around the corner, then whether they have a car would be irrelevant.

We argue that such an interaction can be represented using online learning, where two types of learning are occurring. First, the person making the recommendation is learning about the preferences of the person asking. However, the attributes learned will be *contextual*, based on the likely follow-on answers (such as the car question earlier). Second, the person making the recommendation is learning about which questions allow them to quickly reach a good recommendation in the current context. In this paper, we present a recommendation system that exhibits these two types of learning. Further, the learning is online: It immediately impacts future recommendations for this user, rather than requiring a batch reprocessing of information learned.

We present a bandit-based approach for online recommendation, applied to restaurant recommendation so as to ground it in a specific application. Our approach builds on top of prior work, such as [33], but learns to adapt the recommendation space (user-item embedding) to its users throughout their interactions. We use generalized Thompson Sampling to systematically sample questions to ask the user and to incorporate observed feedback. We further propose and compare a range of alternative question selection strategies to identify characteristics of approaches that most effectively learn users' preferences. We use a matrix factorization approach [21, 29] to learn and adapt the embedding.

Our main contributions are four-fold. (1) We propose a novel view of human-like recommenders that converse with new users to learn their preferences. (2) We successfully demonstrate a fully online learning approach for recommendation – both using absolute and relative feedback. (3) We propose a systematic approach to incorporating offline data to initialize online learning recommenders, and demonstrate performance improvements, even using weakly labeled offline data. (4) We propose a set of item selection strategies for deciding what question to ask to a cold-start user to

*This work was done during an internship at Microsoft.

KDD '16, August 13 - 17, 2016, San Francisco, CA, USA

ISBN 978-1-4503-4232-2/16/08...$15.00

DOI: http://dx.doi.org/10.1145/2939672.2939746

most quickly infer preferences, and demonstrate benefits of bandit-based strategies. Our extensive experiments on both synthetic and real data evaluate each step of our approach.

Importantly, we note that this work is applicable to a wide variety of recommendation scenarios. Here, we focus on one such application, restaurant recommendation, where (1) we study search logs to understand the space of real user needs; (2) we use the insights to collect preference data in a user study; (3) we use online behavioral data to initialize the recommendation system; (4) we use both synthetic and user study data to evaluate our approaches.

We now present related work (Section 2), followed by an analysis of real-live restaurant search (3). We describe our model (4) and empirical setup (5), and validate the model on synthetic data (6). Finally, we evaluate on real data to further empirically analyze our learning framework (7).

2. RELATED WORK

This paper builds on work in multiple active research areas. We review recent work in the most closely related areas.

Offline Recommenders. The wide interest in personalized recommendations has sparked substantial research in this area [14]. The most common approaches are content-based approaches [24] and collaborative filtering (CF) [9, 21]. Collaborative filtering, which powers most modern recommenders, uses an a-priori available set of user-item ratings to learn the interdependencies among users and items. It predicts a user's rating on an item either via the neighboring items' ratings (neighbor-based [9, 28]) or by inferring latent factors in a low-dimensional embedding (latent factor-based [21, 29]). The majority of the work in recommendation has focused on offline recommenders, i.e., building an offline model based on past user-item interactions, periodically retrained to incorporate new observations.

Online Recommenders. Recently, it has been recognized that offline recommender approaches (i) suffer from the cost of retraining the model, (ii) are built to optimize offline performance which does not necessarily match online user behavior and (iii) fail to capture preference drifts. These realizations have initiated developments towards building continuously learning (online) recommenders.

A recent line of work poses the problem in a *contextual bandit* formulation [16, 31, 32], where items are seen as *arms*, users as *contexts*, and the goal is to *explore* the arm space in order to *exploit* the best performing arm for a given context. Most work in this area relies on the availability of user/item features and assumes that the reward of an arm for a given context is a linear/logistic function of the concatenated feature of arm-context [16, 31]. [32] uses Gaussian processes to allow feedback sharing among similar contexts and arms.

Using the CF point of view, [4] introduced an ϵ-greedy online user-user *neighbor-based* CF method. The first *latent-factor* online recommender was introduced in [33], which uses bandit strategies on top of Probabilistic Matrix Factorization (PMF) [21]. This is the most closely related work to ours. However, while [33] fixes the item latent factors to those learned offline, formulating the problem as a linear bandit, our method *fully online* learns *all* user and item parameters, including the biases; [33] can be seen as special case of our framework. In [13], the authors extend Thompson Sampling for PMF with a Kalman filter to track changing preferences over time. This work is orthogonal to ours.

Preference Elicitation. The problem of eliciting user feedback has long been of interest for a variety of tasks (e.g [8]). To elicit the preferences of an existing or new user (cold-start), a range of methods have been proposed, varying from interview-based strategies (e.g [30]), to asking users to rate some items, to active learning [26], entropy minimization [27], picture-based [22], and explore-exploit strategies on top of a latent factor model [33]. Our work is the first to elicit users' preferences by utilizing either absolute or relative feedback in a fully online setting.

Interactive Recommenders. There have been many works (critique-based [7], constraint-based [10], dialog, utility-based recommenders [19]) emphasizing the importance of interactivity in recommenders so that the user has a more active role over the recommendations. However, these works rely on prior modeling of the items' features, preventing the flexibility in adaptation to a different domain; thus a comparison with them is out of the scope of this work.

In contrast, our work, in the same spirit as a recent line of work [18, 11] initiated by [33], learns online the *latent factors* from PMF and uses *these* to do interactive preference elicitation. These methods, although close in principle, have significant differences from our work.[1] Briefly, in [18], the authors focus on set-based feedback and propose a progressive building of the user's latent factor in each question. In contrast, our work focuses on absolute and relative feedback on (pairs of) items, and uses a preference elicitation phase fully integrated with the online updates of the PMF model. The method of [11] focuses on choice-based feedback and updates online only the user's latent factor. Neither of [11, 18] balance the exploration-exploitation tradeoff.

3. UNDERSTANDING REAL USERS

A recommendation system that aims to satisfy real people should reflect how real people look for recommendations. Therefore, we start by analyzing restaurant-related search behavior in a commercial Web search engine. Our goals are two-fold. First, to gain insight into our target domain, namely understand the criteria people use to choose restaurants[2]. Second, to identify questions we must ask users to construct ground truth data for evaluating our system.

Given a large sample of all queries issued between 07/2014 and 07/2015, we filtered for those that contain *restaurant* or *dining*, and terms such as *for*, *near(by)*, *next (to)*, *close (to)*, *with* and *in*. Let $\mathcal{Q}$ be the most frequent 10,000 such queries.

3.1 Query Annotation with Entities

We tagged the top several hundred queries from $\mathcal{Q}$ as containing a location, name, cuisine, food type, or terms such as *best* and *menu*. The dictionary of tags was not pre-specified to avoid biasing our annotations due to prior beliefs about categories people *should* be looking for. Rather, our methodology used content analysis [25] to develop a coding that captures the dominant behaviors involved.

We found that 39% of queries specify a location, 19% a restaurant name, 9% cuisine constraints, 7% have the term *best* or other superlative. More rarely, queries specified food ethnicity (2%), an adjective describing the restaurant (2%), dish name (2%), decoration, etc. The most common term co-

[1] We plan to extend our framework to set and choice-based feedback, to allow the comparison with [18, 11].

[2] Keeping in mind that these criteria to some degree reflect users' perception of the search engine and its capabilities.

Table 1: Contextual terms in restaurant related queries.

IN	NEAR	FOR	WITH
nyc	me	wedding receptions	party room
chicago	by	large group	small private room
las vegas	times square	rich	piano
houston	here	dessert	live music
miami	lax	your 21st birthday	someone
los angeles	miami airport	steak at lunch time	a view
atlanta	airport	gluten free food	play area
brooklyn	fenway park	valentine day in dallas	banquet room

Table 2: Restaurant Feature Dictionaries (note: frequency counts have been rescaled)

Cuisine	Freq.	Adj.	Freq.	Food	Freq.
mexican	475	good	27	seafood	139
chinese	407	famous	13	sushi	40
italian	381	nice	12	steak	32
thai	174	romantic	11	bbq	29
indian	144	upscale	6	fish	24
japanese	125	small	6	tapas	19

occurences are location and name in the same query (29%), cuisine and location (10%), and *best* and location (8%).

3.2 Understanding Common Phrases

The above statistics show that location is an important factor in restaurant search. Hence we zoom in to discover the specific ways in which people constrain locations. Similarly, the context under which users search for a restaurant is a second common constraint. We analyzed the specific terms appearing after a variety of prepositions, and constructed a dictionary of the most frequent contextual constraints.

A sample of these is shown in Table 1. For example, the top places people search for restaurants *in* are nyc, chicago, las vegas. Using the preposition 'near' to indicate location, the majority of terms shows users want a restaurant *near me*. Queries can also be very specific, e.g. searching for a restaurant near points of interest (*times square*), airports (*miami airport, lax*), postal codes or entire addresses. The contexts under which users search for restaurants vary from an occasion (*wedding reception*), to dietary restrictions, to type of meal or a group of people. People also search for restaurants *with live music, piano, a view* etc.

3.3 Restaurant Feature Dictionaries

As user queries can be very specific (e.g., combining constraints, 'adjective & dish & great & location'), we now study the terms that people use to describe restaurants. We annotated the top 1,013 phrases appearing before the word 'restaurant' or 'dining' in 5,000 queries from $\mathcal{Q}$ with a number of traits. The traits identified are related to food (cuisine, meal, dietary restrictions, quality e.g. *organic, healthy,* buffet, menu), rating (e.g michelin star), atmosphere (view, *fancy* or *romantic*), time/location (opening hours, decade theme, time of the day) etc.

For every trait, we collected the most common terms. Table 2 shows a few common examples, giving us a glimpse into the most searched cuisines, food types, and adjectives. Though not shown, top amenities searched are *garden, jazz, patio, ocean* and top restaurant types are *bar, fast food, cafe.*

3.4 Outlook

Besides motivating our application scenario, this search log analysis forms the basis of the user study in Section 7. Given this understanding of *what to ask* people who look for a restaurant, we also focus on *how to ask it.* In this work, among the various combinations of the feedback type (explicit/implicit, absolute/relative/list) on the available content (explicit features/items/latent features), we elicit users' preferences using *explicit feedback* from *absolute* and *relative* questions about *explicit items* (e.g. restaurants).

4. MODEL

We next present our approach for determining 'what to ask' and 'how to ask' as the key pieces of a conversational recommender, starting with a high level picture of the entire algorithm (Section 4.1). Then, we describe the pieces in detail as we require (i) a model exploiting implicit structure among items and users to efficiently propagate feedback (Section 4.2); (ii) an explore-exploit approach to probe the space of items, to allow continuous learning (Section 4.3) and (iii) a feedback elicitation mechanism for selecting absolute (Section 4.3) and relative questions (Section 4.4).

4.1 Overview

Our recommendation pipeline can be summarized as:

1. Pick a model (Absolute/Pairwise) (Sec. 4.2) and preference elicitation mechanism: `Abs` (Sec. 4.3) / `Abs Pos` / `Abs Pos & Neg` / `Pairwise` (Sec. 4.4).
2. Initialize model parameters using offline data.
3. A new user arrives. Now iterate for a few questions[3]:
   (a) Mechanism selects a question to ask
   (b) User answers the question
   (c) All model parameters are updated
   (d) Remove the question from the allowed questions
4. System presents the final recommended list

The inner loop represents the 'human in the loop' present in all interactive systems, i.e., we make an intervention which affects the user and thus the future system decisions.

4.2 Latent Factor Recommendation

Consider how people make recommendations when a friend asks them to suggest a restaurant. They strategically ask each question with the goal of eliminating or confirming strong candidates for dining out. Similarly, when designing a conversational recommender that asks questions about explicit items, a principled way of selecting items is desired.

The implicit structure of the item space that allows us to learn quickly is motivated by *collaborative filtering.* Items that have been co-rated similarly (liked/disliked) by users will lie close in a low dimensional embedding. For our model we use a simplified version of the Matchbox Recommender model [29] – equivalent to Probabilistic Matrix Factorization (PMF) [21]. This is a generative model, in that it specifies a probabilistic procedure by which the observed likes/dislikes of users on items are generated on the basis of latent variables. The model variables are learned so that the model can explain the observed training data.

Formally, throughout the paper we use the convention that i denotes the index over M users, forming the set $\mathcal{I}$, and j denotes the index over N items, forming the set $\mathcal{J}$. Every user $i \in \mathcal{I}$ is modeled by a user bias variable $\alpha_i \in \mathbb{R}$, accounting for users who tend to like/dislike most of the items, and a d-dimensional trait vector $\mathbf{u}_i \in \mathbb{R}^d$. The trait vector represents the latent embedding of user i in a d-dimensional

[3] A study of the right stopping criterion is left for the future.

space, where $d \ll M, N$. Every item $j \in \mathcal{J}$ is modeled with latent variables $\beta_j \in \mathbb{R}$ (the item bias that accounts for item popularity) and a trait vector $\mathbf{v}_j \in \mathbb{R}^d$ that represents the latent embedding of item j in the *same* d-dimensional space.

Given that both users and items trait vectors lie in the same latent space, the similarity between a user i and an item j can be measured with the inner product of their corresponding trait vectors $\mathbf{u}_i^T \mathbf{v}_j$. We now present two models for estimating the latent variables, depending on the type of observations we obtain from users, i.e., absolute or pairwise.

Absolute Model. First, let us assume that we have observed tuples of the form (user i, item j, 1/0).[4] The model estimates the *affinity* of user i to item j based on the biases and traits. The generative procedure is:

1. User i has traits $\mathbf{u}_i \sim \mathcal{N}(\mathbf{0}, \sigma_1^2\mathbf{I})$, bias $\alpha_i \sim \mathcal{N}(0, \sigma_2^2)$.
2. Item j has traits $\mathbf{v}_j \sim \mathcal{N}(\mathbf{0}, \sigma_1^2\mathbf{I})$, bias $\beta_j \sim \mathcal{N}(0, \sigma_2^2)$.
3. (a) The (unobserved) affinity is

$$y_{ij} = \alpha_i + \beta_j + \mathbf{u}_i^T \mathbf{v}_j. \tag{1}$$

Observations are modeled as the noisy estimate $\hat{y}_{ij} \sim \mathcal{N}(y_{ij}, \epsilon_{ij})$, where ϵ_{ij} models the affinity variance, accounting for noise in user preferences. This yields an observation of whether the user likes an item ($\hat{r}_{ij}$):

$$\hat{r}_{ij} = \mathbf{1}[\hat{y}_{ij} > 0]. \tag{2}$$

The hyper-parameters σ_1, σ_2 model the variance in traits and biases. The model variables are learned by maximizing the log-posterior over the item and user variables with fixed hyper-parameters, given the training observations.

Pairwise Model. People are often better at giving relative preferences over items instead of absolute judgments. Such preferences yield tuples of the form (user i, item j, item h) when user i prefers item j over item h (both j and h are indices over $\mathcal{J}$.) We can adapt the generative model to such ground truth data by modifying the third step of the *Absolute* model to yield a pairwise model:

3. (b) For each observation (i, j, h) compute

$$\text{noisy difference: } \hat{y}_{ijh} = \hat{y}_{ij} - \hat{y}_{ih} \tag{3}$$

where the noisy item affinities are defined as before. Using $\hat{y}_{ijh}$, we estimate if user i prefers j over h:

$$j \succ_i h : \hat{r}_{ijh} = \mathbf{1}[\hat{y}_{ijh} > 0] \tag{4}$$

4.3 Continuous Learning Recommender

To generate recommendations, most latent factor based recommender systems use an offline trained model based on past interactions, such as the one described above, that they periodically update to incorporate new data. The parameters for new users are typically initialized based on a combination of explicit attributes and past ratings (e.g [1]). The items with the highest predicted noisy affinity mean comprise the recommendations presented to the user.

In contrast, recent work has moved towards continuously learning recommenders [4, 16, 33]. This optimizes for *online* performance using explore-exploit (EE) strategies. We present our fully online updated recommendation approach with the embedded preference elicitation in Algorithm 1. Following we detail the components of this algorithm for the case of asking absolute questions (`Abs`). In Section 4.4 we show how we extend this framework for relative questions.

[4]We use the convention that 0 denotes dislike and 1 like.

Algorithm 1 Preference Elicitation Algorithm

Input: $\forall i \in \mathcal{I} : \mathbf{u}_i, \alpha_i, \forall j \in \mathcal{J} : \mathbf{v}_j, \beta_j$ (offline embedding)
A new user i arrives. Initialize prior based on Eq. 5.
$\forall j \in \mathcal{J}$, infer noisy affinity y_{ij} (Eq. 1)
while fewer than allowed questions have been asked **do**:
  Pick item(s) for absolute (relative) question (Sec. 4.3/ 4.4).
  Incorporate feedback according to (i) `Abs` (Sec. 4.3), (ii) `Abs Pos`, (iii) `Abs Pos & Neg`, or (iv) `Pairwise`. (Sec. 4.4)
  Update $\mathbf{u}_i$, α_i, $\mathbf{v}$, β (Section 4.3.3) and infer the noisy affinity distribution $\mathbf{y}_i$ (Eq. 1) or noisy difference (Eq. 3).
end while

4.3.1 Initialization from Offline Data

We propose to initialize online learning models using an initial embedding, that is learned offline. We hypothesize that such an initial embedding will allow the system to learn new user's preferences more quickly. Effective learning from few questions is crucial for conversational recommenders.

We start by learning the *offline embedding* of items from logged observations. Then, we initialize the prior of every item $j \in \mathcal{J}$ by setting the trait $\mathbf{v}_j$ and bias β_j from the corresponding offline posterior – assuming that all items in the online phase appeared in the offline data.

For the initialization of the user parameters, we focus on the case when the user is new to the system. Without additional information, we can assume that the new user is similar to the average offline user. We implement this by using as trait and bias the mean value over all offline users:

$$\mathbf{u}^{cold} \sim \mathbf{E}_{i=1,\ldots,M}[\mathbf{u}_i] \qquad \alpha^{cold} \sim \mathbf{E}_{i=1,\ldots,M}[\alpha_i] \tag{5}$$

4.3.2 Question Selection Strategies

When a new user initiates interaction with a continuous recommender, the system asks a few questions to learn about the user's preferences. During this phase, it is important to select questions that lead to learning effectively (i) the user's preferences and (ii) the questions' quality, so that the number of questions asked can be minimized and interactions remain enjoyable. This task can be modeled as an item selection task. Here, we propose approaches that capture characteristics of *active learning* and *bandit learning*. Active learning approaches capture the intuition that learning is fastest when the system queries for labels that provide a high amount of new information [26]. Bandit learning approaches balance the need to learn new information with a focus on what has already been learned [3, 5]. In the context of conversational recommenders, such a balance may help focus questions on the most relevant part of the latent space, while still considering that highly preferred items may lie in as of yet unexplored areas of the space.

The model's confidence in its belief over the user's preferences on items $j \in \mathcal{J}$ at a given time is captured by the current variances of the posterior of the noisy affinities y_j^{cold}. As we ask about an item j^* and observe the user's feedback, the variance of the inferred noisy affinity of this item *and of the nearby items* in the learned embedding is reduced. Also, the means of these items' inferred noisy affinities change. It is this property that allows us to search the space of items quickly. Hence, while in the classic multi-armed bandit scenario the bandit algorithms converge only after all arms are sufficiently explored, in our setting the collaborative structure allows for faster convergence.[5]

[5]A formal regret analysis lies beyond the scope of this work.

Table 3: Question selection strategies evaluated.

Greedy: $j^* = \arg\max_j y_{ij}$
A trivial *exploit*-only strategy: Select the item with highest estimated affinity mean.
Random: $j^* = \text{random}(1,N)$
A trivial *explore*-only strategy.
Maximum Variance (MV): $j^* = \arg\max_j \epsilon_{ij}$
A *explore*-only strategy, variance reduction strategy: Select the item with the highest noisy affinity variance.
Maximum Item Trait (MaxT): $j^* = \arg\max_j \|\mathbf{v}_j\|_2$
Select the item whose trait vector $\mathbf{v}_j$ contains the most information, namely has highest L2 norm $\|\mathbf{v}_j\|_2 = \sqrt{v_{j1}^2 + v_{j2}^2 + \ldots + v_{jd}^2}$.
Minimum Item Trait (MinT): $j^* = \arg\min_j \|\mathbf{v}_j\|_2$
Select the item with trait vector with least information.
Upper Confidence (UCB): $j^* = \arg\max_j y_{ij} + \epsilon_{ij}$
Based on UCB1 [3]: Pick the item with the highest upper confidence bound, namely mean plus variance (95% CI)
Thompson Sampling (TS) [5]: $j^* = \arg\max_j \hat{y}_{ij}$
For each item, sample the noisy affinity from the posterior. Select item with the maximum sampled value.

We compare a number of approaches for question selection that reflect the considerations discussed above, and several baselines. All approaches are listed in Table 3. Each selects an item j^* to obtain user feedback on. While the first few are self-explanatory baselines, we discuss three in more detail. (1) MaxT approximates maximizing information gain, in the vein of active learning: As user-item ratings are observed, the PMF model adds information to the corresponding user and item trait vectors. In the opposite extreme case, if all item trait elements are close to 0, the corresponding item carries no information. As MinT does the opposite from MaxT, it is hypothesized to have low performance and is employed to establish a lower bound on question selection performance. (2) UCB [3] is a popular bandit algorithm that selects the items with the highest confidence bound to avoid missing preferences for promising items. (3) Thompson Sampling (TS) is a bandit algorithm that balances exploration and exploitation by selecting items using a sampling strategy [5]. It samples from its current posterior belief over noisy affinities, and then acts optimally according to this sampled belief. TS focuses on items with high mean affinity, but is also likely to select items with high variance.

4.3.3 Online Updating

After posing a question to the user, the observed response needs to be incorporated into to the recommender to allow for continued learning. As shown in [23], the questions can be incorporated into the model by setting the probability of the question to 1 and incorporating the user's response following standard probability theory.

The user's response thus becomes a new observation that the system uses to update the posterior distributions of *all* latent model parameters related to the incoming user i and the item j asked about, i.e., $\alpha_i, \beta_j, \mathbf{u}_i, \mathbf{v}_j$ (but affecting only user i's interaction session). Due to space constraints, we refer the reader to [29] for the specific Expectation Propagation updates. To select the next question for user i, we use the updated posteriors as the new priors to infer the user's noisy affinity distribution $\hat{y}_{ij}$ for all items $j \in \mathcal{J}$, denoted by $\hat{\mathbf{y}}_i$. As the system keeps asking questions to user i and incorporates his/her feedback, the beliefs about the user, and the item in the question, change. This allows the model to move towards the true underlying affinity distribution. All online updates were implemented in Infer.NET [20].

`Abs`: *Absolute Model, Absolute Questions*

So far we have presented the entire framework for the case where the system poses absolute questions. Before turning to relative feedback, we describe the high-level approach for asking absolute questions (`Abs`). Using TS for illustration purposes, `Abs` asks user i about the item with the largest sampled noisy affinity as inferred by the *Absolute* model:

$$j^* = \arg\max_{j \in \mathcal{J}} \hat{y}_{ij} \tag{6}$$

Based on whether the user (dis)liked item j^*, a new observation (i, j^*,1/0) is incorporated into the Absolute model.

4.4 Extension to Relative Preferences

An alternative is for the system to ask for a preference about a pair of items, i.e., does the user prefer item A (j^*) or item B (h^*)? Therefore, we present here the extension of our framework to the case of asking *relative questions*.

We consider three separate formulations (referred to as `Abs Pos`, `Abs Pos & Neg` and `Pairwise`) for selecting relative questions and incorporating feedback, to identify the best way of asking relative questions. Importantly, in every such formulation there are two choices: (i) the underlying model (*Absolute* vs. *Pairwise*) and (ii) how the user's response to the question is incorporated back into the model. For the first choice, `Abs Pos` and `Abs Pos & Neg` use the Absolute model, while `Pairwise` uses the Pairwise model. The second choice is applicable only for `Abs Pos` and `Abs Pos & Neg`, as they represent two ways of incorporating relative feedback into the absolute model.

4.4.1 Absolute Model, Relative Questions

First, we present `Abs Pos` and `Abs Pos & Neg`. Both use the same mechanism to generate the question "A vs. B" for user i:

1. Select item A as in `Abs` (Equation 6).
2. Virtual observation: Assume user i did not like A.
3. Virtual update: Incorporate the tuple (i, A, 0) into the *Absolute* model, infer the posteriors for all model parameters and set them as the virtual new prior.
4. Select item B, again according to `Abs`, but this time using the virtual prior as prior.

The insight behind this mechanism of constructing the relative question is that the two items the user is asked to give a relative preference on should be relatively far apart in the latent embedding, so that (i) the system can learn users' preferences effectively and (ii) the user is not forced to choose among very similar items. This diversity enforcing mechanism is inspired by the approach in [6].

The two methods introduced here differ only in the way the feedback is incorporated into the Absolute model. `Abs Pos` incorporates only positive information while `Abs Pos & Neg` incorporates both positive and negative information. For example, assume that the user preferred item B to A. Then, `Abs Pos` incorporates only the observation (i, B, 1), interpreting the relative preference on the preferred item B as a like for B. In contrast, `Abs Pos & Neg` incorporates two observations: (i, B, 1) for the preferred item and (i, A, 0) for the less preferred item. This can be seen as a variant of the "sparring" approach to dueling bandits [2], which samples item pairs and updates the model for both items as if an absolute reward were observed.

4.4.2 *Pairwise Model, Relative Questions*

The third method for selecting relative questions, **Pairwise**, uses the *Pairwise* model that directly takes pairwise preferences as input, to generate the relative question and incorporate the observations. Thus, the user's relative feedback is incorporated into the model without any intermediate transformation, i.e., as an observation (i, B, A) when B is preferred over A.

The **Pairwise** method picks A exactly as in **Abs**, and for item B, inspired by the dueling bandit approach in [34], it picks the item with the largest probability of being preferred to item A. We instantiate the latter by selecting the item with the maximum noisy difference from item A (j^*):

$$\text{item B} = h^* = \arg\max_{h \in \mathcal{J}} \hat{y}_{ihj^*} \tag{7}$$

For the selection of item B, any question selection strategy besides TS illustrated here (except for MinT, MaxT), can be employed exactly as in Table 3, with the difference that the noisy *difference* distribution should be used.

Incorporating the 'Neither' Option.

Preliminary experiments showed that when the method asks the user to give a relative preference on two items that he dislikes, forcing him/her to choose one could mislead the model about the user's preferences. Thus, we adjusted all methods so that in such a case the user can specify that he likes neither. We implemented this by (i) incorporating two dislikes in **Abs Pos & Neg** and (ii) omitting the update in **Abs Pos** and **Pairwise**.

5. EXPERIMENTAL SETUP

We now describe our overall empirical setup, used for the experiments described in the next two sections.

Setting. One main difficulty of evaluating conversational recommenders is that it requires the ability to have access to user reactions to any possible system action. We address this requirement using generative user models. The first user model is constructed synthetically and is used to validate our model (Section 6). The second is instantiated from real user preferences, collected via a user study (Section 7).

All experiments consist of an offline and an online phase. During the *offline phase*, the model is presented with data where M users interact with N items. In the subsequent *online phase*, the model is used to interact with cold-start users, asking questions using the pool of the offline N items.

We varied the number of questions from 0 to 15 and report the model's performance after each question. In practice, recommendations could be given after fewer questions, could be integrated with initial recommendations, or could be spread out over several interactions with a given user.

Research Questions. Our experiments are designed to address the following research questions:

RQ 1. Can our model adapt to the user's preferences?
RQ 2. Does our model learn effectively under either absolute or relative feedback?
RQ 3. Which relative question method performs better?
RQ 4. Is absolute or relative feedback more effective?
RQ 5. Does the offline initialization step help?
RQ 6. Which question selection strategy is more effective?

To answer each one of these questions, we need some measure of evaluating the effectiveness of our framework. Given that the goal of preference elicitation is a good recommendation list adhering to the user's preferences, we use *Average Precision@k* (*AP@k*) as our evaluation metric.

Metric. *AP@k* is a widely used, precision-oriented metric [15] for capturing accuracy in the top k (we set $k = 10$). Formally, for user i, we obtain the user's predicted recommendation list by sorting all items by decreasing mean of inferred noisy affinities $\mathbf{y}_i$. We evaluate this list by looking at the ground truth $\mathbf{r}_i^{\text{true}}$, i.e., capturing whether the user liked/disliked each item. *AP@k* is defined as the average of precisions computed at each liked position in the top k items of the user's ranked list. *P@ℓ* (*Precision@ℓ*) is the fraction of liked items out of the top $\ell + 1$ ranked items. Thus,

$$AP@k = \sum_{\ell=0}^{k-1} \frac{P@\ell \cdot r_{i[\ell]}^{\text{true}}}{\min(k, \#\text{ of liked items})} \tag{8}$$

where $[\ell]$ represents the index of the item present in rank ℓ, with $[\ell] = 0$ corresponding to the index of the top recommended item. Higher value (closer to 1) of *AP@k* implies better recommendation list. In our results, we report the average and 95% confidence intervals of AP@10 over all cold-start users. Results in additional metrics, such as ratio of correctly ranked pairs and mean reciprocal rank, were omitted as they showed similar trends as *AP@10*.

6. LEARNING SYNTHETIC USER TYPE PREFERENCES

We begin our experiments with an intentionally simplistic example of restaurant recommendation, as real world high-dimensional data is difficult to visualize. The example is meant to demonstrate concepts of our model and to illustrate the effectiveness of our approach to unlearn initial prior beliefs and tailor recommendations to specific user types, answering *RQ1* affirmatively.

In our framework, we first use observations to learn an offline embedding for users and items in the same low-d space. Here, we generated the offline observations by considering types of users and restaurants as follows:

Restaurant types	%
expensive	15%
cheap & spicy	5%
cheap & not-spicy	10%
only cheap	35%
only not-spicy	15%
only spicy	20%

User types	%
Like expensive	20%
Like spicy	15%
Like not-spicy	25%
Like cheap	30%
Like only not-spicy	5%
Like only spicy	5%

We generated $N = 200$ restaurants, and $M = 200$ users. For each offline user, according to their type, we sampled 10 items from their liked category as likes and 10 items from the rest of the categories as dislikes. We used this intentionally simple synthetic setup to evaluate various parameter choices, and we show results for $\sigma_1^2 = 10$, $\sigma_2^2 = 0.5$, $\epsilon = 0.1$. To allow visualization, we considered only two latent traits (d=2) for this example. We see that in the learned embedding, the first trait indicates spiciness, while the second the price.

In the same space, an embedding for users is also learned (not shown to avoid clutter). The average trait vector over

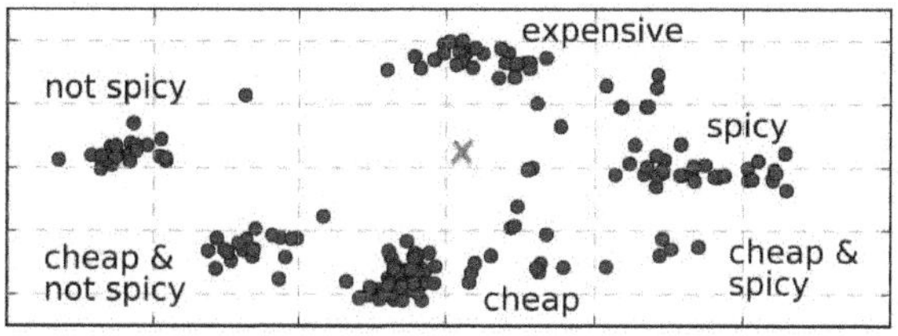

all users is shown with a red cross. This becomes the initial trait vector for the cold-start user. Considering also the learned items' biases and the average user bias (not shown here), the system constructs an initial estimate of the noisy affinity distribution of the incoming user about all items.

Based on the offline observations, the learned prior for this affinity distribution favors user types which were popular in the offline data. The task of selecting restaurants for online users resembling the mean offline user is easy, as the prior already captures valuable information. As Fig. 1, *bottom right* panel shows, even with no questions, a close to perfect recommendation list can be given for *Liking not-spicy* users. Similar is the trend for the *Liking cheap* users (not shown).

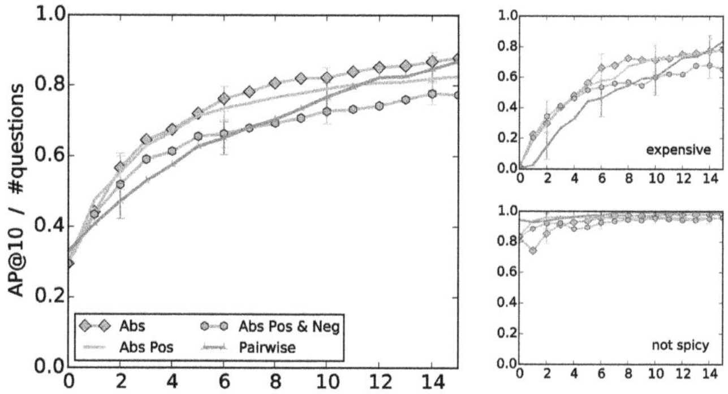

Figure 1: Results on synthetic restaurant data, across user types (*left*), and two of the user types (*right*).

In contrast, when the user is of a type that was rarely seen during the offline phase (e.g., expensive, shown in Fig. 1, *top right* panel), the online recommender has to collect observations that move away from more popular types. The trends for *Liking spicy*, *Liking only-spicy*, and *only not-spicy* user types are similar to the *Liking expensive*. For these types, the model (all four approaches) starts with AP@10 close to 0, but after every question asked, unlearns the initial wrong prior beliefs, and learns the specific user types' preferences.

For the results reported, we considered 60 cold-start users of each type and used TS for the question selection.

All methods learn effectively across all user types, with minor differences (Fig. 1, *left*) answering *RQ 2* positively.

7. RESULTS ON REAL DATA

Having positively answered *RQ 1* and *RQ 2* above, we turn our attention to a real-world setting to address all research questions in the context of 'where to dine in Cambridge, UK'. For the offline initialization of our framework, we use real users' online search behavior in a commercial search engine (Section 7.1). We use the insights from Section 3 to design a user study that is used to collect real restaurant preferences for Cambridge (Section 7.2). The collected responses serve as a basis for evaluating our online recommendation methods. We sketch a novel two-step approach to infer ratings for all restaurants, apart from those asked in the study (Section 7.3). We extensively evaluate our choices for the recommendation pipeline (Section 7.4).

7.1 Search Data for Offline Initialization

We start by describing the data which serve as our offline user-restaurants observations, based on which we learn the embedding used to warm start the question-asking phase.

This data is obtained by identifying restaurant review pages for restaurants in Cambridge (UK) on a major restaurant review service provider. Next, we filter the query and click logs from a major commercial search engine to find (anonymous) cookies that mark a single PC accessing a sequence of these restaurant pages. Each cookie is taken to be a distinct user, and all visits on restaurant review pages are considered to be indicating the user liking the restaurant[6].

In particular, taking logs from 26 March to 26 April 2015, we identified 3,549 cookies (users) who accessed at least one of the 512 distinct Cambridge restaurant review pages identified on the review service provider. This resulted in an index of Cambridge restaurants, each one visited by at least one user. Augmenting each of the restaurants with all known links and metadata associated with it in a proprietary restaurant index, and selecting a further three months back in each of those users' search histories, we recorded every interaction of these users with these restaurant links. During the four month search history of the users, we recorded interactions with 289 unique restaurants out of the 512 Cambridge restaurants. The total number of unique user – restaurant interactions recorded is 9330.

Thus, our offline data consists of $M = 3549$ users, $N = 289$ restaurants, and 9330 positive observations (1). To introduce dislikes (0) to the rating matrix as well, for every user i who has liked n_i^+ items, we sampled uniformly at random $n_i^- = \min(10, n_i^+)$ restaurants as dislikes.

Parameter Setting. To learn the offline embedding, we set the hyper-parameters to the combination that achieved the highest pairwise accuracy in the offline observations: $d = 4$ (i.e., 4 latent traits), $\sigma_1^2 = \sigma_2^2 = 10$, $\epsilon = 0.1$.

7.2 User Study as Basis for Online Evaluation

One of the issues of evaluating a conversational recommender is that one needs to know the user's ground truth on the space of all items (and questions). To obtain this, one needs to implement an interactive recommender asking questions to real users and receiving their responses. As an intermediate step, we conducted a user study and used the collected responses as ground truth for online users.

In the user study conducted, each participant filled in an anonymous web questionnaire about their preferences on a pool of restaurants in Cambridge, UK. The participants were asked "would you consider restaurant X for your next Friday night dinner?", labeling each restaurant with a binary label (yes/no). These responses comprise our ground truth.

For the pool of Cambridge restaurants we carefully selected ten restaurants, diverse in various features (as identified in Section 3). We recruited twenty eight individuals for the study. Given the anonymity of the questionnaire (in order to encourage truthfulness in the responses), demographic information was not recorded. However, the larger

[6]Though URL visitation is a weak positive signal, the experiments indicate it is a reasonable proxy for interest.

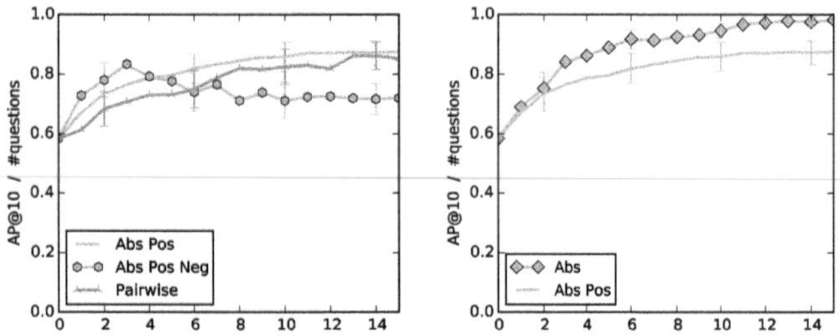

Figure 2: Differences between relative feedback models (*left*); and comparing absolute and relative feedback (*right*).

pool of individuals from which the participants were drawn (65 people working in a research lab) varied in factors such as age, job level, income, time spent in Cambridge.

Each participant was presented with the questionnaire about the same restaurants, but with varying order to avoid presentation bias. The participants were advised to visit the restaurant webpage when unfamiliar with the restaurant.

7.3 Obtaining Ground Truth

In our user study, we obtained restaurant labels for 10 out of the 289 Cambridge restaurants present in the offline data, for 28 participants. However, for reliable evaluation we need labels for the entire item space (rather than limiting our methods to ask about just these 10 restaurants). Therefore, we introduce an approach to fill in complete ground truth labels. Also, to increase the diversity of the user space, inspired by [17], we used bootstrapping to obtain 50 cold-start users based on the 28 participants' ground truth.

In particular, for each cold-start user:

1. Randomly sample one of the 28 participants.
2. Observe the sampled user's labels on the pool of 10 restaurants asked in the user study.
3. Infer user's traits $\mathbf{u}_i$ (prior= learned embedding in 7.1).
4. *Sample* $\hat{\mathbf{u}}_i \sim \mathbf{u}_i$. Set this to be the new prior of $\mathbf{u}_i$.
5. With this prior, infer the ratings $\mathbf{r}_i$ distribution.
6. *Sample* ratings from their distribution $\hat{\mathbf{r}}_i \sim \mathbf{r}_i$.

In this way, for each bootstrapped user we obtain a complete rating list for all 289 restaurants that is consistent with the user study labels of some user, yet is perturbed to account for variety in real user populations.

As far as we are aware, this approach for filling in the missing ratings is novel. It gives us ground truth as close to real as possible given the resources available. Alternatives would be exhaustive labels (not feasible for our study), or rejection/importance sampling (only effective when leveraging logged exploration data from large-scale systems, e.g [16]).

7.4 Results

Having obtained the offline embedding and the online users' ground truth for all items, we now present our experiments on a real restaurant recommendation scenario with the focus of answering the remaining research questions RQ 3 - RQ 6. Each of these questions investigates a separate component of our continuously learning recommender system.

Which method for relative questions is better? (RQ 3)

Recall that we proposed three approaches for modeling relative feedback. The first two incorporate feedback in an absolute model, (a) by incorporating information that the user liked the preferred item (ignoring the non-preferred one, `Abs Pos`), and (b) by incorporating both positive (preferred) and negative (non-preferred) information (`Abs Pos & Neg`). Alternatively, we construct a pairwise model (`Pairwise`). The results of the three methods' comparison are shown in the *left* panel of Figure 2. These results were obtained using TS for question selection and start from the offline embedding.

We see no significant difference among the methods during the first few questions. After only 2 questions, all methods significantly improve over the initial performance of .584 to respectively .734 (`Abs Pos`), .780 (`Abs Pos & Neg`), and .684 (`Pairwise`). However, as we ask more questions, `Abs Pos & Neg` forces negative observations on liked restaurants, thus causing the method to degrade the ranking. Overall, `Abs Pos` is the most effective method for relative questions.[7]

Are absolute or relative questions better? (RQ 4)

To answer this question, we compare the performance of the absolute-question asking method (`Abs`) with the best relative-question asking method (`Abs Pos`). The results are shown in the *right* panel of Figure 2. Until 2 questions, both methods have almost identical performance. But, after 5 questions, `Abs` performs significantly better than the relative feedback method, and achieves close to perfect performance after 15 questions ($AP@10 = .975$). We hypothesize that this result can be explained by the fact that our offline embedding favored absolute feedback.

Although our result shows that very high accuracy can be achieved when users provide accurate feedback on absolute questions, in practice this may not always be possible. Psychological effects such as anchor bias [12] can lead users to implicitly compare items, lowering the quality of absolute feedback. When this is the case, our result shows that high performance can be achieved with relative feedback as well.

Future work could involve hybrid models that automatically learn whether absolute or relative feedback, or a combination, is more accurate in a given setting.

Does offline initialization help? (RQ 5)

Next, we investigate the impact of model initialization, i.e., initializing the online recommender with an initial *offline embedding*, compared to starting from a generic prior (using the optimized hyper-parameters specified in 7.1). We present the results of this comparison in Figure 3 both for the absolute (`Abs`) and the best relative feedback model (`Abs Pos`), in the left and right panel correspondingly.

Our hypothesis is that the offline embedding learned from the weakly labeled data of a search log captures sufficient information to helpfully constrain continued learning, even if it does not exactly match the structure that underlies online users. Indeed, Figure 3 demonstrates great performance improvements when initializing the models from this embedding over generic prior initialization. By placing the new users as the average offline user, performance increases from .217 to .584, even without asking any questions. As the recommender collects more responses, performance continues to improve in both cases.

One observation is that the uninitialized system can ultimately achieve high performance, and for `Abs Pos (Prior)` even pass the offline initialized system. However, this is only achieved after many questions (here: 14). The phenomenon

[7]Studying the effect of alternatives for introducing dislikes in the offline data on `Abs Pos`'s success is left for future work.

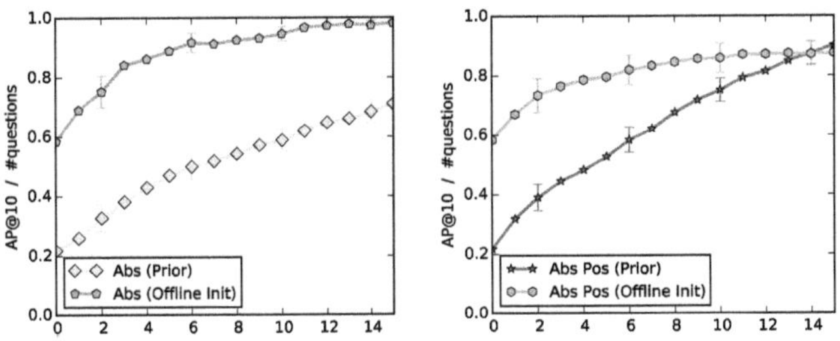

Figure 3: Impact of offline initialization on performance for absolute (**Abs**, *left*) and relative feedback (**Abs Pos**, *right*).

is nevertheless interesting, as it may point to a bias-variance trade-off. Starting from the generic prior allows the system to eventually perfectly fit a given user's preferences, however, learning takes a long time because there is no initial structure to constrain learning outcomes. We conclude that using offline initialization is highly beneficial.

Which question selection strategy is best? (RQ 6)

In Figure 4 we report the comparison results of the various question selection strategies of Section 4.3.2 (except **MaxV** whose performance almost coincides with **UCB**), for the **Abs** and **Abs Pos** methods initialized with the offline embedding.

For the **Abs** model (Figure 4, *top*), we observe that: (i) as expected, lowest AP@10 is achieved by **MinT**, (ii) **Random** learns slowly, likely because it fails to focus on more promising items for effective learning, and (iii) all remaining strategies perform equally well. We hypothesize that **Greedy** performs well thanks to the offline embedding, along with the online updating of all parameters after each response.

Turning to **Abs Pos** (Figure 4, *bottom*), the best performing strategies are those that encourage more diversity across the questions of the interactive session, namely the bandit-based ones and **Random**. **Greedy** and **MaxT** are the worst performing ones, following **MinT**. Our insight why this is the case is that they tend to select questions *A vs B*, followed by *A vs C*, etc. when A is preferred. Given that there is no construction encouraging B and C to be diverse (such as sampling or taking into account uncertainties), the questions focus on comparing parts of the embedding which are similar across questions, thus preventing truly effective learning.

Overall, we find that the bandit-inspired strategies perform the most robustly, achieving top performance across models. In the classic bandit setting, these approaches systematically balance the need to explore new solutions with the need to reap the rewards of what has already been learned. Here, we find that similar principles allow these strategies to collect user feedback that balances the need to not discard any areas of the latent space prematurely with the need to focus questions on the most promising areas. This novel insight is important because it shows that bandit-based question selection strategies can lead to benefits that go beyond the typical bandit problem.

Discussion. All our results show that our methods enable effective learning from interactions with their users, under either feedback type, answering positively *RQ 1* and *RQ 2*.

We show substantial recommendation performance improvements over the performance we would get without adapting to the user; by 25% after only 2 questions.

Although our underlying model can be augmented with external features [29], one key advantage is it does not need

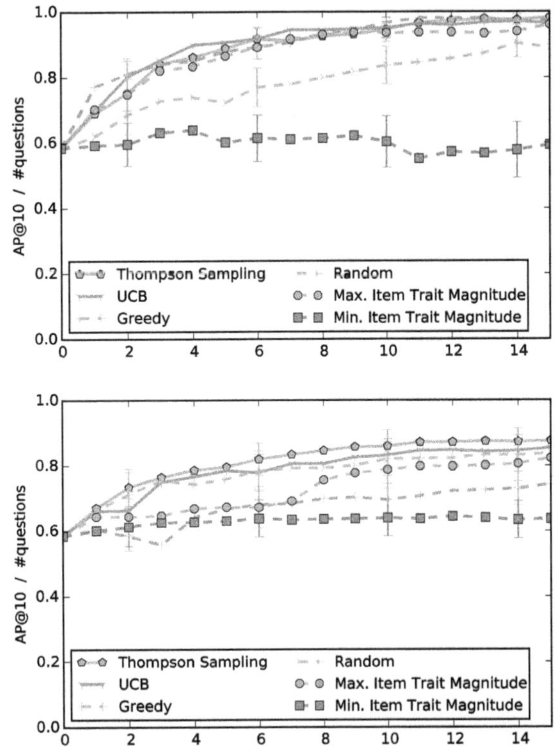

Figure 4: Performance of question selection strategies for absolute (**Abs**, *top*) and relative (**Abs Pos**, *bottom*) models.

them. It learns online both the user's and the items' latent traits. Together with [18] and [33], our findings corroborate the effectiveness of latent-feature interactive recommenders.

A novel insight is that taking into account the uncertainties in the learning of *both* the item and the user embedding, we can adapt to the specific user's preferences, under a certain context. This answers to the question posed by [33] and is key for allowing the system to learn both the user's profile and the questions' effectiveness in a contextual manner.

We have demonstrated effective learning from feedback present in many interactive settings. Thus, our approach is a good candidate for online learning across domains.

8. CONCLUSIONS

In this paper we proposed a novel view of recommendation as an interactive process. Like human recommenders, we envision recommender systems that can converse with new users to learn to know their preferences.

We develop such a conversational recommender, using restaurant recommendation as our motivating example. We start by examining restaurant related queries issued in a commercial search engine. Using these insights, we conducted a user study to elicit ground truth for evaluating our system. We propose a conversational recommender model that is theoretically well anchored in probabilistic matrix factorization models [21, 29]. We show how such models can be extended to support continuous learning. We empirically evaluate our approach using the ground truth based on real dining preferences elicited through our user study.

Our results have important implications for the development of conversational recommender systems. First, we demonstrated that best performance can be achieved with absolute questions. However, even in settings where only relative feedback is available, effective learning is possible. Second, we proposed a systematic approach to initializing conversational recommenders with an offline learned embedding, boosting greatly the performance even when only weakly supervised data is available. Third, we identified question selection strategies that can elicit feedback for very effective learning. Together, these insights pave the way towards conversational recommenders.

A promising future direction is to extend conversational recommenders to use reinforcement learning approaches, for capturing longer-term dependencies [17]. The modular structure of our framework allows various choices in a plug-and-play-manner, considering different feedback types, underlying probabilistic models etc., with the goal of building a suite of conversational recommenders for a variety of settings.

Acknowledgments. We would like to thank Tom Minka and Yordan Zaykov for the very insightful discussions on the model and evaluation. We also thank the participants of our user study.

9. REFERENCES

[1] D. Agarwal and B.-C. Chen. Regression-based latent factor models. In *KDD*, 19–28, 2009.

[2] N. Ailon, Z. Karnin, and T. Joachims. Reducing dueling bandits to cardinal bandits. In *ICML*, 856–864, 2014.

[3] P. Auer. Using confidence bounds for exploitation-exploration trade-offs. In *JMLR*, 3:397–422, 2003.

[4] G. Bresler, G. H. Chen, and D. Shah. A latent source model for online collaborative filtering. In *NIPS*, 3347–3355, 2014.

[5] O. Chapelle and L. Li. An empirical evaluation of thompson sampling. In *NIPS*, 2249–2257, 2011.

[6] H. Chen and D. R. Karger. Less is more: probabilistic models for retrieving fewer relevant documents. In *SIGIR*, 429–436, 2006.

[7] L. Chen and P. Pu. Critiquing-based recommenders: survey and emerging trends. In *User Modeling and User-Adapted Interaction*, 22(1-2):125–150, 2012.

[8] I. J. Cox, M. L. Miller, T. P. Minka, T. V. Papathomas and P. N. Yianilos. The Bayesian image retrieval system, PicHunter: theory, implementation, and psychophysical experiments. In *Image Processing, IEEE transactions*, 9(1):20–37, 2000.

[9] A. S. Das, M. Datar, A. Garg, and S. Rajaram. Google news personalization: scalable online collaborative filtering. In *WWW*, 271–280, 2007.

[10] A. Felfernig, G. Friedrich, D. Jannach and M. Zanker. Developing Constraint-based Recommenders. In *Recommender systems handbook*, 187–212, 2011.

[11] M. P. Graus and M. C. Willemsen. Improving the user experience during cold start through choice-based preference elicitation. In *RecSys*, 273–276, 2015.

[12] D. Kahneman and A. Tversky. Prospect theory: An analysis of decision under risk. In *Econometrica*, 263–291, 1979.

[13] J. Kawale, H. H Bui, B. Kveton, L. Tran-Thanh, and S. Chawla. Efficient Thompson Sampling for Online Matrix-Factorization Recommendation. In *NIPS*, 1297–1305, 2015.

[14] Y. Koren, R. Bell, and C. Volinsky. Matrix factorization techniques for recommender systems. In *Computer*, (8):30–37, 2009.

[15] H. Li. A short introduction to learning to rank. In *IEICE TIS*, 94(10):1854–1862, 2011.

[16] L. Li, W. Chu, J. Langford, and R. E. Schapire. A contextual-bandit approach to personalized news article recommendation. In *WWW*, 661–670, 2010.

[17] E. Liebman, M. Saar-Tsechansky, and P. Stone. Dj-mc: A reinforcement-learning agent for music playlist recommendation. In *AAMAS*, 591–599, 2015.

[18] B. Loepp, T. Hussein, and J. Ziegler. Choice-based preference elicitation for collaborative filtering recommender systems. In *CHI*, 3085–3094, 2014.

[19] T. Mahmood and F. Ricci. Improving recommender systems with adaptive conversational strategies. In *Hypertext*, 73–82, 2009.

[20] T. Minka, J. Winn, J. Guiver, and D. Knowles. Infer .net 2.5. *Microsoft Research Cambridge*, 2012.

[21] A. Mnih and R. Salakhutdinov. Probabilistic matrix factorization. In *NIPS*, 1257–1264, 2007.

[22] J. Neidhardt, R. Schuster, L. Seyfang, and H. Werthner. Eliciting the users' unknown preferences. In *RecSys*, 309–312, 2014.

[23] P. A. Ortega and D. A. Braun. Generalized thompson sampling for sequential decision-making and causal inference. In *Complex Adaptive Systems Modeling*, 2(1):2, 2014.

[24] M. J. Pazzani and D. Billsus. Content-based recommendation systems. In *The adaptive web*, 325–341, 2007.

[25] J. Ritchie and J. Lewis. Qualitative research practice. In *Sage*, 2003.

[26] N. Rubens, D. Kaplan, and M. Sugiyama. Active learning in recommender systems. In *Recommender systems handbook*, 735–767, 2011.

[27] T. Salimans, U. Paquet, and T. Graepel. Collaborative learning of preference rankings. In *RecSys*, 261–264, 2012.

[28] B. Sarwar, G. Karypis, J. Konstan, and J. Riedl. Item-based collaborative filtering recommendation algorithms. In *WWW*, 285–295, 2001.

[29] D. H. Stern, R. Herbrich, and T. Graepel. Matchbox: large scale online bayesian recommendations. In *WWW*, 111–120, 2009.

[30] M. Sun, F. Li, J. Lee, K. Zhou, G. Lebanon, and H. Zha. Learning multiple-question decision trees for cold-start recommendation. In *WSDM*, 445–454, 2013.

[31] L. Tang, Y. Jiang, L. Li, C. Zeng, and T. Li. Personalized recommendation via parameter-free contextual bandits. In *SIGIR*, 323–332, 2015.

[32] H. P. Vanchinathan, I. Nikolic, F. De Bona, and A. Krause. Explore-exploit in top-n recommender systems via gaussian processes. In *RecSys*, 225–232, 2014.

[33] X. Zhao, W. Zhang, and J. Wang. Interactive collaborative filtering. In *CIKM*, 1411–1420, 2013.

[34] M. Zoghi, S. A. Whiteson, M. de Rijke, and R. Munos. Relative confidence sampling for efficient on-line ranker evaluation. In *WSDM*, 73–82, 2014.

TRIÈST: Counting Local and Global Triangles in Fully-Dynamic Streams with Fixed Memory Size

Lorenzo De Stefani
Brown University
Providence, RI, USA
lorenzo@cs.brown.edu

Alessandro Epasto*
Google
New York, NY, USA
aepasto@google.com

Matteo Riondato*
Two Sigma Investments
New York, NY, USA
matteo@twosigma.com

Eli Upfal
Brown University
Providence, RI, USA
eli@cs.brown.edu

"Ogni lassada xe persa"[1] – Proverb from Trieste, Italy.

ABSTRACT

We present TRIÈST, a suite of one-pass streaming algorithms to compute unbiased, low-variance, high-quality approximations of the global and local (i.e., incident to each vertex) number of triangles in a fully-dynamic graph represented as an adversarial stream of edge insertions and deletions.

Our algorithms use reservoir sampling and its variants to exploit the user-specified memory space at all times. This is in contrast with previous approaches, which require hard-to-choose parameters (e.g., a fixed sampling probability) and offer no guarantees on the amount of memory they use. We analyze the variance of the estimations and show novel concentration bounds for these quantities.

Our experimental results on very large graphs demonstrate that TRIÈST outperforms state-of-the-art approaches in accuracy and exhibits a small update time.

1. INTRODUCTION

Exact computation of characteristic quantities of Web-scale networks is often impractical or even infeasible due to the humongous size of these graphs. It is natural in these cases to resort to *efficient-to-compute approximations* of these quantities, which, when of sufficiently high quality, can be used as proxies for the exact values.

In addition to being huge, many interesting networks are *fully-dynamic* and can be represented as a *stream* whose elements are edges/nodes insertions and deletions occurring in an *arbitrary* (even adversarial) order. Characteristic quantities in these graphs are *intrinsically volatile*, hence there is limited added value in maintaining them exactly. The goal is rather to keep track, *at all times*, of a high-quality approximation of these quantities. For efficiency, the algorithms should *aim at exploiting the available memory space as much as possible* and they should *require only one pass over the stream.*

We introduce TRIÈST, a suite of *sampling-based, one-pass algorithms for adversarial fully-dynamic streams to approximate the global number of triangles and the local number of triangles incident to each vertex.* Mining local and global triangles is a fundamental primitive with many applications (e.g., community detection [4], topic mining [10], spam/anomaly detection [3, 27], ego-networks mining [12] and protein interaction networks analysis [29].)

Many previous works on triangle estimation in streams also employ sampling (see Sect. 3), but they usually require the user to specify *in advance* an *edge sampling probability* p that is fixed for the entire stream. This approach presents several significant drawbacks. First, choosing a p that allows to obtain the desired approximation quality requires to know or guess a number of properties of the input (e.g., the size of the stream). Second, a fixed p implies that the sample size grows with the size of the stream, which is problematic when the stream size is not known in advance: if the user specifies a large p, the algorithm may run out of memory, while for a smaller p it will provide a suboptimal estimation. Third, even assuming to be able to compute a p that ensures (in expectation) full use of the available space, the memory would be fully utilized only at the end of the stream, and the estimations computed throughout the execution would be suboptimal.

Contributions. We address all the above issues by taking a significant departure from the fixed-probability, independent edge sampling approach taken even by state-of-the-art methods [27]. Specifically:

- We introduce TRIÈST (*TRI*angle *E*stimation from *ST*reams), a suite of *one-pass streaming algorithms* to approximate, at each time instant, the global and local number of triangles in a *fully-dynamic* graph stream (i.e., a sequence of edges additions and deletions in arbitrary order) using a *fixed amount of memory.* This is the first contribution that enjoys all these properties. TRIÈST only requires the user to specify *the amount of available memory*, an interpretable parameter that is definitively known to the user.
- Our algorithms maintain a sample of edges: they use the *reservoir sampling* [37] and *random pairing* [14] sampling

*Work partially done at Brown University.

[1]Any missed chance is lost forever.

KDD '16, August 13–17, 2016, San Francisco, CA, USA

ISBN 978-1-4503-4232-2/16/08...$15.00

DOI: http://dx.doi.org/10.1145/2939672.2939771

schemes to exploit the available memory as much as possible. To the best of our knowledge, ours is the first application of these techniques to subgraph counting in fully-dynamic, arbitrarily long, adversarially ordered streams. We present an analysis of the unbiasedness and of the variance of our estimators, and establish strong concentration results for them. The use of reservoir sampling and random pairing requires additional sophistication in the analysis, as the presence of an edge in the sample is *not independent* from the concurrent presence of another edge. Hence, in our proofs we must consider the complex dependencies in events involving sets of edges. The gain is worth the effort: we prove that the variance of our algorithms is smaller than that of state-of-the-art methods [27], and this is confirmed by our experiments.

- We conduct an extensive experimental evaluation of TRIÈST on very large graphs, some with billions of edges, comparing the performances of our algorithms to those of existing state-of-the-art contributions [18, 27, 32]. *Our algorithms significantly and consistently reduce the average estimation error by up to* 90% w.r.t. the state of the art, both in the global and local estimation problems, while using the same amount of memory. Our algorithms are also extremely scalable, showing update times in the order of hundreds of microseconds for graphs with billions of edges.

Due to space constraints, the proofs and additional experimental results can be found in the extended version [9].

2. PRELIMINARIES

We study the problem of counting global and local triangles in a fully-dynamic undirected graph as an arbitrary (adversarial) stream of edge insertions and deletions.

Formally, for any (discrete) time instant $t \geq 0$, let $G^{(t)} = (V^{(t)}, E^{(t)})$ be the graph observed up to and including time t. At time $t = 0$ we have $V^{(t)} = E^{(t)} = \emptyset$. For any $t > 0$, at time $t+1$ we receive an element $e_{t+1} = (\bullet, (u,v))$ from a stream, where $\bullet \in \{+,-\}$ and u, v are two distinct vertices. The graph $G^{(t+1)} = (V^{(t+1)}, E^{(t+1)})$ is obtained by *inserting a new edge or deleting an existing edge* as follows:

$$E^{(t+1)} = \begin{cases} E^{(t)} \cup \{(u,v)\} \text{ if } \bullet = \text{“}+\text{”} \\ E^{(t)} \setminus \{(u,v)\} \text{ if } \bullet = \text{“}-\text{”} \end{cases} .$$

If u or v do not belong to $V^{(t)}$, they are added to $V^{(t+1)}$. Nodes are deleted from $V^{(t)}$ when they have degree zero.

Edges can be added and deleted in the graph in an arbitrary adversarial order, i.e., as to cause the worst outcome for the algorithm, but we assume that the adversary has *no access to the random bits* used by the algorithm. We assume that *all operations have effect*: if $e \in E^{(t)}$ (resp. $e \notin E^{(t)}$), $(+, e)$ (resp. $(-, e)$) can not be on the stream at time $t+1$.

Given a graph $G^{(t)} = (V^{(t)}, E^{(t)})$, a *triangle* in $G^{(t)}$ is a *set* of three vertices $\{u, v, w\} \subseteq V^{(t)}$ such that $\{(u,v),(v,w),(w,u)\} \subseteq E^{(t)}$. We refer to the vertices forming a triangle as its *corners*. We denote with $\Delta^{(t)}$ the set of *all* triangles in $G^{(t)}$, and, for any vertex $u \in V^{(t)}$, with $\Delta_u^{(t)}$ the subset of $\Delta^{(t)}$ containing all and only the triangles that have u as a corner.

Problem definition. We study the *Global* (resp. *Local*) Triangle Counting Problem in Fully-dynamic Streams, which requires to compute, at each time $t \geq 0$ an estimation of $|\Delta^{(t)}|$ (resp. for each $u \in V$ an estimation of $|\Delta_u^{(t)}|$).

3. RELATED WORK

The literature on triangle counting is extremely rich, including exact algorithms, graph sparsifiers [35, 36], complex-valued sketches [20, 28], and MapReduce algorithms [30, 31, 33]. Here we restrict the discussion to the works most related to ours, i.e., to those presenting algorithms for counting or approximating the number of triangles from data streams. We refer to the survey by Latapy [25] for an in-depth discussion of other works.

Many previous contributions presented algorithms for more restricted (i.e., less generic) settings than ours, or for which the constraints on the computation are more lax [2, 6, 19, 22]. For example, Becchetti et al. [3] and Kolountzakis et al. [21] present algorithms for approximate triangle counting from *static* graphs by performing multiple passes over the input. Pavan et al. [32] and Jha et al. [18] propose algorithms for approximating only the global number of triangles from *edge-insertion-only* streams. Kutzkov and Pagh [23] present a one-pass algorithm for fully-dynamic graphs, but the triangle count estimation is (expensively) computed only at the end of the stream and the algorithm requires, in the worst case, more memory than what is needed to store the entire graph. Ahmed et al. [1] apply the sampling-and-hold approach to insertion-only graph stream mining to obtain, only at the end of the stream and using non-constant space, an estimation of many network measures including triangles.

None of these works has *all* the features offered by TRIÈST: performs a single pass over the data, handles fully-dynamic streams, uses a fixed amount of memory space, requires a single interpretable parameter, and returns an estimation at each time instant. Furthermore, our experimental results show that we outperform the algorithms from [18, 32] on insertion-only streams.

Lim and Kang [27] present an algorithm for insertion-only streams that is based on independent edge sampling with a fixed probability. Since the memory is not fully utilized during most of the stream, the variance of the estimate is large. Our approach handles fully-dynamic streams and makes better use of the available memory space at each time instant, resulting in a better estimation, as shown by our analytical and experimental results.

Vitter [37] presents a detailed analysis of the reservoir sampling scheme and discusses methods to speed up the algorithm by reducing the number of calls to the random number generator. Random Pairing [14] is an extension of reservoir sampling to handle fully-dynamic streams with insertions and deletions. Cohen et al. [8] generalize and extend the Random Pairing approach to the case where the elements on the stream are key-value pairs, where the value may be negative (and less than -1). In our settings, where the value is not less than -1 (for an edge deletion), these generalizations do not apply and the algorithm presented by Cohen et al. [8] reduces essentially to Random Pairing.

4. ALGORITHMS

We present TRIÈST, a suite of three novel algorithms for approximate global and local triangle counting from edge streams. The first two work on insertion-only streams, while the third can handle fully-dynamic streams where edge deletions are allowed.

Parameters. Our algorithms keep an edge sample $\mathcal{S}$ of up to M edges from the stream, where M is a positive integer parameter. For ease of presentation, we realistically assume $M \geq 6$. In Sect. 1 we motivated the design choice of only requiring M as a parameter and remarked on its advantages over using a fixed sampling probability p. Our algorithms are designed to use the available space as much as possible.

Counters. TRIÈST algorithms keep *counters* to compute the estimations of the global and local number of triangles. They *always* keep one global counter τ for the estimation of the global number of triangles. Only the global counter is needed to estimate the total triangle count. To estimate the local triangle counts, the algorithms keep a set of local counters τ_u for a subset of the nodes $u \in V^{(t)}$. The local counters are created on the fly as needed, and *always* destroyed as soon as they have a value of 0. Hence our algorithms use $O(M)$ space (with one exception, see Sect. 4.2).

Notation. For any $t \geq 0$, let $G^{\mathcal{S}} = (V^{\mathcal{S}}, E^{\mathcal{S}})$ be the subgraph of $G^{(t)}$ containing all and only the edges in the current sample $\mathcal{S}$. We denote with $\mathcal{N}_u^{\mathcal{S}}$ the *neighborhood* of u in $G^{\mathcal{S}}$: $\mathcal{N}_u^{\mathcal{S}} = \{v \in V^{(t)} : (u,v) \in \mathcal{S}\}$ and with $\mathcal{N}_{u,v}^{\mathcal{S}} = \mathcal{N}_u^{\mathcal{S}} \cap \mathcal{N}_v^{\mathcal{S}}$ the *shared neighborhood* of u and v in $G^{\mathcal{S}}$.

4.1 A first algorithm – TRIÈST-BASE

We first present TRIÈST-BASE, which works on insertion-only streams and uses standard reservoir sampling [37] to maintain the edge sample $\mathcal{S}$:

- If $t \leq M$, then the edge $e_t = (u,v)$ on the stream at time t is deterministically inserted in $\mathcal{S}$.
- If $t > M$, TRIÈST-BASE flips a biased coin with heads probability M/t. If the outcome is heads, it chooses an edge $(w,z) \in \mathcal{S}$ uniformly at random, removes (w,z) from $\mathcal{S}$, and inserts (u,v) in $\mathcal{S}$. Otherwise, $\mathcal{S}$ is not modified.

After each insertion (resp. removal) of an edge (u,v) from $\mathcal{S}$, TRIÈST-BASE calls the procedure UPDATECOUNTERS that increments (resp. decrements) τ, τ_u and τ_v by $|\mathcal{N}_{u,v}^{\mathcal{S}}|$, and τ_c by one, for each $c \in \mathcal{N}_{u,v}^{\mathcal{S}}$.

The pseudocode for TRIÈST-BASE is presented in Alg. 1.

Algorithm 1 TRIÈST-BASE

Input: Insertion-only edge stream Σ, integer $M \geq 6$
$\mathcal{S} \leftarrow \emptyset$, $t \leftarrow 0$, $\tau \leftarrow 0$
for each element $(+,(u,v))$ from Σ **do**
  $t \leftarrow t+1$
  if SAMPLEEDGE$((u,v),t)$ **then**
    $\mathcal{S} \leftarrow \mathcal{S} \cup \{(u,v)\}$
    UPDATECOUNTERS$(+,(u,v))$

function SAMPLEEDGE$((u,v),t)$
  if $t \leq M$ **then**
    return True
  else if FLIPBIASEDCOIN$(\frac{M}{t})$ = heads **then**
    $(u',v') \leftarrow$ random edge from $\mathcal{S}$
    $\mathcal{S} \leftarrow \mathcal{S} \setminus \{(u',v')\}$
    UPDATECOUNTERS$(-,(u',v'))$
    return True
  return False

function UPDATECOUNTERS$((\bullet,(u,v)))$
  $\mathcal{N}_{u,v}^{\mathcal{S}} \leftarrow \mathcal{N}_u^{\mathcal{S}} \cap \mathcal{N}_v^{\mathcal{S}}$
  for all $c \in \mathcal{N}_{u,v}^{\mathcal{S}}$ **do**
    $\tau \leftarrow \tau \bullet 1$
    $\tau_c \leftarrow \tau_c \bullet 1$
    $\tau_u \leftarrow \tau_u \bullet 1$
    $\tau_v \leftarrow \tau_v \bullet 1$

Estimation. For any $t \geq 0$, let $\xi^{(t)} = \max\left\{1, \frac{t(t-1)(t-2)}{M(M-1)(M-2)}\right\}$. Let $\tau^{(t)}$ (resp. $\tau_u^{(t)}$) be the value of the counter τ at the end of time step t (i.e., after the edge on the stream at time t has been processed by TRIÈST-BASE) (resp. the value of the counter τ_u at the end of time step t if there is such a counter, 0 otherwise). When queried at the end of time t, TRIÈST-BASE returns $\xi^{(t)}\tau^{(t)}$ (resp. $\xi^{(t)}\tau_u^{(t)}$) as the estimation for the global (resp. local for $u \in V^{(t)}$) triangle count.

Analysis.

THEOREM 1. *We have*

$$\xi^{(t)}\tau^{(t)} = \tau^{(t)} = |\Delta^{(t)}| \text{ if } t \leq M$$
$$\mathbb{E}\left[\xi^{(t)}\tau^{(t)}\right] = |\Delta^{(t)}| \text{ if } t > M \ .$$

The TRIÈST-BASE estimations are not only *unbiased in all cases*, but actually *exact for* $t \leq M$, i.e., for $t \leq M$, they are the true global/local number of triangles in $G^{(t)}$.

We now analyze the variance of the estimation returned by TRIÈST-BASE for $t > M$ (the variance is 0 for $t \leq M$.) Let $t \geq 0$. For any $u \in V^{(t)}$, let $r_u^{(t)}$ be the number of *unordered* pairs of distinct triangles from $\Delta_u^{(t)}$ sharing an edge.[1] Similarly, let $r^{(t)} = \frac{1}{3}\sum_{u \in V^{(t)}} r_u^{(t)}$ be the *total* number of unordered pairs of distinct triangles from $\Delta^{(t)}$ sharing an edge. We also define $w^{(t)} = \binom{|\Delta^{(t)}|}{2} - r^{(t)}$ as the number of unordered pairs of distinct triangles that do not share any edge, and analogously for $w_u^{(t)}$.

THEOREM 2. *For any $t > M$, let $f(t) = \xi^{(t)} - 1$,*

$$g(t) = \xi^{(t)}\frac{(M-3)(M-4)}{(t-3)(t-4)} - 1$$

and

$$h(t) = \xi^{(t)}\frac{(M-3)(M-4)(M-5)}{(t-3)(t-4)(t-5)} - 1 \ (\leq 0).$$

We have:

$$\mathrm{Var}\left[\xi(t)\tau^{(t)}\right] = |\Delta^{(t)}|f(t) + r^{(t)}g(t) + w^{(t)}h(t). \quad (1)$$

In our proofs, we carefully account for the fact that, as we use reservoir sampling [37], the presence of an edge a in $\mathcal{S}$ is *not independent* from the concurrent presence of another edge b in $\mathcal{S}$. This is not the case for samples built using fixed-probability independent edge sampling. When computing the variance, we must consider not only pairs of triangles that share an edge (as for independent edge sampling approaches), but also pairs of triangles sharing no edge, as their respective presences in the sample are not independent events. The gain is worth the additional sophistication needed in the analysis, because the contribution to the variance by triangles not sharing edges is *non-positive* ($h(t) \leq 0$), i.e., it reduces the variance. A comparison of the variance of our estimator with that obtained with a fixed-probability independent edge sampling approach, is discussed below.

Let $h^{(t)}$ denote the maximum number of triangles sharing a single edge in $G^{(t)}$. The following concentration theorem relies on *1.* a result by Hajnal and Szemerédi [15] on graph coloring, *2.* a novel concentration result for fixed-probability independent edge sampling, and *3.* a Poisson-approximation-like result on probabilities of general events under reservoir sampling w.r.t. their probabilities under independent edge sampling. These ingredients are then combined to obtain the following result. The details can be found in our extended online version [9].

[1]Two distinct triangles can share at most one edge.

THEOREM 3. *Let $t \geq 0$ and assume $|\Delta^{(t)}| > 0$.*[2] *For any $\varepsilon, \delta \in (0,1)$, let*

$$\Phi = \sqrt[3]{8\varepsilon^{-2}\frac{3h^{(t)}+1}{|\Delta^{(t)}|}\ln\left(\frac{(3h^{(t)}+1)e}{\delta}\right)} .$$

If

$$M \geq \max\left\{t\Phi\left(1+\frac{1}{2}\ln^{2/3}(t\Phi)\right), 12\varepsilon^{-1}+e^2, 25\right\},$$

then $|\xi^{(t)}\tau^{(t)} - |\Delta^{(t)}|| < \varepsilon|\Delta^{(t)}|$ with probability $> 1-\delta$.

Results analogous to those in Thms. 1, 2, and 3 hold for the local triangle count for any $u \in V^{(t)}$, replacing the global quantities with the corresponding local ones.

Comparison with fixed-probability approaches. We now compare the variance of TRIÈST-BASE to the variance of the fixed probability sampling approach MASCOT-C [27], which samples edges *independently* with a fixed probability p and uses $p^{-3}|\Delta_{\mathcal{S}}|$ as the estimate for the global number of triangles at time t. As shown by Lim and Kang [27, Lemma 2], the variance of this estimator is

$$\mathrm{Var}[p^{-3}|\Delta_{\mathcal{S}}|] = |\Delta^{(t)}|\bar{f}(p) + r^{(t)}\bar{g}(p),$$

where $\bar{f}(p) = p^{-3} - 1$ and $\bar{g}(p) = p^{-1} - 1$.

Assume that we give MASCOT-C the additional information that the stream has finite length T, and assume we run MASCOT-C with $p = M/T$ so that the expected sample size at the end of the stream is M.[3] Let $\mathbb{V}^{(t)}_{\text{fix}}$ be the resulting variance of the MASCOT-C estimator at time t, and let $\mathbb{V}^{(t)}$ be the variance of our estimator at time t (see (1)). For $t \leq M$, $\mathbb{V}^{(t)} = 0$, hence $\mathbb{V}^{(t)} \leq \mathbb{V}^{(t)}_{\text{fix}}$.

For $M < t < T$, we can show the following result.

LEMMA 1. *Let $0 < \alpha < 1$ be a constant. For any constant $M > \max(\frac{8\alpha}{1-\alpha}, 42)$ and any $t \leq \alpha T$ we have $\mathbb{V}^{(t)} < \mathbb{V}^{(t)}_{\text{fix}}$.*

For example, if we set $\alpha = 0.99$ and run TRIÈST-BASE with $M \geq 400$ and MASCOT-C with $p = M/T$, we have that TRIÈST-BASE has strictly smaller variance than MASCOT-C for 99% of the stream.

What about $t = T$? The difference between the definitions of $\mathbb{V}^{(t)}_{\text{fix}}$ and $\mathbb{V}^{(t)}$ is in the presence of $\bar{f}(M/T)$ instead of $f(t)$ (resp. $\bar{g}(M/T)$ instead of $g(t)$) as well as the additional term $w^{(t)}h(M,t) \leq 0$ in our $\mathbb{V}^{(t)}$. Let $M(T)$ be an arbitrary slowly increasing function of T. For $T \to \infty$ we can show that $\lim_{T\to\infty}\frac{\bar{f}(M(T)/T)}{f(T)} = \lim_{T\to\infty}\frac{\bar{g}(M(T)/T)}{g(T)} = 1$, hence, *informally*, $\mathbb{V}^{(T)} \to \mathbb{V}^{(T)}_{\text{fix}}$, for $T \to \infty$.

A similar discussion also holds for the method we present in Sect. 4.2, and explains the results of our experimental evaluations, which show that our algorithms have strictly lower (empirical) variance than fixed probability approaches for most of the stream.

Update time. The time to process an element of the stream is dominated by the computation of the shared neighborhood $\mathcal{N}_{u,v}$ in UPDATECOUNTERS. A MERGESORT-based algorithm for the intersection requires $O(\deg(u) + \deg(v))$ time, where the degrees are w.r.t. the graph $G_{\mathcal{S}}$. By storing the neighborhood of each vertex in a Hash Table (resp. an AVL tree), the update time can be reduced to $O(\min\{\deg(v), \deg(u)\})$ (resp. amortized time $O(\min\{\deg(v), \deg(u)\} + \log\max\{\deg(v), \deg(u)\})$).

[2]If $|\Delta^{(t)}| = 0$, our algorithms correctly estimate 0 triangles.

[3]We are giving MASCOT-C a significant advantage: if only space M were available, we should run MASCOT-C with a sufficiently smaller $p' < p$, otherwise there would be a constant probability that MASCOT-C would run out of memory.

4.2 Improved insertion algorithm – TRIÈST-IMPR

TRIÈST-IMPR is a variant of TRIÈST-BASE with small modifications that result in higher-quality (i.e., lower variance) estimations. The changes are:

1. UPDATECOUNTERS is called *unconditionally for each element on the stream*, before the algorithm decides whether or not to insert the edge into $\mathcal{S}$. W.r.t. the pseudocode in Alg. 1, this change corresponds to moving the call to UPDATECOUNTERS on line 6 to *before* the **if** block. MASCOT [27] uses a similar idea, but TRIÈST-IMPR is significantly different as TRIÈST-IMPR allows edges to be removed from the sample, since it uses reservoir sampling.
2. TRIÈST-IMPR *never* decrements the counters when an edge is removed from $\mathcal{S}$. W.r.t. the pseudocode in Alg. 1, we remove the call to UPDATECOUNTERS on line 13.
3. UPDATECOUNTERS performs a *weighted* increase of the counters using $\eta^{(t)} = \max\{1, (t-1)(t-2)/(M(M-1))\}$ as weight. W.r.t. the pseudocode in Alg. 1, we replace "1" with $\eta^{(t)}$ on lines 19–22 (given change 2 above, all the calls to UPDATECOUNTERS have $\bullet = +$).

Counters. If we are interested only in estimating the global number of triangles in $G^{(t)}$, TRIÈST-IMPR needs to maintain only the counter τ and the edge sample $\mathcal{S}$ of size M, so it still requires space $O(M)$. If instead we are interested in estimating the local triangle counts, at any time t TRIÈST maintains (non-zero) local counters *only* for the nodes u such that at least one triangle with a corner u has been detected by the algorithm up until time t. The number of such nodes may be greater than $O(M)$, but this is the price to pay to obtain estimations with lower variance (Thm. 5).

Estimation. When queried for an estimation, TRIÈST-IMPR returns the value of the corresponding counter, unmodified.

Analysis.

THEOREM 4. *We have $\tau^{(t)} = |\Delta^{(t)}|$ if $t \leq M$ and $\mathbb{E}\left[\tau^{(t)}\right] = |\Delta^{(t)}|$ if $t > M$.*

As in TRIÈST-BASE, the estimations by TRIÈST-IMPR are *exact* at time $t \leq M$ and unbiased for $t > M$.

We now show an *upper bound* to the variance of the TRIÈST-IMPR estimations for $t > M$. The proof relies on a very careful analysis of the covariance of two triangles which depends on the order of arrival of the edges in the stream (which we assume to be adversarial). Let $z^{(t)}$ be the number of unordered pairs (λ, γ) of distinct triangles in $G^{(t)}$ that share an edge g and are such that g is neither the last edge of λ on the stream nor the last edge of γ on the stream. For any node $u \in V^{(t)}$, let $z^{(t)}_u$ be similarly defined, but considering only the triangles incident to u.

THEOREM 5. *Then, for any time $t > M$, we have*

$$\mathrm{Var}\left[\tau^{(t)}\right] \leq |\Delta^{(t)}|(\eta^{(t)} - 1) + z^{(t)}\frac{t-1-M}{M} .$$

For the sake of clarity, in Thm. 5, we chose not to present a stricter but more complex bound involving triangles that do not share any edge, which, as in Thm. 2, would add a *non-positive* term to the variance (i.e., reduce the variance).

The following result relies on Chebyshev's inequality and Thm. 5.

THEOREM 6. *Let $t \geq 0$ and assume $|\Delta^{(t)}| > 0$. For any $\varepsilon, \delta \in (0,1)$, if*

$$M > \max\left\{\sqrt{\frac{2(t-1)(t-2)}{\delta\varepsilon^2|\Delta^{(t)}|+2}+\frac{1}{4}}+\frac{1}{2}, \frac{2z^{(t)}(t-1)}{\delta\varepsilon^2|\Delta^{(t)}|^2+2z^{(t)}}\right\}$$

then $|\tau^{(t)} - |\Delta^{(t)}|| < \varepsilon|\Delta^{(t)}|$ with probability $> 1-\delta$.

In Thms. 5 and 6, it is possible to replace the value $z^{(t)}$ with the more interpretable $r^{(t)}$, which is agnostic to the order of the edges on the stream but gives a looser upper bound to the variance.

Results analogous to those in Thms. 4, 5, and 6 hold for the local triangle count for any $u \in V^{(t)}$, replacing the global quantities with the corresponding local ones.

4.3 Fully-dynamic algorithm – TRIÈST-FD

TRIÈST-FD computes unbiased estimates of the global and local triangle counts in a *fully-dynamic stream where edges are inserted/deleted in any arbitrary, adversarial order.* It is based on *random pairing* (RP) [14], a sampling scheme that extends reservoir sampling and can handle deletions. The idea behind the RP scheme is that edge deletions seen on the stream will be "compensated" by future edge insertions. Following RP, TRIÈST-FD keeps a counter d_i (resp. d_o) to keep track of the number of uncompensated edge deletions involving an edge e that was (resp. was *not*) in $\mathcal{S}$ at the time the deletion for e was on the stream.

When an edge deletion for an edge $e \in E^{(t-1)}$ is on the stream at the beginning of time step t, then, if $e \in \mathcal{S}$ at this time, TRIÈST-FD removes e from $\mathcal{S}$ (effectively decreasing the number of edges stored in the sample by one) and increases d_i by one. Otherwise, it just increases d_o by one. When an edge insertion for an edge $e \notin E^{(t-1)}$ is on the stream at the beginning of time step t, if $d_i + d_o = 0$, then TRIÈST-FD follows the standard reservoir sampling scheme. If $|\mathcal{S}| < M$, then e is deterministically inserted in $\mathcal{S}$ without removing any edge from $\mathcal{S}$ already in $\mathcal{S}$, otherwise it is inserted in $\mathcal{S}$ with probability M/t, replacing an uniformly-chosen edge already in $\mathcal{S}$. If instead $d_i + d_o > 0$, then e is inserted in $\mathcal{S}$ with probability $d_i/(d_i + d_o)$; since it must be $d_i > 0$, then it must be $|\mathcal{S}| < M$ and no edge already in $\mathcal{S}$ needs to be removed. In any case, after having handled the eventual insertion of e into $\mathcal{S}$, the algorithm decreases d_i by 1 if e was inserted in $\mathcal{S}$, otherwise it decreases d_o by 1. TRIÈST-FD also keeps track of $s^{(t)} = |E^{(t)}|$ by appropriately incrementing or decrementing a counter by 1 depending on whether the element on the stream is an edge insertion or deletion. The pseudocode for TRIÈST-FD is presented in Alg. 2 where the UPDATECOUNTERS procedure is the one from Alg. 1.

Estimation. We denote as $M^{(t)}$ the size of $\mathcal{S}$ at the end of time t (we always have $M^{(t)} \leq M$). For any time t, let $d_i^{(t)}$ and $d_o^{(t)}$ be the value of the counters d_i and d_o at the end of time t respectively, and let $\omega^{(t)} = \min\{M, s^{(t)} + d_i^{(t)} + d_o^{(t)}\}$. Define

$$\kappa^{(t)} = 1 - \sum_{j=0}^{2}\binom{s^{(t)}}{j}\binom{d_i^{(t)}+d_o^{(t)}}{\omega^{(t)}-j}\Big/\binom{s^{(t)}+d_i^{(t)}+d_o^{(t)}}{\omega^{(t)}} .$$

Algorithm 2 TRIÈST-FD

```
Input: Fully Dynamic edge stream Σ, integer M ≥ 6
S ← ∅, d_i ← 0, d_o ← 0, t ← 0, s ← 0
for each element (•, (u, v)) from Σ do
    t ← t + 1
    s ← s • 1
    if • = + then
        if SAMPLEEDGE (u, v) then
            UPDATECOUNTERS(+, (u, v))
    else if (u, v) ∈ S then
        UPDATECOUNTERS(−, (u, v))
        S ← S \ {(u, v)}
        d_i ← d_i + 1
    else  d_o ← d_o + 1

function SAMPLEEDGE(u, v)
    if d_o + d_i = 0 then
        if |S| < M then
            S ← S ∪ {(u, v)}
            return True
        else if FLIPBIASEDCOIN(M/t) = heads then
            Select (z, w) uniformly at random from S
            UPDATECOUNTERS(−, (z, w))
            S ← (S \ {(z, w)}) ∪ {(u, v)}
            return True
    else if FLIPBIASEDCOIN(d_i/(d_i + d_o)) = heads then
        S ← S ∪ {(u, v)}
        d_i ← d_i − 1
        return True
    else
        d_o ← d_o − 1
        return False
```

For any three positive integers a, b, c s.t. $a \leq b \leq c$, define

$$\psi_{a,b,c} = \prod_{i=0}^{a-1}\frac{c-i}{b-i} .$$

When queried at the end of time t, for an estimation of the global number of triangles, TRIÈST-FD returns

$$\rho^{(t)} = \begin{cases} 0 \text{ if } M^{(t)} < 3 \\ \frac{\tau^{(t)}}{\kappa^{(t)}}\psi_{3,M^{(t)},s^{(t)}} = \frac{\tau^{(t)}}{\kappa^{(t)}}\frac{s^{(t)}(s^{(t)}-1)(s^{(t)}-2)}{M^{(t)}(M^{(t)}-1)(M^{(t)}-2)} \text{ othw.} \end{cases}$$

When estimating $|\Delta_u^{(t)}|$ for $u \in V^{(t)}$, the definition for $\rho_u^{(t)}$ uses $\tau_u^{(t)}$ and has the additional condition that $\rho_u^{(t)} = 0$ if there is no counter τ_u. TRIÈST-FD can keep track of $\kappa^{(t)}$ during the execution, each update of $\kappa^{(t)}$ taking time $O(1)$. Hence the time to return the estimations is still $O(1)$.

Analysis. Let t^* be the first $t \geq M+1$ such that $|E^{(t)}| = M+1$, if such a time step exists (otherwise $t^* = +\infty$).

THEOREM 7. *We have $\rho^{(t)} = |\Delta^{(t)}|$ for all $t < t^*$, and $\mathbb{E}\left[\rho^{(t)}\right] = |\Delta^{(t)}|$ for $t \geq t^*$.*

The proof relies on properties of RP and on the definitions of $\kappa^{(t)}$ and $\rho^{(t)}$.

THEOREM 8. *Let $t > t^*$ s.t. $|\Delta^{(t)}| > 0$ and $s^{(t)} \geq M$. Suppose we have $d^{(t)} = d_o^{(t)} + d_i^{(t)} \leq \alpha s^{(t)}$ total unpaired deletions at time t, with $0 \leq \alpha < 1$. If $M \geq \frac{1}{2\sqrt{\alpha'-\alpha}}7\ln s^{(t)}$ for some $\alpha < \alpha' < 1$, we have:*

$$\mathrm{Var}\left[\rho^{(t)}\right] \leq (\kappa^{(t)})^{-2}|\Delta^{(t)}|\left(\psi_{3,M(1-\alpha'),s^{(t)}} - 1\right) + (\kappa^{(t)})^{-2}2 + (\kappa^{(t)})^{-2}r^{(t)}\left(\psi^2_{3,M(1-\alpha'),s^{(t)}}\psi^{-1}_{5,M(1-\alpha'),s^{(t)}} - 1\right)$$

The following result relies on Chebyshev's inequality and on Thm. 8.

THEOREM 9. *Let $t \geq t^*$ s.t. $|\Delta^{(t)}| > 0$ and $s^{(t)} \geq M$. Let $d^{(t)} = d_o^{(t)} + d_i^{(t)} \leq \alpha s^{(t)}$ for some $0 \leq \alpha < 1$. For any $\varepsilon, \delta \in (0,1)$, if for some $\alpha < \alpha' < 1$*

$$M > \max\left\{ \frac{1}{\sqrt{a' - \alpha}} 7 \ln s^{(t)}, \right.$$

$$(1-\alpha')^{-1}\left(\sqrt[3]{\frac{2s^{(t)}(s^{(t)}-1)(s^{(t)}-2)}{\delta\varepsilon^2|\Delta^{(t)}|(\kappa^{(t)})^2 + 2\frac{|\Delta^{(t)}|-2}{|\Delta^{(t)}|}}} + 2 \right),$$

$$\left. \frac{(1-\alpha')^{-1}}{3}\left(\frac{r^{(t)}s^{(t)}}{\delta\varepsilon^2|\Delta^{(t)}|^2(\kappa^{(t)})^{-2} + 2r^{(t)}} \right) \right\}$$

then $|\rho^{(t)} - |\Delta^{(t)}|| < \varepsilon|\Delta^{(t)}|$ with probability $> 1 - \delta$.

Results analogous to those in Thms. 7, 8, and 9 hold for the local triangle count for any $u \in V^{(t)}$, replacing the global quantities with the corresponding local ones.

5. EXPERIMENTAL EVALUATION

We evaluated TRIÈST on several real-world graphs with up to a billion edges. The algorithms were implemented in C++, and ran on the Brown University CS department cluster.[4] Each run employed a single core and used at most 4 GB of RAM. We report here only a subset of the results. Additional details are available in the extended online version. The code is available from http://bigdata.cs.brown.edu/triangles.html.

Datasets. We created the streams from the following publicly available graphs (properties in Table 1).

Patent (Co-Aut.) and Patent (Cit.). The *Patent (Co-Aut.)* and *Patent (Cit.)* graphs are obtained from a dataset of $\approx$ 2 million U.S. patents granted between '75 and '99 [16]. In *Patent (Co-Aut.)*, the nodes represent inventors and there is an edge with timestamp t between two co-inventors of a patent if the patent was granted in year t. In *Patent (Cit.)*, nodes are patents and there is an edge (a, b) with timestamp t if patent a cites b and a was granted in year t.

LastFm. The LastFm graph is based on a dataset [7, 34] of $\approx$ 20 million last.fm song listenings, $\approx$ 1 million songs and $\approx$ 1000 users. There is a node for each song and an edge between two songs if ≥ 3 users listened to both on day t.

Yahoo! Answers. The Yahoo! Answers graph is obtained from a sample of $\approx$ 160 million answers to $\approx$ 25 millions questions posted on Yahoo! Answers [38]. An edge connects two users at time $max(t_1, t_2)$ if they both answered the same question at times t_1, t_2 respectively. We removed 6 outliers questions with more than 5000 answers.

Twitter. This is a snapshot [5, 24] of the Twitter followers/following network with $\approx$ 41 million nodes and $\approx$ 1.5 billions edges. We do not have time information for the edges, hence we assign a random timestamp to the edges (of which we ignore the direction).

Ground truth. To evaluate the accuracy of our algorithms, we computed the *ground truth* for our smaller graphs (i.e., the exact number of global and local triangles for each time step), using an exact algorithm. The entire current graph is stored in memory and when an edge u, v is inserted (or deleted) we update the current count of local and global

[4]https://cs.brown.edu/about/system/services/hpc/grid/

Graph	$\lvert V \rvert$	$\lvert E \rvert$	$\lvert E_u \rvert$	$\lvert \Delta \rvert$
Patent (Co-Aut.)	1,162,227	3,660,945	2,724,036	3.53×10^6
Patent (Cit.)	2,745,762	13,965,410	13,965,132	6.91×10^6
LastFm	681,387	43,518,693	30,311,117	1.13×10^9
Yahoo! Answers	2,432,573	1.21×10^9	1.08×10^9	7.86×10^{10}
Twitter	41,652,230	1.47×10^9	1.20×10^9	3.46×10^{10}

Table 1: Properties of the dynamic graph streams analyzed. $|V|$, $|E|$, $|E_u|$, $|\Delta|$ refer respectively to the number of nodes appearing in the graph, the number of edge addition events, the number of distinct edges additions, and the maximum number of triangles in the graph (for Yahoo! Answers and Twitter estimated with TRIÈST-IMPR $M = 1000000$, otherwise computed exactly with the naïve algorithm).

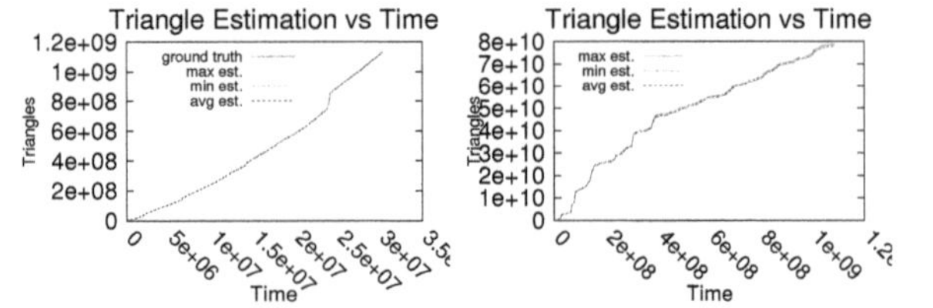

(a) LastFm (b) Yahoo! Answers

Figure 1: Estimation by TRIÈST-IMPR of the global number of triangles over time. Our estimations have very small error and variance: the ground truth is indistinguishable from max/min point-wise estimation over ten runs.

triangles by checking how many triangles are completed (or broken). As exact algorithms are not scalable, computing the exact triangle count is feasible only for small graphs such as Patent (Co-Aut.), Patent (Cit.) and LastFm. Table 1 reports the exact total number of triangles at the end of the stream for those graphs (and an estimate for the larger ones using TRIÈST-IMPR with $M = 1000000$).

5.1 Insertion-only case

We now evaluate TRIÈST on insertion-only streams and compare its performances with those of state-of-the-art approaches [18, 27, 32], showing that TRIÈST has an average estimation error significantly smaller than these methods both for the global and local estimation problems, while using the same amount of memory.

Estimation of the global number of triangles. Starting from an empty graph we add one edge at a time, in timestamp order. Figure 1 illustrates the evolution, over time, of the estimation computed by TRIÈST-IMPR with $M = 1{,}000{,}000$. For smaller graphs for which the ground truth can be computed exactly, the curve of the exact count is practically indistinguishable from our estimation showing the precision of the method. Our estimators have very small variance even on the very large Yahoo! Answers graph (point-wise max/min estimation over ten runs is almost coincident with the average estimation). These results show that TRIÈST-IMPR is very accurate even when storing less than a 0.001 fraction of the total edges of the graph.

Comparison with the state of the art. We compare quantitatively with three state-of-the-art methods: MAS-

			Max. MAPE		Avg. MAPE		
Graph	Impr.	p	MASCOT	TRIÈST	MASCOT	TRIÈST	Change
Patent (Cit.)	N	0.01	0.9231	0.2583	0.6517	0.1811	-72.2%
	Y	0.01	0.1907	0.0363	0.1149	0.0213	-81.4%
	N	0.1	0.0839	0.0124	0.0605	0.0070	-88.5%
	Y	0.1	0.0317	0.0037	0.0245	0.0022	-91.1%
LastFm	N	0.01	0.1525	0.0185	0.0627	0.0118	-81.2%
	Y	0.01	0.0273	0.0046	0.0141	0.0034	-76.2%
	N	0.1	0.0075	0.0028	0.0047	0.0015	-68.1%
	Y	0.1	0.0048	0.0013	0.0031	0.0009	-72.1%

Table 2: Global triangle estimation MAPE for TRIÈST and MASCOT. The rightmost column shows the reduction in terms of the avg. MAPE obtained by using TRIÈST. Rows with Y in column "Impr." refer to improved algorithms (TRIÈST-IMPR and MASCOT-I) while those with N to basic algorithms (TRIÈST-BASE and MASCOT-C).

	Avg. Pearson			Avg. ε Err		
p	MASCOT-I	TRIÈST	Change	MASCOT-I	TRIÈST	Change
0.1	0.99	1.00	+1.18%	0.79	0.30	-62.02%
0.05	0.97	1.00	+2.48%	0.99	0.47	-52.79%
0.01	0.85	0.98	+14.28%	1.35	0.89	-34.24%

Table 3: Comparison of the quality of the local triangle estimations in LastFM between TRIÈST-IMPR and MASCOT-I). We outperform MASCOT-I using the same amount of memory.

COT [27], JHA ET AL. [18] and PAVAN ET AL. [32]. MASCOT is a suite of local triangle counting methods (but provides also a global estimation). The other two are global triangle counting approaches. None of these can handle fully-dynamic streams, in contrast with TRIÈST-FD. We first compare the three methods to TRIÈST for the global triangle counting estimation. MASCOT comes in two memory efficient variants: the basic MASCOT-C variant and an improved MASCOT-I variant.[5] Both variants sample edges with fixed probability p, so there is no guarantee on the amount of memory used during the execution. To ensure fairness of comparison, we devised the following experiment. First, we run both MASCOT-C and MASCOT-I for $\ell = 10$ times with a fixed p using the same random bits for the two algorithms run-by-run (i.e. the same coin tosses used to select the edges) measuring each time the number of edges M'_i stored in the sample at the end of the stream (by construction this the is same for the two variants run-by-run). Then, we run our algorithms using $M = M'_i$ (for $i \in [\ell]$). We do the same to fix the size of the edge memory for JHA ET AL. [18] and PAVAN ET AL. [32].[6] This way, all algorithms use the same amount of memory for storing edges (run-by-run).

We use the *MAPE* (Mean Average Percentage Error) to assess the accuracy of the global triangle estimators over time. The MAPE measures the average percentage of the prediction error with respect to the ground truth, and is widely used in the prediction literature [17]. For $t = 1, \ldots, T$, let $\overline{\Delta}^{(t)}$ be the estimator of the number of triangles at time t, the MAPE is defined as $\frac{1}{T}\sum_{t=1}^{T}\left|\frac{|\Delta^{(t)}|-\overline{\Delta}^{(t)}}{|\Delta^{(t)}|}\right|$.[7]

In Fig. 2(a), we compare the average MAPE of TRIÈST-BASE and TRIÈST-IMPR as well as the two MASCOT variants and the other two streaming algorithms for the Patent (Co-Aut.) graph, fixing $p = 0.01$. TRIÈST-IMPR has the smallest error of all the algorithms compared.

We now turn our attention to the efficiency of the methods. Figure 2(b) shows the average update time per operation in Patent (Co-Aut.) graph, fixing $p = 0.01$. Both JHA ET AL. [18] and PAVAN ET AL. [32] are up to ≈ 3 orders of magnitude slower than the MASCOT variants and TRIÈST. This is expected as both algorithms have an update complexity of $\Omega(M)$ (they have to go through the entire reservoir graph at each step), while both MASCOT algorithms and TRIÈST need only to access the neighborhood of the nodes involved in the edge addition.[8] This allows both algorithms to efficiently exploit larger memory sizes. We can use efficiently M up to 1 million edges in our experiments,

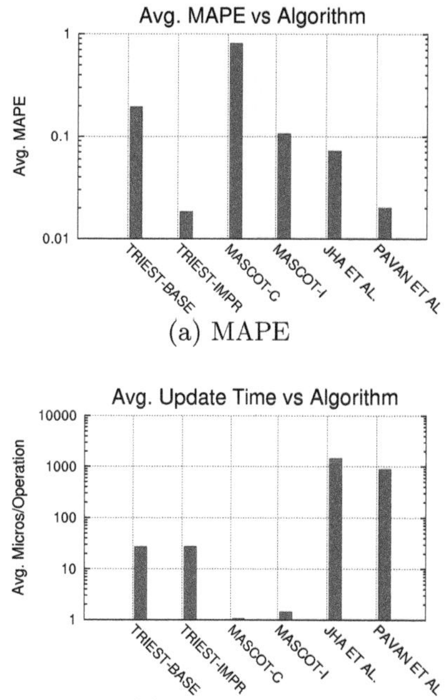

(a) MAPE

(b) Update Time

Figure 2: Average MAPE and average update time of the various methods on the Patent (Co-Aut.) graph with $p = 0.01$ – insertion only. TRIÈST-IMPR has the lowest error. Both PAVAN ET AL. and JHA ET AL. have very high update times compared to our method and the two MASCOT variants.

[5]In the original work [27], this variant had no suffix and was simply called MASCOT. We add the -I suffix to avoid confusion. The variant MASCOT-A can be forced to store the entire graph with probability 1 (using an adversarial edge order) so we do not consider it here.

[6]More precisely, we use $M'_i/2$ estimators in PAVAN ET AL. as each estimator stores two edges. For JHA ET AL. we set the two reservoirs in the algorithm to have each size $M'_i/2$. This way, all algorithms use M'_i cells for storing (w)edges.

[7]The MAPE is not defined for t s.t. $\Delta^{(t)} = 0$ so we compute it only for t s.t. $|\Delta^{(t)}| > 0$. All algorithms we consider are guaranteed to output the correct answer for t s.t. $|\Delta^{(t)}| = 0$.

[8]We observe that PAVAN ET AL. [32] would be more efficient with batch updates. However, we want to estimate the triangles continuously at each update. In their experiments they use batch sizes of million of updates for efficiency.

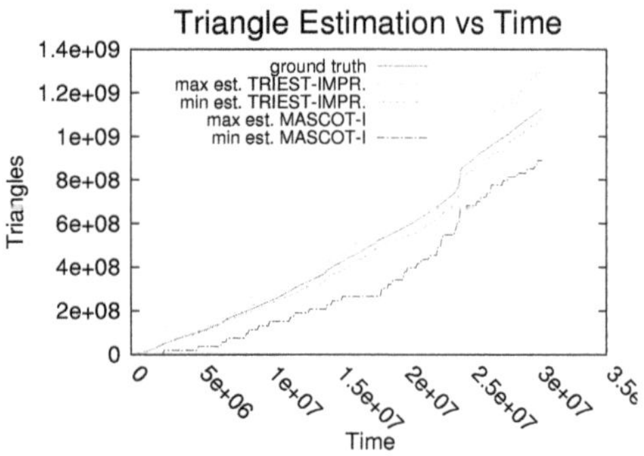

Figure 3: Variance of TRIÈST-IMPR with $M = 10000$ and of MASCOT with same expected memory, on LastFM. TRIÈST-IMPR has a smaller variance: the max/min estimation lines are closer to the ground truth. (Average estimations are qualitatively similar and not shown).

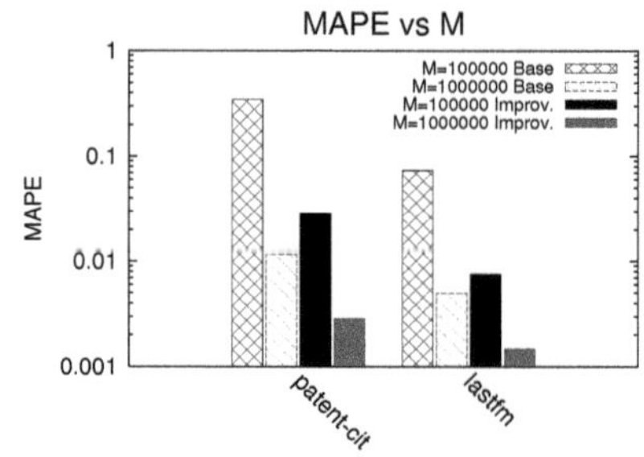

(a) M vs MAPE

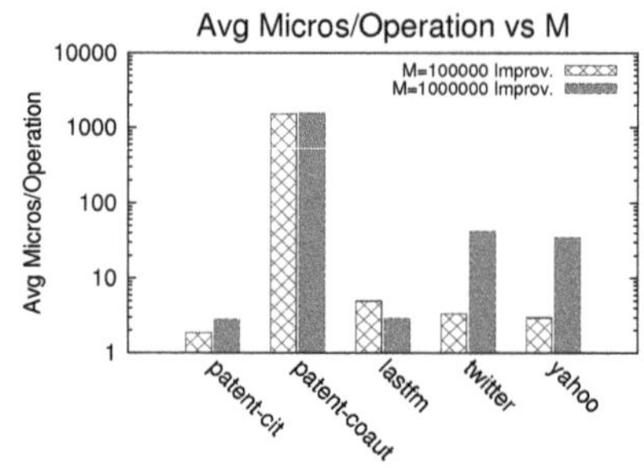

(b) M vs Update Time

Figure 4: Trade-offs between M and MAPE or avg. update time (μs) – edge insertion only. Higher M implies lower errors but higher update times.

which only requires few megabytes of RAM.[9] MASCOT is one order of magnitude faster than TRIÈST (which runs in ≈ 28 micros/op), because it does not have to handle edge removal from the sample, as it offers no guarantees on the used memory. As we will show, TRIÈST has much higher precision and scales well on billion-edges graphs.

Given the slow execution of the other algorithms on the larger datasets we compare in details TRIÈST only with MASCOT.[10] Table 2 shows the average MAPE of the two approaches. The results confirm the pattern observed in Figure 2(a): TRIÈST-BASE and TRIÈST-IMPR both have an average error significantly smaller than that of the basic MASCOT-C and improved MASCOT variant respectively. We achieve up to a 91% (i.e., 9-fold) reduction in the MAPE while using the same amount of memory. This experiment confirms the theory: reservoir sampling has overall lower or equal variance in all steps for the same expected total number of sampled edges. To further validate this observation we run TRIÈST-IMPR and of the improved MASCOT variant using the same (expected memory) $M = 10000$. Figure 3 shows the max-min estimation over 10 runs. TRIÈST-IMPR shows significantly lower variance over the evolution: the maxmin estimation lines are closer to the ground truth virtually all time. This confirms our theoretical observations in the previous sections. Even with very low M (about 2/10000 of the size of the graph) TRIÈST gives a good estimation.

Local triangle counting. We compare the precision in local triangle count estimation of TRIÈST with that of MASCOT [27] using the same approach of the previous experiment. We can not compare with JHA ET AL. and PAVAN ET AL. algorithms as they provide only global estimation. As in [27], we measure the Pearson coefficient and the average ε error (see [27] for definitions). In Table 3 we report the Pearson coefficient and average ε error over all timestamps for the smaller graphs.[11] TRIÈST (significantly) improves (i.e., has higher correlation and lower error) over the state-of-the-art MASCOT, using the same amount of memory.

Memory vs accuracy trade-offs. We study the tradeoff between the sample size M vs the running time and accuracy of the estimators. Figure 4(a) shows the tradeoffs between the accuracy of the estimation and the size M for the smaller graphs for which the ground truth number of triangles can be computed exactly using the naive algorithm. Even with small M TRIÈST-IMPR achieves very low MAPE value. As expected, larger M corresponds to higher accuracy and for the same M TRIÈST-IMPR outperforms TRIÈST-BASE. Figure 4(b) shows the average time per update in microseconds (μs) for TRIÈST-IMPR as function of M. Larger M requires longer update times (a larger sample implies larger graph on which to count triangles). On average a few hundreds of microseconds are sufficient for handling any update even in very large graphs with billions of edges. Our algorithms can handle hundreds of thousands of edge updates per second with very small error (Fig. 4(a)), and therefore can be used efficiently and effectively in high-velocity contexts.

Alternative edge orders. In all previous experiments the edges are added in their natural order (i.e., in order of their appearance).[12] While the natural order is the most important use case, we have assessed the impact of other ordering on the accuracy of the algorithms. We experiment with both the uniform-at-random (u.a.r.) order of the edges and the random BFS order: until all the graph is explored a BFS is started from a u.a.r. unvisited node and edges are added in order of their visit (neighbors are explored in u.a.r. order). The results for the random BFS order (Fig. 5) and for the

[9]The experiments in [18] use M in the order of 10^3, and in [32], large M values require large batches for efficiency.

[10]We attempted to run the other two algorithms but they did not complete after 12 hours for the larger datasets in Table 2 with the prescribed p parameter setting.

[11]For efficiency, in this test we evaluate the local number of triangles of all nodes every 1000 edge updates.

[12]Excluding twitter for which we used the random order, given the lack of timestamps.

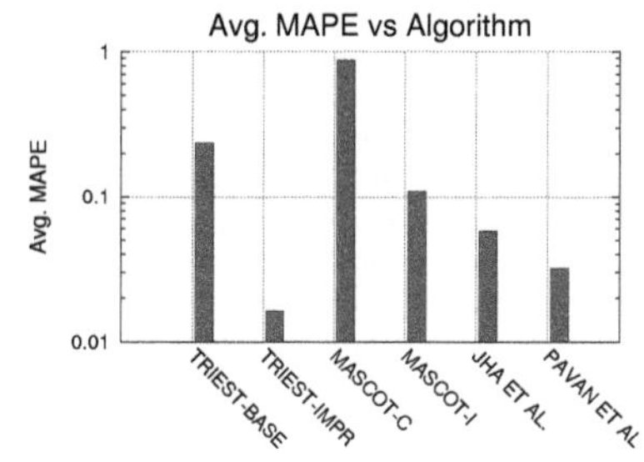

Figure 5: Average MAPE on Patent (Co-Aut.), with $p = 0.01$ – insertion only in Random BFS order. TRIÈST-IMPR has the lowest error.

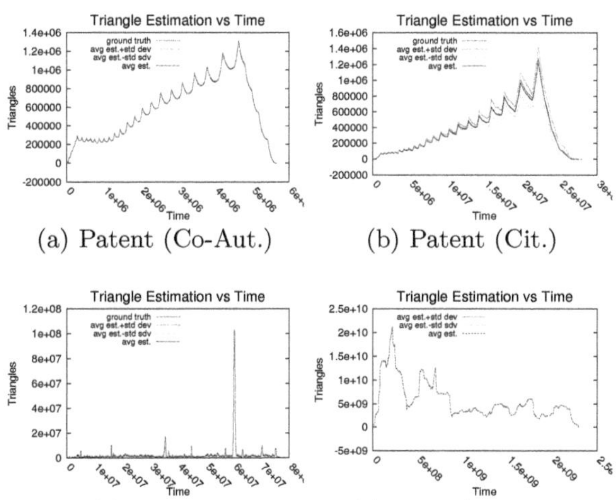

(a) Patent (Co-Aut.) (b) Patent (Cit.)

(c) LastFm (d) Yahoo! Answers

Figure 6: Evolution of the global number of triangles – fully dynamic case.

u.a.r. (omitted for lack of space) confirm that TRIÈST has the lowest error and is very scalable in every tested ordering.

5.2 Fully-dynamic case

We evaluate TRIÈST-FD on fully-dynamic streams. We cannot compare TRIÈST-FD with the algorithms previously used [18, 27, 32] as they only handle insertion-only streams.

In the first set of experiments we model deletions using the widely used *sliding window model*, where a sliding window of the most recent edges defines the current graph. The sliding window model is of practical interest as it allows to observe recent trends in the stream. For Patent (Co-Aut.) & (Cit.) we keep in the sliding window the edges generated in the last 5 years, while for LastFm we keep the edges generated in the last 30 days. For Yahoo! Answers we keep the last 100 millions edges in the window[13].

Figure 6 shows the evolution of the global number of triangles in the sliding window model using TRIÈST-FD using $M = 200{,}000$ ($M = 1{,}000{,}000$ for Yahoo! Answers). The sliding window scenario is significantly more challenging than the addition-only case (very often the entire sample of edges is flushed away) but TRIÈST-FD maintains good variance and scalability even when, as for LastFm and Yahoo! Answers, the global number of triangles varies quickly.

[13]The sliding window model is not interesting for the Twitter dataset as edges have random timestamps. We omit the results for Twitter but TRIÈST-FD is fast and has low variance.

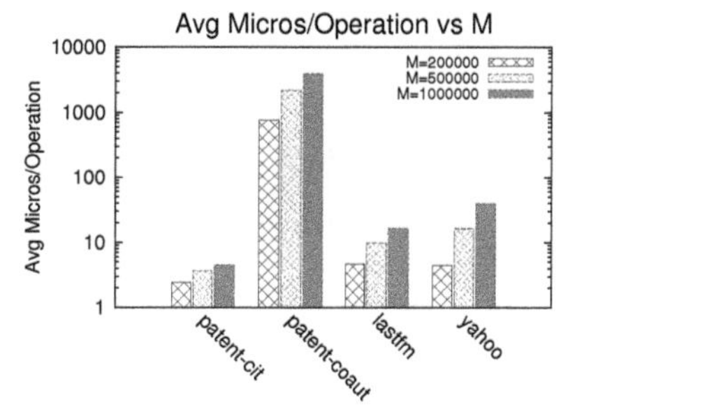

Figure 7: Trade-offs between the avg. update time (μs) and M for TRIÈST-FD.

Graph	M	Avg. Global MAPE	Avg. Local Pearson	Avg. Local ε Err.
LastFM	200000	0.005	0.98	0.02
	1000000	0.002	0.999	0.001
Pat. (Co-Aut.)	200000	0.01	0.66	0.30
	1000000	0.001	0.99	0.006
Pat. (Cit.)	200000	0.17	0.09	0.16
	1000000	0.04	0.60	0.13

Table 4: Estimation errors for TRIÈST-FD.

Continuous monitoring of triangle counts with TRIÈST-FD allows to detect patterns that would otherwise be difficult to notice. For LastFm (Fig. 6(c)) we observe a sudden spike of several order of magnitudes. The dataset is anonymized so we cannot establish which songs are responsible for this spike. In Yahoo! Answers (Fig. 6(d)) a popular topic can create a sudden (and shortly lived) increase in the number of triangles, while the evolution of the Patent co-authorship and co-citation networks is slower, as the creation of an edge requires filing a patent (Fig. 6(a) and (b)). The almost constant increase over time[14] of the number of triangles in Patent graphs is consistent with previous observations of *densification* in collaboration networks as in the case of nodes' degrees [26] and the observations on the density of the densest subgraph [13].

Table 4 shows the results for both the local and global triangle counting estimation provided by TRIÈST-FD. In this case we can not compare with previous works, as they only handle insertions. It is evident that precision improves with M values, and even relatively small M values result in a low MAPE (global estimation), high Pearson correlation and low ε error (local estimation). Figure 7 shows the tradeoffs between memory (i.e., accuracy) and time. In all cases our algorithm is very fast and it presents update times in the order of hundreds of microseconds for datasets with billions of updates (Yahoo! Answers).

Alternative models for deletion. We evaluate TRIÈST-FD using other models for deletions than the sliding window model. To assess the resilience of the algorithm to massive deletions we run the following experiment. We added edges in their natural order but each edge addition is followed with probability q by a mass deletion event where each edge cur-

[14]The decline at the end is due to the removal of the last edges from the sliding window after there are no more edge additions.

rently in the graph is deleted with probability d independently. We run experiments with $q = 3{,}000{,}000^{-1}$ (i.e., a mass deletion expected every 3 millions edges) and $d = 0.80$ (in expectation 80% of edges are deleted). We observe that TRIÈST-FD maintains a good accuracy and scalability even in face of a massive (and unlikely) deletions of the vast majority of the edges: e.g., for LastFM with $M = 200000$ (resp. $M = 1{,}000{,}000$) we observe 0.04 (resp. 0.006) Avg. MAPE. More results are available in our full version online [9].

6. CONCLUSIONS

We presented TRIÈST, the first suite of algorithms that use reservoir sampling and its variants to continuously maintain unbiased, low-variance estimates of the local and global number of triangles in fully-dynamic graphs streams of arbitrary edge/vertex insertions and deletions using a fixed, user-specified amount of space. Our experimental evaluation shows that TRIÈST outperforms state-of-the-art approaches and achieves high accuracy on real-world datasets with more than one billion of edges, with update times of hundreds of microseconds. Interesting directions for future work include the use of color-coding techniques [30], and the extension to 3-profiles and complex graph motifs [11].

Acknowledgments. This work was supported in part by NSF grant IIS-1247581 and NIH grant R01-CA180776.

7. REFERENCES

[1] N. K. Ahmed, N. Duffield, J. Neville, and R. Kompella. Graph Sample and Hold: A framework for big-graph analytics. KDD'14.

[2] Z. Bar-Yossef, R. Kumar, and D. Sivakumar. Reductions in streaming algorithms, with an application to counting triangles in graphs. SODA'02.

[3] L. Becchetti, P. Boldi, C. Castillo, and A. Gionis. Efficient algorithms for large-scale local triangle counting. *TKDD* 4 (3):13:1–13:28, 2010.

[4] J. W. Berry, B. Hendrickson, R. A. LaViolette, and C. A. Phillips. Tolerating the community detection resolution limit with edge weighting. *Phys. Rev. E*, 83(5):056119, 2011.

[5] P. Boldi, M. Rosa, M. Santini, and S. Vigna. Layered label propagation: A multiresolution coordinate-free ordering for compressing social networks. WWW'11.

[6] L. S. Buriol, G. Frahling, S. Leonardi, A. Marchetti-Spaccamela, and C. Sohler. Counting triangles in data streams. PODS'06.

[7] Ò. Celma Herrada. Music recommendation and discovery in the long tail. UPF Technical report, 2009.

[8] E. Cohen, G. Cormode, and N. Duffield. Don't let the negatives bring you down: sampling from streams of signed updates. SIGMETRICS'12.

[9] L. De Stefani, A. Epasto, M. Riondato, and E. Upfal. TRIÈST: Counting local and global triangles in fully-dynamic streams with fixed memory size. *CoRR*, abs/1602.07424, 2016. http://arxiv.org/pdf/1602.07424.pdf.

[10] J.-P. Eckmann and E. Moses. Curvature of co-links uncovers hidden thematic layers in the world wide web. *PNAS*, 99(9):5825–5829, 2002.

[11] E. R. Elenberg, K. Shanmugam, M. Borokhovich, and A. G. Dimakis. Beyond triangles: A distributed framework for estimating 3-profiles of large graphs. KDD'15.

[12] A. Epasto, S. Lattanzi, V. Mirrokni, I. O. Sebe, A. Taei, and S. Verma. Ego-net community mining applied to friend suggestion. *Proceedings of the VLDB Endowment*, 2015.

[13] A. Epasto, S. Lattanzi, and M. Sozio. Efficient densest subgraph computation in evolving graph. WWW'15.

[14] R. Gemulla, W. Lehner, and P. J. Haas. Maintaining bounded-size sample synopses of evolving datasets. *VLDBJ*, 17(2):173–201, 2008.

[15] A. Hajnal and E. Szemerédi. Proof of a conjecture of P. Erdős. *Combinat. theo. and its appl., II*, 601–623, 1970.

[16] B. H. Hall, A. B. Jaffe, and M. Trajtenberg. The NBER patent citation data file: Lessons, insights and methodological tools. NBER Technical report, 2001.

[17] R. J. Hyndman and A. B. Koehler. Another look at measures of forecast accuracy. *Int. J. Forecasting*, 22(4): 679–688, 2006.

[18] M. Jha, C. Seshadhri, and A. Pinar. A space-efficient streaming algorithm for estimating transitivity and triangle counts using the birthday paradox. *TKDD*, 9(3): 15:1–15:21, 2015.

[19] H. Jowhari and M. Ghodsi. New streaming algorithms for counting triangles in graphs. *Computing and Combinatorics*, LNCS 3595, 710–716, 2005.

[20] D. M. Kane, K. Mehlhorn, T. Sauerwald, and H. Sun. Counting arbitrary subgraphs in data streams. ICALP'12.

[21] M. N. Kolountzakis, G. L. Miller, R. Peng, and C. E. Tsourakakis. Efficient triangle counting in large graphs via degree-based vertex partitioning. *Internet Mathematics*, 8 (1–2):161–185, 2012.

[22] K. Kutzkov and R. Pagh. On the streaming complexity of computing local clustering coefficients. WSDM'13.

[23] K. Kutzkov and R. Pagh. Triangle counting in dynamic graph streams. SWAT'14.

[24] H. Kwak, C. Lee, H. Park, and S. Moon. What is Twitter, a social network or a news media? WWW'10.

[25] M. Latapy. Main-memory triangle computations for very large (sparse (power-law)) graphs. *TCS*, 407(1):458–473, 2008.

[26] J. Leskovec, J. Kleinberg, and C. Faloutsos. Graph evolution: Densification and shrinking diameters. *TKDD*, 1 (1):2, 2007.

[27] Y. Lim and U. Kang. MASCOT: Memory-efficient and accurate sampling for counting local triangles in graph streams. KDD'15.

[28] M. Manjunath, K. Mehlhorn, K. Panagiotou, and H. Sun. Approximate counting of cycles in streams. ESA'11.

[29] R. Milo, S. Shen-Orr, S. Itzkovitz, N. Kashtan, D. Chklovskii, and U. Alon. Network motifs: simple building blocks of complex networks. *Science*, 298(5594): 824–827, 2002.

[30] R. Pagh and C. E. Tsourakakis. Colorful triangle counting and a MapReduce implementation. *IPL*, 112(7):277–281, 2012.

[31] H.-M. Park and C.-W. Chung. An efficient MapReduce algorithm for counting triangles in a very large graph. CIKM'13.

[32] A. Pavan, K. Tangwongsan, S. Tirthapura, and K.-L. Wu. Counting and sampling triangles from a graph stream. VLDB'13.

[33] S. Suri and S. Vassilvitskii. Counting triangles and the curse of the last reducer. WWW'11.

[34] The Koblenz Network Collection (KONECT). Last.fm song network dataset. http://konect.uni-koblenz.de/networks/lastfm_song.

[35] C. E. Tsourakakis, U. Kang, G. L. Miller, and C. Faloutsos. Doulion: counting triangles in massive graphs with a coin. KDD'09.

[36] C. E. Tsourakakis, M. N. Kolountzakis, and G. L. Miller. Triangle sparsifiers. *JGAA*, 15(6):703–726, 2011.

[37] J. S. Vitter. Random sampling with a reservoir. *TOMS*, 11 (1):37–57, 1985.

[38] Yahoo! Research Webscope Datasets. Yahoo! Answers browsing behavior version 1.0. http://webscope.sandbox.yahoo.com.

A Subsequence Interleaving Model for Sequential Pattern Mining

Jaroslav Fowkes Charles Sutton

School of Informatics
University of Edinburgh, Edinburgh, EH8 9AB, UK
{jfowkes, csutton}@ed.ac.uk

ABSTRACT

Recent sequential pattern mining methods have used the minimum description length (MDL) principle to define an encoding scheme which describes an algorithm for mining the most compressing patterns in a database. We present a novel subsequence interleaving model based on a probabilistic model of the sequence database, which allows us to search for the most compressing set of patterns without designing a specific encoding scheme. Our proposed algorithm is able to efficiently mine the most relevant sequential patterns and rank them using an associated measure of interestingness. The efficient inference in our model is a direct result of our use of a structural expectation-maximization framework, in which the expectation-step takes the form of a submodular optimization problem subject to a coverage constraint. We show on both synthetic and real world datasets that our model mines a set of sequential patterns with low spuriousness and redundancy, high interpretability and usefulness in real-world applications. Furthermore, we demonstrate that the quality of the patterns from our approach is comparable to, if not better than, existing state of the art sequential pattern mining algorithms.

1. INTRODUCTION

Sequential data pose a challenge to exploratory data analysis, as large data sets of sequences are difficult to visualise. In applications such as healthcare (patterns in patient paths [10]), click streams (web usage mining [18]), bioinformatics (predicting protein sequence function [27]) and source code (API call patterns [30]), a common approach has been *sequential pattern mining*, to identify a set of patterns that commonly occur as subsequences of the sequences in the data.

A natural family of approaches for sequential pattern mining is to mine frequent subsequences [2] or closed frequent subsequences [26], but these suffer from the well-known problem of pattern explosion, that is, the list of frequent subsequences is typically long, highly redundant, and difficult to understand. Recently, researchers have introduced methods to prevent the problem of pattern explosion based on the *minimum description length* (MDL) principle [12, 25]. These methods define an encoding scheme which describes an algorithm for compressing a sequence database based on a library of subsequence patterns, and then search for a set of patterns that lead to the best compression of the database. These MDL methods provide a theoretically principled approach that results in better patterns than frequent subsequence mining, but their performance relies on designing a coding scheme.

In this paper, we introduce an alternate probabilistic perspective on subsequence mining, in which we develop a generative model of the database conditioned on the patterns. Then, following Shannon's theorem, the length of the optimal code for the database under the model is simply the negative logarithm of its probability. This allows us to search for the set of patterns that best compress the database without designing a specific coding scheme. Our approach, which we call the *Interesting Sequence Miner* (ISM)[1], is a novel sequential pattern mining algorithm that is able to efficiently mine the most relevant sequential patterns from a database and rank them using an associated measure of interestingness. ISM makes use of a novel probabilistic model of sequences, based on generating a sequence by interleaving a group of subsequences. It is these learned component subsequences that are the patterns ISM returns.

An approach based on probabilistic machine learning brings a variety of benefits, namely, that the probabilistic model allows us to declaratively incorporate ideas about what types of patterns would be most useful; that we can easily compose the ISM model with other types of probabilistic models from the literature; and that we are able to bring to bear powerful tools for inference and optimization from probabilistic machine learning. Inference in our model involves approximate optimization of a non-monotone submodular objective subject to a submodular coverage constraint. The necessary partition function is intractable to construct directly, however we show that it can be efficiently computed using a suitable lower bound. The set of sequential patterns under our model can be inferred efficiently using a *structural expectation maximization* (EM) framework [8]. This is, to our knowledge, the first use of an expectation-maximization scheme for the subsequence mining problem.

On real-world datasets (Section 4), we find that ISM returns a notably more diverse set of patterns than the recent MDL methods SQS and GoKrimp (Table 2), while retain-

[1]https://github.com/mast-group/sequence-mining

KDD '16, August 13 - 17, 2016, San Francisco, CA, USA

ISBN 978-1-4503-4232-2/16/08... $15.00

DOI: http://dx.doi.org/10.1145/2939672.2939787

ing similar quality. A more diverse set of patterns is, we suggest, especially suitable for manual examination during exploratory data analysis. Qualitatively, the mined patterns from ISM are all highly correlated and extremely relevant, e.g. representing phrases such as *oh dear* or concepts such as *reproducing kernel hilbert space*. More broadly, this new perspective has the potential to open up a wide variety of future directions for new modelling approaches, such as combining sequential pattern mining methods with hierarchical models, topic models, and nonparametric Bayesian methods.

2. RELATED WORK

Sequential pattern mining was first introduced by Agrawal and Srikant [2] in the context of market basket analysis, which led to a number of other algorithms for frequent subsequence, including GSP [23], PrefixSpan [22], SPADE [29], and SPAM [3]. Frequent sequence mining suffers from *pattern explosion*: a huge number of highly redundant frequent sequences are retrieved if the given minimum support threshold is too low. One way to address this is by mining frequent closed sequences, i.e., those that have no subsequences with the same frequency, such as via the BIDE algorithm [26]. However, even mining frequent closed sequences does not fully resolve the problem of pattern explosion. We refer the interested reader to Chapter 11 of [1] for a survey of frequent sequence mining algorithms.

In an attempt to tackle this problem, modern approaches to sequence mining have used the *minimum description length* (MDL) principle to find the set of sequences that best summarize the data. The GoKrimp algorithm [12] directly mines sequences that best compress a database using a MDL-based approach. The goal of GoKrimp is essentially to cover the database with as few sequences as possible, because the dictionary-based description length that is used by GoKrimp favours encoding schemes that cover more long and frequent subsequences in the database. In fact, finding the most compressing sequence in the database is strongly related to the maximum tiling problem, i.e., finding the tile with largest area in a binary transaction database.

SQS-Search (SQS) [25] also uses MDL to find the set of sequences that summarize the data best: a small set of informative sequences that achieve the best compression is mined directly from the database. SQS uses an encoding scheme that explicitly punishes gaps by assigning zero cost for encoding non-gaps and higher cost for encoding larger gaps between items in a pattern. While SQS can be very effective at mining informative patterns from text, it cannot handle interleaving patterns, unlike GoKrimp and ISM, which can be a significant drawback on certain datasets e.g. patterns generated by independent processes that may frequently overlap.

In related work, Mannila and Meek [15] proposed a generative model of sequences which finds partial orders that describe the ordering relationships between items in a sequence database. Sequences are generated by selecting a subset of items from a partial order with a learned inclusion probability and arranging them into a compatible random ordering. Unlike ISM, their model does not allow gaps in the generated sequences and each sequence is only generated from a single partial order, an unrealistic assumption in practice.

There has also been some existing research on probabilistic models for sequences, especially using Markov models. Gwadera et al. [9] use a variable order Markov model to identify statistically significant sequences. Stolcke and Omohundro [24] developed a structure learning algorithm for HMMs that learns both the number of states and the topology. Landwehr [13] extended HMMs to handle a fixed number of hidden processes whose outputs interleave to form a sequence. Wood et al. developed the sequence memoizer [28], a variable order Markov model with a Pitman-Yor process prior. Also, Nevill-Manning and Witten [20] infer a context-free grammar over sequences using the Sequitur algorithm.

3. MINING SEQUENTIAL PATTERNS

In this section we will formulate the problem of identifying a set of interesting sequences that are useful for explaining a sequence database. First we will define some preliminary concepts and notation. An *item* i is an element of a universe $U = \{1, 2, \ldots, n\}$ that indexes symbols. A *sequence* S is simply an ordered list of items $(e_1, \ldots, e_m)$ such that $e_i \in U\ \forall i$. A sequence $S_a = (a_1, \ldots, a_n)$ is a subsequence of another sequence $S_b = (b_1, \ldots, b_m)$, denoted $S_a \subset S_b$, if there exist integers $1 \leq i_1 < i_2 < \ldots < i_n \leq m$ such that $a_1 = b_{i_1}, a_2 = b_{i_2}, \ldots, a_n = b_{i_n}$ (i.e., the standard definition of a subsequence). A sequence *database* is merely a list of sequences $X^{(j)}$. Further, we say that a sequence S is *supported* by a sequence X in the sequence database if $S \subset X$. Note that in the above definition each sequence only contains a single item as this is the most important and popular sequence type (cf. word sequences, protein sequences, click streams, etc.).[2] A *multiset* $\mathcal{M}$ is a generalization of a set that allows elements to occur multiple times, i.e., with a specific *multiplicity* $\#_{\mathcal{M}}(\cdot)$. For example in the multiset $\mathcal{M} = \{a, a, b\}$, the element a occurs twice and so has multiplicity $\#_{\mathcal{M}}(a) = 2$.

3.1 Problem Formulation

Our aim in this work is to infer a set of interesting subsequences $\mathcal{I}$ from a database of sequences $X^{(1)}, \ldots, X^{(N)}$. Here by *interesting*, we mean a set of patterns that are useful for helping a human analyst to understand the important properties of the database, that is, interesting subsequences should reflect the most important patterns in the data, while being sufficiently concise and non-redundant that they are suitable for manual examination. These criteria are inherently qualitative, reflecting the fact that the goal of data mining is to build human insight and understanding. To quantify these criteria, we operationalize the notion of interesting sequence as those sequences that best explain the underlying database under a *probabilistic model* of sequences. Specifically we will use a *generative* model, i.e., a model that starts with a set of interesting subsequences $\mathcal{I}$ and from this set generates the sequence database $X^{(1)}, \ldots, X^{(N)}$. Our goal is then to infer the most likely generating set $\mathcal{I}$ under our chosen generative model. We want a model that is as simple as possible yet powerful enough to capture correlations between items in sequences. A simple such model is as follows: iteratively sample subsequences S from $\mathcal{I}$ and randomly interleave them to form the database sequence X. If we associate each subsequence $S \in \mathcal{I}$ with a probability π_S, we can sample the indicator variable $z_S \sim \text{Bernoulli}(\pi_S)$

[2]Note that we can easily extend our algorithm to mine sequences of sets of items (as defined in the original sequence mining paper [2]) by extending the subsequence operator $\subset$ to handle these more general 'sequences'.

and include it in X if $z_S = 1$. However, we may wish to include a subsequence more than once in the sequence X, that is, we need some way of sampling the multiplicity of S in X. The simplest way to do this is to change our generating distribution from Bernoulli to e.g. Categorical and sample the multiplicity $z_S \sim \text{Categorical}(\boldsymbol{\pi}_S)$ where $\boldsymbol{\pi}_S$ is now a vector of probabilities, with one entry for each multiplicity (up to the maximum in the database). We define the generative model formally in the next section.

3.2 Generative Model

As discussed in the previous section, we propose a simple directed graphical model for generating a database of sequences $X^{(1)}, \ldots, X^{(N)}$ from a set $\mathcal{I}$ of interesting sequences. The generative story for our model is, independently for each sequence X in the database:

1. For each interesting sequence $S \in \mathcal{I}$, decide independently the number of times S should be included in X, i.e., sample the multiplicity $z_S \in \mathbb{N}_0$ as

$$z_S \sim \text{Categorical}(\boldsymbol{\pi}_S),$$

   where $\boldsymbol{\pi}_S$ is a vector of multiplicity probabilities. For clarity we present the Categorical distribution here but one could use a more general distribution if desired.
2. Set $\mathcal{S}$ to be the multiset with multiplicities z_S of all the sequences S selected for inclusion in X:

$$\mathcal{S} := \{S \,|\, z_S \geq 1\}.$$

3. Set $\mathcal{P}$ to be the set of all possible sequences that can be generated by interleaving together all occurrences of the sequences in the multiset $\mathcal{S}$, i.e.,

$$\mathcal{P} := \{X \,|\, \mathcal{S} \text{ partition of } X, S \subset X \; \forall S \in \mathcal{S}\}.$$

   Here by *interleaving* we mean the placing of items from one sequence into the gaps between items in another whilst maintaining the orders of the items imposed by each sequence.
4. Sample X uniformly from $\mathcal{P}$, i.e.,

$$X \sim \mathcal{P}.$$

Note that we never need to construct the set $\mathcal{P}$ in practice, since we only require its cardinality during inference, and we show in the next section how we can efficiently compute an approximation to $|\mathcal{P}|$. We can, however, sample from $\mathcal{P}$ efficiently by merging subsequences $S \in \mathcal{S}$ into X one at a time as follows: splice the elements of S, in order, into X at randomly chosen points (here by splicing S into X we mean the placing of items from S into the gaps between items in X). For example, $\mathcal{S} = \{(1,2),(3,4)\}$ will generate the set of sequences $\mathcal{P} = \{(3,4,1,2),(3,1,4,2),(3,1,2,4),(1,3,4,2),(1,3,2,4),(1,2,3,4)\}$. We could of course learn a transition distribution between subsequences in our model, but we choose not to do so because we want to force the model to use $\mathcal{I}$ to explain the sequential dependencies in the data.

3.3 Inference

Given a set of interesting sequences $\mathcal{I}$, let $\mathbf{z}$ denote the vector of z_S for all sequences $S \in \mathcal{I}$ and similarly, let $\boldsymbol{\Pi}$ denote the list of $\boldsymbol{\pi}_S$ for all $S \in \mathcal{I}$. Assuming $\mathbf{z}, \boldsymbol{\Pi}$ are fully determined, it is evident from the generative model that the probability of generating a database sequence X is

$$p(X, \mathbf{z}|\boldsymbol{\Pi}) = \begin{cases} \frac{1}{|\mathcal{P}|} \prod_{S \in \mathcal{I}} \prod_{m=0}^{|\boldsymbol{\pi}_S|-1} \pi_{S_m}^{[z_S = m]} & \text{if } X \in \mathcal{P}, \\ 0 & \text{otherwise,} \end{cases}$$

where $|\boldsymbol{\pi}_S|$ is the length of $\boldsymbol{\pi}_S$ and $[z_S = m]$ evaluates to 1 if $z_S = m$, 0 otherwise. Intuitively, it helps to think of each $\boldsymbol{\pi}_S$ as being an infinite vector and each $S \in \mathcal{I}$ as being augmented with a Kleene star operator, so that, for example, one can use $(1,2)^*$ and $(3)^*$ to generate the sequence $(1,2,1,3,2)$.

Calculating the normalization constant $|\mathcal{P}|$ is problematic as we have to count the number of possible distinct sequences that could be generated by interleaving together subsequences in $\mathcal{S}$. This is further complicated by the fact that $\mathcal{S}$ is a multiset and so can contain multiple occurrences of the same subsequence, which makes efficient computation of $|\mathcal{P}|$ impractical. However, it turns out that we can compute a straightforward upper bound since $|\mathcal{P}|$ is clearly bounded above by all possible permutations of all the items in all the subsequences $S \in \mathcal{S}$, and this bound is attained when $\mathcal{S}$ contains only distinct singleton sequences without repetition. Formally,

$$|\mathcal{P}| \leq \left(\textstyle\sum_{S \in \mathcal{S}} |S|\right)!$$

Conveniently, this gives us a non-trivial lower-bound on the posterior $p(X, \mathbf{z}|\boldsymbol{\Pi})$ which, as we will want to maximize the posterior, is precisely what we want. Moreover, the lower bound acts as an additional penalty, strongly favouring a non-redundant set of sequences (see Section 4.2).

Now assuming the parameters $\boldsymbol{\Pi}$ are known, we can infer $\mathbf{z}$ for a database sequence X by maximizing the log of the lower bound on the posterior $p(X, \mathbf{z}|\boldsymbol{\Pi})$ over $\mathbf{z}$:

$$\max_{\mathbf{z}} \sum_{S \in \mathcal{I}} \sum_{m=0}^{|\boldsymbol{\pi}_S|-1} [z_S = m] \ln(\pi_{S_m}) - \sum_{j=1}^{\sum_{S \in \mathcal{S}} |S|} \ln j \quad \text{s.t. } X \in \mathcal{P}. \tag{3.1}$$

This is an NP-hard problem in general and so impractical to solve directly in practice. However, we will show that it can be viewed as a special case of maximizing a submodular function subject to a submodular constraint and so approximately solved using the greedy algorithm for submodular function optimization. Now strictly speaking the notion of a submodular function is only applicable to sets, however we will consider the following generalization to multisets:

Definition 1. (Submodular Multiset Function) Let Ω be a finite multiset and let $\mathbb{N}_0{}^{\Omega}$ denote the set of all possible multisets that are subsets of Ω, then a function $f \colon \mathbb{N}_0{}^{\Omega} \to \mathbb{R}$ is *submodular* if for for every $\mathcal{C} \subset \mathcal{D} \subset \Omega$ and $S \in \Omega$ with $\#_{\mathcal{C}}(S) = \#_{\mathcal{D}}(S)$ it holds that

$$f(\mathcal{C} \cup \{S\}) - f(\mathcal{C}) \geq f(\mathcal{D} \cup \{S\}) - f(\mathcal{D}).$$

Let us now define a function f for our specific case: let $\mathcal{T}$ be the multiset of supported interesting sequences, i.e., sequences $S \in \mathcal{I}$ s.t. $S \subset X$ with multiplicity given by the maximum number of occurrences of S in any partition of X. Now, define $f \colon \mathbb{N}_0{}^{\mathcal{T}} \to \mathbb{R}$ as

$$f(\mathcal{C}) := \sum_{S \in \mathcal{C}} \sum_{m=0}^{|\boldsymbol{\pi}_S|-1} [\#_{\mathcal{C}}(S) = m] \ln(\pi_{S_m}) - \sum_{j=1}^{\sum_{S \in \mathcal{C}} |S|} \ln j$$

and $g(\mathcal{C}) := |\cup_{S \in \mathcal{C}} S|$. We can now re-state (3.1) as: Find a non-overlapping multiset covering $\mathcal{C} \subset \mathcal{T}$ that maximizes $f(\mathcal{C})$, i.e., such that $g(\mathcal{C}) = g(\mathcal{T})$ and $f(\mathcal{C})$ is maximized. Note that $g(\mathcal{T}) = |X|$ by construction. Now clearly g is monotone submodular as it is a multiset coverage function, and we will show that f is non-monotone submodular. To see that f is submodular observe that for $\mathcal{C} \subset \mathcal{D}, \#_{\mathcal{C}}(S) = \#_{\mathcal{D}}(S)$

$$\begin{aligned} f(\mathcal{D} \cup \{S\}) - f(\mathcal{D}) &= \ln(\pi_{S_{\#_{\mathcal{D}}(S)+1}}) - \ln(\pi_{S_{\#_{\mathcal{D}}(S)}}) \\ &\quad - \sum_{j=\sum_{D \in \mathcal{D}} |D|+1}^{\sum_{D \in \mathcal{D}} |D|+|S|} \ln j \\ &\leq \ln(\pi_{S_{\#_{\mathcal{C}}(S)+1}}) - \ln(\pi_{S_{\#_{\mathcal{C}}(S)}}) \\ &\quad - \sum_{j=\sum_{C \in \mathcal{C}} |C|+1}^{\sum_{C \in \mathcal{C}} |C|+|S|} \ln j \\ &= f(\mathcal{C} \cup \{S\}) - f(\mathcal{C}) \end{aligned}$$

which is precisely Definition 1. To see that f is non-monotone observe that

$$f(\mathcal{C} \cup \{S\}) - f(\mathcal{C}) = \ln\left(\frac{\pi_{S_{\#_{\mathcal{C}}(S)+1}}}{\pi_{S_{\#_{\mathcal{C}}(S)}}}\right) - \sum_{j=\sum_{C \in \mathcal{C}} |C|+1}^{\sum_{C \in \mathcal{C}} |C|+|S|} \ln j$$

whose sign is indeterminate.

Maximizing the posterior (3.1) is therefore a problem of maximizing a submodular function subject to a submodular coverage constraint and can be approximately solved by applying the greedy approximation algorithm (Algorithm 1). The greedy algorithm builds a multiset covering $\mathcal{C}$ by repeatedly choosing a sequence S that maximizes the profit $f(\mathcal{C} \cup \{S\}) - f(\mathcal{C})$ of adding S to the covering divided by the number of items in S not yet covered by the covering $g(\mathcal{C} \cup \{S\}) - g(\mathcal{C}) = |S|$. In order to minimize CPU time spent solving the problem, we cache the sequences and coverings for each database sequence as needed.

Algorithm 1 GREEDY ALGORITHM

Input: Database sequence X, supported sequences $\mathcal{T}$
  Initialize multiset $\mathcal{C} \leftarrow \emptyset$
  while $g(\mathcal{C}) \neq |X|$ **do**
    Choose $S \in \mathcal{T}$ maximizing $\frac{f(\mathcal{C} \cup \{S\}) - f(\mathcal{C})}{|S|}$
    $\mathcal{C} \leftarrow \mathcal{C} \cup \{S\}$
  end while
  return $\mathcal{C}$

Note that while there are good theoretical guarantees on the approximation ratio achieved by the greedy algorithm when maximizing a *monotone* submodular set function subject to a coverage constraint (e.g. $\ln|X| + 1$ for weighted set cover [5, 7]) the problem of maximizing a *non-monotone* submodular set function subject to a coverage constraint has, to the best of our knowledge, not been studied in the literature. However, as our submodular optimization problem is an extension of the weighted set cover problem, the greedy algorithm is a natural fit and indeed we observe good performance in practice.

Algorithm 2 HARD-EM

Input: Set of sequences $\mathcal{I}$ and initial estimates $\mathbf{\Pi}^{(0)}$
  $k \leftarrow 0$
  do
    $k \leftarrow k + 1$
    E-STEP: $\forall X^{(i)}$ solve (3.1) to get $z_S^{(i)}$ $\forall S \in \mathcal{T}_i$
    M-STEP: $\pi_{S_m}^{(k)} \leftarrow \frac{1}{N} \sum_{i=1}^{N} [z_S^{(i)} = m]$ $\forall S \in \mathcal{I}, \forall m$
  while $\|\mathbf{\Pi}^{(k-1)} - \mathbf{\Pi}^{(k)}\|_F > \varepsilon$
  Remove from $\mathcal{I}$ sequences S with $\pi_{S_0} = 1$
  return $\mathcal{I}, \mathbf{\Pi}^{(k)}$

3.4 Learning

Given a set of interesting sequences $\mathcal{I}$, consider now the case where both variables $\mathbf{z}, \mathbf{\Pi}$ in the model are unknown. In this case we can use the hard EM algorithm [6] for parameter estimation with latent variables. The hard-EM algorithm in our case is merely a simple layer on top of the inference algorithm (3.1). Suppose there are N database sequences $X^{(1)}, \ldots, X^{(N)}$ with multisets of supported interesting sequences $\mathcal{T}^{(1)}, \ldots, \mathcal{T}^{(N)}$, then the hard EM algorithm is given in Algorithm 2 (note that $\|\cdot\|_F$ denotes the Frobenius norm and π_{S_0} is the probability that S does not explain any sequence in the database). To initialize $\mathbf{\Pi}$, a natural choice is simply the support (relative frequency) of each sequence.

3.5 Inferring new sequences

We infer new sequences using structural EM [8], i.e., we add a candidate sequence S' to $\mathcal{I}$ if doing so improves the optimal value $\overline{p}$ of the problem (3.1) averaged across all database sequences. Interestingly, there are two implicit regularization effects here. Firstly, observe from (3.1) that when a new candidate S' is added to the model, a corresponding term $\ln \pi_{S'_0}$ is added to the log-likelihood of all database sequences that S' does not support. For large sequence databases, this amounts to a significant penalty on candidates in practice. Secondly, observe that the last term of (3.1) acts as an additional penalty, strongly favouring a non-redundant set of sequences.

To get an estimate of maximum benefit to including candidate S', we must carefully choose an initial value of $\boldsymbol{\pi}_{S'}$ that is not too low, to avoid getting stuck in a local optimum. To infer a good $\boldsymbol{\pi}_{S'}$, we force the candidate S' to explain all database sequences it supports by initializing $\boldsymbol{\pi}_{S'} = (0, 1, \ldots, 1)^T$ and update $\boldsymbol{\pi}_{S'}$ with the probability corresponding to its actual usage once we have inferred all the coverings. Given a set of interesting sequences $\mathcal{I}$ and corresponding probabilities $\mathbf{\Pi}$ along with database sequences $X^{(1)}, \ldots, X^{(N)}$, each iteration of the structural EM algorithm is given in Algorithm 3 below.

Occasionally the HARD-EM algorithm may assign zero probability to one or more singleton sequences and cause the greedy algorithm to not be able to fully cover a database sequence X using just the interesting sequences in $\mathcal{I}$. In this case we simply re-seed $\mathcal{I}$ with the necessary singletons. Finally, in practice we store the set of candidates that have been rejected by STRUCTURAL-EM and check each potential candidate against this set for efficiency.

3.6 Candidate generation

The STRUCTURAL-EM algorithm (Algorithm 3) requires a

Algorithm 3 STRUCTURAL-EM (one iteration)

Input: Sequences $\mathcal{I}$, $\mathbf{\Pi}$, optima $p^{(i)}$ of (3.1) $\forall X^{(i)}$
  Set profit $\overline{p} \leftarrow \frac{1}{N}\sum_{i=1}^{N} p^{(i)}$
  do
    Generate candidate S' using CANDIDATE-GEN
    $\mathcal{I} \leftarrow \mathcal{I} \cup \{S'\}$, $\boldsymbol{\pi}_{S'} \leftarrow (0, 1, \ldots, 1)^T$
    E-STEP: $\forall X^{(i)}$ solve (3.1) to get $z_S^{(i)}$ $\forall S \in \mathcal{T}_i$
    M-STEP: $\pi'_{S_m} \leftarrow \frac{1}{N}\sum_{i=1}^{N}[z_S^{(i)} = m]$ $\quad\forall S \in \mathcal{I}, \forall m$
    $\forall X^{(i)}$, solve (3.1) using $\boldsymbol{\pi}'_S, z_S^{(i)}$ $\forall S \in \mathcal{T}_i$
      to get the optimum $p^{(i)}$
    Set new profit $\overline{p}' \leftarrow \frac{1}{N}\sum_{i=1}^{N} p^{(i)}$
    $\mathcal{I} \leftarrow \mathcal{I} \setminus \{S'\}$
  while $\overline{p}' \leq \overline{p}$ {until one good candidate found}
  $\mathcal{I} \leftarrow \mathcal{I} \cup \{S'\}$
  return $\mathcal{I}, \mathbf{\Pi}'$

method to generate new candidate sequences S' that are to be considered for inclusion in the set of interesting sequences $\mathcal{I}$. One possibility would be to use the GSP algorithm [23] to recursively suggest larger sequences starting from singletons, however preliminary experiments found this was not the most efficient method. For this reason we take a slightly different approach and recursively combine the interesting sequences in $\mathcal{I}$ with the *highest support first* (Algorithm 4). In this way our candidate generation algorithm is more likely to propose viable candidate sequences earlier and in practice we find that this heuristic works well.

Algorithm 4 CANDIDATE-GEN

Input: Sequences $\mathcal{I}$, cached supports $\boldsymbol{\sigma}$, queue length q
  if $\nexists$ priority queue $\mathcal{Q}$ for $\mathcal{I}$ **then**
    Initialize $\boldsymbol{\sigma}$-ordered priority queue $\mathcal{Q}$
    Sort $\mathcal{I}$ by decreasing sequence support using $\boldsymbol{\sigma}$
    for all ordered pairs $S_1, S_2 \in \mathcal{I}$, highest ranked first
    do
      Generate candidate $S' = S_1 S_2$
      Cache support of S' in $\boldsymbol{\sigma}$ and add S' to $\mathcal{Q}$
      if $|\mathcal{Q}| = q$ **break**
    end for
  end if
  Pull highest-ranked candidate S' from $\mathcal{Q}$
  return S'

3.7 Mining Interesting Sequences

Our complete interesting sequence mining (ISM) algorithm is given in Algorithm 5. Note that the HARD-EM parameter optimization step need not be performed at every iteration, in fact it is more efficient to suggest several candidate sequences before optimizing the parameters. As all operations on database sequences in our algorithm are trivially parallelizable, we perform the E and M-steps in both the hard and structural EM algorithms in parallel.

Algorithm 5 ISM (Interesting Sequence Miner)

Input: Database of sequences $X^{(1)}, \ldots, X^{(N)}$
  Initialize $\mathcal{I}$ with singletons, $\mathbf{\Pi}$ with their supports
  while not converged **do**
    Add sequences to $\mathcal{I}, \mathbf{\Pi}$ using STRUCTURAL-EM
    Optimize parameters for $\mathcal{I}, \mathbf{\Pi}$ using HARD-EM
  end while
  return $\mathcal{I}, \mathbf{\Pi}$

3.8 Interestingness Measure

Now that we have inferred the model variables $\mathbf{z}, \mathbf{\Pi}$, we are able to use them to rank the retrieved sequences in $\mathcal{I}$. There are two natural rankings one can employ, and both have their strengths and weaknesses. The obvious approach is to rank each sequence $S \in \mathcal{I}$ according to its probability under the model $\boldsymbol{\pi}_S$, however this has the disadvantage of strongly favouring frequent sequences over rare ones, an issue we would like to avoid. An alternative is to rank the retrieved sequences according to their *interestingness* under the model, that is the ratio of database sequences they explain to database sequences they support. One can think of interestingness as a measure of how necessary the sequence is to the model: the higher the interestingness, the more supported database sequences the sequence explains. Thus interestingness provides a more balanced measure than probability, at the expense of missing some frequent sequences that only explain some of the database sequences they support. We define interestingness formally as follows.

Definition 2. The *interestingness* of a sequence $S \in \mathcal{I}$ retrieved by ISM (Algorithm 5) is defined as

$$int(S) = \frac{\sum_{i=1}^{N}[z_S^{(i)} \geq 1]}{supp(S)}$$

and ranges from 0 (least interesting) to 1 (most interesting).

Any ties in the ranking can be broken using the sequence probability $p(S \subset X) = p(z_S \geq 1) = 1 - \pi_{S_0}$.

3.9 Correspondence to Existing Models

There is a close and well-known connection between probabilistic modelling and the minimum description length principle used by SQS and GoKrimp (see MacKay [14], §28.3 for a particularly nice explanation). Given a probabilistic model $p(X|\mathbf{\Pi}, \mathcal{I})$ of a single database sequence X, by Shannon's theorem the optimal code for the model will encode X using approximately $-\log_2 p(X|\mathbf{\Pi}, \mathcal{I})$ bits. So by finding a set of patterns that maximizes the probability of the data, we are also finding patterns that minimize description length. Conversely, any encoding scheme implicitly defines a probabilistic model. Given an encoding scheme E that assigns each transaction X to a string of $L(X)$ bits, we can define $p(X|E) \propto 2^{-L(X)}$, and then E is an optimal code for $p(X|E)$. Interpreting the previous subsequence mining methods in terms of their implicit probabilistic models provides interesting insights into these methods.

The encoding of a database sequence used by SQS can be interpreted as a probabilistic model $p(X, \mathbf{z}|\mathbf{\Pi}, \mathcal{I})$, where the SQS analog of $p(X, \mathbf{z}|\mathbf{\Pi}, \mathcal{I})$ is similar to (3.1) with

$$\pi_{S_m} = \left(\frac{\sum_{i=1}^{N} z_S^{(i)}}{\sum_{I \in \mathcal{I}} \sum_{j=1}^{N} z_I^{(j)}}\right)^m,$$

along with additional terms that correspond to the description lengths for indicating the presence and absence of gaps in the usage of a sequence S. Additionally, SQS contains an explicit penalty for the encoding of the set of patterns $\mathcal{I}$, that encourages a smaller number of patterns. In a probabilistic model, this can be interpreted as a prior distribution $p(\mathcal{I})$ over patterns. There is also a prior distribution on the content of the patterns, similar to a unigram model, which encourages the patterns to contain more common elements.

Similarly, GoKrimp uses a variant of the above model, where instead we have

$$\pi_{S_m} = \left(\frac{\sum_{i=1}^{N} z_S^{(i)} + |\{T \in \mathcal{I} \,|\, S \subset T\}|}{\sum_{I \in \mathcal{I}} \sum_{j=1}^{N} z_I^{(j)} + |\{T \in \mathcal{I} \,|\, I \subset T\}|} \right)^m .$$

In addition, the description length used by GoKrimp also has a gap cost that penalizes sequences with large gaps. GoKrimp employs a greedy heuristic to find the most compressing sequence: an empty sequence S is iteratively extended by the most frequent item that is statistically dependent on S. ISM, by contrast, iteratively extends sequences by the most frequent sequence in its candidate generation step which enables it to quickly generate large candidate sequences (Section 3.6). We did consider performing a statistical test between a sequence and its extending sequence, however this proved computationally prohibitive.

The differences between these models and ISM are:

- *Interleaving.* SQS cannot mine subsequences that are interleaved and thus struggles on datasets which consist mainly of interleaved subsequences (for illustration, see Section 4.4). GoKrimp handles interleaving using a pointer scheme that explicitly encodes the location of the subsequence within the database. In ISM, the partition function $|\mathcal{P}|$ allows us to handle interleaving of subsequences without needing to explicitly encode positions, and also serves as an additional penalty on the number of elements in the subsequences used to explain a database sequence.
- *Gap penalties.* Both SQS and GoKrimp explicitly punish gaps in sequential patterns. Adding such a penalty would require only a trivial modification to the algorithm, namely, updating the cost function in Algorithm 1. We did not pursue this as we observe excellent results without it (Section 4).
- *Encoding the set of patterns.* Both SQS and GoKrimp contain an explicit penalty term for the description length of the pattern database, which corresponds to a prior distribution $p(\mathcal{I})$ over patterns. In our experiments with ISM, we did not find in practice that an explicit prior distribution $p(\mathcal{I})$ was necessary for good results. It would be possible to incorporate it with a trivial change to the ISM algorithm, in particular, when computing the score improvement of a new candidate in the structural EM step.
- *Encoding pattern absence.* Also, observe that, if we view ISM as an MDL-type method, not only the presence of a pattern, but also the absence of it is explicitly encoded (in the form of π_{S_0} in (3.1)). As a result, there is an implicit penalty for adding too many patterns to the model and one does not need to use a code table which would serve as an explicit penalty for greater model complexity.

4. NUMERICAL EXPERIMENTS

In this section we perform a comprehensive quantitative and qualitative evaluation of ISM. On synthetic datasets we show that ISM returns a list of sequential patterns that is largely non-redundant, contains few spurious correlations and scales linearly with the number of sequences in the dataset. On a set of real-world datasets we show that ISM finds patterns that are consistent, interpretable and highly relevant to the problem at hand. Moreover, we show that ISM is able to mine patterns that achieve good accuracy when used as binary features for real-world classification tasks.

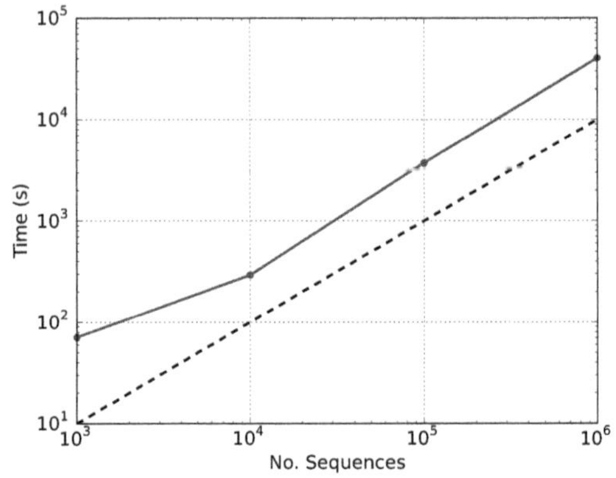

Figure 1: ISM scaling as the number of sequences in our synthetic database increases.

Datasets We use ten real-world datasets in our numerical evaluation (see Table 1). The Alice dataset consists of the text of Lewis Carrol's Alice in Wonderland, tokenized into 1,638 sentences using the Stanford Document Preprocessor [17] with stop words and punctuation deliberately retained. The Gazelle dataset consists of 59,601 sequences of clickstream data from an e-commerce website used in the KDD-CUP 2000 competition [11]. The JMLR dataset consists of 788 abstracts from the Journal of Machine Learning Research and has previously been used in the evaluation of the SQS and GoKrimp algorithms [12, 25]. Each sequence is a list of stemmed words from the text with stop words removed. The Sign dataset is a list of 730 American sign language utterances where each utterance contains a number of gestural and grammatical fields [21]. The last six datasets listed in Table 1 were first introduced in [19] to evaluate classification accuracy when mined sequential patterns are used as features. The datasets were converted from time interval sequences into sequences of items by considering the start and end of each unique interval as distinct items and ordering the items according to time.

ISM Results We ran ISM on each dataset for 1,000 iterations with a priority queue size of 100,000 candidates. The runtime and number of non-singleton sequential patterns returned by ISM is given in the right-hand side of Table 1. We

Dataset	Uniq. Items	Sequences	Subseq.†	Runtime
Alice	2,619	1,638	123	114 min
Gazelle	497	59,601	727	582 min
JMLR	3,846	788	361	230 min
Sign	267	730	159	31 min
aslbu	250	424	144	4 min
aslgt	94	3,464	57	19 min
auslan2	16	200	10	>1 min
context	94	240	19	7 min
pioneer	178	160	86	3 min
skating	82	530	70	9 min

Table 1: Summary of the real datasets used and ISM results after 1,000 iterations. † excluding singleton subsequences.

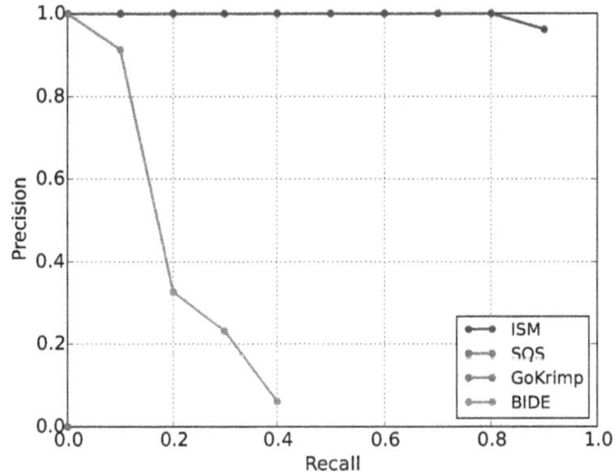

Figure 2: Precision against recall for each algorithm on our synthetic database, using the top-k patterns as a threshold. Note that SQS is a single point at the top-left and GoKrimp has near zero precision and recall. Each plotted curve is the 11-point interpolated precision[3].

also investigated the scaling of ISM as the number of sequences in the database increases, using the model trained on the Sign dataset from Section 4.1 to generate synthetic sequence databases of various sizes. We ran ISM for 100 iterations on these databases and one can see in Figure 1 that the scaling is linear as expected. All experiments were performed on a machine with 16 Intel Xeon E5-2650 2.60Ghz CPUs and 128GB of RAM.

Evaluation criteria We will evaluate ISM along with SQS, GoKrimp and BIDE according to the following criteria:

1. *Spuriousness* – to assess the degree of spurious correlation in the mined set of sequential patterns.
2. *Redundancy* – to measure how redundant the mined set of patterns is.
3. *Classification Accuracy* – to measure the usefulness of the mined patterns.
4. *Interpretability* – to informally assess how meaningful and relevant the mined patterns actually are.

4.1 Pattern Spuriousness

The sequence-cover formulation of the ISM algorithm (3.1) naturally favours adding sequences to the model whose items co-occur in the sequence database. One would therefore expect ISM to largely avoid suggesting sequences of uncorrelated items and so return more meaningful patterns. To verify this is the case and validate our inference procedure, we check if ISM is able to recover the sequences it used to generate a synthetic database. To obtain a realistic synthetic database, we sampled 10,000 sequences from the ISM generative model trained on the Sign dataset (cf. Section 3.2). We were then able to measure the precision and recall for each algorithm, i.e., the fraction of mined patterns that are generating and the fraction of generating patterns that are mined, respectively. Figure 2 shows the precision-recall curve for ISM, SQS, GoKrimp and BIDE using the top-k mined sequences (according to each algorithms ranking) as a threshold. One can clearly see that ISM was able to mine almost all the generating patterns and almost all the patterns mined were generating, despite the fact that the generated database will contain many subsequences not present in the original dataset due to the nature of our 'subsequence interleaving' generative model. This not only provides a good validation of ISM's inference procedure and underlying generative model but also demonstrates that ISM returns few spurious patterns. For comparison, SQS returned a very small set of generating patterns and GoKrimp returned many patterns that were not generating. The set of top-k patterns mined by BIDE contained successively less generating patterns as k increased. It is not our intention to draw conclusions about the performance of the other algorithms as this experimental setup naturally favours ISM. Instead, we compare the patterns from ISM with those from SQS and GoKrimp on real-world data in the next sections.

[3] i.e., the interpolated precision at 11 equally spaced recall points between 0 and 1 (inclusive), see [16], §8.4 for details.

4.2 Pattern Redundancy

We now turn our attention to evaluating how redundant the sets of sequential patterns returned by ISM, SQS, GoKrimp and BIDE actually are. A suitable measure of redundancy for a single sequence is the minimum edit distance between it and the other mined sequences in the set. Averaging this distance across all sequences in the set, we obtain the *average inter-sequence distance* (ISD). Similarly, we can also calculate the average number of sequences containing other mined sequences in the set (CS), which provides us with another measure of redundancy. Finally, we can also look at the number of unique items present in the set of mined sequences which gives us an indication of how diverse it is. We ran ISM, SQS, GoKrimp and BIDE on all the datasets in Table 1 and report the results of the three aforementioned redundancy metrics on the top 50 non-singleton sequential patterns for each algorithm in Table 2. One can see that on average the top ISM sequences have a larger inter-sequence distance, smaller number of containing sequences and larger number of unique items, clearly demonstrating they are less redundant than SQS, GoKrimp and BIDE. Predictably, the top BIDE sequences are the most redundant, with an average inter-sequence distance of 1.00.

4.3 Classification Accuracy

A key property of any set of patterns mined from data is its usefulness in real-world applications. To this end, in keeping with previous work [12], we will focus on classification tasks as they are some of most important applications of pattern mining algorithms. Specifically we will consider the task of classifying sequences in a database using mined sequential patterns as binary features. We therefore performed 10-fold cross validation using a Support Vector Machine (SVM) classifier on the six classification datasets from Table 1 with the top-k patterns mined by ISM, SQS, GoKrimp and BIDE as features. We used the linear classifier from the libSVM library [4] with default parameters. Additionally, we used the top-k most frequent singleton patterns as a baseline for the classification tasks. The resulting plots of k against classification accuracy for all the datasets and algorithms are given in Figure 3. One can see that the patterns mined by SQS perform best, exhibiting the highest classification accuracy on four out of the six datasets, closely followed by ISM and GoKrimp, which performs surprisingly well considering it struggles to return more than 50 patterns. All three consistently outperform BIDE and the singletons baseline which exhibit similar performance to each other. We therefore conclude that the sequential patterns mined by ISM can indeed be useful in real-world applications.

	Alice			Gazelle			JMLR			Sign			aslbu		
	ISD	CS	Items	ISD	CS	Items	ISD	CS	Items	ISD	CS	Items	ISD	CS	Items
ISM	**2.00**	**0.00**	**94**	3.36	**0.00**	167	**1.84**	**0.00**	**96**	**3.64**	**0.00**	**113**	**2.24**	**0.00**	**110**
SQS	1.76	0.10	72	**4.24**	0.38	**183**	1.82	0.02	92	1.26	0.94	57	*1.89	*0.11	*61
GoKrimp	1.24	0.10	52	*4.51	*0.05	*176	*1.40	*0.10	*30	1.72	0.24	63	*2.00	*0.00	*18
BIDE	1.00	0.36	29	1.00	0.36	26	1.00	0.18	12	1.00	0.60	15	1.00	0.00	26

	aslgt			auslan2			context			pioneer			skating		
	ISD	CS	Items	ISD	CS	Items	ISD	CS	Items	ISD	CS	Items	ISD	CS	Items
ISM	**2.08**	0.20	**94**	*2.40	*1.0	*14	*2.16	*0.47	*35	**2.04**	**0.00**	**102**	**2.12**	0.72	**73**
SQS	1.96	0.28	86	*1.42	*1.17	*12	2.14	0.90	**64**	1.64	0.40	78	1.62	0.84	46
GoKrimp	*2.00	*0.00	*89	*2.00	*0.25	*8	*2.07	*0.52	*51	*1.82	*0.00	*33	*1.90	*0.29	*64
BIDE	1.00	0.00	22	*1.00	*3.16	*6	1.00	1.72	12	1.02	0.06	32	1.00	1.06	17

Table 2: Average inter-sequence distance (ISD), average no. containing sequences (CS) and no. unique items for the top 50 non-singleton sequences returned by the algorithms from the datasets. Larger inter-sequence distances and smaller no. containing sequences indicate less redundancy. * returned less than 50 non-singleton sequences.

ISM	SQS	GoKrimp	BIDE
support vector machin	support vector machin	support vector machin	algorithm algorithm
real world	machin learn	machin learn	learn learn
larg scale	state art	real world	learn algorithm
high dimension	data set	state art	algorithm learn
state art	bayesian network	high dimension	data data
first second	larg scale	reproduc hilbert space	learn data
reproduc kernel hilbert space	nearest neighbor	experiment result	model model
maximum likelihood	decis tree	supervis learn	problem problem
wide rang	neural network	neural network	learn result
gene express	cross valid	compon analysi	problem algorithm
princip compon analysi	featur select	well known	method method
random field	graphic model	support vector	algorithm result
maximum entropi	real world	base result	data set
low dimension	high dimension	paper investig	learn learn learn
blind separ	mutual inform	data demonstr	learn problem
wide varieti	sampl size	hilbert space	learn method
acycl graph	learn algorithm	such paper	algorithm data
turn out	princip compon analysi	algorithm demonstr	learn set
markov chain	logist regress	learn result	problem learn
leav out	model select	learn experi	algorithm algorithm algorithm

Table 3: The top twenty non-singleton sequences as found by ISM, SQS, GoKrimp and BIDE for the JMLR dataset.

4.4 Pattern Interpretability

For the two text datasets in Table 1 we can directly interpret the mined patterns and informally assess how meaningful and relevant they are.

JMLR Dataset We compare the top-20 non-singleton patterns mined by ISM, SQS, GoKrimp and BIDE in Table 3. It is immediately obvious from the table that the BIDE patterns are almost exclusively permutations of frequent items and so uninformative. For this reason we omit BIDE from consideration on the next dataset. The patterns mined by ISM, SQS and GoKrimp are all very informative, containing technical concepts such as *support vector machine* and commonly used phrases such as *state (of the) art*.

Alice Dataset We compare the top twenty-20 non-singleton patterns mined by ISM, SQS and GoKrimp in the first three columns Table 4. This time, one can clearly see that the patterns mined by ISM are considerably more informative. They contain collocated words and phrases such as *mock turtle* and *oh dear*, correlated words such as *as spoke* and *off head*, as well as correlated punctuation such as *( )* and *“ ”*. Both SQS and GoKrimp on the other hand mine collocated words with spurious punctuation and stop words, e.g. prepending *the* to nouns and commas to phrases. To further illustrate this notable difference, we also show the top-20 non-singleton patterns that are exclusive to each algorithm (i.e., found by ISM but not SQS/GoKrimp, etc.) in the last three columns of Table 4. One can clearly see that GoKrimp has the least informative exclusive patterns, predominantly combinations of stop words and punctuation, SQS mostly prepends and appends informative exclusive patterns with punctuation and stop words, whereas ISM is the only algorithm that just returns purely correlated words. Note that SQS in particular struggles to return patterns such as balanced parentheses, since it punishes the large gaps between them and cannot handle interleaving them with the patterns they enclose. Here we can really see the power of the statistical model underlying ISM as it is able to discern spurious punctuation from genuine phrases.

Parallel Dataset Finally, we consider a synthetic dataset that demonstrates the ability of ISM to handle interleaving patterns. Following [12], we generate a synthetic dataset where each item in the sequence is generated by five independent parallel processes, i.e., each process i generates one item from a set of five possible items $\{a_i, b_i, c_i, d_i, e_i\}$ in or-

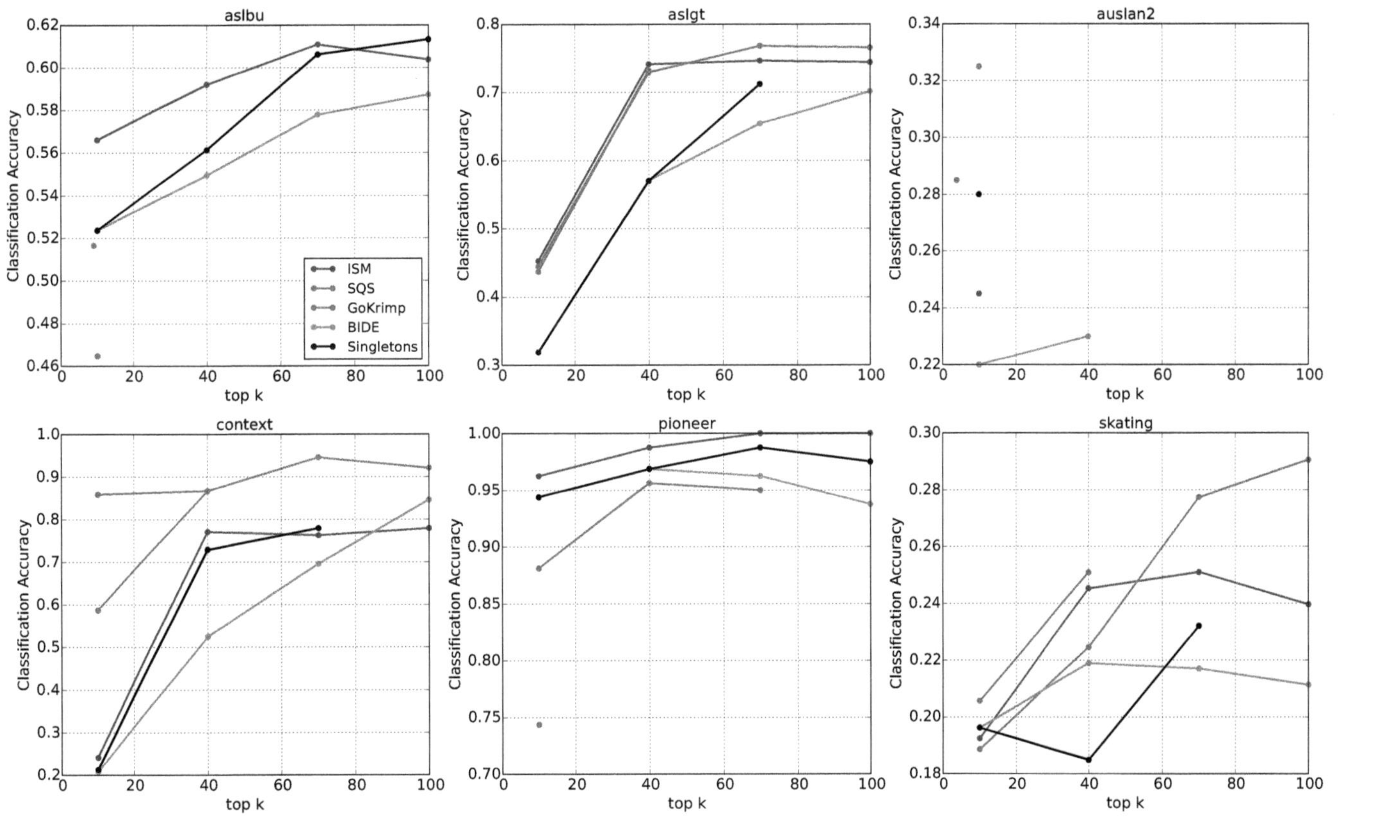

Figure 3: Linear SVM classification accuracy using the top-k sequences returned by each algorithm as binary features. ISM shows consistently good performance, comparable to SQS and GoKrimp.

ISM	SQS	GoKrimp	Exclusive ISM	Exclusive SQS	Exc. GoKrimp
she herself	! ’	‘ ’	she herself	? ’	‘ ’
mock turtle	, and	, and	( )	the mock turtle	, said .
( )	? ’	, said .	he his	the march hare	said the .
went on	. ’	mock turtle	as spoke	* * * *	of the .
“ ”	the mock turtle	said the .	had back	, ’ said alice	i n't ’
ca n't	the march hare	in a	just when	, you know	march hare
he his	* * * *	of the .	off head	it was	alice .
looked at	, ’ said alice	i n't ’	she at once	the white rabbit	what ?
had been	the queen	i 'm	oh dear	, ’	you know
must be	, you know	march hare	never before	; and	‘ !
at last	went on	went on	join dance	she had	you ?
as spoke	it was	a little	might well	beau – ootiful soo – oop !	, , ,
looking at	the white rabbit	! ’	if 'd	i 've	oh , !
had back	, ’	alice .	such thing	minute or two	i ’
just when	; and	to herself	've seen	there was	alice ;
off head	a little	as she	do n't know what	‘ well ,	, !
she at once	i 'm	what ?	going into	– ’	the .
oh dear	do n't	you know	too much	in a tone	alice ,
more than	she had	the queen	soon found	soo – oop of the e – e –	it :
never before	beau – ootiful soo – oop !	the hatter	took its	, ’ said the king	and she

Table 4: The top twenty non-singleton sequences as found by ISM, SQS and GoKrimp for the Alice dataset as well as those found by ISM but not SQS/GoKrimp, SQS not ISM/GoKrimp and GoKrimp not ISM/SQS.

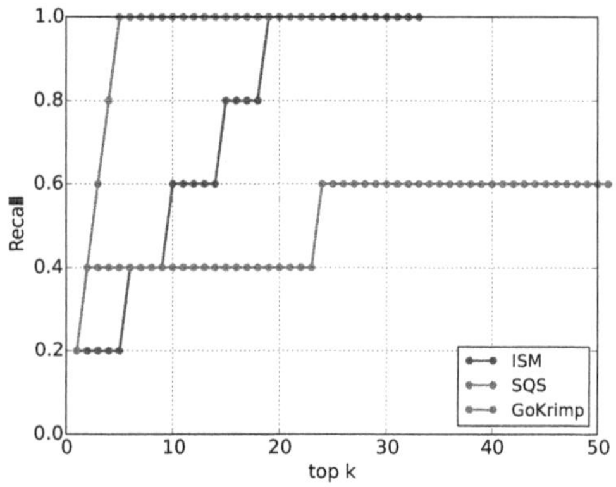

Figure 4: Recall for each algorithm on the synthetic parallel dataset, using the top-k (first-k for SQS) patterns as a threshold. Note that SQS maintains a recall level of 0.6 for the remaining patterns (up to $k = 403$, not shown for clarity).

der. In each step, the generator chooses i at random and generates an item using process i, until the sequence has length 1,000,000. The sequence is then split into 10,000 sequences of length 100. For this dataset we know that all mined sequences containing a mixture of items from different processes are spurious. This enables us to calculate recall, i.e., the fraction of processes present in the set of true patterns mined by each algorithm. We plot the recall for the top-k patterns mined by ISM and GoKrimp in Figure 4 and the first-k patterns mined by SQS (as it was still running after seven days). One can see that while ISM and GoKrimp are able to mine true patterns from all processes, SQS only returns patterns from 3 of the 5 processes.

5. CONCLUSIONS

In this paper, we have taken a probabilistic machine learning approach to the subsequence mining problem. We presented a novel subsequence interleaving model, called the Interesting Sequence Miner, that infers subsequences which best compress a sequence database without having to design a MDL encoding scheme. We demonstrated the efficacy of our approach on both synthetic and real-world datasets, showing that ISM returns a more diverse set of patterns than previous approaches while retaining comparable quality. In the future we would like to extend our approach to the many promising application areas as well as considering more advanced techniques for parallelization.

Acknowledgments

This work was supported by the Engineering and Physical Sciences Research Council (grant number EP/K024043/1).

References

[1] C. Aggarwal and J. Han. *Frequent Pattern Mining.* Springer, 2014.
[2] R. Agrawal and R. Srikant. Mining sequential patterns. In *ICDE*, pages 3–14, 1995.
[3] J. Ayres, J. Flannick, J. Gehrke, and T. Yiu. Sequential pattern mining using a bitmap representation. In *KDD*, pages 429–435, 2002.
[4] C.-C. Chang and C.-J. Lin. LIBSVM: A library for support vector machines. *ACM TIST*, 2:27:1–27:27, 2011. http://www.csie.ntu.edu.tw/~cjlin/libsvm.
[5] V. Chvátal. A greedy heuristic for the set-covering problem. *Math. O.R.*, 4(3):233–235, 1979.
[6] A. Dempster, N. Laird, and D. Rubin. Maximum likelihood from incomplete data via the EM algorithm. *Journal of the Royal Statistical Society: Series B*, pages 1–38, 1977.
[7] U. Feige. A threshold of ln n for approximating set cover. *Journal of the ACM*, 45(4):634–652, 1998.
[8] N. Friedman. The Bayesian structural EM algorithm. In *UAI*, pages 129–138, 1998.
[9] R. Gwadera, M. J. Atallah, and W. Szpankowski. Markov models for identification of significant episodes. In *SDM*, pages 404–414, 2005.
[10] N. Jay, G. Herengt, E. Albuisson, F. Kohler, and A. Napoli. Sequential pattern mining and classification of patient path. In *MEDINFO*, page 1667, 2004.
[11] R. Kohavi, C. E. Brodley, B. Frasca, L. Mason, and Z. Zheng. KDD-Cup 2000 organizers' report: Peeling the onion. *SIGKDD Explorations Newsletter*, 2(2):86–93, 2000.
[12] H. T. Lam, F. Moerchen, D. Fradkin, and T. Calders. Mining compressing sequential patterns. *Statistical Analysis and Data Mining*, 7(1):34–52, 2014.
[13] N. Landwehr. Modeling interleaved hidden processes. In *ICML*, pages 520–527, 2008.
[14] D. J. C. MacKay. *Information Theory, Inference, and Learning Algorithms.* Cambridge University Press, 2003.
[15] H. Mannila and C. Meek. Global partial orders from sequential data. In *KDD*, pages 161–168, 2000.
[16] C. D. Manning, P. Raghavan, and H. Schütze. *Introduction to Information Retrieval.* Cambridge University Press, 2008.
[17] C. D. Manning, M. Surdeanu, J. Bauer, J. Finkel, S. J. Bethard, and D. McClosky. The Stanford CoreNLP natural language processing toolkit. In *ACL System Demonstrations*, pages 55–60, 2014.
[18] B. Mobasher, H. Dai, T. Luo, and M. Nakagawa. Using sequential and non-sequential patterns in predictive web usage mining tasks. In *ICDM*, pages 669–672, 2002.
[19] F. Moerchen and D. Fradkin. Robust mining of time intervals with semi-interval partial order patterns. In *SDM*, pages 315–326, 2010.
[20] C. G. Nevill-Manning and I. H. Witten. Identifying hierarchical structure in sequences: A linear-time algorithm. *Journal of Artificial Intelligence Research*, 7:67–82, 1997.
[21] P. Papapetrou, G. Kollios, S. Sclaroff, and D. Gunopulos. Discovering frequent arrangements of temporal intervals. In *ICDM*, pages 82–89, 2005.
[22] J. Pei, J. Han, B. Mortazavi-Asl, H. Pinto, Q. Chen, U. Dayal, and M.-C. Hsu. PrefixSpan: Mining sequential patterns efficiently by prefix-projected pattern growth. In *ICDE*, pages 0215–0215, 2001.
[23] R. Srikant and R. Agrawal. Mining sequential patterns: Generalizations and performance improvements. In *EDBT*, pages 3–17, 1996.
[24] A. Stolcke and S. Omohundro. Hidden Markov model induction by Bayesian model merging. In *NIPS*, pages 11–18, 1993.
[25] N. Tatti and J. Vreeken. The long and the short of it: summarising event sequences with serial episodes. In *KDD*, pages 462–470, 2012.
[26] J. Wang and J. Han. BIDE: Efficient mining of frequent closed sequences. In *ICDE*, pages 79–90, 2004.
[27] M. Wang, X.-Q. Shang, and Z.-H. Li. Sequential pattern mining for protein function prediction. In *ADMA*, pages 652–658. Springer, 2008.
[28] F. Wood, J. Gasthaus, C. Archambeau, L. James, and Y. W. Teh. The sequence memoizer. *Communications of the ACM*, 54(2):91–98, 2011.
[29] M. J. Zaki. SPADE: An efficient algorithm for mining frequent sequences. *Machine Learning*, 42(1-2):31–60, 2001.
[30] H. Zhong, T. Xie, L. Zhang, J. Pei, and H. Mei. MAPO: Mining and recommending API usage patterns. In *ECOOP*, pages 318–343. 2009.

Efficient Frequent Directions Algorithm for Sparse Matrices

Mina Ghashami
University of Utah
Utah, USA
ghashami@cs.utah.edu

Edo Liberty
Yahoo Research!
NewYork, USA
edo@yahoo-inc.com

Jeff M. Phillips*
University of Utah
Utah, USA
jeffp@cs.utah.edu

ABSTRACT

This paper describes Sparse Frequent Directions, a variant of Frequent Directions for sketching sparse matrices. It resembles the original algorithm in many ways: both receive the rows of an input matrix $A^{n \times d}$ one by one in the streaming setting and compute a small sketch $B \in \mathbb{R}^{\ell \times d}$. Both share the same strong (provably optimal) asymptotic guarantees with respect to the space-accuracy tradeoff in the streaming setting. However, unlike Frequent Directions which runs in $O(nd\ell)$ time regardless of the sparsity of the input matrix A, Sparse Frequent Directions runs in $\tilde{O}\left(\text{nnz}(A)\ell + n\ell^2\right)$ time. Our analysis loosens the dependence on computing the Singular Value Decomposition (SVD) as a black box within the Frequent Directions algorithm. Our bounds require recent results on the properties of fast approximate SVD computations. Finally, we empirically demonstrate that these asymptotic improvements are practical and significant on real and synthetic data.

Keywords

Frequent Directions, Sparse Matrix, Matrix Sketching

1. INTRODUCTION

It is very common to represent data in the form of a matrix. For example, in text analysis under the bag-of-words model, a large corpus of documents can be represented as a matrix whose rows refer to the documents and columns correspond to words. A non-zero in the matrix corresponds to a word appearing in the corresponding document. Similarly, in recommendation systems [13], preferences of users are represented as a matrix with rows corresponding to users and columns corresponding to items. Non-zero entires correspond to user ratings or actions.

A large set of data analytic tasks rely on obtaining a low-rank approximation of the data matrix. These include clustering, dimension reduction, principal component analysis (PCA), signal denoising, etc. Such approximations can be computed using the Singular Value Decompositions (SVD). For an $n \times d$ matrix A ($d \leq n$) computing the SVD requires $O(nd^2)$ time and $O(nd)$ space in memory on a single machine.

In many scenarios, however, data matrices are extremely large and computing their SVD exactly is infeasible. Efficient approximate solutions exist for distributed setting or when data access otherwise is limited. In the row streaming model, the matrix rows are presented to the algorithm one by one in an arbitrary order. The algorithm is tasked with processing the stream in one pass while being severely restricted in its memory footprint. At the end of the stream, the algorithm must provide a sketch matrix B which is a good approximation of A even though it is significantly more compact. This is called matrix sketching.

Matrix sketching methods are designed to be parallelizable, space and time efficient, and easily updatable. Computing the sketch on each machine and then combining the sketches together should be as good as sketching the combined data from all the different machines. The streaming model is especially attractive since a sketch can be obtained and maintained as the data is being collected. Therefore, eliminating the need for data storage altogether.

Often matrices, as above, are sparse; most of their entries are zero. The work of [9] argues that typical term-document matrices are sparse; documents contain no more than 5% of all words. On wikipedia, most words appear on only a small constant number of pages. Similarly, in recommendation systems, in average a user rates or interacts with a small fraction of the available items: less than 6% in some user-movies recommendation tasks [1] and much fewer in physical purchases or online advertising. As such, most of these datasets are stored as sparse matrices.

There exist several techniques for producing low rank approximations of sparse matrices whose running time is $O(\text{nnz}(A)\,\text{poly}(k, 1/\varepsilon))$ for some error parameter $\varepsilon \in (0,1)$. Here $\text{nnz}(A)$ denotes the number of non-zeros in the matrix A. Examples include the power method [19], random projection techniques [35], projection-hashing [6], and instances of column selection techniques [11].

However, for a recent and popular technique Frequent-Directions (best paper of KDD 2013 [24]), there is no known way to take advantage of the sparsity of the input matrix. While it is deterministic and its space-error bounds are known to be optimal for dense matrices in the row-update model [17], it runs in $O(nd\ell)$ time to produce a sketch of

*Thanks to support by NSF CCF-1350888, IIS-1251019, ACI-1443046, and CNS-1514520.

KDD '16, August 13 - 17, 2016, San Francisco, CA, USA

ISBN 978-1-4503-4232-2/16/08...$15.00

DOI: http://dx.doi.org/10.1145/2939672.2939800

size $\ell \times d$. In particular, it maintains a sketch with ℓ rows and updates it iteratively over a stream, periodically invoking a full SVD which requires $O(d\ell^2)$ time. Reliance on exact SVD computations seems to be the main hurdle in reducing the runtime to depend on $O(\text{nnz}(A))$. This paper shows a version of FREQUENTDIRECTIONS whose runtime depends on $O(\text{nnz}(A))$. This requires a new understanding and a more careful analysis of FREQUENTDIRECTIONS. It also takes advantage of block power methods (also known as Subspace Iteration, Simultaneous Iteration, or Orthogonal Iteration) that run in time proportional to nnz(A) but incur small approximation error [29].

1.1 Linear Algebra Notations

Throughout the paper we identify an $n \times d$ matrix A with a set of n rows $[a_1; a_2; \ldots; a_n]$ where each a_i is a vector in $\mathbb{R}^d$. The notation a_i stands for the ith row of the matrix A. By $[A; a]$ we mean the row vector a appended to the matrix A as its last row. Similarly, $[A; B]$ stands for stacking two matrices A and B vertically. The matrices I_n and $0^{n\times d}$ denote the n-dimensional identity matrix and the full zero matrix of dimension $n \times d$ respectively. The notation $\mathcal{N}(0,1)^{d\times\ell}$ denotes the distribution over $d\times\ell$ matrices whose entries are drawn independently from the normal distribution $\mathcal{N}(0,1)$. For a vector x the notation $\|\cdot\|$ refers to the Euclidian norm $\|x\| = (\sum_i x_i^2)^{1/2}$. The Frobenius norm of a matrix A is defined as $\|A\|_F = \sqrt{\sum_{i=1}\|a_i\|^2}$, and the operator (or spectral) norm of it is $\|A\|_2 = \sup_{x\neq 0}\|Ax\|/\|x\|$.

The notation nnz(A) refers to the number of non-zeros in A, and $\rho = \text{nnz}(A)/(nd)$ denotes relative density of A. The Singular Value Decomposition of a matrix $A \in \mathbb{R}^{m\times d}$ for $m \leq d$ is denoted by $[U, \Sigma, V] = \text{SVD}(A)$. It guarantees that $A = U\Sigma V^T$, $U^TU = I_m$, $V^TV = I_m$, $U \in \mathbb{R}^{m\times m}$, $V \in \mathbb{R}^{d\times m}$, and$\Sigma \in \mathbb{R}^{m\times m}$ is a non-negative diagonal matrix such that$\Sigma_{i,i} = \sigma_i$ and $\sigma_1 \geq \sigma_2 \geq \ldots \geq \sigma_m \geq 0$. It is convenient to denote by U_k, and V_k the matrices containing the first k columns of U and V and by$\Sigma_k \in \mathbb{R}^{k\times k}$ the top left $k \times k$ block of Σ. The matrix $A_k = U_k\Sigma_kV_k^T$ is the best rank k approximation of A in the sense that $A_k = \arg\min_{C:\text{rank}(C)\leq k}\|A - C\|_{2,F}$. In places where we use SVD(A, k), we mean rank k SVD of A.

The notation $\pi_B(A)$ denotes the projection of the rows of A on the span of the rows of B. In other words, $\pi_B(A) = AB^\dagger B$ where $(\cdot)^\dagger$ indicates taking the Moore-Penrose psuedoinverse. Alternatively, setting $[U, \Sigma, V] = \text{SVD}(B)$, we have $\pi_B(A) = AVV^T$. We also denote $\pi_B^k(A) = AV_kV_k^T$, the right projection of A on the top k right singular vectors of B.

2. MATRIX SKETCHING PRIOR ART

This section reviews only matrix sketching techniques that run in input sparsity time and whose output sketch is independent of the number of rows in the matrix. We categorize all known results into three main approaches (1) column/row subset selection (2) random projection based techniques and (3) iterative sketching techniques.

Column selection techniques. These techniques, which are also studied under the Column Subset Selection Problem (CSSP) in literature [16, 10, 3, 8, 15, 2], form the sketch B by selecting a subset of "important" columns of the input matrix A. They maintain the sparsity of A and make the sketch B to be more interpretable. These methods are not typically streaming, nor running in input sparsity time. The only method of this group which achieves both is [11] by Drineas *et al.* that uses reservoir sampling to become streaming. They select $O(k/\varepsilon^2)$ columns proportional to their squared norm and achieve the Frobenius norm error bound $\|A - \pi_{B_k}(A)\|_F^2 \leq \|A - A_k\|_F^2 + \varepsilon\|A\|_F^2$ with time complexity of $O((k^2/\varepsilon^4)(d + k/\varepsilon^2) + \text{nnz}(A))$. In addition, they show that the spectral norm error bound $\|A - \pi_{B_k}(A)\|_2^2 \leq \|A - A_k\|_2^2 + \varepsilon\|A\|_F^2$ holds if one selects $O(1/\varepsilon^2)$ columns. Rudelson *et al.* [34] improved the latter error bound to $\|A - \pi_{B_k}(A)\|_2^2 \leq \|A - A_k\|_2^2 + \varepsilon\|A\|_2^2$ by selecting $O(r/\varepsilon^4 \log(r/\varepsilon^4))$ columns, where $r = \|A\|_F^2/\|A\|_2^2$ is the numeric rank of A. Note that in the result by [11], one would need $O(r^2/\varepsilon^2)$ columns to obtain the same bound.

Another similar line of work is the CUR factorization [4, 10, 12, 14, 27] where methods select c columns and r rows of A to form matrices $C \in \mathbb{R}^{n\times c}$, $R \in \mathbb{R}^{r\times d}$ and $U \in \mathbb{R}^{c\times r}$, and constructs the sketch as $B = CUR$. The only instance of this group that runs in input sparsity time is [4] by Boutsidis and Woodruff, where they select $r = c = O(k/\varepsilon)$ rows and columns of A and construct matrices C, U and R with rank(U) $= k$ such that with constant probability $\|A - CUR\|_F^2 \leq (1 + \varepsilon)\|A - A_k\|_F^2$. Their algorithm runs in $O(\text{nnz}(A)\log n + (n + d)\,\text{poly}(\log n, k, 1/\varepsilon))$ time.

Random projection techniques. These techniques [31, 36, 35, 26] operate data-obliviously and maintain a $r \times d$ matrix $B = SA$ using a $r \times n$ random matrix S which has the Johnson-Lindenstrauss Transform (JLT) property [28]. Random projection methods work in the streaming model, are computationally efficient, and sufficiently accurate in practice [7]. The state-of-the-art method of this approach is by Clarkson and Woodruff [6] which was later improved slightly in [30]. It uses a hashing matrix S with only one non-zero entry in each column. Constructing this sketch takes only $O(\text{nnz}(A) + n \cdot \text{poly}(k/\varepsilon) + \text{poly}(dk/\varepsilon))$ time, and guarantees that for any unit vector x that $(1 - \varepsilon)\|Ax\| \leq \|Bx\| \leq (1 + \varepsilon)\|Ax\|$. For these sparsity-efficient sketches using $r = O(d^2/\varepsilon^2)$ also guarantees that $\|A - \pi_B(A)\|_F \leq (1 + \varepsilon)\|A - A_k\|_F$.

Iterative sketching techniques. These operate in streaming model, where random access to the matrix is not available. They maintain the sketch B as a linear combination of rows of A, and update it as new rows are received in the stream. Examples of these methods include different version of iterative SVD [19, 21, 23, 5, 33]. These, however, do not have theoretical guarantees [7]. The FREQUENTDIRECTIONS algorithm [24] is a unique in this group in that it offers strong error guarantees. It is a deterministic sketching technique that processes rows of an $n \times d$ matrix A in a stream and maintains a $\ell \times d$ sketch B (for $\ell < \min(n, d)$) such that the following two error bounds hold for any $0 \leq k < \ell$

$$\|A^TA - B^TB\|_2 \leq \frac{1}{\ell - k}\|A - A_k\|_F^2$$

and

$$\|A - \pi_B(A)\|_F^2 \leq \frac{\ell}{\ell - k}\|A - A_k\|_F^2 .$$

Setting $\ell = k + 1/\varepsilon$ and $\ell = k + k/\varepsilon$, respectively, achieves bounds $\|A^TA - B^TB\|_2 \leq \varepsilon\|A - A_k\|_F^2$ and $\|A - \pi_B(A)\|_F^2 \leq (1 + \varepsilon)\|A - A_k\|_F^2$. Although FREQUENTDIRECTIONS does not run in input sparsity time, we will explain it in detail in the next section, as it is an important building block for the algorithm we introduce.

2.1 Main Results

We present a randomized version of FREQUENTDIRECTIONS, called as SPARSEFREQUENTDIRECTIONS that receives an $n \times d$ sparse matrix A as a stream of its rows. It computes a $\ell \times d$ sketch B in $O(d\ell)$ space.

It guarantees that with probability at least $1 - \delta$ (for $\delta \in (0, 1)$ being the failure probability), for $\alpha = 6/41$ and any $0 \le k < \alpha\ell$,

$$\|A^T A - B^T B\|_2 \le \frac{1}{\alpha\ell - k}\|A - A_k\|_F^2$$

and

$$\|A - \pi_{B_k}(A)\|_F^2 \le \frac{\ell}{\ell - k/\alpha}\|A - A_k\|_F^2.$$

Note that setting $\ell = \lceil 1/(\varepsilon\alpha) + k/\alpha \rceil$ yields

$$\|A^T A - B^T B\|_2 \le \varepsilon\|A - A_k\|_F^2$$

and setting $\ell = \lceil k/(\varepsilon\alpha) + k/\alpha \rceil$ yields

$$\|A - \pi_{B_k}(A)\|_F^2 \le (1 + \varepsilon)\|A - A_k\|_F^2.$$

The expected running time of the algorithm is

$$O(\text{nnz}(A)\ell \log(d) + \text{nnz}(A) \log(n/\delta) + n\ell^2 + n\ell \log(n/\delta))$$

In the likely case where $\text{nnz}(A) = \Omega(n\ell)$ and $n/\delta < d^{O(\ell)}$, the runtime is dominated by $O(\text{nnz}(A)\ell \log(d))$. We also experimentally validate this theory, demonstrating these runtime improvements on sparse data without sacrificing accuracy.

3. PRELIMINARIES

In this section we review some important properties about FREQUENTDIRECTIONS and SIMULTANEOUSITERATION which will be necessary for understanding and proving bounds on SPARSEFREQUENTDIRECTIONS.

3.1 Frequent Directions

The FREQUENTDIRECTIONS algorithm was introduced by Liberty [24] and received an improved analysis by Ghashami et al.[17]. The algorithm operates by collecting several rows of the input matrix and letting the sketch grow. Once the sketch doubles in size, a lossy DENSESHRINK operation reduces its size by a half. This process repeats throughout the stream. The running time of FREQUENTDIRECTIONS and its error analysis are strongly coupled with the properties of the SVD used to perform the DENSESHRINK step.

An analysis of [7] slightly generalized the one in [17]. Let B be the sketch resulting in applying FREQUENTDIRECTIONS with a potentially different shrink operation to A. Then, the FREQUENTDIRECTIONS asymptotic guarantees hold as long as the shrink operation exhibits three properties, for any positive Δ and a constant $\alpha \in (0, 1)$.

1. Property 1:
   For any vector $x \in \mathbb{R}^d$, $\|Ax\|^2 - \|Bx\|^2 \ge 0$.
2. Property 2:
   For any unit vector $x \in \mathbb{R}^d$, $\|Ax\|^2 - \|Bx\|^2 \le \Delta$.
3. Property 3: $\|A\|_F^2 - \|B\|_F^2 \ge \alpha\Delta\ell$.

For completeness, the exact guarantee is stated in Lemma 3.1.

LEMMA 3.1 (LEMMA 3.1 IN [7]). *Given an input $n \times d$ matrix A and an integer parameter ℓ, any sketch $\ell \times d$ matrix B which satisfies the three properties above (for some any $\alpha \in (0, 1]$ and $\Delta > 0$), guarantees the following error bounds*

$$0 \le \|A^T A - B^T B\|_2 \le \frac{1}{\alpha\ell - k}\|A - A_k\|_F^2,$$

and

$$\|A - \pi_B^k(A)\|_F^2 \le \frac{\ell}{\ell - k/\alpha}\|A - A_k\|_F^2,$$

where $\pi_B^k(\cdot)$ represents the projection operator onto B_k, the top k singular vectors of B.

Another important property of FREQUENTDIRECTIONS is that its sketches are mergeable [17]. To clarify, consider partitioning a matrix A into t blocks $A_1, A_2, \cdots, A_t$ so that $A = [A_1; A_2; \cdots; A_t]$. Let $B_i = \text{FD}(A_i, \ell)$ denotes the FD sketch of the matrix block A_i, and $B' = \text{FD}([B_1; B_2; \cdots; B_t], \ell)$ denotes the FD sketch of all B_is combined together. It is shown that B' has at most as much covariance and projection error as $B = \text{FD}(A,\ell)$, i.e. the sketch of the whole matrix A. It follows that this divide-sketch-and-merging can also be applied recursively on each matrix block without increasing the error.

The runtime of FREQUENTDIRECTIONS is determined by the number of shrinking steps. Each of those computes an SVD of B which takes $O(d\ell^2)$ time. Since the SVD is called only every $O(\ell)$ rows this yields a total runtime $O(d\ell^2 \cdot n/\ell) = O(nd\ell)$. This effectively means that on average we are spending $O(d\ell)$ operations per row, even if the row is sparse.

In the present paper, we introduce a new method called as SPARSEFREQUENTDIRECTIONS that uses randomized SVD methods instead of the exact SVD to approximate the singular vectors and values of intermediate matrices B. We show how this new method tolerates the extra approximation error and runs in time proportional to $\text{nnz}(A)$. Moreover, since it received sparse matrix rows, it can observe more the ℓ rows until the size of the sketch doubles. As a remark, Ghashami and Phillips [18] showed that maintaining any rescaled set of ℓ rows of A over a stream is not a feasible approach to obtain sparsity in FREQUENTDIRECTIONS. It was left as an open problem to produce some version of FREQUENTDIRECTIONS that took advantage of the sparsity of A.

3.2 Simultaneous Iteration

Efficiently computing the singular vectors of matrices is one of the most well studies problems in scientific computing. Recent results give very strong approximation guarantees for block power method techniques [32][38][26][20]. Several variants of this algorithm were studied under different names in the literature e.g. Simultaneous Iteration, Subspace Iteration, or Orthogonal Iteration [19]. In this paper, we refer to this group of algorithms collectively as SIMULTANEOUSITERATION. A generic version of SIMULTANEOUSITERATION for rectangular matrices is described in Algorithm 1.

Algorithm 1 SimultaneousIteration

Input: $A \in \mathbb{R}^{n \times d}$, rank $k \leq \min(n, d)$, and error $\varepsilon \in (0, 1)$
$q = \Theta(\log(n/\varepsilon)/\varepsilon)$
$G \sim \mathcal{N}(0, 1)^{d \times k}$
$Z = \text{GramSchmidt}(A(A^T A)^q G)$
return Z # $Z \in \mathbb{R}^{n \times k}$

While this algorithm was already analyzed by [19], the proofs of [32, 20, 29, 37] manage to prove stable results that hold for any matrix independent of spectral gap issues. Unfortunately, an in depth discussion of these algorithms and their proof techniques is beyond the scope of this paper.

For the proof of correctness of SparseFrequentDirections, the main lemma proven by [29] suffices. SimultaneousIteration (Algorithm 1) guarantees the three following error bounds with high probability:

1. Frobenius norm error bound:
$$\|A - ZZ^T A\|_F \leq (1 + \varepsilon)\|A - A_k\|_F$$
2. Spectral norm error bound:
$$\|A - ZZ^T A\|_2 \leq (1 + \varepsilon)\|A - A_k\|_2$$
3. Per vector error bound:
$$|u_i^T AA^T u_i - z_i^T AA^T z_i| \leq \varepsilon\sigma_{k+1}^2$$
for all i. Here u_i denotes the ith left singular vector of A, and σ_{k+1} is the $(k + 1)$th singular value of A, and z_i is the ith column of the matrix Z returned by SimultaneousIteration.

In addition, for a constant ε, SimultaneousIteration runs in $\tilde{O}(\text{nnz}(A))$ time.

In this paper, we show that SparseFrequentDirections can replace the computation of an exact SVD by using the results of [29] with ε being a constant. This alteration does give up the optimal asymptotic accuracy (matching that of FrequentDirections).

4. SPARSE FREQUENT DIRECTIONS

The SparseFrequentDirections (SFD) algorithm is described in Algorithm 2, and is an extension of FrequentDirections to sparse matrices. It receives the rows of an input matrix A in a streaming fashion and maintains a sketch B of ℓ rows. Initially B is empty. On receiving rows of A, SFD stores non-zeros in a buffer matrix A'. The buffer is deemed full when it contains ℓd non-zeros or d rows. SFD then calls BoostedSparseShrink to produce its sketch matrix B' of size $\ell \times d$. Then, it updates its ongoing sketch B of the entire stream by merging it with the (dense) sketch B' using DenseShrink.

Algorithm 2 SparseFrequentDirections

Input: $A \in \mathbb{R}^{n \times d}$, an integer $\ell \leq d$, failure probability δ
$B = 0^{\ell \times d}$, $A' = 0^{0 \times d}$
for $a \in A$ **do**
  $A' = [A'; a]$
  if $\text{nnz}(A') \geq \ell d$ **or** $\text{rows}(A') = d$ **then**
    $B' = \text{BoostedSparseShrink}(A', \ell, \delta)$
    $B = \text{DenseShrink}([B; B'], \ell)$
    $A' = 0^{0 \times d}$
return B

BoostedSparseShrink amplifies the success probability of another algorithm SparseShrink in Algorithm 3. SparseShrink runs SimultaneousIteration instead of a full SVD to take advantage of the sparsity of its input A'. However, as we will discuss, by itself SparseShrink has too high of a probability of failure. Thus we use BoostedSparseShrink which keeps running SparseShrink and probabilistically verifying the correctness of its result using VerifySpectral, until it decides that the result is correct with high enough probability. Each of DenseShrink, SparseShrink, and BoostedSparseShrink produce sketch matrices of size $\ell \times d$.

Algorithm 3 SparseShrink

Input: $A' \in \mathbb{R}^{m \times d}$, an integer $\ell \leq m$
$Z = \text{SimultaneousIteration}(A', \ell, 1/4)$
$P = Z^T A'$, $[H, \Lambda, V] = \text{SVD}(P, \ell)$
$\tilde{\Lambda} = \sqrt{\Lambda^2 - \lambda_\ell^2 I_\ell}$
$B' = \tilde{\Lambda} V^T$
return B'

Algorithm 4 BoostedSparseShrink

Input: $A' \in \mathbb{R}^{m \times d}$, integer $\ell \leq m$, failure probability δ
while True **do**
  $B' = \text{SparseShrink}(A', \ell)$
  $\Delta = (\|A'\|_F^2 - \|B'\|_F^2)/\alpha\ell$ for $\alpha = 6/41$
  if $\text{VerifySpectral}((A'^T A' - B'^T B')/(\Delta/2), \delta)$ **then**
    return B'

Algorithm 5 DenseShrink

Input: $A \in \mathbb{R}^{m \times d}$, an integer $\ell \leq m$
$[H, \Lambda, V] = \text{SVD}(A, \ell)$
$\tilde{\Lambda} = \sqrt{\Lambda^2 - \lambda_\ell^2 I_\ell}$
$B = \tilde{\Lambda} V^T$
Return B

Our main result is stated in the next theorem. It follows from combining the proofs contained in the subsections below.

Theorem 4.1 (main result). *Given a sparse matrix $A \in \mathbb{R}^{n \times d}$ and an integer $\ell \leq d$, SparseFrequentDirections computes a small sketch $B \in \mathbb{R}^{\ell \times d}$ such that with probability at least $1 - \delta$ for $\alpha = 6/41$ and any $0 \leq k < \alpha\ell$,*
$$\|A^T A - B^T B\|_2 \leq \frac{1}{\alpha\ell - k}\|A - A_k\|_F^2$$
and
$$\|A - \pi_{B_k}(A)\|_F^2 \leq \frac{\ell}{\ell - k/\alpha}\|A - A_k\|_F^2.$$
The total memory footprint of the algorithm is $O(d\ell)$ and its expected running time is
$$O\left(\text{nnz}(A)\ell\log(d) + \text{nnz}(A)\log(n/\delta) + n\ell^2 + n\ell\log(n/\delta)\right).$$

4.1 Success Probability

SparseShrink, described in Algorithm 3, calls SimultaneousIteration to approximate the top rank ℓ subspace of A'. As SIMULTANEOUSITERATION is randomized, it fails to converge to a good subspace when the initial choice of the random matrix G does not sufficiently align with the top ℓ singular vectors of A' (see Algorithm 1). This occurs with probability at most $\rho_\ell = O(1/\sqrt{\ell})$. In Section 4.3.1, we prove that with probability of at least $1 - \rho_\ell$ that SPARSESHRINK satisfies the three properties required for Lemma 3.1 using $\alpha = 6/41$ and $\Delta = 41/8\ s_\ell^2$, but replacing Property 2 with a stronger version

- Property 2 (strengthened):

$$\|A'^T A' - B'^T B'\|_2 \leq (\Delta/2) = 41/16\ s_\ell^2$$

where s_ℓ denotes the ℓth singular value of A'.

However, for the proof of SPARSEFREQUENTDIRECTIONS we require that *all* SPARSESHRINK runs to be successful. The failure probability of SPARSESHRINK, which is upper bounded by $O(1/\sqrt{\ell})$, is high enough that a simple union bound would not give a meaningful bound on the failure probability of SPARSEFREQUENTDIRECTIONS. We therefore reduce the failure probability of each BOOSTEDSPARSESHRINK, by wrapping each call of SPARSESHRINK in the verifier VERIFYSPECTRAL. If VERIFYSPECTRAL does not verify the correctness, then it reruns SPARSESHRINK and tries again until it can verify it. But to perform this verification efficiently, we need to loosen the definition of correctness. In particular, we say SPARSESHRINK is successful if the sketch B' computed from its output satisfies $\|A'^T A' - B'^T B'\|_2 \leq \Delta$ (the original Property 2 specification in Section 3.1), where $\Delta = (\|A'\|_F^2 - \|B'\|_F^2)/\alpha\ell$. Combining the two inequalities through Δ, a successful run implies that $\|A'^T A' - B'^T B'\|_2 \leq (\|A'\|_F^2 - \|B'\|_F^2)/\alpha\ell$. VERIFYSPECTRAL verifies the success of the algorithm by approximating the spectral norm of $(A'^T A' - B'^T B')/(\Delta/2)$; it does so by running the power method for $c \cdot \log(d/\delta_i)$ steps for some constant c.

Algorithm 6 VERIFYSPECTRAL

Initialization persistent $i = 0$ (i retains its state between invocations of this method)
Input: Matrix $C \in \mathbb{R}^{d \times d}$, failure probability δ
$i = i + 1$ and $\delta_i = \delta/2i^2$
Pick x uniformly at random from the unit sphere in $\mathbb{R}^d$.
if $\|C^{c \cdot \log(d/\delta_i)} x\| \leq 1$ **return** TRUE
else return FALSE

LEMMA 4.1. *The* VERIFYSPECTRAL *algorithm returns* TRUE *if* $\|C\|_2 \leq 1$. *If* $\|C\|_2 \geq 2$ *it returns* FALSE *with probability at least* $1 - \delta_i$.

PROOF. If $\|C\| \leq 1$ than $\|C^{c \cdot \log(d/\delta_i)} x\| \leq \|C\|^{c \cdot \log(d/\delta_i)} \|x\| \leq 1$. If $\|C\| \geq 2$, consider execution i of the method. Let v_1 denote the top singular vector of C. Then $\|C^{c \cdot \log(d/\delta_i)} x\| \geq |\langle v_1, x\rangle| 2^{c \cdot \log(d/\delta_i)} \geq 1$, for some constant c as long as $|\langle v_1, x\rangle| = \Omega(\text{poly}(\delta_i/d))$. Let$\Phi(t')$ denote the density function of the random variable $t' = \langle v_1, x\rangle$. Then $\Pr[|\langle v_1, x\rangle| \leq t] = \int_{-t}^{t} \Phi(t')dt' \leq 2t\Phi(0) = O(t\sqrt{d})$. Setting the failure probability to be at most δ_i, we conclude that $|\langle v_1, x\rangle| = \Omega(\delta_i/\sqrt{d})$ with probability at least $1 - \delta_i$. □

Therefore, VERIFYSPECTRAL fails with probability at most δ_i during execution i. If any of VERIFYSPECTRAL runs fail, BOOSTEDSPARSESHRINK and hence SPARSEFREQUENTDIRECTIONS potentially fail. Taking the union bound over all invocations of VERIFYSPECTRAL we obtain that SPARSEFREQUENTDIRECTIONS fails with probability at most $\sum \delta_i \leq \sum_{i=1}^{\infty} \delta/2i^2 \leq \delta$, hence it succeeds with probability at least $1 - \delta$.

4.2 Space Usage and Runtime Analysis

Throughout this manuscript we assume the constant-word-size model. Integers and floating point numbers are represented by a constant number of bits. Random access into memory is assumed to require $O(1)$ time. In this model, multiplying a sparse matrix A' by a dense vector requires $O(\text{nnz}(A'))$ operations and storing A' requires $O(\text{nnz}(A'))$ bits of memory.

FACT 4.1. *The total memory footprint of* SPARSEFREQUENTDIRECTIONS *is* $O(d\ell)$.

PROOF. It is easy to verify that, except for the buffer matrix A', the algorithm only manipulates $\ell \times d$ matrices; in particular, observe that the $(\text{rows}(A') = d)$ condition in SPARSEFREQUENTDIRECTIONS ensures that $m = d$ in SPARSESHRINK, and in DENSESHRINK also $m = 2\ell$. Each of these $\ell \times d$ matrices clearly require at most $O(d\ell)$ bits of memory. The buffer matrix A' contains at most $O(d\ell)$ non-zeros and therefore does not increase the space complexity of the algorithm. □

We turn to bounding the expected runtime of SPARSEFREQUENTDIRECTIONS which is dominated by the cumulative running times of DENSESHRINK and BOOSTEDSPARSESHRINK. Denote by T the number of times they are executed. It is easy to verify $T \leq \text{nnz}(A)/d\ell + n/d$. Since DENSESHRINK runs in $O(d\ell^2)$ time deterministically, the total time spent by DENSESHRINK through T iterations is $O(Td\ell^2) = O(\text{nnz}(A)\ell + n\ell^2)$.

The running time of BOOSTEDSPARSESHRINK is dominated by those of SPARSESHRINK and VERIFYSPECTRAL, and its expected number of iterations. Note that, in expectation, they are each executed on any buffer matrix A'_i a small constant number of times because VERIFYSPECTRAL succeeds with probability (much) greater than 1/2. For asymptotic analysis it is identical to assuming they are each executed once.

Note that the running time of SPARSESHRINK on A'_i is $O(\text{nnz}(A'_i)\ell \log(d))$. Since $\sum_i \text{nnz}(A'_i) = \text{nnz}(A)$ we obtain a total running time of $O(\text{nnz}(A)\ell \log(d))$. The ith execution of VERIFYSPECTRAL requires $O(d\ell \log(d/\delta_i))$ operations. This, because it multiplies $A'^T A' - B'^T B'$ by a single vector $O(\log(d/\delta_i))$ times, and both $\text{nnz}(A') \leq O(d\ell)$ and $\text{nnz}(B') \leq d\ell$. In expectation VERIFYSPECTRAL is executed $O(T)$ times, therefore total running time of it is

$$O(d\ell \sum_{i=1}^{O(T)} \log(d/\delta_i)) = O(d\ell \sum_{i=1}^{O(T)} \log(di^2/\delta))$$
$$= O(Td\ell \log(Td/\delta)) = O((\text{nnz} + n\ell) \log(n/\delta)).$$

Combining the above contributions to the total running time of the algorithm we obtain Fact 4.2.

FACT 4.2. *Algorithm* SPARSEFREQUENTDIRECTIONS *runs in expected time of*

$$O(\text{nnz}(A)\ell \log(d) + \text{nnz}(A) \log(n/\delta) + n\ell^2 + n\ell \log(n/\delta)).$$

4.3 Error Analysis

We turn to proving the error bounds of Theorem 4.1. Our proof is divided into three parts. We first show that SPARSESHRINK obtains the three properties needed for Lemma 3.1 with probability at least $1-\rho_\ell$, and with the constraint on Property 2 strengthed by a factor 1/2. Then we show how loosening Property 2 back to its original bound enables BOOSTEDSPARSESHRINK to succeed with probability $1-\delta_i$ for some $\delta_i \ll \rho_\ell$. Finally we show that due to the mergeability of FREQUENTDIRECTIONS [25], discussed in Section 3.1, the SPARSEFREQUENTDIRECTIONS algorithm obtains the same error guarantees as BOOSTEDSPARSESHRINK with probability $1-\delta$ for a small δ of our choice.

In what follows, we mainly consider a single run of SPARSESHRINK or BOOSTEDSPARSESHRINK and let s_ℓ and u_ℓ denote the ℓth singular value and ℓth left singular vector of A', respectively.

4.3.1 *Error Analysis:* SPARSESHRINK

Here we show that with probability at least $1-\rho_\ell$ that B' computed from SPARSESHRINK(A',ℓ) satisfies the three properties discussed in Section 3.1 required for Lemma 3.1.

- Property 1: For any unit vector $x \in \mathbb{R}^d$, $\|A'x\|^2 - \|B'x\|^2 \geq 0$,
- Property 2 (strengthened): For any unit vector $x \in \mathbb{R}^d$, $\|A'x\|^2 - \|B'x\|^2 \leq \Delta/2 = (41/16)s_\ell^2$,
- Property 3: $\|A'\|_F^2 - \|B'\|_F^2 \geq \ell\alpha\Delta = \ell(3/4)s_\ell^2$.

LEMMA 4.2. *Property 1 holds deterministically for* SPARSESHRINK*:* $\|A'x\|^2 - \|B'x\|^2 \geq 0$ *for all* x.

PROOF. Let $P = Z^T A'$ be as defined in SPARSESHRINK. Consider an arbitrary unit vector $x \in \mathbb{R}^d$, and let $y = A'x$.

$$\begin{aligned}\|A'x\|^2 - \|Px\|^2 &= \|A'x\|^2 - \|Z^TA'x\|^2 = \|y\|^2 - \|Z^Ty\|^2 \\ &= \|(I-ZZ^T)y\|^2 \geq 0\end{aligned}$$

and

$$\|Px\|^2 - \|B'x\|^2 = \lambda_\ell^2 \sum_{i=1}^{\ell} \langle x, v_i\rangle^2 \geq 0,$$

therefore $\|A'x\|^2 - \|B'x\|^2 = (\|A'x\|^2 - \|Px\|^2) + (\|Px\|^2 - \|B'x\|^2) \geq 0$. □

LEMMA 4.3. *With probability at least* $1-\rho_\ell$*, Property 2 holds for* SPARSESHRINK*: for any unit vector* $x \in \mathbb{R}^d$*,* $\|A'x\|^2 - \|B'x\|^2 \leq 41/16\ s_\ell^2$.

PROOF. Consider an arbitrary unit vector $x \in \mathbb{R}^d$, and note that

$$\|A'x\|^2 - \|B'x\|^2 = \left(\|A'x\|^2 - \|Px\|^2\right) + \left(\|Px\|^2 - \|B'x\|^2\right).$$

We bound each term individually. The first term is bounded as

$$\begin{aligned}\|A'x\|^2 - \|Px\|^2 &= x^T(A'^TA' - P^TP)x & (1)\\ &\leq \|A'^TA' - P^TP\|_2 & (2)\\ &= \|A'^TA' - A'^TZZ^TA'\|_2 & (3)\\ &= \|A'^T(I-ZZ^T)A'\|_2 & (4)\\ &= \|A'^T(I-ZZ^T)^T(I-ZZ^T)A'\|_2 & (5)\\ &= \|(I-ZZ^T)A'\|_2^2 & (6)\\ &\leq 25/16\ s_{\ell+1}^2 \leq 25/16\ s_\ell^2. & (7)\end{aligned}$$

Where transition 5 is true because $(I-ZZ^T)$ is a projection. Transition 7 also holds by the spectral norm error bound of [29] for $\varepsilon = 1/4$. To bound the second term, note that $\|Px\| = \|Z^TA'x\| = \|\Lambda V^Tx\|$, since $[H,\Lambda,V] = \text{SVD}(P,\ell)$ as defined in SPARSESHRINK.

$$\|Px\|^2 - \|B'x\|^2 = \sum_{i=1}^{\ell}\lambda_i^2\langle x, v_i\rangle^2 - \sum_{i=1}^{\ell}\tilde{\lambda}_i^2\langle x, v_i\rangle^2 =$$

$$\sum_{i=1}^{\ell}(\lambda_i^2 - \tilde{\lambda}_i^2)\langle x, v_i\rangle^2 = \sum_{i=1}^{\ell}\lambda_\ell^2\langle x, v_i\rangle^2 \leq \lambda_\ell^2 \leq s_\ell^2,$$

where last inequality follows by the Courant-Fischer minmax principle, i.e. as λ_ℓ is the ℓth singular value of the projection of A' onto Z, then $\lambda_\ell \leq s_\ell$. Summing the two terms yields $\|A'x\|^2 - \|B'x\|^2 \leq 41/16\ s_\ell^2$. □

The original bound $\|A'^TA' - B'^TB'\|_2 \leq \Delta = 41/8\ s_\ell^2$ discussed in Section 4.1 is also immediately satisfied.

LEMMA 4.4. *With probability at least* $1-\rho_\ell$*, Property 3 holds for* SPARSESHRINK*:* $\|A'\|_F^2 - \|B'\|_F^2 \geq \ell(3/4)s_\ell^2$.

PROOF.

$$\|A'\|_F^2 - \|P\|_F^2 = \|A'\|_F^2 - \|Z^TA'\|_F^2 = \|A' - ZZ^TA'\|_F^2 \geq 0$$

In addition,

$$\|P\|_F^2 - \|B'\|_F^2 = \ell\lambda_\ell^2 \geq \ell(3/4)s_\ell^2\ .$$

The last inequality holds by the per vector error bound of [29] for $i=\ell$ and $\varepsilon = 1/4$, i.e. $|u_\ell^TA'A'^Tu_\ell - z_\ell^TA'A'^Tz_\ell| = |s_\ell^2 - \lambda_\ell^2| \leq 1/4 s_{\ell+1}^2 \leq 1/4 s_\ell^2$, which means $\lambda_\ell^2 \geq 3/4\ s_\ell^2$. Therefore

$$\|A'\|_F^2 - \|B'\|_F^2 = (\|A'\|_F^2 - \|P\|_F^2) + (\|P\|_F^2 - \|B'\|_F^2) \geq \ell(3/4)s_\ell^2.$$

□

4.3.2 *Error Analysis:* BOOSTEDSPARSESHRINK *and* SPARSEFREQUENTDIRECTIONS

We now consider the BOOSTEDSPARSESHRINK algorithm, and the looser version of Property 2 (the original version) as

- Property 2: For any unit vector $x \in \mathbb{R}^d$, $\|A'x\|^2 - \|B'x\|^2 \leq \Delta = (41/8)s_\ell^2$.

By invoking VERIFYSPECTRAL$((A'^TA' - B'^TB')/(\Delta/2), \delta)$, then VERIFYSPECTRAL always returns TRUE if $\|A'^TA' - B'^TB'\|_2 \leq \Delta/2$ (as is true of the input with probability at least $1-\rho_\ell$ by Lemma 4.3), and VERIFYSPECTRAL catches a failure event where $\|A'^TA' - B'^TB'\|_2 \geq \Delta$ with probability at least $1-\delta_i$ by Lemma 4.1. As discussed in Section 4.1 all invocations of VERIFYSPECTRAL succeed with probability at most $1-\delta$, hence all runs of BOOSTEDSPARSESHRINK succeed and satisfy Property 2 (as well as Properties 1 and 3) with $\alpha = 6/41$ and $\Delta = 41/8\ s_\ell^2$, and with probability at least $1-\delta$. Finally, we can invoke the mergeability property of FREQUENTDIRECTIONS [25] and Lemma 3.1 to obtain the error bounds in our main result, Theorem 4.1.

5. EXPERIMENTS

In this section we empirically validate that SPARSEFREQUENTDIRECTIONS matches (and often improves upon) the accuracy of FREQUENTDIRECTIONS, while running significantly faster on sparse real and synthetic datasets.

We do not implement SPARSEFREQUENTDIRECTIONS exactly as described above. Instead we directly call SPARSESHRINK in Algorithm 2 in place of BOOSTEDSPARSESHRINK. The randomized error analysis of SIMULTANEOUSITERATION indicates that we may occasionally miss a subspace within a call of SIMULTANEOUSITERATION and hence SPARSESHRINK; but in practice this is not a catastrophic event, and as we will observe, does not prevent SPARSEFREQUENTDIRECTIONS from obtaining small empirical error.

The empirical comparison of FREQUENTDIRECTIONS to other matrix sketching techniques is now well-trodden [17, 7]. FREQUENTDIRECTIONS (and, as we observe, by association SPARSEFREQUENTDIRECTIONS) has much smaller error than other sketching techniques which operate in a stream. However, FREQUENTDIRECTIONS is somewhat slower by a factor of the sketch size ℓ up to some leading coefficients. We do not repeat these comparison experiments here.

Setup. We ran all the algorithms under a common implementation framework to test their relative performance as accurately as possible. We ran the experiments on an Intel(R) Core(TM) 2.60 GHz CPU with 64GB of RAM running Ubuntu 14.04.3. All algorithms were coded in C, and compiled using gcc 4.8.4. All linear algebra operation on dense matrices (such as SVD) invoked those implemented in LAPACK.

Datasets. We compare the performance of the two algorithms on both synthetic and real datasets. Each dataset is an $n \times d$ matrix A containing n datapoints in d dimensions.

The real dataset is part of the 20 Newsgroups dataset [22], that is a collection of approximately 20,000 documents, partitioned across 20 different newsgroups. However we use the 'by date' version of the data, where features (columns) are tokens and rows correspond to documents. This data matrix is a zero-one matrix with 11,314 rows and 117,759 columns. In our experiment, we use the transpose of the data and picked the first $d = 3000$ columns, hence the subset matrix has $n = 117{,}759$ rows and $d = 3000$ columns; roughly 0.15% of the subset matrix is non-zeros.

The synthetic data generates n rows i.i.d. Each row receives exactly $z \ll d$ non-zeros (with default $z = 100$ and $d = 1000$), with the remaining entries as 0. The non-zeros are chosen as either 1 or -1 at random. Each non-zero location is chosen without duplicates among the columns. The first $1.5z$ columns (e.g., 150), the "head", have a higher probability of receiving a non-zero than the last $d - 1.5z$ columns, the "tail". The process to place a non-zero first chooses the head with probability 0.9 or the tail with probability 0.1. For whichever set of columns it chooses (head or tail), it places the non-zero uniformly at random among those columns.

Measurements. Each algorithm outputs a sketch matrix B of ℓ rows. For each of our experiments, we measure the efficiency of algorithms against one parameter and keep others fixed at a default value. Table 1 lists all parameters along with their default value and the range they vary in for synthetic dataset. We measure the accuracy of the algorithms with respect to:

- Projection Error:
  $\text{proj-err} = \|A - \pi_{B_k}(A)\|_F^2 / \|A - A_k\|_F^2$,
- Covariance Error:
  $\text{cov-err} = \|A^T A - B^T B\|_2 / \|A\|_F^2$,
- Runtime in seconds.

In all experiments, we have set $k = 10$. Note that proj-err is always larger than 1, and for FREQUENTDIRECTIONS and SPARSEFREQUENTDIRECTIONS the cov-err is always smaller than $1/(\frac{6}{41}\ell - k)$ due to our error guarantees.

5.1 Observations

By considering Table 2 on synthetic data and Figure 1 on the real data, we can vary and learn many aspects of the runtime and accuracy of SPARSEFREQUENTDIRECTIONS and FREQUENTDIRECTIONS.

Runtime. Consider the last row of Table 2, the "Run Time" row, and the last column of Figure 1. SPARSEFREQUENTDIRECTIONS is clearly faster than FREQUENTDIRECTIONS for all datasets, except when the synthetic data becomes dense in the last column of the "Run Time" row, where $d = 1000$ and nnz per row $= 500$ in the right-most data point. For the default values the improvement is between about a factor of 1.5x and $2x$, but when the matrix is very sparse the improvement is 10x or more. Very sparse synthetic examples are seen in the left data points of the last column, and in the right data points of the second column, of the "Run Time" row.

In particular, these two plots (the second and fourth columns of the "Run Time" row) really demonstrate the dependence of SPARSEFREQUENTDIRECTIONS on $\text{nnz}(A)$ and of FREQUENTDIRECTIONS on $n \cdot d$. In the last column, we fix the matrix size n and d, but increase the number of non-zeros $\text{nnz}(A)$; the runtime of FREQUENTDIRECTIONS is basically constant, while for SPARSEFREQUENTDIRECTIONS it grows linearly. In the second column, we fix n and $\text{nnz}(A)$, but increase the number of columns d; the runtime of FREQUENTDIRECTIONS grows linearly while the runtime for SPARSEFREQUENTDIRECTIONS is basically constant.

These algorithms are designed for datasets with extremely large values of n; yet we only run on datasets with n up to 60,000 in Table 2, and 117,759 in Figure 1. However, both FREQUENTDIRECTIONS and SPARSEFREQUENTDIRECTIONS have runtime that grows linearly with respect to the number of rows (assuming the sparsity is at an expected fixed rate per row for SPARSEFREQUENTDIRECTIONS). This can also be seen empirically in the first column of the "Run Time" row where, after a small start-up cost, both FREQUENTDIRECTIONS and SPARSEFREQUENTDIRECTIONS grow linearly as a function of the number of data points n. Hence, it is valid to directly extrapolate these results for datasets of increased n.

Accuracy. We will next discuss the accuracy, as measured in Projection Error in the top row of Table 2 and left plot of Figure 1, and in Covariance Error in the middle row of Table 2 and middle plot of Figure 1.

We observe that both FREQUENTDIRECTIONS and SPARSEFREQUENTDIRECTIONS obtain very small error (much smaller than upper bounded by the theory), as has been observed elsewhere [17, 7]. Moreover, the error for SPARSEFREQUENTDIRECTIONS always nearly matches, or improves over FRE-

Table 1: Parameter values

	default	range
datapoints (n)	10000	$[10^4 - 6 \times 10^4]$
dimension (d)	1000	$[10^3 - 6 \times 10^3]$
sketch size (ℓ)	50	$[5 - 100]$
nnz per row	100	$[5 - 500]$

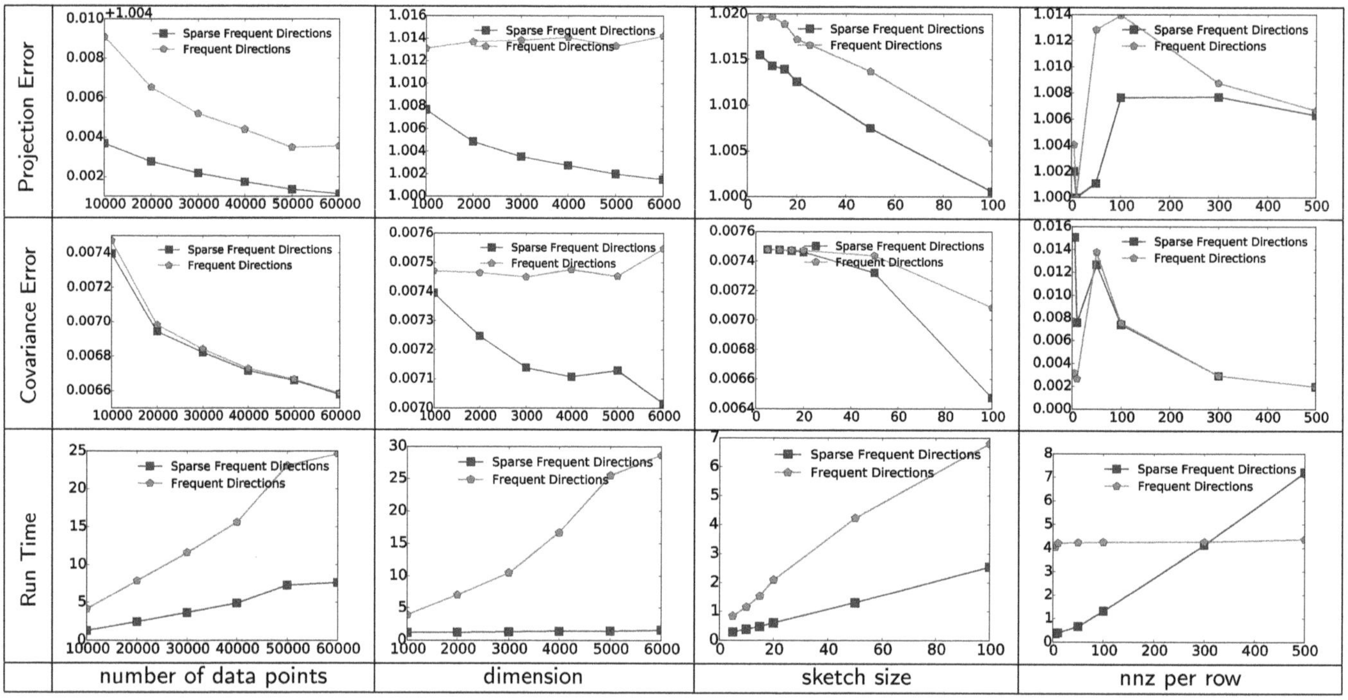

Table 2: Comparing performance of FrequentDirections and SparseFrequentDirections on synthetic data. Each column reports the measurement against one parameter; ordered from left to right it is number of datapoints (n), dimension (d), sketch size (ℓ), and number of non-zeros (nnz) per row. Table 1 lists default value of all parameters.

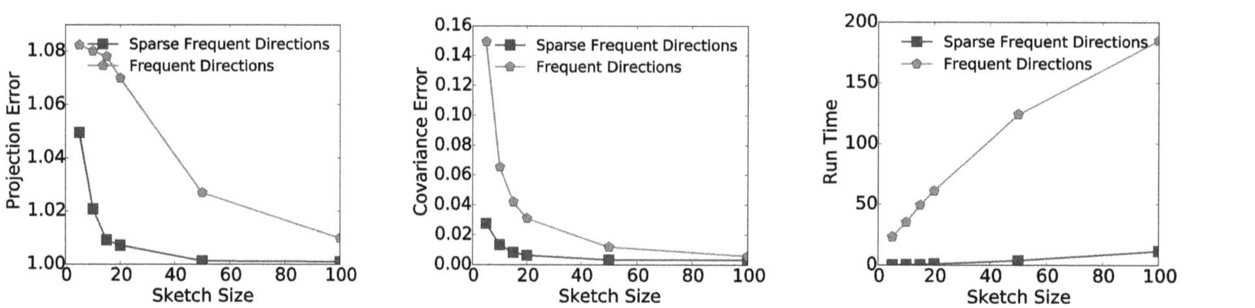

Figure 1: Comparing performance of FrequentDirections and SparseFrequentDirections on 20 Newsgroups dataset. We plot Projection Error, Covariance Error, and Run Time as a function of sketch size (ℓ).

QUENTDIRECTIONS. We can likely attribute this improvement to being able to process more rows in each batch, and hence needing to perform the shrinking operation fewer overall times. The one small exception to SPARSEFREQUENTDIRECTIONS having less Covariance Error than FREQUENTDIRECTIONS is for extreme sparse datasets in the leftmost data points of Table 2, last column – we attribute this to some peculiar orthogonality of columns with near equal norms due to extreme sparsity.

6. REFERENCES

[1] Nick Asendorf, Madison McGaffin, Matt Prelee, and Ben Schwartz. Algorithms for completing a user ratings matrix.

[2] Christos Boutsidis, Petros Drineas, and Malik Magdon-Ismail. Near optimal column-based matrix reconstruction. In *Foundations of Computer Science, 2011 IEEE 52nd Annual Symposium on*, pages 305–314. IEEE, 2011.

[3] Christos Boutsidis, Michael W Mahoney, and Petros Drineas. An improved approximation algorithm for the column subset selection problem. In *Proceedings of the 20th Annual ACM-SIAM Symposium on Discrete Algorithms*, 2009.

[4] Christos Boutsidis and David P Woodruff. Optimal cur matrix decompositions. In *Proceedings of the 46th Annual ACM Symposium on Theory of Computing*, pages 353–362. ACM, 2014.

[5] Matthew Brand. Incremental singular value decomposition of uncertain data with missing values. In *Computer Vision—ECCV 2002*, pages 707–720. Springer, 2002.

[6] Kenneth L. Clarkson and David P. Woodruff. Low rank approximation and regression in input sparsity time. In *Proceedings of the 45th Annual ACM Symposium on Symposium on Theory of Computing*, 2013.

[7] Amey Desai, Mina Ghashami, and Jeff M Phillips. Improved practical matrix sketching with guarantees. *arXiv preprint arXiv:1501.06561*, 2015.

[8] Amit Deshpande and Santosh Vempala. Adaptive sampling and fast low-rank matrix approximation. In *Approximation, Randomization, and Combinatorial Optimization. Algorithms and Techniques*, 2006.

[9] Inderjit S Dhillon and Dharmendra S Modha. Concept decompositions for large sparse text data using clustering. *Machine learning*, 42(1-2):143–175, 2001.

[10] Petros Drineas and Ravi Kannan. Pass efficient algorithms for approximating large matrices. In *Proceedings of the 14th Annual ACM-SIAM Symposium on Discrete Algorithms*, 2003.

[11] Petros Drineas, Ravi Kannan, and Michael W. Mahoney. Fast monte carlo algorithms for matrices ii: Computing a low-rank approximation to a matrix. *SIAM Journal on Computing*, 36(1):158–183, 2006.

[12] Petros Drineas, Ravi Kannan, and Michael W Mahoney. Fast monte carlo algorithms for matrices iii: Computing a compressed approximate matrix decomposition. *SIAM Journal on Computing*, 36(1):184–206, 2006.

[13] Petros Drineas, Iordanis Kerenidis, and Prabhakar Raghavan. Competitive recommendation systems. In *Proceedings of the thiry-fourth annual ACM symposium on Theory of computing*, pages 82–90. ACM, 2002.

[14] Petros Drineas, Michael W. Mahoney, and S. Muthukrishnan. Relative-error cur matrix decompositions. *SIAM Journal on Matrix Analysis and Applications*, 30(2):844–881, 2008.

[15] Petros Drineas, Michael W Mahoney, S Muthukrishnan, and Tamás Sarlós. Faster least squares approximation. *Numerische Mathematik*, 117:219–249, 2011.

[16] Alan Frieze, Ravi Kannan, and Santosh Vempala. Fast monte-carlo algorithms for finding low-rank approximations. *Journal of the ACM (JACM)*, 51(6):1025–1041, 2004.

[17] Mina Ghashami, Edo Liberty, Jeff M Phillips, and David P Woodruff. Frequent directions: Simple and deterministic matrix sketching. *arXiv preprint arXiv:1501.01711*, 2015.

[18] Mina Ghashami and Jeff M Phillips. Relative errors for deterministic low-rank matrix approximations. In *Proceedings of 25th ACM-SIAM Symposium on Discrete Algorithms*, 2014.

[19] Gene H Golub and Charles F Van Loan. *Matrix computations*, volume 3. JHUP, 2012.

[20] Nathan Halko, Per-Gunnar Martinsson, and Joel A Tropp. Finding structure with randomness: Probabilistic algorithms for constructing approximate matrix decompositions. *SIAM review*, 53(2):217–288, 2011.

[21] Peter Hall, David Marshall, and Ralph Martin. Incremental eigenanalysis for classification. In *Proceedings of the British Machine Vision Conference*, 1998.

[22] Ken Lang. Newsweeder: Learning to filter netnews. In *Proceedings of the Twelfth International Conference on Machine Learning*, pages 331–339, 1995.

[23] A Levey and Michael Lindenbaum. Sequential karhunen-loeve basis extraction and its application to images. *Image Processing, IEEE Transactions on*, 9(8):1371–1374, 2000.

[24] Edo Liberty. Simple and deterministic matrix sketching. In *Proceedings of the 19th ACM SIGKDD International Conference on Knowledge Discovery and Data Mining*, 2013.

[25] Edo Liberty. Simple and deterministic matrix sketching. In *Proceedings of the 19th ACM SIGKDD International Conference on Knowledge Discovery and Data Mining*, 2013.

[26] Edo Liberty, Franco Woolfe, Per-Gunnar Martinsson, Vladimir Rokhlin, and Mark Tygert. Randomized algorithms for the low-rank approximation of matrices. *Proceedings of the National Academy of Sciences*, 104(51):20167–20172, 2007.

[27] Michael W Mahoney and Petros Drineas. Cur matrix decompositions for improved data analysis. *Proceedings of the National Academy of Sciences*, 106(3):697–702, 2009.

[28] Jiří Matoušek. On variants of the johnson–lindenstrauss lemma. *Random Structures & Algorithms*, 33(2):142–156, 2008.

[29] Cameron Musco and Christopher Musco. Stronger approximate singular value decomposition via the block lanczos and power methods. *arXiv preprint arXiv:1504.05477*, 2015.

[30] Jelani Nelson and Huy L. Nguyen. OSNAP: Faster numerical linear algebra algorithms via sparser subspace embeddings. In *Proceedings of 54th IEEE Symposium on Foundations of Computer Science*, 2013.

[31] Christos H. Papadimitriou, Hisao Tamaki, Prabhakar Raghavan, and Santosh Vempala. Latent semantic indexing: A probabilistic analysis. In *Proceedings of the 17th ACM Symposium on Principles of Database Systems*, 1998.

[32] Vladimir Rokhlin, Arthur Szlam, and Mark Tygert. A randomized algorithm for principal component analysis. *SIAM Journal on Matrix Analysis and Applications*, 31(3):1100–1124, 2009.

[33] David A Ross, Jongwoo Lim, Ruei-Sung Lin, and Ming-Hsuan Yang. Incremental learning for robust

visual tracking. *International Journal of Computer Vision*, 77(1-3):125–141, 2008.

[34] Mark Rudelson and Roman Vershynin. Sampling from large matrices: An approach through geometric functional analysis. *Journal of the ACM*, 54(4):21, 2007.

[35] Tamas Sarlos. Improved approximation algorithms for large matrices via random projections. In *Proceedings of the 47th Annual IEEE Symposium on Foundations of Computer Science*, 2006.

[36] Santosh S Vempala. *The random projection method*, volume 65. American Mathematical Soc., 2004.

[37] Rafi Witten and Emmanuel Candès. Randomized algorithms for low-rank matrix factorizations: sharp performance bounds. *Algorithmica*, 72(1):264–281, 2013.

[38] Franco Woolfe, Edo Liberty, Vladimir Rokhlin, and Mark Tygert. A fast randomized algorithm for the approximation of matrices. *Applied and Computational Harmonic Analysis*, 25(3):335–366, 2008.

node2vec: Scalable Feature Learning for Networks

Aditya Grover
Stanford University
adityag@cs.stanford.edu

Jure Leskovec
Stanford University
jure@cs.stanford.edu

ABSTRACT

Prediction tasks over nodes and edges in networks require careful effort in engineering features used by learning algorithms. Recent research in the broader field of representation learning has led to significant progress in automating prediction by learning the features themselves. However, present feature learning approaches are not expressive enough to capture the diversity of connectivity patterns observed in networks.

Here we propose *node2vec*, an algorithmic framework for learning continuous feature representations for nodes in networks. In *node2vec*, we learn a mapping of nodes to a low-dimensional space of features that maximizes the likelihood of preserving network neighborhoods of nodes. We define a flexible notion of a node's network neighborhood and design a biased random walk procedure, which efficiently explores diverse neighborhoods. Our algorithm generalizes prior work which is based on rigid notions of network neighborhoods, and we argue that the added flexibility in exploring neighborhoods is the key to learning richer representations.

We demonstrate the efficacy of *node2vec* over existing state-of-the-art techniques on multi-label classification and link prediction in several real-world networks from diverse domains. Taken together, our work represents a new way for efficiently learning state-of-the-art task-independent representations in complex networks.

Categories and Subject Descriptors: H.2.8 **[Database Management]**: Database applications—*Data mining*; I.2.6 **[Artificial Intelligence]**: Learning
General Terms: Algorithms; Experimentation.
Keywords: Information networks, Feature learning, Node embeddings, Graph representations.

1. INTRODUCTION

Many important tasks in network analysis involve predictions over nodes and edges. In a typical node classification task, we are interested in predicting the most probable labels of nodes in a network [33]. For example, in a social network, we might be interested in predicting interests of users, or in a protein-protein interaction network we might be interested in predicting functional labels of proteins [25, 37]. Similarly, in link prediction, we wish to predict whether a pair of nodes in a network should have an edge connecting them [18]. Link prediction is useful in a wide variety of domains; for instance, in genomics, it helps us discover novel interactions between genes, and in social networks, it can identify real-world friends [2, 34].

Any supervised machine learning algorithm requires a set of informative, discriminating, and independent features. In prediction problems on networks this means that one has to construct a feature vector representation for the nodes and edges. A typical solution involves hand-engineering domain-specific features based on expert knowledge. Even if one discounts the tedious effort required for feature engineering, such features are usually designed for specific tasks and do not generalize across different prediction tasks.

An alternative approach is to *learn* feature representations by solving an optimization problem [4]. The challenge in feature learning is defining an objective function, which involves a trade-off in balancing computational efficiency and predictive accuracy. On one side of the spectrum, one could directly aim to find a feature representation that optimizes performance of a downstream prediction task. While this supervised procedure results in good accuracy, it comes at the cost of high training time complexity due to a blowup in the number of parameters that need to be estimated. At the other extreme, the objective function can be defined to be independent of the downstream prediction task and the representations can be learned in a purely unsupervised way. This makes the optimization computationally efficient and with a carefully designed objective, it results in task-independent features that closely match task-specific approaches in predictive accuracy [21, 23].

However, current techniques fail to satisfactorily define and optimize a reasonable objective required for scalable unsupervised feature learning in networks. Classic approaches based on linear and non-linear dimensionality reduction techniques such as Principal Component Analysis, Multi-Dimensional Scaling and their extensions [3, 27, 30, 35] optimize an objective that transforms a representative data matrix of the network such that it maximizes the variance of the data representation. Consequently, these approaches invariably involve eigendecomposition of the appropriate data matrix which is expensive for large real-world networks. Moreover, the resulting latent representations give poor performance on various prediction tasks over networks.

Alternatively, we can design an objective that seeks to preserve local neighborhoods of nodes. The objective can be efficiently optimized using stochastic gradient descent (SGD) akin to backpropogation on just single hidden-layer feedforward neural networks. Recent attempts in this direction [24, 28] propose efficient algorithms but rely on a rigid notion of a network neighborhood, which results in these approaches being largely insensitive to connectivity patterns unique to networks. Specifically, nodes in networks

KDD '16, August 13 - 17, 2016, San Francisco, CA, USA

ISBN 978-1-4503-4232-2/16/08... $15.00

DOI: http://dx.doi.org/10.1145/2939672.2939754

could be organized based on communities they belong to (*i.e.*, *homophily*); in other cases, the organization could be based on the structural roles of nodes in the network (*i.e.*, *structural equivalence*) [7, 10, 36]. For instance, in Figure 1, we observe nodes u and s_1 belonging to the same tightly knit community of nodes, while the nodes u and s_6 in the two distinct communities share the same structural role of a hub node. Real-world networks commonly exhibit a mixture of such equivalences. Thus, it is essential to allow for a flexible algorithm that can learn node representations obeying both principles: ability to learn representations that embed nodes from the same network community closely together, as well as to learn representations where nodes that share similar roles have similar embeddings. This would allow feature learning algorithms to generalize across a wide variety of domains and prediction tasks.

Present work. We propose *node2vec*, a semi-supervised algorithm for scalable feature learning in networks. We optimize a custom graph-based objective function using SGD motivated by prior work on natural language processing [21]. Intuitively, our approach returns feature representations that maximize the likelihood of preserving network neighborhoods of nodes in a d-dimensional feature space. We use a 2nd order random walk approach to generate (sample) network neighborhoods for nodes.

Our key contribution is in defining a flexible notion of a node's network neighborhood. By choosing an appropriate notion of a neighborhood, *node2vec* can learn representations that organize nodes based on their network roles and/or communities they belong to. We achieve this by developing a family of biased random walks, which efficiently explore diverse neighborhoods of a given node. The resulting algorithm is flexible, giving us control over the search space through tunable parameters, in contrast to rigid search procedures in prior work [24, 28]. Consequently, our method generalizes prior work and can model the full spectrum of equivalences observed in networks. The parameters governing our search strategy have an intuitive interpretation and bias the walk towards different network exploration strategies. These parameters can also be learned directly using a tiny fraction of labeled data in a semi-supervised fashion.

We also show how feature representations of individual nodes can be extended to pairs of nodes (*i.e.*, edges). In order to generate feature representations of edges, we compose the learned feature representations of the individual nodes using simple binary operators. This compositionality lends *node2vec* to prediction tasks involving nodes as well as edges.

Our experiments focus on two common prediction tasks in networks: a multi-label classification task, where every node is assigned one or more class labels and a link prediction task, where we predict the existence of an edge given a pair of nodes. We contrast the performance of *node2vec* with state-of-the-art feature learning algorithms [24, 28]. We experiment with several real-world networks from diverse domains, such as social networks, information networks, as well as networks from systems biology. Experiments demonstrate that *node2vec* outperforms state-of-the-art methods by up to 26.7% on multi-label classification and up to 12.6% on link prediction. The algorithm shows competitive performance with even 10% labeled data and is also robust to perturbations in the form of noisy or missing edges. Computationally, the major phases of *node2vec* are trivially parallelizable, and it can scale to large networks with millions of nodes in a few hours.

Overall our paper makes the following contributions:

1. We propose *node2vec*, an efficient scalable algorithm for feature learning in networks that efficiently optimizes a novel network-aware, neighborhood preserving objective using SGD.
2. We show how *node2vec* is in accordance with established principles in network science, providing flexibility in discovering representations conforming to different equivalences.
3. We extend *node2vec* and other feature learning methods based on neighborhood preserving objectives, from nodes to pairs of nodes for edge-based prediction tasks.
4. We empirically evaluate *node2vec* for multi-label classification and link prediction on several real-world datasets.

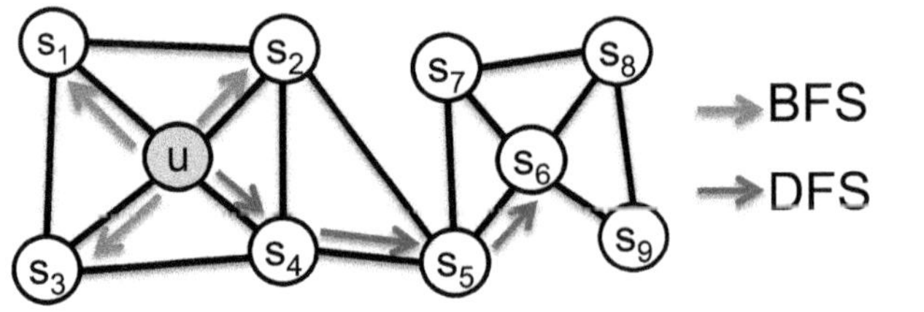

Figure 1: BFS and DFS search strategies from node u ($k = 3$).

The rest of the paper is structured as follows. In Section 2, we briefly survey related work in feature learning for networks. We present the technical details for feature learning using *node2vec* in Section 3. In Section 4, we empirically evaluate *node2vec* on prediction tasks over nodes and edges on various real-world networks and assess the parameter sensitivity, perturbation analysis, and scalability aspects of our algorithm. We conclude with a discussion of the *node2vec* framework and highlight some promising directions for future work in Section 5. Datasets and a reference implementation of *node2vec* are available on the project page: http://snap.stanford.edu/node2vec.

2. RELATED WORK

Feature engineering has been extensively studied by the machine learning community under various headings. In networks, the conventional paradigm for generating features for nodes is based on feature extraction techniques which typically involve some seed hand-crafted features based on network properties [8, 11]. In contrast, our goal is to automate the whole process by casting feature extraction as a representation learning problem in which case we do not require any hand-engineered features.

Unsupervised feature learning approaches typically exploit the spectral properties of various matrix representations of graphs, especially the Laplacian and the adjacency matrices. Under this linear algebra perspective, these methods can be viewed as dimensionality reduction techniques. Several linear (*e.g.*, PCA) and non-linear (*e.g.*, IsoMap) dimensionality reduction techniques have been proposed [3, 27, 30, 35]. These methods suffer from both computational and statistical performance drawbacks. In terms of computational efficiency, eigendecomposition of a data matrix is expensive unless the solution quality is significantly compromised with approximations, and hence, these methods are hard to scale to large networks. Secondly, these methods optimize for objectives that are not robust to the diverse patterns observed in networks (such as homophily and structural equivalence) and make assumptions about the relationship between the underlying network structure and the prediction task. For instance, spectral clustering makes a strong homophily assumption that graph cuts will be useful for classification [29]. Such assumptions are reasonable in many scenarios, but unsatisfactory in effectively generalizing across diverse networks.

Recent advancements in representational learning for natural language processing opened new ways for feature learning of discrete objects such as words. In particular, the Skip-gram model [21] aims to learn continuous feature representations for words by optimizing a neighborhood preserving likelihood objective. The algorithm proceeds as follows: It scans over the words of a document, and for every word it aims to embed it such that the word's features can predict nearby words (*i.e.*, words inside some context window). The word feature representations are learned by optmizing the likelihood objective using SGD with negative sampling [22]. The Skip-gram objective is based on the distributional hypothesis which states that words in similar contexts tend to have similar meanings [9]. That is, similar words tend to appear in similar word neighborhoods.

Inspired by the Skip-gram model, recent research established an analogy for networks by representing a network as a "document" [24, 28]. The same way as a document is an ordered sequence of words, one could sample sequences of nodes from the underlying network and turn a network into a ordered sequence of nodes. However, there are many possible sampling strategies for nodes, resulting in different learned feature representations. In fact, as we shall show, there is no clear winning sampling strategy that works across all networks and all prediction tasks. This is a major shortcoming of prior work which fail to offer any flexibility in sampling of nodes from a network [24, 28]. Our algorithm *node2vec* overcomes this limitation by designing a flexible objective that is not tied to a particular sampling strategy and provides parameters to tune the explored search space (see Section 3).

Finally, for both node and edge based prediction tasks, there is a body of recent work for supervised feature learning based on existing and novel graph-specific deep network architectures [15, 16, 17, 31, 39]. These architectures directly minimize the loss function for a downstream prediction task using several layers of non-linear transformations which results in high accuracy, but at the cost of scalability due to high training time requirements.

3. FEATURE LEARNING FRAMEWORK

We formulate feature learning in networks as a maximum likelihood optimization problem. Let $G = (V, E)$ be a given network. Our analysis is general and applies to any (un)directed, (un)weighted network. Let $f : V \to \mathbb{R}^d$ be the mapping function from nodes to feature representaions we aim to learn for a downstream prediction task. Here d is a parameter specifying the number of dimensions of our feature representation. Equivalently, f is a matrix of size $|V| \times d$ parameters. For every source node $u \in V$, we define $N_S(u) \subset V$ as a *network neighborhood* of node u generated through a neighborhood sampling strategy S.

We proceed by extending the Skip-gram architecture to networks [21, 24]. We seek to optimize the following objective function, which maximizes the log-probability of observing a network neighborhood $N_S(u)$ for a node u conditioned on its feature representation, given by f:

$$\max_f \sum_{u \in V} \log Pr(N_S(u)|f(u)). \tag{1}$$

In order to make the optimization problem tractable, we make two standard assumptions:

- Conditional independence. We factorize the likelihood by assuming that the likelihood of observing a neighborhood node is independent of observing any other neighborhood node given the feature representation of the source:

$$Pr(N_S(u)|f(u)) = \prod_{n_i \in N_S(u)} Pr(n_i|f(u)).$$

- Symmetry in feature space. A source node and neighborhood node have a symmetric effect over each other in feature space. Accordingly, we model the conditional likelihood of every source-neighborhood node pair as a softmax unit parametrized by a dot product of their features:

$$Pr(n_i|f(u)) = \frac{\exp(f(n_i) \cdot f(u))}{\sum_{v \in V} \exp(f(v) \cdot f(u))}.$$

With the above assumptions, the objective in Eq. 1 simplifies to:

$$\max_f \sum_{u \in V} \Big[-\log Z_u + \sum_{n_i \in N_S(u)} f(n_i) \cdot f(u) \Big]. \tag{2}$$

The per-node partition function, $Z_u = \sum_{v \in V} \exp(f(u) \cdot f(v))$, is expensive to compute for large networks and we approximate it using negative sampling [22]. We optimize Eq. 2 using stochastic gradient ascent over the model parameters defining the features f.

Feature learning methods based on the Skip-gram architecture have been originally developed in the context of natural language [21]. Given the linear nature of text, the notion of a neighborhood can be naturally defined using a sliding window over consecutive words. Networks, however, are not linear, and thus a richer notion of a neighborhood is needed. To resolve this issue, we propose a randomized procedure that samples many different neighborhoods of a given source node u. The neighborhoods $N_S(u)$ are not restricted to just immediate neighbors but can have vastly different structures depending on the sampling strategy S.

3.1 Classic search strategies

We view the problem of sampling neighborhoods of a source node as a form of local search. Figure 1 shows a graph, where given a source node u we aim to generate (sample) its neighborhood $N_S(u)$. Importantly, to be able to fairly compare different sampling strategies S, we shall constrain the size of the neighborhood set N_S to k nodes and then sample multiple sets for a single node u. Generally, there are two extreme sampling strategies for generating neighborhood set(s) N_S of k nodes:

- **Breadth-first Sampling (BFS)** The neighborhood N_S is restricted to nodes which are immediate neighbors of the source. For example, in Figure 1 for a neighborhood of size $k = 3$, BFS samples nodes s_1, s_2, s_3.
- **Depth-first Sampling (DFS)** The neighborhood consists of nodes sequentially sampled at increasing distances from the source node. In Figure 1, DFS samples s_4, s_5, s_6.

The breadth-first and depth-first sampling represent extreme scenarios in terms of the search space they explore leading to interesting implications on the learned representations.

In particular, prediction tasks on nodes in networks often shuttle between two kinds of similarities: homophily and structural equivalence [12]. Under the homophily hypothesis [7, 36] nodes that are highly interconnected and belong to similar network clusters or communities should be embedded closely together (*e.g.*, nodes s_1 and u in Figure 1 belong to the same network community). In contrast, under the structural equivalence hypothesis [10] nodes that have similar structural roles in networks should be embedded closely together (*e.g.*, nodes u and s_6 in Figure 1 act as hubs of their corresponding communities). Importantly, unlike homophily, structural equivalence does not emphasize connectivity; nodes could be far apart in the network and still have the same structural role. In real-world, these equivalence notions are not exclusive; networks commonly exhibit both behaviors where some nodes exhibit homophily while others reflect structural equivalence.

We observe that BFS and DFS strategies play a key role in producing representations that reflect either of the above equivalences. In particular, the neighborhoods sampled by BFS lead to embeddings that correspond closely to structural equivalence. Intuitively, we note that in order to ascertain structural equivalence, it is often sufficient to characterize the local neighborhoods accurately. For example, structural equivalence based on network roles such as bridges and hubs can be inferred just by observing the immediate neighborhoods of each node. By restricting search to nearby nodes, BFS achieves this characterization and obtains a microscopic view of the neighborhood of every node. Additionally, in BFS, nodes in the sampled neighborhoods tend to repeat many times. This is also important as it reduces the variance in characterizing the distribution of 1-hop nodes with respect the source node. However, a very small portion of the graph is explored for any given k.

The opposite is true for DFS which can explore larger parts of the network as it can move further away from the source node u (with sample size k being fixed). In DFS, the sampled nodes more accurately reflect a macro-view of the neighborhood which is essential in inferring communities based on homophily. However, the issue with DFS is that it is important to not only infer which node-to-node dependencies exist in a network, but also to characterize the exact nature of these dependencies. This is hard given we have a constrain on the sample size and a large neighborhood to explore, resulting in high variance. Secondly, moving to much greater depths leads to complex dependencies since a sampled node may be far from the source and potentially less representative.

3.2 node2vec

Building on the above observations, we design a flexible neighborhood sampling strategy which allows us to smoothly interpolate between BFS and DFS. We achieve this by developing a flexible biased random walk procedure that can explore neighborhoods in a BFS as well as DFS fashion.

3.2.1 *Random Walks*

Formally, given a source node u, we simulate a random walk of fixed length l. Let c_i denote the ith node in the walk, starting with $c_0 = u$. Nodes c_i are generated by the following distribution:

$$P(c_i = x \mid c_{i-1} = v) = \begin{cases} \frac{\pi_{vx}}{Z} & \text{if } (v, x) \in E \\ 0 & \text{otherwise} \end{cases}$$

where π_{vx} is the unnormalized transition probability between nodes v and x, and Z is the normalizing constant.

3.2.2 *Search bias α*

The simplest way to bias our random walks would be to sample the next node based on the static edge weights w_{vx} *i.e.*, $\pi_{vx} = w_{vx}$. (In case of unweighted graphs $w_{vx} = 1$.) However, this does not allow us to account for the network structure and guide our search procedure to explore different types of network neighborhoods. Additionally, unlike BFS and DFS which are extreme sampling paradigms suited for structural equivalence and homophily respectively, our random walks should accommodate for the fact that these notions of equivalence are not competing or exclusive, and real-world networks commonly exhibit a mixture of both.

We define a 2nd order random walk with two parameters p and q which guide the walk: Consider a random walk that just traversed edge (t, v) and now resides at node v (Figure 2). The walk now needs to decide on the next step so it evaluates the transition probabilities π_{vx} on edges (v, x) leading from v. We set the unnormalized transition probability to $\pi_{vx} = \alpha_{pq}(t, x) \cdot w_{vx}$, where

$$\alpha_{pq}(t, x) = \begin{cases} \frac{1}{p} & \text{if } d_{tx} = 0 \\ 1 & \text{if } d_{tx} = 1 \\ \frac{1}{q} & \text{if } d_{tx} = 2 \end{cases}$$

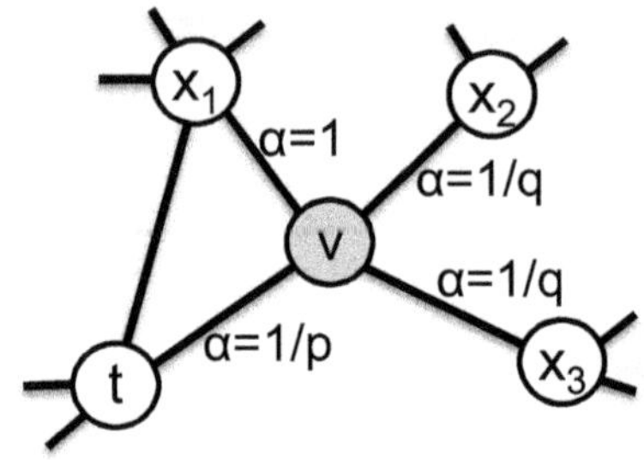

Figure 2: Illustration of the random walk procedure in *node2vec*. The walk just transitioned from t to v and is now evaluating its next step out of node v. Edge labels indicate search biases α.

and d_{tx} denotes the shortest path distance between nodes t and x. Note that d_{tx} must be one of $\{0, 1, 2\}$, and hence, the two parameters are necessary and sufficient to guide the walk.

Intuitively, parameters p and q control how fast the walk explores and leaves the neighborhood of starting node u. In particular, the parameters allow our search procedure to (approximately) interpolate between BFS and DFS and thereby reflect an affinity for different notions of node equivalences.

Return parameter, p. Parameter p controls the likelihood of immediately revisiting a node in the walk. Setting it to a high value ($> \max(q, 1)$) ensures that we are less likely to sample an already-visited node in the following two steps (unless the next node in the walk had no other neighbor). This strategy encourages moderate exploration and avoids 2-hop redundancy in sampling. On the other hand, if p is low ($< \min(q, 1)$), it would lead the walk to backtrack a step (Figure 2) and this would keep the walk "local" close to the starting node u.

In-out parameter, q. Parameter q allows the search to differentiate between "inward" and "outward" nodes. Going back to Figure 2, if $q > 1$, the random walk is biased towards nodes close to node t. Such walks obtain a local view of the underlying graph with respect to the start node in the walk and approximate BFS behavior in the sense that our samples comprise of nodes within a small locality.

In contrast, if $q < 1$, the walk is more inclined to visit nodes which are further away from the node t. Such behavior is reflective of DFS which encourages outward exploration. However, an essential difference here is that we achieve DFS-like exploration within the random walk framework. Hence, the sampled nodes are not at strictly increasing distances from a given source node u, but in turn, we benefit from tractable preprocessing and superior sampling efficiency of random walks. Note that by setting $\pi_{v,x}$ to be a function of the preceeding node in the walk t, the random walks are 2nd order Markovian.

Benefits of random walks. There are several benefits of random walks over pure BFS/DFS approaches. Random walks are computationally efficient in terms of both space and time requirements. The space complexity to store the immediate neighbors of every node in the graph is $O(|E|)$. For 2nd order random walks, it is helpful to store the interconnections between the neighbors of every node, which incurs a space complexity of $O(a^2|V|)$ where a is the average degree of the graph and is usually small for real-world networks. The other key advantage of random walks over classic search-based sampling strategies is its time complexity. In particular, by imposing graph connectivity in the sample generation process, random walks provide a convenient mechanism to increase the effective sampling rate by reusing samples across different source nodes. By simulating a random walk of length $l > k$ we can generate k samples for $l - k$ nodes at once due to the Marko-

Operator	Symbol	Definition
Average	$\boxplus$	$[f(u) \boxplus f(v)]_i = \frac{f_i(u)+f_i(v)}{2}$
Hadamard	$\boxdot$	$[f(u) \boxdot f(v)]_i = f_i(u) * f_i(v)$
Weighted-L1	$\|\cdot\|_{\bar{1}}$	$\|f(u) \cdot f(v)\|_{\bar{1}i} = \|f_i(u) - f_i(v)\|$
Weighted-L2	$\|\cdot\|_{\bar{2}}$	$\|f(u) \cdot f(v)\|_{\bar{2}i} = \|f_i(u) - f_i(v)\|^2$

Table 1: Choice of binary operators $\circ$ for learning edge features. The definitions correspond to the ith component of $g(u, v)$.

vian nature of the random walk. Hence, our effective complexity is $O(\frac{l}{k(l-k)})$ per sample. For example, in Figure 1 we sample a random walk $\{u, s_4, s_5, s_6, s_8, s_9\}$ of length $l = 6$, which results in $N_S(u) = \{s_4, s_5, s_6\}$, $N_S(s_4) = \{s_5, s_6, s_8\}$ and $N_S(s_5) = \{s_6, s_8, s_9\}$. Note that sample reuse can introduce some bias in the overall procedure. However, we observe that it greatly improves the efficiency.

3.2.3 The node2vec algorithm

Algorithm 1 The *node2vec* algorithm.

LearnFeatures (Graph $G = (V, E, W)$, Dimensions d, Walks per node r, Walk length l, Context size k, Return p, In-out q)
  π = PreprocessModifiedWeights(G, p, q)
  $G' = (V, E, \pi)$
  Initialize $walks$ to Empty
  for $iter = 1$ **to** r **do**
    for all nodes $u \in V$ **do**
      $walk$ = node2vecWalk(G', u, l)
      Append $walk$ to $walks$
  f = StochasticGradientDescent(k, d, $walks$)
  return f

node2vecWalk (Graph $G' = (V, E, \pi)$, Start node u, Length l)
  Inititalize $walk$ to $[u]$
  for $walk\_iter = 1$ **to** l **do**
    $curr = walk[-1]$
    V_{curr} = GetNeighbors($curr$, G')
    s = AliasSample(V_{curr}, π)
    Append s to $walk$
  return $walk$

The pseudocode for *node2vec*, is given in Algorithm 1. In any random walk, there is an implicit bias due to the choice of the start node u. Since we learn representations for all nodes, we offset this bias by simulating r random walks of fixed length l starting from *every* node. At every step of the walk, sampling is done based on the transition probabilities π_{vx}. The transition probabilities π_{vx} for the 2nd order Markov chain can be precomputed and hence, sampling of nodes while simulating the random walk can be done efficiently in $O(1)$ time using alias sampling. The three phases of *node2vec*, *i.e.*, preprocessing to compute transition probabilities, random walk simulations and optimization using SGD, are executed sequentially. Each phase is parallelizable and executed asynchronously, contributing to the overall scalability of *node2vec*.

node2vec is available at: http://snap.stanford.edu/node2vec.

3.3 Learning edge features

The *node2vec* algorithm provides a semi-supervised method to learn rich feature representations for nodes in a network. However, we are often interested in prediction tasks involving pairs of nodes instead of individual nodes. For instance, in link prediction, we predict whether a link exists between two nodes in a network. Since our random walks are naturally based on the connectivity structure between nodes in the underlying network, we extend them to pairs of nodes using a bootstrapping approach over the feature representations of the individual nodes.

Given two nodes u and v, we define a binary operator $\circ$ over the corresponding feature vectors $f(u)$ and $f(v)$ in order to generate a representation $g(u, v)$ such that $g : V \times V \rightarrow \mathbb{R}^{d'}$ where d' is the representation size for the pair (u, v). We want our operators to be generally defined for any pair of nodes, even if an edge does not exist between the pair since doing so makes the representations useful for link prediction where our test set contains both true and false edges (*i.e.*, do not exist). We consider several choices for the operator $\circ$ such that $d' = d$ which are summarized in Table 1.

4. EXPERIMENTS

The objective in Eq. 2 is independent of any downstream task and the flexibility in exploration offered by *node2vec* lends the learned feature representations to a wide variety of network analysis settings discussed below.

4.1 Case Study: Les Misérables network

In Section 3.1 we observed that BFS and DFS strategies represent extreme ends on the spectrum of embedding nodes based on the principles of homophily (*i.e.*, network communities) and structural equivalence (*i.e.*, structural roles of nodes). We now aim to empirically demonstrate this fact and show that *node2vec* in fact can discover embeddings that obey both principles.

We use a network where nodes correspond to characters in the novel Les Misérables [13] and edges connect coappearing characters. The network has 77 nodes and 254 edges. We set $d = 16$ and run *node2vec* to learn feature representation for every node in the network. The feature representations are clustered using k-means. We then visualize the original network in two dimensions with nodes now assigned colors based on their clusters.

Figure 3(top) shows the example when we set $p = 1, q = 0.5$. Notice how regions of the network (*i.e.*, network communities) are colored using the same color. In this setting *node2vec* discovers clusters/communities of characters that frequently interact with each other in the major sub-plots of the novel. Since the edges between characters are based on coappearances, we can conclude this characterization closely relates with homophily.

In order to discover which nodes have the same structural roles we use the same network but set $p = 1, q = 2$, use *node2vec* to get node features and then cluster the nodes based on the obtained features. Here *node2vec* obtains a complementary assignment of node to clusters such that the colors correspond to structural equivalence as illustrated in Figure 3(bottom). For instance, *node2vec* embeds blue-colored nodes close together. These nodes represent characters that act as bridges between different sub-plots of the novel. Similarly, the yellow nodes mostly represent characters that are at the periphery and have limited interactions. One could assign alternate semantic interpretations to these clusters of nodes, but the key takeaway is that *node2vec* is not tied to a particular notion of equivalence. As we show through our experiments, these equivalence notions are commonly exhibited in most real-world networks and have a significant impact on the performance of the learned representations for prediction tasks.

4.2 Experimental setup

Our experiments evaluate the feature representations obtained through *node2vec* on standard supervised learning tasks: multilabel classification for nodes and link prediction for edges. For both tasks, we evaluate the performance of *node2vec* against the following feature learning algorithms:

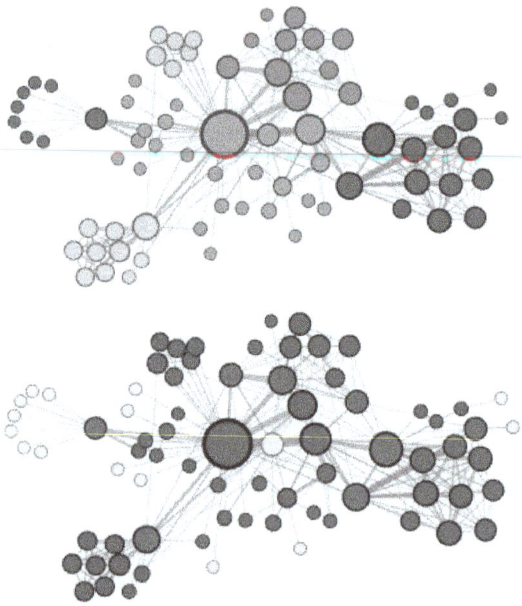

Figure 3: Complementary visualizations of Les Misérables coappearance network generated by *node2vec* with label colors reflecting homophily (top) and structural equivalence (bottom).

- Spectral clustering [29]: This is a matrix factorization approach in which we take the top d eigenvectors of the normalized Laplacian matrix of graph G as the feature vector representations for nodes.
- DeepWalk [24]: This approach learns d-dimensional feature representations by simulating uniform random walks. The sampling strategy in DeepWalk can be seen as a special case of *node2vec* with $p = 1$ and $q = 1$.
- LINE [28]: This approach learns d-dimensional feature representations in two separate phases. In the first phase, it learns $d/2$ dimensions by BFS-style simulations over immediate neighbors of nodes. In the second phase, it learns the next $d/2$ dimensions by sampling nodes strictly at a 2-hop distance from the source nodes.

We exclude other matrix factorization approaches which have already been shown to be inferior to DeepWalk [24]. We also exclude a recent approach, GraRep [6], that generalizes LINE to incorporate information from network neighborhoods beyond 2-hops, but is unable to efficiently scale to large networks.

In contrast to the setup used in prior work for evaluating sampling-based feature learning algorithms, we generate an equal number of samples for each method and then evaluate the quality of the obtained features on the prediction task. In doing so, we discount for performance gain observed purely because of the implementation language (C/C++/Python) since it is secondary to the algorithm. Thus, in the sampling phase, the parameters for DeepWalk, LINE and *node2vec* are set such that they generate equal number of samples at runtime. As an example, if $\mathcal{K}$ is the overall sampling budget, then the *node2vec* parameters satisfy $\mathcal{K} = r \cdot l \cdot |V|$. In the optimization phase, all these benchmarks optimize using SGD with two key differences that we correct for. First, DeepWalk uses hierarchical sampling to approximate the softmax probabilities with an objective similar to the one use by *node2vec*. However, hierarchical softmax is inefficient when compared with negative sampling [22]. Hence, keeping everything else the same, we switch to negative sampling in DeepWalk which is also the de facto approximation in *node2vec* and LINE. Second, both *node2vec* and DeepWalk have

Algorithm	**Dataset**		
	BlogCatalog	PPI	Wikipedia
Spectral Clustering	0.0405	0.0681	0.0395
DeepWalk	0.2110	0.1768	0.1274
LINE	0.0784	0.1447	0.1164
node2vec	**0.2581**	**0.1791**	**0.1552**
node2vec settings (p,q)	0.25, 0.25	4, 1	4, 0.5
Gain of *node2vec* [%]	**22.3**	**1.3**	**21.8**

Table 2: Macro-F_1 scores for multilabel classification on BlogCatalog, PPI (Homo sapiens) and Wikipedia word cooccurrence networks with 50% of the nodes labeled for training.

a parameter for the number of context neighborhood nodes to optimize for and the greater the number, the more rounds of optimization are required. This parameter is set to unity for LINE, but since LINE completes a single epoch quicker than other approaches, we let it run for k epochs.

The parameter settings used for *node2vec* are in line with typical values used for DeepWalk and LINE. Specifically, we set $d = 128$, $r = 10$, $l = 80$, $k = 10$, and the optimization is run for a single epoch. We repeat our experiments for 10 random seed initializations, and our results are statistically significant with a p-value of less than 0.01.The best in-out and return hyperparameters were learned using 10-fold cross-validation on 10% labeled data with a grid search over $p, q \in \{0.25, 0.50, 1, 2, 4\}$.

4.3 Multi-label classification

In the multi-label classification setting, every node is assigned one or more labels from a finite set $\mathcal{L}$. During the training phase, we observe a certain fraction of nodes and all their labels. The task is to predict the labels for the remaining nodes. This is a challenging task especially if $\mathcal{L}$ is large. We utilize the following datasets:

- BlogCatalog [38]: This is a network of social relationships of the bloggers listed on the BlogCatalog website. The labels represent blogger interests inferred through the metadata provided by the bloggers. The network has 10,312 nodes, 333,983 edges, and 39 different labels.
- Protein-Protein Interactions (PPI) [5]: We use a subgraph of the PPI network for Homo Sapiens. The subgraph corresponds to the graph induced by nodes for which we could obtain labels from the hallmark gene sets [19] and represent biological states. The network has 3,890 nodes, 76,584 edges, and 50 different labels.
- Wikipedia [20]: This is a cooccurrence network of words appearing in the first million bytes of the Wikipedia dump. The labels represent the Part-of-Speech (POS) tags inferred using the Stanford POS-Tagger [32]. The network has 4,777 nodes, 184,812 edges, and 40 different labels.

All these networks exhibit a fair mix of homophilic and structural equivalences. For example, we expect the social network of bloggers to exhibit strong homophily-based relationships; however, there might also be some "familiar strangers", *i.e.*, bloggers that do not interact but share interests and hence are structurally equivalent nodes. The biological states of proteins in a protein-protein interaction network also exhibit both types of equivalences. For example, they exhibit structural equivalence when proteins perform functions complementary to those of neighboring proteins, and at other times, they organize based on homophily in assisting neighboring proteins in performing similar functions. The word cooccurence network is fairly dense, since edges exist between words cooccuring in a 2-length window in the Wikipedia corpus. Hence, words having the same POS tags are not hard to find, lending a high degree of homophily. At the same time, we expect some structural equivalence

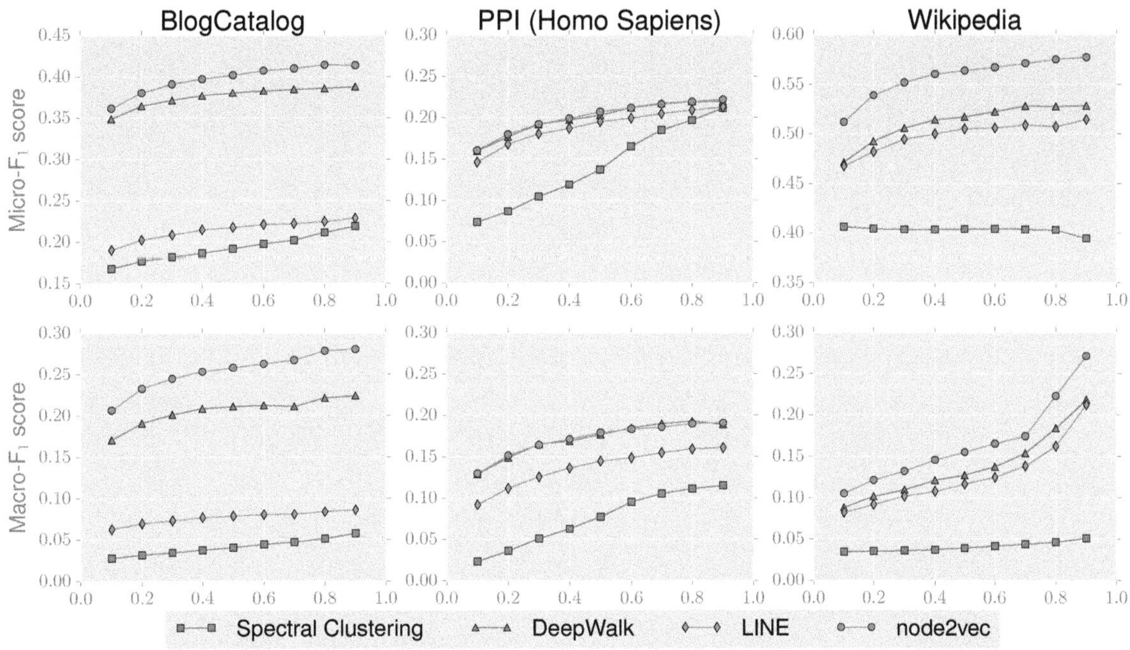

Figure 4: Performance evaluation of different benchmarks on varying the amount of labeled data used for training. The x axis denotes the fraction of labeled data, whereas the y axis in the top and bottom rows denote the Micro-F_1 and Macro-F_1 scores respectively. DeepWalk and *node2vec* give comparable performance on PPI. In all other networks, across all fractions of labeled data *node2vec* performs best.

in the POS tags due to syntactic grammar patterns such as nouns following determiners, punctuations succeeding nouns etc.

Experimental results. The node feature representations are input to a one-vs-rest logistic regression classifier with L2 regularization. The train and test data is split equally over 10 random instances. We use the Macro-F_1 scores for comparing performance in Table 2 and the relative performance gain is over the closest benchmark. The trends are similar for Micro-F_1 and accuracy and are not shown.

From the results, it is evident we can see how the added flexibility in exploring neighborhoods allows *node2vec* to outperform the other benchmark algorithms. In BlogCatalog, we can discover the right mix of homophily and structural equivalence by setting parameters p and q to low values, giving us 22.3% gain over DeepWalk and 229.2% gain over LINE in Macro-F_1 scores. LINE showed worse performance than expected, which can be explained by its inability to reuse samples, a feat that can be easily done using the random walk methods. Even in our other two networks, where we have a mix of equivalences present, the semi-supervised nature of *node2vec* can help us infer the appropriate degree of exploration necessary for feature learning. In the case of PPI network, the best exploration strategy ($p = 4$, $q = 1$) turns out to be virtually indistinguishable from DeepWalk's uniform ($p = 1$, $q = 1$) exploration giving us only a slight edge over DeepWalk by avoiding redudancy in already visited nodes through a high p value, but a convincing 23.8% gain over LINE in Macro-F_1 scores. However, in general, the uniform random walks can be much worse than the exploration strategy learned by *node2vec*. As we can see in the Wikipedia word cooccurrence network, uniform walks cannot guide the search procedure towards the best samples and hence, we achieve a gain of 21.8% over DeepWalk and 33.2% over LINE.

For a more fine-grained analysis, we also compare performance while varying the train-test split from 10% to 90%, while learning parameters p and q on 10% of the data as before. For brevity, we summarize the results for the Micro-F_1 and Macro-F_1 scores graphically in Figure 4. Here we make similar observations. All methods significantly outperform Spectral clustering, DeepWalk outperforms LINE, *node2vec* consistently outperforms LINE and achieves large improvement over DeepWalk across domains. For example, we achieve the biggest improvement over DeepWalk of 26.7% on BlogCatalog at 70% labeled data. In the worst case, the search phase has little bearing on learned representations in which case *node2vec* is equivalent to DeepWalk. Similarly, the improvements are even more striking when compared to LINE, where in addition to drastic gain (over 200%) on BlogCatalog, we observe high magnitude improvements upto 41.1% on other datasets such as PPI while training on just 10% labeled data.

4.4 Parameter sensitivity

The *node2vec* algorithm involves a number of parameters and in Figure 5a, we examine how the different choices of parameters affect the performance of *node2vec* on the BlogCatalog dataset using a 50-50 split between labeled and unlabeled data. Except for the parameter being tested, all other parameters assume default values. The default values for p and q are set to unity.

We measure the Macro-F_1 score as a function of parameters p and q. The performance of *node2vec* improves as the in-out parameter p and the return parameter q decrease. This increase in performance can be based on the homophilic and structural equivalences we expect to see in BlogCatalog. While a low q encourages outward exploration, it is balanced by a low p which ensures that the walk does not go too far from the start node.

We also examine how the number of features d and the node's neighborhood parameters (number of walks r, walk length l, and neighborhood size k) affect the performance. We observe that performance tends to saturate once the dimensions of the representations reaches around 100. Similarly, we observe that increasing the number and length of walks per source improves performance,

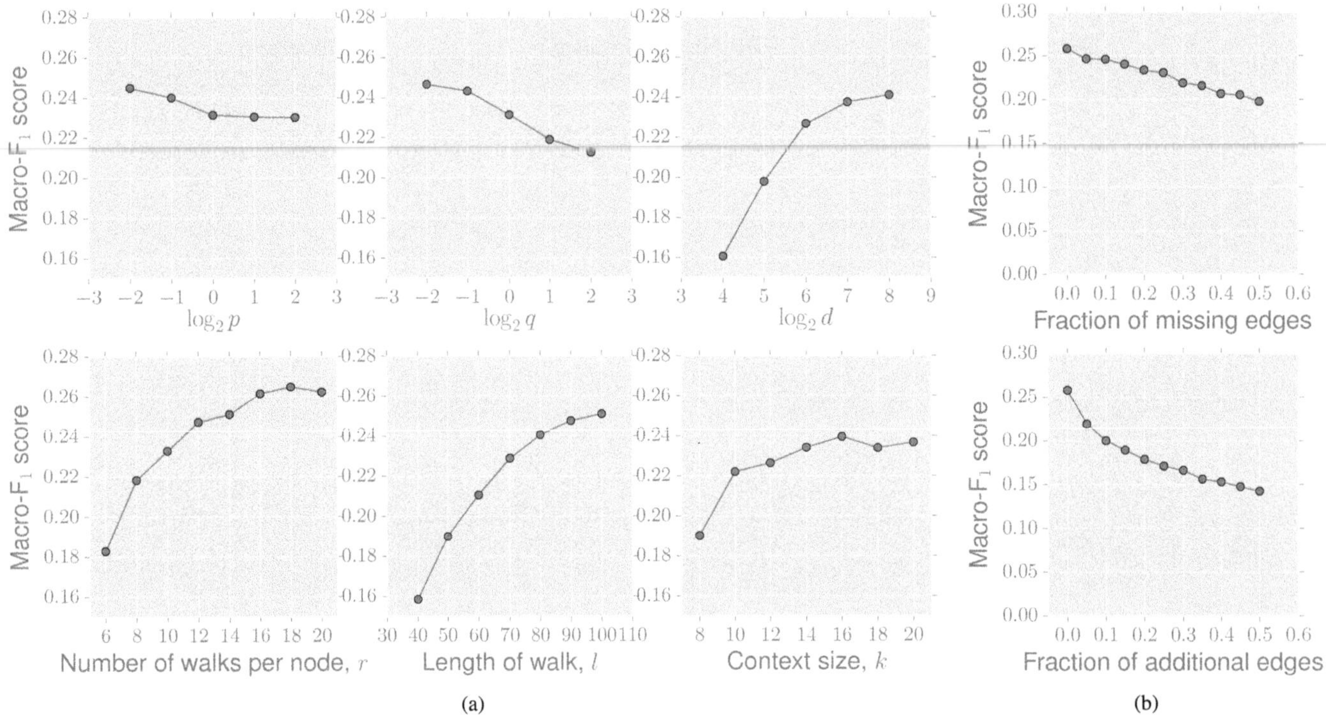

Figure 5: (a). Parameter sensitivity (b). Perturbation analysis for multilabel classification on the BlogCatalog network.

which is not surprising since we have a greater overall sampling budget $\mathcal{K}$ to learn representations. Both these parameters have a relatively high impact on the performance of the method. Interestingly, the context size, k also improves performance at the cost of increased optimization time. However, the performance differences are not that large in this case.

4.5 Perturbation Analysis

For many real-world networks, we do not have access to accurate information about the network structure. We performed a perturbation study where we analyzed the performance of *node2vec* for two imperfect information scenarios related to the edge structure in the BlogCatalog network. In the first scenario, we measure performace as a function of the fraction of missing edges (relative to the full network). The missing edges are chosen randomly, subject to the constraint that the number of connected components in the network remains fixed. As we can see in Figure 5b(top), the decrease in Macro-F_1 score as the fraction of missing edges increases is roughly linear with a small slope. Robustness to missing edges in the network is especially important in cases where the graphs are evolving over time (*e.g.*, citation networks), or where network construction is expensive (*e.g.*, biological networks).

In the second perturbation setting, we have noisy edges between randomly selected pairs of nodes in the network. As shown in Figure 5b(bottom), the performance of *node2vec* declines slightly faster initially when compared with the setting of missing edges, however, the rate of decrease in Macro-F_1 score gradually slows down over time. Again, the robustness of *node2vec* to false edges is useful in several situations such as sensor networks where the measurements used for constructing the network are noisy.

4.6 Scalability

To test for scalability, we learn node representations using *node2vec* with default parameter values for Erdos-Renyi graphs with increasing sizes from 100 to 1,000,000 nodes and constant average degree of 10. In Figure 6, we empirically observe that *node2vec* scales linearly with increase in number of nodes generating representations for one million nodes in less than four hours. The sampling procedure comprises of preprocessing for computing transition probabilities for our walk (negligibly small) and simulation of random walks. The optimization phase is made efficient using negative sampling [22] and asynchronous SGD [26].

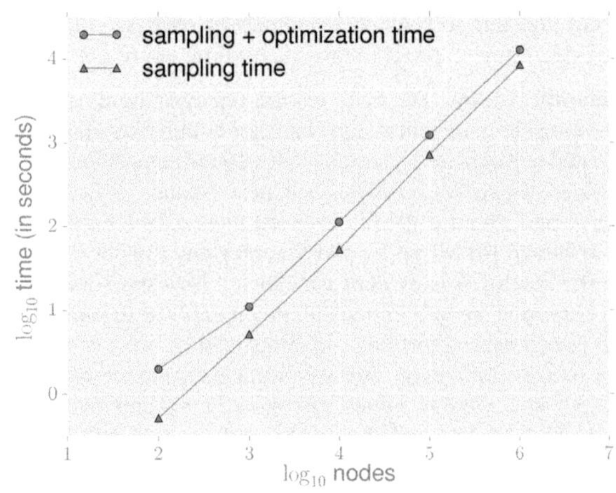

Figure 6: Scalability of *node2vec* on Erdos-Renyi graphs with an average degree of 10.

Many ideas from prior work serve as useful pointers in making the sampling procedure computationally efficient. We showed how random walks, also used in DeepWalk [24], allow the sampled nodes to be reused as neighborhoods for different source nodes appearing in the walk. Alias sampling allows our walks to generalize to weighted networks, with little preprocessing [28]. Though we are free to set the search parameters based on the underlying task and domain at no additional cost, learning the best settings of

Score	Definition
Common Neighbors	$\mid \mathcal{N}(u) \cap \mathcal{N}(v) \mid$
Jaccard's Coefficient	$\frac{\mid\mathcal{N}(u)\cap\mathcal{N}(v)\mid}{\mid\mathcal{N}(u)\cup\mathcal{N}(v)\mid}$
Adamic-Adar Score	$\sum_{t\in\mathcal{N}(u)\cap\mathcal{N}(v)} \frac{1}{\log\mid\mathcal{N}(t)\mid}$
Preferential Attachment	$\mid \mathcal{N}(u) \mid \cdot \mid \mathcal{N}(v) \mid$

Table 3: Link prediction heuristic scores for node pair (u, v) with immediate neighbor sets $\mathcal{N}(u)$ and $\mathcal{N}(v)$ respectively.

our search parameters adds an overhead. However, as our experiments confirm, this overhead is minimal since *node2vec* is semi-supervised and hence, can learn these parameters efficiently with very little labeled data.

4.7 Link prediction

In link prediction, we are given a network with a certain fraction of edges removed, and we would like to predict these missing edges. We generate the labeled dataset of edges as follows: To obtain positive examples, we remove 50% of edges chosen randomly from the network while ensuring that the residual network obtained after the edge removals is connected, and to generate negative examples, we randomly sample an equal number of node pairs from the network which have no edge connecting them.

Since none of feature learning algorithms have been previously used for link prediction, we additionally evaluate *node2vec* against some popular heuristic scores that achieve good performance in link prediction. The scores we consider are defined in terms of the neighborhood sets of the nodes constituting the pair (see Table 3). We test our benchmarks on the following datasets:

- Facebook [14]: In the Facebook network, nodes represent users, and edges represent a friendship relation between any two users. The network has 4,039 nodes and 88,234 edges.
- Protein-Protein Interactions (PPI) [5]: In the PPI network for Homo Sapiens, nodes represent proteins, and an edge indicates a biological interaction between a pair of proteins. The network has 19,706 nodes and 390,633 edges.
- arXiv ASTRO-PH [14]: This is a collaboration network generated from papers submitted to the e-print arXiv where nodes represent scientists, and an edge is present between two scientists if they have collaborated in a paper. The network has 18,722 nodes and 198,110 edges.

Experimental results. We summarize our results for link prediction in Table 4. The best p and q parameter settings for each *node2vec* entry are omitted for ease of presentation. A general observation we can draw from the results is that the learned feature representations for node pairs significantly outperform the heuristic benchmark scores with *node2vec* achieving the best AUC improvement on 12.6% on the arXiv dataset over the best performing baseline (Adamic-Adar [1]).

Amongst the feature learning algorithms, *node2vec* outperforms both DeepWalk and LINE in all networks with gain up to 3.8% and 6.5% respectively in the AUC scores for the best possible choices of the binary operator for each algorithm. When we look at operators individually (Table 1), *node2vec* outperforms DeepWalk and LINE barring a couple of cases involving the Weighted-L1 and Weighted-L2 operators in which LINE performs better. Overall, the Hadamard operator when used with *node2vec* is highly stable and gives the best performance on average across all networks.

Op	Algorithm	Dataset		
		Facebook	PPI	arXiv
	Common Neighbors	0.8100	0.7142	0.8153
	Jaccard's Coefficient	0.8880	0.7018	0.8067
	Adamic-Adar	0.8289	0.7126	0.8315
	Pref. Attachment	0.7137	0.6670	0.6996
(a)	Spectral Clustering	0.5960	0.6588	0.5812
(a)	DeepWalk	0.7238	0.6923	0.7066
(a)	LINE	0.7029	0.6330	0.6516
(a)	*node2vec*	0.7266	0.7543	0.7221
(b)	Spectral Clustering	0.6192	0.4920	0.5740
(b)	DeepWalk	**0.9680**	0.7441	0.9340
(b)	LINE	0.9490	0.7249	0.8902
(b)	*node2vec*	**0.9680**	**0.7719**	**0.9366**
(c)	Spectral Clustering	0.7200	0.6356	0.7099
(c)	DeepWalk	0.9574	0.6026	0.8282
(c)	LINE	0.9483	0.7024	0.8809
(c)	*node2vec*	0.9602	0.6292	0.8468
(d)	Spectral Clustering	0.7107	0.6026	0.6765
(d)	DeepWalk	0.9584	0.6118	0.8305
(d)	LINE	0.9460	0.7106	0.8862
(d)	*node2vec*	0.9606	0.6236	0.8477

Table 4: Area Under Curve (AUC) scores for link prediction. Comparison with popular baselines and embedding based methods bootstapped using binary operators: (a) Average, (b) Hadamard, (c) Weighted-L1, and (d) Weighted-L2 (See Table 1 for definitions).

5. DISCUSSION AND CONCLUSION

In this paper, we studied feature learning in networks as a search-based optimization problem. This perspective gives us multiple advantages. It can explain classic search strategies on the basis of the exploration-exploitation trade-off. Additionally, it provides a degree of interpretability to the learned representations when applied for a prediction task. For instance, we observed that BFS can explore only limited neighborhoods. This makes BFS suitable for characterizing structural equivalences in network that rely on the immediate local structure of nodes. On the other hand, DFS can freely explore network neighborhoods which is important in discovering homophilous communities at the cost of high variance.

Both DeepWalk and LINE can be seen as rigid search strategies over networks. DeepWalk [24] proposes search using uniform random walks. The obvious limitation with such a strategy is that it gives us no control over the explored neighborhoods. LINE [28] proposes primarily a breadth-first strategy, sampling nodes and optimizing the likelihood independently over only 1-hop and 2-hop neighbors. The effect of such an exploration is easier to characterize, but it is restrictive and provides no flexibility in exploring nodes at further depths. In contrast, the search strategy in *node2vec* is both flexible and controllable exploring network neighborhoods through parameters p and q. While these search parameters have intuitive interpretations, we obtain best results on complex networks when we can learn them directly from data. From a practical standpoint, *node2vec* is scalable and robust to perturbations.

We showed how extensions of node embeddings to link prediction outperform popular heuristic scores designed specifically for this task. Our method permits additional binary operators beyond those listed in Table 1. As a future work, we would like to explore the reasons behind the success of Hadamard operator over others, as well as establish interpretable equivalence notions for edges based on the search parameters. Future extensions of *node2vec* could involve networks with special structure such as heterogeneous information networks, networks with explicit domain features for nodes and edges and signed-edge networks. Continuous feature representations are the backbone of many deep learning algorithms, and it would be interesting to use *node2vec* representations as building blocks for end-to-end deep learning on graphs.

Acknowledgements. We are thankful to Austin Benson, Will Hamilton, Rok Sosič, Marinka Žitnik as well as the anonymous reviewers for their helpful comments. This research has been supported in part by NSF CNS-1010921, IIS-1149837, NIH BD2K, ARO MURI, DARPA XDATA, DARPA SIMPLEX, Stanford Data Science Initiative, Boeing, Lightspeed, SAP, and Volkswagen.

6. REFERENCES

[1] L. A. Adamic and E. Adar. Friends and neighbors on the web. *Social networks*, 25(3):211–230, 2003.

[2] L. Backstrom and J. Leskovec. Supervised random walks: predicting and recommending links in social networks. In *WSDM*, 2011.

[3] M. Belkin and P. Niyogi. Laplacian eigenmaps and spectral techniques for embedding and clustering. In *NIPS*, 2001.

[4] Y. Bengio, A. Courville, and P. Vincent. Representation learning: A review and new perspectives. *IEEE TPAMI*, 35(8):1798–1828, 2013.

[5] B.-J. Breitkreutz, C. Stark, T. Reguly, L. Boucher, A. Breitkreutz, M. Livstone, R. Oughtred, D. H. Lackner, J. Bähler, V. Wood, et al. The BioGRID interaction database. *Nucleic acids research*, 36:D637–D640, 2008.

[6] S. Cao, W. Lu, and Q. Xu. GraRep: Learning Graph Representations with global structural information. In *CIKM*, 2015.

[7] S. Fortunato. Community detection in graphs. *Physics Reports*, 486(3-5):75 – 174, 2010.

[8] B. Gallagher and T. Eliassi-Rad. Leveraging label-independent features for classification in sparsely labeled networks: An empirical study. In *Lecture Notes in Computer Science: Advances in Social Network Mining and Analysis*. Springer, 2009.

[9] Z. S. Harris. Word. *Distributional Structure*, 10(23):146–162, 1954.

[10] K. Henderson, B. Gallagher, T. Eliassi-Rad, H. Tong, S. Basu, L. Akoglu, D. Koutra, C. Faloutsos, and L. Li. RolX: structural role extraction & mining in large graphs. In *KDD*, 2012.

[11] K. Henderson, B. Gallagher, L. Li, L. Akoglu, T. Eliassi-Rad, H. Tong, and C. Faloutsos. It's who you know: graph mining using recursive structural features. In *KDD*, 2011.

[12] P. D. Hoff, A. E. Raftery, and M. S. Handcock. Latent space approaches to social network analysis. *J. of the American Statistical Association*, 2002.

[13] D. E. Knuth. *The Stanford GraphBase: a platform for combinatorial computing*, volume 37. Addison-Wesley Reading, 1993.

[14] J. Leskovec and A. Krevl. SNAP Datasets: Stanford large network dataset collection. http://snap.stanford.edu/data, June 2014.

[15] K. Li, J. Gao, S. Guo, N. Du, X. Li, and A. Zhang. LRBM: A restricted boltzmann machine based approach for representation learning on linked data. In *ICDM*, 2014.

[16] X. Li, N. Du, H. Li, K. Li, J. Gao, and A. Zhang. A deep learning approach to link prediction in dynamic networks. In *ICDM*, 2014.

[17] Y. Li, D. Tarlow, M. Brockschmidt, and R. Zemel. Gated graph sequence neural networks. In *ICLR*, 2016.

[18] D. Liben-Nowell and J. Kleinberg. The link-prediction problem for social networks. *J. of the American society for information science and technology*, 58(7):1019–1031, 2007.

[19] A. Liberzon, A. Subramanian, R. Pinchback, H. Thorvaldsdóttir, P. Tamayo, and J. P. Mesirov. Molecular signatures database (MSigDB) 3.0. *Bioinformatics*, 27(12):1739–1740, 2011.

[20] M. Mahoney. Large text compression benchmark. www.mattmahoney.net/dc/textdata, 2011.

[21] T. Mikolov, K. Chen, G. Corrado, and J. Dean. Efficient estimation of word representations in vector space. In *ICLR*, 2013.

[22] T. Mikolov, I. Sutskever, K. Chen, G. S. Corrado, and J. Dean. Distributed representations of words and phrases and their compositionality. In *NIPS*, 2013.

[23] J. Pennington, R. Socher, and C. D. Manning. GloVe: Global vectors for word representation. In *EMNLP*, 2014.

[24] B. Perozzi, R. Al-Rfou, and S. Skiena. DeepWalk: Online learning of social representations. In *KDD*, 2014.

[25] P. Radivojac, W. T. Clark, T. R. Oron, A. M. Schnoes, T. Wittkop, A. Sokolov, K. Graim, C. Funk, Verspoor, et al. A large-scale evaluation of computational protein function prediction. *Nature methods*, 10(3):221–227, 2013.

[26] B. Recht, C. Re, S. Wright, and F. Niu. Hogwild!: A lock-free approach to parallelizing stochastic gradient descent. In *NIPS*, 2011.

[27] S. T. Roweis and L. K. Saul. Nonlinear dimensionality reduction by locally linear embedding. *Science*, 290(5500):2323–2326, 2000.

[28] J. Tang, M. Qu, M. Wang, M. Zhang, J. Yan, and Q. Mei. LINE: Large-scale Information Network Embedding. In *WWW*, 2015.

[29] L. Tang and H. Liu. Leveraging social media networks for classification. *Data Mining and Knowledge Discovery*, 23(3):447–478, 2011.

[30] J. B. Tenenbaum, V. De Silva, and J. C. Langford. A global geometric framework for nonlinear dimensionality reduction. *Science*, 290(5500):2319–2323, 2000.

[31] F. Tian, B. Gao, Q. Cui, E. Chen, and T.-Y. Liu. Learning deep representations for graph clustering. In *AAAI*, 2014.

[32] K. Toutanova, D. Klein, C. D. Manning, and Y. Singer. Feature-rich part-of-speech tagging with a cyclic dependency network. In *NAACL*, 2003.

[33] G. Tsoumakas and I. Katakis. Multi-label classification: An overview. *Dept. of Informatics, Aristotle University of Thessaloniki, Greece*, 2006.

[34] A. Vazquez, A. Flammini, A. Maritan, and A. Vespignani. Global protein function prediction from protein-protein interaction networks. *Nature biotechnology*, 21(6):697–700, 2003.

[35] S. Yan, D. Xu, B. Zhang, H.-J. Zhang, Q. Yang, and S. Lin. Graph embedding and extensions: a general framework for dimensionality reduction. *IEEE TPAMI*, 29(1):40–51, 2007.

[36] J. Yang and J. Leskovec. Overlapping communities explain core-periphery organization of networks. *Proceedings of the IEEE*, 102(12):1892–1902, 2014.

[37] S.-H. Yang, B. Long, A. Smola, N. Sadagopan, Z. Zheng, and H. Zha. Like like alike: joint friendship and interest propagation in social networks. In *WWW*, 2011.

[38] R. Zafarani and H. Liu. Social computing data repository at ASU, 2009.

[39] S. Zhai and Z. Zhang. Dropout training of matrix factorization and autoencoder for link prediction in sparse graphs. In *SDM*, 2015.

Generalized Hierarchical Sparse Model for Arbitrary-Order Interactive Antigenic Sites Identification in Flu Virus Data

Lei Han[†], Yu Zhang[‡], Xiu-Feng Wan[§], Tong Zhang[†¶]
[†]Department of Statistics, Rutgers University
[‡]Department of Computer Science and Engineering, Hong Kong University of Science and Technology
[§]College of Veterinary Medicine, Mississippi State University
[¶]Baidu Inc. Beijing, China
lhan@stat.rutgers.edu; zhangyu@cse.ust.hk; wan@cvm.msstate.edu; tzhang@stat.rutgers.edu

ABSTRACT

Recent statistical evidence has shown that a regression model by incorporating the interactions among the original covariates (features) can significantly improve the interpretability for biological data. One major challenge is the exponentially expanded feature space when adding high-order feature interactions to the model. To tackle the huge dimensionality, Hierarchical Sparse Models (HSM) are developed by enforcing sparsity under heredity structures in the interactions among the covariates. However, existing methods only consider pairwise interactions, making the discovery of important high-order interactions a non-trivial open problem. In this paper, we propose a Generalized Hierarchical Sparse Model (GHSM) as a generalization of the HSM models to learn arbitrary-order interactions. The GHSM applies the ℓ_1 penalty to all the model coefficients under a constraint that given any covariate, if none of its associated kth-order interactions contribute to the regression model, then neither do its associated higher-order interactions. The resulting objective function is non-convex with a challenge lying in the coupled variables appearing in the arbitrary-order hierarchical constraints and we devise an efficient optimization algorithm to directly solve it. Specifically, we decouple the variables in the constraints via both the GIST and ADMM methods into three subproblems, each of which is proved to admit an efficiently analytical solution. We evaluate the GHSM method in both synthetic problem and the antigenic sites identification problem for the flu virus data, where we expand the feature space up to the 5th-order interactions. Empirical results demonstrate the effectiveness and efficiency of the proposed method and the learned high-order interactions have meaningful synergistic covariate patterns in the virus antigenicity.

Keywords

High-Order Interaction; Heredity Structure; Hierarchical Sparsity

1. INTRODUCTION

Fitting a linear regression model to the response based on a number of covariates (features) is a commonly used tool in statistical analysis. However, in numerous situations, a linear model on the covariates may be not sufficiently enough to provide comprehensive explanations for the data and to make accurate predictions. For example, in the influenza antigenic sites identification problem, a mutation at an individual antigenic site (covariate) is less deterministic to change the phenotypic behavior (antigenic change) of the influenza virus. Instead, multiple simultaneous mutations at different antigenic sites will significantly enhance the antigenic drift, and strong interactions among the antigenic sites are observed during the virus evolution.

Actually, recent statistical results have shown that studying the feature interactions in a learning model can significantly enhance its interpretability for the data and improve the prediction accuracy [6, 15, 13]. Generally, the interaction effects are represented as the elementwise product among the covariates and for example, the second-order interaction between two covariates $\mathbf{x}_i$ and $\mathbf{x}_j$ is represented by their elementwise product $\mathbf{x}_i \odot \mathbf{x}_j$. Hence, the interactions can encourage capturing the nonlinearity in the data. The interactions among covariates have been found to play an important role in various areas. For example, strong evidences have been found in [2] that the genetic-environmental interactions have significant effects on conduct disorders, and similar results are reported in [5] that the genetic environmental interactions in serotonin system are highly correlated with the adolescent depression. Moreover, in [19], considering the interaction between the continuance commitment and affective commitment is shown to be effective in predicting the absenteeism. Recently, in the antigenic sites identification problem [23], interactions among co-evolved antigenic sites are proved to be critical to quantify the impact of multiple simultaneous mutations.

As the study of the interactions among covariates gains increasing attentions, a major challenge is the exponentially expanded feature space. That is, when considering the kth-order interactions among covariates, the number of interactions is $O(d^k)$ with respect to the d covariates. Such a large number of interactions make the learning model computationally demanding even when d and k are very small. One promising strategy is to exploit sparse structure under this scenario, since only a subset of the covariates and the interactions could be of interest. A simple way is to directly apply the Lasso [21] method by treating all the covariates and the interactions equally, which is referred to the all-pairs Lasso [1, 23]. Furthermore, since the interaction effects are generated from the covariates and the higher-order interaction effects originate from lower-order ones, logical heredity relationship among those effects could be taken into account instead of treating them equally.

In order to make use of the heredity structure, statisticians favor the sparsity which obeys certain logical heredity constraints,

KDD '16, August 13-17, 2016, San Francisco, CA, USA

DOI: http://dx.doi.org/10.1145/2939672.2939786

referring to the situation that if a set of parameters are estimated as zeros, then the set of its dependent parameters based on some certain heredity relationship should also be set to zeros. Accordingly, a number of Hierarchical Sparse Models (HSM) have been developed. For example, in [15], a convex Lasso-style method named VANISH is proposed by enforcing the *strong heredity* constraint for the second-order interactions that if a second-order interaction is added to the model, then both the corresponding covariates must be included as well. Consequently, many convex formulations, including the glinternet [11], GRESH [16], FAMILY [9], and the hierarchical sparse model [22], incorporate the strong heredity into the second-order interactions with the heredity structure achieved via the group sparsity [25], where the covariate and interactions restricted by a heredity constraint form a group. Similar considerations are discussed by [26, 24]. On the other hand, in contrast to those convex models, the SHIM method [3] adopts a non-convex formulation to achieve the strong heredity by decomposing the coefficient of each interaction into a product of the coefficients for the covariates. In addition to the strong heredity, there is another type of hierarchical relation, the *weak heredity*, which introduces a constraint that a pairwise interaction is considered if either of its corresponding covariates was included. Both the strong and weak heredity are investigated in [1] and an efficient algorithm to handle the weak heredity is introduced in [12].

So far, many interests have been focused on exploring the sparse heredity in the interaction model but none of them can deal with general hierarchies, since all of them study only the second-order interactions and their algorithms are particularly designed for the second-order interactions. On the other hand, there have been sufficient evidences to indicate that higher-order interactions are more important in many applications. For example, in psychological analysis, the third-order interactions among covariates have been shown to be important [4]. Specifically, in antigenicity analysis of influenza virus, a recent study on proteins of the H3N2 influenza virus shows that more than two of the amino acid positions could mutate simultaneously [17] and biological evidences in [14] also demonstrate that the co-evolved antigenic sites are more likely to be physically close in the 3D structure of the protein.

Unfortunately, due to the difficulty in defining and learning with the high-order heredity, we are unaware of any existing work that can deal with general hierarchies with the order of feature interactions larger than two and there is even no formal definition for the arbitrary-order heredity. In this paper, we propose a Generalized Hierarchical Sparse Model (GHSM) to tackle arbitrary-order interactions among features. We first introduce the definition of the *arbitrary-order heredity*, which makes an assumption that given any covariate, if none of its associated kth-order interaction effects contribute to a learning model, then neither do its associated higher-order interaction effects. Based on this definition, we formulate the GHSM model by applying the ℓ_1 penalty to all the coefficients under certain hierarchical chain constraints, which guarantee the arbitrary-order heredity. The resulting problem is non-convex and not easy to be optimized since the number of variables in the optimization problem increases dramatically when the order of interactions becomes bigger, which poses a computational challenge. To optimize the objective function, we use the GIST method [7] where the proximal operator is solved by the ADMM method. In the three subproblems of the ADMM method, the first two need to solve quadratic programming problems and the last one is a least square problem with a hierarchical chain constraint. After analysis, we show that all the three subproblems admit efficiently analytical solutions. In the experiments, we evaluate the GHSM method in both synthetic problem and the antigenic sites identification problem in influenza virus data, and empirical results show that the GHSM method can capture meaningful synergistic covariate patterns, which can be well explained by biological knowledge.

2. PRELIMINARIES

Throughout this paper, we use regular letters to denote scalars, bold-face and lowercase letters for vectors, and bold-face and uppercase letters for matrices or tensors. Suppose the data matrix for training is denoted by $\mathbf{X} = (\mathbf{x}_1, \cdots, \mathbf{x}_d) \in \mathbb{R}^{n\times d}$, where n is the number of samples, d is the feature dimensionality, and $\mathbf{x}_i$ records the values for the ith covariate in the n data samples. The response vector is $\mathbf{y} \in \mathbb{R}^n$. The second-order interaction models [15, 3, 1, 11, 12, 16, 9, 22] commonly consider the following regression model:

$$\mathbf{y} = \sum_{i=1}^{d} \beta_i \mathbf{x}_i + \sum_{i\neq j}^{d} \phi_{i,j}(\mathbf{x}_i \odot \mathbf{x}_j) + \boldsymbol{\varepsilon}, \tag{1}$$

where $\odot$ denotes the elementwise product between vectors, $\boldsymbol{\beta} \in \mathbb{R}^d$ with β_i as its ith element is the coefficient vector for the covariates, $\mathbf{\Phi} \in \mathbb{R}^{d\times d}$ with $\phi_{i,j}$ as its (i,j)th element is the coefficient matrix for the pairwise interaction effects, and $\boldsymbol{\varepsilon} \sim \mathcal{N}(\mathbf{0}, \sigma^2\mathbf{I})$ is a Gaussian noise vector. In the existing works, two types of heredity structure are considered for the second-order interactions, i.e. the strong heredity and the weak heredity, whose definitions are as follows:

$$\begin{aligned}
\text{strong heredity: } & \phi_{i,j} \neq 0 \Longrightarrow \beta_i \neq 0 \text{ and } \beta_j \neq 0, & (2)\\
& \text{or equivalently,} \\
& \beta_i = 0 \text{ or } \beta_j = 0 \Longrightarrow \phi_{i,j} = 0; \\
\text{weak heredity: } & \phi_{i,j} \neq 0 \Longrightarrow \beta_i \neq 0 \text{ or } \beta_j \neq 0, & (3)\\
& \text{or equivalently,} \\
& \beta_i = 0 \text{ and } \beta_j = 0 \Longrightarrow \phi_{i,j} = 0.
\end{aligned}$$

Based on Eqs. (2) and (3), the HSM methods introduced in [1, 12], named as the strong and weak hierNet, explicitly enforce the heredity structure by adding inequality or symmetry constraints to the Lasso method as

$$\begin{aligned}
\text{strong hierNet: } & \min_{\boldsymbol{\beta},\mathbf{\Phi}} l(\boldsymbol{\beta}, \mathbf{\Phi}|\mathbf{X}, \mathbf{y}) + \lambda\|\boldsymbol{\beta}\|_1 + \frac{\lambda}{2}\|\mathbf{\Phi}\|_1 & (4)\\
& \text{s.t. } \mathbf{\Phi} = \mathbf{\Phi}^\top,\ |\beta_i| \geq \|\mathbf{\Phi}_{i,\cdot}\|_1\ \forall i \in \mathbb{N}_d; \\
\text{weak hierNet: } & \min_{\boldsymbol{\beta},\mathbf{\Phi}} l(\boldsymbol{\beta}, \mathbf{\Phi}|\mathbf{X}, \mathbf{y}) + \lambda\|\boldsymbol{\beta}\|_1 + \frac{\lambda}{2}\|\mathbf{\Phi}\|_1 & (5)\\
& \text{s.t. } |\beta_i| \geq \|\mathbf{\Phi}_{i,\cdot}\|_1\ \forall i \in \mathbb{N}_d,
\end{aligned}$$

where $l(\cdot)$ is a loss function based on Eq. (1), λ is a regularization parameter that controls the sparsity, $\mathbb{N}_d$ denotes the set of integers $\{1, \cdots, d\}$, $\|\cdot\|_1$ denotes the ℓ_1 norm of a vector or matrix, and $\mathbf{\Phi}_{i,\cdot}$ denotes the ith row of $\mathbf{\Phi}$. The only difference between problems (4) and (5) is the existence of the symmetry constraint on $\mathbf{\Phi}$. It is not hard to see that the constraints in problems (4) and (5) can guarantee the strong and weak heredity defined in Eqs. (2) and (3). The strong and weak hierNet methods are representatives of the second-order HSM methods which are explicitly enforced to obey the heredity structure.

In the hierNet models, only the second-order interaction is considered. As discussed in the previous section, higher-order interactions are important to model the biological data. To the best of our knowledge, there is no work to even define the high-order interactions. In the next section, we will first provide a formal definition of the arbitrary-order heredity and then introduce our method to model the arbitrary-order interactions.

3. THE GHSM

Here we consider up to the Kth-order interactions among the covariates ($K \ll d$), and the regression model is formulated as

$$
\begin{aligned}
\mathbf{y} = &\sum_{i=1}^{d} \theta_i^{(1)} \mathbf{z}_i^{(1)} + \sum_{i_1<i_2}^{d} \theta_{\langle i_1,i_2\rangle}^{(2)} \mathbf{z}_{\langle i_1,i_2\rangle}^{(2)} + \cdots \\
&+ \sum_{i_1<i_2<\cdots<i_K}^{d} \theta_{\langle i_1,i_2,\cdots,i_K\rangle}^{(K)} \mathbf{z}_{\langle i_1,i_2,\cdots,i_K\rangle}^{(K)} + \boldsymbol{\varepsilon},
\end{aligned} \tag{6}
$$

where $\mathbf{z}_i^{(1)} = \mathbf{x}_i$, $\mathbf{z}_{\langle i_1,i_2,\cdots,i_k\rangle}^{(k)} = \mathbf{x}_{i_1} \odot \mathbf{x}_{i_2} \odot \cdots \odot \mathbf{x}_{i_k}$ denotes a data vector for the kth-order interaction corresponding to $\langle i_1,\cdots,i_k\rangle$, an interaction index $\langle i_1,\cdots,i_k\rangle$, where $i_1 < \cdots < i_k$, is an index to uniquely indicate the interaction among the covariates $i_1,\cdots,i_k$, $\boldsymbol{\theta}^{(k)} \in \mathbb{R}^{\binom{d}{k}}$ for $k = 1,\cdots,K$ is a vector of length $\binom{d}{k} = \frac{d!}{k!(d-k)!}$ with $\theta_{\langle i_1,\cdots,i_k\rangle}^{(k)}$ as its element corresponding to the index $\langle i_1,\cdots,i_k\rangle$. In Eq. (6), each interaction term only corresponds to one model coefficient and hence the number of model parameters is reduced from $O\left(\sum_{k=1}^{K} d^k\right)$ to $O\left(\sum_{k=1}^{K} \binom{d}{k}\right)$.

3.1 Arbitrary-Order Heredity

Based on the regression model in Eq. (6), we will define the arbitrary-order heredity in this section. We first introduce some notations. For $i_1 < \cdots < i_k$ and $j \notin \{i_1,\cdots,i_k\}$, $\langle i_1,\cdots,i_k\rangle \cup j$ and $j \cup \langle i_1,\cdots,i_k\rangle$ are the indices for the interaction effect among covariates $i_1,\cdots,i_k$ and j, which adds j into $\langle i_1,\cdots,i_k\rangle$ by preserving the ascending order. Similarly, $\langle i_1,\cdots,i_k\rangle \backslash j$ defines the index by removing the element j from $\langle i_1,\cdots,i_k\rangle$, where $j \in \{i_1,\cdots,i_k\}$.

If we follow the concept of the strong and weak heredity for the second-order case in Eqs. (2) and (3), a straightforward definition for the strong arbitrary-order heredity can be formulated as

$$\theta_{\langle i_1,\cdots,i_k\rangle}^{(k)} \neq 0 \Longrightarrow \forall j \in \{i_1,\cdots,i_k\},\ \theta_{\langle i_1,\cdots,i_k\rangle\backslash j}^{(k-1)} \neq 0,\ (k \geq 2),$$

or equivalently,

$$\theta_{\langle i_1,\cdots,i_k\rangle}^{(k)} = 0 \Longrightarrow \forall j \notin \{i_1,\cdots,i_k\},\ \theta_{\langle i_1,\cdots,i_k\rangle\cup j}^{(k+1)} = 0,\ (k \geq 1).$$

Similar extension can be made for the weak heredity for arbitrary-order case as well. Unfortunately, the above definition will lead to $\sum_{k=1}^{K-1} \binom{d}{k}$ constraints if the interactions up to the Kth-order are considered, which makes the problem intractable to be solved.

So, in order to represent the heredity structure in arbitrary-order case, we propose a more concise and intuitive definition as follows. First we define an ordering of the elements in $\boldsymbol{\theta}^{(k)}$ in a way following the index principle in Table 1. That is, the 1st element in $\boldsymbol{\theta}^{(k)}$ indicates the element with the interaction index $\langle 1,\cdots,k-1,k\rangle$, the 2nd element in $\boldsymbol{\theta}^{(k)}$ indicates the one with the interaction index $\langle 1,\cdots,k-1,k+1\rangle$, and so on. Based on this ordering, we define $\mathbf{e}_i^{(k)} \in \mathbb{R}^{\binom{d}{k}}$ as a 0/1 binary vector for the ith covariate where if i appears in an interaction index of $\boldsymbol{\theta}^{(k)}$, then the corresponding element in $\mathbf{e}_i^{(k)}$ is set to 1 while the rest entries in $\mathbf{e}_i^{(k)}$ are 0.

Then we introduce the definition for the arbitrary-order heredity.

Definition 1 (Arbitrary-Order Heredity). *Given the regression model in Eq. (6), when up to the Kth-order interactions among the covariates ($K \geq 2$) are considered, the heredity among the K orders is defined as*

$$\mathbf{e}_i^{(k)} \odot \boldsymbol{\theta}^{(k)} = \mathbf{0} \Longrightarrow \mathbf{e}_i^{(k+1)} \odot \boldsymbol{\theta}^{(k+1)} = \mathbf{0},\ \forall i \in \mathbb{N}_d,\ k \in \mathbb{N}_{K-1}.$$

In Definition 1, for any covariate i, if none of its associated kth-order ($k < K$) interaction terms contribute to the regression model, then neither do its associated higher-order interaction terms. The arbitrary-order heredity poses constraints on sets of variables associated with each covariate i instead of each individual interaction coefficient and hence it only leads to $(K-1)d$ constraints, whose size is much smaller than $\sum_{k=1}^{K-1} \binom{d}{k}$, which is the size of constraints induced by the straightforward strong arbitrary-order heredity discussed before, making the learning model have much lower complexity as we will see later.

When K is set to 2, it is easy to see that the arbitrary-order heredity in Definition 1 degenerates to the strong heredity in Eq. (2) and hence the arbitrary-order heredity is a generalization of the strong second-order heredity. Fig. 1 gives an example to explain the relationship among the strong, weak and arbitrary-order heredity where the circle denotes the coefficient of a covariate '1', ovals denote the coefficients of the interactions involving the covariates '1', and the red arrows indicate the heredity. From the figure, we see that when $K = 2$, the top 2 layers in the arbitrary-order heredity degenerates to the strong heredity structure by eliminating the redundancy among the model coefficients.

Table 1: The ordering of elements in $\boldsymbol{\theta}^{(k)}$.

The index in $\boldsymbol{\theta}^{(k)}$	The corresponding interaction index
1	$\langle 1,\cdots,k-1,k\rangle$
2	$\langle 1,\cdots,k-1,k+1\rangle$
$\cdots$	$\cdots$
$d-k+1$	$\langle 1,\cdots,k-2,k-1,d\rangle$
$d-k+2$	$\langle 1,\cdots,k-2,k,k+1\rangle$
$\cdots$	$\cdots$
$\binom{d}{k}$	$\langle d-k+1,\cdots,d-1,d\rangle$

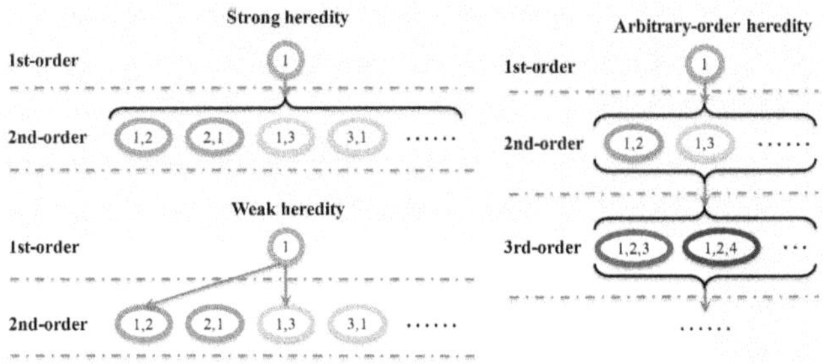

Figure 1: A pictorial illustration of the relationship among the strong, weak and arbitrary-order heredity.

3.2 The Model

Based on Eq. (6) and Definition 1, we formulate the GHSM model for up to the Kth-order interactions as

$$
\begin{aligned}
&\min_{\boldsymbol{\Theta}}\ L(\boldsymbol{\Theta}) + \sum_{k=1}^{K} \frac{\lambda}{\alpha^k} \|\boldsymbol{\theta}^{(k)}\|_1, \\
&\text{s.t. } |\theta_i^{(1)}| \geq \|\mathbf{e}_i^{(2)} \odot \boldsymbol{\theta}^{(2)}\|_1 \geq \cdots \geq \|\mathbf{e}_i^{(K)} \odot \boldsymbol{\theta}^{(K)}\|_1,\ i \in \mathbb{N}_d,
\end{aligned} \tag{7}
$$

where λ and α are two regularization parameters controlling the sparsity and the decay in the coefficients for interactions of different orders, $\boldsymbol{\Theta}$ denotes the set of parameters $\{\boldsymbol{\theta}^{(k)}\}_{k=1}^{K}$, and $L(\cdot)$ is a loss function for regression such as the square loss defined as $L(\boldsymbol{\Theta}) = \frac{1}{2}\|\mathbf{y} - \sum_{k=1}^{K} \sum_{i_1<\cdots<i_k}^{d} \theta_{\langle i_1,\cdots,i_k\rangle}^{(k)} \mathbf{z}_{\langle i_1,\cdots,i_k\rangle}^{(k)}\|_2^2$ where $\|\cdot\|_2$ denotes the ℓ_2 norm of a vector. In problem (7), the constraints associated with each covariate i have a chain of inequality constraints, which contains $(K-1)$ inequality constraints and there are a total of d chains. It is easy to see that these constraints achieve the arbitrary-order hierarchy in Definition 1.

Problem (7) is non-convex due to the chains of inequality constraints. Moreover, the variables are coupled in different chains of constraints, e.g., the variable $\theta^{(3)}_{\langle 1,2,3\rangle}$ appears in three chains associated with the covariates $1, 2, 3$ respectively, which makes the problem more complex. In the next section, we propose an efficient algorithm to solve problem (7).

4. OPTIMIZATION ALGORITHM

In this section, we introduce the optimization algorithm to solve problem (7). The main idea is to combine proximal gradient methods and the ADMM. Since problem (7) is non-convex, we adopt the GIST method [7] whose entire algorithm is shown in Algorithm 1. We define $r(\mathbf{\Theta})$ as

$$r(\boldsymbol{\theta}) = \begin{cases} \sum_{k=1}^{K} \frac{\lambda}{\alpha^k} \|\boldsymbol{\theta}^{(k)}\|_1, & \text{if the constraint in Eq. (7) is satisfied;} \\ +\infty, & \text{otherwise.} \end{cases}$$

Then, the proximal operator at the $(t+1)$th iteration in the GIST method solves the following problem:

$$\mathbf{\Theta}^{(t+1)} = \arg\min_{\mathbf{\Theta}} \frac{\tau_t}{2} \sum_{k=1}^{K} \|\boldsymbol{\theta}^{(k)} - \mathbf{v}^{(k)}\|_2^2 + r(\mathbf{\Theta}), \tag{8}$$

where $[\boldsymbol{\theta}^{(k)}]^{(t)}$ denotes the estimation of $\boldsymbol{\theta}^{(k)}$ in the tth iteration, $\mathbf{v}^{(k)} = [\boldsymbol{\theta}^{(k)}]^{(t)} - \frac{1}{\tau_t}\nabla_{\boldsymbol{\theta}^{(k)}} L(\mathbf{\Theta}^{(t)})$, $\nabla_{\boldsymbol{\theta}^{(k)}} L(\mathbf{\Theta}^{(t)})$ denotes the gradient of $L(\mathbf{\Theta}^{(t)})$ with respect to $\boldsymbol{\theta}^{(k)}$ at $\mathbf{\Theta}^{(t)}$ and it can be easily computed as $[\mathbf{Z}^{(k)}]^\top (\sum_{k'=1}^{K} \mathbf{Z}^{(k')}\boldsymbol{\theta}^{(k')} - \mathbf{y})$ for $k \in \mathbb{N}_K$, $\mathbf{Z}^{(k)} \in \mathbb{R}^{n\times\binom{d}{k}}$ is the matrix containing all the kth-order interaction effects, and τ_t is a step size determined via a line search method by satisfying the following condition:

$$F(\mathbf{\Theta}^{(t+1)}) \le F(\mathbf{\Theta}^{(t)}) - \frac{\varphi\tau_t}{2} \sum_{k=1}^{K} \|[\boldsymbol{\theta}^{(k)}]^{(t+1)} - [\boldsymbol{\theta}^{(k)}]^{(t)}\|_2^2, \tag{9}$$

where $F(\mathbf{\Theta}) = L(\mathbf{\Theta}) + r(\mathbf{\Theta})$ and φ is a constant in $(0, 1)$. Then, the GIST algorithm iteratively solves the proximal problem (8) until convergence.

Algorithm 1 The GIST algorithm for solving problem (7).

Input: $\mathbf{X}, \mathbf{y}, K, \epsilon = 10^{-4}$;
Output: $\hat{\mathbf{\Theta}}$;
Initialize $\mathbf{\Theta}^{(0)}, \eta > 1, 0 < \tau_{min} < \tau_{max}, \varphi \in (0,1), t = 0$;
repeat
  $\tau_t \in [\tau_{min}, \tau_{max}]$;
  repeat
    Solve the proximal problem (8) with $\mathbf{\Theta}^{(t)}$ and τ_t;
    $\tau_t = \eta\tau_t$;
  until condition (9) is satisifed;
  $t = t + 1$;
until $F(\mathbf{\Theta}^{(t)}) - F(\mathbf{\Theta}^{(t+1)}) < \epsilon$;
$\hat{\mathbf{\Theta}} = \mathbf{\Theta}^{(t)}$;

4.1 Solving The Proximal Problem

The key problem in Algorithm 1 is to solve the proximal problem (8). Since $r(\cdot)$ is an extended real-value function, problem (8) can be reformulated as

$$\min_{\mathbf{\Theta}} \frac{\tau}{2} \sum_{k=1}^{K} \|\boldsymbol{\theta}^{(k)} - \mathbf{v}^{(k)}\|_2^2 + \sum_{k=1}^{K} \frac{\lambda}{\alpha^k} \|\boldsymbol{\theta}^{(k)}\|_1, \tag{10}$$
$$\text{s.t. } |\theta_i^{(1)}| \ge \|\mathbf{e}_i^{(2)} \odot \boldsymbol{\theta}^{(2)}\|_1 \ge \cdots \ge \|\mathbf{e}_i^{(K)} \odot \boldsymbol{\theta}^{(K)}\|_1 \ \forall i \in \mathbb{N}_d,$$

where we omit the iterative index t for notational simplicity. Problem (10) is still non-convex due to the chains of inequality constraints. However, the following theorem shows that problem (10) admits an equivalently convex formulation.[1]

THEOREM 1. *Let $\bar{\boldsymbol{\theta}}^{(k)} = |\boldsymbol{\theta}^{(k)}|$, where the operator $|\cdot|$ denotes the elementwise absolute operator on a vector. Then problem (10) is equivalent with the following convex optimization problem:*

$$\min_{\bar{\boldsymbol{\theta}}^{(1)},\ldots,\bar{\boldsymbol{\theta}}^{(K)}} \frac{\tau}{2} \sum_{k=1}^{K} \|\bar{\boldsymbol{\theta}}^{(k)} - \bar{\mathbf{v}}^{(k)}\|_2^2, \tag{11}$$
$$\text{s.t. } \bar{\theta}_i^{(1)} \ge [\mathbf{e}_i^{(2)}]^\top \bar{\boldsymbol{\theta}}^{(2)} \ge \cdots \ge [\mathbf{e}_i^{(K)}]^\top \bar{\boldsymbol{\theta}}^{(K)}, \ \forall i \in \mathbb{N}_d,$$
$$\bar{\boldsymbol{\theta}}^{(k)} \succeq 0, \ \forall k \in \mathbb{N}_K,$$

where $\mathbf{1}$ denotes a column vector of all ones with appropriate size, $\bar{\mathbf{v}}^{(k)} = |\mathbf{v}^{(k)}| - \frac{\lambda}{\alpha^k \tau}\mathbf{1}$, and $\succeq$ denotes the elementwise 'no smaller than' operator. The solution of problem (10) can be obtained as $\boldsymbol{\theta}^{(k)} = \mathrm{sign}(\mathbf{v}^{(k)}) \odot \bar{\boldsymbol{\theta}}^{(k)}$ for $k \in \mathbb{N}_K$, where $\mathrm{sign}(\cdot)$ is the elementwise sign operator.

It is easy to find that problem (11) is a quadratic programming problem, hence many off-the-shelf solvers for convex programming can be used directly to obtain the optimal solution. Nevertheless, instead of using these tools, we propose an efficient algorithm to solve problem (11) by taking advantage of the chain structure in the constraints. In problem (11), the variables are coupled together in the chains of inequality constraints. In order to decouple these parameters, we use the ADMM method to solve problem (11) by introducing new variables.

We define $\mathbf{p}^{(k)} = \bar{\boldsymbol{\theta}}^{(k)}$ for $k \in \mathbb{N}_K$, $\boldsymbol{\delta}_i = ([\mathbf{e}_i^{(2)}]^\top \mathbf{p}^{(2)}, [\mathbf{e}_i^{(3)}]^\top \mathbf{p}^{(3)}, \cdots, [\mathbf{e}_i^{(K)}]^\top \mathbf{p}^{(K)})^\top \in \mathbb{R}^{K-1}$ for $i \in \mathbb{N}_d$, and $\mathbf{q}_i = \boldsymbol{\delta}_i \in \mathbb{R}^{K-1}$. Then, problem (11) can be reformulated as

$$\min_{\{\bar{\boldsymbol{\theta}}^{(k)}\},\{\mathbf{p}^{(k)}\},\{\mathbf{q}_i\}} \frac{\tau}{2} \sum_{k=1}^{K} \|\bar{\boldsymbol{\theta}}^{(k)} - \bar{\mathbf{v}}^{(k)}\|_2^2, \tag{12}$$
$$\text{s.t.} \quad \bar{\boldsymbol{\theta}}^{(k)} \succeq 0, \ \forall k \in \mathbb{N}_K$$
$$\mathbf{p}^{(k)} = \bar{\boldsymbol{\theta}}^{(k)}, \ \forall k \in \mathbb{N}_K$$
$$\mathbf{q}_i = \boldsymbol{\delta}_i, \ \forall i \in \mathbb{N}_d$$
$$p_i^{(1)} \ge q_{1,i} \ge \cdots \ge q_{K-1,i}, \ \forall i \in \mathbb{N}_d,$$

where $p_i^{(1)}$ is the ith element in $\mathbf{p}^{(1)}$ and $q_{j,i}$ is the jth element in $\mathbf{q}_i$. Based on problem (12), we define the augmented Lagrangian function as

$$\bar{L}(\bar{\mathbf{\Theta}}, \mathbf{P}, \mathbf{Q}) = \frac{\tau}{2} \sum_{k=1}^{K} \|\bar{\boldsymbol{\theta}}^{(k)} - \bar{\mathbf{v}}^{(k)}\|_2^2 + \sum_{k=1}^{K} \frac{\rho_1}{2} \|\mathbf{p}^{(k)} - \bar{\boldsymbol{\theta}}^{(k)}\|_2^2$$
$$+ \sum_{k=1}^{K} [\mathbf{a}^{(k)}]^\top (\mathbf{p}^{(k)} - \bar{\boldsymbol{\theta}}^{(k)}) + \sum_{i=1}^{d} \frac{\rho_2}{2} \|\mathbf{q}_i - \boldsymbol{\delta}_i\|_2^2 + \sum_{i=1}^{d} \mathbf{b}_i^\top (\mathbf{q}_i - \boldsymbol{\delta}_i).$$

where $\bar{\mathbf{\Theta}}$ denotes the set of parameters $\{\bar{\boldsymbol{\theta}}^{(k)}\}_{k=1}^{K}$, $\mathbf{P}$ and $\mathbf{Q}$ denote the sets of variables $\{\mathbf{p}^{(k)}\}_{k=1}^{K}$ and $\{\mathbf{q}_i\}_{i=1}^{d}$ respectively, $\{\boldsymbol{a}^{(k)}\}_{k=1}^{K}$ and $\{\boldsymbol{b}_i\}_{i=1}^{d}$ are the Lagrangian multipliers, and ρ_1 and ρ_2 are two penalty parameters. Then we need to solve the following problem:

$$\min_{\bar{\mathbf{\Theta}},\mathbf{P},\mathbf{Q}} \bar{L}(\bar{\mathbf{\Theta}}, \mathbf{P}, \mathbf{Q}) \text{ s.t. } \begin{cases} \bar{\boldsymbol{\theta}}^{(k)} \succeq 0, \ k \in \mathbb{N}_K; \\ p_i^{(1)} \ge q_{1,i} \ge \cdots \ge q_{K-1,i}, \ i \in \mathbb{N}_d. \end{cases}$$

The above problem can be solved via the ADMM algorithm presented in algorithm 2, in which three subproblems in steps 4, 5 and 6 need to be solved. In the next two sections, we will show how to solve those subproblems efficiently.

[1] We put all the proofs in the supplementary material at http://www.stat.rutgers.edu/home/lhan.

Algorithm 2 The ADMM algorithm for solving problem (12).

Input: $\mathbf{X}, \mathbf{y}, K$;
Output: $\hat{\boldsymbol{\Theta}}$;
1: Initialize $\bar{\boldsymbol{\Theta}}^{(0)}$, $\mathbf{Q}^{(0)}$ and $\mathbf{A}^{(0)}$;
2: Set $\rho = 0.1$ and $t = 0$;
3: **repeat**
4: Solve $\bar{\boldsymbol{\Theta}}^{(t+1)}$ with fixed $\mathbf{P}^{(t)}$ and $\mathbf{Q}^{(t)}$;
5: Solve $\{\mathbf{P}^{(t+1)} \backslash [\mathbf{p}^{(1)}]^{(t+1)}\}$ with fixed $\bar{\boldsymbol{\Theta}}^{(t)}$, $\mathbf{Q}^{(t)}$ and $[\mathbf{p}^{(1)}]^{(t)}$;
6: Solve $\mathbf{Q}^{(t+1)}$ and $[\mathbf{p}^{(1)}]^{(t+1)}$ with fixed $\bar{\boldsymbol{\Theta}}^{(t)}$, $\{\mathbf{P}^{(t)} \backslash [\mathbf{p}^{(1)}]^{(t)}\}$;
7: $[\boldsymbol{a}^{(k)}]^{(t+1)} = [\boldsymbol{a}^{(k)}]^{(t)} + \rho_1([\mathbf{p}^{(k)}]^{(t)} - [\bar{\boldsymbol{\theta}}^{(k)}]^{(t)})$ for $k \in \mathbb{N}_K$;
8: $\boldsymbol{b}_i^{(t+1)} = \boldsymbol{b}_i^{(t)} + \rho_2(\mathbf{q}_i^{(t)} - \boldsymbol{\delta}_i^{(t)})$ for $i \in \mathbb{N}_d$;
9: $t = t + 1$;
10: **until** Some convergence criterion is satisfied;

4.2 Analytical Solutions in Steps 4 and 5

In step 4 of Algorithm 2, with fixed $\mathbf{P}$ and $\mathbf{Q}$, the problem with respect to $\bar{\boldsymbol{\Theta}}$ can be rewritten as

$$\min_{\bar{\boldsymbol{\Theta}}} \sum_{k=1}^{K} \|\bar{\boldsymbol{\theta}}^{(k)} - \frac{\tau \bar{\mathbf{v}}^{(k)} + \rho_1 \mathbf{p}^{(k)} + \boldsymbol{a}^{(k)}}{\tau + \rho_1}\|_2^2, \text{ s.t. } \bar{\boldsymbol{\theta}}^{(k)} \succeq 0, \quad (13)$$

which can be easily solved via the following analytical solution:

$$[\bar{\boldsymbol{\theta}}^{(k)}]^* = \max\left(0, \frac{\tau \bar{\mathbf{v}}^{(k)} + \rho_1 \mathbf{p}^{(k)} + \boldsymbol{a}^{(k)}}{\tau + \rho_1}\right), \ \forall k \in \mathbb{N}_K. \quad (14)$$

Given fixed $\bar{\boldsymbol{\Theta}}$, $\mathbf{Q}$ and $\mathbf{p}^{(1)}$, the problem with respect to $\mathbf{p}^{(2)}, \cdots, \mathbf{p}^{(K)}$ corresponding to step 5 of Algorithm 2 can be decomposed into $K-1$ separable problems with the problem for $\mathbf{p}^{(k)}$ formulated as

$$\min_{\mathbf{p}^{(k)}} \frac{1}{2}[\mathbf{p}^{(k)}]^\top \mathbf{H}^{(k)} \mathbf{p}^{(k)} - [\mathbf{c}^{(k)}]^\top \mathbf{p}^{(k)}, \ k = 2, \cdots, K, \quad (15)$$

where $\mathbf{I}$ is an identity matrix with appropriate size, the matrix $\mathbf{E}^{(k)} = (\mathbf{e}_1^{(k)}, \mathbf{e}_2^{(k)}, \cdots, \mathbf{e}_d^{(k)}) \in \mathbb{R}^{\binom{d}{k} \times d}$, and $\mathbf{H}^{(k)}$, $\mathbf{c}^{(k)}$ are defined as

$$\mathbf{H}^{(k)} = \mathbf{I} + \mathbf{E}^{(k)}[\mathbf{E}^{(k)}]^\top,$$

$$\mathbf{c}^{(k)} = \bar{\boldsymbol{\theta}}^{(k)} - \frac{1}{\rho_1}\boldsymbol{a}^{(k)} + \sum_{i=1}^{d}(\frac{1}{\rho_2} b_{k-1,i} + q_{k-1,i})\mathbf{e}_i^{(k)}.$$

Note that $\mathbf{H}^{(k)}$ is positive definite (PD). Hence, $\mathbf{H}^{(k)}$ is invertible and its inverse can be computed efficiently as $[\mathbf{H}^{(k)}]^{-1} = \mathbf{I} - \mathbf{E}^{(k)}(\mathbf{I} + [\mathbf{E}^{(k)}]^\top \mathbf{E}^{(k)})^{-1}[\mathbf{E}^{(k)}]^\top$, where the matrix inverse is actually taken on a $d \times d$ matrix $\mathbf{I} + [\mathbf{E}^{(k)}]^\top \mathbf{E}^{(k)}$ instead of the original $\binom{d}{k} \times \binom{d}{k}$ matrix $\mathbf{H}^{(k)}$. Then, the optimal solution of problem (15) can be computed as

$$\begin{aligned}[\mathbf{p}^{(k)}]^* &= [\mathbf{H}^{(k)}]^{-1}\mathbf{c}^{(k)} \quad (16)\\ &= \mathbf{c}^{(k)} - \left(\mathbf{E}^{(k)}(\mathbf{I} + [\mathbf{E}^{(k)}]^\top \mathbf{E}^{(k)})^{-1}\right)\left([\mathbf{E}^{(k)}]^\top \mathbf{c}^{(k)}\right).\end{aligned}$$

Moreover, given the data, $\mathbf{E}^{(k)}(\mathbf{I} + [\mathbf{E}^{(k)}]^\top \mathbf{E}^{(k)})^{-1} \in \mathbb{R}^{\binom{d}{k} \times d}$ is a constant matrix and so it can be computed only once and stored prior to the model learning. As a consequence, the analytical solution in Eq. (16) only takes $O(d\binom{d}{k})$ time complexity for each $[\bar{\boldsymbol{\theta}}^{(k)}]^*$, which is almost *linear* with respect to the number of the kth-order interactions.

4.3 Efficient Solution in Step 6

With fixed $\bar{\boldsymbol{\Theta}}$ and $\mathbf{p}^{(2)}, \cdots, \mathbf{p}^{(K)}$, the problem w.r.t. $\mathbf{Q}$ and $\mathbf{p}^{(1)}$ can be formulated as

$$\min_{\mathbf{Q}, \mathbf{p}^{(1)}} \frac{\rho_1}{2}\|\mathbf{p}^{(1)} - (\bar{\boldsymbol{\theta}}^{(1)} - \frac{\boldsymbol{a}^{(1)}}{\rho_1})\|_2^2 + \frac{\rho_2}{2}\sum_{i=1}^{d}\|\mathbf{q}_i - (\boldsymbol{\delta}_i - \frac{\boldsymbol{b}_i}{\rho_2})\|_2^2$$

$$\text{s.t. } p_i^{(1)} \geq q_{1,i} \geq \cdots \geq q_{K-1,i}, \ \forall i \in \mathbb{N}_d. \quad (17)$$

Problem (17) can be decomposed into d independent problems with the ith one formulated as

$$\min_{\mathbf{q}_i, p_i^{(1)}} \frac{\rho_1}{\rho_2}\left(p_i^{(1)} - (\bar{\theta}_i^{(1)} - \frac{a_i^{(1)}}{\rho_1})\right)^2 + \sum_{k=1}^{K-1}\left(q_{k,i} - (\delta_{k,i} - \frac{b_{k,i}}{\rho_2})\right)^2$$

$$\text{s.t. } p_i^{(1)} \geq q_{1,i} \geq \cdots \geq q_{K-1,i}, \quad (18)$$

where $\bar{\theta}_i^{(1)}$, $a_i^{(1)}$ are the ith elements in $\bar{\boldsymbol{\theta}}^{(1)}$ and $\boldsymbol{a}^{(1)}$ respectively, and $\delta_{k,i}$, $b_{k,i}$ are the kth elements in $\boldsymbol{\delta}_i$ and $\boldsymbol{b}_i$ respectively.

In problem (18), the chain of inequality constraints still exists. We first rewrite this problem into a more general formulation as

$$\min_{\mathbf{s}} \sum_{k=1}^{K} \omega_k (s_k - u_k)^2 \quad \text{s.t. } s_1 \geq s_2 \geq \cdots \geq s_K, \quad (19)$$

where problem (18) is a special case of problem (19) by setting $\mathbf{s} = (p_i^{(1)}, q_{1,i}, \cdots, q_{K-1,i})^\top \in \mathbb{R}^K$, $\mathbf{u} = (\bar{\theta}_i^{(1)} - \frac{a_i^{(1)}}{\rho_1}, \delta_{1,i} - \frac{b_{1,i}}{\rho_2}, \cdots, \delta_{K-1,i} - \frac{b_{K-1,i}}{\rho_2})^\top \in \mathbb{R}^K$ and $\boldsymbol{\omega} = (\frac{\rho_1}{\rho_2}, 1, \cdots, 1)^\top \in \mathbb{R}^K$.

In the following, we generalize our previous results in [8] to show that an efficient solution exists for problem (19). We first introduce two useful lemmas to reveal some interesting properties of problem (19).

LEMMA 1. *In problem (19), the following properties hold: (1) If $u_1 \geq u_2 \geq \cdots \geq u_K$, then the optimal solution $(s_1^*, s_2^*, \cdots, s_K^*)$ is $(u_1, u_2, \cdots, u_K)$; (2) If $u_1 \leq u_2 \leq \cdots \leq u_K$, then the optimal solution $(s_1^*, s_2^*, \cdots, s_K^*)$ is $(u^*, \cdots, u^*)|_K$, where $u^* = \frac{\sum_{k=1}^K \omega_k u_k}{\sum_{k=1}^K \omega_k}$ and $(u^*, \cdots, u^*)|_K$ denotes a sequence with K identical elements u^*.*

LEMMA 2. *For any two sets of inputs $\{(u_1, \cdots, u_l), (\omega_1, \cdots, \omega_l)\}$ and $\{(u_{l+1}, \cdots, u_n), (\omega_{l+1}, \cdots, \omega_n)\}$, which define two instances of problem (19), if the optimal solutions for them are $(\dot{u}^*, \cdots, \dot{u}^*)|_l$ and $(\ddot{u}^*, \cdots, \ddot{u}^*)|_{n-l}$ respectively, then we have: (1) If $\dot{u}^* \geq \ddot{u}^*$, the optimal solution for the problem defined by the concatenated sequence $(u_1, \cdots, u_l) \bowtie (u_{l+1}, \cdots, u_n)$ and concatenated weights $(\omega_1, \cdots, \omega_l) \bowtie (\omega_{l+1}, \cdots, \omega_n)$ is $(\dot{u}^*, \cdots, \dot{u}^*)|_l \bowtie (\ddot{u}^*, \cdots, \ddot{u}^*)|_{n-l}$; (2) Otherwise, i.e., $\dot{u}^* < \ddot{u}^*$, the optimal solution for the problem defined by the concatenated sequence is $(u^*, \cdots, u^*)|_n$, where $u^* = \frac{\sum_{i=1}^n \omega_i u_i}{\sum_{i=1}^n \omega_i}$.*

Lemma 2 implies that we can immediately obtain the solution of problem (19) defined by the input $(u_1, \cdots, u_n)$ and $(\omega_1, \cdots, \omega_n)$, if $(u_1, \cdots, u_n)$ is a concatenation from two sub-sequences and the optimal solutions corresponding to problems defined by the two sub-sequences have solutions with identical values. Therefore, based on Lemma 2, we devise Algorithm 3 to solve problem (19) with its optimality guaranteed by the following theorem.

THEOREM 2. *For problem (19) defined by $(u_1, \cdots, u_K)$ and $(\omega_1, \cdots, \omega_K)$, Algorithm 3 finds its optimal solution.*

4.4 Time Complexity

We analyze the time complexity of the whole optimization procedure for solving the GHSM model. We first discuss the time complexity of the inner most Algorithm 3. In Algorithm 3, step 1 only needs to scan the input sequence $(u_1, \cdots, u_K)$ once and thus it needs $O(K)$ time. Although there exist two loops from step 3 to step 14, the maximum number of the concatenation operations in step 8 is $M-1$. For the concatenation operation, according to Lemma 2, it only needs to compute the weighted average of the

Algorithm 3 The algorithm for solving problem (19).

Input: $(u_1, \cdots, u_K)$ and $(\omega_1, \cdots, \omega_K)$;
Output: $(s_1^*, \cdots, s_K^*)$;

Scan $(u_1, \cdots, u_K)$ once to split it into M non-decreasing sub-sequences $(\boldsymbol{t}_1, \cdots, \boldsymbol{t}_M)$ and meanwhile split $(\omega_1, \cdots, \omega_K)$ accordingly. Then calculate the solutions for the problems defined by those sub-sequences and sub-weights based on Lemma 1;
Push $\boldsymbol{t}_1$ into a stack;
for $m = 2 : M$ **do**
    Push $\boldsymbol{t}_m$ into the stack;
    while there are at least two sequences in the stack **do**
        Pop the first and second sequences from the stack and denote the solutions for their associated problems by $\ddot{u}^*$ and $\dot{u}^*$ separately;
        if $\dot{u}^* < \ddot{u}^*$ **then**
            Concatenate the two sequences under the second condition in Lemma 2 and then push the concatenated sequence into the stack;
        else
            Push the two sequences back into the stack without any operation;
            Break;
        end if
    end while
end for
Concatenate the solutions of the sequences in the stack from bottom to top and output the concatenated solution;

entries in two sequences and we just need to record the weighted average and the sum of the weights in each sequence, making each concatenation operation cost $O(1)$. Since $M \leq K$, the complexity of Algorithm 3 is $O(K)$.

In Algorithm 2, solving the subproblem in step 4 by using Eq. (14) requires $O\left(\sum_{k=1}^{K}\binom{d}{k}\right)$ time. The computation of step 5 by using the closed-form solution in Eq. (16) takes $O\left(d\sum_{k=2}^{K}\binom{d}{k}\right)$ time. The computation in step 6 needs to execute Algorithm 3 for d times, and hence the time cost is $O(dK)$. Usually, we have $K \ll d$ and hence $dK < d\sum_{k=2}^{K}\binom{d}{k}$. So the total time complexity of each iteration in Algorithm 2 is $O\left(d\sum_{k=2}^{K}\binom{d}{k}\right)$.

By assuming that Algorithms 1 and 2 need N_1 and N_2 iterations to converge respectively, the total time complexity for solving the GHSM model is $O\left(N_1 N_2 d\sum_{k=2}^{K}\binom{d}{k}\right)$, which is almost *linear* with respect to the total number of interaction effects $\sum_{k=2}^{K}\binom{d}{k}$. In our experiments, we empirically find that both N_1 and N_2 are small when convergence. Hence, the overall algorithm for solving the GHSM model is very efficient. Moreover, according to Sections 4.2 and 4.3, the problems in steps 4, 5 and 6 of the ADMM algorithm can be decomposed into a number of independent problems, which can be parallelized to further improve the efficiency.

5. EXPERIMENTS

In this section, we empirically evaluate the proposed GHSM method and compare with a large number of the state-of-the-art methods for hierarchical sparse modeling. Specifically, the competitors include (1) Lasso [21], which is the sparse model using covariates only by applying the ℓ_1 penalty on the model coefficients; (2) All-Interactions Lasso (AIL-k), which is the sparse interaction model using up to the kth-order interactions based on the ℓ_1 penalty. We concatenate all the effects together to form a new data matrix and treat it as a Lasso problem; (3) weak hierNet (w-hierNet) [1], which is the HSM method using up to the 2nd-order interaction effects with the weak heredity, i.e., solving the problem in Eq. (5). Its R package 'hierNet' is available in 'CRAN'; (4) eWHL [12], which is an efficient implementation for the w-hierNet method proposed in [1]; (5) strong hierNet (s-hierNet) [1], which is the HSM method using up to the 2nd-order interaction effects with the strong heredity, i.e., solving the problem in Eq. (4). Its R package 'hierNet' is available in 'CRAN'; (6) FAMILY [9], which is a convex HSM model using up to the 2nd-order interaction effects with the strong heredity, where the sparsity is achieved by using the group lasso. Many methods [11, 16, 9, 22] have similar ideas and we select the FAMILY method as a representative. Its R package 'FAMILY' is available in 'CRAN'; (7) GHSM-k, which is the proposed GHSM models that can deal with up to the arbitrary kth-order interaction effects.

The experimental platform is a 64-bit machine with 2.2 GHz quad-core Intel Core i7 CPU and 16 GB memory.

5.1 Synthetic Study

In this section, we conduct experiments on synthetic datasets.

5.1.1 *Settings*

To study different orders of interactions, we generate 3 synthetic datasets with the highest order being $K = 3, 4, 5$ respectively. In all the datasets, the number of training samples n is set to 200 and the number of covariates d is 20. Each entry in the data matrix for training, $\mathbf{X} \in \mathbb{R}^{n \times d}$, is sampled from the standard normal distribution. The kth-order interaction matrix $\mathbf{Z}^{(k)} \in \mathbb{R}^{n \times \binom{d}{k}}$ is then generated with its column indices following Table 1. All the columns of matrices $\mathbf{X}$ and $\mathbf{Z}^{(k)}$'s are normalized to have zero mean and unit variance.

In all the 3 datasets, we set the first half of the coefficients with respect to $\boldsymbol{\theta}^{(1)}$ to be 1 and the rest to be 0. For the first dataset with $K = 3$, the indices of the non-zero coefficients in the second-order interactions are set to be $\langle 1, 2\rangle$, $\langle 3, 4\rangle$, $\langle 5, 6\rangle$, $\langle 7, 8\rangle$ and $\langle 9, 10\rangle$, i.e., there are 5 non-zero coefficients in $\boldsymbol{\theta}^{(2)}$. Similarly, we set the indices of the non-zero coefficients in the third-order interactions as $\langle 1, 2, 3\rangle$, $\langle 2, 3, 4\rangle$, $\langle 4, 5, 6\rangle$, $\langle 5, 6, 7\rangle$, $\langle 7, 8, 9\rangle$ and $\langle 8, 9, 10\rangle$, i.e., 6 entries in $\boldsymbol{\theta}^{(3)}$ are non-zero. All the non-zero entries in $\boldsymbol{\theta}^{(2)}$ and $\boldsymbol{\theta}^{(3)}$ are set to 0.5. For the second dataset with $K = 4$, we keep the settings for the orders up to the third order as in the case $K = 3$ and set the indices of the non-zero coefficients in the 4th-order interactions as $\langle 1, 2, 3, 4\rangle$, $\langle 2, 3, 4, 5\rangle$, $\langle 5, 6, 7, 8\rangle$ and $\langle 6, 7, 8, 9\rangle$, leading to 4 non-zero coefficients in $\boldsymbol{\theta}^{(4)}$. All the non-zero entries in $\boldsymbol{\theta}^{(4)}$ are also set to 0.5. For the third dataset with $K = 5$, we adopt the same settings for up to the fourth order as in the case $K = 4$ and set the indices of non-zero coefficients in the 5th-order interactions as $\langle 1, 2, 3, 4, 5\rangle$ and $\langle 2, 3, 4, 5, 6\rangle$ with the corresponding entries having values of 0.5. It is easy to check that the above settings of the model coefficients satisfy the arbitrary-order heredity. Finally, the response vector $\mathbf{y}$ is constructed as $\mathbf{y} = \sum_{k=1}^{K}\mathbf{Z}^{(k)}\boldsymbol{\theta}^{(k)} + \boldsymbol{\epsilon}$ where $\mathbf{Z}^{(1)} = \mathbf{X}$ and $\boldsymbol{\epsilon} \sim \mathcal{N}(\mathbf{0}, \mathbf{I}/4)$. The statistic of the interaction effects used in the synthetic data is given in Table 3.

For all the methods in comparison, we choose their regularization parameters from a set $\{0.1, 0.3, 0.5, 1, 3, 5, 10, 30, 50\}$ by using additional 200 data samples as a validation set. For the GHSM method, there is another regularization parameter α, which is selected from a set $\{1, 2, 10\}$. To measure the performance of different methods, we use the sensitivity (Sen.) and the specificity (Spe.) [12], where non-zero entries in the corresponding coefficient vector are treated as positive and zero entries are negative, for each order of interactions to test the recovery performance on the model coefficients and use the root mean square error (RMSE) on a test set having 200 samples for each setting. For each setting, we repeat each configuration for 10 times and report the average results.

Table 2: The recovery and prediction performance of different methods averaged over 10 repetitions on the synthetic data. '–' indicates the value is not available in the corresponding setting. Higher values of Sen. and Spe. indicates better recovery performance on non-zero and zero entries, respectively. The numbers in bold denote the best results.

	Synthetic data 1: with up to the 3rd-order interactions						
	Recovery on training data						Testing RMSE
	1st-order		2nd-order		3rd-order		
Method	Sen.	Spe.	Sen.	Spe.	Sen.	Spe.	
Lasso	**1.00**	0.86	–	–	–	–	2.910±0.283
AIL-2	**1.00**	0.94	**1.00**	0.92	–	–	1.773±0.244
w-hierNet	**1.00**	0.85	**1.00**	0.95	–	–	1.702±0.272
eWHL	**1.00**	0.92	**1.00**	0.94	–	–	1.718±0.241
s-hierNet	**1.00**	0.79	**1.00**	0.96	–	–	1.655±0.257
FAMILY	**1.00**	0.93	**1.00**	0.97	–	–	1.639±0.211
GHSM-2	**1.00**	0.97	**1.00**	**0.99**	–	–	1.672±0.214
AIL-3	**1.00**	0.93	**1.00**	0.94	0.81	0.96	1.027±0.224
GHSM-3	**1.00**	**0.98**	**1.00**	0.97	**1.00**	**0.97**	**0.965±0.246**
AIL-4	–	–	–	–	–	–	–
GHSM-4	–	–	–	–	–	–	–

	Synthetic data 2: with up to the 4th-order interactions								
	Recovery on training data								Testing RMSE
	1st-order		2nd-order		3rd-order		4th-order		
Method	Sen.	Spe.	Sen.	Spe.	Sen.	Spe.	Sen.	Spe.	
Lasso	**1.00**	0.87	–	–	–	–	–	–	3.010±0.225
AIL-2	**1.00**	0.93	**1.00**	0.90	–	–	–	–	2.006±0.308
w-hierNet	**1.00**	0.82	**1.00**	0.94	–	–	–	–	1.929±0.290
eWHL	**1.00**	0.88	**1.00**	0.95	–	–	–	–	1.907±0.273
s-hierNet	**1.00**	0.60	**1.00**	0.89	–	–	–	–	1.868±0.267
FAMILY	**1.00**	0.83	**1.00**	0.92	–	–	–	–	1.891±0.299
GHSM-2	**1.00**	0.88	**1.00**	**0.99**	–	–	–	–	1.856±0.249
AIL-3	**1.00**	0.88	**1.00**	0.86	0.95	0.90	–	–	1.704±0.161
GHSM-3	**1.00**	**0.97**	**1.00**	0.91	**1.00**	0.91	–	–	1.506±0.168
AIL-4	**1.00**	0.95	**1.00**	0.94	0.93	**0.96**	0.85	0.98	1.484±0.226
GHSM-4	**1.00**	0.96	0.98	0.86	0.92	0.91	**0.93**	**0.99**	**1.333±0.271**

	Synthetic data 3: with up to the 5th-order interactions										
	Recovery on training data										Testing RMSE
	1st-order		2nd-order		3rd-order		4th-order		5th-order		
Method	Sen.	Spe.	Sen.	Spe.	Sen.	Spe.	Sen.	Spe.	Sen.	Spe.	
Lasso	**1.00**	0.85	–	–	–	–	–	–	–	–	3.239±0.366
AIL-2	**1.00**	**0.95**	**1.00**	0.88	–	–	–	–	–	–	2.279±0.398
w-hierNet	**1.00**	0.83	**1.00**	0.94	–	–	–	–	–	–	2.157±0.388
eWHL	**1.00**	0.90	**1.00**	**0.95**	–	–	–	–	–	–	2.111±0.372
s-hierNet	**1.00**	0.46	**1.00**	0.89	–	–	–	–	–	–	2.083±0.398
FAMILY	**1.00**	0.78	**1.00**	0.90	–	–	–	–	–	–	1.979±0.361
GHSM-2	**1.00**	0.86	**1.00**	**0.95**	–	–	–	–	–	–	2.081±0.336
AIL-3	**1.00**	0.82	**1.00**	0.85	0.92	0.88	–	–	–	–	2.087±0.280
GHSM-3	**1.00**	0.94	**1.00**	0.92	**0.95**	0.93	–	–	–	–	1.907±0.326
AIL-4	**1.00**	0.84	**1.00**	0.89	0.90	0.94	0.70	0.97	–	–	1.835±0.296
GHSM-4	**1.00**	0.88	**1.00**	0.89	0.88	0.92	**0.88**	**0.98**	–	–	1.813±0.369
AIL-5	**1.00**	0.61	**1.00**	0.68	0.92	0.84	0.58	0.96	0.25	**0.99**	2.074±0.327
GHSM-5	**1.00**	0.91	**1.00**	0.81	0.65	**0.96**	0.78	**0.98**	**0.80**	**0.99**	**1.793±0.377**

Table 3: The statistic of the effects in the synthetic study. '#' indicates 'the number of'.

	1st	2nd	3rd	4th	5th
# effects	20	190	1140	4845	15504
# non-zeros	10	5	6	4	2

5.1.2 Results and Analysis

The detailed results are shown in Table 2. The compared methods can be divided into 5 groups, i.e., {Lasso}, {AIL-2, w-hierNet, eWHL, s-hierNet, FAMILY, GHSM-2}, {AIL-3, GHSM-3}, {AIL-4, GHSM-4} and {AIL-5, GHSM-5}, according to the highest order of interactions that they can handle. From the results, we have several observations: (1) All the methods in comparison can correctly detect the useful covariates, since all the Sen. values in the column for the 1st-order interactions are 1's. Similar results are also observed for the 2nd-order interaction models; (2) In each synthetic dataset, the GHSM method has better recovery performance for different orders of interactions compared with other methods; (3) The prediction performance of each method is usually proportional to its capacity. That is, the methods that can learn higher-order interactions will achieve lower RMSE for prediction; (4) In all the three datasets, the GHSM method always has the best prediction performance and it significantly outperforms the Lasso and the existing second-order interaction models; (5) In the third synthetic dataset, the AIL-5 method performs even worse than the AIL-4 method. One possible reason is that the AIL method does not capture the sparse heredity structure, making it hardly detect the correct higher-order interactions. One evidence is that the AIL-5 method only recovers 58% and 25% of the correct 4th and 5th order interactions, respectively, while our GHSM-5 method achieves 78% and 80%.

The synthetic study demonstrates that as long as significant high-order interaction effects exist in the data, the high-order interaction methods will have better performance compared with the conventional second-order interaction methods, and the proposed GHSM method with high-order interactions can learn the sparse heredity structure and accurately detect those interactions, leading to improved prediction performance.

5.2 H3N2 Influenza A Virus Data

In this section, we study the application of the GHSM method on the antigenic sites identification problem.

5.2.1 Settings

Seasonal influenza A viruses pose great threats to public health, while the vaccination is the primary way to reduce this risk. An effective vaccination program requires an antigenic match between circulating viruses and vaccine strains to be used, and hence a timely identification of emerging influenza virus antigenic variants is critical to the success of influenza vaccination programs. Recent studies have suggested that multiple interactive antigenic sites mutations will significantly enhance the antigenic drift of the influenza viruses to new variants [17, 10, 23]. However, discovering the important interactive patterns among the antigenic sites is not trivial.

In this problem, each site is treated as a covariate of the antigenic distances which are the responses, hence identifying interactive patterns among multiple antigenic sites can be formulated as an interaction model. Here we apply the proposed GHSM method to identify interactive antigenic sites on an influenza H3N2 virus dataset [20, 23].[2] This dataset collects the results from the hemagglutination inhibition (HI) assays, which is a matrix recording the reaction values between 192 viruses in rows and a number of test serums in columns. The 192 H3N2 influenza A viruses are collected during year 2004 to 2007. These reaction values in the HI matrix describe the virus antigenicities, and the Euclidian difference between the reaction values of two viruses describes the antigenic distance between them. A large antigenic distance may induce an antigenic drift and sometimes cause influenza outbreaks due to viral escape from existing immunity. Therefore, accurately predicting the antigenic distances among viruses is a fundamental task. In this dataset, for each virus, its hemagglutinin (HA) protein sequence, i.e., a sequence of amino acid sites (covariates) that are responsible for antigenic changes, is also collected. The number of amino acid sites in the HA sequence of each virus is $d = 329$. By comparing the sites in any two HA sequences, we could obtain a difference vector, in which the unchanged positions have zero values and the mutated positions have integer values between 1 and 5, which is computed via the pattern-induced multi-sequence alignment (PIMA) scheme [20, 23]. Then, each pairwise difference vector is treated as a data sample in the data matrix $\mathbf{X}$, and each pairwise antigenic distance obtained from the HI reaction values is used as a response value in the target $\mathbf{y}$. So there are a total number of $\binom{192}{2} = 18336$ samples.

Table 4: Statistics of the influenza virus data.

	1st	2nd	3rd	4th
# effects	329	53,956	5,881,204	479,318,126
# valid effects	329	4368	37,857	157,462
rate	100%	8.1%	0.64%	0.03%
# samples			18,336	

Since there are 329 features, the number of interaction effects increases drastically with respect to the order. Table 4 gives statistics of the effects in this data. When we consider the 3rd- and 4th-order interactions, the dimension of the entire feature space is around hundreds of millions, which leads to heavy computational demand. Fortunately, in each data sample, we find that only few mutated positions have non-zero values and hence the data matrix $\mathbf{X}$ is sparse. As a consequence, a large number of the interaction effects are useless zero vectors since they are obtained via the product among sparse inputs and we can eliminate them before learning. The number of valid effects for each order is given in Table 4. Here we focus on up to the 4th-order interactions since higher-order interactions cannot bring too much performance improvement.

The entries in $\mathbf{X}$ and $\mathbf{Z}^{(k)}$'s are normalized into $[0, 1]$ and each entry in $\mathbf{y}$ is log-transformed and normalized into $[0, 1]$ as well. The regularization parameters for different methods are selected from a set $\{10^{-5}, 10^{-4}, \cdots, 10^{3}\}$ via the 5-fold cross validation. The parameter α in GHSM methods is chosen in the same way as that in the synthetic data. We randomly split the dataset into a training set and a test set by varying the training ratio from 10% to 90% at an interval of 20%. Each setting is repeated for 10 times. We report both the predictive RMSE on the test set and the running time for all the methods.

5.2.2 Results and Analysis

The predictive RMSE's for different methods are presented in Table 5. From the results, we observe that all the interaction models remarkably outperform the Lasso method, implying that incorporating the feature interactions is important in this dataset. Different from the synthetic case, the AIL methods do not show much improvement over the Lasso and this is possibly because the AIL methods can not make use of the sparse heredity structure and the interactions among the antigenic sites are much more complex than the synthetic case. For the second-order interaction models, the strong heredity based methods, i.e., the s-hierNet, FAMILY, and GHSM-2, show better performance than the weak heredity based methods including the w-hierNet and eWHL methods. This could be an evidence that the strong heredity structure is more useful for this problem. Similar to the results in the synthetic case, the GHSM method with higher-order interactions obtain more accurate prediction results and the GHSM-4 method performs the best in all settings.

In addition to the RMSE, we also provide visualizations for the prediction results of different methods via the antigenic cartography, which is an approach to visualize the virus antigenic evolution process on a 2D/3D space by using the antigenic distance among the viruses and has been widely used for virus antigenicity explanation since its first use by [18]. The idea in the antigenic cartography is to utilize the multi-dimensional scaling technique to obtain the coordinates of each virus on a 2D/3D space given the antigenic distance among them. We plot the embedding results in Fig. 2 when the training rate is 10% and use the predicted antigenic distance to reconstruct the cartography of all the viruses. In Fig. 2(a), the cartography using the true antigenic distance among the viruses is plotted in a 2D space, where each circle represents a virus and all the 192 viruses are divided into four different groups according to the year of their appearance. Figs. 2(b)-2(h) show the cartographies of different methods respectively. Since the cartographies of the AIL methods are similar to that of the Lasso and the eWHL and w-hierNet methods are two solutions of the same model, we omit their cartographies. By comparing with Fig. 2(a), we observe that the Lasso method can hardly reconstruct the antigenic distances among the viruses. The second-order interaction models including the w-hierNet, s-hierNet, FAMILY and GHSM-2 methods show clearer reconstruction but the viruses in different years are still hard to be distinguished. The group structure in the cartographies of the GHSM-3 and GHSM-4 methods is much better than others, which can be confirmed by the Pearson correlation coefficients reported in Fig. 2.

One advantage of the GHSM method is that we can identify important high-order interactions based on the model parameters. Specifically, we take the 4th-order interactions learned from the GHSM-4 method for example to see which 4th-order interactions are detected by the algorithm. We sort the magnitude of the coefficients for the 4th-order interactions in a descending order and then select the top 5 interactions, which are $\langle 157, 159, 242, 246\rangle$, $\langle 186, 193, 242, 246\rangle$, $\langle 94, 145, 189, 219\rangle$, $\langle 145, 189, 198, 219\rangle$ and $\langle 94, 145, 189, 198\rangle$. It is well-known in the H3N2 virus antigenicity analysis that there are 135 important antigenic sites out of the total 329 positions identified as the antibody binding sites, since these sites locate at the surface of the H3N2 virus protein structure and they are more likely to react with the sera. These antibody binding sites are further divided into 5 binding areas A-E according to their locations. Promisingly, we find that all of these detected positions in the 4th-order interactions belong to the binding areas. More interestingly, when we tag the binding areas for these sites in the selected interactions, we get the following patterns: ⟨B, B, D, D⟩, ⟨B, B, D, D⟩, ⟨E, A, B, D⟩, ⟨A, B, B, D⟩ and ⟨E, A, B, B⟩, respectively, from which we see that the antigenicity of the H3N2 virus is more likely to be controlled by the interactions among the sites in different binding regions simultaneously instead of in the same binding region. This observation is reasonable since multiple sites from different binding areas can accurately capture the 3D

[2] http://sysbio.cvm.msstate.edu/research/resources

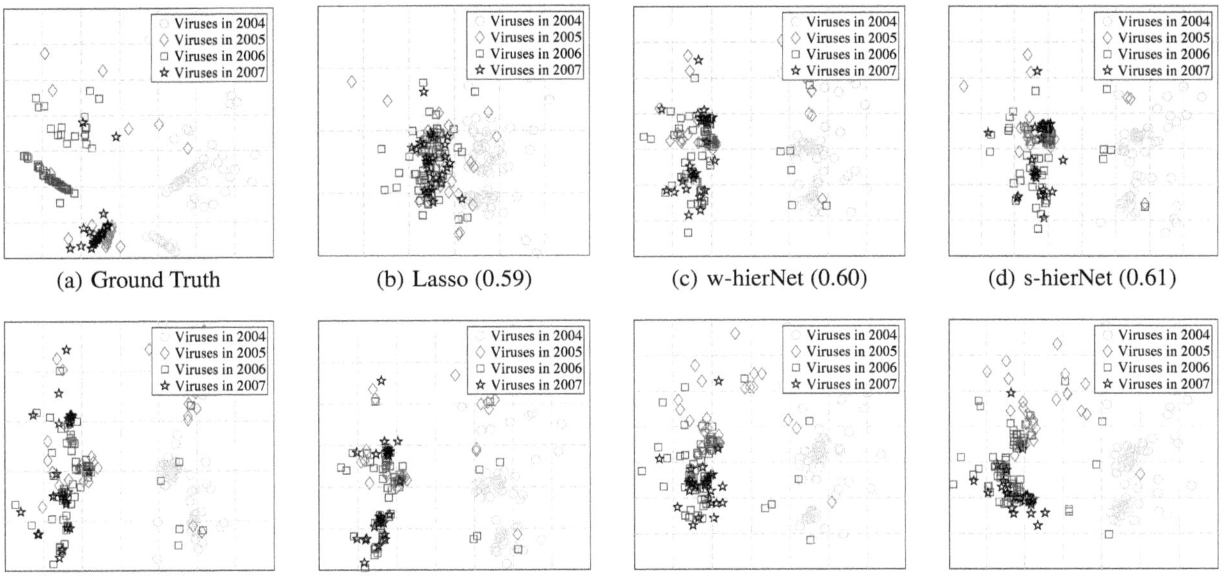

(a) Ground Truth (b) Lasso (0.59) (c) w-hierNet (0.60) (d) s-hierNet (0.61)

(e) FAMILY (0.62) (f) GHSM-2 (0.64) (g) GHSM-3 (0.67) (h) GHSM-4 (**0.70**)

Figure 2: Cartographies of the prediction results of different methods when using 10% samples for training. The number in each bracket of figures (b)-(h) denotes the Pearson correlation coefficient between the true coordinates and the coordinates obtained from each method.

Table 5: The predictive RMSE's on the influenza virus data. '−' indicates that the corresponding algorithm does not return a result after running over 5 hours. The numbers in bold face denotes the best results.

Training Rate	Covariates	Up to 2nd-order interactions					
	Lasso	AIL-2	w-hierNet	eWHL	s-hierNet	FAMILY	GHSM-2
10%	0.3938±0.0076	0.3648±0.0150	0.2025±0.0011	0.2024±0.0023	0.1869±0.0040	0.1823±0.0029	0.1887±0.0018
30%	0.3914±0.0038	0.3622±0.0056	0.2018±0.0019	0.2021±0.0010	0.1855±0.0016	0.1818±0.0016	0.1884±0.0014
50%	0.3935±0.0020	0.3625±0.0027	0.2013±0.0013	0.2019±0.0009	0.1844±0.0040	−	0.1875±0.0014
70%	0.3927±0.0011	0.3634±0.0022	0.1989±0.0024	0.2015±0.0013	0.1835±0.0024	−	0.1873±0.0022
90%	0.3926±0.0027	0.3629±0.0024	0.1958±0.0011	0.2013±0.0022	0.1815±0.0018	−	0.1868±0.0022

Training Rate	Up to 3rd-order interactions		Up to 4th-order interactions	
	AIL-3	GHSM-3	AIL-4	GHSM-4
10%	0.3655±0.0143	0.1742±0.0014	0.3658±0.0163	**0.1737±0.0013**
30%	0.3638±0.0066	0.1735±0.0007	0.3642±0.0065	**0.1725±0.0013**
50%	0.3641±0.0031	0.1733±0.0015	0.3635±0.0034	**0.1714±0.0011**
70%	0.3640±0.0022	0.1732±0.0013	0.3636±0.0025	**0.1718±0.0015**
90%	0.3620±0.0022	0.1723±0.0031	0.3631±0.0029	**0.1697±0.0039**

structure (shape) of the virus. Fig. 3 shows the 3D structure of these binding areas with the sites from the selected interactions. So far, all of the above analysis is considerably useful in influenza vaccine strain selection, and it can significantly reduce the human labor efforts for serological characterization and will increase the probability of correct influenza vaccine candidate selection.

Moreover, we compare the training time of different HSM models on the entire influenza virus dataset and report the results in Table 6. For the 2nd-order HSM, the strong heredity based methods, i.e., the s-hierNet and FAMILY, are computationally much more expensive than the weak heredity based methods such as the w-hierNet and eWHL. The FAMILY method fails to give the solution in reasonable time. Actually, the FAMILY method is computationally intractable even when using only 50% of the samples for training (refer to Table 5). The eWHL method is very efficient since it is specifically designed for the w-hierNet model. The proposed GHSM-2 method, a strong heredity based method, is much more efficient than the s-hierNet and FAMILY methods and comparable with the eWHL algorithm. By increasing the order of interactions, the GHSM-3 and GHSM-4 methods are still very efficient compared with the w-hierNet, s-hierNet and FAMILY methods, while it has much better performance than those methods.

6. CONCLUSION

In this paper, we proposed a generalized hierarchical sparse model to learn arbitrary-order interactions contained in the data via the proposed arbitrary-order heredity structure. An efficient algorithm was developed by decoupling the variables in the complex constraint and all the subproblems have efficient analytical solutions. Empirical results show the effectiveness of the proposed method.

When considering high-order interactions, if the data matrix are not sparse like the influenza virus data, the number of high-order interactions still increases exponentially with respect to the order and solving the GHSM will become intractable even for small d and K. One possible direction to solve this problem is to conduct dimensionality reduction methods before learning the GHSM model via, for example, the feature screening technique. We are also interested in applying the GHSM methods to other biological problems, such as the cancer microarray analysis, to detect important interactions.

Acknowledgments

This work was partially supported by NSF IIS-1250985, NSF IIS-1407939, NIH R01AI116744, NSFC-61305071, NSFC-61473087 and NSF of Jiangsu Province (BK20141340).

Table 6: Training time of all HSMs on the entire flu virus data. '–' indicates that the algorithm does not return a result after running over 5 hours.

	2nd-order interaction models					Higher-order interaction models	
	w-hierNet	eWHL	s-hierNet	FAMILY	GHSM-2	GHSM-3	GHSM-4
Training time (in seconds)	205.6	11.3	5876.9	–	21.3	34.3	76.4

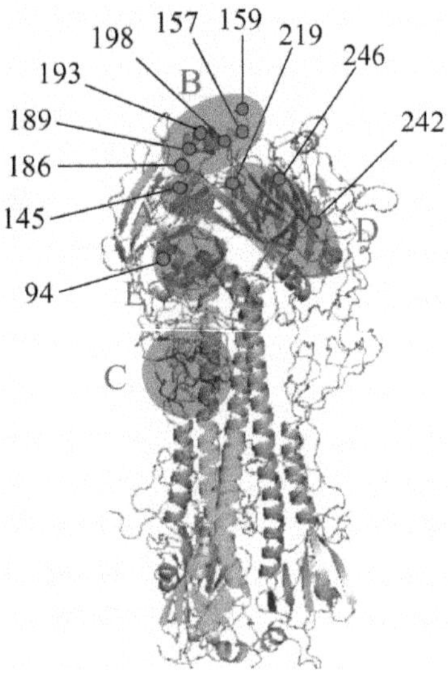

Figure 3: The 3D structure of the H3N2 virus. The red regions denote the anti-body binding regions A-E. The sites from the selected interactions are also labeled.

7. REFERENCES

[1] J. Bien, J. Taylor, and R. Tibshirani. A lasso for hierarchical interactions. *The Annals of Statistics*, 41(3):1111–1141, 2013.

[2] R. J. Cadoret, W. R. Yates, G. Woodworth, and M. A. Stewart. Genetic-environmental interaction in the genesis of aggressivity and conduct disorders. *Archives of General Psychiatry*, 52(11):916–924, 1995.

[3] N. H. Choi, W. Li, and J. Zhu. Variable selection with the strong heredity constraint and its oracle property. *Journal of the American Statistical Association*, 105(489):354–364, 2010.

[4] J. F. Dawson and A. W. Richter. Probing three-way interactions in moderated multiple regression: development and application of a slope difference test. *Journal of Applied Psychology*, 91(4):917, 2006.

[5] T. C. Eley, K. Sugden, A. Corsico, A. M. Gregory, P. Sham, P. McGuffin, R. Plomin, and I. W. Craig. Gene–environment interaction analysis of serotonin system markers with adolescent depression. *Molecular Psychiatry*, 9(10):908–915, 2004.

[6] J. Friedman, T. Hastie, and R. Tibshirani. *The Elements of Statistical Learning*. Springer, Berlin, 2001.

[7] P. Gong, C. Zhang, Z. Lu, J. Z. Huang, and J. Ye. A general iterative shrinkage and thresholding algorithm for non-convex regularized optimization problems. In *ICML*, 2013.

[8] L. Han and Y. Zhang. Learning tree structure in multi-task learning. In *KDD*, pages 397–406, 2015.

[9] A. Haris, D. Witten, and N. Simon. Convex modeling of interactions with strong heredity. *arXiv preprint arXiv:1410.3517*, 2014.

[10] J.-W. Huang, C.-C. King, and J.-M. Yang. Co-evolution positions and rules for antigenic variants of human influenza a/h3n2 viruses. *BMC Bioinformatics*, 10(Suppl 1):S41, 2009.

[11] M. Lim and T. Hastie. Learning interactions through hierarchical group-lasso regularization. *arXiv preprint arXiv:1308.2719*, 2013.

[12] Y. Liu, J. Wang, and J. Ye. An efficient algorithm for weak hierarchical lasso. In *KDD*, pages 283–292, 2014.

[13] D. C. Montgomery, E. A. Peck, and G. G. Vining. *Introduction to Linear Regression Analysis*, volume 821. John Wiley & Sons, 2012.

[14] D. D. Pollock, W. R. Taylor, and N. Goldman. Coevolving protein residues: maximum likelihood identification and relationship to structure. *Journal of Molecular Biology*, 287(1):187–198, 1999.

[15] P. Radchenko and G. M. James. Variable selection using adaptive nonlinear interaction structures in high dimensions. *Journal of the American Statistical Association*, 105(492):1541–1553, 2010.

[16] Y. She and H. Jiang. Group regularized estimation under structural hierarchy. *arXiv preprint arXiv:1411.4691*, 2014.

[17] A. C.-C. Shih, T.-C. Hsiao, M.-S. Ho, and W.-H. Li. Simultaneous amino acid substitutions at antigenic sites drive influenza a hemagglutinin evolution. *PNAS*, 104(15):6283–6288, 2007.

[18] D. J. Smith, A. S. Lapedes, J. C. de Jong, T. M. Bestebroer, G. F. Rimmelzwaan, A. D. Osterhaus, and R. A. Fouchier. Mapping the antigenic and genetic evolution of influenza virus. *Science*, 305(5682):371–376, 2004.

[19] M. J. Somers. Organizational commitment, turnover and absenteeism: An examination of direct and interaction effects. *Journal of Organizational Behavior*, 16(1):49–58, 1995.

[20] H. Sun, J. Yang, T. Zhang, L.-P. Long, K. Jia, G. Yang, R. J. Webby, and X.-F. Wan. Using sequence data to infer the antigenicity of influenza virus. *MBio*, 4(4):e00230–13, 2013.

[21] R. Tibshirani. Regression shrinkage and selection via the lasso. *Journal of the Royal Statistical Society. Series B (Methodological)*, pages 267–288, 1996.

[22] X. Yan and J. Bien. Hierarchical sparse modeling: a choice of two regularizers. *arXiv preprint arXiv:1512.01631*, 2015.

[23] J. Yang, T. Zhang, and X.-F. Wan. Sequence-based antigenic change prediction by a sparse learning method incorporating co-evolutionary information. *PLOS One*, 9(9):e106660, 2014.

[24] M. Yuan, V. R. Joseph, and H. Zou. Structured variable selection and estimation. *The Annals of Applied Statistics*, 3(4):1738–1757, 2009.

[25] M. Yuan and Y. Lin. Model selection and estimation in regression with grouped variables. *Journal of the Royal Statistical Society: Series B (Statistical Methodology)*, 68(1):49–67, 2006.

[26] P. Zhao, G. Rocha, and B. Yu. The composite absolute penalties family for grouped and hierarchical variable selection. *The Annals of Statistics*, 37(6A):3468–3497, 2009.

Joint Community and Structural Hole Spanner Detection via Harmonic Modularity

Lifang He*
Shenzhen University
Shenzhen, China
lifanghescut@gmail.com

Chun-Ta Lu
University of Illinois at Chicago
Chicago, IL, USA
clu29@uic.edu

Jiaqi Ma
Tsinghua University
Beijing, China
mjq12@mails.tsinghua.edu.cn

Jianping Cao
National University of Defense Technology
Changsha, China
caojianping@nudt.edu.cn

Linlin Shen†
Shenzhen University
Shenzhen, China
llshen@szu.edu.cn

Philip S. Yu
University of Illinois at Chicago
Chicago, IL, USA
Tsinghua University
Beijing, China
psyu@uic.edu

ABSTRACT

Detecting communities (or modular structures) and structural hole spanners, the nodes bridging different communities in a network, are two essential tasks in the realm of network analytics. Due to the topological nature of communities and structural hole spanners, these two tasks are naturally tangled with each other, while there has been little synergy between them. In this paper, we propose a novel harmonic modularity method to tackle both tasks simultaneously. Specifically, we apply a harmonic function to measure the smoothness of community structure and to obtain the community indicator. We then investigate the sparsity level of the interactions between communities, with particular emphasis on the nodes connecting to multiple communities, to discriminate the indicator of SH spanners and assist the community guidance. Extensive experiments on real-world networks demonstrate that our proposed method outperforms several state-of-the-art methods in the community detection task and also in the SH spanner identification task (even the methods that require the supervised community information). Furthermore, by removing the SH spanners spotted by our method, we show that the quality of other community detection methods can be further improved.

Keywords

Community detection; structural hole; harmonic function; modularity; social network

*This work was done while the first author was at the University of Illinois at Chicago.

†Corresponding author

KDD '16, August 13–17, 2016, San Francisco, CA, USA.

DOI: http://dx.doi.org/10.1145/2939672.2939807

1. INTRODUCTION

Detecting communities (or modular structures) has been one of the flourishing issues in understanding the characteristics of real-world networks (*e.g.*, computer networks, biological, semantic and social networks). Exemplar applications include recognizing functions of protein in bioinformatics networks [36], and to forecast the information diffusion process in social networks [19]. It is non-trivial mainly because some bridging nodes, which keep the communication between different communities, blur the boundary of communities. From another point of view, these bridging nodes, known as "hubs" in neurology and "structural hole (SH) spanners" in sociology, have more control over the information that is being transmitted among communities [1, 4, 20, 33]. In neurology, examining the function and role of these hubs is of special interest as they play a central role in establishing and maintaining efficient global brain communication, a crucial feature for healthy brain functioning [1, 33]. In sociology, the theory of structural holes [4] suggests that individuals would acquire more potential resources from filling the "holes" between communities that are otherwise disconnected.

Due to the topological nature of communities and SH spanners, both detection tasks are naturally intermingled with each other. To date, however, studies on these two tasks have been performed independently. Traditional community detection approaches focus on finding clusters such that nodes inside a cluster are tightly connected to each other than to nodes in other clusters. Division [11], agglomeration [22], label propagation [8], and optimization [7] which continuously update the network partition to minimize or maximize a given measure of the quality of the network partition (*e.g.*, spectral clustering and modularity) are typical examples for such approaches. However, SH spanners are inherently connected to multiple communities, effectively linking diverse communities into a weakly-knit network. It's not surprising that well defined communities in real world networks are hard to find without considering the existence of SH spanners.

For mining SH spanners, many approaches [5, 13, 18, 20, 28, 32] have been proposed. For example, the authors in [20]

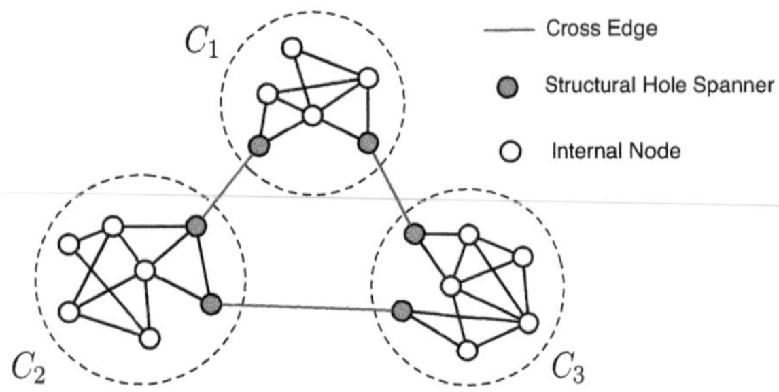

Figure 1: A simple network with three communities and six SH spanners

assume the communities are known in advance and formulate the SH spanners as the nodes such that after removing these nodes, the decrease of minimal cut for communities in network can be maximized. However, for most social networks, it is often difficult to determine the boundaries of communities, as mentioned above. Furthermore, the quality of the identified SH spanners are determined by the communities, which are usually hard to be discovered without removing the SH spanners.

Without given the community information, several importance measures, such as the PageRank [26] and degree centrality [16, 34] have been applied to identify nodes that are important in information diffusion. Some studies [5, 13, 32] utilize the betweenness measure to identify the SH spanners as nodes that have a large number of shortest paths that pass through them. Most recently, [28] proposes to identify the SH spanners by exploiting the bounded inverse closeness centralities of vertices and making use of articulation points of the network. However, the above methods fail to consider one of the most important properties of SH spanners: the information flows between communities are dominated by SH spanners.

Figure 1 illustrates an example of a network with three communities and six SH spanners, where the communities are enclosed by the dashed circles, SH spanners are represented as the red nodes, and the cross edges that connect different communities are marked in blue color. One can notice that these SH spanners are either not having the highest degree centrality or the highest betweenness centrality, but they are the only nodes that can spread information from one community to the other communities. When the community labels (*e.g.*, C_1, C_2 and C_3) are not available, though, it is hard to inspect the information flows between communities.

To unravel the tangled problems regarding community detection and SH spanner detection, we propose to tackle them simultaneously. For the sake of generality, we solely consider the topological structure of the given network. In this paper, we devise a HArmonic Modularity (HAM) scheme to formulate the interaction between communities. Specifically, we apply a harmonic function to measure the harmony between each node and its neighbors, and produce harmonic assignment in each detected community, so that the internal nodes and their intra-community neighbors are as harmonious as possible. By investigating the sparsity level of the interactions between communities, with particular emphasis on the nodes connecting to multiple communities, we are able to discriminate the indicator of SH spanners and assist the community guidance.

Our contributions can be summarized as follows:

- To the best of our knowledge, this is the first attempt to address the problem of joint community and structural hole spanner detection in real-world networks.
- We use the harmonic function to model the topological nature of community and SH spanners, and establish cooperation together. This provides an innovative perspective on the analysis of network structure.
- Through extensive experiments on three real-world network datasets, we present that the proposed HAM method outperforms several state-of-the-art methods in the community detection task and also in the SH spanner detection task (even the methods that require the supervised community information).
- We demonstrate HAM can capture the most intermediate nodes between communities. Furthermore, the SH spanners identified by HAM are more effective in spreading information to different communities than that identified by the alternative methods.
- By removing the SH spanners spotted by our method, we show that the quality of other community detection methods can be further improved.

2. PRELIMINARIES

In this section we establish key definitions and notational conventions that simplify the exposition in later sections. Table 1 lists the important notations used in this paper.

Throughout this paper, matrices are written as boldface capital letters and vectors are denoted as boldface lowercase letters. For a matrix $\mathbf{M} \in \mathbb{R}^{n\times m}$, its elements are denoted by m_{ij}, and its i-th row, j-th column are denoted by $\mathbf{m}^i$, $\mathbf{m}_j$ respectively. The Frobenius norm of $\mathbf{M}$ is defined as $\|\mathbf{M}\|_F = \sqrt{\sum_{i=1}^{n}\|\mathbf{m}^i\|_2^2}$, the $\ell_{2,1}$ norm of $\mathbf{M}$ is defined as $\|\mathbf{M}\|_{2,1} = \sum_{i=1}^{n}\|\mathbf{m}^i\|_2$. For any vector $\mathbf{u} \in \mathbb{R}^n$, $Diag(\mathbf{u}) \in \mathbb{R}^{n\times n}$ is the diagonal matrix whose diagonal elements are u_i. $\mathbf{I}_n$ denotes an identity matrix with size n. $\|\mathbf{u}\|_0$ is the ℓ_0 norm, which counts the number of nonzero elements in the vector $\mathbf{u}$. We assume that there is a social network represented as an undirected graph $G = (V, E)$, where $V = \{v_1, \cdots, v_n\}$ is the set of nodes and $E \subset V \times V$ is the set of edges whose element $e_{ij} = (v_i, v_j)$ represents an interaction between the nodes v_i and v_j. We denote the adjacency matrix of G by $\mathbf{A} = [a_{ij}]$, where $1 \le i, j \le |V| = n$, $a_{ij} = 1$ if node v_i is connected by an edge to node v_j and 0 otherwise. We assume no self loops, thus $a_{ii} = 0$ for all i. In particular, assume that the nodes of the network can be grouped into m communities $C = \{C_1, \cdots, C_m\}$, with $V = C_1 \cup \cdots \cup C_m$ and $C_i \cap C_j = \varnothing$ for every pair i, j with $i \neq j$.

Next, we establish the definitions and main properties of nodes which will be used to formulate the problem.

Definition 1. (Internal Node) For any node $v_i \in C_p$, if all of its neighboring nodes belong to C_p, node v_i is called an internal node.

Table 1: Important Notations

Symbol	Definition
$V = \{v_i\}_{i=1}^n$	set of nodes
$C = \{C_i\}_{i=1}^m$	set of communities
n	total number of nodes ($\|V\|$)
m	number of communities ($\|C\|$)
k	number of top-ranked SH spanners
$\mathbf{A}, \mathbf{D}$	adjacency and degree matrices
$\mathbf{F}$	indicator matrix
d_i	degree of node v_i
$\|\cdot\|_F$	Frobenius norm
$\|\cdot\|_{2,1}$	$\ell_{2,1}$ norm
$\|\cdot\|_0$	ℓ_0 norm

Definition 2. (Structural Hole Spanner) For any node $v_i \in C_p$, if there exists some neighboring nodes $v_j \in C_q (p \neq q)$, node v_i is called a structural hole spanner.

Definition 3. (Intra-Community Neighbor) For any node $v_i \in C_p$, if node v_i connects with node $v_j \in C_p (i \neq j)$, node v_j is called an intra-community neighbor of node v_i. All the intra-community neighbors of node v_i constitute its intra-community neighbor set.

Definition 4. (Inter-Community Neighbor) For any node $v_i \in C_p$, if node v_i connects with node $v_j \in C_q (p \neq q)$, node v_j is called an inter-community neighbor of node v_i. All the inter-community neighbors of node v_i constitute its inter-community neighbor set.

Definition 5. (Cross Edge) For any edge $e_{ij} = (v_i, v_j) \in E$, if v_i and v_j belong to different communities, edge e_{ij} is called a cross edge.

Definition 6. (Harmonic Function) Given a network $G = (V, E)$, a function $h : V \rightarrow \mathbb{R}$ defined on nodes of G is called harmonic if for every $v_i \in V$

$$h(v_i) \equiv \frac{1}{d_i} \sum_{(v_i, v_j) \in E} h(v_j) \tag{1}$$

where $d_i = \sum_j a_{ij}$ denotes the degree of node v_i. Intuitively, at every node $v_i \in V$, the value of a harmonic function is equal to the average of its values at the neighboring nodes.

3. HARMONIC MODULARITY

In this section, we first illustrate the formulation of our harmonic modularity (HAM) scheme. Then a detailed approach is rendered to solve the objective function of HAM. Further, we investigate its convergence and computational complexity.

3.1 Problem Formulation

Key intuitions: In graph theory, a community is described as a group of nodes more densely connected with each other than with the rest of the network. Intuitively, community structure characterizes the neighborhood relationships of the nodes, with nodes that are closer together in the graph having a similar community indicator. As such, the problem of community detection is much more related to the concept of *intra-community neighbor.* On the other hand, as SH spanners play a boundary-spanning role across communities, it is clear that the problem of top-k SH spanner detection is much more related to the concept of *inter-community neighbor.* Most of the existing studies focus on either one or the other of these two assignments. However, by bringing these two assignments together, we can see that although community detection and top-k SH spanner detection assign graph nodes from two different aspects, they both measure neighborhood relationships. Such neighborhood relationships would correspond to the *harmony* and *diversity* of nodes, respectively. From Definition 6, we know the harmonic property provides a systematic way to quantify the harmony and diversity between the indicator value at a given node and the average of its neighboring nodes. Thus, we propose to jointly detect community and top-k SH spanners by measuring the harmonic modularity of the given network. To overcome limitations in prior work, we state the following desiderata:

- **Nonparametric Guidance:** Utilize SH spanner information when inferring community assignment, and vice versa, so that assignment information is able to provide guidance to the detection process in a nonparametric fashion.
- **Harmony:** Produce a harmonic assignment in each community, so that the internal nodes and their intra-community neighbors are as harmonious as possible, even though they connect to the SH spanners.
- **Diversity:** Produce heterogeneous role assignments for internal nodes and SH spanners, so that community and top-k SH spanner assignments are as diverse from each other as possible.

Building upon these desiderata, we proceed to present HAM. We first present how to measure the harmonic modularity, which itself can be used to learn community assignment, of the given network. Since SH spanners involve different communities, we then model and analyze the topology of SH spanners to quantify the influence exerted on communities, which goes with the ability to identify SH spanners and improve community assignment. Let $\mathbf{F} \in \mathbb{R}^{n \times m}$ be the community indicator matrix, where $f_{ij} = 1$ if a node v_i is assigned to the j-th community, and 0 otherwise. The constraints on $\mathbf{F}$ can be written as

$$\mathbf{F} \in \{0,1\}^{n \times m}, \quad \|\mathbf{f}^i\|_0 = 1, \quad \forall i, \; 1 \leq i \leq n, \tag{2}$$

where $\|\mathbf{f}^i\|_0 = 1$ is utilized to indicate the community that the node v_i most likely belongs to.

For each node v_i, its community indicator $\mathbf{f}^i$ should be as harmonious with its neighbors as possible, *i.e.*, the difference between the value of $\mathbf{f}^i$ and the averaged value of its neighbors $\frac{1}{d_i} \sum_{(v_i,v_j) \in E} \mathbf{f}^j$ should be minimized. Hence, a harmonic function can be embedded to learn the community indicator matrix $\mathbf{F}$. On the basis of the Harmonic analysis, we formulate the following minimization problem

$$\begin{aligned} \min_{\mathbf{F}} \quad & \left\|\mathbf{F} - \mathbf{D}^{-1}\mathbf{A}\mathbf{F}\right\|_F^2 \\ \text{s.t.} \quad & \left\|\mathbf{f}^i\right\|_0 = 1, \quad \forall\, i, 1 \leq i \leq n \\ & \mathbf{F} \in \{0,1\}^{n \times m} \end{aligned} \tag{3}$$

One can see if there are no cross edges or SH spanners in the network, the value of the objective function is essentially zero. However, when a node connects with the inter-community neighbors, it will leads to a relatively large value. SH spanner identification is expected to moderate this influence, as the more influential SH spanner is more likely to get involved into interaction between communities. Moreover, to exploit the formulation of (3) on community detection more effectively, it is crucial for the community indicator matrix $\mathbf{F}$ to have discriminative ability for SH spanners, *i.e.*, promoting row-wise sparsity to discriminate relevant SH spanners. We introduce the $\ell_{2,1}$-norm penalty and orthogonality constraint to make it and thus solve the following optimization problem

$$\min_{\mathbf{F}} \|\mathbf{F} - \mathbf{D}^{-1}\mathbf{A}\mathbf{F}\|_{2,1} \quad \text{s.t.} \quad \mathbf{F}^{\mathrm{T}}\mathbf{F} = \mathbf{I}_m \tag{4}$$

Note that the relaxation of orthogonality condition has two benefits: it not only avoids solving the NP-hard problem of ℓ_0 norm, but also allows the sparsity of the community indicator matrix $\mathbf{F}$ to be exploited. It can be seen the sparsity-inducing property of $\ell_{2,1}$ norm pushes $\mathbf{F}$ to be sparse in rows. More specifically, $\mathbf{f}^i$ shrinks to zero if the neighbors of node v_i belongs to different communities. In particular, the more inter-neighbors the node v_i connects to the more different communities, the larger $\|\mathbf{f}_i - \mathbf{D}^{-1}\mathbf{A}\mathbf{f}_i\|_2^2$ is, so the value of $\mathbf{f}^i$ gets penalized more harshly. Therefore, we can obtain the top-k SH spanners corresponding to the top-k smallest values of $\|\mathbf{f}^i\|_2$. Further, the shrinkage of the $\mathbf{f}^i$ diminishes the influence of the node v_i on its neighbors, making them to be more harmonious with their intra-community neighbors.

It is not difficult to see that the formulation of (4) characterizes graph nodes from two different aspects: harmony and diversity. The harmonic modularity provides a measure of the smoothness of $\mathbf{F}$ over the edges in G, and thus help produce harmonic community assignment. The $\ell_{2,1}$ norm provides an investigation on the sparsity level of the interactions between communities, and thus help discriminate SH spanners and assist the community guidance.

3.2 Solution

Directly minimizing Eq. (4) involving $\ell_{2,1}$ norm is non-trivial. Here we propose an iterative algorithm based on the half-quadratic minimization [25] to solve this problem. We start by introducing the following lemma [15].

Lemma 1. *Let $\phi(.)$ be a function satisfying the conditions: $x \to \phi(x)$ is convex on R; $x \to \phi(\sqrt{x})$ is convex on R_+; $\phi(x) = \phi(-x), \forall x \in R$; $\phi(x)$ is C^1 on R; $\phi''(0^+) \geq 0$, $\lim_{x\to\infty} \phi(x)/x^2 = 0$. Then for a fixed $\|\mathbf{u}^i\|_2$, there exists a dual potential function $\varphi(.)$, such that*

$$\phi(\|\mathbf{u}^i\|_2) = \inf_{p\in R}\{p\|\mathbf{u}^i\|_2^2 + \varphi(p)\} \tag{5}$$

where p is determined by the minimizer function $\varphi(.)$ with respect to $\phi(.)$.

Let $\mathbf{P} = \mathbf{F} - \mathbf{D}^{-1}\mathbf{A}\mathbf{F}$. According to the analysis for the $\ell_{2,1}$ norm in [15], if we define $\phi(x) = \sqrt{x^2+\epsilon}$, we can replace $\|\mathbf{P}\|_{2,1}$ with $\sum_{i=1}^n \phi(\|\mathbf{p}^i\|_2)$. Thus, based on Lemma 1, the objective function of Eq. (4) can be reformulated as follows:

$$\min_{\mathbf{F}} \mathrm{Tr}(\mathbf{P}^{\mathrm{T}}\mathbf{Q}\mathbf{P}) \quad \text{s.t.} \quad \mathbf{F}^{\mathrm{T}}\mathbf{F} = \mathbf{I}_m \tag{6}$$

Algorithm 1 Harmonic Modularity (HAM)

Input: $G = (V, E)$, m, k

Output: Assignments to m communities and the top-k SH spanners

1: Initialize $\mathbf{F}_0$ s.t. $\mathbf{F}_0^{\mathrm{T}}\mathbf{F}_0 = \mathbf{I}_m$, $t \leftarrow 0$;
2: **while** not converge **do**
3: Set $\mathbf{Q}_t \leftarrow Diag(\frac{1}{2\sqrt{\|\mathbf{p}_t^i\|_2^2+\epsilon}})$;
4: Compute $\mathbf{R}_t$ according to Eq. (8)
5: Compute $\mathbf{F}_{t+1}$ as the eigenvectors of $\mathbf{R}_t$ corresponding to the first m smallest eigenvalues;
6: $t \leftarrow t+1$;
7: **end while**
8: Sort each node according to $\|\mathbf{f}\|_2$ in **ascending** order and select the top-k ranked ones as SH spanners;
9: Remove the top-k SH spanners from $\mathbf{F}$, and then cluster $\mathbf{F}$ by K-means to obtain clustering communities.

where $\mathbf{Q} = Diag(\mathbf{q})$, and $\mathbf{q}$ is an auxiliary vector of the $\ell_{2,1}$ norm. The elements of $\mathbf{q}$ are computed as follows.

$$q_i = \frac{1}{2\sqrt{\|\mathbf{p}^i\|_2^2 + \epsilon}} \tag{7}$$

where ϵ is a smoothing term that avoids division by zero, which is usually set to be a small constant value (we set $\epsilon = 10^{-4}$ in this paper).

Clearly, the optimal solution of (6) can be computed via solving the eigenvector problem for the matrix:

$$\mathbf{R} = (\mathbf{I}_n - \mathbf{D}^{-1}\mathbf{A})^{\mathrm{T}}\mathbf{Q}(\mathbf{I}_n - \mathbf{D}^{-1}\mathbf{A}) \tag{8}$$

Based on the above analysis, we summarize the detailed optimization algorithm in Algorithm 1.

3.3 Convergence and Complexity

The Algorithm 1 to optimize Eq. (4) is presented from line 2 to line 7. We prove that it converges to the optimal solution $\mathbf{F}$. We begin with the following Lemma [24].

Lemma 2. *For any nonzero vectors $\mathbf{v}_t^i \in \mathbb{R}^c, 1 \leq i \leq r$, where r is an arbitrary number. The following inequality holds:*

$$\sum_i \|\mathbf{v}_{t+1}^i\|_2 - \sum_i \frac{\|\mathbf{v}_{t+1}^i\|_2^2}{2\|\mathbf{v}_t^i\|_2} \leq \sum_i \|\mathbf{v}_t^i\|_2 - \sum_i \frac{\|\mathbf{v}_t^i\|_2^2}{2\|\mathbf{v}_t^i\|_2} \tag{9}$$

Proof. The detailed proof can be found in the work [24]. □

Next, we show that the iterative algorithm shown in Algorithm 1 converges by the following theorem.

Theorem 3. *The iterative approach in Algorithm 1 (line 2 to line 7) monotonically decreases the objective function value of $\min_{\mathbf{F}^{\mathrm{T}}\mathbf{F}=\mathbf{I}_m} \|\mathbf{F} - \mathbf{D}^{-1}\mathbf{A}\mathbf{F}\|_{2,1}$ in each iteration.*

Proof. Let $\mathbf{\Delta} = \mathbf{I}_n - \mathbf{D}^{-1}\mathbf{A}$, then $\mathbf{P} = \mathbf{\Delta}\mathbf{F}$. In line 5 of Algorithm 1, we can see that

$$\mathbf{F}_{t+1} = \arg\min_{\mathbf{F}^{\mathrm{T}}\mathbf{F}=\mathbf{I}_m} \mathrm{Tr}(\mathbf{F}^{\mathrm{T}}\mathbf{\Delta}^{\mathrm{T}}\mathbf{Q}_t\mathbf{\Delta}\mathbf{F}) \tag{10}$$

Therefore, we have

$$\mathrm{Tr}(\mathbf{F}_{t+1}^{\mathrm{T}}\mathbf{\Delta}^{\mathrm{T}}\mathbf{Q}_t\mathbf{\Delta}\mathbf{F}_{t+1}) \leq \mathrm{Tr}(\mathbf{F}_t^{\mathrm{T}}\mathbf{\Delta}^{\mathrm{T}}\mathbf{Q}_t\mathbf{\Delta}\mathbf{F}_t)$$
$$\Rightarrow \sum_i \frac{\|\mathbf{p}_{t+1}^i\|_2^2}{2\|\mathbf{p}_t^i\|_2} \leq \sum_i \frac{\|\mathbf{p}_t^i\|_2^2}{2\|\mathbf{p}_t^i\|_2}$$

Then according to Lemma 2, $\sum_i \|\mathbf{p}_{t+1}^i\|_2 - \sum_i \frac{\|\mathbf{p}_{t+1}^i\|_2^2}{2\|\mathbf{p}_t^i\|_2} \leq \sum_i \|\mathbf{p}_t^i\|_2 - \sum_i \frac{\|\mathbf{p}_t^i\|_2^2}{2\|\mathbf{p}_t^i\|_2}$, we have the following inequality

$$\sum_i \|\mathbf{p}_{t+1}^i\|_2 \leq \sum_i \|\mathbf{p}_t^i\|_2 \quad (11)$$

Based on the definition of $\ell_{2,1}$ norm and $\mathbf{P} = \mathbf{F} - \mathbf{D}^{-1}\mathbf{AF}$, we can obtain

$$\|\mathbf{F}_{t+1} - \mathbf{D}^{-1}\mathbf{AF}_{t+1}\|_{2,1} \leq \|\mathbf{F}_t - \mathbf{D}^{-1}\mathbf{AF}_t\|_{2,1} \quad (12)$$

which indicates that the value of $\min_{\mathbf{F}^T\mathbf{F}=\mathbf{I}_m} \|\mathbf{F} - \mathbf{D}^{-1}\mathbf{AF}\|_{2,1}$ monotonically decreases using the updating rule in Algorithm 1. □

According to Theorem 3, we can see that the iterative approach in Algorithm 1 converges to local optimal $\mathbf{F}$ corresponding to Eq. (4). The proposed optimization algorithm is efficient. In the experiment, we observe that our algorithm usually converges around only 20 iterations.

The complexity is briefly discussed as follows. The complexity of computing $\mathbf{Q}$ is $\mathcal{O}(n^2)$. To obtain $\mathbf{F}$, we need to conduct eigendecomposition of $\mathbf{R}$, which is $\mathcal{O}(n^3)$ in complexity. It can be reduced to $\mathcal{O}(n^{2.376})$ using the Coppersmith-Winograd algorithm. The complexity of identifying communities by K-means is $\mathcal{O}(m^2nt)$, where t is the iterative index required for K-means to converge. The complexity of top-k SH spanner selection is $\mathcal{O}(n\log(n) + nm)$.

4. INTERPRETATION AND CONNECTION

Here we present the special case of our HAM method and relate it to the existing works. These different viewpoints provide a rich and complementary set of techniques for reasoning about this approach to the joint community and SH spanner detection problem.

Perhaps the most interesting and significant aspect of HAM is that it can be viewed as a direct response to the harmonic property. As we use the $\ell_{2,1}$ norm to push the community indicators of SH spanners shrink to zero, this equals to remove SH spanners from the graph. Thus, in our method, the value of the objective function is close to zero, which is consistent with the notion of *harmony*. Moreover, one can see if there are no cross edges or SH spanners in the network, then the auxiliary matrix $\mathbf{Q}$ is always constant, regardless of any changes of community indicator $\mathbf{F}$. In this case, we will solve the minimum Frobenius norm residual problem (*i.e.*, $\min \|\mathbf{F} - \mathbf{D}^{-1}\mathbf{AF}\|_F$, s.t. $\mathbf{F}^T\mathbf{F} = \mathbf{I}_m$), and HAM degenerates into the random walk approach (also called harmonic function learning) [31].

Our HAM uses the eigenvectors of a matrix ($\mathbf{R}$ in Eq. (8)) to reveal the community structure in the graph, therefore it can be regarded as belonging to the category of spectral clustering approaches. However, there are two major differences. The matrix whose eigenvectors are used for clustering plays the key role in spectral clustering. In HAM, this matrix is computed based on the harmonic function learning idea in conjunction with the sparsity-inducing $\ell_{2,1}$-norm, while conventional spectral clustering methods are often based on the graph Laplacian matrices. Second, spectral clustering gives a closed-form solution, and HAM needs to be optimized in a half-quadratic way. In practice, the main computational load of HAM and spectral clustering is to compute the eigenvectors, therefore they have the same order of time complexity.

5. EXPERIMENTS

To evaluate the effectiveness of HAM, we conduct extensive experiments on real-world social networks, and compare them with various baseline methods. As there hardly exist comparative methods that can simultaneously detect communities and SH spanners, we compare our approach to community detection and SH spanner detection methods, respectively. Since the quality of detected communities can be well affected by the spotted SH spanners, we first investigate the effectiveness of HAM on SH spanner detection. We then study the performance of HAM on community detection. Finally, we discuss the results and the reasons behind them.

5.1 Dataset Description

We adopt three real-world social network datasets from different contexts.

- *Karate Club* [38] is the network of friendships between members of a karate club that splits into two clubs due to a dispute between the coach and administrator.
- *DBLP* is a co-authorship network where two authors are connected if they publish at least one paper together. Publication venue defines an individual ground-truth community; authors who published to the same journal or conference form a community.
- *YouTube* is a video-based social network, where users form friendship with each other based on their interactions over videos and users can create groups which other users can join. Such user-defined groups are considered as ground-truth communities.

The *DBLP* and *YouTube* data were obtained from [37]. We sample 5 datasets from each and measure the average performance. Since we focus on detecting distinct communities, the communities of interest should not have too much overlaps with other communities. We compute the number of cross edges between each pair of communities, and divide it by the number of nodes in the smaller community as the cross ratio between the community pair. The sampling rule is: randomly pick a community, and then take all the nodes within the community if the cross ratios between the picked community and the existing selected communities is less than a threshold (set as 0.3 in the experiment). We repeat the sampling process until the number of nodes or the number of communities in the sampled network reaches a predefined limit (set as 2,000 and 20, respectively, in the experiment) or no more community to be picked. Table 2 summarizes the original datasets and also the sampled datasets for the large networks.

5.2 Structural Hole Spanner Detection

5.2.1 *Compared Methods*

We compare HAM with the following seven state-of-the-art methods, each of which represents a different strategy for detecting the top-k SH spanners.

- HAM is our proposed method, which selects the nodes that have neighbors belonging to more different communities as the SH spanners.

Table 2: Summary of experimental datasets. Sampled datasets are listed by the mean ± standard deviation.

Types of data	Datasets	Characteristics # Nodes	# Edges	# Cross edges	# SH spanners	# Communities
Original data	Karate Club	34	78	11	13	2
Sampled data	DBLP	1557.6±362.19	4915.6±451.95	127.4±41.60	189±49.44	15±4.24
	YouTube	1310±133.67	2853.5±289.69	82.5±15.18	91.3±13.57	15.25±2.06

Table 3: Structural hole spanner detection results (average *SHII*). Column 2 indicates the used Information Diffusion model

Datasets	ID model	Comparative Methonds HAM	Constraint	PageRank	BC	2-Step	MaxD	HIS	AP_BICC
Karate Club	LT	**0.343**	0.295	0.159	0.159	0.159	0.159	0.132	0.295
	IC	**0.002**	**0.002**	0.001	0.001	0.001	0.001	0.001	**0.002**
	SH spanners	[3,20,9]	[1,34,3]	[34,1,33]	[1,34,33]	[34,1,33]	[34,1,33]	[32,9,14]	[1,3,34]
DBLP	LT	**5.384**	0.404	0.357	0.958	0.394	0.272	0.718	0.550
	IC	**3.578**	0.229	0.190	0.821	0.203	0.135	0.304	0.495
YouTube	LT	**3.951**	2.447	1.236	1.226	1.935	1.674	3.198	1.630
	IC	**2.452**	1.254	0.662	0.791	1.014	0.798	2.148	0.799

- Constraint [4] uses constraint to estimate the importance of each node and select the top-k nodes with the lowest constraint scores as the SH spanners.

- PageRank [26] is the traditional node ranking algorithm, which returns the nodes with the top-k page rank scores as the SH spanners.

- Betweenness Centrality (BC) [2] assigns each node a score that is the number of shortest paths (between all pairs of nodes) on which the node lies, then selects the top-k nodes with the highest scores as the SH spanners.

- 2-Step [32] assigns each node a score that is the number of pairs of its neighbors without edges between them, and then selects the top-k highest scores as the SH spanners.

- MaxD [20] is a supervised learning strategy, which focuses on predefined communities and minimal cut theory to select the top-k nodes, such that after removing these nodes the decrease of the minimal cut will be maximized.

- HIS [20] is also a supervised method. It assigns each node v a score that simulates the likelihood of v as a structural hole spanner across the given subset of communities, and then selects the top-k nodes with the highest scores as the SH spanners.

- AP_BICC [28] is a recently proposed SH spanner detection method, which selects the top-k SH spanners based on articulation points (AP) (that is, nodes of a graph that connect two or more otherwise unconnected parts of the graph) and bounded inverse closeness centrality (BICC), such that after removing these nodes the increase of the mean distance of the network will be maximized. We set the bounded parameter to $l = 2$, and the number of nodes used in the BICC to $K = 50$, as they suggested.

5.2.2 Evaluation criteria

Currently there is no standard criteria available for evaluating the performance of the top-k SH spanners. Here we base on simulating the information diffusion process [12] in the given network to evaluate the performance. Since a SH spanner usually dominates the spread of information across communities, when using the more effective SH spanner as a seed (source) node, the faster the information would be diffused to different communities. Hence, the number of the influenced outsiders, which are the ones reside in the communities different from the SH spanner's community, should be larger. However, the number of outsiders is related to the size of the given community. Further, considering a well connected node in the center of a community can also propagate its influence to other communities through its neighbors, simply relying on the number of influenced outsiders may not be able to discriminate SH spanners from center nodes. Thus, to give a evaluation criterion that is suitable for a variety of SH spanners and can distinguish SH spanners from center nodes, we consider the proposition of the number of the influenced outsiders to the total number of all the influenced nodes. Formally, we define the *structural hole influence index* under a certain diffusion model as the evaluation criterion.

- *Structural Hole Influence Index (SHII)*: Let s be the given seed, C_p be the community that the given seed belongs to, and I_v be an indicator of whether a node v is influenced by using a certain information diffusion model. We define *SHII* as follows:

$$SHII(s) = \frac{\sum_{C_i \in C \setminus C_p} \sum_{v \in C_i} I_v}{\sum_{C_i \in C} \sum_{v \in C_i} I_v}$$

  where C is the set of all the communities. Generally, higher *SHII* corresponds to better performance.

In this study, we use two different and widely used information diffusion models [17]: Linear Threshold (LT) model and Independent Cascade (IC) model to find the set of influenced nodes. Since it is unlikely to simulate the information diffusion procedure using only one seed, for the given SH spanner

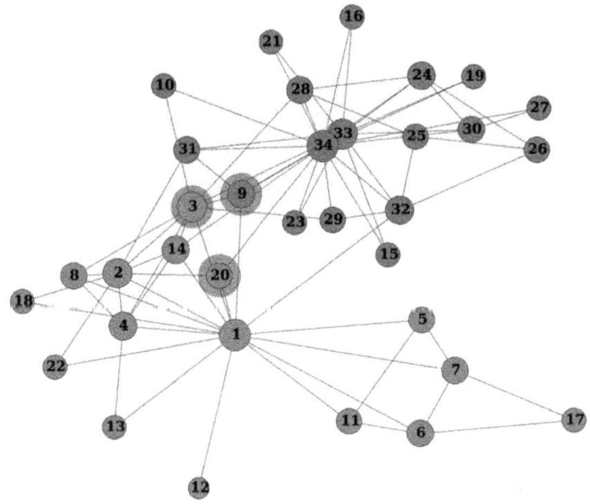

Figure 2: Visualization of the identified SH spanners in Karate Club, where the large blue shadowed nodes represent SH Spanners discovered by HAM.

candidate, we randomly select a certain number (5% of the number of the nodes that are in the same community as the candidate) of the candidate's neighbors along with the candidate as the seed set in the LT/IC model. For each SH spanner candidate, we repeat the random selection for 1,000 times and run the LT and IC models for 100,000 times for each selected seed set. Finally, we report the average *SHII* for each method.

5.2.3 *Experiment Result*

Table 3 reports the performance of each method in terms of the proposed evaluation criterion. From the results, we can observe that HAM significantly outperforms all the other baseline methods even the supervised methods (*i.e.*, MaxD and HIS), which are aware of the ground truth of the communities. Specifically, it can be seen in the DBLP data that the *SHII* achieved by HAM under the LT model is 5.384, which is more than 5 times higher than that obtained by BC and HIS, about 10 times larger than that achieved by Constraint, PageRank, 2-Step, MaxD, and AP_BICC.

For qualitative analysis, in Figure 2, we visualize the network of Karate Club using the tool *Networkx* [14] and mark the identified SH spanners by HAM to see the topological position of them. The nodes with large blue shadow are the top-3 SH spanners spotted and the colors of nodes indicate the different communities they belong to. The results of the other methods are listed in Table 3. We can find that HAM captures the most intermediate nodes between communities. In contrast, most of the compared methods take the nodes with the highest degree as SH spanners, but actually these nodes are usually the center of the communities. It obviously contradicts to the definition of SH spanners. Although HIS does not focus on finding the nodes with the highest degree, its identified SH spanners have less impact on the information diffusion across different communities, as can be seen that HIS has smaller values of *SHII* than all the other methods.

5.3 Community Detection

We apply the results of identified top-k SH spanners by HAM to help predict community structure. To further show the effectiveness of the identified SH spanners, we evaluate the community detection performance before and after removing the top-k SH spanners for each comparative methods. When considering all the nodes in the network as the prediction object, in our HAM method, for each SH spanner we determine its community label via majority voting using its connected nodes' community labels.

5.3.1 *Compared Methods*

We compare HAM with the following commonly used algorithms for community detection.

- Spectral Clustering [23] refers to a class of techniques which rely on the eigenstructure of the graph Laplacian to partition points into disjoint clusters with points in the same cluster having high similarity and points in different clusters having low similarity. Typical graph Laplacians are: the unnormalized Laplacian defined as $\mathbf{L} = \mathbf{D} - \mathbf{A}$, the symmetric normalized Laplacian $\mathbf{L}_{sym} = \mathbf{D}^{-\frac{1}{2}}\mathbf{L}\mathbf{D}^{-\frac{1}{2}}$ and the asymmetric normalized Laplacian $\mathbf{L}_{asym} = \mathbf{D}^{-1}\mathbf{L}$. We use these three matrices based on spectral clustering, and denote them as SP, SP_{sym} and SP_{asym}, respectively.
- Random Walk (RW) [31] is a special case of our approach, when the norm of the objective function is Frobenius norm.
- Q-modularity (Q) [22] is a recently introduced community detection method that greedily computes partitions of networks into communities by maximizing the so-called 'modularity'. In particular, the author has shown in [21] that it can use the largest eigenvectors of the 'modularity' matrix to characterize the community structure in the graph.

5.3.2 *Evaluation criteria*

In order to evaluate the quality of the communities generated by different community detection approaches, we adopt the following measures.

a) Accuracy (ACC) is one of the most frequently used criterion, which evaluates the quality of similarity between resulted cluster labels and ground truth labels. Let c_i represent the clustering label result from a community detection algorithm and y_i represent the corresponding ground truth label of an arbitrary node v_i. Then ACC is defined as follows:

$$ACC = \frac{\sum_{i=1}^{n} \delta(y_i, map(c_i))}{n}$$

where δ is the Kronecker delta function, and $map(c_i)$ is the best mapping function that permutes clustering labels to match the ground truth labels using the KuhnMunkres algorithm. A larger ACC indicates better clustering performance.

b) Normalized Mutual Information (NMI) measures the mutual information entropy between resulted cluster labels and ground truth labels. For any two arbitrary variables P and Q, NMI is defined as follows:

$$NMI = \frac{I(P,Q)}{\sqrt{H(P)H(Q)}}$$

where $I(P,Q)$ computes the mutual information between P and Q, and $H(P)$ and $H(Q)$ are the entropies

Table 4: **Community detection results "average score" on three datasets. "↑" indicates the larger the value the better the performance; "↓" indicates the smaller the value the better the performance.**

Datasets	Evaluations with top-k SH spanners				Evaluations without top-k SH spanners			
	Methods	ACC ↑	NMI ↑	ACE ↓	Methods	ACC ↑	NMI ↑	ACE ↓
Karate Club	HAM	**1.000**	**1.000**	**0.000**	HAM	1.000	1.000	0.000
	SP	0.912	0.646	0.253	SP	1.000	1.000	0.000
	SP_{sym}	0.971	0.837	0.115	SP_{sym}	1.000	1.000	0.000
	SP_{asym}	0.824	0.363	0.448	SP_{asym}	0.968	0.824	0.125
	RW	0.971	0.837	0.115	RW	1.000	1.000	0.000
	Q	1.000	1.000	0.000	Q	1.000	1.000	0.000
DBLP	HAM	**0.879**	**0.885**	**0.114**	HAM	0.879	0.886	0.112
	SP	0.693	0.790	0.162	SP	0.872	0.876	0.120
	SP_{sym}	0.680	0.756	0.179	SP_{sym}	0.821	0.788	0.255
	SP_{asym}	0.307	0.472	0.687	SP_{asym}	0.331	0.497	0.665
	RW	0.790	0.810	0.154	RW	0.916	0.877	0.136
	Q	0.429	0.634	0.373	Q	0.468	0.663	0.342
YouTube	HAM	**0.953**	**0.938**	**0.100**	HAM	0.954	0.940	0.100
	SP	0.888	0.881	0.176	SP	0.909	0.908	0.160
	SP_{sym}	0.802	0.815	0.212	SP_{sym}	0.826	0.857	0.158
	SP_{asym}	0.433	0.583	0.513	SP_{asym}	0.545	0.630	0.499
	RW	0.908	0.905	0.163	RW	0.933	0.922	0.143
	Q	0.492	0.626	0.395	Q	0.515	0.721	0.294

of P and Q. An advantage of *NMI* is that it does not necessarily increase when the number of clusters increase. The larger the value, the better the performance.

c) Average Cluster Entropy (ACE) is based on the impurity of a cluster given the true classes in the data. Let p_{ij} be the fraction of class j in obtained cluster i, and n_i be the size of cluster i, then ACE is defined as:

$$ACE = \sum_{i=1}^{m} \frac{n_i(-\sum_j p_{ij}\log(p_{ij}))}{n}$$

The smallest the value, the better the performance. Particularly, the low values of ACE indicate homogeneous distribution of the nodes within each group [6].

5.3.3 *Experiment Result*

Table 4 summarizes the performance of different methods according to three evaluation criteria. The performance before removing the top-k SH spanners (with top-k SH spanners) are shown in the left column and without top-k SH spanners in the right column. From the left column of Table 4 it can be seen that the performance of each method on different datasets can be quite different. However, the best method that outperforms other methods in all datasets is HAM, especially for DBLP and YouTube datasets. We can see the accuracies achieved by HAM (0.879 and 0.953, respectively) are considerably larger than the second best method (0.790 and 0.888, respectively). Moreover, HAM significantly outperforms RW, which means that the sparsity-inducing $\ell_{2,1}$-norm is effective to increase the harmony within the community. From the right column of Table 4, we can see the performance of each comparative method substantially benefits from the removal of top-k SH spanners. For example, the accuracy performance of SP is improved from 0.693 to 0.872 on the DBLP dataset. These results suggest that our proposed method can guarantee to find more positive structural hole spanners connecting to different communities, and removing them makes the community structure more apparent, thus facilitating better community detection performance.

5.4 Discussion

We now turn to the discussion of the experimental results. Table 3 shows HAM is substantially better than other SH spanner detection methods. The reason is that HAM finds the SH spanners who bridge different communities, while most other methods detect the SH spanners with higher degree, which collaborate with many nodes in their own community. In other words, structural hole spanners are more likely to connect the nodes between communities than higher-degree nodes. Thus they have great potentials to control information flow between communities. Moreover, the left column of Table 4 shows the community detection performance gain of HAM over other methods is significant. This result is due to the absence of SH spanners in our original community detection procedure. Removing SH spanners helps make the community structure more tangible such that different communities are easier to be separated. As can be seen in the right column of Table 4, the performance of each comparative method is improved after removing the identified top-k SH spanners detected by HAM.

In addition, Figure 3 shows convergence curves of HAM. From this figure, we can see that the proposed optimization algorithm converges quickly in the vicinity of the minimum, *i.e.*, only around 20 iterations. At the same time, it can also be seen from Figure 3 that the objective function converges to a very small value, which is consistent with intuitive interpretation of SH spanner selection process. Furthermore, our method needs no parameter tuning, which makes it even more appealing.

6. RELATED WORK

To the best of our knowledge, this is the first work to simultaneously address the problems of community detection and SH spanner detection. Our work is related to both com-

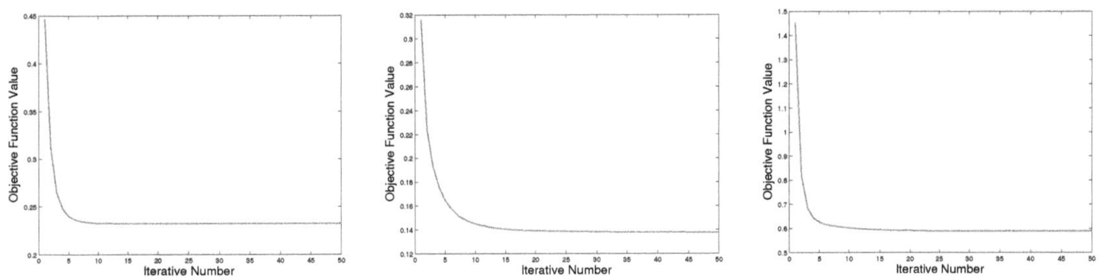

(a) Karate Club (b) DBLP (c) YouTube

Figure 3: : Convergence curve of HAM over Karate Club, DBLP and YouTube datasets

munity detection techniques and SH spanners mining. We briefly discuss both of them.

6.1 Community Detection

Community detection, with its root in graph partitioning and graph clustering, has been pivotal to network science. A plethora of algorithms have been presented to address this task over the years, be it cut-based [9], spectrum-based [23], modularity-based [22], or information theoretic [29]. To cover all community detection algorithms is beyond the scope of this paper, and interested readers can refer to the survey papers such as [10].

In recent years, a variety of methods inspired by different paradigms are put forward for community detection [35]. A prominent one is to consider the structural roles of individual nodes. This desideratum is motivated by the observation on many real-world networks that, by nature, community and structural role discovery are interdependent and complementary to each other. Real-world communities often contain nodes with various roles for it to function, such as ones that interface with other communities and ones that are peripheral to community cores. On the other hand, the role assignment of a node also depends on the communities that the node itself, its neighbors and beyond belong to. Therefore, there exists a strong and crucial need to detect communities and roles jointly. Recent work has leveraged role detection techniques for community detection [30]. None of those methods, however, consider the SH spanner detection.

6.2 Structural Hole Spanner Detection

Structural Hole theory is first introduced by [4] to find the key employees in organizations for integrating operations across functional and business boundaries. A series of empirical studies [3, 27] have demonstrated that advantages accrue to SH spanners who occupy bridging positions between different communities. In the literature, many strategies [13, 18] have been devised to model the property of structural holes in a network. [13] proposed a network formation model that a vertex serves as an intermediary between many vertices. The strategic link formation in their model leads to a star network, while real-world networks are not necessary of the star topology.

In recent years, several approaches have been proposed to find the top-k SH spanners. [13] formulated SH spanners as nodes that reside on large number of shortest paths between different pairs of nodes. Because counting all the shortest paths is time-consuming, [32] proposed a 2-Step approach that only counts the number of shortest paths with length two. Most recently, [28] viewed the SH spanners as a set of vertices whose removal will result in the maximum increase on the mean distance of the network, which is the average of the lengths of all pairs of vertices in the network. They then proposed the AP_BICC model, by exploiting the bounded inverse closeness centrality (BICC) of vertices and making use of articulation points (AP) of the network.

To our best knowledge, there is only one paper that utilized the community information for mining the top-k SH spanners [20], which assumes the communities are given. One instantiation of their proposed model is to find a set of vertices whose removal leads to the maximum decrease in the minimum cut in the given set of communities. However, communities usually are not known in most scenarios, thus the quality of the solution relies on the quality of communities found. In contrast, given only the topological structure of the network, our proposed HAM can detect the communities and the top-k SH spanners simultaneously. Furthermore, as demonstrated in the experiment, HAM captures the most influential intermediate nodes between communities, while most of the previous methods take the nodes in the center of the communities as SH spanners.

7. CONCLUSION

In this work, we proposed a novel Harmonic Modularity (HAM) method for simultaneously detecting the potential communities and the top-k SH spanners, using only the topological structure of the network. Specifically, we applied the harmonic function analysis to measure the harmonic modularity and to obtain the community indicator. We further investigated the sparsity level of the interactions between communities, with particular emphasis on the nodes connecting to multiple communities, to discriminate the indicator of SH spanners and assist the community guidance. Extensive experiments conducted on three real-world social networks demonstrated that HAM can capture the characteristics of structural hole spanners, and the proposed algorithm significantly outperform several comparative methods (even the methods using the supervised community information) in the top-k SH spanner identification problem and also the community detection problem, respectively.

8. ACKNOWLEDGMENTS

The work is supported in part by NSF (III-1526499), NSFC (61272050, 61472089, 61503253), NSFC-Guangdong Joint Found(U1501254), and the Science Foundation of Guangdong Province (2014A030313556).

9. REFERENCES

[1] D. S. Bassett, E. T. Bullmore, A. Meyer-Lindenberg, J. A. Apud, D. R. Weinberger, and R. Coppola. Cognitive fitness of cost-efficient brain functional networks. *PNAS*, 106(28):11747–11752, 2009.

[2] U. Brandes. A faster algorithm for betweenness centrality*. *Journal of Mathematical Sociology*, 25(2):163–177, 2001.

[3] R. S. Burt. Secondhand brokerage: Evidence on the importance of local structure for managers, bankers, and analysts. *Academy of Management Journal*, 50:119–148, 2007.

[4] R. S. Burt. *Structural holes: The social structure of competition.* Harvard university press, 2009.

[5] V. Buskens and A. Van de Rijt. Dynamics of networks if everyone strives for structural holes1. *American Journal of Sociology*, 114(2):371–407, 2008.

[6] K. Ciesielski, D. Czerski, M. Dramiński, M. A. Kłopotek, and S. T. Wierzchoń. Semantic information within the beatca framework. *Control and Cybernetics*, 39(2):377–400, 2010.

[7] A. Clauset, M. E. Newman, and C. Moore. Finding community structure in very large networks. *Physical review E*, 70(6):066111, 2004.

[8] G. Cordasco and L. Gargano. Community detection via semi-synchronous label propagation algorithms. In *BASNA*, pages 1–8, 2010.

[9] I. S. Dhillon, Y. Guan, and B. Kulis. Weighted graph cuts without eigenvectors a multilevel approach. *TPAMI*, 29(11):1944–1957, 2007.

[10] S. Fortunato. Community detection in graphs. *Physics reports*, 486(3):75–174, 2010.

[11] M. Girvan and M. E. Newman. Community structure in social and biological networks. *PNAS*, 99(12):7821–7826, 2002.

[12] A. Goyal, W. Lu, and L. V. Lakshmanan. Celf++: optimizing the greedy algorithm for influence maximization in social networks. In *WWW*, pages 47–48, 2011.

[13] S. Goyal and F. Vega-Redondo. Structural holes in social networks. *Journal of Economic Theory*, 137(1):460–492, 2007.

[14] A. A. Hagberg, D. A. Schult, and P. J. Swart. Exploring network structure, dynamics, and function using NetworkX. In *SciPy*, pages 11–15, 2008.

[15] R. He, T. Tan, L. Wang, and W.-S. Zheng. $\ell_{2,1}$ regularized correntropy for robust feature selection. In *CVPR*, pages 2504–2511, 2012.

[16] U. Kang and C. Faloutsos. Beyond'caveman communities': Hubs and spokes for graph compression and mining. In *ICDM*, pages 300–309, 2011.

[17] D. Kempe, J. Kleinberg, and É. Tardos. Maximizing the spread of influence through a social network. In *KDD*, pages 137–146, 2003.

[18] J. Kleinberg, S. Suri, É. Tardos, and T. Wexler. Strategic network formation with structural holes. In *EC*, pages 284–293, 2008.

[19] S. Lin, Q. Hu, G. Wang, and S. Y. Philip. Understanding community effects on information diffusion. In *PAKDD*, pages 82–95, 2015.

[20] T. Lou and J. Tang. Mining structural hole spanners through information diffusion in social networks. In *WWW*, pages 825–836, 2013.

[21] M. E. Newman. Modularity and community structure in networks. *PNAS*, 103(23):8577–8582, 2006.

[22] M. E. Newman and M. Girvan. Finding and evaluating community structure in networks. *Physical review E*, 69(2):026113, 2004.

[23] A. Y. Ng, M. I. Jordan, Y. Weiss, et al. On spectral clustering: Analysis and an algorithm. *NIPS*, 2:849–856, 2002.

[24] F. Nie, H. Huang, X. Cai, and C. H. Ding. Efficient and robust feature selection via joint $\ell_{2,1}$-norms minimization. In *NIPS*, pages 1813–1821, 2010.

[25] M. Nikolova and M. K. Ng. Analysis of half-quadratic minimization methods for signal and image recovery. *SISC*, 27(3):937–966, 2005.

[26] L. Page, S. Brin, R. Motwani, and T. Winograd. The pagerank citation ranking: bringing order to the web. 1999.

[27] J. M. Podolny and J. N. Baron. Resources and relationships: Social networks and mobility in the workplace. *American Sociological Review*, 62(5):673, 1997.

[28] M. Rezvani, W. Liang, W. Xu, and C. Liu. Identifying top-k structural hole spanners in large-scale social networks. In *CIKM*, pages 263–272, 2015.

[29] M. Rosvall and C. T. Bergstrom. Multilevel compression of random walks on networks reveals hierarchical organization in large integrated systems. *PloS one*, 6(4):e18209, 2011.

[30] Y. Ruan and S. Parthasarathy. Simultaneous detection of communities and roles from large networks. In *COSN*, pages 203–214, 2014.

[31] D. A. Spielman. Algorithms, graph theory, and linear equations in laplacian matrices. In *ICM*, volume 4, pages 2698–2722, 2010.

[32] J. Tang, T. Lou, and J. Kleinberg. Inferring social ties across heterogenous networks. In *WSDM*, pages 743–752, 2012.

[33] M. P. van den Heuvel and O. Sporns. Rich-club organization of the human connectome. *The Journal of neuroscience*, 31(44):15775–15786, 2011.

[34] L. Wang, T. Lou, J. Tang, and J. E. Hopcroft. Detecting community kernels in large social networks. In *ICDM*, pages 784–793, 2011.

[35] Z. Wang, Z. Chen, Y. Zhao, and S. Chen. A community detection algorithm based on topology potential and spectral clustering. *The Scientific World Journal*, 2014.

[36] W. Winterbach, P. Van Mieghem, M. Reinders, H. Wang, and D. de Ridder. Topology of molecular interaction networks. *BMC systems biology*, 7(1):90, 2013.

[37] J. Yang and J. Leskovec. Defining and evaluating network communities based on ground-truth. *KAIS*, 42(1):181–213, 2015.

[38] W. W. Zachary. An information flow model for conflict and fission in small groups. *Journal of anthropological research*, pages 452–473, 1977.

Robust Influence Maximization

Xinran He
University of Southern California
941 Bloom Walk
Los Angeles, CA, United States
xinranhe@usc.edu

David Kempe
University of Southern California
941 Bloom Walk
Los Angeles, CA, United States
dkempe@usc.edu

ABSTRACT

Uncertainty about models and data is ubiquitous in the computational social sciences, and it creates a need for *robust* social network algorithms, which can simultaneously provide guarantees across a spectrum of models and parameter settings. We begin an investigation into this broad domain by studying robust algorithms for the Influence Maximization problem, in which the goal is to identify a set of k nodes in a social network whose joint influence on the network is maximized.

We define a Robust Influence Maximization framework wherein an algorithm is presented with a set of influence functions, typically derived from different influence models or different parameter settings for the same model. The different parameter settings could be derived from observed cascades on different topics, under different conditions, or at different times. The algorithm's goal is to identify a set of k nodes who are simultaneously influential for all influence functions, compared to the (function-specific) optimum solutions.

We show strong approximation hardness results for this problem unless the algorithm gets to select at least a logarithmic factor more seeds than the optimum solution. However, when enough extra seeds may be selected, we show that techniques of Krause et al. can be used to approximate the optimum robust influence to within a factor of $1 - 1/e$. We evaluate this bicriteria approximation algorithm against natural heuristics on several real-world data sets. Our experiments indicate that the worst-case hardness does not necessarily translate into bad performance on real-world data sets; all algorithms perform fairly well.

Categories and Subject Descriptors

[**Human-centered computing**]: Social networks

1. INTRODUCTION

Computational social science is the study of social and economic phenomena based on electronic data, algorithmic approaches and computational models. It has emerged as an important application of data mining and learning, while also invigorating research in the social sciences. Computational social science is frequently envisioned as a foundation for a discipline one could term "computational social engineering," wherein algorithmic approaches are used to change or mitigate individuals' behavior.

Among the many concrete problems that have been studied in this context, perhaps the most popular is Influence Maximization. It is based on the observation that behavioral change in individuals is frequently effected by influence from their social contacts. Thus, by identifying a small set of "seed nodes," one may influence a large fraction of the social network. The desired behavior may be of social value, such as refraining from smoking or drug use, using superior crops, or following hygienic practices. Alternatively, the behavior may provide financial value, as in the case of viral marketing, where a company wants to rely on word-of-mouth recommendations to increase the sale of its products.

1.1 Prevalence of Uncertainty and Noise

Contrary to the "hard" sciences, the study of social networks — whether using traditional or computational approaches — suffers from massive amounts of noise inherent in the data and models. The reasons range from the fundamental to the practical:

- At a fundamental level, it is not even clear what a "social tie" is. Different individuals or researchers operationalize the intuition behind "friendship", "acquaintance", "regular" advice seeking, etc. in different ways (see, e.g., [4]). Based on different definitions, the same real-world individuals and behavior may give rise to different mathematical models of the same "social network."
- Mathematical models of processes on social networks (such as opinion adoption or tie formation) are at best approximations of reality, and frequently mere guesses or mathematically convenient inventions. Furthermore, the models are rarely validated against real-world data, in large part due to some of the following concerns.
- Human behavior is typically influenced by many environmental variables, many of them hard or impossible to measure. Even with the rapid growth of available social data, it is unlikely that data sets will become sufficiently rich to disentangle the dependence of human behavior on the myriad variables that may shape it.

KDD '16, August 13-17, 2016, San Francisco, CA, USA

DOI: http://dx.doi.org/10.1145/2939672.2939760

- Observational data on social behavior is virtually always incomplete. For example, even if API restrictions and privacy were not concerns (which they definitely are at this time) and a "complete" data set of Twitter *and* Facebook *and* e-mail communication were collected, it would still lack in-person and phone interactions.

- Inferring model parameters relies on a choice of model and hyperparameters, many of which are difficult to make. Furthermore, while for many models, parameter inference is computationally efficient, this is not universally the case.

Since none of these issues are likely to be resolved anytime soon, both the models for social network processes and their inferred parameters must be treated with caution. This is true both when one wants to draw scientific insight for its own sake, and when one wants to use the inferred models to make computational social engineering decisions. Indeed, the correctness guarantees for algorithms are predicated on the assumption of correctness of the model and the inferred parameters. When this assumption fails — which is inevitable — the utility of the algorithms' output is compromised. Thus, to make good on the claims of real-world relevance of computational social science, *it is imperative that the research community focus on robustness as a primary design goal.*

1.2 Modeling Uncertainty in Influence Maximization

We take an early step in this bigger agenda, studying robustness in the context of the well-known Influence Maximization problem. (Detailed definitions are given in Section 3.) In Influence Maximization, the algorithm selects a set S_0 of *seed nodes*, of pre-specified size k. The seed nodes are initially exposed to a product or idea; we say that they are *active*. Based on a probabilistic model of influence propagation[1], they cause some of their neighbors to become active, who then cause some of their neighbors to become active, etc.; this process leads to a (random) final set of active nodes. The goal is to maximize the size of this set; we denote this quantity by $\sigma(S_0)$.

The concerns discussed above combine to lead to significant uncertainty about the function σ: different models give rise to very different functional forms of σ, and missing observations or approximations in inference lead to uncertainty about the models' parameters.

To model this uncertainty, we assume that the algorithm is presented with a set Σ of influence functions, and assured that one of these functions actually describes the influence process, but not told *which* one. The set Σ could be finite or infinite. A finite Σ could result from a finite set of different information diffusion models that are being considered, or from of a finite number of different contexts under which the individuals were observed (e.g., word-of-mouth cascades for different topics or products), or from a finite number of different inference algorithms or algorithm settings being used to infer the model parameters from observations. An infinite (even continuous) Σ arises if each model parameter is only known to lie within some given interval; this model of adversarial noise, which we call the Perturbation Interval model, was recently proposed in [19].

Since the algorithm does not know $\hat{\sigma}$, in the Robust Influence Maximization problem, it must "simultaneously optimize" for all objective functions in Σ, in the sense of maximizing $\rho(S_0) = \min_{\hat{\sigma}\in\Sigma} \frac{\hat{\sigma}(S_0)}{\hat{\sigma}(\hat{S})}$, where $\hat{S} \in \text{argmax}_S\, \hat{\sigma}(S)$ is an optimal solution knowing which function $\hat{\sigma}$ is to be optimized. In other words, the selected set should simultaneously get as close as possible to the optimal solutions for all possible objective functions.

1.3 Our Approach and Results

Our work is guided by the following overarching questions:

1. How well can the objective ρ be optimized in principle?
2. How well do simple heuristics perform in theory?
3. How well do simple heuristics perform in practice?
4. How do robustly and non-robustly optimized solutions differ qualitatively?

We address these questions as follows. First, we show (in Section 4) that unless the algorithm gets to exceed the number of seeds k by at least a factor $\ln|\Sigma|$, approximating the objective ρ to within a factor $O(n^{1-\epsilon})$ is NP-hard for all $\epsilon > 0$.

However, when the algorithm does get to exceed the seed set target k by a factor of $\ln|\Sigma|$ (times a constant), much better bicriteria approximation guarantees can be obtained.[2] Specifically, we show that a modification of an algorithm of Krause et al. [23] uses $O(k \ln|\Sigma|)$ seeds and finds a seed set whose influence is within a factor $(1 - 1/e)$ of optimal.

We also investigate two straightforward heuristics:

1. Run a greedy algorithm to optimize ρ directly, picking one node at a time.
2. For each objective function $\sigma \in \Sigma$, find a set S_σ (approximately) maximizing $\sigma(S_\sigma)$. Evaluate each of these sets under $\rho(S_\sigma)$, and keep the best one.

We first exhibit instances on which both of the heuristics perform very poorly. Next (in Section 5), we focus on more realistic instances , exemplifying the types of scenarios under which robust optimization becomes necessary. In the first set of experiments, we infer influence networks on a fixed node set from Twitter cascades on different *topics*. Individuals' influence can vary significantly based on the topic, and for a previously unseen topic, it is not clear which inferred influence network to use. In additional sets of experiments, we derive data sets from the same MemeTracker data [25], but use different *time slices*, different *inference algorithms and parametrizations*, and different samples from confidence intervals.

The main outcome of the experiments is that while the algorithm with robustness as a design goal typically (though not even always) outperforms the heuristics, the margin is often quite small. Hence, heuristics may be viable in practice, when the influence functions are reasonably similar. A visual inspection of the nodes chosen by different algorithms reveals how the robust algorithm "hedges its bets" across models, while the non-robust heuristic tends to cluster selected nodes in one part of the network.

[1] We use the terms "influence propagation" and "diffusion" interchangeably.

[2] A bicriteria algorithm gets to pick more nodes than the optimal solution, but is only judged against the optimum solution with the original bound k on the number of nodes.

1.4 Stochastic vs. Adversarial Models

Given its prominent role in our model, the decision to treat the choice of $\hat{\sigma}$ as adversarial rather than stochastic deserves some discussion.

First, adversarial guarantees are stronger than stochastic guarantees, and will lead to more robust solutions in practice. Perhaps more importantly, inferring a Bayesian prior over influence functions in Σ will run into exactly the type of problem we are trying to address in the first place: data are sparse and noisy, and if we infer an incorrect prior, it may lead to very suboptimal results. Doing so would next require us to establish robustness over the values of the *hyperparameters* of the Bayesian prior over functions.

Specifically for the Perturbation Interval model, one may be tempted to treat the parameters as drawn according to some distribution over their possible range. This approach was essentially taken in [2, 17]: Adiga et al. [2] assume that for each edge e independently, its presence/absence was misobserved with probability ϵ, whereas Goyal et al. [17] assume that for each edge, the actual parameter is perturbed with independent noise drawn uniformly from a known interval. In both cases, under the Independent Cascade model (for example), the edge activation probability can be replaced with the *expected* edge activation probability under the random noise model, which will provably lead to the exact same influence function σ. Thus, independent noise for edge parameters, drawn from a known distribution, does not augment the model in the sense of capturing robustness. In particular, it does not capture uncertainty in a meaningful way.

To model the type of issues one would expect to arise in real-world settings, at the very least, noise must be correlated between edges. For instance, certain subpopulations may be inherently harder to observe or have sparser data to learn from. However, correlated random noise would result in a more complex description of the noise model, and thus make it harder to actually learn and verify the noise model. In particular, as discussed above, this would apply given that the noise model itself must be learned from noisy data.

2. RELATED WORK

Kempe et al. [21] formally defined the problem of finding a set of influential individuals as a discrete optimization problem, proposing a greedy algorithm with a $1 - 1/e$ approximation guarantee for the Independent Cascade and Linear Threshold models. A long sequence of subsequent work focused on more efficient algorithms for Influence Maximization (both with and without approximation guarantees) and on broadening the class of models for which guarantees can be obtained [3, 7, 9, 21, 22, 28, 34, 35]. See the recent book by Chen et al. [5] and the survey in [21] for more detailed overviews.

As a precursor to maximizing influence, one needs to infer the influence function σ from observed data. The most common approach is to estimate the parameters of a particular diffusion model [1, 11, 14, 15, 30, 32, 33]. Theoretical bounds on the required sample complexity for many diffusion models have been established, including [1, 30, 32] for the Discrete-Time Independent Cascade (DIC) model, [11] for the Continuous-Time Independent Cascade (CIC) model, and [30] for the Linear Threshold model. However, it remains difficult to decide which diffusion models fit the observation best. Moreover, the diffusion models only serve as a rough approximation to the real-world diffusion process. In order to sidestep the issue of diffusion models, Du et al. [12] recently proposed to directly learn the influence function σ from the observations, without assuming any particular diffusion model. They only assume that the influence function is a weighted average of coverage functions. While their approach provides polynomial sample complexity, they require a strong technical condition on finding an accurate approximation to the reachability distribution. Hence, their work remains orthogonal to the issue of Robust Influence Maximization.

Several recent papers take first steps toward Influence Maximization under uncertainty. Goyal, Bonchi and Lakshmanan [17] and Adiga et al. [2] study *random* (rather than adversarial) noise models, in which either the edge activation probabilities $p_{u,v}$ are perturbed with random noise [17], or the presence/absence of edges is flipped with a known probability [2].

Another approach to dealing with uncertainty is to carry out multiple influence campaigns, and to use the observations to obtain better estimates of the model parameters. Chen et al. [8] model the problem as a combinatorial multi-armed bandit problem and use the UCB1 algorithm with regret bounds. Lei et al. [24] instead incorporate beta distribution priors over the activation probabilities into the DIC model. They propose several strategies to update the posterior distributions and give heuristics for seed selection in each trial so as to balance exploration and exploitation. Our approach is complementary: even in an exploration-based setting, there will always be residual uncertainty, in particular when exploration budgets are limited.

The adversarial Perturbation Interval model was recently proposed in work of the authors [19]. The focus in that work was not on robust optimization, but on algorithms for detecting whether an instance was likely to suffer from high instability of the optimal solution. Optimization for multiple scenarios was also recently used in work by Chen et al. on tracking influential nodes as the structure of the graph evolves over time [10]. However, the model explicitly allowed updating the seed set over time, while our goal is simultaneous optimization.

Simultaneously to the present work, Chen et al. [6] and Lowalekar et al. [27] have been studying the Robust Influence Maximization problem under the Perturbation Interval model [19]. Their exact formulations are somewhat different. The main result of Chen et al. [6] is an analysis of the heuristic of choosing the best solution among three candidates: make each edge's parameter as small as possible, as large as possible, or equal to the middle of its interval. They prove *solution-dependent* approximation guarantees for this heuristic.

The objective of Lowalekar et al. [27] is to minimize the maximum regret instead of maximizing the minimum ratio. They propose a heuristic based on constraint generation ideas to solve the robust influence maximization problem. The heuristic does not come with approximation guarantees; instead, [27] proposes a solution-dependent measure of robustness of a given seed set. As part of their work, [27] prove a result similar to our Lemma 1, showing that the worst-case instances all have the largest or smallest possible values for all parameters.

3. MODELS AND PROBLEM DEFINITION

3.1 Influence Diffusion Models

For concreteness, we focus on two diffusion models: the discrete time Independent Cascade model (DIC) [21] and the continuous-time Independent Cascade model (CIC) [15]. Our framework applies to most other diffusion models; in particular, most of the concrete results carry over to the discrete and continuous Linear Threshold models [21, 33].

Under the DIC model, the diffusion process unfolds in discrete time steps as follows: when a node u becomes active in step t, it attempts to activate all currently inactive neighbors in step $t+1$. For each neighbor v, it succeeds with a known probability $p_{u,v}$; the $p_{u,v}$ are the parameters of the model. If node u succeeds, v becomes active. Once u has made all its attempts, it does not get to make further activation attempts at later times; of course, the node v may well be activated at time $t+1$ or later by some node other than u.

The CIC model describes a continuous-time process. Associated with each edge (u, v) is a delay distribution with parameter $\alpha_{u,v}$. When a node u becomes newly active at time t_u, for every neighbor v that is still inactive, a delay time $\Delta_{u,v}$ is drawn from the delay distribution. $\Delta_{u,v}$ is the duration it takes u to activate v, which could be infinite (if u does not succeed in activating v). Commonly assumed delay distributions include the Exponential distribution or Rayleigh distribution. If multiple nodes $u_1, \ldots, u_\ell$ attempt to activate v, then v is activated at the earliest time $\min_i t_{u_i} + \Delta_{u_i,v}$. Nodes are considered activated by the process if they are activated within a specified observation window $[0, T]$.

A specific instance is described by the class of its influence model (such as DIC, CIC, or others not discussed here in detail) and the setting of the model's parameters; in the DIC and CIC models above, the parameters would be the influence probabilities $p_{u,v}$ and the parameters $\alpha_{u,v}$ of the edge delay distributions, respectively. Together, they completely specify the dynamic process; and thus a mapping σ from initially active sets S_0 to the expected number[3] $\sigma(S_0)$ of nodes active at the end of the process. We can now formalize the Influence Maximization problem as follows:

DEFINITION 1 (INFLUENCE MAXIMIZATION). *Maximize the objective $\sigma(S_0)$ subject to the constraint $|S_0| \leq k$.*

For most of the diffusion models studied in the literature, including the DIC [21] and CIC [13] models, it has been shown that $\sigma(S_0)$ is a monotone and submodular[4] function of S_0. These properties imply that a greedy approximation algorithm guarantees a $1 - 1/e$ approximation [31].

3.2 Robust Influence Maximization

The main motivation for our work is that often, σ is not precisely known to the algorithm trying to maximize influence. There may be a (possibly infinite) number of candidate functions σ, resulting from different diffusion models or parameter settings. We denote the set of all candidate influence functions[5] by Σ. We now formally define the *Robust Influence Maximization* problem.

DEFINITION 2 (ROBUST INFLUENCE MAXIMIZATION). *Given a set Σ of influence functions, maximize the objective*

$$\rho(S) = \min_{\sigma \in \Sigma} \frac{\sigma(S)}{\sigma(S_\sigma^*)},$$

subject to a cardinality constraint $|S| \leq k$. Here S_σ^* is a seed set with $|S_\sigma^*| \leq k$ maximizing $\sigma(S_\sigma^*)$.

A solution to the Robust Influence Maximization problem achieves a large fraction of the maximum possible influence (compared to the optimal seed set) under all diffusion settings simultaneously. Alternatively, the solution can be interpreted as solving the Influence Maximization problem when the function σ is chosen from Σ by an adversary.

While Definition 2 per se does not require the $\sigma \in \Sigma$ to be submodular and monotone, these properties are necessary to obtain positive results. Hence, we will assume here that all $\sigma \in \Sigma$ are monotone and submodular, as they are for standard diffusion models. Notice that even then, ρ is the minimum of submodular functions, and as such not necessarily submodular itself [23].

A particularly natural and important special case of Definition 2 is the Perturbation Interval model recently proposed in [19]. Here, the influence model is known (for concreteness, DIC), but there is uncertainty about its parameters. For each edge e, we have an interval $I_e = [\ell_e, r_e]$, and the algorithm only knows that the parameter (say, p_e) lies in I_e; the exact value is chosen by an adversary. Notice that Σ is (uncountably) infinite under this model. While this may seem worrisome, the following lemma shows that we only need to consider finitely (though exponentially) many functions:

LEMMA 1. *Under the Perturbation Interval model for DIC[6], the worst case for the ratio in ρ for any seed set S_0 is achieved by making each p_e equal to ℓ_e or r_e.*

PROOF. Fix one edge $\hat{e}$, and a seed set S_0. Fix the activation probabilities on all edges except $\hat{e}$, and consider the function $f_{S_0}(x)$, the expected number of nodes activated by S_0 when the activation probabilities of all edges $e \neq \hat{e}$ are as fixed, and the activation probability of $\hat{e}$ is x.

By explicitly writing the expectation as a distribution over live edge graphs (see [21]), one can observe that $f_{S_0}(x)$ is a linear function of x. Hence, the optimum influence (over all S_0) $g(x)$, being a maximum of linear functions, is convex. This means that the ratio $\frac{f_{S_0}(x)}{g(x)}$ is quasi-concave, which one can show by considering its level sets, and noticing that $\{x \mid f_{S_0}(x)/g(x) \geq \alpha\} = \{x \mid g(x) - 1/\alpha \cdot f_{S_0}(x) \leq 0\}$. The latter is a level set of a convex function, and thus convex.

Finally, because $f_{S_0}(x)/g(x)$ is quasi-concave, it attains its minimum at the smallest or largest value of x. By repeating this argument for all edges $\hat{e}$, we obtain a worst-case setting in which all parameter values are equal to the left or right endpoints of the respective intervals I_e. □

[3]The model and virtually all results in the literature extend straightforwardly when the individual nodes are assigned non-negative importance scores.

[4]Recall that a set function f is monotone iff $f(S) \leq f(T)$ whenever $S \subseteq T$, and is submodular iff $f(S \cup \{x\}) - f(S) \geq f(T \cup \{x\}) - f(T)$ whenever $S \subseteq T$.

[5]For computation purposes, we assume that the functions are represented compactly, for instance, by the name of the diffusion model and all of its parameters.

[6]The result carries over with a nearly identical proof to the Linear Threshold model. We currently do not know if it also extends to the CIC model.

4. ALGORITHMS AND HARDNESS

Even when Σ contains just a single function σ, Robust Influence Maximization is exactly the traditional Influence Maximization problem, and is thus NP-hard. This issue also appears in a more subtle way: *evaluating* $\rho(S_0)$ (for a given S_0) involves taking the minimum of $\frac{\sigma(S_0)}{\sigma(S^*_\sigma)}$ over all $\sigma \in \Sigma$. It is not clear how to calculate the ratio $\frac{\sigma(S_0)}{\sigma(S^*_\sigma)}$ even for one of the σ, since the scaling constant $\sigma(S^*_\sigma)$ (which is independent of the chosen S_0) is exactly the solution to the original Influence Maximization problem, and thus NP-hard to compute.

This problem, however, is fairly easy to overcome: instead of using the true optimum solutions S^*_σ for the scaling constants, we can compute $(1-1/e)$-approximations S^g_σ using the greedy algorithm, because the σ are monotone and submodular [31]. Then, because $(1-1/e)\cdot\sigma(S^*_\sigma) \le \sigma(S^g_\sigma) \le \sigma(S^*_\sigma)$ for all $\sigma \in \Sigma$, we obtain that the "greedy objective function" $\rho^g(S) = \min_{\sigma\in\Sigma} \frac{\sigma(S)}{\sigma(S^g_\sigma)}$, satisfies the following property for all sets S: $(1-1/e)\cdot\rho^g(S) \le \rho(S) \le \rho^g(S)$. Hence, optimizing $\rho^g(S)$ in place of $\rho(S)$ comes at a cost of only a factor $(1-1/e)$ in the approximation guarantee. We will therefore focus on solving the problem of (approximately) optimizing $\rho^g(S)$.

Because each σ is monotone and submodular, and the $\sigma(S^g_\sigma)$, just like the $\sigma(S^*_\sigma)$, are just scaling constants, $\rho^g(S)$ is a minimum of monotone submodular functions. However, we show (in Theorem 2, proved in the full version [20]) that even in the context of Influence Maximization, this minimum is impossible to approximate to within any polynomial factor. This holds even in a bicriteria sense, i.e., the algorithm's solution is allowed to pick $(1-\delta)\ln|\Sigma|\cdot k$ nodes, but is compared only to solutions using k nodes. The result also extends to the seemingly more restricted Perturbation Interval model, giving an almost equally strong bicriteria approximation hardness result there.

THEOREM 2. *Let $\delta, \epsilon > 0$ be any constants, and assume that $P \neq NP$. There are no polynomial-time algorithms for the following problems:*

1. *Given n nodes and a set Σ of influence functions on these nodes (derived from the DIC or CIC models), as well as a target size k. Find a set S of $|S| \le (1-\delta)\ln|\Sigma|\cdot k$ nodes, such that $\rho(S) \ge \rho(S^*)\cdot\Omega(1/n^{1-\epsilon})$, where S^* is the optimum solution of size k.*
2. *Given a graph G on n nodes and intervals I_e for edge activation probabilities under the DIC model (or intervals I_e for edge delay parameters under the CIC model), as well as a target size k. Find a set S of cardinality $|S| \le \epsilon\cdot c\cdot\ln n\cdot k$ (for a sufficiently small fixed constant c) such that $\rho(S) \ge \rho(S^*)\cdot\Omega(1/n^{1-\epsilon})$, where S^* is the optimum solution of size k.*

The hardness results naturally apply to any diffusion model that subsumes the DIC or CIC models. However, an extension to the DLT model is not immediate: the construction relies crucially on having many edges of probability 1 into a single node, which is not allowed under the DLT model.

4.1 Bicriteria Approximation Algorithm

Theorem 2 implies that to obtain any non-trivial approximation guarantee, one needs to allow the algorithm to exceed the seed set size by at least a factor of $\ln|\Sigma|$. In this section, we therefore focus on such bicriteria approximation results, by slightly modifying an algorithm of Krause et al. [23].

Algorithm 1 SATURATE GREEDY (Σ, k, precision γ)

Initialize $c_{\min} \leftarrow 0$, $c_{\max} \leftarrow 1$.
while $(c_{\max} - c_{\min}) \ge \gamma$ **do**
  $c \leftarrow (c_{\max} + c_{\min})/2$.
  Define $H^{(c)}(S) \leftarrow \sum_{\sigma\in\Sigma} \min(c, \frac{\sigma(S)}{\sigma(S^g_\sigma)})$.
  $S \leftarrow$ GREEDY MINTSS$(H^{(c)}, k, c\cdot|\Sigma|, c\cdot\gamma/3)$.
  if $|S| > \beta\cdot k$ **then**
    $c_{\max} \leftarrow c$.
  else
    $c_{\min} \leftarrow c\cdot(1-\gamma/3)$, $S^* \leftarrow S$.
  end if
end while
Return S^*.

The slight difference lies in how the submodular coverage subproblem is solved. Both [23] and the GREEDY MINTSS algorithm [18] greedily add elements. However, the GREEDY MINTSS algorithm adds elements until the desired submodular objective is attained up to an additive ε term, while [23] requires exact coverage. Moreover, directly considering real-valued submodular functions instead of going through fractional values leads to a more direct analysis of the GREEDY MINTSS algorithm [18].

The high-level idea of the algorithm is as follows. Fix a real value c, and define $h^{(c)}_\sigma(S) := \min(c, \frac{\sigma(S)}{\sigma(S^g_\sigma)})$ and $H^{(c)}(S) := \sum_{\sigma\in\Sigma} h^{(c)}_\sigma(S)$. Then, $\rho^g(S) \ge c$ if and only if $\frac{\sigma(S)}{\sigma(S^g_\sigma)} \ge c$ for all $\sigma \in \Sigma$. But because by definition, $h^{(c)}_\sigma(S) \le c$ for all σ, the latter is equivalent to $H^{(c)}(S) \ge |\Sigma|\cdot c$. (If any term in the sum is less than c, no other term can ever compensate for it, because they are capped at c.)

Because $H^{(c)}(S)$ is a non-negative linear combination of the monotone submodular functions $h^{(c)}_\sigma$, it is itself a monotone and submodular function. This enables the use of a greedy $\ln|\Sigma|$-approximation algorithm to find an (approximately) smallest set S with $H^{(c)}(S) \ge c|\Sigma|$. If S has size at most $k\ln|\Sigma|$, this constitutes a satisfactory solution, and we move on to larger values of c. If S has size more than $k\ln|\Sigma|$, then the greedy algorithm's approximation guarantee ensures that there is no satisfactory set S of size at most k. Hence, we move on to smaller values of c. For efficiency, the search for the right value of c is done with binary search and a specified precision parameter.

A slight subtlety in the greedy algorithm is that $H^{(c)}$ could take on fractional values. Thus, instead of trying to meet the bound $c|\Sigma|$ precisely, we aim for a value of $c|\Sigma|-\epsilon$. Then, the analysis of the GREEDY MINTSS algorithm of Goyal et al. [18] (of which our algorithm is an unweighted special case) applies. The resulting algorithm SATURATE GREEDY is given as Algorithm 1. The simple greedy subroutine — a special case of the GREEDY MINTSS algorithm — is given as Algorithm 2.

By combining the discussion at the beginning of this section (about optimizing ρ vs. ρ^g) with the analysis of Krause et al. [23] and Goyal et al. [18], we obtain the following approximation guarantee. The (straightforward) missing details are given in the full version [20].

Algorithm 2 Greedy Mintss (f, k, threshold η, error ε)

```
Initialize S ← ∅.
while f(S) < η − ε do
    u ← argmax_{v∉S} f(S ∪ {v}).
    S ← S ∪ {u}.
end while
Return S.
```

Theorem 3. *Let $\beta = 1 + \ln|\Sigma| + \ln\frac{3}{\gamma}$. Saturate Greedy finds a seed set $\hat{S}$ of size $|\hat{S}| \leq \beta k$ with*

$$\rho(\hat{S}) \geq (1 - 1/e) \cdot \rho(S^*) - \gamma,$$

where $S^* \in \mathrm{argmax}_{S:|S|\leq k}\, \rho(S)$ is an optimal robust seed set of size k.

Theorem 3 holds very broadly, so long as all influence functions are monotone and submodular. This includes the DIC, DLT, and CIC models, and allows mixing influence functions from different model classes. Notice the contrast between Theorems 3 and 2. By allowing the seed set size to be exceeded just a little more (a factor $\ln|\Sigma| + O(1)$ instead of $0.999 \ln|\Sigma|$), we go from $\Omega(n^{1-\epsilon})$ approximation hardness to a $(1 - 1/e)$-approximation algorithm.

4.2 Simple Heuristics

In addition to the Saturate Greedy algorithm, our experiments use two natural baselines. The first is a simple greedy algorithm Single Greedy which adds βk elements to S one by one, always choosing the one maximizing $\rho^g(S \cup \{v\})$. While this heuristic has provable guarantees when the objective function is submodular, this is not the case for the minimum of submodular functions.

The second heuristic is to run a greedy algorithm for each objective function $\sigma \in \Sigma$ separately, and choose the best of the resulting solutions. Those solutions are exactly the sets S^g_σ defined earlier in this section. Thus, the algorithm consists of choosing $\mathrm{argmax}_{\sigma\in\Sigma}\, \rho^g(S^g_\sigma)$. We call the resulting algorithm All Greedy.

In the worst case, both Single Greedy and All Greedy can perform arbitrarily badly, as seen by the following class of examples with a given parameter k. The example consists of k instances of the DIC model for the following graph with $3k + m$ nodes (where $m \gg k$). The graph comprises a directed complete bipartite graph $K_{k,m}$ with k nodes $x_1, \ldots, x_k$ on one side and m nodes $y_1, \ldots, y_m$ on the other side, as well as k separate edges $(u_1, v_1), \ldots, (u_k, v_k)$. The edges (u_i, v_i) have activation probability 1 in all instances. In the bipartite graph, in the ith scenario, only the edges leaving node x_i have probability 1, while all others have 0 activation probability.

The optimal solution for Robust Influence Maximization is to select all nodes x_i, since one of them will succeed in activating the m nodes y_j. The resulting objective value will be close to 1. However, All Greedy only picks one node x_i and the remaining $k - 1$ nodes as u_j. Single Greedy instead picks all of the u_j. Thus, both All Greedy and Single Greedy will have robust influence close to 0 as m grows large. Empirical experiments confirm this analysis. For example, for $k = 2$ and $m = 100$, Saturate Greedy achieves $\rho = 0.985$, while Single Greedy and All Greedy only achieve 0.038 and 0.029, respectively.

Implementation

The most time-consuming step in all of the algorithms is the estimation of influence coverage, given a seed set S. Naïve estimation by Monte Carlo simulation could lead to a very inefficient implementation. The problem is even more pronounced compared to traditional Influence Maximization as we must estimate the influence in multiple diffusion settings. Instead, we use the ConTinEst algorithm of Du et al. [13] for fast influence estimation under the CIC model. For the DIC model, we generalize the approach of Du et al. To accelerate the Greedy Mintss algorithm, we also apply the CELF optimization [26] in all cases. Analytically, one can derive linear running time (in both n and $|\Sigma|$) for all three algorithms, thanks to the fast influence estimation. This is borne out by detailed experiments[7], which also show that Saturate Greedy is slower than the heuristics by about a factor of ten.

5. EXPERIMENTS

We empirically evaluate the Saturate Greedy algorithm and the Single Greedy and All Greedy heuristics. Our goal is twofold: (1) Evaluate how well Saturate Greedy and the heuristics perform on realistic instances. (2) Qualitatively understand the difference between robustly and non-robustly optimized solutions.

Our experiments are all performed on real-world data sets. The data sets span the range of different causes for uncertainty, namely: (1) influences are learned from cascades for different topics; (2) influences are learned with different modeling assumptions; (3) influences are only inferred to lie within intervals I_e (the Perturbation Interval model).

5.1 Different Networks

We first focus on the case in which the diffusion model is kept constant: we use the DIC model, with parameters specified below. Different objective functions are obtained from observing cascades (1) on different topics. We use Twitter retweet networks for different topics. (2) at different times. We use MemeTracker diffusion network snapshots at different times.

The Twitter networks are extracted from a complete collection of tweets between Jan. 2010 and Feb. 2010. We treat each hashtag as a separate cascade, and extract the top 100/250 users with the most tweets containing these hashtags into two datasets (Twitter100 and Twitter250). The hashtags are manually grouped into five categories of about 70–80 hashtags each, corresponding to major events/topics during the data collection period. The five groups are: Haiti earthquake (Haiti), Iran election (Iran), Technology, US politics, and the Copenhagen climate change summit (Climate). Examples of hashtags in each group are shown in Table 1. Whenever user B retweets a post of user A with a hashtag belonging to category i, we insert an edge with activation probability 1 from A to B in graph i. The union of all these edges specifies the ith influence function.

Our decision to treat each hashtag as a separate cascade is supposed to capture that most hashtags "spread" across Twitter when one user sees another use it, and starts posting with it himself. The grouping of similar hashtags captures that a user who may influence another to use the hashtag, say, #teaparty, would likely also influence the other user

[7] omitted here due to space constraints

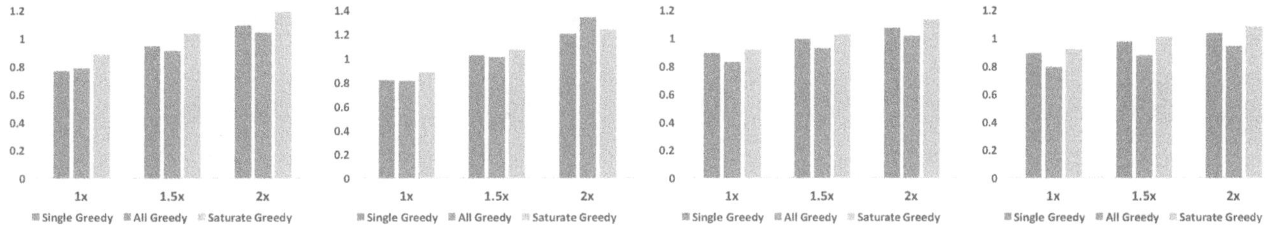

(a) Twitter100 ($k = 10$) (b) Twitter250 ($k = 20$) (c) Meme2000 ($k = 50$) (d) Meme5000 ($k = 100$)

Figure 1: Performance of the algorithms on the four topical/temporal datasets. The x-axis is the number of seeds selected, and the y-axis the resulting robust influence (compared to seed sets of size k).

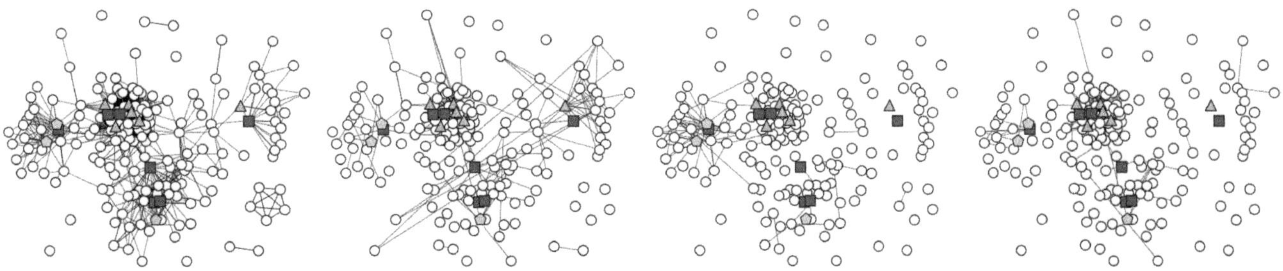

(a) Iran (b) Haiti (c) US politics (d) Climate

Figure 2: Saturate Greedy vs. Iran graph seed nodes. Green/pentagon nodes are selected in both; orange/triangle nodes are selected by Saturate Greedy only; purple/square nodes for Iran only.

to a similar extent to use, say, #liberty. The pruning of the data sets was necessary because most users had showed very limited activity. Naturally, if our goal were to evaluate the algorithmic efficiency rather than the performance with respect to the objective function, we would focus on larger networks, even if the networks were less easily visualized.

Category	Hashtags
Iran	#iranelection, #iran, #16azar, #tehran
Haiti	#haiti, #haitiquake, #supphaiti, #cchaiti
Technology	#iphone, #mac, #microsoft, #tech
US politics	#obama, #conservative, #teaparty, #liberty
Climate	#copenhagen, #cop15, #climatechange

Table 1: Examples of hashtags in each category

The MemeTracker dataset [25] contains memes extracted from the Blogsphere and main-stream media sites between Aug. 2009 and Feb. 2010. In our experiments, we extract the 2000/5000 sites with the most posting activity across the time period we study (Meme2000 and Meme5000). We extract six separate diffusion networks, one for each month. The network for month i contains all the directed links that were posted in month i (in reverse order, i.e., if B links to A, then we add a link from A to B), with activation probability 1. It thus defines the ith influence function.

The parameters of the DIC model used for this set of experiments are summarized in Table 2.

Recalling that in the worst case, a relaxation in the number of seeds is required to obtain robust seed sets, we allow all algorithms to select more seeds than the solution they are compared against. Specifically, we report results in which the algorithms may select k, $1.5 \cdot k$ and $2 \cdot k$ seeds, respectively. The reported results are averaged over three independent runs of each of the algorithms.

Data set	Edge Activation Probability	# Seeds
Twitter100	0.2	10
Twitter250	0.1	20
Meme2000	0.05	50
Meme5000	0.05	100

Table 2: Diffusion model settings

Results: Performance

The aggregate performance of the different algorithms on the four data sets is shown in Figure 1.

The first main insight is that (in the instances we study) getting to over-select seeds by 50%, all three algorithms achieve a robust influence of at least 1.0. In other words, 50% more seeds let the algorithms perform as though they knew exactly which of the (adversarially chosen) diffusion settings was the true one. This suggests that the networks in our data sets share a lot of similarities that make influential nodes in one network also (mostly) influential in the other networks. This interpretation is consistent with the observation that the baseline heuristics perform similarly to (and in one case better than) the SATURATE GREEDY algorithm. Notice, however, that when selecting just k seeds, SATURATE GREEDY does perform best (though only by a small margin) among the three algorithms. This suggests that keeping robustness in mind may be more crucial when

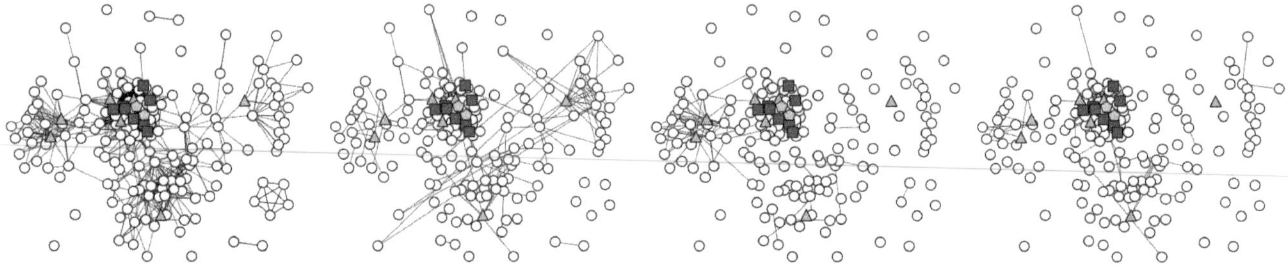

Figure 3: Saturate Greedy vs. Climate graph seed nodes. Green/pentagon nodes are selected in both; orange/triangle nodes are selected by Saturate Greedy only; purple/square nodes for Climate only.

the algorithm does not get to compensate with a larger number of seeds.

Results: Visualization

To further illustrate the tradeoffs between robust and non-robust optimization, we visualize the seeds selected by SATURATE GREEDY (robust seeds) compared to seeds selected non-robustly based on only one diffusion setting. For legibility, we focus only on the Twitter250 data set, and only plot 4 out of the 5 networks. (The fifth network is very sparse, and thus not particularly interesting.)

Figure 2 compares the seeds selected by SATURATE GREEDY with those (approximately) maximizing the influence for the Iran network. Notice that SATURATE GREEDY focuses mostly (though not exclusively) on the densely connected core of the network (at the center), while the Iran-specific optimization also exploits the dense regions on the left and at the bottom. These regions are much less densely connected in the US politics and Climate networks, while the core remains fairly densely connected, leading the SATURATE GREEDY solution to be somewhat more robust.

Similarly, Figure 3 compares the SATURATE GREEDY seeds (which are the same as in Figure 2) with seeds for the Climate network. The trend here is exactly the opposite. The seeds selected based only on the Climate network are exclusively in the core, because the other parts of the Climate network are barely connected. On the other hand, the robust solution picks a few seeds from the clusters at the bottom, left, and right, which are present in other networks. These seeds lead to extra influence in those networks, and thus more robustness.

5.2 Different Diffusion Models

In choosing a diffusion model, there is little convincing empirical work guiding the choice of a model class (such as CIC, DIC, or threshold models) or of distributional assumptions for model parameters (such as edge delay). A possible solution is to optimize robustly with respect to these different possible choices.

In this section, we evaluate such an approach. Specifically, we perform two experiments: (1) learning the CIC influence network under different parametric assumptions about the delay distribution, and (2) learning the influence network under different models of influence (CIC, DIC, DLT). We again use the MemeTracker dataset, restricting ourselves to the data from August 2008 and the 500 most active users. We use the MULTITREE algorithm of Gomez-Rodriguez et al. [16] to infer the diffusion network from the observed cascades. This algorithm requires a parametric assumption for the edge delay distribution. We infer ten different networks G_i corresponding to the Exponential distribution with parameters 0.05, 0.1, 0.2, 0.5, 1.0, and to the Rayleigh distribution with parameters 0.5, 1, 2, 3, 4. The length of the observation window is set to 1.0.

We then use the three algorithms to perform robust influence maximization for $k = 10$ seeds, again allowing the algorithms to exceed the target number of vertices. The influence model for each graph is the CIC model with the same parameters that were used to infer the graphs.

The performance of the algorithms is shown in Figure 4(a). All methods achieve satisfactory results in the experiment; this is again due to high similarity between the different diffusion settings inferred with different parameters.

For the second experiment, we investigate the robustness across different classes of diffusion models. We construct three instances of the DIC, DLT and DIC model from the ground truth diffusion network between the 500 active users. For the DIC model, we set the activation probability uniformly to 0.1. For the DLT model, we follow [21] and set the edge weights to $1/d_v$ where d_v is the in-degree of node v. For the CIC model, we use an exponential distribution with parameter 0.1 and an observation window of length 1.0. We perform robust influence maximization for $k = 10$ seeds and again allow the algorithms to exceed the target number of seeds.

The results are shown in Figure 4(b). Similarly to the case of different estimated parameters, all methods achieve satisfactory results in the experiment due to the high similarity between the diffusion models. Our results raise the intriguing question of which types of networks would be prone to significant differences in algorithmic performance based on which model is used for network estimation.

5.3 Networks sampled from the Perturbation Interval model

To investigate the performance when model parameters can only be placed inside "confidence intervals" (i.e., the Perturbation Interval model), we use the CONNIE algorithm [29] to infer the (fractional) parameters of a DIC model from the same 500-node MemeTracker data set used in the previous section. Following the approach of [19], we then assign "confidence intervals" $I_e = [(1-q)p_e, (1+q)p_e]$, where the p_e are the inferred parameters, and $q \in \{10\%, 20\%, 30\%, \ldots, 100\%\}$.

While Lemma 1 guarantees that the worst-case instances

have activation probabilities $(1-q)p_e$ or $(1+q)p_e$, this still leaves $2^{|E|}$ candidate functions, too many to include. We generate an instance for our experiments by sampling 10 of these functions uniformly, i.e., by independently making each edge's activation probability either $(1-q)p_e$ or $(1+q)p_e$. This collection is augmented by two more instances: one where all edge probabilities are $(1-q)p_e$, and one where all probabilities are $(1+q)p_e$. Notice that with the inclusion of these two instances, the ALL GREEDY heuristic generalizes the LUGreedy algorithm by Chen et al. [6], but might provide strictly better solutions on the *selected* instances because it explicitly considers those additional instances. The algorithms get to select 20 seed nodes; note that in these experiments, we are not considering a bicriteria approximation.

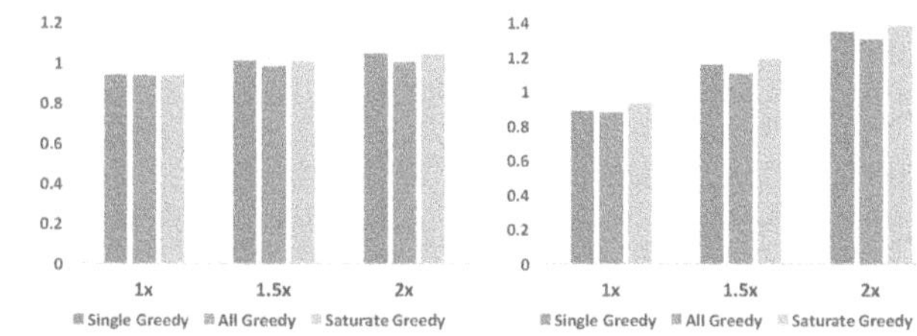

(a) Different Distributions. (b) Different Models

Figure 4: Performance of the algorithms (a) under different delay distributions following the CIC model, and (b) under different classes of diffusion models. The x-axis shows the number of seeds selected, and $k = 10$.

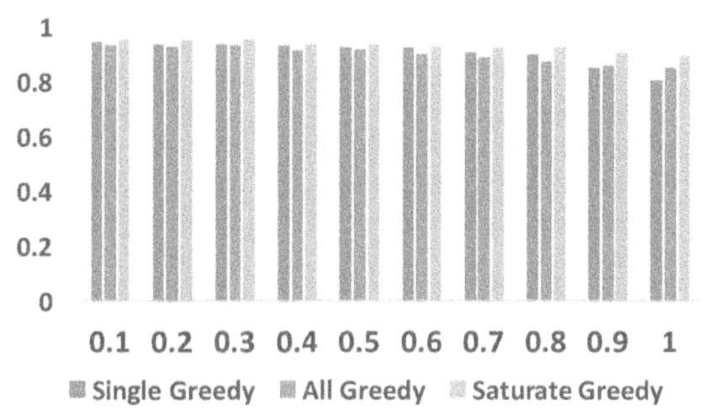

Figure 5: Performance of the algorithms under networks sampled from the Perturbation Interval model. The x axis shows the (relative) size of the perturbation interval I_e, and $k = 20$.

The results are shown in Figure 5. Contrary to the previous results, when there is a lot of uncertainty about the edge parameters (relative interval size 100%), the SATURATE GREEDY algorithm more clearly outperforms the SINGLE GREEDY and ALL GREEDY heuristics. Thus, robust optimization does appear to become necessary when there is a lot of uncertainty about the model's parameters.

Notice that the evaluation of the algorithms' seed sets is performed only with respect to the *sampled* influence functions, not with respect to all $2^{|E|}$ functions. Whether one can efficiently identify a worst-case parameter setting for a given seed set S_0 is an intriguing open question. Absent this ability, we cannot efficiently guarantee that the solutions are actually good with respect to all parameter settings.

6. FUTURE WORK

Our work marks an early step, rather than the conclusion, in devising robust algorithms for social network tasks, and more specifically Influence Maximization. An interesting unresolved question is whether one can efficiently find an (approximately) worst-case influence function in the Perturbation Interval model. This would allow us to empirically evaluate the performance of natural heuristics for the Perturbation Interval model, such as randomly sampling a small number of influence functions. Furthermore, it would allow us to design "column generation" style algorithms for the Perturbation Interval model, where we alternate between finding a near-optimal seed set for all influence functions encountered so far, and finding a worst-case influence function for the current seed set, which will then be added to the encountered functions.

In the context of the bigger agenda, one could conceive of other notions of robustness in Influence Maximization, perhaps tracing a finer line between worst-case and Bayesian models. Also, much more research is needed into identifying which influence models best capture the behavior of real-world cascades, and under what circumstances. It is quite likely that different models will perform differently depending on the type of cascade and many other factors, and in-depth evaluations of the models could give practitioners more guidance on which mathematical models to choose. While our model of robustness allows us to combine instances of different models (e.g., IC and LT), this may come at a cost of decreased performance for each of the models individually. Thus, it remains an important task to identify the influence models that best fit real-world data.

Acknowledgments

We would like to thank Shaddin Dughmi for useful pointers and feedback, Shishir Bharathi and Mahyar Salek for useful discussions, and anonymous reviewers for useful feedback. The research was sponsored in part by NSF research grant IIS-1254206 and by the U.S. Defense Advanced Research Projects Agency (DARPA) under Social Media in Strategic Communication (SMISC) program, Agreement Number W911NF-12-1-0034. The views and conclusions are those of the authors and should not be interpreted as representing the official policies of the funding agency, or the U.S. Government.

7. REFERENCES

[1] B. Abrahao, F. Chierichetti, R. Kleinberg, and A. Panconesi. Trace complexity of network inference. In *Proc. 19th KDD*, pages 491–499, 2013.

[2] A. Adiga, C. J. Kuhlman, H. S. Mortveit, and A. K. S. Vullikanti. Sensitivity of diffusion dynamics to network uncertainty. In *Proc. 28th AAAI*, 2013.

[3] C. Borgs, M. Brautbar, J. Chayes, and B. Lucier. Maximizing social influence in nearly optimal time. In *Proc. 25th ACM SODA*, pages 946–957, 2014.

[4] K. E. Campbell and B. A. Lee. Name generators in surveys of personal networks. *Social Networks*, 13(3):203–221, 1991.

[5] W. Chen, L. V. Lakshmanan, and C. Castillo. *Information and Influence Propagation in Social Networks*. Synthesis Lectures on Data Management. Morgan & Claypool, 2013.

[6] W. Chen, T. Lin, Z. Tan, M. Zhao, and X. Zhou. Robust influence maximization. In *Proc. 22nd KDD*, 2016.

[7] W. Chen, Y. Wang, and S. Yang. Efficient influence maximization in social networks. In *Proc. 15th KDD*, pages 199–208, 2009.

[8] W. Chen, Y. Wang, Y. Yuan, and Q. Wang. Combinatorial multi-armed bandit and its extension to probabilistically triggered arms. *J. Mach. Learn. Res.*, 17(1):1746–1778, 2016.

[9] W. Chen, Y. Yuan, and L. Zhang. Scalable influence maximization in social networks under the linear threshold model. In *Proc. 10th ICDM*, pages 88–97, 2010.

[10] X. Chen, G. Song, X. He, and K. Xie. On influential nodes tracking in dynamic social networks. In *Proc. 15th SDM*, pages 613–621, 2015.

[11] H. Daneshmand, M. Gomez-Rodriguez, L. Song, and B. Schölkopf. Estimating diffusion network structures: Recovery conditions, sample complexity & soft-thresholding algorithm. In *Proc. 31st ICML*, 2014.

[12] N. Du, Y. Liang, M.-F. Balcan, and L. Song. Influence function learning in information diffusion networks. In *Proc. 31st ICML*, 2014.

[13] N. Du, L. Song, M. Gomez-Rodriguez, and H. Zha. Scalable influence estimation in continuous-time diffusion networks. In *Proc. 25th NIPS*, 2013.

[14] M. Gomez-Rodriguez, D. Balduzzi, and B. Schölkopf. Uncovering the temporal dynamics of diffusion networks. In *Proc. 28th ICML*, pages 561–568, 2011.

[15] M. Gomez-Rodriguez, J. Leskovec, and A. Krause. Inferring networks of diffusion and influence. *ACM Transactions on Knowledge Discovery from Data (TKDD)*, 5(4):21, 2012.

[16] M. Gomez-Rodriguez and B. Schölkopf. Submodular inference of diffusion networks from multiple trees. In *Proc. 29th ICML*, 2012.

[17] A. Goyal, F. Bonchi, and L. V. S. Lakshmanan. A data-based approach to social influence maximization. *Proc. VLDB Endowment*, 5(1):73–84, 2011.

[18] A. Goyal, F. Bonchi, L. V. S. Lakshmanan, and S. Venkatasubramanian. On minimizing budget and time in influence propagation over social networks. *Social Network Analysis and Mining*, 3(2):179–192, 2013.

[19] X. He and D. Kempe. Stability of influence maximization. Unpublished Manuscript, available at http://arxiv.org/abs/1501.04579, 2015.

[20] X. He and D. Kempe. Robust influence maximization. Technical Report, http://arxiv.org/abs/1602.05240, 2016.

[21] D. Kempe, J. Kleinberg, and E. Tardos. Maximizing the spread of influence in a social network. *Theory of Computing*, 11(4):105–147, 2015. A preliminary version of the results appeared in KDD 2003 and ICALP 2005.

[22] S. Khanna and B. Lucier. Influence maximization in undirected networks. In *Proc. 25th ACM SODA*, pages 1482–1496, 2014.

[23] A. Krause, H. B. McMahan, C. Guestrin, and A. Gupta. Robust submodular observation selection. In *Journal of Machine Learning Research*, volume 9, pages 2761–2801, 2008.

[24] S. Lei, S. Maniu, L. Mo, R. Cheng, and P. Senellart. Online influence maximization. In *Proc. 21st KDD*, pages 645–654, 2015.

[25] J. Leskovec, L. Backstrom, and J. Kleinberg. Meme-tracking and the dynamics of the news cycle. In *Proc. 15th KDD*, pages 497–506, 2009. Note: updated data sets at http://www.memetracker.org/.

[26] J. Leskovec, A. Krause, C. Guestrin, C. Faloutsos, J. VanBriesen, and N. S. Glance. Cost-effective outbreak detection in networks. In *Proc. 13th KDD*, pages 420–429, 2007.

[27] M. Lowalekar, P. Varakantham, and A. Kumar. Robust influence maximization (extended abstract). In *Proc. 15th AAMAS*, pages 1395–1396, 2016.

[28] E. Mossel and S. Roch. Submodularity of influence in social networks: From local to global. *SIAM J. Comput.*, 39(6):2176–2188, 2010.

[29] S. A. Myers and J. Leskovec. On the convexity of latent social network inference. In *Proc. 22nd NIPS*, pages 1741–1749, 2010.

[30] H. Narasimhan, D. C. Parkes, and Y. Singer. Learnability of influence in networks. In *Proc. 27th NIPS*, pages 3168–3176, 2015.

[31] G. L. Nemhauser, L. A. Wolsey, and M. L. Fisher. An analysis of the approximations for maximizing submodular set functions. *Mathematical Programming*, 14:265–294, 1978.

[32] P. Netrapalli and S. Sanghavi. Learning the graph of epidemic cascades. In *ACM SIGMETRICS Performance Evaluation Review*, pages 211–222, 2012.

[33] K. Saito, M. Kimura, K. Ohara, and H. Motoda. Selecting information diffusion models over social networks for behavioral analysis. In *Proc. 2010 European Conference on Machine Learning and Knowledge Discovery in Databases: Part III, ECML/PKDD 10*, pages 180–195, 2010.

[34] C. Wang, W. Chen, and Y. Wang. Scalable influence maximization for independent cascade model in large-scale social networks. *Data Mining and Knowledge Discovery Journal*, 25(3):545–576, 2012.

[35] Y. Wang, G. Cong, G. Song, and K. Xie. Community-based greedy algorithm for mining top-k influential nodes in mobile social networks. In *Proc. 16th KDD*, pages 1039–1048, 2010.

FRAUDAR: Bounding Graph Fraud in the Face of Camouflage

Bryan Hooi, Hyun Ah Song, Alex Beutel, Neil Shah, Kijung Shin, Christos Faloutsos
Carnegie Mellon University
5000 Forbes Avenue
Pittsburgh PA 15213, USA
bhooi@andrew.cmu.edu, {hyunahs, abeutel, neilshah, kijungs, christos}@cs.cmu.edu

ABSTRACT

Given a bipartite graph of users and the products that they review, or followers and followees, how can we detect fake reviews or follows? Existing fraud detection methods (spectral, etc.) try to identify dense subgraphs of nodes that are sparsely connected to the remaining graph. Fraudsters can evade these methods using *camouflage*, by adding reviews or follows with honest targets so that they look "normal". Even worse, some fraudsters use *hijacked accounts* from honest users, and then the camouflage is indeed organic.

Our focus is to spot fraudsters in the presence of camouflage or hijacked accounts. We propose FRAUDAR, an algorithm that (a) is camouflage-resistant, (b) provides upper bounds on the effectiveness of fraudsters, and (c) is effective in real-world data. Experimental results under various attacks show that FRAUDAR outperforms the top competitor in accuracy of detecting both camouflaged and non-camouflaged fraud. Additionally, in real-world experiments with a Twitter follower-followee graph of 1.47 billion edges, FRAUDAR successfully detected a subgraph of more than 4000 detected accounts, of which a majority had tweets showing that they used follower-buying services.

1. INTRODUCTION

How can we detect if a politician has purchased fake followers on Twitter, or if a product's reviews on Amazon are genuine? More challengingly, how can we *provably* prevent fraudsters who sell fake followers and reviews for various web services from evading our detection systems? In this paper we focus on precisely this problem – specifically, how can we design a fraud detection system with strong, provable guarantees of robustness?

Given the rise in popularity of social networks and other web services in recent years, fraudsters have strong incentives to manipulate these services. On several shady websites, anyone can buy fake Facebook page-likes or Twitter followers by the thousands. Yelp, Amazon and TripAdvisor fake reviews are also available for sale, misleading consumers about restaurants, hotels, and other services and products. Detecting and neutralizing these actions is important for companies and consumers alike.

The tell-tale sign of such fraudulent actions is that fraudsters must add many edges, creating unusually *large* and *dense* regions in the adjacency matrix of the graph (see Figure 2). Smart fraudsters will also try to 'look normal', by adding links to popular items/idols (like famous singers/actors, or well-liked products) - this behavior is called "*camouflage*" in the recent literature. State-of-the-art algorithms, such as SPOKEN [23] and NETPROBE [21] exploit exactly the density signal, but do not account for "camouflage."

We propose FRAUDAR, a novel approach for successfully detecting fraudsters under camouflage, and we give *provable* limits on undetectable fraud. We provide data-dependent limits on the maximum number of edges a group of fraudulent adversaries can have without being detected, on a wide variety of real world graphs. As shown in Figure 1(a), FRAUDAR provides limits on undetectable fraud, and additionally provides novel optimizations that strengthen this bound.

Moreover, our method outperforms competitors and finds real world fraud on Twitter. In Figure 1(b) we find that FRAUDAR detects injected fraud with high accuracy, even in the case of camouflage, where prior methods struggle to detect fraudulent attacks. Additionally, when tested on a Twitter graph from 2009, FRAUDAR finds a 4031 by 4313 subgraph that is 68% dense. As shown in Figure 1(c-d), we find that *a majority* of the detected accounts had tweets showing that they used follower-buying services, and had gone undetected by Twitter for the 7 years since the data was collected. Finally, our method is scalable, with near linear runtime in the data size.

Thus, our main contributions are as follows:

- **Metric**: we propose a novel family of metrics which satisfies intuitive "axioms" and has several advantages as a suspiciousness metric.
- **Theoretical Guarantees**: we provide a provable bound on how much fraud an adversary can have in the graph without being caught, even in the face of camouflage. Additionally, we improve the theoretical bound through novel optimizations that better distinguish fraud and normal behavior in real-world data.
- **Effectiveness**: FRAUDAR outperforms state-of-the-art methods in detecting various fraud attacks in real world graphs, and detects a large amount of previously undetected fraudulent behavior on Twitter.
- **Scalability**: FRAUDAR is scalable, with near-linear time complexity in the number of edges.

Furthermore, FRAUDAR offers natural extensibility and can easily incorporate more complex relations available in certain contexts such as review text, IP addresses, etc.

Reproducibility: Our code is open-sourced at **www.andrew.cmu.edu/user/bhooi/camo.zip**.

KDD '16, August 13-17, 2016, San Francisco, CA, USA
 ISBN 978-1-4503-4232-2/16/08...$15.00
DOI: http://dx.doi.org/10.1145/2939672.2939747

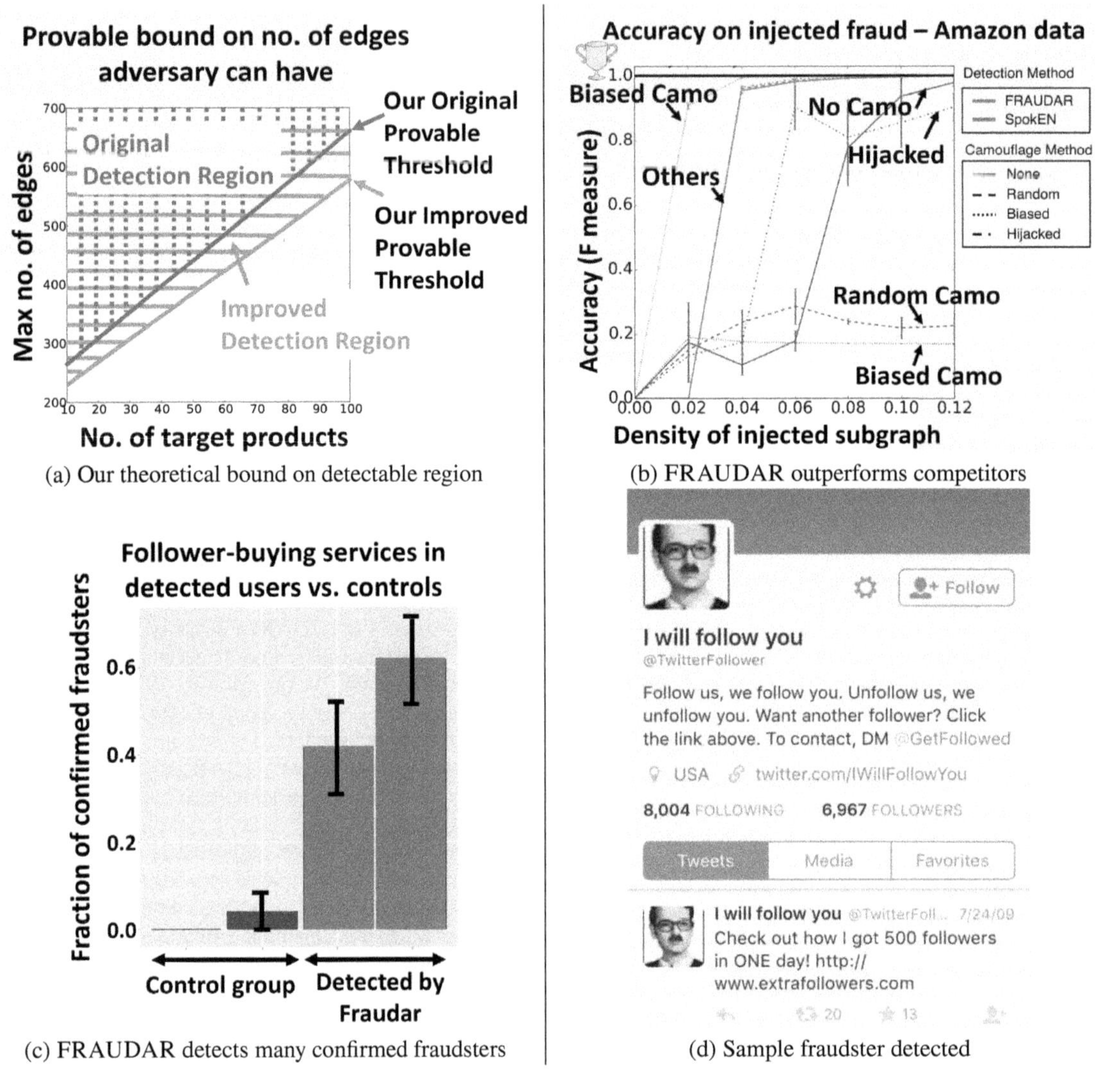

(a) Our theoretical bound on detectable region

(b) FRAUDAR outperforms competitors

(c) FRAUDAR detects many confirmed fraudsters

(d) Sample fraudster detected

Figure 1: **(a) Our theoretical thresholds:** fraudsters in the detection region will be caught by our approach. Our novel optimizations improve the (data-dependent) bounds by lowering it to the green region. **(b) Fraudar outperforms competitors. (c) A large fraction of accounts flagged by our algorithm are confirmed fraudsters**: both among detected followees (left red bar) and followers (right red bar) compared to almost none among non-flagged accounts (2 control groups). Confirmation was done by inspecting Tweets that advertise *TweepMe* or *TweeterGetter*. **(d) Real-life results - a sample fraudster caught.**

2. BACKGROUND AND RELATED WORK

Fraud detection has received significant focus in recent years. Many existing methods aim to detect fraud through review text [13,20]. However, these approaches are typically not adversarially robust: spammers can carefully select their review texts to avoid detection. Even without knowledge of the detection system, they may mimic normal user reviews as closely as possible. Graph-based approaches detect groups of spammers, often by identifying unexpectedly dense regions of the graph of users and products. Such methods are potentially harder to evade, as creating fake reviews unavoidably generates edges in the graph. Graph-based methods may be classified into global and local methods.

Global methods: Building on singular value decomposition (SVD), latent factor models, and belief propagation (BP), these model the entire graph to find fraud. SPOKEN [23] considered the "eigenspokes" pattern produced by pairs of eigenvectors of graphs, and was later generalized for fraud detection [12]. FBOX [25] builds on SVD but focuses on detecting attacks missed by spectral techniques. Several methods have used HITS [15]-like ideas to detect fraud in graphs [3,6,9,11,30]. BP has been used for fraud classification on eBay [21], and fraud detection [1]. All of these methods have been successful in finding fraud but they offer no guarantees of robustness. [25] performs adversarial analysis for spectral algorithms, showing that attacks of small enough scale will necessarily evade detection methods which rely on the top k SVD components.

Local clustering methods: A different direction for fraud detection focuses on local subgraphs, by analyzing the properties of egonets to detect fraud [5,22]. COPYCATCH [2] and GETTHESCOOP [12] use local search heuristics to find relevant dense bipartite subgraphs. However, without guarantees on the search algorithm, the algorithms may not be robust to intelligent adversaries.

Dense subgraph mining: Finding dense subgraphs has been an important focus of graph theory communities and has been studied from a wide array of perspectives [7,14]. Most closely related

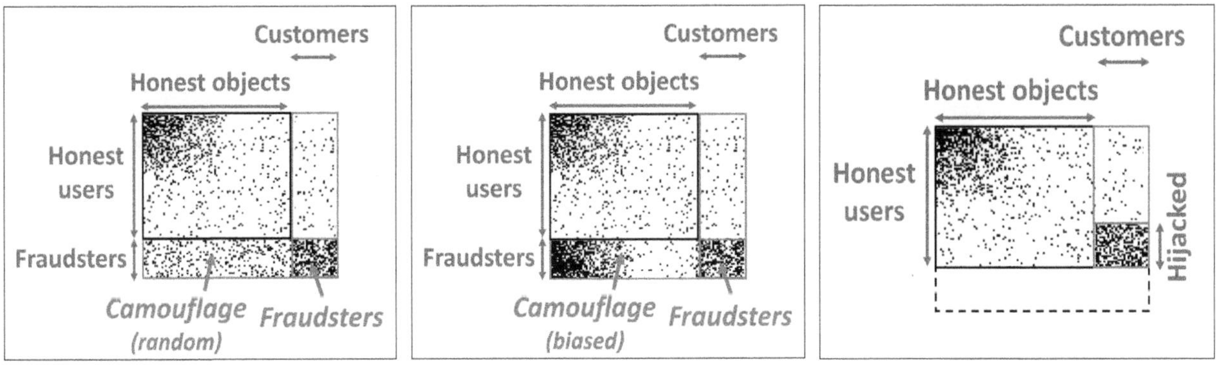

(a) Attacks with random camouflage | (b) Attacks with biased camouflage | (c) Hijacked accounts

Figure 2: **Three examples of possible attacks.**

	COPYCATCH	CatchSync	BP-based methods	SPOKEN	FBOX	GETTHESCOOP	FRAUDAR
Detects dense blocks	✓	✓	✓	✓	✓	✓	✓
Camouflage-resistant	✓	?			?		✓
Theoretical guarantees							✓

Table 1: Comparison between FRAUDAR and other fraud detection algorithms.

Symbol	Interpretation
$\mathcal{U} = \{u_1, \ldots, u_m\}$	Users
$\mathcal{W} = \{w_1, \ldots, w_n\}$	Objects
$\mathcal{V}$	Nodes of bipartite graph: $\mathcal{U} \cup \mathcal{W}$
G	Bipartite graph $G = (\mathcal{V}, \mathcal{E})$
$\mathcal{A}$	Subset of users
$\mathcal{B}$	Subset of objects
$\mathcal{S}$	Subset of nodes, $\mathcal{S} = \mathcal{A} \cup \mathcal{B}$
$g(\mathcal{S})$	Density metric
$f(\mathcal{S})$	'Total suspiciousness' metric (2)
$\mathcal{X}$	Current set of nodes in the greedy algorithm
Δ_i	$f(\mathcal{X} \setminus \{i\}) - f(\mathcal{X})$
$\hat{\mathcal{A}}, \hat{\mathcal{B}}$	Users (resp. objects) returned by FRAUDAR
m_0, n_0	No. of users (resp. objects) in fraud block
d_i	ith column sum of adjacency matrix
λ	Min. fraction of fraud edges per customer
$g_{\log}$	Logarithmic weighted metric

Table 2: Symbols and Definitions

to ours is Charikar's work on finding subgraphs with large average degree [4], which shows that subgraph average degree can be optimized with approximation guarantees. Variants have been proposed to efficiently find large, dense subgraphs [27], with approximation guarantees. To our knowledge, however, this is the first work which adapts this theoretical perspective to the challenges of fraud detection and camouflage resistance, and achieves meaningful bounds for our application. Moreover, our work differs from these in its setting of bipartite graphs, and in the use of edge reweighting to further increase accuracy.

Social network-based Sybil defense: Multiple identity or 'Sybil' attacks pose problems of malicious behavior in distributed systems. SybilGuard [32] and SybilLimit [31] use a decentralized random walk approach to limit the number of Sybil attackers. SumUp [26] and Iolaus [19] adapt this to content rating settings. However, these systems rely on a separate trust network between users; our setting is fundamentally different as our approach works directly with the user-product bipartite graph.

Handling camouflage: [8, 28] consider fraud detection methods that are robust to camouflage attacks. However, both methods focus on the time-series domain, observing changes in the behavior of fraudsters from system access logs rather than graph data.

A comparison between FRAUDAR and other fraud detection algorithms is summarized in Table 1. Our proposed method FRAUDAR is the only one that matches all specifications.

3. PROBLEM DEFINITION

Consider a set of m users $\mathcal{U} = \{u_1, \ldots, u_m\}$ and n objects $\mathcal{W} = \{w_1, \ldots, w_n\}$ connected according to a bipartite graph $G = (\mathcal{U} \cup \mathcal{W}, \mathcal{E})$. We can consider the objects to be followees on Twitter or products on Amazon. Table 2 gives a complete list of the symbols we use throughout the paper. We now describe our attack model and then our problem definition.

Attack model.

We assume that fraudsters are hired to use users they control to add edges pointing to a subset of nodes in $\mathcal{W}$. For example, a business may pay for followers on Twitter or positive reviews on Yelp. In general, fraudsters add a large number of edges, inducing a dense subgraph between the fraudster accounts and customers, as shown in the bottom right corner of each subplot of Figure 2. This general characteristic of fraud was found to be true in our experiments on real datasets, as well as in many other papers which use dense blocks to detect fraud [1,2,12,21,23].

To mask the fraud, fraudster accounts can add arbitrary "camouflage", i.e. edges pointing from their user accounts to any of the nodes in $\mathcal{W}$ that are not customers. We assume that fraudsters have *complete* knowledge of the graph and fraud detection mechanisms, enabling worst-case camouflage for any fraud detection system we create. Examples of the possible types of camouflage are given in Figure 2: (a) adding camouflage edges to random honest users, (b) camouflage biased toward high degree nodes, (c) using hijacked accounts, whereby fraudster accounts have realistic patterns of camouflage essentially similar to that of honest users.

While it is trivial for fraud accounts to add edges to any other node, it is more difficult for customer accounts to get honest edges. In particular, we assume that a customer would try to increase their number of incoming edges by a significant portion, and as a result a fraction, $\lambda \in [0, 1]$, of their incoming edges will be from fraudsters. This assumption would manifest itself as customers wanting to boost their follower count to seem *noticeably* more popular or a restaurant wanting a *significant* number of positive ratings to shift its average "number of stars" on Yelp. We will demonstrate how using this real world pattern significantly improves fraud detection both theoretically and in practice.

Desired properties of detection approach.

Our goal is to detect dense subgraphs in G, typically indicative of fraudulent groups of users and objects, like in the bottom-right of Figure 2.

INFORMAL PROBLEM 1. *Given a bipartite graph, detect attacks so as to minimize the number of edges that fraudsters can add pointing to customers without being detected.*

Given that we want our detection algorithm to be able to handle camouflage, we define the requirements for a *camouflage-resistant* algorithm:

DEFINITION 1. *Let $(\mathcal{A}, \mathcal{B})$ be a block consisting of fraudulent users and objects. A density metric g is* camouflage-resistant *if when any amount of camouflage is added by the adversary, $g(\mathcal{A} \cup \mathcal{B})$ does not decrease.*

That is, fraudsters cannot make themselves less suspicious by adding camouflage. Our goal is to find a fraud detection approach satisfying the following criteria:

PROBLEM DEFINITION 1 (DENSE SUBGRAPH DETECTION). *Design a class of density metrics for bipartite graphs, which can be optimized (1) in near-linear time, (2) within a constant factor of the optimum, and (3) is minimally affected by camouflage edges added by adversaries.*

Obtaining theoretical guarantees on the near-optimality of the returned subgraph is important because, as we will later show, it allows us to offer guarantees against *worst-case* fraudsters.

4. PROPOSED METHOD

Given this problem definition and attack model, we now offer FRAUDAR and our theoretical analysis of FRAUDAR.

4.1 Metric

In this section, we propose a class of metrics g that have particularly desirable properties when used as suspiciousness metrics. Namely, we will show that if g takes the form in (1) and (2), then it can be optimized in a way that is (a) scalable; (b) offers theoretical guarantees, and (c) is robust to camouflage.

Let $\mathcal{A} \subseteq \mathcal{U}$ be a subset of users and $\mathcal{B} \subseteq \mathcal{W}$ be a subset of objects. Let $\mathcal{S} = \mathcal{A} \cup \mathcal{B}$, and $\mathcal{V} = \mathcal{U} \cup \mathcal{W}$. For the rest of this paper, we use g to denote the density metric that the algorithm will optimize, i.e. the algorithm will find $\mathcal{S}$ to (approximately) maximize $g(\mathcal{S})$. Note that g has a single argument, which is the union of the users and objects whose suspiciousness we are evaluating.

We propose using density metrics g of the following form:

$$g(\mathcal{S}) = \frac{f(\mathcal{S})}{|\mathcal{S}|} \tag{1}$$

where total suspiciousness f is:

$$\begin{aligned} f(\mathcal{S}) &= f_{\mathcal{V}}(\mathcal{S}) + f_{\mathcal{E}}(\mathcal{S}) \\ &= \sum_{i \in \mathcal{S}} a_i + \sum_{i,j \in \mathcal{S} \wedge (i,j) \in \mathcal{E}} c_{ij}, \end{aligned} \tag{2}$$

for some constants $a_i \geq 0$ and constants $c_{ij} > 0$.

Intuitively, the node suspiciousness $f_{\mathcal{V}}(\mathcal{S})$ is a sum of constants a_i corresponding to the users and objects in $\mathcal{S}$, which can be thought of as how individually suspicious that particular user or object is. The edge suspiciousness $f_{\mathcal{E}}(\mathcal{S})$ is a sum of constants c_{ij} corresponding to the edges in between $\mathcal{S}$, which can be thought of as how suspicious that particular edge is (e.g. the suspiciousness of the text of a review by user i for object j).

There are many advantages to metrics of this form. Firstly, metrics of this form can be optimized in a way that is (a) scalable; (b) offers theoretical guarantees, and (c) is robust to camouflage, as we demonstrate in the rest of this paper. All 3 of these properties hold due to the particular chosen form in (1) and (2).

Secondly, metrics of this form obey a number of basic properties (or "axioms") that we would intuitively expect a reasonable suspiciousness metric should meet, as we next show. These basic properties are adapted from the "axioms for suspiciousness metrics," proposed in [10], to our setting where node and edge weights exist.

AXIOM 1 (NODE SUSPICIOUSNESS). *A subset consisting of higher suspiciousness nodes is more suspicious than one consisting of lower suspiciousness nodes, if the other conditions are fixed. Formally,*

$$|\mathcal{S}| = |\mathcal{S}'| \wedge f_{\mathcal{E}}(\mathcal{S}) = f_{\mathcal{E}}(\mathcal{S}') \wedge f_{\mathcal{V}}(\mathcal{S}) > f_{\mathcal{V}}(\mathcal{S}') \Rightarrow g(\mathcal{S}) > g(\mathcal{S}')$$

AXIOM 2 (EDGE SUSPICIOUSNESS). *Adding edges within a subset increases the suspiciousness of the subset if the other conditions are fixed. Formally,*

$$e \notin \mathcal{E} \Rightarrow g(\mathcal{S}(\mathcal{V}, \mathcal{E} \cup \{e\})) > g(\mathcal{S}(\mathcal{V}, \mathcal{E}))$$

where $\mathcal{S}(\mathcal{V}, \mathcal{E})$ is the subgraph induced by $\mathcal{S}$ in the graph $(\mathcal{V}, \mathcal{E})$.

The **edge density** $\rho(\mathcal{S})$ of an induced subgraph is its number of edges divided by its maximum possible number of edges.

AXIOM 3 (SIZE). *Assuming node and edge weights are all equal, larger subsets are more suspicious than smaller subsets with the same edge density. Formally, given $a_i = a \; \forall \; i$, and $c_{ij} = b \; \forall \; (i, j) \in \mathcal{E}$:*

$$|\mathcal{S}| > |\mathcal{S}'| \;\wedge\; \mathcal{S} \supset \mathcal{S}' \;\wedge\; \rho(\mathcal{S}) = \rho(\mathcal{S}') \Rightarrow g(\mathcal{S}) > g(\mathcal{S}')$$

AXIOM 4 (CONCENTRATION). *A subset with smaller size is more suspicious than one with the same total suspiciousness but larger size. Formally,*

$$|\mathcal{S}| < |\mathcal{S}'| \;\wedge\; f(\mathcal{S}) = f(\mathcal{S}') \Rightarrow g(\mathcal{S}) > g(\mathcal{S}')$$

Density metrics g of the form defined in Equation (1) satisfy these properties:

THEOREM 1. *The density metric defined in* (1) *satisfies axioms 1 to 4.*

PROOF. See appendix A. ■

Note some simple metrics that violate these axioms: the edge density $\rho(\mathcal{S})$ itself, as a metric, does not increase with the size of $\mathcal{S}$ and hence violates axiom 3. On the opposite end, the total edge weight function $\sum_{i,j\in\mathcal{S}\wedge(i,j)\in\mathcal{E}} c_{ij}$ as a metric violates axiom 4 as it does not consider how concentrated the edge weight is. In contrast, g scales in a reasonable manner as its size or concentration changes.

A simple example of a metric g as defined in (1) and (2) is the bipartite graph average degree:

EXAMPLE 1. *(Bipartite Graph Average Degree) Let $a_i = 0$, and let $c_{ij} = 1$ if $(i,j) \in \mathcal{E}$ and 0 otherwise. In the expression (2) for $f(\mathcal{S})$, we add one term c_{ij} for each edge (i,j) for which i,j are both in the subset $\mathcal{S}$. Thus, $f(\mathcal{S})$ is equal to the number of edges in the subgraph spanned by $\mathcal{S}$, or half the total degree in the subgraph spanned by $\mathcal{S}$. As a result, $g(\mathcal{S}) = \frac{f(\mathcal{S})}{|\mathcal{S}|}$ is half the average degree of the subgraph spanned by $\mathcal{S}$.*

4.2 Algorithm

Let f and g be as given in (1) and (2). In this section, we give an algorithm for optimizing the density metric g in near-linear time.

Algorithm 0 describes our proposed FRAUDAR algorithm, a greedy approach inspired by that of [4] but which covers our broader objective class. We start with the entire set of nodes $\mathcal{U} \cup \mathcal{W}$, then repeatedly remove the node which results in the highest value of g evaluated on the remaining set of nodes. Formally, denote by $\mathcal{X}$ the current set we are optimizing over; initially we set $\mathcal{X} = \mathcal{U} \cup \mathcal{W}$. Let $\Delta_i = f(\mathcal{X}\setminus\{i\}) - f(\mathcal{X})$ be the change in f when we remove i from the current set. At each step, we will select i to maximize Δ_i, i.e. to leave behind the set with highest value of f. We then remove i from $\mathcal{X}$. We then repeat this process: we recompute the values of Δ_j, then choose the next node to delete, and so on. This leads to a shrinking series of sets $\mathcal{X}$ over time, denoted $\mathcal{X}_0, \dots, \mathcal{X}_{m+n}$ of sizes $m+n, \dots, 0$. At the end, we return the one of these that maximizes the density metric g.

The key fact that allows the algorithm to be efficient is the forms for f and g in (1) and (2). When i is removed, the only values of Δ_j which need to be updated are those where j is a neighbor of i. This is because for all other j, the expressions (1) and (2) ensure that Δ_j does not change. Hence, the updates are fast: for each $(i,j) \in \mathcal{E}$, over the lifetime of the algorithm we will perform at most one such update over this edge, for a total of $O(|\mathcal{E}|)$ updates. Using appropriate data structures, as we next describe, each update can be performed in $O(\log|\mathcal{V}|)$ time, totalling $O(|\mathcal{E}|\log|\mathcal{V}|)$ time.

Priority Tree.

Each element $i \in \mathcal{X}$ has a priority that will change as the algorithm progresses: the priority of element i at the tth iteration is $\Delta_i = f(\mathcal{X}_t \setminus \{i\}) - f(\mathcal{X}_t)$. This ensures that in Line 5, the element $i^* = \arg\max_{i\in\mathcal{X}_t} g(\mathcal{X}_t \setminus \{i\})$ we wish to find is exactly the element of highest priority, allowing us to retrieve it quickly (in $O(\log|\mathcal{V}|)$ time, as we explain below). Note that it does not matter if we use f or g in the arg max since the denominator of g in (1), $|\mathcal{X}_t \setminus \{i\}|$, is the same for all possible deletions i.

These priorities are stored in the priority tree T constructed in line 2 of Algorithm 0. This data structure is a binary tree with all $|\mathcal{V}|$ elements as leaves, all at the bottom level of the tree. Each internal node keeps track of the maximum priority of its two children.

The priority tree supports fast retrieval of the maximum priority element (used in Line 5 of Algorithm 0); it does this by starting at the root and repeatedly moving to the child with higher priority. It also supports quickly updating priorities: since all the leaves can be stored in fixed locations, we can easily retrieve the leaf at any index to update its priority. Then, after updating that node's priority, we travel up the tree to update each parent up to the root (used in Line 6). Each of these operations on T takes $O(\log|\mathcal{V}|)$ time.

Scalability.

The bottleneck is the loop in Lines 5 to 7 which runs $m+n$ times. Lines 5 and 6 take $O(\log|\mathcal{V}|)$ as discussed, while Line 7 is constant time. Finally, we need $|\mathcal{E}|$ updates to node priorities, one for each edge. Thus the algorithm takes $O(|\mathcal{E}|\log|\mathcal{V}|)$ time.

4.3 Theoretical Bounds

So far, we have shown that g can be optimized in near-linear time. In this section, we will show that when f and g are of the form (1) and (2), FRAUDAR is guaranteed to return a solution of at least half of the optimum value.

THEOREM 2. *Let $\mathcal{A}, \mathcal{B}$ be the set of users and objects returned by* FRAUDAR. *Then:*

$$g(\mathcal{A} \cup \mathcal{B}) \geq \frac{1}{2} g_{OPT}$$

where g_{OPT} is the maximum value of g, i.e.

$$g_{OPT} = \max_{\mathcal{A}',\mathcal{B}'} g(\mathcal{A}' \cup \mathcal{B}')$$

PROOF. Let the elements of $\mathcal{V}$ be labeled $v_1, v_2, \dots, v_{m+n}$. We define 'weight assigned to node v_i in $\mathcal{S}$' as

$$w_i(\mathcal{S}) = a_i + \sum_{(v_j\in\mathcal{S})\wedge((v_i,v_j)\in\mathcal{E})} c_{ij} + \sum_{(v_j\in\mathcal{S})\wedge((v_j,v_i)\in\mathcal{E})} c_{ji}$$

where $a_i (\geq 0)$ indicates the weight of node v_i and $c_{ij} (> 0)$ indicates that of edge (v_i, v_j) as in (2). Note that when node v_i is removed from the current set $\mathcal{S}$ at some point in the algorithm, $w_i(\mathcal{S})$ is the decrease in the value of f, since it is the sum of all terms excluded in (2) when node v_i is removed.

Now consider the optimal set $\mathcal{S}^*$. For each node $v_i \in \mathcal{S}^*$, we claim that $w_i(\mathcal{S}^*) \geq g(\mathcal{S}^*)$. Otherwise, removing a node with $w_i(\mathcal{S}^*) < g(\mathcal{S}^*)$ results in

$$g' = \frac{f(\mathcal{S}^*) - w_i(\mathcal{S}^*)}{|\mathcal{S}^*| - 1} > \frac{f(\mathcal{S}^*) - g(\mathcal{S}^*)}{|\mathcal{S}^*| - 1} = \frac{f(\mathcal{S}^*) - f(\mathcal{S}^*)/|\mathcal{S}^*|}{|\mathcal{S}^*| - 1} = g(\mathcal{S}^*),$$

which is a contradiction.

Let v_i be the node that FRAUDAR removes first among those in $\mathcal{S}^*$, and let $\mathcal{S}'$ be the set before FRAUDAR removes v_i. Then, since $\mathcal{S}' \supset \mathcal{S}^*$, $w_i(\mathcal{S}') \geq w_i(\mathcal{S}^*)$. Moreover, since FRAUDAR chooses to remove node v_i, for each of the other remaining nodes $v_j \in \mathcal{S}'$, $w_j(\mathcal{S}') \geq w_i(\mathcal{S}')$. Since each term in $f(\mathcal{S}')$ can be assigned to at most two nodes, summing over j gives $f(\mathcal{S}') \geq \frac{|\mathcal{S}'|w_i(\mathcal{S}')}{2}$. Also note that $g(\mathcal{A} \cup \mathcal{B}) \geq g(\mathcal{S}')$ since FRAUDAR returns the best solution that it encounters. We conclude that

$$g(\mathcal{A} \cup \mathcal{B}) \geq g(\mathcal{S}') = \frac{f(\mathcal{S}')}{|\mathcal{S}'|} \geq \frac{w_i(\mathcal{S}')}{2} \geq \frac{w_i(\mathcal{S}^*)}{2} \geq \frac{g(\mathcal{S}^*)}{2}.$$

■

4.4 Edge Weights and Camouflage Resistance

So far, we have seen that metrics of the form: $g(\mathcal{S}) = \frac{f(\mathcal{S})}{|\mathcal{S}|}$, where $f(\mathcal{S}) = \sum_{i\in\mathcal{S}} a_i + \sum_{i,j\in\mathcal{S}\wedge(i,j)\in\mathcal{E}} c_{ij}$ can be optimized efficiently and with approximation guarantees. In this section, we show how we can select metrics within this class that are resistant to camouflage, i.e. they do not allow fraudulent users to make themselves less suspicious by adding *camouflage edges*, i.e. edges toward honest objects.

Recall that a_i and c_{ij} are the weights of node i and edge ij, while $f(\mathcal{S})$ is the total node and edge weight in $\mathcal{S}$. A key idea of

Algorithm 1 FRAUDAR, which greedily removes nodes to maximize a metric g. Line 5 and 6 run in $O(\log|\mathcal{V}|)$ time, using a data structure described in Section 4.2.

Require: Bipartite $G = (\mathcal{U} \cup \mathcal{W}, \mathcal{E})$; density metric g of the form in (1)

1: **procedure** FRAUDAR (G, g)
2: Construct priority tree T from $\mathcal{U} \cup \mathcal{W}$ ▷ see Section 4.2
3: $\mathcal{X}_0 \leftarrow \mathcal{U} \cup \mathcal{W}$ ▷ suspicious set is initially the entire set of nodes $\mathcal{U} \cup \mathcal{W}$
4: **for** $t = 1, \ldots, (m+n)$ **do**
5: $i^* \leftarrow \arg\max_{i \in \mathcal{X}_i} g(\mathcal{X}_i \setminus \{i\})$ ▷ exonerate least suspicious node
6: Update priorities in T for all neighbors of i^*
7: $\mathcal{X}_t \leftarrow \mathcal{X}_{t-1} \setminus \{i^*\}$
8: **end for**
9: **return** $\arg\max_{\mathcal{X}_i \in \{\mathcal{X}_0, \ldots, \mathcal{X}_{m+n}\}} g(\mathcal{X}_i)$ ▷ return most suspicious set $\mathcal{X}_i$
10: **end procedure**

our approach is that instead of treating every edge equally, we assign a lower weight c_{ij} when the target object j has high degree. This is because objects of very high degree are not necessarily suspicious (since highly popular objects commonly exist). Thus, this weighting allows us to put greater emphasis on objects within unexpectedly dense subgraphs, rather than just high degree objects.

If we consider the adjacency matrix with rows representing users and columns representing objects, we would like to downweight columns with high column sum (column-weighting). A simple result we show in this section is that column-weightings are camouflage resistant. Recall that a density metric g is camouflage-resistant if $g(\mathcal{A} \cup \mathcal{B})$ does not decrease when any amount of camouflage is added by an adversary with fraudulent users $\mathcal{A}$ and customers $\mathcal{B}$. Let d_i be the the ith column sum, i.e. the degree of object i.

Formally, define a **column-weighting** as a choice of weighting in which each c_{ij} is a function of the respective column sum, i.e. $c_{ij} = h(d_j)$ for some function h.

THEOREM 3. *Let c_{ij} be a column-weighting. Then g (as defined in (1) and (2)) is camouflage resistant.*

PROOF. Adding camouflage only adds edges in the region between $\mathcal{A}$ (fraudulent users) and $\mathcal{B}^C$ (honest objects). It does not add or remove edges within the fraudulent block; moreover, the weights of these edges do not change either as their weights only depend on the column degrees of $\mathcal{B}$, which do not change when camouflage is added. Thus the value of g does not change. ■

A natural follow-up question is whether camouflage-resistance also holds for row-weightings (i.e. selecting c_{ij} to be a function of the corresponding row sum). It turns out that row-weightings are in general not camouflage resistant. This is because a fraudulent user account can add a large number of camouflage edges, thereby increasing their row sum, decreasing the weight of each of their edges. Thus $g(\mathcal{A} \cup \mathcal{B})$ decreases, meaning that g is not camouflage resistant.

Hence we may choose any column-weighting while ensuring camouflage resistance. The remaining question is what function to choose for the column-weighting, i.e. the function h where $c_{ij} = h(d_j)$. It should be decreasing (so as to downweight columns with high sum). It should shrink more slowly than $h(x) = 1/x$, since $h(x) = 1/x$ allows a single edge to contribute as much as the total contribution of a column with any number of edges, causing us to catch columns with single ones rather than dense blocks.

Within the remaining space of choices, we note that a very similar problem of downweighting based on column frequency appears in deciding the form of the 'inverse document frequency' term of the popular heuristic *tf-idf* weighting scheme [24], in which logarithmic weighting of frequency has been empirically found to perform well. We also show empirical results (in Section 5.1) that logarithmic weighting leads to strong theoretical bounds. For these reasons, we recommend using $h(x) = 1/\log(x + c)$, where c is a small constant (set to 5 in our experiments) to prevent the denominator from becoming zero, or excessive variability for small values of x. We use the resulting density metric (denoted $g_{\log}$) in our experiments.

4.5 Implications: Bounding Fraud

Figure 1(a) shows curves representing our theoretical bounds on the maximum amount of fraud that can be present for each possible size of the fraudulent block, based on Theorem 2. We now explain how such bounds can be computed from Theorem 2. Assume that the fraudulent block contains m_0 user accounts and n_0 customers.

In this section, we assume that no side information is present, so we set the a_i, the prior suspiciousness of each node, to 0. Thus here $g_{\log}(\mathcal{S}) = \frac{1}{|\mathcal{S}|} \sum_{i,j \in \mathcal{S}} \frac{1}{\log(d_j + c)}$, where d_j is the degree of the jth object. Consider a fraudulent subgraph with m_0 user nodes and n_0 object nodes. Assume that each fraudulent customer has at least a certain fraction $0 < \lambda < 1$ of fraudulent edges: each fraudulent customer should be receiving at least a comparable fraction of fraudulent reviews to its actual honest reviews, otherwise it would not be profiting appreciably from the fraud.

THEOREM 4. *Let $(\hat{\mathcal{A}}, \hat{\mathcal{B}})$ be the block detected by* FRAUDAR. *Then the number of edges that a fraudulent block of size (m_0, n_0) can have without being detected is at most $2(m_0 + n_0) g_{\log}(\hat{\mathcal{A}} \cup \hat{\mathcal{B}}) \log(m_0/\lambda + c)$. In other words, our algorithm will detect a fraudulent block without fail if it contains more edges than this threshold.*

PROOF. By Theorem 2, $2g_{\log}(\hat{\mathcal{A}} \cup \hat{\mathcal{B}})$ is an upper bound on the value of $g_{\log}$ on any subgraph of users and objects. Since the fraudulent block has m_0+n_0 nodes in total, thus $2(m_0+n_0)g_{\log}(\hat{\mathcal{A}} \cup \hat{\mathcal{B}})$ is an upper bound on the value of total suspiciousness $f_{\log}$.

Moreover, each fraudulent customer has at most m_0 fraudulent edges joined to it, and since at least λ fraction of its edges must be fraudulent, it can have at most m_0/λ degree in total. Hence the weight of each fraudulent edge is at least $\frac{1}{\log(m_0/\lambda + c)}$. But since the total weighted degree is at most $2(m_0 + n_0) g_{\log}(\hat{\mathcal{A}} \cup \hat{\mathcal{B}})$, it follows that the number of fraudulent edges is at most $2(m_0 + n_0) g_{\log}(\hat{\mathcal{A}} \cup \hat{\mathcal{B}}) \log(m_0/\lambda + c)$. ■

We apply this bound to real data in Section 5.1.

	# of nodes	# of edges	Density	Content
Amazon [18]	28K (24K,4K)	28K	2.7e-4	Review
Trip Advisor [29]	84K (82K,2K)	90K	5.9e-4	Review
Epinion [17]	264K (132K,132K)	841K	4.8e-5	Who-trust-whom
Wiki-vote [17]	16K (8K,8K)	103K	1.5e-3	Vote

Table 3: Bipartite graph datasets used in our experiments.

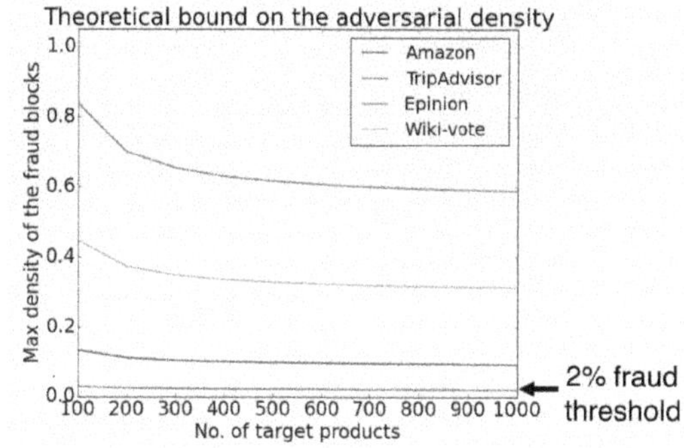

Figure 3: **FRAUDAR's bounds on fraud are stringent, on real graphs:** E.g., on TripAdvisor, the bound says that a fraudulent block containing 50 user accounts and anywhere between 100 and 1000 products must have density of $< 2\%$ to avoid detection.

5. EXPERIMENTS

We design experiments to answer the following questions:
Q1. Illustration of our theorem: How strong are the bounds that FRAUDAR provides in terms of bounding undetectable fraud in the graph? Does column weighting improve those bounds?
Q2. Evaluation on synthetic data: How accurately does FRAUDAR detect injected fraud under different types of camouflage attacks? Does FRAUDAR outperform state-of-the-art competitors?
Q3. Effectiveness in real-world data: Does FRAUDAR detect true fraud in real-world graphs? Have the fraudulent accounts already been detected by previous methods?
Q4. Scalability: Is FRAUDAR scalable with regard to the data size?

We implemented FRAUDAR in Python; all experiments were carried out on a 2.4 GHz Intel Core i5 Macbook Pro, 16 GB RAM, running OS X 10.9.5. The code is available for download at **www.andrew.cmu.edu/user/bhooi/camo.zip**. We test FRAUDAR on a variety of real world datasets. Table 3 offers details on the datasets we used.

To test the accuracy of our method, we use synthetic attacks injected into our Amazon dataset. We structure our "attacks" as shown in Figure 2. We injected a fraudulent block of users and customers with varying densities. We assume $\lambda = 0.5$ for our theoretical bounds.

5.1 Q1. Illustration of our Theorem

In Figure 1 (a), we showed our theoretical bounds (Theorem 4) applied to compute the maximum number of edges an adversary with $m_0 = 50$ user nodes can have for various values of n_0. These are computed by running FRAUDAR under two weighting schemes. First, we use our $g_{\log}$ scheme exactly as in Theorem 4 to get an upper bound $2(m_0 + n_0)g_{log}(\hat{\mathcal{A}} \cup \hat{\mathcal{B}}) \log(m_0/\lambda + c)$ on the number of fraudulent edges; plotting this against n_0 gives the green region ('improved') in Figure 1 (a). The blue region ('original') comes from using the analogous procedure without the log-weighting, i.e. where $g(\mathcal{S})$ is half the average degree, as in Example 1.

In this case, we see that the log-weighted scheme provides stronger bounds, since the bound is lower, i.e. an adversary should have fewer edges in order not to be detected. Intuitively, this happens because down-weighting high degree columns decreases the weight of many of the honest high degree objects in the dataset, so groups of adversaries stand out more, resulting in stronger bounds on how many edges an adversary can have.

Next, we apply our FRAUDAR in the same way over various real-world graphs to analyze the theoretical upper bounds computed by FRAUDAR on the density that fraudulent blocks can have. We run FRAUDAR on four real-world graphs: *Amazon* [18], *Trip Advisor* [29], *Epinions* [17], and *Wiki-vote* [17]. The detailed description of each graph is in Table 3. For all datasets, Figure 3 shows the maximum number of fraudulent edges that an adversary can have without being detected, assuming 50 fraudulent users and varying the number of fraudulent customers. We see that we can detect fraud most easily in *Trip Advisor*, followed by *Epinion, Wiki-vote, Amazon*; even a fairly sparse block of density around 0.05 would stand out strongly in the *Trip Advisor* graph. While density is important in determining how easy it is to detect fraud in each graph (fraudulent blocks stand out more strongly in a sparse graph), it is not the only factor. Indeed, *Wiki-vote* is actually denser than *Amazon*. In fact, the difficulty of detecting fraud in each graph is mainly determined by its densest blocks, since an adversarial block that is significantly less dense than the densest normal blocks in the graph is unlikely to be detected.

5.2 Q2. Evaluation on Synthetic Data

In Figure 1 (b), we demonstrated that FRAUDAR can effectively detect fraud under four types of camouflage attacks: 1) Injection of fraud with no camouflage, 2) random camouflage, 3) biased camouflage and 4) hijacked accounts, more accurately than competitors.

We conduct experiments based on the settings at the beginning of this section, averaged over 5 trials. For the camouflage scenarios 2) and 3), the amount of camouflage added per fraudulent user account was (on average) equal to the amount of actual fraudulent edges for that user. For the 'Random Camo' case, for each fake user node, camouflage edges were chosen at random, with on average the same number of camouflage edges as fraudulent edges, as shown in Figure 2 (a). For the 'Biased Camo' case, for each fake user node, camouflage edges were directed toward each object with probability proportional to the degree of the object as shown in Figure 2 (b). For the 'Hijacked' case, we used a random subset of existing users to form the fraudulent block.

In each case, we injected 200 fraudulent users and 200 fraudulent products with various edge densities to the subsetted Amazon review graph of 2000 users and 2000 products, with a density of 0.0006. We compare FRAUDAR to SPOKEN in their F measure ($= \frac{2 \times \text{precision} \times \text{recall}}{\text{precision} + \text{recall}}$) in detecting the fake users. In the first set of experiments, we assume that no honest user added an edge to the fraudulent target (i.e. object) nodes.

As seen in Figure 1(b), the results demonstrate that FRAUDAR works robustly and efficiently against all four attacks, achieving F-

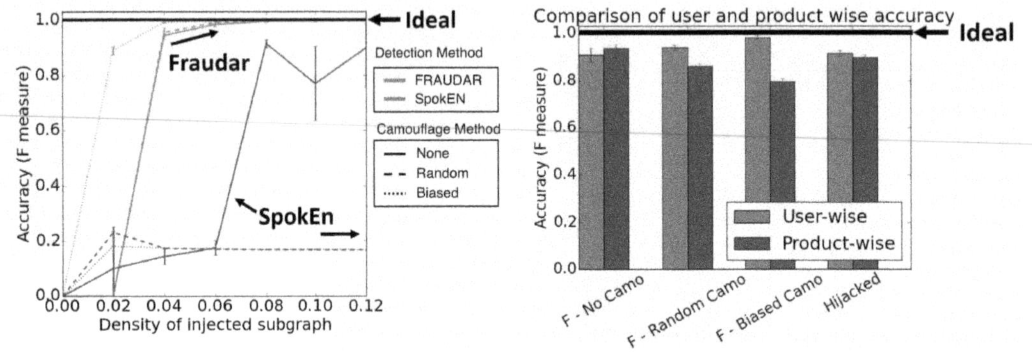

Figure 4: **(a) FRAUDAR outperforms competitors in multiple settings**. Accuracy of fraud detection on Amazon data in the experiment with "reverse camouflage" (edges from honest users to fraudulent products). **(b) FRAUDAR has similar and high accuracy both in detecting fraudulent users and fraudulent customers**. Comparison of accuracy on fake users and targets under four different camouflage attacks.

measures of over 0.95 on all four scenarios for densities of at least 0.04. On the other hand, SPOKEN was able to reach its maximum performance of 0.9 only when fraud blocks had densities of higher than 0.06 and under the 'no camouflage' scenario.

The experimental results in Figure 1(b) were based on the assumption that no honest user added an edge to the fraudulent target nodes. However, in a real-world environment, some honest users may add edges to the fraudulent target nodes (which we refer to as "reverse camouflage"). To incorporate this, we conducted another experiment using an attack model where we add edges between honest users and the fraudulent target nodes, but with sparser density compared to the fraud blocks. We added random edges to this region, with half the density of the fraud blocks. All other experimental settings were unchanged. The experimental results are shown in Figure 4 (a). For FRAUDAR, the results are generally similar. In contrast, SPOKEN shows slightly worse performance under this additional camouflage.

To show that FRAUDAR is effective both at catching fraudulent users accounts as well as fraudulent objects, we next separately evaluate the fraud detection of both fake users and fake targets using F measure. The basic experimental setup is same as before, with the density of the fraudulent blocks now fixed to 0.03. In Figure 4 (b), the bar plots are shown for the comparison. 'User-wise' (red) denotes the F measure of the detecting fake users, and 'target-wise' denotes the F measure of detecting fake target nodes. We see that in general, accuracy is high and fairly similar, but the performance in detecting fake users is slightly higher than that of detecting products.

5.3 Q3. Effectiveness on Real Data

In this section, we verify that FRAUDAR accurately detects a large block of fraudulent accounts in the Twitter follower-followee graph, as verified by hand labelling and by clear signs of fraud exhibited by a majority of the detected users. Indeed, a majority of the detected accounts had tweets advertising follower-buying services, and the tweets had not been removed or the accounts suspended for the 7 years since the data was collected. Figure 1(d) shows a sample fraudster caught by FRAUDAR.

The Twitter graph we use contains 41.7 million users and 1.47 billion follows; it was extracted in July 2009 and first used in [16]. On this graph, FRAUDAR detected a dense subgraph of size 4031 followers by 4313 followees. This subgraph is extremely dense, with 68% density, which is highly suspicious in itself.

To further investigate this block, we randomly sampled 125 followers and 125 followees in the block detected by FRAUDAR for hand labeling to determine how many of them appear fraudulent. To do this, we labeled which users were fraudulent based on the following characteristics of their profile data, chosen based on established criteria in the literature [25] summarized below.

- links on profile associated with malware or scams
- clear bot-like behavior (e.g. replying to large numbers of tweets with identical messages)
- account deleted
- account suspended

For comparison, we also construct two control groups of size 100 containing users that were not detected by the algorithm. The first control group contains randomly selected non-detected users. For the second (degree-matched) control group, we constructed it to match the follower count of users in the detected group; we do this by repeatedly selecting a random detected user, then finding another non-detected user who has at most 10% bigger or smaller follower count. During the labelling process, we shuffled the detected users with the control groups randomly and hid group memberships from labellers, labeling users in a "blind" manner.

Additionally, we also check and report how many of these users have Tweets containing the URLs of two known follower-buying services, *TweepMe* and *TweeterGetter*, showing that they had advertised these follower-buying services through tweets.

Note that this entire labelling process used only profile and tweet data and not follower-followee data, whereas our algorithm uses only follower-followee data, so the labelling is a fair estimate of the algorithm's accuracy. We present two pieces of evidence which strongly indicates fraud in the detected group. Firstly, the percentage of users with tweets advertising *TweepMe* or *Tweetergetter* is much higher among the detected users than among both control groups (Figure 5): 41% of the detected followers, and 26% for the detected followees. These rise to 62% and 42% respectively as shown in Figure 1(c) if we ignore deleted, protected and suspended accounts (for which profile information was unavailable). In the control groups, there were no mentions of *TweepMe* and very few mentions of *TweeterGetter*, as shown in Figure 5. Figure 5 shows the breakdown of our groups in terms of deleted and suspended users. Given the sparsity of *TweepMe* and *TweeterGetter* in the control groups, we see that the detected users are likely charac-

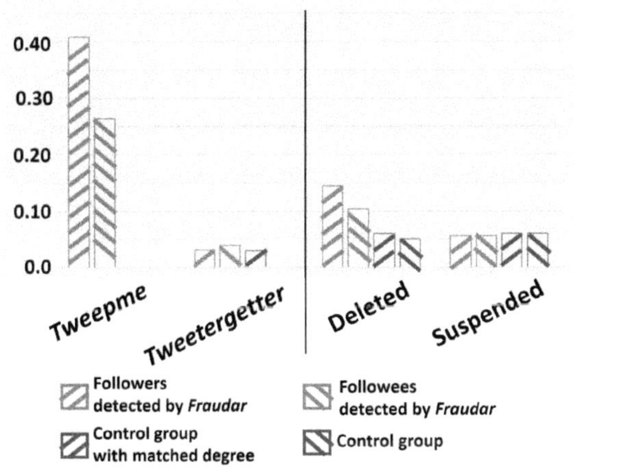

Figure 5: **FRAUDAR detects a large, clearly fraudulent block in Twitter.** A majority of the detected accounts were either deleted, suspended, or contained known follower-buying services, *TweepMe* and *TweeterGetter*. In comparison, the control groups had much less detected fraud.

Figure 6: **Follower-buying services:** a large fraction of detected accounts use *TweepMe* (bottom) or *TweeterGetter* (middle, top).

terized by a large block of users using these and possibly other follower-buying services, resulting in a dense block.

Secondly, we used our hand-labelling using the above criteria to determine how many of each group appear fraudulent. 57% of the detected followers and 40% of the followees were labelled as fraudulent, deleted or suspended accounts, but much fewer in the control groups, with 25% for the degree-matched control group, and 12% for control group with no condition. Thus both these results support the effectiveness of FRAUDAR in detecting fraudulent users in the real-world graphs.

5.4 Q4. Scalability

Figure 7 shows the near-linear scaling of FRAUDAR's running time in the number of edges. Here we used the Trip Advisor dataset, and subsampled user nodes in proportions of $0.7^0, \ldots, 0.7^{12}$. Slopes parallel to the main diagonal indicate linear growth.

6. CONCLUSION

In this paper, we propose FRAUDAR, a fraud detection algorithm which provably bounds the amount of fraud adversaries can have, even in face of camouflage. Our main contributions are as follows.

- **Metric**: we propose a novel family of metrics which satisfies intuitive "axioms" and has several advantages as a suspiciousness metric.
- **Theoretical Guarantees**: we provide theorems (See Theorem 2 in Section 4.3 and Theorem 4 in Section 4.5) on how FRAUDAR gives a provable upper bound on undetectable fraud. We also prove that our proposed metric is camouflage-resistant.
- **Effectiveness**: FRAUDAR was successfully applied on real-world graphs on fraud attacks with various types of camouflage, and outperformed the competitor. It also detected a large block of fraudulent activity in the Twitter follower-followee graph.
- **Scalability**: FRAUDAR runs near-linearly in the input size. (See Figure 7).

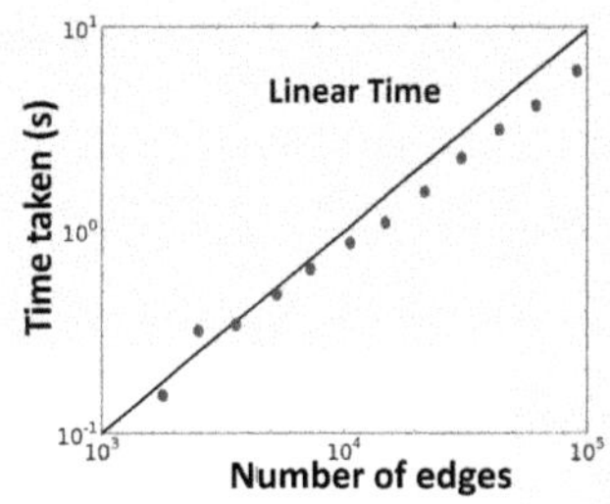

Figure 7: **FRAUDAR runs in near-linear time**: the curve *(blue)* shows the running time of FRAUDAR, compared to a linear function *(black)*.

Acknowledgements

This material is based upon work supported by the National Science Foundation under Grant No. CNS-1314632, DGE-1252522, and IIS-1408924.

Any opinions, findings, and conclusions or recommendations expressed in this material are those of the author(s) and do not necessarily reflect the views of the National Science Foundation, or other funding parties.

7. REFERENCES

[1] L. Akoglu, R. Chandy, and C. Faloutsos. Opinion fraud detection in online reviews by network effects. In *ICWSM*, 2013.

[2] A. Beutel, W. Xu, V. Guruswami, C. Palow, and C. Faloutsos. Copycatch: stopping group attacks by spotting lockstep behavior in social networks. In *22nd WWW*, pages 119–130. International World Wide Web Conferences Steering Committee, 2013.

[3] Q. Cao, M. Sirivianos, X. Yang, and T. Pregueiro. Aiding the detection of fake accounts in large scale social online services. In *NSDI*, 2012.

[4] M. Charikar. Greedy approximation algorithms for finding dense components in a graph. In *Approximation Algorithms for Combinatorial Optimization*, pages 84–95. Springer, 2000.

[5] C. Cortes, D. Pregibon, and C. Volinsky. *Communities of interest*. Springer, 2001.

[6] S. Ghosh, B. Viswanath, F. Kooti, N. K. Sharma, G. Korlam, F. Benevenuto, N. Ganguly, and K. P. Gummadi. Understanding and combating link farming in the twitter social network. In *21st WWW*, pages 61–70. ACM, 2012.

[7] C. Giatsidis, D. M. Thilikos, and M. Vazirgiannis. Evaluating cooperation in communities with the k-core structure. In *Advances in Social Networks Analysis and Mining (ASONAM), 2011 International Conference on*, pages 87–93. IEEE, 2011.
[8] Z. Gu, K. Pei, Q. Wang, L. Si, X. Zhang, and D. Xu. Leaps: Detecting camouflaged attacks with statistical learning guided by program analysis.
[9] Z. Gyöngyi, H. Garcia-Molina, and J. Pedersen. Combating web spam with trustrank. In *VLDB Endowment*, pages 576–587, 2004.
[10] M. Jiang, A. Beutel, P. Cui, B. Hooi, S. Yang, and C. Faloutsos. A general suspiciousness metric for dense blocks in multimodal data. In *Data Mining (ICDM), 2015 IEEE International Conference on*, pages 781–786. IEEE, 2015.
[11] M. Jiang, P. Cui, A. Beutel, C. Faloutsos, and S. Yang. Catchsync: catching synchronized behavior in large directed graphs. In *20th KDD*, pages 941–950. ACM, 2014.
[12] M. Jiang, P. Cui, A. Beutel, C. Faloutsos, and S. Yang. Inferring strange behavior from connectivity pattern in social networks. In *Advances in Knowledge Discovery and Data Mining*, pages 126–138. Springer, 2014.
[13] N. Jindal and B. Liu. Opinion spam and analysis. In *ICDM 2008*, pages 219–230. ACM, 2008.
[14] G. Karypis and V. Kumar. METIS: Unstructured graph partitioning and sparse matrix ordering system. *The University of Minnesota*, 2, 1995.
[15] J. Kleinberg. Authoritative sources in a hyperlinked environment. *Journal of the ACM (JACM)*, 46(5):604–632, 1999.
[16] H. Kwak, C. Lee, H. Park, and S. Moon. What is twitter, a social network or a news media? In *19th WWW*, pages 591–600. ACM, 2010.
[17] J. Leskovec, D. Huttenlocher, and J. Kleinberg. Signed networks in social media. In *Proceedings of the SIGCHI Conference on Human Factors in Computing Systems*, pages 1361–1370. ACM, 2010.
[18] J. McAuley and J. Leskovec. Hidden factors and hidden topics: understanding rating dimensions with review text. In *Proceedings of the 7th ACM conference on Recommender systems*, pages 165–172. ACM, 2013.
[19] A. Molavi Kakhki, C. Kliman-Silver, and A. Mislove. Iolaus: Securing online content rating systems. In *22nd WWW*, pages 919–930. International World Wide Web Conferences Steering Committee, 2013.
[20] M. Ott, Y. Choi, C. Cardie, and J. T. Hancock. Finding deceptive opinion spam by any stretch of the imagination. In *Proceedings of the 49th Annual Meeting of the Association for Computational Linguistics: Human Language Technologies-Volume 1*, pages 309–319. Association for Computational Linguistics, 2011.
[21] S. Pandit, D. H. Chau, S. Wang, and C. Faloutsos. Netprobe: a fast and scalable system for fraud detection in online auction networks. In *16th WWW*, pages 201–210. ACM, 2007.
[22] B. Perozzi, L. Akoglu, P. Iglesias Sánchez, and E. Müller. Focused clustering and outlier detection in large attributed graphs. In *20th KDD*, pages 1346–1355. ACM, 2014.
[23] B. Prakash, M. Seshadri, A. Sridharan, S. Machiraju, and C. Faloutsos. Eigenspokes: Surprising patterns and community structure in large graphs. *PAKDD, 2010a*, 84, 2010.
[24] A. Rajaraman, J. D. Ullman, J. D. Ullman, and J. D. Ullman. *Mining of massive datasets*, volume 1. Cambridge University Press Cambridge, 2012.
[25] N. Shah, A. Beutel, B. Gallagher, and C. Faloutsos. Spotting suspicious link behavior with fbox: An adversarial perspective. *arXiv preprint arXiv:1410.3915*, 2014.
[26] D. N. Tran, B. Min, J. Li, and L. Subramanian. Sybil-resilient online content voting. In *NSDI*, volume 9, pages 15–28, 2009.
[27] C. Tsourakakis. The k-clique densest subgraph problem. In *24th WWW*, pages 1122–1132. International World Wide Web Conferences Steering Committee, 2015.
[28] S. Virdhagriswaran and G. Dakin. Camouflaged fraud detection in domains with complex relationships. In *12th KDD*, pages 941–947. ACM, 2006.
[29] H. Wang, Y. Lu, and C. Zhai. Latent aspect rating analysis without aspect keyword supervision. In *17th KDD*, pages 618–626. ACM, 2011.
[30] B. Wu, V. Goel, and B. D. Davison. Propagating trust and distrust to demote web spam. *MTW*, 190, 2006.
[31] H. Yu, P. B. Gibbons, M. Kaminsky, and F. Xiao. Sybillimit: A near-optimal social network defense against sybil attacks. In *Security and Privacy, 2008. SP 2008. IEEE Symposium on*, pages 3–17. IEEE, 2008.
[32] H. Yu, M. Kaminsky, P. B. Gibbons, and A. Flaxman. Sybilguard: defending against sybil attacks via social networks. *ACM SIGCOMM Computer Communication Review*, 36(4):267–278, 2006.

APPENDIX

A. PROOF OF THEOREM 1

PROOF. **Axiom 1 (Node Suspiciousness)**

$$g(\mathcal{S}) = \frac{f_{\mathcal{V}}(\mathcal{S}) + f_{\mathcal{E}}(\mathcal{S})}{|\mathcal{S}|} > \frac{f_{\mathcal{V}}(\mathcal{S}') + f_{\mathcal{E}}(\mathcal{S}')}{|\mathcal{S}|} = \frac{f_{\mathcal{V}}(\mathcal{S}') + f_{\mathcal{E}}(\mathcal{S}')}{|\mathcal{S}'|} = g(\mathcal{S}').$$

Axiom 2 (Edge Suspiciousness) Let $e = (u, v)$.

$$g(\mathcal{S}(\mathcal{V}, \mathcal{E} \cup \{e\})) = \frac{f_{\mathcal{V}}(\mathcal{S}) + f_{\mathcal{E}}(\mathcal{S}) + c_{uv}}{|\mathcal{S}|} > \frac{f_{\mathcal{V}}(\mathcal{S}) + f_{\mathcal{E}}(\mathcal{S})}{|\mathcal{S}|} = g(\mathcal{S}(\mathcal{V}, \mathcal{E})).$$

Axiom 3 (Size) Let $\mathcal{S} = \mathcal{A} \cup \mathcal{B}$, and ρ be the edge density.

$$g(\mathcal{S}) = \frac{f_{\mathcal{V}}(\mathcal{S}) + f_{\mathcal{E}}(\mathcal{S})}{|\mathcal{S}|} = a + b\left(\frac{\rho|\mathcal{A}||\mathcal{B}|}{|\mathcal{A}| + |\mathcal{B}|}\right) = a + b\rho\left(\frac{1}{|\mathcal{A}|} + \frac{1}{|\mathcal{B}|}\right)^{-1}$$

which is increasing in both $|\mathcal{A}|$ and $|\mathcal{B}|$.

Axiom 4 (Concentration)

$$g(\mathcal{S}) = \frac{f(\mathcal{S})}{|\mathcal{S}|} > \frac{f(\mathcal{S})}{|\mathcal{S}'|} = \frac{f(\mathcal{S}')}{|\mathcal{S}'|} = g(\mathcal{S}').$$

■

Temporal Order-based First-Take-All Hashing for Fast Attention-Deficit-Hyperactive-Disorder Detection

Hao Hu
Department of Computer Science
University of Central Florida
Orlando, Florida
hao_hu@knights.ucf.edu

Joey Velez-Ginorio
Department of Computer Science
University of Central Florida
Orlando, Florida
joeyVelez@knights.ucf.edu

Guo-Jun Qi*
Department of Computer Science
University of Central Florida
Orlando, Florida
guojun.qi@ucf.edu

ABSTRACT

Attention Deficit Hyperactive Disorder (ADHD) is one of the most common childhood disorders and can continue through adolescence and adulthood. Although the root cause of the problem still remains unknown, recent advancements in brain imaging technology reveal there exists differences between neural activities of Typically Developing Children (TDC) and ADHD subjects. Inspired by this, we propose a novel First-Take-All (FTA) hashing framework to investigate the problem of fast ADHD subjects detection through the fMRI time-series of neuron activities. By hashing time courses from regions of interests (ROIs) in the brain into fixed-size hash codes, FTA can compactly encode the temporal order differences between the neural activity patterns that are key to distinguish TDC and ADHD subjects. Such patterns can be directly learned via minimizing the training loss incurred by the generated FTA codes. By conducting similarity search on the resultant FTA codes, data-driven ADHD detection can be achieved in an efficient fashion. The experiments' results on real-world ADHD detection benchmarks demonstrate the FTA can outperform the state-of-the-art baselines using only neural activity time series without any phenotypic information.

Keywords

ADHD detection; First-Take-All; Time series hashing

1. INTRODUCTION

Recent advancements in brain imaging technology, one of the greatest efforts in Neuroscience, aim to uncover features unique to certain neurophysiological phenomena [4, 20]. The intuition is that the neural activity pattern of a healthy human subject ought to appear different from that of a patient suffering from some neural disorder, such as Attention Deficit Hyperactive Disorder (ADHD) and Alzheimer's disease.

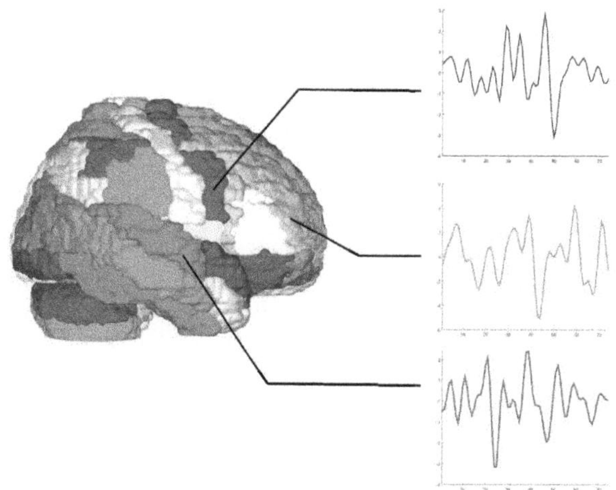

Figure 1: ROIs (AAL[29]) of a human brain and their fMRI time courses. FTA hashes time courses into fixed-size hash codes by encoding temporal order differences between latent patterns among them.

Categorized alongside other neurodevelopmental disorders, ADHD is one of the most common brain diseases. It manifests early and is typically first diagnosed in one's childhood. The predominant effects consist of sustained difficulty in maintaining focus, often offering difficulties assimilating at school, at home, or within the community. Fortunately, despite lacking a cure, brain imaging technology provides an opportunity to timely observe and diagnose ADHD[6, 7].

Several methods for recording sequences of neural activity from the brain exist. Generally, they range from invasive to non-invasive procedures. Whilst the data from invasive techniques such as Electrocorticography (ECoG) or multi-electrode arrays possess higher quality data [24], the opportunity to collect such data seldom arises. By nature of the procedure, it is much more practical for researchers and medical practitioners to opt for non-invasive techniques such as functional Magnetic Resonance Imaging (fMRI). fMRI indirectly measures changes in neural activity by detecting changes in blood flow caused by increased activations of neurons during specific tasks (or resting-state conditions) [27,

*Corresponding author

KDD '16, August 13-17, 2016, San Francisco, CA, USA
© 2016 ACM. ISBN 978-1-4503-4232-2/16/08...$15.00
DOI: http://dx.doi.org/10.1145/2939672.2939774

9]. In this context, fMRI time-courses [1] offer a feature-rich representation of high level functional organization in the brain (Figure 1).

Considering the representations, we aim to exploit its rich nature for the task of ADHD diagnosis as a pattern classification problem [22]. Utilizing the structure of the resting-state fMRI time-courses, we generate hash codes encoding the temporal structure of the data. These hash codes can then be compared to detect similarities and differences between the fMRI time-courses of healthy patients versus those diagnosed with ADHD. It is known that neural connections exist whether or not regions of the brain are functionally active, hence forth the resting-state fMRI provides a controlled dataset to test for fundamental differences in functional neural networks in the brain.

Tasked with hashing time-series data, our approach centers on fast detection based on retrieval of the similar disorder patterns from a database of brain neural imaging activities. Specifically, we propose the First-Take-All (FTA) hashing method for encoding varied-length fMRI sequences into fixed-size hash codes. The problem of fast matching similar fMRI sequences boils down to a fast search of similar hash codes based on their Hamming distances that can be calculated efficiently.

Specifically, the algorithm first projects an input sequence of varied length onto different subspaces, each representing a sequence of latent patterns. After encoding the temporal order of these patterns to hash the fMRI time-courses, the pattern that appears first among a selection of patterns is used to index the time-course [2]. This scheme can yield a compact encoding of temporal relations between the selected patterns that really matter in distinguishing between healthy individuals and those diagnosed with the ADHD. The optimal pattern projections will be learned to result in the hash codes that minimize the diagnosis errors. In this way, FTA allows for not only high detection rates, but a scalable solution for detecting fMRI sequences. Since the projections are learned as opposed to randomly generated, the solution scales well with large-scale input fMRI sequences using compact hash codes.

Suitably, the objective of this paper is to provide a scalable and efficient [18, 28] solution to the problem of detecting neurodevelopmental disorders (specifically ADHD) via fMRI time-courses. Doing so also reverberates to improved success in brain imaging technologies. The proposed temporal order-based hashing algorithms are much more generic, providing a new framework for fast matching and detection to other forms of time-series data. In this paper, the method has implications on functional neural analysis[14, 17]. Being able to reliably infer causal relationships between brain structures and functions presents an interesting opportunity for further investigations, the range of which include areas of classification outside neurodevelopmental disorders [13]. Ultimately, learning the projections to hash a time-series space efficiently provides important practicality to the design.

[1]In medical imaging terminology, a "time course" refers to an obtained sequence for an imaged area. In this paper, we will use this term interchangeably with "time series" when there is no confusion in the context.

[2]Without loss of generality, we can also designate the second or the third appearing pattern or so on to hash a fMRI sequence. As a convention, we choose the first-appearing pattern in this paper.

The contributions of this paper are:

1. We propose a novel FTA hashing algorithm to hash time series with varied length into fixed-size hash codes by encoding the temporal order of the latent patterns inside the time series.

2. In order to acquire the optimal projections, we formulate it as a learning problem whose training loss can be minimized in an efficient fashion.

3. We perform extensive experiment studies on benchmarks of ADHD detection and demonstrate the superior performance of the proposed FTA hashing with several evaluation metrics.

The remainder of this paper is organized as follows: Section 2 briefly reviews the related work. The ADHD detection paradigm including FTA hashing algorithm is introduced and discussed in Section 3. Section 4 includes the learning algorithm for searching optimal projections. Experiments and performance studies are presented in Section 5. Finally, Section 6 concludes the paper.

2. RELATED WORK

In this section, we review several related topics pertinent to the task of ADHD detection. Among these, the overall theme fosters support for classification analysis of fMRI time-courses.

It is known that multivariate data mining and machine learning methods have been used to approach the classification of fMRI data[13, 7]. Similar to the approach in the paper, multivariate methods presume from a core tenet of neuroscience that neural data encodes itself across larger functional regions in the brain. Intriguingly, the motivation behind utilizing multiple ROIs in test and training exists within other works as well; as ROI selection can be viewed as a form of feature selection [13, 25]. Similar works [7] also suggest the widespread adoption of multivariate techniques including Support Vector Machines (SVMs) [5] and Linear Discriminant Analysis (LDA) [3] in spite of the traditional uni-variate alternatives. Fueling this shift was a dissatisfaction with how univariate models rely exclusively on the information contained in time-courses contained in individual voxels[7].

In tune with our method's focus on preserving temporal structure is the Dynamic Time Warping (DTW) to find similar patterns between two time series [2]. The idea is to create a sequence alignment algorithm that preserves and efficiently discovers knowledge from potentially large data archives. The approach used in this paper (FTA) maintains similar motivations, insofar as it aims to solve the task of presenting a model for efficient and scalable knowledge discovery in the domain of neural data.

The related works presented offer several intriguing points of support to our investigation. Foremost, the premise has been set for the intuitions behind fMRI analysis for ADHD detection[7]. For example, [10] extracts features from fMRI time courses to improve the ADHD detection rate. Meanwhile, the method proposed by [12] combines both unsupervised and supervised algorithms and achieves best performance in ADHD-200 Global Competition. This reliably shows that the problem of knowledge discovery in brain imaging can be improved through utilization of Machine

Learning models. In addition, other efforts suggest that a detection scheme for analysis of fMRI time-courses can be expanded to other neural datasets and disorders[10, 7]. This offers an expanded utility to the model presented in this paper, in which the FTA can be used on other problems within Neuroscience and a host of other topic areas, all whilst preserving efficiency. Lastly, DTW offers an element of distinction between former methods in time-series analysis versus those of which focus specifically on preserving temporal order during encoding of time-series data [2]. In doing so, FTA provides clear advantages over methods which eschew these temporal features [16].

3. FIRST-TAKE-ALL: ADHD DETECTION BY TIME-SERIES HASHING

In this paper, we introduce a novel hashing-based paradigm to automatically identify ADHD subjects. The structure of our method can be summarized as following: First, brain atlases containing a number of Regions of Interest (ROIs) will be constructed and corresponding time courses of each ROI will be extracted based on the ADHD subjects' resting state fMRI data of the brain. Then, we propose a new temporal order-preserving hashing algorithm called First-Take-All to hash time courses into binary sequences. With those sequences, we compare the distance (similarity) between them to determine whether a patient is an ADHD subject.

3.1 Brain Atlas Construction and Time Course Extraction

In brain neuroanatomy, many approaches, such as automated anatomical labeling (AAL) [29], Eickhoff-Zilles (EZ) [11], Talairach and Tournoux (TT) [21] and Harvard-Oxford (HO) [15], have been proposed to construct brain atlases by using structural anatomic or functional information. After that, voxels in the regions that have structural or functional similarities will be grouped into Regions of Interest (ROIs) and the time courses of these ROIs can be extracted from the voxels of the subjects' resting state fMRI data. Since the brain atlas construction and time-course extraction are not the focus of this paper, we will employ the existing brain atlases pre-constructed by the neuroanatomy community. The details will be presented in Section 5.

With time courses of ROIs extracted, every subject can be mapped to a unique vector (multivariate) sequence which describes the brain activities of that subject. For example, $\mathbf{X} = [\mathbf{x}_1, \mathbf{x}_2, \cdots, \mathbf{x}_T]$ can be a subject's time-courses of ROIs, where each $\mathbf{x}_t \in \mathbb{R}^D, t = 1, \cdots, T$ represents the brain activities of that subject in D different ROIs. For our convenience, we will refer to Time Courses of ROIs as **TCs** in the rest of this paper for short.

3.2 Temporal Order-Preseving Hashing

Now we propose a hashing algorithm for time-series data which can map a TC into a fixed-size hash codes regardless of its original length. It can be roughly divided into 2 parts. First, a TC will be projected into several subspaces to produce a set of projection sequences. Then, we generate hash codes for entire TC by conducting an operation called First-Take-All (**FTA**) on those projection sequences.

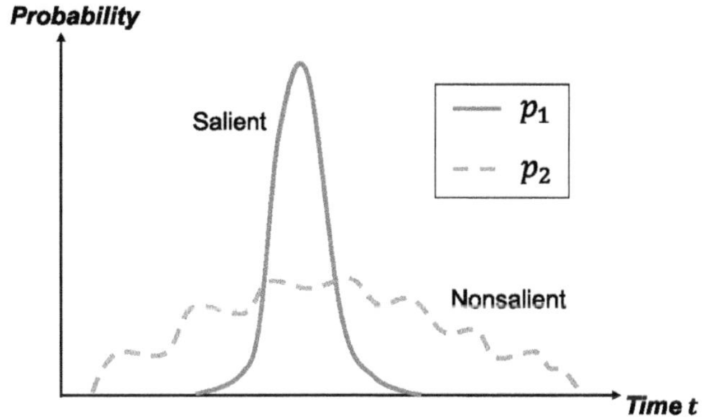

Figure 2: Comparison between projections generated by salient and nonsalient patterns. The red solid line represents the projection of a salient pattern with a small variance, while the blue dotted line represents the projection of a non-salient pattern with a large variance over the time axis.

Sequence Projection

Consider a TC $\mathbf{X} = [\mathbf{x}_1, \mathbf{x}_2, \cdots, \mathbf{x}_T]$ of length T described in Section 3.1. The first step is to project $\mathbf{X}$ into several subspaces defined by an optimized projection matrix $\mathbf{W} = [\mathbf{w}_1, \cdots, \mathbf{w}_K] \in \mathbb{R}^{D\times K}$. Each $\mathbf{w}_k \in \mathbb{R}^D$ is a projection vector taken from $\mathbf{W}$ that generates a sequence $\mathbf{s}_k = \mathbf{w}_k^\intercal \mathbf{X}$ for $k \in \{1, \cdots, K\}$. The way to find the optimal $\mathbf{W}$ will be given in section 4.

Intuitively, each sequence $\mathbf{s}_k$ represents the score over the occurrence of a latent pattern[3] $\mathbf{w_k}$, and any TC is composed of a sequence of temporally-ordered patterns. The **orders** of certain **unknown** neural activation patterns often matter in ADHD detection. Thus, we seek to find these relevant patterns as well as compactly represent their orders in a hash code space, where the similarity between TCs can be directly computed by their Hamming distance.

To model the temporal order of patterns, first we need to locate the moment they appear. Here we use softmax to compute the probability that a pattern k appears at time t:

$$p_{k,t} = \frac{\exp(\mathbf{w}_k^\intercal \mathbf{x}_t)}{\sum_{t'=1}^{T} \exp(\mathbf{w}_k^\intercal \mathbf{x}_{t'})} \tag{1}$$

Let $\mathbf{u} = [1/T, 2/T, \cdots, t/T, \cdots, 1]^\intercal$ be the normalized timescale, each entry of which denotes a relative time moment on the range of $[0, 1]$ in an input sequence of length T. Then, the expected moment m_k that the pattern k appears can be calculated as

$$m_k = \mathbb{E}_{t\sim p_{k,t}}\left[\frac{t}{T}\right] = \sum_{t=1}^{T} \frac{t \cdot p_{k,t}}{T} = \mathbf{u}^\intercal \mathbf{p}_k \tag{2}$$

where $\mathbf{p}_k = [p_{k,1}, \cdots, p_{k,T}]^\intercal$ is a vector containing the probability of pattern k appearing at each moment.

Note that a pattern related with ADHD detection usually corresponds to a salient pattern of neural activation in brain ROIs. Thus, we expect that it should have a sharp appearance in the projection sequence such as the p_1 shown in

[3]These patterns are latent because they are unlabeled.

figure 2. Accordingly, we propose to minimize the **variance of pattern occurrence**

$$v_k = \mathrm{Var}_{t \sim p_{k,t}} \left[\frac{t}{T} \right] = \sum_{t=1}^{T} \frac{(t - m_k)^2 \cdot p_{k,t}}{T^2} \quad (3)$$

together with the other criteria to learn the projection matrix **W** in Section 4. This regularization term is more likely to generate a salient pattern that really matters in detecting ADHD.

First-Take-All Temporal-Order Comparison

Now putting the expected appearing moments of K patterns into $\mathbf{m} = [m_1, \cdots, m_K]$, we wish to develop an ordinal hashing algorithm directly encoding their temporal order for a TC. Specifically, we perform a First-Take-All (FTA) comparison to rank the patterns by their temporal order – the pattern whose expected appearing moment comes first wins the FTA comparison, and its index is used to hash the entire TC.

For example, when we have two projected sequences (i.e., $K = 2$), FTA simply encodes the pairwise order between two corresponding patterns. When $K > 2$, FTA makes a higher-order comparison to decide which pattern appears first. Note that the output FTA hash code is not binary; instead it is a K-ary code. For this reason, we call K the FTA base.

For a pairwise FTA comparison involving only two patterns, knowing the first coming pattern completely encodes the temporal order between these two patterns. This can be generalized to high-order comparison if more than two patterns are involved for choosing the first-coming pattern. Such a high-order FTA comparison could generate more compact code to distinguish between different types of TCs. For example, suppose there are three types of TCs have different orders of patterns 1 – 2 – 3 – 4, 1 – 3 – 2 – 4 and 1 – 4 – 3 – 2, respectively. Then an effective FTA comparison only needs to make a order-3 comparison between the last three patterns 2, 3 and 4, which will output the FTA code 2, 3 and 4 to distinguish these three types of TCs. In this case, there is no need to make comprehensive comparisons between all possible pairs of patterns.

However, the patterns whose orders matter in classifying different types of TCs are unknown a-priori. A suitable group of patterns must be learned so that the same type of TCs will have similar pattern orders. We will discuss the detail about the learning of these patterns in Section 4.

Mathematically, the index of the first-appearing pattern can be expressed as

$$\mathbf{h} = \arg\min_{\boldsymbol{\theta}} \boldsymbol{\theta}^\intercal \mathbf{m} = \boldsymbol{\theta}^\intercal [\mathbf{u}^\intercal \mathbf{p}_1 | \cdots | \mathbf{u}^\intercal \mathbf{p}_K] = \mathbf{u}^\intercal \mathbf{P} \boldsymbol{\theta} \quad (4)$$

where $\boldsymbol{\theta} \in \{0,1\}^K, \mathbf{1}^\intercal \boldsymbol{\theta} = 1$ and $\mathbf{h}$ is an 1-of-K indicator of the FTA winner – its unique nonzero entry is indexed by the first-appearing pattern in the input TC, and $\mathbf{P} = [\mathbf{p}_1, \cdots, \mathbf{p}_K]$.

An algorithmic description for the entire FTA hashing procedure is shown in Algorithm 1. Multiple FTA codes can be generated with a set of projection matrices. The code length L in the algorithm represents the number of hash codes generated for a TC.

Figure 3 illustrates the FTA comparison when K is set to 3. Here p_1, p_2 and p_3 in Figure 3 are the probability of each pattern appearing over the time axis t. From them, we can

Algorithm 1 First-Take-All Hashing

1: **Input:** TC $\mathbf{X}$, code length L, a set of projection matrices $\{\mathbf{W}_i\}_{i=1}^L$
2: **Initialize:** $b \leftarrow$ empty sequence
3: **for** $i = 1$ to L **do**
4: $\quad \mathbf{S} = \mathbf{W}_i^\intercal \mathbf{X}$
5: $\quad$ for each row $\mathbf{s}_k$ of $\mathbf{S}$, calculate m_k through Eq.(1) and Eq. (2)
6: $\quad k^* \leftarrow \arg\min_{1 \le j \le K} m_k$.
7: $\quad b \leftarrow bk^*$ (concatenation)
8: **end for**
9: **return** b

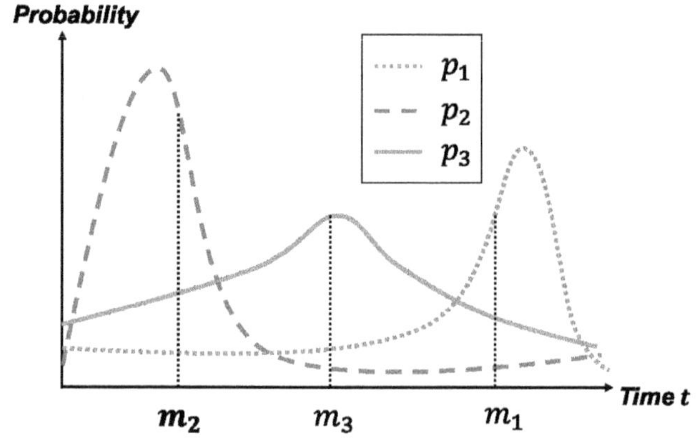

Figure 3: Illustration for First-Take-All Temporal-Order comparison when K is set to 3

get their expected pattern appearing moments m_1, m_2 and m_3, which are approximately shown in the figure, where we have $m_2 < m_3 < m_1$. By the FTA comparison, we choose the index of m_2 as the hash code for the TC, which is 2.

Before the end of this section, let us analyze the computational complexity of hashing a sequence by FTA. First, it costs $O(TDK)$ to apply the projection matrix to an input TC $\mathbf{X}$. Then finding the expected moments of K projected sequences costs $O(TK)$. It also costs $O(K)$ to find the first-appearing pattern which wins FTA comparison out of K candidates. Hence, FTA totally costs $O(TDK)$ to hash an input TC up to a constant factor.

4. LEARNING OPTIMAL PROJECTIONS

A learning algorithm to find out the optimal projections **W** will be presented in this section, including the formulation of the optimizing problem and its efficient solution.

4.1 Training Loss

Given a TC $\mathbf{X}$ and the expected appearing moments of K patterns $\mathbf{m} = [m_1, \cdots, m_K]$, which is acquired from a fixed $\mathbf{W}$. Then we can apply the following softmin to calculate the probability that the kth pattern will appear first:

$$h_k \triangleq P(\text{pattern } k \text{ comes first} | \mathbf{X}) = \frac{\exp(-m_k)}{\sum_{k'=1}^{K} \exp(-m_{k'})} \quad (5)$$

The smaller the m_k, the more likely the pattern k will appear first.

Now consider a pair of TCs $\mathbf{X}^{(i)}$ and $\mathbf{X}^{(j)}$, along with their label s_i and s_j. We hope that through our learning algorithm, the resultant FTA hash codes can reflect the label similarity between two TCs. In other word, when $s_i = s_j$, there is a greater chance that the same pattern will appear first in both $\mathbf{X}^{(i)}$ and $\mathbf{X}^{(j)}$; otherwise, different patterns will appear first if $s_i \neq s_j$ if $s_i \neq s_j$.

Mathematically, it is easy to see that $h_k^{(i)} h_k^{(j)}$ is the probability that the kth pattern will appear first in both $\mathbf{X}^{(i)}$ and $\mathbf{X}^{(j)}$. Suppose h^{ij} represents the probability that the same pattern will appear first in both TCs. It can be computed as by summing up over all patterns

$$h^{ij} = \sum_{k=1}^{K} h_k^{(i)} h_k^{(j)} \tag{6}$$

Our goal is to maximize h^{ij} when $s_i = s_j$ and to minimize it when $s_i \neq s_j$. This results in the following objective function

$$O^{ij} = (1 - h^{ij})^{s_{ij}} (h^{ij})^{(1-s_{ij})} \tag{7}$$

Here, $s_{ij} = 1$ *i.f.f.* $s_i = s_j$; and $s_{ij} = 0$ otherwise. We wish to minimize it for all TC pairs. Suppose the training set is $\mathcal{T} = \{\mathbf{X}^{(i)}, s_i\}_{i=1}^{N}$ with N TCs. Then the total logarithmic training loss over $\mathcal{T}$ becomes

$$\mathcal{L} = \sum_{i=1}^{N} \sum_{j=1}^{N} \left[s_{ij} \log\left(1 - h^{ij}\right) + (1 - s_{ij}) \log\left(h^{ij}\right) \right] \tag{8}$$

Minimizing it can minimize the pairwise diagnosis errors on the training set incurred by the resultant FTA hash codes.

4.2 Projection Orthogonality

In addition to the minimization of training loss, it is worth mentioning that the redundancy between the learned patterns also affects the FTA hashing performance. With a set of redundant patterns learned, their projection sequences would be highly correlated or even identical to one another. This could reduce the degree of the temporal order being distinguished between different patterns. In this case, a smaller perturbation or local warping would change the temporal orders significantly, thereby degenerating the FTA's performance in presence of noises.

To improve the resiliency of FTA against perturbations or noises on TCs, we wish to reduce the redundancy between patterns by minimizing the following normalized inner products between projection vectors

$$\Omega = \sum_{k \neq k'=1}^{K} \left(\frac{\mathbf{w}_k^{\intercal} \mathbf{w}_{k'}}{\|\mathbf{w}_k\| \|\mathbf{w}_{k'}\|} \right)^2 \tag{9}$$

Clearly, minimizing it can make the learned projection vectors as orthogonal to each other as possible, thereby minimizing the redundancy between the corresponding patterns [4].

4.3 Putting Together

In addition to the training loss (8) and the projection orthogonality (9), we also consider to minimize the variance of pattern occurrences as shown in Eq. (3). This can be expressed as the following total variance over the training set:

$$\mathcal{V} = \sum_{i,k=1}^{N,K} v_k^{(i)}$$

where $v_k^{(i)}$ is the occurrence variance of pattern k in the ith TC of training set. As aforementioned, minimizing the variance of pattern occurrences can generate salient patterns for ADHD diagnosis.

Then putting them together, we can define the following minimization problem to learn the projection matrix $\mathbf{W}$

$$\begin{aligned} \min_{\mathbf{W}} \mathcal{F} \triangleq \mathcal{L} & \quad \cdots \text{ training loss} \\ + \gamma\, \Omega & \quad \cdots \text{ Projection Orthogonality} \\ + \eta\, \mathcal{V} & \quad \cdots \text{ Variance of pattern occurences} \end{aligned} \tag{10}$$

where two positive coefficients γ and η are two hyper parameters that control the contributions of the projection orthogonality and the minimization of pattern occurrence variance.

Algorithm 2 Learning Optimal Projections

Input: training TC set $\chi = \{\mathbf{X}^{(i)}, s_i\}_{i=1}^{N}$, K, learning rate α
Initialize: Randomly initialize $\mathbf{W} = [\mathbf{w}_1, \cdots, \mathbf{w}_K]$, $\mathbf{w}_k \in \mathbb{R}^{D \times 1}, k = 1, \cdots, K$
repeat
  Select training pair $\mathbf{X}^{(i)}$, $\mathbf{X}^{(j)}$.
  $P^{(i)} = [p_{k,t}^{(i)}]_{K \times T}$, $P^{(j)} = [p_{k,t}^{(j)}]_{K \times T}$, calculate $p_{k,t}^{(i)}$ and $p_{k,t}^{(j)}$ based on Eq.(1)
  for each $\mathbf{w}_k, k = 1, \cdots, K$, compute $\frac{\partial \mathcal{F}}{\partial \mathbf{w}_k}$ with $p_{k,t}^{(i)}$ and $p_{k,t}^{(j)}$ based on Eq.(12), (13), (14), (15), (16), (17), (18), (19).
  $\nabla_{\mathbf{W}} \mathcal{F} \leftarrow [\frac{\partial \mathcal{F}}{\partial \mathbf{w}_1}, \cdots, \frac{\partial \mathcal{F}}{\partial \mathbf{w}_K}]$
  $\mathbf{W} \leftarrow \mathbf{W} - \alpha \nabla_{\mathbf{W}} \mathcal{F}$
until Convergence.

4.4 Optimization

We adopt the stochastic gradient descent method to minimize $\mathcal{F}$ as to find the optimal projection $\mathbf{W} = [\mathbf{w}_1, \cdots, \mathbf{w}_K] \in \mathbb{R}^{D \times K}$. For each training iteration, we randomly pick up a pair of TCs and their labels and calculate the gradient $\nabla_{\mathbf{W}} \mathcal{F}$. Since $\mathcal{F}$ is differentiable w.r.t. $\mathbf{W}$, it allow us to calculate $\nabla_{\mathbf{W}} \mathcal{F}$, leading to an efficient learning procedure. All equations needed to calculate $\nabla_{\mathbf{W}} \mathcal{F}$ can be found in Appendix A and the entire optimization procedure is described in Algorithm 2.

The above paragraph depicts the training algorithm for a projection matrix resulting in one FTA hash code. The above learning algorithm can be used as a subroutine in a standard ensemble method like AdaBoost. This will yield multiple FTA codes for a TC. The similarity between TCs can be computed with the Hamming distance between their concatenated FTA codes. Then, ADHD can be fast detected by retrieving the similar TCs from a labeled database.

5. EXPERIMENTS

In this section, we demonstrate the effectiveness of the proposed method by conducting experiments on ADHD 200

[4]The projection orthogonality can also be imposed as a hard constraint in the optimization problem. However, by experiments, we found that the performance is more stable by posing it as a soft term that penalizes the projection redundancy in the objective function.

dataset, a dataset developed for ADHD detection. First we give a brief introduction on ADHD dataset. Then we discuss the experiment setting. We compare the proposed method with several supervised and unsupervised baselines with different evaluation metrics. Finally, we study the impact of the hyper-parameters K and L on the performance.

5.1 Datasets and Background

We evaluate the proposed FTA approach on ADHD-200 dataset. ADHD-200 was initially prepared by ADHD-200 Consortium[23] for the ADHD-200 Global Competition, a competition that aimed to improve the understanding of the neural basis of ADHD through the implementation of the scientific discovery. It contains 776 records of the resting-state fMRI and anatomical data across 8 independent imaging sites, 491 of which come from typically developing individuals and 285 from children and adolescents diagnosed with ADHD (ages: 7-21 years old). Accompanying phenotypic information includes: diagnostic status, dimensional ADHD symptom measures, age, sex, intelligence quotient (IQ) and lifetime medication status. Preliminary quality control assessments (usable vs. questionable) based upon visual time-series inspection are included for all resting state fMRI scans. An additional 197 individuals from six imaging sites were released without the diagnosis labels during the competition for testing purposes and their labels were released separately afterwards. More information on the dataset can be found at http://fcon_1000.projects.nitrc.org/indi/adhd200/.

In order to bring the ADHD-200 Global Competition to a wider audience, The Neuro Bureau[5] made preprocessed versions of the competition data freely available to the general public to help those whose specialities lay outside of resting-state fMRI analysis to bypass technical obstacles. There are several preprocessed datasets available which were preprocessed by different pipelines. In order to fairly compare the proposed method with the baselines, we choose the dataset preprocessed by Athena pipeline[1] which is also used by the baseline methods. More information about the Athena pipeline can be found at Neuro Bureau's website[6].

5.2 Experimental Setting and Baselines

For the sake of fair comparison, we follow the experiment setting similar with the baselines. For the proposed FTA hashing, we determine the values of hyper parameters K, L, γ and η by conducting 5-fold cross validation on the training set. As mentioned in section 3.1, the TCs we used for evaluation were extracted from the pre-constructed brain atlas which was built with automated anatomical labeling (AAL)[29]. The way to extract TCs is averaging the time courses within each ROI voxel[6]. Note that the AAL atlas was constructed using anatomic and cyto-architectonic information and did not incorporate functional information. Thus the resultant TCs do not contain any prior phenotypic information which may impact the evaluation. Based on the cross validation, FTA base K and code length L are set to 2 and 200 respectively.

We compare the proposed method with following algorithms:

- Dynamic Time Warping (DTW)[26]: A well known time series alignment technique that computes optimal distance between two time series of different lengths while preserving their temporal order.
- Derivative Dynamic Time Warping (DDTW)[19]: This method uses derivatives of the original time series to improve alignment by DTW.
- Canonical Time Warping (CTW)[31]: This method combines canonical correlation analysis (CCA) with DTW.
- Method from Johns Hopkins University (JHU)[12]: The winner of ADHD-200 Global Competition which achieved the state-of-the-art performance.
- Attributed Graph Distance Measure (AGDM)[10]: This method proposed a graph based feature called Attributed Graph Distance Measure which can be used to classify ADHD subjects.

Note that DTW, DDTW and CTW are unsupervised methods while JHU and AGDM are supervised. Following the settings of these baselines, we evaluate the proposed method with four statistical metrics: Prediction Accuracy, Specificity (= True Negative Rate), Sensitivity (= True Positive Rate) and J-Statistic (= Specificity + Sensitivity - 1). Among them the Prediction Accuracy is the primary metric for scoring. Note that the detection rate used in [10] is identical to prediction accuracy.

5.3 Comparison with Unsupervised Baselines

We begin our evaluation by demonstrating comparison results with the unsupervised baselines. As mentioned in Section 5.1, the training set consists of 8 subsets collected from different sites while the test set consists of 6 subsets. We implement FTA in Matlab and use the Matlab implementation of DTW, DDTW and CTW provided by [30] to conduct the experiments. The training and testing are performed on the training and testing subsets across all the eight imaging sites. The hardware configuration for the experiment is Intel i7-4790 CPU at 3.6GHz and 8GB RAM. Table 1 shows all four evaluation metrics and the computing time of three unsupervised baselines and the FTA.

Metric	DTW	DDTW	CTW	FTA
Accuracy	0.4678	0.4386	0.4678	**0.6140**
Specificity	0.7127	0.6915	0.8085	**0.9149**
Sensitivity	**0.2987**	**0.2987**	0.1818	0.2727
J-Statistics	0.0115	-0.0098	-0.0097	**0.1876**
Time(s)	149.5502	267.8659	47996.5866	**20.771**

Table 1: Performance comparison between the unsupervised baselines and the FTA.

As shown, the FTA outperforms all three baselines by nearly 15% to 18% on the prediction accuracy, a significant improvement to these well known time-series alignment methods. This demonstrates the FTA can better encode the temporal patterns which are important for predicting ADHD subjects than the unsupervised baselines. All four methods have a high specificity but a relatively low sensitivity. The FTA can reach the best specificity of 0.9149 but with a sensitivity of 0.2727. This is reasonable since there are much more TDC subjects than ADHD children diagnosed in the

[5]http://www.neurobureau.org/

[6]http://www.nitrc.org/plugins/mwiki/index.php/neurobureau:AthenaPipeline

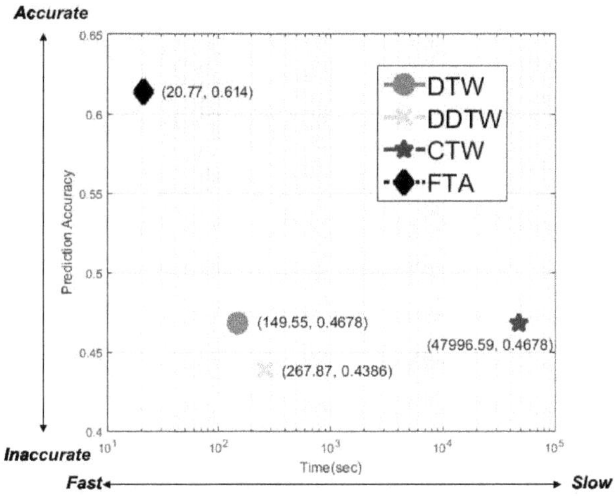

Figure 4: Prediction Accuracy versus Execution Time. Comparison between FTA and unsupervised baselines

training set (491 TDC and 285 ADHD children) thus the ability of a classifier to detect ADHD children is dampened – the prior distribution of TDC is biased by a large number of TDC samples in a general population. Such an unbalance between TDC and ADHD subjects can be relieved by imposing a larger penalty on missing ADHD subjects. However, we do not perform such a re-balance for the sake of a fair comparison with the other baselines.

Next we perform efficiency evaluation for all four methods. Since all three baselines adopt Dynamic Programming (DP) to perform similarity search, it can be expected that they will have a much slower speed than the proposed FTA hashing which performs similarity search by the Hamming distance. Figure 4 shows the Prediction Accuracy versus the Execution Time for all the methods. Compared with the baselines, FTA achieves more than 30% higher prediction accuracy on the entire test set and at least 7 times faster than DP based baselines. That suggests the proposed FTA hashing can be used for fast detection of ADHD subjects.

5.4 Comparison with Supervised Baselines

Now we compare the proposed method with two supervised baselines: JHU[12] and AGDM[10]. The approach proposed by JHU is a weighted combination of several algorithms including CUR decompositions, random forest, gradient boosting and support vector machine et al. It adopts both fMRI data and the accompanying phenotypic information like IQ to predict the ADHD subjects. On the contrary, another baseline AGDM only requires fMRI data to make the prediction. According to [10], features called AGDM were extracted from fMRI data to encode the brain network structure first. Then they were used to train a SVM classifier which made the final prediction. Since two baseline methods have different experiment settings, we follow their individual settings to make a fair comparison.

FTA vs JHU

Similar to Section 5.3, we train and test the FTA on all the training subsets across the eight sites. More specifically, we randomly sample 3,000 pairs from all the 8 training subsets and use them to find the optimal projections. We also report the evaluation metrics following the definitions from the ADHD-200 Global Competition [23]. The comparison results between the JHU and the FTA are summarized in Table 2.

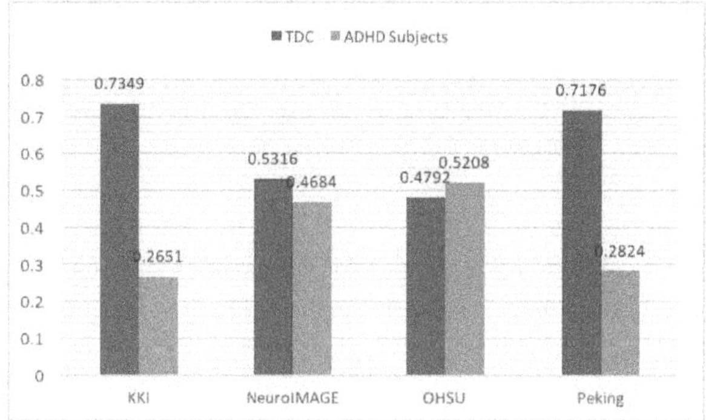

Figure 5: Percentage of TDC/ADHD Subjects in each training subset.

Metric	JHU	FTA
Prediction Accuracy	0.6102	**0.6140**
Specificity	**0.94**	0.9149
Sensitivity	0.21	**0.2727**
J-Statistics	0.15	**0.1876**

Table 2: Performance evaluation of JHU and FTA

From the table, we can see the proposed FTA outperforms the JHU on three metrics – prediction accuracy, sensitivity and J-Statistics. This is an impressive result, considering FTA only uses fMRI time courses to achieve such performance, whereas the JHU method involves both fMRI time courses and phenotypic information. Especially, compared with the JHU result, FTA improves the sensitivity by 29.85% while still keeping a competitive specificity (over 0.9). Such results demonstrate that encoding the temporal orders of the different neural activity patterns is definitely a helpful clue to identify the ADHD subjects.

We further justify this claim by showing some real examples of temporal orders of learned patterns. Figure 6 shows the sequences of two patterns projected from the TCs corresponding to the TDC and ADHD subjects. Figure 6a comes from a TDC subject while Figure 6b is obtained from a ADHD subject. It is clear that these two patterns exhibit different temporal orders between the TDC and ADHD subjects. Since the FTA can encode the temporal order of patterns, the resultant hash codes can characterize the neural activity difference between different types of TCs.

FTA vs AGDM

Unlike the JHU method, the AGDM conducted their experiments on the individual subsets. There are totally eight subsets collected by different imaging sites and AGDM chose four of them to evaluate their approach. The chosen subsets are collected by 1) Kennedy Krieger Institute (KKI), 2) NeuroIMAGE, 3) Oregon Health & Science University (OHSU) and 4) Peking University (Peking) respectively. To evaluate the proposed method, we follow the same experiment setting as the AGDM, and train and test on each subset separately.

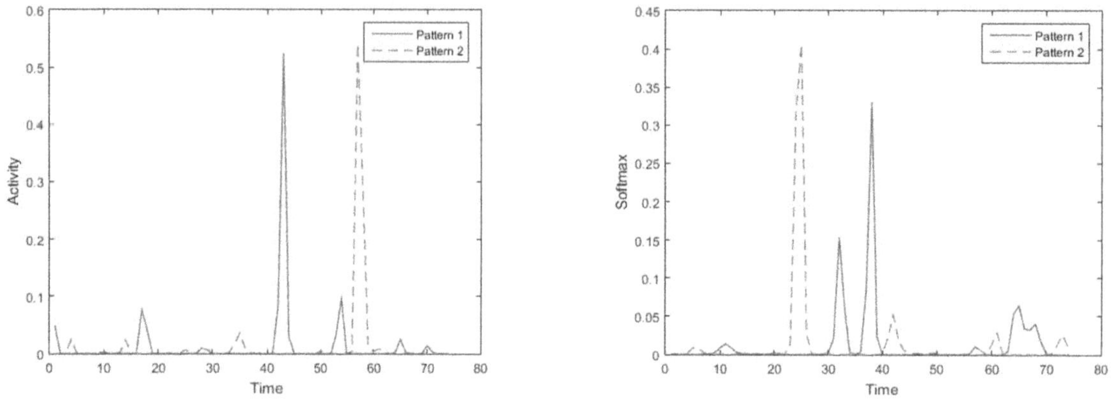

a. Typically Developing Children **b. ADHD Patient**

Figure 6: Comparison of the temporal order of two patterns between the TDC and ADHD subjects. It illustrates how the order of these two patterns matters in detecting ADHD.

Sites	Prediction Accuracy		Specificity		Sensitivity		J-Statistic	
	AGDM	FTA	AGDM	FTA	AGDM	FTA	AGDM	FTA
KKI	0.5455	**0.8182**	0.625	**1**	**0.3333**	**0.3333**	-0.0417	**0.3333**
NeuroImage	0.48	**0.8**	0.6429	**0.8571**	0.2727	**0.7273**	-0.0844	**0.5844**
OHSU	0.8235	**0.8676**	0.8929	**0.9643**	0.5	**0.6667**	0.3929	**0.6310**
Peking	0.5882	**0.6176**	0.9259	**1**	0.2083	**0.25**	0.1342	**0.25**
Average	0.6281	**0.7759**	0.8312	**0.9554**	0.2727	**0.4943**	0.1003	**0.4497**

Table 3: Performance evaluation on individual sets

Table 3 shows the comparison results between the FTA and the AGDM on individual sets. Apparently, the FTA significantly outperforms the AGDM on every evaluation metrics. Specifically, the average prediction accuracy and the average sensitivity of FTA outperform the AGDM by around 15% and 20% respectively. This means more than 75% of subjects can be correctly classified, and nearly half of ADHD patients can be successfully detected by the FTA. Moreover, the specificities of FTA on all four subsets are obviously boosted compared with the AGDM. Especially on KKI and Peking, the specificity achieves 1 – all TDC subjects are correctly identified.

Similar results can be found about the sensitivity. On the NeuroIMAGE and the OHSU subsets, the sensitivities have reached over 0.7 and 0.6, much closer to the corresponding specificity. Consider our discussion in Section 5.3 – the low sensitivity is caused by high ratio of TDC in the training set. We calculated the percentage of TDC and ADHD subjects on each subset, which are illustrated in Figure 5. It shows that the ratio of TDC/ADHD subjects on NeuroIMAGE and OHSU is close to 1, while it is much higher on KKI and Peking. This implies that the low sensitivity is caused by a high ratio of TDC/ADHD.

5.5 Parameter Sensitivity Analysis

Finally, we evaluate the FTA's performance by varying its hyper-parameters. In particular, we study the impact of the code length L and FTA base K on the performance. Besides the AAL, we also conduct experiments with TCs extracted

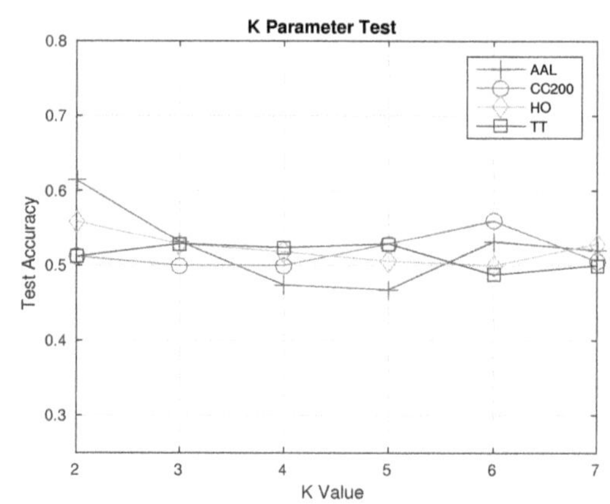

Figure 7: Test accuracy across different ROIs, using different K values

from 3 other pre-built brain atlas: Talairach and Tournoux (TT)[21], Harvard-Oxford (HO)[15] and CC200[8].

Prediction Accuracy vs K

By varying the FTA base K, it can be shown that it affects the test accuracy of the FTA model. For a fixed code length of 200, a variety of K values were used: from 2 through 7. The results show differences in impact of K for different ROI atlases. For instance, with the CC200, an increased K tends to improve the accuracy, whereas an increased K in the AAL results in a subtle decrease in the test accuracy

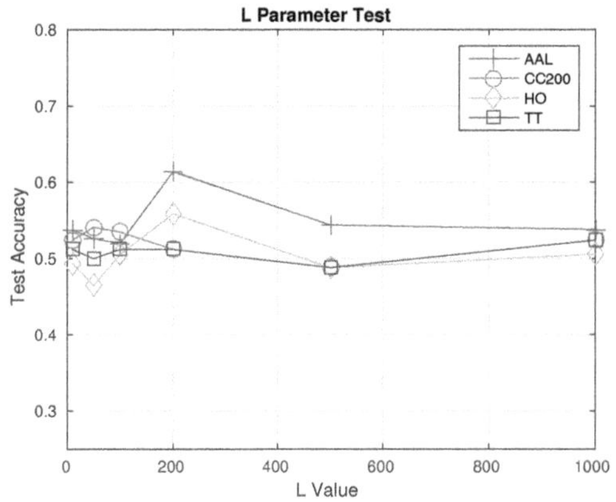

Figure 8: Test accuracy across different ROIs, using different L values

followed by an increase after $K = 6$. Overall, all four ROI atlases, begin to converge to a median of performance when K approaches 7. Throughout the tests, the results indicate only small dependencies contingent on the values of K.

Considering K is the number of patterns involved in generating a hash code, assessing its role offers a way to tune the amount of discriminant information available at any given comparison. From Figure 7, it seems that for slight increases in K (e.g., from K = 4 to K = 6 for CC200) the amount of information increases, offering an increased test accuracy. However, there appears to be a point at which further increasing the value of K no longer improves the test accuracy (beyond $K = 6$). Ultimately, this leads to a decline in performance due to the redundancies in the comparison of a too large number of patterns.

Prediction Accuracy vs L

Now let us assess the code length parameter L. Fixed at $K = 2$, a variety of code lengths were tested, ranging from $L = 10$ to $L = 1000$. In Figure 8, it can be seen that L acts differently across different ROIs, especially between the range of 10 to 200 code length. Incidentally, it is shown that this range experiences the most abrupt shifts in performance, whilst the range 200-1000 shows either constant or steady trends. In the case of AAL and HO, they are particularly sensitive to this parameter. Within the $L = 10$ to $L = 200$ range, the performance reaches its peak and then drops subsequently. Extending to the set of other ROIs, Figure 8 shows that this trend (to a lesser degree) is exhibited on CC200 and TT as well.

Resulting from this experiment, it can be shown that varying code lengths has impact on performance, with tuning required particularly in the range of compact codes from $L = 10$ and $L = 200$. Yet similar to K, simply increasing the value indefinitely does not result in a better test accuracy because of higher redundancies that might exist in longer codes.

6. CONCLUSION

In this paper, we propose a novel FTA algorithm to hash time series of varied length into fixed-size codes. We use the resultant hash codes to efficiently detect the ADHD subjects by fast retrieving the similar subjects. To maximize its performance, we design an effective algorithm to learn the optimal projections $\mathbf{W}$. The results of extensive experimental evaluations show the proposed FTA outperforms both unsupervised and supervised methods on the ADHD-200 dataset for identifying ADHD subjects, beating the winning algorithm in the ADHD-200 Global Competition.

7. ACKNOWLEDGMENT

We gratefully acknowledge the support of NVIDIA Corporation with the donation of the Tesla K40 GPU used for this research.

8. REFERENCES

[1] P. Bellec, C. Chu, F. Chouinard-Decorte, D. S. Margulies, and C. R. Craddock. The neuro bureau adhd-200 preprocessed repository. *bioRxiv*, page 037044, 2016.

[2] D. J. Berndt and J. Clifford. Using dynamic time warping to find patterns in time series. In *KDD workshop*, volume 10, pages 359–370. Seattle, WA, 1994.

[3] D. M. Blei, A. Y. Ng, and M. I. Jordan. Latent dirichlet allocation. *the Journal of machine Learning research*, 3:993–1022, 2003.

[4] G. Buzsaki. *Rhythms of the Brain*. Oxford University Press, 2006.

[5] C. Cortes and V. Vapnik. Support-vector networks. *Machine learning*, 20(3):273–297, 1995.

[6] S. Cortese, C. Kelly, C. Chabernaud, E. Proal, A. Di Martino, M. P. Milham, and F. X. Castellanos. Toward systems neuroscience of adhd: a meta-analysis of 55 fmri studies. *American Journal of Psychiatry*, 2012.

[7] D. D. Cox and R. L. Savoy. Functional magnetic resonance imaging (fmri)"brain reading": detecting and classifying distributed patterns of fmri activity in human visual cortex. *Neuroimage*, 19(2):261–270, 2003.

[8] R. C. Craddock, G. A. James, P. E. Holtzheimer, X. P. Hu, and H. S. Mayberg. A whole brain fmri atlas generated via spatially constrained spectral clustering. *Human brain mapping*, 33(8):1914–1928, 2012.

[9] J. Damoiseaux, S. Rombouts, F. Barkhof, P. Scheltens, C. Stam, S. M. Smith, and C. Beckmann. Consistent resting-state networks across healthy subjects. *Proceedings of the national academy of sciences*, 103(37):13848–13853, 2006.

[10] S. Dey, A. R. Rao, and M. Shah. Attributed graph distance measure for automatic detection of attention deficit hyperactive disordered subjects. *Frontiers in neural circuits*, 8, 2014.

[11] S. B. Eickhoff, K. E. Stephan, H. Mohlberg, C. Grefkes, G. R. Fink, K. Amunts, and K. Zilles. A new spm toolbox for combining probabilistic cytoarchitectonic maps and functional imaging data. *Neuroimage*, 25(4):1325–1335, 2005.

[12] A. Eloyan, J. Muschelli, M. B. Nebel, H. Liu, F. Han, T. Zhao, A. Barber, S. Joel, J. J. Pekar, S. Mostofsky, et al. Automated diagnoses of attention deficit hyperactive disorder using magnetic resonance imaging. 2012.

[13] J. A. Etzel, V. Gazzola, and C. Keysers. An introduction to anatomical roi-based fmri classification analysis. *Brain research*, 1282:114–125, 2009.

[14] M. D. Fox, A. Z. Snyder, J. L. Vincent, M. Corbetta, D. C. Van Essen, and M. E. Raichle. The human brain is intrinsically organized into dynamic, anticorrelated functional networks. *Proceedings of the National Academy of Sciences of the United States of America*, 102(27):9673–9678, 2005.

[15] J. A. Frazier, S. Chiu, J. L. Breeze, N. Makris, N. Lange, D. N. Kennedy, M. R. Herbert, E. K. Bent, V. K. Koneru, M. E. Dieterich, et al. Structural brain magnetic resonance imaging of limbic and thalamic volumes in pediatric bipolar disorder. *American Journal of Psychiatry*, 2005.

[16] T.-c. Fu. A review on time series data mining. *Engineering Applications of Artificial Intelligence*, 24(1):164–181, 2011.

[17] J.-D. Haynes and G. Rees. Decoding mental states from brain activity in humans. *Nature Reviews Neuroscience*, 7(7):523–534, 2006.

[18] E. J. Keogh and M. J. Pazzani. Scaling up dynamic time warping for datamining applications. In *Proceedings of the sixth ACM SIGKDD international conference on Knowledge discovery and data mining*, pages 285–289. ACM, 2000.

[19] E. J. Keogh and M. J. Pazzani. Derivative dynamic time warping. In *Sdm*, volume 1, pages 5–7. SIAM, 2001.

[20] S. Klöppel, A. Abdulkadir, C. R. Jack, N. Koutsouleris, J. Mourão-Miranda, and P. Vemuri. Diagnostic neuroimaging across diseases. *Neuroimage*, 61(2):457–463, 2012.

[21] J. L. Lancaster, M. G. Woldorff, L. M. Parsons, M. Liotti, C. S. Freitas, L. Rainey, P. V. Kochunov, D. Nickerson, S. A. Mikiten, and P. T. Fox. Automated talairach atlas labels for functional brain mapping. *Human brain mapping*, 10(3):120–131, 2000.

[22] S. Lemm, B. Blankertz, T. Dickhaus, and K.-R. Müller. Introduction to machine learning for brain imaging. *Neuroimage*, 56(2):387–399, 2011.

[23] M. P. Milham, D. Fair, M. Mennes, S. H. Mostofsky, et al. The adhd-200 consortium: a model to advance the translational potential of neuroimaging in clinical neuroscience. *Frontiers in systems neuroscience*, 6:62, 2012.

[24] G. A. Ojemann, J. Ojemann, and N. F. Ramsey. Relation between functional magnetic resonance imaging (fmri) and single neuron, local field potential (lfp) and electrocorticography (ecog) activity in human cortex. *Front Hum Neurosci*, 7:34, 2013.

[25] R. A. Poldrack. Region of interest analysis for fmri. *Social cognitive and affective neuroscience*, 2(1):67–70, 2007.

[26] L. Rabiner and B.-H. Juang. Fundamentals of speech recognition. 1993.

[27] R. P. N. Rao. *Brain-Computer Interfacing: An Introduction.* Cambridge University Press, New York, NY, USA, 2013.

[28] C. A. Ratanamahatana and E. Keogh. Making time-series classification more accurate using learned constraints. SIAM, 2004.

[29] N. Tzourio-Mazoyer, B. Landeau, D. Papathanassiou, F. Crivello, O. Etard, N. Delcroix, B. Mazoyer, and M. Joliot. Automated anatomical labeling of activations in spm using a macroscopic anatomical parcellation of the mni mri single-subject brain. *Neuroimage*, 15(1):273–289, 2002.

[30] F. Zhou and F. De la Torre. Generalized time warping for multi-modal alignment of human motion. In *IEEE Conference on Computer Vision and Pattern Recognition (CVPR)*, 2012.

[31] F. Zhou and F. Torre. Canonical time warping for alignment of human behavior. In *Advances in neural information processing systems*, pages 2286–2294, 2009.

APPENDIX

A. EQUATIONS FOR LEARNING OPTIMAL PROJECTIONS

This section contains the equations required to derive the gradient of $\mathcal{F}$ w.r.t. $\mathbf{W}$ in learning the optimal projections.

Here, we use $\mathcal{L}^{ij}$ to denote the logarithmic training loss for a pair of TCs $\mathbf{X}^{(i)}$ and $\mathbf{X}^{(j)}$, i.e.,

$$\mathcal{L}^{ij} = s_{ij} \log\left(1 - h^{ij}\right) + (1 - s_{ij}) \log\left(h^{ij}\right) \tag{11}$$

The following equations can be calculated by applying the chain rule of the derivatives on $\mathcal{F}$ of Eq. (10).

$$\frac{\partial \mathcal{F}}{\partial \mathbf{w}_k} = \sum_{i,j=1}^{N} \frac{\partial \mathcal{L}^{ij}}{\partial \mathbf{w}_k} + \gamma \frac{\partial \Omega}{\partial \mathbf{w}_k} + \eta \frac{\partial \mathcal{V}}{\partial \mathbf{w}_k} \tag{12}$$

$$\frac{\partial \Omega}{\partial \mathbf{w}_k} = \sum_{k \neq k'=1}^{K} \frac{2\mathbf{w}_k^{\intercal}\mathbf{w}_{k'}}{\|\mathbf{w}_k\|^4 \|\mathbf{w}_{k'}\|^2} \left[\left(\mathbf{w}_k^{\intercal}\mathbf{w}_k\right)\mathbf{w}_{k'} - \left(\mathbf{w}_k^{\intercal}\mathbf{w}_{k'}\right)\mathbf{w}_k\right] \tag{13}$$

$$\begin{aligned}\frac{\partial \mathcal{V}}{\partial \mathbf{w}_k} = \sum_{i,k=1}^{N,K} \sum_{t=1}^{T} \frac{1}{T^2} \Bigg[& 2\,(t - m_k)\,(-\frac{\partial m_k^{(i)}}{\partial \mathbf{w}_k}) p_{k,t}^{(i)} \\ & + (t - m_k)^2 (p_{k,t}^{(i)} \mathbf{x}_t^{(i)} - p_{k,t}^{(i)} \left(\sum_{t'=1}^{T} p_{k,t'}^{(i)} \mathbf{x}_{t'}^{(i)}\right)\Bigg]\end{aligned} \tag{14}$$

$$\frac{\partial \mathcal{L}^{ij}}{\partial \mathbf{w}_k} = \begin{cases} -\frac{1}{1-h^{ij}} \frac{\partial h^{ij}}{\partial \mathbf{w}_k} & s_i = s_j \\ \frac{1}{h^{ij}} \frac{\partial h^{ij}}{\partial \mathbf{w}_k} & otherwise \end{cases} \tag{15}$$

$$\frac{\partial h^{ij}}{\partial \mathbf{w}_k} = \sum_{k'=1}^{K} h_{k'}^{(i)} \frac{\partial h_{k'}^{(j)}}{\partial \mathbf{w}_k} + \sum_{k'=1}^{K} h_{k'}^{(j)} \frac{\partial h_{k'}^{(i)}}{\partial \mathbf{w}_k} \tag{16}$$

$$\frac{\partial h_k^{(i)}}{\partial \mathbf{w}_k} = h_k^{(i)}(-\frac{\partial m_k^{(i)}}{\partial \mathbf{w}_k}) - (h_k^{(i)})^2(-\frac{\partial m_k^{(i)}}{\partial \mathbf{w}_k}) \tag{17}$$

$$\frac{\partial h_l^{(i)}}{\partial \mathbf{w}_k} = -h_l^{(i)} h_k^{(i)}(-\frac{\partial m_k^{(i)}}{\partial \mathbf{w}_k}),\ when\ l \neq k \tag{18}$$

$$\frac{\partial m_k^{(i)}}{\partial \mathbf{w}_k} = \sum_{t=1}^{T} \frac{t}{T} \left(p_{k,t}^{(i)} \mathbf{x}_t^{(i)} - p_{k,t}^{(i)} \left(\sum_{t'=1}^{T} p_{k,t'}^{(i)} \mathbf{x}_{t'}^{(i)}\right)\right) \tag{19}$$

When Social Influence Meets Item Inference

Hui-Ju Hung[1], Hong-Han Shuai[2], De-Nian Yang[2],
Liang-Hao Huang[2], Wang-Chien Lee[1], Jian Pei[3], Ming-Syan Chen[4]
[1]The Pennsylvania State University, USA, [2]Academia Sinica, Taiwan
[3]Simon Fraser University, Canada, [4]National Taiwan University, Taiwan
hzh131@cse.psu.edu, hhshuai@citi.sinica.edu.tw, dnyang@iis.sinica.edu.tw
lhhuang@iis.sinica.edu.tw, wlee@cse.psu.edu, jpei@cs.sfu.ca, mschen@cc.ee.ntu.edu.tw

ABSTRACT

Research issues and data mining techniques for product recommendation and viral marketing have been widely studied. Existing works on seed selection in social networks do not take into account the effect of product recommendations in e-commerce stores. In this paper, we investigate the seed selection problem for viral marketing that considers both effects of social influence and item inference (for product recommendation). We develop a new model, *Social Item Graph (SIG)*, that captures both effects in the form of hyperedges. Accordingly, we formulate a seed selection problem, called *Social Item Maximization Problem (SIMP)*, and prove the hardness of SIMP. We design an efficient algorithm with performance guarantee, called Hyperedge-Aware Greedy (HAG), for SIMP and develop a new index structure, called SIG-index, to accelerate the computation of diffusion process in HAG. Moreover, to construct realistic SIG models for SIMP, we develop a statistical inference based framework to learn the weights of hyperedges from data. Finally, we perform a comprehensive evaluation on our proposals with various baselines. Experimental result validates our ideas and demonstrates the effectiveness and efficiency of the proposed model and algorithms over baselines.

Keywords

viral marketing; product recommendation; frequent pattern

1. INTRODUCTION

The ripple effect of social influence [4] has been explored for viral marketing via online social networks. Indeed, studies show that customers tend to receive product information from friends better than advertisements on traditional media [19]. To explore the potential impact of social influence, many research studies on *seed selection*, i.e., selecting a given number of influential customers to maximize the spread of social recommendation for a product, have been reported [7, 17].[1] However, these works do not take into account the effect of product recommendations in online e-commerce stores. We argue that when a customer buys an item due to the social influence (e.g., via Facebook or Pinterest), there is a potential side effect due to the *item inference* recommendations from stores.[2] For example, when Alice buys a DVD of "Star War" due to the recommendation from friends, she may also pick up the original novel of the movie due to an in-store recommendation, which may in turn trigger additional purchases of the novel among her friends. To the best of our knowledge, this additional spread introduced by the item inference recommendations has not been considered in existing research on viral marketing.

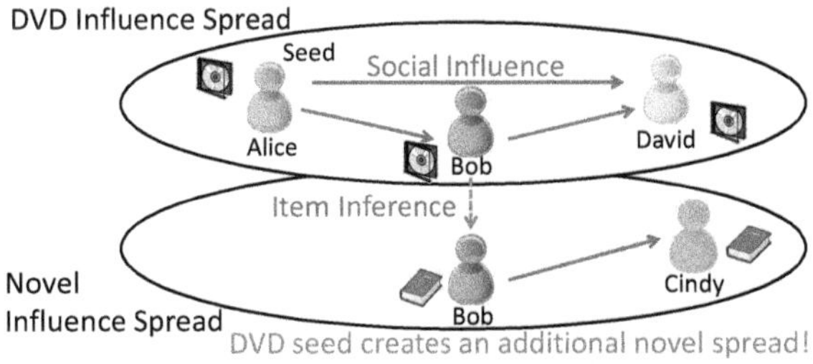

Figure 1: A motivating example

Figure 1 illustrates the above joint effects in a toy example with two products and four customers, where a dash arrow represents the association rule behind the item inference recommendation, and a solid arrow denotes the social influence between two friends upon a product. In the two separate planes corresponding to DVD and novel, social influence is expected to take effect on promoting interests in (and potential purchases of) the DVD and novel, respectively. Meanwhile, the item inference recommendation by the e-commerce store is expected to trigger sales of additional items. Note that the association rules behind item inference are derived without considering the ripple effect of social influence. In the example, when Bob buys the DVD, he may also buy the novel due to the item inference recommendation. Moreover, he may influence Cindy to purchase the novel. However, the association rules behind item inference are derived without considering the ripple effect of social influence. On the other hand, to promote the movie DVD, Alice may be selected as a seed for a viral marketing campaign, hoping to spread her influence to Bob and David to trigger additional purchases of the DVD. Actually, due to the effect of item inference recommendation, having Alice as a seed may additionally trigger purchases of the novel by Bob and Cindy. This is a factor that existing seed selection algorithms for viral marketing do not account for.

[1]All the top 5 online retailers, including Amazon, Staples, Apple, Walmart, and Dell, are equipped with sophisticated recommendation engines. They also support viral marketing by allowing users to share favorite products in Facebook.

[2]In this paper, we refer product/item recommendation based on associations among items inferred from purchase transactions as item inference recommendation.

KDD '16, August 13-17, 2016, San Francisco, CA, USA
© 2016 ACM. ISBN 978-1-4503-4232-2/16/08...$15.00
DOI: http://dx.doi.org/10.1145/2939672.2939758

We argue that to select seeds for maximizing the spread of product information to a customer base (or maximizing the sale revenue of products) in a viral marketing campaign, both effects of item inference and social influence need to be considered. To incorporate both effects, we propose a new model, called *Social Item Graph (SIG)* in the form of hyperedges, for capturing "purchase actions" of customers on products and their potential influence to trigger other purchase actions. Different from the conventional approaches [7, 17] that use links between customers to model social relationship (for viral marketing) and links between items to capture the association (for item inference recommendation), SIG represents a *purchase action* as a node (denoted by a tuple of a customer and an item), while using hyperedges among nodes to capture the influence spread process used to predict customers' future purchases. Unlike the previous influence propagation models [7, 17] consisting of only one kind of edges connecting two customers (in social influence), the hyperedges in our model span across tuples of different customers and items, capturing both effects of social influence and item inference.

Based on SIG, we formulate the *Social Item Maximization Problem* (SIMP) to find a seed set, which consists of selected products along with targeted customers, to maximize the total adoptions of products by customers. Note that SIMP takes multiple products into consideration and targets on maximizing the number of products purchased by customers.[3] SIMP is a very challenging problem, which does not have the submodularity property. We prove that SIMP cannot be approximated within n^c with any $c < 1$, where n is the number of nodes in SIMP, i.e., SIMP is extremely difficult to approximate with a small ratio because the best approximation ratio is almost n.[4]

To tackle SIMP, two challenges arise: 1) numerous combinations of possible seed nodes, and 2) expensive on-line computation of influence diffusion upon hyperedges. To address the first issue, we first introduce the *Hyperedge-Aware Greedy (HAG)* algorithm, based on a unique property of hyperedges, i.e., a hyperedge requires all its source nodes to be activated in order to trigger the purchase action in its destination node. HAG selects multiple seeds in each seed selection iteration to further activate more nodes via hyperedges.[5] To address the second issue, we exploit the structure of Frequent Pattern Tree (FP-tree) to develop *SIG-index* as a compact representation of SIG in order to accelerate the computation of activation probabilities of nodes in online diffusion.

Moreover, to construct a realistic SIG model for SIMP, we also develop a statistical inference based framework to learn the weights of hyperedges from logs of purchase actions. Identifying the hyperedges and estimating the corresponding weights are major challenges for constructing of an SIG due to data sparsity and unobservable activations. To address these issues, we propose a novel framework that employs smoothed expectation and maximization algorithm (EMS) [21], to identify hyperedges and estimate their values by kernel smoothing.

[3]SIMP can be extended to a weighted version with different profits from each product. In this paper, we focus on maximizing the total sales.

[4]While there is no good solution quality guarantee for the worst case scenario, we empirically show that the algorithm we developed achieves total adoptions on average comparable to optimal results.

[5]A hyperedge requires all its source nodes to be activated to diffuse its influence to its destination node.

Our contributions of this paper are summarized as follows.

- We observe the deficiencies in existing techniques for item inference recommendation and seed selection and propose the *Social Item Graph (SIG)* that captures both effects of social influence and item inference in the prediction of potential purchase actions.
- Based on SIG, we formulate a new problem, called *Social Item Maximization Problem (SIMP)*, to select the seed nodes for viral marketing that effectively facilitates the recommendations from both friends and stores simultaneously. In addition, we analyze the hardness of SIMP.
- We design an efficient algorithm with performance guarantee, called Hyperedge-Aware Greedy (HAG), and develop a new index structure, called SIG-index, to accelerate the computation of diffusion process in HAG.
- To construct realistic SIG models for SIMP, we develop a statistical inference based framework to learn the weights of hyperedges from data.
- We conduct a comprehensive evaluation on our proposals with various baselines. Experimental result validates our ideas and demonstrates the effectiveness and efficiency of the proposed model and algorithms over baselines.

The rest of this paper is organized as follows. Section 2 reviews the related work. Section 3 details the SIG model and its influence diffusion process. Section 4 formulates SIMP and designs new algorithms to efficiently solve the problem. Section 5 describes our approach to construct the SIG. Section 6 reports our experiment results and Section 7 concludes the paper.

2. RELATED WORK

To discover the associations among purchased items, frequent pattern mining algorithms find items which frequently appear together in transactions [3]. Some variants, such as closed frequent patterns mining [20], maximal frequent pattern mining [16], have been studied. However, those existing works, focusing on unveiling the common shopping behaviors of individuals, disregard the social influence between customers [26]. On the other hand, it has been pointed out that items recommended by item inference may have been introduced to users by social diffusion [25]. In this work, we develop a new model and a learning framework that consider both the social influence and item inference factors jointly to derive the association among purchase actions of customers. In addition, we focus on seed selection for prevalent viral marketing by incorporating the effect of item inference.

With a great potential in business applications, social influence diffusion in social networks has attracted extensive interests recently [7, 17]. Learning algorithms for estimating the social influence strength between social customers have been developed [10, 18]. Based on models of social influence diffusion, identifying the most influential customers (seed selection) is a widely studied problem [7, 17]. Precisely, those studies aim to find the best k initial seed customers to target on in order to maximize the population of potential customers who may adopt the new product. This seed selection problem has been proved as NP-hard [17]. Based on two influence diffusion models, Independent Cascade (IC) and Linear Threshold (LT), Kempe et al. propose a $1 - 1/e$ approximation greedy algorithm by exploring the submodularity property under IC and LT [17]. Some follow-up studies focus on improving the efficiency of the greedy algorithm using various spread estimation methods,

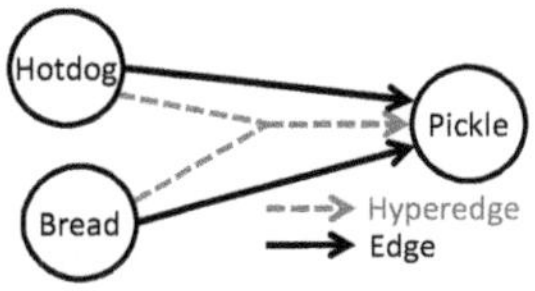

Figure 2: A hyperedge example

e.g., MIA[7] and TIM+[24]. However, without considering the existence of item inference, those algorithms are not applicable to SIMP. Besides the IC and LT model, Markov random field has been used to model social influence and calculate expected profits from viral marketing [9]. Recently, Tang et al. propose a Markov model based on "confluence", which estimates the total influence by combining different sources of conformity [23]. However, these studies only consider the diffusion of a *single* item in business applications. Instead, we incorporate item inference in spread maximization to estimate the influence more accurately.

3. SOCIAL ITEM GRAPH MODEL

Here we first present the social item graph model and then introduce the diffusion process in the proposed model.

3.1 Social Item Graph

We aim to model user purchases and potential activations of new purchase actions from some prior. We first define the notions of the social network and purchase actions.

DEFINITION 1. *A social network is denoted by a directed graph $G = (V, E)$ where V contains all the nodes and E contains all the directed edges in the graph. Accordingly, a social network is also referred to as a* social graph.

DEFINITION 2. *Given a list of commodity items I and a set of customers V, a purchase action (or purchase for short), denoted by (v, i) where $v \in V$ is a customer, and $i \in I$ is an item, refers to the purchase of item i by customer v.*

DEFINITION 3. *A purchase log is a database consisting of all the purchase actions in a given period of time.*

Association-rule mining (called item inference in this paper) has been widely exploited to discover correlations between purchases in transactions. For example, the rule $\{\text{hotdog}, \text{bread}\} \rightarrow \{\text{pickle}\}$ obtained from the transactions of a supermarket indicates that if a customer buys hotdogs and bread together, she is likely to buy pickles. To model the above likelihood, the confidence of a rule $\{\text{hotdog}, \text{bread}\} \rightarrow \{\text{pickle}\}$ is the proportion of the transactions with hotdogs and bread to those also including pickles [12]. It has been regarded as the conditional probability that a customer buying *both* hotdogs *and* bread would trigger the additional purchase of pickles. To model the above rule in a graph, a possible way is to use two separate *edges* (see Figure 2; one from hotdog to pickle, and the other from bread to pickle, respectively), while the probability associated with each of these edges is the confidence of the rule. In the above graph model, however, *either one* of the hotdog or bread may trigger the purchase of pickle. This does not accurately express the intended condition of purchasing *both* the hotdog *and* bread. By contrast, the *hyperedges* in Graph Theory, by spanning multiple source nodes and one destination node, can model the above association rule (as illustrated in Figure 2). The probability associated with the hyperedge represents the likelihood of the purchase action denoted by the destination node when *all* purchase actions denoted by source nodes have happened.

On the other hand, in viral marketing, the traditional IC model activates a new node by the social influence probabilities associated with edges to the node. Aiming to capture both effects of item inference and social influence, we propose a new *Social Item Graph* (SIG). SIG models the likelihood for a purchase (or a set of purchases) to trigger another purchase in the form of *hyperedges*, which may have one or multiple source nodes leading to one destination node. We define a social item graph as follows.

DEFINITION 4. *Given a social graph of customers $G = (V, E)$ and a commodity item list I, a social item graph is denoted by $G_{SI} = (V_{SI}, E_H)$, where V_{SI} is a set of purchase actions and E_H is a set of hyperedges over V_{SI}. A node $n \in V_{SI}$ is denoted as (v, i), where $v \in V$ and $i \in I$. A hyperedge $e \in E_H$ is of the following form:*

$$\{(u_1, i_1), (u_2, i_2), \cdots, (u_m, i_m)\} \rightarrow (v, i)$$

where u_i is in the neighborhood of v in G, i.e., $u_i \in N_G(v) = \{u | d(u, v) \leq 1\}$.[6]

Note that the conventional social influence edge in a social graph with one source and one destination can still be modeled in an SIG as a simple edge associated with a corresponding influence probability. Nevertheless, the influence probability from a person to another can vary for different items (e.g., a person's influence on another person for cosmetics and smartphones may vary.). Moreover, although an SIG may model the purchases more accurately with the help of *both* social influence and item inference, the complexity of processing an SIG with hyperedges is much higher than simple edges in the traditional social graph that denote only social influence.

For simplicity, let $\mathtt{u}$ and $\mathtt{v}$ (i.e., the symbols in Typewriter style) represent the nodes (u, i) and (v, i) in SIG for the rest of this paper. We also denote a hyperedge as $e \equiv \mathtt{U} \rightarrow \mathtt{v}$, where $\mathtt{U}$ is a set of source nodes and $\mathtt{v}$ is the destination node. Let the associated edge weight be p_e, which represents the *activation probability* for $\mathtt{v}$ to be activated if all source nodes in $\mathtt{U}$ are activated. Note that the activation probability is for one single hyperedge $\mathtt{U} \rightarrow \mathtt{v}$. Other hyperedges sharing the same destination may have different activation probabilities. For example, part of the source nodes in a hyperedge $\{\mathtt{a}, \mathtt{b}, \mathtt{c}, \mathtt{d}\} \rightarrow \mathtt{x}$ can still activate $\mathtt{x}$, e.g., by $\{\mathtt{a}, \mathtt{b}, \mathtt{c}\} \rightarrow \mathtt{x}$ with a different hyperedge with its own activation probability.

3.2 Diffusion Process in Social Item Graph

Next, we introduce the diffusion process in SIG, which is inspired by the probability-based approach behind *Independent Cascade* (IC) to capture the word-of-mouth behavior in the real world [7].[7] This diffusion process fits the item inferences captured in an SIG naturally, as we can derive conditional probabilities on hyperedges to describe the trigger (activation) of purchase actions on a potential purchase.

The diffusion process in SIG starts with all nodes inactive initially. Let $\mathtt{S}$ denote a set of seeds (purchase actions). Let a node $\mathtt{s} \in \mathtt{S}$ be a seed. It immediately becomes active. Given all the nodes in a source set $\mathtt{U}$ at iteration $\iota - 1$, if they are all active at iteration ι, a hyperedge $e \equiv \mathtt{U} \rightarrow \mathtt{v}$ has a chance to activate the inactive $\mathtt{v}$ with probability p_e. Each

[6] Notice that when $u_1 = u_2 = \cdots = u_m = v$, the hyperedge represents the item inference of item i. On the other hand, when $i_1 = i_2 = \cdots = i_m = i$, it becomes the social influence of user u on v.

[7] Several variants of IC model have been proposed [5, 6]. However, they focus on modeling the diffusion process between users, such as aspect awareness [6], which is not suitable for social item graph since the topic is embedded in each SIG node.

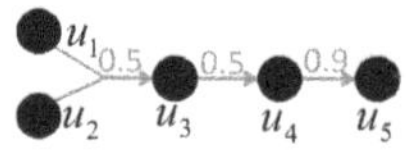

Figure 3: A non-submodular example

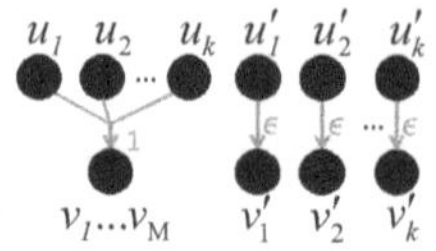

Figure 4: An example of SIMP

(a) Original (b) Transformed

Figure 5: An illustration of graph transformations

node (v, i) can be activated once, but it can try to activate other nodes multiple times, one for each incident hyperedges. For the seed selection problem that we target on, the total number of activated nodes represents the number of items adopted by customers (called *total adoptions* for the rest of this paper).

4. SOCIAL ITEM MAXIMIZATION

Upon the proposed Social Item Graph (SIG), we now formulate a new seed selection problem, called *Social Item Maximization Problem* (SIMP), that selects a set of seed purchase actions to maximize potential sales or revenue in a marketing campaign. In Section 5, we will describe how to construct the SIG from purchase logs by a machine learning approach.

DEFINITION 5. *Given a seed number k, a list of targeted items I, and a social item graph $G_{SI}(V_{SI}, E_H)$, SIMP selects a set $\mathtt{S}$ of k seeds in V_{SI} such that $\alpha_{G_{SI}}(\mathtt{S})$,* **the total adoption *function* of** $\mathtt{S}$, *is maximized.*

Note that a seed in SIG represents the adoption/purchase action of a specific item by a particular customer. The total adoption function $\alpha_{G_{SI}}$ represents the total number of product items ($\in I$) purchased. By assigning prices to products and costs to the selected seeds, an extension of SIMP is to maximize the total revenue subtracted by the cost.

Here we first discuss the challenges in solving SIMP before introducing our algorithm. Note that, for the influence maximization problem based on the IC model, Kempe et al. propose a $1 - 1/e$ approximation algorithm [17], thanks to the submodularity in the problem. Unfortunately, the submodularity does not hold for the total adoption function $\alpha_{G_{SI}}(\mathtt{S})$ in SIMP. Specifically, if the function $\alpha_{G_{SI}}(\mathtt{S})$ satisfies the submodularity, for any node $\mathtt{i}$ and any two subsets of nodes $\mathtt{S}_1$ and $\mathtt{S}_2$ where $\mathtt{S}_1 \subseteq \mathtt{S}_2$, $\alpha_{G_{SI}}(\mathtt{S}_1 \bigcup \{\mathtt{i}\}) - \alpha_{G_{SI}}(\mathtt{S}_1) \geq \alpha_{G_{SI}}(\mathtt{S}_2 \bigcup \{\mathtt{i}\}) - \alpha_{G_{SI}}(\mathtt{S}_2)$ should hold. However, a counter example is illustrated below.

EXAMPLE 1. *Consider an SIMP instance with a customer and five items in Figure 3. Consider the case where $S_1 = \{u_4\}$, $S_2 = \{u_1, u_4\}$, and i corresponds to node u_2. For seed sets $\{u_4\}$, $\{u_2, u_4\}$, $\{u_1, u_4\}$ and $\{u_1, u_2, u_4\}$, $\alpha_{G_{SI}}(\{u_4\}) = 1.9$, $\alpha_{G_{SI}}(\{u_2, u_4\}) = 2.9$, $\alpha_{G_{SI}}(\{u_1, u_4\}) = 2.9$, and $\alpha_{G_{SI}}(\{u_1, u_2, u_4\}) = 4.4$. Thus, $\alpha_{G_{SI}}(S_1 \bigcup \{u_2\}) - \alpha_{G_{SI}}(S_1) = 1 < 1.5 = \alpha_{G_{SI}}(S_2 \bigcup \{u_2\}) - \alpha_{G_{SI}}(S_2)$. Hence, the submodularity does not hold.*

Since the submodularity does not exist in SIMP, the $1 - 1/e$ approximation ratio of the greedy algorithm in [17] does not hold. Now, an interesting question is how large the ratio becomes. Example 2 shows an SIMP instance where the greedy algorithm performs poorly.

EXAMPLE 2. *Consider an example in Figure 4, where nodes v_1, v_2,...,v_M all have a hyperedge with the probability as 1 from the same k sources u_1, u_2,..., u_k, and ϵ is an arbitrarily small edge probability $\epsilon > 0$. The greedy algorithm selects one node in each iteration, i.e., it selects u'_1, u'_2...u'_k as the seeds with a total adoption $k + k\epsilon$. However, the optimal solution actually selects u_1, u_2,..., u_k as the seeds and results in the total adoption $M + k$. Therefore, the approximation ratio of the greedy algorithm is at least $(M+k)/(k+k\epsilon)$, which is close to M/k for a large M, where M could approach $|V_{SI}|$ in the worst case.*

One may argue that the above challenges in SIMP may be alleviated by transforming G_{SI} into a graph with only simple edges, as displayed in Figure 5, where the weight of every $\mathtt{u}_i \rightarrow \mathtt{v}$) with $\mathtt{u}_i \in \mathtt{U}$ can be set independently. However, if a source node $\mathtt{u}_m \in \mathtt{U}$ of $\mathtt{v}$ is difficult to activate, the probability for $\mathtt{v}$ to be activated approaches zero in Figure 5 (a) due to $\mathtt{u}_m$. However, in Figure 5 (b), the destination $\mathtt{v}$ is inclined to be activated by sources in $\mathtt{U}$, especially when $\mathtt{U}$ is sufficiently large. Thus, the idea of graph transformation does not work.

4.1 Hyperedge-Aware Greedy (HAG)

Here, we propose an algorithm for SIMP, *Hyperedge-Aware Greedy (HAG)*, with performance guarantee. The approximation ratio is proved in Section 4.3. A hyperedge requires all its sources activated first in order to activate the destination. Conventional single node greedy algorithms perform poorly because hyperedges are not considered. To address this important issue, we propose *Hyperedge-Aware Greedy (HAG)* to select multiple seeds in each iteration.

A naive algorithm for SIMP would examine $C_k^{|V_{SI}|}$ combinations to choose k seeds. In this paper, as all source nodes of a hyperedge need to be activated in order to activate its destination, an effective way is to consider only the combinations which include the source nodes of any hyperedge. We call the source nodes of a hyperedge as a *source combination*. Based on this idea, in each iteration, HAG includes the source combination leading to *the largest increment on total adoption divided by the number of new seeds added in this iteration*. Note that only the source combinations with no more than k sources are considered. The iteration continues until k seeds are selected. Note that HAG does not restrict the seeds to be the source nodes of hyperedges. Instead, the source node $\mathtt{u}$ of any simple edge $\mathtt{u} \rightarrow \mathtt{v}$ in SIG is also examined.

Complexity of HAG. To select k seeds, HAG takes at most k rounds. In each round, the source combinations of $|E_H|$ hyperedges are tried one by one, and the diffusion cost is c_{dif}, which will be analyzed in Section 4.2. Thus, the time complexity of HAG is $O(k \times |E_H| \times c_{dif})$.

4.2 Acceleration of Diffusion Computation

To estimate the total adoption for a seed set, it is necessary to perform Monte Carlo simulation based on the diffusion process described in Section 3.2 for many times. Finding the total adoption is very expensive, especially when a node $\mathtt{v}$ can be activated by a hyperedge with a large source set $\mathtt{U}$, which indicates that there also exist many other hyperedges with an arbitrary subset of $\mathtt{U}$ as the source set to activate $\mathtt{v}$. In other words, enormous hyperedges need to be examined for the diffusion on an SIG. It is essential to reduce the computational overhead. To address this issue, we propose a new index structure, called *SIG-index*, by exploiting FP-Tree [12] to pre-process source combinations in hyper-

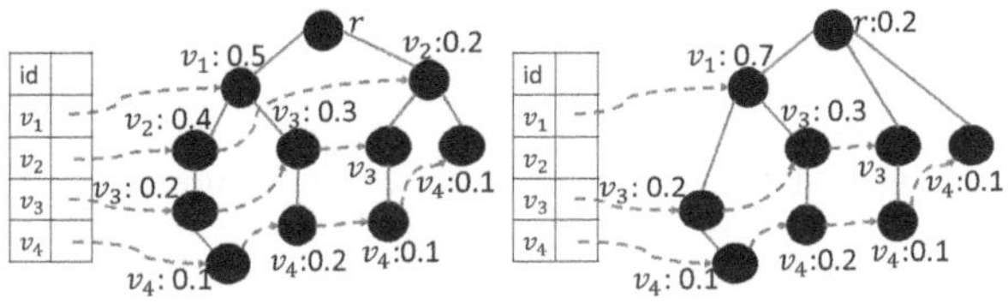

(a) Initial (b) After v_2 is activated

Figure 6: An illustration of SIG-index

edges in a compact form in order to facilitate efficient derivation of activation probabilities during the diffusion process.

The basic idea behind SIG-index is as follows. For each node v with the set of activated in-neighbors $N^a_{v,\iota}$ in iteration ι, if v has not been activated before ι, the diffusion process will try to activate v via every hyperedge $U \to v$ where the last source in U has been activated in iteration $\iota-1$. To derive the activation probability of a node v from the weights of hyperedges associated with v, we first define the activation probability as follows.

DEFINITION 6. *The activation probability of* v *at* ι *is*

$$ap_{v,\iota} = 1 - \prod_{U \to v \in E_H, U \subseteq N_{v,\iota-1}, U \not\subseteq N_{v,\iota-2}} (1 - p_{U \to v}).$$

where $N_{v,\iota-1}$ *and* $N_{v,\iota-2}$ *denote the set of active neighbors of* v *in iteration* $\iota - 1$ *and* $\iota - 2$*, respectively.*

The operations on an SIG-index occur two phases: Index Creation Phase and Diffusion Processing Phase. As all hyperedges satisfying Definition 6 must be accessed, the SIG-index stores the hyperedge probabilities in Index Creation Phase. Later, the SIG-index is updated in Diffusion Processing Phase to derive the activation probability efficiently.

Index Creation Phase. For each hyperedge $U \to v$, we first regard each source combination $U = \{v_1, ... v_{|U|}\}$ as a transaction to build an FP-tree [12] by setting the minimum support as 1. As such, $v_1, ... v_{|U|}$ forms a path $r \to v_1 \to v_2 ... \to v_{|U|}$ from the root r in the FP-tree to node $v_{|U|}$ in U. Different from the FP-Tree, the SIG-index associates the probability of each hyperedge $U \to v$ with the last source node $v_{|U|}$ in U.[8] Initially, the probability associated with the root r is 0. Later the SIG-index is updated during the diffusion process. Example 3 illustrates the SIG-index created based on an SIG.

EXAMPLE 3. *Consider an SIG graph with five nodes,* v_1-v_5*, and nine hyperedges with their associated probabilities in parentheses:* $\{v_1\} \to v_5$ *(0.5),* $\{v_1, v_2\} \to v_5$ *(0.4),* $\{v_1, v_2, v_3\} \to v_5$ *(0.2),* $\{v_1, v_2, v_3, v_4\} \to v_5$ *(0.1),* $\{v_1, v_3\} \to v_5$ *(0.3),* $\{v_1, v_3, v_4\} \to v_5$ *(0.2),* $\{v_2\} \to v_5$ *(0.2),* $\{v_2, v_3, v_4\} \to v_5$ *(0.1),* $\{v_2, v_4\} \to v_5$ *(0.1). Figure 6 (a) shows the SIG-index initially created for node* v_5*.*

Diffusion Processing Phase. The activation probability in an iteration is derived by traversing the initial SIG-index, which takes $O(|E_H|)$ time. However, a simulation may iterate a lot of times. To further accelerate the traversing process, we adjust the SIG-index for the activated nodes in each iteration. More specifically, after a node v^a is activated, accessing an hyperedge $U \to v$ with $v^a \in U$ becomes easier since the number remaining inactivated nodes in $U - \{v^a\}$ is reduced. Accordingly, SIG-index is modified by traversing every vertex labeled as v^a on the SIG-index in the following steps. 1) If v^a is associated with a probability p_a, it is crucial to aggregate the old activation probabilities p_a of v^a and p_p of its parent v^p, and update activation probability associated with v^p as $1 - (1 - p_a)(1 - p_p)$, since the source combination needed for accessing the hyperedges associated with v^a and v^p becomes the same. The aggregation is also performed when v^p is r. 2) If v^a has any children c, the parent of c is changed to be v^p, which removes the processed v^a from the index. 3) After processing every node v^a in the SIG-index, we obtain the activation probability of v in the root r. After the probability is accessed for activating v, the probability of r is reset to 0 for next iteration.

EXAMPLE 4. *Consider an example with* v_2 *activated in an iteration. To update the SIG-index, each vertex* v_2 *in Figure 6 (a) is examined by traversing the linked list of* v_2*. First, the left vertex with label* v_2 *is examined. SIG-index reassigns the parent of* v_2*'s child (labeled as* v_3*) to the vertex labeled as* v_1*, and aggregate the probability 0.4 on the* v_2 *and 0.5 on vertex* v_1*, since the hyperedge* $\{v_1, v_2\} \to v_5$ *can be accessed if the node* v_1 *is activated later. The probability of* v_1 *becomes* $1-(1-p_{v_1})(1-p_{v_2}) = 0.7$*. Then the right vertex with label* v_2 *is examined. The parent of its two children is reassigned to the root* r*. Also, the probability of itself (0.2) is aggregated with the root* r*, indicating that the activation probability of node* v_5 *in the next iteration is 0.2.*

Complexity Analysis. For Index Creation Phase, the initial SIG-index for v is built by examining the hyperedges two times with $O(|E_H|)$ time. The number of vertices in SIG-index is at most $O(c_d|E_H|)$, where c_d is the number of source nodes in the largest hyperedge. During Diffusion Processing Phase, each vertex in SIG-index is examined only once through the node-links, and the parent of a vertex is changed at most $O(c_d)$ times. Thus, the overall time to complete a diffusion requires at most $O(c_d|E_H|)$ time.

4.3 Hardness Results

From the discussion earlier, it becomes obvious that SIMP is difficult. In the following, we will prove that SIMP is inapproximable with a non-constant ratio n^c for all $c < 1$, with a gap-introducing reduction from an NP-complete problem 3-SAT to SIMP, where n is the number of nodes in an SIG. Note that the theoretical result only shows that for any algorithm, there exists a problem instance of SIMP (i.e., a pair of an SIG graph and a seed number k) that the algorithm can not obtain a solution better than $1/n$ times the optimal solution. It does not imply that an algorithm always performs badly in every SIMP instance. Later in Section 6.3, we empirically show that the total adoption obtained by HAG is comparable to the optimal solution.

LEMMA 1. *For a positive integer* q*, there is a gap-introducing reduction from 3-SAT to SIMP, which transforms an* n_{var}*-variables expression* ϕ *to an SIMP instance with the SIG as* $G_{SI}(V_{SI}, E_H)$ *and the* k *as* n_{var} *such that*

- *if* ϕ *is satisfiable,* $\alpha^*_{G_{SI}} \geq (m_{cla} + 3n_{var})^q$*, and*
- *if* ϕ *is not satisfiable,* $\alpha^*_{G_{SI}} < m_{cla} + 3n_{var}$*,*

where $\alpha^*_{G_{SI}}$ *is the optimal solution of this instance,* n_{var} *is the number of Boolean variables, and* m_{cla} *is the number of clauses. Hence there is no* $(m_{cla}+3n_{var})^{q-1}$ *approximation algorithm for SIMP unless* $P = NP$*.*

PROOF. Given a positive integer q, for an instance ϕ of 3-SAT with n_{var} Boolean variables $a_1, \ldots, a_{n_{var}}$ and m_{cla} clauses $C_1, \ldots, C_{m_{cla}}$, we construct an SIG G_{SI} with three node sets X, Y and Z as follows. 1) Each Boolean variable a_i corresponds to two nodes x_i, $\bar{x}_i$ in X and one node y_i in Y. 2) Each clause C_k corresponds to one node c_k in Y. 3) Z has $(|X| + |Y|)^q$ nodes. (Thus, G_{SI} has $(m_{cla} + 3n_{var})^q +$

[8] For ease of explanation, we assume the order of nodes in the SIG-index follows the ascending order of subscript.

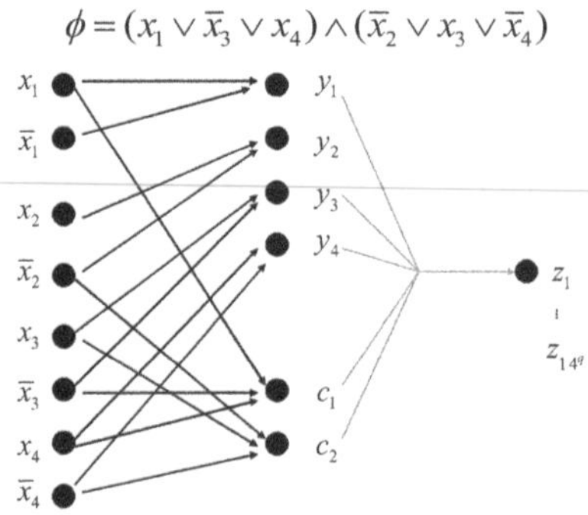

Figure 7: An illustration instance built for 3-SAT

$m_{cla} + 3n_{var}$ nodes.) 4) For each $\mathtt{y}_j$ in Y, we add direct edges $\mathtt{x}_j \rightarrow \mathtt{y}_j$ and $\bar{\mathtt{x}}_j \rightarrow \mathtt{y}_j$. 5) For each $\mathtt{c}_k$ in Y, we add direct edges $\alpha \rightarrow \mathtt{c}_k$, $\beta \rightarrow \mathtt{c}_k$ and $\gamma \rightarrow \mathtt{c}_k$, where α, β, γ are the nodes in X corresponding to the three literals in C_k. 6) We add a hyperedge $\mathtt{Y} \rightarrow \mathtt{z}_v$ from all for every $\mathtt{z}_v \in \mathtt{Z}$. The probability of every edge is set to 1. An example is illustrated in Figure 7.

We first prove that ϕ is satisfiable if and only if G_{SI} has a seed set S with n_{var} seeds and the total adoption of S contains Y. If ϕ is satisfiable, there exists a truth assignment T on Boolean variables $a_1, \ldots, a_{n_{var}}$ satisfying all clauses of ϕ. Let $\mathtt{S} = \{\mathtt{x}_i | T(a_i) = 1\} \cup \{\bar{\mathtt{x}}_j | T(a_j) = 0\}$, and S then has n_{var} nodes and the total adoption of S contains Y. On the other hand, if ϕ is not satisfiable, apparently there exists no seed set S with exactly one of $\mathtt{x}_i$ or $\bar{\mathtt{x}}_i$ selected for every i such that the total adoption of S contains Y. For other cases, 1) all seeds are placed in X, but there exists at least one i with both $\mathtt{x}_i$ and $\bar{\mathtt{x}}_i$ selected. In this case, there must exist some j such that none of $\mathtt{x}_j$ or $\bar{\mathtt{x}}_j$ are selcted (since the seed number is n_{var}), and thus Y is not covered by the total adoption of S. 2) A seed is placed in Y. In this case, the seed can be moved to an adjacent $\mathtt{x}_i$ without reducing the total adoption. Nevertheless, as explained above, there exists no seed set S with all seeds placed in X such that the total adoption of S contains Y, and thus the total adoption of any seed set with a seed placed in Y cannot cover Y, either. With above observations, if ϕ is not satisfiable, G_{SI} does not have a seed set S with n_{var} seeds such that the total adoption of S contains Y. Since the nodes of Z can be activated if and only if the total adoption of S contains Y if and only if ϕ is satisfiable, we have

- if ϕ is satisfiable, $\alpha^*_{G_{SI}} \geq (m_{cla} + 3n_{var})^q$, and
- if ϕ is not satisfiable, $\alpha^*_{G_{SI}} < m_{cla} + 3n_{var}$.

The lemma follows. □

THEOREM 1. *For any $\epsilon > 0$, there is no $n^{1-\epsilon}$ approximation algorithm for SIMP, assuming $P \neq NP$.*

PROOF. For any arbitrary $\epsilon > 0$, we set $q \geq \frac{2}{\epsilon}$. Then, by Lemma 1, there is no $(m_{cla}+3n_{var})^{q-1}$ approximation algorithm for SIMP unless P = NP. Then $(m_{cla} + 3n_{var})^{q-1} \geq 2(m_{cla} + 3n_{var})^{q-2} \geq 2(m_{cla} + 3n_{var})^{q(1-\epsilon)} \geq (2(m_{cla} + 3n_{var})^q)^{1-\epsilon} \geq n^{1-\epsilon}$. Since ϵ is arbitrarily small, thus for any $\epsilon > 0$, there is no $n^{1-\epsilon}$ approximation algorithm for SIMP, assuming P $\neq$ NP. The theorem follows. □

THEOREM 2. *HAG with SIG-index is n-approximated, where n is the number of nodes in SIG.*

PROOF. First, we prove that SIG-index obtains $ap_{\mathtt{v},\iota}$ correctly. Assume that there exists an incorrect $ap_{\mathtt{v},\iota}$, i.e., there exists an hyperedge $\mathtt{U} \rightarrow \mathtt{v}$ satisfying the conditions in Definition 6 (i.e., $\mathtt{U} \not\subseteq N_{\mathtt{v},\iota-2}$ and $\mathtt{U} \subseteq N_{\mathtt{v},\iota-1}$) but its probability is not aggregated to r in ι. However, the probability can not be aggregated before ι since $\mathtt{U} \not\subseteq N_{v,\iota-2}$ and it must be aggregated no later than ι since $\mathtt{U} \subseteq N_{\mathtt{v},\iota-1}$. There is a contradiction.

Proving that HAG with SIG-index is an n-approximation algorithm is simple. The upper bound of total adoption for the optimal algorithm is n, while the lower bound of the total adoption for HAG is 1 because at least one seed is selected. In other words, designing an approximation algorithm for SIMP is simple, but it is much more difficult to have the hardness result for SIMP, and we have proven that SIMP is inapproximable within $n^{1-\epsilon}$ for any arbitrarily small ϵ. □

COROLLARY 1. *HAG with SIG-index is n-approximated, where n is the number of nodes in SIG, because SIG-index only improves the efficiency.*

5. CONSTRUCTION OF SIG

To select seeds for SIMP, we need to construct the SIG from purchase logs and the social network. We first create possible hyperedges by scanning the purchase logs. Let τ be the timestamp of a given purchase $\mathtt{v} = (v, i)$. v's friends purchase and her own purchases that have happened within a given period before τ are considered as candidate source nodes to generate hyperedges to v. For each hyperedge e, the main task is then the estimation of its activation probability p_e. Since p_e is unknown, it is estimated by maximizing the likelihood function based on observations in the purchase logs. Note that learning the activation probability p_e for each hyperedge e faces three challenges.

C1. Unknown distribution of p_e. How to properly model p_e is critical.

C2. Unobserved activations. When v is activated at time τ, this event only implies that at least one hyperedge successfully activates v before τ. It remains unknown which hyperedge(s) actually triggers v, i.e., it may be caused by either the item inference or social influence or both. Therefore, we cannot simply employ the confidence of an association-rule as the corresponding hyperedge probability.

C3. Data sparsity. The number of activations for a user to buy an item is small, whereas the number of possible hyperedge combinations is large. Moreover, new items emerge every day in e-commerce websites, which incurs the notorious cold-start problem. Hence, a method to deal with the data sparsity issue is necessary to properly model an SIG.

To address these challenges, we exploit a statistical inference approach to identify those hyperedges and learn their weights. In the following, we first propose a model of the edge function (to address the first challenge) and then exploit the smoothed expectation and maximization (EMS) algorithm [21] to address the second and third challenges.

5.1 Modeling of Hyperedge Probability

To overcome the first challenge, one possible way is to model the number of success activations and the number of unsuccessful activations by the binomial distributions. As such, p_e is approximated by the ratio of the number of success activations and the number of total activation trials. However, the binomial distribution function is too complex for computing the maximum likelihood of a vast number of data. To handle big data, the previous study reported [14] that the binomial distribution (n, p) can be approximated by the Poisson distribution $\lambda = np$ when the time duration is sufficiently large. According to the above study, it is assumed that the number of activations of a hyperedge e follows the Poisson distribution to handle the social influence and item inference jointly. The expected number of events equals to the intensity parameter λ. Moreover, we use an inhomogeneous Poisson process defined on the space of hyperedges to ensure that p_e varies with different e.

In the following, a hyperedge is of size n, if the cardinality of its source set $\mathtt{U}$ is n. We denote the intensity of the number of activation trials of the hyperedge e as $\lambda_T(e)$. Then the successful activations of hyperedge e follows another Poisson process where the intensity is denoted by $\lambda_A(e)$. Therefore, the hyperedge probability p_e can be derived by parameters $\lambda_A(e)$ and $\lambda_T(e)$, i.e., $p_e = \frac{\lambda_A(e)}{\lambda_T(e)}$.

The maximum likelihood estimation can be employed to derive $\lambda_T(e)$. Nevertheless, $\lambda_A(e)$ cannot be derived as explained in the second challenge. Therefore, we use the expectation maximization (EM) algorithm, which is an extension of maximum likelihood estimation containing latent variables to $\lambda_A(e)$ which is modeled as the latent variable. Based on the observed purchase logs, the E-step first derives the likelihood Q-function of the parameter p_e with $\lambda_A(e)$ as the latent variables. In this step, the purchase logs and p_e are given to find the probability function describing that all events on e in the logs occur according to p_e, whereas the probability function (i.e., Q-function) explores different possible values on latent variable $\lambda_A(e)$. Afterward, The M-step maximizes the Q-function and derives the new p_e for E-Step in the next iteration. These two steps are iterated until convergence.

With the employed Poisson distribution and EM algorithm, data sparsity remains an issue. Therefore, we further exploit a variant of EM algorithm, called *EMS algorithm* [21], to alleviate the sparsity problem by estimating the intensity of Poisson process using *similar hyperedges*. The parameter smoothing after each iteration is called S-Step, which is incorporated in EMS algorithm, in addition to the existing E-Step and M-Step.

5.2 Model Learning by EMS Algorithm

Let p_e and $\hat{p}_e$ denote the true probability and estimated probabilities for hyperedge e in the EMS algorithm, respectively, where $e = U \to v$. Let N_U and K_e denote the number of activations of source set U in the purchase logs and the number of successful activations on hyperedge e, respectively. The EM algorithm is exploited to find the maximum likelihood of p_e, while $\lambda_A(e)$ is the latent variable because K_e cannot be observed (i.e., only N_U can be observed). Therefore, E-Step derives the likelihood function for $\{p_e\}$ (i.e., the Q-function) as follows,

$$Q(p_e, \hat{p}_e^{(i-1)}) = E_{K_e}[\log P(K_e, N_U|p_e)|N_U, \hat{p}_e^{(i-1)}], \quad (1)$$

where $\hat{p}_e^{(i-1)}$ is the hyperedge probability derived in the previous iteration. Note that N_U and $p_e^{(i-1)}$ are given parameters in iteration i, whereas p_e is a variable in the Q-function, and K_e is a random variable governed by the distribution $P(K_e|N_U, p_e^{(i-1)})$. Since p_e is correlated to $\lambda_T(U)$ and $\lambda_A(e)$, we derive the likelihood $P(K_e, N_U|p_e)$ as follows.

$$\begin{aligned} & P(K_e, N_U|p_e) \\ = & P(\{K_e\}_{e\in E_H}, \{N_U\}_{U\subseteq V_{SI}}|\{p_e\}_{e\in E_H}, \{\lambda_T(U)\}_{U\subseteq V_{SI}}) \\ = & P(\{K_e\}_{e\in E_H}|\{p_e\}_{e\in E_H}, \{N_U, \lambda_T(U)\}_{U\subseteq V_{SI}}) \\ & \times P(\{N_U\}_{U\subseteq V_{SI}}|\{\lambda_T(U)\}_{U\subseteq V_{SI}}). \end{aligned}$$

It is assumed that $\{K_e\}$ is independent with $\{N_U\}$, and $Q(p_e, \hat{p}_e^{(i-1)})$ can be derived as follows:

$$\sum_{e\in E_H} \log P(K_e|N_U, p_e) + \log P(\{N_U\}_{U\subseteq V_{SI}}|\{\lambda_T(e)\}_{U\subseteq V_{SI}}).$$

Since only the first term contains the hidden K_e, only this term varies in different iterations of the EMS algorithm, because $\{N_U\}_{U\subseteq V_{SI}}$ in the second term always can be derived by finding the maximum likelihood as follows. Let $p_{U,k}$ denote the probability that the source set U exactly tries to activate the destination node k times, i.e., $p_{U,k} = P\{N_U = k\}$. The log-likelihood of λ_T is

$$\begin{aligned} & \sum_k p_{U,k} \ln(\frac{\lambda_T^k e^{-\lambda_T}}{k!}) = \sum_k p_{U,k}(-\lambda_T + k\ln\lambda_T - \ln k!) \\ = & -\lambda_T + (\ln\lambda_T)\sum_k kp_{U,k} - \sum_k p_{U,k}\ln k!. \end{aligned}$$

We acquire the maximum likelihood by finding the derivative with regard to λ_T:

$$-1 + \frac{1}{\lambda_T}\sum_k kp_{U,k} = 0. \quad (2)$$

Thus, the maximum log-likelihood estimation of $\lambda_T = \sum_k kp_{U,k}$, representing that the expected activation times (i.e., $\hat{\lambda}_T(e)$) is N_U. Let $\mathcal{A} = \{(\mathtt{v}, \tau)\}$ denote the action log set, where each log $(\mathtt{v}, \tau)$ represents that $\mathtt{v}$ is activated at time τ. N_U is calculated by scanning $\mathcal{A}$ and find the times that all the nodes in $\mathtt{U}$ are activated.

Afterward, we focus on the first term of $Q(p_e, \hat{p}_e^{(i-1)})$. Let $p_{e,k} = P\{K_e = k\}$ denote the probability that the hyperedge e exactly activates the destination node k times. In E-step, we first find the expectation for K_e as follows.

$$\begin{aligned} & \sum_{e\in E_H}\sum_{k=1,\cdots,N_U} p_{e,k}\log(k|N_U, p_e) \\ = & \sum_{k=1,\cdots,N_U} p_{e,k}\log P(k|N_U, p_e) \\ = & \sum_{k=1,\cdots,N_U} p_{e,k}\log(\binom{N_U}{k}{p_e}^k(1-p_e)^{N_U-k}) \\ = & \sum_{k=1,\cdots,N_U} p_{e,k}\left(\log\binom{N_U}{k} + k\log p_e + (N_U - k)\log(1-p_e)\right). \end{aligned}$$

Since $\sum_{k=1,\cdots,N_U} p_{e,k}k = E[K_e]$ and $\sum_{k=1,\cdots,N_U} p_{e,k} = 1$, the log-likelihood of the first term is further simplified as

$$\sum_{k=1,\cdots,N_U} p_{e,k}\log\binom{N_U}{k} + N_U\log(1-p_e) + E[K_e](\log p_e - \log(1-p_e)).$$

Afterward, M-step maximizes the Q-function by finding the derivative with regard to p_e:

$$\begin{aligned} & \frac{-N_U}{1-p_e} + E[K_e](\frac{1}{p_e} + \frac{1}{1-p_e}) = 0 \\ & p_e = E[K_e]/N_U \end{aligned}$$

Therefore, the maximum likelihood estimator $\hat{p}_e$ is $\frac{E[K_e]}{N_U}$, $\hat{\lambda}_T(U)$ is N_U, and $\hat{\lambda}_A(e) = E[K_e]$.

The problem remaining is to take expectation of the latent variables $\{K_e\}$ in E-step. Let $\{w_{e,a}\}_{e\in E_H, a=(\mathtt{v},\tau)\in\mathcal{A}}$ be the conditional probability that $\mathtt{v}$ is activated by the source set U of e at τ given $\mathtt{v}$ is activated at τ, and let E_a denote the set of candidate hyperedges containing every possible e with its source set activated at time $\tau - 1$, i.e., $E_a = \{(\mathtt{u}_1, \mathtt{u}_2, \cdots, \mathtt{u}_n) \to \mathtt{v}_i | \forall i = 1, \cdots, n, \mathtt{u}_i \in N(\mathtt{v}_i), (\mathtt{u}_i, \tau-1) \in \mathcal{A}\}$. It's easy to show that given the estimation of the probability of hyperedges, $w_{e,a} = \frac{\hat{p}_e}{1-\prod_{e'\in E_a}(1-\hat{p}_{e'})}$, since $1 - \prod_{e\in E_a}(1 - \hat{p}_{e'})$ is the probability for $\mathtt{v}$ to be activated by any hyperedge at time τ. The expectation of

K_e is $\sum_{a \in A, e \in E_a \cap E_{H,n}} w_{e,a}$, i.e., the sum of expectation of each successful activation of v from hyperedge e, and $E_{H,n} = \{(\mathtt{u}_1, \mathtt{u}_2, \cdots, \mathtt{u}_n; v) \in E_H\}$ contains all size n hyperedges.

To address the data sparsity problem, we leverage information from similar hyperedges (described later). Therefore, our framework includes an additional step to smooth the results of M-Step. Kernel smoothing is employed in S-Step. In summary, we have the following steps:

E-Step:

$$E[K_e] = \sum_{a \in A, e \in E_a \cap E_{H,n}} w_{e,a},$$

$$w_{e,a} = \frac{\hat{p}_e}{1 - \prod_{e' \in E_a} (1 - \hat{p}_{e'})}.$$

M-Step:

$$p_e = \frac{\sum_{a \in A, e \in E_a \cap E_{H,n}} w_{e,a}}{N_U},$$

$$\lambda_A(e) = \sum_{a \in A, e \in E_a \cap E_{H,n}} w_{e,a},$$

$$\lambda_T(U) = N_U.$$

S-Step: To address the data sparsity problem, we leverage information from similar hyperedges (described later). Therefore, in addition to E-Step and M-Step, EMS includes **S-Step**, which smooths the results of M-Step. Kernel smoothing is employed in S-Step as follows:

$$\hat{\lambda}_A(e) = \sum_{a \in A, e' \in E_a \cap E_{H,n}} w_{e',a} L_h(F(e) - F(e'))$$

$$\hat{\lambda}_T(U) = \sum_{U \subseteq V_{SI}} N_U L_h(F(U) - F(U'))$$

where L_h is a kernel function with bandwidth h, and F is the mapping function of hyperedges, i.e., $F(e)$ maps a hyperedge e to a vector. The details of dimension reduction for calculating F to efficiently map hyperedges into Euclidean space are shown in [2] due to space constraint. If the hyperedges e and e' are similar, the distance of the vectors $F(e)$ and $F(e')$ is small. Moreover, a kernel function $L_h(x)$ is a positive function symmetric at zero which decreases when $|x|$ increases, and the bandwidth h controls the extent of auxiliary information taken from similar hyperedges.[9] Intuitively, kernel smoothing can identify the correlation of $\hat{p}_{e_1}$ with $e_1 = \mathtt{U}_1 \to \mathtt{v}_1$ and $\hat{p}_{e_2}$ with $e_2 = \mathtt{U}_2 \to \mathtt{v}_2$ for nearby $\mathtt{v}_1$ and $\mathtt{v}_2$ and similar $\mathtt{U}_1$ and $\mathtt{U}_2$.

6. EVALUATION

We conduct comprehensive experiments to evaluate the proposed SIG model, learning framework and seed selection algorithms. In Section 6.1, we discuss the data preparation for our evaluation. In Section 6.2, we compare the predictive power of the SIG model against two baseline models: i) independent cascade model learned by implementing Variance Regularized EM Algorithm (VAREM) [18] and ii) the generalized threshold (GT) model learned by [11].[10] In addition, we evaluate the learning framework based on the proposed EM and EMS algorithms. Next, in Section 6.3, we evaluate the proposed HAG algorithm for SIMP in comparison to a number of baseline strategies, including random, single node selection, social, and item approaches. Finally, in Section 6.4, we evaluate alternative approaches for diffusion processing, which is essential and critical for HAG, based on SIG-index, Monte Carlo simulations and sorting enhancement.

6.1 Data Preparation

Here, we conduct comprehensive experiments using three real datasets to evaluate the proposed ideas and algorithms. The first dataset comes from Douban [1], a social networking website allowing users to share music and books with friends. Dataset *Douban* contains 5,520,243 users and 86,343,003 friendship links, together with 7,545,432 (user, music) and 14,050,265 (user, bookmark) pairs, representing the music noted and the bookmarks noted by each user, respectively. We treat those (user, music) and (user, bookmark) pairs as purchase actions. In addition to *Douban*, we adopt two public datasets, i.e., *Gowalla* and *Epinions*. Dataset *Gowalla* contains 196,591 users, 950,327 links, and 6,442,890 check-ins [8]. Dataset *Epinions* contains 22,166 users, 335,813 links, 27 categories of items, and 922,267 ratings with timestamp [22]. Notice that we do not have data directly reflecting item inferences in online stores, so we use the purchase logs for learning and evaluations. The experiments are implemented on an HP DL580 server with 4 Intel Xeon E7-4870 2.4 GHz CPUs and 1 TB RAM.

We split all three datasets into 5-fold, choose one subsample as training data, and test the models on the remaining subsamples. Specifically, we ignore the cases when the user and her friends did not buy anything. Finally, to evaluate the effectiveness of the proposed SIG model (and the learning approaches), we obtain the purchase actions in the following cases as the ground truth: 1) item inference - a user buys some items within a short period of time, and 2) social influence - a user buys an item after at least one of her friends bought the item. The considered periods of item inference and social influence are set differently according to [15] and [27], respectively. It is worth noting that only the hyperedges with the probability larger than a threshold parameter θ are considered. We empirically tune θ to obtain the default setting based on optimal F1-Score. Similarly, the threshold parameter θ for the GT model is obtained empirically. The reported precision, recall, and F1 are the average of these tests. Since both SIGs and the independent cascade model require successive data, we split the datasets into continuous subsamples.

6.2 Model Evaluation

Tables 1 present the precision, recall, and F1 of SIG, VAREM and GT on *Douban*, *Gowalla*, and *Epinions*. All three models predict most accurately on *Douban* due to the large sample size. The SIG model significantly outperforms the other two models on all three datasets, because it takes into account both effects of social influence and item inference, while the baseline models only consider the social influence. The difference of F1 score between SIG and baselines is more significant on *Douban*, because it contains more items. Thus, item influence plays a more important role. Also, when the user size increases, SIG is able to extract more social influence information leading to better performance than the baselines. The offline training time is 1.68, 1.28, and 4.05 hours on *Epinions*, *Gowalla*, *Douban*, respectively.

To evaluate the approaches adopted to learn the activation probabilities of hyperedges for construction of SIG, Fig. 8 compares the precision and F1 of EMS and EM algorithms on Epinions (results on other datasets are consistent and

[9] A symmetric Gaussian kernel function is often used [13].
[10] http://people.cs.ubc.ca/~welu/downloads.html

Table 1: Comparison of precision, recall, and F1 for three models on Douban, Gowalla, Epinions

Dataset	Douban			Gowalla			Epinions		
	Precision	Recall	F1-Score	Precision	Recall	F1-Score	Precision	Recall	F1-Score
GT	0.420916	0.683275	0.520927	0.124253	0.435963	0.171214	0.142565	0.403301	0.189999
VAREM	0.448542	0.838615	0.584473	0.217694	0.579401	0.323537	0.172924	0.799560	0.247951
SIG	0.869348	0.614971	0.761101	0.553444	0.746408	0.646652	0.510118	0.775194	0.594529

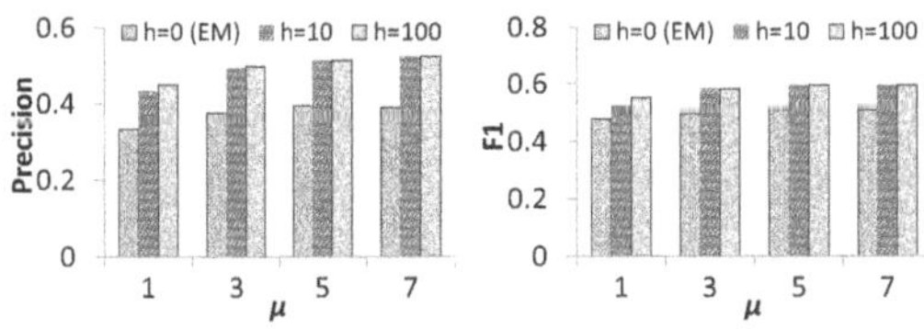

(a) Precision (b) F1-Score

Figure 8: Comparisons of precision and F1 in various μ and h on *Epinions*

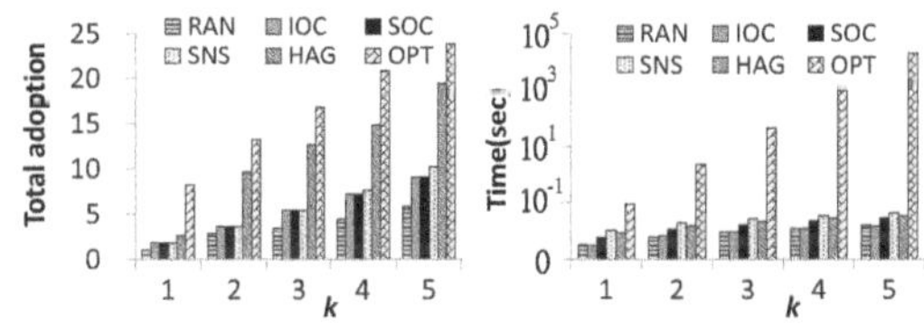

(a) *Sample* (b) Time

Figure 9: Total adopting and running time of *Sample* in various k

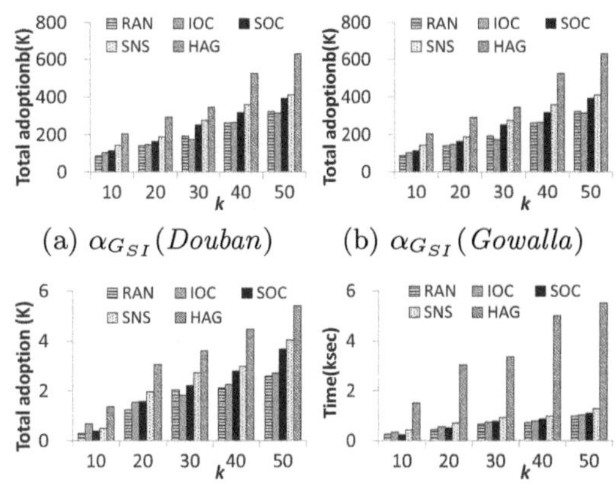

(a) $\alpha_{G_{SI}}$(*Douban*) (b) $\alpha_{G_{SI}}$(*Gowalla*)

(c) $\alpha_{G_{SI}}$(*Epinions*) (d) Time (*Douban*)

Figure 10: Total adoption $\alpha_{G_{SI}}$ and running time in various k

thus not shown due to space limitation). Note that EM is a special case of EMS (with the smoothing parameter $h = 0$, i.e., no similar hyperedge used for smoothing). EMS outperforms EM on both precision and F1-score in all settings of μ (the maximum size of hyperedges) and h tested. Moreover, the precision and F1-score both increases with h as a larger h overcomes data sparsity significantly. As μ increases, more combinations of social influence and item inference can be captured. Therefore, the experiments show that a higher μ improves F1-score without degrades the precision. It manifests that the learned hyperedges are effective for predicting triggered purchases.

6.3 Algorithm Effectiveness and Efficiency

We evaluate HAG proposed for SIMP, by selecting top 10 items as the marketing items to measure their total adoption, in comparison with a number of baselines: 1) *Random approach (RAN)*. It randomly selects k nodes as seeds. Note that the reported values are the average of 50 random seed sets. 2) *Single node selection approach (SNS)*. It selects a node with the largest increment of the total adoption in each iteration, until k seeds are selected, which is widely employed in conventional seed selection problem [6, 7, 17]. 3) *Social approach (SOC)*. It only considers the social influence in selecting the k seeds. The hyperedges with nodes from different products are eliminated in the seed selection process, but they are restored for calculation of the final total adoption. 4) *Item approach (IOC)*. The seed set is the same as HAG, but the prediction is based on item inference only. For each seed set selected by the above approaches, the diffusion process is simulated 300 times. We report the average in-degree of nodes learned from the three datasets in the following: Douban is 39.56; Gowalla is 9.90; Epinions is 14.04. In this section, we evaluate HAG by varying the number of seeds (i.e., k) using two metrics: 1) total adoption, and 2) running time.

To understand the effectiveness, we first compared all those approaches with the optimal solution (denoted as OPT) in a small subgraph sampled, *Sample*, from the SIG of *Douban* with 50 nodes and 58 hyperedges. Figures 9 (a) displays the total adoption obtained by different approaches. As shown, HAG performs much better than the baselines and achieves comparable total adoption with OPT (the difference decreases with increased k). Note that OPT is not scalable as shown in Figures 9 (b) since it needs to examine all combination with k nodes. Also, OPT takes more than 1 day for selecting 6 seeds in *Sample*. Thus, for the rest of experiments, we exclude OPT.

Figures 10 (a)-(c) compare the total adoptions of different approaches in the SIG learned from real networks. They all grow as k increases, since a larger k increases the chance for seeds to influence others to adopt items. Figure 10 (a)-(c) manifest that HAG outperforms all the other baselines for any k in SIG model. Among them, SOC fails to find good solutions since item inference is not examined during seed selection. IOC performs poorly without considering social influence. SNS only includes one seed at a time without considering the combination of nodes that may activate many other nodes via hyperedges.

Figure 10 (d) reports the running time of those approaches. Note that the trends upon *Gowalla* and *Epinions* are similar with *Douban*. Thus we only report the running time of *Douban* due to the space constraint. Taking the source combinations into account, HAG examines source combinations of hyperedges in E_H and obtains a better solution by spending more time since the number of hyperedges is often much higher than the number of nodes.

6.4 Online Diffusion Processing

Diffusion processing is an essential operation in HAG. We evaluate the efficiency of diffusion processing based on SIG-index (denoted as SX), in terms of the running time, in comparison with that based on the original Monte Carlo simulation (denoted as MC) and the sorting enhancement

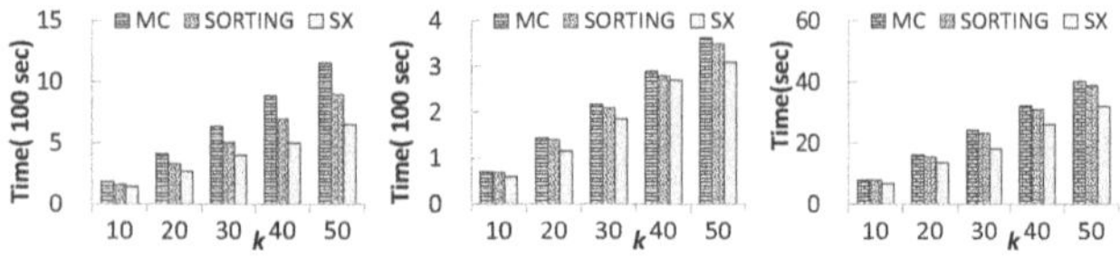

(a) Douban (b) Gowalla (c) Epinions

Figure 11: Running time of different simulation methods

(denoted as SORTING), which accesses the hyperedges in descending order of their weights. Figure 11 plots the running time of SX, SORTING, and MC under various k using the *Douban*, *Gowalla*, and *Epinions*. For each k, the average running times of 50 randomly selected seed sets for SX, SORTING, and MC, are reported. The diffusion process is simulated 300 times for each seed set. As Figure 11 depicts, the running time for all the three approaches grows as k increases, because a larger number of seeds tends to increase the chance for other nodes to be activated. Thus, it needs more time to diffuse. Notice that SX takes much less time than SORTING and MC, because SX avoids accessing hyperedges with no source nodes newly activated while calculating the activation probability. Moreover, the SIG-index is updated dynamically according to the activated nodes in diffusion process. Also note that the improvement by MC over SORTING in *Douban* is more significant than that in *Gowalla* and *Epinions*, because the average in-degree of nodes is much larger in *Douban*. Thus, activating a destination at an early stage can effectively avoid processing many hyperedges later.

7. CONCLUSION

In this paper, we argue that existing techniques for item inference recommendation and seed selection need to jointly take social influence and item inference into consideration. We propose Social Item Graph (SIG) for capturing purchase actions and predicting potential purchase actions. We propose an effective machine learning approach to construct an SIG from purchase action logs and learn hyperedge weights. We also develop efficient algorithms to solve the new and challenging Social Item Maximization Problem (SIMP) that effectively select seeds for marketing. Experimental results demonstrate the superiority of the SIG model over existing models and the effectiveness and efficiency of the proposed algorithms for processing SIMP. We also plan to further accelerate the diffusion process by indexing additional information on SIG-index.

8. REFERENCES

[1] The Douban dataset download. http://arbor.ee.ntu.edu.tw/~hhshuai/Douban.tar.bz2.

[2] When social influence meets association rule learning. In *CoRR (1502.07439)*, 2016.

[3] R. Agrawal, T. Imielinski, and A. N. Swami. Mining association rules between sets of items in large databases. In *SIGMOD*, 1993.

[4] R. M. Bond, C. J. Fariss, J. J. Jones, A. D. Kramer, C. Marlow, J. E. Settle, and J. H. Fowler. A 61-million-person experiment in social influence and political mobilization. *Nature*, 2012.

[5] S. Bourigault, S. Lamprier, and P. Gallinari. Representation learning for information diffusion through social networks: an embedded cascade model. In *WSDM*, 2016.

[6] S. Chen, J. Fan, G. Li, J. Feng, K. Tan, and J. Tang. Online topic-aware influence maximization. In *VLDB*, 2015.

[7] W. Chen, C. Wang, and Y. Wang. Scalable influence maximization for prevalent viral marketing in large-scale social networks. In *KDD*, 2010.

[8] E. Cho, S. A. Myers, and J. Leskovec. Friendship and mobility: user movement in location-based social networks. In *KDD*, 2011.

[9] P. Domingos and M. Richardson. Mining the network value of customers. In *KDD*, 2001.

[10] A. Goyal, F. Bonchi, and L. V. S. Lakshmanan. Learning influence probabilities in social networks. In *WSDM*, 2010.

[11] A. Goyal, W. Lu, and L. V. S. Lakshmanan. SIMPATH: An efficient algorithm for influence maximization under the linear threshold model. In *ICDM*, 2011.

[12] J. Han, M. Kamber, and J. Pei. *Data Mining: Concepts and Techniques*. Morgan Kaufmann, 3rd Edition, 2011.

[13] N. L. Hjort and M. C. Jones. Locally parametric nonparametric density estimation. In *The Annals of Statistics*, 1996.

[14] R. V. Hogg and E. A. Tanis. *Probability and statistical inference*. Prentice Hall, 7th Edition, 2005.

[15] R. Jones and K. Klinkner. Beyond the session timeout: automatic hierarchical segmentation of search topics in query logs. In *CIKM*, 2008.

[16] R. J. B. Jr. Efficiently mining long patterns from databases. In *SIGMOD*, 1998.

[17] D. Kempe, J. M. Kleinberg, and É. Tardos. Maximizing the spread of influence through a social network. In *KDD*, 2003.

[18] H. Li, T. Cao, and Z. Li. Learning the information diffusion probabilities by using variance regularized em algorithm. In *ASONAM*, 2014.

[19] J. Nail. The consumer advertising backlash, 2004. Forrester Research and Intelliseek Market Research Report.

[20] N. Pasquier, Y. Bastide, R. Taouil, and L. Lakhal. Discovering frequent closed itemsets for association rules. In *ICDT*, 1999.

[21] B. W. Silverman, M. C. Jones, J. D. Wilson, and D. W. Nychka. A smoothed em approach to indirect estimation problems, with particular, reference to stereology and emission tomography. *Journal of the Royal Statistical Society. Series B (Methodological)*, 1990.

[22] J. Tang, H. Gao, H. Liu, and A. D. Sarma. etrust: Understanding trust evolution in an online world. In *KDD*, 2012.

[23] J. Tang, S. Wu, and J. Sun. Confluence: conformity influence in large social networks. In *KDD*, 2013.

[24] Y. Tang, X. Xiao, and Y. Shi. Influence maximization: near-optimal time complexity meets practical efficiency. In *SIGMOD*, 2014.

[25] H. Vahabi, I. K. F. Gullo, and M. Halkidi. Difrec: A social-diffusion-aware recommender system. In *CIKM*, 2015.

[26] Z. Wen and C.-Y. Lin. On the quality of inferring interests from social neighbors. In *KDD*, 2010.

[27] J. Yang and J. Leskovec. Modeling information diffusion in implicit networks. In *ICDM*, 2010.

Privacy-preserving Class Ratio Estimation

Arun Iyer
Indian Institute of Technology Bombay,
Mumbai, India. 400076.
aruniyer@cse.iitb.ac.in

J. Saketha Nath*
Indian Institute of Technology Bombay,
Mumbai, India. 400076.
saketh@cse.iitb.ac.in

Sunita Sarawagi†
Indian Institute of Technology Bombay,
Mumbai, India. 400076.
sunita@iitb.ac.in

ABSTRACT

In this paper we present learning models for the class ratio estimation problem, which takes as input an unlabeled set of instances and predicts the proportions of instances in the set belonging to the different classes. This problem has applications in social and commercial data analysis. Existing models for class-ratio estimation however require instance-level supervision. Whereas in domains like politics, and demography, set-level supervision is more common. We present a new method for directly estimating class-ratios using set-level supervision. Another serious limitation in applying these techniques to sensitive domains like health is data privacy. We propose a novel label privacy-preserving mechanism that is well-suited for supervised class ratio estimation and has guarantees for achieving efficient differential privacy, provided the per-class counts are large enough. We derive learning bounds for the estimation with and without privacy constraints, which lead to important insights for the data-publisher. Extensive empirical evaluation shows that our model is more accurate than existing methods and that the proposed privacy mechanism and learning model are well-suited for each other.

1. INTRODUCTION

In this work we study statistical learning models for estimating the proportion of instances belonging to different classes in a given set of instances. Many real-world applications motivate this problem: a health analyst wants to estimate the proportion of individuals susceptible to a disease in a locality, a political analyst wants to estimate the proportion of votes to different parties, and so on. Recent work [13, 29] shows how to train such models when presented with a set of instances each attached with its correct label. Unfortunately, such instance-labeled data is not easily accessible in domains like health and social analysis. Often labels are available only for groups of instances and not individual instances in the group. For instance in voting, we only have access to aggregate number of votes to each party, and not the vote of any one individual. [23] lists other scenarios where instance-level supervision in not plausible. In other cases (example, in health [11]), the labels are private and not easily accessible to an analyst. Much work [15, 24, 4, 14, 16, 1, 30, 7, 27] exists on creating machine learning models over private data. But most of these assume that learning happens within the trust boundary of private data. We are targeting cases where the training data might have to be aggregated from many private organizations for understanding broader trends. Thus, our goal in this work is to learn a model for estimating class proportions under these two constraints: (i) supervision is in the form of label counts on sets of instances, and (ii) the labels of data is private and model training happens outside the trust boundary of owners of private data.

In the first part of the paper we present a new learning model for estimating class ratios with set-labeled data for supervision. Our model directly estimates class ratios in a given set of instances using the principle of Maximum Mean Discrepancy in a Reproducible Kernel Hilbert Space [10]. We show this paradigm to be significantly more accurate than first building classifiers with set-labeled data using the techniques of [22, 28, 23, 25, 21] and then estimating proportions in predicted instance labels. We theoretically analyze our model and show that our model is statistically consistent. More interestingly, the analysis shows that our model performs best when trained on few sets, each with a large number of examples. In contrast, existing models for training with set-labeled data (e.g., [28]) prefer many, small sets. Since large sets imply easier hiding of private labels, our model is particularly compatible with the goals of learning under privacy constraints. More importantly, the existing models assume that the training and test distributions are the same, which defeats the very purpose of class-ratio estimation. Our empirical results confirm that existing models perform poorly when the class-ratios in the training and test are different; while the proposed models handle such distribution shift well.

Next we extend our model to handle data privacy. In this work we focus only on protecting the privacy of the class labels. This setting has been proposed earlier in [3, 21] and is of interest in domains like health and finance where some fields are more private than others. In this work, we consider the popular (ϵ, δ)-differential privacy [8, 2] as the

*Work done while on sabbatical at Microsoft, Hyderabad, India.
†Work done while on sabbatical at Google, Mountain View, USA.

KDD '16, August 13 - 17, 2016, San Francisco, CA, USA

ISBN 978-1-4503-4232-2/16/08...$15.00

DOI: http://dx.doi.org/10.1145/2939672.2939806

definition of privacy. A widely used mechanism for enforcing differential privacy is based on adding a Laplace noise [8, 20, 18]. We show that this mechanism distorts proportions too much. We propose a new label privacy preserving mechanism that is well-suited for the supervised class-ratio estimation problem. We theoretically analyze our mechanism and show that our method guarantees $\epsilon \to 0, \delta \to 0$ as long as each class has large enough counts, independent of the number of classes. In contrast, existing mechanisms based on Lapace noise have a (non-zero) lower bound on ϵ, which worsens with the number of classes. Empirically also, we show that our mechanism provides much lower distortion particularly for large number of classes.

Our privacy mechanism and learning algorithm are designed to be maximally compatible with each other and aligned to the goals of creating an accurate model while guaranteeing differential privacy. Our privacy mechanism preserves class ratios and incurs low distortion when set sizes are large. Our learning algorithm yields high accuracy when each set is large and the number of sets is small. These together lead to much lower estimation error than can be obtained using existing learning models and existing privacy mechanisms.

In summary, the main contributions of this work are:

1. We designed a model for estimating class ratios that can be trained with set-labeled data. We show that the proposed model outperforms existing ones, especially when the distribution-shift between the training and test sets is high.

2. We theoretically bound the estimation error of our model. The bound shows that our model is statistically consistent, and has low error when the number of sets is minimized (equal to number of classes), each set is large, and label proportions in each training set are skewed. In contrast, existing methods of creating classification models from set-labeled data prefer many, small sets.

3. We propose a new mechanism for achieving (ϵ, δ) differential privacy of a multiset of labels. Unlike existing mechanisms that add independent Laplace noise to each label count, our design preserves class proportions more effectively for increasing number of classes. We analyze our mechanism to show conditions for achieving differential privacy (with $\epsilon \approx 0, \delta \approx 0$).

4. We extend the learning model as well as its analysis for privacy-protected data. We show that the proposed learning and privacy mechanisms are well-suited for each other. In particular we show some conditions that are common for achieving efficiency in both these phases. We also identify that the skew in class-ratios across the sets in training data controls the trade-off between learning and privacy protection.

5. Empirical evaluation of our method on several large real-datasets shows that: (i) our learning model incurs much lower error than baselines designed over existing models trained from set-labeled data [28] and can reduce error by as much as 70% for skewed test sets. (ii) Our privacy mechanism achieves much lower distortion than existing methods, particularly for large class sizes. For example, on a 5-class dataset, our method distorts proportions by only 0.06 whereas the best existing method distorts by 0.15. (iii) We show that the combination of our learning algorithm and privacy mechanism is able to provide significantly more accurate estimates than existing methods. On an Mnist dataset, our model with our mechanism incurs 60% lower error than with Laplace.

The rest of the paper is organized as follows. We first present and analyze our learning model for class ratio estimation with set-labeled data in Section 2. Next in Section 3, we present our mechanism of enforcing differential privacy on label proportions and analyze our learning model with privacy protected data. In Section 4 we empirically compare our learning model and privacy mechanism. We present related work and conclusions in Sections 5 and 6 respectively.

2. SUPERVISED CLASS RATIO ESTIMATION

In this section we define the supervised class ratio estimation problem and discuss models for it.

2.1 Problem statement

We start with a formal definition of the supervised class ratio estimation problem. Let $\mathcal{X}$ be the set of all instances and $\mathcal{Y} = \{1, \ldots, c\}$ be the set of all labels. Our goal is to design an estimator $\mathcal{M}$ that for any given set $U(\subset \mathcal{X})$ estimates the true probabilities of the various classes: $\rho_u = [\rho_{u1}, \ldots, \rho_{uc}]^\top$ in the distribution from which U was sampled. In this paper we use class-ratios or class-proportions to refer to such ρ. Since U is a finite sample, in practice we will only be able to estimate the sample proportions $\hat{\rho}_u = [\hat{\rho}_{u1}, \ldots, \hat{\rho}_{uc}]^\top$ that denotes the fraction of instances in U belonging to the various classes.

To facilitate the estimation, supervised training data $\mathcal{D}$ consisting of M sets of instances, $\mathcal{S}_i \subset \mathcal{X}$, $i = 1, \ldots, M$, and the corresponding fractions of instances belong to the various classes, $\hat{\rho}_i$ are provided, i.e., $\mathcal{D} = \{(\mathcal{S}_i, \hat{\rho}_i) : i = 1 \ldots M\}$. We will use n_i to denote the number of instances in set $\mathcal{S}_i$. We call such $\mathcal{D}$ set-labeled data. Such set-labeled supervision is much weaker than in standard classification where labels are associated with each instance in the training data[1].

Needless to say, we need to assume that the affine-hull of the label proportions, $\hat{\rho}_i \; \forall i = 1, \ldots, M$, contains the c-dimensional simplex[2]:

$$\Delta_c \subset \text{Aff}\left(\{\hat{\rho}_i \; \forall i\}\right) \qquad (\mathcal{A}0)$$

If this is not the case, then it is easy to see that some classes may go totally un-represented.

A standard assumption in supervised learning is that the joint-distribution over $\mathcal{X} \times \mathcal{Y}$ is unchanged between training and test data. In contrast, in this setting we allow the distribution of the class labels to differ among the sets in training and test. For instance, the class proportions ρ_u in the unlabeled set U can be arbitrary and be very different

[1]However this setting still falls under standard supervised learning as the prediction/estimation is also over sets and not over instances

[2]The affine hull of a set of vectors V, denoted by Aff(V), is the set of all linear combinations of vectors in V such that the combining coefficients sum to unity.

from those in the training set. Our only distributional assumption about the training and test sets is that the class conditional distribution $P(\mathbf{x}|y)$ is unchanged. That is, for any two sets $\mathcal{S}', \mathcal{S}$ in the training and/or test set

$$P(\mathbf{x}|y, S) = P(\mathbf{x}|y, S') \quad \forall y \in \mathcal{Y}, \qquad (\mathcal{A}1)$$

Note this is a much weaker assumption than in classification and in existing models for class ratio estimation (e.g., [23, 28]) which assume that both $P(\mathbf{x}|y)$ and $P(y)$ are preserved in the training and test sets. Requiring the $P(y)$ distribution to be unchanged defeats the very goal of estimating class proportions.

2.2 Existing models

One method to solve the above problem using existing literature, is to tap into the recent work on learning classifiers from set-labeled training data [22, 28, 23, 25]. The goals of all these work is to create a classifier to predict labels of individual instances given weak supervision in the form of set-labeled data during training. Using such a classifier, we can estimate label proportions in any set U as follows: for each $\mathbf{x}_j \in U$, invoke classifier to get predicted label $\hat{y_j}$ and then estimate/approximate the class proportions as the fractions of instances belonging to the various classes.

Firstly, such methods assume that the training and test distributions are the same and hence will perform poorly. Also, recent work [29, 13] shows that learning methods that directly estimate the class-ratios out-perform such per-instance predictive models. The models of [29, 13] require instance-labeled data and cannot be trained with set-labeled training data, limiting their pragmatic applicability [23]. We are aware of no other work that proposes a method of direct class ratio estimation with set-labeled data. In the next section we present the first such model.

2.3 Our Model

In this section we detail the proposed class ratio estimation algorithm.

We begin by recalling the basic assumption $\mathcal{A}0$, which motivates us to parameterize the class ratios in the unlabeled set using:

$$\rho_u = \sum_{i=1}^{M} \alpha_i \rho_i \qquad (1)$$

Then the problem of class ratio estimation boils down to that of estimating the parameters α_i.

We now make the following identifiability assumption without which the class ratio estimation problem is undefined and no algorithm can identify the true class ratios:

$$\boldsymbol{\theta}_1 \neq \boldsymbol{\theta}_2 \Rightarrow \sum_{y\in\mathcal{Y}} P(\mathbf{x}|y)\theta_{1y} \neq \sum_{y\in\mathcal{Y}} P(\mathbf{x}|y)\theta_{2y}, \qquad (\mathcal{A}2)$$

in other words, we are assuming that the class conditionals are linearly independent. Let us denote the class conditional distribution that is common for all sets by $P(\mathbf{x}|y)$.

With the above in place, we note that:

$$\rho_u = \sum_{i=1}^{M} \alpha_i \rho_i \iff \sum_{y=1}^{c} P(\mathbf{x}|y)\rho_{uy} = \sum_{y=1}^{c} P(\mathbf{x}|y) \sum_{i=1}^{M} \alpha_i \rho_{iy}$$

$$\iff P(\mathbf{x}, U) = \sum_{i=1}^{M} \alpha_i P(\mathbf{x}, \mathcal{S}_i),$$

where $P(\mathbf{x}, \mathcal{S}_i)$ denotes the marginal distribution over $\mathcal{X}$ that generated $\mathcal{S}_i$.

Thus, to solve for α we need a method to represent and compare the distributions of each set. Recently, a powerful tool for such algebraic operations on distributions has been provided by the concept of Maximum Mean Discrepency (MMD) on a Reproducible Kernel Hilbert Space (RKHS) [10]. Examples of some algorithms based on MMD are: handling covariance shift [10], the two-sample problem [9], class ratio estimation [29, 13] and training deep generative neural networks [19]. MMD uses the notion of embedding distributions in the RKHS of a kernel. Using this we find α's by minimizing the distance between $P(\mathbf{x}, U)$ and $\sum_{i=1}^{M} \alpha_i P(\mathbf{x}, \mathcal{S}_i)$.

Accordingly, we define K to be a characteristic kernel and let $\mathcal{H}$ denote the RKHS induced by K. Let $\Phi : \mathcal{X} \mapsto \mathcal{H}$ denote the canonical feature map induced by the kernel onto the RKHS. Let

$$\bar{\Phi}_i(\mathbf{x}) = \mathbb{E}_{P(\mathbf{x},\mathcal{S}_i)}\Phi(\mathbf{x}), \forall i \in [1, \dots, M], \qquad (2)$$

and

$$\bar{\Phi}_U(\mathbf{x}) = \mathbb{E}_{P(\mathbf{x},U)}\Phi(\mathbf{x}), \qquad (3)$$

where $\mathbb{E}_{P(\mathbf{x},\mathcal{S})}h(\mathbf{x})$ denotes the expectation of $h(\mathbf{x})$ taken under the distribution $P(\mathbf{x}, \mathcal{S})$.

Our objective of finding α's such that $\sum_{i=1}^{M} \alpha_i P(\mathbf{x}, \mathcal{S}_i) = P(\mathbf{x}, U)$ can now be posed as the following optimization problem:

$$\min_{\alpha\in\mathbb{R}^M} \left\| \sum_{i=1}^{M} \alpha_i \bar{\Phi}_i(\mathbf{x}) - \bar{\Phi}_U(\mathbf{x}) \right\|_{\mathcal{H}} \qquad (4)$$

The class-ratios can then be computed using $\rho_u = \mathcal{P}\alpha^*$, where $\mathcal{P}$ is the matrix with i^{th} column as ρ_i and α^* is the optimal solution of (4). Now since $\bar{\Phi}_i, \bar{\Phi}_U$ as well as $\mathcal{P}$ are not available, we instead approximate them using the following empirical estimates:

$$\bar{\Phi}_i \approx \hat{\Phi}_i \equiv \frac{1}{n_i} \sum_{\mathbf{x}\in\mathcal{S}_i} \Phi(\mathbf{x})$$

and

$$\bar{\Phi}_U \approx \hat{\Phi}_U \equiv \frac{1}{n_u} \sum_{\mathbf{x}\in U} \Phi(\mathbf{x})$$

where $n_i = |\mathcal{S}_i|$ and $n_u = |U|$. And,

$$\mathcal{P} \approx \hat{\mathcal{P}} \equiv [\hat{\rho}_1 \dots \hat{\rho}_M]$$

This leads to the following estimate for α's:

$$\min_{\alpha\in\mathbb{R}^M} \left\| \sum_{i=1}^{M} \alpha_i \hat{\Phi}_i - \hat{\Phi}_U \right\|_{\mathcal{H}} \qquad (5)$$

and the following for the class-ratios: $\hat{\mathcal{P}}\hat{\alpha}$, where $\hat{\alpha}$ is the optimal solution of (5).

Now, because of the approximations it may as well happen that $\hat{\mathcal{P}}\hat{\alpha} \notin \Delta_c$. Hence we finally propose to employ the following estimate: $\hat{\rho}_u \equiv Proj_{\Delta_c}\left(\hat{\mathcal{P}}\hat{\alpha}\right)$, where $Proj_V(v)$ denotes the projection of vector v onto the set V.

The analysis presented in 2.4 shows that the above two-step approximation indeed leads to a statistically consistent alogrithm. More importantly, it shows that: i) $M = c$ number of sets, each with large number of examples leads to efficient estimation. Note that this is completely in contrast with the ∝-SVM [28]. This feature of our algorithm, as we shall see later, naturally leads to high-levels of label privacy; thus achieving good trade-off between estimation accuracy and label privacy, and, ii) the more the label purity[3] in the sets, the better the estimation.

2.4 Main results from the theoretical analysis

In this section we present the learning bounds associated with the proposed algorithm. We begin by rewriting (4) and (5) respectively as:

$$\min_{\boldsymbol{\alpha}} \|\bar{A}\boldsymbol{\alpha} - \bar{a}\| \quad (6)$$

where $\bar{A} = [\bar{\Phi}_1(\mathbf{x}), \ldots, \bar{\Phi}_M(\mathbf{x})]$ and $\bar{a} = [\bar{\Phi}_U(\mathbf{x})]$ and

$$\min_{\boldsymbol{\alpha}} \left\|\hat{A}\boldsymbol{\alpha} - \hat{a}\right\| \quad (7)$$

where $\hat{A} \equiv [\hat{\Phi}_1, \ldots, \hat{\Phi}_M]$ and $\hat{a} = [\hat{\Phi}_U]$.

For the analysis we make another very mild assumption:

$$\hat{A} \text{ has full column rank.} \quad (\mathcal{A}4)$$

Note that this is satisfied whenever the instances in $\mathcal{D}_x$ are unique, since the kernel is universal. To simplify the notation in the learning bound we assume that the kernel is normalized and hence $\max_{x\in\mathcal{X}} \|\Phi(x)\| = 1$.

THEOREM 1. *Given the notation, and assumptions stated above, the error of our estimated proportions $\hat{\rho}_u$ from the true proportions ρ_u is upper bounded with at least probability $1-\delta$ as follows:*

$$\|\hat{\rho}_u - \rho_u\| \leq \frac{\sqrt{\sum_{i=1}^{M} C_\delta(n_i)^2}}{minsing(\bar{A})}(1 + Q(\mathcal{D})) + Q(\mathcal{D})\, C_\delta(n_u)$$

where $C_\delta(n)$ is a confidence term defined by $C_\delta(n) \equiv \frac{2}{\sqrt{n}} + \sqrt{\frac{\ln(2(2M+1)/\delta)}{2n}}$, $minsing(\bar{A})$ is the minimum singular value of $\bar{A}$ (maxsing is analogously defined), and $Q(\mathcal{D})$ is, what we call the condition number of the training set, defined by $Q(\mathcal{D}) \equiv \frac{maxsing(\hat{\mathcal{P}})}{minsing(\hat{A})}$.

We detail in Section 2.4.1 the valuable insights provided by the bound and then in Section 2.4.2 present a sketch of the proof.

2.4.1 Properties of our estimator

First, the confidence term decays at $O(\frac{1}{\sqrt{n}})$ with growing sizes of the sets, and shows that the estimation error reduces with increasing number of points in both the training and test sets. The model prefers smaller number of sets with large number of points in each set[4]. Note that this is in contrast with ∝-SVM and is an attractive feature of our algorithm wrt. privacy.

Second, we notice that the upper bound vanishes to zero as the training set sizes n_i and test set size n_u approach infinity. This indicates that our estimator is consistent.

[3]Purity of set increases as the proportion of instances with the majority label approaches unity.

[4]However, since we want to span the entire convex hull spanned by the class conditional distributions, the minimum number of sets we must have is c.

The condition number $Q(\mathcal{D})$ brings out more desirable properties of our estimator. This term simply measures how "close-by" the sets are with respect to the y distribution (via the term $\text{maxsing}(\hat{\mathcal{P}})$ in the numerator) and the $\mathbf{x}$ distribution (via the term $\text{minsing}(\hat{A})$ in the denominator). The more diverse the class-ratios are across the sets, less is the condition number and vice-versa. It is easy to see that the condition number is the highest, reaching ∞, when the class-ratios are almost the same across the sets (because the minsing will then be near zero). And is the least, approaching unity, when the class-ratios are orthogonal to each other. This indicates that the estimator performs best when the class proportions in the training set are skewed towards any one class.

2.4.2 Proof of Theorem 1

To prove the theorem, we begin with the observation that[5]:

$$\begin{aligned}
\|\hat{\rho}_u - \rho\| &= \|Proj_{\Delta_c}\left(\hat{\mathcal{P}}\hat{\boldsymbol{\alpha}}\right) - \mathcal{P}\boldsymbol{\alpha}^*\| \\
&\leq \|\hat{\mathcal{P}}\hat{\boldsymbol{\alpha}} - \mathcal{P}\boldsymbol{\alpha}^*\| \\
&\leq \|\boldsymbol{\alpha}^*\|\|\hat{\mathcal{P}} - \mathcal{P}\| + \|\hat{\mathcal{P}}\|\|\hat{\boldsymbol{\alpha}} - \boldsymbol{\alpha}^*\| \\
&\leq \|\boldsymbol{\alpha}^*\|\|\hat{\mathcal{P}} - \mathcal{P}\|_F + \|\hat{\mathcal{P}}\|\|\hat{\boldsymbol{\alpha}} - \boldsymbol{\alpha}^*\| \quad (8)
\end{aligned}$$

We now proceed to bound the two difference terms above. The first difference term accounts for the error that may arise from the errors in the estimates of the class proportions of each set calculated from finite sets. Lemma 1 gives the error bound for this difference term. The proof for the bound for the second difference term proceeds in two steps. In the first step via Lemma 2, we bound the difference term with the difference in the objective function of the respective optimization problems in Equations 6 and 7. In the second step in Lemma 3, we bound the difference in the objective functions in terms of known quantities.

LEMMA 1. *With probability $1 - \delta\frac{M}{2M+1}$*

$$\|\hat{\mathcal{P}} - \mathcal{P}\|_F \leq \sqrt{\sum_{i=1}^{M}\left(\frac{2}{\sqrt{|S_i|}} + \sqrt{\frac{\ln(2(2M+1)/\delta)}{2|S_i|}}\right)^2}$$

PROOF. Notice that, $\|\hat{\mathcal{P}}-\mathcal{P}\|_F = \sqrt{\sum_{i=1}^{M}\|\hat{\rho}_i - \rho_i\|^2}$ where ρ_i is the true class proportion in the set S_i. We can now proceed to bound each term of this summation using Theorem 27 from [17]. □

LEMMA 2. $\|\hat{\boldsymbol{\alpha}} - \boldsymbol{\alpha}^*\| \leq \sqrt{\frac{\|\hat{A}\boldsymbol{\alpha}^* - \hat{a}\|^2 - \|\hat{A}\hat{\boldsymbol{\alpha}} - \hat{a}\|^2}{minsing(\hat{A})}}$

PROOF. The proof for the above lemma is identical to proof of Lemma 1 in [13]. □

LEMMA 3. *With probability $1 - \delta\frac{M+1}{2M+1}$,*

$$\begin{aligned}
&\sqrt{\|\hat{A}\boldsymbol{\alpha}^* - \hat{a}\|^2 - \|\hat{A}\hat{\boldsymbol{\alpha}} - \hat{a}\|^2} \\
&\leq \|\boldsymbol{\alpha}^*\|\sqrt{\sum_{i=1}^{M}\left(\frac{2}{\sqrt{n_i}} + \sqrt{\frac{\ln(2(2M+1)/\delta)}{2n_i}}\right)^2} \\
&\quad + \frac{2}{\sqrt{n_u}} + \sqrt{\frac{\ln(2(2M+1)/\delta)}{2n_u}}
\end{aligned}$$

[5]Here, the matrix norm is the maximum singular value and the Frobenius norm is highlighted with an 'F' subscript.

PROOF. Note that, $\|\hat{A}\boldsymbol{\alpha}^* - \hat{a}\|^2 - \|\hat{A}\hat{\boldsymbol{\alpha}} - \hat{a}\|^2 \leq \|\hat{A}\boldsymbol{\alpha}^* - \hat{a}\|^2$. From our discussion in Section 2.3, we know that $\sum_{i=1}^{M} \alpha_i^* \bar{\Phi}_i(\mathbf{x}) = \bar{\Phi}_U$. With this knowledge, we get,

$$\|\hat{A}\boldsymbol{\alpha}^* - \hat{a}\| \leq \|\boldsymbol{\alpha}^*\| \sqrt{\sum_{i=1}^{M} \|\hat{\Phi}_i(\mathbf{x}) - \bar{\Phi}_i(\mathbf{x})\|^2} + \left\|\bar{\Phi}_U(\mathbf{x}) - \hat{\Phi}_U(x)\right\|$$

Applying Theorem 27 from [17] to each individual difference term gives us the result. □

Combining results from Lemma 1, 2, and 3 and the fact that $\|\alpha^*\| \leq \frac{1}{\text{minsing}(\hat{A})}$ proves the theorem.

3. PRESERVING LABEL PRIVACY

Let $\mathcal{S} = \{(\mathbf{x}_1, y_1), \ldots, (\mathbf{x}_m, y_m)\}$ represent a typical set in the un-published training data. Now, let us denote the set consisting of only the input instances from $\mathcal{S}$ i.e., $\{\mathbf{x}_1, \ldots, \mathbf{x}_m\}$ by $\mathcal{S}^x$. Similary, define $\mathcal{S}^y = \{y_1, \ldots, y_m\}$. Let η and ρ denote the vectors with entries as the number and proportions respectively of the instances belonging to the various classes in $\mathcal{S}$. Note that $\sum_{i=1}^{c} \eta_i = m$ and thus each $\rho_i = \frac{\eta_i}{m}$.

In this section we present a label privacy preserving mechanism g, which takes as input $\mathcal{S}^y$ and outputs a vector $\hat{\theta}$ that is a proxy for ρ, the proportions of instances belonging to the various classes in $\mathcal{S}$. Our goal is for g to satisfy the standard differential privacy requirements [8] which states that the output of g should be randomized such that neighboring data sets assign similar probabilities to any output θ. More formally, let $\mathcal{S}^y_{(i,j)}$ denote the dataset obtained from $\mathcal{S}^y$ by changing the label of an instance from class i to class j. Then g is said to satisfy (ϵ, δ)-differential privacy (DP) iff:

$$P\left[g(\mathcal{S}^y) \in B\right] \leq \delta + e^{\epsilon} P\left[g(\mathcal{S}^y_{(i,j)}) \in B\right], \; \forall\, B \subset \Delta_c, \; \forall\, i \neq j.$$

We seek a mechanism that achieves this privacy while minimally distorting the true ρ-s so that they continue to be useful for the learning algorithm. A popular recipe for (ϵ, δ)-differential privacy is to add to each η_i an independent random noise z_i generated from a Laplace or Gaussian distribution[8]. The resultant $\tilde{\eta_i} = \eta_i + z_i$ may not be positive or sum to m. Recently, [18] proposed a constrained least square step that can be used to convert such $\tilde{\eta_i}$ to a valid output in a post-processing step. Another option is to use the technique of [20] that uses $\tilde{\eta_i}$ to define the parameters of a Dirichlet distribution and sample a valid proportion θ from this distribution. While all these mechanisms achieve (ϵ, δ) privacy, they do so at the cost of a large distortion to the true proportions as we show in Section 4. In this paper we propose a new mechanism that achieves (ϵ, δ) privacy with significantly smaller distortion, provided no class is under-represented. Our mechanism achieves differential privacy with $\epsilon \to 0, \delta \to 0$ asymptotically[6]. In contrast, in the mechanism of [20] ϵ is bounded from below by a value that grows with k.

The key point of our mechanism is to sample θ from a Dirichlet distribution given by:

$$g(\mathcal{S}^y) \sim Dir(\sigma\eta_1, \sigma\eta_2, \ldots, \sigma\eta_k),$$

[6]As $\eta_i \to \infty \; \forall\, i = 1, \ldots, k$.

Here σ is an input-dependent parameter that is tuned to achieve the desired trade-off between the level of privacy and accuracy of the output. We next show how to choose σ for a given (ϵ, δ) and $\mathcal{S}^y$.

Let $f_0 \equiv Dir\left(\sigma\eta_1, \sigma\eta_2, \ldots, \sigma\eta_i, \ldots, \sigma\eta_j, \ldots, \sigma\eta_k\right)$ and $f_{ij} \equiv Dir\left(\sigma\eta_1, \sigma\eta_2, \ldots, \sigma(\eta_i - 1), \ldots, \sigma(\eta_j + 1), \ldots, \sigma\eta_k\right)$ denote the probability density functions of $g(\mathcal{S}^y)$ and $g(\mathcal{S}^y_{(i,j)})$ respectively. The key steps in the analysis are:

1. Finding Θ_{ij} such that $f_0(\theta) \leq e^{\epsilon} f_{ij}(\theta) \; \forall\, \theta \in \Theta_{ij}$. Hence for $B \subset \Theta_{ij}$, we have that differential privacy is satisfied with $\delta = 0$.
2. For $B \not\subset \Theta_{ij}$, it is easy to see that (ϵ, δ)-differential privacy holds if $\delta \geq P\left[g(\mathcal{S}) \notin \Theta_{ij}\right] \; \forall\, i, j$. Hence we need to compute $\max_{i,j} P\left[g(\mathcal{S}) \notin \Theta_{ij}\right]$.

Accordingly, let us first find $\Theta_{i,j}$: Now, $f_0(\theta) \leq e^{\epsilon} f_{ij}(\theta)$

$$\iff \frac{\theta_i^{\sigma}}{\theta_j^{\sigma}} \frac{\Gamma(\sigma\eta_i - \sigma)}{\Gamma(\sigma\eta_i)} \frac{\Gamma(\sigma\eta_j + \sigma)}{\Gamma(\sigma\eta_j)} \leq e^{\epsilon},$$

$$\iff \frac{\theta_i}{\theta_j} \leq \Lambda_{ij}^{\frac{1}{\sigma}} e^{\frac{\epsilon}{\sigma}}$$

where $\Lambda_{ij} \equiv \frac{\Gamma(\sigma\eta_i)}{\Gamma(\sigma\eta_i - \sigma)} \frac{\Gamma(\sigma\eta_j)}{\Gamma(\sigma\eta_j + \sigma)}$. Thus,

$$\Theta_{ij} = \left\{\theta \in \Delta_k \mid \frac{\theta_i}{\theta_j} \leq \Lambda_{ij}^{\frac{1}{\sigma}} e^{\frac{\epsilon}{\sigma}}\right\}.$$

Now, for bounding δ, we calculate

$$\delta = P\left[g(\mathcal{S}) \notin \Theta_{ij}\right] = P\left[\theta_i - \Lambda_{ij}^{\frac{1}{\sigma}} e^{\frac{\epsilon}{\sigma}} \theta_j > 0\right] \tag{9}$$

$$= \int_{\Theta_{ij}} Dir\left(\sigma\eta_i, \sigma\eta_j, \sigma(m - \eta_i - \eta_j)\right)$$

The above integral is not easy to solve in closed form but we can use the Chebyshev's inequality to bound it as follows.

Let Z_{ij} denote the random variable $\theta_i - \Lambda_{ij}^{\frac{1}{\sigma}} e^{\frac{\epsilon}{\sigma}} \theta_j$. The expectation of Z_{ij} is $\mathbb{E}\left[Z_{ij}\right] = \hat{\rho}_i - \Lambda_{ij}^{\frac{1}{\sigma}} e^{\frac{\epsilon}{\sigma}} \hat{\rho}_j$ and its variance is given by

$$var\left(\theta_i\right) + \Lambda_{ij}^{\frac{2}{\sigma}} e^{2\frac{\epsilon}{\sigma}} var\left(\theta_j\right) - 2\Lambda_{ij}^{\frac{1}{\sigma}} e^{\frac{\epsilon}{\sigma}} cov\left(\theta_i, \theta_j\right),$$

$$= \frac{\hat{\rho}_i\left(1 - \hat{\rho}_i\right) + \Lambda_{ij}^{\frac{2}{\sigma}} e^{2\frac{\epsilon}{\sigma}} \hat{\rho}_j\left(1 - \hat{\rho}_j\right) + 2\Lambda_{ij}^{\frac{1}{\sigma}} e^{\frac{\epsilon}{\sigma}} \hat{\rho}_i\hat{\rho}_j}{(\sigma m + 1)}$$

Using the Chebyshev's inequality, we obtain δ as:

$$\max_{i \neq j} \frac{\hat{\rho}_i\left(1 - \hat{\rho}_i\right) + \Lambda_{ij}^{\frac{2}{\sigma}} e^{2\frac{\epsilon}{\sigma}} \hat{\rho}_j\left(1 - \hat{\rho}_j\right) + 2\Lambda_{ij}^{\frac{1}{\sigma}} e^{\frac{\epsilon}{\sigma}} \hat{\rho}_i\hat{\rho}_j}{(\sigma m + 1)\left(\hat{\rho}_i - \Lambda_{ij}^{\frac{1}{\sigma}} e^{\frac{\epsilon}{\sigma}} \hat{\rho}_j\right)^2} \tag{10}$$

For a given ϵ, we perform line search over σ to find the largest σ for which we achieve a target δ. We may find no σ for a given δ when any of the η_i-s is too small, in which case one can fallback to any standard mechanism like [20]. In our experiments we performed the search exactly via Equation 9 but for faster search the approximation in Equation 10 might be more useful.

level (ϵ, δ) for given counts η. When any η_i is too small, not all choices of ϵ, δ, may yield a valid σ. The algorithm detects such cases and returns an error. When all η_i-s are large, our mechanism guarantees that differential privacy with arbitrarily small ϵ, and δ is possible as we show in the asympototic analysis below.

In the asymptotic case i.e., as each $\eta_i \to \infty$, $\Lambda_{ij}^{\frac{1}{\sigma}}$ behaves like $\frac{\hat{\rho}_i}{\hat{\rho}_j}$. Using this substitution we obtain that

$$\delta = \frac{\left(\max_{ij} \frac{1-\hat{\rho}_i}{\hat{\rho}_i} + e^{2\frac{\epsilon}{\sigma}} \frac{1-\hat{\rho}_j}{\hat{\rho}_j}\right) + 2e^{\frac{\epsilon}{\sigma}}}{(\sigma m + 1)\left(1 - e^{\frac{\epsilon}{\sigma}}\right)^2}. \quad (11)$$

From the above it is clear that in the asymptotic case, differential privacy with $\epsilon \to 0, \delta \to 0$ is possible as long as the parameter $\sigma \to 0$ such that $\sigma\eta_i \to \infty \ \forall\ i$ and $\frac{\epsilon}{\sigma} \to \kappa$, for some constant $\kappa > 0$. Also, the above analysis shows that sets with near uniform distribution of labels lead to lower δ, and hence better privacy. However, more interestingly, if σ is chosen properly, low values of δ are achievable even with sets with skewed class-ratios (which lead to better class-ratio estimation).

In Section 4 we show that even in the finite set case our mechanism provides much smaller error for a given (ϵ, δ) requirement than existing methods.

3.1 Estimation under Privacy Constraints

In this section we extend the proposed class-ratio estimation algorithm as well as its analysis for the case where the training set is perturbed using the privacy preserving mechanism proposed in the previous section. Let $\sigma_i(\epsilon, \delta)$ be the Dirichlet mechanism parameter set to achieve (ϵ, δ)-differential privacy over the set $\mathcal{S}_i$.

The estimation algorithm is now given by: $\tilde{\rho}_u \equiv Proj_{\Delta_c}\left(\tilde{\mathcal{P}}\hat{\alpha}\right)$, where $\tilde{\mathcal{P}}$ is the matrix with i^{th} column as $g(\mathcal{S}_i^y)$. In other words, the algorithm simply uses the output of the Dirichlet mechanism as a proxy for the fraction of labels in the set. It is easy to see that the only modification in the analysis is that the $\|\hat{\mathcal{P}} - \mathcal{P}\|_F$ term in (8) is now replaced by $\|\tilde{\mathcal{P}} - \mathcal{P}\|_F$. Again, $\|\tilde{\mathcal{P}} - \mathcal{P}\|_F \leq \|\hat{\mathcal{P}} - \mathcal{P}\|_F + \|\tilde{\mathcal{P}} - \hat{\mathcal{P}}\|_F$. Hence, in the following we analyze only the new term $\|\tilde{\mathcal{P}} - \hat{\mathcal{P}}\|_F$ and leave details of the other analogous terms to the reader. More importantly, analysis of this term illustrates the suitability of the proposed Dirichlet mechanism for estimating class-ratios using the proposed MMD based algorithm. Towards this goal we present the following lemma:

LEMMA 4. *With probability* $1 - \zeta$ *we have:*

$$\|\tilde{\mathcal{P}} - \hat{\mathcal{P}}\|_F \leq \frac{Mc}{\sqrt{\zeta}} \max_{i \in \{1,\dots,M\}; y \in \mathcal{Y}} \sqrt{\frac{\hat{\rho}_{iy}(1 - \hat{\rho}_{iy})}{\sigma_i(\epsilon, \delta)\, m_i + 1}},$$

where all notations are as defined in Section 2.

Before we present the proof, it is insightful to note the following:

- The best case for privacy is when $\epsilon \to 0, \delta \to 0$. From the discussions in section 3, it is known that this is plausible if $\sigma_i(\epsilon, \delta)\, m_i \to \infty$.
- Interestingly, the bound in the above lemma also converges to zero as $\sigma_i(\epsilon, \delta)\, m_i \to \infty$. Hence the proposed Dirichlet mechanism is well-suited for class-ratio estimation using the MMD based algorithm.

PROOF. We begin by noting that:

$$P\left[\|\tilde{\mathcal{P}} - \hat{\mathcal{P}}\| > \tau\right] \leq \sum_{i=1}^{M}\sum_{y=1}^{c} P\left[\|\tilde{\rho}_{iy} - \hat{\rho}_{iy}\|^2 > \frac{\tau^2}{Mc}\right]$$

Also,

$$P\left[\|\tilde{\rho}_{iy} - \hat{\rho}_{iy}\|^2 > \frac{\tau^2}{Mc}\right] \leq \frac{Mc\ var(\tilde{\rho}_{iy})}{\tau^2} = \frac{Mc\ \hat{\rho}_{iy}(1 - \hat{\rho}_{iy})}{\tau^2(\sigma_i(\epsilon, \delta)\, m_i + 1)}$$

The result follows by choosing the RHS of the last inequality to be $\frac{\zeta}{Mc}$. □

We conclude this section by noting that the insights provided from the learning bounds are indeed very useful for the data-publisher, who may have access to instance-level supervised data. The bounds suggest that the data-publisher must create c sets, with almost equal number of instances in each set, and such that each set has moderate level of skew in the class-proportions (while ensuring $\mathcal{A}0$ is satisfied). As the skew increases, the learning becomes more efficient but privacy might suffer. Thus, the data publisher could prefer the largest skew that satisfies his privacy requirements possibly as per guidelines laid in [12].

4. EXPERIMENTS

In this section we first show that our mechanism for enforcing (ϵ, δ) privacy on a set of labels induces less distortion than existing methods (Section 4.1). We next show that our learning model for estimating class proportions is more accurate than existing models for both undistorted training data (Section 4.2) and privacy protected data (Section 4.3)

4.1 Privacy preserving mechanisms

In this section we compare different privacy preserving mechanisms for publishing a set of labels as discussed in Section 3. For these experiments, the input is a set of c counts $\eta = (\eta_1, \dots, \eta_c)$ and we generate perturbed $\hat{\eta}$ via different mechanisms of (ϵ, δ) differential privacy. We measure distortion as the L1 distance between the true and perturbed counts scaled by the size of the set.

We compare the following three methods

1. **Laplace:** In this method we first add Laplace noise [8] to each η_i value using a sensitivity parameter 2. We then post process using constrained least square to make perturbed counts be non-negative and sum to m as described in [18].
2. **Gaussian:** Same as above but with the noise generated via a Gaussian distribution instead of Laplace as described in [8, 2].
3. **Laplace Prior:** This is the mechanism proposed in [20] where the counts distorted with Laplace noise are used to define parameters of a Dirichlet distribution. The output proportions are sampled from this Dirichlet.
4. **Scaled Dirichlet:** This is our mechanism described in Section 3.

For these experiments we set the default value of c to 5, set size (m) to 1000, class proportion for first $c-1$ classes to a $\rho_1 = 0.05$ and the last class to $1 - (c-1)\rho_1$, and (ϵ, δ) to $(0.05, 0.05)$. All reported numbers are averaged over twenty random samples of perturbed outputs for the same input. We study distortion between the true and perturbed proportions under varying values of the default parameters in Figure 1.

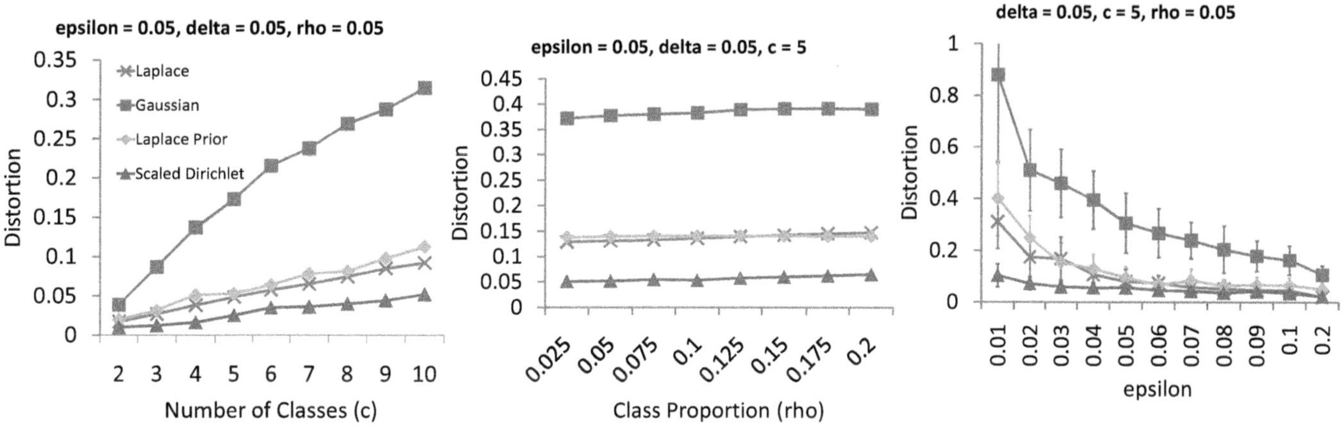

Figure 1: Comparing distortion of privacy mechanisms under varying settings of parameters. The first plot is for increasing number of classes, second plot for changing class proportions on five classes, third plot for increasing ϵ on five classes.

Varying number of classes.

The first plot in Figure 1 shows distortion in the output of different privacy mechanisms with increasing number of classes (c). We observe that as the number of classes increases, our method increasingly scores over all existing approaches. The key reason is that all other methods distort by adding independent noise to each class count. In contrast, our method preserves class ratios by using the same multiplicative parameter to increase variance when required.

Varying class proportions.

Next in the middle plot of Figure 1 we fix the number of classes to 5 and vary the class proportions ($\rho_1, \rho_1, \rho_1, \rho_1, 1-4\rho_1$) by varying ρ_1 from 0.025 (skewed proportions) to 0.2 (uniform proportions). We observe that the distortion achieved by our mechanism is the lowest under all settings.

Varying ϵ.

In the last plot in Figure 1 we vary ϵ from 0.01 to 0.2. As expected, the output is distorted more when the privacy requirements is more stringent (ϵ small). The Laplace mechanism is quite competitive with ours (Scaled Dirichlet) when ϵ is large but for small ϵ, our method provides much smaller distortion. Also, from the error bars we note that the variance of our method is the lowest.

We thus conclude that our privacy model has smaller distortion and smaller variance compared to other models, and is particularly useful when the number of classes is large.

4.2 Class ratio estimation models

In this section we compare various class ratio estimation models on set-labeled data without any perturbation of the class proportions.

We evaluate our method, which we call **MMD**, presented in Section 2.3 using a RBF kernel chosen through cross-validation. We vary the bandwidth of the kernels in the range 2^{-5} to 2^5. The only existing method that we are aware of that can be trained with set-labeled supervision and work with universal kernels is [28]. As discussed in Section 2, we can estimate class ratios using this method by aggregating per-instance predictions from the SVM classifier. We call this the **pSVM** method. The classifier we used was $\propto$SVM[7] [28] which trains a SVM like model from sets of instances and their class proportions. The parameters for this classifier are chosen via cross-validation. We vary the bandwidth of the kernels in the range 2^{-5} to 2^5. The other parameters of varied in the range as per [28].

Dataset	Number Features	Number Instances	$\lvert\mathcal{Y}\rvert$ (c)	n_i	n_u
Census	14	48,842	2	600	600
Youtube	1000	6,431,471	2	600	600
Higgs	28	11,000,000	2	600	600
Mnist	780	60,000	10	3000	3000
Acoustic	50	78,823	3	900	900
Twitter	3600	6,940	3	900	900

Table 1: Summary of Datasets

Datasets.

The method **pSVM** only works for binary classes. So, for the comparisons in this section we restrict to datasets with two classes. Table 1 summarizes the datasets we used.

Census: Census dataset consists of records from 1994 census database with features that include age, workclass, occupation, relationship, race, sex etc. The target label is income which is 1 if the person earns more than 50000 in a year and 0 otherwise. This dataset is available from the UCI repository[8].

Higgs: In a particle accelerator, not all collisions are likely to produce interesting particles. This dataset captures features of several collisions or processes. The label indicates whether a given collision or process is going to produce an interesting particle or not. 21 out of the 28 features are properties measured by the particle detectors in the accelerator and the remaining 7 are abstract features hand-designed by physicists. This dataset is available from the UCI repository.

Youtube: A dataset based on YouTube comments that we created based on this[9] collection. The goal in the YouTube dataset is to estimate the fraction of comments that are

[7] Code taken from https://github.com/felixyu/pSVM

[8] https://archive.ics.uci.edu/ml/datasets/Census+Income

[9] http://mlg.ucd.ie/yt

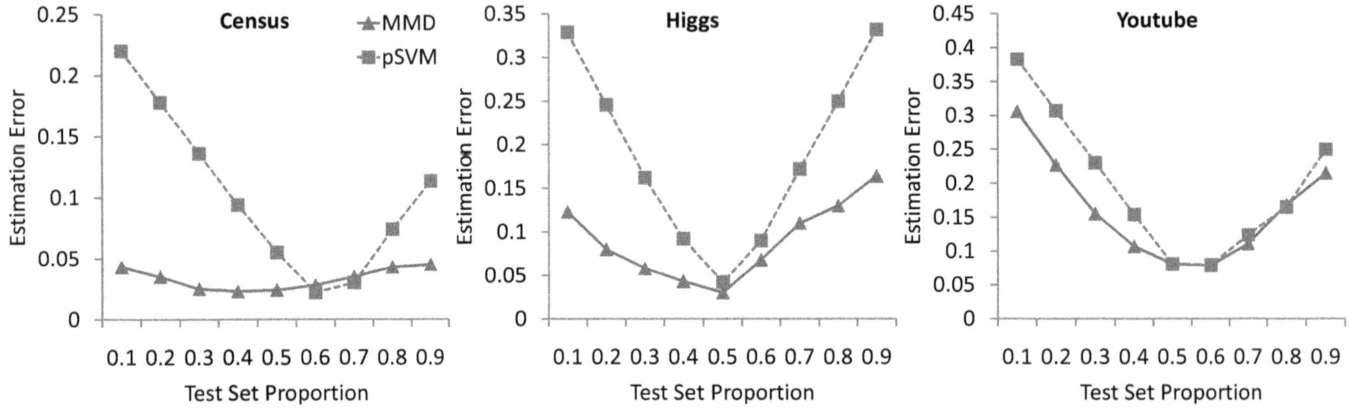

Figure 2: Comparison of models for class ratio estimation. Y-axis is the L1 difference between the true and estimated class ratios, and X-axis is the fraction of instances in class 1 in the test set. Each plot shows results for a different dataset. In all three plots, the method legends is the same.

spams on a YouTube video. The dataset was crawled by tracking 6407 popular YouTube videos over 77 days and comprises of 6,431,471 comments labeled spam or not. The feature set is a normalized TF-IDF vector over 1000 words + a comment length feature.

If the number of classes is c, we create c training sets in the following way: we initially choose a value ρ which is usually 0.05 or 0.1. Then, we create c sets with the following class proportions $[\rho, \rho, \ldots, 1-(c-1)\rho], [\rho, \rho, \ldots, 1-(c-1)\rho, \rho], [\rho, \ldots, 1-(c-1)\rho, \rho, \rho], \ldots, [1-(c-1)\rho, \rho, \ldots, \rho]$. The training sets are all class conditionally sampled. In addition, we add c more sets with the same class proportions as above to support cross validation for kernel selection.

Since, we are dealing with only binary datasets in this experiment, we create 4 sets in training, 2 of them have proportions $(0.1, 0.9)$ and the other 2 had proportions $0.9, 0.1$. This is similar to the process described above with $\rho = 0.1$. For testing, we created various test sets whose positive class proportions varied from 0.1 to 0.9.

For each method we measure estimation error as the L1 distance between the correct class proportions in the test set and the proportions estimated by the method. In Figure 2 we show the errors of the baseline **pSVM** and our **MMD** method on test sizes with increasing fraction of instances in the first class. We observe that **MMD** estimates have much lower error than **pSVM** especially for extreme class skews. The **pSVM** method assumes that the training and test distributions of $P(y)$ remain unchanged, and therefore this method returns accurate class ratios only in the range of ratios where this assumption holds. Our method allows the $P(y)$ distribution to shift and therefore provides lower error on a wider range.

We conclude from this section with set-labeled training data, our proposed **MMD** method provides the lowest error among existing options for a large range of test set ratios.

4.3 Private Class Ratio Estimation

In this section, we evaluate if our estimates continue to remain accurate when the label proportions are distorted to protect privacy. Our experiments in Section 4.1 showed that the distortion is within tolerable limits for binary datasets but is large for non-binary datasets. Therefore, in this section we report experiments on real-world non-binary datasets. The three we considered are described below and summarized in Table 1.

Mnist: This is a handwritten digit recognition dataset. The target labels are the digits 0 to 9 and inputs are fixed size input containing the handwritten image of a digit.

Acoustic: Acoustic is a three class dataset about classifying military vehicles from microphone recordings. This dataset as well as Mnist are available from LibSVM multi-class dataset repository[10].

Twitter: This twitter dataset was created for the task of classifying each tweet into one of three sentiment classes: positive, negative and neutral. We use the dataset and feature extraction mechanism described in [26]. The authors of [26] have made code and data available online[11].

In Figure 3 we show the **MMD** estimation error when trained with data distorted by three privacy mechanisms: ours (scaled dirichlet), Laplace, and Laplace Prior as defined in Section 4.1. We drop the Gaussian method since it provides no advantage over the Laplace method as per our experiments in Section 4.1. Instead we add as a reference the errors when **MMD** is trained with undistorted sets. Note this method does not guarantee any privacy and is just included to get a lower bound. The test set for these experiments where created with varying class proportions using the parameter ρ_1 as described in Section 4.1. The X-axis in Figure 3 indicates these class proportions.

We can make the following observations from these figures.

1. As expected, our estimation model is sensitive to the distortion of training data as revealed by the comparison with the "No distortion" setting. Thus it is important to devise mechanisms that reduce distortion. We showed in Section 4.1 that our method achieves the lowest distortion. These experiments show that the reduced distortion translates to reduced error of our learning algorithm.

2. When the number of classes is large (as in Mnist), existing methods (Laplace) introduce such large distortion that the errors of the learning model become unacceptably large.

[10] https://www.csie.ntu.edu.tw/~cjlin/libsvmtools/datasets/multiclass.html

[11] https://github.com/duytinvo/ijcai2015

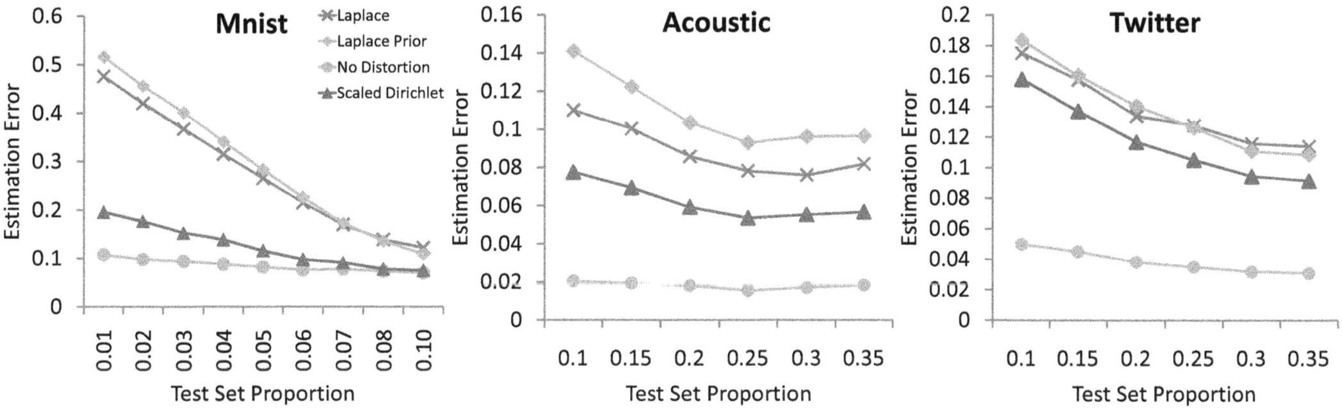

Figure 3: Our MMD estimation model trained with privacy protected data under three different mechanisms. For reference we also include error with correct set proportions (no privacy). The first plot is for Mnist, second for Acoustic and third for twitter. X-axis is increasing test set proportions.

3. The effect of bad training data is more pronounced when the test set has skewed proportions. This trend is very clear for the Mnist dataset where we see a sharp increase in error of Laplace distortion on highly skewed testset.

5. RELATED WORK

In this paper we presented a learning model for estimating proportions of labels in a set of instances using set-labeled training data with privacy constraints on the true label.

Our use of set-labeled data for training is related to the models proposed in [22, 28, 23, 25, 21] for training classification models with the same kind of supervision. However, the way we wrap an MMD objective around set-labeled data allows effective learning from a few, large sets. In contrast, the classification models of [28], while being kernel-based like us, prefer many small sets. Since small sets is anti-thetical to privacy, our method is particularly suitable for learning under privacy constraints.

The use of MMD for estimating class proportions has been explored before in [13, 29]. But these models require instance-labeled data during training which does not work under privacy constraints. One option would have been to train the model with private data while enforcing privacy during the model creation phase as used in [24, 4, 14, 16, 1] and several others [15]. We did not consider this option because we are targeting scenarios where the training data is aggregated from several private organizations and the model creation happens outside the trust boundary.

Another class of methods attempt to first create DP joint distribution of the data [6, 20] and then sample instances from the distribution for down-stream tasks like model-creation. These summaries are for general-purpose analysis, and not a specific classification task, and are expected to be less accurate. Ours and others like [21, 30] of creating summaries is geared for the prediction task at hand while allowing data from multiple agencies to be aggregated. We have shown that our mechanism for publishing label proportions provides much higher accuracy for the same (ϵ, δ) guarantees than existing approaches based adding Gaussian noise to each component as suggested in [8] and sanitizing the output using either the recently proposed constrained least square approach [18] or the Dirichlet samples [20].

A different category of approach attempt to publish combinatorial summaries of data, for instance [5] proposes to create trees to publish set-valued data for differential privacy. Even though the method is designed for publishing sets of items, their raw data is a large set of records each of which is small set of items. Consequently their definition of differential privacy (DP) is to be insensitive to the removal of a record. In contrast, our raw data is a single set of labels and our notion of DP is to be insensitive to the change of any single element of the set.

6. CONCLUSION

In this paper we designed a model for estimating class ratios and devised mechanisms for training it in scenarios where labels are provided on sets of instances and where labels are private. We theoretically analyzed our model and showed it to be consistent and accurate when the number of training sets is large. This is in contrast to existing methods that prefer many, small sets. Empirical evaluation on three real-world datasets show that our estimator provides lower error than existing methods, particularly when test class distributions are skewed.

We proposed a new mechanism for achieving differential privacy of labels that is more effective in preserving class ratios than existing mechanisms, particularly when the number of classes is large. We extend the learning model as well as its analysis for privacy-protected data. We show that the proposed learning and privacy mechanisms are well-suited for each other. In particular we show common conditions for achieving efficiency in both these phases. Empirical evaluation on several large real-datasets shows that the combination of our learning algorithm and privacy mechanism is able to provide significantly more accurate estimates than existing methods.

Our future work includes extending our model for the case of continuous y values (regression setting). Also, we would like to extend our mechanism to protect the privacy of the $\mathbf{x}$ part of an instance. Since our estimator is based on kernels, one idea is to use the technique of [24] for preserving privacy of the $\mathbf{x}$ and our current technique to protect the privacy of the ys.

7. REFERENCES

[1] R. Bassily, A. Smith, and A. Thakurta. Private empirical risk minimization: Efficient algorithms and tight error bounds. In *Foundations of Computer Science (FOCS), 2014 IEEE 55th Annual Symposium on*, pages 464–473. IEEE, 2014.

[2] A. Blum, C. Dwork, F. McSherry, and K. Nissim. Practical privacy: The sulq framework. In *PODS*, 2005.

[3] K. Chaudhuri and D. Hsu. Sample complexity bounds for differentially private learning. In *COLT*, 2011.

[4] K. Chaudhuri, C. Monteleoni, and A. D. Sarwate. Differentially private empirical risk minimization. *Journal of Machine Learning Research*, 12:1069–1109, 2011.

[5] R. Chen, N. Mohammed, B. C. M. Fung, B. C. Desai, and L. Xiong. Publishing set-valued data via differential privacy. *PVLDB*, 4(11), 2011.

[6] R. Chen, Q. Xiao, Y. Zhang, and J. Xu. Differentially private high-dimensional data publication via sampling-based inference. In *Proceedings of the 21th ACM SIGKDD International Conference on Knowledge Discovery and Data Mining*, pages 129–138. ACM, 2015.

[7] J. C. Duchi, M. I. Jordan, and M. J. Wainwright. Privacy aware learning. In *NIPS*. 2012.

[8] C. Dwork and A. Roth. The algorithmic foundations of differential privacy. *Foundations and Trends in Theoretical Computer Science*, 9(3-4):211–407, 2014.

[9] A. Gretton, K. M. Borgwardt, M. J. Rasch, B. Schölkopf, and A. J. Smola. A kernel two-sample test. *Journal of Machine Learning Research*, 13:723–773, 2012.

[10] A. Gretton, A. J. Smola, J. Huang, M. Schmittfull, K. M. Borgwardt, and B. Schölkopf. *Covariate shift and local learning by distribution matching*, pages 131–160. MIT Press, Cambridge, MA, USA, 2 2009.

[11] C. Guttmann, X. Sun, C. Rao, C. Queiroz, and B. I. Rubinstein. On the challenges of balancing privacy and utility of open health data. In *Joint Proceedings of the Workshop on AI Problems and Approaches for Intelligent Environments and Workshop on Semantic Cities*, pages 43–47. ACM, 2013.

[12] J. Hsu, M. Gaboardi, A. Haeberlen, S. Khanna, A. Narayan, B. C. Pierce, and A. Roth. Differential privacy: An economic method for choosing epsilon. In *IEEE 27th Computer Security Foundations Symposium, CSF*, 2014.

[13] A. Iyer, S. Nath, and S. Sarawagi. Maximum mean discrepancy for class ratio estimation: Convergence bounds and kernel selection. In *ICML*, pages 530–538, 2014.

[14] P. Jain and A. Thakurta. Differentially private learning with kernels. In *Proceedings of the 30th International Conference on Machine Learning (ICML-13)*, pages 118–126, 2013.

[15] Z. Ji, Z. C. Lipton, and C. Elkan. Differential privacy and machine learning: a survey and review. *CoRR*, 2014.

[16] D. Kifer, A. Smith, and A. Thakurta. Private convex empirical risk minimization and high-dimensional regression. *JMLR*, 1:41, 2012.

[17] S. Le. *Learning via Hilbert space embedding of distributions*. PhD thesis, University of Sydney, School of Information Technologies, 2008.

[18] J. Lee, Y. Wang, and D. Kifer. Maximum likelihood postprocessing for differential privacy under consistency constraints. In *ACM SIGKDD*, 2015.

[19] Y. Li, K. Swersky, and R. S. Zemel. Generative moment matching networks. In *ICML*, 2015.

[20] A. Machanavajjhala, D. Kifer, J. M. Abowd, J. Gehrke, and L. Vilhuber. Privacy: Theory meets practice on the map. In *ICDE*, 2008.

[21] R. Nock, G. Patrini, and A. Friedman. Rademacher observations, private data, and boosting. In *Proceedings of the 32nd International Conference on Machine Learning, ICML 2015, Lille, France, 6-11 July 2015*, pages 948–956, 2015.

[22] G. Patrini, R. Nock, T. Caetano, and P. Rivera. (almost) no label no cry. In *Advances in Neural Information Processing Systems 27: Annual Conference on Neural Information Processing Systems 2014, December 8-13 2014, Montreal, Quebec, Canada*, pages 190–198, 2014.

[23] N. Quadrianto, A. J. Smola, T. S. Caetano, and Q. V. Le. Estimating labels from label proportions. *Journal of Machine Learning Research*, 10:2349–2374, 2009.

[24] B. I. P. Rubinstein, P. L. Bartlett, L. Huang, and N. Taft. Learning in a large function space: Privacy-preserving mechanisms for svm learning. *Journal of Privacy and Confidentiality*, 4(1), 2012.

[25] S. Rüping. SVM classifier estimation from group probabilities. In *Proceedings of the 27th International Conference on Machine Learning (ICML-10), June 21-24, 2010, Haifa, Israel*, pages 911–918, 2010.

[26] D.-T. Vo and Y. Zhang. Target-dependent twitter sentiment classification with rich automatic features. In *Proceedings of the 24th International Conference on Artificial Intelligence*, IJCAI'15, pages 1347–1353. AAAI Press, 2015.

[27] Y. Xin and T. Jaakkola. Controlling privacy in recommender systems. In *Advances in Neural Information Processing Systems*, pages 2618–2626, 2014.

[28] F. X. Yu, D. Liu, S. Kumar, T. Jebara, and S. Chang. $\propto$SVM for learning with label proportions. In *Proceedings of the 30th International Conference on Machine Learning, ICML 2013, Atlanta, GA, USA, 16-21 June 2013*, pages 504–512, 2013.

[29] K. Zhang, B. Schölkopf, K. Muandet, and Z. Wang. Domain adaptation under target and conditional shift. In *ICML*, 2013.

[30] S. Zhou, J. D. Lafferty, and L. A. Wasserman. Compressed and privacy-sensitive sparse regression. *IEEE Transactions on Information Theory*, 55(2):846–866, 2009.

Extreme Multi-label Loss Functions for Recommendation, Tagging, Ranking & Other Missing Label Applications

Himanshu Jain, Yashoteja Prabhu
Indian Institute of Technology Delhi
himanshu.j689@gmail.com,
yashoteja.prabhu@gmail.com

Manik Varma
Microsoft Research
manik@microsoft.com

ABSTRACT

The choice of the loss function is critical in extreme multi-label learning where the objective is to annotate each data point with the most relevant *subset* of labels from an extremely large label set. Unfortunately, existing loss functions, such as the Hamming loss, are unsuitable for learning, model selection, hyperparameter tuning and performance evaluation. This paper addresses the issue by developing propensity scored losses which: (a) prioritize predicting the few relevant labels over the large number of irrelevant ones; (b) do not erroneously treat missing labels as irrelevant but instead provide unbiased estimates of the true loss function even when ground truth labels go missing under arbitrary probabilistic label noise models; and (c) promote the accurate prediction of infrequently occurring, hard to predict, but rewarding tail labels. Another contribution is the development of the PfastreXML algorithm (code available from [1]) which efficiently scales to large datasets with up to 9 million labels, 70 million points and 2 million dimensions and which gives significant improvements over the state-of-the-art.

This paper's results also apply to tagging, recommendation and ranking which are the motivating applications for extreme multi-label learning. They generalize previous attempts at deriving unbiased losses under the restrictive assumption that labels go missing uniformly at random from the ground truth. Furthermore, they provide a sound theoretical justification for popular label weighting heuristics used to recommend rare items. Finally, they demonstrate that the proposed contributions align with real world applications by achieving superior clickthrough rates on sponsored search advertising in Bing.

1. INTRODUCTION

Extreme multi-label learning addresses the problem of learning a classifier that can annotate a data point with the most relevant *subset* of labels from an extremely large label set. Note that multi-label learning is distinct from multi-class classification which aims to predict a single mutually exclusive label.

KDD '16, August 13 - 17, 2016, San Francisco, CA, USA

ISBN 978-1-4503-4232-2/16/08...$15.00
DOI: http://dx.doi.org/10.1145/2939672.2939756

Extreme multi-label learning is an important research problem as it has many applications in tagging, recommendation and ranking. For instance, there are more than a million labels (tags) on Wikipedia and one might wish to build an extreme multi-label classifier that tags a new article or web page with the subset of most relevant Wikipedia labels. Similarly, given a user's buying or viewing history, one might wish to build an extreme multi-label classifier that recommends the subset of millions of items that the user might wish to buy or view next. In general, one can reformulate ranking and recommendation problems as extreme classification tasks by treating each item to be ranked/recommended as a separate label, learning an extreme multi-label classifier that maps a user's feature vector to a set of labels, and then using the classifier to predict the subset of items that should be ranked/recommended to each user.

Extreme multi-label learning differs from traditional multi-label learning in a number of ways including the need for logarithmic time prediction, training at an extreme scale with millions of data points, features and labels, *etc.* Two aspects are germane to this paper. First, every data point has missing labels in its ground truth labelling since it is impossible for annotators to go through millions of labels and mark out the exact relevant subset. This has a fundamental impact on training, validation and performance evaluation. Second, the notion of what constitutes a good prediction changes when one moves from traditional to extreme multi-label learning. In particular, due to relevant label sparsity, it is more important to accurately predict relevant labels than irrelevant ones. Furthermore, due to the power law distribution over labels, infrequently occurring tail labels have little training data and are harder to predict than frequently occurring ones but might also be more informative and rewarding. As such, design choices made for traditional multi-label learning might not apply at the extreme scale.

One of the most critical design choices is that of the loss function. It determines whether the training algorithm learns a good solution, whether hyper-parameters are tuned appropriately, influences model selection and, perhaps most importantly, ensures that performance evaluation on the test set is aligned with real world application requirements.

This paper argues that traditional multi-label loss functions are unsuitable for extreme multi-label learning even though they have been used extensively thus far. For instance, the popular Hamming loss [5, 7, 10, 11, 14, 19, 22,

40, 43, 48] does not prioritize predicting the few relevant labels over the millions of irrelevant ones, erroneously treats missing labels as irrelevant, treats all relevant labels as being equally important and is biased due to missing ground truth. As a result, extreme multi-label models optimized and selected using traditional loss functions might perform poorly when deployed in real world applications.

The primary contribution of this paper is to develop loss functions suitable for extreme multi-label learning. It is argued that losses which focus on ranking relevant labels as highly as possible are more suitable than the Hamming loss. Propensity scored variants of such losses, including precision@k and nDCG@k, are developed and proved to give unbiased estimates of the true loss function even when ground truth labels go missing under arbitrary probabilistic label noise models. Furthermore, it is shown that the propensity models developed in this paper based on real world applications naturally promote the accurate prediction of infrequently occurring, difficult to predict, but rewarding tail labels. This addresses both the limitations of traditional multi-label loss functions as discussed in this paper. Another contribution is the development of the PfastreXML algorithm that can scale to extreme multi-label datasets with up to 9 million labels, 70 million training points and 2 million dimensional features and achieves significant improvements over the state-of-the-art. The code for PfastreXML is available from [1].

This paper's results generalize beyond extreme multi-label learning and are also relevant to tagging, recommendation and ranking. Previous attempts at developing unbiased loss functions in these areas have been limited to square loss [17], recall [38] and average discounted gain [26] under the restrictive assumption that ground truth labels go missing uniformly at random. Furthermore, the propensity models developed in this paper present a sound theoretical justification for the popular label weighting heuristics [9, 12, 35, 39, 44, 47, 49, 51] used in the recommendation literature to promote the prediction of rare and novel items. Finally, the fact that higher clickthrough rates are achieved while ranking queries for sponsored search advertising in Bing demonstrates that the loss functions and algorithms proposed in this paper are better aligned with real world applications.

2. RELATED WORK

Extreme multi-label learning algorithms typically follow a tree [4, 34, 46] or an embedding based approach [5, 6, 7, 10, 11, 14, 18, 20, 22, 27, 32, 36, 43, 45, 48, 50]. While some algorithms have been proposed for training with missing labels [23, 40, 48] under restrictive settings, aspects such as hyper-parameter tuning, model selection and performance evaluation have not been addressed before. As such, the Hamming loss [5, 7, 10, 11, 14, 19, 22, 40, 43, 48] continues to be one of the most popular losses for extreme multi-label learning along with precision [4, 6, 18, 21, 22, 34, 45, 46] and the F-measure [5, 11, 15, 19, 20, 22, 40, 50]. On the other hand, unbiased estimators for recall [38], average discounted gain [26] and square loss [17] have been developed under the restrictive assumption that labels go missing uniformly at random from the ground truth. By contrast, this paper develops propensity scored variants of precision, nDCG and other loss functions and proves that they are unbiased even under general probabilistic label noise models.

Propensity scoring has been used to develop unbiased estimators for observational data [37]. In machine learning, propensities have been used for bias correction in situations where the training and test data have been drawn from different distributions [3]. Propensities have also been used for off policy evaluation, whereby feedback data from the interaction logs of an existing system is used to evaluate a new system [8, 24, 25, 41, 42].

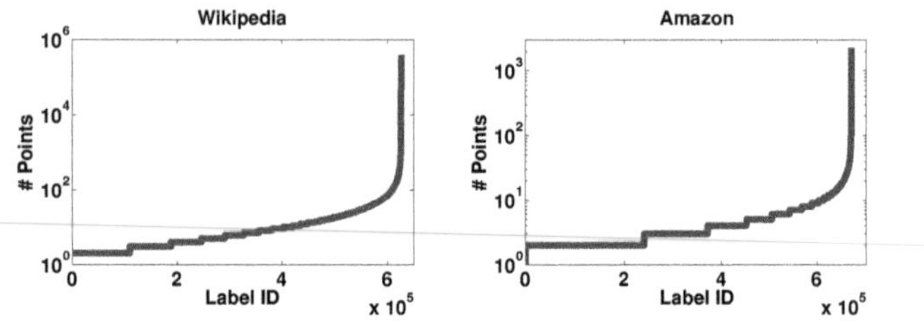

Figure 1: Plot showing the number of times each label occurs in a dataset: 246201 and 452262 labels occur less than 5 times each in Wikipedia and Amazon respectively. Such labels are harder to predict than popular ones but might also be more informative and rewarding in certain applications.

Label (item) weighting loss functions have been proposed to promote the accurate prediction of infrequently occurring labels (rare items) which might delight and surprise the user. For instance, denoting a label's normalized frequency of occurrence by p_l, [9, 44, 47, 49, 51] used the heuristic of weighting each label by $-\log p_l$ whereas [12, 35, 39] recommended a weight of $p_l^{-\gamma/(\gamma+1)}$ where $\gamma \geq 0$ was a user tunable parameter. This paper provides theoretical justification for such heuristics by showing how similar weights can arise from the proposed propensity models.

3. A MOTIVATING EXAMPLE

Consider evaluating the performance of an extreme multi-label algorithm for tagging Wikipedia articles by computing a chosen loss function on the ground truth labels provided by Wikipedia's editors. To take a concrete example, Wikipedia's editors annotated the article for the Divine Comedy with 15 labels such as "14th-century Christian texts", "Epic poems in Italian", "1300 in Italy", *etc.* Note that many relevant labels such as "Dante Alighieri", "Medieval philosophical literature" and "Allegory" are missing since it is impossible for any annotator or expert to go through the entire list of Wikipedia labels and select all the relevant ones. Evaluating performance using the Hamming loss leads to the following issues which can be overcome by the proposed propensity scored nDCG@k and precision@k.

Relevant labels: Table 2 shows that the number of labels relevant to any given data point is far smaller than the number of irrelevant ones. Accurately predicting a relevant label is therefore more important than predicting an irrelevant one. For instance, predicting that "Epic poems in Italian" is relevant to the Divine Comedy is more difficult, and informative, than predicting that "Baseball" is irrelevant. Similarly, it is more important to accurately predict relevant labels to fill the few slots available in typical recommendation applications than it is to predict irrelevant ones. Unfortunately, the Hamming loss charges the same penalty for misclassifying relevant and irrelevant labels. Precision@k and nDCG@k avoid this by promoting the prediction of relevant labels with high ranks.

Missing labels: The Hamming loss would penalize an algorithm for predicting that the label "Dante Alighieri" was relevant to the article for the Divine Comedy since the label was missing from the ground truth. Section 4 addresses this issue by developing propensity scored variants of precision@k and nDCG@k which provide unbiased estimates of the true loss as if computed on the complete ground truth without any missing labels.

Tail labels: Labels follow a power law distribution in extreme multi-label learning applications (see Figure 1). Infrequently occurring labels have little training data and are harder to predict than frequently occurring ones but might also be more informative and rewarding. This is particularly important on a dataset such as Wikipedia where 246201 labels occur in less than 5 articles each. For instance, little information is gained by predicting popular generic labels such as "Poems" for the Divine Comedy article as compared to predicting relatively infrequent labels such as "Epic poems in Italian" (which implies "Poems" and more) or "14th-century Christian texts". Similarly, in certain applications, there is little to be gained by recommending popular items since users might know about them already. Predicting rare items might be more desirable in these cases. While existing losses treat all labels as equal, Section 5 develops a propensity model that naturally promotes the accurate prediction of infrequent labels with high ranks.

4. PROPENSITY SCORED LOSSES

This Section develops propensity scored variants of precision@k, nDCG@k and other popular loss functions (see Table 1 for examples). It is proved that the proposed propensity scored losses computed on the observed labels provide unbiased estimates of the true loss function computed on the complete (but unobtainable) ground truth without any missing labels.

Label representation: Extreme multi-label learning deals with applications having an extremely large number of labels L where it is not possible for any annotator to select the exact relevant label subset for even a single data point. Let $\mathbf{y}^*, \mathbf{y} \in \{0,1\}^L$ denote the complete (but unobtainable) and observed (but with missing labels) ground truth label vectors for a given data point such that $y_l^* = y_l = 1$ for observed relevant labels, $y_l^* = 1, y_l = 0$ for unobserved relevant labels and $y_l^* = y_l = 0$ for irrelevant labels. Continuing with the example of the Divine Comedy from Section 3, $y_l^* = y_l = 1$ for the observed relevant label "Epic poems in Italian", while $y_l^* = 1, y_l = 0$ for the relevant, but missing, label "Dante Alighieri" and $y_l^* = y_l = 0$ for the irrelevant label "Baseball". Furthermore, it is assumed that the noise in the labelling process is one sided and that irrelevant labels are never marked as relevant. For instance, Wikipedia's editors are not malicious and never allow an article to be tagged with an irrelevant label. Note that, even if this mild assumption was violated, it might be possible to hire annotators to weed out the irrelevant tags. Also note that, since $\mathbf{y}^*$ is unavailable, this label representation does not assume that the position of missing labels is known unlike previous work [48]. Finally, let $\hat{\mathbf{y}} \in \{0,1\}^L$ denote an algorithm's predicted label vector for a given data point.

Table 1: (a) presents unbiased propensity scored loss functions $\mathcal{L}(\mathbf{y}, \hat{\mathbf{y}})$ corresponding to precision@k and nDCG@k for an unrestricted probabilistic label noise model which is the focus of this paper. The unbiased losses in (b), including the Mean Reciprocal Rank (MRR) and the Average Discounted Gain (ADG), require either knowledge of $\mathbf{1}^\top\mathbf{y}^*$ or that labels go missing with probability $1 - g_l/\mathbf{1}^\top\mathbf{y}^*$ with known g_l (except for the F-score). Note that $\hat{\mathbf{y}}$ has only k non-zero entries for precision@k, nDCG@k and recall@k and that r_l represents the rank of label l in $\hat{\mathbf{y}}$.

(a) Gain	$-\mathcal{L}(\mathbf{y}, \hat{\mathbf{y}})$	(b) Gain	$-\mathcal{L}(\mathbf{y}, \hat{\mathbf{y}})$
Precision@k	$\frac{1}{k}\sum_l \frac{1}{p_l} y_l \hat{y}_l$	Recall@k	$\frac{1}{\mathbf{1}^\top\mathbf{y}^*}\sum_l \frac{1}{p_l} y_l \hat{y}_l$
nDCG@k	$\frac{\sum_l \frac{y_l \hat{y}_l}{p_l \log(r_l+1)}}{\left(\sum_{l=1}^k \frac{1}{\log(l+1)}\right)}$	MRR	$\frac{1}{\mathbf{1}^\top\mathbf{y}^*}\sum_l \frac{y_l}{p_l r_l}$
		ADG	$\frac{1}{\mathbf{1}^\top\mathbf{y}^*}\sum_l \frac{y_l}{p_l \log(r_l+1)}$
-Hamming Loss	$\left(\frac{1}{p_l}(2\hat{y}_l - 1)\right) y_l - \hat{y}_l^2$	F_β score	$\frac{(1+\beta^2)}{\beta^2(\mathbf{1}^\top\mathbf{y}^*)+\mathbf{1}^\top\hat{\mathbf{y}}}\sum_l \frac{1}{p_l} y_l \hat{y}_l$

Propensities: The propensity $p_{il} \equiv P(y_{il} = 1 | y_{il}^* = 1)$ denotes the marginal probability of a relevant label l being observed for a data point i. No constraints have been placed on the propensities apart from the fact that label noise is one sided – i. e. $P(y_{il} = 1 | y_{il}^* = 0) = 0$. In particular, it is not assumed that labels go missing independently or uniformly at random. Note that, for notational convenience, the subscript i will be dropped from p_{il} even though the propensity depends on both the label l and the data point i.

Propensity scored loss functions: Let $\mathcal{L}^*(\mathbf{y}^*, \hat{\mathbf{y}}) = \sum_{l=1}^L \mathcal{L}_l^*(y_l^*, \hat{y}_l) = \sum_{l:y_l^*=1}^L \mathcal{L}_l^*(1, \hat{y}_l)$ denote the family of loss functions which decompose over individual labels l and are computed over the relevant labels alone ($\{l | y_l^* = 1\}$). $\mathcal{L}^*$ represents the true loss function measuring the loss incurred for predicting $\hat{\mathbf{y}}$ when the complete ground truth vector was $\mathbf{y}^*$. Training and performance evaluation using $\mathcal{L}^*$ is desirable but infeasible as $\mathbf{y}^*$ is unavailable. The propensity scored variant of $\mathcal{L}^*$ computed on the observed ground truth $\mathbf{y}$ is defined to be $\mathcal{L}(\mathbf{y}, \hat{\mathbf{y}}) = \sum_{l:y_l=1}^L \mathcal{L}_l(1, \hat{y}_l) = \sum_{l:y_l=1}^L \mathcal{L}_l^*(1, \hat{y}_l)/p_l$. Then the following theorem implies that $\mathcal{L}$ can be a viable proxy for $\mathcal{L}^*$ for training, model selection, hyperparameter tuning and performance evaluation.

THEOREM 4.1. *The loss function $\mathcal{L}(\mathbf{y}, \hat{\mathbf{y}})$ evaluated on the observed ground truth $\mathbf{y}$ is an unbiased estimator of the true loss function $\mathcal{L}^*(\mathbf{y}^*, \hat{\mathbf{y}})$ evaluated on the complete ground truth $\mathbf{y}^*$. Thus, $\mathbb{E}_{\mathbf{y}}[\mathcal{L}(\mathbf{y}, \hat{\mathbf{y}})] = \mathbb{E}_{\mathbf{y}^*}[\mathcal{L}^*(\mathbf{y}^*, \hat{\mathbf{y}})]$, for any $P(\mathbf{y}^*)$ and $P(\mathbf{y})$ related through propensities p_l and any fixed $\hat{\mathbf{y}}$.*

PROOF. Please click here for the supplementary material containing the proof. □

Theorem 4.1 covers loss functions which decompose over individual labels such as precision@k and nDCG@k which are the primary focus of this paper. Unbiased estimators of recall, average discounted gain, mean reciprocal rank and other relevant non-decomposable loss functions can also be derived if it is assumed that $P(\mathbf{y}^*)$ is a delta function implying that each ground truth label is either definitely relevant or definitely irrelevant (with no uncertainty) to the data point being annotated.

THEOREM 4.2. *If $P(\mathbf{y}^*)$ is a delta function then $\mathbb{E}_{\mathbf{y}}[\mathcal{L}(\mathbf{y}, \hat{\mathbf{y}})] = \mathbb{E}_{\mathbf{y}^*}[\mathcal{L}^*(\mathbf{y}^*, \hat{\mathbf{y}})]$ for non-decomposable loss functions of the form $\mathcal{L}^*(\mathbf{y}^*, \hat{\mathbf{y}}) = \sum_{l:y_l^*=1}^L \frac{\mathcal{L}_l^*(1, \hat{y}_l)}{g^*(\mathbf{y}^*, \hat{\mathbf{y}})}$ and $\mathcal{L}(\mathbf{y}, \hat{\mathbf{y}}) = \sum_{l:y_l=1}^L \frac{\mathcal{L}_l^*(1, \hat{y}_l)}{g^*(\mathbf{y}^*, \hat{\mathbf{y}}) p_l}$ with arbitrary propensities p_l.*

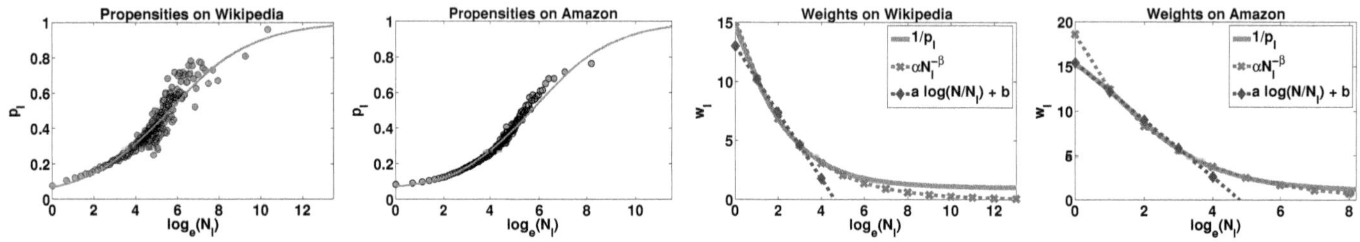

Figure 2: Propensities p_l and their corresponding weights $w_l = 1/p_l$ on Wikipedia and Amazon. The estimated propensities follow a sigmoidal curve on the semi-log plot and provide a principled setting of the weights for recommending rare items as compared to popular heuristics such as $N_l^{-\beta}$ and $\log(N/N_l)$.

PROOF. Please click here for the supplementary material containing the proof. □

Note that Theorem 4.2 is useful only if $g^*(\mathbf{y}^*, \hat{\mathbf{y}})$ can be evaluated even though $\mathbf{y}^*$ is unknown. This is certainly possible in some applications. For instance, in the case of recall, $g^*(\mathbf{y}^*, \hat{\mathbf{y}}) = \mathbf{1}^\top \mathbf{y}^*$ counts how many labels were relevant in the complete ground truth. This can be readily estimated by counting the number of face detections $(\mathbf{1}^\top \mathbf{y}^*)$ in a given image in name tagging applications on Facebook even though the name of each individual might not be known ($\mathbf{y}^*$ is unknown). Alternatively, if $g^*(\mathbf{y}^*, \hat{\mathbf{y}})$ is unknown, the following corollary derives unbiased estimators when $g^*(\mathbf{y}^*, \hat{\mathbf{y}}) = g^*(\mathbf{y}^*)$ and labels go missing with probability $1 - g_l/g^*(\mathbf{y}^*)$ with known g_l. Note that this generalizes the results of [26, 38] which assume that labels go missing uniformly at random with constant $g_l = \mathbf{1}\top\mathbf{y}$.

COROLLARY 4.2.1. *If $P(\mathbf{y}^*)$ is a delta function and labels are retained with propensities $p_l = g_l/g^*(\mathbf{y}^*)$, then $\mathbb{E}_{\mathbf{y}}[\mathcal{L}(\mathbf{y}, \hat{\mathbf{y}})]$ $= \mathbb{E}_{\mathbf{y}^*}[\mathcal{L}^*(\mathbf{y}^*, \hat{\mathbf{y}})]$ for non-decomposable loss functions of the form $\mathcal{L}^*(\mathbf{y}^*, \hat{\mathbf{y}}) = \sum_{l:y_l^*=1}^{L} \frac{\mathcal{L}_l^*(1,\hat{y}_l)}{g^*(\mathbf{y}^*)}$ and $\mathcal{L}(\mathbf{y}, \hat{\mathbf{y}}) = \sum_{l:y_l=1}^{L} \frac{\mathcal{L}_l^*(1,\hat{y}_l)}{g_l}$.*

PROOF. Please click here for the supplementary material containing the proof. □

The theorems so far prove that the propensity scored losses are unbiased in expectation. In practice, one can only compute the propensity scored loss on the observed labels rather than in expectation over $\mathbf{y}$. The following theorem shows that the bias induced by this point estimate depends on the average number of relevant labels rather than the total number of labels and that it reduces as the number of points over which the loss is computed is increased.

THEOREM 4.3. ***(Concentration bound)*** *Let $\mathbf{Y} = \{\mathbf{y}_i \in \{0,1\}^L\}_{i=1}^N$ be a set of N independent observed ground truth random variables. Then with probability at least $1 - \delta$*

$$\left|\mathbb{E}_{\mathbf{Y}}\left[\frac{1}{N}\sum_{i=1}^N \mathcal{L}(\mathbf{y}_i, \hat{\mathbf{y}}_i)\right] - \frac{1}{N}\sum_{i=1}^N \mathcal{L}(\mathbf{y}_i, \hat{\mathbf{y}}_i)\right| \le \rho\bar{L}\sqrt{\frac{1}{2N}\log\left(\frac{2}{\delta}\right)}$$

where $\rho = max_{il}\left|\frac{1}{p_{il}}\frac{\mathcal{L}_l^*(y_{il},\hat{y}_{il})}{g(\mathbf{y}_i^*,\hat{\mathbf{y}}_i)}\right|$, $\bar{L} = \sqrt{\frac{1}{N}\sum_{i=1}^N L_i^{*2}}$ and L_i^* is the maximum number of labels that can be relevant to a data point i in the complete ground truth.

PROOF. Please click here for the supplementary material containing the proof. □

Finally, an unbiased estimator can also be derived for the Hamming loss even though other loss functions, such as precision@k and nDCG@k, might be preferable

THEOREM 4.4. *For any $P(\mathbf{y}^*)$ and $P(\mathbf{y})$ related through propensities p_l and any fixed $\hat{\mathbf{y}}$, $\mathbb{E}_{\mathbf{y}}[\mathcal{L}(\mathbf{y}, \hat{\mathbf{y}})] = \mathbb{E}_{\mathbf{y}^*}[\mathcal{L}^*(\mathbf{y}^*, \hat{\mathbf{y}})]$ where $\mathcal{L}(\mathbf{y}, \hat{\mathbf{y}}) = \sum_l \left(\frac{1}{p_l}(1 - 2\hat{y}_l)\right) y_l + \hat{y}_l^2$ is an unbiased estimator of the Hamming loss $\mathcal{L}^*(\mathbf{y}^*, \hat{\mathbf{y}}) = \sum_l \|y_l^* - y_l\|^2$ with concentration bound $\rho\bar{L}\sqrt{\frac{1}{2N}}\log(2/\delta)$ where $\rho = max_{il}(1/p_{il})$.*

PROOF. Please click here for the supplementary material containing the proof. □

5. PROPENSITY MODEL

The unbiased variants of precision@k, nDCG@k and other loss functions developed in Section 4 require that the marginal propensities of labels being retained is known. Unfortunately, propensities are generally unknown as $\mathbf{y}^*$ is unavailable due to the large label space. Based on empirical observation, this Section proposes that the propensities might be modelled as a sigmoidal function of $\log N_l$

$$p_l \equiv P(y_l = 1 | y_l^* = 1) = \frac{1}{1 + Ce^{-A\log(N_l+B)}} \quad (1)$$

where N_l is the number of data points annotated with label l in the observed ground truth dataset of size N and A, B are application specific parameters and $C = (\log N - 1)(B+1)^A$. In particular, propensities are estimated on Wikipedia and Amazon where meta-data is available for the task and shown to give a close fit to (1) (see Figure 2).

Tagging on Wikipedia ($A = 0.5, B = 0.4$): The marginal propensity of a label can be estimated as $p_l = N_l/N_l^*$ where N_l and N_l^* are the number of times the label occurred in the observed and complete ground truth respectively. Estimates of N_l^* can be obtained for Wikipedia by leveraging its hierarchy. It is assumed that if a label is relevant to a Wikipedia article then so are all its ancestor labels. For instance, the Divine Comedy article has been annotated with "1300 in Italy" and should therefore have also been annotated with its ancestor "14th century in Italy". Examining all Wikipedia articles revealed that 45 articles were annotated with a descendant of the label "14th century in Italy" but only 10 were annotated with the label itself resulting in a propensity estimate of $p_l = 10/(10 + 45) = 0.182$. This procedure was carried out for all labels with more than 4 descendants for robust estimation. Labels with similar frequencies were binned together in an equiheight histogram with 20 labels per bin. Figure 2 plots the average propensity per bin as a function of label frequency on a log scale. As can be seen, the proposed sigmoid propensity model with parameters $A = 0.5$ and $B = 0.4$ is a close fit to the estimated propensities.

Product recommendation on Amazon ($A = 0.6, B = 2.6$)**:** The item-to-item recommendation task on Amazon is to predict the subset of items (labels) that a user might buy along with a given item. In this case, N_l represents the number of items that item l was bought along with in the observed dataset (across all transactions) while N_l^* represents the total number of items that item l could have been bought along with. While N_l is known, N_l^* can be estimated by figuring out which items could have been substituted in place of the ones that item l was bought along with. It has been argued that substitutable products can be inferred from the "also viewed" items while complimentary items can be inferred from the "also bought" items [28, 30]. Following this principle, N_l^* can be estimated as the total number of unique items viewed along with items that item l was "also bought" along with. For robustness, propensities $p_l = N_l/N_l^*$ were estimated only for those items for which "also viewed" information was available for each of the items that item l was "also bought" with . Items with similar N_l were binned together in an equiheight histogram as in the case of Wikipedia. Figure 2 plots the average propensity per bin as a function of item frequency on a log scale. As can be seen, the proposed sigmoid propensity model with parameters $A = 0.6$ and $B = 2.6$ is a close fit to the estimated propensities.

Recommending rare items: It is important to remove the popularity bias and recommend rare/novel items in many applications [9, 12, 35, 39, 44, 47, 49, 51]. A common heuristic is to weight each item inversely to its popularity and to assign weighted rewards for accurate recommendations. Weights have often been set in an ad hoc fashion as $w_l \propto N_l^{-\beta}$ [12, 35, 39] or $w_l \propto \log(N/N_l)$ [9, 44, 47, 49, 51].

Such weights arise naturally as inverse propensities in the unbiased losses developed in this paper. As can be seen from (1) and Table 1, each label in the proposed unbiased losses has a weight given by

$$w_l = 1/p_l = 1 + C(N_l + B)^{-A} \tag{2}$$

which somewhat matches $(N_l + B)^{-A}$ and $\log(N/N_l)$ in different ranges of N_l (see Figure 2). This not only provides a sound theoretical justification of label weighting heuristics for recommending rare items but also leads to a more principled setting of the weights.

Other datasets: Propensity estimation might not be possible on datasets where meta information is not available. In such cases, it is recommended that $A = (0.5 + 0.6)/2 = 0.55$ and $B = (0.4 + 2.6)/2 = 1.5$ are set to their values averaged over Wikipedia and Amazon. This was verified to be reasonably close to the parameter settings on the Wiki10 dataset ($A = 0.55, B = 0.1$).

6. ALGORITHMS

This Section develops the PfastreXML algorithm for extreme multi-label learning. PfastreXML optimizes propensity scored nDCG by leveraging FastXML [34] for nDCG optimization. PfastreXML then further extends FastXML to improve tail label prediction which is the most challenging aspect of extreme multi-label learning. PfastreXML achieves this at scale by making key approximations which increase FastXML's training time by just seconds while retaining the prediction accuracy gains of the extension.

6.1 Propensity scored FastXML

Classifier architecture: Propensity scored FastXML (PfastXML) shares the same architecture as FastXML [34] which learns an ensemble of trees during training. Trees are grown by recursively partitioning nodes starting at the root until each tree is fully grown. Nodes are split by learning a separating hyperplane which partitions training points between a left and a right child. The FastXML hyperplane is learnt by optimizing nDCG such that each training point's relevant labels are ranked as highly as possible in its partition. Node partitioning terminates when a node contains less than a user specified number of points. Leaf nodes contain a probability distribution over labels generated by normalizing the frequency counts of all the training labels reaching the node.

Predictions are made in logarithmic time by passing a test point down each of the balanced trees in the ensemble. The test point is sent to an internal node's left (right) child if it lies on the negative (positive) side of the separating hyperplane at that node. The label distributions of all the leaves containing the test point are aggregated in order to make a prediction as follows:

$$\mathbf{P}_{\text{pf}}(\mathbf{y}^*|\mathbf{x}) = \frac{\sum_{t=1}^{T} \mathbf{P}_t^{\text{leaf}}(\mathbf{x})}{T} \tag{3}$$

Propensity scored objective function: PfastXML improves upon FastXML by replacing the nDCG loss with its propensity scored variant which is unbiased and assigns higher rewards for accurate tail label predictions. Given a set of N training points at a node $\{(\mathbf{x}_i, \mathbf{y}_i)_{i=1}^N\}$ with features $\mathbf{x}_i \in \mathcal{R}^D$ and observed ground truth label vectors $\mathbf{y}_i \in \{0,1\}^L$, PfastXML's separating hyperplane $\mathbf{w}^*$ at the node is given by the optimal solution of

$$\begin{aligned}
\min \quad & \|\mathbf{w}\|_1 + C_\delta \sum_i \log(1 + e^{-\delta_i \mathbf{w}^\top \mathbf{x}_i}) \\
& + C_r \sum_i \tfrac{1}{2}(1 + \delta_i)\mathcal{L}_{\text{PSnDCG@}L}(\mathbf{r}^+, \mathbf{y}_i) \\
& + C_r \sum_i \tfrac{1}{2}(1 - \delta_i)\mathcal{L}_{\text{PSnDCG@}L}(\mathbf{r}^-, \mathbf{y}_i) \\
\text{w. r. t.} \quad & \mathbf{w} \in \mathcal{R}^D, \boldsymbol{\delta} \in \{-1,+1\}^L, \mathbf{r}^+, \mathbf{r}^- \in \Pi(1, L)
\end{aligned} \tag{4}$$

where $\mathcal{L}_{\text{PSnDCG@}L}(\mathbf{r}, \mathbf{y}) = -\frac{\sum_l \frac{y_l}{p_l \log(r_l+1)}}{\sum_{l=1}^L \frac{1}{\log(1+l)}}$, i indexes all the training points present at the node being partitioned, $\delta_i \in \{-1,+1\}$ indicates whether point i was assigned to the negative or positive partition and $\mathbf{r}^+$ and $\mathbf{r}^-$ represent the predicted label rankings for the positive and negative partition respectively.

Optimization: Note that FastXML's objective function can be recovered from PfastXML's by substituting $y_{il}^p = y_{il}/p_{il}$ – i. e. by replacing each label y_{il} with label y_{il}^p. PfastXML's objective function can therefore be optimized by FastXML's iterative alternating optimization applied to y_{il}^p. In each iteration, the algorithm fixes $\mathbf{w}$ and alternates between optimizing $\boldsymbol{\delta}$ and $\mathbf{r}^\pm$ using efficient closed form solutions until a stationary point is reached according to Theorem 1 of [34]. Then $\boldsymbol{\delta}$ and $\mathbf{r}^\pm$ are fixed and $\mathbf{w}$ is optimized by solving a standard l_1 regularized logistic regression binary classification problem using Liblinear [13].

Scale: PfastXML enjoys all the scaling properties of FastXML and is therefore one of the most efficient extreme multi-label

Table 2: Dataset statistics

Dataset	Train N	Features D	Labels L	Test M	Avg. labels per point	Avg. points per label
EUR-Lex	15,539	5,000	3,993	3,809	5.31	25.73
AmazonCat-13K	1,186,239	203,882	13,330	306,782	5.05	566.01
Wiki10-31K	14,149	101,938	30,935	6,613	17.25	11.58
WikiLSHTC-325K	1,778,351	1,617,899	325,056	587,084	3.26	23.74
Amazon-670K	490,449	135,909	670,091	153,025	5.38	5.17
Ads-9M	70,455,530	2,082,698	8,838,461	22,629,136	1.79	14.32

learning algorithm for large scale problems. It could train on WikiLSHTC-325K (325 K labels, 1.7 M training points and 1.6 M dimensions) and Ads-9M (9 M labels, 70 M training points and 2 M dimensions) in less than 30 minutes and 17 hours respectively using a 16 core Intel Xeon 2.6 GHz server. In contrast, MLRF [4] required 4 and 42 hours on a thousand core cluster for training on these datasets and resulted in significantly lower prediction accuracies [34]. No other algorithm has been shown to scale to datasets of the size of Ads-9M to the best of our knowledge. Equally importantly in terms of scaling, PfastXML's predictions required less than 1.5 milliseconds per test point even at the largest scale which is critical for deployment in real world applications.

6.2 PfastreXML

Propensity scoring improves FastXML but tree classifiers are still prone to predicting tail labels with low probabilities as partitioning errors in the internal nodes disproportionately reduce the support of tail labels in the leaf node distributions. PfastreXML addresses this limitation by re-ranking PfastXML's predictions using classifiers designed specifically for tail labels. PfastreXML's training and prediction routines are shown in Algorithms 2 and 3 of the supplementary material while code is available from [1].

Tail label classifiers: It is assumed that each label can be predicted independently based on a hyperspherical decision boundary generated by

$$P(y^*_{il}|\mathbf{x}_i) = 1/(1+v_{il}^{2y^*_{il}-1}) \quad \text{where } v_{il} = e^{\frac{\gamma}{2}\|\mathbf{x}_i-\boldsymbol{\mu}_l\|_2^2} \quad (5)$$

Discriminative MLE estimation of the parameters $\{\boldsymbol{\mu}_l\}$ on the *observed* training data $\{(\mathbf{x}_i, \mathbf{y}_i)_{i=1}^N\}$ with features $\mathbf{x}_i \in \mathcal{R}^D$ and observed ground truth label vectors $\mathbf{y}_i \in \{0,1\}^L$ can be carried out as $\arg\max_{\{\boldsymbol{\mu}_l\}} \prod_{i=1}^N \prod_{l=1}^L \sum_{y^*_{il}=0}^1 P(y_{il}|y^*_{il})P(y^*_{il}|\mathbf{x}_i)$ where it has been reasonably assumed that $P(y_{il}|y^*_{il}, \mathbf{x}_i) = P(y_{il}|y^*_{il})$.

Optimization: Taking the log leads to L independent optimization problems

$$\boldsymbol{\mu}^*_l = \arg\max_{\boldsymbol{\mu}_l} \sum_{i=1}^N \log\left((1-y_{il}) + \frac{p_{il}(2y_{il}-1)}{1+v_{il}}\right) \quad (6)$$

Taking the gradient and equating it to zero yields $\boldsymbol{\mu}^*_l = \frac{\sum_{i=1}^N u_{il}\mathbf{x}_i}{\sum_{i=1}^N u_{il}}$ where $u_{il} = \frac{v_{il}}{1+v_{il}} - \frac{(1-y_{il})v_{il}}{1+v_{il}-p_{il}}$. Note that this is not a closed form solution since v_{il} is a function of $\boldsymbol{\mu}^*_l$ and hence one needs to apply an optimization technique, such as stochastic gradient descent, to obtain $\boldsymbol{\mu}^*_l$.

Approximation: Unfortunately, stochastic gradient descent is too expensive at the scale of Ads-9M. A simple, yet effective, approximation is therefore proposed which allowed training on Ads-9M in 18 minutes on a single core (all other datasets were trained in less than 20 seconds), led to sparse solutions taking up only 2.64 Gigabytes of RAM for Ads-9M and reduced prediction accuracy over the stochastic gradient descent solution by 0.2% as measured on the smaller datasets. In particular, assuming that $\frac{\gamma}{2}\|\mathbf{x}_i - \boldsymbol{\mu}_l\|^2 \gg 0 \forall\, i \in \{1,..,N\}$, led to the simplification $u_{il} \approx y_{il}$ yielding

$$\boldsymbol{\mu}^*_l = \frac{\sum_{i=1}^N y_{il}\mathbf{x}_i}{\sum_{i=1}^N y_{il}} \quad (7)$$

Thus, each $\boldsymbol{\mu}^*_l$ turns out to be the mean of the training points for which the label was observed to be relevant. This implies that solutions preserving data sparsity can be efficiently computed for millions of tail labels as each of them has only a handful of training points.

Re-ranking: The final ranked list of labels is predicted by sorting a linear combination of (3) and (5)

$$s_l = \alpha \log P_{\text{pf}}(y^*_l = 1|\mathbf{x}) + (1-\alpha)\log P(y^*_l = 1|\mathbf{x}) \quad (8)$$

restricted to those l for which $P_{\text{pf}}(y^*_l = 1|x) \neq 0$. Note that the re-ranking takes place in 0.13 milliseconds per point on Ads-9M so that the overall prediction time continues to be less than 1.5 milliseconds per test point.

7. EXPERIMENTS

Experiments were carried out on a synthetic dataset to show that the proposed propensity scored loss functions are unbiased and preferable for both training and performance evaluation. Experiments were also carried out on the largest benchmark datasets demonstrating that PfastreXML could achieve significantly higher prediction accuracies as compared to the state-of-the-art. Improvements in the click-through rates on Bing Ads indicated that the proposed loss functions and algorithms were better suited for real world applications.

Datasets: Experiments were carried out on extreme multi-label datasets including Ads-9M, Amazon-670K [6, 29], Wiki10-31K [6, 52],WikiLSHTC-325K [33, 34], AmazonCat-13K [29] and EUR-Lex [31]. The Ads-9M dataset is proprietary. All the other datasets are publically available and can be downloaded from The Extreme Classification Repository [2]. The tasks include annotating Wikipedia articles with the subset of relevant 325 K Wikipedia tags, item-to-item recommendation on Amazon with 670 K items and ranking 9 M queries for sponsored search advertising on Bing. Table 2 lists the statistics of these datasets.

Baseline algorithms: PfastreXML was compared to a number of baseline extreme multi-label algorithms including FastXML [34] and SLEEC [6] which are the leading tree and embedding based approaches respectively. Other

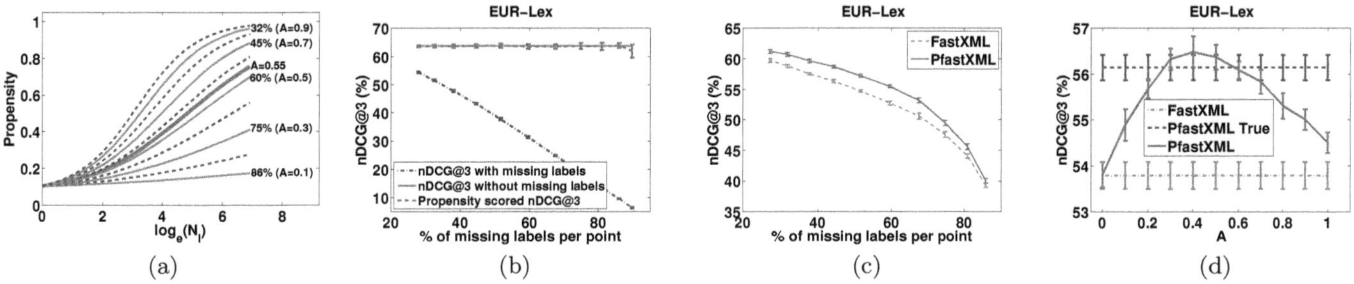

Figure 3: (a) propensity curves used for simulating missing labels on the EUR-Lex dataset with each curve labelled with the corresponding percentage of missing labels; (b) propensity scored nDCG@k is unbiased; (c) propensity scoring improves training; and (d) training using incorrect propensities ($A \neq 0.55$) might be better than training without propensities. See text for details. Figure best viewed under magnification.

baseline algorithms include 1-vs-All [16], LEML [48], WSABIE [45], CPLST [10], CS [18], ML-CSSP [7] and LPSR [46]. A Popularity baseline was also included which predicted a constant ranking of the most frequently occurring labels in each dataset. Unfortunately, some of the algorithms did not scale beyond the EUR-Lex dataset and results are presented in Table 3.

Implementations of SLEEC, FastXML, LEML and 1-vs-All were provided by the authors. The remaining algorithms were implemented by us taking care to ensure that the published results could be reproduced and were verified by the authors wherever possible.

Hyper-parameters: PfastreXML has 2 hyper-parameters α, γ in addition to FastXML's hyper-parameters. These were set to constants $\alpha = 0.8, \gamma = 30$ across all datasets. All of FastXML's hyper-parameters were also set to constant default values across all datasets as was done in [34]. This helps significantly reduce training time by eliminating hyper-parameter tuning. The hyper-parameters for all the other algorithms were set using fine grained validation on each data set so as to achieve the highest possible prediction accuracy.

Evaluation metrics: Given a set of M test points, performance was evaluated using the unbiased propensity scored loss functions of Table 1 as $\mathcal{G}(\{\hat{\mathbf{y}}_i\}) = \frac{-1}{M}\sum_{i=1}^{M}\mathcal{L}(\mathbf{y}_i, \hat{\mathbf{y}}_i)$. Note that the gain $\mathcal{G}$ could be greater than 1 due to the propensities. Therefore, for greater interpretability, Table 3 reports $100*\mathcal{G}(\{\hat{\mathbf{y}}_i\})/\mathcal{G}(\{\mathbf{y}_i\})$ for Precision@k and nDCG@k, referred to as Pk and Nk respectively, for $k = 1, 3$ and 5. Coverage@k measuring the percentage of normalized unique labels present in the top $k = 1, 3$ and 5 predictions made by an algorithm across all test points is also reported as Ck.

Simulations: It was assumed that the complete ground truth was available for the EUR-Lex dataset and missing labels were simulated according to the propensity curves shown in Figure 3a.

In the second experiment, FastXML was trained on missing labels by optimizing nDCG while PfastXML was trained on the same set by optimizing propensity scored nDCG. Both methods were evaluated using nDCG@3 computed on the complete ground truth with no missing labels. As Figure 3c shows, PfastXML consistently outperformed FastXML thereby indicating that propensity scoring could improve training. A related concern might be that PfastXML (or PfastreXML) might outperform FastXML just because it optimizes the loss function being used for evaluation while FastXML does not. This experiment demonstrates otherwise as PfastXML was trained using propensity scored nDCG but evaluated using standard nDCG. Results of similar experiments on the benchmark datasets are provided in the supplementary material.

Finally, Figure 3d demonstrates that training with incorrect propensities might be better than training with no propensities. In this experiment, labels were removed from the training set using a reference propensity curve depicted in bold in Figure 3a. FastXML and PfastXML were trained on this set and their performance evaluated using nDCG@3 computed on the complete test set without any missing labels. PfastXML was then trained on the very same training set but using incorrect propensities (also shown in Figure 3a with $A \neq 0.55$). As can be seen, PfastXML trained on incorrect propensities could outperform FastXML trained without propensities. This indicates that using even incorrect propensity estimates might be beneficial in certain situations as compared to using no propensities.

Benchmark Results: Table 3 compares PfastreXML's performance to that of state-of-the-art SLEEC, FastXML and other baseline algorithms using unbiased precision and nDCG. As can be seen, the proposed PfastXML and PfastreXML lead to significantly better prediction accuracies as compared to the state-of-the-art. PfastreXML's improvements ranged from 3% on Ads-9M to more than 20% on AmazonCat-13K. Figure 4 shows that most of these improvements were made for infrequently occurring tail labels. In addition, Table 4 shows that PfastreXML predicted a larger number of unique labels than SLEEC or FastXML further indicating that PfastreXML had better coverage in the tail.

PfastreXML also improves upon PfastXML's prediction accuracy with negligible training and prediction overheads. For instance, PfastXML could train on WikiLSHTC-325K and Ads-9M in less than 30 minutes and 17 hours respectively using a 16 core Intel Xeon 2.6 GHz server. PfastreXML took an extra 12 seconds and 18 minutes for training on these datasets using a single core. PfastreXML's predictions took an extra 0.13 milliseconds per test point over PfastXML's and continued to be under 1.5 milliseconds.

Sponsored search on Bing: PfastreXML's query rankings were also used to serve ads on the Bing search engine. PfastreXML was observed to give an improvement of sig-

Table 3: The proposed PfastreXML and PfastXML algorithms make significantly more accurate predictions as compared to state-of-the-art SLEEC, FastXML and other baseline algorithms. PfastreXML's predictions are more accurate than PfastXML's with negligible training and prediction overheads. Performance is evaluated according to the unbiased propensity scored Precision@k (Pk) and nDCG@k (Nk) for $k = 1, 3$ and 5.

(a) EUR-Lex $N = 15K, D = 5K, L = 4K$

Algorithm	N1(%)	N3(%)	N5(%)	P1(%)	P3(%)	P5(%)
Popularity	1.80	2.10	2.36	1.80	2.20	2.62
1-vs-All	37.97	42.44	43.97	37.97	44.01	46.17
SLEEC	35.45	39.79	41.97	35.45	41.35	44.62
LEML	24.33	26.45	27.70	24.33	27.22	29.13
WSABIE	31.65	34.12	35.43	31.65	35.04	36.99
CPLST	28.93	31.60	32.92	28.93	32.57	34.55
CS	25.31	26.98	25.71	25.31	27.57	25.13
ML-CSSP	25.25	26.70	27.79	25.25	27.27	28.97
FastXML	27.61	33.22	36.28	27.61	35.35	39.95
LPSR	33.65	38.20	39.82	33.65	39.88	42.17
PfastXML	41.31	44.01	45.13	41.31	45.02	46.67
PfastreXML	**45.38**	**46.42**	**47.25**	**45.38**	**46.79**	**48.08**

(b) AmazonCat-13K $N = 1.18M, D = 203K, L = 13K$

Algorithm	N1(%)	N3(%)	N5(%)	P1(%)	P3(%)	P5(%)
Popularity	14.41	13.08	13.22	14.41	12.59	12.95
SLEEC	46.75	55.19	60.08	46.75	58.46	65.96
FastXML	46.58	55.48	61.59	46.58	59.00	68.50
PfastXML	67.44	70.70	72.27	67.44	71.94	74.32
PfastreXML	**69.05**	**71.79**	**73.33**	**69.05**	**72.83**	**75.21**

(c) Wiki10-31K $N = 14K, D = 101K, L = 31K$

Algorithm	N1(%)	N3(%)	N5(%)	P1(%)	P3(%)	P5(%)
Popularity	2.30	2.26	2.28	2.30	2.25	2.29
SLEEC	13.43	13.66	13.81	13.43	13.75	13.96
FastXML	10.31	10.18	10.35	10.31	10.14	10.42
PfastXML	15.62	16.05	16.42	15.62	16.20	16.71
PfastreXML	**21.32**	**19.97**	**19.48**	**21.32**	**19.53**	**18.93**

(d) WikiLSHTC-325K $N = 1.78M, D = 1.62M, L = 325K$

Algorithm	N1(%)	N3(%)	N5(%)	P1(%)	P3(%)	P5(%)
Popularity	2.56	1.91	1.83	2.56	1.65	1.53
SLEEC	20.51	22.45	23.52	20.51	23.32	25.23
FastXML	16.52	19.70	21.17	16.52	21.12	23.69
PfastXML	25.58	26.55	27.42	25.58	27.01	28.59
PfastreXML	**31.16**	**31.56**	**32.40**	**31.16**	**31.80**	**33.35**

(e) Amazon-670K $N = 490K, D = 136K, L = 670K$

Algorithm	N1(%)	N3(%)	N5(%)	P1(%)	P3(%)	P5(%)
Popularity	0.03	0.04	0.04	0.03	0.04	0.04
SLEEC	20.62	22.63	24.43	20.62	23.32	25.98
FastXML	20.20	22.94	25.26	20.20	23.88	27.28
PfastXML	25.61	26.95	28.09	25.61	27.42	29.09
PfastreXML	**29.93**	**30.91**	**31.94**	**29.93**	**31.26**	**32.80**

(f) Ads-9M $N = 70.45M, D = 2.08M, L = 8.84M$

Algorithm	N1(%)	N3(%)	N5(%)	P1(%)	P3(%)	P5(%)
Popularity	0.05	0.08	0.09	0.05	0.09	0.12
FastXML	12.89	14.86	15.61	12.89	15.88	17.26
PfastXML	13.27	15.39	16.32	13.27	16.49	18.22
PfastreXML	**13.52**	**16.43**	**17.79**	**13.52**	**17.95**	**20.50**

Table 4: PfastreXML has more unique labels Ck in the top $k = 1, 3$ and 5 predictions across all test points in a dataset as compared to SLEEC or FastXML indicating that it has better coverage of tail labels.

(a) EUR-Lex $N = 15K, D = 5K, L = 4K$

Algorithm	C1 (%)	C3 (%)	C5 (%)
1-vs-All	33.50	44.29	53.82
SLEEC	27.21	38.10	49.26
FastXML	16.39	28.39	40.49
PfastreXML	**48.81**	**56.29**	**62.31**

(b) AmazonCat-13K $N = 1.18M, D = 203K, L = 13K$

Algorithm	C1 (%)	C3 (%)	C5 (%)
SLEEC	8.62	23.50	49.16
FastXML	2.13	15.76	53.69
PfastreXML	**83.03**	**85.12**	**86.49**

(c) Wiki10-31K $N = 14K, D = 101K, L = 31K$

Algorithm	C1 (%)	C3 (%)	C5 (%)
SLEEC	5.94	5.73	6.59
FastXML	1.57	2.12	2.88
PfastreXML	**25.67**	**18.48**	**17.67**

(d) WikiLSHTC-325K $N = 1.78M, D = 1.62M, L = 325K$

Algorithm	C1 (%)	C3 (%)	C5 (%)
SLEEC	14.06	24.53	30.11
FastXML	9.52	18.43	23.29
PfastreXML	**29.63**	**36.45**	**40.67**

(e) Amazon-670K $N = 490K, D = 136K, L = 670K$

Algorithm	C1 (%)	C3 (%)	C5 (%)
SLEEC 24.19	26.18	30.97	
FastXML	22.06	25.25	30.94
PfastreXML	**34.58**	**36.41**	**40.13**

(f) Ads-9M $N = 70.45M, D = 2.08M, L = 8.84M$

Algorithm	C1 (%)	C3 (%)	C5 (%)
FastXML	3.26	3.94	4.33
PfastreXML	**6.04**	**7.45**	**8.09**

nificantly more than 5% in the clickthrough rate over both FastXML and the highly specialized system in production (which was a large ensemble of many different ranking techniques). Note that the production system was very good at predicting head queries with high ranks and that PfastreXML was rewarded for making only those predictions which could not be made by the production system. Accurately ranking tail queries highly was therefore critical in this case and PfastreXML was able to successfully serve ads which had never received clicks before. This helps verify that the propensity scored loss functions and proposed algorithm align with the requirements of real world applications.

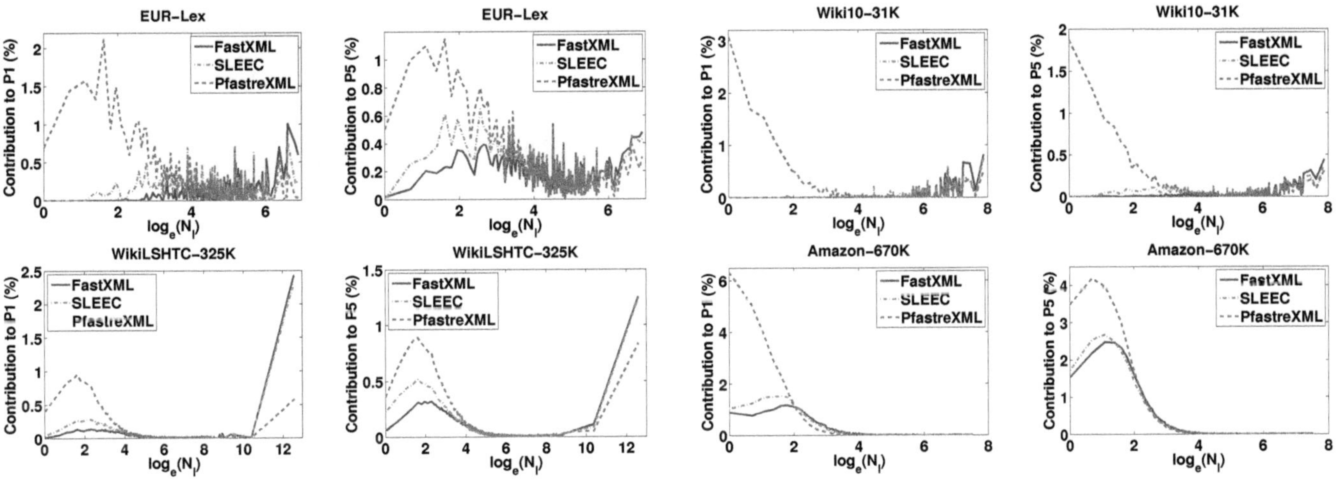

Figure 4: Plot showing the contribution of each label to the overall propensity scored Precision@1 and Precision@5. PfastreXML is significantly more accurate at predicting infrequently occurring (small N_l) tail labels. Figure best viewed under magnification

8. CONCLUSIONS

This paper developed loss functions suitable for extreme multi-label learning and long tail, missing label applications such as ranking, recommendation and tagging. Propensity scored variants of precision and nDCG were developed and proved to give unbiased estimates of the true loss function evaluated on the complete ground truth. No restrictions were placed on the propensities apart from the mild assumption that irrelevant labels were never marked as relevant. Furthermore, propensity models were developed based on real world applications and were shown to naturally promote the accurate prediction of infrequently occurring tail labels. This provides a sound theoretical justification of popular label weighting heuristics used to remove the popularity bias and recommend rare/novel items. The results also provide a more principled setting of the weights as compared to previous heuristics.

This paper also developed the PfastreXML algorithm for optimizing propensity scored nDCG. PfastreXML was shown to make significantly more accurate predictions on all datasets as compared to the state-of-the-art. PfastreXML was demonstrated to be specially well suited to predicting tail labels which is the most challenging aspect of extreme multi-label learning. This helped PfastreXML achieve significantly higher clickthrough rates for sponsored search advertising on Bing as compared to the large ensemble of highly specialized rankers currently in production. In terms of scaling, PfastreXML could train on WikiLSHTC-325K and Ads-9M in less than 30 minutes and 17 hours respectively using a 16 core Intel Xeon 2.6 GHz server. Finally, PfastreXML's predictions were made in under 1.5 milliseconds per test point which is critical for deployment in real world applications. The code for PfastreXML is available from [1].

Acknowledgement

We are grateful to Rahul Agrawal, Samy Bengio, Abhishek Kadian, Shrutendra Harsola, Purushottam Kar, Prateek Jain and Ambuj Tewari for discussions, feedback and help with experiments. Himanshu Jain is supported by a Google PhD Fellowship. Yashoteja Prabhu is supported by a TCS PhD Fellowship and MSR India travel grant. Manik Varma would like to thank the School of Information Technology at IIT Delhi where he holds an adjunct position.

References

[1] Code for PfastreXML. http://research.microsoft.com/en-us/um/people/manik/code/PfastreXML/download.html.

[2] The Extreme Classification Repository. http://research.microsoft.com/en-us/um/people/manik/downloads/XC/XMLRepository.html.

[3] D. Agarwal, L. Li, and A. J. Smola. Linear-time estimators for propensity scores. In *AISTATS*, 2011.

[4] R. Agrawal, A. Gupta, Y. Prabhu, and M. Varma. Multi-label learning with millions of labels: Recommending advertiser bid phrases for web pages. In *WWW*, 2013.

[5] K. Balasubramanian and G. Lebanon. The landmark selection method for multiple output prediction. In *ICML*, 2012.

[6] K. Bhatia, H. Jain, P. Kar, M. Varma, and P. Jain. Sparse local embeddings for extreme multi-label classification. In *NIPS*, 2015.

[7] W. Bi and J. T. Kwok. Efficient multi-label classification with many labels. In *ICML*, 2013.

[8] L. Bottou, J. Peters, J. Quinonero-Candela, D. X. Charles, D. M. Chickering, E. Portugaly, D. Ray, P. Simard, and E. Snelson. Counterfactual reasoning and learning systems: The example of computational advertising. *JMLR*, 2013.

[9] P. Castells, S. Vargas, and J. Wang. Novelty and diversity metrics for recommender systems: choice, discovery and relevance. In *DDR*, 2011.

[10] Y. N. Chen and H. T. Lin. Feature-aware label space dimension reduction for multi-label classification. In *NIPS*, 2012.

[11] M. Cissé, N. Usunier, T. Artières, and P. Gallinari. Robust bloom filters for large multilabel classification tasks. In *NIPS*, 2013.

[12] C. Dhanjal, R. Gaudel, and S. Clémençon. Collaborative filtering with localised ranking. In *AAAI*, 2015.

[13] R. E. Fan, K. W. Chang, C. J. Hsieh, X. R. Wang, and C. J. Lin. LIBLINEAR: A library for large linear classification. *JMLR*, 2008.

[14] C. S. Ferng and H. T. Lin. Multi-label classification with error-correcting codes. In *ACML*, 2011.

[15] S. Gopal and Y. Yang. Recursive regularization for large-scale classification with hierarchical and graphical dependencies. In *KDD*, 2013.

[16] B. Hariharan, S. V. N. Vishwanathan, and M. Varma. Efficient max-margin multi-label classification with applications to zero-shot learning. *ML*, 2012.

[17] C. J. Hsieh, N. Natarajan, and I. Dhillon. PU learning for matrix completion. In *ICML*, 2015.

[18] D. Hsu, S. Kakade, J. Langford, and T. Zhang. Multi-label prediction via compressed sensing. In *NIPS*, 2009.

[19] K. Jasinska and K. Dembczyński. Consistent label tree classifiers for extreme multi-label classification. In *Extreme Classification Workshop, ICML*, 2015.

[20] S. Ji, L. Tang, S. Yu, and J. Ye. Extracting shared subspace for multi-label classification. In *KDD*, 2008.

[21] A. Kapoor, R. Viswanathan, and P. Jain. Multilabel classification using bayesian compressed sensing. In *NIPS*, 2012.

[22] N. Karampatziakis and P. Mineiro. Scalable multilabel prediction via randomized methods. *CoRR*, 2015.

[23] X. Kong, Z. Wu, L. J. Li, R. Zhang, P. S. Yu, H. Wu, and W. Fan. Large-scale multi-label learning with incomplete label assignments. In *SDM*, 2014.

[24] L. Li, S. Chen, J. Kleban, and A. Gupta. Counterfactual estimation and optimization of click metrics in search engines: A case study. In *WWW*, 2015.

[25] L. Li, W. Chu, J. Langford, and X. Wang. Unbiased offline evaluation of contextual-bandit-based news article recommendation algorithms. In *WSDM*, 2011.

[26] D. Lim, J. McAuley, and G. Lanckriet. Top-N recommendation with missing implicit feedback. In *RecSys*, 2015.

[27] Z. Lin, G. Ding, M. Hu, and J. Wang. Multi-label classification via feature-aware implicit label space encoding. In *ICML*, 2014.

[28] J. McAuley, T. Christopher, S. Qinfeng, and A. van den Hengel. Image-based recommendations on styles and substitutes. In *SIGIR*, 2015.

[29] J. McAuley and J. Leskovec. Hidden factors and hidden topics: understanding rating dimensions with review text. In *RecSys*, 2013.

[30] J. McAuley, R. Pandey, and J. Leskovec. Inferring networks of substitutable and complementary products. In *KDD*, 2015.

[31] E. L. Mencia and J. Fürnkranz. Efficient pairwise multilabel classification for large-scale problems in the legal domain. In *SIGIR*, 2008.

[32] P. Mineiro and N. Karampatziakis. Fast label embeddings for extremely large output spaces. In *ECML*, 2015.

[33] I. Partalas, A. Kosmopoulos, N. Baskiotis, T. Artières, G. Paliouras, É. Gaussier, I. Androutsopoulos, M. R. Amini, and P. Gallinari. LSHTC: A benchmark for large-scale text classification. *CoRR*, 2015.

[34] Y. Prabhu and M. Varma. FastXML: A fast, accurate and stable tree classifier for extreme multi-label learning. In *KDD*, 2014.

[35] B. Pradel, N. Usunier, and P. Gallinari. Ranking with non-random missing ratings: Influence of popularity and positivity on evaluation metrics. In *RecSys*, 2012.

[36] P. Rai, C. Hu, R. Henao, and L. Carin. Large-scale bayesian multi-label learning via topic-based label embeddings. In *NIPS*, 2015.

[37] P. R. Rosenbaum and D. B. Rubin. The central role of the propensity score in observational studies for causal effects. *Biometrika*, 1983.

[38] H. Steck. Training and testing of recommender systems on data missing not at random. In *KDD*, 2010.

[39] H. Steck. Item popularity and recommendation accuracy. In *RecSys*, 2011.

[40] Y. Y. Sun, Y. Zhang, and Z. H. Zhou. Multi-label learning with weak label. In *AAAI*, 2010.

[41] A. Swaminathan and T. Joachims. Counterfactual risk minimization: Learning from logged bandit feedback. In *ICML*, 2015.

[42] A. Swaminathan and T. Joachims. The self-normalized estimator for counterfactual learning. In *NIPS*, 2015.

[43] F. Tai and H. T. Lin. Multi-label classification with principal label space transformation. In *MLD*, 2010.

[44] S. Vargas and P. Castells. Rank and relevance in novelty and diversity metrics for recommender systems. In *RecSys*, 2011.

[45] J. Weston, S. Bengio, and N. Usunier. Wsabie: Scaling up to large vocabulary image annotation. In *IJCAI*, 2011.

[46] J. Weston, A. Makadia, and H. Yee. Label partitioning for sublinear ranking. In *ICML*, 2013.

[47] H. Wu, X. Cui, J. He, B. Li, and Y. Pei. On improving aggregate recommendation diversity and novelty in folksonomy-based social systems. *Personal and Ubiquitous Computing*, 2014.

[48] H. F. Yu, P. Jain, P. Kar, and I. S. Dhillon. Large-scale multi-label learning with missing labels. In *ICML*, 2014.

[49] L. Zhang. The definition of novelty in recommendation system. *JESTR*, 2013.

[50] Y. Zhang and J. G. Schneider. Multi-label output codes using canonical correlation analysis. In *AISTATS*, 2011.

[51] T. Zhou, Z. Kuscsik, J. G. Liu, M. Medo, J. R. Wakeling, and Y. C. Zhang. Solving the apparent diversity-accuracy dilemma of recommender systems. *Proc. Nat. Acad. Sci. USA*, 2010.

[52] A. Zubiaga. Enhancing navigation on wikipedia with social tags. *CoRR*, 2012.

CatchTartan: Representing and Summarizing Dynamic Multicontextual Behaviors

Meng Jiang[1], Christos Faloutsos[2], Jiawei Han[1]
[1]Department of Computer Science, University of Illinois Urbana-Champaign, IL, USA
[2]Computer Science Department, Carnegie Mellon University, PA, USA
mjiang89@illinois.edu, christos@cs.cmu.edu, hanj@illinois.edu

ABSTRACT

Representing and summarizing human behaviors with rich contexts facilitates behavioral sciences and user-oriented services. Traditional behavioral modeling represents a behavior as a tuple in which each element is one contextual factor of one type, and the tensor-based summaries look for high-order dense blocks by clustering the values (including timestamps) in each dimension. However, the human behaviors are *multicontextual* and *dynamic*: (1) each behavior takes place within multiple contexts in a few dimensions, which requires the representation to enable non-value and set-values for each dimension; (2) many behavior collections, such as tweets or papers, evolve over time. In this paper, we represent the behavioral data as a two-level matrix (temporal-behaviors by dimensional-values) and propose a novel representation for behavioral summary called Tartan that includes a set of dimensions, the values in each dimension, a list of consecutive time slices and the behaviors in each slice. We further develop a propagation method CATCHTARTAN to catch the dynamic multicontextual patterns from the temporal multidimensional data in a *principled* and *scalable* way: it determines the meaningfulness of updating every element in the Tartan by minimizing the encoding cost in a compression manner. CATCHTARTAN outperforms the baselines on both the accuracy and speed. We apply CATCHTARTAN to four Twitter datasets up to 10 million tweets and the DBLP data, providing comprehensive summaries for the events, human life and scientific development.

Categories and Subject Descriptors

H.3.5 [**Information Systems**]: Information Storage and Retrieval - On-line Information Services; J.4 [**Computer Applications**]: Social and Behavioral Sciences

Keywords

Behavior Representation; Behavior Summarization; Minimum Description Length

1. INTRODUCTION

Behavioral representation and summarization is a fundamental component of behavioral scientific discovery: it supports the systematic analysis and investigation of human behaviors. It is also a fundamental problem in many user-oriented applications for a better understanding of the event from news, human life from tweets, and the scientific development from publications. However, it is rather challenging for the following two characteristics of the behaviors [10, 4]. (Terms and their definitions are given in Table 1.)

Tweeting behavior (Twitter) 20:03:09 @ebekahwsm : this better be the best halftime show ever in the history of halftimes shows. ever. #SuperBowl

Time slice	User	Location	Phrase	Hashtag	URL
20:00-20:30	@ebekahwsm	∅	{best halftime show, in the history, halftimes shows}	{#SuperBowl}	∅

Publishing-paper behavior (DBLP) SIGKDD 2009 "Sentiment analysis of blogs by combining lexical knowledge with text classification"

Time slice	Author	Venue	Keyword	Cited papers
2009	{P. Melville, W. Gryc, R. Lawrence}	SIGKDD	{sentiment analysis, lexical knowledge, text classification}	{p81623, p84395, p95393, p95409, p99073, p116349 ...}

(a) Representing a behavior with dimensional values including non-value and set-values, instead of one guaranteed value.

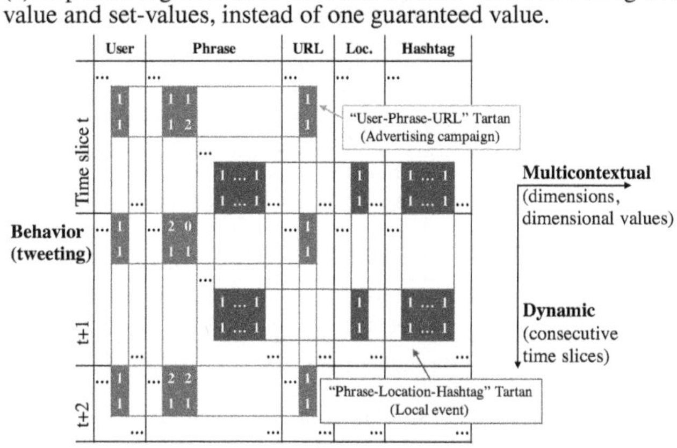

(b) Tartans in a "two-level matrix": dimensions and values on the columns, time slices and behaviors on the rows.

Figure 1: The representation and summarization of dynamic multicontextual behaviors: it takes every behavior while the tensor fails.

First, human behaviors are *multicontextual*: a behavior consists of one or multiple types (i.e., dimensions) of contextual factors [12], and it has one or multiple values in each dimension. Take the "Super Bowl" tweet in Figure 1a as an example: it has several dimensions such as the user, phrase, hashtag and shorten-URL, and this behavior has one user, one hashtag, *several* phrases and *no* URL. The publishing-paper behavior also has multiple values in the author, keyword and cited-paper dimensions. The representation should enable different combinations of the dimensions and a non-value/set-value setting of the dimensional values.

Second, human behaviors are *dynamic*. They naturally evolve with the changing of personality, physical environment and so-

KDD '16, August 13-17, 2016, San Francisco, CA, USA

DOI: http://dx.doi.org/10.1145/2939672.2939749

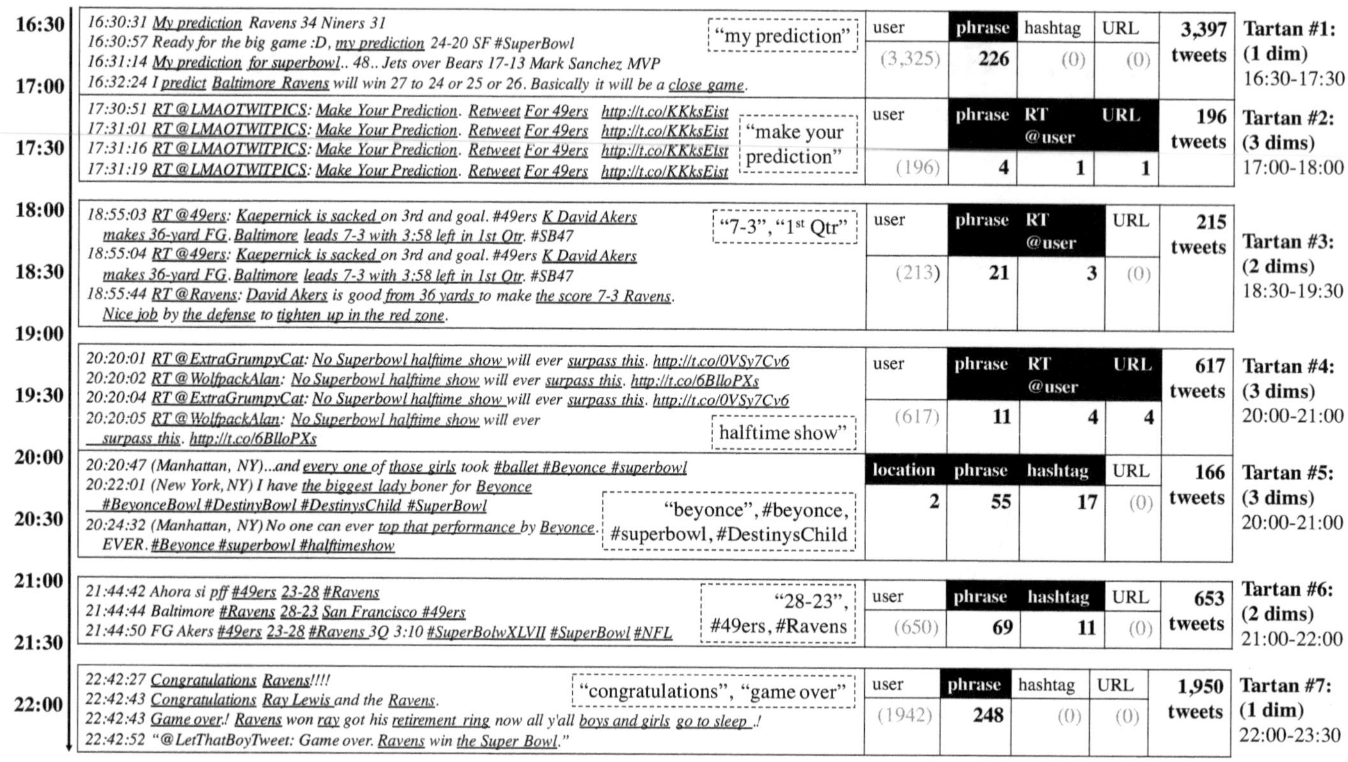

Figure 2: CATCHTARTAN captures multiple phases (e.g., score prediction, half-time show) in the "Super Bowl 2013" event by representing the dynamic and multicontextual patterns with "Tartans" (consecutive time slices, a set of dimensions and dimensional value sets).

Term	Definition
Dimension	The type of a contextual factor (e.g., location, phrase; author, keyword)
(Dimensional) value	The contextual factor in the dimension
Time slice	The period for consecutive behaviors
Behavior	A set of dimensions, a set of values in each dimension, a time slice for the timestamp

Table 1: Terms used throughout the paper and their definitions.

cial interaction [34]. For example, the crowds predicted the score before the Super Bowl, commented the singers and bands at the half-time show, and expressed their happiness or sadness after the match. Therefore, the representation should make the behaviors sortable by their time dimensional values (i.e., timestamps), while the other dimensions are not required to be compared.

Traditional behavior modeling used the "tensor" [15, 30, 11, 9] to represent the multidimensional behaviors and proposed a great line of block detection methods [5, 17, 24] to capture the dense blocks as interesting patterns.

Why not Tensor? FEMA [11] and CROSSSPOT [9] represented the tweets as (user, phrase, hashtag, URL) tuples and used the 4-mode tensor to define the tweet data. However, when the tweet has *neither* a hashtag *nor* a URL, it either has to be moved out or individually creates a 2-mode dense block. Therefore, the tensor representation either loses a large amount of such information or overweights the meaningfulness of the tweet.

Why not Block Detection? SVD and tensor decompositions have been widely used for multidimensional clustering, subgraph mining and community/block detection [17, 24, 9]. However, they mix all the values into one dimension even including the timestamp values. Their blocks cannot select the meaningful dimensions; the grouped timestamps cannot capture the dynamic patterns.

In this paper, we propose novel representations for the behaviors and summaries (see Figure 1b): a *"two-level matrix"* for the behaviors in which the columns are the dimensional values of the contextual types, and the rows are the behaviors in the time slices; a *"Tartan"* for the behavioral summary that includes (1) a set of meaningful dimensions, the meaningful values in each dimension to define the multicontextual patterns; and (2) a list of consecutive time slices and the representative behaviors in each slice to define the dynamic patterns. To address the problem of catching the Tartans (i.e., summarizing the behavioral data), we propose a propagation method called CATCHTARTAN that defines the meaningfulness metric of including or excluding a value, a dimension, a behavior and a time slice by leveraging the Minimum Description Length (MDL) principle. The general philosophy is that saving more bits in compression indicates a more important element in the Tartan. Moreover, CATCHTARTAN is carefully developed with several desired properties: it requires no user-defined parameters, runs in parallel and adapts to the dynamic environment.

Figure 2 shows seven of the Tartans that CATCHTARTAN catches from tweets about the "Super Bowl 2013" event. They summarize its five phases such as the score prediction, first half, half-time show, second half and sentiments after a win/loss. The Tartans consist of different numbers of dimensions from 1 ("Phrase") to 3 ("Location-Phrase-Hashtag","Phrase-RT@User-URL") and different consecutive time slices from 5pm, 8pm to 10pm, indicating the advertising campaigns, local trends and topical discussions.

It is worthwhile to highlight our contributions as follows.

- **The Tartan concept:** we propose a novel representation for behavioral summary to capture the dynamic and multicontextual patterns. It enables the non-value/set-values, the temporal ordering of behaviors and the dimension selectivity.
- **Scalable, parameter-free algorithm:** we propose a scalable and parameter-free method CATCHTARTAN for behavioral summarization, iteratively updating the Tartans with an

	FSG [20]	GRAPH-CUBE [35]	EVENT-CUBE [30]	MDC [22]	BOW [7]	FEMA [11]	COM2 [2]	CROSS-SPOT [9]	GRAPH-SCOPE [28]	VOG [18]	TIME-CRUNCH [27]	**CATCH-TARTAN**
Principled scoring								√	√	√	√	√
Parameter-free	√				√		√	√	√	√	√	√
Multidimensional		√	√	√	√	√	√	√				√
Multicontextual												√
Timestamp value			√	√		√	√	√	√		√	√
Dynamics							√		√		√	√

Table 2: Feature-based comparison of CATCHTARTAN with alternative approaches: it gives a straight line of checks (blanks for "×").

Dataset	**#Tweet**	**#User**	**#Loc**	**#Phrase**	**#Hashtag**	**#URL**	**# RT @User**	**#@User**	**Time Period**
NYC14	10,111,725	329,779	690	1,082,463	587,527	2,766,557	24,439	955,764	113 days
LA14	402,036	14,949	55	257,301	24,711	76,950	795	42,951	113 days
SPB13	2,072,402	1,456,992	9,306	416,461	105,473	140,874	284,647	223,261	25 half-hours
GRM13	2,606,933	1,457,664	5,750	433,548	81,582	334,707	235,097	160,184	52 half-hours
Dataset	**#Paper**	**#Author**	**#Venue**	**#Keyword**	**#Cited paper**				**Time Period**
DBLP	112,157	117,934	55	33,285	62,710				35 years

Table 3: Four Twitter datasets (New York 2014, Los Angeles 2014, Super Bowl 2013 and Grammy Awards 2013) and the DBLP data.

information-theoretically principled metric that defines the meaningfulness of including or excluding any element.

- **Effectiveness:** we evaluate the scalable CATCHTARTAN on synthetic data, four Twitter datasets and the DBLP data. We show both quantitative and qualitative results: CATCHTARTAN provides comprehensive behavioral summaries.

2. RELATED WORK

Traditional approaches model behaviors in three ways: graphs, tensors/cubes and multidimensional itemsets. However, none of the above can represent the dynamic multicontextual patterns in the human behavioral data. Table 2 gives a visual feature-based comparison of CATCHTARTAN with the existing methods.

Graph data summarization. Graph is common to represent the binary relations inside human behaviors. GRAPHSCOPE [28] uses graph search for hard-partitioning of temporal graphs to find dense temporal cliques and bipartite cores. VOG [18] and TIMECRUNCH [27] use MDL to label subgraphs in terms of stars, (near) cliques, (near) bipartite cores and chains: the former approach works on static graphs, while the latter focuses on dynamic graphs. SLASHBURN [16] is a recursive node-reordering approach to leverage run-length encoding for graph compression. Toivonen et al. [31] uses structural equivalence to collapse nodes/edges to simplify graph representation. These approaches work on flat representations, while the behavioral dataset itself is naturally multidimensional.

Tensor decomposition and cube analysis. Tensor decompositions [29, 17, 11] conduct multidimensional analysis; COM2 [2] uses CP/PARAFAC tensor decomposition with MDL. However, the tensor has a big flaw: it has to drop the behaviors in which some dimension is missing. On the cube side, TOPICCUBE [15] proposes a topic-concept cube that supports online multidimensional mining of query log. GRAPHCUBE [35] defines analysis cubes and OLAP operations on cubes over graphs. EVENTCUBE [30] performs multidimensional search and analysis of large collections of free text. Our CATCHTARTAN proposes a totally different representation for the behaviors and it has a principled scoring function to select the dimensions for the summaries.

Frequent pattern mining and multidimensional clustering. We can adopt the concept of itemsets in both the frequent pattern mining [20, 8] and multidimensional data clustering [23, 14, 1, 19] to represent the behavioral contexts. F. Cordeiro et al. [7] proposes BOW method for clustering very large and multidimensional datasets with MAPREDUCE. However, the mixture of the dimensional values (itemsets in the above methods) kills the selectivity of meaningful dimensions and thus fails to describe the multicontextual patterns. The timestamp clustering cannot describe the dynamic patterns either.

MDL theory and applications. Rissanen [25] proposes optimal encoding for integers greater than or equal to 1, which minimizes the description length one obtains estimates of the integer-valued structure parameters. Cilibrasi et al. [3] proposes a hierarchical clustering method on compression using the non-computable notion of Kolmogorov complexity. Faloutsos et al. [6] demonstrates that compression and Kolmogorov complexity can measure structure and order. The MDL principle aims to be a practical version of Kolmogorov Complexity [21]. Vreeken et al. [32] uses the MDL principle to catch large groups of patterns essentially describing the same set of transactions in the data.

To summarize, our CATCHTARTAN is unique for its (1) novel representations for behaviors and summaries to capture dynamic multicontextual patterns; (2) principled scoring function with no user-defined parameters; and (3) scalable propagation algorithm.

3. BEHAVIORAL REPRESENTATION AND SUMMARIZATION

In this section, we first introduce several datasets of behaviors and preliminarily analyze the multicontextual characteristic. Then we propose our representations for the behaviors and summaries, following by the problem definition of behavioral summarization.

3.1 The Multicontextual Behaviors

Datasets. We use four large Twitter datasets as well as the DBLP data (see Table 3). The tweets were collected from different sources: (1) NYC14 and LA14 were crawled using Twitter Streaming API[1] from August 1st to November 30th 2014. The NYC14 dataset consists of 10 million tweets in New York and the LA14 consists of 0.4 million in the Greater Los Angeles Area. (2) SPB13 (Super Bowl 2013) and GRM13 (the Grammy Awards 2013) were collected by Techtunk[2], each of which has over 2 million tweets. We extract many hard-encoded dimensions such as location, hashtag, URL,

[1]https://dev.twitter.com/streaming/overview
[2]http://www.techtunk.com/

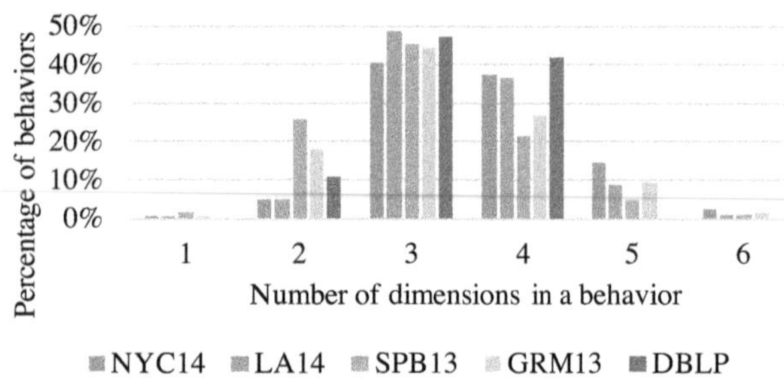

Figure 3: The distribution of #dimensions in human behaviors.

@User, as well as the rich phrase dimension. For the DBLP data, we have the author, venue, keyword and cited-paper dimensions.

Dimension distributions. Given the number of dimensions in a behavior, Figure 3 shows the percentage of the behaviors of that many dimensions in the datasets. The most frequent number in all the datasets is 3: (User, Phrase, Location/Hashtag/URL) in the Twitter data, and (Author, Venue, Keyword) in the DBLP. The behaviors are allowed to have various dimensions and for each dimension, they are allowed to have multiple values (a few phrases or a few keywords). A specific behavioral intention shares a set of specific contextual factors and creates a pattern of specific dimensions and values. For example, advertisers often generate tweets of similar phrases and the same URL; local events often share a group of hashtags and phrases. This is so called "multicontextual".

3.2 "Two-level Matrix" and the Tartan

Now we know that the behavioral data include temporal and contextual information, because every behavior has its timestamp and a set of contexts, or called dimensional values. On the contextual side, suppose the data have D dimensions, and for each dimension $d \in [1, D]$, there are N_d values. On the temporal side, suppose the data can be divided into T time slices, and for each time slice $t \in [1, T]$, there are $E^{(t)}$ behaviors. The symbols are their definitions are given in Table 4.

Figure 1b has illustrated our proposed "two-level matrix" to represent human behaviors. The formal definition is as follows.

DEFINITION 1 (TWO-LEVEL MATRIX (BEHAVIORAL DATA)). *A two-level matrix $\mathcal{X}$ consists of $\sum_{d=1}^{D} N_d$ columns (dimensional values) and $\sum_{t=1}^{T} E^{(t)}$ rows (behaviors), in which $\mathcal{X}_d^{(t)}(b, i)$ denotes how many times the i-th value in the d-th dimension appears in the b-th behavior at the t-th time slice. The top level consists of D dimensions and T time slices.*

Note that our definition can represent any dimensional setting and any type of values including non-value and set-values. A behavioral summary is a subset of the data that creates a representative pattern. Specifically, the definition is as follows.

DEFINITION 2 (TARTAN (BEHAVIORAL SUMMARY)). *A behavioral summary $\mathcal{A}$ has five components:*

- *a set of dimensions $\mathcal{D} \subseteq \{1, \ldots, D\}$;*
- *a set of values $\mathcal{V}_d \subseteq \{1, \ldots, N_d\}$ in the dimension $d \in \mathcal{D}$;*
- *a list of consecutive time slices $\mathcal{T} = [t_{start}, t_{end}] \subseteq [1, T]$;*
- *a set of behavior entries $\mathcal{B}^{(t)} \subseteq \{1, \ldots, E^{(t)}\}$ in the time slice $t \in \mathcal{T}$;*
- *the behavior-value entries $\{\mathcal{X}_d^{(t)}(b, i) | d \in \mathcal{D}, t \in \mathcal{T}, b \in \mathcal{B}^{(t)}, i \in \mathcal{B}^{(t)}\}$*

The size of the first four components are denoted by $1 \leq D^{\mathcal{A}} \leq D$, $1 \leq n_d \leq N_d$, $1 \leq T^{\mathcal{A}} \leq T$ and $1 \leq e^{(t)} \leq E^{(t)}$.

As shown in Figure 1b and 4, the Tartan is named after its particular shape in the two-level matrix.

Symbol	Definition
$\mathcal{X}$	The "two-level" matrix: the behavioral data
$\mathcal{A}$	The Tartan: the behavioral summary
$\mathcal{X}^{\mathcal{A}}$	The first-level submatrix of $\mathcal{X}$ that includes $\mathcal{A}$
D	Number of dimensions in the data
T	Number of time slices in the data
d	The dimension index
t	The time slice index
N_d	The size of the d-th dimension
$E^{(t)}$	The size of the t-th time slice
V	The volume of $\mathcal{X}^{\mathcal{A}}$
C	The sum of non-zero entries in $\mathcal{X}^{\mathcal{A}}$
$\mathcal{D}$	The set of dimensions in $\mathcal{A}$
$\mathcal{T}$	The consecutive time slices in $\mathcal{A}$: $[t_{start}, t_{end}]$
$\mathcal{V}_d$	The set of values on the d-th dimension in $\mathcal{A}$
$\mathcal{B}^{(t)}$	The set of behaviors at the t-th time slice in $\mathcal{A}$
$D^{\mathcal{A}}$	The number of dimensions in $\mathcal{A}$
$T^{\mathcal{A}}$	The number of time slices in $\mathcal{A}$
n_d	The number of values on the d-th dimension in $\mathcal{A}$
$e^{(t)}$	The number of behaviors at the t-th time slice in $\mathcal{A}$
v	The volume of the Tartan $\mathcal{A}$
c	The sum of non-zero entries in $\mathcal{A}$

Table 4: Symbols and their definitions.

3.3 The Behavioral Summarization Problem

In this paper, the ultimate goal is to summarize the behaviors, in other words, to find the behavioral summaries in the temporal multidimensional data. With the above representations for the behavior and summary, we define the problem of behavioral summarization as follows, equally as catching Tartans in the two-level matrix.

PROBLEM 1 (BEHAVIORAL SUMMARIZATION). ***Given*** *the behavioral data (a two-level matrix) $\mathcal{X} = \{D, N_d|_{d=1}^{D}, T, E^{(t)}|_{t=1}^{T}\}$,* ***find*** *a list of behavioral summaries (Tartans) $\tilde{\mathcal{A}} = \{\ldots, \mathcal{A}, \ldots\}$ ordered by a principled metric function $f(\mathcal{A}, \mathcal{X})$ which defines how well the sets of meaningful dimensions, values, time slices and behaviors are partitioned and how well the meaningful subset of data is summarized, where $\mathcal{A} = \{\mathcal{D}, \mathcal{V}_d|_{d \in \mathcal{D}}, \mathcal{T}, \mathcal{B}^{(t)}|_{t \in \mathcal{T}}\}$.*

Good summarization including good partitions will be determined in an information-theoretic manner. We would like to emphasize that we solve the problem in a *parameter-free* and *scalable* way.

4. PROPOSED METHOD: CATCHTARTAN

Our CATCHTARTAN method is based on the Minimum Description Length (MDL) principle and employs a lossless encoding scheme for the temporal multidimensional data. Our objective function estimates the number of bits that encoding the Tartan can save from merging this meaningful knowledge into the data. In this section, we will address the proposed problem in Section 3 by answering three questions: (1) how to derive the cost of encoding the Tartan; (2) how to define the principled scoring function for optimization; (3) how to develop a scalable algorithm to catch the Tartans.

Encoding the Tartan.

Figure 4 illustrates the MDL-based scheme for encoding the five components of the Tartan. The components are (1) first-level columns (dimensions), (2) second-level columns (dimensional values), (3) first-level rows (time slices), (4) second-level rows (behaviors), and (5) the behavior-value entries.

Encoding the dimensions. Suppose $D = 5$ and the set of dimensions in the Tartan $\mathcal{A}$ is $\mathcal{D} = \{1, 2, 4\}$ ($D^{\mathcal{A}} = 3$), the binary string

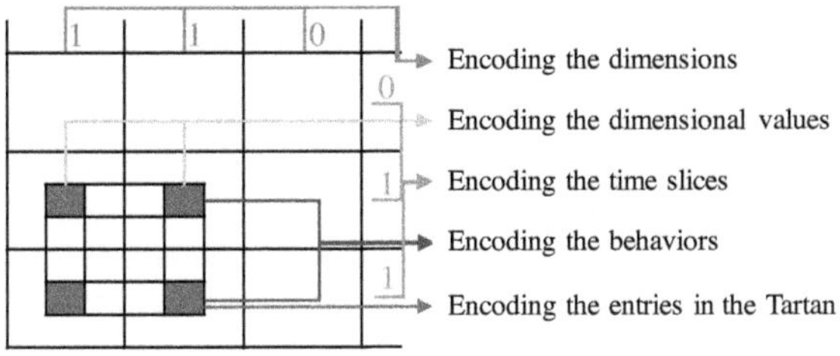

Figure 4: Encoding the 5 components when encoding a Tartan.

to encode the set is 11010. The length of this string is D and the number of 1s is $D^{\mathcal{A}}$. To further save space, we can adopt Huffman coding or arithmetic coding to encode the binary string, which formally can be viewed as a sequence of realizations of a binomial random variable X. We denote by $H_{\mathcal{D}}(X)$ the entropy:

$$\begin{aligned} H_{\mathcal{D}}(X) &= -\sum_{x\in\{0,1\}} P(X=x)\log P(X=x) \\ &= -\left(\frac{D^{\mathcal{A}}}{D}\log\frac{D^{\mathcal{A}}}{D} + \frac{D-D^{\mathcal{A}}}{D}\log\frac{D-D^{\mathcal{A}}}{D}\right). \end{aligned}$$

Additionally, two integers need to be stored: D and $D^{\mathcal{A}}$. The cost for storing these integers is ($\log^* D + \log^* D^{\mathcal{A}}$) bits, where $\log^* x$ is the universal code length for an integer x [26]. Therefore, the description length is

$$\begin{aligned} L_{\mathcal{D}}(\mathcal{A}) &= \log^* D + \log^* D^{\mathcal{A}} + D\cdot H_{\mathcal{D}}(X) \\ &= \log^* D + \log^* D^{\mathcal{A}} + g(D, D^{\mathcal{A}}), \end{aligned}$$

where $g(x,y) = x\log x - (x-y)\log(x-y) - y\log y, y \le x$; x is the total number of values and y is the number of selected values.

Encoding the dimensional values. For each dimension $d \in \mathcal{D}$, the binary string is of the length N_d and has n_d 1s. Therefore, the entropy is

$$H_{\mathcal{V}_d}(X) = -\left(\frac{n_d}{N_d}\log\frac{n_d}{N_d} + \frac{N_d-n_d}{N_d}\log\frac{N_d-n_d}{N_d}\right).$$

The total description length is

$$L_{\mathcal{V}}(\mathcal{A}) = \sum_{d\in\mathcal{D}}\left(\log^* N_d + \log^* n_d + g(N_d, n_d)\right).$$

Encoding the time slices. The set of consecutive time slices in the Tartan $\mathcal{A}$ is $\mathcal{T} = [t_{start}, t_{end}] \subseteq [1, T]$, where $t_{end} = t_{start} + T^{\mathcal{A}} - 1$. Thus, the description length is

$$L_{\mathcal{T}}(\mathcal{A}) = \log^* T + \log^* T^{\mathcal{A}} + \log^* t_{start}$$

Encoding the behaviors. For each time slice $t \in \mathcal{T}$, the binary string is of the length $E^{(t)}$ and has $e^{(t)}$ 1s. The entropy is

$$H_{\mathcal{B}^{(t)}}(X) = -\left(\frac{e^{(t)}}{E^{(t)}}\log\frac{e^{(t)}}{E^{(t)}} + \frac{E^{(t)}-e^{(t)}}{E^{(t)}}\log\frac{E^{(t)}-e^{(t)}}{E^{(t)}}\right).$$

The total description length is

$$L_{\mathcal{B}}(\mathcal{A}) = \sum_{t\in\mathcal{T}}\left(\log^* E^{(t)} + \log^* e^{(t)} + g(E^{(t)}, e^{(t)})\right).$$

Encoding the entries in the Tartan. The entries in the Tartan $\mathcal{A}$ are non-negative counts instead of binary values. The volume, i.e., the length of the non-negative integer string, is

$$v = \left(\sum_{d\in\mathcal{D}} n_d\right)\left(\sum_{t\in\mathcal{T}} e^{(t)}\right).$$

The sum of the non-negative counts is

$$c = \sum_{d\in\mathcal{D}, t\in\mathcal{T}} \sum_{b\in\mathcal{B}^{(t)}, i\in\mathcal{V}_d} \mathcal{X}_d^{(t)}(b,i).$$

It is straightforward to add bits in order to store the integer string as a binary string. For example, if the string is 2 1 0 4 0, it can be stored as 110 10 0 11110 0, where $1\cdots10$ encodes a non-negative integer x with x 1s. Therefore, the binary string is of the length $v+c$ and has c 1s. The entropy is

$$H_{\mathcal{A}}(X) = -\left(\frac{c}{v+c}\log\frac{c}{v+c} + \frac{v}{v+c}\log\frac{v}{v+c}\right).$$

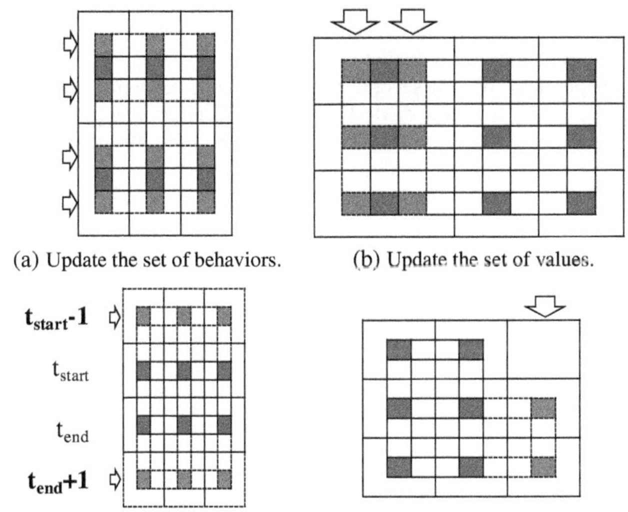

(a) Update the set of behaviors. (b) Update the set of values.

(c) Update the consecutive time slices. (d) Update the set of dimensions.

Figure 5: Updating the four elements of the Tartan till convergence: time slices, behaviors, dimensions and dimensional values.

The description length is

$$L_{\mathcal{A}}(\mathcal{A}) = (v+c)H_{\mathcal{A}}(X) = g(v+c, c).$$

The *entire encoding cost* of the Tartan $\mathcal{A}$ is

$$L(\mathcal{A}) = L_{\mathcal{D}}(\mathcal{A}) + L_{\mathcal{V}}(\mathcal{A}) + L_{\mathcal{T}}(\mathcal{A}) + L_{\mathcal{B}}(\mathcal{A}) + L_{\mathcal{A}}(\mathcal{A}).$$

The principled scoring function.

The goal is to find the Tartan with high "meaningfulness score". The scoring function is defined as the number of bits (description length) that encoding the Tartan $\mathcal{A}$ saves from encoding every individual entry in the first-level matrix $\mathcal{X}^{\mathcal{A}}$:

$$\boxed{f(\mathcal{A},\mathcal{X}) = L(\mathcal{X}^{\mathcal{A}}) - L(\mathcal{A}) - L(\mathcal{X}^{\mathcal{A}}\backslash\mathcal{A}).} \quad (1)$$

where $\mathcal{X}^{\mathcal{A}}\backslash\mathcal{A}$ is the individual entries in $\mathcal{X}^{\mathcal{A}}$ except the Tartan $\mathcal{A}$.

Encoding the individual entries in the first-level matrix. $\mathcal{X}^{\mathcal{A}}$ includes every value from the dimension in the set $\mathcal{D}$ and every behavior from the time slice in the set $\mathcal{T}$:

$$\mathcal{X}^{\mathcal{A}} = \{\mathcal{X}_d^{(t)}(b,i) | d\in\mathcal{D}, t\in\mathcal{T}, i\in\{1,\ldots,N_d\}, b\in\{1,\ldots,E^{(t)}\}\}.$$

The volume of this first-level matrix is

$$V = \left(\sum_{d\in\mathcal{D}} N_d\right)\left(\sum_{t\in\mathcal{T}} E^{(t)}\right).$$

Its sum of the non-negative counts is

$$C = \sum_{d\in\mathcal{D}, t\in\mathcal{T}} \sum_{b\in\{1,\ldots,E^{(t)}\}, i\in\{1,\ldots,N_d\}} \mathcal{X}_d^{(t)}(b,i).$$

Therefore, the description length of $\mathcal{X}^{\mathcal{A}}$ is

$$\begin{aligned} L(\mathcal{X}^{\mathcal{A}}) &= g(V+C, C) + L_{\mathcal{D}}(\mathcal{A}) + L_{\mathcal{T}}(\mathcal{A}) \\ &\quad + \sum_{d\in\mathcal{D}} \log^* N_d + \sum_{t\in\mathcal{T}} \log^* E^{(t)}. \end{aligned}$$

Given the $\mathcal{A}$ and $\mathcal{X}^{\mathcal{A}}$, the #bits to encode the individual entries is

$$L(\mathcal{X}^{\mathcal{A}}\backslash\mathcal{A}) = g(V+C-v-c, C-c);$$

Our proposed scoring function encodes different partitions including the dimensions, dimensional values, as well as the time slices and behaviors in the time slice, in order to achieve a concise description of the data. The fundamental trade-off that decides the "best" summaries is between (1) the number of bits needed to describe the Tartan, and (2) the number of bits needed to describe the individual entries in the data.

Properties. We list several good properties that agree with intuition of the function $f(\mathcal{A}, \mathcal{X})$, which directs us to a propagation algorithm that updates the Tartan for a high score. These properties are proved in the Appendix.

Property 1. A Tartan of a higher sum c saves more bits, when other variables are fixed (which is assumed for all properties).

Property 2. A Tartan of a smaller volume v saves more bits.

Property 3. The first-level data of a smaller sum C saves more bits.

Property 4. The data of a bigger volume V saves more bits.

The scalable algorithm to catch the Tartans.

We propose a greedy search algorithm for optimal partitions in the Tartans. However, finding the optimal solution is NP-hard[3]. So we present an iterative alternating optimization where we find the optimal set of dimensions, values, time slices and behaviors while holding other variables in the Tartan. We run this sequence of updates until convergence. The algorithm is scalable to run on multiple threads sharing the memory of the dataset.

Algorithm 1 CATCHTARTAN : Catching the dynamic multicontextual Tartans for behavioral summaries

Require: the behavioral data $\mathcal{X} = \{D, N_d|_{d=1}^{D}, T, E^{(t)}|_{t=1}^{T}\}$

$\tilde{\mathcal{A}} = \{\}$
while the threads run **do**
  generate a seed Tartan $\mathcal{A} = \{\mathcal{D}, \mathcal{V}_d|_{d\in\mathcal{D}}, \mathcal{T}, \mathcal{B}^{(t)}|_{t\in\mathcal{T}}\}$
  while not converged **do**
    for each time slice $t \in \mathcal{T} = [t_{start}, t_{end}]$ **do**
      Update the set of behaviors $\mathcal{B}^{(t)}$ (see Figure 5a) by maximizing the scoring function $f(\mathcal{A}, \mathcal{X})$
    end for
    for each dimension $d \in \mathcal{D}$ **do**
      Update the set of values $\mathcal{V}_d$ (see Figure 5b)
    end for
    Update the consecutive time slices: check if includes the (t_{start}-1)-th and (t_{end}+1)-th slices (see Figure 5c)
    for each dimension $d \notin \mathcal{D}$ **do**
      Check if includes the dimension (see Figure 5d)
    end for
  end while
  $\tilde{\mathcal{A}} \leftarrow \tilde{\mathcal{A}} \cup \mathcal{A}$ sorted in descending order by $f(\mathcal{A}, \mathcal{X})$
end while
return $\tilde{\mathcal{A}}$: the list of Tartans in $\mathcal{X}$

Seed selection. We recommend three ways of generating seed Tartans: (1) one or several random behaviors in a single time slice, (2) several popular dimensional values, and (3) high-order SVD on the partial data. Experimental results in Section 5 show that the first, simple setting performs well and runs fast.

Complexity. The properties with guarantees ensure that the top behaviors in $\mathcal{B}^{(t)}$ and top dimensional values in $\mathcal{V}_d$. Intuitively, a higher score looks for a better compression, i.e., few behaviors/values in the time slice/dimension that give large sums of counts. Therefore, the optimization can be solved via a quick sorting of the values. The time complexity is $\mathcal{O}(\sum_d N_d \log N_d + \sum_t E^{(t)} \log E^{(t)})$.

5. EXPERIMENTS

In this section, we evaluate CATCHTARTAN and seek to answer the following questions. Can it accurately catch the Tartans from the temporal multidimensional data? Is it scalable? For real-world behaviors, are their patterns dynamic and multicontextual? If they are, what Tartan structures do we see and what do they mean?

5.1 Quantitative Analysis

It is impracticable to evaluate the behavioral summaries in real datasets. Thus, we generate the synthetic datasets and report the quantitative results.

Synthetic datasets and experimental setup. We generate random "behavioral" data and inject a Tartan into it. We set up extensive experiments with many parameters on (1) the Tartan distribution:

1. $T^{\mathcal{A}} \in [2,\ 9]$, the number of consecutive time slices in the Tartan $\mathcal{A}$, 4 as default;
2. $e^{(t)} \in [100,\ 2,000]$, the number of behaviors in the time slice, $1,000$ as default;
3. $D^{\mathcal{A}} \in [2,\ 9]$, the number of dimensions in $\mathcal{A}$, 3 as default;
4. $n_d \in [50,\ 200]$, the number of values per dimension in $\mathcal{A}$, 100 as default;
5. $\rho \in [1,\ 10]$, the average number of values per dimension in the behaviors, 3 as default;

and (2) the data distribution:

6. $T \in [5, 30]$, the total number of time slices in the dataset, 10 as default;
7. $E^{(t)} \in [1,000,\ 10,000]$, the number of behaviors per time slice in the dataset, $5,000$ as default;
8. $N_d \in [1,000,\ 2,000]$, the number of values per dimension in the data, $1,000$ as default.

Our task is to catch the Tartan, which has two binary classification subtasks: (1) detecting the set of behaviors in the Tartan, (2) detecting the set of dimensional values (contexts) in the Tartan.

We adopt the following methods as the baselines:

- FSG (Frequent Subgraph Discovery) [20]: this is a frequent itemset discovery algorithm that discovers subgraphs that occur frequently over the entire set of graphs.
- EIGENSPOKE [24]: this is a SVD-based method that can detect communities from large graphs by reading the singular vectors of the adjacency matrix.
- NMF (Nonnegative Matrix Factorization) [33]: it factorizes the matrices of complex networks to find the close relationship between clustering methods.

The experiments were conducted on a machine with 20 cores of Intel(R) Xeon(R) CPU E5- 2680 v2 @ 2.80GHz. We set up 10 threads and each thread searches the Tartans with 2 seeds.

Note that none of the above methods selects the dimensions nor time slices. The tensor-based methods including decompositions [29, 11] and the CROSSSPOT [9] fail to represent the multicontextual data. They lose lots of information and gave poor performances in the Tartan detection, so we do not show their results in this paper.

We evaluate the performance of our CATCHTARTAN and the baselines from two perspectives, (1) accuracy: F1 score that is the harmonic mean of precision and recall, (2) efficiency: the cost of running time. A high F1 score indicates accurate performance and a small time cost indicates high efficiency.

Accuracy and efficiency. Figure 6 presents the extensive experimental results. As every parameter varies in a big range, it shows the accuracy (on the 1st and 3rd columns in the figure) and the time cost (on the 2nd and 4th columns) of our CATCHTARTAN and the baseline methods. The solid lines are for the behavior detection, and the dashed lines are for the dimensional value detection. The symbols of our CATCHTARTAN is the red triangles. We have the following observations.

- CATCHTARTAN *consistently outperforms the baselines and the F1 score is close to the perfect 1.* FSG performs well

[3]It is NP-hard since, even allowing only column re-ordering, a reduction to the TSP problem can be found [13].

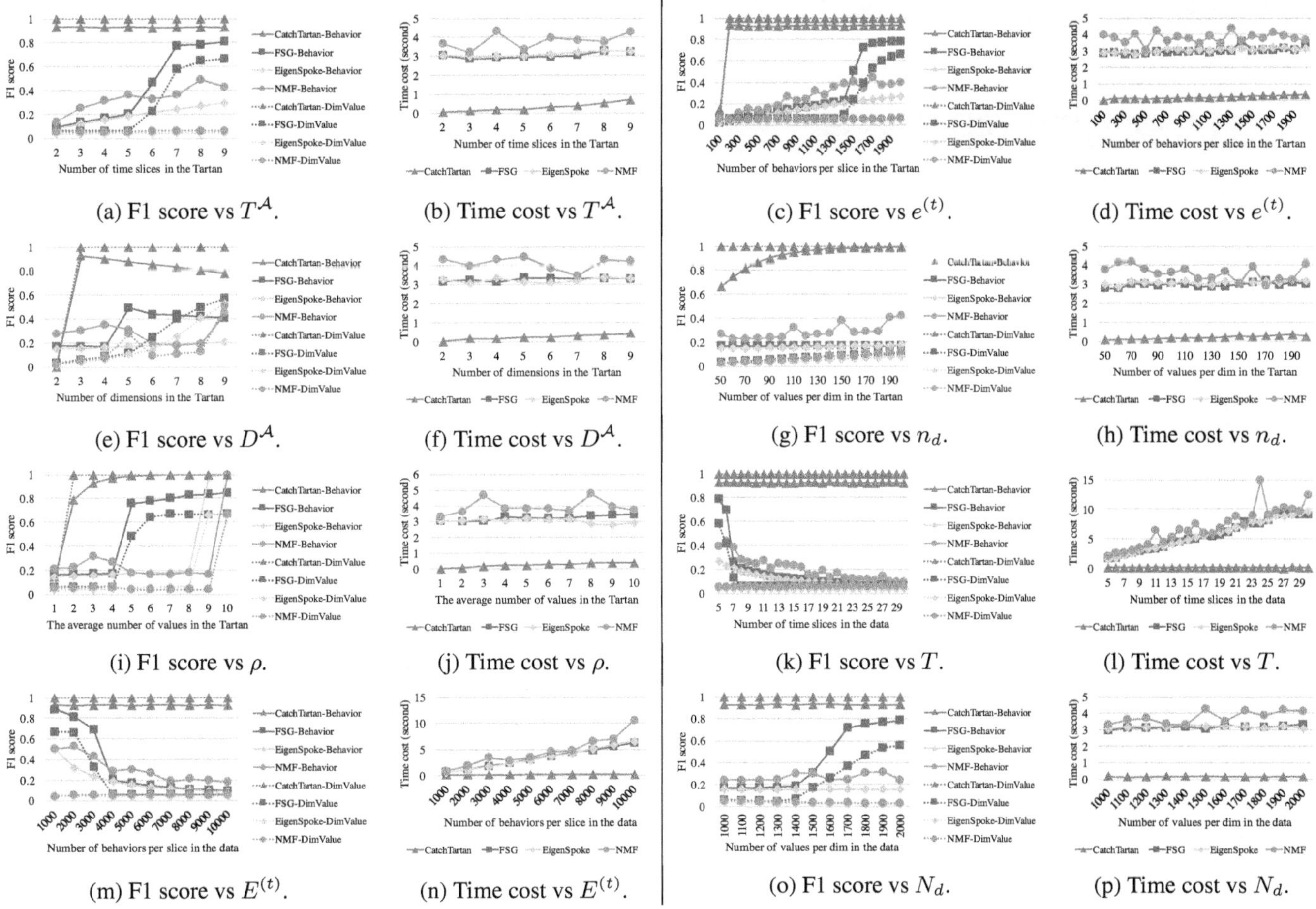

(a) F1 score vs $T^{\mathcal{A}}$. (b) Time cost vs $T^{\mathcal{A}}$. (c) F1 score vs $e^{(t)}$. (d) Time cost vs $e^{(t)}$.

(e) F1 score vs $D^{\mathcal{A}}$. (f) Time cost vs $D^{\mathcal{A}}$. (g) F1 score vs n_d. (h) Time cost vs n_d.

(i) F1 score vs ρ. (j) Time cost vs ρ. (k) F1 score vs T. (l) Time cost vs T.

(m) F1 score vs $E^{(t)}$. (n) Time cost vs $E^{(t)}$. (o) F1 score vs N_d. (p) Time cost vs N_d.

Figure 6: Synthetic experimental results demonstrate the effectiveness and efficiency of our CATCHTARTAN : the red triangle gives high and stable F1 scores on the tasks of both catching the behaviors and catching the values; it also costs much less running time than the baselines.

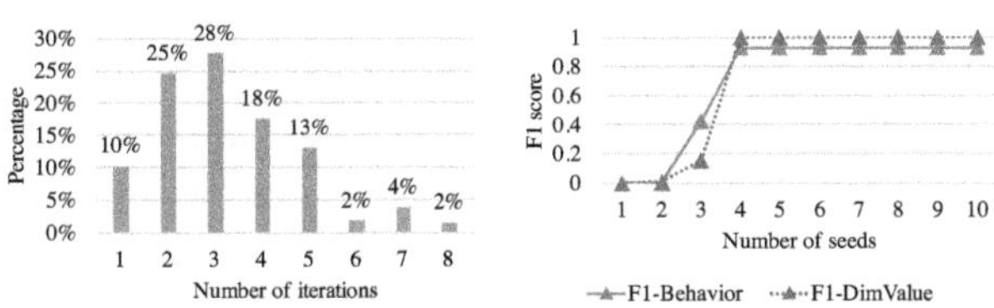

(a) Taking few iterations. (b) Taking few seeds.

Figure 7: Our CATCHTARTAN takes fewer than 5 iterations in over 90% runs; it requires 4 seeds to reach a higher-than-0.92 F1 score.

when the number of time slices $T^{\mathcal{A}}$ or the behaviors $e^{(t)}$ in the Tartan is big, however, CATCHTARTAN can catch the Tartan when the time period is short, which is a common case in real data. When the number of dimensions $D^{\mathcal{A}}$ is bigger or the number of values in the dimension becomes smaller, the F1 score of CATCHTARTAN gradually decreases since the Tartan becomes more like a high-dimensional block but it is still higher than the baselines. Moreover, from Figure 6k, 6m and 6o, we demonstrate that CATCHTARTAN is robust to the data distributions, especially when the baselines are inaccurate for the too big data scale of both the temporal and contextual dimension.

- CATCHTARTAN *consistently costs much less time than the baselines.* Our method is cheaper for its counting and sorting operations instead of the high-order decomposition. It has a quasi-linear complexity while the complexity of the traditional approaches are quadratic. From the 2nd and 4th columns of the figure, we spot that CATCHTARTAN spends less time to reach a much better performance. For the default setting, the CATCHTARTAN uses 0.155 second, while FSG, EIGENSPOKE and NMF use 3.25, 3.08 and 3.98 seconds, respectively: our method has a 20× speed.

The robustness to the number of iterations and seeds. Figure 7a shows that over 92% of the processes of catching the Tartans take fewer than 5 iterations. In Figure 7b, we spot that in the default setting, CATCHTARTAN requires only 4 seeds to reach an as-high-as-0.92 F1 score for both the detection tasks of behaviors and dimensional values. CATCHTARTAN requires no user-defined parameters, and it is robust to the number of iterations and seeds.

5.2 Qualitative Analysis

In this section, we discuss qualitative results from applying CATCHTARTAN to the tweet datasets and DBLP data mentioned in Table 3.

"Super Bowl 2013" event summaries. We have introduced Figure 2 in which the seven of the Tartans summarize the behavioral patterns in the data. They present five phases of the event such as the score prediction, first half, half-time show, second half and sentiments after a win/loss. The Tartans consist of different numbers of dimensions and different consecutive time slices, which indicates the advertising campaigns, local trends and topical discussions.

"Grammys Award 2013" event summaries. Figure 9 presents ten Tartans caught by our method from the GRM13 data. The Tartans have meaningful dimensional settings: (User, Phrase, @User) in-

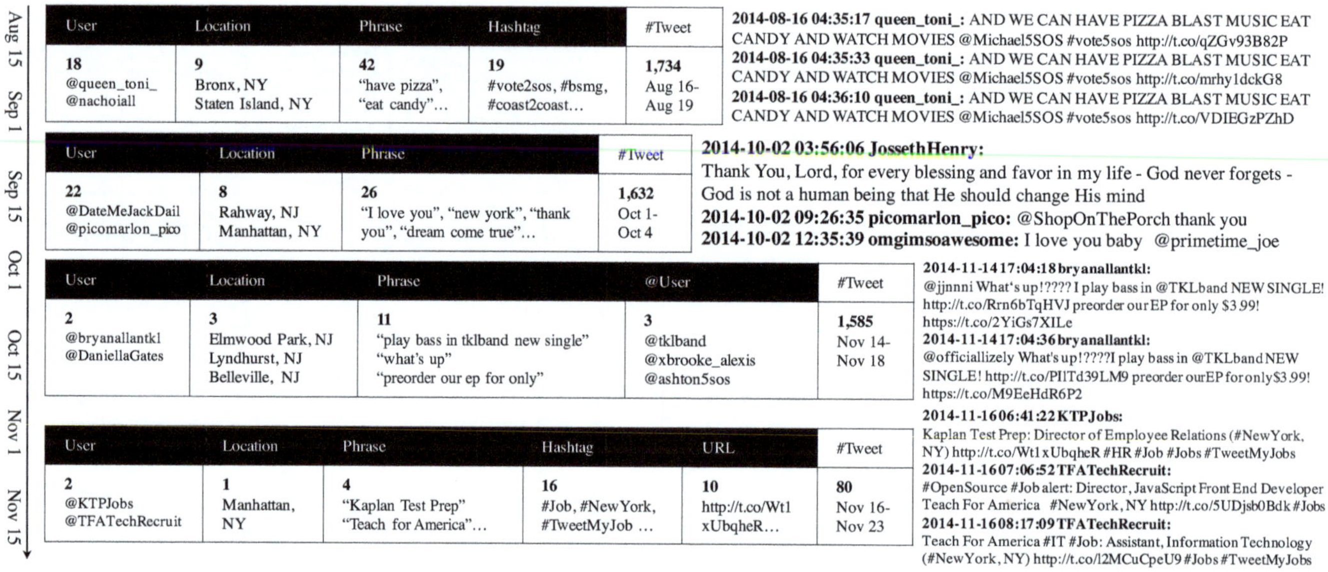

Figure 8: Tweet summaries of the NYC14 data: four Tartans of different sets of dimensions indicate behavioral patterns (e.g., advertising).

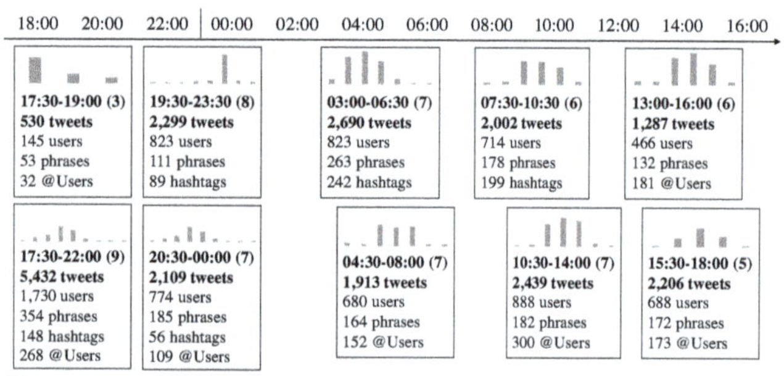

Figure 9: Tweet summaries of the GRM13 (Grammys): Tartans of different consecutive half-hours and different dimensions.

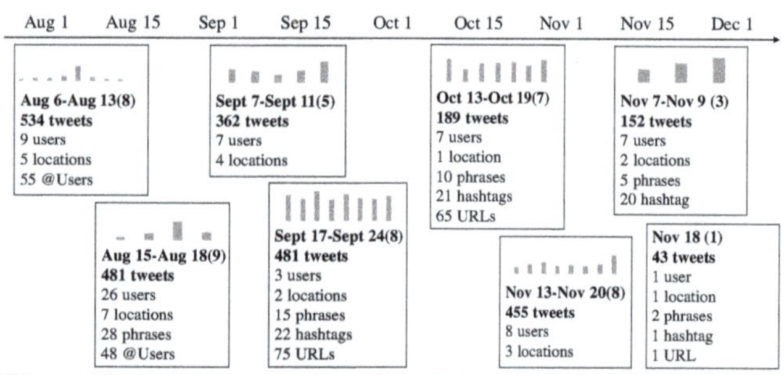

Figure 10: Tweet summaries of the LA14 (Los Angeles): Tartans of different consecutive days and different dimensions.

dicating that a group of users communicated with each other about the same words, (User, Phrase, Hashtag) indicating that the users discussed similar topics with a group of phrases; besides these three-dimensional Tartans, there are two four-dimensional ones. All these Tartans include a list of consecutive time slices for their dynamic behavioral patterns.

"Los Angeles 2014" tweet summaries. Figure 10 presents eight Tartans from the LA14 data. The Tartans have various dimensional settings: three are five-dimensional, (User, Location, Phrase, Hashtag, URL) for well-designed advertising campaigns; two are four-dimensional, (User, Location, Phrase, Hashtag) for local topics and (User, Location, Phrase, URL) for advertisements; one is three-dimensional, (User, Location, @User); and two are two-dimensional, (User, Location). These Tartans show not only the multicontextual view but also the dynamic patterns for 3 days, 5 days or even one

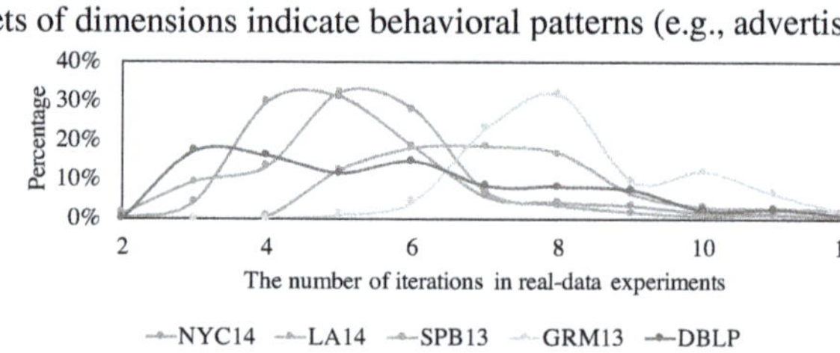

(a) CATCHTARTAN takes fewer than 15 iterations.

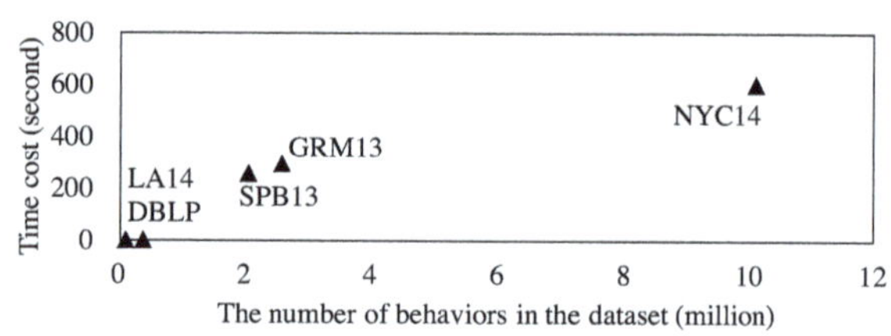

(b) The time cost is linear in the number of behaviors.

Figure 11: The scalability in real-data experiments.

week. CATCHTARTAN provides comprehensive behavioral summaries about the information at the Greater Los Angeles Area.

"New York City 2014" tweet summaries. Figure 8 takes more space to introduce four Tartans in the NYC14 data. The first Tartan has four dimensions. It has 18 users from 9 locations, talking about 42 phrases and 19 hashtags during 4 days in August, 2014. It has as many as 1,734 tweets. The tweets show that this Tartan encodes a campaign that promotes the band *5SOS* (5 Seconds of Summer).

The second Tartan has 1,632 tweets with 22 users, 8 locations and 26 phrases. This 3-dimensional Tartan also takes 4 days but in October, 2014. The tweets encode the positive sentiments of the New York citizens.

The third Tartan has four dimensions, user, location, phrase and @user. The volume is quite small: only 2 users, 3 locations, 11 phrases and 3 users who were mentioned, but the sum of tweet counts is big. The 1,585 tweets were generated from November 14 to November 18, which promoted the EP by the band *TKLband* (The Killing Lights). The messages are too similar to be generated by the two "legitimate" users: they are high probably created by some scripts. We even doubt whether the message "preorder our EP for only $3.99" is true or false or fraudulent.

The last example has five dimensions: 2 users, 1 location, 4

1997 2000 2003 2006 2009 2012

Author	Venue	Keyword	Cited	#Paper
76	**7**	**7**	**68**	**32**
Cheng-xiang Zhai	SIGIR	"information retrieval"	p56743[1]	2003-
Hui Fang	VLDB	"data integration"	p62995	2007
S. Kambhampati	TKDE	"text classification"	p76869	

[1] "A language modeling approach to information retrieval"

Venue	Keyword	#Paper
5	**6**	**40**
ICML	"reinforcement learning"	1997-
NIPS	"machine learning"	2002
...		

Author	Venue	Cited	#Paper
6	**1**	**1**	**22**
Jiawei Han	SIG-	p76095[2]	2004-
Xifeng Yan	MOD		2010

[2] "Frequent subgraph discovery"

Venue	Keyword	#Paper
3	**1**	**25**
ICDM	"anomaly	2005-
AAAI	detection"	2013
TKDE		

Author	Venue	Keyword	#Paper
27	**6**	**12**	**70**
C. Faloutsos	KDD	"large graphs"	2006-
J. Pei	ICDM	"data streams"	2013
P. S. Yu	ICDE	"evolving data"	
X. Lin	TKDE	"evolving graphs"	
C. Aggarwal...	...	...	

Author	Venue	Keyword	Cited	#Paper
12	**5**	**3**	**12**	**32**
Ryen White	SIGIR	"web search"	p82630[3]	2006-
Hang Li	WWW	"click-through data"	p116290	2013
Tie-Yan Liu	WSDM	"sponsored search"	p103899	
Zhaohui Zheng...	CIKM...		p106191...	

[3] "Optimizing search engines using clickthrough data"

Author	Venue	Keyword	#Paper
8	**3**	**6**	**17**
Qiang Yang	KDD	"transfer learning"	2007-
Dou Shen	PAKDD	"data mining"	2010
Sinno Pan...	AAAI	"localization models"	

Figure 12: Publishing-paper behavioral summaries: seven Tartans about DM and ML show the dynamics and contexts of our community.

phrases, 16 hashtags and 10 URLs. The messages are a large group of interesting news about job hunting in the Manhattan, NY. The number of the messages is 80. It looks small but the messages are from a even smaller number of users and locations. Compressing these messages as a whole can save lots of bits from compressing the messages individually.

"DBLP" summaries. Figure 12 presents seven (but not the least) Tartans in the DBLP data. They are shown for their relatedness to the area of database, data mining, machine learning and so on.

The first Tartan has four dimensions, author, venue, keyword and cited paper. From 2003 to 2007, 76 authors published papers about "information retrieval", "data integration" and "text classification" on the SIGIR, VLDB conferences and TKDE journal. The paper *p56743* ("A language modeling approach to information retrieval") was frequently cited by these papers. The authors have all read this paper and explored new techniques to address the problems.

The second Tartan has only two dimensions, the venue and keyword. There were 40 papers about "reinforcement learning" on the ICML and NIPS conferences from 1997 to 2002. The author and cited-paper dimensions are missing as many scholars cited many related papers in their publications. The Tartan automatically excluded both the dimensions because no leading authors nor cited papers could be summarized.

The third Tartan has three dimensions, author, venue and cited paper. A group of six famous researchers, e.g., Dr. Jiawei Han and Dr. Xifeng Yan, published 22 papers on the SIGMOD conference which cited the same paper *p76095* ("Frequent subgraph discovery") from 2004 to 2010. The 22 papers used different phrases because the area of "subgraph mining" or "frequent subgraph pattern mining" was promising but not mature: many different methods, models and algorithms were proposed.

The forth Tartan has two dimensions, venue and keyword. 25 papers about "anomaly detection" were published in the ICDM, AAAI conferences and TKDE journal from 2005 to 2013. The papers were written by a large number of authors to address the detection problem in many applications with different methods.

The fifth Tartan is relatively large. It has 3 dimensions of 27 authors, 6 venues and 12 keywords. These 70 papers were published from 2006 to 2013. The group of researchers studied the "large graphs", "data streams", "evolving data" and "evolving graphs" on the KDD, ICDM, ICDE conferences and TKDE journal.

The sixth Tartan presents the behaviors by the "web search" community. It has four dimensions. A group of 12 authors studied 3 keywords "web search", "click-through data" and "sponsored search" and published 32 papers on the SIGIR, WWW, WSDM, CIKM conferences from 2006 to 2013. These conferences are the major information retrieval conferences. There are 12 highly-cited papers. The most representative paper is *p82630* ("Optimizing search engines using clickthrough data").

Finally, the small but meaningful Tartan represents the "transfer learning" community. 8 authors, e.g., Dr. Qiang Yang and Dr. Dou Shen, published 17 papers about "transfer learning" and " data mining" on the KDD and AAAI conferences. This is a 3-dimensional Tartan during the year 2007-2010.

Efficiency. Figure 11a shows the distributions of the number of iterations until convergence when we apply CATCHTARTAN to different datasets: CATCHTARTAN takes fewer than 15 iterations, and the most frequent number is consistently smaller than 10. Figure 11b shows that the time cost is linear in the number of behaviors in the real-data experiments, which demonstrates the scalability.

6. CONCLUSIONS

In this paper, we uncovered the dynamic and multicontextual patterns of human behaviors and focused on the problem of behavioral summarization. We proposed a novel representation called the Tartan that includes a set of dimensions, sets of dimensional values, consecutive time slices, and sets of behaviors in the slices. We proposed a parameter-free and scalable method CATCHTARTAN to capture the Tartan summaries with a principled scoring function. We applied our CATCHTARTAN to the synthetic data, DBLP data and Twitter datasets. The experimental results including the comprehensive event summaries have demonstrated the effectiveness and efficiency of our proposed CATCHTARTAN .

7. ACKNOWLEDGEMENTS

We thank the reviewers for their insightful comments. This work was sponsored in part by the U.S. Army Research Lab. under Cooperative Agreement No. W911NF-09-2-0053 (NSCTA), National Science Foundation CNS-1314632, IIS-1408924, IIS-1017362, IIS-1320617, IIS-1354329, HDTRA1-10-1-0120, and grant 1U54GM114838 awarded by NIGMS through funds provided by the trans-NIH Big Data to Knowledge (BD2K) initiative (www.bd2k.nih.gov), and

MIAS, a DHS-IDS Center for Multimodal Information Access and Synthesis at UIUC. The views and conclusions contained in this document are those of the authors and should not be interpreted as representing the official policies, either expressed or implied, of the Army Research Laboratory, the U.S. Government, or other funding parties. The U.S. Government is authorized to reproduce and distribute reprints for Government purposes notwithstanding any copyright notation here on.

8. REFERENCES

[1] R. Agrawal, J. Gehrke, D. Gunopulos, and P. Raghavan. Automatic subspace clustering of high dimensional data. *DMKD'05*.

[2] M. Araujo, S. Papadimitriou, S. Günnemann, C. Faloutsos, P. Basu, A. Swami, E. E. Papalexakis, and D. Koutra. Com2: fast automatic discovery of temporal ("comet") communities. In *PAKDD'14*.

[3] R. Cilibrasi and P. Vitanyi. Clustering by compression. *TIT'05*.

[4] P. Cui, H. Liu, C. Aggarwal, and F. Wang. Computational modeling of complex user behaviors: Challenges and opportunities. *IEEE Intelligent Systems*, 31(2):78–81, 2016.

[5] L. De Lathauwer, B. De Moor, and J. Vandewalle. A multilinear singular value decomposition. *SIAM journal on Matrix Analysis and Applications*, 2000.

[6] C. Faloutsos and V. Megalooikonomou. On data mining, compression, and kolmogorov complexity. *DMKD'07*.

[7] R. L. Ferreira Cordeiro, C. Traina Junior, A. J. Machado Traina, J. López, U. Kang, and C. Faloutsos. Clustering very large multi-dimensional datasets with mapreduce. In *KDD'11*.

[8] J. Han, H. Cheng, D. Xin, and X. Yan. Frequent pattern mining: current status and future directions. *DMKD'07*.

[9] M. Jiang, A. Beutel, P. Cui, B. Hooi, S. Yang, and C. Faloutsos. A general suspiciousness metric for dense blocks in multimodal data. In *ICDM'15*.

[10] M. Jiang, P. Cui, and C. Faloutsos. Suspicious behavior detection: Current trends and future directions. *Intelligent Systems, IEEE*, 31(1):31–39, 2016.

[11] M. Jiang, P. Cui, F. Wang, X. Xu, W. Zhu, and S. Yang. Fema: flexible evolutionary multi-faceted analysis for dynamic behavioral pattern discovery. In *KDD'14*.

[12] M. Jiang, P. Cui, F. Wang, W. Zhu, and S. Yang. Scalable recommendation with social contextual information. *TKDE'14*.

[13] D. Johnson, S. Krishnan, J. Chhugani, S. Kumar, and S. Venkatasubramanian. Compressing large boolean matrices using reordering techniques. In *VLDB'04*.

[14] K. Kailing, H.-P. Kriegel, and P. Kröger. Density-connected subspace clustering for high-dimensional data. In *SDM'04*.

[15] D. Kang, D. Jiang, J. Pei, Z. Liao, X. Sun, and H.-J. Choi. Multidimensional mining of large-scale search logs: a topic-concept cube approach. In *WSDM'11*.

[16] U. Kang and C. Faloutsos. Beyond "caveman communities": Hubs and spokes for graph compression and mining. In *ICDM'11*.

[17] T. G. Kolda and B. W. Bader. Tensor decompositions and applications. *SIAM review*, 2009.

[18] D. Koutra, U. Kang, J. Vreeken, and C. Faloutsos. Vog: Summarizing and understanding large graphs. *SDM'14*.

[19] H.-P. Kriegel, P. Kröger, M. Renz, and S. Wurst. A generic framework for efficient subspace clustering of high-dimensional data. In *ICDM'05*.

[20] M. Kuramochi and G. Karypis. An efficient algorithm for discovering frequent subgraphs. *TKDE'04*.

[21] M. Li and P. Vitányi. *An introduction to Kolmogorov complexity and its applications*. 2013.

[22] S. Padmanabhan, B. Bhattacharjee, T. Malkemus, L. Cranston, and M. Huras. Multi-dimensional clustering: a new data layout scheme in db2. In *SIGMOD'03*.

[23] L. Parsons, E. Haque, and H. Liu. Subspace clustering for high dimensional data: a review. *KDD'04*.

[24] B. A. Prakash, A. Sridharan, M. Seshadri, S. Machiraju, and C. Faloutsos. Eigenspokes: Surprising patterns and scalable community chipping in large graphs. In *PAKDD'10*.

[25] J. Rissanen. Modeling by shortest data description. *Automatica*, 14(5), 1978.

[26] J. Rissanen. A universal prior for integers and estimation by minimum description length. *The Annals of statistics*, 1983.

[27] N. Shah, D. Koutra, T. Zou, B. Gallagher, and C. Faloutsos. Timecrunch: Interpretable dynamic graph summarization. In *KDD'15*.

[28] J. Sun, C. Faloutsos, S. Papadimitriou, and P. S. Yu. Graphscope: parameter-free mining of large time-evolving graphs. In *KDD'07*.

[29] J. Sun, D. Tao, and C. Faloutsos. Beyond streams and graphs: dynamic tensor analysis. In *KDD'06*.

[30] F. Tao, K. H. Lei, J. Han, C. Zhai, X. Cheng, M. Danilevsky, N. Desai, B. Ding, J. G. Ge, H. Ji, et al. Eventcube: multi-dimensional search and mining of structured and text data. In *KDD'13*.

[31] H. Toivonen, F. Zhou, A. Hartikainen, and A. Hinkka. Compression of weighted graphs. In *KDD'11*.

[32] J. Vreeken, M. Van Leeuwen, and A. Siebes. Krimp: mining itemsets that compress. *DMKD'11*.

[33] F. Wang, T. Li, X. Wang, S. Zhu, and C. Ding. Community discovery using nonnegative matrix factorization. *DMKD'11*.

[34] T. Zhang, P. Cui, C. Song, W. Zhu, and S. Yang. A multiscale survival process for modeling human activity patterns. *PloS one*, 11(3):e0151473, 2016.

[35] P. Zhao, X. Li, D. Xin, and J. Han. Graph cube: on warehousing and olap multidimensional networks. In *SIGMOD'11*.

APPENDIX

Proofs of the Properties in Section 4. Suppose the partitions have much smaller encoding cost than the data entries, the scoring function can be written as

$$f(\mathcal{A}, \mathcal{X}) = g(V + C, C) - g(v + c, c) - g(V + C - v - c, C - c).$$

Since $g'(x) = \log x - \log(x - y)$ and $g'(y) = \log(x - y) - \log y$, we have the derivatives of the function as follows.

$$\frac{\partial f}{\partial c} = \log \frac{\frac{(C-c-v)c}{Vv} + \frac{c}{v}}{\frac{(C-c-v)c}{Vv} + \frac{C}{V}} \quad , \quad \frac{\partial f}{\partial v} = \log \frac{\frac{V-v-c}{V} + \frac{C}{V}}{\frac{V-v-c}{V} + \frac{c}{v}}$$

$$\frac{\partial f}{\partial C} = \log \frac{\frac{(V+C-c)C}{Vv} - \frac{c}{v}}{\frac{(V+C-c)C}{Vv} - \frac{C}{V}} \quad , \quad \frac{\partial f}{\partial V} = \log \frac{\frac{C+V-v}{v} - \frac{C}{V}}{\frac{C+V-v}{v} - \frac{c}{v}}.$$

In a summary, the density of the Tartan is higher than the data: $\frac{c}{v} > \frac{C}{V}$. Thus, we obtain that $\frac{\partial f}{\partial c} > 0$ (Property 1), $\frac{\partial f}{\partial v} < 0$ (Property 2), $\frac{\partial f}{\partial C} > 0$ (Property 3), and $\frac{\partial f}{\partial V} < 0$ (Property 4).

Smart Reply: Automated Response Suggestion for Email

Anjuli Kannan⋆ Karol Kurach⋆ Sujith Ravi⋆
Tobias Kaufmann⋆ Andrew Tomkins Balint Miklos
Greg Corrado László Lukács Marina Ganea
Peter Young Vivek Ramavajjala

Google
{anjuli, kkurach, sravi, snufkin}@google.com

ABSTRACT

In this paper we propose and investigate a novel end-to-end method for automatically generating short email responses, called Smart Reply. It generates semantically diverse suggestions that can be used as complete email responses with just one tap on mobile. The system is currently used in *Inbox by Gmail* and is responsible for assisting with 10% of all mobile responses. It is designed to work at very high throughput and process hundreds of millions of messages daily. The system exploits state-of-the-art, large-scale deep learning.

We describe the architecture of the system as well as the challenges that we faced while building it, like response diversity and scalability. We also introduce a new method for semantic clustering of user-generated content that requires only a modest amount of explicitly labeled data.

Keywords

Email; LSTM; Deep Learning; Clustering; Semantics

1. INTRODUCTION

Email is one of the most popular modes of communication on the Web. Despite the recent increase in usage of social networks, email continues to be the primary medium for billions of users across the world to connect and share information [2]. With the rapid increase in email overload, it has become increasingly challenging for users to process and respond to incoming messages. It can be especially time-consuming to type email replies on a mobile device.

An initial study covering several million email-reply pairs showed that ~25% of replies have 20 tokens or less. Thus we raised the following question: can we assist users with composing these short messages? More specifically, would it be possible to suggest brief responses when appropriate, just one tap away?

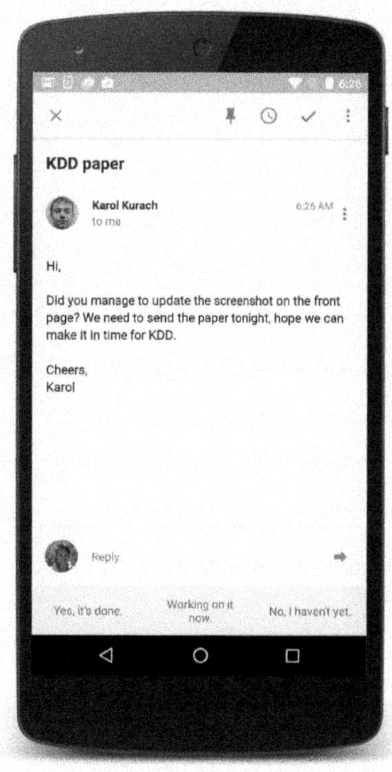

Figure 1: Example Smart Reply suggestions.

⋆Equal contribution.

KDD '16 August 13-17, 2016, San Francisco, CA, USA

ACM ISBN 978-1-4503-4232-2/16/08.
DOI: http://dx.doi.org/10.1145/2939672.2939801

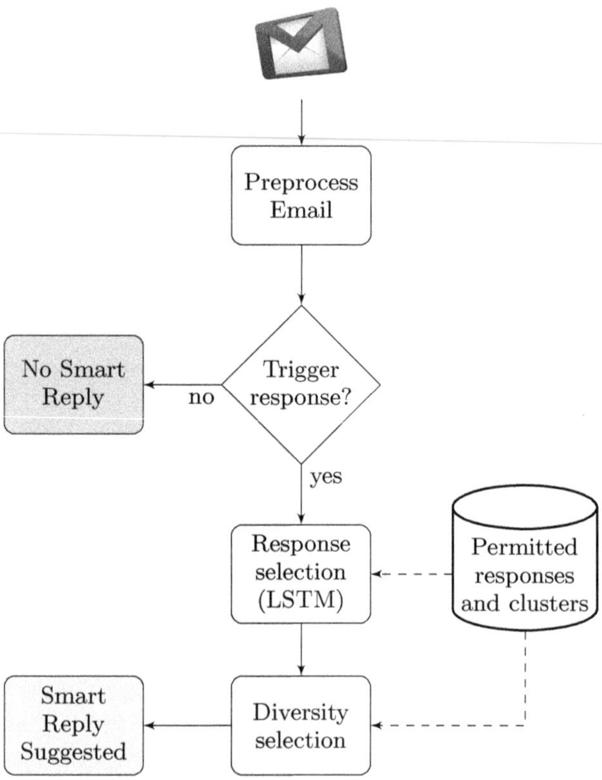

Figure 2: Life of a message. The figure presents the overview of inference.

To address this problem, we leverage the sequence-to-sequence learning framework [23], which uses long short-term memory networks (LSTMs) [10] to predict sequences of text. Consistent with the approach of the Neural Conversation Model [24], our *input* sequence is an incoming message and our *output* distribution is over the space of possible replies. Training this framework on a large corpus of conversation data produces a fully generative model that can produce a response to any sequence of input text. As [24] demonstrated on a tech support chat corpus, this distribution can be used to decode coherent, plausible responses.

However, in order to deploy such a model into a product used globally by millions, we faced several challenges not considered in previous work:

- **Response quality** How to ensure that the individual response options are *always* high quality in language and content.
- **Utility** How to select multiple options to show a user so as to maximize the likelihood that one is chosen.
- **Scalability** How to efficiently process millions of messages per day while remaining within the latency requirements of an email delivery system.
- **Privacy** How to develop this system without ever inspecting the data except aggregate statistics.

To tackle these challenges, we propose Smart Reply (Figure 1), a novel method and system for automated email response suggestion. Smart Reply consists of the following components, which are also shown in Figure 2:

1. **Response selection:** At the core of our system, an LSTM neural network processes an incoming message, then uses it to predict the most likely responses. LSTM computation can be expensive, so we improve *scalability* by finding only the approximate best responses. We explain the model in detail in Section 3.
2. **Response set generation:** To deliver high *response quality*, we only select responses from response space which is generated offline using a semi-supervised graph learning approach. This is discussed in Section 4.
3. **Diversity:** After finding a set of most likely responses from the LSTM, we would like to choose a small set to show to the user that maximize the total *utility*. We found that enforcing diverse semantic intents is critical to making the suggestions useful. Our method for this is described further in Section 5.
4. **Triggering model:** A feedforward neural network decides whether or not to suggest responses. This further improves *utility* by not showing suggestions when they are unlikely to be used. We break this out into a separate component so that we have the option to use a computationally cheaper architecture than what is used for the scoring model; this keeps the system *scalable*. This model is described in Section 6.

The combination of these components is a novel end-to-end method for generating short, complete responses to emails, going beyond previous works. For response selection it exploits state-of-the-art deep learning models trained on billions of words, and for response set generation it introduces a new semi-supervised method for semantic understanding of user-generated content.

Moreover, since it directly addresses all four challenges mentioned above, it has been successfully deployed in *I*nbox. Currently, the Smart Reply system is responsible for assisting with 10% of email replies for *I*nbox on mobile.

Next, we discuss the related work in Section 2, followed by a description of our core system components in Sections 3, 4, 5, and 6. We close by showing modeling results in Section 7 and our conclusions in Section 8.

2. RELATED WORK

As we consider related work, we note that building an automated system to suggest email responses is not a task for which there is existing literature or benchmarks, nor is this a standard machine learning problem to which existing algorithms can be readily applied. However, there is work related to two of our core components which we will review here: predicting responses and identifying a target response space.

Predicting full responses. Much work exists on analyzing natural language dialogues in public domains such as Twitter, but it has largely focused on social media tasks like predicting whether or not a response is made [3], predicting next word only [14], or curating threads [4].

Full response prediction was initially attempted in [16], which approached the problem from the perspective of machine translation: given a Twitter post, "translate" it into a response using phrase-based statistical machine translation (SMT). Our approach is similar, but rather than using

SMT we use the neural network machine translation model proposed in [23], called "sequence-to-sequence learning".

Sequence-to-sequence learning, which makes use of long short-term memory networks (LSTMs) [10] to predict sequences of text, was originally applied to Machine Translation but has since seen success in other domains such as image captioning [25] and speech recognition [6].

Other recent works have also applied recurrent neural networks (RNNs) or LSTMs to full response prediction [21], [20], [19], [24]. In [21] the authors rely on having an SMT system to generate n-best lists, while [19] and [24], like this work, develop fully generative models. Our approach is most similar to the Neural Conversation Model [24], which uses sequence-to-sequence learning to model tech support chats and movie subtitles.

The primary difference of our work is that it was deployed in a production setting, which raised the challenges of response quality, utility, scalability, and privacy. These challenges were not considered in any of these related works and led to our novel solutions explained in the rest of this paper.

Furthermore, in this work we approach a different domain than [21], [20], [19], and [24], which primarily focus on social media and movie dialogues. In both of those domains it can be acceptable to provide a response that is merely related or on-topic. Email, on the other hand, frequently expresses a request or intent which must be addressed in the response.

Identifying a target response space. Our approach here builds on the Expander graph learning approach [15], since it scales well to both large data (vast amounts of email) and large output sizes (many different underlying semantic intents). While Expander was originally proposed for knowledge expansion and classification tasks [26], our work is the first to use it to discover semantic intent clusters from user-generated content.

Other graph-based semi-supervised learning techniques have been explored in the past for more traditional classification problems [27, 5]. Other related works have explored tasks involving semantic classification [12] or identifying word-level intents [17] targeted towards Web search queries and other forums [7]. However, the problem settings and tasks themselves are significantly different from what is addressed in our work.

Finally, we note that Smart Reply is the first work to address these tasks together and solve them in a single end-to-end, deployable system.

3. SELECTING RESPONSES

The fundamental task of the Smart Reply system is to find the most likely response given an original message. In other words, given original message $\mathbf{o}$ and the set of all possible responses R, we would like to find:

$$\mathbf{r}^* = \underset{r \in R}{\operatorname{argmax}}\, P(\mathbf{r}|\mathbf{o})$$

To find this response, we will construct a model that can score responses and then find the highest scoring response.

We will next describe how the model is formulated, trained, and used for inference. Then we will discuss the core challenges of bringing this model to produce high quality suggestions on a large scale.

3.1 LSTM model

Since we are scoring one sequence of tokens $\mathbf{r}$, conditional on another sequence of tokens $\mathbf{o}$, this problem is a natural fit for sequence-to-sequence learning [23]. The model itself is an LSTM. The input is the tokens of the original message $\{o_1, ..., o_n\}$, and the output is the conditional probability distribution of the sequence of response tokens given the input:

$$P(r_1, ..., r_m|o_1, ..., o_n)$$

As in [23], this distribution can be factorized as:

$$P(r_1, ..., r_m|o_1, ..., o_n) = \prod_{i=1}^{m} P(r_i|o_1, ..., o_n, r_1, ..., r_{i-1})$$

First, the sequence of original message tokens, including a special end-of-message token o_n, are read in, such that the LSTM's hidden state encodes a vector representation of the whole message. Then, given this hidden state, a softmax output is computed and interpreted as $P(r_1|o_1, ..., o_n)$, or the probability distribution for the first response token. As response tokens are fed in, the softmax at each timestep t is interpreted as $P(r_t|o_1, ..., o_n, r_1, ..., r_{t-1})$. Given the factorization above, these softmaxes can be used to compute $P(r_1, ..., r_m|o_1, ..., o_n)$.

Training Given a large corpus of messages, the training objective is to maximize the log probability of observed responses, given their respective originals:

$$\sum_{(\mathbf{o},\mathbf{r})} \log P(r_1, ..., r_m|o_1, ..., o_n)$$

We train against this objective using stochastic gradient descent with AdaGrad [8]. Ten epochs are run over a message corpus which will be described in Section 7.1. Due to the size of the corpus, training is run in a distributed fashion using the TensorFlow library [1].

Both our input and output vocabularies consist of the most frequent English words in our training data after preprocessing (steps described in Section 7.1). In addition to the standard LSTM formulation, we found that the addition of a recurrent projection layer [18] substantially improved both the quality of the converged model and the time to converge. We also found that gradient clipping (with the value of 1) was essential to stable training.

Inference At inference time we can feed in an original message and then use the output of the softmaxes to get a probability distribution over the vocabulary at each timestep. These distributions can be used in a variety of ways:

1. To draw a random sample from the response distribution $P(r_1, ..., r_m|o_1, ..., o_n)$. This can be done by sampling one token at each timestep and feeding it back into the model.

2. To approximate the most likely response, given the original message. This can be done greedily by taking the most likely token at each time step and feeding it back in. A less greedy strategy is to use a beam search, i.e., take the top b tokens and feed them in, then retain the b best response prefixes and repeat.

Query	Top generated responses
Hi, I thought it would be great for us to sit down and chat. I am free Tuesday and Wenesday. Can you do either of those days? Thanks! –Alice	I can do Tuesday. I can do Wednesday. How about Tuesday? I can do Tuesday! I can do Tuesday. What time works for you? I can do Wednesday! I can do Tuesday or Wednesday. How about Wednesday? I can do Wednesday. What time works for you? I can do either.

Table 1: Generated response examples.

3. To determine the likelihood of a specific response candidate. This can be done by feeding in each token of the candidate and using the softmax output to get the likelihood of the next candidate token.

Table 1 shows some example of generating the approximate most likely responses using a beam search.

3.2 Challenges

As described thus far, the model can generate coherent and plausible responses given an incoming email message. However, several key challenges arise when bringing this model into production.

Response quality In order to surface responses to users, we need to ensure that they are *always* high quality in style, tone, diction, and content.

Given that the model is trained on a corpus of real messages, we have to account for the possibility that the most probable response is not necessarily a high quality response. Even a response that occurs frequently in our corpus may not be appropriate to surface back to users. For example, it could contain poor grammar, spelling, or mechanics (*your the best!*); it could convey a familiarity that is likely to be jarring or offensive in many situations (*thanks hon!*); it could be too informal to be consistent with other *Inbox* intelligence features (*yup, got it thx*); it could convey a sentiment that is politically incorrect, offensive, or otherwise inappropriate (*Leave me alone*).

While restricting the model vocabulary might address simple cases such as profanity and spelling errors, it would not be sufficient to capture the wide variability with which, for example, politically incorrect statements can be made. Instead, we use semi-supervised learning (described in detail in Section 4) to construct a target response space R comprising only high quality responses. Then we use the model described here to choose the best response in R, rather than the best response from any sequence of words in its vocabulary.

Utility Our user studies showed that suggestions are most useful when they are highly specific to the original message and express diverse intents. However, as column 1 in Table 2 shows, the raw output of the model tends to (1) favor common but unspecific responses and (2) have little diversity.

First, to improve specificity of responses, we apply some light normalization that penalizes responses which are applicable to a broad range of incoming messages. The results of this normalization can be seen in column 2 of Table 2. For example, the very generic "Yes!" has fallen out of the top ten. Second, to increase the breadth of options shown to the user, we enforce diversity by exploiting the semantic structure of R, as we will discuss in Section 5. The results of this are also shown at the bottom of Table 2.

We further improve the utility of suggestions by first passing each message through a triggering model (described in Section 6) that determines whether suggestions should be generated at all. This reduces the likelihood that we show suggestions when they would not be used anyway.

Scalability Our model needs to be deployed in a production setting and cannot introduce latency to the process of email delivery, so scalability is critical.

Exhaustively scoring every response candidate $r \in R$, would require $O(|R|l)$ LSTM steps where l is the length of the longest response. In previous work [23], this could be afforded because computations were performed in a batch process offline. However, in the context of an email delivery pipeline, time is a much more precious resource. Furthermore, given the tremendous diversity with which people communicate and the large number of email scenarios we would like to cover, we can assume that R is very large and only expected to grow over time. For example, in a uniform sample of 10 million short responses (say, responses with at most 10 tokens), more than 40% occur only once. Therefore, rather than performing an exhaustive scoring of every candidate $r \in R$, we would like to efficiently search for the best responses such that complexity is *not* a function of $|R|$.

Our search is conducted as follows. First, the elements of R are organized into a trie. Then, we conduct a left-to-right beam search, but only retain hypotheses that appear in the trie. This search process has complexity $O(bl)$ for beam size b and maximum response length l. Both b and l are typically in the range of 10-30, so this method dramatically reduces the time to find the top responses and is a critical element of making this system deployable. In terms of quality, we find that, although this search only approximates the best responses in R, its results are very similar to what we would get by scoring and ranking all $r \in R$, even for small b. At $b = 128$, for example, the top scoring response found by this process matches the true top scoring response 99% of the time. Results for various beam sizes are shown in Figure 3.

Additionally, requiring that each message first pass through a triggering model, as mentioned above, has the additional benefit of reducing the total amount of LSTM computation.

Privacy Note that all email data (raw data, preprocessed data and training data) was encrypted. Engineers could only inspect aggregated statistics on anonymized sentences that occurred across many users and did not identify any user. Also, only frequent words are retained. As a result, verifying model's quality and debugging is more complex.

Our solutions for the first three challenges are described further in Sections 4, 5, and 6.

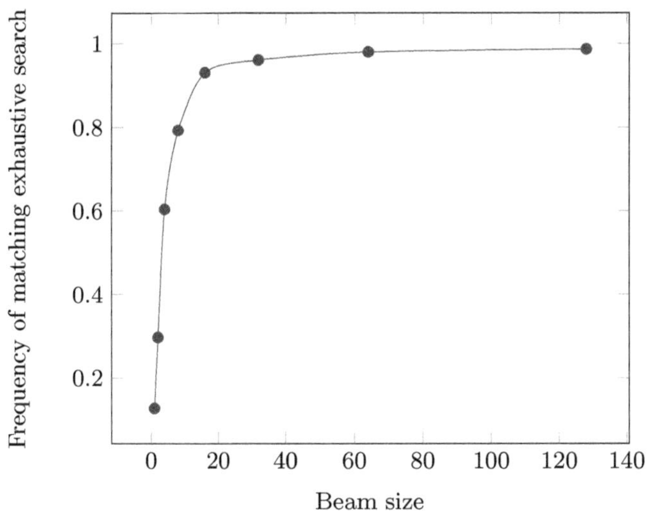

Figure 3: Effectiveness of searching the response space R. For a sample of messages we compute the frequency with which the best candidate found by a beam search over R matches the best candidate found by exhaustively scoring all members of R. We compare various beam sizes. At a beam size of 16, these two methods find the same best response 93% of the time.

4. RESPONSE SET GENERATION

Two of the core challenges we face when building the end to end automated response system are *response quality* and *utility*. Response quality comes from suggesting "high quality" responses that deliver a positive user experience. Utility comes from ensuring that we don't suggest multiple responses that capture the same intent (for example, minor lexical variations such as "*Yes, I'll be there.*" and "*I will be there.*"). We can consider these two challenges jointly.

We first need to define a target response space that comprises high quality messages which can be surfaced as suggestions. The goal here is to generate a structured response set that effectively captures various intents conveyed by people in natural language conversations. The target response space should capture both variability in language and intents. The result is used in two ways downstream—(a) define a response space for scoring and selecting suggestions using the model described in Section 3, and (b) promote diversity among chosen suggestions as discussed in Section 5.

We construct a response set using only the most frequent anonymized sentences aggregated from the preprocessed data (described in Section 7.1). This process yields a few million unique sentences.

4.1 Canonicalizing email responses

The first step is to automatically generate a set of canonical responses messages that capture the variability in language. For example, responses such as "*Thanks for your kind update.*", "*Thank you for updating!*", "*Thanks for the status update.*" may appear slightly different on the surface but in fact convey the same information. We parse each sentence using a dependency parser and use its syntactic structure to generate a canonicalized representation. Words (or phrases) that are modifiers or unattached to head words are ignored.

4.2 Semantic intent clustering

In the next step, we want to partition all response messages into "semantic" clusters where a cluster represents a meaningful response intent (for example, "*thank you*" type of response versus "*sorry*" versus "*cannot make it*"). All messages within a cluster share the same semantic meaning but may appear very different. For example, "*Ha ha*", "*lol*" and "*Oh that's funny!*" are associated with the *funny* cluster.

This step helps to automatically digest the entire information present in frequent responses into a coherent set of semantic clusters. If we were to build a semantic intent prediction model for this purpose, we would need access to a large corpus of sentences annotated with their corresponding semantic intents. However, this is neither readily available for our task nor at this scale. Moreover, unlike typical machine learning classification tasks, the semantic intent space cannot be fully defined a priori. So instead, we model the task as a semi-supervised machine learning problem and use scalable graph algorithms [15] to automatically learn this information from data and a few human-provided examples.

4.3 Graph construction

We start with a few manually defined clusters sampled from the top frequent messages (e.g., *thanks*, *i love you*, *sounds good*). A small number of example responses are added as "seeds" for each cluster (for example, *thanks* → "*Thanks!*", "*Thank you.*").[1]

We then construct a base graph with frequent response messages as nodes (V_R). For each response message, we further extract a set of lexical features (ngrams and skip-grams of length up to 3) and add these as "feature" nodes (V_F) to the same graph. Edges are created between a pair of nodes (u, v) where $u \in V_R$ and $v \in V_F$ if v belongs to the feature set for response u. We follow the same process and create nodes for the manually labeled examples V_L. We make an observation that in some cases an incoming original message could potentially be treated as a response to another email depending on the context. For example, consider the following (original, response) message pairs:

Let us get together soon. → *When should we meet?*
When should we meet? → *How about Friday?*

Inter-message relations as shown in the above example can be modeled within the same framework by adding extra edges between the corresponding message nodes in the graph.

4.4 Semi-supervised learning

The constructed graph captures relationships between similar canonicalized responses via the feature nodes. Next, we learn a semantic labeling for all response nodes by propagating semantic intent information from the manually labeled examples through the graph. We treat this as a semi-supervised learning problem and use the distributed EXPANDER [15] framework for optimization. The learning framework is scalable and naturally suited for semi-supervised graph propagation tasks such as the semantic clustering problem described here. We minimize the following objective function for response nodes in the graph:

[1] In practice, we pick 100 clusters and on average 3–5 labeled seed examples per cluster.

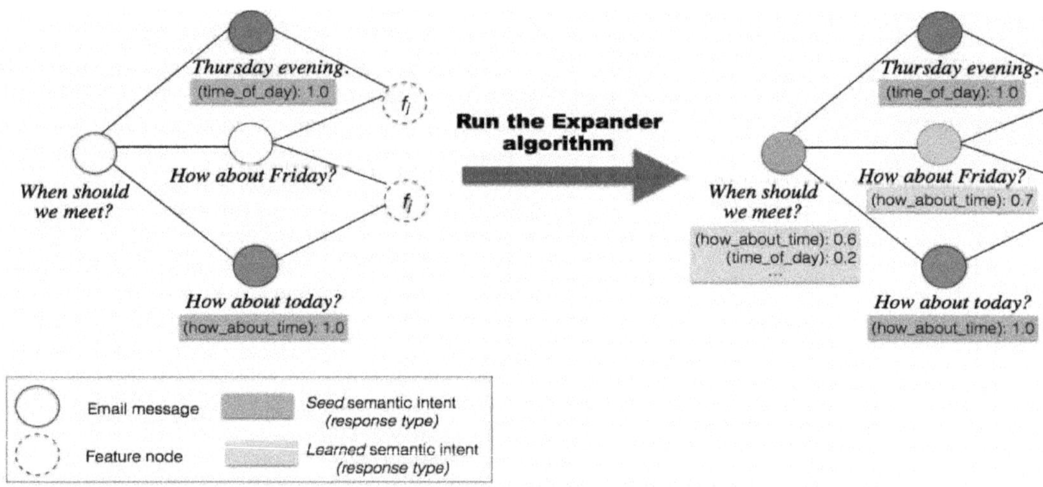

Figure 4: Semantic clustering of response messages.

$$s_i||\hat{C}_i - C_i||^2 + \mu_{pp}||\hat{C}_i - U||^2 + \mu_{np}\Big(\sum_{j\in\mathcal{N}_{\mathcal{F}}(i)} w_{ij}||\hat{C}_i - \hat{C}_j||^2 + \sum_{j\in\mathcal{N}_{\mathcal{R}}(i)} w_{ik}||\hat{C}_i - \hat{C}_k||^2\Big) \quad (1)$$

where s_i is an indicator function equal to 1 if the node i is a seed and 0 otherwise, $\hat{C}_i$ is the learned semantic cluster distribution for response node i, C_i is the true label distribution (i.e., for manually provided examples), $\mathcal{N}_{\mathcal{F}}(i)$ and $\mathcal{N}_{\mathcal{R}}(i)$ represent the feature and message neighborhood of node i, μ_{np} is the predefined penalty for neighboring nodes with divergent label distributions, $\hat{C}_j$ is the learned label distribution for feature neighbor j, w_{ij} is the weight of feature j in response i, μ_{pp} is the penalty for label distribution deviating from the prior, a uniform distribution U.

The objective function for a feature node is alike, except that there is no first term, as there are no seed labels for feature nodes:

$$\mu_{np}\sum_{i\in\mathcal{N}(j)} w_{ij}||\hat{C}_j - \hat{C}_i||^2 + \mu_{pp}||\hat{C}_j - U||^2 \quad (2)$$

The objective function is jointly optimized for all nodes in the graph.

The output from EXPANDER is a learned distribution of semantic labels for every node in the graph. We assign the top scoring output label as the semantic intent for the node, labels with low scores are filtered out. Figure 4 illustrates this process.

To discover new clusters which are not covered by the labeled examples, we run the semi-supervised learning algorithm in repeated phases. In the first phase, we run the label propagation algorithm for 5 iterations. We then fix the cluster assignment, randomly sample 100 new responses from the remaining unlabeled nodes in the graph. The sampled nodes are treated as potential new clusters and labeled with their canonicalized representation. We rerun label propagation with the new labeled set of clusters and repeat this procedure until convergence (i.e., until no new clusters are discovered and members of a cluster do not change between iterations). The iterative propagation method thereby allows us to both expand cluster membership as well as discover (up to 5X) new clusters, where each cluster has an interpretable semantic interpretation.

4.5 Cluster Validation

Finally, we extract the top k members for each semantic cluster, sorted by their label scores. The set of (response, cluster label) pairs are then validated by human raters. The raters are provided with a response R_i, a corresponding cluster label C (e.g., *thanks*) as well as few example responses belonging to the cluster (e.g., "*Thanks!*", "*Thank you.*") and asked whether R_i belongs to C.

The result is an automatically generated and validated set of high quality response messages labeled with semantic intent. This is subsequently used by the response scoring model to search for approximate best responses to an incoming email (described earlier in Section 3) and further to enforce diversity among the top responses chosen (Section 5).

5. SUGGESTION DIVERSITY

As discussed in Section 3, the LSTM first processes an incoming message and then selects the (approximate) best responses from the target response set created using the method described in Section 4. Recall that we follow this by some light normalization to penalize responses that may be too general to be valuable to the user. The effect of this normalization can be seen by comparing columns 1 and 2 of Table 2. For example, the very generic "Yes!" falls out of the top ten responses.

Next, we need to choose a small number of options to show the user. A straight-forward approach would be to just choose the N top responses and present them to the user. However, as column 2 of Table 2 shows, these responses tend to be very similar.

The likelihood of at least one response being useful is greatest when the response options are not redundant, so it would be wasteful to present the user with three variations of, say, *I'll be there.* The job of the diversity component is to select a more varied set of suggestions using two strategies: omitting redundant responses and enforcing negative or positive responses.

5.1 Omitting Redundant Responses

This strategy assumes that the user should never see two responses of the same *intent*. An intent can be thought of as a cluster of responses that have a common communication purpose, e.g. confirming, asking for time or rejecting participation. In Smart Reply, every target response is associated with exactly one intent. Intents are defined based on automatic clustering followed by human validation as discussed in Section 4.

The actual diversity strategy is simple: the top responses are iterated over in the order of decreasing score. Each response is added to the list of suggestions, unless its intent is already covered by a response on the suggestion list. The resulting list contains only the highest-scored representative of each intent, and these representatives are ordered by decreasing score.

5.2 Enforcing Negatives and Positives

We have observed that the LSTM has a strong tendency towards producing positive responses, whereas negative responses such as *I can't make it* or *I don't think so* typically receive low scores. We believe that this tendency reflects the style of email conversations: positive replies may be more common, and where negative responses are appropriate, users may prefer a less direct wording.

Nevertheless, we think that it is important to offer negative suggestions in order to give the user a real choice. This policy is implemented through the following strategy:

> If the top two responses (after omitting redundant responses) contain at least one positive response and none of the top three responses are negative, the third response is replaced with a negative one.

A positive response is one which is clearly affirmative, e.g. one that starts with *Yes*, *Sure* or *Of course*. In order to find the negative response to be included as the third suggestion, a second LSTM pass is performed. In this second pass, the search is restricted to only the negative responses in the target set (refer Table 2 for scored negative response examples). This is necessary since the top responses produced in the first pass may not contain any negatives.

Even though missing negatives are more common, there are also cases in which an incoming message triggers exclusively negative responses. In this situation, we employ an analogous strategy for enforcing a positive response.

The final set of top scoring responses (bottom row in Table 2) are then presented to the user as suggestions.

6. TRIGGERING

The *triggering* module is the entry point of the Smart Reply system. It is responsible for filtering messages that are bad candidates for suggesting responses. This includes emails for which short replies are not appropriate (e.g., containing open-ended questions or sensitive topics), as well as emails for which no reply is necessary at all (e.g., promotional emails and auto-generated updates).

The module is applied to every incoming email just after the preprocessing step. If the decision is negative, we finish the execution and do not show any suggestions (see Figure 2). Currently, the system decides to produce a Smart

Unnormalized Responses	Normalized Responses
Yes, I'll be there.	Sure, I'll be there.
Yes, I will be there.	Yes, I can.
I'll be there.	Yes, I can be there.
Yes, I can.	Yes, I'll be there.
What time?	Sure, I can be there.
I'll be there!	Yeah, I can.
I will be there.	Yeah, I'll be there.
Sure, I'll be there.	Sure, I can.
Yes, I can be there.	Yes. I can.
Yes!	Yes, I will be there.

Normalized Negative Responses
Sorry, I won't be able to make it tomorrow.
Unfortunately I can't.
Sorry, I won't be able to join you.
Sorry, I can't make it tomorrow.
No, I can't.
Sorry, I won't be able to make it today.
Sorry, I can't.
I will not be available tomorrow.
I won't be available tomorrow.
Unfortunately, I can't.

Final Suggestions
Sure, I'll be there.
Yes, I can.
Sorry, I won't be able to make it tomorrow.

Table 2: Different response rankings for the message *"Can you join tomorrow's meeting?"*

Reply for roughly 11% of messages, so this process vastly reduces the number of useless sugestions seen by the users. An additional benefit is to decrease the number of calls to the more expensive LSTM inference, which translates into smaller infrastructure cost.

There are two main requirements for the design of the triggering component. First, it has to be good enough to figure out cases where the response is not expected. Note that this is a very different goal than just scoring a set of responses. For instance, we could propose several valid replies to a newsletter containing a sentence "*Where do you want to go today?*", but most likely all of the responses would be useless for our users. Second, it has to be fast: it processes hundreds of millions of messages daily, so we aim to process each message within milliseconds.

The main part of the triggering component is a feedforward neural network which produces a probability score for every incoming message. If the score is above some threshold, we *trigger* and run the LSTM scoring. We have adopted this approach because feedforward networks have repeatedly been shown to outperform linear models such as SVM or linear regression on various NLP tasks (see for example [9]).

6.1 Data and Features

In order to label our training corpus of emails, we use as positive examples those emails that have been responded to. More precisely, out of the data set described in Section 7.1, we create a training set that consists of pairs $(\mathbf{o}, y)$, where $\mathbf{o}$ is an incoming message and $y \in \{true, false\}$ is a boolean label, which is *true* if the message had a response and *false* otherwise. For the positive class, we consider only messages that were replied to from a mobile device, while for negative we use a subset of all messages. We downsample the negative class to balance the training set. Our goal is to model $P(y = true \mid \mathbf{o})$, the probability that message $\mathbf{o}$ will have a response on mobile.

After preprocessing (described in Section 7.1), we extract content features (e.g. unigrams, bigrams) from the message body, subject and headers. We also use various social signals like whether the sender is in recipient's address book, whether the sender is in recipient's social network and whether the recipient responded in the past to this sender.

6.2 Network Architecture and Training

We use a feedforward multilayer perceptron with an embedding layer (for a vocabulary of roughly one million words) and three fully connected hidden layers. We use feature hashing to bucket rare words that are not present in the vocabulary. The embeddings are separate for each sparse feature type (eg. unigram, bigram) and within one feature type, we aggregate embeddings by summing them up. Then, all sparse feature embeddings are concatenated with each other and with the vector of dense features (those are real numbers and boolean values mentioned in Section 6.1).

We use the ReLu [13] activation function for non-linearity between layers. The dropout [22] layer is applied after each hidden layer. We train the model using AdaGrad [8] optimization algorithm with logistic loss cost function. Similarly to the LSTM, the training is run in a distributed fashion using the TensorFlow library [1].

7. EVALUATION AND RESULTS

In this section, we describe the training and test data, as well as preprocessing steps used for all messages. Then, we evaluate different components of the Smart Reply system and present overall usage statistics.

7.1 Data

To generate the training data for all Smart Reply models from sampled accounts, we extracted all pairs of an incoming message and the user's response to that message. For training the triggering model (see Section 6), we additionally sampled a number of incoming personal messages which the user didn't reply to. At the beginning of Smart Reply pipeline (Figure 2), data is preprocessed in the following way:

Language detection The language of the message is identified and non-English messages are discarded.

Tokenization Subject and message body are broken into words and punctuation marks.

Sentence segmentation Sentences boundaries are identified in the message body.

Normalization Infrequent words and entities like personal names, URLs, email addresses, phone numbers etc. are replaced by special tokens.

Quotation removal Quoted original messages and forwarded messages are removed.

Salutation/close removal Salutations like *Hi John* and closes such as *Best regards, Mary* are removed.

After the preprocessing steps, the size of the training set is 238 million messages, which include 153 million messages that have no response.

7.2 Results

The most important end-to-end metric for our system is the fraction of messages for which it was used. This is currently 10% of all mobile replies. Below we describe in more detail evaluation stats for different components of the system. We evaluate all parts in isolation using both offline analysis as well as online experiments run on a subset of accounts.

7.2.1 *Triggering results*

In order to evaluate the triggering model, we split the data set described in Section 6.1 into train (80%) and test (20%) such that all test messages are delivered after train messages. This is to ensure that the test conditions are similar to the final scenario. We use a set of standard binary classifier metrics: precision, recall and the area under the ROC curve. The AUC of the triggering model is 0.854. We also compute the fraction of triggered messages in the deployed system, which is 11%. We observed that it may be beneficial to slightly over-trigger, since the cost of presenting a suggestion, even if it is not used, is quite low.

7.2.2 *Response selection results*

We evaluate the LSTM scoring model on three standard metrics: Perplexity, Mean Reciprocal Rank and Precision@K.

Perplexity.

Perplexity is a measure of how well the model has fit the data: a model with lower perplexity assigns higher likelihood to the test responses, so we expect it to be better at predicting responses. Intuitively, a perplexity equal to k means that when the model predicts the next word, there are on average k likely candidates. In particular, for the ideal scenario of perplexity equal to 1, we always know exactly what should be the next word. The perplexity on a set of N test samples is computed using the following formula:

$$P_r = \exp(-\frac{1}{W}\sum_{i=1}^{N}\ln(\hat{P}(r_1^i, ..., r_m^i | o_1^i, ..., o_n^i)))$$

where W is the total number of words in all N samples, $\hat{P}$ is the learned distribution and $\mathbf{r}^i$, $\mathbf{o}^i$ are the i-th response and original message. Note that in the equation above only response terms are factored into P_r. The perplexity of the Smart Reply LSTM is 17.0. By comparison, an n-grams language model with Katz backoff [11] and a maximum order of 5 has a perplexity of 31.4 on the same data (again, computed only from response terms).

Response ranking.

While perplexity is a quality indicator, it does not actually measure performance at the scoring task we are ultimately interested in. In particular, it does not take into account the constraint of choosing a response in R. Therefore we also evaluate the model on a response ranking task: for each of N test message pairs (o, r) for which $r \in R$, we compute $s = P(r|o)$ and $\forall_i x_i = P(w_i|o)$, where w_i is the i-th element of R. Then we sort the set $R = \{s, x_1, \ldots, x_N\}$ in descending order. Finally, we define $rank_i = \text{argmin}_j(R_j | R_j = s)$. Put simply, we are finding the rank of the actual response with respect to all elements in R.

Model	Precision@10	Precision@20	MRR
Random	$5.58e-4$	$1.12e-3$	$3.64e-4$
Frequency	0.321	0.368	0.155
Multiclass-BOW	0.345	0.425	0.197
Smart Reply	0.483	0.579	0.267

Table 3: Response ranking

Using this value, we can compute the Mean Reciprocal Rank:

$$MRR = \frac{1}{N}\sum_{i=1}^{N}\frac{1}{rank_i}$$

Additionally we can compute Precision@K. For a given value of K it is computed as the number of cases for which target response r was within the top$K$ responses that were ranked by the model.

We compare the Smart Reply response selection model to three baselines on the same ranking task. The *Random* baseline ranks R randomly. The *Frequency* baseline ranks them in order of their frequency in the training corpus. This baseline captures the extent to which we can simply suggest highly frequent responses without regard for the contents of the original message. The *Multiclass-BOW* baseline ranks R using a feedforward neural network whose input is the original message, represented with bag of words features, and whose output is a distribution over the elements of R (a softmax).

As shown in Table 3, the Smart Reply LSTM significantly improves on the *Frequency* baseline, demonstrating that conditioning on the original message is effective; the model successfully extracts information from the original message and uses it to rank responses more accurately.

It also significantly outperforms the *Multiclass-BOW* baseline. There are a few possible explanations for this. First, the recurrent architecture allows the model to learn more sophisticated language understanding than bag of words features. Second, when we pose this as a mulitclass prediction problem, we can only train on messages whose response is in R, a small fraction of our data. On the other hand, the sequence-to-sequence framework allows us to take advantage of all data in our corpus: the model can learn a lot about original-response relationships even when the response does not appear in R exactly.

Note that an added disadvantage of the multiclass formulation is that it tightly couples the training of the model to the construction of R. We expect R to grow over time, given the incredible diversity with which people communicate. While a simpler application such as chat might only need a small number of possible responses, we find that for email we will need a tremendous number of possible suggestions to really address users' needs.

7.2.3 Diversity results

We justify the need for both the diversity component and a sizable response space R by reporting statistics around unique suggestions and clusters in Table 4. The Smart Reply system generates daily 12.9k unique suggestions that belong to 376 unique semantic clusters. Out of those, people decide to use 4,115, or 31.9% of, unique suggestions and 313, or 83.2% of, unique clusters. Note, however, that many suggestions are never seen, as column 2 shows: the user may not open an email, use the web interface instead of mobile

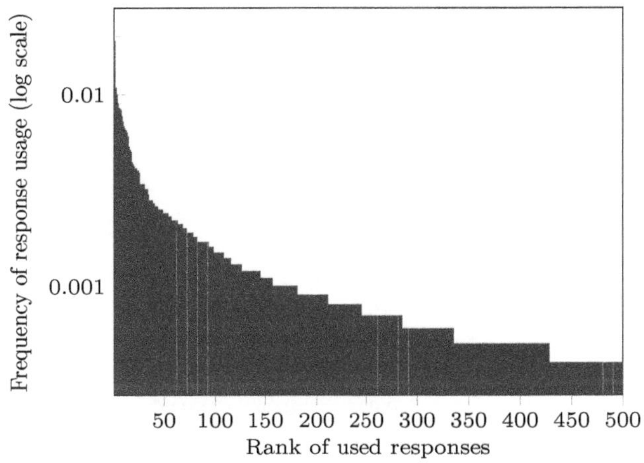

Figure 5: Usage distribution of top responses.

	Daily Count	Seen	Used
Unique Clusters	376	97.1%	83.2%
Unique Suggestions	12.9k	78%	31.9%

Table 4: Unique cluster/suggestions usage per day

or just not scroll down to the bottom of the message. Also, only one of the three displayed suggestions will be selected by the user. These statistics demonstrate the need to go well beyond a simple system with 5 or 10 canned responses.

Figure 5 and Figure 6 present, respectively, the distribution of the rank for suggested responses and the distribution of suggested clusters. The tail of the cluster distribution is long, which explains the poor performance of *Frequency* baseline described in Section 7.2.2.

We also measured how Smart Reply suggestions are used based on their location on a screen. Recall that Smart Reply always presents 3 suggestions, where the first suggestion is the top one. We observed that, out of all used suggestions, 45% were from the 1*st* position, 35% from the 2nd position and 20% from the 3rd position. Since usually the third position is used for diverse responses, we conclude that the diversity component is crucial for the system quality.

Finally, we measured the impact of enforcing a diverse set of responses (e.g., by not showing two responses from the same semantic cluster) on user engagement: when we completely disabled the diversity component and simply suggested the three suggestions with the highest scores, the click-through rate decreased by roughly 7.5% relative.

8. CONCLUSIONS

We presented Smart Reply, a novel end-to-end system for automatically generating short, complete email responses. The core of the system is a state-of-the-art deep LSTM model that can predict full responses, given an incoming email message. To successfully deploy this system in *Inbox by Gmail*, we addressed several challenges:

- We ensure that individual response options deliver *quality* by selecting them from a carefully constructed response space. The responses are identified by a novel method for semantic clustering.
- We increase the total *utility* of our chosen combina-

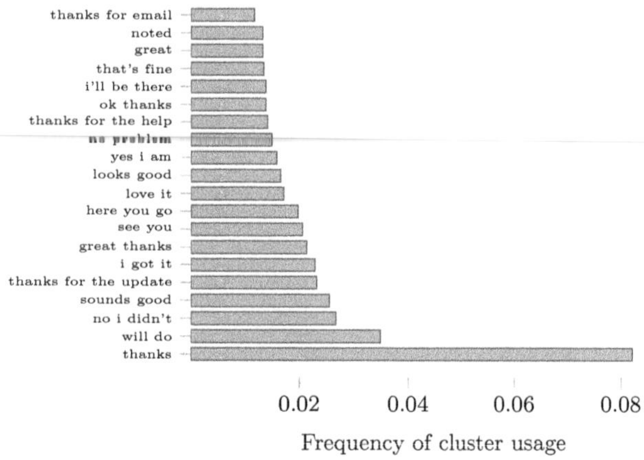

Figure 6: Usage distribution of top clusters.

tion of suggestions by enforcing diversity among them, and filtering traffic for which suggestions would not be useful.

- We build a *scalable* system by efficiently searching the target response space.

Our clearest metric of success is the fact that 10% of mobile replies in *Inbox* are now composed with assistance from the Smart Reply system. Furthermore, we have designed the system in such a way that it is easily extendable to address additional user needs; for instance, the architecture of our core response scoring model is language agnostic, therefore accommodates extension to other languages in addition to English.

9. ACKNOWLEDGMENTS

The authors would like to thank Oriol Vinyals and Ilya Sutskever for many helpful discussions and insights, as well as Prabhakar Raghavan for his guidance and support.

10. REFERENCES

[1] M. Abadi, A. Agarwal, P. Barham, and et al. Tensorflow: Large-scale machine learning on heterogeneous systems. 2015.

[2] I. G. P. Affairs. Interconnected world: Communication & social networking. Press Release, March 2012. http://www.ipsos-na.com/news-polls/pressrelease.aspx?id=5564.

[3] Y. Artzi, P. Pantel, and M. Gamon. Predicting responses to microblog posts. In *Proceedings of the 2012 Conference of the North American Chapter of the Association for Computational Linguistics: Human Language Technologies*, pages 602–606, Montréal, Canada, June 2012. Association for Computational Linguistics.

[4] L. Backstrom, J. Kleinberg, L. Lee, and C. Danescu-Niculescu-Mizil. Characterizing and curating conversation threads: Expansion, focus, volume, re-entry. In *Proceedings of the Sixth ACM International Conference on Web Search and Data Mining*, WSDM '13, pages 13–22, 2013.

[5] Y. Bengio, O. Delalleau, and N. Le Roux. Label propagation and quadratic criterion. In O. Chapelle, B. Schölkopf, and A. Zien, editors, *Semi-Supervised Learning*, pages 193–216. MIT Press, 2006.

[6] W. Chan, N. Jaitly, Q. V. Le, and O. Vinyals. Listen, attend, and spell. *arXiv:1508.01211*, abs/1508.01211, 2015.

[7] Z. Chen, B. Liu, M. Hsu, M. Castellanos, and R. Ghosh. Identifying intention posts in discussion forums. In *Proceedings of the 2013 Conference of the North American Chapter of the Association for Computational Linguistics: Human Language Technologies*, pages 1041–1050, Atlanta, Georgia, June 2013. Association for Computational Linguistics.

[8] J. Duchi, E. Hazad, and Y. Singer. Adaptive subgradient methods for online learning and stochastic optimization. *JMLR*, 12, 2011.

[9] Y. Goldberg. A primer on neural network models for natural language processing. *CoRR*, abs/1510.00726, 2015.

[10] S. Hochreiter and J. Schmidhuber. Long short-term memory. *Neural Computation*, 9(8):1735–1780, 1997.

[11] S. M. Katz. Estimation of probabilities from sparse data for the language model component of a speech recogniser. *IEEE Transactions on Acoustics, Speech, and Signal Processing*, 35:400–401, 1987.

[12] X. Li. Understanding the semantic structure of noun phrase queries. In *Proceedings of the 48th Annual Meeting of the Association for Computational Linguistics (ACL)*, pages 1337–1345, Uppsala, Sweden, July 2010. Association for Computational Linguistics.

[13] V. Nair and G. E. Hinton. Rectified linear units improve restricted boltzmann machines. In *Proceedings of the 27th International Conference on Machine Learning (ICML-10)*, pages 807–814, 2010.

[14] B. Pang and S. Ravi. Revisiting the predictability of language: Response completion in social media. In *Proceedings of the 2012 Joint Conference on Empirical Methods in Natural Language Processing and Computational Natural Language Learning*, pages 1489–1499, Jeju Island, Korea, July 2012. Association for Computational Linguistics.

[15] S. Ravi and Q. Diao. Large scale distributed semi-supervised learning using streaming approximation. In *Proceedings of the 19th International Conference on Artificial Intelligence and Statistics (AISTATS)*, 2016.

[16] A. Ritter, C. Cherry, and W. B. Dolan. Data-driven response generation in social media. In *Proceedings of the 2011 Conference on Empirical Methods in Natural Language Processing*, Edinburgh, UK, July 2011. Association for Computational Linguistics.

[17] R. Saha Roy, R. Katare, N. Ganguly, S. Laxman, and M. Choudhury. Discovering and understanding word level user intent in web search queries. *Web Semant.*, 30(C):22–38, Jan. 2015.

[18] H. Sak, A. Senior, and F. Beaufays. Long short-term memory recurrent neural network architectures for large scale acoustic modeling. In *Proceedings of the Annual Conference of International Speech Communication Association (INTERSPEECH)*, 2014.

[19] I. V. Serban, A. Sordoni, Y. Bengio, A. Courville, and J. Pineau. Hierarchical neural network generative models for movie dialogues. In *arXiv preprint arXiv:1507.04808*, 2015.

[20] L. Shang, Z. Lu, and H. Li. Neural responding machine for short-text conversation. In *In Proceedings of ACL-IJCNLP*, 2015.

[21] A. Sordoni, M. Galley, M. Auli, C. Brockett, Y. Ji, M. Mitchell, J.-Y. Nie, J. Gao, and B. Dolan. A neural network approach to context-sensitive generation of conversation responses. In *In Proceedings of NAACL-HLT*, 2015.

[22] N. Srivastava, G. Hinton, A. Krizhevsky, I. Sutskever, and R. Salakhutdinov. Dropout: A simple way to prevent neural networks from overfitting. *Journal of Machine Learning Research*, 15:1929–1958, 2014.

[23] I. Sutskever, O. Vinyals, and Q. V. Le. Sequence to sequence learning with neural networks. *Advances in Neural Information Processing Systems (NIPS)*, 2014.

[24] O. Vinyals and Q. V. Le. A neural conversation model. In *ICML Deep Learning Workshop*, 2015.

[25] O. Vinyals, A. Toshev, S. Bengio, and D. Erhan. Show and tell: A neural image caption generator. In *Proceedings of IEEE Conference on Computer Vision and Pattern Recognition (CVPR)*, 2015.

[26] J. B. Wendt, M. Bendersky, L. Garcia-Pueyo, V. Josifovski, B. Miklos, I. Krka, A. Saikia, J. Yang, M.-A. Cartright, and S. Ravi. Hierarchical label propagation and discovery for machine generated email. In *Proceedings of the International Conference on Web Search and Data Mining (WSDM) (2016)*, 2016.

[27] X. Zhu, Z. Ghahramani, and J. Lafferty. Semi-supervised learning using gaussian fields and harmonic functions. In *Proceedings of the International Conference on Machine Learning (ICML)*, pages 912–919, 2003.

Mining Subgroups with Exceptional Transition Behavior

Florian Lemmerich
GESIS - Leibniz Institute for the Social Sciences & University of Koblenz-Landau
florian.lemmerich@gesis.org

Martin Becker
University of Würzburg
becker@informatik.uni-wuerzburg.de

Philipp Singer
GESIS - Leibniz Institute for the Social Sciences & University of Koblenz-Landau
philipp.singer@gesis.org

Denis Helic
Graz University of Technology
dhelic@tugraz.at

Andreas Hotho
University of Würzburg and L3S Hannover
hotho@informatik.uni-wuerzburg.de

Markus Strohmaier
GESIS - Leibniz Institute for the Social Sciences & University of Koblenz-Landau
markus.strohmaier@gesis.org

ABSTRACT

We present a new method for detecting interpretable subgroups with exceptional transition behavior in sequential data. Identifying such patterns has many potential applications, e.g., for studying human mobility or analyzing the behavior of internet users. To tackle this task, we employ exceptional model mining, which is a general approach for identifying interpretable data subsets that exhibit unusual interactions between a set of target attributes with respect to a certain model class. Although exceptional model mining provides a well-suited framework for our problem, previously investigated model classes cannot capture transition behavior. To that end, we introduce first-order Markov chains as a novel model class for exceptional model mining and present a new interestingness measure that quantifies the exceptionality of transition subgroups. The measure compares the distance between the Markov transition matrix of a subgroup and the respective matrix of the entire data with the distance of random dataset samples. In addition, our method can be adapted to find subgroups that match or contradict given transition hypotheses. We demonstrate that our method is consistently able to recover subgroups with exceptional transition models from synthetic data and illustrate its potential in two application examples. Our work is relevant for researchers and practitioners interested in detecting exceptional transition behavior in sequential data.

Keywords: Subgroup Discovery; Exceptional Model Mining; Markov chains; Transitions; Sequential data

1. INTRODUCTION

Exceptional Model Mining [13, 31], a generalization of the classic subgroup discovery task [3, 25], is a framework that identifies patterns which contain unusual interactions between multiple target attributes. In order to obtain operationalizable insights, it emphasizes the detection of *easy-to-understand* subgroups, i.e., it aims to find exceptional subgroups with descriptions that are directly interpretable by domain experts. In general, exceptional model mining operates as follows: A target model of a given model class is computed once over the entire dataset, resulting in a set of model parameters. The same parameters are also calculated for each subgroup in a large (often implicitly specified) candidate set, using only the instances covered by the respective subgroup. A subgroup is considered as *exceptional* or *interesting* if its parameter values differ significantly from the ones of the overall dataset. While exceptional model mining has been implemented for a variety of model classes including classification [31], regression [12], Bayesian network [15] and rank correlation [11] models, it has not yet been applied using models for sequential data.

In this paper, we aim to apply exceptional model mining to discover interpretable subgroups with exceptional transition behavior. This enables a new analysis method for a variety of applications. As one example, assume a human mobility dataset featuring user transitions between locations. The overall transition model could for example show that people either move within their direct neighborhood or along main roads. Detecting subgroups with exceptional transition behavior goes beyond this simple analysis: It allows to automatically identify subgroups of people (such as "male tourists from France") or subsegments of time (such as "10 to 11 p.m.") that exhibit unusual movement characteristics, e.g., tourists moving between points-of-interest or people walking along well-lit streets at night. Other application examples could include subgroups of web-users with unusual navigation behavior or subgroups of companies with unusual development over time, cf. [24].

The main contribution of this paper is a new method that enables mining subgroups with exceptional transition behavior by introducing *first-order Markov chains as a novel model class for exceptional model mining.* Markov chains have been utilized for studying sequential data about, e.g., human navigation [37, 44] and mobility [20], meteorology [19], or economics [24]. To apply exceptional model mining with this model, we derive an interestingness measure that quantifies the exceptionality of a subgroup's transition model. It measures how much the distance between the Markov transitions matrix of a subgroup and the respective matrix of the entire data deviates from the distance of random dataset samples. This measure can be integrated into any known search algorithm. We also show how an adaptation of our approach allows to find subgroups specifically matching (or contradicting) given hypotheses about transition behavior (cf. [8, 43, 45]). This enables the use of exceptional model mining for a new type of studies, i.e., the detailed analysis of such hypotheses. We demonstrate the potential of the proposed approach with synthetic as well as real-world data.

KDD '16, August 13 - 17, 2016, San Francisco, CA, USA

ISBN 978-1-4503-4232-2/16/08...$15.00

DOI: http://dx.doi.org/10.1145/2939672.2939752

The remainder of this work is organized as following: We summarize our background in Section 2. Then, the main approach for mining subgroups with exceptional transition behavior is introduced in Section 3. Section 4 presents experiments and results. Finally, we discuss related work in Section 5, before we conclude in Section 6.

2. BACKGROUND

Our solution extends *Exceptional Model Mining* with first-order *Markov Chain Models*. In the following, we give a brief overview of both techniques.

2.1 Exceptional Model Mining

We formally define a dataset D as a multiset of data instances $i \in I$ described by a set of attributes A consisting of describing attributes $A_D \subset A$ and model attributes $A_M \subset A$. A *subgroup* consists of a *subgroup description* $p : D \to \{true, false\}$ that is given by a Boolean function, and a *subgroup cover* $c(p)$, i.e., the set of instances described by p, i.e., $c(p) = \{i \in I | p(i) = true\}$. In principle, our approach works with any *pattern description language* to describe subgroups. As a canonical choice, we focus in our experiments on conjunctions of selection conditions over individual describing attributes, i.e., attribute-value pairs in the case of a nominal attribute, or intervals in the case of numeric attributes. Hence, an example description of a subgroup could be: $Age < 18 \wedge Gender = Male$. Due to combinatorial explosion, a large number of subgroups can be formed even from comparatively few selection conditions.

From this large set of candidate subgroups, exceptional model mining identifies the ones that are unusual ("interesting") with respect to a target model class and the model attributes A_M. While for traditional subgroup discovery the target concept is given by a Boolean expression over a single attribute (e.g., *"Class = Good"*) and a subgroup is considered as interesting if the expressions holds more (or less) often than expected, exceptional model mining considers more complex target concepts. Given a specific *model class* (such as a correlation or a classification model), the *model parameters* for a subgroup can be computed depending on the instances of the respective subgroup. A subgroup is then considered as interesting if its model parameters deviate significantly from the parameters of the model that is derived from all dataset instances. For example, consider a study about the correlation (model class) between the two model attributes exam preparation time of students and the final score they achieve. A finding of exceptional model mining could be: *"While overall there is a positive correlation between the exam preparation time and the score ($\rho = 0.3$), the subgroup of males that are younger than 18 years shows a negative correlation ($\rho = -0.1$)"*.

The goal of finding exceptional subgroups is accomplished by using a quality measure q that maps a subgroup to a real number (a score) based on the supposed interestingness of its model parameters and performing a search for the subgroups with the highest scores.

2.2 Markov Chain Models

In this paper, we introduce first-order Markov chains as a target concept for exceptional model mining. Markov chains are stochastic systems modeling transitions between states $s_1, \ldots, s_m$. Each observed sequence of states corresponds to a sequence of assignments of random variables $X_1, \ldots, X_z$, $X_i \to \{s_1, \ldots, s_m\}$. The commonly employed *first-order* Markov chain model assumes that this process is memoryless, i.e., the probabilities of the next state at time $\tau+1$ only depend on the current state at time τ: $P(X_{\tau+1} = s_j | X_1 = s_{i_1}, \ldots, X_\tau = s_{i_\tau}) = P(X_{\tau+1} = s_j | X_\tau = s_{i_\tau})$, denoted in short as $P(s_j|s_i)$. First-order Markov chain modeling is an established and robust method that underlies many analyses and algorithms [22, 44], one of the most prominent examples being Google's PageRank [37].

The parameters of a first-order Markov chain model can be specified by a stochastic transition matrix $T = (t_{ij})$ with matrix elements $t_{ij} = P(s_j|s_i)$ displaying the conditional probability for a transition from state i to state j; thus, the sum of elements for each matrix row is 1. When working with datasets containing transitions, we can easily derive the stochastic transition matrix (i.e., the model parameters) with the maximum likelihood from a transition matrix containing counts for each transition by normalizing each row. Thus, we use the term transition matrix for both, stochastic matrices and count matrices, if specifics are clear from the context.

3. MAIN APPROACH

Given a set of state sequences and additional information on the sequences or parts of sequences, our main goal is to discover subgroups of transitions that induce exceptional transition models. We formalize this as an exceptional model mining task.

For that purpose, we first prepare the dataset D of transitions with model attributes A_M and describing attributes A_D (see Section 3.1). These allow to form a large set of candidate subgroup descriptions and to filter the dataset accordingly. For each candidate subgroup g, we then determine the corresponding set of transitions and compute its transition matrix T_g. By comparing this matrix to a reference matrix T_D derived from the entire data, we can then calculate a score according to an interestingness measure q (see Section 3.2). In order to detect the subgroups with the highest scores, standard exceptional model mining search algorithms are utilized to explore the candidate space (see Section 3.3). The automatically found subgroups then should be assessed by human experts (see Section 3.4). In a variation of our approach, we do not use the transition matrix of the entire data T_D for comparison with the subgroup matrices T_g, but instead employ a matrix T_H that expresses a user-specified hypothesis. This allows for finding subgroups that specifically match or contradict this hypothesis (see Section 3.5).

3.1 Data Representation

We consider sequences of states and additional background information about them. Since we will perform exceptional model mining on a *transition level*, we split the given state sequences in order to construct a tabular dataset, in which each instance corresponds to a single transition. For each instance, the source and target state represent the values of the model attributes A_M from which the model parameters, i.e., the transition matrix of the Markov chain model, are derived. Each instance is also associated with a set of describing attributes A_D based on the given background information.

Figure 1(a-b) illustrates such a preparation process for a simple example. It shows sequences of states (e.g., certain locations) that users have visited and some background knowledge, i.e., some user information and the time of each visit (Figure 1a). This information is integrated in a single data table (Figure 1b). It contains two columns for the transition model attributes A_M, i.e., for the source and the target state of each transition. Additional describing attributes A_D capture more information on these transitions. This includes information specific to a single transition such as the departure time at the source state but also information on the whole sequence that is projected to all of its transitions, e.g., user data or the sequence length. Example subgroup descriptions that can be expressed based on these attributes are *"all transitions by female users"*, *"all transitions on Saturdays"*, or combinations such as *"all transitions between 13:00h and 14:00h from users older than 30 years that visited at least three locations"*. As different types of information can be considered for the construction of the descriptive attributes, the approach is very flexible.

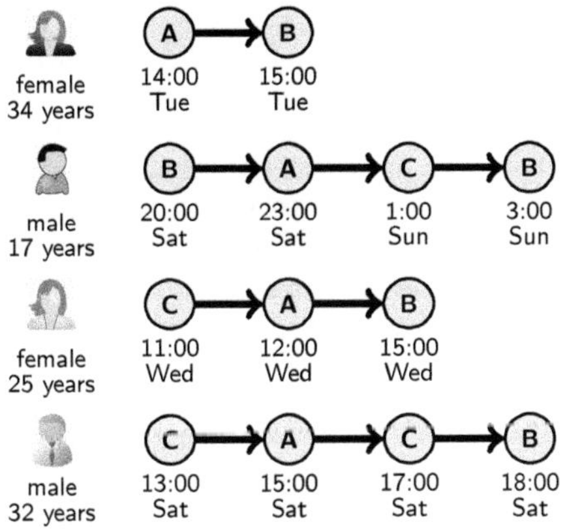

(a) Sequence data with background knowledge

A_M		A_D				
Source State	**Target State**	**Gender**	**Age**	**Hour**	**Weekday**	**# Visits of user**
A	B	f	34	14	Tue	2
B	A	m	17	20	Sat	4
A	C	m	17	23	Sat	4
C	B	m	17	1	Sun	4
C	A	f	25	11	Wed	3
A	B	f	25	12	Wed	3
C	A	m	32	13	Sat	4
A	C	m	32	15	Sat	4
C	B	m	32	17	Sat	4

(b) Transition dataset

$$\begin{pmatrix} 0 & 2 & 2 \\ 1 & 0 & 0 \\ 2 & 2 & 0 \end{pmatrix}$$

(c) Transition matrix T_D (entire dataset)

$$\begin{pmatrix} 0 & 2 & 0 \\ 0 & 0 & 0 \\ 1 & 0 & 0 \end{pmatrix}$$

(d) Transition matrix $T_{Gender=f}$

$$\begin{pmatrix} 0 & 0 & 2 \\ 1 & 0 & 0 \\ 1 & 1 & 0 \end{pmatrix}$$

(e) Transition matrix $T_{Weekday=Sat}$

Figure 1: *Illustrative example.* Sequential data with background information (a) is initially transformed to a transition dataset with transition model attributes A_M and descriptive attributes A_D (b). To discover interesting subgroups, transition matrices for the dataset (c) and for the candidate subgroups, e.g., *Gender=f* (d) or *Weekday=Sat* (e), are computed and compared with each other.

3.2 Interestingness Measure

We aim to find subgroups that are interesting with regard to their transition models. For quantifying interestingness, we employ an *interestingness measure q* that assigns a score to each candidate subgroup. The score is based on a comparison between the transition matrix of the subgroup T_g and a reference transition matrix T_D that is derived from the overall dataset. In short, the interestingness measure that we propose expresses *how unusual the distance between the transition matrix of a subgroup and the reference matrix is in comparison to transition matrices of random samples from the overall dataset.* For that purpose, we first define a distance measure on transition matrices. Then, we show how this distance can be compared against transition matrices built from random dataset samples. We describe those two steps in detail before discussing more specific issues.

Distance measure and weighting. First, we compute the reference transition (count) matrix $T_D = (d_{ij})$ for the overall dataset D as exemplified in Figure 1c. To evaluate a subgroup g, all instances in the tabular dataset that match its subgroup description are identified and a transition matrix $T_g = (g_{ij})$ is determined accordingly (see, e.g., Figure 1d and Figure 1e). Then, a distance measure is employed to measure the difference of transition probabilities in these matrices. For both matrices T_D and T_g, each row i describes a conditional categorical probability distribution for the next state given that state s_i was observed directly before. In literature, several methods have been proposed to compare such distributions. Here, we focus on the *total variation distance* δ_{tv}, also called *statistical distance* or (excluding the constant factor) *Manhattan distance.* For one row, this is computed as the sum of absolute differences between the normalized row entries, i.e., between transition probabilities:

$$\delta_{tv}(g,D,i) = \frac{1}{2}\sum_j \left| \frac{g_{ij}}{\sum_j g_{ij}} - \frac{d_{ij}}{\sum_j d_{ij}} \right|$$

We then aggregate this value over all states (matrix rows). Since in our setting differences in states with many observations in the subgroup should be more important than those with less observations, we weight the rows with the number of transitions $w_i = \sum_j g_{ij}$ from the corresponding source state s_i in the subgroup:

$$\omega_{tv}(g,D) = \sum_i \left(w_i \cdot \sum_j \left| \frac{g_{ij}}{\sum_j g_{ij}} - \frac{d_{ij}}{\sum_j d_{ij}} \right| \right)$$

The factor $\frac{1}{2}$ can be omitted as it is constant across all subgroups. States that do not occur in a subgroup are weighted with 0 and can be ignored in the computation even if transition probabilities are formally not defined in this case.

As an example, consider the transition matrix for the entire example dataset (Figure 1c) and the one for the subgroup $Gender = f$ (Figure 1d). The weighted total variation for this subgroup is computed as follows: $\omega_{tv}(Gender = f,D) = 2 \cdot (|\frac{0}{2} - \frac{0}{4}| + |\frac{2}{2} - \frac{2}{4}| + |\frac{0}{2} - \frac{2}{4}|) + 0 \cdot \mathrm{NA} + 1 \cdot (|\frac{1}{1} - \frac{2}{4}| + |\frac{0}{1} - \frac{2}{4}| + |\frac{0}{1} - \frac{0}{4}|) = 3$.

Of course, there are also alternatives to the total variation distance measure that we can use, e.g., the *Kullback-Leibler divergence* $\delta_{kl}(g,D,i) = \sum_j g_{ij} \cdot \log \frac{g_{ij}}{d_{ij}}$ or the *Hellinger distance* $\delta_{hell}(g,D,i) = \frac{1}{\sqrt{2}}\sqrt{\sum_j(\sqrt{g_{ij}} - \sqrt{d_{ij}})^2}$. However, in this paper, we focus on the weighted total variation as it naturally extends existing approaches for interestingness measures from classical pattern mining: it can be considered as an extension of the *multi-class weighted relative accuracy* measure for multi-class subgroup discovery [1]. Additionally, it can also be interpreted as a special case of *belief update* in a Bayesian approach as it has been proposed in [42] for traditional pattern mining. We provide a proof for this in the Appendix. Despite this focus, we also conducted a large set of experiments with all three distance measures in parallel with overall very similar results.

Comparison with random samples. The measure ω_{tv} describes a weighted distance between transition matrices. Yet, it is heavily influenced by the number of transitions covered by a subgroup. For example, small subgroups might be over-penalized by small weighting factors w_i, while very large subgroups can be expected to reflect the distribution of the overall dataset more precisely. Thus, using ω_{tv} directly as an interestingness measure does not consistently allow for identifying subgroups that actually influence transition behavior in presence of noise attributes, cf. Section 4.2.

To account for these effects, we propose a sampling-based normalization procedure. First, we compute the weighted distance $\omega_{tv}(g,D)$ of the subgroup g to the reference matrix as described before. Then, we draw a set of r random sample transition datasets $R = \{R_1, \ldots, R_r\}$, $R_i \subset D$ from the overall dataset D, each containing as many transitions as the evaluated subgroup g. Then, we compute the weighted distances $\omega_{tv}(R_i)$ for each of these samples, and build a *distribution of false discoveries* (cf. [14]) from the obtained scores. In particular, we compute the mean value $\mu(\omega_{tv}(R_1,D), \ldots, \omega_{tv}(R_r,D))$ and the sample standard deviation $\sigma(\omega_{tv}(R_1,D), \ldots, \omega_{tv}(R_r,D))$ for the distances of the random samples. A subgroup is considered as interesting if the distance of the subgroup strongly deviates from the distances of the random samples. We quantify this by a (marginally adapted) *z-score*, which we will use as the interestingness measure q in our approach:

$$q_{tv}(g,D) = \frac{\omega_{tv}(g,D) - \mu(\omega_{tv}(R_1,D),\ldots,\omega_{tv}(R_r,D))}{\sigma(\omega_{tv}(R_1,D),\ldots,\omega_{tv}(R_r,D)) + \varepsilon},$$

with ε being a very small constant to avoid divisions by zero. Thus, $q_{tv}(g,D)$ quantifies how unusual the difference of the transition matrix of the subgroup g and the reference matrix is *compared to a random set of transitions drawn from the overall data that contains the same number of transitions*.

The rationale for using sampling *without replacement* is that the subgroup itself also cannot contain multiple instances of the same transition. As a consequence, even subgroups selected by random noise attributes would appear to be exceptional compared to samples with replacement in some settings. Sampling without replacement is also equivalent to randomizing (shuffling) the entries of the column for the target state as it has been suggested in pattern mining for the statistical validation of the resulting patterns [14], see also [21].

Stratification of samples. When drawing random samples equally across all states, high scores q_{tv} can exclusively be caused by a peculiar distribution of source states in a subgroup. However, this is not desirable when studying transition behavior. Consider, e.g., a dataset D, where transitions for all but one source state (matrix rows) are deterministic (the transition probability is 1 for a single target state), and all source states have the same number of observed transitions. Then, random transition samples R_i will be drawn mostly from the deterministic states and thus, will consistently have very small weighted distances $\omega_{tv}(R_i,D)$. Now, if any subgroup g only contains transitions from the non-deterministic source state, a random deviation from the underlying transition probabilities is likely. Yet, even if this deviation and thus the distance $\omega_{tv}(g,D)$ is small on an absolute scale, this distance would still be higher than the ones of the random samples. As a consequence, g appears as an exceptional subgroup with respect to its transition probabilities, even if only the distribution of source states differs.

To address this issue, we adapt our sampling procedure: we do not use simple random sampling, but instead apply stratified sampling w.r.t. the source states of the transitions. Thus, we draw the random samples $R_1,\ldots,R_r$ in such a way that for each source state in the data, each random sample contains exactly as many transitions as the evaluated subgroup. Note, that we do *not* stratify with respect to the target states since a different distribution of these states signals different transition behavior.

Significance. To ensure that our findings are not only caused by random fluctuations in the data, the z-score q_{tv} which we employ as our interestingness score can be used as a test statistic for a z-test on statistical significance. Yet, this test requires a normal distribution of the weighted distances $\omega_{tv}(R_i,D)$ obtained from the samples. Although in many practical situations the distribution of the sampled distances is *approximately* normally distributed, this does not necessarily hold in all cases. We thus propose a two-step approach to assess statistical significance of the results. First, we use a normality test such as the *Shapiro-Wilk-Test* [41] on the set of distance scores obtained for the sample set R. If the test does not reject the assumption of normality, a p-value can be directly computed from the z-score. If normality is rejected, a substantially larger set of random samples can be drawn to compute the *empirical p-value* of a specific subgroup [21], i.e., the fraction of samples that show a more extreme distance score than the subgroup. Although this is computationally too expensive to perform for every single candidate subgroup, it can be used for confirming significance for the most interesting subgroups in the result set.

For both methods one must consider the *multiple comparison problem* [23]: if many different subgroups are investigated (as it is usually done in pattern mining), then some candidates will pass standard significance tests with unadapted significance values by pure chance. Therefore an appropriate correction such as *Bonferroni correction* [16] or *layered critical values* [47] must be applied.

Estimate the effect of limited sample numbers. Determining the interestingness score $q_{tv}(g,D)$ requires to choose a number of random samples r. While fewer samples allow faster computation, results might get affected by random outliers in drawn samples. To estimate the potential error in the score computation caused by the limited number of samples, we employ a *bootstrapping approach* [17]: we perform additional sampling on the weighted distances of the original samples $S = \{\omega_{tv}(R_1,D),\ldots,\omega_{tv}(R_r,D)\}$. From this set, we repeatedly draw (e.g., 10,000 times) *"bootstrap replications"*, i.e., we draw r distance values by sampling *with* replacement from S and compute the subgroup score q_{tv} for each replication. The standard deviation of the replication scores provides an approximation of the standard error compared to an infinitely large number of samples, cf. [18]. In other words, we estimate how precise we compute the interestingness score q_{tv} with the chosen value of r compared to an infinite number of samples. If the calculated standard error is high compared to the subgroup score, re-computation with a higher number of samples is recommended.

3.3 Subgroup Search

To detect interesting subgroups, we enumerate all candidate subgroups in the search space in order to find the ones with the highest scores. For this task, a large variety of mining algorithms has been proposed in the pattern mining literature featuring exhaustive as well as heuristic search strategies, e.g., depth-first search [25], best-first search [46, 51], or beam-search [27, 29]. In this paper, we do not focus on efficient algorithms for exceptional model mining, but apply a depth-first mining algorithm as a standard solution.

Candidate evaluation in our approach is computationally slightly more expensive than for traditional subgroup discovery. That is, the runtime complexity for determining the score of a single subgroup in our implementation is $O(r \cdot (N + S^2))$ for a dataset with N transitions, S different states, and a user chosen parameter of r samples: selecting the set of instances from a subgroup as well as drawing a stratified sample requires $O(N)$ operations per subgroup and sample. The transition matrices for each of these transition sets can also be built in linear time. The weighted distance for each of the r samples and the subgroup can then be determined in $O(S^2)$ as a constant number of operations is required for each of the S^2 matrix cells.

A typical problem in pattern mining is redundancy, i.e., the result set often contains several similar subgroups. For example, if the subgroup *male* induces an exceptional transition model and thus achieves a high score, then also the subgroup *males older than 18* can be expected to feature a similarly unusual model and receive a high score—even if age does not influence transition behavior at all. A simple, but effective approach to reduce redundancy in the result set is to adapt a *minimum improvement constraint* [7] as a filter criterion. To that end, we remove a subgroup from the result set if the result also contains a generalization, i.e., a subgroup described by a subset of conditions, with a similar (e.g., less than 10% difference) or a higher score.

3.4 Subgroup Assessment

Automatic discovery algorithms with the proposed interestingness measure can detect subgroups with exceptional transition models. Yet, to interpret the results, manual inspection and assessment of the top findings is crucial as this allows users to identify in what aspects the found "interesting" subgroups differ from the overall data. For that purpose, a comparison between the subgroup transition matrix and the reference matrix is required. Yet, manual comparison can be difficult for large matrices (state spaces). Therefore, we recommend to assess subgroups with summarizing *key statistics*, such as the number of transitions in a subgroup, the weighted distance ω_{tv} between subgroup and reference transition matrices, the unweighted raw distance $\Delta_{tv} = \sum_i \delta_{tv}(sg, D, i)$, or the distribution of source and target states. Additionally, *exemplification*, e.g., by displaying representative sequences, and *visualizations* are helpful tools for subgroup inspection. In that regard, we propose a graph-based visualization to get a quick overview of the differences between subgroup and reference transition matrices, see Figure 3 for an example. Here, each state is represented as a node and directed edges represent the differences of transition probabilities between the states. The width of an edge represents the amount of change in the transition probability, the color indicates if it is a decrease or increase. Edges without significant differences can be removed from the graph to increase visibility. In addition to that, application-specific visualizations often allow a natural view on the data, see Figure 2 for an example featuring geo-spatial data.

3.5 Variation: User-Defined Hypotheses

In addition to comparing subgroups to the overall dataset, our approach can also detect subgroups that specifically contradict or match a user-defined hypothesis. Following the concepts of [43], we can express such a hypothesis as a *belief matrix* $T_H = (h_{ij})$, where higher values h_{ij} indicate a stronger belief in transitions from state s_i to state s_j. An example of a hypothesis considering the example dataset of Figure 1 could be stated as: $\begin{pmatrix} 0&1&0 \\ 1&1&1 \\ 1&1&1 \end{pmatrix}$. This hypothesis formalizes a belief that users from state A (first row) will always go to state B, and users from the states B and C will proceed to any of the three states with equal probability.

Given a hypothesis matrix, the interestingness score of a subgroup is computed analogously to the original case, but instead of using the transition matrix derived from the overall dataset T_D as reference, we use the hypothesis belief matrix T_H for the computation of the weighted distance ω_{tv}. A subgroup g (exceptionally) contradicts a hypothesis H, if its transition matrix T_g has a significantly larger distance to the hypothesis matrix T_H than the stratified random samples of the dataset. To find subgroups that *match* a hypothesis specifically well instead of contradicting it, the inverted interestingness measure $-q_{tv}(g, D)$ can be used instead.

4. EXPERIMENTS

We demonstrate the potential of our approach with synthetic and empirical data. With synthetic data, we show that our approach is able to recover (combinations of) conditions that determine the transition probabilities in presence of noise attributes. With empirical data, we illustrate possible application scenarios and findings.

As selection expressions for subgroup descriptions, we used all attribute-value pairs for nominal attributes, and all intervals obtained by equal-frequency discretization into five groups for numeric attributes. For computing the interestingness measure, we used $r = 1,000$ random samples. If not stated otherwise, we focused on subgroups with simple descriptions, i.e., no combinations of selection conditions were considered. For the empirical studies, we confirmed our top results to be statistically significant on an $\alpha = 0.01$ level using the procedure presented in Section 3.2. Our implementation, an extension of the VIKAMINE data mining environment [4], and the synthetic datasets are publicly available[1].

[1] http://florian.lemmerich.net/paper/subtrails.html

4.1 Synthetic I: Random transition matrices

We start with a synthetic dataset directly generated from two first-order Markov chain transition matrices.

Experimental setup. We created two 5×5 matrices of transition probabilities by inserting uniformly distributed random values in each cell and normalizing the matrices row-wise. Then, for each generated instance, one of the matrices was chosen based on two attributes, a ternary attribute A and a binary attribute B. If both attributes take their first values, i.e., $A = A1$ and $B = B1$, then transitions were generated from the first matrix, otherwise from the second matrix. For each combination of values, we generated $10,000$ transitions, resulting in 60,000 transitions overall. For each transition, we additionally generated random values for 20 binary noise attributes, each with an individual random probability for the value *true*. We employed our approach with a maximum search depth of two selectors to find subgroups with different transition models compared to the overall dataset. Our approach should then detect the subgroup $A = A1 \wedge B = B1$ as the most relevant one.

Results. The top-5 result subgroups are displayed in Table 1. It shows the number of covered transitions (instances), the score of the interestingness measure q_{tv} including the standard error of its computation estimated by bootstrapping ($\pm$), the weighted total variation ω_{tv} between the subgroup and the reference transition matrix, and its unweighted counterpart Δ_{tv}. Result tables for the following experiments will be analogously structured.

We observe that our approach successfully recovered the subgroup of transitions that were generated from a different probability matrix, i.e., the subgroup ($A = A1 \wedge B = B1$). This subgroup receives the best score q_{tv} by a wide margin. The subgroup with the next highest score ($A = A1$) is a generalization of this subgroup. Since it contains transitions generated from both matrices in a different mixture, it also features indeed an unusual transition model compared to the entire dataset. In the same way, the next subgroups all feature the attributes A and B that actually influence the transition behavior, and none of the noise attributes. These top subgroups all pass a Bonferroni-adjusted statistical significance test as described in Section 3.2 with an empirical p-value of $p \ll 10^{-10}$, while all subgroups containing only noise attributes (not among the shown top subgroups) do not pass such a test with a critical value of $\alpha = 0.05$.

4.2 Synthetic II: Random walker

Our second demonstration example features a set of transitions generated by a random walker in a network of colored nodes.

Experimental setup. First, we generated a scale-free network consisting of $1,000$ nodes (states) with a Barabási-Albert model [6]. That is, starting with a small clique of nodes, new nodes with degree 10 were inserted to the graph iteratively using preferential attachment. Then, we assigned one of ten colors randomly to each node. On this network, we generated $200,000$ sequences of random walks with five transitions each, resulting in $1,000,000$ transitions overall. For each sequence, we randomly assigned a walker type. With

Table 1: Top subgroups for random transition matrix data. For each subgroup, we show the number of instances covered by this subgroup, the interestingness score q_{tv}, the weighted total variation ω_{tv} and the unweighted total variation Δ_{tv}.

Description	# Inst.	q_{tv} (score)	ω_{tv}	Δ_{tv}
A = A1 ∧ B = B1	10,000	113.01 ± 2.74	5,783	1.54
A = A1	20,000	67.23 ± 1.60	4,634	0.60
B = B1	30,000	45.52 ± 0.94	3,480	0.33
B = B2	30,000	44.69 ± 1.08	3,480	0.51
A = A3	20,000	32.05 ± 0.77	2,378	0.53

a probability of 0.8, the walk was purely *random*, i.e., given the current node of the walker, the next node was chosen with uniform probability among the neighbouring nodes. Otherwise, the walk was *homophile*, i.e., transitions to nodes of the same color were twice as likely. For each transition, the resulting dataset contains the source node, the target node, the type of the respective walker (random or homophile), and additionally the values for 20 binary noise attributes, which were assigned with an individual random probability each.

With this data, we performed three experiments. In the first, we searched for subgroups with different transition models compared to the entire data. In the second and third experiment, we explored the option of finding subgroups that contradict — respectively match — a hypothesis. For that purpose, we elicited a hypothesis matrix $T_H = (h_{ij})$ that expresses belief in walkers being *homophile*, i.e., in transitions being more likely between nodes of the same color. Towards that end, we set a matrix value h_{ij} to 1 if i and j belong to the same color and $h_{ij} = 0$ otherwise. Edges of the underlying network were ignored for the hypothesis generation.

Results. Table 2 presents the results for the three experiments. As intended, exceptional model mining identified the subgroups that influence the transition behavior as the top subgroups for all three tasks. In the first experiment (see Table 2a) both subgroups described by the *Type* attribute are top-ranked. For the second experiment (see Table 2b), the subgroup *Type=Random* receives the highest score. This subgroup should by construction indeed expose the least homophile behavior since any subgroup described by noise attributes contains transitions from homophile as well as non-homophile walkers. Its complement subgroup *Type=Homophile* does not contradict our hypothesis and thus does not appear in the top subgroups. By contrast and as expected, the subgroup *Type=Homophile* receives the highest score in the third experiment that searches for subgroups matching the homophile hypothesis, while *Type=Random* is not returned as a top result, cf. Table 2c. For all three experiments, the statistical significance of the top subgroups described by the *Type* attribute was decisive ($p \ll 10^{-10}$), while the top findings for the noise attributes were not significant at the Bonferroni-adjusted $\alpha = 0.05$ level.

Table 2: Top subgroups for the random walker datasets. For each subgroup, we show the number of instances covered by this subgroup, the interestingness score q_{tv}, the weighted total variation ω_{tv} and the unweighted total variation Δ_{tv}.

(a) Comparison to the overall dataset

Description	# Inst.	q_{tv} (score)	ω_{tv}	Δ_{tv}
Type = Homophile	200,915	35.67 ± 0.78	51,929	125.96
Type = Random	799,085	34.34 ± 0.80	51,929	31.73
Noise9 = False	681,835	2.25 ± 0.06	51,358	36.27
Noise9 = True	318,165	2.23 ± 0.06	51,358	77.94
Noise2 = False	18,875	1.80 ± 0.05	14,844	394.51

(b) Comparison to the *homophile* hypothesis, contradicting

Description	# Inst.	q_{tv} (score)	ω_{tv}	Δ_{tv}
Type = Random	799,085	26.88± 0.57	1,554,130	981.38
Noise4 = True	519,130	2.28 ± 0.06	1,008,912	981.25
Noise2 = False	18,875	2.25 ± 0.06	37,057	987.49
Noise1 = True	469,290	2.00 ± 0.05	912,032	981.26
Noise19 = True	342,765	1.93 ± 0.05	666,229	981.28

(c) Comparison to the *homophile* hypothesis, matching

Description	# Inst.	q_{tv} (score)	ω_{tv}	Δ_{tv}
Type = Homophile	200,915	12.10 ± 0.27	389,841	981.04
Noise4 = False	480,870	2.69 ± 0.07	934,190	981.20
Noise19 = False	657,235	2.27 ± 0.06	1,276,868	981.20
Noise1 = False	530,710	1.99 ± 0.05	1,031,101	981.20
Noise0 = True	523,410	1.74 ± 0.05	1,016,899	981.21

In additional experiments (no result tables shown), we employed the weighted distance ω_{tv} directly as an interestingness measure. By doing so, we were not able to recover the relevant subgroups as they were dominated by several random noise subgroups. This shows the necessity of a comparison with random samples.

We also experimented extensively with different parametrizations (e.g., different walker type probabilities or different numbers of node colors). Consistently, we were able to identify the two subgroups *Type=Random* and *Type=Homophile* as the top subgroups.

4.3 Flickr

In addition to the synthetic datasets, we present illustrative examples with empirical data; we start with data from Flickr.

Experimental setup. For this dataset, we crawled all photos with geo-spatial information (i.e., latitude and longitude) at street-level accuracy in Manhattan from the years 2010 to 2014 on Flickr. Each photo was mapped according to its geo-location to one of the 288 census tracts (administrative units) that we use as states in our model (see also [20]). Based on this information, we built sequences of different tracts (i.e., no self-transitions) that users have taken photos at. Additionally, we elicited a wide range of describing attributes for each transition, i.e., the number of photos the respective user has uploaded from Manhattan, the number of views the source photo of the transition received on Flickr, as well as the month, the weekday and the hour this photo was taken. We added two more features based on the user's origin, that is, the tourist status and the nationality (country). We considered a user to be a tourist if the time from her first to her last photo does not exceed 21 days, cf. [10]. Country information of a user was derived from the location field in her user profile by extracting the country using a combination

Table 3: Top subgroups for the Flickr dataset. For each subgroup, we show the number of instances covered by this subgroup, the interestingness score q_{tv}, the weighted total variation ω_{tv} and the unweighted total variation Δ_{tv}.

(a) Comparison to the overall dataset

Description	# Inst.	q_{tv} (score)	ω_{tv}	Δ_{tv}
# Photos > 714	76,859	103.83 ± 2.41	42,277	106.68
# Photos ≤ 25	78,254	88.83 ± 2.07	37,555	141.78
Tourist = True	76,667	75.42 ± 1.79	33,418	148.64
Tourist = False	310,314	75.00 ± 1.60	33,418	16.92
Country = US	163,406	64.47 ± 1.39	44,822	70.97
# Photos = 228-715	77,448	46.10 ± 1.02	33,214	115.65
Country = Mexico	2,667	33.22 ± 0.82	3,575	122.83
# PhotoViews > 164	79,218	31.58 ± 0.74	31,461	107.84
# PhotoViews < 12	76,573	30.54 ±0.71	30,881	110.83

(b) Comparison to the *Proximate-PoI* hypothesis, contradicting

Description	# Inst.	q_{tv} (score)	ω_{tv}	Δ_{tv}
# Photos ≤ 25	78,254	64.85 ± 1.37	110,124	221.07
# Photos = 26–81	77,003	23.41 ± 0.53	99,646	207.21
Hour = 22h–23h	14,944	18.26 ± 0.43	20,526	215.69
Hour = 23h–0h	11,726	17.42 ± 0.37	16,404	208.91
Hour = 21h–22h	17,806	16.52 ± 0.33	23,951	211.34
Tourist = False	310,314	16.09 ± 0.35	379,676	185.13
Hour = 0h–1h	9,693	15.12 ± 0.33	13,590	215.42

(c) Comparison to the *Proximate-PoI* hypothesis, matching

Description	# Inst.	$-q_{tv}$ (score)	ω_{tv}	Δ_{tv}
# Photos > 714	76,859	58.59 ± 1.30	80,690	164.16
# PhotoViews < 12	76,573	21.56 ± 0.50	88,948	185.78
Hour = 12h–13h	25,022	14.04 ± 0.32	29,590	187.84
# Photos = 228–714	77,448	10.63 ± 0.23	91,877	193.57
Tourist = True	76,667	10.60 ± 0.24	91,214	197.79
Hour = 14h–15h	27,420	10.51 ± 0.25	33,028	194.40
Hour = 11h–12h	20,323	9.18 ± 0.21	24,613	196.99

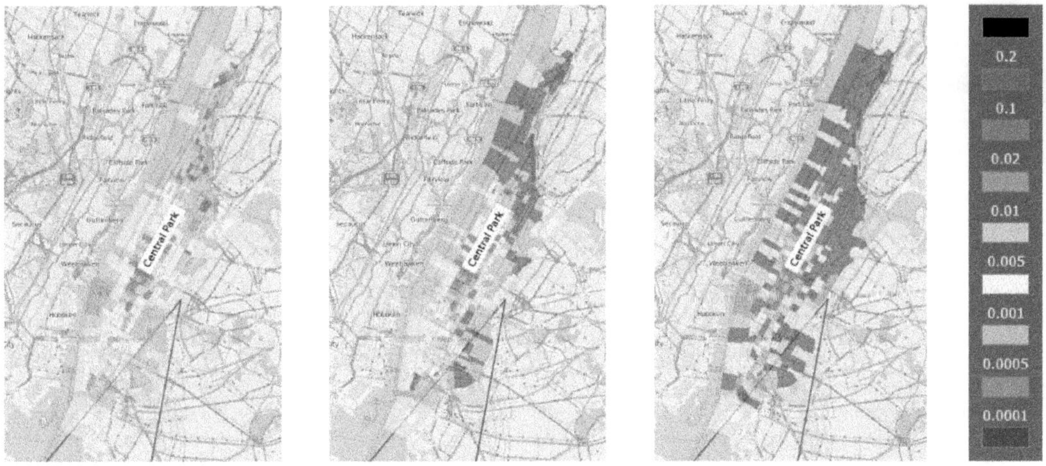

(a) All transitions (b) Transitions of tourists (c) Night transitions (22–23 h)

Figure 2: *Exceptional transition behavior of Flickr users.* The figure shows transition probabilities from Central Park to other tracts in Manhattan for (a) the entire dataset, (b) the subgroup *tourists*, and (c) the subgroup *transitions during night time (22–23 h)*. Cool colors (blue, green) represent small, warm colors (orange, red) high transition probabilities, see the legend on the right hand side.

of querying GeoNames[2] and specialized regular expressions. The country information was only available for about half of the users. Overall, our dataset contained 386,981 transitions and allowed to construct 163 selection conditions.

In a first experiment, we aimed at discovering subgroups with different transition models compared to the entire data. Additionally, we investigated an existing hypothesis about the trails derived from Flickr photos, that is, the *Proximate-PoI* hypothesis. This hypothesis has been shown to be one of the best hypotheses for explaining movements in Flickr photo data [8]. It expresses that users at a certain location are most likely to go to another location that is (a) nearby and (b) contains important points of interest (PoI), such as tourist attractions or transportation hubs. To construct this hypothesis, the locations of points of interest have been extracted from DBPedia [30], see [8] for further construction details.

Results. Table 3 reports our results: the most exceptional subgroups in comparison with the overall data (see Table 3a) describe transitions by users that take either very many (more than 714) or very few (less than 25) photos. We explain this by the fact that users with overall fewer photos are more likely to travel a longer distance before taking another picture, resulting in more long distance transitions. The next two subgroups *Tourist=True* and *Tourist=False* suggest that tourists continue their trip to different locations than locals, e.g., as they are more interested in touristic attractions. Further top subgroups with deviating transition models involve the number of views pictures receive on Flickr and the country of origin.

Table 3b and Table 3c display the top subgroups that contradict the Proximate-PoI hypothesis, respectively match it. We observe that users with small amounts of pictures and non-tourists do not move as the investigated hypothesis suggests. Also, night time mobility (roughly 21h – 1h, see the result table for exact subgroup ordering) does not match this hypothesis, maybe due to the closing of touristic attractions at night times. By contrast, tourists and users with many pictures as well as transitions at midday are especially consistent with the Proximate-PoI hypothesis.

Although we discover these exceptional subgroups from the large set of candidates automatically, it has to be investigated post-hoc *how* the transition models deviate. In that direction, we studied the subgroup *Tourist=True* in detail. For that purpose, we first computed the source state with the most unusual distribution of target states, i.e., the row that contributes the highest value to the weighted total variation q_{tv}. For the tourist subgroup, this state (tract) corresponds to the central park. We then visualized the transition probabilities for this single state for the entire dataset and the subgroup with the *VizTrail* visualization system [9], see Figure 2. It can be observed that tourists are less likely to move to the northern parts of Manhattan, but are more likely to take their next picture in the city center or at the islands south of Manhattan. For a second investigated subgroup, i.e., the subgroup of transitions between 22h and 23h, this effect is even more pronounced as almost no transitions from the central park to the northern or north-eastern tracts can be observed. Note, that this visualization only covers the transition probabilities of a single state, not the overall transition matrix used for detecting interesting subgroups.

4.4 LastFM

Additionally, we analyzed data from the LastFM music service.

Experimental setup. We used the *1K listening data*[3] containing the full listening history of 1,000 LastFM users featuring more than 19,000,000 tracks (songs) by more than 170,000 artists. With this data, we studied sequences of music genres (such as *rock*, *pop*, *rap*, *classical*, etc.) of songs that users listened to, focusing on a list of 16 main genres. Since genre information is difficult to obtain on a track-level, we labeled each track with the best fitting genre for the respective artist as obtained by the EchoNest API[4]. In doing so, we could determine genres for more than 95% of the tracks. We then constructed genre transitions for each user based on the sequence of tracks she had listened to. We filtered subsequent tracks of the same artist to remove cases where the user listened to all songs of a single album. Additionally, we removed all transitions with unknown source or target state (genre). Thus, we obtained a dataset of 9,020,396 transitions between tracks. Background knowledge includes user information about age, gender, origin and the year of signup to LastFM, and the point in time the source song of the transition was played, i.e., the hour of the day, the weekday, the month and the year. This allowed to generate 86 selection conditions. On this data, we applied our approach twice to find subgroups with

[2] http://www.geonames.org/

[3] http://ocelma.net/MusicRecommendationDataset/index.html

[4] http://developer.echonest.com/

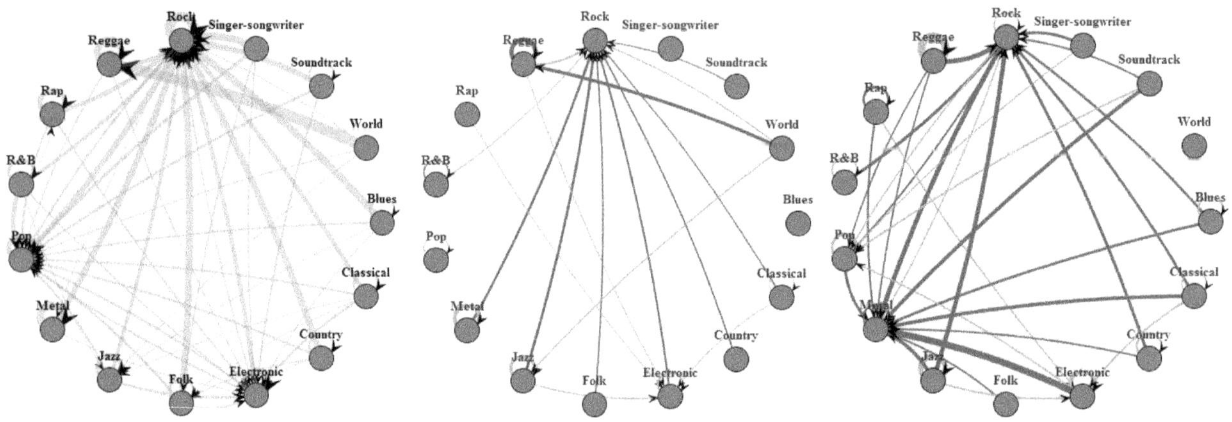

(a) All transitions (b) Users from the United States (c) Users from Finland

Figure 3: *Exceptional transition models of LastFM users.* The figures show transitions between music genres: stronger arrows represent higher transition probabilities. (a) shows all transitions in the data, (b) and (c) illustrate the differences of transition models in two exceptional subgroups. Green arrows indicate that transitions are more probable in the subgroup than in the overall dataset, red arrows the contrary. E.g., it can be observed in (b) that users from the US are more likely to listen to *Reggae* after *World* music; (c) shows that Finnish users have higher transition probabilities to *Metal*. Insignificant differences are removed for visibility.

exceptional transition behavior: once for subgroups described by a single selection condition only, and once including combinations of two selection conditions (search with depth 2).

Results. Results for single selection conditions are displayed in Table 4a. We can see that the country of origin of users is an important factor: the majority of top subgroups is described by this attribute. Specifically, users from the United States, from Finland, and from Argentina exhibit transitions between music genres that are unusual compared to the entire data. By contrast, date and time influence the transitions between genres only little and do not describe any of the top subgroups. For subgroups described by combinations of conditions, see Table 4b, we can see that users with a high number of tracks show unusual transition behavior, especially if they signed up to the system early, or if they are in a certain age group.

Figure 3 visualizes differences in transition behavior in comparison to the overall dataset for two top-subgroups. Here, each node represents a state (genre). The first graph gives an impression on the transition probabilities in the entire dataset. Stronger arrows represent higher probabilities. We omit probabilities below 0.1. The next two graphs show *deviations* from these probabilities in the subgroups *Country=US* and *Country=Finland*. Green arrows indicate transitions that are more likely in the subgroup than in the overall data, red arrows imply less likely transitions. Stronger arrows represent higher deviations; small deviations (< 0.05) are omitted.

Table 4: Top subgroups for the LastFM dataset. For each subgroup, we show the number of instances covered by this subgroup, the interestingness score q_{tv}, the weighted total variation ω_{tv} and the unweighted total variation Δ_{tv}.

(a) Single selection conditions only

Description	# Inst.	q_{tv} (score)	ω_{tv}	Δ_{tv}
Country = US	2,576,652	420.37 ± 9.67	326,435	1.44
Country = Finland	384,214	408.37 ± 8.89	132,378	3.05
Country = Argentina	174,140	360.22 ± 8.62	84,285	4.54
# Tracks > 79277	1,803,363	355.27 ± 8.39	249,634	1.61
Country = Poland	378,003	346.09 ± 7.37	122,155	3.35

(b) Including combinations of selection conditions

Description	# Inst.	q_{tv} (score)	ω_{tv}	Δ_{tv}
# Tracks >=79277 $\wedge$ signup=2005	617,245	425.59 ± 9.30	186,048	3.38
# Tracks >=79277 $\wedge$ age = [23–24]	155,998	421.67 ± 9.78	89,769	4.67
Country = US	2,576,652	420.37 ± 9.67	326,435	1.44
Country = Finland	384,214	408.37 ± 8.89	132,378	3.05
# Tracks >=79277 $\wedge$ signup=2006	658,135	398.40 ± 8.74	182,690	3.38

We observe that users from the US and Finland deviate from the overall behavior in characteristic ways. For example, users from the US tend to skip to *Rock* more often, while the same is true for users from Finland with regard to *Metal*. Also, we observe interesting dynamics between genres that go beyond the different target state distributions: for example, users from the US are more likely to listen to *Reggae* after a song from the *World* genre, while the preference for *Rock* decreases in this case. We can also see, that although *Rock* is overall more popular in the US, it follows a track of *Reggae* less likely than in the entire data.

5. RELATION TO STATE-OF-THE-ART

Mining patterns in sequential data has a long history in data mining. However, large parts of research have been dedicated to the tasks of finding frequent subsequences efficiently, see for example [2, 36, 50]. Other popular settings are sequence classification [33, 49] and sequence labeling [26]. Unlike this work, these methods do not aim to detect subgroups with unusual transition behavior.

Our solution is based on exceptional model mining, a generalization of subgroup discovery [3, 25]. This classical data mining task aims at finding descriptions of data subsets that show an unusual statistical distribution of a target concept. Traditional subgroup discovery focuses on a single attribute as a target concept. Exceptional model mining [13, 31] was proposed as a generalized framework that facilitates more complex target concepts over multiple target attributes. For exceptional model mining, different model classes, e.g., classification [31] and regression models [12], Bayesian networks [15] as well as advanced mining algorithms [28, 29, 32] have been proposed. No models featuring sequential data have been explored for exceptional model mining so far.

We have presented an approach to detect subgroups with exceptional transition models, i.e., subgroups that show unusual distributions of the target states in first order Markov chain models. The results from our approach may correlate with subgroups that could also be obtained by multi-class subgroup discovery [1] that investigates the distribution of target states. However, such a static analysis aims to achieve a different goal than our analysis of behavior dynamics and will not capture all subgroups with exceptional transition models. For example, in the random walker synthetic dataset (see Section 4.2) the distribution of target states is approximately uniform for all subgroups by construction, also for the ones that influence the transition behavior. As a consequence and in contrast to our method, a static analysis could not recover the exceptional subgroups. Furthermore, the task of finding subgroups that match or contradict a hypothesis of dynamic state transitions (e.g., as demonstrated in the Flickr example, see Section 4.3) cannot be formulated as a more traditional subgroup discovery task.

Our interestingness measure is inspired by previous methods. The weighted distance measure can be considered as an adaptation of the multi-class weighted relative accuracy [1] or as a special case of the Bayesian belief update [42]. The randomization/sampling processes to capture significant differences of subgroups also builds upon previous approaches. In that direction, Gionis et al. [21] utilize swap randomization to construct alternative datasets in order to ensure the statistical significance of data mining results. For subgroup discovery, analyzing a distribution of false discoveries obtained by randomization has been proposed to assess subgroups and interestingness measures [14]. We have extended these methods to exceptional model mining with complex targets and have used it directly in the interestingness measure for the subgroup search.

For modeling sequential processes, Markov chains have been used in a wide variety of applications ranging from user navigation [38, 44] to economical settings and meteorological data [19]. The *mixed markov model* extension [39] of classical Markov chains features separate transition matrices for "segments" of users, but these segments are not interpretable, i.e., have no explicit descriptions. The work maybe closest to ours is [40], where the authors detect outliers of user sessions with respect to their probability in a Markov-chain model; outliers are then manually categorized into several interpretable groups. By contrast, our solution allows to identify descriptions of groups that show unusual transition behavior automatically from large sets of candidate subgroups.

Recently, also the comparison of hypotheses about Markov chain models has been popularized [8, 43, 45]. The approach proposed in this paper enables extensions to this line of research with more fine-grained analyses: we cannot only compare hypotheses against each other, but also identify (sets of) conditions under which a given hypothesis is matched or contradicted.

6. CONCLUSION

In this paper, we have introduced first-order Markov chains as a novel model class for exceptional model mining in sequence data with background knowledge. This enables a novel kind of analysis: it allows to detect interpretable subgroups that exhibit exceptional transition behavior, i.e., induce different transition models compared to the entire dataset. In addition, we have presented a variation of the standard task that compares subgroups against user-defined hypotheses, enabling a detailed analysis of given hypotheses about transition behavior. We have illustrated the potential of our approach by applying it to both synthetic and empirical data. For synthetic data, the proposed method successfully recovered exceptional transitions from artificial noise attributes.

In the future, we aim to improve and extend our approach in several directions. First, the proposed interestingness measure is currently based on individual transitions. As a consequence, few very long sequences (e.g., of very active users) can strongly influence the results. To avoid dominance of such sequences, weighting of the transition instances according to the overall activity could be applied in future extensions, cf. [5]. In addition, we intend to investigate ways of speeding-up the mining process, e.g., by optimistic estimate pruning [48] or by using advanced data structures [32], and more sophisticated options to reduce redundancy, cf. [34, 35]. Finally, we would like to generalize the proposed model class to Markov chains of higher order or even more advanced sequential models that potentially also take indirect state transitions into account.

Acknowledgements. This work was partially funded by the German Science Fund project "PoSTs II" and the Austrian Science Fund project "Navigability of Decentralized Information Networks".

References

[1] T. Abudawood and P. Flach. Evaluation Measures for Multi-class Subgroup Discovery. In *European Conference on Machine Learning and Knowledge Discovery in Databases*, 2009.

[2] R. Agrawal and R. Srikant. Mining Sequential Patterns. In *IEEE Int'l Conference on Data Engineering*, 1995.

[3] M. Atzmueller. Subgroup Discovery. *Wiley Interdisciplinary Reviews: Data Mining and Knowledge Discovery*, 5(1):35–49, 2015.

[4] M. Atzmueller and F. Lemmerich. VIKAMINE - Open-Source Subgroup Discovery, Pattern Mining, and Analytics. In *European Conference on Machine Learning and Knowledge Discovery in Databases*, 2012.

[5] M. Atzmueller and F. Lemmerich. Exploratory Pattern Mining on Social Media using Geo-References and Social Tagging Information. *Int'l Journal of Web Science*, 2(1–2):80–112, 2013.

[6] A.-L. Barabási and R. Albert. Emergence of Scaling in Random Networks. *Science*, 286(5439):509–512, 1999.

[7] R. J. Bayardo Jr. Efficiently Mining Long Patterns from Databases. *ACM Sigmod Record*, 27(2):85–93, 1998.

[8] M. Becker, P. Singer, F. Lemmerich, A. Hotho, D. Helic, and M. Strohmaier. Photowalking the City: Comparing Hypotheses about Urban Photo Trails on Flickr. In *Social Informatics*, 2015.

[9] M. Becker, P. Singer, F. Lemmerich, A. Hotho, D. Helic, and M. Strohmaier. VizTrails: An Information Visualization Tool for Exploring Geographic Movement Trajectories. In *Conference on Hypertext and Social Media*, 2015.

[10] M. De Choudhury, M. Feldman, S. Amer-Yahia, N. Golbandi, R. Lempel, and C. Yu. Automatic Construction of Travel Itineraries using Social Breadcrumbs. In *Conference on Hypertext and Hypermedia*, 2010.

[11] L. Downar and W. Duivesteijn. Exceptionally Monotone Models: The Rank Correlation Model Class for Exceptional Model Mining. In *IEEE Int'l Conference on Data Mining*, 2015.

[12] W. Duivesteijn, A. Feelders, and A. Knobbe. Different Slopes for Different Folks: Mining for Exceptional Regression Models with Cook's Distance. In *ACM SIGKDD Int'l Conference on Knowledge Discovery and Data Dining*, 2012.

[13] W. Duivesteijn, A. Feelders, and A. Knobbe. Exceptional Model Mining. *Data Mining and Knowledge Discovery*, 30(1):47–98, 2016.

[14] W. Duivesteijn and A. Knobbe. Exploiting False Discoveries–Statistical Validation of Patterns and Quality Measures in Subgroup Discovery. In *IEEE Int'l Conference on Data Mining*, 2011.

[15] W. Duivesteijn, A. Knobbe, A. Feelders, and M. Van Leeuwen. Subgroup Discovery Meets Bayesian Network – An Exceptional Model Mining Approach. In *IEEE Int'l Conference on Data Mining*, 2010.

[16] O. J. Dunn. Multiple Comparisons Among Means. *Journal of the American Statistical Association*, 56(293):52–64, 1961.

[17] B. Efron. Bootstrap Methods: Another Look at the Jackknife. *The Annals of Statistics*, pages 1–26, 1979.

[18] B. Efron and R. J. Tibshirani. *An Introduction to the Bootstrap*. CRC press, 1994.

[19] K. R. Gabriel and J. Neumann. A Markov Chain Model for Daily Rainfall Occurrence at Tel Aviv. *Quarterly Journal of the Royal Meteorological Society*, 88(375):90–95, 1962.

[20] S. Gambs, M.-O. Killijian, and M. N. del Prado Cortez. Show Me How You Move and I Will Tell You Who You Are. In *Int'l Workshop on Security and Privacy in GIS and LBS*, 2010.

[21] A. Gionis, H. Mannila, T. Mielikäinen, and P. Tsaparas. Assessing Data Mining Results via Swap Randomization. *Transactions on Knowledge Discovery from Data*, 1(3), 2007.
[22] S. Gomez, A. Arenas, J. Borge-Holthoefer, S. Meloni, and Y. Moreno. Discrete-time Markov Chain Approach to Contact-based Disease Spreading in Complex Networks. *Europhysics Letters*, 89(3), 2010.
[23] S. Holm. A Simple Sequentially Rejective Multiple Test Procedure. *Scandinavian Journal of Statistics*, 6(2):65–70, 1979.
[24] G. G. Judge and E. R. Swanson. Markov Chains: Basic Concepts and Suggested Uses in Agricultural Economics. *Australian Journal of Agricultural Economics*, 6(2):49–61, 1962.
[25] W. Klösgen. Explora: A Multipattern and Multistrategy Discovery Assistant. In *Advances in Knowledge Discovery and Data Mining*, pages 249–271. American Association for Artificial Intelligence, 1996.
[26] J. D. Lafferty, A. McCallum, and F. C. N. Pereira. Conditional Random Fields: Probabilistic Models for Segmenting and Labeling Sequence Data. In *Int'l Conference on Machine Learning*, 2001.
[27] N. Lavrač, B. Kavšek, P. A. Flach, and L. Todorovski. Subgroup Discovery with CN2-SD. *Journal of Machine Learning Research*, 5:153–188, 2004.
[28] M. van Leeuwen. Maximal Exceptions with Minimal Descriptions. *Data Mining and Knowledge Discovery*, 21(2):259–276, 2010.
[29] M. van Leeuwen and A. Knobbe. Diverse Subgroup Set Discovery. *Data Mining and Knowledge Discovery*, 25(2):208–242, 2012.
[30] J. Lehmann, R. Isele, M. Jakob, A. Jentzsch, D. Kontokostas, P. N. Mendes, S. Hellmann, M. Morsey, P. van Kleef, S. Auer, et al. DBpedia – A Large-scale, Multilingual Knowledge Base Extracted From Wikipedia. *Semantic Web*, pages 167–195, 2014.
[31] D. Leman, A. Feelders, and A. J. Knobbe. Exceptional Model Mining. In *European Conference on Machine Learning and Knowledge Discovery in Databases*, 2008.
[32] F. Lemmerich, M. Becker, and M. Atzmueller. Generic Pattern Trees for Exhaustive Exceptional Model Mining. In *European Conference on Machine Learning and Knowledge Discovery in Databases*, 2012.
[33] N. Lesh, M. J. Zaki, and M. Ogihara. Mining Features for Sequence Classification. In *ACM SIGKDD Int'l Conference on Knowledge Discovery and Data Mining*, 1999.
[34] J. Li, J. Liu, H. Toivonen, K. Satou, Y. Sun, and B. Sun. Discovering Statistically Non-Redundant Subgroups. *Knowledge-Based Systems*, 67:315–327, 2014.
[35] R. Li, R. Perneczky, A. Drzezga, and S. Kramer. Efficient Redundancy Reduced Subgroup Discovery via Quadratic Programming. *Journal of Intelligent Information Systems*, 44(2):271–288, 2015.
[36] C. Mooney and J. Roddick. Sequential Pattern Mining – Approaches and Algorithms. *ACM Computing Surveys*, 45(2):19:1–19:39, 2013.
[37] L. Page, S. Brin, R. Motwani, and T. Winograd. The PageRank Citation Ranking: Bringing order to the web. 1999.
[38] P. L. Pirolli and J. E. Pitkow. Distributions of Surfers' Paths through the World Wide Web: Empirical Characterizations. *World Wide Web*, 2(1-2):29–45, 1999.
[39] C. S. Poulsen. Mixed Markov and Latent Markov Modelling Applied to Brand Choice Behaviour. *Int'l Journal of Research in Marketing*, 7(1):5–19, 1990.
[40] N. Sadagopan and J. Li. Characterizing Typical and Atypical User Sessions in Clickstreams. In *Int'l World Wide Web Conference*, 2008.
[41] S. S. Shapiro and M. B. Wilk. An Analysis of Variance Test for Normality (Complete Samples). *Biometrika*, 52(3/4):591–611, 1965.
[42] A. Silberschatz and A. Tuzhilin. What Makes Patterns Interesting in Knowledge Discovery Systems. *Transactions on Knowledge and Data Engineering*, 8:970–974, 1996.
[43] P. Singer, D. Helic, A. Hotho, and M. Strohmaier. HypTrails: A Bayesian Approach for Comparing Hypotheses About Human Trails on the Web. In *Int'l World Wide Web Conference*, 2015.
[44] P. Singer, D. Helic, B. Taraghi, and M. Strohmaier. Detecting Memory and Structure in Human Navigation Patterns Using Markov Chain Models of Varying Order. *PLoS ONE*, 9(7):e102070, 2014.
[45] S. Walk, P. Singer, L. E. Noboa, T. Tudorache, M. A. Musen, and M. Strohmaier. Understanding How Users Edit Ontologies: Comparing Hypotheses About Four Real-World Projects. In *Int'l Semantic Web Conference*, 2015.
[46] G. I. Webb. OPUS: An Efficient Admissible Algorithm for Unordered Search. *Journal of AI Research*, 3(1):431–465, 1995.
[47] G. I. Webb. Layered Critical Values: a Powerful Direct-Adjustment Approach to Discovering Significant Patterns. *Machine Learning*, 71(2–3):307–323, 2008.
[48] S. Wrobel. An Algorithm for Multi-relational Discovery of Subgroups. In *European Symposium on Principles of Data Mining and Knowledge Discovery*, 1997.
[49] Z. Xing, J. Pei, and E. Keogh. A Brief Survey on Sequence Classification. *ACM SIGKDD Expl. Newsletter*, 12(1):40–48, 2010.
[50] M. J. Zaki. SPADE: An Efficient Algorithm for Mining Frequent Sequences. *Machine Learning*, 42(1-2):31–60, 2001.
[51] A. Zimmermann and L. De Raedt. Cluster-Grouping: From Subgroup Discovery to Clustering. *Machine Learning*, 77(1):125–159, 2009.

APPENDIX

In Bayesian statistics, one's current beliefs H are expressed by Bayesian probabilities over parameters θ. Given new information I, the *prior* belief $P(\theta|H)$ is updated to a *posterior* belief $P(\theta|H,I)$. Here, we show that the total variation measure $\omega_{tv} = \sum_i \left(\sum_j g_{ij} \cdot \sum_j \left| \frac{g_{i,j}}{\sum_j g_{i,j}} - \frac{d_{i,j}}{\sum_j d_{i,j}} \right|\right)$ (see Section 3.2) is order-equivalent to the *amount of Bayesian belief update* in the setting of Markov chain models if the reference matrix T_D is used as a very strong prior. That means that both measures ultimately imply the same ranking of subgroups. The belief update implied by a subgroup g is defined by the difference between the prior distribution and the posterior distribution after observing the instances covered by g. The amount of belief update was proposed in [42] as an interestingness measure for pattern mining in traditional settings.

As [43] suggests, we can elicit the matrix of a Dirichlet prior $T_A = (a_{ij})$ through a reference matrix of (pseudo-)observations $T_D = (d_{ij})$ using the formula $a_{ij} = (k \cdot d_{ij}) + 1$. Here, k specifies the strength of the belief expressed by the prior. It is updated to a posterior according to observed transitions in a subgroup g given in a transition matrix $T_g = (g_{ij})$. In this context, according to [44], the expected probabilities $E[p_{ij}](X)$ for a state transition from state s_i to state s_j in the prior are $\frac{a_{ij}}{\sum_j a_{ij}}$ and the expected probabilities in the posterior are $c_i \cdot \frac{g_{ij}}{\sum_j g_{ij}} + (1-c_i) \cdot \frac{a_{ij}}{\sum_j a_{ij}}$, with $c_i = \frac{\sum_j g_{ij}}{\sum_j (g_{ij}+a_{ij})}$. To determine the overall belief update BU for all state transitions, we compute the absolute difference between the posterior and the prior for each cell and aggregate over all cells in the matrix:

$$
\begin{aligned}
BU(H,D) &= \sum_i \sum_j \left| \left(c_i \frac{g_{ij}}{\sum_j g_{ij}} + (1-c_i) \frac{a_{ij}}{\sum_j a_{ij}} \right) - \frac{a_{ij}}{\sum_j a_{ij}} \right| \\
&= \sum_i \sum_j \left| c_i \cdot \left(\frac{g_{ij}}{\sum_j g_{ij}} - \frac{a_{ij}}{\sum_j a_{ij}} \right) \right| \\
&= \sum_i c_i \cdot \sum_j \left| \left(\frac{g_{ij}}{\sum_j g_{ij}} - \frac{a_{ij}}{\sum_j a_{ij}} \right) \right| \\
&= \sum_i \frac{1}{\sum_j (g_{ij} + a_{ij})} \sum_j g_{ij} \sum_j \left(\left| \frac{g_{ij}}{\sum_j g_{ij}} - \frac{a_{ij}}{\sum_j a_{ij}} \right| \right)
\end{aligned}
$$

Now, assume that we have a very strong belief in the prior, i.e., $k \to \infty$ and thus $a_{ij} \gg g_{ij}$. Then, the right hand sum converges to the total variation δ_{tv} between the observed transition matrix T_g and the reference matrix T_D. The factor $\sum_j g_{ij}$ corresponds to the weights w_i. The additional factor $\frac{1}{\sum_j (a_{ij}, +g_{ij})}$ is approximately constant across all subgroups if $a_{ij} \gg g_{ij}$ since a_{ij} is independent from the evaluated subgroup. Overall, the weighted total variation ω_{tv} describes the amount of belief update a subgroup induces to a prior that reflects a very strong belief in the transition probabilities given by the reference matrix T_D.

Point-of-Interest Recommendations: Learning Potential Check-ins from Friends

Huayu Li*, Yong Ge+, Richang Hong- and Hengshu Zhu×
*The University of North Carolina at Charlotte, + University of Arizona,
- Hefei University of Technology, ×Baidu Research-Big Data Lab
hli38@uncc.edu, ygestrive@gmail.com, hongrc@hfut.edu.cn, zhuhengshu@baidu.com

ABSTRACT

The emergence of Location-based Social Network (LBSN) services provides a wonderful opportunity to build personalized Point-of-Interest (POI) recommender systems. Although a personalized POI recommender system can significantly facilitate users' outdoor activities, it faces many challenging problems, such as the hardness to model user's POI decision making process and the difficulty to address data sparsity and user/location cold-start problem. To cope with these challenges, we define three types of friends (i.e., social friends, location friends, and neighboring friends) in LBSN, and develop a two-step framework to leverage the information of friends to improve POI recommendation accuracy and address cold-start problem. Specifically, we first propose to learn a set of potential locations that each individual's friends have checked-in before and this individual is most interested in. Then we incorporate three types of check-ins (i.e., observed check-ins, potential check-ins and other unobserved check-ins) into matrix factorization model using two different loss functions (i.e., the square error based loss and the ranking error based loss). To evaluate the proposed model, we conduct extensive experiments with many state-of-the-art baseline methods and evaluation metrics on two real-world data sets. The experimental results demonstrate the effectiveness of our methods.

Keywords

Point-of-Interest; Recommendation; Matrix Factorization

1. INTRODUCTION

Recent years have witnessed the prevalence of smart mobile devices and the convenience of accessing wireless network, which makes people much easier to acquire their real-time location information. This development stimulates the emergence of location-based social network (LBSN) services such as Foursquare, Jiepang, and Facebook Places. These LBSNs allow users to build connections with each other, and share their experience and check-in information associated with a Point-of-Interest (POI). A variety of such user interaction data with LBSNs provide a good opportunity for developing personalized POI recommender systems. Indeed, the accurate and personalized POI recommendation is a crucial demand in LBSN services. It not only helps users to explore new locations, but also facilitates users to find relevant POIs without spending too much time on searching, particularly when they are in a new region.

Although developing a personalized POI recommender system is a crucial task and could benefit users' outdoor activities, it is still a very challenging problem due to three reasons. First, a user's check-in decision making process is very complex and could be influenced by many different kinds of factors. For example, it is difficult to model the influence of social friends on user's check-in behaviours. We do not know which friend will actually influence user's POI decision, not mention to know how she affects user's choice. Also, the geographical distance might affect user's POI decision. A user often prefers a nearby POI to another one far away. Second, POI recommender system usually suffers a severe challenge caused by extreme sparse check-in data. In real system, there are over millions of POIs. However, a single user usually checks-in a limited number of POIs, which significantly increases the difficulty of recommendation. Third, when a new POI or a new user enters the system and we do not have its visitor information or her historical check-in information, it is very difficult to recommend new POI to users or recommend POIs to new user.

In the literature, some related works have been proposed to incorporate social network into POI recommendations. For example, [16] placed a social regularization term to constrain the estimation of user feature vectors with the assumption that friends will share the similar interests. Meanwhile, some researchers also proposed to take the geographical influence into account to assist POI recommendation. For instance, [28] leveraged a linear model to combine user interest, social network and geographical distance for POI prediction. On the other hand, [15] modeled the geographical neighborhood influence in both instance and region level. In instance level, one user's preference for a location is predicted as a combination of her special preference on this location and the nearest neighborhoods of this location. In region level, it places a group lasso penalty to learn location-specific latent vectors. However, few of these models incorporate the influence of geographically close users on each other's check-in activities into matrix factorization. The geographically close users may share similar interests and should have potential influence on check-in behaviors [23].

KDD '16, August 13-17, 2016, San Francisco, CA, USA

 ISBN 978-1-4503-4232-2/16/08...$15.00

DOI: http://dx.doi.org/10.1145/2939672.2939767

Moreover, few of these models could address user cold-start problem in location recommendation. Motivated by these, we first formally define three types of friends for each user: social friends, location friends and neighboring friends. The social friends of a user refer to the set of users who are socially connected with this user in LBSNs. The location friends of a user denote the set of users who check-in the same locations as this user does. The neighboring friends of a user are those users who are geographically close to this user. Then we novelly incorporate their historical check-ins into matrix factorization model with different loss functions.

Through our analysis on two real-world data sets, we find that users share the similar interests with their three types of friends. Consequently, we propose a two-step framework to elaborate friends' check-ins. In the first step, we design two approaches (i.e., a linear aggregation based and a random walk based) to learn a set of friends' locations that each user most potentially prefers and she never visited. Thus, a user's check-ins are divided into observed check-ins, potential check-ins and other unobserved check-ins. In the second step, we develop two loss functions to model these three kinds of check-ins: the square error based loss function and the ranking error based loss function. Specifically, the square error based loss treats user's check-ins as an indication of positive, potential and negative preference with varying confidence. The ranking error based loss assumes that the user prefers an observed location over any potential locations, and also prefers a potential location over any unobserved locations. We extensively evaluate our models with many state-of-the-art baseline models and different validation metrics on two real-world data sets. The experimental results not only demonstrate the improvements of our models on POI recommendation, but also show the effectiveness for cold-start problem.

To summarize, the major contributions of this paper are:

- empirically analyzes the correlations between users and their three type of friends using two check-in datasets;
- designs two approaches to learn a set of locations for each individual user that her friends have checked-in before and she is most interested in;
- develops matrix factorization based models via different error loss functions with the learned potential check-ins, and correspondingly proposes two scalable optimization methods;
- designs three different recommendation strategies for standard recommendation, new location recommendation, and new user recommendation.

2. PRELIMINARIES

In this section, we first introduce some mathematical notions, and then provide the definition of friends. At last, we introduce the recommendation framework.

2.1 Notation

Suppose there are N users and M locations. For convenience we will henceforth refer to i as user, f as friend and j as the location unless stated otherwise. Suppose there are C kinds of categories and the category of location j is denoted as c_j. For user i, $\mathcal{F}_i$ denotes a set of friends which will be further defined and explained in Section 2.2, $\mathcal{M}_i^o$ is a set of locations checked-in by her, $\mathcal{M}_i^p$ is a set of potential locations learned in Section 3, and $\mathcal{M}_i^u$ is the remaining unvisisted locations. r_{ij} is the check-in frequency of user i on location j. In addition, all column vectors are represented by bold lower case letters, all matrices are represented by bold upper case letters, and a numeric value is denoted by lower case letter. A predicted value is denoted with a ˆ (hat) over it. The terms *location* and *POI* are used interchangeably.

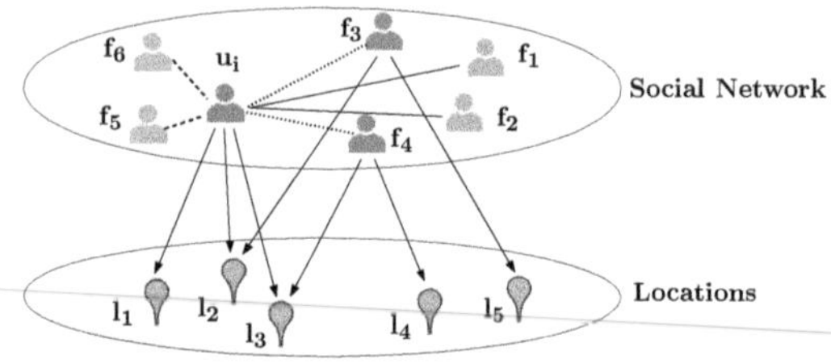

Figure 1: The user u_i's social network and check-ins.

2.2 Definition

To better understand users' check-in behaviours, we examine the check-in data collected from Gowalla and Foursquare (Details can be found in Section 5). To clarify the relation between the similarity of pairwise users and their physical distance, we plot their relations in Figure 2(a) and Figure 2(b). The physical distance of two users refers to the distance between their home locations, and the similarity of user i and user f is measured by cosine similarity, given by:

$$Sim_u(i,f) = (\sum_{j\in\mathcal{M}_i^o} r_{ij}^2 \sum_{j\in\mathcal{M}_f^o} r_{fj}^2)^{-\frac{1}{2}} \sum_{j\in\mathcal{M}_i^o\cap\mathcal{M}_f^o} r_{ij}r_{fj}. \quad (1)$$

Based on the observation, we find that the physically closer two users live, the more similar their POI interests are. It motivates us to leverage neighboring friends, who are physically neighbors, to learn user's interest in POIs. In addition, social friends who build connections online share the similar interests in POI decisions [16, 1, 5, 22]. Users who check-in similar locations are treated as location friends, and also might have similar tastes. Thus, three types of friends of user i, i.e., neighboring friends, social friends and location friends, might affect her check-in activity, defined as:

DEFINITION 1 (SOCIAL FRIENDS). *The social friends of user i are the set of users who have socially connected with her in LBSNs, which is denoted as $\mathcal{F}_i^s$.*

DEFINITION 2 (LOCATION FRIENDS). *Given a set of locations $\mathcal{M}_i^o$, which have been checked-in by user i, her location friends, denoted as $\mathcal{F}_i^l$, are the set of users who have also checked-in these locations, i.e., $\mathcal{F}_i^l = \bigcup_{j\in\mathcal{M}_i^o}\Psi_j$, where Ψ_j is the set of users who also have checked-in location j.*

DEFINITION 3 (NEIGHBORING FRIENDS). *Given the home location of user i, the neighboring friends are the set of users who live physically closest to her and denoted as $\mathcal{F}_i^n$.*

In the example of Figure 1, the target user u_i has checked-in locations $\{l_1, l_2, l_3\}$. $\{f_1, f_2\}$ are her social friends who socially connect with her online. User f_3 has check-ins at locations l_2 and l_5, and user f_4 has check-ins at locations l_3 and l_4. f_4 and f_5 have common POIs with user u_i, i.e., l_2 and l_3, respectively. Thus, both of them are the location friends of user u_i. In addition, f_5 and f_6 are the target user's neighboring friends due to their physically short distance to her. Thus, $\{f_1, \cdots, f_6\}$ are regarded as the friends of user i. In this paper, the **friends** of user i are defined as:

$$\mathcal{F}_i = \mathcal{F}_i^s \cup \mathcal{S}(\mathcal{F}_i^l) \cup \mathcal{S}(\mathcal{F}_i^n), \quad (2)$$

where $\mathcal{S}(\mathcal{F}_i^l)$ is the set of S most similar friends with the highest cosine similarities and $\mathcal{S}(\mathcal{F}_i^n)$ is the set of S physically nearest friends with the shortest distance among their

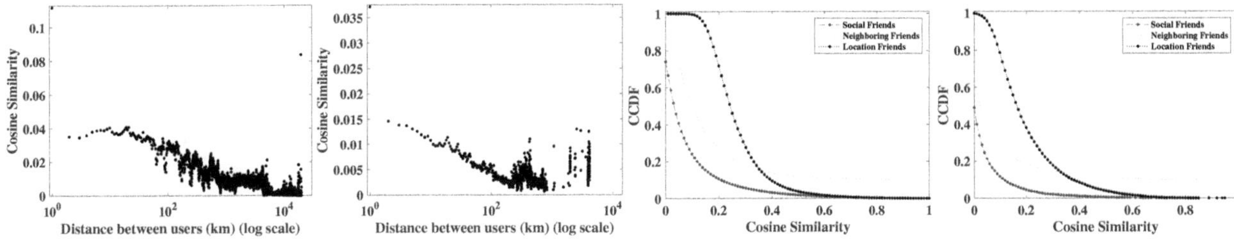

(a) Gowalla Data (b) Foursquare Data (c) Gowalla Data (d) Foursquare Data

Figure 2: (a) $\sim$ (b) Cosine similarity as a function of distance between users' home locations. (c) $\sim$ (d) Complementary Cumulative Distribution Function (CCDF) of cosine similarity between friends.

homes[1]. To examine the correlation between friends, we report the complementary cumulative distributions of their similarities in Figure 2(c) and Figure 2(d) on Gowalla and Foursquare, respectively. There are over 5%, 20% and 40% pairs of social, neighboring and location friends which have similarities larger than 0.2. Particularly, the friends' correlation is much stronger in Gowalla than Foursquare. The observation shows the importance of friends in LBSNs and motivates us to use friends' historical check-ins to improve recommendation accuracy.

2.3 The Recommendation Framework

The recommendation task in this paper is defined as: given users' historical checked-in locations, we aim at recommending each user with top-K locations that she might be interested in but has not visited before. In this paper, we propose a two-step recommendation framework. Specifically, in the first step, we learn a set of potential locations from three types of friends, which will be introduced in Section 3. In the second step, we incorporate the learned potential locations of each individual into matrix factorization model with different error loss functions, which will be presented in Section 4. At last, we introduce different recommendation strategies for standard recommendation, location cold-start recommendation and user cold-start recommendation.

3. LEARNING POTENTIAL LOCATIONS

Social network plays an important role in recommendations [16, 28, 5, 22]. However, only leveraging the historical locations of social friends cannot successfully model user's preference for locations due to that it is difficult to appropriately model the preference of users who have no social friends, not mention to handle user cold-start problem (i.e., a user has never checked-in any location before). To address these problems, we will exploit the characteristics of three types of friends: social friends, location friends and neighboring friends. The earlier section has shown their significance in LBSNs, i.e., friends would share the similar preferences for POIs. In other words, users might be interested in those locations which have been checked-in by their friends, and have a high probability to check-in them next time. However, the extremely large number of these locations will lead to the inefficiency of computation with the increase of locations, and the inaccuracy of prediction with the increase of noise. Hence, the problem in this section is to find the most potential locations for the target user, defined as:

DEFINITION 4 (PROBLEM OF POTENTIAL LOCATIONS). *Given the set of locations $\mathcal{M}_i^f = \bigcup_{f\in\mathcal{F}_i}\mathcal{M}_f^o \backslash \mathcal{M}_i^o$, that the friends of target user i have checked-in before but she never visits, the problem is to find top S most potential locations that she might be interested, denoted as $\mathcal{M}_i^p$.*

To obtain the potential locations of each user i, we propose two methods, i.e., *Linear Aggregation* and *Random Walk*, to estimate the probability p_{ij}^{pot} of this user on each location j that her friends have checked-in. Then we rank them by the estimated probabilities and select S locations with the highest probabilities[2]. The learned potential locations will assist to make accurate recommendation in Section 4.

3.1 Linear Aggregation

In this section, we propose *Linear Aggregation* method, denoted as LA, to predict the probability p_{ij}^{pot} that user i prefers location j which has been visited by her friends. Suppose $Sim(i,f;j)$ is the similarity between user i and friend f on the preference for location j. A location is possibly checked-in by more than one friends, so we define p_{ij}^{pot} as:

$$p_{ij}^{pot} \propto \max_{f\in\mathcal{F}_i^j} \{Sim(i,f;j)\},$$

where $\mathcal{F}_i^j$ is the set of user i's friends who have checked-in location j. The similarity $Sim(i,f;j)$ incorporates two parts: (1) the similarity of user interest, and (2) the similarity of geographical location. The similarity of user interest can be measured by cosine similarity in Eq.(1). Since a user's check-in probability and the distance from her home to the corresponding location follow a power law distribution [9], we exploit this characteristic to model geographical similarity. Hence, we define the probability that a user checks-in a location d-km far away as the following:

$$Pr_G(d) = a\cdot d^b, \tag{3}$$

where a and b are the parameters of power law distribution and could be learned by maximum likelihood estimation. Then the probability of user i to check-in a POI j due to the geographical influence is normalized as:

$$p_{ij}^G = \frac{Pr_G(d(h_i,j))}{Pr_G(d_{min})}, \tag{4}$$

where h_i is the home location of user i, and $d(h_i,j)$ indicates the distance between the home location of user i and the POI j, and d_{min} is the minimum distance. The distance could be computed by Haversine formula with latitude and longitude. Thus, $Sim(i,f;j)$ is the linear aggregation of similarities on both user interest and geographical location, given by

$$Sim(i,f;j) = \zeta\ Sim_u(i,f) + (1-\zeta)\ p_{ij}^G,$$

where $\zeta\in[0,1]$ is a tuning parameter to control the importance of the similarity of user interest.

3.2 Random Walk

Random walk with restart has successfully measured the correlation between two nodes in a graph [7, 24]. In this section, we propose a *Random Walk* method, denoted as RW, to learn the probability p_{ij}^{pot} of user i on location j which has been visited by her friends. We construct a directed

[1]In the experiment, we set S as 10.

[2]In the experiments, we set S as 500.

graph with two kinds of nodes: the users (i.e., the target user and her friends), and the locations checked-in by her and her friends. Let $\mathbf{y}$ be a column vector where y_i refers to the probability that the random walk is at node i. Also let $\mathbf{A}$ be the column normalized transition matrix where a_{ij} denotes the probability that node i jumps to node j. Here we consider three types of transition probabilities: (1) the probability between users measured by the cosine similarity in Eq.(1); (2) the probability from each user to each location which is one if the user checks-in the corresponding location and otherwise is zero; (3) the similarity between a pair of locations (j and k) measured by the normalized power-law function which is defined as the following:

$$Sim_G(j,k) = \frac{Pr_G(d(j,k))}{Pr_G(d_{min})}, \tag{5}$$

where $d(j,k)$ is the distance between these two locations and the power law parameters are learned with the check-in probabilities and corresponding distances of pairwise locations. Hence, the iteration equation for updating the steady-state probability of each node is given as follows:

$$\mathbf{y} = (1-\beta)\mathbf{A}\mathbf{y} + \frac{\beta}{|\mathcal{M}_i^o \cap \mathcal{M}_i^f| + |\mathcal{F}_i| + 1}\mathbf{x}, \tag{6}$$

where $\mathbf{x}$ is the column vector of zeros with the elements corresponding to the target user and her checked-in locations as one, and $\beta \in [0,1]$ is the restart probability to return to the target user and her checked-in locations. The steady-state probability is achieved by recursively performing Eq.(6) until convergence. Thus, the probability p_{ij}^{pot} is the steady-state probability corresponding to the location j.

4. RECOMMENDATION MODELS

In Section 3, for each individual user, we have learned the potential locations from her friends' information. In this section, the learned potential locations are utilized to make accurate recommendation and address user cold-start problem. Overall, for each user i, we have her three kinds of locations: observed locations $\mathcal{M}_i^o$, potential locations $\mathcal{M}_i^p$ and other unobserved locations $\mathcal{M}_i^u$.

In this paper, we build our recommendation models by leveraging the widely-used matrix factorization techniques [20, 19, 8, 6, 11], where both user and location are mapped into latent low-dimension spaces. Let $\mathbf{U} \in \mathbb{R}^{K\times N}$ and $\mathbf{V} \in \mathbb{R}^{K\times M}$ be the latent user and location feature matrices, with column vectors $\mathbf{u}_i$ and $\mathbf{v}_j$ representing the K-dimensional user-specific and location-specific feature vectors of user i and location j, respectively. A typical prediction for the preference of user i to location j is taken by an inner product of latent vectors, i.e., $\hat{p}_{ij} = \mathbf{u}_i^T\mathbf{v}_j$, where $\mathbf{P} \in \mathbb{R}^{N\times M}$ is the preference matrix.

However, in LBSNs the category information of POIs affects user's check-in decision making process. Users are often used to visiting those POIs which belong to the same category due to their specific hobbies. For example, users who like eating would have a much higher probability to choose a new POI relevant to *food* next time, but they have much less chance to check-in a POI about *sight*. Thus, the preference of category is another important factor to affect user's decision on a new POI. Here, we introduce the category feature matrix $\mathbf{Q} \in \mathbb{R}^{N\times C}$, where each entry q_{ic} indicates the preference of user i to category c. Hence, the preference of user i for location j is refined as follows:

$$\hat{p}_{ij} = (q_{ic_j} + \varepsilon)\mathbf{u}_i^T\mathbf{v}_j, \tag{7}$$

where c_j is the category of location j and ε is a tuning parameter to indicate that user has a small probability to prefer one location with another category.

Many of the recent works suppose to only model the observed rating, which is adapted to explicit feedback datasets. However, the check-in dataset is implicit feedback dataset, where we do not have explicit feedback for user's preference to locations. In other words, we lack substantial evidence on which location the user dislikes. To address user cold start problem and data sparseness problem, we propose to model the observed preference, potential preference and unobserved preference of users for location, simultaneously. Let j, k, h denote the observed location, potential location and unobserved location, respectively. The loss function of general form is given as follows:

$$\underset{\mathbf{U},\mathbf{V},\mathbf{Q}}{\operatorname{argmin}} \sum_i E_i(p_{ij}, p_{ik}, p_{ih}, \hat{p}_{ij}, \hat{p}_{ik}, \hat{p}_{ih}) + \Theta(\mathbf{U},\mathbf{V},\mathbf{Q}), \tag{8}$$
$$\forall j \in \mathcal{M}_i^o, \forall k \in \mathcal{M}_i^p, \forall h \in \mathcal{M}_i^u,$$

where $E_i(\cdot)$ is the loss function for the observed, potential and unobserved preference of user i for locations, and $\Theta(\cdot)$ is a regularization term with ℓ_2 norm which is defined as:

$$\Theta(\mathbf{U},\mathbf{V},\mathbf{Q}) = \frac{\lambda_u}{2}||\mathbf{U}||_2^2 + \frac{\lambda_v}{2}||\mathbf{V}||_2^2 + \frac{\lambda_q}{2}||\mathbf{Q}||_2^2, \tag{9}$$

where λ_u, λ_v and λ_q are the regularization constants. We develop two different types of models which use different loss function for $E_i(\cdot)$, i.e., the square error based and the ranking error based loss functions, and will be described in the next two sections, respectively.

4.1 The Square Error based Model

In this section, we present the Augmented Square error based Matrix Factorization (*ASMF*) model constrained with the square error loss function and its optimization method.

4.1.1 The ASMF Model

Due to the similar interests between friends, one user might have opportunity to visit those potential locations that her friends have visited before but she never checks-in. We treat each individual user's check-ins as an indication of positive, potential and negative preference associated with different confidence. One user has a high confidence for the positive preference to their checked-in POIs. However, she will have a low confidence for the potential preference to those potential locations and the negative preference to other unvisited locations. Correspondingly, we augment the binary preference variable p_{ij} to a ternary value as follows:

$$p_{ij} = \begin{cases} 1 & \text{if } j \in \mathcal{M}_i^o \\ \alpha & \text{if } j \in \mathcal{M}_i^p \\ 0 & \text{otherwise,} \end{cases} \tag{10}$$

where $\alpha \in [0,1]$ is a potential preference constant, indicating user i has a probability α to choose an unvisited location j that her friends have visited before.

Therefore, we propose the augmented square error based matrix factorization model (*ASMF*) to compute the loss $E_i(\cdot)$ by using the squared error loss function with the ternary variable defined in Eq.(10), given by:

$$E_i(\cdot) = \sum_{j=1}^{M} w_{ij}\left(p_{ij} - \hat{p}_{ij}\right)^2, \tag{11}$$

where $\mathbf{W}$ is the confidential matrix with element w_{ij} as the confidential weight for user i to location j, given by:

$$w_{ij} = \begin{cases} 1 + \gamma \times r_{ij} & \text{if } j \in \mathcal{M}_i^o \\ 1 & \text{otherwise,} \end{cases} \tag{12}$$

where γ is the tuning parameter.

4.1.2 The Parameter Estimation

In *ASMF* model, based on the Eq.(7), Eq.(8) and Eq.(11), the matrices **U**, **V**, and **Q** are learned by minimizing the following regularized optimization problem:

$$\mathcal{L} = \min_{\mathbf{U},\mathbf{V},\mathbf{Q}} \sum_{i=1}^{N}\sum_{j=1}^{M} w_{ij}\left(p_{ij} - (q_{ic_j} + \varepsilon)\mathbf{u}_i^T\mathbf{v}_j\right)^2 + \Theta(\mathbf{U},\mathbf{V},\mathbf{Q}), \quad (13)$$

To solve the above optimization problem, we adopt Alternating Least Squares (ALS) [8] optimization method due to the accurate parameter estimation and fast convergence rate. We perform ALS method to compute each latent variable by fixing the other variables when minimizing the objective function. The updating formulas with respect to **U**, **V** and **Q** are given as follows:

$$\mathbf{u}_i = (\lambda_u\mathbf{I}_K + \sum_j w_{ij}\tilde{q}_{ic_j}^2\mathbf{v}_j\mathbf{v}_j^T)^{-1}\sum_j \mathbf{w}_{ij}\tilde{q}_{ic_j}p_{ij}\mathbf{v}_j, \quad (14)$$

$$\mathbf{v}_j = (\lambda_v\mathbf{I}_K + \sum_i w_{ij}\tilde{q}_{ic_j}^2\mathbf{u}_i\mathbf{u}_i^T)^{-1}\sum_i w_{ij}\tilde{q}_{ic_j}p_{ij}\mathbf{u}_i, \quad (15)$$

$$\mathbf{q}_{ic} = (\sum_{j\in\mathcal{N}_c} w_{ij}(p_{ij} - \varepsilon)\mathbf{u}_i^T\mathbf{v}_j)/(\lambda_q + \sum_{j\in\mathcal{N}_c} w_{ij}(\mathbf{u}_i^T\mathbf{v}_j)^2), \quad (16)$$

where $\mathbf{I}_K$ is the K-dimension unit matrix, $\mathcal{N}_c$ is the set of locations with category c, and $\tilde{q}_{ic_j}$ is equal to $q_{ic_j} + \varepsilon$. The detailed algorithm is reported in Algorithm 1. Specifically, we place the non-negative constraints on **Q** and project the negative variables to 0 in each iteration.

Algorithm 1: ASMF Optimization

Input: $\mathbf{W}$, $\mathbf{P}$, λ_u, λ_v, λ_q, α, ε, τ, $maxIter$
Output: $\mathbf{U}^{(t)}$, $\mathbf{V}^{(t)}$, $\mathbf{Q}^{(t)}$

```
Randomly initialize U^(0) and V^(0), t ← 1, ω ← ∞
Initialize Q^(0) by using Eq.(16)
while t ⩽ maxIter && ω ⩾ τ do
    Update U^(t) by using Eq.(14)
    Update V^(t) by using Eq.(15)
    Update Q^(t) by using Eq.(16)
    ω ← |L(U^(t),V^(t),Q^(t)) − L(U^(t−1),V^(t−1),Q^(t−1))| / |L(U^(t−1),V^(t−1),Q^(t−1))|
    t ← t + 1
end
return U^(t), V^(t), Q^(t)
```

Complexity Analysis. The complexity of direct computation is $\mathcal{O}(NMK^2)$ which is extremely inefficient particularly with the increase of locations and users. To improve the efficiency, we design the following updating strategies. For updating $\mathbf{u}_i$, we employ the similar trick in [6], i.e., $\sum_j w_{ij}\tilde{q}_{ic_j}^2\mathbf{v}_j\mathbf{v}_j^T = \sum_j \tilde{q}_{ic_j}^2\mathbf{v}_j\mathbf{v}_j^T + \sum_j \gamma r_{ij}\tilde{q}_{ic_j}^2\mathbf{v}_j\mathbf{v}_j^T$. The first term can be written as $\sum_j \tilde{q}_{ic_j}^2\mathbf{v}_j\mathbf{v}_j^T = \sum_c \tilde{q}_{ic}^2\sum_{j\in\mathcal{N}_c}\mathbf{v}_j\mathbf{v}_j^T$. For each category c, $\sum_{j\in\mathcal{N}_c}\mathbf{v}_j\mathbf{v}_j^T$ is independent of i and already pre-computed, so the time complexity of this term is $\mathcal{O}(CK^2)$ and C is usually very small. The cost time of the second term is $\mathcal{O}(n_iK^2)$, where the potential part can be pre-computed and n_i is the number of observed locations for which $r_{ij} > 0$. In addition, the inverse of a $K\times K$ matrix costs $\mathcal{O}(K^3)$. Consequently, the re-computation of $\mathbf{u}_i$ is performed in time $\mathcal{O}(CK^2 + n_iK^2 + K^3)$. This procedure is performed over each user, so the total time is $\mathcal{O}(NCK^2 + nK^2 + NK^3)$, where n is defined as $n = \sum_i n_i$.

Similarly, when updating $\mathbf{v}_j$, we have $\sum_i w_{ij}\tilde{q}_{ic_j}^2\mathbf{u}_i\mathbf{u}_i^T = \sum_i \tilde{q}_{ic_j}^2\mathbf{u}_i\mathbf{u}_i^T + \sum_i \gamma r_{ij}\tilde{q}_{ic_j}^2\mathbf{u}_i\mathbf{u}_i^T$. For each category c, the first term is independent of j and was already pre-computed. Thus, the total cost time over M locations is $\mathcal{O}(nK^2 + MK^3)$.

To update q_{ic}, we can rewrite the crucial expression as $\sum_{j\in\mathcal{N}_c} w_{ij}(\mathbf{u}_i^T\mathbf{v}_j)^2 = \sum_{j\in\mathcal{N}_c}(\mathbf{u}_i^T\mathbf{v}_j)^2 + \sum_{j\in\mathcal{N}_c}\gamma r_{ij}(\mathbf{u}_i^T\mathbf{v}_j)^2$. The first term can be written as $\sum_{j\in\mathcal{N}_c}(\mathbf{u}_i^T\mathbf{v}_j)^2 = \mathbf{u}_i^T(\sum_{j\in\mathcal{N}_c}\mathbf{v}_j\mathbf{v}_j^T)\mathbf{u}_i$, where $\sum_{j\in\mathcal{N}_c}\mathbf{v}_j\mathbf{v}_j^T$ was already pre-computed, so it costs $\mathcal{O}(K^2)$. The second term costs $\mathcal{O}(Kn_{ic})$, where n_{ic} is the number of locations for which $r_{ij} > 0$ and belongs to category c. The total complexity of updating **Q** is $\mathcal{O}(NCK^2 + Kn)$.

In a summary, for each iteration of optimization, the total time is $\mathcal{O}(nK^2)$, where $n > max\{M, N\}K$, and $n > CN$ are usually satisfied. In other words, the time complexity of one optimization iteration is in linear proportion to the number of observed check-ins.

4.2 The Ranking Error based Model

In this section, we present the Augmented Ranking error based Matrix Factorization (*ARMF*) model constrained with the ranking error loss and its optimization method.

4.2.1 The ARMF Model

In check-in dataset, we only have a user's check-in record and do not know how much she dislikes a location. In other words, an unvisited location does not necessarily indicate the user dislikes it. The unobserved data actually is a mixture of negative preference for locations and missing values. It motivates us to consider a ranking error based loss function for modeling the ranking order of user's preference for observed locations, potential locations and unobserved locations. We assume that the user prefers an observed location over all potential locations, and at the same time she prefers a potential location over all other unobserved locations. Thus, for user i, the ranking order of her preference over an observed location $j \in \mathcal{M}_i^o$, a potential location $k \in \mathcal{M}_i^p$ and an unobserved location $h \in \mathcal{M}_i^u$ is given as the following:

$$\begin{cases}\hat{p}_{ij} > \hat{p}_{ik}\\ \hat{p}_{ik} > \hat{p}_{ih}\end{cases} \Rightarrow \begin{cases}(q_{ic_j} + \varepsilon)\mathbf{u}_i^T\mathbf{v}_j > (q_{ic_k} + \varepsilon)\mathbf{u}_i^T\mathbf{v}_k\\ (q_{ic_k} + \varepsilon)\mathbf{u}_i^T\mathbf{v}_k > (q_{ic_h} + \varepsilon)\mathbf{u}_i^T\mathbf{v}_h\end{cases}. \quad (17)$$

To this end, we propose the augmented ranking error based matrix factorization (*ARMF*) to compute the loss $E_i(\cdot)$ by using the ranking error loss function, given by,

$$E_i(\cdot) = -\sum_{j\in\mathcal{M}_i^o}\sum_{k\in\mathcal{M}_i^p}\ln\sigma(\hat{p}_{ij} - \hat{p}_{ik}) - \sum_{k\in\mathcal{M}_i^p}\sum_{h\in\mathcal{M}_i^u}\ln\sigma(\hat{p}_{ik} - \hat{p}_{ih}), \quad (18)$$

where $\sigma(x) = \frac{1}{1+e^{-x}}$ is the logistic sigmoid function which is introduced to penalize the violated constraints in Eq.(17). As we can see in Eq.(18), the error function does not focus on predicting the right value, but on the ordering of the preference for observed, potential and unobserved locations.

4.2.2 The Parameter Estimation

In ARMF model, based on the Eq.(7), Eq.(8) and Eq.(18), the matrices **U**, **V**, and **Q** are learned by minimizing the following regularized optimization problem:

$$\underset{\mathbf{U},\mathbf{V},\mathbf{Q}}{\text{argmin}} -\sum_i\left(\sum_{j\in\mathcal{M}_i^o}\sum_{k\in\mathcal{M}_i^p}\ln\sigma(\hat{p}_{ij} - \hat{p}_{ik}) + \sum_{k\in\mathcal{M}_i^p}\sum_{h\in\mathcal{M}_i^u}\ln\sigma(\hat{p}_{ik} - \hat{p}_{ih})\right) + \Theta(\mathbf{U},\mathbf{V},\mathbf{Q}). \quad (19)$$

As there is no close-form for each variable with ALS approach, a Stochastic Gradient Descent (SGD) using the boostrap sampling with replacement algorithm is employed to solve the optimization problem in Eq.(19). The optimization algorithm is iteratively performed by sampling a tuple

(i, j, k, h) and updating the corresponding variables, where i is a user, $j \in \mathcal{M}_i^o$ is her observed location, $k \in \mathcal{M}_i^p$ is her potential location, and $h \in \mathcal{M}_i^u$ is other unobserved location. More details of optimization are provided in Algorithm 2. Specifically, we define $g'(x) = \sigma(x) - 1$.

Complexity Analysis. The run time of sampling a tuple (i, j, k, h) is quite small in each update and can be neglected. Hence, the complexity of the optimization algorithm is $\mathcal{O}(mK)$, where m is the total iteration number. In the experiments, m is proportional to the number of observed check-ins.

Algorithm 2: ARMF Optimization

Input: λ_u, λ_v, λ_q, η, $maxIter$
Output: $\mathbf{U}$, $\mathbf{V}$, $\mathbf{Q}$

```
Randomly initialize U and V, Q, t ← 1
while t ⩽ maxIter do
    Randomly sample a (i, j, k, h), where i is a user, and j, k, h
      are her one observed, potential, and unobserved location
    ṽ_j^i ← (q_{ic_j} + ε) v_j
    ũ_i^j ← (q_{ic_j} + ε) u_i
    p̃_{ijk} ← g'(p̂_{ij} − p̂_{ik})
    p̃_{ikh} ← g'(p̂_{ik} − p̂_{ih})
    u_i ← u_i − η(p̃_{ijk}(ṽ_j^i − ṽ_k^i) + p̃_{ikh}(ṽ_k^i − ṽ_h^i) + λ_u u_i)
    v_j ← v_j − η(p̃_{ijk} ũ_i^j + λ_v v_j)
    v_k ← v_k − η((p̃_{ikh} − p̃_{ijk}) ũ_i^k + λ_v v_k)
    v_h ← v_h − η(−p̃_{ikh} ũ_i^h + λ_v v_h)
    q_{ic_j} ← q_{ic_j} − η(p̃_{ijk} u_i^T v_j + λ_q q_{ic_j})
    q_{ic_k} ← q_{ic_k} − η((p̃_{ikh} − p̃_{ijk}) u_i^T v_k + λ_q q_{ic_k})
    q_{ic_h} ← q_{ic_h} − η(−p̃_{ikh} u_i^T v_h + λ_q q_{ic_h})
    t ← t + 1
end
return U, V, Q
```

4.3 Incorporating Geographical Influence

Different from online product consuming, a POI's geographical distance significantly affects the user's check-in decision making process. One user would have a small probability to check-in a location far away, even though she is interested in it. In the example shown in Figure 1, user u_i has more chance to check-in the locations in the left side than those in the right side. It motivates us to incorporate the geographical influence into user's decision on POIs. Thus, the probability that user i prefers a POI j is:

$$\hat{p}_{ij} \propto p_{ij}^G \times \sigma(\hat{p}_{ij}) \Rightarrow \hat{p}_{ij} \propto p_{ij}^G \times \sigma((q_{ic_j} + \varepsilon)\mathbf{u}_i^T \mathbf{v}_j), \qquad (20)$$

where p_{ij}^G is the geographical influence shown in Eq.(4).

4.4 Recommendation Strategies

Our goal is to recommend unvisited locations for users which they might be interested in. For each individual user, we first predict the probability that this user would check-in each unvisited location and then recommend the top-K locations with the highest probabilities for her. In particular, we adopt the following strategies for recommendation.

- **Standard Recommendation.** Similar to traditional recommendation, we consider to recommend the existing users with the existing locations. After learning the model from training data, we exploit Eq.(20) to predict the probability that one user prefers each unvisited location.
- **New User Recommendation.** When new users enter the system, we consider to recommend them with the existing locations. First, we need to re-train the models with these new users by leveraging the historical check-ins of their social friends and neighboring friends. As new users do not have check-ins, they do not have location friends but they have neighboring friends. After the latent factors are learned, Eq.(20) is employed for recommendations.
- **New Location Recommendation.** When new locations enter the system, we consider to recommend existed users for them. By utilizing the neighboring location characteristics, the probability that user i checks-in a new location j is defined as follows:

$$\hat{p}_{ij} \propto p_{ij}^G \times \sigma\left(\frac{\sum_{l \in \hat{\psi}_j} Sim_G(j, l)\hat{p}_{il}}{\sum_{l \in \hat{\psi}_j} Sim_G(j, l)}\right),$$

where $\hat{\psi}_j$ is the set of S nearest neighboring locations of location j in the training data and in the experiments S is set as 10. The advantage to exploit the similarity of neighboring locations is that we can handle new locations as soon as they are generated in the system, without needing to re-train the model and estimate new parameters.

5. EXPERIMENTS

In this section, we evaluate the proposed models with baseline methods on two real-world data sets.

5.1 Experimental Setup

Datasets. In this paper, we use Gowalla and Foursquare datasets to evaluate the performance of the proposed models. Gowalla contains check-in data ranging from January 2009 to August 2010, and Foursquare includes the check-in data of users who live in California, ranging from December 2009 to June 2013. Each check-in record in the datasets includes a user ID, a location ID and a timestamp, where each location has latitude, longitude and category information. Totally, there are 262 and 10 categories in Gowalla and Foursquare, respectively. Also, data sets have undirected friendship information and user's home information[3].

To evaluate model's cold-start recommendation performance, for each data set, we divide it in three steps. First, we remove those users who have visited less than 10 locations and those locations which are visited by less than 10 users. These check-ins are used to evaluate our model's performance for standard POI recommendation. In recommendation system, we aim to recommend those unvisited locations for users. Therefore, we split the training and testing data as follows: for each individual user, (1) aggregating the check-ins for each location; (2) sorting the location according to the first time that the user checked-in; (3) selecting the earliest 80% to train the model and using the next 20% as testing. Second, in the rest of check-ins (i.e., locations that are visited by less than 10 users and not included in the training), we use those check-ins whose locations are visited by users in the training data to evaluate the model's performance for new location recommendation. Third, in the rest of check-ins (i.e., users who have visited less than 10 locations), we use those check-ins where users are not in training data to evaluate user cold-start recommendation performance. The data statistics are shown in Table 1.

Experimental Settings. In the experiments, the parameters β, λ_u, λ_v, ζ, η and ε are set to 0.15, 0.015, 0.015, 0.5, 0.001, and 0.1, respectively. In Gowalla dataset, α, and λ_q are set to 0.3 and 500. In Foursquare dataset, α and λ_q are set to 0.1 and 300. We will discuss the influence of α in the Section 5.4.4. The latent feature number is set as 10.

[3]Our model can be applied in the general check-in datasets. The home location can be estimated by using the existing approach in [2, 3]

Table 1: The statistics of data sets.

							New Location Rec		New User Rec	
Data Set	#User	#Location	#Checkin	#Train	#Test	Sparsity	#New Location	#Test	#New User	#Test
Gowalla	52,216	98,351	2,577,336	2,049,630	527,706	0.0399%	78,881	568,937	9,326	79,153
Foursquare	2,551	13,474	124,933	100,033	24,900	0.2910%	93,311	119,876	1,221	17,964

Table 2: The performance comparison of standard recommendation in terms of MAP.

Data Set	ASMF-RW	ASMF-LA	ARMF-RW	ARMF-LA	USG	IRenMF	WRMF	BPR	LOCABAL	RegPMF	PMF
Gowalla	0.05700	0.05713	0.05715	0.05705	0.05205	0.02554	0.02470	0.03652	0.01446	0.01388	0.01357
Foursquare	0.04167	0.04064	0.03857	0.03907	0.03464	0.03683	0.03626	0.01923	0.02344	0.02325	0.02288

5.2 Evaluation Metrics

As POI recommender system only recommends the limited locations for users, we quantitatively evaluate our models versus other models in terms of ranking performance, i.e., Precision@K and Recall@K metrics. MAP metric, the mean of the average precision (AP) over all locations in the testing, is also adopted in the experiments to evaluate models' performance. They are formally defined as follows:

$$Precision@K = \frac{1}{N}\sum_{i=1}^{N}\frac{S_i(K)\cap T_i}{K}, Recall@K = \frac{1}{N}\sum_{i=1}^{N}\frac{S_i(K)\cap T_i}{|T_i|},$$

$$MAP = \frac{1}{N}\sum_{i=1}^{N}\frac{\sum_{j=1}^{\hat{m}_i} p(j)\times rel(j)}{|T_i|},$$

where $S_i(K)$ is a set of top-K unvisited locations recommended to user i excluding those locations in the training, and T_i is a set of locations that are visited by user i in the testing. $\hat{m}_i$ is the number of the returned locations in the list for user i, $p(j)$ is the precision of a cut-off rank list from 1 to j, and $rel(j)$ is an indicator function that equals to 1 if the location is visited in the testing, otherwise equals to 0.

5.3 Baseline Methods

To comparatively demonstrate the effectiveness of our models, we compare them with the following seven models:

- **USG** [28], which combines geographical influence, social network and user interest with collaborative filtering;
- **IRenMF** [15], which models geographical influence by incorporating neighboring characteristics into weighted matrix factorization in both instance level and region level;
- **LOCABAL** [22], which models two types of social relations: social friends and the users with high global reputations, in the framework of matrix factorization;
- **RegPMF** [16], which models the influence of social network by placing a social regularization constraint on learning user-specific feature vectors between friends;
- **PMF** [20], which minimizes the square error loss only using the observed check-ins based on matrix factorization.
- **WRMF** [6], which minimizes the square error loss by assigning both observed and unobserved check-ins with different confidential values based on matrix factorization;
- **BRP** [18], which optimizes the ordering of the preference for the observed location and the unobserved location.

In this paper, we develop two methods to learn the potential locations for each user (i.e., *LA*, *RW*) and then design two loss functions: *ASMF* and *ARMF*. Thus we consider the following combinations: *ASMF + LA*, *ASMF + RW*, *ARMF + LA*, *ARMF + RW*, which are denoted as **ASMF-LA**, **ASMF-RW**, **ARMF-LA**, **ARMF-RW**, respectively.

5.4 Performance Comparison

In this section, we evaluate the proposed models for standard recommendation, new location and new user recommendation in terms of Precision@K, Recall@K and MAP. In addition, we discuss the influence of α in *ASMF-LA* model.

5.4.1 Performance of Standard Recommendation

The performance comparison of our models and baseline models in terms of Precision@K, Recall@K, and Map are shown in Figure 3, Figure 4 and Table 2.

Modeling observed check-ins v.s. modeling all check-ins. From the results, we can see that *WRMF* and *BPR* almost outperform *LOCABAL*, *RegPMF* and *PMF*. Even though *LOCABAL* and *RegPMF* incorporate social network into matrix factorization, the sparseness of data due to only modeling the observed check-ins results in their poor performance. Both *LOCABAL* and *RegPMF* are slightly superior to *PMF*. One possible explanation is that social network assists to make more accurate recommendation. Different from them, *WRMF* not only utilizes the observed check-ins, but also models negative preference for all unvisited locations with a low confidence. But *BPR* easily leads to bias by only sampling some unvisited locations, which explains why it performs not good in Foursquare data set.

Our models v.s. baseline models. Our models achieve the best performance in both data sets with all evaluation metrics, illustrating the superiority of our approaches. Although *USG* exploits social influence, geographical effect and user interest, its simple linear combination results in the poor performance. As Gowalla covers a much larger area than Foursquare, the clustering result is not good, leading to the worse performance of *IRenMF* in Gowalla than in Foursquare. *ARMF* and *ASMF* have different performance in two datasets which is consistent with performance of *WRMF* and *BPR*. Their similar performance in Gowalla is due to the much more evident spatial clustering phenomenon. Two approaches to learn potential locations perform similarly. But *LA* is more efficient than *RW* because it does not require any matrix operation. In addition, the better performance of our models in Gowalla than in Foursquare is for the sake of (1) the stronger correlation in Gowalla which is reflected in Figure 2(c) and Figure 2(d), and (2) the more detailed category in Gowalla than in Foursquare, where Gowalla has 262 kinds of categories while Foursquare only has 10 different categories.

5.4.2 Performance of New POI Recommendation

In this section, we evaluate the model performance of addressing location cold-start problem. To recommend new locations, we predict the check-in probability for each new location and then recommend the top-K locations with the highest probabilities. Note that, among all the baseline methods, only *USG* and *IRenMF* can be applied here. Since new locations are never checked-in by any users, *USG* is reduced to only model the geographical influence. In addition, the latent location vectors for new locations are not learned in the training, so one user's preference for a new location in *IRenMF* model is actually dependent on her preferences for this location's neighborhoods. The model performance in terms of precision, recall and MAP is shown in Table 3.

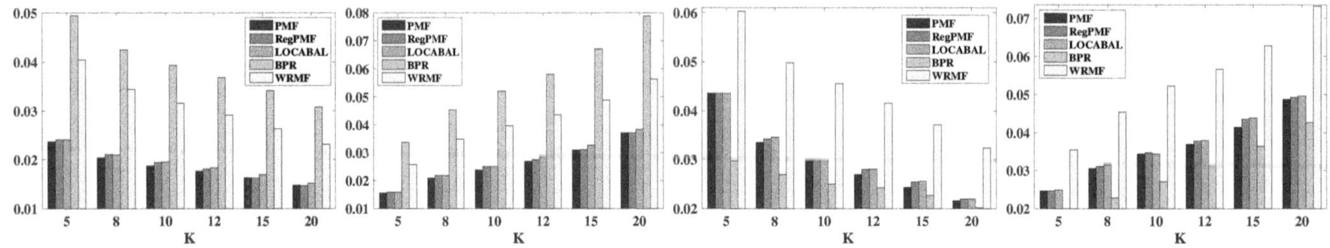

(a) Precision@K on Gowalla (b) Recall@K on Gowalla (c) Precision@K on Foursquare (d) Recall@K on Foursquare

Figure 3: The performance comparison of standard recommendation of basic methods for precision and recall.

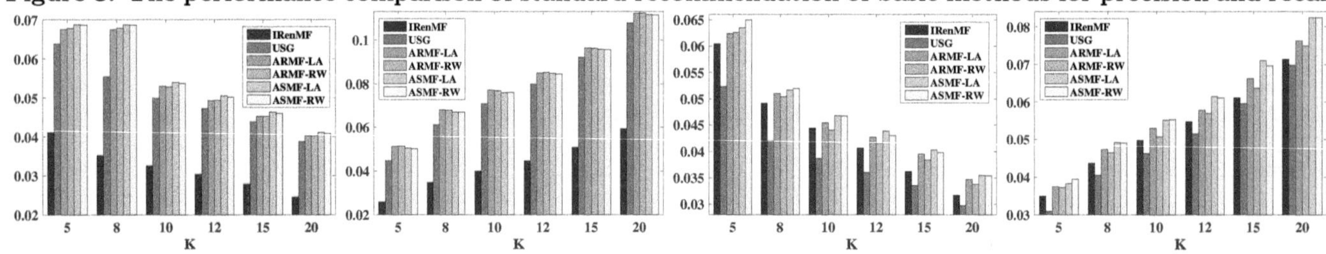

(a) Precision@K on Gowalla (b) Recall@K on Gowalla (c) Precision@K on Foursquare (d) Recall@K on Foursquare

Figure 4: The performance comparison of standard recommendation of our models and other models.

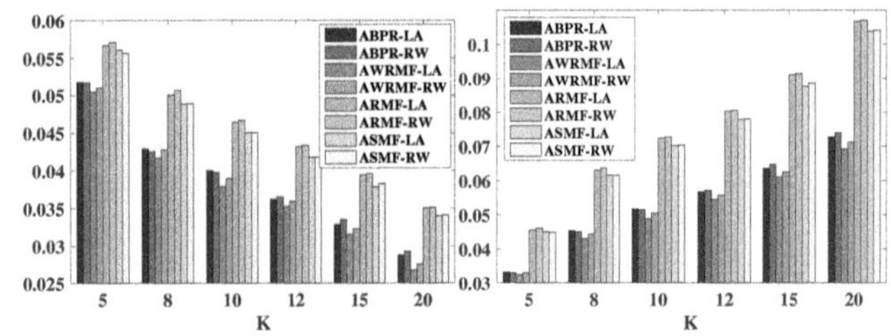

(a) Precision@K (b) Recall@K

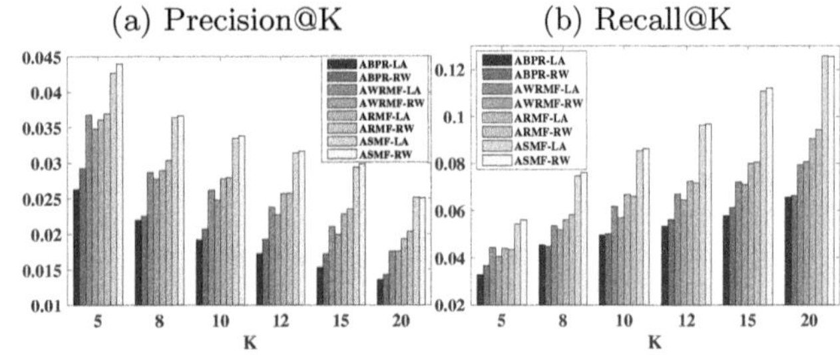

(c) Precision@K (d) Recall@K

Figure 5: The performance comparison of new user recommendation on Gowalla data set (top) and Fousquare data set(bottom).

Based on the results, we can observe that *IRenMF* performs the worst among all methods on both datasets. Although taking advantage of the similarities of neighboring locations, *IRenMF* fails to appropriately model user's check-in behaviours. It happens likely due to that it does not well exploit the inherent characteristics of geographical distance. On the other hand, our models and *USG* utilize the power-law distribution to capture the spatial clustering phenomenon for user's check-in activities, which is based on the observation over data. Therefore, they have much better performance than *IRrenMF* model in location cold-start recommendation. Also, our models gain superior performance over *USG*. A possible reason is that a user's preference latent vector has been learned in the training so that her preference on the target location's neighborhoods can be accurately predicted. However, *USG* only leverages the geographical similarity between a new location and her historical POIs as prediction. In addition, the performance of *ASMF* and *ARMF* is consistent with earlier experimental results.

5.4.3 Performance of New User Recommendation

In this section, we evaluate model's recommendation performance for user cold-start problem. When a new user enters the system, we do not have her historical check-in information. As a result, her latent vector cannot be learned and all of these baseline methods could not address this problem. The proposed models elaborate the historical check-ins of a user's neighboring friends (and social friends if she has) to learn her preference vector. Thus, they can be adopted to cope with user cold-start problem. As the proposed augmenting framework could be adapted to *WRMF* and *BPR* based models, we construct the following baseline methods with the similar loss functions in Eq.(18) and Eq.(11): (1) *WRMF+LA*, denoted as *AWRMF-LA*; (2) *WRMF+RW*, denoted as *AWRMF-RW*; (3) *BPR+LA*, denoted as *ABPR-LA*; (4) *BPR+RW*, denoted as *ABPR-RW*. The precision, recall and MAP of these models over two datasets are shown in Figure 5 and Table 4.

From the results, we find that all models have good performance to address user cold-start problem. The augmenting approach with friends' historical check-ins significantly benefits the location recommendation, in particular user cold-start recommendation. Meanwhile, the successful application of the augmenting strategy in *WRMF* and *BPR* demonstrates that the proposed augmenting strategy can be easily applied in any square error and ranking error based matrix factorization models. Moreover, our models perform much better than the baseline approaches for the sake of exploiting geographical influence and category information. *ARMF* and *ASMF* perform consistently as above results. Overall, we can see that our models can handle user cold-start problem very well.

5.4.4 Study of Influence of Parameter α

The *ASMF* model treats user's check-in as an indication of positive, potential and negative preference with difference confidence. The parameter α shown in Eq.(10) indicates the probability that users will check-in an unvisited location

Table 3: The performance comparison of new location recommendation.

	P@5	P@8	P@10	P@12	P@15	R@5	R@8	R@10	P@12	R@15	MAP
Gowalla Data Set											
ASMF-RW	0.08956	0.08543	0.08320	0.08095	0.07807	0.06032	0.08029	0.09259	0.10344	0.11883	0.08424
ASMF-LA	0.08967	0.08549	0.08323	0.08100	0.07807	0.06020	0.08035	0.09268	0.10353	0.11887	0.08430
ARMF-RW	0.09463	0.08946	0.08666	0.08401	0.08038	0.06457	0.08576	0.09822	0.10914	0.12437	0.08768
ARMF-LA	0.09456	0.08927	0.08643	0.08375	0.08022	0.06449	0.08564	0.09794	0.10901	0.12440	0.08766
USG	0.08632	0.07826	0.07407	0.07044	0.06587	0.05448	0.07645	0.08885	0.10007	0.11515	0.07578
IRenMF	0.00073	0.00094	0.00104	0.00113	0.00120	0.00033	0.00057	0.00079	0.00105	0.00140	0.00271
Foursquare Data Set											
ASMF-RW	0.04195	0.04276	0.04171	0.04144	0.04121	0.00419	0.00697	0.00843	0.01006	0.01247	0.02036
ASMF-LA	0.04171	0.04257	0.04230	0.04111	0.04116	0.00411	0.00680	0.00860	0.00992	0.01257	0.02040
ARMF-RW	0.04061	0.04085	0.04057	0.04052	0.04048	0.00382	0.00664	0.00823	0.00993	0.01296	0.02010
ARMF-LA	0.04022	0.04000	0.04002	0.03951	0.03949	0.00457	0.00701	0.00856	0.01017	0.01258	0.02051
USG	0.03551	0.03594	0.03452	0.03375	0.03301	0.00268	0.00561	0.00714	0.00886	0.01126	0.01592
IRenMF	0.00401	0.00339	0.00314	0.00304	0.00317	0.00038	0.00050	0.00055	0.00068	0.00108	0.00346

Table 4: The performance comparison of new user recommendation in terms of MAP.

Data Set	ASMF-RW	ASMF-LA	ARMF-RW	ARMF-LA	AWRMF-RW	AWRMF-LA	ABPR-RW	ABPR-LA
Gowalla	0.05442	0.05427	0.05589	0.05562	0.03021	0.02921	0.02423	0.02396
Foursquare	0.04831	0.04836	0.03770	0.03718	0.03242	0.03683	0.02971	0.02813

which her friends have checked-in before. In this section, we study the influence of variable α. Due to limited space, we only show the performance of *ASMF* model with *Linear Aggregation.* The precision, recall and MAP of *ASMF-LA* with different α value over two datasets are reported in Figure 6.

Based on the results, we can observe that the performance in all evaluation metrics has similar behaviour with the varying value of α. It is observed that *ASMF-LA* achieves the best performance when α is 0.3 and 0.1 on Gowalla and Foursquare, respectively. The performance then drops dramatically when α goes far away from the maximum point. If the α is set as a very small value, it will have no major difference to optimize those potential check-ins and other unobserved check-ins, which makes *ASMF-LA* difficult to obtain more accuracy prediction. If the α is set with a very large value, it will easily generate noise when optimizing both her own and friends' historical check-ins. It occurs possibly due to some other locations that a user's friends have checked-in but she might be in fact not interested in. As a result, α with a large value would probably affect the entire optimization process. Furthermore, the maximum point of α on Gowalla is larger than the one on Foursqaure, which indicates that users would have a larger chance to check-in their friends' POIs on Gowalla. This result is consistent with the observation that the correlation between users in Gowalla is much stronger than that in Foursquare. At last, we find that the performance with different α value on Gowalla changes much smaller than that on Foursquare. The more evident spatial clustering phenomenon on Gowalla than that on Foursquare is a reasonable explanation why *ASMF-LA* has such small change. On Gowalla dataset, geographical distance plays an extremely important role on affecting user's POI decision so that it compromises the prediction result even though user interest has a big change.

6. RELATED WORK

Related works about POI recommendation can be grouped into two categories. The first category focuses on modeling geographical influence [28, 3, 1, 30, 13, 14, 12, 15, 17]. Specifically, there are several approaches to model geographical distance. For example, some approaches leveraged Gaussian mixture model to characterize user's check-in activities [3, 1]; While some approaches utilized the kernel density estimation (KDE) to study user's check-in behavior and avoid employing a specific distribution[30, 13]. [28] proposed to use a power law distribution to estimate the check-in probability with the distance of any pair of visited POIs due to the spatial clustering phenomenon exhibited in LBSNs. The user's preference for one location is predicted by a linear model with combining users' interest, social friends' interests and geographical influence. Later, [15] considered two types of geographical neighborhood characteristics: instance level and region level. Specifically, in instance level, a user's preference for one location is modeled by a combination of her preference for this location and the nearest neighborhoods of this location. In region level, it places a group lasso penalty to learn location-specific latent vectors and capture the region effect.

The second category throws light on elaborating social network information [16, 5, 22, 28, 25, 4, 27, 7, 21, 9]. For example, [27, 28] proposed user-based collaborative filtering to estimate the unobserved rating by directly using the check-in information of friends. [16] assumed friends would share similar interests and then placed a social regularization term to constrain the objective functions for learning accurate user feature vectors. [5] proposed to model four types of social correlations (i.e., local friends, distant friends, local non-friends and distant non-friends) by using a geo-social correlation model with users' check-in activities, where the check-in probability was measured as a linear combination of these four geo-social correlations and the corresponding coefficients were learned by a group of features in a logistic regression like fashion. [22] modeled local and global social relations for all users. Specifically, in local context, it models the correlation between users and their friends; while in global context, it uses the reputation of a user in the whole social network as weight to fit observed ratings.

In addition, there are some recommendation works based on content, sentiments and temporal effect [10, 14, 26, 17, 29, 31]. However, our work is different from these existing works. To be specific, we first learn user's potential locations with the check-in information of social friends, location friends and neighboring friends, and then incorporate them into matrix factorization model using different error loss functions.

7. CONCLUSION

In this paper, we proposed a two-step framework for POI recommendation problem, which considers the check-in information of three types of friends, i.e., social friends, loca-

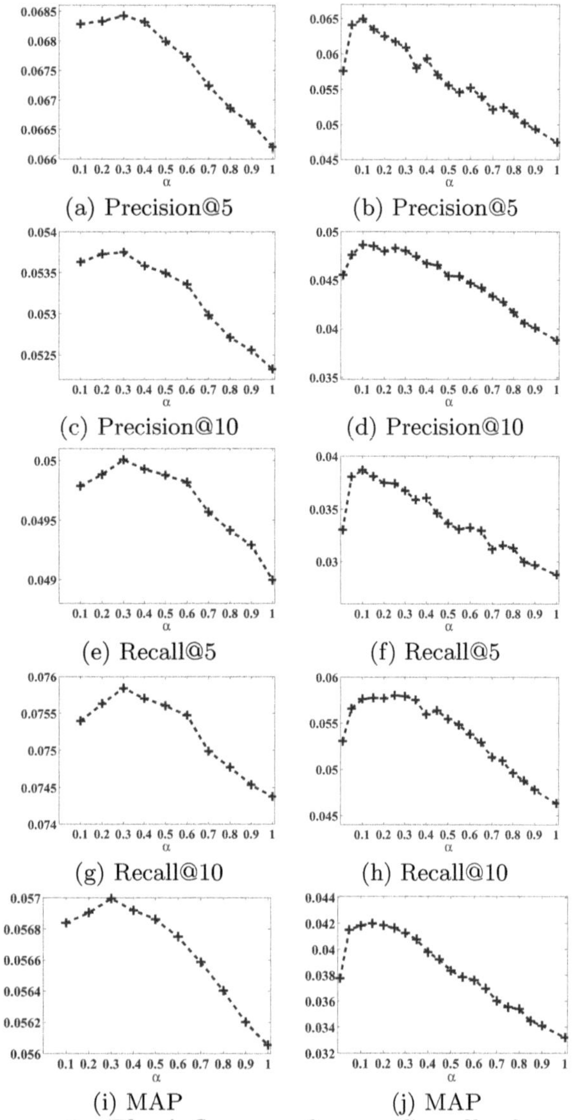

Figure 6: The influence of α on Gowalla data set (left) and Foursquare data set (right).

tion friends and neighboring friends. Specifically, in the first step, we designed two approaches to learn the locations that a user's friends had checked-in before and she was most interested in. In the second step, we developed matrix factorization based models with two different error loss functions using the learned potential locations. Specifically, the square error based loss extended a binary preference to a ternary variable for the observed check-ins, potential check-ins and other unobserved check-ins, and the ranking error based loss modeled the ranking of user's preference for her visited locations, potential locations, and unvisited locations. Finally, experimental results on two real-world data sets clearly validated the improvement of our models over many baseline methods based on different validation metrics.

Acknowledgments

This work is partially supported by NIH (1R21AA023975-01) and NSFC (71571093, 71372188, 61572032).

8. REFERENCES

[1] C. Cheng, H. Yang, I. King, and M. R. Lyu. Fused matrix factorization with geographical and social influence in location-based social networks. In *AAAI*, 2012.

[2] Z. Cheng, J. Caverlee, K. Lee, and D. Z. Sui. Exploring millions of footprints in location sharing services. In *ICWSM*, 2011.

[3] E. Cho, S. A. Myers, and J. Leskovec. Friendship and mobility: User movement in location-based social networks. In *KDD*, pages 1082–1090, 2011.

[4] H. Gao, J. Tang, and H. Liu. Exploring social-historical ties on location-based social networks. In *ICWSM*, 2012.

[5] H. Gao, J. Tang, and H. Liu. gscorr: Modeling geo-social correlations for new check-ins on location-based social networks. In *CIKM*, pages 1582–1586, 2012.

[6] Y. Hu, Y. Koren, and C. Volinsky. Collaborative filtering for implicit feedback datasets. In *ICDM*, pages 263–272, 2008.

[7] I. Konstas, V. Stathopoulos, and J. M. Jose. On social networks and collaborative recommendation. In *SIGIR*, 2009.

[8] Y. Koren, R. Bell, and C. Volinsky. Matrix factorization techniques for recommender systems, 2009.

[9] H. Li, R. Hong, S. Zhu, and Y. Ge. Point-of-interest recommender systems: A separate-space perspective. In *ICDM*, pages 231–240, 2015.

[10] H. Li, Z. W. Richang Hong, and Y. Ge. A spatial-temporal probabilistic matrix factorization model for point-of-interest recommendation. In *SDM*, pages 117–125, 2016.

[11] H. Li, H. Zhu, Y. Ge, Y. Fu, and Y. Ge. Personalized TV recommendation with mixture probabilistic matrix factorization. In *SDM*, pages 352–360, 2015.

[12] D. Lian, C. Zhao, X. Xie, G. Sun, E. Chen, and Y. Rui. Geomf: Joint geographical modeling and matrix factorization for point-of-interest recommendation. In *KDD*, 2014.

[13] M. Lichman and P. Smyth. Modeling human location data with mixture of kernel densities. In *KDD*, 2014.

[14] B. Liu, Y. Fu, Z. Yao, and H. Xiong. Learning geographical preferences for point-of-interest recommendation. In *KDD*, pages 1043–1051, 2013.

[15] Y. Liu, W. Wei, A. Sun, and C. Miao. Exploiting geographical neighborhood characteristics for location recommendation. In *CIKM*, pages 739–748, 2014.

[16] H. Ma, D. Zhou, C. Liu, M. R. Lyu, and I. King. Recommender systems with social regularization. In *WSDM*, 2011.

[17] QuanYuan, G. Cong, and A. Sun. Graph-based point-of-interest recommendation with geographical and temporal influences. In *CIKM*, pages 659–668, 2014.

[18] S. Rendle, C. Freudenthaler, Z. Gantner, and L. Schmidt-Thieme. Bpr: Bayesian personalized ranking from implicit feedback. In *UAI*, pages 452–461, 2009.

[19] S. Ruslan and M. Andriy. Bayesian probabilistic matrix factorization using markov chain monte carlo. In *ICML*, 2008.

[20] R. Salakhutdinov and A. Mnih. Probabilistic matrix factorization. In *NIPS*, pages 1257–1264, 2007.

[21] S. Scellato, A. Noulas, and C. Mascolo. Exploiting place features in link prediction on location-based social networks. In *KDD*, pages 1046–1054, 2011.

[22] J. Tang, X. Hu, H. Gao, and H. Liu. Exploiting local and global social context for recommendation. In *IJCAI*, 2013.

[23] W. Tobler. A computer movie simulating urban growth in the detroit region. *Economic Geography*, pages 234–240, 1970.

[24] H. Tong, C. Faloutsos, and J.-Y. Pan. Fast random walk with restart and its applications. In *ICDM*, pages 613–622, 2006.

[25] H. Wang, M. Terrovitis, and N. Mamoulis. Location recommendation in location-based social networks using user check-in data. In *SIGSPATIAL*, pages 374–383, 2013.

[26] D. Yang, D. Zhang, Z. Yu, and Z. Wang. A sentiment-enhanced personalized location recommendation system. In *HT*, 2013.

[27] M. Ye, P. Yin, and W.-C. Lee. Location recommendation for location-based social networks. In *GIS*, pages 458–461, 2010.

[28] M. Ye, P. Yin, W.-C. Lee, and D.-L. Lee. Exploiting geographical influence for collaborative point-of-interest recommendation. In *SIGIR*, pages 325–334, 2011.

[29] Z. Yu, H. Xu, Z. Yang, and B. Guo. Personalized travel package with multi-point-of-interest recommendation based on crowdsourced user footprints. *IEEE Trans. Human-Machine Systems*, 46(1):151–158, 2016.

[30] J. Zhang and C. Chow. igslr: Personalized geo-social location recommendation - a kernel density estimation approach. In *SIGSPATIAL*, pages 334–343, 2013.

[31] H. Zhu, E. Chen, H. Xiong, K. Yu, H. Cao, and J. Tian. Mining mobile user preferences for personalized context-aware recommendation. *ACM (TIST)*, 5(4):58:1–58:27, 2014.

QUINT: On Query-Specific Optimal Networks

Liangyue Li
Arizona State University
liangyue@asu.edu

Yuan Yao
Nanjing University
targenardy@gmail.com

Jie Tang
Tsinghua University
jietang@tsinghua.edu.cn

Wei Fan
Baidu Big Data Lab
fanwei03@baidu.com

Hanghang Tong
Arizona State University
hanghang.tong@asu.edu

ABSTRACT

Measuring node proximity on large scale networks is a fundamental building block in many application domains, ranging from computer vision, e-commerce, social networks, software engineering, disaster management to biology and epidemiology. The state of the art (e.g., random walk based methods) typically assumes the input network is *given* a priori, with the known network topology and the associated edge weights. A few recent works aim to further infer the *optimal edge weights* based on the side information.

This paper generalizes the challenge in multiple dimensions, aiming to learn optimal networks for node proximity measures. First (*optimization scope*), our proposed formulation explores a much larger parameter space, so that it is able to simultaneously infer the optimal network topology and the associated edge weights. This is important as a noisy or missing edge could greatly mislead the network node proximity measures. Second (*optimization granularity*), while all the existing works assume one common optimal network, be it given as the input or learned by the algorithms, exists for all queries, our method performs optimization at a much finer granularity, essentially being able to infer an optimal network that is specific to a given query. Third (*optimization efficiency*), we carefully design our algorithms with a linear complexity wrt the neighborhood size of the user preference set. We perform extensive empirical evaluations on a diverse set of 10+ real networks, which show that the proposed algorithms (1) consistently outperform the existing methods on *all* six commonly used metrics; (2) empirically scale *sub-linearly* to billion-scale networks and (3) respond in a fraction of a second.

Keywords

Node proximity; Optimal networks

KDD '16, August 13-17, 2016, San Francisco, CA, USA

DOI: http://dx.doi.org/10.1145/2939672.2939768

1. INTRODUCTION

Measuring node proximity (i.e., similarity/relevance) on large scale networks is a fundamental building block in many application domains, ranging from computer vision [23], e-commerce [10, 9], social networks [28, 29], software engineering [27], disaster management [41] to biology [22] and epidemiology [31].

The state of the art has mainly focused on best leveraging the network topology for measuring node proximity. Among others, a prevalent choice for node proximity is random walk based methods (e.g., random walk with restart and many of its variants - see Section 5 for a review), largely due to its flexibility in summarizing multiple weighted relationships between nodes. These methods typically assume the input network is *given* a priori, with the *known*, whether static or dynamic, network topology and the associated edge weights. A few recent works aim to further infer the *optimal edge weights* based on the side information (e.g., user feedback, node/edge attribute information). Representative works include supervised random walk (SRW) [5] and learning to rank methods [2, 3]. Moreover, an implicit assumption behind these existing works is that *one* common (optimal) network, be it given a priori or learned by the algorithms, exists for all queries. Despite much progress has been made, several algorithmic questions have largely remained nascent.

Q1 *Optimal weights or optimal topology?* Both supervised random walks and learning to rank methods assume the topology of the input network is given and fixed. Yet, both the edge weights and the network topology could affect the proximity measures. More often than not, a noisy or missing edge could largely mislead random walks, and thus lead to sub-optimal proximity measures. On the other hand, almost any real-world network is incomplete and/or noisy [15]. How can we design an algorithm that is able to simultaneously learn the optimal network topology as well as the associated edge weights, to better measure node proximity?

Q2 *One-fits-all, or one-fits-one?* Most, if not all, of the existing works implicitly assume there exists *one* common optimal network for measuring node proximity for all the queries. From the optimization perspective, such a *one-(network)-fits-all-(queries)* assumption might be sub-optimal. How can we optimize the input network at the finer granularity, to learn a query-specific network for a given query (i.e., *one-(network)-fits-one-(query)*)?

Q3 *Offline learning or online learning?* Even if we restrict ourselves to only learning the optimal weights for only one single network, it is already a computationally intensive procedure. For example, both supervised random walks and learning to rank methods rely on a costly iterative sub-routine to compute a single gradient vector (a key step in these methods), and consequently the learning process has to be conducted in the off-line stage. The answers to Q1 and Q2 would further intensify the computational challenge. For Q1 (i.e., to learn the optimal network topology), it would require to significantly expand the parameter space to $O(n^2)$, where n is the number of the nodes in the network. For Q2 (i.e., to learn one network for one query), it would require to learn many networks (i.e., one network for one query), and to conduct learning in the on-line query stage. How can we design an effective on-line learning algorithm that simultaneously fulfills both Q1 and Q2, and in the meanwhile scales to billion-scale networks and responds in (near-)real time?

We aim to answer all these questions in this paper. First (*for Q1 - optimizaiton scope*), our proposed formulation explores a much larger parameter space, so that it is able to simultaneously infer the optimal network topology and the associated edge weights. Second (*for Q2 - optimization granularity*), while all the existing works assume there is one common optimal network for all queries, our method performs optimization at a much finer granularity, essentially being able to infer a (different) optimal network that is specific to a given query. Third (*for Q3 - optimization efficiency*), we carefully design our algorithms with a linear complexity wrt the neighborhood size of the user preference sets, which is often sub-linear wrt the size of the input network. Our main contributions can be summarized as follows:

- **Paradigm Shift:** we go beyond the two fundamental assumptions (i.e., Q1 and Q2) and introduce two new design objectives for node proximity measures, including (D1) to simultaneously learn the optimal topology and the associated edge weights, and (D2) to learn an optimal network for a given query node (i.e., one-network-fits-one-query).
- **Algorithms and Analysis:** we propose an optimization based approach to fulfill the two design objectives, and further develop a family of effective and efficient algorithms to solve it, including an on-line algorithm with a linear complexity wrt the neighborhood size of the user preference sets.
- **Empirical Evaluations:** we conduct extensive experiments on a diverse set of 10+ real networks and demonstrate that our algorithms (1) consistently outperform all existing methods on six commonly used evaluation metrics, (2) empirically scale *sub-linearly* to billion-scale networks and (3) respond in a fraction of a second.

The rest of the paper is organized as follows. Section 2 formally defines the query-specific optimal network learning problem. Section 3 introduces the proposed algorithms.

Table 1: Symbols

Symbols	Definition
$\mathbf{G} = (\mathbf{V}, \mathbf{E})$	a network
$\mathbf{A}$	adjacency matrix of the input network
$\mathbf{A}_s$	adjacency matrix of the learned optimal network
s	query node
$\mathbf{r}_s$	ranking vector for node s
$\mathcal{P} = \{x_1, x_2, \ldots, x_p\}$	set of positive nodes
$\mathcal{N} = \{y_1, y_2, \ldots, y_l\}$	set of negative nodes
$g(\cdot)$	loss function
n	number of nodes in the network
m	number of edges in the network
c	decay factor in random walks
b	margin in the loss function
λ, β	trade-off parameters

Section 4 presents the empirical evaluation results. After reviewing related work in Section 5, we conclude the paper in Section 6.

2. PROBLEM DEFINITION AND PRELIMINEARIES

In this section, we present the notations used throughout the paper (summarized in Table 1), formally define the query-specific optimal network learning problem and then give preliminaries on random walk based methods for node proximity.

2.1 Problem Definitions

We use bold upper-case letters for matrices (e.g., $\mathbf{A}$), bold lowercase letters for vectors (e.g., $\mathbf{v}$), and lowercase letters (e.g., α) for scalars. For matrix indexing, we use a convention similar to Matlab as follows. We use $\mathbf{A}(i, j)$ to denote the entry at the intersection of the i-th row and j-th column of matrix $\mathbf{A}$, $\mathbf{A}(i, :)$ to denote the i-th row of $\mathbf{A}$ and $\mathbf{A}(:, j)$ to denote the j-th column of $\mathbf{A}$. Besides, we use prime for matrix transpose (e.g., $\mathbf{A}'$ is the transpose of $\mathbf{A}$).

In our problem setting, we are given a network which is represented by an $n \times n$ normalized adjacency matrix, which has m non-zero elements (i.e., edges). As mentioned earlier, there is often rich information from user provided feedback/preference in some applications [32, 3]. For a user s, s/he could explicitly indicate some nodes that s/he wants to connect with, defined as *positive nodes*, and some other nodes that s/he wants to avoid, defined as *negative nodes*. We use the positive set $\mathcal{P} = \{x_1, x_2, \ldots, x_p\}$ to denote the set of positive nodes, i.e., s likes nodes x_i. Similarly, we use the negative set $\mathcal{N} = \{y_1, y_2, \ldots, y_l\}$ to denote the set of negative nodes, i.e., s dislikes y_i. See [5, 32] on how to select the positive and negative sets. Our goal is to learn an optimal network for this specific query node s, so that, when measured on the *learned network*, the proximities from s to the nodes in $\mathcal{P}$ and those in $\mathcal{N}$ match his/her preference. With these notations, the problem can be formally defined as follows:

PROBLEM 1. *Query-specific Optimal Network Learning*

Given: *a network with adjacency matrix* $\mathbf{A}$, *a query node* s, *positive node set* $\mathcal{P}$ *and negative node set* $\mathcal{N}$.

Learn: *an optimal network* $\mathbf{A}_s$ *specific to the query* s.

2.2 Preliminaries

Random walk based methods (such as random walk with restart [30] and many of its variants) have been a prevalent choice for proximity measures. Here, we present a brief summarization of random walk with restart (RWR), which is the base of our proposed methods. Please refer to Section 5 for detailed review of node proximity measures. For a given network $\mathbf{G}$, RWR works as follows. Consider a random surfer that starts from the node s. At each step, the random surfer has two options: (1) transmits to one of its neighbors with probability proportional to the edge weights; or (2) jumps back to the starting node s with a restart probability $(1-c)$. The proximity score from node s to node i is defined as the steady state probability r_{si} that the random surfer will visit node i. Define the ranking vector $\mathbf{r}_s$ for node s as the vector of proximity scores from node s to all the nodes on the network, RWR recursively computes the ranking vector as follows:

$$\mathbf{r}_s = c\mathbf{A}\mathbf{r}_s + (1-c)\mathbf{e}_s, \tag{1}$$

where $\mathbf{A}$ is the adjacency matrix of the network $\mathbf{G}$ and $\mathbf{e}_s$ is a vector of all zeros except 1 at the s-th position.

The ranking vector $\mathbf{r}_s$ can also be computed in the following closed form: $\mathbf{r}_s = (1-c)(\mathbf{I} - c\mathbf{A})^{-1}\mathbf{e}_s$. Let $\mathbf{Q} = (\mathbf{I} - c\mathbf{A})^{-1}$, we can see that $\mathbf{r}_s$ is the s-th column of $\mathbf{Q}$ with some constant scaling. In other words, we can regard the element $\mathbf{Q}(i,j)$ as the (scaled) proximity score from node j to node i. For the normalized matrix $\mathbf{A}$, it is often chosen as the stochastic matrix of the input network. Nonetheless, from the algorithmic perspective, we can also choose other forms to normalize $\mathbf{A}$, e.g., the so-called normalized graph laplacian [42]. In fact, as long as the leading eigenvalue of $\mathbf{A}$ is less than $1/c$, we can show that Eq. (1) always converges to its closed-form solution. Having this in mind, we will remove this constraint (i.e., $\mathbf{A}$ being a stochastic matrix) to simplify the proposed algorithms. We will also discuss how to impose such a constraint if the stochastic matrix is indeed a desired output in some applications.

3. PROPOSED ALGORITHMS

In this section, we present our algorithm, QUINT, to learn a QUery-specific optImal NeTwork (i.e. Problem 1). We first introduce the proposed formulations and give optimization solutions, followed up with scalable algorithms and some variants.

3.1 QUINT - Formulations

Given the input network with the adjacency matrix $\mathbf{A}$, and a query node s along with its associated positive node set $\mathcal{P}$ and negative node set $\mathcal{N}$, we want to learn an optimal network with adjacency matrix $\mathbf{A}_s$ such that the proximity from s to positive nodes in $\mathcal{P}$ and negative nodes in $\mathcal{N}$ matches the preference. The key ideas behind our proposed formulations can be summarized as follows. First, we want to avoid that the learned network $\mathbf{A}_s$ deviates too far from the input network $\mathbf{A}$. Second, on the *learned* network $\mathbf{A}_s$, the measured proximity should match the user preference. That is, if we compute the ranking vector $\mathbf{r}_s$ for s using the learned adjacency matrix $\mathbf{A}_s$, the proximity from s to any positive node in $\mathcal{P}$ is greater than to any negative node in $\mathcal{N}$, i.e., $\mathbf{r}_s(x) > \mathbf{r}_s(y), \forall x \in \mathcal{P}, \forall y \in \mathcal{N}$. Based on the above intuition, we propose the following formulation to learn a query-specific network:

$$\begin{aligned} \arg\min_{\mathbf{A}_s} \quad & \|\mathbf{A}_s - \mathbf{A}\|_F^2 \\ \text{s.t.,} \quad & \mathbf{Q}(x,s) > \mathbf{Q}(y,s), \forall x \in \mathcal{P}, \forall y \in \mathcal{N}, \end{aligned} \tag{2}$$

where $\mathbf{Q} = (\mathbf{I} - c\mathbf{A}_s)^{-1}$ contains the pairwise node proximities on the learned network. In Eq. (2), the objective function states that the distance from the learned network adjacency matrix $\mathbf{A}_s$ to the original network $\mathbf{A}$ measured by Frobenius norm should be minimized; while in the constraint, we want the proximity from node s to any positive node in $\mathcal{P}$ to be greater than to any negative node in $\mathcal{N}$. This is a hard constraint as we do not allow any exception. In practice, the constraint might not be satisfied by all the possible pairs of positive and negative nodes. Instead, we can relax the constraint and introduce some penalization if violations occur. This relaxed soft version can be formulated as follows:

$$\arg\min_{\mathbf{A}_s} \mathcal{L}(\mathbf{A}_s) = \lambda\|\mathbf{A}_s - \mathbf{A}\|_F^2 + \sum_{x\in\mathcal{P}, y\in\mathcal{N}} g(\mathbf{Q}(y,s) - \mathbf{Q}(x,s)), \tag{3}$$

where λ is the trade-off parameter that balances between the adjacency matrices difference and constraint violations. To penalize the constraint violations, we introduce the loss function $g(\cdot)$. Ideally, we want $\mathbf{Q}(y,s) < \mathbf{Q}(x,s)$. Hence, if $\mathbf{Q}(y,s) < \mathbf{Q}(x,s)$, i.e., the constraint is not violated, then $g(\cdot) = 0$; otherwise if $\mathbf{Q}(y,s) > \mathbf{Q}(x,s)$, then $g(\cdot) > 0$ to penalize such a violation. In the paper, we consider the Wilcoxon-Mann-Whitney (WMW) loss [35] with width b, which is differentiable and was originally proposed to optimize the area under the ROC curve (AUC):

$$g(x) = \frac{1}{1 + exp(-x/b)}.$$

Remarks: The formulation in Eq. (3) bears a high-level resemblance to the supervised random walks (SRW) [5] in terms of the way they encode the user preference. Nonetheless, there are several subtle differences between them. First, we explore a much larger parameter space in the order of $O(n^2)$, whereas SRW only searches in a d-dimensional vector space, where d is the length of the feature vector. The potential benefit is that we are able to search for both the optimal topology and the associated edge weights. Second, our formulation is tailored for a specific query node, and thus is potentially able to learn an optimal network for that specific query (instead of one universal network for all the queries). Third, in our formulation, we drop the typical constraint that requires the learned network $\mathbf{A}_s$ to be a stochastic matrix. We find that such a relaxation will greatly ease the optimization algorithm, without a noticeable empirical performance degradation. For readers who are interested in keeping this constraint in our formulation, we will present a variant to do so in Section 3.4.3.

3.2 QUINT - Optimization Solutions

The objective function in Eq. (3) is non-convex. We aim to solve it using gradient descent based methods by first calculating the derivative of $\mathcal{L}(\mathbf{A}_s)$ w.r.t. $\mathbf{A}_s$ and then updating the adjacency matrix $\mathbf{A}_s$ along the negative direction of the derivative.

The derivative of $\mathcal{L}(\mathbf{A}_s)$ w.r.t. $\mathbf{A}_s$ can be written as fol-

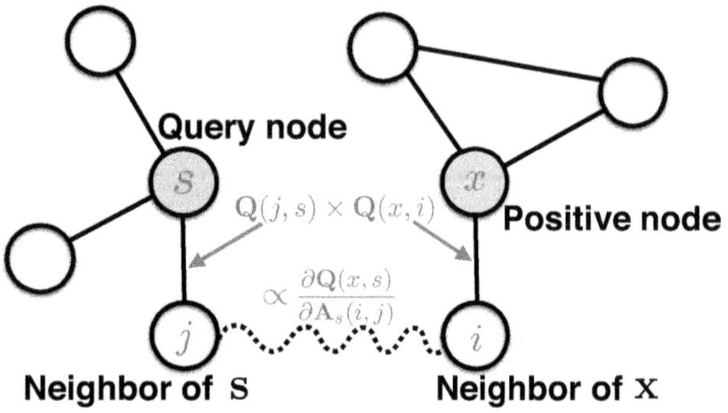

Figure 1: Update on $\mathbf{A}_s(i,j)$.

lows:

$$\begin{aligned}\frac{\partial \mathcal{L}(\mathbf{A}_s)}{\partial \mathbf{A}_s} &= 2\lambda(\mathbf{A}_s - \mathbf{A}) + \sum_{x\in\mathcal{P}, y\in\mathcal{N}} \frac{\partial g(\mathbf{Q}(y,s)-\mathbf{Q}(x,s))}{\partial \mathbf{A}_s} \\ &= 2\lambda(\mathbf{A}_s - \mathbf{A}) + \sum_{x,y} \frac{\partial g(d_{yx})}{\partial d_{yx}} \Big(\frac{\partial \mathbf{Q}(y,s)}{\partial \mathbf{A}_s} - \frac{\partial \mathbf{Q}(x,s)}{\partial \mathbf{A}_s}\Big),\end{aligned} \tag{4}$$

where we denote $d_{yx} = \mathbf{Q}(y,s) - \mathbf{Q}(x,s)$ and we apply chain rule in the second step. The WMW loss function is differentiable and its derivative is computed as: $\frac{\partial g(d_{yx})}{\partial d_{yx}} = \frac{1}{b} g(d_{yx})(1 - g(d_{yx}))$. To compute the derivative of $\frac{\partial \mathbf{Q}(y,s)}{\partial \mathbf{A}_s}$ is more involved, since $\mathbf{Q}$ is an inverse of a matrix, which itself is a function of $\mathbf{A}_s$.

From the basic identity for derivatives of a matrix inverse [24], we have that:

$$\frac{\partial \mathbf{Q}}{\partial \mathbf{A}_s(i,j)} = -\mathbf{Q}\frac{\partial (\mathbf{I} - c\mathbf{A}_s)}{\partial \mathbf{A}_s(i,j)}\mathbf{Q} = c\mathbf{Q}\mathbf{J}^{ij}\mathbf{Q}, \tag{5}$$

where $1 \le i \le n$, $1 \le j \le n$, and $\mathbf{J}^{i,j}$ is a single-entry matrix with $\mathbf{J}(i,j) = 1$ and zeros everywhere else.

Based on the above equation, we have that

$$\frac{\partial \mathbf{Q}(x,s)}{\partial \mathbf{A}_s(i,j)} = c\mathbf{Q}(x,i)\mathbf{Q}(j,s). \tag{6}$$

The intuition behind the formulation is that the update to $\mathbf{A}_s(i,j)$ is proportional to the product of the proximity from i to x and the proximity from s to j. In other words, if i is a close neighbor of x (i.e., large $\mathbf{Q}(x,i)$) and j is a close neighbor of s (i.e., large $\mathbf{Q}(j,s)$), as illustrated in Figure 1, then $\mathbf{A}_s(i,j)$ will have a relatively large update. This makes sense since a larger increase on $\mathbf{A}_s(i,j)$ (i.e., a pair of close neighbors of the query node s and a positive node x, respectively) will increase the chance of reaching x from s by random walks (i.e., increasing $\mathbf{Q}(x,s)$ measured on the updated adjacency matrix $\mathbf{A}_s$).

Following this, we can compute the derivative of $\frac{\partial \mathbf{Q}(x,s)}{\partial \mathbf{A}}$ as:

$$\frac{\partial \mathbf{Q}(x,s)}{\partial \mathbf{A}_s} = c[\mathbf{Q}(x,i)\mathbf{Q}(j,s)]_{1\le i\le n, 1\le j\le n} = c\mathbf{Q}(x,:)'\mathbf{Q}(:,s)'. \tag{7}$$

Similarly, the derivative of $\frac{\partial \mathbf{Q}(y,s)}{\partial \mathbf{A}_s}$ can be computed as:

$$\frac{\partial \mathbf{Q}(y,s)}{\partial \mathbf{A}_s} = c\mathbf{Q}(y,:)'\mathbf{Q}(:,s)'. \tag{8}$$

Therefore, the derivative of $\mathcal{L}(\mathbf{A}_s)$ w.r.t. $\mathbf{A}_s$ can be rewritten as follows:

$$\begin{aligned}\frac{\partial \mathcal{L}(\mathbf{A}_s)}{\partial \mathbf{A}_s} &= 2\lambda(\mathbf{A}_s - \mathbf{A}) + \sum_{x,y} \frac{\partial g(d_{yx})}{\partial d_{yx}} \Big(\frac{\partial \mathbf{Q}(y,s)}{\partial \mathbf{A}_s} - \frac{\partial \mathbf{Q}(x,s)}{\partial \mathbf{A}_s}\Big) \\ &= 2\lambda(\mathbf{A}_s - \mathbf{A}) + \sum_{x,y} c\frac{\partial g(d_{yx})}{\partial d_{yx}} (\mathbf{Q}(y,:)' - \mathbf{Q}(x,:)')\mathbf{Q}(:,s)'.\end{aligned} \tag{9}$$

The above optimization solution for the query-specific network learning is summarized in Algorithm 1. From the algorithm we can see that, we not only update the weights of existing edges, but might also add an unseen edge and/or remove a noisy edge during the update (i.e., changing the original topology).

Algorithm 1 QUINT– Learning a Query-Specific Optimal Network

Input: (1) the initial network adjacency matrix $\mathbf{A}$,
(2) a query node s,
(3) a positive node set $\mathcal{P}$
(4) a negative node set $\mathcal{N}$
(5) parameters c, λ, b, and step size η.
Output: The adjacency matrix $\mathbf{A}_s$ of the optimal network specific to query s.
1: Initialize $\mathbf{A}_s = \mathbf{A}$;
2: **while** not converged **do**
3:   **for** each positive node x from $\mathcal{P}$ **do**
4:     **for** each negative node y from $\mathcal{N}$ **do**
5:       Compute $\mathbf{Q}(:,s)$, $\mathbf{Q}(y,:)$ and $\mathbf{Q}(x,:)$;
6:       Compute $c\frac{\partial g(d_{yx})}{\partial d_{yx}}(\mathbf{Q}(y,:)' - \mathbf{Q}(x,:)')\mathbf{Q}(:,s)'$;
7:     **end for**
8:   **end for**
9:   Compute the derivative $\frac{\partial \mathcal{L}(\mathbf{A}_s)}{\partial \mathbf{A}_s}$ by Eq (9);
10:   Update $\mathbf{A}_s = \mathbf{A}_s - \eta \cdot \frac{\partial \mathcal{L}(\mathbf{A}_s)}{\partial \mathbf{A}_s}$;
11: **end while**
12: **return** the learned network adjacency matrix $\mathbf{A}_s$;

We summarize complexities of Algorithm 1 in Theorem 1.

THEOREM 1. *(Time and Space Complexities of Algorithm 1). Algorithm 1 takes $O(T_1|\mathcal{P}|\cdot|\mathcal{N}|(T_2m+n^2))$ time, where T_1 is the number of iterations to convergence, and T_2 is the number of iterations in the power method for computing ranking vector. It takes additional $O(n^2)$ space.*

PROOF. The inner loop, line 5 and line 6, is executed $|\mathcal{P}|\cdot|\mathcal{N}|$ times. For line 5, it would be too expensive ($O(n^3)$) to first compute $\mathbf{Q} = (\mathbf{I} - c\mathbf{A}_s)^{-1}$. Instead, we can use power method to extract the corresponding column of $\mathbf{Q}$ by Eq. (1) and this line would take $O(T_2m)$ time, where T_2 is the number of iterations in the power method and m is the number of edges. Line 6 involves a multiplication of a column vector and a row vector, which would take $O(n^2)$. As a result, the overall time complexity is $O(T_1|\mathcal{P}|\cdot|\mathcal{N}|(T_2m + n^2))$, where T_1 is the number of iterations to convergence. The two vectors in the multiplication are dense and their multiplication would result in an $n \times n$ dense matrix, taking $O(n^2)$ additional space. □

3.3 QUINT - Scale-up for Online Queries

To learn an optimal network for one query using Algorithm 1, it would take $O(T_1|\mathcal{P}|\cdot|\mathcal{N}|(T_2m + n^2))$, which is not scalable to large real network data (usually in the order of millions or billions of nodes/edges), not to mention that it practically eliminates the possibility to conduct learning in on-line stage. In this subsection, we introduce an effective on-line algorithm to learn the optimal network for each query. The key idea behind the fast solution is that the optimal network can be approximated by a rank-one perturbation to the original network. If we observe more closely at the derivative of $\mathcal{L}(\mathbf{A}_s)$ w.r.t. $\mathbf{A}_s$ in Eq. (9), the second term (the summation over x and y) is exactly a matrix of rank one for a specific query.

Following the rank-one perturbation assumption, we can approximate the optimal network as $\mathbf{A}_s = \mathbf{A} + \mathbf{f}\mathbf{g}'$, where $\mathbf{f}$ and $\mathbf{g}$ are n-dimensional vectors we want to learn. Having this, we can formulate our optimal network learning with rank-one perturbation as follows:

$$\begin{aligned} \arg\min_{\mathbf{f},\mathbf{g}} \mathcal{L}(\mathbf{f},\mathbf{g}) &= \lambda\|\mathbf{f}\mathbf{g}'\|_F^2 + \beta(\|\mathbf{f}\|^2 + \|\mathbf{g}\|^2) \\ &+ \sum_{x\in\mathcal{P},y\in\mathcal{N}} g(\mathbf{Q}(y,s) - \mathbf{Q}(x,s)), \end{aligned} \quad (10)$$

where λ and β are the trade-off parameters. Notice that in this formulation, $\mathbf{Q} = (\mathbf{I} - c\mathbf{A} - c\mathbf{f}\mathbf{g}')^{-1}$ is a function of both $\mathbf{f}$ and $\mathbf{g}$.

We apply an alternating strategy to solve the above formulation. Let us first fix $\mathbf{g}$ and solve for $\mathbf{f}$. The derivative of $\mathcal{L}(\mathbf{f})$ w.r.t. $\mathbf{f}$ can be written as follows:

$$\begin{aligned} \frac{\partial\mathcal{L}(\mathbf{f})}{\partial\mathbf{f}} &= 2\lambda\mathbf{f}\mathbf{g}'\mathbf{g} + 2\beta\mathbf{f} + \sum_{x\in\mathcal{P},y\in\mathcal{N}} \frac{\partial g(\mathbf{Q}(y,s)-\mathbf{Q}(x,s))}{\partial\mathbf{f}} \\ &= 2\lambda\mathbf{f}\mathbf{g}'\mathbf{g} + 2\beta\mathbf{f} + \sum_{x,y} \frac{\partial g(d_{yx})}{\partial d_{yx}}\left(\frac{\partial\mathbf{Q}(y,s)}{\partial\mathbf{f}} - \frac{\partial\mathbf{Q}(x,s)}{\partial\mathbf{f}}\right), \end{aligned} \quad (11)$$

where we denote $d_{yx} = \mathbf{Q}(y,s) - \mathbf{Q}(x,s)$. The question now becomes how to compute the derivative $\frac{\partial\mathbf{Q}(x,s)}{\partial\mathbf{f}}$.

Again, according to the basic identity for derivative of a matrix inverse, we have the following:

$$\frac{\partial\mathbf{Q}}{\partial\mathbf{f}(i)} = -\mathbf{Q}\frac{\partial(\mathbf{I} - c\mathbf{A} - c\mathbf{f}\mathbf{g}')}{\partial\mathbf{f}(i)}\mathbf{Q} = c\mathbf{Q}\mathbf{e}_i\mathbf{g}'\mathbf{Q}. \quad (12)$$

Following this, we obtain

$$\frac{\partial\mathbf{Q}(x,s)}{\partial\mathbf{f}(i)} = c\mathbf{Q}(x,i)\mathbf{Q}(:,s)'\mathbf{g}. \quad (13)$$

Now, we can compute the derivative $\frac{\partial\mathbf{Q}(x,s)}{\partial\mathbf{f}}$ as follows:

$$\frac{\partial\mathbf{Q}(x,s)}{\partial\mathbf{f}} = c[\mathbf{Q}(x,i)\mathbf{Q}(:,s)'\mathbf{g}]_{1\le i\le n} = c\mathbf{Q}(x,:)'\mathbf{Q}(:,s)'\mathbf{g}. \quad (14)$$

Therefore, the derivative of $\mathcal{L}(\mathbf{f})$ w.r.t. $\mathbf{f}$ can be computed as follows:

$$\begin{aligned} \frac{\mathcal{L}(\mathbf{f})}{\partial\mathbf{f}} &= 2\lambda\mathbf{f}\mathbf{g}'\mathbf{g} + 2\beta\mathbf{f} + \sum_{x,y} \frac{\partial g(d_{yx})}{\partial d_{yx}}\left(\frac{\partial\mathbf{Q}(y,s)}{\partial\mathbf{f}} - \frac{\partial\mathbf{Q}(x,s)}{\partial\mathbf{f}}\right) \\ &= 2\lambda\mathbf{f}\mathbf{g}'\mathbf{g} + 2\beta\mathbf{f} + \sum_{x,y} c\frac{\partial g(d_{yx})}{\partial d_{yx}}(\mathbf{Q}(y,:)' - \mathbf{Q}(x,:)')(\mathbf{Q}(:,s)'\mathbf{g}). \end{aligned} \quad (15)$$

The computation for the derivative of $\mathcal{L}(\mathbf{g})$ w.r.t. $\mathbf{g}$ is similar to Eq. (15) with $\mathbf{f}$ substituted with $\mathbf{g}$ and $\mathbf{g}$ substituted with $\mathbf{f}$.

We summarize the above optimization solution for optimal network learning with rank-one perturbation in Algorithm 2, along with its complexity analysis in Theorem 2.

THEOREM 2. *(Time and Space Complexities of Algorithm 2). Algorithm 2 takes $O(T_1|\mathcal{P}|\cdot|\mathcal{N}|(T_2 m+n))$ time, where T_1 is the number of iterations to convergence, and T_2 is the number of iterations in the power method for computing ranking vector. It takes additional $O(n)$ space.*

Algorithm 2 QUINT-rankOne – Learning a Query-Specific Optimal Network

Input: (1) the initial network adjacency matrix $\mathbf{A}$,
(2) a query node s,
(3) a positive node set $\mathcal{P}$
(4) a negative node set $\mathcal{N}$
(5) parameters c, λ, β, b, and step size η.
Output: The rank-one perturbation to the network $\mathbf{f}$ and $\mathbf{g}$.

1: Initialize $\mathbf{f}$ and $\mathbf{g}$;
2: **while** not converged **do**
3:   **for** each positive node x from $\mathcal{P}$ **do**
4:     **for** each negative node y from $\mathcal{N}$ **do**
5:       Compute $\mathbf{Q}(:,s)$, $\mathbf{Q}(y,:)$ and $\mathbf{Q}(x,:)$;
6:       Compute $c\frac{\partial g(d_{yx})}{\partial d_{yx}}(\mathbf{Q}(y,:)' - \mathbf{Q}(x,:)')(\mathbf{Q}(:,s)'\mathbf{g})$;
7:     **end for**
8:   **end for**
9:   Compute the derivative $\frac{\partial\mathcal{L}(\mathbf{f})}{\partial\mathbf{f}}$ by Eq (15);
10:   Compute the derivative $\frac{\partial\mathcal{L}(\mathbf{g})}{\partial\mathbf{g}}$;
11:   Update $\mathbf{f} = \mathbf{f} - \eta\cdot\frac{\partial\mathcal{L}(\mathbf{f})}{\partial\mathbf{f}}$;
12:   Update $\mathbf{g} = \mathbf{g} - \eta\cdot\frac{\partial\mathcal{L}(\mathbf{g})}{\partial\mathbf{g}}$;
13: **end while**
14: **return** the learned rank-one perturbations $\mathbf{f}$ and $\mathbf{g}$;

PROOF. The inner loop, line 5 and line 6, is executed $|\mathcal{P}|\cdot|\mathcal{N}|$ times. For line 5, we can use power method to extract the corresponding column of $\mathbf{Q}$ by Eq. (1) and this line would take $O(T_2 m)$ time, where T_2 is the number of iterations in the power method. Line 6 takes $O(n)$. As a result, the overall time complexity is $O(T_1|\mathcal{P}|\cdot|\mathcal{N}|(T_2 m+n))$, where T_1 is the number of iterations to convergence. The additional space takes $O(n)$, i.e., the length of the vectors. □

Remarks: The major computational overhead of Algorithm 2 comes from line 5 to extract certain columns of $\mathbf{Q}$, which leads to an $O(T_2 m)$ complexity. In the next subsection, we propose additional ways to further speed up the algorithm to scale linearly and even sub-linearly on n.

3.4 QUINT - Variants

In this subsection, we first provide several ways to further speed up the proposed algorithm to scale linearly and even sub-linearly; and then point out a way to satisfy stochasticity of the output and to learn the decay factor c in RWR.

3.4.1 Variant #1: Taylor Approximation for $\mathbf{Q}$

As we mentioned above, the major time complexity of Algorithm 2 is due to the extraction of certain columns of $\mathbf{Q}$ using the power method. In fact, we could approximate $\mathbf{Q}$ using Taylor approximation as follows:

$$\begin{aligned} \mathbf{Q} &= (\mathbf{I} - c\mathbf{A})^{-1} \\ &\approx \mathbf{I} + \textstyle\sum_{i=1}^{k} c^k\mathbf{A}^k. \end{aligned} \quad (16)$$

If we use first order Taylor approximation, i.e. $k = 1$ in Eq. (16), line 5 in Algorithm 2 would only take $O(n)$ instead of $O(T_2 m)$. Therefore, the overall time complexity of Algorithm 2 can be reduced to $O(T_1|\mathcal{P}|\cdot|\mathcal{N}|n)$.

3.4.2 Variant #2: Localized Rank-One Perturbation

It is often not necessary to update the global adjacency matrix, instead, we could focus on certain local zones in the network that will play a more important role to the proximities from the query node s.

In particular, we would update the local structure in the neighborhood of the query node as well as the neighborhood of the preference sets. Denote the neighborhood of node s (including s) by $\mathbb{N}(s) = \{z|(z,s) \in \mathbf{E}\} \cup \{s\}$ and denote the neighborhood of the positive and negative nodes by $\mathbb{N}(\mathcal{P},\mathcal{N}) = \{z|z \in \mathbb{N}(x) \text{ or } z \in \mathbb{N}(y), \forall x \in \mathcal{P}, \forall y \in \mathcal{N}\}$. When we update $\mathbf{f}$ using Eq. (15), we only need to update $\mathbf{f}(i), i \in \mathbb{N}(s)$. Similarly, when we update $\mathbf{g}$, we only need to update $\mathbf{g}(i), i \in \mathbb{N}(\mathcal{P},\mathcal{N})$. This will further bring down the time complexity of Algorithm 2 to $O(T_1|\mathcal{P}| \cdot |\mathcal{N}| \max(|\mathbb{N}(s)|, |\mathbb{N}(\mathcal{P},\mathcal{N})|))$ (Theorem 3).

THEOREM 3. *(Time Complexity of QUINT-rankOne with First-order Taylor Approximation and Localized Rank-One Perturbation.) If we use first-order Taylor approximation for $\mathbf{Q}$ and localized rank-one perturbation in QUINT-rankOne, it would take $O(T_1|\mathcal{P}| \cdot |\mathcal{N}| \max(|\mathbb{N}(s)|, |\mathbb{N}(\mathcal{P},\mathcal{N})|))$ to learn the optimal network.*

PROOF. Omitted for brevity. □

3.4.3 Variant #3: Stochastic Matrix $\mathbf{A}_s$

As mentioned earlier, we do not require the learned network $\mathbf{A}_s$ to be a stochastic matrix, which largely eases the optimization process. If a stochastic matrix is indeed the desired output network, we can naturally modify the proposed algorithms to fulfill it. To be specific, immediately following the gradient descent step in the proposed algorithms, we introduce a *simplex projection* operation for each column of $\mathbf{A}_s$ [33]. In this way, we ensure that matrix $\mathbf{A}_s$ is always a valid stochastic matrix. However, we do not observe a noticeable empirical improvement by the simplex projection operation, yet it introduces an additional $O(n^2 \log n)$ (since we need to do so for n columns) into the overall time complexity. Therefore, we do not recommend it in practice.

3.4.4 variant #4: Learning Decay Factor in RWR

An important parameter in RWR is the decay factor c, which is usually manually set. As a side product, our proposed methods naturally provide a way to learn the parameter c. In this setting, we assume the network structure $\mathbf{A}$ is known and fixed, and we have the following optimization formulation:

$$\arg\min_c \mathcal{L}(c) = \sum_{x\in\mathcal{P}, y\in\mathcal{N}} g(\mathbf{Q}(y,s) - \mathbf{Q}(x,s)).$$

The key to the above optimization problem is to calculate the derivative of $\mathcal{L}(c)$ w.r.t. c. We have that

$$\begin{aligned}\frac{\partial\mathcal{L}(c)}{\partial c} &= \sum_{x\in\mathcal{P}, y\in\mathcal{N}} \frac{\partial g(\mathbf{Q}(y,s)-\mathbf{Q}(x,s))}{\partial c}\\ &= \sum_{x,y} \frac{\partial g(d_{yx})}{\partial d_{yx}}\left(\frac{\partial \mathbf{Q}(y,s)}{\partial \mathbf{c}} - \frac{\partial \mathbf{Q}(x,s)}{\partial \mathbf{c}}\right).\end{aligned}$$

Again, we have the following identity

$$\frac{\partial \mathbf{Q}}{\partial c} = -\mathbf{Q}\frac{\partial(\mathbf{I} - c\mathbf{A})}{\partial c}\mathbf{Q} = \mathbf{QAQ}.$$

Following this, we can get

$$\frac{\partial \mathbf{Q}(x,s)}{\partial c} = \mathbf{Q}(x,:)\mathbf{AQ}(:,s).$$

The derivative of $\mathcal{L}(c)$ w.r.t. c becomes

$$\begin{aligned}\frac{\partial\mathcal{L}(c)}{\partial c} &= \sum_{x,y} \frac{\partial g(d_{yx})}{\partial d_{yx}}\left(\frac{\partial \mathbf{Q}(y,s)}{\partial \mathbf{c}} - \frac{\partial \mathbf{Q}(x,s)}{\partial \mathbf{c}}\right)\\ &= \sum_{x,y} \frac{\partial g(d_{yx})}{\partial d_{yx}}(\mathbf{Q}(y,:) - \mathbf{Q}(x,:))\mathbf{AQ}(:,s).\end{aligned}$$

We omit the detailed algorithm description for learning the parameter c due to the space limit.

4. EMPIRICAL EVALUATIONS

In this section, we design and conduct experiments mainly to answer the following questions:

- *Effectiveness:* How effective are the proposed algorithms for learning a query-specific optimal network?
- *Efficiency:* How fast and scalable are the proposed algorithms?

4.1 Datasets

We test our algorithms on a diverse set of real-world network datasets, including collaboration networks, social networks, infrastructure networks, etc. The statistics of all the datasets used are summarized in Table 2.

COLLABORATION NETWORKS. We use four collaboration networks from arXiv preprint archive[1]. In the networks, the nodes are authors and an edge exists between two authors if they have co-authored the same paper. We consider such collaboration networks from four areas of Physics: Astrophysics (*Astro-Ph*), general relativity and quantum cosmology (*GR-QC*), high energy physics theory (*Hep-TH*) and high energy physics phenomenology (*Hep-PH*).

SOCIAL NETWORKS. Here, nodes are users and edges indicate social relationships. Among them, *Last.fm* provides a music streaming and recommendation service and users can befriend with each other. *LiveJournal* provides social networking service where users can write a blog, journal or diary. *LinkedIn* provides social networking service to professionals and helps people find the right position. *Twitter* is a popular micro-blogging website where people can follow each other. *Email-Enron* is a communication network that covers around half million email communications [17]. The nodes are email addresses and an edge exists between two nodes if they have communicated through emails.

INFRASTRUCTURE NETWORKS. *Oregon* is a network of routers in Autonomous Systems (AS) inferred from Oregon route-views between March 31, 2001 and May 26, 2001 [17]. *Airport* network represents one month of internal US air traffic links between 2,833 airports[2].

SPORTS NETWORKS. *NBA* dataset contains NBA and ABA statistics from the year of 1946 to the year of 2009 [18]. The nodes are players and two players have an edge if they played in the same team before.

BIOLOGY NETWORKS. *Gene* is a human gene regulatory network obtained based on gene expression profiles [3]. *Protein* is a network of proteins obtained by BLAST algorithm [4] for comparing the sequence similarity.

4.2 Experiment Setup

We test the effectiveness of our query-specific optimal network learning algorithms in the task of *link prediction* – to

[1]http://arxiv.org/

[2] http://www.levmuchnik.net/Content/Networks/NetworkData.html

[3]http://www.cise.ufl.edu/research/sparse/matrices/Belcastro/human_gene2.html

Table 2: Statistics of the datasets.

Category	Network	# Nodes	# Edges
COLLABORATION	Astro-Ph	19,144	198,110
	GR-QC	5,242	14,496
	Hep-TH	10,700	25,997
	Hep-PH	12,527	118,515
SOCIAL	Email-Enron	36,692	183,831
	Last.fm	136,420	1,685,524
	LiveJournal	3,017,286	87,037,567
	LinkedIn	6,726,011	19,360,690
	Twitter	40,171,624	1,468,365,182
INFRASTRUCTURE	Oregon	7,352	15,665
	Airport	2,833	7,602
SPORTS	NBA	3,924	126,994
BIOLOGY	Gene	14,340	43,588
	Protein	2,712	25,979

predict links in the network that will be created in the future. We reserve half of the edges as the training set (i.e., the observed network) and the rest as testing set and for choosing the positive and negative node sets. In particular, for each query node s, we choose 5 positive nodes to which it has an edge and 5 negative nodes to which it has no edge. To simulate the noisy edges, we add edges from the query node to its negative nodes with weight 1 and edges from the neighborhood of the query node to the neighborhood of the negative nodes with weight 0.1.

Evaluation metrics: We quantify the performance for link prediction using several metrics. Among them, Mean Average Precision (**MAP**) [36] measures the overall performance based on precision at different recall levels. Mean Percentage Ranking (**MPR**) [13] computes the average percentile-ranking over all node pairs (e.g., a percentile-ranking 0% means that connected node has the highest ranking score). Half-Life Utility (**HLU**) [8] estimates how likely a node will connect to the nodes in the ranking list, and the likelihood would decay exponentially as the rank increases.

In addition, we also consider the commonly used Area under the ROC curve (**AUC**), Precision@K, and Recall@K. Ideally, we want to achieve lower MPR value and higher values on other metrics.

Repeatability of Experimental Results. All the datasets are publicly available. We will release the code of the proposed algorithms through authors' website. For all the results reported, we set $\lambda = \beta = 0.1$ and $b = 1$. The experiments are performed on a Windows machine with four 3.5GHz Intel Cores and 256GB RAM.

4.3 Effectiveness Results

We perform the effectiveness comparisons with the following methods:

1. Random Walk with Restart (RWR): perform RWR on the network with no side information used.
2. Common Neighbors: count the number of common neighbors as ranking scores.
3. Adamic/Adar [1]: similar to Common Neighbors but with more weights given to those common neighbors with fewer degrees.
4. Supervised Random Walk (SRW) [5]: learn a function that assigns weights to edges. For an edge, we use its two nodes' degrees and number of their common neighbors as features.
5. wiZAN_Dual [36]: incorporate node similarities into one-class collaborative filtering.
6. ProSIN [32]: refine the network structure in response to the user feedback.
7. QUINT-Basic: use the power method to extract columns of $\mathbf{Q}$ in Algorithm 1.
8. QUINT-Basic1st: use first order Taylor approximation of $\mathbf{Q}$ for the columns extraction in Algorithm 1.
9. QUINT-rankOne: use first order Taylor approximation of $\mathbf{Q}$ for the columns extraction in Algorithm 2.

The effectiveness comparison results across a diverse set of networks on the six evaluation metrics are shown from Figure 2 to Figure 6. We have the following observations: (1) our QUINT family algorithms consistently outperform other comparison methods across all the datasets on all the six evaluation metrics. For example, on the *Astro* dataset, compared with the best competitor ProSIN, QUINT-rankOne is 21.4% higher on MAP, 13.5% higher on HLU. (2) The QUINT-Basic1st and QUINT-rankOne share a similar performance as QUINT-Basic, indicating that both approximation strategies are effective.

We also perform a t-test between the MAP results of QUINT-rankOne and the best competitor ProSIN on *Astro*. The p-value is 3.7e-44, which suggests the improvement of the proposed methods is indeed statistically significant.

4.4 Efficiency Results

Scalability: We show the running time per query vs. number of nodes (n) and edges (m) on the *LinkedIn*, *LiveJournal* and *Twitter* networks from Figure 8 to Figure 13. We do not report the running time of QUINT-Basic on *Twitter* dataset because of "out of memory" error ($O(n^2)$ space complexity). Our QUINT-rankOne algorithm scales sub-linearly w.r.t. to both n and m on *LinkedIn* and *Twitter*, while scales linearly w.r.t. to n and m on *LiveJournal*. This is in accordance with our complexity analysis, since QUINT-rankOne is linear w.r.t. to the size of neighborhood of the query as well as positive and negative nodes, which is *at most* linear w.r.t. n and m. In addition, it only takes $\sim$ 0.34s for QUINT-rankOne to process one query on the largest dataset (i.e. *Twitter*) with $\sim$ 1.4 billion edges and $\sim$ 40 million nodes.

5. RELATED WORK

In this section, we review the related work.

Node Proximity and RWR. Measuring node proximity in a network is an important task in many real applications, ranging from computer vision [23], e-commerce [10, 9], social networks [28, 29, 11], software engineering [27], disaster management [41] to biology [22] and epidemiology [31]. The state of the art has mostly focused on best exploring the topology information for measuring the proximity. Among others, the random walk based methods have gained prevalence largely due to its superiority in capturing the multiple weighted relationships between nodes. Despite their successes, several limitations still exist.

First (Q1), most of the existing works assume a fixed network topology along with its associated edge weights, although the real networks could be incomplete and noisy. For this reason, Agarwal et al. [3, 2] propose to compute the global rankings of nodes in a network by learning the edge weights; Backstrom and Leskovec [5] propose to learn the optimal edge weights based on the node and edge attributes/features. However, these methods still assume the topology of the given network is fixed. Another work proposes to use side information to refine the network topology

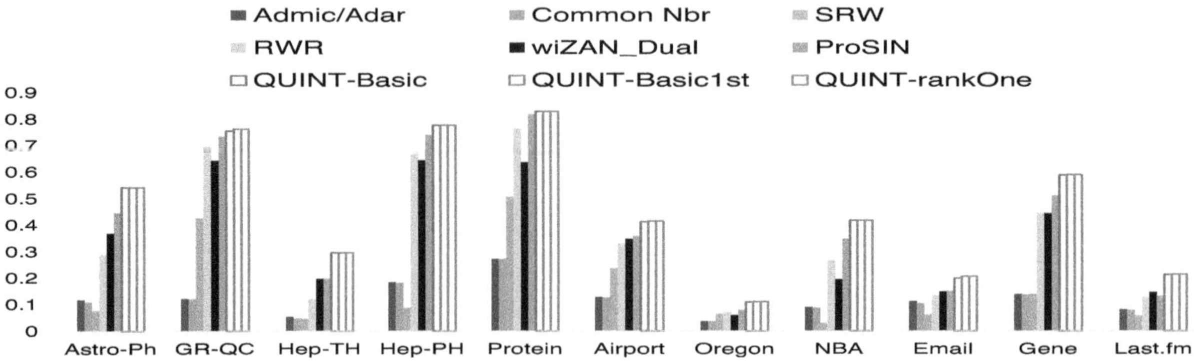

Figure 2: MAP performance comparisons on different network datasets. Higher is better. Best viewed in color.

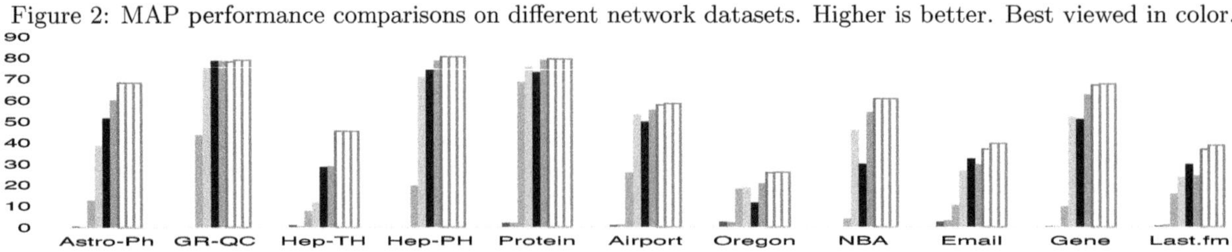

Figure 3: HLU performance comparisons on different network datasets. Higher is better. Best viewed in color.

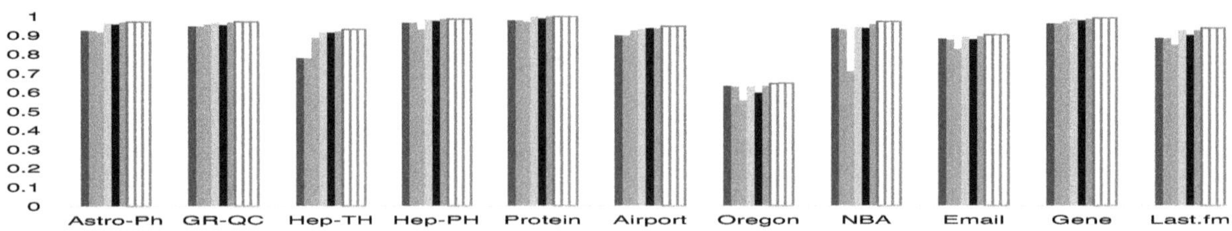

Figure 4: AUC performance comparisons on different network datasets. Higher is better. Best viewed in color.

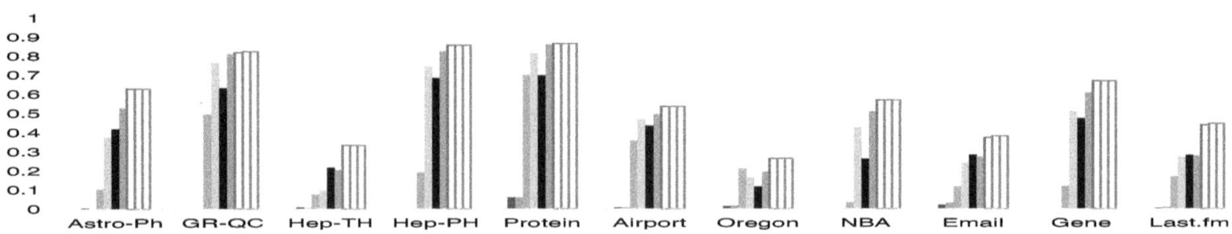

Figure 5: Precision@20 performance comparisons on different network datasets. Higher is better. Best viewed in color.

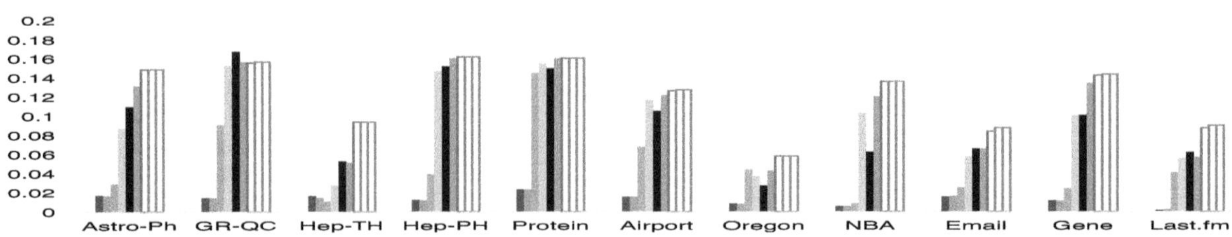

Figure 6: Recall@5 performance comparisons on different network datasets. Higher is better. Best viewed in color.

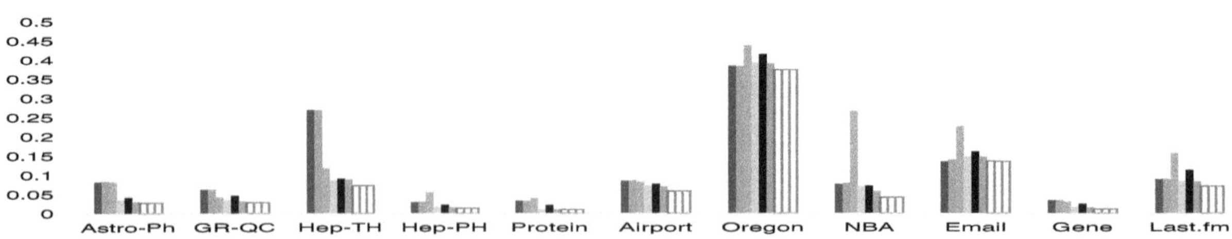

Figure 7: MPR performance comparisons on different network datasets. **Lower** is better. Best viewed in color.

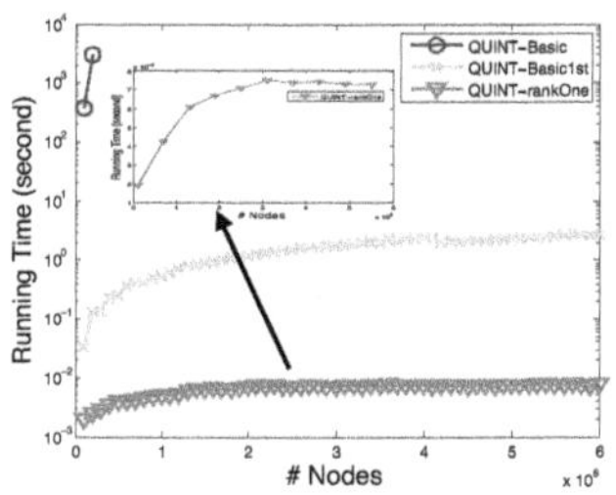

Figure 8: Running time per query vs. number of nodes on LinkedIn dataset (y-axis is in log scale). Inset: scalability of QUINT-rankOne only (y-axis is in linear scale).

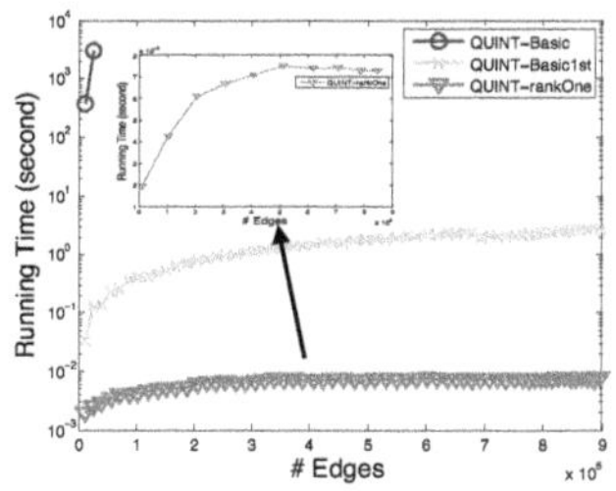

Figure 9: Running time per query vs. number of edges on LinkedIn dataset (y-axis is in log scale). Inset: scalability of QUINT-rankOne only (y-axis is in linear scale).

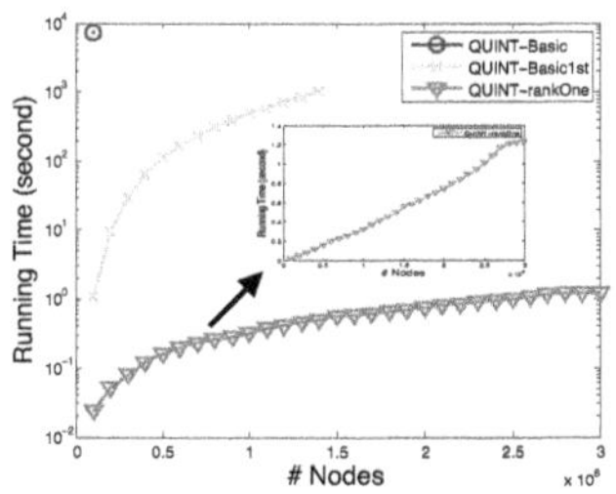

Figure 10: Running time per query vs. number of nodes on LiveJournal dataset (y-axis is in log scale). Inset: scalability of QUINT-rankOne only (y-axis is in linear scale).

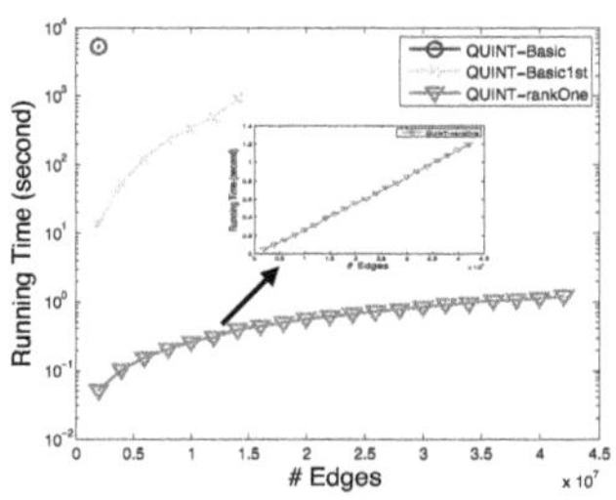

Figure 11: Running time per query vs. number of edges on LiveJournal dataset (y-axis is in log scale). Inset: scalability of QUINT-rankOne only (y-axis is in linear scale).

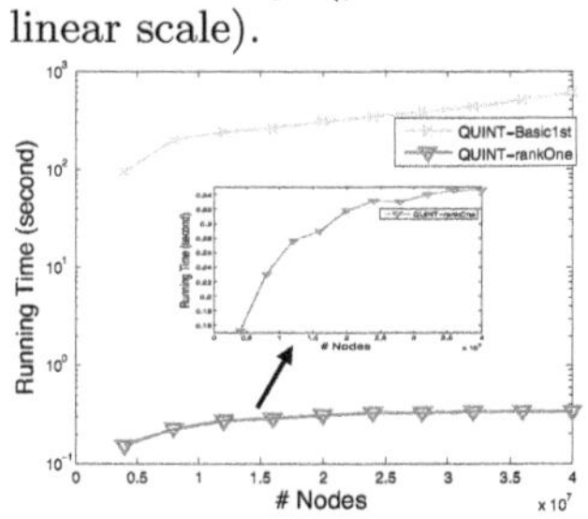

Figure 12: Running time per query vs. number of nodes on Twitter dataset (y-axis is in log scale). Inset: scalability of QUINT-rankOne only (y-axis is in linear scale).

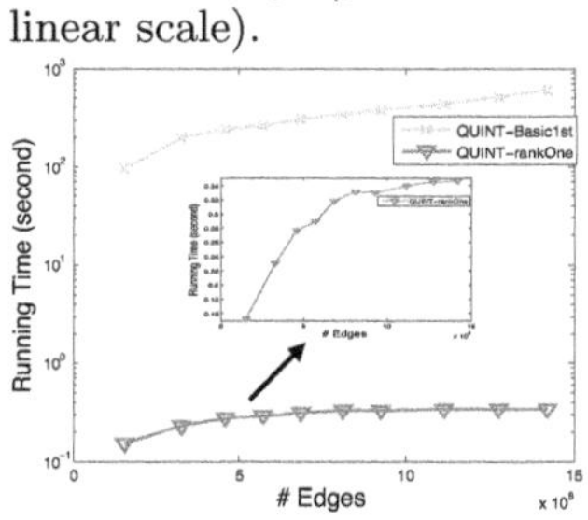

Figure 13: Running time per query vs. number of edges on Twitter dataset (y-axis is in log scale). Inset: scalability of QUINT-rankOne only (y-axis is in linear scale).

[32], so that the random walks can be guided towards/away from certain specific zones in the network.

Second (Q2), an implicit assumption behind most existing works is that one common (optimal) network exists for all queries. In some scenarios, it is desirable to find a query-specific optimal network. Some recent work aim at finding k nearest neighbor nodes without calculating the ranking scores of all nodes for a given query node [7, 34, 39]. However, their focus is more on the computational efficiency.

Third (Q3), scalable computation is a key challenge for node proximity measures, and various solutions have been proposed to alleviate this issue. Lofgren et al. [21] propose to efficiently compute the RWR score between two given nodes under a certain error bound based on a bi-directional search. Yu and Lin [38] incrementally update the RWR scores when the underlying network structure changes without recomputing from scratch. Shin et al. [26] scale up RWR computation by reordering the adjacency matrix so that it contains a large and easy-to-invert submatrix. After the preprocessing, the RWR scores can be efficiently calculated. Zhang et al. [40] design a sampling method to accelerate the proximity computation based on the concept of random path. These efforts are complementary to the proposed algorithms in this paper - *after* we learn a query-specific optimal network, we can leverage these methods to speedup the subsequent proximity score computation.

Overall, none of the existing works simultaneously address all these challenges (i.e., Q1-Q3 summarized in Section 1).

Collaborative Filtering. Considering the problem setting, our work is also related to collaborative filtering [16, 14]. For example, we can apply collaborative filtering to learn the hidden relationships between nodes, and use the recovered weights as node proximity [36]; however, collaborative filtering still uses a fixed observed network/matrix as input. Ruchansky et al. [25] propose to use side information to complete a matrix/network (i.e., to infer user preference) by actively probing a subset of true underlying matrix; in contrast, our goal is to use the user preference to learn the optimal network for a given query.

Link Prediction. Finally, our work is also related to link prediction [19, 6]. While link prediction aims at predicting the existence of a network edge, our goal is to learn an optimal network where edges can be added, strengthened or weakened. RWR score computation based on our *learned* network could be used to improve link prediction. For example, we can directly use the RWR scores to predict links [20], or merge RWR scores with other inputs such as node attributes for link prediction [37, 12].

6. CONCLUSIONS

In this paper, we study the problem of learning query-specific optimal networks for node proximity measures. The proposed QUINT algorithm advances the state of the art in multiple dimensions, with a larger *optimization scope*, at a finer *optimization granularity*, and with a much better *optimization efficiency*. The extensive empirical evaluations on a diverse set of real networks show that the proposed algorithms (1) consistently outperform all the existing methods on all six commonly used metrics; (2) scale (sub)-linearly to billion-scale networks; (3) respond in a fraction of a second.

7. ACKNOWLEDGMENTS

This work is partially supported by the National Science Foundation under Grant No. IIS1017415, by DTRA under the grant number HDTRA1-16-0017, by Army Research Office under the contract number W911NF-16-1-0168, by National Institutes of Health under the grant number R01LM011986, Region II University Transportation Center under the project number 49997-33 25 and a Baidu gift. Jie Tang is supported by the National 863 Program (2014AA015103, 2015AA124102) and NSFC (2014CB340506, 2012CB316006).

8. REFERENCES

[1] L. A. Adamic and E. Adar. Friends and neighbors on the web. *Social networks*, 25(3):211–230, 2003.

[2] A. Agarwal and S. Chakrabarti. Learning random walks to rank nodes in graphs. In *ICML*, 2007.

[3] A. Agarwal, S. Chakrabarti, and S. Aggarwal. Learning to rank networked entities. In *KDD*, pages 14–23. ACM, 2006.
[4] S. F. Altschul, W. Gish, W. Miller, E. W. Myers, and D. J. Lipman. Basic local alignment search tool. *Journal of molecular biology*, 215(3):403–410, 1990.
[5] L. Backstrom and J. Leskovec. Supervised random walks: predicting and recommending links in social networks. In *WSDM*, pages 635–644. ACM, 2011.
[6] N. Barbieri, F. Bonchi, and G. Manco. Who to follow and why: link prediction with explanations. In *KDD*, pages 1266–1275. ACM, 2014.
[7] P. Bogdanov and A. Singh. Accurate and scalable nearest neighbors in large networks based on effective importance. In *CIKM*, pages 1009–1018. ACM, 2013.
[8] J. S. Breese, D. Heckerman, and C. M. Kadie. Empirical analysis of predictive algorithms for collaborative filtering. In *UAI*, 1998.
[9] Y.-C. Chen, Y.-S. Lin, Y.-C. Shen, and S.-D. Lin. A modified random walk framework for handling negative ratings and generating explanations. *ACM Transactions on Intelligent Systems and Technology*, 4(1):12, 2013.
[10] H. Cheng, P.-N. Tan, J. Sticklen, and W. F. Punch. Recommendation via query centered random walk on k-partite graph. In *ICDM*, pages 457–462. IEEE, 2007.
[11] D. F. Gleich and C. Seshadhri. Vertex neighborhoods, low conductance cuts, and good seeds for local community methods. In *KDD*. ACM, 2012.
[12] N. Z. Gong, A. Talwalkar, L. Mackey, L. Huang, E. C. R. Shin, E. Stefanov, E. R. Shi, and D. Song. Joint link prediction and attribute inference using a social-attribute network. *ACM TIST*, 5(2):27, 2014.
[13] Y. Hu, Y. Koren, and C. Volinsky. Collaborative filtering for implicit feedback datasets. In *ICDM*, pages 263–272. IEEE, 2008.
[14] P. Jain, P. Netrapalli, and S. Sanghavi. Low-rank matrix completion using alternating minimization. In *STOC*, pages 665–674. ACM, 2013.
[15] M. Kim and J. Leskovec. The network completion problem: Inferring missing nodes and edges in networks. In *SDM*, pages 47–58, 2011.
[16] Y. Koren. Factorization meets the neighborhood: a multifaceted collaborative filtering model. In *KDD*, pages 426–434. ACM, 2008.
[17] J. Leskovec and A. Krevl. SNAP Datasets: Stanford large network dataset collection. http://snap.stanford.edu/data, June 2014.
[18] L. Li, H. Tong, N. Cao, K. Ehrlich, Y.-R. Lin, and N. Buchler. Replacing the irreplaceable: Fast algorithms for team member recommendation. In *WWW*, pages 636–646, 2015.
[19] D. Liben-Nowell and J. Kleinberg. The link-prediction problem for social networks. In *CIKM*, 2003.
[20] R. N. Lichtenwalter, J. T. Lussier, and N. V. Chawla. New perspectives and methods in link prediction. In *KDD*, pages 243–252. ACM, 2010.
[21] P. A. Lofgren, S. Banerjee, A. Goel, and C. Seshadhri. Fast-ppr: Scaling personalized pagerank estimation for large graphs. In *KDD*, pages 1436–1445. ACM, 2014.
[22] J. Ni, H. Tong, W. Fan, and X. Zhang. Inside the atoms: ranking on a network of networks. In *KDD*, pages 1356–1365, 2014.
[23] J.-Y. Pan, H.-J. Yang, C. Faloutsos, and P. Duygulu. Automatic multimedia cross-modal correlation discovery. In *KDD*, pages 653–658. ACM, 2004.
[24] K. B. Petersen and M. S. Pedersen. The matrix cookbook, nov 2012.
[25] N. Ruchansky, M. Crovella, and E. Terzi. Matrix completion with queries. In *KDD*, pages 1025–1034. ACM, 2015.
[26] K. Shin, J. Jung, S. Lee, and U. Kang. Bear: Block elimination approach for random walk with restart on large graphs. In *SIGMOD*. ACM, 2015.
[27] D. Surian, N. Liu, D. Lo, H. Tong, E.-P. Lim, and C. Faloutsos. Recommending people in developers' collaboration network. In *WCRE*, 2011.
[28] H. Tong and C. Faloutsos. Center-piece subgraphs: problem definition and fast solutions. In *KDD*, pages 404–413, 2006.
[29] H. Tong, C. Faloutsos, B. Gallagher, and T. Eliassi-Rad. Fast best-effort pattern matching in large attributed graphs. In *KDD*, pages 737–746, 2007.
[30] H. Tong, C. Faloutsos, and J. Pan. Fast random walk with restart and its applications. In *ICDM*, pages 613–622, 2006.
[31] H. Tong, B. Prakash, C. Tsourakakis, T. Eliassi-Rad, C. Faloutsos, and D. Chau. On the vulnerability of large graphs. In *ICDM*, pages 1091–1096, 2010.
[32] H. Tong, H. Qu, and H. Jamjoom. Measuring proximity on graphs with side information. In *ICDM*, pages 598–607, 2008.
[33] W. Wang and M. A. Carreira-Perpinán. Projection onto the probability simplex: An efficient algorithm with a simple proof, and an application. *arXiv:1309.1541*, 2013.
[34] Y. Wu, R. Jin, and X. Zhang. Fast and unified local search for random walk based k-nearest-neighbor query in large graphs. In *SIGMOD*, pages 1139–1150. ACM, 2014.
[35] L. Yan, R. Dodier, M. Mozer, and R. Wolniewicz. Optimizing classifier performance via an approximation to the Wilcoxon-Mann-Whitney statistic. *ICML*, pages 848–855, 2003.
[36] Y. Yao, H. Tong, G. Yan, F. Xu, X. Zhang, B. K. Szymanski, and J. Lu. Dual-regularized one-class collaborative filtering. In *CIKM*. ACM, 2014.
[37] Z. Yin, M. Gupta, T. Weninger, and J. Han. A unified framework for link recommendation using random walks. In *ASONAM*, pages 152–159. IEEE, 2010.
[38] W. Yu and X. Lin. Irwr: Incremental random walk with restart. In *SIGIR*, pages 1017–1020. ACM, 2013.
[39] C. Zhang, S. Jiang, Y. Chen, Y. Sun, and J. Han. Fast inbound top-k query for random walk with restart. In *PKDD*, pages 608–624, 2015.
[40] J. Zhang, J. Tang, C. Ma, H. Tong, Y. Jing, and J. Li. Panther: Fast top-k similarity search on large networks. In *KDD*, 2015.
[41] L. Zheng, C. Shen, L. Tang, T. Li, S. Luis, and S.-C. Chen. Applying data mining techniques to address disaster information management challenges on mobile devices. In *KDD*, pages 283–291, 2011.
[42] D. Zhou, B. Schölkopf, and T. Hofmann. Semi-supervised learning on directed graphs. In *NIPS*, 2004.

Dynamic Clustering of Streaming Short Documents

Shangsong Liang† shangsong.liang@ucl.ac.uk
Emine Yilmaz† emine.yilmaz@ucl.ac.uk
Evangelos Kanoulas‡ e.kanoulas@uva.nl
†University College London, London, United Kingdom
‡University of Amsterdam, Amsterdam, The Netherlands

ABSTRACT

Clustering technology has found numerous applications in mining textual data. It was shown to enhance the performance of retrieval systems in various different ways, such as identifying different query aspects in search result diversification, improving smoothing in the context of language modeling, matching queries with documents in a latent topic space in ad-hoc retrieval, summarizing documents etc. The vast majority of clustering methods have been developed under the assumption of a static corpus of long (and hence textually rich) documents. Little attention has been given to streaming corpora of short text, which is the predominant type of data in Web 2.0 applications, such as social media, forums, and blogs. In this paper, we consider the problem of dynamically clustering a streaming corpus of short documents. The short length of documents makes the inference of the latent topic distribution challenging, while the temporal dynamics of streams allow topic distributions to change over time. To tackle these two challenges we propose a new dynamic clustering topic model - DCT - that enables tracking the time-varying distributions of topics over documents and words over topics. DCT models temporal dynamics by a short-term or long-term dependency model over sequential data, and overcomes the difficulty of handling short text by assigning a single topic to each short document and using the distributions inferred at a certain point in time as priors for the next inference, allowing the aggregation of information. At the same time, taking a Bayesian approach allows evidence obtained from new streaming documents to change the topic distribution. Our experimental results demonstrate that the proposed clustering algorithm outperforms state-of-the-art dynamic and non-dynamic clustering topic models in terms of perplexity and when integrated in a cluster-based query likelihood model it also outperforms state-of-the-art models in terms of retrieval quality.

CCS Concepts

•Information systems → Clustering;

Keywords

Clustering; Topic Models; Streaming Text; Cluster-based Retrieval

KDD '16, August 13 - 17, 2016, San Francisco, CA, USA

ISBN 978-1-4503-4232-2/16/08... $15.00

DOI: http://dx.doi.org/10.1145/2939672.2939748

1. INTRODUCTION

New media applications and the increasing prevalence of mobile devices have facilitated the collection and rapid dissemination of news and information by anyone connected to the Internet. Massive amounts of user generated content, often in the form of short text (e.g. microblog posts), typically clustered around real-life events [6, 20], are streaming in, and being consumed by interconnected users. Organizing large text collections around concise topics (or clusters) allows effective summarization and retrieval of information [5, 7, 13]. In the case of a rapidly streaming short text, however, traditional clustering algorithms are either not applicable, or do not tackle the temporal and sparse nature of the text corpus [7, 25]. In this paper we propose a dynamic clustering topic model method – DCT – for short-length streaming text and we demonstrate that it can effectively model both the temporal nature of topics in streaming text and the sparsity problem of short text, improving the performance of clustering and ad-hoc search.

One of the key challenges in clustering streaming data is the dynamic nature of topics (or clusters): topic distributions change with time, with previously salient topics "fading-off" and vice versa [1, 6, 7, 10, 22]. Therefore, techniques developed ought to allow for changes in the topic distribution along time. For example, Twitter posts about Apple Inc. on September 9, 2015, when Apple introduced *iPhone 6s plus*, are expected to be clustered around *Apple iPhone 6s plus*, while this may not be the case on December 3, 2015, when *Apple swift* was announced. The problem of clustering documents in streams has been widely investigated in the past [1, 6, 10, 22]. However, most of the previous work makes the assumption that the content of documents is rich enough to infer a per-document multinomial distribution of topics. The second key challenge in clustering streaming data is that this assumption does not hold for short text, as the number of words in each document is limited, which prohibits the accurate inference of a topic distribution over the document. Our method tackles the two challenges by introducing a collapsed Gibbs sampling algorithm that (a) assigns a single topic to all the words of a short document, and (b) uses the inferred topic distribution of past documents as a prior of the topic distribution of the current documents, while at the same time allowing new evidence (newly streamed documents) to change the posterior distribution of topics. Based on the exact definition of the prior the proposed model enables both short-term and long-term dependencies between the previously and currently inferred distributions.

In this paper, we take a special interest in the application of topic models in the area of information retrieval. Our goal is to infer the relevance of each cluster to a user query by calculating the dynamic topic distribution over short documents and incorporating that in a query likelihood model for ad-hoc retrieval. We evaluate our proposed clustering model on a publicly available Twitter dataset by comparing the retrieval performance achieved with state-of-the-art methods and demonstrate the superiority of our algorithm.

The contribution of this work is threefold:

(1) We propose a Dynamic Dirichlet Multinomial Mixture Model that captures short and long term temporal dependencies, tracking dynamic topic distributions over short document streams.

(2) We propose a collapsed Gibbs sampling algorithm for our Dynamic Dirichlet Multinomial Mixture Model to infer the changes in topic and document probability distributions.

(3) We analyze the effectiveness of the proposed clustering models by using the produced clusters to improve the performance of short text ad-hoc retrieval against a Twitter dataset, and demonstrate that our method significantly outperforms state-of-the-art methods.

The remainder of the paper is organized as follows: §2 discusses related work; §3 details the problem; §4 describes the proposed clustering model; §5 describes our experimental setup; §6 is devoted to our experimental results and we conclude the paper in §7.

2. RELATED WORK

There are two lines of work related to our work, topic modeling and clustering, with a rich literature available on both topics. In the following sections we only discuss the most related models and algorithms.

2.1 Topic Modeling

Topic modeling provides a suite of algorithms to discover hidden thematic structure in a collection of documents. A topic model takes a collection of documents as input, and discovers a set of "latent topics"—recurring themes that are discussed in the collection—and the degree to which each document exhibits those topics [3]. Latent Dirichlet Allocation (LDA) [3] is one of the simplest topic models, and it decomposes a collection of documents into topics—biased probability distributions over terms—and represents each document with a subset of these topics.

Many models that extend LDA have been proposed, such as topic over time model [20], dynamic mixture model [22], topic tracking model [10], online multi-scale dynamic topic model [11] and more recently, (static) Dirichlet multinomial mixture model [25], Dirichlet-hawkes topic model [6] and user-aware sentiment topic model [24]. These models can either infer topics in static collections of short text, e.g. the (static) Dirichlet multinomial mixture model [25], or infer dynamic topics in long documents, e.g. the dynamic mixture model [22], the topic tracking model [10], and the online multi-scale dynamic topic model [11]. Instead, we propose two dynamic Dirichlet multinomial mixture topic models for short text streams: one for short term dependency of the current inference of the topics and another for long term dependency. Based on these topic models we can infer the dynamic changes of the multinomial distribution of the documents in a stream, and the document probabilities to the topics, and we use the inferred topics to cluster the documents. Hence, our model can both infer topics in short text streams and track the dynamic changes in clusters.

2.2 Clustering

Clustering is one of the main technologies that has been applied to tackle many challenges in data mining, text mining, and information retrieval [5]. For instance, [21] proposed a cluster-based document retrieval model where the clusters are generated by LDA. [13] presented a burst-aware approach to fusing document lists retrieved in response to a query via integrating information used by fusion methods with that induced from time-sensitive clusters of documents. Efron et al [7] found that relevant documents tend to cluster together in time and utilizing some existing clustering algorithms can boost the performance of tweet search. In terms of data mining, Botezatu et al. [4] proposed a multi-view incident ticket clustering algorithm for optimal ticket dispatching.

To this date, a large number of clustering algorithms have been proposed with KNN (K-Nearest Neighbours) and K-Means as some of the most famous ones. Among those, given that we want to tackle the problem of clustering short documents in streams, we focus on Dirichlet multinomial mixture clustering model [25], that performs well on short text, and which is based on topic modeling. This model acknowledges that as the number of words in short documents is limited, and thus each word in the same document can be assigned to one topic. Then documents assigned to the same topic are in the same cluster. Their experimental results validated the effectiveness of this assumption. However, this model and more recent short document clustering model based on convolutional neural networks [23] can only cluster a static collection of short documents. Other clustering technologies based on topic modeling include dynamic mixture model [22], topic over time model [20] and topic tracking model [10]. However, until now all of the dynamic topic models make a strong assumption that documents arriving in a data stream are long and provide rich context for the inference. To the best of our knowledge, our proposed clustering algorithm is the first attempt to cluster streams of short text documents.

Table 1: Main notation used in dynamic clustering topic model.

Notation	Gloss
d	document
z	topic
t	time
v	word
V	total number of words
Z	total number of latent topics
$\mathbf{d}'_t$	set of documents arriving at time t
$\mathbf{d}_t$	document stream up to time t, shorten for $\mathbf{d}_{\leq t}$
α_t	parameter of topic Dirichlet prior at time t
β_t	parameter of word Dirichlet prior at time t
$\mathbf{\Theta}_t$	dynamic topic distribution at time t
$\mathbf{\Phi}_t$	dynamic word distribution at time t

3. TASK DESCRIPTION

The task we address in this work is the clustering of short text streaming documents, with clusters changing dynamically, as new documents stream in. The dynamic clustering algorithm is essentially a function f that satisfies:

$$\mathbf{d}_{\leq t} = \{\ldots, \mathbf{d}'_{t-2}, \mathbf{d}'_{t-1}, \mathbf{d}'_t\} \xrightarrow{f} \mathbf{c}_{\leq t} = \{\mathbf{c}'_1, \mathbf{c}'_2, \ldots, \mathbf{c}'_Z\},$$

where $\mathbf{d}_{\leq t}$ represents the *stream* of documents with $\mathbf{d}'_t$ being the most recent *set* of short documents, arrived at time t, and $\mathbf{c}_{\leq t}$ is the resulting set of clusters of documents up to time t, with $\mathbf{c}'_z$ being the z-th cluster in $\mathbf{c}_t$ and Z the total number of clusters. $\mathbf{d}'_t$ comprises a set of short text documents, with each document d being represented by a sequence of words appearing in d, coming from a vocabulary $\mathbf{V} = \{v_1, v_2, \ldots, v_V\}$. We assume that the length of d is no more than a predefined small length (for instance, 140 characters in the case of Twitter). For brievity, in the remainder of the paper, we denote $\mathbf{d}_{\leq t}$ and $\mathbf{c}_{\leq t}$ with $\mathbf{d}_t$ and $\mathbf{c}_t$, respectively.

Table 1 summarizes the main notation used in our dynamic clustering topic model.

4. DYNAMIC CLUSTERING MODEL

In this section, we describe our proposed dynamic clustering topic model, **DCT**, aiming at the effective clustering of short document streams.

4.1 Preliminaries

The goal of the dynamic clustering topic model is to infer the dynamically changing topic distribution and document distribution over topics at any given time t. That is, we want to infer the temporal word probability for a topic, $P(v|t,z)$, and the temporal topic probability over a document, $P(z|t,d)$. Previous work [25] has demonstrated that algorithms that assign a single topic to all the words in a short document outperform those that assign different topics to different words in terms of clustering quality. The intuition behind this observation is that the number of words in short documents is limited and a short document is likely to be associated with one topic. Following [25], our proposed Gibbs sampling – as it will be described in the following sections – assigns a single topic to all the words in each short document.

Following the notation of past topic modeling work [2, 3, 10, 20], we let $\mathbf{\Theta}_t = \{\theta_{t,z}\}_{z=1}^{Z}$be the topic distribution at time t with $\theta_{t,z} = P(z|t) > 0$, and $\sum_{z=1}^{Z} \theta_{t,z} = 1$. We also let $\mathbf{\Phi}_t = \{\phi_{t,z}\}_{z=1}^{Z}$be the word distribution over topics at time t. $\phi_{t,z} = \{\phi_{t,z,v}\}_{v=1}^{V}$ is the (multinomial) distribution of words for topic z at time t, while the probability of a word v belonging to z at t, $\phi_{t,z,v} = P(v|t,z) > 0$, and $\sum_{v=1}^{V} \phi_{t,z,v} = 1$; V is the size of the vocabulary $\mathbf{V}$. In fully bayesian non-dynamic topic models (such as LDA [3]), there is an underlying assumption that the per-document topic distribution is independent of the past distributions, and have a Dirichlet prior with a static set of parameters $\kappa = \{\kappa_z\}_{z=1}^{Z}$, with $\kappa_z > 0$,

$$P(\mathbf{\Theta}_t|\kappa) \propto \prod_{z=1}^{Z} \theta_{t,z}^{\kappa_z - 1}, \tag{1}$$

Similarly, the per-topic word distribution $\phi_{t,z}$ also has a Dirichlet prior with a static set of parameters $\gamma = \{\gamma_v\}_{v=1}^{V}$, with $\gamma_v > 0$,

$$P(\phi_{t,z}|\gamma) \propto \prod_{v=1}^{V} \phi_{t,z,v}^{\gamma_v - 1}, \tag{2}$$

The assumptions made in (1) and (2) are not realistic when it comes to a data stream setting, where the distributions at time t are dependent on past distributions. In the following subsections, we infer $\mathbf{\Theta}_t$ and $\mathbf{\Phi}_t$ by modeling short-term dependency (Section 4.2) and long-term dependency (Section 4.3).

4.2 Short-term Dependency DCT

Modeling short-term dependency. To model the temporal dependencies of the topics in a document stream, and by following the work of past dynamic topic models [10, 11, 22], we propose a *short-term-dependency* DCT model. According to this model, the topic distribution at time t remains the same as the one at time $t-1$ if no new documents are observed, while it is updated on the basis of new evidence when a new set of documents is observed at time t. To achieve that we factorize the parameter κ in (1) into the mean of the distribution at the previous time-step, $\theta_{t-1,z}$, and a set of precision values $\alpha_t = \{\alpha_{t,z}\}_{z=1}^{Z}$. Hence, $\kappa = \alpha_t \mathbf{\Theta}_{t-1}$, which allows the mean of the current distribution $\mathbf{\Theta}_t$ to depend on the mean of the previous distribution $\mathbf{\Theta}_{t-1}$,

$$P(\mathbf{\Theta}_t|\mathbf{\Theta}_{t-1}, \alpha_t) \propto \prod_{z=1}^{Z} \theta_{t,z}^{(\alpha_{t,z}\theta_{t-1,z})-1}, \tag{3}$$

where the precision value $\alpha_{t,z}$ represents the topic persistency, that is how salience is topic z at time t compared to that at time $t-1$. The distribution is a conjugate prior of the Multinomial distribution, hence the inference can be performed by Gibbs sampling [17].

In a similar way, to model the dynamic changes of the multinomial distribution of words specific to topic z, we assume a Dirichlet prior, in which the mean of the current distribution $\mathbf{\Phi}_t$ evolves from the mean of the previous distribution $\mathbf{\Phi}_{t-1}$ with the precision being β_t,

$$P(\phi_{t,z}|\phi_{t-1,z}, \beta_{t,z}) \propto \prod_{v=1}^{V} \phi_{t,z,v}^{(\beta_{t,z,v}\phi_{t-1,z,v})-1}, \tag{4}$$

where as before, the Dirichlet prior parameter γ in (2) is factorized into the mean and precision, $\gamma = \beta_{t,z}\phi_{t-1,z}$, with $\beta_t = \{\beta_{t,z}\}_{z=1}^{Z}$ being the set of precision values at time t for the topics. Here $\beta_{t,z} = \{\beta_{t,z,v}\}_{v=1}^{V}$, with $\beta_{t,z,v}$ representing the persistency of word v in topic z at time t, a measure of how consistently word v belongs to topic z at time t compared to that at the previous time $t-1$. We describe the inference for $\mathbf{\Theta}_t$, $\mathbf{\Phi}_t$, α_t and β_t in later part of this section.

Assuming that we know the topic distribution at time $t-1$, $\mathbf{\Theta}_{t-1}$, and the word distribution over topics at time $t-1$, $\mathbf{\Phi}_{t-1}$, the proposed Dynamic Dirichlet Multinomial Mixture Model is a generative topic model that depends on $\mathbf{\Theta}_{t-1}$ and $\mathbf{\Phi}_{t-1}$. We can initialize (at time $t = 0$) the means of the two distributions to $\theta_{0,z} = 1/Z$ and $\phi_{0,z,v} = 1/V$. The generative process (used by the Gibbs sampler for parameter estimation) of our model for documents in stream $\mathbf{d}_t$ at time t, is as follows,

i. Draw a multinomial distribution $\mathbf{\Theta}_t$ from a Dirichlet prior distribution $\alpha_t \mathbf{\Theta}_{t-1}$;

ii. Draw Z, one for each topic z, multinomial distributions $\phi_{t,z}$ from a Dirichlet prior distribution $\beta_{t,z}\phi_{t-1,z}$;

iii. For each document $d \in \mathbf{d}_t$, draw a topic z_d from the multinomial distribution $\mathbf{\Theta}_t$ and for each word v_d in the document d:

    (a) Draw a word v_d from multinomial ϕ_{t,z_d};

Fig. 1 illustrates the graphical representation of our Dynamic Dirichlet Multinomial Mixture Model; given that documents are short, and following [25], all words in the same document d are drawn from the Multinomial distribution associated with the same topic z_d. The parameterization of the proposed dynamic topic model is as follows:

$$\begin{aligned} \mathbf{\Theta}_t &\sim \text{Dirichlet}(\alpha_t \mathbf{\Theta}_{t-1}) \\ \phi_{t,z}|\beta_{t,z}\phi_{t-1,z} &\sim \text{Dirichlet}(\beta_{t,z}\phi_{t-1,z}) \\ z_d &\sim \text{Multinomial}(\mathbf{\Theta}_t) \\ v_d|\phi_{t,z_d} &\sim \text{Multinomial}(\phi_{t,z_d}) \end{aligned}$$

Note that in the generative process described above, there is a fixed number of latent topics Z. A non-parametric Bayes version of our dynamic topic model that automatically integrates over the number of topics is possible, but we leave this as future work.

Inference for the short-term dependency DCT. The inference of the distribution parameters of the model is intractable. Following [14, 15, 19, 20] we employ a collapsed Gibbs sampler [9] for an approximate inference. We adopt a conjugate prior (Dirichlet) for the multinomial distributions, and thus we can easily integrate out the uncertainty associated with $\phi_{t,z}$ and $\mathbf{\Theta}_t$. In this way we enable sampling since we do not need to sample $\phi_{t,z}$ or $\mathbf{\Theta}_t$.

In the Gibbs sampling procedure we need to calculate the conditional distribution $P(z_d|\mathbf{z}_{t,-d}, \mathbf{d}_t, \mathbf{\Phi}_{t-1}, \mathbf{\Theta}_{t-1}, \alpha_t, \beta_t)$, at time t,

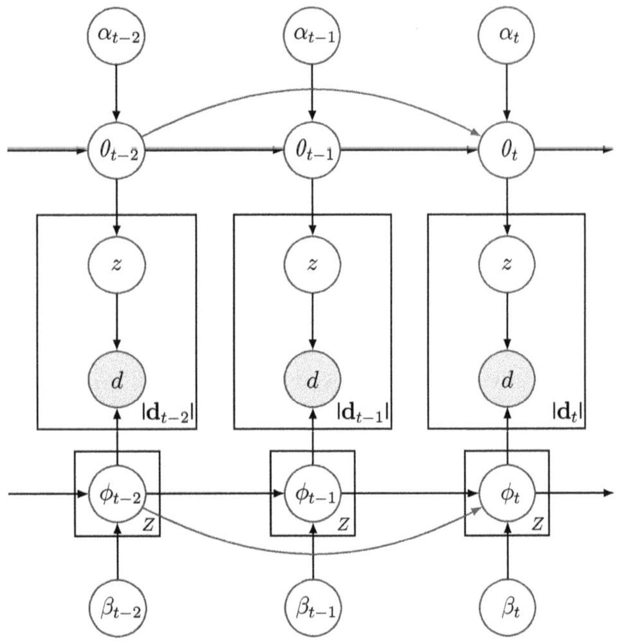

Figure 1: Graphical representation of our dynamic Dirichlet multinomial mixture clustering topic model, DCT. Note that short term dependence DCT model excludes the two blue curved lines; while long term dependence DCT model does include these two lines. The figure is best viewed in color.

where $\mathbf{z}_{t,-d}$ represents the topic assignments for all documents in $\mathbf{d}_t$ except document d. We begin with the joint probability of the current document set $\mathbf{d}_t$, $P(\mathbf{d}_t, \mathbf{z}_t | \mathbf{\Phi}_{t-1}, \mathbf{\Theta}_{t-1}, \alpha_t, \beta_t)$ (see Appendix A for the detail of the join probability), and using the chain rule, we can obtain the following conditional probability,

$$P(z_d|\mathbf{z}_{t,-d}, \mathbf{d}_t, \mathbf{\Phi}_{t-1}, \mathbf{\Theta}_{t-1}, \alpha_t, \beta_t) \propto \frac{m_{t,z} + \alpha_{t,z}\theta_{t-1,z} - 1}{\sum_{z=1}^{Z}(m_{t,z} + \alpha_{t,z}\theta_{t-1,z}) - 1} \times \frac{\prod_{v \in d}\prod_{j=1}^{N_{d,v}}(n_{t,z,v,-d} + \beta_{t,z,v}\phi_{t-1,z,v} + j - 1)}{\prod_{i=1}^{N_d}(n_{t,z,-d} + i - 1 + \sum_{v=1}^{V}\beta_{t,z,v}\phi_{t-1,z,v})}, \quad (5)$$

where $m_{t,z}$ is the total number of documents in $\mathbf{d}_t$ assigned to topic z, $N_{d,v}$ is the number of word v in the document d, $n_{t,z,v,-d}$ is the total number of the word v assigned to topic z except that in d, and $n_{t,z,-d}$ is the total number of documents assigned to z except d. Detailed derivation of Gibbs sampling for our proposed DCT model is provided in Appendix A. During sampling, at each iteration, the precision parameters α_t and β_t can be estimated by maximizing the joint distribution $P(\mathbf{d}_t, \mathbf{z}_t | \mathbf{\Phi}_{t-1}, \mathbf{\Theta}_{t-1}, \alpha_t, \beta_t)$. We apply fixed-point iteration to get the optimal α_t and β_t at time t. The following update rule of α_t for maximizing the joint distribution in our fixed-point iteration is derived by applying two bounds in [18],

$$\alpha_{t,z} \leftarrow \frac{\alpha_{t,z}\left(\Psi(m_{t,z} + \alpha_{t,z}\theta_{t-1,z}) - \Psi(\alpha_{t,z}\theta_{t-1,z})\right)}{\Psi(\sum_{z=1}^{Z} m_{t,z} + \alpha_{t,z}\theta_{t-1,z}) - \Psi(\sum_{z=1}^{Z}\alpha_{t,z}\theta_{t-1,z})},$$

where $\Psi(\cdot)$ defined by $\Psi(x) = \frac{\partial \log \Gamma(x)}{\partial x}$ is the digamma function; whereas the following update rule of β_t is,

$$\beta_{t,z,v} \leftarrow \frac{\sum_{z=1}^{Z}\beta_{t,z,v}\phi_{t-1,z,v}A_{t,z,v}}{\sum_{z=1}^{Z}\phi_{t-1,z,v}B_{t,z,v}},$$

where $A_{t,z,v} = \Psi(n_{t,z,v} + \beta_{t,z,v}\phi_{t-1,z,v}) - \Psi(\beta_{t,z,v}\phi_{t-1,z,v})$, $B_{t,z,v} = \Psi(\sum_{v=1}^{V} n_{t,z,v} + \beta_{t,z,v}\phi_{t-1,z,v}) - \Psi(\sum_{v=1}^{V}\beta_{t,z,v}\phi_{t-1,z,v})$ and $n_{t,z,v}$ is the number of word v assigned to topic z in stream $\mathbf{d}_t$.

Algorithm 1: Inference for the Dynamic Dirichlet Multinomial Mixture Model at time t.

Input : Previous topic distribution $\mathbf{\Theta}_{t-1}$
Previous word distribution specific to topics $\mathbf{\Phi}_{t-1}$
A set of short documents $\mathbf{d}_t$ at time t
Initialized α_t and β_t
Number of iterations N_{iter}

Output: Current topic distribution $\mathbf{\Theta}_t$
Current word distribution specific to topics $\mathbf{\Phi}_t$
Documents' probabilities to each topic at time t, $P(z|t,d)$

1 Initialize topic assignments randomly for all documents in $\mathbf{d}_t$
2 **for** *iteration = 1 to* N_{iter} **do**
3   **for** d = *1 to* $|\mathbf{d}_t|$ **do**
4   draw z_d from $P(z_d|\mathbf{z}_{t,-d}, \mathbf{d}_t, \mathbf{\Phi}_{t-1}, \mathbf{\Theta}_{t-1}, \alpha_t, \beta_t)$
5   update m_{t,z_d} and $n_{t,z_d,v}$
6   update α_t and β_t
7 Compute the posterior estimates $\mathbf{\Theta}_t$ and $\mathbf{\Phi}_t$
8 Compute $P(z|t,d)$

Our derivation of the update rules for α_t and β_t, and the two bounds used in deviating the update rules are detailed in Appendix B. An overview of our proposed collapsed Gibbs sampling algorithm, including the input and output, is shown in Algorithm 1.

4.3 Long-term Dependency DCT

Modeling long-term dependency. So far the distributions $\mathbf{\Theta}_t$ and $\mathbf{\Phi}_t$ depend on the previous time-step distributions. Research has shown that topic distributions - or the interests of a user on a topic when searching for information - may depend on a longer time-step history. We model such a *long-term (L-steps) dependency* DCT model on the basis of the distribution priors as follows:

$$P(\mathbf{\Theta}_t|\{\mathbf{\Theta}_{t-l}, \alpha_{t,l}\}_{l=1}^{L}) \propto \prod_{z=1}^{Z}\theta_{t,z}^{\left(\sum_{l=1}^{L}\alpha_{t,z,l}\theta_{t-l,z}\right)-1}. \quad (6)$$

The mean in this case is proportional to the weighted sum of the past L "topic trends" in the documents, and $\alpha_{t,l} = \{\alpha_{t,z,l}\}_{z=1}^{Z}$ represents how the topics at time t are related to the l-previous topics. For a comparison with the short-term dependency model refer to Eq. (3) and Eq. (6). Further, long-term dependency reduces the information loss and the bias of the inference due to the multiple estimates.

Similarly, the Dirichlet prior of the topic trends $\phi_{t,z}$ at t can be modified such that $\phi_{t,z}$ depends on the past L topic trends $\{\phi_{t-l,z}\}_{l=1}^{L}$ as well. By doing so, we can make the inference more robust. Thus, we have:

$$P(\phi_{t,z}|\{\phi_{t-l,z}, \beta_{t,z,l}\}_{l=1}^{L}) \propto \prod_{v=1}^{V}\phi_{t,z,v}^{\left(\sum_{l=1}^{L}\beta_{t,z,v,l}\phi_{t-l,z,v}\right)-1}, \quad (7)$$

where $\beta_{t,z,l} = \{\beta_{t,z,v,l}\}_{v=1}^{V}$ represents how the word distribution over topics at time t are related to the l-previous one.

Inference for the long-term dependency DCT. The parameters $\mathbf{\Theta}_t$ and $\phi_{t,z}$ in Eq. (6) and Eq. (7) can be integrated in the exact same way as before (since priors are still Dirichlet distributed) and $\mathbf{\Theta}_t$ and $\phi_{t,z}$ at time t are inferred using the proposed Gibbs sampling in Algorithm 1. The only difference lies in the way we sample the latent topic for each document (step 4 in Algorithm 1) and the update rules for the priors (step 6 in Algorithm 1). Similar to Eq.(5), we sample a latent topic for a document d by:

$$P(z_d|\mathbf{z}_{t,-d},\mathbf{d}_t,\{\mathbf{\Phi}_{t-l},\mathbf{\Theta}_{t-l},\alpha_{t,l},\beta_{t,l}\}_{l=1}^{L}) \propto$$
$$\frac{m_{t,z}+\sum_{l=1}^{L}\alpha_{t,z,l}\theta_{t-l,z}-1}{\sum_{z=1}^{Z}(m_{t,z}+\sum_{l=1}^{L}\alpha_{t,z,l}\theta_{t-l,z})-1}\times \tag{8}$$
$$\frac{\prod_{v\in d}\prod_{j=1}^{N_{d,v}}(n_{t,z,v,-d}+\sum_{l=1}^{L}\beta_{t,z,v,l}\phi_{t-l,z,v}+j-1)}{\prod_{i=1}^{N_d}(n_{t,z,-d}+i-1+\sum_{v=1}^{V}\sum_{l=1}^{L}\beta_{t,z,v,l}\phi_{t-l,z,v})}.$$

The derivation of Eq. (8) is similar to that of Eq. (5) (see Appendix A). Again, we update $\alpha_{t,z,l}$ in Eq. (8) using the two bounds in [18] with fixed-point iteration such that:

$$\alpha_{t,z,l}\leftarrow\frac{\alpha_{t,z,l}C_{t,z}}{D_{t,z}-D'_{t,z}},$$

where $C_{t,z}=\Psi(m_{t,z}+\sum_{l=1}^{L}\alpha_{t,z,l}\theta_{t-l,z})-\Psi(\sum_{l=1}^{L}\alpha_{t,z,l}\theta_{t-l,z})$, and $D_{t,z}=\Psi(\sum_{z=1}^{Z}m_{t,z}+\sum_{l=1}^{L}\alpha_{t,z,l}\theta_{t-l,z})$ and $D'_{t,z}=\Psi(\sum_{z=1}^{Z}\sum_{l=1}^{L}\alpha_{t,z,l}\theta_{t-l,z})$. Similarly, we update $\beta_{t,z,v,l}$ in (8) with fixed-point iteration by:

$$\beta_{t,z,v,l}\leftarrow\frac{\sum_{z=1}^{Z}\beta_{t,z,v,l}\phi_{t-l,z,v}A'_{t,z,v}}{\sum_{z=1}^{Z}\phi_{t-l,z,v}B'_{t,z,v}},$$

where $A'_{t,z,v}=\Psi(n_{t,z,v}+\sum_{l=1}^{L}\beta_{t,z,v,l}\phi_{t-l,z,v})-\Psi(\sum_{l=1}^{L}\beta_{t,z,v,l}\phi_{t-l,z,v})$, and $B'_{t,z,v}=\Psi(\sum_{v=1}^{V}n_{t,z,v}+\sum_{l=1}^{L}\beta_{t,z,v,l}\phi_{t-l,z,v})-\Psi(\sum_{v=1}^{V}\sum_{l=1}^{L}\beta_{t,z,v,l}\phi_{t-l,z,v})$. Given the space limitation, we do not show the derivations of the update rules for $\alpha_{t,z,l}$ and $\beta_{t,z,v,l}$, as they are similar to those for $\alpha_{t,z}$ and $\beta_{t,z,v}$ in our short term dependency DCT model (see Appendix B).

4.4 Clustering

Now, we can infer the dynamic topic distribution at time t, $\mathbf{\Theta}_t$ in our short-term dependency DCT model as,

$$\theta_{t,z}=\frac{m_{t,z}+\alpha_{t,z}\theta_{t-1,z}}{\sum_{z=1}^{Z}m_{t,z}+\alpha_{t,z}\theta_{t-1,z}}=\frac{m_{t,z}+\alpha_{t,z}\theta_{t-1,z}}{m_t+\sum_{z=1}^{Z}\alpha_{t,z}\theta_{t-1,z}},$$

where m_t is the total number of documents in $\mathbf{d}_t$, and infer a multinomial distribution over words for topic z at time t as,

$$\phi_{t,z,v}=\frac{n_{t,z,v}+\beta_{t,z,v}\phi_{t-1,z,v}}{n_{t,z}+\sum_{v=1}^{V}\beta_{t,z,v}\phi_{t-1,z,v}}, \tag{9}$$

where $n_{t,z}$ is the number of words assigned to topic z at time t. Similarly, we can infer the dynamic topic distribution at time t in our long-term dependency DCT model as,

$$\theta_{t,z}=\frac{m_{t,z}+\sum_{l=1}^{L}\alpha_{t,z,l}\theta_{t-l,z}}{m_t+\sum_{z=1}^{Z}\sum_{l=1}^{L}\alpha_{t,z,l}\theta_{t-l,z}},$$

and the multinomial distribution over words for topic z at time t,

$$\phi_{t,z,v}=\frac{n_{t,z,v}+\sum_{l=1}^{L}\beta_{t,z,v,l}\phi_{t-l,z,v}}{n_{t,z}+\sum_{v=1}^{V}\sum_{l=1}^{L}\beta_{t,z,v,l}\phi_{t-l,z,v}}. \tag{10}$$

As one can observe in all equations for the two models, the short-term model is just a special case of the long-term one for $L=1$.

Having computed $\theta_{t,z}$ and $\phi_{t,z,v}$, we can compute the probability that a document d is relevant to topic z_d at time t in the stream $\mathbf{d}_t$, $P(z_d|t,d)$ as:

$$P(z_d|t,d)=$$
$$\frac{P(z_d|\mathbf{z}_{t,-d},\mathbf{d}_t,\{\mathbf{\Phi}_{t-l},\mathbf{\Theta}_{t-l},\alpha_{t,l},\beta_{t,l}\}_{l=1}^{L})}{\sum_{z'_d=1}^{Z}P(z'_d|\mathbf{z}_{t,-d},\mathbf{d}_t,\{\mathbf{\Phi}_{t-l},\mathbf{\Theta}_{t-l},\alpha_{t,l},\beta_{t,l}\}_{l=1}^{L})}, \tag{11}$$

where $P(z_d|\mathbf{z}_{t,-d},\mathbf{d}_t,\{\mathbf{\Phi}_{t-l},\mathbf{\Theta}_{t-l},\alpha_{t,l},\beta_{t,l}\}_{l=1}^{L})$ can be obtained by Eq. (5) and Eq. (8) for the short- and long-term dependency DCT model, respectively. Finally, the document d in stream $\mathbf{d}_t$ at t is clustered to cluster $\mathbf{c}'_z$, i.e., the topic $z=\arg\max_{z_d}P(z_d|t,d)$.

5. EXPERIMENTAL SETUP

Ideally, we would like to evaluate the performance of our dynamic clustering model by directly comparing the clustering result with ground truth labels in a streaming short text corpus. However, to the best of our knowledge, there is no such collection available to this date; obtaining cluster labels for all documents in a stream and all points in time is rather expensive. Instead, we perform an extrinsic evaluation of the proposed model: (a) we incorporate the clustering algorithm derived by the DCT model into a cluster-based query likelihood model for ad-hoc retrieval [5, 21], and test the clustering quality on the basis of retrieval performance, and (b) we test the ability of the DCT generative model to predict the observed data on the basis of perplexity [2, 3]. We compare the performance of our model with other state-of-the-art clustering models.

The cluster-based ad-hoc retrieval model [21] used in our experimental setup is the following:

$$P(q|t,d)=\prod_{v\in q}P(v|t,d)^{n(v,q)}, \tag{12}$$

where $n(v,q)$ is the term frequency of term v in query q, and $P(v|t,d)$ is the probability of document $d\in\mathbf{d}_t$ being relevant to the query term v, which is computed by using a Dirichlet smoothing language model [5] as,

$$P(v|t,d)=\lambda P_{\text{Cluster}}(v|t,d)+$$
$$(1-\lambda)\left(\frac{N_d}{N_d+\mu}P_{\text{ML}}(v|t,d)+(1-\frac{N_d}{N_d+\mu})P_{\text{ML}}(v|\mathbf{d}_t)\right) \tag{13}$$

where λ is a free parameter, μ is a Dirichlet prior in language model [5], and $P_{\text{ML}}(v|t,d)$, $P_{\text{ML}}(v|\mathbf{d}_t)$ and $P_{\text{Cluster}}(v|t,d)$ are the maximum likelihood estimates of word v in the document d, in the current short document stream $\mathbf{d}_t$ and in the document d in terms of clusters at time t, respectively. According to the cluster-based retrieval model proposed in [21], $P_{\text{Cluster}}(w|t,d)$ is computed by,

$$P_{\text{Cluster}}(v|t,d)=\sum_{z=1}^{Z}P(v|t,d,z)P(z|t,d),$$

where $P(v|t,d,z)$ is the probability of word v being relevant to topic z at time t, and $P(z|t,d)$ the probability of document d being assigned to topic z. When applying the proposed DCT clustering model, for instance, we set $P(v|t,d,z)=\phi_{t,z,v}$, where $\phi_{t,z,v}$ is defined in Eq. (9) and Eq. (10) for the short and long term dependence DCT models, respectively, while $P(z|t,d)$ is defined in Eq. (11), for the two models, respectively.

5.1 Research Questions

The research questions we investigate in experimental section of the paper are:

On the basis of ranking performance:

RQ1: How does the proposed DCT clustering model perform compared to state-of-the-art clustering algorithms in searching a short-text document stream?

RQ2: Is the performance consistent across different user queries?

RQ3: How does the performance of the long-term dependence DCT model compares to that of the short-term dependence DCT model?

RQ4: What is the impact of the free parameter λ in Eq. (13) when applying the DCT model on cluster-based ad-hoc retrieval?

RQ5: Is the performance of cluster-based ad-hoc retrieval sensitive to the number of clusters used in the DCT model?

On the basis of the generative model:

RQ6: What is the performance of the generative DCT model compared to other baseline topic models in terms of the likelihood of generating the top-k documents (measured by perplexity [3])?

5.2 Data Set

One of the key criteria for a suitable test collection for our ad-hoc retrieval task is the dynamic nature of the intent of a users' query. That is we make the assumption that for the same query, e.g. *Egypt*, the intent may change over time (something that we hope to be reflected in the identified dynamic topic distribution). Publicly available labeled corpora, such as Tweets2011 and Tweets2013 used for ad hoc retrieval in TREC 2011–2015 Microblog track [16], have been constructed however by judging documents against a static query intent; furthermore the time-span of the collection is relatively small (16 and 59 days, respectively).

To allow for a dynamic query intent we construct a new test collection based on a publicly available corpus of Twitter posts (an 1% sample of all tweets). [1] The corpus has been collected between February 1, 2015 and April 30, 2015, covering a period of 90 days. Most of the tweets are written in English; we remove non-English tweets and retweets to end up with 369 million tweets. We follow Fisher et al. [8] and generated queries and relevance labels as follows: (a) Manual selected hashtags on topics of general interest, such as "#Apple" and "#Egypt" are transformed into keyword queries. (b) Given a query at time t, we label the top-k documents retrieved by a time-sensitive language model (see Section 5), resulting in the query-document ground truth used in our experiments. Assessors are university students employed remotely, while no specific intent for a query was provided to them. Therefore, it was up to their own judgment to decide what constitutes relevant and what not. To enable the possibility of query intent drifting relevance judgments were not obtained retrospectively (i.e. at the end of the 90 days period) but we simulated a streaming scenario and obtained labels at 20-day intervals[2]. This resulted in 5 sets of ground truth data: on February 9th, March 1st, March 21st, April 10th, and April 30th of 2015. Our test collection includes 107 queries, and 5 sets of (disjoint) ground truth labels for each one of them.

5.3 Baselines, Evaluation Metrics, and Setting

We compare the DCT [3] model with a number of baselines and state-of-the-art algorithms:

Language Model (LM) [5]: Directly ranks documents by their relevance scores computed by a multinomial query likelihood model - Eq. (12) and (13) after removing $P_{\text{Cluster}}(v|t,d)$.

Time-aware Microblog Search (TMS) [7]: Based on the temporal cluster hypothesis that relevant documents tend to cluster together in time,first adopts a feedback framework where temporal features are extracted from an initial ranked list of documents and then reranks this list to produce a final ranking.

Laten Dirichlet Allocation (LDA) [21]: Clusters documents based on LDA and ranks them by a cluster-based document retrieval model (Eq. (12) and (13)), in the same way DCT ranks documents.

Dirichlet Multinomial Mixture Model (DMM) [25]: Clusters documents based on a vanilla Dirichlet multinomial mixture model (without the temporal dependencies introduced by this paper) and ranks them by Eq. (12) and (13).

Topic Tracking Model (TTM) [10]: Clusters documents based on a dynamic topic tracking model that captures temporal dependencies between long text streams, and ranks them by Eq. (12) and (13).

LDA, DMM, TTM and our proposed DCT use the same retrieval model, i.e., Eq.(13), to compute the relevant scores for the documents; they only differ in the way they perform clustering. For all methods including the vanilla LM, we define the probability of a term given a document and a point in time as $P_{\text{ML}}(v|t,d) = P_{\text{ML}}(v|d) \cdot b^{-(t-t_d)}$, where b is a base parameter that determines the rate of the recency decay and t_d is the creation time of document d. In the remainder of this paper we refer to the cluster-based retrieval models with the name of the clustering method they employ, that is, LDA, DMM, TTM and DCT.

The evaluation metrics used to assess the performance of the ranking algorithms are the ones widely used in TREC 2011—2015 Microblog tracks [16]: NDCG [12], MAP [5], Recall, R-prec, and P@k (Precision at k) [5]. R-Prec is the precision after R documents have been retrieved, where R is the total number of relevant document for the query. We set k to 30 to align with the cut-off used in the TREC Microblog tracks [16]. The statistical significance of the observed differences between the performance of two ranking algorithms across the 107 queries is tested using a two-tailed paired t-test and is denoted using $^{\blacktriangle}$ (or $^{\blacktriangledown}$) for $\alpha = .01$, and $^{\triangle}$ (and $^{\triangledown}$) for $\alpha = .05$.

Experiments are run as follows: First, we obtain the top-k documents, $\mathbf{d}_t$, in response to a user's query using a vanilla query likelihood model at time t. In our experiments we used $k = 500$, but we experimented with other values for k; for any $k > 100$ the results of our experiments remained stable. For cluster-based retrieval, topics are then inferred over the documents in $\mathbf{d}_t$, and (a) documents are re-ranked based on the cluster-based query likelihood model, and rankings are evaluated on the basis of different information retrieval metrics, and (b) we calculate the likelihood of observing these documents in the collection on the basis of the underlying generative model. We use a 60/30/10 split of our collection for training, validation and testing, respectively. We train the vanilla LM, LDA, DMM, TTM, and DCT for different values of the parameters λ, and μ in Eq. (13); λ varies from 0 to 1.0 and μ from 0 to 1000. The optimal λ and μ values are decided based on the validation set, and evaluated on the test set. The training/validation/test splits are permuted until all 107 queries have been chosen once for the test set. We repeat the experiments 10 times and report the average evaluation measures.

6. RESULTS

We start by comparing the retrieval performance of DCT with the rest of the methods in Section 5.3 **(RQ1)**, and the persistence of the performance across queries **(RQ2)**. We then analyse the effect of

[1] https://archive.org/details/twitterstream

[2] Applying shorter intervals requires more efforts of manual labeling and we found that it yielded not significantly different results in many cases.

[3] The code of the DCT topic model is available at https://bitbucket.org/sliang1/dct/get/DCT.zip

Table 2: Mean performance over the five test cutoff days. The best performance per metric is in boldface. Statistically significant differences between DCT and the best baseline, TTM, are marked in the upper right-hand corner of DCT's performance scores.

	NDCG	MAP	Recall	R-prec	P@30
LM	.4446	.2241	.3092	.3534	.2772
LDA	.5018	.2749	.3439	.3976	.3171
TMS	.5286	.2991	.3604	.4152	.3353
DMM	.5715	.3416	.3854	.4460	.3685
TTM	.5936	.3638	.4019	.4648	.3928
DCT	**.6421**$^{\blacktriangle}$	**.4132**$^{\blacktriangle}$	**.4298**$^{\blacktriangle}$	**.5021**$^{\blacktriangle}$	**.4277**$^{\blacktriangle}$

various parameters in our model: the dependency length **(RQ3)**, the mixture parameter λ **(RQ4)**, and the predefined number of topics **(RQ5)**. Last, we test the generalisability of the proposed generative model in terms of perplexity **(RQ6)**.

6.1 The Ranking Performance of DCT

RQ1: We compare the ranking performance of the short term DCT cluster-based retrieval model with the rest of the methods in Section 5.3.

Table 2 reports the performance averaged across all five testing time cutoffs. The ranking of models with respect to the retrieval performance is consistent across the different evaluation measures, and in particular the following order is observed: DCT $>$ TTM $>$ DMM $>$ TMS $\geq$ LDA $>$ LM. Here $>$ denotes statistically significantly better performance at a significance level of 99%, and $\geq$ denotes statistically significantly better performance at a significance level of 95%. To get a better insight on the persistence of the results across the five testing time cutoffs, we compare the performance of the six algorithms on a per cutoff basis. We visualise the results in Fig. 2 in terms of five heat maps, one per metric, so that the relative performance per model and per time cutoff can be observed, by examining the intense of the color (dark blue translates to high measure values, and light blue to low measure values). The five heat maps lead to the exact same findings per time cutoff to those when the average values were considered: in most cases, DCT statistically significantly outperforms TTM, which is followed by DMM, TMS, LDA, and LM.

The finding DCT $>$ TTM in both Table 2 and Fig. 2 illustrates that the way we track the changes of topics specific to a query in DCT works better than the way it is done by TTM which focuses on long documents. The finding DCT $>$ DMM illustrates that DCT integrates time information better in the inference of topics distribution at time t compared to DMM, which ignores time information. An interesting observation in Fig. 2 is that as time progresses, the performance of both DCT and all other baselines slightly decreases due to the fact that more and new intents underlying a given query appear and make the retrieval task more challenging. Instead the performance of DCT remains stable across all the test time cutoffs.

6.2 Query-level Analysis

RQ2: We take an in-depth view of the improvements of DCT performance over the best baseline (TTM) on a per query basis.

Fig. 3 shows the per query performance differences in terms of all the metrics, averaged across all the test days. The number of queries on which DCT outperforms TTM is larger than the number of queries on which TTM outperforms DCT, for every metric. Further, the positive differences of DCT against TTM are larger than the negative differences in most case. Both of these findings further support the conclusion that DCT can effectively capture the topic distribution at a given time and query for clustering short documents in streams compared to state-of-the-art dynamic or non-dynamic clustering topic models for long or short text documents. There are only very few cases in which DCT performs worse than TTM.

6.3 Impact of Dependency Length

RQ3: We compare the short-term DCT with the long-term DCT (DCT-L with L being the length of dependency under consideration). We vary the length of dependency from 1 to 8 time-steps.

Fig. 4 shows the performance on the metrics, averaged across the five test cutoff days. It is clear from the figure that the longer the dependences captured by the model the better the performance of the ranking algorithm. This is especially true for $L = 1, \ldots, 4$, while after that the performance reaches a plato. This illustrates that our DCT model can enhance the performance of clustering when past distribution information is integrated in the model.

In the remaining of the analysis we will focus on the short term DCT model so that we can study the performance of our dynamic topic model independently of the length of the dependency. The performance of DCT-L is at least as good as the performance of the short-term DCT.

6.4 Contribution of Clustering Ingredient

RQ4: We vary λ in Eq. (13) and measure the average performance of our model to analyze the contribution of clustering ingredient in the cluster-based retrieval model.

Fig. 5 depicts the performance on all metrics. For $\lambda = 0$, the performance of DCT and the rest of the methods is identical with the time-sensitive language model (LM) performance, as expected. As λ increases from 0 to 0.6, giving more weight to the cluster terms, the performance of all cluster-based methods improves, with the DCT clusters providing more relevant to the query terms. This leads to a faster improvement of DCT compared to the rest of the methods (TTM, DMM, and LDA), which demonstrates the homogeneity of clusters on the query topic. The performance of all algorithms drops as expected when larger weights are given to the cluster terms. However, even when the query is completely ignored ($\lambda = 1$) the DCT clusters continue to provide good on-topic terms outperforming the language model method in the task of re-ranking. Again, these findings strengthen our conclusion that integrating high quality clustering information, as provided by our dynamic clustering model, can enhance the performance of ad-hoc retrieval in short document streams.

6.5 Effect of the Number of Topics

RQ5: We examine the effect of the number of latent topics passed as an input parameter to DCT and the rest of the clustering models on the overall retrieval performance. We vary the number of latent topics from 2 to 16 for each query, and compare the performance in terms of all the metrics, averaged across all five test cutoff days.

As illustrated by Fig. 6 when only two latent topics are modeled, the four clustering models yields almost the same performance; if the number of available topics to be inferred is small DCT does not offer any improvements compared to other methods. With the number of latent topics increasing to 4 and 8, the positive performance differences between DCT and baseline methods also increases. When the number of latent topics further increases (e.g. between 8 to 16), the performance of all the clustering models reaches a plato. This also demonstrates the merit of the proposed DCT model: it is robust and insensitive to the number of latent topics and once enough latent topics are used it is able to improve the

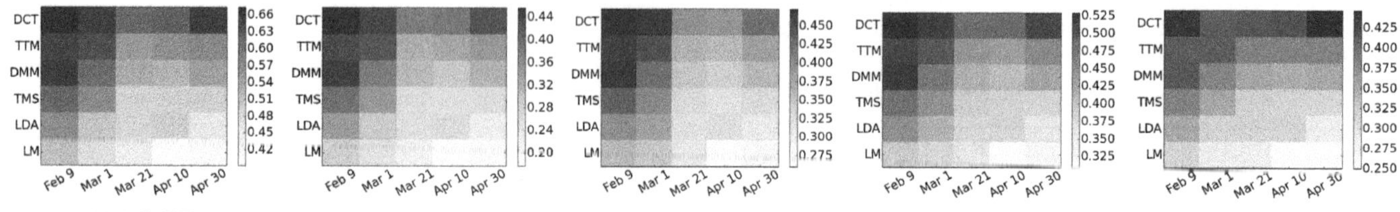

(a) NDCG (b) MAP (c) Recall (d) R-prec (e) P@30

Figure 2: Heat maps of retrieval performance (one per metric); columns represent testing cutoff days (February 9, March 1, March 21, April 10, and April 30, respectively); rows represent methods (DCT, TTM, DMM, TMS, LDA, and LM, going from top to bottom).

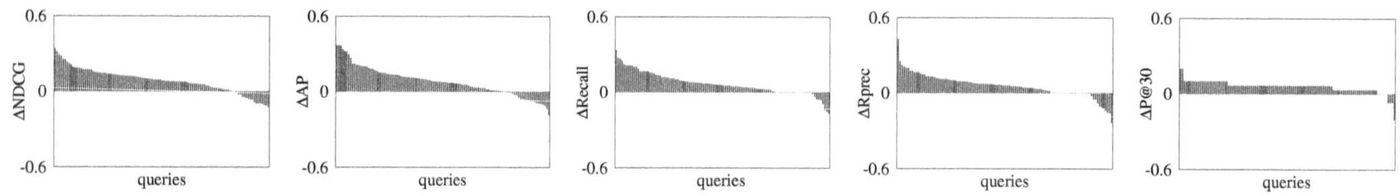

Figure 3: Per-query retrieval performance differences between DCT and TTM, averaged across all test days. A bar above the line y=0 indicates that DCT outperforms TTM, while the opposite is true for bars below y=0.

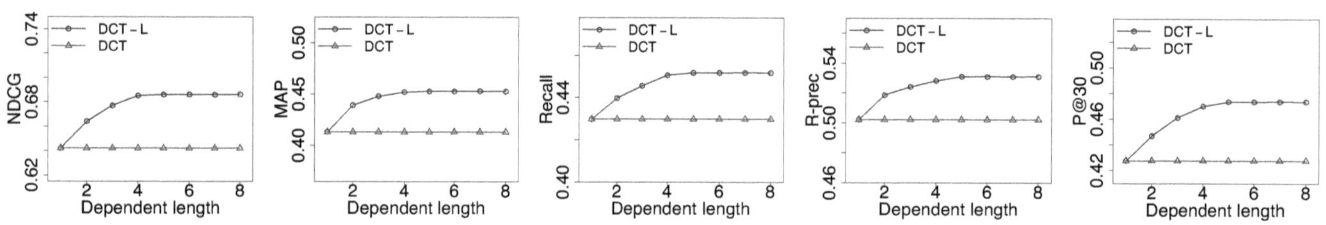

Figure 4: Mean retrieval performance of the short-term and the long-term DCT with the dependency length L varying between 2 and 8.

performance of the cluster-based retrieval model and work better than the state-of-the-art dynamic and non-dynamic clustering models in short document streams.

6.6 Perplexity

RQ6: Last, we evaluate the performance of DCT and the baseline models in terms of perplexity, which is widely used as an evaluation metric in previous topic modeling work [2, 3]. The perplexity used in language modeling, is monotonically decreasing with the likelihood of the documents, and is algebraically equivalent to the inverse of the geometric mean per-word likelihood. The perplexity [3] that is widely used to evaluate the generalization performance of many topic models is computed as $\text{Perplexity}(\mathbf{d}_t) = \exp\Big(-\frac{\sum_{d=1}^{|\mathbf{d}_t|}\sum_{v\in d}\log p(v|t,d)}{\sum_{d=1}^{|\mathbf{d}_t|} N_d}\Big)$, where N_d is the number of words in document d, and $p(v|t,d) = \sum_z p(v|t,d,z)p(z|t,d)$. A lower perplexity score indicates better generalization performance. Fig. 7 shows the mean perplexity performance of DCT and the baseline models, over the five test cutoff days with the number of latent topics ranging between 2 and 16 for each query. As it can be observed, DCT consistently performs better than the rest of the models, with the performance flattening out when the number of topics is equal or more than 8.

7. CONCLUSION

Clustering technologies have been widely used in a number of text related applications including information retrieval, and summarization. In this work we studied the problem of clustering short document streams, and proposed a new dynamic Dirichlet multinomial mixture clustering topic model, DCT, to effectively handle both the textual sparsity of short documents, and the dynamic nature of topics across time. The proposed clustering model can capture short-term and long-term trends in topics. We evaluated the performance of the proposed model in terms of retrieval effectiveness. We conducted experiments over a Twitter streaming dataset, which was manually labeled. To allow possible drifts in the query intent across time we did not provide any static query intent description to the assessors. We compared the performance of the proposed model with a state-of-the-art dynamic topic model that infers clusters in the context of long documents, a static topic model that infers clusters in static short document sets, a state-of-the-art time-aware microblog search model, an LDA topic model, and a time-sensitive language model. Our experimental results demonstrate the effectiveness of the proposed dynamic clustering model.

As future work we intent to automatically estimate the (dynamic) number of topics in our clustering model in the context of short document streams, and use the proposed model to improve the performance of other text-related applications such as tweet summarization, sentiment analysis, and query suggestion in the context of short document streams.

Acknowledgments. We thank Prof. W. Bruce Croft and Stephen M. Harding at the University of Massachusetts, Amherst for helpful discussion and preprocessing the dataset, respectively. This research was partially supported by the UCL Big Data Institute and Elsevier.

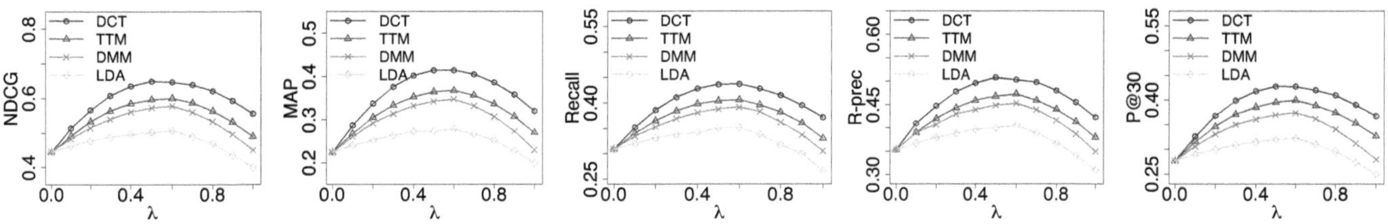

Figure 5: Mean retrieval performance of DCT and the state-of-the-art topic models when varying the smoothing parameter λ.

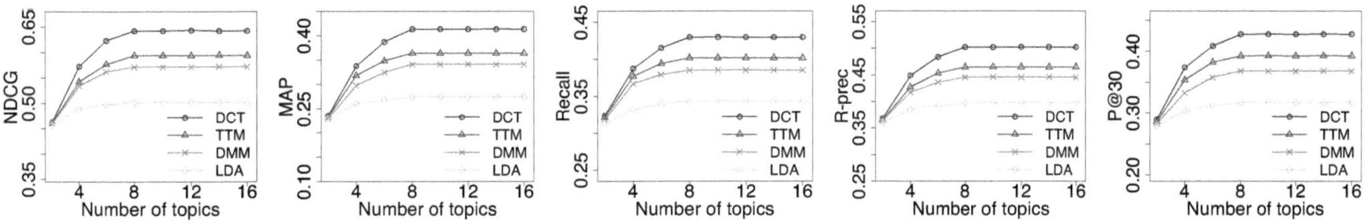

Figure 6: Mean retrieval performance of DCT and the state-of-the-art topic models with the number of latent topics ranging from 2 to 16.

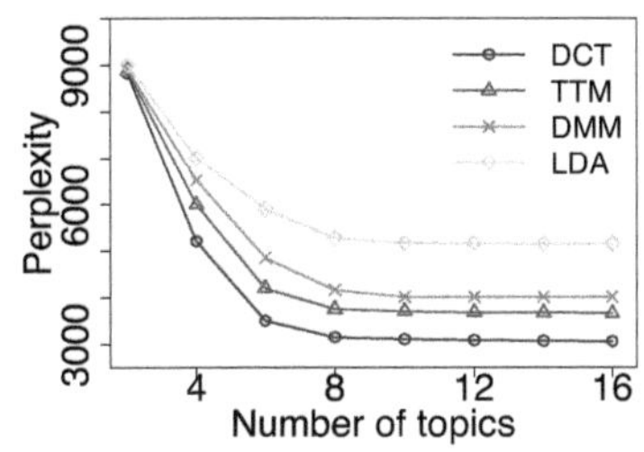

Figure 7: Mean perplexity of DCT and state-of-the-art topic models with varying numbers of latent topics.

8. REFERENCES

[1] N. Begum, L. Ulanova, J. Wang, and E. Keogh. Accelerating dynamic time warping clustering with a novel admissible pruning strategy. In *KDD*, pages 49–58, 2013.

[2] D. M. Blei and J. D. Lafferty. Dynamic topic models. In *ICML*, pages 113–120, 2006.

[3] D. M. Blei, A. Y. Ng, and M. I. Jordan. Latent dirichlet allocation. *J. Mach. Learn. Res.*, 3:993–1022, 2003.

[4] M. Botezatu, J. Bogojeska, I. Giurgiu, H. Voelzer, and D. Wiesmann. Multi-view incident ticket clustering for optimal ticket dispatching. In *KDD*, pages 1711–1720, 2015.

[5] W. B. Croft, D. Metzler, and T. Strohman. *Search engines: Information retrieval in practice*. Addison-Wesley Reading, 2015.

[6] N. Du, M. Farajtabar, A. Ahmed, A. J. Smola, and L. Song. Dirichlet-hawkes processes with applications to clustering continuous-time document streams. In *KDD*, pages 347–362, 2015.

[7] M. Efron, J. Lin, J. He, and A. de Vries. Temporal feedback for tweet search with non-parametric density estimation. In *SIGIR*, pages 33–42, 2014.

[8] D. Fisher, A. Jain, M. Keikha, W. B. Croft, and N. Lipka. Evaluating ranking diversity and summarization in microblogs using hashtags. Technical report, University of Massachusetts, 2015.

[9] T. L. Griffiths and M. Steyvers. Finding scientific topics. *PNAS*, 101: 5228–5235, 2004.

[10] T. Iwata, S. Watanabe, T. Yamada, and N. Ueda. Topic tracking model for analyzing consumer purchase behavior. In *IJCAI*, volume 9, pages 1427–1432, 2009.

[11] T. Iwata, T. Yamada, Y. Sakurai, and N. Ueda. Online multiscale dynamic topic models. In *KDD*, pages 663–672. ACM, 2010.

[12] K. Järvelin and J. Kekäläinen. Cumulated gain-based evaluation of IR techniques. *ACM Trans. Inf. Syst.*, 20(4):422–446, 2002.

[13] S. Liang and M. de Rijke. Burst-aware data fusion for microblog search. *Information Processing & Management*, pages 89–113, 2015.

[14] S. Liang, Z. Ren, and M. de Rijke. Fusion helps diversification. In *SIGIR*, pages 303–312, 2014.

[15] S. Liang, Z. Ren, and M. de Rijke. Personalized search result diversification via structured learning. In *KDD*, pages 751–760, 2014.

[16] J. Lin, M. Efron, Y. Wang, and G. Sherman. Overview of the TREC 2014 Microblog track. In *TREC 2015*. NIST, 2015.

[17] J. S. Liu. The collapsed Gibbs sampler in Bayesian computations with applications to a gene regulation problem. *J. Am. Stat. Assoc.*, 89(427):958–966, 1994.

[18] T. Minka. Estimating a dirichlet distribution, 2000.

[19] X. Quan, Q. Wang, Y. Zhang, L. Si, and L. Wenyin. Latent discriminative models for social emotion detection with emotional dependency. *ACM Trans. Inf. Syst.*, 34(1):2:1–2:19, 2015.

[20] X. Wang and A. McCallum. Topics over time: a non-markov continuous-time model of topical trends. In *KDD*, pages 424–433, 2006.

[21] X. Wei and W. B. Croft. LDA-based document models for ad-hoc retrieval. In *SIGIR*, pages 178–185, 2006.

[22] X. Wei, J. Sun, and X. Wang. Dynamic mixture models for multiple time-series. In *IJCAI*, pages 2909–2914, 2007.

[23] J. Xu, P. Wang, G. Tian, B. Xu, and J. Zhao. Short text clustering via convolutional neural networks. In *NAACL-HLT*, pages 62–69, 2015.

[24] Z. Yang, A. Kotov, A. Mohan, and S. Lu. Parametric and non-parametric user-aware sentiment topic models. In *SIGIR*, pages 413–422, 2015.

[25] J. Yin and J. Wang. A dirichlet multinomial mixture model-based approach for short text clustering. In *KDD*, pages 233–242, 2014.

APPENDIX

A. GIBBS SAMPLING DERIVATION FOR DYNAMIC CLUSTERING TOPIC MODEL

We begin with the joint distribution $P(\mathbf{d}_t, \mathbf{z}_t | \mathbf{\Phi}_{t-1}, \mathbf{\Theta}_{t-1}, \alpha_t, \beta_t)$. We can take advantage of conjugate priors to simplify the integrals. We use the abbreviation $\overline{\phi} = \phi_{t-1,z,v}$ in the following. All other symbols are defined in Section 3 and 4. Due to space limitation, we only provide the derivation for the short term dependence DCT model, and the derivation for the long term DCT model is actually similar.

$$P(\mathbf{d}_t, \mathbf{z}_t | \mathbf{\Phi}_{t-1}, \mathbf{\Theta}_{t-1}, \alpha_t, \beta_t) = P(\mathbf{d}_t | \mathbf{z}_t, \mathbf{\Phi}_{t-1}, \beta_t) P(\mathbf{z}_t | \mathbf{\Theta}_{t-1}, \alpha_t)$$
$$= \int P(\mathbf{d}_t | \mathbf{z}_t, \mathbf{\Phi}_t) P(\mathbf{\Phi}_t | \mathbf{\Phi}_{t-1}, \beta_t) d\mathbf{\Phi}_t \int P(\mathbf{z}_t | \mathbf{\Theta}_t) P(\mathbf{\Theta}_t | \mathbf{\Theta}_{t-1}, \alpha_t) d\mathbf{\Theta}_t$$

$$
\begin{aligned}
&= \int \prod_{d=1}^{|\mathbf{d}_t|}\prod_{i=1}^{N_d} P(v_{t,di}|\phi_{t,z_{di}}) \prod_{z=1}^{Z} P(\phi_{t,z}|\phi_{t-1,z},\beta_t)d\Phi_t \\
&\quad \times \int \prod_{d=1}^{|\mathbf{d}_t|} P(z_{t,d}|\theta_t)P(\theta_t|\theta_{t-1},\alpha_t)d\Theta_t \\
&= \int \prod_{z=1}^{Z}\prod_{v=1}^{V} \phi_{t,z,v}^{n_{t,z,v}} \prod_{z=1}^{Z} P(\phi_{t,z}|\phi_{t-1,z},\beta_t)d\Phi_t \\
&\quad \times \int \prod_{d=1}^{|\mathbf{d}_t|} P(z_{t,d}|\theta_t)P(\theta_t|\theta_{t-1},\alpha_t)d\Theta_t \\
&= \int \prod_{z=1}^{Z}\prod_{v=1}^{V} \phi_{t,z,v}^{n_{t,z,v}} \prod_{z=1}^{Z}\left(\frac{\Gamma(\sum_{v=1}^{V}\beta_{t,z,v}\overline{\phi})}{\prod_{v=1}^{V}\Gamma(\beta_{t,z,v}\overline{\phi})}\prod_{v=1}^{V}\phi_{t,z,v}^{\beta_{t,z,v}\overline{\phi}-1}\right)d\Phi_t \\
&\quad \times \int \prod_{z=1}^{Z}\theta_{t,z}^{m_{t,z}}\left(\frac{\Gamma(\sum_{z=1}^{Z}\alpha_{t,z}\theta_{t-1,z})}{\prod_{z=1}^{Z}\Gamma(\alpha_{t,z}\theta_{t-1,z})}\right)\prod_{z=1}^{Z}\theta_{t,z}^{\alpha_{t,z}\theta_{t-1,z}-1}d\Theta_t \\
&= \prod_{z=1}^{Z}\frac{\Gamma(\sum_{v=1}^{V}\beta_{t,z,v}\overline{\phi})}{\prod_{v=1}^{V}\Gamma(\beta_{t,z,v}\overline{\phi})}\prod_{z=1}^{Z}\int\prod_{v=1}^{V}\phi_{t,z,v}^{n_{t,z,v}+\beta_{t,z,v}\overline{\phi}-1}d\Phi_t \\
&\quad \times \frac{\Gamma(\sum_{z=1}^{Z}\alpha_{t,z}\theta_{t-1,z})}{\prod_{z=1}^{Z}\Gamma(\alpha_{t,z}\theta_{t-1,z})}\int\prod_{z=1}^{Z}\theta_{t,z}^{m_{t,z}+\alpha_{t,z}\theta_{t-1,z}-1}d\Theta_t \\
&= \prod_{z=1}^{Z}\frac{\Gamma(\sum_{v=1}^{V}\beta_{t,z,v}\overline{\phi})}{\prod_{v=1}^{V}\Gamma(\beta_{t,z,v}\overline{\phi})}\prod_{z=1}^{Z}\frac{\prod_{v=1}^{V}\Gamma(n_{t,z,v}+\beta_{t,z,v}\overline{\phi})}{\Gamma(\sum_{v=1}^{V}n_{t,z,v}+\beta_{t,z,v}\overline{\phi})} \\
&\quad \times \frac{\Gamma(\sum_{z=1}^{Z}\alpha_{t,z}\theta_{t-1,z})}{\prod_{z=1}^{Z}\Gamma(\alpha_{t,z}\theta_{t-1,z})}\frac{\prod_{z=1}^{Z}\Gamma(m_{t,z}+\alpha_{t,z}\theta_{t-1,z})}{\Gamma(\sum_{z=1}^{Z}m_{t,z}+\alpha_{t,z}\theta_{t-1,z})}.
\end{aligned}
$$

Applying the chain rule, we can obtain the conditional probability:

$$
\begin{aligned}
&P(z_d=z|\mathbf{z}_{t,-d},\mathbf{d}_t,\mathbf{\Phi}_{t-1},\mathbf{\Theta}_{t-1},\alpha_t,\beta_t) = \frac{P(\mathbf{z}_t,\mathbf{d}_t|\mathbf{\Phi}_{t-1},\mathbf{\Theta}_{t-1},\alpha_t,\beta_t)}{P(\mathbf{z}_{t,-d},\mathbf{d}_t|\mathbf{\Phi}_{t-1},\mathbf{\Theta}_{t-1},\alpha_t,\beta_t)} \\
&\propto \frac{P(\mathbf{z}_t,\mathbf{d}_t|\mathbf{\Phi}_{t-1},\mathbf{\Theta}_{t-1},\alpha_t,\beta_t)}{P(\mathbf{z}_{t,-d},\mathbf{d}_{t,-d}|\mathbf{\Phi}_{t-1},\mathbf{\Theta}_{t-1},\alpha_t,\beta_t)} \\
&= \prod_{z=1}^{Z}\frac{\prod_{v=1}^{V}\Gamma(n_{t,z,v}+\beta_{t,z,v}\overline{\phi})}{\Gamma(\sum_{v=1}^{V}n_{t,z,v}+\beta_{t,z,v}\overline{\phi})}\times\frac{\prod_{z=1}^{Z}\Gamma(m_{t,z}+\alpha_{t,z}\theta_{t-1,z})}{\Gamma(\sum_{z=1}^{Z}m_{t,z}+\alpha_{t,z}\theta_{t-1,z})}\Big/ \\
&\quad \prod_{z=1}^{Z}\frac{\prod_{v=1}^{V}\Gamma(n_{t,z,v,-d}+\beta_{t,z,v}\overline{\phi})}{\Gamma(\sum_{v=1}^{V}n_{t,z,v,-d}+\beta_{t,z,v}\overline{\phi})}\times\frac{\prod_{z=1}^{Z}\Gamma(m_{t,z,-d}+\alpha_{t,z}\theta_{t-1,z})}{\Gamma(\sum_{z=1}^{Z}m_{t,z,-d}+\alpha_{t,z}\theta_{t-1,z})}.
\end{aligned}
$$

Because document d is associated with its own topic z, it becomes

$$
\begin{aligned}
&= \frac{\prod_{v=1}^{V}\Gamma(n_{t,z,v}+\beta_{t,z,v}\overline{\phi})}{\Gamma(\sum_{v=1}^{V}n_{t,z,v}+\beta_{t,z,v}\overline{\phi})}\times\frac{\Gamma(m_{t,z}+\alpha_{t,z}\theta_{t-1,z})}{\Gamma(\sum_{z=1}^{Z}m_{t,z}+\alpha_{t,z}\theta_{t-1,z})}\Big/ \\
&\quad \frac{\prod_{v=1}^{V}\Gamma(n_{t,z,v,-d}+\beta_{t,z,v}\overline{\phi})}{\Gamma(\sum_{v=1}^{V}n_{t,z,v,-d}+\beta_{t,z,v}\overline{\phi})}\times\frac{\Gamma(m_{t,z,-d}+\alpha_{t,z}\theta_{t-1,z})}{\Gamma(\sum_{z=1}^{Z}m_{t,z,-d}+\alpha_{t,z}\theta_{t-1,z})} \\
&= \frac{\Gamma(m_{t,z}+\alpha_{t,z}\theta_{t-1,z})}{\Gamma(m_{t,z}+\alpha_{t,z}\theta_{t-1,z}-1)}\frac{\Gamma(\sum_{z=1}^{Z}(m_{t,z}+\alpha_{t,z}\theta_{t-1,z})-1)}{\Gamma(\sum_{z=1}^{Z}m_{t,z}+\alpha_{t,z}\theta_{t-1,z})} \\
&\quad \times\frac{\prod_{v=1}^{V}\Gamma(n_{t,z,v}+\beta_{t,z,v}\overline{\phi})}{\prod_{v=1}^{V}\Gamma(n_{t,z,v,-d}+\beta_{t,z,v}\overline{\phi})}\frac{\Gamma(\sum_{v=1}^{V}n_{t,z,v,-d}+\beta_{t,z,v}\overline{\phi})}{\Gamma(\sum_{v=1}^{V}n_{t,z,v}+\beta_{t,z,v}\overline{\phi})} \\
&= \frac{\Gamma(m_{t,z}+\alpha_{t,z}\theta_{t-1,z})}{\Gamma(m_{t,z}+\alpha_{t,z}\theta_{t-1,z}-1)}\frac{\Gamma(\sum_{z=1}^{Z}(m_{t,z}+\alpha_{t,z}\theta_{t-1,z})-1)}{\Gamma(\sum_{z=1}^{Z}m_{t,z}+\alpha_{t,z}\theta_{t-1,z})} \\
&\quad \times\frac{\prod_{v\in d}\Gamma(n_{t,z,v}+\beta_{t,z,v})}{\prod_{v\in d}\Gamma(n_{t,z,v,-d}+\beta_{t,z,v})}\frac{\Gamma(n_{t,z,-d}+\sum_{v=1}^{V}\beta_{t,z,v}\overline{\phi})}{\Gamma(n_{t,z,-d}+N_d+\sum_{v=1}^{V}\beta_{t,z,v}\overline{\phi})}.
\end{aligned}
$$

Applying $\Gamma(x)=(x-1)\Gamma(x-1)$ and $\Gamma(x+m)=\prod_{i=1}^{m}(x+i-1)\Gamma(x)$, the above becomes

$$
\begin{aligned}
&= \frac{m_{t,z}+\alpha_{t,z}\theta_{t-1,z}-1}{\sum_{z=1}^{Z}(m_{t,z}+\alpha_{t,z}\theta_{t-1,z})-1}\frac{\frac{\prod_{v\in d}\Gamma(n_{t,z,v}+\beta_{t,z,v}\overline{\phi})}{\prod_{v\in d}\Gamma(n_{t,z,v,-d}+\beta_{t,z,v}\overline{\phi})}}{\prod_{i=1}^{N_d}(n_{t,z,-d}+i-1+\sum_{v=1}^{V}\beta_{t,z,v}\overline{\phi})} \\
&= \frac{m_{t,z}+\alpha_{t,z}\theta_{t-1,z}-1}{\sum_{z=1}^{Z}(m_{t,z}+\alpha_{t,z}\theta_{t-1,z})-1} \\
&\quad \times\frac{\prod_{v\in d}\prod_{j=1}^{N_{d,v}}(n_{t,z,v,-d}+\beta_{t,z,v}\overline{\phi}+j-1)}{\prod_{i=1}^{N_d}(n_{t,z,-d}+i-1+\sum_{v=1}^{V}\beta_{t,z,v}\overline{\phi})}
\end{aligned}
$$

B. DERIVATION OF THE UPDATE RULES

We apply a fixed-point iteration for estimating the parameters α_t and β_t by maximizing the joint distribution $P(\mathbf{d}_t,\mathbf{z}_t|\mathbf{\Phi}_{t-1},\mathbf{\Theta}_{t-1},\alpha_t,\beta_t)$. Here we only show the derivation for short term dependence DCT model, while that for long term dependence DCT model is similar. Instead of maximizing the joint distribution directly, we try to maximize the following:

$$
\begin{aligned}
&\log P(\mathbf{d}_t,\mathbf{z}_t|\mathbf{\Phi}_{t-1},\mathbf{\Theta}_{t-1},\alpha_t,\beta_t) \\
&= \sum_{z=1}^{Z}\log\Gamma(\sum_{v=1}^{V}\beta_{t,z,v}\overline{\phi}) - \sum_{z=1}^{Z}\log\Gamma(\sum_{v=1}^{V}n_{t,z,v}+\beta_{t,z,v}\overline{\phi}) \\
&\quad + \sum_{z=1}^{Z}\sum_{v=1}^{V}\log\Gamma(n_{t,z,v}+\beta_{t,z,v}\overline{\phi}) - \sum_{z=1}^{Z}\sum_{v=1}^{V}\log\Gamma(\beta_{t,z,v}\overline{\phi}) \\
&\quad + \log\Gamma(\sum_{z=1}^{Z}\alpha_{t,z}\theta_{t-1,z,v}) - \log\Gamma(\sum_{z=1}^{Z}m_{t,z}+\alpha_{t,z}\theta_{t-1,z}) \\
&\quad + \sum_{z=1}^{Z}\log\Gamma(m_{t,z}+\alpha_{t,z}\theta_{t-1,z}) - \sum_{z=1}^{Z}\log\Gamma(\alpha_{t,z}\theta_{t-1,z})
\end{aligned}
$$

Using the bounds [18]: for any $x^*\in\mathbb{R}^+$, $n\in\mathbb{Z}^+$ and x^*'s estimation x:

$$
\begin{aligned}
\log\Gamma(x^*)-\log\Gamma(x^*+n) \geq{}& \log\Gamma(x)-\log\Gamma(x+n) \\
&+(\Psi(x+n)-\Psi(x))(x-x^*),
\end{aligned}
$$

and

$$
\begin{aligned}
\log\Gamma(x^*+n)-\log\Gamma(x^*) \geq{}& \log\Gamma(x+n)-\log\Gamma(x) \\
&+x(\Psi(x+n)-\Psi(x))(\log x^*-\log x),
\end{aligned}
$$

supposing $\alpha^*_{t,z}$ is the optimal parameter in the next fixed-point iteration, it follows that

$$
\begin{aligned}
&\log P(\mathbf{d}_t,\mathbf{z}_t|\mathbf{\Phi}_{t-1},\mathbf{\Theta}_{t-1},\{\alpha_{t,1},\dots\alpha^*_{t,z},\dots,\alpha_{t,Z}\},\beta_t)\geq B(\alpha^*_{t,z}) \\
&=\alpha_{t,z}\theta_{t-1,z}(\Psi(m_{t,z}+\alpha_{t,z}\theta_{t-1,z})-\Psi(\alpha_{t,z}\theta_{t-1,z}))\log\alpha^*_{t,z}\theta_{t-1,z} \\
&\quad -\alpha^*_{t,z}\theta_{t-1,z}\left(\Psi(\sum_{z=1}^{Z}m_{t,z}+\alpha_{t,z}\theta_{t-1,z})\right)+C,
\end{aligned}
$$

where C is function not containing the term $\alpha^*_{t,z}$ and thus will be integrated out by taking $\frac{\partial(\cdot)}{\partial\alpha^*_{t,z}}$ to $\alpha^*_{t,z}$. Then, we let

$$
\begin{aligned}
\frac{\partial B(\alpha^*_{t,z})}{\partial\alpha^*_{t,z}} ={}& \frac{\alpha_{t,z}\theta_{t-1,z}(\Psi(m_{t,z}+\alpha_{t,z}\theta_{t-1,z})-\Psi(\alpha_{t,z}\theta_{t-1,z}))}{\alpha^*_{t,z}} \\
&-\theta_{t-1,z}\left(\Psi(\sum_{z=1}^{Z}m_{t,z}+\alpha_{t,z}\theta_{t-1,z})-\Psi(\sum_{z=1}^{Z}\alpha_{t,z}\theta_{t-1,z})\right) \\
={}&0,
\end{aligned}
$$

which results in

$$
\alpha^*_{t,z}=\frac{\alpha_{t,z}(\Psi(m_{t,z}+\alpha_{t,z}\theta_{t-1,z})-\Psi(\alpha_{t,z}\theta_{t-1,z}))}{\Psi(\sum_{z=1}^{Z}m_{t,z}+\alpha_{t,z}\theta_{t-1,z})-\Psi(\sum_{z=1}^{Z}\alpha_{t,z}\theta_{t-1,z})},
$$

where $\Psi(\cdot)$ is the digamma function defined by $\Psi(x)=\frac{\partial\log\Gamma(x)}{\partial x}$.

Following the same derivation, again supposed $\beta^*_{t,z,v}$ is the optimal parameter in the next fixed-point iteration, we have

$$
\beta^*_{t,z,v}=\frac{\sum_{z=1}^{Z}\beta_{t,z,v}\overline{\phi}\left(\Psi(n_{t,z,v}+\beta_{t,z,v}\overline{\phi})-\Psi(\beta_{t,z,v}\overline{\phi})\right)}{\sum_{z=1}^{Z}\overline{\phi}\left(\Psi(\sum_{v=1}^{V}n_{t,z,v}+\beta_{t,z,v}\overline{\phi})-\Psi(\sum_{v=1}^{V}\beta_{t,z,v}\overline{\phi})\right)}.
$$

Rebalancing Bike Sharing Systems: A Multi-source Data Smart Optimization

Junming Liu[1], Leilei Sun[2], Weiwei Chen[3], Hui Xiong[1]*
[1]Management Science and Information Systems, Rutgers University, USA, {jl1433, hxiong}@rutgers.edu
[2]Institute of Systems Engineering, Dalian University of Technology, China, leisun@mail.dlut.edu.cn
[3]Supply Chain Management, Rutgers University, USA, wchen@business.rutgers.edu

ABSTRACT

Bike sharing systems, aiming at providing the missing links in public transportation systems, are becoming popular in urban cities. A key to success for a bike sharing systems is the effectiveness of rebalancing operations, that is, the efforts of restoring the number of bikes in each station to its target value by routing vehicles through pick-up and drop-off operations. There are two major issues for this bike rebalancing problem: the determination of station inventory target level and the large scale multiple capacitated vehicle routing optimization with outlier stations. The key challenges include demand prediction accuracy for inventory target level determination, and an effective optimizer for vehicle routing with hundreds of stations. To this end, in this paper, we develop a Meteorology Similarity Weighted K-Nearest-Neighbor (MSWK) regressor to predict the station pick-up demand based on large-scale historic trip records. Based on further analysis on the station network constructed by station-station connections and the trip duration, we propose an inter station bike transition (ISBT) model to predict the station drop-off demand. Then, we provide a mixed integer nonlinear programming (MINLP) formulation of multiple capacitated bike routing problem with the objective of minimizing total travel distance. To solve it, we propose an Adaptive Capacity Constrained K-centers Clustering (AdaCCKC) algorithm to separate outlier stations (the demands of these stations are very large and make the optimization infeasible) and group the rest stations into clusters within which one vehicle is scheduled to redistribute bikes between stations. In this way, the large scale multiple vehicle routing problem is reduced to inner cluster one vehicle routing problem with guaranteed feasible solutions. Finally, the extensive experimental results on the NYC Citi Bike system show the advantages of our approach for bike demand prediction and large-scale bike rebalancing optimization.

*Contact Author.

KDD '16, August 13-17, 2016, San Francisco, CA, USA

DOI: http://dx.doi.org/10.1145/2939672.2939776

CCS Concepts

•**Applied computing** → **Transportation;** *Forecasting;*
•**Information systems** → Clustering;

Keywords

Bike Sharing System; Optimization; Clustering

1. INTRODUCTION

Recent years have witnessed worldwide prevalence of public bike sharing systems [5, 21], which provide short-term bike rental services with many bike stations scattering over an urban city. Indeed, these bike sharing systems offer an environment-friendly solution for the first-and-last mile connection and help bridge the gap between existing transportation modes such as subways and bus systems.

However, despite the significant benefits from bike sharing systems, it is very challenging to operate these systems in an effective and efficient way. The dynamics of human mobility often lead to inevitable bike supply/demand imbalance. Thus, it is crucial for service providers to redistribute bikes among stations in a proactive and economical way in order to ensure the system functioning effectively. To this end, in this paper, we study the bike rebalancing problem, where the assumption is that the number of bikes at each station is known in advance and will not be changed during the rebalancing operation (when system is closed or during midnight). There are two major challenges for this problem. First, it is necessary to determine the desired inventory level at each station. However, this depends on the accurate prediction of station-level pick-up and drop-off demands, which can be impacted by multiple factors, such as time, location, weather conditions, and traffic situations. Second, the bike rebalancing problem is a large-scale multiple capacitated vehicle routing problem, which is intractable due to the existence of the outlier stations with extremely large target inventory levels. Also, the scales of bike sharing systems, consisting of hundreds of stations, are too large to be solved by traditional route optimization techniques.

A number of recent researches have studied the bike rebalancing problem. Most studies on bike demand prediction are based on historical demand mean [10] or stochastic process [20, 1] with historical pick-up (drop-off) rate, without considering the impact of other influential factors. A promising way to improve bike demand prediction accuracy is to leverage a variety of data that is directly or indirectly related to the public bike sharing service. For instance, Yexin, etc (2015) [14] propose a multi-factor hierarchical prediction model to predict the bike demands of the clusters of stations in a future period. However, it requires an accurate station-level bike usage prediction to determine the desired inventory level. For the problem of station rebalancing optimization problem, the small-scale (up to 60 stations) bike rebalancing problem has been investigated by solving feasible optimization models with the assumption that there exists at least one route for covering all targeted stations [4, 6, 3]. In practice, especially in large scale bike sharing systems, it is expected to determine the optimal number of the relocated bikes and to deal with large number of stations with some outlier stations which make traditional routing optimization infeasible.

Indeed, the emergence of multi-source big data enables a new paradigm for enhancing bike sharing services. Along this line, we exploit multi-source data related to bike sharing services, such as trip records, station status records, and weather reports, for developing data smart bike rebalancing solutions. Specifically, we first propose a Meteorology Similarity Weighed K-Nearest-Neighbor (MSWK) regression model to predict the hourly bike pick-up demand at each station. The weight of different factors are carefully learned to improve the accuracy of bike pick-up demand prediction. Also, for predicting the drop-off demand at each station, we provide an inter station bike transition (ISBT) predictor which considers the surrounding station pick-up information and the connection information between stations (station-station trip frequencies and trip durations). The predicted pick-up and drop-off demands can then be used to determine the station inventory targets.

Moreover, to solve the large scale multi-capacitated bike routing optimization problem for rebalancing, a hierarchical optimization model is proposed by exploring multi-source data. The optimization model first performs Adaptive Capacity Constrained K-centers Clustering (AdaCCKC) which separates outlier stations and groups the rest stations into different clusters, within which the stations are rebalanced by one vehicle with optimal route. Here, a mixed integer nonlinear programming (MINLP) model with lazy constrains is conducted to optimize the inner cluster rebalancing routes.

Finally, we carry out extensive experiments on a real world data set including trip records of 698 days collected from the NYC Citi Bike system and the experimental results clearly show the effectiveness of the proposed methods.

2. PROBLEM FORMULATION

In this section, we first define some preliminaries. Then, we introduce the rebalancing problem of multiple capacitated vehicles route optimization in bike sharing systems.

2.1 Preliminaries

Here, we first introduce some preliminaries, which will be used throughout this paper.

2.1.1 *Station network.*

A bike station network is represented by a directed graph $G = (S, E)$. With each station $s \in S$ as a node, the edges in E are directed connections of bike stations $e_{ij} = (s_i, s_j) \in E$. Each node and edge have several attributes. For example, $e_{ij}.f$ represents the frequency of bike trip records from station i to station j.

The station network is constructed by tracking a set of trip records. A trip record $tr = (s_0, s_d, \tau_0, \tau_0)$ is a bike usage record from an origin station s_0 to a destination station s_d. τ_0 is the pick-up time and and τ_d is the drop-off time. Only trips with duration $\tau_d - \tau_0$ larger than 1 min are recorded.

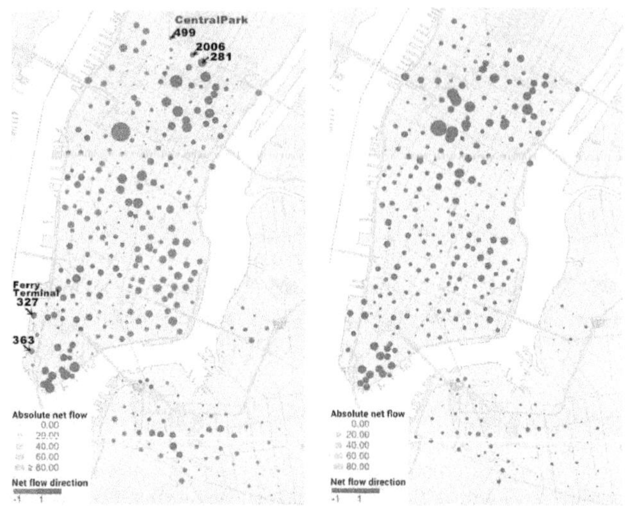

(a) Net flow 9 am ~ 10 am (b) Net flow 6pm ~ 7 pm

Figure 1: A net flow distribution of the NYC Citi Bike System during rush hours.

2.1.2 *Station pick-up/drop-off demand.*

The station bike demand is defined as the pick-up (drop-off) frequency per unit time when the station is available. Station availability means the station is in service and there are bikes available for pick-up (drop-off). Station unavailability is usually due to maintenance, empty dock (for pick-up) and full dock (for drop-off). We do not consider the station demand during its unavailable period.

Definition 1: *Station pick-up (drop-off) demand.* Let $s_i.pf(t)$ ($s_i.df(t)$) and $s_i.pa(t)$ ($s_i.da(t)$) represent the pick-up (drop-off) frequency and the pick-up (drop-off) available time of station i during time slot t. Each day is separated into 24 time slots of one hour duration, $t \in \{0, 1, ..., 23\}$. The station pick-up (drop-off) demand $s_i.pd(t)$ ($s_i.dd(t)$) and the bike net flow $s_i.nf(t)$ is defined as follows:

$$\begin{aligned} s_i.pd(t) &= \frac{s_i.pf(t)}{s_i.pa(t)} \quad (s_i.dd(t) = \frac{s_i.df(t)}{s_i.da(t)}) \\ s_i.nf(t) &= s_i.dd(t) - s_i.pd(t) \end{aligned} \tag{1}$$

The one month (July. 2014) averaged station net flow distribution during weekday rush hours (9 am ~ 10 am and 6 pm ~ 7 pm) of the NYC CitiBike sharing system is presented in Figure 1 as an example. In Figure 1, each dot represents a bike station in NYC with its size representing the absolute value of net flow. The red color represents a positive net flow (drop-off frequency is larger than pick-up frequency) and the blue color represents a negative net flow. As we can see from Figure 1, the station demand distribution is unbalanced both geographically and temporally.

2.1.3 *Station rebalancing target*

Definition 2: *Station Rebalancing Target.* Given the station capacity $s_i.c$, the current number of bikes $s_i.cn$ and the station bike net flow $s_i.nf(t)$, the station rebalancing target $s_i.rt$ is defined as the number of bikes that need to be picked-up or delivered by rebalancing vehicle. The optimal inventory level aims at maximizing the time duration T within which the station remains balanced during its in-service time period. Thus the station rebalancing target $s_i.rt$ is decided by the following calculation:

$$\arg\max_{s_i.rt}\{T || s_i.cn + s_i.rt + \sum_{t=0}^{T} s_i.nf| \leq s_i.c\} \tag{2}$$

2.2 Problem Definition

2.2.1 *Station level bike demand prediction*

Given a set of bike trip records $TR_H = \{tr_1, tr_2, ...tr_H\}$ and weather report R_t, the problem of station level bike pick-up (drop-off) prediction is to predict the hourly pick-up (drop-off) demand $s_i.pd(t)$ ($s_i.dd(t)$) defined by Definition 1 of each station during a day.

2.2.2 *Static bike rebalancing optimization*

Given a set of bike station locations s_i of size m, rebalancing target $s_i.rt$, their inter vehicle transportation distance TD_{ij} and the number of operating vehicles $|V|$ with specified capacity limit VC, the problem of bike rebalancing optimization is to decide the optimal vehicle rebalancing routes, which is mathematically formulated as follows:

$$\min \quad \mathcal{F}(\mathbf{x}) = \sum_{i=1}^{m}\sum_{j=1}^{m}\sum_{v\in V} x_{ijv} TD_{ij} \tag{3}$$

$$s.t. \quad y_i + \sum_{j\neq i}\sum_{v\in V} x_{ijv} s_j.rt = \sum_{j\neq i}\sum_{v\in V} x_{ijv} y_j \quad \forall i \tag{4}$$

$$0 \leq y_i \leq VC \qquad \forall i \tag{5}$$

$$x_{ijv} \in \{0,1\} \qquad \forall i \neq j, \forall v \in V \tag{6}$$

$$\sum_{j\neq i, v\in V} x_{ijv} = 1 \quad \forall i \tag{7}$$

$$\sum_{i\neq j, v\in V} x_{ijv} = 1 \quad \forall j \tag{8}$$

Binary decision variable $x_{ijv} = 1$ indicates vehicle $v \in V$ redistributes bikes from station i to station j, otherwise $x_{ijv} = 0$. Integer decision variable y_i indicates the number of bikes carried by a vehicle after visiting station i. The objective function (3) minimizes the total traveling distance of vehicles for re-balancing. Quadratic constrain (4) implies bike flow conservation. Constrain (5) is for the vehicle capacity limit and (7, 8) indicate that a vehicle must enter and leave a station only once (no self loop). This MINLP formulation for vehicle route optimization is not completed because there exists outlier stations making this model infeasible and subtours have not been eliminated. We could add subtour elimination constrains (SEC) directly into our MINLP formulation. However, the number of SEC increases exponentially with the number of stations. Thus, for a large scale bike sharing system, considering all SEC is unsolvable.

2.3 An overview of the framework

Figure 2 shows the framework of our proposed method, which consists of two major phases: the station level bike demand (pick-up and drop-off) prediction and the AdaCCKC based bike rebalancing optimization.

Station level bike demand prediction. We first extract bike history records and station inventory status data from bike sharing systems, from which the station level bike

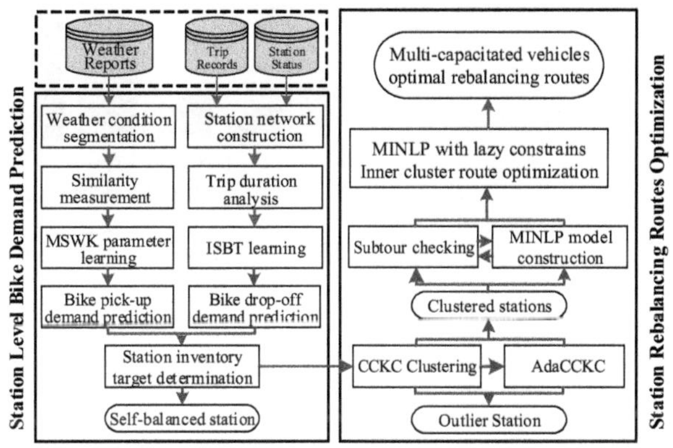

Figure 2: An overview of the framework.

demands defined by Definition 1 are calculated as benchmark data. The weather reports of each time slot are extracted, and the unbalanced weather condition records and missing records are preprocessed. In this step, weather conditions are clustered into four categories according to their suitability for outdoor bicycling: U_1={heavy snow, heavy rain}, U_2={snow, rain, light snow, light rain}, U_3={fog, mist, haze}, U_4={Cloudy, Sunny}. A meteorology similarity function is learned to build the meteorology similarity weighted KNN (MSWK) regression for station bike pick-up demand prediction. The station bike drop-off demand is predicted by the Inter Station Bike Transition (ISBT) predictor which estimates the drop-off station and drop-off time after a pick-up event according to the station-station connected network. Based on the predicted station bike net flow defined by Definition 1 and current inventory level, the station inventory target is then determined by Equation 2.

Bike station rebalancing optimization. According to the station level target, several self-balanced stations (stations with net-flow close to zero) are excluded. The remaining stations are clustered by (Adaptive) Capacity Constrained K-centers Clustering (CCKC or AdaCCKC) and some outlier stations are discovered. We then implement one-vehicle routing MINLP model with lazy constrains to optimize the vehicle rebalancing routes for the rest stations within each cluster.

3. THE REBALANCING APPROACH

In this section, we provide the technical details of our bike demand prediction model and AdaCCKC based bike rebalancing optimization model. Weekdays and weekends are studied separately since the bike demand and the net flows are very different (see the example of CitiBike 24-hour net flow as an example in Figure 3(a)).

3.1 Station Bike Pick-up Prediction

The MSWK regressor is built to predict the station level bike pick-up demand $s_i.pd(D^t)$ during time slot t of any given day D that is on the basis of a meteorology multi-similarity function.

3.1.1 *Similarity measurement*

Given the weather reports R_D^t of each time slot t, which contains weather condition $W_{D_p^t}$ (sunny, raining, etc.), temperature $F_{D_p^t}$, humidity $H_{D_p^t}$, wind speed $S_{D_p^t}$ and visibility

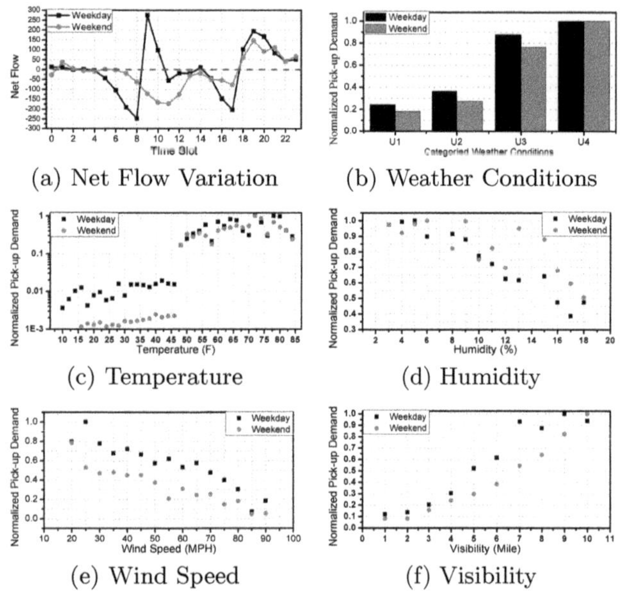

Figure 3: Demand net flow (a) and the effect of multiple factors on bike pick-up demand (b)-(f).

$V_{D_p^t}$ of time slot t on day D_p, the similarity between 2 different days D_p^t and D_q^t is calculated as the linear combination of three units: weather similarity, temperature similarity and humidity-wind speed-visibility similarity. Each unit is associated with an effective coefficient a that is learned to improve the prediction accuracy.

Weather similarity. The weather conditions are first manually segmented into different levels according to their suitability for outdoor bicycling (see Figure 3(b)): ((heavy snowy, heavy rainy), (snowy, rainy), (hazy, foggy), (clear, cloudy))=(1, 0.75, 0.5, 0.25). Then the weather similarity is defined as follows:

$$\lambda_1(W_{D_p^t}, W_{D_q^t}) = \frac{1}{2\pi\sigma_1} e^{-\frac{(W_{D_p^t} - W_{D_q^t})^2}{\sigma_1^2}} \tag{9}$$

Temperature similarity. As can be seen from Figure 3(c), the bike pick-up demand is sensitive to the temperature, especially when temperature is below 47 F during the weekends. We extract the temperature information and calculate its similarity based on a Gaussian Kernel function:

$$\lambda_2(F_{D_p}^t, F_{D_q}^t) = \frac{1}{2\pi\sigma_2} e^{-\frac{(F_{D_p^t} - F_{D_q^t})^2}{\sigma_2^2}} \tag{10}$$

Humidity, wind speed and visibility similarity. Different from the effect of temperature, the humidity, wind speed and visibility affect bike pick-up demand with similar effects (see Figure 3(d)-3(f)). We choose a 3-D Gaussian Kernel to calculate the similarity between $(H_{D_p^t}, S_{D_p^t}, V_{D_p^t})$ and $(H_{D_q^t}, S_{D_q^t}, V_{D_q^t})$:

$$\lambda_3 = \frac{1}{2\pi\sigma} e^{-\left(\frac{(H_{D_p^t} - H_{D_q^t})^2}{\sigma_3^2} + \frac{(S_{D_p^t} - S_{D_q^t})^2}{\sigma_4^2} + \frac{(V_{D_p^t} - V_{D_q^t})^2}{\sigma_5^2}\right)} \tag{11}$$

Similarity function. To uniform these similarity calculations, we normalize the temperature, humidity, wind speed and visibility into range $[0, 1]$ and simplify equation (9)-(11) by setting $\sigma_k = 1$ $(k = 1, 2, 3, 4, 5)$. The similarity function is then defined as a linear combination of λ:

$$M(D_p^t, D_q^t; a) = \delta_w(D_p, D_q) \sum_{i=1}^{3} a_i \lambda_i \tag{12}$$

where $\delta_w(D_p, D_q)$ is the delta function. $\delta_w(D_p, D_q) = 1$ if D_p and D_q are both weekdays or weekends, otherwise $\delta_w(D_p, D_q) = 0$.

3.1.2 MSWK learning

Given K and a, we select top K days $\{D_1^t, D_2^t, ..., D_K^t\}$ with the highest similarity to our target day D_n^t according to the similarity function. Then the $s_i.pd(D_q^t)$ is predicted by a similarity weighed KNN:

$$s_i.pd(D_q^t; a) = \frac{\sum_{p=1}^{K} M(D_p^t, D_q^t; a) s_i.pd(D_p^t)}{\sum_{p=1}^{K} M(D_p^t, D_q^t; a)} \tag{13}$$

The weight of different similarity function a in equation (12) is trained to reach the minimum prediction absolute error of predicted value $\hat{s}_i.pd(D_q^t; a)$ and ground truth $s_i.pd(D_q^t)$ by brute force searching:

$$a* = \arg\min_a \frac{1}{N} \sum_{i=1}^{N} |\hat{s}_i.pd(D_q^t; a) - s_i.pd(D_q^t)| \tag{14}$$

3.2 Station bike drop-off prediction

The inter station bike transition (ISBT) predictor for bike drop-off demand prediction investigates that for a pick-up event at station i during time slot t, the possibility that it will be dropped-off at station j during the same time slot t and next time slot $t + 1$.

3.2.1 Station-station inter transportation analysis

Given predicted station bike pick-up demand during time slot t ($s_i.pd(t)$), the number of bikes that will be dropped-off at station s_j from s_i is estimated from trip history records:

$$e_{ij}^t = s_i.pd(t) \frac{e_{ij}.f}{s_i.pd} \tag{15}$$

where $s_i.pd$ is the total pick-up demand at station s_i and $e_{ij}.f$ is the total number of trips from station s_i to s_j.

Among all the trips from station s_i to s_j which start during time slot t, not all of them will be dropped-off during the same time slot due to the unestimated trip duration. For commuters, they will find the fastest path to reach station s_j. For tourists or bike exercisers, the trip duration will vary. Figure 4 presents 3 typical station-station connections (the station IDs are indexed by the NYC Citi Bike System). The trip duration distributions are fitted by a 2-Gaussian functions (see fitting results in Table 1). Among the 3 typical station-station trip connections, the commuters construct the first left gaussian peak with a mean trip duration close to the fastest route estimated by Google Maps (second column of Table 1). The second right gaussian peak reveals the tourists or bike exercisers. Most trips from station 2006 to 281 (the large dot marker with black fit line) are not for the fastest route commuting and about half trips from station 281 to 499 (the diamond marker with red fit line) are for commuting. The trips from station 327 to 363 (the small dot marker with blue line) are mostly commuting trips. It is interesting that the station 2006 and 281 are near Central Park where most bike users are tourists or exercisers. The

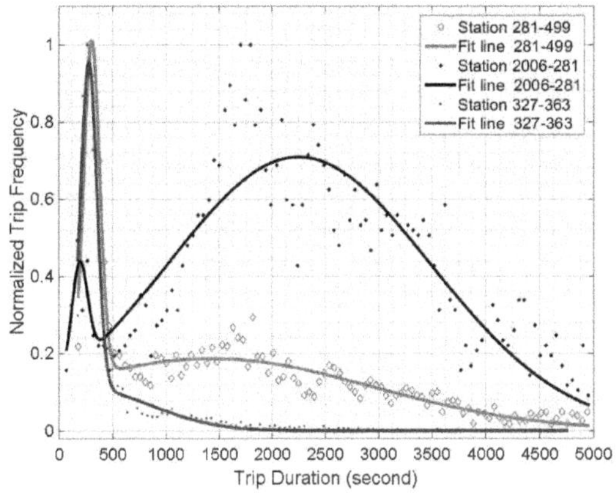

Figure 4: Trip duration distributions of three typical station-station connections.

Table 1: Fitting Results and P_{ij}^T, P_{ij}^{T+1} estimation function: $f(x) = a_1 exp^{-(\frac{x-x_{c1}}{b_1})^2} + a_2 exp^{-(\frac{x-x_{c2}}{b_2})^2}$

Edges	Map	x_{c1} (95% CI)	x_{c2} (95% CI)	R^2	P_{ij}^T
281-499	300	304.5±5	1424±237	0.9569	0.89
2006-281	120	194.3±55.5	2250±92	0.7532	0.73
327-363	180	212.9±30.5	278.1±6.1	0.9728	0.96

station 327 and 363 are located near World Financial Center Ferry Terminal where most bike users are commuters (see Figure 1 for station locations). Therefore, we estimate the trip duration (in unite of second) of each two pair of stations s_i and s_j by a 2-peak Gaussian function:

$$D_{ij}(t) = g_1(t; \mu_1, \sigma_1) + g_2(t; \mu_2, \sigma_2) \tag{16}$$

Let t_1 represent the actual pick-up time and t_2 represent trip duration from station s_i to s_j during time slot t of length $|t|$, the possibility that the picked-up bike will arrive at station j at the same time slot is calculated as:

$$\begin{aligned} P_{ij}^t &= P(t_1 + t_2 \leq |t|) \\ &= \int_0^{|t|} dt_1' P(t_2 \leq |t| - t_1 | t_1 = t_1') P(t_1 = t_1') \end{aligned} \tag{17}$$

Assuming the pick-ups arrive with uniform distribution, the same slot arrival possibility P_{ij}^T and next slot arrival possibility P_{ij}^{T+1} are calculated as following:

$$\begin{aligned} P_{ij}^t &= \frac{1}{|t|} \int_0^{|t|} \int_0^{|t|-t_1'} dt_1' dt_2 D_{ij}(t_2) \\ P_{ij}^{t+1} &= \frac{1}{|t|} \int_0^{|t|} \int_{|t|-t_1'}^{+\infty} dt_1' dt_2 D_{ij}(t_2) \end{aligned} \tag{18}$$

The slot arrival probability has the property of $P_{ij}^t + P_{ij}^{t+1} = 1$ since we neglect the possibility that a pick-up will be dropped off after 2 time slot periods (2 hours).

3.2.2 *Station level drop-off prediction*

The drop-off at station j is then estimated as:

$$s_j.dd(t) = \sum_{i \neq j} e_{ij}^t P_{ij}^t + e_{ij}^{t-1} P_{ij}^{t+1} \tag{19}$$

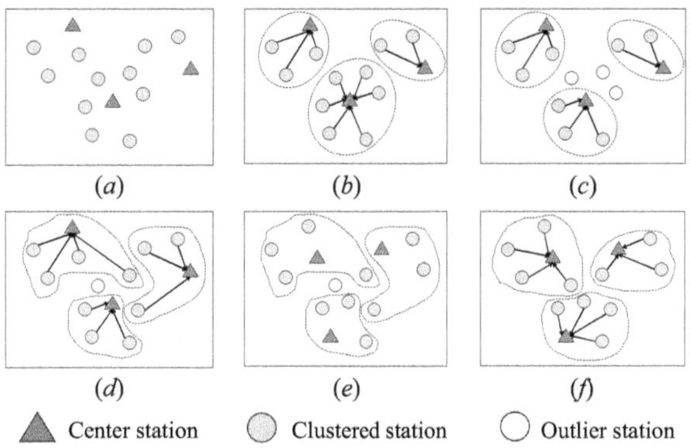

Figure 5: Constrained K-Centers Clustering procedure illustration.

The first term represents the estimated drop-offs during the same time slot as their pick-ups and the second term represents the estimated drop-offs one time slot later than their origin pick-ups from other stations.

3.3 Station rebalancing optimization

After we predict the station bike demand and determine their station inventory targets from Equation (2), the MINLP model for capacitated vehicle route optimization (Equation (3)-(8)) is still not solvable due to the following challenges: 1. the optimization problem is not feasible if the number of vehicles is not large enough to cover all stations; 2. the problem scale is too large to be solved efficiently; 3. direct solution of our MINLP model formulation contains subtours. In this section, we propose an AdaCCKC based hierarchial optimization model to solve the aforementioned challenges.

3.3.1 *Station clustering*

Clustering can be used to reduce the complexity of large-scale optimization problem. However, it has not arouse enough attention to reduce the scale of rebalancing optimization problem in bike sharing systems. Recently, Forma (2015) [9] proposed a heuristic algorithm and Schuijbroek (2013) [20] implemented the Maximum Spanning Star approximation for station clustering. However, in real large scale bike sharing systems, none of their methods are practical to deal with outlier stations. The implementation of clustering algorithms for bike rebalancing optimization problem has two challenges: 1) not only distances between stations should be taken into account, the station inventory target should also be considered for inventory constrains (Constrain (5)); 2) outlier stations should be discovered to guarantee inner cluster feasible routes. Although constrained clustering algorithms have been detailed studied, the constrained conditions in previous studies are mainly in the manner of *must-link* or *cannot link* pairs under the name of semi-supervised clustering [23, 2]. In this problem, whether two stations belong to the same cluster is not determined by themselves, but is affected by the total balance of stations in the same cluster. To the best of our knowledge, such kind of constrained clustering algorithm has not been studied ever before. In this paper, we propose a constrained K-Centers Clustering algorithm for bike stations to fill the research gap.

Algorithm 1 presents the proposed algorithm. It begins

Algorithm 1 $CCKC(\mathbf{TD},\mathbf{b},VN,VC,\delta,E)$

Input: TD_{ij}, b_i, VN, VC, δ, E;
Output: $\mathbf{c}$;

1: **for all** stations **do**
2: $\quad c(i) = \arg\min_{j \in E}(TD_{ij})$;
3: **for each** cluster $C_k = \{i|c(i) = E(k)\}$, **if** $B(C_k) > VC$ **do**
4: $\quad$ **while** $B(C_k) > VC$ **do**
5: $\quad\quad q = \arg\min_{i \in C_k^*} (\sum_{j \in E} TD_{ij})$, where $C_k^* = \{i|B(C_k \setminus i) < B(C_k)\}$;
6: $\quad\quad c(q) = 0, C_k = C_k \setminus q$;
7: **find** $l = \arg\max_{i,c(i)=0} (\sum_{j \in E} TD_{ij})$
8: $\quad$ **if** $\exists\ S_l = \{k|B(C_k \bigcup l) < VC, \min_{j \in C_k} TD_{lj} < \delta\}$
9: $\quad$ **then do** $c(l) = E(k)$, $k = \arg\min_{q \in S_l}(\min_{j \in C_q} TD_{lj})$
10: $\quad$ **else do** $c(l) = -1$;
11: **go to** step 7 **till** $\nexists\ i$ that $c(i) = 0$;
12: **for each** cluster C_k
13: $\quad E'(k) = \arg\min_{i,c(i)=E_k} \sum_{j,c(j)=E_k} TD_{ij}$;
14: **if** $E' \neq E$ **then** $E = E'$ **go to** step 1, **else go to** step 15;
15: **return** clustering result $\mathbf{c}$.

with an initial center set E, and assigns each station to its nearest stations. Then for a cluster, if the balance condition is not satisfied ($B(C_k) > VC$, where $B(C_k) = |\sum_{i \in C_k} b_i|$), we pick some stations out of the cluster. The stations, which are able to reduce the total balance of the cluster and close to other centers, are firstly picked out. In step 7~11, the unlabeled stations are assigned with new cluster label. For each unlabeled station, the new cluster label is determined by the total balance of a cluster and the distance between the station and its nearest station in the cluster. The unlabeled outlier stations that are far from cluster centers are preferentially processed. This step ensures these outliers scattered at the central region of the studied area, and can be easily covered by other clusters. After adjusting clustering result according to balance conditions, new centers are selected in Step 12~13. Step 1~13 are iterated until convergence (centers are unchanged). Step 15 outputs the clustering result.

Figure 5 presents a toy example of the capacity constrained K-centers algorithm. Fourteen stations are given in Figure 5(a), and three stations are marked as initial centers by triangles. All other stations are assigned to their nearest centers in (b). Capacity condition is examined in (c). If the capacity of a cluster is over the vehicle capacity, then some stations are pressed out as temporary outliers. Stations near other centers are preferentially excluded as they are much easier to be visited by vehicles from other clusters. The outliers are assigned to other centers with respect to cluster capacity and traveling distance in (d). New centers are generated according to the current clustering result in (e) and stations are assigned to new centers in (f). This procedure is repeated till convergence.

The clustering result obtained by Algorithm 1 has the following features: 1) the total balance of a cluster is under the capacity of vehicle; 2) stations in a same cluster are close to each other; 3) clusters are overlapped, their boundaries are not discriminative; 4) outliers (if any) are at the central region of the studied area. All the features mentioned above are very helpful for designing bicycle station rebalancing routes. Feature 1) guarantees that there exists feasible solutions in the optimization of inner cluster, while Feature 2) means the traveling cost can be largely reduced as most of the routes are internal/short-term travels. Feature 3) shows vehicles can travel in an overlapping manner to serve as many stations as possible. Feature 4) means outliers are surrounded by a lot of vehicles. Therefore, the stations can be easily served by adding the capacity of vehicles nearby or by assigning two or more vehicles from other clusters to serve them. Although these features show advantages of Algorithm 1 in solving the bicycle station rebalancing problem, this algorithm still has some shortages as a K-Centers based method. On the one hand, the number of clusters needs to be specified. On the other hand, the clustering result is influenced by the initial center set. We further improve Algorithm 1 by proposing an Adaptive Capacity Constrained K-centers Clustering (AdaCCKC) to overcome these shortages.

Algorithm 2 $AdaCCKC(\mathbf{TD},\mathbf{b},VC,\delta,VNmax, NI)$

Input: TD_{ij}, b_i, VC, δ, $VNmax$, NI;
Output: $\mathbf{c}$;

1: $VNbest = VNmax$, $zbest = \sum_p \sum_q TD_{pq}$;
2: **for** i **from** 1 **to** $VNmax$ **do**
3: $\quad$ Generate initial center set E;
4: $\quad$ **for** j **from** i **to** $VNmax$ **do**
5: $\quad\quad \mathbf{c}=CCKC(\mathbf{TD}, \mathbf{b}, VN, VC, \delta, E)$;
6: $\quad\quad$ **if** $\nexists\ h$ that $c(h) = 0$ **then break**
7: $\quad\quad$ **else** $l = \arg\min_{p,c(p)=0} \sum_{q,c(q)=0} TD_{pq}$,
8: $\quad\quad\quad E = unique(\mathbf{c})$, $E = E \bigcup l$;
9: $\quad$ **end**
10: $\quad VN = |E|$, $z = \sum_{k=1}^{|E|} \sum_{p,q \in C(k)} TD_{pq}$;
11: $\quad$ **if** $(VN < VNbest)\&(z < zbest)$ **then**
12: $\quad\quad VNbest = VN$, $zbest = z$, $\mathbf{c}^* = \mathbf{c}$;
13: Repeat Step 2~12 NI times;
14: **return** $\mathbf{c}^*$.

Algorithm 2 presents the proposed AdaCCKC algorithm. In each round, it begins with a randomly generated initial center set in Step 3. In step 4~9, Algorithm 1 CCKC is implemented to get a temporary clustering result. If there exists unlabeled bicycle stations, a new cluster center is added to the current center set. The new added center is determined by all unlabeled stations as shown in Step 7. The break condition in Step 6 can also be activated if the number of outliers is below a specified threshold instead of 0, which makes the proposed algorithm more flexible for bicycle stations rebalancing problem. Considering the effect of initial center set on the final clustering result, the number of initial centers is set to vary from 1 to $VNmax$ in Step 2, where $VNmax$ is the maximum number of available vehicles. Step 12 picks out the best clustering result. Steps 2~12 are repeated many times to reduce the influence of initial center set. As a result, Algorithm 2 can automatically determine the optimal number of vehicles in a smarter way, and users do not need to provide an initial center set.

3.3.2 *Inner cluster route optimization*

After our AdaCCKC clustering, the large scale multiple capacitated vehicles route optimization problem is simplified to one capacitated vehicle route optimization problem of small or median problem sizes:

$$\min \quad \mathcal{F}_C(\mathbf{x}) = \sum_{i=1}^{m}\sum_{j=1}^{m} x_{ij} TD_{ij} \tag{20}$$

$$s.t. \quad y_i + \sum_{j \neq i} x_{ij} s_j.rt = \sum_{j \neq i} x_{ij} y_j \quad \forall i \tag{21}$$

$$y_i \leq VC \qquad \forall i \tag{22}$$

$$x_{ij} \in \{0,1\} \qquad \forall i \neq j \tag{23}$$

$$\sum_{j \neq i} x_{ij} = 1 \quad \forall i \tag{24}$$

$$\sum_{i \neq j} x_{ij} = 1 \quad \forall j \tag{25}$$

However, this formulation is not complete since it allows multiple cycles (subtours) rather than one big route through all stations within one cluster. To handle this condition, subtour elimination constrains (SEC) should be included to provide one complete feasible rebalancing route.

$$\sum_{i \in S_C} \sum_{j \notin S_C} x_{ij} \geq 2 \qquad \forall S$$

where S_C is a subset of stations in cluster C. The SEC enforces that at least one route is going from a station in subset S_C to a station outside S_C. The number of SEC increases exponentially with the number of stations. For the bike sharing system with clusters of size up to 50 stations, generating all SECs is therefore impossible.

To solve this problem, we build SECs as lazy constrains. Unlike normal constrains which are generated in advance, lazy constrains are activated and added when a violated SEC is found from a feasible solution. We add the lazy constraints inside a callback function on the platform of Gurobi 6.5.0 Optimizer [17]. The callback function checks whether the candidate feasible solution is one complete tour. If not, a SEC is added for each subtour.

4. EXPERIMENTAL RESULTS

To validate the efficiency and effectiveness of our proposed method, extensive experiments are performed on real world NYC CitiBike trajectory data of 328 stations from July 2013 to May 2015. Among the 499 weekdays and 199 weekends, three sets of 40 weekdays and 40 weekends are randomly selected as testing set and the rest are selected as training set for bike usage demand prediction. For the problem of vehicle route optimization, a set of randomly selected 100 days records are selected to test the effectiveness and efficiency of our AdaCCKC algorithm and one day case study is conducted to test our optimization method. All experiments are conducted on a PC 7 with an Intel(R) Core i7-4790 CPU, 3.6 GHz, and 16 GB RAM running 64-bit Windows 10 system.

4.1 Experimental Data

We conduct our experiments on trip history data, station status data and meteorology data from NYC with their statistics presented in Table 2.

Citi Bike Data. Citibike transactions are generated by NYC Bike Sharing System which is public available from Citibike official website. 15.24 million transactions are extracted from July 1st 2013 to May 28_{th} 2015. This data set contains the following information: station id, bicycle pick-up station, bicycle pick-up time, bicycle drop-off station and bicycle drop-off time. The station status is monitored every 5 minutes which contains the information of station in service status, current available bikes and station capacity. The capacity of all rebalancing vehicles is set to be $VC = 25$ in our experiments.

Table 2: Details of the datasets

Data Source		New York City
Time Span		7/1/13 to 5/28/15
weekdays (weekends)		499 (199) days
Bike Data	# Stations	328
	# Bikes	6,000
	# Trips	15+ million
Meteo-rology Data	Heavy snowy (rainy)	60 hours
	snowy (rainy)	927 hours
	Foggy (mist)	739 hours
	Cloudy (sunny)	13,495 hours
	Temperature	[1.9, 97] ^oF
	Visibility	[0.2, 10] mile
	Wind Speed	[3.5, 65] mph
	Humidity	[11%, 100%]

Hourly Weather Reports. The NYC weather report data covers the time period from July 2013 to May 2015 which consists of the hourly weather report formatted as (time, weather condition, temperature, humidity, wind speed, visibility). The missing meteorology data is completed according to the previous weather report and the missing wind speed is estimated by the average value of its previous and next report. Due to the unbalanced weather condition records, weather conditions are clustered into four categories based on their suitability for outdoor bicycling (see Section 3.1.1).

4.2 Baselines & Metric

The methods proposed in our work to predict the station level pick-up demand and drop-off demand are denoted as multi-similarity-weighed KNN (**MSWK**) predictor and inter station bike transition (**ISBT**) predictor. In order to confirm the effectiveness of our models, we conduct experiments to compare our methods with the following baselines:

Multi-similarity-based inference (MSI) [14]: The MSI considers the similarity of weather, temperature, wind speed and time. Its similarity function is the multiplication of these three similarities and the weight of different factors are not studied.

Multi-similarity-equally-weighted KNN (MSEWK): The MSEWK method treats different factors ($\lambda_1, \lambda_2, \lambda_3$ see Section 3.1.1) with equally weight. This baseline is conducted to test the effectiveness of factors weight learning (Equation (14)).

Inhomogeneous Poisson Process Inference (IPPI) [1]: The IPPI method simulates the time between pick-up (or drop-off) events based on inhomogeneous Poisson process, choosing the estimated average rate of pick-ups and drop-offs from history trip records.

Historical Mean (HM) [10]: The HM method takes the average bike demand of historical records as prediction value without considering other influential factors.

The multi-similarity-weighed KNN (MSWK) predictor is also studied as a baseline to compare our inter station bike transition (ISBT) predictor for drop-off demand prediction.

Metric: The metric we adopt to measure the performance is the mean absolute error of bike demand of each time slot.

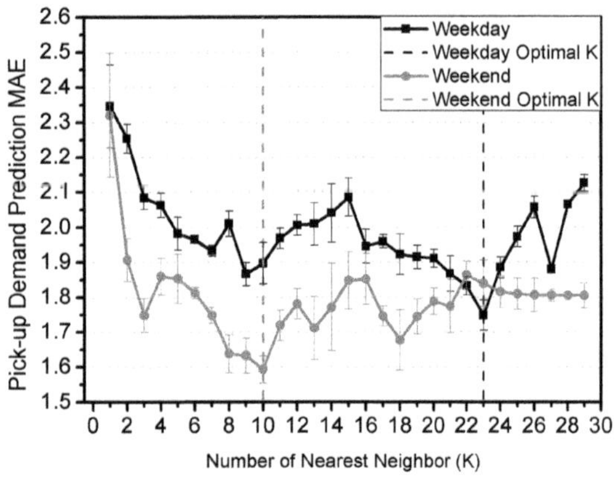

Figure 6: Performance comparison of MSWK predictor with different K.

The metric is denoted as MAE which is defined as follows:

$$MAE = \frac{1}{T}\sum_{t=1}^{T}\frac{\sum_{i=1}^{m}|\hat{s}_i.d(t) - s_i.d(t)|}{m}$$

Here $s_i.d(t)$ is our ground truth of bike pick-up or drop-off demand of station i during time slot t while $\hat{s}_i.d(t)$ and is the corresponding prediction value.

4.3 Performance Comparison

4.3.1 Station level bike demand prediction.

Station level bike pick-up demand prediction. As can be seen from Figure 6, the optimal number of nearest neighbor K for weekday pick-up demand prediction is 23 with minimum MAE of 1.74905 and the optimal number of nearest neighbor for weekend pick-up demand prediction is 10 with minimum MAE of 1.59323. A small K takes insufficient records to provide an accurate prediction result while a large K introduces unnecessary abnormal records. The performance comparison for pick-up demand prediction between our proposed MSWK and baselines is summarized in Figure 7(a). From Figure 7(a), we can see that the error rate obtained under our proposed MSWK is much lower than all the baselines with a significant margin. The performance comparison between MSWK and MSBI indicates that it is not necessary to consider the weighted records of all training data pool, which introduces abnormal records and lowers prediction accuracy. The comparison between MSWK and MSEWK proves the effectiveness of our similarity weight training process. Moreover, the multi-source prediction models (MSWK, MSBI and MSEWK) are better than the traditional one-factor statistical prediction models (IPPI, HM) by introducing multiple meteorology factors.

Station level bike drop-off demand prediction. The proposed ISBT method for bike drop-off demand prediction lowers the error rate for weekdays prediction with $MAE = 1.9133$ and for weekends prediction with $MAE = 1.5889$ compared to MSWK and other baseline algorithms (see Figure 7(b)). The performance of ISBT can be further improved by collecting more sufficient trip data to generate better 2-Gaussian fits for station-station connections.

4.3.2 Station inventory rebalancing optimization.

Constrained K-centers Clustering. The effectiveness and efficiency of our proposed CCKC are presented in Figure 8.

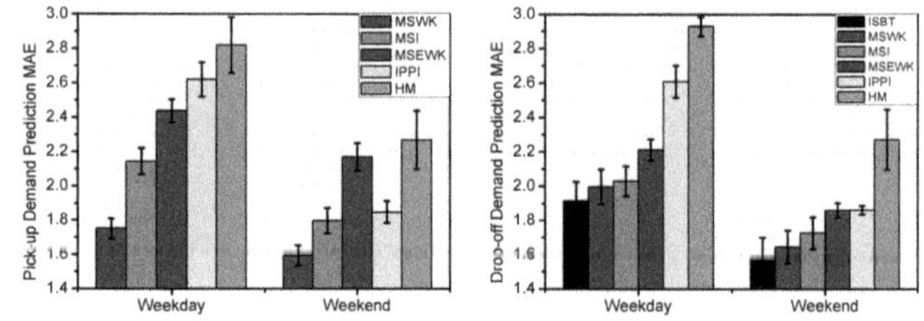

(a) Pick-up demand (b) Drop-off demand

Figure 7: A performance comparison of bike pick-up and drop-off demand prediction.

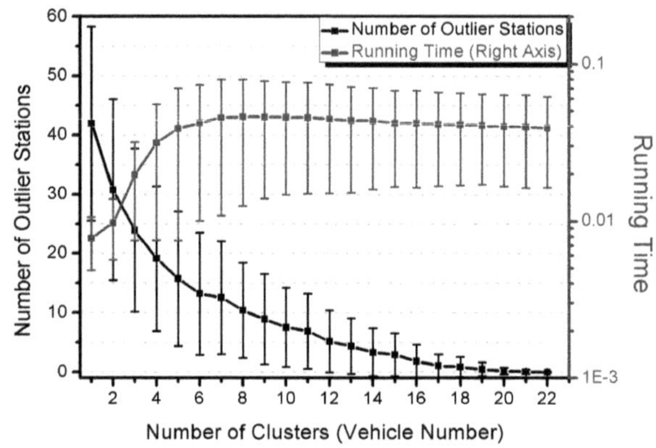

Figure 8: The efficiency of CCKC clustering

As can be seen, For a given number of vehicles, we are able to cluster the optimizable stations and discover outlier station efficiently with CPU running time less than 0.1 second. As the number of scheduled vehicles increases, the number of outlier stations decreases fast. The CCKC algorithm can help decide the minimum number of vehicles to cover all target stations or to balance the operation cost and the number of outlier stations.

Inner Cluster route optimization (A case study). We present one day NYC Citi Bike sharing system of 328 stations with their station inventory target calculated (see Figure 9(a)) as an example. In Figure 9(a), the red dots represent stations that need vehicle deliveries and blue dots represent stations that need vehicle pick-ups. 70 stations with zero inventory targets marked as gray dots in Figure 9(a)) are self-balanced stations and are not studied in our clustering and optimization progress. Figure 9(b) presents our optimization results based on CCKC algorithm with specified 8 vehicles. The CCKC algorithm clusters stations into different groups but 8 vehicles can not cover all stations. 22 outlier stations are discovered and marked as "X" when only 8 vehicles are scheduled (see Figure 9(b)). The self-balanced stations are marked as "diamond". The stations belong to the same cluster have the same color and are rebalanced by one vehicle with its routes represented by the lines. The first visited stations are marked as "star" from which an arrow is pointed out toward the second visited station that specifies the rebalancing route direction. Figure 9(c) represents the situation when all stations are optimized with 12 vehicles based on our AdaCCKC clustering and optimization models. Table 3 summarizes the optimization results including number of Lazy Constrains (LC), optimal objectives (Obj), CPU running times (CT) and objective gap (Gap) between baselines and MINLP model for inner cluster route optimiza-

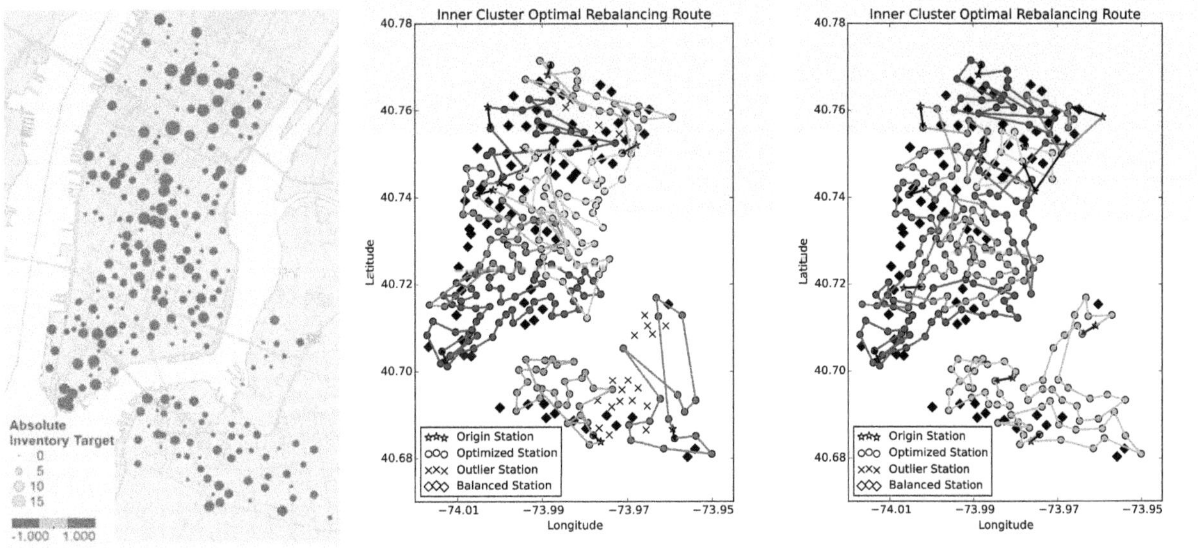

(a) Station Target Distribution (b) Route with outliers ($VN = 8$) (c) Route without outliers ($VN = 12$)

Figure 9: Vehicle Rebalancing Route Optimization (Case Study)

tions of 12 vehicles in Figure 9(c). The sizes of the station clusters range from 5 to 48. As can be seen from our case study, the optimization is very efficient for cluster size under 30 and it is able to solve for cluster of size up to 48. The effectiveness of our optimization model is compared to Nearest Neighbor Insertion Algorithm (NNIA) [12] and Genetic Algorithm (GA) [8], which are supposed to be efficient for vehicle routing optimization problems. In our case, our proposed MINLP model with lazy constrains is much more effective than NNIA and GA by providing optimal routs with much smaller traveling distances.

Table 3: Efficiency of inner cluster optimization

Cluster Size	MINLP with LC			NNIA		GA	
	LC	Obj (mile)	CT (s)	Obj (mile)	Gap (%)	Obj (mile)	Gap (%)
5	0	4.48	<1	4.48	0	4.48	0
6	2	4.23	<1	4.75	**12.3**	4.23	0
8	6	4.91	<1	5.07	3.3	4.91	0
21	10	9.58	40	14.75	5.4	9.84	2.7
20	37	10.21	210	10.39	1.8	10.97	7.4
25	26	11.21	271	11.73	4.6	12.2	8.8
22	36	8.32	401	9.49	**14.1**	8.87	6.6
23	35	17.83	752	21.4	**20.0**	18.28	2.5
19	29	12.16	1299	13.78	**13.3**	12.38	1.8
23	47	15.25	3469	16.64	9.1	15.84	3.9
38	69	18.96	7623	20.17	6.4	21.45	**13.1**
48	67	16.25	10163	19.44	**19.6**	18.81	**15.8**

5. RELATED WORK

There is an increasing interest in optimization problems arising in bike sharing systems. Below we describe some related studies that have been accomplished on bike demand prediction and rebalancing optimization.

Bike Demand Prediction. The early research on bike sharing system focused on the studies of daily bike demand forecasting using data mining techniques and classical empirical statistical methods. Yutaka [16] and Juan [11] built multi-factor statistical models for bicycle demand prediction by considering the influence of weather and geography. Liu et al.(2015) [15] built a spatial station demand prediction model by combining multiple static factors of surrounding environment and public transportation networks. The dynamic bike demand prediction for station inventory target requirements were investigated by implementing statistical models on historical trip data [1, 20]. The weather conditions were considered as influence factors on bike demands and integrated into prediction models [24, 14, 24]. However, among these multi-factor prediction models, the effectiveness of different influential factors has not been carefully studied and the different types of trips (commuters and exercisers) with different trip durations have not been considered to further improve the bike demand prediction accuracy.

Bike Rebalancing Optimization. For re-balancing the inherent asymmetry bicycle demand with minimum operation cost, Kaspi [13] explored bicycle reservation policies and suggested users visit the least loaded stations. Reservation could be denied or the destination could be diverted if no vacant lockers were expected to be available at the original destination. Also, Waserhole [25] and Singla [22] presented different dynamic pricing mechanisms that incentivized users to redistribute bikes by providing alternate rental prices.

Recent work on bike station re-balancing problem mainly focused on minimizing the total dispatching travel distance. Most bike station re-balancing problems focused on the static cases. Chemla [3] proposed a heuristic method for the single-vehicle static re-balancing problem, where each station could be visited more than once and could be used as a buffer in which bicycles are stored for a later visit. Their algorithm was based on a solution of the relaxed problem solved by a branch-and-cut procedure for system scale up to 60 stations. Erdogan [7] investigated a single capacitated vehicle routing problem that allowed the final bicycle inventory at each station to be between given lower and upper bounds. Rainer et. al [18] presented neighborhood search heuristics that considered optimal loading operations. For large scale problems, Forma [9] proposed a 3-step model. The stations were first clustered according to geographic information as well as inventory capacity, and then the routing problem was solved within each cluster and consecutive clusters. In addition, Raviv (2013) [19] studied an extended objective that minimized a weighted sum of expected number of un-served stations and traveling distance simultaneously. However, rebalancing optimization with outlier stations for large scale bike systems has not been studied.

6. CONCLUSION

In this paper, we developed a multi-source data smart optimization approach for addressing the station rebalancing problem in bike sharing systems. Specifically, we first proposed a Meteorology Similarity Weighted KNN (MSWK) regressor for predicting station pick-up demand. Also, we provided an Inter Station Bike Transition (ISBT) model to predict the drop-off demand. Then, the station inventory target levels were determined based on the predicted traffic flows, and were used for the following rebalancing task. Moreover, we developed an AdaCCKC clustering algorithm that can separate infeasible outlier stations and group the remaining stations into different clusters. With AdaCCKC, the large-scale multiple vehicle routing problem is reduced to inner cluster one vehicle routing problem with guaranteed feasible solutions. The vehicle rebalancing route is then optimized by a MINLP model with lazy constrains. Finally, the extensive experiments on real-world weather data as well as the trip data from the NYC Citi Bike System of 328 stations showed the advantages of our approach for bike demand prediction and large-scale bike rebalancing optimization.

7. ACKNOWLEDGMENTS

This research was partially supported by Futurewei Technologies, Inc. Also, it was supported in part by Natural Science Foundation of China (71329201) and the Rutgers 2015 Chancellor's Seed Grant Program.

8. REFERENCES

[1] R. Alvarez-Valdes, J. M. Belenguer, E. Benavent, J. D. Bermudez, F. Muñoz, E. Vercher, and F. Verdejo. Optimizing the level of service quality of a bike-sharing system. *Omega*, 2015.

[2] S. Basu, M. Bilenko, and R. J. Mooney. A probabilistic framework for semi-supervised clustering. In *SIGKDD 2004*, pages 59–68. ACM, 2004.

[3] D. Chemla, F. Meunier, and R. W. Calvo. Bike sharing systems: Solving the static rebalancing problem. *Discrete Optimization*, 10(2):120–146, 2013.

[4] M. Dell'Amico, E. Hadjicostantinou, M. Iori, and S. Novellani. The bike sharing rebalancing problem: Mathematical formulations and benchmark instances. *Omega*, 45:7–19, 2014.

[5] P. DeMaio. Bike-sharing: History, impacts, models of provision, and future. *J PUBLIC TRANSPORT*, 2009.

[6] G. Erdoğan, M. Battarra, and R. W. Calvo. An exact algorithm for the static rebalancing problem arising in bicycle sharing systems. *EJOR*, 2015.

[7] G. Erdoğan, G. Laporte, and R. W. Calvo. The one-commodity pickup and delivery traveling salesman problem with demand intervals. 2013.

[8] Z. Fanggeng, L. Sujian, S. Jiangsheng, and M. Dong. Genetic algorithm for the one-commodity pickup-and-delivery traveling salesman problem. *COMPUT IND ENG*, 2009.

[9] I. A. Forma, T. Raviv, and M. Tzur. A 3-step math heuristic for the static repositioning problem in bike sharing systems. *TRANSPORT RES B-METH*, 2015.

[10] J. Froehlich, J. Neumann, and N. Oliver. Sensing and predicting the pulse of the city through shared bicycling. In *IJCAI' 2009.*

[11] J. C. GarcÍla-Palomares, J. GutiÍęrrez, and M. Latorre. Optimizing the location of stations in bike-sharing programs: A {GIS} approach. *Applied Geography*, 35(1ÍC2):235 – 246, 2012.

[12] S. Joshi and S. Kaur. Nearest neighbor insertion algorithm for solving capacitated vehicle routing problem. In *INDIACom*, pages 86–88. IEEE, 2015.

[13] M. Kaspi, T. Raviv, and M. Tzur. Parking reservation policies in one-way vehicle sharing systems. *TRANSPORT RES B-METH*, 2014.

[14] Y. Li, Y. Zheng, H. Zhang, and L. Chen. Traffic prediction in a bike-sharing system. In *23rd SIGSPATIAL*, GIS '15, 2015.

[15] J. Liu, Q. Li, M. Qu, W. Chen, J. Yang, X. Hui, H. Zhong, and Y. Fu. Station site optimization in bike sharing systems. In *ICDM 2015.* IEEE, 2015.

[16] Y. Motoaki and R. A. Daziano. A hybrid-choice latent-class model for the analysis of the effects of weather on cycling demand. *Transportation Research Part A: Policy and Practice*, 75:217 – 230, 2015.

[17] G. Optimization et al. Gurobi optimizer reference manual. *URL: http://www.gurobi.com*, 2016.

[18] M. Rainer-Harbach, P. Papazek, B. Hu, and G. R. Raidl. *Balancing bicycle sharing systems: A variable neighborhood search approach.* Springer, 2013.

[19] T. Raviv, M. Tzur, and I. A. Forma. Static repositioning in a bike-sharing system: models and solution approaches. *EURO Journal on Transportation and Logistics*, 2(3):187–229, 2013.

[20] J. Schuijbroek, R. Hampshire, and W.-J. van Hoeve. Inventory rebalancing and vehicle routing in bike sharing systems. 2013.

[21] S. A. Shaheen, S. Guzman, and H. Zhang. Bikesharing in europe, the americas, and asia. *Transportation Research Record: Journal of the Transportation Research Board*, 2143(1):159–167, 2010.

[22] A. Singla, M. Santoni, G. Bartók, P. Mukerji, M. Meenen, and A. Krause. Incentivizing users for balancing bike sharing systems. In *29th AAAI Conference on Artificial Intelligence*, 2015.

[23] K. Wagstaff, C. Cardie, S. Rogers, S. Schrödl, et al. Constrained k-means clustering with background knowledge. In *ICML*, volume 1, pages 577–584, 2001.

[24] W. Wang. Forecasting bike rental demand using new york citi bike data. 2016.

[25] A. Waserhole and V. Jost. Pricing in vehicle sharing systems: Optimization in queuing networks with product forms. *EURO Journal on Transportation and Logistics*, pages 1–28, 2014.

Unified Point-of-Interest Recommendation with Temporal Interval Assessment

Yanchi Liu
Management Science and Information Systems
Rutgers University
yanchi.liu@rutgers.edu

Chuanren Liu
Decision Sciences and MIS
LeBow College of Business
Drexel University
chuanren.liu@drexel.edu

Bin Liu
Management Science and Information Systems
Rutgers University
binben.liu@rutgers.edu

Meng Qu
Management Science and Information Systems
Rutgers University
meng.qu@rutgers.edu

Hui Xiong*
Management Science and Information Systems
Rutgers University
hxiong@rutgers.edu

ABSTRACT

Point-of-interest (POI) recommendation, which helps mobile users explore new places, has become an important location-based service. Existing approaches for POI recommendation have been mainly focused on exploiting the information about user preferences, social influence, and geographical influence. However, these approaches cannot handle the scenario where users are expecting to have POI recommendation for a specific time period. To this end, in this paper, we propose a unified recommender system, named the 'Where and When to gO' (WWO) recommender system, to integrate the user interests and their evolving sequential preferences with temporal interval assessment. As a result, the WWO system can make recommendations dynamically for a specific time period and the traditional POI recommender system can be treated as the special case of the WWO system by setting this time period long enough. Specifically, to quantify users' sequential preferences, we consider the distributions of the temporal intervals between dependent POIs in the historical check-in sequences. Then, to estimate the distributions with only sparse observations, we develop the low-rank graph construction model, which identifies a set of bi-weighted graph bases so as to learn the static user preferences and the dynamic sequential preferences in a coherent way. Finally, we evaluate the proposed approach using real-world data sets from several location-based social networks (LBSNs). The experimental results show that our method outperforms the state-of-the-art approaches for POI recommendation in terms of various metrics, such as F-measure and NDCG, with a significant margin.

*Contact Author

KDD '16, August 13-17, 2016, San Francisco, CA, USA

DOI: http://dx.doi.org/10.1145/2939672.2939773

CCS Concepts

•**Information systems** → **Location based services;** *Geographic information systems;* •**Computing methodologies** → **Factor analysis;** •**Human-centered computing** → *Mobile computing;*

Keywords

POI Recommendation; Sequential Preference

1. INTRODUCTION

The successful development of location-aware services, such as location-based social networks (LBSNs), has changed people's lives. For example, Foursquare[1] reported 8 billion check-ins at 65 million point-of-interests (POIs) by over 55 million users as of December, 2015. Even in one local area, there are often multiple competing POIs with similar utilities, and individual users are not capable to make fully informed choices. Based on collective intelligence, recommending the right POIs to the right users thus becomes beneficial for users exploring new places with higher satisfactory level. The POI recommendations are also essential for service providers to improve service quality and attract new customers.

As we know, POI recommendation is a time-critical task [4, 19]. First of all, some POIs need more time to plan than others due to the capacity and budget issues. Let us consider to recommend a visit to a museum, such type of POI recommendation is preferred to be provided several days in advance so as to allow the user to be more prepared (e.g., learning the background of the museum). More importantly, the users' needs and preferences often vary from time to time, and we need to capture the users' dynamic needs and evolving preferences to deliver the right recommendations at the right time. For instance, if one visits a museum in one day, he/she might be more interested in going for shopping instead of visiting another museum in the following day. The *right POI (e.g., a shopping center) for the coming trip* or the *right time for the next visit to a museum* could be inferred from the historical check-in records. In summary, it

[1]https://foursquare.com/

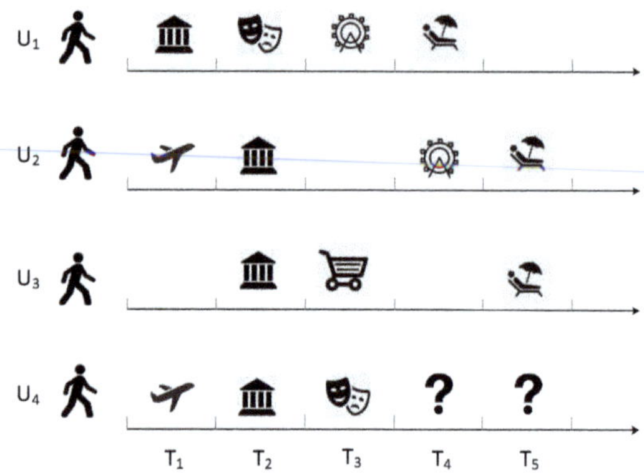

Figure 1: Examples of users check-in sequences.

is critical to investigate how to recommend the right POIs for a specific time period by learning the users' evolving sequential preferences from their historical check-in records.

In the literature, various methods have been proposed for POI recommendation in recent years [3, 22, 12, 13]. Also, there are studies taking temporal factors into consideration for the purpose of improving the algorithm efficiency and/or effectiveness. For example, Yuan et al. [29] and Gao et al. [7] proposed to separate each day into different time slots and learn the users' preferences for each slot for time-aware POI recommendations. However, these methods do not consider the temporal relationship between the related check-ins by considering all check-ins as 'a bag of words'. Thus, they may recommend *museums in the morning* and *bars at night*, but the same recommendations will be provided for the same time period on different days. Indeed, these methods cannot capture the evolving changes of user preferences. The assumption of unchanging user preferences across several days may not hold due to the temporal relationship between dependent POI check-ins. More recently, the importance of the sequential relationships/patterns hidden in the historical check-in sequences has been realized for 'next' POI recommendations [2, 4, 6, 30]. In particular, given the current check-in POI, the 'next' POI recommendation predicts the next interested POI which is most likely to be visited. However, these studies are unable to recommend POI for a specific time period due to the lack of modeling temporal interval information in their methods.

To better motivate this work, let us consider the example in Figure 1. For illustration purpose, we assume the time unit is day, i.e. T_1 is the first day and T_5 is the fifth day in the records of each user. Given users' check-ins to airport, museum, theater, shopping mall, amusement park and beach, what POIs should we recommend to user U_4 at time T_4 and T_5? Traditional POI recommender systems may recommend beach for both time periods since beach appears most frequently with museum and theater, and the existing 'next' POI recommender systems will recommend amusement park for both since amusement park appears mostly after theater. However, intuitively, we can see amusement park should be more likely to be recommended for time T_4, and beach for T_5 because users went to amusement park mostly two days after going to museum according to the history records, and followed by going to beach. The possible reason could be that, after spending one day in museum, one would prefer to do something else to refresh the mind, e.g., by watching a show. Then, he/she would do something fun, e.g., going to amusement park, followed by relaxing on beach.

Indeed, in this paper, we investigate how to do POI recommendations for a specific time period in LBSNs by capturing users' evolving sequential preferences from their historical check-in records. This task is much harder than the traditional POI recommendation due to the following challenges. First, it is necessary to model the sequential check-in patterns with temporal intervals between dependent POIs. Second, the sequential check-in data is very sparse. Only limited observations are available for estimating the distributions of the temporal intervals between dependent POIs in the historical check-in sequences.

To address these challenges, we propose a unified recommender system, named 'Where and When to gO' (WWO), to integrate the static user interests and evolving sequential preferences with temporal interval assessment. Specifically, given POI sequences consisting of check-in POIs ordered by check-in time, we first assess the temporal intervals between POIs from check-in sequences of each user as a POI-POI transition matrix, where each item is a set of observed intervals for a POI-POI pair. Then, we develop a bi-weighted low-rank graph construction model to learn individual user's behavioral preferences by identifying a set of common graph bases. The graph is bi-weighted so that the static user interests used by the traditional recommender systems are simultaneously learned with their evolving sequential preferences.[2] Finally, the main contributions of this paper can be summarized as follows:

- A new recommender system, named WWO, is developed for providing POI recommendations for a specific time period. WWO exploits user check-in sequential patterns with temporal interval assessment based on all historical user check-ins. Moreover, WWO is able to capture both static user interests and their evolving sequential preferences for POI recommendations.

- A bi-weighted low-rank graph construction model is proposed to estimate the distributions with only sparse observations. The model helps to identify a set of bi-weighted graph bases, which in turn can be leveraged for learning the user interests and their sequential preferences in a coherent way.

- The WWO recommender system has been evaluated on large-scale real-world data for POI recommendations. The experimental results show that our method outperforms state-of-the-art methods in terms of multiple metrics such as F-measure and Normalized Discounted Cumulative Gain (NDCG).

2. THE WWO RECOMMENDER SYSTEM

In this section, we introduce our WWO (Where and When to gO) recommender system. Assume that we have M POIs denoted by the set $\mathcal{P}$ and N users. For simplicity, we let $\mathcal{P} = \{1, 2, \cdots, M\}$, i.e., we use integers to represent the POIs. For the n-th user, $n = 1, 2, \cdots, N$, we have his/her

[2]In this way, the traditional recommendation methods can be treated as the special cases of our approach.

Table 1: Descriptions of mathematical notations.

Notation	Description
M, N	The number of POIs and users, respectively.
$\mathcal{P} = \{1, 2, \cdots, M\}$	The set of POIs.
$s^n = (s_1^n, s_2^n, \cdots, s_{L_n}^n)$	The check-in sequence of n-th user.
$s_l^n = (p_l^n, t_l^n)$	The l-th check-in event with POI $p_l^n \in \mathcal{P}$ and time t_l^n.
d_{ij}^n	The observed temporal intervals from POI i to POI j in the sequence s^n.
$\mathcal{N}(\mu_{ij}^n, \sigma_\mu^2)$	The distribution of d_{ij}^n.
c_p^n	The observed visiting frequency to POI p in the sequence s^n.
$\text{Poisson}(\nu_p^n)$	The distribution of c_p^n.
$\alpha \in \mathbb{R}^{N\times K}$	The approximating coefficients in low-rank graph construction.
$\beta^k \in \mathbb{R}^{M\times M}$	The edge weight matrix of the k-th graph basis, for $k = 1, 2, \cdots, K$.
$\gamma \in \mathbb{R}^{K\times M}$	The node weights of all graph bases.
$\mathcal{N}(0, \sigma_\alpha^2), \mathcal{N}(0, \sigma_\beta^2), \Gamma(\eta, \theta)$	The priors of α, β, and γ, respectively.

check-in records represented as a sequence of check-in events $s^n = (s_1^n, s_2^n, \cdots, s_{L_n}^n)$ with the length L_n. Each check-in event s_l^n, $l = 1, 2, \cdots, L_n$, is a tuple $s_l^n = (p_l^n, t_l^n)$ where $p_l^n \in \mathcal{P}$ is the l-th POI in the check-in records ordered by the corresponding event time t_l^n. Therefore, we have $t_{l'}^n \geq t_l^n$ when $l' > l$. Table 1 lists some notations used in this paper.

Given the historical check-in records of all the users $\mathcal{S} = \{s^n | n = 1, 2, \cdots, N\}$ and a future time t, we predict the n-th user's possible check-in, e.g. $p \in \mathcal{P}$, based on not only the user interest on p but also the temporal dependency between the prediction (p, t) and the historical records $s_l^n = (p_l^n, t_l^n)$.

Formally, our idea of WWO recommendations is to maximize the likelihood of check-in $p \in \mathcal{P}$ at time t, $\Pr(p, t|s^n)$, which is computed as:

$$\Pr(p, t|s^n) \propto f^n(p) \cdot g^n(t|p). \quad (1)$$

The term $f^n(p)$ computes the user's *interest* on p, which is the focus of traditional POI recommender systems. The term $g^n(t|p)$ computes the user's *evolving sequential preference*, which is the likelihood of the predicted check-in event (p, t) at time t. In other words, we aim at recommending the right POI at the right time to the right user. As such, we distribute the ongoing recommendations over time based on the historical temporal interval patterns so as to make the recommendation less disturbing and more favorable. In the following, we provide the details about computing these two terms with probability density functions.

Figure 2 shows the framework of our WWO recommender system. We construct a POI transition cube by extracting sequential patterns from user check-in sequences, then the user interests and their evolving sequential preferences are modeled and learned simultaneously with a low-rank graph construction model. Finally, by ranking the potential POIs according to both sequential preferences and user interests for specific time period, we have our WWO POI recommender system.

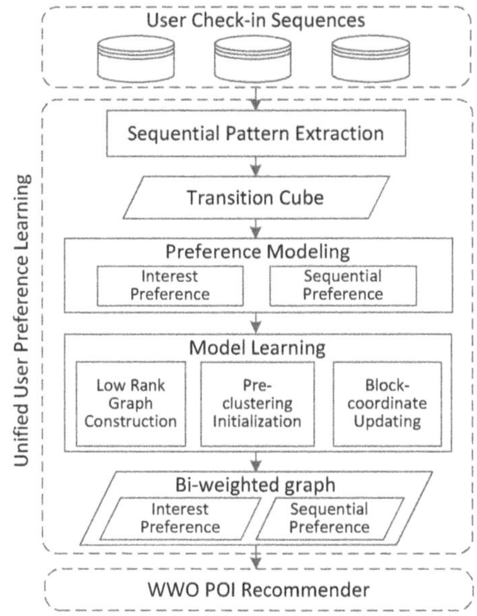

Figure 2: The WWO recommendation framework.

2.1 Sequential Pattern Extraction

To extract the sequential patterns from historical check-in records, we first define:

DEFINITION 1 (**Observed Temporal Intervals**). *The observed temporal intervals from i to j in s^n are represented by a set:*

$$d_{ij}^n = \{ \min_{\substack{l'>l \\ s_{l'}^n = j}} t_{l'}^n - t_l^n \mid l = 1, 2, \cdots, L_n, s_l^n = i \}. \quad (2)$$

Note that we use the min operator with several constraints in Equation 2 because both i and j can be visited by the same user multiple times. As a result, we consider only the soonest visit of j after each recent visit of i. With the temporal intervals between POI pairs extracted for user n, a POI-POI transition interval matrix is constructed, with each item d_{ij}^n as a set of intervals from POI i to POI j of user n. By combining the transition matrices for all the users, a transition interval cube can be obtained, which unifies both user interests and their sequential preferences. To provide an intuitive understanding, an example is shown in Figure 3 about how to generate the transition matrix for one user from a sequence of user check-ins.

2.2 Preference Modeling

Sequential Preference: $g^n(t|p)$. We compute the sequential preference term as: $g^n(t|p) = \max_{1\leq l\leq L_n} g_l^n(t|p)$, where $g_l^n(p, t)$ is the probability density of temporal interval $(t - t_l^n)$ from the check-in of p_l^n at time t_l^n to the check-in of p at time t. We use the max operator to identify the historical check-in event s_l^n having the strongest temporal dependency with the recommendation (p, t).

Generally, by letting $s_l^n = i$ and $p = j$, we want to estimate a distribution of the temporal intervals when the user

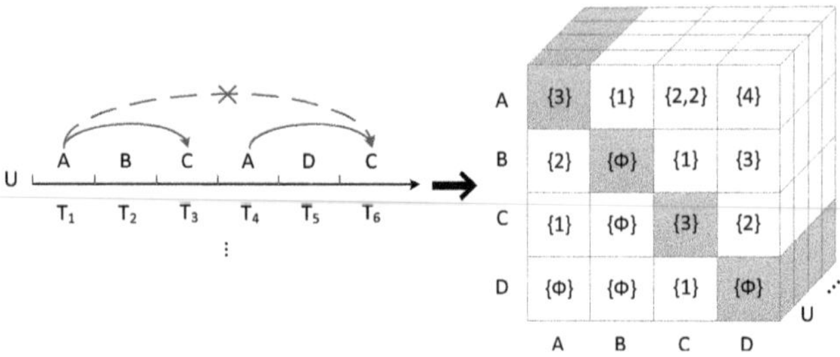

Figure 3: Example of observed temporal intervals. For the POI pair A to C, the temporal intervals with solid lines are counted, and we get $\{2, 2\}$ as d^U_{AC}.

would visit j after visiting i. In this paper, we approximate this distribution using $\mathcal{N}(\mu^n_{ij}, \sigma^2_\mu)$. It follows that:

$$g^n_l(t|p) = \mathcal{N}(\delta|\mu^n_{ij}, \sigma^2_\mu) = \frac{1}{\sqrt{2\pi}\sigma_\mu} \exp(-\frac{(\delta - \mu^n_{ij})^2}{2\sigma^2_\mu}),$$

where $s^n_l = i, p = j$ and $t - t^n_l = \delta$. We have a histogram of one random POI pair in Figure 4 which shapes like a Gaussian distribution and indicates our model specifications are appropriate.

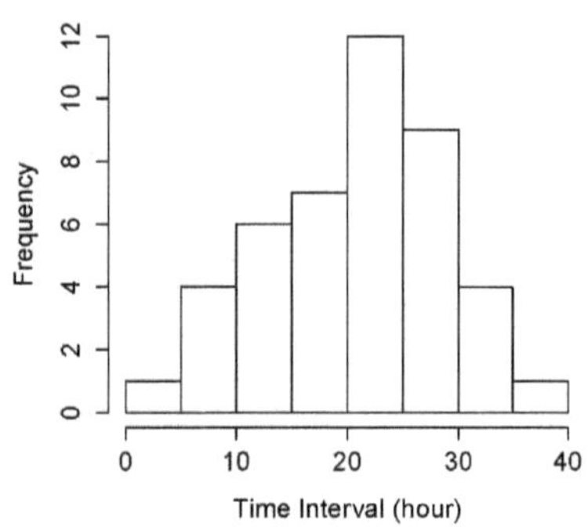

Figure 4: Histogram of the temporal interval of one POI pair

Interest Preference: $f^n(p)$. To compute the interest preference term, we also fit the observed visiting frequency with a distribution, e.g., Gaussian. However, the visiting frequencies in our data is polarized as shown in Figure 5, which does not shape like a Gaussian. As noticed by [1, 13], the nature of Poisson distribution is more suitable and effective for modeling the skewed interest preference in terms of visiting counts, which provide implicit feedback for better POI recommendations. Therefore, we adopt the Poisson distribution Poisson(ν^n_p) to estimate $f^n(p)$:

$$f^n(p) = \text{Poisson}(c^n_p|\nu^n_p) = \frac{(\nu^n_p)^{c^n_p}}{c^n_p!} \exp(-\nu^n_p),$$

where c^n_p is the observed visiting frequency:

DEFINITION 2 (**Observed Visiting Frequency**). *The observed visiting frequency to $p \in \mathcal{P}$ of the user in s^n is the cardinality of visiting records:*

$$c^n_p = |\{\, l \mid l = 1, 2, \cdots, L_n, s^n_l = p \,\}|, \qquad (3)$$

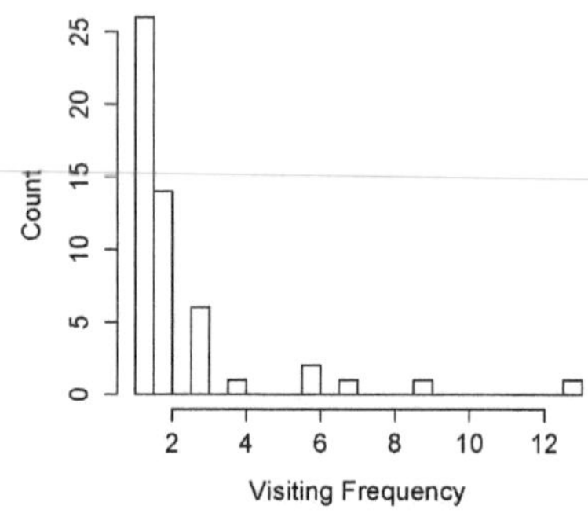

Figure 5: Histogram of the visiting frequency of one user

2.3 Model Learning

Both the observed temporal intervals and visiting frequency can be very sparse. Therefore, 1) we have empty $d^n_{ij} = \emptyset$ or $|d^n_{ij}|$ is too small, for many pairs of POI (i, j); 2) we have $c^n_p = 0$ for many unobserved check-ins $p \in \mathcal{P}$. As a result, using these observations directly does not suffice to robustly estimate the temporal interval distributions and the user preferences. To address these issues, we develop the low-rank graph construction model in Section 3.

2.4 Recommendation

In practice, we aim to recommend the historically unvisited POIs within a time duration T instead of a single timestamp t. This can be achieved by ranking the options p according to the expected visiting frequency within the time duration $T = [t, t + \Delta]$:

$$\mathbb{E}[c^n_p|\nu^n_p] \cdot \max_{1 \le l \le L_n} \int_t^{t+\Delta} g^n_l(t|p)\mathrm{d}t \qquad (4)$$
$$= \nu^n_p \cdot \max_{1 \le l \le L_n} \left(\Phi(\frac{t + \Delta - t^n_l - \mu^n_{s^n_l p}}{\sigma_\mu}) - \Phi(\frac{t - t^n_l - \mu^n_{s^n_l p}}{\sigma_\mu}) \right)$$

where $c^n_p \sim$ Poisson(ν^n_p) and the integral term can be easily computed with the cumulative distribution function (CDF) $\Phi(\cdot)$ of standard $\mathcal{N}(0, 1)$. The top ranked options can then be recommended to the user. It's worthy to note that, when $t \to t^n_{L_n}$ and $\Delta \to \infty$, the computation of Equation 4 will be dominated by the interest preference ν^n_p. In other words, our unified recommender system is a proper generalization of the existing approaches.

3. LOW-RANK GRAPH CONSTRUCTION

Since the observations for specific users are sparse, we estimate the distribution parameters μ^n and ν^n for all users $n = 1, 2, \cdots, N$ collaboratively. To this end, we define the bi-weighted graph $G^n = \langle \mathcal{P}, E, \mu^n, \nu^n \rangle$ with $\mathcal{P}$ as graph nodes, where each graph node $p \in \mathcal{P}$ is weighted by ν^n_p and each graph edge $(i, j) \in E$ is weighted by μ^n_{ij}. In other words, the bi-weighted graph G^n is a unified representation of two aspects in the POI check-in behaviors of the n-th user: 1) The node weight vector $\nu^n \in \mathbb{R}^M$ characterizes the distribution of user interests. 2) The edge weight matrix $\mu^n \in \mathbb{R}^{M \times M}$ characterizes the distribution of the temporal intervals between the check-in events.

With this definition, we estimate the distribution parameters by collaboratively constructing the bi-weighted graphs for all the users. Specifically, we assume there are K graph bases B^k for $k = 1, 2, \cdots, K$ and each user-specific graph G^n can be approximated by:

$$G^n \leftarrow \sum_{k=1}^{K} \alpha_{nk} B^k. \tag{5}$$

Equivalently, by letting the edge weight matrix and the node weight vector of the graph basis B^k be $\beta^k \in \mathbb{R}^{M \times M}$ and $\gamma^k \in \mathbb{R}^M$, respectively, it follows that:

$$\mu^n = \sum_{k=1}^{K} \alpha_{nk} \beta^k, \tag{6}$$

$$\nu^n = \sum_{k=1}^{K} \alpha_{nk} \gamma^k. \tag{7}$$

Here, α_{nk} are the approximating coefficients. Note that, the number of graph bases, K, can be deemed the rank of the graph construction, which is set to be much smaller than the number of user-specific graphs, i.e., $K \ll N$.

Now we can compute the probability density of the observations in d_{ij}^n and c_p^n:

$$\begin{aligned}
&\Pr(d, c|\alpha, \beta, \gamma, \sigma_\mu) \\
=&\prod_{n=1}^{N}\prod_{i=1}^{M}\prod_{j=1}^{M}\prod_{\delta \in d_{ij}^n} \frac{1}{\sqrt{2\pi}\sigma_\mu} \exp(-\frac{(\delta - \mu_{ij}^n)^2}{2\sigma_\mu^2}) \\
&\prod_{n=1}^{N}\prod_{p=1}^{M} \frac{(\nu_p^n)^{c_p^n}}{c_p^n!} \exp(-\nu_p^n)
\end{aligned}$$

Therefore the log-likelihood is:

$$\begin{aligned}
&\ln \Pr(d, c|\alpha, \beta, \gamma, \sigma_\mu) \\
=&-\frac{1}{2\sigma_\mu^2}\sum_{n=1}^{N}\sum_{i=1}^{M}\sum_{j=1}^{M}\sum_{\delta \in d_{ij}^n} (\delta - \mu_{ij}^n)^2 \\
&-\frac{1}{2}\sum_{n=1}^{N}\sum_{i=1}^{M}\sum_{j=1}^{M}\sum_{t \in d_{ij}^n} \ln(2\pi\sigma_\mu^2) \\
&+\sum_{n=1}^{N}\sum_{p=1}^{M}(c_p^n \ln(\nu_p^n) - \nu_p^n) - \sum_{n=1}^{N}\sum_{p=1}^{M} \ln(c_p^n!)
\end{aligned}$$

Maximizing this log-likelihood is equivalent to minimize the following objective function:

$$\begin{aligned}
\mathcal{L}(\alpha, \beta, \gamma) =& \frac{1}{2\sigma_\mu^2}\sum_{n=1}^{N}\sum_{i=1}^{M}\sum_{j=1}^{M}\sum_{\delta \in d_{ij}^n} (\delta - \mu_{ij}^n)^2 \\
&-\sum_{n=1}^{N}\sum_{p=1}^{M}(c_p^n \ln(\nu_p^n) - \nu_p^n),
\end{aligned}$$

where the hyperparameter σ_μ is fixed. With the low-rank graph construction Equation 6 and Equation 7, it follows that

$$\begin{aligned}
\mathcal{L}(\alpha, \beta, \gamma) =& \frac{1}{2\sigma_\mu^2}\sum_{n=1}^{N}\sum_{i=1}^{M}\sum_{j=1}^{M}\sum_{\delta \in d_{ij}^n} (\delta - \sum_{k=1}^{K} \alpha_{nk}\beta_{ij}^k)^2 \\
&-\sum_{n=1}^{N}\sum_{p=1}^{M}(c_p^n \ln(\sum_{k=1}^{K} \alpha_{nk}\gamma_p^k) - \sum_{k=1}^{K} \alpha_{nk}\gamma_p^k).
\end{aligned}$$

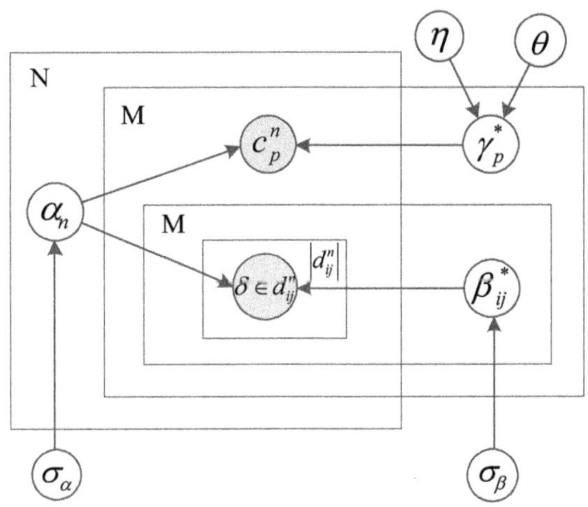

Figure 6: The probabilistic graphical model.

Indeed, the above factorization can be demonstrated as a probabilistic graphical model shown in Figure 6. Moreover, in order to reduce the generalization error (accuracy on unseen data), priors of the latent variables (α, β, γ) can be used as regularizations:

$$\alpha \sim \mathcal{N}(0, \sigma_\alpha^2),$$
$$\beta \sim \mathcal{N}(0, \sigma_\beta^2),$$
$$\gamma \sim \Gamma(\eta, \theta).$$

In particular, we use the Gamma distribution $\gamma \sim \Gamma(\eta, \theta)$ since it is the conjugate one with Poisson. Then the joint log-likelihood to be minimized is as follows:

$$\begin{aligned}
\mathcal{L}(\alpha, \beta, \gamma) =& \frac{1}{2\sigma_\mu^2}\sum_{n=1}^{N}\sum_{i=1}^{M}\sum_{j=1}^{M}\sum_{\delta \in d_{ij}^n} (\delta - \sum_{k=1}^{K} \alpha_{nk}\beta_{ij}^k)^2 \\
&-\sum_{n=1}^{N}\sum_{p=1}^{M}(c_p^n \ln(\sum_{k=1}^{K} \alpha_{nk}\gamma_p^k) - \sum_{k=1}^{K} \alpha_{nk}\gamma_p^k) \\
&+\frac{1}{2\sigma_\alpha^2}\|\alpha\|_F^2 + \frac{1}{2\sigma_\beta^2}\sum_{k=1}^{k}\|\beta^k\|_F^2 \\
&-\sum_{k=1}^{K}\sum_{p=1}^{M}((\eta - 1)\ln \gamma_p^k - \theta\gamma_p^k),
\end{aligned} \tag{8}$$

where $\alpha \in \mathbb{R}^{N \times K}$ is the matrix of approximating coefficients α_{nk}, $\beta^k \in \mathbb{R}^{M \times M}$ is the edge weight matrix of graph basis B^k, and $\gamma \in \mathbb{R}^{K \times M}$ is the matrix of node weights γ_p^k in all graph bases.

4. LEARNING ALGORITHM

We use an alternative algorithm to solve α, β, and γ iteratively. Here, we let

$$D_{ij}^n = \sum_{\delta \in d_{ij}^n} \delta, C_{ij}^n = |d_{ij}^n|.$$

Also, at the beginning of each iteration, we compute μ and ν with Equation 6 and Equation 7 with current solution (α, β, γ). Then we have

$$\frac{\partial \mathcal{J}}{\partial \alpha_{nk}} = \frac{\sum_{ij}(D_{ij}^n - C_{ij}^n \mu_{ij}^n)\beta_{ij}^k}{-\sigma_\mu^2} - \sum_p (\frac{c_p^n}{\nu_p^n} - 1)\gamma_p^k + \frac{\alpha_{nk}}{\sigma_\alpha^2},$$

$$\frac{\partial \mathcal{J}}{\partial \beta_{ij}^k} = \frac{\sum_n (D_{ij}^n - C_{ij}^n \mu_{ij}^n)\alpha_{nk}}{-\sigma_\mu^2} + \frac{\beta_{ij}^k}{\sigma_\beta^2},$$

$$\frac{\partial \mathcal{J}}{\partial \gamma_p^k} = -\sum_n (\frac{c_p^n}{\nu_p^n} - 1)\alpha_{nk} - (\frac{\eta - 1}{\gamma_p^k} - \theta).$$

Although it is straightforward to update one entry at a time with arbitrary initialization for all entries in α, β, and γ, we improve the robustness of the alternative algorithm using: 1) the pre-clustering initialization based on spherical KMeans; and 2) the block-coordinate updating [21].

4.1 Pre-clustering Initialization

Specifically, we first propose a novel clustering method to initialize the graph bases and the approximating coefficients. Note that, since the graph bases are used to approximate the distribution parameters μ and ν, the bases can be initialized with the representative observed distribution samples. Therefore, we aggregate and cluster the observed temporal intervals and visiting frequencies. To aggregate the observations, we construct the feature matrix $X \in \mathbb{R}^{N \times (M^2+M)}$, where each row X_n corresponds to one sequence s^n. The first M^2 entries of X_n encodes the average temporal interval:

$$X_{n,(i-1)M+j} = D_{ij}^n / C_{ij}^n.$$

The last M entries of X_n encodes the observed visiting frequency:

$$X_{n,M^2+p} = c_p^n.$$

Then, we apply the spherical KMeans algorithm to group the rows of X into K clusters, where K is the number of graph bases for the low-rank graph construction. Here, we use spherical KMeans with cosine similarity instead of Euclidean distance since the dimension of X is high.

Although the results of this pre-clustering may not be the true graph bases, we believe the clustering results can provide positive guidance for the graph basis learning algorithm. Thus, given the centroid $\widehat{X}_k$ of the k-th cluster in the pre-clustering solution, we initialize the graph basis B^k by reformatting the first M^2 entries of $\widehat{X}_k$ as the matrix β^k and the last M entries as the vector γ^k. Moreover, we initialize the approximating coefficients α with the cosine similarity between X_n and $\widehat{X}_k$ used by the spherical clustering:

$$\alpha_{nk} = \frac{\cos(X_n, \widehat{X}_k)}{\sum_{k'} \cos(X_n, \widehat{X}_{k'})}.$$

4.2 Block-coordinate Updating

With the above pre-clustering initialization, we then iteratively update rows in α where each row corresponds to one user. Then we update each graph basis B^k with the edge weight matrix β^k and the node weight vector γ^k. For each updating, the learning rate ϵ is determined to make sure the objective function $\mathcal{J}(\alpha, \beta, \gamma)$ is decreasing. The overall algorithm repeats until the value of $\mathcal{J}(\alpha, \beta, \gamma)$ keeps stable or the limitation on the number of iterations is reached. More details are shown in Algorithm 1.

Algorithm 1 Block-coordinate Optimization

```
Initialize α, β, and γ with pre-clustering.
repeat
  for n = 1, ···, N do
    Update the row α_n ← α_n − ε ∂J/∂α_n.
  end for
  for k = 1, ···, K do
    Update the base β^k ← β^k − ε ∂J/∂β^k.
  end for
  for k = 1, ···, K do
    Update the ror γ_p^k ← γ_p^k − ε ∂J/∂γ_p^k.
  end for
until Convergence
```

5. EXPERIMENTAL RESULTS

In this section, we evaluate the performances of the proposed WWO recommender system.

5.1 The Experimental Data

All the experiments were performed on real-world datasets including two LBSN datasets collected from Foursquare and Gowalla[3], which are shown in Figure 7.

The Foursquare dataset includes 2,932 users for 4,194 POIs with 121,678 check-in observations. Each user checked into 41.5 POIs on average. Each check-in contains the user ID, check-in time, venue ID and the venue's geo-coordinates.

The Gowalla dataset includes 1,313 users for 2,196 POIs with 45,410 check-in observations. Each user checked into 34.58 POIs on average. Note that, for Foursquare and Gowalla data, we remove those POIs with less than 10 users and remove users with less than 10 check-ins.

5.2 Evaluation Metrics

In our experiments, the first 80% check-ins are used as the training data, and the other 20% are used as the testing data. We learn the models and obtain the recommendation POI list for a future time period $T_n = [t_n + \delta, t_n + \Delta]$ for each user n, where t_n is the latest check-in time in the training data. Specifically, we are interested in investigating the following questions: (1) How WWO performs with different lengths of time period from now, which means $\delta = 0$ and Δ varies; (2) How WWO performs with specific time period from different future time, which means $\Delta - \delta$ is a constant and δ varies.

Note that if there is no check-in existing in the T_n period, this user will not be included for evaluation. Also, the visited POIs in the training data have been removed in the testing data since recommending new POIs is our target. Finally,

[3]https://snap.stanford.edu/data/loc-gowalla.html

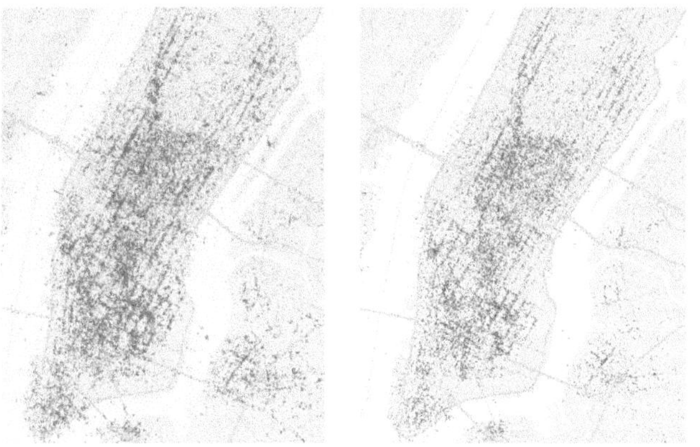

(a) Foursquare (b) Gowalla

Figure 7: Data visualization

the evaluation metrics include F-measure and the NDCG of the newly visited POIs.

F-measure. F-measure combines precision and recall together with a harmonic mean. Here we use the F_β measure with $\beta = 0.5$ which puts more emphasis on precision than recall [13],

$$F_\beta@P = (1+\beta^2)\frac{Precision@P \times Recall@P}{\beta^2 \cdot Precision@P + Recall@P}. \quad (9)$$

Given a top-P recommendation list S_{rec} sorted in a descending order based on the prediction values, precision and recall can be obtained as follows: $Precision@P = \frac{S_{rec} \bigcap S_{new}}{P}$, $Recall@P = \frac{S_{rec} \bigcap S_{new}}{S_{new}}$, where S_{new} are the POIs a user newly visited in the test data. The precision and recall for the entire recommender system are computed by averaging all the precision and recall values of all the users.

Normalized Discounted Cumulative Gain (NDCG). Given a top-P recommendation list sorted in a descending order of the prediction values, NDCG [10] is defined as

$$NDCG@P = \frac{1}{IDCG} \times \sum_{i=1}^{N} \frac{2^{rel_i} - 1}{log(i+1)}, \quad (10)$$

where IDCG is the maximum possible DCG for a given set of recommendations, and rel_i is 1 if the recommended POI at position i is visited by the user and 0 otherwise. NDCG measures the ranking quality of the recommender system based on a graded relevance scale of recommendations, which assumes more interested POIs should appear earlier in the recommendation list. The NDCG for the entire recommender system are computed by averaging all the NDCG values of all the users.

5.3 Baselines

Our proposed system focuses on assessing user evolving sequential preferences together with user interests for POI recommendation. We thus introduce the following baseline methods for comparison.

- Probabilistic Matrix Factorization (PMF) [18] is a generalized matrix factorization model, which has been widely used for recommendation tasks.
- Factorized Personalized Markov Chains (FPMC) [20] embeds users' preferences and their personalized Markov chain to provide next basket item recommendation. An extended factorized personalized Markov chain with localized region constraint (FPMC-LR) [4] was proposed for POI recommendation while considering only the neighborhood locations. Since we only focus on POI recommendation and try to explore the time interval influence, so we do not consider the location constraint here.
- Purchase Interval based Matrix Factorization (PIMF) [32] shows that the intervals between user purchases have an influence on a user's purchase decision, and thus PIMF incorporates this purchase interval factor into matrix factorization for recommendation.

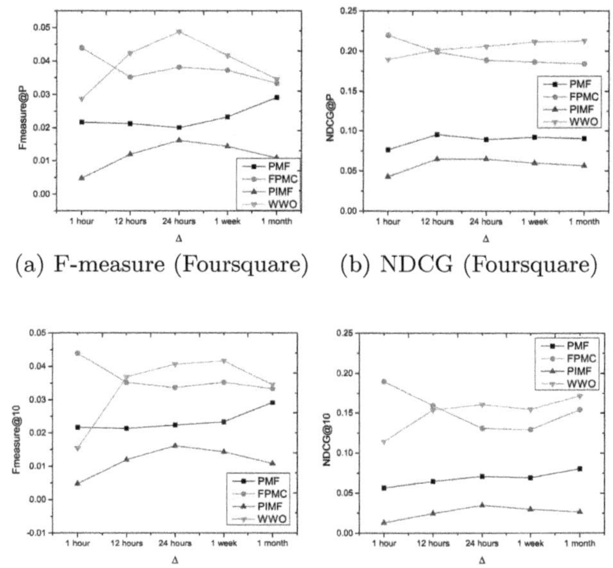

(a) F-measure (Foursquare) (b) NDCG (Foursquare)

(c) F-measure (Gowalla) (d) NDCG (Gowalla)

Figure 8: The performances for different Δ, with $\delta = 0$.

5.4 POI Recommendation Performances

In this subsection, we present the performance comparison on the recommendation accuracy between WWO and baselines. The results are based on Foursquare and Gowalla data by setting the latent dimensions to $K = 10$.

We first investigate how WWO performs with different lengths of time period from now. When $\delta = 0$ (recommending for the next Δ time period), the performances in terms of F-measure and NDCG with respect to Δ (from 1 hour to 1 month) on Foursquare and Gowalla data are shown in Figure 8. In the figures, we can see that FPMC and WWO obtain better overall performances than PMF and PIMF. For a short next time period, such as 1 hour, FPMC outperforms others significantly. When Δ is increased to 24 hours and 1 week, WWO achieves the best performance. This implies that the temporal interval information between check-ins can be helpful for identifying the temporal relationship between POIs, especially better captured for a granularity of several days. This result is consistent with the observation for the time interval histogram shown in Figure 9, where we can see that the intervals between POIs are mostly dis-

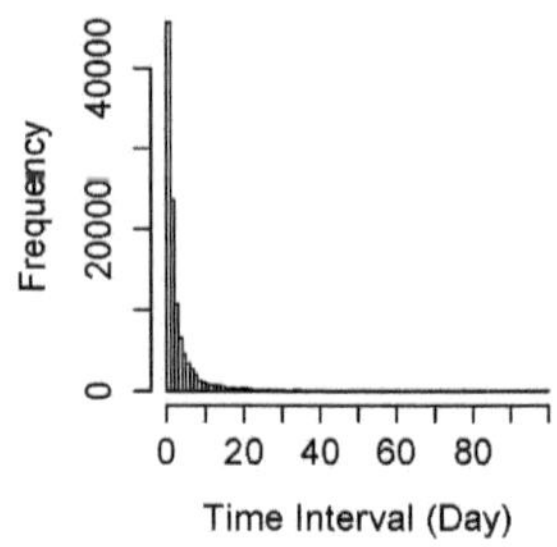

(a) Foursquare

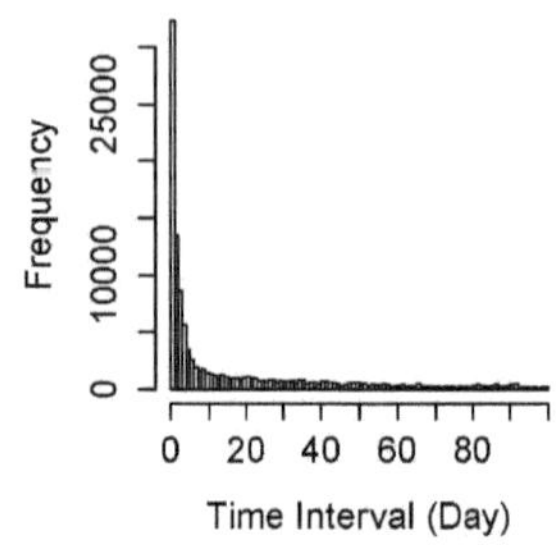

(b) Gowalla

Figure 9: The histogram of all user check-in intervals

tributed in the first 7 days. Moreover, as the increase of Δ, the performance of PMF is getting closer to FPMC and WWO. This is because PMF does not consider sequential preferences. POI recommendation for a long term is mainly determined by user preferences and the temporal factor is no longer significant. Finally, PIMF does not work well in POI recommendation, mainly because check-in data include higher level of noise and are very sparse compared to purchase data. In fact, PIMF cannot capture the intervals between POIs without considering the interval distribution.

We then investigate how WWO performs with specific time period from different future time. The recommendation results for one specified day (i.e., $\Delta - \delta = 24$ hours) with respect to various δ are shown in Figure 10. We illustrate the results of δ from 0 to 6 because these are the most effective time periods to recommend. In the figure, we can see that WWO obtains better performances than others. The reason is that all the other methods cannot make recommendations for a specific time period.

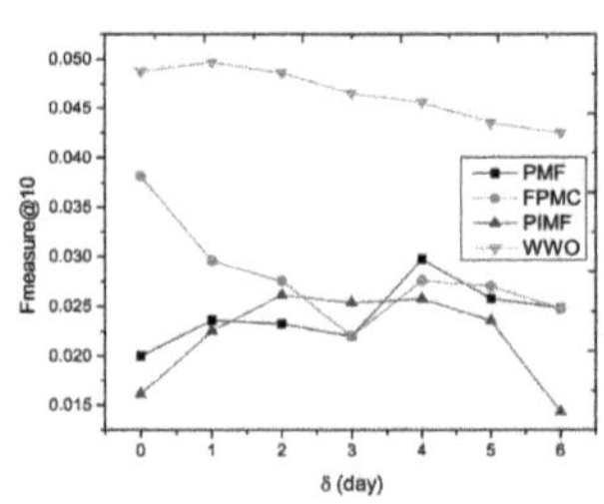

(a) F-measure (Foursquare)

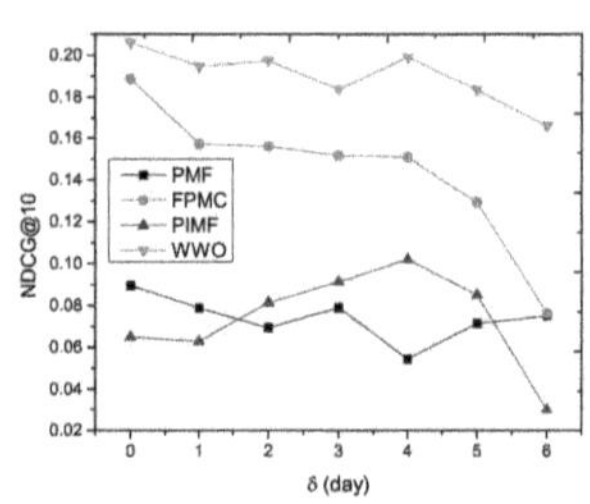

(b) NDCG (Foursquare)

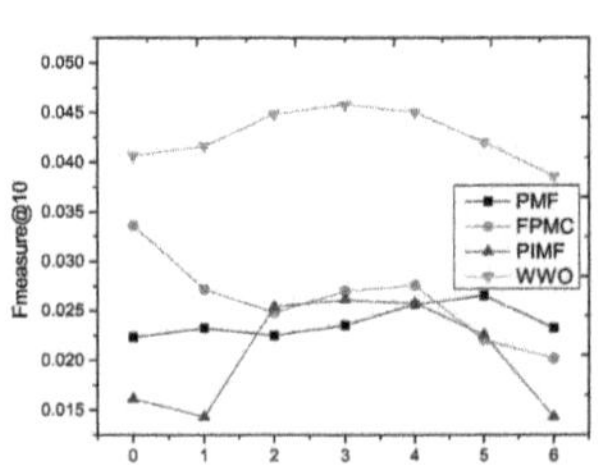

(c) F-measure (Gowalla)

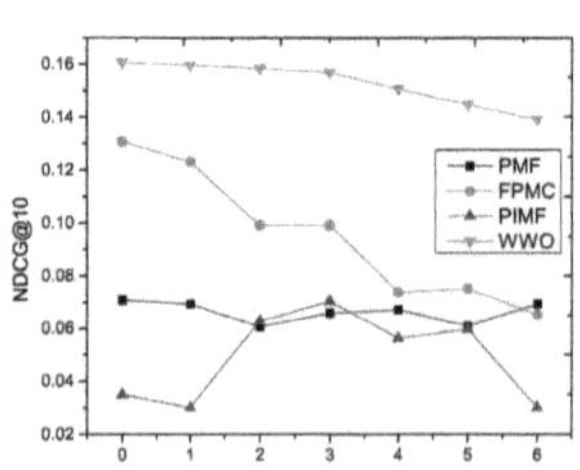

(d) NDCG (Gowalla)

Figure 10: The performances for different δ, with $\Delta - \delta = 24hours$.

5.5 Parameter Selection

For simplicity, we only present the parameter selection results on Foursquare data. First, we use the empirical standard deviation in $\cup_{n,i,j} d_{ij}^{n}$ as σ_μ in $\mathcal{N}(\mu_{ij}^{n}, \sigma_\mu^2)$. Then, we determine the number of graph bases K based on the recommendation performances. As shown in Figure 11 (a), we plot the results with increasing number of graph bases. It is worthwhile to note that the performance might not increase with more bases. The reason is that more bases imply higher modeling complexity and may lead to overfitting in the training data and decreasing generality of the identified graph bases. From Figure 11, we see that $K = 10$ is a feasible trade off between the modeling complexity and the empirical accuracy. Thus, we choose $K = 10$.

Due to space limitations, we omit the similar procedures for tuning the prior parameters such as σ_α, σ_β, η, and θ.

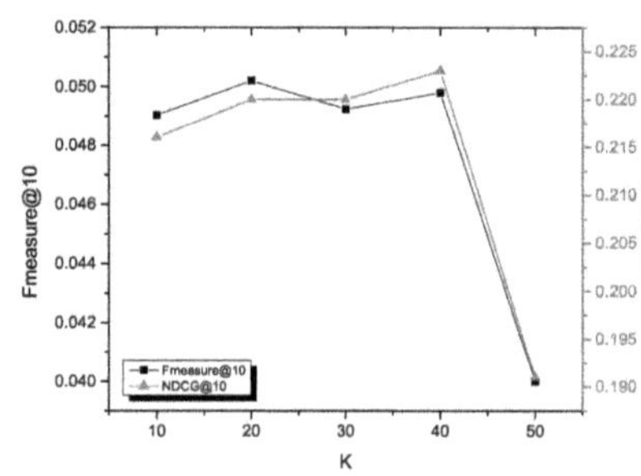

Figure 11: The performances at different number of graph bases K when $\delta = 0, \Delta = 24hours$

5.6 Time Complexity

The overall asymptotic computational complexity of Algorithm is $O(NM^2K^2T)$ where T is the number of iterations. Although the complexity is higher than the conventional static recommender systems, it is comparable with other state-of-the-art approaches utilizing the temporal patterns. Moreover, due to the pre-clustering initialization proposed in Section 4.1, our method converges quickly. Table 2 reports the running time of all methods.

Table 2: The running time (seconds).

Data	PMF	FPMC	PIMF	WWO
Foursquare	79.34	1431.67	27416.5	1378.03
Gowalla	17.96	273.97	4301.62	287.56

6. RELATED WORK

In this section, we will first introduce relevant studies on POI recommendation, followed by the general recommendation tasks with sequential information.

6.1 POI Recommendation

POI recommendation, targeting at recommending the right POIs to the target users, has been an important task in understanding user mobility [33, 11, 28, 17]. Unlike other recommender systems based on explicit user feedback, such as user ratings, POI recommendation is developed based on implicit user feedback, such as the check-in frequency. Recently, other implicit information, such as check-in locations, check-in time, and transition between POIs, have been exploited for POI recommendations.

Among methods proposed in previous studies, latent factor model is the most used algorithm to solve this task. Specifically, each user's check-in times for every POI are counted, which serve as the preferences of POIs. With this user-POI check-in matrix constructed, Collaborative Filtering (CF) methods such as probabilistic matrix factorization (PMF) [18] are used to detect and recommend potential POIs which may be interested by users. Collaborative filtering algorithm is also used to fuse the check-in information, e.g., user interest preferences, social influence, temporal influence and geographical influence [29, 7, 34]. In [27], Ye et al. considered the social influence under the framework of a user-based CF model, and modeled the geographical influence by a model-based method (a Bayesian CF algorithm). To exploit the social influence, the authors made use of the users' friends for recommendation rather than all the users. On the other hand, to explore the geographical influence, they assumed that the probability that a user visited two POIs was determined by their distance, the larger the distance the smaller the probability. Moreover, Yuan et al. [29] and Gao et al. [7] introduced temporal preference to enhance the algorithm efficiency and effectiveness. The authors separated a day into different time slots and user preferences were learned for each slot, thus POIs can be recommended according to different times of a day. Cheng et al. [3] considered more comprehensive information, such as the multi-center of user check-in patterns, and the skewed user check-in frequency. However, this work lacked an integrated consideration of factors that can influence POI recommendation. To improve the ad hoc integration between them, Liu et al. [13] proposed a geographical probabilistic factor analysis framework to analyze the joint effects of multiple factors by considering user preference for locations as a multiplication of interest in the locations, location popularity and distance between user and POIs.

The above works focus on evaluating the relationships between POIs and check-in features, such as location or time, while the relationship between POIs has rarely been considered. Recent works have shown the fact that human movement exhibits sequential patterns [9, 23, 5], suggesting that users usually follow some sequential behaviors when visiting POIs. In light of this, Cheng et al. [4] considered the task of next POI recommendation, in an attempt to recommend POIs to users for their next visits. This work took user check-in sequential information into account, assuming the next check-in is dependent on last check-in. Zheng et al. [31] further extended the next POI recommendation with sequential information by considering not only the latest visited POI but also the earlier visited POIs with a n-order Markov chain, and integrating geographical and social influence into the proposed method. Feng et al. [6] also proposed a metric embedding model to learn the personalized sequential information for next POI recommendation. However, these methods did not consider the temporal interval information between dependent POIs, thus cannot capture the sequential interval patterns to make recommendations for a specified future time period.

Different from the above works, we consider the sequential preferences with temporal interval assessment between check-ins. And, the temporal interval distribution for different users and POI pairs are estimated with a novel factorization method, which enables our method to make recommendation for a specific time period.

6.2 Sequential Information and Recommendation

Most recommender systems rely on statistical models that use the event history of users on items to produce recommendations. Also, as an important information source for understanding user preferences, the information about user sequential behaviors have often been utilized in recommender systems. Indeed, sequential information is critical for many time-sensitive data mining tasks [15, 14], such as travel package recommendations [16, 8] and marketing campaign recommendations [25], since users' preferences change over time in those application scenarios.

Recent works have shown that sequential patterns can be utilized to improve personalized recommendations at the right time. For example, Rendle et al. [20] proposed a factorized personalized Markov chain (FPMC) model to recommend the products which user will probably buy in the next visit. Specifically, a transition matrix from product to product was constructed for each user, thus a transition cube is formed for all the users. Then, the transition tensor was estimated by a factorization model to propagate information among similar users, similar items and similar transitions. Additionally, Wang et al. [24] proposed an opportunity model to estimate the follow-up purchase probability of a user at a specific time. To recommend the best next-items to each target user, Yap et al. [26] learned user-specific sequential knowledge through personalized sequential pattern mining. Moreover, the time interval information between purchase transactions was used to improve the performance of next-product recommendations [32].

Similarly, POI recommendation is also a time-sensitive task, since people's interests for POIs are drifting over time. Therefore, the POI recommendations will be more effective if the recommender system can capture the users' evolving sequential preferences. In order to make recommendations at the right time, the interval information between check-ins should be considered. Along this line, this paper focuses on POI recommendations for a specific time period by considering users' evolving sequential preferences with temporal interval assessment.

7. CONCLUDING REMARKS

In this paper, we investigated how to exploit both user interests and their evolving sequential preferences for recommending POIs for a specific time period. Along this line, we first proposed a unified framework to integrate user interests and their sequential preferences. Specifically, the distributions of the temporal intervals between dependent POIs were studied for measuring users evolving sequential preferences based on their historical check-in sequences. Here, to address the challenge of estimating the distributions with only sparse observations, we developed a bi-weighted low-rank graph construction model to identify a set of bi-weighted graph bases, which in turn can be leveraged for learning user interests and their sequential preferences in a coherent way. As shown in the experimental results on real-world data, unlike existing POI recommender systems, the proposed WWO recommender system can provide effective POI recommendations for a future specified time period by capturing user evolving sequential preferences.

8. ACKNOWLEDGEMENT

This research was partially supported by Futurewei Technologies, Inc. Also, it was supported in part by Natural Science Foundation of China (71329201) and the Rutgers 2015 Chancellor's Seed Grant Program.

References

[1] J. Canny. Gap: a factor model for discrete data. In *SIGIR*, pages 122–129. ACM, 2004.

[2] Z. Chen, H. T. Shen, and X. Zhou. Discovering popular routes from trajectories. In *ICDE*, pages 900–911. IEEE, 2011.

[3] C. Cheng, H. Yang, I. King, and M. R. Lyu. Fused matrix factorization with geographical and social influence in location-based social networks. In *AAAI*, pages 17–23, 2012.

[4] C. Cheng, H. Yang, M. R. Lyu, and I. King. Where you like to go next: Successive point-of-interest recommendation. In *IJCAI*, 2013.

[5] E. Cho, S. A. Myers, and J. Leskovec. Friendship and mobility: user movement in location-based social networks. In *KDD*, pages 1082–1090, 2011.

[6] S. Feng, X. Li, Y. Zeng, G. Cong, Y. M. Chee, and Q. Yuan. Personalized ranking metric embedding for next new poi recommendation. In *IJCAI*, pages 2069–2075. AAAI Press, 2015.

[7] H. Gao, J. Tang, X. Hu, and H. Liu. Exploring temporal effects for location recommendation on location-based social networks. In *RecSys*, 2013.

[8] Y. Ge, Q. Liu, H. Xiong, A. Tuzhilin, and J. Chen. Cost-aware travel tour recommendation. In *KDD*, pages 983–991. ACM, 2011.

[9] M. C. Gonzalez, C. A. Hidalgo, and A.-L. Barabasi. Understanding individual human mobility patterns. *Nature*, 453(7196):779–782, 2008.

[10] K. Järvelin and J. Kekäläinen. Cumulated gain-based evaluation of ir techniques. *TOIS*, 20(4):422–446, 2002.

[11] D. Lian, C. Zhao, X. Xie, G. Sun, E. Chen, and Y. Rui. Geomf: joint geographical modeling and matrix factorization for point-of-interest recommendation. In *KDD*, pages 831–840, 2014.

[12] B. Liu and H. Xiong. Point-of-interest recommendation in location based social networks with topic and location awareness. In *SDM*, 2013.

[13] B. Liu, H. Xiong, S. Papadimitriou, Y. Fu, and Z. Yao. A general geographical probabilistic factor model for point of interest recommendation. *TKDE*, 27(5):1167–1179, 2015.

[14] C. Liu, F. Wang, J. Hu, and H. Xiong. Temporal phenotyping from longitudinal electronic health records: A graph based framework. In *KDD*, pages 705–714. ACM, 2015.

[15] C. Liu, K. Zhang, H. Xiong, G. Jiang, and Q. Yang. Temporal skeletonization on sequential data: patterns, categorization, and visualization. *TKDE*, 28(1):211–223, 2016.

[16] Q. Liu, E. Chen, H. Xiong, Y. Ge, Z. Li, and X. Wu. A cocktail approach for travel package recommendation. *TKDE*, 26(2):278–293, 2014.

[17] Y. Liu, C. Liu, N. J. Yuan, L. Duan, Y. Fu, H. Xiong, S. Xu, and J. Wu. Intelligent bus routing with heterogeneous human mobility patterns. *KAIS*, pages 1–33, 2016.

[18] A. Mnih and R. Salakhutdinov. Probabilistic matrix factorization. In *NIPS*, pages 1257–1264, 2007.

[19] A. Noulas, S. Scellato, N. Lathia, and C. Mascolo. Mining user mobility features for next place prediction in location-based services. In *ICDM*, 2012.

[20] S. Rendle, C. Freudenthaler, and L. Schmidt-Thieme. Factorizing personalized markov chains for next-basket recommendation. In *WWW*, pages 811–820, 2010.

[21] P. Richtárik and M. Takáč. Iteration complexity of randomized block-coordinate descent methods for minimizing a composite function. *Math. Prog.*, 144(1-2):1–38, 2014.

[22] J. Sang, T. Mei, J.-T. Sun, C. Xu, and S. Li. Probabilistic sequential pois recommendation via check-in data. In *GIS*, 2012.

[23] C. Song, Z. Qu, N. Blumm, and A.-L. Barabási. Limits of predictability in human mobility. *Science*, 327(5968):1018–1021, 2010.

[24] J. Wang and Y. Zhang. Opportunity model for e-commerce recommendation: right product; right time. In *SIGIR*, pages 303–312. ACM, 2013.

[25] J. Yang, C. Liu, M. Teng, H. Xiong, M. Liao, and V. Zhu. Exploiting temporal and social factors for b2b marketing campaign recommendations. In *ICDM*, pages 499–508. IEEE, 2015.

[26] G.-E. Yap, X.-L. Li, and S. Y. Philip. Effective next-items recommendation via personalized sequential pattern mining. In *Database Systems for Advanced Applications*, pages 48–64. Springer, 2012.

[27] M. Ye, P. Yin, W.-C. Lee, and D.-L. Lee. Exploiting geographical influence for collaborative point-of-interest recommendation. In *SIGIR*, 2011.

[28] Z. Yu, H. Xu, Z. Yang, and B. Guo. Personalized travel package with multi-point-of-interest recommendation based on crowdsourced user footprints. *IEEE T HUM-MACH SYST*, 46(1), 2015.

[29] Q. Yuan, G. Cong, Z. Ma, A. Sun, and N. M. Thalmann. Time-aware point-of-interest recommendation. In *SIGIR*, 2013.

[30] J.-D. Zhang and C.-Y. Chow. Spatiotemporal sequential influence modeling for location recommendations: A gravity-based approach. *TIST*, 7(1):11, 2015.

[31] J.-D. Zhang, C.-Y. Chow, and Y. Li. Lore: Exploiting sequential influence for location recommendations. In *GIS*, 2014.

[32] G. Zhao, M. L. Lee, W. Hsu, and W. Chen. Increasing temporal diversity with purchase intervals. In *SIGIR*, pages 165–174, 2012.

[33] V. W. Zheng, B. Cao, Y. Zheng, X. Xie, and Q. Yang. Collaborative filtering meets mobile recommendation: A user-centered approach. In *AAAI*, 2010.

[34] H. Zhu, E. Chen, H. Xiong, K. Yu, H. Cao, and J. Tian. Mining mobile user preferences for personalized context-aware recommendation. *TIST*, 5(4):58, 2015.

AnyDBC: An Efficient Anytime Density-based Clustering Algorithm for Very Large Complex Datasets

Son T. Mai
Aarhus University
mtson@cs.au.dk

Ira Assent
Aarhus University
ira@cs.au.dk

Martin Storgaard
Aarhus University
martin@cs.au.dk

ABSTRACT

The density-based clustering algorithm DBSCAN is a state-of-the-art data clustering technique with numerous applications in many fields. However, its $O(n^2)$ time complexity still remains a severe weakness. In this paper, we propose a novel *anytime* approach to cope with this problem by reducing both the range query and the label propagation time of DBSCAN. Our algorithm, called AnyDBC, compresses the data into smaller density-connected subsets called primitive clusters and labels objects based on connected components of these primitive clusters for reducing the label propagation time. Moreover, instead of *passively* performing the range query for all objects like existing techniques, AnyDBC *iteratively* and *actively* learns the current cluster structure of the data and selects a few most promising objects for refining clusters at each iteration. Thus, in the end, it performs substantially fewer range queries compared to DBSCAN while still guaranteeing the *exact* final result of DBSCAN. Experiments show speedup factors of orders of magnitude compared to DBSCAN and its fastest variants on very large real and synthetic complex datasets.

Keywords

Density-based clustering, anytime clustering, active learning

1. INTRODUCTION

The density-based clustering algorithm DBSCAN [5] is a fundamental data clustering technique for finding arbitrary shape clusters as well as for detecting outliers. In DBSCAN, an object is dense if it has more than μ objects inside an ϵ radius. A cluster is formed as a connected set of dense objects separated from other clusters by low density regions. Since its invention, the density-based paradigm of DBSCAN has seen numerous extensions, e.g. [2,6], as well as applications in, e.g. neuroscience [10], and astronomy [16]. However, many challenges remain, especially when facing massive complex datasets, as described below.

First, for grouping data, DBSCAN [5] performs ϵ-range queries for all objects and determines their neighbors during the cluster expansion process. The overall complexity of DBSCAN thus comes from two sources (1) the range query process with exactly n range queries, resulting in $O(\theta n^2)$ worst case complexity in general, where n is the number of objects and θ is the complexity of the distance measure and (2) the label propagation process with $O(n^2)$ time complexity for assigning labels to objects. When the volume increases, these sources quickly become a severe computational bottleneck and thus have been targets for numerous works for enhancing DBSCAN. Besides techniques that approximate the result of DBSCAN for acquiring speedups like [4], most previous exact techniques for enhancing DBSCAN generally aim at either (1) or (2) in *passive* ways, i.e., knowledge of the data is not learned and exploited to enhance the performance. For example, [2] uses fast lower-bound distances as a filter for reducing slow true distance calculations with the cost of increasing the label propagation time for maintaining the order of its seed list. Grid-based techniques, e.g. [9], divide the data space by grids, perform clustering in each cell locally and merge the results thereby saving runtime. For all these techniques, since knowledge of data is fully not utilized, they incur many redundant distance calculations thus limiting their performance. In contrast, our algorithm, called AnyDBC, introduces a *unique* approach to cope with both problems above in an *active* way. Generally, it consists of an *active learning* [15] scheme to *iteratively* study the current cluster structure of the data and to *actively* select only a small subset of objects for refining clusters at each iteration. As a result, it performs substantially fewer range queries and distance calculations compared to existing techniques, while still guaranteeing to have the *exact* final result of DBSCAN at the end. Moreover, in AnyDBC, objects are assigned into clusters via the labels of their representatives instead of directly propagating labels among them. Thus, the label propagation time is significantly reduced.

Second, most existing methods work in a *batch* scheme, i.e., they run till the end and do not allow user interaction during their execution, e.g. [2,6]. In contrast, *anytime* algorithms [20] quickly produce an approximate result and continuously refine it during their runtime. Moreover, they allow users to suspend them for examining the result and to resume them for finding better results until a satisfactory result is reached. Due to this scheme, *anytime* algorithms have become a useful approach and are widely employed in many fields [20]. However, there are only few density-based clustering algorithms that have this useful property, e.g. [11]. Unfortunately, all of them are mainly designed to cope with small datasets due to their high time and space complexity. In contrast, AnyDBC is an *anytime* algorithm aiming at providing efficient interactive clustering scheme for very large datasets with millions of objects or more.

KDD '16, August 13-17, 2016, San Francisco, CA, USA

DOI: http://dx.doi.org/10.1145/2939672.2939750

Third, most efficient techniques for DBSCAN are built in a grid scheme that limits them to vector data and the L_p norm, e.g. [6, 7]. There are only few algorithms that are capable of handling complex data such as images, graphs or trajectories, e.g. [2, 11]. However, they all suffer from scalability problems on very large datasets. AnyDBC, on the other hand, does not follow a grid scheme. Thus, it can be applied to such complex data. Moreover, it does not require high time and space complexity data structures like [2] or special conditions such as a sequence of lower-bounding functions [12], thus, it scales well with very large complex data and arbitrary metric distance measures for these data.

Contributions. In this paper, we introduce a novel approach for clustering large datasets that addresses all the problems described above. Concretely, our algorithm, called AnyDBC, has the following advantages:

- AnyDBC *actively* learns knowledge of data and uses it to reduce both the total number of range queries as well as the label propagation time. This scheme significantly speeds up the runtime of up to orders of magnitude compared to DBSCAN and its variants.
- AnyDBC is an *anytime* algorithm which requires very small initial runtime for acquiring similar results as DBSCAN. Thus, it not only allows user interaction but also can be used to obtain good approximations under arbitrary time constraints.
- AnyDBC can be applied for any complex dataset and any metric distance measure, e.g., Edit Distance [3].

The rest of this paper is organized as follows. In Section 2, we briefly introduce the algorithm DBSCAN and some characteristics of anytime algorithms. The algorithm AnyDBC is presented in Section 3. We introduce distance measures used in our experiments in Section 4. Section 5 analyzes the performance of our algorithm. Related works are discussed in Section 6. Finally, Section 7 concludes the paper.

2. BACKGROUND

2.1 Density-based Clustering Algorithm

We assume a set of objects O with n objects, a distance function $d : O \times O \to \mathbb{R}$, and two parameters $\epsilon \in \mathbb{R}^+$ (radius) and $\mu \in \mathbb{N}^+$ (density threshold).

DEFINITION 1. *(ϵ-neighborhood) The ϵ-neighborhood of an object $p \in O$, denoted as $N_\epsilon(p)$, is the set of objects inside an ϵ radius around p.*

$$N_\epsilon(p) = \{q \in O | d(p, q) \leq \epsilon\}$$

DEFINITION 2. *(Core property) An object p is called a:*

1. *Core object, denoted as $core(p)$, iff $|N_\epsilon(p)| \geq \mu$*
2. *Border object, denoted as $border(p)$ iff $|N_\epsilon(p)| < \mu \wedge \exists q \in N_\epsilon(p) : |N_\epsilon(q)| \geq \mu$*
3. *Noise object, denoted as $noise(p)$, else*

DEFINITION 3. *(Density-reachability) An object q is directly density-reachable from object p, denoted as $p \triangleright q$, iff $core(p)$ and $d(q, p) \leq \epsilon$.*

Two objects p and q are density-connected if they are density-reachable through a chain of connected core objects.

DEFINITION 4. *(Density-connectedness) Two objects p and q are density-connected, denoted as $p \bowtie q$, iff there is a sequence of objects $(x_1, \ldots, x_m)$, where $\forall x_i : core(x_i)$ and $p \triangleleft x_1 \triangleleft \cdots \triangleright x_m \triangleright q$.*

A cluster is a maximal set of density-connected objects [5].

DEFINITION 5. *(Cluster) A subset $C \subseteq O$, which contains core and border objects, is a density-based cluster iff it satisfies two conditions:*

1. *Maximality: $\forall p \in C, \forall q \subset O \setminus C : \neg p \bowtie q$*
2. *Connectivity: $\forall p, q \in C : p \bowtie q$*

For constructing clusters, DBSCAN randomly draws an unlabeled object p and performs the ϵ-range query on p. If p is a core object, the ϵ-range query is executed for all $q \in N_\epsilon(p)$ to expand the cluster until there is no core object found. Then, p and all of its density-connected objects are assigned a cluster label. And, the next unlabeled objects are processed for expanding new clusters.

2.2 Anytime Algorithms

Anytime algorithms provide an effective way to cope with time consuming problems in many fields, e.g. robotics [20], and object recognition [8]. Their general idea is quickly producing an approximate result and continuously refining it until a satisfactory solution is reached or it is terminated by the user. While running, they can be interrupted for examining intermediate results and resumed for finding better solutions at any time. Figure 1 shows the progress of different anytime algorithms. Among three algorithms A, B, and C, C obviously has the worst performance, while it is harder to evaluate the performances of A and B. However, A is preferred by many other works, e.g. [20], since it has better quality improvement in the beginning.

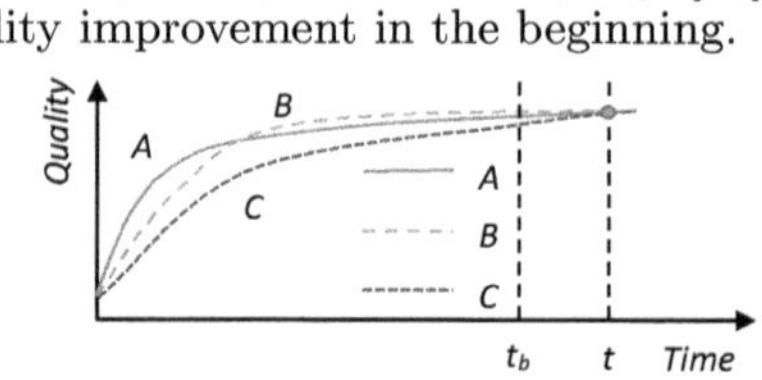

Figure 1: Common progress of anytime algorithms. Generally, the quality of results increases over time. At time $t > t_b$ the results of anytime algorithms are equal to those of the batch ones, where t_b is the runtime of the batch algorithm

3. OUR PROPOSED ALGORITHM

We illustrate the general idea of our algorithm in Section 3.1. In Section 3.2, we present the algorithms and theories behind AnyDBC. Section 3.3 summarizes the algorithm AnyDBC and its characteristics.

3.1 General idea

Figure 2 illustrates the general idea of our algorithm. Assume that we have already performed the range query on objects a, b, c, d, and e. As we can see, their neighborhoods almost determine the final clustering result of DBSCAN with two clusters C_1 and C_2. Here, a, b, and their neighbors form two small clusters inside the cluster C_1, d, e, and their neighbors form two other small clusters inside the cluster C_2, and c is an outlier. Now, if we select the next two objects, say f and g, for querying and updating the current cluster structure, a and b are thus density-connected together since f is a core object. At this time, cluster C_1 is completely determined. Though g is a border object, it allows to determine that h is a core object without having to perform a range query on h since h has at least μ neighbors. Similarly, cluster C_2 is now determined due to the density-connectedness

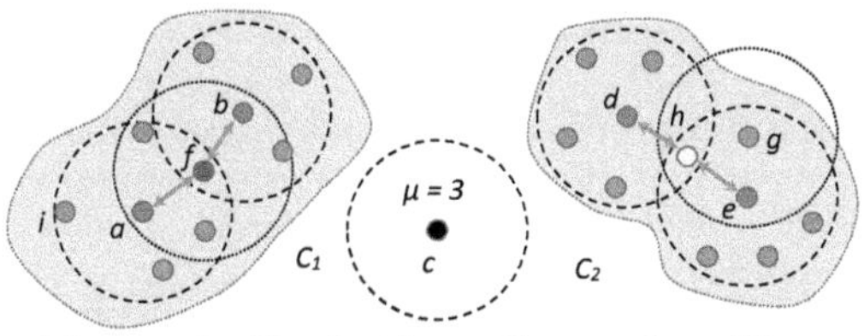

Figure 2: Basic idea of our algorithm

between d and e. The algorithm can be stopped and produces *exactly the same result as DBSCAN* without having to execute all range queries like DBSCAN. Obviously, using fewer range queries means that the clustering time is reduced. This leads to a question: (1) *how do we build an initial cluster structure and select objects for updating?* For example, if we choose object i instead of f, it clearly does not help to identify the cluster C_1. For approximating DBSCAN's result, we can simply stop the algorithm at any given time in the update step. However, producing the exact result of DBSCAN is a non-trivial task. Here another question needs to be solved: (2) *when can we stop the algorithm while guaranteeing that the final result is exactly that of DBSCAN?* For example, all additional queries after f and h are redundant since the cluster structure is identified.

3.2 The major steps of AnyDBC

Since AnyDBC is an anytime algorithm, we use T for denoting an arbitrary time point during its execution. We obmit T whenever it is clear from the context. As illustrated in Section 3.1, at a given time T, the core properties of objects are only partly determined since some range queries may not have been executed. Consequently, we start by formally defining the states of objects as follows.

DEFINITION 6. *(Object state) The state of an object p, denoted as state(p), represents the knowledge about p at a given time T. Starting with the* untouched *state at the beginning, if a range query is performed on an object p, it is marked as* processed. *Otherwise it is* unprocessed. *Depending on its current core property, p is additionally labeled as* core, border, *or* noise.

Basically, Definition 6 is an extension of Definition 2, which takes into account that a range query may not have been performed on an object p at T. At $T+1$, p may change its state via interacting with new performed range queries. For example, object h becomes a core object after the range query on object g in Figure 2. Figure 3 summarizes the transition states of objects in our algorithm. Note that the *unprocessed-noise* state does not exist since there is no way to confirm that p is noise without examining its neighbors.

THEOREM 1. *At any given time T, an object p may only change its state following the transition schema in Figure 3.*

PROOF. (Sketch) Let's take an *unprocessed-border* object p. If a range query is carried out on p confirming that p is a core, its state is changed to *processed-core*. Otherwise p is marked as *processed-border* following Definition 2 since it already lies inside the neighborhood of a core object, i.e., there is no way p moves to the *processed-noise* state. The other cases can be proven similarly. □

At any given time T, AnyDBC produces clusters following the density-based notions of DBSCAN described in Section 2.1 and the current states of objects described above. Generally, AnyDBC consists of the following major steps.

Step 1: Building an initial structure. In this step, some range queries are performed to build a preliminary cluster structure of the data. AnyDBC starts by randomly choosing an object p with *untouched* state for querying. If object p has fewer than μ neighbors, it is marked as *processed-noise* and is stored in a noise list L for a post processing procedure at the last step. If p is a core object, p is marked as *processed-core*, and all *unprocessed* objects $q \in N_\epsilon(p)$ are marked as *unprocessed-border.* If q is *processed-noise*, its state will be changed to *processed-border.* If q is *processed-core* or *unprocessed-core*, its status remains unchanged. If an *unprocessed-border* object $r \in N_\epsilon(p)$ has more than μ neighbors, it surely is a core object regardless of further range queries, thus it is marked as *unprocessed-core.* The whole process is repeated until there is no *untouched* object left, i.e., all objects are either in *processed* or *unprocessed* state.

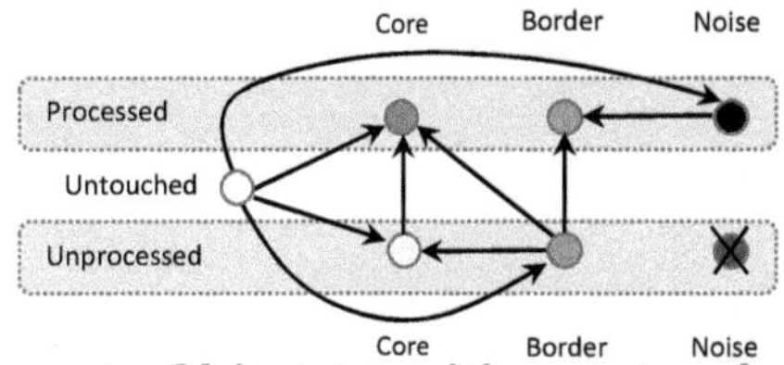

Figure 3: Object transition state schema

Since queries are performed only for *untouched* objects, the total number of range queries in this step is much smaller than the total number of range queries in DBSCAN (see Section 5 for a comprehensive study). At the end of step 1, all objects $p \in O$ are grouped into small, potentially overlapping sets of objects called *primitive clusters.*

DEFINITION 7. *(Primitive cluster) At a given time T, a* processed-core *object $p \in O$ together with its known density-connected neighbors form a so-called* primitive cluster, *denoted as pclu(p), where p is the cluster representative. If a primitive cluster consists of only p and its ϵ-neighborhood $N_\epsilon(p)$, it is called a* primitive circle *and is denoted as pcir(p).*

COROLLARY 1. *At any given time T, all objects $q \in pclu(p)$ belong to the same cluster.*

PROOF. Straightforward from Definitions 5. □

Note that, at the end of Step 1 and 2, we only have *primitive circles.* At the next steps, *primitive circles* will be merged to form the more general *primitive clusters.*

Step 2: Creating a graph. In this step, we use a graph G, called the *cluster graph,* for capturing the relationships among primitive clusters and representing the current cluster structure. Two primitive clusters are directly density-connected at a given time T iff there is a chain of objects inside them that makes their representatives density-connected.

DEFINITION 8. *(Direct cluster connectivity) Two primitive clusters pclu(p) and pclu(q) are directly density-connected at a given time T, denoted as $pclu(p) \bowtie pclu(q)$, iff $\exists X = \{x_1, \cdots, x_m\} \in pclu(p) \cup pclu(q)$ so that $p \lhd x_1 \lhd \cdots \rhd x_m \rhd q$.*

COROLLARY 2. *At any given time T, if $pclu(p) \bowtie pclu(q)$, all objects $x \in pclu(p) \cup pclu(q)$ belong to the same cluster.*

PROOF. Deriving from Definition 5 and 7. □

LEMMA 1. *Given two primitive circles pcir(p) and pcir(q), we have:*

- *Case A:* $d(p,q) > 3\epsilon \Rightarrow \forall T : \neg pcir(p) \bowtie pcir(q)$
- *Case B:* $d(p,q) > \sqrt{3}\epsilon \wedge |pcir(p) \cap pcir(q)| \geq \mu \Rightarrow pcir(p) \bowtie pcir(q)$
- *Case C:* $\exists k \in pcir(p) \cap pcir(q) : state(k) = processed\text{-}core \vee state(k) = unprocessed\text{-}core \Rightarrow pcir(p) \bowtie pcir(q)$.

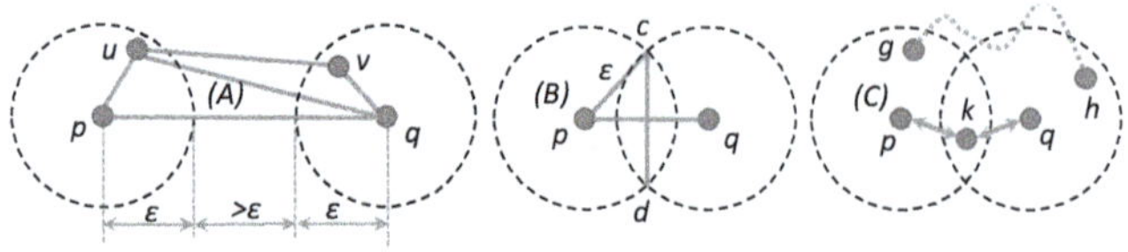

PROOF. The above picture illustrates the three cases A, B, and C of Lemma 1. For simplicity, we use uv for denoting the distance $d(u, v)$ between two objects u and v here.

Case A: Let u and v be arbitrary objects in $pcir(p)$ and $pcir(q)$, respectively. We have $pu+uq \geq pq$ and $uv+vq \geq uq$ (triangle inequality). Thus $uv + vq + pu \geq pq$ or $uv \geq pq - pu - vq$. Since $pq > 3\epsilon$ and $pu, vq \leq \epsilon$, we have $uv > \epsilon \Rightarrow u \notin N_\epsilon(v) \Rightarrow \neg u \bowtie v$ (due to Definition 4) $\Rightarrow \forall T$: $\neg pcir(p) \bowtie pcir(q)$ (following Definition 8).

Case B: We have $pq^2 + cd^2 = 4\epsilon^2 \Rightarrow cd \leq \epsilon$ (since $pq > \sqrt{3}\epsilon$). Therefore, $\forall x \in pcir(p) \cap pcir(q) \Rightarrow pcir(p) \cap pcir(q) \subseteq N_\epsilon(x) \Rightarrow core(x)$ (since $|pcir(p) \cap pcir(q)| \geq \mu$) $\Rightarrow p \lhd x \rhd q$ (Definition 3) $\Rightarrow pcir(p) \bowtie pcir(q)$ (Definition 8).

Case C: We have, $core(k) \Rightarrow p \lhd k \rhd q$ (due to Definition 3) $\Rightarrow pcir(p) \bowtie pcir(q)$ (following Definition 8). □

DEFINITION 9. *(Cluster graph) A cluster graph is a graph $G = (V, E)$, where each vertex $v \in V$ corresponds to a primitive cluster pclu(v), and each edge (u, v) is assigned a state, denoted as state(u, v), that represents the connectivity status of the two primitive clusters pclu(u) and pclu(v).*

- *if $\forall T : \neg pclu(u) \bowtie pclu(v)$, $(u, v) \notin E$ (state(u, v) = no)*
- *else if $pclu(u) \bowtie pclu(v)$, state(u, v) = yes*
- *else if $pclu(u) \cap pclu(v) \neq \emptyset$, state(u, v) = weak*
- *else state(u, v) = unknown*

Generally, each edge of G connects two primitive clusters that may belong to the same cluster. And its state reflects how strong the connection is. For example, at the time T, if $pclu(u)$ and $pclu(v)$ share an object p and they are currently not directly density-connected, $state(u, v)$ is thus *weak*. Obviously, they have more chance to be in the same cluster than the *unknown* case. The state of an edge also changes overtime. Assume that at time $T+1$, some additional range queries reveal that p is a core object, then $state(u, v)$ thus becomes *yes* at time $T+1$ since $pclu(u)$ and $pclu(v)$ are now directly density-connected following Lemma 1. If $state(u, v)$ is *no*, it means that $pclu(u)$ and $pclu(v)$ will never be directly connected even when all range queries have been performed. Thus, (u, v) will not belong to the edge set E of G. To build the graph G, AnyDBC first puts all the primitive clusters found in step 1 into V. Then the states of all edges are determined following Lemma 1 and Definition 9 above.

LEMMA 2. *Given two nodes pcir(u) and pcir(v) of G, if u and v are truly density-connected, there must exist a path that connects pcir(u) and pcir(v) in G.*

PROOF. (Sketch) Assume that for all chains of nodes $\{u, \cdots, x, y, \cdots, v\}$ of G, there always exist two adjacent nodes x and y so that $state(x, y) = no$. According Lemma 1 Case A, $\forall p \in x\ \forall q \in y : d(p, q) > \epsilon$. Thus, there is no chain of objects that connect u and v (following Definition 4). This lead to a contradiction. □

Lemma 2 directly implies that the connectivity of u and v can be determined via examining all the edges of G.

Step 3: Finding connected components. AnyDBC determines chains of directly density-connected primitive clusters by finding connected components of the graph G'.

DEFINITION 10. *(Cluster connection graph) A cluster connection graph $G' = (V, E')$ is the subgraph of cluster graph G, where $E' = \{(u, v) | (u, v) \in E \wedge state(u, v) = yes\}$.*

COROLLARY 3. *Given two nodes u and v in a connected component C of G', pclu(u) and pclu(v) belong to the same cluster at a given time T.*

PROOF. Deriving from Definition 9 and Corollary 2. □

Following Corollary 3, at any given time T, an intermediate clustering result of AnyDBC can be produced by labeling all nodes of G' according to their connected components. Objects are then labeled according to the labels of their representative nodes. This is an advantage of AnyDBC compared to other techniques. Since the size of G is very small, the label propagation time is significantly reduced. Thus, we obtain high quality approximations efficiently (Section 5).

Step 4: Merging connected components. All primitive clusters on a connected component will be merged together to reduce the number of nodes in G, thus enhancing the performance, e.g., reducing the time for finding connected components in subsequence steps. For each component, we randomly select the representative of a node inside it as a representative for the whole group. In experiments, the total number of graph nodes decreases extremely fast at the first few iterations due to this merging scheme (see Section 5).

THEOREM 2. *Each connected component $C \in G'$ represented by an object p is a primitive cluster after merging.*

PROOF. (Sketch) $\forall q \in C$ and $\forall x \in pclu(q)$, we have $x \bowtie q$ (Definition 7). Since p and q belong C, there is a path of nodes $X = \{p = x_1, \cdots, x_m = q\}$, where $state(x_i, x_{i+1}) = yes$, i.e., $x_i \bowtie x_{i+1}$ (Definition 8 and 9). Thus, $x \bowtie p$. Therefore, $pclu(p)$ is a primitive cluster (Definition 7). □

The states of edges of the new graph still follow Definition 9, and can be directly inferred from G following Lemma 3.

LEMMA 3. *Given two connected components $C = \{c_1, \cdots, c_2\}$ and $D = \{d_1, \cdots, d_2\}$ of G' at a given time T. We have:*

- *Case A: $\forall c_i \in C, d_j \in D : state(c_i, c_j) = no \Rightarrow state(C, D) = no$*
- *Case B: $\exists c_i \in C, d_j \in D : state(c_i, c_j) = weak \Rightarrow state(C, D) = weak$*
- *Case C: otherwise state(C, D) = unknown*

PROOF. Since we only merge nodes in each connected component of G', we have for all $c_i \in C$ and $d_j \in D \Rightarrow \neg pclu(c_i) \bowtie pclu(d_j)$ ($state(c_i, d_j) \neq yes$) $\Rightarrow \neg \cup pclu(c_i) \bowtie \cup pclu(d_j) \Rightarrow \neg pclu(C) \bowtie pclu(D)$.

Case A: $\forall c_i, d_j : state(c_i, d_j) = no \Rightarrow \forall T : \neg pclu(c_i) \bowtie pclu(d_j)$ (Definition 9) $\Rightarrow \forall T : \neg pclu(C) \bowtie pclu(D) \Rightarrow state(C, D) = no$ (Definition 9).

Case B: $state(c_i, d_j) = weak \Rightarrow pclu(c_i) \cap pclu(d_j) \neq \emptyset$ (Definition 9) $\Rightarrow pclu(C) \cap pclu(D) \neq \emptyset \Rightarrow state(C, D) = weak$ (Definition 9).

Case C: directly inferred from Case A and B. □

Step 5: Checking the stopping condition. As presented in Section 3.1, knowing when to stop the algorithm is crucial for improving the performance of AnyDBC.

THEOREM 3. *At a given time T, if $\forall (u, v) \in E : state(u, v) = yes$, then $\forall T' > T\ \forall (u, v) \in E : state_T(u, v) = state_{T'}(u, v)$, where $state_T(u, v)$ and $state_{T'}(u, v)$ are the states of the edge (u, v) at time T and T'.*

PROOF. If $state_T(u,v) = yes$, we have $pclu(u) \bowtie pclu(v)$ (Definition 9). Due to Theorem 1, the state of an object p only changes from noise to border to core, i.e., not from core to border to noise. Thus, there is no way that a chain of object $u \triangleleft x_1 \triangleleft \cdots \triangleright x_m \triangleright v$ that connects u and v (Definition 8) be broken at any time $T' > T$, i.e., $state_{T'}(u,v) = yes$. $\square$

Following Theorem 3, if all edges of the graph G have states *yes*, AnyDBC can stop without examining all range queries since there will be no change in the graph G and thus in the final clustering result following Corollary 3. As a result, its performance is significantly enhanced. In the next following Section, we will prove that the final results of AnyDBC and DBSCAN are identical.

Step 6: Selecting objects for range queries. A naive way is randomly choosing an unprocessed object for performing a range query. However, as we demonstrate in Section 5, it is inefficient since the current cluster structure is not exploited. Thus, we introduce an *active learning* [15] scheme to significantly reduce the number of used range queries for building the final clustering result. The general idea is letting the algorithm *iteratively and actively* learn the current cluster structure from the graph G and choose objects that it *considers* most effective for updating the cluster structure. According to Theorem 3, the faster we eliminate all *weak* and *unknown* edges from G, the sooner AnyDBC reaches its final state, i.e., the fewer queries are used. To do so, AnyDBC first evaluates the importance of each node of G. Then, it ranks all unprocessed objects according to its current neighbors and its position inside G. Thoses with highest scores are chosen as targets for performing range queries.

DEFINITION 11. *(Node statistic) At a given time T, the statistical information of a node $u \in V$, denoted as $stat(u)$, is defined as follows:*

$$stat(u) = \frac{usize(u)}{|pclu(u)|} + \frac{|pclu(u)|}{n}$$

where $usize(u)$ is the number of unprocessed objects inside $pclu(u)$ and n is the number of objects.

DEFINITION 12. *(Node degree) Given a node u and its adjacent nodes $N(u)$ in the graph G. The degree of u, denoted as $deg(u)$, at a given time T is defined as follows:*

$$deg(u) = w(\textstyle\sum_{v \in N(u) \wedge state(u,v)=weak} stat(v)) + \sum_{v \in N(u) \wedge state(u,v)=unknown} stat(v) - \psi(u)$$

where $\psi(u) = 0$ if u does not contain border objects otherwise it is the total number of weak *and* unknown *edges of u.*

The degree of a node u measures how certain the node u is wrt. its adjacent nodes. Intuitively, high $deg(u)$ means that u lies inside a highly uncertain area with many undetermined connections. Thus, if a range query is performed on u, it has higher change to either connect u and its adjacent nodes v ($state(u,v) = yes$) or to separate u from its adjacent nodes ($state(u,v) = no$). Moreover, if two nodes u and v have some common objects, they are more likely to be directly density connected. In contrast, if $state(u,v) = unknown$, it is much harder to determine the true connection status of u and v. Therefore, we assign a higher weight $w = |V|$ for edges with *weak* states than edges with *unknown* states. Moreover, if node u contains border objects, it should be processed later due to the effect of Lemma 5 and the merging scheme of each new query in Step 7 for ensuring an earlier termination of the algorithm. The general idea is surrounding a promising node with *processed* objects so that any future queries can bring it closer to the empty state as stated in Lemma 5.

DEFINITION 13. *(Object score) The score of an unprocessed object p, denoted as $score(p)$, at a given time T is defined as follows:*

$$score(p) = \textstyle\sum_{u \in V \wedge p \in pclu(u)} deg(u) + \frac{1}{nei(p)}$$

where $nei(p)$ is the number of neighbors of p at time T.

The score of an object p is calculated based on the sum of degrees of all nodes $v \in V$ that contain p and its current number of neighbors. Beside the node degrees discussed above, we prefer objects with lower numbers of neighbors since performing range queries on them would lead to more core objects to be revealed with each query. Moreover, since q has fewer neighbors, it is more likely to be in a highly uncertain area. Thus, examining it earlier can help to eliminate this uncertainty faster. Note that only *unprocessed-border* and *unprocessed-core* objects need to be examined.

Step 7: Performing range queries. Assume that an object p is selected for performing range queries. If p is not a core object, it is marked as *processed-border* since it is already inside a cluster. Otherwise, it is marked as *processed-core*. And for all objects $q \in N_\epsilon(p)$, the status of q changes following the transition schema in Figure 3. Moreover, $N_\epsilon(p)$ is merged into all nodes u that contain p.

THEOREM 4. *At a given time T, if $core(p) \wedge p \in pclu(u)$, $N_\epsilon(p) \cup pclu(u)$ is a primitive cluster.*

PROOF. Since $p \in pclu(u) \Rightarrow p \bowtie u$ (Definition 7) $\Rightarrow$ $\forall q \in N_\epsilon(p)$: $p \bowtie q$ (Definition 4) $\Rightarrow q \bowtie u$ $(core(p)) \Rightarrow$ $N_\epsilon(p) \cup pclu(u)$ is a primitive cluster (Definition 7). $\square$

Step 8: Updating the cluster graph. In this step, the graph G is updated to reflect changes in the current cluster structure after the new queries q following Definition 10, and Lemma 4 and 5 described below.

LEMMA 4. *Given two nodes u and v at a given time T, if $usize(u) = 0 \vee usize(v) = 0$ and $\neg pclu(u) \bowtie pclu(v)$, then $\forall T' > T : state(u,v) = no$, where $usize(u)$ and $usize(v)$ are the numbers of unprocessed objects of $pclu(u)$ and $pclu(v)$.*

PROOF. Assume that a node u is fully processed wlog. and $\exists T' > T : pclu(u) \bowtie pclu(v)$, there exists a chain of core objects $X = \{v, \cdots, d, e, \cdots, u\}$ that connects the two core objects v and u at T' (Definition 8). However, if e is a core object, all of its neighbors including d are merged into $pclu(u)$ at a time $T_1 \leq T$ in step 7. Thus, $pclu(u) \bowtie pclu(v)$ at the time T. This leads to a contradiction. $\square$

According to Lemma 4, if a node u is fully processed, all of its adjacent nodes v, where $state(u,v) = weak$ or $unknown$, end up having their link broken, i.e., removed from E ($state(u,v) = no$). This pushes the algorithm moving faster to the stop condition described in Theorem 3.

LEMMA 5. *Given two primitive clusters $pclu(u)$ and $pclu(v)$, if $\exists k \in pcir(u) \cap pcir(v)$: $state(k) = processed\text{-}core$ $\vee$ $state(k) = unprocessed\text{-}core \Rightarrow pcir(u) \bowtie pcir(v)$.*

PROOF. Similar to the case C of Lemma 1. $\square$

Step 9: Processing outliers. In Step 1, any noise object p together with its neighbors is stored in a noise list L for a post processing procedure in this step. The goal here is to determine whether p is a true outlier or it is a border object of a cluster. To do so, AnyDBC scans all objects p in L to see whether p has been placed inside the nodes of the graph

```
function C = AnyDbClu (O, d, μ, ε, α, β)
input:   dataset O, distance function d, and parameters μ, ε of DBSCAN
         the query block size α, β
output:  the final clustering result C
begin
   /* step 1: building an initial cluster structure */
   while there exist untouched objects in O do
      S = set of α untouched objects
      for all objects o in S do
         perform range query on o and mark the state of o
         if o is a core object then mark the states of its neighbors in Nε(o)
         if o is a noise object then put o and Nε(o) into the noise list L
   /* step 2: creating a cluster graph G = (V, E)*/
   put all primitive clusters into V as nodes
   determine the states of all edges e in E
   /* repeatedly select objects for range queries until terminated */
   do
      /* step 3: finding connected components */
      find all connected components of G via the yes states
      /* step 4: merging connected components */
      merge each connected component of G into a single node
      calculate the state of each edge of the new graph G
      return an intermediate clustering result C' if required
      /* step 5: checking the stopping condition */
      b = check if G only contains edges with yes or no states
      if b = false then
         /* step 6: selecting objects for range queries */
         for all nodes v in V do
            calculate the node statistic for v
            calculate the node degree for v
         calculate object scores for all unprocessed objects in O
         S = set of β objects with highest scores
         /* step 7: performing range queries */
         for all objects o in S do
            perform range queries on the object o
            update the states of o and its neighbors Nε(o)
            merge Nε(o) to all nodes that contain o
         /* step 8: updating the cluster graph */
         update the states of all edges e in E
   while the stopping condition is not reached (b = false)
   /* step 9: processing outliers */
   for all objects o in L do
      check if o is truly a noise or a border object
return the final clustering result C
```

Figure 4: The pseudo code of AnyDBC

G, i.e., $state(p) = processed\text{-}border$. If so, we do not need to process p anymore. Otherwise, if there exists an object $q \in N_\epsilon(p)$ so that $state(q) = unprocessed\text{-}core$, p is surely a border object connected to q and its cluster. Conversely, we sequentially perform range queries on *unprocessed* objects $q \in N_\epsilon(p)$ looking for a core object. If a core object q is found, p is determined as a border object and has the same label as q. Otherwise, p is a noise object. It is worth recalling that any object $p \in L$ has fewer than μ neighbors, thus the overhead of this step is very small. Note that, for a shared border object p of two different core objects a and b, depending on the object examining order, it will be assign the label of a or b as in DBSCAN.

3.3 The algorithm AnyDBC

Figure 4 shows the pseudo code of the algorithm AnyDBC following the nine main steps described above. However, while we illustrate the operation of AnyDBC in Section 3.2 using a single query for each iteration for clarity, AnyDBC actually queries objects in blocks of size α for step 1 and β for step 6 and 7, i.e., it chooses α and β objects for performing queries at each iteration of step 1, 6 and 7. This provides major benefits: (1) enhancing the intermediate clustering qualities at earlier steps by allowing overlapping primitive circles, and (2) reducing the overall overhead of the anytime scheme of AnyDBC (e.g., merging nodes and finding connected components), which is the major bottleneck of AnyDBC, thus significantly enhancing the performance. Unless otherwise stated, we always use $\alpha = \beta$ for simplicity. In Section 5, we will extensively analyze the effect of the block sizes α and β on the performance of our algorithm.

Correctness of the algorithm. Unlike most techniques for enhancing DBSCAN, AnyDBC is an exact technique, i.e., it produces the same final results as DBSCAN.

LEMMA 6. *Assume that AnyDBC is run to the end, its final result is completely identical to that of DBSCAN.*

PROOF. (Sketch) As described in Section 3.2, AnyDBC produces clusters following the notion of DBSCAN. Therefore, if all queries are performed, AnyDBC and DBSCAN obviously produce the same results. Though AnyDBC only uses a small sets of all range queries at each iteration, it still produces clusters following the density-connected notion of DBSCAN as demonstrated by Corollary 1, 2, and 3. According to Theorem 3, at a given time T when all edges of G have *yes* or *no* states, there is no more change in the graph G and thus the cluster structure regardless of how many additional queries will be performed. Thus the clustering result of AnyDBC at T is similar to that at T_∞ when all queries are executed with only a minor difference on some shared border objects, which are assigned to clusters based on the examined order of objects in both DBSCAN and AnyDBC. □

Complexity analysis. For simplicity, we analyze here a worst case complexity of AnyDBC. Let n be the number of objects, $v = |V|$ be the number of initial nodes of G (after Step 2), $l = |L|$ be the size of the noise list L, and b is the total number of update iterations of AnyDBC. Step 1 needs $O(vn)$ time for querying and marking objects. Creating the graph in Step 2 consumes $O(v^2 n)$ time. $O(\sum_{i=1}^{b} v_{i-1}^2)$ is the time needed to find connected components in Step 3, where v_i is the number of graph nodes at iteration i and $v_0 = v$. Merging nodes in Step 4 costs $O(\sum_{i=1}^{b} v_{i-1} n)$ time for merging nodes, $O(\sum_{i=1}^{b} v_i^2)$ time for relabeling the states of edges, and $O(\sum_{i=1}^{b} v_i n)$ time for updating the number of unprocessed objects inside each node. Step 5 simply requires $O(\sum_{i=1}^{b} v_i^2)$ time for checking the stopping condition. Step 6 needs $O(\sum_{i=1}^{b} v_i^2)$ time for calculating node degrees, $O(\sum_{i=1}^{b} v_i(n-v-(i-1)\beta))$ time for calculating object scores, $O(\sum_{i=1}^{b}(n-v-(i-1)\beta)log(n-v-(i-1)\beta))$ time for sorting unprocessed objects. Step 7 has $O(b\beta n)$ time for querying, $O(\sum_{i=1}^{b} v_i \beta n)$ time for merging nodes, and $O(\sum_{i=1}^{b} v_i n)$ for updating the node size. It takes $O(\sum_{i=1}^{b} v_i^2 n)$ time to update the graph in Step 8. The last Step 9 consumes $O(l\mu n)$ time for detecting true outliers. It is important to note that the true time complexities at all steps of AnyDBC are much smaller than those described above if indexing techniques are used. Moreover, in the experiments (see Section 5.1 for an experimental analysis), $v_i \ll v \ll n$ and $b \ll b_{max}$, where $b_{max} = (n-v)/\beta$ is the maximal number of iterations of AnyDBC. Consequently, the final complexity of AnyDBC is much smaller than $O(n^2)$ time of DBSCAN.

AnyDBC needs $O(v^2 + vn + n + v + l\mu)$ space for storing the graph G, objects inside nodes, the number of neighbors for unprocessed objects, the number of unprocessed objects inside nodes, and the noise list L. Since $v \ll n$ (see Section 5.1), the overall space complexity of AnyDBC is thus $O(vn)$ in the worst case, which is linear to the number of objects.

4. DISTANCE FUNCTION

In this paper, we use two different kinds of distance measures for assessing the performance of our algorithm including L_p distances and Edit Distance.

L_p distances are among the most well-known distance measures for traditional vector data. Most state-of-the-art techniques for enhancing DBSCAN, e.g. [6], are specifically designed for these data under the L_p distance.

For complex data such as time series or trajectories, there are many kinds of complex distance measures [3], which is more effective than L_p. However, all of them have quadratic complexity in contrast to the linear time of L_p, which is a major bottleneck during the clustering process. There are only few extensions of DBSCAN which are capable of dealing with these complex data and distances, e.g., [2,12]. Here we use some trajectory datasets and Edit distance with Real Penalty (ERP) [3] as a distance measure for demonstrating the performance of our algorithm. Due to space limitation, interested reader please refer to [3] for more details.

5. EXPERIMENTS

In Section 5.1, we study important characteristics of AnyDBC. Then, we study its performance in comparison with state-of-the-art techniques on vector data and complex data in Section 5.2 and 5.3. All experiments are conducted on a Linux workstation with 3.1 GHz CPU and 128 GB RAM using C++. Averaged runtimes of all rival algorithms as well as averaged cumulative runtimes of AnyDBC are reported over 10 runs. For speeding up the range query process, we use *kd*-trees [14] for indexing data. However, any other indexing techniques like R-tree [5] can also be used.

5.1 Characteristics

For studying the behavior of AnyDBC, we create four synthetic 2D datasets DS1-DS4, which contain from 3254 to 9554 points belonging to 16 to 32 clusters. Based on them, we can construct bigger datasets by randomly placing additional points in the unit circle of each existing object inside each cluster (except outliers). Here, DS1x100 means 99 more objects are additionally placed for each object of the original dataset DS1. Thus, we can visually study the effect of arbitrarily shaped clusters on AnyDBC. We can also study the behavior of AnyDBC when the number of objects increases while the cluster structures are preserved. Moreover, we have ground truths for assessing the intermediate clustering results of AnyDBC. Experiments on higher dimensional datasets will be conducted in next Sections. Unless otherwise stated, we use $\mu = 5$, $\epsilon = 1.0$, and $\alpha = \beta = 512$.

Performance of AnyDBC. Figure 5 shows the performances of AnyDBC with increasing numbers of objects for DS1-DS4. As we can see from (B), AnyDBC is much faster than DBSCAN. Moreover, the denser the clusters, i.e., the more objects in the datasets, the higher the speedup factors (compared to DBSCAN (see (B)). The reasons can be found in (C) and (D). First, AnyDBC consumes much fewer queries than DBSCAN, e.g., it requires only 6964.4 (0.25%) range queries on average for clustering DS1x300 with 2783567 objects. Second, the initial numbers of graph nodes are also very small, e.g., there are only 3441.6 (0.12%) initial nodes on average for clustering DS1x300. Moreover, during its runtime, the number of graph nodes is significantly reduced at

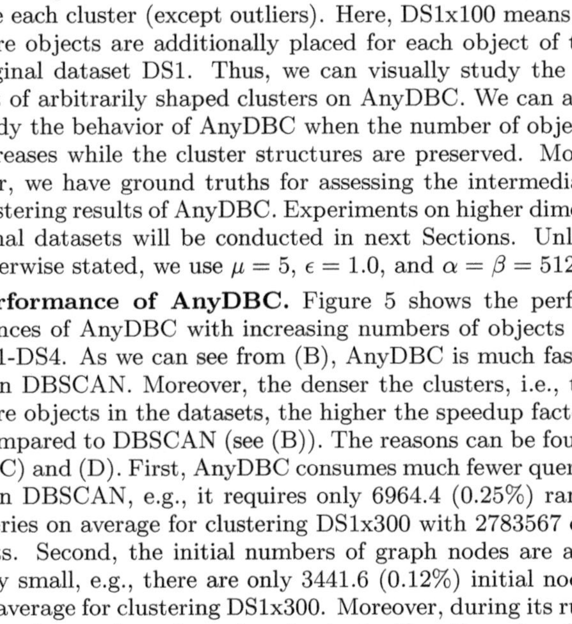

Figure 5: Performances of AnyDBC with increasing number of objects for DS1-DS4.

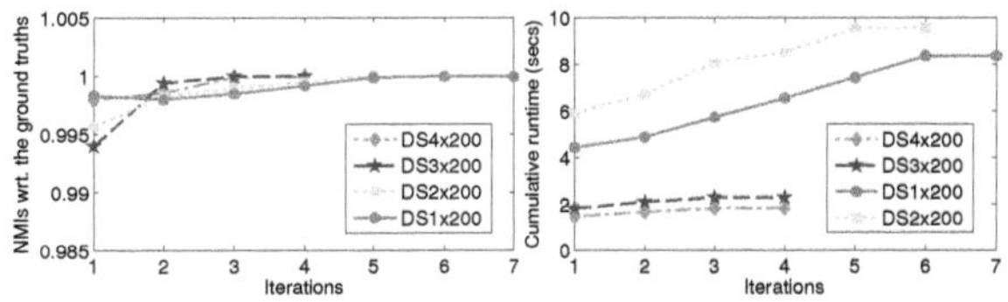

Figure 6: NMI scores and cumulative runtimes of AnyDBC at each iteration for DS1-DS4. It acquires near perfect clustering results at the first iteration.

each iteration of AnyDBC (see Figure 8 (D)). Thus, the label propagation time is significantly reduced compared to DBSCAN. These two reasons make AnyDBC orders of magnitude faster than DBSCAN at the end. Moreover, when we increase the number of objects, the total number of queries as well as the number of graph nodes does not change much. And so do the runtimes of AnyDBC (see (A)). However, the runtimes of DBSCAN change significantly due to its full quadratic complexity. Thus, the speedup factors increase.

Anytime property of AnyDBC. For assessing the intermediate clustering results of AnyDBC, we use Normalized Murtual Information (NMI) [17] to compare them with the ground truths. NMI results are in [0,1] where 1 means a perfect clustering result and vice versa. As we can see from Figure 6, AnyDBC acquires almost perfect clustering results indicated by very high NMI scores even at the first step. For DS1x200 (with 1855767 points) as an example, AnyDBC starts with a NMI = 0.998 which is almost identical to the NMI = 0.999 of DBSCAN. However, while DBSCAN requires 252.4 secs, AnyDBC needs only 4.4 secs, which is 57.3 times faster. Even if AnyDBC runs till the end, it only consumes 8.3 secs, around 30.4 times faster. This anytime scheme of AnyDBC thus provides a very efficient and effective approach for coping with very large datasets.

The *active* selection scheme of AnyDBC. Figure 7 shows the NMI scores and cumulative runtimes of the *active* scoring scheme of AnyDBC for selecting objects in Step 6 and a random scheme, i.e., objects are randomly selected, for DS1x0200. Due to its efficient scheme, AnyDBC stops after only 7 iterations, 8.3 secs and 6149 queries while the random scheme requires 225 iterations 87.7 secs and 117761 queries to finish.

The role of the block sizes α and β. Figure 8 shows the effects of the block sizes α and β on the performance of AnyDBC. Obviously, increasing α will increase the number of initial nodes in G due to the overlap between primitive circles in step 1 (see (B)). This overlap, however, leads to the faster reduction of the graph nodes due to the merging scheme in Step 4. Beside, since more queries are performed in each step, the number of nodes also decreases faster at each iteration (see (D)) due to the node merging scheme (Step 4) and so do the overall operation costs on graph G. Thus, the final cumulative runtimes of AnyDBC are significantly reduced (see (A)). However, since nodes are merged earlier, they become bigger and therefore more queries are required for clearly identifying the *no* states of edges (Lemma 4). Consequently, the total numbers of required queries in-

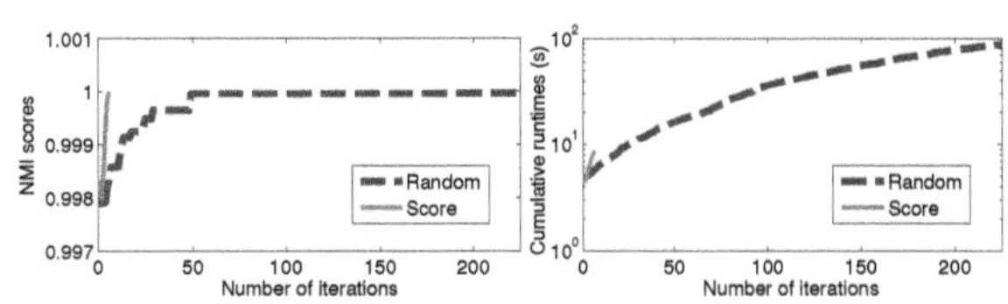

Figure 7: Performance of the active selection scheme of AnyDBC for DS1x0200

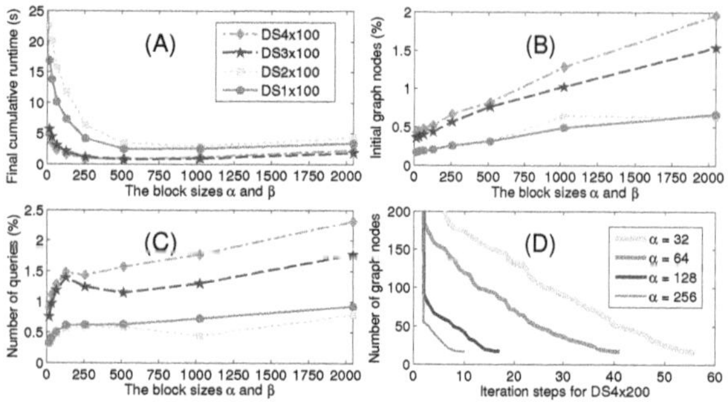

Figure 8: The effects of the block sizes α and β ($\alpha = \beta$) on the performance of AnyDBC

crease and remain relatively stable if β is large enough since more core objects are detected at each step also leading to faster identifying the *yes* states of edges (Lemma 5) (see (C)). However, the additional costs for performing queries are still small enough to be dominated by the operation cost reductions described above. Thus, overall, the cumulative runtimes of AnyDBC are still reduced ((A)). When α and β are too big, redundant queries will happen, thus leading to the moderate degradation of the overall performance. For DS4 as an example, when $\alpha = \beta = 1024$, AnyDBC requires only 1.1 secs to finish, while it consumes 2.2 secs when $\alpha = \beta = 2048$. Thought 512 seems to be a good choice, the larger a dataset, the bigger value of α, β we should choose. One simple scheme is choosing $\alpha = \beta$ so that the maximal number of iterations should be several thousands at most.

The effects of the parameters μ and ϵ. Figure 9 (bottom) shows the effect of the parameter μ on the performance of AnyDBC. As we can see, increasing μ slightly increases the runtimes of AnyDBC since more queries are required to identify the core properties of unprocessed objects. However, the change diminishes with larger μ since the size of graph G decreases, thus leading to the reduction of the operation cost. In contrast, the number of initial graph nodes is slightly reduced since there are more noise objects.

The parameter ϵ has a stronger impact than μ on AnyDBC. Obviously, increasing ϵ will reduce the number of initial graph nodes since more objects are marked inside each primitive circle. Moreover, more unprocessed objects will be determined as core ones with each additional range query. Thus, the runtimes as well as the total numbers of queries are also reduced. However, when ϵ is large enough, the states *weak* and *unknown* may occur more frequently as replacements for the *no* state. Consequently, more range queries are required for breaking these edges according to Lemma 4. Thus, the runtime of AnyDBC increases as we can see from Figure 9 (top). However, it is interesting to note that, the bigger the ϵ, the faster AnyDBC reaches the final clustering result of DBSCAN at each iteration. Thus, in term of the

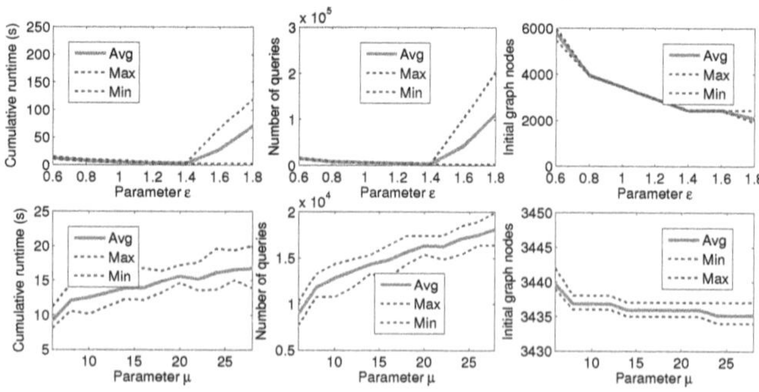

Figure 9: The effects of the parameters μ ($\epsilon = 1.0$) and ϵ ($\mu = 5$) for DS1x200 (1855767 points)

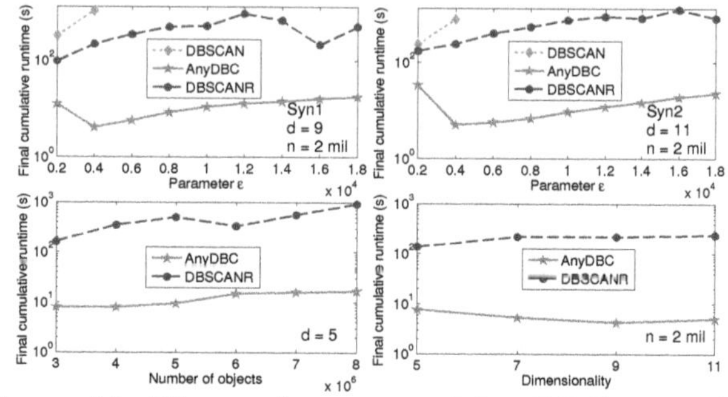

Figure 10: The performance of AnyDBC on various synthetic datasets

anytime scheme, users can stop the algorithm sooner for acquiring higher speed up factors. Due to the space constrain, we do not show a Figure for this experiment here.

5.2 Performance on vector data

We compare the performances of AnyDBC in with state-of-the-art techniques including the original DBSCAN [5] and its fastest variant in [6] (here denoted as DBSCANR) using the binary file provided by the authors. We include the building time for *kd*-tree into the final runtimes of AnyDBC and DBSCAN since DBSCANR does not use indexing techniques for maximal comparison fairness. A-DBSCAN [11] is another variant of DBSCAN. However, it must store the whole ϵ-neighborhood graph and repeatedly performs clustering at each level using DBSCAN. Obviously, it is both memory and time consuming, especially for large datasets. Thus, we exclude it from the comparison for clarity.

Figure 10 (top) shows the performance on synthetic datasets, generated by the data generator scheme of DBSCANR [6] with 2 million points in 9 (Syn1) and 11 (Syn2) dimensions, with different values of ϵ ($\mu = 5$). AnyDBC is much faster than and DBSCANR and DBSCAN, e.g., for the Syn1 dataset and $\epsilon = 4000$, AnyDBC requires 3.68 secs, which is 60 and 297.1 times faster than DBSCANR (221 secs) and DBSCAN (1093.6 secs), respectively. Overall, AnyDBC is up to 82.2 times faster than DBSCANR. It is mainly due to its efficient range query reduction and label propagation reduction scheme as explained above. Figure 10 (bottom) shows the scalability of AnyDBC and DBSCANR wrt. the numbers of objects ($\mu = 5$ and $\epsilon = 5000$) and dimension of data ($\mu = 5$ and $\epsilon = 4000$). The higher the number of objects and dimensions, the better the performance of AnyDBC. For clustering 5 million objects, AnyDBC finishes within 9.3 secs while DBSCANR and DBSCAN take 505.4 secs and 19388.8 secs, respectively. Thus, it is 54.3 times and 2084.8 times faster than DBSCANR and DBSCAN, respectively. Overall AnyDBC is up to 55.5 times faster than DBSCANR and several thousand times faster than DBSCAN.

Figure 11 (top) shows the performance of AnyDBC wrt. different values of ϵ on two real datasets: the Gas sensor array data (4208261 points in 16D - $\mu = 50$ and $\alpha = \beta = 2048$) and the PAMAP2 dataset (974479 points in 39D - $\mu = 50$ and $\alpha = \beta = 512$) acquired from the UCI archive (http://archive.ics.uci.edu/ml/). AnyDBC significantly outperforms the others. For Gas data with $\epsilon = 6000$, AnyDBC requires 69.1 secs which is 89.0 and 245.2 times faster than DBSCANR (6151.4 secs) and DBSCAN (16946.6 secs), respectively. For the PAMAP2 dataset, we stop DBSCANR after 24 hours and thus the speedup factors should be greater than 297.9 times overall. If we stop AnyDBC right after Step 1 (while still having nearly optimal results as demonstrated in Figure 6), the speedup factors are much higher. For $\epsilon = 30000$ as an example, AnyDBC Step 1 and AnyDBC

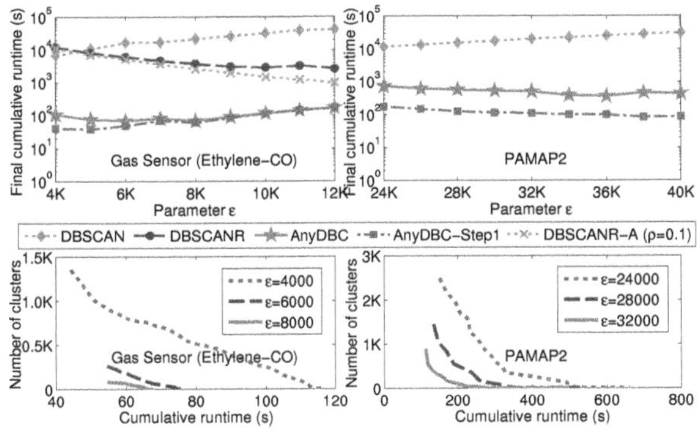

Figure 11: The performance of AnyDBC on real datasets

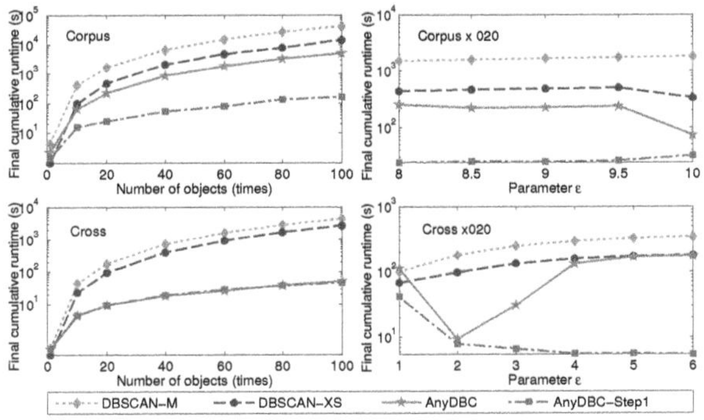

Figure 12: The performance of AnyDBC on trajectory datasets

requires 112.6 and 521.6 secs, which are 155.6 and 34.4 times faster than DBSCAN (17520.9 secs), respectively. Overall, AnyDBC is up to 267.6 and more than 298.6 times faster than DBSCAN and DBSCANR on both datasets. Though DBSCANR is an elegant algorithm and works very well on low dimensional datasets ($d \leq 5$), it has problems when coping with high dimensional ones due to its grid-based scheme. The number of cells increases exponentially with the dimension of data and thus significantly affects its performance.

Approximation. We further compare AnyDBC with one of the best approximation techniques for DBSCAN (denoted as DBSCANR-A) with different approximation factors $\rho = 0.001, 0.01, 0.1$ as suggested in [6]. For the Gas data, DBSCANR-A is up to 2.7 times faster than DBSCANR. For $\epsilon = 4000$ and $\rho = 0.1$ as an example, it requires 11114.3 secs (compared with 12247.7 secs of DBSCANR) and discovers 8 clusters like DBSCAN. AnyDBC requires 104.8 secs to produce 8 clusters like DBSCANR-A and ends after 105.2 secs, which is around 105 times faster than DBSCANR-A. Overall, AnyDBC is up to 105.2 times faster than DBSCANR-A. If we increase ρ to 1 (extremely coarse), the runtime of DBSCANR-A slightly decreases to 10814.2 secs. However, it discovers only 7 instead of 8 clusters like DBSCAN. For the PAMAP2 dataset, we have to stop DBSCANR-A after 12 hours running each.

Anytime. Since we do not have ground truths, we plot the numbers of clusters vs. the runtimes at each iteration of AnyDBC in Figure 11 (bottom). As we can see, the numbers of clusters decrease quickly at each iteration and remain stable when they are close to the results of DBSCAN. This implies that the intermediate results of AnyDBC comes very quickly to the final results as studied in Section 5.1.

5.3 Performance on complex data

We study the performance of AnyDBC on two trajectory datasets under the ERP distance [3]. The synthetic Cross dataset contains 410 trajectories consisting 21 to 23 points in 3D. The Corpus dataset [12] consists of the Corpus Callosum bundle, one of the biggest white matter structures in human brain that connects left and right hermit spheres. It has 1103 fibers consisting of 22 to 73 3D points each. Based on them, we produce bigger datasets by adding some Gaussian noise to each trajectory and inserting them into the dataset. Here Crossx10 means each trajectory is duplicated 9 times. There are some variants of DBSCAN for coping with complex datasets such as DBSCAN-XS [2]and A-DBSCAN-XS [12], which uses LB distances and a data structure called Xseedlist to reduce the distance calculations, and DBSCAN-M [12], which uses a LB distance for speeding up the range query process in a *filter-and-refinement* scheme. Thus, they are our comparison targets. We use LB_{ERP} [3] as a LB distance for ERP [3].

Figure 12 (left) illustrates the performance of these algorithms when the sizes of the datasets increase from 1 to 100 times ($\mu = 5$, $\alpha = 128$, and $\epsilon = 9$ for Corpus and 2 for Cross). The bigger the datasets, the better the performance enhancement of AnyDBC. The performances of AnyDBC and DBSCAN-M are not different much on the original Cross dataset. However, if we increase the size of Cross by 100 times, AnyDBC is 86 times faster than DBSCAN-M due to its calculation reduction scheme. DBSCAN-XS is slightly faster than AnyDBC on the original datasets. However, when the sizes of the datasets increase, DBSCAN-XS performs worse than AnyDBC (52.5 times on Crossx100). The reasons are: (1) it requires much distance calculation than AnyDBC, especially when the data volume increases and (2) the high operation cost of its Xseedlist. Moreover, it consumes quadratic memory wrt. the number of objects. Thus, it is only applicable for small datasets. The final cumulative runtimes of A-DBSCAN-XS are almost similar to those of DBSCAN-XS. Thus, we exclude it from the Figure for clarity. Figure 12 (right) shows the performances of all algorithms on Crossx020 and Corpusx020 datasets with different values of ϵ. AnyDBC is up to 29 and 10.2 times faster than DBSCAN-M and DBSCAN-XS, respectively. Moreover, if AnyDBC is stopped after Step 1, it acquires much higher speedup factors compared to others. For Corpusx020 (38000 trajectories), AnyDBC requires 25.3 secs at Step 1 (with $\epsilon = 8.5$) which is 8.9, 177.3, 18.7 times faster than AnyDBC (225.1 secs), DBSCAN-M (1631.9 secs), and DBSCAN-XS (473.1 secs), respectively.

6. RELATED WORKS AND DISCUSSION

Approximation techniques. Many techniques such as BRIDGE [4] accelerate DBSCAN by compressing data into smaller subsets using k-Means. Then DBSCAN is performed on features of subsets for reducing runtimes. AnyDBC also summarizes data into primitive clusters using range queries. However, instead of performing clustering on features and consequently approximating the result of DBSCAN, AnyDBC uses these primitive clusters as a guideline for studying the potential cluster structure and producing clustering results but does not disregard the original object representation. DBRS [18] only performs range queries on some objects and merges the neighborhoods of two core objects to form clusters if they share some arbitrary objects. SDBSCAN [19] only selects a subset of objects to perform clustering. Then, the rest is assigned labels according to their nearest clusters. IDBSCAN [1] divides the neighborhood of an object p into smaller quadrants. For each quadrant, IDBSCAN identifies its nearest object and only use this one as a seed for expanding the cluster. Though these techniques are fast, they can only coarsely approximate the results of DBSCAN as pointed out in [18]. AnyDBC follows a total different approach from these techniques. It consists of an unique *active learning* scheme for *iteratively* examining the cluster structure, and using the acquired knowledge for minimizing the number of required range queries for producing the same clustering result as DBSCAN at the end. Moreover, none of these techniques has an *anytime* property like AnyDBC.

Exact techniques. Most exact techniques for enhancing DBSCAN use grids. For example, Gunawan et al. [7] introduce an $O(nlogn)$ algorithm for clustering points in 2D by dividing the data space into grid cell of width $\epsilon/\sqrt{2}$. Gan et al. [6] significantly extend the work of [7] for higher dimensional data using the Bichromatic Closest Pair (BCP) problem for finding density-connected grid cells. For these methods, since the number of cells is exponential wrt. the dimensionality of the data, their performance significantly decreases when facing high dimensional data, while AnyDBC still works well as illustrated in Section 5. Due to their grid scheme, they are limited to vector data and the L_p metric and cannot deal with complex data. Moreover, they do not utilize knowledge of data and are not *anytime* techniques.

Complex data. In [2], a fast lower bound distance is used for guiding the clustering process in a complex database such as CADs and trajectories, thus reducing the total number of slow true distance calculations. This technique relies on a data structure called XSeedlist to sort objects according to their distances to processed objects. A-DBSCAN [11] and A-DBSCAN-XS [12] are anytime techniques that operate in multiple steps and rely on a sequence of LB distances and the monotonicity of cluster structures for enhancing performance. Act-DBSCAN [13] is an active clustering algorithm which aims at maximizing the clustering quality of DBSCAN under a pairwise distance calculation budget. AnyDBC can also be regarded as an active clustering algorithm. However, it does not focus on a pairwise distance budget like Act-DBSCAN but on minimizing the total numbers of queries instead. Similar to [2], all these techniques are mainly designed to cope with small datasets and expensive distance measures due to their high time and space complexity, while AnyDBC focuses on clustering large complex datasets. Moreover, AnyDBC do not require special conditions like LB distances [2,11,13] which may not be available.

Parallelism. AnyDBC consists of high degree parallelism steps, thus allowing the design of a scalable parallel method. The detail, however, is left out due to the space constraint.

7. CONCLUSION

Though DBSCAN is a fundamental clustering algorithm with many applications, its quadratic time complexity still remains a major challenge. AnyDBC proposes a unique approach to cope with this problem. The heart of AnyDBC is an *active learning* scheme that allows AnyDBC to actively learn the current cluster structure and to select only the most meaningful objects for performing range queries. As a result, it produces the same clustering result as DBSCAN with much fewer queries, thus significantly improving the performance. Moreover, its anytime property provides a very efficient approach for coping with large datasets. Experiments on real and synthetic datasets show that AnyDBC is orders of magnitudes faster than competing techniques, even if it is run until the end.

Acknowledgment We special thank Prof. Yufei Tao for providing us the binary file of DBSCANR and anonymous reviewers for their invaluable comments. Part of this research was funded by a Villum postdoc fellowship.

8. REFERENCES

[1] B. Borah and D. K. Bhattacharyya. An Improved Sampling-Based DBSCAN for Large Spatial Databases. *ICISIP*, 2004.

[2] S. Brecheisen, H. Kriegel, and M. Pfeifle. Efficient density-based clustering of complex objects. In *ICDM*, pages 43–50, 2004.

[3] L. Chen and R. T. Ng. On The Marriage of Lp-norms and Edit Distance. In *VLDB*, pages 792–803, 2004.

[4] M. Dash, H. Liu, and X. Xu. '1 + 1 > 2': Merging distance and density based clustering. In *DASFAA*, pages 32–39, 2001.

[5] M. Ester, H.-P. Kriegel, J. Sander, and X. Xu. A Density- Based Algorithm for Discovering Clusters in Large Spatial Databases with Noise. In *KDD*, pages 226–231, 1996.

[6] J. Gan and Y. Tao. DBSCAN Revisited: Mis-Claim, Un-Fixability, and Approximation. In *SIGMOD*, pages 519–530, 2015.

[7] A. Gunawan. A Faster Algorithm for DBSCAN. Msc thesis, TU Eindhoven, 2013.

[8] T. Kobayashi, M. Iwamura, T. Matsuda, and K. Kise. An Anytime Algorithm for Camera-Based Character Recognition. In *ICDAR*, pages 1140–1144, 2013.

[9] S. Mahran and K. Mahar. Using grid for accelerating density-based clustering. In *CIT*, pages 35–40, 2008.

[10] S. T. Mai, S. Goebl, and C. Plant. A Similarity Model and Segmentation Algorithm for White Matter Fiber Tracts. In *ICDM*, pages 1014–1019, 2012.

[11] S. T. Mai, X. He, J. Feng, and C. Böhm. Efficient Anytime Density-based Clustering. In *SDM*, pages 112–120, 2013.

[12] S. T. Mai, X. He, J. Feng, C. Plant, and C. Böhm. Anytime density-based clustering of complex data. *Knowl. Inf. Syst.*, 45(2):319–355, 2015.

[13] S. T. Mai, X. He, N. Hubig, C. Plant, and C. Böhm. Active Density-Based Clustering. In *ICDM*, pages 508–517, 2013.

[14] M. M. A. Patwary, D. Palsetia, A. Agrawal, W. keng Liao, F. Manne, and A. N. Choudhary. A new scalable parallel DBSCAN algorithm using the disjoint-set data structure. In *SC*, page 62, 2012.

[15] B. Settles. Active learning literature survey. Computer Sciences Technical Report 1648, University of Wisconsin–Madison, 2009.

[16] A. Tramacere and C. Vecchio. gamma-ray dbscan: a clustering algorithm applied to fermi-lat gamma-ray data. i. detection performances with real and simulated data. 2012.

[17] N. X. Vinh, J. Epps, and J. Bailey. Information theoretic measures for clusterings comparison: is a correction for chance necessary? In *ICML*, pages 1073–1080, 2009.

[18] X. Wang and H. J. Hamilton. DBRS: A Density-Based Spatial Clustering Method with Random Sampling. In *PAKDD*, pages 563–575, 2003.

[19] S. Zhou, A. Zhou, J. Cao, W. Jin, Y. Fan, and Y. Hu. Combining Sampling Technique with DBSCAN Algorithm for Clustering Large Spatial Databases. In *PAKDD*, pages 169–172, 2000.

[20] S. Zilberstein. Using Anytime Algorithms in Intelligent Systems. *AI Magazine*, 17(3):73–83, 1996.

Fast Memory-efficient Anomaly Detection in Streaming Heterogeneous Graphs

Emaad Manzoor*
Stony Brook University
Department of Computer Science
emanzoor@cs.stonybrook.edu

Sadegh M. Milajerdi†
University of Illinois at Chicago
Department of Computer Science
smomen2@uic.edu

Leman Akoglu
Stony Brook University
Department of Computer Science
leman@cs.stonybrook.edu

ABSTRACT

Given a stream of heterogeneous graphs containing different types of nodes and edges, how can we spot anomalous ones in real-time while consuming bounded memory? This problem is motivated by and generalizes from its application in security to host-level advanced persistent threat (APT) detection. We propose StreamSpot, a clustering based anomaly detection approach that addresses challenges in two key fronts: (1) *heterogeneity*, and (2) *streaming nature*. We introduce a new similarity function for heterogeneous graphs that compares two graphs based on their relative frequency of local substructures, represented as short strings. This function lends itself to a vector representation of a graph, which is (a) fast to compute, and (b) amenable to a *sketched* version with bounded size that preserves similarity.

StreamSpot exhibits desirable properties that a streaming application requires—it is (i) fully-streaming; processing the stream one edge at a time as it arrives, (ii) memory-efficient; requiring constant space for the sketches and the clustering, (iii) fast; taking constant time to update the graph sketches and the cluster summaries that can process over $100K$ edges per second, and (iv) online; scoring and flagging anomalies in real time. Experiments on datasets containing simulated system-call flow graphs from normal browser activity and various attack scenarios (ground truth) show that StreamSpot is *high-performance*; achieving above 95% detection accuracy with small delay, as well as competitive time and memory usage.

1. INTRODUCTION

Anomaly detection is a pressing problem for various critical tasks in security, finance, medicine, and so on. In this work, we consider the anomaly detection problem for streaming heterogeneous graphs, which contain different types of nodes and edges. The input is a stream of timestamped and typed edges, where the source and destination nodes are also typed. Moreover, multiple such graphs may be arriving over the stream simultaneously, that is, edges that belong to different graphs may be interleaved. The goal is to accurately and quickly identify the anomalous graphs that are significantly different from what has been observed over the stream thus far, while meeting several important needs of the driving applications including fast real-time detection and bounded memory space usage.

The driving application that motivated our work is the advanced persistent threat (APT) detection problem in security, although the above abstraction can appear in numerous other settings (e.g., software verification). In the APT scenario, we are given a stream of logs capturing the events occurring in the system. These logs are used to construct what is called *information flow graphs*, in which edges depict data or control dependencies. Both the nodes and edges of the flow graphs are typed. Examples of node types are `file`, `process`, etc. and edge types include various system calls such as `read`, `write`, `fork`, etc. as well as other parent-child relations. Within a system, an information flow corresponds to a unit of functionality (e.g., checking email, watching video, software updates, etc.). Moreover, multiple information flows may be occurring in the system simultaneously. The working assumption for APT detection is that the information flows induced by malicious activities in the system are sufficiently different from the normal behavior of the system. Ideally, the detection is to be done in real-time with small computational overhead and delay. As the system-call level events occur rapidly in abundance, it is also crucial to process them in memory while also incurring low space overhead. The problem then can be cast as real-time anomaly detection in streaming heterogeneous graphs with bounded space and time, as stated earlier.

Graph-based anomaly detection has been studied in the past two decades. Most work is for static homogeneous graphs [5]. Those for typed or attributed graphs aim to find deviations from frequent substructures [26, 12, 22], anomalous subgraphs [16, 27], and community outliers [13, 28], all of which are designed for static graphs. For streaming graphs various techniques have been proposed for clustering [3] and connectivity anomalies [4] for plain graphs, which are recently extended to graphs with attributes [35, 24]. (See Sec. 6) Existing approaches are not, at least directly, applicable to our motivating scenario as they do not exhibit all of the desired properties simultaneously; namely, handling heterogeneous graphs, streaming nature, low computational and space overhead, and real-time anomaly detection.

---

*Primary author.

†This author has contributed with the creation of the datasets used in this work (i.e., collecting and preprocessing system-call traces for the benign/malicious scenarios).

KDD '16, August 13-17, 2016, San Francisco, CA, USA

DOI: `http://dx.doi.org/10.1145/2939672.2939783`

To address the problem for streaming heterogeneous graphs, we introduce a new clustering-based anomaly detection approach called StreamSpot[1] that (*i*) can handle temporal graphs with typed nodes and edges, (*ii*) processes incoming edges fast and consumes bounded memory, as well as (*iii*) dynamically maintains the clustering and detects anomalies in real time. In a nutshell, we propose a new shingling-based similarity function for heterogeneous graphs, which lends itself to graph sketching that uses fixed memory while preserving similarity. We show how to maintain the graph sketches efficiently as new edges arrive. Based on this representation, we employ and dynamically maintain a centroid-based clustering scheme to score and flag anomalous graphs. The main contributions of this work are listed as follows:

- **Novel formulation and graph similarity:** We formulated the host-level APT detection problem as a clustering-based anomaly detection task in streaming heterogeneous graphs. To enable an effective clustering, we designed a new similarity function for timestamped typed graphs, based on *shingling*, which accounts for the frequency of different substructures in a graph. Besides being efficient to compute and effective in capturing similarity between graphs, the proposed function lends itself to comparing two graphs based on their *sketches*, which enables memory-efficiency.
- **Dynamic maintenance:** We introduce efficient techniques to keep the various components of our approach up to date as new edges arrive over the stream. Specifically, we show how to maintain (*a*) the graph sketches, and (*b*) the clustering incrementally.
- **Desirable properties:** Our formulation and proposed techniques are motivated by the requirements and desired properties of the application domain. As such, our approach is (*i*) *fully streaming*, where we perform a continuous, edge-level processing of the stream, rather than taking a snapshot-oriented approach; (*ii*) *time-efficient*, where the processing of each edge is fast with constant complexity to update its graph's sketch and the clustering; (*iii*) *memory-efficient*, where the sketches and cluster summaries consume constant memory that is controlled by user input, and (*iv*) *online*, where we score and flag the anomalies in real-time.

We quantitatively validate the effectiveness and efficiency (time and space) of StreamSpot on simulated datasets containing normal host-level activity as well as abnormal attack scenarios (i.e., ground truth). We also design experiments to study the approximation quality of our sketches, and the behavior of our detection techniques under varying parameters, such as memory size.

2. PROBLEM & OVERVIEW

For host-level APT detection, a host machine is instrumented to collect system logs. These logs essentially capture the events occurring in the system, such as memory accesses, system calls, etc. An example log sequence is illustrated in Figure 1. Based on the control and data dependences, information flow graphs are constructed from the system logs. In the figure, the **tag** column depicts the ID of the information flow (graph) that an event (edge) belongs to.

[1]Code/data at http://www3.cs.stonybrook.edu/~emanzoor/streamspot/

time	pid	event	arg/data	tag
100	10639	fork	NULL	1
200	10640	execve	/bin/sh	1
300	10650	read	STDIN	2
400	10640	fstat	0xbfc5598	1
500	10660	sock_wr	0.0.0.0	2
...	...	...	...	...

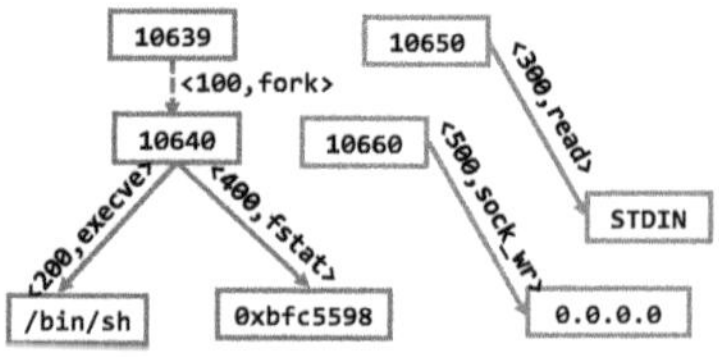

Figure 1: Example stream of system logs, and two resulting information flow graphs (red vs. blue). Both nodes and edges are typed. Edges arriving to different flows may interleave.

The streaming graphs are heterogeneous where edge types correspond to system calls such as **read**, **fork**, **sock_wr**, etc. and node types include **socket**, **file**, **memory**, etc. As such, an edge can be represented in the form of:

< source-id, source-type ϕ_s, dest-id, dest-type ϕ_d, timestamp t, edge-type ϕ_e, flow-tag >

These edges form dynamically evolving graphs, where the edges sharing the same flow-tag belong to the same graph. Edges arriving to different graphs may be interleaved, that is, multiple graphs may be evolving simultaneously.

Our goal is to detect anomalous graphs at any given time t, i.e., in real time as they occur. To achieve this goal, we follow a clustering-based anomaly detection approach. In a nutshell, our method maintains a small, memory-efficient representation of the evolving graphs in main memory, and uses a new similarity measure that we introduce to cluster the graphs. The clustering is also maintained dynamically as existing graphs evolve or as new ones arrive. Anomalies are flagged in real time through deviations from this clustering model that captures the normal flow patterns.

The main components of StreamSpot are as follows, which are detailed further in the noted (sub)sections:

- **Similarity of heterogeneous graphs:** (§3.1) We introduce a new similarity measure for heterogeneous graphs with typed nodes and edges as well as timestamped edges. Each graph G is represented by a what we call shingle-frequency vector (or shortly *shingle vector*) $\mathbf{z}_G$. Roughly, a k-shingle $s(v,k)$ is a string constructed by traversing edges, in their temporal order, in the k-hop neighborhood of node v. The shingle-vector contains the counts of unique shingles in a graph. Similarity between two graphs is defined as the cosine similarity between their respective shingle vectors. Intuitively, the more the same shingles two graphs contain in common, the more similar they are.
- **Memory-efficient sketches:** (§3.2) The number of unique shingles can be arbitrarily large for heterogeneous graphs with hundreds to thousands of node and edge types. We show how to instead use a *sketch* representation of a graph. Sketches are small, constant-size vector representations of graphs whose pairwise similarities also approximate the (cosine) similarities of the shingle vectors of those graphs.
- **Efficient maintenance of sketches:** (§3.3) As new edges arrive, shingle counts of a graph change. As such, the shingle vector entries need to be updated. Recall that we do not explicitly maintain this vector in memory, but rather its (much smaller) sketch. In this paper, we show how to update the sketch of a graph efficiently, (*i*) in *constant* time and (*ii*) without incurring *any* additional memory overhead.

- **Clustering graphs (dynamically):** (§4) We employ a centroid-based clustering of the graphs to capture normal behavior. We show how to update the clustering as the graphs change and/or as new ones emerge, that again, exhibit small memory footprints.
- **Anomaly detection (in real time):** We score an incoming or updated graph by its distance to the closest centroid in the clustering. Based on a distribution of distances for the corresponding cluster, we quantify the significance of the score to flag anomalies. Distance computation is based on (fixed size) sketches, as such, scoring is fast for real time detection.

3. SKETCHING TYPED GRAPHS

We require a method to represent and compute the similarity between heterogeneous graphs that also captures the temporal order of edges. The graph representation must permit efficient online updates and consume bounded space with new edges arriving in an infinite stream.

Though there has been much work on computing graph similarity efficiently, existing methods fall short of our requirements. Methods that require knowing node correspondence [20] are inapplicable, as are graph kernels that precompute a fixed space of substructures [31] to represent graphs, which is infeasible in a streaming scenario. Methods that rely on *global* graph metrics [7] cannot accommodate edge order and are also inapplicable. Graph-edit-distance-based [9] methods approximate hard computational steps with heuristics that provide no error guarantees, and are hence unsuitable.

We next present a similarity function for heterogenous graphs that captures the local structure and respects temporal order of edges. The underlying graph representation permits efficient updates as new edges arrive in the stream and consumes bounded space, without needing to compute or store the full space of possible graph substructures.

3.1 Graph Similarity by Shingling

Analogous to *shingling* text documents into k-grams [8] to construct their vector representations, we decompose each graph into a set of *k-shingles* and construct a vector of their frequencies. The similarity between two graphs is then defined as the cosine similarity between their k-shingle frequency vectors. We formalize these notions below.

DEFINITION 1 (k-shingle). *Given a graph $G = (V, E)$ and node $v \in V$, the k-shingle $s(v, k)$ is a string constructed via a k-hop breadth-first traversal starting from v as follows:*

1. *Initialize k-shingle as type of node v: $s(v, k) = \phi_v$.*
2. *Traverse the outgoing edges from each node in the order of their timestamps, t.*
3. *For each traversed edge e having destination w, concatenate the types of the edge and the destination node with the k-shingle: $s(v, k) = s(v, k) \oplus \phi_e \oplus \phi_w$.*

We abbreviate the **O**rdered **k**-hop **B**readth **F**irst **T**raversal performed during the k-shingle construction defined above as OKBFT. It is important to note that the k-hop neighborhood constructed by an OKBFT is *directed*.

DEFINITION 2 (*shingle (frequency) vector* $\mathbf{z}_G$). *Given the k-shingle universe S and a graph $G = (V, E)$, let $S_G = \{s(v, k), \forall v \in V\}$ be the set of k-shingles of G. $\mathbf{z}_G$ is a vector of size $|S|$ wherein each element $\mathbf{z}_G(i)$ is the frequency of shingle $s_i \in S$ in S_G.*

Shingling is illustrated for two example graphs in Figure 2, along with their corresponding shingle vectors.

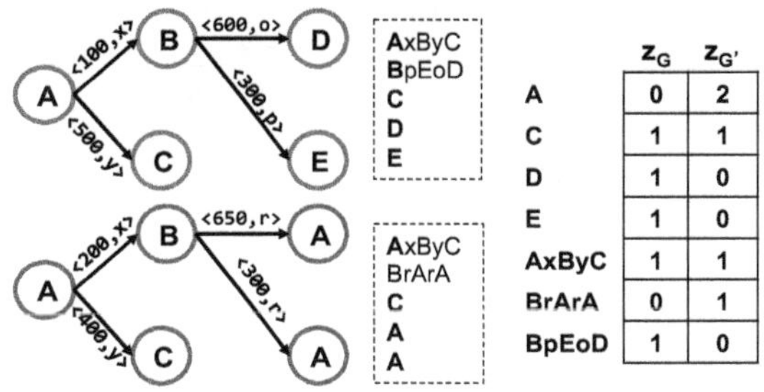

Figure 2: Shingling: (left) two example graphs with their shingles listed in dashed boxes (for $k = 1$), (right) corresponding shingle frequency vectors.

The similarity between two graphs G and G' is then the cosine similarity between their shingle vectors $\mathbf{z}_G$ and $\mathbf{z}_{G'}$.

Representing graphs by shingle vectors captures both their local graph structure and edge order. It also permits efficient online updates, since the local nature of k-shingles ensures that only a few shingle vector entries need to be updated for each incoming edge (§3.3). The parameter k controls the trade-off between expressiveness and computational efficiency. A larger k produces more expressive local neighborhoods, whereas a smaller one requires fewer entries to be updated in the shingle vector per incoming edge.

3.2 Graph Sketches by Hashing

With a potentially large number of node and edge types, the universe S of k-shingles may explode combinatorially and render it infeasible to store $|S|$-dimensional shingle vectors for each graph. We now present an alternate *constant*-space graph representation that approximates the shingle count vector via *locality-sensitive hashing* (LSH) [17].

An LSH scheme for a given similarity function enables efficient similarity computation by projecting high-dimensional vectors to a low-dimensional space while preserving their similarity. Examples of such schemes are MINHASH [8] for the Jaccard similarity between sets and SIMHASH [10] for the cosine similarity between real-valued vectors, which we detail further in this section.

3.2.1 SIMHASH

Given input vectors in $\mathbb{R}^d$, SIMHASH is first instantiated with L projection vectors $\mathbf{r}_1, \ldots, \mathbf{r}_L \in \mathbb{R}^d$ chosen uniformly at random from the d-dimensional Gaussian distribution. The LSH $h_{\mathbf{r}_l}(\mathbf{z})$ of an input vector $\mathbf{z}$ for a given random projection vector $\mathbf{r}_l$, $l = 1 \ldots, L$, is defined as follows:

$$h_{\mathbf{r}_l}(\mathbf{z}) = \begin{cases} +1, & \text{if } \mathbf{z} \cdot \mathbf{r}_l \geq 0 \\ -1, & \text{if } \mathbf{z} \cdot \mathbf{r}_l < 0 \end{cases} \quad (1)$$

In other words $h_{\mathbf{r}_l}(\mathbf{z}) = sign(\mathbf{z} \cdot \mathbf{r}_l)$, which obeys the property that the probability (over vectors $\mathbf{r}_1, \ldots, \mathbf{r}_L$) that any two input vectors $\mathbf{z}_G$ and $\mathbf{z}_{G'}$ hash to the same value is proportional to their cosine similarity:

$$P_{l=1\ldots L}[h_{\mathbf{r}_l}(\mathbf{z}_G) = h_{\mathbf{r}_l}(\mathbf{z}_{G'})] = 1 - \frac{cos^{-1}(\frac{\mathbf{z}_G \cdot \mathbf{z}_{G'}}{\|\mathbf{z}_G\| \|\mathbf{z}_{G'}\|})}{\pi} \quad (2)$$

Since computing similarity requires only these hash values, each d-dimensional input vector $\mathbf{z}$ can be replaced with an L-dimensional *sketch vector* $\mathbf{x}$ containing its LSH values, i.e.,

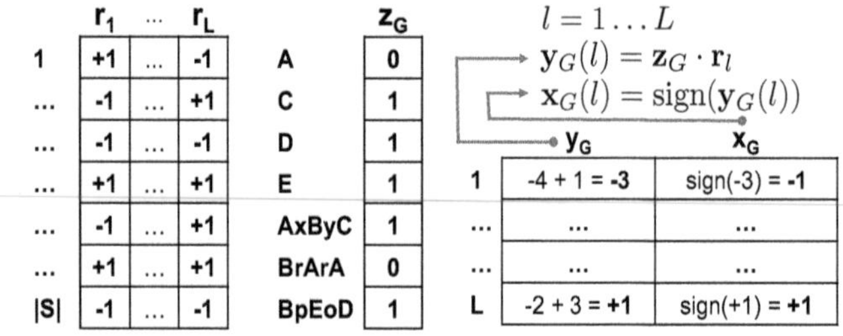

Figure 3: Sketching: (left) L random vectors, (center) shingle vector $\mathbf{z}_G$ of graph G, (right) corresponding projection vector $\mathbf{y}_G$ and sketch vector $\mathbf{x}_G$.

$\mathbf{x} = [h_{\mathbf{r}_1}(\mathbf{z}), \ldots, h_{\mathbf{r}_L}(\mathbf{z})]$. As such, each sketch vector can be represented with just L bits, where each bit corresponds to a value in $\{+1, -1\}$.

The similarity between two input vectors then can be estimated by empirically evaluating the probability in Eq. (2) as the proportion of hash values that the input vectors agree on when hashed with L random vectors. That is,

$$sim(G, G') \propto \frac{|\{l : \mathbf{x}_G(l) = \mathbf{x}_{G'}(l)\}|}{L} \quad (3)$$

In summary, given a target dimensionality $L \ll |S|$, we can represent each graph G with a sketch vector of dimension L, discard the $|S|$-dimensional shingle vectors and compute similarity in this new vector space.

3.2.2 *Simplified* SIMHASH

Note that we need to perform the *same* set of random projections on the changing or newly emerging shingle vectors, with the arrival of new edges and/or new graphs. As such, we would need to maintain the set of L projection vectors in main memory (for now, later we will show that we do not need them explicitly).

In practice, the random projection vectors $\mathbf{r}_l$'s remain sufficiently random when each of their $|S|$ elements are drawn uniformly from $\{+1, -1\}$ instead of from a $|S|$-dimensional Gaussian distribution [29]. With this simplification, just like the sketches, each projection vector can also be represented using $|S|$ *bits*, rather than $32 \times |S|$ bits (assuming 4 bytes per float), further saving space.

Figure 3 illustrates the idea behind sketching (for now in the static case). Given $|S|$-dimensional random $\mathbf{r}_l$ vectors, $l = 1 \ldots L$, with elements in $\{+1, -1\}$ (left) and a shingle vector $\mathbf{z}_G$ (center), the L-dimensional sketch $\mathbf{x}_G$ is obtained by taking the sign of the dot product of $\mathbf{z}$ with each $\mathbf{r}_l$ (right).

However, three main shortcomings of SIMHASH remain: (1) it requires explicit projection vectors in memory, (2) $|S|$ can still get prohibitively large, and (3) it requires knowing the size of the complete shingle universe $|S|$ to specify the dimension of each random vector. With new shingles continuously being formed from the new node and edge types arriving in the stream, the complete shingle universe (and hence its size) always remains *unknown*. As such, SIMHASH as proposed cannot be applied in a streaming setting.

3.2.3 STREAMHASH

To resolve the issues with SIMHASH for the streaming setting, we propose STREAMHASH which, rather than L $|S|$-dimensional random bit vectors (with entries corresponding to $\{+1, -1\}$ as described above), is instead instantiated with L hash functions $h_1, \ldots, h_L$ picked uniformly at random from a family $\mathcal{H}$ of hash functions, mapping shingles to $\{+1, -1\}$. That is, a $h \in \mathcal{H}$ is a *deterministic* function that maps a fixed/given shingle s to either $+1$ or -1.

Properties of $\mathcal{H}$. We require a family that exhibits three key properties; uniformity with respect to shingles and hash functions, and pairwise-independence, as described below.

First, it should be equally probable for a given shingle to hash to $+1$ or -1 over all hash functions in the family:

$$\Pr_{h \in \mathcal{H}}[h(s) = +1] = \Pr_{h \in \mathcal{H}}[h(s) = -1], \ \forall s \in S. \quad (4)$$

Second, to disallow trivially uniform families such as $\mathcal{H} = \{\forall s \in S : h_1(s) = +1,\ h_2(s) = -1\}$, we also require that for a given hash function, hash values in $\{+1, -1\}$ are equiprobable over all shingles in the universe:

$$\Pr_{s \in S}[h(s) = +1] = \Pr_{s \in S}[h(s) = -1], \ \forall h \in \mathcal{H}. \quad (5)$$

To further disallow uniform families with correlated uniform hash functions such as $\mathcal{H} = \{h_1(s),\ h_2(s) = -h_1(s)\}$ (where h_1 is some uniform hash function), we require the hash functions in the family to be pairwise-independent:

$$\forall s, s' \in S \text{ s.t. } s \neq s' \text{ and } \forall t, t' \in \{+1, -1\},$$
$$\Pr_{h \in \mathcal{H}}[h(s') = t' | h(s) = t] = \Pr_{h \in \mathcal{H}}[h(s') = t']. \quad (6)$$

If the shingle universe is fixed and known, picking a hash function h_l at random from $\mathcal{H}$ is equivalent to picking some vector $\mathbf{r}_l$ at random from $\{+1, -1\}^{|S|}$, with each element $\mathbf{r}_l(i)$ equal to the hash value $h_l(s_i)$.

If we overload the "dot-product" operator for an input vector $\mathbf{z}$ and a hash function h_l as follows:

$$\mathbf{y}(l) = \mathbf{z} \cdot h_l = \sum_{i=1,\ldots,|S|} \mathbf{z}(i) h_l(s_i), \quad l = 1 \ldots L \quad (7)$$

we can define the LSH $g_{h_l}(\mathbf{z})$ of the input vector $\mathbf{z}$ for the given hash function similar to Eq. (1):

$$g_{h_l}(\mathbf{z}) = \begin{cases} +1, & \text{if } \mathbf{z} \cdot h_l \geq 0 \\ -1, & \text{if } \mathbf{z} \cdot h_l < 0 \end{cases} \quad (8)$$

The $\mathbf{y}$ vector is called the *projection vector* of a graph. Each entry $\mathbf{y}(l)$ as given in Eq. (7) essentially holds the sum of the counts of shingles that map to $+1$ by h_l minus the sum of the counts of shingles that map to -1 by h_l.

The L-bit sketch can then be constructed for each input vector $\mathbf{z}$ by $\mathbf{x} = sign(\mathbf{y})$ and used to compute similarity the same way as in SIMHASH. Unlike SIMHASH, the sketches in STREAMHASH can be constructed and maintained *incrementally* (§3.3), as a result of which, we no longer need to know the complete shingle universe S or maintain $|S|$-dimensional random vectors in memory.

Choosing $\mathcal{H}$. A family satisfying the aforementioned three properties is said to be *strongly universal* [34]. We adopt the strongly universal multilinear family for strings [21]. In this family, the input string s (i.e., shingle) is divided into $|s|$ components (i.e., "characters") as $s = c_1 c_2 \ldots c_{|s|}$. A hash function h_l is constructed by first choosing $|s|$ random numbers $m_1^{(l)}, \ldots, m_{|s|}^{(l)}$, and s is then hashed as follows:

$$h_l(s) = 2 \times \left((m_1^{(l)} + \sum_{i=2}^{|s|} m_i^{(l)} \times int(c_i)) \bmod 2 \right) - 1. \quad (9)$$

where $int(c_i)$ is the ASCII value of c_i and $h_l(s) \in \{+1, -1\}$.

Note that the hash value for a shingle s of length $|s|$ can be computed in $\Theta(|s|)$ time.

We represent each hash function by $|s|_{\max}$ random numbers, where $|s|_{\max}$ denotes the maximum possible length of a shingle. These numbers are fixed per hash function h_l, as it is a deterministic function that hashes a fixed/given shingle to the same value each time. In practice, L hash functions can be chosen uniformly at random from this family by generating $L \times |s|_{\max}$ uniformly random 64-bit integers using a pseudorandom number generator.

Merging sketches. Two graphs G and G' will merge if an edge arrives in the stream having its source node in G and destination node in G', resulting in a graph that is their union $G \cup G'$. The centroid of a cluster of graphs is also represented by a function of their union (§4). Both scenarios require constructing the *sketch of the union of graphs*, which we detail in this subsection.

The shingle vector of the union of two graphs G and G' is the sum of their individual shingle vectors:

$$\mathbf{z}_{G \cup G'} = \mathbf{z}_G + \mathbf{z}_{G'}. \tag{10}$$

As we show below, the projection vector of the union of two graphs $\mathbf{y}_{G \cup G'}$ also turns out to be the sum of their individual projection vectors $\mathbf{y}_G$ and $\mathbf{y}_{G'}$; $\forall l = 1, \ldots, L$:

$$\begin{aligned} \mathbf{y}_{G \cup G'}(l) &= \mathbf{z}_{G \cup G'} \cdot h_l && \text{(by Eq. (7))} \\ &= \sum_{i=1,\ldots,|S|} (\mathbf{z}_G(i) + \mathbf{z}_{G'}(i))\, h_l(s_i) && \text{(by Eq. (10))} \\ &= \sum_{i=1,\ldots,|S|} \mathbf{z}_G(i) h_l(s_i) + \sum_{i=1,\ldots,|S|} \mathbf{z}_{G'}(i) h_l(s_i) \\ &= \mathbf{y}_G(l) + \mathbf{y}_{G'}(l). && (11) \end{aligned}$$

Hence, the L-bit sketch of $G \cup G'$ can be computed as $\mathbf{x}_{G \cup G'} = sign(\mathbf{y}_G + \mathbf{y}_{G'})$. This can trivially be extended to construct the sketch of the union of any number of graphs.

3.3 Maintaining Sketches Incrementally

We now describe how StreamHash sketches are updated on the arrival of a new edge in the stream. Each new edge being appended to a graph gives rise to a number of *outgoing* shingles, which are removed from the graph, and *incoming* shingles, which are added to the graph. These shingles are constructed by OkBFT traversals from certain nodes of the graph, which we detail further in this section.

Let $e(u, v)$ be a new edge arriving in the stream from node u to node v in some graph G. Let $\mathbf{x}_G$ be the L-bit sketch vector of G. We also associate with each graph a length-L *projection vector* $\mathbf{y}_G$, which contains "dot-products" (Eq. (7)) for the hash functions $h_1, \ldots, h_L$. For an empty graph, $\mathbf{y}_G = \mathbf{0}$ and $\mathbf{x}_G = \mathbf{1}$ since $\mathbf{z}(i)$'s are all zero.

For a given incoming shingle s_i, the corresponding $\mathbf{z}(i)$ implicitly[2] increases by 1. This requires each element of the projection vector $\mathbf{y}_G(l)$ to be updated by simply adding the corresponding hash value $h_l(s_i) \in \{+1, -1\}$ due to the nature of the dot-product in Eq. (7). Updating $\mathbf{y}_G$ for an outgoing shingle proceeds similarly but by subtracting the hash values. For each element $\mathbf{y}_G(l)$ of the projection vector that is updated *and* that changes sign, the corresponding bit of the sketch $\mathbf{x}_G(l)$ is updated using the new sign (Eq. (8)). Updating the sketch for an incoming or outgoing shingle s is formalized by the following update equations. $\forall l = 1, \ldots, L$:

$$\mathbf{y}_G(l) = \begin{cases} \mathbf{y}_G(l) + h_l(s), & \text{if } s \text{ an incoming shingle} \\ \mathbf{y}_G(l) - h_l(s), & \text{if } s \text{ an outgoing shingle} \end{cases} \tag{12}$$

$$\mathbf{x}_G(l) = \text{sign}(\mathbf{y}_G(l)). \tag{13}$$

Now that we can update the sketch (using the updated projection vector) of a graph for both incoming and outgoing shingles, without maintaining any shingle vector explicitly, we need to describe the construction of the incoming and outgoing shingles for a new edge e.

Appending e to the graph updates the shingle for every node that can reach e's destination node v in at most k hops, due to the nature of k-shingle construction by OkBFT. For each node w to be updated, the incoming shingle is constructed by an OkBFT from w that considers e during traversal, and the outgoing shingle is constructed by an OkBFT from w that ignores e during traversal. In practice, both shingles can be constructed by a single modified-OkBFT from w parameterized with the new edge.

Since the incoming shingle for a node may be the outgoing shingle for another, combining and further collapsing the incoming and outgoing shingles from all the updated nodes will enable updating the sketch while minimizing the number of redundant updates.

3.4 Time and Space Complexity

Time. Since sketches are constructed incrementally (§3.3), we evaluate the running time for each new edge arriving in the stream. This depends on the largest directed k-hop neighborhood possible for the nodes in our graphs. Since the maximum length of a shingle $|s|_{\max}$ is proportional to the size of this neighborhood, we specify the time complexity in terms of $|s|_{\max}$.

A new edge triggers an update to $O(|s|_{\max})$ nodes, each of which results in an OkBFT that takes $O(|s|_{\max})$ time. Thus, it takes $O(|s|^2_{\max})$ time to **construct** the $O(|s|_{\max})$ incoming and outgoing shingles for a new edge. Hashing each shingle takes $O(|s|_{\max})$ time (§3.2.3) resulting in a total **hashing** time of $O(|s|^2_{\max})$. Updating the projection vector elements and bits in the sketch takes $O(L)$ time.

This leads to an overall sketch update time of $O(L + |s|^2_{\max})$ per edge. Since L is a constant parameter and $|s|_{\max}$ depends on the value of the parameter k, the per-edge running time can be controlled.

Space. Each graph (of size at most $|G|_{\max}$) with its sketch and projection vectors consumes $O(L + |G|_{\max})$ space.[3] However, the number of graphs in the stream is unbounded, as such the overall space complexity is dominated by storing graphs. Hence, we define a parameter N to limit the maximum number of edges we retain in memory at any instant. Once the total number of edges in memory exceeds N, we evict the oldest edge incident on the least recently *touched* node. The rationale is that nodes exhibit locality of reference by the edges in the stream that touch them (i.e., that have them as a source or destination). With up to N edges, we also assume a *constant* number c of graphs is maintained and processed in memory at any given time.

The total space complexity is then $O(cL + N)$ which can also be controlled. Specifically, we choose N proportional to the available memory size, and L according to the required quality of approximation of graph similarity.

[2] As we do not maintain the shingle vector $\mathbf{z}$'s explicitly.

[3] Note that the projection vector holds L positive and/or negative *integers*, and the sketch is a length-L *bit* vector.

4. ANOMALY DETECTION

Bootstrap Clusters. StreamSpot is first initialized with bootstrap clusters obtained from a training dataset of benign flow-graphs. The training graphs are grouped into K clusters using the K-medoids algorithm, with K chosen to maximize the silhouette coefficient [30] of the resulting clustering. This gives rise to compact clusters that are well-separated from each other. An *anomaly threshold* for each cluster is set to 3 standard deviations greater than the mean distance between the cluster's graphs and medoid. This threshold is derived from Cantelli's inequality [14] with an upper-bound of 10% on the false positive rate.

Provided the bootstrap clusters, StreamSpot constructs StreamHash projection vectors for each training graph, and constructs the projection vector of the centroid of each cluster as the average of the projection vectors of the graphs it contains. In essence, the centroid of a cluster is the "average graph" with shingle vector counts formed by the union (§3.2.3) of the graphs it contains divided by the number of graphs. The sketch of each centroid is then constructed and the bootstrap graphs are discarded from memory.

Streaming Cluster Maintenance. Apart from the cluster centroid sketches and projection vectors, we maintain in memory the number of graphs in each cluster and, for each observed and unevicted graph, its anomaly score and assignment to either one of K clusters or an "attack" class. Each new edge arriving at a graph G updates its sketch $\mathbf{x}_G$ and projection vector $\mathbf{y}_G$ to $\mathbf{x}'_G$ and $\mathbf{y}'_G$ respectively (§3.3). $\mathbf{x}'_G$ is then used to compute the distance of G to each cluster centroid. Let Q be the nearest cluster to G, of size $|Q|$ and with centroid sketch $\mathbf{x}_Q$ and centroid projection vector $\mathbf{y}_Q$.

If G was previously unassigned to any cluster and the distance of G to Q is lesser than its corresponding cluster threshold, then G is assigned to Q and its size and projection vector are updated $\forall l = 1, \ldots, L$ as:

$$\mathbf{y}_Q(l) = \frac{\mathbf{y}_Q(l) \times |Q| + \mathbf{y}'_G(l)}{|Q| + 1}, \qquad |Q| = |Q| + 1 \,. \tag{14}$$

If the graph was previously already assigned to Q, its size remains the same and its projection vector is updated as:

$$\mathbf{y}_Q(l) = \mathbf{y}_Q(l) + \frac{\mathbf{y}'_G(l) - \mathbf{y}_G(l)}{|Q|} \,. \tag{15}$$

If the graph was previously assigned to a different cluster $R \neq Q$, Q is updated using Eq. 14 and the size and projection vector of R are updated as:

$$\mathbf{y}_R(l) = \frac{\mathbf{y}_R(l) \times |R| - \mathbf{y}_G(l)}{|R| - 1}, \qquad |R| = |R| - 1 \,. \tag{16}$$

If the distance from G to Q is greater than its corresponding cluster threshold, G is removed from its assigned cluster (if any) using Eq. (16) and assigned to the "attack" class. In all cases where the projection vector of Q (or R) is updated, the corresponding sketch is also updated as:

$$\mathbf{x}_Q(l) = sign(\mathbf{y}_Q(l)), \quad \forall l = 1, \ldots, L. \tag{17}$$

Finally, the anomaly score of G is computed as its distance to Q after Q's centroid has been updated.

Time and Space Complexity. With K clusters and L-bit sketches, finding the nearest cluster takes $O(KL)$ time and computing the graph's anomaly score takes $O(L)$ time. Adding a graph to (Eq. (14)), removing a graph from (Eq. (16)) and updating (Eq. (15)) a cluster each take $O(L)$ time, leading to a total time complexity of $O(KL)$ per-edge.

With a maximum of c graphs retained in memory by limiting the maximum number of edges to N (§3.4), storing cluster assignments and anomaly scores each consume $O(c)$ space. The centroid sketches and projection vectors each consume $O(KL)$ space, leading to a total space complexity of $O(c + KL)$ for clustering and anomaly detection.

5. EVALUATION

Datasets. Our datasets consist of flow-graphs derived from 1 attack and 5 benign scenarios. The benign scenarios involve normal browsing activity, specifically watching YouTube, downloading files, browsing `cnn.com`, checking Gmail, and playing a video game. The attack involves a drive-by download triggered by visiting a malicious URL that exploits a Flash vulnerability and gains root access to the visiting host. For each scenario, Selenium RC[4] was used to automate the execution of a 100 tasks on a Linux machine. All system calls on the machine from the start of a task until its termination were traced and used to construct the flow-graph for that task. The flow-graphs were compiled into 3 datasets whose properties are shown in Table 1.

Experiment Settings. We evaluate StreamSpot in the following settings:

(1) *Static*: We use p% of all the benign graphs for training, and the rest of the benign graphs along with the attack graphs for testing. We find an offline clustering of the training graphs and then score and rank the test graphs based on this clustering. Graphs are represented by their shingle vectors and all required data is stored in memory. The goal is to quantify the effectiveness of StreamSpot before introducing approximations to optimize for time and space.

(2) *Streaming*: We use p% of the benign graphs for training to first construct a bootstrap clustering offline. This is provided to initialize StreamSpot, and the test graphs are then streamed in and processed online one edge at a time. Hence, test graphs may be seen only partially at any given time. For each edge, StreamSpot updates the corresponding graph sketch, clusters, cluster assignments and anomaly scores, and a snapshot of the anomaly scores is retained every 10,000 edges for evaluation. StreamSpot is also evaluated under memory constraints by limiting the sketch size and maximum number of stored edges.

5.1 Static Evaluation

We first cluster the training graphs based on their shingle-vector similarity. Due to the low diameter and large out-degree exhibited by flow-graphs, the shingles obtained tend to be long (even for $k = 1$), and similar pairs of shingles from two graphs differ only by a few characters; this results in most pairs of graphs appearing dissimilar.

To mitigate this, we 'chunk' each shingle by splitting it into fixed-size units. The chunk length parameter C controls the influence of graph structure and node type frequency on the pairwise similarity of graphs. A small C reduces the effect of structure and relies on the frequency of node types, making most pairs of graphs similar. A large C tends to make pairs of graphs more dissimilar. This variation is evident in Figure 4, showing the pairwise-distance distributions for different chunk lengths.

[4] http://www.seleniumhq.org/projects/remote-control/

Table 1: **Dataset summary: Training scenarios and test edges (attack + 25% benign graphs).**

Dataset	Scenarios	# Graphs	Avg. |V|	Avg. |E|	# Test Edges
YDC	YouTube, Download, CNN	300	8705	239648	21,857,899
GFC	GMail, VGame, CNN	300	8151	148414	13,854,229
ALL	YouTube, Download, CNN, GMail, VGame	500	8315	173857	24,826,556

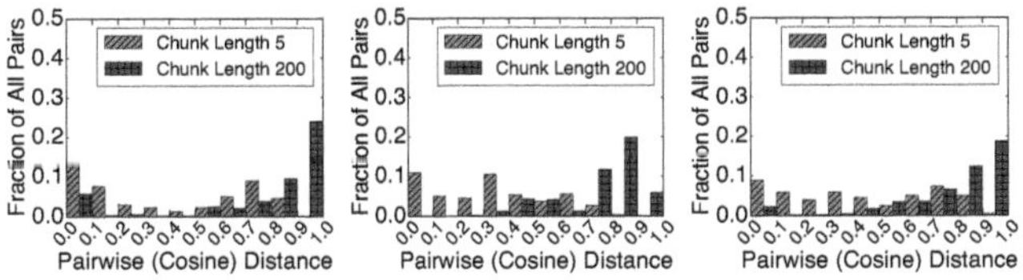

(a) YDC (b) GFC (c) ALL

Figure 4: Distribution of pairwise cosine distances for different values of chunk lengths.

We aim to choose a C that neither makes all pairs of graphs too similar or dissimilar. Figure 5 shows the entropy of pairwise-distances with varying C for each dataset. At the point of maximum entropy, the distances are near-uniformly distributed. A safe region to choose C is near and to the right of this point; intuitively, this C sufficiently differentiates dissimilar pairs of graphs, while not affecting similar ones. For our experiments, we pick $C = 25, 100, 50$ respectively for YDC, GFC, and ALL. After xing C, we cluster the training graphs with K-medoids and pick K with the maximum silhouette coefficient [30] for the resulting clustering; these are $K = 5, 5, 10$ respectively for YDC, GFC, and ALL.

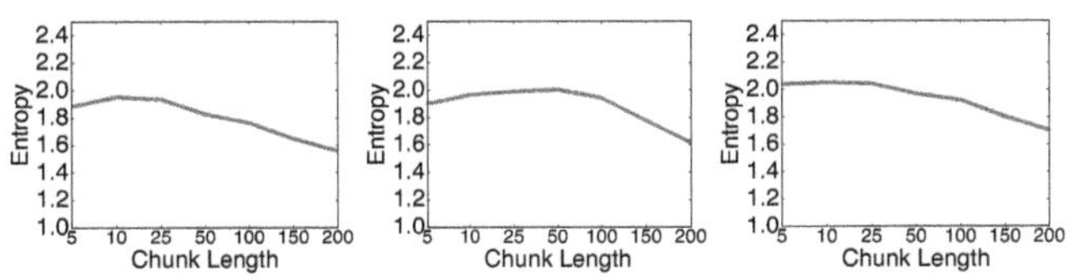

(a) YDC (b) GFC (c) ALL

Figure 5: Variation in entropy of the pairwise cosine distance distribution. ($p = 75\%$)

To validate our intuition for picking C, Figure 6 shows a heatmap of the average precision obtained after clustering and anomaly-ranking on the test data (the attack and remaining 25% benign graphs), for varying C and K. We can see that for our chosen C and K, StreamSpot achieves near-ideal performance. We also nd that the average precision appears robust to the number of clusters when chunk length is chosen in the safe region .

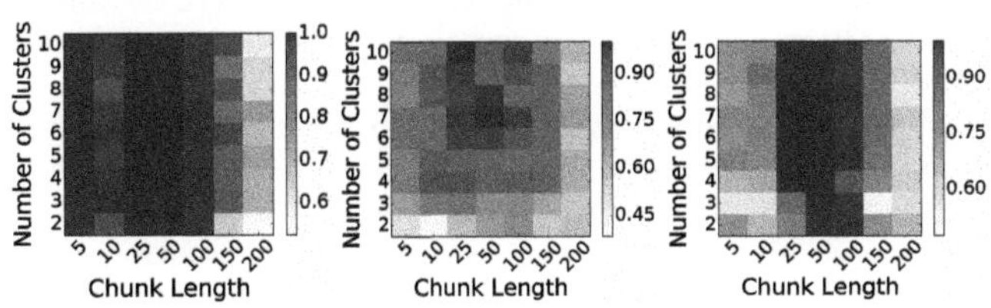

(a) YDC (b) GFC (c) ALL

Figure 6: Average precision for different chunk-length C and number of clusters K. ($p = 75\%$)

To quantify anomaly detection performance in the static setting, we set $p = 25\%$ of the data as training and cluster the training graphs based on their shingle vectors, following the aforementioned steps to choose C and K. We then score each test graph by its distance to the closest centroid in the clustering. This gives us a ranking of the test graphs, based on which we plot the precision-recall (PR) and ROC curves.

As a baseline, we use iForest [23] with 100 trees and 75% subsampling rate with each graph represented by a vector of 10 structural features: the average/maximum degree and distinct-degree[5], the average eccentricity and shortest-path length, and the diameter, density and number of nodes/edges.

The curves (averaged over 10 independent random samples) for all the datasets are shown in Figure 7. Note that even with 25% of the data, static StreamSpot is effective in correctly ranking the attack graphs and achieves an average precision (AP, area under the PR curve) of more then 0.9 and a near-ideal AUC (area under ROC curve).

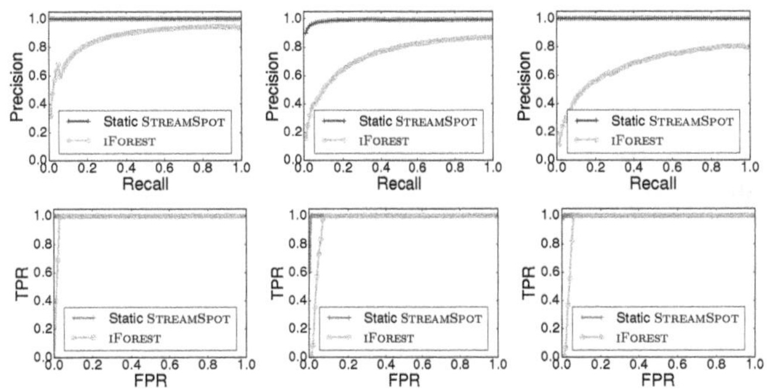

(a) YDC (b) GFC (c) ALL

Figure 7: (top) Precision-Recall (PR) and (bottom) ROC curves averaged over 10 samples. ($p = 25\%$)

Finally, in Figure 8 we show how the AP and AUC change as the training data percentage p is varied from $p = 10\%$ to $p = 90\%$. We note that with sufficient training data, the test performance reaches an acceptable level for GFC.

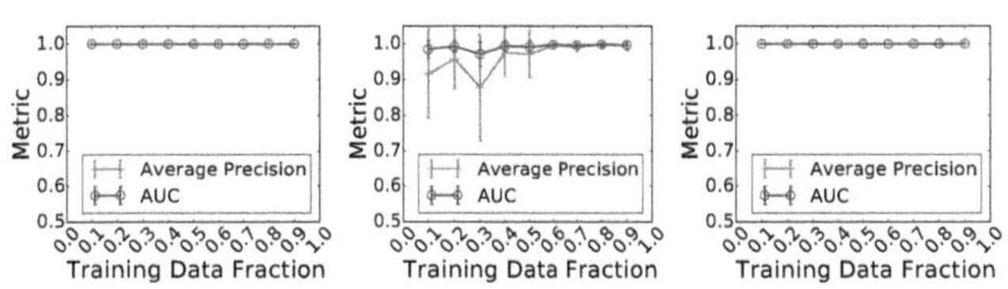

(a) YDC (b) GFC (c) ALL

Figure 8: AP and AUC with varying training % p.

The results in this section demonstrate a proof of concept that our proposed method can effectively spot anomalies provided offline data and unbounded memory. We now move on to testing StreamSpot in the streaming setting, for which it was designed.

5.2 Streaming Evaluation

We now show that StreamSpot remains both accurate in detecting anomalies and efficient in processing time and memory usage in a streaming setting. We control the number of graphs that arrive and grow *simultaneously* with parameter B, by creating groups of B graphs at random from the test

[5] Ignoring multi-edges to the same destination node.

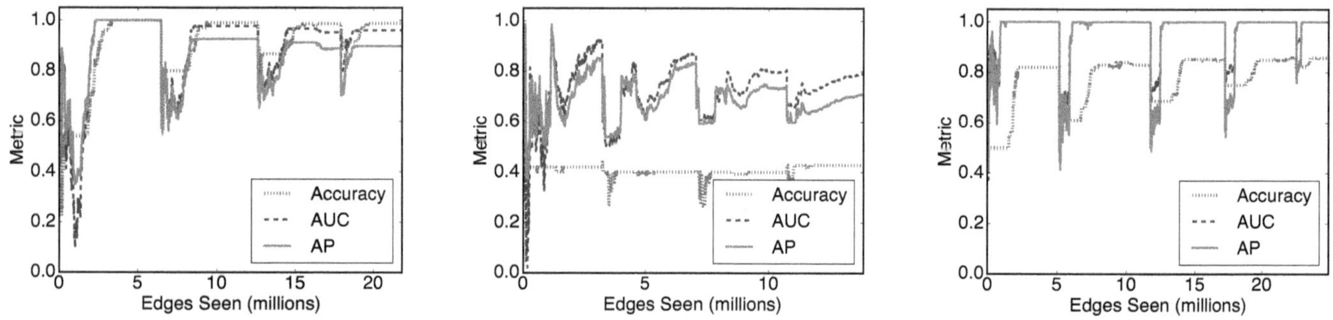

(a) YDC (b) GFC (c) ALL

Figure 9: Performance of StreamSpot at different instants of the stream for all datasets ($L = 1000$).

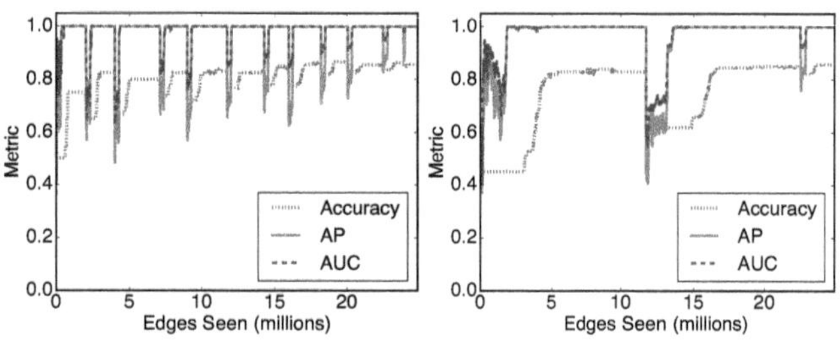

Figure 10: StreamSpot performance on ALL (measured at every 10K edges) when (left) $B = 20$ graphs and (right) $B = 100$ graphs arrive simultaneously.

graphs, picking one group at a time and interleaving the edges from graphs within the group to form the stream.

In all experiments, 75% of the benign graphs where used for bootstrap clustering. Performance metrics are computed on the instantaneous anomaly ranking every 10,000 edges.

Detection performance. Fig. 10 shows the anomaly detection performance on the ALL dataset, when $B = 20$ graphs grow in memory simultaneously (left) as compared to $B = 100$ graphs (right). We make the following observations: (*i*) The detection performance follows a trend, with periodic dips followed by recovery. (*ii*) Each dip corresponds to the arrival of a new group of graphs. Initially, only a small portion of the new graphs are available and the detection performance is less accurate. However, performance recovers quickly as the graphs grow; the steep surges in performance in Fig. 10 imply a small anomaly detection delay. (*iii*) The average precision after recovery indicates a near-ideal ranking of attack graphs at the top. (*iv*) The dips become less severe as the clustering becomes more 'mature' with increasing data seen; this is evident in the general upward trend of the accuracy. (*v*) The accuracy loss is not due to the ranking (since both AP and AUC remain high) but due to the chosen anomaly thresholds derived from the bootstrap clustering, where the error is due to false negatives.

Similar results hold for $B = 50$ as shown in Figure 9 (c) for ALL, and (a) and (b) for YDC and GFC respectively.

Sketch size. Figures 9 and 10 show StreamSpot's performance for sketch size $L = 1000$ bits. When compared to the number of unique shingles $|S|$ in each dataset (649,968, 580,909 and 1,106,684 for YDC, GFC and ALL), sketching saves considerable space. Reducing the sketch size saves further space but increases the error of cosine distance approximation. Figure 11 shows StreamSpot's performance on ALL for smaller sketch sizes. Note that it performs equally well for $L = 100$ (compared to Fig. 9(c)), and reasonably well even with sketch size as small as $L = 10$.

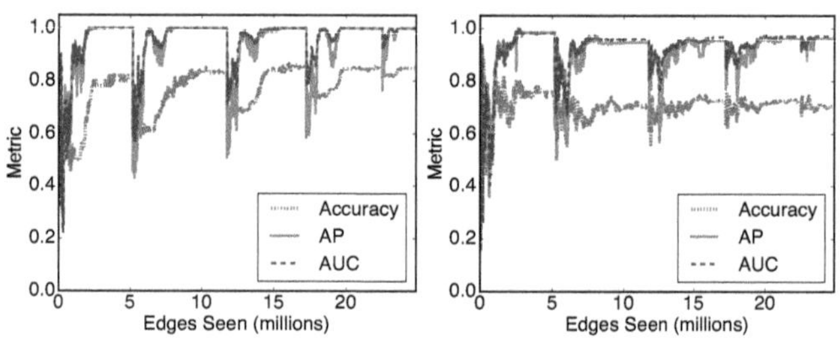

(a) $L = 100$ (b) $L = 10$

Figure 11: Performance of StreamSpot on ALL for different values of the sketch size.

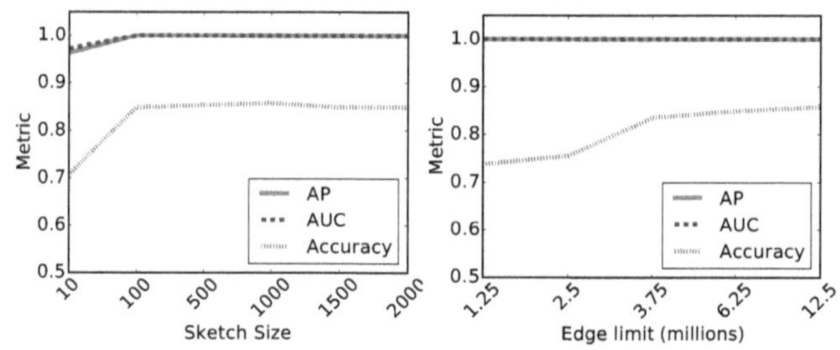

Figure 13: StreamSpot performance on ALL with (left) sketch size L and (right) memory limit N.

Memory limit. Now we investigate StreamSpot's performance by limiting the memory usage using N: the maximum number of allowed edges in memory at any given time. Figures 12 (a)–(c) show the performance when N is limited to 15%, 10%, and 5% of the incoming stream of ~25M edges, on ALL (with $B = 100$, $L = 1000$). The overall performance decreases only slightly as memory is constrained. The detection delay (or the recovery time) increases, while the speed and extent of recovery decays slowly. This is expected, as with small memory and a large number of graphs growing simultaneously, it takes longer to observe a certain fraction of a graph at which effective detection can be performed.

These results indicate that StreamSpot continues to perform well even with limited memory. Figure 13 shows performance at the end of the stream with (a) increasing sketch size L (N fixed at 12.5M edges) and (b) increasing memory limit N (L fixed at 1000). StreamSpot is robust to both parameters and demonstrates stable performance across a wide range of settings.

Running time[6]. To evaluate the scalability of StreamSpot for high-volume streams, we measure its per-

[6] On an Intel Xeon® E7 4830 v3 at 2.1Ghz with 1TB RAM.

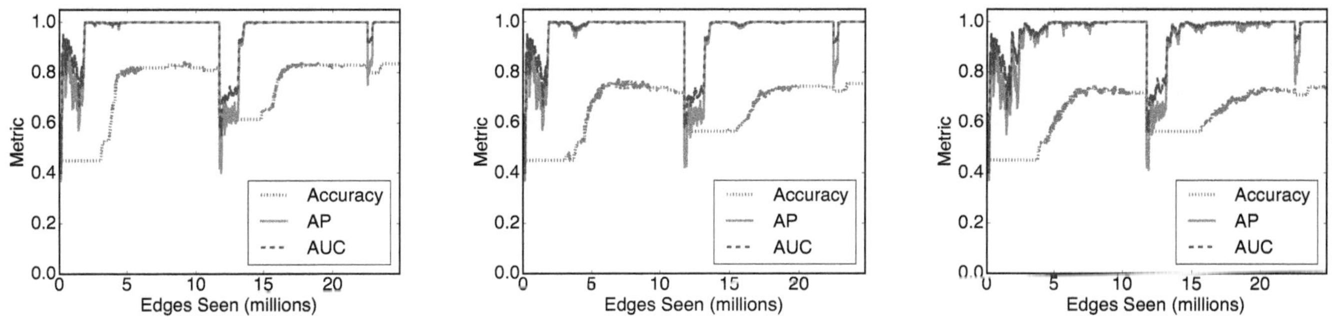

(a) Limit = 15% (b) Limit = 10% (c) Limit = 5%

Figure 12: Performance of STREAMSPOT on ALL ($L = 1000$), for different values of the memory limit N (as a fraction of the number of incoming edges).

edge running time on ALL for sketch sizes $L = 1000, 100$ and 10 averaged over the stream of ~25M edges in Fig. 14 (left). Each incoming edge triggers four operations: updating the graph adjacency list, constructing shingles, updating the sketch/projection vector and updating the clusters. We observe that the running time is dominated by the sketch-update time (distribution in Fig. 14 (right)), but the total per-edge running time is under $70\mu s$ when $L = 1000$. Thus, STREAMSPOT can scale to process over 14,000 edges per second. For $L = 100$, which performs comparably (see Fig. 11 (a)), it can further scale to over 100,000 edges per second.

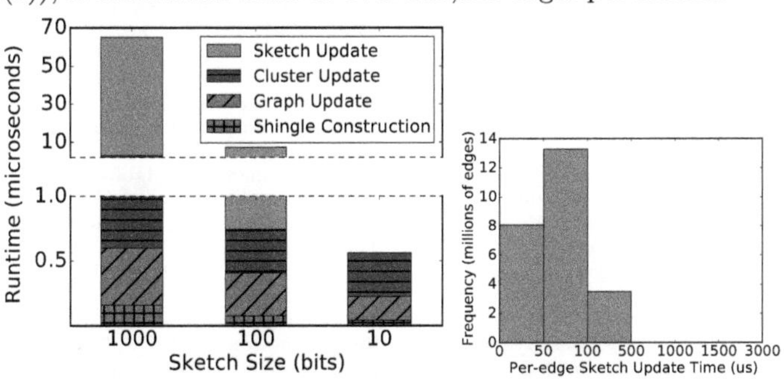

Figure 14: (left) Average runtime of STREAMSPOT per edge, for various sketch sizes on ALL. (right) Distribution of sketch processing times for ~25M edges.

Memory usage. Finally, we quantify the memory usage of STREAMSPOT. Table 2 shows the total memory consumed for ALL by graph edges (M_G) in megabytes and by the projection and sketch vectors (M_Y, M_X) in kilobytes with increasing N (the maximum number of edges stored in memory). We also mention the number of graphs retained memory at the end of the stream. Note that M_G grows in proportion to N, and M_Y is 32 times M_X, since projection vectors are 32-bit integer vectors of the same length as the sketch vectors. Overall, STREAMSPOT's memory consumption for $N = 12.5$M and $L = 1000$ is as low as 240 megabytes, which is comparable to the memory consumed by an average process on a commodity machine.

In summary, these results demonstrate the effectiveness as well as the time and memory-efficiency of STREAMSPOT.

6. RELATED WORK

Our work is related to a number of areas of study, including graph similarity, graph sketching and anomaly detection in streaming and typed graphs, which we detail further in this section.

Table 2: STREAMSPOT memory use on ALL ($L = 1000$). $|G|$: final # graphs in memory. Memory used by M_G: graphs, M_Y: projection vectors, M_X: sketches

N	$\|G\|$	M_G	M_Y	M_X
1.25 M	8	23.84 MB	31.25 KB	0.98 KB
2.5 M	29	47.68 MB	113.28 KB	3.54 KB
3.75 M	42	71.52 MB	164.06 KB	5.13 KB
6.25 M	56	119.20 MB	218.75 KB	6.84 KB
12.5 M	125	238.41 MB	488.28 KB	15.26 KB

Graph similarity. There exists a large body of work on graph similarity, which can be used for various tasks including clustering and anomaly detection. Methods that require knowing the node correspondence between graphs are inapplicable to our scenario, as are methods that compute a vector of *global* metrics [7] for each graph (such as the average properties across all nodes), since they cannot take into account the temporal ordering of edges.

Graph-edit-distance (GED) [9] defines the dissimilarity between two graphs as the minimum total cost of operations required to make one graph isomorphic to the other. However, computing the GED requires finding an inexact matching between the two graphs that has minimum cost. This is known to be NP-hard and frequently addressed by local-search heuristics [19] that provide no error bound.

Graph kernels [33, 31] decompose each graph into a set of local substructures and the similarity between two graphs is a function of the number of substructures they have in common. However, these methods require knowing a fixed universe of the substructures that constitute all the input graphs, which is unavailable in a streaming scenario.

Heterogeneous/typed graphs. An early method [26] used an information-theoretic approach to find anomalous node-typed graphs in a large static database. The method used the SUBDUE [11] system to first discover frequent substructures in the database in an offline fashion. The anomalies are then graphs containing only a few of the frequent substructures. Subsequent work [12] defined anomalies as graphs that were mostly similar to normative ones, but differing in a few GED operations. Frequent typed subgraphs were also leveraged as features to identify non-crashing software bugs from system execution flow graphs [22]. Work also exists studying anomalous communities [16, 27] and community anomalies [13, 28] for attributed graphs. All of these approaches are designed for static graphs.

Streaming graphs. GMicro [3] clustered untyped graph streams using a centroid-based approach and a distance function based on edge frequencies. It was extended to graphs with whole-graph-level attributes [35], and node-level attributes [24] where the goal was to cluster nodes. GOutlier [4] introduced structural reservoir sampling to maintain summaries of untyped, undirected graph streams and detect anomalous graphs as those having unlikely edges. Classy [19] implemented a scalable distributed approach to clustering streams of untyped call graphs by employing simulated annealing to approximate the GED between pairs of graphs, and GED lower bounds to prune away candidate clusters.

There also exist methods that detect changes in graphs that evolve through community evolution, by processing the edge stream to determine expanding and contracting communities [2] and by applying information-theoretic [32] and probabilistic [15] approaches on graph snapshots to find time points of global community-structure change. Methods also exist to find temporal patterns called graph evolution rules [6], which are subgraphs with similar structure, types of nodes, and order of edges. All the aforementioned methods are primarily suited to untyped graphs.

Graph skeletons and sketches. Graph "skeletons" [18] were introduced to approximately solve a number of common graph-theoretic problems such as finding the global min-cut and max-flow with provable error-bounds. Skeletons were also applied [1] to construct compressed representations of disk-resident graphs for efficiently approximating and answering minimum s-t cut queries. Work on sketching graphs has primarily focused on constructing specialized sketches that enable approximate solutions to specific graph problems such as finding testing reachability and finding the densest subgraph [25]; the proposed sketches cannot be applied directly to detect graph-based anomalies.

7. CONCLUSION

We have presented StreamSpot to cluster and detect anomalous heterogeneous graphs originating from a stream of typed edges, in which new graphs emerge and existing graphs evolve as the stream progresses. We introduced representing heterogeneous ordered graphs by shingling and devised StreamHash to maintain summaries of these representations online with constant-time updates and bounded memory consumption. Exploiting the mergeability of our summaries, we devised an online centroid-based clustering and anomaly detection scheme to rank incoming graphs by their anomalousness that obtains over 90% average precision for the course of the stream. We showed that performance is sustained even under strict memory constraints, while being able to process over 100,000 edges per second.

While designed to detect APTs from system log streams, StreamSpot is applicable to other scenarios requiring scalable clustering and anomaly-ranking of typed graphs arriving in a stream of edges, for which no method currently exists. It has social media applications in event-detection using streams of sentences represented as syntax trees, or biochemical applications in detecting anomalous entities in streams of chemical compounds or protein structure elements.

Acknowledgments

This research is sponsored by the DARPA Transparent Computing Program under Contract No. FA8650-15-C-7561, NSF CAREER 1452425 and IIS 1408287, an R&D grant from Northrop Grumman, and a faculty gift from Facebook. Any conclusions expressed in this material are of the authors and do not necessarily reflect the views, expressed or implied, of the funding parties.

8. REFERENCES

[1] C. C. Aggarwal, Y. Xie, and P. S. Yu. Gconnect: A connectivity index for massive disk-resident graphs. *PVLDB*, 2009.
[2] C. C. Aggarwal and P. S. Yu. Online analysis of community evolution in data streams. In *SDM*, 2005.
[3] C. C. Aggarwal, Y. Zhao, and P. S. Yu. On clustering graph streams. In *SDM*, 2010.
[4] C. C. Aggarwal, Y. Zhao, and P. S. Yu. Outlier detection in graph streams. In *ICDE*, 2011.
[5] L. Akoglu, H. Tong, and D. Koutra. Graph based anomaly detection and description: a survey. *Dat. Min. Know. Disc.*, 2015.
[6] M. Berlingerio, F. Bonchi, B. Bringmann, and A. Gionis. Mining graph evolution rules. In *ECML/PKDD*, 2009.
[7] M. Berlingerio, D. Koutra, T. Eliassi-Rad, and C. Faloutsos. Network similarity via multiple social theories. In *ASONAM*, 2013.
[8] A. Z. Broder. On the resemblance and containment of documents. In *Compression and Complex. of Sequences*, 1997.
[9] H. Bunke and G. Allermann. Inexact graph matching for structural pattern recognition. *Pattern Recogn. Letters*, 1983.
[10] M. S. Charikar. Similarity estimation techniques from rounding algorithms. In *STOC*, 2002.
[11] D. J. Cook and L. B. Holder. Graph-based data mining. *IEEE Intelligent Systems*, 2000.
[12] W. Eberle and L. B. Holder. Discovering structural anomalies in graph-based data. In *ICDMW*, 2007.
[13] J. Gao, F. Liang, W. Fan, C. Wang, Y. Sun, and J. Han. On community outliers and their efficient detection in information networks. In *KDD*, 2010.
[14] G. Grimmett and D. Stirzaker. *Probability and random processes*. Oxford University Press, 2001.
[15] M. Gupta, C. C. Aggarwal, J. Han, and Y. Sun. Evolutionary clustering and anal. of bibliographic networks. *ASONAM*, 2011.
[16] M. Gupta, A. Mallya, S. Roy, J. H. D. Cho, and J. Han. Local learning for mining outlier subgraphs from network datasets. In *SDM*, 2014.
[17] P. Indyk and R. Motwani. Approximate nearest neighbors: towards removing the curse of dimensionality. In *STOC*, 1998.
[18] D. R. Karger. Random sampling in cut, flow, and network design problems. In *STOC*, 1994.
[19] O. Kostakis. Classy: fast clustering streams of call-graphs. *Data Min. Knowl. Discov.*, 2014.
[20] D. Koutra, J. T. Vogelstein, and C. Faloutsos. Deltacon: A principled massive-graph similarity function. In *SDM*, 2013.
[21] D. Lemire and O. Kaser. Strongly universal string hashing is fast. *The Computer Journal*, 2014.
[22] C. Liu, X. Yan, H. Yu, J. Han, and P. S. Yu. Mining behavior graphs for "backtrace" of noncrashing bugs. In *SDM*, 2005.
[23] F. T. Liu, K. M. Ting, and Z.-H. Zhou. Isolation forest. In *ICDM*, 2008.
[24] R. McConville, W. Liu, and P. Miller. Vertex clustering of augmented graph streams. In *SDM*, 2015.
[25] A. McGregor. Graph stream algorithms: a survey. *SIGMOD Record*, 2014.
[26] C. C. Noble and D. J. Cook. Graph-based anomaly detection. In *KDD*, 2003.
[27] B. Perozzi and L. Akoglu. Scalable anomaly ranking of attributed neighborhoods. In *SDM*, 2016.
[28] B. Perozzi, L. Akoglu, P. Iglesias Sánchez, and E. Müller. Focused clustering and outlier detection in large attributed graphs. In *KDD*, 2014.
[29] A. Rajaraman and J. D. Ullman. *Mining of Massive Datasets*. Cambridge University Press, 2011.
[30] P. Rousseeuw. Silhouettes: a graphical aid to the interpretation and validation of cluster analysis. *J. Comp. Appl. Math.*, 1987.
[31] N. Shervashidze, P. Schweitzer, E. J. Van Leeuwen, K. Mehlhorn, and K. M. Borgwardt. Weisfeiler-Lehman graph kernels. *JMLR*, 2011.
[32] J. Sun, C. Faloutsos, S. Papadimitriou, and P. S. Yu. Graphscope: Parameter-free mining of large time-evolving graphs. In *KDD*, 2007.
[33] S. V. N. Vishwanathan, N. N. Schraudolph, R. Kondor, and K. M. Borgwardt. Graph kernels. *JMLR*, 2010.
[34] M. N. Wegman and J. L. Carter. New hash functions and their use in authentication and set equality. *J. of Comp. & Sys. Sciences*, 1981.
[35] P. S. Yu and Y. Zhao. On graph stream clustering with side information. In *SDM*, 2013.

Regime Shifts in Streams: Real-time Forecasting of Co-evolving Time Sequences

Yasuko Matsubara
Kumamoto University
yasuko@cs.kumamoto-u.ac.jp

Yasushi Sakurai
Kumamoto University
yasushi@cs.kumamoto-u.ac.jp

ABSTRACT

Given a large, online stream of multiple co-evolving event sequences, such as sensor data and Web-click logs, that contains various types of non-linear dynamic evolving patterns of different durations, how can we efficiently and effectively capture important patterns? How do we go about forecasting long-term future events?

In this paper, we present REGIMECAST, an efficient and effective method for forecasting co-evolving data streams. REGIMECAST is designed as an adaptive non-linear dynamical system, which is inspired by the concept of "regime shifts" in natural dynamical systems. Our method has the following properties: (a) *Effective*: it operates on large data streams, captures important patterns and performs long-term forecasting; (b) *Adaptive*: it automatically and incrementally recognizes the latent trends and dynamic evolution patterns (i.e., regimes) that are unknown in advance; (c) *Scalable*: it is fast and the computation cost does not depend on the length of data streams; (d) *Any-time*: it provides a response at any time and generates long-range future events.

Extensive experiments on real datasets demonstrate that REGIMECAST does indeed make long-range forecasts, and it outperforms state-of-the-art competitors as regards accuracy and speed.

Categories and Subject Descriptors: H.2.8 [**Database management**]: Database applications–*Data mining*
Keywords: Time series; Real-time forecasting; Regime shifts;

1. INTRODUCTION

Time-series event analysis is an important topic that has attracted huge interest in countless domains such as sensor network monitoring [10, 24], financial and economic analysis [37, 35], social activity mining [13, 18], online text [6, 7], and medical and health record data analysis [9, 4, 19]. In the real applications, a massive volume and variety of time-stamped data is generated and collected at a very high logging rate, and this situation provides various new demands and opportunities for data scientists and analysts.

In this paper, we focus on the most important and challenging time-series analysis task, namely, the real-time forecasting of co-evolving event streams, and specifically, we present REGIMECAST, an efficient forecasting method for co-evolving time sequences. REGIMECAST is designed as an adaptive non-linear dynamical system, inspired by the concept of "regime shifts" in natural ecological systems [31, 3].

Intuitively, the problem we wish to solve is as follows:

INFORMAL PROBLEM 1. **Given** *a data stream* X, *which consists of event entries of* d*-dimensional data, i.e.,* $X = \{\boldsymbol{x}(1), \ldots, \boldsymbol{x}(t_c)\}$, *where* t_c *is the current time tick,* **forecast** l_s*-steps-ahead future event* $\boldsymbol{x}(t_c + l_s)$*, immediately, at any point in time.*

What is real-time forecasting over data streams? Assume that we have a data stream X, which is a semi-infinite sequence of event entries of d-dimensional data, $\{\boldsymbol{x}(1), \boldsymbol{x}(2), \ldots, \boldsymbol{x}(t_c), \ldots\}$, where $\boldsymbol{x}(t_c)$ is the most recent event, and t_c increases with every new time tick. So, what would be the real requirements for forecasting data streams? We need an efficient algorithm that reports upcoming unknown future events, immediately, at any point in time, while discarding redundant information. In short, the ideal solution would satisfy the following requirements.

- l_s**-steps-ahead forecasting**: Assume that we have multiple sensors (e.g., accelerometers in automobiles or motion sensors in public areas), which generate d-dimensional co-evolving event entries, every millisecond. Given such a huge collection of event sequences, we want to forecast future events, efficiently and effectively, (e.g., to perform traffic accident prevention or home security monitoring and intrusion detection). Basically, our forecasting algorithm should be (a) *long-term*: it should generate more than, say, $l_s = 100$ steps-ahead predictions, every time tick; and (b) *continuous*: it should estimate future events, smoothly and continuously, by monitoring current trends and dynamic evolving patterns. With respect to the first property (a), it is very important to predict long-range future events. For example, if we receive an alert message, such as *"there will be a traffic accident in a second"*, it would be too late to avoid the accident. That is, faced with real-time forecasting problems, short-term (say, $1, 2, 3, \ldots$-steps-ahead) prediction is *meaningless*. The second property, i.e., (b) continuous processing is a requirement for data streams. Unlike the traditional time-series forecasting approaches (e.g., ARIMA), which are *static* (as opposed to dynamic), the ideal method should report future events, at every point in time, by capturing and updating the current dynamic evolving patterns, flexibly and continuously.
- **Adaptive non-linear modeling**: As we will see later (e.g., in Figure 1 (a)), real-life time-series event streams contain various types of distinct, dynamic evolving patterns of different durations, e.g., the walking and house-cleaning motion patterns in Figure 1 (a), the normal and abnormal patterns seen in network traffic monitoring streams, and the patterns

KDD '16, August 13-17, 2016, San Francisco, CA, USA

DOI: http://dx.doi.org/10.1145/2939672.2939755

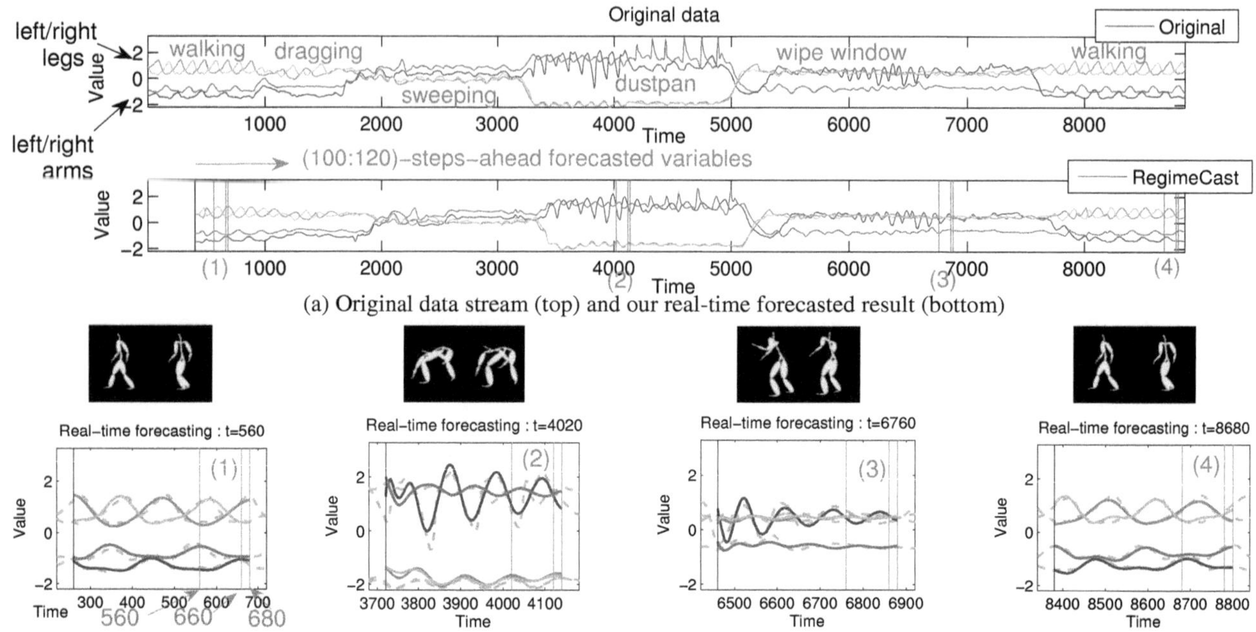

(a) Original data stream (top) and our real-time forecasted result (bottom)

(b-1) Walking ($t_c = 560$) (b-2) Dustpan ($t_c = 4020$) (b-3) Wipe a window ($t_c = 6760$) (b-4) Walking ($t_c = 8680$)

Figure 1: Forecasting power of REGIMECAST for a "house cleaning" motion event stream: (a) The original data (top), our (100:120)-steps-ahead forecasted results (bottom), and (b) snapshots of video clips (top) and REGIMECAST outputs (bottom) at four different time ticks. Given an original data stream, REGIMECAST incrementally and automatically identifies typical motions (such as "walking" and "using a dustpan"), and also forecasts long-range future events (e.g., in figure (b-1), at the current time tick $t_c = 560$, it makes (100:120)-steps-ahead predictions, i.e., from $t_s = 660$ to $t_e = 680$). We note that our algorithm requires no prior training and no hint regarding the number of motions (i.e., regimes). For a more detailed explanation of our forecasting mechanism, please see Figure 3.

of growth, maturity and decline seen in product sales or Web-based online user activities (e.g., Figure 7). Hereafter, we refer to such a distinct dynamic evolving pattern as a *"regime"*. As shown in Figure 1 (a), a single event stream X consists of multiple regimes, where there are some abrupt changes of regimes, namely, *"regime shifts"*, such as, $t = 1,000$, from a walking motion to a dragging motion. Consequently, our algorithm should identify any sudden discontinuity in an event stream, and recognize the current regime, immediately, so that it can forecast l_s-steps-ahead future events, adaptively, at any time. We should also emphasize that these regimes are unknown in advance, and thus the algorithm should incrementally learn all arrived events, summarize them into a compact yet powerful representation. We thus propose using an *adaptive* non-linear modeling approach that satisfies all the above requirements. We will discuss this further in subsection 3.2.

Preview of our results. Figure 1 (a) shows the original event stream of a "house cleaning" motion (top) and the result we obtained with REGIMECAST (bottom). The original data stream consists of four co-evolving motion capture sensors: left/right arms and left/right legs. As shown in the figure, the original event stream is composed of several consecutive motions, including "walking", "dragging a mop", "using a dustpan" and "wiping a window".

The bottom of Figure 1 (a) shows our (100:120)-steps-ahead forecasting results, and specifically, REGIMECAST forecasts (100:120)-steps-ahead future events, for every (reporting) time [1]. Figure 1 (b-1)-(b-4) shows original video clips (top) and snapshots of REGIMECAST outputs (bottom) at four different time ticks (i.e., $t_c = 560$, 4020, 6760, 8680, respectively). In figures (b-1)-(b-4), the estimated events are shown by bold colored lines, and the original sequences are shown by dotted gray lines. The red vertical axes show the time ticks $\{t_c, t_s, t_e\}$, where, t_c is the current time tick. At each time tick t_c, the algorithm tries to forecast (100:120)-steps-ahead future events, that is, from t_s to t_e. For example, in the figure (b-1), at the current time tick $t_c = 560$, it predicts future events from $t_s = 660$ to $t_e = 680$. We will see this snapshot-plot so often that we have given it a name, "REGIMESNAP". Also, We will explain our detailed forecasting mechanism later in Figure 3 in subsection 4.1.

Consequently, given a large collection of co-evolving events, our method identifies important motion patterns (e.g., "walking" and "wiping"), and forecasts l_s-steps-ahead future events, incrementally and automatically. Most importantly, our algorithm requires no prior training and no hint regarding the number of motions (i.e., regimes) or trend-changing (i.e., regime shift) positions.

Contributions. In this paper, we present REGIMECAST, which is a real-time forecasting method for large co-evolving data streams. Our method has the following desirable properties:

1. **Effective**: it operates on a large collection of time series and performs long-term event forecasting.
2. **Adaptive**: it incrementally and automatically recognizes latent trends and non-linear dynamic patterns (i.e., regimes) while these patterns are unknown in advance.
3. **Scalable**: the computation cost does not depend on data stream length.
4. **Any-time**: it generates long-range predictions, immediately, at any point in time.

Outline. The rest of the paper is organized in the conventional way: Next we describe related work, followed by our proposed model and algorithms, experiments, discussion and conclusions.

[1] The reporting-time window l_p can be set by the user (e.g., $l_p = 20$). If it is set at $l_p = 1$, the algorithm reports a l_s-steps-ahead single event, every 1 time tick.

2. RELATED WORK

In recent years, there has been an explosion of interest in mining time-stamped data [29, 30, 24, 23, 33]. Similarity search and pattern discovery in time sequences have attracted huge interest [32, 21, 28, 24, 25, 20, 2]. Rakthanmanon et al. [27] proposed a similarity search algorithm for "trillions of time series" under the dynamic time warping (DTW) distance. The work in [17] proposed a scalable method for forecasting complex time-stamped events, while, [14] developed AutoPlait, which is a fully-automatic mining algorithm for co-evolving sequences. Traditional approaches applied to time series data mining typically use linear method, such as auto-regression (AR), autoregressive integrated moving average (ARIMA), linear dynamical systems (LDS), Kalman filters (KF) and their derivatives including AWSOM [22], TBATS [12], PLiF [11] and TriMine [17]. Note that these methods are fundamentally unsuitable for our setting: they are all based on *linear* equations, and are thus incapable of modeling data governed by non-linear equations. Existing non-linear methods for forecasting tend to be hard to interpret and cannot be used easily for long-term prediction, because they rely on a nearest-neighbor search [36, 1]. Non-linear mining and analyses of epidemics and social activities have attracted a lot of interest [4, 15, 16, 26, 18]. The work described in [18] studied the rise and fall patterns in the information diffusion process through online social media.

3. DESIGN PHILOSOPHY OF REGIMECAST

In this section, we present the fundamental concepts and design philosophy behind our method.

3.1 Regime shifts in natural systems

Large, abrupt, long-lasting changes in the structure of complex systems – regime shift– it is a key concept for understanding real-world dynamical phenomena. Because of its importance and substantial impact on human society, regime shift has been widely studied over recent decades in various research domains, especially, in the field of environmental ecology [31, 5, 3, 34].

In ecology, a *regime* is defined as a characteristic behavior of a natural phenomenon over time, and a *regime shift* implies an abrupt change, in relation to the duration of a regime, from one characteristic behavior to another [5]. Typically, regime shifts are triggered either by internal processes, e.g., weakening of stability, or by external shocks that exceed the stabilizing capacity of a system. Also, these transition patterns are sometimes gradual, rather than abrupt [34].

For example, let us consider biological ecosystems, such as lakes, coral reefs and woodlands, where biotic/abiotic components (e.g., fishes, corals, water, mineral soils) are interacting with each other, as a complex, adaptive non-linear system. In such a natural ecosystem, we can observe several sudden changes of states. For example, one of the most dramatic state shifts is the the sudden loss of transparency and vegetation in shallow lakes caused by human-induced eutrophication. Similarly, in a marine ecosystem, there is a transition from a coral dominated system to an fleshy brown macroalgae dominated system, which is possibly induced by hurricane or climate change. Also, as described in Figure 2 (a), a woodland ecosystem can be alternated with a grassy open landscape. Landscapes can be kept open by herbivores (or, fires and tree cutting), while woodlands, once established, are stable because adult trees cannot be destroyed by herbivores [31] [2].

Theoretical analysis and mathematical modeling. The most basic and minimum form of an ecological dynamical system can be

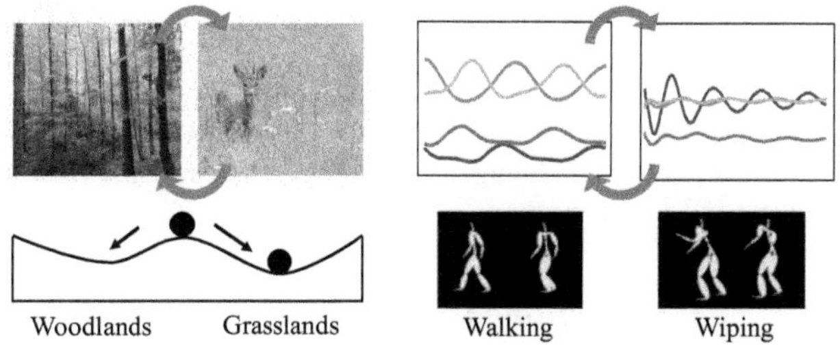

(a) Ecological system (b) Motion sensors

Figure 2: Illustration of regime shifts in an ecological system vs. sensor stream: (a) Regime shifts between two alternative stable states: woodlands and grasslands, and (b) regime shifts in motion sensors, between walking and wiping activities.

described with the following ordinary differential equation (ODE) [31]:

$$\frac{ds(t)}{dt} = a_0 + a_1 s(t) + a_2 f(s(t)), \qquad (1)$$

where, $s(t)$ shows the time-evolving ecosystem property, such as nutrients or soils at time tick t, and a_0 describes an environmental factor that promotes $s(t)$, (e.g., nutrient loading), a_1 is the rate at which $s(t)$ grows/decays in the system (e.g., nutrient removal rate, for $a_1 < 0$). The last term, a_2 represents the rate at which $s(t)$ recovers again as a function $f(s(t))$, (e.g., internal nutrient recycling), and the function f can cause alternative stable states.

Because of its simplicity and generality, the above dynamical equation and the concept of regime shifts have been applied outside ecology, to sociology, economics, political science and beyond. Next we present our proposed method, REGIMECAST, which is inspired by the regime shifts in natural dynamical systems.

3.2 Proposed model

Given a large event stream X, which contains various dynamic evolving patterns (i.e., regimes), our goal is to find important trends and summarize them as a compact but powerful and adaptive representative model, to perform, long-term event forecasting.

So, what exactly are the most important properties for forecasting the event stream X? Specifically, we want to describe the following three important properties:

- **(P1)** Latent non-linear dynamics
- **(P2)** Regime shifts in event streams
- **(P3)** Nested structure

Similar to the natural dynamical systems described in subsection 3.1, real event streams evolve naturally over time, depending on many latent factors, such as traffic, weather and driver's condition for automobile sensors, or user's preferences and customs for online Web-click activities. We need to capture the complicated and hidden dynamics of real time-series events that involve *non-linear* phenomena. To handle **(P1)**, we propose using latent non-linear differential equations. We also want to automatically detect the switching positions of dynamic evolution patterns, that is, **(P2)** regime shifts in event streams. Figure 2 compares regime shifts in an ecological system vs. an event stream (i.e., a motion sensor stream). We conjecture that event streams behave as a complex, adaptive non-linear dynamical system in the same way that biotic/abiotic components in a natural ecosystem evolve and interact over time, where there are multiple alternative stable states (i.e., regimes), that can be switched to one another. We should also note that real event streams are composed of multi-level nested systems, each of which has a different time scale, and can be integrated as a part of a larger system, that is, we need **(P3)**. For example, as shown in Figure 7, Web-click activities exhibit long-term evolution such as ten-year

[2] Image courtesy of dan at FreeDigitalPhotos.net.

patterns of growth and decline, as well as short-term, say weekly, daily and hourly patterns. Similar behavior can be observed in natural systems, e.g., both long-term climate change and sudden hurricanes can affect a coral reef system [31]. We thus propose using a multi-level nested modeling structure that enables more effective modeling and forecasting.

Now, we describe our concept in steps, adding complexity.

3.2.1 Latent non-linear dynamical systems (P1)

We begin with the simplest case, where we have only a single dynamical pattern (i.e., regime), e.g., walking motion in a sensor event stream, where, there are no regime shifts in the sequence (**P1**). In our basic model, we assume that there are two classes of time-evolving activities:

- $\boldsymbol{s}(t)$: Potential activity, i.e., k-dimensional latent activity at time tick t, ($\boldsymbol{s}(t) = \{s_i(t)\}_{i=1}^{k}$).
- $\boldsymbol{v}(t)$: Estimated event, i.e., d-dimensional actual activity that can be observed at time tick t, ($\boldsymbol{v}(t) = \{v_i(t)\}_{i=1}^{d}$).

Here, we can only observe the actual event $\boldsymbol{v}(t)$ at time tick t, (such as, actual variables generated by d sensors), while $\boldsymbol{s}(t)$ is a hidden vector that evolves over time as a dynamical system. Consequently, a single regime can be described with the following equations:

MODEL 1. *Let $\boldsymbol{s}(t)$ be the k-dimensional potential activity at time tick t, and $\boldsymbol{v}(t)$ be the d-dimensional estimated event at time tick t. Our base model is governed by the following equations,*

$$\frac{d\boldsymbol{s}(t)}{dt} = \boldsymbol{p} + \mathbf{Q}\boldsymbol{s}(t) + \mathcal{A}\mathbf{S}(t) \qquad (2)$$

$$\boldsymbol{v}(t) = \boldsymbol{u} + \mathbf{V}\boldsymbol{s}(t) \qquad (3)$$

with initial conditions $\boldsymbol{s}(0) = \boldsymbol{s}_0$, where, $d\boldsymbol{s}(t)/dt$ is the derivative with respect to time tick t and $\mathbf{S}(t)$ shows the quadratic form matrix of $\boldsymbol{s}(t)$, i.e., $\mathbf{S}(t) = \boldsymbol{s}(t)^T\boldsymbol{s}(t)$.

Here, $\boldsymbol{p}$, $\mathbf{Q}$, $\mathcal{A}$ describe the potential activity $\boldsymbol{s}(t)$, each of which captures linear, exponential, and non-linear dynamical activities [3], while, $\boldsymbol{u}$, $\mathbf{V}$ show the observation projection, which generates the estimated event $\boldsymbol{v}(t)$ at each time tick t. Also note that the non-linear activity tensor $\mathcal{A}$ should be *sparse*, to eliminate the complexity of the system. We will explain this later in section 4.

Consequently, we have the following:

DEFINITION 1 (SINGLE REGIME PARAMETER SET: $\boldsymbol{\theta}$). *Let $\boldsymbol{\theta}$ be a parameter set of a single non-linear dynamical system, i.e., $\boldsymbol{\theta} = \{\boldsymbol{s}_0, \boldsymbol{p}, \mathbf{Q}, \mathcal{A}, \boldsymbol{u}, \mathbf{V}\}$. We refer to $\boldsymbol{\theta}$ as a single regime parameter set.*

3.2.2 Regime shifts in event streams (P2)

Our next step is to answer the most important question, namely, how can we describe regime shifts in an event stream (**P2**)? Assume that we have a sensor stream that consists of $c = 2$ regimes, e.g., walking and wiping motions (Figure 2 (b)). We want an adaptive model that can generate c distinct time-evolving patterns, such as walking and wiping motions, where these patterns appear interchangeably, that is, the regimes can be switched to others. So what would be the best way to describe the dynamic evolving regime shift patterns among c distinct regimes? We thus introduce an additional time-evolving activity, namely,

- $\boldsymbol{w}(t)$: Regime activity, i.e., c-dimensional latent regime shift activity among c regimes at time tick t.

[3] In this paper, for simplicity, we use a quadratic function for the non-linear activity tensor $\mathcal{A}$.

Here, $\boldsymbol{w}(t)$ describes the dynamical activity for each i-th regime ($1 \leq i \leq c$) at time tick t.

Consequently, we extend Model 1, and propose the following model, which is designed as a complex and adaptive dynamical system:

MODEL 2. *Let $\boldsymbol{s}_i(t)$ be the k dimensional latent activity of i-th regime at time tick t (i.e., $\boldsymbol{s}_i(t) = \{s_{ij}(t)\}_{j=1}^{k}$), $\boldsymbol{w}(t)$ be the contribution strength of each i-th regime at time tick t (i.e., $\boldsymbol{w}(t) = \{w_i(t)\}_{i=1}^{c}$), and $\boldsymbol{v}(t)$ be the d-dimensional estimated event at time tick t. Our full model can be described as the following equations,*

$$\frac{d\boldsymbol{s}_i(t)}{dt} = \boldsymbol{p}_i + \mathbf{Q}_i\boldsymbol{s}_i(t) + \mathcal{A}_i\mathbf{S}_i(t) \quad (i = 1, \ldots, c) \qquad (4)$$

$$\frac{d\boldsymbol{w}(t)}{dt} = \boldsymbol{r}(t) \qquad (5)$$

$$\boldsymbol{v}(t) = \sum_{i=1}^{c} w_i(t)\,[\boldsymbol{u}_i + \mathbf{V}_i\boldsymbol{s}_i(t)] \qquad (6)$$

where, $d\boldsymbol{w}(t)/dt$ shows the derivative with respect to time tick t.

In Model 2, we need an additional parameter, $\boldsymbol{r}(t)$, which is a c-dimensional vector at time tick t. Let $\mathbf{R}$ be a parameter set of regime shift dynamics, i.e., $\mathbf{R} = \{\boldsymbol{r}(t)\}_{t=1}^{t_c}$, where t_c shows the length of the event sequence. We refer to $\mathbf{R}$ as a regime shift matrix. Please note that if there is a single regime (i.e., $c = 1$), our full model is identical to Model 1. Consequently, we have the following:

DEFINITION 2 (REGIME SET: $\boldsymbol{\Theta}$). *Let $\boldsymbol{\Theta}$ be a parameter set of regime set, namely, $\boldsymbol{\Theta} = \{\boldsymbol{\theta}_1, \ldots, \boldsymbol{\theta}_c, \mathbf{R}\}$, that describes non-linear co-evolving patterns of c regimes.*

3.2.3 With nested structure (P3)

Until now, we have assumed a single-level dynamical system, which consists of a regime set $\boldsymbol{\Theta}$. In reality, however, we should consider multi-level, nested structure to describe multi-scale dynamical activities, such as long-term evolution (e.g., ten-year pattern) and short-term (e.g., weekly) dynamical events in online activities. So, is there any simple solution to capture this phenomenon? To handle (**P3**), we propose using multi-level regime set $\mathcal{M} = \{\boldsymbol{\Theta}^{(1)}, \boldsymbol{\Theta}^{(2)}, \ldots\}$, where each regime set $\boldsymbol{\Theta}^{(i)}$ in $\mathcal{M}$ describes a dynamical system at a different time scale. The idea is that, given a set of multi-level regimes in $\mathcal{M}$, we generate the local estimated event $\boldsymbol{v}^{(i)}(t)$ at the i-th level. The estimated event $\boldsymbol{v}(t)$ can be organized simply by gathering all the local event set together.

Full model parameter set of RegimeCast. Our complete model consists of the following:

DEFINITION 3 (COMPLETE SET OF REGIMECAST: $\mathcal{M}$). *Let $\mathcal{M}$ be a full parameter set, namely, $\mathcal{M} = \{\boldsymbol{\Theta}^{(1)}, \ldots, \boldsymbol{\Theta}^{(h)}\}$, that describes multi-level time evolving patterns.*

4. STREAMING ALGORITHM

We now introduce our full algorithm, namely, REGIMECAST, which is an efficient and effective forecasting method for large co-evolving event streams.

4.1 Problem formulation

We first define some key concepts.

DEFINITION 4 (EVENT STREAM: X). *Let X be a data stream that consists of event entries of d-dimensional data, i.e., $X = \{\boldsymbol{x}(1), \ldots, \boldsymbol{x}(t_c)\}$, where t_c is the current time tick. We refer to X as an event stream.*

Table 1: Symbols and definitions.

Symbol	Definition
d	Number of dimensions
t_c	Current time tick
X	d co-evolving event stream, i.e., $X = \{\boldsymbol{x}(1), \dots, \boldsymbol{x}(t_c)\}$
$\boldsymbol{x}(t)$	d-dimensional event at time tick t, i.e., $\boldsymbol{x}(t) = \{x_i(t)\}_{i=1}^{d}$
$\boldsymbol{s}(t)$	Potential activity at time tick t, i.e., $\boldsymbol{s}(t) = \{s_i(t)\}_{i=1}^{k}$
$\boldsymbol{w}(t)$	Regime activity at time tick t, i.e., $\boldsymbol{w}(t) = \{w_i(t)\}_{i=1}^{c}$
$\boldsymbol{v}(t)$	Estimated event at time tick t, i.e., $\boldsymbol{v}(t) = \{v_i(t)\}_{i=1}^{d}$
X_C	Current window, i.e., $X_C = X[t_m : t_c]$
V_F	Forecast window, i.e., $V_F = V[t_s : t_e]$
$c^{(i)}$	Number of regimes at i-th level
$\boldsymbol{\theta}_j{}^{(i)}$	Parameter set of j-th regime at i-th level
$\mathbf{R}^{(i)}$	Parameter set of regime shift matrix at i-th level
$\boldsymbol{\Theta}^{(i)}$	Full parameter set at i-th level
$\mathcal{M}$	Complete set of REGIMECAST, i.e., $\mathcal{M} = \{\boldsymbol{\Theta}^{(i)}\}_{i=1}^{h}$

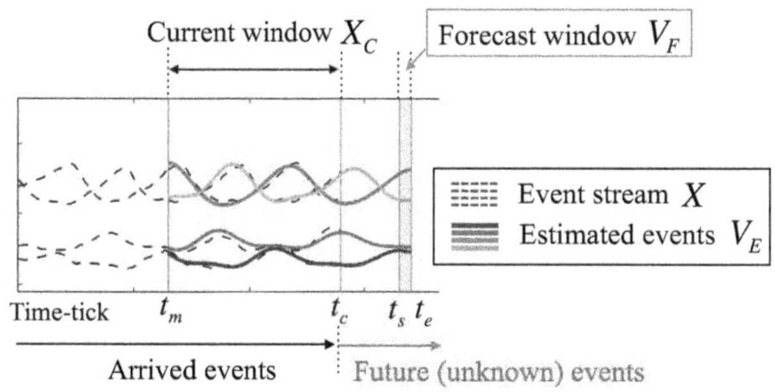

Figure 3: Illustration of REGIMESNAP: Given an event stream X (black dotted lines), our algorithm estimates the current time-series pattern V_E (colored bold lines), and reports l_s-steps-ahead future events V_F (in a red box), incrementally and continuously. Here, $X_C = X[t_m : t_c]$ is a current window (i.e., recently arrived events) and $V_F = V[t_s : t_e]$ is a l_s-steps-ahead future (i.e., unknown) event set.

Assume that we receive a new event $\boldsymbol{x}(t_c)$, continuously, and t_c increases with every new time tick. It would be convenient to treat the most recently arrived events, as a current window.

DEFINITION 5 (CURRENT WINDOW: X_C). *Let $X_C = X[t_m : t_c]$ be the subsequence of length l_c, starting from time tick t_m and ending at t_c ($1 \le t_m \le t_c$)*[4].

Given the current window X_C, our next step is to find the optimal regimes in $\mathcal{M}$, and predict l_s-steps-ahead future activities: $V_F = \{\boldsymbol{v}(t_s), \dots, \boldsymbol{v}(t_e)\}$ using Model 2.

DEFINITION 6 (l_s-STEPS-AHEAD FORECAST WINDOW: V_F). *Let $V_F = V[t_s : t_e]$ denote the l_s-steps-ahead future events starting from time-tick t_s and ending at t_e ($t_c \le t_s \le t_e$), where, $t_s = t_c + l_s$, $t_e = t_s + l_p$, and l_p is the length of the reporting window.*

Figure 3 shows a snapshot of REGIMECAST at the current time tick t_c, namely, REGIMESNAP. Here, the black dotted lines show the original event stream X, which consists of a $d = 4$ dimensional event sequence. The bold colored lines show our estimated events V_E from time tick t_m to t_e. Note that the subsequence from t_c to t_e is future (unknown) events, and we need to estimate these hidden dynamical patterns, incrementally and continuously.

[4]We set $l_c = 3 \cdot l_s$ in our setting.

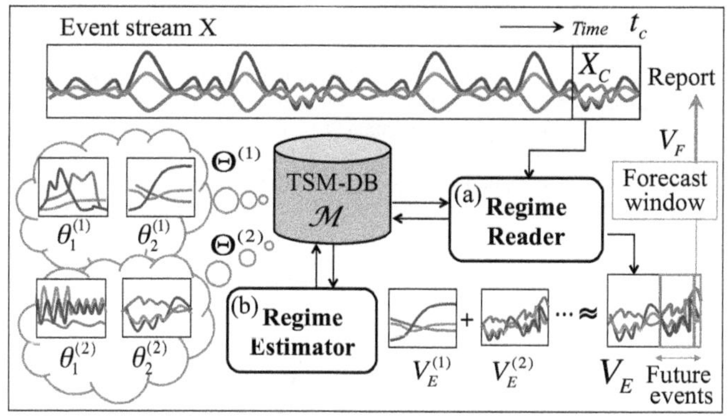

Figure 4: Overview of the REGIMECAST algorithm: Given an event stream X, it first extracts the current window X_C, and then (a) searches for the optimal regime patterns in the time-series model database, and generates the l_s-steps-ahead events V_F. If there is a new (i.e., unknown) regime pattern in X_C, (b) it also estimates the new regime model parameter set $\boldsymbol{\theta}$, and inserts it into the database.

Consequently, given an event stream X, our goal is to capture the current time-evolving patterns in X_C, as a complex, non-linear dynamical system, and predict the l_s-steps-ahead forecast window V_F, at any point in time. We formally define our problem as follows:

PROBLEM 1. **Given** *a data stream $X = \{\boldsymbol{x}(1), \dots, \boldsymbol{x}(t_c), \dots\}$ at regular time intervals,* **report** *l_s-steps-ahead future events V_F at any point in time, i.e.,*

- *identify the optimal regime patterns in X_C,*
- *update the model parameter set $\mathcal{M}$ that describe the dynamic patterns in X_C,*
- *report l_s-steps-ahead future events, i.e., V_F.*

4.2 Overview

We now introduce our forecasting algorithm, REGIMECAST, which consists of the following algorithms.

- REGIMEREADER: Estimates good regime dynamics and generates the estimated events $V_E = V[t_m : t_e]$, when we are given the current window X_C and the model parameters $\boldsymbol{\Theta}$.
- REGIMEESTIMATOR: Estimates a good regime parameter set $\boldsymbol{\theta}$ for X_C, when the current window X_C contains a new regime pattern (if required).
- REGIMECAST: Estimates the optimal event set $V_E{}^{(i)}$ at each level i ($i = 1, \dots, h$), computes estimated event event set $V_E = V_E{}^{(1)} + V_E{}^{(2)} + \dots$, and reports the l_s-steps-ahead future events i.e., forecast window V_F. It also maintains the full model parameter set $\mathcal{M}$.

Figure 4 illustrates how the REGIMECAST algorithm works. Given an event stream $X = \{\boldsymbol{x}(1), \dots, \boldsymbol{x}(t_c)\}$, where t_c is the current time tick, our algorithm incrementally extracts the current window X_C, estimates the current regime pattern $V_E = V_E{}^{(1)} + V_E{}^{(2)} + \dots$, and reports l_s-steps-ahead future events V_F, at any point in time. It also maintains the time-series model database (TSM-DB), and updates model parameters in $\mathcal{M}$, if required.

4.3 Proposed algorithms

Here we present our proposed algorithms in steps. To simplify the discussion, let us focus on a simple step first, where we have a single-level window X_C and a regime parameter set $\boldsymbol{\Theta}$ (that is, we have a single-level structure, $h = 1$).

Algorithm 1 REGIMEREADER $(X_C, \boldsymbol{\Theta})$

Input: current window X_C and current regime parameters $\boldsymbol{\Theta}$
Output: Estimated events $V_E = V[t_m : t_e]$ and updated regimes $\boldsymbol{\Theta}$
/* (I) Individual regime estimation */
for $i = 1 : c$ **do**
  /* Estimate $\boldsymbol{s}'_0$ and activity $V_C{}'_i$ for i-th regime $\boldsymbol{\theta}_i$ */
  $\{\boldsymbol{\theta}_i[\boldsymbol{s}_0], V_{Ci}\} = \arg\min_{\boldsymbol{s}'_0, V_C{}'_i} ||X_C - V_C{}'_i||$; // $V_C{}'_i = f_C(\boldsymbol{s}'_0|\boldsymbol{\theta}_i)$;
end for
/* (II) Estimate regime activity at current time tick t_c */
$\boldsymbol{w}(t_c) = \arg\min_{w_1,\dots,w_c} ||X_C - \sum_{i=1}^{c} w_i V_{Ci}||$;
$\boldsymbol{r}(t_c) = \boldsymbol{w}(t_c) - \boldsymbol{w}(t_c - 1)$; // Calculate regime shift variable
$\mathbf{R} = \mathbf{R} \cup \boldsymbol{r}(t_c)$; $\boldsymbol{\Theta} = \{\boldsymbol{\theta}_1, \dots, \boldsymbol{\theta}_c, \mathbf{R}\}$; // Update full parameters
$V_E = f_E(\boldsymbol{\Theta})$; // Calculate estimated event V_E
return $\{V_E, \boldsymbol{\Theta}\}$;

4.3.1 *RegimeReader*

Assume that we are given the current window X_C and the current regime parameter set $\boldsymbol{\Theta} = \{\boldsymbol{\theta}_1, \dots, \boldsymbol{\theta}_c, \mathbf{R}\}$. Our first goal is to estimate the dynamical event sequence $V_E = V[t_m : t_e]$, as shown in Figure 4 (a). So, how can we estimate events V_E, given the current regime set $\boldsymbol{\Theta}$? The most straightforward solution would be simply to use the fixed parameters in $\boldsymbol{\Theta}$ and calculate $\boldsymbol{v}(t_m), \boldsymbol{v}(t_m + 1), \dots$, using Model 2. However, in real event streams, the latent trends of the current window X_C would dynamically and continuously change over time. That is, We should identify the optimized regimes in $\boldsymbol{\Theta}$ that describe the characteristics of the current window X_C. Most importantly, the algorithm needs to adaptively update parameters in $\boldsymbol{\Theta}$, so that it can describe the current activities in X_C. Algorithm 1 shows the overall procedure for the adaptive regime detection, namely, REGIMEREADER. In short, the algorithm consists of two parts, namely, (I) individual regime optimization, and (II) regime shift identification.

(I) Individual regime optimization. For each i-th regime parameters $\boldsymbol{\theta}_i \in \boldsymbol{\Theta}$ $(i = 1, \dots, c)$, the algorithm tries to optimize the initial condition of potential activity, i.e., $\boldsymbol{s}_0$ in $\boldsymbol{\theta}_i$, so that it minimizes the mean square errors between the original events and the estimated events, i.e., $\min ||X_C - V_{Ci}||$. Here, let $f_C(\boldsymbol{s}_0|\boldsymbol{\theta})$ be a function that generates estimated events $V_C = \{\boldsymbol{v}(t_m), \dots, \boldsymbol{v}(t_c)\}$ in Model 2, given regime parameters $\boldsymbol{s}_0$ and $\boldsymbol{\theta}$.

(II) Regime shift identification. Given a set of c optimized event sequences $\{V_{Ci}\}_{i=1}^{c}$, the algorithm estimates the latent dynamics of regime shifts at time tick t_c, and specifically, it computes regime activity $\boldsymbol{w}(t_c)$ to optimize the regime set in $\boldsymbol{\Theta}$, and updates regime shift matrix $\mathbf{R}$ in $\boldsymbol{\Theta}$, according to Equation 6 (i.e., $\min ||X_C - f_C(\boldsymbol{\Theta})||$). Finally, it computes the estimated event $V_E = f_E(\boldsymbol{\Theta})$ as the optimal events for the current window X_C.

Here, we use the Levenberg-Marquardt (LM) algorithm to minimize the mean square errors $||\cdot||$.

4.3.2 *RegimeEstimator*

Next, let us tackle the next question, namely, what if there is a new, unknown regime in X_C? We want to estimate the new regime parameter set $\boldsymbol{\theta}$ that describes the dynamical patterns in X_C, and insert it into the full parameter set $\boldsymbol{\Theta}$ (Figure 4 (b)). Since $\boldsymbol{\theta}$ consists of a large number of parameters, it is extremely expensive to optimize all the parameters simultaneously. Also, as we mentioned in subsubsection 3.2.1, the non-linear activity tensor $\mathcal{A}$ should be *sparse*, to avoid overfitting, and to simplify the dynamical patterns in a single regime. We thus propose an efficient and effective algorithm, namely, REGIMEESTIMATOR, which searches for the optimal solution in terms of both the linear and non-linear parameters. The idea is that we split parameter set $\boldsymbol{\theta}$ into two subsets, i.e., $\boldsymbol{\theta}_L = \{\boldsymbol{p}, \mathbf{Q}, \boldsymbol{u}, \mathbf{V}\}$ and $\boldsymbol{\theta}_N = \{\mathcal{A}\}$, each of which corresponds to a linear/non-linear parameter set, and try to fit the parameter sets separately. Algorithm 2 shows the steps performed by REGIMEESTIMATOR in detail. Given a current window X_C, it first set $\mathcal{A} = 0$, and estimates the initial condition $\boldsymbol{s}_0$ and linear parameters $\boldsymbol{\theta}_L$ that describe linear dynamical patterns in X_C. Here, we use the expectation-maximization (EM) algorithm to optimize the parameters. It then estimates non-linear elements in $\mathcal{A}$ to minimize the errors between X_C and potential activity V_C, using the LM algorithm. Also note that, for the non-linear tensor $\mathcal{A}$, we only estimate parameters for the diagonal elements $a_{ijk} \in \mathcal{A}$ $(i = j = k)$ to eliminate the complexity.

Algorithm 2 REGIMEESTIMATOR (X_C)

Input: current window X_C
Output: Estimated model parameter set $\boldsymbol{\theta} = \{\boldsymbol{s}_0, \boldsymbol{p}, \mathbf{Q}, \mathcal{A}, \boldsymbol{u}, \mathbf{V}\}$
/* Estimate linear dynamical parameters $\boldsymbol{\theta}_L = \{\boldsymbol{p}, \mathbf{Q}, \boldsymbol{u}, \mathbf{V}\}$*/
$\mathcal{A} = 0$; // Initialize tensor $\mathcal{A}$
$\{\boldsymbol{s}_0, \boldsymbol{\theta}_L\} = \arg\min_{\boldsymbol{s}'_0, \boldsymbol{\theta}'_L} ||X_C - V_C||$; $//V_C = f_C(\boldsymbol{s}'_0, \boldsymbol{\theta}'_L, \boldsymbol{\theta}_N)$
/* Estimate non-linear dynamical parameters $\boldsymbol{\theta}_N = \{\mathcal{A}\}$ */
$\{\boldsymbol{s}_0, \boldsymbol{\theta}_N\} = \arg\min_{\boldsymbol{s}'_0, \boldsymbol{\theta}'_N} ||X_C - V_C||$; $//V_C = f_C(\boldsymbol{s}'_0, \boldsymbol{\theta}_L, \boldsymbol{\theta}'_N)$
$\boldsymbol{\theta} = \{\boldsymbol{s}_0, \boldsymbol{\theta}_L, \boldsymbol{\theta}_N\}$; // Full parameter set
return $\boldsymbol{\theta} = \{\boldsymbol{s}_0, \boldsymbol{p}, \mathbf{Q}, \mathcal{A}, \boldsymbol{u}, \mathbf{V}\}$;

4.3.3 *RegimeCast*

Until now, we have discussed how to generate the estimated event sequence V_E at a single-level regimes $\boldsymbol{\Theta}$. Our final goal is to capture multi-level dynamical patterns $\mathcal{M} = \{\boldsymbol{\Theta}^{(1)}, \dots, \boldsymbol{\Theta}^{(h)}\}$, and predict l_s-steps-ahead forecast window V_F (see Figure 4). As we described in subsubsection 3.2.3, given a event stream X, we want to describe multi-level dynamical activities, e.g., yearly, weekly, and daily patterns. We thus propose multi-scale modeling approach that enables more effective forecasting. The idea is that we decompose the current window X_C into a set of multi-scale event sequences $X_C = X_C{}^{(1)} + \dots X_C{}^{(h)}$, where $X_C{}^{(i)}$ shows the current event sequence at the i-th level. Specifically, the i-th level sequence can be computed as follows: $X_C{}^{(i)} = g(X_C - \sum_{j=1}^{i} X_C{}^{(j)} | H(i))$, where $g(\cdot|t)$ denotes the moving average of length t.[5]

The detailed REGIMECAST algorithm is shown in Algorithm 3. Given a new event $\boldsymbol{x}(t_c)$, it extracts the current window $X_C{}^{(i)}$ at the i-th level, and (I) estimates event sequence $V_E{}^{(i)}$. If there is no appropriate regime in $\boldsymbol{\Theta}^{(i)}$ (i.e., the error between the current window and estimated events is more than ϵ, e.g., $\epsilon = 1/2||X_C{}^{(i)}||$), (II) it creates a new regime $\boldsymbol{\theta}$ and update the regime set $\boldsymbol{\Theta}^{(i)}$. Finally, (III) it reports l_s-steps-ahead forecast window V_F.

Efficient event generation and dynamic point set (DPS). Since our estimation algorithm, REGIMEREADER, is based on a complex dynamical system, described in Model 2, it requires $O(l_e)$ time to calculate the potential activity $S_E = \{\boldsymbol{s}(t_m), \dots, \boldsymbol{s}(t_e)\}$ at every time tick t_c, where l_e shows the length of S_E. However, it is a potential bottleneck for the real-time processing. We thus propose an efficient approach for the dynamic event generation. Specifically, instead of computing all events $S_E = \{\boldsymbol{s}(t_m), \boldsymbol{s}(t_m + 1), \boldsymbol{s}(t_m + 2), \dots, \boldsymbol{s}(t_e)\}$, we generate a subset of S_E, namely, a dynamic point set (DPS): $\hat{S}_E = \{\boldsymbol{s}(t_m), \boldsymbol{s}(t_m + \delta), \boldsymbol{s}(t_m + 2\delta), \dots, \boldsymbol{s}(t_e)\}$, where δ shows the time interval of the potential activity (say, $\delta = 0.1 \cdot l_s$). We use a simple yet powerful, numerical integration method, namely, the forth-order Runge-Kutta method [8], to generate the dynamic point set $\hat{S}_E$:

[5] In this paper, we set $H = \{2 \cdot l_s, 1\}$.

Algorithm 3 REGIMECAST ($\boldsymbol{x}(t_c)$)

```
Input: a new event x(t_c) at time tick t_c
Output: l_s-steps-ahead future events V_F
/* Initialize forecast window V_F = 0 */
for i = 1 : h do
    Compute X_C^(i); // current window at i-level
    /* (I) Parameter fitting for regime activities */
    {V_E^(i), Θ^(i)} = REGIMEREADER(X_C^(i), Θ^(i));
    /* (II) Regime estimation (if required) */
    V_C^(i) = V^(i)[t_m : t_c]; // Estimated events from t_m to t_c
    if ||X_C^(i) − V_C^(i)|| > ε then
        θ = REGIMEESTIMATOR(X_C^(i)); Θ^(i) = {Θ^(i) ∪ θ};
    end if
end for
/* (III) l_s-steps-ahead future event generation */
V_E = V_E^(1) + ..., V_E^(h); V_F = V[t_s : t_e];
return V_F;
```

$$\boldsymbol{s}(t+\delta) = \boldsymbol{s}(t) + \frac{1}{6}(K_1 + 2K_2 + 2K_3 + K_4) + O(\delta^5) \quad (7)$$

where, we define $d\boldsymbol{s}(t)/dt = F(\boldsymbol{s}(t))$, and $K_1 = \delta F(\boldsymbol{s}(t))$, $K_2 = \delta F(\boldsymbol{s}(t) + \frac{1}{2}K_1)$, $K_3 = \delta F(\boldsymbol{s}(t) + \frac{1}{2}K_2)$, $K_4 = \delta F(\boldsymbol{s}(t) + K_3)$. Consequently, the algorithm requires $O(l_e/\delta)$ time to compute $\hat{S}_E$, where l_e/δ shows the length of $\hat{S}_E$.

Theoretical analysis. Let l_e be the length of the estimate event set V_E, and c be the number of regimes in $\mathcal{M}$.

LEMMA 1. *The computation time of* REGIMECAST *is at least* $O(c \cdot l_e/\delta)$ *time per time tick, at most* $O(c \cdot l_e/\delta + l_c)$ *time per time tick.*

PROOF. For each time tick t_c, REGIMEREADER requires $O(c \cdot l_e/\delta)$ time to estimate c optimal regimes V_E. If there is a new regime in the current window X_C, REGIMEESTIMATOR requires $O(l_c)$ to estimate parameter set $\boldsymbol{\theta}$. Thus, we have at least $O(c \cdot l_e/\delta)$ time at most $O(c \cdot l_e/\delta + l_c)$ time per time tick. □

5. EXPERIMENTS

In this section we demonstrate the effectiveness of REGIMECAST with real event streams. The experiments were designed to answer the following questions:

- Q1 *Effectiveness*: How successful is our method in forecasting long-term events in given input streams?
- Q2 *Accuracy*: How well does our method forecast future event entries?
- Q3 *Scalability*: How does our method scale in terms of computational time?

Our experiments were conducted on an Intel Core i7-3770K 3.50GHz with 32GB of memory, running Linux. We normalized the values of each dataset so that they had the same mean and variance (i.e., z-normalization), and set $k = 4$ for all datasets.

5.1 Q1: Effectiveness

We demonstrate the forecasting power of REGIMECAST in terms of capturing important patterns of event streams.

Sensor event streams. We first examine our forecasting results on real motion event streams. Figure 1, Figure 5 and Figure 6 show our real-time forecasting results for three motion capture steams: *"house-cleaning"*, *"exercise"* and *"chicken-dance"*, respectively. The datasets were obtained from the CMU motion capture database[6]. Each event stream consists of $d = 4$ dimensional vectors (left-right legs and arms), and it contains various motions (i.e., regimes), such as walking and dancing. One of the results has already been presented in section 1 (i.e., Figure 1). It automatically and effectively identifies multiple regime shift positions (such as from the wiping motion to the walking motion), and forecasts long-range future activities.

Figure 5 shows our real-time forecasting results and some snapshots obtained at several different time ticks. Specifically, Figure 5 (a) consists of several regimes, which correspond to some exercise activities. The bottom of Figure 5 (a) shows the output for (100:120)-steps-ahead real-time predictions, where we set the reporting window $l_p = 20$. More specifically, REGIMECAST generates (100:120)-steps-ahead future events for every $l_p = 20$ time tick, (e.g., at time tick $t_m = 100$, it reports $X[200 : 220]$, at time tick $t_m = 120$, it reports $X[220 : 240]$, and so on). Figure 5 (b) shows four examples of REGIMESNAP at different time points, each of which belongs to one of four different regimes. As shown in the figures, our modeling approach successfully captures dynamical regime shift patterns, as well as the non-linear dynamical evolving activities of four different regimes.

Figure 6 shows REGIMECAST for the chicken-dance stream. Specifically, the top of Figure 6 (a) shows the original stream, which is composed of four steps in the following order: "beaks", "wings", "tail feathers" and "claps", and these steps are repeated again. It is a much more challenging task to forecast upcoming dance steps because the event stream contains several nested multi-scale regimes. As shown at the top of Figure 6 (b), each step can be decomposed into several basic movements, where each movement has a different tempo/speed. For example, "tail feathers" consists of "moving arms, quickly" and "bending knees, once", The bottom of Figure 6 (a) and (c-1)-(c-3) show our entire output of (30:35)-steps-ahead forecasting results, and REGIMESNAP at several time ticks, respectively. As shown in the figures, our proposed method captures complicated dynamical activities, which consist of multiple hidden regimes, and successfully generates long-range upcoming motion patterns. We should also note that our algorithm does not use any prior training or hint regarding the steps. It incrementally finds important dynamical patterns (i.e., regimes), estimates the parameters of the new regime and inserts it into the model database.

Online activity streams. Next, we demonstrate our forecasting power as regards Web-click activities. Figure 7 shows our results for *GoogleTrend* event streams, which consist of the search volumes for various queries (i.e., words) on Google[7]. Each query represents the search volumes related to keywords over time (over twelve years, on a weekly basis). We performed our real-time forecasts on four event streams, which were taken from the following domains: (a) *OnlineTV*, (b) *Beer*, (c) *Social media* and (d) *Software*. For each event stream, it continuously generates three-months-ahead predictions, every time tick.

Figure 7 (a) shows our forecasting result for *OnlineTV*, which contains $d = 4$ dimensional events: Netflix ($\boldsymbol{x}_1$), Hulu ($\boldsymbol{x}_2$), YouTube ($\boldsymbol{x}_3$) and Amazon Prime ($\boldsymbol{x}_4$). Recently, there has been a rapid increase in new video streaming services, and REGIMECAST successfully captures the long-range evolution and exponential rising patterns in all co-evolving keywords. Note that there was a regime shift point from 2011 to 2012, i.e., Hulu ($\boldsymbol{x}_2$, shown as the green line) has had a declining pattern since 2011, which coincided with the ascent of Netflix ($\boldsymbol{x}_1$, shown as the blue line), possibly indicating that there was competition/interaction between the two services, and Netflix has been drawing customers' attention away from Hulu. Most importantly, our algorithm, REGIMECAST, can auto-

[6] *MoCap*: http://mocap.cs.cmu.edu/

[7] *GoogleTrend*: http://www.google.com/trends/

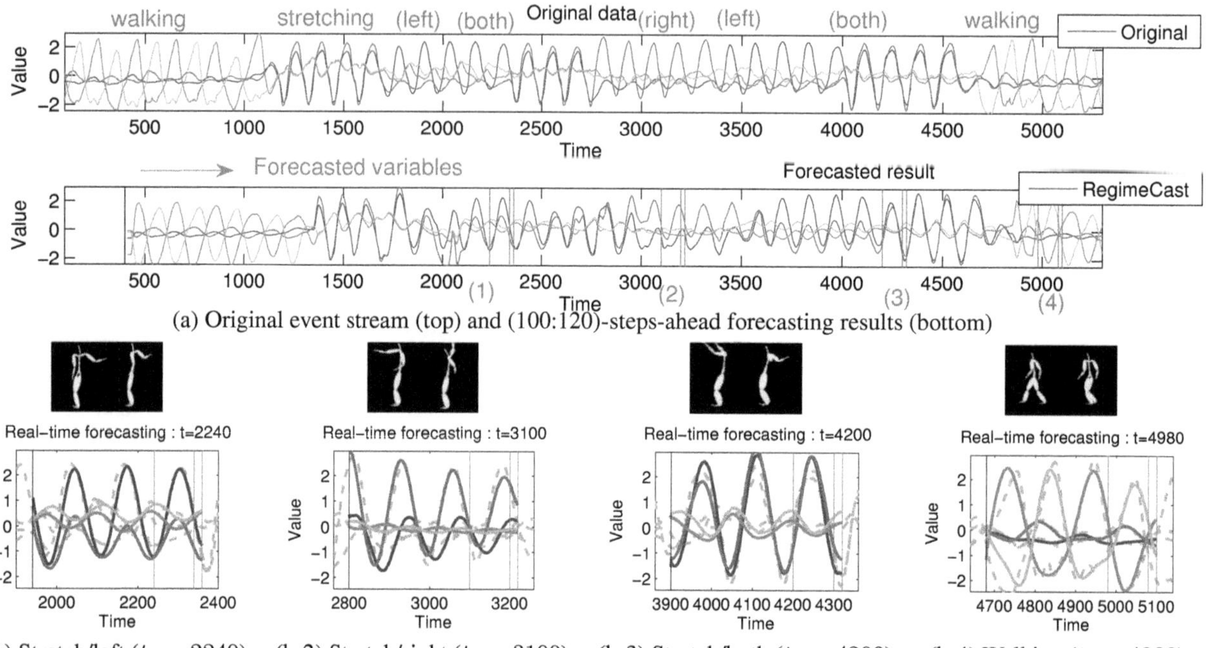

(a) Original event stream (top) and (100:120)-steps-ahead forecasting results (bottom)

(b-1) Stretch/left ($t_c = 2240$) (b-2) Stretch/right ($t_c = 3100$) (b-3) Stretch/both ($t_c = 4200$) (b-4) Walking ($t_c = 4980$)

Figure 5: REGIMECAST is effective: Forecasting power of REGIMECAST for the motion event stream (*"exercise"*). (a) The original data (top), our (100:120)-steps-ahead predictions (bottom), and (b) snapshots of video clips (top) and REGIMESNAP (bottom) at four different time ticks. REGIMECAST automatically identifies important regime patterns (e.g., "stretching" and "walking"), and also forecasts future events, incrementally, and effectively.

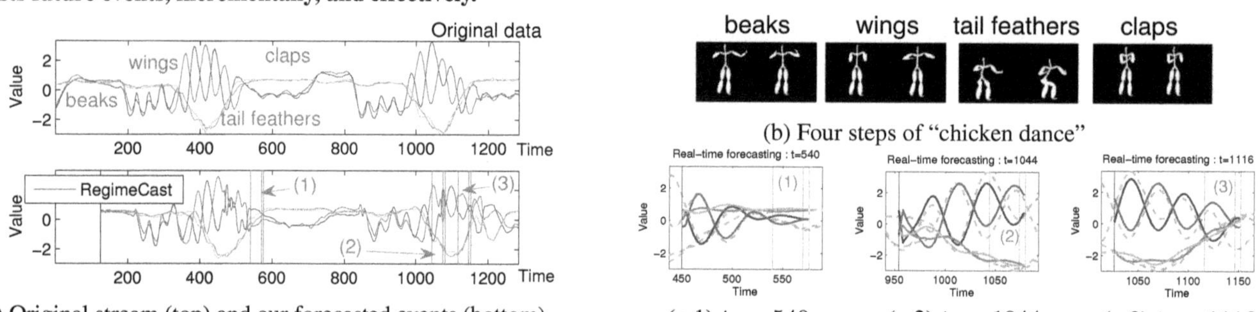

(a) Original stream (top) and our forecasted events (bottom)

(b) Four steps of "chicken dance"

(c-1) $t_c = 540$ (c-2) $t_c = 1044$ (c-3) $t_c = 1116$

Figure 6: Real-time forecasting of REGIMECAST for "chicken dance": (a) Given the dance motion stream (bottom), our proposed method incrementally identifies four basic steps, i.e., (b) "beaks", "wings", "tail feathers" and "claps" in the sequence, and adaptively forecasts long-range future patterns. (c) REGIMESNAP for four different time points. Here, it generates (30:35)-steps-ahead future events. We emphasize that our algorithm does not need any prior training or knowledge regarding the motions (i.e., regimes).

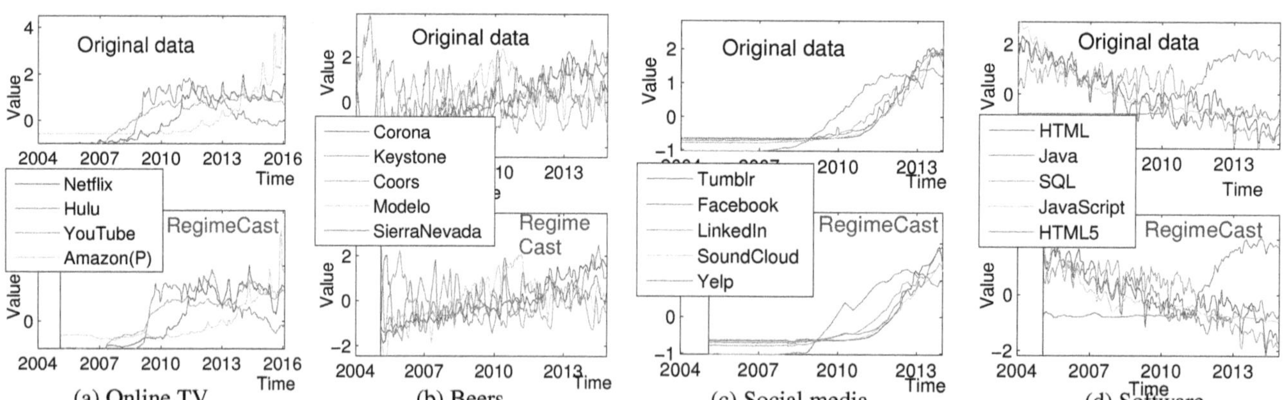

(a) Online TV (b) Beers (c) Social media (d) Software

Figure 7: REGIMECAST successfully forecasts 3-months-ahead future events of online user activities: Each event sequence consists of the Google search volume for several keywords (from 2004 to the present), i.e., (a) *OnlineTV* (1:Netflix, 2:Hulu, 3:YouTube, 4:Amazon Prime), (b) *Beer* (1:Corona, 2:Keystone, 3:Coors, 4:Modelo, 5:Sierra Nevada), (c) *Social media* (1:Tumblr, 2:Facebook, 3:LinkedIn, 4:SoundCloud, 5:Yelp), (d) *Software* (1:HTML, 2:Java, 3:SQL, 4:JavaScript, 5:HTML5). Given the online user activities (top), it incrementally forecasts events three months (i.e., 13 weeks) ahead, at every reporting window $l_p = 2$ weeks (bottom).

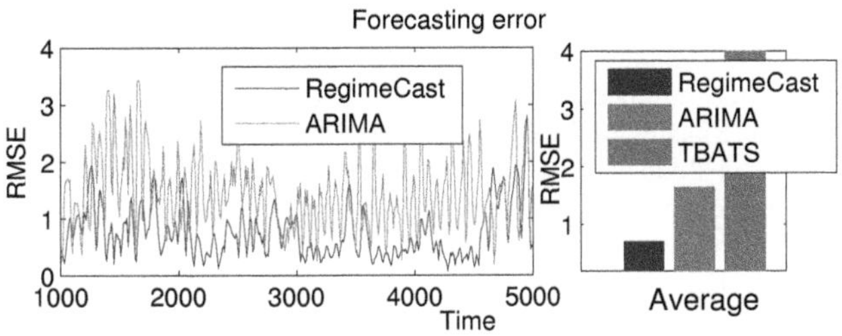

(a) Forecasting error for each time tick (left) and average (right)

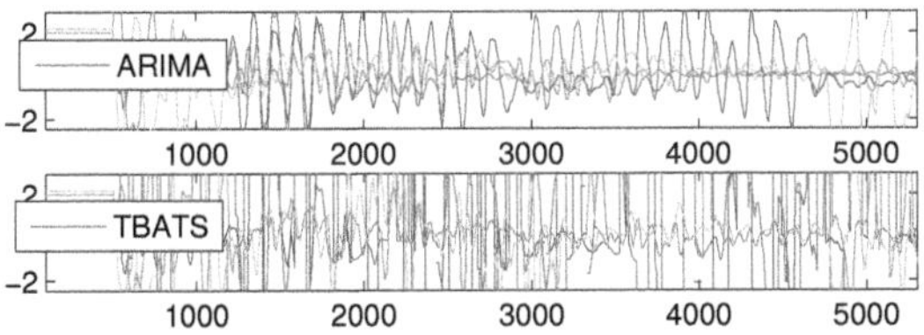

(b) Forecasting results of ARIMA (top) and TBATS (bottom)

Figure 8: Forecasting error (RMSE) for the motion event stream: REGIMECAST consistently outperforms the state-of-the-art methods with respect to accuracy between real values and the (100:120)-steps-ahead forecasted results. (a) Forecasting error for each time tick (left) and the average (right). Lower is better. (b) Forecasting results of our competitors. Please also see the original stream and our result shown in Figure 5 (a).

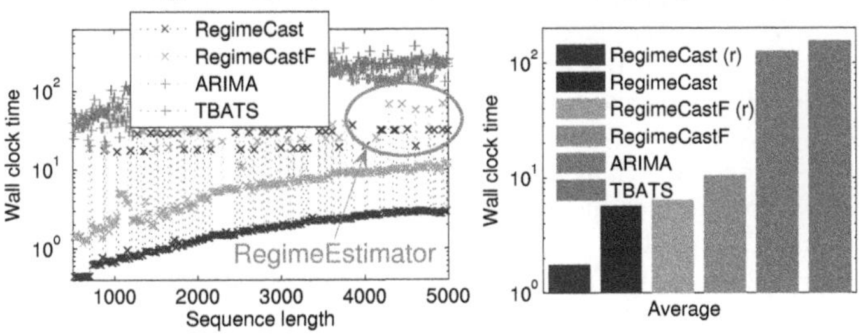

(a) "Exercise"

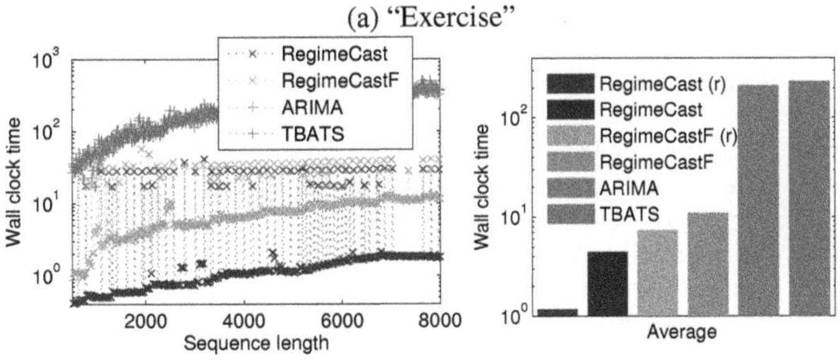

(b) "House-cleaning"

Figure 9: Wall clock time vs. sequence length t_c (left) and average (right): REGIMECAST consistently wins. It is up to 270 times faster than TBATS.

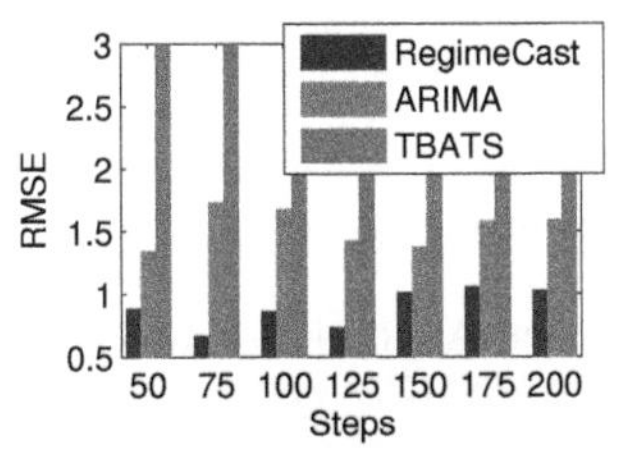

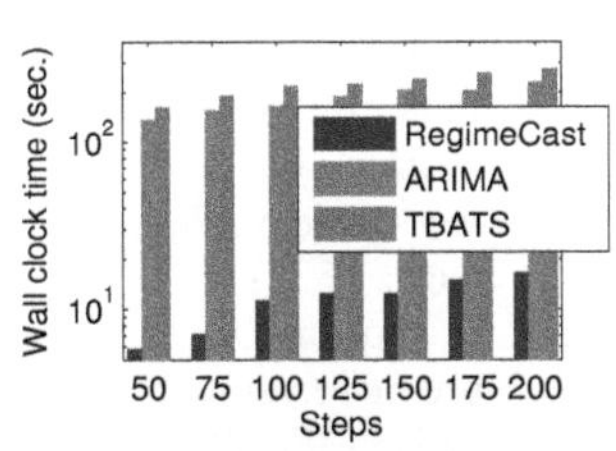

(a) forecasting error (b) computation time

Figure 10: l_s-steps-ahead forecasting over the motion event stream (*"exercise"*): REGIMECAST consistently wins. (a) Forecasting error (RMSE) vs. prediction length l_s; (b) Wall clock time vs. prediction length l_s. Lower is better.

matically identify sudden changes of regimes, and forecast upcoming events, adaptively and immediately.

Figure 7 (b) shows our result for *Beer*, which successfully captures the long-term non-linear dynamical evolution of the beer industry. There is significant growth of all the keywords with one exception, Coors (shown as the red line), which is a popular beer, brewed in Colorado, US. Similarly, as shown in Figure 7 (c) and (d), our proposed method also successfully identifies non-linear dynamic patterns of *Social media* and *Software*, including growing and competing activities, and estimates optimal regimes. Our forecasted results are very close to the real event streams.

5.2 Q2. Accuracy

Next, we discuss the quality of REGIMECAST in terms of forecasting accuracy. We compared our method with the following methods: (a) ARIMA, where we determined the optimal parameter set using AIC, and (b) TBATS [12], which is a state-of-the-art forecasting algorithm for complex seasonal time series.

Figure 8 shows the forecasting power of REGIMECAST for the motion event stream: "exercise", which is shown in Figure 5 (a). Specifically, Figure 8 (a) shows the root mean square error (RMSE) between the original and the (100:120)-steps-ahead forecasted events, where the left figure shows the RMSE for each time tick, and the right figure shows the average errors. A lower value indicates a better forecasting accuracy. Note that we omit the TBATS result for the left figure, due to high error values.

Figure 8 (b) shows the actual forecasting results of ARIMA and TBATS. Compared to our forecasted result, shown in Figure 5 (a), ARIMA and TBATS are *unsuitable* for capturing complex, non-linear dynamics and regime shifts; they are *linear* models, and failed to forecast abrupt changes of regimes.

5.3 Q3. Scalability

We also evaluate the efficiency of our forecasting algorithm. Figure 9 compares REGIMECAST with ARIMA and TBATS in terms of computation time for varying sequence lengths t_c. Note that the figures are shown in linear-log scales. To evaluate the efficiency of the dynamic point set (DPS), which is described in section 4, we also compared them with special versions of our method, REGIMECAST-F, which uses full point set (i.e., it sets the time interval $\delta = 1$). As we expected, REGIMECAST generates long-range future events, significantly faster than the competitors for the large streams (i.e., up to two orders of magnitude). In the left column of Figure 9, each spike corresponds to REGIMEESTIMATOR process, which creates a new regime (please see the red circle). The right column of Figure 9 shows the average computation time of entire event streams. Here, REGIMECAST/REGIMECAST-F (r) shows the average computation time of REGIMEREADER, and REGIMECAST/REGIMECAST-F is the computation time of REGIMECAST.

Discussion: l_s-steps-ahead prediction. As we mentioned in the introduction section, one of our motivations is the long-range forecasting over data streams. So, how long ahead can our method forecast future events? Is there any difference between, say, 50-steps-ahead and 200-steps-ahead forecasting results? We thus examine the forecasting power of REGIMECAST in terms of the future event length l_s. Figure 10 shows the forecasting errors and speeds of REGIMECAST for varying the steps: $l_s = 50, 75, \ldots, 200$. Specifically, Figure 10 compares our method with other methods in terms of (a) forecasting accuracy and (b) computation time. Thanks to our carefully designed models and algorithms, our method achieved a large reduction in both computation time and forecasting error for every step l_s.

6. CONCLUSIONS

In this paper, we focused on the problem of real-time forecasting over co-evolving event streams. Our proposed method, REGIMECAST exhibits all the desirable properties:

1. It is **Effective**: It captures complex non-linear dynamic patterns in event streams and forecasts long-term future events.
2. It is **Adaptive**: It incrementally and automatically recognizes the current regimes and finds regime shift points immediately, while it requires no prior training.
3. It is **Scalable**: Thanks to our efficient streaming algorithms, the computation time does not depend on data stream length.
4. It is **Any-time**: It provides a response at any time and generates long-range future events, immediately.

Acknowledgement. This work was supported by JSPS KAKENHI Grant-in-Aid for Scientific Research Number JP15H02705, JP16K12430, JP26730060, JP26280112, and the MIC/SCOPE #162110003.

7. REFERENCES

[1] D. Chakrabarti and C. Faloutsos. F4: Large-scale automated forecasting using fractals. *CIKM*, 2002.
[2] V. Chandola, A. Banerjee, and V. Kumar. Anomaly detection: A survey. *ACM Comput. Surv.*, 41(3):15:1–15:58, July 2009.
[3] C. Folke, S. Carpenter, B. Walker, M. Scheffer, T. Elmqvist, L. Gunderson, and C. S. Holling. Regime shifts, resilience and biodiversity in ecosystem management. *Annual Review of Ecology, Evolution, and Systematics*, 35:557–581, 2004.
[4] J. Ginsberg, M. Mohebbi, R. Patel, L. Brammer, M. Smolinski, and L. Brilliant. Detecting influenza epidemics using search engine query data. *Nature*, 457:1012–1014, 2009.
[5] S. Hare and N. Mantua. Empirical evidence for North Pacific regime shifts in 1977 and 1989. *Progress in oceanography*, 47(2000):103–145, 2000.
[6] M. D. Hoffman, D. M. Blei, and F. R. Bach. Online learning for latent dirichlet allocation. In *NIPS*, pages 856–864, 2010.
[7] T. Iwata, T. Yamada, Y. Sakurai, and N. Ueda. Online multiscale dynamic topic models. In *KDD*, pages 663–672, 2010.
[8] E. Jackson. *Perspectives of Nonlinear Dynamics:*. Cambridge University Press, 1992.
[9] E. J. Keogh, S. Chu, D. Hart, and M. J. Pazzani. An online algorithm for segmenting time series. In *ICDM*, pages 289–296, 2001.
[10] J. Letchner, C. Ré, M. Balazinska, and M. Philipose. Access methods for markovian streams. In *ICDE*, pages 246–257, 2009.
[11] L. Li, B. A. Prakash, and C. Faloutsos. Parsimonious linear fingerprinting for time series. *PVLDB*, 3(1):385–396, 2010.
[12] A. M. D. Livera, R. J. Hyndman, and R. D. Snyder. Forecasting time series with complex seasonal patterns using exponential smoothing. *Journal of the American Statistical Association*, 106(496):1513–1527, 2011.
[13] M. Mathioudakis, N. Koudas, and P. Marbach. Early online identification of attention gathering items in social media. In *WSDM*, pages 301–310, 2010.
[14] Y. Matsubara, Y. Sakurai, and C. Faloutsos. Autoplait: Automatic mining of co-evolving time sequences. In *SIGMOD*, pages 193–204, 2014.
[15] Y. Matsubara, Y. Sakurai, and C. Faloutsos. The web as a jungle: Non-linear dynamical systems for co-evolving online activities. In *WWW*, pages 721–731, 2015.
[16] Y. Matsubara, Y. Sakurai, and C. Faloutsos. Non-linear mining of competing local activities. In *WWW*, 2016.
[17] Y. Matsubara, Y. Sakurai, C. Faloutsos, T. Iwata, and M. Yoshikawa. Fast mining and forecasting of complex time-stamped events. In *KDD*, pages 271–279, 2012.
[18] Y. Matsubara, Y. Sakurai, B. A. Prakash, L. Li, and C. Faloutsos. Rise and fall patterns of information diffusion: model and implications. In *KDD*, pages 6–14, 2012.
[19] Y. Matsubara, Y. Sakurai, W. G. van Panhuis, and C. Faloutsos. FUNNEL: automatic mining of spatially coevolving epidemics. In *KDD*, pages 105–114, 2014.
[20] A. Mueen and E. J. Keogh. Online discovery and maintenance of time series motifs. In *KDD*, pages 1089–1098, 2010.
[21] T. Palpanas, M. Vlachos, E. Keogh, and D. Gunopulos. Streaming time series summarization using user-defined amnesic functions. *IEEE Transactions on Knowledge and Data Engineering*, 20(7):992–1006, 2008.
[22] S. Papadimitriou, A. Brockwell, and C. Faloutsos. Adaptive, hands-off stream mining. In *VLDB*, pages 560–571, 2003.
[23] S. Papadimitriou, J. Sun, and C. Faloutsos. Streaming pattern discovery in multiple time-series. In *VLDB*, pages 697–708, 2005.
[24] S. Papadimitriou and P. S. Yu. Optimal multi-scale patterns in time series streams. In *SIGMOD*, pages 647–658, 2006.
[25] P. Patel, E. J. Keogh, J. Lin, and S. Lonardi. Mining motifs in massive time series databases. In *Proceedings of ICDM*, pages 370–377, 2002.
[26] B. A. Prakash, A. Beutel, R. Rosenfeld, and C. Faloutsos. Winner takes all: competing viruses or ideas on fair-play networks. In *WWW*, pages 1037–1046, 2012.
[27] T. Rakthanmanon, B. J. L. Campana, A. Mueen, G. E. A. P. A. Batista, M. B. Westover, Q. Zhu, J. Zakaria, and E. J. Keogh. Searching and mining trillions of time series subsequences under dynamic time warping. In *KDD*, pages 262–270, 2012.
[28] Y. Sakurai, C. Faloutsos, and M. Yamamuro. Stream monitoring under the time warping distance. In *ICDE*, pages 1046–1055, Istanbul, Turkey, April 2007.
[29] Y. Sakurai, Y. Matsubara, and C. Faloutsos. Mining and forecasting of big time-series data. In *SIGMOD, Tutorial*, pages 919–922, 2015.
[30] Y. Sakurai, S. Papadimitriou, and C. Faloutsos. Braid: Stream mining through group lag correlations. In *SIGMOD*, pages 599–610, 2005.
[31] M. Scheffer, J. A. Foley, S. R. Carpenter, C. Folke, and B. H. Walker. Catastrophic shifts in ecosystems. *Nature*, 413(6856):591–6, 2001.
[32] M. Vlachos, D. Gunopulos, and G. Kollios. Discovering similar multidimensional trajectories. In *ICDE*, pages 673–684, 2002.
[33] M. Vlachos, G. Kollios, and D. Gunopulos. Elastic translation invariant matching of trajectories. *Mach. Learn.*, 58(2-3):301–334, Feb. 2005.
[34] Y. R. Zelnika, E. Meron, and G. Bel. Gradual regime shifts in fairy circles. *PNAS*, 2015.
[35] Y. Zhao, N. Sundaresan, Z. Shen, and P. S. Yu. Anatomy of a web-scale resale market: a data mining approach. In *WWW*, pages 1533–1544, 2013.
[36] J. Zhou and A. K. H. Tung. Smiler: A semi-lazy time series prediction system for sensors. In *SIGMOD*, pages 1871–1886, 2015.
[37] Y. Zhu and D. Shasha. Statstream: Statistical monitoring of thousands of data streams in real time. In *VLDB*, pages 358–369, 2002.

Skinny-dip: Clustering in a Sea of Noise

Samuel Maurus, Claudia Plant
Helmholtz Zentrum München/Technische Universität München, University of Vienna, Vienna, Austria
samuel.maurus@helmholtz-muenchen.de, claudia.plant@univie.ac.at

ABSTRACT

Can we find heterogeneous clusters hidden in data sets with 80% noise? Although such settings occur in the real-world, we struggle to find methods from the abundance of clustering techniques that perform well with noise at this level. Indeed, perhaps this is enough of a departure from classical clustering to warrant its study as a separate problem. In this paper we present SkinnyDip which, based on Hartigan's elegant dip test of unimodality, represents an intriguing approach to clustering with an attractive set of properties. Specifically, SkinnyDip is highly noise-robust, practically parameter-free and completely deterministic. SkinnyDip never performs multivariate distance calculations, but rather employs insightful recursion based on "dips" into univariate projections of the data. It is able to detect a range of cluster shapes and densities, assuming only that each cluster admits a unimodal shape. Practically, its run-time grows linearly with the data. Finally, for high-dimensional data, continuity properties of the dip enable SkinnyDip to exploit multimodal projection pursuit in order to find an appropriate basis for clustering. Although not without its limitations, SkinnyDip compares favorably to a variety of clustering approaches on synthetic and real data, particularly in high-noise settings.

Keywords

Clustering; modality-testing; parameter-free; high-noise

1. INTRODUCTION

Depending on the nature of the measurements in a data set, it is not uncommon for patterns to be found swimming in a global sea of "clutter" or noise. In the clustering literature, however, we typically see methods showcased on data where the *majority* of objects shape the *signal*. Indeed, many clustering approaches are deficient of a clear "noise" concept. Our work hence begins with the question: what happens when there are *considerably* more "noise" objects in the data set than "clustered" objects?

KDD '16, August 13-17, 2016, San Francisco, CA, USA
© 2016 ACM. ISBN 978-1-4503-4232-2/16/08...$15.00
DOI: http://dx.doi.org/10.1145/2939672.2939740

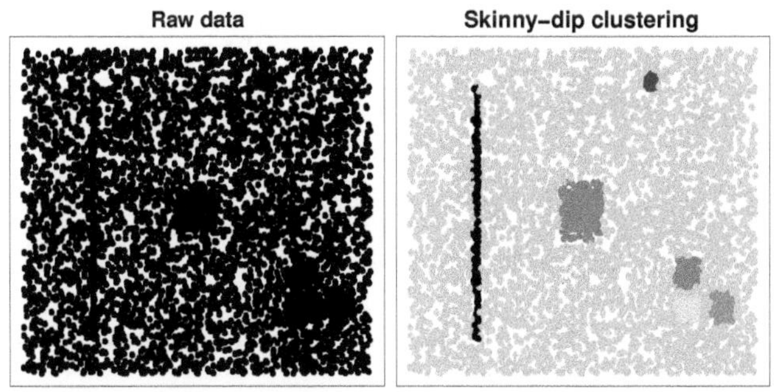

Figure 1: Our running example.

To tackle this question, we assume in this paper that the **clusters in a data set coincide with the modes of its multivariate distribution**, and design recursive heuristics based on the formal statistical *dip* test of unimodality in order to extract them. The resulting algorithm exhibits properties mirroring those of the dip: deterministic, parameter-free, highly robust to noise, free from the need to perform distance calculations, no strict model assumptions, and fast.

Consider with Figure 1 our illustrative running example[1]. It is clear that this is a rather turbulent data set: 80% of the objects are sampled from a uniform "noise" distribution. Despite this, our six clusters (Gaussians of varying size, a square, and a tall, thin rectangle) stand out as patterns. Our goal with this data set is to separate the signal (exposing each of the six shapes) from the noise.

An experienced data scientist would suspect centroid-based clustering approaches to be a poor choice here. They tend to lack a clear notion of "noise", so the Adjusted Mutual Information (AMI) value[2] (a clustering quality metric ranging from 0 at worst to 1 at best) of 0.18 for standard k-means, even when it is given the correct k, is unsurprising (visualization in supplement[1]). Model-based approaches like EM also fail because our cluster shapes do not follow a simple model (AMI of 0.22, Figure 2, reproducible[1]).

Suspecting that the clusters may have heterogeneous form, our scientist decides to begin with *spectral* clustering – a technique known to perform well with non-Gaussian clusters. The popular Self-Tuning [15] variant automatically detects six clusters and assigns labels as shown in Figure

[1]Supplement: github.com/samhelmholtz/skinny-dip
[2]Noise points are assigned a seventh class label. Normalized Mutual Information (NMI) measurements are provided for reference in the supplement.

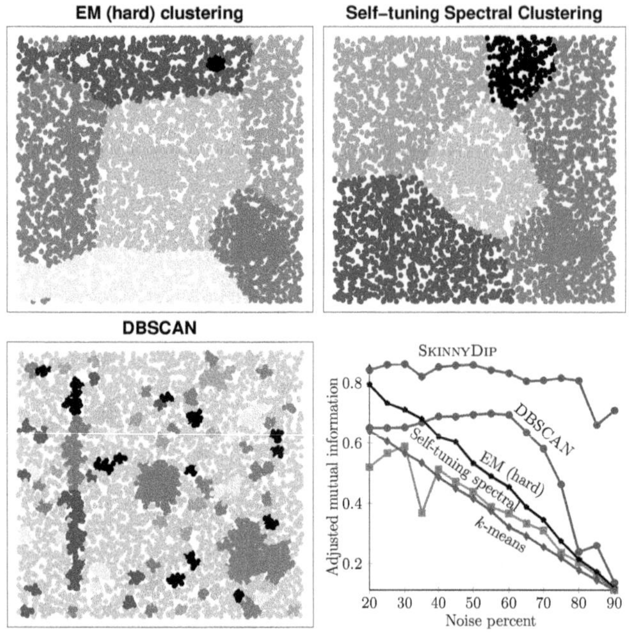

Figure 2: Further results for our running example.

2. The result, which again sees clusters composed purely of noise points, is not surprising given the known limitations of spectral clustering in the presence of significant noise.

Undiscouraged, our scientist wonders if density-based approaches can help. The popular DBSCAN method is known to robustly discover clusters of varying shape in noisy environments. After fine-tuning its parameters[3] (requiring graphical inspection), the DBSCAN result in Figure 2 is produced. This result is an improvement, however leaves much to be desired. DBSCAN detects 95 clusters in this case (AMI 0.24), primarily because there are various areas in which, through the randomness of noise, the local density threshold is exceeded. We need this threshold to prevent fragmentation of our tall rectangular cluster, but it causes our three neighboring Gaussians to merge. No parameter combination for DBSCAN can solve these problems.

Enter SkinnyDip[4], which pairs the formal dip test with efficient recursive heuristics. Requiring **practically no parameters** other than a threshold α for statistical significance (which for *all* our work is fixed at $\alpha = 0.05$), SkinnyDip detects all six clusters plus noise (back in Figure 1) to achieve an AMI of 0.81. SkinnyDip does this **deterministically and quickly**. It requires **no manual intervention, no convergence-based processes, no multivariate distance calculations, and no model-order selection techniques** (like the Bayesian Information Criterion).

Although we focus more on experiments in Section 6, we can briefly see in Figure 2 that SkinnyDip is able to defend its result the longest on this running-example data as we vary the noise percentage up to 90% (where nine of the ten-thousand data set objects are noise points).

Situations involving oddly-shaped clusters embedded in a sea of noise are not only of theoretical interest. For a **real-world example** we need look no further than Figure 3, which shows a simplified and annotated version of the North Jutland (Denmark) Road Network data from the UCI repository (data in the supplement). The data points represent road segments, which are generally denser in highly-populated areas (cities like Aalborg, Hjørring and Frederikshavn – with populations over 20,000). The majority of the road segments, however, could be termed "noise": long arterials connecting cities, or less-dense road networks in the relatively sparsely-populated countryside. We also appreciate the heterogeneity of cluster shapes, especially around the coastal and island regions, stemming from the topographical restrictions (lakes, shorelines) on habitation.

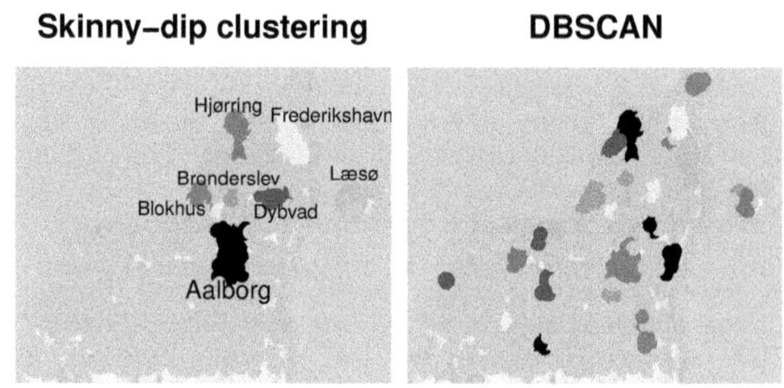

Figure 3: Clustering road segments in North Jutland. Background courtesy of Google Maps.

Without having to tune any parameters, SkinnyDip quickly produces an intuitive result in which the aforementioned three major cities of the region are found. The island of Læsø and particularly dense areas around Bronderslev (population over 12,000) are also found. The best result we were able to achieve by tuning the parameters of DBSCAN is displayed to its right ($minPts = 10$, $\epsilon = 0.03$, replicable[1]). It detects over 20 additional and insignificant "countryside" (noise) clusters.

Contributions:

We consider the (often neglected) problem of clustering in extreme-noise settings, showing real examples.

We present SkinnyDip to cluster such data. SkinnyDip is deterministic and requires no distance computations, strict model assumptions, obscure parameters or convergence processes. As far as we know, it is the first clustering algorithm with this combination of properties.

We show that the core recursive heuristics on which SkinnyDip is based can be used to complement existing statistical tests of unimodality in order to answer the additional question of *where are the modes?* (not just: *is it multimodal?*) for arbitrary continuous samples.

We show the interpretation benefits that come from pursuing the maximum-dip directions in the data and clustering with them as a basis.

2. THE DIP TEST

Relatively unknown in the data-mining community, the *dip* [9] is a prominent formal statistical test for measuring the unimodality of a sample from a continuous random variable. Before introducing SkinnyDip, we briefly review the dip's fundamentals (rigorous treatment in [9]).

---

[3] Here $minPts = 10$ and $\epsilon = 0.019$.

[4] So named because it uses the dip test and is "skinny" in the sense that it is lean (few assumptions/parameters).

Consider Figure 4, which shows the histogram we obtain after projecting our running-example data[5] onto its horizontal axis. To its right is the sample's empirical cumulative distribution function (ECDF), denoted F. The colored regions correspond to the modes (**A-E**) of the sample, and we can see that F's gradient is larger where modes exist. Note that the histogram is for visual comparison only – the dip only needs F (which requires no bin-width parameter).

To measure the unimodality of the sample, the dip uses a common definition of unimodality: a distribution is unimodal if its ECDF takes a *convex* form up to its mode (or *modal interval* in general) and a *concave* form after it. The dip hence tries to assert that F is unimodal by fitting a piecewise-linear function G of this form onto it and taking a measure for its "goodness of fit". This statistic, the "dip" $d \in (0, \frac{1}{4}]$, is defined as the minimum achievable vertical offset for two copies of F (one above, one below, shown as dashed lines in the bottom graphic) such that G does not violate its unimodal rules ("convex then concave").

With our depicted analogy we imagine that the two offset copies of F form the edges of a racing track (birds-eye view). The racer, who follows the trajectory of G, *must* drive as though she were navigating a chicane, that is, "first steer to the left, then optionally straight, then to the right"[6]. The smallest possible width of the track which still enables the driver to follow these rules and remain on the track[7] is twice the dip statistic d. The farther F strays from unimodality, the larger the required width of the track.

After comparing d with that of a suitable reference unimodal distribution (null distribution), a p-value is reported for the null hypothesis H_0 ="F is unimodal". For our example we have $p < 10^{-10}$. Using the common threshold of $\alpha = 0.05$ we hence reject H_0 and favor the alternative ("F is *at least* bimodal").

The dip test hence gives us a measure for F's *departure from unimodality* – a useful insight if we assume that clusters are the modes of a distribution. Importantly though, the dip communicates one more piece of information: the location of the *modal interval* $[x_L, x_U]$. This is the interval in which G is prescribed maximum slope (shown as the gray region). As we will see shortly, SkinnyDip exploits this information when searching for all modes of a distribution.

Based purely on the geometry of the ECDF, the dip has convenient properties. Firstly, it is nonparametric – any continuous distributions with this abstract "convex then concave" shape are supported (Gaussian, beta, uniform and so on). The dip is invariant to shifting and scaling and, as we have hinted, is particularly robust to noise and outliers. It requires no input parameters. Finally, it is deterministic and *fast* – the standard algorithm on a sorted sample requires $\mathcal{O}(n)$ operations in the worst case. These properties mirror much of what we would like to see in a clustering technique.

Taken in its existing form, however, the dip test is of little use for clustering. The reasons for this are twofold: 1) it is only applicable to univariate data[8], and 2) it can only help us accept or reject the hypothesis that *the distribution is unimodal*[9], and thus cannot help us find the count and location of *all* modes in a distribution.

Despite this, we propose that the test is a promising and intriguing formal foundation from which we can commence exploring novel heuristics for the task of clustering.

3. DIP-BASED UNIVARIATE CLUSTERING

We take the first step towards our goal by considering a simpler problem: how can we cluster noisy *univariate* data? In this section we propose a solution in the form of a dip-based heuristic. Our approach is a recursive one, and at a high level is analogous to the traversing mechanism used by the dip in computing its statistic. In our case, however, it is used to "pick off" one mode at a time from the sample. We refer to this core part of SkinnyDip with the name UniDip and describe it now for our running example with the aid of Figure 4 and Algorithm 1.

We begin by "dipping" over the sorted univariate ($m = 1$) sample $x_1 \leq \ldots \leq x_n$ of size n (line 2). The dip result tells us two things. Firstly, from the p-value of $p < 10^{-10}$ we learn (based on the significance threshold of $\alpha = 0.05$) that the distribution has *at least* two modes. Secondly, we learn

[5]For visual clarity we use the version with 30% noise.

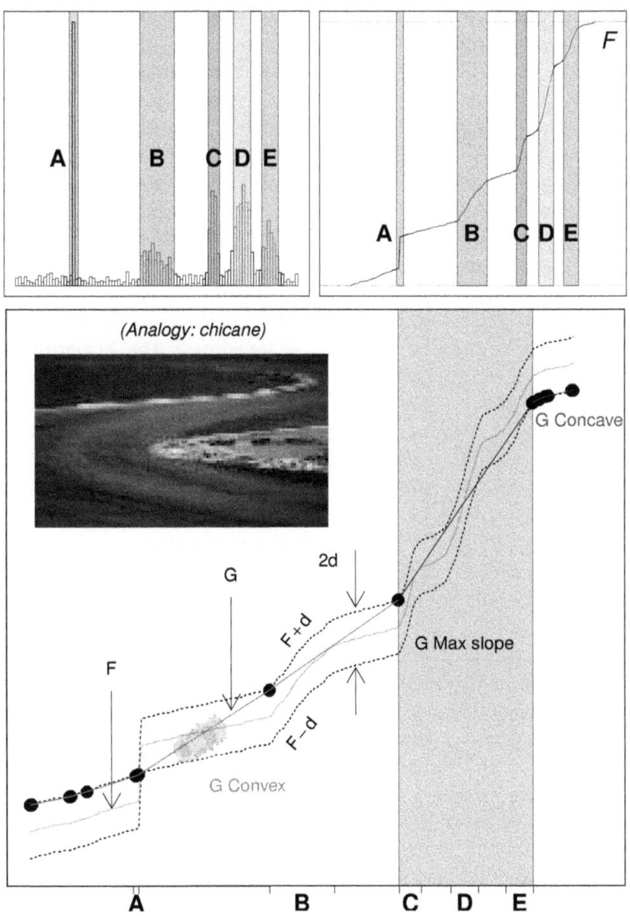

Figure 4: Histogram, ECDF (top) and dip solution (bottom) for the horizontal-axis projection of our running-example data.

[6]Strictly speaking, the steering must be such that the car's trajectory follows the exact restrictions imposed on G.

[7]The driver can leave the track inside the modal interval.

[8]A measure of distance on the space, as well as a means for generalizing empirical distribution functions, would be required for the multivariate case.

[9]The alternate hypothesis is hence the relatively unspecific statement of *the distribution is at least bimodal.*

the location of the modal interval $[x_L, x_U]$ for this sample. In the context of the dip this represents the interval for G's prescribed maximum constant slope. In our concrete case this first modal interval spans our modes **C**,**D** and **E** (the gray region in Figure 4). Intuitively, the dip lumps these into one modal interval because they lie close together in the ECDF (mathematically, doing so allows it to achieve a minimum d). We recurse into the modal interval to extract these three modes (line 5), which gives us three individual modal intervals $[x_{L_\mathbf{C}}, x_{U_\mathbf{C}}], [x_{L_\mathbf{D}}, x_{U_\mathbf{D}}], [x_{L_\mathbf{E}}, x_{U_\mathbf{E}}]$.

Knowing that there is at least one more mode, our search is not over. To find the next, we recognize that it must lie outside the gray interval $[x_L, x_U]$. At this point we heuristically assert that if a mode were to exist to its right, then dipping over $[x_{L_\mathbf{E}}, x_n]$ (that is, mode **E** and everything to its right) would yield a significant result. The choice of this interval is key. Consider if we were instead to dip over $[x_U, x_n]$ (everything to the right of the gray region). For our example, where that region only contains uniform noise, the dip would give a non-significant (unimodal) result. However, we would *equally* get a unimodal result if a single "cluster" (another Gaussian, for example) resided in that region. Clearly we need to be able to distinguish between these cases, so we include mode **E**. This way, if the dip concludes unimodality, we can assume that the single mode to which it refers is simply mode **E** again, and thus there is nothing "interesting" to its right. If the dip concludes multimodality, we know there *is* something interesting to its right. At the other end, if a mode were to exist to the *left* of x_L, then dipping analogously over $[x_1, x_{U_\mathbf{C}}]$ (this time including mode **C**) would yield a significant result.

For our example we find that the right part $[x_{L_\mathbf{E}}, x_n]$ is unimodal ($p \approx 0.97$, line 10), so we need not search right of x_U. The left part $[x_1, x_{U_\mathbf{C}}]$ *is* significantly multimodal ($p < 10^{-10}$, line 9), so we recurse into the region $[x_1, x_L]$ to continue searching. Through this recursive call the intervals $[x_{L_\mathbf{A}}, x_{U_\mathbf{A}}], [x_{L_\mathbf{B}}, x_{U_\mathbf{B}}]$ for modes **A** and **B** are obtained.

UniDip thus recursively exploits the dip's ability to 1) make a binary decision (unimodal or not), and 2) identify the primary modal interval. Assuming the procedure is provided with a sorted sample, its worst-case time complexity is in $\mathcal{O}(n \cdot k)$, where k is the number of modes found ($k \leq n$, typically $k \ll n$). For interest, Figure 5 demonstrates UniDip on a somewhat busier sample ($k = 17$).

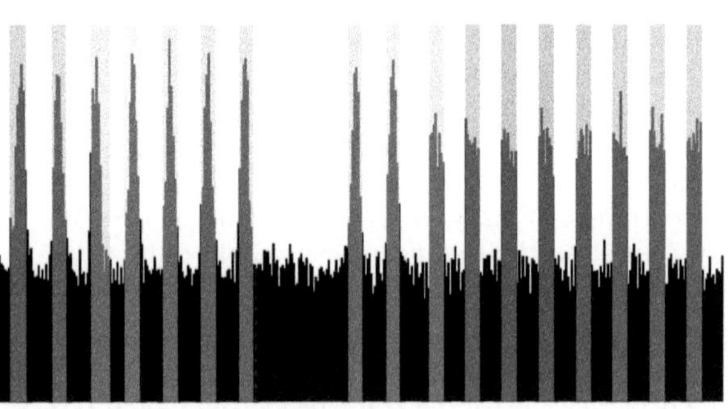

Figure 5: UniDip finds the 17 modes in this univariate sample (Gaussian and uniform clusters in a sea of 75% noise). Replication code in supplement.

input : Sorted univariate sample $x_1, \ldots, x_n$, significance level α, indicator $\delta = 1$ if $\vec{x}$ was identified as modal interval, else $\delta = 0$

output: Modal intervals $\mathcal{M} = \{[x_{L_1}, x_{U_1}], \ldots\}$

1 /* Dip over the sample, obtaining modal interval estimate and p-value */

2 $\{x_L, x_U, p\} \leftarrow$ `dip`$(\vec{x})$;

3 **if** $p > \alpha$ **then return** δ ? $\{[x_1, x_n]\}$: $\{[x_L, x_U]\}$;

4 /* Recall using the modal interval to find the list $\mathcal{M}_m$ of modal intervals within */

5 $\mathcal{M}_m \leftarrow$ `recall`$(\forall x_j : x_L \leq x_j \leq x_U,\ \alpha,\ \delta = 1)$;

6 /* Check to the left and right of the modal interval, recursing to extract additional modes where appropriate */

7 $u \leftarrow \min_{x_U \in \mathcal{M}_m}(x_U), l \leftarrow \max_{x_L \in \mathcal{M}_m}(x_L)$;

8 $p_l \leftarrow$ `dip`$(\forall x_j : x_j \leq u)$, $p_u \leftarrow$ `dip`$(\forall x_j : x_j \geq l)$;

9 $\mathcal{M}_l \leftarrow p_l \leq \alpha$? `recall`$(\forall x_j : x_j < x_L,\ \alpha,\ 0)$: $\emptyset$;

10 $\mathcal{M}_r \leftarrow p_u \leq \alpha$? `recall`$(\forall x_j : x_j > x_U,\ \alpha,\ 0)$: $\emptyset$;

11 **return** $\mathcal{M}_l \cup \mathcal{M}_m \cup \mathcal{M}_r$;

Algorithm 1: UniDip

4. THE MULTIVARIATE CASE

We wrap UniDip with another recursive heuristic, this time over the dimensions of the data space, in order to extract the modal hyperintervals from a continuous *multivariate* distribution. More specifically, we construct our hyperintervals one edge at a time, with each edge corresponding to a modal interval found from clustering the univariate projection of appropriately-filtered data. Again we explain using our running example (Figure 6 and Algorithm 2).

We begin by assuming for now that each cluster in the space forms a unimodal shape in all coordinate directions (like the rectangles and circles in our running example) – this assumption will be relaxed in Section 5. We consider the first direction in our data (line 4 of Algorithm 2, the horizontal-axis in our running example) onto which we project all data. Note that information may be lost in this step – considering Figures 1 and 4 we see that mode **D** (green) is formed from the projection of two separate clusters and much noise. We cluster this projection (lines 6 and 7) using our approach from Section 3, which yields the set of five modal intervals $\mathcal{M} = \{[x_{L_\mathbf{A}}, x_{U_\mathbf{A}}], \ldots, [x_{L_\mathbf{E}}, x_{U_\mathbf{E}}]\}$ for our example.

In Figure 6 we see the recursive step in action for the example modal interval $[x_{L_\mathbf{D}}, x_{U_\mathbf{D}}]$ (it is done analogously for the others). The values $x_{L_\mathbf{D}}$ and $x_{U_\mathbf{D}}$ represent the bounds of the hyperinterval in the first dimension. To find the bounds in the second dimension, we consider the subset of data objects whose coordinates in the first dimension lie within $[x_{L_\mathbf{D}}, x_{U_\mathbf{D}}]$ (line 10; that is, all objects within the green region in Figure 6). For these data points, we take a univariate projection onto the *second* direction (line 4, one recursive layer deeper, the vertical direction in our running example), the density of which is shown superimposed in Figure 6. We then cluster this projection, again using our approach from Section 3. This time we find two modal intervals (labeled D_1 and D_2 in Figure 6), from which we generate two modal hyperintervals (dark boxes in Figure 6), each with bounds of $[x_{L_\mathbf{D}}, x_{U_\mathbf{D}}]$ in the first direction. The procedure is repeated recursively for each of these hyper-

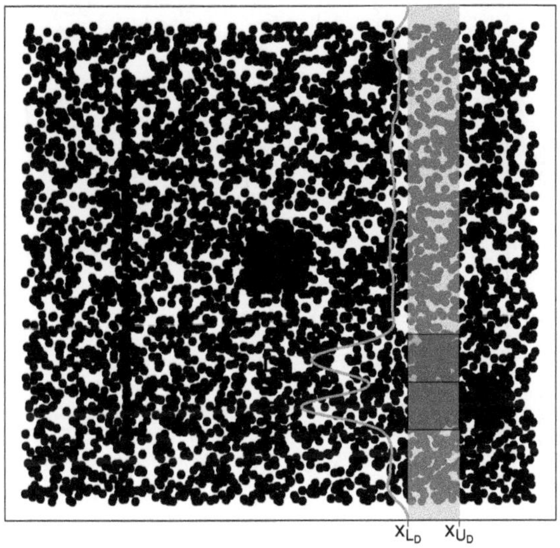

Figure 6: Dipping into the second dimension to find the modal hyperintervals.

input : Data $X \in \mathbb{R}^{n \times m}$, significance level α, bounds for current hyperinterval $(\vec{x}_L \in \mathbb{R}^d, \vec{x}_U \in \mathbb{R}^d)$ ($d = 0$ on first call)

output: Modal hyperintervals (clusters) $\{[\vec{x}_{L_1}, \vec{x}_{U_1}], [\vec{x}_{L_2}, \vec{x}_{U_2}], \ldots\}$

1 `/* We are done if all dimensions checked */`
2 **if** $d == m$ **then return** $\{[\vec{x}_L, \vec{x}_U]\}$;
3 `/* Otherwise, take next projection */`
4 $\vec{x} \leftarrow X_{\cdot,(d+1)}$;
5 `/* Sort/cluster this univariate projection (yields set of modal intervals` $\mathcal{M}$`) */`
6 $\vec{x} \leftarrow$ `sort(`$\vec{x}$`)` ; `/* (`*ascending* `sort). */`
7 $\mathcal{M} \leftarrow$ UNIDIP($\vec{x}$, α, $\delta = 0$);
8 $\mathcal{H} \leftarrow \emptyset$;
9 **for** $[x_L, x_U] \in \mathcal{M}$ **do**
10 $\quad Y \leftarrow \left[\forall X_{i,\cdot} : \left(x_L \leq X_{i,(d+1)} \leq x_U\right)\right]$;
11 $\quad \mathcal{H}$`.add(recall(`Y, α, $\vec{x}_L$`.push(`x_L`),` $\vec{x}_U$`.push(`x_U`)));`
12 **end**
13 **return** $\mathcal{H}$;

Algorithm 2: SKINNYDIP

intervals for the remaining dimensions in the space (in our running example we would be finished).

On line 6 we must sort the data before clustering. The overall worst-case run-time complexity of SKINNYDIP hence depends on the run-time complexity to sort a vector of n real numbers. We note that the sort mappings can be computed for each feature vector in advance (an optimized implementation would then refactor line 6 to use global sort-mappings). We also observe that we never have more than m levels of recursion, and due to the strict partitioning the maximum count of data objects considered across SKINNYDIP function invocations for any given recursion level is n. Assuming the use of a comparison-based sorting algorithm like merge- or heap-sort (worst-case run-time in $\mathcal{O}(n \cdot \log(n))$), we thus find SKINNYDIP's **worst-case time complexity** as a full-space clustering technique to be in $\mathcal{O}(n \cdot \log(n) \cdot m + n \cdot m \cdot k)$, where m is the dimension of the data space and k is the maximum number of modes found from a call to UNIDIP. It is clear that SKINNYDIP involves **no "convergence"-style processes** (e.g. meeting an accuracy threshold, or iterating until the local maximum of an objective function is obtained). Section 6.3 shows that *practical* run-time growth is *linear* in nm.

5. FINDING A SUITABLE BASIS

In the previous section we assumed that each cluster forms a unimodal shape in *all* coordinate directions. This is often unrealistic – many features of a data set may be irrelevant to a clustering. In this section we show how we can use the idea of *multimodal projection pursuit* to find an appropriate basis in which to cluster. Our dip-based search strategy complements our dip-based algorithm SKINNYDIP. It is motivated by the insight that *the directions which depart the most from unimodality are promising when searching for a clustering.* To be clear, we are *not* searching for arbitrary subspaces *per cluster*, but rather a *single basis* in which clustering is to be performed (discussed further in Section 7).

We thus seek directions in our data that *maximize* the dip, thereby generating a basis in which the SKINNYDIP algorithm can exploit these maximal-multimodal directions in order to find clusters. Fortunately, continuity properties of the dip enable us to exploit gradient ascent to help find the directions we seek. Specifically, for m-dimensional data, Krause [11] showed that the dip varies smoothly with respect to a changing projection vector $\vec{a} \in \mathbb{R}^m$. If we denote by d the dip of the projection of our data $D \in \mathbb{R}^{n \times m}$ with respect to $\vec{a}$, the partial derivatives[10] of d with respect to the elements of the projection vector are given by:

$$\frac{\partial d}{\partial a_i}(\vec{a}) = \begin{cases} -\frac{i_3 - i_1}{n} \cdot \frac{\vec{a} \cdot (\beta_i \vec{\gamma} - \gamma_i \vec{\beta})}{(\vec{a} \cdot \vec{\gamma})^2} & \text{if } \eta > 0, \\ \frac{i_3 - i_1}{n} \cdot \frac{\vec{a} \cdot (\beta_i \vec{\gamma} - \gamma_i \vec{\beta})}{(\vec{a} \cdot \vec{\gamma})^2} & \text{if } \eta \leq 0, \end{cases} \tag{1}$$

where $\vec{\beta} = (\beta_1, \ldots, \beta_m) = D_{i_2\cdot} - D_{i_1\cdot}$, $\vec{\gamma} = (\gamma_1, \ldots, \gamma_m) = D_{i_3\cdot} - D_{i_1\cdot}$ and $\cdot$ for two vectors is their scalar product. The indices i_1, i_2, i_3 correspond to the location of the so-called *modal triangle*, the height h of which satisfies $h = 2d$. The value $\eta = i_2 - i_1 - (i_3 - i_1)\left(\vec{a} \cdot \vec{\beta}\right) / (\vec{a} \cdot \vec{\gamma})$ simply accounts for the case when the modal triangle points in the negative direction. See [11] for full details.

Of course, gradient ascent will not identify the global maximum-dip direction in the general case. Indeed, looking at Figure 8, which shows the dip variation for projection vector angles in the range $[0, \pi]$ for our running example data, we see valleys with numerous maxima. Although the surface becomes more smooth with increasing n, it is clear that gradient ascent would profit from a good initialization.

We therefore require a mechanism for choosing a *starting point* for gradient-ascent. Simple random sampling, that is, randomly generating a number w of unit vectors in the space and greedily taking the one giving a data projection with maximum dip, is clearly a straight forward option here that is trivial to support. However, it is undesirable to introduce an element of randomness into our work at this stage

[10] We note that a syntax error appears to be present in the original paper. Our version contains the suggested correction.

(SkinnyDip and UniDip are deterministic and involve no random-sampling). We hence sample from the nodes of a *sparse grid* [3, 13] – a structured and scalable way to span high-dimensional spaces. Sparse grids are based on a multiscale basis which is derived from a one-dimensional multiscale basis by a tensor product construction. Discretizing a function on a sparse grid requires only $\mathcal{O}(q \cdot (\log q)^{m-1})$ nodes, where q is the number of grid points in one coordinate direction at the boundary. Unlike simple random sampling, the nodes of a sparse grid are generated deterministically. Furthermore, although we cannot make any theoretical guarantees that the use of sparse grids will in *every* case produce more favorable candidate nodes for arbitrary dip surfaces (we may well "get lucky" using simple random sampling), reproducible results in our supplement[1] show that their use directly leads to better clustering results for *all ten* of the real-world data sets we present in Section 6.2. On a more general level, systematic experiments on numerous high-dimensional benchmark optimization surfaces[1] (such as the Rosenbrock and Michalewicz functions in Figure 7) additionally show the benefits of this sampling strategy.

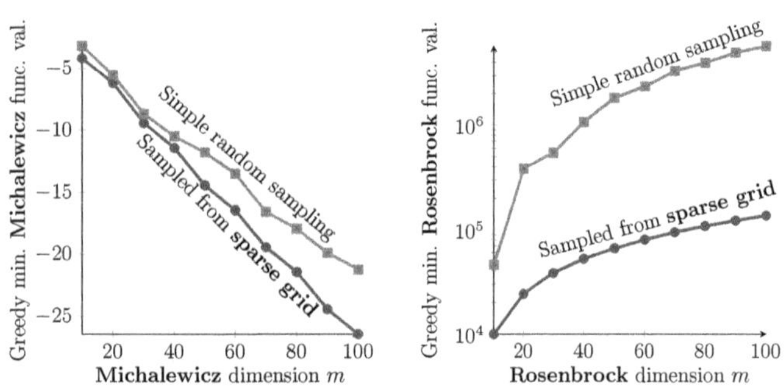

Figure 7: Simple random sampling versus sparse-grids sampling: a comparison of the greedy minimum value obtained over an equally-sized (large) sample by varying function dimension. Note that the global minimum value of the Michalewicz function decreases with increasing dimension.

With SparseDip (Algorithm 3) we hence sample from a sparse grid rather than randomly. As we only require unit vectors and can exploit symmetry, we can for an m-dimensional data space construct a sparse grid in $[0, \pi]^{m-1}$ "angle" space (line 6) in order to obtain sparsely-positioned unit vectors lying on a $(m-1)$-sphere in m-dimensional space (line 8, where SphToCart converts spherical coordinates to Cartesian). Figure 9 shows a concrete example for $m = 3$.

To maintain efficiency, our implementation of SparseDip uses a bound for the number of grid nodes to evaluate. When asked to generate a grid of dimension m, the method SgGen returns the regular sparse grid over $[0, \pi]^m$ of level l whose node-count is closest to w (i.e. $\mathcal{O}(w)$, line 6). In general, exploring higher-dimensional spaces would call for the use of a higher value for w, however for simplicity and efficiency we use a default of $w = 1000$ for all our work.

For each unit vector we project the data and compute the dip (requiring us to sort the sample), greedily taking the maximum as the starting point for gradient ascent (line 10). The worst-case run-time complexity for finding the starting point is easily shown to be in $\mathcal{O}(n \cdot \log(n) \cdot m \cdot w)$.

Having greedily selected a starting point (the sparse-grid-

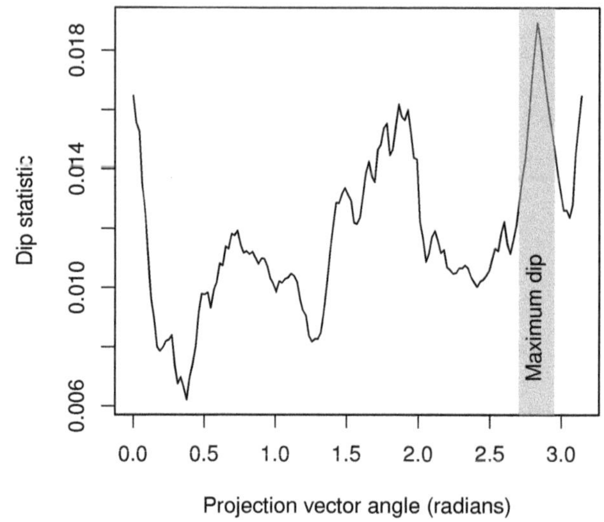

Figure 8: Dip variation against angle of the projection vector (running-example data).

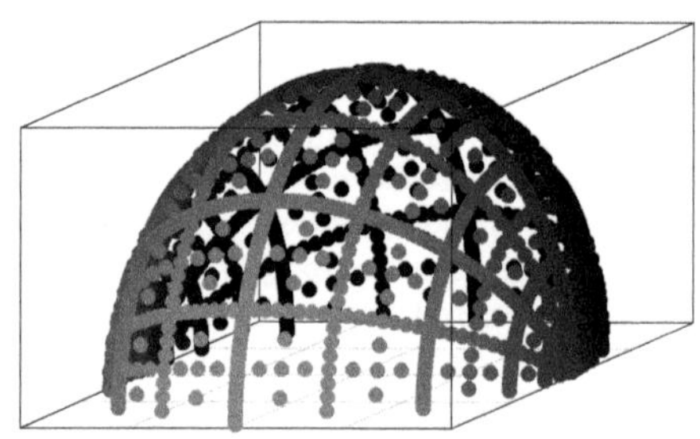

Figure 9: The two-dimensional regular sparse grid of level 8 can be used to define sparsely-distributed unit vectors lying on the 2-(hemi)sphere.

based unit vector with largest dip), we proceed with gradient ascent (line 11) on the hypersphere to "fine tune" this vector, obtaining a unit vector with a locally-maximum dip. This vector becomes the first in the set $\mathcal{B}$ of orthonormal vectors defining the basis in which we plan to cluster. The basis is expanded one direction at a time by repeating this process on the data's projection to the orthogonal complement of this basis (line 4), in which we find the next direction (orthogonal to our existing directions) maximizing the dip. The process terminates when a maximum-dip direction is found for which H_0 cannot be rejected (i.e. we can't find an "interesting" direction in the remaining space, line 13), or if the basis obtains the cardinality m (the dimension of the original data). SkinnyDip (the full-space clustering technique from Section 4) can then be applied to the data's projection onto the found basis. In the case where there are as many "interesting" directions in the data as original features m, the overall worst-case run-time complexity for finding a basis using SparseDip is in $\mathcal{O}(n \cdot \log(n) \cdot \frac{m(m-1)}{2} \cdot w)$.

6. EXPERIMENTAL EVALUATION

We now turn to a practical evaluation of SkinnyDip, comparing it to state-of-the-art *automated* representatives from different families (in Section 7 we elaborate on the moti-

```
input : Data D ∈ ℝ^{n×m}, significance level α,
        sparse grid point count w.
output: Orthonormal basis set 𝓑 s.t. |𝓑| ≤ m.
𝓑 ← ∅;
while |𝓑| < m do
    /* Project data to orthogonal complement
       of our existing basis                              */
    D_c ← D · (𝓑^⊥) ;          /* (D_c ∈ ℝ^{n×(m−|𝓑|)}) */
    /* Sparse grid points over angle space                */
    {θ⃗_1, ..., θ⃗_{O(w)}} ← SGGen(m − |𝓑| − 1, w);
    /* Cartesian candidate vectors (lengths
       m − |𝓑|) for gradient ascent                       */
    {v⃗_1, ..., v⃗_{O(w)}} ← SphToCart({θ⃗_1, ..., θ⃗_{O(w)}});
    /* Gradient ascent starting from
       candidate with maximum dip                         */
    v⃗_m ←      arg max        (dip(sort(D_c · v⃗)));
          v⃗∈{v⃗_1,...,v⃗_{O(w)}}
    v⃗_m ← GradAsc(v⃗_m, D_c) ;               /* See [11] */
    /* Done if result not significant                     */
    p ← dip(sort(D_c · v⃗_m));
    if p > α then return 𝓑 ;
    𝓑.push(v⃗_m);
end
return 𝓑;
```

Algorithm 3: SparseDip

vation for our selection). We begin with RIC [1], which fine-tunes an initial coarse clustering based on the Minimum Description Length principle (a model-selection strategy based on balancing accuracy with complexity through data-compression). PgMeans [8] and DipMeans [10] are wrappers for automating EM and k-means respectively. Self-tuning spectral clustering (STSC) [15] is the popular automated approach to spectral clustering from Zelnik-Manor and Perona. With DBSCAN [5] we have the popular member of the density-based family. Sync [2] is a more recent automated algorithm which combines density-based concepts with a novel approach inspired by phase-oscillators.

We thank various peers[11] for sharing code implementations. In our supplement[1] we share our code as well as all data sets, generative models and results which follow.

6.1 Synthetic Data

We choose our generative model such that the data sets exhibit the challenging properties on which we focus. Specifically, we desire high levels of noise around clusters of varying shape that may only be separated by a small distance. That is, our generative model creates data with properties similar to our running example. By default, we choose six clusters of 200 objects each in three dimensions. Half of the clusters are Gaussian with a standard deviation of 0.005. The remaining half are rectangular (one thin side of width 0.005; the remaining sides of width 0.25). The centers of the three Gaussians are pairwise-separated by a distance of 6σ (similar to the bottom Gaussians in our running example), and are otherwise randomly placed in the space. The three rectangles are similarly separated by a distance of 0.03. By default, 80% of the objects in the data set are "noise", that is, objects which have been sampled from the uniform distribution over the unit hypercube. With our default parameters, we hence obtain data sets with $n = 6000$ and $m = 3$.

Relative to the default parameters, we systematically vary the number of clusters $k = \{3, 6, \ldots, 15\}$, the noise percentage $\eta = \{20, 25, \ldots, 90\}$ and the dimensionality $m = \{2, 3, \ldots, 8\}$. For each parameter combination we randomly generate 20 data sets (560 data sets in total).

SkinnyDip uses its default value of $\alpha = 0.05$ in all cases. We likewise use the default parameter values for the provided implementations of the comparison algorithms. To automate DBSCAN, we fix *minPts*= 10 and run DBSCAN for all $\epsilon = \{0.01, 0.02, \ldots, 0.2\}$, reporting the best AMI result from these parameter combinations in each case.

Figure 10 presents the results for SkinnyDip and the comparison techniques on these data. A point in a plot series is the mean AMI value from the 20 data sets corresponding to that parameter combination, and the error bars span one standard deviation in each direction (omitted on every second point to reduce clutter). In fairness to the techniques which have no concept of noise (e.g. centroid-based techniques), the AMI only considers the objects which truly belong to a cluster (non-noise points). The results are discussed in Section 7.

6.2 Real-World Data

In Table 1 we present results (AMI value) for **ten real-world data sets** of varying size from the UCI and Comprehensive R Archive Network (CRAN) repositories. These classification-style data are often used to quantitatively evaluate clustering techniques in real-world settings; however it should be noted that *every* point is assigned a semantic class label (none of the data include a noise label). For this reason we run the k-means iteration (based on Euclidean distance) on the final SkinnyDip result to assign any detected noise objects to a "true" cluster.

As some of the data exhibit high dimensionality, SkinnyDip makes use of the SparseDip basis-search (Section 5), noting of course that it can yield the full space when appropriate. Particularly for the high-dimensional data sets, our use of SparseDip is somewhat unfair on the methods which are not able to perform such a search, and for this reason we additionally evaluate the recent FOSSCLU [6] method here. FOSSCLU is a state-of-the-art technique which, like SkinnyDip, searches for a *single* basis in which to perform clustering in an automated manner. For DBSCAN we automate in the same way as for our synthetic experiments, reporting the best AMI value achieved from $\epsilon \in \{0.05, 0.10, \ldots, 5.00\}$ in each case[12]. RIC is always provided with a starting value of $k = 10$ (for all data sets we have $k \leq 10$), which it seeks to refine through cluster-merging. For all of the other automated techniques we use the default parameters as given by their provided implementations.

In a *quantitative* sense, SkinnyDip's results are promising compared to the competition. It achieves the strongest AMI value on seven of the ten data sets, and is ranked second on

[11] Warm thanks to Greg Hamerly, Christian Böhm and Junming Shao for PgMeans, RIC and Sync respectively. For each of DipMeans and STSC we used the implementation from the author's website.

[12] Here our range for ϵ needs to be larger because the data are in general of higher dimension than in the synthetic cases. *minPts* was again fixed at 10 (much smaller than any data set cluster).

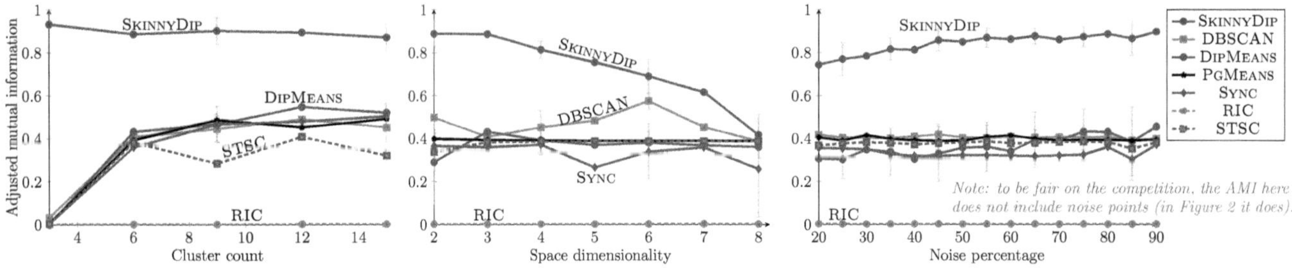

Figure 10: Synthetic experiment results.

two of the remaining sets. On the Pen Digits data set it ranks fourth.

As a *qualitative* supplement, we investigate two of the results in detail. Figure 11 depicts the case of the Whiteside data. Recorded at a house in England, the horizontal and vertical axes represent weekly average external temperature and gas consumption respectively. The class labels record whether cavity-wall insulation had been installed (blue) or not (red). Intuitively we expect a negative association between gas consumption and temperature (heating costs are lower when it is warmer), and also see that the insulation factor introduces a negative vertical offset (the use of insulation is associated with a reduced overall gas consumption). From a clustering perspective we can view this data as two elongated and neighboring clusters, which SKINNYDIP is able to automatically detect (with an optimal AMI value of 1) by finding the direction of maximum dip and clustering in the corresponding projection.

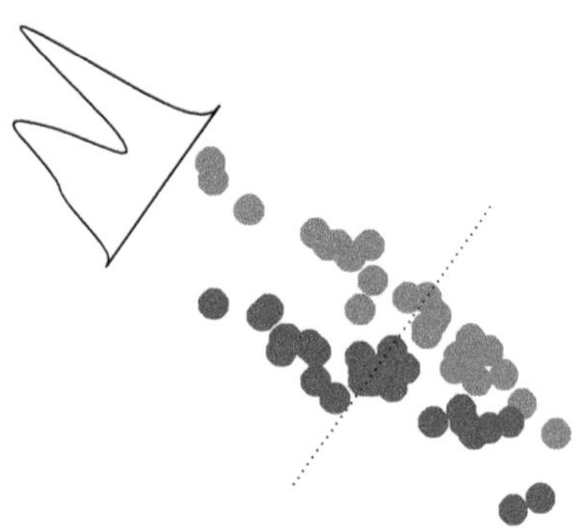

Figure 11: The projection vector and corresponding univariate distribution found by SkinnyDip on the Whiteside data. Subsequent SkinnyDip clustering yields the optimal result.

SKINNYDIP's subspace-identification for the Image Segmentation data is also noteworthy. It finds a three-dimensional space for clustering, the projections for two directions of which are displayed in Figure 12. The first direction has a high loading for the feature *value-mean* and a large *negative* loading for *short-line-density-2*. It cleanly separates the *sky* images, which is sensible because images of sky and clouds typically contain few lines. The second direction has large positive and negative loadings for the features *hue-mean* and *exblue-mean* respectively. It cleanly separates the *grass* images, which we intuitively expect to have a large hue and significantly lack the color blue.

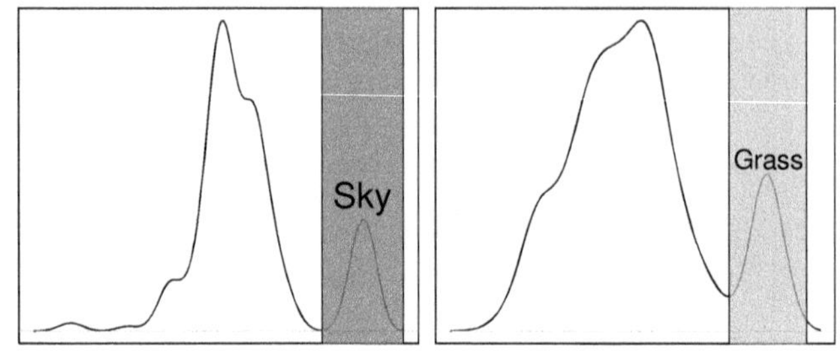

Figure 12: Densities along two of the basis directions found for the image-segmentation data.

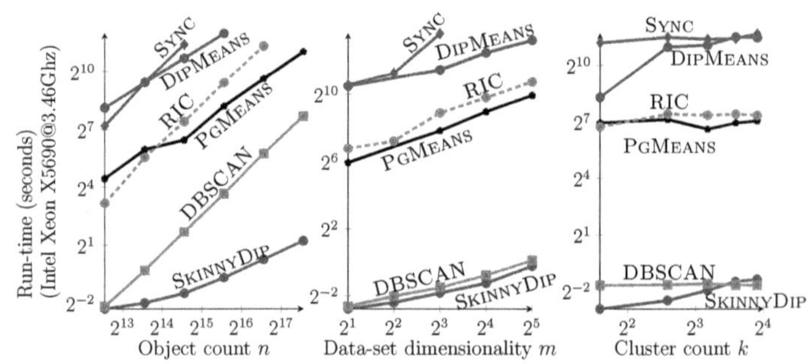

Figure 13: Run-time for varying n, m and k.

6.3 Run-Time Experiments

We support our stated theoretical run-time bounds with measurements and comparisons on synthetic data with scaled n, m and k. SKINNYDIP is implemented in R, and we use the R implementation[13] of DBSCAN. RIC and SYNC were provided in Java, and the remaining algorithms were provided in MATLAB. Given the heterogeneous implementations (interpreted vs compiled languages, and varied levels of optimization), we focus only on the asymptotic trends.

We use the same generative model as that described in Section 6.1. By scaling the number of objects per cluster we are able to scale n (the noise percentage is fixed at 80%).

We see linear run-time behavior in m for all algorithms (except perhaps SYNC). Run-time growth for increasing k is between zero (e.g. DBSCAN) and linear. SKINNYDIP's run-time grows sub-linearly with k (linear growth is only expected for pathological cases).

Interestingly, the SKINNYDIP results show a practically *linear* growth in n. Our theoretical bound has an additional

[13]Package *dbscan* on CRAN.

Data set (n, m)	Whites. 56,2	Derm. 358,34	Im-seg. 210,19	Maps 429,3	Seeds 210,7	Coalit. 340,7	Motor 94,3	Soy. Lg. 266,62	Prest. 98,5	Pen dig. 7494,16
SkinnyDip	**1.000**	**0.638**	**0.552**	**0.804**	0.534	**0.579**	**1.000**	0.554	**0.540**	0.647
STSC	0.272	0.296	0.211	0.434	0.436	0.297	**1.000**	0.238	0.311	**0.769**
PgMeans	0.000	0.571	*0.000	0.801	0.043	0.317	**1.000**	*0.000	0.365	0.619
DipMeans	0.000	0.296	0.210	0.066	0.000	0.313	**1.000**	0.319	0.448	0.605
Sync	0.122	0.608	*0.000	0.649	0.483	0.340	0.727	0.005	0.517	0.537
DBSCAN	0.254	0.620	0.399	0.754	0.453	0.385	**1.000**	0.294	0.479	0.692
RIC	0.000	0.053	0.444	0.001	0.000	0.575	0.536	**0.611**	0.000	0.002
FOSSCLU	0.493	0.324	0.000	0.536	**0.566**	0.271	0.727	0.000	0.410	0.694

Table 1: Real-world results (AMI value). *Three failed due to non-trivial bugs in provided implementations.

logarithmic factor which we expected to materlialize from the need to sort. This curious result was explained by isolated tests of the optimized R sorting routine used in our SkinnyDip implementation: it appears to manage ("near")-linear run-time growth in many "average" practical cases.

We see *quadratic* growth in n for many of the comparison techniques (e.g. DBSCAN and Sync). We note that the use of appropriate data structures (e.g. *kd*-tree) can reduce the growth of DBSCAN to sub-quadratic in n. The "slowest" of the competition based on our measurements is STSC: the computation of its locally-scaled affinity matrix is very expensive. The run-time growth of the provided implementation is cubic in n, rendering it intractable for us to collect enough measurements on the scale used.

Overall, the practical run-time growth of SkinnyDip is within our predicted bounds. These low bounds, coupled with its freedom from convergence-based processes, renders it a strong candidate for work on the large-scale.

7. DISCUSSION AND RELATED WORK

We now turn to a discussion of SkinnyDip and its results in the context of related work. Many papers have been published on the broad subject of clustering, so we must filter known techniques considering the properties of our proposed technique and the kinds of data on which it performs well.

Perhaps the most practically-relevant criteria by which to filter algorithms is the nature and count of the required parameters. SkinnyDip is practically parameter-free, so we select prominent representatives that require neither obscure parameters nor additional processing (e.g. hierarchical methods require some additional mechanism for transforming a dendrogram to a flat clustering). It is in this light that we find PgMeans [8], a wrapper for automating EM clustering. It uses the Kolmogorov-Smirnov statistical test for selecting the most appropriate model, and was shown to outperform the earlier techniques G-Means [7] and X-Means [12]. We also find the recent DipMeans [10] technique – a wrapper for automating techniques of the k-means family. DipMeans is one of the few data-mining contributions that has explored the use of the dip test, albeit in a different manner. In DipMeans, data points are *viewers* and the dip is used to test whether or not the distribution of distance measurements (e.g. Euclidean) from a viewer is multimodal. Information about the cluster structure can be extracted by these means, however the technique suffers from the *viewer-selection* problem which requires enumeration of all data set objects and the computation of multivariate distances for each (time complexity unfortunately quadratic in n). It is also clear that such techniques do not have a clear concept of noise, but even if we ignore noise in our quality measurements (as in our synthetic experiments) we still see these techniques fail because of model- and distance-assumptions.

We also find Sync [2] and RIC [1] as two further approaches to automated clustering. Sync regards each object as a kind of "phase oscillator" which can change its position as clusters (the count of which is determined automatically through the MDL principle) converge toward so-called *local perfect synchronization* over time. Sync uses ideas from density-based clustering (like the ϵ-neighborhood) and exhibits some the same weaknesses (reliance on distance calculations, standard time complexity in $\mathcal{O}(n^2)$). RIC is designed to be a wrapper for arbitrary clustering techniques, starting with a preliminary clustering and refining it based on information-theoretical concepts. Unfortunately it meets difficulties when the amount of noise in the data set is non-trivial: for almost all our experiments the number of clusters detected was one (giving an AMI value of zero).

In the area of spectral clustering, we compare to the prominent *self-tuning* method (STSC) of Zelnik-Manor and Perona [15], which is automatically able to select the appropriate scale of analysis and the number of clusters using a *local* scale approach with affinities. STSC obtained a good result on the Pen-Digits data set, but was otherwise unable to differentiate itself from the other techniques (particularly on the challenging, highly-noisy synthetic cases).

The density-based technique DBSCAN is not strictly automatic (arguably unfair on the other techniques), but is nonetheless a useful comparison because is has a clear concept of noise. DBSCAN requires the parameters ϵ and *minPts*. Our running example showed that the well-known limitations of DBSCAN (finding clusters of varying density) are magnified when the data set also contains large amounts of noise. Run-time can additionally be a limiting factor for implementations without optimized index structures.

We are aware of two techniques which specifically focus on high levels of noise. In [4] the authors consider the problem of detecting minefields and seismic faults from "cluttered" data. Despite it being restricted to the two-dimensional case ($m = 2$), we provide the results for a core part of their algorithm on our running-example data in the supplement for reference (its performance is similar to EM). The authors of the second work [14] likewise only provide demonstrations on problems with low-dimensionality (up to $m = 5$), but more critically require execution "with a sequence of hundreds of different values" for unwieldy algorithm parameters.

Our results on synthetic data showed that SkinnyDip has the ability to outperform the comparison techniques by a large margin. Here we focused on data of the kind where

SkinnyDip shines, that is, data which 1) contain clusters each taking a unimodal form in each coordinate direction (otherwise are arbitrarily shaped), 2) contain clusters potentially "close" to others, and 3) contain a very high percentage (e.g. 80%) of noise. The large margin by which SkinnyDip outperforms the competition on this data is more or less maintained as the cluster count and level of noise are varied. Large differences *between* the comparison techniques are not evident. One main reason for their failure can be seen with an investigation into the $k = 3$ case: the clusters here are three long rectangles (similar to that in our running example), which the comparison methods tend to group together as one (giving an AMI of zero). In the noise plot the performance of all methods stays relatively constant as noise is varied. The reason for this is that the AMI in this case is only considering those objects truly belonging to a cluster (Figure 2, in comparison, provides results for the case in which noise points are also considered).

With increasing dimension m, however, the limitations of SkinnyDip's heuristic begin to surface. Practically though, we argue that "real" clusterings seldom require representation in such a high-dimensional space. The results of our real-world experiments showed, for example, that the use of SparseDip on high-dimensional data achieved dimensionality reduction to levels at which SkinnyDip's heuristics function well.

These SkinnyDip results on the real-world data were generally pleasing. Here we also compared to the recent FOSSCLU (*Finding the optimal subspace for clustering*) technique [6] which likewise tames high-dimensional data sets by searching for an appropriate clustering basis. Here it is necessary to draw a line between *generalized subspace clustering* techniques (which we do not address) and techniques like SkinnyDip and FOSSCLU. Subspace clustering techniques seek a separate subspace for each cluster in the general case. SkinnyDip and FOSSCLU, in contrast, argue that it is more valuable to find a *single* basis for clustering as *both* the intra- and inter-cluster relationships can be interpreted [6].

Like all clustering techniques, SkinnyDip has **limitations**. Firstly, it is clear that the dip is designed for univariate data. At a fundamental level there will thus exist cases of information-loss through our univariate projections. With some work we can construct pathological examples where SkinnyDip fails (consider $D \in [0,1]^{n\times 2}$ with one uniform cluster filling $[0, \frac{1}{2}]^2$ and another filling $[\frac{1}{2}, 1]^2$). The use of these projections, however, clearly also has its advantages: through them SkinnyDip is faster and is liberated from the need to perform multivariate distance computations.

It is also clear that SkinnyDip starts as a "global" technique but becomes increasingly "local" as the recursion progresses. That is, as the depth of recursion increases, the fraction of data points that are actually considered by the dip decreases. Practically this is seldom a problem, but again we can construct pathological examples which exploit this weakness (consider a univariate sample with successive modes that are each 50% the height of their predecessor, for example). Other limitations of SkinnyDip are that 1) a permutation of the features in the data may affect the outcome, 2) its modal hyper-intervals cannot precisely model "rounded" patterns, and 3) it is generally restricted to continuous data.

8. CONCLUSION

As a novel approach to clustering, SkinnyDip has a unique set of properties. It is deterministic, makes no strict model assumptions, and performs no distance calculations. Practically it is automatic (requiring only a statistical significance threshold) and *fast*. Its secret is the multi-level exploitation of the statistical *dip test* of unimodality on univariate projections of the data, enabling it to fundamentally distinguish itself from centroid-, distribution-, density- and connectivity-based approaches. This same test can be used to find an intuitive and interpretation-friendly basis for clustering through the concept of multimodal projection pursuit.

SkinnyDip outperforms competing automated techniques particularly well when clusters have heterogeneous unimodal shapes and the environment is extremely noisy. Future work shall explore possibilities for mitigating some of the undesirable effects of using univariate projections.

9. REFERENCES

[1] C. Böhm, C. Faloutsos, J.-Y. Pan, and C. Plant. Robust information-theoretic clustering. In *KDD*, pages 65–75, 2006.

[2] C. Böhm, C. Plant, J. Shao, and Q. Yang. Clustering by synchronization. In *KDD*, pages 583–592, 2010.

[3] H.-J. Bungartz and M. Griebel. Sparse grids. *Acta numerica*, 13:147–269, 2004.

[4] A. Dasgupta and A. E. Raftery. Detecting features in spatial point processes with clutter via model-based clustering. *Journal of the American Statistical Association*, 93(441):294–302, 1998.

[5] M. Ester, H.-P. Kriegel, J. Sander, and X. Xu. A density-based algorithm for discovering clusters in large spatial databases with noise. In *KDD*, 1996.

[6] S. Goebl, X. He, C. Plant, and C. Bohm. Finding the optimal subspace for clustering. In *ICDM*, 2014.

[7] G. Hamerly and C. Elkan. Learning the k in k-means. *Advances in neural information processing systems*, 16:281, 2004.

[8] Y. F. G. Hamerly. Pg-means: learning the number of clusters in data. *Advances in neural information processing systems*, 19:393–400, 2007.

[9] J. A. Hartigan and P. Hartigan. The dip test of unimodality. *The Annals of Statistics*, 1985.

[10] A. Kalogeratos and A. Likas. Dip-means: an incremental clustering method for estimating the number of clusters. In *Advances in neural information processing systems*, pages 2393–2401, 2012.

[11] A. Krause and V. Liebscher. Multimodal projection pursuit using the dip statistic. *Preprint-Reihe Mathematik*, 13, 2005.

[12] D. Pelleg, A. W. Moore, et al. X-means: Extending k-means with efficient estimation of the number of clusters. In *ICML*, pages 727–734, 2000.

[13] D. Pflüger. *Spatially Adaptive Sparse Grids for High-Dimensional Problems.* Verlag Dr. Hut, München, Aug. 2010.

[14] W.-K. Wong and A. Moore. Efficient algorithms for non-parametric clustering with clutter. In *Proceedings of the 34th Interface Symposium*, 2002.

[15] L. Zelnik-Manor and P. Perona. Self-tuning spectral clustering. In *Advances in neural information processing systems*, pages 1601–1608, 2004.

Semi-Markov Switching Vector Autoregressive Model-Based Anomaly Detection in Aviation Systems

Igor Melnyk[1], Arindam Banerjee[1], Bryan Matthews[2], Nikunj Oza[2]
[1]Department of Computer Science and Engineering, Minneapolis, MN
[2]NASA Ames Research Center, Moffett Field, CA
{melnyk, banerjee}@cs.umn.edu, {bryan.l.matthews, nikunj.c.oza}@nasa.gov

ABSTRACT

In this work we consider the problem of anomaly detection in heterogeneous, multivariate, variable-length time series datasets. Our focus is on the aviation safety domain, where data objects are flights and time series are sensor readings and pilot switches. In this context the goal is to detect anomalous flight segments, due to mechanical, environmental, or human factors in order to identifying operationally significant events and highlight potential safety risks. For this purpose, we propose a framework which represents each flight using a semi-Markov switching vector autoregressive (SMS-VAR) model. Detection of anomalies is then based on measuring dissimilarities between the model's prediction and data observation. The framework is scalable, due to the inherent parallel nature of most computations, and can be used to perform online anomaly detection. Extensive experimental results on simulated and real datasets illustrate that the framework can detect various types of anomalies along with the key parameters involved.

Keywords

Graphical Model; Anomaly Detection; Time Series Analysis

1. INTRODUCTION

It is estimated that by 2040 the United States alone can expect an increase of more than 60% in the commercial air traffic [12]. The anticipated air traffic growth can lead to increased congestion on the ground and air, creating conditions for possible accidents. Noting this problem, air transportation authorities are engaged in research and development of the Next Generation Air Transportation System [13], the initiative to improve the air traffic control system by increasing its capacity and utilization. A part of this effort is devoted to the processing and analysis of the air traffic flight information, also known as Flight Operations Quality Assurance (FOQA) data [11], to detect issues in aircraft operation, study pilot-automation interaction problems, propose corrective actions and design new training procedures.

KDD '16, August 13-17, 2016, San Francisco, CA, USA
© 2016 ACM. ISBN 978-1-4503-4232-2/16/08...$15.00
DOI: http://dx.doi.org/10.1145/2939672.2939789

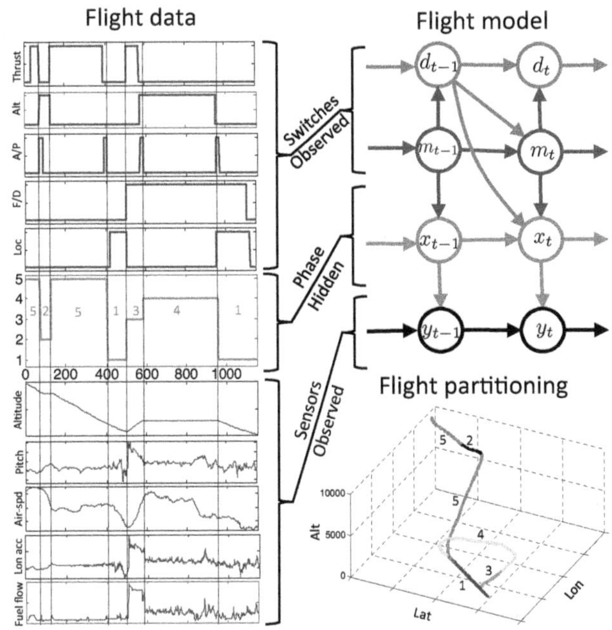

Figure 1: Representing heterogeneous flight data using SMS-VAR model. Left plot shows time evolution of several pilot switches, phase and sensor measurements during aircraft's landing. Top right plot shows the proposed model to represent such data. The bottom right graph shows the trajectory of aircraft, where its path is partitioned into phases. The value of the phases is obtained after constructing SMS-VAR on such data and running Viterbi algorithm to recover most probable phase path.

Therefore, the objective of our work is to develop a general framework to detect operationally significant events in the flight data due to mechanical, environmental or human factors. We are specifically interested in the scenarios when the data is *unlabeled*, i.e., there is no information which flights are normal and anomalous. Moreover, our interest is focused on the algorithms which can handle *variable-length*, *multivariate* and *heterogeneous* datasets.

The currently deployed automated methods for the analysis of FOQA data are exceedance-based approaches [32], [27], monitoring the normal operation of the flight using predefined ranges on the parameters. Although simple and fast, this approach is limited since it examines each feature independently, ignoring potential correlations among the parameters. Moreover, since the thresholds need to be defined upfront, the method can fail to discover previously unknown abnormal events. The proposed algorithms in current research literature (see Section 2) are also not adequate since they either cannot work with the data of mixed type or their approaches for handling such data still failing to uncover the underlying problem structure and thus achieve high anomaly detection performance.

To motivate our proposed approach, consider Figure 1, showing a real flight data and a model to represent it. On the left we plot a part of flight related to landing and show time series of several *pilot switches* (from top: thrust, altitude, autopilot, flight director, localizer) as well as some of the *sensors* (altitude, pitch angle, airspeed, longitudinal acceleration, fuel flow). The switches act as controls, determining the behavior of aircraft and sensors measure the effects of the controls on the system. A combination of the switches set by a pilot determines the aircraft's behavior for a certain period of time after which a different combination of switches defines another flight period and so on. Within each flight period, called a *phase* (shown in red on the left in Figure 1), the aircraft's dynamics usually remains consistent and steady, while across phases the dynamics change.

As an example, consider a lower right plot in Figure 1, showing aircraft's path as it descends from 10000 feet to a runway. The descent is interrupted by some event, causing it to fly back to a certain altitude, make a circle and repeat the landing. The path is partitioned into phases shown with different colors and numbers. For instance, phase 5 corresponds to a steady descent, where aircraft constantly loses altitude while maintaining its airspeed. This phases is interrupted by phase 2 of duration about 50 seconds, caused by a switch off in auto thrust system and activating hold altitude switch. In phase 2 the aircraft levels off by steadily increasing its pitch angle and losing airspeed.

Thus, if a flight is partitioned into multiple phases, determined by the pilot controls (switches), then the continuous dynamics of each phase can be represented separately by its own model. We propose to model such data with a dynamic Bayesian network - *semi-Markov switching vector autoregressive* (SMS-VAR) model, shown on the right plot of Figure 1. We note that our motivation comes from a rich literature of systems identification [23], where a standard approach for modeling continuous system dynamics (in our case the flight's sensor measurements) is a vector autoregressive model (VAR) [24]. However, as we discussed above, using a single VAR model for the entire flight is inappropriate, thus we employ multiple VARs. A change from one VAR process to another, i.e., the switching behavior, is modeled with a hidden variable x_t, representing a flight phase.

To model the dynamics of flight switches, we convert their representation from binary categorical into discrete, i.e., at each time stamp t a vector of zeros and ones (values of switches at t) is converted into an integer. We call the resulting variable a flight mode m_t and represent it using semi-Markov model (SMM) [19]. SMM is an extension of a simple Markov chain, allowing to model arbitrary state durations. A simple Markov chain has implicit geometric state duration distribution [29], causing fast state transitions and is inappropriate for our case. SMM fixes this by introducing a variable d_t which controls the duration of mode m_t.

To summarize, in this work we (i) propose to model multivariate, heterogeneous, variable-length flight data using SMS-VAR model (see Section 3 for a model description and parameter learning); (ii) present anomaly detection framework, based on the dissimilarity of one-step ahead predicted and filtered phase distributions, showing advantage over the standard likelihood-based approach (see Section 4 for details); (iii) provide extensive evaluations on synthetic and real data, including 20000 unlabeled flights, showing SMS-VAR outperforming many base line algorithms and accurately detecting different types of anomalies (see Section 6).

2. RELATED WORK

The problem of anomaly detection in aviation is an active area of research in the data mining community and has attracted attention of many researchers. For example, [31] considered a problem of detecting abnormal fuel consumption in jet engines. The method is based on using regression models to estimate consumed fuel and compare it to the observed to detect the abnormal behavior. It is a supervised approach since training requires anomaly-free data, limiting its practical application in cases when the labeled data is unavailable, as is the case in the present work.

In [16] the authors proposed an approach based on a specially designed linear regression model to describe the aerodynamic forces acting on an aircraft. However, the postulated model requires significant domain knowledge and careful design, limiting its generalization and usage in other anomaly detection problems.

The work of [21] presented a model-based framework to identify flight human-automation issues using switches data and sensor measurements. The anomaly is identified if there is a difference between inferred intents of the automation and the observed pilot actions. The limitation of this approach is that it assumes the data is noise-free and does not account for parameter uncertainties. Moreover, it is not clear how the algorithm performs on large flight data, since the presented evaluations are limited to a few examples.

Das et. al. [7] introduced MKAD, a multiple kernel learning approach for heterogeneous anomaly detection problems. The method constructs a kernel matrix as a convex combination of a kernel over discrete sequences and continuous time series. One-class SVM [30] is then used to detect anomalies. This method was applied to the FOQA dataset [26] to detect operationally significant events. Although it showed good results, the algorithm lacks scalability since the kernel matrix has to be updated for each new test flight.

The work of Li et. al. [22] proposed to detect anomalies in the flight data based on continuous and discrete features using a clustering approach, called ClusterAD. Their idea is to represent each flight as a vector, by concatenating all feature across time. After dimensionality reduction, the data is clustered based on Euclidean distance measure to identify outliers and groups of similar flights. A potential issue with this approach is a misalignment between time series from different flights. Since the size of the vectors needs to be the same for all flights, forcing such equality can introduce spurious dissimilarities, increasing false positives in the detected anomalies. Moreover, the study in [6] revealed that ClusterAD does not perform well on discrete anomalies as compared to MKAD. Partially, this is due to the use of Euclidean similarity measure on heterogeneous data vectors, making it less effective in finding discrete anomalies.

Summarizing the above literature and comparing to the proposed SMS-VAR model, we can make several remarks.

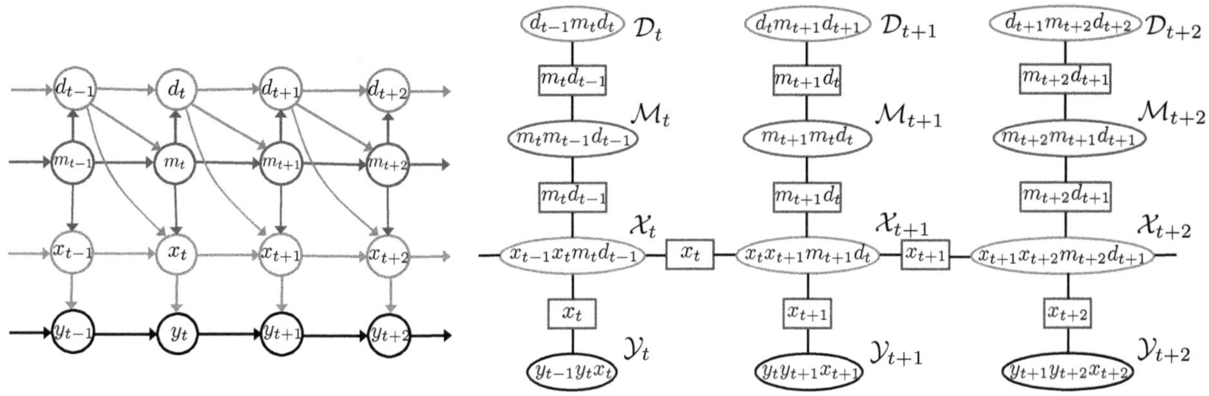

Figure 2: Left: Dynamic Bayesian Network of Semi-Markov Switching Vector Autoregressive Model (SMS-VAR). Right: Junction Tree for SMS-VAR. Ovals represent graph cliques, denoted by calligraphic letters $\mathcal{D}_t, \mathcal{M}_t, \mathcal{X}_t$, and $\mathcal{Y}_t$, rectangles denote separators. Symbols within shapes show variables on which the corresponding objects depend.

First, our method is unsupervised, thus it does not require a training set of labeled normal flights. Moreover, our framework works with multivariate and heterogeneous data, where each data sample can be of variable length. As compared to data-driven methods, our framework is model-based and therefore can be computationally more efficient in the detection stage by not requiring to recompute the model for each test flight. At the same time, the model construction requires only basic knowledge about the considered parameters and can easily be extended to other domains.

In particular, we would like to emphasize that the proposed SMS-VAR model is generic enough to be applicable in many other applications dealing with dynamic, multivariate, heterogeneous data streams, whose objective is to monitor behavior of the objects, discover meaningful patterns or detect anomalous events. For example, in healthcare applications [19] an SMS-VAR-type model using a record of many vital signs of a patient can be used to monitor the patient's health or detect any changes in his/her history. In activity recognition domain [10], multiple wearable sensors such as accelerometer, gyroscope or barometer can be used to track and recognize people's activities using similar types of models. In economics, detection of regime changes, patterns or trends in the financial markets [2] is frequently addressed with a semi-Markov switching autoregressive modeling.

3. SEMI-MARKOV SWITCHING VAR

In this Section we formally introduce the SMS-VAR model and show details about the parameter learning algorithm.

3.1 Model Specification

In this work we propose to model the flight of an aircraft using semi-Markov switching vector autoregressive model (SMS-VAR), whose Dynamic Bayesian Network (DBN) is shown in Figure 2. From the graphical model perspective, SMS-VAR has four classes of variables: continuous sensor measurements $y_t \in \mathbb{R}^{n_y}$, discrete phase $x_t \in \{1, \dots, n_x\}$, discrete mode, $m_t \in \{1, \dots, n_m\}$ and a positive real variable $d_t \in \mathbb{Z}_{\geq 0}$, determining the time duration of the mode and phase in a particular state. The SMS-VAR model is then fully defined by specifying the probability distributions which govern the time evolution of the above four variables. In particular, the probability distribution of mode transition is modeled as

$$p(m_t|m_{t-1}, d_{t-1}) = \begin{cases} p(m_t|m_{t-1}) & \text{if } d_{t-1} = 1 \\ \delta(m_t, m_{t-1}) & \text{if } d_{t-1} > 1 \end{cases}, \tag{1}$$

where $\delta(a, b)$ denotes the Dirac delta function: $\delta(a, b) = 1$ if $a = b$ and 0 otherwise. In essence, in this expression d_{t-1} works as a down counter for mode persistence, i.e., when $d_{t-1} > 1$, the mode is forced to remain unchanged: $m_t = m_{t-1}$. On the other hand, when $d_{t-1} = 1$, a new mode state m_t is determined by sampling from $p(m_t|m_{t-1}) \in \mathbb{R}^{n_m \times n_m}$, which is a 2-dimensional multinomial distribution. Note that to disallow self-transitions and ensure that mode changes to another state whenever $d_{t-1} = 1$, we set all the diagonal entries in $p(m_t|m_{t-1})$ to zero.

The duration variable d_t is modeled as

$$p(d_t|m_t, d_{t-1}) = \begin{cases} p(d_t|m_t) & \text{if } d_{t-1} = 1 \\ \delta(d_t, d_{t-1} - 1) & \text{if } d_{t-1} > 1 \end{cases}, \tag{2}$$

which means that as long as $d_{t-1} > 1$, we simply set $d_t = d_{t-1} - 1$. On the other hand, for $d_{t-1} = 1$, the new duration d_t is determined by sampling from $p(d_t|m_t)$, based on the current value of mode m_t. In this work we assume that

$$p(d_t|m_t) := P(d_t = k|m_t) = \frac{\lambda_{m_t}^k e^{-\lambda_{m_t}}}{k!}$$

is a Poisson distribution with $\lambda_{m_t} > 0$ and $k = 0, 1, 2, \dots$. Observe that d_t together with m_t define a semi-Markov process [19] (top two chains shown in the left plot of Figure 2), which has more flexibility in modeling mode durations as opposed to a simple Markov process, whose implicit mode duration is constrained to a geometric distribution [29].

The phase x_t is distributed according to the following transition model

$$p(x_t|x_{t-1}, m_t, d_{t-1}) = \begin{cases} p(x_t|x_{t-1}, m_t) & \text{if } d_{t-1} = 1 \\ \delta(x_t, x_{t-1}) & \text{if } d_{t-1} > 1 \end{cases}. \tag{3}$$

Here $p(x_t|x_{t-1}, m_t) \in \mathbb{R}^{n_x \times n_x \times n_m}$ is a 3-dimensional multinomial distribution of x_t: for each value of the mode m_t, there is a separate transition matrix defining the distribution of x_t, given x_{t-1}: $p(x_t|x_{t-1})$. It is invoked whenever the counter $d_{t-1} = 1$, otherwise the phase is forced to stay in the same state. We note that in contrast to the mode distribution in (1), here we allow self-transitions even when $d_{t-1} = 1$, i.e., $p(x_t|x_{t-1}, m_t)$ for each m_t can have non-zero diagonal. The idea behind this modeling step comes from the motivation to enable long-lasting phase persistence. In other words, although the mode can switch quickly to another state, the phase, on the other hand, has a flexibility to either remain unchanged or transition to another phase. In fact, this property of our model is precisely what enables to compress many mode states into a single phase, allowing the use of only a few VAR processes to model the data.

Finally, the sensor measurements are modeled using first-order VAR process:

$$y_t = A_{x_t} y_{t-1} + \epsilon_{x_t}, \tag{4}$$

where $A_{x_t} \in \mathbb{R}^{n_y \times n_y}$ is the VAR transition matrix and $\epsilon_{x_t} \sim \mathcal{N}(0, \Sigma_{x_t})$ is a Gaussian noise, uncorrelated in time t. The probability distribution of y_t then takes the form

$$p(y_t|y_{t-1}, x_t) \propto C e^{-\frac{1}{2}(y_t - A_{x_t} y_{t-1})^T \Sigma_{x_t}^{-1} (y_t - A_{x_t} y_{t-1})}, \tag{5}$$

for some normalization constant C. Note that for each value of the phase variable x_t, there is a separate VAR process with its own transition matrix and noise characteristics, which determines the time evolution of the vector y. In this work we assume that Σ_{x_t} is identity, thus the only unknown parameter in (5) is a transition matrix A_{x_t}. Each VAR process is assumed to be stable [24], i.e., all the eigenvalues of A_{x_t} have magnitude less than 1.

We remark on several important points about our model. (i) SMS-VAR is similar but different from Markov switching autoregressive model [17], also known in literature as hybrid, switching state-space models or jump-linear systems [14]. The main difference is that the switching dynamics is governed by a hierarchy of observed, m_t, and unobserved, x_t semi-Markov processes, rather than a single unobserved Markov process. (ii) We could have defined our model without a phase x_t, where the mode m_t would directly determine the active VAR process. However, whenever any of the switches change its state, there would be a transition to a different VAR. This is a bad design since the transitions would be too frequent and the number of VARs would be too large. Including phase x_t, which depends on mode m_t and duration d_t, enables data compression since not every switch change would result in the phase change. This behavior is observed on the left of Figure 1, where phase 5 is insensitive to a change in auto thrust around $t = 50$, similarly phase 1 around $t = 1200$ stays same, although some switches change. (iii) Evaluations of the flight dataset based on correlogram [24] revealed that sample autocorrelation functions of the time series exhibit a fast decay beyond the first lag. i.e., there are no long-range interaction between two events far away from each other. Therefore, the use of first-order dependency in our model is adequate to represent the data. Based on this, we position SMS-VAR as a short-memory model [18] and the proposed anomaly detector in Section 4 specifically targets short-term anomaly events.

3.2 Parameter Learning

Given data $D = \{F^1, \ldots, F^N\}$, consisting of N time series $F^i = \{\bar{d}_1^i, \ldots, \bar{d}_{T_i}^i, \bar{m}_1^i, \ldots, \bar{m}_{T_i}^i, \bar{y}_1^i, \ldots, \bar{y}_{T_i}^i\}$, (bar over the variable means that it is observed), our objective here is to estimate the parameters of SMS-VAR model:

$$\Theta = \{p(m_t|m_{t-1}), p(x_t|x_{t-1}, m_t), \lambda_{m_t}, A_{x_t}\}. \tag{6}$$

Since the data related to hidden phase $X^i = \{x_1^i, \ldots, x_{T_i}^i\}$ is unobservable, the standard approach is to use Expectation-Maximization (EM) algorithm [9]. The idea is to find Θ, which maximizes likelihood of all the observed and unobserved data $p\left(F^{1:N}, X^{1:N} \middle| \Theta\right)$. Assuming that we have an initial estimate of parameters Θ_0, the EM algorithm consists of iterating the following two steps until convergence:

- *E*-step: $Q(\Theta,\Theta_k) = \mathbb{E}_{X^{1:N}}\left[\log p\left(F^{1:N}, X^{1:N} \middle| \Theta\right) \middle| F^{1:N}, \Theta_k\right]$
- *M*-step: $\Theta_{k+1} = \arg\max_{\Theta} Q(\Theta, \Theta_k)$.

Note that the *E*-step is executed for each flight independently, while in *M*-step the resulting probability information from all flights is collected to update the model parameters.

Also, observe that the execution of EM for the considered model can be challenging since the nodes in DBN are of mixed data type, complicating the inference in *E* and optimization in *M* steps. However, exploiting the fact that d_t, m_t and y_t are observable, we can compute both steps very efficiently.

3.2.1 E-step

Given the parameter specifications in Section 3.1, the *E*-step can be efficiently computed using Junction Tree algorithm [3]. Specifically, based on the DBN structure of the model on the left plot of Figure 2, we construct its junction tree (JT), shown on the right plot of Figure 2. JT is simply a tree-structured representation of the graph, which helps to decompose the global computations of joint probability $p\left(F^{1:N}, X^{1:N} \middle| \Theta\right)$ into a linked set of local computations.

Each oval node in junction tree in Figure 2, representing cliques in the graph of SMS-VAR, is initialized with a value of the corresponding probability distribution. For example, a node $\mathcal{D}_t$ is initialized with the value of duration distribution $p(\bar{m}_t|\bar{m}_{t-1}, \bar{d}_{t-1})$ in (2). Similarly, $\mathcal{M}_t$, $\mathcal{X}_t$, and $\mathcal{Y}_t$ are initialized by evaluating (1), (3) and (5) on the data.

After all the N trees are initialized with the data $D = \{F^1, \ldots, F^N\}$, the operation of Junction Tree algorithm to compute *E*-step consists of propagating messages forward in time (form $t = 1$ to $t = T_i$) and backward in time (form $t = T_i$ to $t = 1$). For example, at iteration k, the result of forward propagation is the computation of likelihood of data $p(F^{1:N}|\Theta_k)$, while the backward propagation computes $p(x_t, x_{t+1}|F^{1:N}, \Theta_k)$ and $p(x_t|F^{1:N}, \Theta_k)$ for each t.

Note that since d_t, m_t and y_t are observable, the computational complexity of the *E*-step is $\mathcal{O}(n_x^2 \sum_i^N T_i)$, mainly determined by the operations on the messages involving x_t.

3.2.2 M-step

The result of *E*-step is now used to update the parameter estimates Θ in (6). We note that since phase x_t is the only unobservable part of the model, the only parameters that are re-estimated are phase transition distribution $p(x_t|x_{t-1}, m_t)$ and VAR transition matrices A_{x_t}. The other parameters, i.e., mode and duration distributions, depend on variables which are completely observable and estimated directly from data once and never re-estimated during EM iterations.

To estimate phase transition distribution $p(x_t|x_{t-1}, m_t)$, it can be shown that optimization problem $\arg\max_{\Theta} Q(\Theta, \Theta_k)$ amounts to estimating for each value of m_t the transition matrix $p(x_t|x_{t-1})$ by multiplying matrices $p(x_t, x_{t+1}|F^1 : F^N, \Theta_k)$ across those time steps t at which m_t matches the mode value $\bar{m}_t$ in the data.

The solution of $\arg\max_{\Theta} Q(\Theta, \Theta_k)$ for A_{x_t} can be shown to be equivalent to a solution of a least-square problem for each $x_t \in \{1, \ldots, n_x\}$. Specifically, using $p(x_t|F^{1:N}, \Theta)$ from the results of E-step, we weight each sample vector $\bar{y}_t$ with a scalar $w_t = p(x_t|F^{1:N}, \Theta)$ for one of the x_t: $\bar{y}'_t = w_t\bar{y}_t$. Then for each weighted data sequence $\bar{y}'_t, \ldots, \bar{y}'_{T_i}$, $i = 1 \ldots, N$ we can stack the vectors as in expression (4) in a matrix form and write the following system of equations

$$\begin{bmatrix}\bar{y}_2'^T & \bar{y}_3'^T & \ldots & \bar{y}_{T_i}'^T\end{bmatrix}^T = \begin{bmatrix}\bar{y}_1'^T & \bar{y}_2'^T & \ldots & \bar{y}_{T_i-1}'^T\end{bmatrix}^T A_{x_t}^T.$$

In compact notations above can be written as $Y_i = M_iB$, where $Y_i, M_i \in \mathbb{R}^{L_i \times n_y}$ and $B = A_{x_t}^T \in \mathbb{R}^{n_y \times n_y}$ for $L_i = T_i - 1$. Now stacking together the equations for all N data sequences, we get $[Y_1^T, \ldots, Y_N^T]^T = [M_1^T, \ldots, M_N^T]^T B$, which again can be compactly written as a matrix equation $Y = MB$, where $Y, M \in \mathbb{R}^{L \times n_y}$ for $L = \sum_{i=1}^N L_i$. Now vectorizing (column-wise) each matrix in $Y = MB$, we get

$$\begin{aligned}\text{vec}(Y) &= (I_{n_y \times n_y} \otimes M)\text{vec}(Y)\\ \mathbf{y} &= Z\boldsymbol{\beta},\end{aligned}$$

where now $\mathbf{y} \in \mathbb{R}^{Ln_y}$, $Z = (I_{n_y \times n_y} \otimes M) \in \mathbb{R}^{Ln_y \times n_y^2}$, $\boldsymbol{\beta} \in \mathbb{R}^{n_y^2}$ and $\otimes$ is the Kronecker product. Consequently, $\boldsymbol{\beta}$ (rows of A_{x_t} stacked in a vector) is estimated by solving

$$\arg\min_{\boldsymbol{\beta}} \frac{1}{L}\|\mathbf{y} - Z\boldsymbol{\beta}\|_2^2. \tag{7}$$

Note that matrix Z in (7) can become very tall in cases when there are many data sequences N, each of large length T_i. The standard approaches of estimating $\boldsymbol{\beta}$, based on regular QR decomposition [15], become impractical. For this purpose, in practice, we use the approach of [8] based on Tall and Skinny QR (TSQR), which enables to perform QR of a tall matrix in a block-by-block manner. The computational cost of the M-step is $\mathcal{O}(Ln_y^5 n_x)$ determined by the solution of (7) for each of n_x phases.

To summarize, the execution of the above two steps can be computed in an efficient, parallel manner. For instance, E step is completely separable across flights and although M step (main computation is (7)), requires synchronization, it can also be distributed with the use of parallel QR [8].

4. ANOMALY DETECTION FRAMEWORK

Given a dataset of N *unlabeled* flights our objective is to detect which of them deviate from the normal behavior the most. Since there is no a-priori knowledge on which flights belong to which category, we cannot build a separate model for each class. Our approach is to construct a single SMS-VAR model using *all* flight data and then evaluate the built model on *all* the flights to detect anomalies. Assuming that the fraction of anomalous flights in the dataset is small, we expect that the constructed model mostly represents a typical normal aircraft behavior and is not significantly influenced by the abnormal data. See Section 6.1.2 for further discussion of this point.

Evaluation of the constructed model on the flights is a critical step of the approach since it determines the detection accuracy of the framework. One simple and straightforward choice is the computation of likelihood of each flight. For example, given estimated model parameters Θ, we can compute the likelihood of the data of flight i (dropping i related to the numbering of time series to avoid clutter)

$$\begin{aligned}p(F) &= p(\bar{d}_{1:T}, \bar{m}_{1:T}, \bar{y}_{1:T}) = \\ &= p(\bar{d}_1, \bar{m}_1, \bar{y}_1) \prod_{t=2}^{T} p(\bar{d}_t, \bar{m}_t, y_t|\bar{d}_{1:t-1}, \bar{m}_{1:t-1}, \bar{y}_{1:t-1})\end{aligned} \tag{8}$$

where $p(\bar{d}_t, \bar{m}_t, \bar{y}_t|\bar{d}_{1:t-1}, \bar{m}_{1:t-1}, \bar{y}_{1:t-1})$ is the likelihood of observation at t given data seen so far. At each time stamp we can monitor the flight and flag down the times when probability drops to small values, signaling of anomalous activity. However, as we subsequently show in Section 6, this metric did not perform well as compared to the approach we propose in this work and discuss below.

Our proposed method to monitor flight behavior is based on evaluating a discrepancy between one-step ahead predicted and the filtered phase distribution, i.e., after data observation. Specifically, assume that the current phase distribution x_t over $\{1, \ldots, n_x\}$ is $p(x_t|\bar{d}_{1:t}, \bar{m}_{1:t}, \bar{y}_{1:t})$. Then we can propagate this probability one step forward using estimated model parameters to get prior estimate of phase distribution at $t + 1$ (see left plot of Figure 2 for details):

$$\begin{aligned}&p(x_{t+1}|\bar{d}_{1:t}, \bar{m}_{1:t}, \bar{y}_{1:t}) = \\ &= \sum_{d_{t+1}, m_{t+1}, x_t, y_{t+1}} p(d_{t+1}, m_{t+1}, x_t, x_{t+1}, y_{t+1}|\bar{d}_{1:t}, \bar{m}_{1:t}, \bar{y}_{1:t}) \\ &= \sum_{d_{t+1}, m_{t+1}, x_t, y_{t+1}} p(x_t|\bar{d}_{1:t}, \bar{m}_{1:t}, \bar{y}_{1:t})\ p(d_{t+1}|m_{t+1}, \bar{d}_t) \times \\ &\times p(m_{t+1}|\bar{m}_t, \bar{d}_t)\ p(x_{t+1}|x_t, m_{t+1}, \bar{d}_t)\ p(y_{t+1}|\bar{y}_t, x_{t+1}).\end{aligned} \tag{9}$$

At time $t + 1$ we observe data $\bar{m}_{t+1}$, $\bar{d}_{t+1}$, $\bar{y}_{t+1}$, and so the posterior (filtered) distribution of the phase changes to

$$\begin{aligned}&p(x_{t+1}|\bar{d}_{1:t+1}, \bar{m}_{1:t+1}, \bar{y}_{1:t+1}) = \\ &= \frac{p(\bar{d}_{t+1}, \bar{m}_{t+1}, x_{t+1}, \bar{y}_{t+1}|\bar{d}_{1:t}, \bar{m}_{1:t}, \bar{y}_{1:t})}{\sum_{x_{t+1}} p(\bar{d}_{t+1}, \bar{m}_{t+1}, x_{t+1}, \bar{y}_{t+1}|\bar{d}_{1:t}, \bar{m}_{1:t}, \bar{y}_{1:t})},\end{aligned} \tag{10}$$

where we computed

$$\begin{aligned}&p(\bar{d}_{t+1}, \bar{m}_{t+1}, x_{t+1}, \bar{y}_{t+1}|\bar{d}_{1:t}, \bar{m}_{1:t}, \bar{y}_{1:t}) = \\ &= \sum_{x_t} p(\bar{d}_{t+1}, \bar{m}_{t+1}, x_t, x_{t+1}, \bar{y}_{t+1}|\bar{d}_{1:t}, \bar{m}_{1:t}, \bar{y}_{1:t}) \\ &= \sum_{x_t} p(x_t|\bar{d}_{1:t}, \bar{m}_{1:t}, \bar{y}_{1:t})\ p(\bar{d}_{t+1}|\bar{m}_{t+1}, \bar{d}_t) \times \\ &\times p(\bar{m}_{t+1}|\bar{m}_t, \bar{d}_t)\ p(x_{t+1}|x_t, \bar{m}_{t+1}, \bar{d}_t)\ p(\bar{y}_{t+1}|\bar{y}_t, x_{t+1}).\end{aligned} \tag{11}$$

Next, given (9) and (10), i.e., the distribution of the hidden phase before and after observations at time $t + 1$, we compare these two distributions and measure their difference. For this purpose, we use Kullback–Leibler (KL) divergence, which is defined as

$$\begin{aligned}&D_{t+1}\left[p(x_{t+1}|F_{1:t})\middle\|p(x_{t+1}|F_{1:t+1})\right] = \\ &= \sum_{x_{t+1} \in \{1, \ldots, n_x\}} p(x_{t+1}|F_{1:t}) \log \frac{p(x_{t+1}|F_{1:t})}{p(x_{t+1}|F_{1:t+1})},\end{aligned} \tag{12}$$

where $F_{1:t}$ is a shorthand for $\{\bar{d}_{1:t}, \bar{m}_{1:t}, \bar{y}_{1:t}\}$, and similarly for $F_{1:t+1}$. Observe from (9) and (11) that information about all the observed variables, $\bar{d}_t$, $\bar{m}_t$ and $\bar{y}_t$ participate in the computation of the phase distribution. The prior $p(x_{t+1}|F_{1:t})$ reflects the model's belief based on data seen so far about the probability of which phase (i.e., VAR process) currently is active. After data observation, if the posterior $p(x_{t+1}|F_{1:t+1})$ shows a different phase distribution, then the distance measure (12) captures this by producing a large D_t. On the other hand, when both distributions are similar, it means the observed data are likely to have been generated from the model and the computed value D_t is small. Moreover, observe that incremental nature of the computation of D_t values implies that our approach can be used for *online* anomaly detection, i.e., algorithm can monitor a flight in real time, without the need to wait for all the data to arrive.

Finally, once we compute D_t's, the anomaly score S, characterizing the flight's abnormality, is obtained by computing a standard deviation (STD) of all D_t, i.e.,

$$S_{\text{KL}} = \frac{1}{T}\sum_{t=1}^{T}(D_t - \mu_D)^2, \quad (13)$$

where $\mu_D = \frac{1}{T}\sum_{t=1}^{T} D_t$. Thus, small values of S indicate normal flights, while large S correspond to anomalies. The computational complexity of the proposed detection step is $\mathcal{O}(Tn_x^2)$ to get (9) and (10) and $\mathcal{O}(Tn_x)$ to evaluate (13).

To motivate our choice for using STD, note that the first-order SMS-VAR is a short-memory model (see Section 3), which usually detects short-duration anomalies. Moreover, the values D_t, comparing phases at neighboring times, are sensitive to short-duration anomalies, and so for a typical abnormal flight, D_t usually stay small except for a few time stamps, at which anomaly events occurs and D_t spike. Therefore, STD which uses a sum of quadratic deviations, is sufficiently sensitive to outliers and can serve as an adequate summary measure. We note that detecting abnormal flights based on D_t values can be viewed as a separate outlier detection problem in univariate time-series. Various sophisticated approaches can be used for this, e.g., based on support vector regression [25], mixture transition distribution approach of [20] or a median information from the neighborhood [4], although we observed that a simple standard deviation performed well in practice.

5. COMPARED ALGORITHMS

In this Section we present an overview of the algorithms which we used in the comparison studies in Section 6.The five algorithms we considered were: SMS-VAR KL, based on KL divergence (discussed in Section 4), SMS-VAR based on log-likelihood, vector autoregressive (VAR) model, semi-Markov switching (SMM) model and the multiple kernel anomaly detector (MKAD).

SMS-VAR LL. This approach is based on estimating SMS-VAR using all the data points and evaluating the flights based on log-likelihood of data. However, instead of using $p(F)$ from (8) directly as a measure of abnormality, which usually washes out the events of interest and makes them undetectable; similarly as in (13) we used standard deviation, i.e., $S_{\text{LL}} = \frac{1}{T}\sum_{t=2}^{T}(\log \ell_t - \mu_\ell)^2$, where $\ell_t = p(\bar{d}_t, \bar{m}_t, \bar{y}_t|\bar{d}_{1:t-1}, \bar{m}_{1:t-1}, \bar{y}_{1:t-1})$ and μ_ℓ is the mean of ℓ_t's.

VAR. In this approach we modeled only the continuous part of the data using a single first-order VAR process $y_t = Ay_{t-1} + \epsilon_t$. The anomaly detection is based on computing $S_{\text{VAR}} = \frac{1}{T}\sum_{t=2}^{T}(r_t - \mu_r)^2$, where $r_t = \|y_t - \hat{A}y_{t-1}\|_2$ is a one-step-ahead prediction error, $\hat{A}$ is the estimated VAR matrix using all the data and μ_r is the mean.

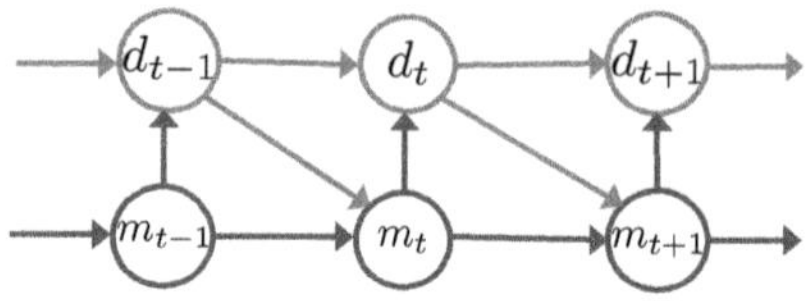

Figure 3: Semi-Markov Model.

SMM. An approach based on modeling only the discrete part of data is based on semi-Markov model shown in Figure 3. Here, similarly as in SMS-VAR, we modeled m_t and d_t using (1) and (2), respectively. The anomaly score is then computed as $S_{\text{SMM}} = \frac{1}{T}\sum_{t=2}^{T}(\ell_t - \mu_\ell)^2$, where $\ell_t = p(\bar{d}_t, \bar{m}_t|\bar{d}_{1:t-1}, \bar{m}_{1:t-1})$.

MKAD. This algorithm was designed to detect anomalies in the heterogeneous multivariate time series, where both discrete and continuous features are present. Let F^i and F^j denote the multivariate time series of two flights. The algorithm constructs a kernel of the form $K\left(F^i, F^j\right) = \alpha K_d\left(F^i, F^j\right) + (1-\alpha)K_c\left(F^i, F^j\right)$, where K_d is a kernel over discrete sequences and K_c is a kernel over continuous time series and $\alpha \in [0,1]$ is a weight, usually set to $\alpha = 0.5$. For discrete sequences, the normalized longest common subsequence (LCS) is used, i.e., $K_d\left(F^i, F^j\right) = \frac{|LCS(F^i,F^j)|}{\sqrt{T_i T_j}}$, where $|LCS(F^i, F^j)|$ denotes the length of LCS. For continuous sequences, the kernel $K_c\left(F^i, F^j\right)$ is inversely proportional to the distance between symbolic aggregate approximation (SAX) representation [28] of continuous sequences in F^i and F^j. The constructed kernel $K \in \mathbb{R}^{N \times N}$, N is the number of flights, is then used in one-class support vector machine (SVM) to construct a hyperplane to separate anomalous and normal flights.

6. EXPERIMENTAL RESULTS

In this Section we present extensive evaluations of the SMS-VAR model on both synthetic as well as real flight data. We compare the performance of the proposed approach with the four alternatives described in Section 5.

6.1 Synthetic Data

In the first simulation scenario we study detection accuracy of all the algorithms when presented with different types of anomalies, while in the second study we examine how the proportion of anomalous to normal flights affects the detection accuracy of SMS-VAR algorithm. We note that the synthetic data was generated by sampling from a set of suitably defined SMS-VAR models.

6.1.1 Detecting Different Types of Anomalies

We generated three synthetic datasets consisting of 100 normal flights and 10 anomalous, each of length 200 time stamps. The number of phases and sensor measurements in the generation model was set, respectively, to $n_x = 3$ and $n_y = 4$. The number of binary switches was set to 5, which corresponds to $n_m = 2^5 = 32$. In each dataset, the 10 abnormal flights represented a different type of anomaly.

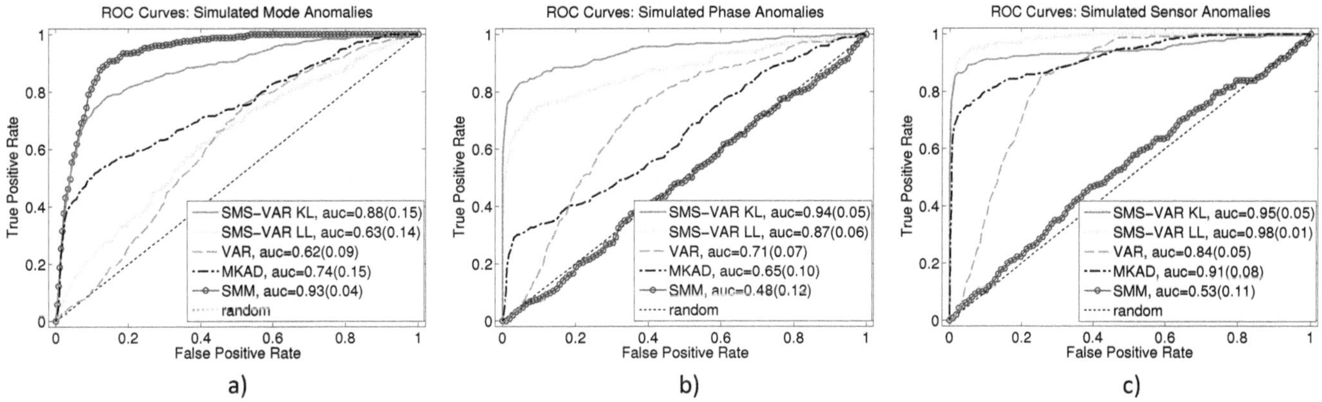

Figure 4: Performance of the five algorithms at detecting three simulated types of anomaly events: a) Mode anomaly, b) Phase anomaly, c) Sensor anomaly. There were 100 normal and 10 anomalous flights in each considered scenario. The evaluation was done using the area under ROC curve (AUC). The AUC values are shown after averaging the results over 30 runs, the values in parenthesis show one standard deviation.

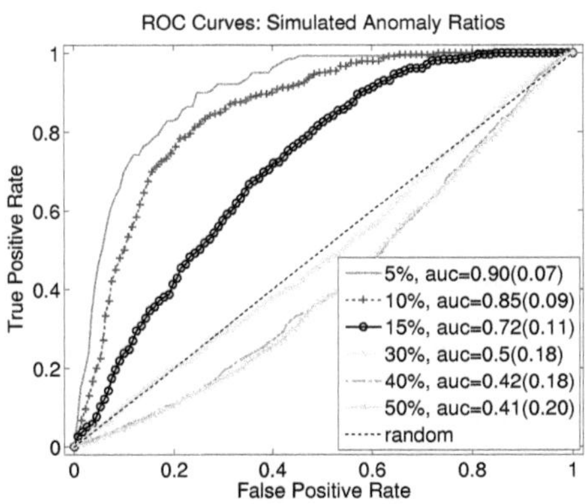

Figure 5: Anomaly detection accuracy of SMS-VAR KL when applied to datasets with different proportion of anomalous data ($5\% - 50\%$ of normal data is replaced with anomalous). Total number of flights in all scenarios is 100.

In the first dataset, each anomalous flight contained several mode anomalies, i.e., unusual flips of switches, while the continuous sensor measurements behaved normally. In the second dataset, we simulated unusual change of unobserved phases, i.e., at several time stamps one VAR process switched to another VAR process. Note that in this scenario all the measurements related to a particular VAR process were normal except that the change in underlying dynamics was abnormal. Finally, in the third dataset we simulated errors in sensor measurements (continuous data), while the mode transitions behaved normally.

The results are shown in Figure 4. It can be seen from Figure 4-a that the discrete anomaly detector SMM had the highest accuracy for detecting mode anomalies, followed by SMS-VAR and others. Since the dataset contained only discrete anomalies, it is expected that SMM performed the best. It was also expected that SMM would do poorly on the other two datasets since it could not use the information from sensor measurements. Similarly, the VAR model-based anomaly detector did not do well on the first dataset in Figure 4-a but improved its accuracy in Figures 4-b, c. MKAD algorithm, using both discrete and continuous data, achieved medium level accuracy in detecting discrete anomalies and did well on the dataset with errors in sensor measurements (we used a SAX window of size 2, since anomalies are of short duration). The algorithm, on the other hand, was insensitive to unusual phase changes in the data.

In contrast, the SMS-VAR-based algorithm, which fuses information from both sources of measurements is able to detect the anomalous flights with high accuracy across all the datasets. Moreover, the anomaly detection approach based on KL measure performed better than the log-likelihood measure (LL) on first and second datasets and did slightly worse on the third one, confirming that it is a viable method to detect abnormal activities.

6.1.2 Effect of Anomaly Proportion on Accuracy

In this study we investigate the validity of the assumption made in Section 4, where we mentioned that for our anomaly detection approach to be accurate, the fraction of anomalous flights should not be large. For this purpose we generated a set of datasets of same size but with different proportion ($5\% - 50\%$) of anomalous sequences. The simulated anomaly type was related to unusual switch changes; the parameter dimensions in the generation model remained the same as above. Results are shown in Figure 5. It can be seen that when the number of irregular data sequences is small ($5\% - 15\%$), the algorithm's detection accuracy is high (AUC value is $0.9 - 0.7$). On the other hand, as we replace more and more normal flights with anomalous, the accuracy drops. This can be explained by noting that SMS-VAR is built using all the data, so when the fraction of anomalous flights is large, the constructed model represents now a typical *anomalous* behavior. For example, in Figure 5 we see that when 50% or more flights are anomalous, the algorithm prediction flips and it starts classifying normal flights as anomalous.

6.2 Real Flight Data

In this section we present the evaluation results of the considered approaches on the FOQA flight dataset from a partner airline company (a similar, publicly available flight dataset can be found at [1]). The data contains over a million flights, each having a record of about 300 parameters, including sensor readings, control inputs and weather information, sampled at 1 Hz. Out of 300 parameters, we selected 31 continuous ones related to aircraft's sensor measurements and 18 discrete binary parameters related to pilot switches.

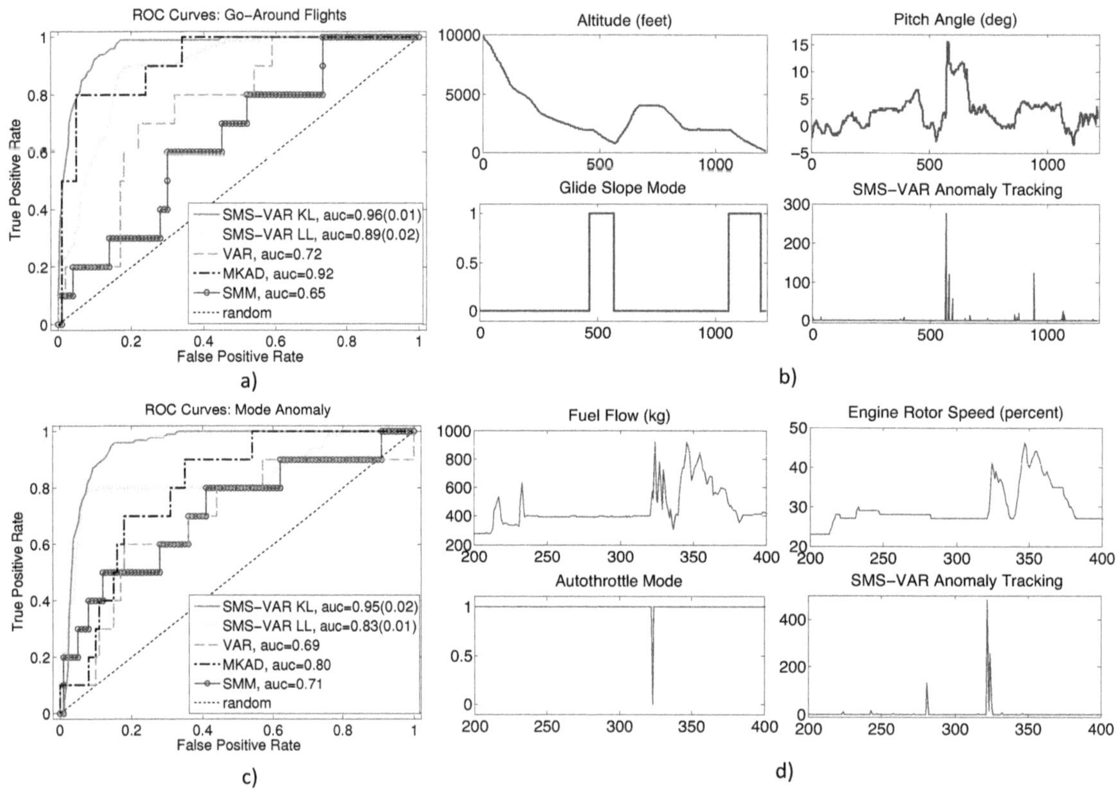

Figure 6: Performance of the five approaches at detecting go-around (top) and mode anomaly (bottom) flights. There were 100 regular and 10 anomalous flights in each dataset. Figures a) and c) show ROC curves for each method. AUCs shown after averaging over 30 runs for SMS-VAR, for other methods no averaging is done since they are deterministic. Figure b) shows an example of SMS-VAR KL detecting a typical go-around flight with a history of some of the parameters. Figure d) shows detection of a typical mode anomaly flight.

Therefore, the model dimensions are $n_y = 18$ and $n_m = 2^{18}$. Note that although 18 binary features correspond potentially to $2^{18} = 262144$ unique combinations, however the number of such values in real data is much smaller, since only few combinations of binary flight switches are possible. For example, in the dataset consisting of 20000 flights, used in Section 6.2.2, only 673 unique modes exist (0.3% of 262144). The number of hidden phases was set to $n_x = 5$, after some preliminary experiments in which we tested several n_x in range $[3, 20]$ and selected n_x balancing a good prediction accuracy with low computational complexity of algorithm. We have selected flights with landings at the same destination airport with aircrafts of the same fleet and type, so that we eliminate potential differences related to aircraft dynamics or landing patterns. Data analysis focused on a portion of the flight below 10000 feet until touchdown (duration 600-1500 time stamps), usually having the highest rates of accidents [5].

The evaluation of the algorithms is first done by using two small datasets (110 flights each) of manually labeled flights (Section 6.2.1), while in the second study we use a large dataset in a more realistic scenario with no information about flights' labels (Section 6.2.2). In the second case the shown results are only qualitative since no ground truth is available but the discoveries were validated by the domain experts.

6.2.1 Labeled Flights

Go-Around. For this study we manually selected flights, which abort their normal landing, fly back up to a certain altitude and try to repeat the landing again (see Figure 1 for an example). These flights are considered operationally significant anomalies since they could be executed in response to an emergency or unsafe conditions in the air or on the runway. The dataset included 10 go-around and 100 normal flights. The results are shown in Figure 6. In particular, from Figure 6-a we see that SMS-VAR and MKAD performed similar, with SMS-VAR based on KL measure achieving the highest accuracy of detection. Both SMM and VAR-based approaches, which used only part of data, performed worse, missing many go-around flights.

In Figure 6-b we also show a typical go-around flight and the corresponding history of D_t (see definition in (12)) values across the flight. Note that the go-around happens shortly after $t = 500$, when the altitude increases to about 5000 feet, coupled with unusual behavior in other parameters. For example, a glide slope mode was switched off, which typically is used to safely descend aircraft to a runway. Also, there was a sharp rise of pitch angle, corresponding to airplane's nose lifting up during ascent. The SMS-VAR KL model correctly detected these unusual changes with multiple spikes around the time the go-around was initiated.

Mode Anomaly. Additionally, we tested the performance of the algorithms on the real flight anomaly related to unusual auto-throttle switchings, whose example is shown in Figure 6-d. In particular, around $t = 400$ during aircraft's descent, one of the switches related to throttle control is switched off briefly ($2-5$ seconds). This action led to a fast

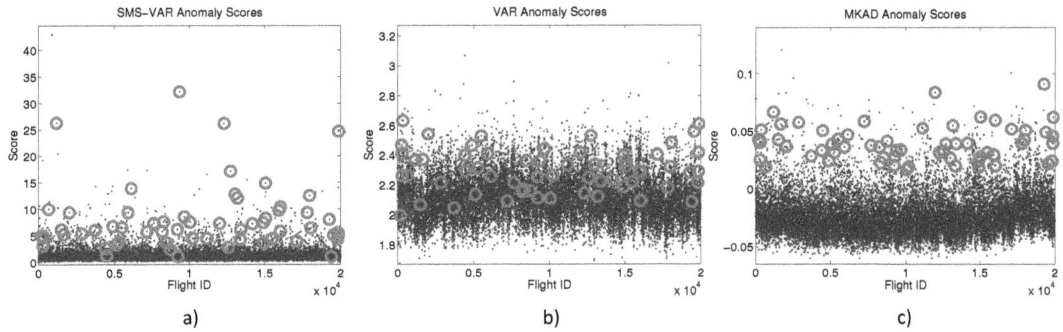

Figure 7: Anomaly scores of SMS-VAR KL, VAR and MKAD on unlabeled dataset consisting of 20000 flights. Red circles in all plots denote all the 61 go-around flights present in the 20000 flights.

SMS-VAR KL	VAR	MKAD
go-around (19)	go-around (3)	go-around (17)
high speed in approach (5)	fast approach (2)	high pitch at touch down (1)
high rate of descent in approach (4)	high speed in approach (5)	high speed in approach (2)
bounced landing (2)	high rate of descent in approach (4)	low speed at touch down (1)
delayed braking at landing(2)	bank cycling in approach(2)	low path in approach (1)
late retraction of landing gear (4)	high pitch at touch down (1)	flaps retracted in approach (1)
deviation from glide-slope (2)		unusual flight switch changes (15)
unusual flight switch changes (11)		

Table 1: Anomalies discovered in the top 100 anomalous flights, ranked by each anomaly detection method in the set of 20000 unlabeled flights. The distribution of anomaly scores for each method is shown in Figure 7.

spool up of engines (from 25% to 40% within few seconds). This abnormal behavior usually causes a quick increase of longitudinal acceleration leading to an abrupt forward motion of the aircraft. Similarly as before, we created a dataset consisting of 10 anomalous and 100 normal flights and the results are shown in Figure 6-c.

Interestingly, although the anomaly type was discrete, the simple SMM approach, which looks only at discrete part of data, did not perform well. Similarly, using only continuous features, the VAR algorithm also did poorly. When the information from both sources is combined, as was done in SMS-VAR KL or MKAD, the detection accuracy increased. Still, it can be seen that SMS-VAR KL performed better than other methods by a margin, justifying our proposed approach to track anomalies using the phase information.

6.2.2 Unlabeled Flights

Finally, we compared the algorithms' performance on a dataset containing 20000 unlabeled flights. We tested SMS-VAR KL and compared its performance with MKAD and VAR. Figure 7 shows the anomaly scores for the three approaches. For each method, we examined the top 100 flights with the highest anomaly scores to determine the flights with operationally significant events. In Table 1 we present a summary of the discovered anomalies, examined and validated by the experts. Note that since there is no ground truth available, the presented results are only *qualitative*.

As can be seen, among the top 100 flights, we found that the most common type of anomaly were the go-around flights, shown as red circles in Figure 7, as well as anomalies related to unusual pilot switches. The number of go-arounds detected by SMS-VAR and MKAD was similar, 19 and 17, respectively. The VAR-based approach only identified 3 such flights in its 100 top anomalous flight list. SMS-VAR and MKAD algorithms have additionally identified many flights with unusual changes in pilot switches, although these flights did not overlap. In particular, the anomalies identified by SMS-VAR are characterized by quick changes in the flight parameters (few seconds), e.g., the switchings in auto throttle system as in Figure 6-d or the flights when the localizer switch was turned off during approach resulting in large deviation from glide slope and these are difficult to detect using MKAD. The discrete anomalies identified by MKAD are of longer duration. For example, it found several flights when the flight director was switched off for over 2 minutes during the approach. It is an unusual behavior since, typically, flight director is used throughout the approach to assist the pilot with vertical and horizontal cues. Therefore, we can conclude that although achieving better performance in detecting certain types of anomalies, the proposed framework can be positioned as complementary to the existing state-of-the-art approaches, enabling the discoveries of more diverse spectrum of operationally significant events.

7. CONCLUSION

In this work we presented a novel framework for identifying operationally significant anomalies in the aviation systems based on representing each flight as SMS-VAR model. The anomaly detection is performed using a proposed approach comparing the phase distribution predicted by the model and the one suggested by the data. Extensive experimental tests have shown that the proposed approach has high detection accuracy of various aviation safety events. Moreover, the comparison to several algorithms showed that the proposed approach outperforms many baseline methods, it also achieves similar or better detection accuracy than MKAD, identifying itself as complimentary to current state-of-the-art methods. Going forward, we plan to extend our anomaly detection approach to include the ability to model long-duration anomaly events.

Acknowledgements

This work was supported by NASA grant NNX12AQ39A, NSF Grants IIS-0953274, IIS-1029711, IIS-0916750. We acknowledge the computing support from Minnesota Supercomputing Institute (MSI). A. B. acknowledges support from Adobe, IBM, and Yahoo.

8. REFERENCES

[1] NASA Flight Dataset. Available at https://c3.nasa.gov/dashlink/projects/85/.

[2] A. Ang and A. Timmermann. Regime changes and financial markets. Technical report, National Bureau of Economic Research, 2011.

[3] D. Barber. *Bayesian Reasoning and Machine Learning*. Cambridge University Press, 2012.

[4] S. Basu and M. Meckesheimer. Automatic outlier detection for time series: an application to sensor data. *Knowledge and Information Systems*, 11(2):137–154, 2007.

[5] Boeing. Statistical summary of commercial jet airplane accidents. Available at www.boeing.com/news/techissues/pdf/statsum.pdf, 2013.

[6] S. Das, L. Li, A. N. Srivastava, and R. J. Hansman. Comparison of algorithms for anomaly detection in flight recorder data of airline operations. In *AIAA Aviation Technology, Integration, and Operations Conference*, 2012.

[7] S. Das, B. Matthews, A. Srivastava, and N. Oza. Multiple kernel learning for heterogeneous anomaly detection: Algorithm and aviation safety case study. In *International Conference on Knowledge Discovery and Data Mining*, pages 47–56, 2010.

[8] J. Demmel, L. Grigori, M. Hoemmen, and J. Langou. Communication-optimal parallel and sequential QR and LU factorizations. *SIAM Journal on Scientific Computing*, 34(1):206–239, 2012.

[9] A. P. Dempster, N. M. Laird, and D. B. Rubin. Maximum likelihood from incomplete data via the EM algorithm. *Journal of the Royal Statistical Society*, pages 1–38, 1977.

[10] T. V. Duong, H. H. Bui, D. Q. Phung, and S. Venkatesh. Activity recognition and abnormality detection with the switching hidden semi-Markov model. In *Computer Vision and Pattern Recognition*, volume 1, pages 838–845, 2005.

[11] Federal Aviation Administration. Advisory circular. Flight operational quality assurance. *Federal Aviation Administration*, 12(2), 2004.

[12] Federal Aviation Administration. FAA Terminal area forecast summary report. Available at http://www.faa.gov/about/office_org/headquarters_offices/apl/aviation_forecasts/taf_reports/media/TAF_Summary_Report_FY2013-2040.pdf, 2013.

[13] Federal Aviation Administration. Next Generation Air Transportation System. Available at http://www.faa.gov/nextgen/, 2016.

[14] Z. Ghahramani and G. E. Hinton. Variational learning for switching state-space models. *Neural computation*, 12(4):831–864, 2000.

[15] G. H. Golub and C. F. Van Loan. *Matrix computations*. John Hopkins University Press, 3 edition, 2012.

[16] D. Gorinevsky, B. Matthews, and R. Martin. Aircraft anomaly detection using performance models trained on fleet data. In *Conference on intelligent data understanding*, pages 17–23, 2012.

[17] J. D. Hamilton. A new approach to the economic analysis of nonstationary time series and the business cycle. *Econometrica: Journal of the Econometric Society*, pages 357–384, 1989.

[18] U. Hassler. *Stochastic Processes and Calculus: An Elementary Introduction with Applications*. Springer, 2015.

[19] J. Janssen and N. Limnios. *Semi-Markov models and applications*. Springer Science & Business Media, 2013.

[20] N. D. Le, R. D. Martin, and A. E. Raftery. Modeling flat stretches, bursts outliers in time series using mixture transition distribution models. *Journal of the American Statistical Association*, 91(436):1504–1515, 1996.

[21] S. Lee, I. Hwang, and K. Leiden. Flight deck human-automation issue detection via intent inference. In *International Conference on Human-Computer Interaction in Aerospace*, 2014.

[22] L. Li, S. Das, H. John, R. Palacios, and A. Srivastava. Analysis of flight data using clustering techniques for detecting abnormal operations. *Journal of Aerospace Information Systems*, 12(9):587–598, 2015.

[23] L. Ljung. *System identification: theory for the user*. Springer, 1998.

[24] H. Lutkepohl. *New introduction to multiple time series analysis*. Springer, 2007.

[25] J. Ma and S. Perkins. Online novelty detection on temporal sequences. In *International Conference on Knowledge Discovery and Data Mining*, pages 613–618, 2003.

[26] B. Matthews, S. Das, K. Bhaduri, K. Das, R. Martin, and N. Oza. Discovering anomalous aviation safety events using scalable data mining algorithms. *Journal of Aerospace Information Systems*, 10(10):467–475, 2013.

[27] R. Nehl and J. Schade. Update: Concept and operation of the performance data analysis and reporting system (PDARS). In *Aerospace Conference*, pages 1–16, 2007.

[28] P. Patel, E. Keogh, J. Lin, and S. Lonardi. Mining motifs in massive time series databases. In *International Conference on Data Mining*, pages 370–377, 2002.

[29] S. M. Ross. *Introduction to probability models*. Academic press, 2014.

[30] B. Scholkopf, J. C. Platt, J. C. Shawe-Taylor, A. J. Smola, and R. C. Williamson. Estimating the support of a high-dimensional distribution. *Neural Computation*, 13(7):1443–1471, 2001.

[31] A. N. Srivastava. Greener aviation with virtual sensors: a case study. *Data Mining and Knowledge Discovery*, 24(2):443–471, 2012.

[32] I. C. Statler and D. A. Maluf. NASA's aviation system monitoring and modeling project. Technical report, NASA/TP–2007–214556, 2003.

Continuous Experience-aware Language Model

Subhabrata Mukherjee[†] Stephan Günnemann[‡] Gerhard Weikum[†]
[†]Max Planck Institute for Informatics, [‡]Technical University of Munich
smukherjee@mpi-inf.mpg.de, guennemann@in.tum.de, weikum@mpi-inf.mpg.de

Abstract

Online review communities are dynamic as users join and leave, adopt new vocabulary, and adapt to evolving trends. Recent work has shown that recommender systems benefit from explicit consideration of user experience. However, prior work assumes a fixed number of discrete experience levels, whereas in reality users gain experience and mature continuously over time.

This paper presents a new model that captures the *continuous evolution* of user experience, and the resulting *language model* in reviews and other posts. Our model is unsupervised and combines principles of Geometric Brownian Motion, Brownian Motion, and Latent Dirichlet Allocation to trace a smooth temporal progression of user experience and language model respectively. We develop practical algorithms for estimating the model parameters from data and for inference with our model (e.g., to recommend items). Extensive experiments with five real-world datasets show that our model not only fits data better than discrete-model baselines, but also outperforms state-of-the-art methods for predicting item ratings.

CCS Concepts

•Information systems → Recommender systems; •Mathematics of computing → Dimensionality reduction; •Human-centered computing → *Collaborative filtering; Social recommendation;*

Keywords

Review Community; User Experience; Language Evolution; Recommendation; Topic Modeling; Brownian Motion

1. INTRODUCTION

Motivation: Review communities about items like movies, cameras, restaurants, beer, newspapers and more are a key asset for recommender systems. State-of-the-art methods harness different signals for predictions: user-user and item-item similarities in addition to user-item ratings. These are typically cast into latent factor models [12] that exploit user-user interactions, user bias, bursty posting behavior and other community-level features (e.g., [11, 14, 7]). None of the above methods, however, consider the role of *user experience* and the *evolution* of how users mature over time. These dimensions have been recognized, investigated and incorporated into recommender models only recently by [15, 18].

KDD '16, August 13-17, 2016, San Francisco, CA, USA
© 2016 ACM. ISBN 978-1-4503-4232-2/16/08...$15.00
DOI: http://dx.doi.org/10.1145/2939672.2939780

Example: Experienced users often appreciate certain facets of an item differently from novices and amateurs. As users gain experience they mature, and may later appreciate these more intricate facets. Consider the following reviews about Christopher Nolan movies. The facet of interest is the (non-linear) narrative style.

- *User 1 on Memento (2001): "A story does not become interesting if told backwards."*
- *User 2 on The Dark Knight (2008): "Memento was very complicated. The Dark Knight was flawless. Heath Ledger rocks!"*
- *User 3 on Inception (2010): "Inception is a triumph of style over substance. It is complex only in a structural way, not in terms of plot. It doesn't unravel in the way Memento does."*

The first user does not appreciate complex narratives. The second user prefers simpler blockbusters. The third user seems to appreciate the non-linear narration style of Inception and, more so of Memento. In terms of maturity, we would consider User 3 to be more experienced in the underlying facet, and use this assessment when generating future recommendations to her or similar users.

State-of-the-Art and its Limitations: The evolution of user experience and how it affects ratings has first been studied in [15, 18]. However, these works make the simplifying assumption that user experience is categorical with discrete levels (e.g. $[1, 2, 3, \ldots, E]$), and that users progress from one level to the next in a discrete manner. As an artifact of this assumption, the experience level of a user changes abruptly by one transition. Also, an undesirable consequence of the discrete model is that all users at the same level of experience are treated similarly, although their maturity could still be far apart (if we had a continuous scale of measuring experience). Therefore, the assumption of *exchangeability* of reviews, for the latent factor model in [18], for users at the same level of experience may not hold as the language model changes.

The prior work [15] assumes user *activity* (e.g., number of reviews) to play a major role in experience evolution, which biases the model towards highly active users (as opposed to an experienced person who posts only once in a while). In contrast, our own prior work [18] captures *interpretable* evidence for a user's experience level using her vocabulary, cast into a language model with latent facets. However, this approach also exhibits the drawbacks of discrete levels of experience, as discussed above.

The current paper overcomes these limitations by modeling the evolution of user experience, and the corresponding language model, as a *continuous-time* stochastic process. We model time *explicitly* in this work, in contrast to the prior works.

Other prior work on item recommendation that considered review texts (e.g., [16], [23], [17]) did this with the sole perspective of learning topical similarities in a static snapshot-oriented manner, without considering time at all.

Approach and Technical Challenges: This paper is the first work to develop a continuous-time model of user experience and language evolution. Unlike prior work, we do not rely on explicit features like ratings or number of reviews. Instead, we capture a user's experience by a latent language model learned from the user-specific vocabulary in her review texts. We present a generative model where the user's experience and language model evolve according to a Geometric Brownian Motion (GBM) and Brownian Motion process, respectively. Analysis of the GBM trajectory of users offer interesting insights; for instance, users who reach a high level of experience progress faster than those who do not, and also exhibit a comparatively higher variance. Also, the number of reviews written by a user does not have a strong influence, unless they are written over a long period of time.

The facets in our model (e.g., narrative style, actor performance, etc. for movies) are generated using Latent Dirichlet Allocation. User experience and item facets are latent variables, whereas the observables are *words* at explicit *timepoints* in user reviews.

The parameter estimation and inference for our model are challenging since we combine discrete multinomial distributions (generating words per review) with a continuous Brownian Motion process for the language models' evolution, and a continuous Geometric Brownian Motion (GBM) process for the user experience.

Contributions: To solve this technical challenge, we present an inference method consisting of three steps: a) estimation of user experience from a user-specific GBM using the Metropolis Hastings algorithm, b) estimation of the language model evolution by Kalman Filter, and c) estimation of latent facets using Gibbs sampling. Our experiments, with real-life data from five different communities on movies, food, beer and news media, show that the three components *coherently* work together and yield a better fit of the data (in terms of log-likelihood) than the previously best models with discrete experience levels. We also achieve an improvement of ca. 11% to 36% for the mean squared error for predicting user-specific ratings of items compared to the baseline of [15, 18]. Finally, we present a use-case study with a news-media community, where experience-aware models can be used to identify experienced *citizen journalists* — where our method performs well in capturing user maturity.

In summary, our contributions are:

- Model: We devise a probabilistic model for tracing *continuous* evolution of *user experience*, combined with a language model for facets that explicitly captures smooth evolution over time.
- Algorithm: We introduce an effective learning algorithm, that infers each users' experience progression, time-sensitive language models, and latent facets of each word.
- Experiments: We perform extensive experiments with five real-word datasets, together comprising of 12.7 million ratings from 0.9 million users on 0.5 million items, and demonstrate substantial improvements of our method over state-of-the-art baselines.

The rest of the paper is organized as follows. Section 2 introduces the fundamental components for modeling the continuous evolution of user experience and language. Section 3 presents the generative model for the joint evolution of facets, experience, and language, and also our inference methods based on Markov Chain Monte Carlo (MCMC) sampling. Section 4 shows our experimental results, comparing our model against a variety of baselines. Section 5 discusses the use-case study, followed by related prior work.

2. MODEL COMPONENTS

2.1 Importance of Time

Previous works on experience evolution [15, 18] model time only implicitly by assuming the (discrete) latent experience to progress from one review to the next. In contrast, this current paper models time explicitly, and allows experience to *continuously* evolve over time — so that we are able to trace the joint evolution of experience, and vocabulary. This is challenging as the discrete Multinomial distribution based language model (to generate words) needs to be combined with a continuous stochastic process for experience evolution.

We use two levels of temporal granularity. Since experience is naturally continuous, it is beneficial to model its evolution at a very fine resolution (say, minutes or hours). On the other hand, the language model has a much coarser granularity (say, days, weeks or months). We show in Section 3 how to smoothly merge the two granularities using continuous-time models. Our model for language evolution is motivated by the seminal work of Wang and Blei et al. [21], with major differences and extensions. In the following subsections, we formally introduce the two components affected by time: the experience evolution and the language model evolution.

2.2 Continuous Experience Evolution

Prior works [15, 18] model experience as a discrete random variable . At each timepoint, a user is allowed to stay at level l, or move to level $l + 1$. As a result the transition is abrupt when the user switches levels. Also, the model does not distinguish between users at the same level of experience, (or even for the same user at beginning or end of a level) even though their experience can be quite far apart (if measured in a continuous scale). For instance, in Figure 1b the language model uses the same set of parameters as long as the user stays at level 1, although the language model changes. In order to address these issues, our goal is to develop a continuous experience evolution model with the following requirements:

- The experience value is always positive.
- Markovian assumption for the continuous-time process: The experience value at any time t depends only on the value at the *most recent observed time prior to t*.
- Drift: It has an overall *trend* to increase over time.
- Volatility: The evolution may not be smooth with occasional volatility. For instance, an experienced user may write a series of expert reviews, followed by a sloppy one.

To capture all of these aspects, we model each user's experience as a *Geometric Brownian Motion* (GBM) process (also known as Exponential Brownian Motion).

GBM is a natural continuous state alternative to the discrete-state space based Hidden Markov Model (HMM) used in our previous work [18]. Figure 1 shows a real-world example of the evolution of an experienced and amateur user in the BeerAdvocate community, as traced by our proposed model — along with that of its discrete counterpart from our previous work. The GBM is a stochastic process used to model population growth, financial processes like stock price behavior (e.g., Black-Scholes model) with random noise. It is a continuous time stochastic process, where the logarithm of the random variable (say, X_t) follows Brownian Motion with a *volatility* and *drift*. Formally, a stochastic process X_t, with an arbitrary initial value X_0, for $t \in [0, \infty)$ is said to follow Geometric Brownian Motion, if it satisfies the following Stochastic Differential Equation (SDE) [9]:

$$dX_t = \mu X_t dt + \sigma X_t dW_t \tag{1}$$

where, W_t is a Wiener process (Standard Brownian Motion); $\mu \in \mathbb{R}$ and $\sigma \in (0, \infty)$ are constants called the *percentage trend* and

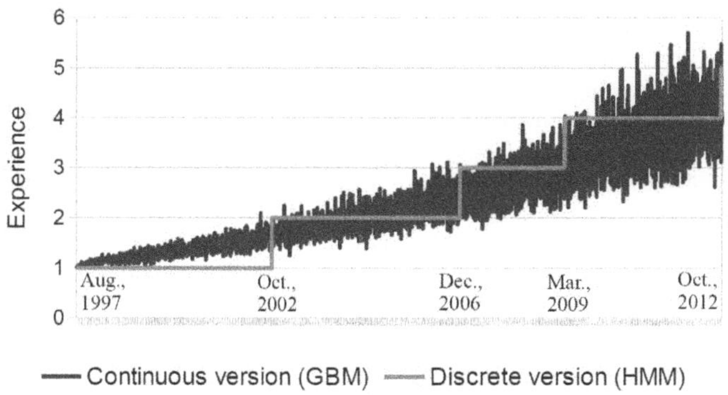

(a) Evolution of an experienced user.

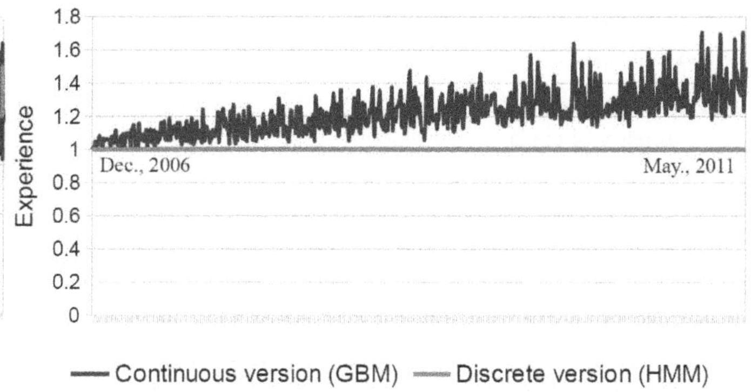

(b) Evolution of an amateur user.

Figure 1: Discrete state and continuous state experience evolution of some typical users from the BeerAdvocate community.

percentage volatility respectively. The former captures deterministic trends, whereas the latter captures unpredictable events occurring during the motion.

In a Brownian Motion trajectory, $\mu X_t dt$ and $\sigma X_t dW_t$ capture the "trend" and "volatility", as is required for experience evolution. However, in real life communities each user might show a different experience evolution; therefore our model considers a *multivariate* version of this GBM – we model one trajectory *per-user*. Correspondingly, during the inference process we learn μ_u and σ_u for each user u.

Properties: A straightforward application of *Itô's* formula yields the following analytic solution to the above SDE (Equation 1):

$$X_t = X_0\ exp((\mu - \frac{\sigma^2}{2})t + \sigma W_t) \tag{2}$$

Since $log(X_t)$ follows a Normal distribution, X_t is Log-Normally distributed with mean $\left(log(X_0) + (\mu - \frac{\sigma^2}{2})t\right)$ and variance $\sigma\sqrt{t}$. The probability density function $f_t(x)$, for $x \in (0, \infty)$, is given by:

$$f_t(x) = \frac{1}{\sqrt{2\pi t}\sigma x} exp\Big(- \frac{\left(log(x) - log\ (x_0) - (\mu - \frac{\sigma^2}{2})t\right)^2}{2\sigma^2 t} \Big) \tag{3}$$

It is easy to show that GBM has the Markov property. Consider $U_t = (\mu - \frac{\sigma^2}{2})t + \sigma W_t$.

$$\begin{aligned} X_{t+h} &= X_0 exp(U_{t+h}) \\ &= X_0 exp(U_t + U_{t+h} - U_t) \\ &= X_0 exp(U_t) exp(U_{t+h} - U_t) \\ &= X_t exp(U_{t+h} - U_t) \end{aligned} \tag{4}$$

Therefore, future states depend only on the future increment of the Brownian Motion, which satisfies our requirement for experience evolution. Also, for $X_0 > 0$, the GBM process is always positive. *Note* that the start time of the GBM of *each* user is relative to her first review in the community.

2.3 Experience-aware Language Evolution

Once the experience values for each user are generated from a Log-Normal distribution (more precisely: the experience of the user at the times when she wrote each review), we develop the language model whose parameters evolve according to the Markov property for experience evolution.

As users get more experienced, they use more sophisticated words to express a concept. For instance, experienced cineastes refer to a movie's "protagonist" whereas amateur movie lovers talk about the "hero". Similarly, in a Beer review community (e.g., BeerAdvocate, RateBeer) experts use more *fruity* words to describe a beer like "caramel finish, coffee roasted vanilla", "and citrus hops". Facet preferences of users also evolve with experience. For example, users at a high level of experience prefer "hoppiest" beers which are considered too "bitter" by amateurs [15]. Encoding explicit time in our model allows us to trace the evolution of vocabulary and trends *jointly* on the temporal and experience dimension.

Latent Dirichlet Allocation (LDA): In the traditional LDA process [2], a document is assumed to have a distribution over Z facets (a.k.a. topics) $\beta_{1:Z}$, and each of the facets has a distribution over words from a fixed vocabulary collection. The per-facet word (a.k.a topic-word) distribution β_z is drawn from a Dirichlet distribution, and words w are generated from a Multinomial(β_z).

The process assumes that documents are drawn *exchangeably* from the same set of facets. However, this process neither takes experience nor the evolution of the facets over *time* into account.

Discrete Experience-aware LDA: Our previous work [18] incorporates a layer for *experience* in the above process. The user experience is manifested in the set of facets that the user chooses to write on, and the vocabulary and writing style used in the reviews. The experience levels were drawn from a *Hidden Markov Model* (HMM). The reviews were assumed to be exchangeable for a user at the same level of experience – an assumption which generally may not hold; since the language model of a user at the same discrete experience level may be different at different points in time (refer to Figure 1b) (if we had a continuous scale for measuring experience). The process considers *time* only *implicitly* via the transition of the latent variable for experience.

Continuous Time LDA: The seminal work of Blei et. al in [1, 21] captures evolving content, for instance, in scholarly journals and news articles where the themes evolve over time, by considering time *explicitly* in the generative LDA process. Our language model evolution is motivated by their Continuous Time Dynamic Topic Model [1], with the major difference that the facets, in our case, evolve over both *time* and *experience*.

Continuous Experience-aware LDA (this work): Since the assumption of exchangeability of documents at the same level of experience of a user may not hold, we want the language model to explicitly evolve over experience and time. To incorporate the effect of changing experience levels, our goal is to condition the parameter evolution of β on the experience progression.

In more detail, for the language model evolution, we desire the following properties:

- It should *smoothly* evolve over time preserving the Markov property of experience evolution.
- Its variance should *linearly increase* with the *experience change* between successive timepoints. This entails that if the experience of a user does not change between successive timepoints, the language model remains almost the same.

To incorporate the temporal aspects of data, in our model, we use multiple distributions $\beta_{t,z}$ for each time t and facet z. Furthermore, to capture the smooth temporal evolution of the facet language model, we need to chain the different distributions to sequentially evolve over time t: the distribution $\beta_{t,z}$ should affect the distribution $\beta_{t+1,z}$.

Since the traditional parametrization of a Multinomial distribution via its mean parameters is not amenable to sequential modeling, and inconvenient to work with in gradient based optimization – since any gradient step requires the projection to the feasible set, the simplex — we follow a similar approach as [21]: instead of operating on the mean parameters, we consider the natural parameters of the Multinomial. The natural parameters are unconstrained and, thus, enable an easier sequential modeling.

From now on, we denote with $\beta_{t,z}$ the natural parameters of the Multinomial at time t for facet z. For *identifiability* one of the parameters $\beta_{t,z,w}$ needs to be fixed at zero. By applying the following mapping we can obtain back the mean parameters that are located on the simplex:

$$\pi(\beta_{t,z,w}) = \frac{exp(\beta_{t,z,w})}{1 + \sum_{w=1}^{V-1} exp(\beta_{t,z,w})} \quad (5)$$

Using the natural parameters, we can now define the facet-model evolution: The underlying idea is that strong changes in the users' experience can lead to strong changes in the language model, while low changes should lead to only few changes. To capture this effect, let $l_{t,w}$ denote the average experience of a word w at time t (e.g. the value of $l_{t,w}$ is high if many experienced users have used the word). That is, $l_{t,w}$ is given by the average experience of all the reviews D_t containing the word w at time t.

$$l_{t,w} = \frac{\sum_{d \in D_t : w \in d} e_d}{|D_t|} \quad (6)$$

where, e_d is the experience value of review d (i.e. the experience of user u_d at the time of writing the review).

The language model evolution is then modeled as:

$$\beta_{t,z,w} \sim Normal(\beta_{t-1,z,w}, \sigma \cdot |l_{t,w} - l_{t-1,w}|) \quad (7)$$

Here, we simply follow the idea of a standard dynamic system with Gaussian noise, where the mean is the value at the previous timepoint, and the variance increases linearly with increasing change in the experience. Thereby, the desired properties of the language model evolution are ensured.

3. JOINT MODEL FOR EXPERIENCE-LANGUAGE EVOLUTION

3.1 Generative Process

Consider a corpus $D = \{d_1, \ldots, d_D\}$ of review documents written by a set of users U at timestamps T. For each review $d \in D$, we denote u_d as its user, t'_d as the fine-grained timestamp of the review (e.g. minutes or seconds; used for experience evolution) and with t_d the timestamp of coarser granularity (e.g. yearly or monthly; used for language model evolution). The reviews are assumed to be ordered by timestamps, i.e. $t'_{d_i} < t'_{d_j}$ for $i < j$. We denote with $D_t = \{d \in D \mid t_d = t\}$ all reviews written at timepoint t. Each review $d \in D$ consists of a sequence of N_d words denoted by $d = \{w_1, \ldots, w_{N_d}\}$, where each word is drawn from a vocabulary V having unique words indexed by $\{1 \ldots V\}$. The number of facets corresponds to Z.

Let $e_d \in (0, \infty)$ denote the experience value of review d. Since each review d is associated with a unique timestamp t'_d and unique user u_d, the experience value of a review refers to the experience of the user at the time of writing it. In our model, each user u follows her own Geometric Brownian Motion trajectory – starting time of which is relative to the first review of the user in the community – parametrized by the mean μ_u, variance σ_u, and her *starting experience* value $s_{0,u}$. As shown in Equation 3, the analytical form of a GBM translates to a Log-Normal distribution with the given mean and variance. We use this user-dependent distribution to generate an experience value e_d for the review d written by her at timestamp t'_d.

Following standard LDA, the facet proportion θ_d of the review is drawn from a Dirichlet distribution with concentration parameter α, and the facet $z_{d,w}$ of each word w in d is drawn from a Multinomial(θ_d).

Having generated the experience values, we can now generate the language model and individual words in the review. Here, the language model $\beta_{t,z,w}$ uses the state-transition Equation 7, and the actual word w is based on its facet $z_{d,w}$ and timepoint t_d according to a Multinomial($\pi(\beta_{t_d,z_{d,w}})$), where the transformation π is given by Equation 5.

Note that technically, the distribution β_t and word w have to be generated simultaneously: for β_t we require the terms $l_{t,w}$, which depend on the experience and the words. Thus, we have a joint distribution $P(\beta_t, w|\ldots)$. Since, however, words are *observed* during inference, this dependence is not crucial, i.e. $l_{t,w}$ can be computed once the experience values are known using Equation 6.

We use this observation to simplify the notations and illustrations of Algorithm 1, which outlines the generative process, and Figure 2, which depicts it visually in plate notation for graphical models.

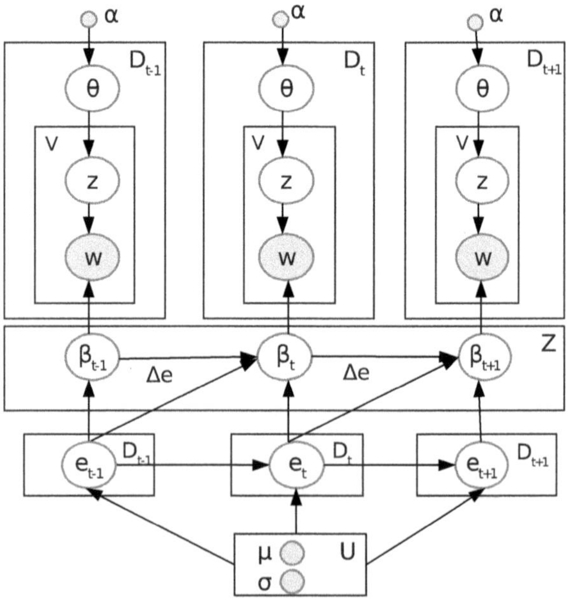

Figure 2: Continuous experience-aware language model. Words (shaded in blue), and timestamps (not shown for brevity) are observed.

Algorithm 1: Generative model for continuous experience-aware language model.

1. Set granularity t for language model evolution (e.g., years, months, days)
2. Set granularity for experience evolution, timestamp t' (e.g., minutes, seconds)

for *each coarse timepoint t* **do**
  for *each review* $d \in D_t$ **do**
    // retrieve user $u = u_d$ and fine-grained timepoint $t' = t'_d$
    3. Draw $e_d \sim \text{Log-Normal}((\mu_u - \frac{\sigma_u^2}{2})t' + log(s_{0,u}), \sigma_u\sqrt{t'})$
    4. Draw $\theta_d \sim \text{Dirichlet}(\alpha)$
    for *each word w in d* **do**
      5. Draw $z_{d,w} \sim \text{Multinomial}(\theta_d)$
    end
  end
  6. Draw $\beta_{t,z,w} \sim \text{Normal}(\beta_{t-1,z,w}, \sigma \cdot |l_{t,w} - l_{t-1,w}|)$
  for *each review* $d \in D_t$ **do**
    for *each word w in d* **do**
      7. Draw $w \sim \text{Multinomial}(\pi(\beta_{t_d, z_{d,w}}))$
    end
  end
end

3.2 Inference

Let E, L, Z, T and W be the set of experience values of all reviews, experience values of words, facets, timestamps and words in the corpus, respectively. In the following, d denotes a review and j indexes a word in it. θ denotes the per-review facet distribution, and β the language model respectively.

The joint probability distribution is given by:

$$P(E, L, Z, W, \theta, \beta | U, T; \alpha, \langle\mu\rangle, \langle\sigma\rangle) \propto \prod_{t \in T} \prod_{d \in D_t} P(e_d; s_{0,u_d}, \mu_{u_d}, \sigma_{u_d})$$
$$\cdot \left(P(\theta_d; \alpha) \cdot \prod_{j=1}^{N_d} P(z_{d,j}|\theta_d) \cdot P(w_{d,j}|\pi(\beta_{z_{d,j},t}))\right)$$
$$\cdot \left(\prod_{z \in Z} \prod_{w \in W} P(l_{t,w}; e_d) \cdot P(\beta_{t,z,w}; \beta_{t-1,z,w}, \sigma \cdot |l_{t,w} - l_{t-1,w}|)\right) \tag{8}$$

The exact computation of the above distribution is intractable, and we have to resort to approximate inference. Exploiting conjugacy of the Multinomial and Dirichlet distributions, we can integrate out θ from the above distribution. Assuming θ has been integrated out, we can decompose the joint distribution as:

$$P(Z, \beta, E, L | W, T) \propto P(Z, \beta | W, T) \cdot P(E | Z, \beta, W, T) \cdot P(L | E, W, T) \tag{9}$$

The above decomposition makes certain conditional independence assumptions in line with our generative process.

3.2.1 *Estimating Facets Z*

We use Collapsed Gibbs Sampling [5], as in standard LDA, to estimate the conditional distribution for each of the latent facets $z_{d,j}$, which is computed over the current assignment for all other hidden variables, after integrating out θ. Let $n(d, z)$ denote the count of the topic z appearing in review d. In the following equation, $n(d, .)$ indicates the summation of the above counts over all possible $z \in Z$. The subscript $-j$ denotes the value of a variable excluding the data at the jth position.

The posterior distribution $P(Z|\beta, W, T; \alpha)$ of the latent variable Z is given by:

$$\begin{aligned} &P(z_{d,j} = k | z_{d,-j}, \beta, w_{d,j}, t, d; \alpha) \\ &\propto \frac{n(d,k) + \alpha}{n(d,.) + Z \cdot \alpha} \cdot P(w_n = w_{d,j} | \beta, t, z_n = k, z_{-n}, w_{-n}) \\ &= \frac{n(d,k) + \alpha}{n(d,.) + Z \cdot \alpha} \cdot \pi(\beta_{t,k,w_n}) \end{aligned} \tag{10}$$

where, the transformation π is given by Equation 5.

3.2.2 *Estimating Language Model* β

In contrast to θ, the variable β cannot be integrated out by the same process, as Normal and Multinomial distributions are not conjugate. Therefore, we refer to another approximation technique to estimate β.

In this work, we use *Kalman Filter* [8] to model the sequential language model evolution. It is widely used to model linear dynamic systems from a series of observed measurements over time, containing statistical noise, that produces robust estimates of unknown variables over a single measurement. It is a continuous analog to the Hidden Markov Model (HMM), where the state space of the latent variables is continuous (as opposed to the discrete state-space HMM); and the observed and latent variables evolve with Gaussian noise.

We want to estimate the following state-space transition model:

$$\begin{aligned} \beta_{t,z,w} | \beta_{t-1,z,w} &\sim N(\beta_{t-1,z,w}, \sigma \cdot |l_{t,w} - l_{t-1,w}|) \\ w_{d,j} | \beta_{t,z,w} &\sim Mult(\pi(\beta_{t,z,w})) \text{ where, } z = z_{d,j}, t = t_d. \end{aligned} \tag{11}$$

However, unlike standard Kalman Filter, we do not have any *observed* measurement of the variables — due to the presence of *latent* facets Z. Therefore, we resort to *inferred* measurement from the Gibbs sampling process.

Let $n(t, z, w)$ denote the number of times a given word w is assigned to a facet z at time t in the corpus. Therefore,

$$\beta^{inf}_{t,z,w} = \pi^{-1}\left(\frac{n(t,z,w) + \gamma}{n(t,z,.) + V \cdot \gamma}\right) \tag{12}$$

where, we use the inverse transformation of π given by Equation 5, and γ is used for smoothing.

Update Equations for Kalman Filter: Let p_t and g_t denote the *prediction error*, and *Kalman Gain* at time t respectively. The variance of the process noise and measurement is given by the difference of the experience value of the word observed at two successive timepoints. Following standard Kalman Filter calculations [8], the predict equations are given by:

$$\begin{aligned} \widehat{\beta}_{t,z,w} &\sim N(\beta_{t-1,z,w}, \sigma \cdot |l_{t,w} - l_{t-1,w}|) \\ \widehat{p_t} &= p_{t-1} + \sigma \cdot |l_{t-1,w} - l_{t-2,w}| \end{aligned} \tag{13}$$

and the update becomes:

$$\begin{aligned} g_t &= \frac{\widehat{p_t}}{\widehat{p_t} + \sigma \cdot |l_{t,w} - l_{t-1,w}|} \\ \beta_{t,z,w} &= \widehat{\beta}_{t,z,w} + g_t \cdot (\beta^{inf}_{t,z,w} - \widehat{\beta}_{t,z,w}) \\ p_t &= (1 - g_t) \cdot \widehat{p_t} \end{aligned} \tag{14}$$

Thus, the new value for $\beta_{t,z,w}$ is given by Eq. 14.

If the experience does not change much between two successive timepoints, i.e. the variance is close to zero, the Kalman Filter just emits the counts as estimated by Gibbs sampling (assuming, $P_0 = 1$). This is then similar to the Dynamic Topic Model [1]. Intuitively, the Kalman Filter is smoothing the estimate of Gibbs sampling taking the experience evolution into account.

3.2.3 *Estimating Experience E*

The experience value of a review depends on the user and the language model β. Although we have the state-transition model of β, the previous process of estimation using Kalman Filter cannot be applied in this case, as there is no observed or inferred value of E. Therefore, we resort to Metropolis Hastings sampling. Instead of sampling the E's from the complex true distribution, we use a proposal distribution for sampling the random variables — followed by an acceptance or rejection of the newly sampled value. That is, at each iteration, the algorithm samples a value of a random variable — where the current estimate depends only on the previous estimate, thereby, forming a Markov chain.

Assume all reviews $\{\cdots d_{i-1}, d_i, d_{i+1} \cdots\}$ from all users are sorted according to their timestamps. As discussed in Section 2.1, for computational feasibility, we use a coarse granularity for the language model β. For the inference of E, however, we need to operate at the fine temporal resolution of the reviews' timestamps (say, in minutes or seconds). Note that the process defined in Eq. (7) represents the aggregated language model over multiple fine-grained timestamps. Accordingly, its corresponding fine-grained counterpart is $\beta_{t'_{d_i},z,w} \sim Normal(\beta_{t'_{d_{i-1}},z,w}, \sigma \cdot |e_{d_i} - e_{d_{i-1}}|)$ — now operating on t' and the review's individual experience values. Since the language model is given (i.e. previously estimated) during the inference of E , we can now easily refer to this fine-grained definition for the Metropolis Hastings sampling.

As the proposal distribution for the experience of review d_i at time t'_{d_i} , we select the corresponding user's GBM ($u = u_d$) and sample a new experience value $\widehat{e_{d_i}}$ for the review:

$$\widehat{e}_{d_i} \sim \text{Log-Normal}((\mu_u - \frac{\sigma_u^2}{2})t'_{d_i} + log(s_{0,u}), \sigma_u \sqrt{t'_{d_i}})$$

The language model $\beta_{t'_{d_i}}$ at time t'_{d_i} depends on the language model $\beta_{t'_{d_{i-1}}}$ at time $t'_{d_{i-1}}$, and experience value difference $|e_{d_i} - e_{d_{i-1}}|$ between the two timepoints. Therefore, a change in the experience value at any timepoint affects the language model at the *current* and next timepoint, i.e. $\beta_{t'_{d_{i+1}}}$ is affected by $\beta_{t'_{d_i}}$, too.

Thus, the acceptance ratio of the Metropolis Hastings sampling becomes:

$$Q = \prod_{w,z} \left[\frac{N(\beta_{t'_b,z,w}; \beta_{t'_a,z,w}, \sigma \cdot |\widehat{e_b} - e_a|)}{N(\beta_{t'_b,z,w}; \beta_{t'_a,z,w}, \sigma \cdot |e_b - e_a|)} \cdot \frac{N(\beta_{t'_c,z,w}; \beta_{t'_b,z,w}, \sigma \cdot |e_c - \widehat{e_b}|)}{N(\beta_{t'_c,z,w}; \beta_{t'_b,z,w}, \sigma \cdot |e_c - e_b|)} \right] \quad (15)$$

where $a = d_{i-1}$, $b = d_i$ and $c = d_{i+1}$. The numerator accounts for the modified distributions affected by the updated experience value, and the denominator discounts the old ones. Note that since the GBM has been used as the proposal distribution, its factor cancels out in the term Q.

Overall, the Metropolis Hastings algorithm iterates over the following steps:

1. Randomly pick a review d at time $t' = t'_d$ by user $u = u_d$ with experience e_d
2. Sample $\widehat{e_d} \sim \text{Log-Normal}\Big((\mu_u - \frac{\sigma_u^2}{2})t' + log(s_{0,u}), \sigma_u \sqrt{t'} \Big)$
3. Accept $\widehat{e_d}$ as the new experience with probability $P = min(1, Q)$

3.2.4 *Estimating Parameters for the Geometric Brownian Motion*

For each user u, the mean μ_u and variance σ_u of her GBM trajectory are estimated from the sample mean and variance.

Consider the set of all reviews $\langle d_t \rangle$ written by u, and $\langle e_t \rangle$ be the corresponding experience values of the reviews.

Let $\widehat{m}_u = \frac{\sum_{d_t} log(e_t)}{|d_t|}$, and $\widehat{s}_u^2 = \frac{\sum_{d_t} (log(e_t) - \widehat{m}_u)^2}{|d_t - 1|}$.

Furthermore, let Δ be the average length of the time intervals for the reviews of user u.

Now, $log(e_t) \sim N\big((\mu_u - \frac{\sigma_u^2}{2})\Delta + log(s_{0,u}), \sigma_u \sqrt{\Delta}\big)$.

From the above equations we can obtain the following estimates using Maximum Likelihood Estimation (MLE):

$$\begin{aligned} \widehat{\sigma}_u &= \frac{\widehat{s}_u}{\sqrt{\Delta}} \\ \widehat{\mu}_u &= \frac{\widehat{m}_u - log(s_{0,u})}{\Delta} + \frac{\widehat{\sigma}_u^2}{2} \\ &= \frac{\widehat{m}_u - log(s_{0,u})}{\Delta} + \frac{\widehat{s}_u^2}{2\Delta} \end{aligned} \quad (16)$$

3.2.5 *Overall Processing Scheme*

Exploiting the results from the above discussions, the overall inference is an iterative process consisting of the following steps:

1. Estimate facets Z using Equation 10.
2. Estimate β using Equations 13 and 14.
3. Sort all reviews by timestamps, and estimate E using Equation 15 and the Metropolis Hastings algorithm, for a random subset of the reviews.
4. Once the experience values of all reviews have been determined, estimate L using Equation 6.

4. EXPERIMENTS

We perform experiments with data from five communities in different domains:

- BeerAdvocate (`beeradvocate.com`) and RateBeer (`ratebeer.com`) for beer reviews
- Amazon (`amazon.com`) for movie reviews
- Yelp (`yelp.com`) for food and restaurant reviews
- NewsTrust (`newstrust.net`) for reviews of news media

Table 1 gives the dataset statistics[1]. We have a total of 12.7 million reviews from 0.9 million users over 16 years from all of the five communities combined. The first four communities are used for product reviews, from where we extract the following quintuple for our model $< userId, itemId, timestamp, rating, review >$. NewsTrust is a special community, which we discuss in Section 5.

4.1 Data Likelihood, Smoothness and Convergence

Inference of our model is quite involved with different Markov Chain Monte Carlo methods. It is imperative to show that the resultant model is not only stable, but also improves the log-likelihood of the data. Although there are several measures to evaluate the quality

[1] http://snap.stanford.edu/data/, http://www.yelp.com/dataset_challenge/, http://resources.mpi-inf.mpg.de/impact/credibilityanalysis/data.tar.gz

Dataset	#Users	#Items	#Ratings	#Years
Beer (BeerAdvocate)	33,387	66,051	1,586,259	16
Beer (RateBeer)	40,213	110,419	2,924,127	13
Movies (Amazon)	759,899	267,320	7,911,684	16
Food (Yelp)	45,981	11,537	229,907	11
Media (NewsTrust)	6,180	62,108	89,167	9
TOTAL	885,660	517,435	12,741,144	-

Table 1: Dataset statistics.

of facet models, we report the following from [20]: $LL = \sum_d \sum_{j=1}^{N_d} log\ P(w_{d,j}|\beta; \alpha)$. A higher likelihood indicates a better model.

Figure 3 contrasts the log-likelihood of the data from the continuous experience model and its discrete counterpart [18]. We find that the continuous model is stable and has a *smooth* increase in the data log-likelihood *per iteration.* This can be attributed to how smoothly the language model evolves over time, preserving the Markov property of experience evolution. Empirically our model also shows a fast convergence, as indicated by the number of iterations.

On the other hand, the discrete model not only has a worse fit, but is also less smooth. It exhibits abrupt state transitions in the Hidden Markov Model, when the experience level changes (refer to Figure 1). This leads to abrupt changes in the language model, as it is coupled to experience evolution.

4.2 Experience-aware Item Rating Prediction

In the first task, we show the effectiveness of our model for item rating prediction. Given a user u, an item i, time t, and review d with words $\langle w \rangle$ — the objective is to predict the rating the user would assign to the item based on her *experience*.

For prediction, we use the following features: The experience value e of the user is taken as the last experience attained by the user during training. Based on the learned language model β, we construct the language feature vector $\langle F_w = log(max_z(\beta_{t,z,w})) \rangle$ of dimension V (size of the vocabulary). That is, for each word w in the review, we consider the value of β corresponding to the best facet z that can be assigned to the word at the time t. We take the log-transformation of β which empirically gives better results.

Furthermore, as also done in the baseline works [15, 18], we consider: γ_g, the average rating in the community; γ_u, the offset of the average rating given by user u from the global average; and γ_i, the rating bias for item i.

Thus, combining all of the above, we construct the feature vector $\langle \langle F_w \rangle, e, \gamma_g, \gamma_u, \gamma_i \rangle$ for each review with the user-assigned ground rating for training. We use Support Vector Regression [4], with the same set of default parameters as used in our discrete model [18], for rating prediction.

4.2.1 Baselines

We consider baselines [b – e] from [15], and use their code[2] for experiments. Baseline (f) is our prior discrete experience model[18].

a) *LFM*: A standard latent factor recommendation model [10].

b) *Community at uniform rate*: Users and products in a community evolve using a single "global clock" [11, 26, 25], where the different stages of the community evolution appear at uniform time intervals.

c) *Community at learned rate*: This extends b) by learning the rate at which the community evolves with time, eliminating the uniform rate assumption.

d) *User at uniform rate*: This extends b) to consider individual users, by modeling the different stages of a user's progression based on preferences and experience levels evolving over time. The model assumes a uniform rate for experience progression.

e) *User at learned rate*: This extends d) by allowing the *experience* of each user to evolve on a "personal clock", where the time to reach certain (*discrete*) experience levels depends on the user [15]. This is reportedly the best version of their experience evolution models.

f) *Discrete experience model*: This is our prior work [18] on the discrete version of the experience-aware language model, where the experience of a user depends on the evolution of the user's maturing rate, facet preferences, and writing style.

4.2.2 Quantitative Results

Table 2 compares the *mean squared error (MSE)* for rating predictions in this task, generated by our model versus the six baselines. Our model outperforms all baselines — except in the NewsTrust community, performing slightly worse than our prior work [18] (discussed in Section 5) — reducing the MSE by ca. 11% to 36%. Our improvements over the baselines are statistically significant at 99% level of confidence determined by *paired sample t-test.*

For all models, we used the three most recent reviews of each user as withheld test data. All experience-based models consider the *last* experience value reached by each user during training, and the corresponding learned parameters for rating prediction. Similar to the setting in [15], we consider users with a minimum of 50 reviews. Users with less than 50 reviews are grouped into a background model, and treated as a single user. We set $Z = 5$ for BeerAdvocate, RateBeer and Yelp facets; and $Z = 20$ for Amazon movies and $Z = 100$ for NewsTrust which have richer latent dimensions. All *discrete* experience models consider $E = 5$ experience levels. In the continuous model, the experience value $e \in (0, \infty)$. We initialize the parameters for our joint model as: $s_{0,u} = 1, \alpha = 50/Z, \gamma = 0.01$. Our performance improvement is strong for the *BeerAdvocate* community due to large number of reviews per-user for a long period of time, and low for NewsTrust for the converse.

4.3 Qualitative Results

User experience progression: Figure 4 shows the variation of the users' *most recent* experience (as learned by our model), along with the number of reviews posted, and the number of years spent in the community. As we would expect, a user's experience increases with the amount of *time* spent in the community. On the contrary, number of reviews posted does not have a strong influence on experience progression. Thus, if a user writes a large number of reviews in a short span of time, her experience does not increase much; in contrast to if the reviews are written over a long period of time.

Figure 5 shows the variation of the users' *most recent* experience, along with the mean μ_u and variance σ_u of her Geometric Brownian Motion (GBM) trajectory — all learned during inference. We observe that users who reach a high level of experience progress faster (i.e. a higher value of μ_u) than those who do not. Experienced users also exhibit comparatively higher variance than amateur ones. This result also follows from using the GBM process, where the mean and variance tend to increase with time.

Language model evolution: Figure 6 shows the variation of the frequency of a word — used in the community in "2011" — with the *learned* experience value $l_{t,w}$ associated to each word. The plots depict a bell curve. Intuitively, the experience value of a word does not increase with general usage; but increases if it has been used by experienced users. Highlighted words in the plot give some interesting insights. For instance, the words "beer, head, place, food,

[2] Code available from http://cseweb.ucsd.edu/ jmcauley/code/

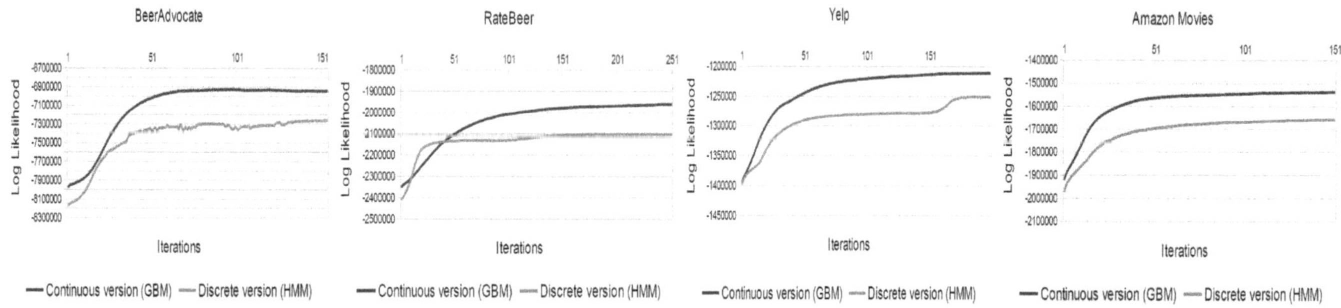

Figure 3: Log-likelihood per iteration of discrete [18] vs. continuous experience model (this work).

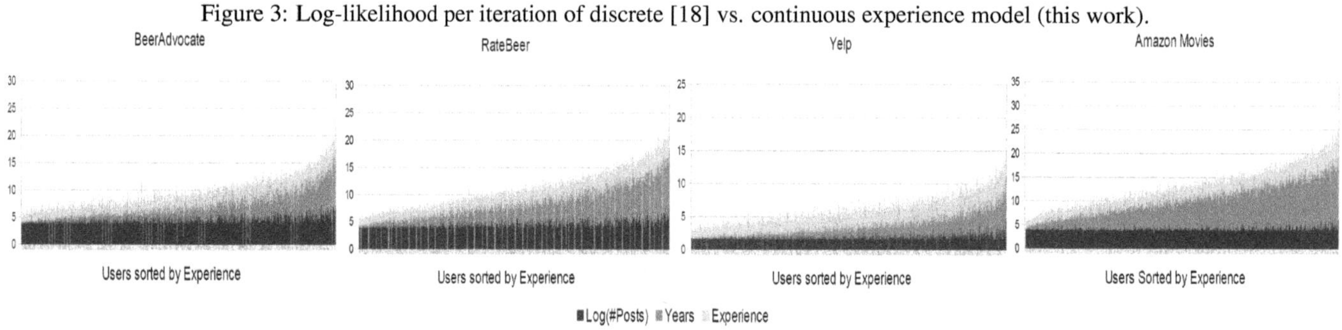

Figure 4: Variation of *experience* (e) with *years* and *reviews* of each user. Each bar in the above stacked chart corresponds to a user with her most recent experience, number of years spent, and number of reviews posted in the community.

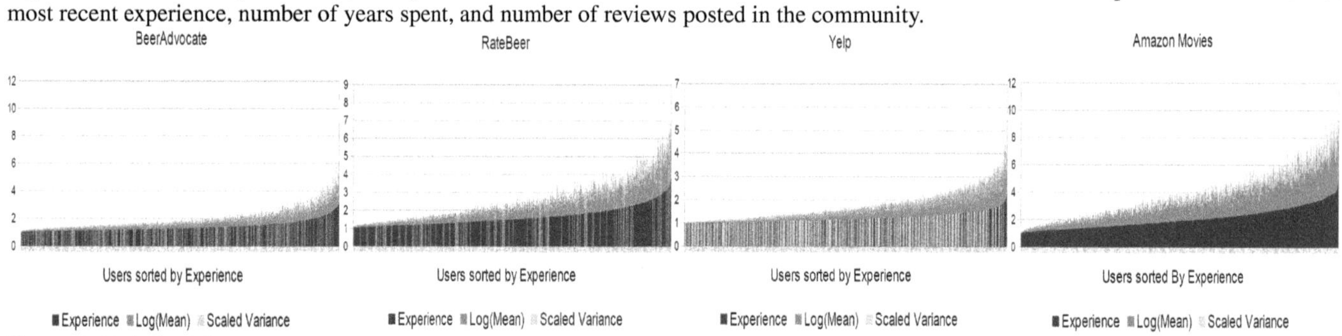

Figure 5: Variation of *experience* (e) with *mean* (μ_u) and *variance* (σ_u) of the GBM trajectory of each user (u). Each bar in the above stacked chart corresponds to a user with her most recent experience, mean and variance of her experience evolution.

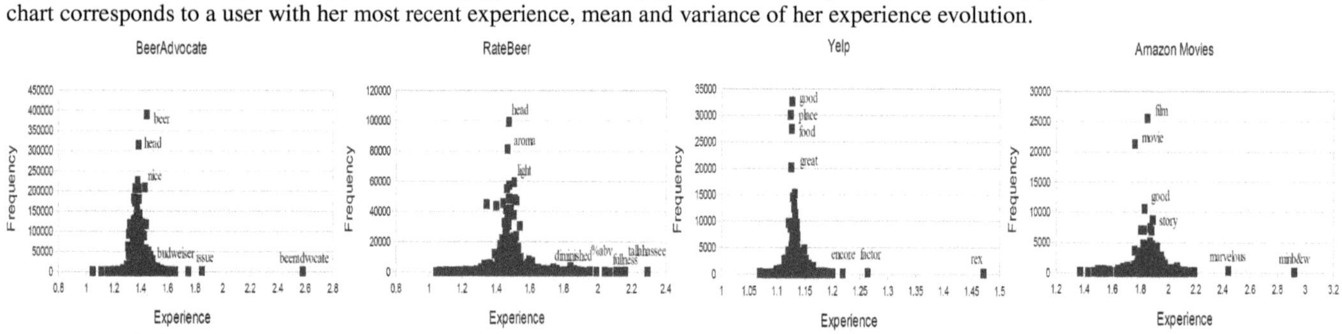

Figure 6: Variation of *word frequency* with *word experience*. Each point in the above scatter plot corresponds to a word (w) in "2011" with corresponding frequency and experience value ($l_{t=2011,w}$).

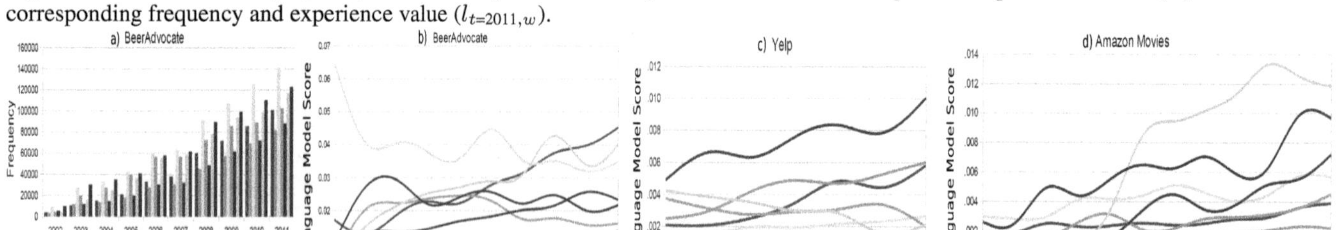

Figure 7: *Language model* score ($\beta_{t,z,w} \cdot l_{t,w}$) variation for sample words with *time*. Figure a) shows the count of some sample words over time in BeerAdvocate community, whose evolution is traced in Figure b). Figures c) and d) show the evolution in Yelp and Amazon Movies.

Models	BeerAdvocate	RateBeer	NewsTrust	Amazon	Yelp
Continuous experience model (this work)	**0.247**	**0.266**	0.494	**1.042**	**0.940**
Discrete experience model [18]	0.363	0.309	**0.464**	1.174	1.469
User at learned rate [15]	0.379	0.336	0.575	1.293	1.732
Community at learned rate [15]	0.383	0.334	0.656	1.203	1.534
Community at uniform rate [15]	0.391	0.347	0.767	1.203	1.526
User at uniform rate [15]	0.394	0.349	0.744	1.206	1.613
Latent factor model [12]	0.409	0.377	0.847	1.248	1.560

Table 2: Mean squared error (MSE) for rating prediction. Our model performs better than competing methods.

movie, story" etc. are used with high frequency in the beer, food or movie community, but have an average experience value. On the other hand specialized words like "beeradvocate, budweiser, %abv, fullness, encore, minb&w" etc. have high experience value.

Table 3 shows some top words used by *experienced* users and amateur ones in different communities, as learned by our model. Note that this is a ranked list of words with numeric values (not shown in the table). We see that experienced users are more interested about fine-grained facets like the mouthfeel, "fruity" flavors, and texture of food and drinks; narrative style of movies, as opposed to popular entertainment themes; discussing government policies and regulations in news reviews etc.

The word "rex" in Figure 6 in Yelp, appearing with low frequency and high experience, corresponds to a user "Rex M." with "Elite" status who writes humorous reviews with *self* reference.

Figure 7 shows the evolution of some sample words over *time* and experience (as given by our model) in different communities. The score in the *y-axis* combines the language model probability $\beta_{t,z,w}$ with the experience value $l_{t,w}$ associated to each word w at time t. Figure 7 a) illustrates the frequency of the words in BeerAdvocate, while their evolution is traced in Figure 7 b). It can be seen that the overall usage of each word increases over time; but the evolution path is different for each word. For instance, the "smell" convention started when "aroma" was dominant; but the latter was less used by *experienced* users over time, and slowly replaced by (increasing use of) "smell". This was also reported in [3] in a different context. Similarly "caramel" is likely to be used more by *experienced* users, than "flavor". Also, contrast the evolution of "bitterness", which is used more by experienced users, compared to "bitter".

In Yelp, we see certain food trends like "grilled" and "crispy" increasing over time; in contrast to a decreasing feature like "casino" for restaurants. For Amazon movies, we find certain genres like "horror, thriller" and "contemporary" completely dominating other genres in recent times.

5. USE-CASE STUDY

So far we have focused on traditional item recommendation for items like beers or movies. Now we switch to different kind of items - newspapers and news articles - by analyzing the NewsTrust online community (`newstrust.net`) (data available from [19]). It features news stories posted and reviewed by members, some of whom are professional journalists and content experts. Stories are reviewed based on their objectivity, rationality, and general quality of language to present an unbiased and balanced narrative of an event with focus on *quality journalism*. Unlike the other datasets, NewsTrust contains expertise of members that can be used as ground-truth for evaluating our model-generated *experience* values.

In our framework, each story is an item, which is rated and reviewed by a user. The facets are the underlying topic distribution of the reviews, with topics being *Healthcare, Obama Administration, NSA*, etc. The facet preferences can be mapped to the (political) polarity of users in this news community.

Most Experience	Least Experience
BeerAdvocate	
chestnut_hued near_viscous rampant_perhaps faux_foreign cherry_wood sweet_burning bright_crystal faint_vanilla boned_dryness woody_herbal citrus_hops mouthfeel	originally flavor color didnt favorite dominated cheers tasted review doesnt drank version poured pleasant bad bitter sweet
Amazon	
aficionados minimalist underwritten theatrically unbridled seamless retrospect overdramatic diabolical recreated notwithstanding oblivious featurettes precocious	viewer entertainment battle actress tells emotional supporting evil nice strong sex style fine hero romantic direction superb living story
Yelp	
rex foie smoked marinated savory signature contemporary selections bacchanal delicate grits gourmet texture exotic balsamic	mexican chicken salad love better eat atmosphere sandwich local dont spot day friendly order sit
NewsTrust	
health actions cuts medicare oil climate major jobs house vote congressional spending unemployment citizens events	bad god religion iraq responsibility questions clear jon led meaningful lives california powerful

Table 3: Top words used by experienced and amateur users.

Recommending News Articles. Our first objective is to recommend news to readers catering to their viewpoints, and experience. We apply our model with the same setting as with earlier datasets. The mean squared error (MSE) results were reported in Section 4. Our model clearly outperforms most of the baselines; it performs only slightly worse regarding our prior work [18] in this task — possibly due to high rating sparsity in face of a large number of model parameters.

Identifying Experienced Users. Our second task is to find experienced members of this community, who have the potential of being *citizen journalists*. In order to evaluate the quality of the ranked list of experienced users generated by our model, we consider the following proxy measure for user experience. In NewsTrust, users have *Member Levels* determined by the NewsTrust staff based on community engagement, time in the community, other users' feedback on reviews, profile transparency, and manual validation. We use these member levels to categorize users as *experienced* or *inexperienced*. This is treated as the ground truth for assessing the ranking quality of our model against the baseline models [15, 18] — considering top 100 users from each model ranked by experience. Here we consider the top-performing baseline models from the previous task. We report the *Normalized Discounted Cumulative Gain (NDCG)* and the *Normalized Kendall Tau Distance* for the ranked lists of users generated by all the models. The better model should exhibit higher *NDCG*, and lower *Kendall Tau Distance*. As Table 4 shows, our model outperforms baseline models in capturing user maturity.

6. RELATED WORK

State-of-the-art recommender systems [10, 12] harness user-user and item-item similarities by means of latent factor models. Time-dependent phenomena such as bursts in item popularity, bias in ratings, and the temporal evolution of user community are investigated in [11, 26, 25]. There is also prior work on anomaly detection [6,

Models	NDCG	Kendall Tau Normalized Distance
Continuous experience model (this work)	**0.917**	**0.113**
Discrete experience model [18]	0.898	0.134
User at learned rate [15]	0.872	0.180

Table 4: Performance on identifying experienced users.

7], capturing changes of social links [14] and linguistic norms [3]. None of these prior works take into account the evolving experience and behavior of individual users.

Prior work that analyzed user review texts focused on sentiment analysis [13], learning latent aspects and their ratings [23, 17, 16], and user-user interactions [24]. However, all of these prior approaches operate in a static, snapshot-oriented manner, without considering time at all.

The work [15], one of our baselines, has modeled and studied the influence of evolving user experience on rating behavior and for targeted recommendations. However, it disregards the vocabulary in the users' reviews. Our own recent work [18] addressed this very limitation, by means of language models that are specific to the experience level of an individual user, and by modeling transitions between experience levels with a Hidden Markov Model. However, both of these works are limited to *discrete* experience levels leading to abrupt changes in both experience and language model. To address the above, and other related drawbacks, the current paper introduces continuous-time models for the smooth evolution of both user experience and language model.

Wang et al. [22] modeled topics over time. However, the topics themselves were constant, and time was only used to better discover them. Dynamic topic models have been introduced by Blei et al. in [1, 21]. This prior work developed generic models based on Brownian Motion, and applied them to news corpora. [21] argues that the continuous model avoids making choices for discretization and is also more tractable compared to fine-grained discretization. Our language model is motivated by the latter. We substantially extend it to capture evolving user behavior and experience in review communities using Geometric Brownian Motion.

7. CONCLUSION

In this paper, we have proposed an experience-aware language model that can trace the *continuous* evolution of user experience and language explicitly over *time*. We combine principles of Geometric Brownian Motion, Brownian Motion, and Latent Dirichlet Allocation to model a smooth temporal progression of user experience, and language model over time. This is the first work to develop a continuous and generalized version of user experience evolution.

Our experiments – with data from domains like beer, movies, food, and news – demonstrate that our model effectively exploits user experience for item recommendation that substantially reduces the mean squared error for predicted ratings, compared to the state-of-the-art baselines [15, 18].

We further demonstrate the utility of our model in a use-case study about identifying experienced members in the NewsTrust community, where these users would be top candidates for being citizen journalists. Another similar use-case for our model can be to detect experienced medical professionals in the health community.

8. REFERENCES

[1] David M. Blei and John D. Lafferty. Dynamic topic models. ICML '06, 2006.

[2] David M. Blei, Andrew Y. Ng, and Michael I. Jordan. Latent dirichlet allocation. *J. Mach. Learn. Res.*, 3, 2003.

[3] Cristian Danescu-Niculescu-Mizil, Robert West, Dan Jurafsky, Jure Leskovec, and Christopher Potts. No country for old members: User lifecycle and linguistic change in online communities. WWW, 2013.

[4] Harris Drucker, Chris J. C. Burges, Linda Kaufman, Alex Smola, and Vladımır Vapnik. Support vector regression machines. NIPS, 1997.

[5] Tom Griffiths. Gibbs sampling in the generative model of latent dirichlet allocation. Technical report, 2002.

[6] Nikou Günnemann, Stephan Günnemann, and Christos Faloutsos. Robust multivariate autoregression for anomaly detection in dynamic product ratings. In *WWW*, 2014.

[7] Stephan Günnemann, Nikou Günnemann, and Christos Faloutsos. Detecting anomalies in dynamic rating data: A robust probabilistic model for rating evolution. KDD, 2014.

[8] R. E. Kalman. A new approach to linear filtering and prediction problems. *Transactions of the ASME*, 1960.

[9] Ioannis Karatzas and Steven Eugene Shreve. *Brownian motion and stochastic calculus*. Graduate texts in mathematics. 1991.

[10] Yehuda Koren. Factorization meets the neighborhood: A multifaceted collaborative filtering model. KDD, 2008.

[11] Yehuda Koren. Collaborative filtering with temporal dynamics. *Commun. ACM*, 53(4), 2010.

[12] Yehuda Koren and Robert Bell. Advances in collaborative filtering. In *Recommender systems handbook*. 2011.

[13] Chenghua Lin and Yulan He. Joint sentiment/topic model for sentiment analysis. CIKM, 2009.

[14] Hao Ma, Dengyong Zhou, Chao Liu, Michael R. Lyu, and Irwin King. Recommender systems with social regularization. WSDM, 2011.

[15] J. J. McAuley and J. Leskovec. From amateurs to connoisseurs: modeling the evolution of user expertise through online reviews. WWW, 2013.

[16] Julian McAuley and Jure Leskovec. Hidden factors and hidden topics: Understanding rating dimensions with review text. RecSys, 2013.

[17] Subhabrata Mukherjee, Gaurab Basu, and Sachindra Joshi. Joint author sentiment topic model. SDM, 2014.

[18] Subhabrata Mukherjee, Hemank Lamba, and Gerhard Weikum. Experience-aware item recommendation in evolving review communities. ICDM, 2015.

[19] Subhabrata Mukherjee and Gerhard Weikum. Leveraging joint interactions for credibility analysis in news communities. CIKM, 2015.

[20] Hanna M. Wallach, Iain Murray, Ruslan Salakhutdinov, and David Mimno. Evaluation methods for topic models. ICML, 2009.

[21] Chong Wang, David M. Blei, and David Heckerman. Continuous time dynamic topic models. UAI, 2008.

[22] Xuerui Wang and Andrew McCallum. Topics over time: A non-markov continuous-time model of topical trends. KDD, 2006.

[23] Hongning Wang et al. Latent aspect rating analysis without aspect keyword supervision. KDD, 2011.

[24] Robert West, Hristo S. Paskov, Jure Leskovec, and Christopher Potts. Exploiting social network structure for person-to-person sentiment analysis. *TACL*, 2(2), 2014.

[25] Liang Xiang and et al. Temporal recommendation on graphs via long- and short-term preference fusion. KDD, 2010.

[26] L. Xiong, X. Chen, T. K. Huang, J. Schneider, and J. G. Carbonell. Temporal collaborative filtering with bayesian probabilistic tensor factorization. SDM, 2010.

Structural Neighborhood Based Classification of Nodes in a Network

Sharad Nandanwar
Department of Computer Science and Automation
Indian Institute of Science
Bangalore, India
sharadnandanwar@csa.iisc.ernet.in

M. N. Murty
Department of Computer Science and Automation
Indian Institute of Science
Bangalore, India
mnm@csa.iisc.ernet.in

ABSTRACT

Classification of entities based on the underlying network structure is an important problem. Networks encountered in practice are sparse and have many missing and noisy links. Statistical learning techniques have been used in intra-network classification; however, they typically exploit only the local neighborhood, so may not perform well. In this paper, we propose a novel structural neighborhood-based classifier learning using a random walk. For classifying a node, we take a random walk from the node and make a decision based on how nodes in the respective k^{th}-level neighborhood are labeled. We observe that random walks of short length are helpful in classification. Emphasizing role of longer random walks may cause the underlying Markov chain to converge to a stationary distribution. Considering this, we take a lazy random walk based approach with variable termination probability for each node, based on the node's structural properties including its degree. Our experimental study on real world datasets demonstrates the superiority of the proposed approach over the existing state-of-the-art approaches.

CCS Concepts

•Computing methodologies → Semi-supervised learning settings; Statistical relational learning; •Human-centered computing → Social networks;

Keywords

Graph-based semi-supervised learning; Relational learning; Collective classification

1. INTRODUCTION

With widespread availability and exponential growth of network data in recent years, there has been a surge of interest in mining network and graph data; this has shown up in many guises. Classification, although a well defined problem in machine learning and pattern recognition literature, has not been studied extensively in the context of networks. In the network domain, the classification problem, often addressed as relational classification, is to assign each node of the network to a well defined community (based on interests, demographics, concepts, etc.) in the presence of its intrinsic features as well as the link structure. Some of the popular applications of node classification are, `Wikipedia` page categorization based on intra-wiki links, genre identification of movies in a movie-actor network, social circle learning in a friendship network etc. [25, 17]

To motivate the problem, we use a toy example of a citation network shown in figure 1, where nodes in the network represent papers published in the past proceedings of a conference, and edges depict the citations made by these papers. Each track in the conference where papers are published represents a class, which are distinguished by the color in figure 1. Nodes with missing color information correspond to new submissions which are unlabeled. For a new submission in an upcoming conference, the classification task is to identify the track based on the citations made by the authors in the paper. Networks generally observe homophily, i.e., nodes have a tendency to connect to other nodes that are similar to them. Because of this, it can be claimed that citations made in a paper are from an identical or a correlated track. Further, citations made by authors may range over multiple publishers who opt for different schema standards. This leads to heterogeneity in the metadata. Obtaining precise track information for such papers may have its own cost overheads. In the real world, getting labeled data for learning a supervised model is always expensive and the process involved is also tedious. So, the problem boils down to learning from a small set of labeled examples.

Generally, the study of networks revolves around social networking websites because of their popularity. However, in this paper, by "network" we refer to a generic network, be it a co-citation network, friendship network, biological network, hyper-link structure of the Internet, astronomical network, etc. Network Analysis is not only limited to data showing linked structure; other unstructured data expressed in high dimensional space can also be transformed into weighted graphs so as to understand the topology of the data in a better way. Several approaches have been suggested in the literature for transforming non-graph data into graph data, by using measures like Gaussian similarity [15].

KDD '16, August 13-17, 2016, San Francisco, CA, USA
© 2016 ACM. ISBN 978-1-4503-4232-2/16/08. . . $15.00
DOI: http://dx.doi.org/10.1145/2939672.2939782

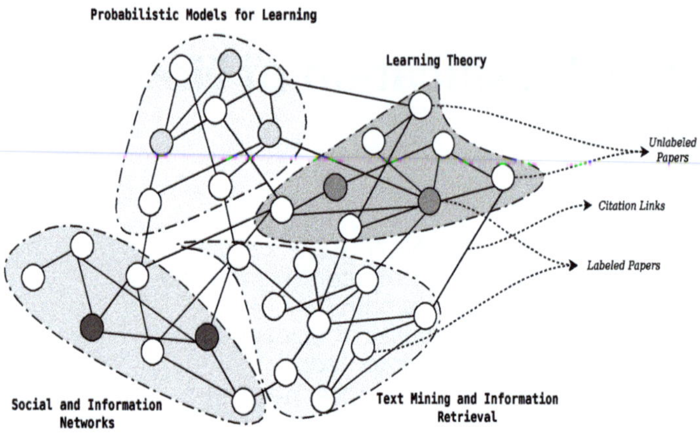

Figure 1: Illustration of multi-class classification in a Citation Network

Conventionally, networks are represented by graphs, defined as follows.

DEFINITION 1. *A network is modeled as a graph* $\mathcal{G}(\mathcal{V}, \mathcal{E}, \mathcal{W})$, *where* $\mathcal{V}$ *is the set of* $|\mathcal{V}| = n$ *interacting units (nodes or actors), and* $\mathcal{E} \subseteq \mathcal{V} \times \mathcal{V}$ *is the set of edges indicating relationship or interactions among the nodes.* $\mathcal{W} \in \mathbb{R}^{n \times n}$, *where* $\mathcal{W}_{ij}$ *indicates affinity or strength of the relationship between nodes* $v_i, v_j \in \mathcal{V}$.

For a sparsely labeled network, the classification problem is formally stated as follows.

DEFINITION 2. *Given a graph* $\mathcal{G}(\mathcal{V}, \mathcal{E})$ *and a set of labeled nodes* $\mathcal{V}_l$ ($\subsetneq \mathcal{V}$) *with corresponding (ordered) set of labels* $\mathcal{Y}_l \in \mathcal{C}^{|\mathcal{V}_l|}$, *where* $\mathcal{C} = \{\mathcal{C}_1, \mathcal{C}_2, \ldots, \mathcal{C}_k\}$ *, the set of* k *labels* $\mathcal{C}_1$ *to* $\mathcal{C}_k$. *The objective is to learn a model for inferring labels of the unlabeled nodes* $\mathcal{V}_u = \mathcal{V} \setminus \mathcal{V}_l$.

Many times, structure of the graph is noisy because of missing and noisy edges. While using traditional statistical learning tools like Support Vector Machines (SVM), we may be losing crucial information if we learn on the basis of a node's local neighborhood alone. Such locally oriented models may not be able to capture global or long distance relationships. Techniques from link prediction (another sub-domain in network analysis) can be leveraged to make the representation more precise. On these lines, many graph kernels [8, 9, 19] were proposed, which compute global structural similarity between pairs of nodes. However, when the network size is in the order of millions, such graph kernel based approaches also suffer due to the high computational requirements and overhead involved in searching over the parameter space.

Unlike the traditional supervised learning techniques, the features in a relational data scenario correspond to the data instances themselves. Hence, since features and instances are interdependent, so are the data instances, rendering the otherwise usual *i.i.d.* assumption invalid. Even though the network is sparsely labeled ($|\mathcal{V}_l| << |\mathcal{V}|$), the connectivity between nodes imparts additional knowledge, strengthening the case for a classifier. In accordance with the principle of homophily [1], neighboring nodes in a network are supposed to be similar to each other. Also, as per the clustering hypothesis, nodes forming a dense sub-network should be correlated [1]. These assumptions, along with the knowledge of connectivity, can be used to formulate the problem as a semi-supervised or transductive learning problem in graph. To exploit homophily in networks, we take a comprehensive view of classification, where a node is classified based on how other nodes in its extended neighborhood are labeled. A random walk in the limit gets attracted towards dense sub-networks in the graph. Hence, a majority of nodes in such a dense sub-network share the same class label.

The principal contributions of our work are as follows:

- *We propose a novel approach for intra-network classification, which enriches the adjacency structure of a node by exploiting its global neighborhood.*
- *We formulate this as an optimization problem that exploits the network structure.*
- *We provide a learning algorithm based on the stochastic gradient descent approach for the same.*
- *We show effectiveness of the proposed approach by making an exhaustive comparative study with state-of-the-art approaches for intra-network classification.*

Rest of the paper is organized as follows: section 2 describes some of the state-of-the-art techniques in the field of relational classification including collective classification, graph kernels, and social representation learning. The proposed approach for discriminative learning, viz. *Structural Neighborhood Based Classification*, is described in section 3. Section 4 describes how to extend the proposed framework from exploiting the local neighborhood to that of the global neighborhood. A detailed comparative study with existing baseline approaches is made in section 5, followed by discussion and conclusion in section 6 and section 7 respectively. All the source code and datasets used for evaluation are available at `https://github.com/sharadnandanwar/snbc`.

2. STATE-OF-THE-ART

Traditional statistical relational learning methods may not work well in cases where the data is sparsely labeled. In the past decade, several approaches that exploit the relational dependency among the nodes have been proposed. We summarize some of the influential methods below.

Lu and Getoor [12] proposed an approach on the lines of logistic regression, which computes the conditional probability of a class as the product of posterior probabilities conditioned on the node attributes and the node links respectively, and finds a MAP estimate for the class variable. However, similar to the other local classifiers like the k-Nearest Neighbor Classifier and SVM, this approach too cannot view beyond the local neighborhood of the nodes and is hence not robust to noise.

Collective Classification: Collective classification approaches utilize additional knowledge about attributes and class information, based on relationships among entities. Macskassy and Provost [13] introduced a simple relational classifier for network data, the weighted-vote relational neighbor (wvRN) classifier. It computes the class membership as a weighted average of the estimated class membership probabilities of the neighboring nodes. Multi Rank Walk [11], yet another relational classifier, is based on the principle of random graph walks similar to Page Rank [16]. The class of any unlabeled node is decided as the one which has the highest probability of containing terminal nodes of the random walk.

Social Dimensions for Classification: Networks encountered in practice generally exhibit a community structure, i.e. a certain group of nodes or entities have stronger connections among themselves, as compared to rest of the network. SocioDim [24] is a framework which exploits the cluster hypothesis, which posits that the nodes in the same community are likely to be of the same class. SocioDim attempts to find the latent social dimensions of the network corresponding to the communities and performs classification in these dimensions. However, in networks where community structure has a high conductance, the obtained social dimensions would be inexact, leading to poor classification performance. Wang et al. [25] propose relational learning in a multi-label setting by extracting social context based features. The extracted social context features correspond to hidden causes which make nodes collaborate among themselves. Based on these features, an iterative probabilistic process similar to wvRN is adopted. DeepWalk [17] and LINE [22] are recently proposed approaches for Social Representation Learning based on random walks. These methods try to capture neighborhood similarity and community membership in latent representations. These label independent representations are then used in multi-label classification.

Random Walk based approaches: Zhou et al. [27] proposed a globally consistent learning approach on the lines of spectral clustering. The proposed iterative method updates the label of a node using information the node receives from its neighbors. Label propagation algorithm [28] adapts a probabilistic perspective using Markov random walks, wherein structure is used to compute transition probabilities. Hidden labels of a node are thereafter inferred using its ancestors' hidden/observed labels. In [2], Baluja et al. proposed a controlled random walk over a graph, with three possible actions (*inject, continue, abandon*) at each step. *Inject* causes the random walk to stop and return its current label, *continue* continues the random walk to its neighbors, and *abandon* terminates the walk without performing any labeling. [21] proposed a modification to this by defining a well-behaved objective function which such a framework minimizes, thus guaranteeing convergence.

Learning using Graph Kernels: In addition to the above schemes, many graph kernels that exploit structural information have also been proposed. Link prediction techniques based on Common Neighbors, Adamic-Adar, Resource Allocation Index, etc. [10] provide means for computing similarity between nodes. They, however, consider only the local neighborhood of nodes and neglect long range relationships. Graph kernels, on the other hand, capture the notion of global similarity between the nodes. A simple kernel would count the number of paths of fixed length between the nodes. It is well-known that longer paths between two nodes are less significant compared to shorter ones. Exponential and von-Neumann graph kernels [8] compute a weighted mean of all such path counts giving higher weights to shorter paths. The number of paths of length n between nodes v_i and v_j are reflected in A^n_{ij}, where A is the adjacency matrix. Then, a von Neumann kernel is defined as,

$$\sum_{i=0}^{\infty} \gamma^i A^i = (I - \gamma A)^{-1},$$

where $\gamma \in (0, 1)$. Exponential graph kernel, very similar to the above, is defined as,

$$\sum_{i=0}^{\infty} \frac{\gamma^i}{i!} A^i = \exp(\gamma A).$$

Laplacian counterparts of the above kernels have also been defined, namely, regularized Laplacian kernel [19] and heat diffusion kernel [9] respectively. Graph kernels usually work well on smaller networks. For learning on large networks, these approaches require inverting large matrices, which is not feasible when the resources are limited.

On a side note, relational classifiers described above do not have good generalization abilities and suffer when the given network is sparsely labeled.

A heterogeneous information network [20] is a network composed of multiple types of nodes and relationships between them. Study of these networks has lately gained prominence. Chakrabarti et al. [3] showed that making use of hyper-links along with hypertext while classifying linked text content leads to an enhanced performance. Ming Ji et al. [7] proposed a framework for transductive learning in heterogeneous networks based on two assumptions: local consistency (class assignment of neighbors is similar) and ground truth (pre-assigned class labels are correct). In [6], ranking and classification in heterogeneous information networks are combined based on the intuition that highly ranked objects within a class should play a more important role in classification.

3. STRUCTURAL NEIGHBORHOOD BASED CLASSIFICATION (SNBC)

Traditional learning approaches like the k-Nearest Neighbor classifier and SVM use local adjacency information in classification. In a sparsely labeled network, it becomes difficult to classify a node if there are not sufficient number of labeled nodes in its vicinity. In accordance with homophily, two nodes connected by an edge are expected to be similar to each other. We assume that the behavior of a node is defined by the average behavior of its neighboring nodes, and come up with a novel way of learning in networks. Most of the statistical classifier learning problems are inherently binary classification problems, which can be easily extended for multi-class classification using standard approaches like one-vs-one and one-vs-all [14]. Henceforth, in this paper, we will be working with a binary classification problem, which can be extended to deal with multi-class classification like others.

Let $\mathcal{C}^+$ and $\mathcal{C}^-$ represent the sets of positive and negative examples respectively in the binary classification problem under consideration. A simple approach to classify a node would be to count the number of neighbors from the respective classes and label the node based on majority voting. However, this approach has its own limitations. If the network is sparsely labeled, nodes may lack sufficient number of labeled neighbors. Macskassy [13] showed that instead of counting votes, taking a weighted vote of each neighbor is more useful. The weight of a vote expresses the confidence with which a neighbor can be assigned to a class. In a probabilistic model, this confidence can be measured using conditional class probabilities. In classifiers where a real decision function is learned, a larger distance from the decision boundary signifies a higher weight.

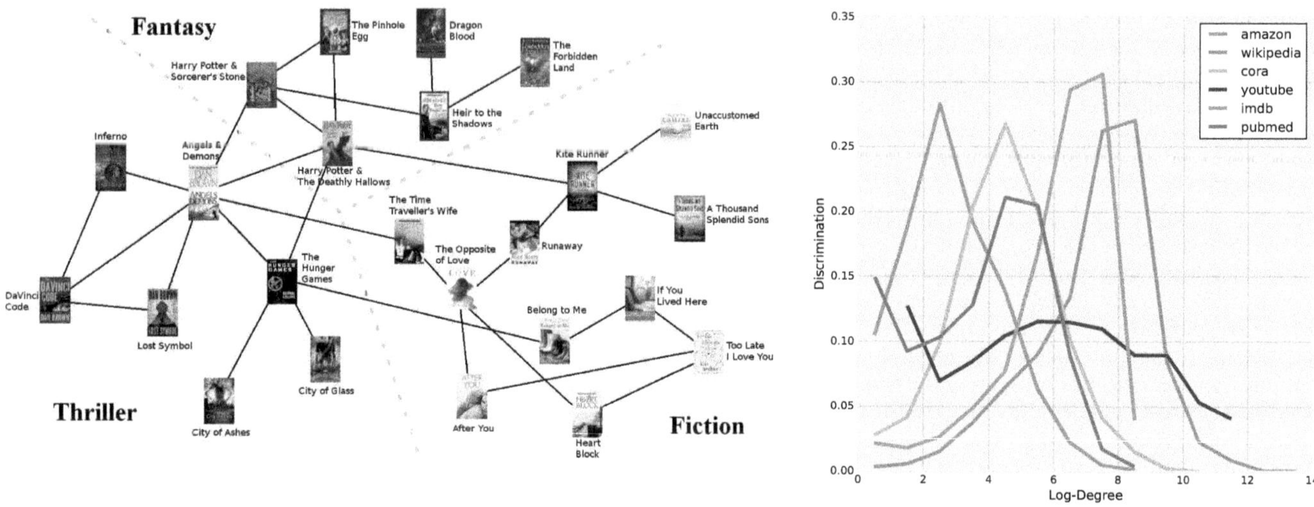

(a) (b)

Figure 2: (a)Toy network of books modeling similarity relationship among books based on user preferences. (b)Plot showing expected contribution of nodes with degree d towards discrimination i.e. $\Delta(d)$

We start by defining the adjacency based representation of a graph. Given an undirected and binary-weighted graph $\mathcal{G}(\mathcal{V},\mathcal{E})$, where $\mathcal{V} = \{v_1, v_2, \ldots, v_n\}$ and $\mathcal{E} \subseteq \mathcal{V} \times \mathcal{V}$, the corresponding adjacency matrix A is defined as follows,

$$A_{ij} = \begin{cases} 1, & \text{if } (v_i, v_j) \in \mathcal{E} \\ 0, & \text{otherwise} \end{cases} .$$

In the case of a weighted graph $\mathcal{G}(\mathcal{V},\mathcal{E},\mathcal{W})$, links carry a non-negative weight specified by $\mathcal{W}$. Adjacency Matrix A for these graphs is modified as $A_{ij} = \mathcal{W}_{ij}$. Based on the link attributes of a node, we define node v_i in vector space notation as $a_i = [A_{ji}]_{n\times 1}$ where $j \in \{1, 2, \cdots, n\}$. For node v_i, we define the first-level/local neighborhood as follows:

DEFINITION 3. ***First-Level Neighborhood*** *of a node* v_i *is the set* $\mathcal{N}_i^1$ *s.t.* $v_j \in \mathcal{N}_i^1$ *if and only if there exists an edge in the graph connecting* v_i *and* v_j*, i.e.,* $(v_i, v_j) \in \mathcal{E}$*.*

Further, let $\mathcal{N}_{i,+}^1 \subseteq \mathcal{C}^+$ and $\mathcal{N}_{i,-}^1 \subseteq \mathcal{C}^-$ denote the sets of neighboring nodes from positive class and negative class respectively in the binary labeled network. In this setting, we assume a linear separating hyperplane (like the one in perceptron, logistic regression, SVM) of the form $w^\mathsf{T} \cdot x + b$. Then, given the parameters w and b of an optimal decision boundary, for an unknown example x_u, the predicted label is given by

$$\hat{y}_u = sign(w^\mathsf{T} \cdot x_u + b)$$

Because of homophily in the network, a node is expected to have its class label (defined by its properties) similar to majority of its neighbors. For a target node v_i, the above scoring function assigns a positive or negative value ($\hat{y}_j$) to its neighboring node (v_j). As most of the neighboring nodes are expected to have their class label same as that of the target node, the aggregated sum of scores from these neighboring nodes should also have the same sign as the target label (y_i).

Also, in real networks, variability in the node degree is inherent and follows a power law distribution. It is observed that high degree nodes are generally the source of linkage noise in networks. For example consider the toy network of books shown in figure 2a. The network models "users who liked this also liked" similarity relation among books. In the graph, **Angels and Demons** shares a similarity relation with most of the books in the **Thriller** category. This entices one to become prejudiced that any book that shares such a relation with **Angels and Demons** will belong to the **Thriller** category. However, contrary to this intuition, the same book shares many relations with books in other categories too, as is visible in the graph. This can be attributed to the *"rich getting richer"* phenomenon in networks, i.e., the book went popular and was enjoyed by readers across the genres. Based on this observation, we argue that a link to a low or medium degree node should be considered more reliable in comparison with a link to a high degree node. Thus, while learning the weight vector w, if an almost equivalent performance can be achieved by (1) assigning larger weights to a large number of medium degree nodes, than (2) assigning larger weights to a small number of high degree nodes, then the former should be preferred. Figure 2b shows the expected discriminatory power (defined below) with varying degree. The graph shows how the relative average mutual information varies for nodes lying in different degree zones. We define a measure of discrimination Δ for degree d as follows:

$$\Delta(d) = \frac{1}{Z} \sum_{i\in\{j:d_j=d\}} \max_{c\in\mathcal{C}} MI(a_i, y_c),$$

where Z is the normalization constant, and $MI(X,Y)$ computes the mutual information of random variables X and Y, d_j is the degree of node v_j, and y_c refers to the label vector of class c. We observe a consistent behavior across all datasets considered in our experiments, however the peaking range is different for each dataset, which would depend on the network size and its structure, more specifically on its sparsity. Based on these observations, we state the following conjectures:

Conjecture 1. *For a node v, its neighbors $\mathcal{N}_v$ and the decision boundary ($\mathcal{H}$), sum of distances between $\mathcal{H}$ and neighbors $\mathcal{N}_v^{(s)}$ similar to v (i.e., of the same class as v) should be greater than the same for other neighbors ($\mathcal{N}_v \setminus \mathcal{N}_v^{(s)}$).*

Conjecture 2. *The role of high degree nodes in discrimination is smaller compared to that of medium degree nodes.*

We formalize our intuition as follows:

(1) Structural Neighborhood: For a node v_i having class label $y_i \in \{-1, 1\}$, the aggregated scores from the nodes having label y_i in the first-level neighborhood ($\mathcal{N}_i^1$) should be more than the aggregated scores from rest of the nodes in the first-level neighborhood. Thus, for optimal w and b, we have, for all i,

$$y_i \sum_{j\in\mathcal{N}_{i,y_i}^1} A(v_i,v_j)(w^\top \cdot a_j + b) \;\geq\; -y_i \sum_{j\in\mathcal{N}_{i,-y_i}^1} A(v_i,v_j)(w^\top \cdot a_j + b),$$

where $A(v_i, v_j) = A_{ij}$ indicates the weight of edge joining nodes v_i and v_j. This can be equivalently rewritten as,

$$y_i \left(\sum_{j\in\mathcal{N}_{i,y_i}^1} A_{ij}(w^\top \cdot a_j + b) + \sum_{j\in\mathcal{N}_{i,-y_i}^1} A_{ij}(w^\top \cdot a_j + b) \right) \geq 0,$$

$$\Longrightarrow y_i \left(\sum_{j\in\mathcal{V}} A_{ij}(w^\top \cdot a_j + b) \right) \geq 0.$$

Rearranging the terms, we get,

$$y_i \;\left(\; w^\top \cdot A \cdot a_i + d_i\, b \;\right) \;\geq\; 0,$$

where $d_i = \sum_{j\in\mathcal{V}} A_{ij}$.

$$\Longrightarrow y_i \left(\frac{1}{d_i} w^\top \cdot A \cdot a_i + b \right) \geq 0$$

Let $M = [m_1, m_2, \cdots, m_n] = A^2 D^{-1}$, where $D \in \mathbb{R}n \times n$ defined as $D_{ij} = \begin{cases} d_i & \text{if } i = j \\ 0 & \text{otherwise} \end{cases}$.

Then, we have the following in a linearly separable case:

$$y_i(w^\top m_i + b) \geq 0.$$

The above can be interpreted as mapping the adjacency information a_i to a new space as $m_i = A\frac{a_i}{d_i}$, and then learning a decision boundary. For node v_i, we define empirical loss ε_i (≥ 0) such that

$$y_i(w^\top m_i + b) \geq 1 - \varepsilon_i.$$

Mean empirical loss, that is to be minimized, is given by

$$f(w,b) = \frac{1}{|\mathcal{V}_l|} \sum_{i\in\mathcal{V}_l} \varepsilon_i. \qquad (1)$$

(2) Degree Dependent Regularization: Weight w_i for node v_i with degree d_i should be affected in a manner directly proportional to a monotonically increasing function of d_i. Let $g : (\mathbb{R}^+ \bigcup\{0\}) \times \mathbb{Z}^+ \to \mathbb{R}$ be the penalty function such that penalty for node v_i is $p_i = g(w_i, d_i)$. We define penalty for the network as a whole by the ℓ_2 norm of vector $p = (p_1, p_2, \ldots, p_n)$, and try to minimize the squared penalty. In this work we consider the following penalty functions:

- Linear Weighted Degree **(LWD):**

$$g(w_i, d_i) := |w_i| d_i$$

- Linear Weighted Root Degree **(LWRD):**

$$g(w_i, d_i) := |w_i|\sqrt{d_i}$$

- Linear Weighted Root Log Degree **(LWRLD):**

$$g(w_i, d_i) := |w_i|\sqrt{\log_2 d_i}$$

Regularizing the objective in (1) corresponding to empirical loss with the above penalty using regularization parameter λ would lead to,

$$\min_{w,b} \quad \frac{\lambda}{2}||p||^2 \;+\; \frac{1}{|\mathcal{V}_l|}\sum_{i\in\mathcal{V}_l} \varepsilon_i \qquad (2)$$

$$\text{such that} \quad y_i(w^\top m_i + b) \geq 1 - \varepsilon_i\,, \quad \varepsilon_i \geq 0\,, \text{ and} \quad m_i = A\frac{a_i}{d_i}$$

4. DIVING DEEP INTO THE NETWORK

The objective in (2) attempts to learn parameters (w and b), while labeling the node under consideration based on the collective behavior of its first-level neighborhood. We further explore the significance of far away neighbors in this setting. We begin by giving a recursive definition of the rth-level neighborhood of a node:

Definition 4. ***r^{th}-Level Neighborhood*** *of a node v_i is defined as a multiset $\mathcal{N}_i^r$ s.t. $v_k \in \mathcal{N}_i^r$ if and only if there is an edge in graph $\mathcal{G}$ connecting nodes v_k and v_j where node $v_j \in \mathcal{N}_i^{r-1}$, and multiplicity of v_k in $\mathcal{N}_i^r$ is given by the cardinality of set $\{v_j | (v_k, v_j) \in \mathcal{E}$ and $v_j \in \mathcal{N}_i^{r-1}\}$.*

Note that the multiplicity of a node v_k in multiset $\mathcal{N}_i^r$ indicates the number of paths of length r possible between nodes v_i and v_k. Proceeding on similar lines as in section 3, we deal with the second-level neighborhood, which can be generalized for any depth in the network. While considering the first-level neighborhood $\mathcal{N}^1$, we were interested in how nodes in $\mathcal{N}^1$ get classified based on adjacency information they have. When using second-level neighborhood, we first accumulate scores at first-level neighbors using decision values of second-level neighbors. These scores from first-level neighbors are further propagated to the node under consideration to perform classification. Figure 3 illustrates the involved process (3a) for first-level neighborhood based classification, and (3b) when using second-level neighborhood in classification.

In section 3 we have derived the representation m_i for node v_i based on its first-level neighborhood as $m_i = A\frac{a_i}{d_i}$. We carry forward this representation while delving into higher level neighborhoods. Using similar homophily arguments at each node, we have,

$$y_i \left(\sum_{j\in\mathcal{N}_{i,y_i}^1} A_{ij}(w^\top \cdot m_j + b) + \sum_{j\in\mathcal{N}_{i,-y_i}^1} A_{ij}(w^\top \cdot m_j + b) \right) \geq 0, \quad \forall i = 1, \ldots, n$$

which simplifies to

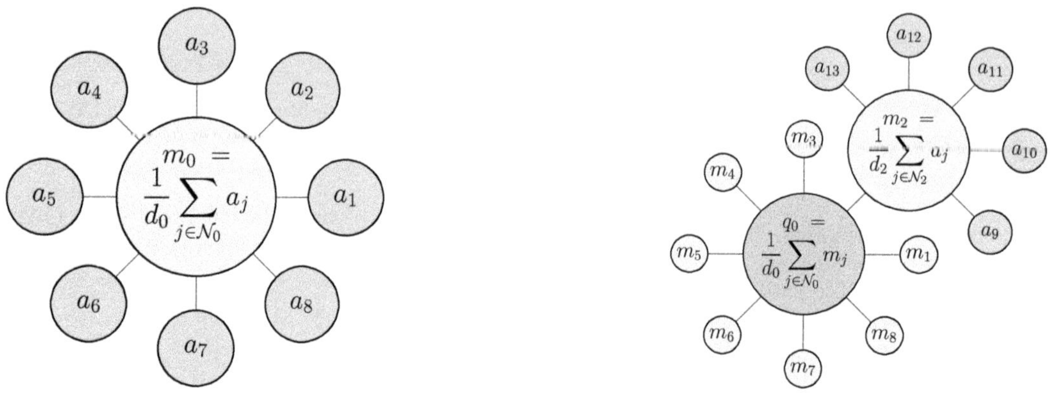

(a) First-Level Neighborhood

(b) Second-Level Neighborhood

Figure 3: For an unweighted graph Figure 3(a) illustrates how representation for node v_0 based on its first-level neighbors is derived while 3(b) illustrates the representation for the same based on its second level neighbors. $\mathcal{N}_i$ denotes the set of first-level neighbors for node v_i with degree $d_i = |\mathcal{N}_i|$

$$y_i \left(\frac{1}{d_i} w^\top \cdot A \cdot m_i + b\right) \geq 0, \quad \forall i = 1, \ldots, n$$

where, $d_i = \sum_{j\in\mathcal{V}} A_{ij}$.

Let $Q = [q_1, q_2, \cdots, q_n] = MAD^{-1} = A(AD^{-1})^2$, where M and D are defined in section 3. Then, for the linearly separable case, we have,

$$y_i(w^\top q_i + b) \geq 0, \quad \forall i = 1, \ldots, n$$

where $q_i = A^2 D^{-1} \frac{a_i}{d_i}$ based on second-level neighborhood of a node. We can argue using inductive logic that while using r-level neighbors, the same will be mapped to $A(AD^{-1})^{r-1} \frac{a_i}{d_i}$. For classification using r-level neighbors, the adjacency information contained in the matrix A as a whole gets mapped to $A(AD^{-1})^r$.

Random Walk Based View: The above scheme can also be viewed as taking random walks of fixed length r starting from the node under consideration, and classifying the node by accumulating the decision values for respective neighbor nodes. With higher values of r, the representation derived above tends to become more global. However, with increasing values of r, the transition probabilities between any pair of nodes start converging towards the stationary probability distribution. Because of this, in a connected graph for sufficiently large values of r, every node will eventually end up having a similar representation. Because of this, one can expect some loss in discrimination for higher values of r.

Lazy Random Walk: To avoid the situation where all nodes have identical representation, we consider taking lazy random walks of arbitrary lengths instead of a fixed length r. We start by introducing a dampening factor at each hop, which controls the termination of the random walk. If dampening factor is denoted by $\gamma \in [0, 1]$, the random walk terminates at each hop with probability $(1 - \gamma)$, and continues to the next hop with probability γ. The representation q_i for node v_i obtained using the above procedure is given by

$$q_i = (1-\gamma)A\Big(e_i + \gamma\frac{a_i}{d_i} + \gamma^2(AD^{-1})\frac{a_i}{d_i} + \gamma^3(AD^{-1})^2\frac{a_i}{d_i} + \ldots\Big), \tag{3}$$

e_i being a n-dimensional unit vector with i^{th} entry as 1 and remaining as zeros. Other notations used have already been defined. This closely resembles the regularized graph laplacian kernel [19] using unnormalized graph laplacian. However, instead of computing structure based similarity matrix, we are interested in a structural similarity based representation. In equation 3, if γ is chosen to be close to zero, it is equivalent to learning with the given adjacency representation alone. On the other extreme, if gamma is large (≈ 1), higher powers will dominate. This may lead to every node having similar representation as mentioned previously. We empirically find that taking such an approach does not lead to a significant improvement in the performance of the learned classifier.

Structured Random Walk: As stated earlier, networks observed in practice exhibit a variability in degree. It is easier to classify higher degree nodes than it is to classify low degree nodes, since the former have a richer local neighborhood. Low degree nodes have limited information owing to their smaller local neighborhood. In addition, if the dampening factor is high, then continuing from a high degree node may lead to accumulation of more noise at each successive hop. Considering these consequences, we decide upon having a separate dampening factor specific to a node, based on its structural property. Intuitively, on encountering a high degree node, a random walk should observe higher termination probability $(1 - \gamma)$, and the same should be lower in case of low degree nodes. We use randomness of a node as a measure to derive respective dampening factors, which is defined for node v_i as follows:

$$H_i = -\sum_{j\in\mathcal{N}_i} p_{ij} \log_2(p_{ij}),$$

where $\mathcal{N}_i$ denotes the set of neighbors of node v_i, as defined earlier. Assuming uniform transition probabilities for all neighbors of a node, we have $p_{ij} = \frac{1}{|\mathcal{N}_i|}$, which gives

$$H_i = \log_2 |\mathcal{N}_i| = \log_2 d_i$$

As stated earlier, higher randomness implies a higher termination probability and a lesser dampening factor. Taking this into account, we choose

$$\gamma_i = \frac{1}{\log_2 d_i}.$$

We define matrix Γ as,

$$\Gamma = diag(\gamma_1, \gamma_2, \dots, \gamma_{|\mathcal{V}|}).$$

The representation then becomes

$$q_i = A\Big(e_i + \Gamma\tfrac{a_i}{d_i} + (AD^{-1})\Gamma^2\tfrac{a_i}{d_i} + (AD^{-1})^2\Gamma^3\tfrac{a_i}{d_i} + \dots\Big)(I-\Gamma).$$

Let Q be the matrix obtained by stacking column vectors q_i corresponding to all the nodes. Then, we have

$$Q = A(I - AD^{-1}\Gamma)^{-1}(I - \Gamma).$$

4.1 Structural Neighborhood Based Classification (SNBC) Algorithm

Taking structured random walk into account the objective in (2) is modified as:

$$\min_{w,b} \quad \frac{\lambda}{2}||p||^2 \; + \; \frac{1}{|\mathcal{V}_l|}\sum_{i\in\mathcal{V}_l} \varepsilon_i \qquad (4)$$

$$\text{s.t.} \quad y_i(w^\top q_i + b) \geq 1 - \varepsilon_i \; , \quad \varepsilon_i \geq 0 \; , \text{ and}$$

$$q_i = A\Big(e_i + \Gamma\tfrac{a_i}{d_i} + (AD^{-1})\Gamma^2\tfrac{a_i}{d_i} + (AD^{-1})^2\Gamma^3\tfrac{a_i}{d_i} + \dots\Big)(I-\Gamma)$$

Subgradient of the above is given by,

$$\nabla_t = \lambda p\frac{\partial p}{\partial w} - \frac{1}{|\mathcal{V}_l|}\sum_{i\in\mathcal{V}_l} \mathbb{1}[y_i w_t^\top q_i < 1] y_i q_i,$$

where $\mathbb{1}$ denotes indicator function. Using gradient descent, the iterative update rule for w is given by

$$w_{t+1} = w_t - \eta_t \nabla_t$$

where η_t is the learning rate for the tth iteration. We use stochastic gradient descent mini-batch update algorithm with a variable learning rate η_t given by $\eta_t = \dfrac{1}{2+\lambda t}$. Algorithm 1 provides the pseudocode for the adopted approach with a LWRLD penalty function.

Algorithm 1 Training Structural Neighborhood Based Classifier with LWRLD penalty using stochastic gradient descent

procedure SNBC_TRAIN $(\boldsymbol{A}, \boldsymbol{y}, \lambda, imax, k)$

Input:
- $\boldsymbol{A}_{n\times n}$ ▷ Adjacency matrix representation of network
- $\boldsymbol{y}_{n\times 1}$ ▷ Label vector, $\boldsymbol{y}_i \in \{-1, 1\}$ if i^{th} node is labeled, $\boldsymbol{y}_i = 0$ otherwise
- λ ▷ Regularization parameter
- $imax$ ▷ Maximum number of iterations for SGD
- k ▷ Sample size for SGD

Output:
- $\boldsymbol{w}_{imax}, b$ ▷ Learned decision function parameter

$Tr \leftarrow \{i : \boldsymbol{y}_i \neq 0\}$ ▷ Set of training points
$\boldsymbol{d}_{n\times 1} \leftarrow \boldsymbol{A}\,\boldsymbol{1}$ ▷ Degree Vector
$\boldsymbol{D} \leftarrow diag(\boldsymbol{d})$
Define log degree vector $\boldsymbol{l}_{n\times 1}$ s.t. $\boldsymbol{l}_i \leftarrow \log_2(2 + \boldsymbol{d}_i)$
$\boldsymbol{L} \leftarrow diag(\boldsymbol{l})$
$\boldsymbol{\Gamma} \leftarrow diag^{-1}(\boldsymbol{l})$
$\boldsymbol{X} \leftarrow \boldsymbol{A}(\boldsymbol{I} - \boldsymbol{A}\boldsymbol{D}^{-1}\boldsymbol{\Gamma})^{-1}(\boldsymbol{I} - \boldsymbol{\Gamma})$
$\boldsymbol{w}_0 \leftarrow \boldsymbol{0}_{n\times 1}, b \leftarrow 0$ ▷ Initialization
for $t = 1, 2, \dots, imax$ **do**
  $b \leftarrow \frac{1}{k}\sum_{i\in Tr}(\boldsymbol{y}_i - \boldsymbol{x}_i^\top \boldsymbol{w}_{t-1})$
  Choose $Smp \subseteq Tr$, where $|Smp| = k$, at random
  $Mc \leftarrow \{i \in Smp : \boldsymbol{y}_i(\boldsymbol{x}_i^\top \boldsymbol{w}_{t-1} + b) < 1\}$
  $\boldsymbol{w}_t \leftarrow (\boldsymbol{I} - \eta_t \boldsymbol{L})\boldsymbol{w}_{t-1} + \frac{\eta_t}{k}\sum_{i\in Mc} \boldsymbol{y}_i \boldsymbol{x}_i$
end for
return $\boldsymbol{w}_{imax}, b$
end procedure

5. EXPERIMENTS

We empirically evaluate the results of the proposed approach SNBC over various real world datasets. In order to show the effectiveness of SNBC we compare it with some of the recent and state-of-the-art intra-network classification schemes.

5.1 Datasets:

We used some of the popular relational datasets described below.

Youtube: A subset of Youtube users with grouping information made available by Lei Tang[1] is used. The graph models *"knows"* friendship relations amongst users who are assigned to multiple groups according to their interests.

PubMed: The PubMed data set[2] consists of scientific publications from the PubMed database pertaining to diabetes, where each publication is classified into one of three classes: "Diabetes Mellitus, Experimental", "Diabetes Mellitus Type 1", "Diabetes Mellitus Type 2".

CoRA: A collection of research articles[3] in the computer science domain classified into pre-defined research topics. For our study, we ignored the citations for which complete information is not available.

IMDb: We crawled information about movies from IMDb[4]. For generating the graph, we took a subset of English movies released after the year 1990. Then, we defined the similarity between the movies based on the top 5 billed stars in them. Genre assigned to the movies is used as the target variable.

Amazon Books: We extracted a subset of books from the amazon co-purchasing network data[5]. Books having less than 5 reviews were ignored. For each book, the dataset also provides a list of other similar books, which is used to build a network. The Genre of books gives a natural

[1] leitang.net/code/social_dimension/data/youtube.mat

[2] linqs.cs.umd.edu/projects/projects/lbc/index.html

[3] people.cs.umass.edu/~mccallum/data/CoRA-classify.tar.gz

[4] www.imdb.com/interfaces

[5] snap.stanford.edu/data/amazon-meta.html

categorization, which we use as class labels in our learning problem.

`Wikipedia:` We use a crawled dump of `Wikipedia` pages from different areas of computer science using the Wikimedia API[6]. For crawling, we choose 16 top level category pages, and recursively crawled subcategories up to a depth of 3. The top level categories are used as class labels.

Some of the statistics of the datasets are summarized in Table 1.

Dataset	#Nodes	#Edges	#Classes	Label Cardinality
Amazon	83742	190097	30	1.546
CoRA	24519	92207	10	1.004
IMDb	19359	362079	21	2.300
PubMed	19717	44324	3	1.000
Wikipedia	35633	495388	16	1.312
Youtube	22693	96361	47	1.707

Table 1: Datasets used for experiments

5.2 Comparative Study:

There is a lot of work on semi-supervised learning in graphs and on collective classification. However, we focus on comparing our work with the state-of-the-art approaches. We restrict our study to some of the recent advances in the field of intra-network classification, and use linear Support Vector Machine (SVM) as the baseline classifier. We briefly describe below, the approaches considered by us for the empirical study.

Linear SVM [4]: We learn from local adjacency vector using Support Vector Machine(SVM) and use this as a benchmark.

SocioDim-Modularity [23]: This approach uses modularity matrix and tries to extract social dimensions hidden in relations among nodes by computing eigenvectors of the modularity matrix. We fix the number of social dimensions as 200 for our experiments.

SocioDim-EdgeClustering [24]: As an extension to SocioDim-Modularity, this approach performs edge clustering by using incidence matrix of the given graph. The hard clusters for edges thus obtained are used to compute latent dimensions of the node. In our experiment, we partition edges into 5000 clusters.

SCRN [25]: SCRN, an approach for collective classification, exploits social context features in relational learning. The social features are computed using edge clustering, in a way similar to SocioDim-EdgeClustering.

Deepwalk [17]: Deepwalk is a recently proposed approach for deep learning in networks. The approach is useful for learning low dimensional embeddings in large networks. We obtain 128 dimensional embeddings for a node using Deepwalk, and use these embeddings further in classification.

5.3 Setup and Parameter-tuning:

To study the robustness of the proposed framework on a sparsely labeled network, we learn a model by holding out the labels of 90%, 70%, 50%, 30% and 10% of nodes respectively. However, because of lack of space here, we show results obtained on using 10% of the labeled nodes for training. Set of nodes used for training is sampled using the Snowball sampling [5] technique. For datasets having directed edges, we remove directionality by adding an edge in the opposite direction also. The datasets used in experiments are multi-labeled, i.e., a node can belong to more than one class. To train SVM in this setting, we use the one-vs-all approach for training a model corresponding to each class. For tuning linear SVM, we restricted the search space to $2^{-10} < \lambda < 2^5$. For each node in the test set, decision values are obtained from the respective class models. We assign s most probable classes to the node using these decision values, where s is equal to the number of labels assigned to the node originally. However, the decision values given by different SVM models cannot be compared directly. We use Platt's Scaling [18] to convert these decision values into probability scores. Probability scores from different models, being on the same scale, can be compared. For validating our results, we use three popular evaluation measures for multi-label classification: Hamming Score, Micro-F_1 Score, and Macro-F_1 Score [26]. If for the ith node, T_i is the set of true labels, and P_i is set of predicted labels, then we have

$$\text{Hamming Score} = \sum_i \frac{|T_i \cap P_i|}{|T_i \cup P_i|}$$

$$\text{Micro-}F_1 \text{ Score} = \frac{2\sum_i |T_i \cap P_i|}{\sum_i |T_i| + \sum_i |P_i|}$$

$$\text{Macro-}F_1 \text{ Score} = \frac{1}{k}\sum_{j=1}^{k} \frac{2\sum_{i\in\mathcal{C}_j} |T_i \cap P_i|}{\sum_{i\in\mathcal{C}_j} |T_i| + \sum_{i\in\mathcal{C}_j} |P_i|}$$

To verify robustness of various approaches, we take 100 random splits of the network into test and train datasets. We report average Hamming Score, Micro-F_1 Score, and Macro-F_1 Score over these random splits.

6. RESULTS AND DISCUSSION

In this section, we explain the behavior of the proposed approach SNBC based on a systematic experimental study described above. Table 2 reports the results using different penalty functions. We choose the functions LWD, LWRD, and LWRLD as described in section 3. Although the penalty function can have many more forms, our purpose of choosing these functions is to demonstrate the impact of rate of increase of function value with degree. In all the cases, we found LWRLD penalty to be outperforming. The reason is that the other two functions, in addition to penalizing high degree nodes, also heavily penalize medium degree nodes that carry maximum discriminative power. This heavy penalization inhibits learning larger weights for medium degree nodes. However, LWRD was found to be competent in case of small networks like `IMDb` and `PubMed`, where the average degree is small. The behavior can be seen as an implication of $\sqrt{d_{avg}} \approx \log_2(d_{avg})$ for small average degree (d_{avg}).

Figures 4, 5, and 6 show respectively the Hamming Score, Macro-F_1 Score, and Micro-F_1 score for multi-label classification of the datasets. In most of the cases, the proposed approach improves over the existing ones. We investigate the reason behind this. As we move from local neighborhood to global neighborhood, the ratio of number of between-class

[6] `en.wikipedia.org/w/api.php`

Dataset → Penalty Func. ↓	*Measure*	Youtube	PubMed	CoRA	IMDb	Amazon	Wikipedia
LWD	*Hamming Sc.*	18.27 ± 0.09	41.13 ± 1.28	37.74 ± 0.10	32.77 ± 0.15	15.18 ± 0.03	16.13 ± 0.04
	Micro-F1 Sc.	24.29 ± 0.16	41.12 ± 1.37	37.71 ± 0.10	40.93 ± 0.55	17.60 ± 0.15	21.32 ± 0.11
	Macro-F1 Sc.	8.09 ± 0.08	21.63 ± 2.39	6.33 ± 0.11	9.84 ± 0.25	2.84 ± 0.02	7.32 ± 0.19
LWRD	*Hamming Sc.*	35.05 ± 2.79	78.55 ± 0.37	60.46 ± 2.56	32.76 ± 0.12	61.08 ± 0.36	16.08 ± 0.16
	Micro-F1 Sc.	40.64 ± 1.12	78.55 ± 0.37	60.45 ± 2.55	40.91 ± 0.46	61.53 ± 0.45	21.26 ± 0.22
	Macro-F1 Sc.	33.43 ± 2.20	76.35 ± 0.77	49.33 ± 4.38	9.82 ± 0.22	59.67 ± 0.74	7.22 ± 0.27
LWRLD	*Hamming Sc.*	**36.15 ± 2.58**	**80.04 ± 0.19**	**67.39 ± 2.23**	**32.90 ± 0.36**	**61.24 ± 0.19**	**69.93 ± 0.16**
	Micro-F1 Sc.	**41.26 ± 1.34**	**80.04 ± 0.19**	**67.39 ± 2.24**	**41.30 ± 0.44**	**61.71 ± 0.25**	**71.32 ± 0.12**
	Macro-F1 Sc.	**35.66 ± 3.31**	**78.28 ± 0.24**	**57.47 ± 3.06**	**16.56 ± 0.31**	**59.69 ± 0.31**	**61.37 ± 1.58**

Table 2: Evaluation of multi-label classification with different penalty functions, using 10% of labeled data for training.

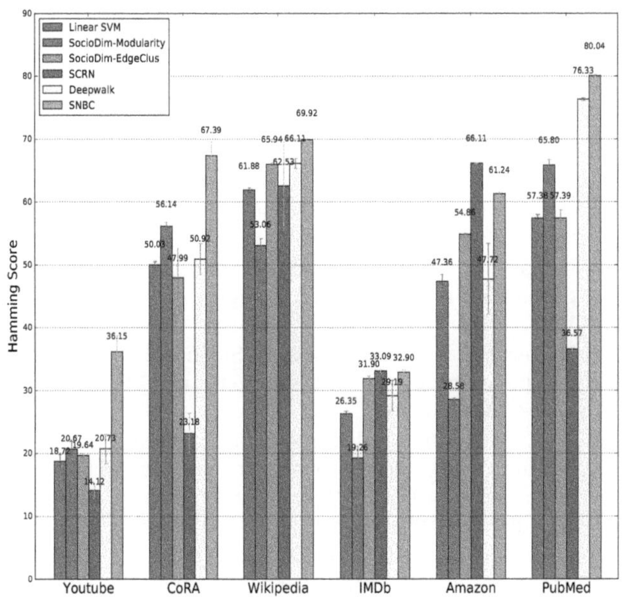

Figure 4: Hamming score for multi-label classification compared with the state-of-the-art approaches using 10% of nodes for training

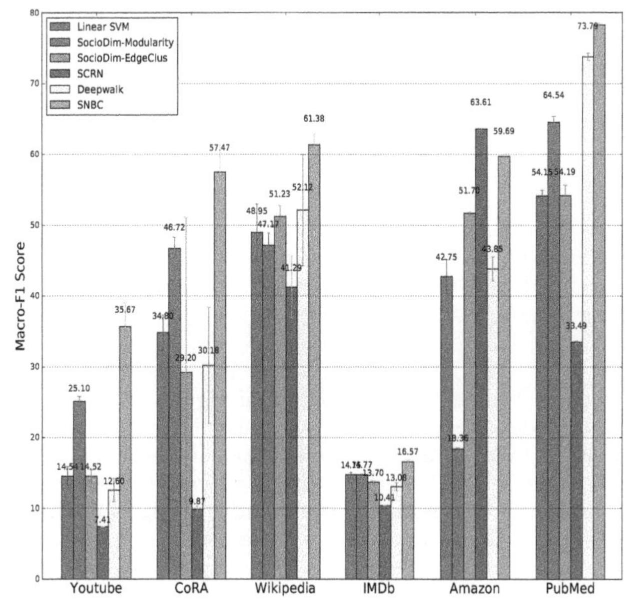

Figure 5: Macro-F1 score for multi-label classification compared with the state-of-the-art approaches using 10% of nodes for training

to within-class paths keeps increasing, i.e., the boundary between classes starts diminishing in an expected sense. Despite all this, SNBC is able to perform well. The reason is that even though inter-class separability diminishes in an expected sense, low degree nodes which earlier had very less information for classification, now have a better representation.

Citation networks are generally sparse, and many low degree nodes can be expected to occur in such a network. In our experimental results, we find that SNBC was able to improve remarkably over all other techniques in both `CoRA` and `PubMed` citation networks. In our setting, where the network is sparsely labeled, some of the features important to low degree nodes got ignored, leading to misclassification. While learning using global neighborhood, these features are extended by exploiting neighborhood information, which leads to improved performance. Similar to citation networks, in case of the `Youtube` social network also, we record a significant improvement for all metrics. `Youtube` data being a real world data, has a similar behavior, i.e., presence of large number of low degree nodes, which get aided when we look into global neighborhood. However, networks like `Amazon` and `IMDb` are synthesized based on similarity. These networks have enough link information for most of the nodes. For example, in the `Amazon` network, for each book, we have a list of five similar books; this makes most of the books to have almost the same degree. Expanding representation using global neighborhood in such a case will only lead to accumulation of noise and hence, will show only marginal or no improvement. Similar is the case for `IMDb` movie network. The `Wikipedia` hyperlink network is a highly noisy network with lots of between-class edges. We find performance of the proposed approach to be significantly better in this case also. In the `Wikipedia` network, most of the noisy links come out of high degree nodes. But the adopted structured walk approach causes the random walk not to move further from high degree nodes, thus inhibiting accumulation of noise.

7. CONCLUSION

The work here proposes and demonstrates an approach for classifying network data based on homophily, cluster hypothesis, and structural properties including degrees of nodes. We propose a structured random walk based ap-

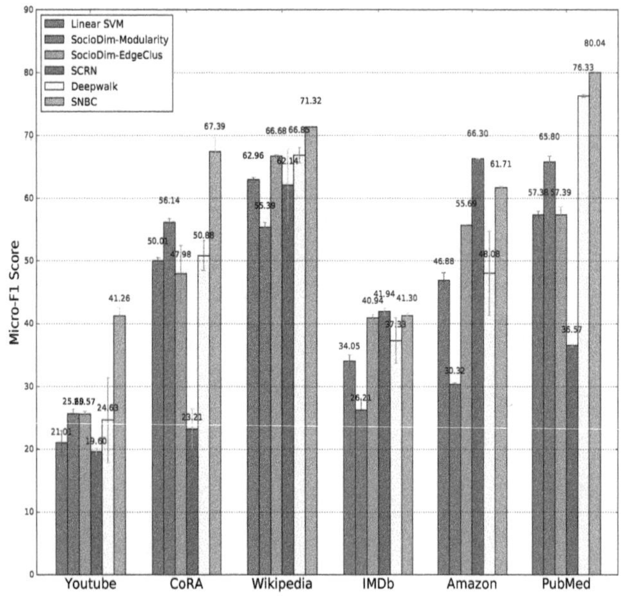

Figure 6: Micro-F1 score for multi-label classification compared with the state-of-the-art approaches using 10% of nodes for training

proach to classification, while emphasizing the role of medium degree nodes in classification. A regularizer that underplays the importance of high degree and low degree nodes is implicitly used. This helps us in achieving robust classification by regulating the noise. A comparative study is made using some of the state-of-the-art intra-network classification approaches, and a baseline classifier demonstrates the effectiveness of our approach.

8. REFERENCES

[1] A. Anagnostopoulos, R. Kumar, and M. Mahdian. Influence and correlation in social networks. In *KDD*, pages 7–15. ACM, 2008.

[2] S. Baluja, R. Seth, D. Sivakumar, Y. Jing, J. Yagnik, S. Kumar, D. Ravichandran, and M. Aly. Video suggestion and discovery for youtube: taking random walks through the view graph. In *WWW*, pages 895–904. ACM, 2008.

[3] S. Chakrabarti, B. Dom, and P. Indyk. Enhanced hypertext categorization using hyperlinks. 27(2):307–318, 1998.

[4] R.-E. Fan, K.-W. Chang, C.-J. Hsieh, X.-R. Wang, and C.-J. Lin. Liblinear: A library for large linear classification. *JMLR*, 9:1871–1874, 2008.

[5] L. A. Goodman. Snowball sampling. *The annals of mathematical statistics*, pages 148–170, 1961.

[6] M. Ji, J. Han, and M. Danilevsky. Ranking-based classification of heterogeneous information networks. In *KDD*, pages 1298–1306. ACM, 2011.

[7] M. Ji, Y. Sun, M. Danilevsky, J. Han, and J. Gao. Graph regularized transductive classification on heterogeneous information networks. In *ECML PKDD*, pages 570–586. Springer, 2010.

[8] J. Kandola, N. Cristianini, and J. S. Shawe-taylor. Learning semantic similarity. In *NIPS*, pages 657–664, 2002.

[9] R. I. Kondor and J. Lafferty. Diffusion kernels on graphs and other discrete input spaces. In *ICML*, pages 315–322, 2002.

[10] D. Liben-Nowell and J. Kleinberg. The link-prediction problem for social networks. *JASIST*, 58(7):1019–1031, 2007.

[11] F. Lin and W. W. Cohen. Semi-supervised classification of network data using very few labels. In *ASONAM*, pages 192–199. IEEE, 2010.

[12] Q. Lu and L. Getoor. Link-based classification. In *ICML*, pages 496–503, 2003.

[13] S. A. Macskassy and F. Provost. A simple relational classifier. In *MRDM at KDD*, 2003.

[14] C. Manning, P. Raghavan, and H. Schütze. *Introduction to Information Retrieval.* Cambridge University Press, 2008.

[15] A. Y. Ng, M. I. Jordan, Y. Weiss, et al. On spectral clustering: Analysis and an algorithm. In *NIPS*, pages 849–856. MIT; 1998, 2002.

[16] L. Page, S. Brin, R. Motwani, and T. Winograd. The pagerank citation ranking: bringing order to the web. 1999.

[17] B. Perozzi, R. Al-Rfou, and S. Skiena. Deepwalk: Online learning of social representations. In *KDD*, pages 701–710. ACM, 2014.

[18] J. C. Platt. Probabilistic outputs for support vector machines and comparisons to regularized likelihood methods. *Advances in large margin classifiers*, 10(3):61–74, 1999.

[19] A. J. Smola and R. Kondor. Kernels and regularization on graphs. In *Learning theory and kernel machines*, pages 144–158. Springer, 2003.

[20] Y. Sun and J. Han. Mining heterogeneous information networks: a structural analysis approach. *ACM SIGKDD Explorations Newsletter*, 14(2):20–28, 2013.

[21] P. P. Talukdar and K. Crammer. New regularized algorithms for transductive learning. In *ECML PKDD*, pages 442–457. Springer, 2009.

[22] J. Tang, M. Qu, M. Wang, M. Zhang, J. Yan, and Q. Mei. Line: Large-scale information network embedding. In *WWW*, pages 1067–1077, 2015.

[23] L. Tang and H. Liu. Relational learning via latent social dimensions. In *KDD*, pages 817–826. ACM, 2009.

[24] L. Tang and H. Liu. Leveraging social media networks for classification. *DMKD*, 23(3):447–478, 2011.

[25] X. Wang and G. Sukthankar. Multi-label relational neighbor classification using social context features. In *KDD*, pages 464–472. ACM, 2013.

[26] M.-L. Zhang and Z.-H. Zhou. A review on multi-label learning algorithms. *TKDE*, 26(8):1819–1837, 2014.

[27] D. Zhou, O. Bousquet, T. N. Lal, J. Weston, and B. Schölkopf. Learning with local and global consistency. In *NIPS*, pages 321–328, 2004.

[28] X. Zhu and Z. Ghahramani. Learning from labeled and unlabeled data with label propagation. Technical report, Citeseer, 2002.

Modeling Precursors for Event Forecasting via Nested Multi-Instance Learning

Yue Ning*, Sathappan Muthiah*, Huzefa Rangwala†, Naren Ramakrishnan*
* Discovery Analytics Center, Department of Computer Science, Virginia Tech, Arlington, VA 22203
† Department of Computer Science, George Mason University, Fairfax, VA 22030
* yning, sathap1, naren@vt.edu
† rangwala@cs.gmu.edu

ABSTRACT

Forecasting large-scale societal events like civil unrest movements, disease outbreaks, and elections is an important and challenging problem. From the perspective of human analysts and policy makers, forecasting algorithms must not only make accurate predictions but must also provide supporting evidence, e.g., the causal factors related to the event of interest. We develop a novel multiple instance learning based approach that jointly tackles the problem of identifying evidence-based precursors and forecasts events into the future. Specifically, given a collection of streaming news articles from multiple sources we develop a nested multiple instance learning approach to forecast significant societal events such as protests. Using data from three countries in Latin America, we demonstrate how our approach is able to consistently identify news articles considered as precursors for protests. Our empirical evaluation demonstrates the strengths of our proposed approach in filtering candidate precursors, in forecasting the occurrence of events with a lead time advantage and in accurately predicting the characteristics of civil unrest events.

Keywords

Multi-Instance Learning; Event Detection; Text Mining

1. INTRODUCTION

Forecasting societal uprisings such as civil unrest movements is an important and challenging problem. Open source data (e.g., social media and news feeds) have been proven to serve as surrogates in forecasting a broad class of events, e.g., disease outbreaks [1], election outcomes [18, 22], stock market movements [6] and protests [19]. While many of these works focus on predictive performance, there is a critical need to develop methods that also yield insight by identifying precursors to events of interest.

This paper focuses on the problem of identifying precursors (evidence) for forecasting significant societal events, specifically protests. Modeling and identifying the precursors for a given protest is useful for human analysts and policy makers as it discerns the underlying reasons behind the civil unrest movement. In particular, the objective of this paper is to study and forecast protests across different cities in three Latin American countries (Argentina, Brazil and Mexico). 6000 news outlets are tracked daily across these countries with the goal of forecasting protest occurrences with at least one day of lead time. From the news feeds, we also aim to identify the specific news articles that can be considered as precursors for the target event.

Figure 1 shows an example of precursors identified by our model. On the right of the timeline is a news report about a protest event in Argentina. The connected dots denotes the generated probabilities of a protest event over the days leading upto this protest. From this example, we find that within 10 days before the event, there are multiple precursor events identified as highly probable leading indicators of a protest. Most significant societal events are a consequence of several factors that affect different entities within communities and their relationships with each other (or the government) over time. In this specific example, the leading precursor was an article commenting on standards of living in Argentina and rising poverty levels. The International Court of Justice also delivered a verdict on the debt crisis. All these factors led to the final protest involving the general population across the country demanding better work opportunities.

We formulate the precursor identification and forecasting problem in a novel multiple instance learning algorithm (MIL) setting. Multiple instance learning algorithms [3, 28] are a class of supervised learning techniques that accept labels for groups of instances, but where labels for individual instances are not avaialble. In our formulation, instances denote news articles and while class labels are not associated with individual news articles, a group of news articles is attached with a label (indicating the occurrence of a protest). We further extend the standard MIL formulation by introducing a nested structure, wherein we group news articles published in a given day at the first level and then group the collection of individual days at the second level. This nested MIL approach allows for modeling the sequential constraints between the news articles (grouped by days) published on different days and also provides a probabilistic estimate for every news article and the collection of news article. This estimate is significant because it indicates for a given news article the probability of it signaling a protest event. Recall that in our datasets we do not have any training labels to associate a protest per news article.

KDD '16, August 13-17, 2016, San Francisco, CA, USA

DOI: http://dx.doi.org/10.1145/2939672.2939802

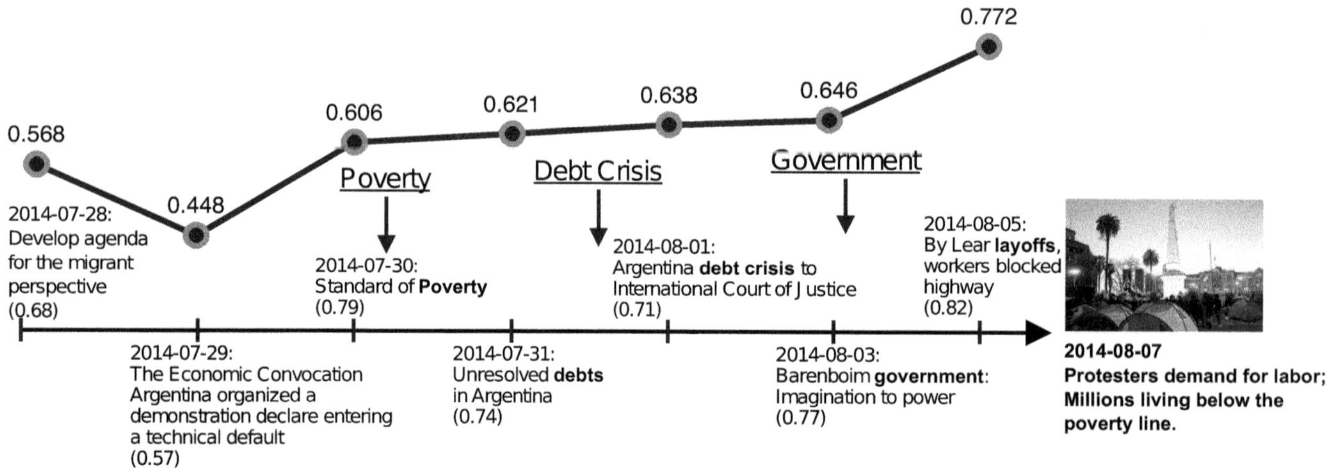

Figure 1: Precursor story line for a protest event in Argentina. The x-axis is the timeline. The dots above with numbers are the probabilities for each day that the model generated for the target event. Each precursor document is titled in the timeline.

The main contributions of this study are summarized as follows:

1. **A novel nested framework of multi-instance learning for event forecasting and precursor mining.** We formulate event forecasting and precursor mining for multiple cities in a country as a multi-instance learning problem with a nested structure. By estimating a prediction score for each instance in the history data, we automatically detect significant precursors for different events.

2. **Harness temporal constraints in multi-instance learning.** We explore different penalty function and regularizations where we employ the temporal information in our dataset under assumption that most events of interest are follow-up reports of other events that happened before, and most planned events are developing over time.

3. **Modeling for various event categories in multiple geo-locations.** We extend the nested MIL formulation for general purpose multi-class classification to determine necessary attributes of events in terms of their underlying population.

4. **Application and evaluation with comprehensive experiments.** We evaluate the proposed methods using news data collected from July 2012 to December 2014 in three countries of Latin America: Argentina, Mexico, and Brazil. For comparison, we implement other multi-instance algorithms, and validate the effectiveness and efficiency of the proposed approach. We also perform qualitative and quantitative analysis on the precursors inferred by our model.

The rest of this paper is organized as follows. We discuss related work in Section 2. Section 3 introduces the problem setup and our proposed model based on multi-instance learning is presented in Section 4. This section is then followed by experiments and evaluations on real world datasets, presented in Section 5 and Section 6 . Finally, we conclude with a summary of the research in Section 7.

2. RELATED WORK

Event Detection and Forecasting. Event detection and forecasting from online open source datasets has been an active area of research in the past decade. Both supervised and unsupervised machine learning techniques have been developed to tackle different challenges. Linear regression models use simple features to predict the occurrence time of future events [4, 6, 10, 18]. Advanced techniques use a combination of sophisticated features such as topic related keywords, as input to support vector machines, LASSO and multi-task learning approaches [23, 20]. Ramakrishnan *et al.* [19] designed a framework (EMBERS) for predicting civil unrest events in different locations by using a wide combination of models with heterogeneous input sources ranging from social media to satellite images. Zhao *et al.* [27] combine multi-task learning and dynamic features from social networks for spatial-temporal event forecasting. Generative models have also been used in [26] to jointly model the temporal evolution in semantics and geographical burstiness within social media content. Laxman *et al.* [13] designed a generative model for categorical event prediction in event streams using frequent episodes. However, few existing approaches provide evidence and interpretive analysis as support for event forecasting.

Identifying Precursors. Identifying precursors for significant events is an interesting topic and has been used extensively for interpretive narrative generation and in storytelling algorithms [11]. Rong *et al.* [21] developed a combinational mixed Poisson process (CMPP) model to learn social, external and intrinsic influence in social networks.

Multiple Instance Learning. In the multiple instance learning (MIL) paradigm, we are given labels for sets of instances commonly referred as *bags* or *groups*. However, individual instance-level labels are unknown or missing. The bag-level labels are assumed to be an association function (e.g., OR, average) of the unknown instance level labels. One approach to MIL adapts support vector machines (SVMs) by: (i) modifying the maximum margin formulation to discriminate between bags rather than individual instances [3], and (ii) developing kernel functions that operate directly on bags [9]. Other multiple instance learning approaches

Table 1: Notation.

Variable	Meaning
$\mathcal{S} = \{\mathbb{S}\}$	a set of n "super bags" in our dataset
$\mathbb{S} = [\mathcal{X}_i], i \in \{1, ..., t\}$	an ordered set of t "bags" in $\mathbb{S}$
$\mathcal{X}_i = \{\mathbf{x}_{ij}\}, j \in \{1, ..., n_i\}$	a set of instances with $n_i = \vert\mathcal{X}_i\vert$, number of instance in a bag $\mathcal{X}_i$
$\mathbf{x}_{ij} \in \Re^{V \times 1}$	the j-th instance in set $\mathcal{X}_i$, a V-dimension vector
$Y \in \{-1, +1\}$	label of super bag
$P \in [0, 1]$	estimated probability for a super bag
$\mathbb{P}_i \in [0, 1]$	the probability of bag i in super bag to be positive
$p_{ij} \in [0, 1]$	the probability of an instance $\mathbf{x}_{ij}$ in bag $\mathcal{X}_i$ in super bag to be positive
$C \in \{1, 2, ..., K\}$	multi-class label of super bag

and various applications are found in a detailed survey [2]. Specifically, the generalized MIL [25] formulation assumes the presence of multiple concepts and a bag is classified as positive if there exists instances from every concept. Relevant to our work, besides predicting bag labels, Liu *et al.* [15] seek to identify the key instances within the positively-labeled bags using nearest neighbor techniques. Recent work [12] has focused on instance-level predictions from group labels (GICF) and allowed for the application of general aggregation functions with applications to detecting sentiments associated with sentences within reviews.

The methods proposed in this paper can be viewed as complementary to prior work, casting the forecasting and precursor discovery problems within novel extensions of multiple instance learning.

3. PROBLEM FORMULATION

Given a collection of streaming media sources (e.g., news feeds, blogs and social network streams), the objective of our study is to develop a machine learning approach to forecast the occurrence of an event of interest in the near future. Specifically, we focus on forecasting protests or civil unrest movements in Latin America from a daily collection of published news articles. Besides forecasting the protest, we aim to identify the specific news articles from the streaming news outlets that can be considered as supporting evidence for further introspection by an intelligence analyst. We refer to these identified articles as *precursors* for a specific protest.

Figure 2 provides an overview of our proposed approach and problem formulation. Here, we show groups of news articles collected daily, five days prior to the specific protest event (being forecast). Within our proposed MIL-based formulation, each news article is an individual instance, the collection of news articles published on a given day is a bag, and the ordered collection of bags (days) is denoted as a super-bag (explained in detail later). For this study, each individual news article is represented by a distributed representation for text derived using a framework such as text embedding [14]. Figure 2 shows that for certain days within the collection we attempt to identify news articles (highlighted) that are considered as precursors from the entire collection of input news articles used for forecasting the occurrence of a specific target.

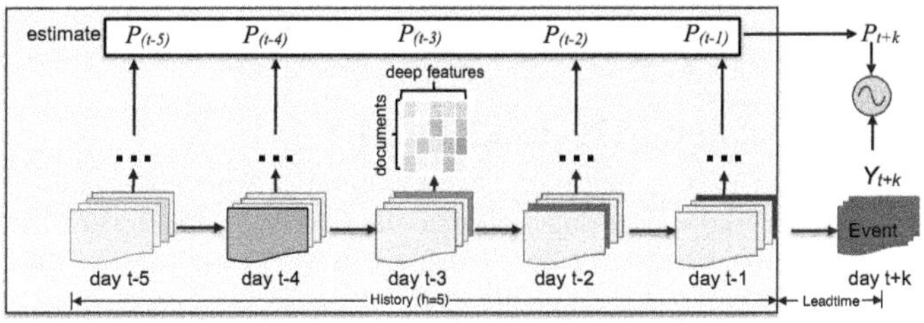

Figure 2: Overview of proposed approach to forecasting and precursor discovery.

3.1 Formal Definition and Notation

For a given protest event e occurring on day $t + k$, we assume that for each day before the event we are tracking a multitude of news sources. We represent the collection of n_i news articles published on a given day i by $\mathcal{X}_i = \{\mathbf{x}_{i,1} \dots \mathbf{x}_{i,n_i}\}$, where the j-th news article is represented by $\mathbf{x}_{ij}$. The ordered collection of news articles for the protest event up to day t can be represented as a super-bag, $\mathbb{S}_{1:t} = \{\mathcal{X}_1, \dots, \mathcal{X}_t\}$. The occurrence of the protest event at time $t + k$ is denoted by $\mathcal{Y}_{t+k} \in \{-1, +1\}$ where 1 denotes a protest and -1, otherwise.

The forecasting problem can be formulated as learning a mathematical function $f(\mathbb{S}_{1:t}) \rightarrow \mathcal{Y}_{t+k}$ that maps the input, an ordered collection of news articles extracted per day to a protest indicator k days in the future from the day t. To identify the news articles considered as precursors (evidence), we aim to estimate a probability for each news article on any given day that signifies the occurrence of a given protest. For a news article $\mathbf{x}_{ij}$, we denote this estimated probability value by p_{ij}. As such, given the collection of news articles we identify the precursor set as the ones with p_{ij} greater than a fixed threshold τ. We represent this precursor set of documents as a subset of the original super-bag, given by $\{\mathbf{x}_{ij} \in \mathbb{S}_{1:t} \mid p_{ij} > \tau\}$. As a secondary objective, we aim to forecast the occurrence of an event with a long lead time i.e., large values of k. Table 1 captures the notation and definitions used in this study.

4. METHODS

We first provide our intuition behind formulating the precursor discovery and forecasting problem within a novel extension of multiple instance learning algorithm. Parallel to the standard multiple instance learning algorithms we have a group of news articles (bags) with labels available only for the entire bag (i.e., leading to a protest); and one of the objectives is to train a classifier to predict the bag-level label. In addition to predicting the group-level labels, we also care about predicting the labels for individual news articles (instances) since they signify the precursor. Various MIL formulations extend the basic definition with a similar motivation, i.e., to estimate the key instances within a bag or provide instance-level labels. However, our problem setting has a two-level grouping structure with sequential constraints, i.e., we capture news articles per day (bags) and group the days to form a super-bag with labels only available at the super-bag level. As such, we propose a nested multiple instance learning formulation for predicting the super bag level labels (forecast) and then estimate the bag-level and instance-level probabilities for identifying association of the bag and instance with the event, respectively. We developed various extensions of our proposed approach to tie the different sequential and group constraints.

4.1 Nested MIL model (nMIL)

We model the instance level probability estimates p_{ij} for a news article j on day i to associate with a targeted event e with a logistic function. These probability estimates indicate how related the specific instance is to the target event, e. Higher the probability value, the more related the document is to the target event and most probably represents a precursor that contains information about causes of the target event.

$$p_{ij} = \sigma(\mathbf{w}^T \mathbf{x}_{ij}) = \frac{1}{1+e^{-\mathbf{w}^T \mathbf{x}_{ij}}}. \quad (1)$$

Here, $\mathbf{w}$ denotes the learned weight vector for our model. The probability for a day (or bag) is then modeled as the average of probability estimates of all instances in a day [12]. Hence, for each bag:

$$\mathbb{P}_i = \mathcal{A}(\mathcal{X}_i, \mathbf{w}) = \frac{1}{n_i}\sum_{j}^{n_i} p_{ij}, \quad (2)$$

where $\mathcal{A}$ is an aggregation function.

We then model the probability of a super-bag $\mathbb{S}$ (associated with an event e) being positive as the average of the probability of all t bags within the super bag to be positive (related to the target event). Thus:

$$P = \mathcal{A}(\mathbb{S}, \mathbf{w}) = \frac{1}{t}\sum_{i}^{t} \mathbb{P}_i \quad (3)$$

For a given super bag $\mathbb{S}$, as all the t bags within it are temporally ordered, the probability estimates for a given bag (day) is assumed to be similar to its immediate predecessor. This consistency in consecutive bag probabilities is modeled by minimizing the following cross-bag cost as below:

$$g(\mathcal{X}_i, \mathcal{X}_{i-1}) = (P_i - P_{i-1})^2 \quad (4)$$

Finally, given a set of true labels Y for the super bags, we can train our model by minimizing the following cost function w.r.t to $\mathbf{w}$:

$$J(\mathbf{w}) = \frac{\beta}{n}\sum_{\mathbb{S}\in\mathcal{S}} f(\mathbb{S}, Y, \mathbf{w}) + \frac{1}{n}\sum_{\substack{\mathbb{S}\in\mathcal{S};\\ \mathcal{X}_i,\mathcal{X}_{i-1}\in\mathbb{S}}} \frac{1}{t}\sum_{i=1}^{t} g(\mathcal{X}_i, \mathcal{X}_{i-1}, \mathbf{w})$$
$$+ \frac{1}{n}\sum_{\substack{\mathbb{S}\in\mathcal{S};\mathcal{X}_i\in\mathbb{S}\\ \mathbf{x}_{ij}\in\mathcal{X}_i}} \frac{1}{t}\sum_{i=1}^{t}\frac{1}{n_i}\sum_{j=1}^{n_i} h(\mathbf{x}_{ij}, \mathbf{w}) + \lambda R(\mathbf{w}) \quad (5)$$

Here,

- $f(\mathbb{S}, Y, \mathbf{w}) = -\mathbf{I}(Y=1)logP - \mathbf{I}(Y=-1)(log(1-P))$ is the negative log-likelihood function that penalizes the difference between prediction and the true label for super bag $\mathbb{S}$ where $\mathbf{I}(\cdot)$ is the indicator function.
- $g(\mathcal{X}_i, \mathcal{X}_{i-1}, \mathbf{w})$ is the cross-bag cost defined in Equation. 4
- $h(\mathbf{x}_{ij}, \mathbf{w}) = max(0, m_0 - sgn(p_{ij} - p_0)\mathbf{w}^T\mathbf{x}_{ij})$ represents the instance level cost. Here, sgn is the sign function; m_0 is a crucial margin parameter used to separate the positive and negative instances from the hyper line in the feature space; p_0 is a threshold parameter to determine positiveness of instance.
- $R(\mathbf{w})$ is the regularization function.
- β, λ are constants that control the trade-offs between the loss function and regularization function.

4.1.1 *Cross-bag Similarity* (nMIL$^{\Delta}$)

The cross-bag similarity $g(,)$ in the above equation does not allow for sudden changes in the day-level probabilities caused due to newer events happening on the current day. We update the cost function across days (bags) (Equation 4) as follows:

$$g(\mathcal{X}_i, \mathcal{X}_{i-1}) = \Delta(\mathcal{X}_i, \mathcal{X}_{i-1})(P_i - P_{i-1})^2 \quad (6)$$

The objective function above allows for label information to spread over the manifold in the feature-space. As such, we compute $\Delta(,)$ as the pairwise cosine similarity between the news articles in $\mathcal{X}_i$ and $\mathcal{X}_{i-1}$. Since we do not have ground truth labels for the bag level (day) we make this consistency assumption that estimated probabilities for consecutive days should be similar if the news articles have similarity in the feature space as well. This model is referred by **nMIL**$^{\Delta}$and allows for sudden changes in how events unfold.

4.2 Sequential Model (nMIL$^{\Omega}$)

The basic **nMIL** models assume that there exists a single weight vector across all the days (bags) within a super bag. To model the sequential characteristics of the articles published across consecutive days, we extend this formulation by learning individual weight vectors for each of the historical days. Assuming t days within a super bag $\mathbb{S}$ we learn a weight vector for each individual day represented as $\Omega = [\mathbf{w}_1, \ldots, \mathbf{w}_t]$; where $\mathbf{w}_i$ is the weight vector learned for day i. In this setting, the individual weight vectors are still learned together in a joint fashion akin to multi-task learning approaches [7]. However, the probability of a news article j on day i will be given by $p_{ij} = \sigma(\mathbf{w}_i^T\mathbf{x}_{ij})$. This formulation is called **nMIL**$^{\Omega}$and given by:

$$J(\mathbf{\Omega}) = \underbrace{\frac{\beta}{n}\sum_{\mathbb{S}\in\mathcal{S}} f(\mathbb{S}, \mathbf{\Omega}, Y)}_{\text{empirical loss}} + \underbrace{\frac{1}{n}\sum_{\substack{\mathbb{S}\in\mathcal{S};\\ \mathcal{X}_i,\mathcal{X}_{i-1}\in\mathbb{S}}} \frac{1}{t}\sum_{i=1}^{t} g(\mathcal{X}_i, \mathcal{X}_{i-1}, \mathbf{w}_i)}_{\text{sequential loss}}$$
$$+ \underbrace{\frac{1}{n}\sum_{\substack{\mathbb{S}\in\mathcal{S};\mathcal{X}_i\in\mathbb{S}\\ \mathbf{x}_{ij}\in\mathcal{X}_i}} \frac{1}{t}\sum_{i=1}^{t}\frac{1}{n_i}\sum_{j=1}^{n_i} h(\mathbf{x}_{ij}, \mathbf{w}_i)}_{\text{unsupervised loss}} + \lambda R(\mathbf{\Omega}) \quad (7)$$

Just like the multi-task learning algorithms, the regularization term $R(\mathbf{\Omega})$ can be modified to capture the various relationship-based constraints. However, in this study we ignore these specialized approaches focusing only on the MIL paradigm.

4.3 Multiclass Classification

We also extend our developed **nMIL** formulations to solve general purpose multiclass classification problems rather than binary classification problems. Within our domain, each labeled event is manually attached with event population.

Event population indicates the size/community of people who participated in the protest event.

For multiclass classification problems, we train one-versus-rest classifiers for each of the classes learning a separate weight vector per class. When classifying a super bag to a specific event population we first forecast the binary protest indicator label for a super bag. Next, we apply the multi-class classification only on the predicted positive examples.

4.4 Optimization

We perform online stochastic gradient decent optimization to solve our cost function and test our model on new data to predict super bag label. For every iteration in our algorithm, we randomly choose a super-bag $(\mathbb{S}, Y)$ from the training dataset $\mathcal{S}$ by picking an index $r \in \{1, \ldots, n\}$ using a standard uniform distribution. Then we optimize an approximation based on the sampled super-bag by:

$$J(\mathbf{w}; \mathbb{S}) = \beta f + \frac{1}{t}\sum_{i}^{t} g_i + \frac{1}{t}\sum_{i}^{t}\frac{1}{n_i}\sum_{j}^{n_i} h_{ij} + \lambda R(\mathbf{w}) \quad (8)$$

The gradient of the approximate function is given by:

$$\begin{aligned}\nabla J(\mathbf{w}) &= \frac{\partial J(\mathbf{w}; \mathbb{S})}{\partial \mathbf{w}} = \lambda \mathbf{w} \quad (9)\\ &- \frac{Y-P}{P(1-P)}\frac{\beta}{t}\sum_{i}^{t}\frac{1}{n_i}\sum_{k}^{n_i} p_{ij}(1-p_{ij})\mathbf{x}_{ij}\\ &+ \frac{1}{t}\sum_{i}^{t} 2(P_i - P_{i-1})\frac{1}{n_i}\sum_{j}^{n_i} p_{ij}(1-p_{ij})\mathbf{x}_{ij}\\ &- \frac{1}{t}\sum_{i}^{t} 2(P_i - P_{i-1})\frac{1}{n_{i-1}}\sum_{j}^{n_{i-1}} p_{vj}(1-p_{vj})\mathbf{x}_{vj}\\ &- \frac{1}{t}\sum_{i}^{t}\frac{1}{n_i}\sum_{j}^{n_i} sgn(p_{ij} - p_0)\mathbf{x}_{ij}(o_{ij})\end{aligned}$$

where $v = i - 1, o_{ij} = I(sgn(p_{ij} - p_0)\mathbf{w}\mathbf{x}_{ij} < m_0)$. We update the weight vector using a varied learning rate and $\mathbf{w}' = \mathbf{w} - \eta\nabla(\mathbf{w})$ using mini-batch stochastic gradient descent where η is the learning rate at current iteration.

4.5 Precursor discovery using nMIL

In the **nMIL** model, each super-bag consists of an ordered set of bags and each bag represents the documents in one day in the city for which we are forecasting a protest event. We present in Algorithm 1 the steps to identify news articles as precursors based on their estimated probability given by $p_{ij} > \tau$.

Algorithm 1 Precursor Discovery in **nMIL**

procedure PD-**nMIL**
  Input: $\mathcal{S} = \{(\mathbb{S}_r, Y_r)\}_{r \in n^+}, \mathcal{M}$
  Output: $\{(ps_r, Y_r)\}_{r \in n^+}$
  for super bag (S_r, Y_r) **do**
    $ps_r = []$
    for t = 1,2,...,h(history days) **do**
      $y_t = []$
      for $\mathbf{x}_{tm} \in \mathcal{X}_t$ **do**
        $\hat{y}_{tm} = \sigma(\hat{\mathbf{w}}\mathbf{x}_{tm})$
        if $\hat{y}_{tm} > \tau$ **then**
          $y_t \leftarrow (m, \hat{y}_{tm})$
      sort(y_t) by $\hat{y}_{tm}$ in descending order
      $ps_r \leftarrow$ m where m in top(y_t)
  return $\{(ps_r, Y_r)\}_{r \in n^+}$

5. EXPERIMENTS

5.1 Datasets

The experimental evaluation was performed on news documents collected from around 6000 news agencies between July 2012 to December 2014 across three countries in South America, viz. Argentina, Brazil, and Mexico. For Argentina and Mexico, the input news articles were primarily in Spanish and for Brazil, the news articles were in Portuguese.

The ground truth information about protest events, called the gold standard report (GSR) is exclusively provided by MITRE [19]. The GSR is a manually created list of civil unrest events that happened during the period 2012-2014. A labeled GSR event provides information about the geographical location at the city level, date, type and population of a civil unrest news report extracted from the most influential newspaper outlets within the country of interest. These GSR reports are the target events that are used for validation of our forecasting algorithm. We have no ground truth available for verifying the validity of the precursors.

Argentina: We collected data for Argentina from newspaper outlets including *Clarin* and *Lanacion* for the period of July 2010 to December 2014. There are multiple protest events in Argentina during this period. For instance, people protested against the government and utility/electricity-providing companies because of heatwaves in Dec. 2013.

Brazil: For Brazil, we obtained data from news agencies including the three leading news agencies in Brazil; *O Globo, Estadao,* and *Jornal do Brasil* from November 2012 to September 2013. During this period Brazil faced several mass public demonstrations across several Brazilian cities stemming from a variety of issues ranging from transportation costs, government corruption, and police brutality. These mass protests were initiated due to a local entity advocating for free public transportation. This period had an unusually high social media activity and news coverage and is also known as the "Brazilian Spring" [1].

Mexico: For Mexico, we tracked news agencies including the top outlets: *Jornada, Reforma, Milenio* from January 2013 to December 2014. Over 619 days, we noticed 71 news articles per day on average. There were more than 2000 protest events in this two-year period with major unrest movements in 2013 led by teachers and students demanding education reforms by protesting against the government.

5.2 Experimental Protocol

The GSR signifies the occurrence of a protest event on a given day at a specific location. To evaluate the MIL-based forecasting and precursor discovery algorithms, for each protest event we extract all the published news articles for up to 10 days before the occurrence of the specific event. This ordered collection of per-day news documents up to the protest day are considered as positive super bags. For negative samples, we identify consecutive sets of five days within our studied time periods for the different countries when no

[1]http://abcnews.go.com/ABC_Univision/brazilian-spring-explainer/story?id=19472387

protest was reported by the GSR. The ordered collection of per-day news documents not leading to a protest are considered as negative super bags for the nMIL approach. For any news article (i.e., an individual instance) within a positive/negative super-bag we have no label (or ground truth). As part of the precursor discovery algorithm, we estimate a probability for an individual instance to signal a protest (by showing evidence). It is important to note that the GSR linked news article for a protest is never used for training purposes. Having identified the positive and negative samples, we split our datasets into training and testing partitions and perform 3-fold cross-validation. A single run of the model on a machine with 4 cores and 16 GB memory takes about 250 seconds.

We study the performance of forecasting models with varying lead time and varying historical days. Lead time (l) indicates the number of days in advance the model makes predictions and historical days (h) denotes the number of days over which the news articles are extracted as input to the prediction algorithms. As an example, if l is set to 1, then the model forecasts if a protest event is planned for the next day. Setting the historical days, h, to 5 denotes that we use news from five days before the current day to make the forecast. We varied l from 1 to 5 and h from 1 to 10 and trained 50 different models for the different approaches to study the characteristics of the developed approaches with varying lead time and historical days.

For event forecasting, we evaluate the performance by standard metrics including precision, recall, accuracy and F1-measure.

5.3 Comparative Approaches

We compare the proposed **nMIL** models to the following approaches:

- **SVM** : We use the standard support vector machine formulation [8] by collapsing the nested grouping structure and assigning the same label for each news article as its super-bag (for training). During the prediction phase, the SVM yields the final super-bag prediction (forecast) by averaging the predicted label obtained for each of the instances.

- **MI-SVM** [3]: The MI-SVM model extends the notion of a margin from individual patterns to bags. Notice that for a positive bag the margin is defined by the margin of the "most positive" instance, while the margin of a negative bag is defined by the "least negative" instance. In our case, we collapse the news articles from the different historical days into one bag and apply this standard MIL formulation.

- **Relaxed-MIL** (**rMIL^{nor}**) [24]: Similar to the MI-SVM baseline, we collapse the news articles into one bag. However, unlike the MI-SVM formulation the **rMIL^{nor}** model can provide a probabilistic estimate for a given document within a bag to be positive or negative.

- **Modified Relaxed-MIL** (**rMIL^{avg}**): This approach is similar to the **rMIL^{nor}** , except we compute the probability of a bag being positive by taking average of estimate of each instance in the bag rather than using the Noisy-OR model discussed above.

- **GICF** [12]: This model optimizes a cost function which parameterized the whole-part relationship between groups and instances and pushes similar items across different groups to have similar labels.

5.4 Feature Description

In practice, finding good feature representations to model the news articles is not a trivial problem. Traditionally the bag-of-words representation allows for easy interpretation but also requires pre-processing and feature selection. Several researchers have developed efficient and effective neural network representations for language models [5, 16, 17]. Specifically, we learn deep features for documents by taking advantage of the existing doc2vec model. For each document, we generate a 300 dimension vector for training with a contextual window size of 10 in an unsupervised version [14]. We compared the performance of deep features with traditional TF-IDF features but the results showed little difference. Thus, we only report the evaluation of models with deep features.

6. RESULTS AND DISCUSSION

In this section, we evaluate the performance of the proposed models. First, we evaluate the effectiveness and efficiency of the methods on real data in comparison with baseline methods on multiple configurations of forecasting tasks. Then, we study and analyze the quality of precursors with respect to quantitative and qualitative measures. Multi-class forecasting evaluation is also provided for one of the countries. Finally, we perform a sensitivity analysis of performance regarding parameters in the proposed model.

6.1 How well does nMIL forecast protests?

6.1.1 Comparative Evaluation

Table 2 reports the prediction performance of the **nMIL** approach in comparison to other baseline approaches for the task of forecasting protests. Specifically, we use set $\beta = 3.0$, $\lambda = 0.05$, $m_0 = 0.5$ and $p_0 = 0.5$ (β, λ chosen by sensitivity analysis, m_0, p_0 by default setting in hinge loss) and report the average accuracy and F1 score along with standard deviation for predicting protests across multiple runs of varying historical days with lead time set to 1. We observe that the **nMIL** approaches outperform the baseline approaches across all the three countries. The **rMIL^{nor}** approach performs poorly because the the noisy-OR aggregation function associating the bag-level labels to instance-level labels forces most of the news articles within the positive bags to have probability values close to 1. However, given the large collection of news articles available per day only a subset of them will provide a signal/evidence for a protest. For Argentina, the **nMIL** and **nMIL$^{\triangle}$**approaches outperformed the best baseline (**MI-SVM**), by **7%** and **8%** with respect the average F1 score, respectively.

Figure 3 shows the changes to F1 score for the proposed **nMIL** approach in comparison to **SVM** , **MI-SVM** and **rMIL^{avg}** for different number of historical days that are used in training with lead time set to 2. We trained 10 different models that use different number of historical days respectively varying from 1 to 10. These results show that the methods that utilize the nested structure (**nMIL** ,**nMIL$^{\triangle}$**) within the multi-instance learning paradigm generally performed better than others. Moreover, the proposed **nMIL**

Table 2: Event forecasting performance comparison based Accuracy (Acc) and F-1 score w.r.t to state-of-the-art methods. The proposed **nMIL** , **nMIL$^{\Delta}$**, **nMIL$^{\Omega}$**method outperform state-of-the-art methods across the three countries.

	Argentina		Brazil		Mexico	
	Acc	F-1	Acc	F-1	Acc	F-1
SVM	0.611(±0.034)	0.406(±0.072)	0.693(±0.040)	0.598(±0.067)	0.844(±0.062)	0.814(±0.091)
MI-SVM	0.676(±0.026)	0.659(±0.036)	0.693(±0.040)	0.503(±0.087)	0.880(±0.025)	0.853(±0.040)
rMIL^{nor}	0.330(±0.040)	0.411(±0.092)	0.505(±0.012)	0.661(±0.018)	0.499(±0.009)	0.655(±0.025)
rMIL^{avg}	0.644(±0.032)	0.584 (±0.055)	0.509(±0.011)	0.513(±0.064)	0.785(±0.038)	0.768(±0.064)
GICF	0.589(±0.058)	0.624(±0.048)	0.650(±0.055)	0.649 (±0.031)	0.770(±0.041)	0.703(±0.056)
nMIL	**0.709**(±0.036)	0.702(±0.047)	**0.723**(±0.039)	0.686(±0.055)	**0.898**(±0.031)	**0.902**(±0.030)
nMIL$^{\Delta}$	0.708(±0.039)	**0.714**(±0.034)	0.705(±0.048)	**0.698**(±0.045)	0.861(±0.014)	0.868(±0.014)
nMIL$^{\Omega}$	0.687(±0.038)	0.680(±0.045)	0.713(±0.028)	0.687(±0.038)	0.871(±0.013)	0.879(±0.014)

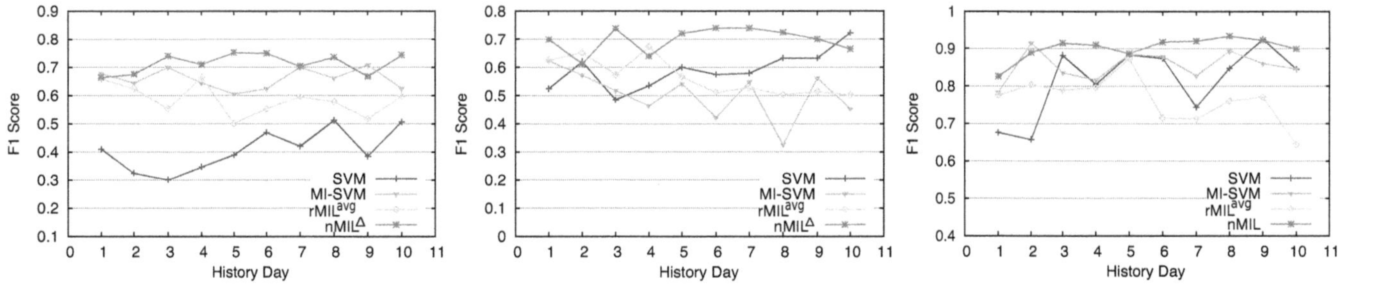

(a) Argentina (b) Brazil (c) Mexico

Figure 3: Forecasting evaluation on 3 countries with respect to F1 score for **SVM** , **rMIL^{nor}** , **rMIL^{avg}** and **nMIL** . X-axis is the number of historical days used in the training process. Y-axis shows the average F1 score of 10 runs of experiments.

models performed well consistently across different countries with different number of history days.

6.1.2 *How early can* nMIL *forecast?*

In order to study the changes of performance with and without the nested structure, we show the F1 score with varying lead times and historical days from 1 to 5 for **rMIL^{avg}** and **nMIL$^{\Delta}$**models in Table 3, respectively. We observe that with larger lead time (i.e., forecasting earlier than later), the **nMIL** model does not necessarily lose forecasting accuracy, but is sometimes even better. This can be explained by the fact that several times protests are planned a few days in advance and that civil unrest unfold as a series of actions taken by multiple participating entities over a sequence of days. As the lead time increases, F1 score for forecasting initially drops and then increases back. This behavior is also noted in prior work by Ramakrishnan et. al [19], which includes protest related data from these countries. In comparison to the **nMIL** model, the **rMIL^{avg}** approach, (which collapses the sequential structure encoded within the history of days) seems to perform inconsistently with increasing lead time.

6.2 Do the precursors tell a story?

Quantitative Evaluation. Figures 4a and 4b show the distribution of the estimated probabilities for instances within positive and negative super bags for Argentina and Mexico, respectively.

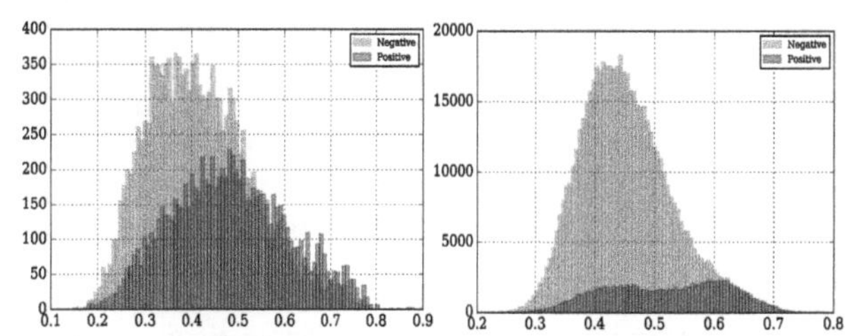

(a) Argentina (b) Mexico

Figure 4: Estimated probabilities for negative examples (purple) and positive examples (green) for Argentina and Mexico.

The instances within the negative super bags show lower probability estimates by the proposed model and the instances within the positive super bags show higher probability estimates. For Mexico, fewer instances within the positives are assigned high probabilities indicating strength of the proposed model to identify and rank the precursors.

Relative cosine similarity is computed as the pairwise normalized cosine similarity, scaled relative to each event. Figures 5a and 5b show the average cosine similarity value for the precursor documents (probability estimate greater than 0.7) with the target GSR documents.

For Argentina, we observe that on average, the documents on day 5 have the highest semantic similarity to the target event documents (GSR). The documents on day 3 and day 10 have lower similarity compared to the target event.

Table 3: F1-measure for $\mathbf{rMIL^{avg}}$ and $\mathbf{nMIL^{\triangle}}$models on Argentina, Brazil, and Mexico with history days from 1 to 5.

	Country	Argentina					Brazil					Mexico				
	History Days	1	2	3	4	5	1	2	3	4	5	1	2	3	4	5
Leadtime 1	$\mathbf{rMIL^{avg}}$	0.719	0.714	0.690	0.710	0.705	0.717	0.692	0.696	0.662	0.680	0.815	0.803	0.789	0.796	0.873
	$\mathbf{nMIL^{\triangle}}$	**0.745**	**0.735**	**0.722**	0.691	**0.716**	**0.734**	**0.768**	**0.721**	**0.735**	**0.717**	**0.842**	**0.868**	**0.863**	**0.884**	**0.884**
Leadtime 2	$\mathbf{rMIL^{avg}}$	0.659	0.624	0.554	0.665	0.500	0.695	0.651	0.573	0.672	0.565	0.846	0.875	0.860	0.878	0.912
	$\mathbf{nMIL^{\triangle}}$	**0.664**	**0.675**	**0.740**	**0.710**	**0.751**	**0.699**	0.611	**0.738**	0.639	**0.721**	0.825	**0.889**	**0.914**	**0.909**	0.886
Leadtime 3	$\mathbf{rMIL^{avg}}$	0.674	0.606	0.622	0.543	0.578	0.694	0.682	0.620	0.715	0.622	0.819	0.787	0.808	0.750	0.853
	$\mathbf{nMIL^{\triangle}}$	0.649	**0.669**	0.560	**0.669**	**0.737**	**0.687**	0.639	**0.674**	**0.717**	**0.742**	**0.856**	**0.903**	**0.884**	**0.909**	**0.900**
Leadtime 4	$\mathbf{rMIL^{avg}}$	0.656	0.558	0.588	0.556	0.476	0.729	0.712	0.720	0.628	0.621	0.809	0.822	0.798	0.878	0.772
	$\mathbf{nMIL^{\triangle}}$	**0.676**	**0.693**	**0.670**	**0.712**	**0.631**	**0.754**	0.584	**0.736**	**0.735**	**0.725**	**0.872**	**0.888**	**0.894**	**0.916**	**0.874**
Leadtime 5	$\mathbf{rMIL^{avg}}$	0.669	0.676	0.590	0.567	0.575	0.710	0.588	0.616	0.548	0.570	0.828	0.845	0.810	0.733	0.889
	$\mathbf{nMIL^{\triangle}}$	0.626	0.676	**0.687**	**0.773**	**0.737**	0.683	**0.665**	**0.657**	**0.697**	**0.735**	**0.833**	**0.937**	**0.878**	**0.935**	**0.931**

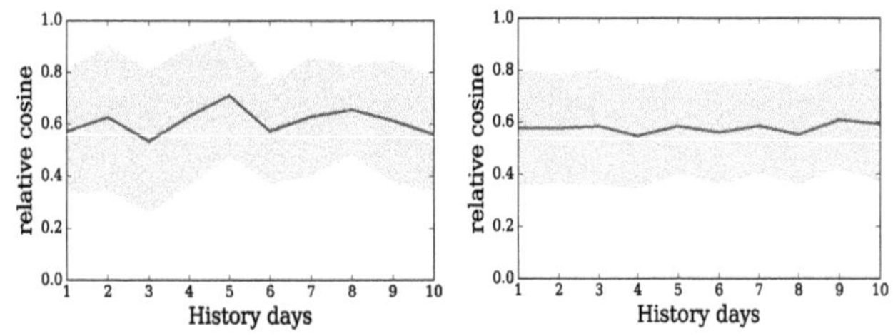

(a) Argentina (b) Mexico

Figure 5: Mean of relative cosine values w.r.t target events in history days for Argentina and Mexico.

In order to investigate the relationship between the semantic similarity and the estimated probability by the proposed models, we compare the distribution of relative cosine similarity and relative entity hit score of the precursor documents with the target GSR documents with respect to bag of words features. Entity words in each news document are extracted by an enrichment tool for natural language processing. The relative entity hit score is calculated as the the intersection of entity set of precursor document and the target event divided by the relative minimum length of these two sets.

Figures 6a and 6b show the fitted Gaussian distribution of relative cosine similarities for all documents (green lines) and precursor documents (blue lines) for Argentina and Mexico, respectively. Figures 6c and 6d show the distribution of relative entity hit score for Argentina and Mexico, respectively. These distribution figures demonstrate that the proposed model assigns higher probability to news articles with higher semantic similarity to the GSR articles representing the protests events. These results show the strength of our proposed models in identifying the precursor articles.

Case Studies. We present findings about the identified precursors based on the probability estimate by **nMIL** across three observed protests. In Figure 1, we present a protest event against government in Argentina, and the selected precursors before its occurrence with their estimated probabilities. The titles of news reports as precursors are shown in the timeline.

In Figures 8a and 8b, we present story lines by precursors that were discovered for two different protest events in Argentina and Mexico, respectively. Figure 8a showcases the story line about a protest event in Argentina in December 2014. In this case, the police were protesting against government for better salaries. Before this event, clashes between police and gendarmerie (military policy) had occurred leading to the involvement of several policemen from different parts of the country. The text from news articles

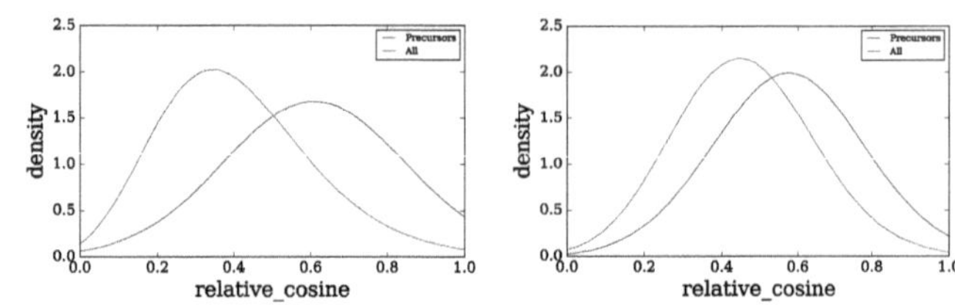

(a) Argentina (b) Mexico

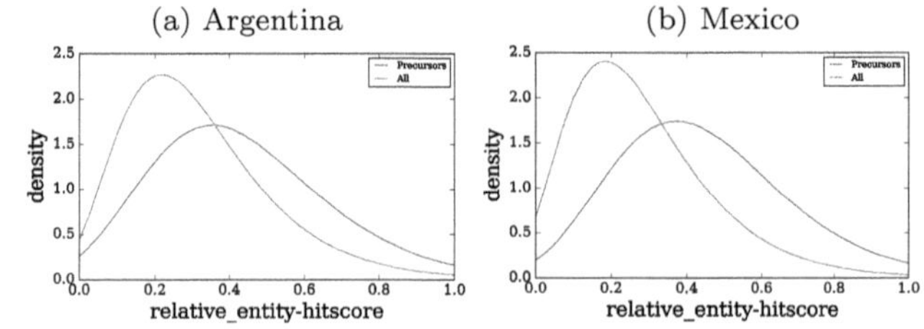

(c) Argentina (d) Mexico

Figure 6: The figures on top depict the distribution of relative cosine similarity for all documents (green line) and for precursor documents (blue line) with probability greater than 0.7. The figures in the bottom row depict the distribution of relative entity hit score for all documents (green line) and for precursor documents (blue line) with probability greater than 0.7.

demonstrate the tense situation between the police and government in La Pampa, Argentina identified as precursors.

Figure 8b shows another story line of a continuous protest event in Mexico regarding the infamous case of 43 missing students [2]. The resulting outrage triggered constant protests which were identified by our proposed model. The figure shows a timeline of how the events turned violent leading up to the burning of congressional offices and depicts how different communities joined the movement.

6.3 Can nMIL forecast event populations?

We also evaluated the performance of our **nMIL** approaches for predicting the event populations by solving a multi-class classification problem. In Table 4 we depict the weighted-average F1 score for event populations (here, with categories such as *Government, Wages, Energy, Others* drawn from the GSR). Due to space limitations, we only depict the performance of weighted average F1 score on event population across 1 to 5 historical days with lead time of 1.

The proposed multi-class **nMIL** model outperforms the multi-class $\mathbf{rMIL^{avg}}$ model. On average, for event population, **nMIL** outperformed $\mathbf{rMIL^{avg}}$ by 10.5% and 10.6% for Argentina and Mexico, respectively.

[2]https://en.wikipedia.org/wiki/2014_Iguala_mass_kidnapping

Table 4: Multi-Class F1-Measure for **rMIL**^{avg} and **nMIL** models on Argentina and Mexico with historical days from 1 to 5.

	History Days	1	2	3	4	5	Average(Variance)
Argentina	rMIL^{avg}	0.512	0.512	0.473	0.417	0.457	0.474(1e-3)
	nMIL	0.523	0.552	0.515	0.485	0.537	**0.524(7e-4)**
Mexico	rMIL^{avg}	0.576	0.526	0.447	0.547	0.493	0.518(3e-3)
	nMIL	0.570	0.583	0.560	0.615	0.545	**0.575(7e-4)**

6.4 How sensitive is nMIL to parameters?

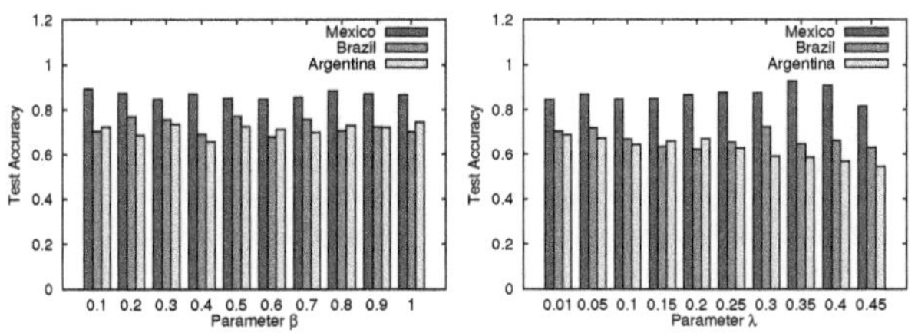

(a) β in **nMIL** (b) λ in **nMIL**

Figure 7: Sensitivity analysis on β and λ. x-axis represents the varying values for the parameter and y-axis denotes the test accuracy.

There are three main parameters in the proposed **nMIL** model, which are the regularization parameter λ, weight for super bag loss β and threshold for instance level hinge loss m_0. Figures 7a and 7b illustrate the performance of the proposed **nMIL** by varying β and λ, respectively. The test accuracy for different values of λ and β is relatively stable.

7. CONCLUSION AND FUTURE WORK

This paper has presented a novel extension of the multi-instance learning framework for event forecasting and for identifying precursors for protest events. Most existing multi-instance approaches solve problems in object detection in images, drug activity prediction or identify sentimental sentences in text reviews. In contrast, we provide a novel application of MIL algorithms that require a two-level nested structure for event forecasting and precursor modeling.

We have also studied the strengths of our developed methods on open source news datasets from three Latin American countries. Through extensive evaluation and analysis, we illustrate the strong forecasting performance of the proposed methods with varying lead time and historical data. We also show qualitatively via several case studies, the richness of the identified precursors for different protests across different cities. In the future, we plan to incorporate heterogeneous data sources like social media streams for event forecasting within the developed framework. We will also extend our nested multi-instance learning framework by exploring regularized multi-task learning approaches for enforcing similarity of learned parameters, while enforcing spatial and temporal constraints.

Acknowledgments

Supported by the Intelligence Advanced Research Projects Activity (IARPA) via DoI/NBC contract number D12PC000337, the US Government is authorized to reproduce and distribute reprints of this work for Governmental purposes notwithstanding any copyright annotation thereon. Disclaimer: The views and conclusions contained herein are those of the authors and should not be interpreted as necessarily representing the official policies or endorsements, either expressed or implied, of IARPA, DoI/NBC, or the US Government.

8. REFERENCES

[1] H. Achrekar, A. Gandhe, R. Lazarus, S.-H. Yu, and B. Liu. Predicting flu trends using twitter data. In *IEEE Conference on Computer Communications Workshops (INFOCOM WKSHPS)*, pages 702–707, April 2011.

[2] J. Amores. Multiple instance classification: Review, taxonomy and comparative study. *Artificial Intelligence*, 201:81–105, 2013.

[3] S. Andrews, I. Tsochantaridis, and T. Hofmann. Support vector machines for multiple-instance learning. In *Advances in neural information processing systems*, pages 561–568, 2002.

[4] M. Arias, A. Arratia, and R. Xuriguera. Forecasting with twitter data. *ACM Transactions on Intelligent Systems and Technology (TIST)*, 5(1):8:1–8:24, Jan. 2014.

[5] Y. Bengio, R. Ducharme, P. Vincent, and C. Janvin. A neural probabilistic language model. *J. Mach. Learn. Res.*, 3:1137–1155, Mar. 2003.

[6] J. Bollen, H. Mao, and X. Zeng. Twitter mood predicts the stock market. *Journal of Computational Science*, 2(1):1 – 8, 2011.

[7] R. Caruana. Multitask learning. *Machine Learning*, 28(1):41–75, July 1997.

[8] C. Cortes and V. Vapnik. Support-vector networks. *Machine Learning*, 20(3):273–297, Sept. 1995.

[9] T. Gartner, P. A. Flach, A. Kowalczyk, and A. J. Smola. Multi-instance kernels. In *Proceedings of the Nineteenth International Conference on Machine Learning, ICML*, pages 179–186, San Francisco, CA, USA, 2002.

[10] J. He, W. Shen, P. Divakaruni, L. Wynter, and R. Lawrence. Improving traffic prediction with tweet semantics. In *Proceedings of the Twenty-Third International Joint Conference on Artificial Intelligence*, IJCAI, pages 1387–1393, 2013.

[11] M. S. Hossain, P. Butler, A. P. Boedihardjo, and N. Ramakrishnan. Storytelling in entity networks to support intelligence analysts. In *Proceedings of the 18th ACM SIGKDD International Conference on Knowledge Discovery and Data Mining*, KDD, pages 1375–1383, New York, NY, USA, 2012.

[12] D. Kotzias, M. Denil, N. de Freitas, and P. Smyth. From group to individual labels using deep features. In *Proceedings of the 21th ACM SIGKDD International Conference on Knowledge Discovery and Data Mining*, KDD, pages 597–606, New York, NY, USA, 2015.

[13] S. Laxman, V. Tankasali, and R. W. White. Stream prediction using a generative model based on frequent episodes in event sequences. In *Proceedings of the 14th ACM SIGKDD International Conference on Knowledge Discovery and Data Mining*, KDD, pages 453–461, New York, NY, USA, 2008.

[14] Q. V. Le and T. Mikolov. Distributed representations of sentences and documents. *CoRR*, abs/1405.4053, 2014.

[15] G. Liu, J. Wu, and Z.-H. Zhou. Key instance detection in multi-instance learning. In *ACML*, volume 25 of *JMLR Proceedings*, pages 253–268. JMLR.org, 2012.

[16] T. Mikolov, K. Chen, et al. Efficient estimation of word representations in vector space. *CoRR*, abs/1301.3781, 2013.

[17] T. Mikolov, I. Sutskever, K. Chen, G. Corrado, and J. Dean. Distributed representations of words and phrases and their compositionality. *CoRR*, abs/1310.4546, 2013.

[18] B. O'Connor, R. Balasubramanyan, B. R. Routledge, and N. A. Smith. From tweets to polls: Linking text sentiment

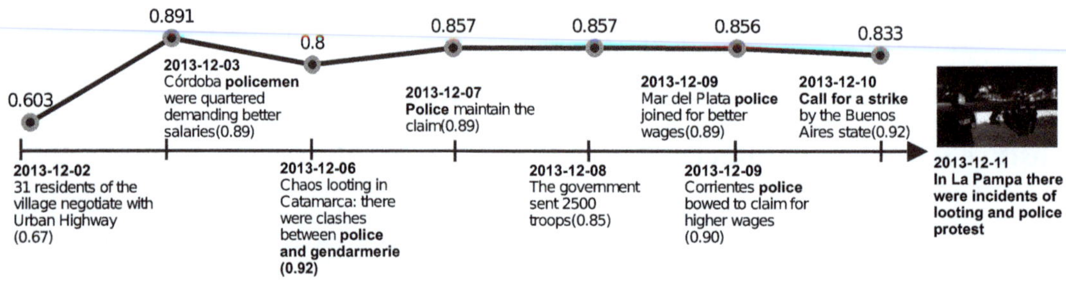

(a) A continuous police protest in Argentina against government for better salary. In the beginning, policemen at Cordoba were requesting for better salaries. Later on, police in Catamarca were involved in clashes with gendarmerie. Three days before the target event, the government sent out troops and more and more police joined for the same purpose. One day before the event, Buenos Aires state call for a strike.

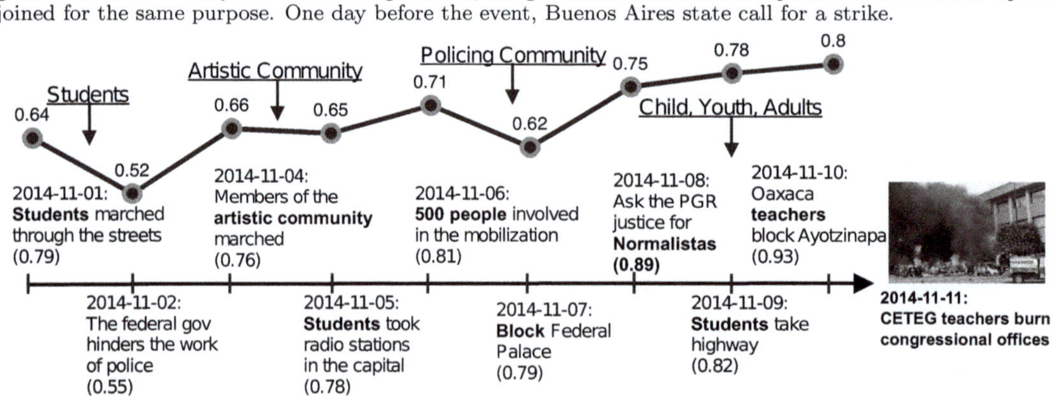

(b) Protester in Mexico burned the congressional offices for justice for the missing students. In the beginning, students were marching for justice. Gradually, more communities such as artistic and policing community joined the event. Later on, children, youth, adults, students and teachers blocked traffic for protest.

Figure 8: Case Studies

to public opinion time series. In *Proceedings of the Fourth International Conference on Weblogs and Social Media (ICWSM)*. The AAAI Press, 2010.

[19] N. Ramakrishnan, P. Butler, S. Muthiah, and et al. "Beating the News" with EMBERS: Forecasting Civil Unrest Using Open Source Indicators. In *Proceedings of the 20th ACM SIGKDD International Conference on Knowledge Discovery and Data Mining*, KDD, pages 1799–1808, New York, NY, USA, 2014.

[20] J. Ritterman, M. Osborne, and E. Klein. Using prediction markets and twitter to predict a swine flu pandemic. In *Proceedings of the 1st International Workshop on Mining Social*, 2009.

[21] Y. Rong, H. Cheng, and Z. Mo. Why it happened: Identifying and modeling the reasons of the happening of social events. In *Proceedings of the 21th ACM SIGKDD International Conference on Knowledge Discovery and Data Mining*, KDD '15, pages 1015–1024, New York, NY, USA, 2015. ACM.

[22] A. Tumasjan, T. Sprenger, P. Sandner, and I. Welpe. Predicting elections with twitter: What 140 characters reveal about political sentiment. In *Proceedings of the Fourth International AAAI Conference on Weblogs and Social Media*, pages 178–185, 2010.

[23] X. Wang, M. S. Gerber, and D. E. Brown. Automatic crime prediction using events extracted from twitter posts. In *Proceedings of the 5th International Conference on Social Computing, Behavioral-Cultural Modeling and Prediction*, SBP, pages 231–238, Berlin, Heidelberg, 2012.

[24] X. Wang, Z. Zhu, C. Yao, and X. Bai. Relaxed multiple-instance SVM with application to object discovery. *CoRR*, abs/1510.01027, 2015.

[25] N. Weidmann, E. Frank, and B. Pfahringer. A two-level learning method for generalized multi-instance problems. In *The European Conference on Machine Learning and Principles and Practice of Knowledge Discovery in Databases*, pages 468–479, 2003.

[26] L. Zhao, F. Chen, C. Lu, and N. Ramakrishnan. Spatiotemporal event forecasting in social media. In *Proceedings of the SIAM International Conference on Data Mining, Vancouver, BC, Canada*, pages 963–971, 2015.

[27] L. Zhao, Q. Sun, J. Ye, F. Chen, C.-T. Lu, and N. Ramakrishnan. Multi-task learning for spatio-temporal event forecasting. In *Proceedings of the 21th ACM SIGKDD International Conference on Knowledge Discovery and Data Mining*, KDD, pages 1503–1512, New York, NY, USA, 2015.

[28] Z.-H. Zhou and J.-M. Xu. On the relation between multi-instance learning and semi-supervised learning. In *Proceedings of the 24th International Conference on Machine Learning (ICML)*, volume 227, pages 1167–1174, 2007.

Asymmetric Transitivity Preserving Graph Embedding

Mingdong Ou
Tsinghua University
oumingdong@gmail.com

Peng Cui
Tsinghua University
cuip@tsinghua.edu.cn

Jian Pei
Simon Fraser University
jpei@cs.sfu.ca

Ziwei Zhang
Tsinghua University
zhangziwei1993@126.com

Wenwu Zhu
Tsinghua University
wwzhu@tsinghua.edu.cn

ABSTRACT

Graph embedding algorithms embed a graph into a vector space where the structure and the inherent properties of the graph are preserved. The existing graph embedding methods cannot preserve the asymmetric transitivity well, which is a critical property of directed graphs. Asymmetric transitivity depicts the correlation among directed edges, that is, if there is a directed path from u to v, then there is likely a directed edge from u to v. Asymmetric transitivity can help in capturing structures of graphs and recovering from partially observed graphs. To tackle this challenge, we propose the idea of preserving asymmetric transitivity by approximating high-order proximity which are based on asymmetric transitivity. In particular, we develop a novel graph embedding algorithm, *High-Order Proximity preserved Embedding* (*HOPE* for short), which is scalable to preserve high-order proximities of large scale graphs and capable of capturing the asymmetric transitivity. More specifically, we first derive a general formulation that cover multiple popular high-order proximity measurements, then propose a scalable embedding algorithm to approximate the high-order proximity measurements based on their general formulation. Moreover, we provide a theoretical upper bound on the RMSE (Root Mean Squared Error) of the approximation. Our empirical experiments on a synthetic dataset and three real-world datasets demonstrate that *HOPE* can approximate the high-order proximities significantly better than the state-of-art algorithms and outperform the state-of-art algorithms in tasks of reconstruction, link prediction and vertex recommendation.

Keywords

asymmetric transitivity, directed graph, high-order proximity, graph embedding

1. INTRODUCTION

Nowadays, more and more applications are based on larger and larger networks and graphs. It is well recognized that

KDD '16, August 13-17, 2016, San Francisco, CA, USA

DOI: http://dx.doi.org/10.1145/2939672.2939751

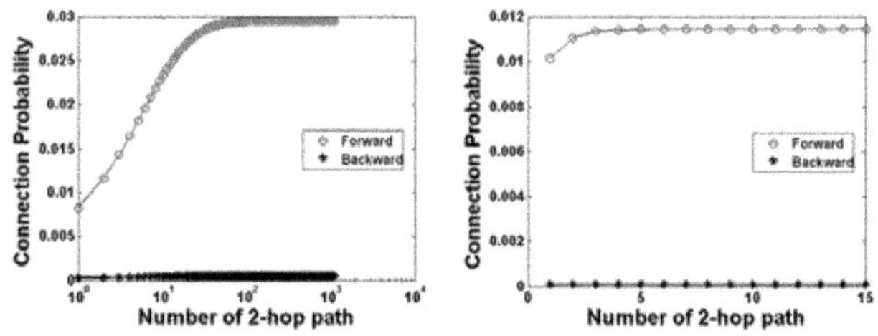

Figure 1: Asymmetric Transitivity in Real Data. Given a pair of vertexes (u, v), the horizontal axis is the Number of 2-hop paths from u to v. For the red (or black) curve with circle (or star) marker, the vertical axis represents the cumulative forward (or backward) transiting probability, that is the connection probability from u (or v) to v (or u), when the number of 2-hop paths is less than corresponding horizontal axis value. The left figure is the statistics from the social network of Tencent Weibo, and the right figure is the statistics from the social network of Twitter. As the two red curves increases monotonically, we can claim that the more paths from u to v there are, the more probable it is that there exists an edge from u to v, which reflects the transitivity assumption. The forward connection probability is much larger than the backward connection probability, which reflects the asymmetry assumption. In summary, asymmetric transitivity can be widely observed in real datasets.

graph data is sophisticated and challenging. To process graph data effectively, the first critical challenge is graph data representation, that is, how to represent graphs properly so that advanced analytic tasks, such as pattern discovery, analysis, and prediction, can be conducted efficiently in both time and space. However, graph representation in general remains an open problem.

Recently, the graph embedding paradigm [35] is proposed to represent vertices of a graph in a low-dimensional vector space while the structures (i.e. edges and other high-order structures) of the graph can be reconstructed in the vector space. With proper graph embedding, we can easily apply classic vector-based machine learning techniques to process graph data. Meanwhile, it effectively facilitates the parallelization of graph analysis by decoupling highly correlated vertices into independent vectors. However, most of the existing graph embedding methods target on undirected

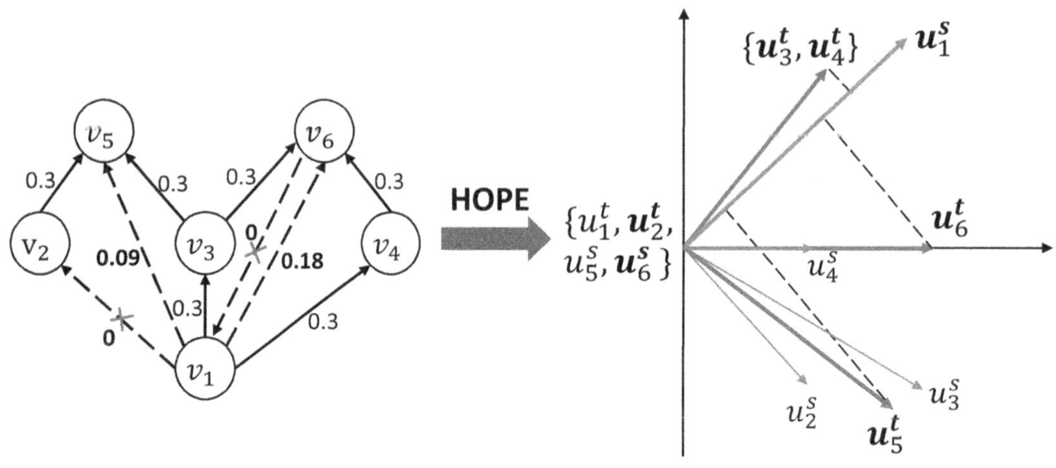

Figure 2: Framework of Asymmetric Transitivity Preserving Graph Embedding. The left is a input directed graph, and the right is the embedding vector space of the left graph, which is learned by our algorithm. In the left directed graph, the solid arrows represent observed directed edges and the numbers along with the solid arrows are the edge weights. The numbers along with the dashed arrows is the Katz proximity, which is highly correlated with asymmetric transitivity. For example, according to asymmetric transitivity, the two paths, $v_1 \to v_3 \to v_6$ and $v_1 \to v_4 \to v_6$, suggest that there may exist $v_1 \to v_6$. Then, the Katz proximity from v_1 to v_6 is relatively large, i.e. 0.18. On the other hand, because $v_6 \to v_1$ is in the opposite direction, $v_1 \to v_3 \to v_6$ and $v_1 \to v_4 \to v_6$ do not suggest $v_6 \to v_1$. Then, the Katz proximity from v_6 to v_1 is small, i.e. 0. In the embedding space, the arrows represent the embedding vectors of vertices, where row vectors $\mathbf{u}_i^s$ and $\mathbf{u}_i^t$ represent the source vector and target vector of v_i respectively. We use the inner product between $\mathbf{u}_i^s$ and $\mathbf{u}_j^t$ (i.e. $\mathbf{u}_i^s \cdot {\mathbf{u}_j^t}^\top$) as the approximated proximity from v_i to v_j. Note that $\mathbf{u}_1^t$, $\mathbf{u}_2^t$, $\mathbf{u}_5^s$ and $\mathbf{u}_6^s$ are all zero vectors. We can find that the approximated proximity perfectly preserve the Katz proximity. For example, with respect to source vector $\mathbf{u}_1^s$, the inner product with target vector $\mathbf{u}_6^t$ is larger than with $\mathbf{u}_5^t$, which preserves the rank order of corresponding Katz proximities.

graphs. Directed graphs, a natural and popularly used representation of data in many applications, such as social networks and webpage networks, are largely untouched.

Can we straightforwardly apply undirected graph embedding methods on directed graphs? The answer is no due to a fundamentally different characteristic of directed graphs: asymmetric transitivity.

Transitivity is a common characteristic of undirected and directed graphs [29] (see Figure 1). In undirected graphs, if there is an edge between vertices u and w, and one between w and v, then it is likely that u and v are connected by an edge. Transitivity plays a key role in graph inference and analysis tasks, such as calculating similarities between nodes [16, 14] and measuring the importance of nodes. Transitivity is symmetric in undirected graphs. However, transitivity is asymmetric in directed graphs. If there is a directed link from u to w and a directed link from w to v, there is likely a directed link from u to v, but not from v to u. More generally, If there is a directed path from u to v, there is likely a directed link from u to v, but not from v to u.

Preserving the symmetric transitivity in undirected graphs in an embedding space is natural and straightforward, as most of the distance metrics defined in the vector space possess the property of symmetric transitivity. However, how to preserve the asymmetric transitivity of directed graphs in a vector space is much more challenging.

Recently, a paucity of studies [37, 20, 3, 2, 24] focus on directed graph embedding. In order to reflect the asymmetric property in vector space, these methods design asymmetric metrics on the embedding vectors. Unfortunately, those asymmetric metrics are not fully transitive, which severely limit the capability of the learned embedding space in reflecting the structure of graphs as well as supporting graph inference and analysis.

In this paper, we tackle the challenging problem of asymmetric transitivity preserving graph embedding. Our major idea is that we learn two embedding vectors, source vector and target vector, for each node to capture asymmetric edges, as illustrated in Figure 2. Then, for a directed link from v_1 to v_2 without the reverse link from v_2 to v_1, we can assign similar values to v_1's source vector and v_2's target vector, and assign very different values to v_1's target vector and v_2's source vector. In this way, the feasibility of asymmetry transitivity is preserved. The key challenge is how well the asymmetric transitivity of directed graphs can be preserved in the embedding learning.

From the learning perspective, a good way is to let the learned embedding vectors directly approximate a target measure reflecting asymmetric transitivity of graphs. From the graph embedding pserspective, the property of asymmetric transitivity leads to the assumption that the more and the shorter paths from v_i to v_j, the more similar should be v_i's source vector and v_j's target vector. This assumption coincides with high-order proximities of nodes in graphs, such as Katz [16] and rooted pagerank [30]. What is more, these high-order proximities are defined to be asymmetric in directed graphs. Thus, in its place, we propose to use high-order proximities of nodes as the target measure, resulting in a novel directed graph embedding algorithm, High Order Proximity preserved Embedding (HOPE).

In this model, we theoretically derive a general form covering multiple high-order proximities. Interestingly, the general form is consistent with the formulation of generalized SVD. Based on this, we propose a scalable embedding algorithm for large-scale graphs by avoiding the time-consuming computation of high-order proximities. Moreover, we derive a theoretical upper bound on the approximation error of HOPE, which is used to estimate the embedding quality in theory and determine embedding dimensions automatically.

To verify the advantages of our algorithm, we conduct experiments on both synthetic data and 3 real datasets. The experiments show that our method consistently and significantly outperforms the state-of-the-art baselines in several tasks, including high-order proximity approximation, graph reconstruction, link prediction and vertex recommendation.

The main contributions of this paper are as follows:

- We propose a high-order proximity preserved embedding (HOPE) method to solve the challenging problem of asymmetric transitivity in directed graph embedding.
- We derive a general form covering multiple commonly used high-order proximities, enabling the scalable solution of HOPE with generalized SVD.
- We provide an upper bound on the approximation error of HOPE.
- Extensive experiments are conducted to verify the usefulness and generality of the learned embedding in various applications.

The rest of the paper is organized as follows. In Section 2, we review the related work. We develop our method in Section 3 and report the experimental results in Section 4. We conclude the paper in Section 5.

2. RELATED WORK

2.1 Graph Embedding

Graph embedding technology has been widely studied in the fields of dimensionality reduction [15, 27, 33, 1, 8], natural language processing [18], network analysis [11] and so on.

For dimensionality reduction, adjacency matrices of graphs are constructed from the feature similarity (distance) between samples [35]. And the graph embedding algorithms aim to preserve the feature similarity in the embedded latent space. For example, Laplacian Eigenmaps (LE) [1] aims to learn the low-dimensional representation to expand the manifold where data lie. Locality Preserving Projections (LPP) [8] is a linearization variant of LE which learns a linear projection from feature space to embedding space. Besides, there are many other graph embedding algorithms for dimensionality reduction, including non-linear [33, 27], linear [15, 6], kernlized [28] and tensorized [36] algorithms. All of these algorithms are based on undirected graphs derived from symmetric similarities. Thus, they cannot preserve asymmetric transitivity.

In the field of natural language processing, the graph of words is often used to learn the representation of words [19, 18, 23]. Mikolov et. al. [19] propose to ultilize the context of words to learn representation, which has been proved equivalent to factorizing word-context matrix [18]. Pennington et. al. [23] exploit a word-word co-occurrance matrix.

In network analysis, Hoff et. al. [11] first propose to learn latent space representation of vertexes in graph and the probability of a relation depends on the distance between vertexes in the latent space, and they apply it to link prediction problem [10]. Handcock et. al. [7] propose to apply the latent space approach to clustering in graph. And Zhu et. al. [37] propose to address the classification problem in graph with graph embedding model. While early graph embedding works focus on modeling the observed first-order relationship (i.e. edges in graph) between vertexes, some recent works try to model the directed higher order relationships between vertexes in sparse graphs [24, 2]. GraRep [2] is related to our work. But, it cannot fully capture transitivity. Moreover, it is not scalable for large-scale graph.

2.2 Directed Graph

Theoretically, any type (undirected and directed) of graph can be represented as directed graph. So, modeling directed graph is a critical problem for graph analysis. Holland et. al. [12] propose the p_1 distribution model to capture the structural properties in directed graph, including the atrractiveness and expansiveness of vertexes and the reciprocation of edges. Besides these properties, Wang et. al. [34] take the group information of vertexes into consideration. Recently, some works adopt graph embedding [4, 26, 25, 21] to model directed graphs. Chen et. al. [4] learn the embedding vectors in Euclidean space with locality property preserved. Perrault-Joncas et. al. [26, 25] and Mousazadeh et. al. [21] learn the embedding vectors based on Laplacian type operators and preserve the asymmetry property of edges in a vector field. However, all of these methods cannot preserve asymmetry property in embedding vector space.

3. HIGH-ORDER PROXIMITY PRESERVED EMBEDDING

In this section, we will derive how to preserve high-order proximities in the embedding space. Before introducing the detailed derivation, we will clarify the symbols and definition that will be used.

3.1 Notations

We define a directed graph as $\mathbf{G} = \{\mathbf{V}, \mathbf{E}\}$. $\mathbf{V}$ is the vertex set. Let $\mathbf{V} = \{v_1, \cdots, v_i, \cdots, v_N\}$ where N is the number of vertexes. $\mathbf{E}$ is the directed edge set. $\mathbf{e}_{ij} = (\mathbf{v}_i, \mathbf{v}_j) \in \mathbf{E}$ represents a directed edge from $\mathbf{v}_i$ to $\mathbf{v}_j$. The adjacency matrix is denoted as $\mathbf{A}$. We define a high-order proximity matrix as $\mathbf{S}$, where S_{ij} is the proximity between $\mathbf{v}_i$ and $\mathbf{v}_j$. And $\mathbf{U} = [\mathbf{U}^s, \mathbf{U}^t]$ is the embedding matrix, where the i-th row, $\mathbf{u}_i$, is the embedding vector of v_i. $\mathbf{U}^s, \mathbf{U}^t \in \mathcal{R}^{N \times K}$ are the source embedding vectors and target embedding vectors respectively, where K is the embedding dimensions. For any matrix $\mathbf{B}$, the lowercase symbol $\mathbf{b}_i$ represents the i-th row of $\mathbf{B}$, and B_{ij} represents the element at i-th row and j-th column.

Table 1: General Formulation for High-order Proximity Measurements

Proximity Measurement	$\mathbf{M}_g$	$\mathbf{M}_l$
Katz	$\mathbf{I} - \beta \cdot \mathbf{A}$	$\beta \cdot \mathbf{A}$
Personalized Pagerank	$\mathbf{I} - \alpha\mathbf{P}$	$(1-\alpha) \cdot \mathbf{I}$
Common neighbors	$\mathbf{I}$	$\mathbf{A}^2$
Adamic-Adar	$\mathbf{I}$	$\mathbf{A} \cdot \mathbf{D} \cdot \mathbf{A}$

3.2 Problem Definition

In this paper, we focus on the directed graph embedding problem. It aims to represent the vertexes in the numerical vector space, where asymmetric transitivity is preserved. As high-order proximities are derived from asymmetric transitivity, we propose to preserve the asymmetric transitivity by approximating high-order proximity. Formally, we adopt the L2-norm below as the loss function which need to be minimized:

$$\min \|\mathbf{S} - \mathbf{U}^s \cdot \mathbf{U}^{t^\top}\|_F^2 \quad (1)$$

.

As Figure 2 shows, the embedding vectors can well preserve the asymmetric transitivity.

3.3 High order proximities

Many high-order proximity measurements in graph can reflect the asymmetric transitivity. Moreover, we found that many of them share a general formulation which will facilitate the approximation of these proximities, that is:

$$\mathbf{S} = \mathbf{M}_g^{-1} \cdot \mathbf{M}_l \quad (2)$$

, where $\mathbf{M}_g$ and $\mathbf{M}_l$ are both polynomial of matrices. Below, we will introduce some popular proximity measurements and transform them into this formulation.

Katz Index [16]. This index is an ensemble of all paths, which is a weighted summation over the path set between two vertexes. The weight of a path is a exponential function of its length. Actually, the formula of Katz index can also be written as a recurrent formula:

$$\mathbf{S}^{Katz} = \sum_{l=1}^{\infty} \beta \cdot \mathbf{A}^l = \beta \cdot \mathbf{A} \cdot \mathbf{S}^{Katz} + \beta \cdot \mathbf{A} \quad (3)$$

, where β is a decay parameter. It determines how fast the weight of a path decay when the length of path grows. β should be properly set to preserve the series converging. Actually, β must be smaller than the spectral radius of adjacency matrix.

Then, we can get that:

$$\mathbf{S}^{Katz} = (\mathbf{I} - \beta \cdot \mathbf{A})^{-1} \cdot \beta \cdot \mathbf{A} \quad (4)$$

, where $\mathbf{I}$ is a identity matrix.

For Katz index,

$$\mathbf{M}_g = \mathbf{I} - \beta \cdot \mathbf{A} \quad (5)$$

$$\mathbf{M}_l = \beta \cdot \mathbf{A} \quad (6)$$

Rooted PageRank (RPR). $\mathbf{S}_{ij}^{RPR}$ is the probability that a random walk from node v_i will locate at v_j in the steady state. Consider one step of a random walk from v_i, the random walker randomly jumps to one of the neighbor of current node with probability α, and jumps back to v_i with probability α. The fomula is:

$$\mathbf{S}^{RPR} = \alpha \cdot \mathbf{S}_{ij}^{RPR} \cdot \mathbf{P} + (1-\alpha) \cdot \mathbf{I} \quad (7)$$

, where $\alpha \in [0, 1)$ is the probability to randomly walk to a neighbor, and $\mathbf{P}$ is the probability transition matrix satisfying that $\sum_{i=1}^{N} P_ij = 1$.

Then, we can get:

$$\mathbf{S}^{RPR} = (1-\alpha) \cdot (\mathbf{I} - \alpha\mathbf{P})^{-1} \quad (8)$$

So, for rooted PageRank,

$$\mathbf{M}_g = \mathbf{I} - \alpha\mathbf{P} \quad (9)$$

$$\mathbf{M}_l = (1-\alpha) \cdot \mathbf{I} \quad (10)$$

.

Common Neighbors (CN). $\mathbf{S}_{ij}^{CN}$ counts the number of vertexes connecting to both v_i and v_j. For directed graph, $\mathbf{S}_{ij}^{CN}$ is the number of vertexes which is the target of an edge from v_i and the source of an edge to v_j. Formally,

$$\mathbf{S}^{CN} = \mathbf{A}^2 \quad (11)$$

So, for common neighbors,

$$\mathbf{M}_g = \mathbf{I} \quad (12)$$

$$\mathbf{M}_l = \mathbf{A}^2 \quad (13)$$

Adamic-Adar (AA). Adamic-Adar is a variant of common neighbors. Unlike common neighbors, Adamic-Adar assigns each neighbor a weight, that is the reciprocal of the degree of the neighbor. This means that the more vertexes one vertex connected to, the less important it is on evaluating the proximity between a pair of vertex. Formally,

$$\mathbf{S}^{AA} = \mathbf{A} \cdot \mathbf{D} \cdot \mathbf{A} \quad (14)$$

, where $\mathbf{D}$ is a diagonal matrix,

$$\mathbf{D}_{ii} = 1/\sum_j (A_{ij} + A_{ji}) \quad (15)$$

.

So, for Adamic-Adar,

$$\mathbf{M}_g = \mathbf{I} \quad (16)$$

$$\mathbf{M}_l = \mathbf{A} \cdot \mathbf{D} \cdot \mathbf{A} \quad (17)$$

We list the corresponding formula of $\mathbf{M}_g$ and $\mathbf{M}_l$ of each proximity measurement in Table 1. Note that $\mathbf{M}_g$ and $\mathbf{M}_l$ are both the polynomial of adjacency matrix or its variants. The above proximity measurements can be classified into two types, i.e. global proximity and local proximity. Global proximities, i.e. Katz index and rooted PageRank, are derived from a recurrent formula, which make the proximity can preserve global asymmetric transitivity. And local proximities, i.e. common neighbors and Adamic-Adar, have no recurrent structure and just preserve the asymmetric transitivity in the local structure, which we call it local asymmetric transitivity. Intuitively, $\mathbf{M}_g$ is highly related to global asymmetric transitivity. $\mathbf{M}_g$ has a formulation like $\mathbf{I} - \alpha \cdot \mathbf{B}$, where α is a parameter and $\mathbf{B}$ is a transition matrix. The larger the alpha is, the easier the observed relationship (the edges of the graph) is to be transited in the graph. When $\alpha = 0$, the observed relationship can just transit in a subgraph whose range is limited by the order of $\mathbf{M}_l$.

3.4 Approximation of High-Order Proximity

The objective in Equation (1) aims to find an optimal rank-K approximation of the proximity matrix $\mathbf{S}$. According to [13], the solution is to perform SVD (Singular Value Decomposition) on $\mathbf{S}$ and use the largest K singular value and corresponding singular vectors to construct the optimal embedding vectors. Formally, if

$$\mathbf{S} = \sum_{i=1}^{N} \sigma_i \mathbf{v}_i^s \mathbf{v}_i^{t\top} \quad (18)$$

, where $\{\sigma_1, \sigma_2, \cdots, \sigma_N\}$ is the singular values sorted in decreasing order, $\mathbf{v}_i^s$ and $\mathbf{v}_i^t$ are corresponding singular vectors of σ_i,

then, we can get the optimal embedding vectors as:

$$\mathbf{U}^s = [\sqrt{\sigma_1} \cdot \mathbf{v}_1^s, \cdots, \sqrt{\sigma_K} \cdot \mathbf{v}_K^s] \quad (19)$$

$$\mathbf{U}^t = [\sqrt{\sigma_1} \cdot \mathbf{v}_1^t, \cdots, \sqrt{\sigma_K} \cdot \mathbf{v}_K^t] \quad (20)$$

.

However, this solution need to calculate the proximity matrix $\mathbf{S}$. Even for sparse adjacency matrix, the time complexity of matrix inversion is up to $O(N^3)$. And the matrix polynomial operation on adjacency matrix will make $\mathbf{S}$ much denser than adjacency matrix $\mathbf{A}$ which will also make the SVD on $\mathbf{S}$ very expensive. Thus, the solution is not feasible for large scale graphs.

As the calculation of $\mathbf{S}$ is the efficiency bottleneck and $\mathbf{S}$ is just the intermediate product in our problem, we propose a novel algorithm to avoid the calculation of $\mathbf{S}$ and learn the embedding vectors directly. As many proximity measurements have the general formulation in Equation (2), we transform the original SVD problem into a generalized SVD problem [22] for proximity measurements with the general formulation.

According to [22], it is easy to derive the following theorem:

THEOREM 1. *If we have the singular value decomposition of the general formulation*

$$\mathbf{M}_g^{-1} \cdot \mathbf{M}_l = \mathbf{V}^s \Sigma \mathbf{V}^{t\top}$$

, where $\mathbf{V}^t$ and $\mathbf{V}^s$ are two orthogonal matrices,

$$\Sigma = diag(\sigma_1, \sigma_2, \cdots, \sigma_N)$$

.

Then, there exists a nonsingular matrix $\mathbf{X}$ and two diagonal matrices, i.e. Σ^l and Σ^g, satisfying that

$$\mathbf{V}^{t\top} \mathbf{M}_l^\top \mathbf{X} = \Sigma^l$$
$$\mathbf{V}^{s\top} \mathbf{M}_g^\top \mathbf{X} = \Sigma^g$$

, where

$$\Sigma^l = diag(\sigma_1^l, \sigma_2^l, \cdots, \sigma_N^l)$$
$$\Sigma^g = diag(\sigma_1^g, \sigma_2^g, \cdots, \sigma_N^g)$$
$$\sigma_1^l \geq \sigma_2^l \geq \cdots \geq \sigma_K^l \geq 0$$
$$0 \leq \sigma_1^g \leq \sigma_2^g \leq \cdots \leq \sigma_K^g$$
$$\forall i \quad {\sigma_i^l}^2 + {\sigma_i^g}^2 = 1$$

,

and

$$\sigma_i = \frac{\sigma_i^l}{\sigma_i^g} \quad (21)$$

Algorithm 1 High-order Proximity preserved Embedding

Require: adjacency matrix $\mathbf{A}$, embedding dimension K, parameters of high-order proximity measurementθ.

Ensure: embedding source vectors $\mathbf{U}^s$ and target vectors $\mathbf{U}^t$.

1: calculate $\mathbf{M}_g$ and $\mathbf{M}_l$.
2: perform JDGSVD with $\mathbf{M}_g$ and $\mathbf{M}_l$, and obtain the generalized singular values $\{\sigma_1^l, \cdots, \sigma_K^l\}$ and $\{\sigma_1^g, \cdots, \sigma_K^g\}$, and the corresponding singular vectors, $\{\mathbf{v}_1^s, \cdots, \mathbf{v}_K^s\}$ and $\{\mathbf{v}_1^t, \cdots, \mathbf{v}_K^t\}$.
3: calculate singular values $\{\sigma_1, \cdots, \sigma_K\}$ according to Equation (21).
4: calculate embedding matrices $\mathbf{U}^s$ and $\mathbf{U}^t$ according to Equation (19) and (20).

As the generalized SVD can also derive the results of SVD, we can still use Equation (19) (20) to get the embedding vectors.

Complete generalized SVD will also achieve $O(N^3)$ time complexity, which is not feasible for large scale graphs. As we only need the largest K singular values and corresponding singular vectors, we adopt a partial generalized SVD algorithm [9], which we call it JDGSVD. This is an iterative Jacobi-Davidson type algorithm which is very scalable when $K \ll N$. Algorithm 1 lists the steps of our algorithm.

3.4.1 Complexity Analysis

In this algorithm, we do not explicitly perform the polynomial operation on adjacency matrix in $\mathbf{M}_l$ and $\mathbf{M}_g$, whose time complexity is up to $O(N^3)$. Because, in JDGSVD, we only need to multiply $\mathbf{M}_g$ and $\mathbf{M}_l$ with some thin matrices whose size is $N \times K$. If we change the multiplication order, and first perform multiplication between adjacency matrix and thin matrix, the time complexity of this operation will reduce to $O(m \cdot K)$, where m is the number of non-zero elements in adjacency matrix (i.e. the number of edges in the graph) and much smaller than N^2 in sparse graph. And, the total time complexity of JDGSVD is $O(m \cdot K^2 \cdot L)$, where L is the iteration number. We can see that the time complexity is just linear with respect to the volumn of data (i.e. the number of edges), which means that it is scalable for large scale graphs.

3.4.2 Approximation Error

Finally, we give the error bound of our algorithm:

THEOREM 2. *Given the proximity matrix, $\mathbf{S}$, of a directed graph, and the embedding vectors, $\mathbf{U}^s$ and $\mathbf{U}^t$, learned by* HOPPE. *Then the approximation error is*

$$\|\mathbf{S} - \mathbf{U}^s \cdot \mathbf{U}^t\|_F^2 = \sum_{i=K+1}^{N} \sigma_i^2$$

, and the relative approximation error is:

$$\frac{\|\mathbf{S} - \mathbf{U}^s \cdot \mathbf{U}^t\|_F^2}{\|\mathbf{S}\|_F^2} = \frac{\sum_{i=K+1}^{N} \sigma_i^2}{\sum_{i=1}^{N} \sigma_i^2} \quad (22)$$

where $\{\sigma_i\}$ are the singular values of $\mathbf{S}$ in descend order.

Prove:

$$\|\mathbf{S} - \mathbf{U}^s \cdot \mathbf{U}^t\|_F^2 = \|\sum_{i=1}^{N} \sigma_i \cdot \mathbf{v}_i^s {\mathbf{v}_i^t}^\top - \sum_{j=1}^{K} \sigma_j \cdot \mathbf{v}_j^s {\mathbf{v}_j^t}^\top\|_F^2$$
$$= \|\sum_{i=K+1}^{N} \sigma_i \cdot \mathbf{v}_i^s {\mathbf{v}_i^t}^\top\|_F^2$$
$$= \sum_{i=K+1}^{N} \sigma_i^2$$

and we have:

$$\|\mathbf{S}\| = \|\sum_{i=1}^{N} \sigma_i \cdot \mathbf{v}_i^s {\mathbf{v}_i^t}^\top\| = \sum_{i=1}^{N} \sigma_i^2$$

So, the relative approximation error is:

$$\frac{\|\mathbf{S} - \mathbf{U}^s \cdot \mathbf{U}^t\|_F^2}{\|\mathbf{S}\|_F^2} = \frac{\sum_{i=K+1}^{N} \sigma_i^2}{\sum_{i=1}^{N} \sigma_i^2}$$

If $\mathbf{S}$ is low-rank, then the singular values $\{\sigma_{K+1}, \cdots, \sigma_N\}$ will be close to zero and the error will be very small. That is, the lower the rank of $\mathbf{S}$ is, the smaller the error is.

4. EXPERIMENTS

We conduct experiments on a synthetic data and three real-world datasets. We will first introduce the experiment setting, then show the results and analysis on the two types of datasets respectively.

4.1 Experiment Setting

4.1.1 Datasets

We use four datasets, whose statistics are summarized in Table 2.

Table 2: Statistics of datasets. $|V|$ denotes the number of vertexes and $|E|$ denotes the number of edges.

	Syn	Cora	SN-Twitter	SN-TWeibo
$\|\mathbf{V}\|$	10,000	23166	465,017	1,944,589
$\|\mathbf{E}\|$	144,555	91500	834,797	50,655,143

- Synthetic Data (Syn): We generate the synthetic data by the forest fire model [17]. The model can generate powerlaw graphs. We can observe asymmetric transitivity in the generated graphs. As the time complexity of computation of some high-order proximities (e.g. Katz, RPR) is too high, we generate small-scaled synthetic data to allow for the computation of high-order proximities, so that we can evaluate the accuracy of high-order proximity approximation. We randomly generate ten synthetic datasets.
- Cora[1] [31]: This is a citation network of academic papers. The vertexes are academic papers and the directed edges are the citation relationship between papers.
- Twitter Social Network[2] (SN-Twitter) [5]: This dataset is a subnetwork of Twitter. The vertexes are users of Twitter, and the directed edges are following relationships between users.
- Tencent Weibo Social Network[3] (SN-TWeibo): This dataset contains a subnetwork of the social network in Tencent Weibo[4], a Twitter-style social platform in China. The vertexes are users and the directed edges are following relationship between users.

Due to high time complexity of calculating high-order proximity measurements, we first evaluate the high-order proximity approximation error on two small datasets, i.e. Synthetic Data and Cora, where it is feasible to calculate high-order proximity. Furthermore, we conduct other application experiments on two large datasets, i.e. SN-Twitter and SN-TWeibo, to evaluate the performance of our algorithm in real large-scale graphs. For Synthetic Data and Cora, the graph in each dataset is randomly separated into training set and testing set, and training set contains 80% edges. All the reported performances are the average value on these ten datasets. For SN-Twitter and SN-TWeibo, we generate three datasets by randomly separated the graph into training graph and testing graph, where training graph contains 80% edges and testing graph contains the rest edges.

4.1.2 Baseline Methods

- LINE [32]: This algorithm preserves the first-order and second-order proximity between vertexes. but it only can preserve symmetric second-order proximity when applied to directed graph. We use vertex vectors as source vectors and context vectors as target vectors. We use LINE1 to represent LINE preserving first-order proximity and LINE2 to represent LINE preserving second-order proximity.
- DeepWalk [24]: this algorithm first randomly walks on the graph, and assumes a pair of vertexes similar if they are close in the random path. Then, the embedding is learned to preserve these pairwise similarities in the embedding.
- PPE (Partial Proximity Embedding) [30]: This algorithm first selects a small subset of vertexes as landmarks, and learns the embedding by approximating the proximity between vertexes and landmarks.
- Common Neighbors: We rank the links by the number of common neighbors. We use it for link prediction and vertex recommendation.
- Adamic-Adar: We rank the links by the Adamic-Adar values. We use it for link prediction and vertex recommendation.

In graph reconstruction, link prediction and vertex recommendation experiments, we adopt Katz as the target high-order proximity for HOPE and PPE methods, as Katz has shown superior performance in related tasks in previous works, to approximate for HOPE and PPE. For PPE, we sample 1000 landmarks. For LINE and DeepWalk, we search the parameters grid search.

[1]http://konect.uni-koblenz.de/networks/subelj_cora

[2]http://konect.uni-koblenz.de/networks/munmun_twitter_social

[3]http://www.kddcup2012.org/c/kddcup2012-track1/data

[4]http://t.qq.com/

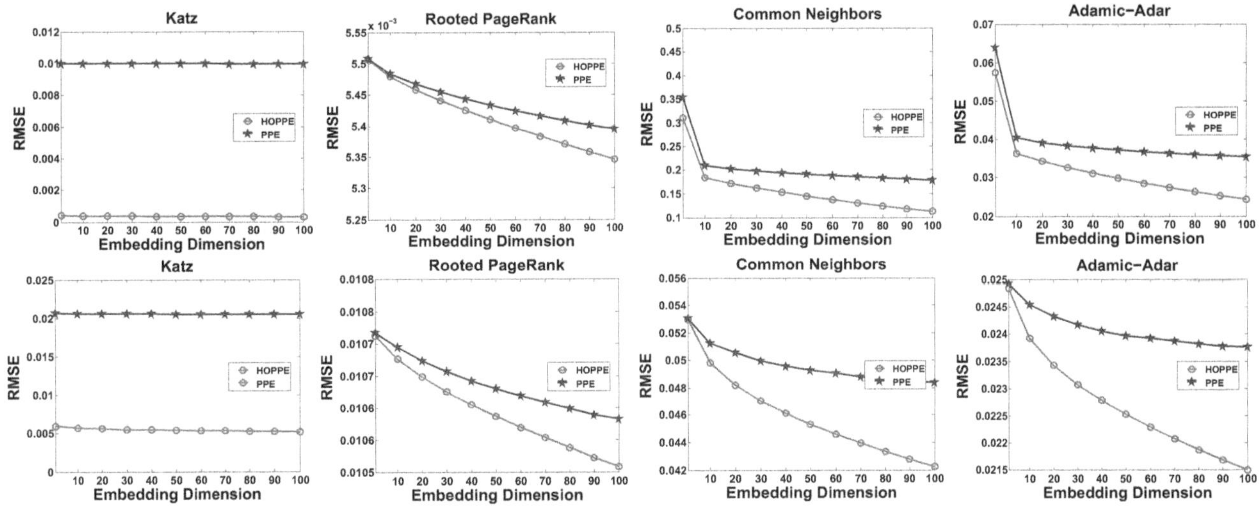

Figure 3: Error of proximity approximation. We evaluate the errors of HOPE and PPE in approximating four proximity measurements, including Katz, RPR, Common Neighbors and Adamic-Adar. First row is the results on Synthetic Data, and second row is the results on Cora. For Katz, $\beta = 0.1$; for RPR, $\alpha = 0.5$.

4.1.3 Evaluation Metrics

In the experiments, we adopt RMSE, Precision@k and MAP (Mean Average Precision) as the evaluation metrics.

RMSE is used to evaluate the approximation error of the proximity approximation algorithms, including HOPE and PPE. The formula of RMSE in our problem is:

$$RMSE = \sqrt{\frac{\|\mathbf{S} - \mathbf{U}^s\mathbf{U}^{t\top}\|_F^2}{N^2}}$$

NRMSE (Normalized RMSE) is used to evaluate the relative error of the proximity approximation algorithms. The formula of NRMSE in our problem is:

$$NRMSE = \frac{\sqrt{\frac{\|\mathbf{S} - \mathbf{U}^s\mathbf{U}^{t\top}\|_F^2}{N^2}}}{\sqrt{\frac{\|\mathbf{S}\|_F^2}{N^2}}} = \sqrt{\frac{\|\mathbf{S} - \mathbf{U}^s\mathbf{U}^{t\top}\|_F^2}{\|\mathbf{S}\|_F^2}}$$

Precision@k is used to evaluate the performance of link prediction, which measures the prediction precision of top k links. The formula of Precision@k is:

$$Precision@k = \frac{|\{(i,j)|(i,j) \in \mathbf{E}_p \cap \mathbf{E}_o\}|}{|\mathbf{E}_p|}$$

where $\mathbf{E}_p$ is the set of top k predicted links, $\mathbf{E}_o$ is the set of observed links and $|\cdot|$ represents the size of set.

MAP is used to evaluate the performance of vertex recommendation, which measures the rank accuracy of recommended vertex list. The formula of MAP@k is:

$$AP@k(i) = \frac{\sum_{j=1}^{k} P_i(j) \cdot \delta_i(j)}{\sum_{j=1}^{k} \delta_i(j)}$$

$$MAP@k = \frac{\sum_{v_i \in \mathbf{V}_t} AP(i)}{|\mathbf{V}_t|}$$

4.2 High-order Proximity Approximation

As we preserve asymmetric transitivity by approximating high-order proximity, the error of approximation can evaluate how well we preserve asymmetric transitivity.

We evaluate the approximation error on Synthetic Data and Cora. Besides our algorithms, PPE can also approximate high-order proximity. Here, we compare HOPE with PPE on four proximity measurements, including Katz, RPR, Common Neighbors and Adamic-Adar. Figure 3 shows the RMSE with different number of embedding dimensions. When the number of embedding dimensions grows, the approximation error, RMSE, will decrease. We can see that HOPE achieves much lower RMSE than PPE on all the proximity measurements, which is stable in the ten randomly selected datasets. Especially on Katz, the error of HOPE is one order of magnitude smaller than the error of PPE. With the number of embedding dimensions growing, the error of both algorithms decreases but the margin between HOPE and PPE becomes larger. Although more embedding dimensions can make these two methods be able to incorporate more proximity information, PPE can only approximate a sub-block of the proximity matrix, while HOPE can approximate the whole proximity matrix. Thus HOPE can take more advantage of the increased embedding dimension.

Furthermore, we evaluate how the rank (more precisely, the condition number) of proximity matrix will influence the approximation error. In section 3.4.2, we have theoretically proven that the approximation error of our method is related to the rank of the promixity matrix. Here, we take Rooted PageRank as an example to empirically demonstrate the claim. The parameter α of RPR is highly related to the rank of RPR matrix (i.e. $\mathbf{S}^{RPR}$). When $\alpha = 0$, $\mathbf{S}^{RPR} = \mathbf{I}$, which is full rank. When $\alpha = 1$, all the rows of $\mathbf{S}^{RPR}$ are the stationary distribution of transition matrix $\mathbf{P}$, and the rank of $\mathbf{S}^{RPR}$ is 1. Intuitively, the larger α is, the lower the rank of $\mathbf{S}^{RPR}$ tends to be. We use NRMSE to evaluate the relative error of RPR approximation. Figure 4 shows the NRMSE of HOPE with different α. The larger α is,

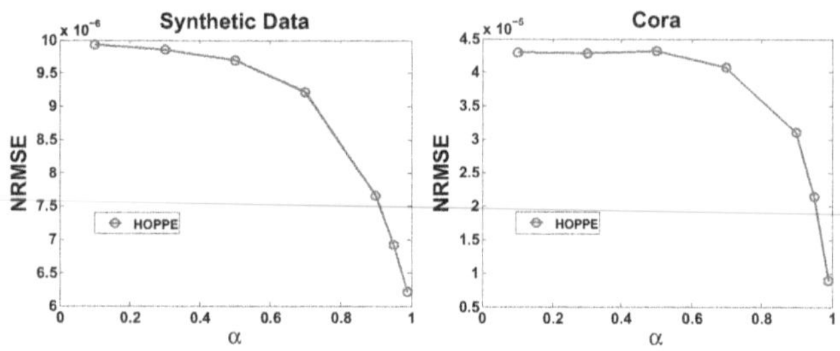

Figure 4: Correlation between relative approximation error and the rank of proximity matrix. The parameter α of Rooted PageRank is highly related to the rank of proximity matrix. Here, we use α to simulate the rank of proximity matrix. The embedding dimension is 100.

the smaller the NRMSE is. This suggests that HOPE can achieve better performance on lower-rank proximity matrix.

4.3 Graph Reconstruction

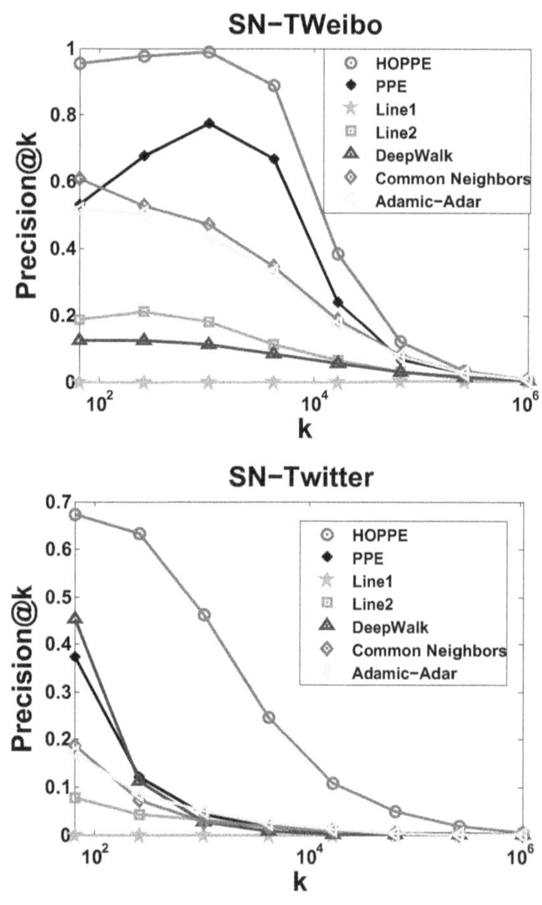

Figure 5: Precision@k of graph reconstruction on SN-TWeibo and SN-Twitter. We rank pairs of vertexes according to their reconstructed proximity and evaluate the reconstruction precision in top k pairs of vertexes.

As the representation of a graph, embedding vectors are expected to well reconstruct the graph. We evaluate the reconstruction ability on training sets of SN-TWeibo and SN-Twitter. We reconstruct the graph edges based on the reconstructed proximity between vertexes. For graph embedding algorithms (i.e. HOPE, PPE, Line and DeepWalk), we use the inner product between embedding vectors to reconstruct the proximity matrix. For Common Neighbors and Adamic-Adar, we directly calculate the proximity matrix. We rank the pairs of vertexes according to their corresponding reconstructed proximity. Then, we calculate the ratio of real links in top k pairs of vertexes as the reconstruction precision. As the number of possible pairs of vertexes $(N \cdot (N-1))$ is too large in SN-TWeibo and SN-Twitter, we randomly sample about 0.1% pairs of vertexes for evaluation.

Figure 5 shows the Precision@k with different k. HOPE significantly outperforms baselines. As mentioned above, PPE just approximates a sub-block of proximity matrix. So, it works poorer than HOPE. Comparing with Line2 which directly reconstructs the directed links, HOPE still achieves much better performance. It may because HOPE uses high-order proximity as weight of directed edges, but LINE2 assigns equivalent weight for each directed edges. The edges in densely connected vertex clusters will obtain higher weights. Thus, these edges will be preserved first. Moreover, the number of these edges is larger than that in sparsely connected vertex clusters. Thus, HOPE may reconstruct more edges than Line2.

4.4 Link Prediction

As asymmetric transitivity captures the correlation among edges, we can use it to predict missing edges in graphs. On the other hand, the performance of HOPE on link prediction can also reflect how well the asymmetric transitivity is preserved. This experiment is conducted on SN-TWeibo and SN-TWitter. We train the embedding vectors on training graphs, and evaluate the prediction performance on testing graphs. We randomly sample about 0.1% pairs of vertexes for evaluation. Then, we rank them according to the inner product between embedding vectors (for HOPE, LINE1, LINE2 and PPE) or the calculated proximity (for Common Neighbors and Adamic-Adar), and evaluate the prediction precision in top k pairs of vertexes.

Figure 6 shows the precision@k of link prediction with different k. Our algorithm, HOPE, outperforms the baselines significantly. Compared to Section 4.3, the performance of PPE significantly decreases in prediction task. This is mainly because PPE only trains on partial proximity matrix, which is easy to overfit. Besides, we can see that all the curves converges to a point when k is large. This is because almost all the real edges have been correctly predicted by all the algorithms.

4.5 Vertex Recommendation

The setting of training procedure in this experiment is the same as link prediction. But, we evaluate the performance of algorithms from the vertex view, i.e. vertex recommendation performance. We randomly sample 1000 vertexes. For each vertex v_i, we randomly hide 20% outgoing links as groundtruth. Then we derive the top 100 vertexes with the highest proximity with v_i as the candidates that v_i will possible point to. After that, we use MAP@10, MAP@50 and MAP@100 to evaluate the quality of recommendation. Table 3 shows the MAPs of different algorithms. HOPE outperforms the baseline algorithms.

Table 3: MAP of vertex recommendation on SN-TWeibo and SN-Twitter. For each vertex, the recommended vertex list is ranked according to the predicted proximity between vertexes. For embedding algorithms, we calculate the predicted proximity by performing inner product between embedding vectors.

Method	SN-TWebio			SN-Twitter		
	MAP@10	MAP@50	MAP@100	MAP@10	MAP@50	MAP@100
HOPE	**0.2295**	**0.1869**	**0.169**	**0.1000**	**0.0881**	**0.0766**
PPE	0.0928	0.0845	0.077	0.0061	0.0077	0.0081
LINE1	0	0	0.005	0.0209	0.0221	0.0221
LINE2	0.051	0.051	0.048	0.0044	0.0043	0.0035
DeepWalk	0.0635	0.0583	0.004	0.0006	0.0008	0.001
Common Neighbors	0.1217	0.1031	0.155	0.0394	0.0379	0.0369
Adamic-Adar	0.1173	0.0990	0.156	0.0455	0.0442	0.0423

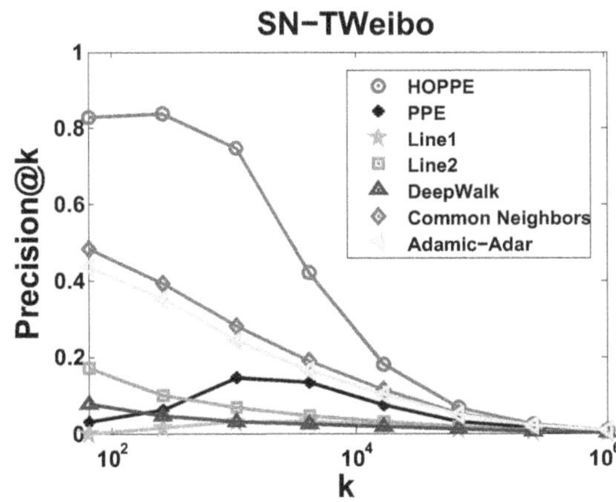

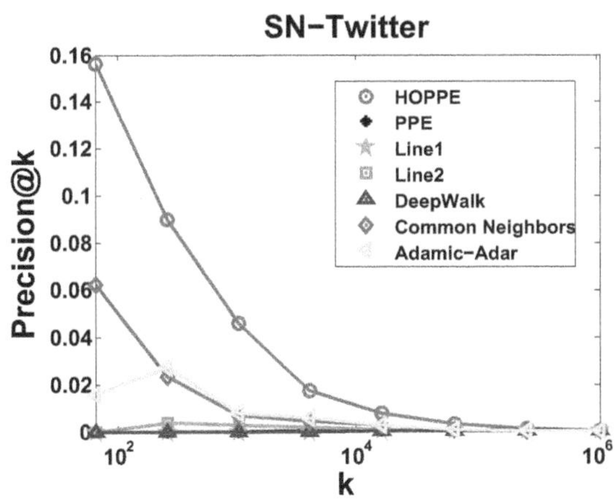

Figure 6: Precision@k of link prediction on SN-TWeibo and SN-Twitter. We rank pairs of vertexes according to their reconstructed proximity and evaluate the reconstruction precision in largest k pairs of vertexes.

Especially, the MAP@10 of HOPE achieves at least 88.5% improvement and the MAP@50 of HOPE achieves at least 81.2% improvement over all baseline algorithms. In most settings, the algorithms preserving directed high-order relationship, including HOPE, Common Neighbors, Adamic-Adar and PPE, outperforms LINE2 which only preserves directed first-order relationship. This proves that preserving directed high-order relationship is critical to capture the structure of directed graphs.

5. CONCLUSION

In this paper, we aim to preserve asymmetric transitivity in directed graphs, and propose to preserve asymmetric transitivity by approximating high-order proximities. We propose a scalable approximation algorithm , called High-Order Proximity preserved Embedding (HOPE). In this algorithm, we first derive a general formulation of a class of high-order proximity measurements, then apply generalized SVD to the general formulation, whose time complexity is linear with the size of graph. The empirical study demonstrates the superiority of asymmetric transitivity and our proposed algorithm, HOPE. Our future direction is to develop a nonlinear model to better capture the complex structure of directed graphs.

6. ACKNOWLEDGEMENTS

This work was supported by National Program on Key Basic Research Project, No. 2015CB352300; National Natural Science Foundation of China, No. 61370022, No. 61531006, No. 61472444 and No. 61210008. Thanks for the research fund of Tsinghua-Tencent Joint Laboratory for Internet Innovation Technology.

7. REFERENCES

[1] M. Belkin and P. Niyogi. Laplacian eigenmaps and spectral techniques for embedding and clustering. In *NIPS*, volume 14, pages 585–591, 2001.

[2] S. Cao, W. Lu, and Q. Xu. Grarep: Learning graph representations with global structural information. In *Proceedings of the 24th ACM International on Conference on Information and Knowledge Management*, pages 891–900. ACM, 2015.

[3] S. Chang, G.-J. Qi, C. C. Aggarwal, J. Zhou, M. Wang, and T. S. Huang. Factorized similarity learning in networks. In *Data Mining (ICDM), 2014 IEEE International Conference on*, pages 60–69. IEEE, 2014.

[4] M. Chen, Q. Yang, and X. Tang. Directed graph embedding. In *IJCAI*, pages 2707–2712, 2007.

[5] M. De Choudhury, Y.-R. Lin, H. Sundaram, K. S. Candan, L. Xie, A. Kelliher, et al. How does the data sampling strategy impact the discovery of information diffusion in social media? *ICWSM*, 10:34–41, 2010.

[6] R. A. Fisher. The use of multiple measurements in taxonomic problems. *Annals of eugenics*, 7(2):179–188, 1936.

[7] M. S. Handcock, A. E. Raftery, and J. M. Tantrum. Model-based clustering for social networks. *Journal of the Royal Statistical Society: Series A (Statistics in Society)*, 170(2):301–354, 2007.

[8] X. He, S. Yan, Y. Hu, P. Niyogi, and H.-J. Zhang. Face recognition using laplacianfaces. *Pattern Analysis and Machine Intelligence, IEEE Transactions on*, 27(3):328–340, 2005.

[9] M. Hochstenbach. A jacobi–davidson type method for the generalized singular value problem. *Linear Algebra and its Applications*, 431(3):471–487, 2009.

[10] P. D. Hoff. Multiplicative latent factor models for description and prediction of social networks. *Computational and Mathematical Organization Theory*, 15(4):261–272, 2009.

[11] P. D. Hoff, A. E. Raftery, and M. S. Handcock. Latent space approaches to social network analysis. *Journal of the american Statistical association*, 97(460):1090–1098, 2002.

[12] P. W. Holland and S. Leinhardt. An exponential family of probability distributions for directed graphs. *Journal of the american Statistical association*, 76(373):33–50, 1981.

[13] J. Hopcroft and R. Kannan. Foundations of data science. 2014.

[14] G. Jeh and J. Widom. Simrank: a measure of structural-context similarity. In *Proceedings of the eighth ACM SIGKDD international conference on Knowledge discovery and data mining*, pages 538–543. ACM, 2002.

[15] I. Jolliffe. *Principal component analysis.* Wiley Online Library, 2002.

[16] L. Katz. A new status index derived from sociometric analysis. *Psychometrika*, 18(1):39–43, 1953.

[17] J. Leskovec, J. Kleinberg, and C. Faloutsos. Graphs over time: densification laws, shrinking diameters and possible explanations. In *Proceedings of the eleventh ACM SIGKDD international conference on Knowledge discovery in data mining*, pages 177–187. ACM, 2005.

[18] O. Levy and Y. Goldberg. Neural word embedding as implicit matrix factorization. In *Advances in Neural Information Processing Systems*, pages 2177–2185, 2014.

[19] T. Mikolov, I. Sutskever, K. Chen, G. S. Corrado, and J. Dean. Distributed representations of words and phrases and their compositionality. In *Advances in neural information processing systems*, pages 3111–3119, 2013.

[20] K. Miller, M. I. Jordan, and T. L. Griffiths. Nonparametric latent feature models for link prediction. In *Advances in neural information processing systems*, pages 1276–1284, 2009.

[21] S. Mousazadeh and I. Cohen. Embedding and function extension on directed graph. *Signal Processing*, 111:137–149, 2015.

[22] C. C. Paige and M. A. Saunders. Towards a generalized singular value decomposition. *SIAM Journal on Numerical Analysis*, 18(3):398–405, 1981.

[23] J. Pennington, R. Socher, and C. D. Manning. Glove: Global vectors for word representation. *Proceedings of the Empiricial Methods in Natural Language Processing (EMNLP 2014)*, 12:1532–1543, 2014.

[24] B. Perozzi, R. Al-Rfou, and S. Skiena. Deepwalk: Online learning of social representations. In *Proceedings of the 20th ACM SIGKDD international conference on Knowledge discovery and data mining*, pages 701–710. ACM, 2014.

[25] D. Perrault-Joncas and M. Meila. Estimating vector fields on manifolds and the embedding of directed graphs. *arXiv preprint arXiv:1406.0013*, 2014.

[26] D. C. Perrault-Joncas and M. Meila. Directed graph embedding: an algorithm based on continuous limits of laplacian-type operators. In *Advances in Neural Information Processing Systems*, pages 990–998, 2011.

[27] S. T. Roweis and L. K. Saul. Nonlinear dimensionality reduction by locally linear embedding. *Science*, 290(5500):2323–2326, 2000.

[28] B. Scholkopft and K.-R. Mullert. Fisher discriminant analysis with kernels. *Neural networks for signal processing IX*, 1:1, 1999.

[29] T. A. Snijders, P. E. Pattison, G. L. Robins, and M. S. Handcock. New specifications for exponential random graph models. *Sociological methodology*, 36(1):99–153, 2006.

[30] H. H. Song, T. W. Cho, V. Dave, Y. Zhang, and L. Qiu. Scalable proximity estimation and link prediction in online social networks. In *Proceedings of the 9th ACM SIGCOMM conference on Internet measurement conference*, pages 322–335. ACM, 2009.

[31] L. Šubelj and M. Bajec. Model of complex networks based on citation dynamics. In *Proceedings of the 22nd international conference on World Wide Web companion*, pages 527–530. International World Wide Web Conferences Steering Committee, 2013.

[32] J. Tang, M. Qu, M. Wang, M. Zhang, J. Yan, and Q. Mei. Line: Large-scale information network embedding. In *Proceedings of the 24th International Conference on World Wide Web*, pages 1067–1077. International World Wide Web Conferences Steering Committee, 2015.

[33] J. B. Tenenbaum, V. De Silva, and J. C. Langford. A global geometric framework for nonlinear dimensionality reduction. *Science*, 290(5500):2319–2323, 2000.

[34] Y. J. Wang and G. Y. Wong. Stochastic blockmodels for directed graphs. *Journal of the American Statistical Association*, 82(397):8–19, 1987.

[35] S. Yan, D. Xu, B. Zhang, H.-J. Zhang, Q. Yang, and S. Lin. Graph embedding and extensions: a general framework for dimensionality reduction. *Pattern Analysis and Machine Intelligence, IEEE Transactions on*, 29(1):40–51, 2007.

[36] J. Ye, R. Janardan, and Q. Li. Two-dimensional linear discriminant analysis. In *Advances in neural information processing systems*, pages 1569–1576, 2004.

[37] S. Zhu, K. Yu, Y. Chi, and Y. Gong. Combining content and link for classification using matrix factorization. In *Proceedings of the 30th annual international ACM SIGIR conference on Research and development in information retrieval*, pages 487–494. ACM, 2007.

PTE: Enumerating Trillion Triangles On Distributed Systems

Ha-Myung Park
KAIST
hamyung.park@kaist.ac.kr

Sung-Hyon Myaeng
KAIST
myaeng@kaist.ac.kr

U Kang*
Seoul National University
ukang@snu.ac.kr

ABSTRACT

How can we enumerate triangles from an enormous graph with billions of vertices and edges? Triangle enumeration is an important task for graph data analysis with many applications including identifying suspicious users in social networks, detecting web spams, finding communities, etc. However, recent networks are so large that most of the previous algorithms fail to process them. Recently, several MapReduce algorithms have been proposed to address such large networks; however, they suffer from the massive shuffled data resulting in a very long processing time.

In this paper, we propose PTE (*Pre-partitioned Triangle Enumeration*), a new distributed algorithm for enumerating triangles in enormous graphs by resolving the structural inefficiency of the previous MapReduce algorithms. PTE enumerates trillions of triangles in a billion scale graph by decreasing three factors: the amount of shuffled data, total work, and network read. Experimental results show that PTE provides up to 47× faster performance than recent distributed algorithms on real world graphs, and succeeds in enumerating more than 3 *trillion* triangles on the ClueWeb12 graph with 6.3 billion vertices and 72 billion edges, which any previous triangle computation algorithm fail to process.

CCS Concepts

•**Information systems** → Data mining; •**Theory of computation** → **Parallel algorithms; Distributed algorithms;** *MapReduce algorithms; Graph algorithms analysis;*

Keywords

triangle enumeration; big data; graph algorithm; scalable algorithm; distributed algorithm; network analysis

1. INTRODUCTION

How can we enumerate trillion triangles from an enormous graph with billions of vertices and edges? The problem of *triangle enumeration* is to discover every triangle in a graph one by one where a triangle is a set of three vertices connected to each other. The problem has numerous graph mining applications including detecting suspicious accounts like advertisers or fake users in social networks [29, 16], uncovering hidden thematic layers on the web [8], discovering roles [5], detecting web spams [3], finding communities [4, 24], etc. A challenge in triangle enumeration is handling big real world networks, such as social networks and WWW, which have millions or billions of vertices and edges. For example, Facebook and Twitter have 1.39 billion [9] and 300 million active users [27], respectively, and at least 1 trillion unique URLs are on the web [1].

Even recently proposed algorithms, however, fail to enumerate triangles from such large graphs. The algorithms have been proposed in different ways: I/O efficient [13, 21, 19], distributed memory [2, 11], and MapReduce algorithms [6, 22, 23, 26]. These algorithms have a limited scalability. The I/O efficient algorithms use only a single machine, and thus they cannot process a graph exceeding the external memory space of the machine. The distributed memory algorithms use multiple machines, but they also cannot process a graph whose intermediate data exceed the capacity of distributed-memory. The state of the art MapReduce algorithm [23], named CTTP, significantly increases the size of processable dataset by dividing the entire task into several sub-tasks and processing them in separate MapReduce rounds. Even CTTP, however, takes a very long time to process an enormous graph because, in every round, CTTP reads the entire dataset and shuffles a lot of edges. Indeed, shuffling a large amount of data in a short time interval causes network congestion and heavy I/O to disks which decrease the scalability and the fault tolerance, and prolong the running time significantly. Thus, it is desirable to shrink the amount of shuffled data.

In this paper, we propose PTE (*Pre-partitioned Triangle Enumeration*), a new distributed algorithm for enumerating triangles in an enormous graph by resolving the structural inefficiency of the previous MapReduce algorithms. We show that PTE successfully enumerates trillions of triangles in a billion scale graph by decreasing three factors: the amount of shuffled data, total work, and network read. The main contributions of this paper are summarized as follows:

*Corresponding Author

KDD '16, August 13-17, 2016, San Francisco, CA, USA

DOI: http://dx.doi.org/10.1145/2939672.2939757

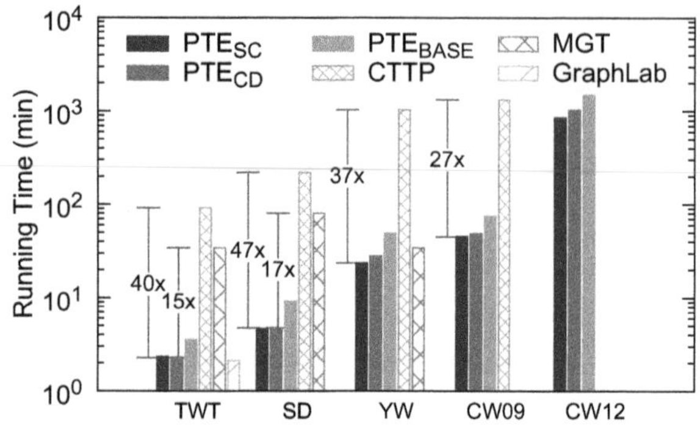

Figure 1: The running time of proposed methods (PTE$_{SC}$, PTE$_{CD}$, PTE$_{BASE}$) and competitors (CTTP, MGT, GraphLab) on real world datasets (log scale). GraphX is not shown since it failed to process any of the datasets. Missing methods for some datasets mean they failed to run on the datasets. PTE$_{SC}$ shows the best performances outperforming CTTP and MGT by up to 47× and 17×, respectively. Only the proposed algorithms succeed in processing the ClueWeb12 graph containing 6.3 billion vertices and 72 billion edges.

- We propose PTE, a new distributed algorithm for enumerating triangles in an enormous graph, which is designed to minimize the amount of shuffled data, total work, and network read.
- We prove the efficiency of the proposed algorithm: the algorithm operates in $O(|E|)$ shuffled data, $O(|E|^{3/2}/\sqrt{M})$ network read, and $O(|E|^{3/2})$ total work, the worst case optimal, where $|E|$ is the number of edges of a graph and M is the available memory size of a machine.
- Our algorithm is experimentally evaluated using large real world networks. The results demonstrate that our algorithm outperforms the best previous distributed algorithms by up to 47× (see Figure 1). Moreover, PTE successfully enumerates more than 3 trillion triangles in the ClueWeb12 graph containing 6.3 billion vertices and 72 billion edges. Any previous algorithms, including GraphLab, GraphX, and CTTP, fail to process the graph because of massive intermediate data.

The codes and datasets used in this paper are provided in `http://datalab.snu.ac.kr/pte`. The remaining part of the paper is organized as follows. In Section 2, we review the previous researches related to the triangle enumeration. In Section 3, we formally define the problem and introduce important concepts and notations used in this paper. We introduce the details of our algorithm in Section 4. The experimental results are given in Section 5. Finally, we conclude in Section 6. The symbols frequently used in this paper are summarized in Table 1.

2. RELATED WORK

In order to handle enormous graphs, several triangle enumeration algorithms have been proposed recently. In this section, we introduce the distinct approaches of the algorithms, including recent MapReduce algorithms related to our work. We also outline the MapReduce model and emphasize the importance of reducing the amount of shuffled data in improving the performance.

Table 1: Table of symbols.

Symbol	Definition
$G = (V, E)$	Simple graph with the set V of vertices and the set E of edges.
u, v, n	Vertices.
i, j, k	Vertex colors.
(u, v)	Edge between u and v where $u \prec v$.
(u, v, n)	Triangle with vertices u, v, and n where $u \prec v \prec n$.
$(i, j, k), (i, j)$	Subproblems.
$d(u)$	Degree (number of neighbors) of u.
$id(u)$	Vertex number of u, a unique identifier.
$\prec$	Total order on V. $u \prec v$ means u precedes v.
ρ	Number of vertex colors.
ξ	Coloring function: $V \to \{0, \cdots, \rho - 1\}$. $\xi(u)$ is the color of vertex u.
E_{ij}	Set of edges (u, v) where $(\xi(u), \xi(v)) = (i, j)$ or (j, i).
$E^{\star}_{ij}$	Set of edges (u, v) where $(\xi(u), \xi(v)) = (i, j)$.
M	Available memory size of a machine.
P	Number of processors in a distributed system.

2.1 I/O Efficient Triangle Algorithms

Recently, several triangle enumeration algorithms have been proposed in I/O efficient ways to handle graphs that do not fit into the main memory [13, 21, 19]. Hu et al. [13] propose Massive Graph Triangulation (MGT) which buffers a certain number of edges on the memory and finds all triangles containing one of these edges by traversing every vertex. Pagh and Silvestri [21] propose a cache oblivious algorithm which colors the vertices of a graph hierarchically so that it does not need to know the cache structure of a system. Kim et al. [19] present a parallel external-memory algorithm exploiting the features of a solid-state drive (SSD).

These algorithms, however, cannot process a graph exceeding the external memory space of a single machine. Moreover, these algorithms cannot output all the triangles in a large graph containing numerous triangles; for example, the ClueWeb12 graph (see Section 5) has 3 trillion triangles requiring 70 Terabytes of storage.

2.2 Distributed-Memory Triangle Algorithms

The triangle enumeration problem has been recently targeted in the distributed-memory model which assumes a multi-processor system where each processor has its own memory. We call a processor with a memory *a machine*. Arifuzzaman et al. [2] propose a distributed-memory algorithm based on *Message Passing Interface* (MPI). The algorithm divides a graph into overlapping subgraphs and finds triangles in each subgraph in parallel. GraphLab-PowerGraph (shortly GraphLab) [11], which is an MPI-based distributed graph computation framework, provides an implementation for triangle enumeration. GraphLab copies each vertex and its outgoing edges γ times on average to multiple machines where γ is determined by the characteristic of the input graph and the number of machines. Thus, $\gamma|E|$ data are replicated in total, and GraphLab fails when $\gamma|E|/P \geq M$ where P is the number of processors and M is the available memory size of a machine. GraphX, a graph computation library for Spark, also provides an implementation of the same algorithm as in GraphLab; thus it has the same limitation in scalability. PDTL [10] is a parallel and distributed extension of MGT. The experiment of the paper shows impressive speed of PDTL, but it has limited scalability: 1) every machine must hold a copy of an entire graph, 2) a part of PDTL runs on a single machine, which can be a performance bottleneck, and 3) it stores entire triangles in a single machine. In summary, all the previous distributed memory algorithms are limited in handling large graphs.

2.3 MapReduce

MapReduce [7] is a programming model supporting parallel and distributed computation to process large data. MapReduce is highly scalable and easy to use, and thus it has been used for various important graph mining and data mining tasks such as radius [18], graph queries [17], triangle [16, 22, 23], visualization [15], and tensors [14]. A MapReduce round transforms an input set of key-value pairs to an output set of key-value pairs by three steps: it first transforms each pair of the input to a set of new pairs (*map step*), groups the pairs by key so that all values with the same key are aggregated together (*shuffle step*), and processes the values by each key separately and outputs a new set of key-value pairs (*reduce step*).

The amount of shuffled data significantly affects the performance of a MapReduce task because shuffling includes heavy tasks of writing, sorting, and reading the data [12]. In detail, each map worker buffers the pairs from the map step in memory (collect). The buffered pairs are partitioned into R regions and written to local disk periodically where R is the number of reduce workers (spill). Each reduce worker remotely reads the buffered data from the local disks of the map workers via a network (shuffle). When a reduce worker has read all the pairs for its partition, the reduce worker sorts the pairs by keys so that all values with the same key are grouped together (merge and sort). Because of such heavy I/O and network traffic, a large amount of shuffled data decreases the performance significantly. Thus, it is desirable to shrink the amount of shuffled data as much as possible.

2.4 MapReduce Triangle Algorithms

Several triangle computation algorithms have been designed in MapReduce. We review the algorithms in terms of the amount of shuffled data. The first MapReduce algorithm is proposed by Cohen [6]. The algorithm is a variant of node-iterator [25], a well-known sequential algorithm. It shuffles $O(|E|^{3/2})$ length-2 paths (also known as wedges) in a graph. Suri and Vassilvitskii [26] reduce the amount of shuffled data to $O(|E|^{3/2}/\sqrt{M})$ by proposing a graph partitioning based algorithm *Graph Partition* (GP). Considering types of triangles, Park and Chung [22] improve GP by a constant factor in their algorithm, *Triangle Type Partition* (TTP). That is, TTP also shuffles $O(|E|^{3/2}/\sqrt{M})$ data during the process. Aforementioned algorithms cause an out of space error when the size of shuffled data is larger than the total available space. Park et al. [23] avoid the out of space error by introducing a multi-round algorithm, namely Colored TTP (CTTP). CTTP limits the shuffled data size of a round, and thus significantly increases the size of processable data. However, CTTP still shuffles the same amount of data as TTP does, that is, $O(|E|^{3/2}/\sqrt{M})$. Note that our proposed algorithm in this paper reduces the amount of shuffled data to $O(|E|)$, improving the performance significantly.

3. PRELIMINARIES

In this section, we define the problem that we are going to solve, introducing several terms and notations formally. We also describe two previously introduced major algorithms for distributed triangle enumeration.

3.1 Problem Definition

We first define the problem of triangle enumeration.

DEFINITION 1. (Triangle enumeration) Given a simple graph $G = (V, E)$, the problem of *triangle enumeration* is to discover every triangle in the graph G one by one, where a simple graph is an undirected graph containing no loops or no duplicate edges, and a triangle is a set of three vertices fully connected to each other.

Note that we do not require the algorithm to retain or emit each triangle (u, v, n) into any memory system, but to call a local function `enum(·)` with the triangle as the parameter.

On a vertex set V, we define a total order to uniquely express an edge or a triangle.

DEFINITION 2. (Total order on V) The order of two vertices u and v is determined as follows:

- $u \prec v$ if $d(u) < d(v)$ or $(d(u) = d(v)$ and $id(u) < id(v))$

where $d(u)$ is the degree, and $id(u)$ is the unique identifier of a vertex u.

We denote by (u, v) an edge between two vertices u and v, and by (u, v, n) a triangle consisting of three vertices u, v, and n. Unless otherwise noted, the vertices in an edge (u, v) have the order of $u \prec v$, and we presume it has a *direction*, from u to v, even though the graph is undirected. Similarly, the vertices in a triangle (u, v, n) also has the order of $u \prec v \prec n$, and we give each edge a name to simplify the description as follows (see Figure 2):

DEFINITION 3. For a triangle (u, v, n) where the vertices are in the order of $u \prec v \prec n$, we call (u, v) *pivot edge*, (u, n) *port edge*, and (v, n) *starboard edge*.

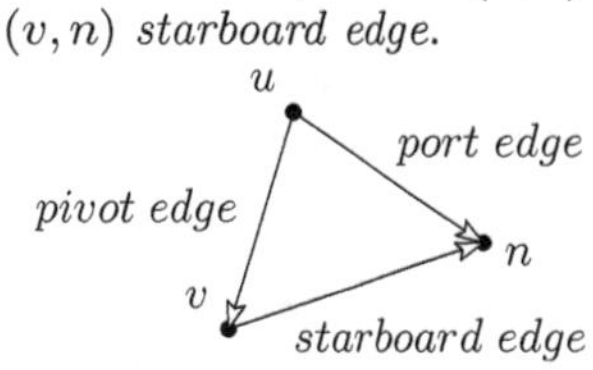

Figure 2: A triangle with directions by the total order on the three vertices.

3.2 Triangle Enumeration in TTP and CTTP

Park and Chung [22] propose a MapReduce algorithm, named *Triangle Type Partition* (TTP), for enumerating triangles. We introduce TTP briefly because of its relevance to our work, and we show that it shuffles $O(|E|^{3/2}/\sqrt{M})$ data.

The first step of TTP is to color the vertices with $\rho = O(\sqrt{|E|/M})$ colors by a hash function $\xi : V \rightarrow \{0, \cdots, \rho - 1\}$. Let E_{ij} with $i, j \in \{0, \cdots, \rho - 1\}$ and $i \leq j$ be the set $\{(u, v) \in E \mid i = \min(\xi(u), \xi(v))$ and $j = \max(\xi(u), \xi(v))\}$. A triangle is classified as *type-1* if all the vertices in the triangle have the same color, *type-2* if there are exactly two vertices with the same color, and *type-3* if no vertices have the same color. TTP divides the entire problem into $\binom{\rho}{2} + \binom{\rho}{3}$ subproblems of two types:

(i, j) **subproblem**, with $i, j \in \{0, \cdots, \rho - 1\}$ and $i < j$, is to enumerate triangles in an edge-induced subgraph on $E'_{ij} = E_{ij} \cup E_{ii} \cup E_{jj}$. It finds every triangle of type-1 and type-2 where the vertices are colored with i and j. There are $\binom{\rho}{2}$ subproblems of this type.

(i, j, k) **subproblem**, with $i, j, k \in \{0, \cdots, \rho - 1\}$ and $i < j < k$, is to enumerate triangles in an edge-induced subgraph on $E'_{ijk} = E_{ij} \cup E_{ik} \cup E_{jk}$. It finds every triangle of type-3 where the vertices are colored with i, j and k. There are $\binom{\rho}{3}$ subproblems of this type.

Algorithm 1: Graph Partitioning

/* ψ is a meaningless dummy key */

Map : input $\langle \psi; (u,v) \in E \rangle$

emit $\langle (\xi(u), \xi(v)); (u,v) \rangle$

Reduce : input $\langle (i,j); E^\star_{ij} \rangle$

emit $E^\star_{ij}$ to a distributed storage

Each map task of TTP gets an edge $e \in E$ and emits $\langle (i,j); e \rangle$ and $\langle (i,j,k); e \rangle$ for every E'_{ij} and E'_{ijk} containing e, respectively. Thus, each reduce task gets a pair $\langle (i,j); E'_{ij} \rangle$ or $\langle (i,j,k); E'_{ijk} \rangle$, and finds all triangle in the edge-induced subgraph. For each edge, a map task emits $\rho - 1$ key-value pairs (Lemma 2 in [22]); that is, $O(|E|\rho) = O(|E|^{3/2}/\sqrt{M})$ pairs are shuffled in total. TTP fails to process a graph when the shuffled data size is larger than the total available space. CTTP [23] avoids the failure by dividing the tasks into multiple rounds and limiting the shuffled data size of a round. However, CTTP still shuffles exactly the same pairs as TTP; hence CTTP also suffers from the massive shuffled data resulting in a very long running time.

4. PROPOSED METHOD

In this section, we propose PTE (*Pre-partitioned Triangle Enumeration*), a distributed algorithm for enumerating triangles in an enormous graph. There are several challenges in designing an efficient and scalable distributed algorithm for triangle enumeration.

1. **Minimize shuffled data.** Massive data are shuffled for generating subgraphs by the previous algorithms. How can we minimize the amount of shuffled data?
2. **Minimize computations.** The previous algorithms contain several kinds of redundant operations (details in Section 4.2). How can we remove the redundancy?
3. **Minimize network read.** In previous algorithms, each subproblem reads necessary sets of edges via network, and the amount of network read is determined by the number of vertex colors. How can we decrease the number of vertex colors to minimize network read?

We have the following main ideas to address the above challenges, which are described in detail in later subsections.

1. **Separating graph partitioning from generating subgraphs** decreases the amount of shuffled data to $O(|E|)$ from $O(|E|^{3/2}/\sqrt{M})$ of the previous MapReduce algorithms (Section 4.1).
2. **Considering the color-direction of edges** removes redundant operations and minimizes computations (Section 4.2).
3. **Carefully scheduling triangle computations** in subproblems shrinks the amount of network read by decreasing the number of vertex colors (Section 4.3).

In the following we first describe PTE$_{\text{BASE}}$ which exploits pre-partitioning to decrease the shuffled data (Section 4.1). Then, we describe PTE$_{\text{CD}}$ which improves on PTE$_{\text{BASE}}$ to remove redundant operations (Section 4.2). After that, we explain our desired method PTE$_{\text{SC}}$ which further improves on PTE$_{\text{CD}}$ to shrink the amount of network read (Section 4.3). The theoretical analysis of the methods and implementation issues are discussed in the end (Sections 4.4 and 4.5). Note that although we describe PTE using MapReduce primitives for simplicity, PTE is general enough to be implemented in any distributed framework (discussions in Section 4.5 and experimental comparisons in Section 5.2.3).

Algorithm 2: Triangle Enumeration (PTE$_{\text{BASE}}$)

/* ψ is a meaningless dummy key */

Map : input $\langle \psi; problem = (i,j) \text{ or } (i,j,k) \rangle$

initialize E'

if *problem is of type* (i,j) **then**

  /* $E_{ij} = E^\star_{ij} \cup E^\star_{ji}$, and $E_{ii} = E^\star_{ii}$ */

  read E_{ij}, E_{ii}, E_{jj}

  $E' \leftarrow E_{ij} \cup E_{ii} \cup E_{jj}$

else if *problem is of type* (i,j,k) **then**

  /* $E_{ij} = E^\star_{ij} \cup E^\star_{ji}$, $E_{ik} = E^\star_{ik} \cup E^\star_{ki}$, and $E_{jk} = E^\star_{jk} \cup E^\star_{kj}$ */

  read E_{ij}, E_{ik}, E_{jk}

  $E' \leftarrow E_{ij} \cup E_{ik} \cup E_{jk}$

enumerateTriangles(E')

/* enumerate triangles in the edge-induced subgraph on E */

Function enumerateTriangles(E)

  foreach $(u,v) \in E$ **do**

    foreach $n \in \{n_u | (u, n_u) \in E\} \cap \{n_v | (v, n_v) \in E\}$ **do**

      if $\xi(u) = \xi(v) = \xi(n)$ **then**

        if *($\xi(u) = i$ and $i+1 \equiv j \mod \rho$) or ($\xi(u) = j$ and $j+1 \equiv i \mod \rho$)* **then**

          enum((u,v,n))

      else

        enum((u,v,n))

4.1 PTE$_{\text{BASE}}$: Pre-partitioned Triangle Enumeration

In this section we propose PTE$_{\text{BASE}}$ which rectifies the massive shuffled data problem of previous MapReduce algorithms. The main idea is partitioning an input graph into sets of edges before enumerating triangles, and storing the sets in a distributed storage like *Hadoop Distributed File System* (HDFS) of Hadoop, or *Resilient Distributed Dataset* (RDD) of Spark. We observe that the subproblems of TTP require each set E_{ij} of edges as a unit. It implies that if each edge set E_{ij} is directly accessible from a distributed storage, we need not shuffle the edges like TTP does. Consequently, we partition the input graph into $\rho + \binom{\rho}{2} = \frac{\rho(\rho+1)}{2}$ sets of edges according to the vertex colors in each edge; ρ and $\binom{\rho}{2}$ are for E_{ij} when $i = j$ and $i < j$, respectively. Each edge $(u,v) \in E_{ij}$ keeps the order $u \prec v$. Each vertex is colored by a coloring function ξ which is randomly chosen from a pairwise independent family of functions [28]. The pairwise independence of ξ guarantees that edges are evenly distributed. PTE$_{\text{BASE}}$ sets ρ to $\lceil \sqrt{6|E|/M} \rceil$ to fit the three edge sets for an (i,j,k) subproblem into the memory of size M in a processor: the expected size of an edge set is $2|E|/\rho^2$, and the sum $6|E|/\rho^2$ of the size of the three edge sets should be less than or equal to the memory size M.

After the graph partitioning, PTE$_{\text{BASE}}$ reads edge sets and finds triangles in each subproblem. In each (i,j) subproblem, it reads E_{ij}, E_{ii}, and E_{jj}, and enumerates triangles in the union of the edge sets. In each (i,j,k) subproblem, similarly, it reads E_{ij}, E_{ik}, and E_{jk}, and enumerates triangles in the union of the edge sets. The edge sets are read from a distributed storage via a network, and the total amount of network read is $O(|E|\rho)$ (see Section 3.2). Note that the network read is different from the data shuffle; the data shuffle is a much heavier task since it requires data collecting and writing in senders, data transfer via a network, and data merging and sorting in receivers (see Section 2.3). However, the network read contains data transfer via a network only.

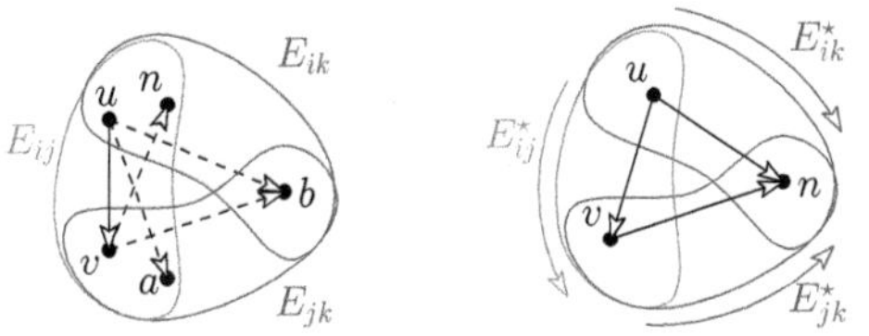

(a) (b)

Figure 3: (a) An example of finding type-3 triangles containing an edge $(u,v) \in E_{ij}$ in an (i,j,k) subproblem. PTE$_{\text{BASE}}$ finds the triangle (u,v,b) by intersecting u's neighbor set $\{v,a,b\}$ and v's neighbor set $\{n,b\}$. However, it is unnecessary to consider the edges in E_{ij} since the other two edges of a type-3 triangle containing (u,v) must be in E_{ik} and E_{jk}, respectively. (b) `enumerateTrianglesCD(`$E^\star_{ij}$, $E^\star_{ik}$, $E^\star_{jk}$`)` in PTE$_{\text{CD}}$ finds every triangle whose pivot edge, port edge, and starboard edge have the same color-directions as those of $E^\star_{ij}$, $E^\star_{ik}$, and $E^\star_{jk}$, respectively. The arrows denote the color-directions.

Pseudo codes for PTE$_{\text{BASE}}$ are listed in Algorithm 1 and Algorithm 2. The graph partitioning is done by a pair of map and reduce steps (Algorithm 1). In the map step, PTE$_{\text{BASE}}$ transforms each edge (u,v) into a pair $\langle(\xi(u),\xi(v));(u,v)\rangle$ (line 1). The edges of the pairs are aggregated by the keys; and for each key (i,j), a reduce task receives $E^\star_{ij}$ and emits it to a separate file in a distributed storage (line 2), where $E^\star_{ij}$ is $\{(u,v) \in E | (\xi(u),\xi(v)) = (i,j)\}$. Note that the union of $E^\star_{ij}$ and $E^\star_{ji}$ is E_{ij}, that is, $E^\star_{ij} \cup E^\star_{ji} = E_{ij}$.

Thanks to the pre-partitioned edge sets, the triangle enumeration is done by a single map step (see Algorithm 2). Each map task reads edge sets needed to solve a subproblem (i,j) or (i,j,k) (lines 3, 6), makes the union of the edge sets (lines 4, 7), and enumerates triangles with a sequential algorithm `enumerateTriangles` (line 8). Although any sequential algorithm for triangle enumeration can be used for `enumerateTriangles`, we use CompactForward [20], one of the best sequential algorithms, with a modification (lines 9-16): we skip the vertex sorting procedure of CompactForward because the edges are already ordered by the degrees of its vertices. Given a set E' of edges, `enumerateTriangles` runs in $O(|E'|^{3/2})$ total work, the same as that of CompactForward. Note that we propose a specialized algorithm to reduce the total work in Section 4.2. Note also that although every type-1 triangle appears $\rho - 1$ times, PTE$_{\text{BASE}}$ emits the triangle only once: for each type-1 triangle of color i, PTE$_{\text{BASE}}$ emits the triangle if and only if $i+1 \equiv j \mod \rho$ given a subproblem (i,j) or (j,i) (lines 12-14). Still, a type-1 triangle is computed $\rho - 1$ times which is unnecessary. We completely resolve the issue in Section 4.2.

4.2 PTE$_{\text{CD}}$: Reducing the Total Work

PTE$_{\text{CD}}$ improves on PTE$_{\text{BASE}}$ to minimize the amount of computations by exploiting *color-direction*. We first give an example (Figure 3(a)) to show that the function `enumerateTriangles` in Algorithm 2 performs redundant operations. Let us consider finding type-3 triangles containing an edge $(u,v) \in E_{ij}$ in an (i,j,k) subproblem. `enumerateTriangles` finds such triangles by intersecting the two outgoing neighbor sets of u and v. In the figure, the neighbor sets are $\{v,a,b\}$ and $\{n,b\}$; and we find the triangle (u,v,b). However, it is unnecessary to consider edges in E_{ij} (that is, (u,v), (u,a), (v,n)) since the other two edges of a type-3 triangle containing (u,v) must be in E_{ik} and E_{jk}, respectively. The redundant operations can be removed by intersecting u's neighbors only in E_{ik} and v's neighbors only in E_{jk} instead of looking at all the neighbors of u and v. In the figure, the two neighbor sets are both $\{b\}$; and we find the same triangle (u,v,b). PTE$_{\text{CD}}$ removes the redundant operations by adopting a new function `enumerateTrianglesCD` (lines 11-14 in Algorithm 3). We define the *color-direction* of an edge (u,v) to be from $\xi(u)$ to $\xi(v)$; and we also define the *color-direction* of $E^\star_{ij}$ to be from i to j. Then, `enumerateTrianglesCD(`$E^\star_{ij}$, $E^\star_{ik}$, $E^\star_{jk}$`)` finds every triangle whose pivot edge, port edge, and starboard edge have the same color-directions as those of $E^\star_{ij}$, $E^\star_{ik}$, and $E^\star_{jk}$, respectively (see Figure 3(b)). Note that the algorithm does not look at any edges in E_{ij} for the intersection in the example of Figure 3(a) by separating the input edge sets.

Redundant operations of another type appear in (i,j) subproblems; PTE$_{\text{BASE}}$ outputs a type-1 triangle exactly once but still computes it multiple times: *type*-1 triangles with a color i appears $\rho - 1$ times in (i,j) or (j,i) subproblems for $j \in \{0,\cdots,\rho-1\} \setminus \{i\}$. PTE$_{\text{CD}}$ resolves the duplicate computation by performing `enumerateTrianglesCD(`$E^\star_{ii}$, $E^\star_{ii}$, $E^\star_{ii}$`)` exactly once for each vertex color i; and thus, every type-1 triangle appears only once.

Algorithm 3 shows PTE$_{\text{CD}}$ using the new function `enumerateTrianglesCD`. To find type-3 triangles in each (i,j,k) subproblem, PTE$_{\text{CD}}$ calls the function `enumerateTrianglesCD` 6 times for every possible color-direction (lines 10, 15-18) (see Figure 4(a)). To find type-2 triangles in each (i,j) subproblem, similarly, PTE$_{\text{CD}}$ calls `enumerateTrianglesCD` 6 times (lines 7-8) (see Figure 4(b)). For type-1 triangles

Algorithm 3: Triangle Enumeration (PTE$_{\text{CD}}$)

```
   /* ψ is a meaningless dummy key                                  */
   Map        : input ⟨ψ; problem = (i,j) or (i,j,k)⟩
1  if problem is of type (i,j) then
2      read E*_ij, E*_ji, E*_ii, E*_jj
       /* enumerate Type-1 triangles                                */
3      if i+1 = j then
4          enumerateTrianglesCD(E*_ii, E*_ii, E*_ii)
5      else if j = ρ−1 and i = 0 then
6          enumerateTrianglesCD(E*_jj, E*_jj, E*_jj)
       /* enumerate Type-2 triangles                                */
7      foreach
       (x,y,z) ∈ {(i,i,j),(i,j,i),(j,i,i),(i,j,j),(j,i,j),(j,j,i)}
       do
8          enumerateTrianglesCD(E*_xy, E*_xz, E*_yz)
9  else if problem is of type (i,j,k) then
10     enumerateType3Triangles((i,j,k))

   /* enumerate every triangle (u,v,n) such that ξ(u) = i,
      ξ(v) = j and ξ(n) = k                                         */
11 Function enumerateTrianglesCD(E*_ij, E*_ik, E*_jk)
12     foreach (u,v) ∈ E*_ij do
13         foreach
           n ∈ {n_u|(u,n_u) ∈ E*_ik} ∩ {n_v|(v,n_v) ∈ E*_jk} do
14             enum((u,v,n))

15 Function enumerateType3Triangles(i, j, k)
16     read E*_ij, E*_ik, E*_ji, E*_jk, E*_ki, E*_kj
17     foreach (x,y,z) ∈
       {(i,j,k),(i,k,j),(j,i,k),(j,k,i),(k,i,j),(k,j,i)} do
18         enumerateTrianglesCD(E*_xy, E*_xz, E*_yz)
```

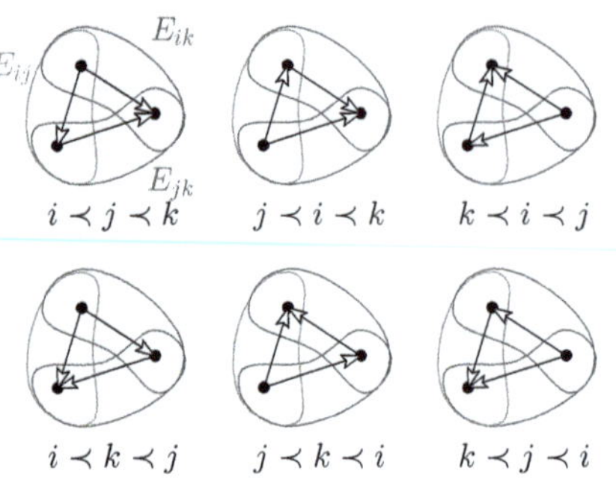

(a) The six color-directions of a type-3 triangle in an (i, j, k) subproblem.

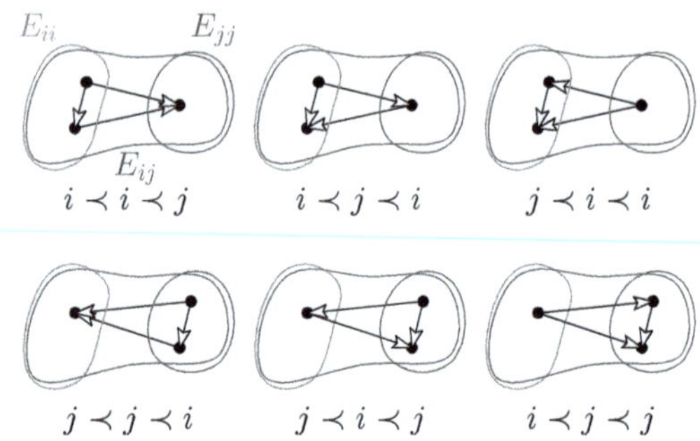

(b) The six color-directions of a type-2 triangle in an (i, j) subproblem.

Figure 4: The color-directions of a triangle according to its type. The function enumerateTrianglesCD is called for each color-direction; that is, PTE$_{\text{CD}}$ calls it 6 times for type-3 triangles and type-2 triangles, respectively.

whose vertices have a color i, PTE$_{\text{CD}}$ performs `enumerateTrianglesCD(`$E^\star_{ii}$, $E^\star_{ii}$, $E^\star_{ii}$`)` only if $i + 1 \equiv j \mod \rho$ given a subproblem (i, j) or (j, i) so that `enumerateTrianglesCD(`$E^\star_{ii}$, $E^\star_{ii}$, $E^\star_{ii}$`)` operates exactly once (lines 3-6). As a result, the algorithm emits every triangle exactly once.

Removing the two types of redundant operations, PTE$_{\text{CD}}$ decreases the number of operations for intersecting neighbor sets by more than $2 - \frac{2}{\rho}$ times from PTE$_{\text{BASE}}$ in expectation. As we will see in Section 5.2.1, PTE$_{\text{CD}}$ decreases the operations by up to 6.83× than PTE$_{\text{BASE}}$ on real world graphs.

THEOREM 1. *PTE$_{CD}$ decreases the number of operations for intersecting neighbor sets by more than $2 - \frac{2}{\rho}$ times compared to PTE$_{BASE}$ in expectation.*

PROOF. To intersect the sets of neighbors of u and v in an edge (u, v) such that $\xi(u) = i$, $\xi(v) = j$ and $i \neq j$, the function `enumerateTriangles` in PTE$_{\text{BASE}}$ performs $d^\star_{ij}(u) + d^\star_{ik}(u) + d^\star_{ji}(v) + d^\star_{jk}(v)$ operations while `enumerateTrianglesCD` in PTE$_{\text{CD}}$ performs $d^\star_{ik}(u) + d^\star_{jk}(v)$ operations for each color $k \in \{0, \cdots, \rho - 1\} \setminus \{i, j\}$ where $d^\star_{ij}(u)$ is the number of u's neighbors in $E^\star_{ij}$. Thus, PTE$_{\text{BASE}}$ performs $(\rho - 2) \times (d^\star_{\xi(u)\xi(v)}(u) + d^\star_{\xi(v)\xi(u)}(v))$ additional operations compared to PTE$_{\text{CD}}$ for each $(u, v) \in E^{out}$ where E^{out} is the set of edges $(u, v) \in E$ such that $\xi(u) \neq \xi(v)$; that is,

$$(\rho - 2) \times \sum_{(u,v) \in E^{out}} \left(d^\star_{\xi(u)\xi(v)}(u) + d^\star_{\xi(v)\xi(u)}(v) \right) \quad (1)$$

Given an edge (u, v) such that $\xi(u) = \xi(v) = i$, PTE$_{\text{BASE}}$ performs $d^\star_{ii}(u) + d^\star_{ij}(u) + d^\star_{ii}(v) + d^\star_{ij}(v)$ operations for each color $j \in \{0, \cdots, \rho - 1\} \setminus \{i\}$; meanwhile, PTE$_{\text{CD}}$ performs $d^\star_{ij}(u) + d^\star_{ij}(v)$ operations for each color $j \in \{0, \cdots, \rho - 1\}$. Thus, PTE$_{\text{BASE}}$ performs $(\rho - 2) \times (d^\star_{\xi(u)\xi(v)}(u) + d^\star_{\xi(v)\xi(u)}(v))$ more operations than PTE$_{\text{CD}}$ for each $(u, v) \in E^{in}$ where E^{in} is $E \setminus E^{out}$; that is,

$$(\rho - 2) \times \sum_{(u,v) \in E^{in}} \left(d^\star_{\xi(u)\xi(v)}(u) + d^\star_{\xi(v)\xi(u)}(v) \right) \quad (2)$$

Then, the total number of *additional* operations performed by PTE$_{\text{BASE}}$, compared to PTE$_{\text{CD}}$, is the sum of (1) and (2):

$$(\rho - 2) \times \sum_{(u,v) \in E} \left(d^\star_{\xi(u)\xi(v)}(u) + d^\star_{\xi(v)\xi(u)}(v) \right) \quad (3)$$

The expected value of $d^\star_{\xi(u)\xi(v)}(u)$ is $d^\star(u)/\rho$ where $d^\star(u)$ is the number of neighbors v of u such that $u \prec v$, since the coloring function ξ is randomly chosen from a pairwise independent family of functions. Thus, (3) becomes as follows:

$$\frac{(\rho - 2)}{\rho} \times \sum_{(u,v) \in E} (d^\star(u) + d^\star(v) + O(\rho)) \quad (4)$$

We add $O(\rho)$ because $(d^\star(u) + d^\star(v))/\rho$ can be less than 1 but $d^\star_{\xi(u)\xi(v)}(u) + d^\star_{\xi(v)\xi(u)}(v)$ is always larger than or equal to 1. Meanwhile, the number of operations by PTE$_{\text{CD}}$ for intersecting neighbor sets is $\sum_{(u,v) \in E} (d^\star(u) + d^\star(v))$ as we will see in Theorem 5. Thus, PTE$_{\text{CD}}$ reduces the number of operations by more than $2 - \frac{2}{\rho}$ times from PTE$_{\text{BASE}}$ in expectation. □

4.3 PTE$_{\text{SC}}$: Reducing the Network Read

PTE$_{\text{SC}}$ further improves on PTE$_{\text{CD}}$ to shrink the amount of network read by *scheduling* calls of the function `enumerateTrianglesCD`. Reading each $E^\star_{ij}$ in $\rho - 1$ subproblems, PTE$_{\text{CD}}$ (as well as PTE$_{\text{BASE}}$) reads $O(|E|\rho)$ data via a network in total. For example, $E^\star_{01}$ is read in every $(0, 1, k)$ subproblem for $2 \leq k < \rho$, and the $(0, 1)$ subproblem. It implies that the amount of network read depends on ρ, the number of vertex colors. PTE$_{\text{BASE}}$ and PTE$_{\text{CD}}$ set ρ to $\lceil \sqrt{6|E|/M} \rceil$ as mentioned in Section 4.1. In PTE$_{\text{SC}}$, we reduce it to $\lceil \sqrt{5|E|/M} \rceil$ by setting the sequence of triangle computation as in Figure 5 which represents the schedule of data loading for an (i, j, k) subproblem. We denote by Δ_{ijk} the set of triangles enumerated by `enumerateTrianglesCD(`$E^\star_{ij}$, $E^\star_{ik}$, $E^\star_{jk}$`)`. PTE$_{\text{CD}}$ handles the triangle sets one by one from left to right in the figure. The check-marks (✓) show the relations between edge sets and triangle sets. For example, $E^\star_{ij}$, $E^\star_{ik}$, and $E^\star_{jk}$ should be retained in the memory together to enumerate Δ_{ijk}. When we restrict to read an edge set only once in a subproblem, the shaded areas represent when the edge sets are in the memory. For example, $E^\star_{ij}$ is read before Δ_{ijk}, and is released after Δ_{kij}. Then, we can easily see that the maximum number of edge sets which are retained in the memory together at a time is 5, and it leads to setting ρ to $\lceil \sqrt{5|E|/M} \rceil$. The pro-

	Δ_{ijk}	Δ_{ikj}	Δ_{jik}	Δ_{jki}	Δ_{kij}	Δ_{kji}
$E^\star_{ij}$	✓	✓			✓	
$E^\star_{ik}$	✓	✓	✓			
$E^\star_{ji}$			✓	✓		✓
$E^\star_{jk}$	✓		✓	✓		
$E^\star_{ki}$				✓	✓	✓
$E^\star_{kj}$		✓			✓	✓

Figure 5: The schedule of data loading for an (i, j, k) subproblem. PTE$_{\text{SC}}$ enumerates triangles in columns one by one from left to right. Each check-mark (✓) shows the relations between edge sets and triangle types. Each shaded area denotes when the edge set is in the memory, when we restrict to read an edge set only once in a subproblem.

Algorithm 4: Type-3 triangle enumeration in PTE$_{SC}$

```
Function enumerateType3Triangles(i, j, k)
    read E*_ij, E*_ik, E*_ji, E*_jk, E*_kj
    foreach (x, y, z) ∈ {(i, j, k), (i, k, j), (j, i, k)} do
        enumerateTrianglesCD(E*_xy, E*_xz, E*_yz)
    release E*_ik
    read E*_ki
    foreach (x, y, z) ∈ {(j, k, i), (k, i, j), (k, j, i)} do
        enumerateTrianglesCD(E*_xy, E*_xz, E*_yz)
```

cedure of type-3 triangle enumeration with the scheduling method is described in Algorithm 4 which replaces the function `enumerateType3Triangles` in Algorithm 3. Note that the number 5 of edge sets loaded in the memory at a time is optimal as shown in the following theorem.

THEOREM 2. *Given an (i, j, k) subproblem, the maximum number of edge sets retained in the memory at a time cannot be smaller than 5, if each edge set can be read only once.*

PROOF. Suppose that there is a schedule to make the maximum number of edge sets retained in the memory at a time less than 5. Then, we first read 4 edge sets in the memory. Then, 1) any edge set in the memory cannot be released until all triangles containing an edge in the set have been enumerated, and 2) we cannot read another edge set until we release one in the memory. Thus, for at least one edge set in the memory, it should be able to process all triangles containing an edge in the edge set without reading an additional edge set. However, it is impossible because enumerating all triangles containing an edge in an edge set requires 5 edge sets but we have only 4 edge sets. For example, the triangles in Δ_{ijk}, Δ_{ikj}, and Δ_{kij}, which are related to an edge set $E^\star_{ij}$, require $E^\star_{ij}$, $E^\star_{ik}$, $E^\star_{jk}$, $E^\star_{kj}$, and $E^\star_{ki}$. Thus, there is no schedule to make the maximum number of edge sets retained in the memory at a time less than 5. □

4.4 Analysis

In this section we analyze the proposed algorithm in terms of the amount of shuffled data, network read, and total work. We first prove the claimed amount of shuffled data generated by the graph partitioning in Algorithm 1.

THEOREM 3. *The amount of shuffled data for partitioning a graph is $O(|E|)$ where $|E|$ is the number of edges in the graph.*

PROOF. The pairs emitted from the map operation is exactly the data to be shuffled. For each edge, a map task emits one pair; accordingly, the amount of shuffled data is the number $|E|$ of edges in the graph. □

We emphasize that while the previous MapReduce algorithms shuffle $O(|E|^{3/2}/\sqrt{M})$ data, we reduce it to be $O(|E|)$. Instead of data shuffle requiring heavy disk I/O, network read, and massive intermediate data, we only require the same amount of network read, that is $O(|E|^{3/2}/\sqrt{M})$.

THEOREM 4. *PTE requires $O(|E|^{3/2}/\sqrt{M})$ network read.*

PROOF. We first show that every $E^\star_{ij}$ for $(i, j) \in \{0, \cdots, \rho-1\}^2$ are read $\rho - 1$ times. It is clear that $E^\star_{ij}$ such that $i = j$ is read $\rho-1$ times in (i, k) or (k, i) subproblems for $k \in \{0, \cdots, \rho-1\} \setminus \{i\}$. We now consider $E^\star_{ij}$ for $i \neq j$. Without loss of generality, we assume $i < j$. Then, $E^\star_{ij}$ is read $\rho - 2$ times in (i, j, k) or (i, k, j) or (k, i, j) subproblems where $k \in \{0, \cdots, \rho-1\} \setminus \{i, j\}$, and once in an (i, j) subproblem; $\rho - 1$ times in total. The total amount of data read by PTE is as follows:

$$(\rho-1)\sum_{i=0}^{\rho-1}\sum_{j=0}^{\rho-1}|E^\star_{ij}| = |E|(\rho-1) = |E|\left(\sqrt{\frac{5|E|}{M}}-1\right) = O\left(\frac{|E|^{3/2}}{\sqrt{M}}\right)$$

where $|E^\star_{ij}|$ is the number of edges in $E^\star_{ij}$. □

Finally, we prove the claimed total work of the proposed algorithm.

THEOREM 5. *PTE requires $O(|E|^{3/2})$ total work.*

PROOF. Intersecting two sets requires comparisons as many times as the number of elements in the two sets. Accordingly, the number of operations performed by `enumerateTrianglesCD(`$E^\star_{ij}, E^\star_{ik}, E^\star_{jk}$`)` is

$$\sum_{(u,v)\in E^\star_{ij}} \left(d^\star_{ik}(u) + d^\star_{jk}(v) + O(1)\right)$$

where $d^\star_{ik}(u)$ is the number of u's neighbors in $E^\star_{ik}$. We put $O(1)$ since $d^\star_{ik}(u)+d^\star_{jk}(v)$ can be smaller than 1. PTE$_{SC}$ (as well as PTE$_{CD}$) calls `enumerateTrianglesCD` for every possible triple $(i, j, k) \in \{0, \cdots, \rho-1\}^3$; thus the total number of operations is as follows:

$$\sum_{i=0}^{\rho-1}\sum_{j=0}^{\rho-1}\sum_{k=0}^{\rho-1}\sum_{(u,v)\in E^\star_{ij}} \left(d^\star_{ik}(u) + d^\star_{jk}(v) + O(1)\right)$$
$$=O(E\rho) + \sum_{(u,v)\in E} \left(d^\star(u) + d^\star(v)\right)$$

The left term $O(|E|\rho)$ is $O(|E|^{3/2}/\sqrt{M})$ for checking all edges in each subproblem, which occurs also in PTE$_{BASE}$. The right summation is the number of operations for intersecting neighbors, and it is $O(|E|^{3/2})$ when the vertices are ordered by Definition 2 because the maximum value of $d^\star(u)$ for every $u \in V$ is $2\sqrt{|E|}$ as proved in [25]. □

Note that it is the worst case optimal and the same as one of the best sequential algorithms [20].

4.5 Implementation

In this section, we discuss practical implementation issues of PTEs. We focus on the most famous distributed computation frameworks, Hadoop and Spark. Note that PTEs can be implemented for any distributed framework which supports map and reduce functionalities.

PTE on Hadoop. We describe how to implement PTE on Hadoop which is the de facto standard of MapReduce framework. The graph partitioning method (Algorithm 1) of PTE is implemented as a single MapReduce round. The result of the graph partitioning method has a custom output format that stores each edge set as a separate file in *Hadoop Distributed File System* (HDFS); and thus each edge set is accessible by the path. The triangle enumeration method (Algorithms 2 or 3) of PTE is implemented as a single map step where each map task processes an (i, j) or (i, j, k) subproblem. For this purpose, we generate a text file where each line is (i, j) or (i, j, k), and make each map task read a line and solve the subproblem.

PTE on Spark. We describe how to implement PTE on Spark, which is another popular distributed computing

Table 2: The summary of datasets.

Dataset	Vertices	Edges	Triangles
Twitter (TWT)[1]	42M	1.2B	34824916864
SubDomain (SD)[2]	101M	1.9B	417761664336
YahooWeb (YW)[3]	1.4B	6.4B	85782928684
ClueWeb09 (CW09)[4]	4.8B	7.9B	31012381940
ClueWeb12 (CW12)[5]	6.3B	72B	3064499157291
ClueWeb12/256	287M	260M	184494
ClueWeb12/128	457M	520M	1458207
ClueWeb12/64	679M	1.0B	11793453
ClueWeb12/32	947M	2.1B	94016252
ClueWeb12/16	1.3B	4.2B	750724625
ClueWeb12/8	1.8B	8.2B	6015772801
ClueWeb12/4	2.6B	17B	48040237257
ClueWeb12/2	4.0B	35B	384568217900

framework. The reduce operation of Algorithm 1 is replaced by a pair of *partitionBy* and *mapPartitions* operations of general *Resilient Distributed Dataset* (RDD). The partitionBy operation uses a custom partitioner that partitions edges according to their vertex colors. The mapPartition operation outputs an RDD (namely edgeRDD) where each partition contains an edge set. A special RDD where each partition is in charge of a subproblem (i, j) or (i, j, k) wraps the edgeRDD; the edge sets used in each partition of the special RDD are loaded directly from the edgeRDD.

5. EXPERIMENTS

In this section, we experimentally evaluate our algorithms and compare them to recent single machine and distributed algorithms. We aim to answer the following questions.

- **Q1** How much do the three methods of PTE contribute to the performance improvement? (Section 5.2.1)
- **Q2** How does PTE scale up in terms of the number of machines? (Section 5.2.2)
- **Q3** How does the performance of PTE change depending on the underlying distributed framework (MapReduce or Spark)? (Section 5.2.3)

We first introduce datasets and experimental environment in Section 5.1. After that, we answer the questions in Section 5.2 presenting the result of the experiments.

5.1 Setup

5.1.1 Datasets

We use real world datasets to evaluate the proposed algorithms. The datasets are summarized in Table 2. *Twitter* is a followee-follower network in the social network service Twitter. *SubDomain* is a hyperlink network among domains where an edge exists if there is at least one hyperlink between two subdomains. *YahooWeb*, *ClueWeb09*, and *ClueWeb12* are page level hyperlink networks on the Web. *ClueWeb12/k* is a subgraph of ClueWeb12. We use random edge sampling to make ClueWeb12/k, with the sampling probability $1/k$ where k varies from 2 to 256.

Each dataset is preprocessed to be a simple graph. We reorder the vertices in each edge (u, v) to be $u \prec v$ using an algorithm in [6]. These tasks are done in $O(E)$.

[1] `http://an.kaist.ac.kr/traces/WWW2010.html`

[2] `http://webdatacommons.org/hyperlinkgraph`

[3] `http://webscope.sandbox.yahoo.com`

[4] `http://boston.lti.cs.cmu.edu/clueweb09/wiki/tiki-index.php?page=Web+Graph`

[5] `http://www.lemurproject.org/clueweb12/webgraph.php`

5.1.2 Experimental Environment

We implement PTE on Hadoop (open source version of MapReduce) and Spark. Results described in Sections 5.2.1 and 5.2.2 are from Hadoop implementation of PTE; we also describe the Spark results in Section 5.2.3. We compare PTEs with previous algorithms: CTTP [23], MGT [13] and the triangle counting implementations on GraphLab and GraphX. CTTP is the state of the art MapReduce algorithm. MGT is an I/O efficient external memory algorithm. GraphX is a graph processing API on Spark, a distributed computing framework. GraphLab is another distributed graph processing framework using MPI.

All experiments were conducted on a cluster with 41 machines where each machine is equipped with an Intel Xeon E3-1230v3 CPU (quad-core at 3.30GHz), and 32GB RAM. The cluster runs Hadoop v1.2.1, and consists of a master node, and 40 slave nodes. Each slave node can run 3 mappers and 3 reducers (120 mappers and 120 reducers in total) concurrently. The memory size for each mapper and reducer is set to 4GB. Spark v1.5.1 is also installed at the cluster where each slave is set to use 30GB memory and 3 cores of CPU; one core is for system maintenance. We operate GraphLab PowerGraph v2.2 on OpenRTE v1.5.4 at the same cluster servers.

5.2 Experimental Results

In this section, we present experimental results to answer the questions listed at the beginning of Section 5.

5.2.1 Effect of PTE's three methods

Effect of pre-partitioning. We compare the amount of shuffled data between PTE and CTTP to show the effect of pre-partitioning (Section 4.1). Figure 6(a) shows the results on ClueWeb12 with various numbers of edges. It shows that PTE shuffles far fewer data than CTTP, and the difference gets larger as the data size increases; as the number of edges varies from 0.26 billions to 36 billions, the difference increases from 30× to 245×. The slopes for PTE and CTTP are 0.99 and 1.48, respectively. They reflect the claimed complexity of shuffled data size, $O(|E|)$ of PTE and $O(|E|^{1.5}/\sqrt{M})$ of CTTP. Figure 6(b) shows the results on real world graphs; PTE shuffles far fewer data by up to 175× than CTTP does.

Effect of color-direction. To show the effect of color-direction (Section 4.2), we count the number of all oper-

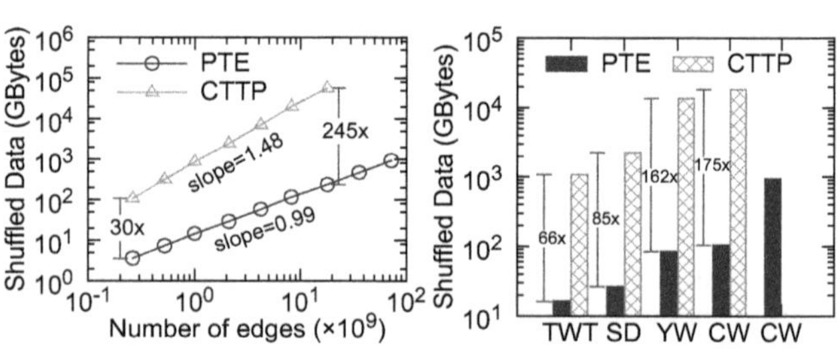

(a) (b)

Figure 6: The shuffled data size of PTE and CTTP (a) on ClueWeb12 with various numbers of edges, and (b) on real world graphs. PTE shuffles up to 245× fewer data than CTTP on ClueWeb12; the gap grows when the data size increases. On real world graphs, PTE shuffles up to 175× fewer data than CTTP on ClueWeb09.

Table 3: The number of operations by PTE_{CD} and PTE_{BASE} on various graphs. PTE_{CD} decreases the number of operations by up to 6.85× from PTE_{BASE}.

Dataset	PTE_{BASE}	PTE_{CD}	$\frac{PTE_{BASE}}{PTE_{CD}}$
CW12/256	1.5×10^8	2.1×10^7	6.85
CW12/128	6.2×10^8	1.0×10^8	6.22
CW12/64	2.7×10^9	4.6×10^8	5.83
CW12/32	1.2×10^{10}	2.2×10^9	5.10
CW12/16	4.9×10^{10}	1.1×10^{10}	4.44
CW12/8	2.1×10^{11}	5.4×10^{10}	3.90
CW12/4	8.9×10^{11}	2.6×10^{11}	3.47
CW12/2	3.7×10^{12}	1.2×10^{12}	3.18
CW12	1.6×10^{13}	4.9×10^{12}	3.14
TWT	1.1×10^{12}	5.4×10^{11}	2.03
SD	8.3×10^{12}	4.0×10^{12}	2.06
YW	7.4×10^{11}	2.9×10^{11}	2.55
CW09	2.7×10^{11}	6.9×10^{10}	3.94

Table 4: The amount of data read via a network on various graphs. The ratio ($\frac{PTE_{CD}}{PTE_{SC}}$) is about $1.10 \approx \sqrt{6/5}$ for all datasets, as expected.

Dataset	PTE_{CD}	PTE_{SC}	$\frac{PTE_{CD}}{PTE_{SC}}$
CW12/256	22.5GB	18.7GB	1.20
CW12/128	58.8GB	51.5GB	1.14
CW12/64	174GB	162GB	1.08
CW12/32	485GB	426GB	1.14
CW12/16	1.3TB	1.2TB	1.09
CW12/8	3.7TB	3.3TB	1.10
CW12/4	9.9TB	9.0TB	1.10
CW12/2	26.9TB	24.1TB	1.12
CW12	72.9TB	64.3TB	1.13
TWT	102GB	83GB	1.23
SD	206GB	191GB	1.08
TW	1.9TB	1.7TB	1.13
CW09	2.9TB	2.6TB	1.11

ations in intersecting two neighbor sets (line 13 in Algorithm 3) in Table 3. PTE_{CD} reduces the number of comparisons by up to 6.85× from PTE_{BASE} by the color-direction.

Effect of scheduling computation. We also show the effect of scheduling calls of the function `enuerateTrianglesCD` (Section 4.3) by comparing the amount of data read via a network by PTE_{CD} and PTE_{SC} in Table 4. As expected, for every dataset, the ratio ($\frac{PTE_{CD}}{PTE_{SC}}$) is about $1.10 \approx \sqrt{6/5}$.

Running time comparison. We now compare the running time of PTEs, and competitors (CTTP, MGT, GraphLab, GraphX) in Figure 7. PTE_{SC} shows the best performance and PTE_{CD} follows it very closely. CTTP fails to run when edges are more than 20 billions within 5 days. GraphLab, GraphX and MGT also fail when the number of edges is larger than 600 million, 3 billion and 10 billion, respectively, because of out of memory or out of range error. The out of range error occurs when a vertex id exceeds the range of 32-bit integer limit. Note that, even when MGT can treat vertex ids exceeding the integer range, the performance of MGT would worsen as the graph size increases since MGT performs massive I/O ($O(|E|^2/M)$) when the input data size is large. The slope of the PTEs is 1.26, which is smaller than 1.5. It means that the practical time complexity is smaller than the worst case $O(|E|^{3/2})$.

Figure 1 shows the running time of various algorithms on real world datasets. PTE_{SC} shows the best performances outperforming CTTP and MGT by up to 47× and 17×, respectively. Only the proposed algorithms succeed in processing ClueWeb12 with 6.3 billion vertices and 72 billion edges while all other algorithms fail to process the graph.

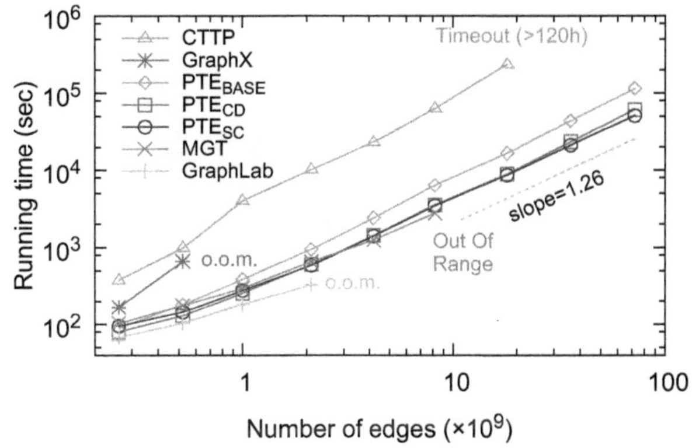

Figure 7: The running time on ClueWeb12 with various numbers of edges. o.o.m.: out of memory. PTE_{SC} shows the best data scalability; only PTEs succeed in processing the subgraphs containing more than 20B edges. The pre-partitioning (CTTP vs PTE_{BASE}) significantly reduces the running time while the effect of the scheduling function (PTE_{CD} vs PTE_{SC}) is relatively insignificant.

5.2.2 Machine Scalability

We evaluate the machine scalability of PTEs by measuring the running time of them and CTTP on YahooWeb varying the number of machines from 5 to 40 in Figure 8. Note that GraphX and GraphLab are omitted because they fail to process YahooWeb on our cluster. Every PTE shows strong scalability: the slope -0.94 of the PTEs is very close to the ideal value -1. It means that the running time decreases $2^{0.94} = 1.92$ times as the number of machines is doubled. On the other hand, CTTP shows weak scalability when the number of machine increases from 20 to 40.

5.2.3 PTE on Spark

We implemented PTE_{SC} on Spark as well as on Hadoop to show that PTEs are general enough to be implemented in any distributed system supporting map and reduce functionalities. We compare the running time of the two implementations in Figure 9. The result indicates that the Spark implementation does not show a better performance than the Hadoop implementation even though the Spark implementation uses a distributed memory as well as disks. The reason is that PTE is not an iterative algorithm; thus, there are little data to reuse from memory. Even reading data

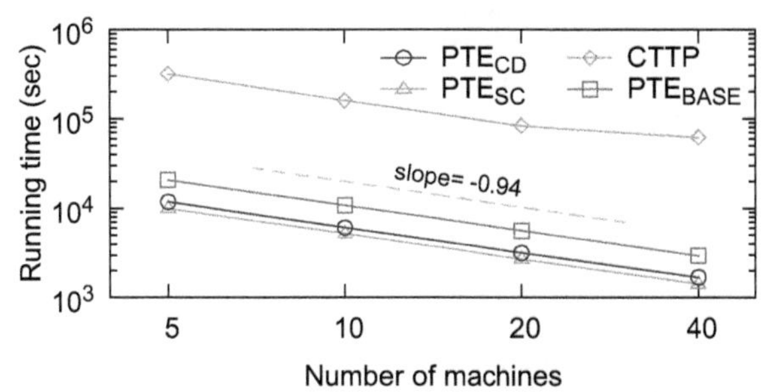

Figure 8: Machine scalability of PTEs and CTTP on YahooWeb. GraphLab and GraphX are excluded because they failed to process YahooWeb. PTEs show very strong scalability with exponent -0.94 which is very close to -1, the ideal.

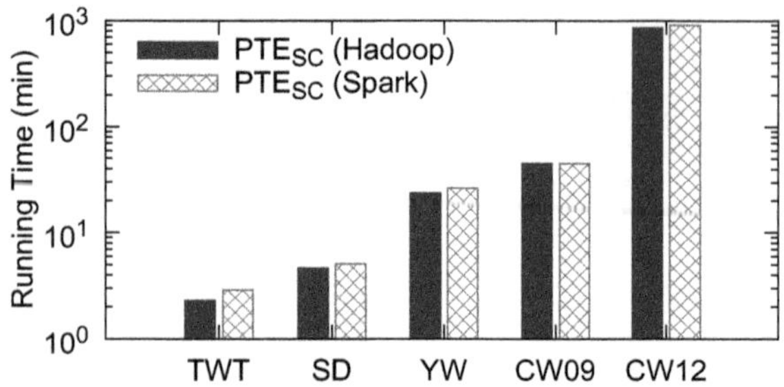

Figure 9: The running time of PTE$_{SC}$ on Hadoop and Spark. There is no significant difference between them.

from distributed memory, not from remote disk, does not contribute to performance improvement of PTE; they take similar time since disk reading and network transmission occur simultaneously.

6. CONCLUSION

In this paper, we propose PTE, a scalable distributed algorithm for enumerating triangles in very large graphs. We carefully design PTE so that it minimizes the amount of shuffled data, total work, and network read. PTE operates in $O(|E|)$ shuffled data, $O(|E|^{3/2}/\sqrt{M})$ network read, and $O(|E|^{3/2})$ total work, the worst case optimal. PTE shows the best performances in real world data: it outperforms the state-of-the-art scalable distributed algorithm by up to 47×. Also, PTE is the only algorithm that successfully enumerates more than 3 trillion triangles in ClueWeb 12 graph with 72 billion edges while all other algorithms including GraphLab, GraphX, MGT, and CTTP fail. Future research directions include extending the work to support general subgraphs.

Acknowledgments

This work was supported by IT R&D program of MSIP/IITP [R0101-15-0176, Development of Core Technology for Human-like Self-taught Learning based on Symbolic Approach]. This work was also funded by Institute for Information communications Technology Promotion (IITP) grant funded by the Korea government (MSIP) (No.R0190-15-2012, "High Performance Big Data Analytics Platform Performance Acceleration Technologies Development"). The ICT at Seoul National University provides research facilities for this study.

7. REFERENCES

[1] Jesse Alpert and Nissan Hajaj. `http://googleblog.blogspot.kr/2008/07/we-knew-web-was-big.html`, 2008.

[2] Shaikh Arifuzzaman, Maleq Khan, and Madhav V. Marathe. PATRIC: a parallel algorithm for counting triangles in massive networks. In *CIKM*, 2013.

[3] Luca Becchetti, Paolo Boldi, Carlos Castillo, and Aristides Gionis. Efficient algorithms for large-scale local triangle counting. *TKDD*, 2010.

[4] Jonathan W Berry, Bruce Hendrickson, Randall A LaViolette, and Cynthia A Phillips. Tolerating the community detection resolution limit with edge weighting. *Phys. Rev. E*, 83(5):056119, 2011.

[5] Bin-Hui Chou and Einoshin Suzuki. Discovering community-oriented roles of nodes in a social network. In *DaWaK*, pages 52–64, 2010.

[6] Jonathan Cohen. Graph twiddling in a mapreduce world. *CiSE*, 11(4):29–41, 2009.

[7] Jeffrey Dean and Sanjay Ghemawat. Mapreduce: Simplified data processing on large clusters. In *OSDI*, pages 137–150, 2004.

[8] Jean-Pierre Eckmann and Elisha Moses. Curvature of co-links uncovers hidden thematic layers in the world wide web. *PNAS*, 99(9):5825–5829, 2002.

[9] Facebook. `http://newsroom.fb.com/company-info`, 2015.

[10] Ilias Giechaskiel, George Panagopoulos, and Eiko Yoneki. PDTL: parallel and distributed triangle listing for massive graphs. In *ICPP*, 2015.

[11] Joseph E. Gonzalez, Yucheng Low, Haijie Gu, Danny Bickson, and Carlos Guestrin. Powergraph: Distributed graph-parallel computation on natural graphs. In *OSDI*, pages 17–30, 2012.

[12] Herodotos Herodotou. Hadoop performance models. *arXiv*, 2011.

[13] Xiaocheng Hu, Yufei Tao, and Chin-Wan Chung. Massive graph triangulation. In *SIGMOD*, pages 325–336, 2013.

[14] ByungSoo Jeon, Inah Jeon, Lee Sael, and U Kang. Scout: Scalable coupled matrix-tensor factorization - algorithm and discoveries. In *ICDE*, 2016.

[15] U Kang, Jay-Yoon Lee, Danai Koutra, and Christos Faloutsos. Net-ray: Visualizing and mining billion-scale graphs. In *PAKDD*, 2014.

[16] U Kang, Brendan Meeder, Evangelos E. Papalexakis, and Christos Faloutsos. Heigen: Spectral analysis for billion-scale graphs. *TKDE*, pages 350–362, 2014.

[17] U Kang, Hanghang Tong, Jimeng Sun, Ching-Yung Lin, and Christos Faloutsos. Gbase: an efficient analysis platform for large graphs. *VLDB J.*, 21(5):637–650, 2012.

[18] U Kang, Charalampos E. Tsourakakis, and Faloutsos Faloutsos. Pegasus: A peta-scale graph mining system - implementation and observations. *ICDM*, 2009.

[19] Jinha Kim, Wook-Shin Han, Sangyeon Lee, Kyungyeol Park, and Hwanjo Yu. OPT: A new framework for overlapped and parallel triangulation in large-scale graphs. In *SIGMOD*, pages 637–648, 2014.

[20] Matthieu Latapy. Main-memory triangle computations for very large (sparse (power-law)) graphs. *Theor. Comput. Sci.*, pages 458–473, 2008.

[21] Rasmus Pagh and Francesco Silvestri. The input/output complexity of triangle enumeration. In *PODS*, pages 224–233, 2014.

[22] Ha-Myung Park and Chin-Wan Chung. An efficient mapreduce algorithm for counting triangles in a very large graph. In *CIKM*, pages 539–548, 2013.

[23] Ha-Myung Park, Francesco Silvestri, U Kang, and Rasmus Pagh. Mapreduce triangle enumeration with guarantees. In *CIKM*, pages 1739–1748, 2014.

[24] Filippo Radicchi, Claudio Castellano, Federico Cecconi, Vittorio Loreto, and Domenico Parisi. Defining and identifying communities in networks. *PNAS*, 101(9):2658–2663, 2004.

[25] Thomas Schank. Algorithmic aspects of triangle-based network analysis. *Phd thesis, University Karlsruhe*, 2007.

[26] Siddharth Suri and Sergei Vassilvitskii. Counting triangles and the curse of the last reducer. In *WWW*, pages 607–614, 2011.

[27] Twitter. `https://about.twitter.com/company`, 2015.

[28] Mark N. Wegman and Larry Carter. New hash functions and their use in authentication and set equality. *J. Comput. Syst. Sci.*, 22(3):265–279, 1981.

[29] Zhi Yang, Christo Wilson, Xiao Wang, Tingting Gao, Ben Y. Zhao, and Yafei Dai. Uncovering social network sybils in the wild. *TKDD*, 2014.

Robust Large-Scale Machine Learning in the Cloud

Steffen Rendle, Dennis Fetterly, Eugene J. Shekita, Bor-yiing Su
Google Inc.
1600 Amphitheatre Parkway
Mountain View, CA 94043, USA
{srendle,fetterly,shekita,boryiingsu}@google.com

ABSTRACT

The convergence behavior of many distributed machine learning (ML) algorithms can be sensitive to the number of machines being used or to changes in the computing environment. As a result, scaling to a large number of machines can be challenging. In this paper, we describe a new scalable coordinate descent (SCD) algorithm for generalized linear models whose convergence behavior is always the same, regardless of how much SCD is scaled out and regardless of the computing environment. This makes SCD highly robust and enables it to scale to massive datasets on low-cost commodity servers. Experimental results on a real advertising dataset in Google are used to demonstrate SCD's cost effectiveness and scalability. Using Google's internal cloud, we show that SCD can provide near linear scaling using thousands of cores for 1 trillion training examples on a petabyte of compressed data. This represents 10,000x more training examples than the 'large-scale' Netflix prize dataset. We also show that SCD can learn a model for 20 billion training examples in two hours for about $10.

Keywords

Distributed Machine Learning; Coordinate Descent; Linear Regression

1. INTRODUCTION

Although distributed machine learning (ML) algorithms have been extensively studied [22, 12, 10, 9], scaling to a large number of machines can still be challenging. Most fast converging single machine algorithms update model parameters at a very high rate which makes them hard to distribute without compromises. For example, single-machine stochastic gradient descent (SGD) [7] updates model parameters after processing each training example, while coordinate descent (CD) [18] updates them after processing a single feature. Common approaches to distribute SGD or CD break the basic flow of the single-machine algorithm by letting updates occur with some delay or by batching [16, 22, 8, 23, 12]. However, this changes the convergence behavior of the algorithm, making it sensitive to the number of machines as well to the computing environment. As a result, scaling can become non-linear and the benefit from adding more machines can tail off early [16].

Because of these scaling problems, some authors [9] have argued that it is better to scale out ML algorithms using just a few 'fat' servers with lots of memory, networking cards, and GPUs. While this may be an appealing approach for some problems, it has obvious scaling limitations in terms of I/O bandwidth. Generally speaking, it is also more expensive than scaling out using low-cost commodity servers. GPUs in particular are not always a cost effective solution for sparse datasets.

In this paper, we describe a new scalable coordinate descent (SCD) algorithm for generalized linear models that does not suffer from the scaling problems outlined above. SCD is highly robust, having the same convergence behavior regardless of how much it is scaled out and regardless of the computing environment. This allows SCD to scale to thousands of cores and makes it well suited for running in a cloud environment with low-cost commodity servers. A key observation of our work is that, by using a natural partitioning of parameters into blocks, updates can be performed in parallel a block at a time without compromising convergence. In fact, on many real-world problems, SCD has the same convergence behavior as the popular single-machine coordinate descent algorithm.

In addition to the SCD algorithm, we describe a distributed system that addresses the specific challenges of scaling SCD in a cloud computing environment. Straggler handling ends up being the biggest challenge to achieving linear scaling with SCD. Experimental results using a real advertising dataset in Google are used to demonstrate SCD's cost effectiveness and scalability.

To summarize, the main contributions of this paper are as follows:

- We describe a new scalable coordinate descent algorithm (SCD) whose convergence behavior is always the same, regardless of how much SCD is scaled out and regardless of the computing environment.
- We describe a distributed system for SCD that can provide near linear scaling using thousands of cores.
- We provide experimental results from Google's internal cloud using low-cost preemptible virtual machines to show that SCD can solve large-scale ML problems with 1 trillion training examples.

KDD '16 August 13-17, 2016, San Francisco, CA, USA

ACM ISBN 978-1-4503-4232-2/16/08.
DOI: http://dx.doi.org/10.1145/2939672.2939790

2. PROBLEM STATEMENT

In this section, we discuss the machine learning and computing environments that are the focus of our work. Then we state the main goals of our work.

2.1 Machine Learning Environment

We focus on generalized linear models with large sparse datasets. Linear models are popular in industry for large-scale prediction tasks [24, 21, 12, 20] because of their high prediction quality and interpretability.

2.1.1 Linear Model

Let $\boldsymbol{x} \in \mathbb{R}^p$ be a feature vector and y an unknown variable of interest, e.g. click/non-click, rating, etc. A linear model $\hat{y} : \mathbb{R}^p \to \mathbb{R}$ assumes a linear dependency between the input feature vector $\mathbb{R}$ and the variable of interest y

$$\hat{y}(\boldsymbol{x}) = \langle \boldsymbol{\theta}, \boldsymbol{x} \rangle = \sum_{i=1}^{p} \theta_i x_i \tag{1}$$

where $\boldsymbol{\theta} \in \mathbb{R}^p$ are the model parameters that parameterize the dependency. Using a link function, linear models can be generalized (GLM) [18] to prediction tasks such as logistic regression (binary classification), Poisson regression (count data), etc. Note that even though a linear model assumes a linear dependency in $\boldsymbol{x}$, non-linearity can be introduced by preprocessing $\boldsymbol{x}$, e.g., using polynomial expansions or log-transformations. Preprocessing allows linear models to be very expressive and highly non-linear in the original space. The remainder of the paper assumes that a proper preprocessing has been done and that $\boldsymbol{x}$ is the feature vector after transformation.

2.1.2 Optimization Task

ML algorithms learn the values of the model parameters $\boldsymbol{\theta}$ given a set S of labeled *training examples* $(\boldsymbol{x}, y)$. In matrix notation, $X \in \mathbb{R}^{|S| \times p}$ is the *design matrix* with labels $\boldsymbol{y} \in \mathbb{R}^{|S|}$. The optimization task is to find the model parameters that minimize a loss:

$$\operatorname*{argmin}_{\boldsymbol{\theta} \in \mathbb{R}^p} \sum_{(\boldsymbol{x},y) \in S} l(y, \hat{y}(\boldsymbol{x})) + \lambda ||\boldsymbol{\theta}||^2 \tag{2}$$

where l is a loss function that depends on the optimization task, e.g., using a squared loss $l(y, \hat{y}) := (y - \hat{y})^2$, or using a logistic loss $l(y, \hat{y}) := -y\hat{y} + \ln(1 + exp(\hat{y}))$. λ is a regularization value for generalization. For simplicity, we will assume L2 regularization, but all the results in this paper can be extended to L1 regularization.

2.1.3 Large-Scale Learning and Sparse Datasets

We focus on datasets with potentially trillions of training examples, that is, $|S| \in \mathcal{O}(10^{12})$. Consequently, the training data does not fit in memory. We also focus on models with billions of features, that is, $p \in \mathcal{O}(10^9)$. The model will usually fit in memory, but our proposed solution can also handle models that are larger than memory.

Typically, a training dataset with lots of features will also have a lot of sparsity. There might be billions of features, but only a small number (e.g., hundreds) of non-zero features per example. The reason for high sparsity is usually because of one-hot encoded categorical variables. For example, part of the feature vector $\boldsymbol{x}$ might contain a country variable that is represented by a binary vector with as many entries as there are countries. But each binary vector will contain only one non-zero entry, corresponding to the selected country. For variables like countries, there might be only hundreds of entries, whereas for variables like video ids or user ids, there might be billions of entries leading to very high sparsity. Note that our approach is not limited to categorical variables but supports any kind of real-valued feature vector $\boldsymbol{x} \in \mathbb{R}^p$.

Let $N_Z(\boldsymbol{x})$ be the number of non-zeros in a feature vector $\boldsymbol{x}$ or design matrix X. ML algorithms can make use of the sparsity and usually have a runtime in the order of $N_Z(X)$ instead of $|S| \times p$.

2.2 Computing Environment

Cloud computing has become a cost effective solution for many applications, particularly for batch applications that need to scale with their data size. Although our work can be applied to any large-scale distributed computing environment, we focus on a cloud with the following properties:

- *Shared Machines*: To increase utilization, each physical machine can be shared by multiple virtual machines (VMs).
- *Distributed File System*: A fault tolerant distributed file system (DFS), such as the Google File System [19], is available to store data. In addition to training data, the DFS can be used to save any application state needed for fault tolerance.
- *Preemptible VMs*: The cloud scheduler is free to preempt a low-priority VM in favor of a higher-priority one. All of a VM's state is lost when it is preempted. However, a notification is sent to a VM before it is preempted. This includes a grace period that is long enough for the application to save its state to the DFS for fault tolerance, if necessary.
- *Machine Failures*: Physical machines can fail without any notification. Failures are assumed to be rare, but do happen. Consequently, long-running jobs need to checkpoint their state to the DFS for fault tolerance.

Other than preemptible VMs, these are fairly standard properties for most modern clouds. Preemptible VMs are available on Google's Cloud Platform (GCP) [1] and as "spot instances" from Amazon Web Services (AWS) [2]. They are an attractive way to lower costs for long-running batch jobs. For example, a preemptible VM is about 70% less expensive than a standard VM on GCP.

In terms of cost, a cloud with the above properties is particularly appealing for running distributed ML jobs. However, scaling a distributed ML algorithm on such a cloud becomes even more challenging. This is because there can be wide variations in machine performance because of contention for physical resources such as CPU and networking, or contention for software resources such as access to the DFS. Preemptions also create headaches. All these things can negatively impact convergence behavior.

2.3 Goals of Distributed Learning

In terms of the learning algorithm and its distributed system design, the main goals of our work are as follows:

1. *Robust Distribution*: The algorithm's convergence behavior should always be the same, regardless of how

much it is scaled out and regardless of the computing environment.

2. *Linear Scale-out*: If the number of training examples $|S|$ as well as the number of computing resources grow by a factor of M, the time to solve the learning problem should stay constant. This is also known as "weak scaling".

3. *Linear Speed-up*: If the number of computing resources grows by a factor of M, the same learning problem should be solved M times faster in wall time. This is also known as "strong scaling".

The learning algorithm and distributed system that we describe in this paper satisfies all three of these goals for a wide range of problem sizes and scaling factors.

3. LEARNING ALGORITHMS

In this section, we review the popular coordinate descent (CD) algorithm [18, 26, 11], which is inherently restricted to a single machine. Then we describe our new scalable coordinate descent (SCD) algorithm. Note that this section focuses on the abstract SCD algorithm. In Section 4, we describe SCD's distributed system design and implementation.

3.1 Coordinate Descent (CD)

CD looks at a single model parameter or *coordinate* θ_j at a time, assuming that the values of other model parameters $\boldsymbol{\theta} \setminus \theta_j$ are known and fixed. Under this assumption, the optimum for θ_j has a closed form solution:

$$\theta_j^* = \frac{T_j}{T_j' + \lambda}. \tag{3}$$

For linear regression, the *sufficient statistics* T_j and T_j' are:

$$T_j := \sum_{(\boldsymbol{x},y)\in S} x_j \left(y - \sum_{i \neq j} \theta_i \, x_i \right), \quad T_j' := \sum_{(\boldsymbol{x},y)\in S} x_j^2. \tag{4}$$

To simplify the discussion, we use linear regression in all the algorithm descriptions, but other loss functions can be handled similarly, such as logistic regression using a second-order Taylor expansion [18]. For sparse data, the computation for T_j and T_j' can be accelerated by only iterating over examples $\boldsymbol{x}$ where $x_j \neq 0$.

From this analysis follows Algorithm 1. As shown, CD iterates over one model parameter θ_j at a time. In each iteration, the sufficient statistics T_j and T_j' are aggregated (lines 8-11), and the local optimum θ_j^* is calculated (line 12). To make the cost of computing T_j independent of the other features $\boldsymbol{x} \backslash x_j$, the current prediction $\hat{y}(\boldsymbol{x})$ of each example is precomputed. Using $\hat{y}(\boldsymbol{x})$, the computation of T_j simplifies to:

$$T_j = \sum_{(\boldsymbol{x},y)\in S} x_j \, (y - \hat{y}(\boldsymbol{x}) + \theta_j \, x_j). \tag{5}$$

The precomputed prediction $\hat{y}(\boldsymbol{x})$ for each example also needs to be updated each iteration (lines 13-15). Finally, the model parameter is updated with its local optimum (line 16).

CD is known as a fast-converging algorithm for problems that fit on a single machine [11]. Variations on Algorithm 1 include cyclic coordinate descent [18] and stochastic coordinate descent [26].

Algorithm 1 Coordinate Descent

1: **procedure** CD(S)
2: $\quad \hat{\boldsymbol{y}} \leftarrow (0, \dots, 0)$ ▷ Precomputed predictions
3: $\quad \boldsymbol{\theta} \leftarrow (0, \dots, 0)$
4: $\quad$ **repeat**
5: $\quad\quad$ **for** $j \in \{1, \dots, p\}$ **do**
6: $\quad\quad\quad T_j \leftarrow 0$
7: $\quad\quad\quad T_j' \leftarrow 0$
8: $\quad\quad\quad$ **for** $(\boldsymbol{x}, y) \in S$ where $x_j \neq 0$ **do**
9: $\quad\quad\quad\quad T_j \leftarrow T_j + x_j \, (y - \hat{y}(\boldsymbol{x}) + \theta_j \, x_j)$
10: $\quad\quad\quad\quad T_j' \leftarrow T_j' + x_j^2$
11: $\quad\quad\quad$ **end for**
12: $\quad\quad\quad \theta_j^* \leftarrow \frac{T_j}{T_j' + \lambda}$
13: $\quad\quad\quad$ **for** $(\boldsymbol{x}, y) \in S$ where $x_j \neq 0$ **do**
14: $\quad\quad\quad\quad \hat{y}(\boldsymbol{x}) \leftarrow \hat{y}(\boldsymbol{x}) + x_j(\theta_j^* - \theta_j)$
15: $\quad\quad\quad$ **end for**
16: $\quad\quad\quad \theta_j \leftarrow \theta_j^*$
17: $\quad\quad$ **end for**
18: $\quad$ **until** converged
19: **end procedure**

3.1.1 CD Analysis

Recall that CD processes one parameter at a time. We define a CD *iteration* as the update of one parameter and an *epoch* as a pass over all parameters. The amount of computation per iteration is on average $\mathcal{O}(N_Z(X)/p)$ and per epoch $\mathcal{O}(N_Z(X))$.

A straightforward distributed version of Algorithm 1 would require a system-wide synchronization *barrier* just after aggregating the sufficient statistics T_j and T_j' (lines 8-11). In general, distributing work only pays off if the overhead in terms of communication and barriers is small compared to the amount of work that is parallelized. However, with a large number p of parameters and a high sparsity ($N_Z(\boldsymbol{x}) \ll p$) per feature vector $\boldsymbol{x}$, there is relatively little work to be done in an iteration of CD. Consequently, a straightforward distributed version of Algorithm 1 would neither scale-out nor speed-up.

3.2 Scalable Coordinate Descent (SCD)

SCD increases the amount of work per iteration by carefully partitioning the parameters and by iterating a block of parameters at a time. Scaling is achieved by computing the sufficient statistics over examples in parallel across machines. Robustness is achieved by keeping the partition fixed and independent of the number of machines. Fast convergence is achieved by a clever partitioning of parameters.

We start with discussing the algorithm, assuming a partition is given and later show how to choose a good partition.

3.2.1 Robust and Scalable Algorithm

Let $\mathcal{P}$ be a partition of feature or parameter indices $\{1, .., p\}$. We refer to $B \in \mathcal{P}$ as a *block*. We denote the subset of parameters $\boldsymbol{\theta}$ associated with the block B by $\boldsymbol{\theta}^B$, the subvector of the feature vector $\boldsymbol{x}$ by $\boldsymbol{x}^B$, and the submatrix of the design matrix X by X^B. The basic flow of SCD (see Algorithm 2) is similar to CD, but instead of iterating over one model parameter at a time, SCD iterates over one block B of parameters at a time (line 7). In each iteration, partial sums for the sufficient statistics T and T' are computed in parallel (lines 8-13). These are aggregated across machines

Algorithm 2 Scalable Coordinate Descent

1: **procedure** SCD($S, \mathcal{P}$)
2: $\quad \boldsymbol{\theta} \leftarrow (0, \ldots, 0)$
3: $\quad \hat{\boldsymbol{y}} \leftarrow (0, \ldots, 0)$ $\qquad \triangleright$ Precomputed predictions
4: $\quad$ **repeat**
5: $\quad\quad \boldsymbol{T} \leftarrow (0, \ldots, 0)$
6: $\quad\quad \boldsymbol{T}' \leftarrow (0, \ldots, 0)$
7: $\quad\quad B \leftarrow$ SelectBlock($\mathcal{P}$)
8: $\quad\quad$ **for** $(\boldsymbol{x}, y) \in S$ **do** $\triangleright$ In parallel, across machines
9: $\quad\quad\quad$ **for** $j \in B$ where $x_j \neq 0$ **do**
10: $\quad\quad\quad\quad T_j \leftarrow T_j + x_j\,(y - \hat{y}(\boldsymbol{x}) + \theta_j\, x_j)$
11: $\quad\quad\quad\quad T'_j \leftarrow T'_j + x_j^2$
12: $\quad\quad\quad$ **end for**
13: $\quad\quad$ **end for**
14: $\quad\quad$ Aggregate $\boldsymbol{T}$ and $\boldsymbol{T}'$ across machines.
15: $\quad\quad$ **for** $j \in B$ **do**
16: $\quad\quad\quad \theta_j^* \leftarrow (1-\alpha)\,\theta_j + \alpha \frac{T_j}{T'_j + \lambda}$
17: $\quad\quad$ **end for**
18: $\quad\quad$ **for** $(\boldsymbol{x}, y) \in S$ **do** $\triangleright$ In parallel, across machines
19: $\quad\quad\quad$ **for** $j \in B$ where $x_j \neq 0$ **do**
20: $\quad\quad\quad\quad \hat{y}(\boldsymbol{x}) \leftarrow \hat{y}(\boldsymbol{x}) + x_j\,(\theta_j^* - \theta_j)$
21: $\quad\quad\quad$ **end for**
22: $\quad\quad$ **end for**
23: $\quad\quad$ **for** $j \in B$ **do**
24: $\quad\quad\quad \theta_j \leftarrow \theta_j^*$
25: $\quad\quad$ **end for**
26: $\quad$ **until** converged
27: **end procedure**

(line 14), and the new value θ_j^* of each parameter in B is calculated (lines 15-17).

Because the sufficient statistics of several features have been computed in parallel, the independence assumptions of the CD update step (eq. 3) are violated. To ensure convergence, we use the common line-search method to find a step size $\alpha \in [0, 1]$ and update each parameter with:

$$\theta_j^* = (1-\alpha)\,\theta_j + \alpha \frac{T_j}{T'_j + \lambda}. \tag{6}$$

Obviously, the smaller the step size α, the slower the convergence in comparison to CD. In Section 3.2.3, we will show that by using a clever partitioning, SCD can usually take optimal steps, in which case $\alpha = 1$. After the new value has been calculated, the precomputed predictions $\hat{y}(\boldsymbol{x})$ for each example are updated (lines 18-22). Finally, each model parameter in B is updated with its new value (lines 23-25).

In Algorithm 2, it is important to note that parallel execution is done over examples, i.e., *sharding* is by example. This means that each machine is responsible for computing the partial sufficient statistics T and T' for all the parameters $\boldsymbol{\theta}^B$ in the selected block B but only for a subset of examples. Consequently, the more machines, the faster sufficient statistics are computed. As long as the amount of work for a block is large enough, SCD scales with more machines. Moreover, as the partition is fixed and does not change with the number of machines, SCD is robust.

3.2.2 *Optimal Updates with Pure Blocks*

So far we have discussed the robustness and scalability, now we focus on convergence speed. The key idea is to partition the model parameters into what we call *pure blocks* of independent parameters. We prove that parallel updates within a pure block are equivalent to processing the updates sequentially and consequently, full update steps $\alpha = 1$ can be taken.

DEFINITION 1 (PURE BLOCK). *A block B is* pure *iff the feature subvector $\boldsymbol{x}^B$ of every example $(\boldsymbol{x}, y) \in S$ has at most one non-zero entry:*

$$B \text{ pure} :\Leftrightarrow \forall (\boldsymbol{x}, y) \in S : N_Z(\boldsymbol{x}^B) \leq 1.$$

Similarly, a partition $\mathcal{P}$ of $\{1, \ldots, p\}$ is *pure* if all the blocks in the partition $B \in \mathcal{P}$ are pure.

LEMMA 1 (INDEPENDENCE OF UPDATES). *All parameter updates for a pure block are independent.*

PROOF. The well known closed form solution of a regularized least-squares problem is $\boldsymbol{\theta} = (X^t\, X + \lambda\, I)^{-1}\, X\, \boldsymbol{y}$. Let $\tilde{B} := \{1, \ldots, p\} \setminus B$. Consequently, the closed form solution for the parameters of the block B is $\boldsymbol{\theta}^B = ((X^B)^t\, X^B + \lambda\, I)^{-1}\, X^B\, (\boldsymbol{y} - X^{\tilde{B}}\, \boldsymbol{\theta}^{\tilde{B}})$. Because B is pure, the Gramian $(X^B)^t\, X^B$ is a diagonal matrix diag$(T'_1, T'_2, \ldots)$. It follows that the standard CD update (eq. 3) is identical to the joined closed form solution for all parameters $\boldsymbol{\theta}^B$ of the block. This means that, within a pure block B, the update of one parameter does not influence the update of another parameter. $\square$

The upshot of Lemma 1 is that, within a pure block, processing parameter updates in parallel is equivalent to processing the updates sequentially. In other words, SCD on pure partitions is equivalent to CD while allowing scaling.

Note that purity and robustness are two different concepts. SCD is robust no matter if a pure or impure partition has been chosen. Pure partitions are preferred because optimal step sizes can be taken.

3.2.3 *Generating a Partition*

Now we describe how to construct a good partition for a training set $S = (X, \boldsymbol{y})$. Based on our analysis, a good partition has two properties: (1) pure blocks for convergence speed and (2) a large amount of work per block for system speed. Both properties can easily be met individually but at first glance fulfilling both looks hard. However, most real-world datasets have a natural partition with good properties. As mentioned in Section 2.1.3, input feature vectors $\boldsymbol{x}$ are usually generated from several variables. We suggest to partition the features by variable. For each variable v, a block is constructed that corresponds to the features generated from v. The properties of this partition are: (1) For many variable types the resulting blocks are pure. This includes categorical variables, a cross product of categorical variables, bucketized numerical variables, dense numerical variables, etc. (2) For these variables each resulting block is of equal computational complexity with $N_Z(X^B) = |S|$. To summarize, a natural partition by underlying variable often has all desired properties. Many real-world datasets are composed of these variable types. In fact, these are the most common variable types in regression datasets at Google.

Some datasets contain variable types with suboptimal properties. An example is a set-valued variable, such as the genres of a movie, where several genres can be assigned to one movie. In this case a split by variable would result in an *impure* block. We propose splitting the features of such a

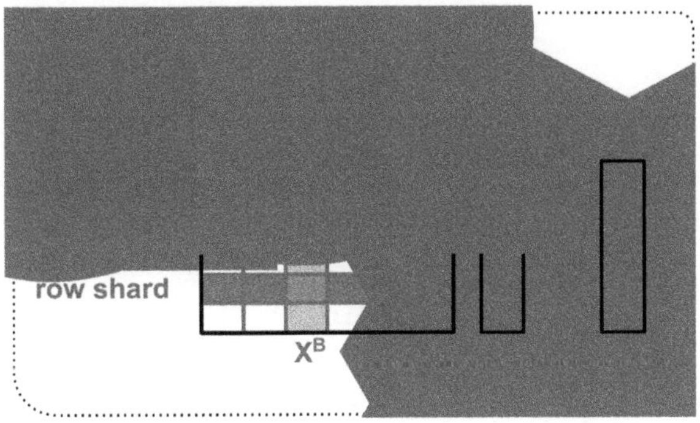

Figure 1: Data is sharded in both the feature and example dimensions. Each cell in the grid is stored as a separate file that holds the data of many examples for one block.

variable v into $N_Z(X^v)/|S|$ blocks. Splitting the features this way means there will be one active feature per block on average. However, there can still be training examples with more than one active feature. That means the blocks of a set variable can be impure and a step size $\alpha < 1$ is used.

3.2.4 SCD Analysis

An SCD *iteration* processes one block B of model parameters at a time. The computational complexity for an iteration is $\mathcal{O}(N_z(X^B))$. Updating all parameters, that is, one SCD *epoch*, takes $|\mathcal{P}|$ iterations, so the overall complexity of one epoch is $\mathcal{O}(N_Z(X))$. Although it is not shown in Algorithm 2, a small number of synchronization barriers are required in each SCD iteration. More will be said about this in Section 4 when SCD's implementation is described. Consequently, the number of barriers per SCD epoch is $\mathcal{O}(|\mathcal{P}|)$. Compared to CD, SCD decreases the number of barriers from $\mathcal{O}(p)$ to $\mathcal{O}(|\mathcal{P}|)$. On a large sparse dataset, this can mean hundreds of barriers instead of billions of barriers. The decrease in the number of barriers, along with an increase in the amount of work per barrier, is what makes it feasible to distribute SCD over a large number of machines.

The SCD algorithm meets the three goals of Section 2.3. First, SCD is robust in the sense that it performs exactly the same update computations no matter how many machines it uses. Moreover, the outcome of each SCD update step is deterministic and unaffected by the computing environment. Second, the increase of work per iteration allows SCD to scale linearly – at least in theory. In practice, various system overheads and stragglers become a limiting factor. More will be said about this shortly.

4. DISTRIBUTED SCD SYSTEM

In this section, we describe a distributed system that addresses the specific challenges of scaling SCD in a cloud computing environment.

4.1 Storage Format

As shown in Figure 1, the training data $S = (X, \boldsymbol{y})$ for SCD is sharded in both the feature and example dimensions. It is sharded in the feature dimension using the block partition $\mathcal{P}$ (i.e., the sharding follows $\mathcal{P}$), while it is sharded in the example dimension using *row sharding*. Feature sharding enables SCD to process the data corresponding to one block

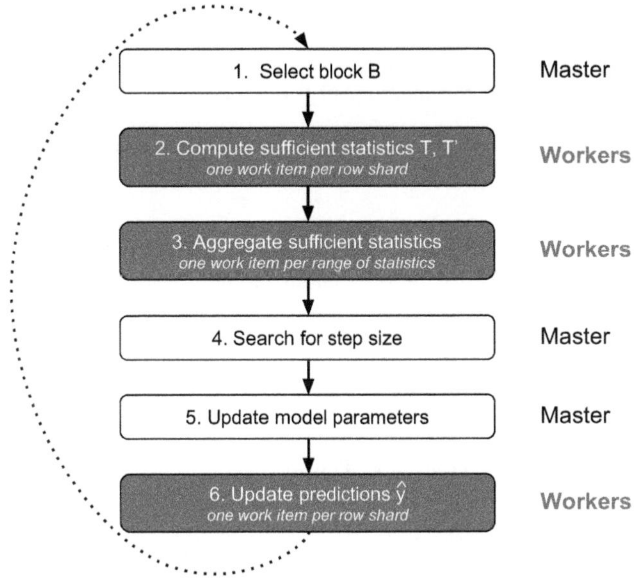

Figure 2: The system flow for one iteration of the SCD algorithm. The computationally expensive steps are distributed over the workers.

independently of the other blocks, while example sharding enables SCD to process different shards of X^B in parallel.

The remaining data is sharded as follows. The model parameters $\boldsymbol{\theta}$ are sharded in just the feature dimension (following $\mathcal{P}$), while the labels $\boldsymbol{y}$ and predictions $\hat{\boldsymbol{y}}$ are sharded in just the example dimension (following the row sharding).

As noted in Figure 1, each cell in the grid is stored in a separate file. For example, if there were $p = 10^9$ features partitioned into $|\mathcal{P}| = 100$ blocks and $|S| = 10^{10}$ examples sharded in 10^4 rows with 10^6 examples each, then the design matrix X would be stored in $10^4 * 100 = 10^6$ files.

4.2 System Architecture

Our system architecture is based on a single *master* and multiple *workers*. The master acts as the orchestrator and is responsible for assigning work, while the workers execute the computationally expensive parts of the SCD algorithm. To assign work, the master hands out *work items* to workers. Each work item corresponds to a small unit of work that usually takes only a few hundred milliseconds to execute. Both the master and workers are multi-threaded to take advantage of multi-core parallelism.

A single master obviously becomes a scaling bottleneck at some point. But as the performance experiments in Section 5 will show, even a single master can scale to hundreds of workers with thousands of cores.

4.3 System Flow

Recall that the main loop of the SCD algorithm iterates over one block of parameters at a time (see Algorithm 2, lines 4-26). One iteration of this loop translates into the following steps:

1. Select block: The master selects a block B based on various heuristics that try to estimate which block will have the largest impact on convergence.

2. Compute sufficient statistics: The workers compute the partial sums of sufficient statistics T and T' over the row shards of block B. These partial sums are stored in the memory of the workers.

3. Aggregate sufficient statistics: The sufficient statistics of the workers are aggregated and sent back to the master.

4. Search for step size: The master chooses a step size according to the line-search method described in Section 3.2.1.

5. Update model parameters: The master updates the model parameters $\boldsymbol{\theta}$ of block B using the chosen step size and the sufficient statistics.

6. Update predictions: The workers update their predictions $\hat{\boldsymbol{y}}$ to reflect the change in the model parameters.

The steps in this flow are depicted in Figure 2. The master executes the steps sequentially, either by performing the step itself (steps 1, 4, and 5) or by assigning work items to the workers for the steps that are computationally expensive (steps 2, 3, and 6). The latter are distributed over the workers and executed in parallel.

The sequential execution of the steps effectively creates a system-wide barrier for the workers after steps 2, 3, and 6. Typically, a whole iteration of SCD takes less than a minute, which means there is a system-wide barrier every few seconds. Handling stragglers, preempted and/or failed workers and executing a system-wide barrier at this rate is challenging. The steps assigned to workers are now described in more detail.

4.3.1 *Computing Sufficient Statistics*

The workers compute the partial sums for the sufficient statistics over row shards of the selected block (see Algorithm 2, lines 8-13). Each worker is multi-threaded and the threads execute work items in parallel. Each work item refers to one row shard in this case. Given a work item, a worker thread needs the training data, labels $\boldsymbol{y}$, and predictions $\hat{\boldsymbol{y}}$ for the corresponding row shard in order to compute the statistics. These can be found in the worker's cache, in another worker's cache, or in the DFS. Section 4.4.2 will provide more detail about the caches maintained by each worker.

Sufficient statistics are stored in the memory of each worker using a thread-local store for the 100K most-frequent features and a worker-level store (over all threads) for the remaining features. This two-level scheme improves hardware cache locality and also enables lock-free updates [25] of the statistics. Update collisions can occur in the worker-level store, but they have a very low probability of happening since it is only used for infrequent features.

4.3.2 *Aggregating Sufficient Statistics*

After the partial sums for the sufficient statistics have been computed by the workers, they need to be aggregated across workers (see Algorithm 2, line 14). If each worker sent back its statistics to the master, it would create a scaling bottleneck due to the TCP Incast problem [13]. Instead, the statistics are partitioned into ranges and the aggregation is distributed among the workers (see Figure 3).

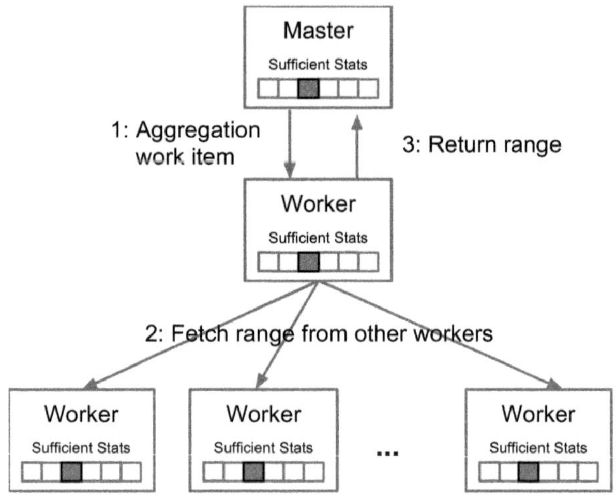

Figure 3: Aggregating Sufficient Statistics: The statistics are partitioned into ranges. For a particular range, an 'aggregator' worker collects the statistics from the other 'leaf' workers and sends the summation to the master. A worker can simultaneously be an aggregator and leaf for different ranges.

Each work item refers to one range of the sufficient statistics in this case. For load balancing, each range is sized to be about 128KB. The worker thread assigned a particular work item becomes the aggregator for the corresponding range of statistics. It collects the statistics for the range from the other workers, performs the aggregation, then sends the aggregated range to the master. Multiple ranges are aggregated in parallel across the workers to take advantage of all the available networking bandwidth.

Let $|W|$ be the number of workers, and let $r > \frac{|B|}{|W|}$ be the number of aggregation ranges, where $|B|$ is the number of features in a block. The size of each range is $\frac{|B|}{r}$. Each range creates $|W|\frac{|B|}{r}$ inbound network traffic for the aggregator, $\frac{|B|}{r}$ outbound traffic for each (leaf) worker, and $\frac{|B|}{r}$ inbound traffic for the master. This means that, over all ranges, each worker has $|B|$ inbound and outbound network traffic, while the master has $|B|$ inbound traffic. Consequently, the network traffic of the workers and the master remains constant, no matter how many workers there are.

4.3.3 *Updating Predictions*

After the master updates the model parameters, the predictions $\hat{\boldsymbol{y}}$ need to be updated to reflect the change in the model parameters (see Algorithm 2, lines 18-22). Each work item refers to one row shard in this case. Given a work item, a worker thread needs the training data and labels $\boldsymbol{y}$ for the corresponding row shard in order to update the predictions. Again, these can be found in the worker's cache, in another worker's cache, or in the DFS.

4.4 Straggler Handling

In theory, SCD should scale perfectly. However, in practice, various overheads and stragglers become a limiting factor. Up to about 1K workers, stragglers are by far the biggest limiting factor. After that, the single master design becomes the limiting factor.

Recall that there is a system-wide barrier for the workers after steps 2, 3, 6 in the SCD system flow (see Figure 2). Therefore, the time it takes to execute these steps is gated by the slowest worker, that is, the worst straggler. It is well known that straggler effects get amplified the more a system is scaled-out [15]. Stragglers are especially challenging in SCD because there is a barrier every few seconds. Moreover, the more SCD is sped-up, the shorter the time between barriers.

Stragglers are usually caused by variations in CPU, networking, or DFS performance. Dynamic load balancing is the main mechanism used to deal with stragglers. It eliminates most of the stragglers caused by CPU and networking performance. However, because of tail latencies, load balancing alone is not sufficient to handle some DFS stragglers. Caching and prefetching are added to deal with these tail latencies.

4.4.1 *Dynamic Load Balancing*

The DFS enables any worker to work on any work item. Any time a worker thread is idle, it asks the master for a new work item. This results in dynamic load balancing similar to that in a multithreaded program [6], where faster workers get assigned more work items, and vice versa for slower workers. To facilitate load balancing, the system is configured so that there are at least four work items per worker thread.

4.4.2 *Caching*

In a cloud computing environment with shared access to the DFS, tail latencies can be as bad as several seconds. The best way to mitigate these tail latencies is to avoid the DFS as much as possible using caching. Files for the training data, labels $\boldsymbol{y}$, and predictions $\hat{\boldsymbol{y}}$ are cached in each worker using an LRU eviction strategy. Compressed files are cached in memory and decompressed when a worker needs to access them.

To improve caching, the master tries to assign the same row shard to a given worker in each iteration of its main loop. If a row shard ends up being "stolen" by a different worker because of load balancing, the new worker can avoid accessing the DFS by requesting the row shard's files from the old worker's cache. When this happens, hedged-requests [15] are used to avoid a worker that is slow to respond. A request is sent to both the old worker and the DFS. The first request to finish is the "winner" and the "loser" is canceled.

4.4.3 *Prefetching*

Using compression, even a small cache for the labels $\boldsymbol{y}$ and predictions $\hat{\boldsymbol{y}}$ can be highly effective. However, caching is less effective for the training data. This is because each iteration of the SCD algorithm accesses the training data associated with a different block B. As a result, the cache hit rate for training data tends to be much lower. This means that workers have to frequently access the DFS for training data. To minimize the impact of tail latencies in this case, training data for the next iteration is prefetched. As a result, even a very slow DFS access has no effect as long as it is shorter than a whole iteration.

4.5 Dealing with VM Preemptions

Recall that a notification is sent to a VM before it is preempted. This includes a grace period that is long enough for the application to save its state to the DFS for fault tolerance, if necessary. We use this grace period to drain a worker that will be preempted. When a worker is notified that it will be preempted, it simply stops asking for new work items. As a result, other workers end up stealing all the preempted worker's row shards and associated data.

The master is usually configured using a standard VM to prevent preemptions. But even if it is configured with a preemptible VM, there is only one master and many workers, so the chances of it being preempted are low. If the master is preempted, it is treated as a machine failure (see below).

4.6 Dealing with Machine Failures

Machine failures are very rare but do happen. The predictions $\hat{\boldsymbol{y}}$ for a row shard are only written to the DFS when they are evicted from a worker's cache. Consequently, predictions can be lost if a worker fails. When this happens, a recovery phase orchestrated by the master simply recomputes the lost predictions.

Of course, the master can also fail. At the end of each iteration, the master takes a checkpoint of its state to the DFS which includes the current value of the model parameters $\boldsymbol{\theta}$. If the master fails and is restarted, it uses the last checkpoint to recovery its state and resume from where it left off.

5. EXPERIMENTS

In this section, we investigate the performance of SCD on a large-scale advertising dataset. The dataset has 1.7 billion parameters ($p = 1.7 * 10^9$) with a pure partition in $|\mathcal{P}| = 194$ blocks. We experimented with several scales of the dataset from 20 billion examples with 4 trillion non-zero elements in the design matrix up to one trillion examples ($|S| = 10^{12}$) and 200 trillion non-zero elements ($N_Z(X) = 2 * 10^{14}$).

CD is considered a fast solver for linear models (e.g., [11, 18]) and is a popular choice for single machine implementations, e.g., LIBLINEAR [3] or glmnet [4]. As shown in Section 3.2.2, on pure partitions, SCD produces the same models with an identical convergence behavior as CD and thus, we focus on runtime and scaling questions. In particular, we investigate the scale-out and speed-up of SCD.

All experiments are run in the internal Google cloud [27] using low-priority, preemptible VMs. Each VM uses 8 cores and less than 30GB of memory. A comparable preemptible VM in Google's external cloud is the *n1-standard-8* with an hourly price of $0.12. The workers are overthreaded by a ratio of 2:1 to hide I/O latency.

5.1 Scale-out

As defined in Section 2.3, scale-out refers to a system's behavior when the problem as well as the number of machines grows. We experimented with $M \in \{1, 2, 4, 8, 16, 32, 50\}$ scales of the dataset and increased the number of machines accordingly by the same factor M. For each of the M scale-out variants, we ran SCD for one epoch, i.e., 194 iterations, and report the average iteration time. The baseline 1x experiment uses 20 machines for 20 billion training examples, the 2x scale-out 40 machines for 40 billion training examples, etc. Note that on the 50x scale, the dataset consists of 1 trillion examples which is 10,000x more data points than the 'large-scale' Netflix prize dataset [5]. The compressed 50x dataset takes about one petabyte on the DFS including standard replication. Figure 4 shows the scale-out behavior

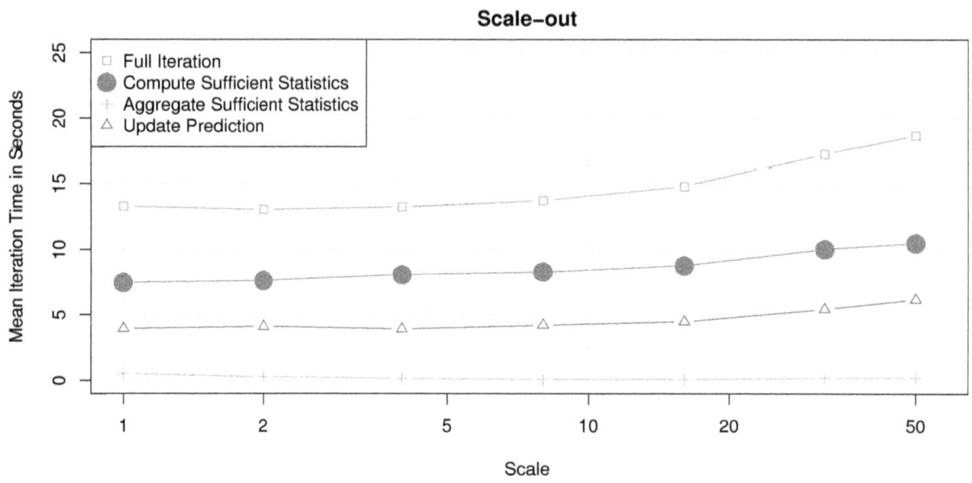

Figure 4: Scale-out behavior of SCD: 1x corresponds to 20 billion training examples and 20 machines, 2x to 40 billion examples and 40 machines, and 50x to 1 trillion examples and 1000 machines. The average total time for an iteration as well as the average time for the main phases of the SCD algorithm are shown.

of SCD. Compared to a perfect linear scaling, SCD shows less than 10% degradation for a 16x (=1600%) scale-out and about 35% degradation for a 50x scale-out. One of the main reasons for the degradation are stragglers caused by the very short barriers of SCD. The larger the data set, and consequently the more files, the higher the chance to hit a severe straggler. E.g., in the *update prediction* phase, the system orchestrates a thousand workers with 8000 cores and hundreds of thousands of work items in about 6 seconds. We conclude that SCD allows near linear scale-out to extremely large datasets.

5.2 Speed-up

The second gain from a distributed system is speed-up, i.e., increasing the number of machines while the problem size stays the same. We study the speed-up of our system on 20 billion training examples and vary the number of machines from 1 to 128 workers. Again, we run each variant of the system for one epoch and report the mean iteration time. As SCD is robust, every configuration learns exactly the same model.

The left plot of Figure 5 shows the average iteration time versus the number of workers. As can be seen, SCD provides a close to linear speed-up behavior. Actually, all configurations outperform the theoretical linear speed-up of a single worker. The reason for the super-linear speed-up is that the amount of data that can be cached increases with more workers. For example, if one worker has 1 GB of memory for caching label data and there are 10 GB of label files, then with one worker at most 10% of the label requests are cache hits, whereas with 32 workers, overall 32 GB of labels can be cached, which results in a much higher cache hit rate. In Figure 5, the super-linear speed-up has its optimum with 16 to 32 workers and moves closer to a linear speed-up with more workers. This is expected because the more machines, the faster the iterations, the shorter the barriers and consequently, the stronger straggler effects. For example, having a straggler of 1 second might not have any effect on a run with 32 machines because barriers are every 3 seconds, whereas for 64 machines, where a perfect speed-up means 1.5 second barriers, the same straggler has more impact. More aggressive prefetching, e.g., two iterations ahead, might solve this tail latency issue.

Speeding-up a system implies getting the results faster when using more resources. If the cost for a resource is constant as in common cloud environments, a theoretical linear speed-up implies getting the result faster with exactly the same cost. In reality, speed-ups are not exactly linear and additional costs can occur. The right plot of Figure 5 shows the time vs. cost trade-off for speeding up the SCD algorithm. The number of resources was varied from 1 to 128 workers and the plot shows the time to converge, i.e., in this case running SCD for five epochs, vs. the costs of the machines. For instance, running SCD for five epochs with 128 machines takes about one hour whereas the time with one worker is about 140 hours. The cost for running 128 workers for about one hour is about $16 whereas the cost for running one worker for 140 hours is about $17. Because SCD is robust, this means SCD can get the same model 100x faster with the same resource bill as a single machine. Factoring in the cost for the master, running SCD with 128 workers is actually much cheaper. In particular, the same result is achieved 100x faster with 2x less cost. If cost alone should be minimized, the optimal choice would be using 16 workers which costs less than $10 and requires about five hours. Spending a dollar more and running with 32 machines, would give the results in 2.5 hours.

Besides the resource costs, learning models is also associated with other costs such as the time (=salary) of the end user who is waiting for the results, the number of experiments that can be explored, etc. That means reducing the runtime is usually much more valuable than the computation costs. Factoring in such other costs, SCD provides a substantial speed-up at marginally higher compute costs. Finally, we want to highlight, that running very large datasets on low-priority cloud environments is very inexpensive, e.g., running the 20 billion example version of the *advertising* dataset to convergence would cost about $10 in the Google cloud. Given the value that such a model provides when it is applied, the costs are many orders of magnitude smaller.

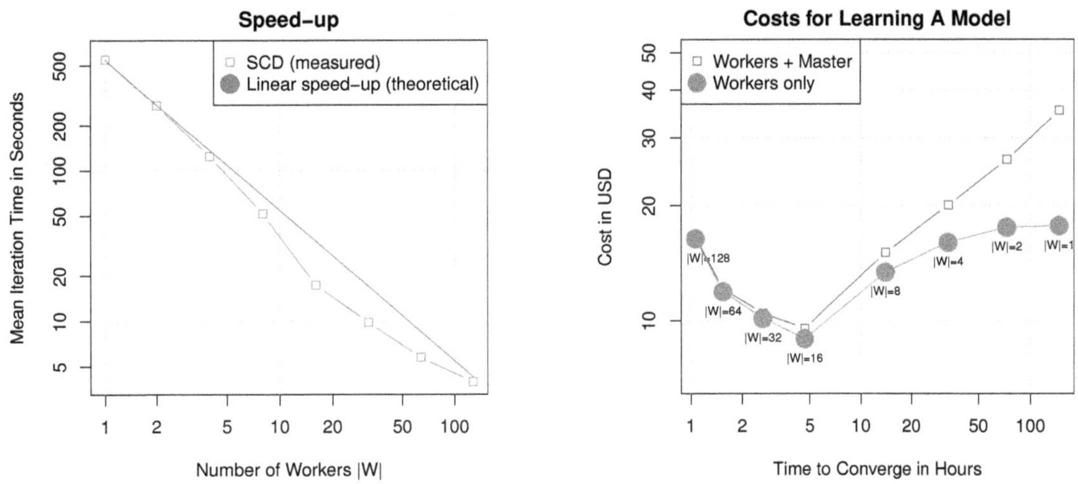

Figure 5: Speed-up behavior of SCD: Increasing the number of workers $|W|$ decreases the runtime close to linearly. The super linear speed-up is due to a larger overall cache size when running with more machines. The right plot shows the time vs. cost trade-off for learning the advertisement model to convergence with a varying number of workers $|W|$.

6. RELATED WORK

Block or parallel coordinate descent (BCD), e.g., [8, 23], and SCD share the idea of updating several coordinates in parallel but differ in important aspects. BCD [8, 23] assigns features to computing resources, e.g., cores or machines, and computes the sufficient statistics in parallel. This has consequences on both robustness and scalability.

First, the more computing resources, the more model parameters are updated in parallel with BCD. Consequently, BCD is not robust with respect to our goal in Section 2.3. In contrast to BCD, SCD parallelizes over examples while keeping the partitioning constant, which makes SCD robust.

Second, the frequency of a feature being non-zero is usually non-uniform distributed. Typically, the distribution is Zipfian, e.g., a popular video occurs in much more examples than a niche video. Moreover, imbalance occurs not only within the same variable, e.g., popular vs. non popular videos, but also over variables, e.g., high vs. low cardinality variables. For example, in the advertisement data set of Section 5, the bias feature occurs in 1 trillion example, other frequent features appear billions or millions of times but most features appear only a few times. Consequently, a parallel execution where each feature is a unit of work is impossible to load balance even in a perfect distributed environment. This means BCD will not have linear scaling properties in sparse datasets. In contrast to this, SCD parallelizes work over examples and does not care about the number of features that are updated in parallel. For example, the block sizes in Section 5 range from 1 feature per block to 240,000,000 features per block but in each block the number of non-zeros is constant $N_Z(X^B) \approx |S|$. That means, row shards are balanced in terms of computational costs.

Third, we introduce pure partitions which allow us to scale the popular single-machine CD algorithm without compromising convergence. Finally, we demonstrate the effectiveness of SCD on truly large-scale datasets. The distributed BCD algorithm [23] was evaluated on less than 10M examples using 400 machines. This dataset is 100,000 times smaller than our datasets. A single core in our system processes 10M examples in less than a second end-to-end including all synchronization work.

Another related line of work is Sibyl [10], a widely used ML platform in Google that distributes the parallel boosting algorithm [14]. Parallel boosting updates all features in one iteration and is comparable to SCD with a single non-pure block $B = \{1, \ldots, p\}$. The parallelism is achieved similar to SCD over examples. This makes Sibyl both robust and scalable. Parallel boosting fits very well a standard framework such as MapReduce [17] because iterations are long. The downside is that it requires many more epochs to converge than SCD and the memory consumption is much higher because all parameters and statistics are in each mapper. On various datasets, SCD showed an improvement of one to two orders of magnitude in convergence speed and computing resources. We omit these results due to space restrictions.

The orthogonal approach to CD is stochastic gradient descent (SGD) that iterates over examples. As described in Section 1, the single-machine SGD algorithm [7] accesses and updates parameters at a very high rate. This makes standard SGD inherently a single-machine algorithm. Many distributed SGD modifications have been proposed, e.g., using combinations of delayed updates and batching (e.g. [22, 12, 16]). Distributed SGD algorithms do not scale linearly and the behavior is more complex to control when changing the number of machines. This makes them harder to use than the SCD system – especially in a shared cloud environment where the system behavior is less predictable. In consequence, distributed SGD does not meet the design goals of robustness and linear scaling that motivated our work (see Section 2.3).

7. CONCLUSION

In this paper, we described a new scalable coordinate descent (SCD) algorithm for generalized linear models. SCD is highly robust, having the same convergence behavior regardless of how much it is scaled out and regardless of the computing environment. This allows SCD to scale to thousands of cores and makes it well suited for running in a cloud environment with low-cost commodity servers. On many real-world problems, SCD has the same convergence behavior as the popular single-machine coordinate descent algorithm. In addition to the SCD algorithm, we described a distributed system that addresses the specific challenges of scaling SCD in a cloud computing environment. Using Google's internal cloud, we showed that SCD can provide near linear scaling using thousands of cores for 1 trillion training examples on a petabyte of compressed data.

8. ACKNOWLEDGMENTS

We would like to thank our colleagues Tushar Chandra, Mike Gunter, Judah Jacobson, Gus Katsiapis, Lukasz Lew, Alex Passos, Tal Shaked, and Greg Steuck of the Sibyl team for their insightful discussions about the SCD algorithm and system design.

9. REFERENCES

[1] https://cloud.google.com/.
[2] https://aws.amazon.com/.
[3] https://www.csie.ntu.edu.tw/~cjlin/liblinear/.
[4] https://cran.r-project.org/web/packages/glmnet/.
[5] J. Bennet and S. Lanning. The Netflix prize. In *KDD Cup and Workshop*, 2007.
[6] R. D. Blumofe and C. E. Leiserson. Scheduling multithreaded computations by work stealing. *J. ACM*, 46(5):720–748, Sept. 1999.
[7] L. Bottou. Stochastic learning. In *Advanced Lectures on Machine Learning*, Lecture Notes in Artificial Intelligence, LNAI 3176, pages 146–168. Springer Verlag, 2004.
[8] J. K. Bradley, A. Kyrola, D. Bickson, and C. Guestrin. Parallel coordinate descent for l1-regularized loss minimization. In *Proceedings of the International Conference on Machine Learning (ICML 2011)*, June 2011.
[9] J. Canny and H. Zhao. Big data analytics with small footprint: Squaring the cloud. In *Proceedings of the 19th ACM SIGKDD International Conference on Knowledge Discovery and Data Mining*, KDD '13, pages 95–103, 2013.
[10] T. Chandra. Sibyl: A system for large scale machine learning at Google. *Keynote talk at the 44th Annual IEEE/IFIP International Conference on Dependable Systems and Networks*, 2014.
[11] K.-W. Chang, C.-J. Hsieh, and C.-J. Lin. Coordinate descent method for large-scale l2-loss linear support vector machines. *J. Mach. Learn. Res.*, 9:1369–1398, June 2008.
[12] O. Chapelle, E. Manavoglu, and R. Rosales. Simple and scalable response prediction for display advertising. *ACM Trans. Intell. Syst. Technol.*, 5(4):61:1–61:34, Dec. 2014.
[13] Y. Chen, R. Griffit, D. Zats, and R. H. Katz. Understanding TCP incast and its implications for big data workloads. Technical report, DTIC Document, 2012.
[14] M. Collins, R. E. Schapire, and Y. Singer. Logistic regression, Adaboost and Bregman distances. *Mach. Learn.*, 48(1-3):253–285, Sept. 2002.
[15] J. Dean and L. A. Barroso. The tail at scale. *Commun. ACM*, 56(2):74–80, Feb. 2013.
[16] J. Dean, G. Corrado, R. Monga, K. Chen, M. Devin, M. Mao, M. A. Ranzato, A. Senior, P. Tucker, K. Yang, Q. V. Le, and A. Y. Ng. Large scale distributed deep networks. In *Advances in Neural Information Processing Systems 25*, pages 1223–1231. 2012.
[17] J. Dean and S. Ghemawat. Mapreduce: Simplified data processing on large clusters. *Commun. ACM*, 51(1):107–113, Jan. 2008.
[18] J. Friedman, T. Hastie, and R. Tibshirani. Regularization paths for generalized linear models via coordinate descent. *Journal of Statistical Software*, 33(1):1–22, 2010.
[19] S. Ghemawat, H. Gobioff, and S.-T. Leung. The Google file system. In *Proceedings of the Nineteenth ACM Symposium on Operating Systems Principles*, SOSP '03, pages 29–43, 2003.
[20] T. Graepel, J. Q. Candela, T. Borchert, and R. Herbrich. Web-scale bayesian click-through rate prediction for sponsored search advertising in microsoft's bing search engine. In *Proceedings of the 27th International Conference on Machine Learning*, pages 13–20, 2010.
[21] X. He, J. Pan, O. Jin, T. Xu, B. Liu, T. Xu, Y. Shi, A. Atallah, R. Herbrich, S. Bowers, and J. Q. n. Candela. Practical lessons from predicting clicks on ads at Facebook. In *Proceedings of the Eighth International Workshop on Data Mining for Online Advertising*, ADKDD'14, pages 5:1–5:9, 2014.
[22] M. Li, D. G. Andersen, J. W. Park, A. J. Smola, A. Ahmed, V. Josifovski, J. Long, E. J. Shekita, and B.-Y. Su. Scaling distributed machine learning with the parameter server. In *Proceedings of the 11th USENIX Conference on Operating Systems Design and Implementation*, OSDI'14, pages 583–598, 2014.
[23] D. Mahajan, S. S. Keerthi, and S. Sundararajan. A distributed block coordinate descent method for training l1 regularized linear classifiers. *CoRR*, abs/1405.4544, 2014.
[24] H. B. McMahan, G. Holt, D. Sculley, M. Young, D. Ebner, J. Grady, L. Nie, T. Phillips, E. Davydov, D. Golovin, S. Chikkerur, D. Liu, M. Wattenberg, A. M. Hrafnkelsson, T. Boulos, and J. Kubica. Ad click prediction: A view from the trenches. In *Proceedings of the 19th ACM SIGKDD International Conference on Knowledge Discovery and Data Mining*, KDD '13, pages 1222–1230, 2013.
[25] B. Recht, C. Re, S. Wright, and F. Niu. Hogwild: A lock-free approach to parallelizing stochastic gradient descent. In *Advances in Neural Information Processing Systems 24*, pages 693–701. 2011.
[26] S. Shalev-Shwartz and A. Tewari. Stochastic methods for l1-regularized loss minimization. *J. Mach. Learn. Res.*, 12:1865–1892, July 2011.
[27] A. Verma, L. Pedrosa, M. R. Korupolu, D. Oppenheimer, E. Tune, and J. Wilkes. Large-scale cluster management at Google with Borg. In *Proceedings of the European Conference on Computer Systems (EuroSys)*, 2015.

"Why Should I Trust You?" Explaining the Predictions of Any Classifier

Marco Tulio Ribeiro
University of Washington
Seattle, WA 98105, USA
marcotcr@cs.uw.edu

Sameer Singh
University of Washington
Seattle, WA 98105, USA
sameer@cs.uw.edu

Carlos Guestrin
University of Washington
Seattle, WA 98105, USA
guestrin@cs.uw.edu

ABSTRACT

Despite widespread adoption, machine learning models remain mostly black boxes. Understanding the reasons behind predictions is, however, quite important in assessing *trust*, which is fundamental if one plans to take action based on a prediction, or when choosing whether to deploy a new model. Such understanding also provides insights into the model, which can be used to transform an untrustworthy model or prediction into a trustworthy one.

In this work, we propose LIME, a novel explanation technique that explains the predictions of *any* classifier in an interpretable and faithful manner, by learning an interpretable model locally around the prediction. We also propose a method to explain models by presenting representative individual predictions and their explanations in a non-redundant way, framing the task as a submodular optimization problem. We demonstrate the flexibility of these methods by explaining different models for text (e.g. random forests) and image classification (e.g. neural networks). We show the utility of explanations via novel experiments, both simulated and with human subjects, on various scenarios that require trust: deciding if one should trust a prediction, choosing between models, improving an untrustworthy classifier, and identifying why a classifier should not be trusted.

1. INTRODUCTION

Machine learning is at the core of many recent advances in science and technology. Unfortunately, the important role of humans is an oft-overlooked aspect in the field. Whether humans are directly using machine learning classifiers as tools, or are deploying models within other products, a vital concern remains: *if the users do not trust a model or a prediction, they will not use it.* It is important to differentiate between two different (but related) definitions of trust: (1) *trusting a prediction*, i.e. whether a user trusts an individual prediction sufficiently to take some action based on it, and (2) *trusting a model*, i.e. whether the user trusts a model to behave in reasonable ways if deployed. Both are directly impacted by how much the human understands a model's behaviour, as opposed to seeing it as a black box.

Determining trust in individual predictions is an important problem when the model is used for decision making. When using machine learning for medical diagnosis [6] or terrorism detection, for example, predictions cannot be acted upon on blind faith, as the consequences may be catastrophic.

Apart from trusting individual predictions, there is also a need to evaluate the model as a whole before deploying it "in the wild". To make this decision, users need to be confident that the model will perform well on real-world data, according to the metrics of interest. Currently, models are evaluated using accuracy metrics on an available validation dataset. However, real-world data is often significantly different, and further, the evaluation metric may not be indicative of the product's goal. Inspecting individual predictions and their explanations is a worthwhile solution, in addition to such metrics. In this case, it is important to aid users by suggesting which instances to inspect, especially for large datasets.

In this paper, we propose providing explanations for individual predictions as a solution to the "trusting a prediction" problem, and selecting multiple such predictions (and explanations) as a solution to the "trusting the model" problem. Our main contributions are summarized as follows.

- LIME, an algorithm that can explain the predictions of *any* classifier or regressor in a faithful way, by approximating it locally with an interpretable model.
- SP-LIME, a method that selects a set of representative instances with explanations to address the "trusting the model" problem, via submodular optimization.
- Comprehensive evaluation with simulated and human subjects, where we measure the impact of explanations on trust and associated tasks. In our experiments, non-experts using LIME are able to pick which classifier from a pair generalizes better in the real world. Further, they are able to greatly improve an untrustworthy classifier trained on 20 newsgroups, by doing feature engineering using LIME. We also show how understanding the predictions of a neural network on images helps practitioners know when and why they should not trust a model.

2. THE CASE FOR EXPLANATIONS

By "explaining a prediction", we mean presenting textual or visual artifacts that provide qualitative understanding of the relationship between the instance's components (e.g. words in text, patches in an image) and the model's prediction. We

KDD 2016 San Francisco, CA, USA

ISBN 978-1-4503-4232-2/16/08...$15.00

DOI: http://dx.doi.org/10.1145/2939672.2939778

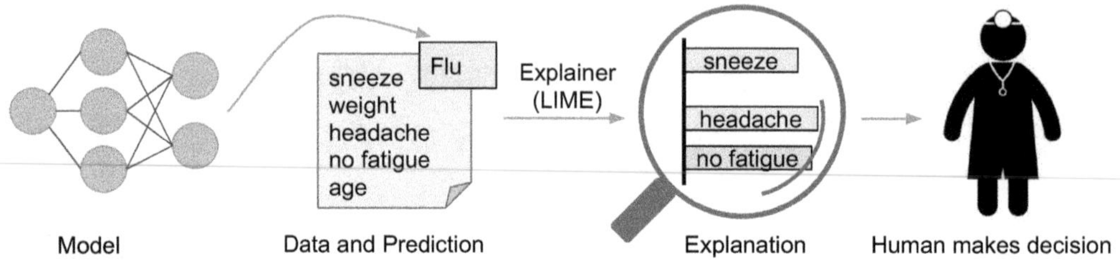

Figure 1: Explaining individual predictions. A model predicts that a patient has the flu, and LIME highlights the symptoms in the patient's history that led to the prediction. Sneeze and headache are portrayed as contributing to the "flu" prediction, while "no fatigue" is evidence against it. With these, a doctor can make an informed decision about whether to trust the model's prediction.

argue that explaining predictions is an important aspect in getting humans to trust and use machine learning effectively, if the explanations are faithful and intelligible.

The process of explaining individual predictions is illustrated in Figure 1. It is clear that a doctor is much better positioned to make a decision with the help of a model if intelligible explanations are provided. In this case, an explanation is a small list of symptoms with relative weights – symptoms that either contribute to the prediction (in green) or are evidence against it (in red). Humans usually have prior knowledge about the application domain, which they can use to accept (trust) or reject a prediction if they understand the reasoning behind it. It has been observed, for example, that providing explanations can increase the acceptance of movie recommendations [12] and other automated systems [8].

Every machine learning application also requires a certain measure of overall trust in the model. Development and evaluation of a classification model often consists of collecting annotated data, of which a held-out subset is used for automated evaluation. Although this is a useful pipeline for many applications, evaluation on validation data may not correspond to performance "in the wild", as practitioners often overestimate the accuracy of their models [21], and thus trust cannot rely solely on it. Looking at examples offers an alternative method to assess truth in the model, especially if the examples are explained. We thus propose explaining several representative individual predictions of a model as a way to provide a global understanding.

There are several ways a model or its evaluation can go wrong. Data leakage, for example, defined as the unintentional leakage of signal into the training (and validation) data that would not appear when deployed [14], potentially increases accuracy. A challenging example cited by **(author?)** [14] is one where the patient ID was found to be heavily correlated with the target class in the training and validation data. This issue would be incredibly challenging to identify just by observing the predictions and the raw data, but much easier if explanations such as the one in Figure 1 are provided, as patient ID would be listed as an explanation for predictions. Another particularly hard to detect problem is dataset shift [5], where training data is different than test data (we give an example in the famous 20 newsgroups dataset later on). The insights given by explanations are particularly helpful in identifying what must be done to convert an untrustworthy model into a trustworthy one – for example, removing leaked data or changing the training data to avoid dataset shift.

Machine learning practitioners often have to select a model from a number of alternatives, requiring them to assess the relative trust between two or more models. In Figure

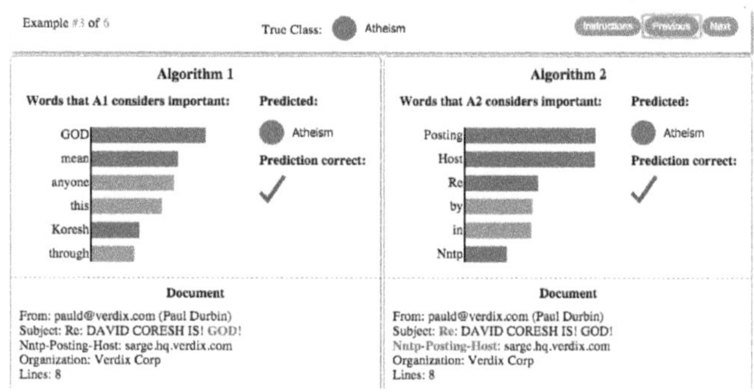

Figure 2: Explaining individual predictions of competing classifiers trying to determine if a document is about "Christianity" or "Atheism". The bar chart represents the importance given to the most relevant words, also highlighted in the text. Color indicates which class the word contributes to (green for "Christianity", magenta for "Atheism").

2, we show how individual prediction explanations can be used to select between models, in conjunction with accuracy. In this case, the algorithm with higher accuracy on the validation set is actually much worse, a fact that is easy to see when explanations are provided (again, due to human prior knowledge), but hard otherwise. Further, there is frequently a mismatch between the metrics that we can compute and optimize (e.g. accuracy) and the actual metrics of interest such as user engagement and retention. While we may not be able to measure such metrics, we have knowledge about how certain model behaviors can influence them. Therefore, a practitioner may wish to choose a less accurate model for content recommendation that does not place high importance in features related to "clickbait" articles (which may hurt user retention), even if exploiting such features increases the accuracy of the model in cross validation. We note that explanations are particularly useful in these (and other) scenarios if a method can produce them for *any* model, so that a variety of models can be compared.

Desired Characteristics for Explainers

We now outline a number of desired characteristics from explanation methods.

An essential criterion for explanations is that they must be **interpretable**, i.e., provide qualitative understanding between the input variables and the response. We note that interpretability must take into account the user's limitations. Thus, a linear model [24], a gradient vector [2] or an additive model [6] may or may not be interpretable. For example, if hundreds or thousands of features significantly contribute to a prediction, it is not reasonable to expect any user to comprehend why the prediction was made, even if individual weights can be inspected. This requirement further implies that explanations should be easy to understand, which is not necessarily true of the features used by the model, and thus the "input variables" in the explanations may need to be different than the features. Finally, we note that the notion of interpretability also depends on the target audience. Machine learning practitioners may be able to interpret small Bayesian networks, but laymen may be more comfortable with a small number of weighted features as an explanation.

Another essential criterion is **local fidelity**. Although it is often impossible for an explanation to be completely faithful unless it is the complete description of the model itself, for an explanation to be meaningful it must at least be *locally faithful*, i.e. it must correspond to how the model behaves in the vicinity of the instance being predicted. We note that local fidelity does not imply global fidelity: features that are globally important may not be important in the local context, and vice versa. While global fidelity would imply local fidelity, identifying globally faithful explanations that are interpretable remains a challenge for complex models.

While there are models that are inherently interpretable [6, 17, 26, 27], an explainer should be able to explain *any* model, and thus be **model-agnostic** (i.e. treat the original model as a black box). Apart from the fact that many state-of-the-art classifiers are not currently interpretable, this also provides flexibility to explain future classifiers.

In addition to explaining predictions, providing a **global perspective** is important to ascertain trust in the model. As mentioned before, accuracy may often not be a suitable metric to evaluate the model, and thus we want to *explain the model*. Building upon the explanations for individual predictions, we select a few explanations to present to the user, such that they are representative of the model.

3. LOCAL INTERPRETABLE MODEL-AGNOSTIC EXPLANATIONS

We now present Local Interpretable Model-agnostic Explanations (**LIME**). The overall goal of LIME is to identify an **interpretable** model over the *interpretable representation* that is **locally faithful** to the classifier.

3.1 Interpretable Data Representations

Before we present the explanation system, it is important to distinguish between features and interpretable data representations. As mentioned before, **interpretable** explanations need to use a representation that is understandable to humans, regardless of the actual features used by the model. For example, a possible *interpretable representation* for text classification is a binary vector indicating the presence or absence of a word, even though the classifier may use more complex (and incomprehensible) features such as word embeddings. Likewise for image classification, an *interpretable representation* may be a binary vector indicating the "presence" or "absence" of a contiguous patch of similar pixels (a super-pixel), while the classifier may represent the image as a tensor with three color channels per pixel. We denote $x \in \mathbb{R}^d$ be the original representation of an instance being explained, and we use $x' \in \{0,1\}^{d'}$ to denote a binary vector for its interpretable representation.

3.2 Fidelity-Interpretability Trade-off

Formally, we define an explanation as a model $g \in G$, where G is a class of potentially *interpretable* models, such as linear models, decision trees, or falling rule lists [27], i.e. a model $g \in G$ can be readily presented to the user with visual or textual artifacts. The domain of g is $\{0,1\}^{d'}$, i.e. g acts over absence/presence of the *interpretable components*. As not every $g \in G$ may be simple enough to be interpretable - thus we let $\Omega(g)$ be a measure of *complexity* (as opposed to *interpretability*) of the explanation $g \in G$. For example, for decision trees $\Omega(g)$ may be the depth of the tree, while for linear models, $\Omega(g)$ may be the number of non-zero weights.

Let the model being explained be denoted $f : \mathbb{R}^d \to \mathbb{R}$. In classification, $f(x)$ is the probability (or a binary indicator) that x belongs to a certain class[1]. We further use $\pi_x(z)$ as a proximity measure between an instance z to x, so as to define locality around x. Finally, let $\mathcal{L}(f, g, \pi_x)$ be a measure of how unfaithful g is in approximating f in the locality defined by π_x. In order to ensure both **interpretability** and **local fidelity**, we must minimize $\mathcal{L}(f, g, \pi_x)$ while having $\Omega(g)$ be low enough to be interpretable by humans. The explanation produced by **LIME** is obtained by the following:

$$\xi(x) = \underset{g \in G}{\operatorname{argmin}} \ \mathcal{L}(f, g, \pi_x) + \Omega(g) \qquad (1)$$

This formulation can be used with different explanation families G, fidelity functions $\mathcal{L}$, and complexity measures Ω. Here we focus on sparse linear models as explanations, and on performing the search using perturbations.

3.3 Sampling for Local Exploration

We want to minimize the locality-aware loss $\mathcal{L}(f, g, \pi_x)$ without making any assumptions about f, since we want the explainer to be **model-agnostic**. Thus, in order to learn the local behavior of f as the interpretable inputs vary, we approximate $\mathcal{L}(f, g, \pi_x)$ by drawing samples, weighted by π_x. We sample instances around x' by drawing nonzero elements of x' uniformly at random (where the number of such draws is also uniformly sampled). Given a perturbed sample $z' \in \{0,1\}^{d'}$ (which contains a fraction of the nonzero elements of x'), we recover the sample in the original representation $z \in R^d$ and obtain $f(z)$, which is used as a *label* for the explanation model. Given this dataset $\mathcal{Z}$ of perturbed samples with the associated labels, we optimize Eq. (1) to get an explanation $\xi(x)$. The primary intuition behind LIME is presented in Figure 3, where we sample instances both in the vicinity of x (which have a high weight due to π_x) and far away from x (low weight from π_x). Even though the original model may be too complex to explain globally, LIME presents an explanation that is locally faithful (linear in this case), where the locality is captured by π_x. It is worth noting that our method is fairly robust to sampling noise since the samples are weighted by π_x in Eq. (1). We now present a concrete instance of this general framework.

3.4 Sparse Linear Explanations

For the rest of this paper, we let G be the class of linear models, such that $g(z') = w_g \cdot z'$. We use the locally weighted square loss as $\mathcal{L}$, as defined in Eq. (2), where we let $\pi_x(z) = exp(-D(x,z)^2/\sigma^2)$ be an exponential kernel defined on some

[1]For multiple classes, we explain each class separately, thus $f(x)$ is the prediction of the relevant class.

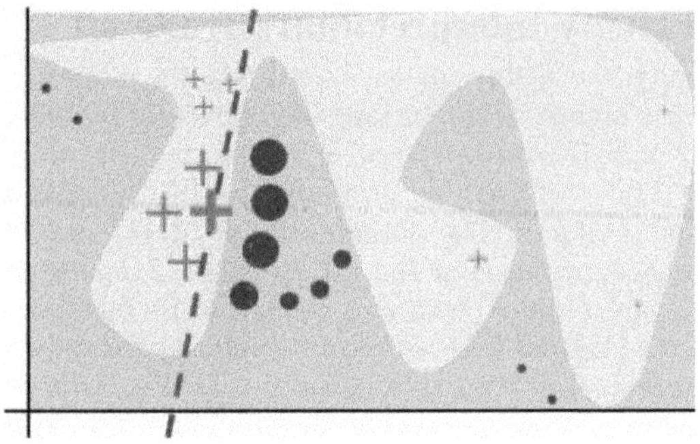

Figure 3: Toy example to present intuition for LIME. The black-box model's complex decision function f (unknown to LIME) is represented by the blue/pink background, which cannot be approximated well by a linear model. The bold red cross is the instance being explained. LIME samples instances, gets predictions using f, and weighs them by the proximity to the instance being explained (represented here by size). The dashed line is the learned explanation that is locally (but not globally) faithful.

Algorithm 1 Sparse Linear Explanations using LIME

Require: Classifier f, Number of samples N
Require: Instance x, and its interpretable version x'
Require: Similarity kernel π_x, Length of explanation K
  $\mathcal{Z} \leftarrow \{\}$
  for $i \in \{1, 2, 3, ..., N\}$ **do**
    $z'_i \leftarrow sample\_around(x')$
    $\mathcal{Z} \leftarrow \mathcal{Z} \cup \langle z'_i, f(z_i), \pi_x(z_i) \rangle$
  end for
  $w \leftarrow$ K-Lasso$(\mathcal{Z}, K)$ ▷ with z'_i as features, $f(z)$ as target
  return w

distance function D (e.g. cosine distance for text, $L2$ distance for images) with width σ.

$$\mathcal{L}(f, g, \pi_x) = \sum_{z, z' \in \mathcal{Z}} \pi_x(z) \left(f(z) - g(z')\right)^2 \tag{2}$$

For text classification, we ensure that the explanation is **interpretable** by letting the *interpretable representation* be a bag of words, and by setting a limit K on the number of words, i.e. $\Omega(g) = \infty \mathbb{1}[\|w_g\|_0 > K]$. Potentially, K can be adapted to be as big as the user can handle, or we could have different values of K for different instances. In this paper we use a constant value for K, leaving the exploration of different values to future work. We use the same Ω for image classification, using "super-pixels" (computed using any standard algorithm) instead of words, such that the interpretable representation of an image is a binary vector where 1 indicates the original super-pixel and 0 indicates a grayed out super-pixel. This particular choice of Ω makes directly solving Eq. (1) intractable, but we approximate it by first selecting K features with Lasso (using the regularization path [9]) and then learning the weights via least squares (a procedure we call K-LASSO in Algorithm 1). Since Algorithm 1 produces an explanation for an individual prediction, its complexity does not depend on the size of the dataset, but instead on time to compute $f(x)$ and on the number of samples N. In practice, explaining random forests with 1000 trees using scikit-learn (http://scikit-learn.org) on a laptop with $N = 5000$ takes under 3 seconds without any optimizations such as using gpus or parallelization. Explaining each prediction of the Inception network [25] for image classification takes around 10 minutes.

Any choice of interpretable representations and G will have some inherent drawbacks. First, while the underlying model can be treated as a black-box, certain interpretable representations will not be powerful enough to explain certain behaviors. For example, a model that predicts sepia-toned images to be *retro* cannot be explained by presence of absence of super pixels. Second, our choice of G (sparse linear models) means that if the underlying model is highly non-linear even in the locality of the prediction, there may not be a faithful explanation. However, we can estimate the faithfulness of the explanation on $\mathcal{Z}$, and present this information to the user. This estimate of faithfulness can also be used for selecting an appropriate family of explanations from a set of multiple interpretable model classes, thus adapting to the given dataset and the classifier. We leave such exploration for future work, as linear explanations work quite well for multiple black-box models in our experiments.

3.5 Example 1: Text classification with SVMs

In Figure 2 (right side), we explain the predictions of a support vector machine with RBF kernel trained on unigrams to differentiate "Christianity" from "Atheism" (on a subset of the 20 newsgroup dataset). Although this classifier achieves 94% held-out accuracy, and one would be tempted to trust it based on this, the explanation for an instance shows that predictions are made for quite arbitrary reasons (words "Posting", "Host", and "Re" have no connection to either Christianity or Atheism). The word "Posting" appears in 22% of examples in the training set, 99% of them in the class "Atheism". Even if headers are removed, proper names of prolific posters in the original newsgroups are selected by the classifier, which would also not generalize.

After getting such insights from explanations, it is clear that this dataset has serious issues (which are not evident just by studying the raw data or predictions), and that this classifier, or held-out evaluation, cannot be trusted. It is also clear what the problems are, and the steps that can be taken to fix these issues and train a more trustworthy classifier.

3.6 Example 2: Deep networks for images

When using sparse linear explanations for image classifiers, one may wish to just highlight the super-pixels with positive weight towards a specific class, as they give intuition as to why the model would think that class may be present. We explain the prediction of Google's pre-trained Inception neural network [25] in this fashion on an arbitrary image (Figure 4a). Figures 4b, 4c, 4d show the superpixels explanations for the top 3 predicted classes (with the rest of the image grayed out), having set $K = 10$. What the neural network picks up on for each of the classes is quite natural to humans - Figure 4b in particular provides insight as to why acoustic guitar was predicted to be electric: due to the fretboard. This kind of explanation enhances trust in the classifier (even if the top predicted class is wrong), as it shows that it is not acting in an unreasonable manner.

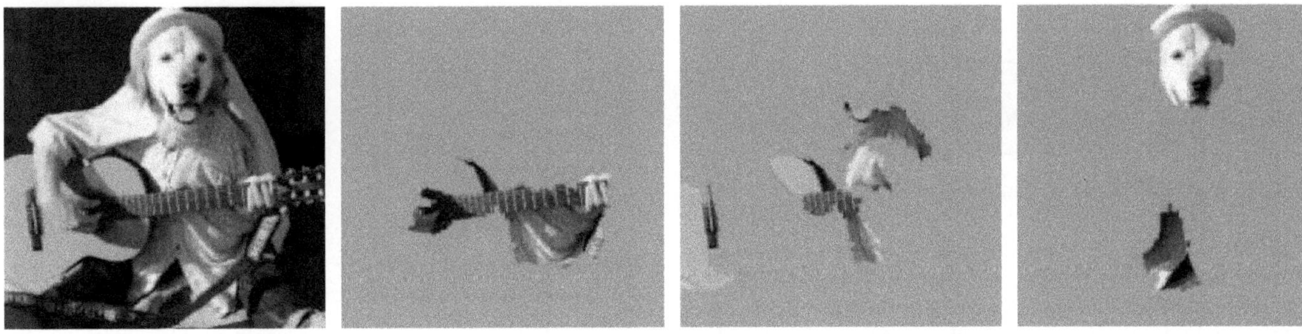

(a) Original Image (b) Explaining *Electric guitar* (c) Explaining *Acoustic guitar* (d) Explaining *Labrador*

Figure 4: Explaining an image classification prediction made by Google's Inception neural network. The top 3 classes predicted are "Electric Guitar" ($p = 0.32$), "Acoustic guitar" ($p = 0.24$) and "Labrador" ($p = 0.21$)

4. SUBMODULAR PICK FOR EXPLAINING MODELS

Although an explanation of a single prediction provides some understanding into the reliability of the classifier to the user, it is not sufficient to evaluate and assess trust in the model as a whole. We propose to give a global understanding of the model by explaining a set of individual instances. This approach is still model agnostic, and is complementary to computing summary statistics such as held-out accuracy.

Even though explanations of multiple instances can be insightful, these instances need to be selected judiciously, since users may not have the time to examine a large number of explanations. We represent the time/patience that humans have by a budget B that denotes the number of explanations they are willing to look at in order to understand a model. Given a set of instances X, we define the **pick step** as the task of selecting B instances for the user to inspect.

The pick step is not dependent on the existence of explanations - one of the main purpose of tools like Modeltracker [1] and others [11] is to assist users in selecting instances themselves, and examining the raw data and predictions. However, since looking at raw data is not enough to understand predictions and get insights, the pick step should take into account the explanations that accompany each prediction. Moreover, this method should pick a diverse, representative set of explanations to show the user – i.e. non-redundant explanations that represent how the model behaves globally.

Given the explanations for a set of instances X ($|X| = n$), we construct an $n \times d'$ *explanation matrix* $\mathcal{W}$ that represents the local importance of the interpretable components for each instance. When using linear models as explanations, for an instance x_i and explanation $g_i = \xi(x_i)$, we set $\mathcal{W}_{ij} = |w_{g_{ij}}|$. Further, for each component (column) j in $\mathcal{W}$, we let I_j denote the *global* importance of that component in the explanation space. Intuitively, we want I such that features that explain many different instances have higher importance scores. In Figure 5, we show a toy example $\mathcal{W}$, with $n = d' = 5$, where $\mathcal{W}$ is binary (for simplicity). The importance function I should score feature f2 higher than feature f1, i.e. $I_2 > I_1$, since feature f2 is used to explain more instances. Concretely for the text applications, we set $I_j = \sqrt{\sum_{i=1}^{n} \mathcal{W}_{ij}}$. For images, I must measure something that is comparable across the super-pixels in different images, such as color histograms or other features of super-pixels; we leave further exploration of these ideas for future work.

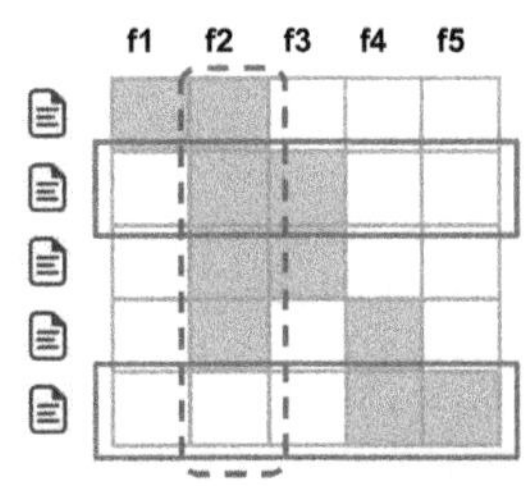

Figure 5: Toy example $\mathcal{W}$. Rows represent instances (documents) and columns represent features (words). Feature f2 (dotted blue) has the highest importance. Rows 2 and 5 (in red) would be selected by the pick procedure, covering all but feature f1.

Algorithm 2 Submodular pick (SP) algorithm

Require: Instances X, Budget B
  for all $x_i \in X$ **do**
    $\mathcal{W}_i \leftarrow$ **explain**(x_i, x'_i) ▷ Using Algorithm 1
  end for
  for $j \in \{1 \ldots d'\}$ **do**
    $I_j \leftarrow \sqrt{\sum_{i=1}^{n} |\mathcal{W}_{ij}|}$ ▷ Compute feature importances
  end for
  $V \leftarrow \{\}$
  while $|V| < B$ **do** ▷ Greedy optimization of Eq (4)
    $V \leftarrow V \cup \text{argmax}_i\, c(V \cup \{i\}, \mathcal{W}, I)$
  end while
  return V

While we want to pick instances that cover the important components, the set of explanations must not be redundant in the components they show the users, i.e. avoid selecting instances with similar explanations. In Figure 5, after the second row is picked, the third row adds no value, as the user has already seen features f2 and f3 - while the last row exposes the user to completely new features. Selecting the second and last row results in the coverage of almost all the features. We formalize this non-redundant coverage intuition in Eq. (3), where we define coverage as the set function c that, given $\mathcal{W}$ and I, computes the total importance of the features that appear in at least one instance in a set V.

$$c(V, \mathcal{W}, I) = \sum_{j=1}^{d'} \mathbb{1}_{[\exists i \in V : \mathcal{W}_{ij} > 0]} I_j \quad (3)$$

The pick problem, defined in Eq. (4), consists of finding the set $V, |V| \leq B$ that achieves highest coverage.

$$Pick(\mathcal{W}, I) = \underset{V, |V| \leq B}{\operatorname{argmax}}\, c(V, \mathcal{W}, I) \quad (4)$$

The problem in Eq. (4) is maximizing a weighted coverage function, and is NP-hard [10]. Let $c(V \cup \{i\}, \mathcal{W}, I) - c(V, \mathcal{W}, I)$ be the marginal coverage gain of adding an instance i to a set V. Due to submodularity, a greedy algorithm that iteratively adds the instance with the highest marginal coverage gain to the solution offers a constant-factor approximation guarantee of $1 - 1/e$ to the optimum [15]. We outline this approximation in Algorithm 2, and call it **submodular pick**.

5. SIMULATED USER EXPERIMENTS

In this section, we present simulated user experiments to evaluate the utility of explanations in trust-related tasks. In particular, we address the following questions: (1) Are the explanations faithful to the model, (2) Can the explanations aid users in ascertaining trust in predictions, and (3) Are the explanations useful for evaluating the model as a whole. Code and data for replicating our experiments are available at https://github.com/marcotcr/lime-experiments.

5.1 Experiment Setup

We use two sentiment analysis datasets (*books* and *DVDs*, 2000 instances each) where the task is to classify product reviews as positive or negative [4]. We train decision trees (**DT**), logistic regression with L2 regularization (**LR**), nearest neighbors (**NN**), and support vector machines with RBF kernel (**SVM**), all using bag of words as features. We also include random forests (with 1000 trees) trained with the average word2vec embedding [19] (**RF**), a model that is impossible to interpret without a technique like LIME. We use the implementations and default parameters of scikit-learn, unless noted otherwise. We divide each dataset into train (1600 instances) and test (400 instances).

To explain individual predictions, we compare our proposed approach (**LIME**), with **parzen** [2], a method that approximates the black box classifier globally with Parzen windows, and explains individual predictions by taking the gradient of the prediction probability function. For parzen, we take the K features with the highest absolute gradients as explanations. We set the hyper-parameters for parzen and LIME using cross validation, and set $N = 15,000$. We also compare against a **greedy** procedure (similar to **(author?)** [18]) in which we greedily remove features that contribute the most to the predicted class until the prediction changes (or we reach the maximum of K features), and a **random** procedure that randomly picks K features as an explanation. We set K to 10 for our experiments.

For experiments where the pick procedure applies, we either do random selection (random pick, **RP**) or the procedure described in §4 (submodular pick, **SP**). We refer to pick-explainer combinations by adding RP or SP as a prefix.

5.2 Are explanations faithful to the model?

We measure faithfulness of explanations on classifiers that are by themselves interpretable (sparse logistic regression

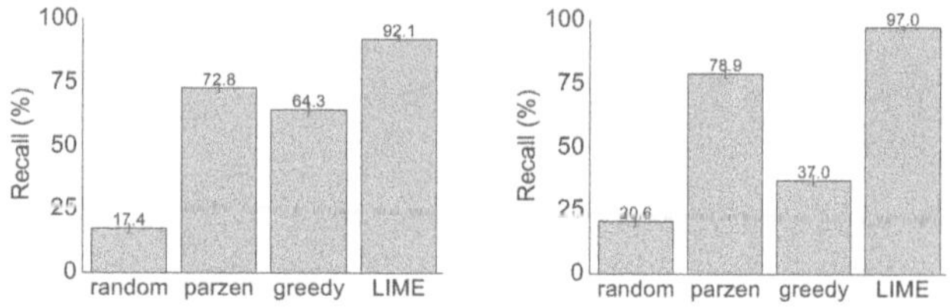

(a) Sparse LR (b) Decision Tree

Figure 6: Recall on truly important features for two interpretable classifiers on the books dataset.

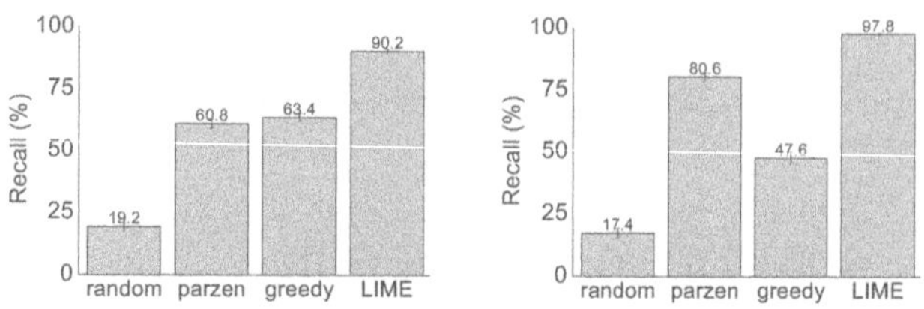

(a) Sparse LR (b) Decision Tree

Figure 7: Recall on truly important features for two interpretable classifiers on the DVDs dataset.

and decision trees). In particular, we train both classifiers such that the maximum number of features they use for any instance is 10, and thus we know the *gold* set of features that the are considered important by these models. For each prediction on the test set, we generate explanations and compute the fraction of these *gold* features that are recovered by the explanations. We report this recall averaged over all the test instances in Figures 6 and 7. We observe that the greedy approach is comparable to parzen on logistic regression, but is substantially worse on decision trees since changing a single feature at a time often does not have an effect on the prediction. The overall recall by parzen is low, likely due to the difficulty in approximating the original high-dimensional classifier. LIME consistently provides $> 90\%$ recall for both classifiers on both datasets, demonstrating that LIME explanations are faithful to the models.

5.3 Should I trust this prediction?

In order to simulate trust in individual predictions, we first randomly select 25% of the features to be "untrustworthy", and assume that the users can identify and would not want to trust these features (such as the headers in 20 newsgroups, leaked data, etc). We thus develop *oracle* "trustworthiness" by labeling test set predictions from a black box classifier as "untrustworthy" if the prediction changes when untrustworthy features are removed from the instance, and "trustworthy" otherwise. In order to simulate users, we assume that users deem predictions untrustworthy from LIME and parzen explanations if the prediction from the linear approximation changes when all untrustworthy features that appear in the explanations are removed (the simulated human "discounts" the effect of untrustworthy features). For greedy and random, the prediction is mistrusted if any untrustworthy features are present in the explanation, since these methods do not provide a notion of the contribution of each feature to the prediction. Thus for each test set prediction, we can evaluate whether the simulated user trusts it using each explanation method, and compare it to the trustworthiness oracle.

Using this setup, we report the F1 on the trustworthy

Table 1: Average F1 of *trustworthiness* for different explainers on a collection of classifiers and datasets.

	Books				DVDs			
	LR	NN	RF	SVM	LR	NN	RF	SVM
Random	14.6	14.8	14.7	14.7	14.2	14.3	14.5	14.4
Parzen	84.0	87.6	94.3	92.3	87.0	81.7	94.2	87.3
Greedy	53.7	47.4	45.0	53.3	52.4	58.1	46.6	55.1
LIME	**96.6**	**94.5**	**96.2**	**96.7**	**96.6**	**91.8**	**96.1**	**95.6**

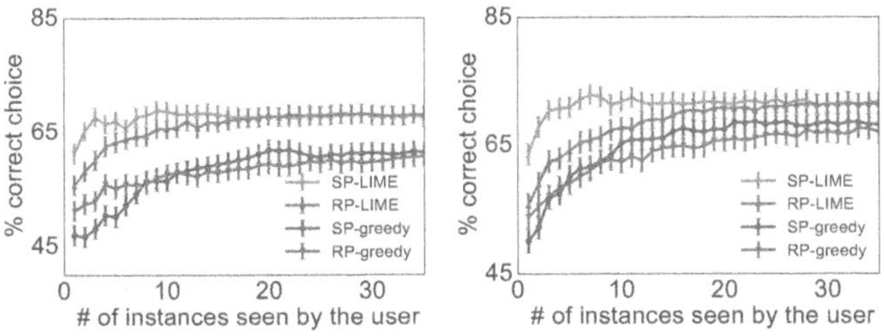

(a) Books dataset (b) DVDs dataset

Figure 8: Choosing between two classifiers, as the number of instances shown to a simulated user is varied. Averages and standard errors from 800 runs.

predictions for each explanation method, averaged over 100 runs, in Table 1. The results indicate that LIME dominates others (all results are significant at $p = 0.01$) on both datasets, and for all of the black box models. The other methods either achieve a lower recall (i.e. they mistrust predictions more than they should) or lower precision (i.e. they trust too many predictions), while LIME maintains both high precision and high recall. Even though we artificially select which features are untrustworthy, these results indicate that LIME is helpful in assessing trust in individual predictions.

5.4 Can I trust this model?

In the final simulated user experiment, we evaluate whether the explanations can be used for model selection, simulating the case where a human has to decide between two competing models with similar accuracy on validation data. For this purpose, we add 10 artificially "noisy" features. Specifically, on training and validation sets (80/20 split of the original training data), each artificial feature appears in 10% of the examples in one class, and 20% of the other, while on the test instances, each artificial feature appears in 10% of the examples in each class. This recreates the situation where the models use not only features that are informative in the real world, but also ones that introduce spurious correlations. We create pairs of competing classifiers by repeatedly training pairs of random forests with 30 trees until their validation accuracy is within 0.1% of each other, but their test accuracy differs by at least 5%. Thus, it is not possible to identify the *better* classifier (the one with higher test accuracy) from the accuracy on the validation data.

The goal of this experiment is to evaluate whether a user can identify the better classifier based on the explanations of B instances from the validation set. The simulated human marks the set of artificial features that appear in the B explanations as untrustworthy, following which we evaluate how many total predictions in the validation set should be trusted (as in the previous section, treating only marked features as untrustworthy). Then, we select the classifier with fewer untrustworthy predictions, and compare this choice to the classifier with higher held-out test set accuracy.

We present the accuracy of picking the correct classifier as B varies, averaged over 800 runs, in Figure 8. We omit SP-parzen and RP-parzen from the figure since they did not produce useful explanations, performing only slightly better than random. LIME is consistently better than greedy, irrespective of the pick method. Further, combining submodular pick with LIME outperforms all other methods, in particular it is much better than RP-LIME when only a few examples are shown to the users. These results demonstrate that the trust assessments provided by SP-selected LIME explanations are good indicators of generalization, which we validate with human experiments in the next section.

6. EVALUATION WITH HUMAN SUBJECTS

In this section, we recreate three scenarios in machine learning that require trust and understanding of predictions and models. In particular, we evaluate LIME and SP-LIME in the following settings: (1) Can users choose which of two classifiers generalizes better (§ 6.2), (2) based on the explanations, can users perform feature engineering to improve the model (§ 6.3), and (3) are users able to identify and describe classifier irregularities by looking at explanations (§ 6.4).

6.1 Experiment setup

For experiments in §6.2 and §6.3, we use the "Christianity" and "Atheism" documents from the 20 newsgroups dataset mentioned beforehand. This dataset is problematic since it contains features that do not generalize (e.g. very informative header information and author names), and thus validation accuracy considerably overestimates real-world performance.

In order to estimate the real world performance, we create a new *religion dataset* for evaluation. We download Atheism and Christianity websites from the DMOZ directory and human curated lists, yielding 819 webpages in each class. High accuracy on this dataset by a classifier trained on 20 newsgroups indicates that the classifier is generalizing using semantic content, instead of placing importance on the data specific issues outlined above. Unless noted otherwise, we use SVM with RBF kernel, trained on the 20 newsgroups data with hyper-parameters tuned via the cross-validation.

6.2 Can users select the best classifier?

In this section, we want to evaluate whether explanations can help users decide which classifier generalizes better, i.e., which classifier would the user deploy "in the wild". Specifically, users have to decide between two classifiers: SVM trained on the original 20 newsgroups dataset, and a version of the same classifier trained on a "cleaned" dataset where many of the features that do not generalize have been manually removed. The original classifier achieves an accuracy score of 57.3% on the *religion dataset*, while the "cleaned" classifier achieves a score of 69.0%. In contrast, the test accuracy on the original 20 newsgroups split is 94.0% and 88.6%, respectively – suggesting that the worse classifier would be selected if accuracy alone is used as a measure of trust.

We recruit human subjects on Amazon Mechanical Turk – by no means machine learning experts, but instead people with basic knowledge about religion. We measure their ability to choose the better algorithm by seeing side-by-side explanations with the associated raw data (as shown in Figure 2). We restrict both the number of words in each explanation (K) and the number of documents that each

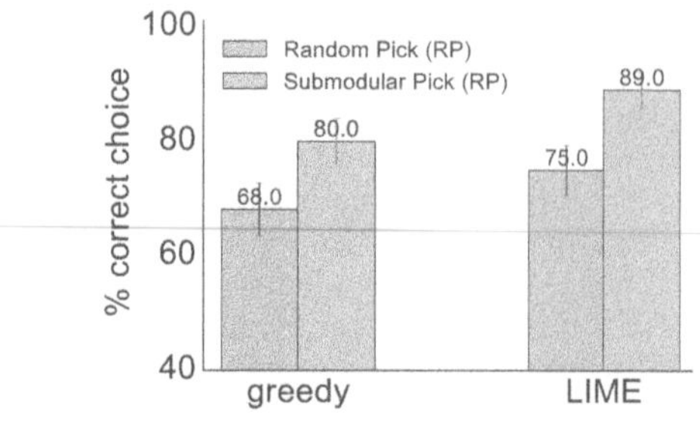

Figure 9: Average accuracy of human subject (with standard errors) in choosing between two classifiers.

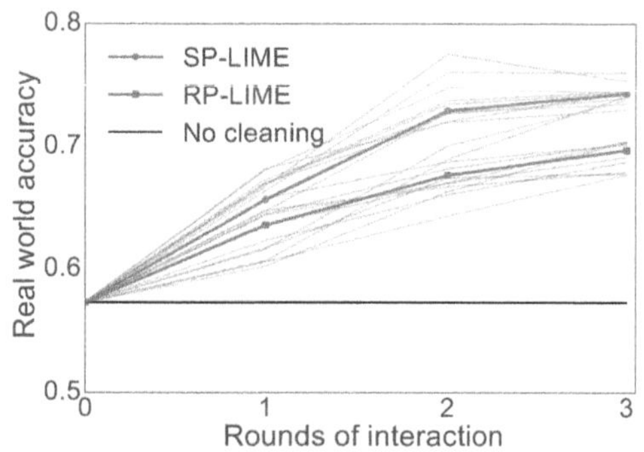

Figure 10: Feature engineering experiment. Each shaded line represents the average accuracy of subjects in a path starting from one of the initial 10 subjects. Each solid line represents the average across all paths per round of interaction.

person inspects (B) to 6. The position of each algorithm and the order of the instances seen are randomized between subjects. After examining the explanations, users are asked to select which algorithm will perform best in the real world. The explanations are produced by either greedy (chosen as a baseline due to its performance in the simulated user experiment) or LIME, and the instances are selected either by random (RP) or submodular pick (SP). We modify the greedy step in Algorithm 2 slightly so it alternates between explanations of the two classifiers. For each setting, we repeat the experiment with 100 users.

The results are presented in Figure 9. Note that all of the methods are good at identifying the better classifier, demonstrating that the explanations are useful in determining which classifier to trust, while using test set accuracy would result in the selection of the wrong classifier. Further, we see that the submodular pick (SP) greatly improves the user's ability to select the best classifier when compared to random pick (RP), with LIME outperforming greedy in both cases.

6.3 Can non-experts improve a classifier?

If one notes that a classifier is untrustworthy, a common task in machine learning is feature engineering, i.e. modifying the set of features and retraining in order to improve generalization. Explanations can aid in this process by presenting the important features, particularly for removing features that the users feel do not generalize.

We use the 20 newsgroups data here as well, and ask Amazon Mechanical Turk users to identify which words from the explanations should be removed from subsequent training, for the worse classifier from the previous section (§6.2). In each round, the subject marks words for deletion after observing $B = 10$ instances with $K = 10$ words in each explanation (an interface similar to Figure 2, but with a single algorithm). As a reminder, the users here are not experts in machine learning and are unfamiliar with feature engineering, thus are only identifying words based on their semantic content. Further, users do not have any access to the *religion* dataset – they do not even know of its existence. We start the experiment with 10 subjects. After they mark words for deletion, we train 10 different classifiers, one for each subject (with the corresponding words removed). The explanations for each classifier are then presented to a set of 5 users in a new round of interaction, which results in 50 new classifiers. We do a final round, after which we have 250 classifiers, each with a path of interaction tracing back to the first 10 subjects.

The explanations and instances shown to each user are produced by **SP-LIME** or **RP-LIME**. We show the average accuracy on the *religion* dataset at each interaction round for the paths originating from each of the original 10 subjects (shaded lines), and the average across all paths (solid lines) in Figure 10. It is clear from the figure that the crowd workers are able to improve the model by removing features they deem unimportant for the task. Further, **SP-LIME** outperforms **RP-LIME**, indicating selection of the instances to show the users is crucial for efficient feature engineering.

Each subject took an average of 3.6 minutes per round of cleaning, resulting in just under 11 minutes to produce a classifier that generalizes much better to real world data. Each path had on average 200 words removed with **SP**, and 157 with **RP**, indicating that incorporating coverage of important features is useful for feature engineering. Further, out of an average of 200 words selected with SP, 174 were selected by at least half of the users, while 68 by *all* the users. Along with the fact that the variance in the accuracy decreases across rounds, this high agreement demonstrates that the users are converging to similar *correct* models. This evaluation is an example of how explanations make it easy to improve an untrustworthy classifier – in this case easy enough that machine learning knowledge is not required.

6.4 Do explanations lead to insights?

Often artifacts of data collection can induce undesirable correlations that the classifiers pick up during training. These issues can be very difficult to identify just by looking at the raw data and predictions. In an effort to reproduce such a setting, we take the task of distinguishing between photos of Wolves and Eskimo Dogs (huskies). We train a logistic regression classifier on a training set of 20 images, hand selected such that all pictures of wolves had snow in the background, while pictures of huskies did not. As the features for the images, we use the first max-pooling layer of Google's pre-trained Inception neural network [25]. On a collection of additional 60 images, the classifier predicts "Wolf" if there is snow (or light background at the bottom), and "Husky" otherwise, regardless of animal color, position, pose, etc. We trained this *bad* classifier intentionally, to evaluate whether subjects are able to detect it.

The experiment proceeds as follows: we first present a balanced set of 10 test predictions (without explanations), where one wolf is not in a snowy background (and thus the prediction is "Husky") and one husky is (and is thus predicted as "Wolf"). We show the "Husky" mistake in Figure 11a. The other 8 examples are classified correctly. We then ask the subject three questions: (1) Do they trust this algorithm

(a) Husky classified as wolf (b) Explanation

Figure 11: Raw data and explanation of a bad model's prediction in the "Husky vs Wolf" task.

	Before	After
Trusted the bad model	10 out of 27	3 out of 27
Snow as a potential feature	12 out of 27	25 out of 27

Table 2: "Husky vs Wolf" experiment results.

to work well in the real world, (2) why, and (3) how do they think the algorithm is able to distinguish between these photos of wolves and huskies. After getting these responses, we show the same images with the associated explanations, such as in Figure 11b, and ask the same questions.

Since this task requires some familiarity with the notion of spurious correlations and generalization, the set of subjects for this experiment were graduate students who have taken at least one graduate machine learning course. After gathering the responses, we had 3 independent evaluators read their reasoning and determine if each subject mentioned snow, background, or equivalent as a feature the model may be using. We pick the majority to decide whether the subject was correct about the insight, and report these numbers before and after showing the explanations in Table 2.

Before observing the explanations, more than a third trusted the classifier, and a little less than half mentioned the snow pattern as something the neural network was using – although all speculated on other patterns. After examining the explanations, however, almost all of the subjects identified the correct insight, with much more certainty that it was a determining factor. Further, the trust in the classifier also dropped substantially. Although our sample size is small, this experiment demonstrates the utility of explaining individual predictions for getting insights into classifiers knowing when not to trust them and why.

7. RELATED WORK

The problems with relying on validation set accuracy as the primary measure of trust have been well studied. Practitioners consistently overestimate their model's accuracy [21], propagate feedback loops [23], or fail to notice data leaks [14]. In order to address these issues, researchers have proposed tools like Gestalt [20] and Modeltracker [1], which help users navigate individual instances. These tools are complementary to LIME in terms of explaining models, since they do not address the problem of explaining individual predictions. Further, our submodular pick procedure can be incorporated in such tools to aid users in navigating larger datasets.

Some recent work aims to anticipate failures in machine learning, specifically for vision tasks [3, 29]. Letting users know when the systems are likely to fail can lead to an increase in trust, by avoiding "silly mistakes" [8]. These solutions either require additional annotations and feature engineering that is specific to vision tasks or do not provide insight into why a decision should not be trusted. Furthermore, they assume that the current evaluation metrics are reliable, which may not be the case if problems such as data leakage are present. Other recent work [11] focuses on exposing users to different kinds of mistakes (our pick step). Interestingly, the subjects in their study did not notice the serious problems in the 20 newsgroups data even after looking at many mistakes, suggesting that examining raw data is not sufficient. Note that **(author?)** [11] are not alone in this regard, many researchers in the field have unwittingly published classifiers that would not generalize for this task. Using LIME, we show that even non-experts are able to identify these irregularities when explanations are present. Further, LIME can complement these existing systems, and allow users to assess trust even when a prediction seems "correct" but is made for the wrong reasons.

Recognizing the utility of explanations in assessing trust, many have proposed using interpretable models [27], especially for the medical domain [6, 17, 26]. While such models may be appropriate for some domains, they may not apply equally well to others (e.g. a supersparse linear model [26] with $5 - 10$ features is unsuitable for text applications). Interpretability, in these cases, comes at the cost of flexibility, accuracy, or efficiency. For text, EluciDebug [16] is a full human-in-the-loop system that shares many of our goals (interpretability, faithfulness, etc). However, they focus on an already interpretable model (Naive Bayes). In computer vision, systems that rely on object detection to produce candidate alignments [13] or attention [28] are able to produce explanations for their predictions. These are, however, constrained to specific neural network architectures or incapable of detecting "non object" parts of the images. Here we focus on general, model-agnostic explanations that can be applied to any classifier or regressor that is appropriate for the domain - even ones that are yet to be proposed.

A common approach to model-agnostic explanation is learning a potentially interpretable model on the predictions of the original model [2, 7, 22]. Having the explanation be a gradient vector [2] captures a similar locality intuition to that of LIME. However, interpreting the coefficients on the gradient is difficult, particularly for confident predictions (where gradient is near zero). Further, these explanations approximate the original model *globally*, thus maintaining local fidelity becomes a significant challenge, as our experiments demonstrate. In contrast, LIME solves the much more feasible task of finding a model that approximates the original model *locally*. The idea of perturbing inputs for explanations has been explored before [24], where the authors focus on learning a specific *contribution* model, as opposed to our general framework. None of these approaches explicitly take cognitive limitations into account, and thus may produce non-interpretable explanations, such as a gradients or linear models with thousands of non-zero weights. The problem becomes worse if the original features are nonsensical to humans (e.g. word embeddings). In contrast, LIME incorporates interpretability both in the optimization and in our notion of *interpretable representation*, such that domain and task specific interpretability criteria can be accommodated.

8. CONCLUSION AND FUTURE WORK

In this paper, we argued that trust is crucial for effective human interaction with machine learning systems, and that explaining individual predictions is important in assessing trust. We proposed LIME, a modular and extensible approach to faithfully explain the predictions of *any* model in an interpretable manner. We also introduced SP-LIME, a method to select representative and non-redundant predictions, providing a global view of the model to users. Our experiments demonstrated that explanations are useful for a variety of models in trust-related tasks in the text and image domains, with both expert and non-expert users: deciding between models, assessing trust, improving untrustworthy models, and getting insights into predictions.

There are a number of avenues of future work that we would like to explore. Although we describe only sparse linear models as explanations, our framework supports the exploration of a variety of explanation families, such as decision trees; it would be interesting to see a comparative study on these with real users. One issue that we do not mention in this work was how to perform the pick step for images, and we would like to address this limitation in the future. The domain and model agnosticism enables us to explore a variety of applications, and we would like to investigate potential uses in speech, video, and medical domains, as well as recommendation systems. Finally, we would like to explore theoretical properties (such as the appropriate number of samples) and computational optimizations (such as using parallelization and GPU processing), in order to provide the accurate, real-time explanations that are critical for any human-in-the-loop machine learning system.

Acknowledgements

We would like to thank Scott Lundberg, Tianqi Chen, and Tyler Johnson for helpful discussions and feedback. This work was supported in part by ONR awards #W911NF-13-1-0246 and #N00014-13-1-0023, and in part by TerraSwarm, one of six centers of STARnet, a Semiconductor Research Corporation program sponsored by MARCO and DARPA.

9. REFERENCES

[1] S. Amershi, M. Chickering, S. M. Drucker, B. Lee, P. Simard, and J. Suh. Modeltracker: Redesigning performance analysis tools for machine learning. In *Human Factors in Computing Systems (CHI)*, 2015.

[2] D. Baehrens, T. Schroeter, S. Harmeling, M. Kawanabe, K. Hansen, and K.-R. Müller. How to explain individual classification decisions. *Journal of Machine Learning Research*, 11, 2010.

[3] A. Bansal, A. Farhadi, and D. Parikh. Towards transparent systems: Semantic characterization of failure modes. In *European Conference on Computer Vision (ECCV)*, 2014.

[4] J. Blitzer, M. Dredze, and F. Pereira. Biographies, bollywood, boom-boxes and blenders: Domain adaptation for sentiment classification. In *Association for Computational Linguistics (ACL)*, 2007.

[5] J. Q. Candela, M. Sugiyama, A. Schwaighofer, and N. D. Lawrence. *Dataset Shift in Machine Learning*. MIT, 2009.

[6] R. Caruana, Y. Lou, J. Gehrke, P. Koch, M. Sturm, and N. Elhadad. Intelligible models for healthcare: Predicting pneumonia risk and hospital 30-day readmission. In *Knowledge Discovery and Data Mining (KDD)*, 2015.

[7] M. W. Craven and J. W. Shavlik. Extracting tree-structured representations of trained networks. *Neural information processing systems (NIPS)*, pages 24–30, 1996.

[8] M. T. Dzindolet, S. A. Peterson, R. A. Pomranky, L. G. Pierce, and H. P. Beck. The role of trust in automation reliance. *Int. J. Hum.-Comput. Stud.*, 58(6), 2003.

[9] B. Efron, T. Hastie, I. Johnstone, and R. Tibshirani. Least angle regression. *Annals of Statistics*, 32:407–499, 2004.

[10] U. Feige. A threshold of ln n for approximating set cover. *J. ACM*, 45(4), July 1998.

[11] A. Groce, T. Kulesza, C. Zhang, S. Shamasunder, M. Burnett, W.-K. Wong, S. Stumpf, S. Das, A. Shinsel, F. Bice, and K. McIntosh. You are the only possible oracle: Effective test selection for end users of interactive machine learning systems. *IEEE Trans. Softw. Eng.*, 40(3), 2014.

[12] J. L. Herlocker, J. A. Konstan, and J. Riedl. Explaining collaborative filtering recommendations. In *Conference on Computer Supported Cooperative Work (CSCW)*, 2000.

[13] A. Karpathy and F. Li. Deep visual-semantic alignments for generating image descriptions. In *Computer Vision and Pattern Recognition (CVPR)*, 2015.

[14] S. Kaufman, S. Rosset, and C. Perlich. Leakage in data mining: Formulation, detection, and avoidance. In *Knowledge Discovery and Data Mining (KDD)*, 2011.

[15] A. Krause and D. Golovin. Submodular function maximization. In *Tractability: Practical Approaches to Hard Problems*. Cambridge University Press, February 2014.

[16] T. Kulesza, M. Burnett, W.-K. Wong, and S. Stumpf. Principles of explanatory debugging to personalize interactive machine learning. In *Intelligent User Interfaces (IUI)*, 2015.

[17] B. Letham, C. Rudin, T. H. McCormick, and D. Madigan. Interpretable classifiers using rules and bayesian analysis: Building a better stroke prediction model. *Annals of Applied Statistics*, 2015.

[18] D. Martens and F. Provost. Explaining data-driven document classifications. *MIS Q.*, 38(1), 2014.

[19] T. Mikolov, I. Sutskever, K. Chen, G. S. Corrado, and J. Dean. Distributed representations of words and phrases and their compositionality. In *Neural Information Processing Systems (NIPS)*. 2013.

[20] K. Patel, N. Bancroft, S. M. Drucker, J. Fogarty, A. J. Ko, and J. Landay. Gestalt: Integrated support for implementation and analysis in machine learning. In *User Interface Software and Technology (UIST)*, 2010.

[21] K. Patel, J. Fogarty, J. A. Landay, and B. Harrison. Investigating statistical machine learning as a tool for software development. In *Human Factors in Computing Systems (CHI)*, 2008.

[22] I. Sanchez, T. Rocktaschel, S. Riedel, and S. Singh. Towards extracting faithful and descriptive representations of latent variable models. In *AAAI Spring Syposium on Knowledge Representation and Reasoning (KRR): Integrating Symbolic and Neural Approaches*, 2015.

[23] D. Sculley, G. Holt, D. Golovin, E. Davydov, T. Phillips, D. Ebner, V. Chaudhary, M. Young, and J.-F. Crespo. Hidden technical debt in machine learning systems. In *Neural Information Processing Systems (NIPS)*. 2015.

[24] E. Strumbelj and I. Kononenko. An efficient explanation of individual classifications using game theory. *Journal of Machine Learning Research*, 11, 2010.

[25] C. Szegedy, W. Liu, Y. Jia, P. Sermanet, S. Reed, D. Anguelov, D. Erhan, V. Vanhoucke, and A. Rabinovich. Going deeper with convolutions. In *Computer Vision and Pattern Recognition (CVPR)*, 2015.

[26] B. Ustun and C. Rudin. Supersparse linear integer models for optimized medical scoring systems. *Machine Learning*, 2015.

[27] F. Wang and C. Rudin. Falling rule lists. In *Artificial Intelligence and Statistics (AISTATS)*, 2015.

[28] K. Xu, J. Ba, R. Kiros, K. Cho, A. Courville, R. Salakhutdinov, R. Zemel, and Y. Bengio. Show, attend and tell: Neural image caption generation with visual attention. In *International Conference on Machine Learning (ICML)*, 2015.

[29] P. Zhang, J. Wang, A. Farhadi, M. Hebert, and D. Parikh. Predicting failures of vision systems. In *Computer Vision and Pattern Recognition (CVPR)*, 2014.

ABRA: Approximating Betweenness Centrality in Static and Dynamic Graphs with Rademacher Averages

Matteo Riondato
Two Sigma Investments, LP
New York, NY, USA
matteo@twosigma.com

Eli Upfal
Dept. of Computer Science – Brown University
Providence, RI, USA
eli@cs.brown.edu

ΑΒΡΑΞΑΣ (ABRAXAS): Gnostic word of mystic meaning

ABSTRACT

We present ABRA, a suite of algorithms to compute and maintain probabilistically-guaranteed, high-quality, approximations of the betweenness centrality of all nodes (or edges) on both static and fully dynamic graphs. Our algorithms use progressive random sampling and their analysis rely on Rademacher averages and pseudodimension, fundamental concepts from statistical learning theory. To our knowledge, this is the first application of these concepts to the field of graph analysis. Our experimental results show that ABRA is much faster than exact methods, and vastly outperforms, in both runtime and number of samples, state-of-the-art algorithms with the same quality guarantees.

Keywords

betweenness; centrality; pseudodimension; Rademacher averages; sampling;

1. INTRODUCTION

Centrality measures are fundamental concepts in graph analysis: they assign to each node or edge in the network a score that quantifies some notion of importance of the node/edge in the network [21]. Betweenness Centrality (BC) is a very popular centrality measure that, informally, defines the importance of a node or edge z in the network as proportional to the fraction of shortest paths in the network that go through z [2, 13] (see Sect. 3 for formal definitions).

Brandes [9] presented an algorithm (denoted BA) to compute the exact BC values for all nodes or edges in a graph $G = (V, E)$ in time $O(|V||E|)$ if the graph is unweighted, or time $O(|V||E| + |V|^2 \log |V|)$ if the graph has positive weights. The cost of BA is excessive on modern networks with millions of nodes and tens of millions of edges. Moreover, having the exact BC values may often not be needed, given the exploratory nature of the task, and a high-quality approximation of the values is usually sufficient, provided it comes with stringent guarantees.

Today's networks are not only large, but also *dynamic*: edges are added and removed continuously. Keeping the BC values up-to-date after edge insertions and removals is a challenging task, and proposed algorithms [15, 17–19] have worst-case time and space complexities not better than from-scratch-recomputation using BA. Maintaining a high-quality approximation up-to-date is more feasible and more *sensible*: there is little added value in keeping track of exact BC values that change continuously.

Contributions. We focus on developing algorithms for approximating the BC of all nodes and edges in static and dynamic graphs. Our contributions are the following.

- We present ABRA (for "Approximating Betweenness with Rademacher Averages"), the first family of algorithms based on *progressive sampling* for approximating the BC of all nodes in static and dynamic graphs, where node and edge insertions and deletions are allowed. The BC approximations computed by ABRA are *probabilistically guaranteed* to be within an user-specified additive error from their exact values. We also present variants with relative error (i.e., within a multiplicative factor ε of the true value) for the top-k nodes with highest BC, and variants that use refined estimators to give better approximations with a slightly larger sample size.
- Our analysis relies on Rademacher averages [28] and pseudodimension [23], fundamental concepts from the field of statistical learning theory [30]. Exploiting known and novel results using these concepts, ABRA computes the approximations without having to keep track of any global property of the graph, in contrast with existing algorithms [4, 6, 24]. ABRA performs only "real work" towards the computation of the approximations, without having to obtain such global properties or update them after modifications of the graph. To the best of our knowledge, ours is the first application of Rademacher averages and pseudodimension to graph analysis problems, and the first to use *progressive* random sampling for BC computation. Using pseudodimension, we derive new analytical results on the sample complexity of the BC computation task, generalizing previous contributions [24], and formulating a conjecture on the connection between pseudodimension and the distribution of shortest path lengths.
- The results of our experimental evaluation on real networks show that ABRA outperforms, in both speed and

KDD '16, August 13–17, 2016, San Francisco, CA, USA

ISBN 978-1-4503-4232-2/16/08...$15.00

DOI: http://dx.doi.org/10.1145/2939672.2939770

number of samples, the state-of-the-art methods offering the same guarantees [24].

Due to space constraints, some details and additional results have been deferred to the extended online version [25].

2. RELATED WORK

The definition of Betweenness Centrality comes from the sociology literature [2, 13], but the study of efficient algorithms to compute it started only when graphs of substantial size became available to the analysts, following the emergence of the Web. The **BA** algorithm by Brandes [9] is currently the asymptotically fastest algorithm for computing the exact BC values for all nodes in the network. A number of works also explored heuristics to improve **BA** [12, 27], but retained the same worst-case time complexity.

The use of random sampling to approximate the BC values in static graphs was proposed independently by Bader et al. [3] and Brandes and Pich [10], and successive works explored the tradeoff space of sampling-based algorithms [4–6, 24]. We focus here on related works that offer approximation guarantees similar to ours. For an in-depth discussion of previous contributions approximating BC on static graphs, we refer the reader to [24, Sect. 2].

Riondato and Kornaropoulos [24] present algorithms that employ the Vapnik-Chervonenkis (VC) dimension [30] to compute what is currently the tightest upper bound on the sample size sufficient to obtain guaranteed approximations of the BC of all nodes in a static graph. Their algorithms offer the same guarantees as ours but, to compute the sample size, they need to compute an upper bound on a characteristic quantity of the graph (the vertex diameter, namely the maximum number of nodes on any shortest path). Thanks to our use of Rademacher averages in a progressive random sampling setting, **ABRA** does not need to compute any characteristic quantity of the graph, and instead uses an efficient-to-evaluate stopping condition to determine when the approximated BC values are close to the exact ones. This allows **ABRA** to use smaller samples and be much faster than the algorithms by Riondato and Kornaropoulos [24].

A number of works [15, 17–19] focused on computing the *exact* BC for all nodes in a dynamic graph, taking into consideration different update models. None of these algorithm is provably asymptotically faster than a complete computation from scratch using Brandes' algorithm [9] and they all require significant amount of space (more details about these works can be found in [4, Sect. 2]). In contrast, Bergamini and Meyerhenke [4, 5] built on the work by Riondato and Kornaropoulos [24] to derive an algorithm for maintaining high-quality approximations of the BC of all nodes when the graph is dynamic and both additions and deletions of edges are allowed. Due to the use of the algorithm by Riondato and Kornaropoulos [24] as a building block, the algorithm must keep track of the vertex diameter after an update to the graph. Our algorithm for dynamic graphs, instead, does not need this piece of information, and therefore can spend more time in computing the approximations, rather than in keeping track of global properties of the graph. Moreover, our algorithm can handle directed graphs, which is not the case for the algorithms by Bergamini and Meyerhenke [4, 5].

Hayashi et al. [16] recently proposed a data structure called *Hypergraph Sketch* to maintain the shortest path DAGs between pairs of nodes following updates to the graph. Their algorithm uses random sampling and this novel data structure allows them to maintain a high-quality, probabilistically guaranteed approximation of the BC of all nodes in a dynamic graph. Their guarantees come from an application of the simple uniform deviation bounds (i.e., the union bound) to determine the sample size, as previously done by Bader et al. [3] and Brandes and Pich [10]. As a result, the resulting sample size is excessively large, as it depends on the *number of nodes in the graph.* Our improved analysis using the Rademacher averages allows us to develop an algorithm that uses the Hypergraph Sketch with a much smaller number of samples, and is therefore faster.

Progressive random sampling with Rademacher Averages has been used by Elomaa and Kääriäinen [11] and Riondato and Upfal [26] in completely different settings.

3. PRELIMINARIES

We now introduce the formal definitions and basic results that we use throughout the paper.

3.1 Graphs and Betweenness Centrality

Let $G = (V, E)$ be a graph. G may be directed or undirected and may have non-negative weights on the edges. For any ordered pair (u, v) of different nodes $u \neq v$, let $\mathcal{S}_{uv}$ be the set of *Shortest Paths* (SPs) from u to v, and let $\sigma_{uv} = |\mathcal{S}_{uv}|$. Given a path p between two nodes $u, v \in V$, a node $w \in V$ is *internal to p* iff $w \neq u$, $w \neq u$, and p goes through w. We denote as $\sigma_{uv}(w)$ the number of SPs from u to v that w is internal to.

Definition 1 (Betweenness Centrality (BC) [2, 13]). *Given a graph* $G = (V, E)$, *the* Betweenness Centrality (BC) of a node $w \in V$ *is defined as*

$$\mathsf{b}(w) = \frac{1}{|V|(|V|-1)} \sum_{\substack{(u,v)\in V\times V\\ u\neq v}} \frac{\sigma_{uv}(w)}{\sigma_{uv}} \quad (\in [0,1]) \ .$$

Many variants of BC have been proposed in the literature, including one for edges [21]. Our results can be extended to these variants, following the reduction by Riondato and Kornaropoulos [24, Sect. 6], but we do not discuss them here due to space constraints.

In this work we focus on computing an (ε, δ)*-approximation* of the collection $B = \{\mathsf{b}(w), w \in V\}$.

Definition 2 ((ε, δ)-approximation). *Given* $\varepsilon, \delta \in (0, 1)$, *an* (ε, δ)-approximation to B *is a collection* $\tilde{B} = \{\tilde{\mathsf{b}}(w), w \in V\}$ *such that*

$$\Pr(\forall w \in v, |\tilde{\mathsf{b}}(w) - \mathsf{b}(w)| \leq \varepsilon) \geq 1 - \delta \ .$$

In Sect. 4.2 we discuss a relative (i.e., multiplicative) error variant for the top-k nodes with highest BC.

3.2 Rademacher Averages

Rademacher Averages are fundamental concepts to study the rate of convergence of a set of sample averages to their expectations. They are at the core of statistical learning theory [30] but their usefulness extends way beyond the learning framework [26]. We present here only the definitions and results that we use in our work and we refer the readers to, e.g., the book by Shalev-Shwartz and Ben-David [28] for in-depth presentation and discussion.

While the Rademacher complexity can be defined on an arbitrary measure space, we restrict our discussion here to a sample space that consists of a finite domain $\mathcal{D}$ and a uniform distribution over that domain. Let $\mathcal{F}$ be a family of functions from $\mathcal{D}$ to $[0,1]$, and let $\mathcal{S} = \{c_1, \ldots, c_\ell\}$ be a sample of ℓ elements from $\mathcal{D}$, sampled uniformly and independently at random. For each $f \in \mathcal{F}$, the *true average* and the *sample average* of f on a sample $\mathcal{S}$ are, respectively,

$$\mathsf{m}_{\mathcal{D}}(f) = \frac{1}{|\mathcal{D}|}\sum_{c\in\mathcal{D}}^{\ell} f(c) \quad\text{and}\quad \mathsf{m}_{\mathcal{S}}(f) = \frac{1}{\ell}\sum_{i=1}^{\ell} f(c_i) \ . \quad (1)$$

Given $\mathcal{S}$, we are interested in bounding the *maximum deviation of* $\mathsf{m}_{\mathcal{S}}(f)$ *from* $\mathsf{m}_{\mathcal{D}}(f)$ *among all* $f \in \mathcal{F}$, i.e.,

$$\sup_{f\in\mathcal{F}} |\mathsf{m}_{\mathcal{S}}(f) - \mathsf{m}_{\mathcal{D}}(f)| \ . \quad (2)$$

For $1 \le i \le \ell$, let σ_i be a Rademacher r.v., i.e., a r.v. that takes value 1 with probability 1/2 and -1 with probability 1/2. The r.v.'s σ_i are independent. Consider the quantity

$$\mathsf{R}(\mathcal{F},\mathcal{S}) = \mathbb{E}_\sigma\left[\sup_{f\in\mathcal{F}} \frac{1}{\ell}\sum_{i=1}^{\ell}\sigma_i f(c_i)\right] , \quad (3)$$

where the expectation is taken w.r.t. the Rademacher r.v.'s, i.e., conditionally on $\mathcal{S}$. The quantity $\mathsf{R}(\mathcal{F},\mathcal{S})$ is known as the *(conditional) Rademacher average of* $\mathcal{F}$ *on* $\mathcal{S}$. The following is a key result in statistical learning theory, connecting $\mathsf{R}(\mathcal{F},\mathcal{S})$ to the maximum deviation (2).

THEOREM 1 (THM. 26.5 [28]). *Let $\eta \in (0,1)$ and let $\mathcal{S}$ be a collection of ℓ elements of $\mathcal{D}$ sampled independently and uniformly at random. Then, with probability at least $1-\eta$,*

$$\sup_{f\in\mathcal{F}} |\mathsf{m}_{\mathcal{S}}(f) - \mathsf{m}_{\mathcal{D}}(f)| \le 2\mathsf{R}(\mathcal{F},\mathcal{S}) + \sqrt{\frac{2\ln(2/\eta)}{\ell}} \ . \quad (4)$$

Thm. 1 is how the result is classically presented, but better although more complex bounds than (4) are available [22].

THEOREM 2 (THM. 3.11 [22]). *Let $\eta \in (0,1)$ and let $\mathcal{S}$ be a collection of ℓ elements of $\mathcal{D}$ sampled independently and uniformly at random. Let*

$$\alpha = \frac{\ln\frac{2}{\eta}}{\ln\frac{2}{\eta} + \sqrt{\left(2\ell\mathsf{R}(\mathcal{F},\mathcal{S}) + \ln\frac{2}{\eta}\right)\ln\frac{2}{\eta}}}, \quad (5)$$

then, with probability at least $1-\eta$,

$$\sup_{f\in\mathcal{F}} |\mathsf{m}_{\mathcal{S}}(f) - \mathsf{m}_{\mathcal{D}}(f)| \le \frac{\mathsf{R}(\mathcal{F},\mathcal{S})}{1-\alpha} + \frac{\ln\frac{2}{\eta}}{2\ell\alpha(1-\alpha)} + \sqrt{\frac{\ln\frac{2}{\eta}}{2\ell}} \ . \quad (6)$$

Computing, or even estimating, the expectation in (3) w.r.t. the Rademacher r.v.'s is not straightforward and can be computationally expensive, requiring a time-consuming Monte Carlo simulation [7]. For this reason, *upper bounds to the Rademacher average* are usually employed in (4) and (6) in place of $\mathsf{R}(\mathcal{F},\mathcal{S})$. A powerful and efficient-to-compute bound is presented in Thm. 3. Given $\mathcal{S}$, consider, for each $f \in \mathcal{F}$, the vector $\mathbf{v}_{f,\mathcal{S}} = (f(c_1), \ldots, f(c_\ell))$, and let $\mathcal{V}_\mathcal{S} = \{\mathbf{v}_f, f \in \mathcal{F}\}$ be the *set* of such vectors ($|\mathcal{V}_\mathcal{S}| \le |\mathcal{F}|$).

THEOREM 3 ([26]). *Let $\mathsf{w} : \mathbb{R}^+ \to \mathbb{R}^+$ be the function*

$$\mathsf{w}(s) = \frac{1}{s}\ln\sum_{\mathbf{v}\in\mathcal{V}_\mathcal{S}} \exp(s^2\|\mathbf{v}\|^2/(2\ell^2)), \quad (7)$$

where $\|\cdot\|$ denotes the Euclidean norm. Then

$$\mathsf{R}(\mathcal{F},\mathcal{S}) \le \min_{s\in\mathbb{R}^+} \mathsf{w}(s) \ . \quad (8)$$

The function w is convex, continuous in $\mathbb{R}^+$, and has first and second derivatives w.r.t. s everywhere in its domain, so it is possible to minimize it efficiently using standard convex optimization methods [8]. In future work, we plan to explore how to obtain a tighter bound than the one presented in Thm. 3 using recent results by Anguita et al. [1].

4. STATIC GRAPH BC APPROXIMATION

We now present and analyze ABRA-s, our *progressive sampling algorithm* for computing an (ε,δ)-approximation to the collection of exact BC values in a *static* graph. Many of the details and properties of ABRA-s are shared with the other ABRA algorithms we present.

Progressive Sampling. Progressive sampling algorithms are intrinsically *iterative*. At a high level, they work as follows. At iteration i, the algorithm extracts an approximation of the values of interest (in our case, of the BC of all nodes) from a collection $\mathcal{S}_i$ of $S_i = |\mathcal{S}_i|$ random samples from a suitable domain $\mathcal{D}$ (in our case, the samples are pairs of different nodes). Then, the algorithm checks a specific *stopping condition* that uses information obtained from the sample $\mathcal{S}_i$ and from the computed approximation. If the stopping condition is satisfied, then the approximation has, with the required probability, the desired quality (in our case, it is an (ε,δ)-approximation). The approximation is then returned in output and the algorithm terminates. If the stopping condition is not satisfied, ABRA-s builds a collection $\mathcal{S}_{i+1}$ by adding random samples to $\mathcal{S}_i$ until it has size S_{i+1}. Then it computes a new approximation from the so-created collection $\mathcal{S}_{i+1}$, and checks the stopping condition again and so on.

There are two main challenges for the algorithm designer: deriving a "good" stopping condition and determining good choices for the initial sample size S_1 and the subsequent sample sizes S_{i+1}, $i \ge 1$.

Ideally, a good stopping condition is such that:

1. when satisfied, guarantees that the computed approximation has the desired quality properties (in our case, it is an (ε,δ)-approximation); and
2. can be evaluated efficiently; and
3. is tight, in the sense that is satisfied at small sample sizes.

The stopping condition for ABRA-s is based on Thm. 2 and Thm. 3, and has all the above desirable properties.

The second challenge is determining the *sample schedule* $(S_i)_{i>0}$. Any monotonically increasing sequence of positive numbers can act as sample schedule, but the goal in designing a good sample schedule is to minimize the number of iterations that are needed before the stopping condition is satisfied, while minimizing the sample size S_i at the iteration i at which this happens. The sample schedule may be fixed in advance, but an *adaptive approach* that ties the sample schedule to the stopping condition can give better results, as the sample size S_{i+1} for iteration $i+1$ can be computed using information obtained in (or up-to) iteration i. ABRA uses such an adaptive approach (see Sect. 4.1.1.)

4.1 Algorithm Description and Analysis

ABRA-s takes as input a graph $G = (V,E)$, which may be directed or undirected, and may have non-negative weights on the edges, and two parameters $\varepsilon, \delta \in (0,1)$. It outputs a collection $\widetilde{B} = \{\widetilde{\mathsf{b}}(w), w \in V\}$ that is an (ε,δ)-approximation of the betweenness centralities $B = \{\mathsf{b}(w), w \in V\}$. The algorithm samples from $\mathcal{D} = V \times V, u \neq v\}$.

For each node $w \in V$, let $f_w : \mathcal{D} \to [0,1]$ be the function

$$f_w(u,v) = \frac{\sigma_{uv}(w)}{\sigma_{uv}}, \tag{9}$$

i.e., $f_w(u,v)$ is the fraction of shortest paths (SPs) from u to v that go through w. Let $\mathcal{F} = \{f_w, w \in V\}$ be the set of these functions. Given this definition, we have that

$$\begin{aligned}\mathsf{m}_{\mathcal{D}}(f_w) &= \frac{1}{|\mathcal{D}|}\sum_{(u,v)\in\mathcal{D}} f_w(u,v)\\ &= \frac{1}{|V|(|V|-1)}\sum_{\substack{(u,v)\in V\times V\\ u\neq v}} \frac{\sigma_{uv}(w)}{\sigma_{uv}}\\ &= \mathsf{b}(w) \ .\end{aligned}$$

Let now $\mathcal{S} = \{(u_i,v_i), 1 \leq i \leq \ell\}$ be a collection of ℓ pairs (u,v) from $\mathcal{D}$. For the sake of clarity, we define

$$\widetilde{\mathsf{b}}(w) = \mathsf{m}_{\mathcal{S}}(f_w) = \frac{1}{\ell}\sum_{i=1}^{\ell} f_w((u_i,v_i)) \ .$$

For each $w \in V$ consider the vector

$$\mathbf{v}_w = (f_w(u_1,v_1),\ldots,f_w(u_\ell,v_\ell)) \ .$$

It is easy to see that $\widetilde{\mathsf{b}}(w) = \|\mathbf{v}_w\|_1/\ell$. Let now $\mathcal{V}_{\mathcal{S}}$ be the *set* of these vectors:

$$\mathcal{V}_{\mathcal{S}} = \{\mathbf{v}_w, w \in V\} \quad (|\mathcal{V}_{\mathcal{S}}| \leq |V|) \ .$$

If we have complete knowledge of this set of vectors, then we can compute the quantity

$$\omega^* = \min_{s\in\mathbb{R}^+} \frac{1}{s}\ln\sum_{\mathbf{v}\in\mathcal{V}_{\mathcal{S}}} \exp\left(s^2\|\mathbf{v}\|^2/(2\ell^2)\right),$$

then use ω^* in (5) in place of $\mathsf{R}(\mathcal{F},\mathcal{S})$ to obtain α, and combine (6), (7), and (8) to obtain

$$\Delta_{\mathcal{S}} = \frac{\omega^*}{1-\alpha} + \frac{\ln\frac{2}{\eta}}{2\ell\alpha(1-\alpha)} + \sqrt{\frac{\ln\frac{2}{\eta}}{2\ell}},$$

and finally check whether $\Delta_{\mathcal{S}} \leq \varepsilon$. This is ABRA-s's stopping condition. When it holds, we can just return the collection $\widetilde{B} = \{\widetilde{\mathsf{b}}(w) = \|\mathbf{v}_w\|_1/\ell, w \in V\}$ since, from the definition of $\Delta_{\mathcal{S}}$ and Thms. 2 and 3, we have that $\widetilde{B}$ is an (ε,δ)-approximation to the exact betweenness values.

ABRA-s works as follows. Suppose for now that we fix a priori a monotonically increasing sequence $(S_i)_{i>0}$ of sample sizes (we show in Sect. 4.1.1 how to compute the sample schedule adaptively on the fly). The algorithm builds a collection $\mathcal{S}$ by sampling pairs (u,v) independently and uniformly at random from $\mathcal{D}$ until $\mathcal{S}$ has size S_1. After each pair of nodes has been sampled, ABRA-s performs an $s-t$ SP computation from u to v and then backtracks from v to u along the SPs just computed, to keep track of the set $\mathcal{V}_{\mathcal{S}}$ of vectors (details given below). For clarity of presentation, let $\mathcal{S}_1$ denote $\mathcal{S}$ when it has size exactly S_1, and analogously for $\mathcal{S}_i$ and S_i, $i > 1$. Once $\mathcal{S}_i$ has been built, ABRA-s computes $\Delta_{\mathcal{S}_i}$ using $\eta = \delta/2^i$ and checks whether $\Delta_{\mathcal{S}_i}$ is at most ε. If so, then it returns $\widetilde{B}$. Otherwise, ABRA-s iterates and continues adding samples from $\mathcal{D}$ to $\mathcal{S}$ until it has size S_2, and so on until $\Delta_{\mathcal{S}_i} \leq \varepsilon$ holds. The pseudocode for ABRA-s is presented in Alg. 1, including the steps to update $\mathcal{V}_{\mathcal{S}}$ and to adaptively choose the sample schedule (Sect. 4.1.1). We now prove the correctness of the algorithm.

Algorithm 1: ABRA-s: absolute error approximation of BC on static graphs

input : Graph $G = (V,E)$, accuracy parameter $\varepsilon \in (0,1)$, confidence parameter $\delta \in (0,1)$
output: Set $\widetilde{B}$ of BC approximations for all nodes in V

$\mathcal{D} \leftarrow \{(u,v) \in V \times V, u \neq v\}$
$S_0 \leftarrow 0$, $S_1 \leftarrow \frac{(1+8\varepsilon+\sqrt{1+16\varepsilon})\ln(2/\delta)}{4\varepsilon^2}$
$\mathbf{0} = (0)$
$\mathcal{V} = \{\mathbf{0}\}$
foreach $w \in V$ **do** $M[w] = \mathbf{0}$
$\mathsf{c}_{\mathbf{0}} \leftarrow |V|$
$i \leftarrow 1$, $j \leftarrow 1$
while *True* **do**
  for $\ell \leftarrow 1$ **to** $S_i - S_{i-1}$ **do**
    $(u,v) \leftarrow$ `uniform_random_sample(`$\mathcal{D}$`)`
    `compute_SPs(`u,v`)  //Truncated SP computation`
    if *reached* v **then**
      foreach $z \in \mathsf{P}_u[v]$ **do** $\sigma_{zv} \leftarrow 1$
      foreach *node* w *on a SP from* u *to* v*, in reverse order by* $\mathsf{d}(u,w)$ **do**
        $\sigma_{uv}(w) \leftarrow \sigma_{uw}\sigma_{wv}$
        $\mathbf{v} \leftarrow M[w]$
        $\mathbf{v}' \leftarrow \mathbf{v} \cup \{(j, \sigma_{uv}(w)\}$
        if $\mathbf{v}' \notin \mathcal{V}$ **then**
          $\mathsf{c}_{\mathbf{v}'} \leftarrow 1$
          $\mathcal{V} \leftarrow \mathcal{V} \cup \{\mathbf{v}'\}$
        else $\mathsf{c}_{\mathbf{v}'} \leftarrow \mathsf{c}_{\mathbf{v}'} + 1$
        $M[w] \leftarrow \mathbf{v}'$
        if $\mathsf{c}_{\mathbf{v}} > 1$ **then** $\mathsf{c}_{\mathbf{v}} \leftarrow \mathsf{c}_{\mathbf{v}} - 1$
        else $\mathcal{V} \leftarrow \mathcal{V} \setminus \{\mathbf{v}\}$
        foreach $z \in \mathsf{P}_u[w]$ **do** $\sigma_{zv} \leftarrow \sigma_{zv} + \sigma_{wv}$
      end
    end
    $j \leftarrow j + 1$
  end
  $\omega_i^* \leftarrow \min_{s\in\mathbb{R}^+} \frac{1}{s}\ln\sum_{\mathbf{v}\in\mathcal{V}_{\mathcal{S}}} \exp\left(s^2\|\mathbf{v}\|^2/(2S_i^2)\right)$
  $\alpha_i \leftarrow \frac{(i+1)\ln\frac{2}{\delta}}{(i+1)\ln\frac{2}{\delta} + \sqrt{(2S_i\omega_i^* + (i+1)\ln\frac{2}{\delta})(i+1)\ln\frac{2}{\delta}}}$
  $\Delta_{\mathcal{S}_i} \leftarrow \frac{\omega_i^*}{1-\alpha_i} + \frac{(i+1)\ln\frac{2}{\delta}}{2S_i\alpha_i(1-\alpha_i)} + \sqrt{(i+1)\frac{\ln\frac{2}{\delta}}{2S_i}}$
  if $\Delta_{\mathcal{S}_i} \leq \varepsilon$ **then break**
  else
    $S_{i+1} \leftarrow$ `nextSampleSize()`
    $i \leftarrow i + 1$
  end
end
return $\widetilde{B} \leftarrow \{\widetilde{\mathsf{b}}(w) \leftarrow \|M[w]\|_1/S_i, w \in V\}$

THEOREM 4 (CORRECTNESS). *The collection $\widetilde{B}$ returned by ABRA-s is a (ε,δ)-approximation.*

PROOF. The claim follows from the definitions of $\mathcal{S}$, $\mathcal{V}_{\mathcal{S}}$, $\mathcal{F}$, f_w for $w \in V$, $\widetilde{\mathsf{b}}(w)$, $\Delta_{\mathcal{S}_i}$, Thm. 3, and from the fact that, at each iteration i, Thm. 2 holds with probability $\delta/2^i$. □

Computing and maintaining the set $\mathcal{V}_{\mathcal{S}}$. We now discuss in details how ABRA-s efficiently maintain the set $\mathcal{V}_{\mathcal{S}}$ of vectors, which is used to compute the value $\Delta_{\mathcal{S}}$ and the values $\widetilde{\mathsf{b}}(w) = \|\mathbf{v}_w\|_1/|\mathcal{S}|$ in $\widetilde{B}$. In addition to $\mathcal{V}_{\mathcal{S}}$, ABRA-s also maintains a map M from V to $\mathcal{V}_{\mathcal{S}}$ (i.e., $M[w]$ is a vector $\mathbf{v}_w \in \mathcal{V}_{\mathcal{S}}$), and a counter $\mathsf{c}_{\mathbf{v}}$ for each $\mathbf{v} \in \mathcal{V}_{\mathcal{S}}$, denoting how many nodes $w \in V$ have $M[w] = \mathbf{v}$.

At the beginning of the execution of the algorithm, we have $\mathcal{S} = \emptyset$ and also $\mathcal{V}_{\mathcal{S}} = \emptyset$. Nevertheless, ABRA-s initializes $\mathcal{V}_{\mathcal{S}}$ to contain one special empty vector $\mathbf{0}$, with no components, and M so that $M[w] = \mathbf{0}$ for all $w \in V$, and $\mathsf{c}_{\mathbf{0}} = |V|$ (lines 3 and following in Alg. 1).

After having sampled a pair (u, v) from $\mathcal{D}$, ABRA-s updates $\mathcal{V}_{\mathcal{S}}$, M and the counters as follows. First, it performs (line 11) a $s-t$ SP computation from u to v using any SP algorithm (e.g., BFS or Dijkstra) modified, as discussed by Brandes [9, Lemma 3], to keep track, for each node w encountered during the computation, of the SP distance $\mathsf{d}(u, w)$ from u to w, of the number σ_{uw} of SPs from u to w, and of the set $\mathsf{P}_u(w)$ of (immediate) predecessors of w along the SPs from u.[1] Once v has been reached (and only if it has been reached), the algorithm starts backtracking from v towards u along the SPs it just computed (line 14). During this backtracking, the algorithm visits the nodes along the SPs in inverse order of SP distance from u, ties broken arbitrarily. For each visited node w different from u and v, ABRA-s computes the value $f_w(u, v) = \sigma_{uv}(w)$ of SPs from u to v that go through w, which is obtained as

$$\sigma_{uv}(w) = \sigma_{uw} \times \sum_{z \,:\, w \in \mathsf{P}_u(z)} \sigma_{zv}$$

where the value σ_{uw} is obtained during the $s-t$ SP computation, and the values σ_{zw} are computed recursively during the backtracking (line 25) [9]. After computing $\sigma_{uv}(w)$, the algorithm takes the vector $\mathbf{v} \in \mathcal{V}_{\mathcal{S}}$ such that $M[w] = \mathbf{v}$ and creates a new vector $\mathbf{v}'$ by appending $\sigma_{uv}(w)$ to the end of $\mathbf{v}$.[2] Then it adds $\mathbf{v}'$ to the *set* $\mathcal{V}_{\mathcal{S}}$, updates $M[w]$ to $\mathbf{v}'$, and increments the counter $\mathsf{c}_{\mathbf{v}'}$ by one (lines 16 to 22). Finally, the algorithm decrements the counter $\mathsf{c}_{\mathbf{v}}$ by one, and if $\mathsf{c}_{\mathbf{v}}$ becomes equal to zero, ABRA-s removes $\mathbf{v}$ from $\mathcal{V}_{\mathcal{S}}$ (line 24). At this point, the algorithm moves to analyzing another node w' with distance from u less or equal to the distance of w from u. It is easy to see that when the backtracking reaches u, the set $\mathcal{V}_{\mathcal{S}}$, the map M, and the counters, have been correctly updated.

We remark that to compute $\Delta_{\mathcal{S}_i}$ and $\widetilde{B}$ and to keep the map M up to date, ABRA-s does not actually need to store the vectors in $\mathcal{V}_{\mathcal{S}}$ (even in sparse form), but it is sufficient to maintain their ℓ_1- and Euclidean norms, which require much less space.

4.1.1 Computing the sample schedule

We now discuss how to compute the initial sample size S_1 at the beginning of ABRA-s (line 2 of Alg. 1) and the sample size S_{i+1} at the end of iteration i of the main loop (line 35). We remark that any sample schedule $(S_i)_{i>0}$ can be used, and our method is an heuristic that nevertheless exploits all available information at the end of each iteration to the most possible extent, with the goal of increasing the chances that the stopping condition is satisfied at the next iteration.

As initial sample size S_1 we choose

$$S_1 \geq \frac{(1 + 8\varepsilon + \sqrt{1 + 16\varepsilon}) \ln(4/\delta)}{4\varepsilon^2} \quad . \tag{10}$$

To understand the intuition behind this choice, recall (6), and consider that, at the beginning of the algorithm, we obviously have no information about $\mathsf{R}(\mathcal{F}, \mathcal{S}_1)$, except that it is *non negative*. Consequently we also cannot compute α as in (5) using $\eta = \delta/2$, but we can easily see that $\alpha \in [0, 1/2]$. From the fact that $\mathsf{R}(\mathcal{F}, \mathcal{S}) \geq 0$, we have that, for the r.h.s. of (6) to be at most ε (i.e., for the stopping condition to be satisfied after the first iteration of the algorithm), it is necessary that

$$\frac{\ln \frac{4}{\delta}}{2S_1\alpha(1-\alpha)} + \sqrt{\frac{\ln \frac{4}{\delta}}{2S_1}} \leq \varepsilon \ .$$

Then, using the fact that the above expression decreases as α increases, we use $\alpha = 1/2$, i.e., its maximum attainable value, to obtain the following inequality, where S_1 acts as the unknown:

$$\frac{2\ln(4/\delta)}{S_1} + \sqrt{\frac{\ln(4/\delta)}{2S_1}} \leq \varepsilon \ .$$

Solving for S_1 under the domain constraints $S_1 \geq 1$, $\delta \in (0, 1)$, and $\varepsilon \in (0, 1)$ gives the unique solution in (10).

Computing the next sample size S_{i+1} at the end of iteration i (in the pseudocode in Alg. 1, this is done by calling `nextSampleSize()` on line 35) is slightly more involved. The intuition is to assume that ω_i^*, which is an upper bound on $\mathsf{R}(\mathcal{F}, \mathcal{S}_i)$, is also an upper bound on $\mathsf{R}(\mathcal{F}, \mathcal{S}_{i+1})$, whatever $\mathcal{S}_{i+1}$ will be, and whatever size it may have. At this point, we can ask what is the minimum size $S_{i+1} = |\mathcal{S}_{i+1}|$ for which $\Delta_{\mathcal{S}_{i+1}}$ would be at most ε, under the assumption that $\mathsf{R}(\mathcal{F}, \mathcal{S}_{i+1}) \leq \omega_i^*$. More formally, we want to solve the inequality

$$\left(1 + \frac{(i+2)\ln\frac{2}{\delta}}{\sqrt{(2S_{i+1}\omega_i^* + (i+2)\ln\frac{2}{\delta})(i+2)\ln\frac{2}{\delta}}}\right) \times \left(\omega_i^* + \frac{(i+2)\ln\frac{2}{\delta} + \sqrt{(2S_{i+1}\omega_i^* + (i+2)\ln\frac{2}{\delta})(i+2)\ln\frac{2}{\delta}}}{2S_{i+1}}\right) + \sqrt{\frac{(i+2)\ln\frac{2}{\delta}}{2S_{i+1}}} \leq \varepsilon \tag{11}$$

where S_{i+1} acts as the unknown. The l.h.s. of this inequality is obtained by plugging (5) into (6) and using ω_i^* in place of $\mathsf{R}(\mathcal{F}, \mathcal{S})$, S_{i+1} in place of ℓ, $\delta/2^{i+1}$ in place of η, and slightly reorganize the terms for readability. Finding the solution to the above inequality requires computing the roots of the cubic equation (in x)

$$-8\left((i+2)\ln\frac{2}{\delta}\right)^3 + \left((i+2)\ln\frac{2}{\delta}\right)^2(-16\omega_i^* + (1+4\varepsilon)^2)x - 4\left((i+2)\ln\frac{2}{\delta}\right)(\omega_i^* - \varepsilon)^2(1+4\varepsilon)x^2 + 4(b-f)^4x^3 = 0 \ . \tag{12}$$

One can verify that the roots of this equation are all reals. The roots are presented in Table 1. The solution to inequality (11) is that S_{i+1} should be larger than one of these roots,

[1] Storing the set of immediate predecessors is not necessary. By not storing it, we can reduce the space complexity from $O(|E|)$ to $O(|V|)$, at the expense of some additional computation at runtime.

[2] ABRA-s uses a sparse representation for the vectors $\mathbf{v} \in \mathcal{V}_{\mathcal{S}}$, storing only the non-zero components of each $\mathbf{v}$ as pairs (j, g), where j is the component index and g is the value of that component.

but which of the roots it should be larger than depends on the values of ω_i^*, δ, and ε. In practice, we compute each of the roots and then choose the smallest positive one such that, when S_{i+1} equals to this root, then (11) is satisfied.

The assumption $\mathsf{R}(\mathcal{F}, \mathcal{S}_{i+1}) \le \omega_i^*$, which is not guaranteed to be true, is what makes our procedure for selecting the next sample size an *heuristics*. Nevertheless, using information available at the current iteration to compute the sample size for the next iteration is more sensible than having a fixed sample schedule, as it tunes the growth of the sample size to the quality of the current sample. Moreover, it removes from the user the burden of choosing a sample schedule, effectively eliminating one parameter of the algorithm.

4.2 Relative-error Top-k Approximation

In practical applications it is usually necessary (and sufficient) to identify the nodes with highest BC, as they act, in some sense, as the "primary information gateways" of the network. In this section we present a variant ABRA-k of ABRA-s to compute a high-quality approximation of the set $\mathsf{TOP}(k, G)$ of the top-k nodes with highest BC in a graph G. The approximation $\widetilde{\mathsf{b}}(w)$ returned by ABRA-k for a node w is within a *multiplicative* factor ε from its exact value $\mathsf{b}(w)$, rather than an additive factor ε as in ABRA-s. This higher accuracy has a cost in terms of the number of samples needed to compute the approximations.

Formally, assume to order the nodes in the graph in decreasing order by BC, ties broken arbitrarily, and let b_k be the BC of the k-th node in this ordering. Then the set $\mathsf{TOP}(k, G)$ is defined as the set of nodes with BC at least b_k, and can contain more than k nodes:

$$\mathsf{TOP}(k, G) = \{(w, \mathsf{b}(w) \ : \ v \in V \text{ and } \mathsf{b}(w) \ge b_k\} \ .$$

The algorithm ABRA-k follows the same approach as the algorithm for the same task by Riondato and Kornaropoulos [24, Sect. 5.2] and works in two phases. Let δ_1 and δ_2 be such that $(1-\delta_1)(1-\delta_2) \ge (1-\delta)$. In the first phase, we run ABRA-s with parameters ε and δ_1. Let ℓ' be the k-th highest value $\widetilde{\mathsf{b}}(w)$ returned by ABRA-s, ties broken arbitrarily, and let $\tilde{b}' = \ell' - \varepsilon$.

In the second phase, we use a variant ABRA-r of ABRA-s with a modified stopping condition based on relative-error versions of Thms. 1 and 3 (Thms. 11 and 12 from Appendix D of the extended online version [25]) , which take ε, δ_2, and $\lambda = \tilde{b}'$ as parameters. The parameter λ plays a role in the stopping condition. Indeed, ABRA-r is the same as ABRA-s, with the only crucial difference in the definition of the quantity $\Delta_{\mathcal{S}_i}$, which is now:

$$\Delta_{\mathcal{S}_i} = 2 \min_{s \in \mathbb{R}^+} \frac{1}{s} \ln \sum_{\mathbf{v} \in \mathcal{V}} \exp\left(\frac{s^2 \|\mathbf{v}\|^2}{\lambda 2 S_i^2}\right) + \frac{3}{\lambda}\sqrt{i\frac{\ln(4/\delta)}{2S_i}} \ . \tag{13}$$

THEOREM 5. *Let $\widetilde{B} = \{\widetilde{\mathsf{b}}(w), w \in V\}$ be the output of ABRA-r. Then $\widetilde{B}$ is such that*

$$\Pr\left(\exists w \in V \ : \ \frac{|\widetilde{\mathsf{b}}(v) - \mathsf{b}(v)|}{\max\{\lambda, \mathsf{b}(v)\}} > \varepsilon\right) < \delta \ .$$

The proof follows the same steps as the proof for Thm. 4, using the above definition of $\Delta_{\mathcal{S}_i}$ and applying Thms. 11 and 12 from Appendix D of the extended online version [25] instead of Thms. 2 and 3.

Let ℓ'' be the kth highest value $\widetilde{\mathsf{b}}(w)$ returned by ABRA-r (ties broken arbitrarily) and let $\tilde{b}'' = \ell''/(1+\varepsilon)$. ABRA-k then returns the set

$$\widetilde{\mathsf{TOP}}(k, G) = \{(w, \widetilde{\mathsf{b}}(w)) \ : \ w \in V \text{ and } \widetilde{\mathsf{b}}(w) \ge \tilde{b}''\} \ .$$

We have the following result showing the properties of the collection $\widetilde{\mathsf{TOP}}(k, G)$.

THEOREM 6. *With probability at least $1-\delta$, the set $\widetilde{\mathsf{TOP}}(k, G)$ is such that:*

1. *for any pair $(v, \mathsf{b}(v)) \in \mathsf{TOP}(k, G)$, there is one pair $(v, \widetilde{\mathsf{b}}(v)) \in \widetilde{\mathsf{TOP}}(k, G)$ (i.e., we return a superset of the top-k nodes with highest betweenness) and this pair is such that $|\widetilde{\mathsf{b}}(w) - \mathsf{b}(w)| \le \varepsilon \mathsf{b}(w)$;*
2. *for any pair $(w, \widetilde{\mathsf{b}}(w)) \in \widetilde{\mathsf{TOP}}(k, G)$ such that $(w, \mathsf{b}(w)) \notin \mathsf{TOP}(k, G)$ (i.e., any false positive) we have that $\widetilde{\mathsf{b}}(w) \le (1+\varepsilon)b_k$ (i.e., the false positives, if any, are among the nodes returned by ABRA-k with lower BC estimation).*

The proof and the pseudocode for ABRA-k can be found in Appendix A of the extended online version [25].

4.3 Special Cases

In this section we consider some special restricted settings that make computing an high-quality approximation of the BC of all nodes easier. One example of such restricted settings is when the graph is *undirected* and every pair of distinct nodes is either connected with a *single* SP or there is no path between the two nodes (because they belong to different connected components). Examples of these settings are many road networks, where the unique SP condition is often enforced [14]. Riondato and Kornaropoulos [24, Lemma 2] showed that, in this case, the number of samples needed to compute a high-quality approximation of the BC of all nodes is *independent* of any property of the graph, and only depends on the quality controlling parameters ε and δ. The algorithm by Riondato and Kornaropoulos [24] works differently from ABRA-s, as it samples one SP at a time and only updates the BC estimation of nodes along this path, rather than sampling a pair of nodes and updating the estimation of all nodes on any SPs between the sampled nodes. Nevertheless, as shown in the following theorem, we can actually even generalize the result by Riondato and Kornaropoulos [24], as shown in Thm. 7. The statement and the proof of this theorem use pseudodimension [23], an extension of the Vapnik-Chervonenkis (VC) dimension to real-valued functions. Details about pseudodimension and the proof of Thm. 7 can be found in Appendix B of the extended online version [25]. Corollary 1 shows how to modify ABRA-s to take Thm. 7 into account.

THEOREM 7. *Let $G = (V, E)$ be a graph such that it is possible to partition the set $\mathcal{D} = \{(u, v) \in V \times V, u \ne v\}$ in two classes: a class $A = \{(u^*, v^*)\}$ containing a single pair of different nodes (u^*, v^*) such that $\sigma_{u^*v^*} \le 2$ (i.e., connected by either at most two SPs or not connected), and a class $B = \mathcal{D} \setminus A$ of pairs (u, v) of nodes with $\sigma_{uv} \le 1$ (i.e., either connected by a single SP or not connected). Then the pseudodimension of the family of functions*

$$\{f_w \ : \ \mathcal{D} \to [0,1], w \in V\},$$

where f_w is defined as in (9), is at most 3.

Let	$\begin{cases} z = 48\omega_i^* + (1+4\varepsilon)^2 \\ w = -1 - 12\varepsilon + 8(27(\omega_i^*)^2 + (21-8\varepsilon)\varepsilon^2 + 18\omega_i^*(1+\varepsilon) \\ y = 12\sqrt{3}\lvert -1 + 2\omega_i^* + 2\varepsilon\rvert\sqrt{-(27(\omega_i^*)^2 - \varepsilon^2(1+16\varepsilon) - \omega_i^*(1+18\varepsilon))} \\ \theta = \arg(-w+jy)/3 \text{ where } j \text{ is the imaginary unity and } \arg(\ell) \text{ is the argument of the complex number } \ell \end{cases}$
Root 1	$\frac{1}{3}(i+2)(\ln\frac{2}{\delta})((1+4\varepsilon) - \sqrt{z}\cos\theta)(\omega_i^* - \varepsilon)^{-2}$
Root 2	$\frac{1}{6}(i+2)(\ln\frac{2}{\delta})(2(1+4\varepsilon) + \sqrt{z}(\cos\theta + \sqrt{3}\sin\theta))(\omega_i^* - \varepsilon)^{-2}$
Root 3	$\frac{1}{6}(i+2)(\ln\frac{2}{\delta})(2(1+4\varepsilon) + \sqrt{z}(\cos\theta - \sqrt{3}\sin\theta))(\omega_i^* - \varepsilon)^{-2}$

Table 1: Roots of the cubic equation (12) for the computation of the next sample size.

COROLLARY 1. *Suppose to augment* **ABRA-s** *with the additional stopping condition instructing to return the set* $\tilde{B} = \{\tilde{\mathsf{b}}(w), w \in V\}$ *after a total of*

$$r = \frac{c}{\varepsilon^2}\left(3 + \ln\frac{1}{\delta}\right)$$

pairs of nodes have been sampled from $\mathcal{D}$. *The set* $\tilde{B}$ *is an* (ε, δ)*-approximation.*

The bound in Thm. 7 is strict, i.e., there exists a graph for which the pseudodimension is exactly 3 [24, Lemma 4]. Moreover, as soon as we relax the requirement in Thm. 7 and allow two pairs of nodes to be connected by two SPs, there are graphs with pseudodimension 4 (Lemma 4 in Appendix B of the extended online version [25]).

For the case of *directed* networks, it is currently an open question whether a high-quality (i.e., within ε) approximation of the BC of all nodes can be computed from a sample whose size is independent of properties of the graph, but it is known that, even if possible, the constant would not be the same as for the undirected case [24, Sect. 4.1].

We conjecture that, given some information on how many pair of nodes are connected by x shortest paths, for $x \geq 0$, it should be possible to derive a strict bound on the pseudodimension associated to the graph.

4.4 Improved Estimators

Geisberger et al. [14] present an improved estimator for BC using random sampling. Their experimental results show that the quality of the approximation is significantly improved, but they do not present any theoretical analysis. Their algorithm, which follows the work of Brandes and Pich [10] differs from ours as it samples nodes and performs a Single-Source-Shortest-Paths (SSSP) computation from each of the sampled nodes. We can use an adaptation of their estimator in a variant of our algorithm, and we can prove that this variant is still probabilistically guaranteed to compute an (ε, δ)-approximation of the BC of all nodes, therefore removing the main limitation of the original work, which offered no quality guarantees. We now present this variant considering, for ease of discussion, the special case of the linear scaling estimator by Geisberger et al. [14]. This technique can be extended to the generic parameterized estimators they present.

The intuition behind the improved estimator is to increase the estimation of the BC for a node w proportionally to the ratio between the SP distance $\mathsf{d}(u, w)$ from the first component u of the pair (u, v) to w and the SP distance $\mathsf{d}(u, v)$ from u to v. Rather than sampling pairs of nodes, the algorithm samples triples (u, v, d), where d is a *direction*, (either $\leftarrow$ or $\rightarrow$), and updates the betweenness estimation differently depending on d, as follows. Let $\mathcal{D}' = \mathcal{D} \times \{\leftarrow, \rightarrow\}$ and for each $w \in V$, define the function g_w from $\mathcal{D}'$ to $[0, 1]$ as:

$$g_w(u, v, d) = \begin{cases} \frac{\sigma_{uv}(w)}{\sigma_{uv}} \frac{\mathsf{d}(u,w)}{\mathsf{d}(u,v)} & \text{if } d = \rightarrow \\ \frac{\sigma_{uv}(w)}{\sigma_{uv}}\left(1 - \frac{\mathsf{d}(u,w)}{\mathsf{d}(u,v)}\right) & \text{if } d = \leftarrow \end{cases}$$

Let $\mathcal{S}$ be a collection of ℓ elements of $\mathcal{D}'$ sampled uniformly and independently at random with replacement. Our estimation $\tilde{\mathsf{b}}(w)$ of the BC of a node w is

$$\tilde{\mathsf{b}}(w) = \frac{2}{\ell} \sum_{(u,v,d)\in\mathcal{S}} g_w(u, v, d) = 2\mathsf{m}_{\mathcal{S}}(f_w) .$$

The presence of the factor 2 in the estimator calls for a single minor adjustment in the definition of $\Delta_{\mathcal{S}_i}$ which, for this variant of **ABRA-s**, becomes

$$\Delta_{\mathcal{S}_i} = \frac{\omega_i^*}{1 - \alpha_i} + \frac{(i+1)\ln\frac{2}{\delta}}{2\mathcal{S}_i\alpha_i(1-\alpha_i)} + \sqrt{(i+1)\frac{2\ln\frac{2}{\delta}}{\mathcal{S}_i}}$$

i.e., w.r.t. the original definition of $\Delta_{\mathcal{S}_i}$, there is an additional factor 4 inside the square root of the third term on the r.h.s..

The output of this variant of **ABRA-s** is still a high-quality approximation of the BC of all nodes, i.e., Thm. 4 still holds with this new definition of $\Delta_{\mathcal{S}_i}$. This is due to the fact that the results on the Rademacher averages presented in Sect. 3.2 can be extended to families of functions whose codomain is an interval $[a, b]$, rather than just $[0, 1]$ [28].

5. DYNAMIC GRAPH BC APPROXIMATION

In this section we present an algorithm, named **ABRA-d**, that computes and keeps up to date an high-quality approximation of the BC of all nodes in a *fully dynamic graph*, i.e., in a graph where nodes and edges can be added or removed over time. Our algorithm builds on the recent work by Hayashi et al. [16], who introduced two fast data structures called the Hypergraph Sketch and the Two-Ball Index: the Hypergraph Sketch stores the BC estimations for all nodes, while the Two-Ball Index is used to store the SP DAGs and to understand which parts of the Hypergraph Sketch needs to be modified after an update to the graph (i.e., an edge or node insertion or deletion). Hayashi et al. [16] show how to populate and update these data structures to maintain an (ε, δ)-approximation of the BC of all nodes in a fully dynamic graph. Using the novel data structures results in orders-of-magnitude speedups w.r.t. previous contributions [4, 5]. The algorithm by Hayashi et al. [16] is based on a static random sampling approach which is identical to the one described for **ABRA-s**, i.e., pairs of nodes are sampled and the BC estimation of the nodes along the SPs between the two nodes are updated as necessary. Their analysis on the number of samples necessary to obtain an (ε, δ)-approximation of the

BC of all nodes uses the union bound, resulting in a number of samples that depends on the logarithm of the number of nodes in the graph, i.e., $O(\varepsilon^{-}2(\log(|V|/\delta)))$ pairs of nodes must be sampled.

ABRA-d builds and improves over the algorithm presented by Hayashi et al. [16] as follows. Instead of using a static random sampling approach with a fixed sample size, we use the progressive sampling approach and the stopping condition that we use in ABRA-s to understand when we sampled enough to first populate the Hypegraph Sketch and the Two-Ball Index. Then, after each update to the graph, we perform the same operations as in the algorithm by Hayashi et al. [16], with the crucial addition, after these operation have been performed, of keeping the set $\mathcal{V}_S$ of vectors and the map M (already used in ABRA-s) up to date, and checking whether the stopping condition is still satisfied. If it is not, additional pairs of nodes are sampled and the Hypergraph Sketch and the Two-Ball Index are updated with the estimations resulting from these additional samples. The sampling of additional pairs continues until the stopping condition is satisfied, potentially according to a sample schedule either automatic, or specified by the user. As we show in Sect. 6, the overhead of additional checks of the stopping condition is minimal. On the other hand, the use of the progressive sampling scheme based on the Rademacher averages allows us to sample much fewer pairs of nodes than in the static sampling case based on the union bound: Riondato and Kornaropoulos [24] already showed that it is possible to sample much less than $O(\log|V|)$ nodes, and, as we show in our experiments, our sample sizes are even smaller than the ones by Riondato and Kornaropoulos [24]. The saving in the number of samples results in a huge speedup, as the running time of the algorithms are, in a first approximation, linear in the number of samples, and in a reduction in the amount of space required to store the data structures, as they now store information about fewer SP DAGs.

THEOREM 8. *The set $\widetilde{B} = \{\widetilde{\mathsf{b}}(w), w \in V\}$ returned by ABRA-d after each update has been processed is such that*

$$\Pr(\exists w \in V \text{ s.t. } |\widetilde{\mathsf{b}}(w) - \mathsf{b}(w)| > \varepsilon) < \delta \ .$$

The proof follows from the correctness of the algorithm by Hayashi et al. [16] and of ABRA-s (Thm. 4).

6. EXPERIMENTAL EVALUATION

In this section we presents the results of our experimental evaluation. We measure and analyze the performances of ABRA-s in terms of its runtime and sample size and accuracy, and compared them with those of the exact algorithm BA [9] and the approximation algorithm RK [24], which offers the same guarantees as ABRA-s (computes an (ε, δ)-approximation the BC of all nodes).

Implementation and Environment. We implement ABRA-s and ABRA-d in C++, as an extension of the NetworKit library [29]. The code is available from http://matteo.rionda.to/software/ABRA-radebetw.tbz2. We performed the experiments on a machine with a AMD Phenom^{TM} II X4 955 processor and 16GB of RAM, running FreeBSD 11.

Datasets and Parameters. We use graphs of various nature (communication, citations, P2P, and social networks) from the SNAP repository [20]. The characteristics of the graphs are reported in the leftmost column of Table 2.

In our experiments we varied ε in the range $[0.005, 0.3]$, and we also evaluate a number of different sampling schedules (see Sect. 6.2). In all the results we report, δ is fixed to 0.1. We experimented with different values for this parameter, and, as expected, it has a very limited impact on the nature of the results, given the logarithmic dependence of the sample size on δ. We performed five runs for each combination of parameters. The variance between the different runs was essentially insignificant, so we report, unless otherwise specified, the results for a random run.

6.1 Runtime and Speedup

Our main goal was to develop an algorithm that can compute an (ε, δ)-approximation of the BC of all nodes as fast as possible. Hence we evaluate the runtime and the speedup of ABRA-s w.r.t. BA and RK. The results are reported in columns 3 to 5 (from the left) of Table 2 (the values for $\varepsilon = 0.005$ are missing for Email-Enron and Cit-HepPh because in these case both RK and ABRA-s were slower than BA). As expected, the runtime is a perfect linear function of the sample size (column 9), which in turns grows as ε^{-2}. The speedup w.r.t. the exact algorithm BA is significant and naturally decreases quadratically with ε. More interestingly ABRA-s is always faster than RK, sometimes by a significant factor. At first, one may think that this is due to the reduction in the sample size (column 10), but a deeper analysis shows that this is only one component of the speedup, which is almost always greater than the reduction in sample size. The other component can be explained by the fact that RK must perform an expensive computation (computing the vertex diameter [24] of the graph) to determine the sample size before it can start sampling, while ABRA-s can immediately start sampling and rely on the stopping condition, whose computation is inexpensive, as we will discuss. The different speedups for different graphs are due to different characteristics of the graphs: when the SP DAG between two nodes has many paths, ABRA-s does more work per sample than RK, which only backtracks along a single SP of the DAG, hence the speedup is smaller.

Runtime breakdown. The main challenge in designing a stopping condition for progressive sampling algorithm is striking the right balance between the strictness of the condition (i.e., it should stop early) and the efficiency in evaluating it. We now comment on the efficiency, and will report about the strictness in Sect. 6.2 and 6.3. In columns 6 to 8 of Table 2 we report the breakdown of the runtime into the main components. It is evident that evaluating the stopping condition amounts to an insignificant fraction of the runtime, and most of the time is spent in computing the samples (selection of nodes, execution of SP algorithm, update of the BC estimations). The amount in the "Other" column corresponds to time spent in logging and checking invariants. We can then say that our stopping condition is extremely efficient to evaluate, and ABRA-s is almost always doing "real" work to improve the estimation.

6.2 Sample Size and Sample Schedule

We evaluate the final sample size of ABRA-s and the performances of the "automatic" sample schedule (Sect. 4.1.1). The results are reported in columns 9 and 10 of Table 2.

Graph	ε	Runtime (sec.)	Speedup w.r.t. BA	Speedup w.r.t. RK	Runtime Breakdown (%) Sampling	Runtime Breakdown (%) Stop Cond.	Runtime Breakdown (%) Other	Sample Size	Reduction w.r.t. RK	Absolute Error ($\times 10^5$) max	Absolute Error ($\times 10^5$) avg	Absolute Error ($\times 10^5$) stddev
Soc-Epinions1 Directed $\lvert V\rvert = 75,879$ $\lvert E\rvert = 508,837$	0.005	483.06	1.36	2.90	99.983	0.014	0.002	110,705	2.64	70.84	0.35	1.14
	0.010	124.60	5.28	3.31	99.956	0.035	0.009	28,601	2.55	129.60	0.69	2.22
	0.015	57.16	11.50	4.04	99.927	0.054	0.018	13,114	2.47	198.90	0.97	3.17
	0.020	32.90	19.98	5.07	99.895	0.074	0.031	7,614	2.40	303.86	1.22	4.31
	0.025	21.88	30.05	6.27	99.862	0.092	0.046	5,034	2.32	223.63	1.41	5.24
	0.030	16.05	40.95	7.52	99.827	0.111	0.062	3,668	2.21	382.24	1.58	6.37
P2p Gnutella31 Directed $\lvert V\rvert = 62,586$ $\lvert E\rvert = 147,892$	0.005	100.06	1.78	4.27	99.949	0.041	0.010	81,507	4.07	38.43	0.58	1.60
	0.010	26.05	6.85	4.13	99.861	0.103	0.036	21,315	3.90	65.76	1.15	3.13
	0.015	11.91	14.98	4.03	99.772	0.154	0.074	9,975	3.70	109.10	1.63	4.51
	0.020	7.11	25.09	3.87	99.688	0.191	0.121	5,840	3.55	130.33	2.15	6.12
	0.025	4.84	36.85	3.62	99.607	0.220	0.174	3,905	3.40	171.93	2.52	7.43
	0.030	3.41	52.38	3.66	99.495	0.262	0.243	2,810	3.28	236.36	2.86	8.70
Email-Enron Undirected $\lvert V\rvert = 36,682$ $\lvert E\rvert = 183,831$	0.010	202.43	1.18	1.10	99.984	0.013	0.003	66,882	1.09	145.51	0.48	2.46
	0.015	91.36	2.63	1.09	99.970	0.024	0.006	30,236	1.07	253.06	0.71	3.62
	0.020	53.50	4.48	1.05	99.955	0.035	0.010	17,676	1.03	290.30	0.93	4.83
	0.025	31.99	7.50	1.11	99.932	0.052	0.016	10,589	1.10	548.22	1.21	6.48
	0.030	24.06	9.97	1.03	99.918	0.061	0.021	7,923	1.02	477.32	1.38	7.34
Cit-HepPh Undirected $\lvert V\rvert = 34,546$ $\lvert E\rvert = 421,578$	0.010	215.98	2.36	2.21	99.966	0.030	0.004	32,469	2.25	129.08	1.72	3.40
	0.015	98.27	5.19	2.16	99.938	0.054	0.008	14,747	2.20	226.18	2.49	5.00
	0.020	58.38	8.74	2.05	99.914	0.073	0.013	8,760	2.08	246.14	3.17	6.39
	0.025	37.79	13.50	2.02	99.891	0.091	0.018	5,672	2.06	289.21	3.89	7.97
	0.030	27.13	18.80	1.95	99.869	0.108	0.023	4,076	1.99	359.45	4.45	9.53

Table 2: Runtime, speedup, breakdown of runtime, sample size, reduction, and absolute error

As expected, the sample size grows with ε^{-2}. We already commented on the fact that ABRA-s uses a sample size that is consistently (up to 4×) smaller than the one used by RK and how this is part of the reason why ABRA-s is much faster than RK. In Fig. 1 we show the behavior (on P2p-Gnutella31, figures for other graphs can be found in Appendix C of the extended online version [25]) of the final sample size chosen by the automatic sample schedule in comparison with *static geometric sample schedules*, i.e., schedules for which the sample size at iteration $i+1$ is c times the size of the sample size at iteration i. We can see that the *automatic sample schedule is always better than the geometric ones*, sometimes significantly depending on the value of c (e.g., more than 2× decrease w.r.t. using $c = 3$ for $\varepsilon = 0.05$). Effectively this means that the automatic sample schedule really frees the user from having to selecting a parameter whose impact on the performances of the algorithm may be devastating (larger final sample size implies higher runtime). Moreover, thanks to the automatic sample schedule, ABRA-s always terminates after just two iterations, while this was not the case for the geometric sample schedules (taking even 5 iterations in some cases): this means that effectively the automatic sample schedules "jumps" directly to a sample size for which the stopping condition will be verified. We can sum up the results and say that the stopping condition of ABRA-s stops at small sample sizes, smaller than those used in RK, and the automatic sample schedule we designed is extremely efficient at choosing the right successive sample size.

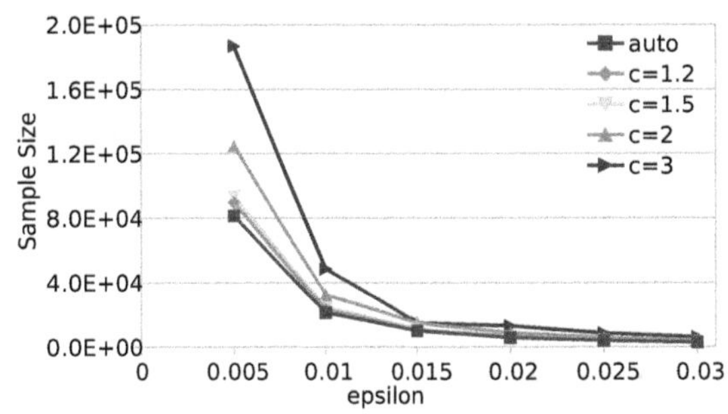

Figure 1: Final sample size for different sample schedules on P2p-Gnutella

6.3 Accuracy

We evaluate the accuracy of ABRA-s by measuring the absolute error $|\widetilde{\mathsf{b}}(v) - \mathsf{b}(v)|$. The theoretical analysis guarantees that this quantity should be at most ε for all nodes, with probability at least $1 - \delta$. A first important result is that in *all* the thousands of runs of ABRA-s, the maximum error was *always* smaller than ε (not just with probability $> 1-\delta$). We report statistics about the absolute error in the three rightmost columns of Table 2 and in Fig. 2 (figures for the other graphs are in Appendix C of the extended online version [25]. The minimum error (not reported) was always 0. The maximum error is *an order of magnitude smaller than* ε, and the average error is around *three orders of magnitude* smaller than ε, with a very small standard deviation. As expected, the error grows as ε^{-2}. In Fig. 2 we show the behavior of the maximum, average, and average plus three standard deviations (approximately corresponding to the 95% percentile) for Soc-Epinions1 (the vertical axis has a logarithmic scale), to appreciate how most of the errors are almost two orders of magnitude smaller than ε.

All these results show that ***ABRA-s*** *is very accurate, more than what is guaranteed by the theoretical analysis.* This can be explained by the fact that the bounds to the sampling size, the stopping condition, and the sample schedule are *conservative*, in the sense that ABRA-s may be sampling more than necessary to obtain an (ε, δ)-approximation. Tightening any of these components would result in a less

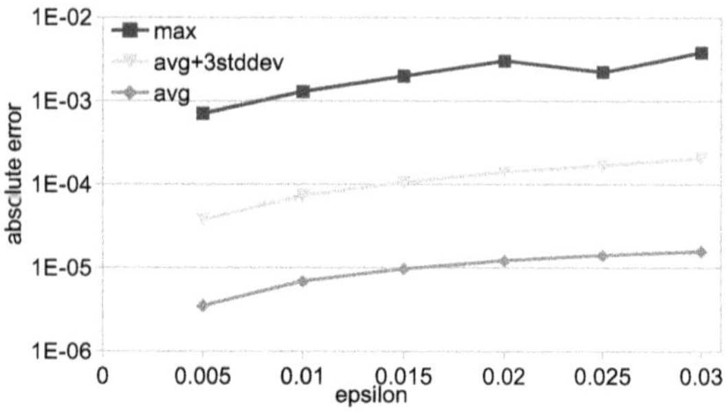

Figure 2: Absolute error evaluation – Soc-Epinions1

conservative algorithm that offers the same approximation quality guarantees, and is an interesting research direction.

6.4 Dynamic BC Approximation

We did not evaluate ABRA-d experimentally, but, given its design, it is reasonable to expect that, when compared to previous contributions offering the same quality guarantees [5, 16], it would exhibit similar or even larger speedups and reductions in the sample size than what ABRA-s had w.r.t. RK. Indeed, the algorithm by Bergamini and Meyerhenke [4] uses RK as a building block and it needs to constantly keep track of (an upper bound on) the vertex diameter of the graph, a very expensive operation. On the other hand, the analysis of the sample size by Hayashi et al. [16] uses very loose simultaneous deviation bounds (the union bound). As already shown by Riondato and Kornaropoulos [24], the resulting sample size is extremely large and they already showed how RK can use a smaller sample size. Since we built over the work by Hayashi et al. [16] and ABRA-s improves over RK, we can reasonably expect it to have better performances than the algorithm by Hayashi et al. [16]

7. CONCLUSIONS

We presented ABRA, a family of sampling-based algorithms for computing and maintaining high-quality approximations of (variants of) the BC of all nodes in static and dynamic graphs with updates (both deletions and insertions). We discussed a number of variants of our basic algorithms, including finding the top-k nodes with higher BC, using improved estimators, and special cases when there is a single SP. ABRA greatly improves, theoretically and experimentally, the current state of the art. The analysis relies on Rademacher averages and on pseudodimension. To our knowledge this is the first application of these concepts to graph mining. In the future we plan to investigate stronger bounds to the Rademacher averages, give stricter bounds to the sample complexity of BC by studying the pseudodimension of the class of functions associated to it, and extend our study to other network measures.

Acknowledgements. This work was supported in part by NSF grant IIS-1247581 and NIH grant R01-CA180776.

8. REFERENCES

[1] D. Anguita, A. Ghio, L. Oneto, and S. Ridella. A deep connection between the Vapnik-Chervonenkis entropy and the Rademacher complexity. *IEEE Trans. Neural Netw. Learn. Sys.*, 25(12):2202–2211, 2014.

[2] J. M. Anthonisse. The rush in a directed graph. TR BN 9/71, Stichting Mathematisch Centrum, 1971.

[3] D. A. Bader, S. Kintali, K. Madduri, and M. Mihail. Approximating betweenness centrality. *Algorithms and Models for the Web-Graph*, 124–137, 2007.

[4] E. Bergamini and H. Meyerhenke. Fully-dynamic approximation of betweenness centrality. ESA'15.

[5] E. Bergamini and H. Meyerhenke. Approximating betweenness centrality in fully-dynamic networks. *Internet Mathematics*, to appear.

[6] E. Bergamini, H. Meyerhenke, and C. L. Staudt. Approximating betweenness centrality in large evolving networks. ALENEX'15, 2015.

[7] S. Boucheron, O. Bousquet, and G. Lugosi. Theory of classification : A survey of some recent advances. *ESAIM: Probability and Statistics*, 9:323–375, 2005.

[8] S. Boyd and L. Vandenberghe. *Convex optimization.* Cambridge university press, 2004.

[9] U. Brandes. A faster algorithm for betweenness centrality. *J. Math. Sociol.*, 25(2):163–177, 2001.

[10] U. Brandes and C. Pich. Centrality estimation in large networks. *Int. J. Bifurc. Chaos*, 17(7):2303–2318, 2007.

[11] T. Elomaa and M. Kääriäinen. Progressive Rademacher sampling. AAAI'2001, 2001.

[12] D. Erdős, V. Ishakian, A. Bestavros, and E. Terzi. A divide-and-conquer algorithm for betweenness centrality. SDM'15, 2015.

[13] L. C. Freeman. A set of measures of centrality based on betweenness. *Sociometry*, 40:35–41, 1977.

[14] R. Geisberger, P. Sanders, and D. Schultes. Better approximation of betweenness centrality. ALENEX'08, 2008.

[15] O. Green, R. McColl, and D. Bader. A fast algorithm for streaming betweenness centrality. PASSAT'12, 2012.

[16] T. Hayashi, T. Akiba, and Y. Yoshida. Fully dynamic betweenness centrality maintenance on massive networks. VLDB'16, 2015.

[17] M. Kas, M. Wachs, K. M. Carley, and L. R. Carley. Incremental algorithm for updating betweenness centrality in dynamically growing networks. ASONAM'13, 2013.

[18] N. Kourtellis, G. D. F. Morales, and F. Bonchi. Scalable online betweenness centrality in evolving graphs. *IEEE Trans. Knowl. Data Eng.*, 27(9):2494–2506, 2015.

[19] M.-J. Lee, J. Lee, J. Y. Park, R. H. Choi, and C.-W. Chung. QUBE: A quick algorithm for updating betweenness centrality. WWW'12, 2012.

[20] J. Leskovec and A. Krevl. SNAP Datasets http://snap.stanford.edu/data, 2014.

[21] M. E. J. Newman. *Networks – An Introduction.* Oxford University Press, 2010.

[22] L. Oneto, A. Ghio, D. Anguita, and S. Ridella. An improved analysis of the Rademacher data-dependent bound using its self bounding property. *Neur. Netw.*, 44:0, 2013.

[23] D. Pollard. *Convergence of stochastic processes.* Springer-Verlag, 1984.

[24] M. Riondato and E. M. Kornaropoulos. Fast approximation of betweenness centrality through sampling. *Data Mining Knowl. Disc.*, 30:(2) 438–475, 2015.

[25] M. Riondato and E. Upfal. Approximating betweenness centrality in static and dynamic graphs with Rademacher averages (extended version) http://rionda.to/papers/RiondatoUpfal-ABRA-ext.pdf, 2016.

[26] M. Riondato and E. Upfal. Mining frequent itemsets through progressive sampling with Rademacher averages. KDD'15, 2015.

[27] A. E. Sarıyüce, E. Saule, K. Kaya, and U. V. Çatalyürek. Shattering and compressing networks for betweenness centrality. SDM'15, 2015.

[28] S. Shalev-Shwartz and S. Ben-David. *Understanding Machine Learning: From Theory to Algorithms.* Cambridge University Press, 2014.

[29] C. Staudt, A. Sazonovs, and H. Meyerhenke. NetworKit: A tool suite for high-performance network analysis. *Network Science*, to appear.

[30] V. N. Vapnik. *The Nature of Statistical Learning Theory.* Springer-Verlag, 1999.

Sampling of Attributed Networks from Hierarchical Generative Models

Pablo Robles
Purdue University
West Lafayette, IN USA
problesg@purdue.edu

Sebastian Moreno
Universidad Adolfo Ibañez
Viña del Mar, Chile
sebastian.moreno@uai.cl

Jennifer Neville
Purdue University
West Lafayette, IN USA
neville@cs.purdue.edu

ABSTRACT

Network sampling is a widely used procedure in social network analysis where a random network is sampled from a generative network model (GNM). Recently proposed GNMs, allow generation of networks with more realistic structural characteristics than earlier ones. This facilitates tasks such as hypothesis testing and sensitivity analysis. However, sampling of networks with correlated vertex attributes remains a challenging problem. While the recent work of [16] has provided a promising approach for attributed-network sampling, the approach was developed for use with relatively simple GNMs and does not work well with more complex hierarchical GNMs (which can model the range of characteristics and variation observed in real world networks more accurately). In contrast to simple GNMs where the probability mass is spread throughout the space of edges more evenly, hierarchical GNMs concentrate the mass to smaller regions of the space to reflect dependencies among edges in the network—this produces more realistic network characteristics, but also makes it more difficult to identify candidate networks from the sampling space.

In this paper, we propose a novel sampling method, CSAG, to sample from hierarchical GNMs and generate networks with correlated attributes. CSAG constrains every step of the sampling process to consider the structure of the GNM—in order to bias the search to regions of the space with higher likelihood. We implemented CSAG using *mixed Kronecker Product Graph Models* and evaluated our approach on three real-world datasets. The results show that CSAG jointly models the correlation and structure of the networks better than the state of the art. Specifically, CSAG maintains the variability of the underlying GNM while providing a ≥ 5X reduction in attribute correlation error.

Keywords

Complex Networks; Network Sampling; Statistical Network Models; Attributed Networks

KDD '16, August 13-17, 2016, San Francisco, CA, USA
© 2016 ACM. ISBN 978-1-4503-4232-2/16/08...$15.00
DOI: http://dx.doi.org/10.1145/2939672.2939808

1 Introduction

Since many complex systems can be represented as networks (where nodes and edges represent entities and their relations, respectively), there has been increased scientific interest in how to model observed network structure effectively—to analyze the properties of the associated systems. Recently many network analyses have focused on data that comprise a single large network (e.g., Facebook, Twitter). Moreover, algorithms are often developed using a small number of network datasets gathered from different domains. Thus, it is critical to have generative network models that can produce data samples that exhibit the natural characteristics of real world networks. Models that generate realistic networks can be used for a variety of analytic tasks. For instance, they enable hypothesis testing (by facilitating assessment of data variability), sensitivity analysis (by facilitating model evaluation under different settings), and benchmark testing (by providing semi-synthetic datasets that preserve privacy) [5].

The ability to generate network structure has served to support research in the basic area of network science but to date there are few methods to generate networks with correlated node attributes [10][16]. Furthermore, few can replicate the range of complex characteristics that occur in real world networks. More precisely, the problem of modeling graph structure with correlated node attributes corresponds to modeling the joint distribution $P(G, \mathbf{X})$ where $P(G)$ and $P(\mathbf{X})$ refer to the marginal distributions of the network structure G and node attributes $\mathbf{X}$, respectively. Most of current methods in network science focus on the problem of modeling $P(G)$ without considering node-attributes $P(\mathbf{X})$[11][18]. Other methods in statistical relational learning focus on the problem of modeling the attribute distribution *conditioned* on the network structure [4]. However, no method effectively represents and samples from the joint distribution $P(G, \mathbf{X})$, due to the complexities of modeling both structure and correlated node attributes (e.g., high-dimensionality, sparse graphs, few sample graphs, etc.). While $P(G, \mathbf{X})$ could be described by combining these efforts to use $P(\mathbf{X}|G)P(G)$, it is typically impractical to draw samples from $P(\mathbf{X}|G)$ due to cyclic attribute dependencies.

More formally, in this work we explore the following–
Problem Definition: Let $G_{IN} = (\mathbf{V}, \mathbf{E})$ be an input network with node attributes $\mathbf{X}_{IN}$, where $\mathbf{x}_i$ refers to the attribute value of node i (e.g., $\mathbf{x}_i \in \{0, 1\}$ for binary attributes). Let $\mathbf{P} = P(G, \mathbf{X})$ be the unknown target distribution which generated $< G_{IN}, \mathbf{X}_{IN} >$. If $P(G)$ is the marginal distribution of the network structure estimated with a generative network model $\mathcal{M}$ with parameter Θ^G, and $P(\mathbf{X})$ is

the marginal distribution of node attributes with estimated parameter Θ^X, then our objective is to learn a model using the marginals $P(\mathbf{X}), P(G)$ to construct a proposal distribution Q and sample a pair $<G_{OUT}, \mathbf{X}_{OUT}> \sim Q$ such that it is likely to have been drawn from P.[1]

The *Attributed Graph Model* (AGM [16]) is a new approach to solve this problem, which approximates sampling from the joint distribution of structure and attributes $P(G, \mathbf{X})$ using rejection sampling. The AGM uses $Q = P(G)P(\mathbf{X})$ as a proposal distribution—by first sampling the node attributes from $P(\mathbf{X})$ and then using a probabilistic *generative network model* (GNM) to sample edges efficiently from $P(G)$. The proposed edges are accepted with probability proportional to $P(G|\mathbf{X})$ (learned from observed data). The AGM is simple to use and performs well with several edge-based GNMs, such as the Chung Lu (CL) model [2] and the Kronecker product graph model (KPGM) [11].

However, the AGM approximation is only accurate when all edge probabilities in the associated GNM are non-zero, and performance degrades if the edge probability mass is more concentrated over a subset of node pairs, instead of being spread more evenly over all pairs of nodes. As we will discuss later, some hierarchical GNMs that model more complex dependencies among graph edges produce more concentrated probability mass over smaller regions of node pairs. Thus, the AGM will not perform as well with these GNMs.

In this paper, we explore the issue of using hierarchical GNMs to generate attributed networks with correlated attributes and network structure that reflects the characteristics of real world graphs. Namely, we use the *mixed Kronecker product graph model* (mKPGM [14]), a sub-class of hierarchical generative models that overcome known limitations [19] of KPGMs. This hierarchical GNM creates networks by *iteratively* sampling from a hierarchy of latent variables that represent edges, blocks, and superblocks of edges. The hierarchical process restricts the space of possible networks, conditioned on the sampling of the blocks. Specifically, if a block is not sampled, the associated edges have zero probability (i.e., they cannot be sampled). This has significant impact on the model's effective sampling space and makes it difficult to use AGM's rejection sampling process.

We propose *Constrained Sampling for Attributed Graphs* (CSAG), a new method to approximate sampling structure and attributes from $P(G, \mathbf{X})$ using mKPGMs as the generative network model in the proposal distribution. As in AGM, we use a proposal Q composed by the network distribution and the attribute distribution, i.e. $Q = P(G)P(\mathbf{X})$. However, due to the complex GNM hierarchy, we cannot model the target joint $\mathbf{P} = P(G|\mathbf{X})P(\mathbf{X})$ directly (i.e., we cannot efficiently calculate the likelihood of a sample, nor can we effectively use rejection sampling). Instead, we develop a two-stage constrained sampling process to generate from a distribution $Q' \sim \mathbf{P}$: a block-sampling stage to generate from the hierarchy, and an edge-sampling stage to generate edges, using constraints based on the maximum entropy principle [7]. The combination increases the accuracy of the sampling process, producing samples with correlated node-attribute values and complex network structure that match the marginal models.

To summarize, our contributions are twofold. First, we show both a discussion and empirical evidence of the reduction in sampling space that results from the use of a hierarchical GNM such as mKPGM—which makes it difficult to model $P(G, \mathbf{X})$ with the recently developed AGM sampling method. Second, to address the issue above, we propose CSAG, a 2-stage constrained sampling method that samples a set of blocks from a region of feasibility and then samples edges from the selected block-space. CSAG is appropriate to use with mKPGM and other hierarchical GNMs. We provide a detailed implementation of CSAG for mKPGMs. Our experiments on three real datasets show that CSAG outperforms the state of the art by jointly matching attribute correlations and network structure—using orders of magnitude fewer parameters than competing methods. The experiments also show a ≥ 5X reduction in the attribute correlation error with respect to the state-of-the-art.

[1] This likelihood depends on the goodness of fit of $P(G)$ and $P(\mathbf{X})$.

2 Background and Related Work

2.1 Generative Network Models

Let $G = (\mathbf{V}, \mathbf{E})$ be a graph with set of vertices $\mathbf{V}$ and edges $\mathbf{E} \subset \mathbf{V} \times \mathbf{V}$. Generative network models sample random networks G from a distribution $P(G)$. Let $\mathcal{M}(\Theta^G)$ refer to a generative network model with parameters Θ^G, which generates a network G through a random sampling process as follows. We define E_{ij} to be a binary random variable, where $E_{ij} = 1$ indicates that an edge between $V_i, V_j \in \mathbf{V}$ exists (i.e., $e_{ij} \in \mathbf{E}$), and $E_{ij} = 0 \Rightarrow e_{ij} \notin \mathbf{E}$. Many GNMs sample networks from a $|\mathbf{V}| \times |\mathbf{V}|$ probability matrix $\mathcal{P}$, where $\mathcal{P}_{ij} = p_{ij}$ is the probability of the edge e_{ij} existing in the network, i.e., $P(E_{ij} = 1) = p_{ij}$. We will denote as $\mathcal{P}^+$ the subset $\mathcal{P}_{ij} > 0$. Some examples of generative network models appear below.

Unique Bernoulli probabilities. An important abstraction/property of GNMs that use the probability matrix $\mathcal{P}$ is the fact that they can be simply represented with the pair $<\mathbf{U}, \mathbf{T}>$. $\mathbf{U}$ is the set of unique Bernoulli probabilities that appear in the matrix $\mathcal{P}$, i.e. $\mathbf{U} = \{\pi_1, \pi_2, \ldots, \pi_u, \ldots\} = \texttt{unique}(\mathcal{P})$. The function **unique** returns the set of all p_{ij} (i.e. without repetitions). $\mathbf{T}$ is a set of lists $\mathbf{T}_u$, which lists the positions where the probability π_u appears in $\mathcal{P}$. Later we will see that $\mathbf{T}$ can be indexed also by other criteria (e.g. by the node attributes). For now, it is enough to understand that u indexes $\mathbf{T}$ ($\mathbf{T}_u$).

Erdős-Rényi Model (ER) [3]. In an ER model, random graphs are formed by creating edges between each pair of nodes independently with probability p. It is easy to see that $\mathbf{U} = \{\pi = p\}$ has only one unique probability and $\mathbf{T}$ consists of a single list with all the positions in $\mathcal{P}$.

Chung-Lu Model (CL) [2]. In a CL model $\mathcal{P}_{ij} = w_i w_j / \sum w_k$ for a sequence of expected degrees of nodes $\mathbf{w} = (w_1, \ldots, w_{|\mathbf{V}|})$ (CL assumes $\max_k w_k^2 < \sum w_k$ so that $0 \leq \mathcal{P}_{ij} \leq 1$). In the worst case, although very unlikely, there could be $|\mathbf{V}|^2$ unique probabilities π_i and $\mathbf{T}$ would consist of $|\mathbf{V}|^2$ lists of a single element each.

Transitive Chung Lu Model (TCL) [17]. TCL is a generalization of CL. Both CL and TCL model the expected degree via a set of weights w_i proportional to degree of node i. However, while CL samples each edge independently with probability proportional to $w_i w_j$, TCL rewires edges to match clustering coefficient of the original network. The same criteria applies for the size of $\mathbf{U}$ and $\mathbf{T}$ as for CL.

Block two-level Erdős-Rényi Model (BTER) [18]. Sampling for BTER is done in two phases. First, affinity blocks are created in a preprocessing step, where edges in each block are linked with an ER model. Second, connections between blocks are created with a CL model. Since the phase-2 uses a CL model $\mathbf{U}$ and $\mathbf{T}$ could have the same worst case scenario than CL.

Kronecker Product Graph Model (KPGM) [11]. Given a $b \times b$ parameter matrix Θ^G where $\forall i,j\ \theta^G_{ij} \in [0,1]$, and K (the number of Kronecker products), KPGM samples graphs as follows. First, it computes $\mathcal{P}$ a matrix equal to $K-1$ Kronecker products of Θ^G with itself. Second, it samples $G=(\mathbf{V},\mathbf{E})$ from $\mathcal{P}$ by sampling each cell independently from $Bernoulli(\mathcal{P}_{ij})$. In KPGM, $\mathbf{U}$ is $|\mathbf{U}| = \binom{b^2+K-1}{K}$ and $\mathbf{T}$ consists of $|\mathbf{U}|$ lists of edges (more details in [15]).

mixed Kronecker Product Graph Model (mKPGM) [14]. mKPGM is a hierarchical generative network model that overcomes known limitations [19] of the KPGM. Given a $b \times b$ parameters Θ^G where $\forall i,j\ \theta^G_{ij} \in [0,1]$, the number of Kronecker products K, and the number of untied levels ℓ, mKPGM samples a network as follows. First, it computes $\mathcal{P}^{[0]}$, a $b^\ell \times b^\ell$ matrix, equal to $\ell-1$ Kronecker products of Θ^G with itself, i.e., it computes a KPGM model with parameters Θ^G, ℓ. Second, it samples $G^{[0]}=(\mathbf{V}^{[0]},\mathbf{E}^{[0]})$ from $\mathcal{P}^{[0]}$ by sampling each cell independently via $Bernoulli(\mathcal{P}^{[0]}_{ij})$. Note, $|\mathbf{V}^{[0]}| = b^\ell$. Third, it calculates $\mathcal{P}^{[l]} = G^{[l-1]} \otimes \Theta^G$ and samples $G^{[l]}$ for $l=1\ldots K-\ell$. The iterations increase the variability in the sampled network $G^{[K-\ell]}$ (where $|\mathbf{V}^{[K-\ell]}| = b^K$).

Since $G^{[0]} \ldots G^{[K-\ell-1]}$ represent auxiliary graphs (in matrices of increasing size), where each edge influences a *block* of possible edges in the next iteration of the hierarchical sampling process (and they are not present in the final output network) we refer to them as block matrices: $\mathbf{B}^{[0]} \ldots \mathbf{B}^{[K-\ell-1]}$. To simplify notation we will refer to the final sampled network $G^{[K-\ell]} = (\mathbf{V}^{[K-\ell]}, \mathbf{E}^{[K-\ell]})$ as $G_{OUT} = (\mathbf{V}_{OUT}, \mathbf{E}_{OUT})$. Figure 1 illustrates the hierarchical sampling process from $\mathcal{P}$s to $\mathbf{B}$s, of increasing size. In mKPGMs, the size of $\mathbf{U}$ is b^2 for each level of the hierarchy and $\mathbf{T}$ consists of b^2 lists of edges.

2.2 Attributed Networks and Related Work

When developing models to sample attributed networks, it is worth highlighting the importance of accurately modeling the correlation observed among the attributes of linked nodes (or *autocorrelation*). Autocorrelation is typically observed in networks due to processes such as *social influence* and *homophily* [13, 20], and is an important feature exploited in statistical relational learning to improve classification and other statistical inference tasks in network domains [4].

The Attributed Graph Model (AGM) [16] approximates sampling from the joint distribution of network structure and node attributes $P(G, \mathbf{X})$ using rejection sampling. AGM combines structure and attributes independently in a proposal distribution $Q = P(G)P(\mathbf{X})$, by first sampling the node attributes from a distribution $P(\mathbf{X};\Theta^X)$ with parameters Θ^X and then using a generative network model $P(G;\Theta^G)$ with parameters Θ^G to sample attributed edges, based on:

$$P(E_{ij}|\mathbf{X}) \approx P(E_{ij}|\Theta^G) \cdot A(f(\mathbf{x}_i,\mathbf{x}_j)|\Theta^G,\Theta^X)$$

where $P(E_{ij}=1|\Theta^G) = \mathcal{P}_{ij}$ is the edge probability defined by the generative network model and $A(\cdot)$ is the acceptance probability based on features between nodes $f(\mathbf{x}_i,\mathbf{x}_j)$. The acceptance probability ensures that we add edges e_{ij} with correlated attribute values.

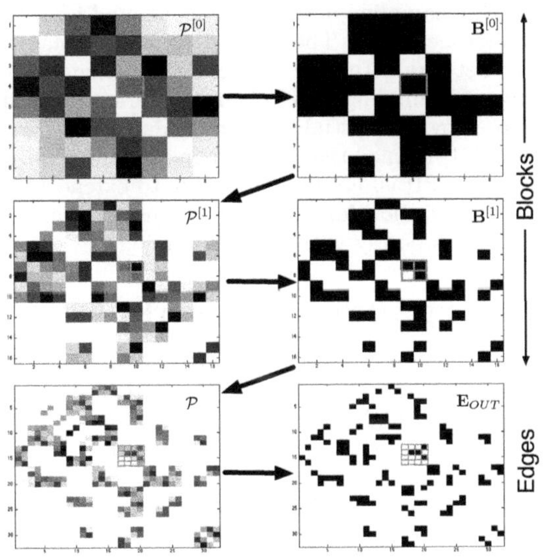

Figure 1: mKPGM sampling process with $b=2$, $\ell=3$, $K=5$. $\mathcal{P}^{[0]}$ is generated as a KPGM. Left: Matrices of probabilities $\mathcal{P}^{[l]}$ (white: $\mathcal{P}_{ij}=0$ black: $\mathcal{P}_{ij}=1$). Right: Adjacency matrices $\mathbf{B}^{[0]} \ldots \mathbf{B}^{[K-\ell-1]}$, E_{OUT} (black $\Rightarrow$ block/edge sampled).

For training, AGM uses an input network G_{IN} and attributes $\mathbf{X}_{IN}$, to learn Θ^X, Θ^G, and $A(\cdot)$. To illustrate AGM's process consider a network where nodes have a single attribute. AGM learns a GNM model from the network structure (i.e., $P(G)$), fits a Bernoulli distribution to the observed attribute values (i.e., $P(\mathbf{X})$), and learns $A(\cdot)$ by comparing the attribute correlations observed in G_{IN} to those produced by an independent sampling process (i.e., $P(G)P(\mathbf{X})$). Then, AGM produces a new set of nodes, samples attribute values from $P(\mathbf{X})$ for each node, generates candidate edges from the GNM, and accepts/rejects based on the attributes of the incident nodes using $A(\cdot)$. AGM has been implemented for GNMs: FCL [17], TCL, and KPGM.

Another approach to generate samples of attributed-networks is to develop a probabilistic model that jointly incorporates both attributes and structure. There is work in this direction. One example is the *multiplicative attribute graph* (MAG) model [10]. However, the evaluation of AGM [16] showed that MAG underperformed AGM for sampling new networks because MAG considers latent node attributes instead of learning from observed node attributes.

As we will describe below, the insight of our CSAG method is that sampling from the full joint is difficult due to its high dimensional space, but much of the space has essentially zero probability in some hierarchical GNMs, such as mKPGMs. Our CSAG approach uses constrained sampling to effectively explore only parts of the network space that are likely. It discards random variables with zero probability and exploits information about the desired level of autocorrelation to further constrain the search using the maximum entropy (MaxEnt) principle. We will compare CSAG only to AGM since [16] showed that AGM was significantly better than MAG and other methods.

Finally, it is important to note some existing applications of MaxEnt to related problems. While it has not been used for sampling attributed networks, MaxEnt has been extensively used in sampling of structure alone, and for inference in attributed networks. The earliest example of MaxEnt for sampling network structure is the Erdős-Rényi model [3]. Modeling and sampling of scale-free networks with MaxEnt was explored by [8], [5] studied anomaly detection (i.e., inference), and [21] learned the structure in attributed networks. We note that [21] is, however, not easy to extend to model the joint distribution for sampling because it prunes away data and scales poorly without this pruning.

3 Sampling Attributed Networks

Naive application of AGM with mKPGM

A full description of the joint distribution of structure and attributes $P(G, \mathbf{X})$ remains an open problem [16] and AGM is one of the first methods to approximate attributed-network sampling (i.e. sampling from $P(G, \mathbf{X})$). Thus, one could naively apply AGM using mKPGMs as the component GNM as follows. First, learn an mKPGM from G_{IN} to model $P(G)$, fit a distribution $P(\mathbf{X})$ to the observed attributes $\mathbf{X}_{IN}$, and learn $A(\cdot)$ as usual. Next, produce a new set of nodes and sample their attribute values from $P(\mathbf{X})$. Then, sample blocks from the mKPGM and generate candidate edges based on the sampled blocks (i.e., the results of the penultimate iteration of mKPGM sampling process: $\mathbf{B}^{[K-\ell-1]}$). Finally, accept/reject the candidate edges based on the attribute values of the incident nodes.

While this implementation will preserve the network structure modeled by the mKPGM, it will be difficult for the process to match the correlations observed in G_{IN}. AGM assumes the set of non-zero edge-probabilities in $\mathcal{P}$ where $p_{ij} > 0$, which we will denote $\mathcal{P}^+$, has a large cardinality and is as close as possible to $|\mathbf{V}|^2$ (i.e., $|\mathcal{P}^+| \simeq |\mathcal{P}|$). However, in mKPGMs there is a high probability that many blocks will not be sampled (see Fig. 1), thus $E[|\mathcal{P}^+|] << |\mathcal{P}|$, as shown by Lemma 1 below. The restricted space of possible edges in mKPGM limits the possibilities considered in the AGM's rejection process and as a result degrades its ability to match the targeted attribute correlations.

Impact of the Generative Sampling Space

As we discussed before, mKPGM sampling comprises a hierarchical structure of edges, blocks, and super-blocks of edges. A block ij at level l has an associated random variable (r.v.) $B_{ij}^{[l]}$ which represents its state: sampled ($B_{ij}^{[l]} = 1$) or not ($B_{ij}^{[l]} = 0$). Here $l \in \{0, \ldots, K-\ell\}$, with $l = 0$ corresponding to the root of the hierarchy and $l = K-\ell$ to the level of edges. A block or edge can be sampled iff its parent is sampled—if a superblock is not sampled, sampling of sub-blocks or edges is inhibited. In this case, the conditional $P(E_{ij} \mid pa(E_{ij}) = 0) = 0$, but the marginal $P(E_{ij}) > 0$. As a consequence, mKPGMs have a reduced conditional space. Specifically, $|\mathcal{P}^+| < |\mathcal{P}|$ given the set of sampled blocks in the hierarchy of an mKPGM model:

Lemma 1. *Let $\mathcal{P}$ be the matrix of edge probabilities and $\mathcal{P}^+$ the matrix of non-zero edge-probabilities conditioned on the sampled blocks in the level $K-\ell-1$ of an mKPGM. If $\sum \Theta^G < b^2$, then $E[|\mathcal{P}^+|] << |\mathcal{P}|$, where $K-\ell-1$ is the last block-iteration (before the generation of edges) (figure 1).*

Proof. Let $\Theta_s = \sum \Theta^G$ be the sum of the mKPGM parameters, then $E[|\mathcal{P}^+|] = (\Theta_s)^{K-1} \cdot b^2$ and $|\mathcal{P}| = (b^2)^K$. Then $\frac{E[|\mathcal{P}^+|]}{|\mathcal{P}|} = \frac{(\Theta_s)^{K-1}}{(b^2)^{K-1}}$. Since $\Theta_s < b^2$, then $\frac{E[|\mathcal{P}^+|]}{|\mathcal{P}|} << 1$, i.e. mKPGM has a reduced sampling space. □

In sparse networks $|\mathbf{E}| = O(|\mathbf{V}|)$ and for KPGM-family models $E[|\mathbf{E}|] = (\Theta_s)^K$. Thus, $(\Theta_s)^K = O(|\mathbf{V}|) \Rightarrow (\Theta_s)^{K-1} \approx \frac{|\mathbf{V}|}{\Theta_s}$. Consequently, for mKPGMs $\frac{E[|\mathcal{P}^+|]}{|\mathcal{P}|} \approx \frac{|\mathbf{V}|/\Theta_s}{|\mathbf{V}|^2} = \frac{1}{\Theta_s |\mathbf{V}|}$. Our empirical analysis in Table 2 shows that $|\mathcal{P}^+|$ for mKPGMs is up to 6 orders of magnitude smaller than $|\mathcal{P}^+|$ for other GNM models. In general, for non-hierarchical GNMs: $|\mathcal{P}| \simeq |\mathcal{P}^+| \simeq |\mathbf{V}|^2$.

The reduced sampling space for mKPGMs constrains the ability to generate edges with correlation between the attributes of the incident nodes (e.g., autocorrelation). This is because the correlation is jointly produced by the attribute distribution and the sampling of edges from the GNM. When $|\mathcal{P}^+| < |\mathcal{P}|$, the potential edges may not exhibit the combinations of attribute values needed to produce (auto)correlation. For instance, if an unsampled block contain nodes with particular values of an attribute, the correlation that can be obtained will be determined by the values in the remaining blocks. In comparison to GNMs with matrices where $|\mathcal{P}^+| \simeq |\mathcal{P}|$, for iterative sampling methods like AGM, it will be difficult to produce the target level of correlation when using hierarchical GNMs like mKPGM.

Our approach

As we describe next, we develop a 2-stage constrained sampling method to address the problem of sampling from $P(G, \mathbf{X})$ with hierarchical GNMs. First, we use linear programming (LP) to sample blocks from the latent space. Then, we sample edges from the sampled blocks. We use MaxEnt [7] via constraints, maintained through the method of moments.

4 CSAG Sampling Method

To solve the problem defined in Section 1, we propose a novel sampling method to draw the network structure conditioned on the attribute values. Specifically, we fit a distribution $P(\mathbf{X})$ to the attributes $\mathbf{X}_{IN}$, and estimate the structure $P(G)$ by learning a model $\mathcal{M}$ from G_{IN}, where G_{IN} and X_{IN} are the input data by problem definition. Then we use the structure conditioned on the attributes, as a proposal $Q = P(G)P(\mathbf{X})$. Although Q is easy to sample from (because assumes independence) it is not a good approximation of the joint $\mathbf{P}$ because $P(G)$ and $P(\mathbf{X})$ are not independent. To solve this, we calculate the moments $\mathbf{f} = \{f_o(G_{IN}, \mathbf{X}_{IN})\}$ of the training data (attributes and structure), and sample a network from Q that matches those moments i.e. we sample from $Q' \subset Q : Q' = P(G|\mathbf{X}, \mathbf{f})P(\mathbf{X})$.

The general goal of the algorithm is to maintain the marginals $P(G)$ and $P(\mathbf{X})$ and keep only the sampled networks that maintain the characteristics of networks in the joint distribution $\mathbf{P}$. In other words, from the candidate edges we keep only those that match the moments $\mathbf{f}$.

Here we describe the intuition behind our 2-stage sampling algorithm while its full description is provided in 4.1. First, let us define the moments used for sampling. The set of attributes $\mathbf{X} = \{\mathbf{X}^1, \mathbf{X}^2, ..., \mathbf{X}^m\}$ create the pairs $(\mathbf{x}_i^m, \mathbf{x}_j^{m'})$ for $e_{ij} \in \mathbf{E}\ \forall i, j, m, m'$. We refer the set of unique labels $(\mathbf{x}_i^m, \mathbf{x}_j^{m'})$ as the edge-types Ψ (e.g., for an undirected network with a single binary node attribute $\Psi = \{00, 01, 11\}$), and the fraction of edges of each type Ψ

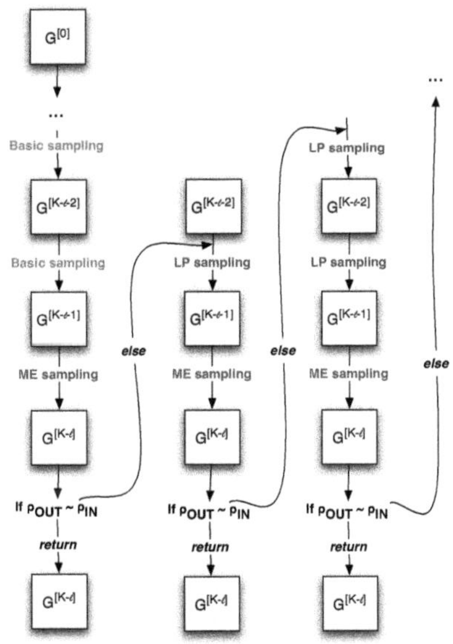

Figure 2: Example illustration of the sampling process which combines basic sampling with MaxEnt sampling, and LP search at different levels of the hierarchy, depending on whether the output network meets the desired constraints.

Algorithm *GraphSampling*

Input: $G_{IN} = (\mathbf{V}, \mathbf{E})$, node attrs $\mathbf{X}_{IN}$, GNM $\mathcal{M}$, error ϵ
Ouput: $G_{OUT}, \mathbf{X}_{OUT}, \rho_{OUT}$
$[\Psi, \beta, \Theta^{\mathbf{X}}, \Theta^{G}] \leftarrow$ *LearnParameters*$(G_{IN}, \mathbf{X}_{IN})$
Sample $\mathbf{X}_{OUT}$ from $P(\mathbf{X}|\Theta^{\mathbf{X}})$
Initialize $\rho_{OUT} = \infty$ and $l_o = K - \ell - 1$
while $(|\rho_{IN} - \rho_{OUT}| > \epsilon)$ AND $(l_o \geq 0)$ **do**
  Sample $\mathbf{B}^{[l_o]}_{sample} \sim \mathcal{M}(\Theta^G)$ using *basic sampling* [2]
  for $l = l_o + 1$ **to** $K - \ell - 1$ **do**
    $\mathbf{B}^{[l+1]}_{sample} \leftarrow$ *LPBlockSearch*$(\mathcal{M}, \Theta^G, \mathbf{B}^{[l]}_{sample}, \Psi, \beta)$
  $G_{OUT} \leftarrow$ *MEEdgeSampling*$(\mathcal{M}, \Theta^G, \mathbf{B}^{[K-\ell-1]}_{sample}, \Psi, \beta)$
  Calculate ρ_{OUT} using G_{OUT} and $\mathbf{X}_{OUT}$
  $l_o = l_o - 1$

---

in G as $\beta = \{\beta_1, \ldots, \beta_{|\Psi|}\}$. The moments $\mathbf{f} = \beta$ model the Pearson correlation ρ of the attribute vectors $\mathbf{X}^m = \{\mathbf{x}^m_i\}$ and $\mathbf{X}^{m'} = \{\mathbf{x}^{m'}_j\}$ over the pairs $e_{ij} \in \mathbf{E}\ \forall i, j$. When $m = m'$, this corresponds to the autocorrelation of a single attribute across edges in the network. We will denote the target correlation as ρ_{IN} and the sample correlation as ρ_{OUT}. Since ρ is function of β (and $|\mathbf{E}|$) we will use β instead of ρ in our discussion. It is worth to note that ρ is jointly defined by the GNM and the distribution of node attribute values. Thus in hierarchical GNMs where the graph structure is constrained, the possible values of ρ in the sample are also constrained.

Given an input graph and its attributes $(G_{IN}, \mathbf{X}_{IN})$, and a GNM $\mathcal{M}$, we sample in a two stage process to generate the attributed network $(G_{OUT}, \mathbf{X}_{OUT})$ with correlation ρ_{OUT}, as outlined in Algorithm *GraphSampling*. The task of *GraphSampling* is to sample the network structure conditioned on the attribute values to match ρ_{IN}. The general idea of this two-stage sampling method is to apply moment matching whenever possible while sampling edges. When the sampling space is too restrictive however (i.e., it is not possible to sample edges with the target correlations), a second stage sampling is used to steer the search towards parts of the space with blocks of edges that make the target correlations more likely. Specifically, when the *basic unconstrained sampling* of the GNM[2] results in a space (of sampled blocks) where it is possible to match $\mathbf{f}$, then the first stage sampling (with MaxEnt moment matching) will be sufficient to sample edges with the target correlations. Otherwise, sampling will require a second stage linear program (LP sampling), to sample blocks before the first stage—replacing the basic sampling of that iteration. This is repeated for as many previous iterations as needed (see Figure 2). Since the number of iterations where second stage sampling is needed is generally small ($\leq K/2$), the process is relatively efficient.

The first-stage sampling, described by Algorithm *MEEdge-Sampling*, is a general procedure to sample edges and works under the assumption that β can be achieved with the sampled blocks. Consider the case where sampling from an mKPGM leads to a space where a network with the target correlation is feasible. In such case, the edges can be sampled from a set of blocks $\mathbf{B}^{K-\ell-1}_{sample}$ sampled at the iteration $K-\ell-1$ of the sampling process. The **constraints** that must be enforced to sample edges (at iteration $K-\ell$) are two-fold: (1) the *structure of the sampled network* is the one defined by the GNM, and (2) the *correlations obtained* are the same as the input correlations. CSAG constrains every step of the sampling process by including these two restrictions. The former restriction (to maintain the structure of the GNM) is guaranteed by using group probability sampling [15] as follows. Given the set of unique Bernoulli probabilities π_u from the GNM[3], we need to guarantee that the resulting samples follow the exact same Bernoulli distribution of the edges. This is accomplished by ensuring the number of edges sampled per π_u follows a binomial distribution, as proved in [15]. The later restriction (to maintain the correlation) is guaranteed by matching the moments β_j of edges of each type ψ_j to the moments of the input data.

The second-stage sampling, described in Algorithm *LP-BlockSearch*, is used to draw blocks, i.e. it can be applied to *all iterations except the last*, as opposed to the previous stage that only applies to the *last iteration* for sampling edges. This stage is necessary to deal with cases where the network-space obtained using the generative network model does not allow for networks with the target correlation. In such cases the set of blocks from which edges will be sampled must be realized from regions of high(er) likelihood such that the edges sampled fulfill the constraints that produce the target correlation.

The objective in the second stage is to find the set χ of blocks to sample in a particular iteration. As we will describe, χ must fulfill **constraints** so that the blocks selected will maintain both the *network structure* of the GNM and the *attribute structure* of $P(\mathbf{X})$, based on the training data. To express these two types of constraints mathematically, we will consider certain conditions that the sampled blocks must follow. Thus, our objective function $f(\chi)$ is an error function (to minimize) that measures how far the samples are from a region that satisfies the conditions.

Since both sampling stages respect the original distribution of the GNM, the structure and the variability of the GNM is maintained in the output network. Both stages are also designed to sample from a region that has non-trivial

---

[2]Section 2.1 describes mKPGM's *basic unconstrained sampling.*

[3]As described in 2.1, GNMs are equivalent to a set of unique Bernoulli probabilities $\pi_u \in \mathbf{U}$ and their positions $\mathbf{T}_u$.

mass in the joint distribution—because many networks with high likelihood w.r.t. the GNM will typically not exhibit the desired attribute correlations.

Learning

Learning $\Theta^{\mathbf{X}}$ and Θ^{G} is straightforward. In our evaluation, we estimate $\Theta^{\mathbf{X}}$ using the MLE of the multinomial distribution for $\mathbf{X}$, while for Θ^{G} we use the simulated method of moments of [14]. Likewise, estimating ρ_{IN} is a trivial MLE. In our example, for instance, it simply consists in calculating the fraction of edges with labels $\Psi = \{00, 01, 11\}$.

Algorithm *LearnParameters*

1: **Input:** $G_{IN} = (\mathbf{V}, \mathbf{E})$, node attrs $\mathbf{X}_{IN}$, model $\mathcal{M}$
2: **Ouput:** Ψ, β, $\Theta^{\mathbf{X}}$, Θ^{G}
3: Compute Ψ and β (that define ρ_{IN}) from G_{IN} and $\mathbf{X}_{IN}$
4: Compute the MLE of $\Theta^{\mathbf{X}}$ using $\mathbf{X}_{IN} \sim f(X)$
5: Estimate Θ^{G} from $G_{IN} \sim \mathcal{M}$

4.1 Algorithmic details

Algorithm *GraphSampling* describes CSAG's overall framework. *GraphSampling* first determines the correlation ρ_{IN} of the input graph (the edge-types Ψ, and the fraction of edges per type β), and learns $\Theta^{\mathbf{X}}$ and Θ^{G} for the attributes $P(\mathbf{X})$ and model $\mathcal{M}(\Theta^{G})$ (line 3). $\Theta^{\mathbf{X}}$ is estimated using the MLE of the multinomial distribution of $\mathbf{X}$, while Θ^{G} is estimated with the learning algorithm of the GNM (e.g. [14] is used to learn Θ^{G} for mKPGM). The algorithm samples attribute values X_{OUT} for the output nodes with $\Theta^{\mathbf{X}}$ (line 4). G_{OUT} is sampled using the two stage-sampling based on Θ^{G}. The LP-search starts from the set of blocks $\mathbf{B}^{[l_o]}_{sample}$ sampled from $\mathcal{M}$ at layer l_o (line 7). Then, it searches through the hierarchy ($l = l_o \ldots K - \ell - 1$) to ultimately sample $\mathbf{B}^{[K-\ell-1]}_{sample}$ (lines 8-9). Then the method of moments uses $\mathbf{B}^{[K-\ell-1]}_{sample}$ to sample edges (line 10). l_o moves one level up in the hierarchy if the space cannot match ρ_{IN}. This process is repeated until $|\rho_{IN} - \rho_{OUT}| \leq \epsilon$, for some predefined error ϵ. The LP search is not realized if ρ_{IN} is feasible to obtain (e.g. in non-hierarchical GNMs)—then G_{OUT} is sampled directly. It is important to note that there are configurations of attribute values, and target correlations, for which sampling may not be possible. If this is the case, *GraphSampling* will not satisfy the constraints and the algorithm will terminate (with $l_o = 0$). In practice, because the networks are sparse and the attributes are low-dimensional it is generally possible to find a sample of edges that satisfy the constraints.

Algorithm *LPBlockSearch* describes the LP block-sampling stage. This stage focuses the sampling on relevant regions of the space where networks with the target correlation of node attributes are possible to be drawn. Given the GNM $\mathcal{M}$ with parameters Θ^{G}, the set of sampled blocks $\mathbf{B}^{[l]}_{sample}$, the list of edge-types Ψ, and the fraction of edges of each type β, *LPBlockSearch* returns the set of sample blocks $\mathbf{B}^{[l+1]}_{sample}$ at level $l+1$ such that all possible edges descendent from $\mathbf{B}^{[l+1]}_{sample}$ have the same proportions as β. *LPBlockSearch* first calculates $\mathbf{U} = \{\pi_1, \ldots, \pi_k\}$, and $\mathbf{T}$—the set of unique probabilities of $\mathcal{M}$ and the locations of possible sample blocks per unique probability π_u, respectively, which can be generated by $\mathbf{B}^{[l]}_{sample}$. The FOR loop (lines 4-14) performs a linear search per π_u. Specifically, it calculates the number of blocks to be sampled (line 5). The next FOR loop computes

Algorithm *LPBlockSearch*

1: **Input:** $\mathcal{M}, \Theta^{G}, \mathbf{B}^{[l]}_{sample}, \Psi, \beta$
2: **Ouput:** $\mathbf{B}^{[l+1]}_{sample}$ sampled blocks in $l+1$:
3: $(\mathbf{U}, \mathbf{T})$=*getUniquePr_BLocations*$(\mathcal{M}, \Theta^{G}, \mathbf{B}^{[l]}_{sample})$
4: **for** $u = 1$ **to** $|\mathbf{U}|$ **do**
5: Draw $n_u \sim Bin(|\mathbf{T}_u|, \pi_u)$ {# of blocks to sample per π_u}
6: **for** $j = 1$ **to** $|\Psi|$ **do**
7: $\mathbf{e}_j = \beta_j \times n_u$ {fraction of possible edges leading to ρ_{IN}}
8: Determine A_{jk} {# of descendent edges of type $\psi_j \in \Psi$ per position $t_k \in \mathbf{T}_u$}
9: **for** $j = 1$ **to** N_Ω **do**
10: $ub_j = \sum_{k=1}^{|\Psi|} A_{jk}$ {max # of sampled blocks per $A_{\cdot k}$}
11: Solve the LP of eq 1: find min χ using n_u, $\mathbf{e}$, A, and ub
12: **for** $j = 1$ **to** N_Ω **do**
13: $\mathbb{B}'_{sample}$= Randomly sample χ_j blocks from ub_j places
14: $\mathbf{B}^{[l+1]}_{sample} = \mathbf{B}^{[l+1]}_{sample} \cup \mathbb{B}'_{sample}$

the fraction of edges per type $\psi_j \in \Psi$ that would lead to ρ_{IN} (lines 6-7). Then, the algorithm determines the matrix A with the number of descendent edges of type $\psi_j \in \Psi$ per position $t_k \in \mathbf{T}_u$ (line 8). Thus, A is a look-ahead structure for the possible edges of the blocks sampled with probability π_u. In theory the dimension of A is $|\Psi| \times |\mathbf{T}_u|$. However, in practice we take only the set of unique columns which makes A much smaller ($|\Psi| \times N_\Omega$). Let χ be the indices of the blocks to be sampled, then $A \cdot \chi$ is (a $|\Psi|$-dimensional vector with) the total number of possible descendent edges per edge-type $\psi_j \in \Psi$. Next, the algorithm computes the maximum number of blocks that can be sampled per column in A, which we refer to as a configuration (lines 9-10). Using these restrictions, the number of edges to sample χ is obtained through LP search (line 11, we used Matlab's interior-point algorithm *fmincon* [9]). Given χ, the last FOR loop (lines 12-14) samples the desired number of blocks per configuration (line 13), generating $\mathbf{B}^{[l+1]}_{sample}$ (line 14).

In summary, *LPBlockSearch* applies the following process per probability π_u.

(a) Number of samples according to the GNM $P(G)$. Since π_u is Bernoulli, the number of blocks to sample per π_u is $n_u \sim Bin(|\mathbf{T}_u|, \pi_u)$, where $\mathbf{T}$ is the *set* of locations of possible blocks per unique probability π_u

(b) Number of samples according to correlation in $P(\mathbf{X})$. Let $\mathbf{e}_j = \beta_j \times n_u$ be the fraction of edges per type $\psi_j \in \Psi$ that would lead to ρ_{IN}. Let $A \cdot \chi$ be (a $|\Psi|$-dimensional vector with) the total number of possible descendent edges per edge-type $\psi_j \in \Psi$, where matrix A is a look-ahead structure on the possible edges for the blocks sampled with probability π_u. Then, $e_j - A_{j\cdot} \cdot \chi$ must be as small as possible $\forall j \in [1, |\Psi|]$; where χ is a N_Ω-dimensional vector with the set of blocks to sample per configuration $A_{\cdot k}$. The value of χ can be found by minimizing the objective function:

$$\begin{aligned} \text{minimize} \quad & f(\chi) = \sum_{j}^{|\Psi|} (\mathbf{e}_j - A_{j\cdot} \cdot \chi) \times \mathbb{1}[(\mathbf{e}_j - A_{j\cdot} \cdot \chi) > 0] \\ \text{subject to} \quad & \textstyle\sum_j \chi_j = n_u \\ & 0 \leq \chi_j \leq ub_j \quad \forall j \end{aligned} \tag{1}$$

Minimizing $f(\chi)$ gives a solution where the fraction of possible descendent edges per type is similar to the fraction of edges β of the input network, which leads to the target correlation ρ_{IN}. Notice $f(\chi)$ is the summation of the differences

Algorithm *MEEdgeSampling*

1: **Input:** $\mathcal{M}, \Theta^G, \mathbf{B}^{[K-\ell-1]}_{sample}, \Psi, \beta$
2: **Output:** G_{OUT}
3: $(\mathbf{U},\mathbf{T})$=*getUniquePr_ELocations*$(\mathcal{M}, \Theta^G, \mathbf{B}^{[l]}_{sample}, \Psi)$
4: **for** $u = 1$ **to** $|\mathbf{U}|$ **do**
5: Draw $n_u \sim Bin(|\mathbf{T}_{u\cdot}|, \pi_u)$ {# edges per unique probabil}
6: Set $N_e = N_e + n_u$ {Total # edges to be sample}
7: Draw $\mathbf{\Gamma} = [\gamma_1, \ldots, \gamma_{|\Psi|}] \sim Mult\,(N_e; \beta)$ {# edges per edge-type to match ρ_{IN}}
8: **for** $u = 1$ **to** $|\mathbf{U}|$ **do**
9: Draw $\mathbf{Y} = [Y_1, ..., Y_{|\Psi|}] \sim Mult\left(n_u; \frac{\mathbf{\Gamma}}{N_e}\right)$ {# edges per edge-type for π_u}
10: **for** $j = 1$ **to** $|\Psi|$ **do**
11: $\mathbf{E}'$ = Sampling Y_j edges at random from $\mathbf{T}_{uj}$ locations.
12: $\mathbf{E}_{OUT} = \mathbf{E}_{OUT} \cup \mathbf{E}'$
13: $\gamma_j = \gamma_j - Y_j$ {Adaptative process to match the moments}
14: $N_e = N_e - Y_j$

between the expected number of possible edges according to β and the actual number of descendent edges per edge-type. If $(\mathbf{e}_j - A_{j\cdot} \cdot \chi)$ is negative, the value $(\mathbb{1}[(\mathbf{e}_j - A_{j\cdot} \cdot \chi) > 0])$ is zero and the term is not considered (i.e., enough edges exist satisfying the condition). This forces the function to apply constraints for all conditions where not enough edges exist.

The constraint $\sum_j \chi_j = n_u$ guarantees that the sum of the number of blocks to sample, per edge type, is equal to the desired number of blocks to sample n_u. This constraint forces sampling a network with a high likelihood with respect to $P(G|\mathcal{M}(\Theta^G))$, because n_u edges are sampled from the unique π_u. The inequalities $0 \leq \chi_j \leq ub_j \; \forall j$ ensure that χ is a valid solution, i.e. each χ_j is greater than zero and less than the number of possible blocks.

Algorithm *MEEdgeSampling* describes the edge sampling stage. In this stage of the sampling process, the network is sampled by drawing edges from the graph-model $\mathcal{M}$ conditioned on the node attributes. The edges accepted must respect a sampling-invariant of the sampling-process, namely, that the fraction of edges of each type are the same as those in the input-network. Given the GNM $\mathcal{M}$ with parameter Θ^G, the set of sample blocks $\mathbf{B}^{[K-\ell-1]}_{sample}$, the list of edge-types Ψ, and the fraction of edges of each type β, *MEEdgeSampling* returns the sampled graph G_{OUT}. *MEEdgeSampling* calculates $\mathbf{U} = \{\pi_1, \ldots, \pi_k\}$ and $\mathbf{T}$—the set of unique probabilities and the locations of possible sample edges. In order to optimize sampling we transform $\mathbf{T}$ from a vector to a matrix indexed not only per unique probability π_u but also per edge type $\psi_j \in \Psi$. Thus, $\mathbf{T}_{uj}$ contains a matrix with the position of edges sampled with probability π_u that correspond to edge type ψ_j, i.e dim($\mathbf{T}$) = $|\mathbf{U}| \times |\Psi|$. Then, *MEEdgeSampling* computes the number of edges n_u per unique probability and the total number of edges N_e to sample in the final network (lines 4-6). With N_e and β, it determines $\mathbf{\Gamma}$ (the total number of edges per type that must be sampled to match ρ_{IN}). Edge sampling is realized by the FOR loop (lines 8-14). This loop calculates the number of edges per edge-type $\mathbf{Y}$ to be sampled given a unique probability π_u (line 9). This matches moments by sampling networks with the original proportion of edges β, i.e. ρ_{IN}. Lines 10 to 14 sample edges per edge-type given $\mathbf{Y}$. Specifically, Y_j edges are sampled from the $|\mathbf{T}_{uj}|$ possible locations with probability π_u and edge-type Ψ_j. The sampled edges are added to the sampled G_{OUT}. Finally, the number of edges per edge-type γ_j, and N_e are updated to avoid possible errors given the multinomial sampling process (lines 13-14). Lines 13 and 14 are crucial to generate networks able to match ρ_{IN} for all unique probabilities and edge-types, unless the number of edges to sample $(\mathbf{Y})$ is smaller than the possible positions T_{uj}. For a unique probability π_u consider $Y_j > T_{uj}$, (i.e. it is impossible to sample the required number of edges). These lines distribute $Y_j - T_{uj}$ edges among the other edge-types, to obtain the number of edges n_u for π_u. Since other edge-types may be oversampled for π_u, the lines recalculate the proportion of edges for the next unique probabilities such that $\rho_{OUT} \approx \rho_{IN}$.

In summary, algorithm *MEEdgeSampling* performs the edge sampling stage, as follows:

(a) The structure of the GNM $P(G)$ is maintained by sampling the target number of edges $n_u \sim Bin(|\mathbf{T}_{u\cdot}|, \pi_u)$, because π_u is Bernoulli-distributed [15].

(b) The attribute distribution $P(\mathbf{X})$ is guaranteed by maintaining the correlation as defined by β, N_e: $\mathbf{\Gamma} = [\gamma_1, \ldots, \gamma_{|\Psi|}] \sim Mult\,(N_e; \beta)$.

These two criteria are combined to sample the number of edges per unique probability π_u and per type ψ_j: $\mathbf{Y} = [Y_1, ..., Y_{|\Psi|}] \sim Mult\left(n_u; \frac{\mathbf{\Gamma}}{N_e}\right)$.

As in *LPBlockSearch*, G_{OUT} has high probability with respect to $P(G|\mathcal{M}(\Theta^G))$. By respecting the original distribution of the GNM, the structure is maintained as well as the variability of the sample networks.

5 Experimental Results

We compare our sampling method, CSAG, using mixed Kronecker Product Graph Model (CSAG-mKPGM), with AGM-mKPGM, AGM Chung Lu (AGM-CL), and AGM Transitive Chung Lu (AGM-TCL)[4]. We note that AGM-TCL is the state of the art, outperforming AGM-CL and MAG [16]. However, AGM-TCL can not be applied to directed networks [17]. The results confirm that CSAG-mKPGM accurately captures the structure and correlation of the input networks, while creating networks with enough variability.

5.1 Datasets

We evaluate our framework on three real world datasets: CoRA citations network [12], Facebook wall postings from Purdue University, and the US patent citation network [6]. The CoRA network comprises 11,881 papers with 31,482 citations between them. We use the categorical attribute *AI* (*AI*=1 iff a paper's topic is in the field of Artificial Intelligence). The Facebook network contains wall postings of 449,748 users with 1,016,621 posting edges. We use two profile attributes: Religion (*R*=1 indicates a user's *Religious Views* contains "christ") and Politics (*P*=1 indicates a user's *Political Views* contains "conservative"). The US patent citation network contains 3,774,768 patents with 16,528,948 citation edges. We use the attribute Category with six possible values: Chemical, Computers and Communications, Drugs and Medical, Electrical and Electronic, Mechanical, and Others. For all networks, we model the attribute distributions with multinomials and use MLE estimation.

[4]Code and data available at www.dropbox.com/s/rdppd1qvqwjgj29/CSAG.zip?dl=0

Table 1: Correlation modeled for CoRA, Facebook, and Patents using AGM and CSAG. Best performers: Values closest to original are bolded. Values corresponding to non-rejected hypothesis under $\alpha = 0.01$ are marked with *

Model	Correlations				
	CoRA	Facebook			Patent
	AI	R	P	RP	
Original	0.8373	0.1319	0.2231	0.1873	0.7097
AGM-TCL	0.8388*	0.1369	0.2364	0.1945	–
AGM-CL	–	–	–	–	**0.7111**
mKPGM	0.2884	0.0311	0.0076	0.0391	0.6310
AGM-mKPGM	0.6945	0.1253	0.0286	0.0807	0.7260
CSAG-mKPGM	**0.8370***	**0.1317***	**0.2225***	**0.1870***	0.7074

5.2 Models

Since AGM is the best performer in [17], we compare CSAG-mKPGM against AGM-mKPGM and AGM-TCL (AGM-CL was used for directed network). We use TCL as described in [17]. We trained mKPGM using the simulated method of moments [14] with the following features: average number of edges, clustering coefficient, geodesic distance (approximated by a sample of nodes), size of largest connected component, and number of non-zero-degree nodes. Table 3 shows the values of the learned parameters. As we will discuss, due to its use of mKPGM, CSAG requires significantly fewer parameters than AGM.

Our sampling method introduces a constraint on the order of attribute values that are generated for the output nodes. To understand the rationale for this choice, we note that in practice random attribute samples can result in a scenario where networks with the desired structure and correlation have probability close to zero due to the specifics of Θ^G. This is because the GNMs create edges at particular locations in the adjacency matrix. Thus it can be difficult for CSAG to produce high correlations with arbitrary orderings of the attribute values (over the random nodes). While this issue could be solved more generally by iteratively reassigning attribute values as part of the search process, for this work we randomly generated the attribute values and then partially sorted (over the nodes in the matrix) before randomly sampling the edges. Sorting starts the sampling from a location that might likely, although not always, result in a successful search. Although this process introduces a bias in a selection of edges geared to match the target correlation, sorting the labels does not affect the distribution nor the sampled graph because the nodes are all random.

5.3 Evaluation and Results

With the learned parameters (Table 3), we sampled 50 networks for CoRA with attribute AI, 20 networks for Facebook with both attributes (Religion and Politics), and a single network for Patent because of AGM's run-time limitations. We analyze both the attribute correlations and the graph structures of the sampled networks.

Figure 3 summarizes both network structure and attribute correlation errors in a single plot. The x-axis comprises the 3-dimensional Kolmogorov-Smirnov distance of the CDFs of the three network characteristics described before, between the models and the original data. The y-axis comprises the relative error of the correlation, i.e. $|\rho_{IN} - \rho_{OUT}|/\rho_{IN}$. As the figure shows, CSAG (enclosed by the triangle) has the lowest errors in all three datasets for both graph-structure and attribute correlation. As we will discuss, CSAG also provides relatively faster performance than AGM and uses orders of magnitude fewer parameters.

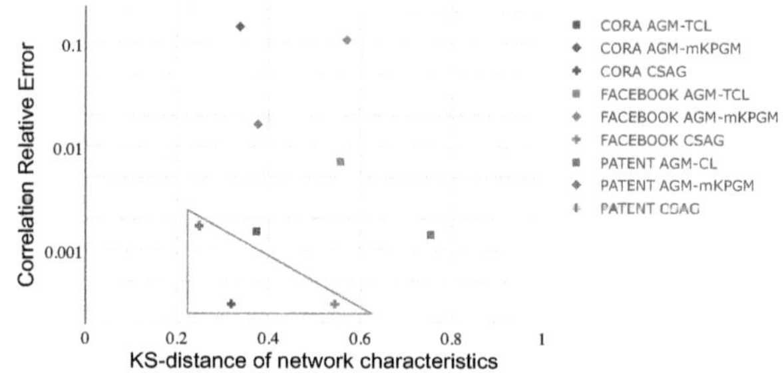

Figure 3: Performance of methods (shape-coded) per dataset (color-coded). Values towards the bottom-left are better.

Table 2: Non-zero edge-probabilities for mKPGM and TCL/CL modeling the three datasets.

Dataset	count of $p(e_{ij}) \neq 0$	
	mKPGM	CL and TCL
CoRA	2.60×10^5	1.41×10^8
Facebook	6.35×10^6	2.02×10^{11}
Patent	4.53×10^7	1.42×10^{13}

5.3.1 *Feature Correlations*

Our first set of evaluations are based on the mean attribute-correlation of the sampled networks. The measurements of the mean-correlation are shown in Table 1. These results show that, though mKPGM has a very restricted sample space (Table 2), in all cases CSAG-mKPGM can capture attribute correlation. Indeed, CSAG-mKPGM is the best model to capture correlation except for AGM-CL in Patents data where CSAG-mKPGM gives competitive performance. The results confirm the importance of our CSAG framework to search over the space of possible networks to sample edges that match the target correlations. Moreover, we can observe that AGM-mKPGM performs badly when AGM's assumptions are violated, producing quite different correlations from the input. We verified these results statistically. Since population variance is unknown for the original networks, we used a T-test with $\alpha = 0.01$ and null hypothesis H_0: true correlation=model's correlation (assuming the true correlation to be that of the original network). H_0 is never rejected for our framework while H_0 is rejected for TCL (values with non-rejected H_0 are marked with $*$ in Table 1). The test cannot be applied to Patents because there is only one network available. This confirms that CSAG in combination with mKPGM provides the closest match to the correlations in the original network datasets.

5.3.2 *Graph Structure*

In our second set of evaluations, we investigated whether the models capture three important structure characteristics of real networks: degree, clustering coefficient (CC), and hop-plot (HP). To evaluate the ability of the models to capture these characteristics, we compared the cumulative distribution functions (CDFs) of the sampled vs. the original networks, visualizing not only the median but the variability of the sampled networks through the plot of the first and ninety nine percentiles (in the case of CoRA and Facebook). Additionally, we compared two more undirected-network characteristics, not included in the mKPGM learning process: the K-core distribution [1] and eigenvalue distances. We measured the maximum absolute distance between the K-core

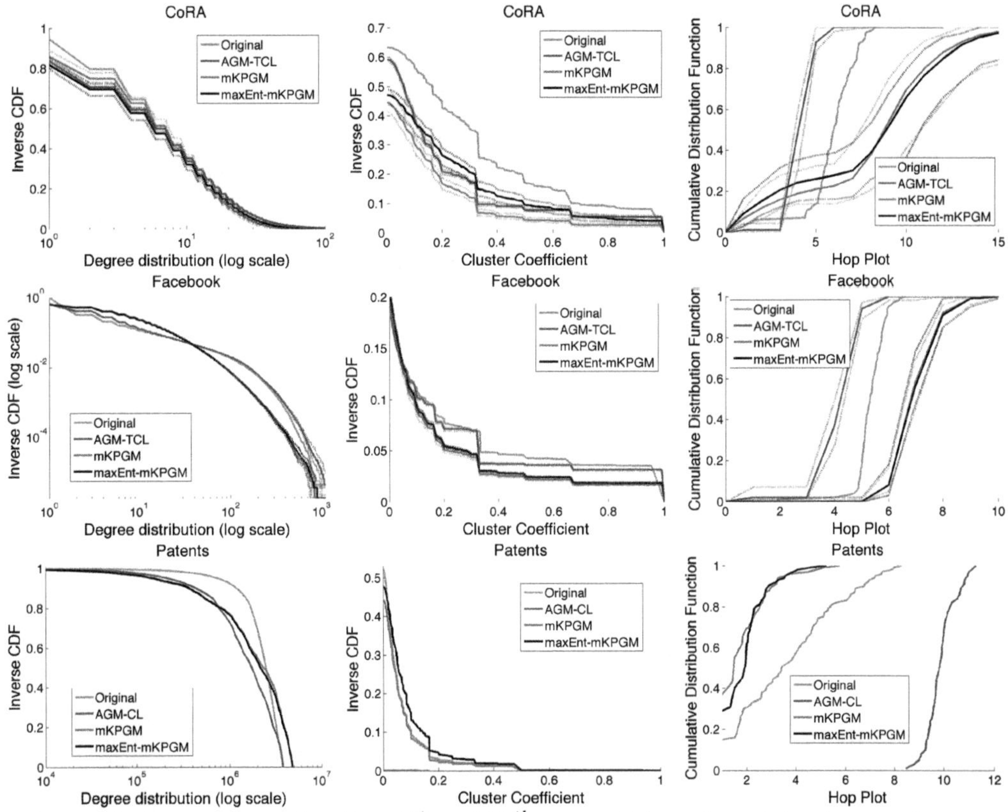

Figure 4: CDF of network characteristics (median, 1st, and 99th percentile). Left-to-right: degree, cluster coefficient, and hop plot. Top-to-bottom: CoRA, Facebook, and Patents.

Table 3: Learned parameters for mKPGMs in CoRA: $K=9, \ell=6$, Facebook: $K=12, \ell=9$, and Patent: $K=14, \ell=10$

$$\Theta^G_{CoRA} = \begin{bmatrix} .94 & .01 & .03 \\ - & .86 & .40 \\ - & - & .95 \end{bmatrix} \quad \Theta^G_{Facebook} = \begin{bmatrix} .99 & .01 & .07 \\ - & .01 & .65 \\ - & - & .98 \end{bmatrix} \quad \Theta^G_{Patents} = \begin{bmatrix} .99 & .01 & .01 \\ .01 & .81 & .01 \\ .46 & .01 & .98 \end{bmatrix}$$

CDFs of the sampled vs. the original networks, and compared the largest 10 eigenvalues of each network using the standardized absolute distance between them.

Figure 4 shows the cumulative distribution function (CDF) of three different characteristics. We compare CSAG with the best performing AGM (i.e. AGM-TCL, which outperforms MAG [10]). The results show CSAG with mKPGM captures most characteristics of the real networks using only 9 parameters. Moreover, the results also show variability in the generated networks, as can be observed in the dashed lines of the plots in the first two rows, which represent the 1st and 99th percentile of the set of samples. (Recall, we generated only a single network for Patents due to AGM's restrictive sampling time.)

While AGM also captures the characteristics of the original networks, AGM requires 11881, 449748, and 3774768 parameters to model CoRA, Facebook, and Patents respectively. One exception is the surprisingly poor fit of AGM for Patents HP and CC (recall, we did not use TCL because it is only defined for undirected networks). As expected, AGM-TCL also shows significantly less variability than CSAG with mKPGM.

We further analyze the variability in network characteristics in two ways. First, we compare CSAG-mKPGM's with

Table 4: K-core and eigVal distances [**undirected** networks] CoRA and Facebook (smallest distances to original bolded).

Model	CoRA		Facebook	
	K-core	eigenvalue	K-core	eigenvalue
AGM-TCL	0.1069	0.5438	**0.3281**	0.6608
mKPGM	**0.0838**	0.2737	0.3398	**0.2707**
AGM-mKPGM	0.1073	0.3059	0.3458	0.2825
CSAG-mKPGM	0.1255	**0.1647**	0.3409	0.3008

mKPGM's variance, using an F-test ($\alpha = 0.01$) for distinct values (vertical slice) of the characteristics in Figure 4. We assume normality for each slice. In this case H_0: the variance of a model is equal to the variance of mKPGM. For CC, HP, and degree CSAG fails to reject H_0 (i.e. maintains mKPGM's variance) for 100% 80% and 91% of the slices for CoRA. Facebook's results were similar. Second, we asses the variance reduction of AGM vs. CSAG. AGM's average variance reduction (compared to CSAG) is as follows: (1) For CoRA, the CC, degree, and HP, is reduced by 88%, 76%, and 70% respectively; (22) For Facebook, CC is reduced by 19%, but degree and HP are similar for AGM and CSAG.

Table 4 shows the K-core and eigenvalue distances for CoRA and Facebook using all models. The K-core distances for CoRA and Facebook are similar across models, confirming that both models (mKPGM and TCL) show similar connectivity and community structure in the sampled graphs compared to the original network. In contrast, mKPGMs have considerably smaller eigenvalue distance than AGM-TCL. In fact, CSAG-mKPGM obtains the lowest eigenvalue distance across models in CoRA, which indicates the similarity of the most important nodes compared to the original network. In contrast, AGM-TCL shows surprisingly high eigenvalue distances for both CoRA and Facebook. Once again, there are no results for Patents dataset because these measures are calculated only for undirected networks.

Finally, sampling with CSAG is faster than with AGM. For Facebook the mean ± 1 stdev runtimes using a MATLAB implementation on a laptop with 2.8 GHz Intel Core i7 and 16 GB in RAM are: CSAG:12.42 ± 0.55s vs AGM:59.15 ± 4.07s, respectively. In the more restricted scenario of CoRA, AGM is faster (CSAG:9.9 ± 0.65s vs AGM:1.5 ± 0.15s) but AGM does not match the correlation. CSAG is an order of magnitude faster in Patents (CSAG:100.7s vs AGM: 1361.6s).

In summary, the results show that CSAG achieves: (1) Overall best fit of attribute correlation (smallest relative error) and network structure (smallest KS-distance). Specifically, CSAG produces $\geq$ 5X reduction in attribute correlation error compared to AGM-TCL. Moreover, AGM-TCL cannot model correlation consistently and cannot be used with directed networks; (2) More effective sampling—the exponential complexity of sampling from the full joint is relieved in CSAG by having a proposal distribution and few rejected samples. This is reflected in the improvement in runtime compared to AGM; (3) Variability of the GNM is maintained for $80\% - 100\%$ of the values of the characteristics; (4) Fewer parameters required compared to AGM.

6 Discussion and Conclusion

There are two main contributions of this paper. First, we showed that hierarchical GNMs, such as mKPGM, have a limited size of the matrix of conditional edge-probabilities which restricts iterative sampling of edges with targeted attribute correlation. This constrains AGM's performance as a result. Second, we proposed CSAG, a novel method to samples networks using mKPGM as the structural component of a proposal distribution. Our method uses a two-stage constrained sampling: an LP stage to sample blocks and a moment matching stage to sample edges. While the LP stage is strictly for models with constrained space, the moment matching is general enough to work with other types of models as well. CSAG's implementation with mKPGM provides the following benefits, as verified experimentally with 3 real datasets: (1) It jointly models network structure and correlated attributes, obtaining cumulative distribution functions (CDFs) and correlations close to the original networks. (2) It does not affect the network variability of the original GNM, as observed in the CDFs. (3) It captures the attribute correlations better than AGM, when using the same GNM.

Acknowledgements

The authors thank the reviewers for their useful comments. This research is supported by NSF under contracts IIS-1149789, IIS-1219015, and CCF-0939370. Sebastian Moreno acknowledges the support of "CONICYT + PAI/Concurso nacional de apoyo al retorno de investigadores/as desde el extranjero, convocatoria 2014 + folio 82140043".

7 References

[1] J. I. Alvarez-Hamelin, A. Barrat, A. Vespignani, and et al. k-core decomposition of internet graphs: hierarchies, self-similarity and measurement biases. *Networks and Heterogeneous media*, 3(2):371, 2008.

[2] F. Chung and L. Lu. The average distances in random graphs with given expected degrees. *PNAS*, 99(25):15879–15882, 2002.

[3] P. Erdos and A. Renyi. On the evolution of random graphs. In *Publication of the Mathematical Institute of the Hungarian Academy of Sciences*, pages 17–61, 1960.

[4] L. Getoor, N. Friedman, D. Koller, and A. Pfeffer. Learning probabilistic relational models. In *Relational Data Mining*, pages 307–335. Springer-Verlag, 2001.

[5] Y. Gu, A. McCallum, and D. Towsley. Detecting anomalies in network traffic using maximum entropy estimation. In *Proceedings of the 5th ACM SIGCOMM Conference on Internet Measurement*, IMC '05, pages 32–32, Berkeley, CA, USA, 2005. USENIX Association.

[6] B. Hall, A. Jaffe, and M. Trajtenberg. The NBER patent citation data file: Lessons, insights and methodological tools. *NBER working paper 8498*, 2001.

[7] E. T. Jaynes. On the rationale of maximum-entropy methods. *Proceedings of the IEEE*, 70(9):939–952, June 1982.

[8] K. Judd, M. Small, and T. Stemler. What exactly are the properties of scale-free and other networks? *EPL (Europhysics Letters)*, 103(5):58004, 2013.

[9] N. Karmarkar. A new polynomial-time algorithm for linear programming. In *Proceedings of the 16th Annual ACM Symposium on Theory of Computing*, STOC '84, pages 302–311, 1984.

[10] M. Kim and J. Leskovec. Multiplicative attribute graph model of real-world networks. In *Algorithms and Models for the Web-Graph*, volume 6516 of *LNCS*, pages 62–73, 2010.

[11] J. Leskovec, D. Chakrabarti, J. Kleinberg, C. Faloutsos, and Z. Ghahramani. Kronecker graphs: An approach to modeling networks. *JMLR*, 11(Feb):985–1042, 2010.

[12] A. McCallum, K. Nigam, J. Rennie, and K. Seymore. Automating the construction of internet portals with machine learning. *Information Retrieval*, 3(2):127–163, 2000.

[13] M. McPherson, L. Smith-Lovin, and J. Cook. Birds of a feather: Homophily in social networks. *Annual Review of Sociology*, 27:415–445, 2001.

[14] S. Moreno, J. Neville, and S. Kirshner. Learning mixed kronecker product graph models with simulated method of moments. In *Proceedings of the 19th ACM SIGKDD International Conference on Knowledge Discovery and Data Mining*, pages 1052–1060, 2013.

[15] S. Moreno, J. Pfeiffer III, S. Kirshner, and J. Neville. A scalable method for exact sampling from kronecker family models. In *IEEE 14th International Conference on Data Mining (ICDM)*, Dec 2014.

[16] J. J. Pfeiffer, III, S. Moreno, T. La Fond, J. Neville, and B. Gallagher. Attributed graph models: Modeling network structure with correlated attributes. In *Proceedings of the 23rd International Conference on World Wide Web*, WWW '14, pages 831–842, 2014.

[17] J. J. Pfeiffer III, T. La Fond, S. Moreno, and J. Neville. Fast generation of large scale social networks while incorporating transitive closures. In *4th ASE/IEEE International Conference on Social Computing*, 2012.

[18] C. Seshadhri, T. Kolda, and A. Pinar. Community structure and scale-free collections of Erdős-Rényi graphs. *Physical Review E*, 85(5), 2012.

[19] C. Seshadhri, A. Pinar, and T. Kolda. An in-depth analysis of stochastic Kronecker graphs. *Journal of the ACM*, 60(2), 2013.

[20] C. R. Shalizi and A. C. Thomas. Homophily and contagion are generically confounded in observational social network studies. *Sociological methods & research*, 40(2):211?239, May 2011.

[21] E. Spyropoulou, T. De Bie, and M. Boley. Interesting pattern mining in multi-relational data. *Data Mining and Knowledge Discovery*, 28(3):808–849, 2014.

Goal-Directed Inductive Matrix Completion

Si Si
Dept. of Computer Science
University of Texas at Austin
ssi@cs.utexas.edu

Kai-Yang Chiang
Dept. of Computer Science
University of Texas at Austin
kychiang@cs.utexas.edu

Cho-Jui Hsieh
Depts. of Statistics and Computer Science
University of California, Davis
chohsieh@ucdavis.edu

Nikhil Rao
Technicolor R&I
nikhilrao86@gmail.com

Inderjit S. Dhillon
Dept. of Computer Science
University of Texas at Austin
inderjit@cs.utexas.edu

ABSTRACT

Matrix completion (MC) with additional information has found wide applicability in several machine learning applications. Among algorithms for solving such problems, Inductive Matrix Completion(IMC) has drawn a considerable amount of attention, not only for its well established theoretical guarantees but also for its superior performance in various real-world applications. However, IMC based methods usually place very strong constraints on the quality of the features(side information) to ensure accurate recovery, which might not be met in practice. In this paper, we propose Goal-directed Inductive Matrix Completion(GIMC) to learn a nonlinear mapping of the features so that they satisfy the required properties. A key distinction between GIMC and IMC is that the feature mapping is learnt in a supervised manner, deviating from the traditional approach of unsupervised feature learning followed by model training. We establish the superiority of our method on several popular machine learning applications including multi-label learning, multi-class classification, and semi-supervised clustering.

1. INTRODUCTION

Matrix completion methods are widely used in several applications, ranging from collaborative filtering for recommender systems [8], to social network analysis [4] and clustering [25]. In these applications, a particular entry of the observed matrix is modeled as a linear interaction between factors corresponding to the row and column variables. For example, a rating provided by user i for movie j in a recommender system is modeled as $r_{ij} = \boldsymbol{w}_i^T \boldsymbol{h}_j$, where $\boldsymbol{w}_i, \boldsymbol{h}_j$ are low dimensional user and movie embeddings.

Modern applications typically involve large amounts of data (often in the millions or more), and several scalable algorithms have been proposed to solve matrix completion problems in such large data regimes [27, 21]. As a consequence of large-scale data acquisition methods, these applications involving large amounts of data also involve side information. Fast and scalable methods have been proposed in [30, 19] when the side information is in the form of pairwise relationships, such as product co-purchasing networks or social networks for recommender systems, or gene–gene interaction networks in computational biology.

In several applications of interest, one is not aware of the relational information in the form of graphs, but is given direct information in the form of features. These might correspond to demographic information (gender, occupation) for users and product information (genre, year of release) in a movie recommender system for example. When such features are provided, one can model an observation as a specific interaction between the features. For example in the recommender system case considered above, we would have $r_{ij} = \boldsymbol{x}_i^T Z \boldsymbol{y}_j$ where Z is the learnt model and $\boldsymbol{x}_i(\boldsymbol{y}_j)$ are the user (movie) features [5] [1]. These methods two advantages over traditional matrix completion applications:

- The target matrix to be estimated (Z above) can be significantly smaller than the partially observed data matrix, thus lowering the number of parameters to learn and speeding up computation.
- The presence of features allows the practitioner to generalize to previously unseen users and/or items, which is something standard matrix completion cannot do.

While such methods have been considered before in [24, 5], the authors in [2] showed that a significant drawback of feature-based matrix completion methods–Inductive Matrix Completion(IMC)– is that there need to be extremely strict constraints placed on the features to ensure accurate recovery of the underlying matrix. Specifically, the space spanned by the row (column) features must correspond to the row (column) space of the matrix to be factorized. In practice, such constraints are seldom met, which might result in poor performance of IMC. One way to solve this problem is by constructing mappings of the features so that the mapped features are more aligned to the subspaces in question. Moreover, the mappings should be constructed so that the methods are scalable, to be applicable to modern datasets. This brings us to the questions we wish to answer in this paper:

[1]We expound on this in more detail in the sequel

KDD '16, August 13 - 17, 2016, San Francisco, CA, USA

ISBN 978-1-4503-4232-2/16/08...$15.00
DOI: http://dx.doi.org/10.1145/2939672.2939809

1. Can a (possibly nonlinear) mapping be constructed for the features so that we can retain the gains provided by IMC given noisy features?

2. Can the resulting method be scaled to large datasets?

We answer both the above questions in the affirmative. To answer the first question, we aim to construct (nonlinear) embeddings of the row (or column) features so that they are better aligned to the task at hand. Specifically, we develop a minimization scheme called Goal-Directed Inductive Matrix Completion (GIMC) that alternates between learning the low-rank factors of the target matrix, and the aforementioned embeddings. A key contribution of this work is that the embeddings are learned in a supervised manner. This is a significant deviation from several other feature learning methodologies that learn the features in an unsupervised setting and use the learned features to solve the machine learning task.

To answer the second question, we resort to performing linear approximations of the nonlinear mappings that we aim to learn. Linear approximations of kernel-based methods have spawned large amounts of interest, either by using random Fourier features [17] or via Nyström approximations [23]. Such methods are attractive since they facilitate the use of highly scalable existing methods for learning with linear models. However, the dimension of these approximate kernel mappings could be very high, which induces a significant computational burden. We show that since we can learn the features based on the task at hand, we can use significantly fewer Fourier features or Nyström landmark points to achieve the same error as classical, unsupervised kernel approximation methods.

Viewed from a different perspective, our proposed Goal-Directed Inductive Matrix Completion framework could be viewed as a three-layer neural network. In this shallow neural network, the objective is a least squares loss and $cos(\cdot)$ and $sin(\cdot)$ are the activation functions. Interestingly, with such a shallow neural network, we achieve state-of-the-art performance in various matrix completion applications. Note that instead of using gradient descent in our algorithm to optimize the loss function, similar to neural networks, we could use back-propagation and SGD as an optimization scheme, and also use other activation functions such as the sigmoid function or hyperbolic tangent.

We consider three applications to test our proposed method: Multi-Label learning, Multi-Class classification, and Semi-supervised Clustering. In these three cases, we show that GIMC achieves state of the art results, while using far fewer features than what would be required to achieve the same performance using unsupervised feature learning methods. We verify that we achieve orders of magnitude speedups over existing methods.

The rest of the paper is organized as follows: in the next Section, we summarize related work. In Section 3 we detail the Inductive Matrix Factorization formulation and summarize known results. We propose our model in Section 4 and show how to apply our framework for solving three popular machine learning applications: Multi-Label learning, Multi-Class classification, and Semi-supervised Clustering in Section 5. We provide extensive empirical results on several real-world datasets in Section 6 before concluding our paper in Section 7.

2. RELATED WORK

We categorize related work into three categories, based on the core contribution of the corresponding works:

2.1 Scalable Matrix Factorization

Stochastic gradient descent(SGD) is widely used in matrix factorization due to its efficiency and ease of implementation. Various update schemes to parallelize SGD have been proposed: HogWild [21] uses lock free approach and DSGD [20] partitions the rating matrix into independent blocks to avoid conflict in the distributed system. [15] takes I/O cost and the CPU utility into consideration and proposed a fast and robust parallel SGD matrix factorization algorithm to deal with the situation when data cannot fit into memory. On a different note, [27][26] proposed to use coordinate descent instead of SGD to optimize the loss function, and the corresponding parallel solvers are shown to have superior performance in both multi-core and distributed settings.

2.2 Matrix Completion with Side Information

Matrix completion with side information has drawn much attention for improving the performance of traditional matrix completion. For instance, [19, 30] incorporates graph information as a regularization term into matrix completion framework, where the graph encodes pairwise relationships among variables. Along similar lines, [13] uses a social network among users to bias the recommender system. Instead of these pairwise relationships, in scenarios where one is provided with features for the rows and/or columns of the matrix, [5, 24, 10] proposed an Inductive Matrix Completion formulation. The method is "Inductive", in that it generalizes to previously unobserved data points, which is a drawback in traditional recommender systems. These methods have since been applied to predict gene-disease relationships [14] and semi-supervised clustering [25].

2.3 Non-Linear Kernel Mappings

To overcome the computational barrier of applying kernel methods to very large datasets, linear approximations have become popular, common among them being Nyström based methods [23] [29] [11] and random feature based methods [18] [12] [3, 7]. It has been shown that these approximate kernel mappings can speed up the training and prediction for kernel machines such as kernel SVM and Gaussian processes. To achieve a "good" approximation to the underlying kernel, these methods require the generation of many random features or landmark points. Thus, while such methods can in principle alleviate the computational costs associated with kernel machines, achieving a good approximation requires generation of many random features or landmark points which contributes to increased costs.

3. INDUCTIVE MATRIX COMPLETION

In this section, we first introduce traditional matrix completion and inductive matrix completion, and then formally set up the problem we are interested in solving. Consider a standard matrix completion setup, where we observe entries from an $n_x \times n_y$ matrix A. Let $\Omega : \ |\Omega| \ll n_x n_y$ be the set of observed entries in A. Traditional matrix completion models A to be low rank, meaning that the row and column variables of A share a low dimensional latent space.

Standard matrix completion tries to recover the low-rank

matrix by solving one of the following optimization problems:

$$\min_{Z} \frac{1}{2}\|P_\Omega(A-Z)\|_F^2 + \lambda_z\|Z\|_*, \quad (1)$$

$$\min_{W,H} \frac{1}{2}\|P_\Omega(A-WH^T)\|_F^2 + \lambda_{WH}(\|W\|_F^2+\|H\|_F^2), \quad (2)$$

where $W \in \mathbb{R}^{n_x\times k}$ and $H \in \mathbb{R}^{n_y\times k}$, and $P_\Omega(\cdot)$ is the projection operator that only retains those entries of the matrix that lie in the set Ω, It has been shown that these two problems are in fact equivalent when the chosen $k \geq \text{rank}(A)$ [22]. In addition, although the factorization objective (2) is non-convex, it turns out that the (local optimal) solution given by this non-convex form is usually comparable to the global optimum in (1). To solve (2), note that when either W or H is fixed, the above optimization becomes convex with respect to the other variable, so that one can solve (2) by alternating minimization. Various optimization techniques, for example, coordinate descent and stochastic gradient descent, have been proposed to solve (2) efficiently.

One challenge for traditional matrix completion is that it cannot directly use side information and apply it to predict new and unseen data, or to simplify computation. Inductive Matrix Completion [5] alleviates this issue. Specifically, suppose we are given a set of features $X \in \mathbb{R}^{n_x\times d_x}$ for the rows of A, and similarly for the columns, $Y \in \mathbb{R}^{n_y\times d_y}$. Each row of X (denoted as $\boldsymbol{x}_i$) and each row of Y (denoted as $\boldsymbol{y}_j$) are features for the i-th row and j-th column entity respectively. Then, IMC incorporates the feature information into matrix completion by solving the following problem:

$$\min_{Z} \frac{1}{2}\|P_\Omega(A-XZY^T)\|_F^2 + \lambda_z\|Z\|_*,$$
$$\min_{W,H} \frac{1}{2}\|P_\Omega(A-XWH^TY^T)\|_F^2 + \lambda_{WH}(\|W\|_F^2+\|H\|_F^2), \quad (3)$$

where now $W \in \mathbb{R}^{d_x\times k}$ and $H \in \mathbb{R}^{d_y\times k}$.

Note that the number of unknown parameters are $k(d_x + d_y)$ which can be significantly smaller than $k(n_x+n_y)$. This has the potential to speed up computations by non-trivial amounts. Furthermore, besides recovering unseen entries in A, (3) can also be used to deal with cold start problem in recommendation systems. For example, for a movie recommendation problem, given a new user where only its features $\boldsymbol{x}_{\text{new}}$ are available, IMC could predict the score for the movies to be $\boldsymbol{x}_{\text{new}}^T ZY^T$. We refer the interested reader to [5] for details.

We consider a comparison between MC and IMC on a synthetic example. We generate the underlying matrix A as $XY^T + N$, where $X, Y \in \mathbb{R}^{200\times 50}$ are two rank-50 random matrices with each entry drawn from Gaussian distribution $\mathcal{N}(0,1)$, and $N \in \mathbb{R}^{200\times 200}$ is the noise matrix with each entry drawn from $\mathcal{N}(0,0.1)$. X and Y are provided as features to IMC, and rank k is set to be 20 for both MF and IMC. We vary the number of observed entries from 5% to 30% and recover the remaining entries of the target matrix. The approximately recovered matrix $\hat{A}$ will be WH^T in MF and XWH^TY^T in IMC. We then evaluate the recovered matrix $\hat{A}$ using the relative approximation error $\frac{\|\hat{A}-A\|_F}{\|A\|_F}$. As shown in Figure 1, IMC results in lower error than MC, suggesting that incorporating side information is useful for better recovery given a small perturbed observations.

While Figure 1 shows that IMC could outperform MC, the quality of the features plays a significant role in determining the accuracy of the recovered matrix. Indeed, the authors in [24] showed that to guarantee exact recovery in IMC, the features X, Y should be perfectly aligned with the row and column spaces of the target matrix A. Specifically, we require that

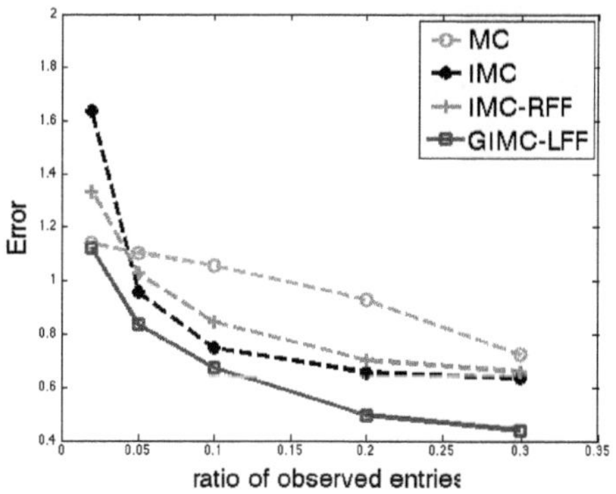

Figure 1: Toy example comparing MC, IMC, IMC-RFF, and GIMC-LFF. MC is the traditional model (Eq (2)); IMC is the model in Eq (3); IMC-RFF is a modification of IMC with random Fourier feature based side information as in Eq (5). GIMC-LFF learns the Fourier projections and the model simultaneously by solving Eq (9) side information is the random Fourier features from X and Y as in Eq (5); GIMC-LFF is to learn the projections of Fourier feature and model in IMC simultaneously. Using side information (IMC and IMC-RFF) improves performance, but not as significantly as learning both the projections and the model (GIMC-LFF)

$$Col(A) \subseteq Col(X), \quad Row(A) \subseteq Col(Y), \quad (4)$$

where $Col(\cdot)$ and $Row(\cdot)$ correspond to the column and row space respectively. That is, to achieve good performance, the features X and Y should be strongly related to the underlying problem, which might not be satisfied in practice. This motivates us to ask if, given noisy features X and Y, one can learn an embedding of the features so that we can retain the gains provided by IMC given noisy features.

4. PROPOSED FRAMEWORK: GIMC

In this section, we introduce our framework–Goal-directed Inductive Matrix Completion (GIMC). We first show how to employ nonlinear mappings into IMC, and then introduce the proposed GIMC model where we add supervision into nonlinear mappings throughout the learning process.

4.1 Nonlinear Feature Mapping for IMC

As discussed previously, performance of IMC may suffer if condition (4) is not satisfied. One way to address this issue is to generate features based on X and Y; that is, mapping X to $\Phi_X(X)$ and Y to $\Phi_Y(Y)$ via two mappings $\Phi_X : \mathbb{R}^{d_x} \to \mathbb{R}^{d'_x}$ and $\Phi_Y : \mathbb{R}^{d_y} \to \mathbb{R}^{d'_y}$. Notice that to overcome the violation of (4), such mapping has to be *nonlinear*, since for any linear mapping L, $Col(L(X)) \subseteq Col(X)$ and thus cannot help to relieve the violation of (4). By doing so, the IMC problem can modified to be:

$$\min_{Z} \frac{1}{2}\|P_{\Omega}(A - \Phi_X(X)Z\Phi_Y(Y)^T)\|_F^2 + \lambda_z\|Z\|_*, \quad (5)$$

where $\Phi_X(X)$ and $\Phi_Y(Y)$ are new set of features generated by the non-linear mapping of X and Y respectively. For simplicity, here we again consider Z to be low rank, but in general, the term $\|Z\|_*$ could be further replaced by other regularizations for different applications. From now on, we will focus our discussion on the mapping of X, and use n, d to represent n_x, n_d. All subsequent discussions could be applied to Y as well with $n = n_y, d = d_y$.

Indeed, the specific mapping to be used can be varied, and the choices are many. A popular choice of such mappings are kernel mappings where we map $\boldsymbol{x}$ to $\varphi(\boldsymbol{x})$ which could be infinite dimensional. Recently, scalable alternatives to using exact kernels (either directly in the primal or via the Gram matrix in the dual) have been proposed where the exact mapping is replaced by an approximation. For instance, for shift-invariant kernels, based on Bochner's theorem[17], the feature mapping $\varphi(\cdot)$ can be written as (with high probability):

$$\boldsymbol{x}_i \rightarrow \varphi_U(\boldsymbol{x}_i) = \frac{1}{\sqrt{m}}[\cos(\boldsymbol{u}_1^T\boldsymbol{x}_i), \cdots, \cos(\boldsymbol{u}_m^T\boldsymbol{x}_i), \sin(\boldsymbol{u}_1^T\boldsymbol{x}_i), \cdots, \sin(\boldsymbol{u}_m^T\boldsymbol{x}_i)] \quad (6)$$

where $U = \{\boldsymbol{u}_1, \cdots, \boldsymbol{u}_m\}$ are the m projection directions sampled according to the distribution from the Fourier transform of the kernel function. For the RBF kernel ($k(\boldsymbol{x}_i, \boldsymbol{x}_j) = e^{-\gamma\|\boldsymbol{x}_i - \boldsymbol{x}_j\|^2}$ with γ representing kernel width), the sampling distribution is a Gaussian distribution $p(\boldsymbol{u}) = N(0, 2\gamma I)$. Since there are infinite number of data points from that distribution, the feature mapping is infinite dimensional, and cannot be used in practice. [17] proposed to randomly sample a few projections from the distribution, and used the approximate feature mapping to speed up kernel machines.

Another popular kernel mapping is Nyström features that approximate the kernel matrix G by sampling $m \ll n$ landmark points $\{\boldsymbol{u}_r\}_{r=1}^m$, and forming two matrices $C \in \mathbb{R}^{n\times m}$ and $E \in \mathbb{R}^{m\times m}$ based on the kernel function. Here $C_{ir} = K(\boldsymbol{x}_i, \boldsymbol{u}_r)$ and $E_{ij} = K(\boldsymbol{u}_i, \boldsymbol{u}_j)$, and the kernel matrix can be approximated as

$$G \approx \bar{G} := CE^{\dagger}C^T, \quad (7)$$

where $E^{\dagger}$ denotes the pseudo-inverse of E. From the feature point of view, the Nyström method may be viewed as constructing features for $\boldsymbol{x}_i$; with m landmark points $\boldsymbol{u}_1, \cdots, \boldsymbol{u}_m$, the feature mapping is

$$\boldsymbol{x}_i \rightarrow \varphi_U(\boldsymbol{x}_i) = [k(\boldsymbol{x}_i, \boldsymbol{u}_1), k(\boldsymbol{x}_i, \boldsymbol{u}_2), \cdots, k(\boldsymbol{x}_i, \boldsymbol{u}_m)]M, \quad (8)$$

where $M = (E^{\dagger})^{\frac{1}{2}}$ and $U = \{\boldsymbol{u}_1, \cdots, \boldsymbol{u}_m, M\}$.

However, when using the above feature mappings for solving IMC, as shown in the experiment, we need large number of projections or landmark points (large m), to achieve good performance. The memory requirement for storing these new set of features $\varphi_U(\boldsymbol{x}_i)$ for all $\boldsymbol{x}_i$ is $O(nm)$. This can be infeasible in many applications, for example, when $m > 10,000$ and n approaches 1 million. A natural question to ask is if we can reduce the number of samples needed to perform the approximation.

4.2 Goal-directed IMC

To overcome the issue with large number of nonlinear features, we propose Goal-directed Inductive Matrix Completion(GIMC), which aims to learn the feature mapping automatically to benefit the model. Instead of constructing a mapping $\varphi_U(\cdot)$ in an unsupervised setting which ignores the task at hand, we propose to learn the feature mappings and the model parameters simultaneously in a supervised manner. This can be attempted by solving the following joint optimization problem:

$$\min_{Z,U,V} \left\{\lambda_z\|Z\|_* + \sum_{(i,j)\in\Omega} \ell(\varphi_U(\boldsymbol{x}_i)^T Z\varphi_V(\boldsymbol{y}_j), A_{ij})\right\} := f(Z,U,V), \quad (9)$$

where ℓ is the loss function, Z represents the model, and the feature mapping of X and Y are $\varphi_U(\cdot), \varphi_V(\cdot)$ which are parameterized by U and V respectively. For simplicity, in this paper we focus on squared loss $\ell(b,a) = \frac{1}{2}(b-a)^2$, but in general we can extend the algorithm to any loss function. The main difference between problems (5) and (9) is that the former only considers the model parameters Z given a fixed feature mapping since U, V are predetermined, while the latter considers to learn Z and U, V simultaneously. As a result, we have the flexibility to optimize the kernel mapping according to the objective function that is defined by different machine learning applications with IMC.

Again, we can define the feature mapping $\varphi_U(\cdot)$ in (9) using various functions. In our first algorithm, Goal-directed IMC with Learned Fourier Features (GIMC-LFF) approach, we define the feature mapping according to (6), and the parameters $U = \{\boldsymbol{u}_r\}_{r=1}^m$ are the projection directions in Fourier Features. Compared to the original RFF that samples $\{\boldsymbol{u}_r\}_{r=1}^m$ randomly from a distribution, we can learn the projection directions $\{\boldsymbol{u}_r\}_{r=1}^m$ by minimizing the final objective function in IMC.

Our second proposed algorithm, Goal-directed IMC with Learned Nyström approximation (GIMC-LNYS), uses $\varphi_U(\cdot)$ defined in (8). In this case, the parameters $U = \{\boldsymbol{u}_1, \ldots, \boldsymbol{u}_m, M\}$, where each $\boldsymbol{u}_i$ is a landmark point, and $M \in \mathbb{R}^{m\times m}$ is a linear transformation. Although gradient descent updates discussed below can be applied to two set of variables ($\{\boldsymbol{u}_r\}_{r=1}^m$ and M), we observe no improvement by learning two sets of parameters, so in the following we assume $M = I$ in GIMC-LNYS. Thus, $U = \{\boldsymbol{u}_r\}_{r=1}^m$ for both GIMC-LNYS and GIMC-LFF, where each $\boldsymbol{u}_r \in \mathbb{R}^d$.

Problem (9) is non-convex and can be solved via alternating minimization, where we alternatively optimize the model parameters Z and feature mapping parameters U and V. The update of model Z varies through applications, and we will discuss how to update model parameters under specific applications shortly in Section 5. To update nonlinear mapping parameters $\boldsymbol{u}_1, \ldots, \boldsymbol{u}_m$, we use gradient descent and update the parameters as:

$$\boldsymbol{u}_r^{t+1} \leftarrow \boldsymbol{u}_r^t - \eta\nabla_{\boldsymbol{u}_r} f(Z,U,V), \ \forall r = 1, \ldots, m \quad (10)$$

where η is the step size and we adopt the Armijo-rule based step size selection to perform line search. Assume $B_{ij} = \varphi_U(\boldsymbol{x}_i)^T Z\varphi_V(\boldsymbol{y}_j)$ is the current prediction on (i,j) element, the gradient for each $\boldsymbol{u}_r$ can be computed by chain rule:

$$\begin{aligned}\nabla_{\boldsymbol{u}_r} f(Z,U,V) &= \sum_{(i,j)\in\Omega} \ell'(B_{ij},A_{ij}) \frac{\partial \varphi_U(\boldsymbol{x}_i)}{\partial \boldsymbol{u}_r} \frac{\partial B_{ij}}{\partial \varphi_U(\boldsymbol{x}_i)} \\ &= \sum_{(i,j)\in\Omega} \ell'(B_{ij},A_{ij}) \frac{\partial \varphi_U(\boldsymbol{x}_i)}{\partial \boldsymbol{u}_r} Z \varphi_V(\boldsymbol{y}_j)\end{aligned} \quad (11)$$

where $\frac{\partial \varphi_U(\boldsymbol{x}_i)}{\partial \boldsymbol{u}_r}$ is a $d \times m$ Jacobian matrix. For GIMC-LFF, each $\boldsymbol{u}_r$ only correlates with two features (see (6)), so the Jacobian matrix has only two nonzero columns; where for GIMC-LNYS each Jacobian matrix has only one nonzero column. The update of V could be conducted similarly.

The time complexity of computing (11) can be analyzed as follows. (1) Computing $\varphi_V(\boldsymbol{y}_j)$ for all j: Assume the computation of each element in $\varphi_V(\boldsymbol{y}_j)$ requires $O(d)$ time (one inner product for both GIMC-LNYS and GIMC-LFF), so constructing $\varphi_V(\boldsymbol{y}_j)$ for all j requires $O(dmn)$ time. This can be further reduced to $O(\text{nnz}(Y)m)$ if the original feature matrix Y is sparse. (2) Computing $\varphi_U(\boldsymbol{x}_i)$ for all i: similarly this requires $O(\text{nnz}(X)m)$ time. (3) Computing eq (11): Since only one or two columns of $\frac{\partial \varphi_U(\boldsymbol{x}_i)}{\partial \boldsymbol{u}_r}$ are nonzero, each term in eq (11) requires $O(m)$ time. In summary, the overall time complexity for evaluating $\nabla_{\boldsymbol{u}_r} f(Z,U,V)$ is

$$O\Big((\text{nnz}(X) + \text{nnz}(Y) + \text{nnz}(A))m\Big),$$

which is similar to the original matrix completion if m is small.

Details of the method are given in Algorithm 1. Since we employ alternating minimization scheme for solving (9), one can show that with the same number of landmark points or projection directions m, our method can achieve lower objective function values compared to the one achieved by using IMC with unsupervised Nyström (IMC-NYS) or random Fourier features(IMC-RFF). Specifically, let U^0 and V^0 be the initial set of mapping directions, Z^0 be the model trained using IMC-RFF or IMC-NYS, and U^t be the updated directions at iteration t of Algorithm 1, we will have

$$f(Z^t,U^t,V^t) \le f(Z^0,U^0,V^0),$$

which potentially implies a lower generalization error. In the toy example in Figure 1, we can clearly see that GIMC-LFF performs better than IMC-RFF, because we learn the feature and model together and thus construct a better set of non-linear features to benefit IMC. In our real-world experiments, we will also show that for a fixed number of features, our method outperforms IMC using both traditional Nyström and random Fourier feature mappings.

5. APPLICATIONS

We now state how to apply our proposed GIMC model to three machine learning applications: multi-label/multi-class learning problems, and semi-supervised clustering problem.

5.1 Multi-label and Multi-class Learning

Modern multi-label learning algorithms have to deal with problems with a very large number of samples, features and labels [2] For example in our experiments, the largest dataset we used has more than a hundred thousand samples, features, and labels.

[2]called "extreme multi-label learning" http://research.microsoft.com/en-us/um/people/manik/events/xc15/

Algorithm 1: Goal-Directed Inductive Matrix Factorization (GIMC)

Input : Partially observed set $\{A_{ij} \mid (i,j) \in \Omega\}$, feature set $X = \{\boldsymbol{x}_i\}_{i=1}^{n_x}$ and $Y = \{\boldsymbol{y}_i\}_{i=1}^{n_y}$, number of landmark points or projection directions m_x, m_y for X and Y.

Output: The model Z, $U = \{\boldsymbol{u}_r\}_{r=1}^{m_x}$ and $V = \{\boldsymbol{v}_r\}_{r=1}^{m_y}$ which parameterize the goal-directed feature mapping for $X : \varphi_U(\cdot)$ and mapping for $Y : \varphi_V(\cdot)$ respectively.

[For GIMC-LFF]: Initialize $\{\boldsymbol{u}_r\}_{r=1}^{m_x}$, $\{\boldsymbol{v}_r\}_{r=1}^{m_y}$ by original random Fourier features
[For GIMC-LNYS]: Initialize $\{\boldsymbol{u}_r\}_{r=1}^{m_x}$, $\{\boldsymbol{v}_r\}_{r=1}^{m_y}$ by kmeans sampling or random sampling from training data
for $t = 1, \dots, maxiter$ **do**
  Update Z by existing IMC with $\{\varphi_U(\boldsymbol{x}_i)\}_{i=1}^{n_x}$ and $\{\varphi_V(\boldsymbol{y}_i)\}_{i=1}^{n_y}$
  // Learn feature map for X
  Compute $\boldsymbol{g}_r \leftarrow \nabla_{\boldsymbol{u}_r} f(Z,U,V)$, $\forall r = 1,\dots,m_x$
  Line search to find a step size η
  Update $\boldsymbol{u}_r \leftarrow \boldsymbol{u}_r - \eta \boldsymbol{g}_r$, $\forall r = 1,\dots,m_x$
  // Learn feature map for Y
  Compute $\boldsymbol{g}_r \leftarrow \nabla_{\boldsymbol{v}_r} f(Z,U,V)$, $\forall r = 1,\dots,m_y$
  Line search to find a step size η
  Update $\boldsymbol{v}_r \leftarrow \boldsymbol{v}_r - \eta \boldsymbol{g}_r$, $\forall r = 1,\dots,m_y$

Traditional multi-label learning approaches usually only consider linear models due to computational concerns, especially when the number of labels is huge (see [28, 16]). Using our goal-directed kernel approximation framework, we can not only learn the non-linear features, but also make computation efficient in both training and prediction phases.

Given training data $X = \{\boldsymbol{x}_i\}_{i=1}^n$, we use $A \in \mathbb{R}^{n \times L}$ to denote the 0/1 label matrix, where each row of A represents the L labels associated with $\boldsymbol{x}_i$. We can formulate a simple model that assumes no correlation among labels, and solve for each label independently:

$$\min_{\boldsymbol{w}_1 \dots \boldsymbol{w}_L} \sum_{j=1}^{L} \Big(\frac{\lambda}{2}\|\boldsymbol{w}_j\|^2 + \sum_{i=1}^{n} \ell(\boldsymbol{w}_j^T \varphi_U(\boldsymbol{x}_i), A_{ij})\Big),$$

where each $\boldsymbol{w}_j$ is the parameters for predicting whether the data has label j. This can be reduced to L binary classification problems, but this approach is very time consuming. For example, the Delicious dataset with 983 labels requires more than 1 day for training. Generally speaking, a method cannot scale to large n and large L if the time complexity grows with $O(nL)$.

We now show that we can apply GIMC-LFF and GIMC-LNYS to solve this problem. As ℓ is chosen to be the squared loss, the objective function can be rewritten as

$$\min_{W,U} \frac{\lambda}{2}\|W\|_F^2 + \frac{1}{2}\|A - \varphi_U(X)W\|_F^2,$$
$$\text{where} \quad \varphi_U(X) := [\varphi_U(\boldsymbol{x}_1) \dots \varphi_U(\boldsymbol{x}_n)]^T, \quad (12)$$

and $W \in \mathbb{R}^{m \times L}$ are model parameters. We can see that (12) is a special case of (9), where $\varphi_V(Y) = I$ and Ω is all the nL elements in A. [3] Therefore, we can solve it by the alternating minimization algorithm. Unfortunately, as analyzed in Section 4.2, directly computing (11) will lead to $O(|\Omega| m) = O(Lmn)$, which will not scale to problems with $L, n \geq 100,000$.

Interestingly, in the following we show that by carefully arranging the computation, the computational complexity can be reduced to $O(m^2(n+L)+m\|X\|_0+m\|A\|_0))$, which leads to a scalable algorithm that only depends on the number of nonzero elements in feature and label matrices.

When U is fixed, the subproblem with respect to W is a standard linear regression problem, which can be solved by a linear system solver: $W \leftarrow (\lambda\varphi_U(X)^T\varphi_U(X)+\lambda I)^{-1}\varphi_U(X)^T A$. This costs $O(m^3 + m\|A\|_0 + m^2 L)$ time complexity.

When W is fixed, for GIMC-LFF the subproblem with respect to U can be written as

$$\nabla_{\boldsymbol{u}_r} f(\boldsymbol{w}, U) = \frac{1}{\sqrt{m}} \sum_{i=1}^{n} \sum_{j=1}^{L} (\boldsymbol{w}_j^T \varphi_U(\boldsymbol{x}_i) - A_{i,j})(W_{r,j} \sin(\boldsymbol{u}_r^T \boldsymbol{x}_i) - W_{r+m,j} \cos(\boldsymbol{u}_r^T \boldsymbol{x}_i))\boldsymbol{x}_i,$$

which can be written in a compact form as

$$\nabla_U f(\boldsymbol{w}, U) = \frac{1}{\sqrt{m}} X^T \big((\varphi_U(X) W W_{(2)}^T - A W_{(2)}^T) \circ \cos(XU)) - (\varphi_U(X) W W_{(1)}^T - A W_{(1)}^T) \circ \sin(XU)) \big),$$

where $U \in \mathbb{R}^{d \times m}$, $W^T = [W_{(1)}^T \; W_{(2)}^T]$ and $\circ$ is the element-wise product. This can be computed in $O(m^2 n + m\|X\|_0 + m\|A\|_0)$ time where $\|\cdot\|_0$ is number of nonzeroes in the matrix.

In the line search step, we use the following formulation to compute the objective function value,

$$\|A - \varphi_U(X)W\|_F^2 = \sum_{1\leq i,j\leq m} \left((WW^T) \circ (\varphi_U(X)^T \varphi_U(X))\right)_{ij} + \|A\|_F^2 - 2 \sum_{1\leq i,j\leq m} (AW^T \circ \varphi_U(X))_{ij},$$

which only requires $O(m\|A\|_0 + nm^2 + Lm^2)$ time. The complexity will not grow as $O(nL)$, which means it can use large number of samples and labels when A is sparse. A similar update rule can be derived for GIMC-LNYS.

As a final remark, we can also use (12) for solving multi-class classification problem, where A is a $n \times L$ matrix with L to be the number of classes. $A_{ij} = 1$ when $\boldsymbol{x}_i$ belong to j-th class. The algorithm and analysis remain the same.

5.2 Semi-supervised Clustering

We now show that we can apply our GIMC framework for semi-supervised clustering as well. The semi-supervised clustering problem can be stated as follows: Suppose we are given n items and a feature matrix $X \in \mathbb{R}^{n\times d}$ where the i-th row $\boldsymbol{x}_i$ is the feature of i-th item, and a set of pairwise constraints $\mathcal{C} = \{S_{ij} \mid (i,j) \in \Omega\}$ where each constraint S_{ij} is in the following form:

$$S_{ij} = \begin{cases} 1, & \text{if item } i \text{ and } j \text{ are similar,} \\ 0, & \text{if item } i \text{ and } j \text{ are dissimilar.} \end{cases}$$

[3] Rigorously speaking, it is a special case for the "generalized" GIMC model where regularization of model parameter is replaced with $\|\cdot\|_F^2$.

Then the goal is to find a clustering of items such that most similar items are within the same cluster. A state-of-the-art approach MCCC [25] models this problem using IMC framework. Specifically, let $S = \sum_{i=1}^{k} \boldsymbol{c}_i \boldsymbol{c}_i^T$ be the rank-k similarity matrix, where $\boldsymbol{c}_i$ is the indicator of the i-th cluster. Then the constraint set $\mathcal{C}$ could be thought of as partial observations of S. MCCC first tries to complete the low rank matrix S using IMC (3), and then uses its top-k singular vectors, which ideally will be the cluster indicators, to derive a partition.

Although it has been shown that MCCC outperforms traditional semi-supervised clustering algorithms [25], one issue is that it only considers linear mapping of features in matrix completion step, while the clustering may be revealed by some non-linear mapping of features. Thus, to overcome this problem, we propose to apply our GIMC framework to solve the semi-supervised clustering by learning both non-linear mapping of features and the underlying similarity S by solving the following optimization problem:

$$\min_{W,H,U,V} \frac{1}{2} \|P_\Omega(S - \varphi_U(X) W H^T \varphi_V(X)^T)\|_F^2 + \frac{\lambda}{2}(\|W\|_F^2 + \|H\|_F^2) \tag{13}$$

which is a special case of the GIMC framework (9) with $Y = X$ and $A = S$ [4]. To solve above optimization problem, we alternate between learning the nonlinear mapping (i.e. solve U, V with fixed W, H) and the model (i.e. solve W, H with fixed U, V). Once converged, we can derive a clustering by running k-means on top-k singular vectors of $\varphi_U(X) W H^T \varphi_V(X)^T$.

We now briefly discuss how to solve each subproblem efficiently using GIMC under semi-supervised clustering context. First, fixing U, V, solving W, H becomes a standard IMC problem, and one can use existing efficient algorithms (e.g. alternating minimization with conjugate gradient [28] as used in our experiment) to solve for W and H. The method addressed in [28] only requires $O((|\Omega| + nm)k)$ for each update of W or H.

Fixing W, H, we could solve U, V alternatively by gradient descent with line search. For example, let us first consider (13) to be GIMC-LFF where U, V are parameters for projections in Fourier Features, then the learning process of U is similar to the one in multilabel learning, except here we only consider the loss on a subset Ω. The gradient of each projection $\boldsymbol{u}_r$ could be written as:

$$\nabla_{\boldsymbol{u}_r} f(U, V, W, H) = \sum_{(i,j)\in\Omega} (\varphi(\boldsymbol{x}_i)^T \boldsymbol{q}_j - S_{ij})(-Q_{j,r} \sin(\boldsymbol{u}_r^T \boldsymbol{x}_i) + Q_{j,r+k} \cos(\boldsymbol{u}_r^T \boldsymbol{x}_i))\boldsymbol{x}_i, \tag{14}$$

where $Q = \varphi_V(X) H W^T$. The gradient of U could be computed in $O((|\Omega| + nd)m)$ as discussed in Section 4.2. In addition, for each line search iteration, evaluating objective function also takes $O((|\Omega| + nd)m)$ since only $|\Omega|$ inner products have to be computed. Similar update rule and time complexity analysis could also be derived if we consider Nyström features for U and V. Typically, $m, d \ll n, |\Omega| \ll n^2$, the overall time complexity for learning mappings grows at a rate much smaller than $O(n^2)$, especially if the available constraints are sparse. Using GIMC-LFF for semi-supervised

[4] Here we consider the equivalent nonconvex form of IMC objective (see Section 3).

clustering is shown in Algorithm 2. We can derive similar algorithm using GIMC-LNYS.

Algorithm 2: Semi-supervised Clustering with GIMC-LFF

Input : feature matrix X, constraint set $\mathcal{C} = \{S_{ij} \mid (i,j) \in \Omega\}$, number of clusters k, regularization parameter λ, number of projections m.

Output: Clustering result π.

```
// Solve for GIMC-LFF model (13)
Initialize random projections U, V ∈ R^{d×m}, model parameter W, H ∈ R^{2m×k}.
for t = 1, ..., maxiter do
    // Learning IMC model
    [W, H] ← min_{W,H} 1/2 ||P_Ω(S − φ_U(X) W H^T φ_V(X)^T)||_F^2 + λ/2 (||W||_F^2 + ||H||_F^2)
    // Learning non-linear mapping
    Update U with gradient descent (using (14)).
    Update V with gradient descent (similar to (14)).
// Use left side of matrix to approximate top-k singular vectors
T ← svds(φ_U(X) W, k)
π ← kmeans(T, k)
```

6. EXPERIMENTS

We consider the three applications mentioned in the preceding section. We compare the following methods:

1. IMC-NYS: IMC with Nyström features. Here the landmark points in Nyström features are sampled uniformly at random from the dataset [23].

2. IMC-RFF: IMC with random Fourier features [18]. Random Fourier features are constructed based on the Fourier transform of the shift-invariant kernel function.

3. LEML[28]: state-of-the-art multi-label solver using IMC framework.

4. FastXML[16]: state-of-the-art multi-label solver using a random forest approach, where each tree is constructed by jointly optimizing both the ranking loss and tree structure.

5. SLEEC[1]: state-of-the-art multi-label solver which learns an ensemble of local distance preserving embeddings to preserve the pairwise distance between the neighbors' label vector.

6. k-means: traditional k-means clustering, which only considers data points as features.

7. MCCC[25]: a semi-supervised clustering method using IMC framework.

8. GIMC-LNYS: our proposed framework GIMC which learns Nyström features.

9. GIMC-LFF: our proposed framework GIMC which learns Fourier features.

Note that we compare with SLEEC, FastXML, and LEML for the multi-label learning task, and k-means and MCCC for semi-supervised clustering problem. SLEEC, FastXML, and LEML are highly optimized C++ implementation published along with the original papers. We use the parameters along with the released code for these three methods. We use Gaussian kernel as the basis kernel function used in Nyström feature and random Fourier features. The kernel width γ in Gaussian kernel and the regularization term λ in IMC are chosen by cross-validation. All experiments are conducted on a machine with an Intel Xeon X5440 2.83GHz CPU and 32G RAM.

6.1 Multi-label and Multi-class Learning

First, we show that our proposed algorithms can be applied to large-scale multi-label and multi-class classification problems. The datasets are listed in Table 1. The four multi-label datasets are from [1]. We evaluate the results by averaged precision at top 1, 3, and 5.

For multi-label learning problem, firstly we compare with IMC using Nyström features (IMC-NYS) and random Fourier features(IMC-RFF) in Figure 2. Here we vary m, i.e., the number of projections or landmark points in the feature mapping, which is directly related to the memory usage and prediction time of our method, and show the top-3 accuracy. It shows that GIMC-LFF and GIMC-LNYS are much better than IMC-NYS and IMC-RFF. This shows that with the same number of features, learning feature mapping and models together will benefit IMC. Furthermore, we compare with three state-of-the-art multi-label learning approaches: SLEEC [1], FastXML [16] and LEML [28] in the same figures. For these three algorithms, we compare with the best accuracy using the best parameters reported in their papers. Also, GIMC-LFF achieves better test accuracy compared to state-of-the-art multi-label solvers on all these three datasets.

The detailed comparison in terms of precision at $1, 3, 5$ are shown in Table 2. In addition, the efficiency of our algorithms is competitive to state-of-the-art algorithms, SLEEC and FastXML. On the NUS-WIDE dataset, using 500 features with 100 iterations, our GIMC-LFF achieves a 17.27% accuracy taking 6,482 seconds, while FastXML achieves a 16.32% using 17,774 seconds and SLEEC takes 68,232 seconds and achieves 17.67% accuracy.

We can also use our proposed methods for multi-class classification. We treat it as a special case of multi-label learning problem where the label matrix Y has only one 1 in each row. Here we test on one popular multi-class classification dataset: CIFAR-10.

CIFAR-10: We benchmark our method on the CIFAR-10[9], a popular multi-class classification dataset with 10 classes of natural images including 50,000 training samples and 10,000 testing samples. Each image is an 32× 32 RGB image. For each image, we extracted 12,288-dimensional features using CAFFE, a popular deep learning framework[6]. We then apply our proposed method GIMC-LFF and GIMC-LNYS on these new set of features for classification. The result is in Figure 2. In our experiment, linear SVMs with the new set of features achieves 81.73% accuracy, while our proposed methods achieve around 84% accuracy using 2000 features which is also much better than IMC with random Fourier features and Nyström features.

Table 1: Data set statistics for multi-label and multi-class classification problems.

Dataset	type	# training samples	# testing samples	# features	# labels
Bibtex	multi-label	4,880	2,515	1,836	159
Delicious	multi-label	12,920	3,185	500	983
NUS-WIDE	multi-label	161,789	107,859	1,134	1,000
Delicious-large	multi-label	196,606	100,095	782,585	205,443
CIFAR-10	multi-class	50,000	10,000	12,288	10

Table 2: Comparison between our proposed method GIMC with SLEEC, FastXML, and LEML for multi-label learning problem. Note that P1, P3, and P5 indicates Precision at top 1, top 3, and top 5 respectively. GIMC means GIMC-LFF for BibTex, Delicious, and NUS-WIDE datasets. For Delicious-large, we combine GIMC-LFF and GIMC-LNYS, that is, we concatenate the non-linear features learned from both GIMC-LFF and GIMC-LNYS, to make the final prediction. We can see that for the first three datasets, GIMC achieves the best performance comparing with other methods. On Delicious-large dataset, GIMC has similar accuracy with SLEEC, but takes much less time: 4,724 vs 25,289 seconds.

	Bibtex			Delicious			NUS-WIDE			Delicious-large		
	P1 (%)	P3 (%)	P5 (%)	P1 (%)	P3 (%)	P5 (%)	P1 (%)	P3 (%)	P5 (%)	P1 (%)	P3 (%)	P5 (%)
GIMC	**65.85**	**41.17**	**30.01**	**71.40**	**65.16**	**59.79**	**22.49**	**17.40**	**14.70**	46.13	40.32	38.15
SLEEC [1]	65.29	39.60	28.63	68.38	61.50	56.35	17.67	14.20	12.07	**47.03**	**41.67**	**38.88**
FastXML[16]	64.53	40.17	29.27	69.65	63.93	59.36	21.00	16.32	13.66	42.81	38.76	36.34
LEML[16]	62.53	38.40	28.21	65.66	61.15	56.08	20.76	16.00	13.11	40.30	37.76	36.66

6.2 Semi-Supervised Clustering

Since GIMC-LFF and GIMC-LNYS perform similarly well, we mainly compare our proposed GIMC-LFF for semi-supervised clustering with three popular clustering methods. We consider using simple k-means on data points' features (and ignore pairwise constraints) as the baseline, and also compare with state-of-the-art clustering method MCCC [25], and IMC-RFF which first generates random Fourier features, and then applies MCCC with these nonlinear features. We take $m = 500$ for both IMC-RFF and GIMC-LFF. Note that (1) MCCC is based on the IMC framework; (2) since MCCC has been shown to outperform many traditional methods (see [25] for details), we thus focus on comparing with MCCC to demonstrate the effectiveness of our model.

In this experiment, we consider three real-world datasets: Mushroom, Segment and Covtype [5] from classification benchmarks. Items with the same label are regarded as in the same cluster which is the general setting for semi-supervised clustering. We randomly sample $|\Omega|$ pairs of items and generate the pairwise constraints based on these pairs, with $|\Omega| = [1, 5, 10, 15, 20] \times n$, where n is the number of data points. For each choice of $|\Omega|$, we apply each method several times with different regularization parameters λ chosen from the set $\{0.1, 0.5, 1, 5, 10\}$, and take the parameter (and the corresponding clustering π) that achieves the smallest empirical clustering error on the validation set:

$$\frac{1}{|\Omega|}\Big(\sum_{(i,j)\in\Omega:\pi_i=\pi_j} \mathbf{1}(S_{ij}=0) + \sum_{(i,j)\in\Omega:\pi_i\neq\pi_j} \mathbf{1}(S_{ij}=1)\Big).$$

Then we use the parameter λ to train the model and generate the clustering π, and evaluate π using the clustering error rate to the ground-truth clustering defined by:

$$\frac{2}{n(n-1)}\Big(\sum_{(i,j):\pi_i^*=\pi_j^*} \mathbf{1}(\pi_i\neq\pi_j) + \sum_{(i,j):\pi_i^*\neq\pi_j^*} \mathbf{1}(\pi_i=\pi_j)\Big)$$

where π_i^* is the ground-truth cluster of item i.

The result is shown in Table 3. First, we observe that MCCC, IMC-RFF, and GIMC-LFF all perform well on Mushroom as perfect clustering could be (almost) derived. This confirms that MCCC is indeed effective when clustering is linearly dependent on features (100% training classification accuracy could be attained by a linear SVM on this dataset). However, in Segment and Covtype where features are not linearly separable for clustering, MCCC is trapped and both IMC-RFF and GIMC-LFF perform better than MCCC on these two datasets. This shows that considering nonlinear mapping of features improves the clustering result when data points are not linearly separable. Furthermore, we see that GIMC-LFF can further improve IMC-RFF with sufficient constraints. This is because when constraints are sufficient, GIMC-LFF could reliably *learn* a better nonlinear mapping based on constraints, and thus a better clustering could be obtained. The results show that our framework outperforms both state-of-the-art MCCC algorithm and IMC-RFF by learning a better nonlinear mapping of features for clustering.

7. CONCLUSION

We propose a family of Goal-directed Inductive Matrix Completion (GIMC) algorithms. Instead of constructing non-linear features without any supervision to the final goal, we formulate the non-linear mapping finding stage and the model learning stage together as a unified function. As a result, out algorithms find the non-linear mapping that is good for Inductive Matrix Completion. We apply our two algorithms, GIMC based on Fourier features (GIMC-LFF) and GIMC based on Nyström features(GIMC-LNYS), to multi-label learning, multi-class classification, and semi-supervised clustering problems. Experimental results show that our algorithms significantly reduce the number of non-linear features needed, and we obtain a better prediction accuracy and lower clustering error rate compared to state-of-the-art methods.

[5]We subsample from the entire dataset to make clusters have balanced size.

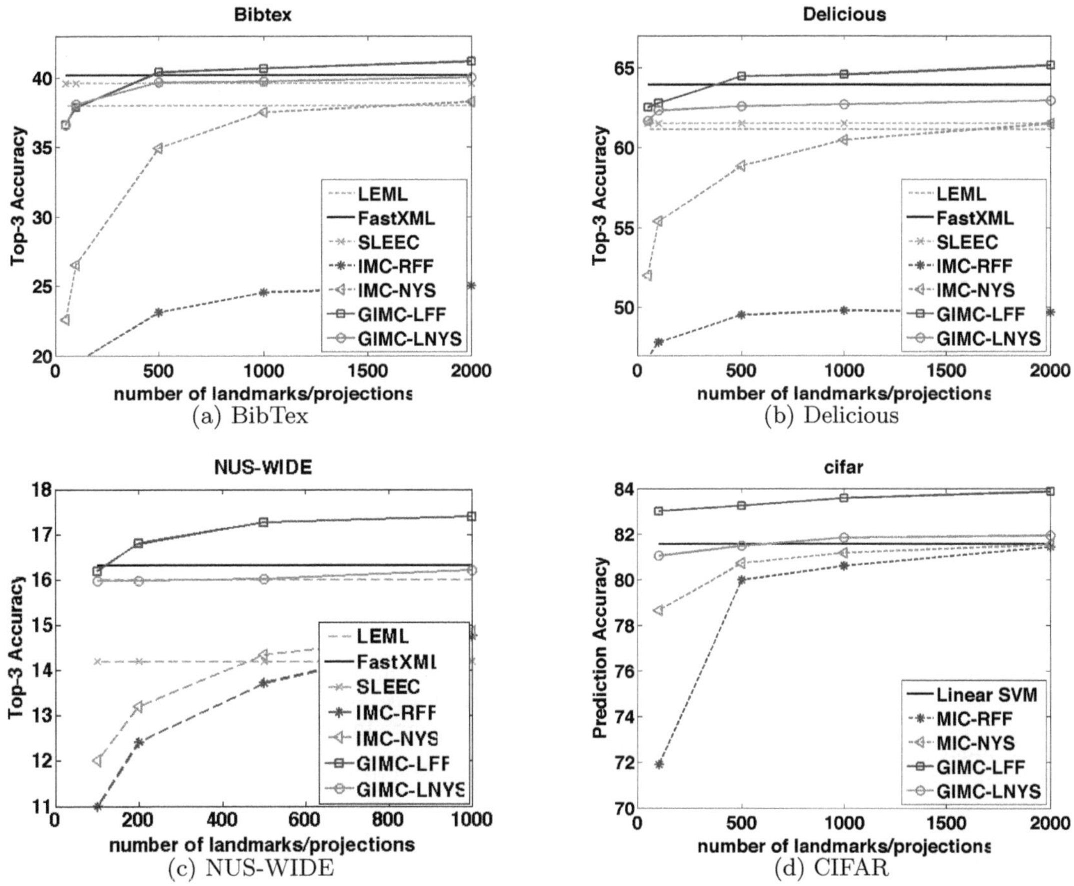

Figure 2: The comparison on multi-label and multi-class classification problems. Figures 2(a),2(b), and 2(c) show results for multi-label learning problem and Figure 2(d) shows results for multi-class classification problem. x-axis shows the number of projections in GIMC-LFF or number of landmark points in GIMC-LNYS. y-axis shows the Top-3 accuracy for multi-label learning or prediction accuracy for multi-class classification. In Figure 2(b) and 2(c) we can observe GIMC-LFF and GIMC-LNYS are much better than IMC-RFF and IMC-NYS for multi-label learning. GIMC-LFF even outperforms state-the-art multi-label solvers (LEML, FastXML, and SLEEC). In Figure 2(d), our algorithms also have good performance when applying to multi-class problems such as the CIFAR-10 dataset.

As future work, we are planning to exploit (1) different non-linear features mapping, e.g., polynomial kernel feature mapping; (2) different optimization techniques in our framework to speed up the computation, e.g., using coordinate descent and stochastic gradient descent; (3) other machine learning applications, such as classification and regression.

Acknowledgments

This research was supported by NSF grants CCF-1320746 and IIS-1546459. We also thank Dinesh Jayaraman for help on CAFFE installation, Hsiang-Fu Yu for help on LEML code, Prateek Jain and Manik Varma for sharing the code and parameters for FastXML and SLEEC.

References

[1] K. Bhatia, H. Jain, P. Kar, M. Varma, and P. Jain. Sparse local embeddings for extreme multi-label classification. In *NIPS*. 2015.

[2] K.-Y. Chiang, C.-J. Hsieh, and I. S. Dhillon. Matrix completion with noisy side information. In *NIPS*, 2015.

[3] B. Dai, B. Xie, N. He, Y. Liang, A. Raj, M. Balcan, and L. Song. Scalable kernel methods via doubly stochastic gradients. In *NIPS*, 2014.

[4] C. Hsieh, K. Chiang, and I. S. Dhillon. Low rank modeling of signed networks. In *KDD*, pages 507–515, 2012.

[5] P. Jain and I. S. Dhillon. Provable inductive matrix completion. *CoRR*, abs/1306.0626, 2013.

[6] Y. Jia, E. Shelhamer, J. Donahue, S. Karayev, J. Long, R. Girshick, S. Guadarrama, and T. Darrell. Caffe: Convolutional architecture for fast feature embedding. *arXiv preprint arXiv:1408.5093*, 2014.

[7] P. Kar and H. Karnick. Random feature maps for dot product kernels. *arXiv preprint arXiv:1201.6530*, 2012.

[8] Y. Koren, R. Bell, and C. Volinsky. Matrix factorization techniques for recommender systems. *IEEE Computer*, 42(8):30–37, 2009.

Dataset	n	d	k	# constraints $\|\Omega\|$	k-means	MCCC	IMC-RFF	GIMC-LFF
Mushroom	8142	112	2	n	0.1897	0.0007	0.0034	**0.0002**
				$5n$	0.1897	0.0010	0.0005	**0.0000**
				$10n$	0.1897	0.0007	**0.0000**	**0.0000**
				$15n$	0.1897	0.0007	0.0002	**0.0000**
				$20n$	0.1897	0.0007	0.0002	**0.0000**
Segment	2319	19	7	n	0.1433	0.0891	**0.0683**	0.0724
				$5n$	0.1347	0.0800	0.0580	**0.0570**
				$10n$	0.1363	0.0809	0.0650	**0.0446**
				$15n$	0.1362	0.0872	0.0678	**0.0402**
				$20n$	0.1330	0.0837	0.0564	**0.0380**
Covtype-sub	1711	54	7	n	0.2523	0.2498	**0.1840**	0.1898
				$5n$	0.2112	0.1772	0.1930	**0.1592**
				$10n$	0.2068	0.1708	0.1722	**0.1388**
				$15n$	0.2203	0.1677	0.1687	**0.1262**
				$20n$	0.2124	0.1607	0.1561	**0.1078**

Table 3: Semi-supervised clustering results. Here n is the number of data points, d is the dimension of the data, and k is the number of clusters. In this table, we vary $|\Omega|$ pairwise constraints with $|\Omega| = [1, 5, 10, 15, 20] \times n$ and report the clustering error rate achieved by each method. We can see that our proposed method GIMC-LFF achieves the best performance among almost all settings in these three datasets. This shows that learning non-linear mappings and models jointly will benefit IMC.

[9] A. Krizhevsky. Learning Multiple Layers of Features from Tiny Images. Master's thesis, 2009.

[10] R. Kueng, H. Rauhut, and U. Terstiege. Low rank matrix recovery from rank one measurements. *Applied and Computational Harmonic Analysis*, 2015.

[11] S. Kumar, M. Mohri, and A. Talwalkar. Ensemble Nyström methods. In *NIPS*, 2009.

[12] Q. V. Le, T. Sarlos, and A. J. Smola. Fastfood – approximating kernel expansions in loglinear time. In *ICML*, 2013.

[13] H. Ma, D. Zhou, C. Liu, M. R. Lyu, and I. King. In *WSDM*, pages 287–296.

[14] N. Natarajan and I. S. Dhillon. Inductive matrix completion for predicting gene-disease associations. *Bioinformatics*, 30(12):60–68, 2014.

[15] J. Oh, W.-S. Han, H. Yu, and X. Jiang. Fast and robust parallel sgd matrix factorization. In *KDD*, 2015.

[16] Y. Prabhu and M. Varma. Fastxml: A fast, accurate and stable tree-classifier for extreme multi-label learning. In *KDD*, 2014.

[17] A. Rahimi and B. Recht. Random features for large-scale kernel machines. In *NIPS*, 2007.

[18] A. Rahimi and B. Recht. Weighted sums of random kitchen sinks: Replacing minimization with randomization in learning. *NIPS*, 2009.

[19] N. Rao, H.-F. Yu, P. Ravikumar, and I. S. Dhillon. Collaborative filtering with graph information: Consistency and scalable methods. In *NIPS*, 2015.

[20] B. Recht and C. Ré. Parallel stochastic gradient algorithms for large-scale matrix completion. *Mathematical Programming Computation*, 5(2):201–226, 2013.

[21] B. Recht, C. Re, S. Wright, and F. Niu. Hogwild: A lock-free approach to parallelizing stochastic gradient descent. In *NIPS*, pages 693–701. 2011.

[22] N. Srebro and A. Shraibman. Rank, trace-norm and max-norm. In *COLT*, pages 545–560, 2005.

[23] C. K. I. Williams and M. Seeger. Using the Nyström method to speed up kernel machines. In *NIPS*, 2001.

[24] M. Xu, R. Jin, and Z.-H. Zhou. Speedup matrix completion with side information: Application to multi-label learning. In *NIPS*, pages 2301–2309, 2013.

[25] J. Yi, L. Zhang, R. Jin, Q. Qian, and A. Jain. Semi-supervised clustering by input pattern assisted pairwise similarity matrix completion. In *ICML*, pages 1400–1408, 2013.

[26] H.-F. Yu, C.-J. Hsieh, S. Si, and I. S. Dhillon. Scalable coordinate descent approaches to parallel matrix factorization for recommender systems. In *ICDM*, 2012.

[27] H.-F. Yu, C.-J. Hsieh, S. Si, and I. S. Dhillon. Parallel matrix factorization for recommender systems. *Knowledge and Information Systems (KAIS)*, 41(3):793–819, 2014.

[28] H. F. Yu, P. Jain, P. Kar, and I. S. Dhillon. Large-scale multi-label learning with missing labels. In *ICML*, 2014.

[29] K. Zhang, I. W. Tsang, and J. T. Kwok. Improved Nyström low rank approximation and error analysis. In *ICML*, 2008.

[30] T. Zhou, H. Shan, A. Banerjee, and G. Sapiro. Kernelized probabilistic matrix factorization: Exploiting graphs and side information. In *SDM*, 2012.

Graph Wavelets via Sparse Cuts

Arlei Silva †, Xuan-Hong Dang †, Prithwish Basu *, Ambuj Singh †, Ananthram Swami ‡
†Computer Science Department, University of California, Santa Barbara, CA, USA
*Raytheon BBN Technologies, Cambridge, MA, USA
‡Army Research Laboratory, Adelphi, MD, USA
{arlei,xdang,ambuj}@cs.ucsb.edu, phasu@bbn.com, ananthram.swami.civ@mail.mil

ABSTRACT

Modeling information that resides on vertices of large graphs is a key problem in several real-life applications, ranging from social networks to the Internet-of-things. Signal Processing on Graphs and, in particular, graph wavelets can exploit the intrinsic smoothness of these datasets in order to represent them in a compact and accurate manner. However, how to discover wavelet bases that capture the geometry of the data with respect to the signal as well as the graph structure remains an open problem. In this paper, we study the problem of computing graph wavelet bases via sparse cuts in order to produce low-dimensional encodings of data-driven bases. This problem is connected to known hard problems in graph theory (e.g. multiway cuts) and thus requires an efficient heuristic. We formulate the basis discovery task as a relaxation of a vector optimization problem, which leads to an elegant solution as a regularized eigenvalue computation. Moreover, we propose several strategies in order to scale our algorithm to large graphs. Experimental results show that the proposed algorithm can effectively encode both the graph structure and signal, producing compressed and accurate representations for vertex values in a wide range of datasets (e.g. sensor and gene networks) and significantly outperforming the best baseline.

Categories and Subject Descriptors: H.2.8 [**Database Management**]: Database applications – *data mining*
General Terms: Algorithms, Experimentation
Keywords: Graph mining, Spectral Theory, Wavelets

1. INTRODUCTION

Graphs are the model of choice in several applications, ranging from social networks to the *Internet-of-things (IoT)*. In many of these scenarios, the graph represents an underlying space in which information is generated, processed and transferred. For instance, in social networks, opinions propagate via social interactions and might produce large cascades across several communities. In IoT, different objects (e.g. cars) collect data from diverse sources and communicate with each other via the network infrastructure. As a consequence, exploiting the underlying graph structure in order to manage and process data arising from these applications has become a key challenge.

Signal processing on graphs (SPG) is a framework for the analysis of data residing on vertices of a graph [28, 26]. The idea generalizes traditional signal processing (e.g. compression, sampling) as means to support the analysis of high-dimensional datasets. In particular, SPG has been applied in the discovery of traffic events using speed data collected by a sensor network [22]. Moreover, graph signals are a powerful representation for data in machine learning [13, 11]. As in traditional signal processing, the fundamental operation in SPG is the *transform*, which projects the graph signal in the frequency (or other convenient) domain. Real signals are expected to be smooth with respect to the graph structure—values at nearby vertices are similar—and an effective transform should lead to rapidly decaying coefficients for smooth signals. The most popular transform in SPG, known as Graph Fourier Transform [25, 28], represents a signal as a linear combination of the eigenvectors of the graph Laplacian. However, as its counterpart in traditional signal processing, Graph Fourier fails to localize signals in space (i.e. within graph regions). This limitation has motivated recent studies on graph wavelets [6, 16, 5].

An open issue in SPG is how to link properties of the signal and underlying graph to properties of the transform [28]. Gavish et al. [13] makes one of the first efforts in this direction, by relating the smoothness of the signal with respect to a tree structure of increasingly refined graph partitions and the fast decay of the wavelet coefficients in a Haar-like expansion. However, as explicitly stated in their paper, their approach *"raises many theoretical questions for further research, in particular regarding construction of trees that best capture the geometry of these challenging datasets"*.

In this paper, we study the problem of computing wavelet trees that encode both the graph structure and the signal information. A wavelet tree defines a hierarchical partitioning used as basis for a graph wavelet transform. Good wavelet trees should produce fast decaying coefficients, which support a low-dimensional representation of the graph signal. The particular application scenario we consider is the lossy graph signal compression. This task arises in many relevant data management and analytics applications, including IoT and social networks, where values associated to interconnected entities have to be represented in a compact form.

KDD '16, August 13-17, 2016, San Francisco, CA, USA

DOI: http://dx.doi.org/10.1145/2939672.2939777

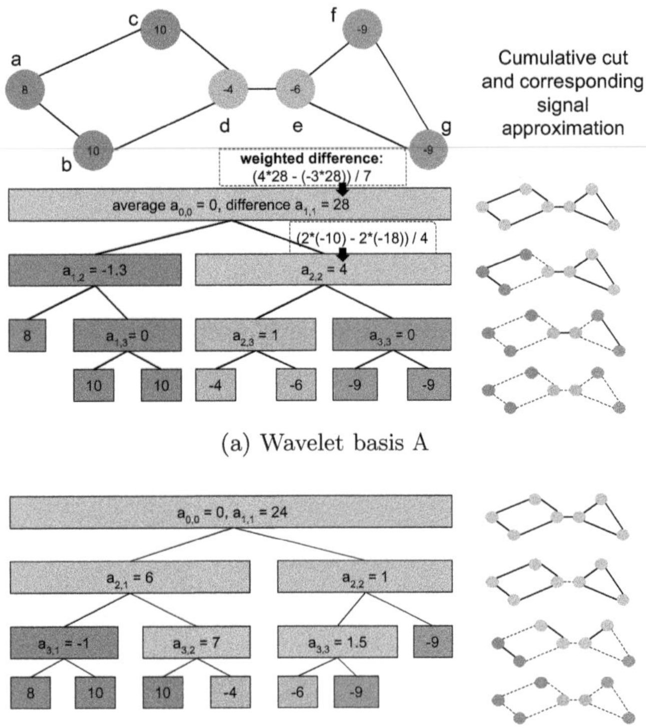

(a) Wavelet basis A

(b) Wavelet basis B

Figure 1: Graph wavelet transforms for two different wavelet trees and the same piecewise smooth graph signal (values set to vertices). A wavelet tree contains one *average coefficient* and several *weighted difference coefficients* associated with vertex partitions. Basis A is better than B because it produces fast decaying difference coefficients. Moreover, basis A can be approximately encoded as a sequence of sparse graph cuts (first $\{(b,d),(c,d)\}$ then $\{(e,f),(e,g)\}$), which leads to a compact and accurate representation of the graph signal.

Figure 1 shows two wavelet trees, A and B, and their respective transforms for a piecewise smooth graph signal defined over seven vertices. The wavelet transform contains a single *average coefficient* and a set of *weighted difference coefficients* associated to each node of the tree. Weighted difference coefficients are computed as a function of the values in each partition and the partition sizes (see Equation 2 for a formal definition). Notice that these two bases produce very different wavelet transforms for the same signal. While tree A is characterized by fast decaying difference coefficients, tree B has relatively large coefficients at every level. This indicates that tree A supports a better representation for the signal than does tree B. However, good wavelet trees must also capture properties of the graph structure.

We measure the relationship between a wavelet tree and the graph structure using the notion of sparse cuts. A graph cut is a set of edges that connect two disjoint sets of vertices and sparse cuts (i.e. those with a small number of edges) are a natural way to model graph partitions [9]. As each node of the wavelet tree separates a set of vertices into two subsets, a sparse wavelet tree can be approximately encoded by a sequence of sparse cuts. This work is the first effort to connect graph cuts and graph signal processing. In particular, we show how problems that arise in the construction of optimal wavelet trees are related to hard cut problems, such as *graph bisection* [2] and *multiway-cuts* [7].

In Figure 1, we also show the cuts associated to each level of the wavelet tree together with the signal approximation for the respective level. Basis A can be approximately encoded by the cutting four edges: $\{(b,d),(c,d)\}$ (level 1) and $\{(e,f),(e,g)\}$ (level 2). The resulting compact wavelet tree can effectively represent the graph signal using only the two top wavelet coefficients, leading to a relative L_2 error of 1%. On the other hand, basis B does not have such a compact approximation with small error via sparse cuts.

In this paper, we formalize the problem of computing sparse wavelet bases (or trees) for graph wavelet transforms. This problem, which we call *sparse graph wavelet transform* (SWT) consists of identifying a sequence of sparse graph cuts that leads to the minimum error in the reconstruction of a given graph signal. We show that this problem is NP-hard, even to approximate by a constant. In fact, we are able to show that computing each individual cut in the tree construction is an NP-hard problem.

As the main contribution of this paper, we propose a novel algorithm for computing an SWT via spectral graph theory. The algorithm design starts by formulating a relaxation of our problem as an eigenvector problem, which follows the lines of existing approaches for *ratio-cuts* [15], *normalized-cuts* [27] and *max-cuts* [33]. We further show how the proposed relaxation leads to a regularization of pairwise values by the graph Laplacian, which relates to existing work on graph kernels [31, 19]. In order to improve the computational efficiency of our algorithm, we design a *fast graph wavelet transform* (FSWT) using several techniques including *Chebyshev Polynomials* and the *Power method*.

2. RELATED WORK

Generalizing the existing signal processing framework to signals that reside on graphs is the main focus of *Signal Processing on Graphs (SPG)* [28, 26]. Operations such as filtering, denoising, and downsampling, which are well-defined for signals in regular Euclidean spaces, have several applications also when signals are embedded in sparse irregular spaces that can be naturally modeled as graphs. For instance, sensor networks [22], brain imaging [20], computer network traffic [6], and statistical learning [31, 19, 11], are examples of scenarios where graph signals have been studied. The main idea in SPG is the so called *Graph Fourier Transform (GFT)* [25], which consists of applying eigenvectors of the Laplacian matrix of a graph as a basis for graph signals. Laplacian eigenvectors oscillate at different frequencies over the graph structure, capturing a notion of frequency similar to complex exponentials in the standard Fourier Transform.

As is the case for its counterpart for Euclidean spaces, GFT fails to localize graph signals, i.e. capture differences within graph regions. This aspect has motivated the study of graph wavelets [6, 13, 16, 5]. Crovella and Kolaczyk [6] introduced wavelets on graphs for the analysis of network traffic. Their design extracts differences in values within a disc (i.e. a center node and a fixed radius) and a surrounding ring as means to identify traffic anomalies. Coiffman and Maggioni [5] proposed a more sophisticated design, known as *diffusion wavelets*, based on compressed representations of dyadic powers of a diffusion operator. In [16], Hammond et al. present a wavelet design using kernel functions that modulate eigenvectors around vertices at multiple scales.

An assumption shared by existing work on graph wavelets is that good bases can be computed based solely on the graph structure. However, as shown in Figure 1, a proper choice of graph wavelet bases can lead to significantly more effective transforms. In this paper, we study the problem of computing optimal graph wavelet bases for a given signal via sparse graph cuts. A graph cut partitions the vertices of a graph into two disjoint subsets and optimization problems associated with graph cuts are some of the most traditional problems in graph theory [8, 12]. In particular, graph cuts (e.g. min-cut, max-cut) are a natural way to formulate graph partitioning problems [9]. Here, we constraint the size of the cut, in number of edges, associated to a graph wavelet basis in order to discover bases that are well-embedded in the graph. A similar constraint also appears in the min-cut [8], graph bisection [2], and multiway-cut [7] problems.

Learning bases tailored for classes of signals is an important problem in signal processing, known as *dictionary learning* [32]. This problem differs from ours since our wavelet bases are adapted to each signal, which leads to more compact representations. In [29], the authors show how importance sampling can support the discovery of center-radius partitions for attribute compression. However, their approach does not generalize to arbitrarily shaped partitions.

Many relevant problems on graphs have been solved using the framework of Spectral Graph Theory (SPG) [4], which studies combinatoric graph properties via the spectrum of matrices associated with them. For instance, the relationship between eigenvectors of the Laplacian and graph partitions can be traced back to Cheeger's inequality [3]. More recently, SPG has led to efficient graph partitioning algorithms (e.g. ratio-cuts [15], normalized-cuts [27]). In this paper, we propose a spectral algorithm for computing sparse graph wavelet bases. Interestingly, our analysis show that these bases are related to existing work on graph kernels [31, 19], including the wavelet design by Hammond et al. [16].

3. WAVELETS ON GRAPHS

A graph is a tuple $G(V, E)$, where V is a set of n vertices and E is a set of m (unweighted) edges, respectively. A signal $W{:}V \rightarrow \mathbb{R}$ is a real-valued function defined on the set of vertices V. In other words, $W(v)$ is the value of the signal for a vertex $v \in V$. In Figure 1 we show an example of a graph G for which we define a signal W.

A graph wavelet tree is a binary tree structure $\mathcal{X}(G)$ that partitions the graph recursively as follows. A root node X_1^1 contains all the vertices in the graph (i.e. $X_1^1 = V$). In general, $X_k^\ell \subseteq V$ is the k-th node at level ℓ with children $X_i^{\ell+1}$ and $X_j^{\ell+1}$ at level $\ell+1$ such that $X_i^{\ell+1} \cap X_j^{\ell+1} = \emptyset$ and $X_i^{\ell+1} \cup X_j^{\ell+1} = X_k^\ell$. We focus on binary trees since they have the same encoding power as n-ary trees in this model.

The tree $\mathcal{X}(G)$ defines spaces of functions, $\mathcal{V}_\ell$ and $\mathcal{W}_\ell$, analogous to Haar wavelet spaces in harmonic analysis [21]. The space $\mathcal{V}_1$ contains functions that are constant on V. And, in general, $\mathcal{V}_\ell$ contains functions that are piecewise constant on nodes in X_k^ℓ at the ℓ-level of $\mathcal{X}(G)$. Let $\mathcal{V}$ be the space of functions that are constant on individual nodes in V. Bases to span such spaces can be constructed using functions $\mathbf{1}_{X_k^\ell}$ equal to 1 for $v \in X_k^\ell$ and 0, otherwise (box functions). This formulation leads to a multiresolution $\mathcal{V}_1 \subset \mathcal{V}_2 \subset \ldots \mathcal{V}$ for function spaces. Another set of function spaces in the form $\mathcal{W}_\ell$ contains *wavelet functions* $\psi_{k,\ell}$ with the following properties: (1) are piecewise constant on $X_i^{\ell+1}$ and $X_j^{\ell+1}$, (2) are orthogonal to $\mathbf{1}_{X_k^\ell}$ defined on X_k^ℓ and (3) are 0 everywhere else. It follows that any function in $\mathcal{W}_\ell$ can be represented using $\mathcal{V}_{\ell+1}$. Also, for any level ℓ, $\mathcal{V}_\ell \perp \mathcal{W}_\ell$ and $\mathcal{V}_\ell \oplus \mathcal{W}_\ell = \mathcal{V}_{\ell+1}$, where $\oplus$ is the orthogonal sum.

We combine wavelet functions with $\mathbf{1}_V$ to produce an orthonormal basis for G. Intuitively, this basis supports the representation of any graph signal W as a linear combination of the average $\mu(W)$ plus piecewise functions defined on recursive partitions of the vertices V (see Figure 1). A graph wavelet transform φW is a set of difference coefficients $a_{k,\ell}$:

$$a_{k,\ell} = \begin{cases} \mu(W), & \text{if } \ell = k = 0 \\ \langle W, \psi_{k,\ell} \rangle, & \text{otherwise} \end{cases} \tag{1}$$

In particular, except for $a_{0,0}$, we can write $a_{k,\ell}$ as:

$$a_{k,\ell} = \frac{|X_j^{\ell+1}|}{|X_k^\ell|} \sum_{v \in X_i^{\ell+1}} W(v) - \frac{|X_i^{\ell+1}|}{|X_k^\ell|} \sum_{v \in X_j^{\ell+1}} W(v) \tag{2}$$

The sizes $|X_k^\ell|$, $|X_i^{\ell+1}|$ and $|X_j^{\ell+1}|$ are taken into account because partitions might be unbalanced. Analogously, the wavelet inverse $\varphi^{-1}W$ is defined as:

$$\varphi^{-1}W(v) = a_{0,0} + \sum_k \sum_\ell \nu_{k,\ell}(v) a_{k,\ell} \tag{3}$$

where:

$$\nu_{k,\ell}(v) = \begin{cases} 1/|X_i^{\ell+1}|, & \text{if } v \in X_i^{\ell+1} \\ -1/|X_j^{\ell+1}|, & \text{if } v \in X_j^{\ell+1} \\ 0, & \text{otherwise} \end{cases} \tag{4}$$

Figure 1a shows the graph wavelet transform for a toy example. For instance, the value of $a_{2,2} = (2.(-4 + (-6)) - 2.(-9 + (-9)))/4 = 4$ and the inverse $\varphi^{-1}W(e) = 0 + (-28)/4 + 4/2 + (-1)/1 = -6 = W(e)$. An important property of the graph wavelet transform, known as Parseval's relation, is that the signal and its transform are equivalent representations (i.e. $\varphi^{-1}\varphi W = W$) for any signal W and wavelet tree $\mathcal{X}(G)$. More formally, we can define the L_2 energy of a graph wavelet coefficient as:

$$||a_{k,\ell}||_2 = \frac{|X_i^{\ell+1}|.a_{k,\ell}^2}{|X_i^{\ell+1}|^2} + \frac{|X_j^{\ell+1}|.a_{k,\ell}^2}{|X_j^{\ell+1}|^2} = \frac{a_{k,\ell}^2}{|X_i^{\ell+1}|} + \frac{a_{k,\ell}^2}{|X_j^{\ell+1}|} \tag{5}$$

Using Equation 2, we can show the Parseval's relation:

$$\sum_k \sum_\ell ||a_{k,\ell}||_2 = \sum_v |W(v)|^2 \tag{6}$$

In particular, a lossy compressed representation of W can be constructed by the following procedure: (1) Compute transform φW, (2) set the lowest energy coefficients $a_{k,\ell}$ to 0, (3) return the non-zero wavelet coefficients $\varphi' W$ from φW. In this setting, the error of the compression is the sum of the energies of the dropped coefficients. If W has a sparse representation in the transform (frequency domain), where most of the energy is concentrated in a few high-level coefficients, it can be compressed with small error.

Figure 1a illustrates a sparse representation of a graph signal W (basis A). The fast decay of the difference coefficients

$a_{k,\ell}$ in the wavelet transform as the level ℓ increases leads to a high compression using the aforementioned algorithm. The signal can be approximated within L_2 error of 1% using the top coefficients $a_{1,1}$ and $a_{2,2}$. However, by keeping the top coefficients for basis B (Figure 1b), the error is 22%.

In [13] (see theorems 1-3), the authors show that, if the energy of a wavelet coefficient $a_{k,\ell}$ is bounded as a function of the size of its corresponding vertex set X_k^ℓ and the tree $\mathcal{X}(G)$ is almost balanced, then there is a sparse representation of W as a wavelet transform. Here, we tackle the problem from a more practical and data-driven perspective, where a tree $\mathcal{X}(G)$ that leads to a sparse representation of W is unknown. Moreover, we add sparsity constraints to the description size of $\mathcal{X}(G)$ in order to enforce wavelet bases that are embedded in the graph structure. In the next section, we formalize the problem of computing wavelet basis using sparse cuts and characterize its hardness.

4. WAVELET BASES VIA SPARSE CUTS

The existence of a good basis (or tree) for a signal W in a graph G provides relevant information about both W and G. We measure the description length of a wavelet tree $\mathcal{X}(G)$ as the size $|\mathcal{X}(G)|_E$ of its edge cut. The edge cut of a wavelet tree is the number of edges in the set $E' \subseteq E$ that, if removed, separates the leaf nodes of $\mathcal{X}(G)$. In other words, there is no path between any pair of vertices $u \in X_i^a$, $v \in X_j^b$ in $G(V, E - E')$ whenever X_i^a and X_j^b are leaves of $\mathcal{X}(G)$. A tree $\mathcal{X}(G)$ associated with a *sparse cut* requires a few edges to be removed in order to disconnect its leaf nodes.

If $|\mathcal{X}(G)|_E < |E|$, the energy of at least one coefficient a_k^ℓ of any transform φW will be always set to 0 and, as a consequence, the inverse $\varphi^{-1}\varphi W(v)$ will be the same for any vertex $v \in X_k^\ell$. As graphs have a combinatorial number of possible cuts, we formalize the problem of finding an optimal sparse wavelet basis in terms of (L_2) error minimization.

DEFINITION 1. ***Optimal graph wavelet basis via sparse cuts.*** *Given a graph $G(V, E)$, a signal W, and a cut size q compute a wavelet tree $\mathcal{X}(G)$ with a cut $|\mathcal{X}(G)|_E$ of size q that minimizes $||W - \varphi^{-1}\varphi W||_2$.*

Figure 2 shows two candidate wavelet trees with cut size $q = 4$ for the same graph signal shown previously in Figure 1a. While the tree from Figure 2b achieves an error of 22%, the one from Figure 2a is the optimal basis of cut size 4 for our example, with an error of 1%. As discussed in Section 3, a good basis generates sparse transforms, which maximize the amount of energy from the signal that is conserved in a few coefficients. In the remainder of this section, we analyze the hardness of computing sparse wavelet bases by connecting it to well-known problems in graph theory.

THEOREM 1. *Computing an optimal graph wavelet basis is NP-hard.*

Please refer to the extended version of this paper [30] for proofs of Theorems 1, 2 and 5. Theorem 1 shows that finding an optimal basis is NP-hard using a reduction from the 3-multiway cut problem [7], which leads to the question of whether such problem can be approximated within a constant factor in polynomial time. Theorem 2 shows that our problem is also NP-hard to approximate by any constant.

THEOREM 2. *Computing an optimal graph wavelet basis is NP-hard to approximate by a constant.*

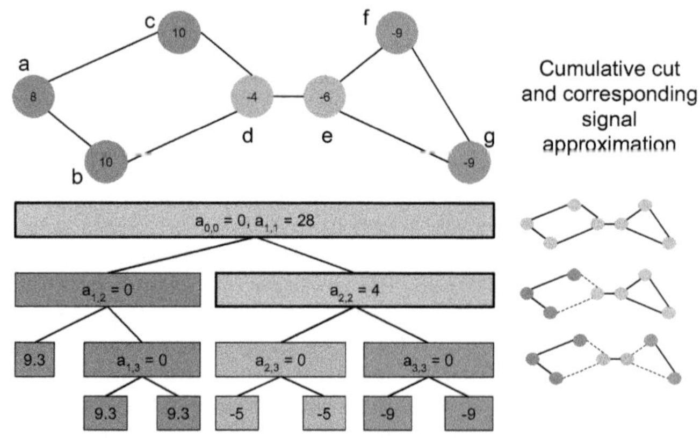

(a) Optimal wavelet basis

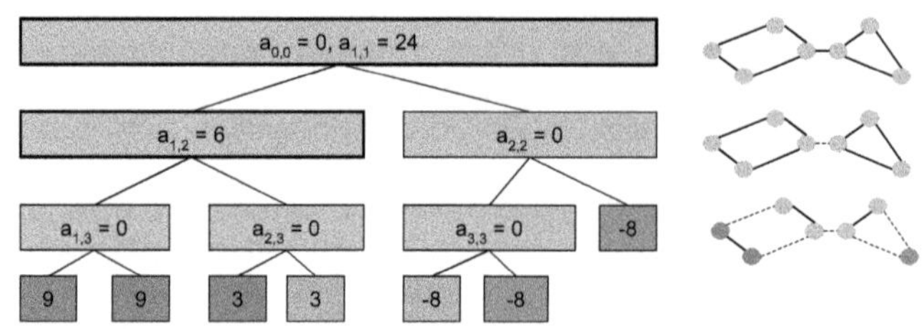

(b) Alternative wavelet basis

Figure 2: Two graph wavelet bases with cut of size 4 for the same signal. Reconstructed values are set to leaf nodes. The basis from Figure 2a achieves 1% error and is optimal. An alternative basis with 22% error is shown in Figure 2b.

Connecting the construction of sparse wavelet basis to a hard problem such as the 3-multiway cut is a key step for proving Theorems 1 and 2. However, these constructions assume wavelet trees $\mathcal{X}(G)$ with a number of levels ℓ strictly larger than 2 (i.e. more than two partitions are generated). A final question we ask regarding the hardness of our problem is whether there is an efficient algorithm for partitioning a set of nodes X_k^ℓ into children $X_i^{\ell+1}$ and $X_j^{\ell+1}$. If so, one could apply such an algorithm recursively in a top-down manner in order to construct a reasonably good wavelet basis. We can pose such a problem using the notion of L_2 energy of graph wavelet coefficients from Equation 5.

DEFINITION 2. ***Optimal graph wavelet cut.*** *Given a graph $G(V, E)$, a signal W, a constant k, and a set of nodes $X_k^\ell \subseteq V$, compute a partition of X_k^ℓ into $X_i^{\ell+1}$ and $X_j^{\ell+1}$ that maximizes $||a_{k,\ell}||_2$.*

Theorem 3 rules out the existence of an efficient algorithm that solves the aforementioned problem optimally.

THEOREM 3. *Computing an optimal sparse graph wavelet cut is NP-hard.*

Our proof (in the appendix) is based on a reduction from the graph bisection [12] and raises an interesting aspect of good graph wavelet bases, which is *balancing.* The problem of finding balanced partitions in graphs has been extensively studied in the literature, specially in the context of VLSI design [15], image segmentation [27] and other applications of spectral graph theory [4]. In the next section, we propose a spectral algorithm for computing graph wavelet bases.

5. SPECTRAL ALGORITHM

Our approach combines structural and signal information as a vector optimization problem. By leveraging the power of spectral graph theory, we show how a relaxed version of this formulation is a regularized eigenvalue problem, which can be solved using 1-D search and existing eigenvalue computation procedures. Our discussion focuses on computing a single cut (Definition 2) and extends to the computation of a complete basis. Section 5.3 is focused on performance.

5.1 Formulation

First, we introduce some notation. The degree d_v of a vertex v is the number of vertices $u \in V$ such that $(u, v) \in E$. The degree matrix $\mathcal{D}$ of G is an $n \times n$ diagonal matrix with $D_{v,v} = d_v$ for every $v \in V$ and $D_{u,v} = 0$, for $u \neq v$. The adjacency matrix A of G is an $n \times n$ matrix such that $A_{u,v} = 1$ if $(u, v) \in E$ and $A_{u,v} = 0$, otherwise[1]. The Laplacian of G is defined as $L = D - A$. We also define a second matrix $C = n\mathbf{I} - \mathbf{1}_{n \times n}$, where $\mathbf{I}$ is the identity matrix and $\mathbf{1}_{n \times n}$ is an $n \times n$ matrix of 1's. The matrix C can be interpreted as the Laplacian of a complete graph with n vertices. The third matrix, which we call S, is a matrix of pairwise squared differences with $S_{u,v} = (W(u) - W(v))^2$ for any pair of nodes $u, v \in V$. Notice that these matrices can also be computed for an induced subgraph $G'(X_k^\ell, E')$, where $E' = \{(u, v) | u \in X_k^\ell \wedge v \in X_k^\ell\}$.

In order to formulate the problem of finding an optimal sparse wavelet cut in vectorial form, we define a $|X_k^\ell|$ dimensional indicator vector x for the partition of X_k^ℓ into $X_i^{\ell+1}$ and $X_j^{\ell+1}$. For any $v \in X_k^\ell$, $x_v = -1$ if $v \in X_i^{\ell+1}$ and $x_v = 1$ if $v \in X_j^{\ell+1}$. By combining the matrices (C, S, L) and the indicator vector x, the following Theorem shows how the problem from Definition 2 can be rewritten as an optimization problem over vectors (see appendix for the proof).

THEOREM 4. *The problem of finding an optimal sparse graph wavelet partition (Definition 2) can be written as:*

$$x* = \min_{x \in \{-1,1\}^n} a(x) \qquad st. \quad x^\intercal L x \leq 4q \tag{7}$$

where $a(x) = \frac{x^\intercal CSCx}{x^\intercal Cx}$ *and q is the maximum cut size.*

Theorem 4 does not make the problem of computing an optimal wavelet basis any easier. However, we can now define a relaxed version of our problem by removing the constraint that $x_i \in \{-1, 1\}$. Once real solutions ($x_i \in \mathbb{R}$) are allowed, we can compute an approximate basis using eigenvectors of a well-designed matrix. The next corollary follows directly from a variable substitution and properties of Lagrange multipliers in eigenvalue problems [10, chapter-12].

COROLLARY 1. *A relaxed version of the problem from Definition 2 can be solved as a regularized eigenvalue problem:*

$$\begin{aligned} x* &= \min_x a(x) \\ &= \min_x \frac{x^\intercal CSCx}{x^\intercal Cx + \beta x^\intercal Lx} \\ &= ((C + \beta L)^+)^{\frac{1}{2}} y* \end{aligned} \tag{8}$$

where $y* = \min_y \frac{y^\intercal My}{y^\intercal y}$, $M = ((C + \beta L)^+)^{\frac{1}{2}} CSC((C + \beta L)^+)^{\frac{1}{2}}$, $y = (C + \beta L)^{\frac{1}{2}} x$, $(C + \beta L)^+$ *is the pseudoinverse of* $(C + \beta L)$ *and* β *is a regularization factor.*

This eigenvalue problem is well-defined due to properties of the matrix M, which is real and symmetric. In fact, M is negative semidefinite, since the energy $||a_{k,\ell}||_2$ of a wavelet coefficient is non-negative. We apply the pseudoinverse $(C + \beta L)^+$ because C and L are positive semidefinite and thus their standard inverses are not well-defined—they both have at least one zero eigenvalue.

At this point, it is not clear how the matrix M captures both signal and structural information as means to produce high-energy sparse wavelet cuts. In particular, we want to provide a deeper insight into the role played by the regularization factor β in preventing partitions that are connected by many edges in G. To simplify the notation and without loss of generality, let us assume that $X_k^\ell = V$ and that V has 0-mean. The next theorem gives an explicit form for the entries of M based on the node values and graph structure:

THEOREM 5. *The matrix M is in the form:*

$$M_{ij} = 2n^2 \sum_{v=1}^{n} \left(\sum_{u=1}^{n} \left(\sum_{r=2}^{n} \left(\frac{1}{\sqrt{\lambda_r}} e_{r,i} e_{r,u} \right) W(u).W(v) \right) \sum_{r=2}^{n} \frac{1}{\sqrt{\lambda_r}} e_{r,v} e_{r,j} \right) \tag{9}$$

where (λ_r, e_r) is an eigenvalue-eigenvector pair of the matrix $(C + \beta L)$ such that $\lambda_r > 0$.

Based on Theorem 5, we can interpret M as a Laplacian regularized matrix and Expression 8 as a relaxation of a maximum-cut problem in a graph with Laplacian matrix $-M$. In this setting, the largest eigenvalue of $-M$ is known to be a relaxation of the maximum cut in the corresponding graph. The matrix $(C + \beta L)$ is the Laplacian of a graph G'' associated to G with the same set of vertices but edge weights $w_{u,v} = 1 + \beta$ if $(u, v) \in G$, and $w_{u,v} = 1$, otherwise. Intuitively, as β increases, G'' becomes a better representation of a weighted version of G with Laplacian matrix βL. For instance, if $\beta = 0$, G'' is a complete graph with all non-zero eigenvalues equal to n and G has no effect over the weights of the cuts in M. In other words, the wavelet cut selected will simply maximize the sum of (negative) products $-W(u).W(v)$ and separate nodes with different values. On the other hand, for large β, the eigenvalues λ_r will capture the structure of G and have a large magnitude. The relative importance of a product $-W(u).W(v)$ will be reduced whenever u and v are well-connected to nodes i and j, respectively, in G. As a consequence, the cuts selected will rather cover edge pairs (i, j) for which far away nodes u and v in G have different values for the signal W.

Expressions in the form $\sum_r g(\lambda_r) e_i e_i^\intercal$ define regularizations via the Laplacian, which have been studied in the context of kernels on graphs [31, 19] and also wavelets [16, 20].

Notice that the regularization factor β is not known a priori, which prevents the direct solution of the relaxation given by Expression 8. However, we can apply a simple 1-D search algorithm (e.g. golden section search [18]) in order to compute an approximate optimal β within a range $[0, \beta_{max}]$.

$$(x*, \beta*) = \min_\beta \min_x a(x) \qquad st. \quad x^\intercal Lx \leq 4q \tag{10}$$

[1]Our method can be generalized to weighted graphs.

Algorithm 1 Spectral Algorithm

Require: Graph G, values W, set X_k^ℓ, regularization constant β, cut size q
Ensure: Partitions $X_i^{\ell+1}$ and $X_j^{\ell+1}$
1: $C \leftarrow n \times n$ Laplacian of complete graph
2: $L \leftarrow n \times n$ Laplacian of G
3: $S \leftarrow n \times n$ squared difference matrix of G
4: $x* \leftarrow \min_x a(x)$
5: $(X_1, X_2)_z \leftarrow$ cut $(\{1, 2 \ldots z\}, \{z+1 \ldots n\})$
6: $(X_i^{\ell+1}, X_j^{\ell+1}) \leftarrow \max_{(X_1,X_2)_j} ||a_{k,\ell}||_2$ st. cut size $|(X_1, X_2)| \leq q$

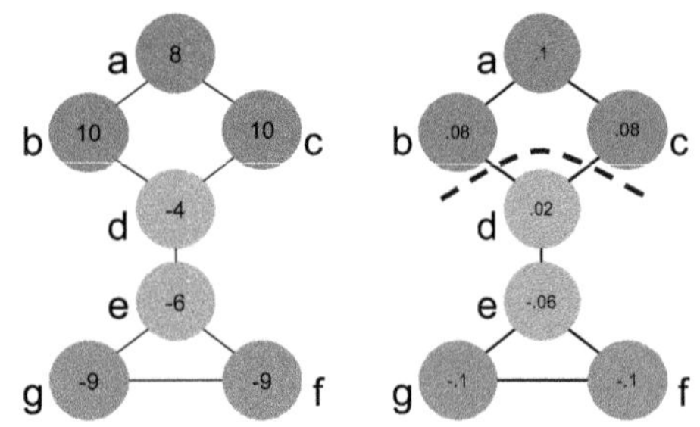

(a) Graph signal (b) Eigenvector/cut

Figure 3: Example of a cut of size $q = 2$ found by the spectral algorithm. The eigenvector x is rounded using a sweep procedure and the best wavelet cut is selected.

5.2 Algorithm

Algorithm 1 describes our spectral algorithm for computing sparse graph wavelet cuts. Its inputs are the graph G, the signal W, a set of nodes X_k^ℓ from G, the regularization constant β, and the cut size q. As a result, it returns a cut $(X_i^{\ell+1}, X_j^{\ell+1})$ that partitions X_k^ℓ by maximizing the energy $||a_{k,\ell}||_2$ and has at most q edges. The algorithm starts by constructing matrices C, L and S based on G and W (lines 1-3). The best relaxed cut $x*$ is computed using Equation 8 (line 4) and a wavelet cut is obtained using a standard *sweeping approach* [27] (lines 5-6). Vertices in X_k^ℓ are sorted in non-decreasing order of their value in $x*$. For each value x_u, the algorithm generates a candidate cut $(X_1, X_2)_j$ by setting $x_v = -1$ if $v < u$, and $x_v = 1$, otherwise (line 5). The cut with size $|(X_i^{\ell+1}, X_j^{\ell+1})|$ at most q that maximizes the energy $||a_{k,\ell}||$ is selected among the candidate ones (line 6) and is returned by the algorithm.

Figure 3 illustrates a wavelet cut of size $q = 2$ discovered by our spectral algorithm. The input graph and its signal are given in Figure 3a. Moreover, we show the value of the eigenvector x that maximizes Expression 8 for each vertex and the resulting cut after rounding in Figure 3b. Notice that x captures both signal and structural information, assigning similar values to vertices that have small difference regarding the signal and are near in the graph. The energy $||a_{k,\ell}||_2$ associated with the cut is 457 (96% of the energy of the signal), which is optimal in this particular setting.

We evaluate Algorithm 1 using several datasets in our experiments. However, an open question is whether such an algorithm provides any quality guarantee regarding its solution (for a single cut). One approach would be computing a lower bound on the L_2 energy of the wavelet cuts generated by the rounding algorithm, similar to the *Cheeger's inequality* for the sparsest cut [4]. Unfortunately, proving such a bound has shown to be quite challenging and will be left as future work. For a similar proof regarding an approximation for the max-cut problem, please refer to [33].

We apply Algorithm 1 recursively in order to construct a complete graph wavelet basis. Starting with the set of nodes V, we repeatedly compute new candidate wavelet cuts and select the one with maximum L_2 energy (i.e. it is a greedy algorithm). Once there is no feasible cut given the remaining budget of edges, we compute the remaining of the basis using ratio-cuts, which do not depend on the signal.

5.3 Efficient Approximation

Here, we study the performance of the algorithm described in the previous section and describe how it can be approximated efficiently. Although performance is not the main focus of this paper, we still need to be able to compute wavelets on large graphs. The most complex step of Algorithm 1 is computing the matrix M (see Corollary 1), which involves (pseudo-)inverting and multiplying dense matrices. Moreover, the algorithm also requires the computation of the smallest eigenvalue/eigenvector of M.

A naive implementation of our spectral algorithm would take $O(n^3)$ time to compute the pseudo-inverse $(C + \beta L)^+$, $O(n^3)$ time for computing matrix products, and other $O(n^3)$ time for the eigen-decomposition of M. Assuming that the the optimal value of β (Equation 10) is found in s iterations, the total complexity of this algorithm is $O(sn^3)$, which would hardly enable the processing of graphs with more than a few thousand vertices. Therefore, we propose a fast approximation of our algorithm by removing its dependence of β and using Chebyshev polynomials and the Power Method.

Our original algorithm searches for the optimal value of the regularization constant β using golden-search, which requires several iterations of Algorithm 1. However, our observations have shown that typical values of β found by the search procedure are large, even for reasonable values of q, compared to the number of edges in G. Thus, we propose simplifying Equation 8 to the following:

$$\frac{x^\intercal CSCx}{x^\intercal Lx} \tag{11}$$

As a consequence, we can compute a wavelet cut with a single execution of our spectral algorithm. Using Theorem 5, we can show that dropping the matrix C from the denominator has only a small effect over the resulting matrix M. First, consider the eigenvalue-eigenvector pairs (λ_r, e_r) of $(C + \beta L)$ and let (λ_l, e_l) and (λ_c, e_c) be the eigenvalue-eigenvector pairs for non-zero eigenvalues of L and C, respectively. Given that C is the Laplacian of a complete graph, we know that $\lambda_c = n$, for any c, and every vector orthogonal to the constant vector $\mathbf{1}_n$ is an eigenvector of C. In particular, any eigenvector e_l of L is an eigenvector of C. From the definition of eigenvalues/eigenvectors, we get that $(C + \beta L)e_l = (n + \beta\lambda_l)e_l$ and thus $(n + \beta\lambda_l, e_l)$ is an eigenvalue-eigenvector pair of $(C + \beta L)$.

Nevertheless, computing all the eigenvalues of the graph Laplacian L might still be prohibitive in practice. Thus, we avoid the eigen-decomposition by computing an approximated version of M using Chebyshev polynomials [16]. These polynomials can efficiently approximate an expression in the form $\langle v, f \rangle$, where $v_i = \sum_r g(\lambda_r)e_{r,i}e_{r,j}$ and f is a real vector. We can apply the same approach to approximate the product $((L^+)^{\frac{1}{2}} \times CSC)_{i,j}$ by setting g and f as:

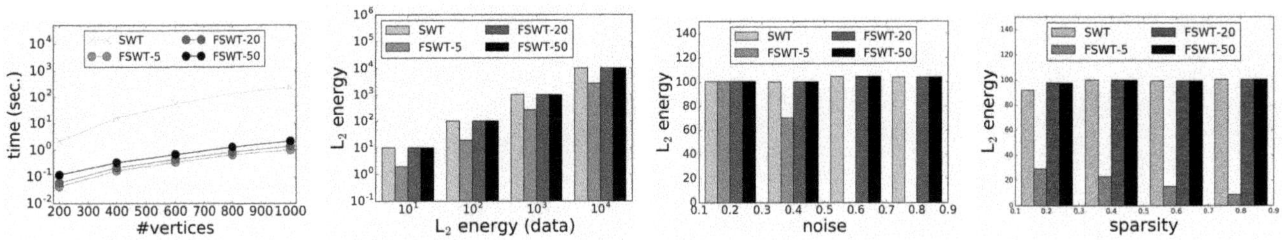

(a) Scalability (b) Energy (c) Noise (d) Sparsity

Figure 4: Scalability and L_2 energy associated to the cuts discovered by the sparse wavelet transform (**SWT**) and its fast approximation (**FSWT-p**) for different number of polynomial coefficients (p) and varying the graph size (a), the energy of the cut in the data (b), the noise level (c), and the sparsity of the cut (d) using synthetic datasets. Our fast approximation is up to 100 times faster than the original algorithm and achieves accurate results even when p is relatively small (20).

$$g(\lambda_r) = \frac{1}{\sqrt{\lambda_r}}, \quad f = CSC_{:,j} \tag{12}$$

where $\lambda_r \in [1, n]$ and $:, j$ is an index for a matrix column.

Chebyshev polynomials can be computed iteratively with cost dominated by a matrix-vector multiplication by L. By truncating these polynomials to p terms (i.e. iterations), each one with cost $O(mn)$, where m is the number of edges, and n is the number of nodes, we can approximate this matrix product in $O(pmn)$ time. For sparse matrices ($m = O(n)$) and small p, $pmn \ll n^3$, which leads to significant performance gains over the naive approach. In order to compute M, we can repeat the same process with $f = ((L^+)^{\frac{1}{2}} \times CSC)_{j,:}$, where $j, :$ is an index for a matrix row.

Once the matrix M is constructed, it remains to compute its eigenvector associated to the smallest eigenvalue. A trivial solution would be computing all the eigenvectors of M, which can be performed in time $O(n^3)$. However, due to the fact that our matrix is negative semidefinite, its smallest eigenvector can be approximated more efficiently using the Power Method [14], which requires a few products of a vector and M. Assuming that such method converges to a good solution in t iterations, we can approximate the smallest eigenvalue of M in time $O(tn^2)$. Moreover, the computation of x from y using $(L^+)^{\frac{1}{2}}$ can also be performed via Chebyshev polynomials in time $O(pm)$.

The time taken by our improved algorithm to compute a single cut is $O(pmn + tn^2)$, where p is the number of terms in the Chebyshev polynomial, $m = |E|$, $n = |V|$, and t is the number of iterations of the Power method. This complexity is a significant improvement over the $O(sn^3)$ time taken by its naive version whenever p, m, and t are small compared to n. For computing all the cuts, the total worst-case time complexity of the algorithm is $O(qpmn + qtn^2)$, where q is the size of the cut of the wavelet tree $\mathcal{X}(G)$. However, notice that good bases tend to be balanced (see Theorem 3) and in such case our complexity decreases to $O(pmn + tn^2)$.

6. EXPERIMENTS

We evaluate our algorithms for computing sparse wavelet bases using synthetic and real datasets. We start by analyzing the scalability and quality of our efficient approximation compared to the original algorithm. Next, we compare our approach against different baselines and using four real datasets in the signal compression task. This section ends with some visualizations of the sparse wavelet formulation, which provides further insights into our algorithm. All the implementations are available as open-source and we also provide the datasets applied in this evaluation[2].

6.1 Scalability and Approximation

The results discussed in this section are based on a synthetic data generator for both the graph and an associated signal. Our goal is to produce inputs for which the best wavelet cut is known. The data generator can be summarized in the following steps: (1) Generate sets of nodes V_1 and V_2 such that $|V_1| = |V_2|$; (2) Generate m edges such that the probability of an edge connecting vertices in V_1 and V_2 is given by a sparsity parameter h; (3) Assign average values μ_1 and μ_2 to V_1 and V_2, respectively, so that the energy of the cut (V_1, V_2) is equal to an energy parameter α; (4) Draw values from a Gaussian distribution $N(\mu_i, \sigma)$ for each vertex set V_i, where σ is a noise parameter.

Proper values for the averages are computed using Equation 13. We set default values for each parameter as follows: number of vertices $n = 500$ and edges $m = 3n$, sparsity $h = .5$, and noise $\sigma = |\mu_i|$. These parameters are varied in each experiment presented in Figure 4. For SWT, we fix the value of β_{max} in the golden search to 1000 and, for the fast approximation (FSWT), we vary the number of Chebyshev polynomials applied (5, 20, and 50). The number of iterations of the Power method to approximate the eigenvectors of M is fixed at 10, which achieved good results in our experiments. Figure 4a compares FSWT and the original algorithm (SWT) varying the graph size (n), showing that FSWT is up to 100 times faster than SWT. In Figures 4b-4d, we compare the approaches in terms of the energy $||a_{1,1}||_2$ of the first wavelet cut discovered varying the synthetic signal parameters. The results show that FSWT achieves similar or better results than SWT for relatively few coefficients ($p = 20$) in all the settings.

6.2 Compression

We evaluate our spectral algorithm for sparse wavelet bases in the signal compression task. Given a graph G and a signal W, the goal is to compute a compact representation W' that minimizes the L_2 error ($||W - W'||_2$). For the baselines, the *size* of the representation is the number of coefficients of the transform kept in the compression, relative to the size of the

[2] https://github.com/arleilps/sparse-wavelets

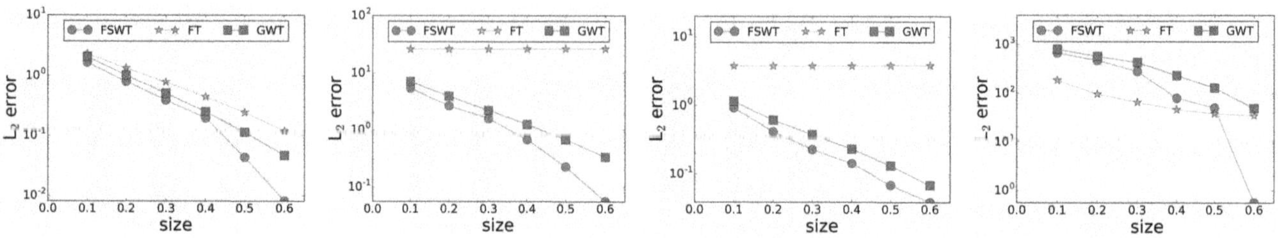

(a) Traffic (b) Human (c) Wiki (d) Blogs

Figure 5: Compression results for the *Traffic*, *Human*, *Wiki*, and *Blogs*. Our approach (FSWT) outperforms the baselines in most of the settings considered. In particular, FSWT achieves up to 80 times lower error than the best baseline (GWT).

dataset. We also take into the account the representation cost of the cuts ($\log(m)$ bits/edge) for our approach.

Datasets: Four datasets are applied in our evaluation. *Small Traffic* and *Traffic* are road networks from California for which vehicle speeds –measured by sensors– are modeled as a signal, with $n = 100$ and $m = 200$, and $n = 2K$ and $m = 6K$, respectively [23]. *Human* is a gene network for *Homo Sapiens* with expression values as a signal where $n = 1K$ and $m = 1K$ [24]. *Wiki* is a sample of Wikipedia pages where the (undirected) link structure defines the graph and the signal is the number of page views for each page with $n = 5K$ and $m = 25K$. *Blogs* is a network of blogs with political leaning (-1 for left and 1 for right) as vertex attributes [1] ($n = 1K$ and $m = 17K$). Notice that these graphs have sizes in the same scale as the ones applied by existing work on signal processing on graphs [28, 13, 11]. We normalize the values to the interval $[0, 1]$ to make the comparisons easier.

Baselines: We consider the Graph Fourier Transform (FT) [25, 28] and the wavelet designs by Hammond et al. (HWT) [16] and Gavish et al. (GWT) [13] as baselines. Instead of the original bottom-up partitioning algorithm proposed for GWT, we apply ratio-cuts [15], which is more scalable and achieves comparable results in practice.

Figure 6a shows compression results for *Small Traffic*. The best baselines (GWT and FT) incur up to 5 times larger error than our approaches (SWT and FSWT). Figures 5a-5d show the results for FSWT, GWT, and FT using the remaining datasets. Experiments for HWT and SWT took too long to finish and were terminated. FSWT outperforms the baselines in most of the settings, achieving up to 5, 6, 2, and 80 times lower error than the best baseline (GWT) for *Traffic*, *Human*, *Wikipedia*, and *Blogs*, respectively. FT performs surprisingly well for *Blogs* because vertex values are almost perfectly separated into two communities, and thus some low frequency eigenvectors are expected to approximately match the separation (see [1, Fig. 3]). As the size of the representation increases, FSWT is the only method able to separate values at the border of the communities.

These results offer strong evidence that our sparse wavelet bases can effectively encode both the graph structure and the signal. The main advantage of our approach is building bases that are adapted to the signal by cutting few edges in the graph. The compression times of our algorithm are comparable with the baselines, as shown in Table 6b.

6.3 Visualization

Finally, we illustrate some interesting features of our sparse wavelet formulation using graph drawing. Eigenvectors of

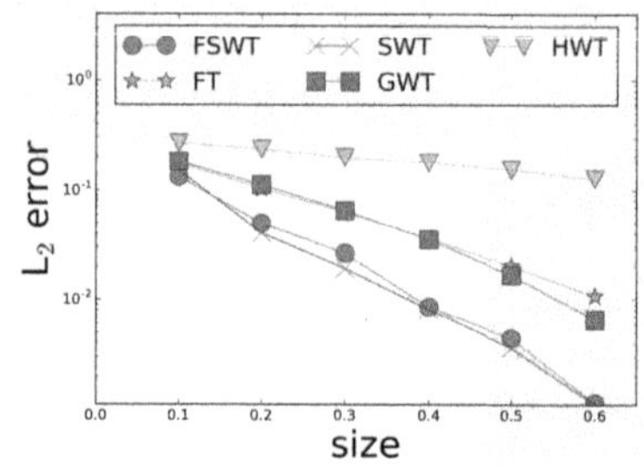

(a) Compression for *Small Traffic*

	Small Traffic	*Traffic*	*Human*	*Wiki*	*Blogs*
HWT	8	-	-	-	-
FT	1	35	2	381	7
GWT	1	5	11	386	47
SWT	1	-	-	-	-
FSWT	1	18	14	425	38

(b) Average compression times (in secs).

Figure 6: Compression results for *Small Traffic* and compression times for all methods and the datasets. Our approaches (SWT and FSWT) outperform the baselines while taking comparable compression time.

the Laplacian matrix are known to capture the community structure of graphs, and thus can be used to project vertices in space. In particular, if e_2 and e_3 are the second (*Fiedler*) and the third eigenvectors of the Laplacian matrix, we can draw a graph in 2-D by setting each vertex $v_i \in V$ to the position $(e_2(i), e_3(i))$. Following the same approach, we apply the smallest eigenvectors of the matrix M (see Corollary 1) to draw graphs based on both the structure and a signal.

Figure 7 presents drawings for two graphs, one is the traditional Zachary's Karate club network with a synthetic heat signal starting inside one community and the other is *Small Traffic*. Three different drawing approaches are applied: (1) The Scalable Force Directed Placement (SFDP) [17][3], the Laplacian eigenvectors, and the wavelet eigenvectors. Both SFDP and the Laplacian are based on the graph structure only. The drawings demonstrate how our wavelet formulation separates vertices based on both values and structure.

7. CONCLUSION

Signal Processing in Graphs (SPG) is a powerful framework for modeling complex data arising from several applica-

[3]Implemented by *GraphViz*: http://www.graphviz.org/

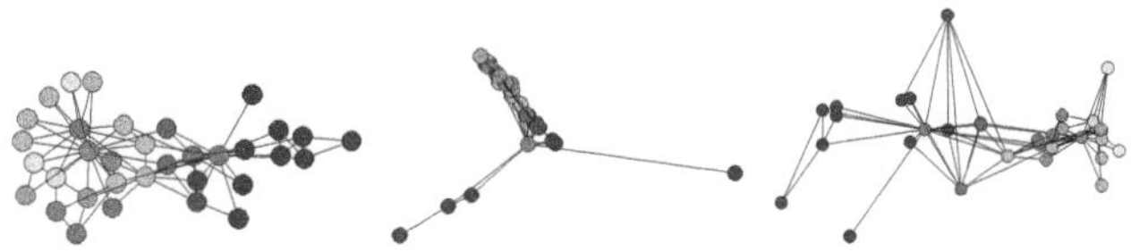

(a) SFDP (b) Laplacian (c) Wavelet

Zachary's karate club.

(d) SFDP (e) Laplacian (f) Wavelet

Traffic.

Figure 7: Drawing graphs using SFDP (a,d) and Laplacian (b,e) and wavelet eigenvectors (c,f). Vertices are colored based on values (red=high, green=average and blue=low). Different from the other schemes, wavelet eigenvectors are based on both signal and structure (better seen in color).

tions. A major challenge in SPG is relating properties of the graph signal, the graph structure and the transform. Graph wavelets are able to effectively model a smooth graph signal conditioned to the existence of a hierarchical partitioning of the graph that captures the geometry of the graph structure as well as the signal. Our work is the first effort to build such hierarchies in a compact fashion. We first introduced the problem of computing graph wavelet bases via sparse cuts and show that it is NP-hard—even to approximate by a constant—by connecting it to existing problems in graph theory. Then, we proposed a novel algorithm for computing sparse wavelet bases by solving regularized eigenvalue problems using spectral graph theory. While naively considering both structure and values can lead to computationally intensive operations, we introduced an efficient solution using several techniques. These approaches are extensively evaluated using real and synthetic datasets and the results provide strong evidence that our solution produces compact and accurate representations for graph signals in practice.

This work opens several lines for future investigation: (i) It remains an open question whether approximating a single optimal wavelet cut is NP-hard. (ii) The wavelet design applied in this work maps only to a particular type of wavelets (*Haar*); extending our approach to other wavelet functions (e.g. *Mexican hat, Meyer* [21]) might lead to better representations for particular classes of signals. (iii) Generalizing the ideas presented here to time-varying graph signals might lead to novel algorithms for anomaly detection, event discovery, and data compression.

Acknowledgment. Research was sponsored by the Army Research Laboratory and was accomplished under Cooperative Agreement Number W911NF-09-2-0053 (the ARL Network Science CTA). The views and conclusions contained in this document are those of the authors and should not be interpreted as representing the official policies, either expressed or implied, of the Army Research Laboratory or the U.S. Government. The U.S. Government is authorized to reproduce and distribute reprints for Government purposes notwithstanding any copyright notation here on.

8. REFERENCES

[1] L. A. Adamic and N. Glance. The political blogosphere and the 2004 us election: divided they blog. In *Workshop on Link Discovery*, 2005.

[2] T. Bui, S. Chaudhuri, F. Leighton, and M. Sipser. Graph bisection algorithms with good average case behavior. *Combinatorica*, 7:171–191, 1987.

[3] J. Cheeger. A lower bound for the smallest eigenvalue of the laplacian. *Problems in analysis*, 625:195–199, 1970.

[4] F. R. Chung. *Spectral graph theory.* American Mathematical Society, 1997.

[5] R. Coifman and M. Maggioni. Diffusion wavelets. *Applied and Computational Harmonic Analysis*, 21:53–94, 2006.

[6] M. Crovella and E. Kolaczyk. Graph wavelets for spatial traffic analysis. In *INFOCOM*, 2003.

[7] E. Dahlhaus, D. Johnson, C. Papadimitriou, P. Seymour, and M. Yannakakis. The complexity of multiway cuts. In *STOC*, 1992.

[8] J. Edmonds and R. M. Karp. Theoretical improvements in algorithmic efficiency for network flow problems. *Journal of the ACM*, 19:248–264, 1972.

[9] S. Fortunato. Community detection in graphs. *Physics Reports*, 486:75–174, 2010.

[10] J. Friedman, T. Hastie, and R. Tibshirani. *The elements of statistical learning.* Springer, 2001.

[11] A. Gadde, A. Anis, and A. Ortega. Active semi-supervised learning using sampling theory for graph signals. In *SIGKDD*, 2014.

[12] M. R. Garey and D. S. Johnson. *Computers and intractability.* WH Freeman, 2002.

[13] M. Gavish, B. Nadler, and R. Coifman. Multiscale wavelets on trees, graphs and high dimensional data. In *ICML*, 2010.

[14] G. H. Golub and C. F. Van Loan. *Matrix computations.* JHU Press, 2012.

[15] L. Hagen and A. B. Kahng. New spectral methods for ratio cut partitioning and clustering. *IEEE Transactions on Computer-aided Design of Integrated Circuits and Systems*, 11(9):1074–1085, 1992.

[16] D. Hammond, P. Vandergheynst, and R. Gribonval. Wavelets on graphs via spectral graph theory. *Applied and Computational Harmonic Analysis*, 30:129–150, 2011.

[17] Y. Hu. Efficient, high-quality force-directed graph drawing. *Mathematica*, 10:37–71, 2005.

[18] J. Kiefer. Sequential minimax search for a maximum. In *Proceedings of the AMS*, 1953.

[19] J. Lafferty and G. Lebanon. Diffusion kernels on statistical manifolds. *JMLR*, 6:129–163, 2005.

[20] N. Leonardi and D. Van De Ville. Tight wavelet frames on multislice graphs. *IEEE Transactions on Signal Processing*, 61:3357–3367, 2013.

[21] S. Mallat. *A wavelet tour of signal processing.* Academic Press, 1999.
[22] D. Mohan, M. T. Asif, N. Mitrovic, J. Dauwels, and P. Jaillet. Wavelets on graphs with application to transportation networks. In *ITSC*, 2014.
[23] M. Mongiovi, P. Bogdanov, and A. Singh. Mining evolving network processes. In *ICDM*, 2013.
[24] F. Moser, R. Colak, A. Rafiey, and M. Ester. Mining cohesive patterns from graphs with feature vectors. In *SDM*, 2009.
[25] A. Sandryhaila and J. Moura. Discrete signal processing on graphs. In *ICASSP*, 2013.
[26] A. Sandryhaila and J. Moura. Big data analysis with signal processing on graphs. *IEEE Signal Processing Magazine*, 31:80–90, 2014.
[27] J. Shi and J. Malik. Normalized cuts and image segmentation. *IEEE Transactions on Pattern Analysis and Machine Intelligence*, 22:888–905, 2000.
[28] D. Shuman, S. Narang, P. Frossard, A. Ortega, and P. Vandergheynst. The emerging field of signal processing on graphs. *IEEE Signal Processing Magazine*, 2013.
[29] A. Silva, P. Bogdanov, and A. K. Singh. Hierarchical in-network attribute compression via importance sampling. In *ICDE*, 2015.
[30] A. Silva, X.-H. Dang, P. Basu, A. Singh, and A. Swami. Graph wavelets via sparse cuts. http://arxiv.org/abs/1602.03320, 2016.
[31] A. Smola and R. Kondor. Kernels and regularization on graphs. In *Learning theory and kernel machines*, volume 2777, pages 144–158. 2003.
[32] I. Tošić and P. Frossard. Dictionary learning. *IEEE Signal Processing Magazine*, 28:27–38, 2011.
[33] L. Trevisan. Max cut and the smallest eigenvalue. *SIAM Journal on Computing*, 41:1769–1786, 2012.

APPENDIX

Proofs for Theorems 1, 2 and 5 are provided in [30].

Proof of Theorem 3

PROOF. We use a reduction from *graph bisection*, which given a graph $G'(V',E')$ and a constant q, asks whether there is a set of q edges in E' that, if removed, would break G into two equal parts (assume $|V'|$ is even). Graph bisection is NP-complete [12]. By substituting Expression 2 in Expression 5, we obtain the following expression:

$$||a_{k,\ell}||_2 = (\mu(X_i^{\ell+1}) - \mu(X_j^{\ell+1}))^2 \frac{|X_i^{\ell+1}||X_j^{\ell+1}|}{|X_k^{\ell}|} \tag{13}$$

For a given instance of the graph bisection problem, we generate $|V'|(|V'|-1)/2$ instances of the sparse wavelet basis problem, one for each pair of vertices (u,v) in V. Set $V = V' \cup \{s,t\}$, $E = E' \cup \{(s,u),(v,t)\}$, $W(s)=1$, $W(t)=-1$, and $W(u)=0$ for $u \in V'$. From Expression 13, we get that s and t have to be separate from each other in an optimal partitioning. Moreover, since $|X_i^{\ell+1}|+|X_j^{\ell+1}|$ is fixed, the energy is maximized when the partitions have equal size, with value $4(|V'|+1)^2/(|V'|+2)^2$. □

Proof of Theorem 4

PROOF. We start by rewriting Expression 5 in terms of pairwise differences (we drop the index ℓ):

$$\begin{aligned}||a_k||_2 = & \frac{-1}{2|X_i||X_j||X_k|}\Bigg(-2|X_i||X_j|\sum_{u\in X_i}\sum_{v\in X_j}(W(u)-W(v))^2 \\ & + |X_j|^2\sum_{u,v\in X_i}(W(u)-W(v))^2 \\ & + |X_i|^2\sum_{u,v\in X_j}(W(u)-W(v))^2\Bigg)\end{aligned} \tag{14}$$

$|X_k|$ is a constant and can be dropped from the denominator. $x^\intercal Cx$ is the quadratic form of the Laplacian C, thus:

$$x^\intercal Cx = \sum_{u,v\in C}(x_u - x_v)^2 = 4|X_i||X_j|$$

Similarly, $x^\intercal Lx$ is the standard quadratic form for the size of the cut between two partitions in G:

$$x^\intercal Lx = \sum_{u,v\in E}(x_u - x_v)^2 = 4|\{(u,v)\in E | u\in X_i \wedge v \in X_j\}|$$

Regarding $x^\intercal CSCx$:

$$\begin{aligned} x^\intercal C &= [x_1 \dots x_n] \times \begin{pmatrix} (n-1) & -1 & \dots & -1 \\ -1 & (n-1) & \dots & -1 \\ \vdots & & \ddots & \vdots \\ -1 & -1 & \dots & (n-1) \end{pmatrix} \\ &= \begin{pmatrix} x_1(n-1) - \sum_{i\neq 1} x_i \\ \vdots \\ x_n(n-1) - \sum_{i\neq n} x_i \end{pmatrix} \end{aligned} \tag{15}$$

$(x^\intercal C)_b$ can take two possible values, depending on x_b:

$$x_b(n-1) - \sum_{i\neq b} x_i = \begin{cases} -2|X_j|, & \text{if } x_b = -1 \\ 2|X_i|, & \text{otherwise} \end{cases} \tag{16}$$

Also $Cx = (x^\intercal C^\intercal)^\intercal = (x^\intercal C)^\intercal$. Therefore, $x^\intercal CSCx$ is also a quadratic form for the matrix S:

$$\begin{aligned} z^\intercal Sz &= \sum_{u\in X_k}\sum_{v\in X_k}(w_v - w_u)^2 z_v z_u \\ &= -4\sum_{u\in X_i}\sum_{v\in X_i}(w_v - w_u)^2|X_j|^2 \\ &\quad -4\sum_{u\in X_j}\sum_{v\in X_j}(w_v - w_u)^2|X_i|^2 \\ &\quad +8\sum_{u\in X_i}\sum_{v\in X_j}(w_v - w_u)^2|X_i||X_j| \end{aligned} \tag{17}$$

where $z = Cx$. This ends the proof. □

Lexis: An Optimization Framework for Discovering the Hierarchical Structure of Sequential Data

Payam Siyari
GeorgiaTech
Atlanta, GA, USA
payamsiyari@gatech.edu

Bistra Dilkina
GeorgiaTech
Atlanta, GA, USA
bdilkina@cc.gatech.edu

Constantine Dovrolis
GeorgiaTech
Atlanta, GA, USA
constantine@gatech.edu

ABSTRACT

Data represented as strings abounds in biology, linguistics, document mining, web search and many other fields. Such data often have a hierarchical structure, either because they were artificially designed and composed in a hierarchical manner or because there is an underlying evolutionary process that creates repeatedly more complex strings from simpler substrings. We propose a framework, referred to as *Lexis*, that produces an optimized hierarchical representation of a given set of "target" strings. The resulting hierarchy, "Lexis-DAG", shows how to construct each target through the concatenation of intermediate substrings, minimizing the total number of such concatenations or DAG edges. The Lexis optimization problem is related to the smallest grammar problem. After we prove its NP-hardness for two cost formulations, we propose an efficient greedy algorithm for the construction of Lexis-DAGs. We also consider the problem of identifying the set of intermediate nodes (substrings) that collectively form the "core" of a Lexis-DAG, which is important in the analysis of Lexis-DAGs. We show that the Lexis framework can be applied in diverse applications such as optimized synthesis of DNA fragments in genomic libraries, hierarchical structure discovery in protein sequences, dictionary-based text compression, and feature extraction from a set of documents.

1. INTRODUCTION

In both nature and technology, information is often represented in sequential form, as strings of characters from a given alphabet [11]. Such data often exhibit a hierarchical structure in which previously constructed strings are re-used in composing longer strings [21]. In some cases this hierarchy is formed "by design" in synthetic processes where there are some cost savings associated with the re-use of existing modules [15, 19]. In other cases, the hierarchy emerges naturally when there is an underlying evolutionary process that repeatedly creates more complex strings from simpler ones, conserving only those that are being re-used [19, 21]. For instance, language is hierarchically organized starting from phonemes to stems, words, compound words, phrases, and so on [20]. In the biological world, genetic information is also represented sequentially and there is ample evidence that evolution has led to a hierarchical structure in which sequences of DNA bases are first translated into amino acids, then form motifs, regions, domains, and this process continues to create many thousands of distinct proteins [8].

In the context of synthetic design, an important problem is to construct a minimum-cost Directed Acyclic Graph (DAG) that shows how to produce a given set of "target strings" from a given "alphabet" in a hierarchical manner, through the construction of intermediate substrings that are re-used in at least two higher-level strings. The cost of a DAG should be related somehow to the amount of "concatenation work" (to be defined more precisely in the next setion) that the corresponding hierarchy would require. For instance, in *de novo* DNA synthesis [4, 7], biologists aim to construct target DNA sequences by concatenating previously synthesized DNAs in the most cost-efficient manner.

In other contexts, it may be that the target strings were previously constructed through an evolutionary process (not necessarily biological), or that the synthetic process that was followed to create the targets is unknown. Our main premise is that even in those cases it is still useful to construct a cost-minimizing DAG that composes the given set of targets hierarchically, through the creation of intermediate substrings. The resulting DAG shows the most parsimonious way to represent the given targets hierarchically, revealing substrings of different lengths that are highly re-used in the targets and identifying the dependencies between the re-used substrings. Even though it would not be possible to prove that the given targets were actually constructed through the inferred DAG, this optimized DAG can be thought of as a plausible hypothesis for the unknown process that created the given targets as long as we have reasons to believe that that process cares to minimize, even heuristically, the same cost function that the DAG optimization considers. Additionally, even if our goal is not to reverse engineer the process that generated the given targets, the derived DAG can have practical value in the applications such as compression or feature extraction.

In this paper, we propose an optimization framework, referred to as *Lexis*,[1] that designs a minimum-cost hierarchical representation of a given set of target strings. The resulting hierarchy, referred to as "Lexis-DAG", shows how to construct each target through the concatenation of intermediate substrings, which themselves might be the result

KDD '16, August 13-17, 2016, San Francisco, CA, USA

DOI: http://dx.doi.org/10.1145/2939672.2939741

[1]Lexis means "word" in Greek.

of concatenation of other shorter substrings, all the way to a given alphabet of elementary symbols. We consider two cost functions: minimizing the total number of concatenations and minimizing the number of DAG edges. The choice of cost function is application-specific. The Lexis optimization problem is related to the smallest grammar problem [6, 14]. We show that Lexis is NP-hard for both cost functions, and propose an efficient greedy algorithm for the construction of Lexis-DAGs. Interestingly, the same algorithm can be used for both cost functions. We also consider the problem of identifying the set of intermediate nodes (substrings) that collectively form the "core" of a Lexis-DAG. This is the minimal set of DAG nodes that can cover a given fraction of source-to-target paths, from alphabet symbols to target strings. The core of a Lexis-DAG represents the most central substrings in the corresponding hierarchy. We show that the Lexis framework can be applied in diverse applications such as optimized synthesis of DNA fragments in genomic libraries, hierarchical structure discovery in protein sequences, dictionary-based text compression, and feature extraction from a set of documents.

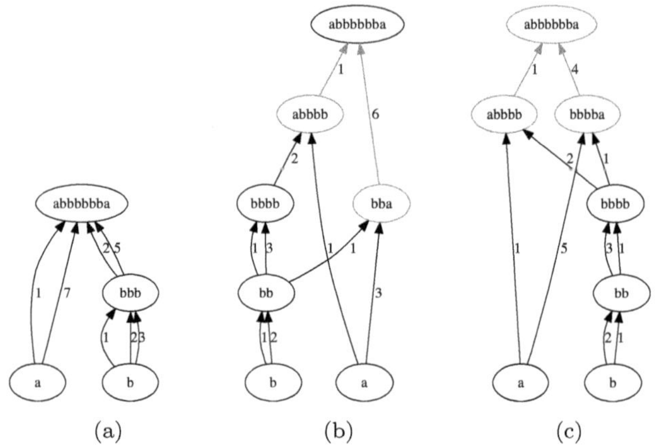

Figure 1: Illustration of the Lexis-DAG for targets $T = \{abbbbbba\}$ and sources $S = \{a, b\}$. Edge-labels indicate the occurrence indices: **(a)** A valid Lexis-DAG having both minimum number of concatenations and edges. **(b)** An invalid Lexis-DAG: two intermediate nodes are re-used only once. **(c)** An invalid Lexis-DAG: the top-layer string is not equal to the concatenation of its two in-neighbors (best viewed in color).

2. PROBLEM STATEMENT

2.1 Lexis-DAG

Given an alphabet S and a set of "target" strings T over the alphabet S, we need to construct a Lexis-DAG. A Lexis-DAG D is a directed acyclic graph $D(V, E)$, where V is the set of nodes and E the set of edges, that satisfies the following three constraints.[2]

First, each node $v \in V$ in a Lexis-DAG represents a string $\mathcal{S}(v)$ of characters from the alphabet S. The nodes V_S that represent characters of S are referred to as *sources*, and they have zero in-degree. The nodes V_T that represent target strings $T = \{t_1, t_2, \ldots, t_m\}$ are referred to as *targets*, and they have zero out-degree. V also includes a set of *intermediate nodes* V_M, which represent substrings that appear in the targets T. So, $V = V_S \cup V_M \cup V_T$.

Second, each node in $V_M \cup V_T$ of a Lexis-DAG represents a string that is the concatenation of two or more substrings, specified by the incoming edges from other nodes to that node. Specifically, an edge $e \in E$ from node u to node v is a triplet (u, v, i) such that the string $\mathcal{S}(u)$ appears as substring of $\mathcal{S}(v)$ at index i (the first character of a string has index 1). Note that there may be more than one edges from node u to node v. The number of incoming and outgoing edges for v is denoted by $d_{in}(v)$ and $d_{out}(v)$, respectively. $I(v)$ is the sequence of nodes u that appear in the incoming edges (u, v, i) of v, ordered by edge index i. We require that for each node v in $V_M \cup V_T$ replacing the sequence of nodes in $I(v)$ with their corresponding strings results in exactly $\mathcal{S}(v)$.

Third, a Lexis-DAG should only include intermediate nodes that have an out-degree of at least two,

$$\forall v \in V_M, d_{out}(v) \geq 2. \tag{1}$$

In other words, every intermediate node $v \in V_M$ in a Lexis-DAG should be such that the string $\mathcal{S}(v)$ is re-used in at least two concatenation operations. Otherwise, $\mathcal{S}(v)$ is either not used in any concatenation operation, or it is used only once and so the outgoing edge from v can be replaced by re-wiring the incoming edges of v straight to the single occurrence of $\mathcal{S}(v)$. In both cases node v can be removed from the Lexis-DAG, resulting in a more parsimonious hierarchical representation of the targets. Fig. 1 illustrates the concepts introduced in this section.

[2]To simplify the notation, even though D is a function of S and T, we do not denote it as such.

2.2 The Lexis Optimization Problem

The *Lexis* optimization problem is to construct a minimum-cost Lexis-DAG for the given alphabet S and target strings T. In other words, the problem is to determine the set of intermediate nodes V_M and all required edges E so that the corresponding Lexis-DAG D is optimal in terms of a given cost function $C(D)$.

$$\begin{aligned} &\min_{(E, V_M)} \; C(D) \\ &s.t.\; D = (V, E) \text{ is a Lexis-DAG for } S \text{ and } T \end{aligned} \tag{2}$$

The selection of an appropriate cost function is somewhat application-specific. A natural cost function to consider is the number of edges in the Lexis-DAG. In certain applications, such as DNA synthesis, the cost is usually measured in terms of the number of required concatenation operations. In the following, we consider both cost functions. Note that we choose to not explicitly minimize the number of intermediate nodes in V_M; minimizing the number of edges or concatenations, however, tends to also reduce the number of required intermediate nodes. Additionally, the constraint (1) means that the optimal Lexis-DAG will not have redundant intermediate nodes that can be easily removed without increasing the concatenation or edge cost. More general cost formulations, such as a variable edge cost or a weighted average of a node cost and an edge cost, are interesting but they are not pursued in this paper.

2.2.1 *Edge cost*

Suppose that the cost of each edge is one. The *edge cost* to construct a node $v \in V$ is defined as the number of incoming edges required to construct $\mathcal{S}(v)$ from its in-neighbors, which is equal to $d_{in}(v)$. The edge cost of source nodes is obviously zero. The edge cost $\mathcal{E}(D)$ of Lexis-DAG D is defined as the edge cost of all nodes, equal to the number of edges in D:

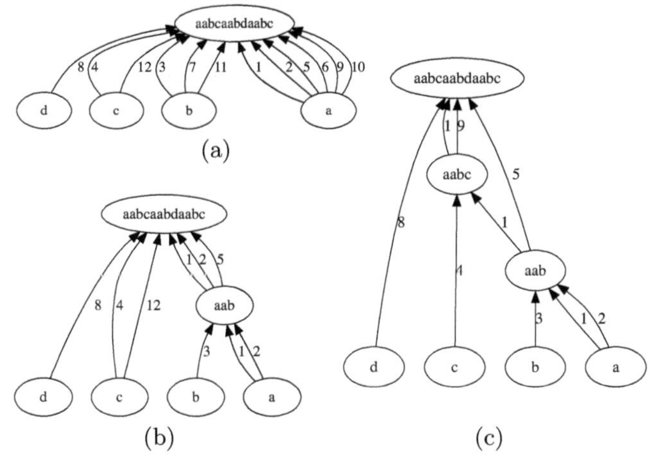

Figure 2: Illustration of G-Lexis given target $T = \{aabcaabdaabc\}$ and sources $S = \{a, b, c, d\}$. - **(a)** Initial Lexis-DAG: The string passed to the suffix tree is $I(aabcaabdaabc) = aabcaabdaabc$. **(b)** Substring aab has maximum *SavedCost*. The target can be now written as $I(aabcaabdaabc) = \sigma_{aab} c \sigma_{aab} d \sigma_{aab} c$ where σ_{aab} is the substring aab of the new intermediate node. We also have that $I(aab) = aab$. The strings passed to the suffix tree are $\{I(aabcaabdaabc), I(aab)\}$. **(c)** Substring $\sigma_{aab} c$ has maximum *SavedCost* and is chosen for a new intermediate node. In this example, this would be the last iteration.

$$\mathcal{E}(D) = \sum_{v \in V} d_{in}(v) = |E| \tag{3}$$

2.2.2 Concatenation cost

Suppose that the cost of each concatenation operation is one. The *concatenation cost* to construct a node $v \in V_M \cup V_T$ is defined as the number of concatenations required to construct $\mathcal{S}(v)$ from its in-neighbors, which is equal to $d_{in}(v) - 1$. The concatenation cost $\mathcal{C}(D)$ of Lexis-DAG D is defined as the concatenation cost of all non-source nodes; it is easy to see that this is equal to the number of edges in D minus the number of non-source nodes,

$$\mathcal{C}(D) = \sum_{v \in V \setminus V_S} (d_{in}(v) - 1) = |E| - |V \setminus V_S| \tag{4}$$

Theorem 1. *The optimization problem in Eq.* (2) *is NP-hard for both the edge cost of Eq.* (3) *and the concatenation cost of Eq.* (4).

The proof is given in the Appendix. Note that the objective in Eq. (4) is an explicit function of the number of intermediate nodes in the Lexis-DAG. Hence the optimal solutions for the concatenation cost can be different than those for the edge cost. An example is shown in the Appendix.

3. THE GREEDY LEXIS ALGORITHM

In this section, we describe a greedy algorithm, referred to as G-Lexis, for both previous optimization problems. The basic idea in G-Lexis is that it searches for the substring ξ that will lead, under certain assumptions, to the maximum cost reduction when added as a new intermediate node in the Lexis-DAG. The algorithm starts from the trivial Lexis-DAG with no intermediate nodes and edges from the source nodes representing alphabet symbols to each of their occurrences in the target strings.

Recall that for every node $v \in V_T \cup V_M$, $I(v)$ is the sequence of nodes appearing in the incoming edges of v, i.e., the sequence of nodes whose string concatenation results in the string $\mathcal{S}(v)$ represented by v. The sequences $I(v)$ can be interpreted as strings over the "alphabet" of Lexis-DAG nodes. Note that every symbol in a string $I(v)$ has a corresponding edge in the Lexis-DAG. We look for a repeated substring ξ in the strings $I_{T \cup M} = \{I(v) | v \in V_T \cup V_M\}$ that can be used to construct a new intermediate node. We can construct a new intermediate node for ξ, create incoming edges based on the symbols in ξ (remember ξ is a substring over the alphabet of nodes), and replace the incoming edges to each of the non-overlapping repeated occurrences of ξ with a single outgoing edge from the new node.

Consider the edge cost first. Suppose that ξ is repeated $R_{T \cup M, \xi}$ times in the strings $I_{T \cup M}$. If these occurrences of ξ are non-overlapping, the number of required edges would be $|\xi| \, R_{T \cup M, \xi}$. After we construct a new intermediate node for ξ as outlined above, the edge cost will be $|\xi| + R_{T \cup M, \xi}$. So, the reduction in edge cost from re-using ξ would be $(R_{T \cup M, \xi} - 1)(|\xi| - 1) - 1$. Under the stated assumptions about ξ, this reduction is non-negative if ξ is repeated at least twice and its length is at least two.

Consider the concatenation cost now. If these occurrences of ξ are non-overlapping, the number of required concatenations for all the repeated occurrences would be $(|\xi| - 1) \, R_{T \cup M, \xi}$. After we construct a new intermediate node for ξ as outlined above, the concatenation cost will be $|\xi| - 1$. We expect a reduction in the number of required concatenations by $(R_{T \cup M, \xi} - 1)(|\xi| - 1)$.

So, the greedy choice for both cost functions is the same: select the substring ξ that maximizes the term *SavedCost* $= (R_{T \cup M, \xi} - 1)(|\xi| - 1)$. For this reason, our G-Lexis algorithm can be used for both cost functions we consider. It starts with the trivial Lexis-DAG, and at each iteration it chooses a substring of $I_{T \cup M}$ in the Lexis-DAG that maximizes *SavedCost*, creates a new intermediate node for that substring and updates the edges of the Lexis-DAG accordingly. The algorithm terminates when there are no more substrings of $I_{T \cup M}$ with length at least two and repeated at least twice. The pseudocode for G-Lexis is shown in Algorithm 1. An example of application of the G-Lexis algorithm is shown in Fig. 2.

Algorithm 1. G-Lexis

Input: Alphabet S, Targets T **Output:** Lexis-DAG D

1. Initialize $V \leftarrow V_T \cup V_S$ and E, constructing each target in T from characters in S. $V_M \leftarrow \varnothing$.
2. Repeat:
   (a) $I_{T \cup M} \leftarrow \{I(v) | v \in (V_T \cup V_M)\}$;
   (b) Select ξ with maximum $(R_{T \cup M, \xi} - 1)(|\xi| - 1)$, where $R_{T \cup M, \xi}$ is the number of repeats of substring ξ in $I_{T \cup M}$; #GreedyChoice
   (c) If $(R_{T \cup M, \xi} - 1)(|\xi| - 1) = 0$, *break;*
   (d) $V \leftarrow V \cup \{\sigma_\xi\}$, where σ_ξ is the new intermediate node, and update E accordingly; #UpdateLexis-DAG

At each iteration of G-Lexis, we need to find efficiently the substring of $I_{T \cup M}$ with maximum *SavedCost*. We observe that the substring that maximizes *SavedCost* is a "maximal repeat". Maximal repeats are substrings of length at least two, whose extension to the right or left would reduce its occurrences in the given set of strings. Suppose that it is not. Then, there is a substring $\hat{\sigma}$, which is not a maximal repeat, that maximizes *SavedCost*. If we can extend $\hat{\sigma}$ to the left or right we can increase its length without reducing its number of occurrences. By doing so, we construct a new substring with higher *SavedCost* than $\hat{o}$, violating our initial assumption. So, the substring that maximizes *SavedCost* is a maximal repeat. A suffix tree over a set of input strings captures all right-maximal repeats, and right-maximal repeats are a superset of all maximal repeats [11]. To pick the one with maximum *SavedCost*, we need the count of non-overlapping occurrences of these substrings. A Minimal Augmented Suffix Tree [5] over $I_{T \cup M}$ can be constructed and used to count the number of non-overlapping occurrences of all right-maximal repeats in overall $O(L \log L)$ time, where L is the total length of target strings. Using a regular suffix tree instead, this can be achieved in only $O(L)$ time; but suffix tree may count overlapping occurrences. In our implementation we prefer to use regular suffix tree, following related work [10] that has shown that this performance optimization has negligible impact on the solution's quality. So, the substring that is chosen for the new Lexis-DAG node is based on length and overlapping occurrence count. We then use the suffix tree to iterate over all occurrences of the selected substring, skipping overlapping occurrences. If a selected substring has less than two non-overlapping occurrences, we skip to the next best substring. Using the suffix tree, we can update the Lexis-DAG with the new intermediate node, and with the corresponding edges for all occurrences of that substring, in $O(L)$ time. The maximum number of iterations of G-Lexis is $O(L)$ because each iteration reduces the number of edges (or concatenations), which at the start is $O(L)$. So, the overall run-time complexity using suffix tree is $O(L^2)$.

We have also experimented with other algorithms, such as a greedy heuristic that selects the longest repeat in each iteration of building the DAG, i.e., it chooses based on length among all substrings that appear at least twice in the targets or intermediate node strings. This heuristic can be efficiently implemented to run in only $O(L)$ time [13]. Our evaluation shows that G-Lexis performs significantly better than the longest repeat heuristic in terms of solution quality, despite some running time overhead. Running both algorithms on a machine with an Intel Core-i7 2.9 GHz CPU and 16GB of RAM on the NSF abstracts dataset (introduced in Section 5) of 2,309 target strings with total length 245,968 symbols takes 562 sec for G-Lexis and 408 sec for the longest repeat algorithm. The edge cost with G-Lexis is 169,060 compared to 183,961 with the longest repeat algorithm. More detailed results can be found in the Appendix.

4. PATH-CENTRALITY AND THE CORE OF A LEXIS-DAG

After constructing a Lexis-DAG, an important question is to rank the constructed intermediate nodes in terms of significance or *centrality*. Even though there are many related metrics in the network analysis literature, such as closeness, betweenness or eigenvector centrality [22], none of them captures well the semantics of a Lexis-DAG. In a Lexis-DAG, a path that starts from a source and terminates at a target represents a dependency chain in which each node depends on all previous nodes in that path. So, the higher the number of such source-to-target paths traversing an intermediate node v is, the more important v is in terms of the number of dependency chains it participates in. More formally, let $P_D(v)$ be the number of source-to-target paths that traverse node $v \in V_M$; we refer to $P_D(v)$ as the *path centrality* of intermediate node v. The path centrality of sources and targets is zero by definition. First, note that:

$$P(v) = P_S(v)\, P_T(v) \tag{5}$$

where $P_S(v)$ is the number of paths from any source to v, and $P_T(v)$ is the number of paths from v to any target. This suggests an efficient way to calculate the path centrality of all nodes in a Lexis-DAG in $O(|E|)$ time: perform two DFS traversals, one starting from sources and following the direction of edges, and another starting from targets and following the opposite direction. The first DFS traversal will recursively produce $P_S(v)$ while the second will produce $P_T(v)$, for all intermediate nodes.

Second, it is easy to see that $P_T(v)$ is equal to the number of times string $\mathcal{S}(v)$ is used for replacement in the target strings T. Similarly, $P_S(v)$ is equal to the number of times any source node is repeated in $\mathcal{S}(v)$, which is simply the length of $\mathcal{S}(v)$. So, the path centrality $P(v)$ of a node in a Lexis-DAG can be also interpreted as its "re-use count" (or number of replaced occurrences in the targets) times its length. Thus, an intermediate node will rank highly in terms of path centrality if it is both long and frequently re-used.

An important follow-up question is to identify the *core* of a Lexis-DAG, i.e., a set of intermediate nodes that represent, as a whole, the most important substrings in that Lexis-DAG. Intuitively, we expect that the core should include nodes of high path centrality, and that almost all source-to-target dependency chains of the Lexis-DAG should traverse at least one of these core nodes.

More formally, suppose K is a set of intermediate nodes and $\mathcal{P}^-(K)$ is the set of source-to-target paths after we remove the nodes in K from D. The core of D is defined as the minimum-cardinality set of intermediate nodes $\hat{K}$ such that the fraction of remaining source-to-target paths after the removal of $\hat{K}$ is at most τ:

$$\begin{aligned} \min_{K \subseteq V_M} \quad & |K| \\ s.t.\ & |\mathcal{P}^-(K)| \leq \tau\, |\mathcal{P}^-(\varnothing)| \end{aligned} \tag{6}$$

where $|\mathcal{P}^-(\varnothing)|$ is the number of source-to-target paths in the original Lexis-DAG, without removing any nodes.[3]

Note that if $\tau = 0$ the core identification problem becomes equivalent to finding the min-vertex-cut of the given Lexis-DAG. In practice a Lexis-DAG often includes some *tendril-like* source-to-target paths traversing a small number of intermediate nodes that very few other paths traverse. These paths can cause a large increase in the size of the core. For this reason, we prefer to consider the case of a positive, but potentially small, value of the threshold τ.

We solve the core identification problem with a greedy algorithm referred to as G-Core. This algorithm adds in each iteration the node with the highest path-centrality value to the core set, updates the Lexis-DAG by removing that node and its edges, and recomputes the path centralities before the next iteration. The algorithm terminates when the desired fraction of source-to-target paths has been achieved. G-Core requires at most $O(|V|)$ iterations, and in each it-

[3]It is easy to see that $|\mathcal{P}^-(\varnothing)|$ is equal to the cumulative length of all target strings L.

eration we update the path centralities in $O(|E|)$ time. So the run-time complexity of G-CORE is $O(|V||E|)$.

5. APPLICATIONS OF LEXIS

We now discuss a variety of applications of the proposed framework. Note that in all experiments, we use the library from [10] for extracting the maximal repeats and NetworkX [12] as the graph library in our implementation.

5.1 Optimized String Hierarchies

Lexis can be used as an optimization tool for the hierarchical synthesis of sequences. One such application comes from synthetic biology, where novel DNA sequences are created by concatenating existing DNA sequences in a hierarchical process [7]. The cost of DNA synthesis is considerable today due to the biochemical operations that are required to perform this "genetic merging" [7, 4]. Hence, it is desirable to re-use existing DNA sequences, and more generally, to perform this design process in an efficient hierarchical manner.

Biologists have created a library of synthetic DNA sequences, referred to as iGEM [2]. Currently, there are 787 elementary "BioBrick parts" from which longer composite sequences can be created. Longer sequences are submitted to the Registry of Standard Biological Parts in the annual iGEM competition, then functionally evaluated and labeled. In the following, we analyze a subset of the iGEM dataset. In particular, this dataset contains 1,375 composite DNA sequences that are labeled as iGEM *devices* because they have distinct biological functions; we treat these sequences as Lexis targets. The cumulative length of the target sequences is 6,957 symbols. The 787 elementary BioBrick parts are treated as the Lexis sources. The iGEM dataset also includes other BioBrick parts that are neither devices nor elementary, and that have been used to construct more complex parts in iGEM; we ignore those because they do not have a distinct biological function (i.e., they should not be viewed as targets but as intermediate sequences that different teams of biologists have previously constructed).

We constructed an optimized Lexis-DAG for the given sets of iGEM sources and targets. To quantify the gain that results from using a hierarchical synthesis process, we compare the number of edges and concatenations in the Lexis-DAG versus a flat synthesis process in which each target is independently constructed from the required sources. The *Lexis* solution requires only 52% of the edges (or 56% of the concatenations) that the flat process would require. The sequence with the highest path centrality in the Lexis-DAG is *B0010-B0012*.[4] This part is registered as *B0015* in the iGEM library and it is the most common "terminator" in iGEM devices. *Lexis* identified several more high centrality parts that are already in iGEM, such as *B0032-E0040-B0010-B0012*, registered as *E0240*. Interestingly, however, the Lexis-DAG also includes some high centrality parts that have not been registered in iGEM yet, such as *B0034-C0062-B0010-B0012-R0062*. A list of the top-15 nodes in terms of path centrality is given in the Appendix.

To explore the hierarchical nature of the iGEM sequences, we compared the *"Original"* Lexis-DAG, the one we constructed with the actual iGEM devices as targets, with *"Randomized"* Lexis-DAGs. *"Randomized"* Lexis-DAG is the result of applying G-LEXIS to a target set where each iGEM

[4] BioBricks start with *BBa_* prefix that are omitted here.

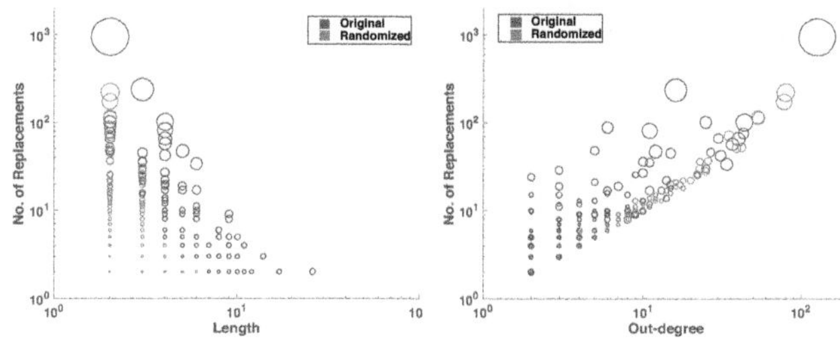

Figure 3: Comparison of the Lexis-DAGs that result from the Original and Randomized iGEM devices (best viewed in color). The size of each point represents the path-centrality of that node.

device sequence is randomly reshuffled. We compare the Original Lexis-DAG characteristics to the average Lexis-DAG characteristics over ten randomized experiments. The Original Lexis-DAG has fewer intermediate nodes than the Randomized ones (169 in Original vs 359 in Randomized), and its depth is twice as large (8 vs 4.4). Importantly, the Randomized DAGs are significantly more costly: 44% higher cost in terms of edges and 52% in terms of concatenations.

To further understand these differences from the topological perspective, Fig. 3 shows scatter plots for the length, path centrality, and re-use (number of replacements) of each intermediate node in the Original Lexis-DAG vs one of the Randomized Lexis-DAGs. With randomized targets, the intermediate nodes are short (mostly 2-3 symbols), their re-use is roughly equal to their out-degree, and their path centrality is determined by their out-degree; in other words, most intermediate nodes are directly connected to the targets that include them, and the most central nodes are those that have the highest number of such edges. On the contrary, with the original targets we find longer intermediate nodes (up to 11-12 symbols) and their number of replacements in the targets can be up to an order of magnitude higher than their out-degree. This happens when intermediate nodes with a large number of replacements are not only used directly to construct targets but they are repeatedly combined to construct longer intermediate nodes, creating a deeper hierarchy of re-use. In this case, the high path centrality nodes tend to be those that are both relatively long and common, achieving a good trade-off between specificity and generality.

5.2 Structure Discovery

As mentioned in the introduction, it is often the case that the hierarchical process that creates the observed sequences is unknown. *Lexis* can be used to discover underlying hierarchical structure as long as we have reasons to believe that that hierarchical process cares to minimize, even heuristically, the same cost function that Lexis considers (i.e., number of edges or concatenations). A related reason to apply Lexis in the analysis of sequential data is to identify the most parsimonious way, in terms of number of edges or concatenations, to represent the given sequences hierarchically. Even though this representation may not be related to the process that generated the given targets, it can expose if the given data have an inherent hierarchical structure.

As an illustration of this process, we apply Lexis on a set of protein sequences. Even though it is well-known that such sequences include conserved and repeated subsequences (such as motifs) of various lengths, it is not currently known whether these repeats form a hierarchical structure. That would be the case if one or more short conserved sequences are often combined to form longer conserved sequences, which can themselves be combined with others to form even longer sequences, etc. If we accept the premise that a conserved sequence serves a distinct biological function, the discovery of hierarchical structure in protein sequences would suggest that elementary biological functions are combined in a Lego-like manner to construct the complexity and diversity of the proteome. In other words, the presence of hierarchical structure would suggest that proteins satisfy, at least to a certain extent, the *composability* principle, meaning that the function of each protein is composed of, and it can be understood through, the simpler functions of hierarchical components.

Our dataset is the proteome of baker's Yeast[5], which consists of 6,721 proteins. However, this includes many protein homologues. It is important that we replace each cluster of homologues with a single protein; otherwise Lexis can detect repeated sequences within two or more homologues. To remedy this issue, we use the *UCLUST* sequence clustering tool [1], which is based on the *USEARCH* similarity measure (or identity search) [9]. The Percentage of Identity (PID) parameter controls how similar two sequences should be so that they are assigned to the same cluster. We set PID to 50%, which reduces the number of proteins to 6,033. Much higher PID values do not cluster together some obvious homologues, while lower PID values are too restrictive.[6] To reduce the running time associated with the randomization experiments described next, we randomly sample 1,500 proteins from the output of *UCLUST*.

The total length of the protein targets is about 344K amino acids. The resulting Lexis-DAG has about 151K edges and 5,171 intermediate nodes, and its maximum depth is 7. Fig. 4(a) shows a scatter plot of the length and number of replacements of these intermediate Lexis nodes (repeated sequences discovered by Lexis).

Of course some of these sequences may not have any biological significance because their length and number of replacements may be so low that they are likely to occur just based on chance. For instance, a sequence of two amino acids that is repeated just twice in a sequence of thousands of amino acids is almost certain (the distribution of amino acids is not very skewed). To filter out the sequences that are *not* statistically significant, we rely on the following hypothesis test. Consider a node that corresponds to a sequence with length l and number of replacements r in the given targets. The null-hypothesis is that sequences with these values of l and r will occur in a Lexis-DAG that is constructed for a random permutation of the given targets. To evaluate this hypothesis, we randomize the given target sequences multiple times, and construct a Lexis-DAG for each randomized sequence. We then estimate the probability that sequences of length l and number of replacements r occur in the randomized target Lexis-DAG, as the fraction of 500 experiments in which this is true. For a given significance level $\alpha = 0.1$, we can then identify the pairs (l, r) for which we can reject the null-hypothesis; these pairs correspond to the nodes that we view as statistically significant.[7]

On average, the randomized target Lexis-DAGs have a smaller depth (5.0) and more edges ($155K$) than the original Lexis-DAG. Fig. 4(b) shows the intermediate nodes of the original Lexis-DAG that pass the previous hypothesis test.

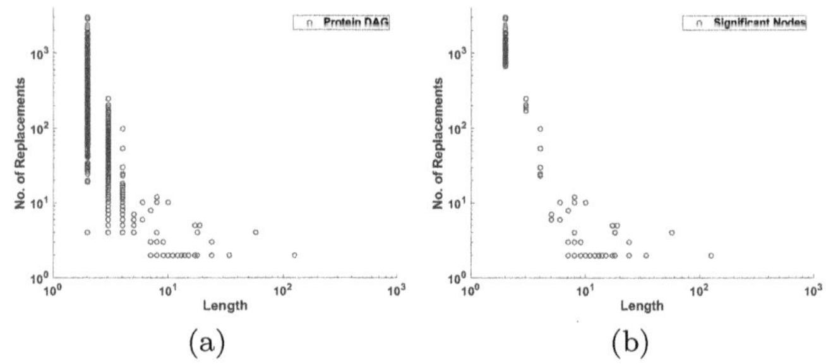

Figure 4: Length and number of replacements for the intermediate nodes in the protein sequence Lexis-DAG (a) before and (b) after we filter out the nodes that are not statistically significant.

Fig. 5 shows a small subgraph of the Lexis-DAG, showing only about 30 intermediate nodes; all these nodes have passed the previous significance test. The grey lines represent indirect connections, going through nodes that have not passed the significance test (not shown), while the bold lines represent direct connections. Interestingly, there seems to be a non-trivial hierarchical structure with several long paths, and with sequences of several amino acids that repeat several times even in this relatively small sample of proteins. Despite these preliminary results, it is clearly still early to draw any hard conclusions about the presence of hierarchical structure in protein sequences. We are planning to further pursue this question using Lexis in collaboration with domain experts.

5.3 Compression

Recent work has highlighted the connection between pattern mining and sequence compressibility [16]. Data compression looks for regularities that can be used to compress the data, while patterns are often useful as such regularities. In dictionary-based lossless compression, the original sequence is encoded with the help of a dictionary, which is a subset of the sequence's substrings as well as a series of pointers indicating the location(s) at which each dictionary element should be placed to fully reconstruct the original sequence. Following the Minimum Description Principle, one strives for a compression scheme that results in the smallest size for the joint representation of both the dictionary and the encoding of the data using that dictionary. The size of this joint representation is the total space needed to store the dictionary entries plus the total space needed for the required pointers. We assume for simplicity that the space to store an individual character and a pointer are the same.

We now evaluate the use of a Lexis-DAG for compression (or compact representation) of strings. To do so, we need to decide 1) how to choose the patterns that will be used for compression, and 2) if a pattern appears more than once, which occurrences of that pattern to replace. A naive approach is to simply use the set of substrings that appear in the Lexis-DAG as dictionary entries, and compare them to sets of patterns found by other substring mining algorithms.

[5]http://www.uniprot.org/proteomes/UP000002311

[6]http://drive5.com/usearch/manual/uclust_algo.html

[7]Another way to conduct this hypothesis test would be to estimate the probability that a specific sequence of length l will be repeated r times in a permutation of the targets. The number of randomization experiments would need to be much higher in that case, however, to cover all sequences that we see in the actual Lexis-DAG, each with a given value of r.

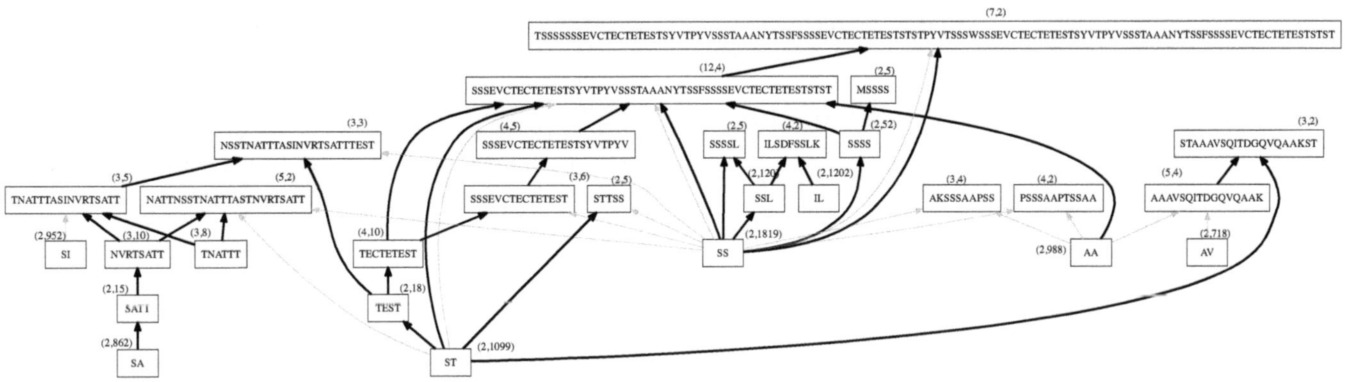

Figure 5: A small subgraph of the Lexis-DAG for 1,500 Yeast proteins. This plot only shows statistically significant nodes. Bold edges represent a direct connection between two nodes, while grey edges represent indirect connections (through nodes that are not shown in this plot). The label on top of each node shows the tuple (in-degree, number of replacements).

Given a set of patterns as potential dictionary entries, selecting the best dictionary and pointer placement is NP-hard. A simple greedy compression scheme, that we refer to as *CompressLR*, is to iteratively add to the dictionary the substring that gives the highest compression gain when replacing all Left-to-Right non-overlapping occurrences of that substring with pointers. We re-evaluate the compression gain of candidate dictionary entries in each iteration. For a substring v with length $|v|$ and number of left-to-right non-overlapping occurrences R_v, the compression gain is:

$$R_v \times |v| - R_v - |v| = (R_v - 1) \times (|v| - 1) - 1 \quad (7)$$

We compare the substrings identified by Lexis with the substrings generated by a recent contiguous pattern mining algorithm called *ConSgen* [27] (we could only run it on the smallest available dataset). Additionally, we compare the *Lexis* substrings with the set of patterns containing all 2- and 3-grams of the data. The comparisons are performed on six sequence datasets: the "Yeast" and iGEM datasets of the previous sections, as well as four "NSF CS awards" datasets that will be described in more detail in the next section.

Table 1 shows the comparison results under the headings: Lexis-CompressLR, 2+3grams-CompressLR and ConSgen-CompressLR. These naive approaches are all on par with each other. This comparison, however, treats G-Lexis as a mere pattern mining algorithm. Instead, the G-Lexis algorithm constructs a Lexis-DAG that puts the generated patterns in a hierarchical context. One can think of the Lexis-DAG as the instructions in constructing a hierarchical "Lego-like" sequence. The edges into the targets tell us how to place the final pointers, i.e., which occurrences of a dictionary entry to replace in the targets. Further, the rest of the DAG shows how to compress the patterns that appear in the targets using smaller patterns. It is easy to see that using this strategy the compressed size becomes equal to the number of edges in the DAG. Using this strategy that is encoded in the Lexis-DAG results in an additional 2%-20% reduction in the compressed size over the CompressLR approaches.

5.4 Feature Extraction

The Lexis-DAG can also be used to extract machine learning features for sequential data. The intermediate nodes that form the core of a Lexis-DAG, in particular, correspond to sequences that are both relatively long and frequently re-

Dataset	Lexis DAG	Lexis CompressLR	2+3-gram CompressLR	ConSgen CompressLR
Know&Cog	**68.69**	76.58	77.13	—
Networks	**78.48**	86.47	86.43	—
Robotics	**73.19**	80.62	79.69	—
Theory	**79.41**	81.89	82.63	—
Yeast	**44.28**	51.08	50.71	—
iGEM	**47.86**	67.47	67.75	67.47

Table 1: Compression ratio (i.e., percentage of compressed data size over original data size).

used in the targets. We hypothesize that such sequences will be good features for machine learning tasks such as classification or clustering because they can discriminate different classes of objects (due to their longer length) and at the same time they are general within the same class of objects (due to their frequent occurrence in the targets of that class).

To test this hypothesis, we used Lexis to extract text features for four classes of NSF research award abstracts during the 1990–2003 time period.[8] We pre-processed each award's abstract through stopword removal and Porter stemming. The alphabet S is the set of word stems that appear at least once in any of these abstracts. Table 2 describes this dataset in terms of number of abstracts, cumulative abstract length, and average length per abstract for each class.

Table 2: Description of 4 classes of NSF award abstracts

Class	$\|T\|$	L	$L/\|T\|$	$\|V_M\|$
Knowledge &Cog Sci	411	47,858	116	2,902
Networks	836	74,738	89	3,730
Robotics	496	56,481	113	4,560
Theory	566	66,891	118	4,247

We constructed the Lexis-DAG for each class of abstracts, and then used the G-Core algorithm to identify the core for each DAG. We stopped G-Core at the point where 95% of indirect paths in the Lexis-DAG are covered. The strings in each core are the extracted features for the corresponding class of abstracts. Table 3 shows the 5 strings extracted by G-Core for each class. We create a common set of G-Core features by taking the union of the sets of core substrings derived for each class. The next step is to construct the

[8]archive.ics.uci.edu/ml/machine-learning-databases/nsfabs-mld/nsfawards.data.html

feature vector for each abstract. We do so by representing each abstract as a vector of counts, with a count for each substring feature.

Table 3: 5 word stems in the Lexis-DAG core of each class of abstracts.

Knowledge & Cog	Networks
machine learn	request support nsf connect
knowledg base	bit per second
natur languag	two year
artifici intellig	provide partial support
neural network	high perform
Robotics	**Theory**
comput vision	comput scienc
first year	real world
robot system	complex class
object recognit	complex theori
real time	approxim algorithm

Table 4: SVM classification accuracy. # nonzeros is the number of nonzero elements in the term-document matrix with each feature set. The accuracies and the parameters are fit based on 10-fold cross-validation for each feature set.

Method (# Features)	# Nonzeros	(γ, c)	Accuracy
Bag-of-words (9,7k)	190,2k	*(0.0015,3)*	88.3%
G-Core (14,4k)	**55,5k**	*(0.02,1)*	90.0%
2-Gram (124,9k)	228,0k	*(0.0015,3)*	**91.3%**
3-Gram (186,3k)	234,5k	*(0.001,1)*	75.8%
1+2-Gram (134,6k)	418,2k	*(0.001,1)*	90.9%
1+2+3-Gram (321,0k)	652,8k	*(0.001,1)*	89.2%

To assess how good these features are, we compare the classification accuracy obtained using the Lexis features with more mainstream representations in text mining on NSF data: "bag-of-words", 2-gram, 3-gram, and two combinations of these representations. We use a basic SVM classifier with an RBF kernel. We used the SVM implementation in MATLAB. The accuracy results are similar to those with a KNN classifier that we tried with a Cosine distance, and the accuracy is evaluated with 10-fold cross-validation.

Table 4 shows that the Lexis features result in a much sparser term-document matrix, and so in smaller data overhead in learning tasks, without sacrificing classification accuracy. Lexis also results in a lower feature dimensionality (with the exception of the 1-gram method but the accuracy of that method is much lower). Note that most *Lexis* features are 2-grams but the *Lexis* core (for 95% of path coverage) may also include longer n-grams. Lexis becomes better, relative to the other feature sets, as we decrease the number of considered features. For instance, with 3,000 features the accuracy with Lexis is 74%, while the accuracy with the 1-gram and 2-gram features is 69% and 64%, respectively.

6. RELATED WORK

Lexis is closely related to the *Smallest Grammar Problem* (SGP), which focuses on the following question: *What is the smallest context-free grammar that only generates a given string?* The constraint that the grammar should generate only one string is important because otherwise we could simply consider a Σ^* as the generator of any string over Σ. The SGP is NP-hard, and inapproximable beyond a ratio of $\frac{8569}{8568}$ [6]. Algorithms for SGP have been used for string compression [18] and structure discovery [21] (for a survey see [10]). There are major differences between *Lexis* and SGP. First, in *Lexis* we are given a set of several target strings, not only one string. Second, *Lexis* infers a network representation (a DAG) instead of a grammar, and so it is a natural tool for questions relating to the hierarchical structure of the targets. For instance, the centrality analysis of intermediate nodes or the core identification question are well understood problems in network analysis, while it is not obvious how to approach them with a grammar-based approach.

One can also relate *Lexis* to the body of work on *sequence pattern mining*, where one is interested in discovering frequent or interesting patterns in a given sequence. Most work in this area has focused on mining subsequences, i.e., a set of ordered but not necessarily adjacent characters from the given sequence. In Lexis, we focus on identifying substrings, also known as *contiguous sequence patterns*. A couple of recent papers develop algorithms for mining substring patterns [27, 26], since sequence mining algorithms do not readily apply to the contiguous case. However, they rely on the methodology of candidate generation (commonly used in sequence pattern mining), where all patterns meeting a certain criterion are found, such as having frequency of at least two or being maximal. In the sequence mining literature, it has been recently observed that the size of the discovered set of patterns as well as their redundancy can be better controlled by mining for a set of patterns that meet a criterion collectively, as opposed to individually. This is useful when these patterns are used as features in other tasks such as summarization or classification. Algorithms for such set-based pattern discovery have been recently developed for sequence pattern mining [16, 25]. In the context of substring pattern mining, Paskov et al [24] show how to identify a set of patterns with optimal lossless compression cost in an unsupervised setting, to be then used as features in supervised learning for classification. In a follow-up paper [23], DRACULA provides a "deep variant" of [24] that is similar to Lexis, in terms of the general problem setup. DRACULA's focus is mostly on complexity and learning aspects of the problem, while Lexis focuses on network analysis of the resulting optimized hierarchy. For instance, DRACULA considers how to take into account how dictionary strings are constructed to regularize learning problems, and how the optimal Dracula solution behaves as the cost varies. We have shown that, although not specifically designed for feature extraction or compression, the *Lexis* framework also results in a small and non-redundant set of substring patterns that can be used in classification and compression tasks.

Optimal DNA synthesis is a new application domain, and we are only aware of the work by Blakes et. al. [4]; they describe DNALD, an algorithm that greedily attempts to maximize DNA re-use for multistage assembly of DNA libraries with shared intermediates. Even though the *Lexis* framework was not specifically designed for DNA synthesis, the Lexis-DAGs can be seemlessly used as solutions for this task. In our illustrative example with the iGEM dataset, G-Lexis returns solutions with 11% lower synthesis cost (equivalent to concatenation cost) than DNALD.

Structure discovery in strings has been explored from several different perspectives. For example, the grammar-based algorithm SEQUITIR [21] presents interesting possible applications in natural language and musical structure identification. In an information-theoretic context, Lancot et. al. [17] shows how to distinguish between coding and noncoding regions by analyzing the hierarchical structure of genomic sequences.

7. CONCLUSIONS AND FUTURE WORK

Lexis is a novel optimization-based framework for exploring the hierarchical nature of sequence data. In this paper, we stated the corresponding optimization problems in the admittedly limited context of two simple cost functions (number of edges and concatenations), proved their NP-hardness, and proposed a greedy algorithm for the construction of Lexis-DAGs. This research can be extended in the direction of more general cost formulations and more efficient algorithms. Additionally, we are working on an incremental version of Lexis in which new targets are added to an existing Lexis-DAG, without re-designing the hierarchy.

We also applied network analysis in Lexis-DAGs, proposing a new centrality metric that can be used to identify the most important intermediate nodes, corresponding to substrings that are both relatively long and frequently occurring in the target sequences. This network analysis connection raises an interesting question: are there certain topological properties that are common across Lexis-DAGs that have resulted from long-running evolutionary processes? We have some evidence that one such topological property is that these DAGs exhibit the *hourglass effect* [3].

Finally, we gave four examples of how Lexis can be used in practice, applied in optimized hierarchical synthesis, structure discovery, compression and feature extraction. In future work, we plan to apply Lexis in various domain-specific problems. In biology, in particular, we can use Lexis in comparing the hierarchical structure of protein sequences between healthy and cancerous tissues. Another related application is *generalized phylogeny inference*, considering that horizontal gene transfers (which are common in viruses and bacteria) result in DAG-like phylogenies (as opposed to trees).

8. ACKNOWLEDGEMENTS

This research was supported by the National Science Foundation under Grant No. 1319549.

9. REFERENCES

[1] *drive5.com/usearch/manual/uclust_algo.html.*

[2] *igem.org/main_page.*

[3] S. Akhshabi and C. Dovrolis. The evolution of layered protocol stacks leads to an hourglass-shaped architecture. In *Dynamics On and Of Complex Networks, Volume 2.* Springer, 2013.

[4] J. Blakes, O. Raz, U. Feige, J. Bacardit, P. Widera, T. Ben-Yehezkel, E. Shapiro, and N. Krasnogor. Heuristic for maximizing DNA re-use in synthetic DNA library assembly. *ACS Synthetic Biology*, 3(8):529–542, 2014.

[5] G.S. Brodal, R.B. Lyngso, A. Ostlin, and C.N.S. Pedersen. Solving the string statistics problem in time $o(n \log n)$. In *ICALP*, pages 728–739, 2002.

[6] M. Charikar, E. Lehman, D. Liu, R. Panigrahy, M. Prabhakaran, A. Sahai, and A. Shelat. The Smallest Grammar Problem. *IEEE Trans. on Inf. Theory*, 51(7), 2005.

[7] D. Densmore, T.H. Hsiau, J.T. Kittleson, W. DeLoache, C. Batten, and J.C. Anderson. Algorithms for automated DNA assembly. *Nucleic Acids Res.*, 38(8):2607–2616, 2010.

[8] W. Dubitzky, M. Granzow, and D. P. Berrar. *Fundamentals of data mining in genomics and proteomics.* Springer Science & Business Media, 2007.

[9] R. C. Edgar. Search and clustering orders of magnitude faster than BLAST. *Bioinformatics*, 26(19):2460–2461, 2010.

[10] M. Gallé. *Searching for compact hierarchical structures in DNA by means of the Smallest Grammar Problem.* PhD thesis, Université Rennes 1, 2011.

[11] D. Gusfield. Algorithms on strings, trees, and sequences: Computer science and computational biology. Cambridge Univ. Press, 1997.

[12] A. A. Hagberg, D. A. Schult, and P. J. Swart. Exploring network structure, dynamics, and function using NetworkX. In *Proceedings of the 7th Python in Science Conference*, pages 11–15, 2008.

[13] S. Inenaga, T. Funamoto, M. Takeda, and A. Shinohara. Linear-time off-line text compression by longest-first substitution. In *String Processing and Information Retrieval*, pages 137–152, 2003.

[14] J.C. Kieffer and E. Yang. Grammar based codes: A new class of universal lossless source codes. *IEEE Trans. on Inf. Theory*, 46:2000, 2000.

[15] J. Kleinberg. Bursty and hierarchical structure in streams. In *KDD*, pages 91–101, 2002.

[16] H. T. Lam, F. Mörchen, D. Fradkin, and T. Calders. Mining compressing sequential patterns. *Statistical Analysis and Data Mining*, 7(1):34–52, 2014.

[17] J.K. Lanctot, M. Li, and E. Yang. Estimating DNA sequence entropy. In *ACM-SIAM Symposium on Discrete Algorithms*, 2000.

[18] N.J. Larsson and A. Moffat. Offline dictionary-based compression. In *Data Compression Conference, 1999. Proceedings.*, pages 296–305, 1999.

[19] H. Mengistu, J. Huizinga, J.B. Mouret, and J. Clune. The evolutionary origins of hierarchy. *CoRR*, abs/1505.06353, 2015.

[20] S. Miyagawa, R.C. Berwick, and K. Okanoya. The emergence of hierarchical structure in human language. *Frontiers in Psychology*, 4(71), 2013.

[21] C.G. Nevill-Manning and I.H. Witten. Identifying hierarchical structure in sequences: A linear-time algorithm. *J. Artif. Int. Res.*, 7(1):67–82, 1997.

[22] M. Newman. *Networks: An introduction.* Oxford University Press, Inc., 2010.

[23] H. S. Paskov, J. C. Mitchell, and T. J. Hastie. Data representation and compression using linear-programming approximations. In *ICLR*, 2016.

[24] H. S. Paskov, R. West, J. C. Mitchell, and T. Hastie. Compressive feature learning. In *NIPS*, pages 2931–2939, 2013.

[25] N. Tatti and J. Vreeken. The long and the short of it: Summarising event sequences with serial episodes. In *KDD*, pages 462–470, 2012.

[26] J. Zhang, Y. Wang, and D. Yang. CCSpan: Mining closed contiguous sequential patterns. *Knowledge-Based Systems*, 89:1 – 13, 2015.

[27] J. Zhang, Y. Wang, C. Zhang, and Y. Shi. Mining contiguous sequential generators in biological sequences. *IEEE/ACM Transactions on Computational Biology and Bioinformatics*, PP(99):1–1, 2015.

Appendix

NP-hardness of Lexis Problem

We prove that the Lexis problem is NP-hard through a reduction from the *Smallest Grammar Problem* (SGP) [6].

Formally, *The Smallest Grammar Problem* for a string s is to identify a *Straight-Line Grammar* (SLG) G^* such that $L(G^*) = \{s\}$ and $|G^*| \leq |G|$ for any other G with $L(G) = \{s\}$, where $|G|$ denotes the size of grammar G. Charikar et al. [6] define the size of a grammar as the cumulative length of the right-hand side of all rules, i.e., $|G| = \sum_{T \to \alpha \in \Delta} |\alpha|$ where $|\alpha|$ is the number of symbols appearing in the term α of a grammar rule. Under this grammar size, Charikar et al. show that the Smallest Grammar Problem is NP-hard [6].

THEOREM 1. *The Lexis problem in Eq. (2) is NP-hard for $C(D)$ being edge cost (Eq. (3)) or concatenation cost (Eq. (4)).*

Proof: Let us first start with edge cost. Consider an instance of SGP in which we are given string s and we are asked to compute an SLG G such that $L(G) = \{s\}$ and $|G| \leq m$, where $|G| = \sum_{T \to \alpha \in \Delta} |\alpha|$. We reduce it to an instance of the Lexis problem with a single target string $T = \{s\}$, in which we are asked to compute a Lexis-DAG D with $\mathcal{E}(D) \leq m$.

Given a grammar $G = (\Sigma, \Gamma, S, \Delta)$ as a solution to the SGP problem, we construct a solution D for the reduced Lexis problem. For each symbol in $\Sigma \cup \Gamma$, construct a node. For a non-terminal $T \in \Gamma$, we refer to the corresponding node also as T, and associate that node with the string $\mathcal{S}(T)$ that is produced by expanding rule T according to grammar G. Also, for each rule $T \to \alpha$ in G, we scan α and add an edge in D from every node that corresponds to a terminal or nonterminal in α to the node that corresponds to T (along with the corresponding index). It is easy to see that D is acyclic since G is a straight-line grammar and that the number of edges in D is: $\mathcal{E}(D) = \sum_{T \to \alpha \in \Delta} |\alpha| \leq m$.

Conversely, consider a Lexis-DAG $D = (V_S \cup V_M \cup V_T, E)$ which is a solution to the Lexis problem from our reduction above , i.e., it has a single target string s, and $\mathcal{E}(D) \leq m$. We can construct a corresponding grammar G for the SGP as follows. For each source node in V_S, construct a terminal in Σ. For each node v in $V_T \cup V_M$, construct a nonterminal $NT(v)$ in Γ. For the single target node v in V_T, designate $NT(v)$ as the start symbol S. For each node v in $V_T \cup V_M$, add a rule in Δ with the right-hand side listing the corresponding $\Sigma \cup \Gamma$ symbols for all nodes in the sequence $I(v)$ (i.e., ordered as their respective strings appear concatenated in $\mathcal{S}(v)$). The constructed grammar is straight-line, since every nonterminal has one rule associated with it, and the grammar is also acyclic because the Lexis-DAG D is acyclic. It is easy to see that $|G| \leq m$.

The NP-hardness proof of the Smallest Grammar Problem with grammar size defined as $|G| = \sum_{T \to \alpha \in \Delta} |\alpha|$ [6] can be adapted for a modified grammar size definition, i.e., $|G| = \sum_{T \to \alpha \in \Delta} (|\alpha| - 1) = (\sum_{T \to \alpha \in \Delta} |\alpha|) - |\Delta|$. We can then use the same reduction from SGP to Lexis as in the case of edge cost to show that Lexis with concatenation cost is also NP-hard. ■

Lexis-DAGs: Edge Cost vs Concatenation Cost

Fig. 6 illustrates an example that the Lexis-DAG when optimizing for the edge cost function may be different than the Lexis-DAG when optimizing for concatenation cost.

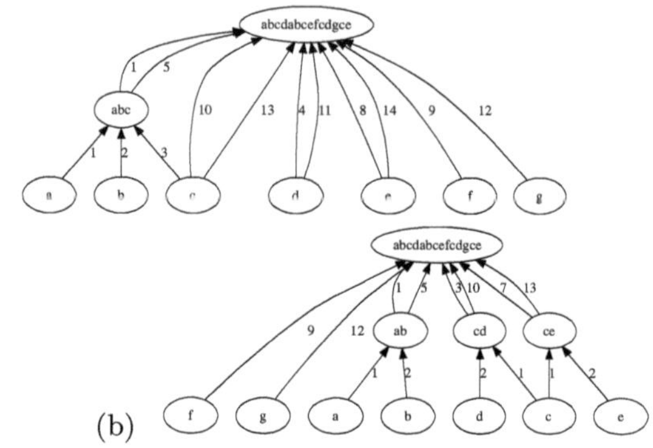

Figure 6: Illustration of Lexis-DAGs for target $T = \{abcdabcefcdgce\}$ and sources $S = \{a, b, c, d, e, f, g\}$ - **(a)** Lexis-DAG D_1 with $\mathcal{E}(D_1) = 13$ (optimal) and $\mathcal{C}(D_1) = 11$ (suboptimal). **(b)** Lexis-DAG D_2 with $\mathcal{E}(D_2) = 14$ (suboptimal) and $\mathcal{C}(D_2) = 10$ (optimal).

Comparison of G-Lexis with Longest Substring Replacement Algorithm

We compare G-Lexis with an algorithm that greedily replaces the longest repeated substring, in terms of both runtime and cost. We implemented the latter, originally proposed in [13] using suffix trees, using our own efficient linked-suffix array. We used the NSF data described in the main text and ran the two algorithms on different fractions of the total dataset, repeating the experiments 10 times and recording the average runtime and edge cost. As seen in Fig. 7, the Longest Substring Replacement heuristic offers a better runtime but its cost becomes increasingly worse than G-Lexis as the size of the dataset grows. Also, G-Lexis is still reasonably fast on all datasets we have analyzed so far.

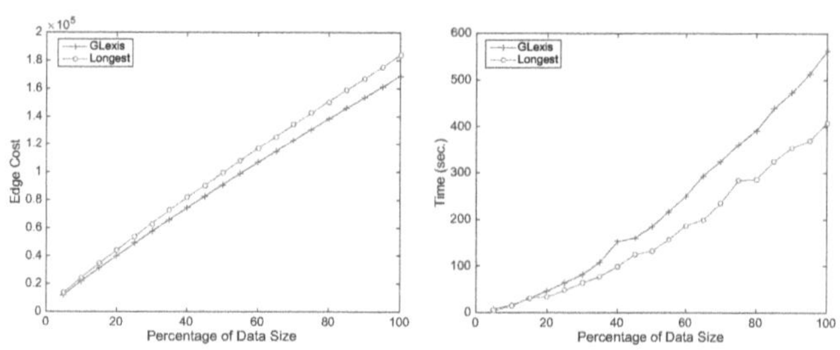

(a) Cost Comparison (b) Runtime Comparison

Figure 7: Comparison of G-Lexis with Longest Substring Replacement algorithm.

Central DNA Parts in iGEM Dataset

Table 5: Top-15 nodes with highest path-centrality iGEM dataset's Lexis-DAG. Nodes shown in bold are already registered in the iGEM library.

B0010-B0012	**E0040-B0010-B0012**
B0034-E0040-B0010-B0012	**B0034-C0062-B0010-B0012**
B0032-E0040-B0010-B0012	B0034-C0062-B0010-B0012-R0062
B0034-E1010-B0010-B0012	**B0034-E1010**
B0034-I732006-B0034-E0040-B0010-B0012	**B0034-C0062**
B0030-E0040-B0010-B0012	**R0010-B0034**
K228000-B0010-B0012	**R0040-B0034**
C0051-B0010-B0012	

Towards Optimal Cardinality Estimation of Unions and Intersections with Sketches

Daniel Ting
Facebook
1730 Minor Ave
Seattle, WA
dting@fb.com

ABSTRACT

Estimating the cardinality of unions and intersections of sets is a problem of interest in OLAP. Large data applications often require the use of approximate methods based on small sketches of the data. We give new estimators for the cardinality of unions and intersection and show they approximate an optimal estimation procedure. These estimators enable the improved accuracy of the streaming MinCount sketch to be exploited in distributed settings. Both theoretical and empirical results demonstrate substantial improvements over existing methods.

CCS Concepts

•Mathematics of computing → Probabilistic algorithms; •Theory of computation → Sketching and sampling; •Computing methodologies → *Distributed algorithms;*

Keywords

cardinality estimation; data sketching; randomized algorithms

1. INTRODUCTION

Consider a dataset $\mathcal{D}$. The basic approximate distinct count problem is to construct a memory efficient summarization S of $\mathcal{D}$ and to estimate the cardinality of the set of unique items A using just the sketch S. Under this basic formulation, a sketch answers a cardinality question that must be specified before computing the sketch. We consider the extended problem of estimating the cardinality of set unions, $|A_1 \cup A_2|$, and intersections, $|A_1 \cap A_2|$, using multiple sketches. This has two important consequences. First, combinatorially many cardinality questions can be accurately answered by sketches. Second, the significant improvements in accuracy using the HIPS or optimal martingale estimator of [10] and [23] can be realized in distributed settings. More specifically, we wish to define union $\tilde{\cup}$ and intersection $\tilde{\cap}$ operations on sketches and derive cardinality estimates that are optimal or nearly optimal.

This problem of estimating the number of distinct elements in a dataset in a memory efficient manner appears in a wide range of applications. For example, in data analytics and OLAP, a web company may count distinct users accessing a service [21]. The summarizations are used in networking to detect denial of service attacks by counting network flows [15], and in databases to optimize query plans [22]. Other applications include graph analysis where they are used to estimate the diameter of a graph [9], [5].

The extended problem for unions has particular importance in OLAP and distributed settings. The streaming cardinality estimator given by [23], [10] is optimal in the sense that no unbiased estimator has lower asymptotic variance. This is much stronger than typical space-complexity results in the theory literature [2], [19] that just guarantee an optimal rate. It guarantees optimality of the constant in front of the rate. This optimality is evident in practice as the estimators require half the space of existing methods to achieve the same error on MinCount sketches. The streaming estimator, however, cannot be applied directly in distributed settings. In a map-reduce setting, the mappers computing efficient streamed sketch summaries need a method to combine them at a reducer. A union operation on the sketches would allow the efficiency gains to be transfered to distributed settings and turn the streamed sketch into a mergeable summary [1]. These efficiency gains can be tremendous as empirical results show efficient cardinality estimation for unions can reduce variance and the space requirements by an order of magnitude when many sketches are merged.

In OLAP settings, one is often interested in cardinality estimates on multi-dimensional data, for example counting the number of users accessing a web service by geographic location, time window, and other factors [21]. This results in exponentially many cardinalities to estimate. Unions and intersections allow a limited number of sketches to answer a multitude of cardinality questions.

Cardinality estimates for intersections are not as well studied as for unions. While most sketches for approximate distinct counting have a natural but inefficient union operation, they do not have one for intersections. Intersection cardinality estimates are often computed using the inclusion-exclusion principle or by using Jaccard similarity [13], [4] when an estimator is available. These methods still require first accurately estimating the cardinality of the union or the Jaccard similarity of a set with the union.

KDD '16, August 13 - 17, 2016, San Francisco, CA, USA

ISBN 978-1-4503-4232-2/16/08...$15.00

DOI: http://dx.doi.org/10.1145/2939672.2939772

Our contributions are as follows. We introduce two techniques for computing unions and intersections on approximate distinct counting sketches: pseudo-likelihood based methods and re-weighting component estimators. These are applied to Streaming MinCount sketches in this paper but may be applied to other sketches as well. The resulting estimators demonstrate state of the art performance on both real and synthetic datasets. The pseudo-likelihood based MinCount method is conjectured to be asymptotically efficient as it is nearly the same as the asymptotically efficient maximum likelihood estimator. This establishes a nearly ideal baseline for comparison. Re-weighted component estimators are much simpler to implement and generalize, and they are empirically shown to be as efficient as the pseudo-likelihood based estimators. We also derive variance estimates which allow confidence intervals to be given for the cardinality estimates. In the special case where the streams are different permutations of the same set, we show that merging the streaming estimates yields a more accurate estimate than the estimator on a single stream. Thus, unlike existing methods, the union operation on streaming sketches exploits information about the order of elements in each stream. The variance after averaging over all possible orderings is shown to be $2/3$ the variance of the streaming MinCount estimator. In addition to improved estimation, the resulting methods yield mergeable summaries [1] under both union and intersection operations unlike existing methods.

2. EXISTING BASIC METHODS

The basic approximate distinct counting problem has been well studied in the literature beginning with the seminal paper by Flajolet and Martin [17]. Methods include Linear Probabilistic Counting (LPCA) [25], HyperLogLog [16], the Multiresolution Bitmap [15], the S-bitmap [7], α-stable distribution methods [12], and MinCount [18]. Kane, et al [19] also gave a method that is optimal in terms of space-complexity.

As described in [23], all these methods generate a stochastic process called the area process that is governed solely by the number of distinct elements encountered. A sketch S can be mapped to a set $\mathcal{R}(S) \subset (0,1)$ called the remaining area. Given a random hash, each element in a stream is hashed to some value U. If U is still in the remaining area, $U \in \mathcal{R}(S)$, the sketch is updated by cutting out a portion of the remaining area containing U. Otherwise, it does not affect the sketch. Since a value U cannot be cut out twice, duplicates do not affect the sketch. Under the assumption that the hash function is a strong universal hash, the original distribution of the data is irrelevant. A sketch is a function of the independent $Uniform(0,1)$ random variates that are the hashed distinct items. It is a random quantity whose distribution depends only on the number of distinct items. Cardinality estimation is thus a statistical parameter estimation problem where the sketch is the observed data.

Using an optimal estimation procedure can lead to substantial efficiency gains. For example, the LogLog and SuperLogLog methods [14] share the same sketch as HyperLogLog and differ only in the estimation procedure. However, LogLog requires 1.56 times the memory of HyperLogLog to achieve the same error and 2.4 times the memory of Streaming HyperLogLog. Likewise, the original cardinality estimation method for the α-stable sketch proposed in [12] uses over twice the memory as that used in [8]. The disadvantage of using the optimal streaming methods described in [23] and [10] is that they require the data to arrive in a single stream. They are not immediately applicable in distributed settings or in OLAP settings where the sketches are pre-aggregations that need to be further merged.

3. NAIVE ESTIMATION

We first consider basic estimation procedures for unions and intersections on distinct counting sketches. Many sketches used in approximate distinct counting have a natural union operation. For example, the LPCA sketch is a bitmap and is equivalent to a Bloom filter with the number of hashes $k = 1$. Taking the union of LPCA sketches simply takes the bitwise OR of the sketches. The resulting sketch is identical to the sketch computed on the union of the original sets. This property holds for other sketches such as HyperLogLog [16] and MinCount [18] as well. In other words, there is an operation $\tilde{\cup}$ such that $S(A_1)\tilde{\cup}S(A_2) = S(A_1 \cup A_2)$ where S is the function that generates a sketch from a streamed set. For notational convenience, we will denote $S_i = S(A_i)$.

Unlike the union, typically no natural intersection operation exists for approximate distinct counting sketches. A simple method to obtain cardinality estimates for the intersection is to use union estimates and the inclusion-exclusion principle, $|A_1 \cap A_2| = |A_1| + |A_2| - |A_1 \cup A_2|$. In the case where there is an estimate $\hat{J}(S_1, S_2)$ for the Jaccard similarity, two existing intersection cardinality estimator are given by [4] and [13]. Throughout, we will use a hat to denote estimated quantities, with $\hat{N}(S)$ denoting a cardinality estimate using sketch S. The naive and Jaccard based estimates of the cardinality of the union and intersection are given by

$$\begin{aligned}
\hat{N}_{naive}(S_1 \tilde{\cup} S_2) &= \hat{N}(S(A_1 \cup A_2)) \qquad (1)\\
\hat{N}_{naive}(S_1 \tilde{\cap} S_2) &= \hat{N}(S_1) + \hat{N}(S_2) - \hat{N}(S(A_1 \cup A_2))\\
\hat{N}_{Jaccard,1}(S_1 \tilde{\cap} S_2) &= \hat{J}(S_1, S_2)\hat{N}(S_1 \tilde{\cup} S_2)\\
\hat{N}_{Jaccard,2}(S_1 \tilde{\cap} S_2) &= \frac{\hat{J}(S_1, S_2)}{1 + \hat{J}(S_1, S_2)}\left(\hat{N}(S_1) + \hat{N}(S_2)\right)
\end{aligned}$$

These estimation strategies turn out to be suboptimal. For the intersection estimators, one reason is that the error is often roughly proportional to the size of the union or the larger set, while a good procedure should give error that is bounded by the size of the smaller set. This can also lead to pathologies where the naive cardinality estimate of the intersection is negative. If a simple correction to replace these negative estimates by zero is used, the resulting estimator is provably biased.

4. STREAMING MINCOUNT

In this paper we focus on applying new estimation techniques to Streaming MinCount sketches. The techniques may be used for other sketches, and their application is discussed in section 13. The choice of Streaming MinCount is driven by two reasons. The first is that it simplifies the calculations since collision probabilities are negligible. The second is that the uniqueness of hash values allows for a closed intersection operation and gives more flexibility to the sketch.

The basic MinCount sketch stores the k minimum hash values and is also known as the K-minimum values [2] or bottom-k [11] sketch. When the hash values are uniformly distributed on $(0,1)$, the estimator for the MinCount sketch is $(k-1)/\tau$ where τ is the largest stored hash value. It is easy to see that this estimator approximates the cardinality since the kth smallest hash value out of n roughly uniformly spaced values is approximately k/n. It can be shown that the estimator is the unique minimum variance unbiased estimator [6] when only the final set of hash values is observed.

The Streaming MinCount sketch augments the basic MinCount sketch with a running estimate of the cardinality. This estimate is given by

$$\hat{N}(S) = \sum_{t=1}^{n} \frac{Z_t}{\tau_t} \tag{2}$$

where τ_t is the threshold for sketch S after encountering t elements and $Z_t = 1$ if the sketch changed at time t. The threshold for a sketch is the largest stored hash value. The streaming estimator operates by incrementing the running estimate by 1 in expected value for each newly encountered element. By exploiting the sequence of sketches rather than just the final sketch, the streaming update procedure reduces the variance of the estimator by half.

5. IMPROVED ESTIMATORS

The usual union operation throws away valuable information for the MinCount sketch. To see this consider the case where the sets A_1, A_2 are disjoint and of equal cardinality. The best estimator would simply add $\hat{N}(S_1 \cup S_2) = \hat{N}(S_1) + \hat{N}(S_2)$ which has variance $(|A_1|^2 + |A_2|^2)/k = |A_1 \cup A_2|^2/2k$. However, the MinCount sketch throws away half of the hash values to maintain the size limit of k hash values. The resulting union estimate correspondingly has twice the variance, $|A_1 \cup A_2|^2/k$. This is the strategy employed by [4].

We introduce a simple improvement by constructing the largest possible merged MinCount sketch rather than fixing the size at k. Let $\tau(S)$ be the threshold, the largest stored hash, for sketch S. Let $h(S)$ denote the set of hashes stored in sketch S and $h(S,\tau')$ be the set that is $\leq \tau'$. For convenience, denote $\tau_i = \tau(S_i)$. Improved union and intersection operators $\cup_0, \cap_0$ on MinCount sketches are defined by

$$\tau_{min} := \tau(S_1 \cup_0 S_2) := \tau(S_1 \cap_0 S_2) := \min\{\tau_1, \tau_2\}$$
$$h(S_1 \cup_0 S_2) := h(S_1, \tau_{min}) \cup h(S_2, \tau_{min})$$
$$h(S_1 \cap_0 S_2) := h(S_1) \cap h(S_2)$$

In other words, the hash values larger than the minimum threshold are discarded, and the sketches are merged by taking the union or intersection of the remaining hash values.

The resulting union sketch is exactly the same as a MinCount sketch of size $|h(S_1 \cup S_2)|$ constructed from $A_1 \cup A_2$. The intersection sketch is similar but allows for the threshold to not be in the intersection. This yields a closed intersection operator. It generates a new sketch and not just an estimate of the cardinality. The union and intersection estimators are

$$\hat{N}_{improved}(S_1 \cup_0 S_2) = \frac{|h(S_1 \cup_0 S_2)| - 1}{\tau_{min}} \tag{3}$$

$$\hat{N}_{improved}(S_1 \cap_0 S_2) = \frac{|h(S_1 \cap_0 S_2)| - \delta(S_1, S_2)}{\tau_{min}} \tag{4}$$

where $\delta(S_1, S_2) = 1$ if $\tau_{min} \in h(S_1 \cap_0 S_2)$ and is 0 otherwise.

This improvement may also be applied to the Discrete MaxCount sketch introduced by [23]. However, there is no obvious generalization of this improvement to the HyperLogLog sketch. For the Streaming MinCount sketch, although it does not define a union or intersection cardinality estimator that exploits the gains from the streaming estimates $\hat{N}(S_i)$, it allows a closed intersection operation to be defined.

6. STATISTICAL EFFICIENCY

The improvements proposed in the previous section are suboptimal in terms of statistical efficiency. Statistical efficiency is a far more stringent optimality criterion than optimal space-complexity when comparing estimators. A consistent estimator $\hat{\theta}_n$ of a parameter θ is asymptotically (statistically) efficient if its asymptotic variance is equal to the Cramer-Rao lower bound on the variance [24]. Whereas space-complexity ensures that the error rate is optimal, asymptotic efficiency ensures both the rate and the constant factor governing the rate are optimal. This is an important distinction, since the rate is typically meaningless for estimation. Under mild regularity conditions, parameter estimation problems on i.i.d. observations invariably have an optimal rate of $\Theta(1/\sqrt{n})$, and almost any reasonable estimation procedure achieves that rate. Only the constant governing the rate yields meaningful comparisons for estimators. By contrast, space-complexity is meaningful when considering the problems of constructing and encoding a sketch but not for estimation [23].

Under mild regularity conditions, the maximum-likelihood estimator (MLE) is an asymptotically efficient estimator. Although we are not able to derive the exact MLE, in section 8.2 we derive both the conditional likelihood given the cardinality of the input sets as well as a full pseudo-likelihood. We conjecture that maximizing the full pseudo-likelihood gives an estimator that is asymptotically equivalent to the MLE. Although a full proof is out of the scope of this paper, we give a heuristic proof sketch that may be able to establish the asymptotic efficiency.

In addition to the class of likelihood based estimators, we derive a class of re-weighted estimators based on linear combinations of the streaming cardinality estimates. These estimators have the advantage of being easy to implement and easy to generalize to other sketches. Although we show how to optimally weight the linear combinations, the resulting estimators are not theoretically guaranteed to be asymptotically efficient, but empirical results suggest that they are efficient or close to efficient.

7. NOTATION AND ASSUMPTIONS

The remainder of the paper focuses on exploiting the efficiency gains from streaming estimation to improve cardinality estimation for union and intersection.

To fix some notation, suppose each sketch S_i contains k_i hash values and estimates the cardinality $|A_i| = n_i$. The total cardinality is $n_{tot} = |\cup_i A_i|$. The threshold τ_i for a sketch S_i is the maximum stored hash value. The proportion of the total that belongs to set A_i is denoted by $p_i = |A_i|/n_{tot}$. For simplicity, only pairwise unions and intersections are analyzed in detail, but merging multiple sketches is discussed in section 11 In the pairwise case, define $q_0 = |A_1 \cap A_2|/n_{tot}, q_1 = |A_1 \backslash A_2|/n_{tot}$, and $q_2 = |A_2 \backslash A_1|/n_{tot}$.

For the analysis of the methods, we consider the asymptotic regime where for each i, $k_i/n_{tot} \to 0$ and $q_i \to c_i > 0$

as $n_{tot} \to \infty$ for some constants c_i. The hash function is assumed to be a strong universal hash that generates i.i.d. $Uniform(0, 1)$ random variates.

8. LIKELIHOOD BASED METHODS

As described in section 2, cardinality estimation is a statistical parameter estimation problem. Under this formulation, statistical theory provides two important results. The useful pieces of information in the sketch are encoded by sufficient statistics, and the maximum likelihood estimator is an asymptotically efficient estimator.

8.1 Sufficient statistics

The notions of sufficiency and ancillarity are important in statistical estimation. A statistic is sufficient if it contains all the information necessary to reconstruct the likelihood function. Under the likelihood principle, the likelihood contains everything useful for parameter estimation. A statistic is ancillary if it is irrelevant for estimating the parameter. More formally, it is a statistic whose distribution does not depend on the parameter of interest. This gives a basic strategy for finding good estimators. Find the smallest sufficient statistic containing as few ancillary statistics as possible. Propose an estimator that is a function of the sufficient statistic.

For the MinCount sketch, the exact values of the stored hashes relative to the threshold are irrelevant for estimation and, hence, ancillary statistics. The value of the threshold, the largest stored hash, is a sufficient statistic when only the final set of hashed values is observed. Furthermore, this threshold is a complete and minimal sufficient statistic, so by the Lehman-Scheffe theorem, the usual MinCount estimator is a minimum variance unbiased estimator as shown by [6].

Likewise, the exact values of the stored hashes are irrelevant when estimating the cardinality of the union or intersection of two sets. Assuming the sizes of the sketches for A_1, A_2 are fixed at k, a set of sufficient statistics for the cardinality of the union and intersection is given by the thresholds of the individual sketches, τ_1 and τ_2, the number of common stored hashes $|h(S_1 \cap_0 S_2)|$, the total number of hashes less than or equal to the smaller of the two thresholds $|h(S_1 \cup_0 S_2)|$, and the streaming estimates of the cardinality $\hat{N}(S_i)$ and variance $\hat{\text{Var}}(S_i)$.

8.2 Likelihood

The first class of estimators we present are the likelihood based estimators. Given a sufficient statistic, the parameter of interest may be estimated using the asymptotically efficient maximum likelihood estimator (MLE). The asymptotic variance of the MLE is given by the inverse Fisher information. Under mild regularity conditions, this is the expected Hessian of the negative log-likelihood evaluated at the true parameters. This yields a natural estimate for the variance of the MLE as well. Compute the Hessian of the negative log-likelihood at the estimated rather than the true parameters and take its inverse.

A closed form for the full likelihood of the Streaming MinCount sketch is not known. Instead, we first derive the likelihood function for the basic MinCount sketch. By plugging in the streaming estimates into this likelihood, it can be used to construct a surrogate likelihood or a pseudo-likelihood [3] for the intersection or union. This surrogate is a form of profile-likelihood for the Streaming Mincount sketches that include the streaming estimates as part of the sketches. We then derive an approximation to the full likelihood.

We first derive the generative process for a pair of basic MinCount sketches from sets A_1, A_2 in lemma 1. This allows derivation of the likelihood. A rough description of the process is as follows. First, generate a threshold τ_1 and propose values for $|h(S_1 \cap_0 S_2)|$ and $|h(S_2, \tau_1) \backslash h(S_1, \tau_1)|$ without considering the constraint that S_2 contains at most k_2 hash values. If their total is less than k_2 and the constraint on S_2 is not violated, then $\tau_1 = \tau_{min}$, and to complete sketch S_2, simply draw the requisite number of additional points above τ_1 to compute τ_2. Otherwise, $\tau_2 < \tau_1$ and the proposed values are thinned using sub-sampling.

LEMMA 1. *Given sets A_1, A_2 and a random universal hash, MinCount generates random sketches S_1, S_2 of sizes k_1, k_2 respectively. The sufficient statistics for the parameters $|A_1|$, $|A_2|$, and $|A_1 \cap A_2|$ are τ_1, τ_2, $|S_1 \cup_0 S_2|$, and $|S_1 \cap_0 S_2|$. These statistics have the distribution given by the following process.*

$$\begin{aligned} \tau_1 &\sim Beta(k_1, |A_1| - k_1 + 1) \\ U &\sim HyperGeometric(|A_1 \cap A_2|, |A_1 \backslash A_2|, k_1) \\ V &\sim Binomial(|A_2| - U, \tau_1) \\ C &\sim Bernoulli(U/k_1) \end{aligned}$$

If $U + V < k_2$ then

$$|S_1 \cap_0 S_2| = U, \quad |S_1 \cup_0 S_2| = k_1 + V$$
$$\frac{\tau_2 - \tau_1}{1 - \tau_1} \sim Beta(k_2 - U - V, |A_2| - k_2 + 1)$$

If $U + V = k_2$ and $C = 1$,

$$|S_1 \cap_0 S_2| = U, \quad |S_1 \cup_0 S_2| = k_1 + V, \quad \tau_2 = \tau_1$$

Otherwise, $\tau_2 < \tau_1$ and

$$\begin{aligned} |S_1 \cap_0 S_2| &\sim HyperGeometric(U, V, k_2) \\ \tau_2 &\sim \tau_1 \times Beta(k_2, U + V - C - k_2 + 1) \\ |S_1 \cup_0 S_2| &\sim k_2 + Binomial(k_1 - U - (1 - C), \tau_2/\tau_1) \end{aligned}$$

PROOF. The order statistics of the hash values determine the MinCount sketch. The order statistics of n uniform random variates are jointly Dirichlet distributed with parameter $1 \in \mathbb{R}^n$, and the marginal distributions are Beta distributed. The labeling of uniform random variates as belonging to $A_1 \backslash A_2$, $A_2 \backslash A_1$, or $A_1 \cap A_2$ follows a multinomial distribution. The lemma follows from conditional distributions for the Dirichlet and multinomial distributions and their properties. □

Note that in the case where $U + V - C < k_2$ or, equivalently $\tau_2 \geq \tau_1$, every generated variable is also observed in the final sketch. There are no hidden variables that need to be integrated out to form the likelihood. By symmetry, exchanging the indices of the variables and parameters does not change the likelihood. This observation reduces the computation of the log-likelihood to the simple case with no hidden variables and gives the following theorem.

THEOREM 2. *Let variables $x_1, x_2, x_{1 \cap 2}$ represent estimates of $|A_1|, |A_2|, |A_1 \cap A_2|$, respectively. The log-likelihood of the*

MinCount sketch may be written as follows.

$$\ell_0(x_1, x_2, x_{1\cap 2}; S_1, S_2)$$
$$= 1(\tau_2 \geq \tau_1) \log p\left(\tau_1, \tau_2, H \middle| x_1, x_2, x_{1\cap 2}\right)$$
$$+ 1(\tau_1 > \tau_2) \log p\left(\tau_2, \tau_1, H \middle| x_1, x_2, x_{1\cap 2}\right)$$

where $H = (|S_1 \cap_0 S_2|, |S_1 \cup_0 S_2|)$ and the conditional probabilities are given by the generative process in lemma 1.

To obtain an estimator that exploits the streaming cardinality estimates, simply replace $x_1 = \hat{N}(S_1)$ and $x_2 = \hat{N}(S_2)$ to obtain a marginal profile likelihood.

$$\hat{N}_{profile}(S_1 \cap S_2) = \arg\max_{x_{1\cap 2}} \ell_0(\hat{N}(S_1), \hat{N}(S_2), x_{1\cap 2}) \quad (5)$$
$$\hat{N}_{profile}(S_1 \cup S_2) = \hat{N}(S_1) + \hat{N}(S_2) - \hat{N}_{profile}(S_1 \cap S_2).$$

After taking a union or intersection, the resulting sketch contains the new cardinality estimate along with the hash values stored by the improved MinCount sketch. Note that although the union cardinality estimate uses the inclusion-exclusion principle, it is simply a reparameterization of the intersection cardinality, and maximum likelihood estimates are invariant under reparameterization.

Since some of the distributions have discrete parameter spaces, we relax the optimization of the log-likelihood by replacing factorials with the corresponding continuous gamma function when doing maximum likelihood estimation.

8.3 Full pseudo-likelihood

The profile-likelihood given above has a deficiency. It is asymptotically inefficient as it not a sufficiently good approximation to the true likelihood and does not account for the distribution $p(\hat{N}(S_1), \hat{N}(S_2)|h(S_1), h(S_2))$. Unfortunately, this conditional distribution of the streaming estimates given the final hash values is intractable to compute. Instead, we approximate it with a tractable distribution to form what we refer to as a full pseudo-likelihood.

We use a bivariate normal as the tractable distribution. This choice is well-motivated as one would expect that the central limit theorem to yield this as the limit distribution. The mean of this distribution is given by the streaming cardinality estimates. An approximate covariance matrix $\Sigma(S_1, S_2)$ for the streaming cardinality estimates is derived in section 10. To simplify calculations, one may also use other choices such as a diagonal matrix.

Mathematically, the likelihood is given by

$$\ell(x_1, x_2, x_{1\cap 2}; S_1, S_2) = \ell_0(x_1, x_2, x_{1\cap 2}; S_1, S_2)$$
$$+ \log\phi\left(n_A, n_B | \hat{N}(S_1), \hat{N}(S_2), \Sigma(S_1, S_2)\right)$$

where ϕ is a bivariate normal density and $\Sigma(S_1, S_2)$ is an approximate covariance matrix for the streaming cardinality estimates. The resulting pseudo-likelihood cardinality estimators for the intersection and union are

$$\hat{N}_{pseudo}(S_1 \cap S_2) = \arg\max_{x_{1\cap 2}} \max_{x_1, x_2} \ell(x_1, x_2, x_{1\cap 2}) \quad (6)$$
$$\hat{N}_{pseudo}(S_1 \cup S_2) = \arg\max_{x_1 + x_2 - x_{1\cap 2}} \max_{x_1, x_2} \ell(x_1, x_2, x_{1\cap 2}). \quad (7)$$

Note that this also allows the estimates of $|A_1|$ and $|A_2|$ to be improved when there is substantial overlap between the sets. In particular, when $A_1 = A_2$, the estimate of $|A_1|$ will be an average of the estimates $\hat{N}(S_1)$ and $\hat{N}(S_2)$.

The variance estimates for the pseudo-likelihood cardinality estimators are

$$\hat{\mathrm{Var}}(\hat{N}_{pseudo}(S_1 \cap S_2)) = D^2_{x_{1\cap 2}} \ell \Big|_{\hat{N}_{pseudo}} \quad (8)$$

$$\hat{\mathrm{Var}}(\hat{N}_{pseudo}(S_1 \cup S_2)) = D^2_{x_1 + x_2 - x_{1\cap 2}} \ell \Big|_{\hat{N}_{pseudo}} \quad (9)$$

where D denotes the directional derivative and $\hat{N}_{pseudo}$ is the maximizer of the pseudo-likelihood.

8.4 Optimality of pseudo-likelihood

Since the pseudo-likelihood is a surrogate for the true likelihood, asymptotic efficiency results for the maximum likelihood estimator do not directly apply. However, we conjecture that the pseudo-likelihood estimator is asymptotically equivalent to the maximum likelihood estimator. This result would not be surprising since one would expect that the streaming cardinality estimates converge to a bivariate normal distribution by the central limit theorem. Furthermore, by asymptotic results for M-estimators [24], such as the MLE, if the quadratic approximation of the pseudo-log-likelihood and log-likelihood converge to the same limit, their asymptotic distributions are the same. Since we estimate the conditional covariance for the streaming estimates given the basic sketch, we have approximated all the quadratic terms of the log-likelihood.

9. RE-WEIGHTED ESTIMATORS

We provide a second class of union and intersection cardinality estimators that are easier to implement than the pseudo-likelihood based estimators. They are also easier generalize to sketches other than MinCount and to set operations on multiple sets. These estimators are formed by taking the weighted average of several unbiased or consistent estimators of the cardinality. We derive how to optimally combine these component estimators to obtain an estimator that performs nearly identically to the pseudo-likelihood based estimator. For the estimators presented in this paper, we use component estimators where each estimator is a multiplicative scaling of a single streaming cardinality estimate.

We first describe the optimal procedure for combining multiple component estimators. Then we propose a set of component estimators and derive the variances and covariances needed to combine them. The procedure to optimally combine estimators is given by the following lemma.

LEMMA 3 (OPTIMAL WEIGHTING). *Given unbiased (or consistent) estimators $\hat{N}_1, ..., \hat{N}_m$ with non-singular covariance matrix Σ, the optimal weights that sum to 1 and minimize variance are given by*

$$w_{opt} \propto \Sigma^{-1} 1_m \quad (10)$$

where 1_m is the m-vector of all ones. The resulting estimator is unbiased (or consistent) and has variance $(1_m^T \Sigma^{-1} 1_m)^{-1}$.

PROOF. Since all the estimators are unbiased (or consistent), the re-weighted estimator is also unbiased (or consistent). Given unnormalized weights v, the variance of the estimator $v^T \hat{N} / v^T 1$ is $\mathrm{Var}(v^T \hat{N} / v^T 1) = v^T \Sigma v / v^T 1 1^T v$. Minimizing this Rayleigh quotient give the optimal weights. □

Typically, the covariance Σ is not known, so a plug-in estimate of Σ is used to generate the weights. An alternate weighting is to treat the estimators as being independent and simply use the diagonal of the covariance. In this case, the simple re-weighted estimator is

$$\hat{N}_{simple} = \sum_{i=1}^{m} \frac{z\hat{N}_i(S)}{\text{Var}(\hat{N}_i(S))} \tag{11}$$

where z is a normalization constant that ensures weights sum to 1. Although this does not provide guarantees on the improvement, we find that this performs nearly as well as the optimal weighting.

We now consider the two ingredients needed to define a re-weighted estimator: a set of consistent estimators that form the components of the combined estimator and the covariance of these estimators to determine the weights.

9.1 Component estimators

The idea for defining the component estimators is to have maximally uncorrelated estimators. We minimize correlation by using component estimators which make use of only one of the streaming cardinality estimate in each component. This gives that the resulting weighted estimator is expressed as a linear combination of streaming cardinality estimates. These component estimators are shown to be unbiased or consistent and, hence, suitable candidates for a re-weighted estimator. The approximate variance of the estimators is computed in order to allow for computation of the weights.

To derive the component estimators, note that both the cardinality of the union and the intersection may be decomposed into a ratio times the cardinality of one of the sets in the operation.

$$|A_1 \cup A_2| = \frac{|A_1 \cup A_2|}{|A_i|}|A_i|, \quad |A_1 \cap A_2| = \frac{|A_1 \cap A_2|}{|A_i|}|A_i|.$$

Define $\alpha_i = |A_1 \cap A_2|/|A_i|$ and $\beta_i = |A_1 \cup A_2|/|A_i|$. Simple estimators for α_i and β_i are

$$\begin{aligned} \hat{\alpha}_i &= |h(S_1 \cap_0 S_2)|/|h(S_i, \tau_{min})| \\ \hat{\beta}_i &= |h(S_1 \cup_0 S_2)|/|h(S_i, \tau_{min})| \end{aligned} \tag{12}$$

These give a consistent, plug-in estimator for the cardinality of an intersection and union as shown in the following lemma, proven in the long version of the paper, and theorem.

LEMMA 4. *The estimator $\hat{\alpha}_i$ is an unbiased estimator of $|A_1 \cap A_2|/|A_i|$ conditional on $|h(S_i, \tau_{min})|$ being non-zero. It is consistent under the conditions in section 7. Similarly, $\hat{\beta}_i$ is a consistent estimator of $|A_1 \cup A_2|/|A_i|$ under the conditions in section 7.*

THEOREM 5. *The estimators*

$$\hat{N}_i(S_1 \cap S_2) = \hat{\alpha}_i \hat{N}(S_i), \quad \hat{N}_i(S_1 \cup S_2) = \hat{\beta}_i \hat{N}(S_i)$$

are consistent estimators of the $|A_1 \cap A_2|, |A_1 \cup A_2|$ under the conditions given in section 7.

PROOF. This immediately follows from Slutzky's theorem since $\hat{\alpha}_i, \hat{\beta}_i, \hat{N}(S_i)$ are consistent. □

Another possible choice for component estimators is to pretend that all items in A_2 appear after A_1 in the stream. A more accurate streaming cardinality estimate can be calculated by not updating the threshold. However, the resulting re-weighted estimator is suboptimal when A_1 and A_2 are disjoint and equal in size. It is equivalent to averaging the suboptimal improved union estimate with optimal sum of streaming estimates.

9.2 Component variances

The variance of each component estimator is required to apply the simple re-weighting scheme. This is approximated by decomposing the component estimator so that the multipliers and cardinality estimates can be treated as essentially independent. Write $\sqrt{k_i}(\hat{\alpha}_i\hat{N}(S_i) - n_i\alpha_i) = \sqrt{k_i}\hat{\alpha}_i(\hat{N}(S_i) - n_i) + \sqrt{k_i}(\alpha_i - \alpha_i)n_i$. Assuming the central limit theorem applies to $\hat{N}(S_i)$, Slutzky's lemma and the central limit theorem imply that the quantity converges in distribution to a normal distribution with variance less than or equal to $\alpha_i^2 k\text{Var}(\hat{N}(S_i)) + n_i^2 k\text{Var}(\hat{\alpha}_i)$. The missing term measuring $Cov(\hat{N}(S_i), \hat{\alpha}_i)$ is excluded as the terms are negatively correlated. The same argument applies to $\hat{\beta}_i$.

In this case, the expectation and variance of $\hat{N}(S_i)$ are already given in [23] and the expectations are known or approximated by lemma 4. The only remaining quantities to compute are $\text{Var}(\hat{\alpha}_i)$ and $\text{Var}(\hat{\beta}_i)$. The variances of $\hat{\alpha}_i, \hat{\beta}_i$ may be approximated using the following formulas.

$$\begin{aligned} \text{Var}(\hat{\alpha}_i) &\approx \frac{\alpha_i(1-\alpha_i)}{|h(S_i, \tau_{min})|} \\ \text{Var}\left(\hat{\beta}_i\right) &\approx \frac{1-p_i}{p_i^2|h(S_i, \tau_{min})|} = \frac{\beta_i(\beta_i - 1)}{|h(S_i, \tau_{min})|}. \end{aligned} \tag{13}$$

These approximate variances may be used in the simple re-weighting scheme given in equation 11.

$$\hat{\text{Var}}(\hat{N}_i(S_1 \cap S_2)) \approx \hat{N}_i(S_1 \cap S_2)^2 \left(\frac{(1-\hat{\alpha}_i)}{\hat{\alpha}_i|h(S_i, \tau_{min})|} + \frac{1}{2k_i} \right)$$

$$\hat{\text{Var}}(\hat{N}_i(S_1 \cup S_2))) = \hat{N}_i(S_1 \cup S_2)^2 \left(\frac{(\hat{\beta}_i - 1)}{\hat{\beta}_i|h(S_i, \tau_{min})|} + \frac{1}{2k_i} \right)$$

The component estimators may be compared to the improved intersection and union estimators given in section 5. Since $\alpha_i|h(S_i, \tau_{min})| \approx |h(S_1 \cap_0 S_2)|$ and $\beta_i|h(S_i, \tau_{min})| \approx |h(S_1 \cup_0 S_2)|$, the variance of the improved intersection estimator is approximately $|A_1 \cap A_2|^2/\alpha_i|h(S_i, \tau_{min})|$. The variance of the component intersection estimator, and similarly the component union estimator, can be approximated by

$$\begin{aligned} \text{Var}(\hat{N}_i(S_1 \cap S_2)) &\approx \text{Var}(\hat{N}_{improved}(S_1 \cap S_2)) \\ &\quad - |A_1 \cap A_2|^2 \left(\frac{1}{|h(S_i, \tau_{min})|} - \frac{1}{2k_i} \right) \end{aligned} \tag{14}$$

$$\begin{aligned} \text{Var}(\hat{N}_i(S_1 \cup S_2)) &\approx \text{Var}(\hat{N}_{improved}(S_1 \cup S_2)) \\ &\quad - |A_1 \cup A_2|^2 \left(\frac{2-\beta_i}{|h(S_i, \tau_{min})|} - \frac{1}{2k_i} \right) \end{aligned} \tag{15}$$

For the intersection estimates, since $|h(S_i, \tau_{min})| \leq k_i$, both component estimators are better than the than the basic improved estimator even though they exploit the accuracy of only one of the streaming cardinality estimates $\hat{N}(S_i)$. Furthermore, the component with the smaller $|h(S_i, \tau_{min})|$ has the greater improvement over the basic improved estimator. A surprising consequence of this approximation is that this component should represent an improvement over the basic improved estimator even when the streaming cardinality estimate is not even used. In that case, the $1/2k_i$ term is replaced by $1/k_i$ in the improvement term. We believe the reason is that the basic improved estimator loses information about the size of the smaller set which constrains the size of the intersection. For the union estimates, the improvement depends on the multiplier β_i. If $\beta_i \leq 3/2$, then the component estimator beats the basic improved estimator.

10. COVARIANCE ANALYSIS

Computing the covariance of the streaming estimates is a necessary step for obtaining the full quadratic approximation to the log-likelihood used by the pseudo-likelihood estimator. It is also needed to compute the weights for the full re-weighted estimator. We present the main ideas and results for calculating the covariance and leave the detailed calculations to the long version of the paper.

In the streaming formulation of MinCount, the remaining area process $\mathcal{R}(S_t) = \tau_t$ implicitly depends on the order π in which elements arrive. This dependency is difficult to analyze. We consider an alternative formulation that expands and extends the proof ideas in [10] and is based on the ranks of the hash values. The Streaming MinCount estimator can be expressed as

$$\hat{N}(S) = k + \sum_{i=k+1}^{n} \frac{Z_i}{U_{(i)}} \tag{16}$$

where $U_{(i)}$ is the ith smallest hash value and $Z_i = 1$ if and only if the estimator was incremented by $1/U_{(i)}$. Equivalently, $Z_i = 1$ if and only if fewer than k of the $i-1$ smallest hash values appear before the ith smallest value. Mathematically, $Z_i = 1(|\{j < i : \pi_j < \pi_i\}| < k)$ where π_i is the position of $U_{(i)}$ in the stream.

When considering multiple sketches, denote the ath streaming estimate by $\hat{N}(S_a) = k_a + \sum_{i=k_a+1}^{n_{tot}} Z_i^{(a)}/U_{(i)}$ where $U_{(i)}$ are the order statistics for all the hash values for $A_1 \cup A_2$. This rank formulation is the key to the analysis in this section. It separates the analysis into three independent components: the order statistics for the hash values $U_{(\cdot)}$, the random orderings $\pi^{(a)}$, and an indicator $Y_i^{(a)}$ denoting if $U_{(i)}$ belongs to stream a. By the independence of Z and U and bilinearity of the covariance operator, the covariance $Cov(\hat{N}(S_1), \hat{N}(S_2))$ of two streaming cardinality estimates can then decomposed into the cross terms

$$Cov\left(\frac{Z_i^{(1)}}{U_{(i)}}, \frac{Z_i^{(1)}}{U_{(i)}}\right) = Cov\left(Z_i^{(1)}, Z_j^{(2)}\right) \mathbb{E}\left(\frac{1}{U_{(i)}} \frac{1}{U_{(j)}}\right) + \mathbb{E}Z_i^{(1)} \mathbb{E}Z_j^{(2)} Cov\left(\frac{1}{U_{(i)}}, \frac{1}{U_{(j)}}\right) \tag{17}$$

Of these terms, $Cov\left(Z_i^{(1)}, Z_j^{(2)}\right)$ depends on the order of elements in both streams. In particular, it depends on whether the common elements $A_1 \cap A_2$ appear in the same order or different orders in the streams. We consider two cases: the orders are the same and the orders are independent random permutations.

The covariances of the cardinality estimates are given by

$$\Sigma_{independent} \approx \frac{n_{tot}^2 k_1 k_2}{\kappa_{max}^2} \frac{q_0}{p_1 p_2} \left(\frac{1}{2\kappa_{min}} - \frac{1}{6\kappa_{max}}\right) \tag{18}$$

$$\Sigma_{identical} \approx \Sigma_{independent} + q_0 \left(\frac{1}{2} - \frac{q_0}{3p_1 p_2}\right) \frac{n_{tot}^2 \kappa_{min}}{\kappa_{max}^2}$$

where $\kappa_{min} = \left\lfloor \min\left\{\frac{k_1}{p_1}, \frac{k_2}{p_2}\right\}\right\rfloor$ and $\kappa_{max} = \left\lfloor \max\left\{\frac{k_1}{p_1}, \frac{k_2}{p_2}\right\}\right\rfloor$.

The covariance $\Sigma_{independent}$ is of particular interest when $q_0 = 1$ so that the sets $A_1 = A_2$. The best estimate when the hash function is fixed takes the average of Streaming MinCount estimates over all possible orderings of the same set. This limit estimator reduces the variance to $\Sigma_{independent} = \frac{n^2}{3k}$. By contrast, when applied to a single stream the Streaming MinCount estimator has variance $\frac{n^2}{2k}$. Thus, even in the case where every cardinality estimate is for exactly the same set, the estimates can be improved by combining them. This result is borne out in figure 2 as the basic MinCount sketch requires 3 times the space as the averaged Streaming MinCount sketches when $q_0 = 1$ and the sets are all the same.

10.1 Conditional covariance

For the pseudo-likelihood described in section 8.2, the required normal approximation is for the conditional distribution $p(\hat{N}(S_1), \hat{N}(S_2)|\tau)$ rather than the unconditional covariance. Under a multivariate normal approximation, this conditional distribution is easy to approximate. Let $\hat{N}_{mincount}$ be the non-streaming MinCount estimator that is based only on the offset τ. Assume that the joint distribution of $\hat{N}(S_1)$, $\hat{N}(S_2)$, $\hat{N}_{mincount}(S_1)$, and $\hat{N}_{mincount}(S_2)$ is multivariate normal. The covariance may be denoted in block form by

$$\begin{pmatrix} \Sigma_{ss} & \Sigma_{sm} \\ \Sigma_{sm}^T & \Sigma_{mm} \end{pmatrix} \tag{19}$$

where s, m denote the streaming and non-streaming MinCount estimators.

Since the streaming estimate is optimal, it cannot be improved upon by conditioning on the threshold. In particular, under a re-weighting scheme a linear combination of the streaming and non-streaming estimators does not improve the variance. Hence, the non-streaming estimator is approximately equal to the streaming estimator plus uncorrelated noise, $\Sigma_{sm} \approx \Sigma_{ss}$. The last component is the covariance of the non-streaming MinCount estimates which is $Cov(\hat{N}_{mincount}(S_1), \hat{N}_{mincount}(S_2)) \approx q_0 \text{Var}(\hat{N}_{mincount}(S_\ell))$ where ℓ is the sketch with the higher threshold. Under a multivariate normality approximation where $\hat{n}_i$ denotes the current estimate for n_i, the conditional variance and mean $\mu_{ss,i|\tau} = \mathbb{E}(\hat{N}(S_i)|\tau)$ are given by

$$\Sigma_{ss|\tau} \approx \Sigma_{ss} - \Sigma_{ss}\Sigma_{mm}^{-1}\Sigma_{ss}$$

$$\mu_{ss|\tau} \approx \begin{pmatrix} \hat{N}(S_1) \\ \hat{N}(S_2) \end{pmatrix} - \Sigma_{ss}\Sigma_{mm}^{-1} \begin{pmatrix} \hat{N}_{mincount}(S_1) - \hat{n}_1 \\ \hat{N}_{mincount}(S_2) - \hat{n}_2 \end{pmatrix}.$$

10.2 Multiplier covariance

The covariance of the multipliers may be approximated by first conditioning on the value in the denominator. This gives rough estimates

$$Cov(\hat{\alpha}_1, \hat{\alpha}_2) \approx \frac{\rho_2(1-\rho_2)}{k_1} \tag{20}$$

$$Cov(\hat{\beta}_1, \hat{\beta}_2) \approx \frac{\rho_2(1-\rho_2)}{k_1} - \frac{\rho_2}{k_1}\left(\frac{p_1}{p_2} - \frac{q_0^2}{p_2^2}\right) \tag{21}$$

where $\rho_2 = q_2/p_2$ and $\tau_1 < \tau_2$. The multiplier covariances may be incorporated by the same argument as in section 9.2.

11. MULTI-SET OPERATIONS

Oftentimes the query of interest merges many sketches together rather than pairs. For example, if the data is processed on d mappers in a map-reduce framework, d sketches must be merged to estimate the cardinality.

Merging multiple estimators using re-weighting is simple. The component estimators are slightly modified, and the re-weighting is virtually unchanged since covariance calculations are pairwise calculations. The multipliers α_i, β_i estimate the size of a set relative to the intersection or union of all the sets. The only difference is that the minimum threshold $\tau_{min} = \min_i\{\tau_i\}$ and the number of relevant hashes $|h(\cap_0 S_i)|, |h(\cup_0 S_i)|$ are taken over all the sets rather than a pair.

Generalizing pseudo-likelihood based methods is more difficult. Although the same technique of ordering the thresholds to compute the likelihood may be used, the likelihood itself contains exponentially many parameters when there are more than two sketches. The intersection of any subset of the sets $\{A_i\}$ is a parameter. This makes the optimization problem difficult, and the finite sample performance of likelihood based methods is not well understood.

Another strategy is to exploit that pairwise intersections and unions are closed operations. The result of intersecting or taking the union of two sketches results in another sketch. These sketches may be further merged. For the profile-likelihood, which does not utilize any variance or covariance information for the estimates $\hat{N}(S_1)$ and $\hat{N}(S_2)$, the merge operation is straightforward. For other methods, a surrogate for the covariances of the merged estimates needed for computation of the cardinality estimate.

12. EMPIRICAL RESULTS

The new estimators were evaluated on both real and simulated data. The results on real data exactly match the theory and empirically demonstrate there is no difference between applying the methods on real or simulated data. We examine the behavior of the estimators in a variety of cases. In all cases, the pseudo-likelihood and re-weighted estimators that exploit the streaming cardinality estimates had the best performance and performed similarly. To assess the performance of the estimators, we computed the Relative Efficiency (RE) of the estimators and the relative size required. The RE is defined as $RE(\hat{N}^{(1)}, \hat{N}^{(2)}) = \text{Var}(\hat{N}^{(2)})/\text{Var}(\hat{N}^{(1)})$. Since the variance of an estimator typically scales as $1/m$ where m is the number of samples used in the estimator, the RE measures how much more data $\hat{N}^{(2)}$ needs to achieve the same accuracy as $\hat{N}^{(1)}$. An estimator with RE of $1/2$ requires twice as many samples to match the variance of the baseline estimator. The relative size is the space required to achieve the same error and is $1/RE$. Figure 1 show that, analogous to the improvement of streaming estimators in the single stream problem, the new methods require half the space of the improved union estimator. They achieve even greater reductions in space when compared to basic MinCount estimator. When intersection sizes are small, the new estimators require less than $1/15^{th}$ of the space of inclusion-exclusion based estimators. Compared to the basic improved estimator, the merged streamed intersection sketches require half the space when and one set is nearly a subset of the other.

In simulations for pairwise unions and intersections, we let $|A_1| = 2^{20}$ and considered cases with both balanced, $|A_2| = |A_1|$, or unbalanced, $|A_2| = |A_1|/4$, cardinalities. The size of the intersection was allowed to vary. Unless otherwise noted, the order of common elements in the streams was the less favorable order for our methods; the elements appear in the same order. We tried different sketch sizes in our simulations but only present the results where the size $k = 1024$ as there was no material difference when $k = 256$ or 4196.

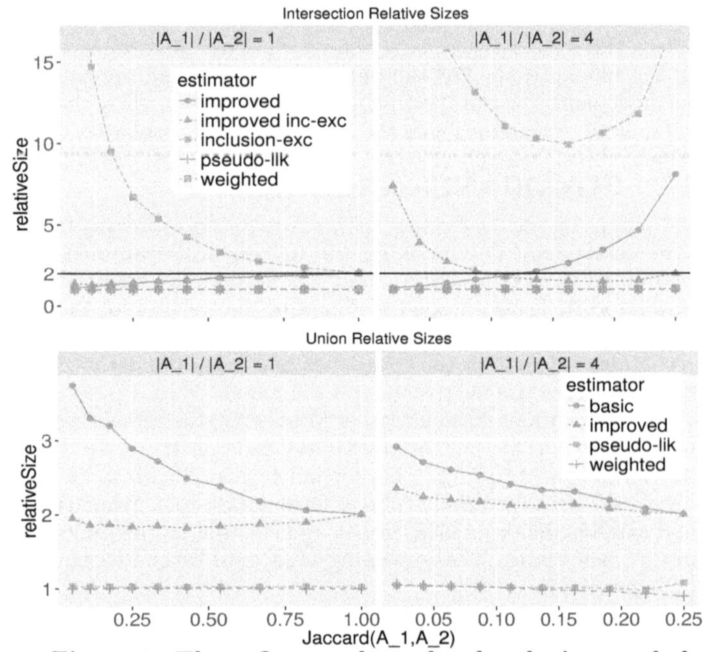

Figure 1: These figures show the sketch size needed by different estimators to achieve a given error relative to the profile-likelihood estimator. For intersections on sets with significantly different cardinalities, the new likelihood and re-weighted estimators require far less space.

For real data, we used the MSNBC dataset from the UCI machine learning repository [20] to validate our simulation results. This dataset consists of 1 million users' browsing history of 17 web page categories. We consider the problem of estimating how many users visited a pair of categories using only the 17 sketches counting unique visits to each category. For comparison, we simulated data using parameters that match the real set and intersection cardinalities. For each set of parameters 10,000 sketches were generated with independent random hashes. Figure 3 shows, as expected, that the estimated cardinalities using the real data have the same distribution as the simulated data. A p-value was computed for each set of parameters testing if the RRMSE for real and simulated data are different. Under the null hypothesis that there is no difference in distributions, the p-values are uniformly distributed. A Kolmogorov-Smirnov test yields a p-value > 0.6, so there is statistically no evidence in the test that the simulated data behaves differently from the real data.

There were only small difference in performance between the simple re-weighted estimator in equation 11 and the optimally weighted estimator in equation 10 except when the cardinalities were unbalanced and the smaller set was nearly a subset of the larger one. This difference only observed for intersections. For unions, the simple re-weighting performed marginally better than the optimal re-weighting, possibly due to additional error in estimating the covariance of the component estimators. We explain this asymmetry by noting that in the case where $A_2 \subset A_1$ and the order elements

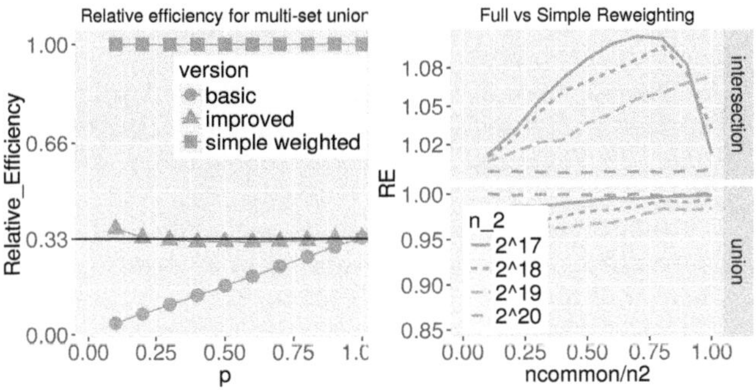

Figure 2: The left figure shows the RE with respect to the simple re-weighted estimator when taking the union of 100 random subsets A_i drawn with probability p from A_{tot}. The right figure shows the RE of the full re-weighted estimator to the simple re-weighted estimator. Using the full covariance structure improves intersection estimates but error in the covariance estimate hurts unions very slightly.

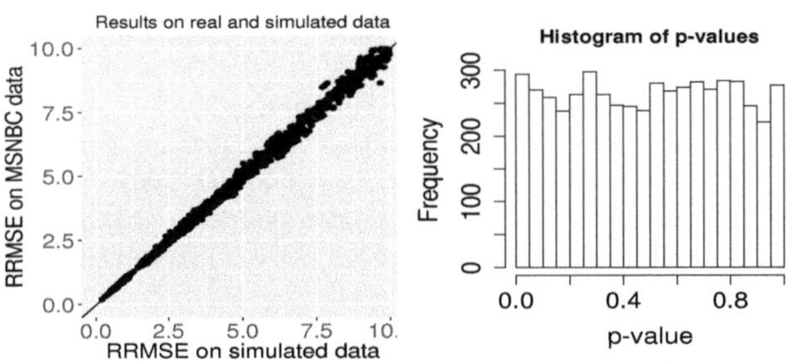

Figure 3: The left figure shows the RRMSE when estimators are run on real data versus simulated data. There is an exact correspondence, The right figure shows the distribution of p-values testing if there is a difference between the real versus simulated data. The distribution fits the null uniform distribution.

appear is the same, every item in A_2 that updates sketch S_1 must also update S_2. Thus, S_1 contains almost no information about the intersection that is not already in S_2. The simple re-weighting adds noise by giving nonzero weight to component $\hat{N}_1(S_1 \cap_0 S_2)$. The reverse for unions is not true; S_2 contains useful information not in S_1 for estimating $|A_1|$. We note that the covariance estimate for the component estimators is imperfect as it does not simply select the smaller set when A_2 is a proper subset of A_1. However, the full re-weighted estimator empirically has relative efficiency $\geq 95\%$ of an optimal re-weighting, so any improvement would be small.

To simulate the distributed map-reduce setting, the simple re-weighted estimator was compared to the basic and improved MinCount estimators when taking the union of 100 sketches. Each sketch was generated by sub-sampling with probability p from a set of 10^6 elements. The sampled items were then randomly permuted before computing the sketch. Figure 2 shows the simple re-weighted estimator has high relative efficiency compared to the naive union estimator, especially when the size of the pairwise intersections is small. Likewise, the improved estimator has high relative efficiency compared to the basic estimator in those cases. Here, the re-weighted estimator requires $1/3$ the space of the improved estimator rather than $1/2$ due to the accuracy gains from averaging over independent permutations.

13. DISCUSSION

Although the calculations presented are specialized for the MinCount sketch, the techniques apply to other sketches as well such as the Flajolet-Martin (FM) sketch used in HyperLogLog or the Discrete Max-Count sketch in [23]. In particular, the simple re-weighted estimator can be easily derived for the FM sketch. The only ingredients needed are estimates of the Jaccard similarities $J(A_1 \cap A_2, A_i)$ and $J(A_i, A_1 \cup A_2)$ and their variances. The FM sketch, however, does not lead to a closed intersection operation that allows for further merging.

Another possible generalization is to estimate set differences. For the likelihood based methods, this is exactly the same as estimating the intersection since it is simply another re-parameterization. For the re-weighting methods, the multipliers change but the analysis remains the same.

For the methods described in this paper, cardinality estimation for the union or intersection only requires constant space. There are a finite number of sufficient statistics and that these can be tabulated with constant memory if the hash values in each sketch can be accessed in sorted order. If a merged sketch and not just a cardinality estimate is required, a closed union operation may result in a larger sketch where the size is proportional to the number of sets in the union. The sketch can be truncated to have k hash values to reduce the space requirements while cardinality estimation is still performed with all the hash values.

One unexplored area is determining the optimal order of pairwise merges. If many sketches cannot be merged simultaneously, the desired cardinalities may still be computed using a sequence pairwise unions and intersections that exploit the closed union and set operations.

13.1 Running times

For all the improved methods in this paper, computing the sufficient statistic requires $O(km)$ time where m is the number of sketches. If the hash values are stored in sorted order, this is reduced to $O(k)$. For the naive estimators, the running time is $O(mk \log k)$ if a heap is used to select the k values. For the pairwise likelihood based methods, the pseudo-likelihood function is from an exponential family and hence, log-concave. Evaluating the gradient and Hessian take constant time, so the running time is proportional to the number of iterations needed to solve this concave optimization problem. For the re-weighted component estimators, if the estimated covariance matrix is diagonal, computing the re-weighted estimator takes $O(m)$ time. If a full covariance matrix is used, then inverting the matrix can take $O(m^3)$ time.

14. CONCLUSION

This paper presents and analyzes two new classes of methods for estimating cardinalities of intersections and unions from sketches. These methods are applied to Streaming MinCount sketches, and variance estimates are derived as well. All the methods theoretically and empirically outperform existing methods for estimating unions and intersections. The new methods also lead to mergeable summaries under intersection and union operations. This allows both intersections and unions on sketches to be chained together while existing methods only allow unions to be chained. Extensions to sketches other than the MinCount sketch are also discussed.

The pseudo-likelihood based estimators are derived as approximations to the asymptotically optimal maximum likelihood estimator. We conjecture that the full pseudo-likelihood estimator is asymptotically equivalent to the maximum likelihood estimator. The re-weighted component estimators are derived as near optimally weighted linear combinations of the streaming estimates. Empirically, the near optimally re-weighted component estimator matches the performance of the full maximum pseudo-likelihood estimator.

The derived estimators are useful in a variety of different settings. The re-weighted estimators can be easily generalized to handle multiple set unions rather than just pairwise unions. The simple re-weighted estimators can be easily generalized to other sketches. The profile-likelihood can be used for sequences of pairwise merges.

The theoretical analysis also allows us to separate and identify the information contained in different parts of the sketch. Since the full re-weighted and the conjectured optimal pseudo-likelihood methods perform nearly identically and since the multipliers for component estimators can be treated as nearly independent from the streaming cardinality estimates, we see that the stored hash values encode information about the proportional sizes of the sets relative to their union and intersection while the streaming cardinality estimate contain information about the absolute size. Section 10 shows that each streaming estimate contains information about the order of elements in the stream since the streaming cardinality variance can be decomposed into an irreducible component that depends on the order statistics for the hash values and a reducible component that depends on the ordering of elements in the stream. In the case of identical sets, averaging streaming estimates over all possible orderings variance reduces the variance to $n^2/3k$. In section 9.2, the single non-streaming component estimator based on the smaller set is shown to dominate the improved MinCount estimator that throws away the larger threshold. All these relevant pieces of information useful for estimation are contained in the sufficient statistics given in section 8.1 which the pseudo-likelihood estimator makes full use of.

Together these contributions advance the methodology, theory, and understanding for the approximate distinct counting problem.

15. REFERENCES

[1] P. K. Agarwal, G. Cormode, Z. Huang, J. M. Phillips, Z. Wei, and K. Yi. Mergeable summaries. *ACM Transactions on Database Systems*, 38(4):26, 2013.

[2] Z. Bar-Yossef, T. Jayram, R. Kumar, D. Sivakumar, and L. Trevisan. Counting distinct elements in a data stream. In *Randomization and Approximation Techniques in Computer Science*, pages 1–10. Springer, 2002.

[3] J. Besag. Statistical analysis of non-lattice data. *The Statistician*, pages 179–195, 1975.

[4] K. Beyer, R. Gemulla, P. J. Haas, B. Reinwald, and Y. Sismanis. Distinct-value synopses for multiset operations. *Communications of the ACM*, 52(10):87–95, 2009.

[5] P. Boldi, M. Rosa, and S. Vigna. Hyperanf: Approximating the neighbourhood function of very large graphs on a budget. In *WWW*, 2011.

[6] P. Chassaing and L. Gerin. Efficient estimation of the cardinality of large data sets. *arXiv preprint math/0701347*, 2011.

[7] A. Chen, J. Cao, L. Shepp, and T. Nguyen. Distinct counting with a self-learning bitmap. *Journal of the American Statistical Association*, 106(495):879–890, 2011.

[8] P. Clifford and I. Cosma. A statistical analysis of probabilistic counting algorithms. *Scandinavian Journal of Statistics*, 39(1):1–14, 2012.

[9] E. Cohen. Size-estimation framework with applications to transitive closure and reachability. *Journal of Computer and System Sciences*, 55(3):441–453, 1997.

[10] E. Cohen. All-distances sketches, revisited: HIP estimators for massive graphs analysis. In *PODS*, 2014.

[11] E. Cohen and H. Kaplan. Summarizing data using bottom-k sketches. In *PODC*, 2007.

[12] G. Cormode, M. Datar, P. Indyk, and S. Muthukrishnan. Comparing data streams using hamming norms (how to zero in). *IEEE Trans. Knowledge and Data Engineering*, 15(3):529–540, 2003.

[13] T. Dasu, T. Johnson, S. Muthukrishnan, and V. Shkapenyuk. Mining database structure; or, how to build a data quality browser. In *SIGMOD*, 2002.

[14] M. Durand and P. Flajolet. Loglog counting of large cardinalities. In *Algorithms-ESA 2003*, pages 605–617. Springer, 2003.

[15] C. Estan, G. Varghese, and M. Fisk. Bitmap algorithms for counting active flows on high speed links. In *Internet Measurement Conference*, 2003.

[16] P. Flajolet, É. Fusy, O. Gandouet, and F. Meunier. Hyperloglog: the analysis of a near-optimal cardinality estimation algorithm. In *AofA*, 2007.

[17] P. Flajolet and G. Nigel Martin. Probabilistic counting algorithms for data base applications. *Journal of computer and system sciences*, 31(2):182–209, 1985.

[18] F. Giroire. Order statistics and estimating cardinalities of massive data sets. *Discrete Applied Mathematics*, 157(2):406–427, 2009.

[19] D. Kane, J. Nelson, and D. Woodruff. An optimal algorithm for the distinct elements problem. In *PODS*, 2010.

[20] M. Lichman. UCI machine learning repository, 2013.

[21] A. Metwally, D. Agrawal, and A. E. Abbadi. Why go logarithmic if we can go linear?: Towards effective distinct counting of search traffic. In *EDBT*, 2008.

[22] P. G. Selinger, M. M. Astrahan, D. D. Chamberlin, R. A. Lorie, and T. G. Price. Access path selection in a relational database management system. In *Proceedings of SIGMOD*, pages 23–34. ACM, 1979.

[23] D. Ting. Streamed approximate counting of distinct elements: beating optimal batch methods. In *KDD*, 2014.

[24] A. van der Vaart. *Asymptotic Statistics*. Cambridge Series in Statistical and Probabilistic Mathematics. Cambridge University Press, 2000.

[25] K. Whang, B. Vander-Zanden, and H. Taylor. A linear-time probabilistic counting algorithm for database applications. *TODS*, 1990.

Overcoming Key Weaknesses of Distance-based Neighbourhood Methods using a Data Dependent Dissimilarity Measure

Kai Ming Ting
Federation University
Victoria 3842, Australia
kaiming.ting@federation.edu.au

Ye Zhu, Mark Carman
Monash University
Victoria 3800, Australia
{yale.zhu, mark.carman}@monash.edu

Yue Zhu, Zhi-Hua Zhou
Nanjing University
Nanjing 210023, China
{zhuy,zhouzh}@lamda.nju.edu.cn

ABSTRACT

This paper introduces the first generic version of data dependent dissimilarity and shows that it provides a better closest match than distance measures for three existing algorithms in clustering, anomaly detection and multi-label classification. For each algorithm, we show that by simply replacing the distance measure with the data dependent dissimilarity measure, it overcomes a key weakness of the otherwise unchanged algorithm.

Keywords

Data dependent dissimilarity; distance measure; distance-based neighbourhood; probability-mass-based neighbourhood; k nearest neighbours.

1. INTRODUCTION AND MOTIVATION

Many data mining algorithms rely on a distance measure to provide the closest match between a test instance and instances in a database in order to find its nearest neighbours. The distance calculation is the core process that has been applied to all aspects of data mining tasks, including density estimation, clustering, anomaly detection and classification.

Despite its widespread applications, research in psychology has pointed out since 1970's that distance measures do not possess the key property of dissimilarity as judged by humans [12, 20], i.e., the characteristic where two instances in a dense region are less similar to each other than two instances of the same interpoint distance in a sparse region. Researchers have suggested that this *data dependent dissimilarity* is a better measure than the data independent geometric model based distance measure in psychological tests [12]. For example, two Caucasians will be judged as less similar when compared in Europe (where there are many Caucasians) than in Asia (where there are few Caucasians and many Asians.)

KDD '16, August 13 - 17, 2016, San Francisco, CA, USA

ISBN 978-1-4503-4232-2/16/08. . . $15.00

DOI: http://dx.doi.org/10.1145/2939672.2939779

We introduce a data dependent dissimilarity which has the above-mentioned characteristic, and we provide concrete evidence that it is a better measure than standard distance measures for three existing algorithms which rely on distance. Using probability mass rather than distance as the means to find the closest match neighbourhood heralds a fundamental change of perspective.

The neighbourhood of an instance has been used for different functions in various data mining tasks. Table 1 shows the key functions and key weaknesses of three existing algorithms relying on distance measure. It is instructive to see that a mere replacement of distance with the data dependent dissimilarity in these algorithms changes the perspective. The corresponding 'new' functions are described in the last column of Table 1. Although the rest of the procedures in each algorithm are unchanged, it overcomes the key weaknesses of these algorithms.

This paper makes the following contributions:

1. A generic data dependent dissimilarity, named mass-based dissimilarity, is proposed to allow for different implementations.

2. Deriving a new neighbourhood function from the data dependent dissimilarity and showing that it can replace an existing neighbourhood density function to overcome a key weakness in density-based clustering, i.e., its inability to find all clusters of varying densities.

3. Through our empirical evaluation, we demonstrate that the data dependent dissimilarity provides a better closest match than distance measure for k-nearest neighbour algorithms in anomaly detection and multi-label classification tasks.

The remainder of the paper is organised as follows. Section 2 introduces the related work. Sections 3 and 4 present the proposed dissimilarity and the new neighbourhood function. Section 5 describes an existing similarity which is a special case of the proposed dissimilarity. Section 6 introduces how the dissimilarity can be applied to three existing algorithms. Section 7 presents the empirical evaluation results. A discussion of related issues and conclusions are provided in the last two sections.

Software download: The source code of mass-based dissimilarity can be obtained at https://sourceforge.net/projects/mass-based-dissimilarity/.

Table 1: Key functions and key weaknesses of algorithms that rely on distance in three tasks and their replacement functions due to mass-based dissimilarity. Details of kNN and MLkNN are provided in Section 6.

Algorithm	Key function	Key weakness	Replacement function
Density-based clustering	Identify core points which have high density using distance-based neighbourhood estimation	Inability to find all clusters of varying densities	Identify core points which have high probability mass using probability mass-based neighbourhood estimation
kNN anomaly detector	Identify anomalies as points with the longest distance to the kth nearest neighbours	Inability to detect local anomalies	Identify anomalies as points having the highest probability mass of the kth lowest probability mass neighbours
Multi-label kNN classifier (MLkNN)	Estimate class-conditioned likelihoods using a frequency estimate based on k nearest neighbours	Poor likelihood estimation in cases where the local neighbourhood covers regions of varied density	Estimate class-conditioned likelihoods using a frequency estimate based on k lowest probability mass neighbours

2. RELATED WORK

Psychologists since 1970's have expressed their concerns on the use of geometric model for dissimilarity measure [12, 20]. The psychological tests they have conducted have clearly shown that the dissimilarity between two instances, as judged by humans, is influenced by the context of measurements and other instances in proximity. It is suggested that a dissimilarity measure which is akin to human's judged dissimilarity is one that interprets two instances in a dense region to be less similar than two instances of equal interpoint distance but located in a less dense region [12].

The first version of data dependent similarity [2], which has the characteristic prescribed by psychologists above, has been shown to provide a more effective match than distance measures in nearest neighbour search for k nearest neighbour classifiers and information retrieval. It is named m_p-dissimilarity and defined in the same form as the ℓ_p-norm, except that the dissimilarity in dimension i is probability mass in a region $P(R_i(x,y))$ rather than distance $|x_i - y_i|$. Region $R_i(x,y)$ is defined as an interval from $min(x_i,y_i) - \delta$ to $max(x_i,y_i) + \delta$, where δ is some small constant value.This implementation requires a search to find all instances in the region, and is not efficient.

This paper presents a general definition of data dependent dissimilarity in which m_p-dissimilarity [2] is a special case. The proposed implementation is efficient and robust for more applications.

A recent definition of mass estimation [7] is the basis of the proposed dissimilarity. We effectively extend from the mass estimation of one point to a dissimilarity measure of two points.

Based on information theory, Lin [14] suggests a probabilistic measure of similarity in ordinal domain as follows:

$$sim(o_a, o_b) = \frac{2 \times \log \sum_{j=\min(a,b)}^{\max(a,b)} P(o_j)}{\log P(o_a) + \log P(o_b)}$$

where o_j is an ordinal random variable.

Like most distance measures, Lin's measure [14] yields a constant maximum value for self similarity; and it has the opposite characteristic of the judged dissimilarity, i.e., two instances are more similar in a dense region than two instances of equal interpoint distance in a sparse region.

Another existing data dependent dissimilarity is shared nearest neighbour (SNN) which has been investigated in clustering only thus far [9, 11]. A detailed discussion of the relationship between SNN and the proposed mass-based dissimilarity is devoted in Section 5.

3. MASS-BASED DISSIMILARITY

Geometric model based measures solely depend on geometric positions to derive their distance measures. Instead, a data dependent dissimilarity mainly depends on data distribution, i.e., the probability mass of the (smallest) region covering the two instances. We use the terms: probability mass or mass or probability, interchangeably hereafter; and name the proposed measure: **mass-based dissimilarity**.

Let D be a data sample from pdf (probability density function) F; and $H \in \mathcal{H}(D)$ be a hierarchical partitioning model of the space into non-overlapping and non-empty regions. The definitions for the domain of $\mathbb{R}^d$, where d is the number of dimensions, are given as follows.

Definition 1. $R(x,y|H;D)$ is the smallest local region covering x and y wrt H and D is defined as:

$$R(x,y|H;D) = \underset{r \subset H \ s.t. \{x,y\} \in r}{\arg\min} \sum_{z \in D} \mathbb{1}(z \in r) \quad (1)$$

where $\mathbb{1}(\cdot)$ is an indicator function.

Definition 2. Mass-based dissimilarity of x and y wrt D and F is defined as the expected probability of $R(x,y|H;D)$:

$$m(x,y|D,F) = E_{\mathcal{H}(D)}[P_F(R(x,y|H;D))] \quad (2)$$

where $P_F(\cdot)$ is the probability wrt F; and the expectation is taken over all models in $\mathcal{H}(D)$.

In practice, the mass-based dissimilarity would be estimated from a finite number of models $H_i \in \mathcal{H}(D), i = 1, \dots, t$ as follows:

$$m_e(x,y|D) = \frac{1}{t} \sum_{i=1}^{t} \tilde{P}(R(x,y|H_i;D)) \quad (3)$$

where $\tilde{P}(R) = \frac{1}{|D|} \sum_{z \in D} \mathbb{1}(z \in R)$.

Note that $R(x,y|H;D)$ is the smallest local region covering x and y, it is analogous to the shortest distance between x and y used in the geometric model. Hereafter D is dropped in the notations when the context is clear.

3.1 Self-dissimilarity

One key difference of the mass-based dissimilarity is self-dissimilarity. Unlike self-dissimilarity of other measures (which usually take a constant value equal to the minimum dissimilarity or 0 in [0,1]), $m_e(x,x)$ is not a constant and ranges over [0,1], depending on the data distribution and the partitioning strategy used.

Table 2: m_e versus ℓ_p. $\partial(\cdot,\cdot)$ is a dissimilarity function. $m_e(x,y)=0$ when both x and y are in an empty region.

	$\partial(x,x)$	$\partial(x,y), \forall y \neq x$	Properties
m_e	[0,1]	[0,1]	$\forall x \neq y, m_e(x,x) \leq m_e(x,y)$ $\exists x \neq y; x \neq z, m_e(x,x) > m_e(z,y)$
ℓ_p	0	(0,1]	$\forall x; y \neq z, \ell_p(x,x) < \ell_p(z,y)$

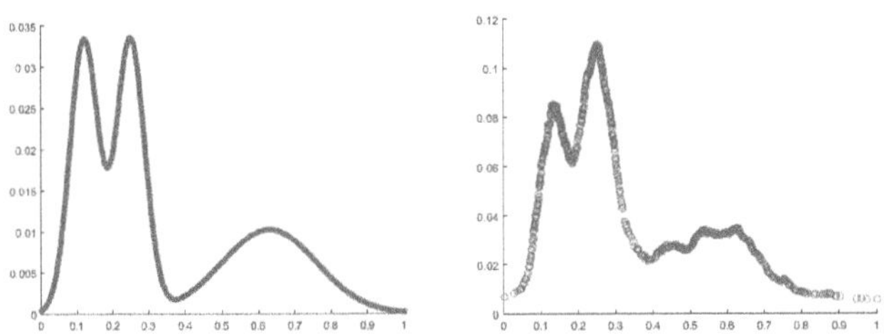

(a) True density distribution (b) Distribution of $m_e(x,x|D)$

Figure 1: (a) A true density distribution; (b) $m_e(x,x|D)$ based on Random Trees (level=8), where D has 1500 instances randomly sampled from (a)

The differences between m_e and ℓ_p are shown in Table 2. The reasons of the two properties of m_e are given below:

- $\forall x \neq y, m_e(x,x) \leq m_e(x,y)$: because $R(x,x|H) \subseteq R(x,y|H)$.
- $\exists x \neq y; x \neq z, m_e(x,x) > m_e(z,y)$: As the mass distribution of $m_e(x,x)$ is not a constant[1]; if x is in the region that includes the maximum mass point, then its mass value will be larger than the dissimilarity of some points which are close to the fringe or have the minimum mass values.

The distribution of the self-dissimilarity is equivalent to mass distribution [18], and its properties depend on the models $\mathcal{H}$ used:

- Half-space is used to define R. Here $m_e(x,y|D)$ reduces to half-space mass [7] if $x=y$. The mass distribution is always concave within the area bounded by the data, irrespective of the density distribution of the given data set [7].
- Random Trees: Here $m_e(x,y|D)$ reduces to level-h mass estimation [19] if $x=y$. An example is shown in Figure 1(b).

3.2 Model used to define a region

Though there are many methods to implement a model to define regions for mass estimation [19], we employ a method based on completely random trees[2] to implement mass-based dissimilarity in this paper.

We use a recursive partitioning scheme called *iForest* (isolation Forest) [15] to define regions. Though *iForest* was initially designed for anomaly detection [15], it has been shown that it is a special case of mass estimation [19].

[1]Note that mass distribution is not uniform even for a uniformly distributed pdf. See [7, 18] for details.

[2]Note that the random trees are not RandomForests [5] because the trees are completely random, built without class labels and any attribute selection criterion.

The implementation can be divided into two steps. There are two input parameters to this procedure. They are: t - the number of *iTrees* (isolation Trees); and ψ - the sub-sampling size used to build each *iTree*. The height limit h of each *iTree* is automatically set by ψ : $h = \lceil log_2 \psi \rceil$.

The first step is to build an *iForest* consisting of t *iTrees* as the partitioning structure R. Each *iTree* is built independently using a subset $\mathcal{D} \subset D$, where $|\mathcal{D}| = \psi$. A randomly selected split is employed at each internal node of an *iTree* to partition the sample set at the node into two non-empty subsets until every point is isolated or the maximum tree height h is reached. In the experiments described in Section 7, we perform axis-parallel split at each node of an *iTree* to build *iForest*. The details of the axis-parallel split *iTree* building process can be found in the Appendix.

After an *iForest* is built, all instances in D are traversed through each tree in order to record the mass of each node.

The second step is the evaluation step. Test points x and y are parsed through each *iTree* to calculate the sum of mass of the lowest nodes containing both x and y, i.e., $\sum_i |R(x,y|H_i)|$. Finally, $m_e(x,y)$ is the mean of these mass values over t *iTrees* as defined below:

$$m_e(x,y) = \frac{1}{t}\sum_{i=1}^{t}\frac{|R(x,y|H_i)|}{|D|} \quad (4)$$

4. μ-NEIGHBOURHOOD MASS

We introduce a new function: μ-neighbourhood mass, which denotes the number of points in a region defined by the mass-based dissimilarity, is defined as follows:

$$M_\mu(x) = \#\{y \in D \mid m_e(x,y) \leq \mu\}$$

Like ϵ-neighbourhood density[3], μ-neighbourhood mass produces an estimate based on a region defined by a dissimilarity measure. However, the region is defined by the expected probability mass (instead of distance.) Like ϵ, the parameter μ controls the size of the region: large (small) μ defines a large (small) region.

Figures 2(a) and 2(b) compare ϵ-neighbourhood with μ-neighbourhood on a dataset having three areas of different densities. Note that the volume of the region defined by μ-neighbourhood mass depends on data distribution—small in dense area and large in sparse area, shown as areas A, B and C in Figure 2(b). Note that the overall shape is not symmetrical. In contrast, ϵ-neighbourhood forms a region which is independent of data distribution with constant volume, in addition to regular and symmetrical shape.

Figure 3(a) shows that a μ-neighbourhood region becomes symmetrical only in the case of a uniform density distribution. Figure 3 shows that the shape depends on the implementation: axis-parallel and non axis-parallel random trees yield diamond and spherical shapes, respectively.

A conceptual comparison between the two neighbourhood functions is given in Table 3. In order to obtain non-zero M_μ, μ must be set higher than $\max_{z \in D} m_e(z,z)$. In other words, μ-neighbourhood mass employs mass distribution (i.e., the distribution of self-dissimilarity) as the reference.

For the purpose of clustering, mass can be used in a similar way as density to identify core points, i.e., instances having high mass values are core points; and those having low mass values are noise.

[3]As used in DBSCAN [10].

Table 3: μ-neighbourhood mass versus ϵ-neighbourhood density

	μ-neighbourhood mass	ϵ-neighbourhood density
Definition	$M_\mu(x) = \#\{y \in D \mid m_e(x,y) \leq \mu\}$	$N_\epsilon(x) = \#\{y \in D \mid \ell_p(x,y) \leq \epsilon\}$
	$M_\mu(x) = 0$ if $m_e(x,x) > \mu$	$\forall x; 0 < \epsilon \leq 1, N_\epsilon(x) \geq 1$
	$M_\mu(x) \geq 0$ if $m_e(x,x) \leq \mu$	
Region	$m_e(x,x)$ is the reference; not symmetrical; volume unfixed	Distance from x; symmetrical; constant volume

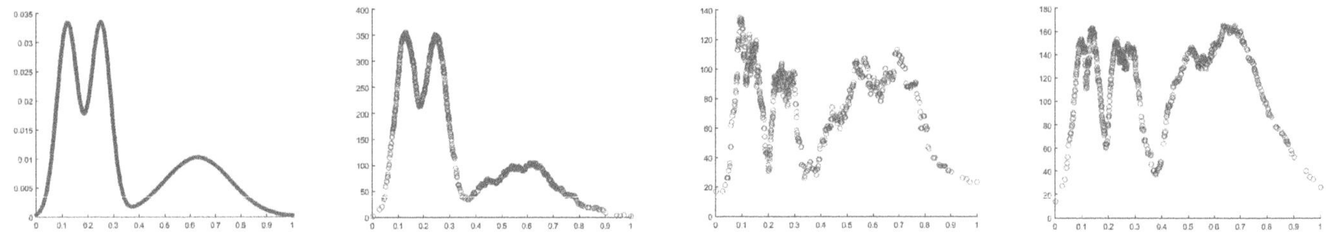

(a) True density distribution (b) ϵ-neighbourhood density (c) μ-neighbourhood mass (d) σ-neighbourhood mass

Figure 4: Density distribution of a "hard distribution" and its estimations using ϵ-neighbourhood density ($\epsilon = 0.03$), μ-neighbourhood mass based on *iForest* (level=8 and $\mu = 0.2$) and σ-neighbourhood mass based on *SNN* ($k = 200$ and $\sigma = 0.3$) from a sample of 1500 instances of (a).

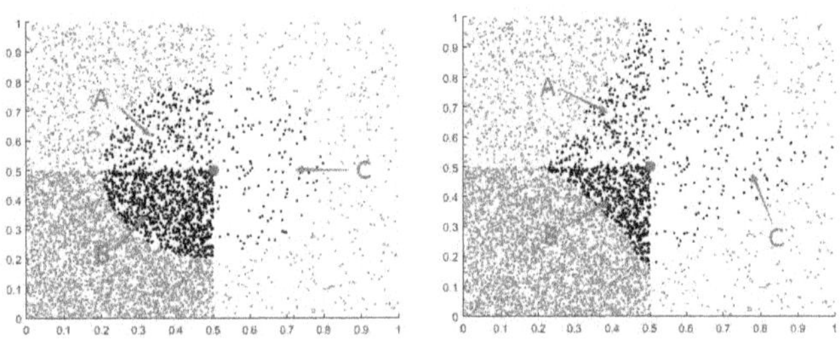

(a) ϵ-neighbourhood region (b) μ-neighbourhood region

Figure 2: (a) and (b) show the two regions defined by ϵ-neighbourhood density ($\epsilon = 0.25$) and μ-neighbourhood mass ($\mu = 0.55$), respectively, on a dataset having three areas of different densities, with reference to the red point (0.5,0.5). The blue-coloured dots denotes the points and the dark-coloured dots denotes the points within the region defined by the ϵ- or μ-neighbourhood estimator.

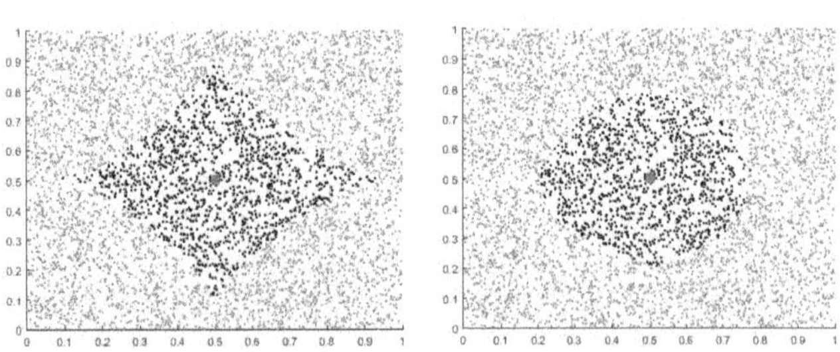

(a) μ-neighbourhood region-A (b) μ-neighbourhood region-B

Figure 3: (a) and (b) show the two regions defined by μ-neighbourhood mass ($\mu = 0.55$) using axis-parallel *iForest* and non axis-parallel *iForest*, respectively, on a dataset with uniform density distribution with reference to the red point (0.5,0.5).

The next subsection describes a characteristic of μ-neighbourhood mass which makes it a better candidate than ϵ-neighbourhood density to identify core points, especially in a dataset which has clusters of varying densities.

4.1 Characteristic of μ-neighbourhood mass

One interesting characteristic of μ-neighbourhood mass is that valleys of a data distribution can be constrained within a small range of mass values by setting an appropriate μ, where a valley is the area surrounding a local minimum in the distribution. This characteristic is especially important in clustering algorithms which rely on a global threshold to identify core points before grouping the core points into separate clusters. Having all the valleys close to a small mass value, a global threshold slightly larger than this value will identify the majority of the core points of all clusters, irrespective of the densities of the clusters.

In contrast, ϵ-neighbourhood density does not possess this characteristic as it estimates density distribution and its valleys can have huge varying densities. As a result, a clustering algorithm, such as DBSCAN [10] which employs the ϵ-neighbourhood density estimator and relies on a global threshold to identify core points, is unable to detect all clusters of varying densities. This kind of distribution, shown in Figure 4(a), is called hard distribution because it is hard for DBSCAN [10] to identify all the clusters in the distribution.

Possessing the above-mentioned characteristic, the hard distribution (in terms of density) will exhibit as easy distribution (in terms of mass). Examples of ϵ-neighbourhood density and μ-neighbourhood mass are given in Figures 4(b) and 4(c), respectively.

In summary, μ-neighbourhood mass converts all valleys of different densities to become valleys of almost equal low mass by using an appropriate μ, if it exists.

The same applies to peaks, i.e., the difference in mass between peaks at dense and sparse regions can be reduced to a smaller value close to zero with an appropriate μ. However, in the clustering context, it is more important to have valleys reduced to about the same value so that a global threshold can be used to easily identify all clusters.

5. RELATION TO *SNN* SIMILARITY

A measure based on shared nearest neighbours (SNN) in k nearest neighbours has been proposed for clustering [11]:

> "Data points are similar to the extent that they share the same nearest neighbours; in particular, two data points are similar to the extent that their respective k nearest neighbour lists match. In addition, for this similarity measure to be valid, it is required that the tested points themselves belong to the common neighbourhood."

SNN (dis)similarity has been used to replace the distance measure in DBSCAN as a way to overcome its inability to find all clusters of varying densities [9].

Let $s_k(x, y) = SNN(x, y)/k$, where $SNN(x, y)$ is the number of shared nearest neighbours of k nearest neighbours of x and y, which include both x and y; $SNN(x, y) = 0$ if both x and y are not included.

The neighbourhood function based on the SNN similarity can be expressed as:

$$M_\sigma(x) = \#\{y \in D \mid s_k(x, y) \geq \sigma\}$$

Note that $M_\sigma(x)$, like $M_\mu(x)$, cannot be treated as densities as the volume used to compute M_σ for every x is not a constant. In other words, we reveal that SNN clustering algorithm is a mass-based method, and not a density-based method as previously thought [9, 17]. This is despite the fact that SNN employs the same DBSCAN procedure by simply replacing the distance measure with the (inverse) SNN similarity [9, 17].

Using the same notation, let $R(x, y|H)$ be the (implicit) region which covers the shared nearest neighbours of x and y, where H is kNN. $SNN(x, y)$ can be defined as follows:

$$SNN(x, y) = |R(x, y|H)| \tag{5}$$

An example of $M_\sigma(x)$ due to SNN is given in Figure 4(d).

The advantages of using $iForest$ instead of k nearest neighbour to estimate the neighbourhood mass are:

- The SNN similarity matrix is sensitive to the parameter of neighbourhood list size k. In contrast, $iForest$ works well with a default setting.
- SNN clustering [9] has $O(k^2n^2)$ time complexity or $O(n^3)$ when $k = \sqrt{n}$ or larger and $n = |D|$. Yet, our solution (see Section 6.1) has the same $O(n^2)$ time complexity as DBSCAN, except an additional preprocessing to compute the dissimilarity matrix which takes $O(t \log \psi(\psi + n^2))$ or $O(n^2)$ since $\psi \ll n$.

6. APPLICATIONS TO THREE EXISTING ALGORITHMS RELYING ON DISTANCE

Here we show that the mass-based dissimilarity can simply replace the distance measure used in existing algorithms in three tasks: clustering, anomaly detection, and multi-label classification. The pertinent details are described in the following three subsections.

6.1 Density-based clustering

DBSCAN [10] is a natural choice not only because it is a commonly used clustering algorithm, but also it employs ϵ-neighbourhood density estimation. Here we convert DBSCAN to MBSCAN, i.e., from density based to mass based, by simply replacing distance measure with mass-based dissimilarity, leaving the rest of the procedure unchanged. This effectively changes the use of ϵ-neighbourhood density estimation to μ-neighbourhood mass estimation, as described in Section 4. This enables a global threshold to be used to identify all clusters of varying densities in hard distribution as shown in Figure 4.

6.2 k-nearest neighbour anomaly detection

Here we use one of the simplest anomaly detector which is based on k^{th} nearest distance [4]. The anomaly score for a test instance x is defined as the distance between x and its kth nearest neighbour. Anomalies are instances which have the largest scores, i.e., they have the longest distances to their k^{th} nearest neighbours in a given data set.

This distance-based anomaly detector is used to show that a simple replacement of the distance measure with the mass-based dissimilarity can overcome its inability to detect local anomalies and improve its overall detection performance.

The replacement of ℓ_p with m_e effectively converts the entire operation from distance-based to mass-based. Anomalies are redefined as those which have the highest probability mass to their k^{th} lowest probability mass neighbours in a given data set.

The advantage of using mass is that fringes of any clusters with the same structure but different densities will have about the same probability mass. This enables (local) anomalies of dense clusters to be ranked at similar positions as anomalies of sparse clusters. The mass-based version is denoted as M-kNN [4] to contrast it with kNN.

6.3 Multi-label kNN classification

In multi-label classification tasks, each instance is associated with several class labels simultaneously. MLkNN [22] has been proposed to adapt the (single-label) kNN approach to multi-label problems, which makes a prediction via the maximum a posteriori rule. The rule is defined as follows.

In the context of multi-label learning, let $y_{i,j} \in \{1, 0\}$ be the j-th label of the i-th instance, where 1 and 0 indicate the instance's association and dissociation, respectively. The prediction rule of the j-th label for $\boldsymbol{x}_i$ is given by [22]:

$$y_{i,j} = \begin{cases} 1 & \text{if } \mathbb{P}(y_{i,j} = 1|c_{i,j})/\mathbb{P}(y_{i,j} = 0|c_{i,j}) > 1 \\ 0 & \text{otherwise} \end{cases},$$

where $c_{i,j}$ denotes the number of instances in the neighbourhood (i.e., k nearest neighbours) of $\boldsymbol{x}_i$ with the jth-label, $\mathbb{P}(y_{i,j} = 1|c_{i,j})$ is the posterior probability of $y_{i,j} = 1$ given that $\boldsymbol{x}_i$ has $c_{i,j}$ neighbours with the jth-label; and $\mathbb{P}(y_{i,j} = 0|c_{i,j})$ is similarly defined.

Bayes theorem yields that $\mathbb{P}(y_{i,j} = 1|c_{i,j}) \propto \mathbb{P}(y_{i,j} = 1)\mathbb{P}(c_{i,j}|y_{i,j} = 1)$, where $\mathbb{P}(y_{i,j} = 1)$ is the prior probability of $y_{i,j} = 1$ and $\mathbb{P}(c_{i,j}|y_{i,j} = 1)$ is the likelihood that $\boldsymbol{x}_i$ has $c_{i,j}$ neighbours when $y_{i,j} = 1$. Both $\mathbb{P}(y_{i,j} = 1)$ and $\mathbb{P}(c_{i,j}|y_{i,j} = 1)$ can be estimated via frequency counting on the training set. In the same manner, we can obtain $\mathbb{P}(y_{i,j} = 0|c_{i,j})$ via $\mathbb{P}(y_{i,j} = 0)$ and $\mathbb{P}(c_{i,j}|y_{i,j} = 0)$.

[4] Though there is a fundamental change of perspective, we have opted to reuse the same name of the original algorithm to emphasize that the same algorithm is employed with the exception of dissimilarity measure only.

Getting an effective closest match neighbourhood of a test instance is of prime importance in MLkNN, which directly influences the calculation of the likelihood. Thus, the dissimilarity measure employed plays a critical role in this process. In the original MLkNN, Euclidean distance is applied. The use of mass-based dissimilarity has the potential to enhance the nearest neighbour search and leads to a better multi-label classification result. We denote the version employing mass-based dissimilarity, M-MLkNN.

7. EMPIRICAL EVALUATION

7.1 Clustering

We evaluated the mass-based version of DBSCAN, named MBSCAN, and compared it with DBSCAN, SNN [9] and OPTICS [1]. Note that the only difference among DBSCAN, SNN and MBSCAN is the dissimilarity matrix, which is pre-processed and serves as input to these algorithms. We used *iForest* with the default setting (i.e., $\psi = 256$ and $t = 100$) [15] to generate the mass-based dissimilarity matrix as the input for MBSCAN.

Th evaluation is conducted on 2 synthetic and 8 real-world datasets from UCI Machine Learning Repository [13]. Table 4 presents the properties of the datasets.

Table 4: Properties of clustering datasets

Dataset	Size	Dimensions	Clusters
Libras	360	90	15
WDBC	569	30	2
Thyroid	215	5	3
Segment	2310	19	7
Wine	178	13	3
Seeds	210	7	3
Pendig	10992	16	10
Iris	150	4	3
S1	900	2	3
S2	1500	2	3

S1 and S2 are synthetic datasets. S1 is a "hard distribution" which contains 3 Gaussian clusters $N(mean, std)$ with means located at $(x^{(1)}, x^{(2)})$=(3.3, 9.3), (8, 5), (12, 12), and standard deviations $std = 3, 3, 8$ in each dimension; and each cluster has 300 instances. S2 is an "easy distribution" which has 3 Gaussian clusters $N(mean, std)$ with means located at $(x^{(1)}, x^{(2)}) = (10, 10), (20, 20), (60, 60)$, and $std = 2, 2, 11$ in each dimension; and each cluster has 500 instances. The density plots of S1 and S2 are shown in Figure 5.

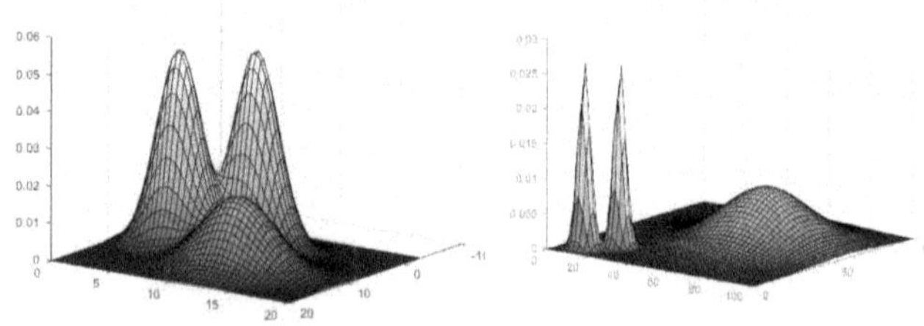

(a) S1: "hard distribution" (b) S2: "easy distribution"

Figure 5: Density distributions of S1 and S2.

We recorded the best F-measure[5] of a clustering algorithm on a dataset. Because *iForest* is a randomised method, we reported the average result over 10 trials.

For each clustering algorithm, the search range of either ϵ, μ or σ was from the minimum to the maximum value of pairwise dissimilarity in the given dataset. The search range of $MinPts$ in DBSCAN, SNN and MBSCAN was in the range $\{2, 3, \ldots, 10\}$. The parameter k in SNN was set to the square root of the data size as suggested by some researchers [16]. For OPTICS, we searched $MinPts$ to produce the required hierarchical plots, and then searched threshold ξ[6] in the range $\{0.01, 0.02, \ldots, 0.99\}$ to extract clusters from each plot.

Figure 6 shows the best F-measure of DBSCAN, OPTICS, SNN and MBSCAN. The counts in the last column of the table reveal that MBSCAN and SNN performed the best in 5 and 3 datasets, respectively.

Table 5 shows the performance ratio of OPTICS, SNN, and MBSCAN with reference to DBSCAN. The geometric mean reveals that MBSCAN enhances DBSCAN the most by 27%; and SNN enhances DBSCAN by 21%.

Although MBSCAN and SNN have similar F-measures in many datasets, MBSCAN is significantly better than SNN in two datasets: S1 and WDBC. For example, MBSCAN enhances DBSCAN by more than 80% compared with less than 50% achieved by SNN on S1. Because S1 is a hard distribution for DBSCAN, this shows that mass-based dissimilarity provides a much better solution than shared nearest neighbour similarity in finding clusters of varying densities. Except for S1, WDBC and Thyroid, other datasets appear to have a lesser degree of hard distribution since their enhancements over DBSCAN are less than 40%.

The post-hoc Nemenyi test[7] reveals that both MBSCAN and SNN are significantly better than both DBSCAN and OPTICS. Figure 7 shows the average rank of each algorithm and its critical difference.

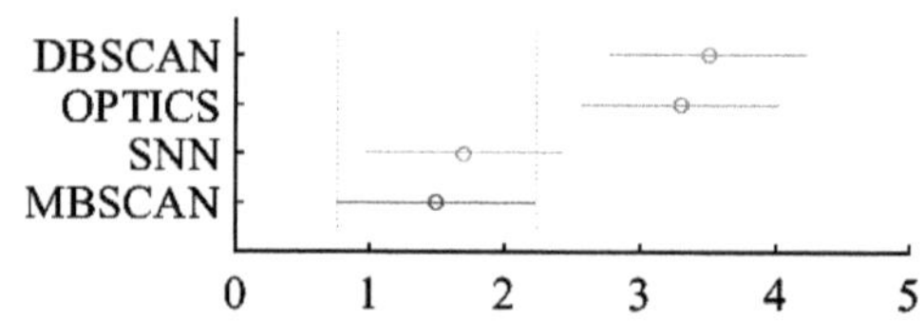

Figure 7: Critical difference (CD) diagram of the post-hoc Nemenyi test ($\alpha = 0.05$). The difference between two algorithms is significant if their CDs do not overlap.

[5]Given a clustering result, we calculate the precision score p_i and the recall score r_i for each cluster based on the confusion matrix, and then the overall F-measure is the average over all clusters: F-measure$= \frac{1}{m}\sum_{i=1}^{m}\frac{2P_iR_i}{P_i+R_i}$.

[6]Parameter ξ is used to identify downward and upward areas of a hierarchical plot in order to extract clusters. This hierarchical extraction method was proposed in the original OPTICS paper [1].

[7]This test (after the Friedman test) [8] is conducted to examine whether the performance difference between any two algorithms is significant. Firstly, the algorithms were ranked on each dataset according to their F-measures, where the best one is rank 1. Then, the post-hoc Nemenyi test is used to calculate the critical difference value (CD) for each algorithm.

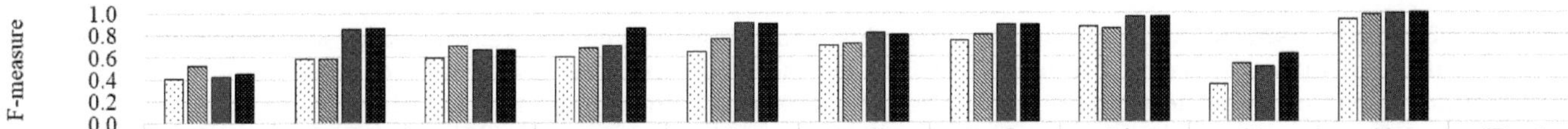

	Libras	Thyroid	Segment	WDBC	Wine	Pendig	Seeds	Iris	S1	S2	#Top 1
□DBSCAN	0.40	0.58	0.59	0.60	0.65	0.70	0.75	0.87	0.34	0.94	0/10
▨OPTICS	0.52	0.59	0.70	0.68	0.76	0.72	0.80	0.85	0.53	0.98	2/10
■SNN	0.42	0.85	0.66	0.70	0.91	0.82	0.89	0.96	0.50	0.99	3/10
■MBSCAN	0.45	0.86	0.67	0.86	0.90	0.80	0.889	0.963	0.62	0.993	5/10

Figure 6: Best F-measures of DBSCAN, OPTIC, SNN and MBSCAN on 10 datasets. The best performer on each dataset is underlined.

Table 5: Performance ratio of OPTICS, SNN, and MBSCAN with reference to DBSCAN on 10 datasets.

	Libras	Thyroid	Segment	WDBC	Wine	Pendig	Seeds	Iris	S1	S2	Geomean
OPTICS	1.30	1.02	1.19	1.13	1.17	1.03	1.07	.98	1.56	1.04	1.14
SNN	1.05	1.47	1.12	1.17	1.40	1.17	1.19	1.10	1.47	1.06	1.21
MBSCAN	1.13	1.48	1.14	1.43	1.38	1.14	1.19	1.11	1.82	1.06	1.27

7.2 Anomaly detection

In this section, we evaluate M-kNN in two experiments.

We first examined the ability of kNN and M-kNN to detect local anomalies on a synthetic dataset. The dataset contains one sparse cluster and one dense cluster, and each cluster has 500 instances. The instances at the fringes of the dense cluster are anomalies relative to this cluster only because they have higher densities than most instances in the sparse cluster; that is why they are called local anomalies.

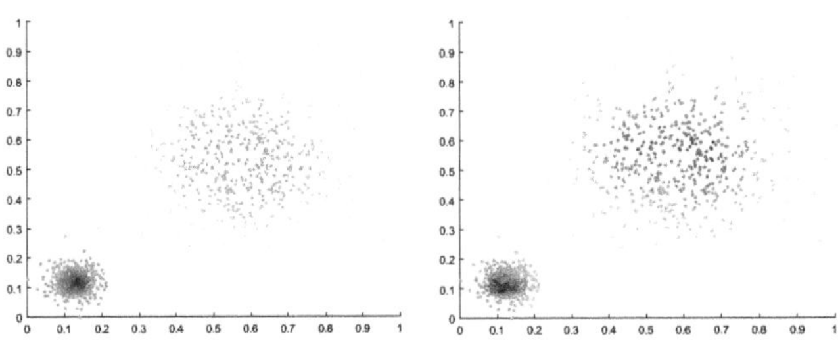

(a) kNN (b) M-kNN

Figure 8: The ability to detect local anomalies in the dense cluster. Contour of the scores of k-nearest neigbour anomaly detectors using ℓ_p and m_e, with k = 100 on a synthetic dataset. The lighter the colour, the higher the anomaly score.

Figure 8 shows the contour of anomaly scores on the dataset. As expected, kNN is unable to detect local anomalies. Yet, M-kNN is able to detect all instances at the fringes of the dense cluster as anomalies. Note that the fringes of both dense and sparse clusters have similar high scores, allowing all of them to be identified as anomalies.

In the second experiment, we compared the performance on 6 real-world benchmark datasets[8]. The data size, dimensions and percentage of anomalies are shown in Table 6. A state-of-the-art local anomaly detector named Local Outlier Factor (LOF) [6] is also used in the comparison.

[8]Velocity is from http://openscience.us/repo/defect/ck/ and others are from UCI Machine Learning Repository [13].

Table 6: Properties of benchmark datasets

Dataset	Size	Dimensions	% Anomaly
Velocity	229	20	34.06%
Mfeat	410	649	2.44%
BloodDonation	604	4	5.63%
Diabetes	768	8	34.9%
annThyroid	7200	6	7.42%
p53Mutant	10387	5408	0.51%

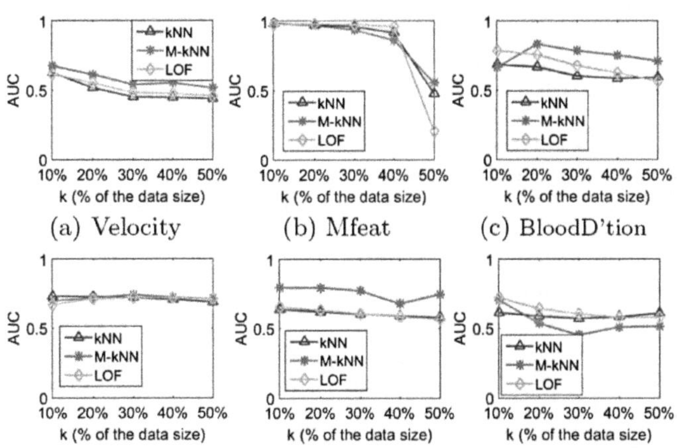

(a) Velocity (b) Mfeat (c) BloodD'tion
(d) Diabetes (e) annThyroid (f) p53Mutant

Figure 9: AUC of kNN, M-kNN and LOF.

We search k from 10% to 50% of the data size and present the result in terms of AUC (Area Under ROC Curve.)

M-kNN was run over 10 trials using different random seeds in computing the dissimilarity matrix for each dataset. kNN yields a deterministic result for a given data set; thus, it is run once only for each data set.

Comparing their best AUC values in Figure 9, M-kNN performs equivalent to or better than kNN on every dataset. M-kNN always outperforms kNN on Velocity and annThyroid with any k. On BloodDonation, M-kNN with a high k value performs better than kNN. Compared with LOF, M-KNN performs equally or better than kNN on 5 out of 6 datasets in terms of the highest AUC.

Table 8: **M-MLkNN versus MLkNN on hamming loss, ranking loss, coverage, one error and average precision. Each result is an average over 10 trials of 10-fold cross-validation and its standard error. For the first four performance measures, the lower the better; for the last one, the higher the better.**

		HammingLoss	RankingLoss	Coverage	OneError	AveragePrecision
Birds	MLkNN	0.051 ± 0.001	0.298 ± 0.004	3.507 ± 0.084	0.713 ± 0.017	0.392 ± 0.010
	M-MLkNN	$\mathbf{0.046} \pm 0.001$	$\mathbf{0.167} \pm 0.007$	$\mathbf{2.008} \pm 0.067$	$\mathbf{0.473} \pm 0.006$	$\mathbf{0.600} \pm 0.005$
CAL500	MLkNN	0.139 ± 0.001	0.187 ± 0.002	132.467 ± 0.489	0.131 ± 0.005	0.489 ± 0.002
	M-MLkNN	0.139 ± 0.001	0.187 ± 0.001	131.731 ± 0.538	0.125 ± 0.005	0.489 ± 0.001
Emotions	MLkNN	0.269 ± 0.007	0.278 ± 0.011	2.358 ± 0.071	0.419 ± 0.013	0.692 ± 0.011
	M-MLkNN	$\mathbf{0.208} \pm 0.004$	$\mathbf{0.180} \pm 0.005$	$\mathbf{1.857} \pm 0.025$	$\mathbf{0.309} \pm 0.008$	$\mathbf{0.776} \pm 0.006$
Enron	MLkNN	0.053 ± 0.000	0.099 ± 0.001	13.850 ± 0.095	0.340 ± 0.013	0.604 ± 0.005
	M-MLkNN	$\mathbf{0.052} \pm 0.000$	$\mathbf{0.094} \pm 0.001$	$\mathbf{13.477} \pm 0.103$	$\mathbf{0.288} \pm 0.008$	$\mathbf{0.640} \pm 0.004$
Scene	MLkNN	0.175 ± 0.002	0.198 ± 0.003	1.065 ± 0.023	0.338 ± 0.008	0.774 ± 0.003
	M-MLkNN	$\mathbf{0.168} \pm 0.002$	$\mathbf{0.175} \pm 0.003$	$\mathbf{0.978} \pm 0.021$	$\mathbf{0.310} \pm 0.008$	$\mathbf{0.794} \pm 0.004$

Table 7: Properties of multi-label datasets. W is the average number of labels per instance.

Dataset	Size	Dimensions	Labels	W
Birds	645	260	19	1.014
CAL500	502	68	174	26.044
Emotions	593	72	6	1.869
Enron	1702	1001	53	3.378
Scene	2407	294	6	1.074

7.3 Multi-label classification

In this section, we compare the original distance-based MLkNN[22] with the mass-based version M-MLkNN. The best k is searched in the range: 1,3,5,10,15 via 5-fold cross-validation on the training set.

We evaluate their performance in terms of Hamming loss, ranking loss, coverage, one error and average precision on five datasets[9], commonly used for multi-label classifier evaluations. Table 7 shows the properties of these datasets.

The result presented in Table 8 shows that M-MLkNN is significantly better (by two standard errors) than MLkNN in four out of the five datasets in terms of all five performance measures. The improvement of M-MLkNN over MLkNN is noteworthy (range between 30% and 50%) on the Birds dataset in terms of the last four measures.

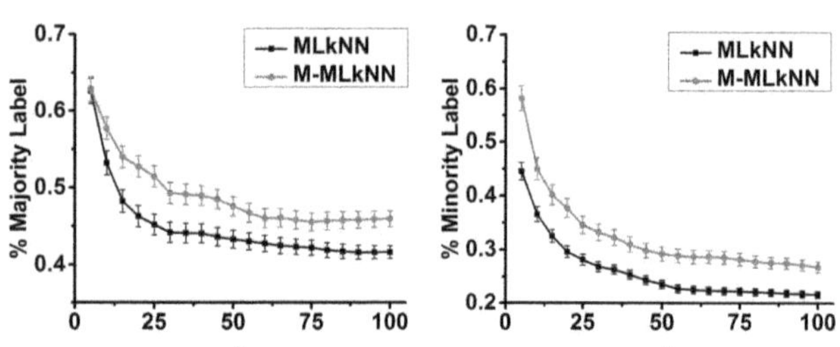

Figure 10: The proportion of k nearest neighbours having a particular label on the Emotions dataset for different k. The left and right figures show the proportions for the majority and minority labels (i.e., the labels which have the largest and smallest number of instances), respectively, on the dataset.

The improvement is due to the fact that mass-based dissimilarity provides a better closest match neighbourhood, where instances are more likely to hold the same label and the proportion of the majority label is larger. Figure 10 provides an insight into two of the labels individually. Each of the majority and minority labels (in the dataset) has a higher proportion in the k nearest neighbours found using mass-based dissimilarity than that using the distance measure. In fact, this occurs for every label on this dataset.

Visualisation provides another perspective of the advantage, i.e., how far apart instances are from one another according to each of the two dissimilarity measures. Here we performed multidimensional scaling (MDS)[10]. The MDS plot based on ℓ_2 is shown in Figure 11(a); and the one based on m_e is shown in Figure 11(b). It shows that instances of different labels are easier to separate using m_e.

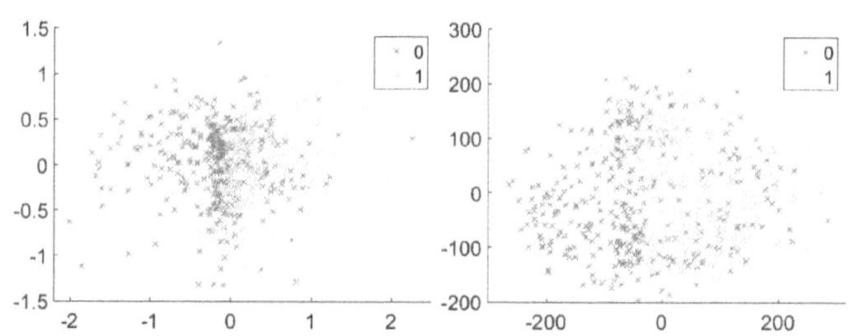

(a) MDS using ℓ_2 (b) MDS using m_e

Figure 11: MDS plots using distance matrix and mass-based dissimilarity matrix on Emotions. Green and red points represent the positive and negative instances of the majority label, respectively.

7.4 Evaluation in runtime

The only difference between the ℓ_p and m_e versions of the algorithms in the above three subsections is the computation time for dissimilarity matrix. After the matrix is computed and served as input, the algorithm has the same runtime regardless of the dissimilarity used to compute the matrix.

Using ℓ_p to compute the dissimilarity matrix has $O(dn^2)$ time complexity. m_e builds *iForest* and computes the dissimilarity matrix based on *iForest*, which yields $O(t\psi log\psi + n^2 t log\psi)$ time complexity. For large datasets, $\psi \ll n$, the time cost is $O(n^2)$. The time complexity of SNN similarity is $O(n^3)$ in the worst case when $k = \sqrt{n}$ or larger. Table 9

[9]Source: http://mulan.sourceforge.net/datasets-mlc.html.

[10]Multidimensional scaling is a technique for visualising the information contained in a dissimilarity matrix [21]. An MDS algorithm aims to place each data point in a p-dimensional space ($p = 2$ is used here), while preserving as much as possible pairwise dissimilarities between them.

gives the time and space complexities of dissimilarity matrix calculation based on ℓ_p, m_e and SNN.

Table 9: Time and space complexities of dissimilarity matrix calculation based on ℓ_p, m_e and SNN.

Measure	Time complexity	Space complexity
ℓ_p	$O(dn^2)$	$O(dn)$
m_e	$O(t\psi log\psi + n^2 tlog\psi)$	$O(t\psi log\psi + dn)$
SNN	$O(k^2n^2 + dn^2)$	$O(dn + kn)$

Table 10: Runtime of the dissimilarity matrix calculation for the three dissimilarities (in seconds).

Data set (Data size) (Dimension)	Segment (2310) (19)	annThyroid (7200) (6)	Pendig (10992) (16)	p53Mut (10387) (5408)
ℓ_p	5	42	110	8182
m_e	31	259	600	548
SNN	26	243	573	9141

Table 10 shows the runtime of the dissimilarity matrix calculation for the three dissimilarities on four real-world datasets. In small dimensional datasets, m_e has almost the same runtime as SNN, but takes longer to compute than ℓ_p due to the use of $iForest$. However, in large and high dimensional datasets such as p53Mutant, m_e is much faster than both ℓ_p and SNN because it is independent of the data dimensionality, i.e., each split node of a tree chooses one attribute randomly up to the certain height limit only.

8. DISCUSSION

Concepts. Dissimilarity measures are assumed to be a metric or a pseudo-metric as a necessary criterion for all data mining tasks. This work shows for the first time that this assumption is incorrect in three tasks.

We show that distance measures are the source of key weaknesses in three existing algorithms, highlighted in Table 1. Having recognised the source issue and created an effective alternative to distance measure, the solution becomes simple—merely replacing the distance measure with the data dependent dissimilarity; the otherwise unchanged algorithm can now overcome its weakness.

The result of not recognising the source issue can often lead to a solution which is more complicated than necessary and may not resolve the issue completely. An example is the inability of density-based clustering to find all clusters of varying densities. This issue is well-known and many suggestions have focused on density-based solutions [1, 9]. The fact that the ϵ-neighbourhood density estimator employed relies on distance measure, which is the source of the weakness, has been overlooked.

It is interesting to note that one of the existing solutions, i.e., SNN clustering has been incorrectly designated as density-based [9, 17] thus far. Our analysis in Section 5 has revealed that when replacing SNN (dis)similarity with the distance measure in ϵ-neighbourhood density estimator, the result is a mass estimator, not a density estimator.

Viewed from the conceptual perspective, simply changing the distance measure to a data dependent measure converts a density-based algorithm to a mass-based algorithm.

μ-neighbourhood mass can be viewed as a more general version of ϵ-neighbourhood density. However, the shape of ϵ-neighbourhood density region is fixed while the shape of μ-neighbourhood mass region depends on data distribution. We provide an example in Figure 3 that μ-neighbourhood mass has a regular shape region like ϵ-neighbourhood estimator in uniform density distribution only.

Implementations. An efficient implementation of m_p dissimilarity [2] employs a fixed-width one-dimensional histogram [3]. It partitions each attribute space into a fixed-number of cells independently, and the dissimilarity of any two instances is the total number of instances in the cells between the two instances in each attribute. In the experiments we have done in clustering and anomaly detection tasks, we found that using m_p with this implementation performs better than using distance on most datasets. However, their overall results are worse than those using m_e with the $iForest$ implementation.

The use of $iForest$ can be viewed as estimating probability from multiple variable-size multi-dimensional histograms.

Parameter ψ in iForest, used in the μ-neighbourhood estimator, is a smoothing parameter similar to k in a k-nearest neighbour density estimator. High ψ yields large trees which are sensitive to local variations in data distribution—similar effect of setting small k.

Since the default setting of $iForest$ ($\psi = 256$ and $t = 100$) can be used to provide good performance on many datasets, the implementation of mass-based dissimilarity based on $iForest$ does not create additional limitations, i.e., each existing algorithm, which has been transformed with the mass-based dissimilarity, has the same time complexity and the same number of parameters as in the original algorithm.

The generic formulation of mass-based dissimilarity allows different implementations, including different variants of $iForest$; and m_p dissimilarity [2] and SNN (dis)similarity are its special cases—all of them possess the characteristic of judged dissimilarity as prescribed by psychologists [12].

It is possible to use SNN in the contexts of kNN anomaly detection and MLkNN. However, its use has two issues. First, there are two k parameters as kNN is employed separately in the dissimilarity matrix calculation and the decision making process. Second, the high time complexity shown in Table 9 makes it prohibitive in large datasets.

Note that a mass-based neighbourhood function can be implemented using distance measure, as in the case of SNN. But, it is not only an indirect way to estimate mass but also an expensive one, as mentioned in Section 5.

Our implementation of data-dependent dissimilarity using trees opens up new research directions that worth investigating. kNN-based methods are traditionally regarded as distance-based methods; they become tree-based methods, though still employ dissimilarity measures, as we have shown here. The distinction between tree-based and distance-based methods are not clear-cut any more. Tree-based methods are usually thought to be less amenable than distance-based methods in dealing with high-dimensional datasets, especially when they consists of mostly relevant attributes. This research raises the question whether this is still true when data-dependent dissimilarity is used.

9. CONCLUDING REMARKS

We introduce a generic mass-based dissimilarity which is readily applied to existing algorithms in different tasks. The data dependent dissimilarity implemented with $iForest$ overcomes key weaknesses of three existing algorithms that rely on distance, and effectively improves their task-specific performance on density-based clustering, kNN anomaly detection and multi-label classification.

These existing algorithms are transformed by simply replacing the distance measure with the mass-based dissimilarity, leaving the rest of the procedures unchanged.

As the transformation heralds a fundamental change of perspective in finding the closest match neighbourhood, the converted algorithms are more aptly called lowest probability mass neighbour algorithms than nearest neighbour algorithms, since the lowest mass represents the least dissimilar.

In the future, we will further explore other implementations of data dependent dissimilarity and investigate their influence in different data mining tasks.

10. ACKNOWLEDGMENTS

This material is based upon work partially supported by the Air Force Office of Scientific Research, Asian Office of Aerospace Research and Development (AOARD) under award number: #FA2386-13-1-4043 and 111 Project (B14020) (Kai Ming Ting); and NSFC (61333014) and the Collaborative Innovation Center of Novel Software Technology and Industrialization (Zhi-Hua Zhou). The anonymous reviewers have provided many helpful suggestions to improve this paper.

11. REFERENCES

[1] M. Ankerst, M. M. Breunig, H.-P. Kriegel, and J. Sander. OPTICS: ordering points to identify the clustering structure. In *ACM Sigmod Record*, volume 28, pages 49–60. ACM, 1999.

[2] S. Aryal, K. M. Ting, G. Haffari, and T. Washio. m_p-dissimilarity: A data dependent dissimilarity measure. In *Proceedings of the IEEE International Conference on Data Mining*, pages 707–712, 2014.

[3] S. Aryal, K. M. Ting, G. Haffari, and T. Washio. Beyond tf-idf and cosine distance in documents dissimilarity measure. In *Proceedings of the 11th Asia Information Retrieval Societies Conference*, pages 400–406. Springer, 2015.

[4] S. D. Bay and M. Schwabacher. Mining distance-based outliers in near linear time with randomization and a simple pruning rule. In *Proceedings of the Ninth ACM International Conference on Knowledge Discovery and Data Mining*, pages 29–38. ACM, 2003.

[5] L. Breiman. Random forests. *Machine Learning*, 45(1):5–32, 2001.

[6] M. M. Breunig, H.-P. Kriegel, R. T. Ng, and J. Sander. LOF: identifying density-based local outliers. In *ACM sigmod record*, volume 29, pages 93–104. ACM, 2000.

[7] B. Chen, K. M. Ting, T. Washio, and G. Haffari. Half-space mass: a maximally robust and efficient data depth method. *Machine Learning*, 100(2-3):677–699, 2015.

[8] J. Demšar. Statistical comparisons of classifiers over multiple data sets. *The Journal of Machine Learning Research*, 7:1–30, 2006.

[9] L. Ertöz, M. Steinbach, and V. Kumar. Finding clusters of different sizes, shapes, and densities in noisy, high dimensional data. In *Proceedings of the SIAM Data Mining Conference*, pages 47–58, 2003.

[10] M. Ester, H.-P. Kriegel, J. S, and X. Xu. A density-based algorithm for discovering clusters in large spatial databases with noise. In *Proceedings of the Second International Conference on Knowledge Discovery and Data Mining*, pages 226–231, 1996.

[11] R. A. Jarvis and E. A. Patrick. Clustering using a similarity measure based on shared near neighbors. *IEEE Transactions on Computers*, 100(11):1025–1034, 1973.

[12] C. L. Krumhansl. Concerning the applicability of geometric models to similarity data: The interrelationship between similarity and spatial density. *Psychological Review*, 85(5):445–463, 1978.

[13] M. Lichman. UCI machine learning repository, 2013.

[14] D. Lin. An information-theoretic definition of similarity. In *Proceedings of the Fifteenth International Conference on Machine Learning*, pages 296–304, San Francisco, CA, USA, 1998. Morgan Kaufmann.

[15] F. T. Liu, K. M. Ting, and Z.-H. Zhou. Isolation forest. In *Proceedings of the IEEE International Conference on Data Mining*, pages 413–422, 2008.

[16] B. W. Silverman. *Density estimation for statistics and data analysis*, volume 26. CRC press, 1986.

[17] P.-N. Tan, M. Steinbach, and V. Kumar. *Introduction to Data Mining, (First Edition)*. Addison-Wesley Longman Publishing, Boston, MA, USA, 2005.

[18] K. M. Ting, G.-T. Zhou, F. T. Liu, and J. S. C. Tan. Mass estimation and its applications. In *Proceedings of the 16th ACM SIGKDD International Conference on Knowledge Discovery and Data Mining*, pages 989–998, New York, NY, USA, 2010. ACM.

[19] K. M. Ting, G.-T. Zhou, F. T. Liu, and S. C. Tan. Mass estimation. *Machine Learning*, 90(1):127–160, 2013.

[20] A. Tversky. Features of similarity. *Psychological Review*, 84(4):327–352, 1977.

[21] F. Wickelmaier. An introduction to MDS. *Sound Quality Research Unit, Aalborg University*, 2003.

[22] M.-L. Zhang and Z.-H. Zhou. ML-KNN: A lazy learning approach to multi-label learning. *Pattern Recognition*, 40(7):2038–2048, 2007.

Appendix: Algorithm for random trees

iForest consists of t *iTrees*, each built independently using a subset $\mathcal{D}$, sampled without replacement from D, where $|\mathcal{D}| = \psi$. The maximum tree height $h = \lceil log_2 \psi \rceil$. Note that the parameter e in *iTree* is initialised to 0 at the beginning of the tree building process.

Algorithm 1 *iTree*(X, e, h)

Input: X - input data; e - current height; h - height limit.
Output: an *iTree*.

```
if e ⩾ h OR |X| ⩽ 1 then
    return exNode{Size ← |X|};
else
    Randomly select an attribute q;
    Randomly select a split point p between min and
  max values of attribute q in X;
    X_l ← filter(X, q < p), X_r ← filter(X, q ⩾ p);
    return inNode{ Left ← iTree(X_l, e + 1, h),
                   Right ← iTree(X_r, e + 1, h),
                   SplitAttr ← q, SplitValue ← p};
end if
```

Just One More: Modeling Binge Watching Behavior

William Trouleau*
EPFL

Azin Ashkan
Technicolor Research

Weicong Ding
Technicolor Research

Brian Eriksson
Technicolor Research

ABSTRACT

Easy accessibility can often lead to over-consumption, as seen in food and alcohol habits. On video on-demand (VOD) services, this has recently been referred to as "binge watching", where potentially entire seasons of TV shows are consumed in a single viewing session. While a user viewership model may reveal this binging behavior, creating an accurate model has several challenges, including censored data, deviations in the population, and the need to consider external influences on consumption habits. In this paper, we introduce a novel statistical mixture model that incorporates these factors and presents a "first of its kind" characterization of viewer consumption behavior using a real-world dataset that includes playback data from a VOD service. From our modeling, we tackle various predictive tasks to infer the consumption decisions of a user in a viewing session, including estimating the number of episodes they watch and classifying if they continue watching another episode. Using these insights, we then identify binge watching sessions based on deviation from normal viewing behavior. We observe different types of binging behavior, that binge watchers often view certain content out-of-order, and that binge watching is not a consistent behavior among our users. These insights and our findings have application in VOD revenue generation, consumer health applications, and customer retention analysis.

Keywords

Binge Watching, Censored Poisson Regression, Mixture Model

1. INTRODUCTION

In recent years, the ability to record user behavior has given rise to datasets containing consumption patterns of individuals for activities as diverse as alcohol consumption [1] and gambling [2]. Of course, not all users consume at the same rate, with some users specifically over-consuming during a single session. This is a compelling problem, as the ability to identify the over consumption of food, alcohol, or gambling behavior has applications in public health [18]. The focus of this paper is on modeling and inferring the user consumption behavior in order to identify abnormal over-consumption, or "binging" behavior from real-world consumption data. Specifically, we focus on user binging of video content, or "binge watching".

For years television episodes were consumed in a standard network broadcast format, where each new episode was released once a week and then consumed one-at-a-time. In recent years, with the advent of video on-demand (VOD) services, consumers now have the ability to access full seasons of television episodes at once. This has led to the rise of binge watching, where multiple TV episodes, and potentially entire seasons, are consumed in a single viewing session. Recent market research studies have shown that over 60% of consumers binge watch on a regular basis [17]. This change in watching habits, and consumers demands to continue binge watching, has resulted in modified viewership numbers, content release schedules, and consumer expectations.

Unfortunately, the precise modeling of user binge watching behavior is difficult. While the popular press usually defines binge watching with respect to a specific number of episodes consumed for all scenarios (*e.g.,* between two and six episodes in one sitting [3]), this ignores factors such as behavior changes due to the type of content or the day of the week. To create an accurate viewership model from real-world VOD playback data, several factors must be considered. The first factor is incorporating when the user has consumed all their available items, resulting in "censored" data, where the user cannot possibly consume more but may desire to. The second is the lack of homogeneous behavior among all users, where the binge users may behave considerably different than those that consume only a handful of episodes. Finally, external factors, such as the time of day, or details about the specific object being consumed – such as, what specific show is being watched – can determine different behavioral patterns.

In this paper, we model, characterize, and infer consumption behavior of users by accommodating all the factors mentioned above using real-world playback observations. We reject a one-size-fits-all approach and create a statistical mixture model that adapts to the many sub-populations of the observed user base. Additionally, we account for the possibility of censored data and learn the contribution of covariates (*i.e.,* external factors) on the number of items consumed. The result is framing our user viewership problem as *censored Poisson regression with latent factors.* To estimate the relevant parameters of this model, we derive a novel Expectation-Maximization (EM) algorithm that incorporates these features.

Given our model, we infer various aspects of the user consumption behavior. This includes predicting the total number of episodes a user will consume from the start of a viewing session. Our technique results in an improvement of 4% in RMSE and 9% in MAE over other tested techniques. Additionally, we show how this model

*This work was completed while at Technicolor Research.

KDD '16, August 13 - 17, 2016, San Francisco, CA, USA

ISBN 978-1-4503-4232-2/16/08...$15.00

DOI: http://dx.doi.org/10.1145/2939672.2939792

can predict if the user will continue watching another episode during the session. For this application, our model results in classification AUC over 7% better than off-the-shelf techniques. These consistent improvements demonstrate the accuracy of our viewing model.

Finally, we demonstrate how this model can be used to detect binge watching sessions. We determine what constitutes "binge watching", identify sessions that involve binge watching, and show how behavior of users in such sessions deviates from normal behavior. We describe the particular television show titles and genres that cause binge watching, with the observation that comedies (like "The Big Bang Theory" and "How I Met Your Mother") result in more and longer binge watching sessions than dramatic shows (like "Homeland" and "The Walking Dead"). We also discover that users binge differently dependent on the content. On story-driven television shows (such as many dramas or "How I Met Your Mother"), a vast majority of users binge the episodes sequentially, allowing them to complete, or catch-up on, episodes quickly. On shows without a dominant storyline across episodes (such as "The Big Bang Theory" or "Modern Family"), almost half the binge sessions view episodes out-of-order, possibly as a background activity. Our insights demonstrate how binge watching is a distinctly different activity compared with regular viewing behavior.

2. RELATED WORK

Characterizing aggregate traffic on Video On-Demand (VOD) services has been a well studied area. Prior work often focused on detailing the traffic patterns from a specific service, such as TeliaSonera [4], China Telecom [22], or YouTube [7]. These specific papers focused on content popularity and viewing trends for the purposes of service improvements. This has direct application on content caching and availability, but is separate from our focus on individual user sessions. The modeling of individual user sessions in VOD was the focus of [6]. This study analyzed content popularity and how it changes as a result of individual user behavior. To the best of our knowledge, no prior VOD study targets viewer consumption patterns with the consideration of the application of binge-watching characterization and inference. To this date, the primary source of binge watching characterization has come from explicit market research surveys.

Netflix conducted a survey on the binge watching behavior of 3,078 adults aged 18 and older, of whom 1,496 people (48.6% of respondents) stream TV shows at least once a week [3]. Among these participants, 61% reported they binge watch regularly, where binge watching is defined as watching two to three episodes of a single TV series in one session. More recently, TiVo conducted a similar survey on a group of 15,196 users [17]. They define binge watching as watching 3 or more episodes in one day. The results of this survey indicate that 91% of users report binge watching as a common behavior, of whom 40% and 69% reporting they had at least one binge watching session within a week and within a month of the survey, respectively. According to the responses from both surveys, factors driving binge watching include catching up on TV shows and compensating for the delay in learning about a show since the first time it was aired. We note that all of these prior research has focused on qualitative user responses, and not on actual user playback information.

Our focus on modeling user episode playback takes the form of building regression models on event counts. Parametric regression models, such as Poisson regression model and its variants [15], have been extensively used for modeling event data. Extensions, such as censored Poisson regression model in medical and biological studies [21], and mixtures of Poisson regression has also been applied in various fields [10, 11, 16]. These extensions can be viewed as a limited case of our proposed model of censored Poisson regression with latent factors. Recently Karlis et al. [13] proposed a censored mixture Poisson regression model which is similar to our model. In contrast, we focus on session dependent censorship while this prior work considered the traditional setting where censorship threshold is fixed for all observations. Additionally, Karlis et al. simplifies their model parameter estimation, whereas our algorithm optimizes the exact likelihood. Finally, our regression model is a more general form of survival analysis, which has been commonly used in various other time-to-event domains, such as user engagement modeling and churn prediction [12], patient treatment studies [14], and auction price inference [20].

3. VIDEO ON-DEMAND DATASET

We received a sampled set of anonymized users from a US-based streaming video on-demand service across a timespan of 16 months from January 2014 to April 2015. This service is pay-per-content and consists of user interactions (*e.g.,* content play actions, pause actions, etc.) from TV, tablet, and phone devices. Our focus throughout the remainder of the paper is on modeling television consumption habits via this dataset, specifically with assessing abnormal binge consumption patterns. In order to assess viewing consumption patterns, we must first define a discrete television viewing session. Informed by prior work, we use the following definition,

DEFINITION 1. *A watching* **session** *consists of all interactions of a user containing watching at least one episode of television and with less than an hour between interactions.*

As a result, we created user viewing sessions over our sample of VOD data. We then removed the least popular shows and kept television series that have been watched in more than 100 sessions. In order to filter out infrequent users, we only kept sessions of users who purchased five or more episodes. The resulting dataset contains 65 popular television titles, 3,488 users, and 26,404 total viewing sessions across these users, with each session lasting an average of 91.8 minutes and a median of 62.0 minutes.

Considering just the number of episodes consumed in each session, the histogram can be seen in Figure 1a presented in log scale. As expected, we find a majority of users consume only a handful of episodes during each session. We also find that this distribution has a relatively heavy tail, indictating potential abnormal overconsumption behavior in some sessions.

Using this actual VOD playback dataset, we find that viewing behavior is not a consistent phenomenon. For example, in Figure 1b, we show the average number of episodes viewed per session given the day of the week. This plot indicates that viewers have shorter viewing sessions on weekdays compared with the weekend (*i.e.,* Friday, Saturday, and Sunday). Additionally, we show the average number of episodes consumed relative to the start hour of the session in Figure 1c for both weekday and weekend. Again, we find that the time context changes user behavior. In particular, there are more viewing activities during weekend nights as opposed to weekend days, and the difference between weekend and weekday views appears to be higher later in the day. Finally, our dataset also reveals different behaviors relative to the mechanism the viewer uses to consume content. We find that on mobile devices users consume on-average 1.58 episodes per session, while on televisions they consume 2.00 episodes on average.

In addition to the user context of time and device, viewing behavior is also modified by the content itself. We find that TV shows generally fall in two categories in terms of the length of their

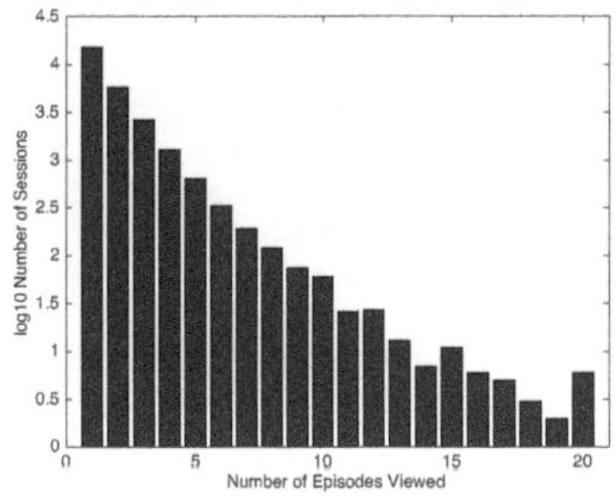

(a) Histogram with respect to the number of episodes viewed per session in log scale.

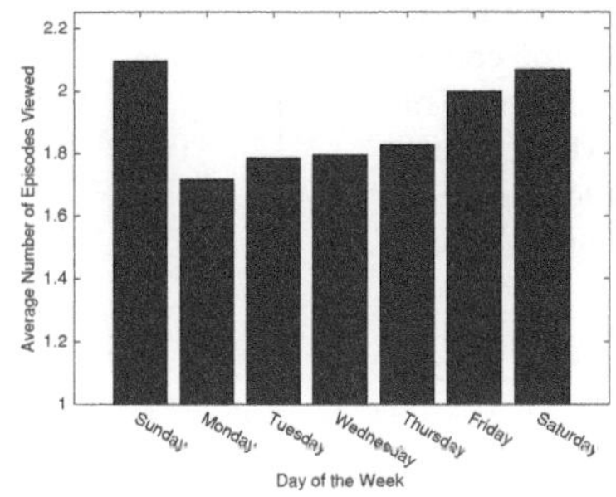

(b) Average number of episodes viewed per session relative to the day of the week.

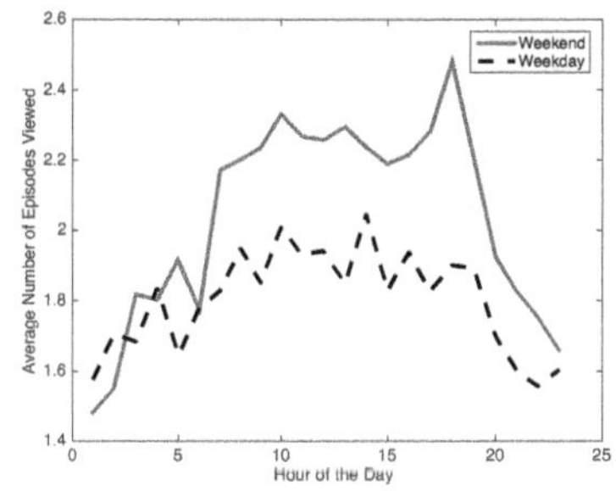

(c) Average number of episodes viewed per session relative to the hour of day.

Figure 1: Viewing statistics.

individual episodes; with episodes commonly either 22 minutes or 44 minutes in length, such that with commercials the episodes would be either a half-hour or one hour in length, respectively. In our VOD data, the average number of episodes per session is reported to be 1.79 for longer episodes whereas it is 2.54 for shorter episodes.

In Table 1, we also show the average number of episodes consumed for specific television shows. We find that this changes dramatically between different titles and different genres. For example, genres of drama/horror/action tended to have fewer episodes viewed per session compared with television shows in the comedy genre. Additionally, we find that even shows in the same genre can have different behavior, such as the more narrative driven comedy show "How I Met Your Mother" resulting in viewers watching on-average half an episode more per session compared with the less story-focused comedy of "The Big Bang Theory".

Table 1: Average Number of episodes consumed per session for given television shows.

Title	Genre	Mean Episodes per Session	Running Time per Episode
Walking Dead	Horror	1.72	44 min.
Breaking Bad	Drama	1.78	49 min.
Arrow	Action	2.01	44 min.
Big Bang Theory	Comedy	2.51	22 min.
How I Met Your Mother	Comedy	3.07	22 min.

We also need to consider the availability of content for particular television shows. For example, consider there are only three episodes of a particular television series available for the user, and the user consumes all three episodes. This is *censoring* behavior. In our dataset, we find that 20.9% of all sessions are censored, indicating that the termination of a session may not have been by user choice. We find this phenomena is not uniformly distributed across television shows, with 41.1% of "The Walking Dead" sessions censored, only 6.04% of "The Big Bang Theory" censored, and 17.4% of "How I Met Your Mother" sessions censored.

Our observations from this dataset indicate considerable differences in viewing behavior due to user context (*e.g.,* time of the day, day of the week) and the television show content. In addition, the frequent occurrence of session censorship indicates that many of the session terminations may be forced by content availability. These insights indicate the need to consider these multitude of factors in order to accurately model user viewing behavior.

4. CONSUMPTION BEHAVIOR MODEL

The characterization of our playback dataset indicates predictable patterns in user behavior. We find that certain timing, content, and metadata all result in distinct differences in viewing patterns. This points to the ability to model user behavior by incorporating these factors. An accurate viewing model allows for user behavior inference, such as, prediction of consumption, estimation of session length, and the extraction of binge watching events.

In this section, we present the assumptions and details of the proposed model of the consumption behavior of users. As mentioned earlier, a key point in our model is to account for the possibility of censorship for sessions where the user cannot consume more episodes but may, in fact, desire to. We also consider the impact of external factors, such as content and context features, on user consumption behavior. Finally, to account for the variability of behavior among user population, the proposed model consists of a mixture of components. A novel Expectation-Maximization (EM) algorithm is proposed to estimate the parameters that correspond to these factors.

4.1 Distribution Assumptions

Let v_i denote the number of episode views in the session i [1]. As defined previously, a session is the unit of interaction time of the user with the VOD in a single sitting, and the number of views is the discrete value of interest on which our model focuses. An initial assumption is that this value follows a Poisson distribution with parameter λ, whose probability mass function is,

$$f(v_i) = \Pr(v_i; \lambda) = \frac{\lambda^{v_i}}{e^{\lambda} v_i!} \quad (1)$$

We choose the Poisson distribution for this purpose mainly because it is suitable to express the probability of counting events, such as the number of episodes viewed. While different discrete distributions could be used here, such as a geometric distribution, we later find in Section 5 that this offers no improvements.

4.2 Censorship in Consumption Behavior

In the VOD domain of our interest, we consider censorship to occur if the last episode watched in a session is the latest episode of the corresponding television series that is aired and available on the VOD service at the time of viewing [2] Therefore, the act of censorship in our setting varies and depends on the current status of the show at the time of a session. For ease of notation, we introduce

[1]For ease of notation, we consider v_i to be the number of episodes consumed in session i, minus one (*e.g.,* viewing one episode would result in $v_i = 0$.)

[2]It is noted this concept of censorship is different from that of used in media content which is known as the act of suppressing unwanted parts from the content.

the value h_i to denote the number of episodes available to the user during session i. This *censorship threshold* depends on the content that is viewed in the session; hence, it is session dependent. This is different from the standard censorship setting in which a fixed censorship threshold across all observations is induced by, for instance, the ending of a clinical trial [14] or user inactivity after a certain point on the study [9].

4.3 Censored Poisson Regression with Latent Factors

We now define our consumption model that incorporates *(1)* - session censorship, *(2)* - the contribution of user context in the form of covariates, and *(3)* - the heterogeneous nature of the user population.

Censorship – We define $c_i = \mathbb{I}(v_i = h_i)$ as a binary variable indicating whether the ith session is censored, where the user has consumed the latest available episodes in the session. By assuming independence across N observed sessions, the likelihood of single Poisson distribution with censorship is obtained as:

$$\Pr(\boldsymbol{v};\lambda) = \prod_{i=1}^{N}\left[\frac{\lambda^{v_i}}{e^{\lambda}v_i!}\right]^{1-c_i}\left[\Pr(v_i \geq h_i)\right]^{c_i} \quad (2)$$

Note that in Equation (2), the likelihood of viewership for a censored observation is considered as $\Pr(v_i \geq h_i)$ to take into account the chance that the user could continue watching any further episode(s) of the series, had the episode(s) been available for viewing at the time.

External Factors – Each session i can be represented by a group of external factors, such as the viewing device used, the time of day, etc. These constitute the vector of d covariates $\mathbf{x}_i = (x_{i,1},\ldots,x_{i,d})^\top$. Instead of assuming a fixed λ parameter for all sessions (as in Eq. (1) and (2)), a session dependent parameter λ_i is introduced to capture the dependency of consumption rate on these factors as discussed in Section 3. We use the log-linear function commonly used as the link function in Poisson regressions,

$$\log\lambda_i = \mathbf{x}_i^\top\boldsymbol{\beta} \quad (3)$$

where $\boldsymbol{\beta} = (\beta_1,\ldots,\beta_d)^\top$ is the corresponding coefficient vector. This facilitates the derivation of our EM algorithm presented later.

Mixture Components – Finally, to account for the variability in the behavior of the user population, we consider a mixture of Poisson distributions to model the heterogeneous consumption behavior between sessions.

Let K denote the number of mixture components, and $k \in \{1\ldots K\}$ denote the index of each component. The probability mass for v_i can be written as follows:

$$\Pr(v_i;\boldsymbol{\beta},\boldsymbol{\pi}) = \sum_{k=1}^{K}\pi_k\left[\frac{\lambda_{i,k}^{v_i}}{e^{\lambda_{i,k}}v_i!}\right]^{1-c_i}\left[\Pr_k(v_i \geq h_i)\right]^{c_i} \quad (4)$$

where π_k is the weight of the mixture component k, $\pi_k \geq 0$, $\sum_{k=1}^{K}\pi_k = 1$, and $\Pr_k(v_i \geq h_i)$ is the likelihood of watching at least h_i episodes in the session according to component k of the mixture model. Finally, the likelihood of all N sessions is:

$$\Pr(\boldsymbol{v};\boldsymbol{\beta},\boldsymbol{\pi}) = \prod_{i=1}^{N}\sum_{k=1}^{K}\pi_k\left[\frac{\lambda_{i,k}^{v_i}}{e^{\lambda_{i,k}}v_i!}\right]^{1-c_i}\left[\Pr_k(v_i \geq h_i)\right]^{c_i} \quad (5)$$

Note that, the session dependent Poisson parameter and the coefficient vector, respectively denoted by $\lambda_{i,k}$ and $\boldsymbol{\beta}_k$, both depend on the component k. In other words, the heterogeneity of the user population results in various behavioral patterns that are captured by different variants of these parameters. Similar to Equation (3), the log-linear relation holds between these two parameters in each component k: $\log(\lambda_{i,k}) = \mathbf{x}_i^\top\boldsymbol{\beta}_k$. It is noted that the censored likelihood $\Pr_k(v_i \geq h_i)$ is calculated using the session dependent consumption rate $\lambda_{k,i}$, hence, it is also a function of $\boldsymbol{\beta}_k$. A summary of notations is provided in Table 2.

Table 2: List of notations.

Notation	Definition
$\mathbf{x}_i$	Covariate vector of each session i
v_i	The number of views in each session i
h_i	The number of episodes available for session i
c_i	Censorship indicator for each session i
$\lambda_{i,k}$	Poisson parameter for component $k \in \{1,\ldots,K\}$ and corresponding to session i
$\boldsymbol{\beta}_k$	Coefficient vector for component $k \in \{1,\ldots,K\}$
π_k	Mixture weight for component $k \in \{1,\ldots,K\}$

4.4 Parameter Estimation

We consider Maximum Likelihood Estimation (MLE) for the model parameters $\Theta = \{\boldsymbol{\beta}_k,\pi_k\}_{k=1}^{K}$ given N observed sessions, their covariates, and the session dependent censorship thresholds.

A closed-form MLE is intractable in our mixture model, hence we instead use an Expectation-Maximization (EM) based approximation [5, 8]. We note that the introduction of covariates and session dependent censorship requires the derivation of a specific EM algorithm for our model.

Let $z_i \in \{1,\ldots,K\}$ be the mixture assignment of session i. Our goal is to lower bound the data likelihood function by,

$$\log\Pr(v_i;\Theta) \geq \sum_{k=1}^{K} q(z_i = k)\log\frac{\Pr(v_i, z_i = k;\Theta)}{q(z_i = k)} \quad (6)$$

and maximize this lower-bound. In the E-Step of the iteration t of the algorithm, we fix $\Theta = \Theta^{(t-1)}$ from M-Step of the previous iteration and maximize the lower-bound with respect to all distributions $q(z)$; in the M-Step, we fix $q(z)$ and find the optimum $\Theta^{(t)}$ that maximizes the lower-bound. The E-Step and M-Step are conducted alternatively.

E-Step: By Jensen's inequality, the optimal solution for $q(z)$ is $q(z_i = k) = \Pr(z_i = k|v_i;\Theta^{(t-1)})$ with $\Theta^{(t-1)}$ from previous iteration. This can be calculated explicitly,

$$\tau_{i,k}^{(t-1)} := \Pr(z_i = k|v_i;\Theta^{(t-1)}) \quad (7)$$

$$= \frac{\pi_k^{(t-1)}\left[\frac{(\lambda_{i,k}^{(t-1)})^{v_i}}{e^{\lambda_{i,k}^{(t-1)}}\,v_i!}\right]^{1-c_i}\left[\Pr_k^{(t-1)}(v_i \geq h_i)\right]^{c_i}}{\sum_{j=1}^{K}\pi_j^{(t-1)}\left[\frac{(\lambda_{i,j}^{(t-1)})^{v_i}}{e^{\lambda_{i,j}^{(t-1)}}\,v_i!}\right]^{1-c_i}\left[\Pr_k^{(t-1)}(v_i \geq h_i)\right]^{c_i}}$$

where $\Pr_k^{(t-1)}$ is calculated using $\Theta^{(t-1)}$. Note that $\tau_{i,k}$ is the posterior probability of the session i being sampled from mixture component k.

M-Step: Using Eq (7), the lower-bound in Eq. (6) after E-Step can be written as:

$$Q(\Theta;\Theta^{(t-1)}) = \sum_{i=1}^{N}\sum_{k=1}^{K}\tau_{i,k}^{(t-1)}\Big[\log(\pi_k) + c_i\log(\Pr_k(v_i \geq h_i))$$
$$+(1-c_i)(v_i\log(\lambda_{i,k}) - \log(v_i!) - \lambda_{i,k})\Big] \quad (8)$$

Now we optimize $\Theta^{(t)} = \arg\max Q(\Theta;\Theta^{(t-1)})$. For π_k:

$$\pi_k^{(t)} = \arg\max \sum_{i=1}^{N} \tau_{i,k}^{(t-1)} \log(\pi_k) + \gamma(1 - \sum_j \pi_j) \quad (9)$$

where γ is the Lagrange multiplier to take into account the constraint that π_j values must sum to one. For $\boldsymbol{\beta}_k$, we numerically solve the following problem:

$$\boldsymbol{\beta}_k^{(t)} = \arg\max \sum_{i=1}^{N} \tau_{i,k}^{(t-1)} \Big[(1 - c_i)(v_i \log(\lambda_{i,k}) - \lambda_{i,k}) \quad (10)$$
$$+ c_i \log(\Pr_k(v_i \geq h_i))\Big]$$

The detailed derivations can be found in Appendix.

Algorithm 1 Censored EM Algorithm: `EM-fit`

Input: Session covariates $\{x_i\}$, consumption observations $\{v_i\}$, censorship thresholds $\{h_i\}$, number of iterations T, number of components K.
Initialize parameters $\Theta^{(0)} = (\boldsymbol{\pi}^{(0)}, \boldsymbol{\beta}^{(0)})$
for $t \in 1 \dots T$ **do**
  E-Step: Compute $\tau_{i,k}^{(t)}$ using Equation 7, for $i = 1 \dots N$, $k = 1 \dots K$.
  M-Step: Compute $\pi_k^{(t)}$ using Equation 9, and $\boldsymbol{\beta}_k^{(t)}$ using Equation 10, for $k = 1 \dots K$
end for
Output: Estimated parameter values, $\widehat{\Theta} = (\boldsymbol{\pi}^{(T)}, \boldsymbol{\beta}^{(T)})$

We present the pseudocode of the estimation algorithm, called `EM-fit` , in Algorithm 1. `EM-fit` receives three session dependent inputs: covariates $\mathbf{x}_i$, episode counts v_i, and the corresponding censorship criterion h_i for sessions $i = 1, \dots, N$, and the number of components K. `EM-fit` iterates over the E-Step and M-Step for T steps, where T is the index of the step in which the convergence criterion is satisfied. We use the common convergence criterion that the algorithm is deemed to have converged when the change in the data log-likelihood falls below some threshold, which we specify in Section 5.

5. EXPERIMENTAL STUDY

In this section, we present results on the real-world VOD viewership dataset described in Section 3. We first show that our model can fit better than simpler models and that each of our factors contribute to a more accurate fit to our observed data. We then show that our model can be used to predict user behaviors in two application scenarios: inferring the number of episodes viewed in a session and classifying if the user will continue to watch the next episode.

To infer our model parameters, we run Algorithm 1. For the specific choice of covariates, $\mathbf{x}_i$, we consider the following:

– The title of television series, *e.g., Arrow*, *Homeland*
– The hour in the day when a session starts, *e.g.,* 7 AM, 10 PM
– The day of week when a session starts, *e.g.,* Monday
– The device used in the session, *e.g.,* iPad, iPhone, television

All these features are binarized and concatenated, resulting in a feature vector for each session of dimension 104.

We run Algorithm 1 until the change of the log-likelihood on training data is below 0.01%. For updating the coefficient vectors, $\boldsymbol{\beta}_k$, we use gradient descent and stop when the frobenius norm of gradient is below 0.01. Parameter vector $\boldsymbol{\beta}_k^{(0)}$ is randomly initialized and $\boldsymbol{\pi}^{(0)}$ is uniformly initialized from the $K - 1$ dimensional simplex. To avoid local minimas, we use 10 random initialization for Algorithm 1. Finally, all results in this section are presented with respect to 5-fold cross validation.

5.1 Model Selection

First the hypothesis of using the Poisson distribution is tested. We compare the Poisson distribution against another candidate, geometric distribution. The estimation for geometric distribution with covariates, censorship, and latent factors can be similarly derived as we performed for the Poisson case in Section 4. Figure 2 compares the empirical probabilities of the observed number of episodes per session with the fitted models for a single Poisson, single geometric distribution, mixture Poisson ($K = 3$) and mixture geometric ($K = 3$). We find the average log-likelihood to be -1.30 for single Geometric, -1.34 for single Poisson, -1.27 for mixture of Geometric, and -1.12 for mixture of Poisson. We find that although a single geometric distribution can fit better than a single Poisson distribution, the mixture of Poisson can fit best to the data. The figure demonstrates that this is especially true with respect to the tail of the distribution. It is also known that mixture of Poisson distributions often have thick tails which make them suitable for long-tailed data [19]. This reinforces our decision to use the Poisson distribution in our model.

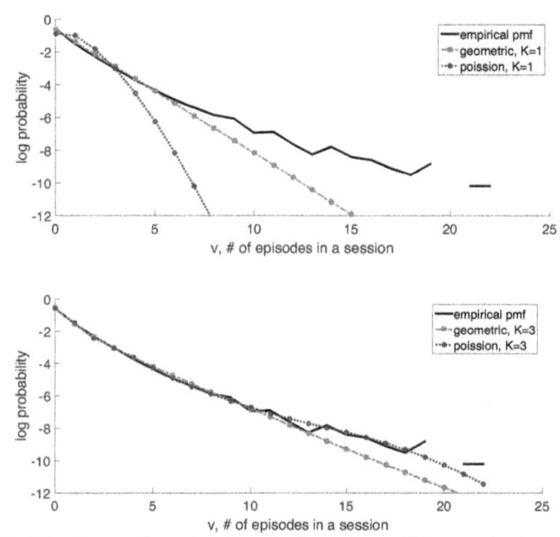

Figure 2: The learned model for single Poisson/Geometric (upper), and mixture Poisson/Geometric (bottom) on the VOD data.

Next, we consider the choice of the number of mixture components K. The *predictive log-likelihood* is used as a performance metric and evaluated using 5-fold cross-validation. Specifically, we estimate the model parameters $\{\boldsymbol{\beta}_k, \pi_k\}_{k=1}^K$ from the training set and then evaluate the log-likelihood of the hold-out validation set for various values of K. We also normalize the log-likelihood by the number of sessions in the validation set.

The average predictive log-likelihood across 5-fold cross-validation as well as the standard deviation of this value are depicted in Figure 3. We observe that $K = 3$ is the knee point of the curve: by increasing $K = 1$ to $K = 3$ the likelihood improves by a large margin. Meanwhile, for $K > 3$ there is no significant change in likelihood. This suggests that $K = 3$ is a good candidate. As a result, we fix $K = 3$ for the rest of the paper.

5.2 Model Component Performance

We next compare the performance of our proposed model against multiple baselines in fitting to the real-world data. These baselines can be viewed as different combinations of the three key factors - *mixture*, *censorship*, and *covariates*. They are summarized in Ta-

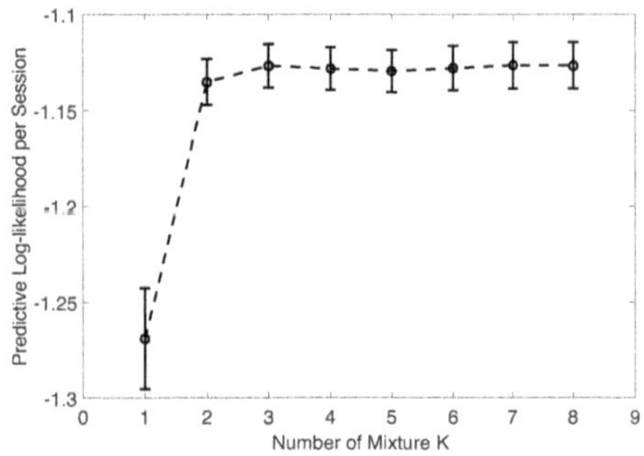

Figure 3: Predictive log-likelihood for various values of K.

Table 3: Settings of the proposed model and various baselines. 'Y' represents the existence of mixture, censorship or covariates in the model. 'N' represents their absence. Our model is 'H'.

Description	ID	Mixture	Censoring	Covariate
Single Poisson	A	N	N	N
Poisson Regression	B	N	N	Y
Mixture Poisson	C	Y	N	N
Poisson Regression with Latent Factors	D	Y	N	Y
Censored Poisson	E	N	Y	N
Censored Single Poisson Regression	F	N	Y	Y
Censored Mixture Poisson	G	Y	Y	N
Proposed Model	H	Y	Y	Y

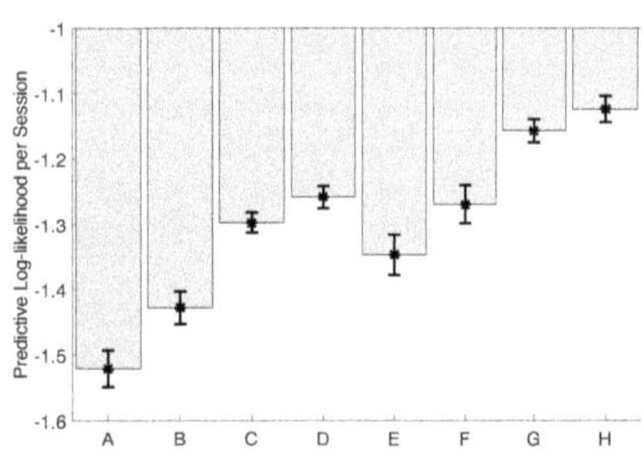

Figure 4: Predictive log-likelihood of the proposed model comparing to various baselines as detailed in Table 3. The predictive log-likelihood measures the goodness of fit of each model.

ble 3. For instance, the censored Poisson regression model (F) is a special case of our model when $K = 1$. As a consequence, we can understand the importance and significance of these components of our model. We note that EM-based estimation algorithms can similarly be derived for these models.

We use predictive log-likelihood on 5-fold cross-validation as the performance metric to evaluate the robustness of different settings as adding modeling complexity does not necessarily improve the predictive likelihood. The results are shown in Figure 4. The log-likelihoods are normalized by the number of sessions in each validation set and the standard deviations over 5-folds are reported.

Overall, our model achieves the best predictive accuracy compared to all the baselines. We find that introduction of latent factors, the censorship, and the covariates all contribute significantly to improving modeling accuracy. One can compare the proposed model (H) against the model without mixtures (F) and observe that adding these mixture components can improve the modeling accuracy by a large margin. Additionally, the improvement of our model (H) versus one without censoring (D) shows that incorporating censorship knowledge also significantly enhances the modeling accuracy.

5.3 Use Case: Predicting the number of episodes in a session

We consider predicting the number of episodes a user will watch given information available at the beginning of a session. Noting that we observe the covariates $\mathbf{x}_i$ and the censorship threshold h_i when session starts, we predict the number of episodes a user will watch $\hat{v}_i$ as,

$$\hat{v}_i = \mathbb{E}(v; \boldsymbol{\beta}, \boldsymbol{\pi}) = \sum_{k=1}^{K} \pi_k \mathbb{E}(v; \boldsymbol{\beta}_k) \tag{11}$$

where $\mathbb{E}(v; \boldsymbol{\beta}_k) = \sum_{j=0}^{h_i-1} j \Pr(j;\ \lambda_{i,k}) + h_i \Pr_k(v \geq h_i;\ \lambda_{i,k})$ is the censored expectation of a single Poisson distribution, with $\lambda_{i,k} = \exp(\mathbf{x}_i^\top \boldsymbol{\beta}_k)$ as the session dependent Poisson rates and the parameters $\boldsymbol{\beta}_k$ and π_k are learned from the training set.

We predict the number of episodes viewed in a session as the expectation based on the session dependent covariates and censorship threshold. It is noted that Eq. (11) guarantees that $\hat{v}_i \leq h_i$ in prediction using our censored model.

Table 4: The predictive root-mean-square-error (Pred.RMSE) and the predictive mean absolute error (Pred.MAE) of the proposed model against various statistical and regression baselines.

Description	ID	Pred.RMSE	Pred.MAE
Single Poisson	A	1.573 ± 0.048	1.027 ± 0.011
Poisson Regression	B	1.513 ± 0.047	0.995 ± 0.009
Mixture Poisson	C	1.573 ± 0.048	1.027 ± 0.011
Poisson Regression with Latent Factors	D	1.513 ± 0.049	0.993 ± 0.009
Censored Poisson	E	1.517 ± 0.049	0.920 ± 0.016
Censored Poisson Regression	F	1.456 ± 0.051	0.895 ± 0.015
Censored Mixture Poisson	G	1.514 ± 0.050	0.926 ± 0.017
Proposed Model	H	$\mathbf{1.452 \pm 0.052}$	$\mathbf{0.895 \pm 0.016}$
Linear Regression	L2	1.517 ± 0.047	0.993 ± 0.008
Thresholded Linear Regression	TL2	1.512 ± 0.046	0.988 ± 0.008
ℓ_1-Regularized Linear Regression	Lasso	1.624 ± 0.048	0.924 ± 0.015

The problem of predicting v_i when a session starts can be viewed as a regression problem where the response variable is v_i and the regression features are $\mathbf{x}_i$ and h_i. Therefore, we compare our algorithm against standard linear regression, ℓ_1 regularized linear regression (Lasso), and Poisson regression (log-linear regression, the setting 'B' as in Table 3). Additionally, we perform a version of linear regression that considers the censorship threshold h_i, such that for linear coefficients $\boldsymbol{\beta}$, the inferred value is $\hat{v}_i = \min\left(h_i, \mathbf{x}_i^\top \boldsymbol{\beta}\right)$, we refer to this as *Thresholded Linear Regression*.

As evaluation metrics, we compute the predictive root mean square error (**RMSE**) and mean absolute error (**MAE**) on the validation set using 5-fold cross-validation. We compare our model against the statistical baselines in Section 5.2 and the regression baselines, using the same setting id as in Table 3 for consistency. The mean and standard deviation across 5-fold cross-validation for Predictive RMSE and MAE are summarized in Table 4.

As it is observed in the table, the proposed model ('H') outperforms the regression baselines (linear regression, Lasso, Poisson regression) in both RMSE and MAE metrics. We note that all linear regression methods directly minimize the square error as training objective, hence they are given the advantage in term of RMSE metric. Therefore the improvement is not expected to be significant. Our model, however, outperforms these baselines in prediction while not explicitly optimizing RMSE or MAE. This suggests that our model can better predict the user behavior given the external factors. We note that the censored Poisson Regression ('F') can predict as accurate as our model, due to the fact the we use the expectation in Eq. (11) and the latent mixture assignment is marginalized.

5.4 Use Case: Predicting if the user will watch the next episode

Another application of our viewership model is to predict the continuation of a viewing session. Specifically, given the number of episodes a user has already watched in the middle of a session v_c, we would like to predict if they will continue to watch the next episode. Given our model, we use $\Pr(v > v_c | v_c; \boldsymbol{\beta}, \boldsymbol{\pi})$ as the probability of continuation, where $\boldsymbol{\beta}, \boldsymbol{\pi}$ are learned from the training set. This conditional probability can be calculated as,

$$\begin{aligned} \Pr(v > v_c | v_c; \boldsymbol{\beta}, \boldsymbol{\pi}) &= \sum_{z=1}^{K} p_z(v > v_c | v_c; \boldsymbol{\beta}, \boldsymbol{\pi}) p(z | v_c; \boldsymbol{\beta}, \boldsymbol{\pi}) \\ &= \sum_{z=1}^{K} \frac{p_z(v > v_c; \boldsymbol{\beta}, \boldsymbol{\pi})}{p_z(v \geq v_c; \boldsymbol{\beta}, \boldsymbol{\pi})} p(z | v_c; \boldsymbol{\beta}, \boldsymbol{\pi}) \end{aligned} \quad (12)$$

where $p(z|v_c; \boldsymbol{\beta}, \boldsymbol{\pi})$ is the posterior likelihood of component membership given the current watched episodes as in Eq. (7).

We then predict the event of continuation by thresholding this conditional probability. Note that this prediction problem is a standard binary classification problem where class labels are 1 if the user continued to watch or 0 if the user stopped. Therefore, we compare our model against the standard classification algorithms using logistic regression and support vector machines (SVMs).

Table 5: The Area Under Curve (AUC) and Cross Entropy of the proposed model compared against various statistical and classification baselines.

Description	ID	AUC	Cross Entropy
Single Poisson	A	0.438 ± 0.003	-0.803 ± 0.006
Poisson Regression	B	0.539 ± 0.004	-0.754 ± 0.006
Mixture Poisson	C	0.530 ± 0.009	-0.727 ± 0.004
Poisson Regression with Latent Factors	D	0.618 ± 0.003	-0.703 ± 0.004
Censored Poisson	E	0.572 ± 0.006	-0.711 ± 0.009
Censored Poisson Regression	F	0.642 ± 0.008	-0.670 ± 0.009
Censored Mixture Poisson	G	0.631 ± 0.007	-0.652 ± 0.005
Proposed model	H	$\mathbf{0.687 \pm 0.005}$	$\mathbf{-0.636 \pm 0.006}$
ℓ_2-Regularized Logistic Regression	LR	0.631 ± 0.005	-0.664 ± 0.002
Linear SVM	SVM	0.617 ± 0.005	NA

For each session i with v_i television episodes, we can construct v_i training or testing samples at the end of each episode. We first create 5-fold cross-validation on the sessions and further convert each session in training and validation sets into continuation data. We consider a collection of performance metrics: the Area Under Curve (AUC), the predictive cross entropy, and the correct classification rate evaluated on validation sets. The cross entropy can be computed as $\sum_i \sum_{j=1}^{v_i} y_j \log(p_j^+) + (1 - y_j) \log(1 - p_j^+)$ averaged over all test samples, where y_j is the label of continuation and p_j^+ is the probability of continuation for j-th test sample.

Table 5 summarizes the prediction result for our model against the statistical baselines summarized in Section 5.2 and the classification baselines. The mean and standard deviation across the 5-folds are reported. We observe that in Table 5, the proposed model outperforms the compared approaches in all performance metrics.

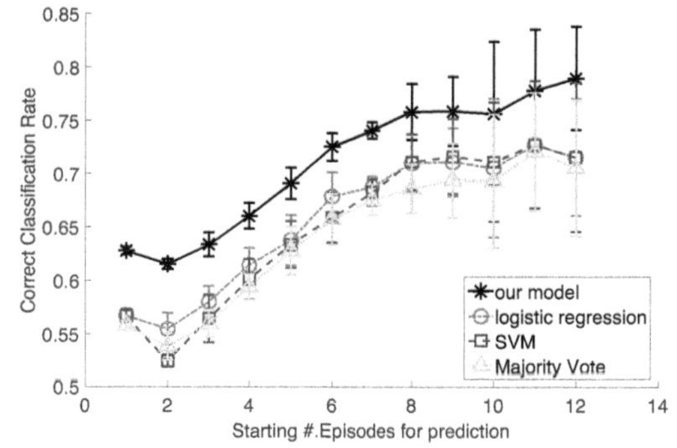

Figure 5: Classification rates on validation set when considering the current episode for the user.

We also investigate how the prediction accuracy changes as the user watches more episodes. Specifically, we design the experiment to only predict the continuation when v_c is above a certain threshold. Figure 5 summarizes the results for our model and standard classification algorithms. Note that the number of training/validation samples are smaller and more biased when the threshold for v_c increases. Therefore, we also include the simple majority votes rules as baselines. For simple majority vote, we predict a user would continue after watching v episodes if most training samples at the end of v episodes continued. As we can see in Figure 5, the prediction accuracy increases as the threshold on v_c increases. This matches the intuition that the event of continuation is easier to predict if we have more observation history in a single session. However, our algorithm consistently outperforms the baselines. This shows that our model can accurately infer the behavior type of a session and make predictions as we gather more observations in a session.

6. BINGE WATCHING CHARACTERIZATION AND DISCUSSION

The experimental study in Section 5 validates that our proposed model both fits to the data and also has applications in inferring user viewing behavior. We can also use this model to segment particular behaviors automatically from our model inference algorithm. In this section, we discuss how our model can be used to categorize and interpret distinct types of viewing behavior. In particular, we focus on the over-conusumption of content, or "binge watching" behavior.

6.1 Identifying Binge Watching Behavior

We begin by considering the real-world implications of our learned mixture model. Given $K = 3$ mixture components, Figure 6 depicts the distribution of each component of the learned model for the three most popular television series in the dataset, "Walking Dead", "Homeland", and "The Big Bang Theory".

We find that the learned mixture components reveal three distinct behaviors that are consistent across the dataset. (1) The component with the smallest λ captures the sessions where the user watches a few (*i.e.,* one or two) episodes in a session. (2) The component with the λ value in between those of the other two corresponds to the sessions in which user consumes an above average number of episodes (*i.e.,* 3 to 7) as indicated by the green curves in Figure 6. (3) The third component with the largest consumption rate λ (the red curves in Figure 6) represents users who watch an extreme number of episodes in a session.

We find these different types of behavior to be consistent not only across the examples in Figure 6 but also hold for all data sam-

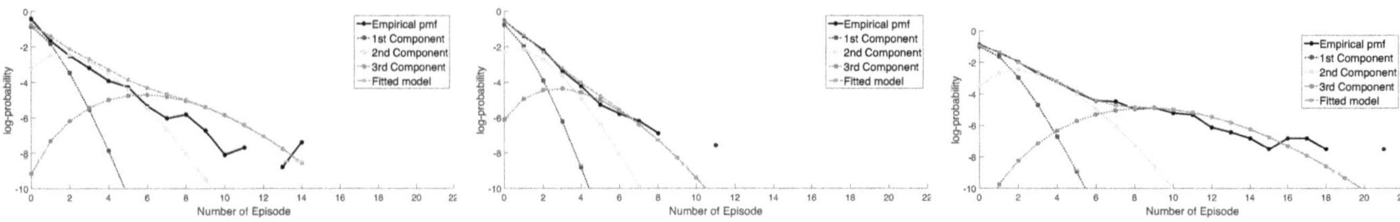

Figure 6: Empirical pmf and the fitted distribution of our model of television watching sessions for "The Walking Dead" (left), "Homeland" (middle), and "The Big Bang Theory" (right). The $K = 3$ mixture components are shown.

ples. This is validated by Figure 7 in which we plot the distributions for the learned Poisson parameters $\lambda_{i,k}$ for each component ($k = 1, 2, 3$) and across all viewing sessions[3]. Overall, the consumption rates for the three components are distinct. The average consumption rate for the second component is 2.9 episodes per session and is 6.8 for the third component. These two components are in accordance with the "*binge watching*" in prior studies [3, 17]. This motivates us to define these two component as the binge-watching components.

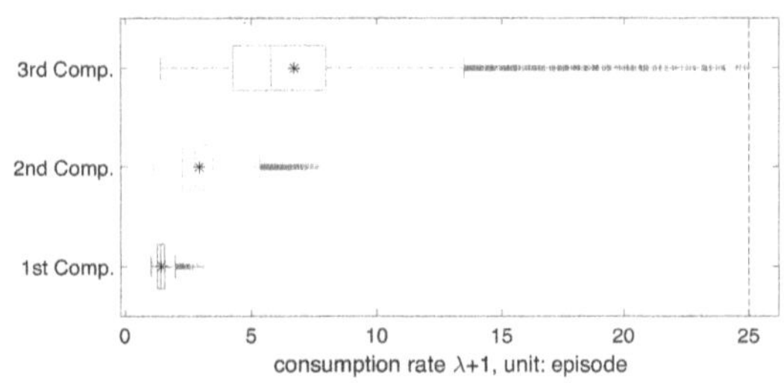

Figure 7: Box-plot of the distribution of $\lambda_{i,k} + 1$ across the three compoenents. The central mark is the median, the edges of the box are the 25th and 75th percentiles. * indicates the mean. The color scheme is consistent with Figure 6.

A Data-Driven Binge Watching Definition - Given the two components associated with binge watching behavior, we then identify a binge-watching session by calculating $\Pr(z_i = k|v_i; \boldsymbol{\beta}, \boldsymbol{\pi})$ according to (7), the posterior mixture assignment of session i to component k. Formally, we define a session to be a binge-watching session if $k = 2$ or $k = 3$ is the most likely mixture assignment of the session. This provides a fully data-driven approach to define and infer binge-watching behavior.

Different Types of Binge Watching - While existing studies characterize binge-watching as a single type of viewing behavior [3, 17], our model reveals that there are in fact two sub-classes of binge-watching. Specifically, the component $k = 3$ captures the sessions in which a significantly large number of episodes is consumed. This is a rather extreme behavior than the component $k = 2$. Therefore, we define the component $k = 3$ as "hyper-binge" watching and corresponding sessions as "hyper-binge" watching sessions. We believe this gives a finer-grain analysis of binge-watching behavior. Similarly, we refer to sessions corresponding to component $k = 2$ as the "binge" watching sessions, and the ones corresponding to component $k = 1$ as the "regular" sessions.

Using this definition, we find that 22.2% of all watching sessions fall in one category of binge watching, *i.e.,* binge watching sessions or hyper-binge watching sessions. To be more explicit, 20.1% of sessions are binging sessions and 2.1% of sessions are hyper-binging sessions. This indicates that "hyper-binging" is a rare yet extreme viewing behavior.

[3]Noting that we subtract 1 from v_i to simplify the model derivation, we plot $\lambda + 1$.

Content and Context-Aware Binge Watching Definition - Our model learns differences between the viewing behavior for different types of shows, days of the week, and devices used for watching. These are summarized in Figures 8, 9, and 10. In these figures, the distributions of $\lambda_{i,k}$ across the three components are shown.

Recall that in most binge-watching studies so far, a one-size-fits-all definition of binging is used [17]. However, Figure 8 shows that binge-watching in our model is adapted to the content of specific watching sessions. For example, in Figure 8, a binge watching session ($k = 2$) for the 20-minutes-long comedy "How I Met Your Mother" has on average more than five episodes while the 1-hour long action drama "Homeland" has on average only two episodes when binging. Similarly, a hyper-binge watching session ($k = 3$) for "How I Met Your Mother" has on average more than 10 episodes per session while that of "Homeland" reveals only four episodes. We can also observe that the less story-focused comedy, "The Big Bang Theory", is binge-watched and hyper-binge watched with a smaller consumption rate than "How I Met Your Mother", which is narrative-driven (*i.e.,* the episodes are connected by a common storyline).

Figures 9 and 10 demonstrate that our binge watching definition is context-aware. We observe that binge and hyper-binge watching sessions on Friday, Saturday, and Sunday have more episodes viewed compared to that of weekdays. Similarly, the dominance of using TV devices (*i.e.,* tv and blu-ray) over mobile (*i.e.,* iPad, and iPhone) appears to be more significance for binge watching and hyper-binge watching sessions compared to regular sessions.

Finally, we consistently observe the distinction between the hyper-binge component $k = 3$ and the binge component $k = 2$ in terms of consumption rate across different contents and context in Figures 8, 9, and 10. In addition, we note that the consumption rates for the first component are between one and two episodes per session. This suggests that the regular component $k = 1$ captures a uniform behavior across all sessions.

6.2 Binge Watching Behavior Characterization

A characterization of binge watching behavior is presented here in terms of *(1)* binge watching behavior across individual users, *(2)* difference in viewing patterns between binging and non-binging sessions, and *(3)* the transition patterns among different viewing behavior types.

User Characterization - Given the most likely component assignment for all sessions of a particular user, we calculate the fraction of sessions that correspond to one of the three components. For each component, we sort the fraction of users in ascending order and summarize the results in Figure 11. We note that the points on different curves with the same x-value may not correspond to the same user. Figure 11 indicates that binge-watching is not a uniform behavior across the user-population. We find that 64% of users in our dataset binge-watched at least once while 11% of users hyper-

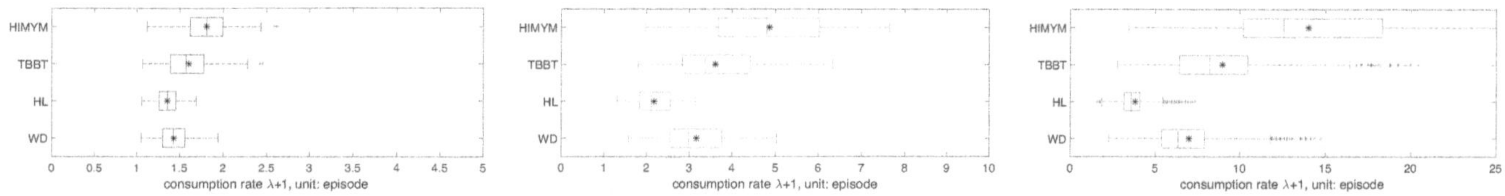

Figure 8: Box-plot of the distribution of $\lambda_{i,k}$ across the three components for four TV series: "The Walking Dead" (WD), "Homeland" (HL), "The Big Bang Theory" (TBBT), and "How I Met Your Mother" (HIMYM). $*$ indicates the mean. **Left:** Regular, **Middle:** Binge, **Right:** Hyper-binge.

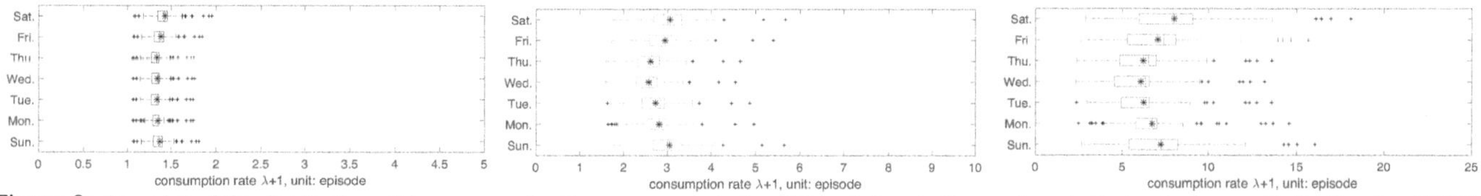

Figure 9: Box-plot of the distribution of $\lambda_{i,k}$ across the three components for different days in the week. $*$ indicates the mean. **Left:** Regular, **Middle:** Binge, **Right:** Hyper-binge.

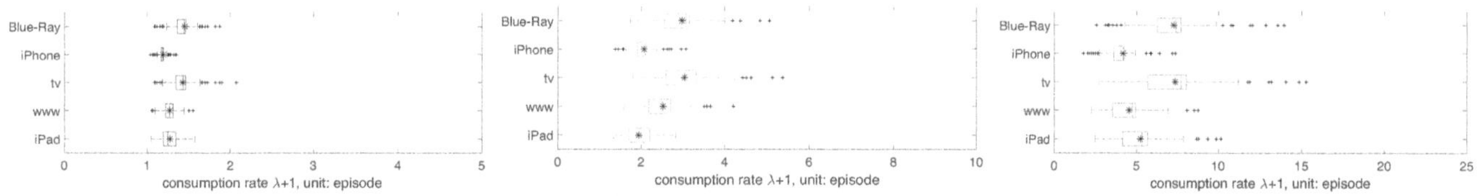

Figure 10: Box-plot of the distribution of $\lambda_{i,k}$ across the three components for a group of devices. $*$ indicates the mean. 'www' denotes watching sessions on web-browsers from non-mobile devices. **Left:** Regular, **Middle:** Binge, **Right:** Hyper-binge.

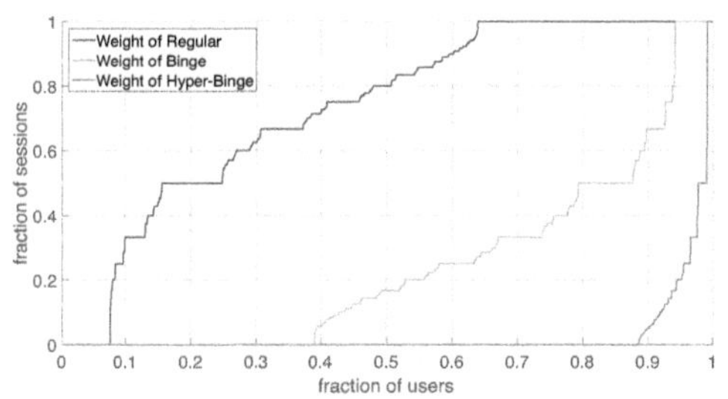

Figure 11: Distribution of different types of viewing sessions across users.

binged at least once. These numbers are consistent with the ones reported in prior user studies [3, 17], conveying that binge watching is popular among viewers. We also observe that for 7.6% of users, all their watching sessions are binge-watching. Similarly, 20% of users binge-watch in more than half of their sessions.

Viewing Patterns - While it is common that episodes are watched in a sequential order in a session to catch-up content, we find that this is not necessarily true for binge-watching. For instance, user might watch episode 10 and then go back to episode 7 or jump to episode 15 in a session. Table 6 summarizes the percentage of sessions that are watched in a sequential order across different components. While regular sessions are almost entirely sequential (97%), we observe 84% of binge watching sessions and only 76% of the hyper-binge watching sessions are sequential, indicating that binge viewers are more likely to watch content out-of-order.

A detailed investigation shows that this distinction in viewing patterns also depends on specific content. For example, story-driven series "Walking Dead", "Homeland", and "How I Met Your Mother" are more likely to be watched in sequential order for both binge and non-binge watching sessions. In contrast, binge-watching implies a different viewing pattern for series like "The Big Bang Theory", "Modern Family", and "NCIS" where each episode is self-contained. We find that only 56% of binge watching and 52% of hyper-binge watching sessions of "The Big Bang Theory" are viewed in a sequential order. In other words, potentially half of the binge-watching sessions of "The Big Bang Theory" are not primarily for "catching-up" on the series.

Table 6: Fraction of sessions with sequential viewing across components.

Title	Regular	Binge	Hyper-binge
All Series	97%	84%	76%
Walking Dead	98%	87%	85%
Homeland	98%	94%	96%
HIMYM	97%	88%	77%
Big Bang Theory	87%	56%	52%
Modern Family	83%	59%	78%
NCIS	98%	71%	67%

Table 7: Transition probability of next session being type j (j-th column) given current session being type i (i-th row).

	Regular	Binge	Hyper-binge
Regular	0.82	0.16	0.02
Binge	0.66	0.30	0.04
Hyper-binge	0.59	0.32	0.09

Transition between Behavior Types - Given the component assignment of each session, we can calculate the probability of the next session being type j given the previous session being type i of the same user. This standard transition probability matrix is illustrated in Table 7. We find that a user currently binging is twice as likely to binge in their next session compared with someone currently in a regular session. We also observe that a majority of binge watchers will not binge on content in their next session, indicating that binge watching is not a consistent behavior for users.

7. CONCLUSION

The combination of video on-demand services and access to entire collections of television episodes has led to the rise of binge watching behavior. In this paper, we offered a "first of its kind" study of viewer binge watching habits from real-world video on-demand records. We characterized the real-world observations to determine relevant context covariates and limitations – such as data censorship. Using these insights, we constructed a statistical viewership model and validated that it fits better to the data than all other tested models. We then showed how this viewership model can be used to infer features of the user viewing session, such as the number of episodes viewed and whether the user will continue watching. Finally, we exploit the properties of this model to introduce a methodology that automatically extracts attributes of binge watching behavior. Our characterization reveals different types of binging behavior, the prevalence of binge watchers viewing content out-of-order, and that binge watching is not a consistent behavior among our users. Next steps include modeling user-level behavior, examination of mechanisms to influence binge watching behavior, analysis of binge consumption of other types of products (*e.g.,* video games, gambling, etc.) and how it differs from television binge watching.

8. REFERENCES

[1] Alcohol Research Group Datasets. http://arg.org/resources-tools/databases/.

[2] The Transparency Project. http://www.thetransparencyproject.org/.

[3] Netflix declares binge watching is the new normal. http://www.prnewswire.com/news-releases/netflix-declares-binge-watching-is-the-new-normal-235713431.html, 2013.

[4] H. Abrahamsson and M. Nordmark. Program popularity and viewer behavior in a large TV-on-demand system. In *ACM Internet Measurement Conference*, pages 199–210, 2012.

[5] C. M. Bishop. *Pattern Recognition and Machine Learning*. Springer-Verlag New York, 2006.

[6] L. Carlinet, T. Huynh, B. Kauffmann, F. Mathieu, L. Noirie, and S. Tixeuil. Four months in daily motion: Dissecting user video requests. In *IEEE Wireless Communications and Mobile Computing Conference*, pages 613–618, 2012.

[7] M. Cha, H. Kwak, P. Rodriguez, Y.-Y. Ahn, and S. Moon. Analyzing the video popularity characteristics of large-scale user generated content systems. *IEEE/ACM Transactions on Networking*, 17(5):1357–1370, 2009.

[8] A. Dempster, N. Laird, and D. Rubin. Maximum likelihood from incomplete data via the EM algorithm. *Journal of the Royal Statistical Society*, pages 1–38, 1977.

[9] G. Dupret and M. Lalmas. Absence time and user engagement: evaluating ranking functions. In *ACM international conference on Web search and Data Mining*, pages 173–182, 2013.

[10] L. A. Hannah, D. M. Blei, and W. B. Powell. Dirichlet process mixtures of generalized linear models. *The Journal of Machine Learning Research*, 12:1923–1953, 2011.

[11] Y. He and K. Wang. Inferring search behaviors using partially observable markov model with duration. In *Proceedings of the fourth ACM International Conference on Web search and Data Mining*, pages 415–424, 2011.

[12] K. Kapoor, M. Sun, J. Srivastava, and T. Ye. A hazard based approach to user return time prediction. In *ACM SIGKDD International Conference on Knowledge Discovery and Data Mining*, pages 1719–1728, 2014.

[13] D. Karlis, P. Papatla, and S. Roy. Finite mixtures of censored Poisson regression models. *Statistica Neerlandica*, 2015.

[14] R. Kay. Proportional hazard regression models and the analysis of censored survival data. *Applied Statistics*, pages 227–237, 1977.

[15] C. McCulloch and S. Searle. *Generalized linear and mixed Models*. John Wiley and Sons, 2004.

[16] S. Nagano, Y. Ichikawa, N. Takaya, T. Uchiyama, and M. Abe. Nonparametric hierarchal Bayesian modeling in non-contractual heterogeneous survival data. In *ACM SIGKDD International Conference on Knowledge Discovery and Data Mining*, pages 668–676, 2013.

[17] TiVO. Viewers' New TV Reality: A "Season" = One Day. http://pr.tivo.com/press-releases, 2014.

[18] R. A. Volberg. The prevalence and demographics of pathological gamblers: implications for public health. *American Journal of Public Health*, 84(2):237–241, 1994.

[19] G. Willmot. Mixed compound Poisson distributions. *Astin Bulletin*, 16(S1):S59–S79, 1986.

[20] W. C.-H. Wu, M.-Y. Yeh, and M.-S. Chen. Predicting winning price in real time bidding with censored data. In *ACM SIGKDD International Conference on Knowledge Discovery and Data Mining*, pages 1305–1314, 2015.

[21] H. Yeh, B. Gajewski, P. Mukhopadhyay, and F. Behbod. The zero-truncated Poisson with right censoring: an application to translational breast cancer research. *Statistics in Biopharmaceutical Research*, 4(3):252–263, 2012.

[22] H. Yu, D. Zheng, B. Y. Zhao, and W. Zheng. Understanding user behavior in large-scale video-on-demand systems. In *ACM SIGOPS Operating Systems Review*, volume 40, pages 333–344, 2006.

APPENDIX

We present the details of derivation for Algorithm 1 for parameter estimation in M-step. Recall that the overall objective is,

$$\Theta^{(t)} = \arg\max \textstyle\sum_{i=1}^{N} \sum_{k=1}^{K} \tau_{i,k}^{(t-1)} [\log(\pi_k) + (1-c_i)(v_i \log(\lambda_{i,k}) - \log(v_i\,!) - \lambda_{i,k}) + c_i \log(\Pr_k(v_i \geq h_i))] \quad (13)$$

subject to $\sum_k \pi_k = 1, \pi_k \geq 0$. For mixture weights it is straightforward to show $\pi_k^{(t)} \propto \sum_i \tau_{i,k}^{(t-1)}$. For $\boldsymbol{\beta}_k$'s, we optimize,

$$\max_{\boldsymbol{\beta}_k} \textstyle\sum_{i=1}^{N} \tau_{i,k}^{(t-1)} [(1-c_i)(v_i \log(\lambda_{i,k}) - \lambda_{i,k}) + c_i \log(\Pr_k(v_i \geq h_i)$$

where $\lambda_{i,k} = \exp(\mathbf{x}_i^\top \boldsymbol{\beta}_k)$ and $\Pr_k$'s also depend on $\boldsymbol{\beta}_k$. We solve this optimization numerically using gradient descent. We first calculate $\nabla_{\boldsymbol{\beta}_k} \log(\Pr_k(v_i \geq h_i))$. For $h_i > 0$, we have,

$$\nabla_{\boldsymbol{\beta}_k} \log(\Pr_k(v_i \geq h_i)) = \frac{1}{\Pr_k(v_i \geq h_i)} \nabla_{\boldsymbol{\beta}_k} \{\textstyle\sum_{j=h_i}^{\infty} \frac{\lambda_{i,k}^j}{e^{\lambda_{i,k}} j\,!}\}$$

$$= \frac{1}{\Pr_k(v_i \geq h_i)} \textstyle\sum_{j=h_i}^{\infty} \frac{\lambda_{i,k}^j \nabla e^{-\lambda_{i,k}} + e^{-\lambda_{i,k}} \nabla \lambda_{i,k}^j}{j\,!} \quad (14)$$

$$= \frac{\lambda_{i,k} \mathbf{x}_i}{\Pr_k(v_i \geq h_i)} \textstyle\sum_{j=h_i}^{\infty} - \frac{\lambda_{i,k}^j e^{-\lambda_{i,k}}}{j\,!} + \frac{\lambda_{i,k}^{j-1} e^{-\lambda_{i,k}}}{(j-1)\,!} \quad (15)$$

$$= \frac{\lambda_{i,k} \Pr_k(v_i = h_i - 1)}{\Pr_k(v_i \geq h_i)} \mathbf{x}_i \quad (16)$$

On the other hand, $\nabla_{\boldsymbol{\beta}_k} \log(\Pr_k(v_i \geq h_i)) = 0$ if $h_i = 0$. Overall, we have,

$$\nabla_{\boldsymbol{\beta}_k} l(\Theta) = \sum_{i=1}^{N} \tau_{i,k}^{t-1} [(1-c_i)(v_i - \lambda_{i,k}) + c_i \lambda_{i,k} \frac{\Pr_k(v_i = h_i - 1)}{\Pr_k(v_i \geq h_i)}]\mathbf{x}$$

Structural Deep Network Embedding

Daixin Wang[1], Peng Cui[1], Wenwu Zhu[1]
[1]Tsinghua National Laboratory for Information Science and Technology
Department of Computer Science and Technology, Tsinghua University. Beijing, China
dxwang0826@gmail.com,cuip@tsinghua.edu.cn,wwzhu@tsinghua.edu.cn

ABSTRACT

Network embedding is an important method to learn low-dimensional representations of vertexes in networks, aiming to capture and preserve the network structure. Almost all the existing network embedding methods adopt shallow models. However, since the underlying network structure is complex, shallow models cannot capture the highly non-linear network structure, resulting in sub-optimal network representations. Therefore, how to find a method that is able to effectively capture the highly non-linear network structure and preserve the global and local structure is an open yet important problem. To solve this problem, in this paper we propose a Structural Deep Network Embedding method, namely *SDNE*. More specifically, we first propose a semi-supervised deep model, which has multiple layers of non-linear functions, thereby being able to capture the highly non-linear network structure. Then we propose to exploit the first-order and second-order proximity jointly to preserve the network structure. The second-order proximity is used by the unsupervised component to capture the global network structure. While the first-order proximity is used as the supervised information in the supervised component to preserve the local network structure. By jointly optimizing them in the semi-supervised deep model, our method can preserve both the local and global network structure and is robust to sparse networks. Empirically, we conduct the experiments on five real-world networks, including a language network, a citation network and three social networks. The results show that compared to the baselines, our method can reconstruct the original network significantly better and achieves substantial gains in three applications, i.e. multi-label classification, link prediction and visualization.

Keywords

Network Embedding, Deep Learning, Network Analysis

1. INTRODUCTION

Nowadays, networks are ubiquitous and many real-world applications need to mine the information within these networks. For example, recommendation system in Twitter aims to mine the preferred tweets for users from the social network. Online advertisement targeting often needs to cluster the users into communities in the social network. Therefore, mining the information in the network is very important. One of the fundamental problems is how to learn useful network representations [5]. An effective way is to embed networks into a low-dimensional space, i.e. learn vector representations for each vertex, with the goal of reconstructing the network in the learned embedding space. As a result, mining information in networks, such as information retrieval [34], classification [15], and clustering [20], can be directly conducted in the low-dimensional space.

Learning network representations faces the following great challenges: (1) **High non-linearity**: As [19] stated, the underlying structure of the network is highly non-linear. Therefore, how to design a model to capture the *highly non-linear* structure is rather difficult. (2) **Structure-preserving**: To support applications analyzing networks, network embedding is required to preserve the network structure. However, the underlying structure of the network is very *complex* [24]. The similarity of vertexes is dependent on both the local and global network structure. Therefore, how to simultaneously preserve the local and global structure is a tough problem. (3) **Sparsity**: Many real-world networks are often so *sparse* that only utilizing the very limited observed links is not enough to reach a satisfactory performance [21].

In the past decades, many network embedding methods have been proposed, which adopted shallow models, such as IsoMAP [29], Laplacian Eigenmaps (LE) [1] and Line [26]. However, due to the limited representation ability of shallow models [2], it is difficult for them to capture the highly nonlinear network structure [30]. Although some methods adopt kernel techniques [32], as [36] stated, kernel methods are also shallow models and cannot capture the highly non-linear structure well.

In order to capture the **highly non-linear** structure well, in this paper we propose a new deep model to learn vertex representations for networks. This is motivated by the recent success of deep learning, which has been demonstrated to have a powerful representation ability to learn complex structures of the data [2] and has achieved substantial success in dealing with images [15], text [25] and audio [10] data. In particular, in our proposed model we design a multi-layer architecture which consists of multiple non-linear functions. The composition of multiple layers of non-linear functions can map the data into a highly non-linear latent space, thereby being able to capture the highly non-linear network structure.

In order to address the **structure-preserving** and **sparsity** problems in the deep model, we further propose to exploit the first-order and second-order proximity [26] jointly into the learning process. The first-order proximity is the local pairwise similarity only between the vertexes linked by edges, which characterizes the local network structure. However, due to the sparsity of the network,

KDD '16, August 13-17, 2016, San Francisco, CA, USA

DOI: http://dx.doi.org/10.1145/2939672.2939753

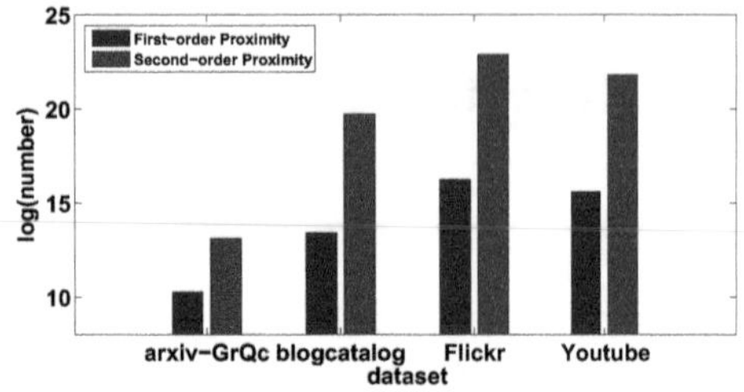

Figure 1: The number of pairs of vertexes which have first-order and second-order proximity in different datasets.

many legitimate links are missing. As a result, the first-order proximity is not sufficient to represent the network structure. Therefore, we further propose the second-order proximity, which indicates the similarity of the vertexes' neighborhood structures, to capture the global network structure. With the first-order and second-order proximity, we can well characterize the local and global network structure, respectively. To preserve both the local and global network structure in the deep model, we propose a semi-supervised architecture, in which the unsupervised component reconstructs the second-order proximity to preserve the global network structure while the supervised component exploits the first-order proximity as the supervised information to preserve the local network structure. As a result, the learned representations can well preserve both the local and global network structure. In addition, as shown in Figure 1, the number of pairs of vertexes which have second-order proximity is much huger than those have first-order proximity. Therefore, the import of second-order proximity is able to provide much more information in term of characterizing the network structure. As a result, our method is robust to sparse networks.

Empirically, we conduct the experiments on five real-world networked datasets and four real-world applications. The results show that compared with baselines, the representations generated by our method can reconstruct the original networks significantly better and achieve substantial gains on various tasks and various networks, including very sparse networks. It demonstrates that our representations learned in the highly non-linear space can preserve the network structure well and are robust to sparse networks.

In summary, the contributions of this paper are listed as follows:

- We propose a Structural Deep Network Embedding method, namely *SDNE*, to perform network embedding. The method is able to map the data to a highly non-linear latent space to preserve the network structure and is robust to sparse networks. To the best of our knowledge, we are among the first to use deep learning to learn network representations.

- We propose a new deep model with a semi-supervised architecture, which simultaneously optimizes the first-order and second-order proximity. As a result, the learned representations preserve the local and global network structure and are robust to sparse networks.

- The proposed method is extensively evaluated on five real datasets and four application scenarios. The results demonstrate the superior usefulness of the method in multi-label classification, reconstruction, link prediction and visualization. Specifically, our method can achieve more significant improvements (20%) over baselines when labelled data is scarce. In some cases we only need 60% less training samples but still achieve better performance.

2. RELATED WORK

2.1 Deep Neural Network

Representation learning has long been an important problem of machine learning and many works aim at learning representations for samples [3, 35]. Recent advances in deep neural networks have witnessed that they have powerful representations abilities [12] and can generate very useful representations for many types of data. For example, [15] proposed a seven-layer convolutional neural network to generate image representations for classification. [33] proposed a multimodal deep model to learn image-text unified representations to achieve cross-modality retrieval task.

However, to the best of our knowledge, there have been few deep learning works handling networks, especially learning network representations. In [9], Restricted Boltzmann Machines were adopted to do collaborative filtering. [30] adopted deep autoencoder to do graph clustering. [5] proposed a heterogeneous deep model to do heterogeneous data embedding. We differ from these works in two aspects. Firstly, the goals are different. Our work focuses on learning low-dimensional structure-preserved network representations which can be utilized among tasks. Secondly, we consider both the first-order and second-order proximity between vertexes to preserve the local and global network structure. But they only focus on one-order information.

2.2 Network Embedding

Our work solves the problem of network embedding, which aims to learn representations for networks. Some earlier works like Local Linear Embedding (LLE) [22], IsoMAP [29] first constructed the affinity graph based on the feature vectors and then solved the leading eigenvectors as the network representations. More recently, [26] designed two loss functions attempting to capture the local and global network structure respectively. Furthermore, [4] extended the work to utilize high-order information. Despite the success of these network embedding approaches, they all adopt shallow models. As we have explained earlier, it is difficult for shallow models to effectively capture the highly non-linear structure in the underlying network. In addition, although some of them attempt to use first-order and high-order proximity to preserve the local and global network structure, they learn the representations for them separately and simply concatenate the representations. Obviously, it is sub-optimal than simultaneously modeling them in a unified architecture to capture both the local and global network structure.

DeepWalk [21] combined random walk and skip-gram to learn network representations. Although empirically effective, it lacks a clear objective function to articulate how to preserve the network structure. It is prone to preserving only the second-order proximity. However, our method designs an explicit objective function, which aims at simultaneously preserving the local and global structure by preserving both the first-order and second-order proximity.

3. STRUCTURAL DEEP NETWORK EMBEDDING

In this section, we first define the problem. Then we introduce the proposed semi-supervised deep model of *SDNE*. At last we present some discussions and analysis on the model.

3.1 Problem Definition

We first give the definition of a Graph.

DEFINITION 1. *(Graph) A graph is denoted as* $G = (V, E)$, *where* $V = \{v_1, ..., v_n\}$ *represents* n *vertexes and* $E = \{e_{i,j}\}_{i,j=1}^{n}$ *represents the edges. Each edge* $e_{i,j}$ *is associated with a weight*

$s_{i,j} \geq 0$ [1]. *For v_i and v_j not linked by an edge, $s_{i,j} = 0$. Otherwise, for unweighted graph $s_{i,j} = 1$ and for weighted graph, $s_{i,j} > 0$.*

Network embedding aims to map the graph data into a low-dimensional latent space, where each vertex is represented as a low-dimensional vector and the network computing can be directly realized. As we have explained, both local and global structure are essential to be preserved. Then we first define the first-order proximity, which characterizes the local network structure.

DEFINITION 2. *(First-Order Proximity) The first-order proximity describes the pairwise proximity between vertexes. For any pair of vertexes, if $s_{i,j} > 0$, there exists positive first-order proximity between v_i and v_j. Otherwise, the first-order proximity between v_i and v_j is 0.*

Naturally, it is necessary for network embedding to preserve the first-order proximity because it implies that two vertexes in real-world networks are always similar if they are linked by an observed edge. For example, if a paper cites another paper, they should contain some common topic. However, real-world datasets are often so sparse that the observed links only account for a small portion. There exist many vertexes which are similar with each other but not linked by any edges. Therefore, only capturing the first-order proximity is not sufficient. We introduce the second-order proximity to capture the global network structure.

DEFINITION 3. *(Second-Order Proximity) The second-order proximity between a pair of vertexes describes the proximity of the pair's neighborhood structure. Let $\mathcal{N}_u = \{s_{u,1}, ..., s_{u,|V|}\}$ denote the first-order proximity between v_u and other vertexes. Then, second-order proximity is determined by the similarity of $\mathcal{N}_u$ and $\mathcal{N}_v$.*

Intuitively, the second-order proximity assumes that if two vertexes share many common neighbors, they tend to be similar. Such an assumption has been proved reasonable in many fields [6, 14]. For example, in linguistics words will be similar if they are always surrounded by similar contexts [6]. People will be friends if they have many common friends [14]. The second-order proximity has been demonstrated to be a good metric to define the similarity of a pair of vertexes, even if they are not linked by an edge [17], and thus can highly enrich the relationship of vertexes. Therefore, by introducing the second-order proximity, it is able to characterize the global network structure and alleviate the sparsity problem.

With the first-order and second-order proximity, we investigate the problem of how to integrate them simultaneously to preserve both the local and global structure when we perform network embedding. Such a problem is defined as follows:

DEFINITION 4. *(Network Embedding) Given a graph denoted as $G = (V, E)$, network embedding aims to learn a mapping function $f : v_i \longmapsto \mathbf{y_i} \in \mathbb{R}^d$, where $d \ll |V|$. The objective of the function is to make the similarity between $\mathbf{y_i}$ and $\mathbf{y_j}$ explicitly preserve the first-order and second-order proximity of v_i and v_j.*

3.2 The Model

3.2.1 Framework

In this paper, we propose a semi-supervised deep model to perform network embedding, whose framework is shown in Figure 2. In detail, to capture the highly non-linear network structure, we propose a deep architecture, which is composed of multiple non-linear mapping functions to map the input data to a highly non-linear latent space to capture the network structure. Furthermore, in

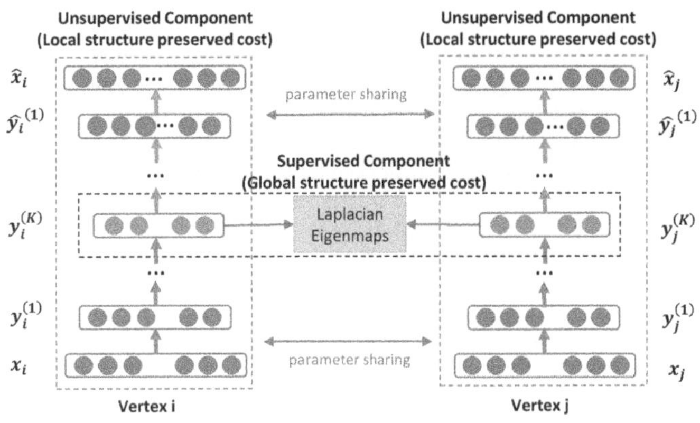

Figure 2: The framework of the semi-supervised deep model of *SDNE*

order to address the structure-preserving and sparsity problems, we propose a semi-supervised model to exploit both the second-order and first-order proximity. For each vertex, we are able to obtain its neighborhood. Accordingly, we design the unsupervised component to preserve the second-order proximity, by reconstructing the neighborhood structure of each vertex. Meanwhile, for a small portion of pairs of nodes, we can obtain their pairwise similarities, i.e. the first-order proximities. Therefore, we design the supervised component to exploit the first-order proximity as the supervised information to refine the representations in the latent space. By jointly optimizing them in the proposed semi-supervised deep model, *SDNE* can preserve the highly-nonlinear local-global network structure well and is robust to sparse networks. In the following section, we will introduce how to realize the semi-supervised deep model in detail.

3.2.2 Loss Functions

Before introducing the loss functions, we define some of the terms and notations in Table 1 which will be used later. Note that ^ above the parameters represents the parameters of the decoder.

Table 1: Terms and Notations

Symbol	Definition
n	number of vertexes
K	number of layers
$S = \{\mathbf{s}_1, ..., \mathbf{s}_n\}$	the adjacency matrix for the network
$X = \{\mathbf{x}_i\}_{i=1}^n, \hat{X} = \{\hat{\mathbf{x}}_i\}_{i=1}^n$	the input data and reconstructed data
$Y^{(k)} = \{\mathbf{y}_i^{(k)}\}_{i=1}^n$	the k-th layer hidden representations
$W^{(k)}, \hat{W}^{(k)}$	the k-th layer weight matrix
$\mathbf{b^{(k)}}, \hat{\mathbf{b}}^{(\mathbf{k})}$	the k-th layer biases
$\theta = \{W^{(k)}, \hat{W}^{(k)}, \mathbf{b}^{(k)}, \hat{\mathbf{b}}^{(k)}\}$	the overall parameters

Now we introduce the loss functions for the semi-supervised model. We first describe how the unsupervised component exploits the second-order proximity to preserve the global network structure.

The second-order proximity refers to how similar the neighborhood structure of a pair of vertexes is. Thus, to model the second-order proximity, it is required to model the neighborhood of each vertex. Given a network $G = (V, E)$, we can obtain its adjacency matrix S, which contains n instances $\mathbf{s}_1, ..., \mathbf{s}_n$. For each instance $\mathbf{s}_i = \{s_{i,j}\}_{j=1}^n$, $s_{i,j} > 0$ if and only if there exists a link between v_i and v_j. Therefore, $\mathbf{s}_i$ describes the neighborhood structure of the vertex v_i and S provides the information of the neighborhood structure of each vertex. With S, we extend the traditional deep autoencoder [23] to preserve the second-order proximity.

For the consideration of being self-contained, we briefly review the key idea of deep autoencoder. It is an unsupervised model

[1]For signed network, negative links exist. But in this paper we only consider non-negative links.

which is composed of two parts, i.e. the encoder and decoder. The encoder consists of multiple non-linear functions that map the input data to the representation space. The decoder also consists of multiple non-linear functions mapping the representations in representation space to reconstruction space. Then given the input $\mathbf{x}_i$, the hidden representations for each layer are shown as follows [2]:

$$\begin{aligned}\mathbf{y}_i^{(1)} &= \sigma(W^{(1)}\mathbf{x}_i + \mathbf{b}^{(1)})\\ \mathbf{y}_i^{(k)} &= \sigma(W^{(k)}\mathbf{y}_i^{(k-1)} + \mathbf{b}^{(k)}), k = 2, ..., K\end{aligned} \tag{1}$$

After obtaining $\mathbf{y}_i^{(K)}$, we can obtain the output $\hat{\mathbf{x}}_i$ by reversing the calculation process of encoder. The goal of the autoencoder is to minimize the reconstruction error of the output and the input. The loss function is shown as follows:

$$\mathcal{L} = \sum_{i=1}^{n} \|\hat{\mathbf{x}}_i - \mathbf{x}_i\|_2^2 \tag{2}$$

As [23] proved, although minimizing the reconstruction loss does not explicitly preserve the similarity between samples, the reconstruction criterion can smoothly capture the data manifolds and thus preserve the similarity between samples. Then considering our case that if we use the adjacency matrix S as the input to the autoencoder, i.e. $\mathbf{x}_i = \mathbf{s}_i$, since each instance $\mathbf{s}_i$ characterizes the neighborhood structure of the vertex v_i, the reconstruction process will make the vertexes which have similar neighborhood structures have similar latent representations.

Nevertheless, such a reconstruction process cannot be directly applied to our problem because of some specific characteristics of networks. In the networks, we can observe some links but simultaneously many legitimate links are not observed, which means that the links between vertexes do indicate their similarity but no links do not necessarily indicate their dissimilarity. Moreover, due to the sparsity of networks, the number of non-zero elements in S is far less than that of zero elements. Then if we directly use S as the input to the traditional autoencoder, it is more prone to reconstruct the zero elements in S. However, this is not what we want. To address this problem, we impose more penalty to the reconstruction error of the non-zero elements than that of zero elements. The revised objective function is shown as follows:

$$\begin{aligned}\mathcal{L}_{2nd} &= \sum_{i=1}^{n} \|(\hat{\mathbf{x}}_i - \mathbf{x}_i) \odot \mathbf{b}_i\|_2^2\\ &= \|(\hat{X} - X) \odot B\|_F^2\end{aligned} \tag{3}$$

where $\odot$ means the Hadamard product, $\mathbf{b}_i = \{b_{i,j}\}_{j=1}^{n}$. If $s_{i,j} = 0$, $b_{i,j} = 1$, else $b_{i,j} = \beta > 1$. Now by using the revised deep autoencoder with the adjacency matrix S as input, the vertexes which have similar neighborhood structure will be mapped near in the representations space, guaranteed by the reconstruction criterion. In other words, the unsupervised component of our model can preserve the global network structure by reconstructing the second-order proximity between vertexes.

It is not only necessary to preserve the global network structure, but also essential to capture the local structure. We use the first-order proximity to denote the local network structure. The first-order proximity can be regarded as the supervised information to constrain the similarity of the latent representations of a pair of vertexes. Therefore, we design the supervised component to exploit the first-order proximity. The loss function for this goal is defined as follows [3]:

$$\begin{aligned}\mathcal{L}_{1st} &= \sum_{i,j=1}^{n} s_{i,j}\|\mathbf{y}_i^{(K)} - \mathbf{y}_j^{(K)}\|_2^2\\ &= \sum_{i,j=1}^{n} s_{i,j}\|\mathbf{y}_i - \mathbf{y}_j\|_2^2\end{aligned} \tag{4}$$

The objective function of Eq. 4 borrows the idea of Laplacian Eigenmaps [1], which incurs a penalty when similar vertexes are mapped far away in the embedding space. Some works about social networks [13] also use the similar idea. We differentiate them in the aspect that we incorporate the idea in the deep model to make the vertexes linked by an edge be mapped near in the embedding space. As a result, the model preserves the first-order proximity.

To preserve the first-order and second-order proximity simultaneously, we propose a semi-supervised model, which combines Eq. 4 and Eq. 3 and joint minimizes the following objective function:

$$\begin{aligned}\mathcal{L}_{mix} &= \mathcal{L}_{2nd} + \alpha\mathcal{L}_{1st} + \nu\mathcal{L}_{reg}\\ &= \|(\hat{X} - X) \odot B\|_F^2 + \alpha\sum_{i,j=1}^{n} s_{i,j}\|\mathbf{y}_i - \mathbf{y}_j\|_2^2 + \nu\mathcal{L}_{reg}\end{aligned} \tag{5}$$

where $\mathcal{L}_{reg}$ is an $\mathcal{L}2$-norm regularizer term to prevent overfitting, which is defined as follows:

$$\mathcal{L}_{reg} = \frac{1}{2}\sum_{k=1}^{K}(\|W^{(k)}\|_F^2 + \|\hat{W}^{(k)}\|_F^2)$$

3.2.3 *Optimization*

To optimize the aforementioned model, the goal is to minimize $\mathcal{L}_{mix}$ as a function of θ. In detail, the key step is to calculate the partial derivative of $\partial\mathcal{L}_{mix}/\partial\hat{W}^{(k)}$ and $\partial\mathcal{L}_{mix}/\partial W^{(k)}$. The detailed mathematical form of the partial derivative is shown as follows:

$$\begin{aligned}\frac{\partial\mathcal{L}_{mix}}{\partial\hat{W}^{(k)}} &= \frac{\partial\mathcal{L}_{2nd}}{\partial\hat{W}^{(k)}} + \nu\frac{\partial\mathcal{L}_{reg}}{\partial\hat{W}^{(k)}}\\ \frac{\partial\mathcal{L}_{mix}}{\partial W^{(k)}} &= \frac{\partial\mathcal{L}_{2nd}}{\partial W^{(k)}} + \alpha\frac{\partial\mathcal{L}_{1st}}{\partial W^{(k)}} + \nu\frac{\partial\mathcal{L}_{reg}}{\partial W^{(k)}}, k = 1, ..., K\end{aligned} \tag{6}$$

We first look at $\partial\mathcal{L}_{2nd}/\partial\hat{W}^{(K)}$. It can be rephrased as follows:

$$\frac{\partial\mathcal{L}_{2nd}}{\partial\hat{W}^{(K)}} = \frac{\partial\mathcal{L}_{2nd}}{\partial\hat{X}} \cdot \frac{\partial\hat{X}}{\partial\hat{W}^{(K)}} \tag{7}$$

For the first term, according to Eq. 3 we have:

$$\frac{\partial\mathcal{L}_{2nd}}{\partial\hat{X}} = 2(\hat{X} - X) \odot B \tag{8}$$

The calculation of the second term $\partial\hat{X}/\partial\hat{W}$ is easy since $\hat{X} = \sigma(\hat{Y}^{(K-1)}\hat{W}^{(K)} + \hat{b}^{(K)})$. Then $\partial\mathcal{L}_{2nd}/\partial\hat{W}^{(K)}$ is accessible. Based on back-propagation, we can iteratively obtain $\partial\mathcal{L}_{2nd}/\partial\hat{W}^{(k)}, k = 1, ...K-1$ and $\partial\mathcal{L}_{2nd}/\partial W^{(k)}, k = 1, ...K$. Now the calculation of the partial derivative of $\mathcal{L}_{2nd}$ is finished.

Then we continue to calculate the partial derivative of $\partial\mathcal{L}_{1st}/\partial W^{(k)}$. The loss function of $\mathcal{L}_{1st}$ can be rephrased as follows:

$$\mathcal{L}_{1st} = \sum_{i,j=1}^{n} s_{i,j}\|\mathbf{y}_i - \mathbf{y}_j\|_2^2 = 2tr(Y^T LY) \tag{9}$$

[2]In this work, we use the sigmoid function $\sigma(x) = \frac{1}{1+exp(-x)}$ as the non-linear activation function

[3]For simplicity of notations, we denote network representations $Y^{(K)} = \{\mathbf{y}_i^{(K)}\}_{i=1}^{n}$ as $Y = \{\mathbf{y}_i\}_{i=1}^{n}$.

where $L = D - S$, $D \in \mathbb{R}^{n \times n}$ is a diagonal matrix, $D_{i,i} = \sum_j s_{i,j}$.

Then we first focus on the calculation of $\partial \mathcal{L}_{1st} / \partial W^{(K)}$:

$$\frac{\partial \mathcal{L}_{1st}}{\partial W^{(K)}} = \frac{\partial \mathcal{L}_{1st}}{\partial Y} \cdot \frac{\partial Y}{\partial W^{(K)}} \tag{10}$$

Since $Y = \sigma(Y^{(K-1)} W^{(K)} + b^{(K)})$, the calculation of the second term $\partial Y / \partial W^{(K)}$ is easy. For the first term of $\partial \mathcal{L}_{1st} / \partial Y$, we have:

$$\frac{\partial \mathcal{L}_{1st}}{\partial Y} = 2(L + L^T) \cdot Y \tag{11}$$

Similarly, by using back-propagation we can finish the calculation of partial derivative of $\mathcal{L}_{1st}$.

Now we have obtained the partial derivatives of the parameters. With an initialization of the parameters, the proposed deep model can be optimized by using stochastic gradient descent. Note that due to the high nonlinearity of the model, it suffers from many local optimal in the parameter space. Therefore, in order to find a good region of parameter space, we use Deep Belief Network to pretrain the parameters at first [11], which has been demonstrated as an essential initialization of parameters for deep learning in literature [7]. The full algorithm is presented in Alg. 1.

Algorithm 1 Training Algorithm for the semi-supervised deep model of *SDNE*

Input: the network $G = (V, E)$ with adjacency matrix S, the parameters α and ν

Output: Network representations Y and updated Parameters: θ

1: Pretrain the model through deep belief network to obtain the initialized parameters $\theta = \{\theta^{(1)}, ..., \theta^{(K)}\}$
2: $X = S$
3: **repeat**
4: Based on X and θ, apply Eq. 1 to obtain $\hat{X}$ and $Y = Y^K$.
5: $\mathcal{L}_{mix}(X; \theta) = \|(\hat{X} - X) \odot B\|_F^2 + 2\alpha tr(Y^T L Y) + \nu \mathcal{L}_{reg}$.
6: Based on Eq. 6, use $\partial L_{mix} / \partial \theta$ to back-propagate through the entire network to get updated parameters θ.
7: **until** converge
8: Obtain the network representations $Y = Y^{(K)}$

3.3 Analysis and Discussions

In this section, we present some analysis and discussions of the proposed semi-supervised deep model of *SDNE*.

New vertexes: A practical issue for network embedding is how to learn representations for newly arrived vertexes. For a new vertex v_k, if its connections to the existing vertexes is known, we can obtain its adjacency vector $\mathbf{x} = \{s_{1,k}, ..., s_{n,k}\}$, where $s_{i,k}$ indicates the similarity between the existing v_i and the new vertex v_k. Then we can simply feed the $\mathbf{x}$ into our deep model and use the trained parameters θ to get the representations for v_k. The complexity for such a process is $O(1)$. If there exist no connections between v_i and the existing vertexes in the network, our method and state-of-the-art network embedding methods cannot handle. To handle such case, we can resort to other side information, such as the content features of the new vertexes, which we leave as the future work.

Training Complexity: It is not difficult to see that the training complexity of our model is $O(ncdI)$, where n is the number of vertexes, d is the maximum dimension of the hidden layer, c is the average degree of the network and I is the number of iterations. Parameter d is usually related to the dimension of embedding vectors but not related to the number of vertexes. I is also independent with n. For c, it usually can be regarded as a constant in real-world applications. For example, in the social network, the maximum number of friends for a people is always bounded [30]. In top-k similarity graph, $c = k$. Therefore, cdI is independent with n and thus the overall training complexity is linear to the number of vertexes in the network.

4. EXPERIMENTS

In this section, we evaluate our proposed method on several real-world datasets and applications. The experimental results demonstrate significant improvements over baselines.

4.1 Datasets

In order to comprehensively evaluate the effectiveness of the representations, we use five networked datasets, including three social networks, one citation network and one language network, for three real-world applications, i.e. multi-label classification, link prediction and visualization. Considering the characteristics of these datasets, for each application we use one or more datasets to evaluate the performances. The detailed descriptions are listed as follows.

- BLOGCATALOG [27], FLICKR [27] and YOUTUBE [28]: They are social network of online users. Each user is labelled by at least one category. There are overall 39 different categories for BLOGCATALOG, 195 categories for FLICKR and 47 categories for categories. These categories can be used as the ground-truth of each vertex. Therefore, they can be evaluated on the multi-label classification task.

- ARXIV GR-QC [16]: It is a paper collaboration network which covers papers in the field of General Relativity and Quantum Cosmology from arXiv. In this network, the vertex represents an author and the edge indicates that the authors have coauthored a scientific paper in arXiv. The dataset is used for the link-prediction task since we have no category information of each vertex.

- 20-NEWSGROUP[4]: This dataset is a collection of approximate 20000 newsgroup documents and each document is labelled by one of the 20 different groups. We use the tf-idf vectors of each word to represent the document and the cosine similarity as the similarity between two documents. We can construct the network according to such similarities. We select the documents labelled as *comp.graphics*, *rec.sport.baseball* and *talk.politics.gums* to perform the visualization task.

To summarize, we conduct experiments on both weighted and unweighted, sparse and dense, small and large networks. Therefore, the datasets can comprehensively reflect the characteristics of the network embedding methods. The detailed statistics of the datasets can be summarized in Table 2.

Table 2: Statistics of the dataset

Dataset	#(V)	#(E)
BLOGCATALOG	10312	667966
FLICKR	80513	11799764
YOUTUBE	1138499	5980886
ARXIV GR-QC	5242	28980
20-NEWSGROUP	1720	Full-connected

[4]http://qwone.com/ jason/20Newsgroups/

4.2 Baseline Algorithms

We use the following five methods as the baselines. The first four are network embedding methods. *Common Neighbor* directly predicts the links over the networks, which has been demonstrated to be an effective method to perform link prediction [17].

- *DeepWalk* [21]: It adopts random walk and skip-gram model to generate network representations.
- *LINE* [26]: It defines loss functions to preserve the first-order or second-order proximity separately. After optimizing the loss functions, it concatenates these representations.
- *GraRep* [4]: It extends to high-order proximity and uses the SVD to train the model. It also directly concatenates the representations of first-order and high-order.
- *Laplacian Eigenmaps (LE)* [1]: It generates network representations by factorizing the Laplacian matrix of the adjacency matrix. It only exploits the first-order proximity to preserve the network structure.
- *Common Neighbor* [17]: It only uses the number of common neighbors to measure the similarity between vertexes. It is used as the baseline only in the task of link prediction.

4.3 Evaluation Metrics

In our experiment, we perform the task of reconstruction, link prediction, multi-label classification and visualization. For reconstruction and link prediction, we use *precision@k* and *Mean Average Precision (MAP)* to evaluate the performance. Their definitions are listed as follows:

- *precision@k* is a metric which gives equal weight to the returned instance. It is defined as follows:

$$precision@k(i) = \frac{|\{j \mid i, j \in V, index(j) \le k, \Delta_i(j) = 1\}|}{k}$$

where V is the vertex set, $index(j)$ is the ranked index of the j-th vertex and $\Delta_i(j) = 1$ indicates that v_i and v_j have a link.

- *Mean Average Precision (MAP)* is a metric with good discrimination and stability. Compared with *precision@k*, it is more concerned with the performance of the returned items ranked ahead. It is calculated as follows:

$$\begin{aligned} AP(i) &= \frac{\sum_j precision@j(i) \cdot \Delta_i(j)}{|\{\Delta_i(j) = 1\}|} \\ MAP &= \frac{\sum_{i \in Q} AP(i)}{|Q|}, \end{aligned}$$

where Q is the query set.

For the multi-label classification task, we adopt *micro-*$F1$ and *macro-*$F1$ as many other works do [27]. In detail, for a label A, we denote TP(A), FP(A) and FN(A) as the number of true positives, false positives and false negatives in the instances which are predicted as A, respectively. Suppose $\mathcal{C}$ is the overall label set. *Micro-*$F1$ and *Macro-*$F1$ are defined as follows:

- *Macro-*$F1$ is a metric which gives equal weight to each class. It is defined as follows:

$$Macro - F1 = \frac{\sum_{A \in \mathcal{C}} F1(A)}{|\mathcal{C}|}$$

where $F1(A)$ is the $F1$-measure for the label A.

- *Micro-*$F1$ is a metric which gives equal weight to each instance. It is defined as follows:

$$Pr = \frac{\sum_{A \in \mathcal{C}} TP(A)}{\sum_{A \in \mathcal{C}} (TP(A) + FP(A))}, R = \frac{\sum_{A \in \mathcal{C}} TP(A)}{\sum_{A \in \mathcal{C}} (TP(A) + FN(A))}$$

$$Micro - F1 = \frac{2 * Pr * R}{Pr + R}$$

4.4 Parameter Settings

We propose a multi-layer deep structure in this paper and the number of layers varies with different datasets. The dimension of each layer is listed in Table 3. The neural networks have three layers for BLOGCATALOG, ARXIV GR-QC and 20-NEWSGROUP and four layers for FLICKR and YOUTUBE. If we use deeper model, the performance almost remains unchanged or even becomes worse.

Table 3: Neural Network Structures

Dataset	#nodes in each layer
BLOGCATALOG	10300-1000-100
FLICKR	80513-5000-1000-100
YOUTUBE	22693-5000-1000-100
ARXIV GR-QC	5242-500-100
20-NEWSGROUP	1720-200-100

For our method, the hyper-parameters of α, β and ν are tuned by using grid search on the validation set. The parameters for baselines are tuned to be optimal. For *LINE*, the *mini-batch size* of the stochastic gradient descent is set to 1. The *learning rate* of the starting value is 0.025. The *number of negative samples* is set as 5 and the *total number of samples* is 10 billion. In addition, according to [26], *LINE* yields better results when concatenating both 1-step and 2-step representations to form the final embedding vectors and do $\mathcal{L}2$ normalization to the final embedding vectors. We follow their way to get the results of the *LINE*. For *DeepWalk*, we set *window size* as 10, *walk length* as 40, *walks per vertex* as 40. For *GraRep*, we set *maximum matrix transition step* as 5.

4.5 Experiment Results

In this section, we first evaluate the reconstruction performance. Then we report the results of the generalization of the network representations generated by different embedding methods on three classic data mining and machine learning applications, i.e. multi-label classification, link prediction and visualization.

4.5.1 Network Reconstruction

Before proceeding to evaluate the generalization of the proposed method on real-world applications, we first provide a basic evaluation on different network embedding methods with respect to their capability of network reconstruction. The reason for this experiment is that a good network embedding method should ensure that the the learned embeddings can preserve the original network structure. We use a language network ARXIV GR-QC and a social network BLOGCATALOG as representatives. Given a network, we use different network embedding methods to learn the network representations and then predict the links of the original networks. As the existing links in the original network are known and can serve as the ground-truth, we can evaluate the reconstruction performance, i.e. the training set error, of different methods. The *precision@k* and *MAP* are used as the evaluation metrics. The result on the *precision@k* is presented in Figure 3. The result on *MAP* is shown in Table 4.

From the results, we have the following observations and analysis:

Table 4: MAP on ARXIV-GRQC and BLOGCATALOG on reconstruction task

Method	ARXIV-GRQC					BLOGCATALOG				
	SDNE	*GraRep*	*LINE*	*DeepWalk*	*LE*	*SDNE*	*GraRep*	*LINE*	*DeepWalk*	*LE*
MAP	**0.836****	0.05	0.69	0.58	0.23	**0.63****	0.42	0.58	0.28	0.12

Significantly outperforms GraRep at the: ** 0.01 level.

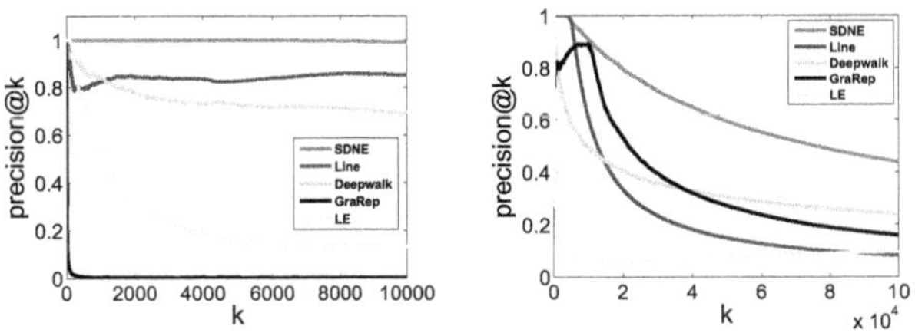

(a) ARXIV GR-QC (b) BLOGCATALOG

Figure 3: precision@k on (a) ARXIV GR-QC and (b) BLOGCATALOG. The results show that our method achieves better reconstruction performance than that of baselines.

- Table 4 shows that our method achieves significant improvements in *MAP* over the baselines in both datasets. Figure 3 shows that the *precision@k* of our method is consistently the highest when k increases. It demonstrates that our method is able to preserve the network structure well.
- Specifically, for the network of ARXIV GR-QC, the *precision@k* of our method can reach 100% and maintain around 100% until the k increases to 10000. This indicates that our method can almost perfectly reconstruct the original network in this dataset, especially considering that the total number of links in this dataset is 28980.
- Although *SDNE* and *LINE* both exploit the first-order and second-order proximity to preserve the network structure, *S-DNE* achieves better performance. The reasons may be t-wofold. Firstly, *LINE* adopts shallow structure, which is d-ifficult to capture the highly non-linear structure in the underlying network. Secondly, *LINE* directly concatenates the representations for the first-order and second-order proximity, which is sub-optimal than jointly optimizing them in *S-DNE*.
- The result that both *SDNE* and *LINE* perform better than *LE*, which only exploits the first-order proximity to preserve the network structure, demonstrates that the import of second-order proximity can help preserve the network structure better.

4.5.2 Multi-label Classification

Classification is a so important task among many applications that the related algorithm and theories have been investigated by many works [18]. Therefore, we evaluate the effectiveness of d-ifferent network representations through a multilabel classification task in this experiment. The representations for the vertexes are generated from the network embedding methods and are used as features to classify each vertex into a set of labels. Specifically, we adopt the LIBLINEAR package [8] to train the classifiers. When training the classifier, we randomly sample a portion of the labeled nodes as the training data and the rest as the test. For BLOGCATALOG, we randomly sample 10% to 90% of the vertexes as the training samples and use the left vertexes to test the performance. For FLICKR and for YOUTUBE, we randomly sample 1% to 10% of the vertexes as the training samples and use the left vertexes to test the performance. In addition, we remove the vertexes which are not labelled by any categories in YOUTUBE. We repeat such a process 5 times and report the averaged *Micro-F1* and *Macro-F1*. The results are shown in Figure 4 and Figure 5, respectively.

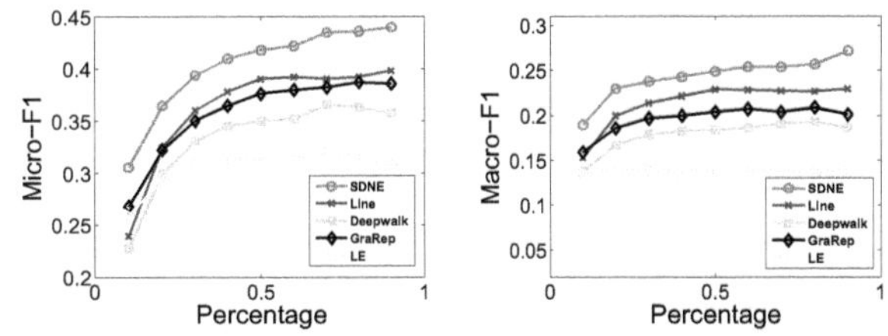

Figure 4: Micro-F1 and Macro-F1 on BLOGCATALOG. The results show that our method achieves better classification performance than that of baselines.

From the results, we have the following observations and analysis[5]:

- In Figure 4 and Figure 5, the curve of our method is consistently above the curves of baselines. It demonstrates that the learned network representations of our method can better generalize to the classification task than baselines.
- In Figure 4 (BLOGCATALOG), the improvement margin of our method over the baselines is more obvious when the training percentage decreases from 60% to 10%. It demonstrates that our method can achieve a more significant improvement than baselines when the labelled data is limited. Such an advantage is especially important for real-world applications because the labelled data is usually scarce.
- In most cases, the performance of *DeepWalk* is the worst a-mong the network embedding methods. The reasons are t-wofold. First of all, *DeepWalk* does not have an explicit objective function to capture the network structure. Secondly, *DeepWalk* uses a random walk to enrich the neighbors of vertexes, which introduces a lot of noises due to the randomness, especially for vertexes which have high degrees.

4.5.3 Link Prediction

In this section, we concentrate on the link prediction task and conduct two experiments. The first evaluates the overall performance and the second evaluates that how different sparsity of the networks affects the performance of different methods.

We use the dataset ARXIV GR-QC in this section. To conduct the link prediction task in a network, we randomly hide a portion of the existing links and use the left network to train the network embedding model. After the training, we can obtain the representations for each vertex and then use the obtained representations

[5] Some results such as the observation that our method outperforms *LINE* have been listed and explained in Section 4.5.1. Therefore, we only list some particular observations of this experiment.

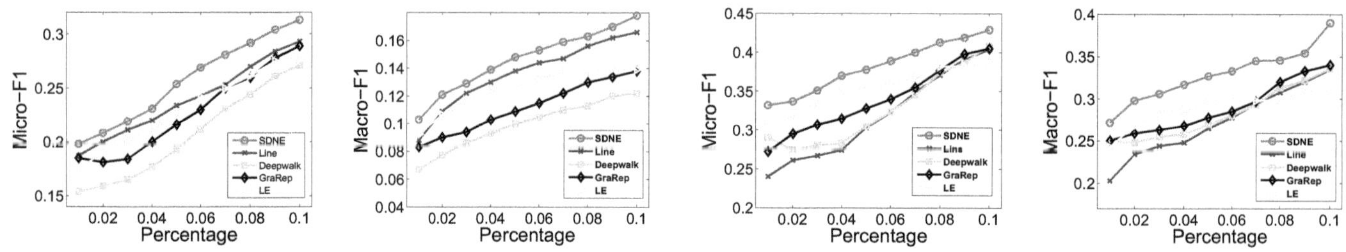

(a) Micro-F1 and Macro-F1 on FLICKR

(b) Micro-F1 and Macro-F1 on YOUTUBE

Figure 5: Micro-F1 and Macro-F1 on (a) FLICKR and (b) YOUTUBE. The results show that our method achieves the best classification performance among baselines.

Table 5: *precision@k* on ARXIV GR-QC for link prediction

Algorithm	P@2	P@10	P@100	P@200	P@300	P@500	P@800	P@1000	P@10000
SDNE	**1**	**1**	**1**	**1**	**1***	**0.99****	**0.97****	**0.91****	**0.257****
LINE	1	1	1	1	0.99	0.936	0.74	0.79	0.2196
DeepWalk	1	0.8	0.6	0.555	0.443	0.346	0.2988	0.293	0.1591
GraRep	1	0.2	0.04	0.035	0.033	0.038	0.035	0.035	0.019
Common Neighbor	1	1	1	0.96	0.9667	0.98	0.8775	0.798	0.192
LE	1	1	0.93	0.855	0.827	0.66	0.468	0.391	0.05

Significantly outperforms Line at the: ** 0.01 and * 0.05 level, paired t-test.

to predict the unobserved link. Unlike the reconstruction task, this task predicts the future links instead of reconstructing the existing links. Therefore, this task can show the performance of predictability of different network embedding methods. In addition, we add *Common Neighbor* in this task because it has been proved as an effective method to do link prediction [17].

For the first experiment, we randomly hide 15 precentage of existing links (about 4000 links) and use the *precision@k* as the evaluation metric of predicting the hidden links. We gradually increase the k from 2 to 10000 and report the result in Table 5. The best performance is highlighted in bold. Some of the observations and analysis on Table 5 are listed as follows:

- The result shows that when k increases, the performance of our method is consistently better than other network embedding methods. It demonstrates that the representations learned by our method have much better predicting power for new link formation.
- When $k = 1000$, the precision of our method is still higher than 0.9, but that of other methods quickly drops below 0.8. It demonstrates that our method can keep a high precision for links ranking ahead. Such an advantage is very important for some real-world applications such as recommendation and information retrieval, because users care more about the results ranked ahead in such applications.

In the second experiment, we change the sparsity of the networks by randomly removing a portion of links in the original network and then follow the aforementioned procedure to report the results of different network embedding methods. The result is shown in Figure 6.

The result shows that the margin between *LE* and *SDNE* or between *LE* and *LINE* becomes larger when the network is sparser. It demonstrates that the import of second-order proximity is able to make the learned representations more robust to sparse networks. Moreover, when we remove 80% of the links, our method still performs significantly better than baselines. It also demonstrates the power of *SDNE* in dealing with sparse networks.

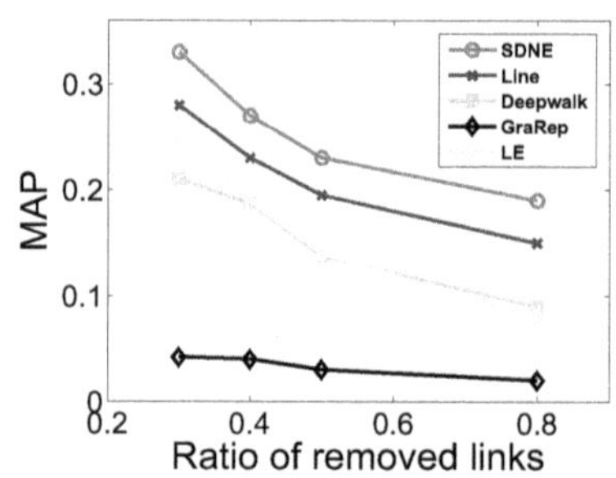

Figure 6: Performance of network embedding on networks of different sparsity. It shows that *SDNE* is more robust to the sparse network.

4.5.4 *Visualization*

Another important application for network embedding is to generate visualizations of a network on a two-dimensional space. Therefore, we visualize the learned representations of the 20-NEWSGROUP network. We use the low-dimensional network representations learned by different network embedding methods as the input to the visualization tool *t-SNE* [31]. As a result, each newsgroup document is mapped as a two-dimensional vector. Then we can visualize each vector as a point on a two dimensional space. For documents which are labelled as different categories, we use different colors on the corresponded points. Therefore, a good visualization result is that the points of the same color are near from each other. The visualization figure is shown in Figure 7. Besides the visualization figure, similar to [4] we use the Kullback-Leibler divergence as a quantitative evaluation metric. The lower the KL divergence, the better the performance. The result is shown in Table 6.

From Figure 7, we can see that the results of *LE* and *DeepWalk* are not satisfactory because the points belonging to different categories are mixed with each other. For *LINE*, the clusters of different categories are formed. However, in the center part the documents

(a) *SDNE* (b) *LINE* (c) *DeepWalk* (d) *GraRep* (e) *LE*

Figure 7: Visualization of 20-NEWSGROUP. Each point indicates one document. Color of a point indicates the category of the document. The blue indicates the topic of rec.sport.baseball, the red indicates the topic of comp.graphics and the green indicates the topic of talk.politics.guns

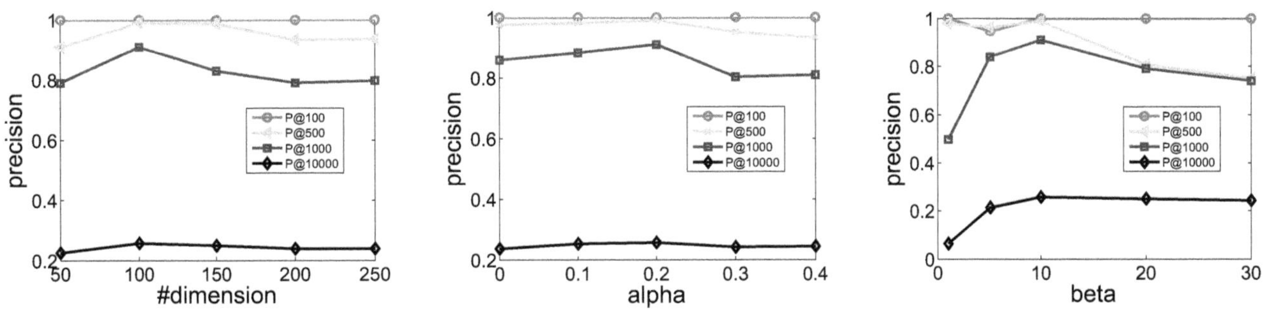

(a) #dimension (b) α (c) β

Figure 8: Parameter w.r.t. the number of embedding dimensions, the value of α and the value of β

Table 6: KL-divergence for the 20-NEWSGROUP dataset

Algorithm	*SDNE*	*GraRep*	*LINE*	*DeepWalk*	*LE*
KL divergence	**0.68****	0.73	0.87	2.6	2.95

Significantly outperforms GraRep at the: ** 0.01 level.

of different categories are still mixed with each other. For *GraRep*, the result looks better because points of the same color form segmented groups. However, the boundaries of each group are not very clear. Obviously, the visualization of *SDNE* performs best in both the aspects of group separation and boundary aspects. The results shown in Table 6 also quantitatively demonstrate the superiority of our method in the visualization task.

4.6 Parameter Sensitivity

We investigate the parameter sensitivity in this section. Specifically, we evaluate how different numbers of the embedding dimensions and different values of hyper-parameter α and β can affect the results. We report *precision@k* on the dataset of ARXIV-GRQC.

Choose an appropriate number of embedding dimensions: We first show how the dimension of the embedding vectors affects the performance in Figure 8(a). We can see that initially the performance raises when the number of dimension increases. This is intuitive as more bits can encode more useful information in the increasing bits. However, when the number of dimensions continuously increases, the performance starts to drop slowly. The reason is that too large number of dimensions may introduce noises which will deteriorate the performance. Overall, it is always important to determine the number of dimensions for the latent embedding space, but our method is not very sensitive to this parameter.

Find a good balanced point between first-order and second-order proximity: Then we show how the value of α affects the performance in Figure 8(b). The parameter of α balances the weight of the first-order proximity and second-order proximity between vertexes. When $\alpha = 0$, the performance is totally determined by the second-order proximity. And the larger the α, the more the model concentrates on the first-order proximity. From Figure 8(b), we can see that the performance of $\alpha = 0.1$ and $\alpha = 0.2$ are better than that of $\alpha = 0$. It demonstrates that both first-order and second-order proximity are essential for network embedding methods to characterize the network structure.

Concentrate more on the reconstruction error for the non-zero elements: At last, we show how the value of β affects the performance. The β controls the reconstruction weight of the non-zero elements in the training graph. The larger the β, the model will more prone to reconstruct the non-zero elements. The result is shown in Figure 8(c). We can see that when $\beta = 1$, the result is not good. Because in this case, the model will equally reconstruct the non-zero and zero elements in the training network. As we have explained before, no link between two nodes does not indicate dissimilarity of these two nodes, but the existence of a link between two nodes does indicate similarity of these two nodes. Therefore, the reconstruction of zero elements will introduce noises and thus deteriorate the performance. However, when β is too large, the performance decreases too. The reason is that, in this case, the model almost ignores the zero-elements when perform reconstruction and is prone to maintain similarity between any pair of nodes. However, many zero elements still indicate the dissimilarity between vertexes. Therefore, the performance drops. This experiment suggests that we should concentrate more on the reconstruction error of none-zero elements in the training networks but cannot totally omit the reconstruction error of zero elements when we perform network embedding.

5. CONCLUSIONS

In this paper, we propose a Structural Deep Network Embedding, namely *SDNE*, to perform network embedding. Specifically, to capture the highly non-linear network structure, we design a semi-supervised deep model, which has multiple layers of non-linear functions. To further address the structure-preserving and sparsity problem, we jointly exploit the first-order proximity and second-order proximity to characterize the local and global network structure. By jointly optimizing them in the semi-supervised deep model, the learned representations are local-global structure-preserved and are robust to sparse networks. Empirically, we evaluate the generated network representations in a variety of network datasets and applications. The results demonstrate substantial gains of our method compared with state-of-the-art.

Our future work will focus on how to learn representations for a new vertex which has no linkage to existing vertexes.

6. ACKNOWLEDGMENTS

This work was supported by National Program on Key Basic Research Project, No. 2015CB352300; National Natural Science Foundation of China, No. 61370022, No. 61531006, No. 61472444 and No. 61210008. Thanks for the research fund of Tsinghua-Tencent Joint Laboratory for Internet Innovation Technology.

7. REFERENCES

[1] M. Belkin and P. Niyogi. Laplacian eigenmaps for dimensionality reduction and data representation. *Neural computation*, 15(6):1373–1396, 2003.

[2] Y. Bengio. Learning deep architectures for ai. *Foundations and trends® in Machine Learning*, 2(1):1–127, 2009.

[3] Y. Bengio, A. Courville, and P. Vincent. Representation learning: A review and new perspectives. *Pattern Analysis and Machine Intelligence, IEEE Transactions on*, 35(8):1798–1828, 2013.

[4] S. Cao, W. Lu, and Q. Xu. Grarep: Learning graph representations with global structural information. In *Proceedings of the 24th ACM International on Conference on Information and Knowledge Management*, pages 891–900. ACM, 2015.

[5] S. Chang, W. Han, J. Tang, G.-J. Qi, C. C. Aggarwal, and T. S. Huang. Heterogeneous network embedding via deep architectures. In *Proceedings of the 21th ACM SIGKDD International Conference on Knowledge Discovery and Data Mining*, pages 119–128. ACM, 2015.

[6] N. S. Dash. Context and contextual word meaning. *SKASE Journal of Theoretical Linguistics*, 5(2):21–31, 2008.

[7] D. Erhan, Y. Bengio, A. Courville, P.-A. Manzagol, P. Vincent, and S. Bengio. Why does unsupervised pre-training help deep learning? *The Journal of Machine Learning Research*, 11:625–660, 2010.

[8] R.-E. Fan, K.-W. Chang, C.-J. Hsieh, X.-R. Wang, and C.-J. Lin. Liblinear: A library for large linear classification. *The Journal of Machine Learning Research*, 9:1871–1874, 2008.

[9] K. Georgiev and P. Nakov. A non-iid framework for collaborative filtering with restricted boltzmann machines. In *ICML-13*, pages 1148–1156, 2013.

[10] G. Hinton, L. Deng, D. Yu, G. E. Dahl, A.-r. Mohamed, N. Jaitly, A. Senior, V. Vanhoucke, P. Nguyen, T. N. Sainath, et al. Deep neural networks for acoustic modeling in speech recognition: The shared views of four research groups. *Signal Processing Magazine, IEEE*, 29(6):82–97, 2012.

[11] G. E. Hinton, S. Osindero, and Y.-W. Teh. A fast learning algorithm for deep belief nets. *Neural computation*, 18(7):1527–1554, 2006.

[12] G. E. Hinton and R. R. Salakhutdinov. Reducing the dimensionality of data with neural networks. *Science*, 2006.

[13] M. Jamali and M. Ester. A matrix factorization technique with trust propagation for recommendation in social networks. In *Proceedings of the fourth ACM conference on Recommender systems*, pages 135–142. ACM, 2010.

[14] E. M. Jin, M. Girvan, and M. E. Newman. Structure of growing social networks. *Physical review E*, 64(4):046132, 2001.

[15] A. Krizhevsky, I. Sutskever, and G. E. Hinton. Imagenet classification with deep convolutional neural networks. In *Advances in neural information processing systems*, pages 1097–1105, 2012.

[16] J. Leskovec, J. Kleinberg, and C. Faloutsos. Graph evolution: Densification and shrinking diameters. *ACM Transactions on Knowledge Discovery from Data (TKDD)*, 1(1):2, 2007.

[17] D. Liben-Nowell and J. Kleinberg. The link-prediction problem for social networks. *Journal of the American society for information science and technology*, 58(7):1019–1031, 2007.

[18] T. Liu and D. Tao. Classification with noisy labels by importance reweighting. *TPAMI*, (1):1–1.

[19] D. Luo, F. Nie, H. Huang, and C. H. Ding. Cauchy graph embedding. In *Proceedings of the 28th International Conference on Machine Learning (ICML-11)*, pages 553–560, 2011.

[20] A. Y. Ng, M. I. Jordan, Y. Weiss, et al. On spectral clustering: Analysis and an algorithm. *Advances in neural information processing systems*, 2:849–856, 2002.

[21] B. Perozzi, R. Al-Rfou, and S. Skiena. Deepwalk: Online learning of social representations. In *SIGKDD*, pages 701–710. ACM, 2014.

[22] S. T. Roweis and L. K. Saul. Nonlinear dimensionality reduction by locally linear embedding. *Science*, 290(5500):2323–2326, 2000.

[23] R. Salakhutdinov and G. Hinton. Semantic hashing. *International Journal of Approximate Reasoning*, 50(7):969–978, 2009.

[24] B. Shaw and T. Jebara. Structure preserving embedding. In *Proceedings of the 26th Annual International Conference on Machine Learning*, pages 937–944. ACM, 2009.

[25] R. Socher, A. Perelygin, J. Y. Wu, J. Chuang, C. D. Manning, A. Y. Ng, and C. Potts. Recursive deep models for semantic compositionality over a sentiment treebank. In *Proceedings of the conference on empirical methods in natural language processing (EMNLP)*, volume 1631, page 1642. Citeseer, 2013.

[26] J. Tang, M. Qu, M. Wang, M. Zhang, J. Yan, and Q. Mei. Line: Large-scale information network embedding. In *Proceedings of the 24th International Conference on World Wide Web*, pages 1067–1077. International World Wide Web Conferences Steering Committee, 2015.

[27] L. Tang and H. Liu. Relational learning via latent social dimensions. In *Proceedings of the 15th ACM SIGKDD international conference on Knowledge discovery and data mining*. ACM, 2009.

[28] L. Tang and H. Liu. Scalable learning of collective behavior based on sparse social dimensions. In *Proceedings of the 18th ACM conference on Information and knowledge management*, pages 1107–1116. ACM, 2009.

[29] J. B. Tenenbaum, V. De Silva, and J. C. Langford. A global geometric framework for nonlinear dimensionality reduction. *Science*, 290(5500):2319–2323, 2000.

[30] F. Tian, B. Gao, Q. Cui, E. Chen, and T.-Y. Liu. Learning deep representations for graph clustering. In *Proceedings of the Twenty-Eighth AAAI Conference on Artificial Intelligence*, pages 1293–1299, 2014.

[31] L. Van der Maaten and G. Hinton. Visualizing data using t-sne. *Journal of Machine Learning Research*, 9(2579-2605):85, 2008.

[32] S. V. N. Vishwanathan, N. N. Schraudolph, R. Kondor, and K. M. Borgwardt. Graph kernels. *The Journal of Machine Learning Research*, 11:1201–1242, 2010.

[33] D. Wang, P. Cui, M. Ou, and W. Zhu. Deep multimodal hashing with orthogonal regularization. In *Proceedings of the 24th International Conference on Artificial Intelligence*, pages 2291–2297. AAAI Press, 2015.

[34] Y. Weiss, A. Torralba, and R. Fergus. Spectral hashing. In *Advances in neural information processing systems*, pages 1753–1760, 2009.

[35] C. Xu, D. Tao, and C. Xu. Multi-view intact space learning. *Pattern Analysis and Machine Intelligence, IEEE Transactions on*, 37(12):2531–2544, 2015.

[36] J. Zhuang, I. W. Tsang, and S. Hoi. Two-layer multiple kernel learning. In *International conference on artificial intelligence and statistics*, pages 909–917, 2011.

Targeted Topic Modeling for Focused Analysis

Shuai Wang†, Zhiyuan Chen†, Geli Fei†, Bing Liu† and Sherry Emery‡
†Department of Computer Science
‡Institute of Health Research and Policy
University of Illinois at Chicago
Chicago, IL, USA
shuaiwanghk@gmail.com, czyuanacm@gmail.com,
gfei2@uic.edu, liub@cs.uic.edu, slemery@uic.edu

ABSTRACT

One of the overarching tasks of document analysis is to find what topics people talk about. One of the main techniques for this purpose is topic modeling. So far many models have been proposed. However, the existing models typically perform full analysis on the whole data to find all topics. This is certainly useful, but in practice we found that the user almost always also wants to perform more detailed analyses on some specific aspects, which we refer to as *targets* (or *targeted aspects*). Current full-analysis models are not suitable for such analyses as their generated topics are often too coarse and may not even be on target. For example, given a set of tweets about e-cigarette, one may want to find out what topics under discussion are specifically related to *children*. Likewise, given a collection of online reviews about a camera, a consumer or camera manufacturer may be interested in finding out all topics about the camera's *screen*, the targeted aspect. As we will see in our experiments, current full topic models are ineffective for such targeted analyses. This paper studies this problem and proposes a novel *targeted topic model* (TTM) to enable focused analyses on any specific aspect of interest. Our experimental results demonstrate the effectiveness of the TTM.

Keywords

Targeted Topic Modeling; Targeted Aspect; Targeted Analysis; Focused Analysis; Targeted Modeling; Topic Modeling

1. INTRODUCTION

One of the important text mining tasks is to discover the topics discussed in a collection of text documents (or a corpus). Topic modeling is one of the main techniques used for this purpose. So far numerous topic models have been proposed in the literature, which may mine topics only or jointly mine topics and other types of useful information, for example, sentiment information [17, 5, 32].

However, existing models typically perform full analysis on the entire corpus to discover all topics. This is certainly useful, but it is inevitably coarse. In practice we found that the user almost always also wants to perform deeper and more focused analysis on some specific aspects of the data, which we refer to as *targets*, or *targeted aspects* in this paper. For example, given a set of tweets about *e-cigarette*, the user (or researcher) wants to gain insight into topics that have been discussed about *children*. Here *children* is the targeted aspect. If a topic model can find topics such as *regulations* and *fears* about children smoking e-cigarette that are specifically related to this target, it will be very useful. Formally, the proposed targeted analysis problem is defined as follows (note that we use targeted analysis and focused analysis in this paper interchangeably).

Problem Definition: Given a corpus C of documents of a broad area/domain, discover related topics T of a user-interested aspect (called targeted aspect) represented with a set of keywords S provided by the user.

To solve this problem, a natural approach to start with is to use a regular full-analysis topic model such as LDA [4]. Following the previous example, we can see that e-cigarette is a broad area (with corpus C provided) and *children* is the targeted aspect. Note that the target *children* is represented by some keywords S (e.g., S = {"children," "kids"}). After applying LDA on the corpus C to produce a set of topics Q, we find those topics in Q that contain some keywords from S in their top ranked words and study them in order to find the target-related topics T ($T \subseteq Q$). However, this approach is often unsatisfactory due to a few reasons (or *issues*).

1. The user does not know all the keywords that can represent a targeted aspect. In the above example, if the user specifies "children" as the only keyword and miss out other related keywords such as "young" and "minors", he may lose some important topics.

2. It may not find any topics for the user-interested aspect. Because there may be many other more prevalent or dominating topics in the data, the model may not find the related topics of some less frequent aspects. For example, when our targeted aspect is *weight* represented by the keyword "weight" in camera reviews, the word "weight" has a relatively low occurrence frequency as people often mention this concept implicitly in the sentences like "the lens is so heavy" or "its battery is light". A full-analysis topic model such as LDA may not find any topic about *weight* at all.

3. Even if the keywords are frequent, one still may not find good coherent topics due to two reasons: (1) *Topic suppression*: Since the targeted aspect is only one of many aspects discussed in a broad area and a full-analysis topic

KDD '16, August 13-17, 2016, San Francisco, CA, USA
© 2016 ACM. ISBN 978-1-4503-4232-2/16/08...$15.00
DOI: http://dx.doi.org/10.1145/2939672.2939743

model generates all topics for all aspects, the related topics of the targeted aspect may be suppressed. Many general words may be ranked at the top. For example, a topic about *children* (the targeted aspect) with topical words like "children", "kids", "young" is not informative. (2) *Word intrusion*: Words from other non-targeted aspects' topics may be *intruder* words appearing in the related topics of the targeted aspect, which makes the detection and understanding of the target-related topics difficult.

The cause of the above problems is related to some properties of topic modeling. First, useful information may not be easily detected under the condition of data sparsity or small data size. That is because classic topic models are unsupervised and governed by the phenomena called *higher order co-occurrence* [13]. As a result, some informative but infrequent words may be ranked low or even can not be correctly grouped. Second, the existing models are not targeted towards any user interest. As identified in [6], the objective functions of topic models may not correlate well with human judgments and needs. For example, a given broad corpus often cover a large number of topics, the topics for the user-interested aspect (i.e., target) may be mixed up with other non-target related topics and become incoherent. Although increasing the number of topics may help, the problem remains and other problems like information fragmentation may show up (the problems will be further discussed in Section 4.4). One may use knowledge-based models for targeted modeling [23, 32], but these models only try to put words related to the user specified keywords in the same topic. They do not distill the topics related to target aspect represented by keywords as we do. They still suffer from the aforementioned issues.

Another intuitive approach to solving the proposed problem is to select a subset of documents from the corpus C that contains at least one keyword $s \in S$ (denoted by C') and apply LDA to the resulting documents in C'. Clearly, this approach has the problem as illustrated in *Issue* 1. It also has *Issue* 2 but manifested differently. For example, when the keyword set S is {"weight"} the number of document C' might be so small that a topic model is unable to produce many good topics. Moreover, since it discards many potentially relevant documents, it diminishes the quality of topics and also loses many potentially related topics.

Recently, topic modeling with sparsity has been proposed. Sparse topic models such as those in [8, 33, 18] can (a) identify focused topics of a document, or (b) extract focused words of a topic. However, they are still full-analysis models and not for targeted modeling, and thus still suffer from the aforementioned issues. More discussions will be given in Section 2. Inspired by them, we employ the sparsity idea in designing our new model for targeted/focused analysis.

To address the proposed problems, we designed a new model called the *targeted topic model* (TTM). It is used for focused analysis as it can directly generate related topics of a given targeted aspect. The novelty of TTM is that it models using the entire corpus C while targeted at the user-specified aspect. This enables TTM to discover more related topics and also improve the topic quality because it can better exploit the information from other relevant documents in C that do not contain the given keywords in S.

In summary, this paper makes the following contributions:

1. It proposes the new problem of targeted topic modeling to discover only topics that are related to a user-specified aspect. To the best of our knowledge, no existing topic model can perform this task. Such targeted/focused analysis is important because not everyone is interested in everything in a corpus. When one is interested in a particular aspect, he/she often wants to perform deeper and focused analysis.

2. It proposes a new probabilistic topic model called *Targeted Topic Model* (TTM) that is able to perform the proposed focused analysis, which is also the first such model.

3. Our experimental results using five real-life datasets and a set of aspects show the effectiveness of the proposed model. It outperforms state-of-art baseline models markedly.

2. RELATED WORK

To our knowledge, there is no existing topic model that is able to perform the proposed targeted analysis as we do. Our work is, however, clearly related to the classic topic models such as PLSA [14] and LDA [4] and their variants. These models have been used to discover hidden thematic structures in a collection of documents or corpus. There are numerous existing models (e.g., [25, 24, 34, 23, 8, 11, 27]). They either identify topics only or jointly identify both topics and other types of information. For example, while both LDA and PLSA only identify topics, [30, 22] jointly model both topics and ratings in reviews. [24, 10] model labeled data with the class information. [19, 15] conduct time-series analysis of topics. However, as we indicated in the introduction section, all these models and their variants are full analysis models. They aim to find all topics in the corpus, and none of them is able to perform targeted analysis based on only a specific aspect that is of interest to users. Existing research also proposed several knowledge-based topic models, which can incorporate prior domain knowledge in topic modeling [1, 23, 9, 32] to generate better results. But they are also full-analysis models, and do not help discover related topics of the user interested aspect.

Our work is also related to sparse topic models. The modeling of sparsity can represent skewed distributions, e.g., a topic usually focuses on a narrow range of words instead of a wide range of them in the vocabulary [18]. This type of models is inspired by the influential power of the asymmetric Dirichlet prior [28]. Existing sparse topic models can be categorized into two types: (1) those that discover the salient (focused) topics of a specific document [8, 33], and (2) those that discover representative (focused) terms of a particular topic [29]. Researchers also tried to achieve both at the same time in a hybrid manner [18, 2]. However, it is important to note that focused topics or terms in sparse models are entirely different from our targeted analysis because they aim to achieve very high probabilities for a small number of topics in a document or for a small set of words/terms in a topic. They are still full-analysis models and cannot focus their modeling only on a user-specified aspect.

Although not directly related, there are other works of non-probabilistic models with sparse coding [35, 20, 7, 31]. However, they function quite differently in the goal or the methodology compared to probabilistic generative models. For example, they do not need to tackle the knotty issue of decoupling sparsity and smoothing [29] for sparsity realization in probabilistic models. Furthermore, they have been shown with poorer performances as the number of topics increases and are inferior compared to the probabilistic sparse topic models reported in [18]. Most importantly, like other models, they do not do targeted analysis like we do.

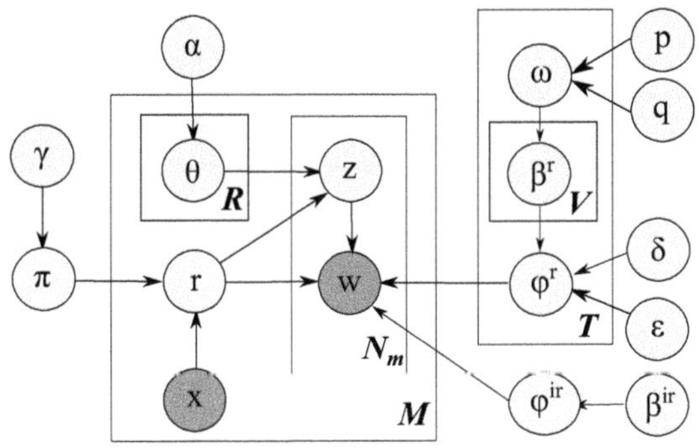

Figure 1: The graphical model of TTM

3. PROPOSED MODEL

As discussed in the introduction section, our problem statement is that given a corpus C of a broad area, the proposed model can generate topics of the targeted aspect specified by the user using a set of keywords S.

Since the proposed model needs to discover fine-grained topics (also called topics of the targeted aspect), we treat each sentence as a document in topic modeling like several other fine-grained models [5, 26]. Following previous work in [26, 5, 34, 23, 17], we also assume that each sentence focuses on only one aspect. Since we regard each sentence as a document in modeling, each document focuses on only one aspect. Although it might not always be correct, it holds up well in practice [17, 34] and generates good results (shown in section 4). The graphical model of the proposed TTM is given in Figure 1. Since a document talks about one aspect, when the targeted aspect is specified, there can be two possible statuses for a document, that is, relevant or irrelevant to the targeted aspect. The status variable is denoted by r.

3.1 Generative Process

Here we present and illustrate the generative process:

1. Draw $\varphi^{ir} \sim Dirichlet(\boldsymbol{\beta^{ir}})$ as a word distribution of a irrelevant topic to the targeted aspect;
2. For each target-relevant topic $t \in \{1, 2, ..., T\}$:
   (a) Draw a prior distribution $\omega_t \sim Beta(p, q)$;
   (b) For each term $v \in \{1, 2, ..., V\}$:
      i. Draw a term selector $\beta^r_{t,\,v} \sim Bernoulli(\omega_t)$;
   (c) Draw a word distribution $\varphi^r_t \sim Dirichlet(\boldsymbol{\beta^r_t \delta} + \boldsymbol{\epsilon})$;
3. For each document $m \in \{1, 2, ..., M\}$:
   (a) Draw a prior distribution $\pi_m \sim Beta(\boldsymbol{\gamma})$;
   (b) Draw relevance status r based on keyword indicator x and $Bernoulli(\pi_m)$;
   (c) If the document is relevant to the targeted aspect, i.e., $r = 1$:
      i. Draw a topic $z \sim Multinomial(\theta^r)$;
      ii. Emit a word $w_i \sim Multinomial(\varphi^r_z)$.
   (d) If the document is irrelevant to the targeted aspect, i.e., $r = 0$:
      i. Emit a word $w_i \sim Multinomial(\varphi^{ir})$

For better understanding, we use three sample documents from the *e-cigarette* (*e-cig* for short) domain for illustration:

(*d*1) *e-cig is a gateway to smoking for children.*
(*d*2) *it explores gateway effect of e-cig for kids.*
(*d*3) *I saw a woman smoking e-cig on the street.*

As we assumed above, a document talks about one aspect. Then when the targeted aspect is given by a user, a document can be identified as relevant or irrelevant to the targeted aspect. r represents this relevance. $r \in \{0, 1\}$, where r=1 means the document is relevant to the target and r=0 is irrelevant. Another related variable is x, which represents whether a document contains at least one keyword $s \in S$. $x \in \{0, 1\}$, where x=1 indicates the document contains the keyword(s) and x=0 indicates it does not. For example, when S is {"children"} and a document m says "e-cigarette is a gateway to smoking for *children*" (i.e., example *d*1), the keyword indicator x_m=1 because the document m contains the keyword "children". In this case (x_m=1), m is regarded as relevant (r_m=1) because it is unlikely that a short sentence contains the word "children" and is not talking about *children*. However, this is a soft constraint that can be relaxed by adjusting a control factor λ (presented in Equation 1) and $0 \leqslant \lambda \leqslant 1$, i.e., λ controls how much we believe a document contains a keyword is actually relevant. When it comes to the opposite situation that there is no keyword found in a documents m (i.e., x_m=0), it is a different case because the document can be either relevant or irrelevant. For instance, the above example *d*2 is clearly relevant to target *children* while example *d*3 is not and they both do not contain the keyword "children". We will discuss how to handle this case (x_m=0) in the following sub-sections.

After the relevance r of a document is drawn, we see how a word w_i is generated. As discussed above, there are two types of relevance status for each document. When r=1, a

T	the number of topics
M	the number of documents
N_m	the number of words in document m
V	the number of words (or terms) in vocabulary
R	the number of the relevance status
m, z, v	document, topic, word
w_i, z_i,	word in position i (word i), topic of word i
x, r	keyword indicator, relevance status
p, q	beta prior for ω
δ, ϵ	smoothing prior, weak smoothing prior
β^r	term selector (value of term selector $\in$ {0,1})
θ	multinomial distribution over topics
π	bernoulli distribution over relevance status
ω	bernoulli distribution over term selector
φ^r	multinomial distribution over topical words
φ^{ir}	multinomial distribution over irrelevant topical words
α, β^{ir}, γ	Dirichlet prior for θ, φ^{ir}, Beta prior for π
x_m, r_m,	keyword indicator, relevance status of document m
β^r_v, $\beta^r_{t,v}$	term selector of term v under relevance status r, term selector of term v in topic t
$\boldsymbol{w}$, $\boldsymbol{z}$, $\boldsymbol{r}$	all words, assigned topics and relevance status
$\boldsymbol{z}^{-i}$	all assigned topics except the one for word i
$\boldsymbol{\beta}^{r(-v)}$	all selected terms except the term v under relevance status r
$\boldsymbol{\beta}_t^{r(-v)}$	all selected terms except the term v in topic t
$f_{r,m,v}$	the frequency of vocabulary term v in document m under relevance status r
$C_r^{R(-m)}$	the number of documents under relevance r except document m
$C^{RW}_{r,\,v}$	the number of words of vocabulary term v under relevance status r
$C^{RMT(-i)}_{r,m,t}$	the number of words under relevance r and topic t in document m except word i
$C^{RTW}_{r,\,t,\,v}$	the number of words of vocabulary term v under relevance r and topic t

Table 1: Definitions of notations

topic t is chosen from θ^r. The total number of topics is $|T|$ and these topics are the topics related to the target. After that a word is emitted from the selected topic by φ^r_t. When r=0 the generative process is similar but TTM does not further generate multiple topics of the non-targeted aspects because they are not related to the user-interested aspect. Thus a word w_i is emitted directly from φ^{ir}. In other words, the words in the irrelevant documents are drawn from only one (irrelevant) topic.

3.2 Targeted Modeling with Sparsity

This sub-section presents how TTM achieves the targeted modeling by exploiting the idea of sparsity. Traditionally, sparsity in topic modeling indicates that a topic usually focuses on a narrow range of words rather than a wide range of them in the vocabulary, or a document focuses on a very small number of topics [29, 18]. Similarly, in TTM we use a similar concept called *aspect sparsity*, which consists of two parts: *document-aspect sparsity* and *targeted-aspect sparsity*, which are detailed below.

Since a sentence is regarded as a document, TTM already assumes that each document focuses on only one aspect. The document-aspect sparsity is then naturally achieved. Additionally, the idea of targeted modeling with sparsity is based on two importance observations.

First, the targeted aspect may only be a small part or a minority among all aspects in a given corpus. For example, *Children* is only one aspect in the e-cigarette domain, which has a large number of other aspects such as *Elderly*, *Vaporizer* and *Health*. This observation gives raise to the targeted-aspect sparsity.

Second, since each document is coupled to one aspect (using document-aspect sparsity), if we can better represent the targeted aspect, we should be able to better extract its relevant documents. If we can extract more relevant documents for the targeted aspect, we are likely to discover other more important words to better represent the target. As a result, better and more topics are more likely to be generated because of better representative words and more relevant documents about the target are identified. Thus, we believe jointly modeling of relevance status r and the targeted aspect can benefit the topic discovery.

As introduced in section 2, sparsity has been used to represent the skewed data distribution in topic modeling. It provides a possible way to represent the property of minority (the first observation above) and to model the targeted aspect with document relevance in a unified framework (the second observation above). We therefore follow this direction and propose the idea of *biased sparsity* to help achieve the targeted modeling and the aspect sparsity.

3.2.1 Biased Sparsity

Note that a target (aspect) is essentially represented by words. So the problem is how to automatically discover representative words of the targeted aspect in a joint modeling manner. As discussed above, a targeted aspect is sparse among all aspects. From it we can further posit that (in most cases) a targeted aspect is also sparse compared to the combination of all non-targeted aspects. When combining this statement with the scenario that *a targeted aspect is represented by words*, we can conclude that the number of important words for distinguishing the targeted aspect from non-targeted aspects is in a narrow range. That is, the representative words for the targeted aspect are sparse. These words are denoted by $V_{r=1}$. However, the representative words from the combination of all other non-targeted aspects are probably not sparse because that combination needs to contain almost all possible words for describing all other aspects. These words are denoted by $V_{r=0}$. Now we introduce the proposed *biased sparsity*, which is used for realizing the above idea.

The proposed *biased sparsity* approach is to make the word sparsity biased much more towards the targeted aspect (i.e., $|V_{r=1}| \ll |V|$) and keep the non-targeted aspects almost non-sparse (i.e., $|V_{r=0}| \approx |V|$). In other words, the word distribution of the targeted aspect (demoted by φ^r) only focuses on a small number of representative words. But the word distribution of non-targeted aspects (denoted by φ^{ir}, where ir means a unified irrelevant topic) contains almost all possible words. With this setting, only those words that simultaneously satisfy both the following two conditions can be selected as representative words for the targeted aspect: (a) they are semantically correlated with the known words of the target (achieved by the power of topic modeling) and (b) they can distinguish the targeted aspect from non-targeted aspects (constrained by *biased sparsity*).

3.2.2 Targeted Modeling

This sub-section demonstrates the targeted modeling in TTM, with the incorporation of biased sparsity. Here we follow the previous examples in section 3.1 to illustrate. Recall that S={"children"} and the document $d1$ containing the keyword (x_{d1}=1) is known to be relevant (r_{d1}=1). Although the word "children" is not in document $d2$, the word "gateway" (also in $d1$) serves as a bridge to connect the words in $d2$ via topic modeling. If the "gateway" has been identified as a discriminative word for target *children*, it makes $d2$ more probable to be relevant (r_{d2}=1) as $d2$ also contains the word "gateway". In this case, even though $d2$ has no keyword "children" it still has a high probability to be relevant. In contrast, although "smoking" appears in both documents $d1$ and $d3$, if "smoking" is not identified as a discriminative word for aspect *children*, $d3$ will be mostly treated as irrelevant (r_{d3}=0).

Biased sparsity is the key to identify discriminative words for the targeted aspect, which is done by imposing the sparse constraint ($|V_{r=1}| \ll |V|$ and $|V_{r=0}| \approx |V|$) discussed above. Specifically, when the target is *children*, "gateway" will be a word included in φ^r and "smoking" will not be. An explanation is that "smoking" is also widely used by other non-targeted aspects like *Elderly* and *Health*, while "gateway" is used in *Children* more often. Thus, "gateway" is more discriminative for *children* but "smoking" is too genreal.

Another crucial factor is the relevance status r. When more discriminative words (like "gateway") are included in φ^r, they in return increase the overall probability of the documents (like $d2$) that contain those words (like "gateway") to be relevant (r=1). When those documents are identified as relevant, new representative words (like "kids" in $d2$) for the target aspect are also found and added to φ^r. Note that the growing of words in φ^r will not be an endless process because of the sparsity constraint. After that these new words (like "kids") in φ^r will help detect other relevant documents. This process shows the strength of joint modeling of the target aspect (using biased sparsity) and the relevance status r in TTM. It also explains why TTM can finally shape better topics. Because it is able to exploit the information in other relevant documents in C even without knowing the additional keywords such as "kids", "young" and "minors", as they are automatically found and involved in the modeling process.

In a nutshell, the relevance variable r and the biased-sparsity related variable φ^r and φ^{ir} function together to ensure the property of aspect sparsity. Specifically, the encoding of φ^r and φ^{ir} to achieve *biased sparsity* is based on the implementation of spike-and-slab prior.

3.2.3 Spike-and-Slab Prior

The spike-and-slab prior is incorporated in the probabilistic topic model to realize a switcher-like "on" and "off" selector. This prior is first introduced in [21] and is recently reported as an effective way to reduce the model uncertainty [16]. It can also be used to decouple the sparsity and smoothing problem in Dirichlet distribution [3]. It has been used in topic modeling for word sparsity [29, 18]. In brief, "spike" controls the selection of a word, while "slab" smooths the word selected by "spike".

The spike-and-slab prior and other related components are together formulated as random variables in our model for the implementation of the biased sparsity. The related variables are ω, p, q, β^r, δ, ϵ and φ^r. For every word $v \in V$, $\beta^r_v \in \{0,1\}$ is the specific word selector. When β^r_v=1 a word is selected and β^r_v=0 a word is not selected. Note that in TTM, for a keyword $s \in S$ the β^r_s is set to 1. It is intuitive as those keywords are given by the user for specifying the targeted aspect. Different from β^r, β^{ir} is a predefined prior. It is symmetric for all other words except the known keywords $s \in S$, because the known keywords given by the user is very unlikely to be irrelevant to the target.

Unlike non-probabilistic models, one knotty issue for probabilistic models is the decoupling of sparsity and smoothing [29]. Motivated by [18], we incorporate a weak smoothing prior ϵ in addition to the regular smoothing prior δ.

Double Sparsity: In addition to the *target sparsity*, the words for a specific topic related to the targeted aspect is also sparse. That is reasonable because TTM aim at discovering more fine-grained topics and the words for describing such a topic are naturally sparse. Likewise, the $\varphi^r_{t,v}$ where $t \in T$ and $v \in V$ is also encoded with a slpike-and-slab prior in TTM. Together with the target sparsity, the sparsity of topical words enables the model to generate more coherent topics of the targeted aspect.

3.3 Inference

We use Gibbs Sampling [12] for model inference. The conditional distributions are shown in Equations 1, 2, 3, 4 and 5 (see Table 1 for the meanings of notations). The * symbol means the summation of all instances of the corresponding variable, for example, $C^{RTW(-i)}_{r,\,t,\,*}$ is the number of all words under relevance status r and topic t except the word in position i.

First, we sample the relevance status r for every document m, where $r \in R$ and $m \in M$.

$$P(r_m = c|x_m = d, \boldsymbol{\Theta}), \boldsymbol{\Theta} = \{\boldsymbol{r_m^{-i}}, \boldsymbol{w}, \boldsymbol{\pi}, \boldsymbol{\beta^r}, \boldsymbol{\beta^{ir}}, \gamma, \delta, \epsilon\}$$
$$\propto \begin{cases} g(c,\boldsymbol{\Theta}) & d=0, c=0 \textit{ or } 1 \\ \lambda \times g(c,\boldsymbol{\Theta}) & d=1, c=1 \\ (1-\lambda)\times g(c,\boldsymbol{\Theta}) & d=1, c=0 \end{cases} \tag{1}$$

$$g(c,\boldsymbol{\Theta}) =$$
$$\begin{cases} \frac{C_c^{R(-m)}+\gamma}{C_*^{R(-m)}+|R|\gamma} \times \frac{\prod_v^V \Gamma(\beta_v^r C_{c,\,v}^{RW(-m)}+\beta_v^r\delta+\epsilon+f_{c,m,v})}{\Gamma(\sum_v^V(\beta_v^r C_{c,\,v}^{RW(-m)}+f_{c,m,v})+|\beta_*^r|\delta+|V|\epsilon)} \\ c=1 \\ \frac{C_c^{R(-m)}+\gamma}{C_*^{R(-m)}+|R|\gamma} \times \frac{\prod_v^V \Gamma(C_{c,\,v}^{RW(-m)}+\beta_v^{ir}+f_{c,m,v})}{\Gamma(\sum_v^V C_{c,\,v}^{RW(-m)}+f_{c,m,v}+\beta_j^{ir})} \\ c=0 \end{cases} \tag{2}$$

Second, we sample the term selector β^r_v, where $v \in V$. $|\beta^r_*|$ is the sum of the values of all such term selectors.

$$P(\beta^r_v = b|\boldsymbol{\beta^{r(-v)}}, \boldsymbol{r}, \boldsymbol{w}, \delta, \epsilon, p, q) \propto$$
$$\begin{cases} \Gamma(C^{RW}_{r=1,\,v}+\delta+\epsilon)\times\Gamma(|\beta_*^{r(-v)}|\delta+|V|\epsilon+C^{RW(-v)}_{r=1,\,*}) \\ \times\,\Gamma(|\beta_*^{r(-v)}|\delta+\delta+|V|\epsilon)\times(p+|\beta_*^{r(-v)}|) & b=1 \\ \Gamma(\delta+\epsilon)\times\Gamma(|\beta_*^{r(-v)}|\delta+\delta+|V|\epsilon+C^{RW(-v)}_{r=1,\,*}) \\ \times\,\Gamma(|\beta_*^{r(-v)}|\delta+|V|\epsilon)\times(q+|V|-|\beta_*^{r(-v)}|-1) & b=0 \end{cases} \tag{3}$$

Third, we sample a topic of the word in position i. We do it for all words in the corpus. $|\beta^r_{t,*}|$ is the sum of the values of all such term selectors in topic t.

$$P(z_i = t|\boldsymbol{z}^{-i}, \boldsymbol{r}, \boldsymbol{w}, \alpha, \boldsymbol{\beta^r}, \boldsymbol{\beta^{ir}}, \delta, \epsilon) \propto$$
$$\begin{cases} \frac{C^{RMT(-i)}_{r_i,m,t}+\alpha}{C^{RMT(-i)}_{r_i,m,*}+|T|\alpha} \times \frac{(\beta^r_{t,v}C^{RTW(-i)}_{r_i,\,t,\,w_i}+\beta^r_{t,v}\delta+\epsilon)}{C^{RTW(-i)}_{r_i,t,*}+|\beta^r_{t,*}|\delta+|V|\epsilon} & r_i=1 \\ \frac{C^{RMT(-i)}_{r_i,m,t}+\alpha}{C^{RMT(-i)}_{r_i,m,*}+|T|\alpha} \times \frac{(C^{RTW(-i)}_{r_i,\,t,\,w_i}+\beta^{ir}_{t,v})}{C^{RTW(-i)}_{r_i,t,*}+|\beta^{ir}_{t,*}|} & r_i=0 \end{cases} \tag{4}$$

Last, we sample the term selector $\beta_{t,v}$, where $t \in T$ and $v \in V$.

$$P(\beta^r_{t,v} = s|\boldsymbol{\beta_t^{r(-v)}}, \boldsymbol{z}, \boldsymbol{r}, \boldsymbol{w}, \delta, \epsilon, p, q) \propto$$
$$\begin{cases} \Gamma(C^{RTW}_{r=1,\,t,\,v}+\delta+\epsilon)\times\Gamma(|\beta_{t,*}^{r(-v)}|\delta+|V|\epsilon+C^{RTW(-v)}_{r=1,\,t,\,*}) \\ \times\,\Gamma(|\beta_{t,*}^{r(-v)}|\delta+\delta+|V|\epsilon)\times(p+|\beta_{t,*}^{r(-v)}|) & s=1 \\ \Gamma(\delta+\epsilon)\times\Gamma(|\beta_{t,*}^{r(-v)}|\delta+\delta+|V|\epsilon+C^{RTW(-v)}_{r=1,\,t,\,*}) \\ \times\,\Gamma(|\beta_{t,*}^{r(-v)}|\delta+|V|\epsilon)\times(q+|V|-|\beta_{t,*}^{r(-v)}|-1) & s=0 \end{cases} \tag{5}$$

4. EXPERIMENT

4.1 Experimental Setup

Data and targeted aspects: Five real-world data sets in different domains are used in our experiments, namely, E-Cigarette, Cigar, Camera, Cell-Phone and Computer. The first two data sets are tweets collected from Twitter in October 2014. Specifically, E-Cigarette and Cigar are two types of tobacco-related products, which are the research areas of the last author from health science. The last three datasets are product reviews of three popular electronic products. We crawled the reviews from Amazon.com. More detailed information about the data sets is presented in Table 2.

Three targeted aspects are picked from each domain for targeted analysis. The aspects cover a wide range of diverse areas: Some of them are typical or frequent aspects in its domain like *Children* in E-Cigarette and *Lens* in Camera. Some are small or infrequent aspects like *Weight*, *Warranty* and *Horse*[1]. Note that one infrequent topic is specially chosen for each domain, listed as the last one in Table 2.

Dataset (Area)	Source	Size	Targeted Aspects
E-Cigarette	Twitter	50k	Children, Vape, Health
Cigar	Twitter	50k	Event, Box, Horse[1]
Camera	Amazon	10k	Lens, Screen, Weight
Cell-Phone	Amazon	10k	Sound, Case, Battery
Computer	Amazon	10k	Monitor, Software, Warranty

Table 2: Five datasets, targeted aspects, and initial documents (tweets or review sentences)

Parameter Setting: For the hyper-parameter setting, we place: $q = p = 1$ for a uniform Beta; $\gamma = 1$, $\alpha = 1$, $\beta^{ir} = \delta = 0.001$ and $\epsilon = 1.0 \times 10^{-7}$. The models for comparison are also with the same setting. λ in Equation 1 is set to 1 for TTM.

4.2 Baseline Models for Comparison

To evaluate our proposed targeted topic model TTM, we compare it with the following baseline models:

LDA: LDA is a well-known topic model [4]. It finds all topics in a corpus. To identify topics that are relevant to the targeted aspect, we manually inspect all resulting topics from LDA and find the subset of relevant topics. Note that the targeted aspect may be split into multiple topics by LDA. This is a labor-intensive and tedious process if there is a large number of topics from LDA.

LDA*: We still use LDA for topic generation, but instead of manual inspection to find related topics, we use keywords in S to search for relevant topics. We refer to this as the *search strategy*, which eliminates the tedious manual process. In this approach the number of topics T can be set large because only the retrieved topics will be analyzed. We search only the top 20 words of each topic.

DS-LDA: This is a state-of-art probabilistic sparse topic model [18] that models both the sparsity of topic mixtures (mining salient topics of a document) and topical words (mining representative words of a topic). We follow the implementation in [18] and refer to this as dual-sparse topic model, DS-LDA, in this paper. Like that for LDA, the relevant topics for DS-LDA are found via manual inspection.

DS-LDA*: Like LDA*, we use keywords S and adopt the *search strategy* to find possible relevant topics from all topics generated by DS-LDA.

SS-LDA: We also use a single-sparse topic model named SS-LDA in this paper for comparison, to see whether the direct injection of the word sparsity can help our task, because it enables the topical word to be more focused. The realization is similar to DS-LDA but it only addresses the sparsity of topical words. Likewise, it requires manual inspection.

SS-LDA*: Like DS-LDA*, a *search strategy* is adopted to find possible relevant topics from all topics.

LDA-PD: This model runs LDA only on the documents in each dataset that contains one or more keywords from S. For instance, to find topics about targeted aspect *Children*, we use the keyword "children" to search for tweets in the *E-Cigarette* tweet corpus. After that we run LDA on the resulting tweets to find topics. We name this approach LDA-PD (where PD means Partial Data) for short.

[1]A special topic: there was an well-known race horse called "Cigar" who died in October 2014. It is covered in the *Cigar* dataset as people talked about it in social media using its name. It is an evidently infrequent aspect in the Cigar data.

4.3 Quantitative Evaluation

Since our goal is to discover topics for a given targeted aspect but the correct number of topics and the number of terms/words under each topic are unknown, a natural evaluation metric is to give the precision results at different rank position n, called *Precision@n* (or *P@n* for short).

For the evaluation of the first two datasets, two experts from our health science collaborator's team who are specialized in the tobacco-related products and social media were invited to judge the results. Two human labelers who are familiar with Amazon product reviews labeled the results from the other three datasets. Cohen's Kappa scores of the two genres are 0.792 and 0.822 respectively.

Evaluation Measure: We use a normalized form of precision (defined in Equation 6) that can evaluate both the correctness of the topical words and the number of detected topics in a unified manner as both are important. Specifically, after the human judgment of all models results, the number of Maximum Unique Topics (MUT) can be obtained. For example, when the target is X, *Model-1* finds one unique topic A (which is correct), *Model-2* finds two unique topics A, B and *Model-3* finds three unique topics A, B, C then MUT is 3. In another case, when *Model-1* finds two unique topics A, B, *Model-2* finds two unique topics B, C and *Model-3* finds topics B, C then the MUT is also 3.

$$P_{(i)}@n = \frac{\sum_{st}^{ST} \#C_{(i)st}(correct@n)}{\sum_{mt}^{MUT} \#C_{mt}(words@n)} \quad (6)$$

In Equation 6, $P_{(i)}@n$ indicates the *precision@n* for model (i), given the targeted aspect. $\#C_{(i)st}(correct@n)$ is the number of correct words found in the topic st, given that there are ST topics found by model i. $\#C_{mt}(words@n)$ is the maximum number of correct words from all models.

This evaluation measure is fair and reasonable because a model may only find one correct topic with high topical word precision but miss some correct topics. Note that if there are more than one identical topics generated by a model, their average score is used. If there are multiple topics mixed in a single topic generated by a model, we use the best topic based on the number of relevant words in the top 20 words.

Two Comparison Settings: Two different experiment settings are used for comparison due to different properties of the candidate models. The reasons and differences will be elaborated in the following sub-sections.

4.3.1 Precision in Setting One

Here we compare LDA, DS-LDA, SS-LDA and LDA-PD with TTM. In this setting the *search strategy* is not used. Instead, the annotators were asked to go through all top (20) words in the generated topics. For LDA-PD, we use the target keyword itself (e.g., "children") to extract documents. For TTM, we also use the target keyword for targeted modeling. The topic number T in LDA-PD and TTM is set to 5 or 10 because we have no prior information about the number of target-related topics but we know that it intuitively depends on the prevalence of the targeted aspect (e.g., in the Camera domain the targeted aspect *Screen* is likely to be frequent and have more topics than the infrequent aspect *Weight*). In general, T is set to 5 for *infrequent* targets and to 10 for other more *frequent* targets. Although T could be 5 or 10 according to the targeted aspect, the same value of T is used for the comparison of results for both LDA-PD and TTM. Likewise, for LDA, DS-LDA and SS-LDA, T is

Data Set	Aspects	LDA (T-15|30)			DS-LDA (T-15|30)			SS-LDA (T-15|30)			LDA-PD (T-5|10)			TTM (T-5|10)		
		P@5	P@10	P@20	P@5	P@10	P@20	P@5	P@10	P@20	P@5	P@10	P@20	P@5	P@10	P@20
E-Cig	children	0.15	0.14	0.13	0.15	0.10	0.07	0.15	0.11	0.09	0.48	0.35	0.27	0.73	0.59	0.41
	vape	0.23	0.30	0.24	0.16	0.10	0.09	0.36	0.32	0.22	0.59	0.42	0.22	0.76	0.57	0.30
	health	0.48	0.39	0.30	0.32	0.19	0.18	0.38	0.25	0.17	0.38	0.28	0.20	0.55	0.42	0.30
Cigar	box	0.46	0.35	0.22	0.15	0.13	0.08	0.20	0.23	0.15	0.53	0.51	0.34	0.65	0.54	0.41
	event	0.30	0.28	0.31	0.24	0.14	0.09	0.36	0.18	0.15	0.30	0.39	0.33	0.64	0.58	0.45
	horse	0.27	0.20	0.26	0.15	0.10	0.06	0.55	0.43	0.24	0.73	0.46	0.34	0.88	0.61	0.37
Camera	screen	0.51	0.35	0.35	0.12	0.15	0.13	0.30	0.25	0.15	0.44	0.31	0.27	0.74	0.61	0.40
	lens	0.25	0.16	0.13	0.21	0.17	0.12	0.31	0.27	0.19	0.36	0.34	0.30	0.53	0.36	0.34
	weight	0.20	0.20	0.15	0.04	0.02	0.04	0.16	0.10	0.08	0.56	0.44	0.25	0.72	0.60	0.44
Cell-Phone	sound	0.58	0.40	0.30	0.27	0.17	0.14	0.50	0.35	0.21	0.52	0.37	0.29	0.75	0.60	0.40
	case	0.56	0.59	0.53	0.14	0.18	0.15	0.23	0.16	0.14	0.61	0.44	0.38	0.66	0.56	0.40
	battery	0.41	0.30	0.20	0.30	0.20	0.14	0.16	0.12	0.12	0.48	0.38	0.25	0.60	0.42	0.42
Computer	monitor	0.72	0.60	0.42	0.11	0.11	0.06	0.57	0.39	0.26	0.66	0.54	0.43	0.70	0.56	0.45
	software	0.48	0.39	0.35	0.24	0.21	0.14	0.36	0.30	0.33	0.36	0.34	0.30	0.60	0.39	0.35
	warranty	0.31	0.23	0.19	0.03	0.03	0.04	0.23	0.13	0.08	0.47	0.38	0.31	0.63	0.53	0.43
average score		0.39	0.32	0.27	0.18	0.13	0.10	0.32	0.24	0.17	0.50	0.40	0.30	0.68	0.53	0.39
improvement by TTM		+0.28	+0.21	+0.12	+0.50	+0.40	+0.29	+0.35	+0.29	+0.22	+0.18	+0.13	+0.09	n/a	n/a	n/a

Table 3: Precisions of setting one. The last two rows are (a) the average scores of all targeted aspects of all topics and (b) the improvement achieved by TTM over other models respectively

set to 15 or 30 (and choose the one produces higher precision results). The numbers are larger because they do not directly generate topics for the targeted aspect like LDA-PD and TTM. They also produce topics for other non-targeted aspects.

The precision results at the rank position of 5, 10 and 20 are reported in Table 3 and we observe the following:

1. TTM significantly outperforms other models. The average scores and the improvements by TTM are presented in the last two rows in Table 3. Among them, LDA-PD obtains the second best scores. Compared to LDA-PD, TTM has two key advantages, which are also the main reasons for the higher scores. (a) TTM can identify and use other relevant documents in modeling the topics of the targeted aspect with the power of biased sparsity, while LDA-PD can only generate topics from the subset of documents selected by user-specified keywords. (b) TTM can find more or better topics for the targeted aspect than LDA-PD because LDA-PD discards many relevant documents, resulting in information loss. Concrete examples will be further given in sub-section 4.4.
2. LDA-PD is the second best because it rules out the irrelevant documents that can interfere with good topic identification. But then it also loses relevant information as we discussed above. Thus, it results in inferior performance to TTM. Moreover, LDA-PD works poorly when it comes to some *infrequent* targets because relevant documents about these targets are not easy to extract as they may not contain the keywords.
3. LDA is neither as good as TTM nor LDA-PD. But it is better than both DS-LDA and SS-LDA. The DS-LDA that models both the sparsity of topic mixture and topical words has the worse performance. We will analyze the reason in the next sub-section.

One might argue that we can keep increasing T to a larger number to make further improvement. That is possible, but it becomes rather messy and impractical (labor intensive and time consuming) for the user to manually inspect all generated topics. An alternative is to apply the *search strategy* with increased T, which leads to our following evaluation of setting two.

4.3.2 *Precision in Setting Two*

This subsection compares LDA*, DS-LDA* and SS-LDA* against TTM. Different from setting one, here the annotators utilize the *search strategy* to identify relevant topics from all models except TTM. That is, the targeted aspect keyword is used to search in the top 20 topical words in each topic to find possibly relevant topics to the target. Only those resulting topics are evaluated. Since search is used, the number of topics T can be large. For LDA* we set T to 15, 30 and 50. For DS-LDA* and SS-LDA* we follow the same setting but their results are not good as LDA*. Due to the limited space we show the T=50 for DS-LDA* and SS-LDA* only.

The precision results at the rank position of 5, 10 and 20 are reported in Table 4 and we observe the following:

1. TTM again outperforms the other models by a large margin. We can see that the results from the search strategy is also poor. TTM generates better topics without human invention.
2. The increase of T for LDA* helps improve the performance but the enhancement is in a decreasing trend. Although the precision scores improve with increased T, the improvement from LDA*(T-30) to LDA*(T-50), which are 5.0%, 2.5%, 0.3% for $P@5$, $P@10$, $P@15$, drops from LDA*(T-15) to LDA*(T-30), which are 7.1%, 5.5%, 3.7% respectively. One reason is that with the increment of T, although more possible relevant topics may be generated, the *search strategy* can only find a subset of the relevant topics because the complete set of keywords for the targeted aspect is unknown. For instance, for aspect *Children* there might be new topics formed about children with a larger T but they do not contain the keyword "children". Instead, the new topics may contain other related keywords such as "kids", "young", and "minors".
3. Neither SS-LDA nor SS-LDA* can produce better results than LDA or LDA*. The reason is that when

Data Set	Aspects	LDA*(T-15)			LDA*(T-30)			LDA*(T-50)			DS-LDA*(T-50)			SS-LDA*(T-50)		
		P@5	P@10	P@20	P@5	P@10	P@20	P@5	P@10	P@20	P@5	P@10	P@20	P@5	P@10	P@20
E-Cig	children	0.08	0.05	0.04	0.13	0.13	0.11	0.20	0.13	0.08	0.05	0.30	0.04	0.16	0.12	0.08
	vape	0.12	0.14	0.13	0.17	0.14	0.17	0.28	0.30	0.23	0.08	0.06	0.06	0.36	0.32	0.19
	health	0.13	0.13	0.12	0.17	0.12	0.06	0.32	0.23	0.16	0.14	0.11	0.11	0.13	0.15	0.8
Cigar	box	0.30	0.25	0.20	0.20	0.24	0.20	0.43	0.26	0.16	0.08	0.06	0.08	0.33	0.29	0.18
	event	0.16	0.08	0.12	0.24	0.20	0.18	0.19	0.18	0.14	0.12	0.08	0.05	0.8	0.60	0.70
	horse	0.05	0.10	0.11	0.25	0.18	0.24	0.50	0.42	0.31	0.05	0.04	0.03	0.5	0.28	0.16
Camera	screen	0.08	0.06	0.08	0.08	0.06	0.06	0.08	0.05	0.06	0.23	0.20	0.14	0.15	0.11	0.06
	lens	0.13	0.10	0.08	0.18	0.16	0.12	0.12	0.11	0.10	0.17	0.13	0.11	0.27	0.16	0.11
	weight	0.08	0.08	0.08	0.16	0.14	0.10	0.12	0.10	0.07	0.04	0.04	0.03	0.13	0.1	0.13
Cell-Phone	sound	0.20	0.15	0.13	0.47	0.37	0.27	0.63	0.45	0.28	0.17	0.12	0.10	0.3	0.2	0.15
	case	0.38	0.35	0.31	0.55	0.51	0.36	0.39	0.37	0.30	0.13	0.11	0.21	0.2	0.2	0.18
	battery	0.16	0.12	0.08	0.32	0.22	0.16	0.32	0.20	0.16	0.16	0.08	0.06	0.12	0.12	0.11
Computer	monitor	0.59	0.56	0.40	0.61	0.51	0.38	0.61	0.46	0.38	0.20	0.10	0.09	0.31	0.24	0.18
	software	0.32	0.24	0.19	0.12	0.11	0.09	0.18	0.15	0.11	0.08	0.04	0.04	0.16	0.12	0.1
	warranty	0.10	0.08	0.05	0.30	0.23	0.18	0.33	0.30	0.20	0.07	0.03	0.03	0.23	0.18	0.11
average score		0.19	0.17	0.14	0.26	0.22	0.18	0.31	0.25	0.18	0.12	0.10	0.08	0.28	0.21	0.22
improvement by TTM		+0.49	+0.37	+0.26	+0.41	+0.31	+0.22	+0.36	+0.28	+0.22	+0.56	+0.43	+0.32	+0.40	+0.32	+0.18

Table 4: Precisions of setting two. The last two rows are (a) the average scores of all targeted aspects of all topics and (b) the improvement achieved by TTM over other models respectively.

the word sparsity can find focused words to represent a topic, the number of related topics (to the target) found by SS-LDA is fewer than that by LDA. In other words, SS-LDA might form better topics but they are less related to the targeted aspect. DS-LDA has the worse results because it may find more focused topics for individual documents but not for the targeted aspect of user interest.

4.4 Qualitative Evaluation

This section presents the qualitative evaluation. We show several resulting topics in Tables 5 and 6 to give a flavor of each system. The domain and the targeted aspect are shown at top of the tables above the model names and topic names (given by us). Incorrect words of a topic are italicized and marked in red. Notice that the targeted aspect keyword itself is also shown but it is excluded from the computation of precision in the previous section because it is already known.

4.4.1 Example One: E-Cigarette and Children

E-Cigarette (e-cig) is a key area studied by our collaborators from the health science and *Children* is one aspect that they are highly interested in and thus want to know its topics discussed on Twitter. Table 5 shows the topical words discovered by different models. The models are attached with the setting in the previous section so the topic number T is not explicitly given in the table. We explain the results below.

(1) Topic *fears*: It means the fears or concerns about children using e-cig. By comparison, we see that TTM generates a clearer and more reasonable topic. While the other methods generate incoherent topics with many wrong words, the words in TTM are more informative and interpretable, because the words like "nicotine", "gateway", and "sale" can better indicate the reasons of the fears as well as what people are actually concerned about for the children. That is, people worry about the "nicotine" in e-cig that is bad for kids; they are afraid that e-cig becomes a "gateway" for their kids to smoking, and the increasing "sale" to the young.

(2) Topic *regulation*: It is about the regulation of e-cig for children, mostly about the policy of purchase. Similar to topic *fears*, TTM finds more informative words like "laws" and "safe". Particularly, the word "young" is also included in the topic *regulation* of TTM, which is meaningful. It can infer that other documents that contain the unknown/unprovided keyword "young" are probably identified by TTM as relevant to the targeted aspect children (i.e., r=1) and thus involved in the topic generation of the target. Because one short sentence is unlikely to mention the keyword "children" and unknown keyword "young" at the same time (they are semantically similar). The documents containing the word "young" is unlikely to also contain "children" and vice versa. This is an advantage that LDA-PD cannot achieve. Those documents (containing "young") identified by TTM as relevant help generate a more coherent topic for the targeted aspect.

Here we also analyze the topics formed by LDA and LDA* (T-50) to demonstrate some aforementioned problems. (a) Although the topic *regulation* in LDA looks good with many good words grouped, the topic is actually not very informative as the words "children, kids, minors" all ranked high but they do not tell anything about a topic related to e-cig and children. (b) Since these words are grouped together, it may lead to missing of some good topics of the targeted aspect. (c) When comes to LDA*, although T is set to 50 this method actually finds only 2 topics that contain "children" by using the *search strategy*. (d) Also in the *regulation* topics, one may notice that the word "minors" which is in LDA (where its topic number is 15 or 30) is not included in LDA*(T-50) any more. However, since we did not previously know all those keywords (e.g.,"minors", "young"), the topic is not found with $T = 50$, i.e., a related topic is unfortunately lost.

4.4.2 Example Two: Camera, Screen and Weight

The previous sub-section presents the example from tweets, which mainly reveals the trend of a discussed topic in Twitter. Now let us take a look at online reviews in the Camera domain. The data is from Amazon.com and the analysis is also related to opinion mining and sentiment analysis.

Domain: E-Cigarette											
Targeted aspect: Children											
TTM		LDA-PD		LDA* (T-50)		LDA		DS-LDA		SS-LDA	
fears	**regulation**	**fears**	**regulation**	**fear**	**regulation**	**fears**	**regulation**	**fears**	**regulation**	**fears**	**regulation**
children	states	children	buy	fears	buy	fears	buy	children	*vaping*	*lacks*	regulation
fears	buy	fears	states	*research*	legally	*city*	kids	*evidence*	regulation	fears	*trending*
nicotine	live	smoked	children	concerns	children	*ban*	legally	nicotine	*vaporizer*	*report*	*two*
nightmare	legally	sale	live	*cloud*	kids	*council*	children	*pour*	*view*	*stories*	*kanavape*
sales	*atlanta*	*real*	legally	*parents*	purchase	*media*	minors	*starter*	*prisoner*	*watch*	washington
data	young	*report*	*online*	*fulled*	state	*social*	*columbia*	*council*	*cut*	prison	safer
age	smoked	easy	*press*	*batteries*	live	*public*	*district*	*fire*	*part*	*slapped*	*drinking*
gateway	*online*	*figures*	*washington*	experimenting	*nocotine*	*study*	*states*	*television*	washington	*world*	*thing*
reason	laws	*top*	*smokeless*	*progress*	*nightmare*	addition	purchase	virus	state	evaporation	*cells*
fight	safe	*make*	*post*	smoked	*press*	*bans*	live	*business*	*social*	*set*	data

Table 5: Topics of aspect *children* under E-Cig. Errors are italicized and marked in red.

Domain: Camera											
Targeted aspect: Screen						Targeted aspect: Weight					
TTM			LDA-PD		LDA	TTM			LDA-PD		DS-LDA*
picture	**menu**	**imaging**	**picture**	**menu**	**picture**	**lens**	**battery**	**carrying**	**lens**	**battery**	**-**
picture	easy	image	picture	screen	picture	lens	battery	easy	weight	weight	*picture*
color	control	shutter	photo	*touch*	photo	weight	weight	carry	lens	battery	compact
shot	manual	speed	*computer*	control	*easy*	*canon*	light	*picture*	*zoom*	light	*stabilization*
sharp	photo	stabilization	video	menu	*video*	size	*life*	compact	*extra*	*image*	weight
feature	function	shooting	black	button	feature	heavy	travel	case	size	*easy*	*place*
clear	menu	*lens*	*show*	easy	clear	smaller	*rechargeable*	small	*add*	*shot*	*absolute*
resolution	condition	picture	full	*small*	pic	long	lightweight	*extra*	light	*life*	*ease*
grainy	macro	frame	*turn*	*comcorder*	*fun*	*digital*	*video*	big	*carry*	*control*	*instruction*
action	*learn*	*feature*	*record*	*change*	*wonderful*	*zoom*	*image*	light	heavy	*focus*	*average*
video	*situation*	produce	*print*	*lcd*	*beautiful*	*trap*	*control*	bulky	*battery*	*flash*	*release*

Table 6: Topics of two aspects *screen* and *weight* under Camera. Errors are italicized and marked in red.

Since a full/comprehensive comparison has been done in the E-Cig domain, this subsection shows two different aspects (a popular aspect and an infrequent aspect) instead of repeating the full comparison with all models. Thus we only select some good models for comparison. Since LDA-PD achieves the second best score most of the time, it is included in our comparison. In addition, we pick one additional model that can also find the same topic. We analyze the two aspects *screen* and *weight* in the camera domain.

(1) Aspect *Screen*: When the target is screen, we first pick up the topic of *picture* for analysis. It discusses the features of the picture displayed on the *Screen*. From Table 6 we observe that TTM produces a good result. LDA also has a topic about *picture* but it has an issue (though it might look good at the first glance). The problem is that it groups the words "picture", "photo", "pic" together as they are synonyms but the topic becomes vague because these words may belong to different fine-grained topics. In addition, while LDA finds some more general features like "wonderful", "beautiful" and "fun" (these words can be regarded as *general* opinion words) because they actually can modify many different aspects) but TTM finds more specific (or coherent) features like "sharp" and "clear". This is an important property in opinion mining because people always want to know the specific reasons for opinions. Further illustration about this property in opinion mining can be found in our previous work in [32].

The quality of commonly found topics like *menu* is also improved. Additionally, it is worth noting that TTM identifies a new unique topic called *imaging*, which is not found by any other model, but is in fact related to aspect *screen*.

(2) Infrequent Aspect *Weight*: Only LDA-PD and TTM find meaningful related topics for the aspect Weight. Here *lens* and *battery* are two detected topics for demonstration. Because people often complain the heavy weight of these two components. However, they usually mention it in an implicit manner like "the lens is so heavy" or "the heavy weight battery is annoying". On the contrary, the topic generated by DS-LDA*(T-50) is not so clear. Moreover, TTM solely detects other interesting topics like "carrying", which is also closely related to the aspect Weight.

5. CONCLUSION

In this paper, we studied the novel problem of targeted modeling. Instead of finding all topics from a corpus like existing models based on full modeling, the proposed model focuses on finding topics of a targeted aspect to help the user perform deeper or finer-grained analysis. This is motivated by real-life applications that researchers are often not interested in everything in a corpus but only some aspects of it in order to answer their research questions. Existing full models are not the most effective methods for such focused analysis because their results are often too coarse and they may not find topics that the user is really interested in and/or miss many details. Experimental results showed that this is indeed the case and the proposed new model outperforms the state-of-the-art existing models markedly.

6. ACKNOWLEDGEMENT

Shuai Wang and Sherry Emery's research was supported by the National Science Foundation (NSF) under award number NSF1524750 and the National Cancer Institute of the National Institutes of Health (NIH) and FDA Center for Tobacco Products (CTP) under Award Number P50CA179546. Bing Liu's research was supported in part by a grant from National Science Foundation (NSF) under grant no. IIS-1407927, a NCI grant under grant no. R01CA192240, and a gift from Bosch. The content is solely the responsibility of the authors and does not necessarily represent the official views of the NSF, NIH, FDA, or Bosch.

7. REFERENCES

[1] D. Andrzejewski, X. Zhu, and M. Craven. Incorporating domain knowledge into topic modeling via dirichlet forest priors. In *ICML*, pages 25–32. ACM, 2009.

[2] C. Archambeau, B. Lakshminarayanan, and G. Bouchard. Latent ibp compound dirichlet allocation. *Pattern Analysis and Machine Intelligence, IEEE Transactions on*, 37(2):321–333, 2015.

[3] Y. Bengio, A. C. Courville, and J. S. Bergstra. Unsupervised models of images by spike-and-slab rbms. In *ICML*, pages 1145–1152, 2011.

[4] D. M. Blei, A. Y. Ng, and M. I. Jordan. Latent dirichlet allocation. *the Journal of machine Learning research*, 3:993–1022, 2003.

[5] S. Brody and N. Elhadad. An unsupervised aspect-sentiment model for online reviews. In *NAACL*, pages 804–812. Association for Computational Linguistics, 2010.

[6] J. Chang, S. Gerrish, C. Wang, J. L. Boyd-Graber, and D. M. Blei. Reading tea leaves: How humans interpret topic models. In *NIPS*, pages 288–296, 2009.

[7] X. Chen, Y. Qi, B. Bai, Q. Lin, and J. G. Carbonell. Sparse latent semantic analysis. In *SDM*, pages 474–485. SIAM, 2011.

[8] X. Chen, M. Zhou, and L. Carin. The contextual focused topic model. In *KDD*, pages 96–104. ACM, 2012.

[9] Z. Chen and B. Liu. Mining topics in documents: standing on the shoulders of big data. In *KDD*, pages 1116–1125. ACM, 2014.

[10] J. Eisenstein, A. Ahmed, and E. P. Xing. Sparse additive generative models of text. 2011.

[11] D. Griffiths and M. Tenenbaum. Hierarchical topic models and the nested chinese restaurant process. *NIPS*, 16:17, 2004.

[12] T. L. Griffiths and M. Steyvers. Finding scientific topics. *PNAS*, 101(suppl 1):5228–5235, 2004.

[13] G. Heinrich. A generic approach to topic models. In *ECML-PKDD*, pages 517–532. Springer, 2009.

[14] T. Hofmann. Probabilistic latent semantic indexing. In *SIGIR*, pages 50–57. ACM, 1999.

[15] L. Hong, D. Yin, J. Guo, and B. D. Davison. Tracking trends: incorporating term volume into temporal topic models. In *KDD*, pages 484–492. ACM, 2011.

[16] H. Ishwaran and J. S. Rao. Spike and slab variable selection: frequentist and bayesian strategies. *Annals of Statistics*, pages 730–773, 2005.

[17] Y. Jo and A. H. Oh. Aspect and sentiment unification model for online review analysis. In *WSDM*, pages 815–824. ACM, 2011.

[18] T. Lin, W. Tian, Q. Mei, and H. Cheng. The dual-sparse topic model: mining focused topics and focused terms in short text. In *WWW*, pages 539–550. ACM, 2014.

[19] Q. Mei and C. Zhai. Discovering evolutionary theme patterns from text: an exploration of temporal text mining. In *KDD*, pages 198–207. ACM, 2005.

[20] K. Min, Z. Zhang, J. Wright, and Y. Ma. Decomposing background topics from keywords by principal component pursuit. In *CIKM*, pages 269–278. ACM, 2010.

[21] T. J. Mitchell and J. J. Beauchamp. Bayesian variable selection in linear regression. *Journal of the American Statistical Association*, 83(404):1023–1032, 1988.

[22] S. Moghaddam and M. Ester. The flda model for aspect-based opinion mining: Addressing the cold start problem. In *WWW*, 2013.

[23] A. Mukherjee and B. Liu. Aspect extraction through semi-supervised modeling. In *ACL*, pages 339–348. Association for Computational Linguistics, 2012.

[24] D. Ramage, D. Hall, R. Nallapati, and C. D. Manning. Labeled lda: A supervised topic model for credit attribution in multi-labeled corpora. In *EMNLP*, pages 248–256. Association for Computational Linguistics, 2009.

[25] M. Rosen-Zvi, T. Griffiths, M. Steyvers, and P. Smyth. The author-topic model for authors and documents. In *UAI*, pages 487–494. AUAI Press, 2004.

[26] I. Titov and R. McDonald. Modeling online reviews with multi-grain topic models. In *WWW*, pages 111–120. ACM, 2008.

[27] H. M. Wallach. Topic modeling: beyond bag-of-words. In *ICML*, pages 977–984. ACM, 2006.

[28] H. M. Wallach, D. M. Mimno, and A. McCallum. Rethinking lda: Why priors matter. In *NIPS*, pages 1973–1981, 2009.

[29] C. Wang and D. M. Blei. Decoupling sparsity and smoothness in the discrete hierarchical dirichlet process. In *NIPS*, pages 1982–1989, 2009.

[30] H. Wang, Y. Lu, and C. Zhai. Latent aspect rating analysis on review text data: a rating regression approach. In *KDD*, pages 783–792. ACM, 2010.

[31] Q. Wang, J. Xu, H. Li, and N. Craswell. Regularized latent semantic indexing. In *SIGIR*, pages 685–694. ACM, 2011.

[32] S. Wang, Z. Chen, and B. Liu. Mining aspect-specific opinion using a holistic lifelong topic model. In *WWW*, pages 167–176. WWW, 2016.

[33] S. Williamson, C. Wang, K. A. Heller, and D. M. Blei. The ibp compound dirichlet process and its application to focused topic modeling. In *ICML*, pages 1151–1158, 2010.

[34] W. X. Zhao, J. Jiang, H. Yan, and X. Li. Jointly modeling aspects and opinions with a maxent-lda hybrid. In *EMNLP*, pages 56–65. Association for Computational Linguistics, 2010.

[35] J. Zhu and E. P. Xing. Sparse topical coding. *arXiv preprint arXiv:1202.3778*, 2012.

Structured Doubly Stochastic Matrix for Graph Based Clustering

Xiaoqian Wang
Department of Computer Science and Engineering
University of Texas at Arlington
Texas, USA
xqwang1991@gmail.com

Feiping Nie
Department of Computer Science and Engineering
University of Texas at Arlington
Texas, USA
feipingnie@gmail.com

Heng Huang*
Department of Computer Science and Engineering
University of Texas at Arlington
Texas, USA
heng@uta.edu

ABSTRACT

As one of the most significant machine learning topics, clustering has been extensively employed in various kinds of area. Its prevalent application in scientific research as well as industrial practice has drawn high attention in this day and age. A multitude of clustering methods have been developed, among which the graph based clustering method using the affinity matrix has been laid great emphasis on. Recent research work used the doubly stochastic matrix to normalize the input affinity matrix and enhance the graph based clustering models. Although the doubly stochastic matrix can improve the clustering performance, the clustering structure in the doubly stochastic matrix is not clear as expected. Thus, post-processing step is required to extract the final clustering results, which may not be optimal. To address this problem, in this paper, we propose a novel convex model to learn the structured doubly stochastic matrix by imposing low-rank constraint on the graph Laplacian matrix. Our new structured doubly stochastic matrix can explicitly uncover the clustering structure and encode the probabilities of pair-wise data points to be connected, such that the clustering results are enhanced. An efficient optimization algorithm is derived to solve our new objective. Also, we provide theoretical discussions that when the input differs, our method possesses interesting connections with K-means and spectral graph cut models respectively. We conduct experiments on both synthetic and benchmark datasets to validate the performance of our proposed method. The empirical results demonstrate that our model provides an approach to better solving the K-mean clustering problem. By using the cluster indicator provided by our model as initialization, K-means converges to a smaller objective function value with better clustering performance. Moreover, we compare the clustering performance of our model with spectral clustering and related double stochastic model. On all datasets, our method performs equally or better than the related methods.

*To whom all correspondence should be addressed. This work was partially supported by US NSF-IIS 1117965, NSF-IIS 1302675, NSF-IIS 1344152, NSF-DBI 1356628, NIH R01 AG049371.

KDD '16, August 13-17, 2016, San Francisco, CA, USA
© 2016 ACM. ISBN 978-1-4503-4232-2/16/08. . . $15.00
DOI: http://dx.doi.org/10.1145/2939672.2939805

CCS Concepts

•Theory of computation → Unsupervised learning and clustering;

Keywords

Doubly Stochastic Matrix; Graph Laplacian; K-means Clustering; Spectral Clustering

1. INTRODUCTION

Graph based learning is one of the central research topics in machine learning. These models use similarity graph as input and perform learning tasks over the graph, such as spectral clustering [17], manifold based dimensional reduction [2, 12], graph-based semi-supervised learning [30, 31], *etc*. Because the input data graph is often associated to the affinity matrix (the pair-wise similarities between data points), graph based learning methods show promising performance and have been introduced to many applications in data mining [20, 19, 18, 1, 6]. The graph-based learning methods depend on the input affinity matrix, thus the quality of the input data graph is crucial in achieving the final superior learning solutions.

To enhance the learning results, graph based learning methods often need pre-processing on the affinity matrix. The doubly stochastic matrix (also called bistochastic matrix) was utilized to normalize the affinity matrix and showed promising clustering results [29]. A doubly stochastic matrix $S \in \Re^{n\times n}$ is a square matrix and all elements in S satisfy:

$$s_{ij} \geq 0, \sum_{j=1}^{n} s_{ij} = 1, \sum_{i=1}^{n} s_{ij} = 1, 1 \leq i,j \leq n\,. \qquad (1)$$

Some previous works have been proposed to learn the best doubly stochastic approximation to a given affinity matrix [29, 26, 11]. Imposing the double stochastic constraints can properly normalize the affinity matrix such that the data graph is more suitable for clustering tasks. However, even with using the doubly stochastic matrix, the final clustering structure is still not obvious in the data graph. The graph based clustering methods often use K-means algorithm to post-process the clustering results to get the clustering indicators, thus the final clustering results are dependent on and sensitive to the initializations.

To address these challenges, in this paper, we propose a novel model to learn the structured doubly stochastic matrix, which encodes the probability of each pair of data points to be connected. We explicitly constrain the rank of the graph Laplacian and guarantee the number of connected components in the graph to be exactly k, *i.e.* the number of clusters. Thus, the clustering results can be directly obtained without the post-processing step, such that the clustering results are superior and stable. To solve the proposed new objective, we introduce an efficient optimization algorithm. Meanwhile, we also provide theoretical analysis on the connection between our method and K-means clustering as well as spectral clustering, respectively.

We conduct extensive experiments on both synthetic and benchmark datasets to evaluate the performance of our method. We find that our method provides a good initialization for K-means clustering such that a smaller objective function value can be achieved for the K-means problem. Also, we compare the clustering performance of our model with other methods. On all datasets, our method performs equally or better than related methods.

Notations: Throughout this paper, matrices are all written as uppercase letters while vectors as bold lower case letters. For a matrix $M \in \Re^{d \times n}$, its i-th row, j-th column and ij-th element are denoted by $\mathbf{m}^i$, $\mathbf{m}_j$ and m_{ij} respectively. The Frobenius norm of M is defined as $\|M\|_F = \sqrt{\sum_{i=1}^{d}\sum_{j=1}^{n} m_{ij}^2}$. The trace norm (also known as the nuclear norm) is defined as $\|M\|_* = \sum_{i=1}^{min\{d,n\}} \sigma_i$, where σ_i is the i-th singular value of M. For a vector $\mathbf{v} \in \Re^n$, when $p \neq 0$, its ℓ_p-norm $\|\mathbf{v}\|_p$ is defined as $\|\mathbf{v}\|_p = (\sum_{i=1}^{n} |v_i|^p)^{\frac{1}{p}}$. Specially, $\mathbf{1}$ represents a vector whose elements are 1 consistently and I stands for the identity matrix.

2. CLUSTERING WITH NEW STRUCTURED DOUBLY STOCHASTIC MATRIX

To achieve good clustering results, doubly stochastic matrix is usually utilized to approximate the given affinity matrix such that the clustering structure in data graph can be maintained. However, final clustering structures are still not obvious in the data graph and post-processing step has to be employed, which leads the clustering results to be not optimal. To address this problem and learn a more powerful doubly stochastic matrix, we propose a new structured doubly stochastic model to capture clustering structure and encode probabilistic data similarity.

2.1 New Structured Doubly Stochastic Matrix

The ideal clustering structure of a graph with n data points is to have exactly k connected components, where k is the number of clusters. If we reshuffle the n data points in the similarity matrix of the ideal graph such that points in the same connected components are arranged together, then the k connected components form k blocks ranging along the diagonal of the similarity matrix. With such ideal structure we can immediately obtain clustering indicators without post-processing steps. Thus, we propose a novel method to learn the new structured doubly stochastic matrix which has such ideal clustering structure with exactly k blocks. From [15, 8], we know that each connected component in the graph W corresponds to an eigenvalue 0 in the Laplacian matrix $L_W = D_W - W$. D_W is the degree matrix of graph W defined as $D_W = Diag(\sum_j w_{ij})$, where $Diag(\mathbf{a})$ denotes a diagonal matrix with diagonal elements formed by the entries of vector $\mathbf{a}$. If W has exactly k blocks, then k eigenvalues of L_W are zeros, *i.e.* the rank of L_W is equal to $n - k$.

Therefore, given the affinity matrix W, we propose to learn a new structured doubly stochastic matrix $M \in \Re^{n \times n}$ such that its Laplacian matrix $L_M = D_M - M$ is restricted to be $rank(L_M) = n - k$. With this constraint, the learnt M has the clustering block structure along the diagonal with proper permutation, based on which we can directly partition the data points into k clusters.

Moreover, to make M encode the probability of each pair of data points to be connected in the graph, we normalize $M\mathbf{1} = \mathbf{1}$. As a result, the entire probability for a point to connect with others is 1. Consequently, we have $D_M = I$. Meanwhile, since M represents the probability of each pair of data points to be connected, we naturally expect the learnt M is symmetric and nonnegative. These constraints validate the doubly stochastic property of matrix M.

Under our new constraints, we learn a structured doubly stochastic matrix M to best approximate the affinity matrix W by solving:

$$\min_M \|M - W\|_F^2 \quad s.t. \quad M \geq 0, M = M^T, M\mathbf{1} = \mathbf{1}, rank(L_M) = n - k\,. \tag{2}$$

Theoretically, in the ideal case the probability of a certain point to correlate with points in the same cluster should be the same. That is, suppose there are n_i points in the i-th cluster, for any two points p_s and p_n in the i-th cluster, the probability of p_s and p_n to be connected is $m_{sn} = \frac{1}{n_i}$. Consistently, for point p_s, we have $m_{ss} = \frac{1}{n_i}$. Toward this end we add another term $r\|M\|_F^2$, where according to Lemma 1 a large enough parameter r forces the elements in each block of matrix M to be the same.

LEMMA 1. *In the following problem:*

$$\min_M \|M - W\|_F^2 + r\|M\|_F^2 \quad s.t. \quad M \geq 0, M = M^T, M\mathbf{1} = \mathbf{1}, rank(L_M) = n - k\,,$$

if the value of r tends to be infinity, the matrix M is block diagonal with elements in each block to be the same. The number of blocks in matrix M is k.

Proof: If r tends to infinity, the following optimization problem

$$\min_M \|M - W\|_F^2 + r\|M\|_F^2 \quad s.t. \quad M \geq 0, M = M^T, M\mathbf{1} = \mathbf{1}, rank(L_M) = n - k \tag{3}$$

is equivalent to

$$\min_M \|M\|_F^2 \quad s.t. \quad M \geq 0, M = M^T, M\mathbf{1} = \mathbf{1}, rank(L_M) = n - k\,. \tag{4}$$

According to the previous discussion, with proper rearrangement of rows and columns of M, the constraint $rank(L_M) = n - k$ require the structure of M to be k blocks diagonally arranged like:

$$\begin{bmatrix} M_1 & & 0 \\ & M_2 & \\ & & \ddots & \\ 0 & & & M_k \end{bmatrix}.$$

Meanwhile, let's we denote a random row (or column) of one block in M as $\mathbf{m}^T$(or $\mathbf{m}$). Since $\sum_i m_i^2 \geq \frac{(\sum_i m_i)^2}{length(\mathbf{m})}$, and only when all m_i are of the same value makes the left and right sides be equal. Thus, the solution to minimize Problem (4) is that M is a block diagonal matrix with elements in each block to be the same. □

In addition, to highlight the constraint that M has exactly k blocks, we add another constraint as $Tr(M) = k$ and have:

$$\begin{aligned} \min_M \ & \|M - W\|_F^2 + r\|M\|_F^2 \\ s.t. \ & M \geq 0, M = M^T, M\mathbf{1} = \mathbf{1}, \\ & rank(L_M) = n - k, Tr(M) = k\,. \end{aligned} \tag{5}$$

The constraint $rank(L_M) = n - k$ makes Problem (5) non-convex. Therefore, we use the trace norm of L_M as a relaxation form of $rank(L_M)$. Our final objective is to solve:

$$J_{opt} = \min_M \|M - W\|_F^2 + \gamma \|L_M\|_* + r\|M\|_F^2$$
$$s.t. \quad M \geq 0, M = M^T, M\mathbf{1} = \mathbf{1}, Tr(M) = k\,. \tag{6}$$

It is not trivial to solve our new objective J_{opt} in Eq. (6). We will propose a novel algorithm to solve the new objective. Before that, we first show the interesting connection between our model and spectral clustering.

2.2 Connections to Spectral Graph Cut Models

THEOREM 1. *In Problem (5), if $r \to \infty$ and W is doubly stochastic, then Problem (5) is equivalent to spectral clustering.*

Proof: As illustrated in [25], given a graph G with n points and its affinity matrix $W \in \Re^{n\times n}$, the definition of graph cut is:

$$\begin{aligned} J &= \sum_{1\leq p\leq q\leq k} \frac{s(C_p, C_q)}{\rho(C_p)} + \frac{s(C_p, C_q)}{\rho(C_q)} \\ &= \sum_{l=1}^{k} \frac{s(C_l, \bar{C}_l)}{\rho(C_l)}\,, \end{aligned} \tag{7}$$

where k is the number of clusters, C_l is the l-th cluster and $\bar{C}_l$ is the complement subset of cluster C_l in graph G, $s(M, N) = \sum_{m\in M}\sum_{n\in N} W_{mn}$.

For Ratio Cut, the function $\rho(C_l)$ in Eq. (7) is defined as:

$$\rho_{RCut}(C_l) = |C_l|\,. \tag{8}$$

We introduce an indicator vector $\mathbf{q}_l \in \Re^n (l = 1, 2, \cdots, k)$, such that the i-th element of $\mathbf{q}_l$ equals to 1 if the i-th point in graph G belongs to the l-th cluster, and 0 otherwise.

With the indicator vector $\mathbf{q}_l$, we have:

$$s(C_l, \bar{C}_l) = \sum_{i\in C_l}\sum_{j\in \bar{C}_l} W_{ij} = \mathbf{q}_l^T(D_W - W)\mathbf{q}_l\,.$$

Along with Eq. (8), we can rewrite the cut function of Ratio Cut in Eq. (7) as:

$$J_{RCut} = \sum_{l=1}^{k} \frac{\mathbf{q}_l^T(D_W - W)\mathbf{q}_l}{\mathbf{q}_l^T\mathbf{q}_l}\,. \tag{9}$$

Define matrix $G \in \Re^{n\times k}$ such that $\mathbf{g}_l = \mathbf{q}_l$. We introduce an indicator matrix F:

$$F = G(G^TG)^{-\frac{1}{2}}\,, \tag{10}$$

Assume $x_i \in C_i$ and $x_j \in C_j$. For the F matrix in Eq. (10), we can observe that if $C_i = C_j$, then $f_{ij} = \frac{1}{\sqrt{n_i}}$; otherwise $f_{ij} = 0$, where n_i denotes the number of data points in the i-th cluster.

Thus, the cut function (9) can be written as:

$$J_{RCut} = Tr(F^T(D_W - W)F)\,. \tag{11}$$

If W is doubly stochastic, then $D_W = I$. In this case, Normalized Cut is equivalent to Ratio Cut and tackles the following problem:

$$\begin{aligned} &\min_F Tr(F^T(I - W)F) \\ \Longrightarrow\ &\max_F Tr(F^TWF) \\ \Longrightarrow\ &\min_F \left\|FF^T - W\right\|_F^2\,. \end{aligned} \tag{12}$$

Let $M = FF^T$, the Problem (12) becomes:

$$\min_M \|M - W\|_F^2\,. \tag{13}$$

We can directly find that $m_{ij} = \frac{1}{n_i}$ when $C_i = C_j$; while $m_{ij} = 0$ when $C_i \neq C_j$, where $x_i \in C_i$ and $x_j \in C_j$.

Thus, the spectral clustering problem is to find a matrix M minimizing Problem (13). From the definition of M, we can obtain some properties of M that $M \geq 0$, $M^T = M$ and $M\mathbf{1} = \mathbf{1}$, thus it is doubly stochastic. As for $Tr(M)$, we have:

$$Tr(M) = Tr(FF^T) = Tr(G(G^TG)^{-1}G) = k\,. \tag{14}$$

□

In practice, matrix W may not always be doubly stochastic. Given affinity matrix W_0, we can learn a doubly stochastic matrix W as the initialization by solving:

$$\min_{W\geq 0, W=W^T, W\mathbf{1}=\mathbf{1}} \|W - W_0\|_F^2\,. \tag{15}$$

The above problem is the same as the problem solved in [29] and also a special case of our proposed objective in Eq. (6) when both parameter γ and r are set as 0.

Previous method in [29] can only learn a doubly stochastic matrix without clear clustering structure. After adding the regularization terms, our new objective can achieve a better doubly stochastic matrix with clear clustering structure to improve the clustering results.

3. OPTIMIZATION ALGORITHM

We use the Augmented Lagrange Multiplier (ALM) optimization strategy [4] to solve our new objective J_{opt} in Eq. (6).

Here we introduce a slack variable L that $L = I - M$, then Problem (6) can be rewritten as:

$$\begin{aligned} &\min_M \|M - W\|_F^2 + \gamma\|L\|_* + r\|M\|_F^2 \\ s.t.\quad &M \geq 0, M = M^T, M\mathbf{1} = \mathbf{1}, Tr(M) = k, \\ &I - M = L\,, \end{aligned} \tag{16}$$

and Problem (16) is equivalent to:

$$\begin{aligned} &\min_M \|M - W\|_F^2 + \gamma\|L\|_* \\ &+\frac{\mu}{2}\left\|I - M - L + \frac{1}{\mu}\Lambda\right\|_F^2 + r\|M\|_F^2 \\ s.t.\quad &M \geq 0, M = M^T, M\mathbf{1} = \mathbf{1}, Tr(M) = k\,, \end{aligned} \tag{17}$$

where $\Lambda \in \Re^{n\times n}$ is the Lagrange multiplier and μ is the penalty parameter for Eq. (17).

Compared with Problem (6), Problem (17) is easier to solve since the trace norm term $\gamma\|L\|_*$ is now independent to M. We introduce an efficient alternating algorithm to tackle Problem (17).

The first step is fixing L and solving M, thus Problem (17) becomes:

$$\begin{aligned} &\min_M \|M - W\|_F^2 + \frac{\mu}{2}\left\|I - M - L + \frac{1}{\mu}\Lambda\right\|_F^2 \\ &+r\|M\|_F^2 \\ s.t.\quad &M \geq 0, M = M^T, M\mathbf{1} = \mathbf{1}, Tr(M) = k\,. \end{aligned} \tag{18}$$

Let

$$T = \frac{1}{\mu + 2r}(2W + \mu(I - L + \frac{1}{\mu}\Lambda))\,,$$

the Problem (18) can be rewritten as:

$$\min_{M} \|M - T\|_F^2 \quad s.t. \quad M \geq 0, M = M^T, M\mathbf{1} = \mathbf{1}, Tr(M) = k. \tag{19}$$

Since the constraint on $Tr(M)$ is only concerned with the diagonal elements, Problem (19) can be divided into two subproblems:

$$\min_{M} \|M - T\|_F^2, \; s.t. \; M = M^T, M\mathbf{1} = \mathbf{1}, \tag{20}$$

and

$$\min_{M} \|M - T\|_F^2, \; s.t. \; M \geq 0, \mathbf{m}^T\mathbf{1} = k, \tag{21}$$

where $\mathbf{m} = diag(M)$ and $diag(M)$ denotes a vector formed by the diagonal elements of M.

Our strategy is to solve two subproblems, Problem (20) and Problem (21) alternately, and let their solutions project mutually. In each iteration, we solve Problem (20) first and let its solution M_1 to be the T matrix in Problem (21), afterwards we solve Problem (21) and let its solution M_2 play the role of matrix T in Problem (20). We solve these two problems alternately and iteratively until M converges.

According to Von Neumann's successive projection lemma [16], this mutual projection strategy we use will converge to the cross of two subspaces formed by Problems (20) and (21). The lemma theoretically ensures that the solution of the alternate projection strategy ultimately converges onto the global optimal solution of Problem (19).

According to Lemma 2 in Appendix A, the optimal solution of Problem (20) is as follows:

$$M = K + \frac{n + \mathbf{1}^T K \mathbf{1}}{n^2}\mathbf{1}\mathbf{1}^T - \frac{1}{n}K\mathbf{1}\mathbf{1}^T - \frac{1}{n}\mathbf{1}\mathbf{1}^T K, \tag{22}$$

where $K = \frac{T+T^T}{2}$.

As far as Problem (21) is concerned, firstly we let matrix T in Problem (21) equal to the solution of M to Problem (20) (shown in Eq. (22)). Then according to Lemma 3 in Appendix B, the optimal solution of Problem (21) is:

$$M = T_+, \quad \mathbf{m} = (\mathbf{t} - \lambda\mathbf{1})_+. \tag{23}$$

Alternately we solve Problems (20) and (21) till M converges onto its global optimal solution.

The second step is fixing M and solving L, then Problem (17) becomes:

$$\min_{L} \gamma \|L\|_* + \frac{\mu}{2}\left\|I - M - L + \frac{1}{\mu}\Lambda\right\|_F^2. \tag{24}$$

Let $N = (I - M + \frac{1}{\mu}\Lambda)$, Problem (24) becomes

$$\min_{L} \frac{\gamma}{\mu}\|L\|_* + \frac{1}{2}\|L - N\|_F^2. \tag{25}$$

According to [5], the solution of Problem (25) is:

$$L = U Diag((\sigma_i - \frac{\gamma}{\mu})_+)V^T, \tag{26}$$

where the singular value decomposition of N is $N = U\Sigma V^T$. $Diag((\sigma_i - \frac{\gamma}{\mu})_+)$ is a diagonal matrix with i-th diagonal element as $(\sigma_i - \frac{\gamma}{\mu})_+$.

Our algorithm to solve the new objective is summarized in Algorithm 1.

Convergence and Complexity Analysis: The convergence of ALM algorithm was proved and discussed in previous papers. Please refer to the literature therein [3, 22]. Because our new objective is convex, our algorithm converges to the global optimum.

In Algorithm 1, the slowest step is Step 2 for updating L. It requires $O(n^3)$ time to implement the singular vector decomposition, where n is the number of samples in the dataset. This time complexity is comparable to that of spectral clustering.

Algorithm 1 Proposed Algorithm

Input:
The given affinity matrix $W \in \Re^{n \times n}$;
The number of clusters k;
Output:
The learnt similarity matrix M^*;
Initialization:
Let the count number of iteration $t = 0$. Randomly initialize matrix $L^{(0)} \in \Re^{n \times n}$ and set the Lagrange multiplier matrix $\Lambda^{(0)} = \mathbf{0} \in \Re^{n \times n}$. Set the penalty parameter $\mu^{(0)} = 0.1$, and the increment step parameter $\rho > 1$;
Preprocessing:
Solve Problem (15) to pre-process W and get a doubly stochastic matrix $M^{(0)}$. Let $W = M^{(0)}$.
while not converge **do**
1. Update $M^{(t+1)}$ using Eq. (22) Eq. (23) alternatively via the successive projection strategy;
2. Update $L^{(t+1)}$ by Eq. (26);
3. Update $\Lambda^{(t+1)} = \Lambda^{(t)} + \mu^{(t)}(I - M^{(t+1)} - L^{(t+1)})$;
4. Update $\mu^{(t+1)} = \rho\mu^{(t)}$;
5. Update $t = t + 1$;
end while
Return: M^*;

4. CONNECTIONS TO K-MEANS CLUSTERING

Here in this section, we will further discuss the connection between our model and the K-means clustering problem.

THEOREM 2. *In Problem (5), if $r \to \infty$ and $W = X^T X$, then Problem (5) is equivalent to K-means clustering.*

Proof: Given a set of data points $X = [\mathbf{x}_1, \mathbf{x}_2, ..., \mathbf{x}_n] \in \Re^{d \times n}$, the K-means clustering problem is meant to partition X into k $(1 \leq k \leq n)$ clusters $C = \{C_1, C_2, ..., C_k\}$ such that the sum of the within cluster variance is minimized [13]. That is to say, the objective function of the K-means problem is:

$$\min_{C} \sum_{i=1}^{k} \sum_{\mathbf{x}_j \in \mathbf{s}_i} \|\mathbf{x}_j - \mu_i\|^2 \tag{27}$$

where μ_i is the mean of data points belonging to C_i.

If we introduce two matrix $U \in \Re^{d \times k}$ and $G \in \Re^{n \times k}$, where $U = [\mu_1, \mu_2, ..., \mu_k]$ and G indicates the clustering indices , then Eq. (27) can be reformulated as:

$$\begin{aligned} &\min_{G \in Ind, U} \left\|X - UG^T\right\|_F^2 \\ \Longleftrightarrow &\min_{G \in Ind, U} Tr(GU^T UG^T) - 2Tr(X^T UG^T) \end{aligned} \tag{28}$$

Since the solution of U w.r.t. X and G is $U = XG(G^T G)^{-1}$, we have $Tr(GU^T UG^T) = Tr(X^T UG^T)$, thus Eq. (28) can be written as:

$$\begin{aligned}&\max_{G\in Ind,U} Tr(X^TUG^T)\\ \Longleftrightarrow &\max_{G\in Ind} Tr((G^TG)^{-\frac{1}{2}}G^T(X^TX)G(G^TG)^{-\frac{1}{2}}) \\ \Longleftrightarrow &\max_{F} Tr(F^T(X^TX)F)\end{aligned} \tag{29}$$

where $F = G(G^TG)^{-\frac{1}{2}}$.

Note that the $Tr(FF^TFF^T) = Tr(FF^T) = Tr(G(G^TG)^{-1}G)$ $= k$, so Problem (29) is equivalent to:

$$\min_{F} \left\|FF^T - X^TX\right\|_F^2 \tag{30}$$

Let $M = FF^T$, then Problem (30) can be rewritten as:

$$\min_{M\in\mathcal{D}} \left\|M - X^TX\right\|_F^2 \tag{31}$$

where $M \in \mathcal{D}$ indicates some constraints on the M matrix. So the K-means clustering problem is to find a matrix M meeting some requirements such that M can minimize Problem (31).

Let's take further observe the properties of M.

From the definition of M, where $M = FF^T$, we can directly find that $m_{ij} = \frac{1}{n_i}$, if $\mathbf{x}_i$ and $\mathbf{x}_j$ belongs to the same cluster; and $m_{ij} = 0$ otherwise. Also, it's apparent that $M \geq 0$, $M^T = M$ and $M\mathbf{1} = \mathbf{1}$, that is to say, M is doubly stochastic. Moreover, we have $Tr(M) = Tr(FF^T) = k$. □

5. EXPERIMENTAL RESULTS

Our structured doubly stochastic model (SDS) can uncover the clustering structure and directly provide the clustering results, thus the clustering performance using doubly stochastic matrix can be enhanced. In this section we evaluate the clustering performance of our method on both synthetic and benchmark datasets, and compare them to the related doubly stochastic model and spectral clustering methods.

Moreover, according to the discussion in the previous section, our model possesses interesting connection with K-means clustering, we also conduct experiments to test whether our model provides an approach to better solving the K-means clustering problem.

5.1 Experiments on Clustering

In this subsection, we conduct clustering experiments on our method and several related method. Our goal is to test whether the structured doubly stochastic matrix learned in our model is beneficial to improve the clustering performance under different circumstances.

5.1.1 Experimental Settings on Clustering

To evaluate the clustering performance of our method, we compare with spectral clustering, *i.e,* Ratio Cut and Normalized Cut, as well as the doubly stochastic normalization (DSN) method [29].

All comparing methods require an affinity matrix as the input. We construct the input affinity matrix with the self-tune Gaussian method [7], where the number of neighbors is set to be 5 and the value of σ is self-tuned. Moreover, we let the input matrix W of our method to be initialized as shown in Eq. (15) such that W is doubly stochastic. In the experiment, we set the number of clusters to be the ground truth in each dataset. In our method, we set parameter μ = 0.1, ρ = 1.1 and r to be tuned in the range of $\{10^0, 10^{0.5}, ..., 10^5\}$.

For all methods requiring K-means as the post-processing step, including Ratio Cut, Normalized Cut and DSN, we give them the same 100 random initializations and compute their respective best initialization vector w.r.t K-means objective function value. Since their performance is unstable with different initialization, we only report their respective best results in the 100 times repetition. For DSN method, we set the number of iteration as 3000 so as to get a good doubly stochastic matrix for clustering.

All experiments are conducted on a Windows system with Intel Core i7-3770 Processor (8M Cache, 3.40 GHz).

The evaluation of different methods is based on two clustering metrics: accuracy and NMI (Normalized Mutual Information).

Accuracy is the percentage of the correctly assigned labels. NMI is short for the normalized mutual information. Let L denote the real label vector in a certain dataset, while L' denotes the predicted one, then

$$NMI(L, L') = \frac{I(L, L')}{\max(H(L), H(L'))}\,, \tag{32}$$

where $I(L, L')$ is the mutual information between L and L':

$$I(L, L') = \sum_{l_i\in L}\sum_{l'_j\in L'} p(l_i, l'_j)\log\frac{p(l_i, l'_j)}{p(l_i)p(l'_j)}\,, \tag{33}$$

and $H(L)$ is the entropy of L:

$$H(L) = -\sum_{i=1}^{n} p(l_i)\log p(l_i)\,. \tag{34}$$

5.1.2 Clustering Experiments on Synthetic Data

First of all, we conduct clustering experiments on the synthetic data as a sanitary check. The synthetic dataset is a 100×100 matrix with four 25×25 block matrices diagonally arranged. The data within each block denotes the probability of two corresponding points from one same cluster to be connected; while the data outside all the blocks denotes the probability of pair-wise data points from different clusters to be connected, *i.e.,* noise (which should be 0 in the ideal clustering data). The probability values within each block are randomly generated in the range of $(0,\ 1)$; while the noise data is randomly generated in the range of $(0,\ c)$, where c is set to be 0.5 and 0.6 respectively. What's more, to make this clustering task more challenging, we randomly pick out 25 noise data and set their value to be 1.

Fig. 1 shows the original random matrix and corresponding clustering results of SDS. We can notice that our model performs well in this task. In our approach, we successfully learn a structured doubly stochastic matrix with explicit block structure, which divides the data into exactly four clusters. After adding high-level disturbance in the random data, our method still effectively recovers the clustering structure, which indicates the robustness of our model.

When the noise ratio is 0.5, our method works out an almost perfect structured doubly stochastic matrix with four clear blocks. As the noise increases, the block structure in the original data blurs, but our model is still able to detect the intrinsic cluster structure from the data.

5.1.3 Clustering Experiments on Benchmark Datasets

We evaluated the proposed double stochastic method on 7 benchmark datasets: AR [14], FERET [21], Yale [9], ORL [23], Carcino-

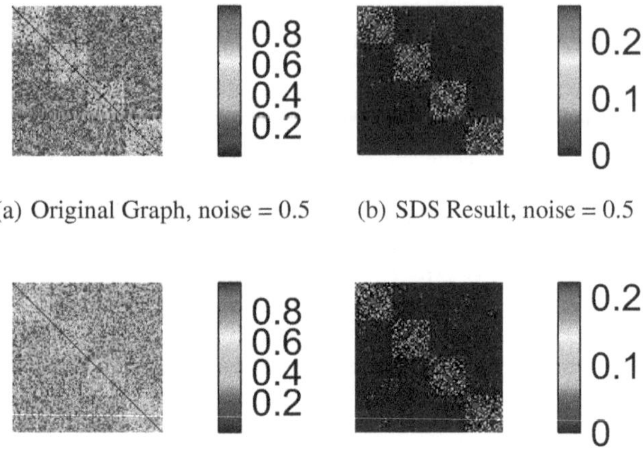

(a) Original Graph, noise = 0.5 (b) SDS Result, noise = 0.5

(c) Original Graph, noise = 0.6 (d) SDS Result, noise = 0.6

Figure 1: Illustration of our clustering results on the block diagonal synthetic data with different settings of noise. On the left column shows the graph structure of the original data generated in the experiment. Figures on the right denote the structure of the doubly stochastic matrix obtained in our SDS model.

Table 1: Descriptions of benchmark datasets used in our experiments.

Datasets	Number of Instances	Dimensions	Classes
AR	840	768	120
FERET	1400	1296	200
Yale	2414	1024	38
ORL	400	1024	40
Carcinomas	174	9182	11
SRBCTML	83	2308	4
LEUML	72	3571	2

mas [24, 28], SRBCTML [10] and LEUML[1]. The detailed description of these datasets is summarized in Table 1.

The clustering performance comparison is summarized in Table 2. Results in Table 2 suggest that our method works very well on real benchmark datasets. Our SDS method maintains a high potential to outperform other methods on these distinct datasets. The theoretical proof in the methodology section indicates the connection between our our model and spectral clustering problem, while the experimental results here verify SDS's better clustering performance. This suggests SDS has the ability to better solve the spectral clustering problem. Compared with the up-to-date method, our method gains an obvious advantage over DSN. DSN only holds constraints on the doubly stochastic property of the learned graph but not its cluster structure, thus cannot get the optimal clustering results. On the contrary, our model learns a novel doubly stochastic matrix with explicit block structure, which performs better in clustering.

5.1.4 Clustering Results Analysis

To further analyze the clustering performance, we draw the graph learned from different methods and compare their structure. We compare the graphs represented by the doubly stochastic matrix learned in DSN and SDS, respectively, and also, we display the graph constructed via self-tune Gaussian method, which is the input for spectral clustering. To explicitly view the graph structure, here we use the two datasets with relatively small number of classes and samples as the example, *i.e.,* LEUML and SRBCTML. We present the graphs in Fig. 2. In each graph, row and columns are reshuffled such that samples from the same cluster are put together, which makes the cluster structure more clear to observe in the graph. For LEUML and SRBCTML, the r value we set for SDS is 10^0 and $10^{0.5}$, respectively. We can notice that the graph learned by SDS maintains the most clear block structure, and elements in each cluster tend to have similar value. These observations coincide with our theoretical analysis. Especially in the LEUML dataset, the doubly stochastic matrix learned by DSN is quite noisy, which leads to bad clustering performance shown in Table 2. Whereas, due to the low-rank constraint on the graph Laplacian matrix, the doubly stochastic matrix learned in our SDS model has more clear block structure, which accounts for the better clustering results obtained from SDS.

[1] http://www2.stat.duke.edu/courses/Spring01/sta293b/datasets.html

5.2 Experiments on K-means Task

In the K-means clustering problem, a "better" solution signifies a smaller objective function value as well as a higher clustering accuracy. Since K-means problem is non-convex, the quality of initialization is crucial in performing K-means clustering. In this subsection, we conduct experiments on both synthetic and real benchmark datasets to demonstrate the contribution of our method in better solving the K-means problem.

5.2.1 Experimental Settings on K-means Task

The experimental settings are similar to the settings in the clustering experiments. The different part is that in this section, we assign the clustering indicator obtained in our method as an initialization for K-means and see if the K-means clustering problem can be better solved with our initialization. For our method, we use $W = X^T X$ as the input matrix.

Still, the number of clusters is set to be the ground truth in each dataset. When implementing K-means clustering, unless specified otherwise, the following settings are adopted: we use 100 random initializations and record the average as well as best result w.r.t. K-means objective function value in the 100 times repetition.

The evaluation is based on three metrics: accuracy, NMI and the K-means objective function value.

5.2.2 K-means Experiments on Synthetic Data

In the synthetic experiment, our toy data is a randomly generated multi-cluster matrix. Data points in each cluster are sampled i.i.d. from the Gaussian distribution $\mathcal{N}(0, 1)$. In our experiment, we set the number of clusters to be 100, number of samples to be 1000, while the dimensionality to be $\{2, 50, 1000\}$ respectively. Our goal is to partition these clusters apart with K-means method. In the beginning we run K-Means for 10000 times and record the minimum K-means objective value and the corresponding clustering accuracy. Then we run our method once by setting the input matrix to be $W = X^T X$ and use the obtained clustering results as an initialization index vector for K-means and compute the same metrics. Comparison results are summarized in Table 3, which indicates apparent superiority of our method over K-means. It shows that even after 10000 times run, the minimum K-means objective value and clustering accuracy obtained by K-means are still far behind the result obtained by our method with just one run. This verifies that our method is able to better solve the K-means problem.

5.2.3 K-means Experiments on Benchmark Datasets

Still, we evaluate our model on the 7 benchmark datasets shown

Table 2: Experimental results comparison of clustering on benchmark datasets.

		Ratio Cut	Normalized Cut	DSN	SDS
ACCURACY	AR	0.358	0.358	0.382	**0.404**
	FERET	0.249	0.255	0.279	**0.280**
	Yale	0.387	0.396	0.439	**0.448**
	ORL	0.653	0.625	0.605	**0.663**
	Carcinomas	**0.724**	0.695	0.690	0.718
	SRBCTML	0.434	0.434	0.410	**0.446**
	LEUML	0.903	0.903	0.542	**0.917**
		Ratio Cut	Normalized Cut	DSN	SDS
NMI	AR	0.677	0.700	0.705	**0.706**
	FERET	0.647	0.674	0.682	**0.683**
	Yale	0.561	0.570	0.604	**0.605**
	ORL	0.799	0.794	0.783	**0.814**
	Carcinomas	**0.719**	0.697	0.707	0.712
	SRBCTML	0.169	0.160	0.132	**0.187**
	LEUML	0.547	0.547	0.079	**0.585**

Table 3: K-means objective function value and clustering results comparison on synthetic datasets.

	K-means Min_obj	K-means Min_obj with SDS Initialization	K-means Accuracy (min_obj)	K-means Accuracy with SDS Initialization
d = 2	1.60	**1.15**	0.713	**0.822**
d = 50	420.08	**0.14**	0.861	**1.000**
d = 1000	10292.00	**2.7305**	0.863	**1.000**

Table 4: Experimental results comparison for K-means problem on benchmark datasets.

		K-means Min_obj	K-means Average	K-means with SDS Initialization
K-means Objective Function Value	AR	7982.58	8395.09 ± 124.98	**7562.62**
	FERET	28684.82	29101.97 ± 215.69	**26420.99**
	Yale	39578.65	40398.72 ± 337.14	**39381.64**
	ORL	6223.80	6633.50±156.62	**5943.80**
	Carcinomas	47160.00	48682.00±692.63	**46787.00**
	SRBCTML	**5747.30**	5982.00±161.18	**5747.30**
	LEUML	**11364.00**	11398.00±78.78	**11364.00**
		K-means Min_obj	K-means Average	SDS
Accuracy	AR	0.310	0.285 ± 0.011	**0.343**
	FERET	0.206	0.200 ± 0.005	**0.234**
	Yale	0.111	0.110 ± 0.006	**0.114**
	ORL	0.568	0.490±0.031	**0.638**
	Carcinomas	0.672	0.571±0.050	**0.695**
	SRBCTML	0.374	0.446±0.070	**0.458**
	LEUML	0.708	0.740±0.058	**0.736**
		K-means Min_obj	K-means Average	SDS
NMI	AR	0.640	0.621 ± 0.009	**0.688**
	FERET	0.598	0.581 ± 0.006	**0.638**
	Yale	0.170	0.163 ± 0.009	**0.178**
	ORL	0.754	0.711±0.018	**0.781**
	Carcinomas	0.648	0.591±0.042	**0.704**
	SRBCTML	0.106	0.187±0.081	**0.261**
	LEUML	0.182	0.225±0.112	**0.237**

in Table 1. We summarize the K-means performance comparison of K-means clustering and our method in Table 4. From Table 4, we can notice that our method improves the performance of K-means on real benchmark datasets. On all dataset, our SDS method performs equally or even better than K-means clustering. These results demonstrates that our model makes a good way to better solve the K-means clustering problem. By adopting the cluster indicator learned in our model as the initialization, not only is the K-means objective function value reduced, but the clustering performance is also boosted to a large extent.

5.3 Experiments on Convergence Analysis

In this subsection, we analyze the influence of parameter r in Eq. (6) to the convergence of our algorithm. To save space, we just take two datasets, Carcinomas and ORL, as an example. We apply our method to these benchmark datasets with three different r values (*i.e.*, 10, 10^3 and 10^5) and record the objective value of our model in each iteration.

The convergence results are presented in Fig. 3. We can notice that no matter what the r value is, our model always converges within about 80 iterations, which indicates the fast convergence of our algorithm.

6. CONCLUSIONS

In this paper, we proposed a novel structured doubly stochastic model with rank constraint on the graph Laplacian matrix. The doubly stochastic matrix learned in our model possesses explicit clustering structure, from which we can immediately partition data points into k connected components, where k is the number of clusters. The doubly stochastic property guarantees the effectiveness of the learnt similarity matrix while the rank constraint on the graph Laplacian matrix enhances the clustering ability. The quality of the learnt graph was verified by extensive experimental results, which suggested the feasibility of our model. What's more, we theoretically and empirically proved that our method made its own contribution in better solving the K-means and spectral clustering problem.

Appendix A

LEMMA 2. *The following gives the global optimal solution to Problem (20):*

$$M = K + \frac{n + \mathbf{1}^T K \mathbf{1}}{n^2}\mathbf{1}\mathbf{1}^T - \frac{1}{n}K\mathbf{1}\mathbf{1}^T - \frac{1}{n}\mathbf{1}\mathbf{1}^T K,$$
$$K = \frac{T + T^T}{2}.$$

Proof: With the Lagrangian function, Problem (20) can be rewritten as:

$$\min_M \frac{1}{2}\|M - T\|_F^2 - (\lambda^T(M\mathbf{1} - \mathbf{1})) - Tr(\Lambda^T(M^T - M)), \quad (35)$$

where $\Lambda \in \Re^{n\times n}$ and $\lambda \in \Re^n$ are Lagrange multipliers.

Taking derivative w.r.t. M and set it to 0, we have:

$$M - T - (\Lambda^T - \Lambda) - \lambda\mathbf{1}^T = 0. \quad (36)$$

Compute transpose on both sides of Eq. (36), we have:

$$M - T^T + (\Lambda^T - \Lambda) - \mathbf{1}\lambda^T = 0. \quad (37)$$

Subtracting Eq. (36) from Eq. (37), we get:

$$T - T^T + 2(\Lambda^T - \Lambda) + \lambda\mathbf{1}^T - \mathbf{1}\lambda^T = 0$$
$$\Longrightarrow -(\Lambda^T - \Lambda) = \tfrac{1}{2}(T - T^T + \lambda\mathbf{1}^T - \mathbf{1}\lambda^T). \quad (38)$$

Combining Eq. (36) with Eq. (38), we further get:

$$2(M - T) + (T - T^T + \lambda\mathbf{1}^T - \mathbf{1}\lambda^T) - 2\lambda\mathbf{1}^T = 0$$
$$\Longrightarrow 2M - T - T^T - \lambda\mathbf{1}^T - \mathbf{1}\lambda^T = 0. \quad (39)$$

Multiply the vector $\mathbf{1}$ on both sides of Eq. (39), we have:

$$2\mathbf{1} - T\mathbf{1} - T^T\mathbf{1} - n\lambda - \mathbf{1}\lambda^T\mathbf{1} = 0. \quad (40)$$

Since $\lambda^T\mathbf{1}$ is a number, it is apparent that $(\lambda^T\mathbf{1})^T = \lambda^T\mathbf{1}$, thus:

$$2\mathbf{1} - T\mathbf{1} - T^T\mathbf{1} - n\lambda - \mathbf{1}\mathbf{1}^T\lambda = 0. \quad (41)$$

From Eq. (41) we can obtain the solution of λ as follows:

$$\lambda = (\mathbf{1}\mathbf{1}^T + nI)^{-1}(2\mathbf{1} - T\mathbf{1} - T^T\mathbf{1}). \quad (42)$$

To enhance the computing speed, we compute the inverse term in Eq. (42) by means of the Woodbury formula [27]:

$$(A+UCV)^{-1} = A^{-1} - A^{-1}U(C^{-1} + VA^{-1}U)^{-1}VA^{-1}. \quad (43)$$

Thus the inverse term in Eq. (42) can be rewritten as:

$$(\mathbf{1}\mathbf{1}^T + nI)^{-1} = (-\frac{1}{2n^2}\mathbf{1}\mathbf{1}^T + \frac{1}{n}I). \quad (44)$$

From Eq. (44), we can rewrite Eq. (42) as follows:

$$\begin{aligned}\lambda &= (-\frac{1}{2n^2}\mathbf{1}\mathbf{1}^T + \frac{1}{n}I)(2\mathbf{1} - T\mathbf{1} - T^T\mathbf{1}) \\ &= \frac{1}{n}\mathbf{1} - (-\frac{1}{2n^2}\mathbf{1}\mathbf{1}^T + \frac{1}{n}I)(T + T^T)\mathbf{1}. \quad (45)\end{aligned}$$

Plugging the solution of λ in Eq. (45) to Eq. (39), we get:

$$\begin{aligned}2M &= T + T^T + \lambda\mathbf{1}^T + \mathbf{1}\lambda^T \\ &= T + T^T + \frac{2}{n}\mathbf{1}\mathbf{1}^T - (-\frac{1}{2n^2}\mathbf{1}\mathbf{1}^T + \frac{1}{n}I)(T + T^T)\mathbf{1}\mathbf{1}^T \\ &\quad -\mathbf{1}\mathbf{1}^T(T + T^T)(-\frac{1}{2n^2}\mathbf{1}\mathbf{1}^T + \frac{1}{n}I) \\ &= T + T^T + \frac{2}{n}\mathbf{1}\mathbf{1}^T + \frac{\mathbf{1}^T T^T \mathbf{1}}{n^2}\mathbf{1}\mathbf{1}^T + \frac{\mathbf{1}^T T \mathbf{1}}{n^2}\mathbf{1}\mathbf{1}^T \\ &\quad -\frac{1}{n}T\mathbf{1}\mathbf{1}^T - \frac{1}{n}T^T\mathbf{1}\mathbf{1}^T - \frac{1}{n}\mathbf{1}\mathbf{1}^T T^T - \frac{1}{n}\mathbf{1}\mathbf{1}^T T\end{aligned}$$

Let $K = \frac{T+T^T}{2}$, then we can rewrite the above equation as:

$$M = K + \frac{n + \mathbf{1}^T K\mathbf{1}}{n^2}\mathbf{1}\mathbf{1}^T - \frac{1}{n}K\mathbf{1}\mathbf{1}^T - \frac{1}{n}\mathbf{1}\mathbf{1}^T K, \quad (46)$$

which is the global optimal solution of Problem (20). Obviously, M is symmetric and

$$M\mathbf{1} = K\mathbf{1} + \frac{n + \mathbf{1}^T K\mathbf{1}}{n}\mathbf{1} - K\mathbf{1} - \frac{1}{n}\mathbf{1}\mathbf{1}^T K\mathbf{1} = \mathbf{1}, \quad (47)$$

which means that the solution of M in Eq. (46) meets the requirements of Problem (20).

Specially, when T is symmetric, the solution of M is:

$$M = T + \frac{n + \mathbf{1}^T T\mathbf{1}}{n^2}\mathbf{1}\mathbf{1}^T - \frac{1}{n}T\mathbf{1}\mathbf{1}^T - \frac{1}{n}\mathbf{1}\mathbf{1}^T T. \quad (48)$$

□

Appendix B

LEMMA 3. *The following gives the global optimal solution to Problem (21):*

$$M = T_+,$$
$$\mathbf{m} = (\mathbf{t} - \lambda\mathbf{1})_+.$$

where $\mathbf{m} = diag(M)$.

Proof: Require $M = T_+$, then Problem (21) could be rewritten as follows:

$$\min_{\mathbf{m}} \|\mathbf{m} - \mathbf{t}\|_2^2 \quad (49)$$
$$s.t. \quad \mathbf{m} \geq 0, \mathbf{m}^T\mathbf{1} = k, \quad (50)$$

where $\mathbf{m} = diag(S)$ and $\mathbf{t} = diag(T)$.

Similarly, we can use the Lagrangian function to solve Problem (49) and define:

$$G(\mathbf{m}, \lambda, \eta) = \frac{1}{2} \|\mathbf{m} - \mathbf{t}\|_2^2 - \lambda(\mathbf{m}^T\mathbf{1} - k) - \eta\mathbf{m}^T , \quad (51)$$

where $\lambda \in \Re^n$ and $\eta \in \Re^n$ are Lagrange multipliers.

Taking derivative w.r.t. $\mathbf{m}$ and set it to 0, then we can solve $\mathbf{m}$ in Problem (51) as follows:

$$\begin{aligned} & \mathbf{m} - \mathbf{t} - \lambda\mathbf{1} - \eta = 0 \\ \Longrightarrow \quad & \mathbf{m} = (\mathbf{t} - \lambda\mathbf{1})_+ . \end{aligned} \quad (52)$$

□

7. REFERENCES

[1] R. Angelova and G. Weikum. Graph-based text classification: Learn from your neighbors. *annual international ACM SIGIR conference on Research and development in information retrieval*, pages 485–492, 2006.

[2] M. Belkin and P. Niyogi. Laplacian eigenmaps for dimensionality reduction and data representation. *Neural Computation*, 15(6):1373–1396, 2003.

[3] D. P. Bertsekas. *Constrained optimization and lagrange multiplier methods*. Athena Scientific, 1996.

[4] D. P. Bertsekas et al. Augmented lagrangian and differentiable exact penalty methods. 1981.

[5] J.-F. Cai, E. J. Candès, and Z. Shen. A singular value thresholding algorithm for matrix completion. *SIAM Journal on Optimization*, 20(4):1956–1982, 2010.

[6] A. Celikyilmaz, M. Thint, and Z. Huang. A graph-based semi-supervised learning for question-answering. *the Joint Conference of the 47th Annual Meeting of the ACL and the 4th International Joint Conference on Natural Language Processing of the AFNLP*, pages 719–727, 2009.

[7] W.-Y. Chen, Y. Song, H. Bai, C.-J. Lin, and E. Y. Chang. Parallel spectral clustering in distributed systems. *IEEE Transactions on Pattern Analysis and Machine Intelligence*, 33(3):568–586, 2011.

[8] F. R. K. Chung. *Spectral Graph Theory*. CBMS Regional Conference Series in Mathematics, No. 92, American Mathematical Society, February 1997.

[9] A. Georghiades, P. Belhumeur, and D. Kriegman. From few to many: Illumination cone models for face recognition under variable lighting and pose. *IEEE Trans. Pattern Anal. Mach. Intelligence*, 23(6):643–660, 2001.

[10] J. Khan, J. S. Wei, M. Ringner, L. H. Saal, M. Ladanyi, F. Westermann, F. Berthold, M. Schwab, C. R. Antonescu, C. Peterson, et al. Classification and diagnostic prediction of cancers using gene expression profiling and artificial neural networks. *Nature medicine*, 7(6):673–679, 2001.

[11] D. Luo, C. Ding, and H. Huang. Forging The Graphs: A Low Rank and Positive Semidefinite Graph Learning Approach. *Advances in Neural Information Processing Systems (NIPS)*, pages 2969–2977, 2012.

[12] D. Luo, C. Ding, F. Nie, and H. Huang. Cauchy graph embedding. *International Conference on Machine Learning*, pages 553–560, 2011.

[13] J. MacQueen et al. Some methods for classification and analysis of multivariate observations. In *Proceedings of the fifth Berkeley symposium on mathematical statistics and probability*, volume 1, pages 281–297. Oakland, CA, USA., 1967.

[14] A. Martinez and R. Benavente. The ar face database. Technical report, CVC Technical report, 1998.

[15] B. Mohar. The laplacian spectrum of graphs. In *Graph Theory, Combinatorics, and Applications*, pages 871–898. Wiley, 1991.

[16] J. V. Neumann. *Functional Operators*, volume 2. 1950.

[17] A. Y. Ng, M. I. Jordan, and Y. Weiss. On spectral clustering: Analysis and an algorithm. In *NIPS*, pages 849–856, 2001.

[18] F. Nie, H. Wang, H. Huang, and C. Ding. Unsupervised and semi-supervised learning via l1-norm graph. In *IEEE Conference on Computer Vision*, pages 2268–2273, 2011.

[19] F. Nie, X. Wang, and H. Huang. Clustering and projected clustering via adaptive neighbor assignment. *The 20th ACM SIGKDD Conference on Knowledge Discovery and Data Mining (KDD 2014)*, pages 977–986, 2014.

[20] F. Nie, X. Wang, M. Jordan, and H. Huang. The constrained laplacian rank algorithm for graph-based clustering. *Thirtieth AAAI Conference on Artificial Intelligence (AAAI 2016)*, pages 1969–1976, 2016.

[21] P. Phillips, H. Wechsler, J. Huang, and P. Rauss. The FERET database and evaluation procedure for face-recognition algorithms. *Image and Vision Computing*, 16(5):295–306, 1998.

[22] M. J. D. Powell. *A method for nonlinear constraints in minimization problems*. In R. Fletcher, editor, Optimization. Academic Press, London and New York, 1969.

[23] F. S. Samaria and A. C. Harter. Parameterisation of a stochastic model for human face identification. In *Applications of Computer Vision, 1994., Proceedings of the Second IEEE Workshop on*, pages 138–142. IEEE, 1994.

[24] A. I. Su, J. B. Welsh, L. M. Sapinoso, S. G. Kern, P. Dimitrov, H. Lapp, P. G. Schultz, S. M. Powell, C. A. Moskaluk, H. F. Frierson, and G. M. Hampton. Molecular Classification of Human Carcinomas by Use of Gene Expression Signatures. *Cancer Res.*, 61(20):7388–7393, 2001.

[25] U. Von Luxburg. A tutorial on spectral clustering. *Statistics and computing*, 17(4):395–416, 2007.

[26] F. Wang, P. Li, and A. Konig. Learning a bi-stochastic data similarity matrix. *IEEE International Conference on Data Mining*, pages 551–560, 2010.

[27] M. A. Woodbury. *Inverting modified matrices*. 1950.

[28] K. Yang, Z. Cai, J. Li, and G. Lin. A stable gene selection in microarray data analysis. *BMC bioinformatics*, 7(1):228, 2006.

[29] R. Zass and A. Shashua. Doubly stochastic normalization for spectral clustering. In *NIPS*, pages 1569–1576, 2006.

[30] D. Zhou, O. Bousquet, T. N. Lal, J. Weston, and B. Schölkopf. Learning with local and global consistency. In *NIPS*, 2004.

[31] X. Zhu, Z. Ghahramani, and J. D. Lafferty. Semi-supervised learning using Gaussian fields and harmonic functions. In *ICML*, pages 912–919, 2003.

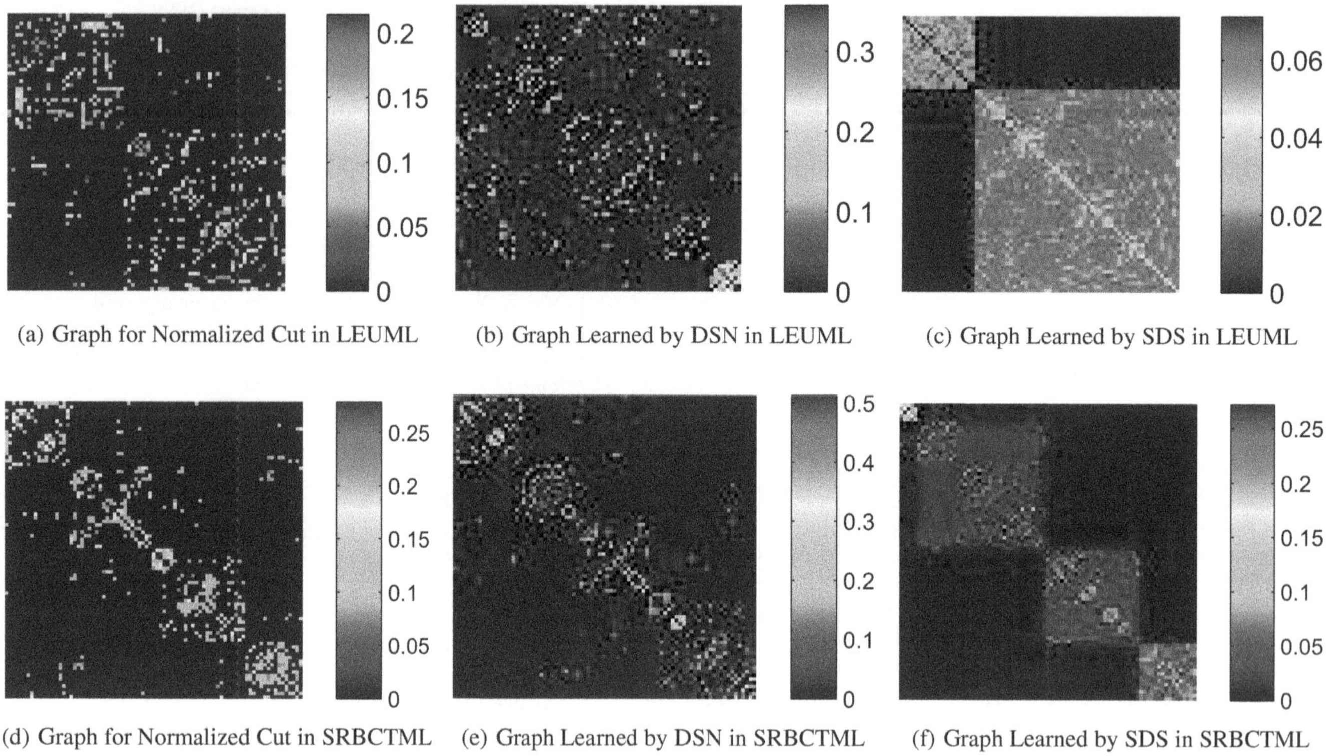

(a) Graph for Normalized Cut in LEUML (b) Graph Learned by DSN in LEUML (c) Graph Learned by SDS in LEUML

(d) Graph for Normalized Cut in SRBCTML (e) Graph Learned by DSN in SRBCTML (f) Graph Learned by SDS in SRBCTML

Figure 2: Illustration of the graph learned from different methods on LEUML and SRBCTML datasets. Rows and columns of the graph are reshuffled respectively such that data points belonging to the same cluster are put together.

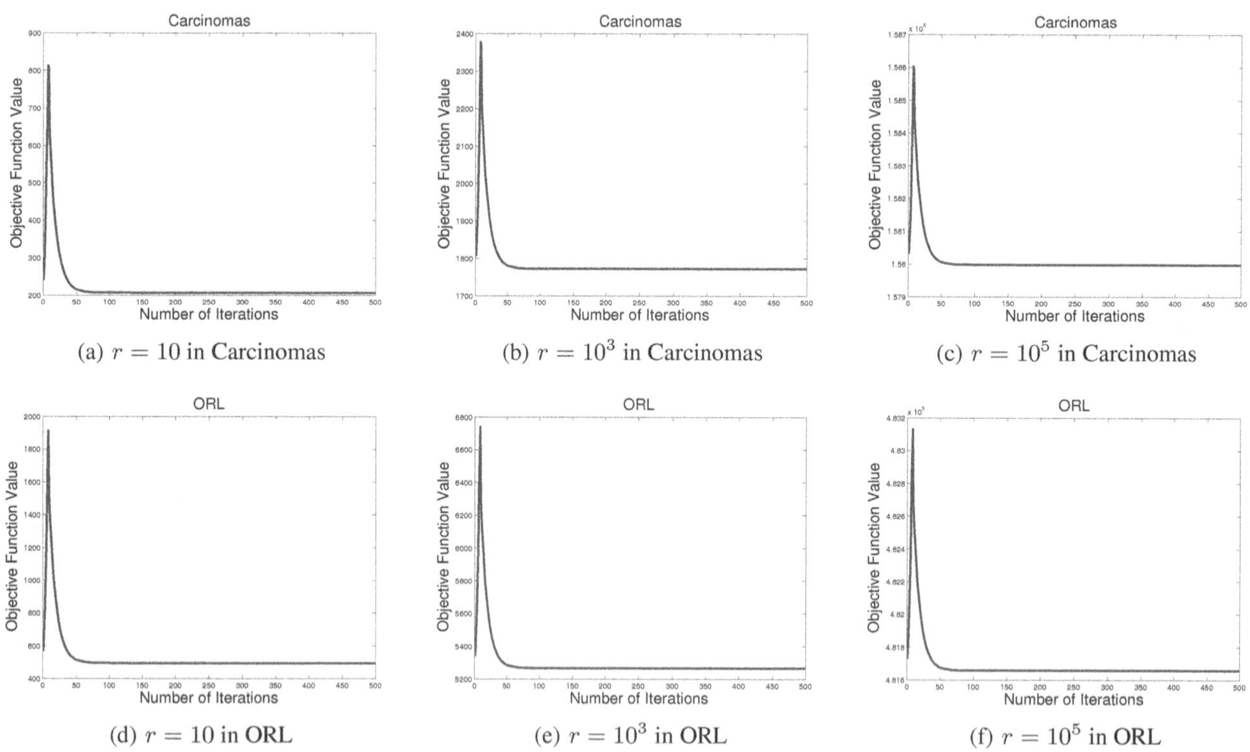

(a) $r = 10$ in Carcinomas (b) $r = 10^3$ in Carcinomas (c) $r = 10^5$ in Carcinomas

(d) $r = 10$ in ORL (e) $r = 10^3$ in ORL (f) $r = 10^5$ in ORL

Figure 3: Objective function value of Eq. (6) with different r parameters in each iteration on Carcinomas and ORL datasets.

A Multiple Test Correction for Streams and Cascades of Statistical Hypothesis Tests

Geoffrey I. Webb
Faculty of Information Technology
Monash University
Clayton, Australia
geoff.webb@monash.edu

François Petitjean
Faculty of Information Technology
Monash University
Clayton, Australia
francois.petitjean@monash.edu

ABSTRACT

Statistical hypothesis testing is a popular and powerful tool for inferring knowledge from data. For every such test performed, there is always a non-zero probability of making a false discovery, i.e. rejecting a null hypothesis in error. Familywise error rate (FWER) is the probability of making at least one false discovery during an inference process. The expected FWER grows exponentially with the number of hypothesis tests that are performed, almost guaranteeing that an error will be committed if the number of tests is big enough and the risk is not managed; a problem known as the multiple testing problem. State-of-the-art methods for controlling FWER in multiple comparison settings require that the set of hypotheses be predetermined. This greatly hinders statistical testing for many modern applications of statistical inference, such as model selection, because neither the set of hypotheses that will be tested, nor even the number of hypotheses, can be known in advance.

This paper introduces Subfamilywise Multiple Testing, a multiple-testing correction that can be used in applications for which there are repeated pools of null hypotheses from each of which a single null hypothesis is to be rejected and neither the specific hypotheses nor their number are known until the final rejection decision is completed.

To demonstrate the importance and relevance of this work to current machine learning problems, we further refine the theory to the problem of model selection and show how to use Subfamilywise Multiple Testing for learning graphical models.

We assess its ability to discover graphical models on more than 7,000 datasets, studying the ability of Subfamilywise Multiple Testing to outperform the state of the art on data with varying size and dimensionality, as well as with varying density and power of the present correlations. Subfamilywise Multiple Testing provides a significant improvement in statistical efficiency, often requiring only half as much data to discover the same model, while strictly controlling FWER.

KDD '16, August 13 - 17, 2016, San Francisco, CA, USA

ISBN 978-1-4503-4232-2/16/08...$15.00

DOI: http://dx.doi.org/10.1145/2939672.2939775

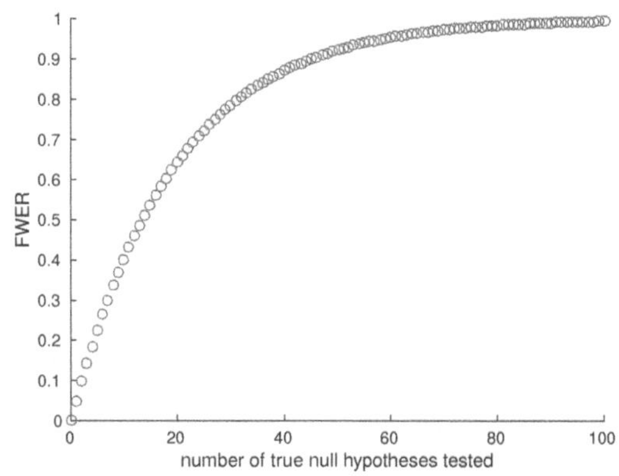

Figure 1: Evolution of the FWER as a function of the number of tested true null hypotheses if no multiple testing correction procedure is used with significance level $\alpha = 0.05$.

Keywords

Hypothesis testing, multiple testing, model selection

1. INTRODUCTION

Statistical hypothesis testing was developed in a context of assessing a single proposition with respect to some data while strictly controlling the risk of type 1 error – the risk of rejecting the null hypothesis, and thus *incorrectly* accepting the hypothesis of interest. This is an extremely powerful approach to knowledge discovery from data. However, in the digital age, where data are almost omnipresent, it is often desirable to employ this approach to test not just a single proposition but massive numbers of propositions. In this case it is not sufficient to simply control in isolation the risk of type one error for each null hypothesis, as even if the individual risk is low, the cumulative risk rapidly approaches near certainty; as shown in Figure 1 which plots the evolution of the FWER as the number of independent true null hypotheses tested m increases. This has led to multiple testing procedures, that can directly control the Familywise Error Rate (FWER), the cumulative risk of any type 1 error when testing a set of null hypotheses [2, 3, 9, 14].

However, these powerful techniques are restricted in that the set of null hypotheses (or at least an upper bound on their number) must be known in advance. This limits their applicability in a growing range of applications where there is a need to test some hypotheses before other hypotheses are known (*hypothesis streams*) and the special case of these streams where the rejection of one hypothesis changes the null hypotheses to be tested subsequently (*hypotheses cascades*).

One context in which hypothesis streams are encountered is online controlled experiments, where many tests are conducted in parallel, with new tests commencing while others are still in progress [19].

Hypothesis streams and cascades also confront scientific research [34]. Scientists increasingly accumulate large datasets at great expense, and it is imperative that these be used to maximum advantage. As a result, it is important to be able to undertake statistical testing of initial hypotheses, and then follow these up with further tests that arise from the initial discoveries.

A further complication is that many datasets are continually growing. It is not possible to wait until all astronomical data are collected, for example, because new observations are made all the time. Nonetheless, we want to be able to derive conclusions from the data. We also want to be able to reconsider hypotheses in the light of additional data as it becomes available. Further, conclusions that we reach with respect to initial hypotheses are likely to lead to the formulation of further hypotheses that we also want to test. If we just keep testing null hypotheses without controlling for the multiple testing problem, then eventually some will be rejected by chance. There is a pressing need for statistical methods that can support science in the age of big data.

Hypothesis streams and cascades are also serious challenges in many data science contexts, including forward stepwise feature selection [8], backward stepwise feature elimination [8], association discovery [38, 39] and model selection [27]. We use this latter application as a case study.

Let us motivate why hypotheses cascades can occur in model selection. Graphical model forward selection traditionally starts with a reference model over n nodes (one node per variable) with no edges. At step s of the process, the reference model contains s edges, and the addition of one edge among e_s has to be considered.[1] The number of possible steps is equal to the maximum number of edges $M = n \cdot (n-1)/2$, and at each step s, there are $M - s + 1$ edges to consider. In consequence, the greatest number of models that we may need to test is $M \cdot (M+1)/2$, which means that discovering a model with $n = 1,000$ leads to the possibility of more than 100 billion tests to be performed, and thus to control against.

This highlights several key motivations of this work:

1. With more than 100 billion tests, even using a recommended flat critical value $\alpha = 0.001$ [17], this is potentially 100 million hypotheses that could correspond to false discoveries. Therefore, controlling for multiple testing is critical.

2. It would be more natural to consider the set of hypotheses as a stream than as a complete set, because many of the hypotheses might never be considered. We are in fact very likely to stop at step $s_k, k \ll M$, which means that controlling for all the hypotheses that might have been present after step s_k is needlessly strict and as we will show, often prevents the acceptance of many true discoveries. We only want to control for the risk with respect to hypotheses that are actually assessed.

   In consequence, the multiple testing procedure should be able to consider new hypotheses to be tested that were not present at the start of the process, without having any knowledge about the hypotheses and their number in advance.

[1] It is important to note that the addition of edge (a, b) at step s and at step s' are two separate hypotheses, because the reference models to which (a, b) would be added is different; we will detail this element in Section 4.

This paper introduces Subfamilywise Multiple Testing (SMT): a multiple testing correction procedure that strictly controls FWER in settings where we have no prior knowledge about the set of hypotheses that will be tested or of their number.

2. SUBFAMILYWISE TESTING

2.1 Problem statement

Let $\mathcal{F} = \bigcup_{i=1}^{n} \mathcal{F}_i$ be a family of n subfamilies of null hypotheses. For any null hypothesis $h \in \mathcal{F}$, let κ_h be an associated test statistic and $p_h = Px(\kappa_h \mid istrue(h))$ be the probability of obtaining the test statistic κ_h or more extreme if h were true, where $Px(\kappa_h \mid istrue(h))$ represents the probability of obtaining the test statistic or more extreme under some predetermined probability distribution for h. Classical hypothesis testing rejects each null hypothesis h if $p_h \leq \alpha$, where α is a predefined critical value.

The probability of making a false discovery when testing a unique null hypothesis h (*i.e.*, the probability of rejecting h when it is true) is no greater than $Pr(h)p_h$, the prior probability that the null hypothesis is true times the p-value p_h. Thus, p_h is an upper bound on the probability of a false discovery when a single hypothesis is tested.

DEFINITION 1. *The familywise error rate (FWER), is the probability of making at least one false discovery — or Type I error — when testing family $\mathcal{F}$. Let $\mathcal{R} \subseteq \mathcal{F}$ be the rejected null hypotheses and $\mathcal{T} \subseteq \mathcal{F}$ be the true null hypotheses. We have*

$$FWER = Pr(\mathcal{R} \cap \mathcal{T} \neq \emptyset) = 1 - Pr(\mathcal{R} \cap \mathcal{T} = \emptyset). \quad (1)$$

A multiple testing correction procedure provides *strict control over the FWER* if it is a function from families of null hypotheses (together with their associated test statistics) and a critical value to a subset of the family, $\mathcal{F}, \alpha \to \mathcal{R} \subseteq \mathcal{F}$ such that no matter which subset of the null hypotheses is true, the probability of rejecting any true null hypothesis is less than α —

$$Pr(\mathcal{R} \cap \mathcal{T} \neq \emptyset) \leq \alpha. \quad (2)$$

We wish to control FWER while iterating over the subfamilies of $\mathcal{F}$, selecting a single null hypothesis for rejection from each subfamily. When considering subfamily $\mathcal{F}_i$ we have knowledge of the subfamilies previously considered, but no information about subsequent subfamilies to be encountered. We allow that the selection of the null hypothesis for rejection in $\mathcal{F}_i$ might determine the null hypotheses that are contained in subsequent subfamilies, as is the case with forward sequential model selection, where the components considered for subsequent inclusion in a model may depend on the components already included.

2.2 SMT Procedure

THEOREM 1. *Let $h_i^{\min}$ be the null hypotheses in $\mathcal{F}_i$ with the lowest p-value, $h_i^{\min} = \arg\min_{h\in\mathcal{F}_i}(p_h)$. Let $\mathcal{R}$ contain the null hypothesis with the lowest p-value from each of the first r subfamilies, $\mathcal{R} = \{h_1^{\min},\ldots,h_r^{\min}\}$. Let $p_i^{\min} = p_{h_i^{\min}} = \min_{h\in\mathcal{F}_i}(p_h)$ be the minimum p-value of a null hypotheses in $\mathcal{F}_i$.*

$$Pr(\mathcal{R}\cap\mathcal{T}\neq\emptyset) \leq \sum_{i=1}^{r} p_i^{\min}\cdot|\mathcal{F}_i|. \tag{3}$$

PROOF.

$$Pr(\mathcal{R}\cap\mathcal{T}\neq\emptyset) = Pr\left(\bigvee_{i=1}^{r}\bigvee_{h\in\mathcal{F}_i\cap\mathcal{T}} p_h \leq p_i^{\min}\right) \tag{4}$$

$$\leq \sum_{i=1}^{r}\sum_{h\in\mathcal{F}_i\cap\mathcal{T}} Pr(p_h \leq p_i^{\min}) \tag{5}$$

$$\leq \sum_{i=1}^{r}\sum_{h\in\mathcal{F}_i\cap\mathcal{T}} p_i^{\min} \tag{6}$$

$$\leq \sum_{i=1}^{r}\sum_{h\in\mathcal{F}_i} p_i^{\min} \tag{7}$$

$$= \sum_{i=1}^{r} p_i^{\min}\cdot|\mathcal{F}_i|. \tag{8}$$

□

Comments. (4) recasts the probability of FWER as the probability of any p-value being less than or equal to $p_i^{\min}$ for any true null hypothesis in any subfamily $\mathcal{F}_i$ from which a null hypothesis is rejected. (5) follows from the consequence of the general disjunction rule that the probability of a disjunction of events cannot exceed the sum of the probabilities of the individual events. For any true null hypothesis h, the probability that the p-value from a valid test procedure is less than or equal to a given p is no greater than p. This justifies (6). The sum over a set of probabilities can be no less than the sum over a superset of those values, justifying (7). (8) re-expresses the equation in terms of $|\mathcal{F}_i|$.

The Subfamilywise Multiple Testing Procedure (SMT) provides strict control over the FWER in a multiple testing situation where there are successive pools of null hypotheses from each of which a single null hypothesis is to be rejected. The procedure has two steps. Step 1 finds

$$r^\star = \arg\max_r\left(\sum_{i=1}^{r} p_i^{\min}\cdot|\mathcal{F}_i| \leq \alpha\right). \tag{9}$$

Step 2 rejects $h_1^{\min},\ldots,h_{r^\star}^{\min}$. That this procedure strictly controls FWER to be no greater than α follows directly from Theorem 1.

3. MONTE CARLO SIMULATIONS

To elucidate the statistical power of the technique, we conducted Monte Carlo simulations, generating sets of null hypotheses, which were randomly assigned to be either true or false and were randomly assigned simulated p-values. These simulations were governed by three parameters — *subfamilySize*: the size of each subfamily; *pTrue*: the probability

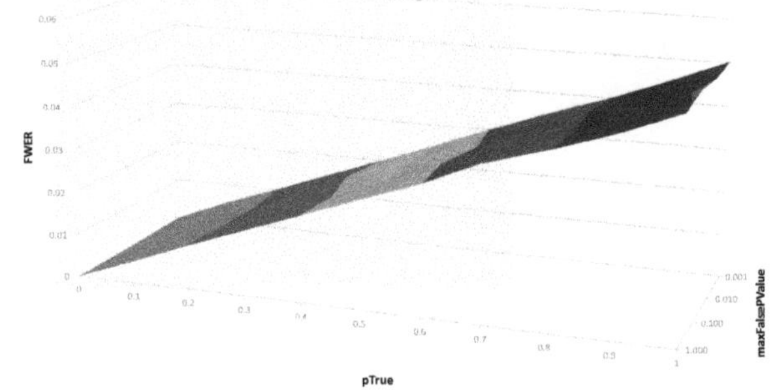

Figure 2: The FWER of SMT as the relative frequency of true to false null hypotheses is increased and the relative p-values of false relative to true null hypotheses is decreased

that a null hypothesis should be designated to be true; and *maxFalsePVal*: the maximum simulated p-value to be assigned to a false null hypothesis.

The following is the procedure used for each simulation.

$\mathcal{R} \leftarrow \emptyset$
$sumP \leftarrow 0.0$
$i \leftarrow 0$
repeat
  $i \leftarrow i+1$
  Generate $\mathcal{F}_i$
  $sumP \leftarrow sumP + |\mathcal{F}_i|\cdot p_i^{\min}$
  if $sumP \leq \alpha$ **then**
    $\mathcal{R} \leftarrow \mathcal{R}\cup\{h_i^{\min}\}$
  end if
until $sumP > \alpha$

To generate each $\mathcal{F}_i$, *subfamilySize* simulated null hypotheses were generated. Each was designated as either true or false, with probability *pTrue* of being designated true. Each true null hypothesis was assigned a simulated p-value drawn uniformly at random from $[0, 1]$ and each false null hypothesis was assigned a simulated p-value drawn uniformly at random from $[0, maxFalsePVal]$. Having lower p-values for false null hypotheses simulates the use of a test statistic that is useful for discriminating between true and false null hypotheses.

We performed two experiments. In the first experiment *subfamilySize* was set to 100, *pTrue* was varied from 0.00 to 1.00 in steps of 0.1 and *maxFalsePVal* was set to each of the values 1.0, 0.1, 0.01 and 0.001, creating a total of 44 treatments. 100,000 Monte Carlo simulations were conducted for each treatment and the FWER and average number of true discoveries per simulation determined.

Figure 2 presents a surface chart that shows the impact on FWER as the relative frequency of true to false null hypotheses is increased and as the p-values of false null hypotheses decrease relative to those of true null hypotheses. As the probability of a true null hypothesis increases, so too does the FWER. This is to be expected, as FWER must be zero when all null hypotheses are false and should be more likely when all null hypotheses are true. Indeed, when all null hypotheses are true, FWER only occurs for family $\mathcal{F}$ if a null hypothesis is rejected from its first subfamily, $\mathcal{F}_1$.

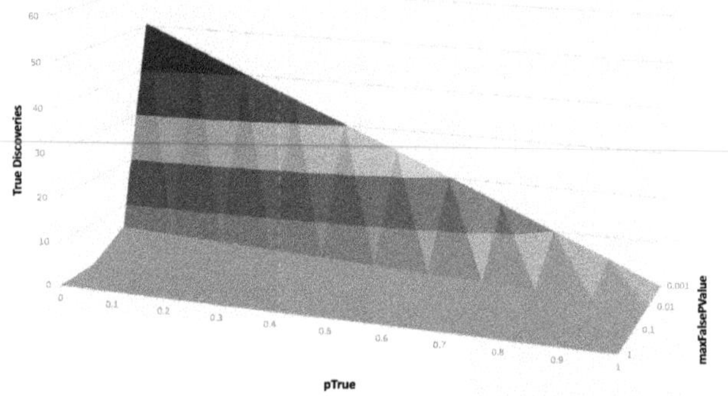

Figure 3: The true discoveries of SMT as the relative frequency of true to false null hypotheses is increased and the relative p-values of false relative to true null hypotheses is decreased

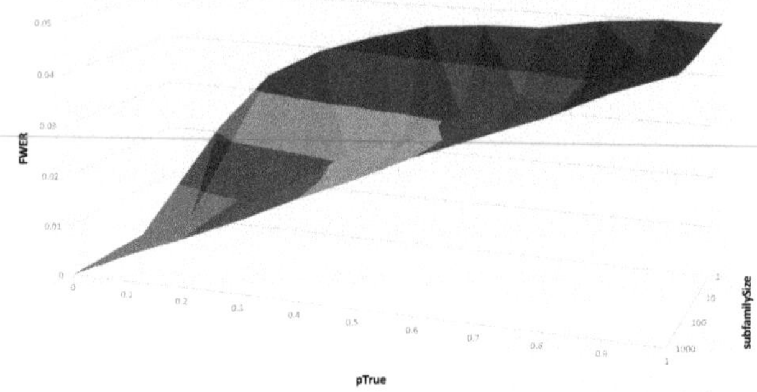

Figure 4: The FWER of SMT as the relative frequency of true to false null hypotheses is increased and the relative p-values of false relative to true null hypotheses is decreased

As the test for the first subfamily is a conventional Bonferroni correction, the FWER must be strictly controlled when all null hypotheses are true.

In contrast, the relative p-values of true and null hypotheses (that is, the power of the simulated test statistic) has little impact on FWER.

Figure 3 shows the effect on true discoveries of the same factors. As can be seen, true discoveries increase as the ratio of false to true null hypotheses increases and as the relative p-value of a false null hypothesis decreases. Recall that true discoveries occur when a false null hypothesis is rejected and hence the true alternative hypothesis is accepted. Clearly there can be no true discoveries when all null hypotheses are true. Conversely, when all null hypotheses are false, all rejected null hypotheses will be true discoveries. In all cases where there are false null hypotheses, the number that are rejected will be determined by their relative p-values, which is why the number of rejections rises as *maxFalsePVal* decreases.

As *maxFalsePVal* had negligible effect on FWER, in the second experiment *maxFalsePVal* was set to 0.01, *pTrue* was again varied from 0.00 to 1.00 in steps of 0.05 and *subfamilySize* was set to each of the values 1, 10, 100 and 1,000, again creating a total of 44 treatments. As in the first experiment, 100,000 Monte Carlo simulations were conducted for each treatment and the FWER and average number of true discoveries per simulation determined.

Figure 4 presents a surface chart showing the effect on FWER as the relative frequency of true to false null hypotheses is increased and as the subfamily size varies. Again, when pTrue is 1.0 and FWER is determined by whether a null hypothesis is rejected for the first subfamily or not, the probability of FWER is strictly controlled by the equivalent of a Bonferroni correction for the first subfamily. Like the first experiment, and for the same reasons, FWER falls as the proportion of false null hypotheses rises.

However, the speed at which FWER falls is greatly affected by the subfamily size. Consider a scenario in which each subfamily contains only a single null hypothesis. If the first null hypothesis is true, the probability of FWER will be exactly α. If the first null hypothesis is false and the second is true, the probability of FWER will be exactly $\alpha/2$, and so on. Hence, when the probability of each null hypothesis being true is high, FWER will be relatively high.

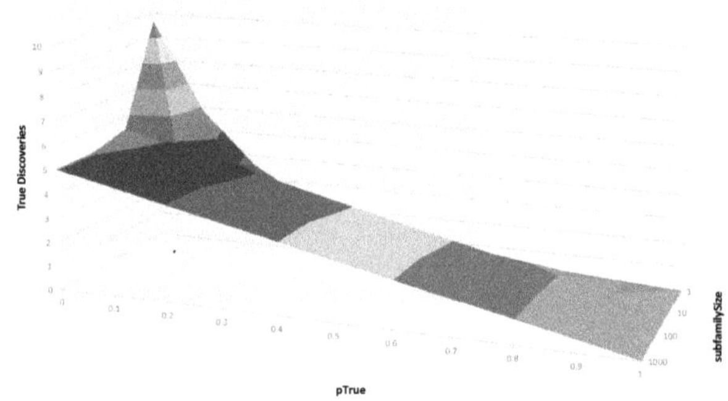

Figure 5: The true discoveries of SMT as the relative frequency of true to false null hypotheses is increased and the relative p-values of false relative to true null hypotheses is decreased

In contrast, as the size of the subfamilies increases, the probability of a subfamily containing false as well as true null hypotheses increases, and the probability increases that the hypothesis with the lowest p-value is false. As familywise error only occurs when the lowest p-value for a subfamily belongs to a true null hypothesis, the FWER correspondingly decreases.

Figure 5 shows the effect on true discoveries of the same factors. Again, true discoveries increase as the ratio of false to true null hypotheses increases. When the probability of each null hypotheses being false is low, true discoveries are highest when the subfamilies are largest, as this gives the greatest chance of each subfamily containing some false null hypotheses to correctly reject. However, as the ratio of false to true null hypotheses increases, the smaller subfamilies begin to reject the greatest number of false null hypotheses, as most subfamilies will include false null hypotheses for rejection, but the smaller subfamilies result in much higher adjusted critical values, making it more likely that the false null hypotheses will be rejected.

These simulations demonstrate the power of SMT, and show that it is most effective when the ratio of false to true hypotheses is highest and the relative p-values of false null hypotheses is lowest. The impact of subfamily size is less straightforward, however, depending on the other factors.

4. SMT FOR MODEL SELECTION

We demonstrate the power of SMT in the context of hill-climbing search for graphical model selection, specifically, where it is used to select interactions for inclusion in a log-linear model within the Chordalysis system [27, 25, 26]. We have made the source-code available for SMT within Chordalysis at https://github.com/fpetitjean/Chordalysis.

4.1 Background

The use of statistical tests and multiple correction methods for learning the structure of graphical models responds to the need for explainable models (see e.g. [22] for genomics). Although long recognized by the data mining community, this highlights again that building an *explanatory* model from data has a different objective to building a *predictive* model [31]. Learning graphical models for which we place greater weight on being confident in the structure is often called log-linear analysis in the statistical community [4], which comes from the fact that the search is often performed among log-linear models. Log-linear models that are graphical are equivalent to Markov Random Fields (or Markov Networks).

Both statistical and machine learning communities have studied the use of statistical methods to learn the structure of graphical models, from the well-known PC algorithm [18, 32], to recent work scaling statistical procedures to high-dimensional data [5, 27, 40].

It is here also interesting to mention MML/MDL methods [28, 37] which, by building on Shannon theory of information, often produce an explanatory model. This is intuitively because every additional parameter has to be explained away by enough data. Several works have studied these approaches for learning Bayesian Networks and Markov Random Fields [1, 6, 25, 30].

It is finally interesting to mention methods based on ℓ_1-regularizers, because they are often claimed to produce understandable models, by biasing the search towards models for which many parameters are zero. Different configurations have been studied: performing a logistic regression for every variable independently [36], focusing on a reduced subset of features [20] or finding a set of variables that best divides the graph [11]. Note that these methods place great weight on the predictivity of the model, which often leads to a significant number of false discoveries (see for example the precision trend depicted in [36] – Section 6). For this reason, we will not consider these methods as being directly related to statistical testing methods.

4.2 Using SMT for model selection

The refined algorithm is given in Table 1. We start with a reference model $\mathcal{M}$ corresponding to the independence model (no edges). We then collect the set E of all potential edges at this stage, *i.e.*, all the $V(V-1)/2$ edges. We then iterate until either there are no edges in E that can be added to the current reference model $\mathcal{M}$ (which happens if all edges have been added), or the addition of the best edge does not satisfy our multiple correction. The process can then be compared to the use of a budget of FWER risk. Starting with the budget being α, at each iteration, we remove from the budget the p-value associated with the accepted edge times the number of concurrent hypotheses that were assessed at the same time as the best edge.

Table 1: Forward selection with SMT

Require: α: the requested FWER
Require: $\mathcal{D}$: a dataset over V variables
Require: $pval(\mathcal{M}, edge)$: a statistical testing procedure returning the p-value associated with the addition of an edge to a model
  $\mathcal{M} \leftarrow (V, \emptyset)$ {independence model (empty graph)}
  $E \leftarrow \{(v_1, v_2) : \forall v_1, v_2 \in V, v_1 \neq v_2\}$
  $budget \leftarrow \alpha$
  while $E \neq \emptyset$ **do**
    bestEdge $\leftarrow \arg\min_{e \in E} pval(\mathcal{M}, e)$
    $p \leftarrow pval(\mathcal{M}, bestEdge)$
    $\alpha' = budget/|E-1|$
    if $p > \alpha'$ **then**
      return $\mathcal{M}$ {would not be valid to add bestEdge}
    end if
    $E \leftarrow E \setminus bestEdge$
    $\mathcal{M} \leftarrow \mathcal{M} \cup bestEdge$
    $budget \leftarrow budget - p \cdot |E|$
  end while

4.3 Experiments with synthetic data

Assessing the quality of model selection techniques requires having knowledge about the multi-way interactions that take place in data. Therefore we start by evaluating the discovery with data that is sampled from known distributions (sets of interactions and associated probability tables). This allows us to compare the discovered interactions to the true structure from which the data was sampled.

Then, we show some results on real-world data.

4.3.1 *Description of experiments*

The task is, given some categorical data, to find the set of correlations that were planted in the distribution from which the data was drawn; all in an unsupervised manner. There are two components to generating the data; first we have to choose a graph structure that describes those correlations, and then we have to parametrize the graphical model. Note that, to ensure reproducibility of the experiments described below, we have made the source-code for generating the parameterized models and data available at http://bit.ly/SourceDataGeneration.

Generation of the data.

To form graphs that are representative of the real-world, we generate random scale-free graphs using the Barabási–Albert (BA) model. This has desirable properties including that the degree distribution follows a power law. BA models are parameterized with (1) the number of nodes (i.e. the number of variables) and (2) the degree, which controls the edge density in the graph. We add an additional condition that the graph be chordal, in order to match the class of models explored by the model selection method that we use: Chordalysis.

Having the graph structure, all we need to generate data is to parameterize the associated graphical model. Chordal graphs each correspond to an equivalence class of Bayesian Networks (BN); we can then use standard procedures for BN parametrization. Each line of every Conditional Probability

Table (CPT) in the network encodes a multinomial distribution. All we need is to control for the strength of the encoded correlations. To this end, we use a flat Dirichlet prior with concentration S ($\text{Dir}(\vec{S})$ for each multinomial). The higher the value of α, the closer the multinomial will be to a uniform distribution, and hence the more subtle the correlation will be.

Finally, the last parameter corresponds to the number of samples to generate. Each data sample is generated independently by sampling the associated Bayesian Network and using a secure pseudo-random number generator (SHA1PRNG).

We thus have four parameters for each experiment:

1. V the number of variables
2. D the degree/density of the edges in the graph
3. S the subtlety of the correlations (inverse of strength)
4. N the number of samples

To assess the statistical efficiency of our proposed SMT, we vary each of those parameters in turn, having set the others to values we assessed as being reasonable: $V = 100$, $D = 3$, $S = 200$ and $N = 50,000$.

Evaluation measure.

The task is unsupervised recovery of the edges[2] that were introduced in the graphical model that generated the data. The number of true/false positives/negatives are thus sufficient statistics for the evaluation; we can then study the *precision*, which is the proportion of discoveries that are true discoveries (rejected null hypotheses that are false), and *recall*, which is the proportion of false null hypotheses that are rejected. The precision obtained across all experiments is consistently 100%; for clarity we thus only report the recall and made all precision graphs available at http://bit.ly/SyntheticResults for cross-check.

We generated over 7,000 datasets in order to study the influence of each parameter on statistical efficiency; each experiment is run 20 times. We report mean and standard deviation.

We compare our novel multiple testing procedure (SMT) to the state of the art:

1. Bonferroni correction [8]
2. *layered critical values* introduced in [29] and integrated in Chordalysis in [27]; we then use different layering 'consuming', at each step either 50%, 1% or 1‰ of the budget. Note that this reformulation in terms of budget is one of the novel contributions of this paper; layered critical values typically uses 50% [27].
3. an MDL/MML scoring technique [25]; MDL and MML are known for their low false-discovery rates, because intuitively, each parameter has to be justified in terms of gain in the compression of the data.

We use a critical value of $\alpha = 0.05$; note that we have also ensured that our results hold for $\alpha = 0.001$ (as per recent recommendations in [17]).

[2]Note that the original graph structure is undirected, actually forming an equivalence class of Bayesian Networks. The use of any BN within this class would result in the same joint probability under maximum likelihood.

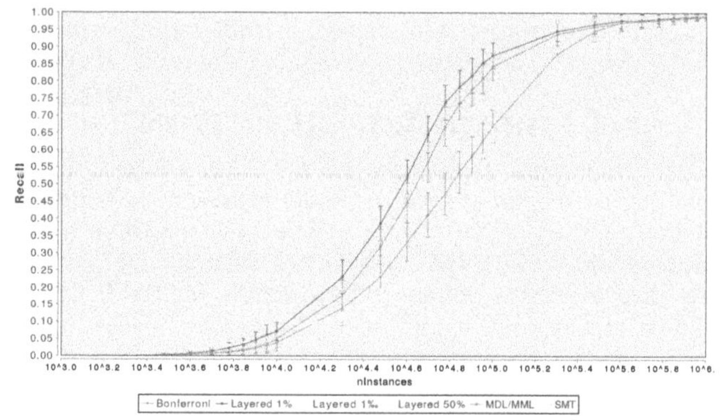

Figure 6: Study of the variation on the number of instances. Note that the x-axis is in log-scale.

4.3.2 Varying the number of instances

We vary N from $1,000$ to $1,000,000$. Results are depicted in Figure 6. Recall generally increases as the data quantity increases, as more data provides more evidence of the planted correlations. SMT uniformly dominates state-of-the-art methods by recovering significantly more of the true structure. The performance of the remaining approaches is uniformly ordered Layered-1%, Layered-1‰, Bonferroni, MML/MDL and then Layered-50%.

We can observe from these results that most parameterizations of the layered correction can beat the full Bonferroni correction. This was to be expected given that the Bonferroni gives a uniform weight to any test in the search, while layering puts more weight on the start of the search. Setting the right layering value is however extremely complicated, because it corresponds to giving a prior as per the number of edges to be found and the distributions of their p-values. For instance, if only few edges are to be discovered, then a high layering value will perform well, while low values should be preferred if many edges are to be discovered. This however raises an important obstacle to the discovery, because there is no way to correctly set this value. By contrast, our proposed SMT does not require to set any parameter, and also significantly dominates all other methods. We will see in the next section that this superiority is substantial for real-world data where the amount of data is fixed.

4.3.3 Varying the number of variables

We vary V from 10 to $1,000$. Results are depicted in Figure 7. Recall generally decreases with the number of variables, which is due to the fact that the density is kept constant; a higher number of variables translates into more and higher-order correlations to be found.

Here again, SMT dominates Layered and MML, with recall declining as the number of variables increases. It is however interesting to note that while SMT uniformly dominates, the relative positioning of other methods differs depending on the number of variables. For instance, MML/MDL performs quite poorly in this experiment when the number of variables is low, but substantially beats Layered-50% from 40 ($10^{1.6} \approx 40$) variables. Similarly, Layered-1% performs well for medium size graphs, but is outperformed by Layered-1‰ when the number of variables is high. This is because with more variables and the density kept constant, there are more correlations to find, which

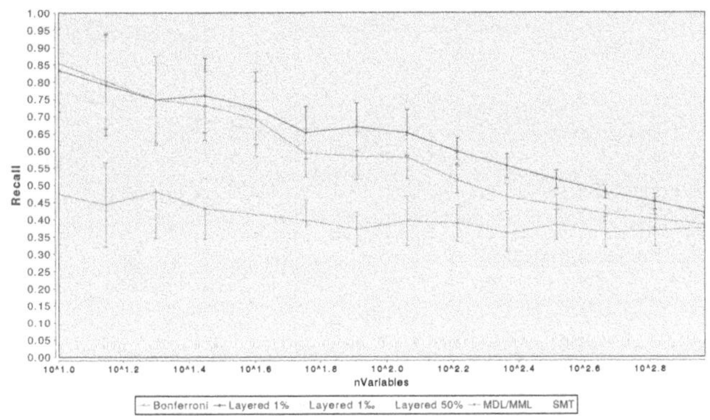

Figure 7: Study of the variation on the number of variables. Note that the x-axis is in log-scale.

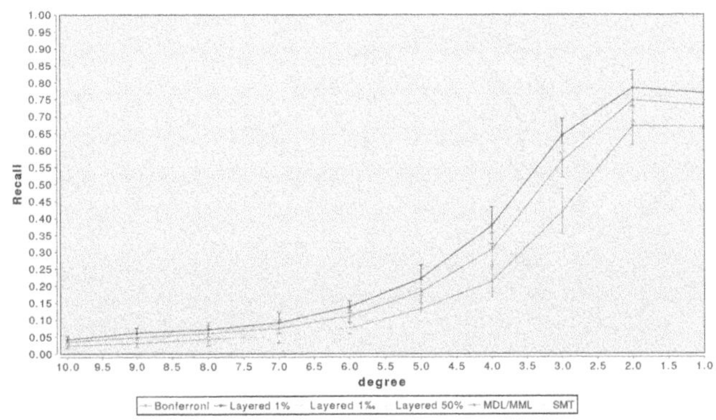

Figure 8: Study of the variation of the density; the x-axis corresponds to the degree in the Barabási–Albert (BA) graph model. High value means more complex graph.

calls for a more 'spread out' use of the budget. Here again, SMT not only outperforms all approaches, but does so without having any parameter to set.

4.3.4 Varying the density of edges in the graph

We vary D from 10 to 1 in steps of 1. Note that D controls for the size of the largest cliques in the graph, which means that the complexity of finding edges grows exponentially with D. Results are depicted in Figure 8. Again, SMT uniformly dominates all other methods; observations are similar to the experiment varying the number of instances.

4.3.5 Varying the subtlety of the correlations

We vary S from 50 to 500 in steps of 50; recall that S corresponds to the concentration parameter of a Dirichlet prior put on the multinomial probabilities of the parameterized model. Intuitively, low values of S lead to peaked multinomial distributions (thus easier to find), while high values lead to multinomials that are close to uniform (thus difficult to find). Results are depicted in Figure 9. SMT uniformly dominates other methods. Observations are similar to the experiment varying the number of instances with the slight difference for $S \geqslant 450$ where Layered-50% slightly outperforms MML/MDL approaches. This is because the absolute value of the recall is very low for high S. We posit that it might then favor statistical approaches that are able to

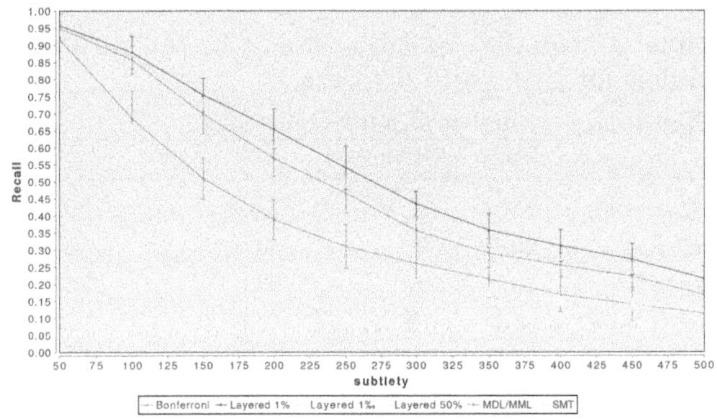

Figure 9: Study of the variation on the strength of correlation. Low values in the x-axis represent strong correlations (thus easier to find).

"spend most of the risk budget," even though one single edge might not be extremely significant. In contrast, MML/MDL approaches decide upon acceptance without looking at the risk that has been spent at previous steps: a model is accepted if it is more probable without any consideration of the multiple testing problem.

4.3.6 General comment

It is clear from these experiments that SMT significantly outperforms state-of-the-art approaches for explanatory model selection (also known as log-linear analysis). We have also drawn a few interesting observations as per the statistical efficiency of other methods. We showed that the setting of the layering parameter makes the layered search method range from very poor performance to second-best. Such parametrization is however problematic because it equates to a prior on the distribution of the p-values for the hypotheses that will be tested. This shows a second advantage to SMT, which outperforms all other methods, without requiring tuning of any parameter.

4.4 Real-world data

We use a broad range of real-world datasets, with both various number of variables and various quantities of data:

Mushroom the classical mushroom dataset, 22 variables, 8k examples [21].

EPESE epidemiological study of the elderly, 25 variables, 14k examples [33].

Internet demographic information on internet users, 70 variables, 10k examples [13].

CoIL2000 insurance customer management, 86 variables, 6k examples [35].

MITFace face recognition dataset, discretized to 4 bins using equal frequency, 362 variables, 31k examples [23].

Finance stock performance of the companies listed in the S&P500 over 20 years of trading, 500 variables.

Protein Multiple alignment of the Serpin family of proteins, 750 variables, 212 proteins [16].

Table 2: **Number of edges found in the resulting models for real-world datasets.**

Name	Number of interactions found			
	MDL	Bonferroni	Best Layered	SMT
Mushroom	21	76	78	**79**
EPESE	26	50	50	**53**
Internet	137	219	230	**247**
CoIL2000	67	168	169	**173**
MITFace	722	1,449	1,456	**1,487**
Finance	864	1,320	1,465	**1,640**
Protein	4	321	399	**471**
Orphamine	**650**	283	394	506
ABC	1,408	1,842	2,102	**2,426**
NYT	9,352	15,778	15,429	**17,741**

Orphamine Frequency of occurrence of 1,260 symptoms for 2,600 rare diseases (1,260 variables and 2,600 examples) [24].

ABC Use of the 500 most interesting (as per $tf\star idf$) words in all the news articles about Melbourne published by the Australian Broadcasting Network (ABC), 500 variables, 35k examples.

NYT Use of the 2,000 most interesting words in 10% of the articles published by the New York Times from 1987 to 2007, 2,000 variables, 180k examples [29].

Where licensing restrictions permit us to do so, we have made these datasets available at http://bit.ly/RealWorldResults.

We report in Table 2 the number of interactions found by the Chordalysis framework using the SMT, layered critical values and MML/MDL frameworks. Note that for clarity of the presentation, we report the best result obtained by the three parameterizations of the layered framework; note that this is significantly 'helping' it.

The results show that SMT significantly outperforms state-of-the-art approaches that control for FWER.

The only possibly surprising result is for the *Orphamine* dataset where the MDL/MML approach retrieves more edges than SMT. It is here important to remind the reader that we included MML/MDL approaches for reference only. MDL/MML approaches neither explicitly control for FWER, nor offer guarantees about it, as opposed to layered critical values and SMT. We thus posit that for the *Orphamine* dataset, the distribution of the successive tested hypotheses lead to MDL/MML having a high FWER. *Orphamine* is indeed a particular dataset with high number of variables and few examples; this translates into a high number of weak associations to find, because the number of samples is too low to have strong indications of the interactions. This has different consequences for statistical and MDL/MML frameworks:

- For SMT, it means that a significant part of the 'risk budget' is consumed for each edge that is found. Quickly after 500 edges, all of the budget has been consumed.

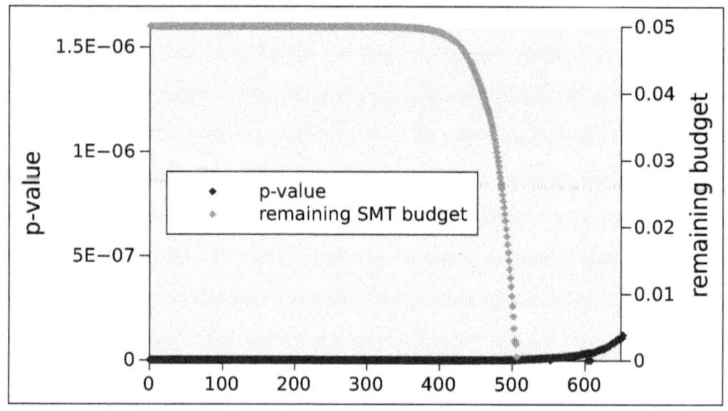

Figure 10: Study of SMT's use of the statistical significance 'budget' compared to p-values of the interactions up to 650 edges.

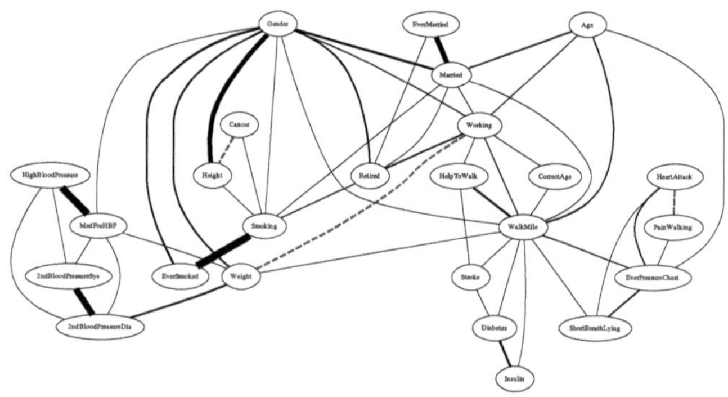

Figure 11: Compared graphs of correlations extracted from the EPESE dataset by the all statistical methods and SMT. Edges found by both frameworks are depicted in black. The three edges found by SMT but not using layered critical values are depicted in dashed blue lines. Edge weights correspond to the decrease in entropy associated with their addition — a proxy for strength of correlation.

- Conversely for MDL/MML, the decision of accepting an edge does not take into account any of the previous decisions. This means that they do not control for the fact that many weak correlations might have already been accepted in the search, resulting in a potential high FWER.

This interpretation is confirmed by Figure 10, where we plot the p-value of the first 650 steps of the process (without stopping criterion on FWER). We can see that the p-values of edges accepted at step 506 (when SMT stops) are not substantially different to the ones that would be accepted at step 650 (when MML/MDL stops) and increase slowly. SMT doesn't stop because of the significance of the current edges, but only because of the previous actions that have consumed the budget. Because MML/MDL decides upon acceptance without looking at what has been done in the previous steps, it naturally follows that it would be able to keep finding edges.

We make all the graphs obtained for all methods and all datasets at http://bit.ly/RealWorldResults. We give an example of results on the medical dataset EPESE in Figure 11.

EPESE corresponds to an epidemiological study of the elderly conducted by [33] in the U.S. between 1981 and 1987, and named *Established Populations for Epidemiologic Studies of the Elderly* (EPESE). The study goals were to describe and to identify predictors of mortality, hospitalization, and placement in long-term care facilities and to investigate risk factors for chronic diseases and loss of functioning. The survey elicited information from persons 65 years of age and older in four geographic locations in the U.S. The publicly available baseline data covers demographic characteristics (age, sex, race, income, education, marital status, number of children, employment, and religion), height, weight, social and physical functioning, chronic conditions, related heath problems, health habits, self-reported use of dental, hospital and nursing home services, and depression.

Many of the multi-way relationships that have been retrieved have supporting evidence. For example, the obvious interaction between being married and having been married is included in the selected model. Many high-order interactions including age and gender and a third variable have been identified by Chordalysis. This is for example the case for the `Married` variable. The corresponding interpretation is simple: it is more likely to be married for an old patient than a young one, and it is well-known that women get married earlier than men. More generally, if the patient is older, then there has been a longer period over which they have had the opportunity to have smoked, been married or have retired (and hence be not working). Moreover, many medical conditions or social behaviors depend upon the gender. It is thus consistent that our approach identified many high-order interactions including age and gender.

Most identified interactions also have a direct medical interpretation. This is the case for the relationship between diabetes and taking insulin, between smoking (or having smoked) and having had cancer, between ability to walk and having had a stroke, between diastolic and systolic blood pressure, between having high blood pressure and taking medications for it, or between having had a heart attack and experiencing shortness of breath.

More interestingly, we can note the direct correlation between smoking and being married, which finds some supporting evidence in [7, 15]; and the one between diabetes and stroke, which is now suggested by several medical studies (see http://bit.ly/DiabetesStroke), because untreated diabetes tends to narrow blood vessels.

Finally, SMT finds 3 more edges than any other method:

- correlation between weight and working; this is supported by recent studies suggesting a tendency to gain weight for women when retiring [10].
- correlation between heart attack and having pain walking; Manesh Patel, MD. says that 'some forms of leg pain can be the first sign of heart disease [...] when leg pain occurs each time you engage in exercise or movement, and it stops soon after you stop, it could be a sign of peripheral arterial disease' (see http://bit.ly/LegPainHeartAttack).
- height and cancer; although this might seem like a very unexpected correlation, a recent large-scale study in the Lancet journal of Oncology found that, for women, 'every 10 cm increase in height [...] risk increased for 15 of the 17 cancers studied' [12].

5. CONCLUSIONS

We have introduced the first multiple testing correction for streams and cascades of statistical hypothesis tests. Monte Carlo simulations demonstrate the statistical power of the approach. A case study of its application in model selection demonstrates its practical utility.

This work opens up multiple avenues of research. Is it possible to improve the power of the technique? Can it be extended to rejecting multiple null hypotheses for each subfamily? Is it possible to allow the decision of whether to reject a null hypothesis to be revisited in the light of null hypotheses and evidence encountered when assessing subsequent subfamilies?

It would also be interesting to study how to guarantee the FWER with MML/MDL approaches. Our experiments have repeatedly shown that such approaches lead to a significantly reduced statistical efficiency. We believe that this could be due to the fact that information theoretic methods implicitly set the significance threshold very low, and hence do not use the whole "risk budget" that one might be willing to spend. We believe that exploring how such a tolerance can be integrated in Bayesian discovery processes constitutes a very promising avenue of research.

Finally, our new type of multiple test correction opens the possibility of new scientific experimental designs, where multiple hypotheses are identified for assessment, that are then assessed in order, with the exact hypotheses to be assessed being determined by which are rejected as the process unfolds. For example, a social science experiment might first test the hypotheses that either a) a particular group suffers from a specific disadvantage, or b) that the group enjoys a specific advantage. If one of the associated null hypothesis is rejected, then the researchers would assess alternative sets of hypotheses that may reveal reasons for the advantage or disadvantage that has been revealed in the first set of tests. The results of these tests might open up further sets of more detailed hypotheses to be explored in turn.

6. ACKNOWLEDGMENTS

This research has been supported by the Australian Research Council under grant DP140100087. We are grateful to Bart Goethals for helpful comments and suggestions.

7. REFERENCES

[1] S. Altmueller and R. Haralick. Approximating high dimensional probability distributions. In *IEEE Int. Conf. on Pattern Recognition*, pages 299–302, 2004.

[2] Y. Benjamini and Y. Hochberg. Controlling the false discovery rate: A practical and powerful approach to multiple testing. *Journal of the Royal Statistical Society. Series B (Methodological)*, 57(1):289–300, 1995.

[3] C. E. Bonferroni. Teoria statistica delle classi e calcolo delle probabilità. *Pubblicazioni del R Istituto Superiore di Scienze Economiche e Commerciali di Firenze*, 8:3–62, 1936.

[4] R. Christensen. *Log-Linear Models and Logistic Regression Second Edition.* Springer, 1997.

[5] C. Dahinden, M. Kalisch, and P. Bühlmann. Decomposition and model selection for large contingency tables. *Biometrical Journal*, 52(2):233–252, 2010.

[6] L. M. De Campos. A scoring function for learning Bayesian networks based on mutual information and conditional independence tests. *The Journal of Machine Learning Research*, 7:2149–2187, 2006.
[7] E. W. Doherty and W. J. Doherty. Smoke gets in your eyes: Cigarette smoking and divorce in a national sample of American adults. *Families, Systems, & Health*, 16(4):393, 1998.
[8] N. Draper and H. Smith. *Applied regression analysis.* John Wiley, 1981.
[9] O. J. Dunn. Estimation of the medians for dependent variables. *The Annals of Mathematical Statistics*, 30(1):192–197, 1959.
[10] V. L. Forman-Hoffman, K. K. Richardson, J. W. Yankey, S. L. Hillis, R. B. Wallace, and F. D. Wolinsky. Retirement and weight changes among men and women in the health and retirement study. *The Journals of Gerontology Series B: Psychological Sciences and Social Sciences*, 63(3):S146–S153, 2008.
[11] V. Gogate, W. Webb, and P. Domingos. Learning Efficient Markov Networks. In *Advances in Neural Information Processing Systems*, pages 748–756, 2010.
[12] J. Green, B. J. Cairns, D. Casabonne, F. L. Wright, G. Reeves, V. Beral, and Million Women Study collaborators. Height and cancer incidence in the million women study: prospective cohort, and meta-analysis of prospective studies of height and total cancer risk. *The Lancet Oncology*, 12(8):785–794, 2011.
[13] S. Hettich and S. Bay. UCI KDD archive, 1999.
[14] S. Holm. A simple sequentially rejective multiple test procedure. *Scandinavian Journal of Statistics*, 6(2):65–70, 1979.
[15] G. G. Homish and K. E. Leonard. Spousal influence on smoking behaviors in a us community sample of newly married couples. *Social science & medicine*, 61(12):2557–2567, 2005.
[16] J. Irving, R. Pike, A. Lesk, and J. Whisstock. Phylogeny of the serpin superfamily: Implications of patterns of amino acid conservation for structure and function. *Genome Research*, 10(12):1845–1864, 2000.
[17] V. E. Johnson. Revised standards for statistical evidence. *Proc. of the National Academy of Sciences of the USA*, 110(48):19313–19317, 2013.
[18] M. Kalisch and P. Bühlmann. Estimating high-dimensional directed acyclic graphs with the pc-algorithm. *The Journal of Machine Learning Research*, 8:613–636, 2007.
[19] R. Kohavi and R. Longbotham. Online controlled experiments and a/b testing. In C. Sammut and G. I. Webb, editors, *Encyclopedia of Machine Learning and Data Mining.* Springer US, in-press.
[20] S.-I. Lee, V. Ganapathi, and D. Koller. Efficient Structure Learning of Markov Networks using ℓ_1-Regularization. In *Advances in Neural Information Processing Systems*, pages 817–824, 2006.
[21] M. Lichman. UCI machine learning repository. http://archive.ics.uci.edu/ml, 2013.
[22] S. F. Meisel, D. A. Carere, J. Wardle, S. S. Kalia, T. A. Moreno, J. L. Mountain, J. S. Roberts, R. C. Green, P. S. Group, et al. Explaining, not just predicting, drives interest in personal genomics. *Genome Medicine*, 7(1):1–7, 2015.
[23] MIT Center For Biological and Computation Learning. CBCL Face Database #1. http://www.ai.mit.edu/projects/cbcl, 2000.
[24] Orphanet. An online database of rare diseases and orphan drugs. http://www.orpha.net, 2014.
[25] F. Petitjean, L. Allison, G. Webb, and A. Nicholson. A statistically efficient and scalable method for log-linear analysis of high-dimensional data. In *IEEE Int. Conf. on Data Mining*, pages 480–489, 2014.
[26] F. Petitjean and G. Webb. Scaling log-linear analysis to datasets with thousands of variables. In *SIAM Int. Conf. on Data Mining*, pages 469–477, 2015.
[27] F. Petitjean, G. Webb, and A. Nicholson. Scaling log-linear analysis to high-dimensional data. In *IEEE Int. Conf. on Data Mining*, pages 597–606, 2013.
[28] J. Rissanen. Modeling by shortest data description. *Automatica*, 14(5):465–471, 1978.
[29] E. Sandhaus. The New York Times Corpus. https://catalog.ldc.upenn.edu/LDC2008T19, 2008.
[30] M. Schmidt, A. Niculescu-Mizil, K. Murphy, et al. Learning graphical model structure using l1-regularization paths. In *AAAI*, volume 7, pages 1278–1283, 2007.
[31] G. Shmueli. To explain or to predict? *Statistical Science*, 25(3):289–310, 2010.
[32] P. Spirtes, C. N. Glymour, and R. Scheines. *Causation, prediction, and search.* MIT press, 2000.
[33] J. Taylor, R. Wallace, A. Ostfeld, and D. Blazer. Established Populations for Epidemiologic Studies of the Elderly, 1981-1993. http://dx.doi.org/10.3886/ICPSR09915, 1998.
[34] A. Terada, M. Okada-Hatakeyama, K. Tsuda, and J. Sese. Statistical significance of combinatorial regulations. *Proc. National Academy of Sciences*, 110(32):12996–13001, 2013.
[35] P. van der Putten and M. van Someren. A Bias-Variance Analysis of a Real World Learning Problem: The CoIL Challenge 2000. *Machine Learning*, 57(1–2):177–195, 2004.
[36] M. Wainwright, P. Ravikumar, and J. Lafferty. High-dimensional graphical model selection using ℓ_1-regularized logistic regression. In *Advances in Neural Information Processing Systems*, pages 1465–1472, 2007.
[37] C. S. Wallace and D. M. Boulton. An information measure for classification. *The Computer Journal*, 11(2):185–194, 1968.
[38] G. I. Webb. Discovering significant patterns. *Machine Learning*, 68(1):1–33, 2007.
[39] G. I. Webb. Layered critical values: a powerful direct-adjustment approach to discovering significant patterns. *Machine Learning*, 71(2–3):307–323, 2008.
[40] X. Wu, D. Barbará, and Y. Ye. Screening and interpreting multi-item associations based on log-linear modeling. In *Int. Conf. on Knowledge Discovery and Data Mining*, pages 276–285, 2003.

Revisiting Random Binning Features: Fast Convergence and Strong Parallelizability

Lingfei Wu *
College of William and Mary
Williamsburg, VA 23185
lfwu@cs.wm.edu

Ian E.H. Yen *
Unversity of Texas at Austin
Austin, TX 78712
ianyen@cs.utexas.edu

Jie Chen
IBM Research
Yorktown Heights, NY 10598
chenjie@us.ibm.com

Rui Yan
Baidu Inc.
Beijing 100085, China
yanrui02@baidu.com

ABSTRACT

Kernel method has been developed as one of the standard approaches for nonlinear learning, which however, does not scale to large data set due to its quadratic complexity in the number of samples. A number of kernel approximation methods have thus been proposed in the recent years, among which the random features method gains much popularity due to its simplicity and direct reduction of nonlinear problem to a linear one. Different random feature functions have since been proposed to approximate a variety of kernel functions. Among them the Random Binning (RB) feature, proposed in the first random-feature paper [21], has drawn much less attention than the Random Fourier (RF) feature proposed also in [21]. In this work, we observe that the RB features, with right choice of optimization solver, could be orders-of-magnitude more efficient than other random features and kernel approximation methods under the same requirement of accuracy. We thus propose the first analysis of RB from the perspective of optimization, which by interpreting RB as a Randomized Block Coordinate Descent in the infinite-dimensional space, gives a faster convergence rate compared to that of other random features. In particular, we show that by drawing R random grids with at least κ number of non-empty bins per grid in expectation, RB method achieves a convergence rate of $O(1/(\kappa R))$, which not only sharpens its $O(1/\sqrt{R})$ rate from Monte Carlo analysis, but also shows a κ times speedup over other random features under the same analysis framework. In addition, we demonstrate another advantage of RB in the L1-regularized setting, where unlike other random features, a RB-based Coordinate Descent solver can be parallelized with guaranteed speedup proportional to κ. Our extensive experiments demonstrate the superior performance of the RB features over other random features and kernel approximation methods.

*Both authors contributed equally to this manuscript

KDD '16, August 13 - 17, 2016, San Francisco, CA, USA

ISBN 978-1-4503-4232-2/16/08...$15.00

DOI: http://dx.doi.org/10.1145/2939672.2939794

Keywords

Kernel approximation, Random Binning Features, large-scale machine learning, faster convergence, strong parallelizability

1. INTRODUCTION

Kernel methods have great promise for learning non-linear model from simple data input representations and have been demonstrated successful for solving various learning problems such as regression, classification, feature extraction, clustering and dimensionality reduction [26, 30]. However, they are typically not first choice for large-scale nonlinear learning problems, since large number of samples (N) presents significant challenges in terms of computation and memory consumptions to Kernel methods for computing the dense kernel matrix $K \in \mathcal{R}^{N\times N}$ which requires at least a $O(N^2)$ complexity. To scale up the kernel methods, there have been great efforts addressing this challenge from various perspectives such as numerical linear algebra, sampling approximation, optimization and functional analysis [4, 5, 7, 21, 27, 33].

A line of research [7, 27, 28, 31] approximates the kernel matrix K using low-rank factorizations, $K \approx Z^T Z$, where $Z \in \mathcal{R}^{N\times R}$ matrix with $R \ll N$. Among them, Nyström method [5, 8, 11, 27, 31] is probably one of the most popular approaches, which reduces the total computational costs to $O(NRd + NR^2 + R^3)$ or $O(NRd + NRm)$ depending whether the algorithm performs on K explicitly or implicitly through Z, where d and m are the input data dimension and the number of iterations of an iterative solver respectively. However, the convergence of the low-rank approximation is proportional to $O(1/\sqrt{R} + 1/\sqrt{N})$ [5, 33], which implies that the rank R may need to be near-linear to the number of data points in order to achieve comparable generalization error compared to the vanilla kernel method. For large-scale problems, the low-rank approximation could become almost as expensive as the exact kernel method to maintain competitive performance [29].

Another popular approach for scaling up kernel method is random features approximation [21, 22]. Unlike previous approach that approximates kernel matrix, Random Features approximate the kernel function directly via sampling from an explicit feature map. Random Fourier (RF) is one of the feature maps that attracted considerable interests due to its easy implementation and fast execution time [4, 12, 20, 22, 32], which has total computational cost and storage requirement as $O(NRd + NRm)$ and $O(NR)$ respectively, for computing feature matrix Z and operating the subsequent algorithms on Z. A *Fastfood* approach and its extension [12, 32] was proposed to reduce the time of computing Fourier features from $O(Rd)$ to $O(R\log d)$ by leveraging Hadamard basis functions, which improves the efficiency for prediction but not necessarily for training if $d \ll m$. Although RF has been successfully applied to speech recognition and vision classifications on very large datasets [3, 10, 17], a drawback is that a significant large number of random features are needed to achieve a comparable performance to exact kernel method. This is not surprising since the convergence of approximation error is in the order $O(1/\sqrt{R}+1/\sqrt{N})$ [4, 22], which is the same as that of low-rank kernel approximations.

Mercer's theorem [19] guarantees that any positive-definite kernel permits a feature-map decomposition. However, the decomposition is not unique. One may find different feature maps to construct the same kernel function [21, 33]. Therefore, we ask following question: do some of the feature maps lead to faster convergence than the others in terms of approximation? In this paper, we address this question by reconsidering the Random Binning (RB) feature map, which was proposed in the first Random-Feature paper [21] but has drawn much less attentions since then compared to the RF feature. Our main contributions are fourfold.

First, we propose the first analysis of RB from the perspective of optimization. By interpreting RB as a *Randomized Block Coordinate Descent* (RBCD) in the infinite-dimensional space induced from the kernel, we prove that RB enjoys faster convergence than other random features. Specifically, by drawing R grids with expected number of non-empty bins per grid lower bounded by κ, RB can achieve a solution comparable to exact kernel method with $O(1/(\kappa R))$ precision in terms of the objective function, which is not only better than the existing $O(1/\sqrt{R})$ rate from Monte Carlo analysis [21], but also shows a κ times speedup over the rate of other random features under the same analysis framework [33].

Second, we exploit the sparse structure of the feature matrix Z, which is the key to rapidly transform the data features into a very high-dimension feature space that is linearly separately by any regressors and classifiers. In addition, we discuss how to efficiently perform the computation for a large, sparse matrix by using state-of-the-art iterative solvers and advanced matrix storage techniques. As a result, the computational complexity and storage requirements in training are still $O(NRd + NRm)$ and $O(NR)$, respectively.

Third, we show that Random Binning features is particularly suitable for *Parallel Coordinate Descent* solver. Unlike other random features, RB guarantees a speedup proportional to κ due to a sparse feature matrix. This is particularly useful in the *Sparse Random Feature* setting [33], where L1 regularization is used to induce a compact nonlinear predictor and *Coordinate Descent* is presumably the state-of-the-art solver in such setting.

Finally, we provide extensive experiments to demonstrate the faster convergence and better parallelizability of RB in practice. Compared to other popular low-rank approximations, RB shows superior performance on both regression and classification tasks under the same computational budgets, and achieves same performance with one to three orders of magnitude reduction in time and memory consumptions. When combined with Coordinate Descent to solve an L1-regularized objective, RB shows an almost linear speedup, in contrast to RF that has almost no speedup.

2. RANDOM BINNING FEATURE AS KERNEL APPROXIMATION

In this work, we consider the problem of fitting a nonlinear prediction function $f : \mathcal{X} \to \mathcal{Y}$ in Reproducing Kernel Hilbert Space $\mathcal{H}$ from training data pairs $\{(\boldsymbol{x}_n, y_n)\}_{n=1}^N$ via regularized Empirical Risk Minimization (ERM)

$$f^* = \underset{f\in\mathcal{H}}{argmin} \quad \frac{\lambda}{2}\|f\|_{\mathcal{H}}^2 + \frac{1}{N}\sum_{n=1}^{N} L(f(\boldsymbol{x}_n), y_n), \tag{1}$$

where $L(z, y)$ is a convex loss function with Lipschitz-continuous derivative satisfying $|L'(z_1, y) - L'(z_2, y)| \le \beta|z_1 - z_2|$, which includes several standard loss functions such as the *square-loss* $L(z, y) = \frac{1}{2}(z - y)^2$, *square-hinge loss* $L(z, y) = \max(1 - zy, 0)^2$ and *logistic loss* $L(z, y) = \log(1 + \exp(-yz))$.

2.1 Learning with RKHS

The RKHS $\mathcal{H}$ can be defined via a positive-definite (PD) kernel function $k(\boldsymbol{x}_1, \boldsymbol{x}_2)$ that measures similarity between samples as

$$\mathcal{H} = \left\{ f(\cdot) = \sum_{i=1}^{K} \alpha_i k(\boldsymbol{x}_i, \cdot) \mid \alpha_i \in \mathbb{R}, \boldsymbol{x}_i \in \mathcal{X} \right\}. \tag{2}$$

One can also define the RKHS via a possibly infinite-dimensional feature map $\{\bar{\phi}_h(\boldsymbol{x})\}_{h\in H}$ with each $h \in H$ defining a feature function $\bar{\phi}_h(\boldsymbol{x}) : \mathcal{X} \to \mathbb{R}$. The space can be expressed as

$$\mathcal{H} = \left\{ f(\cdot) = \int_{h\in H} w(h)\bar{\phi}_h(\cdot)dh = \langle \boldsymbol{w}, \bar{\boldsymbol{\phi}}(\cdot)\rangle_{\mathcal{H}} \mid \|f\|_{\mathcal{H}}^2 < \infty \right\}, \tag{3}$$

where $w(h)$ specifies weights over the set of features $\{\phi_h(\boldsymbol{x})\}_{h\in\mathcal{H}}$. The Mercer's theorem [19] connects the above two formulations of RKHS by stating that every PD kernel $k(.,.)$ can be expressed as an integration over some basis functions $\{\phi_h(.)\}_{h\in H}$

$$k(\boldsymbol{x}_1, \boldsymbol{x}_2) = \int_{h\in H} p(h)\phi_h(\boldsymbol{x}_1)\phi_h(\boldsymbol{x}_2)dh = \langle \bar{\boldsymbol{\phi}}(\boldsymbol{x}_1), \bar{\boldsymbol{\phi}}(\boldsymbol{x}_2)\rangle_{\mathcal{H}}, \tag{4}$$

However, the decomposition (4) is not unique, so one can find different feature maps $\{\bar{\phi}_h(.)\}_{h\in H}$ satisfying (4) for the same kernel $k(.,.)$. In particular, as an example used extensively in this work, the Laplacian Kernel

$$k(\boldsymbol{x}_1, \boldsymbol{x}_2) = \exp\left(-\frac{\|\boldsymbol{x}_1 - \boldsymbol{x}_2\|_1}{\sigma} \right), \tag{5}$$

allows decomposition based on (i) Fourier basis map [21], (ii) RB map [21], and also (iii) map based on infinite number of decision trees [15] to name a few. On the other hand, different kernels can be constructed using the same set of basis function $\{\phi_h(.)\}$ with different distribution $p(h)$. For example, the RB feature map can be used to construct any shift-invariant kernel of the form [21]

$$K(\boldsymbol{x}_1, \boldsymbol{x}_2) = K(\boldsymbol{x}_1 - \boldsymbol{x}_2) = \prod_{j=1}^{d} k_j(x_{1j} - x_{2j}), \tag{6}$$

by sampling the "width" of bins δ_j for each feature j from a distribution proportional to $\delta k_j''(\delta)$, where $k_j''(\delta)$ is the second derivative of $k_j(\delta)$, assuming the kernel has a non-negative second derivative.

2.2 Random Binning Features

In this section, we describe the Random Binning (RB) feature map, which has decomposition of the form

$$K(\boldsymbol{x}_1, \boldsymbol{x}_2) = \int_{\boldsymbol{\delta}} p(\boldsymbol{\delta})\boldsymbol{\phi}_{B_{\boldsymbol{\delta}}}(\boldsymbol{x}_1)^T \boldsymbol{\phi}_{B_{\boldsymbol{\delta}}}(\boldsymbol{x}_2)\, d\boldsymbol{\delta} \tag{7}$$

where $B_{\boldsymbol{\delta}}$ is a grid parameterized by $\boldsymbol{\delta} = (\delta_1, u_1, ..., \delta_d, u_d)$ that specifies the *width* and *bias* of the grid w.r.t. the d dimensions, and $\boldsymbol{\phi}_{B_{\boldsymbol{\delta}}}(\boldsymbol{x})$ is a vector which has

$$\phi_b(\boldsymbol{x}) = 1, \; if\, b = (\lfloor \frac{x_1 - u_1}{\delta_1} \rfloor, ..., \lfloor \frac{x_d - u_d}{\delta_d} \rfloor),$$

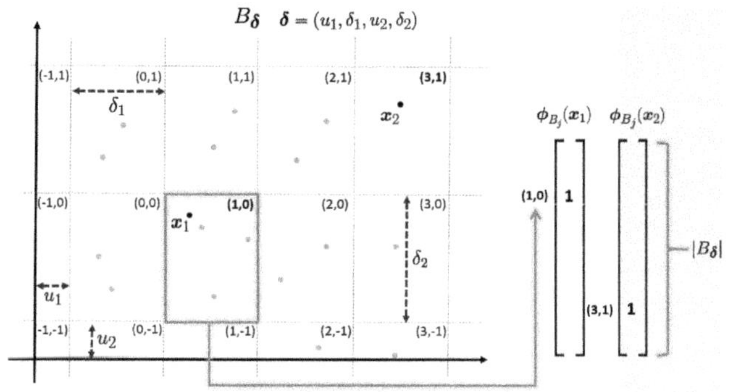

Figure 1: Generating process of RB features.

Algorithm 1 Random Binning Features

Given a kernel function $k(\boldsymbol{x}_1, \boldsymbol{x}_2) = \prod_{j=1}^{d} k_j(|x_{1j} - x_{2j}|)$. Let $p_j(\delta) \propto \delta k_j''(\delta)$ be a distribution over δ.

for $r = 1...R$ **do**

1. Draw $\delta_{rj} \sim p_j(\delta), \forall j \in [d]$. $u_{rj} \in [0, \delta_{rj}], \forall j \in [d]$.
2. Compute feature $\boldsymbol{z}_r(\boldsymbol{x}_n)$ as the the indicator vector of bin index $(\lfloor \frac{x_{n1}-u_1}{\delta_1} \rfloor, ..., \lfloor \frac{x_{nd}-u_d}{\delta_d} \rfloor)$, for $\forall n \in [N]$.

end for.

Return $\boldsymbol{z}(\boldsymbol{x}_n) = \frac{1}{\sqrt{D}}[\boldsymbol{z}_1(\boldsymbol{x}_n); ...; \boldsymbol{z}_D(\boldsymbol{x}_n)]$ $\forall n \in [N]$ as the data with RB Features.

---

and $\phi_b(\boldsymbol{x}) = 0$ otherwise for any $b \in B_{\boldsymbol{\delta}}$. Note for each grid $B_{\boldsymbol{\delta}}$, the number of bins $|B_{\boldsymbol{\delta}}|$ is countably infinite, so $\boldsymbol{\phi}_{B_{\boldsymbol{\delta}}}(\boldsymbol{x})$ has infinite dimension but only 1 non-zero entry (at the bin $\boldsymbol{x}$ lies in). Figure 1 illustrates an example when the raw dimension $d = 2$. The kernel $K(\boldsymbol{x}_1, \boldsymbol{x}_2)$ is thus interpreted as the *collision probability* that two data points $\boldsymbol{x}_1, \boldsymbol{x}_2$ fall in the same bin, when the grid is generated from distribution $p(\boldsymbol{\delta})$. In [21], it is pointed out for any kernel of form (6) with *nonnegative second derivative* $k_j''(\delta)$, one can derive distribution $p(\boldsymbol{\delta}) = \prod_{j=1}^{d} p_j(\delta_j) U(u_j; 0, \delta_j)$, where $p_j(\delta_j) \propto \delta k_j''(\delta_j)$ and $U(\cdot, a, b)$ is uniform distribution in the range $[a, b]$.

To obtain a kernel approximation scheme from the feature map (7), a simple Monte Carlo method can be used to approximate (7) by averaging over R grids $\{B_{\boldsymbol{\delta}_r}\}_{r=1}^{R}$ with each grid's parameter $\boldsymbol{\delta}_r$ drawn from $p(\boldsymbol{\delta})$. The procedure for generating R RB features from raw data $\{\boldsymbol{x}_n\}_{n=1}^{N}$ is given in Algorithm 1.

Using a Monte-Carlo analysis, one can show the approximation to (7) yields approximation error of order $O(1/\sqrt{R})$. From the Representer theorem, one can further bound error of the learned predictor

$$\left|\boldsymbol{w}_{RF}^T \boldsymbol{z}(\boldsymbol{x}) - f^*(\boldsymbol{x})\right| = \left|\sum_{n=1}^{N} \alpha_n^{RF} \boldsymbol{z}(\boldsymbol{x}_n)^T \boldsymbol{z}(\boldsymbol{x}) - \sum_{n=1}^{N} \alpha_n^* k(\boldsymbol{x}_n, \boldsymbol{x})\right|$$

as shown in [21] (appendix C). Unfortunately, the rate of convergence suggests that to achieve small approximation error ϵ, one needs significant amount of random features proportional to $\Omega(1/\epsilon^2)$, and furthermore, the Monte-Carlo analysis does not explain why empirically RB feature achieves faster convergence than other random feature map like Fourier basis by orders of magnitude.

3. FASTER CONVERGENCE OF RANDOM BINNING

In this section, we first illustrate the sparse structure of the feature matrix Z of RB and discuss how to make efficient computation and storage format of Z. Then by interpreting RB features as Randomized Block Coordinate Descent in the infinite-dimensional space, we prove that RB has a faster convergence rate than other random features. We illustrate them accordingly in the following sections.

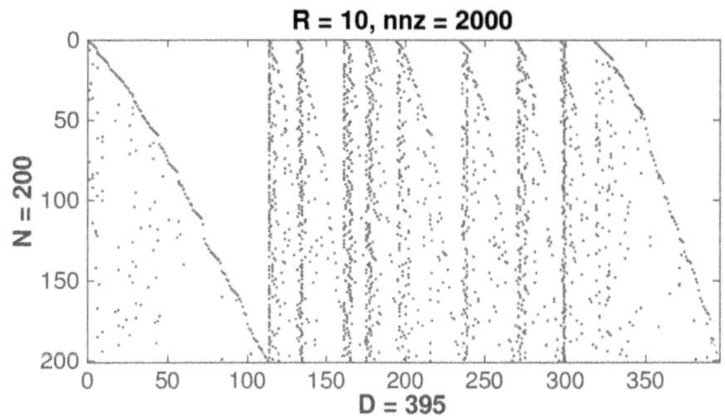

Figure 2: Example of the sparse feature matrix $Z_{N \times D}$ generated by RB. In this special case, Z has the number of rows $N = 200$ and columns $D = 395$, respectively. The number of grids $R = 10$ and the $nnz(Z) = 2000$. Note that for ith row of $Z, nnz(Z(i, :)) = R$ and $R \leq D \leq NR$.

3.1 Sparse Feature Matrix & Iterative Solvers

A special characteristic of RB compared to other low-rank approximations is the fact that the feature matrix generated by RB is typically a large, sparse binary matrix $Z \in \mathbb{R}^{N \times D}$, where the value of D is determined by both number of grids R and the kernel width parameter (ex. σ in the case of Laplacian Kernel). Different from other random features, D, rather than R, is the actual number of columns of Z. A direct connection between D and R is that the matrix has each row i satisfying $nnz(Z(i, :)) = R$ and therefore $R \leq D \leq NR$. Intuitively speaking, RB has more expressive power than RF since it generates a large yet sparse feature matrix to rapidly transform the data space to a very high dimension space, where data could become almost linearly separable by the classifiers. Fig. 2 gives an example to illustrate the sparse structure of Z.

In the case of *Kernel Ridge Regression* (L2-regularization with square loss), if using RB feature to approximate the RKHS, one can solve (1) directly in its primal form. The weighting vector is simply the solution of the linear system:

$$(Z^T Z + \lambda I)\boldsymbol{w}_{RB} = Z^T y. \tag{8}$$

Note since Z is a large sparse matrix, there is no need to explicitly compute the covariance matrix $Z^T Z$, which is much denser than Z itself. One can apply state-of-the-art sparse iterative solvers such as Conjugate Gradient (CG) and GMRES to directly operate on Z [25]. The main computation in CG or GMRES is the sparse matrix-vector products. Let m be the number of iterations, then the total computational complexity of iterative solver is $O(m\, nnz(Z)) = O(mNR)$. In addition, since most elements in Z are zeros, the Compressed Sparse Row type matrix storage format should be employed for economically storing Z [9], which gives computational cost and memory requirement as $O(mNR)$ and $O(NR)$ respectively, a similar cost to that of other low-rank approximations despite its much higher dimension. In testing phase, each point produces a sparse feature vector $z(x) \in \mathcal{R}^D$ based on the grids stored during training, yielding a sparse vector $z(x)$ with $nnz(z(x))) =$

R and computing the decision function $z(x)^T w_{RB}$ onlyl requires $O(dR + R)$.

When the ERM is smooth but not quadratic, a *Newton-CG* method that solves smooth problem via a series of local quadratic approximation gives the same complexity per CG iteration [14], and note that most of state-of-the-art linear classification algorithms have complexity linear to $nnz(Z)$, the number of nonzeros of feature matrix [6]. In section 4, we further discuss cases of L1-regularized problem, where a Coordinate Descent algorithm of cost $O(nnz(Z))$ per iteration is discussed.

3.2 Random Binning Features as Block Coordinate Descent

In [33], a new approach of analysis was proposed, which interpreted Random Features as Randomized Coordinate Descent in the infinite dimensional space, and gives a better $O(1/R)$ rate in the convergence of objective function. In this section, we extend the approach of [33] to show that, RB Feature can be interpreted as RBCD in the infinite-dimensional space, which by drawing *a block of features* at a time, produces a number of features D significantly more than the number of blocks R, resulting a provably faster convergence rate than other RF. While at the same time, by exploiting state-of-the-art iterative solvers introduced in section 3.1, the computational complexity of RB does not increase with number of features D but only with the number of blocks R. Consequently, to achieve the same accuracy, RB requires significantly less training and prediction time compared to other RF.

A key quantity to our analysis is an upper bound on the *collision probability* $\nu_{\boldsymbol{\delta}}$ which specifies how unlikely data points will fall into the same bin, and its inverse $\kappa_{\boldsymbol{\delta}} := 1/\nu_{\boldsymbol{\delta}}$ which lower bounds the number of bins containing at least one data point. We define them as follows.

Definition 1. *Define collision probability of data $\mathcal{D}$ on bin $b \in B_{\boldsymbol{\delta}}$ as*

$$\nu_b := \frac{|\{n \in [N] \mid \phi_b(\boldsymbol{x}_n) = 1\}|}{N}. \tag{9}$$

Let $\nu_{\boldsymbol{\delta}} := \max_{b \in B_{\boldsymbol{\delta}}} \nu_b$ be an upper bound on (9), and $\kappa_{\boldsymbol{\delta}} := 1/\nu_{\boldsymbol{\delta}}$ be a lower bound on the number of nonempty bins of grid $\boldsymbol{\delta}$.

$$\kappa := E_{\boldsymbol{\delta}}[\kappa_{\boldsymbol{\delta}}] = E_{\boldsymbol{\delta}}[1/\nu_{\boldsymbol{\delta}}] \tag{10}$$

is denoted as the lower bound on the expected number of (used) bins w.r.t the distribution $p(\boldsymbol{\delta})$.

In the RB matrix, the empirical collision probability is simply the average number of non-zeros per column, divided by N, a number much smaller than 1 as in the example of Fig. 2. Our analysis assumes a smooth loss function satisfying the following criteria.

Assumption 1. *The loss function $L(z, y)$ is smooth w.r.t. response z so difference between function difference and its linear approximation can be bounded as*

$$L(z_2, .) - L(z_1, .) \leq \nabla L(z_1, .)(z_2 - z_1) + \frac{\beta}{2}(z_2 - z_2)^2.$$

for some constant $0 \leq \beta \leq \infty$.

This assumption is satisfied for a wide range of loss such as square loss ($\beta = 1$), logistic loss ($\beta = 1/4$) and L2-hinge loss ($\beta = 1$).

We interpret RB as a *Fully Corrective Randomized Block Coordinate Descent (FC-RBCD)* on the objective function

$$\min_{\bar{\boldsymbol{w}}} \quad F(\bar{\boldsymbol{w}}) := \mathcal{R}(\bar{\boldsymbol{w}}) + Loss(\bar{\boldsymbol{w}}; \boldsymbol{\phi}) \tag{11}$$

where $Loss(\bar{\boldsymbol{w}}; \phi) = \frac{1}{N}\sum_{n=1}^{N} L(\langle \bar{\boldsymbol{w}}, \boldsymbol{\phi}(\boldsymbol{x}_n)\rangle, y_n)$ and

$$\bar{\boldsymbol{\phi}} := \sqrt{p} \circ \boldsymbol{\phi} = (\sqrt{p(\boldsymbol{\delta})}\boldsymbol{\phi}_{B_{\boldsymbol{\delta}}}(.))_{\boldsymbol{\delta} \in H}$$

with "$\circ$" denoting the component-wise product. The goal is to show that, by performing R steps of FC-RBCD on (11), one can obtain a $\bar{\boldsymbol{w}}^R$ with comparable regularized loss to that from optimal solution of (1). Note one advantage of analysis from this optimization perspective is: it does not rely on Representer theorem, and thus $R(\boldsymbol{w})$ can be L2 regularizer $\frac{\lambda}{2}\|\boldsymbol{w}\|^2$ or L1 regularizer $\lambda\|\boldsymbol{w}\|_1$, where the latter has advantage of giving sparse predictor of faster prediction [33]. The FC-RBCD algorithm maintains an active set of blocks $\mathcal{A}^{(r)}$ which is expanded for R iterations. At each iteration r, the FC-RBCD does the following:

1. Draw $\boldsymbol{\delta}$ from $p(\boldsymbol{\delta})$ (derived from the kernel $k(.,.)$).
2. Expand active set $\mathcal{A}^{(r+1)} := \mathcal{A}^{(r)} \cup B_{\boldsymbol{\delta}}$.
3. Minimize (11) subject to a limited support $supp(\bar{\boldsymbol{w}}) \subseteq \mathcal{A}^{(r+1)}$.

Note this algorithm is only used for analysis. In practice, one can draw R blocks of features at a time, and solve (11) by any optimization algorithm such as those mentioned in section 3.1 or the CD method we introduce in section 4.

Due to space limit, here we prove the case when $\mathcal{R}(.)$ is the non-smooth L1 regularizer $\lambda\|\bar{\boldsymbol{w}}\|_1$. The smooth case for $\mathcal{R}(\boldsymbol{w}) = \frac{\lambda}{2}\|\bar{\boldsymbol{w}}\|^2$ can be shown in a similar way. Note the objective function (11) can be written as

$$\bar{F}(\boldsymbol{w}) := F(\sqrt{\boldsymbol{p}} \circ \boldsymbol{w}) = \mathcal{R}(\sqrt{\boldsymbol{p}} \circ \boldsymbol{w}) + Loss(\boldsymbol{w}, \bar{\boldsymbol{\phi}}). \tag{12}$$

by a scaling of variable $\bar{\boldsymbol{w}} = \sqrt{p} \circ \boldsymbol{w}$.

The below theorem states that, running FC-RBCD for R iterations, it generates a solution $\bar{\boldsymbol{w}}^R$ close to any reference solution $\boldsymbol{w}^*$ in terms of objective (12) with their difference bounded by $O(\frac{1}{\kappa R})$.

Theorem 1. *Let R be the number of blocks (grids) generated by FC-RBCD, and $\boldsymbol{w}^*$ be any reference solution, we have*

$$E[\bar{F}(\boldsymbol{w}^{(R)})] - \bar{F}(\boldsymbol{w}^*) \leq \frac{\beta\|\boldsymbol{w}^*\|^2}{\kappa R'} \tag{13}$$

for $R' := R - c > 0$, where $c = \lceil \frac{2\kappa(\bar{F}(\mathbf{0}) - \bar{F}(\boldsymbol{w}^*))}{\beta\|\boldsymbol{w}^*\|^2} \rceil$.

Proof. Firstly, we obtain an expression for the progress made by each iteration of FC-RBCD. Let $B := B_{\boldsymbol{\delta}^{(r)}}$ be the block drawn at step 1 of FC-RBCD, and $\bar{\boldsymbol{w}}^{(r+1)}$ be the minimizer of (11) subject to support $supp(\bar{\boldsymbol{w}}) \subseteq \mathcal{A}^{(r+1)}$ given by the step 3. Since $B \subseteq \mathcal{A}^{(r+1)}$, we have

$$F(\bar{\boldsymbol{w}}^{(r+1)}) - F(\bar{\boldsymbol{w}}^{(r)}) \leq F(\bar{\boldsymbol{w}}^{(r)} + \boldsymbol{\eta}_B) - F(\bar{\boldsymbol{w}}^{(r)}) \tag{14}$$

for any $\boldsymbol{\eta}_B$: $supp(\boldsymbol{\eta}) \subseteq B$. Then denote b_i as the bin $\boldsymbol{x}_i$ falling in and $L_i' = \nabla L(\bar{\boldsymbol{w}}^{(r)T}\boldsymbol{\phi}(\boldsymbol{x}_i), y_i)$, by smoothness of the loss (Assumption 1), we have

$$\begin{aligned} Loss(\bar{\boldsymbol{w}}^{(r)} + \boldsymbol{\eta}_B) - Loss(\bar{\boldsymbol{w}}^{(r)}) &\leq \frac{1}{N}\sum_{i=1}^{N} L_i'\phi_{b_i}\eta + \frac{\beta}{2}(\eta_{b_i}\phi_{b_i})^2 \\ &\leq \langle \boldsymbol{g}_B, \boldsymbol{\eta}_B\rangle + \frac{\beta\nu_{\boldsymbol{\delta}^{(r)}}}{2}\|\boldsymbol{\eta}_B\|^2 \end{aligned} \tag{15}$$

where the second inequality uses the fact $\phi_{b_i} = 1$ and

$$\boldsymbol{g}_B := \nabla_B Loss(\bar{\boldsymbol{w}}^{(r)}, \boldsymbol{\phi}).$$

Now consider the regularization term, note since block B is drawn from an inifinite-dimensional space, the probability that B is in active set is 0. Therefore, we have $B \cap \mathcal{A}^{(r)} = \emptyset$, $\bar{\boldsymbol{w}}_B^{(r)} = \mathbf{0}$ and $\mathcal{R}_B(\bar{\boldsymbol{w}}_B^{(r)}) = 0$. As a result,

$$\begin{aligned} &F(\bar{\boldsymbol{w}}^{(r)} + \boldsymbol{\eta}_B) - F(\bar{\boldsymbol{w}}^{(r)}) \\ &\leq \mathcal{R}_B(\boldsymbol{\eta}_B) + \langle \boldsymbol{g}_B, \boldsymbol{\eta}_B \rangle + \frac{\beta \nu_{\boldsymbol{\delta}^{(r)}}}{2} \|\boldsymbol{\eta}_B\|^2 \end{aligned} \tag{16}$$

Let $\boldsymbol{\eta}_B$ be the minimizer of RHS of (16). It satisfies $\boldsymbol{\rho}_B + \boldsymbol{g}_B + \beta v_{\boldsymbol{\delta}^{(r)}} \boldsymbol{\eta}_B = \mathbf{0}$ for some $\boldsymbol{\rho}_B \in \partial \mathcal{R}(\boldsymbol{\eta}_B)$, and thus,

$$\begin{aligned} &F(\bar{\boldsymbol{w}}^{(r)} + \boldsymbol{\eta}_B) - F(\bar{\boldsymbol{w}}^{(r)}) \\ &\leq \langle \boldsymbol{\rho}_B, \boldsymbol{\eta}_B \rangle + \langle \boldsymbol{g}_B, \boldsymbol{\eta}_B \rangle + \frac{\beta \nu_{\boldsymbol{\delta}^{(r)}}}{2} \|\boldsymbol{\eta}_B\|^2 \\ &= -\frac{1}{2\beta \nu_{\boldsymbol{\delta}^{(r)}}} \|\boldsymbol{\rho}_B + \boldsymbol{g}_B\|^2 \end{aligned} \tag{17}$$

Now taking expectation w.r.t. $p(\boldsymbol{\delta})$ on both sides of (17), we have

$$\begin{aligned} E[F(\bar{\boldsymbol{w}}^{(r)} + \boldsymbol{\eta}_B)] - F(\bar{\boldsymbol{w}}^{(r)}) &\leq -\frac{1}{2\beta} E\left[\frac{1}{\nu_{\boldsymbol{\delta}^{(r)}}} \|\boldsymbol{\rho}_B + \boldsymbol{g}_B\|^2\right] \\ &\leq -\frac{1}{2\beta} E\left[\frac{1}{\nu_{\boldsymbol{\delta}^{(r)}}}\right] E\left[\|\boldsymbol{\rho}_B + \boldsymbol{g}_B\|^2\right] \\ &\leq -\frac{\kappa}{2\beta} \|\bar{\boldsymbol{\rho}}_B + \bar{\boldsymbol{g}}_B\|^2 \end{aligned} \tag{18}$$

where $\bar{\boldsymbol{\rho}} := \sqrt{\boldsymbol{p}} \circ \boldsymbol{\rho}$, $\bar{\boldsymbol{g}} := \sqrt{\boldsymbol{p}} \circ \boldsymbol{g}$, and the second inequality uses the fact that the number of used bins $\kappa_{\boldsymbol{\delta}^{(r)}} = 1/\nu_{\boldsymbol{\delta}^{(r)}}$ has non-negative correlation with the discriminative power of block B measured by the magnitude of gradient with soft-thresholding $\|\bar{\boldsymbol{\rho}}_B + \bar{\boldsymbol{g}}_B\|$ (i.e. fewer collisions on grid B implies B to be a better block of features).

The result of (18) expresses descent amount in terms of the proximal gradient of the reparameterized objective (12). Note for B : $B \cap \mathcal{A}^{(r)} = \emptyset$, we have $\boldsymbol{w}_B^{(r)} = \mathbf{0}$, and $\mathcal{R}_B(\bar{\boldsymbol{\eta}}) - \mathcal{R}_B(\mathbf{0}) = \langle \bar{\boldsymbol{\rho}}, \bar{\boldsymbol{\eta}} \rangle$; on the other hand, for $B \subseteq \mathcal{A}^{(r)}$, we have

$$\mathbf{0} \in arg\min_{\bar{\boldsymbol{\eta}}_B} \ \mathcal{R}_B(\sqrt{\boldsymbol{p}_B}\boldsymbol{w}_B + \bar{\boldsymbol{\eta}}_B) + \langle \bar{\boldsymbol{g}}_B, \sqrt{\boldsymbol{p}_B}\boldsymbol{w}_B + \bar{\boldsymbol{\eta}}_B \rangle$$

since they are solved to optimality in the previous iteration. Then

$$\begin{aligned} &E[F(\bar{\boldsymbol{w}}^{(r)} + \boldsymbol{\eta})] - F(\bar{\boldsymbol{w}}^{(r)}) \\ &\leq -\frac{\kappa}{2\beta} \|\bar{\boldsymbol{\rho}}_B + \bar{\boldsymbol{g}}_B\|^2 = \langle \bar{\boldsymbol{\rho}}, \bar{\boldsymbol{\eta}} \rangle + \langle \bar{\boldsymbol{g}}, \bar{\boldsymbol{\eta}} \rangle + \frac{\beta}{2\kappa} \|\bar{\boldsymbol{\eta}}_{\bar{\mathcal{A}}^{(r)}}\|^2 \\ &= \mathcal{R}(\sqrt{\boldsymbol{p}} \circ (\boldsymbol{w}^{(r)} + \bar{\boldsymbol{\eta}})) - \mathcal{R}(\sqrt{\boldsymbol{p}} \circ \boldsymbol{w}^{(r)}) + \langle \bar{\boldsymbol{g}}, \bar{\boldsymbol{\eta}} \rangle + \frac{\beta}{2\kappa} \|\bar{\boldsymbol{\eta}}_{\bar{\mathcal{A}}^{(r)}}\|^2 \end{aligned} \tag{19}$$

where $\bar{\boldsymbol{\eta}}_{\bar{\mathcal{A}}^{(r)}} := (\bar{\boldsymbol{\eta}}_B)_{B: B \cap \mathcal{A}^{(r)} = \emptyset}$ and $\bar{\boldsymbol{\eta}} := \sqrt{\boldsymbol{p}} \circ \boldsymbol{\eta}$. Thus the final step is to show the descent amount given by RHS of (19) decreases the suboptimality $\bar{F}(\boldsymbol{w}^{(r)}) - \bar{F}(\boldsymbol{w}^*)$ significantly. This can be achieved by considering $\bar{\boldsymbol{\eta}}$ of the form $\alpha(\boldsymbol{w}^* - \boldsymbol{w}^{(r)})$ for some $\alpha \in [0, 1]$ as follows:

$$\begin{aligned} &E[\bar{F}(\boldsymbol{w}^{(r)} + \bar{\boldsymbol{\eta}})] - \bar{F}(\boldsymbol{w}^{(r)}) \\ &\leq \min_{\bar{\boldsymbol{\eta}}} \mathcal{R}(\sqrt{\boldsymbol{p}} \circ (\boldsymbol{w}^{(r)} + \bar{\boldsymbol{\eta}})) - \mathcal{R}(\sqrt{\boldsymbol{p}} \circ \boldsymbol{w}^{(r)}) + \langle \bar{\boldsymbol{g}}, \bar{\boldsymbol{\eta}} \rangle + \frac{\beta}{2\kappa} \|\bar{\boldsymbol{\eta}}_{\bar{\mathcal{A}}^{(r)}}\|^2 \\ &\leq \min_{\bar{\boldsymbol{\eta}}} \bar{F}(\boldsymbol{w}^{(r)} + \bar{\boldsymbol{\eta}}) - \bar{F}(\boldsymbol{w}^{(r)}) + \frac{\beta}{2\kappa} \|\bar{\boldsymbol{\eta}}_{\bar{\mathcal{A}}^{(r)}}\|^2 \\ &\leq \min_{\alpha \in [0,1]} \bar{F}((1-\alpha)\boldsymbol{w}^{(r)} + \alpha \boldsymbol{w}^*) - \bar{F}(\boldsymbol{w}^{(r)}) + \frac{\beta \alpha^2}{2\kappa} \|\boldsymbol{w}^*\|^2 \\ &\leq \min_{\alpha \in [0,1]} -\alpha(\bar{F}(\boldsymbol{w}^{(r)}) - \bar{F}(\boldsymbol{w}^*)) + \frac{\beta \alpha^2}{2\kappa} \|\boldsymbol{w}^*\|^2, \end{aligned} \tag{20}$$

where the second and fourth inequalities are from convexity of $\bar{F}(.)$. The α minimizing (20) is $\alpha^* := \min(\frac{\kappa(\bar{F}(\boldsymbol{w}^{(r)}) - \bar{F}(\boldsymbol{w}^*))}{\beta \|\boldsymbol{w}^*\|^2}, 1)$, which leads to

$$E[\bar{F}(\boldsymbol{w}^{(r)} + \bar{\boldsymbol{\eta}})] - \bar{F}(\boldsymbol{w}^{(r)}) \leq -\frac{\kappa(\bar{F}(\boldsymbol{w}^{(r)}) - \bar{F}(\boldsymbol{w}^*))^2}{2\beta \|\boldsymbol{w}^*\|^2} \tag{21}$$

if $\bar{F}(\boldsymbol{w}^{(r)}) - \bar{F}(\boldsymbol{w}^*) \leq \frac{\beta}{\kappa} \|\boldsymbol{w}^*\|^2$; otherwise, we have $E[\bar{F}(\boldsymbol{w}^{(r)} + \bar{\boldsymbol{\eta}})] - \bar{F}(\boldsymbol{w}^{(r)}) \leq -\frac{\beta}{2\kappa} \|\boldsymbol{w}^*\|^2$. Note the latter case cannot happen more than $c = \lceil \frac{2\kappa(\bar{F}(\mathbf{0}) - \bar{F}(\boldsymbol{w}^*))}{\beta \|\boldsymbol{w}^*\|^2} \rceil$ times since FC-RBCD is a descent method. Therefore, for $r' := r - c > 0$, solving the recursion (21) leads to the conclusion. □ □

Note we have $\|\sqrt{\boldsymbol{p}} \circ \boldsymbol{w}^*\|_1 \leq \|\sqrt{\boldsymbol{p}}\| \|\boldsymbol{w}^*\| = \|\boldsymbol{w}^*\|$ in the L1-regularized case, and thus the FC-RBCD guarantees convergence of the L1-norm objective to the (non-square) L2-norm objective. The convergence result of Theorem 1 is of the same form to the rate proved in [33] for other random features, however, with an additional multiplicative factor $\kappa \geq 1$ that speeds up the rate by κ times. Recall that κ is the lower bound on the expected number of bins being used by data samples for each block of features $B_{\boldsymbol{\delta}}$, which in practice is a factor much larger than 1, as shown in the Figure 2 and also in our experiments. In particular, in case each grid $B_{\boldsymbol{\delta}}$ has similar number of bins being used, we have $D \approx \kappa R$, and thus obtain a rate of the form

$$E[\bar{F}(\boldsymbol{w}^{(R)})] - \bar{F}(\boldsymbol{w}^*) \lesssim \frac{\beta \|\boldsymbol{w}^*\|^2}{D}. \tag{22}$$

Note for a fixed R, the total number of features D is increasing with kernel parameter $1/\sigma$ in the case of Laplacian Kernel, which means the less smooth the kernel, the faster convergence of RB. A simple extreme case is when $\sigma \to 0$, where one achieves 0 training loss, and the RB, by putting each sample in a separate bin, converges to 0 loss with $R = 1$, $D = N$. On the other hand, other random features, such as Fourier, still require large R for convergence to 0 loss. In practice, there are many data that require a small kernel bandwidth σ to avoid underfitting, for which RB has dramatically faster convergence than other RF.

4. STRONG PARALLELIZABILITY OF RANDOM BINNING FEATURES

In this section, we study another strength of RB Features in the context of *Sparse Random Feature* [33], where one aims to train a sparse nonlinear predictor that has faster prediction and more compact representation through an L1-regularized objective. In this case, the CD method is known as state-of-the-art solver [23, 34], and we aim to show that the structure of RB allows CD to be parallelized with much more speedup than that of other random features.

4.1 Coordinate Descent Method

Given the $N \times D$ data matrix produced by the RB Algorithm 1, a RCD Method solves

$$\min_{\boldsymbol{w} \in \mathbb{R}^D} \ \lambda \|\boldsymbol{w}\|_1 + \frac{1}{N} \sum_{n=1}^{N} L(\boldsymbol{w}^T \boldsymbol{z}_i, y_i) \tag{23}$$

by minimizing (23) w.r.t. a single coordinate j

$$\min_{d_j} \ \lambda |w_j + d_j| + g_j d_j + \frac{M_j}{2} d_j^2 \tag{24}$$

Algorithm 2 Sparse Random Binning Features via Parallel RCD

0. Generate RB feature matrix Z by Algorithm 1
1. $\boldsymbol{z}^1 = \boldsymbol{0}, \boldsymbol{w}^1 = \boldsymbol{0}$.

for t=1......T (with τ threads in parallel) **do**

2. Draw j from $[D]$ uniformly at random.
3. Compute d_j^* by (26).
4. $\boldsymbol{w}^{t+1} := \boldsymbol{w}^t + d_j^* \boldsymbol{e}_j$.
5. Maintain $\hat{y}_i, \forall i \in [N]$ to satisfy (27).

end for

at a time, where

$$g_j := \frac{1}{N}\sum_{n=1}^{N}(\nabla_j L(\boldsymbol{w}^T \boldsymbol{z}_i, y_i))z_{ij} \tag{25}$$

is the gradient of loss term in (23) w.r.t. the j-th coordinate, and $M_j := \beta \frac{1}{N}\sum_{i=1}^{N} z_{ij}^2$ is an upper bound on $\nabla_{jj}L(.)$. Note, by focusing on single coordinate, (24) has a tighter quadratic upper bound than other algorithms such as Proximal Gradient Method, and allows simple closed-form solution

$$d_j^* := \mathbf{prox}_{R/M_j}(w_j - \frac{g_j}{M_j}) - w_j \tag{26}$$

where

$$\mathbf{prox}_R(v_j) := \begin{cases} 0, & |v_j| \le \lambda \\ v_j - \lambda, & v_j > \lambda \\ v_j + \lambda, & v_j < \lambda \end{cases}.$$

To have efficient evaluation of the gradient (25), a practical implementation maintain the responses

$$\hat{y}_i := \boldsymbol{w}^T z_i \tag{27}$$

after each update $\boldsymbol{w}^{t+1} := \boldsymbol{w}^t + d_j^* \boldsymbol{e}_j$, so the cost for each coordinate-wise minimization takes $O(nnz(\boldsymbol{z}_j))$ time for both gradient evaluation and maintenance of (27), where $\boldsymbol{z}_j := (z_{ij})_{i\in[N]}$. The algorithm is summarized in Alg. 2, which just like the iterative solver introduced in section 3.1, has cost $O(nnz(Z))$ for one pass of all variables $j \in [D]$.

4.2 Parallel Randomized Coordinate Descend on Random Binning Features

The RCD, however, is hard to parallelize [23]. It is known that simultaneous updates of two coordinates j_1, j_2 could lead to divergence, and although one can enforce convergence by shortening the step size $\frac{1}{M_p} \ll \frac{1}{M_j}$, the convergence rate will not be improved with parallelization without additional assumption [1, 24].

On the other hand, in [24], it is shown that a function with *partially separable* smooth term plus a separable non-smooth term

$$\min_{\boldsymbol{w}\in\mathbb{R}^D} F(\boldsymbol{w}) := \Omega(\boldsymbol{w}) + \sum_{i=1}^{N} f_i(\boldsymbol{w}) \tag{28}$$

can be parallelized with guaranteed speedup in terms of overall complexity, where $\Omega(\boldsymbol{w})$ is a non-smooth separable function and each function $f_i(\boldsymbol{w})$ is a smooth depends only on at most ω number of variables. The form (28), fortunately, fits our objective (23) with features $\boldsymbol{z}_i$ generated by RB. In particular, the generating process of RB guarantees that, for each block of feature B_δ, the i-th sample can fall in exactly one bin $b = (\lfloor \frac{x_{n1}-u_1}{\delta_1} \rfloor, ..., \lfloor \frac{x_{nd}-u_d}{\delta_d} \rfloor)$, therefore each sample inolves at most R features out of D. Specifically, let $\Omega(\boldsymbol{w}) := \lambda\|\boldsymbol{w}\|_1$ and

$$f_i(\boldsymbol{w}) := \frac{1}{N} L(\boldsymbol{w}^T \boldsymbol{z}_i, y_i),$$

we have $\omega = R$. Then by Theorem 19 of [24], a parallel RCD of τ threads that selects coordinate j uniformly at random achieves a speed-up (i.e. time-of-sequential/time-of-parallel) of

$$\textit{speedup-ratio} = \frac{\tau}{1 + \frac{(R-1)(\tau-1)}{D-1}}. \tag{29}$$

When $D, R \gg 1$, and $\tau = a\bar{\kappa}+1$ where $\bar{\kappa} := D/R$, (29) becomes

$$\textit{speedup-ratio} = \frac{a\bar{\kappa}+1}{1+a}, \tag{30}$$

which equals $(\bar{\kappa}+1)/2$ when $a = 1$ and approaches $\bar{\kappa}$ when $a \to \infty$. Therefore, it is guaranteed in theory that parallelization can speedup RCD significantly as long as $\bar{\kappa} = D/R \gg 1$. We give our sparse RB Features algorithm based on parallel RCD in Alg. 2. Note for other Random Features, there is no speedup guaranteed and our experiment shows that Parallel RCD performed on Random Fourier features could even have no speedup.

Note that the speedup achieved in this section is orthogonal to the faster convergence rate achieved in section 3, so by increasing κ, the advantage of RB over other Random Features is super-linearly increasing if a parallel RCD is used. Note also that the results (29), (30) also apply to algorithms that utilize Coordinate Descent as subproblem solvers such as Proximal (Quasi) Newton Method [13, 35]. Those methods are typically employed for computationally expensive loss functions.

5. EXPERIMENTS

In this section, we present extensive sets of experiments to demonstrate the efficiency and effectiveness of RB. The datasets are chosen to overlap with those in other papers in the literature, where the details are shown in the table 1. All sets except census are available at LIBSVM data set [2]. All computations are carried out on a DELL dual socket with Intel Xeon processors at 2.93GHz for a total of 16 cores and 250 GB of memory running the SUSE Linux operating system. We implemented all methods in C++ and all dense matrix operations are performed by using the optimized BLAS and LAPACK routines provided in the OpenBLAS library. Due to the limited space, we only choose subsets of our results to present in each subsection. However, these results are objective and unbiased.

Table 1: Properties of the datasets.

Name	C: Classes	d: Features	N: Train	M: Test
cadata	1	8	16,512	4,128
census	1	119	18,186	2,273
ijcnn1	2	22	35,000	91,701
cod_rna	2	8	49,437	271,617
covtype	2	54	464,809	116,203
SUSY	2	18	4,000,000	1,000,000
mnist	10	780	60,000	10,000
acoustic	3	50	78,823	19,705
letter	26	16	10,500	5,000

5.1 Effects of σ and R on Random Binning

We perform experiments to investigate the characteristics of RB by varying the kernel parameter λ and the rank R, respectively. We use a regularization $\lambda = 0.01$ to make sure the reasonable performance of RB and other low-rank kernels, although we found that RB is not sensitive to this parameter. We increase the σ in the large interval from $1e-2$ to $1e2$ so that the optimal σ locates within the interval. We apply CG iterative solver to operate on Z directly.

In order to make fair runtime comparison in each run, we set the $tol = 1e - 15$ to force similar CG iterations with different σ.

We evaluate the training and testing performance of regression and classification, when varying σ with fixed R. In [21], it does not consider the effect of σ in their analysis, which however has a large impact on the performance since D depends on the number of bins which is controlled by σ. Fig. 3 shows that the training and testing performance coincidentally decrease (increase) before they diverge when D grows by increasing σ. This confirms with our analysis in Theorem 1 that the larger κ, the faster convergence of RB Feature (recall that the convergence rate is $O(1/(\kappa R))$).

Second, one should not be surprised that the empirical training time increases with D. The operations involving the weighting vector w_{RB} could become as expensive as a sparse matrix-vector operation in an iterative solver. However, the total computational costs are still bounded by $O(NR)$ but the constant factor may vary with different datasets. Fortunately, in most of cases, the training time corresponding to the peak performance is just slightly higher than the smallest one. In practice, there are several ways to improve the computation costs by exploiting more advanced sparse matrix techniques such as preconditioning and efficient storage scheme, which is out scope of this paper and left for future study.

Finally, we evaluate the training and testing performance when varying R with fixed σ. Fig.4 shows that the training and testing performance converge almost linearly with D, which again confirms our analysis in Theorem 1. In addition, we observe that RB has strong overfit ability which turns out to be a strong attribute, especially when the hypothesis space has not yet saturated.

5.2 Performance Comparisons of All Methods

We present a large sets of experiments to compare RB with other most popular low-rank kernel approximations, including RF [21], Nyström [31], and recently proposed independent block approximation [29]. We also compare all methods with the exact kernel as a benchmark [26]. We do not report the results of the vanilla kernel on covtype and SUSY since the programs run out of memory. To make a fair comparison, we also apply CG on RB and Nyström directly on Z to admit similar computational costs. Since the independent block kernel approximation approximates the kernel matrix directly, we employ direct solver of dense matrix for this method. In practice, the CG iterative solver has no need to solve in high precision [3], which has also been observed in our experiments. Thus, we set the tolerance to $1e - 3$.

Fig.5 clearly demonstrates the superiority of RB compared to other low-rank kernels. For example, in the first column, RB significantly outperforms other methods in testing performance on all of these datasets, especially when R is relatively small. This is because RB enjoys much faster convergence rate to the optimal function than other methods. The advantage generally diminishes when R increases to reasonably large. However, for some large datasets such as covtype and SUSY, increasing number of random features or R boosts the performance extremely slow. This is consistent with our analysis that RB enjoys its fast convergence rate of $O(1/(\kappa R))$ while other methods has slow convergence rates $O(1/\sqrt{R})$. The third and fourth columns further promote the insights about how many number of random features or how large rank R that is needed for achieving similar performance of RB. In particular, RB is often between one and three orders of magnitude faster and less memory consumptions than other methods.

In the second column, we also observe that the training time of all low-rank kernels are linear with R, which is expected since all these methods has computational complexity of $O(kNR)$. The difference in training time between these low-rank kernels is only within some constant factors. However, we point out that the computations of RF, Nyström and independent block approximation are mainly carried out by the high-optimized BLAS library since they are dense matrices. In contrast, the computations of RB are most involved in sparse matrix operations, which are self-implemented and not yet optimized. In addition, more advanced sparse matrix techniques such as preconditioning can be explored to significantly accelerate the computation, which we leave it as future work.

5.3 Parallel Performance of Random Binning and Random Fourier

We perform experiments to compare RB with RF when using RCD to solve L1-regularized Lasso and kernel SVM for both regression and binary classification problems. Since the goal is to demonstrate the strong parallel performance of RB, we implement the basic parallel implementation of RCD based on simple shared memory parallel programming model with OpenMP. We leave the high-performance distributed RCD implementation as one of the future works. We define the speedup of RCD on multicore implementation as follows:

$$speedup = \frac{\textit{runtime of RCD using single core}}{\textit{runtime using } P \textit{ cores}}$$

As shown in Fig.6, when the sparsity level of the feature matrix Z is high, the near-linear speedup can be achieved [16, 18]. This is because the minimization problem can almost be separated along the coordinate axes, then higher degrees of parallelism are possible. In contrast, if Z is lack of sparsity, then the penalty for data correlations slows the speedup to none. This is confirmed by no gain of parallel speedup of RF since Z is always fully dense. Obviously, in order to empower strong parallel performance of RB, a very large D is expected, which interestingly coincides with power of its faster convergence. Therefore, one can enjoy the double benefits of fast convergence and strong parallelizability of RB, which is especially useful for very large-scale problems.

6. CONCLUSIONS

In this paper, we revisit RB features, an overlooked yet very powerful random features, which we observe often to be orders of magnitude faster than other random features and kernel approximation methods to achieve the same accuracy. Motivated by these impressive empirical results, we propose the first analysis of RB from the perspective of optimization, to make a solid attempt to quantify its faster convergence, which is not captured by traditional Monte-Carlo analysis. By interpreting RB as a RBCD in the infinite-dimensional space, we show that by drawing R grids with at least κ expected number of non-empty bins per grid, RB achieves a convergence rate of $O(1/(\kappa R))$. In addition, in the L1-regularized setting, we demonstrate the sparse structure of RB features allows RCD solver to be parallelized with guaranteed speedup proportional to κ. Our extensive experiments demonstrate the superior performance of the RB features over other random feature and kernel approximation methods.

7. ACKNOWLEDGEMENT

This work was done while L. Wu was a research intern at IBM Research. J. Chen is supported in part by the XDATA program of the Advanced Research Projects Agency (DARPA), administered through Air Force Research Laboratory contract FA8750-12-C-0323.

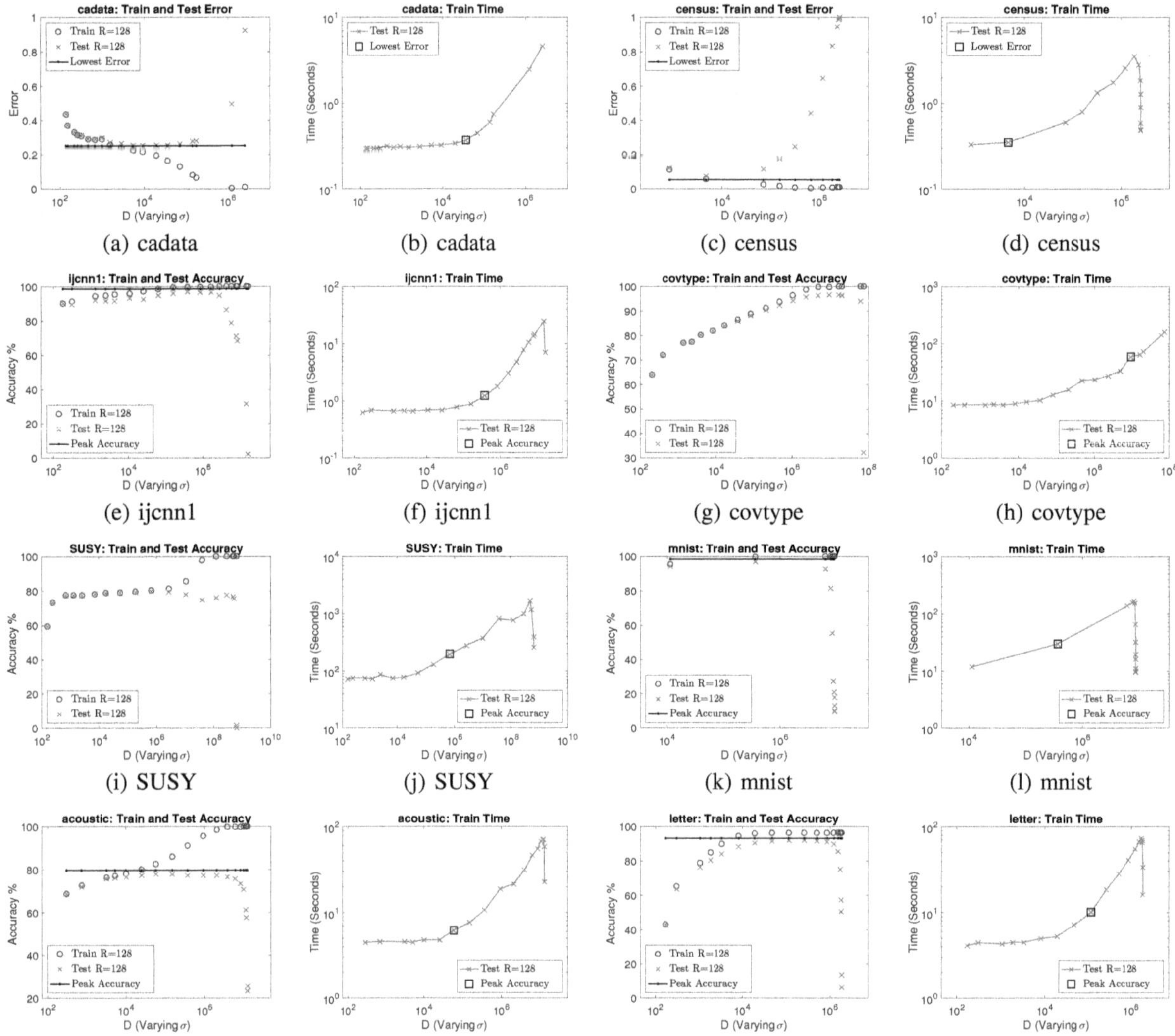

(a) cadata (b) cadata (c) census (d) census

(e) ijcnn1 (f) ijcnn1 (g) covtype (h) covtype

(i) SUSY (j) SUSY (k) mnist (l) mnist

(m) acoustic (n) acoustic (o) letter (p) letter

Figure 3: Train and test performance, and train time when varying σ with fixed R. The black line and square box represent the best test performance of the exact kernel and RB respectively.

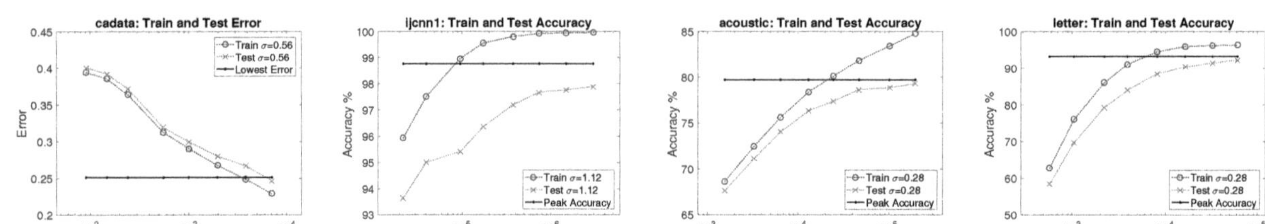

(a) cadata (b) ijcnn1 (c) acoustic (d) letter

Figure 4: Train and test performance when varying R with fixed σ.

References

[1] J. K. Bradley, A. Kyrola, D. Bickson, and C. Guestrin. Parallel coordinate descent for l1-regularized loss minimization. *CoRR, abs/1105.5379*, 2011.

[2] C. Chang and C. Lin. Libsvm: a library for support vector machines. *ACM Transactions on Intelligent Systems and Technology*, 2:27:1–27:27, 2011.

[3] J. Chen, L. Wu, K. Audhkhasi, B. Kingsbury, and B. Ramabhadran. Efficient one-vs-one kernel ridge regression for speech recognition. In *ICASSP*, 2016.

[4] B. Dai, B. Xie, N. He, Y. Liang, A. Raj, M.-F. F. Balcan, and L. Song. Scalable kernel methods via doubly stochastic gradients. In *NIPS*. Curran Associates, Inc., 2014.

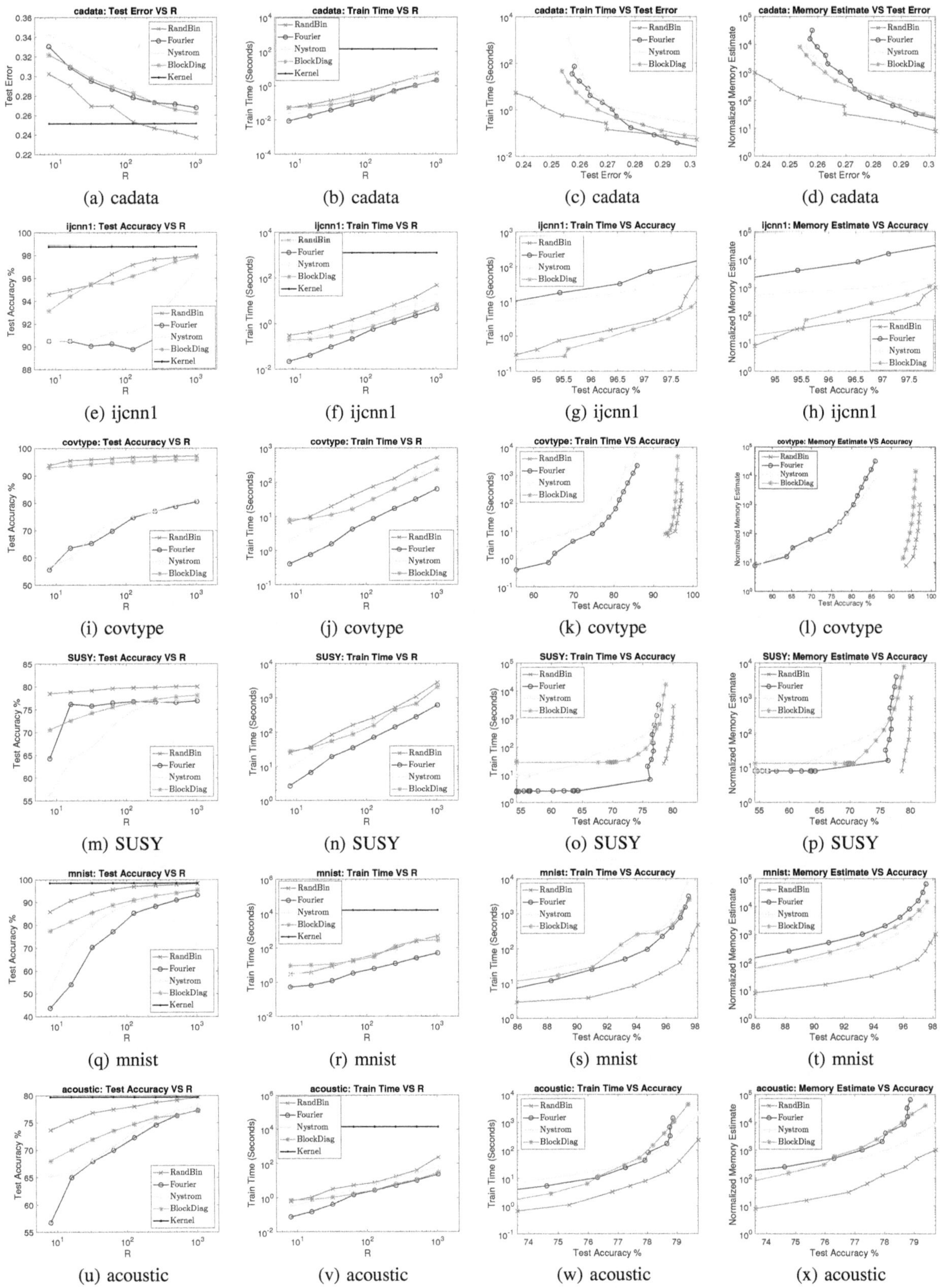

(a) cadata (b) cadata (c) cadata (d) cadata

(e) ijcnn1 (f) ijcnn1 (g) ijcnn1 (h) ijcnn1

(i) covtype (j) covtype (k) covtype (l) covtype

(m) SUSY (n) SUSY (o) SUSY (p) SUSY

(q) mnist (r) mnist (s) mnist (t) mnist

(u) acoustic (v) acoustic (w) acoustic (x) acoustic

Figure 5: Comparisons among RB, RF, Nyström and Independent Block approximation. The first and second columns plot test performance and train time when increasing R. The third and fourth columns plot the train time and memory consumptions when achieving the desired test performance.

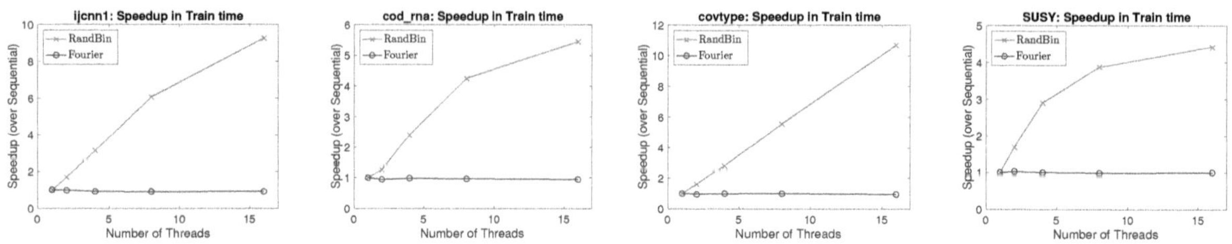

(a) ijcnn1 (b) cod_rna (c) covtype (d) SUSY

Figure 6: Comparisons of parallel performance between RB and RF using RCD when increasing the number of threads.

[5] P. Drineas and M. W. Mahoney. On the nyström method for approximating a gram matrix for improved kernel-based learning. *JMLR*, 6:2153–2175, Dec. 2005.

[6] R.-E. Fan, K.-W. Chang, C.-J. Hsieh, X.-R. Wang, and C.-J. Lin. Liblinear: A library for large linear classification. *JMLR*, 9:1871–1874, 2008.

[7] S. Fine and K. Scheinberg. Efficient svm training using low-rank kernel representations. *JMLR*, 2:243–264, Mar. 2002.

[8] A. Gittens and M. W. Mahoney. Revisiting the nyström method for improved large-scale machine learning. *CoRR*, abs/1303.1849, 2013.

[9] G. H. Golub and C. F. Van Loan. *Matrix Computations*. Johns Hopkins University Press, Baltimore, MD, USA, 1996.

[10] P.-S. Huang, H. Avron, T. Sainath, V. Sindhwani, and B. Ramabhadran. Kernel methods match deep neural networks on timit. In *ICASSP*, 2014.

[11] S. Kumar, M. Mohri, and A. Talwalkar. Sampling methods for the nyström method. *JMLR*, 13:981–1006, Apr. 2012.

[12] Q. V. Le, T. Sarlós, and A. J. Smola. Fastfood: Approximate kernel expansions in loglinear time. *ICML*, 2013.

[13] J. Lee, Y. Sun, and M. Saunders. Proximal newton-type methods for convex optimization. In *Advances in Neural Information Processing Systems*, pages 836–844, 2012.

[14] C.-J. Lin, R. C. Weng, and S. S. Keerthi. Trust region newton method for logistic regression. *JMLR*, 9:627–650, 2008.

[15] H.-T. Lin and L. Li. Support vector machinery for infinite ensemble learning. *JMLR*, 9:285–312, 2008.

[16] J. Liu, S. J. Wright, C. Ré, and V. Bittorf. An asynchronous parallel stochastic coordinate descent algorithm. *JMLR*, 32(1):469–477, 2014.

[17] Z. Lu, A. May, K. Liu, A. B. Garakani, D. Guo, A. Bellet, L. Fan, M. Collins, B. Kingsbury, M. Picheny, and F. Sha. How to scale up kernel methods to be as good as deep neural nets. *CoRR*, abs/1411.4000, 2014.

[18] J. Mareček, P. Richtárik, and M. Takáč. Distributed block coordinate descent for minimizing partially separable functions. *Numerical Analysis and Optimization*, 134:261–288, 2014.

[19] J. Mercer. Functions of positive and negative type, and their connection with the theory of integral equations. *Royal Society London*, A 209:415–446, 1909.

[20] M. Raginsky and S. Lazebnik. Locality-sensitive binary codes from shift-invariant kernels. In Y. Bengio, D. Schuurmans, J. D. Lafferty, C. K. I. Williams, and A. Culotta, editors, *Advances in Neural Information Processing Systems 22*, pages 1509–1517. Curran Associates, Inc., 2009.

[21] A. Rahimi and B. Recht. Random features for large-scale kernel machines. In *NIPS*. Curran Associates, Inc., 2007.

[22] A. Rahimi and B. Recht. Weighted sums of random kitchen sinks: Replacing minimization with randomization in learning. In *NIPS*. Curran Associates, Inc., 2008.

[23] P. Richtárik and M. Takáč. Iteration complexity of randomized block-coordinate descent methods for minimizing a composite function. *Mathematical Programming*, 144(1-2):1–38, 2014.

[24] P. Richtárik and M. Takáč. Parallel coordinate descent methods for big data optimization. *Mathematical Programming*, pages 1–52, 2015.

[25] Y. Saad. *Iterative Methods for Sparse Linear Systems*. Society for Industrial and Applied Mathematics, Philadelphia, PA, USA, 2nd edition, 2003.

[26] B. Scholkopf and A. J. Smola. *Learning with Kernels: Support Vector Machines, Regularization, Optimization, and Beyond*. MIT Press, Cambridge, MA, USA, 2001.

[27] S. Si, C. Hsieh, and I. S. Dhillon. Memory efficient kernel approximation. In *ICML*, 2014.

[28] A. J. Smola and B. Schökopf. Sparse greedy matrix approximation for machine learning. In *ICML*, ICML '00, San Francisco, CA, USA, 2000. Morgan Kaufmann Publishers Inc.

[29] M. L. Stein. Limitations on low rank approximations for covariance matrices of spatial data. *Spatial Statistics*, 8:1 – 19, 2014. Spatial Statistics Miami.

[30] B. Taskar, C. Guestrin, and D. Koller. Max-margin markov networks. In *NIPS*. MIT Press, 2004.

[31] C. K. I. Williams and M. Seeger. Using the nyström method to speed up kernel machines. In *NIPS*. MIT Press, 2001.

[32] Z. Yang, A. G. Wilson, A. J. Smola, and L. Song. A la carte - learning fast kernels. In *AISTATS*, 2015.

[33] I. E.-H. Yen, T.-W. Lin, S.-D. Lin, P. K. Ravikumar, and I. S. Dhillon. Sparse random feature algorithm as coordinate descent in hilbert space. In *JMLR*, 2014.

[34] G.-X. Yuan, K.-W. Chang, C.-J. Hsieh, and C.-J. Lin. A comparison of optimization methods and software for large-scale l1-regularized linear classification. *JMLR*, 11:3183–3234, 2010.

[35] K. Zhong, I. E.-H. Yen, I. S. Dhillon, and P. K. Ravikumar. Proximal quasi-newton for computationally intensive l1-regularized m-estimators. In *Advances in Neural Information Processing Systems*, pages 2375–2383, 2014.

Robust Extreme Multi-label Learning

Chang Xu[*†] xuchang@pku.edu.cn
Dacheng Tao[†] Dacheng.Tao@uts.edu.au
Chao Xu[*] xuchao@cis.pku.edu.cn

Key Laboratory of Machine Perception, Cooperative Medianet Innovation Center, Peking University[*], Beijing, China
Centre for Quantum Computation and Intelligent Systems, University of Technology[†], Sydney

ABSTRACT

Tail labels in the multi-label learning problem undermine the low-rank assumption. Nevertheless, this problem has rarely been investigated. In addition to using the low-rank structure to depict label correlations, this paper explores and exploits an additional sparse component to handle tail labels behaving as outliers, in order to make the classical low-rank principle in multi-label learning valid. The divide-and-conquer optimization technique is employed to increase the scalability of the proposed algorithm while theoretically guaranteeing its performance. A theoretical analysis of the generalizability of the proposed algorithm suggests that it can be improved by the low-rank and sparse decomposition given tail labels. Experimental results on real-world data demonstrate the significance of investigating tail labels and the effectiveness of the proposed algorithm.

CCS Concepts

•**Computing methodologies** → *Supervised learning;*

Keywords

Multi-label Learning; Low-rank Algorithm

1. INTRODUCTION

In contrast to conventional single-label learning, in which each example is assigned only one label, multi-label learning evaluates examples with multiple labels. Many real-world applications use multi-label learning [31] including text categorization and image/video annotation [7]. The rapid evolution of information techniques has fueled the emergence of large-scale multi-label applications with huge numbers of labels. For example, given over a million labels (categories) on Wikipedia, one might wish to build a classifier to annotate a new article or web page with a subset of the most relevant categories. In another example, taking billions of YouTube videos as distinct labels, a task might be to recommend a ranked list of labels to a single user. Hence, extreme multi-label learning with an extremely large number of labels has become an important research focus.

Binary relevance (BR) [24] seeks to independently train a classifier for each label. BR is a straightforward approach for multi-label learning, but due to prohibitive training and prediction costs arising from large numbers of labels, this method becomes less useful. A number of embedding-based approaches have been proposed to overcome this extreme multi-label learning problem that reduce the effective number of labels. The approaches assume that the label matrix is low rank. Different techniques can be used to compress and decompress label vectors, including compressed sensing [15], Bloom filters [9], SVD [23], landmark labels [2, 5], and output codes [32].

The low-rank label matrix assumption in embedding methods is violated in many real-world applications due to the presence of tail labels occurring in a handful of data points. Histograms of the label matrices on the *wiki10*, *Delicious-L* and *Amazon* datasets are shown in Figure 1. There are more than 10^4 labels which occur in at most 2 examples on each dataset, such that they are not well approximated by any linear low-dimensional basis. This tail label issue is frequently and persistently neglected in multi-label learning. Recently, instead of projecting label vectors into a linear low-rank subspace, [4] addressed the tail label problem by learning embeddings that non-linearly captured label correlations by preserving the pairwise distances between label vectors. Although this provides an alternative approach to handling tail labels, we must also ask whether low-rank based approaches really are now redundant.

Here we revisit the classical low-rank principle in multi-label learning and suppress the influence of tail labels. Tail labels can be regarded as label matrix outliers, inspiring us to decompose the label matrix into a low-rank part that depicts label correlations and a sparse part that captures tail labels. Various effective embedding techniques are then applicable. To improve scalability and leverage the growing availability of parallel computing architectures, the divide-and-conquer approach is adopted to optimize the resulting objective function, whose performance can be theoretically guaranteed with high probability. Our theoretical analysis shows that the proposed low-rank and sparse decomposition is useful for improving the generalizability of multi-label learning algorithms. Experiments on real-world data demonstrate the significance of studying tail labels in multi-label learning and the effectiveness of the proposed algorithm.

KDD '16, August 13-17, 2016, San Francisco, CA, USA

DOI: http://dx.doi.org/10.1145/2939672.2939798

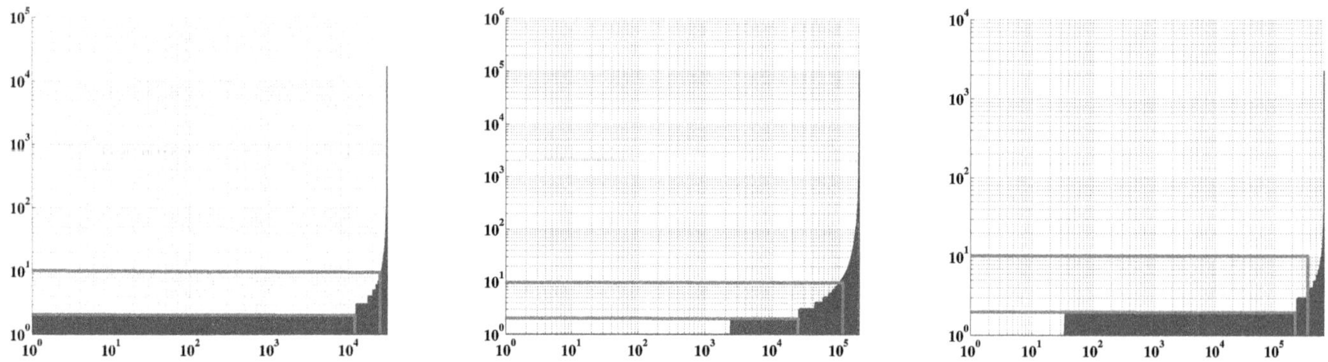

(a) (b) (c)

Figure 1: The number of examples in which each label is present on the (a) Wiki10 (b) Delicious-L and (c) Amazon datasets. The horizontal axis indicates the index of label, while the vertical axis indicates the number of associated examples.

2. RELATED WORK

The multi-label learning problem has been extensively studied in practice [31] and theory [13, 27]. Broadly speaking, existing multi-label learning algorithms can be categorized into two groups: algorithm adaptation and problem transformation methods. Algorithm adaptation methods adapt, extend and customize an existing machine learning algorithms for the task of multi-label learning, while problem transformation methods transform the multi-label learning problem into one or more single-label classification or regression problems. Representative examples include boosting [20, 26, 16], decision trees [25, 17], neural networks [29, 10], support vector machines [12, 14] and k nearest neighbors classifier [30, 21].

The key in multi-label learning is modeling inter-label correlations and using them for label vector prediction. In many applications such as text categorization and functional genomics, the labels are often organized in the form of a tree or directed acyclic graph, so that label relationship can be exploited from the knowledge resources as prior knowledge for multi-label learning [6, 14]. In most real-world tasks, however, prior knowledge of label relationship is often unavailable. It is thus necessary to model the label relationship directly. For example, Sun et al. [22] proposed to employ hypergraphs to exploit the higher-order relations among multiple instances sharing the same label in multi-label learning. They constructed a hyperedge for each label, and included all instances annotated with a common label into one hyperedge, thus capturing their joint similarity. Zhang and Zhang [28] used a Bayesian network to characterize the dependence structure between multiple labels, and learned a binary classifier for each label by treating its parental labels in the dependence structure as additional input features. However, as the number of labels keeps growing, these algorithms are usually computationally infeasible.

Embedding-based approaches are significant for handling extreme multi-label learning problem by reducing the effective number of labels. Generally, they assume that the label matrix is low-rank, and then project label vectors into a low-dimensional subspace. Hence, instead of directly learning to predict the original high-dimensional label vector of each example, the training complexity is largely decreased by first learning the predictor of embedded label vectors, and then a decompression operation is employed to lift the embedded label vectors back to the original label space.

Various compression and decompression techniques have been exploited by existing embedding methods. Hsu et al. [15] addressed classification problem with a large number of labels via a three-step approach. First, random transformation is used to project the high-dimensonal label vector into a low-dimensional space; next, a regression model is trained to predict each dimension of the transformed label vector; finally, for a test example, its predicted label vector in the low-dimensional space is projected back to the original label space. Considering the drawback of random transformation in [15], Tai and Lin [23] proposed the principal label space transformation, which uses principal component analysis (PCA) to accomplish the compression operation on the high-dimensional label vector. Since PCA in the label space only focuses on minimizing the encoding error between high-dimensional feature vectors and their low-dimensional representations [23], Chen and Lin [8] proposed conditional principal label space transformation, which improves [23] by simultaneously considering the label encoding error and training error in the low-dimensional label space. Based on canonical correlation analysis (CCA), Zhang and Schneider [32] also took both feature matrix and label matrix into consideration. After that, a maximum margin formulation was developed to learn an output coding, which is predictive and discriminative so that the codings for different label vectors are easy to predict and significantly different from each other. Instead of using label transformation, Balasubramanian and Lebanon [2] proposed to train only a small subset of the labels, which come from the original labels, so that the difficulty of the learning problems can be decreased. Supposing that the non-selected labels are to be faithfully and easily constructed from the selected ones, a group-sparse learning problem is investigated to discover the optimal label subset [2]. However, the structured sparsity optimization problem in [2] is computationally expensive, especially when there are a lot of labels to select from. Bi and Kwok [5] alleviated this problem by proposing an efficient label selection method based on randomized sampling. Following the assumption in [2], Bi and Kwok [5] designed the sampling probability of each label using its leverage score in the best rank-k subspaces of the label matrix.

Recently, Yu et al. [27] modeled multi-label classification as a general empirical risk minimization (ERM) problem with a low-rank constraint, which generalizes both label and feature dimensionality reduction. Given squared-L_2 loss, LEML algorithm in [27] has a closed form solution, and can be reduced to the conditional principal label space transformation algorithm in [8]. Various loss functions and regularizers are applicable in this ERM framework for preventing overfitting and increasing scalability. However, as suggested by [4], the low-rank assumption in embedding-based approaches is easily violated by tail labels in real-world datasets with a large number of labels. Instead of globally projecting high-dimensional label vectors into a low-rank subspace, SLEEC algorithm in [4] learns low-dimensional embedding which non-linearly capture label correlations by preserving the pairwise distances between only the closest label vectors. Regressors are then trained to predict the embedded label vector for each example. During prediction, rather than using a decomposition matrix, SLEEC uses a k-nearest neighbor (kNN) classifier in the embedding space, which leverages the fact that nearest neighbors have been preserved during training.

3. PROBLEM FORMULATION

Given a training data set $\{(x_1, y_1), \cdots, (x_n, y_n)\}$, where $x_i \in \mathbb{R}^d$ is the feature vector of the i-th example, and $y_i \in \{-1,1\}^L$ is the corresponding label vector, the feature matrix is denoted as $X = [x_1; \cdots; x_n] \in \mathbb{R}^{n\times d}$ and the label matrix is $Y = [y_1; \cdots; y_n] \in \{-1,1\}^{n\times L}$. If $Y_{ij} = 1$, example x_i will have label-j; otherwise, there is no label-i for example x_j. Multi-label learning aims to learn a hypothesis $f : \mathbb{R}^d \to \{-1,1\}^L$ that accurately predicts the label vector for a given example.

There are a large number of labels in the extreme multi-label learning setting. Tail labels, which only occur with several examples, cannot be ignored, and a number of rows in the label matrix Y will have plenty of -1-valued entries while occasionally being dotted with several 1-valued entries. Due to the existence of these rows, the classical low-rank assumption on the label matrix is violated. We attempt to modernize the low-rank principle by carefully formulating the tail labels in the extreme multi-label learning problem.

3.1 Robust Extreme Multi-label Learning

One reasonable approach to interpret the label matrix in multi-label learning is to assume that the label matrix can be well approximated using a low-dimensional subspace. This assumption has been well justified in many practical situations. A general model can be written as

$$\begin{aligned} &\min_{\widehat{Y},W} \|Y - \widehat{Y}\|_F^2 + \lambda \ell(f(X,W), \widehat{Y}) \\ &\text{s.t. } rank(\widehat{Y}) \le k. \end{aligned} \tag{1}$$

where $\widehat{Y}$ is the low-rank approximation of Y, and loss function $\ell(\cdot)$ is employed to penalize the loss generated by a multi-label predictor parameterized by W.

Problem (1) has been studied for decades, and various techniques have been used to formulate the low-rank $\widehat{Y}$, the predictor $f(\cdot)$ and the loss function $\ell(\cdot)$. However, as mentioned above, tail labels damage the low-rank assumption over Y and render the estimated $\widehat{Y}$ arbitrarily far from the true Y; the learned multi-label predictor is, therefore, seriously influenced as a result. A method that can extract the low-rank components from Y even in the presence of tail labels would be desirable.

To achieve this, we treat tail labels as outliers and decompose the label matrix to

$$Y = \widehat{Y}_L + \widehat{Y}_S, \tag{2}$$

where $\widehat{Y}_L$ is of low rank and depict label correlations and $\widehat{Y}_S$ is the sparse component capturing the influence of tail labels. These two components can be obtained by solving the following objective:

$$\begin{aligned} &\min_{\widehat{Y}_L,\widehat{Y}_S} \|Y - \widehat{Y}_L - \widehat{Y}_S\|_F^2 \\ &\text{s.t. } rank(\widehat{Y}_L) \le k, \quad card(\widehat{Y}_S) \le s. \end{aligned} \tag{3}$$

Given the low rank and sparse components $\widehat{Y}_L$ and $\widehat{Y}_S$, we expect to learn regression models that predict them using the input features. That is, we require that $\widehat{Y}_L \approx WX$ and $\widehat{Y}_S \approx HX$, where $W, H \in \mathbb{R}^{d\times L}$. Hence, problem (3) can be reformulated as:

$$\begin{aligned} &\min_{W,H} \|Y - XW - XH\|_F^2 \\ &\text{s.t. } rank(XW) \le k, \quad card(XH) \le s. \end{aligned} \tag{4}$$

Since the rank and card constraints tend to increase the optimization complexity, we employ two popular matrix factorization heuristics (to encourage low-rankness) and $L1$-norm minimization (to encourage sparsity) to relax the constraints in problem (4), such that

$$\begin{aligned} \min_{U,V,H} &\|Y - XUV - XH\|_F^2 + \lambda_1\|H\|_F^2 \\ &+ \lambda_2(\|U\|_F^2 + \|V\|_F^2) + \lambda_3\|XH\|_1, \end{aligned} \tag{5}$$

where $\{\lambda_1, \lambda_2, \lambda_3\}$ are positive constants, W is supposed to have $W = UV$ given $U \in \mathbb{R}^{d\times k}$ and $V \in \mathbb{R}^{k\times L}$, and an $L2$-regularization has been included for H. It is expected that by solving problem (5), we can obtain a low-rank function (i.e., $W = UV$) and a sparse function (i.e., H), which together are used for multi-label prediction.

4. OPTIMIZATION

In this section, we first present the basic optimization method for problem (5) and then adopt the divide-and-conquer strategy to develop an optimization method applicable to extreme multi-label learning.

4.1 Basic Optimization Method

Problem (5) can be solved by alternatively solving the following three subproblems until convergence:

$$V = \arg\min_V \|Y - XUV - XH\|_F^2 + \lambda_2\|V\|_F^2 \tag{6a}$$

$$U = \arg\min_U \|Y - XUV - XH\|_F^2 + \lambda_2\|U\|_F^2 \tag{6b}$$

$$\begin{aligned} H = \arg\min_H &\|Y - XUV - XH\|_F^2 + \lambda_1\|H\|_F^2 \\ &+ \lambda_3\|XH\|_1. \end{aligned} \tag{6c}$$

In the following, we illustrate the optimization of these three subproblems respectively.

4.1.1 Solving V

In problem (6a), updating V is simple since each column v_j of V can be independently updated:

$$\min_{v_j} \sum_{i=1}^{n} \|Y_{ij} - x_i U v_j - (XH)_{ij}\|^2 + \lambda_2 \|v_j\|_2^2, \quad (7)$$

which is easy to solve in a closed form as the dimension of v_j (i.e. k) is generally small. Setting the gradient of Eq. (7) w.r.t. v_j to zero, the optimal v_j^* corresponding to the j-th label can be obtained as

$$v_j^* = \left[\sum_{i=1}^{n} (x_i U)^T x_i U + \lambda_2 I\right]^{-1} \left[\sum_{i=1}^{n} (Y_{ij} - (XH)_{ij})(x_i U)^T\right]$$

4.1.2 Solving U

Problem (6b) is equivalent to

$$\min_{u} \sum_{i=1}^{n} \sum_{j=1}^{L} \|Y_{ij} - u^T \widetilde{X}_{ij} - (XH)_{ij}\|^2 + \lambda_2 \|u\|^2, \quad (8)$$

where $u \in \mathbb{R}^{dk}$ denotes $vec(U)$, and $\widetilde{X}_{ij} = vec(x_i v_j)$. There is a closed form solution for this problem,

$$u^* = \left[\sum_{i=1}^{n} \sum_{j=1}^{L} \widetilde{X}_{ij} (\widetilde{X}_{ij})^T + \lambda_2 I\right]^{-1} \left[\sum_{i=1}^{n} \sum_{j=1}^{L} (Y_{ij} - (XH)_{ij}) \widetilde{X}_{ij}\right]$$

However, it is inefficient to compute the closed form solution for the above problem when d is large due to the huge computational cost of inverting a $dk \times dk$ matrix. Instead, it is more appropriate to employ efficient gradient descent methods (e.g. conjugate gradient descent) for optimization.

4.1.3 Solving H

In problem (6c), given $\widetilde{Y} = Y - XUV$, each column H_j can be independently solved,

$$\min_{H_j} \sum_{i=1}^{n} \|\widetilde{Y}_{ij} - x_i H_j\|_F^2 + \lambda_1 \|H_j\|_F^2 + \lambda_3 \|XH_j\|_1. \quad (9)$$

The $L1$ norm in problem (9) involves both H_j and X, which makes the problem non-smooth and disallows the standard proxy function-based optimization methods. One way to circumvent this difficulty is by introducing an auxiliary variable $Z_j = XH_j$ and transforming problem (9) into

$$\begin{aligned} \min_{H_j, Z_j, \mu} \; & \sum_{i=1}^{n} \|\widetilde{Y}_{ij} - x_i H_j\|_F^2 + \lambda_1 \|H_j\|_F^2 + \lambda_3 \|Z_j\|_1 \\ & + \rho \|XH_j - Z_j + \mu\|_F^2, \end{aligned} \quad (10)$$

where $\rho > 0$ is the penalty parameter, and μ is the scaled dual variable.

Fixing H_j and μ, problem (10) is reduced to

$$\min_{Z_j} \|XH_j - Z_j + \mu\|_F^2 + \frac{\lambda_3}{\rho} \|Z_j\|_1. \quad (11)$$

The optimal Z_j^* can be obtained via soft thresholding operation [11],

$$Z_j^* = soft(XH_j + \mu, \frac{\lambda_3}{\rho}), \quad (12)$$

where

$$soft(a, b) = sign(a) \max(|a| - b, 0). \quad (13)$$

Algorithm 1 Robust Extreme Multi-label Learning

Input: X, Y, $t \geq 1$
For $i = 1, \cdots, t$ **do In Parallel**
  Sample $(Y)_i \subseteq Y$
  repeat
    Solve $(\widehat{V})_i$ from Problem (6a)
    Solve $(\widehat{U})_i$ from Problem (6b)
    Solve $(\widehat{H})_i$ from Problem (6c)
  until Convergence
  $(\widehat{W})_i = (\widehat{U})_i (\widehat{V})_i$
End
ColumnProjection $([(\widehat{W})_1, \cdots, (\widehat{W})_t], (\widehat{W})_1)$

Fixing Z_j and μ, H_j can be solved from the following objective function:

$$\min_{H_j} \sum_{i=1}^{n} \|\widetilde{Y}_{ij} - x_i H_j\|_F^2 + \lambda_1 \|H_j\|_F^2 + \rho \|XH_j - Z_j + \mu\|_F^2. \quad (14)$$

The gradient w.r.t. H_j is calculated as

$$\begin{aligned} \nabla_{H_j} \mathcal{J} = & \, 2(\sum_{i=1}^{n} x_i^T x_i + \lambda_1 I + \rho X^T X) H_j \\ & - 2(\sum_{i=1}^{n} x_i^T \widetilde{Y}_{ij} + \rho X^T (Z_j - \mu)). \end{aligned} \quad (15)$$

By setting Eq. (15) to zero, H_j can be easily solved out in a closed form. On the other hand, if the dimension of H_j is great, cheap gradient descent optimization method can be applied. μ can be updated via

$$\mu \leftarrow \mu + XH - Z. \quad (16)$$

Through alternatively updating H_j, Z_j and μ, the optimal H_j for problem (9) can be achieved.

4.2 Divide-and-Conquer Optimization

The divide-and-conquer strategy can be employed to increase the algorithm's capability for handling extremely large numbers of labels. The original optimization problem is first divided into cheaper sub-problems that can be efficiently solved in parallel. The solutions to these subproblems can then be combined to achieve the final solution. The whole optimization procedure is summarized in Algorithm 1.

Divide Step. Given the label matrix $Y \in \{-1, 1\}^{n \times L}$, we randomly partition the matrix Y into t m-column submatrices $\{(Y)_i\}_{i=1}^t$, where we suppose $L = tm$ and each $(Y_i) \in \{-1, 1\}^{n \times m}$. Hence, the original problem is divided into t sub-problems regarding $\{(Y)_1, \cdots, (Y)_t\}$, respectively. The basic optimization method described in Section 4.1 can be adopted to solve these sub-problems in parallel, which outputs the solutions $\{((\widehat{W})_1, (\widehat{H})_1), \cdots, ((\widehat{W})_t, (\widehat{H})_t)\}$.

Conquer Step. This conquer step exploits column projection to integrate the solutions of sub-problem solutions. The final approximation W to problem (5) can thus be obtained by projecting $[(\widehat{W})_1, \cdots, (\widehat{W})_t]$ onto the column space of $(\widehat{W})_1$. After obtaining $\widehat{W}$, we can then launch the optimization over each each column of $\widehat{H}$ in parallel to obtain the sparse component of the resulting multi-label predictor.

5. THEORETICAL ANALYSIS

In this section, we prove the upper bounds on the estimation error of the basic and divide-and-conquer optimization methods, respectively. The generalizability of our learning model is also analyzed.

5.1 Estimation Error

Given a feature matrix $X \in \mathbb{R}^{n \times d}$ and the corresponding label matrix $Y \in \{-1, 1\}^{n \times L}$ for n training points of L labels, we suppose that

$$Y = XW_0 + Y_S + \epsilon, \tag{17}$$

where $W_0 \in \mathbb{R}^{d \times L}$ is the ground truth weight, Y_S is the sparse component to formulate the influence of tail labels, and ϵ is a data-independent noise term. Given this training data, we aim to estimate W_0 by performing empirical risk minimization:

$$\widehat{W} = \arg\min_{W} = \|\widetilde{Y} - XW\|_F^2 + \lambda\|W\|_*, \tag{18}$$

where $\widetilde{Y} = Y - Y_S$. Note that although the method in Eq. (4) uses a regularized rank-constrained formulation, we analyze the trace norm-regularized version without the rank constraint for simplicity. Since the class of rank-constrained matrices is smaller than the class of trace norm-constrained matrices, we can in fact expect better theoretical results here.

We generically denote the estimator for Σ_{XX} by $X^T X$, and the estimator for $\Sigma_{X\widetilde{Y}}$ by $X^T\widetilde{Y}$. We require Σ_{XX} to be positive semidefinite. Thus, the estimator for $\widehat{W}$ naturally becomes,

$$\widehat{W} = \arg\min_{W} \langle W, \Sigma_{XX}W\rangle - 2\langle \Sigma_{X\widetilde{Y}}, W\rangle + \lambda\|W\|_*. \tag{19}$$

We use the following theorem to show that $\widehat{W}$ solved in Eq. (19) is an approximated estimation of the true W_0.

Theorem 1. *Suppose the smallest eigenvalue of Σ_{XX} is bounded by $\sigma_{min}(\Sigma_{XX}) \geq \sigma > 0$. The estimation error satisfies*

$$\|\widehat{W} - W_0\|_F \leq \frac{1}{\sigma}(2\|\Sigma_{X\widetilde{Y}} - \Sigma_{XX}W_0\|_* - \lambda). \tag{20}$$

Proof. Let $\Delta = \widehat{W} - W_0$. Considering the optimality of $\widehat{W}$ for problem (19), we have

$$\begin{aligned}&\langle W_0 + \Delta, \Sigma_{XX}(W_0 + \Delta)\rangle - 2\langle \Sigma_{X\widetilde{Y}}, W_0 + \Delta\rangle + \lambda\|W_0 + \Delta\|_* \\ &\leq\langle W_0, \Sigma_{XX}W_0\rangle - 2\langle \Sigma_{X\widetilde{Y}}, W_0\rangle + \lambda\|W_0\|_*,\end{aligned}$$

which can be rearranged to

$$\langle \Delta, \Sigma_{XX}\Delta\rangle \leq 2\langle \Sigma_{XY} - \Sigma_{XX}W_0, \Delta\rangle - \lambda\|\Delta\|_*. \tag{21}$$

Since the smallest eigenvalue of Σ_{XX} is bounded, we have

$$\langle \Delta, \Sigma_{XX}\Delta\rangle \geq \sigma\|\Delta\|_F^2. \tag{22}$$

Given $\|\Delta\|_* \geq \|\Delta\|_F$, the right hand side of Eq. (21) can be upper-bounded by

$$\begin{aligned}&2\langle \Sigma_{X\widetilde{Y}} - \Sigma_{XX}W_0, \Delta\rangle - \lambda\|\Delta\|_* \\ &\leq 2\|\Sigma_{X\widetilde{Y}} - \Sigma_{XX}W_0\|_*\|\Delta\|_F - \lambda\|\Delta\|_F.\end{aligned} \tag{23}$$

Combining all the above results, we get

$$\sigma\|\Delta\|_F^2 \leq 2\|\Sigma_{X\widetilde{Y}} - \Sigma_{XX}W_0\|_*\|\Delta\|_F - \lambda\|\Delta\|_F. \tag{24}$$

The result then follows. □

According to Theorem 1, the estimation error bound depends on $\Sigma_{X\widetilde{Y}} = X^T(Y - Y_S)$, and thus Y_S can be interpreted as the perturbations of $\Sigma_{X\widetilde{Y}}$. Since the magnitude of Y_S is no greater than that of Y, the tail labels will not overwhelm the estimation over W.

We next analyze the estimation error in the divide-and-conquer optimization method. Suppose the compact singular value decomposition (SVD) of W is $U_W \Sigma V_W^T$, where Σ is diagonal and contains k non-zero singular values of W, and $U_W \in \mathbb{R}^{d \times k}$ and $V_W \in \mathbb{R}^{L \times k}$ are the corresponding left and right singular vectors of W. We assume the true weight W_0 is (μ, k)-coherent, whose definition is given as below,

Definition 1. *Given $\mu_0(V_W) = \frac{d}{k}\max_{1\leq i\leq d}\|(V_W)_i\|^2$ and $\mu_1(W) = \sqrt{\frac{dL}{k}}\max_{i,j}|e_i^T U_W V_W^T e_j|$, for any $\mu > 0$, if $rank(W) = k$, $\max(\mu_0(V_W), \mu_0(V_W)) \leq \mu$ and $\mu_1(W) \leq \mu$, we call W is (μ, k)-coherent.*

We first invoke a lemma from [18] to show that column projection can produce an approximation that is nearly as good as a given rank-k target by sampling a number of columns proportional to the coherence.

Lemma 1. *[18]. Given a matrix $W \in \mathbb{R}^{d \times L}$ and a rank-k approximation $A \in \mathbb{R}^{d \times L}$, choose $m \geq ck\mu\log(L)\log(1/\delta)/\epsilon^2$, where c is a fixed positive constant, and let $\widetilde{W} \in \mathbb{R}^{d \times m}$ be a matrix of m columns of W sampled uniformly without replacement. Then, with probability at least $1 - \delta$,*

$$\|W - \widetilde{W}^{proj}\|_F \leq (1 + \epsilon)\|W - A\|_F, \tag{25}$$

where $\widetilde{W}^{proj} \in \mathbb{R}^{d \times L}$ is derived by projecting $\widetilde{W}$ onto the space of W.

Recall that the true weight W_0 has been partitioned into t sub-matrices $\{(W_0)_1, \cdots, (W_0)_t\}$ that are solved by optimizing distinct sub-problems in parallel and correspond to t estimated sub-matrices $\{(\widehat{W})_1, \cdots, (\widehat{W})_t\}$. We employ column projection to derive the approximation of W_0 with the help of $\widehat{W}$, and denote it as $\widehat{W}^{proj}$. The difference between W_0 and $\widehat{W}^{proj}$ can be bounded by the following theorem.

Theorem 2. *For $m \geq ck\mu\log(L)\log(1/\delta)/\epsilon^2$, where c is a fixed positive constant. The original problem has been divided into t sub-problems. If a basic optimization method yields the estimation error satisfying Theorem 1 for each sub-problem, then with probability at least $1 - \delta$, the estimation error in the divide-and-conquer method is bounded by*

$$\|W_0 - \widehat{W}^{proj}\|_F \leq \frac{2+\epsilon}{\sigma}\sum_{i=1}^{t}(2\|\Sigma_{X(\widetilde{Y})_i} - \Sigma_{XX}(W_0)_i\|_* - \lambda)$$

Proof. According to Lemma 1, with probability at least $1 - \delta$, the following inequality holds:

$$\|\widehat{W} - \widehat{W}^{proj}\|_F \leq (1 + \epsilon)\|\widehat{W} - W_0\|_F. \tag{26}$$

By adding $\|\widehat{W} - W_0\|_F$ to both sides of the above inequality, we get

$$\begin{aligned}(2 + \epsilon)\|\widehat{W} - W_0\|_F &\geq \|\widehat{W} - \widehat{W}^{proj}\|_F + \|\widehat{W} - W_0\|_F \\ &\geq \|W_0 - \widehat{W}^{proj}\|_F,\end{aligned}$$

which implies that

$$\|W_0 - \widehat{W}^{proj}\|_F \le (2+\epsilon)\|\widehat{W} - W_0\|_F$$
$$\le (2+\epsilon)\sum_{i=1}^{t} \|(W_0)_i - (\widehat{W})_i\|_F$$
$$\le \frac{2+\epsilon}{\sigma}\sum_{i=1}^{t}\left(2\|\Sigma_{X(\widetilde{Y})_i} - \Sigma_{XX}(W_0)_i\|_* - \lambda\right).$$

This ends the proof. □

Compared to the estimation error bound derived by applying a basic optimization method to estimate W_0 in Theorem 1, Theorem 2 exhibits an approximate recovery error with appropriate probability. It is instructive to note that the divide-and-conquer approach provides a controlled increase in error and a controlled decrease in the probability of success. Users can, therefore, adjust the optimization speed and accuracy.

5.2 Generalization Error

Given n multi-label points sampled i.i.d. from the distribution $\mathcal{Q} = \mathcal{X} \times \mathcal{Y}$, the proposed model aims to learn $(\widehat{W}, \widehat{H}) \in \mathcal{F} = \mathcal{W} \times \mathcal{H}$ by performing ERM as follows:

$$\inf_{\substack{rank(W)\le k \\ card(XH)\le s}} \widehat{\mathcal{L}}(W,H) = \frac{1}{n}\sum_{i=1}^{n} \ell(y_i, f(x_i, W, H)), \quad (27)$$

where $\widehat{\mathcal{L}}(W,H)$ is the empirical risk of the predictor (W,H). Our goal would be to show that $(\widehat{W}, \widehat{H})$ has good generalization properties, that is:

$$\mathcal{L}(\widehat{W}, \widehat{H}) \le \inf_{\substack{rank(W)\le k \\ card(XH)\le s}} \widehat{\mathcal{L}}(W,H) + \epsilon, \quad (28)$$

where $\mathcal{L}(W,H) = \mathbb{E}_{(x,y)}[\ell(y, f(x,W,H))]$ is the population risk of the predictor.

The Rademacher complexity is an effective way to measure the richness (complexity) of the function class $\mathcal{F}$, based on which the generalization error bound of the learning algorithm can easily be obtained using standard approaches [3].

DEFINITION 2. *Given a sample $S = \{x_1, \cdots, x_n\} \in \mathcal{X}^n$ and a real-valued function class $\mathcal{F}$ defined on a space $\mathcal{X}$, the empirical Rademacher complexity of $\mathcal{F}$ is defined as*

$$\widehat{R}_n(\mathcal{F}) = \mathbb{E}_\sigma\left[\sup_{f\in\mathcal{F}}\left|\frac{2}{n}\sum_{j=1}^{n}\sigma_j f(x_j)\right| x_1, \cdots, x_n\right],$$

where $\sigma = (\sigma_1, \cdots, \sigma_n)$ are independent uniform $\{\pm 1\}$-valued Rademacher random variables. The Rademacher complexity of $\mathcal{F}$ is

$$R_n(\mathcal{F}) = \mathbb{E}_s(\widehat{R}_n(\mathcal{F})) = \mathbb{E}_{x,\sigma}\left[\sup_{f\in\mathcal{F}}\left|\frac{2}{n}\sum_{j=1}^{n}\sigma_j f(x_j)\right|\right].$$

The Rademacher complexity of the proposed multi-label learning algorithm can thus be written as:

$$R_n(\mathcal{F}) = \frac{2}{n}\mathbb{E}_{x,\sigma}\left[\sup_{(W,H)\in\mathcal{F}}\sum_{i=1}^{n}\sigma_i\sum_{j=1}^{L} x_i(w_j + h_j)\right],$$

where w_j and h_j correspond the j-th columns of W and H, respectively, and together determine the predictor for the j-th label. We denote $\widetilde{x}$ as the weighted summarization $\sum_{i=1}^{n}\sigma_i x_i$. L copies of $\widetilde{x}$ are then stacked into $\widetilde{X}$. Hence, the multi-label Rademacher complexity can be simply written as

$$R_n(\mathcal{F}) = \frac{2}{n}\mathbb{E}_{x,\sigma}\left[\sup_{(W,H)\in\mathcal{F}}\langle W+H, \widetilde{X}\rangle\right], \quad (29)$$

whose upper bound can be revealed by the following theorem.

THEOREM 3. *The proposed algorithm learns W and H over n training points with L labels i.i.d. sampled from distribution $\mathcal{Q} = \mathcal{X}\times\mathcal{Y}$. For any data point, $\|x\|_2 \le \Lambda$. The learning algorithm encourages that $rank(W) \le k$ and $\|XH\|_1 \le \Omega$. $\|W\|_F$ is assumed to be upper bounded by Θ. Then, the Rademacher complexity of F is*

$$R_n(\mathcal{F}) \le 2\frac{\sqrt{nkL}\Theta\Lambda + L^{3/2}\Omega}{n}. \quad (30)$$

PROOF. According to Eq. (29), we have

$$R_n(\mathcal{F}) = \frac{2}{n}\mathbb{E}_{x,\sigma}\sup_{(W,H)\in\mathcal{F}}\left[\langle W+H, \widetilde{X}\rangle\right]$$
$$= \frac{2}{n}\mathbb{E}_{x,\sigma}\sup_{(W,H)\in\mathcal{F}}\left[\langle W, \widetilde{X}\rangle + \langle H, \widetilde{X}\rangle\right]$$
$$\le \frac{2}{n}\mathbb{E}_{x,\sigma}\sup_{(W,H)\in\mathcal{F}}\left[\|W\|_*\|\widetilde{X}\|_F + \|\widetilde{X}H\|_*\right]$$
$$\le \frac{2}{n}\mathbb{E}_{x,\sigma}\sup_{(W,H)\in\mathcal{F}}\left[\sqrt{k}\|W\|_F\|\widetilde{X}\|_F + \sqrt{L}\|\widetilde{X}H\|_1\right].$$

Then the following bounds can be easily obtained,

$$\mathbb{E}_{x,\sigma}\|\widetilde{X}\|_F^2 = \mathbb{E}_{x,\sigma}L\|\widetilde{x}\|_2^2 = \mathbb{E}_{x,\sigma}L[\sum_{i=1}^{n}\sigma_i x_i]_2^2 \le nL\Lambda^2,$$

and

$$\mathbb{E}_{x,\sigma}\|\widetilde{X}H\|_1 \le \mathbb{E}_x L\|XH\|_1 \le L\Omega.$$

This proves

$$R_n(\mathcal{F}) \le 2\frac{\sqrt{nkL}\Theta\Lambda + L^{3/2}\Omega}{n}. \quad (31)$$

□

To make conclusions of Theorem 3, consider a typical algorithm that neglects tail labels and attempts to minimize the trace norm of $W' = W + H$ for multi-label learning and with corresponding Rademacher complexity of $\mathcal{O}(\sqrt{rank(W')/n})$. As shown above, tail labels will significantly violate the low-rank assumption on W', and thus the large $rank(W')$ will lead to a greater Rademacher complexity. In contrast, the bound revealed in Theorem 3 is composed of two components corresponding to the low rank W and sparse XH, respectively. By separating the influence of tail labels, the rank of W (i.e., k) will be smaller. Although tail labels might influence multi-label learning, its significance on the bound can be dramatically decreased by constraining the sparsity of XH (i.e. $\|XH\|_1 \le \Omega$). Hence, decomposing the multi-label model into low-rank and sparse parts to handle tail labels is helpful for decreasing the Rademacher complexity of the function class, which in turn improves the generalization error bound of the algorithm.

Table 1: Statistics of the datasets used in experiments.

Dataset	#training	#test	#features	#labels	#card-label	#card-feature
Bibtex	4,880	2,515	1,836	159	2.40	68.74
Delicious-S	12, 920	3,185	500	983	19.03	18.17
Mediamill	30, 993	12,914	120	101	4.38	120.00
Wiki10	14, 146	6,616	101,938	30,938	18.64	673.45
Delicious-L	196,606	100,095	782,585	205,443	75.54	301.17
Amazon	490,449	153,025	135,909	670,091	5.45	75.68

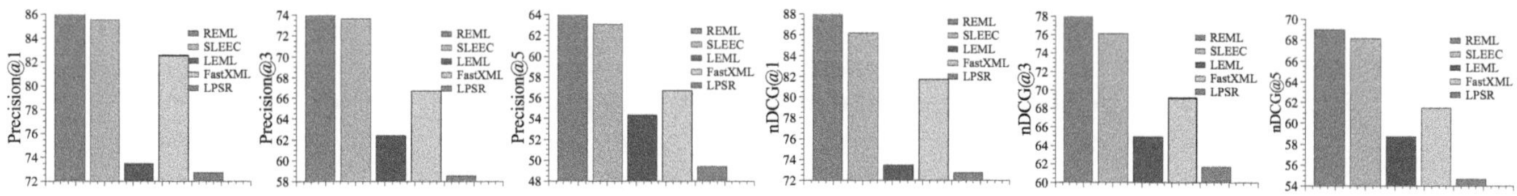

Figure 2: Top k precision and nDCG@k of multi-label learning algorithms on the Wiki10 dataset.

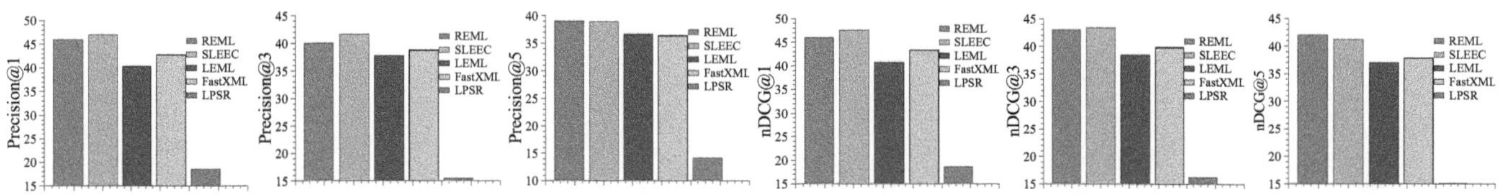

Figure 3: Top k precision and nDCG@k of multi-label learning algorithms on the Delicious-L dataset.

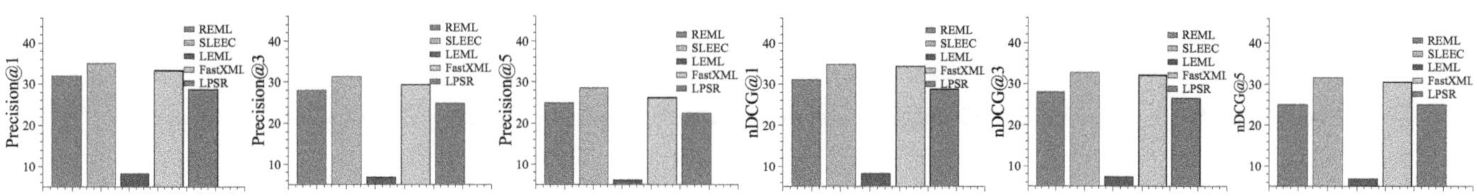

Figure 4: Top k precision and nDCG@k of multi-label learning algorithms on the Amazon dataset.

6. EXPERIMENTS

In this section, we evaluate the proposed algorithm on six benchmark multi-label datasets: *Bibtex*, *Delicious-S*, *Mediamill*, *Wiki10*, *Delicious-L* and *Amazon*. All these datasets were provided by [4], and have already been pre-separated into training and test sets. A summary of the statistics of datasets is shown in Table 1. #training is the number of training examples; #test is the number of test examples; #features is the number of features; #labels is the number of labels; #card-label is the average number of positive labels per example; #card-feature is the average number of nonzero features per example. The first three datasets with less than 1,000 labels are regarded as small datasets, while the last three are large datasets. We set the embedding dimension in REML algorithm as $0.8L$ for the small datasets, and 200 for the large datasets. Since the *Delicious-L* and *Amazon* datasets are rather large, in optimizing REML we divided the original problems into 2 and 4 subproblems respectively using the divide-and-conquer strategy. For the other datasets, we directly solve REML using the basic optimization method.

In experiments, we compared our proposed Robust Extreme Multi-label Learning (REML) algorithm with LEML [27], which is the state-of-the-art label embedding method based on the low-rank assumption over label matrix, and SLEEC [4], which is a recently developed method using the neighborhood embedding technique to handle tail labels. Other representative multi-label learning algorithms, such as CS [15], CPLST [8], ML-CSSP [5] and 1-vs-All [1], which are only applicable for small datasets, are included in comparison experiments as well.

We used two metrics to evaluate the multi-label classification performance in the experiments, both of which have been widely used in the fields of multi-label learning and ranking. Precision at k measures the fraction of true positive predictions in the top k scoring labels, given the predicted score vector $\widehat{y} \in \mathbb{R}^L$. nDCG at k measures the usefulness, or gain, of a label based on its position in the predicted label list. We refer readers to [19] for more detailed information.

6.1 Results on Large Datasets

We compare the classification performance of the proposed REML algorithm with those of leading methods on three large datasets: *Wiki10*, *Delicious-L* and *Amazon*. The classification results measured in Precision@k and nDCG@k are presented in Figures 2-4. It can be seen that REML stably performs better than LEML on these large datasets. For example, REML improves over LEML by as much as

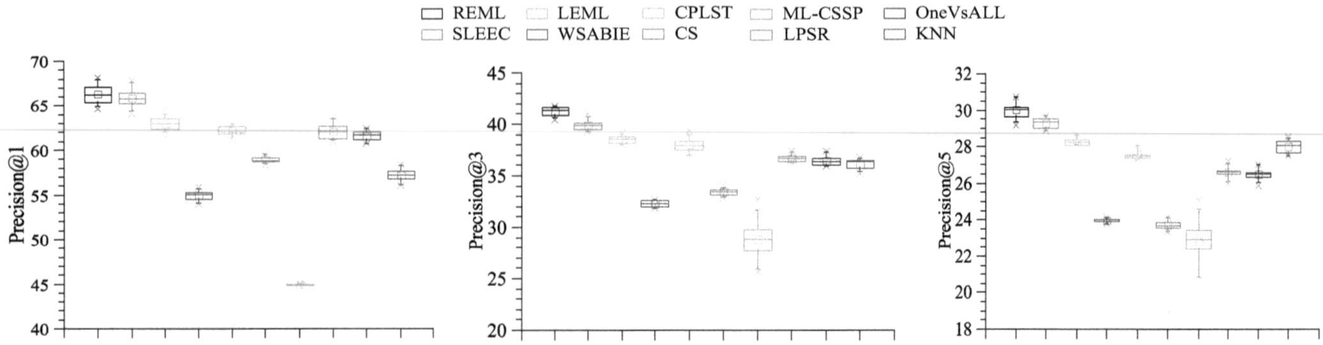

Figure 5: Top k precision of multi-label learning algorithms on the Bibtex dataset.

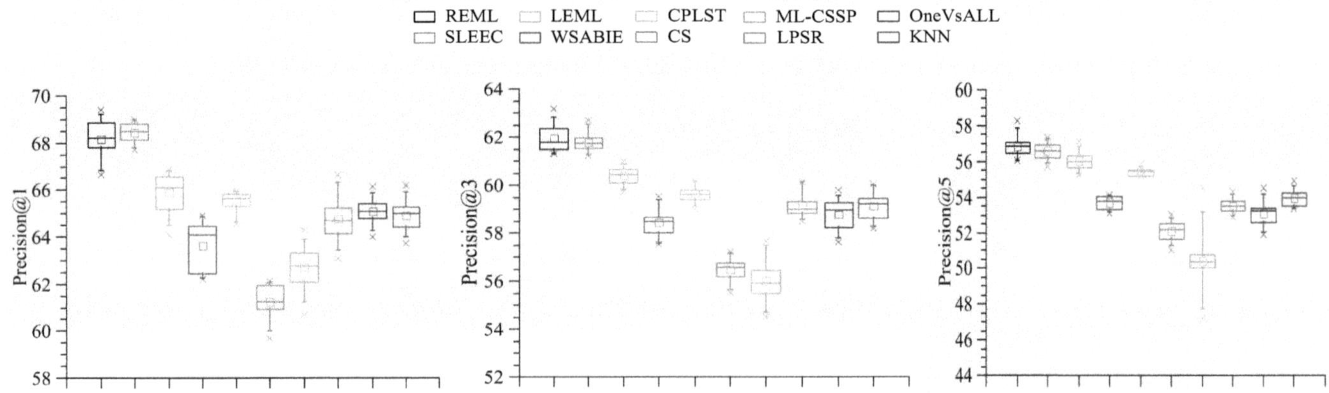

Figure 6: Top k precision of multi-label learning algorithms on the Delicious-S dataset.

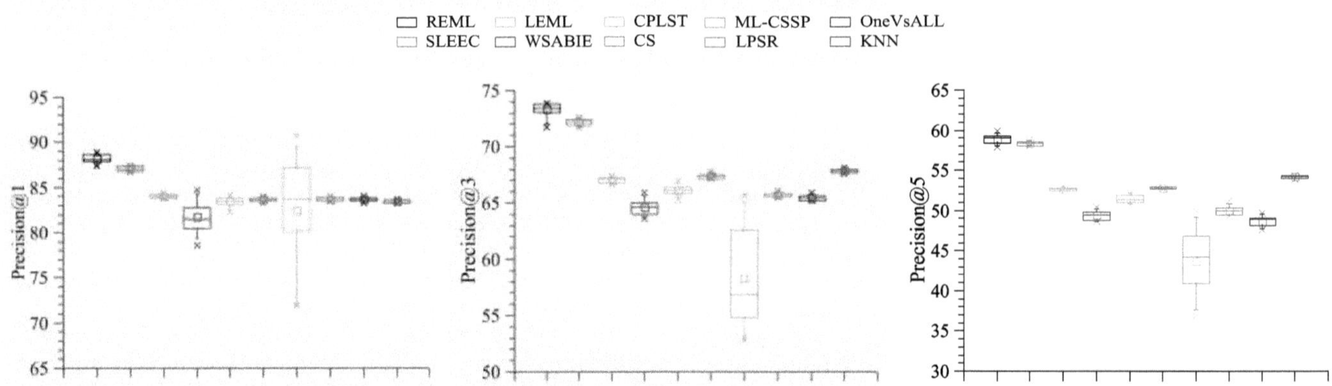

Figure 7: Top k precision of multi-label learning algorithms on the MediaMill dataset.

18% and 20% in terms of Precision@3 and nDCG@3 on the *Wiki10* dataset. This is because that the success of LEML mainly depends on the low-rank assumption, which tends to be violated on the large dataset with lots of tail labels (see Figure 1). REML provides an appropriate approach to preserve the validity of low-rank assumption by elegantly handling the tail labels as outliers. Hence, REML is able to achieve satisfactory classification results when faced with a number of tail labels, which is evidenced by its comparable performance with respect to the SLEEC method.

6.2 Results on Small Datasets

We next conduct multi-label classification over three small datasets: *Bibtex*, *Delicious-S*, *MediaMill*, which can be handled by more leading multi-label learning algorithms, such as CPLST and CS. The classification results in Precision@k are shown in Figures 5-7, while Table 2 presents the results in nDCG@k. Since the tail label problem is not acute on these small datasets, LEML and other comparison algorithms can achieve fine classification results. However, LEML is inferior to SLEEC, which uses neighborhood embedding to get rid of the influence of tail labels. Hence, SLEEC improves LEML

Table 2: nDCG@k of multi-label learning algorithms on the Bibtex, Delicious-S, Mediamill datasets.

Algorithm	Bibtex			Delicious-S			Mediamill		
	nDCG@1	nDCG@3	nDCG@5	nDCG@1	nDCG@3	nDCG@5	nDCG@1	nDCG@3	nDCG@5
KNN	57.81	52.36	54.57	64.80	60.71	57.02	82.59	75.62	72.76
OneVsAll	62.62	59.44	61.73	64.90	60.94	56.54	83.67	73.90	67.75
LPSR	62.98	57.11	58.76	64.46	60.47	56.19	83.65	74.12	69.12
ML-CSSP	56.86	52.54	54.81	63.96	59.07	54.86	83.21	72.67	65.05
CS	59.60	53.08	53.74	61.26	57.85	54.44	83.97	75.29	71.99
CPLST	61.99	57.66	59.71	65.65	61.52	58.00	83.79	74.44	70.49
WSABIE	55.03	50.26	52.33	63.67	59.47	56.37	79.86	72.51	69.31
LEML	63.10	58.84	61.06	64.96	61.80	58.42	83.09	75.23	71.96
SLEEC	64.49	59.90	62.29	67.41	62.46	59.02	86.61	80.04	77.71
REML	65.13	60.01	62.46	66.30	62.65	59.10	86.73	82.67	78.32

Table 3: Time and performance of REML with varying numbers of subproblems.

#subproblems	Time (s)	Precision@1	Precision@3	Precision@5	nDCG@1	nDCG@3	nDCG@5
1	3,739	86.17	74.30	64.37	88.09	78.44	69.38
2	2,190	84.07	72.70	62.92	85.26	76.52	68.94
5	1,495	82.80	71.20	62.78	83.79	75.47	66.23
8	923	78.45	69.53	58.76	81.92	72.07	64.42
10	764	76.68	67.75	56.68	80.01	70.30	63.32

by 4.8% in terms of Precision@1 on the *Bibtex* dataset and 7.8% in terms of Precision@3 on the *MediaMill* dataset. We suggest that the performance gap between LEML and SLEEC can be bridged by the REML algorithm, which is able to suppress the influence of tail labels and activate the low-rank assumption on multiple labels. On the *Delicious-S* dataset, REML is the closest competitor of SLEEC, while on the *Bibtex* dataset, REML takes a lead ahead of SLEEC in terms of Precision@5. This demonstrates that the low-rank assumption is powerful for processing multiple labels, and its performance can be further strengthened by carefully investigating the tail labels as outliers in the low-rank formulation.

6.3 Algorithm Analysis

We next perform experiments on the *Wiki10* dataset, to explore the trade-off between computation and accuracy when using divide-and-conquer technique to optimize the proposed REML algorithm (denoted as 'DC-REML'). Table 3 presents the time required to solve REML with different numbers of subproblems (i.e., t), and the corresponding classification results in Precision@k and nDCG@k. From this table, we find that DC-REML performs comparably to REML for smaller values of t, and the performance gradually degrades for larger subproblem number, which is consistent with the theoretical analysis in Section 5.1. Most importantly, DC-REML have significantly sped up REML by dividing the original problem into 5 subproblems, with an acceptable performance degradation of 4% relative to REML in terms of Precision@3. Hence, given the scalability provided by the divide-and-conquer optimization technique, we can flexibly manage the optimization accuracy and time cost in solving large-scale multi-label learning problems.

7. CONCLUSION

In this paper, we study the tail labels problem in multi-label learning, where the scarce labels associate with limited number of examples. To prevent the damage of tail labels on the low-rank assumption over multiple labels, we treat tail labels as outliers and develop a robust extreme multi-label learning algorithm. Divide-and-conquer approach applied to optimize the resulting objective function is beneficial for improving the scalability, and its advantages in balancing accuracy and computation have been theoretically demonstrated. We analyze the generalization error of the proposed algorithm, and suggest that it can be improved by the low-rank and sparse decomposition given tail labels. Experimental results on real-world datasets demonstrate the significance of investigating tail labels and the promising performance of the proposed algorithm.

Acknowledgment

We greatly thank anonymous reviewers for their positive support and constructive comments for improving the paper quality. The work was supported in part by Australian Research Council Projects FT-130101457, DP-140102164 and LE140100061, NSFC61375026 and 2015BAF15B00.

References

[1] S. V. N. V. B. Hariharan and M. Varma. Efficient max-margin multi-label classification with applications to zero-shot learning. *Machine Learning*, 2012.

[2] K. Balasubramanian and G. Lebanon. The landmark selection method for multiple output prediction. In *ICML*, 2012.

[3] P. L. Bartlett and S. Mendelson. Rademacher and gaussian complexities: Risk bounds and structural results. *The Journal of Machine Learning Research*, 3:463–482, 2003.

[4] K. Bhatia, H. Jain, P. Kar, M. Varma, and P. Jain. Sparse local embeddings for extreme multi-label classification. In *Advances in Neural Information Processing Systems*, pages 730–738, 2015.

[5] W. Bi and J. Kwok. Efficient multi-label classification with many labels. In *Proceedings of the 30th International Conference on Machine Learning (ICML-13)*, pages 405–413, 2013.

[6] W. Bi and J. T. Kwok. Multi-label classification on tree-and dag-structured hierarchies. In *Proceedings of the 28th International Conference on Machine Learning (ICML-11)*, pages 17–24, 2011.

[7] G. Carneiro, A. B. Chan, P. J. Moreno, and N. Vasconcelos. Supervised learning of semantic classes for image annotation and retrieval. *Pattern Analysis and Machine Intelligence, IEEE Transactions on*, 29(3):394–410, 2007.

[8] Y.-N. Chen and H.-T. Lin. Feature-aware label space dimension reduction for multi-label classification. In *Advances in Neural Information Processing Systems*, pages 1538–1546, 2012.

[9] M. M. Cisse, N. Usunier, T. Artieres, and P. Gallinari. Robust bloom filters for large multilabel classification tasks. In *Advances in Neural Information Processing Systems*, pages 1851–1859, 2013.

[10] K. Crammer and Y. Singer. A family of additive online algorithms for category ranking. *The Journal of Machine Learning Research*, 3:1025–1058, 2003.

[11] D. L. Donoho. De-noising by soft-thresholding. *Information Theory, IEEE Transactions on*, 41(3):613–627, 1995.

[12] A. Elisseeff and J. Weston. A kernel method for multi-labelled classification. In *Advances in neural information processing systems*, pages 681–687, 2001.

[13] W. Gao and Z.-H. Zhou. On the consistency of multi-label learning. *Artificial Intelligence*, 199:22–44, 2013.

[14] B. Hariharan, L. Zelnik-Manor, M. Varma, and S. Vishwanathan. Large scale max-margin multi-label classification with priors. In *Proceedings of the 27th International Conference on Machine Learning (ICML-10)*, pages 423–430, 2010.

[15] D. Hsu, S. Kakade, J. Langford, and T. Zhang. Multi-label prediction via compressed sensing. In *NIPS*, volume 22, pages 772–780, 2009.

[16] S.-J. Huang, Y. Yu, and Z.-H. Zhou. Multi-label hypothesis reuse. In *Proceedings of the 18th ACM SIGKDD international conference on Knowledge discovery and data mining*, pages 525–533. ACM, 2012.

[17] C.-L. Li and H.-T. Lin. Condensed filter tree for cost-sensitive multi-label classification. In *Proceedings of the 31st International Conference on Machine Learning (ICML-14)*, pages 423–431, 2014.

[18] L. W. Mackey, M. I. Jordan, and A. Talwalkar. Divide-and-conquer matrix factorization. In *Advances in Neural Information Processing Systems*, pages 1134–1142, 2011.

[19] C. D. Manning, P. Raghavan, H. Schütze, et al. *Introduction to information retrieval*, volume 1. Cambridge university press Cambridge, 2008.

[20] R. E. Schapire and Y. Singer. Boostexter: A boosting-based system for text categorization. *Machine learning*, 39(2-3):135–168, 2000.

[21] E. Spyromitros, G. Tsoumakas, and I. Vlahavas. An empirical study of lazy multilabel classification algorithms. In *Artificial Intelligence: Theories, Models and Applications*, pages 401–406. Springer, 2008.

[22] L. Sun, S. Ji, and J. Ye. Hypergraph spectral learning for multi-label classification. In *Proceedings of the 14th ACM SIGKDD international conference on Knowledge discovery and data mining*, pages 668–676. ACM, 2008.

[23] F. Tai and H.-T. Lin. Multilabel classification with principal label space transformation. *Neural Computation*, 24(9):2508–2542, 2012.

[24] G. Tsoumakas, I. Katakis, and I. Vlahavas. Mining multi-label data. In *Data mining and knowledge discovery handbook*, pages 667–685. Springer, 2010.

[25] C. Vens, J. Struyf, L. Schietgat, S. Džeroski, and H. Blockeel. Decision trees for hierarchical multi-label classification. *Machine Learning*, 73(2):185–214, 2008.

[26] R. Yan, J. Tesic, and J. R. Smith. Model-shared subspace boosting for multi-label classification. In *Proceedings of the 13th ACM SIGKDD international conference on Knowledge discovery and data mining*, pages 834–843. ACM, 2007.

[27] H.-F. Yu, P. Jain, and I. S. Dhillon. Large-scale multi-label learning with missing labels. In *Proceedings of the twenty-first international conference on Machine learning*, 2014.

[28] M.-L. Zhang and K. Zhang. Multi-label learning by exploiting label dependency. In *Proceedings of the 16th ACM SIGKDD international conference on Knowledge discovery and data mining*, pages 999–1008. ACM, 2010.

[29] M.-L. Zhang and Z.-H. Zhou. Multilabel neural networks with applications to functional genomics and text categorization. *Knowledge and Data Engineering, IEEE Transactions on*, 18(10):1338–1351, 2006.

[30] M.-L. Zhang and Z.-H. Zhou. Ml-knn: A lazy learning approach to multi-label learning. *Pattern recognition*, 40(7):2038–2048, 2007.

[31] M.-L. Zhang and Z.-H. Zhou. A review on multi-label learning algorithms. *Knowledge and Data Engineering, IEEE Transactions on*, 26(8):1819–1837, 2014.

[32] Y. Zhang and J. G. Schneider. Multi-label output codes using canonical correlation analysis. In *International Conference on Artificial Intelligence and Statistics*, pages 873–882, 2011.

Taxi Driving Behavior Analysis in Latent Vehicle-to-Vehicle Networks: A Social Influence Perspective

Tong Xu[1], Hengshu Zhu[2], Xiangyu Zhao[1], Qi Liu[1]
Hao Zhong[3], Enhong Chen[1], Hui Xiong[3]

[1] University of Science and Technology of China
{tongxu, zxy1105}@mail.ustc.edu.cn, {qiliuql, cheneh}@ustc.edu.cn

[2] Baidu Research-Big Data Lab
zhuhengshu@baidu.com

[3] Rutgers, the State University of New Jersey
{h.zhong31, hxiong}@rutgers.edu

ABSTRACT

With recent advances in mobile and sensor technologies, a large amount of efforts have been made on developing intelligent applications for taxi drivers, which provide beneficial guide and opportunity to improve the profit and work efficiency. However, limited scopes focus on the latent *social interaction* within cab drivers, and corresponding *social propagation* scheme to share driving behaviors has been largely ignored. To that end, in this paper, we propose a comprehensive study to reveal how the social propagation affects for better prediction of cab drivers' future behaviors. To be specific, we first investigate the correlation between drivers' skills and their mutual interactions in the latent vehicle-to-vehicle network, which intuitively indicates the effects of social influences. Along this line, by leveraging the classic *social influence theory*, we develop a two-stage framework for quantitatively revealing the latent *driving pattern propagation* within taxi drivers. Comprehensive experiments on a real-word data set collected from the New York City clearly validate the effectiveness of our proposed framework on predicting future taxi driving behaviors, which also support the hypothesis that social factors indeed improve the predictability of driving behaviors.

Keywords

Mobile Data Mining, Social Influence, Taxi Trajectories

1. INTRODUCTION

Recent years have witnessed the growing interests on data-driven technologies for developing new paradigms of taxi business. On the one hand, the dramatic expansion of urban areas results in the urge demand of efficient taxi services, which cannot be solved by simply increasing the amount of cabs or drivers. On the other hand, thanks to the rapid development of wireless sensor technologies in mobile environments, such as GPS, Wi-Fi and RFID, the abundant real-time trajectories could be promptly collected [40]. Therefore, through the analysis of trajectory data from taxi drivers, a variety of intelligent services can be enabled, which will not only lead to the improvement of work efficiency and profit of taxi drivers [10], but also help to strike a balance between the needs of taxi drivers and passengers [33].

In the literature, most of the research efforts on taxi business focus on extracting effective transportation patterns, e.g., the fastest driving route like [32] and [38], sequence of pick-up points [23] or customers within the shortest driving distance [10]. However, although the above works can effectively enhance taxi business, they may still suffer some defects due to the ignorance of drivers' behaviors. First, the case-by-case recommendation are sensitive to the context, thus frequent update is required, which results in heavy burden of computation. Second, as drivers tend to be attracted by popular routes, it will be difficult to distribute the cabs for keeping regional balances. Last but not least, predictability of taxi route is still limited as individual factors of taxi drivers have been largely ignored, i.e., neither the self-learning ability, nor the social sharing scheme are considered in the system design.

Indeed, though related techniques could highly support the intellectual services, cab drivers could also rely on themselves to well fit the taxi business. For the experienced drivers who are sensitive to the route and rules, they could effectively summarize the patterns and regulate the lines. At the same time, for those inexperienced ones, thanks to rapid development of intelligent mobile devices and social network services (SNS), not only offline (e.g., refueling or lunching) but also online (e.g., forum, or twitter) gatherings are now available, where driving experience could be shared within drivers, which results in the "*social propagation*" of driving behaviors. For instance, an motivating example below, which summarizes a real post in a online taxi forum [1], could intuitively illustrate this phenomenon.

A Motivating Story. *A new taxi driver, who was unfamiliar with the traffic in New York City, posted a question*

[1] http://www.nycitycab.com/forum/Replies.aspx?postid=649

KDD '16, August 13-17, 2016, San Francisco, CA, USA

DOI: http://dx.doi.org/10.1145/2939672.2939799

in online forum to ask for sharing driving experience. Then, an experienced driver replied with several detailed suggestions on how to drive in Manhattan to avoid the rush hour or earn more tips. Based on these recommended patterns, the new driver could better adjust his driving trajectory to improve the work efficiency.

The true story above indicates that social interactions existing to influence drivers' driving behaviors. Intuitively, if we treat taxi drivers as "social agent" in the mobile social networks, and simulate how the "social propagation" scheme functions to interpret their future behaviors, taxi route will be more predictable, and further social-oriented taxi services, e.g., social-based "tutor" or pattern recommendations could be effectively conducted. Unfortunately, due to the constraint of user privacy, there is no exposed signal for social interactions to be observed. Thus, techniques to reveal latent connections within taxi drivers are required.

To deal with this task, in this paper, we aim at exploring latent vehicle-to-vehicle networks among taxi drivers based on the analysis of their driving behaviors. To be specific, we propose a two-stage framework to capture the latent propagation of driving behaviors among taxi drivers. We assume that the increasing proportion of certain behavior patterns may be caused by stronger influence, and vice versa. Therefore, sequential driving behaviors with integrating social propagation could be formulated as time series and solved as partial ranking tasks. Based on the framework, we could better model the historical driving behaviors to predict their future trends, and also discover the latent social connections within taxi drivers. To the best of our knowledge, we are the first to investigate the impact of social factors on taxi driving patterns to explain drivers' behaviors.

Finally, extensive experiments are conducted on a real-world data set collected from the New York City. The experimental results clearly verify that our framework can better predict driving behaviors of taxi drivers with dramatic margin outperforming the baselines, which validates the hypothesis that social factors indeed affect the driving pattern decisions, and also demonstrates the capability of social analytics in intelligent taxi services.

Overview. The rest of this paper is organized as follows. Section 2 further illustrates the motivation with some intuitive statistics. In Section 3, we propose the novel framework for driving behavior analysis with integrating social factors. Afterwards, we comprehensively evaluate the performances in Section 4, and then conduct some further discussion in Section 5. Related works are summarized in Section 6. Finally, in Section 7, we conclude the paper.

2. DOES "SOCIAL FACTORS" AFFECT TAXI DRIVERS?

As we propose the idea of driving behavior propagation within cab drivers, in this section, we will intuitively discuss the effects of social propagation with related statistical analysis to further support our motivation.

2.1 Data Set Description

We conduct our study on a real-world data set collected from the taxi driving transactions in New York City during the whole year of 2013, which is provided by NYC Taxi and Limousine Commission (NYC TLC). This is a large-scale data set that totally consists of more than 169 million transaction records of 43,191 drivers in 14,144 cabs. For each transaction, we have the spatial and temporal information for both pick-up and drop-off, as well as fares including tip and toll. The statistical details are shown in Table 1.

Table 1: Data Set Description

	Data Statistic
Number of Taxis	14,144
Number of Drivers	43,191
Average Num. of Transactions	3,928.86
Average Num. of Passengers	1.68
Average Trip Time	15.05 min
Average Trip Distance	8.86 miles
Average Trip Fare	$15.39

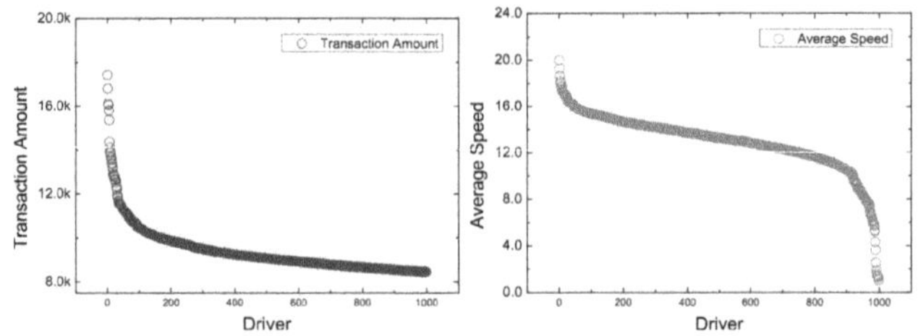

(a) (b)

Figure 1: The distribution of transaction amount and average driving speed of taxi drivers.

As mentioned above that usually there is no explicit signal of social interactions. In the following sections, we will conduct our two-stage framework to reveal the latent social connections via simulating the driving behavior propagation. However, for the intuitive statistics here, we choose the heuristic method which is widely used in *"ephemeral social networks"* study such as [31] and [39], i.e., co-occurrences lead connections, and the frequency indicates the strength. Along this line, if two cabs stop at the same place for a relatively long time (e.g., more than 10 minutes), we guess that a short-term communication may occur, which probably results in social interactions. Therefore, to be the same with the prior arts like [39], an undirected edge will be built between two drivers if long-time co-parking happened, and the frequency will be counted as the link strength.

2.2 Social Effects on Taxi Driver Skill

With the above *"ephemeral vehicle-to-vehicle networks"*, we could now discuss about the social effects on taxi drivers. In details, two questions remain to be answered: 1) if drivers with similar skills hold stronger connections, and 2) if drivers with better skills hold stronger influences. To measure cor-

Table 2: Correlations between social link strength and driving skill of taxi drivers.

Term	Transactions		Speed		Income	
3-4 Driver	T10	R10	T10	R10	T10	R10
Correlation	0.093	0.018	0.177	0.011	0.094	0.021
Significant*	7	0	9	3	7	2
Positive	0	5	0	2	1	3

*P-Value<0.05

Table 3: Mathematical Notations

Symbol	Description
$\mathbf{U} = \{u_i\}$	the set of taxi drivers
w_{ij}	social connection strength from u_i to u_j
$\mathbf{s}_i^t$	pattern frequency vector of u_i in time t
$s_{i,k}^t$	proportion of k-th pattern in time t
$p_{i,k}^t$	social influence of k-th pattern in time t
N_i	social neighbors of driver u_i
$\mathbf{R}_i^t$	the pattern of u_i that raise in time t
$\mathbf{D}_i^t$	the pattern of u_i that decrease in time t

relations of driving skills, here we choose three evaluation metrics, i.e., the *transaction amount*, the *average driving speed* and the *total income*, to study on this issue. Particularly, we choose these three metrics since they can be regarded as the representative symbols of work effectiveness (i.e., more business), efficiency (i.e., faster trip) and profit (higher benefits). Specifically, the distributions of further two metrics are shown in Figure 1, while the curve for total income is quite similar with the first one.

For better understand the correlation between skill level and social influence, here for each evaluation metric, the top 10 drivers are ranked, compared with other 10 randomly selected drivers. Afterwards, for each driver, we list his/her "friends" with two values: *connection strength* and *skill similarity* (absolute value of difference), and then measure correlation between them. Also, we have *P-Value* presents the significance of correlation. Besides, those with positive coefficients, i.e., strong social connection leads to higher difference, are individually listed as they may violate the assumption that social effects encourage similar driving patterns.

The statistical results are shown in Table 2, in which "T10" presents the top 10 drivers and "R10" indicates the random ones for comparison. For each group, we list average correlation, count of significant correlations, and count of positive correlations. Expectedly, we find that for all the three metrics, the top-ranked drivers reflect more significant correlation, and further almost no positive correlation occur. As random selected drivers reflect no significant correlation between skill level and social connections, "homogeneity" may fail to explain this phenomenon. Thus, we may draw the conclusion that skilled drivers may act as the influential nodes to share expertise, and stronger connections lead to better skills via "social learning" scheme, which further supports our motivation.

3. SIMULATING DRIVING BEHAVIORS WITH SOCIAL PROPAGATION

As significance of social effects have been revealed, in this section, we will introduce our two-stage framework to capture the driving behavior propagation within taxi drivers, in which the technical solution for social influence modeling and optimization task will be explained in detail.

3.1 Preliminary and Problem Statement

In this paper, we focus on the social interaction which affects the driving behaviors. Thus, some other factors, e.g., the profit, traffic flow or festivals that may also influence the routes will be temporally ignored, and more complicated framework will be studied in future work.

Though we intuitively discover the social factors with introducing heuristic "ephemeral vehicle-to-vehicle networks", however, it could hardly summarize the complete social interactions due to the following reasons. First, co-occurrences do not necessarily means face-to-face communication, thus they are not adequate clues to reveal latent social connections. Second, occasional co-occurrences are indeed events of small probability ($\ll 1\%$), while majority of interactions might be neglected. To deal with these challenges, in this section, we target at formulating social propagation of driving behaviors within taxi drivers, and then the social interactions could be revealed conversely.

Firstly, to describe the social effects on driving behaviors, we define the vector $\mathbf{s_i}$ to present the driving behaviors of a certain taxi driver u_i, in which each element corresponds to a kind of driving patterns. Specially, each pattern here will be described as a triple contains the information about pick-up area, drop-off area and pick-up time period, such as (*Central Park, JFK Airport, 10:00AM-11:00AM*). The details of extracting these patterns will be introduced in experimental part. Then, we have $s_{i,k}$ to indicate the proportion of k-th pattern in u_i's driving behaviors, and definitely, the vector is normalized by $\sum_k s_{i,k} = 1$.

Further, to integrate social factors, we assume that the driving behaviors could be represented as temporal consequences, and in each round, the effects of social propagation will be reflected by the fluctuation in next round. Thus, timestamp information should be introduced into the driving behavior vectors as $\mathbf{s_i^t}$, which indicates the driving behavior of driver u_i in t-th round. And intuitively, if we could accurately reveal the latent social connections, we will precisely predict drivers' behavior in the future, i.e., $\mathbf{\Delta s_i^{t+1}}$ will be well estimated.

At the same time, to describe the social factors within taxi drivers, i.e., to draw the latent vehicle-to-vehicle network, similar with traditional social network, we introduce e_{ij} to present the edge from u_i to u_j, and correspondingly, w_{ij} indicates the edge weight, or the influential strength, which will be estimated during the training stage. What should be noted is that the social network here is asymmetric and all edges are directional. Afterwards, we have N_i to present the entire social "neighbors" of driver u_i. Furthermore, different from the traditional social propagation problems, to integrate drivers' own opinion into this framework, here we treat each driver as *neighbor of itself*, i.e., $u_i \in N_i$, and then introduce w_{ii} to measure how the drivers insist their own habits. Obviously, higher w_{ii} indicates less propagation and more succession, and vice versa.

Along this line, finally, we could now formally define our research problem as "*social-driven behavior prediction*" as a typical time series analysis as follows.

Problem Statement. *Given the target group of taxi drivers* $\mathbf{U}$, *and for each* $u_i \in \mathbf{U}$, *we have corresponding pattern vectors* $\mathbf{s_i^t}$ *during the time period* $t = 1, 2, ..., T$. *The problem of driving behavior prediction is to accurately reveal weighted social connections* w_{ij} *within each pair of drivers* u_i *and* u_j, *then the fluctuation of driving behavior vector* $\mathbf{\Delta s_i^{T+1}}$ *in* $T+1$ *could be estimated.*

Technical details to solve the problem will be introduced in following subsections, and the mathematical notations used throughout this paper are summarized in Table 3.

3.2 Loss Function for Behavior Prediction

With problem defined and notations summarized, now we turn to formulate the behavior prediction task in detail. Firstly, to describe the social propagation, for each pattern, we have the accumulated **social influence** $p_{i,k}^t$ of k-th pattern to driver u_i, while the technical solution will be explained in next subsection.

As we assume that fluctuation of driving behavior vectors is due to the social propagation within cab drivers, specially, for a certain cab driver i_i, if k-th pattern is holding an increasing proportion in round $T+1$, we conclude that the social influence $p_{i,k}^t$ could be relatively higher, and vice versa. Following this assumption, as it could be difficult to exactly estimate the value of $s_{i,k}^{T+1}$, here to ease the modeling, we target at predicting whether $s_{i,k}^{T+1}$ will increase or decrease in the $T+1$ round, and how the increment $\Delta s_{i,k}^{T+1}$ ranks among all the patterns, which may reflect the rank of corresponding social influence.

Therefore, the problem defined above could be intuitively transformed as a partial ranking problem, i.e., rank $\Delta s_{i,k}^{t+1}$ and label the top results in the list as increased. Here, we define the set of patterns whose frequency are raised in time t as $\mathbf{R}_i^t$, i.e., $\forall r \in \mathbf{R}_i^t, \Delta s_{i,r}^{t+1} = s_{i,r}^{t+1} - s_{i,r}^t > 0$. Similarly, $\mathbf{D}_i^t$ presents set of decreased ones. Then, for each pair $\forall \langle r, d\rangle_{i,t}$ where $r \in \mathbf{R}_i^t$ and $d \in \mathbf{D}_i^t$, the fluctuation is due to the pairwise ranking of corresponding social influence, i.e., $p_{i,d}^t < p_{i,r}^t$.

With the assumption above, finally, we realize that if we could accurately reveal the latent social interactions, we could achieve the optimal ranking results of social influence $\mathbf{p_i^t}$. Correspondingly, optimization of the ranking task will leads to the solution of social connections. Thus, the task of learning latent social connections w_{ij} will be summarized as a pairwise ranking problem as follows:

Ranking Objective. *Finding appropriate w_{ij}, so that for $\forall\langle r, d\rangle_{i,t}$ where $r \in \mathbf{R}_i^t$, we will have $p_{i,d}^t < p_{i,r}^t$.*

To deal with this task, we formulate the loss function of pairwise ranking problem as follows:

$$min_w \mathcal{F}(w) = \sum_{i,t} \sum_{r\in\mathbf{R}_i^t, d\in\mathbf{D}_i^t} h(p_{i,d}^t - p_{i,r}^t), \tag{1}$$

where $h(\gamma_{rd})$ is a loss function to assign a non-negative penalty according to the difference of social influence $\gamma_{rd} = p_{i,d}^t - p_{i,r}^t$. Usually, we have the penalty $h(\gamma_{rd}) = 0$ when $p_{i,d}^t \le p_{i,r}^t$. While for $p_{i,d}^t > p_{i,r}^t$, we have $h(\gamma_{rd}) > 0$ as loss. To ease the computation, here we utilize the squared loss function as follow:

$$h(x) = \max\{x, b\}^2. \tag{2}$$

In this framework, we have a soft margin parameter b to tolerate a small error. To ease the computation, here we simply treat $b = 0$, and $h(x)$ could be rewritten as

$$\sum_{r\in\mathbf{R}_i^t, d\in\mathbf{D}_i^t} h(p_{i,d}^t - p_{i,r}^t) = \sum_{r,d:p_{i,d}^t > p_{i,r}^t} (p_{i,d}^t - p_{i,r}^t)^2. \tag{3}$$

3.3 Social Propagation Simulation

As ranking objective is proposed, now we turn to formulate the *social influence* within taxi drivers. Traditionally, to simulate the propagation, or so-called "social influence" process, classic models like Independent Cascade or Linear Threshold model [16] might be selected, in which each nodes usually has only two statuses, i.e., activated or inactivated. However, in our task, the proportion of a certain driving pattern may never jump from 0 to 1 sharply. Thus, here we adapt the Steady State Spread (SSS) model [1] to simulate the social propagation, in which each node holds its own *activating probability*. Then, in each round, all the nodes (but not only activated nodes in IC model) attempt influence their neighbors, and then influence will be measured not only by strength of social connections, but also their activating probabilities. With adapting the formulation by introducing pattern proportion $s_{I,k}^t$ instead of activating probability, we have the equation as follow:

$$p_{i,k}^t = 1 - \prod_{j\in N_i} (1 - w_{ji} \cdot \delta_{i,j,k}^{t-1}), \tag{4}$$

For $\delta_{i,j,k}^{t-1}$, we design it to present pairwise influential probability sensitive to the pattern, which is different with the overall social connection strength w_{ji}. Similar with the Sigmoid function, we have the formulation as follow:

$$\delta_{i,j,k}^t = \frac{1}{1 + e^{-(s_{j,k}^t - s_{i,k}^t)}}. \tag{5}$$

Based on the formulation, $\delta_{i,j,k}^{t-1}$ will be controlled within [0,1], and the relation between $s_{j,k}^t$ and $s_{i,k}^t$ will affect the influence, i.e., if $s_{j,k}^t > s_{i,k}^t$, we will have $\delta_{i,j,k}^{t-1}$ near 1 to enhance the influence, while for $s_{j,k}^t < s_{i,k}^t$, the pairwise influence will be impaired.

3.4 Optimization Task

As all the formulations established, we could now optimize the loss function Equation 1 to estimate latent social factors w_{ij}. To be specific, we approach the latent social factors w_{ji} by first deriving the gradient of $\mathcal{F}(w)$ with respect to w_{ji}, and then use a gradient based optimization method to find proper $\{w\}$ that minimize $\mathcal{F}(w)$. Specially, as defining $\gamma_{rd} = p_{i,d}^t - p_{i,r}^t$, we have the derivative as follow:

$$\frac{\partial\mathcal{F}(w)}{\partial w_{ji}} = \sum_t \sum_{r\in\mathbf{R}_i^t, d\in\mathbf{D}_i^t} \frac{\partial h(\gamma_{rd})}{\partial\gamma_{rd}} \left(\frac{\partial p_{i,d}^t}{\partial w_{ji}} - \frac{\partial p_{i,r}^t}{\partial w_{ji}}\right), \tag{6}$$

where $h'(x)$ could be easily achieved as derivation of square function, while for the social influence model, we have:

$$\frac{\partial p_{i,k}^t}{\partial w_{ji}} = \prod_{l\in N_i^t, l\neq j} (1 - w_{li} \cdot \delta_{i,l,k}^{t-1}) \cdot \delta_{i,j,k}^{t-1}. \tag{7}$$

According to the formulations, finally gradient descent methods could be exploited to deal with the optimization task.

3.5 Two-stage Framework

Based on the formulations above, we could now formally define our two-stage framework as follows.

Training Stage. Given a group of taxi drivers $\mathbf{U} = \{u_i\}$ as well as their pattern vectors $\mathbf{s_i^t}$ during the time period $t = 1, 2, ..., T$, in the training stage, we aim at inferring the latent social connections $\{w_{ij}\}$ within drivers, which achieve the best explanation for the ranking of driving behavior vector fluctuation $\mathbf{\Delta s_i^{T+1}}$.

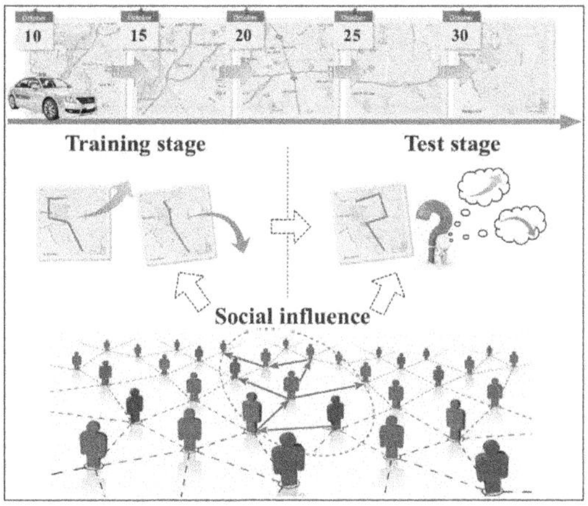

Figure 2: Two-stage framework.

Test Stage. After obtaining the latent connections $\{w_{ij}\}$ in the training stage, in the test stage, given the taxi drivers group $\mathbf{U} = \{u_i\}$ with their pattern vectors $\mathbf{s}_i^t$ during the certain **p-time lag** as $t = T - p + 1, ..., T - 1, T$, we aim at predicting the driving behavior vector fluctuation $\mathbf{\Delta s_i^{T+1}}$ with accurate sign and ranking.

With these definitions, for the training stage, we target at optimizing the Equation 1 to achieve the latent social connections w_{ij}. For the test stage, we could directly calculate $p^t_{i,k}$ according to Equation 4 for each pattern of driver u_i, and then rank the propagation to estimate the ranking of driving pattern proportions, or classify the increment sign. According to the framework, social interactions will be discovered and social propagation scheme will be simulated, which will be beneficial for further discussion on intellectual taxi services.

Based on the definitions above, in training stage, latent social connections will be revealed to support the social-driven behavior prediction task in test stage. The data flow of two-stage framework is summarized in Figure 2.

4. EXPERIMENTS: SOCIAL INFLUENCE INDEED AFFECTS

To verify our hypothesis that social factors may affect the driving behaviors of taxi drivers, which result in the change of pattern frequency, in this section, we conduct extensive experiments on a real-world data set. And further, some related discussion will be conducted.

4.1 Experimental Setup

Here, we introduce the data set pre-processing and baseline algorithms for evaluation.

4.1.1 Data Set Pre-processing

Similar with the statistical analysis in pre-study, our experiments were conducted on the real-world taxi data set collected from New York City. To generalize the driving patterns, we first clustered all the pick-up and drop-off locations in the historical transaction records. Specially, we conducted a bottom-up hierarchial with minimum variance criterion until only 30 clusters were left (indeed, the number of zones doesn't disturb the results if around 20-50). The

Figure 3: Clustering results of New York City Locations.

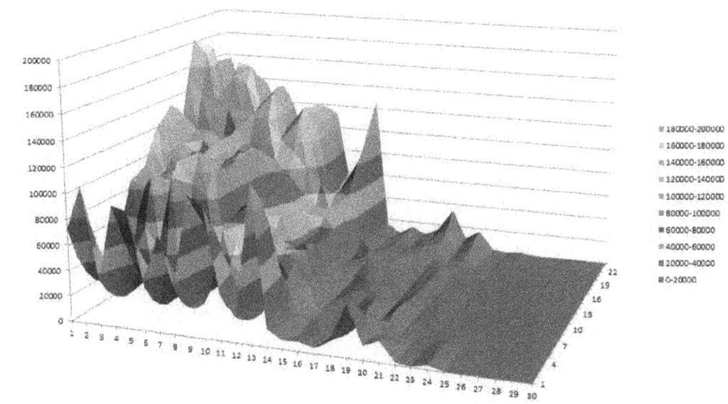

Figure 4: Pattern frequency in each hour, in which X-axis presents the label of area, and Y-axis presents the hour.

clustering results are shown in Figure 3. Interestingly, we find some landmarks have been distinguished, such as the JFK Airport (i.e., the orange part in the southeastern corner) and EWR Airport (i.e., the brownish-green part in the west), as well as some key regions in Manhattan, e.g., the red region around the Central Park, and the pale green in Lower Manhattan representing the Wall Street.

After location clustering, we counted pattern frequency in each hour with respect to different pick-up locations, which is shown in Figure 4. We could find except for the check out time around 18:00 PM, in Manhattan downtown (e.g., area No. 8 and 13), the peak time usually happen around midnight when passengers finish their night life. But for the suburb area (e.g., area No. 3 and 6), the peak time happen around 8:00 AM for those who take taxi for work. Also, only a few areas attract most of the taxi transactions, while some other areas, especially for area No. 25-30, may attract even completely no transactions.

Furthermore, we generalized the patterns by dividing the time period into every 2 hours, e.g., 7:00 AM to 9:00 AM, then 24 hours lead to 12 intervals. Figure 5 shows the most frequent patterns appear around 8:00 AM, which is the peak of the morning rush hour. We can see many passengers take taxi from WTC station to the downtown for work, or return

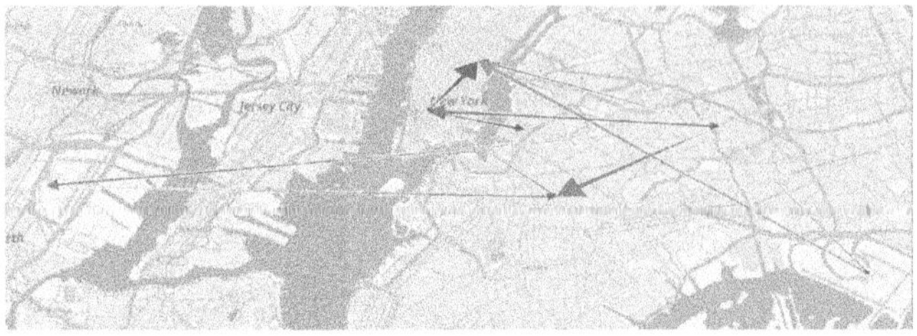

Figure 5: Frequent patterns in NYC taxi driving around 8:00 AM

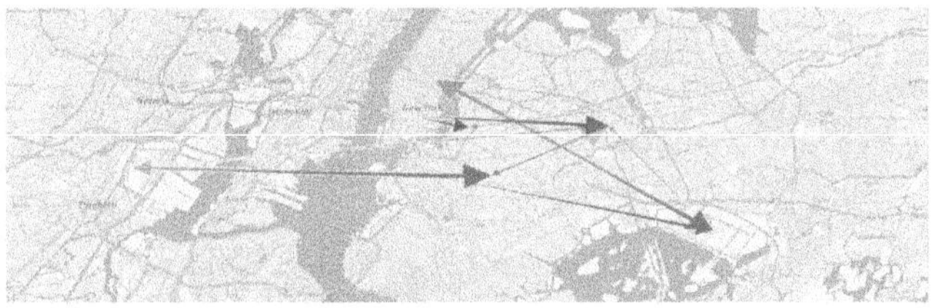

Figure 6: Frequent patterns in NYC taxi driving around 6:00 PM

home from JFK Airport after the long-time international flight. While on the contrary, in Figure 6, which indicates the most frequent patterns around 6:00 PM, passengers return home in Queens and Brooklyn after one day's work. As Figure 4 shows, due to the imbalance distribution of transaction amount with respect to different areas, only the most frequent patterns are considered in order to reduce the interference of data sparsity. The sensitiveness of pattern amount will be discussed in Section 4.3.

4.1.2 Evaluating Metrics

In this paper, we target at discussing the social factors within taxi drivers which may affect their driving behaviors. As mentioned above, we assume that accurate estimation of social propagation leads to better explanation of future driving behaviors. Thus, here we indirectly validate the prediction results of driving pattern fluctuation to measure the performance of our framework.

As mentioned in Section 3.5, to predict the pattern change, we indeed have two tasks, i.e., the **binary classification** to distinguish the sign (positive / negative) of pattern increment, and then **ranking** the patterns with respect to their increments. For each task, related metrics will be selected to measure the performance. For the binary classification task, typically, we select the common used **Precision** and **Recall** rates for validation.

For the ranking task, similar with the state-of-the-art learning to rank problems, **NDCG** and **MAP** are selected. Specially, we get NDCG following the equation $\frac{DCG}{iDCG}$, in which $iDCG$ presents the ideal results and DCG will be calculated based on the formulation as below:

$$DCG = \sum_{i} \frac{2^{r_i} - 1}{\log(1+i)}, \tag{8}$$

where r_i denotes the relevance of result, which is set as reversal order in our experiments. Furthermore, when calculating **MAP**, we treat the top 10 patterns in ground truths as *"expected results"*, and the score will be calculated based on their ranks in the result list.

Table 4: Overall Performance

	SPC	Ave	Pop	VAR
NDCG	0.3502	0.1603	0.2211	**0.3619**
Improve (%)	-	+118.46	+58.39	-3.23
P-Value	-	0.000	0.000	0.755
MAP@10	**0.2128**	0.0254	0.1042	0.2018
Improve (%)	-	+737.79	+104.22	+5.45
P-Value	-	0.000	0.000	0.472
Precision	**0.1579**	0.0134	0.0474	0.0192
Improve (%)	-	+1078.35	+233.12	+722.39
P-Value	-	0.000	0.000	0.000
Recall	**0.6892**	0.0298	0.4151	0.0875
Improve (%)	-	+2212.75	+66.03	+687.66
P-Value	-	0.000	0.000	0.000

4.1.3 Selected Baselines

As mentioned in preliminary, the prediction task could be generally regarded as a time-series analysis problem. Thus, here we exploit three related baselines in our experiments.

1) Personalized Average (Ave). As the basic time-series analytical tool, we follow the simple assumption that drivers' pattern ratio will only fluctuate around the average value of each dimension. Thus, this baseline uses the average value of previous p intervals (i.e., the selected time lag), to predict the change of pattern frequency in next time interval.

2) Overall Popularity (Pop). Another heuristic assumption is that drivers will follow the overall popularity to update their own patterns. Based on this assumption, we intuitively rank the overall popularity within time lag for ranking task. For the binary classification, we compare the ranking with last time lag, and the raising ones will be labeled as positive, while falling ones as negative.

3) Vector Autoregression (VAR) [20]. Vector AutoregRession (VAR) is a classical econometric model to capture the linear interdependencies among multiple time series, which suits modeling the autoregression for more than one evolving variable. As we extracted the driving records into pattern vectors, it will be appropriate to analyze the time-series with VAR model. What should be noted is that there will be one VAR model trained for a certain driver, and the estimation will also be normalized.

In summary, we select two baselines, i.e., personalized average and VAR model that are based on time-series estimation, while one more baseline according to the overall popularity, which follows the similar assumption of our framework that taxi drivers tend to follow suggestions from external information source. With these baselines, comprehensive analysis comparing different assumptions will be achieved.

4.2 Overall Results

Here, we show the overall prediction performance of our approach **SPC** (**S**ocial-aware **P**attern-**C**hange prediction) and other baselines. To be specific, the top 300 patterns were studied and the time lag was set as 5 months (i.e., we have transactions in 5 months as training data to predict the variance of 6th month), while the parameter sensitiveness will be discussed later. Similarly, to ensure the data quality

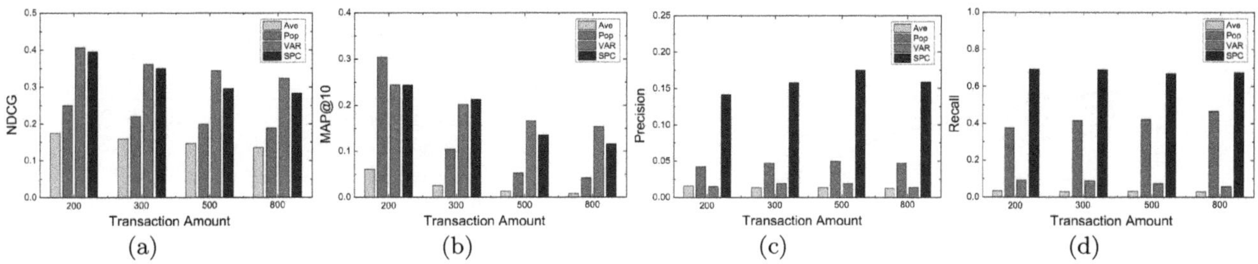

Figure 7: The verification on robustness with different set of patterns in terms of different metrics, a) NDCG, b) MAP@10, c) Precision, d) Recall.

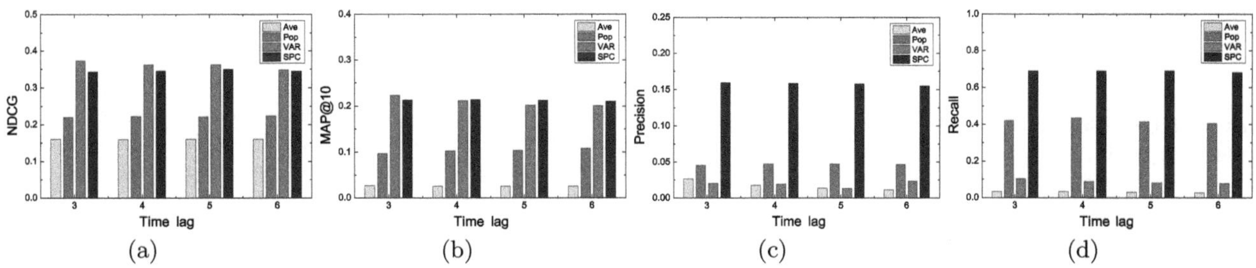

Figure 8: The verification on robustness with different time lag in terms of different metrics, a) NDCG, b) MAP@10, c) Precision, d) Recall.

with reducing sparsity, we selected top 100 taxi drivers with the most records in our experiments. Besides, we set the top 20% of results in ranking list as positive, while the detailed ROC curve will be studied at the end of this section.

The overall results are shown in Table 4. According to the results, we realize that behavior patterns of cab drivers could be largely random, as all the performance are relatively poor. However, we can find that except for the comparison with VAR on ranking problem, our approach outperforms the other baselines with dramatic margin, even 20 times better in some experiments. The performance highly supports our assumption that with introducing the latent social factors, drivers' behaviors could be better explained. The conclusion could also be partially supported by the comparison between overall popularity and personalized average, as the former one beats the later on all the metrics, and achieves a relatively good result in terms of MAP, which indicates that, especially for the most popular patterns, taxi drivers will be glad to follow the trend.

Another interesting finding is that for VAR model, it performs truly great in ranking task, but terribly fails for binary classification. With deep looking of the output of VAR, we realize that usually VAR predicts the proportion as 0 or negative, not only for those patterns that the drivers never try (i.e., no training data), but also for those drivers tried for once but never reappear. With considering auto correlation, VAR model indeed "refused" to change. Combined with the terrible performance on binary classification, we could conclude that the ranking list of VAR might be meaningless as it fails to reveal the real pattern but only maintains the outmoded ones.

According to the results, we may finally draw the conclusion that the heuristic methods might not be appropriate to estimate driving patterns of taxi drivers if without considering additional factors, like financial benefits or running speed. This phenomenon might further explains why our model could outperforms the baselines, as we do not *"teach the model"* how to predict the change, but intuitively "simulate the social propagation scheme", which is finally proved as effective. Clearly, except for those intellectual services, taxi drivers themselves could be the **"best learner"**.

4.3 Parameter Robustness

As the overall performance has been validated, in this subsection, we evaluate the sensitiveness of parameters. In this task, two parameters are concerned, i.e., the amount of pattern, as well as the time lag.

For the amount of pattern, we conducted our experiments on four sets of patterns, which contains 200, 300, 500 and 800 patterns separately. The results are shown in Figure 7. We realize that for the ranking task, the metrics become worse with more patterns that may be due to the following two reasons: 1) more patterns results in more sparse data set, especially when those unpopular ones are studied; 2) more patterns raise the difficulty of ranking. Interestingly, we find that for the overall popularity method, the performance dramatically deteriorates when patterns increase from 200 to 300, which may further prove our conclusion that drivers will be glad to follow the popular trend, but for the unpopular ones, it will be difficult to predict. On the other hand, though data sparsity will also disturb the binary classification, the precision and recall rates keep relatively stable when patterns increase.

For the time lag, similarly, four sets of experiments are conducted with lag as 3, 4, 5 and 6. The results are shown in Figure 8. It seems that for our approach as well as overall popularity, the time lag does not reflect significant effect. However, for personalized average and the VAR model, which are based on time-series estimation, when time lag increases, the performance seems slightly worsen. It is inter-

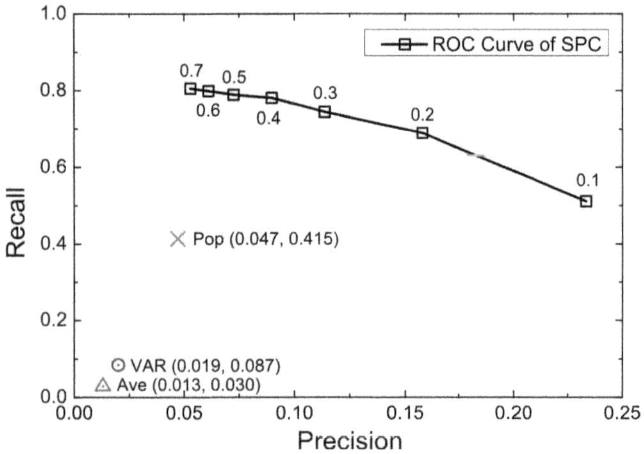

Figure 9: ROC Curve of our framework with different positive ratio.

esting as for time-series analysis, longer lag is usually better to catch the trend, but for taxi driving patterns, as proved above that it might be even a random event, thus time-dependent rules may suffer the over-fitting problem.

4.4 ROC Curve for SPC

Finally, we discuss about the ROC curve of our approach. In former experiments, we treated the top 20% of ranking list as positive. Here we conducted experiments with the same parameters of overall result, while the threshold fluctuates from 10% to 70% with interval as 10%. The ROC curve is shown in Figure 9, in which numbers near the line present the percentage of positive labels. From the figure, we can clearly find that for any threshold, our framework could outperform all the baselines in binary classification task with significant margin. However, we also realize that the recall may hardly pass 0.8 no matter how we regulate the threshold, which indicates that social influence from other taxi drivers or overall popularity may explain at most 80% for pattern selected, while for 20% left, they may be caused by other factors, like municipal engineering or festivals.

5. DISCUSSION: POTENTIAL RULES

In this section, we will further conduct discussions on the estimated social connections for revealing the potential rules of how taxi drivers connect and how driving patterns spread.

5.1 Social Skills: Quantity v.s. Quality

Firstly, we attempt to discover whether the driving skill levels will affect the social connections. What should be noted is that all the connections here are indeed in-edge. Similar with the statistics in pre-study, *average speed* and *total income* will be selected to measure the skills. Generally, with some interesting rules found by statistical analysis, we realize that though the driving skills may not affect how many connections you have, they can determine who you will connect to or study from.

When checking the correlation between the amount of connections and two skills, we find it as completely insignificant by statistical analysis, with P-Value even larger than 0.5 for all the tests. It may indicate that better skills do not necessarily mean more in-edge connections. Clearly, "number" of "tutors" is not a critical factor.

However, since we treat the drivers themselves as one of their connections, when we check the correlation between connection amount and their own position in the ranking list of connection strength. Indeed, it surprisingly results in significantly negative correlation (with the Pearson's coefficient as -0.17), meaning that for those who have better skills are even more willing to learn from the others and update the patterns, while for the ordinary ones, they tend to insist past patterns and refuse to change.

And finally, we check the correlation between driver's skill level, as well as their difference (of rank) with "authorities", i.e., "tutors" with top 5 strongest connection strength. We find a significant correlation with Pearson's coefficient as 0.323 and P-Value 0.001, which indicates that all the drivers tend to learn from those top drivers with best skills, and those with worse driving skills will be more dependent on shared experience from top drivers.

Table 5: Social Metrics for Pattern Spread Graph

	Statistics
Average Edges	327.9122
Average Longest Path	8.5676
Average Max Out-degree	12.5878
Average Density	0.2244

5.2 Pattern with Profit: Effectiveness v.s. Efficiency

Then, we discuss about the spread trend of driving patterns. Similar with traditional social spread analysis, we build one spread graph for each pattern, and for each driver u_i, if the proportion of k-th pattern is increased in time t compared with $t-1$, we defined it as u_i is **activated** in time t. Further, if u_i is activated in t and one of the in-edge connection u_j was activated in $t-1$, it is defined as u_j successfully **activates** u_i in time t and there exists an directed edge from u_j to u_i in k-th spread graph. Based on these definitions, we could draw the pattern spread track similar with traditional social influence analysis.

Then, we count four metrics to measure the graph structure of pattern spread, i.e., the *amount of edges*, which indicates the pattern's popularity; the *longest path*, which indicates the depth of spread; the *maximal out-degree*, which indicates the width of spread; and finally the *density*, which indicates the frequency of spread.

We conduct our study with the same setting of overall experiments in Section 4.2, i.e., top 300 patterns with time lag as 5 for 100 drivers. Table 5 shows the average statistics of this four metrics. With these four metrics, we could now evaluate the correlation between social spread and pattern profit. Specially, to measure the profit, we select the average speed, the average distance and total fare.

The correlation statistics are shown in Table 6. Interestingly, we find that for almost all the pairs, no matter significant or not, the co-efficient is negative. In other words, higher metrics lead to lower social attraction. Indeed, this phenomenon could be reasonable. Take the "distance" metric as an example since all the correlations are significant, we can conclude that long-range trip might not be popular among taxi drivers. Similar conclusion could be drawn for

Table 6: Correlation within Pattern Spread and Profit Metrics

Term	Edge	Long Path	Out Degree	Density
Speed	-0.026	-0.041	-0.040	0.010
P-Value	0.756	0.617	0.631	0.908
Distance	-0.202	-0.182	-0.194	-0.280
P-Value	0.014	0.027	0.018	0.001
Fare	-0.060	-0.044	-0.066	-0.235
P-Value	0.468	0.597	0.426	0.004

the "fare" metric, it seems that experienced drivers are not so willing to share patterns with high rewards.

6. RELATED WORK

In this paper, we deeply analyze taxi driving patterns with considering latent social factors. Indeed, plenty efforts have been made on understanding behaviors of taxi drivers, and further developing intelligent systems, e.g., recommending hotspots that are more likely to pick up passengers quickly [34], planning practically fastest route to a given destination [33] or route which provides a optimal sequence of pick-up points [10], and even constructing the spatio-temporal profitability map for drivers to select profit locations [22]. On the other hand, for passengers to take taxi, prior arts may also list location to easily achieve vacant taxi [34], or support them to share taxi with optimal candidate [21]. Besides, though not directly generating recommendation, some other works also focus on the taxi analysis. For instance, [17] discussed about the comparison of top and ordinary drivers based on several ranking schemes, while [15] studied the strategy to pick up passengers with creating tree structure with highest probability. For the anomaly detection, historical trajectories maintained for fast distinguishing new trajectories that are isolated [36], and similar way was also utilized to detect the taxi fraud [11] or outlier trajectories [9]. Further, some applications were designed based on the taxi driving analysis, e.g., [12] proposed the method to detect traffic jams by searching the GPS records that are close together, and [4] constructed a model to automatically determine the capacity of each road segment using taxi GPS data. Finally, [5] leveraged taxi GPS traces to suggest nightly bus routes.

Another related topic of this paper is social network analysis, to be specific, the social influence or spread analysis, and the location-based social network analysis. Since social network structures are analyzed for marketing in [7] for the first time, the social-based "word-of-mouth" effect, has become one of the hottest issue in recent years, and several prior arts, e.g., [16], [1], and [19] were proposed following [7] that explicitly represent the step-by-step dynamics of influence. Among them, Independent Cascade (IC) model [16] is treated as one of the most widely-studied models with intuitive simulation and simple computation, which motivated several linear approximation like [29] and [26]. Based on the definition, some related works targeted at estimating the influence probability, i.e., the edge strength, like [14] discussed effectiveness of several heuristic method to reveal link strength, [24] predicted diffusion probabilities by using the EM algorithm, and [35] investigated the relationship between the tie strength and information propagation with several strategies of tie selection. Recently, due to the complexity of evolving social network, more issues were discussed, e.g., [28] studied on how to model the implicit social diffusion with time decay, and [2] discussed about differentiation of social influence and homogeneity, as well as the effects of weak ties in social spread.

For the location based social network analysis, the basic issue is whether human mobility indeed reflects social characteristics. Recent studies showed that human mobility is highly repetitive and non-random [13], so did [6] which revealed that 10%-30% of human movement could be explained by social factors, even more evident on long-ranged travel. Also, as comparing the social structure between online and offline social network, prior arts [18] announced that more cohesive communities will be found for offline event-driven social networks than the ordinary ones. Since social ties lead to similar mobility patterns and frequent physical contacts, mobility patterns, in return, shape and impact social connections like [8] and [25]. For instance, [3] indicated that the place of gather may benefit community detection. Also, prior arts like [37] discussed about the homogeneity and influence in location based network, and [27] further discussed the dynamic social influence within decision-making of event participation. Finally, some related work studied the offline user behaviors in the perspective of *ephemeral social networks*, e.g., [39] developed a factor graph model based framework to infer the likelihood of future encounter, and [31] recommended offline geo-friends based on pattern-based heterogeneous information network analysis.

Different from the prior arts, to the best of our knowledge, we are the first to investigate the impact of latent social factors within taxi drivers, and leverage it to explain drivers' future behaviors. Also, to reveal the social connection strength, we formulate the social influence from difference patterns in the perspective of pairwise ranking optimization, which is novel compared with related works.

7. CONCLUSION AND FUTURE WORK

In this paper, we investigated the latent social factors within the latent vehicle-to-vehicle network with simulating the social-driven behaviors pattern change of taxi drivers. To be specific, we proposed a social-driven two-stage framework to simulate latent social interactions within taxi drivers, which could better explain drivers' future behaviors. A unique characteristic of our framework is that it can transfer the problem of driving behavior prediction into the form of partial ranking with social influence, which can be regarded as a pairwise ranking problem for optimization. Extensive experiments conducted on a large-scale real-world data clearly validate the effectiveness of the proposed framework, which also prove the hypothesis that social factors indeed affect the driving behaviors of taxi drivers.

As we discussed that though social factors could better explain the pattern fluctuation at most for around 80%, there are still some other key factors, e.g., financial profit or traffic environment. In the future, we would like to investigate these factors with more comprehensive prediction framework. Also, social-oriented taxi services, e.g., social-based "tutor" or pattern recommendations will be considered. Finally, we will discover whether similar solutions could be used for other service-oriented professions.

Acknowledgments

This research was partially supported by grants from the National Science Foundation for Distinguished Young Scholars of China (61325010), the Natural Science Foundation of China (61403358), the Natural Science Foundation of China (71329201), the Science and Technology Program for Public Wellbeing (2013GS340302) and the National High Technology Research and Development Program of China (2014AA015203). Also, Qi Liu gratefully thanks the support of CCF-Intel Young Faculty Researcher Program (YFRP). Finally, Tong gratefully thanks for Guangyi Lv's kind help during the paper writing.

8. REFERENCES

[1] C. Aggarwal, A. Khan, and X. Yan, On flow authority discovery in social networks, in *Proc. SDM'11*, pp. 522-533, 2011.

[2] E. Bakshy, I. Rosenn, C. Marlow, and L. Adamic, The role of social networks in information diffusion, in *Proc. WWW'12*, pp. 519-528, 2012.

[3] C. Brown, V. Nicosia, S. Scellato, et al., Where online friends meet: social communities in location-based networks, in *Proc. ICWSM'12*, pp. 415-418, 2012.

[4] P. Castro, D. Zhang, and S. Li, Urban traffic modelling and prediction using large scale taxi GPS traces, in *Pervasive Computing*, 2012: 57-72.

[5] C. Chen, D. Zhang, Z. Zhou, et al., B-Planner: Night bus route planning using large-scale taxi GPS traces, in *Proc. IEEE PerCom'13*, pp. 225-233, 2013.

[6] E. Cho, S.A. Myers, and J. Leskovec, Friendship and mobility: user movement in location-based social networks, in *Proc. ACM KDD'11*, pp. 1082-1090, 2011.

[7] P. Domingos, and M. Richardson, Mining the network value of customers, in *Proc. KDD'01*, pp. 57-66, 2001.

[8] N. Eagle, A. Pentland, and D. Lazer, Inferring friendship network structure by using mobile phone data, in *PNAS*, 106(36):15274-15278, 2009.

[9] Y. Ge, H. Xiong, Z. Zhou, H. Ozdemir, J. Yu, and K.C. Lee, Top-eye: Top-k evolving trajectory outlier detection, in *Proc. ACM KDD'10*, pp. 899-908, 2010.

[10] Y. Ge, H. Xiong, A. Tuzhilin, K. Xiao, M. Gruteser, and M. Pazzani, An energy-efficient mobile recommender system, in *Proc. ACM KDD'10*, pp. 899-908, 2010.

[11] Y. Ge, H. Xiong, C. Liu, and Z. Zhou, A taxi driving fraud detection system, in *Proc. IEEE ICDM'11*, pp. 181-190, 2011.

[12] F. Giannotti, M. Nanni, D. Pedreschi, et al., Unveiling the complexity of human mobility by querying and mining massive trajectory data, in *VLDB Journal*, 20(5): 695-719, 2011.

[13] M. Gonzalez, C. Hidalgo, and A. Barabasi., Understanding individual human mobility patterns, in *Nature*, 453(7196):779-782, 2008.

[14] A. Goyal, F. Bonchi, and L. Lakshmanan, Learning influence probabilities in social networks, in *Proc. ACM WSDM'10*, pp. 241-250 2010.

[15] H. Hu, Z. Wu, B. Mao, Y. Huang, J. Cao, and J. Pan, Pick-up tree based route recommendation, in *Proc. WAIM'12*, pp. 471-483, 2012.

[16] D. Kempe, J. Kleinberg, and É. Tardos, Maximizing the spread of influence through a social network, in *Proc. ACM KDD'03*, pp. 137–146, 2003.

[17] L. Liu, C. Andris, A. Biderman, and C. Rattt, Uncovering taxi driver's mobility intelligence through his trace, in *IEEE Pervasive Computing*, 2009, pp. 1-17.

[18] X. Liu, Q. He, Y. Tian, W.C. Lee, J. McPherson, and J. Han, Event-based social networks: linking the online and offline social worlds, in *Proc. ACM KDD'12*, pp. 1032–1040, 2012.

[19] Q. Liu, B. Xiang, E. Chen, H. Xiong, F. Tang, and J. Yu, Influence Maximization over Large-Scale Social Networks: A Linear Approach with Bound, in *Proc. ACM CIKM'14*, pp. 171-180, 2014.

[20] H. Lutkepohl. New introduction to multiple time series analysis. Springer, 2005.

[21] S. Ma, Y. Zheng, and O. Wolfson, T-share: A large-scale dynamic taxi ridesharing service, in *Proc. IEEE ICDE'13*, pp. 410-421, 2013.

[22] J. Powell, Y. Huang, F. Bastani, and M. Ji, Towards reducing taxicab cruising time using spatio-temporal profitability maps, in *Proc. SSTD'11*, pp. 242-260, 2011.

[23] M. Qu, H. Zhu, J. Liu, G. Liu, and H. Xiong, A cost-effective recommender system for taxi drivers, in *Proc. ACM KDD'14*, pp. 45-54, 2014.

[24] K. Saito, R. Nakano, and M. Kimura, Prediction of information diffusion probabilities for independent cascade model, in *Springer KES*, 2008: 67-75.

[25] D. Wang, D. Pedreschi, C. Song, , et al., Human mobility, social ties, and link prediction, in *Proc. ACM KDD'11*, pp. 1100-1108, 2011.

[26] B. Xiang, Q. Liu, E. Chen, H. Xiong, Y. Zheng, and Y. Yang, PageRank with Priors: An Influence Propagation Perspective, in *Proc. IJCAI'13*, pp. 2740-2746, 2013.

[27] T. Xu, H. Zhong, H. Zhu, H. Xiong, E. Chen, and G. Liu, Exploring the Impact of Dynamic Mutual Influence on Social Event Participation, in *Proc. SDM'15*, pp. 262-270, 2015.

[28] J. Yang, and J. Leskovec, Modeling information diffusion in implicit networks, in *Proc. IEEE ICDM'10*, pp. 599-608, 2010.

[29] Y. Yang, E. Chen, Q. Liu, B. Xiang, T. Xu, and S. Shad, On Approximation of Real-World Influence Spread, in *Proc. ECML-PKDD'12*, pp. 548-564, 2012.

[30] D. Yang, H. Hung, W. Lee, and W. Chen, Maximizing acceptance probability for active friending in online social networks, in *Proc. ACM KDD'13*, pp. 713-721, 2013.

[31] X. Yu, A. Pan, L.A. Tang, Z. Li, and J. Han, Geo-friends recommendation in gps-based cyber-physical social network, in *Proc. ASONAM'11*, 2011, pp. 361–368.

[32] J. Yuan, Y. Zheng, C. Zhang, W. Xie, X. Xie, G. Sun, and Y. Huang. T-drive: Driving directions based on taxi trajectories, in *Proc. ACM SIGSPATIAL'10*, pp. 99-108, 2010.

[33] J. Yuan, Y. Zheng, X. Xie, and G. Sun, T-drive: Enhancing driving directions with taxi drivers' intelligence, in *IEEE TKDE*, 25(1):220-232, 2013.

[34] J. Yuan, Y. Zheng, L. Zhang, and X. Xie, T-finder: A recommender system for finding passengers and vacant taxis, in *IEEE TKDE*, 25(10): 2390-2403, 2013.

[35] J. Zhao, J. Wu, X. Feng, H. Xiong, and K. Xu, Information propagation in online social networks: a tie-strength perspective, in *Springer KAIS*, 32(3): 589-608, 2012.

[36] D. Zhang, N. Li, Z. Zhou, C. Chen, L. Sun, and S. Li, iBAT: Detecting anomalous taxi trajectories from GPS traces, in *Proc. UbiComp'11*, pp. 99-108, 2011.

[37] K. Zhang, and K. Pelechrinis, Understanding spatial homophily: the case of peer influence and social selection, in *Proc. WWW'14*, pp. 271-282, 2014.

[38] Y. Zheng, Y. Liu, J. Yuan, and X. Xie, Urban computing with taxicabs, in *Proc. ACM Ubicomp'11*, pp. 89-98, 2011.

[39] H. Zhuang, A. Chin, S. Wu, W. Wang, X. Wang, and J. Tang, Inferring geographic coincidence in ephemeral social networks, in *Proc. ECML-PKDD'12*, 2012, pp. 613–628.

[40] H. Zhu, E. Chen, H. Xiong, K. Yu, H. Cao, and J. Tian, Mining mobile user preferences for personalized context-aware recommendatio, in *ACM TIST*, 5(4): 58, 2015.

DeepIntent: Learning Attentions for Online Advertising with Recurrent Neural Networks

Shuangfei Zhai*
Dept. of Computer Science
Binghamton University
Binghamton, NY, USA
szhai2@binghamton.edu

Keng-hao Chang
Microsoft
Sunnyvale, CA, USA
kenchan@microsoft.com

Ruofei Zhang
Microsoft
Sunnyvale, CA, USA
bzhang@microsoft.com

Zhongfei (Mark) Zhang
Dept. of Computer Science
Binghamton University
Binghamton, NY, USA
zhongfei@cs.binghamton.edu

ABSTRACT

In this paper, we investigate the use of recurrent neural networks (RNNs) in the context of search-based online advertising. We use RNNs to map both queries and ads to real valued vectors, with which the relevance of a given (query, ad) pair can be easily computed. On top of the RNN, we propose a novel attention network, which learns to assign attention scores to different word locations according to their intent importance (hence the name DeepIntent). The vector output of a sequence is thus computed by a weighted sum of the hidden states of the RNN at each word according their attention scores. We perform end-to-end training of both the RNN and attention network under the guidance of user click logs, which are sampled from a commercial search engine. We show that in most cases the attention network improves the quality of learned vector representations, evaluated by AUC on a manually labeled dataset. Moreover, we highlight the effectiveness of the learned attention scores from two aspects: query rewriting and a modified BM25 metric. We show that using the learned attention scores, one is able to produce sub-queries that are of better qualities than those of the state-of-the-art methods. Also, by modifying the term frequency with the attention scores in a standard BM25 formula, one is able to improve its performance evaluated by AUC.

Keywords

Deep Learning; RNN; Attention Mechanism; Online Advertising; Sponsored Search; Query Rewriting; BM25

*This work was completed during the first author's internship at Microsoft.

KDD '16, August 13-17, 2016, San Francisco, CA, USA

DOI: http://dx.doi.org/10.1145/2939672.2939759

1. INTRODUCTION

In the domain of sponsored search, it is essential to understand the search intent from queries as well as the selling intent from ads. Precise representation for both the queries and the ads is the foundation for quality retrieval and a stepping stone for higher user engagement. Succinct representations for queries is also important as it allows more ads to be selected, implying denser bidding landscape and stronger marketplace horsepower. For example, for the query "surface pro 3 keyboard", ads retrieved for shortened sub-queries "surface pro 3" and "surface 3" are not desirable as they do not precisely capture the user intent, which is in fact a keyboard instead of a tablet. On the other hand, if a user queries "Microsoft office for Mac", ignoring the term "Microsoft" does not cause any intent shift and enables one to retrieve more related ads. Representing ads is equally important for the success of a sponsored ads search engine due to a similar reasoning.

In this paper, we adopt recurrent neural networks (RNNs) as the building block to learn desired representations from massive user click logs. RNNs fall into the family of deep learning models which specifically focus on learning multiple levels of representations. RNNs are very suitable for modeling sequential data (such as natural language), and have recently achieved remarkable performance on tasks such as machine translation [22, 1] and image annotation [24]. In this paper, we propose a novel attention network which is stacked on top of an RNN and learns to assign attention scores to words within a sequence (either a query or an ad). Methodology-wise, we interpret attention as a pooling method, similar to mean pooling and max pooling, which compresses a sequence of vectors to a single vector. In contrast to mean pooling and max pooling however, attention based pooling is adaptive, which is able to assign large weights to "important" words and vice versa. Compared with using the last state of an RNN as the output (which we denote as last pooling in this paper), attention based pooling has no difficulty modeling long sequences, as it considers different word locations in an even manner. We consider several types of the underlying RNN, varying from both the one directional and bidirectional versions of vanilla RNN and LSTM [7]. We train our model with a large amount of click logs sampled from a commercial search engine, in the same fashion as [9]. Specifically, we push the model to learn vector representations for both queries and ads such that the click behavior can be well predicted.

We conduct two types of evaluations. The first one is directly taking the output of the RNN as the vector representation of queries and ads. We show that the attention layer improves the quality of learned vector representations by a vanilla RNN. On LSTM, the vectors learned by attention based pooling match those by last pooling, but with the additional advantage of much better model interpretability (which is directly used in the subsequent tasks). In the second set of evaluation, we investigate the quality of the learned attention scores. In particular, we perform query rewriting by selecting the sub-queries corresponding to terms that are assigned high attention. We show that we are able to outperform two existing query rewriting methods by a large margin. We further propose a novel way of utilizing the attention scores to enhance the term space representations, by modifying the term frequency part of the standard BM25 metric with the attention scores. We show that the learned attention scores are able to improve the AUC of BM25, with bidirectional LSTM being the model yielding the largest improvement.

The contribution of the paper is summarized as follows:

- We introduce an attention and RNN based deep architecture for modeling queries and ads in online advertising, and we have verified that using the attention based pooling successfully helps RNNs learn better vector representations for queries and ads.
- We propose novel ways of utilizing the attention scores learned from the deep model. We show that our learned query attention scores can be successfully applied to a query rewriting task, yielding quality rewrites that outperform existing methods. We also propose to use the learned ads attention scores to modify the term frequency of the standard BM25 metric, and demonstrate improved performance.

2. MODEL

As shown in Figure 1, DeepIntent consists of two parts: 1) a query and an ad encoder that take a word sequence as input and outputs a real-valued vector 2) a loss function that provides the signal to guide the learning of the two encoders. The encoders for both the query and ads share the same architecture, which is shown in Figure 2. We will first introduce each component of the encoder in detail, then discuss the construction of the loss function.

2.1 Input Layer

The input to an encoder is a word sequence $\mathbf{x} = \{x_1, ..., x_T\}$ where $x_t \in R^V$ is a one-hot-vector representation of the t-th word and V is the vocabulary size. T is the length of the sequence, which varies for different sequences. Note the difference from the traditionally used BoW representations, as we strictly consider the sequential order.

2.2 Word Embedding Layer

The second layer is a word embedding layer. For each time step t, the word embedding layer transforms the one-hot-vector x_t into a low-dimensional dense vector e_t via a linear mapping

$$e_t = W_{emb} x_t, \; s.t. \; W_{emb} \in R^{d_{emb} \times V}, \tag{1}$$

where each column of W_{emb} corresponds to a word in the vocabulary. The word embedding layer reduces the dimensionality of the input from the vocabulary size which could be up to millions to d_{emb} which is usually several hundreds, thus regularizing the model size.

2.3 RNN Layer

The output of the word embedding layer $\{e_1, ..., e_T\}$ is then fed into an RNN layer. An RNN updates a hidden state $h_t \in R^{d_h}$ given e_t at the t-th time step and the previous hidden state h_{t-1} in a recurrent formula:

$$h_t = \mathcal{H}(e_t, h_{t-1}), \tag{2}$$

where $\mathcal{H}$ is a nonlinear transformation of choice. The simplest form of an RNN is:

$$h_t = \sigma(W_{eh} e_t + W_{hh} h_{t-1} + b_h), \tag{3}$$

where $W_{eh} \in R^{d_h \times d_{emb}}$, $W_{hh} \in R^{d_h \times d_h}$, $b_h \in R^{d_h}$ are the parameters to be learned; $\sigma(\cdot)$ is a nonlinear activation function, eg., ReLU $max(0, x)$. In this case, $\mathcal{H}$ takes a fairly simple form consisting of a linear mapping followed by a simple nonlinear function. There are also more sophisticated forms of $\mathcal{H}$ available. For example, LSTM [7] has recently attracted much attention due to its ability to model long term dependency in sequences, which updates its hidden state as well as a cell state as follows:

$$\begin{aligned}
i_t =& \sigma(W_{ei} e_t + W_{hi} h_{t-1} + b_i) \\
f_t =& \sigma(W_{ef} e_t + W_{hf} h_{t-1} + b_f) \\
c_t =& f_t \cdot c_{t-1} + i_t \cdot tanh(W_{ec} e_t + W_{hc} h_{t-1} + b_c) \\
o_t =& \sigma(W_{eo} e_t + W_{ho} h_{t-1} + b_o) \\
h_t =& o_t \cdot tanh(c_t),
\end{aligned} \tag{4}$$

where $\cdot$ denotes the element-wise product between vectors; $tanh$ is the hyperbolic tangent function. LSTM works by maintaining a cell vector c_t in addition to the hidden state h_t, and introduces input gate i_t, forget gate f_t, output gate o_t to control the update dynamics of the cell and hidden units. Detailed discussions of the advantages of LSTM can be found in [7, 6], which is omitted in this paper due to the space limit.

Besides, it is also useful to build two RNNs taking a sequence in the forward and backward directions, respectively. This results in a bidirectional recurrent neural network (BRNN):

$$\begin{aligned}
\overrightarrow{h}_t = \overrightarrow{\mathcal{H}}(e_t, h_{t-1}),\; \overleftarrow{h}_t = \overleftarrow{\mathcal{H}}(e_t, h_{t+1}) \\
h_t = concatenate(\overrightarrow{h}_t, \overleftarrow{h}_t),
\end{aligned} \tag{5}$$

where the hidden state h_t is achieved by concatenating the corresponding hidden states from the forward and backward passes. BRNN breaks the asymmetry along the time steps and leverages the context around each step in a more balanced way.

Now each h_t can be considered as a representation of the t-th word. Due to the recurrent update of hidden states, h_t also takes the whole sequence into consideration. Hence, h_t is conceptually able to better characterize the semantics of the t-th word location than e_t, which is unaware of the local context. This is especially important for words that

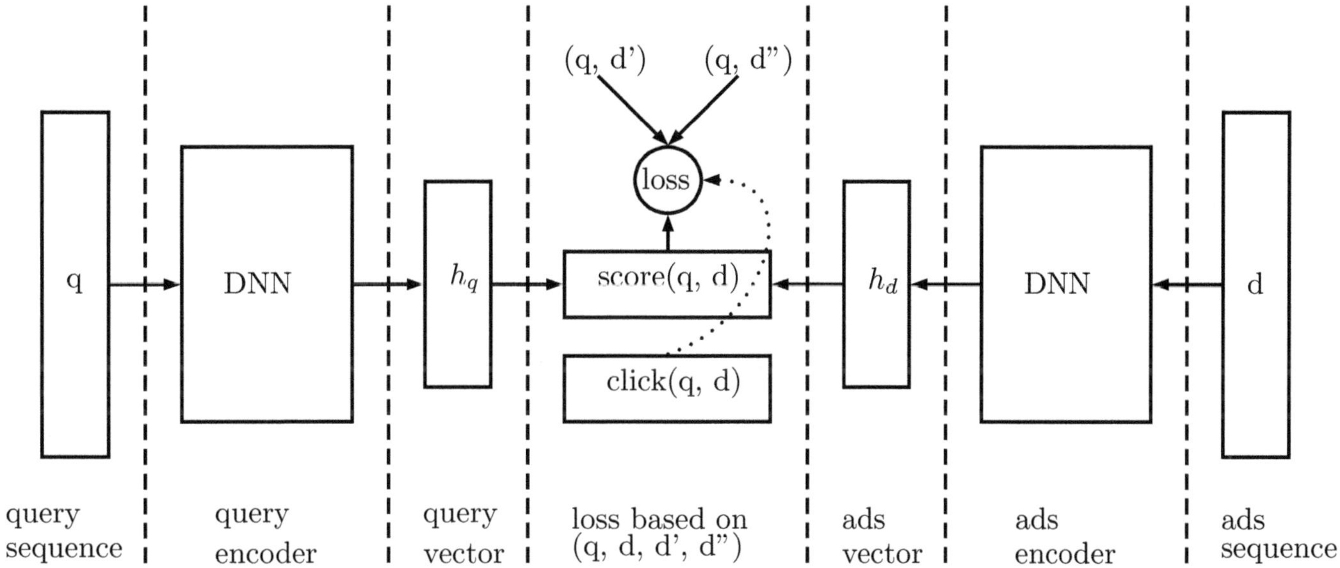

Figure 1: The architecture of the model, which consists of a query and an ad encoder, followed by a loss guided by the click.

have multiple senses, where only with the exact context one is able to tell the meaning of a particular occurrence.

2.4 Attention Based Pooling

The output of an RNN is another sequence of vectors $\mathbf{h} = \{h_1, ..., h_T\}$ with $h_t \in R^{d_h}$. It is thus desirable to further compress the sequence to a single vector to make it easy to build a loss function to facilitate training. In this paper, we denote this step as *pooling*.

The most straightforward approach is to take the last hidden state h_T as the representation for the sequence (for BRNN, this corresponds to *concatenate*$(\overrightarrow{h}_T, \overleftarrow{h}_1)$). In order to make this comparable to other pooling methods, we denote this approach as last pooling which is a slightly unorthodox notation. Note that as in Equation 2, h_T is a function of the whole sequence $\mathbf{x}$; thus theoretically h_T should be able to capture all the information contained in $\mathbf{x}$. However, this simple approach causes the long term dependency problem where the last state is forced to remember inputs that are many steps away. LSTM suffers less from this problem, thanks to its sophisticated update scheme with the help of cell and gate units.

Mean pooling is another popular choice which takes the mean of the hidden states from all time steps: $h = \frac{1}{T}\sum_{t=1}^{T} h_t$. It is obvious that long term dependency is no longer the main issue as every time step is taken into account in the first place. This is especially intuitive when considering a BRNN as conceptually every word contributes equally to the final vector representation, without any bias towards the last (or first) few words. However, this property is also a drawback of mean pooling, as it is unable to distinguish words that dominate the intent of a query or an ad from those that do not.

Max pooling is similar to mean pooling where instead of taking the average it takes the element-wise max of all the hidden states: $h = \max(h_1, ..., h_T)$. The max operation also provides an additional level of nonlinearity, making it a nonlinear transformation. As a result, max pooling typically works better and is arguably more widely used than mean pooling in practice. Despite this, max pooling suffers from the same problem as mean pooling being unable to perform proper credit assignment for individual words.

Motivated by the drawbacks of the above mentioned methods, we propose a novel attention based pooling, which constitutes the main contribution of this paper. We adopt the idea from the sequence to sequence learning machine translation literature [1], but extend it to a more general setting that makes it applicable to cases whenever a global pooling is needed. To be concrete, attention based pooling represents a sequence by a weighted sum of the vector representations of all time steps. In particular, the weights are adaptive to the content of each time step, which makes it able to perform proper credit assignment to time steps according to their importance. Mathematically, it takes the form as follows:

$$h = \sum_{t=1}^{T} a_t h_t, \; a_t = \frac{\exp(s(h_t;\theta))}{\sum_{t=1}^{T}\exp(s(h_t;\theta))}. \tag{6}$$

Here $s(\cdot;\theta)$ (which we call the attention network) is a function that maps a vector h_t to a real valued score. a_t, which we call *attention*, is the normalized score across the whole sequence, which indicates the importance of the corresponding time step t. Compared with mean pooling, Equation 6 replaces the static weight for each time step $\frac{1}{T}$ with a_t, which is adapted to the content of step t. This allows the model to pay higher attention to important words and vice versa. There are two key ingredients that make this possible. First is that h_t should form a precise representation of the t-th word with the context in consideration, and this is achieved by the underlying RNN. Second is that $s(\cdot;\theta)$ must have enough capacity to be able to distinguish between important and unimportant words. For example, a simple linear function would not be able to do so due to the large volume of the semantic space spanned by queries and ads. As a result, we implement $s(\cdot;\theta)$ with yet another neural net-

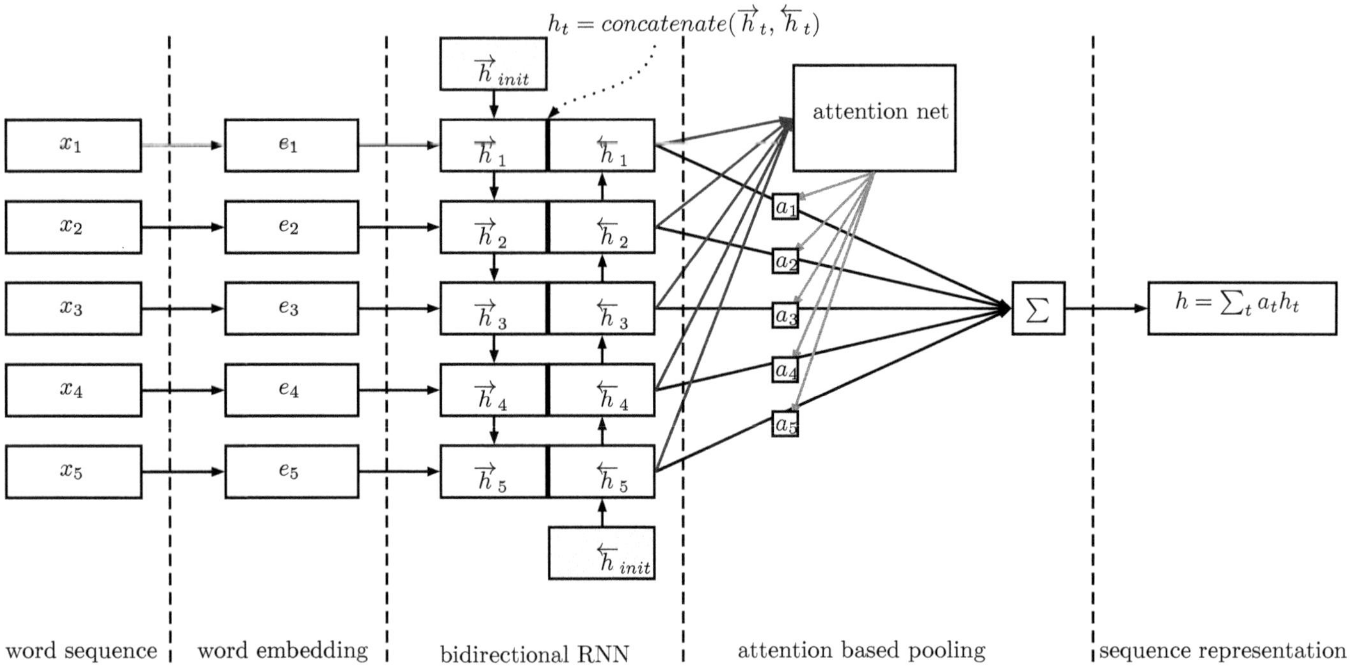

Figure 2: The encoding architecture of attention based pooling, demonstrated with a bidirectional RNN.

work, whose parameters are learned jointly with those of the underlying RNN (hence the name attention network).

The attention scores give us a straightforward way for visualizing a deep neural network based model. This greatly enhances the interpretability of a deep model and allows one to perform deeper analysis of its behavior. In addition, one is also able to extract the words with high attention scores as the dominant intent of a sequence, which can be later fed to existing keyword based information retrieval systems. As the attention scores are computed with a deep architecture which directly models local context, they provide more precise and informative weightings of the words in a sequence. In the experiments, we conduct a series of qualitative and quantitative evaluations and demonstrate that we are able to learn meaningful and useful attention scores.

2.5 Loss Function

As shown in Figure 1, after obtaining the vector representations from query and ad encoders defined previously, we need to define a proper loss function to make learning possible. We first observe that unsupervised learning is unsuitable as it is difficult to make the distinction between important and unimportant contents without supervision. Luckily, for commercial search engines, large amounts of user click logs are available, which provide valuable information about the relevance of a given query and ad pair. Intuitively, the more clicks a pair has, the better a match it is. To this end, we adopt a loss function that is similar to that in [9] which tries to maximize the similarity of the query and ad pairs that have large click counts. Formally, let (q, d^+) be a clicked (query, ad) pair, and $\{d_1^-, ..., d_n^-\}$ be a set of ads that have zero click count with q. We denote $h_q(\cdot)$ and $h_d(\cdot)$ as the encoding functions according to Equation 6 for query and ad sequences, respectively. We then formulate our loss function as follows:

$$J(\theta) = - \sum_{(q,d^+)} \log \frac{\exp(score(q, d^+))}{\exp(score(q, d^+)) + \sum_{i=1}^{n} \exp(score(q, d_i^-))}$$
$$s.t.\ score(q, d) = h_q(q)^T h_d(d), \tag{7}$$

where we have slighted overloaded the notation to let $\theta = \{W_{q,emb}, \theta_{q,rnn}, \theta_{q,attention}, W_{d,emb}, \theta_{d,rnn}, \theta_{d,attention}\}$ be the union of the parameters for both the query and ad encoder. In this way, all the parameters defined previously are learned with the goal to correctly match related (query, ad) pairs. Note that in Equation 7, the summation is denoted as summing over only (q, d^+), where $\{d_1^-, ..., d_n^-\}$ are not explicitly expressed. This is to highlight our implementation where for each (q, d^+), we randomly sample n ads $\{d_1^-, ..., d_n^-\}$ that are not clicked by q; we then form a pseudo $n + 1$ way classification problem where d^+ is considered the positive class, and all the rest are negative. The probability is computed according to the inner product of the vector representation of the query with all of those ads. The adoption of negative sampling greatly reduces the cost of computing the loss, which makes it scale linearly with the number of clicks. In this way, we can directly apply maximum likelihood estimation and minimize $J(\theta)$ with standard gradient descent, and train our model on a large set of click logs.

3. EXPERIMENTS

3.1 Training Dataset

We use user click logs sampled from a commercial "product ads" search engine as training data, where only queries with clear product intent are selected. A total of about 15 million clicks are sampled from a month long of click logs,

	size	vocabulary	average length	clicks
query	6.4M	68K	4.1	15M
ads	5.1M	114K	9.3	15M

Table 1: The statistics of the training set.

which ends up with 6.4 million distinct user queries and 5.1 million distinct ads. We tokenize and represent each query (and ad) as a sequence of uni-gram terms. This yields a dictionary size of around 68 thousand and 114 thousand for queries and ads, respectively. The average length of queries and ads are 4.1 and 9.3 words, respectively. We summarize the statistics of the training dataset in Table 1.

3.2 Implementation Details

We use Theano [2] for the implementation and experiments are run on a Tesla K20 GPU. For all the models, we implement the attention network as a fully connected neural network with one hidden layer. $\sigma(\cdot)$ is set as ReLU for all the cases except for LSTM, where sigmoid is used. We train all the models with mini-batch gradient descent with Adadelta [25]. We use a held out validation set to monitor the training progress, and all the models are trained till the validation loss stops decreasing.

3.3 Evaluation of Vector Representations

We train a variety of models with different architectures to highlight the effectiveness of each component of our model. We summarize the description of all the models we have compared in Table 2. Here we choose the underlying encoding methods from the set {BoW, RNN, BRNN, LSTM, BLSTM}; and pooling methods from the set {max pooling, last pooling, attention based pooling} when applicable. For BoW, the word order is ignored and the corresponding h_t is computed simply as $h_t = \sigma(Wx_t + b)$. And a proper pooling method is then applied to $\{h_1, ..., h_T\}$ as for RNNs. Note that it does not make sense to apply last pooling for BoW, so it is ignored in our experiments. For LSTM and BLSTM, max pooling is ignored as it does not give competitive performance to last pooling in practice. For all the combinations, the dimension of the final vector representation is fixed as 400; the activation function σ is set as ReLU for all the models except for LSTM where we use the sigmoid function. All of them are trained with the same loss function defined in Section 2.5.

As a quantitative evaluation, we test all the models on a fully annotated test set. The test set contains around 966 thousand (query, ad) pairs where each pair is labeled by a group of trained human judges according to the relevance between the query and the ad. Each label ranges in {bad, fair, good, excellent}. The pairs are sampled from the early selection stage of a commercial ads search engine, where there are a significant amount of low quality selected ads to be pruned out in downstream processing. We use AUC (area-under-curve of the receiver operating characteristic plot) [20] as the metric for evaluation, by considering the bad label as the negative class and the rest labels as the positive class (fair, good and excellent). This results in a test set consisting of 318 thousand positive and 597 thousand negative pairs. We briefly summarize the statistics of the testset in Table 3. For each model, we use the cosine similarity $\frac{<h_q(q),h_d(d)>}{\sqrt{\|h_q(q)\|_2^2}\sqrt{\|h_d(d)\|_2^2}}$ instead of the inner product as the relevance score for a pair (q, d). The AUC is then computed according to the scores for all the pairs in the test set. Our results are presented in Figure 3.

The first thing we observe from Figure 3 is that all the models that consider word order significantly outperform BoW, regardless of the pooling method being used. Given that all the models output vectors with the same dimensionality, this demonstrates the benefit of considering word order. Moreover, bidirectional models tend to work comparable to or better than the corresponding one directional variants. In particular, we observe an improvement of BRNN over RNN with all the three pooling methods. BLSTM on the other hand achieves comparable performance compared with LSTM. Note that with the same output dimensionalty, bidirectional models have less parameters compared with their one directional counterpart. To see this, consider an RNN with input dimension d_{in} and hidden size d_h, the number of total parameters are $d_{in} \times d_h + d_h \times d_h$, ignoring the bias term. The number of parameters for the corresponding BRNN is $2 \times d_{in} \times \frac{d_h}{2} + 2 \times \frac{d_h}{2} \times \frac{d_h}{2} = d_{in} \times d_h + \frac{1}{2} d_h \times d_h$. The comparison between LSTM and BLSTM can be seen similarly.

When comparing different pooling methods, we see that for BoW, RNN and BRNN, attention based pooling significantly outperforms max pooling and last pooling. For LSTM, it is interesting to see that attention based pooling is slightly worse than last pooling; on BLSTM, attention based pooling matches last pooling. Also, LSTM and BLSTM achieve the best results evaluated by the vector representations, which makes LSTM the most effective encoder.

In order to gain further insight of the behavior of attention based pooling, we have visualized a sample query and the top five matched ads by a BRNN in Figure 4. The query is chosen from the validation set, which is not seen by the model during training. The height of the bar indicates the value of the attention scores. From Figure 4, we see that all returned ads are of good quality which correctly match the intent of the query. In particular, the attention net correctly assigns larger weights to words that are interesting/important. This suggests that, our BRNN model is able to learn meaningful representations for words at each time; on the other hand, the attention net is able to perform correct credit assignment to different words according to their local contents. As a comparison, we have also visualized the attention scores assigned by LSTM and BLSTM on three ads in Figure 5. Interestingly, we see that for LSTM, the attention scores are obviously skewed to the right, which essentially puts most of the weights on the words that are close to the end of a sequence. Note that in the extreme case if all the attention is assigned on the last word, attention based pooling is equivalent to last pooling. This explains our observation that attention based pooling fails to improve upon last pooling on LSTM. For BLSTM, on the other hand, the attention net is able to perform correct credit assignment, highlighting words mostly related to the product type or brand. This consolidates our speculation about the benefit of using a bidirectional model to break the bias towards the later states of a recurrent neural network.

3.4 Query Intent Extraction with Attention

In the next set of experiments, we focus on the quality of the attention scores for queries. In particular, we evaluate its effect in query intent extraction systems. As we pointed

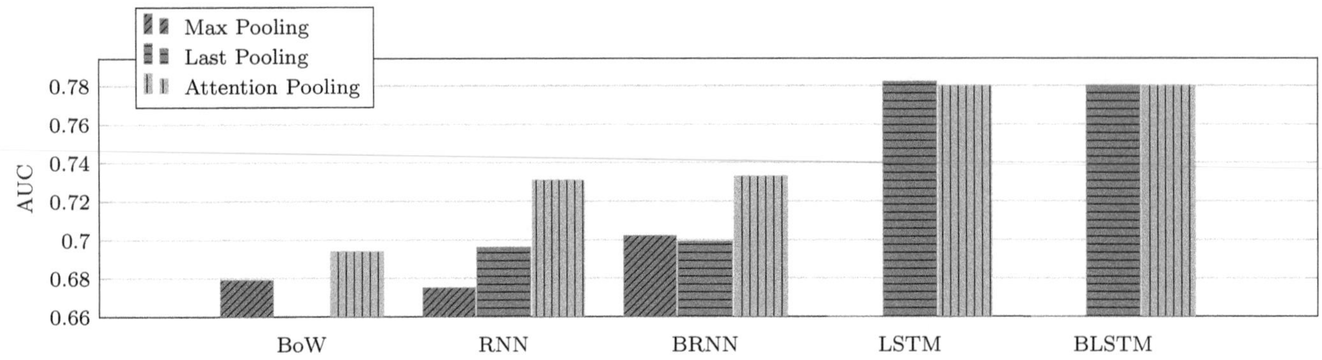

Figure 3: AUC evaluated on the test set of different models.

Model	Word Order	Max Pooling	Last Pooling	Attention Pooling
BoW	None	Yes	No	Yes
RNN	Forward	Yes	Yes	Yes
BRNN	Forward and Backward	Yes	Yes	Yes
LSTM	Forward	No	Yes	Yes
BLSTM	Forward and Backward	No	Yes	Yes

Table 2: The comparison of all the models.

# queries	# ads	# pairs	# positive	# negative
23K	915K	966K	318K	597K

Table 3: Statistics of the testset.

out earlier, the attention layer can be used to determine a subset of query words, which can then be used as query rewrites to increase ads selection density.

We compare the quality of rewrites chosen by attention layer against two baseline algorithms, by asking human judges to evaluate the relevance of the sub-queries. We choose two existing algorithms, namely PartialDrop (with an idea similar to [18]) and SmartIntent [15]. Both baseline algorithms use click information to identify term importance to generate sub-queries as rewrites. PartialDrop considers a term to be important and representing the query intent if dropping it leads to significant reduction of click-through rate (CTR). Removing such terms from a query thus are likely to cause intent shift. PartialDrop then works by choosing to remove certain terms while maintaining the CTR. SmartIntent, on the other hand, leverages query-ad click data by training a machine learning model to rank sub-queries. With the assumption that the distribution of ad bidded keywords is similar to that of queries, a model learned to rank keywords using CTR can then be applied to ranking sub-queries. SmartIntent first parses the query-ad bipartite click graph to summarize the CTR contribution of each pair of terms on both ends: (query term, ad bidded-keyword term). Given a pair of a query and a bidded keyword (or a sub-query), it then represents the relationship using mutual information of seen term pairs and graph walk [4] as features, and train a logistic regression on clicks as the prediction model.

As the test set for this task, we sample 1000 queries with product intent, and apply PartialDrop, SmartIntent on it, respectively. Note that as one shortens a query, the information carried in a sub-query monotonically decreases as the number of words remaining decreases. As a result, we use the following experiment protocol: for each sub-query that PartialDrop or SmartIntent generates, we generate an attention-based counterpart: a sub-query with the same number of words as the baseline, selected according to the assigned attention scores. That is, if a baseline algorithm generates a sub-query of length K, we are interested in whether the attention net is able to choose another set of K query words with higher quality. For example, if a query is "awesome lego star wars sets", a 4-word sub-query "lego star wars sets" is considered more relevant compared to "awesome star wars sets". For this experiment, we use the attention scores from a BRNN trained on the dataset described in Section 3.1.

As a quantitative evaluation, we submit all the (query, rewrite) pairs produced by different algorithms to human judges to label the query-rewrite quality. Each time a judge is presented with a pair of a query and a rewrite (a sub-query in our case), the judge needs to rate whether the rewrite is relevant to the query, with rating label ranges in {same, superset, subset, overlap, disjoint}. This rating system is designed to analyze whether the "product intent space" of a query is intact compared to that of a rewrite. If the product space of a query has the "same" or is a "superset" of that of a rewrite, the rewrite is considered of good quality. On the other hand, if the query product space is a "subset" of the rewrite product space, the query intent is shifting wider in the rewrite. The rewrite could select widened, poor results. The same concept applies to "overlap" and "disjoint".

We summarize the comparison results in Table 4. We see that compared with both PartialDrop and SmartIntent, attention scores yield substantially larger portions of rewrites with good quality. We have also conducted paired t-tests on the labeling results, by considering "same" and "superset" labels as good quality rewrites (quality score = 1), and the rest as bad quality (quality score = 0), which indicates that attention-based rewrite has significant better qualities than both PartialDrop ($p = 0.002, t = 3.102, n = 877$, two-tailed) and SmartIntent ($p = 0.001, t = 3.302, n = 787$, two-tailed).

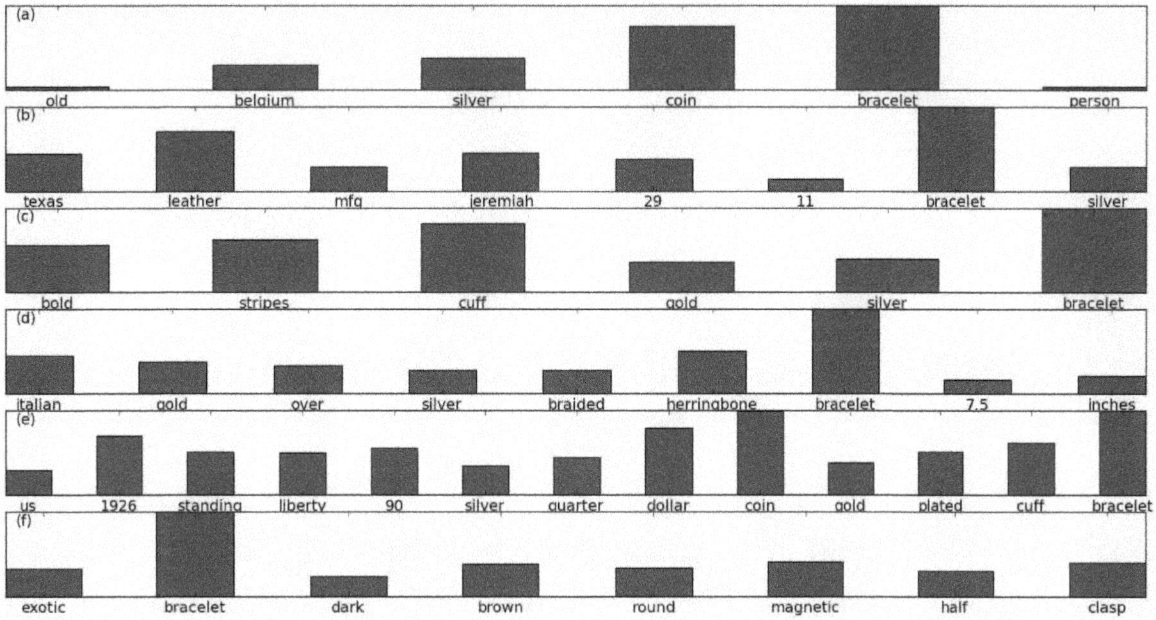

Figure 4: Attention score visualization of a query (a) and 5 top ranked ads (b)(c)(d)(e)(f) by BRNN.

method	# good	% good	method	# good	% good
attention	228	0.275	attention	212	0.286
PD	192	0.222	SI	170	0.225

Table 4: The comparison of our method (attention) with PartialDrop (PD) and SmartIntent (SI).

This strongly confirms that the attention network is able to perform correct credit assignment to words within a query. Also, the large improvement over the two baselines indicates the effectiveness of a deep model that directly models sequences over their shallow BoW based competitors.

3.5 Modified BM25 with Attention

In the next set of experiments, we proceed to evaluate the attention scores learned for ads. In particular, we propose a novel usage of the attention scores by incorporating it with the standard BM25 ranking function [21]. BM25 scores each document based on the query terms appearing in the document as follows:

$$score(q,d) = \sum_{i=1}^{n} IDF(q_i) \frac{TF(q_i,d)(k_1+1)}{TF(q_i,d) + k_1(1-b+b\frac{|d|}{avgdl})}, \quad (8)$$

where $TF(q_i, d)$ is term q_i's term frequency in document d, $|d|$ is the length of document d, and $avgdl$ is the average document length in corpus.

Attention scores can be used to calculate non-uniform, more representative term frequencies. Terms with higher importance should be rewarded with larger term frequency, and vice versa. As in Equation 9, we redistribute the term frequencies using the attention scores as weights, i.e. the component $a_j|d|$. In addition, we add a hyper-parameter λ to balance between the attention-based term frequency and the uniform term frequency (i.e. value = 1) of a document term. This "attention significance" parameter λ serves as a smoothing factor to avoid attention scores being too sharp to force certain term frequency to zero. A zero term frequency implies that matching such a term has no contribution to the relevancy between a query and a document, which is intuitively not desirable [16]. In addition, the optimal λ value (decided by validation set) indicates how useful the learned attention is to the BM25 application. If the λ is zero, it falls back to the uniform term frequencies. We then propose the modified BM25 by replacing the $TF(q_i, d)$ in Equation 8 with attention-based $TF'(q_i, d)$ as follows:

$$TF'(q_i,d) = \sum_{j:d_j=q_i} \lambda \cdot a_j|d| + (1-\lambda)\cdot 1 \quad (9)$$

We compute the AUC of the modified BM25 using the same labeled test set as in Section 3.3 (Table 3). We take 70% of the dataset as the validation set, on which grid search is applied in the range $\lambda = \{0, 0.1, 0.2, ..., 1\}$. The AUC is then computed with the selected optimal λ on the 30% remaining subset, with k_1 set to 2.0 and b set to 0.75 in Equation 8. We compare the attention scores learned by RNN, BRNN, LSTM and BLSTM. The test AUC numbers along with the optimal λ's for each model can be found in Figure 6.

The optimal λ values for RNN, BRNN, and BLSTM are equal or close to one, indicating the attention learned with RNN, BRNN, and BLSTM are good quality. In addition, BLSTM achieves the highest AUC gain, outperforming the standard BM25 by over one absolute percent. This is also

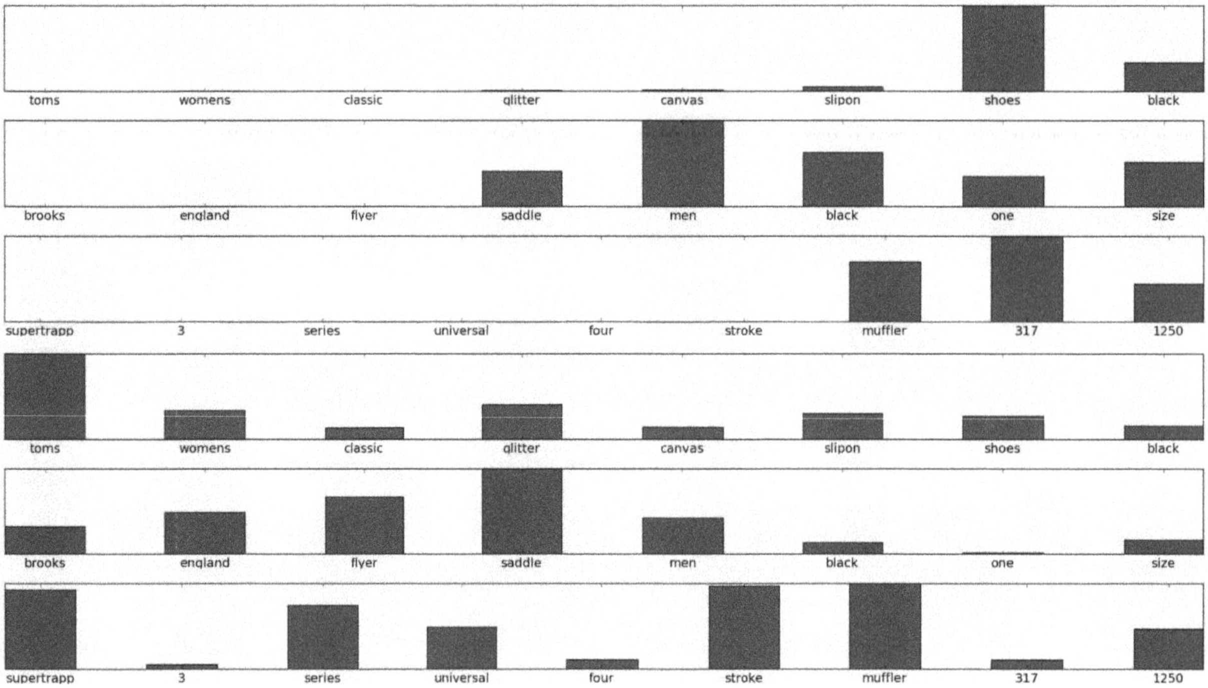

Figure 5: Visualization of the attention scores assigned on three ads. Top three: LSTM, bottom three: BLSTM.

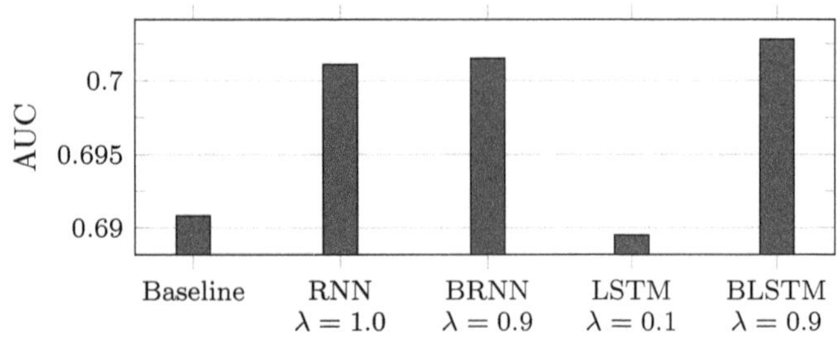

Figure 6: The test AUC of BM25 modified with attention under different architectures, with optimal attention significance factor λ grid-searched in training split

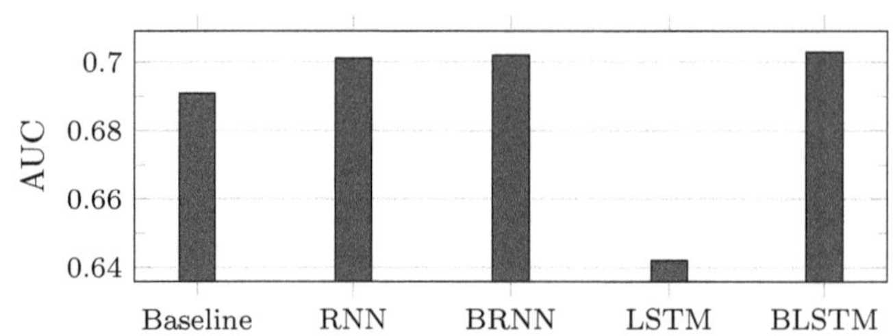

Figure 7: The test AUC of BM25 modified with attention under different architectures, with attention significance factor λ blindly set to 1.0

consistent with Figure 3 where BLSTM yields better vector representations than RNN and BRNN. On the contrary, the λ factor for LSTM is close to zero (which actually hurts the performance), implying the attention scores learned with LSTM is not useful. Figure 7 shows the test AUC where we blindly set λ to 1. Without any factor of smoothing, the attention learned with LSTM significantly degrade the AUC. This also correlates with our findings in Figure 3, where the attention based pooling does not provide improvement over last pooling.

Figure 5 gives an intuitive explanation of the behavior of the attention network on LSTM and BLSTM, where we see that the attention scores learned on LSTM commonly skew to the right. This is sensible because with the usage of gating units and cell units, LSTM is able to (and hence tend to) use the last hidden state to capture the information presented in the whole sequence. As a result, the effect of the attention network is compromised where it can lazily assign high attentions to the rightmost states, while incorrectly ignoring the ones further to the left. On the contrary, with BLSTM, the skewness problem does not exist, as shown in Figure 5. The attention scores are meaningful. For example, the important brand word "toms" for the first shoes ad and "superstrapp" for the third muffler ad are recognized, whereas with LSTM in Figure 5 they have close to 0 attention. Here the bidirectional recurrence helps recognize the intent that stands out in a position, without being biased by the history as in unidirectional recurrence. Plus with the quality control gates provided by LSTM, BLSTM attention modifies BM25 to achieve highest AUC compared to RNN and BRNN.

4. RELATED WORK

There has been a long thread of learning representations for information retrieval systems. Bag of words and its variants such as TF-IDF played a central role due to its simplicity and effectiveness. Vector space models (VSMs) [23] take a step further from BoW by mapping documents into a low dimensional vector space, which form more compact representations. Examples of VSMs include Latent Semantic Indexing [5], Probabilistic Latent Semantic Indexing [8] and Latent Dirichlet Allocation [3]. From one particular perspective, our work also falls into this category, as we are able to produce vector based representations for both queries and ads.

Recently, there has been a thrive to learn deep representations for natural language. The idea is that by using a deep architecture, one is able to learn highly nonlinear transformations of data, thus can exploit much more complicated patterns than simply using simple linear mappings. There has been successful approaches [10, 9, 19] demonstrating that deep architectures can significantly boost the performance of commercial search engines. Among these, [19] is closely related to our work, which corresponds to LSTM + Last pooling in our experiments. Our work further extends it by introducing the attention layer, which enables us to use the deep model to enhance term based tasks such as query rewriting and modified BM25. From this perspective, our work can be considered as enhancing the traditional term based IR systems with latent space deep models trained in an end-to-end fashion, which is to the best of our knowledge the first of its kind.

Methodology wise, our work extends the recently proposed attention mechanism [1, 14] from the NLP tasks such as machine translation and language modeling to the web search applications. Compared with [1], our attention module is static, that is able to directly compute the attention score without knowing the matching candidates. In a more general view, our attention based pooling is an extension of the pooling methods. As a result, it is also applicable in general wherever traditional pooling methods are needed.

There has been plenty query rewriting work for online advertising and information retrieval. Deleting query terms can help increase coverage and selection density. Substituting query terms or phrases solves the problem that a user search query may be an imperfect description of their information need. Both realm of work requires understanding the importance of a term or phrase in a query. Part of [12] simply considers query reformulation feedback by users. A term is considered not as important if a user removes the term from the previously issued query and resubmits. [13] uses point-wise mutual information to determine whether a phrase stands out comparing to adjacent terms. Using user click information [15] or pseudo relevance feedback [18] is also a good way to identify term importance. Intuitively speaking if dropping a term leads to significant reduction of click-through rate (CTR), or leads to reduced ability at discriminating relevant documents, such term is considered important. Both [15] and [18] leverages random walk algorithm [4] on a bipartite query-document graph to identify important query terms contributing CTR or relevance. Our work encompasses the essence of the prior work mentioned above. It leverages user clicks to guide the term importance so that a term with high attention (1) matches the intent of the whole query and (2) contributes to the clicks to relevant ads (and vice versa for the ad side attention). Instead of using bipartite graph, random walk algorithm, and some feature engineering, our attention learning is done through through DNN and embedding.

Okapi BM25 [21, 17] is a well known and widely used document ranking method in information retrieval. BM25 is a bag-of-words retrieval function that ranks a set of documents based on the query terms appearing in each document, through TF-IDF normalization. A known problem to BM25 is that many term weighting practices are insufficient in distinguishing informative words from uninformative ones. [11] addresses this problem by adjusting term frequencies in proportion to their semantic correlation to the categorical information of documents. Our work follows the same idea and takes a simplistic approach: we use attention to redistribute document length into term frequencies. This not only allows us to systematically evaluate attention scores, but also demonstrates the applicability of attention to TF-based information retrieval tasks.

5. CONCLUSIONS AND FUTURE WORK

We have proposed an attention based pooling on top of RNNs to model queries and ads in online advertising. The RNN module allows us to model word sequence, which is shown to be of great importance to accurately capture the meaning of a sequence. The attention based pooling module gives our model the ability to perform correct credit assignment to words within a sequence. We investigate various RNN architectures and conduct large scale experimental evaluation w.r.t. both the vector representations and the attention scores. In particular, we propose a novel way of applying the attention scores to query rewriting as well as a modified BM25 metric, and demonstrate the effectiveness of the learned attention for both queries and ads.

Possible extensions to our work also exist. For example, the fact that using the learned attention scores as term frequency yielding better BM25 metrics is actually a byproduct of our model. In other words, it is the result of optimizing a closely related objective. As a result, it is possible that we can formulate an objective function using the attention enhanced BM25 directly, while with the underlying encoder unchanged. We leave this as future work.

6. REFERENCES

[1] D. Bahdanau, K. Cho, and Y. Bengio. Neural machine translation by jointly learning to align and translate. *arXiv preprint arXiv:1409.0473*, 2014.

[2] J. Bergstra, O. Breuleux, F. Bastien, P. Lamblin, R. Pascanu, G. Desjardins, J. Turian, D. Warde-Farley, and Y. Bengio. Theano: a CPU and GPU math expression compiler. In *Proceedings of the Python for Scientific Computing Conference (SciPy)*, June 2010.

[3] D. M. Blei, A. Y. Ng, and M. I. Jordan. Latent dirichlet allocation. *the Journal of machine Learning research*, 3:993–1022, 2003.

[4] K. Collins-Thompson and J. Callan. Query expansion using random walk models. In *Proceedings of the 14th ACM International Conference on Information and Knowledge Management*, CIKM '05, pages 704–711, New York, NY, USA, 2005. ACM.

[5] S. C. Deerwester, S. T. Dumais, T. K. Landauer, G. W. Furnas, and R. A. Harshman. Indexing by latent semantic analysis. *JAsIs*, 41(6):391–407, 1990.

[6] K. Greff, R. K. Srivastava, J. Koutník, B. R.

Steunebrink, and J. Schmidhuber. LSTM: A search space odyssey. *CoRR*, abs/1503.04069, 2015.

[7] S. Hochreiter and J. Schmidhuber. Long short-term memory. *Neural computation*, 9(8):1735–1780, 1997.

[8] T. Hofmann. Probabilistic latent semantic indexing. In *Proceedings of the 22nd annual international ACM SIGIR conference on Research and development in information retrieval*, pages 50–57. ACM, 1999.

[9] P.-S. Huang, X. He, J. Gao, L. Deng, A. Acero, and L. Heck. Learning deep structured semantic models for web search using clickthrough data. In *Proceedings of the 22nd ACM International Conference on Information & Knowledge Management*, pages 2333–2338. ACM, 2013.

[10] P.-S. Huang, X. He, J. Gao, L. Deng, A. Acero, and L. Heck. Learning deep structured semantic models for web search using clickthrough data. In *Proceedings of the 22Nd ACM International Conference on Information & Knowledge Management*, CIKM '13, pages 2333–2338, New York, NY, USA, 2013. ACM.

[11] R. Jin, J. Y. Chai, and L. Si. Learn to weight terms in information retrieval using category information. In *Proceedings of the 22Nd International Conference on Machine Learning*, ICML '05, pages 353–360, New York, NY, USA, 2005. ACM.

[12] R. Jones and D. C. Fain. Query word deletion prediction. In *Proceedings of the 26th Annual International ACM SIGIR Conference on Research and Development in Informaion Retrieval*, SIGIR '03, pages 435–436, New York, NY, USA, 2003. ACM.

[13] R. Jones, B. Rey, O. Madani, and W. Greiner. Generating query substitutions. In *Proceedings of the 15th International Conference on World Wide Web*, WWW '06, pages 387–396, New York, NY, USA, 2006. ACM.

[14] W. Ling, Y. Tsvetkov, S. Amir, R. Fermandez, C. Dyer, A. W. Black, I. Trancoso, and C.-C. Lin. Not all contexts are created equal: Better word representations with variable attention. In *Proceedings of the 2015 Conference on Empirical Methods in Natural Language Processing*, pages 1367–1372, Lisbon, Portugal, September 2015. Association for Computational Linguistics.

[15] P. Liu, J. Azimi, and R. Zhang. Contextual query intent extraction for paid search selection. In *Proceedings of the 24th International Conference on World Wide Web Companion, WWW 2015, Florence, Italy, May 18-22, 2015 - Companion Volume*, pages 71–72, 2015.

[16] Y. Lv and C. Zhai. Lower-bounding term frequency normalization. In *Proceedings of the 20th ACM International Conference on Information and Knowledge Management*, CIKM '11, pages 7–16, New York, NY, USA, 2011. ACM.

[17] M. E. Maron and J. L. Kuhns. On relevance, probabilistic indexing and information retrieval. *J. ACM*, 7(3):216–244, July 1960.

[18] K. T. Maxwell and W. B. Croft. Compact query term selection using topically related text. In *Proceedings of the 36th International ACM SIGIR Conference on Research and Development in Information Retrieval*, SIGIR '13, pages 583–592, New York, NY, USA, 2013. ACM.

[19] H. Palangi, L. Deng, Y. Shen, J. Gao, X. He, J. Chen, X. Song, and R. Ward. Deep sentence embedding using the long short term memory network: Analysis and application to information retrieval. *arXiv preprint arXiv:1502.06922*, 2015.

[20] F. Provost, T. Fawcett, and R. Kohavi. The case against accuracy estimation for comparing induction algorithms. In *In Proceedings of the Fifteenth International Conference on Machine Learning*, pages 445–453. Morgan Kaufmann, 1997.

[21] S. Robertson, S. Walker, S. Jones, M. Hancock-Beaulieu, and M. Gatford. Okapi at trec-3. pages 109–126, 1996.

[22] I. Sutskever, O. Vinyals, and Q. V. Le. Sequence to sequence learning with neural networks. In *Advances in neural information processing systems*, pages 3104–3112, 2014.

[23] P. D. Turney, P. Pantel, et al. From frequency to meaning: Vector space models of semantics. *Journal of artificial intelligence research*, 37(1):141–188, 2010.

[24] K. Xu, J. Ba, R. Kiros, A. Courville, R. Salakhutdinov, R. Zemel, and Y. Bengio. Show, attend and tell: Neural image caption generation with visual attention. *arXiv preprint arXiv:1502.03044*, 2015.

[25] M. D. Zeiler. Adadelta: An adaptive learning rate method. *arXiv preprint arXiv:1212.5701*, 2012.

GMove: Group-Level Mobility Modeling Using Geo-Tagged Social Media

Chao Zhang[1], Keyang Zhang[1], Quan Yuan[1], Luming Zhang[2], Tim Hanratty[3], and Jiawei Han[1]
[1]Dept. of Computer Science, University of Illinois at Urbana-Champaign, Urbana, IL, USA
[2]Dept. of CSIE, Hefei University of Technology, Hefei, China
[2]Information Sciences Directorate, Army Research Laboratory, Adelphi, MD, USA
[1]{czhang82, kzhang53, qyuan, hanj}@illinois.edu [2]zglumg@gmail.com
[3]timothy.p.hanratty@mail.mil

ABSTRACT

Understanding human mobility is of great importance to various applications, such as urban planning, traffic scheduling, and location prediction. While there has been fruitful research on modeling human mobility using tracking data (*e.g.*, GPS traces), the recent growth of geo-tagged social media (GeoSM) brings new opportunities to this task because of its sheer size and multi-dimensional nature. Nevertheless, how to obtain quality mobility models from the highly sparse and complex GeoSM data remains a challenge that cannot be readily addressed by existing techniques.

We propose GMOVE, a *group-level mobility modeling* method using GeoSM data. Our insight is that the GeoSM data usually contains multiple user groups, where the users within the same group share significant movement regularity. Meanwhile, user grouping and mobility modeling are two intertwined tasks: (1) better user grouping offers better within-group data consistency and thus leads to more reliable mobility models; and (2) better mobility models serve as useful guidance that helps infer the group a user belongs to. GMOVE thus alternates between user grouping and mobility modeling, and generates an ensemble of Hidden Markov Models (HMMs) to characterize group-level movement regularity. Furthermore, to reduce text sparsity of GeoSM data, GMOVE also features a text augmenter. The augmenter computes keyword correlations by examining their spatiotemporal distributions. With such correlations as auxiliary knowledge, it performs sampling-based augmentation to alleviate text sparsity and produce high-quality HMMs.

Our extensive experiments on two real-life data sets demonstrate that GMOVE can effectively generate meaningful group-level mobility models. Moreover, with context-aware location prediction as an example application, we find that GMOVE significantly outperforms baseline mobility models in terms of prediction accuracy.

1. INTRODUCTION

Understanding human mobility has been widely recognized as a corner-stone task for various applications, ranging from urban planning and traffic scheduling to location prediction and personalized activity recommendation. In the past few decades, the importance of this task has led to fruitful research efforts in the data mining community [7, 27, 13, 4, 26]. While most of the previous works use tracking data (*e.g.*, GPS traces) to discover human movement regularity, the recent explosive growth of *geo-tagged social media* (GeoSM) brings new opportunities to this task. Nowadays, as GPS-enabled mobile devices and location-sharing apps are penetrating into our daily life, every single day is witnessing millions of geo-tagged tweets, Facebook checkins, *etc.* Compared with conventional tracking data, GeoSM possesses two unique advantages for mobility modeling: (1) First, in addition to spatial and temporal information, each GeoSM record also includes text. Hence, a user's GeoSM history reveals not only how she moves from one location to another, but also what activities she does at different locations. (2) Second, the GeoSM data has a much larger size and coverage. Due to privacy concerns, gathering tracking data typically requires a huge amount of time and money to engage sufficient volunteers. In contrast, the GeoSM data naturally covers hundreds of millions of users and has a much larger volume.

KDD '16, August 13-17, 2016, San Francisco, CA, USA

 ISBN 978-1-4503-4232-2/16/08...$15.00
DOI: http://dx.doi.org/10.1145/2939672.2939793

Considering its multi-dimensional nature and sheer size, it is clear that GeoSM serves as an unprecedentedly valuable source for human mobility modeling. Hence, we study the problem of using large-scale GeoSM data to unveil human movement regularity. Specifically, we answer the following two questions:

- *What are the intrinsic states underlying people's movements?* To name a few, a state could be working at office in the morning, exercising at gym at noon, or having dinner with family at night. We want each state to provide a unified view regarding a user's activity: (1) where is the user; (2) what is the user doing; and (3) when does this activity happen.

- *How do people move sequentially between those latent states?* For example, where do people working in Manhattan usually go to relax after work? and what are the popular sightseeing routes for a one-day trip in Paris? We aim to summarize people's transitions between the latent states in a concise and interpretable way.

Unveiling human mobility using GeoSM data can greatly benefit various applications. Consider traffic jam prevention as an example. While existing techniques [7, 26, 25] can detect sequential patterns to reflect the populace flow between geographical regions, the GeoSM data allows us understand populace flow beyond that. Suppose severe traffic jams occur frequently in a region R. With the mobility model learnt from massive GeoSM data, we can understand what are people's typical activities in R, which regions do people come from, and why do people take those trips. Such understandings can guide the government to better diagnose the root causes of traffic jams and take prevention actions accordingly. Another example application is context-aware location prediction.

Previous studies [15, 14, 4] typically use the spatiotemporal regularity of human mobility to predict the next location a person may visit. By leveraging GeoSM data, we can incorporate activity-level transitions to infer what activities a user will engage subsequently. As such, the mobility models learnt from GeoSM can potentially improve context-aware location prediction remarkably.

Despite its practical importance, the task of modeling human mobility with GeoSM data is nontrivial due to several challenges: (1) *Integrating diverse types of data.* The GeoSM data involves three different data types: location, time, and text. Considering the totally different representations of those data types and the complicated correlations among them, how to effectively integrate them for mobility modeling is difficult. (2) *Constructing reliable models from sparse and complex data.* Unlike intentionally collected tracking data, the GeoSM data is low-sampling in nature, because a user is unlikely to report her activity at every visited location. Such data sparsity makes it unrealistic to train a mobility model for each individual. On the other hand, one may propose to aggregate the data of all users to train one single model, but the obtained model could then suffer from severe data inconsistency because different users can have totally different moving behaviors. (3) *Extracting interpretable semantics from short GeoSM messages.* The GeoSM messages are usually short. For example, any geo-tagged tweets contain no more than 140 characters, and most geo-tagged Instagram photos are associated with quite short text messages. It is nontrivial to extract reliable knowledge from short GeoSM messages and build high-quality mobility models.

We propose GMOVE, an effective method that models human mobility from massive GeoSM data. GMOVE relies on the Hidden Markov Model (HMM) to learn the multi-view latent states and people's transitions between them. To obtain quality HMMs from the highly sparse and complex GeoSM data, we propose a novel idea of *group-level* mobility modeling. The key is to group the users that share similar moving behaviors, *e.g.*, the students studying at the same university. By aggregating the movements of like-behaved users, GMOVE can largely alleviate data sparsity without compromising the within-group data consistency.

To achieve effective user grouping and mobility modeling, we find that these two sub-tasks can mutually enhance each other: (1) better user grouping offers better within-group data consistency, which helps produce more reliable mobility models; and (2) better mobility models can serve as useful knowledge, which helps infer the group a user belongs to. Based on this observation, we develop an iterative framework, in which we alternate between user grouping and group-level mobility modeling. We theoretically and empirically show that, such a process leads to better user grouping and mobility models after each iteration, and finally generates an ensemble of high-quality HMMs.

Another important component of GMOVE is a text augmenter, which leverages keyword spatiotemporal correlations to reduce text sparsity. While each raw GeoSM message is short and noisy, we find that using millions of GeoSM records, we are able to extract the intrinsic correlations between keywords by examining their spatiotemporal distributions. Consider two users who are having dinner at the same Italian restaurant and posting tweets with two different keywords: "pasta" and "pizza". Although these two keywords do not co-occur in the same tweet, they are spatially and temporally close. We hence quantify the spatiotemporal correlations between keywords, and use such correlations as auxiliary knowledge to augment raw GeoSM messages. We show that such augmentation can largely reduce text sparsity and lead to highly interpretable states.

To summarize, we make the following contributions:

1. We formulate the problem of mobility modeling using massive geo-tagged social media (Section 2). To the best of our knowledge, this is the first study that attempts to use the multi-dimensional (spatial, temporal, textual) information in GeoSM data to unveil human movement regularity.

2. We propose a novel group-level mobility modeling framework. Built upon an ensemble of HMMs (Section 4), it enables user grouping and mobility modeling to mutually enhance each other. As such, it effectively alleviates data sparsity and inconsistency to generate reliable mobility models.

3. We design a strategy that leverages the spatiotemporal distributions to quantify keyword correlations as auxiliary knowledge (Section 3). By augmenting raw GeoSM messages with such knowledge, our method largely reduces text sparsity to produce interpretable latent states.

4. We perform extensive experiments using two real data sets (Section 5). The results show that our method can produce high-quality group-level mobility models. Meanwhile, with context-aware location prediction as an example application, we observe that our method achieves much better prediction accuracy compared with baseline mobility models.

2. PRELIMINARIES

In this section, we formulate the problem of mobility modeling using geo-tagged social media, and explore several characteristics of this problem to motivate the design of GMOVE.

2.1 Problem Description

A GeoSM record x is defined as a tuple $\langle u_x, t_x, l_x, e_x \rangle$ where: (1) u_x is the user id; (2) t_x is the creating timestamp (in second); (3) l_x is a two-dimensional vector representing the user's location when x is created; and (4) e_x, which is a bag of keywords from a vocabulary V, denotes the text message of x.

Let us consider a set of users $U = \{u_1, u_2, \ldots, u_M\}$. For a user $u \in U$, her GeoSM history is a sequence of chronologically ordered GeoSM records $S_u = x_1 x_2 \ldots x_n$. To understand u's mobility, one may propose to use the entire sequence S_u. Nevertheless, the sequence S_u is low-sampling in nature, and the temporal gaps between some pairs of consecutive records can be very large, *e.g.*, several days. To generate reliable mobility models, we only use the dense parts in S_u, which we define as *trajectories*.

DEFINITION 1 (TRAJECTORY). *Given a GeoSM sequence $S = x_1 x_2 \ldots x_n$ and a time gap threshold $\Delta t > 0$, a subsequence $S' = x_i x_{i+1} \ldots x_{i+k}$ is a length-k trajectory of S if S' satisfies: (1) $\forall 1 < j \le k$, $t_{x_j} - t_{x_{j-1}} \le \Delta t$; and (2) there are no longer subsequences in S that contains S' and meanwhile also satisfies condition (1).*

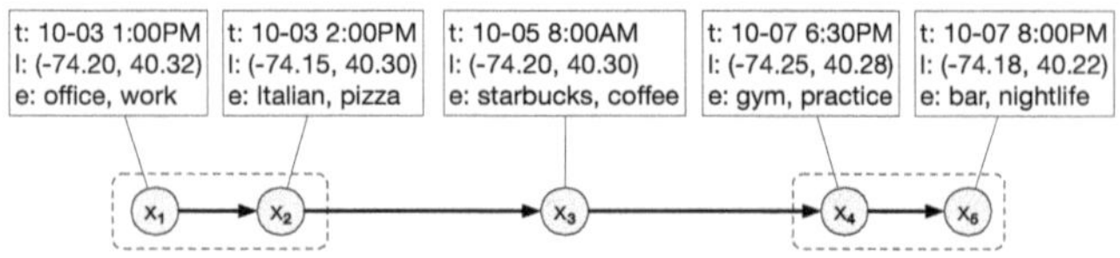

Figure 1: An illustration of *trajectory* ($\Delta t = 3$ hours).

EXAMPLE 1. *In Figure 1, given a user's GeoSM history $S = x_1 x_2 x_3 x_4 x_5$ and $\Delta t = 2$ hours, there are two trajectories: $x_1 x_2$ and $x_4 x_5$. These trajectories correspond to the user's two moving behaviors: (1) having dinner at an Italian restaurant after work; and (2) going to bar after taking exercises.*

A trajectory essentially leverages the time constraint to extract reliable moving behaviors in the GeoSM history. With the extracted trajectories, our general goal is to use them to understand the mobility of the users in U. Nevertheless, the number of trajectories of one single user is usually too limited to train a mobility model, while aggregating the trajectories of all the users in U could suffer from severe data inconsistency and result in an ambiguous model.

To address the dilemma, we propose to study *group-level user mobility*. Our key observation is that, aggregating the trajectories of like-behaved users can largely alleviate data sparsity and inconsistency, and thus unveil the movement regularity for that group. Consider a group of students studying at the same university, they may share similar hotspots like classrooms, gyms, and restaurants. Many students also have similar moving behaviors, *e.g.*, moving from the same residence hall to classrooms, and having lunch together after classes. As another example, a group of tourists in New York may all visit locations like the JFK Airport, the Metropolitan Museum, the 5th Avenue, *etc.*. While the data of one individual is limited, the collective movement data from a group of like-behaved people can be informative about their latent hotspots and the movement regularity. It is important to note that, one user can belong to several different groups, *e.g.*, a student may also go sightseeing in the city on weekends. Therefore, the users should be grouped softly instead of rigidly.

Based on the above observation, we formulate the problem of *group-level mobility modeling* as follows. Given the set U of users and their trajectories extracted from historical GeoSM records, the task of group-level mobility modeling consists of two sub-tasks: (1) ***user grouping***: softly group the users in U such that the members in the same group have similar moving behaviors; and (2) ***mobility modeling***: for each user group, discover the latent states that reflect the users' activities from a multidimensional (where-what-when) view, and find out how the users move between those latent states.

2.2 Overview of GMOVE

GMOVE is built upon the Hidden Markov Model (HMM), an effective statistical model for sequential data. Given an observed sequence $S = x_1 x_2 \ldots x_n$, HMM defines K latent states $Z = \{1, 2, \ldots, K\}$ that are not observable. Each record $x_i (1 \le i \le n)$ corresponds to a latent state $z_i \in Z$, which has a probabilistic distribution that governs the generation of x_i. In addition, the latent state sequence $z_1 z_2 \ldots z_n$ follows the Markov process, namely, the state z_i only depends on the previous state z_{i-1}.

As discussed above, there exists a dilemma when applying HMM to understand the mobility of the users in U: training an HMM for each user is unrealistic due to data sparsity, while training one single HMM for all the users leads to an ambiguous model due to data inconsistency. Therefore, GMOVE performs group-level mobility modeling by coupling the subtasks of user grouping and mobility modeling. It aims at dividing the users in U into like-behaved user groups and training an HMM for each group. By aggregating the movement data within the same group, we can alleviate data sparsity without compromising data consistency.

Now the question is, how can we group the users such that the users within the same group have similar moving behaviors? Our idea is that the sub-tasks of *user grouping* and *mobility modeling* can mutually enhance each other: (1) better user grouping leads to more consistent movement data within each group, which can improve the quality of the HMM; and (2) high-quality HMMs more accurately describe the true latent states and the transitions between them, which helps infer which group a user should belong to. Hence, GMOVE employs an iterative framework that alternates between user grouping and HMM training. Later we will see, as the iteration continues, the user grouping gets more and more accurate, and the mobility models get more and more reliable, and such a process will finally converge to a stable solution.

Another important component of GMOVE is a text augmenter. When training an HMM for each group, we model each latent state to generate multidimensional (spatial, temporal, and textual) observations of the user's activity. While the spatial and temporal observations are clean, the major challenge in obtaining high-quality latent states is that the text messages are mostly short and noisy. To address this problem, we observe that keywords' spatiotemporal distributions can reveal their intrinsic correlations. The text augmenter thus quantifies the spatiotemporal correlations between keywords to obtain auxiliray knowledge. With such knowledge, it performs a weighted sampling process to augment raw text messages. Such augmentation can largely overcome text sparsity and suppress noise to help produce high-quality HMMs.

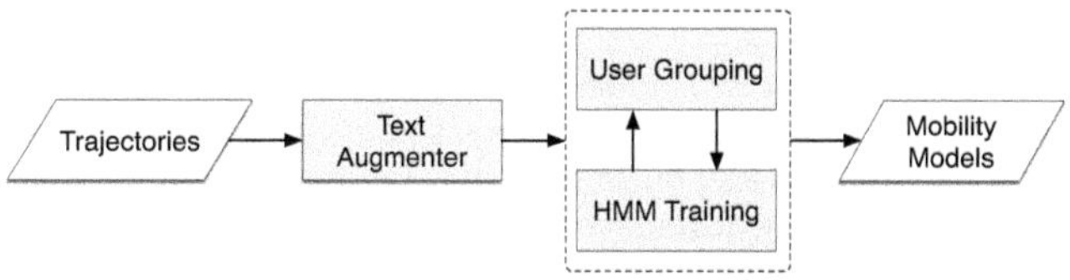

Figure 2: The framework of GMOVE.

Figure 2 summarizes the framework of GMOVE. Given the input trajectories, GMOVE consists of two major modules to produce group-level mobility models. The first module is the text augmenter, which examines the spatiotemporal correlations between keywords to augment raw messages. With the augmented trajectories, the second module obtains an ensemble of HMMs by alternating between user grouping and HMM training. In the following, we elaborate these two module in Section 3 and 4, respectively.

3. TEXT AUGMENTATION

In this section, we describe GMOVE's text augmenter, which first computes keyword correlations and then performs sampling-based text augmentation.

Keyword correlation computation. Our computation of keyword correlation relies on spatiotemporal discretization. Let us consider a spatiotemporal space D that consists of three dimensions: (1) the longitude dimension x; (2) the latitude dimension y; and (3) the time dimension t. We partition D into $N_x \times N_y \times N_t$ equal-size grids, where N_x, N_y and N_t are pre-specified integers that control discretization granularity. Based on such discretization, we define the concepts of *grid density* and *signature* for each keyword.

DEFINITION 2 (GRID DENSITY). *Given a keyword w, the density of w in grid $\langle n_x, n_y, n_t \rangle$ $(1 \le n_x \le N_x, 1 \le n_y \le N_y, 1 \le n_t \le N_t)$ is defined as w's frequency in that grid, namely*

$$d_w(n_x, n_y, n_t) = \frac{c_w(n_x, n_y, n_t)}{\sum_{n_x, n_y, n_t} c_w(n_x, n_y, n_t)},$$

where $c_w(n_x, n_y, n_t)$ is the number of GeoSM records that contain w and meanwhile fall in grid $\langle n_x, n_y, n_t \rangle$.

DEFINITION 3 (SIGNATURE). *Given a keyword w, its signature s_w is a $N_x N_y N_t$-dimensional vector, where $d_w(n_x, n_y, n_t)$ is the value for the $((n_t - 1)N_x N_y + (n_y - 1)N_x + n_x)$-th dimension.*

The signature of a keyword encodes how frequently that keyword appears in different spatiotemporal grids. Intuitively, if two keywords are semantically correlated (*e.g.*, "pasta" and "pizza"), they are more likely to frequently co-occur in the same grid and thus have similar signatures. Below, we measure the spatiotemporal correlation between two keywords by simply computing the similarity of their signatures.

DEFINITION 4 (KEYWORD CORRELATION). *Given two keywords w_i and w_j, let s_{w_i} and s_{w_j} be their signatures. The spatiotemporal correlation between w_i and w_j, denoted as $corr(w_i, w_j)$, is the cosine distance between s_{w_i} and s_{w_j}.*

Sampling-based augmentation. Definition 4 quantifies keyword correlations based on their spatiotemporal distributions. With Definition 4, we further select out a set of vicinity keywords from the vocabulary for each keyword.

DEFINITION 5 (VICINITY). *For any keyword $w \in V$, its vicinity $\mathcal{N}_w$ is $\mathcal{N}_w = \{v | v \in V \wedge corr(w, v) \geq \delta\}$ where $\delta \geq 0$ is a pre-specified correlation threshold.*

The vicinity concept is important as it identifies other keywords that are highly correlated to the target keyword and suppresses noisy keywords. Based on Definition 5, we are now ready to describe the text augmentation process. Given an input GeoSM record x, our goal is to augment the original text message e_x by incorporating many other keywords that are semantically relevant to e_x. As shown in Algorithm 1, the augmentation simply performs sampling by using keyword correlation as auxiliary knowledge. Specifically, we first sample a keyword w from the original message based on normalized TF-IDF weights, and then sample a relevant keyword v from w's vicinity. The probability of a keyword v being sampled is proportional to its spatiotemporal correlation with w, namely $corr(w, v)$. We repeat the sampling process until the augmented message reaches a pre-specified length L.

Algorithm 1: Text augmentation.

Input: A GeoSM record x, the target length L.
Output: The augmented text message of x.

```
A_x ← The original text message e_x;
while len(A_x) < L do
    Sample a word w ∈ e_x with probability TF-IDF(w) / Σ_{v∈e_x} TF-IDF(v);
    Sample a word v ∈ N_w with probability corr(w,v) / Σ_{u∈N_w} corr(w,u);
    Add v into A_x;
return A_x;
```

4. HMM ENSEMBLE LEARNING

In this section, we describe GMOVE's second module that learns an ensemble of HMMs. Below, we first present an iterative refinement framework in Section 4.1, Then we introduce the procedures for the HMM training and user grouping in Section 4.2 and 4.3, respectively. Finally, we prove the convergence of GMOVE and analyze its time complexity in Section 4.4.

4.1 The Iterative Refinement Framework

To generate high-quality group-level HMMs, GMOVE employs an iterative refinement framework that performs the following steps:

1. **Initialization:** Let $U = \{u_1, u_2, \ldots, u_M\}$ be the user set, and $\mathcal{G} = \{1, 2, 3, \ldots, G\}$ be the G underlying user groups.
   (a) $\forall u \in U$, randomly generate an initial membership vector M_u *s.t.* $\sum_{g=1}^{G} M_u(g) = 1$, where $M_u(g)$ denotes the probability that user u belongs to group g.
   (b) $\forall g \in \mathcal{G}$, randomly initialize an HMM H_g. The ensemble of the HMMs are denoted as $\mathcal{H} = \{H_g | g \in \mathcal{G}\}$.
2. **HMM Training:** $\forall g \in \mathcal{G}$, use the membership vectors to reweigh all input trajectories, such that the weights of user u's trajectories are set to $M_u(g)$. Then refine every H_g to generate a new HMM ensemble, $\mathcal{H}^{\text{new}} = \{H_g^{\text{new}} | g \in \mathcal{G}\}$.
3. **User Grouping:** $\forall u \in U$, use $\mathcal{H}^{\text{new}}$ to update u's membership vector such that the g-th dimension is the posterior probability that user u belongs to group g, namely $M_u^{\text{new}}(g) = p(g|u; \mathcal{H}^{\text{new}})$.
4. **Iterating:** Check for convergence using the log-likelihood of the input trajectories. If the convergence criterion is not met, then let
$$\forall g, H_g \leftarrow H_g^{\text{new}}; \ \forall u, M_u \leftarrow M_u^{\text{new}};$$
and return to Step 2.

4.2 HMM Training

In the HMM training step, the task is to use weighted trajectories to train a new HMM for each group. Below, we first define the HMM for generating the trajectories, and then discuss how to infer model parameters.

4.2.1 *Group-Level HMM*

Let us consider a trajectory $S = x_1 x_2 \ldots x_N$. Each observation $x_n (1 \leq n \leq N)$ is multidimensional: (1) l_n is a two-dimensional vector denoting latitude and longitude; (2) t_n is a timestamp; and (3) e_n is a bag of keywords denoting the augmented message.

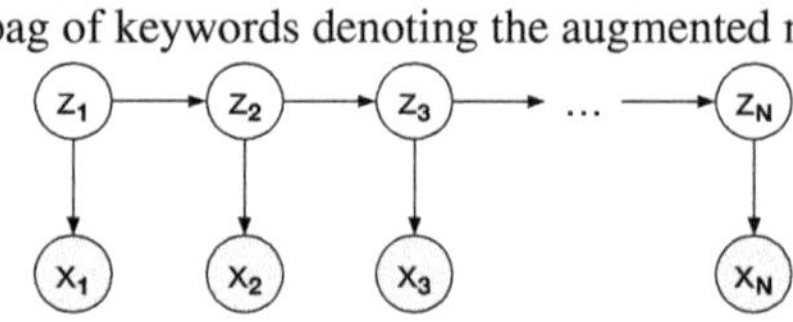

Figure 3: An illustration of the HMM.

To generate the sequence $x_1 x_2 \ldots x_N$, we assume there are K latent states $Z = \{1, 2, \ldots, K\}$. As shown in Figure 3, each observation x_n corresponds to a latent state $z_n \in Z$, and the sequence of the latent states $z_1 z_n \ldots z_N$ follows a Markov process parameterized by: (1) a K-dimensional vector π that defines the initial distribution over the K latent states, *i.e.*, $\pi_k = p(z_1 = k)$ $(1 \leq k \leq K)$; and (2) a $K \times K$ matrix $\mathbf{A}$ that defines the transition probabilities among the K latent states. Suppose the $(n-1)$-th $(n > 1)$ latent sate is $z_{n-1} = j$, then the n-th state z_n depends only on z_{n-1}. More formally, if the state z_{n-1} is j, the probability for the state z_n to be k is given by $\mathbf{A}_{jk}$, *i.e.*, $p(z_n = k | z_{n-1} = j) = \mathbf{A}_{jk}$.

Meanwhile, a state z_n generates x_n by generating the location l_n, the timestamp t_n, and the keywords e_n independently, *i.e.*,
$$p(x_n | z_n = k) = p(l_n | z_n = k) \cdot p(t_n | z_n = k) \cdot p(e_n | z_n = k).$$
For each observation x_n, we assume the following spatial, temporal, and textual distributions: (1) The location l_n is generated from a bi-variate Gaussian, *i.e.*, $p(l_n | z_n = k) = N(l_n | \mu_{lk}, \Sigma_{lk})$ where μ_{lk} and Σ_{lk} are the mean and variance matrix for state k. (2) The timestamp t_n is generated from a uni-variate Gaussian, *i.e.*, $p(t_n | z_n = k) = N(t_n \mod 86400 | \mu_{tk}, \sigma_{tk})$, where μ_{tk} and σ_{tk} are the mean and variance for state k. Note that we convert the raw absolute timestamp t_n (in second) into the relative timestamp in one day. (3) The keywords e_n are generated from a multinomial distribution, *i.e.*, $p(e_n | z_n = k) \propto \prod_{v=1}^{V} \theta_{kv}^{e_n^v}$, where θ_{kv} is the probability of choosing word v for state k, and e_n^v is the number of v's occurrences in e_n.

4.2.2 *Parameter Inference*

When training the HMM for group g, let us use $\{S_1, S_2, \ldots, S_R\}$ to denote the input trajectories, and each trajectory $S_r (1 \leq r \leq R)$ is associated with a weight w_r, denoting the probability that the user of S_r belongs to group g. The group-level HMM is parameterized by $\Phi = \{\pi, \mathbf{A}, \mu_l, \Sigma_l, \mu_t, \sigma_t, \theta\}$. We use the Expectation-Maximization (EM) algorithm to estimate these parameters. It is important to note that, when applying EM to train the HMM for group g, we use the previous HMM H_g to initialize model parameters. Later we will see, such an initialization ensures the iterative framework of GMOVE obtains better HMMs after each iteration and finally converge.

Starting with the initial parameters, the EM algorithm alternates between the E-step and the M-step round by round[1] to generate a new HMM. In the $(t+1)$-th round E-step, it utilizes the estimated parameters at the t-th round $\Phi^{(t)}$, and computes the expectation of the complete likelihood $Q(\Phi)$. In the M-step, it finds a new estimation $\Phi^{(t+1)}$ that maximizes the Q-function. Below, we present the details of the E-step and the M-step.

E-Step. In the E-step, the key is to compute the distribution of the latent states based on the old parameter set $\Phi^{(t)}$. Given a trajectory $S_r = x_{r,1}x_{r,2}\ldots x_{r,N}, \forall 1 \leq n \leq N$, we first use the Baum-Welch algorithm to compute two distributions:

$$\alpha(z_{r,n}) = p(x_{r,1}, x_{r,2}, \ldots, x_{r,n}, z_{r,n}; \Phi^{(t)}),$$
$$\beta(z_{r,n}) = p(x_{r,n+1}, \ldots, x_{r,N} | z_{r,n}; \Phi^{(t)}).$$

Here, $\alpha(z_{r,n})$ can be computed in a forward fashion, and $\beta(z_{r,n})$ can be computed in a backward fashion:

$$\alpha(z_{r,n}) = p(x_{r,n}|z_{r,n}) \sum_{z_{r,n-1}} \alpha(z_{r,n-1}) p(z_{r,n}|z_{r,n-1}),$$
$$\beta(z_{r,n}) = \sum_{z_{r,n+1}} \beta(z_{r,n+1}) p(x_{r,n+1}|z_{r,n+1}) p(z_{r,n+1}|z_{r,n}).$$

where the initial distributions $\alpha(z_{r,1})$ and $\beta(z_{r,N})$ are:

$$\alpha(z_{r,1} = k) = \pi_k p(x_{r,1}|z_{r,1} = k), \quad \beta(z_{r,N} = k) = 1.$$

Based on $\alpha(z_{r,n})$ and $\beta(z_{r,n})$, we are now able to compute the following distributions for the latent states: (1) $\gamma(z_{r,n})$: the distribution of the n-th latent state for the r-th trajectory; and (2) $\xi(z_{r,n-1}, z_{r,n})$: the joint distribution of two consecutive latent states in the r-th trajectory. These two distributions are given by

$$\gamma(z_{r,n}) = p(z_{r,n}|S_r) = \alpha(z_{r,n})\beta(z_{r,n})/p(S_r),$$
$$\xi(z_{r,n-1}, z_{r,n}) = p(z_{r,n-1}, z_{r,n}|S_r)$$
$$= \alpha(z_{r,n-1}) p(x_{r,n}|z_{r,n}) p(z_{r,n}|z_{r,n-1}) \beta(z_{r,n})/p(S_r),$$

where $p(S_r) = \sum_{z_{r,N}} \alpha(z_{r,N})$.

M-Step. In the M-step, we derive the best estimation for the parameter set $\Phi^{(t+1)} = \{\pi, \mathbf{A}, \mu_g, \Sigma_g, \mu_t, \sigma_t, \theta\}$. Based on $\gamma(z_{r,n})$ and $\xi(z_{r,n-1}, z_{r,n})$, let us define

$$\Gamma_k = \sum_{r=1}^{R}\sum_{n=1}^{N} w_r \gamma(z_{r,n}^k); \quad \Xi_j = \sum_{r=1}^{R}\sum_{n=2}^{N}\sum_{i=1}^{K} w_r \xi(z_{r,n-1}^j, z_{r,n}^i).$$

We update the parameters in $\Phi^{(t+1)}$ as follows (please see Appendix for the detailed derivation):

$$\pi_k^{(t+1)} = \sum_{r=1}^{R} w_r \gamma(z_{r,1}^k); \tag{1}$$

$$A_{jk}^{(t+1)} = \frac{1}{\Xi_j} \sum_{r=1}^{R}\sum_{n=2}^{N} w_r \xi(z_{r,n-1}^j, z_{r,n}^k) \tag{2}$$

$$\mu_{lk}^{(t+1)} = \frac{1}{\Gamma_k} \sum_{r=1}^{R}\sum_{n=1}^{N} w_r \gamma(z_{r,n}^k) l_{r,n} \tag{3}$$

$$\Sigma_{lk}^{(t+1)} = \frac{1}{\Gamma_k} \sum_{r=1}^{R}\sum_{n=1}^{N} w_r \gamma(z_{r,n}^k)(l_{r,n} - \mu_{lk}^{(t+1)})(l_{r,n} - \mu_{lk}^{(t+1)})^T; \tag{4}$$

$$\mu_{tk}^{(t+1)} = \frac{1}{\Gamma_k} \sum_{r=1}^{R}\sum_{n=1}^{N} w_r \gamma(z_{r,n}^k) t_{r,n}; \tag{5}$$

$$\sigma_{tk}^{(t+1)} = \frac{1}{\Gamma_k} \sum_{r=1}^{R}\sum_{n=1}^{N} w_r \gamma(z_{r,n}^k)(t_{r,n} - \mu_{tk}^{(t+1)})^2; \tag{6}$$

$$\theta_{kv}^{(t+1)} = \frac{1}{\Gamma_k} \sum_{r=1}^{R}\sum_{n=1}^{N} w_r \gamma(z_{r,n}^k) e_{r,n}^v. \tag{7}$$

4.3 User Grouping

Once the new ensemble of HMMs, $\mathcal{H}^{\text{new}}$, are obtained, we use them to softly assign each user into the G groups. For each user u, we update the membership vector M_u such that the g-th dimension is the posterior probability that u belongs to group g. Let us denote the set of u's trajectories as J_u, in which the j-th $(1 \leq j \leq |J_u|)$ trajectory is S_u^j. Based on the new HMM ensemble $\mathcal{H}^{\text{new}}$, the probability of observing S_u^j given group g, $p(S_u^j|g; \mathcal{H}^{\text{new}})$, can be computed using the forward scoring algorithm of HMM. Accordingly, the probability of observing J_u is given by:

$$p(u|g; \mathcal{H}^{\text{new}}) = \prod_{j=1}^{|J_u|} p(S_u^j|g; \mathcal{H}^{\text{new}}). \tag{8}$$

Using the Bayes' theorem, we further derive the posterior probability that user u belongs to group g as follows:

$$p(g|u; \mathcal{H}^{\text{new}}) \propto p(g) p(u|g; \mathcal{H}^{\text{new}}),$$

where $p(u|g; \mathcal{H}^{\text{new}})$ is given by Equation 8, and $p(g)$ is estimated from the membership vectors: $p(g) = \sum_{u \in U} M_u(g)/|U|$. Finally, we obtain the new membership vector M_u^{new} as $M_u^{\text{new}}(g) = p(g|u; \mathcal{H}^{\text{new}})$.

4.4 Discussions

Now we proceed to prove the convergence of GMOVE.

THEOREM 1. *The iterative refinement framework of* GMOVE *is guaranteed to converge.*

PROOF. With Jensen's inequality, the log-likelihood of the input trajectory data satisfies:

$$l(\mathcal{H}) = \sum_{u \in U} \log \sum_{g=1}^{G} p(u, g; \mathcal{H}) \tag{9}$$

$$= \sum_{u \in U} \log \sum_{g=1}^{G} M_u(g) \frac{p(u, g; \mathcal{H})}{M_u(g)} \tag{10}$$

$$\geq \sum_{u \in U} \sum_{g=1}^{G} M_u(g) \log \frac{p(u, g; \mathcal{H})}{M_u(g)} \tag{11}$$

[1]We intentionally use two different terms, namely *iteration* and *round*, to distinguish the two different iterative processes: (1) GMOVE's iterative refinement framework; and (2) the EM algorithm for HMM training.

Recall that, after each iteration, GMOVE sets $M_u(g)$ to the posterior probability $p(g|u;\mathcal{H})$. The quantity $p(u,g;\mathcal{H})/M_u(g)$ is thus a constant, and hence the equality in Equation 11 is guaranteed to hold. Such a property allows us to prove the log-likelihood is non-decreasing after each iteration. More formally, we have

$$l(\mathcal{H}) = \sum_{u\in U}\sum_{g=1}^{G} M_u^t(g)\log\frac{p(u,g;H_g)}{M_u^t(g)} \quad (12)$$

$$\leq \sum_{u\in U}\sum_{g=1}^{G} M_u^t(g)\log\frac{p(u,g;H_g^{\text{new}})}{M_u^t(g)} \leq l(\mathcal{H}^{\text{new}}) \quad (13)$$

In the above, the key step is Equation 13. It holds because in its iterative refinement framework, GMOVE uses the parameters of the previous HMM ensemble to initialize the current HMM ensemble, which guarantees $p(u,g;\mathcal{H})$ to be non-decreasing after the HMM refinement. As the total likelihood is non-decreasing after every iteration, we have proved the convergence of our algorithm. □

There is a tight connection between our iterative refinement framework and the traditional EM algorithm. The only difference between the two is that, in the EM algorithm, the constructed lower bound is typically convex and thus can be easily optimized to global optimum; while in our case, the constructed lower bound is still non-convex and we need to use yet another EM algorithm (HMM refinement) to optimize this lower bound. As the lower bound is non-convex, we have to make sure the HMM training of every iteration initialize with the parameters learnt from the previous iteration, otherwise we may risk running into different local optimums and thus break the convergence guarantee of our algorithm.

5. EXPERIMENTS

In this section, we evaluate the empirical performance of GMOVE. All the algorithms were implemented in JAVA and the experiments were conducted on a computer with Intel Core i7 2.4Ghz CPU and 8GB memory.

5.1 Data Sets

Our experiments are based on two real-life data sets, both of which are crawled using Twitter Streaming API during 2014.10.10 — 2014.10.30. The first data set, referred to as LA, consists of 0.6 million geo-tagged tweets in Los Angeles. After grouping the tweets by user id and extracting trajectories with a time constraint of three hours (Definition 1), we obtain around 30 thousand trajectories. The second data set, referred to as NY, consists of 0.7 million geo-tagged tweets in New York, and there are 42 thousand trajectories after extracting with the three-hour time constraint. The reason we choose these two cities is because we want to verify the performance of GMOVE on the data sets that have quite different population distributions — the populace of Los Angeles is spread out in many different districts, while the populace of New York is relatively concentrated in Manhattan and Brooklyn.

5.2 Illustrative Cases

In this subsection, we run GMOVE on LA and NY and use several illustrative cases to verify its effectiveness.

5.2.1 Text Augmentation Results

In the first set of experiments, we demonstrate the effectiveness of the text augmentation module of GMOVE. To this end, we randomly choose several tweets in both LA and NY, and use GMOVE to augment the raw tweet messages. Table 1 shows the augmentation results for four example tweets (two from LA and two from NY). As a preprocessing step, we performed stemming and stopwords removal for the raw tweets, and also discretize the spatiotemporal space by partitioning each dimension into ten bins. When augmenting each tweet, the correlation threshold is set to $\delta = 0.2$ and the augmentation size is set to $L = 100$.

Table 1: Text augmentation examples on LA and NY. The number beside each word in the augmented message denotes that word's number of occurrences in the augmented message.

Data	Raw tweet message	Augmented message
LA	Y'all just kobe fans not lakers. Let's go lakers!!	fans(11), game(7), kobe(19), jeremy(6), lakers(26), injury(8), staples(8), center(4), nba(9), bryant(12)
LA	Fun night! @ Universal Studios Hollywood http://t.co/wMibfyleTW	fun(4), universal(20), studio(16), hollywood(18), night(5), party(7), fame(6), people(13), play(11)
NY	Nothing better...fresh off the oven! #Italian #bakery #pizza	fresh(7), oven(21), italian(19), bakery(12), pizza(14), bread(6), cook(5), food(12), kitchen(4)
NY	My trip starts now! @ JFK Airport	jfk(24), international(5), trip(9), travel(6), john(13), kennedy(14), terminal(8), start(6), now(3), airport(12)

Examining Table 1, we find that GMOVE's text augmenter is quite effective: given the short raw tweets, GMOVE generates semantically comprehensive messages by including relevant keywords that are not mentioned in the raw tweets. Consider the first tweet as an example. A fan of the Lakers (a basketball team) was posting to support his team. The original tweet message contains only three meaningful keywords: "kobe", "lakers", and "fan". By computing the spatiotemporal correlations between different keywords, GMOVE successfully identifies several other keywords (*e.g.*, "game", "staples", "center") that are relevant to the three seed keywords. The augmented tweet becomes much more semantically comprehensive, making it possible to connect with other Lakers-related tweets to form high-quality latent states. Similar phenomena are also observed on the other three tweets.

5.2.2 Group-Level Mobility Models

In this set of experiments, we exemplify the group-level mobility models generated by GMOVE on LA and NY. We are interested in the following questions: (1) can GMOVE indeed discover high-quality latent states and meaningful transitions among them? and (2) do different group-level mobility models reflect different mobility patterns? To answer the above questions, we ran GMOVE on LA and NY with the following parameter settings: $\delta = 0.2$, $L = 100$, $G = 80$, and $K = 10$. While GMOVE discovers 80 group-level mobility models on both LA and NY, we choose two representative mobility models learnt on LA due to space limit. In Figure 4(a) and 4(b), we visualize those two example mobility models.

Based on the keywords and locations of the latent states, we can say the mobility model in Figure 4(a) likely corresponds to the trajectories of a group of UCLA students. This is because most latent states are centered around the UCLA campus, and meanwhile carry college-life semantics (*e.g.*, home, school, gym, friends). We have the following interesting findings from the mobility model: (1) *First, the latent states are highly interpretable.* For instance, the top keywords of state 1 are "school", "ucla", "course", *etc.*. It clearly reflects the students' on-campus activities, such as attending classes, taking exams, and staying with friends. (2) *Second, the transitions between latent states are practically meaningful.* Still consider state 1 as an example. As shown by the transition matrix, after taking classes at campus, the top subsequent activities are go-

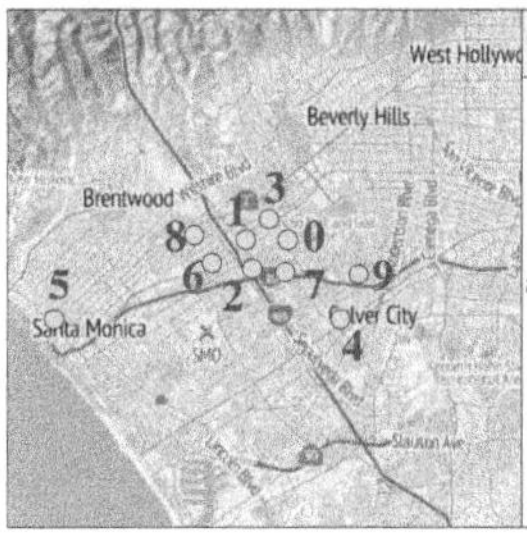

State 0	State 1	State 2	State 3	State 4	State 5	State 6	State 7	State 8	State 9
home	school	food	friend	buy	santa	wait	suck	home	night
morning	ucla	restaurant	hahaha	shop	monica	dinner	gym	rest	music
coffee	course	dinner	dream	mall	beach	food	football	sleep	tonight
dude	midterm	grill	song	beautiful	sunset	worst	team	live	bar
apartment	class	love	child	happy	dinner	grill	game	game	tbh
day	food	deli	birthday	mine	baby	restaurant	play	drink	nightlife
hall	drink	worst	drink	apparel	venice	delicious	buster	bed	evening
run	damn	come	kiss	bag	shore	amazing	let	show	movie
house	friend	waiter	bday	clothes	life	gather	beat	time	beer
sleep	stay	chipotle	snapchat	day	please	love	boy	miss	like

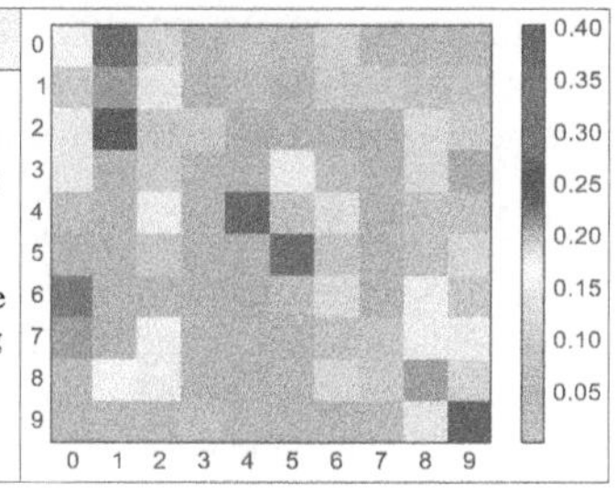

(a) The mobility model for the first user group (students).

State 0	State 1	State 2	State 3	State 4	State 5	State 6	State 7	State 8	State 9
hotel	restaurant	lax	universal	food	venice	shopping	night	food	club
sleep	food	travel	studio	restaurant	beach	buy	hotel	table	night
miss	amazing	airport	night	chinese	people	shop	live	taste	music
building	eat	international	party	mexican	life	clothes	lounge	salad	girl
center	lunch	come	hollywood	spicy	spa	cheap	place	quiet	nightclub
plaza	grill	flylax	buster	hometown	sunshine	sales	taxi	deli	money
flight	american	arrival	friend	taste	beautiful	nice	shower	hot	drink
home	deli	terminal	happy	china	santa	women	sleep	steak	sleep
city	together	train	haloween	town	monica	mall	queen	dining	dance
inn	pancake	depart	club	delicious	food	men	terminal	fame	rock

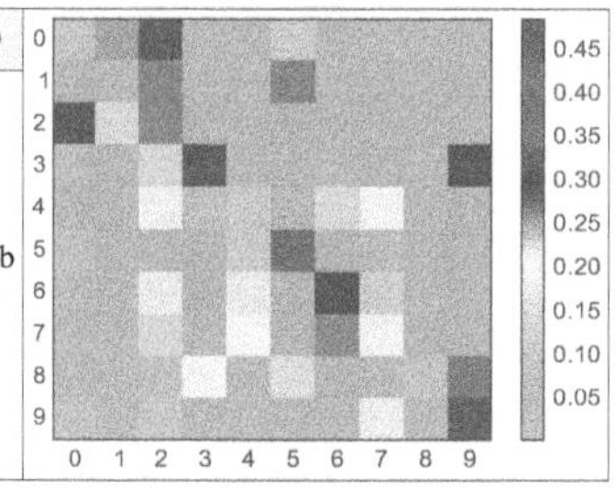

(b) The mobility model for the second user group (tourists).

Figure 4: Two group-level mobility models learnt by GMOVE on LA. For each model, we show (1) the geographical center of each latents state; (2) the top eight keywords of each latent state; and (3) the transition probability matrix among the ten states.

ing back home (state 0 & 8), having dinner (state 2 & 6), and doing sports (state 7). Those transitions are all highly consistent with a student's lifestyle in real life, and thus reflects the high quality of the underlying group-level HMM.

The mobility model shown in Figure 4(b) probably corresponds to the activities of tourists in LA. Again, we find that the latent states (*e.g.*, airport, hotel, Hollywood, beach) are highly interpretable and the transitions (*e.g.*, going to hotel from airport, having food after sightseeing) are intuitive. More importantly, when comparing the mobility models in Figure 4(a) and 4(b), one can clearly observe that these two models reflect totally different hotspots and moving behaviors. This phenomenon suggests that GMOVE can indeed effectively partition the users based on their behaviors, and generate highly descriptive HMMs for different groups.

5.3 Quantitative Evaluation

While GMOVE can be used for various real-life applications, we choose *context-aware location prediction* as an example to quantitatively evaluate the performance of GMOVE.

5.3.1 Experimental Setup

Task description. Context-aware location prediction aims at predicting the next location of a user, given the current observation of the user's movement. Formally, given a ground-truth trajectory $x_1 x_2 \dots x_N$, we assume the sequence $x_1 x_2 \dots x_{N-1}$ is already known, and try to recover x_N from a pool of candidate locations. The candidate pool, denoted as C_x is formed as follows: from all the geo-tagged tweets, we select the ones whose geographical distance to x_N is no larger than three kilometers and the temporal difference to x_N is no larger than five hours. Once the candidate pool is obtained, we use the given mobility model to rank all the candidates in the descending order of visiting probability, and check whether the grouth-truth record x_N appears in the top-k results (k is an integer that controls the result list size).

Intuitively, the better a mobility model is, the more likely it can recover the ground-truth record x_N (*i.e.*, x_N should be ranked higher in the result list). Hence, we use the prediction accuracy to measure the performance of the given mobility model. Given T test trajectories, for each test trajectory, we use a mobility model to retrieve the top-k results and see whether the ground truth record x_N appears in the result list. Let T' denote the number of trajectories for which the ground-truth records are successfully recovered, then the prediction accuracy is $Acc@k = T'/T$. On both LA and NY, we randomly choose 30% trajectories as test data, and use the rest 70% data for model training.

Compared Methods. To compare with GMOVE, we implemented the following mobility models for context-aware location prediction: (1) **LAW** [2] is a prevailing mobility model. Based on the displacement distribution, it models human mobility as a Lévy flight with long-tailed distributions. (2) **GEO** is based on existing works [14, 4] that train one HMM from the input trajectories. It uses only spatial information by assuming each latent state generates the location from a bi-variate Gaussian. (3) **SINGLE** is an adaption of GMOVE, which does not perform user grouping, but trains one HMM using all the trajectories. (4) **NOAUG** is another adaption of GMOVE, which does not perform text augmentation.

When computing the visiting probability for any candidate location, both GEO and SINGLE simply use the obtained HMM and the forward scoring algorithm to derive the likelihood of the sequence. For GMOVE and NOAUG, they both produce an ensemble of HMMs, and each HMM provides a visiting probability for the candidate location. Hence, GMOVE and NOAUG need to first compute the membership vector for the target user based on her historical trajectories, and then use membership values as weights to derive a weighted score.

Note that, while there are other methods [15, 16, 6, 21] optimized for location prediction (*e.g.*, by using a supervised learning framework), we have not included them for comparison. This is because GMOVE is designed for mobility modeling, and we use context-aware location prediction as a quantitatively evaluation for the quality of the obtained mobility models. We do not claim GMOVE can outperform state-of-the-art location prediction techniques.

Parameter Settings. GMOVE has four major parameters: (1) the correlation threshold δ; (2) the augmentation size L; (3) the number of user groups G; and (4) the number of latent states K. We study the effects of different parameters as follows: (1) δ = 0, 0.1, **0.2**, 0.3, 0.4, 0.5; (2) L = 0, 20, **40**, 60, 80, 100; (3) G = 5, 10, 20,

30, 40, 50, 60, 70, **80**, 90, 100; (4) $K = 3, 4, 5, \mathbf{10}, 15, 20, 25, 30$. When studying the effect of one parameter, we fix the other parameters to their default values, as denoted by the bold numbers.

5.3.2 *Prediction Accuracy Comparison.*

Figure 5 reports the accuracies of different mobility models for top-k prediction on LA and NY. The parameters of GMOVE are set to the default values as such a setting offers the highest prediction accuracy. The parameters of all the other compared models are also carefully tuned to achieve the best performance.

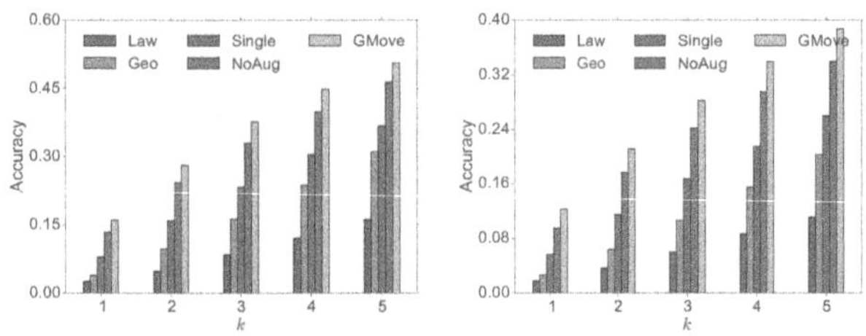

(a) LA (b) NY

Figure 5: Prediction accuracy *v.s.* k.

As shown in Figure 5(a) and 5(b), GMOVE significantly outperforms all the baseline methods on both LA and NY for different k values. Comparing the performance of GMOVE and SINGLE, we find that the prediction accuracy of GMOVE is about 12.7% better on average. This suggests that there indeed exist multiple groups of people that have different moving behaviors. As SINGLE trains one model for all the input trajectories, it suffers from severe data inconsistency and mixes different mobility regularities together. In contrast, GMOVE employs the iterative refinement framework to perform group-level mobility modeling. Such a framework effectively distinguishes different mobility regularities and thus achieves much better accuracy. Meanwhile, by examining the performance of GMOVE and NOAUG, we find that the text augmenter of GMOVE is also effective and improves the prediction accuracy by about 3%. As aforementioned, while each raw tweet message is very short, the augmented message becomes much more semantically comprehensive. The augmentation process allows us to connect the tweets that are intrinsically relevant and thus generate higher-quality HMMs. Another interesting finding is that the performance of SINGLE is consistently better than GEO and LAW. Such a phenomenon verifies the fact that integrating multiple (spatial, temporal, and textual) signals can better describe the users' moving behaviors than using only spatial information, and thus achieve better location prediction accuracy.

5.3.3 *Effects of Parameters.*

As mentioned earlier, there are four major parameters in GMOVE: δ, L, K, and G. After tuning those parameters on LA and NY, we find that the trends for all the four parameters are very similar on LA and NY. We only report the results on LA to save space.

We first study the effects of δ and L. Figure 6(a) shows the prediction accuracy of GMOVE when δ varies from 0 to 0.5. As shown, the performance of GMOVE first increases with δ and then decreases. This phenomenon is expected: a too small correlation threshold tends to include irrelevant keywords in the augmentation process; while a too large threshold constrains a keyword's vicinity to include almost only itself, making the augmentation ineffective. Figure 6(b) shows the performance of GMOVE when the augmentation size L varies. We find that the prediction accuracy first increases with L and quickly becomes stable. This suggest that the augmentation size should not be set to a too small value in practice.

We proceed to study the effects of G and K. Figure 6(c) reports

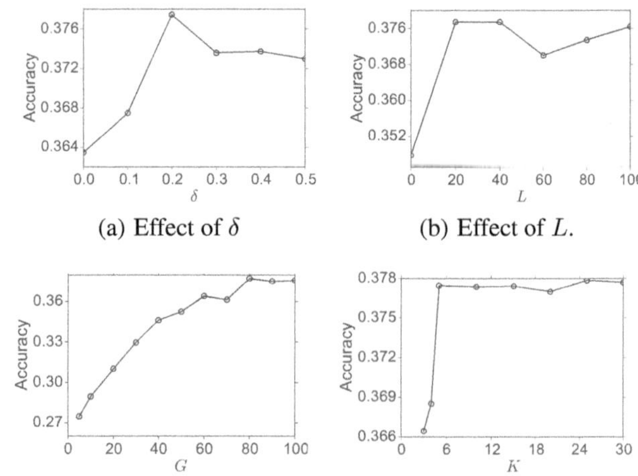

(a) Effect of δ (b) Effect of L.

(c) Effect of G. (d) Effect of K.

Figure 6: Effects of parameters (LA, $k = 3$).

results when G increase from 5 to 100. Not hard to observe, the prediction accuracy increases significantly with G before it gradually becomes stable. This is expected. In big cities like Los Angeles and New York, it is natural that there are a large number of user groups that have totally different lifestyles. When G increases, the GMOVE model fits better with the intrinsic data complexity, and thus improves the prediction accuracy. Figure 6(d) shows the effect of K on the performance of GMOVE. Interestingly, we observe the performance of GMOVE is not sensitive to the number of latent states as long as $K \geq 5$. This suggests that when the user groups are fine-grained enough (*e.g.*, $G = 80$), the number of "hotspots" for each group is usually limited in practice.

5.4 Efficiency Study

In the final set of experiments, we report the training time of GMOVE. When tuning the four parameters of GMOVE, we find that the training time of GMOVE does not change much with δ and L. Therefore, we only report the effects of G and K. Figure 7(a) and 8(a) show that the time cost of GMOVE generally increases with G, but scales well. This is a good property of GMOVE in situations where G needs to be set to a large number. In Figure 7(b) and 8(b), we can see that the time cost increases superlinearly with K. This is mainly because of the intrinsic nature for HMM training, where time complexity of the EM algorithm is quadratic in K.

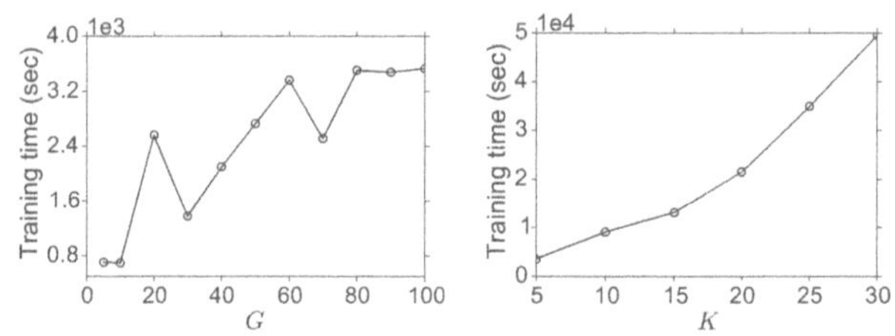

(a) Running time *v.s.* G. (b) Running time *v.s.* K.

Figure 7: Running time of GMOVE on LA.

6. RELATED WORK

Generally, existing approaches on mobility modeling can be classified into three classes: *pattern-based*, *law-based*, and *model-based*.

Pattern-based approaches mine regular mobility patterns from movement data. Existing studies have designed effective methods for mining different types of movement patterns. Specifically,

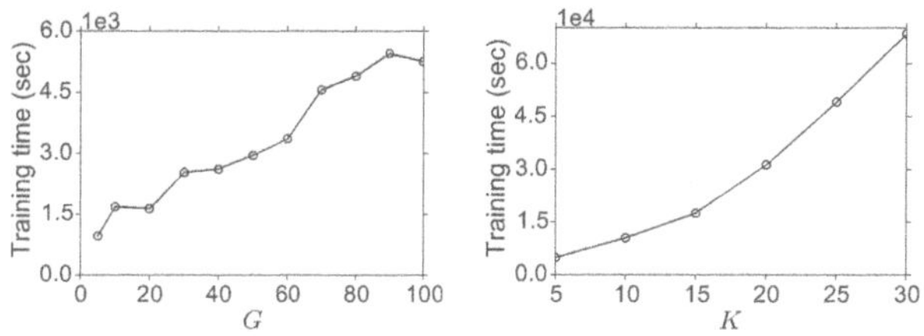

(a) Running time *v.s.* G. (b) Running time *v.s.* K.

Figure 8: Running time of GMOVE on NY.

Giannotti *et al.* [7] define a T-pattern as Region-of-Interest (RoI) sequence that frequently appears in the input trajectories. By partitioning the space, they use frequent sequential pattern mining to extract all the T-patterns. Several studies have attempted to find a set of objects that are frequently co-located. Efforts along this line include mining *flock* [11], *swarm* [12], and *gathering* [26] patterns. Meanwhile, there has also been study on mining periodic movement patterns. For instance, Li *et al.* [13] first use density-based clustering to extract reference spots from GPS trajectories, and then detect periodic visiting behaviors at those spots.

While the above studies focus on pure GPS trajectory data, a number of studies mine mobility patterns from semantic trajectories [17, 1, 5, 25]. Alvares *et al.* [1] first map the stops in trajectories to semantic places using a background map, and then extract frequent place sequences as sequential patterns. Zhang *et al.* [25] introduce a top-down approach to mine fine-grained movement patterns from semantic trajectories. Our work differs from these studies in two aspects. First, we consider unstructured text instead of structured category information. Second, instead of extracting a large number of patterns, we develop a statistical model that comprehensively and concisely summarizes people's moving behaviors.

Law-based approaches investigate the physical laws that govern human's moving behaviors. Brockmann *et al.* [2] find that human mobility can be approximated by a continuous-time random-walk model with long-tail distributions. Gonzalez *et al.* [8] study human mobility using mobile phone data. They find that people periodically return to a few previously visited locations, and the mobility can be modeled by a stochastic process centered at a fixed point. Song *et al.* [20] report that around 93% human movements are predictable due to the high regularity of people's moving behaviors. They [19] further propose a self-consistent microscopic model to predict individual mobility.

Model-based approaches attempt to learn statistical models from movement data. Cho *et al.* [3] observe that a user usually moves around several centers (*e.g.*, home and work) at fixed time slots, and thus propose to model a user's movement as a mixture of Gaussians. Their model can further incorporate social influence based on the fact that a user is more likely to visit a location that is close to the locations of her friends. Wang *et al.* [21] propose a hybrid mobility model that uses heterogeneous mobility data for better location prediction. There are some studies [18, 23, 9, 10, 24] on geographical topic discovery, aiming to discover people's activities in different geographical regions and/or time periods. While our work also uses statistical models to unveil human mobility, it differs from the above studies in that it focuses on extracting the latent states of human movements as well as the *sequential transitions*.

The most relevant works to our study are those HMM-based approaches [4, 22]. Mathew *et al.* [14] discretize the space into equal-size triangles using Hierarchical Triangular Mesh. By assuming each latent state has a multinomial distribution over the triangles, they train an HMM on the input GPS trajectories. Deb *et al.* [4] propose the probabilistic latent semantic model, which essentially uses HMM to extract latent semantic locations from cell tower and bluetooth data. Ye *et al.* [22] use HMM to model user check-ins on location-based social networks. By incorporating the category information of places, their obtained HMM is capable of predicting the category of the next location for the user.

Although our proposed GMOVE method also relies on HMM, it differs from the above works in two aspects. First, none of the above studies consider text data for mobility modeling. In contrast, we simultaneously model spatial, temporal, and textual information to obtain interpretable latent states. Second, they perform HMM training with the movement data of either one individual or a given collection of users. GMOVE, however, couples the subtasks of user grouping and mobility modeling, and generates high-quality user groups as well as group-level HMMs.

7. CONCLUSION

In this paper, we studied the novel problem of modeling human mobility using geo-tagged social media (GeoSM). To effectively unveil mobility regularities from the sparse and complex GeoSM data, we proposed the GMOVE method. Our method distinguishes itself from existing mobility models in three aspects: (1) it enables the mutual enhancement between the subtasks of user grouping and mobility modeling, so as to generate high-quality user groups and reliable mobility models; (2) it leverages keyword spatiotemporal correlations as auxiliary knowledge to perform text augmentation, which effectively reduces text sparsity present in most GeoSM data; and (3) it integrates multiple (spatial, temporal, and textual) signals to generate a comprehensive view of users' moving behaviors. Our experiments on two real-life data sets show that the strategies employed by GMOVE are highly effective in generating quality mobility models. Meanwhile, using context-aware location prediction as an example task, we found GMOVE can achieve much better prediction accuracy than baseline mobility models.

There are several future directions based on this work. First, we currently use a pre-specified time constraint to extract reliable trajectories from raw GeoSM history. In the future, it is interesting to adapt GMOVE such that it can automatically infer the reliability of the transitions and extract trajectories from the raw data. Second, besides context-aware location prediction, we plan to apply GMOVE for other tasks in the urban computing context. By the year 2030, it is estimated over 60% of the world population will be located within a city's boundary. One of the huge challenges facing many government organizations, including the US military, is understanding and preparing for complex urban environments. From disaster relief to anomaly movement detection, the challenges associated with operating within the so-called mega-cities are many. The ability to accurately model group-level human mobility will dramatically improve the understanding of normal urban life patterns and help address such challenges.

8. ACKNOWLEDGEMENTS

This work was sponsored in part by the U.S. Army Research Lab. under Cooperative Agreement No. W911NF-09-2-0053 (NSCTA), National Science Foundation IIS-1017362, IIS-1320617, and IIS-1354329, HDTRA1-10-1-0120, and Grant 1U54GM114838 awarded by NIGMS through funds provided by the trans-NIH Big Data to Knowledge (BD2K) initiative (www.bd2k.nih.gov), and MIAS, a DHS-IDS Center for Multimodal Information Access and Synthesis at UIUC. Luming Zhang is supported by the National Nature Science Foundation of China (Grant No. 61572169) and the Fundamental Research Funds for the Central Universities. The views and conclusions contained in this document are those of the author(s) and should not be interpreted as representing the official policies of the U.S. Army Research Laboratory or the U.S. Government. The U.S. Government is authorized to reproduce and distribute reprints for Government purposes notwithstanding any copyright notation hereon.

9. REFERENCES

[1] L. O. Alvares, V. Bogorny, B. Kuijpers, B. Moelans, J. A. Fern, E. D. Macedo, and A. T. Palma. Towards semantic trajectory knowledge discovery. *Data Mining and Knowledge Discovery*, 2007.

[2] D. Brockmann, L. Hufnagel, and T. Geisel. The scaling laws of human travel. *Nature*, 439(7075):462–465, 2006.

[3] E. Cho, S. A. Myers, and J. Leskovec. Friendship and mobility: User movement in location-based social networks. In *KDD*, pages 1082–1090, 2011.

[4] B. Deb and P. Basu. Discovering latent semantic structure in human mobility traces. In *Wireless Sensor Networks*, pages 84–103. Springer, 2015.

[5] R. Fileto, V. Bogorny, C. May, and D. Klein. Semantic enrichment and analysis of movement data: probably it is just starting! *SIGSPATIAL Special*, 7(1):11–18, 2015.

[6] H. Gao, J. Tang, and H. Liu. Mobile location prediction in spatio-temporal context. In *Nokia mobile data challenge workshop*, volume 41, page 44, 2012.

[7] F. Giannotti, M. Nanni, F. Pinelli, and D. Pedreschi. Trajectory pattern mining. In *KDD*, pages 330–339, 2007.

[8] M. C. Gonzalez, C. A. Hidalgo, and A.-L. Barabasi. Understanding individual human mobility patterns. *Nature*, 453(7196):779–782, 2008.

[9] L. Hong, A. Ahmed, S. Gurumurthy, A. J. Smola, and K. Tsioutsiouliklis. Discovering geographical topics in the twitter stream. In *WWW*, pages 769–778, 2012.

[10] B. Hu and M. Ester. Spatial topic modeling in online social media for location recommendation. In *RecSys*, pages 25–32, 2013.

[11] P. Laube and S. Imfeld. Analyzing relative motion within groups of trackable moving point objects. In *GIScience*, pages 132–144, 2002.

[12] Z. Li, B. Ding, J. Han, and R. Kays. Swarm: Mining relaxed temporal moving object clusters. *PVLDB*, 3(1):723–734, 2010.

[13] Z. Li, B. Ding, J. Han, R. Kays, and P. Nye. Mining periodic behaviors for moving objects. In *KDD*, pages 1099–1108, 2010.

[14] W. Mathew, R. Raposo, and B. Martins. Predicting future locations with hidden markov models. In *UbiComp*, pages 911–918, 2012.

[15] A. Monreale, F. Pinelli, R. Trasarti, and F. Giannotti. Wherenext: a location predictor on trajectory pattern mining. In *KDD*, pages 637–646, 2009.

[16] A. Noulas, S. Scellato, N. Lathia, and C. Mascolo. Mining user mobility features for next place prediction in location-based services. In *ICDM*, pages 1038–1043, 2012.

[17] C. Parent, S. Spaccapietra, C. Renso, G. L. Andrienko, N. V. Andrienko, V. Bogorny, M. L. Damiani, A. Gkoulalas-Divanis, J. A. F. de Macêdo, N. Pelekis, Y. Theodoridis, and Z. Yan. Semantic trajectories modeling and analysis. *ACM Comput. Surv.*, 45(4):42, 2013.

[18] S. Sizov. Geofolk: latent spatial semantics in web 2.0 social media. In *WSDM*, pages 281–290, 2010.

[19] C. Song, T. Koren, P. Wang, and A.-L. Barabási. Modelling the scaling properties of human mobility. *Nature Physics*, 6(10):818–823, 2010.

[20] C. Song, Z. Qu, N. Blumm, and A.-L. Barabási. Limits of predictability in human mobility. *Science*, 327(5968):1018–1021, 2010.

[21] Y. Wang, N. J. Yuan, D. Lian, L. Xu, X. Xie, E. Chen, and Y. Rui. Regularity and conformity: Location prediction using heterogeneous mobility data. In *KDD*, pages 1275–1284, 2015.

[22] J. Ye, Z. Zhu, and H. Cheng. What's your next move: User activity prediction in location-based social networks. In *SDM*, 2013.

[23] Z. Yin, L. Cao, J. Han, J. Luo, and T. S. Huang. Diversified trajectory pattern ranking in geo-tagged social media. In *SDM*, pages 980–991, 2011.

[24] Q. Yuan, G. Cong, Z. Ma, A. Sun, and N. M. Thalmann. Who, where, when and what: discover spatio-temporal topics for twitter users. In *KDD*, pages 605–613, 2013.

[25] C. Zhang, J. Han, L. Shou, J. Lu, and T. F. L. Porta. Splitter: Mining fine-grained sequential patterns in semantic trajectories. *PVLDB*, 7(9):769–780, 2014.

[26] K. Zheng, Y. Zheng, N. J. Yuan, and S. Shang. On discovery of gathering patterns from trajectories. In *ICDE*, pages 242–253, 2013.

[27] Y. Zheng, L. Zhang, X. Xie, and W.-Y. Ma. Mining interesting locations and travel sequences from gps trajectories. In *WWW*, pages 791–800, 2009.

APPENDIX

We derive the updating rules for the HMM parameters in the M-step as follows. Given the weighted trajectories $\{S_1, S_2, \ldots, S_R\}$ and the old paramter set $\Phi^{(t)}$, the expectation of the complete likelihood is

$$Q(\Phi) = \sum_{r=1}^{R} \sum_{z_r} w_r p(z_r|S_r;\Phi^{(t)}) \ln p(S_r, z_r|\Phi) \tag{14}$$

$$= \sum_{r=1}^{R} \sum_{z_r} w_r p(z_r|S_r;\Phi^{(t)}) \ln p(z_{r,1}|\pi) \tag{15}$$

$$+ \sum_{r=1}^{R} \sum_{z_r} \sum_{n=2}^{N} w_r p(z_r|S_r;\Phi^{(t)}) \ln p(z_{r,n}|z_{r,n-1}, \mathbf{A}) \tag{16}$$

$$+ \sum_{r=1}^{R} \sum_{z_r} \sum_{n=1}^{N} \sum_{k=1}^{K} w_r p(z_r|S_r;\Phi^{(t)}) z_{r,n}^k \ln p(x_{r,n}|\Phi). \tag{17}$$

Meanwhile, since $z_{r,n}^k$ is a binary variable, we have:

$$\gamma(z_{r,n}^k) = \sum_{z^r} p(z^r|S_r;\Phi^{(t)}) z_{r,n}^k \tag{18}$$

$$\xi(z_{r,n-1}^j, z_{r,n}^k) = \sum_{z^r} p(z^r|S_r;\Phi^{(t)}) z_{r,n-1}^j z_{r,n}^k \tag{19}$$

The three terms in Equation 15, 16, and 17 are independent, we can thus optimize the parameters π, $\mathbf{A}$, and $\{\mu_l, \Sigma_l, \mu_t, \sigma_t, \theta\}$ separately. To optimize π, we need to maximize Equation 15, namely

$$f(\pi) = \sum_{r=1}^{R} \sum_{z_r} w_r p(z_r|S_r;\Phi^{(t)}) \sum_{k=1}^{K} z_{r,1}^k \ln \pi_k \tag{20}$$

$$= \sum_{r=1}^{R} \sum_{k=1}^{K} w_r \gamma(z_{r,1}^k) \ln \pi_k. \tag{21}$$

Using the Lagrange multiplier, we can easily obtain the updating rule for π (Equation 1) that maximizes the above objective function.

Now consider the optimization of A. With Equation 16 and 19, we can write down the following objective function, which can be similarly optimized using use the Lagrange multiplier to produce Equation 2:

$$g(A) = \sum_{r=1}^{R} \sum_{n=2}^{N} \sum_{k=1}^{K} \sum_{j=1}^{K} \xi(z_{r,n-1}^j, z_{r,n}^k) \ln A_{jk} \tag{22}$$

Finally, as the spatial, temporal, and textual observations are independent, the parameter sets $\{\mu_{kg}, \Sigma_{kg}\}$, $\{\mu_{kt}, \Sigma_{kt}\}$, and θ_k can be derived separately based on 17. Recall that the spatial and temporal distributions are assumed to be Gaussian, we simply take the derivatives of the objective function and set them to zeros, which produces the updating rules in Equation 3, 4, 5, and 6. To optimize θ_k, we again combine Equation 18 with the Lagrange multiplier, and obtain the maximizer shown in Equation 7.

Approximate Personalized PageRank on Dynamic Graphs

Hongyang Zhang
Department of Computer Science
Stanford University
hongyang@cs.stanford.edu

Peter Lofgren
Department of Computer Science
Stanford University
plofgren@cs.stanford.edu

Ashish Goel
Department of Management Science and Engineering
Stanford University
ashishg@stanford.edu

ABSTRACT

We propose and analyze two algorithms for maintaining approximate Personalized PageRank (PPR) vectors on a dynamic graph, where edges are added or deleted. Our algorithms are natural dynamic versions of two known local variations of power iteration. One, Forward Push, propagates probability mass forwards along edges from a source node, while the other, Reverse Push, propagates local changes backwards along edges from a target. In both variations, we maintain an invariant between two vectors, and when an edge is updated, our algorithm first modifies the vectors to restore the invariant, then performs any needed local push operations to restore accuracy.

For Reverse Push, we prove that for an arbitrary directed graph in a random edge model, or for an arbitrary undirected graph, given a uniformly random target node t, the cost to maintain a PPR vector to t of additive error ε as k edges are updated is $O(k + \overline{d}/\varepsilon)$, where $\overline{d}$ is the average degree of the graph. This is $O(1)$ work per update, plus the cost of computing a reverse vector once on a static graph. For Forward Push, we show that on an arbitrary undirected graph, given a uniformly random start node s, the cost to maintain a PPR vector from s of degree-normalized error ε as k edges are updated is $O(k + 1/\varepsilon)$, which is again $O(1)$ per update plus the cost of computing a PPR vector once on a static graph.

Categories and Subject Descriptors

G.2.2 [**Mathematics of Computing**]: Discrete Mathematics—*Graph Algorithms*

Keywords

Personalized PageRank; Online algorithm; Local push.

1. INTRODUCTION

Personalized PageRank (PPR) models the relevance of nodes in a network from the point of view of a given node. It has applications in search [13, 12], friend recommendations [4, 11], community detection [22, 2], video recommendations [6], and other applications. Because PPR is expensive to compute at query time, several authors have proposed pre-computing it for each user and storing it [13, 7, 8]. However, in practice graphs are dynamic, for example on a social network users are constantly adding new edges to the network, so we need a method of updating pre-computed PPR values. In this work, we propose two new algorithms for updating pre-computed PPR vectors and give the first rigorous analysis of their running time.

There are four main algorithms for computing PPR [15], of which only one has an analysis for dynamic graphs prior to our work. The first is power iteration [21], but it is very slow, requiring $\Omega(m)$ time per user (where m is the number of edges), so it can't be used efficiently for PPR even on static graphs. The second, Forward Push [7, 2], is a local variation of power iteration which starts from the source user (the node whose point of view we take) and pushes probability mass forwards along edges. Berkin [7] proposed pre-computing Forward Push vectors from many source nodes, and Ohsaka et al. [20] proposed an algorithm for updating it on dynamic graphs, however no past work has analyzed the running time for maintaining Forward Push. The third, Reverse Push [13, 2], is an alternative variation of power iteration which starts at each target node and pushes values backwards along edges to improve estimates. Jeh and Widom [13] and Lofgren et al. [17] propose pre-computing Reverse Push vectors (or a variation on them), to enable efficient search, but no past work has proposed an algorithm for updating Reverse Push vectors on dynamic graphs. Finally, a fourth method of computing PPR is Monte-Carlo [3, 9], and for that algorithm Bahmani et al. [5] give an efficient algorithm for updating it on dynamic graphs, with running time analysis in a random edge arrival order model. In experiments, Ohsaka et al. [20] find that when maintaining very accurate PPR vectors, Monte-Carlo is slower than Forward-Push, motivating the analysis of updating Forward Push.

Our contribution is the first running time guarantees for updating Forward Push on undirected graphs and for updating Reverse Push on directed as well as undireted graphs. The analysis is challenging because a new edge at one node can cause that node to push, which can cause a cascade of other nodes to push. Understanding and bounding the size of this cascade required a novel amortized analysis. We allow for a worst case graph, but we assume that edge updates arrive in a random order to better capture performance in practice. The same assumption was used in the analysis of Monte Carlo [5] where the bounds it leads to were found

KDD '16, August 13-17, 2016, San Francisco, CA, USA

© 2016 ACM. ISBN 978-1-4503-4232-2/16/08...$15.00

DOI: http://dx.doi.org/10.1145/2939672.2939804

to model the running time in practice on Twitter. Alternatively, for undirected graphs we prove a worst-case amortized running time. In addition, for undirected graphs, we strengthen the analysis of Monte-Carlo on dynamic graphs [5] to a worst-case edge arrival order.

Our algorithms are simple to implement, and we present two experiments for forward push. One insight from our theoretical analysis is a different way of updating Forward Push values than the previously proposed method [20], and we find that our variation is 1.5-3.5 times faster than that method without sacrificing accuracy. In the second experiment, we evaluate forward push for the problem of finding the top K highest personalized PageRank from a source node. We compare to the Monte-Carlo method of Bahmani et al. [5] and found that the forward push is 4.5-12 times more efficient in storage compared to Monte-Carlo, and is able to do edge update 1.5 - 2.5 times faster.

The main idea of our algorithms is that both Forward Push and Reverse Push maintain an invariant between a pair of vectors, and when an edge is added or deleted, we first restore the invariant with an efficient change to the vectors, then perform local push operations as needed to control the error. One limitation of our analysis is that it applies to the pure versions of Forward Push and Reverse Push, while some prior work [13, 7] proposes combining Forward or Reverse push vectors together, but we believe our analysis would extend to that case. It would also be interesting to extend our analysis adapt the Personalized PageRank search index of [17] to dynamic graphs.

Results.

For the Reverse Push algorithm, we show that on a worst-case graph, for a uniform random target, the expected time required to maintain PPR estimates at accuracy ε to that target as k edge updates arrive in a random order is $O(k + k/(n\varepsilon) + \bar{d}/\varepsilon)$. Here ε is the desired additive error of the estimates, and $\bar{d}$ is the average degree of nodes in the graph. Since a random PPR value is $1/n$, values smaller than $1/n$ are not very meaningful. Hence typically $\varepsilon = \Omega(1/n)$ and our running time is $O(k + \bar{d}/\varepsilon)$. Since $\bar{d}/\varepsilon$ is the expected time required to compute Reverse Push from scratch [1, 15], we see that our incremental algorithm can maintain estimates after every edge update using $O(1)$ time per update and the time required to compute a single Reverse Push vector.

For the Forward Push algorithm, we show that on an arbitrary undirected graph and arbitrary edge arrival order, for a uniform random source node s, the worst-case running time to maintain a PPR vector from that source node is $O(k + k/(n\varepsilon) + 1/\varepsilon)$. Here ε is a bound on the degree-normalized error (which we define later). Typically $\varepsilon = \Omega(1/n)$, so this is $O(k + 1/\varepsilon)$. The cost of computing such a PPR vector from scratch is $O(1/\varepsilon)$ [2] so we again see that the cost to maintain the PPR vector over k updates is $O(1)$ per update plus the cost of computing it once from scratch.

One observation that follows from our work is that for Monte-Carlo, for an arbitrary undirected graph and arbitrary edge arrival order, the time required to maintain r random walks from every source node over k arrivals is $O(rk)$. This contrasts with a worst-case example constructed on directed graphs where the total running time to maintain these walks grows super-linear in k [14]. Our observation suggests a weaker yet still meaningful bound without the random edge assumption made in Bahmani et al. [5] for Monte-Carlo methods on undirected graphs.

2. PRELIMINARIES

Let $G = (V, E)$ be an unweighted directed graph. Let A denote the adjacency matrix of G and let D denote the diagonal matrix representing the outdegrees of all vertices in G. For a vertex v, let $N^{\text{OUT}}(v)$ denote the set of out neighbors of v and let $N^{\text{IN}}(v)$ denote the set of in neighbors of v. The personalized PageRank vector $\vec{\pi}_s$ for a source node s is defined as the unique solution of the following linear system ([21]):

$$\vec{\pi}_s = \alpha \cdot \vec{e}_s + (1-\alpha) \cdot A^{\mathsf{T}} D^{-1} \vec{\pi}_s \quad (1)$$

where α (a.k.a. the teleport probability) is a constant between 0 and 1, and $\vec{e_s}$ is the indicator vector with a single nonzero entry of 1 at s. For a pair of vertices s and t on G, we will use $\pi(s,t)$ to denote the personalized PageRank from s to t. This linear algebraic definition of personalized PageRank is equivalent to simulating a random walk. Start from the source node s, with probability $(1-\alpha)$, go to a uniformly chosen neighbor of the current node, or with probability α stop at the current node: $\pi(s,t)$ is the probability that a random walk from s stops at t [21]. In the above definitions, we assumed that the outdegree of every vertex is at least one for simplicity. If a vertex has no out neighbors, then the random walk transitions to s with probability $(1-\alpha)$ (cf. Gleich [10] for other ways to handle dangling nodes).

2.1 The edge arrival model

In the dynamic edge arrival model, we start with an initial graph and there is a sequence of edge updates one by one. Let $G_0 = (V_0, E_0)$ denote the initial graph. Let k denote the number of edge updates. When the i-th edge $e_i = (u_i, v_i)$ arrives, if e_i is already in G_{i-1}, then it will be deleted; else it will be added to G_{i-1}. Let $G_i = (V_i, E_i)$ denote the updated graph. Note that V_i can differ from V_{i-1} by at most two vertices. Let $d_i^{\text{OUT}}(u)$ denote the outdegree of $u \in V$ on G_i and $d_i^{\text{IN}}(u)$ denote its indegree. Also let D_i denote the diagonal matrix of the outdegrees of V_i. Let $\pi_i(s,t)$ denote the personalized PageRank from s to t on G_i. Let $n = |V|_0$ denote the number of vertices and $m = |E_0|$ denote the number of edges in the initial graph G_0. We will analyze the following two edge arrival models:

Random edge permutations of directed graphs [5].

To introduce this graph model in our notation, consider a uniformly random edge permutation of E_k. Then G_0 is the subgraph consisting of the first m edges in the permutation. And e_i is defined as the $(m+i)$-th edge in this permutation, for $i = 1, \ldots, k$. In a uniformly random edge stream, the personalized PageRank vector does not change by "too much" after an edge update [5]. This intuition is not true in the worst case — there exists a sequence of edge insertions such that for a single source node, the aggregate l_1 difference between the personalized PageRank vector before and after every edge insertion grows superlinear in the number of of nodes [14].

Arbitrary edge updates of undirected graphs.

For undirected graph, we observe a few interesting properties for personalized PageRank, which will be used later.

The first one exploits the fact that on an undirected graph, a random walk can be in either direction.

PROPOSITION 1 (CF. LEMMA 1 IN LOFGREN ET AL. [16]). *Let G be an undirected graph. Let s and t be two vertices of G. Then $\pi(s,t) \times d(s) = \pi(t,s) \times d(t)$.*

Here we dropped the superscript on d since there is no direction for undireced edges.

PROPOSITION 2. *Let $G = (V, E)$ be an undirected graph and let t be a vertex of V, then $\sum_{x \in V} \pi(x,t)/d(t) \leq 1$.*

PROOF. Note that,

$$\sum_{x \in V} \frac{\pi(x,t)}{d(t)} = \sum_{x \in V} \frac{\pi(t,x)}{d(x)} \leq \sum_{x \in V} \pi(t,x) = 1.$$

where we used Proposition 1. □

2.2 Local push algorithms

The random walk interpretation of personalized PageRank leads to the following general class of local computation algorithms: start with all the probability mass on the source node of the graph, and iteratively push this mass out to neighboring nodes, getting progressively better approximations. In these "local push" algorithms, we typically maintain a "residual" at every node, which is mass that has been received but not yet been pushed out from that node, as well as an "estimate", which is mass that has been both received and pushed out (after accounting for the teleport probability and the outdegrees), we will now precisely describe how this local approach can be used in the forward and reverse direction.

2.2.1 *Forward push*

Given a source node s, the forward push algorithm maintains an estimate $\vec{P}(s,t)$ of $\pi(s,t)$ for each target $t \in V$. It also maintains a residual $\vec{R}(s,t)$ for t. Let $\vec{P}(s) = \vec{P}(s,\cdot)$ denote the the vector of estimates and $\vec{R}(s)$ the vector of residuals. The estimates and residuals satisfy the following invariant property (cf. Section 3 in Lofgren [2]):

$$\pi(s,t) = \vec{P}(s,t) + \sum_{x \in V} \vec{R}(s,x) \times \pi(x,t), \forall t \in V. \quad (2)$$

Algorithm 1 described below is a variant of the classic forward local push algorithm [2], the difference being that we added negative residuals. As we will see later on, an edge arrival can result in negative residuals — the edge update affects the amount of residuals a vertex have pushed out. During a forward push iteration for vertex u (Step 6 in Algorithm 1), an α fraction of u's residual will be added to u's estimate. For the rest of $(1-\alpha)$ fraction, each out neighbor of u receives an equal proportion of $(1-\alpha)/d^{\text{OUT}}(u)$. Algorithm 1 repeatedly perform forward push iterations, first for vertices with positive residuals and then for vertices with negative residuals, until for every vertex, its residual divided by the outdegree is within $-\varepsilon$ and ε. It's clear that while we work on vertices with negative residuals, no vertices whose residual is positive and below ε will increase above ε.

2.2.2 *Reverse push*

Given a target node t, the reverse push algorithm maintains an estimate $\overleftarrow{P}(s,t)$ of $\pi(s,t)$, for every node s in G. It also maitains a residual $\overleftarrow{R}(s,t)$ for s. Let $\overleftarrow{P}(t) = \overleftarrow{P}(\cdot,t)$ denote the vector of estimates and $\overleftarrow{R}(t) = \overleftarrow{R}(\cdot,t)$ for the vector of residuals. Similar to forward push, estimates and residuals satisfy an invariant property [1, 18]:

$$\pi(s,t) = \overleftarrow{P}(s,t) + \sum_{x \in V} \pi(s,x) \times \overleftarrow{R}(x,t), \forall s \in V. \quad (3)$$

In Algorithm 2 below, we've also added negative residuals. A reverse push iteration on vertex u works backward (step 6): an α fraction of u's residuals goes to u's estimate; to push back the other $1-\alpha$ fraction to an in neighbor v of u, it takes into account the outdegree of v, hence the amount is the residual amount times $(1-\alpha)/d^{\text{OUT}}(v)$. Algorithm 2 keeps pushing residuals back from each vertex, until the residual of every vertex is within $-\varepsilon$ and ε. When this happens, it is guaranteed that $|\pi(s,t) - P(s,t)| \leq \varepsilon$ (cf. Theorem 1 in Anderson et al. [1]).

Algorithm 1 FORWARDLOCALPUSH

INPUT: $(s, \vec{P}(s), \vec{R}(s), G, \varepsilon)$

1: **while** $\max_u \frac{\vec{R}(s,u)}{d^{\text{OUT}}(u)} > \varepsilon$ **do**
2:     FwdPush(u)
3: **while** $\min_u \frac{\vec{R}(s,u)}{d^{\text{OUT}}(u)} < -\varepsilon$ **do**
4:     FwdPush(u)
5: **return** $(\vec{P}(s), \vec{R}(s))$
6: **procedure** FWDPUSH(u)
7:     $\vec{P}(s,u) \mathrel{+}= \alpha \times \vec{R}(s,u)$
8:     **for** $v \leftarrow u$ **do**
9:         $\vec{R}(s,v) \mathrel{+}= (1-\alpha) \times \vec{R}(s,u)/d^{\text{OUT}}(u)$
10:     $\vec{R}(s,u) \leftarrow 0$

Algorithm 2 REVERSELOCALPUSH

INPUT: $(t, \overleftarrow{P}(t), \overleftarrow{R}(t), G, \varepsilon)$

1: **while** $\max_u \overleftarrow{R}(u,t) > \varepsilon$ **do**
2:     RevPush(u)
3: **while** $\min_u \overleftarrow{R}(u,t) < -\varepsilon$ **do**
4:     RevPush(u)
5: **return** $(\overleftarrow{P}(t), \overleftarrow{R}(t))$
6: **procedure** REVPUSH(u)
7:     $\overleftarrow{P}(u,t) \mathrel{+}= \alpha \times \overleftarrow{R}(u,t)$
8:     **for** $v \rightarrow u$ **do**
9:         $\overleftarrow{R}(v,t) \mathrel{+}= (1-\alpha) \times \overleftarrow{R}(u,t)/d^{\text{OUT}}(v)$
10:     $\overleftarrow{R}(u,t) \leftarrow 0$

3. DYNAMIC LOCAL PUSH ALGORITHMS

Given a node, we can run push algorithms to initialize its data structures that include the estimates and residuals. If an edge is inserted/deleted, we can obtain a new pair of estimates and residuals, by adjusting them locally at the updated edge using the invariant equations. Since this adjustment can create residuals that gets above ε or below $-\varepsilon$, we then invoke Algorithm 1 (or Algorithm 2) to push residuals from such nodes. While the idea is simple, the analysis of the number of push iterations is quite intricate. For the rest of this section, we describe an approach to obtain dynamic local push algorithms and show how to analyze their running time. We will introduce a dynamic reverse push algorithm in the first part. Then we will introduce a dynamic forward push algorithm in the second part. Finally we will consider how to extend the algorithms to handle node arrivals and other issues.

3.1 Reverse push

Let t be a (target) vertex of G. Let ε be a parameter between 0 and 1. Our goal is to maintain a pair of estimates and residuals, denoted by $\overleftarrow{P}(t)$ and $\overleftarrow{R}(t)$, such that $\|\overleftarrow{R}(t)\|_\infty \leq \varepsilon$. As mentioned in Section 2.2.2, this will ensure that $|\overleftarrow{P}(s,t) - \pi(s,t)| \leq \varepsilon$, for any node $s \in V$. We start with an equivalent formulation of Equation 3.

LEMMA 3. *Equation* (3) *implies*

$$\overleftarrow{P}(s,t)+\alpha\cdot\overleftarrow{R}(s,t) = \sum_{x\in N^{\text{OUT}}(s)} (1-\alpha)\times\frac{\overleftarrow{P}(x,t)}{d^{\text{OUT}}(s)}+\alpha\times\mathbf{1}_{s=t},\ \forall s\in V,$$

and vice versa.

PROOF. Let $\vec{\pi}^t = \pi(\cdot,t)$ denote the vector with personalized PageRank from every node of G to t. Let $\Pi = (I-(1-\alpha)D^{-1}A)/\alpha$. It follows from the work of Haveliwala [12] that Π is invertible, and $\vec{\pi}^t = \Pi^{-1}\cdot\vec{e}_t$. This implies that the (s,t)-th entry of Π^{-1} is equal to $\pi(s,t)$, since the s-th entry of $\vec{\pi}^t$ is $\pi(s,t)$, Now, we can write Equation (3) in vector form:

$$\begin{aligned}
&\vec{\pi}^t = \overleftarrow{P}(t) + \Pi^{-1}\cdot\overleftarrow{R}(t)\\
\Leftrightarrow\ &\Pi\cdot\vec{\pi}^t = \Pi\cdot\overleftarrow{P}(t) + \overleftarrow{R}(t)\\
\Leftrightarrow\ &\vec{e}_t = \Pi\cdot\overleftarrow{P}(t) + \overleftarrow{R}(t)\\
\Leftrightarrow\ &\overleftarrow{P}(t) + \alpha\times\overleftarrow{R}(t) = (1-\alpha)D^{-1}A\cdot\overleftarrow{P}(t) + \alpha\times\vec{e}_t
\end{aligned}$$

□

Hence it follows if one can maintain the equivalent invariant in Lemma 3, then one obtains a feasible pair of estimates and residuals for the updated graph. And the question becomes how to maintain the invariant between the estimate and the residual vectors. We will only do it for edge insertions, and it's not hard to work out the details for edge deletions using the same approach. Suppose that an edge $u\to v$ is inserted into G. Then the only vertex that doesn't satisfy the invariant in Lemma 3 is u. In this case, it suffices to update $\overleftarrow{R}(u,t)$ without changing any entries of $\overleftarrow{P}(t)$, because the only variable that has been changed is u's out-degree. The precise formula is obtained by calculating u's correct new residual minus its old residual amount. To simplify the expression below, we take out a common factor of $1/\alpha$, which comes from dividing the α multiplier of $\overleftarrow{R}(u,t)$ as in Lemma 3:

$$\begin{aligned}
&\left(\sum_{x\in N^{\text{OUT}}(u)}\frac{(1-\alpha)\times\overleftarrow{P}(x,t)}{d^{\text{OUT}}(u)+1}\right)+\frac{(1-\alpha)\times\overleftarrow{P}(v,t)}{d^{\text{OUT}}(u)+1}\\
&+\alpha\times\mathbf{1}_{u=t}-\overleftarrow{P}(u,t)\\
&-\left(\sum_{x\in N^{\text{OUT}}(u)}\frac{(1-\alpha)\times\overleftarrow{P}(x,t)}{d^{\text{OUT}}(u)}\right)-\alpha\times\mathbf{1}_{u=t}+\overleftarrow{P}(u,t)\\
&=\frac{(1-\alpha)\times\overleftarrow{P}(v,t)}{d^{\text{OUT}}(u)+1}-\sum_{x\in N^{\text{OUT}}(u)}\frac{(1-\alpha)\times\overleftarrow{P}(x,t)}{d^{\text{OUT}}(u)\times(d^{\text{OUT}}(u)+1)}\\
&=\frac{(1-\alpha)\times\overleftarrow{P}(v,t)}{d^{\text{OUT}}(u)+1}-\frac{\overleftarrow{P}(u,t)+\alpha\times\overleftarrow{R}(u,t)-\alpha\times\mathbf{1}_{u=t}}{d^{\text{OUT}}(u)+1}
\end{aligned}$$

Hence the insertion procedure in Algorithm 3 described below correctly generates a pair of estimates and residuals for the updated graph. Similarly for deletions. It is worth mentioning that we haven't described how to handle nodes whose indegree is zero (also known as dangling nodes): since they do not have in neighbors, their residuals cannot be pushed out. We put off this issue until Section 3.3. Another issue is, if one works with undirected graphs, one needs to apply the insert/delete procedure for both direction of an edge.

Algorithm 3 UPDATEREVERSEPUSH

INPUT: $(t, \overleftarrow{P}(t), \overleftarrow{R}(t), u, v, G, \varepsilon)$
Require: G is a directed graph. Let $u\to v$ be the previous edge update, with G being the updated graph.
1: Apply Insert/Delete to $\overleftarrow{P}(t)$ and $\overleftarrow{R}(t)$.
2: **return** REVERSELOCALPUSH$(t, \overleftarrow{P}(t), \overleftarrow{R}(t), G, \varepsilon)$.
3: **procedure** INSERT(u, v)
4: $\quad\overleftarrow{R}(u,t) \mathrel{+}= \frac{(1-\alpha)\times\overleftarrow{P}(v,t)-\overleftarrow{P}(u,t)-\alpha\times\overleftarrow{R}(u,t)+\alpha\times\mathbf{1}_{u=t}}{d^{\text{OUT}}(u)}\times\frac{1}{\alpha}$
5: **procedure** DELETE(u, v)
6: $\quad\overleftarrow{R}(u,t) \mathrel{-}= \frac{(1-\alpha)\times\overleftarrow{P}(v,t)-\overleftarrow{P}(u,t)-\alpha\times\overleftarrow{R}(u,t)+\alpha\times\mathbf{1}_{u=t}}{d^{\text{OUT}}(u)}\times\frac{1}{\alpha}$

For the rest of this section, our goal is presenting an analysis of Algorithm 3. Based on previous work of Bahmani et al. [5], it is not difficult to observe that the updated amount of residuals from step 4 and 6) should be small in expectation in a random edge permutation model. However, one can observe that there are already a lot of nonzero residuals in $\overleftarrow{R}(t)$. While these residuals have all been reduced below ε, it gets unclear if they couple with the updated amount of residuals. Our intuition is to solve this problem with amortized analysis.

THEOREM 4. *Let $\langle G_i = (V_i, E_i)\rangle$ be a sequence of $k+1$ graphs such that each graph is obtained from the previous graph with one edge update. Let $\bar{d}$ denote the average degree of G_0. Let t be a random vertex of G_0. Then the total running time of maintaining a reverse push solution $\overleftarrow{P}_i(t)$ for each graph G_i such that $|\overleftarrow{P}_i(s,t)-\pi_i(s,t)|\leq\varepsilon$, for any $s\in V_i$, using Algorithm 2 and 3, is at most $O(k/\alpha + k/(n\varepsilon\alpha^2)+\bar{d}/(\alpha\varepsilon))$ for the following two dynamic graph models:*

- *Arbitrary edge updates of an undirected graph.*
- *Random edge permutation of a directed graph, under the assumption that the indegree of every vertex of G_0 is at least one, and no new nodes are added during the edge arrivals.*

Remark: the assumptions under the case of directed graphs is because our proof does not deal with issues of bounding the running time of handling dangling nodes, and this can happen a node of G_0 has no in neighbors, or when a new node arrives, thus creating a node without in neighbors.

We prove this theorem in three steps. First of all, we derive a bound on the running time of Algorithm 2. Secondly, we present a bound on the running time of Algorithm 3 and derive the total running time. Finally, we bound the total running time using properties of the graph model. Due to space limit, we only include the proofs for the case of undirected graphs, and refer the reader to the full version for proofs of the other case.

We start with the running time of Algorithm 2. Lemma 5 below is a Corollary of Theorem 2 in the work of Lofgren et al. [18], the difference being that we subtracted a part that corresponds to the total cost of pushing all the remaining residuals, since these residuals have not yet been pushed out. As we will see later on, this part naturally arises in dynamic settings. Let

$$(\overleftarrow{P}_0(t), \overleftarrow{R}_0(t)) \triangleq \text{REVERSELOCALPUSH}(t, \vec{e}_t, \mathbf{0}, G_0, \varepsilon),$$

and

$$\vec{\Phi}_i(x) \triangleq \sum_{s \in V_i} d_i^{\text{IN}}(s) \times \pi_i(s, x), \text{ and} \tag{4}$$

$$\vec{\Phi}_i \triangleq \vec{\Phi}_i(\cdot), \text{ its vector form} \tag{5}$$

LEMMA 5. *The running time of Algorithm 2 is at most:*

$$\frac{\vec{\Phi}_0(t) - \|\vec{\Phi}_0 \cdot \overleftarrow{R}_0(t)\|_1}{\alpha\varepsilon}. \tag{6}$$

PROOF. To see this, note that every time a node pushes, its estimate increases by $\alpha\varepsilon$, hence the total cost of Algorithm 2 is bounded by:

$$\sum_{s \in V_i} \frac{d_0^{\text{IN}}(s) \times \overleftarrow{P}_0(s,t)}{\alpha\varepsilon}$$

$$= \frac{\sum_{s \in V_i} d_0^{\text{IN}}(s) \times (\pi_0(s,t) - \sum_{x \in V_i} \pi_0(s,x) \times \overleftarrow{R}(x,t))}{\alpha\varepsilon}$$

$$= \frac{\vec{\Phi}_0(t) - \|\vec{\Phi}_0 \cdot \overleftarrow{R}_0(t)\|_1}{\alpha\varepsilon}$$

□

Now consider the i-th edge update, for $i = 1, \ldots, k$. That is, we have had the updated graph G_i, after updating G_{i-1} with $e_i = u_i \to v_i$. Then we run Algorithm 3 to update $\overleftarrow{P}_{i-1}(t)$ and $\overleftarrow{R}_{i-1}(t)$. Let

$$(\overleftarrow{P}_i(t), \overleftarrow{R}_i(t)) \triangleq$$
$$\text{UPDATEREVERSEPUSH}(t, \overleftarrow{P}_{i-1}, \overleftarrow{R}_{i-1}(t), u_i, v_i, G_i, \varepsilon).$$

For simplicity, let $\Delta_i(t)$ denote the updated amount of residuals for this edge update. That is, if we are inserting e_i, then from step 4 of Algorithm 3, $\Delta_i(u_i, v_i, t)$ is defined to be $1/\alpha$ times:

$$\left| \frac{(1-\alpha) \times \overleftarrow{P}_{i-1}(v_i,t) - \overleftarrow{P}_{i-1}(u_i,t) - \alpha \times \overleftarrow{R}_{i-1}(u_i,t) + \alpha \times \mathbf{1}_{u_i = t}}{d_i^{\text{OUT}}(u_i)} \right|$$

and it could be similarly defined for deletion.

Lemma 6 is the heart of our amortized analysis. The key observation is that one can take care of the cost of an edge update, by comparing the amount of residuals that we pushed out, to the amount of new residuals that get created. Note that the difference between these two masses is precisely the amount of mass that has been received into the estimates. Another useful property of push algorithms is monotonicity: this property has played a crucial role in all the running time analysis of push algorithms. As long as we only push positive residuals or only negative residuals, then the estimates will only change in one way but not the other. This ensures that we could use estimates as a potential function to bound the number of push operations a vertex does.

LEMMA 6. *The running time of Algorithm 3 for updating $\overleftarrow{P}_{i-1}(t)$ and $\overleftarrow{R}_{i-1}(t)$ for G_i is at most*

$$\frac{\vec{\Phi}_i(u_i) \times \Delta_i(u_i, v_i, t)}{\alpha\varepsilon} + \frac{\|\vec{\Phi}_i - \vec{\Phi}_{i-1}\|_1}{\alpha}$$
$$+ \frac{\|\vec{\Phi}_{i-1} \cdot \overleftarrow{R}_{i-1}(t)\|_1 - \|\vec{\Phi}_i \cdot \overleftarrow{R}_i(t)\|_1}{\alpha\varepsilon}$$

PROOF. Let $\overleftarrow{P}'(t)$ and $\overleftarrow{R}'(t)$ denote the updated values of $\overleftarrow{P}_{i-1}(t)$ and $\overleftarrow{R}_{i-1}(t)$ after step 1 in Algorithm 3. Note that when we invoke Algorithm 2 to reduce the maximum residual of $\overleftarrow{R}'(t)$, we first work on positive residuals and then work on negative residuals. We bound the cost of the two phases separately.

We first bound the cost of pushing out positive residuals (step 1 and 2 in Algorithm 2). Let $\overleftarrow{P}''(t)$ and $\overleftarrow{R}''(t)$ denote the estimate and residual vector after step 2. Since only positive residuals are pushed out, $\overleftarrow{P}''(s,t) \geq \overleftarrow{P}'(s,t)$, for any $s \in V_i$. Hence the cost of this reverse local push is at most:

$$T^+ \triangleq \sum_{s \in V_i} \frac{d_i^{\text{IN}}(s) \times (\overleftarrow{P}''(s,t) - \overleftarrow{P}'(s,t))}{\alpha\varepsilon} \tag{7}$$

By Equation (3),

$$\overleftarrow{P}''(s,t) = \pi_i(s,t) - \sum_{x \in V_i} \pi_i(s,x) \times \overleftarrow{R}''(x,t)$$

Similarly,

$$\overleftarrow{P}'(s,t) = \pi_i(s,t) - \sum_{x \in V_i} \pi_i(s,x) \times \overleftarrow{R}'(x,t)$$

Hence the difference is:

$$\sum_{x \in V_i} \pi_i(s,x) \times (\overleftarrow{R}'(x,t) - \overleftarrow{R}''(x,t))$$

Apply the above expression into Equation (7), we get:

$$T^+ = \sum_{s \in V_i} \sum_{x \in V_i} \frac{d_i^{\text{IN}}(s) \times \pi_i(s,x) \times (\overleftarrow{R}'(x,t) - \overleftarrow{R}''(x,t))}{\alpha\varepsilon}$$
$$= \sum_{x \in V_i} \frac{\vec{\Phi}_i(x) \times (\overleftarrow{R}'(x,t) - \overleftarrow{R}''(x,t))}{\alpha\varepsilon}$$

Here we used $\vec{\Phi}_i(x)$ to simplify the above expression. Now we show that the above expression is at most:

$$T^+ \leq \frac{\|\vec{\Phi}_i \times \overleftarrow{R}'(t)\|_1 - \|\vec{\Phi}_i \cdot \overleftarrow{R}''(t)\|_1}{\alpha\varepsilon}$$

To check this, we compare each vertex $x \in V_i$ and their corresponding entries in the above expression. Since $\vec{\Phi}_i(x)$ is positive for every $x \in V_i$, if $\overleftarrow{R}''(x,t) \geq 0$, then clearly

$$\vec{\Phi}_i(x) \times (\overleftarrow{R}'(x,t) - \overleftarrow{R}''(x,t))$$
$$\leq \vec{\Phi}_i(x) \times (|\overleftarrow{R}'(x,t)| - |\overleftarrow{R}''(x,t)|)$$

If $\overleftarrow{R}''(x,t) < 0$, then we infer that x has not performed any push operation: otherwise $\overleftarrow{R}''(x,t)$ should be nonnegative. Note that x only received positive residual updates during this phase of forward push. This shows $\overleftarrow{R}'(x,t) \leq \overleftarrow{R}''(x,t) < 0$. Therefore:

$$\vec{\Phi}_i(x) \times (\overleftarrow{R}'(x,t) - \overleftarrow{R}''(x,t))$$
$$\leq 0 \leq \vec{\Phi}_i(x) \times (|\overleftarrow{R}'(x,t)| - |\overleftarrow{R}''(x,t)|)$$

We then bound the cost of pushing out negative residuals (step 3 and 4 in Algorithm 2). Since only negative residuals are pushed out, $\overleftarrow{P}_i(s,t) \leq \overleftarrow{P}''(s,t)$, for any $s \in V_i$. By the same argument we used to derive Equation (7), the total cost of this reverse local push is at most:

$$T^- \triangleq \sum_{x \in V_i} \frac{\vec{\Phi}_i(x) \times (\overleftarrow{R}_i(x,t) - \overleftarrow{R}''(x,t))}{\alpha\varepsilon} \tag{8}$$

We claim that:

$$T^- \leq \frac{\|\vec{\Phi}_i \cdot \overleftarrow{R}''(t)\|_1 - \|\vec{\Phi}_i \cdot \overleftarrow{R}_i(t)\|_1}{\alpha\varepsilon} \tag{9}$$

To see this, we compare each vertex $x \in V_i$ and their corresponding entries between Equation (8) and (9). If $\overleftarrow{R}_i(x,t) \leq 0$, then clearly:

$$\begin{aligned}&\vec{\Phi}_i(x) \times (\overleftarrow{R}_i(x,t) - \overleftarrow{R}''(x,t))\\ \leq&\vec{\Phi}_i(x) \times (|\overleftarrow{R}''(x,t)| - |\overleftarrow{R}_i(x,t)|)\end{aligned}$$

If $\overleftarrow{R}_i(x,t) > 0$, then we infer that x does not push out any negative residuals, otherwise $\overleftarrow{R}_i(x,t)$ will be non-positive. This further implies that $\overleftarrow{R}''(x,t) \geq \overleftarrow{R}_i(x,t) > 0$, since x may only receive negative residual updates during this phase. Therefore,

$$\begin{aligned}&\vec{\Phi}_i(x) \times (\overleftarrow{R}_i(x,t) - \overleftarrow{R}''(x,t))\\ &\leq 0 \leq \vec{\Phi}_i(x) \times (|\overleftarrow{R}''(x,t)| - |\overleftarrow{R}_i(x,t)|)\end{aligned}$$

Finally, we obtain a bound on the total running time of invoking Algorithm 2 to reduce the maximum residual:

$$T \triangleq T^+ + T^- \leq \|\vec{\Phi}_i \cdot \overleftarrow{R}'(t)\|_1 - \|\vec{\Phi}_i \cdot \overleftarrow{R}_i(t)\|_1 \tag{10}$$

We work on the above equation to finish the proof. First, since $\overleftarrow{R}'(t)$ is $\overleftarrow{R}_{i-1}(t)$ with an update of $\Delta_i(u_i, v_i, t)$ on vertex u_i, we can separate out $\Delta_i(u_i, v_i, t)$ from $\overleftarrow{R}'(t)$:

$$\|\vec{\Phi}_i \cdot \overleftarrow{R}'(t)\|_1 \leq \vec{\Phi}_i(u_i) \times \Delta_i(u_i, v_i, t) + \|\vec{\Phi}_i \cdot \overleftarrow{R}_{i-1}(t)\|_1$$

Applying the above equation into Equation (10), we found that

$$T \leq \frac{\|\vec{\Phi}_i \cdot \overleftarrow{R}_{i-1}(t)\|_1 + \vec{\Phi}_i(u_i) \times \Delta_i(u_i, v_i, t) - \|\vec{\Phi}_i \cdot \overleftarrow{R}_i(t)\|_1}{\alpha\varepsilon} \tag{11}$$

Then, since $\|\overleftarrow{R}_{i-1}(t)\|_\infty$ is at most ε,

$$\begin{aligned}\|\vec{\Phi}_i \cdot \overleftarrow{R}_{i-1}(t)\|_1 \leq&\|(\vec{\Phi}_i - \vec{\Phi}_{i-1}) \cdot \overleftarrow{R}_{i-1}(t)\|_1 + \|\vec{\Phi}_{i-1} \cdot \overleftarrow{R}_{i-1}(t)\|_1\\ \leq&\varepsilon \times \|\vec{\Phi}_i - \vec{\Phi}_{i-1}\|_1 + \|\vec{\Phi}_{i-1} \cdot \overleftarrow{R}_{i-1}(t)\|_1\end{aligned}$$

Applying the above equation into equation (11) gives us the desired conclusion. □

Lemma 6 naturally suggests that there is a way to amortize per edge update costs, by cancelling out the weighted residual terms. Hence, by summing up the initialization cost in Lemma 5, and the edge update cost in Lemma 6, for $i = 1, \ldots, k$, we obtained the total cost of maintaining the estimates and residuals for every graph G_i, from $i = 0, \ldots, k$:

$$\psi(t) \triangleq \frac{\vec{\Phi}_0(t)}{\alpha\varepsilon} + \sum_{i=1}^{k} \frac{\vec{\Phi}_i(u_i) \times \Delta_i(u_i, v_i, t)}{\alpha\varepsilon} + \sum_{i=1}^{k} \frac{\|\vec{\Phi}_i - \vec{\Phi}_{i-1}\|_1}{\alpha}$$

Now we are ready to present an average case analysis, by summing up $\psi(t)$ over all the target vertices. First, we know from the work of Lofgren et al. (Theorem 1, [18]) that:

$$\sum_{t \in V_0} \vec{\Phi}_0(t) = m.$$

Therefore, the total running time of maintaining a pair of estimates and residuals with threshold ε for every node $t \in V_0$, starting from G_0 with m edges, during k edge updates, is at most:

$$\Psi \triangleq \sum_{t \in V_0} \psi(t) = \frac{m}{\alpha\varepsilon} + \sum_{i=1}^{k} \sum_{t \in V_0} \frac{\vec{\Phi}_i(u_i) \times \Delta_i(u_i, v_i, t)}{\alpha\varepsilon} \tag{12}$$

$$+ \sum_{i=1}^{k} \left(\sum_{t \in V_0} \frac{\|\vec{\Phi}_i - \vec{\Phi}_{i-1}\|_1}{\alpha} \right) \tag{13}$$

where we have changed the order of summation for the second and third term.

LEMMA 7. *Let t be any vertex of V_i. Then*

$$\sum_{t \in V_i} \Delta_i(u_i, v_i, t) \leq (2n\varepsilon + 2)/(\alpha \times d_i^{\text{OUT}}(u_i)),$$

for any $i = 1, \ldots, k$.

PROOF. We deal with the sum of numerators of $\Delta_i(u_i, v_i, t)$ first, since the denominator of $\Delta_i(u_i, v_i, t)$ does not depend on t. We first take out each term from the absolute value to obtain an upper bound of $\Delta_i(u_i, v_i, t)$:

$$\begin{aligned}&(1-\alpha) \times \overleftarrow{P}_{i-1}(v_i, t) + \overleftarrow{P}_{i-1}(u_i, t)\\ &+ \alpha \times \overleftarrow{R}_{i-1}(u_i, t) + \alpha \times \mathbf{1}_{u_i = t}\\ \leq&(1-\alpha) \times (\pi_{i-1}(v_i, t) + \varepsilon) + (\pi_{i-1}(u_i, t) + \varepsilon)\\ &+ \alpha \times \varepsilon + \alpha \times \mathbf{1}_{u_i = t}\end{aligned}$$

We used the fact that $\overleftarrow{P}_{i-1}(u_i, t) \leq \pi_{i-1}(u_i, t) + \varepsilon$ (similarly for v_i) and $\overleftarrow{R}_{i-1}(u_i, t) \leq \varepsilon$. If we sum up the above expression over $t \in V_i$, and take the denominator back to the expression, it leads to the following much simplified conclusion:

$$\sum_{t \in V_i} \Delta_i(u_i, v_i, t) \leq \frac{2n\varepsilon + 2}{\alpha \times d_i^{\text{OUT}}(u_i)}$$

□

Arbitrary edge update on an undirected graph.

Proof of Theorem 4, Part 1: Note that Lemma 5 (initialization cost) holds for undirected graphs as well. When we update an edge, We need to take into account that we applied insertion/deletion twice (step 4 and 6 in Algorithm 3), for each direction of the edge. This makes a difference when we separate out the difference between $\overleftarrow{R}'(t)$ and $\overleftarrow{R}_{i-1}(t)$. Hence, it suffices to add

$$\frac{\vec{\Phi}_i(v_i) \times \Delta_i(v_i, u_i, t)}{\alpha\varepsilon}$$

into the bound of Lemma 6: the rest of the proof holds for undirected graphs. In conclusion, we found that the total running time of maintaining $\overleftarrow{P}_i(t)$ and $\overleftarrow{R}_i(t)$ is at most:

$$\begin{aligned}\Psi \triangleq&\frac{m}{\alpha\varepsilon} + \sum_{i=1}^{k} \sum_{t \in V_0} \frac{\vec{\Phi}_i(u_i) \times \Delta_i(u_i, v_i, t) + \vec{\Phi}_i(v_i) \times \Delta_i(v_i, u_i, t)}{\alpha\varepsilon}\\ &+ \sum_{i=1}^{k} \sum_{t \in V_0} \frac{\|\vec{\Phi}_i - \vec{\Phi}_{i-1}\|_1}{\alpha}\end{aligned}$$

Now we claim that with $\vec{\Phi}_i(x) = d_i(x)$, for any $x \in V_i$ and $i = 0, \ldots, k$. By Proposition 1,

$$\vec{\Phi}_i(x) = \sum_{s \in V_i} d_i(s) \times \pi_i(s, x) = \sum_{s \in V_i} d_i(x) \times \pi_i(x, s). = d_i(x).$$

Combined with Lemma 7, the second term of Φ is at most $k \times (\frac{4n}{\alpha^2} + \frac{4}{\alpha^2 \varepsilon})$.

It also follows that $\vec{\Phi}_i$ is equal to the degree vector of G_i, and the l_1 difference between $\vec{\Phi}_i$ and $\vec{\Phi}_{i-1}$ is equal to 2, since only the degrees of u_i and v_i changed by one.

To sum up,

$$\Psi \leq \frac{m}{\alpha\varepsilon} + k \times (\frac{4n}{\alpha^2} + \frac{4}{\alpha^2\varepsilon}) + \frac{2nk}{\alpha}.$$

3.2 Forward push

Now we apply a similar approach to derive a dynamic forward push algorithm. Let s be a source vertex of G. Let ε be a threshold parameter between 0 and 1. Our goal is to maintain a pair of estimates $\vec{P}(s)$ and residuals $\vec{R}(s)$ such that $\vec{R}(s,t)/d^{\text{OUT}}(t) \leq \varepsilon$, for any $t \in V$. We begin by describing an equivalent invariant property to Equation 2.

LEMMA 8. *Equation 2 implies*

$$\vec{P}(s,t) + \alpha \times \vec{R}(s,t) = \sum_{x \in N^{\text{IN}}(t)} \frac{\vec{P}(s,x)}{d^{\text{OUT}}(x)} + \alpha \times \mathbf{1}_{t=s}, \forall t \in V,$$

and vice versa.

PROOF. Let $\vec{\pi}_s = \pi(s,\cdot)$ denote a vector with personalized PageRank from s to every node of G. Let $\Pi = \alpha \times (I - (1-\alpha)A^\intercal D^{-1})^{-1}$: the fact that Π exists follows from Definition 1, and $\vec{\pi}_s$ is equal to $\Pi \cdot \vec{e}_s$. Therefore equation 2 in vector form is equivalent to:

$$\begin{aligned}
&\vec{\pi}_s = \vec{P}(s) + \Pi \cdot \vec{R}(s) \\
\Leftrightarrow\ &\Pi^{-1} \cdot \vec{\pi}_s = \Pi^{-1}\vec{P}(s) + \vec{R}(s) \\
\Leftrightarrow\ &\vec{e}_s = \frac{I - (1-\alpha)A^\intercal D^{-1}}{\alpha} \cdot \vec{P}(s) + \vec{R}(s) \\
\Leftrightarrow\ &\vec{P}(s) + \alpha \times \vec{R}(s) = (1-\alpha)A^\intercal D^{-1}\vec{P}(s) + \alpha \times \vec{e}_s
\end{aligned}$$

□

Now we use Lemma 8 to derive the update procedure. Consider when an edge $u \to v$ is inserted to G. Since the outdegree of u increases by 1, the invariant does not hold for the out neighbors of u any more: the reason being that every out neighbor receives an equal proportion of mass from u which is $(1-\alpha)$ divided by the outdegree of u times the amount of mass that u pushed. To solve this imbalance, clearly a simple solution is to scale $\vec{P}(s,u)$ by a factor of $(d^{\text{OUT}}(u)+1)/d^{\text{OUT}}(u)$. This ensures the invariant for every out neighbor of u, except v. This is because we need to take into account the amount of residuals v should have received previously, had the edge $u \to v$ existed. Finally, since we have increased $\vec{P}(s,u)$, this will break the invariant for u. Hence we will reduce $\vec{R}(s,u)$ by the increased amount on $\vec{P}(s,u)$, divided by α. See Algorithm 4 below for details. To work with an undirected graph, we will apply insert/delete twice, for both direction between u and v. It's not hard to see this, following our discussion above.

Next we prove a theorem on the update cost of Algorithm 4. We will prove it on undirected graphs. It's not clear to us how to analyze directed graphs with forward push: the difficulty being that there is no clean bound on the error of Algorithm 1, between the estimates and the true personalized PageRank value.

Algorithm 4 UPDATEFORWARDPUSH

INPUT: $(s, \vec{P}(s), \vec{R}(s), u, v, G, \varepsilon)$
Require: G is a directed graph. Let $u \to v$ be the previous edge update, with G being the updated graph.
1: Apply Insert/Delete to $\vec{P}(s)$ and $\vec{R}(s)$.
2: **return** FORWARDLOCALPUSH$(s, \vec{P}(s), \vec{R}(s), G, \varepsilon)$
3: **procedure** INSERT(u, v)
4: $\quad \vec{P}(s,u)$ *= $\frac{d^{\text{OUT}}(u)}{d^{\text{OUT}}(u)-1}$
5: $\quad \vec{R}(s,u)$ −= $\frac{\vec{P}(s,u)}{d^{\text{OUT}}(u)} \cdot \frac{1}{\alpha}$
6: $\quad \vec{R}(s,v)$ += $\frac{(1-\alpha) \times \vec{P}(s,u)}{d^{\text{OUT}}(u)} \cdot \frac{1}{\alpha}$
7: **procedure** DELETE(u, v)
8: $\quad \vec{P}(s,u)$ *= $\frac{d^{\text{OUT}}(u)}{d^{\text{OUT}}(u)+1}$
9: $\quad \vec{R}(s,u)$ += $\frac{\vec{P}(s,u)}{d^{\text{OUT}}(u)} \cdot \frac{1}{\alpha}$
10: $\quad \vec{R}(s,v)$ −= $\frac{(1-\alpha) \times \vec{P}(s,u)}{d^{\text{OUT}}(u)} \cdot \frac{1}{\alpha}$

THEOREM 9. *Let $\langle G_i = (V_i, E_i) \rangle$ be a sequence of $k+1$ undirected graphs, such that each graph is obtained from the previous graph by one edge update. Let s be a random vertex of V_0. And let ε be a parameter between 0 and 1. Then the total running time of maintaining a forward local push solution $\vec{P}_i(s)$ for each graph G_i such that $|\vec{P}_i(s,t) - \pi_i(s,t)|/d_i(t) \leq \varepsilon$, for any $t \in V_i$, using Algorithms 4 is at most $O(k/(\alpha^2) + k/(n\alpha^2\varepsilon) + 1/(\alpha\varepsilon))$.*

As long as $|\vec{R}_i(s,t)|/d_i(t) \leq \varepsilon$, for any $t \in V_i$ and $i = 0, \ldots, k$, then $|\vec{P}_i(s,t) - \pi_i(s,t)|/d_i(t) \leq \varepsilon$. This accuracy guarantee follows from the work of Anderson et al. and Lofgren et al. [2, 15]. Hence, we will focus on analyzing running time. To derive this theorem, we divide the arguments into three parts: first, we present a bound on the initiation cost as well as the update cost per edge; secondly, we amortize the costs together, cancelling out the residual terms; finally, we use properties from undirected graphs to bound the total cost. The proof can be found in the full version of this paper.

3.3 Discussions

The algorithms presented in the previous sections do not handle dangling nodes. We consider how to take care of this situation. We also extend the algorithms to handle newly arrived nodes.

Dangling nodes.

There are two possible ways to handle dangling nodes. The first way is to create a separate sink node. Consider the case of doing reverse push (similarly for forward push). If a node u does not have any in neighbors and need to perform a push operation, then the amount of mass will be pushed to the sink node. These mass will stay at the sink node. Another way is to insert an edge from t to u, if t is the target node for maintaining reverse push solutions. Later on if an edge is added from v to u, so that u is not a dangling node anymore, then we first delete the edge from t to u and then insert an edge from v to u.

Node arrivals.

When a new node arrives, one can insert the edges one by one using the procedures in Algorithm 3 (line 3) and Algorithm 4 (line 3), and then invoke the local push algorithms to reduce the maximum absolute values of residuals. Similarly for node deletions.

4. NUMERICAL RESULTS

In this section, we evaluate our approach in experiments. We first compare our dynamic forward local push algorithm (Algorithm 4) to the previous work of Ohsaka et al. [20]. Our dynamic Forward Push algorithm differs from Ohsaka et. al.'s in an important way. When an edge (u, v) arrives, they propose to push the change in residual immediately to all of u's neighbors, requiring $\Omega(d(u))$ time, in addition to any pushes needed to restore the invariant. In contrast, we modify the estimate and residual values only at u and v, taking only $O(1)$ time, before performing any pushes needed to restore the invariant. We found that this simple optimization decreased the number of residual values updated and led to a 1.5 - 3.5 times improvement in running time, without sacrificing accuracy.

We then make a comparison to the random walk approach of Bahmani et al. [5]. We consider the problem of identifying the top-K vertices that have the highest personalized PageRank from a source node, with random walks being commonly used to solve it on social networks [11, 19]. We found that the random walk algorithm uses 4.5 to 12 times as much storage compared to forward local push algorithm, and requires 1.5 to 2.5 times as much time to update as well, to achieve the same level of precision.

Finally, we evaluate our dynamic reverse push algorithm. We compare against the baseline where we recompute the reverse push from scratch after every edge update. We found that our approach is 100x faster than this baseline.

4.1 Experimental setup

We implement the experiments in Scala. We use an Amazon EC2 Ubuntu machine with 64GB of RAM and 16 processors of Intel(R) Xeon(R) CPU E5-2676 v3 @ 2.40GHz. We tested with three undirected social networks graphs, all downloaded from https://snap.stanford.edu/data/. The statistics are listed in Table 1 below. For each social network, we generate a uniformly random edge stream of the graph. Given a test vertex, we initialize its data structures using the subgraph that consists of the first half of the edges in the random edge stream. After that, for each new edge arrival, we update its data structure depending the approach we are using. The teleport probability α is set to 0.2 in all the experiments. For ease of comparison, we use LazyFwdUpdate to refer to Algorithm 4 (because it "lazily" avoids pushing from vertices that receive new edges), Ohsaka et al.'s Algorithm TrackingPPR and the random walk update Algorithm by RandomWalk.

graph	# nodes	# edges
DBLP	317,080	1,049,866
LiveJournal	3,997,962	34,681,189
Orkut	3,072,441	117,185,083

Table 1: Basic statistics of graphs that we experimented with.

4.2 Residual updates and running time

We compare LazyFwdUpdate and TrackingPPR over 100 uniformly sampled source vertices from each graph. In our implementation, we first update the previous estimate vectors and residual vectors based on LazyFwdUpdate and TrackingPPR, respectively. We then invoke the same forward local push routine (Algorithm 1) to reduce any residual that is outside the desired threshold. At the end of the edge stream, we compare the performance of each algorithm, using measurements described below:

- Residual update: the number of times that a vertex's residual is updated. Each residual update corresponds to an update in the priority queue of residuals.
- Push iterations: the number of times that Algorithm 1 performs a push operation in step 6. The cost of a push iteration is the degree of the pushed vertex times the cost of a residual update.
- Running time: the amount of update time it takes to maintain estimates and residuals. We exclude the amount of time it takes to initialize the data structure. Note that this cost is negligible compared to the amount of update time in our experiment.
- l_1 error: the l_1 distance between the computed estimates and the benchmark values. To get the benchmark, we ran the local push algorithm with threshold $0.02/n$, where n is the number of vertices of the graph.
- Storage: the number of nonzero estimates and residuals maintained.

For residual update, push iteraions and running time, we computed the average value over the 100 samples. For l_1 error, we compute the median error over the 100 samples. The test results is shown in Table 2. We found that TrackingPPR does more residual updates than LazyFwdUpdate, for all three graphs, and the improvement is more significant for denser graphs. While Algorithm 4 does more push operations than TrackingPPR, since the latter already does a push operation before invoking Algorithm 1, the compound effect is that we achieved 1.5 to 5 times speed up, without sacrificing accuracy.

4.3 Comparison to random walks

We compare LazyFwdUpdate and RandomWalk for the problem of finding top-K vertices ranked by their personalized Pagerank from a source vertex. We sample 100 test vertices uniformly at random. For each test vertex, the correct top-K solution is the set of K vertices with highest personalized Pagerank from that vertex. The performance of each algorithm is measured by:

- Accuracy: the number of correctly identified vertices (among its computed K vertices with highest personalized Pagerank) divided by K.
- Running time: the amount of time to maintain/update the data structures.
- Storage: to compare storage used by RandomWalk, we multiply the number of random walks by the expected length of a walk (5 in our experiment) times 4 (number of bytes to store an integer vertex ID). [1] For LazyFwdUpdate, we multiply the number of nonzero

[1] To allow for efficient update, it's necessary to build an inverted index for each vertex that quickly finds to the set of random walks crossing it. In our implementation we built a hashmap for this purpose, resulting in an additional fac-

	DBLP		LiveJournal		Orkut	
	LazyFwd Update	Tracking PPR	LazyFwd Update	Tracking PPR	LazyFwd Update	Tracking PPR
Residual updates	1.5×10^6	2.4×10^6	2.5×10^6	1.8×10^7	2.9×10^6	6.2×10^7
Push iterations	2.3×10^5	1.8×10^5	1.5×10^5	1.0×10^5	5.3×10^4	2.6×10^4
Running time	$2.9s$	$4.7s$	17.1	51.4	49.8	176.4
l_1 error	0.031	0.031	0.145	0.150	0.238	0.244

Table 2: Test results between LazyFwdUpdate with $\varepsilon = 7 \times 10^{-7}$ and TrackingPPR with $\varepsilon = 10^{-6}$. For each graph, we sampled 100 vertices uniformly at random.

	DBLP		LiveJournal		Orkut	
	LazyFwd Update	Random Walk	LazyFwd Update	Random Walk	LazyFwd Update	Random Walk
Storage	2.6×10^4	3.2×10^5	5.3×10^4	3.2×10^5	6.3×10^4	3.2×10^5
Accuracy	0.96	0.92	0.88	0.88	0.74	0.78
Running time	0.32s	0.88s	8.8s	15.3s	29.7s	53.0s

Table 3: Test results for top-50 between LazyFwdUpdate with $\varepsilon = 5 \times 10^{-5}$ and RandomWalk with 16000 walks. For each graph, we sampled 100 vertices uniformly at random. The parameters are chosen so that the median accuracy of both algorithms are around 0.9 on LiveJournal.

	DBLP		LiveJournal		Orkut	
	LazyFwd Update	Random Walk	LazyFwd Update	Random Walk	LazyFwd Update	Random Walk
Storage	6.0×10^4	5.0×10^5	1.2×10^5	5.0×10^5	1.5×10^5	5.0×10^5
Accuracy	0.96	0.91	0.91	0.88	0.75	0.80
Running time	0.41s	1.24s	8.6s	16.0s	30.1s	59.7s

Table 4: Test results for top-100 between LazyFwdUpdate with $\varepsilon = 2 \times 10^{-5}$ and RandomWalk with 25000 walks. For each graph, we sampled 100 vertices uniformly at random. The parameters are chosen so that the median accuracy of both algorithms are around 0.9 on LiveJournal.

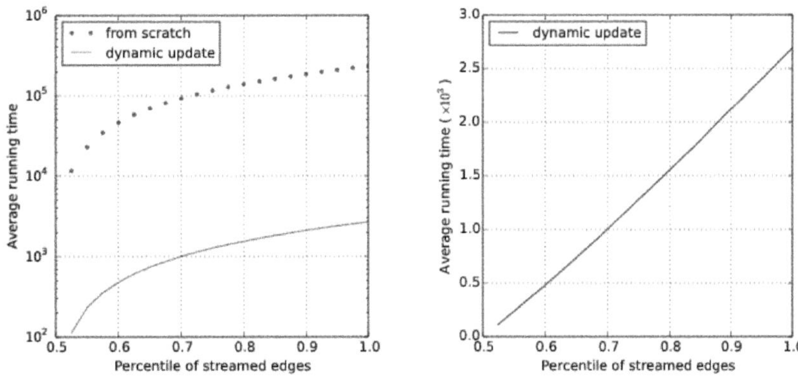

Figure 1: Running time comparisons on LiveJournal, between maintaining reverse push using Algorithm 3 and computing reverse push from scratch for every edge insertion with $\varepsilon = 10^{-4}$. We take 100 random test nodes and compute the average running time for each algorithm.

estimates and residuals by 8 (number of bytes to store a pair of integer and floating point number).

Table 3 and 4 below describe the results with K being 50 and 100, respectively. We take the average of running time and storage, and median of accuracy over the 100 sampled vertices. For the problem of identifying top-50 nodes, we found that RandomWalk uses 4.5 to 12 times as much storage compared to LazyFwdUpdate, and uses 1.6 to 2.7 as much running time. On Orkut graph, when accuracy is controlled to be at the same level as RandomWalk for LazyFwdUpdate (with $\varepsilon = 4 \times 10^{-5}$), the average amount of storage becomes 7.0×10^4 and the average running time becomes $33.3s$. When K is 100, the test results are qualitatively consistent with the above conclusion.

tor of 2 in the amount of storage used. Since there might be more efficient implementation, we do not take this additional factor into account in our comparison.

4.4 Evaluation of dynamic reverse push algorithm

In this section we evaluate the performance of our dynamic reverse push algorithm. We compare our proposed solution (Algorithm 3) to the baseline, where we recompute reverse push from scratch after every edge insertion using Algorithm 2. We sample 100 target vertices uniformly at random and take the average of the running time over these 100 samples. We have chosen the maximum residual parameter $\varepsilon = 10^{-4}$ so that at the end of the edge stream, the median l_1 error over the 100 samples between the maintained reverse push estimates and the true values is less than 0.1. Because it takes too long to compute reverse push from scratch after every edge insertion for 100 sampled vertices, we only computed reverse push from scratch for the first 1000 edge insertions. We take the average running time for performing reverse push during 1000 edge updates, and use this average value times the number of inserted edges as an approximation to the true running time, if we have computed reverse push from scratch for every edge insertion. Figure 1 shows the experiment result on the LiveJournal graph. We found that our approach is 100x faster than the baseline. The aggregate running time for updating reverse push has a linear correlation with the number of edges added. This is consistent with the theoretical bound from Theorem 4.

Acknowledgement.

Research supported by the DARPA GRAPHS program via grant FA9550-12-1-0411, and by NSF grant 1447697.

5. REFERENCES

[1] Reid Andersen, Christian Borgs, Jennifer Chayes, John Hopcraft, Vahab S Mirrokni, and Shang-Hua Teng. Local computation of pagerank contributions. In *Algorithms and Models for the Web-Graph*, pages 150–165. Springer, 2007.

[2] Reid Andersen, Fan Chung, and Kevin Lang. Local graph partitioning using pagerank vectors. In *Foundations of Computer Science, 2006. FOCS'06. 47th Annual IEEE Symposium on*, pages 475–486. IEEE, 2006.

[3] Konstantin Avrachenkov, Nelly Litvak, Danil Nemirovsky, and Natalia Osipova. Monte carlo methods in pagerank computation: When one iteration is sufficient. *SIAM Journal on Numerical Analysis*, 2007.

[4] Lars Backstrom and Jure Leskovec. Supervised random walks: predicting and recommending links in social networks. In *Proceedings of the fourth ACM international conference on Web search and data mining*. ACM, 2011.

[5] Bahman Bahmani, Abdur Chowdhury, and Ashish Goel. Fast incremental and personalized pagerank. *Proceedings of the VLDB Endowment*, 4(3):173–184, 2010.

[6] Shumeet Baluja, Rohan Seth, D Sivakumar, Yushi Jing, Jay Yagnik, Shankar Kumar, Deepak Ravichandran, and Mohamed Aly. Video suggestion and discovery for youtube: taking random walks through the view graph. In *Proceedings of the 17th international conference on World Wide Web*, pages 895–904. ACM, 2008.

[7] Pavel Berkhin. Bookmark-coloring algorithm for personalized pagerank computing. *Internet Mathematics*, 3(1):41–62, 2006.

[8] Soumen Chakrabarti. Dynamic personalized pagerank in entity-relation graphs. In *Proceedings of the 16th international conference on World Wide Web*, pages 571–580. ACM, 2007.

[9] Dániel Fogaras, Balázs Rácz, Károly Csalogány, and Tamás Sarlós. Towards scaling fully personalized pagerank: Algorithms, lower bounds, and experiments. *Internet Mathematics*, 2005.

[10] David F Gleich. Pagerank beyond the web. *SIAM Review*, 57(3):321–363, 2015.

[11] Pankaj Gupta, Ashish Goel, Jimmy Lin, Aneesh Sharma, Dong Wang, and Reza Zadeh. Wtf: The who to follow service at twitter. In *Proceedings of the 22nd international conference on World Wide Web*. International World Wide Web Conferences Steering Committee, 2013.

[12] Taher H Haveliwala. Topic-sensitive pagerank: A context-sensitive ranking algorithm for web search. *Knowledge and Data Engineering, IEEE Transactions on*, 15(4):784–796, 2003.

[13] Glen Jeh and Jennifer Widom. Scaling personalized web search. In *Proceedings of the 12th international conference on World Wide Web*. ACM, 2003.

[14] Peter Lofgren. On the complexity of the monte carlo method for incremental pagerank. *Information Processing Letters*, 114(3):104–106, 2014.

[15] Peter Lofgren. Efficient algorithms for personalized pagerank. *arXiv preprint arXiv:1512.04633*, 2015.

[16] Peter Lofgren, Siddhartha Banerjee, and Ashish Goel. Bidirectional pagerank estimation: From average-case to worst-case. In *Algorithms and Models for the Web Graph*, pages 164–176. Springer, 2015.

[17] Peter Lofgren, Siddhartha Banerjee, and Ashish Goel. Personalized pagerank estimation and search: A bidirectional approach. In *WSDM*, 2016.

[18] Peter A Lofgren, Siddhartha Banerjee, Ashish Goel, and C Seshadhri. Fast-ppr: Scaling personalized pagerank estimation for large graphs. In *Proceedings of the 20th ACM SIGKDD international conference on Knowledge discovery and data mining*, pages 1436–1445. ACM, 2014.

[19] Ioannis Mitliagkas, Michael Borokhovich, Alexandros G Dimakis, and Constantine Caramanis. Frogwild!: fast pagerank approximations on graph engines. *Proceedings of the VLDB Endowment*, 8(8):874–885, 2015.

[20] Naoto Ohsaka, Takanori Maehara, and Ken-ichi Kawarabayashi. Efficient pagerank tracking in evolving networks. In *Proceedings of the 21th ACM SIGKDD International Conference on Knowledge Discovery and Data Mining*, pages 875–884. ACM, 2015.

[21] Lawrence Page, Sergey Brin, Rajeev Motwani, and Terry Winograd. The pagerank citation ranking: bringing order to the web. 1999.

[22] Jaewon Yang and Jure Leskovec. Defining and evaluating network communities based on ground-truth. In *Proceedings of the ACM SIGKDD Workshop on Mining Data Semantics*, page 3. ACM, 2012.

Annealed Sparsity via Adaptive and Dynamic Shrinking

Kai Zhang[§], Shandian Zhe[†], Chaoran Cheng[♯], Zhi Wei[♯], Zhengzhang Chen[§]
Haifeng Chen[§], Guofei Jiang[§], Yuan Qi[†], Jieping Ye[‡]
[§]NEC Laboratories America, Princeton NJ
[†]Dept. Computer Science, Purdue University
[♯]Dept. Computer Science, New Jersey Institute of Technology
[‡]Dept. Computational Medicine & Bioinformatics, University of Michigan, Ann Arbor
[§]{kzhang,zchen,haifeng,gfj}@nec-labs.com, [†]{szhe,alanqi}@purdue.edu
[♯]{cc424,zhi.wei@njit.edu}, [‡]jpye@umich.edu

ABSTRACT

Sparse learning has received tremendous amount of interest in high-dimensional data analysis due to its model interpretability and the low-computational cost. Among the various techniques, adaptive ℓ_1-regularization is an effective framework to improve the convergence behaviour of the LASSO, by using varying strength of regularization across different features. In the meantime, the adaptive structure makes it very powerful in modelling grouped sparsity patterns as well, being particularly useful in high-dimensional multi-task problems. However, choosing an appropriate, global regularization weight is still an open problem. In this paper, inspired by the annealing technique in material science, we propose to achieve "annealed sparsity" by designing a dynamic shrinking scheme that simultaneously optimizes the regularization weights and model coefficients in sparse (multi-task) learning. The dynamic structures of our algorithm are twofold. Feature-wise ("spatially"), the regularization weights are updated interactively with model coefficients, allowing us to improve the global regularization structure. Iteration-wise ("temporally"), such interaction is coupled with gradually boosted ℓ_1-regularization by adjusting an equality norm-constraint, achieving an "annealing" effect to further improve model selection. This renders interesting shrinking behaviour in the whole solution path. Our method competes favorably with state-of-the-art methods in sparse (multi-task) learning. We also apply it in expression quantitative trait loci analysis (eQTL), which gives useful biological insights in human cancer (melanoma) study.

Keywords

Sparse regression, adaptive LASSO, multi-task LASSO, regularization path, sparse multi-task learning

1. INTRODUCTION

With the rapid development of data acquisition technologies in various science and engineering domains such as imaging, physics, biology, and computer networks, we are having access to digital data of unprecedented amount and quality. In this modern paradigm, a significant challenge for data discovery is the huge number of features in representing objects. For example, a high-resolution image is composed of millions of pixels; the micro-array data in human genomic study typically includes tens of thousands of gene expressions; in movie recommendation systems the number of movies can be tens of millions. How to identify truly relevant features in the huge feature pools for accurate learning and prediction has become one of the key challenges in data mining.

Sparse regression has recently emerged as a powerful tool for high-dimensional data analysis, especially in removing irrelevant variables and identifying a parsimonious subset of covariates for predicting the target [29, 38, 39]. Given a response vector $\mathbf{y} = [y_1, y_2, ..., y_n]^\top$ and predictors $\mathbf{X} \in \mathbb{R}^{n\times D}$, where without loss of generality the data is centered, sparse regression and in particular the LASSO solves the following regularized linear regression problem:

$$\min_{\beta} \|\mathbf{X}\beta - \mathbf{y}\|_2^2 + \lambda|\beta|_1, \tag{1}$$

where $\beta \in \mathbb{R}^{D\times 1}$ is the regression coefficient vector. The ℓ_1-norm $|\beta|_1$ is used to enforce the sparsity of solution, making the model easy to interpret. In the meantime, recent advances in solving the non-smooth, convex LASSO problem has made it computationally extremely efficient [14, 12]. Therefore the LASSO and related methods have been applied with great success in a number of domains including bioinformatics [17, 24, 35, 36], imaging and computer vision [33, 21, 9], and signal processing [5, 6].

It is shown that LASSO can perform automatic variable selection because the ℓ_1-penalty is singular at the origin [11]. It was also shown that variable selection with the LASSO is consistent only under certain conditions [22, 37]. Namely, there are scenarios in which the LASSO selection is not consistent. To fix this problem, [38] proposes to use adaptive weights to regularize the model coefficients along different features, as

$$\min_{\beta} \|\mathbf{X}\beta - \mathbf{y}\|_2^2 + \lambda\cdot|\hat{\mathbf{w}}\odot\beta|_1, \tag{2}$$

where $\hat{\mathbf{w}} \in \mathbb{R}^{D\times 1}$ is the regularization weight, and $|\hat{\mathbf{w}}\odot\beta|_1 = \sum_i \hat{w}_i|\beta_i|$, namely each dimension of β is penalized differently instead of sharing a single regularization parameter λ as in LASSO (1). The regularization weights $\hat{\mathbf{w}}$ can be chosen as $\hat{\mathbf{w}} = |\beta_{ols}|^{-\gamma}$, where β_{ols} is the ordinal least-square solution,

KDD '16, August 13–17, 2016, San Francisco, CA, USA.

DOI: http://dx.doi.org/10.1145/2939672.2939769

and γ is a positive number. Such choice renders the oracle property of the adaptive LASSO estimator in simultaneous variable selection and prediction.

Besides improving the asymptotic behaviour of sparse model estimation, the adaptive LASSO can also be quite useful in imposing structured sparsity patterns, in particular in high-dimensional multi-task learning by sharing the same adaptive weight across different tasks. Therefore it has gained a lot of research interest from various domains [10, 17, 19]. However, choosing an optimal regularization weight vector $\hat{\mathbf{w}}$ (2) can be much more challenging than selecting a single regularization parameter λ (1). The former has a significantly larger search space, and is the key to the superior performance of adaptive LASSO.

In this paper, we propose a novel approach to simultaneously compute the model coefficients and adaptive regularization weights in ℓ_1-regularized regression, in comparison to most existing methods that address them separately. The basic idea is to adopt an alternating optimization framework to establish the closed-form relations between model coefficients and regularization weights (under an equality norm-constraint of the latter). By doing this, the two sets of parameters can then be optimized iteratively, until an equilibrium state is obtained upon convergence.

The interactive updating scheme can acquire greater flexibility in tuning the sparse model. In the meantime, to further improve its convergence and reduce the sensitivity on initial conditions, we borrow the idea from material science and propose an "annealed" shrinking procedure. Specifically, throughout the interactive updates between model coefficients and regularization weights, we gradually strengthen the global magnitude of ℓ_1-penalization by adjusting the equality norm-constraint on the regularization weight vector. Then, by starting from a dense solution, the system will go through a series of micro-stages that continuously sparsify and ameliorate itself. In this "annealing" process, features are like particles: in the "high-temperature" beginning, all features have the freedom to compete with each other and position themselves in the model; however, when the system gradually cools down, fewer and fewer features could preserve their energy; finally, only those features that survive the dynamic competing process will be selected.

We find that such a dynamic shrinking scheme leads to an interesting mechanism of feature selection and competition, which favors the choice of truly relevant features. Through extensive experiments, we compare our approach with a number of state-of-the-art techniques in sparse learning, and obtain promising results. The contribution of the paper is summarized as follows:

1. We introduce the concept of "annealing" in sparse learning, and propose an annealed, dynamic shrinking framework to improve the model selection in ℓ_1-regression;

2. We extend our approach to solve high-dimensional multi-task learning problems to improve state-of-the-art;

3. We apply our approach in eQTL, which successfully identifies significant and relevant pathways to help understand the P53 regulation mechanism for melanoma.

The rest of the paper is structured as follows. Section 2 discusses the proposed method. Section 3 extends it to multi-task learning scenario. Section 4 describes related methods. Empirical results are presented in Section 5, and the last section concludes the paper.

2. METHOD

Consider the following linear regression problem with the design matrix $\mathbf{X} \in \mathbb{R}^{n \times D}$, where n is the sample size and D is the dimensionality, and the target response vector $\mathbf{y} \in \mathbb{R}^{n \times 1}$. We use an adaptive weight vector $\mathbf{w} = [w_1, w_2, ..., w_D]^\top$ to regularize over different covariates, as

$$\min_{\mathbf{w},\mathbf{B}} \quad \|\mathbf{X}\beta - \mathbf{y}\|_2^2 + |\mathbf{w}^{-\gamma} \odot \beta| \tag{3}$$

$$s.t. \sum_d w_d = \omega, \quad w_d \geq 0. \tag{4}$$

Here, $\beta \in \mathbb{R}^{D\times 1}$ is the model, $\mathbf{w} \in \mathbb{R}^{D\times 1}$ is the regularization weight vector, and $|\mathbf{w}^{-\gamma} \odot \beta| = \sum_{d=1}^{D} w_d^{-\gamma} \cdot |\beta_d|$. Both parameters will be optimized in our learning procedures.

The equality norm-constraint $\sum_d w_d = \omega$ is quite useful in controlling the global strength of regularization (in an average sense). To see this, note that the regularization imposed on the dth feature is $w_d^{-\gamma}$ (3) . Therefore, if γ is positive: then the larger the ω, the smaller the average strength of the ℓ_1-penalty; on the other hand, if γ is negative: then the larger the ω, the larger the average strength of ℓ_1-penalty. Later we shall see that, it is exactly because of this equality norm-constraint (4) that we acquire the flexibility of "annealing" the whole system to improve the state of solution. The power parameter γ can be chosen either as a positive or negative real number, in comparison to the power parameter that can only be positive in the adaptive LASSO [39].

2.1 Interactive Update

We first consider ω as a pre-defined constant. Then the problem (1) can be solved by alternating optimization. Namely we first fix $\mathbf{w}$ and solve β, and then fix β and solve $\mathbf{w}$, and keep iterating until convergence. Here we use β_d to denote the dth entry of β.

Fix w and solve β. Then this becomes an adaptive LASSO problem,

$$\min_{\beta} \|\mathbf{X}\beta - \mathbf{y}\|_2^2 + |\mathbf{w}^{-\gamma} \odot \beta|, \tag{5}$$

which can be computationally converted to a standard LASSO problem [38].

Fix β **and solve w.** This then become the following constrained optimization problem

$$\min_{\mathbf{w}} \sum_d \beta_d \cdot w_d^{-\gamma}, \tag{6}$$

$$\theta_d = |\beta_d|.$$

Problem (6) has a closed form solution,

$$w_d = \left(\frac{\theta_d^{\frac{1}{1+\gamma}}}{\sum_{j=1}^{D} \theta_j^{\frac{1}{1+\gamma}}} \right) \omega. \tag{7}$$

The derivations are in the appendix.

Choice of the γ Parameter. Based on equation (7), we can examine the relation between the actual regularization imposed in (3), $w^{-\gamma}$, and the (absolute) value of the model coefficient, θ_d (4). We discuss the following scenarios:

1. $\gamma > 0$: if θ_d is larger (compared with $\theta_{d'}, d' \neq d$), then w_d (7) will also be larger due to the positive power term

$\frac{1}{1+\gamma}$, and as a result the regularization term $w_d^{-\gamma}$ in (3) will be smaller, leading to a weaker regularization on the d feature in the next iteration;

2. $\gamma < -1$: if θ_d is larger (compared with $\theta_{d'}, d' \neq d$), then w_d will be smaller due to the negative power $\frac{1}{1+\gamma}$; as a result $w_d^{-\gamma}$ will also be smaller since $-\gamma > 0$, leading to a weaker regularization in the next iteration;

3. $-1 < \gamma < 0$: if θ_d is larger (compared with $\theta_{d'}, d' \neq d$), then w_d will be larger due to the positive power $\frac{1}{1+\gamma}$; so $w_d^{-\gamma}$ will be larger since $-\gamma > 0$, leading to a stronger regularization in the next iteration.

As can be seen, in case $\gamma > 0$ or $\gamma < -1$, the regularization term $w_d^{-\gamma}$ and the model coefficient θ_d are inversely related to each other: larger θ_d will lead to smaller regularization coefficient $w_d^{-\gamma}$, and vice versa. In practice, we update w_d and θ_d iteratively. As a result, important features in the current iteration will tend to be penalized less in the next iteration; on the contrary, less important features will be confronted with strong penalty in future iterations. The system reaches a stationary point upon convergence.

In case $-1 < \gamma < 0$, however, $w_d^{-\gamma}$ and θ_d will be favorably associated with each other. In other words, relevant features in the current step will be strongly penalized in the next iteration. This obviously leads to unstable iterations and therefore we will exclude it from our parameter choice.

In the adaptive LASSO [38], the regularization weight is also inversely related to some pre-computed model coefficient. The difference of our method is that, first, our weights are carefully tuned based on previous model coefficients through norm-regularization (7); second, we keep alternating instead of using a single update; third, as will be discussed, we have the freedom of annealing the strength of global regularization via the equality norm-constraint (4).

2.2 Multi-Stage Shrinking

The interactive updates between models and the adaptive weights mimic a self adapting process that is expected to drive the whole system to a desired state. However, this optimization problem is non-convex, therefore in case of bad initialization, the iterations might quickly get stuck into a local optimum. In this case, dimensions with large model coefficients will keep being dominant and and dimensions with small coefficients may never have a chance to regain their magnitudes.

In order to prevent pre-mature convergence, we propose a multi-stage shrinking procedure. The basic idea is to introduce strong perturbations in the beginning, such that all features have the chance to be selected and compete with each other. Then we gradually "cool down" the system by using stronger and stronger ℓ_1-penalties. Namely fewer and fewer features can survive in the progressive shrinking. By doing this, the system will go a series of self-adjusting micro-stages sequentially before reaching the final solution.

Suppose we initialize $\mathbf{w}$ with $|\mathbf{w}| = \omega^{\tau}$, $\tau = 0$. Then we interactively update β (5) and $\mathbf{w}$ (6) under this equality norm constraint until convergence. When this stage ends, we will start next stage of iterations with an updated norm constraint $|\mathbf{w}| = \omega^{\tau}$, $\tau = 1$, which imposes a stronger ℓ_1-penalty. Then we iterate between β and $\mathbf{w}$ until the second stage ends. By repeating this, we keep strengthening the global ℓ_1-norm regularization stage by stage, achieving an "annealing" effect. Here each stage is indexed by τ and is composed of iterations under $|\mathbf{w}| = \omega^{\tau}$.

Depending on the choice of γ, in order to guarantee that the global regularization strength $\mathbf{w}^{-\gamma}$ will gradually increase, we need different strategies in tuning the ω parameter. (1) $\gamma > 0$: ω will start from a large value (corresponding to a weak regularization) and gradually decrease; (2) $\gamma < -1$: ω will start from a small value and gradually increase throughout the iterations.

2.3 Relation with Annealing

In material science, annealing is a powerful heat treatment technique [31] to improve physical and chemical properties of a metal. It heats the metal to a high temperature, which gives the energy for its atoms to break the bond and diffuse actively within crystal lattices; a suitable temperature is then maintained and gradually cooled down, allowing the material to progress towards equilibrium state. Annealing can reduce the Gibbs-Free-Energy of the metal.

The dynamic shrinking method in Algorithm 1 very much resembles (and is indeed inspired by) an annealing process. The strength of the ℓ_1-regularization can be deemed as controlling the temperature of the system: in the beginning stages when regularization is weak, all features have the freedom to compete and position themselves in the model, meaning that the solution is dense and the system has a high energy. When the regularization gradually enhances, the system begins to cool down, model coefficients start shrinking progressively, and the system energy decreases as well. The norm-constraint $|\mathbf{w}| = \omega$ can be deemed exactly as the as controlling the "temperature" of the system: a larger ω imposes a weak regularization, meaning high temperature and energy status; a smaller ω, on the contrary, enforces low temperature and energy status.

The initial temperature of annealing should be higher than metal recrystallization temperature. Similarly, we also start from a high temperature, i.e., a weak regularization such that initial model parameters are dense. This allows different features to fully compete with each other; if the solution is already sparse in the beginning, the iterations will quickly get trapped into a poor local optima. In our context, the densest initial solution is the ordinary least-square solution, namely a sparse regression with vanishing ℓ_1-penalties.

It is worthwhile to point out the difference between our method and simulated annealing [15]. Simulated annealing is a probabilistic searching technique that can be applied to any pre-defined objective function to find its global optimum [25]; in comparison, we target on more effective sparse regression and feature selection by reformulating the adaptive LASSO with a progressive, multi-stage shrinking mechanism, thus bearing an analogy to the "annealing" process.

3. MULTI-TASK REGRESSION

Suppose we have a number of k tasks, each task is composed of the design matrix $\mathbf{X}^k \in \mathbb{R}^{n^k \times D}$ and target $\mathbf{y}^k \in \mathbb{R}^{n^k \times 1}$; we use shared adaptive weight $\mathbf{w} = [w_1, w_2, ..., w_D]^\top$ to regularize over all the K tasks, as

$$\min_{\mathbf{w},\mathbf{B}} \sum_{k=1}^{K} \left(\left\| \mathbf{X}^k \beta^k - \mathbf{y}^k \right\|_2^2 + |\mathbf{w}^{-\gamma} \odot \beta^k| \right) \quad (8)$$

$$s.t. \sum_d w_d = \omega, \ \ w_d \geq 0. \quad (9)$$

Algorithm 1: Adaptive LASSO + dynamic shrinking

Input: multi-task data $\mathbf{Z} = \{\mathbf{X}^k, \mathbf{y}^k\}_{k=1}^K$; initial norm constraint ω^0; shrinking factor δ; $\tau = 0$; initial regularization weight $\mathbf{w}_0^0 = [\frac{\omega^0}{D}, \frac{\omega^0}{D}, ... \frac{\omega^0}{D}]$;

Output: solution path for all the k tasks

begin
  while *model is unempty* **do**
    $t = 0$;
    while *Convergence* **do**
      $\mathbf{B}_{t+1}^\tau$ =ModelUpdate($\mathbf{w}_t^\tau, \mathbf{Z}$);
      $\mathbf{w}_{t+1}^\tau$ =WeightUpdate($\mathbf{B}_{t+1}^\tau, \omega^\tau$);
      $t = t + 1$;
    $\omega^{\tau+1} = \omega^\tau \cdot \delta$;
    $\mathbf{w}_0^{\tau+1} = \mathbf{w}_t^\tau$;
    $\tau = \tau + 1$

Here, $\beta^k \in \mathbb{R}^{D\times 1}$ is the model coefficients for the kth task for $k = 1, 2, ..., K$, and $\mathbf{B} = [\beta^1, \beta^2, ..., \beta^k]$. Through similar derivations, we have the following procedures.

Fix w and solve β^k's. Then this becomes K independent adaptive LASSO problems, for $k = 1, 2, ..., K$

$$\min_{\beta^k} \left\| \mathbf{X}^k \beta^k - \mathbf{y}^k \right\|_2^2 + |\mathbf{w}^{-\gamma} \odot \beta^k| \tag{10}$$

which can be easily converted to a standard LASSO.

Fix β^k's and solve w. This then becomes the following constrained optimization problem

$$\min_{\mathbf{w}} \sum_d \theta_d \cdot w_d^{-\gamma} \tag{11}$$

$$\theta_d = \sum_{k=1}^K |\beta_d^k|. \tag{12}$$

Problem (11) has a closed form solution,

$$w_d = \left(\frac{\theta_d^{\frac{1}{1+\gamma}}}{\sum_{j=1}^D \theta_j^{\frac{1}{1+\gamma}}} \right) \omega. \tag{13}$$

As can be seen, the proposed method can conveniently handle multi-task learning scenarios, thanks to the flexibility of using an adaptive regularization weight. In the following we introduce two routines to simplify our presentation of the algorithm.

- **B** =ModelUpdate(**w**, **Z**). This denotes training an adaptive LASSO with weights **w** (10) for each of the k tasks in $\mathbf{Z} = \{\mathbf{X}_k, \mathbf{y}_k\}_{k=1}^K$, independently, and obtaining the model coefficients $\mathbf{B} = [\beta^1, \beta_2, ..., \beta^K]$;
- **w** =WeightUpdate(**B**, ω). This denotes the process of using current models **B** and a specified value of ω to update the regularization weights **w**, as in (11) to (13).

Using these notations, we summarize the algorithm in Algorithm 1, which is applicable to both single and multiple tasks. Here the upper index τ denotes outer iterations, where each iteration τ corresponds to a stage with distinct value of ω; the lower index t indexes the inner iterations inside each stage. The δ is a shrinking factor that is smaller than 1 when $\gamma > 0$, and a growing factor that is larger than 1 when $\gamma < -1$. The iteration will keep going until all features are removed from the model. Then a cross-validation can be used to select the best model along the solution path.

In case of classification tasks with high-dimensional features, one can consider the sparse logistic regression [27], $\min -\sum_{i=1}^n \ln\left(1 + \exp[-\beta^\top x_i \cdot y_i]\right) + |\mathbf{w} \odot \beta|_1$which can benefit from our dynamic shrinking approach as well. Similarly, the iterative procedures will decompose into two subproblems: when fixing **w**, it becomes a standard logistic regression with adaptive ℓ_1-regression; and when fixing β, the problem is identical to (6) and can be solved accordingly.

4. RELATED METHODS

4.1 Re-weighted LASSO

In [4], an interesting, re-weighted LASSO algorithm was proposed to improve the sparsity of LASSO. After solving a standard LASSO at time t (starting from $t = 0$), it will compute a set of adaptive regularization weights $w_i^{(t+1)} = 1/(|\beta_i^{(t)}| + \epsilon)$, and then use $w_i^{(t+1)}$'s to adaptively penalize the ℓ_1 regularization. Here ϵ is a small number to ensure that a zero component in β does not strictly prohibit a nonzero estimate at the next step. As can be seen, the algorithm repeatedly performs the adaptive LASSO by using the absolute value of the inverse of previous model coefficients as the regularization weights for the next iteration. Such iterations may easily get trapped in local optimal solution due to the sensitivity of the convergence on initial values. In comparison, our approach avoids pre-mature convergence by continuously adjusting the global regularization strength.

4.2 Mixed-norm Regularization

4.2.1 Univariate Regression Cases

In case there exists grouping structures among input variables, the LASSO algorithm has been extended to recover such grouping. For example, the elastic net algorithm penalizes both the ℓ_1 and ℓ_2 norm of the model [39], which encourages a grouping effect such that strongly correlated predictors tend to be in or out of the model together. When the groupings of the inputs are available as prior knowledge, the group LASSO [34] penalizes the ℓ_2-norm of each group as a unit for variable selection, using the following optimization framework,

$$\min \left\| \sum_{l=1}^L \mathbf{X}_l \beta_l - y \right\|_F^2 + \lambda \sum_{i=1}^L \cdot \sqrt{p_l} \|\beta_l\|_2.$$

Here, the predictors are assumed to have l groups with group size p_l; $\mathbf{X}_l$ represents predictors of the lth group, with corresponding coefficient β_l. The group LASSO achieves sparse feature selection at the group level: depending on λ, an entire group of predictors is either selected simultaneously in the model, or will be removed together.

4.2.2 Multi-variate/Multi-task Cases

Multi-task learning has drawn considerable interest in data mining [2, 3]. It assumes that different tasks share some common structures, and enforcing the task relatedness can help improve the learning performance. We focus on sparse multi-task learning [16, 23, 34, 17], namely joint feature selection in multiple tasks needs to be performed.

The ℓ_1/ℓ_2 penalty of group lasso has been used to recover inputs that are jointly relevant to all of the outputs, or tasks, by applying the ℓ_2-norm to outputs instead of groups of inputs.For example, [23] proposed to penalize the sum of the ℓ_q-norms of the blocks of coefficients associated with each feature across tasks, which is called mixed-norm or ℓ_1/ℓ_q regularization. One appealing property is that it encourages multiple predictors from different tasks to share similar parameter sparsity patterns. Let $\mathbf{B} = [\beta^1, \beta^2, ..., \beta^k]$, and define $\mathbf{B}^i \in R^{1\times K}$ as the ith row in the model coefficient matrix $\mathbf{B}$. Then the objective function of the ℓ_1/ℓ_q regularization is as follows:

$$\min_{\mathbf{B}} \sum\nolimits_{k=1}^{K} \left\| \mathbf{X}^k \beta^k - \mathbf{y}^k \right\| + \lambda \sum\nolimits_{i=1}^{D} \|\mathbf{B}\|_{\ell_1/\ell_q}.$$

Here $\|\mathbf{B}\|_{\ell_1/\ell_q}$ = is the block ℓ_1/ℓ_q norm

$$\|\mathbf{B}\|_{\ell_1/\ell_q} = \sum\nolimits_{i=1}^{D} \left(\sum\nolimits_{j=1}^{K} \mathbf{B}_{ij}{}^q \right)^{\frac{1}{q}}.$$

When $q = 2$, we have a block ℓ_1/ℓ_2 norm, which is identical to the group LASSO [34]. Other choices have also been studied such as ℓ_1/ℓ_∞ [30]. The mixed-norm regularization encourages simultaneous feature selection across tasks. Namely, a given feature is either selected as relevant for all the tasks' output simultaneously, or is excluded all-together for all the tasks. Such regularization is very effective if the underlying task relation satisfies such assumption. However it can be too restrictive in some other applications.

In [17], an adaptive multi-task LASSO framework was proposed which combines adaptive regularization with the mixed-norm regularization, as

$$\min_{\beta,\theta,\rho} \mathcal{L}(\beta) + \lambda_1 \sum_{j=1}^{D} \theta_j \sum_{i=1}^{K} |\beta_j^k| + \lambda_2 \sum_{j=1}^{D} \rho_j \|\beta_j\|_2 + \log Z(\theta, \rho).$$

Here $\mathcal{L}$ is the loss function; the second term is an adaptive LASSO that imposes ℓ_1-norm penalty with strength $\lambda_1 \cdot \theta_j$ on $|\beta_j|_1$ from all tasks; the third term is a mixed-norm regularization together with an adaptive weights, which imposes the penalty $\lambda_2 \cdot \rho_j \; \|\beta_j\|_2$; the last term is a normalization factor on the conditional probability $p(\beta|\theta, \rho)$. The whole framework has an elegant Bayesian interpretation. It achieves sparsity both across tasks and within each task. However, the regularization weights are assumed to be spanned by features from extra domains with prior knowledge, which might not be available in general multi-task learning; on the other hand, it separates the learning of the model and the regularization profile.

4.3 Regularization Path

The dynamic shrinking process of the proposed algorithm is illustrated in Figure 1, where the strength of the ℓ_1-regularization gradually increases, leading to a solution path. Due to the interplay between adaptive weights $\mathbf{w}$ and models coefficients $\mathbf{B}$, the whole solution path of $\mathbf{B}$ is connected: each solution $\mathbf{B}$ is affected by its predecessor. This means, the effect of system evolution is inherited from one stage τ to the next stage $\tau + 1$, or from one iteration t to the next iteration $t + 1$ inside a single stage. In other words, the solutions have to be obtained in a sequential manner. For the standard LASSO, in comparison, the solution path can actually be obtained by training a number of independent LASSO's with different λ's.

Note that the solution path of LASSO can also be obtained in a sequential manner by using the least angle regression [8], which fully exploits the piecewise linear structures of the solutions. However, an important difference is that, our approach will *re-define* the LASSO regression in each iteration. To see this, note that any adaptive LASSO problem $\min \|\mathbf{X}\beta - \mathbf{y}\|_2^2 + |\mathbf{w} \odot \beta|_1$ can be converted to a LASSO $\min \|\mathbf{X}\mathbf{W}^{-1}\overline{\beta} - \mathbf{y}\|_2^2 + |\overline{\beta}|_1$ where $\overline{\beta} = \mathbf{w} \odot \beta$ and $\mathbf{W} = diag(\mathbf{w})$. In our approach, since the regularization weight vector $\mathbf{w}$ keeps updating, therefore each iteration is equivalent to a LASSO problem with continuously rectified data $\mathbf{X}\mathbf{W}^{-1}$, making it different from traditional solution path. It will be a very interesting topic to explore the solution path structures of our dynamic shrinking approach, so as to make it more computationally efficient.

5. EMPIRICAL RESULTS

In this section, we perform extensive experiments to examine the performance of our approach, in both simulation data sets and real-world bioinformatics application.

5.1 Competing Methods

Altogether, we implement and compare the following algorithms:

1. Standard LASSO algorithm [29]: We use the LARS algorithm to generate the solution path;

2. Adaptive LASSO [38]: We use inverse of ridge regression coefficient to compute $\mathbf{w}$ for each task and average them as the shared regularization. Then we rescale $\mathbf{w}$ to generate the solution path;

3. Adaptive LASSO-II [13]: We use inverse of the marginal regression coefficient to compute $\mathbf{w}$ for each task and average them as the shared regularization, then we rescale the regularization to generate the solution path;

4. Multi-task LASSO [23]: We choose different values of the initial λ to compute the solution path;

5. Re-weighted LASSO [4]: We choose different values of the initial λ (each initiates a series of iterations till convergence) to generate the solution path;

6. Our approach: We simply choose $\gamma = 1$, an initial norm $\omega^0 = 1e8$, and shrinking factor $\delta = 0.8$; we can generate a solution path throughout the iterations until all features are removed. Results on using negative power $\gamma < -1$ is similar and therefore removed due to space limit.

We use the following measurements to evaluate the performance of different methods:

1. Specificity (SPC) versus true-positive-rate (TPR) (SPC VS TPR) curve based on solution paths from different algorithms;

2. Cross-validated mean-squared-error (CV-MSE): we report 5-fold cross-validated error of different methods;

3. Cross-validated F-score (CV-Fscore): we comput the 5-fold cross-validated F-score for different methods;

We use the SLEP sparse learning package [18] to implement our approach. All codes are written in Matlab and run on a cluster server with 2.2 $\sim$ 2.8 GHz CPU.

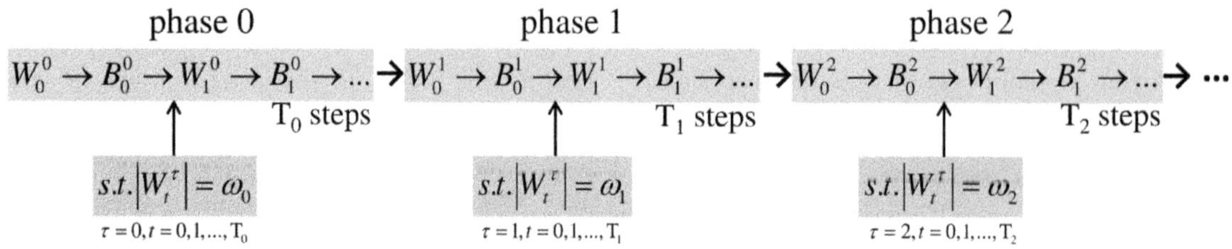

Figure 1: Illustration of the regularization path of our approach. Here, $\{\omega_0, \omega_1, \omega_2, ...\}$ is a sequence such that the global strength of ℓ_1-regularization grows stronger.

5.2 Single Task Regression

First we use single task sparse regression problem to test the performance of different methods. Following the details in [4], we simulate the data set of $n = 100$ samples with dimensionality $D = 256$, and the design matrix is an n-by-d i.i.d. Gaussian entries. Among the 256 features, only $p = 20$ are relevant features with randomly chosen non-zero β entries from a zero-mean unit-variance Gaussian distribution. We then use the linear relation $\mathbf{y}_i = \mathbf{x}_i\beta + \mathcal{N}(0, \sigma^2)$ to generate the response $\mathbf{y}$.

Results are shown in Figure 2, where each algorithm is marked by their indexes specified in Section 5.1. In this data set, multi-task LASSO (method (4)) is identical to s-tandard LASSO (method (1)) and therefore is removed. As can be seen, our approach is superior in terms of picking out relevant covariates throughout the whole solution path, demonstrating the effectiveness of annealed sparsity in improving the sparse model selection. In the meantime, the cross-validated mean-squared-error and F-score of our approach are also the best among competing methods.

5.3 Multi-task Regression

In this experiment we simulate data with $K = 5$ tasks, each task has $n = 40$ samples with dimension $D = 100$. For each task design matrix is an i.i.d Gaussian distribution, and we assume the linear relation $\mathbf{y}_i^k = \mathbf{x}_i^k\beta^k + \mathcal{N}(0, \sigma^2)$, and for the relevant features, the corresponding entries in β^k's are randomly chosen from the distribution $3 + \mathcal{N}(0, 1)$. Here we generate two types of multi-task data.

1. Multitask-I: strict group-wise sparsity. We choose $p = 20$ relevant features for all tasks, and each row of the model coefficient matrix $\mathbf{B}$ is either all zeros or all non-zeros, meaning that one feature is either relevant to all tasks, or excluded from all tasks;
2. Multitask-II: mixed sparsity patterns. We then introduce a perturbation on the model coefficients $\mathbf{B}$: for each non-zero row of $\mathbf{B}$, we randomly pick one entry and set it to zero; in this case, each row of $\mathbf{B}$ can have both zero and non-zero entries. Namely it has a mixed sparsity pattern (across-group and within-group).

We report the results in Figure 3 and Figure 4. We can observe that our approach has the best performance in terms of both feature selection (F-score) and regression (predicting error), on both types of multi-task data sets. The adaptive LASSO-II [13] using the inverse of the marginal regression coefficients as adaptive weights seems to perform better than the adaptive LASSO using ordinary-least-squares coefficients. The LASSO considers each task separately and can be less accurate. Another observation is that, in case of mixed sparsity patterns, all algorithms perform worse than in the case of strict group-wise sparsity, in particularly judged by feature selection accuracy (F-score). Nevertheless, our approach still performs the best among competing methods.

We also experiment with different noise levels to test the noise tolerance shown in Figure 5. As can be observed, our approach is competitive under different noise levels.

5.4 Algorithm Behaviors

In this section, we study properties of the proposed method from different perspectives.

5.4.1 Solution Path

First, to have a direct picture on the shrinking behaviour of our method, we plot the solution path of our approach in Figure 6. Here we use the multi-task simulation data with group wise sparsity under the highest noise level ($\delta = 3$). To prevent visual cluttering, we only plot the solution path for one task, and we only demonstrate 10 of the 20 relevant features and all the rest 80 irrelevant features.

We have several interesting observations. First, note that when the regularization is relatively weak, the solution paths are all smooth; when the regularization becomes stronger, solution paths begin to show clear stage-wise behaviour: the coefficient value is relatively stable within each stage, but may change significantly across stages (due to the change of ω), indicating that the system state goes through significant changes. Second, the solution path is quite non-monotonic. With the growing strength of regularization ($\frac{1}{\omega}$), we can observe that the model coefficients first expand and then gradually shrink. This is in sharp contrast to the solution path of the LASSO, whose solution path almost monotonically shrinks with growing regularization.

The non-monotonic shrinking can be quite beneficial in practice. Note that in the beginning stage, both relevant and irrelevant features have large model coefficients, meaning that they are difficult to differentiate. When the regularization grows stronger, interestingly, we can see that most relevant features begin to expand, while most irrelevant features begin to shrink. This becomes particularly obvious around $\frac{1}{\omega} \approx 10^{-4.5}$, where the majority of irrelevant features suddenly shrink to zero, while relevant features have a jump increase in their coefficients. This is quite beneficial in practical feature selection problems.

Competing mechanism of annealing. In the beginning, under weak global ℓ_1-penalty, model coefficients are dense, indicating that the "energy" of the system is distribut-

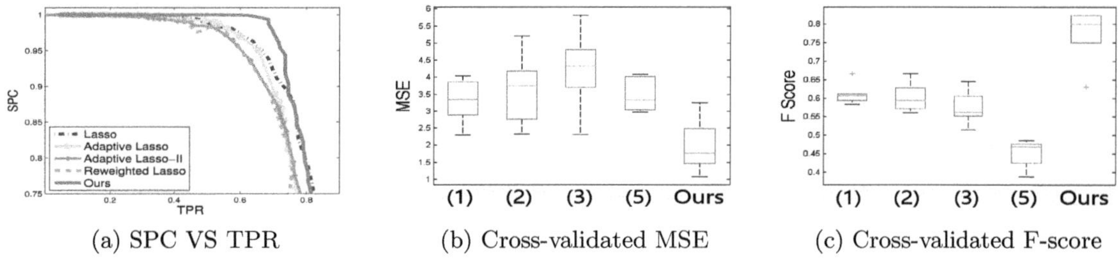

(a) SPC VS TPR (b) Cross-validated MSE (c) Cross-validated F-score

Figure 2: Performance for different methods on single task data, with noise $\sigma = 1$.

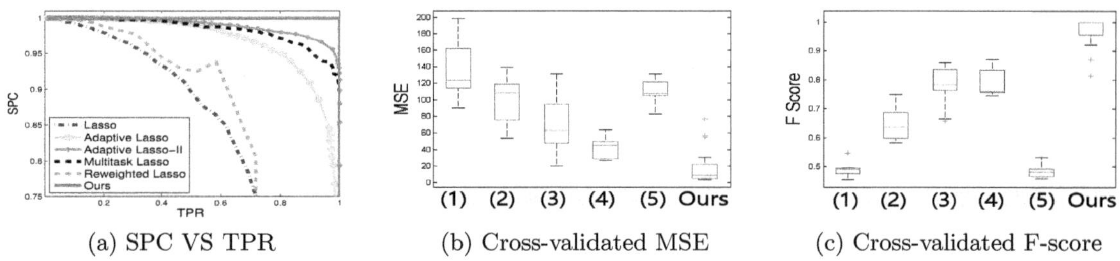

(a) SPC VS TPR (b) Cross-validated MSE (c) Cross-validated F-score

Figure 3: Results on multitask-I data (strict group sparsity), with noise $\sigma = 1$.

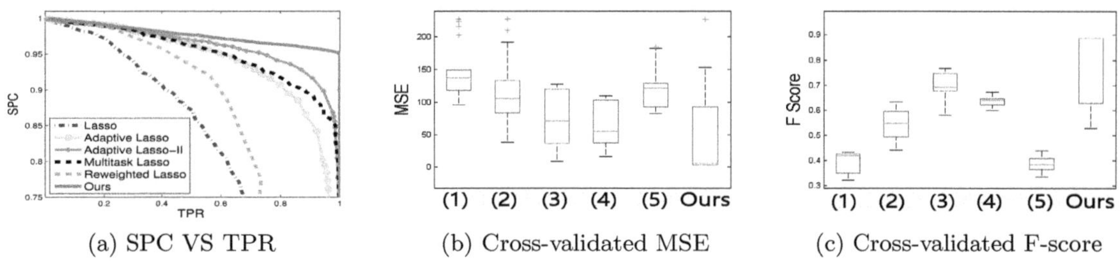

(a) SPC VS TPR (b) Cross-validated MSE (c) Cross-validated F-score

Figure 4: Results on multitask-II data (mixed sparsity pattern), with noise $\sigma = 1$.

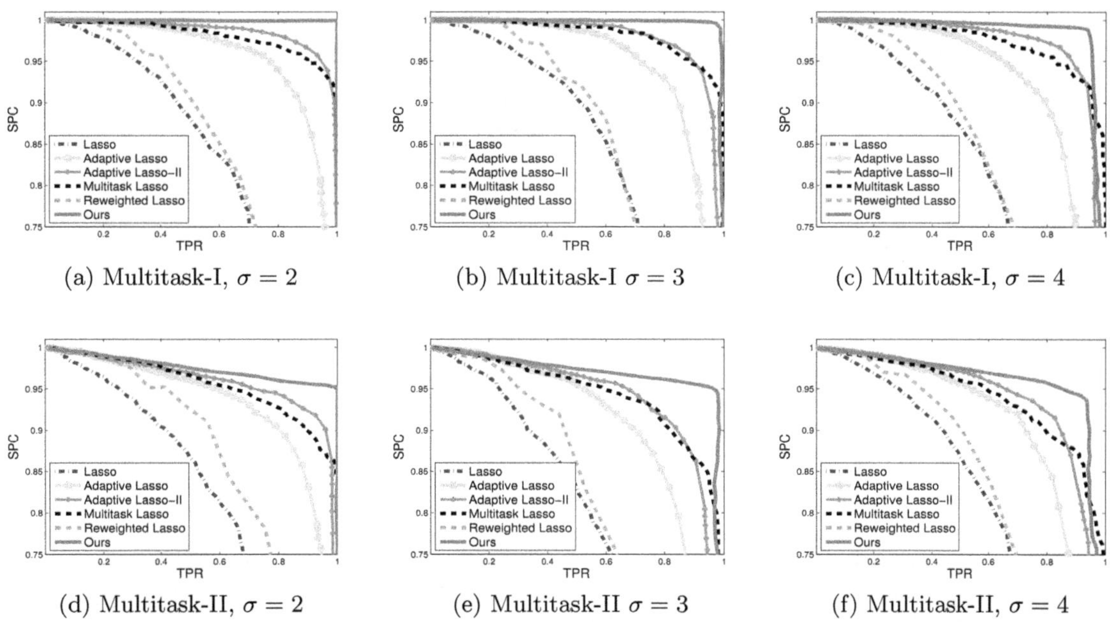

(a) Multitask-I, $\sigma = 2$ (b) Multitask-I $\sigma = 3$ (c) Multitask-I, $\sigma = 4$

(d) Multitask-II, $\sigma = 2$ (e) Multitask-II $\sigma = 3$ (f) Multitask-II, $\sigma = 4$

Figure 5: Results on different noise levels for multitask-I (1st row) and multitask-II (2nd row).

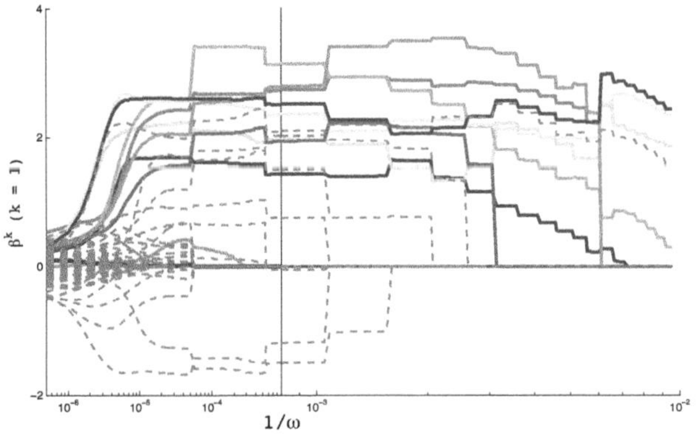

Figure 6: Solution path for dynamic shrinking. Thick colored lines represent relevant features, and dashed lines for irrelevant features. Vertical line in the middle marks change of display scales (for visual clarity). Regularization increases from left to right.

ed somewhat uniformly among competing features. As the regularization grows, the system begins cooling toward a lower-energy state; in the meantime, energy distribution becomes more concentrated. That is, competitive features (in terms of better prediction in the least-square) will attract more energy from irrelevant features, making the latter shrink. This is why we observe significant growth of some feature magnitude even though the global sparsity enhances. Such energy re-allocation through annealing solves the feature selection problem in an effective manner.

5.4.2 Parameter Selection

In this section, we study how the performance of our approach is affected by the following two parameters: the ω^0 that controls the initial "temperature" of the system; the shrinking factor δ that controls the "cooling rate" of the system. The performance is measured by the F-score using the multitask-I data set with $\sigma = 1$.

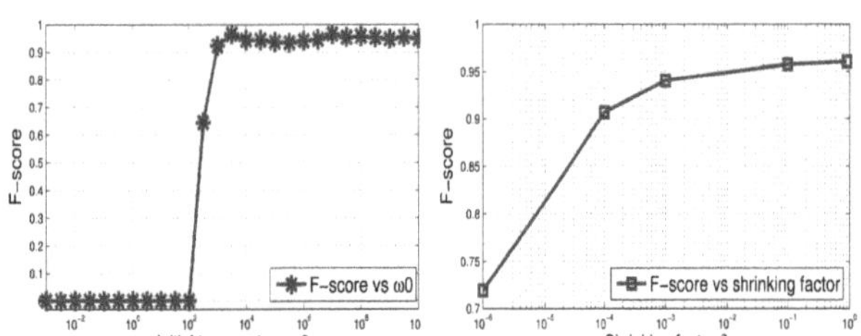

(a) Initial temperature (ω^0) (b) Shrinking factor (δ)

Figure 7: Performance of our method versus different parameters.

First, we examine the performance w.r.t. ω^0 chosen from some grid points $\{10^{10}, 10^9, ..., 10^{-3}\}$. As can be seen from Figure 7(a), in a wide range of high initial temperatures, the performance of our approach is quite satisfactory; when the initial temperature is below a certain value, the performance quickly drops. This coincides with our expectation, since a low initial temperature fails to start the whole system with sufficient energy and as a result the iterations could quickly stop at a local optima. In practice, we simply choose ω^0 as a large value such as $1e8$.

In Figure 7(b), we examine the performance of our approach w.r.t. the shrinking factor. As can be observed, more aggressive shrinking scheme ($\delta \to 0$) makes the performance worse; in comparison, milder shrinking scheme ($\delta \to 1$) allows the system to evolve slowly such that the "annealing" is sufficient, but it is computationally more expensive. In practice, we find that $0.2 < \delta < 0.8$ can strike a balance between efficiency and the quality of annealing.

5.5 Bioinformatics Application

In this section, our task of expression quantitative trait loci (eQTL) is to identify genes whose DNA copy (DNA copy-number data as *input*) are associated with the mRNA expression level of six `P53` target genes (normalized expression data as *response*). Note that `P53` is a well-known tumor suppressor gene. The data set is obtained from Cancer Cell Line Encyclopedia (CCLE) project[1], with DNA copy-number of 23316 genes across 1011 samples. The six target genes include **CDKN1A, PMAIP1, BBC3, MSH2, PML** and **PRKAA2**, which are of particular relevance to melanoma as suggested by biological experts [32]. The regulatory genes identified through our regression analysis will then help understand the whole `P53` regulation mechanism for cancer, and in particular melanoma.

In the application, we treat the eQTL of six `P53` target genes as six tasks, since we believe that the regulating processes on all these melanoma-related genes should share some underlying mechanism. We have used the 5-fold cross-validated error to select the best model. Table 1 reports the 5-fold CV-MSE for all competing methods, from which we can see that our method achieves the lowest fitting error. This fully illustrates the superior performance of the proposed dynamic shrinking scheme in high-dimensional, real-world multi-task learning problems.

We further explore whether the selected genes by our method makes biological sense, by following the common practice of gene set enrichment analysis (GSEA) [28]. Specifically, we rank the selected genes in each task based on the regression coefficients and feed the ranking to `GSEA2-2.2.2` software. We consider the canonical pathways/gene sets provided by the Molecular Signatures Database[2]. For each task, GSEA returns a number of significant pathways/gene-sets under false discovery rate (FDR) 5%, and we pick one example pathway to illustrate in Figure 8. Here, the pathway name is marked on top of each figure; the red bar denotes the ranking of the β-coefficient for each task, and the black lines mark the genes belonging to selected pathway. Our approach identifies more than 100 significant pathways for each task, which is much larger than other methods.

These significant pathways based on our computed gene ranking are very relevant to cancers and/or melanoma, as discussed below:

- The gene **CDKN1A**, cyclin-dependent kinase inhibitor 1A, itself is relevant to cell cycle. The significant pathway "**REACTOME_P53_INDEPENDENT_G1_S**..." includes genes in p53-Independent G1/S DNA damage checkpoint, which has been shown to be quite relevant to dysfunctional cell cycle causing cancer [20].

[1] http://www.broadinstitute.org/ccle/home

[2] http://software.broadinstitute.org/gsea/msigdb/collections.jsp.

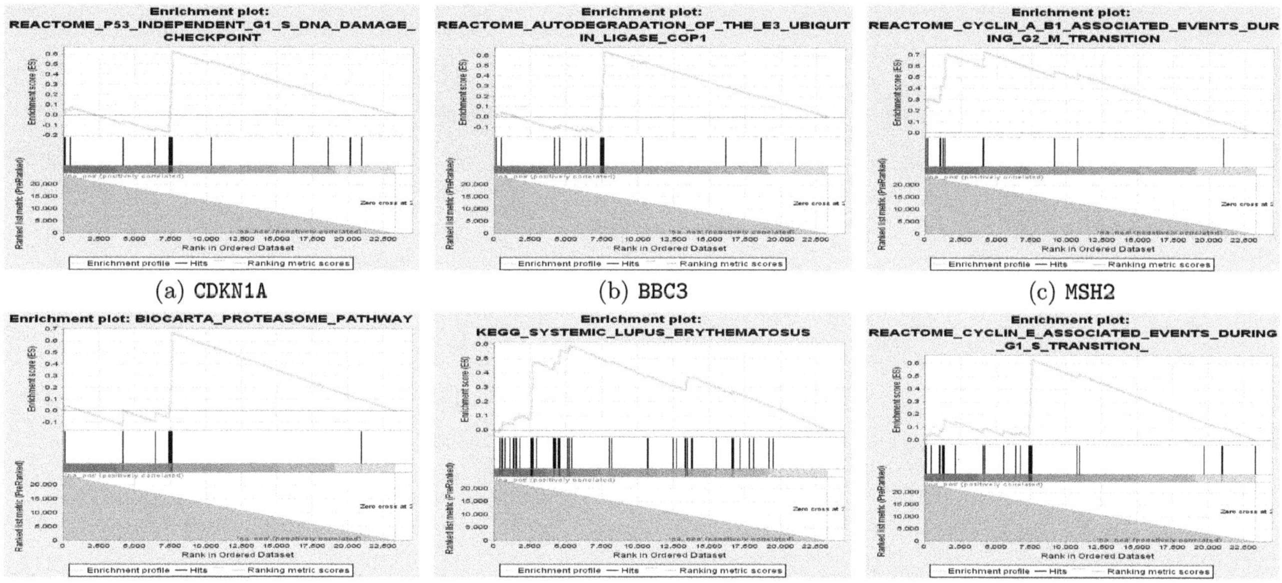

(a) CDKN1A (b) BBC3 (c) MSH2

(d) PMAIP (e) PML (f) PRKAA2

Figure 8: Our ranking of the genes, as well as one example of the identified pathways for each task based on this ranking, via gene enrichment analysis on the CCLE data.

Table 1: CV-MSE on CCLE data set

Method	5 fold Cross-validated MSE
LASSO	3.2530
Adaptive LASSO	1.3078
Adaptive LASSO-II	1.3701
Multitask LASSO	3.2451
Re-weighted LASSO	1.5507
Ours	1.1165

- The gene BBC3 is a protein that cooperates with direct activator proteins to induce mitochondrial outer membrane permeabilization and apoptosis. The pathway "REACTOME_AUTODEGRADATION_OF_THE..." include genes involved in autodegradation of the E3 ubiquitin ligase COP1. Destruction of COP1 results in abrogation of the ubiquitination and degradation of p53 [7].
- The gene MSH2 is involved in cyclin A/B1 associated events during G2/M transition and is a protein coding gene. In literatures, its related pathways are all about cancer and cell cycle, or checkpoint control. The pathway we find, "REACTOME_CYCLIN_A_B1_ASSOCIATED...", is also a cell cycle gene set. It is responsible for phosphorylation of nuclear lamins and histones [26], which in turn regulates G2/M transition, thus controlling cell cycle progression by cyclin-dependent protein kinases in G1/S and G2/M transitions.
- The gene PAMIP promotes activation of caspases and apoptosis. It contributes to p53/TP53-dependent apoptosis after radiation exposure. In the proteasome pathway "BIOCARTA_PROTEASOME_PATHWAY", the regulated proteolysis of proteins by proteasomes removes damaged or improperly translated proteins from cells, and aids caspases and apoptosis [1].

The above results show that our approach not only predicts target gene expressions more accurately, but also identifies biologically meaningful molecular predictors.

6. CONCLUSIONS

In this paper, we propose a dynamic shrinking framework to compute adaptive regularization in sparse (multi-task) regression. Our key contribution is to introduce the concept of annealing in sparse model estimation and feature selection, through an iterative, self-adapting and self-competing mechanism. Empirically, the annealing process can improve the accuracy of models in particular in multi-task problems. In the future, we will study how to explore underlying structures of the dynamic solution path to make it computationally more efficient; we also want to incorporate explicit, task-level constraints to make the learned model coefficients more useful for subsequent learning tasks. Finally, we are trying to build a more rigorous, mathematical connection between our approach and annealing so as to fully characterize the behaviour of system evolutions.

Appendix

To derive (7), we use the Lagrangian of (6). We first drop the non-negativity constraint. Then the Lagrangian can be written as

$$J = \sum_d \theta_d w_d^{-\gamma} + \alpha \left(\sum_d w_d - \omega \right).$$

By setting $\frac{\partial J}{\partial w_d} = 0$, we have

$$\alpha = \frac{\theta_d \gamma}{w_d^{1+\gamma}}. \tag{14}$$

Plugging the above relation in the constraint $\sum_d w_d = \omega$, then we have

$$\alpha = \left(\frac{\sum_d (\theta_d \gamma)^{\frac{1}{1+\gamma}}}{\omega} \right)^{1+\gamma},$$

so we have

$$w_d^{1+\gamma} = \frac{\theta_d \gamma}{\alpha} = \frac{\theta_d \gamma \cdot \omega^{1+\gamma}}{\left(\sum_d (\theta_d \gamma)^{\frac{1}{1+\gamma}}\right)^{1+\gamma}}.$$

Plugging the above equation in (14), we finally have

$$w_d = \frac{\theta_d^{\frac{1}{1+\gamma}}}{\sum_d \theta_d^{\frac{1}{1+\gamma}}} \omega.$$

Since $\theta_d = \sum_k |\beta_k^d| \geq 0$, and $\omega \geq 0$, the solution will satisfy the non-negative constraints automatically. This completes the proof of solution (13).

References

[1] I. Amm, T. Sommer, and D. H. Wolf. Protein quality control and elimination of protein waste: The role of the ubiquitin–proteasome system. *Biochimica et Biophysica Acta (BBA)-Molecular Cell Research*, 1843(1):182–196, 2014.

[2] A. Argyriou, T. Evgeniou, and M. Pontil. Convex multi-task feature learning. *Machine Learning*, 73(3):243–272, 2008.

[3] S. Ben-david and R. Schuller. Exploiting task relatedness for multiple task learning. In *Proceedings of the 16th Annual Conference on Learning Theory*, pages 567–580, 2003.

[4] E. J. Candes, M. B. Wakin, and S. Boyd. Enhancing sparsity by reweighted l1 minimization. *Journal of Fourier Analysis and Applications, special issue on sparsity*, 14(5):877–905, 2008.

[5] S. Chen, D. L. Donoho, and M. A. Saunders. Atomic decomposition by basis pursuit. *SIAM Review*, 43(1):129–159, 2001.

[6] D. Donoho. Compressed sensing. *IEEE Transactions on Information Theory*, 52(4):1289–1304, 2006.

[7] D. Dornan, H. Shimizu, A. Mah, T. Dudhela, M. Eby, K. O'Rourke, S. Seshagiri, and V. M. Dixit. Atm engages autodegradation of the e3 ubiquitin ligase cop1 after dna damage. *Science*, 313(5790):1122–1126, 2006.

[8] B. Efron, T. Hastie, I. Johnstone, and R. Tibshirani. Least angle regression. *Annals of Statistics*, 32(2):407–499, 2004.

[9] M. Elad and M. Aharon. Image denoising via sparse and redundant representations over learned dictionaries. *IEEE Transactions on Image Processing*, 37(4):3736 – 3745, 2006.

[10] J. Fan, Y. Feng, and Y. Wu. Network exploration via the adaptive lasso and scad penalties. *The Annals of Applied Statistics*, 3(2):521–541, 2009.

[11] J. Fan and R. Li. Variable selection via nonconcave penalized like- lihood and its oracle properties. *Journal of the American Statistical Association*, 96:1348–1360, 2001.

[12] M. Figueiredo, R. Nowak, and S. Wright. Gradient projection for sparse reconstruction: Application to compressed sensing and other inverse problems. *IEEE Journal on Selected Topics in Signal Processing*, 1(4):586 –597, 2007.

[13] J. Huang, S. Ma, and C.-H. Zhang. Adaptive lasso for sparse high-dimensional regression models. *Statistica Sinica*, pages 1603–1618, 2008.

[14] S. Kim, K. Koh, M. Lustig, S. Boyd, and D. Gorinevsky. An interior-point method for large-scale l1-regularized least squares. *IEEE Transactions on Signal Processing*, 1(4):606–617, 2007.

[15] S. Kirkpatrick, C. Gelatt, and M. Vecchi. Optimization by simulated annealing. *Science*, 220(4598):671–680, 1993.

[16] M. Kowalski. Sparse regression using mixed norms. *Applied and Computational Harmonic Analysis*, 27(3):303–324, 2009.

[17] S. Lee, J. Zhu, and E. P. Xing. Adaptive multi-task lasso: with application to eqtl detection. In *Advances in Neural Information Processing Systems*, pages 1306–1314, 2010.

[18] J. Liu, S. Ji, and J. Ye. Slep: Sparse learning with efficient projections. *Arizona State University*, 2009.

[19] A. C. Lozano and G. Świrszcz. Multi-level lasso for sparse multi-task regression. In *Proceedings of the International Conference on Machine Learning*, 2012.

[20] N. Mailand, J. Falck, C. Lukas, R. G. Syljuåsen, M. Welcker, J. Bartek, and J. Lukas. Rapid destruction of human cdc25a in response to dna damage. *Science*, 288(5470):1425–1429, 2000.

[21] J. Mairal, F. Bach, J. Ponce, G. Sapiro, and A. Zisserman. Supervised dictionary learning. In *Advances in Neural Information Processing Systems*, 2009.

[22] N. Meinshausen and P. Bühlmann. High-dimensional graphs and variable selection with the lasso. *The Annals of Statistics*, 34(3):1436–1462, 2006.

[23] G. Obozinski, M. J. Wainwright, and M. I. Jordan. High-dimensional union support recovery in multivariate regression. In *Neural Information Processing Systems*, pages 1217–1224, 2008.

[24] S. Puniyani, S. Kim, and E. P. Xing. Multi-population gwa mapping via multi-task regularized regression. *Bioinformatics*, 26(12):208–216, 2010.

[25] S. Raman and V. Roth. Sparse point estimation for bayesian regression via simulated annealing. *Lecture Notes in Computer Science*, 7476:317–326, 2012.

[26] B. M. Sefton and S. Shenolikar. Overview of protein phosphorylation. *Current Protocols in Protein Science*, pages 13–1, 2001.

[27] S. K. Shevade and S. S. Keerthi. A simple and efficient algorithm for gene selection using sparse logistic regression. *Bioinformatics*, 19(17):2246–2253, 2003.

[28] A. Subramanian et al. Gene set enrichment analysis: a knowledge-based approach for interpreting genome-wide expression profiles. *Proceedings of the National Academy of Sciences*, 102(43):15545–15550, 2005.

[29] R. Tibshirani. Regression shrinkage and selection via the lasso. *Journal of the Royal Statistical Society. Series B (Methodological)*, 58(1):267–288, 1996.

[30] J. Tropp, A. Gilbert, and M. Strauss. Algorithms for simultaneous sparse approximation, part ii: Convex relaxation. *Signal Processing*, 86:572–588, 2006.

[31] L. H. V. Vlack. *Elements of Materials Science and Engineering*. Addison-Wesley, 1985.

[32] C. Wei et al. A global map of p53 transcription-binding sites in the human genome. *Cell*, 124(1):207–219, 2006.

[33] J. Wright, A. Yang, A. Ganesh, S. Sastry, and Y. Ma. Robust face recognition via sparse representation. *IEEE Transactions on Pattern Analysis and Machine Intelligence*, 2009.

[34] M. Yuan and Y. Lin. Model selection and estimation in regression with grouped variables. *Journal of the Royal Statistical Society Series B*, 68(1):49–67, 2006.

[35] J. Zhang, W. Cheng, Z. Wang, Z. Zhang, W. Lu, G. Lu, and J. Feng. Pattern classification of large-scale functional brain networks: Identification of informative neuroimaging markers for epilepsy. *PLoS ONE*, 7(5):e36733, 2012.

[36] K. Zhang, J. Gray, and B. Parvin. Sparse multitask regression for identifying common mechanism of response to therapeutic targets. *Bioinformatics*, 26(12):97 – 105, 2010.

[37] P. Zhao and B. Yu. On model selection consistency of lasso. *Journal of Machine Learning Research*, 7:2541–2563, 2007.

[38] H. Zou. The adaptive lasso and its oracle properties. *Journal of the American Statistical Association*, 101(476):1418–1429, 2006.

[39] H. Zou and T. Hastie. Regularization and variable selection via the elastic net. *Journal of the Royal Statistical Society: Series B (Statistical Methodology)*, 67(2):301–320, 2005.

Partial Label Learning via Feature-Aware Disambiguation

Min-Ling Zhang [1,2] Bin-Bin Zhou [1,2] Xu-Ying Liu [1,2]
[1] School of Computer Science and Engineering, Southeast University, Nanjing 210096, China
[2] Key Laboratory of Computer Network and Information Integration (Southeast University), Ministry of Education, China
{zhangml, zhoubinbin, liuxy}@seu.edu.cn

ABSTRACT

Partial label learning deals with the problem where each training example is represented by a feature vector while associated with a set of *candidate* labels, among which only one label is valid. To learn from such ambiguous labeling information, the key is to try to disambiguate the candidate label sets of partial label training examples. Existing disambiguation strategies work by either identifying the ground-truth label iteratively or treating each candidate label equally. Nonetheless, the disambiguation process is generally conducted by focusing on manipulating the label space, and thus ignores making full use of potentially useful information from the feature space. In this paper, a novel two-stage approach is proposed to learning from partial label examples based on *feature-aware disambiguation*. In the first stage, the manifold structure of feature space is utilized to generate normalized labeling confidences over candidate label set. In the second stage, the predictive model is learned by performing regularized multi-output regression over the generated labeling confidences. Extensive experiments on artificial as well as real-world partial label data sets clearly validate the superiority of the proposed feature-aware disambiguation approach.

Keywords

weak supervision; partial label learning; disambiguation; manifold

1. INTRODUCTION

Partial label (PL) learning refers to the problem where each training example is represented by a single instance (feature vector) while associated with a set of *candidate* labels [8, 26]. Among the candidate label set, only one label is assumed to be valid and not directly accessible to the learning algorithm. The need to learn from data with partial labeling information naturally arises in many real-world applications such as automatic image annotation [7, 25], web mining [14], ecoinformatics [16], etc.[1]

[1]In some literatures, the partial label learning framework is also named as *ambiguous label learning* [5, 13] or *superset label learning* [17].

KDD '16, August 13-17, 2016, San Francisco, CA, USA
 ISBN 978-1-4503-4232-2/16/08...$15.00
DOI: http://dx.doi.org/10.1145/2939672.2939788

Formally speaking, let $\mathcal{X} = \mathbb{R}^d$ denote the d-dimensional feature space and $\mathcal{Y} = \{y_1, y_2, \ldots, y_q\}$ denote the label space with q class labels. The task of partial label learning is to learn a *multi-class* classifier $f : \mathcal{X} \mapsto \mathcal{Y}$ from the partial label training set $\mathcal{D} = \{(\boldsymbol{x}_i, S_i) \mid 1 \leq i \leq m\}$. Here, for each PL training example $(\boldsymbol{x}_i, S_i)$, $\boldsymbol{x}_i = (x_{i1}, x_{i2}, \ldots, x_{id})^\top$ is a d-dimensional feature vector and $S_i \subseteq \mathcal{Y}$ is the set of candidate labels associated with $\boldsymbol{x}_i$. Partial label learning takes the basic assumption that the ground-truth label y_i for $\boldsymbol{x}_i$ resides in its candidate label set (i.e. $y_i \in S_i$) but unknown to the learning algorithm.

Apparently, the available labeling information in the training set is ambiguous as the ground-truth label is concealed in the candidate label set. The key for successful partial label learning is therefore trying to disambiguate the set of candidate labels, where existing strategies include disambiguation by identification or disambiguation by averaging. For identification-based disambiguation, the ground-truth label is regarded as latent variable and identified through iterative refining procedure such as EM [5, 15, 16, 18, 24]. For averaging-based disambiguation, all the candidate labels are treated equally and the prediction is made by averaging their modeling outputs [8, 13, 27].

By taking specific views on the candidate labels, both of the existing strategies conduct disambiguation by only focusing on the manipulation of label space. Nonetheless, it is natural to postulate that the potentially useful information from feature space should also be exploited to facilitating the disambiguation process. Specifically, to help disambiguate the candidate label set, one might make use of the *smoothness assumption* that examples close to each other in the feature space will tend to share identical label in the label space. For instance, suppose we have three PL training examples $(\boldsymbol{x}, \{y_2, y_3\})$, $(\boldsymbol{x}', \{y_1, y_2\})$ and $(\boldsymbol{x}'', \{y_3, y_4\})$ where $\boldsymbol{x}$ is shown to be close to $\boldsymbol{x}'$ while far from $\boldsymbol{x}''$ in the feature space. Then, it is reasonable to assign higher labeling confidence on y_2 than y_3 for $\boldsymbol{x}$ (i.e. $\mathbb{P}(y_2 \mid \boldsymbol{x}) > \mathbb{P}(y_3 \mid \boldsymbol{x})$), as y_2 is a shared candidate label between close instances ($\boldsymbol{x}$ and $\boldsymbol{x}'$) while y_3 is a shared candidate label between distant instances ($\boldsymbol{x}$ and $\boldsymbol{x}''$).

In light of the above observation, a novel two-stage approach named PL-LEAF, i.e. *Partial Label LEArning via Feature-aware disambiguation*, is proposed in this paper. In the first stage, the manifold structure among training examples is analyzed in the feature space and then utilized to generate normalized labeling confidences over candidate label set. In the second stage, a multi-class predictive model is learned by fitting a regularized multi-output regressor with the generated labeling confidences. Extensive experiments on controlled UCI data sets as well as real-world PL data sets clearly show the effectiveness of feature-aware disambiguation for partial label learning.

The rest of this paper is organized as follows. Section 2 briefly reviews related work in partial label learning. Section 3 introduces the proposed PL-LEAF approach. Section 4 reports experimental results of comparative studies. Finally, Section 5 concludes the paper and discusses future research issues.

2. RELATED WORK

Due to the ambiguous labeling information conveyed by PL training examples, partial label learning can be regarded as a *weakly-supervised* learning framework. It situates between two ends of the supervision spectrum, i.e. standard supervised learning with explicit supervision and unsupervised learning with blind supervision. Furthermore, partial label learning is related to other well-studied weakly-supervised learning frameworks, including *semi-supervised learning*, *multi-instance learning* and *multi-label learning*, while the weak supervision scenario for partial label learning is different to those counterpart frameworks.

Semi-supervised learning [4, 29] aims to learn a predictive model $f : \mathcal{X} \mapsto \mathcal{Y}$ from few labeled data together with abundant unlabeled data. For unlabeled data the ground-truth label assumes the entire label space, while for PL data the ground-truth label is confined within its candidate label set. Multi-instance learning [1, 9] aims to learn a predictive model $f : 2^{\mathcal{X}} \mapsto \mathcal{Y}$ from training examples each represented as a labeled bag of instances. For multi-instance data the label is assigned to bag of instances, while for PL data the label is assigned to single instance. Multi-label learning [11, 28] aims to learn a predictive model $f : \mathcal{X} \mapsto 2^{\mathcal{Y}}$ from training examples each associated with multiple labels. For multi-label data the associated labels are all valid ones, while for PL data the associated labels are only candidate ones.

Existing approaches learn from PL training examples by trying to disambiguate their candidate label sets. One disambiguation strategy is to assume certain parametric model $F(\boldsymbol{x}, y; \boldsymbol{\theta})$ where the ground-truth label is regarded as latent variable and identified as $\hat{y}_i = \arg\max_{y \in S_i} F(\boldsymbol{x}_i, y; \boldsymbol{\theta})$. Generally, the latent variable is refined iteratively via EM procedure which optimizes objective function defined according to the maximum likelihood criterion: $\sum_{i=1}^{m} \log \left(\sum_{y \in S_i} F(\boldsymbol{x}_i, y; \boldsymbol{\theta}) \right)$ [15, 16], or the maximum margin criterion: $\sum_{i=1}^{m} (\max_{y \in S_i} F(\boldsymbol{x}_i, y; \boldsymbol{\theta}) - \max_{y \notin S_i} F(\boldsymbol{x}_i, y; \boldsymbol{\theta}))$ [18, 24]. One potential drawback of the identification-based disambiguation strategy lies in that, rather than recovering the ground-truth label y_i, the identified label $\hat{y}_i$ might turn out to be false positive label in the candidate label set (i.e. $S_i \setminus \{y_i\}$).

Another disambiguation strategy is to assume equal importance of each candidate label and then make prediction by averaging their modeling outputs. Under discriminative learning setting, the averaged output from all candidate labels, i.e. $\frac{1}{|S_i|} \sum_{y \in S_i} F(\boldsymbol{x}_i, y; \boldsymbol{\theta})$, is distinguished from the outputs from non-candidate labels, i.e. $F(\boldsymbol{x}_i, y; \boldsymbol{\theta})$ $(y \notin S_i)$ [8]. Under instance-based learning setting, the predicted label for unseen instance is determined by averaging the candidate labeling information from its neighboring examples in the PL training set [13, 27]. One potential drawback of the averaging-based disambiguation strategy lies in that the essential modeling output from ground-truth label y_i might be overwhelmed by the distractive outputs from false positive labels.

In the next section, a novel partial label learning approach named PL-LEAF will be introduced. Other than disambiguation by identification or averaging, PL-LEAF facilitates the disambiguation process by making use of local topological information from the feature space. The candidate label set is disambiguated in the form of normalized labeling confidences, which differs from the crisp-style disambiguation of identifying a single candidate label or the uniform-style disambiguation of averaging all candidate labels.

3. THE PROPOSED APPROACH

As shown in Section 1, the task of partial label learning is to learn a multi-class classifier $f : \mathcal{X} \mapsto \mathcal{Y}$ from the PL training set $\mathcal{D} = \{(\boldsymbol{x}_i, S_i) \mid 1 \leq i \leq m\}$. For the proposed PL-LEAF approach, its key novelty lies in how the disambiguation procedure is conducted. Specifically, for each PL training example $(\boldsymbol{x}_i, S_i)$, PL-LEAF aims to disambiguate its candidate label set S_i via a normalized real-valued vector $\boldsymbol{\lambda}_i = (\lambda_{i1}, \lambda_{i2}, \ldots, \lambda_{iq})^\top$. Here, each component λ_{ik} $(1 \leq k \leq q)$ represents the *labeling confidence* of y_k being the ground-truth label for $\boldsymbol{x}_i$, which satisfies the following constraints:

- $\lambda_{ik} = 0 \ \ (\forall\, y_k \notin S_i)$
- $\lambda_{ik} \geq 0 \ \ (\forall\, y_k \in S_i)$ and $\sum_{y_k \in S_i} \lambda_{ik} = 1$

Once the normalized labeling confidence vectors have been generated, the predictive model will be induced by utilizing the disambiguation results.

In the next subsections, the two basic stages of PL-LEAF, i.e. *feature-aware disambiguation* and *predictive model induction*, will be scrutinized respectively.

3.1 Feature-Aware Disambiguation

In the first stage, PL-LEAF aims to disambiguate the candidate label set by exploiting useful information from the feature space. To fulfill this task, the popular smoothness assumption is adopted to enable information exploitation from the feature space to the label space. Given the PL training set $\mathcal{D} = \{(\boldsymbol{x}_i, S_i) \mid 1 \leq i \leq m\}$, a weighted graph $\mathcal{G} = (V, E, \mathbf{W})$ is constructed over the training examples to characterize the manifold structure of feature space. Here, $V = \{\boldsymbol{x}_i \mid 1 \leq i \leq m\}$ corresponds to the set of vertices and $E = \{(\boldsymbol{x}_i, \boldsymbol{x}_j) \mid \boldsymbol{x}_i \in \mathrm{KNN}(\boldsymbol{x}_j),\ i \neq j\}$ corresponds to the set of directed edges from $\boldsymbol{x}_i$ to $\boldsymbol{x}_j$ iff $\boldsymbol{x}_i$ is among the K-nearest neighbors of $\boldsymbol{x}_j$. Furthermore, $\mathbf{W} = [W_{ij}]_{m \times m}$ corresponds to the non-negative weight matrix where $W_{ij} = 0$ if $(\boldsymbol{x}_i, \boldsymbol{x}_j) \notin E$. For the weight matrix, its j-th column $\mathbf{W}_{\cdot j} = (W_{1j}, W_{2j}, \ldots, W_{mj})^\top$ is determined by solving the following linear least square problem:

$$\begin{aligned} \min_{\mathbf{W}_{\cdot j}} \quad & \left\| \boldsymbol{x}_j - \textstyle\sum_{(\boldsymbol{x}_i, \boldsymbol{x}_j) \in E} W_{ij} \cdot \boldsymbol{x}_i \right\|^2 \\ \text{s.t.}: \quad & \textstyle\sum_{(\boldsymbol{x}_i, \boldsymbol{x}_j) \in E} W_{ij} = 1 \\ & W_{ij} \geq 0 \ \ (\forall\, (\boldsymbol{x}_i, \boldsymbol{x}_j) \in E) \end{aligned} \tag{1}$$

Conceptually, the weight value W_{ij} $((\boldsymbol{x}_i, \boldsymbol{x}_j) \in E)$ characterizes the relative importance of neighboring example $\boldsymbol{x}_i$ in reconstructing $\boldsymbol{x}_j$. According to the constraint $\sum_{(\boldsymbol{x}_i, \boldsymbol{x}_j) \in E} W_{ij} = 1$, the above optimization problem (**OP**) can be re-written as:

$$\begin{aligned} \min_{\mathbf{W}_{\cdot j}} \quad & \mathbf{W}_{\cdot j}^\top \mathbf{G}^j \, \mathbf{W}_{\cdot j} \\ \text{s.t.}: \quad & \mathbf{1}^\top \mathbf{W}_{\cdot j} = 1 \\ & W_{ij} \geq 0 \ \ (\forall\, (\boldsymbol{x}_i, \boldsymbol{x}_j) \in E) \\ & W_{ij} = 0 \ \ (\forall\, (\boldsymbol{x}_i, \boldsymbol{x}_j) \notin E) \end{aligned} \tag{2}$$

Here, $\mathbf{G}^j = [G^j_{ab}]_{m \times m}$ is the local Gram matrix for $\boldsymbol{x}_j$ with elements $G^j_{ab} = (\boldsymbol{x}_j - \boldsymbol{x}_a)^\top (\boldsymbol{x}_j - \boldsymbol{x}_b)$. Apparently, **OP**(2) corresponds to a standard quadratic programming (QP) problem whose optimal solution can be obtained by any off-the-shelf QP solver. The weight matrix $\mathbf{W}$ is constructed by solving **OP**(2) column-wisely and the resulting matrix is generally not symmetric. Accordingly, based on the local topological information embodied in $\mathcal{G}$, the manifold structure in the feature space will be exploited to help disambiguate the candidate label set.

Here, in order to generate the labeling confidence vectors $\boldsymbol{\Lambda} = [\boldsymbol{\lambda}_1, \boldsymbol{\lambda}_2, \ldots, \boldsymbol{\lambda}_m]$, PL-LEAF exploits the smoothness assumption

Table 1: The pseudo-code of PL-LEAF.

Inputs:

$\mathcal{D}$: the partial label training set $\{(\boldsymbol{x}_i, S_i) \mid 1 \le i \le m\}$ $(\boldsymbol{x}_i \in \mathcal{X}, S_i \subseteq \mathcal{Y}, \mathcal{X} = \mathbb{R}^d, \mathcal{Y} = \{y_1, y_2, \ldots, y_q\})$

K: the number nearest neighbors used for weighted graph construction

C_1, C_2: the regularization parameters for regression loss function

$\boldsymbol{x}$: the unseen instance $(\boldsymbol{x} \in \mathcal{X})$

Outputs:

y: the predicted label for $\boldsymbol{x}$

Process:

Set the weighted graph $\mathcal{G} = (V, E, \mathbf{W})$ with $V = \{\boldsymbol{x}_i \mid 1 \le i \le m\}$ and $E = \{(\boldsymbol{x}_i, \boldsymbol{x}_j) \mid \boldsymbol{x}_i \in \text{KNN}(\boldsymbol{x}_j),\ i \ne j\}$;
for $j = 1$ **to** m **do**
    Instantiate the j-th column $\mathbf{W}_{\cdot j}$ of the weight matrix $\mathbf{W}$ by solving **OP**(2) with QP procedure;
end for
Generate the labeling confidence vectors $\boldsymbol{\Lambda}$ by solving **OP**(4) with QP procedure, or by solving **OP**(5) with alternating optimization;
Calculate the kernel matrix $\mathbf{K} = [\kappa(\boldsymbol{x}, \boldsymbol{x}_j)]_{m \times m}$ over training examples;
Calculate $\boldsymbol{\Psi} = [\boldsymbol{\psi}_1, \boldsymbol{\psi}_2, \ldots, \boldsymbol{\psi}_m]$ with $\boldsymbol{\psi}_i = -\left(\frac{1}{|S_i|} \cdot \mathbf{1}_{S_i} - \frac{1}{|\hat{S}_i|} \cdot \mathbf{1}_{\hat{S}_i}\right)$ $(1 \le i \le m)$
Set $t = 0$;
Initialize $\boldsymbol{\Theta}^{(0)}$ and $\boldsymbol{b}^{(0)}$ with $\boldsymbol{\alpha}_k^{(0)} = \mathbf{0}$ and $b_k^{(0)} = 0$ $(1 \le k \le q)$;
repeat
    Calculate $\boldsymbol{\rho} = [\rho_1, \rho_2, \ldots, \rho_m]^\top$ according to Eq.(11), and set $\mathbf{D}_\rho = [d_{ij}]_{m \times m}$ with $d_{ij} = \rho_i \delta_{ij}$;
    for $k = 1$ **to** q **do**
        Obtain the solution $\tilde{\boldsymbol{\alpha}}_k$ and $\tilde{b}_k$ by solving Eq.(17);
    end for
    Set the descending direction $\mathbf{P}^{(t)}$ according to Eq.(16);
    Update $\{\boldsymbol{\Theta}^{(t+1)}, \boldsymbol{b}^{(t+1)}\}$ by invoking line search procedure from $\{\boldsymbol{\Theta}^{(t)}, \boldsymbol{b}^{(t)}\}$ along $\mathbf{P}^{(t)}$;
    $t = t + 1$;
until $L(\boldsymbol{\Theta}^{(t-1)}, \boldsymbol{b}^{(t-1)}) - L(\boldsymbol{\Theta}^{(t)}, \boldsymbol{b}^{(t)}) < \tau \cdot L(\boldsymbol{\Theta}^{(t-1)}, \boldsymbol{b}^{(t-1)})$
Set the final predictive model with $\boldsymbol{\Theta}^* = \boldsymbol{\Theta}^{(t)}$ and $\boldsymbol{b}^* = \boldsymbol{b}^{(t)}$;
Return $y = f(\boldsymbol{x})$ according to Eq.(18).

that the manifold structure in the feature space should also be preserved in the label space:

$$\begin{aligned} \min_{\boldsymbol{\Lambda}} \quad & \sum_{j=1}^m \left\| \boldsymbol{\lambda}_j - \sum_{(\boldsymbol{x}_i, \boldsymbol{x}_j) \in E} W_{ij} \cdot \boldsymbol{\lambda}_i \right\|^2 \\ \text{s.t.}: \quad & \lambda_{jk} = 0 \ \ (\forall 1 \le j \le m,\ y_k \notin S_j) \\ & \lambda_{jk} \ge 0 \ \ (\forall 1 \le j \le m,\ y_k \in S_j) \\ & \textstyle\sum_{y_k \in S_j} \lambda_{jk} = 1 \ \ (\forall 1 \le j \le m) \end{aligned} \tag{3}$$

According to the constraint $\sum_{(\boldsymbol{x}_i, \boldsymbol{x}_j) \in E} W_{ij} = 1$, the above **OP**(3) can be re-written as:

$$\begin{aligned} \min_{\boldsymbol{\Lambda}} \quad & \sum_{i=1}^m \sum_{j=1}^m \gamma_{ij} \cdot \boldsymbol{\lambda}_i^\top \boldsymbol{\lambda}_j \\ \text{s.t.}: \quad & \lambda_{jk} = 0 \ \ (\forall 1 \le j \le m,\ y_k \notin S_j) \\ & \lambda_{jk} \ge 0 \ \ (\forall 1 \le j \le m,\ y_k \in S_j) \\ & \textstyle\sum_{y_k \in S_j} \lambda_{jk} = 1 \ \ (\forall 1 \le j \le m) \end{aligned} \tag{4}$$

Here, $\gamma_{ij} = \mathbf{W}_{i\cdot} \mathbf{W}_{j\cdot}^\top + \delta_{ij} \mathbf{W}_{\cdot i}^\top \mathbf{1}_{m \times m} \mathbf{W}_{\cdot i} - 2W_{ij}$ where $\mathbf{W}_{i\cdot}$, δ_{ij} and $\mathbf{1}_{m \times m}$ represent the i-th row of weight matrix $\mathbf{W}$, the Kronecker's delta and the $m \times m$ matrix of 1's respectively.

Note that **OP**(4) corresponds to a standard QP problem with mq variables and $m(q+1)$ constraints, whose computational complexity would be demanding when mq is large. To improve efficiency, we can choose to solve **OP**(4) with *alternating optimization* strategy where a series of QP subproblems with q variables and $q + 1$ constraints are optimized iteratively. Without loss of generality, in each alternating optimization iteration, one labeling confidence vector $\boldsymbol{\lambda}_i$ is optimized by fixing the values of other labeling confidence vectors $\boldsymbol{\lambda}_j$ $(j \ne i)$:

$$\begin{aligned} \min_{\boldsymbol{\lambda}_i} \quad & r_{ii} \cdot \boldsymbol{\lambda}_i^\top \boldsymbol{\lambda}_i + \left(\sum_{j=1, j \ne i}^m (r_{ij} + r_{ji}) \cdot \boldsymbol{\lambda}_j^\top\right) \boldsymbol{\lambda}_i \\ \text{s.t.}: \quad & \lambda_{ik} = 0 \ \ (\forall\, y_k \notin S_i) \\ & \lambda_{ik} \ge 0 \ \ (\forall\, y_k \in S_i) \\ & \textstyle\sum_{y_k \in S_i} \lambda_{ik} = 1 \end{aligned} \tag{5}$$

It is interesting to notice that, to some extent, the disambiguation results returned by existing strategies can be viewed as simplified versions of PL-LEAF's normalized labeling confidence vectors. For identification-based disambiguation [16, 18], a single label $y_{\hat{k}}$ in S_i is identified as the ground-truth label leading to *unimodal* labeling confidence vector with $\lambda_{i\hat{k}} = 1$ and $\lambda_{ik} = 0$ $(k \ne \hat{k})$. For averaging-based disambiguation [8, 13], all candidate labels in S_i are treated equally leading to *uniform* labeling confidence vector with $\lambda_{ik} = \frac{1}{|S_i|}$ $(y_k \in S_i)$. Therefore, the normalized labeling confidence vector considered by PL-LEAF would accommodate

Table 2: Characteristics of the experimental data sets.

Controlled UCI Data Sets				
Data set	# Examples	# Features	# Class Labels	Configurations
vehicle	846	18	4	
segment	2,310	18	7	(I) $p=1, r=1, \varepsilon \in \{0.1, 0.2, \ldots, 0.7\}$ **[Figure 1]**
abalone	4,177	7	29	(II) $r=1, p \in \{0.1, 0.2, \ldots, 0.7\}$ **[Figure 2]**
satimage	6,345	36	7	(III) $r=2, p \in \{0.1, 0.2, \ldots, 0.7\}$ **[Figure 3]**
usps	9,298	256	10	(IV) $r=3, p \in \{0.1, 0.2, \ldots, 0.7\}$ **[Figure 4]**
pendigits	10,992	16	10	

Real-World Data Sets					
Data set	# Examples	# Features	# Class Labels	Avg. # CLs	Task Domain
FG-NET	1,002	262	78	7.48	*facial age estimation* [20]
Lost	1,122	108	16	2.23	*automatic face naming* [8]
MSRCv2	1,758	48	23	3.16	*object classification* [16]
BirdSong	4,998	38	13	2.18	*bird song classification* [3]
Soccer Player	17,472	279	171	2.09	*automatic face naming* [25]
Yahoo! News	22,991	163	219	1.91	*automatic face naming* [12]

more flexibility in modeling the disambiguation results compared to the unimodal or uniform setup.

3.2 Predictive Model Induction

Following the first stage of feature-aware disambiguation, the original PL training set $\mathcal{D}$ has been transformed into its disambiguated counterpart: $\mathcal{D}_{\text{dis}} = \{(\boldsymbol{x}_i, \boldsymbol{\lambda}_i) \mid 1 \le i \le m\}$. In the second stage, PL-LEAF aims to induce the predictive model $f: \mathcal{X} \mapsto \mathcal{Y}$ based on $\mathcal{D}_{\text{dis}}$. Considering that the response variables (normalized labeling confidences) for each training example in $\mathcal{D}_{\text{dis}}$ are actually real-valued, it is natural to induce the predictive model by performing *multi-output regression*. Among various choices of multi-output regression techniques, we choose to adapt the multi-regression support vector machines (MSVR) [6, 21, 23] such that kernel trick can be readily incorporated to accommodate nonlinear modeling.

Let $\phi(\cdot): \mathbb{R}^d \mapsto \mathbb{R}^{\mathcal{H}_\kappa}$ be the (implicit) nonlinear mapping from the original feature space to the higher-dimensional Reproducing Kernel Hilbert Space (RKHS) via kernel function $\kappa: \mathcal{X} \times \mathcal{X} \mapsto \mathbb{R}$. Furthermore, let $\{(\boldsymbol{\theta}_k, b_k) \mid 1 \le k \le q\}$ denote the multi-output regression model in the RKHS with one linear predictor $(\boldsymbol{\theta}_k, b_k)$ for each class label $y_k \in \mathcal{Y}$. Then, PL-LEAF induces the regression model by minimizing the following loss function:

$$L(\boldsymbol{\Theta}, \boldsymbol{b}) = \frac{1}{2}\sum_{k=1}^{q} ||\boldsymbol{\theta}_k||^2 + C_1 \sum_{i=1}^{m} L_1(u_i) + C_2 \sum_{i=1}^{m} v_i \quad (6)$$

Here, $\boldsymbol{\Theta} = [\boldsymbol{\theta}_1, \boldsymbol{\theta}_2, \ldots, \boldsymbol{\theta}_q]$ and $\boldsymbol{b} = [b_1, b_2, \ldots, b_q]^\top$ represent the regression model's weight matrix and bias vector respectively.

As shown in Eq.(6), the first term of $L(\boldsymbol{\Theta}, \boldsymbol{b})$ controls the complexity of the induced model. In addition, the second term of $L(\boldsymbol{\Theta}, \boldsymbol{b})$ is defined based on the ϵ-insensitive loss function:

$$L_1(u) = \begin{cases} 0, & u < \epsilon \\ (u-\epsilon)^2, & u \ge \epsilon \end{cases} \quad (7)$$

For each example $(\boldsymbol{x}_i, \boldsymbol{\lambda}_i)$ in $\mathcal{D}_{\text{dis}}$, the corresponding input to the ϵ-insensitive loss function $L_1(\cdot)$ is set as: $u_i = ||\boldsymbol{e}_i|| = \sqrt{\boldsymbol{e}_i^\top \boldsymbol{e}_i}$ with $\boldsymbol{e}_i = \boldsymbol{\lambda}_i - \boldsymbol{\Theta}^\top \phi(\boldsymbol{x}_i) - \boldsymbol{b}$. In this way, the outputs of all linear predictors are considered simultaneously to yield a unique input to $L_1(\cdot)$ such that the dependencies among all the class labels can be exploited by the ϵ-insensitive term. The third term of $L(\boldsymbol{\Theta}, \boldsymbol{b})$ considers the partial label loss for each example which is set as:

$$v_i = -\left(\frac{1}{|S_i|} \cdot \mathbf{1}_{S_i}^\top - \frac{1}{|\hat{S}_i|} \cdot \mathbf{1}_{\hat{S}_i}^\top\right)\left(\boldsymbol{\Theta}^\top \phi(\boldsymbol{x}_i) + \boldsymbol{b}\right) \quad (8)$$

Here, for candidate label set S_i and its complementary set $\hat{S}_i$ in $\mathcal{Y}$, $\mathbf{1}_{S_i}$ ($\mathbf{1}_{\hat{S}_i}$) corresponds to a q-dimensional vector whose k-th element equals to 1 if $y_k \in S_i$ ($y_k \in \hat{S}_i$) and 0 otherwise. In other words, the third term enforces the property that the average output from candidate labels should be larger than the average output from non-candidate ones, which has been widely-used in designing effective partial label learning algorithms [8, 13, 26].

To minimize $L(\boldsymbol{\Theta}, \boldsymbol{b})$, PL-LEAF employs the gradient-based iterative method named Iterative Re-Weighted Least Square (IRWLS) [21, 23]. Specifically, in each iteration the descending direction is determined analytically by solving linear systems of equations. Let $\{\boldsymbol{\Theta}^{(t)}, \boldsymbol{b}^{(t)}\}$ denote the current model after t-th iteration, the ϵ-insensitive function $L_1(u_i)$ is firstly approximated by its first-order Taylor expansion:

$$\bar{L}_1(u_i) = L_1(u_i^{(t)}) + \left.\frac{dL_1(u)}{du}\right|_{u_i^{(t)}} \frac{(\boldsymbol{e}_i^{(t)})^\top}{u_i^{(t)}}\left(\boldsymbol{e}_i - \boldsymbol{e}_i^{(t)}\right) \quad (9)$$

Here, $u_i^{(t)}$ and $\boldsymbol{e}_i^{(t)}$ are calculated based on the current model $\{\boldsymbol{\Theta}^{(t)}, \boldsymbol{b}^{(t)}\}$. Then, a quadratic approximation to $\bar{L}(u_i)$ is further constructed to ease analytical solution to the descending direction:

$$\begin{aligned} \tilde{L}_1(u_i) &= L_1(u_i^{(t)}) + \left.\frac{dL_1(u)}{du}\right|_{u_i^{(t)}} \frac{u_i^2 - (u_i^{(t)})^2}{2u_i^{(t)}} \\ &= \frac{1}{2}\rho_i u_i^2 + T_i \end{aligned} \quad (10)$$

where

$$\rho_i = \frac{1}{u_i^{(t)}} \left.\frac{L_1(u)}{du}\right|_{u_i^{(t)}} = \begin{cases} 0, & u_i^{(t)} < \epsilon \\ \frac{2\left(u_i^{(t)} - \epsilon\right)}{u_i^{(t)}}, & u_i^{(t)} \ge \epsilon \end{cases} \quad (11)$$

and T_i is a constant which does not depend on $\{\boldsymbol{\Theta}, \boldsymbol{b}\}$.

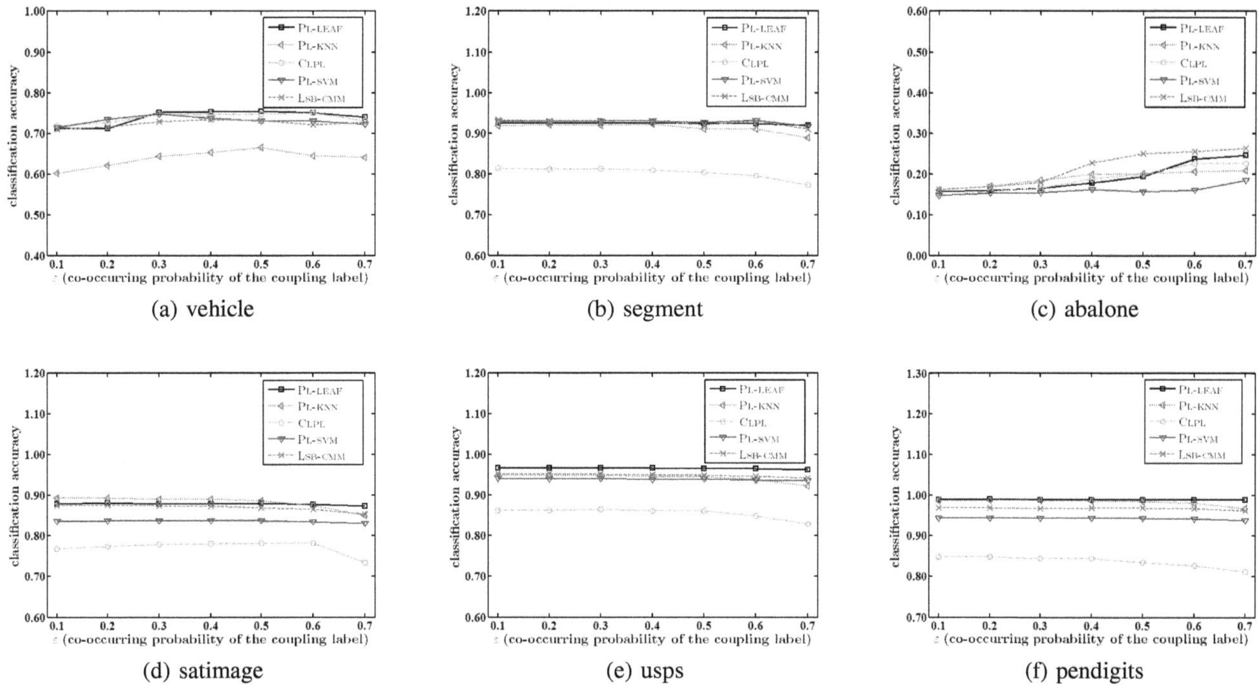

Figure 1: Classification accuracy of each comparing algorithm changes as ε (co-occurring probability of the coupling label) increases from 0.1 to 0.7 (with 100% partially labeled examples [$p = 1$] and one false positive candidate label [$r = 1$]).

Based on Eqs.(10) and (11), the objective function $L(\mathbf{\Theta}, \boldsymbol{b})$ can be re-written as:

$$\tilde{L}(\mathbf{\Theta}, \boldsymbol{b}) = \frac{1}{2}\sum_{k=1}^{q} ||\boldsymbol{\theta}_k||^2 + C_1\sum_{i=1}^{m}\frac{\rho_i}{2}u_i^2 + C_2\sum_{i=1}^{m}v_i + C_1\sum_{i=1}^{m}T_i \tag{12}$$

In contrast to standard least square objective function $\frac{1}{2}\sum_{k=1}^{q}||\boldsymbol{\theta}_k||^2 + C_1\sum_{i=1}^{m}u_i^2$, the minimization of Eq.(12) can be regarded as a *weighted* least square problem along with partial label loss regularization. Minimization of $\tilde{L}(\mathbf{\Theta}, \boldsymbol{b})$ can be decoupled for each class label, whose solution for each $(\boldsymbol{\theta}_k, b_k)$ $(1 \leq k \leq q)$ is found by equating the corresponding gradient to zero:

$$\nabla_{\boldsymbol{\theta}_k}\tilde{L}(\mathbf{\Theta}, \boldsymbol{b}) = \boldsymbol{\theta}_k - C_1\sum_{i=1}^{m}\rho_i\phi(\boldsymbol{x}_i)(\lambda_{ik} - \phi(\boldsymbol{x}_i)^\top\boldsymbol{\theta}_k - b_k) + C_2\sum_{i=1}^{m}\psi_{ik}\phi(\boldsymbol{x}_i) = \mathbf{0} \tag{13}$$

$$\nabla_{b_k}\tilde{L}(\mathbf{\Theta}, \boldsymbol{b}) = -C_1\sum_{i=1}^{m}\rho_i(\lambda_{ik} - \phi(\boldsymbol{x}_i)^\top\boldsymbol{\theta}_k - b_k) + C_2\sum_{i=1}^{m}\psi_{ik} = 0 \tag{14}$$

Here, ψ_{ik} corresponds to the k-th component of the q-dimensional vector $\boldsymbol{\psi}_i = -\left(\frac{1}{|S_i|}\cdot\mathbf{1}_{S_i} - \frac{1}{|\hat{S}_i|}\cdot\mathbf{1}_{\hat{S}_i}\right)$. Accordingly, Eqs.(13) and (14) can be expressed as a linear system of equations:

$$\begin{bmatrix} C_1\mathbf{\Phi}^\top\mathbf{D}_\rho\mathbf{\Phi} + \mathbf{I} & C_1\mathbf{\Phi}^\top\boldsymbol{\rho} \\ C_1\boldsymbol{\rho}^\top\mathbf{\Phi} & C_1\mathbf{1}^\top\boldsymbol{\rho}\end{bmatrix}\begin{bmatrix}\boldsymbol{\theta}_k \\ b_k\end{bmatrix} = \begin{bmatrix} C_1\mathbf{\Phi}^\top\mathbf{D}_\rho\boldsymbol{\lambda}^k - C_2\mathbf{\Phi}^\top\boldsymbol{\psi}^k \\ C_1\boldsymbol{\rho}^\top\boldsymbol{\lambda}^k - C_2\mathbf{1}^\top\boldsymbol{\psi}^k\end{bmatrix} \tag{15}$$

Here, $\mathbf{\Phi} = [\phi(\boldsymbol{x}_1), \phi(\boldsymbol{x}_2), \ldots, \phi(\boldsymbol{x}_m)]^\top$, $\mathbf{D}_\rho = [d_{ij}]_{m\times m}$ with $d_{ij} = \rho_i\delta_{ij}$, $\boldsymbol{\rho} = [\rho_1, \rho_2, \ldots, \rho_m]^\top$, $\boldsymbol{\lambda}^k = [\lambda_{1k}, \lambda_{2k}, \ldots, \lambda_{mk}]^\top$, $\boldsymbol{\psi}^k = [\psi_{1k}, \psi_{2k}, \ldots, \psi_{mk}]^\top$.

Let $\tilde{\mathbf{\Theta}} = [\tilde{\boldsymbol{\theta}}_1, \tilde{\boldsymbol{\theta}}_2, \ldots, \tilde{\boldsymbol{\theta}}_q]$ and $\tilde{\boldsymbol{b}} = [\tilde{b}_1, \tilde{b}_2, \ldots, \tilde{b}_q]^\top$ be the solution obtained by solving Eq.(15) for each class label, the descending direction for the next iteration would be:

$$\mathbf{P}^{(t)} = \begin{bmatrix}\tilde{\mathbf{\Theta}} - \mathbf{\Theta}^{(t)} \\ (\tilde{\boldsymbol{b}} - \boldsymbol{b}^{(t)})^\top\end{bmatrix} \tag{16}$$

The subsequent model $\{\mathbf{\Theta}^{(t+1)}, \boldsymbol{b}^{(t+1)}\}$ is then updated by invoking line search procedure from $\{\mathbf{\Theta}^{(t)}, \boldsymbol{b}^{(t)}\}$ along the descending direction $\mathbf{P}^{(t)}$ [19].

According to the Representer Theorem [22], under fairly general conditions, the predictive model can be expressed by a linear combination of the training examples in the RKHS, i.e. $\boldsymbol{\theta}_k = \sum_{i=1}^{m}\alpha_{ik}\phi(\boldsymbol{x}_i) = \mathbf{\Phi}^\top\boldsymbol{\alpha}_k$. By introducing the kernel trick into Eqs.(13) and (14), the linear system of Eq.(15) can be expressed as follows:

$$\begin{bmatrix} C_1\mathbf{K} + \mathbf{D}_\rho^{-1} & C_1\mathbf{1} \\ C_1\boldsymbol{\rho}^\top\mathbf{K} & C_1\mathbf{1}^\top\boldsymbol{\rho}\end{bmatrix}\begin{bmatrix}\boldsymbol{\alpha}_k \\ b_k\end{bmatrix} = \begin{bmatrix} C_1\boldsymbol{\lambda}^k - C_2\mathbf{D}_\rho^{-1}\boldsymbol{\psi}^k \\ C_1\boldsymbol{\rho}^\top\boldsymbol{\lambda}^k - C_2\mathbf{1}^\top\boldsymbol{\psi}^k\end{bmatrix} \tag{17}$$

Here, $\mathbf{K} = [\kappa(\boldsymbol{x}_i, \boldsymbol{x}_j)]_{m\times m}$ is the kernel matrix over training examples. Based on the kernel trick, the line search procedure can be readily performed in terms of $\boldsymbol{\alpha}_k$ and b_k as well.

Let $\mathbf{\Theta}^*$ and $\boldsymbol{b}^*$ be the resulting model after the whole iterative optimization process, PL-LEAF makes prediction on the class label of unseen instance $\boldsymbol{x}$ as follows:

$$\begin{aligned} f(\boldsymbol{x}) &= \arg\max\nolimits_{y_k\in\mathcal{Y}}\ {\boldsymbol{\theta}_k^*}^\top\phi(\boldsymbol{x}) + b_k^* \\ &= \arg\max\nolimits_{y_k\in\mathcal{Y}}\ \sum\nolimits_{i=1}^{m}\alpha_{ik}^*\kappa(\boldsymbol{x}_i, \boldsymbol{x}) + b_k^* \end{aligned} \tag{18}$$

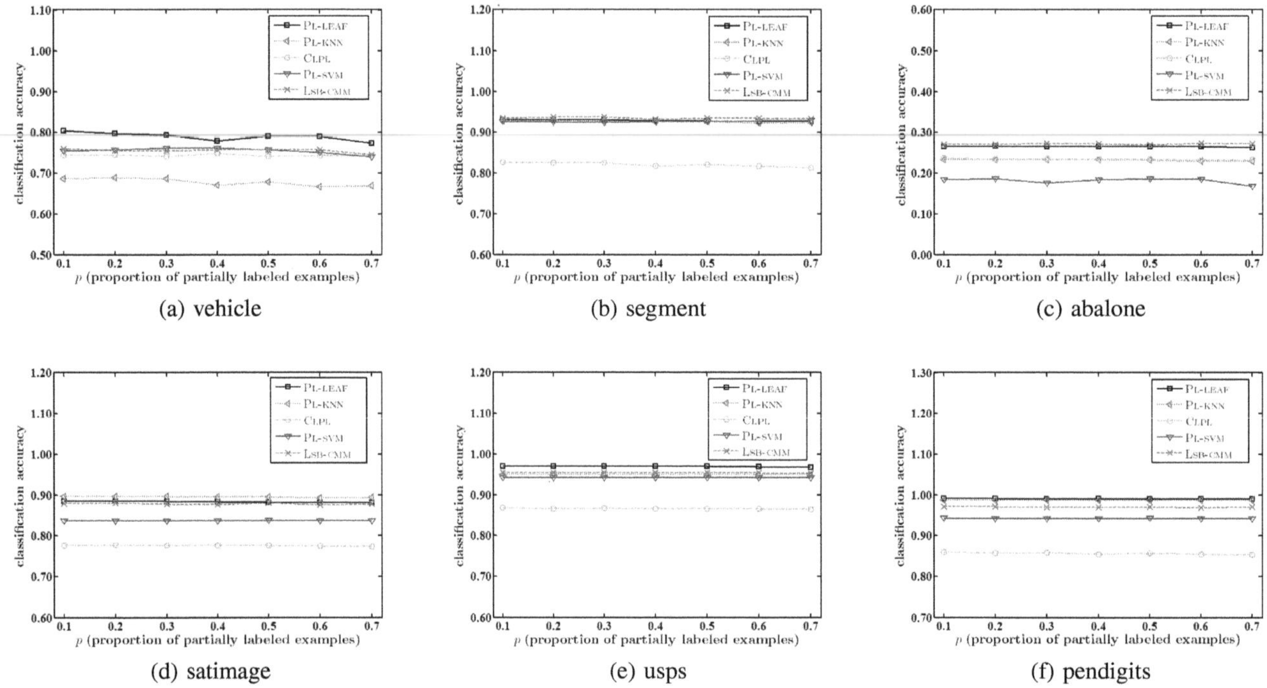

(a) vehicle (b) segment (c) abalone

(d) satimage (e) usps (f) pendigits

Figure 2: Classification accuracy of each comparing algorithm changes as p (proportion of partially labeled examples) increases (with one false positive candidate label $[r = 1]$).

Table 1 summarizes the pseudo-code of PL-LEAF.[2] Given the PL training set, a weighted graph is constructed to characterize the manifold structure of feature space which is then utilized to disambiguate the candidate label set (Steps 1-5). After that, a predictive model based on kernelized multiregression SVR is learned via gradient-based iterative optimization (Steps 6-18).[3] Finally, prediction on the unseen instance is made via the learned predictive model (Steps 19-20).

4. EXPERIMENTS

4.1 Experimental Setup

To evaluate the performance of PL-LEAF, two series of comparative experiments are conducted on controlled UCI data sets [2] as well as real-world partial label data sets. Characteristics of the experimental data sets are summarized in Table 2.

Following the widely-used controlling protocol in partial label learning research [5, 8, 16, 24, 27], an artificial PL data set can be generated from a multi-class UCI data set with three controlling parameters p, r and ε. Here, p controls the proportion of examples which are partially labeled (i.e. $|S_i| > 1$), r controls the number of false positive labels in the candidate label set (i.e. $|S_i| = r + 1$), and ε controls the co-occurring probability between one coupling candidate label and the ground-truth label. As shown in Table 2, a total of 28 (4x7) parameter configurations have been considered for each UCI data set.

In addition to artificial data sets, a number of real-world PL data sets have been collected from several task domains.[4] For the task of *facial age estimation* (`FG-NET` [20]), human faces with landmarks are represented as instances while ages annotated by ten crowd-sourced labelers together with the ground-truth age are regarded as candidate labels. For the task of *automatic face naming* (`Lost` [8], `Soccer Player` [25] and `Yahoo! News` [12]), faces cropped from an image or video frame are represented as instances while names extracted from the associated captions or subtitles are regarded as candidate labels. For the task of *bird song classification* (`BirdSong` [3]), singing syllables of the birds are represented as instances while bird species jointly singing during a 10-seconds period are regarded as candidate labels. For the task of *object classification* (`MSRCv2` [16]), image segmentations are represented as instances while objects appearing within the same image are regarded as candidate labels. The average number of candidate labels (Avg. #CLs) for each real-world PL data set is also recorded in Table 2.

To show the effectiveness of feature-aware disambiguation, PL-LEAF is compared against four state-of-the-art partial label learning approaches with diverse properties, each configured with parameters suggested in respective literatures:

- PL-KNN [13]: A K-nearest neighbor approach to partial label learning via averaging-based disambiguation [suggested configuration: $K = 10$];
- CLPL [8]: A discriminative approach to partial label learning via averaging-based disambiguation [suggested configuration: SVM with squared hinge loss];
- PL-SVM [18]: A maximum-margin approach to partial label learning via identification-based disambiguation [suggested

[2] Code package for PL-LEAF is publicly-available at: http://cse.seu.edu.cn/PersonalPage/zhangml/Resources.htm#kdd16

[3] In this paper, the ϵ-insensitive function $L_1(\cdot)$ is instantiated with $\epsilon = 0.1$ and the convergence condition in Step 18 is instantiated with $\tau = 10^{-10}$.

[4] These data sets are publicly-available at: http://cse.seu.edu.cn/PersonalPage/zhangml/Resources.htm#partial_data

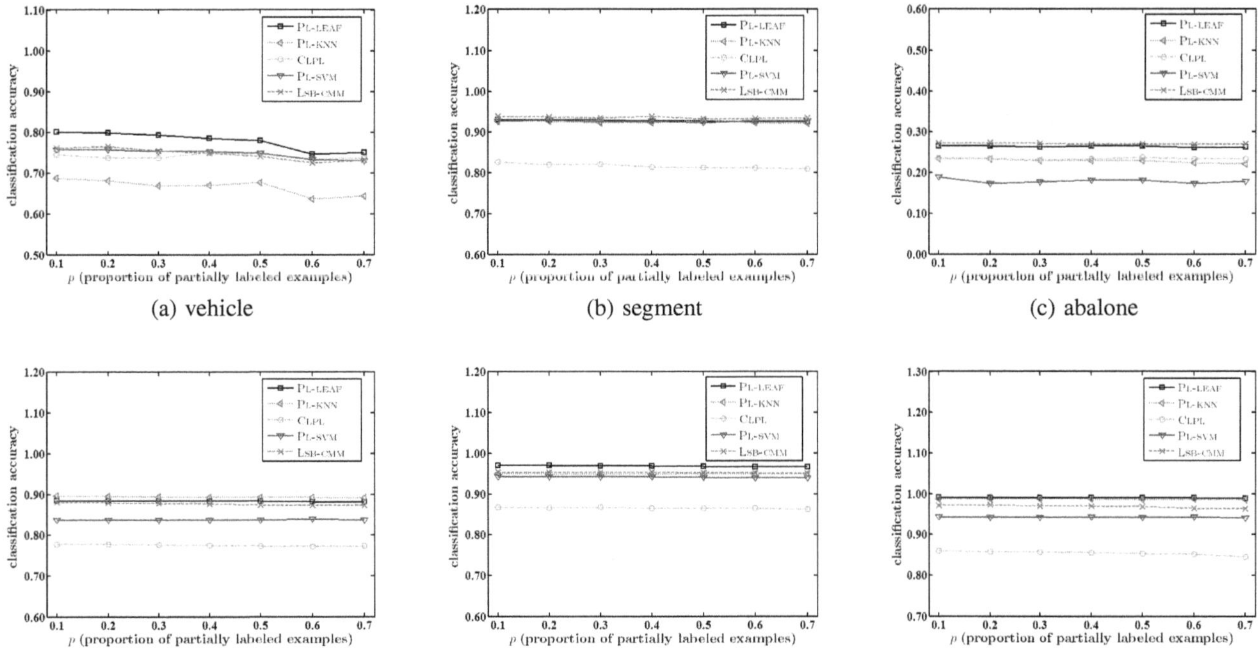

(a) vehicle (b) segment (c) abalone

(d) satimage (e) usps (f) pendigits

Figure 3: Classification accuracy of each comparing algorithm changes as p (proportion of partially labeled examples) increases (with two false positive candidate labels $[r = 2]$).

configuration: regularization parameter pool with $\{10^{-3}, \ldots, 10^{3}\}$];

- LSB-CMM [16]: A maximum-likelihood approach to partial label learning via identification-based disambiguation [suggested configuration: q mixture components].

Parameters for PL-LEAF (Table 1) are set as $K = 10$, $C_1 = 10$ and $C_2 = 1$.[5] In this paper, ten runs of 50%/50% random train/test splits are performed on each artificial as well as real-world PL data set. Accordingly, the mean predictive accuracies (with standard deviation) are recorded for all comparing algorithms.

4.2 Experimental Results

4.2.1 Controlled UCI Data Sets

In Figure 1, the classification accuracy of each comparing algorithm is illustrated where the co-occurring probability ε varies from 0.1 to 0.7 with step-size 0.1 ($p = 1, r = 1$). For any ground-truth label $y \in \mathcal{Y}$, one extra label $y' \neq y$ is designated as the coupling label which co-occurs with y in the candidate label set with probability ε. Otherwise, any other class label would be chosen to co-occur with y. In Figures 2 to 4, the classification accuracy of each comparing algorithm is illustrated where the proportion p varies from 0.1 to 0.7 with step-size 0.1 ($r = 1, 2, 3$). Together with the ground-truth label, r class labels in $\mathcal{Y}$ will be randomly picked up to constitute the candidate label set for each partially labeled example.

As shown in Figures 1 to 4, in most cases, PL-LEAF achieves superior or competitive performance against the comparing algorithms. Based on pairwise t-test at 0.05 significance level, Table 3 summarizes the win/tie/loss counts between PL-LEAF and each comparing algorithm. Out of the 168 statistical tests (28 configurations $\times$ 6 UCI data sets), it is shown that:

- Comparing to averaging-based disambiguation approaches, PL-LEAF achieves superior performance against PL-KNN and CLPL in 66.0% and 90.4% cases respectively. Furthermore, the performance of PL-LEAF is inferior to PL-KNN in only 17.9% cases and has never been outperformed by CLPL.

- Comparing to identification-based disambiguation approaches, PL-LEAF achieves superior performance against PL-SVM and LSB-CMM in 75.5% and 54.7% cases. Furthermore, the performance of PL-LEAF is inferior to LSB-CMM in only 11.9% cases and has been outperformed by PL-SVM in only 2 out of 168 cases.

Table 3: Win/tie/loss counts (pairwise t-test at 0.05 significance level) on the classification performance of PL-LEAF against each comparing algorithm.

	PL-LEAF **against**			
	PL-KNN	CLPL	PL-SVM	LSB-CMM
[Figure 1]	26/7/9	31/11/0	27/13/2	20/16/6
[Figure 2]	28/7/7	42/0/0	35/7/0	23/16/3
[Figure 3]	28/7/7	40/2/0	33/9/0	23/12/7
[Figure 4]	29/6/7	39/3/0	32/10/0	26/12/4
In Total	**111/27/30**	**152/16/0**	**127/39/2**	**92/56/20**

[5]For PL-LEAF, Gaussian kernel $\kappa(\boldsymbol{x}_i, \boldsymbol{x}_j) = \exp\left(-\frac{||\boldsymbol{x}_i - \boldsymbol{x}_j||^2}{\sigma^2}\right)$ is employed in Step 6 with σ being the average distance among each pair of training examples. Furthermore, on the two artificial (`usps`, `pendigits`) and two real-world (`Soccer Player`, `Yahoo! News`) data sets with large scale, alternating optimization is employed in Step 5. Sensitivity analysis on PL-LEAF's parameter configuration is conducted in Subsection 4.3.

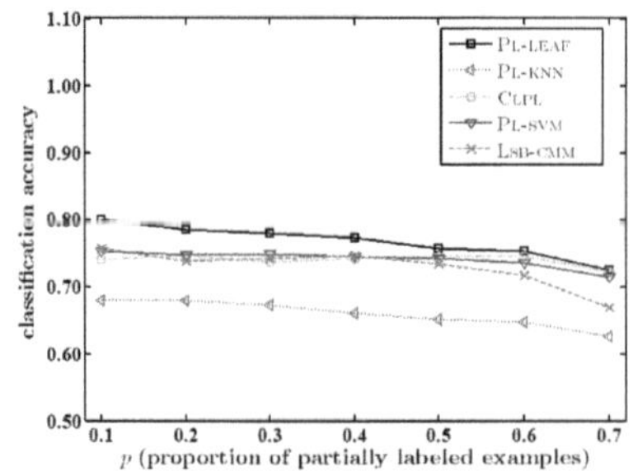

(a) vehicle

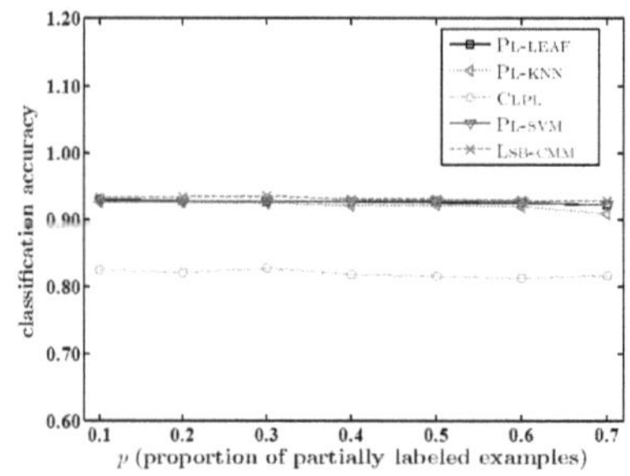

(b) segment

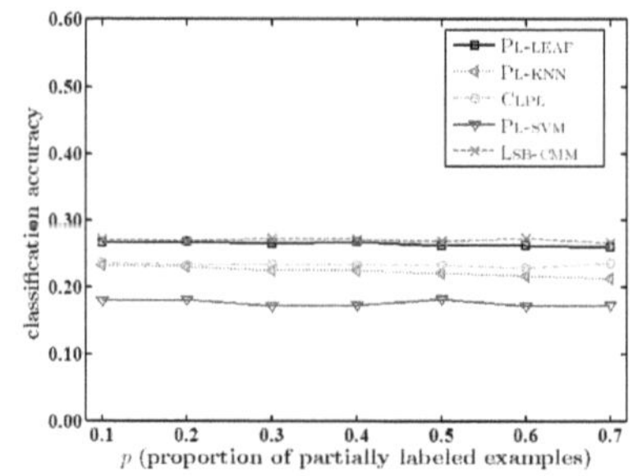

(c) abalone

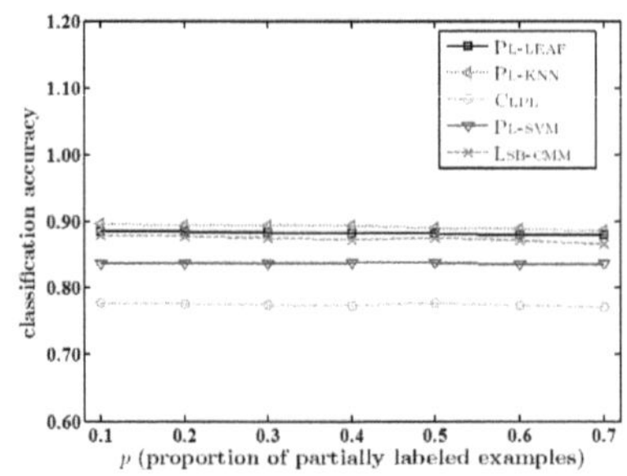

(d) satimage

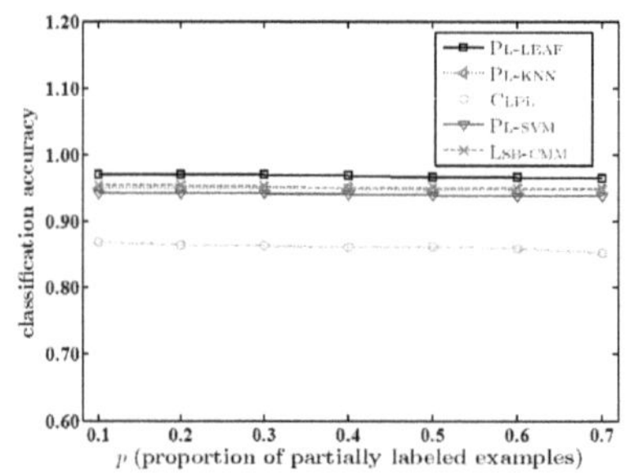

(e) usps

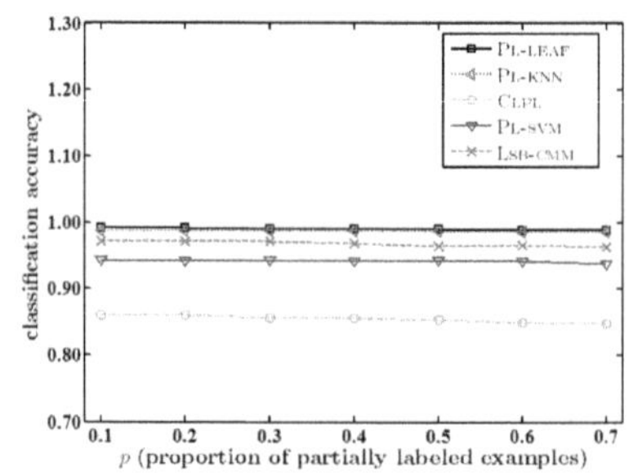

(f) pendigits

Figure 4: Classification accuracy of each comparing algorithm changes as p (proportion of partially labeled examples) increases (with three false positive candidate labels $[r = 3]$).

Table 4: Classification accuracy (mean$\pm$std) of each comparing algorithm on the real-world partial label data sets. In addition, $\bullet/\circ$ indicates whether the performance of PL-LEAF is statistically superior/inferior to the comparing algorithm on each data set (pairwise t-test at 0.05 significance level).

	PL-LEAF	PL-KNN	CLPL	PL-SVM	LSB-CMM
FG-NET	0.072±0.010	0.037±0.008•	0.047±0.017•	0.058±0.010•	0.056±0.008•
FG-NET (MAE3)	0.411±0.012	0.284±0.035•	0.240±0.045•	0.343±0.022•	0.344±0.026•
FG-NET (MAE5)	0.550±0.018	0.438±0.033•	0.343±0.055•	0.473±0.016•	0.478±0.025•
Lost	0.664±0.020	0.332±0.030•	0.670±0.024	0.639±0.056	0.591±0.019•
MSRCv2	0.459±0.013	0.417±0.012•	0.375±0.020•	0.417±0.027•	0.431±0.008•
BirdSong	0.706±0.012	0.637±0.009•	0.624±0.009•	0.671±0.018•	0.692±0.015•
Soccer Player	0.515±0.004	0.494±0.004•	0.347±0.004•	0.430±0.004•	0.506±0.006•
Yahoo! News	0.597±0.004	0.403±0.004•	0.457±0.005•	0.615±0.002∘	0.594±0.007

4.2.2 Real-World Data Sets

Table 4 reports the detailed predictive performance of each comparing algorithm on the real-world PL data sets, where the outcomes of pairwise t-tests at 0.05 significance level are also recorded. Note that the average number of candidate labels (Avg. #CLs) for the `FG-NET` data set (i.e. 7.48 as shown in Table 2) is quite large, which makes the task of facial age estimation (based on training examples with partial labels) rather challenging. Furthermore, the state-of-the-art performance on this data set (based on training examples with ground-truth labels) corresponds to more than 3 years of mean average error (MAE) between the predicted age and the ground-truth age [20]. In Table 4, two extra classification accuracies are reported on the `FG-NET` data set where an unseen example is regarded to be correctly classified if the difference between the predicted age and the ground-truth age is less than 3 years (MAE3) or 5 years (MAE5).

As shown in Table 4, it is impressive to observe that:

- On the `FG-NET` (with its MAE3 and MAE5 variants), `MSRCv2`, `BirdSong` and `Soccer Player` data sets, the performance of PL-LEAF is superior to all the other comparing algorithms.
- On the `Lost` data set, the performance of PL-LEAF is superior to PL-KNN and LSB-CMM, and comparable to CLPL and PL-SVM.
- On the `Yahoo! News` data set, the performance of PL-LEAF is superior to PL-KNN and CLPL, comparable to LSB-CMM, and inferior to PL-SVM.

4.3 Further Analysis

In addition to Table 4 reporting inductive performance on test examples, it is also interesting to study the *transductive* performance of each comparing algorithm on classifying training examples [8, 24]. For each PL training example $(\boldsymbol{x}_i, S_i)$, its ground-truth label is predicted by consulting the candidate label set S_i, i.e. predicting $\hat{y}_i \in S_i$ with largest modeling output. In other words, transductive

Table 5: **Transductive accuracy (mean±std) of each comparing algorithm on the real-world partial label data sets. In addition, •/∘ indicates whether the performance of PL-LEAF is statistically superior/inferior to the comparing algorithm on each data set (pairwise t-test at 0.05 significance level).**

	PL-LEAF	PL-KNN	CLPL	PL-SVM	LSB-CMM	PL-LEAF†
FG-NET	0.148±0.009	0.173±0.017∘	0.158±0.018	0.136±0.021	0.138±0.019	0.142±0.010
FG-NET (MAE3)	0.567±0.015	0.559±0.023	0.548±0.017•	0.502±0.030•	0.541±0.022•	0.556±0.014
FG-NET (MAE5)	0.710±0.014	0.721±0.021	0.684±0.021•	0.644±0.021•	0.684±0.018•	0.698±0.010
Lost	0.809±0.022	0.596±0.018•	0.855±0.007∘	0.814±0.033	0.755±0.018•	0.788±0.025
MSRCv2	0.645±0.015	0.603±0.015•	0.612±0.035•	0.656±0.026	0.603±0.016•	0.629±0.016
BirdSong	0.822±0.014	0.766±0.015•	0.820±0.014	0.831±0.013	0.827±0.017	0.787±0.016
Soccer Player	0.702±0.003	0.674±0.002•	0.742±0.005∘	0.733±0.007∘	0.688±0.003•	0.669±0.003
Yahoo! News	0.827±0.002	0.720±0.003•	0.832±0.002∘	0.861±0.003∘	0.861±0.002∘	0.822±0.002

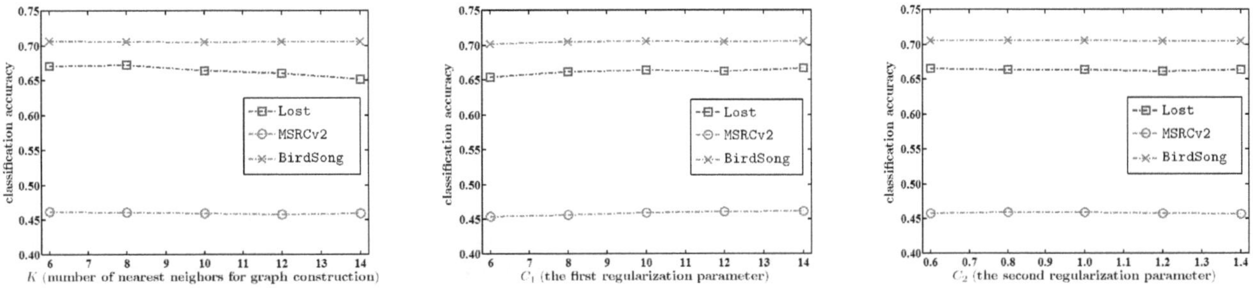

(a) Varying K ($C_1 = 10, C_2 = 1$) (b) Varying C_1 ($K = 10, C_2 = 1$) (c) Varying C_2 ($K = 10, C_1 = 10$)

Figure 5: Parameter sensitivity analysis for PL-LEAF on the `Lost`, `MSRCv2` and `BirdSong` data sets. (a) Classification accuracy of PL-LEAF changes as K increases from 6 to 14 with step-size 2; (b) Classification accuracy of PL-LEAF changes as C_1 increases from 6 to 14 with step-size 2; (c) Classification accuracy of PL-LEAF changes as C_2 increases from 0.6 to 1.4 with step-size 0.2.

performance of the partial label learning algorithm reflects its ability in disambiguating the candidate label set. Accordingly, Table 5 reports the transductive accuracy of each comparing algorithm together with the outcomes of pairwise t-tests at 0.05 significance level. Out of the 32 statistical tests (8 data sets × 4 comparing algorithm), it is shown that:

- Comparing to averaging-based disambiguation approaches, PL-LEAF is outperformed by PL-KNN on the `FG-NET` data set, and outperformed by CLPL on the `Lost`, `Soccer Player` and `Yahoo! News` data sets. In the rest 12 statistical tests, the performance of PL-LEAF is superior or at least comparable to PL-KNN and CLPL.

- Comparing to identification-based disambiguation approaches, PL-LEAF is outperformed by PL-SVM on the `Soccer Player` and `Yahoo! News` data sets, and outperformed by LSB-CMM on the `Yahoo! News` data set. In the rest 13 statistical tests, the performance of PL-LEAF is superior or at least comparable to PL-SVM and LSB-CMM.

As the feature-aware disambiguation stage of PL-LEAF finishes, the generated labeling confidence vector $\boldsymbol{\lambda}_i$ can also be used to predict the ground-truth label of $\boldsymbol{x}_i$ as $\hat{y}_i = \arg\max_{y_k \in S_i} \lambda_{ik}$. The resulting transductive performance is reported in Table 5 (denoted as PL-LEAF†) for referencee purpose. In most cases, the transductive performance of PL-LEAF† is close to PL-LEAF indicating the usefulness of generated labeling confidence vectors.

As shown in Table 1, to study the sensitivity of PL-LEAF w.r.t. its parameters K, C_1 and C_2, Figure 5 illustrates how PL-LEAF performs under different parameter configurations. For clarity of illustration, three data sets (`Lost`, `MSRCv2` and `BirdSong`) are chosen here for sensitivity analysis while similar observations also hold on other data sets.

It is obvious from Figure 5 that the performance of PL-LEAF is stable across a broad range of each parameter. This property is quite desirable as one can make use of PL-LEAF to achieve robust classification performance without the need of parameter fine-tuning. Therefore, the parameter configuration for PL-LEAF in Subsection 4.1 (K=10, C_1=10, C_2=1) naturally follows from these observations.

5. CONCLUSION

In this paper, a novel approach named PL-LEAF is proposed to learning from partial label examples. Different from existing strategies, PL-LEAF aims to disambiguate the candidate label set by manipulating useful information in the feature space. Specifically, PL-LEAF generates normalized labeling confidence vectors based on manifold relationships among training examples, and then induces the predictive model based on multi-output regression analysis. Comparative studies across comprehensive partial label data sets clearly verify the effectiveness of the proposed approach.

For PL-LEAF, an important future work is to investigate ways to perform manifold structure discovery and labeling confidence generation simultaneously. Secondly, it is worth studying whether there are better techniques to exploit the generated labeling confidence vectors, such as fitting probabilistic models [10]. Thirdly, it is also interesting to explore other ways to fulfill the feature-aware disambiguation strategy.

Acknowledgements

The authors wish to thank the anonymous reviewers for their constructive comments and suggestions. This work was supported by the National Science Foundation of China (61222309, 61573104, 61473087), the Natural Science Foundation of Jiangsu Province (BK20141340), the MOE Program for New Century Excellent Talents in University (NCET-13-0130), and the Collaborative Innovation Center of Wireless Communications Technology.

6. REFERENCES

[1] J. Amores. Multiple instance classification: Review, taxonomy and comparative study. *Artificial Intelligence*, 201:81–105, 2013.

[2] K. Bache and M. Lichman. UCI machine learning repository. School of Information and Computer Sciences, University of California, Irvine, 2013.

[3] F. Briggs, X. Z. Fern, and R. Raich. Rank-loss support instance machines for MIML instance annotation. In *Proceedings of the 18th ACM SIGKDD International Conference on Knowledge Discovery and Data Mining*, pages 534–542, Beijing, China, 2012.

[4] O. Chapelle, B. Schölkopf, and A. Zien, editors. *Semi-Supervised Learning*. MIT Press, Cambridge, MA, 2006.

[5] Y.-C. Chen, V. M. Patel, R. Chellappa, and P. J. Phillips. Ambiguously labeled learning using dictionaries. *IEEE Transactios on Information Forensics and Security*, 9(12):2076–2088, 2014.

[6] W. Chung, J. Kim, H. Lee, and E. Kim. General dimensional multiple-output support vector regressions and their multiple kernel learning. *IEEE Transactions on Cybernetics*, 45(11):2572–2584, 2015.

[7] T. Cour, B. Sapp, C. Jordan, and B. Taskar. Learning from ambiguously labeled images. In *Proceedings of the IEEE Computer Society Conference on Computer Vision and Pattern Recognition*, pages 919–926, Miami, FL, 2009.

[8] T. Cour, B. Sapp, and B. Taskar. Learning from partial labels. *Journal of Machine Learning Research*, 12(May):1501–1536, 2011.

[9] T. G. Dietterich, R. H. Lathrop, and T. Lozano-Pérez. Solving the multiple-instance problem with axis-parallel rectangles. *Artificial Intelligence*, 89(1-2):31–71, 1997.

[10] X. Geng, C. Yin, and Z.-H. Zhou. Facial age estimation by label distribution learning. *IEEE Transactions on Pattern Analysis and Machine Intelligence*, 35(10):2401–2412, 2013.

[11] E. Gibaja and S. Ventura. A tutorial on multilabel learning. *ACM Computing Surveys*, 47(3):Article 52, 2015.

[12] M. Guillaumin, J. Verbeek, and C. Schmid. Multiple instance metric learning from automatically labeled bags of faces. In K. Daniilidis, P. Maragos, and N. Paragios, editors, *Lecture Notes in Computer Science 6311*, pages 634–647. Springer, Berlin, 2010.

[13] E. Hüllermeier and J. Beringer. Learning from ambiguously labeled examples. *Intelligent Data Analysis*, 10(5):419–439, 2006.

[14] L. Jie and F. Orabona. Learning from candidate labeling sets. In J. Lafferty, C. K. I. Williams, J. Shawe-Taylor, R. S. Zemel, and A. Culotta, editors, *Advances in Neural Information Processing Systems 23*, pages 1504–1512. MIT Press, Cambridge, MA, 2010.

[15] R. Jin and Z. Ghahramani. Learning with multiple labels. In S. Becker, S. Thrun, and K. Obermayer, editors, *Advances in Neural Information Processing Systems 15*, pages 897–904. MIT Press, Cambridge, MA, 2003.

[16] L. Liu and T. Dietterich. A conditional multinomial mixture model for superset label learning. In P. Bartlett, F. C. N. Pereira, C. J. C. Burges, L. Bottou, and K. Q. Weinberger, editors, *Advances in Neural Information Processing Systems 25*, pages 557–565. MIT Press, Cambridge, MA, 2012.

[17] L. Liu and T. Dietterich. Learnability of the superset label learning problem. In *Proceedings of the 31st International Conference on Machine Learning*, pages 1629–1637, Beijing, China, 2014.

[18] N. Nguyen and R. Caruana. Classification with partial labels. In *Proceedings of the 14th ACM SIGKDD International Conference on Knowledge Discovery and Data Mining*, pages 381–389, Las Vegas, NV, 2008.

[19] J. Nocedal and S. Wright. *Numerical Optimization*. Springer, Berlin, 2nd edition, 2006.

[20] G. Panis and A. Lanitis. An overview of research activities in facial age estimation using the FG-NET aging database. In L. Agapito, M. M. Bronstein, and C. Rother, editors, *Lecture Notes in Computer Science 8926*, pages 737–750. Springer, Berlin, 2015.

[21] M. Sánchez-Fernández, M. de Prado-Cumplido, J. Arenas-García, and F. Pérez-Cruz. SVM multiregression for nonliear channel estimation in multiple-input multiple-output systems. *IEEE Transactions on Signal Processing*, 52(8):2298–2307, 2004.

[22] B. Schölkopf and A. J. Smola. *Learning with Kernels: Support Vector Machines, Regularization, Optimization and Beyond*. MIT Press, Camridge, MA, 2001.

[23] D. Tuia, J. Verrelst, L. Alonso, F. Pérez-Cruz, and G. Camps-Valls. Multioutput support vector regression for remote sensing biophysical parameter estimation. *IEEE Geoscience and Remote Sensing Letters*, 8(4):804–808, 2011.

[24] F. Yu and M.-L. Zhang. Maximum margin partial label learning. In *Proceedings of the 7th Asian Conference on Machine Learning*, pages 96–111, Hong Kong, China, 2015.

[25] Z. Zeng, S. Xiao, K. Jia, T.-H. Chan, S. Gao, D. Xu, and Y. Ma. Learning by associating ambiguously labeled images. In *Proceedings of the IEEE Computer Society Conference on Computer Vision and Pattern Recognition*, pages 708–715, Portland, OR, 2013.

[26] M.-L. Zhang. Disambiguation-free partial label learning. In *Proceedings of the 14th SIAM International Conference on Data Mining*, pages 37–45, Philadelphia, PA, 2014.

[27] M.-L. Zhang and F. Yu. Solving the partial label learning problem: An instance-based approach. In *Proceedings of the 24th International Joint Conference on Artificial Intelligence*, pages 4048–4054, Buenos Aires, Argentina, 2015.

[28] M.-L. Zhang and Z.-H. Zhou. A review on multi-label learning algorithms. *IEEE Transactions on Knowledge and Data Engineering*, 26(8):1819–1837, 2014.

[29] X. Zhu and A. B. Goldberg. Introduction to semi-supervised learning. In R. J. Brachman and T. G. Dietterich, editors, *Synthesis Lectures to Artificial Intelligence and Machine Learning*, pages 1–130. Morgan & Claypool Publishers, San Francisco, CA, 2009.

FINAL: Fast Attributed Network Alignment

Si Zhang
Arizona State University
szhan172@asu.edu

Hanghang Tong
Arizona State University
hanghang.tong@asu.edu

ABSTRACT

Multiple networks naturally appear in numerous high-impact applications. Network alignment (i.e., finding the node correspondence across different networks) is often the very first step for many data mining tasks. Most, if not all, of the existing alignment methods are solely based on the *topology* of the underlying networks. Nonetheless, many real networks often have rich attribute information on nodes and/or edges. In this paper, we propose a family of algorithms (FINAL) to align *attributed* networks. The key idea is to leverage the node/edge attribute information to guide (topology-based) alignment process. We formulate this problem from an optimization perspective based on the alignment consistency principle, and develop effective and scalable algorithms to solve it. Our experiments on real networks show that (1) by leveraging the attribute information, our algorithms can significantly improve the alignment accuracy (i.e., up to a 30% improvement over the existing methods); (2) compared with the exact solution, our proposed fast alignment algorithm leads to a more than 10× speed-up, while preserving a 95% accuracy; and (3) our on-query alignment method scales *linearly*, with an around 90% ranking accuracy compared with our exact full alignment method and a near real-time response time.

Categories and Subject Descriptors

H.2.8 [**Database Management**]: Database Applications—*Data Mining*

Keywords

Attributed network alignment; Alignment consistency; On-query alignment

1. INTRODUCTION

Multiple networks naturally appear in many high-impact application domains, ranging from computer vision, bioinformatics, web mining, chemistry to social network analysis. More often than not, network alignment (i.e., to find node correspondence across different networks) is virtually the very first step for any data mining task in these applications. For example, by linking users from different social network sites, we could recommend the products from one site (e.g., `eBay`) to the users from another site (e.g., `Facebook`) [29]. In bioinformatics, integrating different tissue-specific protein-protein interaction (PPI) networks has led to a significant improvement for candidate gene prioritization [16].

Despite the extensive research on network alignment (see Section 6 for a review), most, if not all, of those work focus on inferring the node correspondence *solely* based on the *topology*. For instance, *IsoRank* [21] propagates pairwise topology similarities in the product graph. *NetAlign* utilizes max-product belief propagation based on the network topology [2]. *BigAlign* and *UniAlign* [11] aim to infer the soft alignment based on the assumption that the adjacency matrix of one network is a noisy permutation of another network. A fundamental assumption behind these existing methods is the *topology consistency*. That is, the same node has a consistent connectivity structure across different networks (e.g., connecting to the same or similar set of the neighbors). However, such an assumption could be easily violated in some applications. For example, a user might be very active on one social network site (e.g., `Facebook`), but behaves more quietly on another site (e.g., `LinkedIn`) [11]; the same gene might exhibit dramatically different behaviors across different tissue-specific PPI network [16]. In these cases, the topology-based methods could lead to sub-optimal or even misleading alignment results.

At the same time, many real networks often have rich accompanying attributes on the nodes and/or edges (e.g., demographic information of the users, the communication types between different users), which might provide a complementary solution to address the node topology consistency assumption violation. Nonetheless, it remains a daunting task to align such attributed networks. To be specific, the following questions have largely remained open. First (*Q1. Formulation*), it is not clear how to assimilate node/edge attribute information into the topology-based network alignment formulation. For instance, many topology-based alignment approaches can often be formulated from the optimization perspective, yet it is unknown what its attributed counterpart is. Second (*Q2. Algorithms*), the optimization problem behind the topology-based network alignment is often non-convex or even NP-hard. Introducing attributes into the alignment process could only further complicate the corresponding optimization problem. How can we develop an effective solver for the attributed network alignment, with a similar or comparable time complexity to its topology-only counterpart? Third (*Q3. Scalable Computation*), how can we scale up the attributed network align-

KDD '16, August 13-17, 2016, San Francisco, CA, USA

DOI: http://dx.doi.org/10.1145/2939672.2939766

ment process by taking advantage of some intrinsic properties (e.g., low-rank) of real networks? For some applications (e.g., cross-network search), we might be interested in finding similar nodes across different networks (e.g., to find similar users on `LinkedIn` for a given user on `Facebook`). How can we further speed up the computation for such an *on-query attributed network alignment* process, without solving the full alignment problem?

In this paper, we address the attributed network alignment problem, aiming to answer all these questions. The main contributions of this paper are as follows:

1. **Formulation.** We formulate the attributed network alignment from the optimization perspective. The key idea behind the proposed formulation is to leverage the node/edge attribute information to guide (topology-based) alignment process based on the *alignment consistency* principle. As a side product, our formulation helps reveal the quantitative relationships between the (attributed) network alignment problem and several other network mining problems (e.g., graph kernel, node proximity).
2. **Algorithms and Analysis.** We propose a family of algorithms FINAL to solve the attributed network alignment problem. Our analysis shows that the proposed FINAL algorithms are both effective and efficient - they converge to the global optima with a complexity that is comparable to the topology-only counterpart.
3. **Computations.** We further develop (1) an approximate algorithm FINAL-N+ to solve the full attributed network alignment problem, which reduces the time complexity from $O(mn)$ to $O(n^2)$ (where m and n are number of edges and nodes in the network, respectively); and (2) a *linear* algorithm to solve the on-query attributed network alignment, which achieves a good quality-speed trade-off.
4. **Evaluations.** We perform extensive experiments to validate the effectiveness and the efficiency of the proposed algorithms. Our experimental evaluations demonstrate that (1) our FINAL algorithms significantly improve the alignment accuracy by up to 30% over the existing methods; (2) the proposed FINAL-N+ algorithm leads to a more than 10× speed-up, while preserving a 95% accuracy compared with the exact method; and (3) our on-query alignment method scales *linearly*, with an around 90% ranking accuracy compared with the exact full alignment method and a near real-time response time.

The rest of the paper is organized as follows. Section 2 defines the attributed network alignment problem and the on-query attributed network alignment problem. Section 3 presents the proposed optimization formulation of FINAL and its solutions. Section 4 proposes two speed-up methods for approximate full alignment and on-query alignment. Section 5 presents the experimental results. Related work and conclusion are given in Section 6 and Section 7.

2. PROBLEM DEFINITIONS

Table 1 summarizes the main symbols and notations used throughout the paper. We use bold uppercase letters for matrices (e.g., $\mathbf{A}$), bold lowercase letters for vectors (e.g., $\mathbf{s}$), and lowercase letters (e.g., α) for scalars. For matrix indexing, we use a convention similar to Matlab's syntax as follows. We use $\mathbf{A}(i,j)$ to denote the entry at the intersection of the i-th row and j-th column of matrix $\mathbf{A}$, $\mathbf{A}(i,:)$ to denote the i-th row of $\mathbf{A}$ and $\mathbf{A}(:,j)$ to denote the j-th column of $\mathbf{A}$. We denote the transpose of a matrix by the superscript T (e.g., $\mathbf{A}^T$ is the transpose of $\mathbf{A}$). We use $\sim$ on top to denote the symmetric normalization of a matrix (e.g., $\tilde{\mathbf{A}} = \mathbf{D}^{-1/2}\mathbf{A}\mathbf{D}^{-1/2}$, where $\mathbf{D}$ is the degree matrix of $\mathbf{A}$). The vectorization of a matrix (in the column order) is denoted by vec(.), and the resulting vector is denoted by the corresponding bold lowercase letter (e.g., $\mathbf{a} = \text{vec}(\mathbf{A})$).

Table 1: Symbols and Notation

Symbols	Definition
$\mathcal{G} = \{\mathbf{A}, \mathbf{N}, \mathbf{E}\}$	an attributed network
$\mathbf{A}$	the adjacency matrix of the network
$\mathbf{N}$	the node attribute matrix of the network
$\mathbf{E}$	the edge attribute matrix of the network
n_1, n_2	# of nodes in $\mathcal{G}_1$ and $\mathcal{G}_2$
m_1, m_2	# of edges in $\mathcal{G}_1$ and $\mathcal{G}_2$
K, L	# of the node and edge labels
a, b	node/edge indices of $\mathcal{G}_1$
x, y	node/edge indices of $\mathcal{G}_2$
v, w	node-pair indices of the vectorized alignment $\mathbf{s} = \text{vec}(\mathbf{S})$
k, l	node/edge label indices
$\mathbf{I}, \mathbf{1}$	an identity matrix and a vector of 1s, respectively
$\mathbf{H}$	$n_2 \times n_1$ prior alignment preference
$\mathbf{S}$	$n_2 \times n_1$ alignment matrix
r, p	reduced ranks
α	the parameter, $0 < \alpha < 1$
$\mathbf{a} = \text{vec}(\mathbf{A})$	vectorize a matrix $\mathbf{A}$ in column order
$\mathbf{Q} = \text{mat}(\mathbf{q}, n_2, n_1)$	reshape vector $\mathbf{q}$ into a $n_2 \times n_1$ matrix in column order
$\tilde{\mathbf{A}}$	symmetrically normalize matrix $\mathbf{A}$
$\mathbf{D} = \text{diag}(\mathbf{d})$	diagonalize a vector $\mathbf{d}$
$\otimes$	Kronecker product
$\odot$	element-wise matrix product

We represent an attributed network by a triplet: $\mathcal{G} = \{\mathbf{A}, \mathbf{N}, \mathbf{E}\}$, where (1) $\mathbf{A}$ is the adjacency matrix, and (2) $\mathbf{N}$ and $\mathbf{E}$ are the node attribute matrix and the edge attribute matrix, respectively[1]. The attribute of node-a corresponds to the value of $\mathbf{N}(a,a)$, and $\mathbf{E}(a,b)$ describes the edge attribute of the edge between node-a and node-b. For a given node attribute value k, we define $\mathbf{N}^k$ as a diagonal matrix with the same size as $\mathbf{N}$, where $\mathbf{N}^k(a,a) = 1$ if node-a has the attribute value k and $\mathbf{N}^k(a,a) = 0$ otherwise. For a given edge attribute value l, we define $\mathbf{E}^l$ as a matrix of the same size with $\mathbf{E}$, where $\mathbf{E}^l(a,b) = 1$ if edge (a,b) has the attribute value l and $\mathbf{E}^l(a,b) = 0$ otherwise.

Figure 1 presents an illustrative example. We can see from Figure 1(a), the set of nodes (2, 3, 4 and 5) from the first network share the exact same topology with another set of nodes (2′, 3′, 4′ and 5′). The topology alone would be inadequate to differentiate these two sets. On the other hand, we can see that (1) 2, 2′, 5 and 5′ share the same node attribute value; (2) 3, 3′, 4 and 4′ share the same node attribute value; and (3) the two edges incident to 3 share the same edge attribute value with those incident to 4′. These node/edge attributes could provide vital information to establish the accurate node-level alignment (i.e., 2 aligns to 5′, 5 aligns to 2′, 3 aligns to 4′ and 4 aligns to 3′). This is exactly what this paper aims to address. Formally, the attributed network alignment problem is defined as follows.

PROBLEM 1. ATTRIBUTED NETWORK ALIGNMENT.
Given: *(1) two attributed networks* $\mathcal{G}_1 = \{\mathbf{A}_1, \mathbf{N}_1, \mathbf{E}_1\}$

[1] In this paper, we use 'graph' and 'network' interchangeably, and '(categorical) attribute' and 'label' interchangeably.

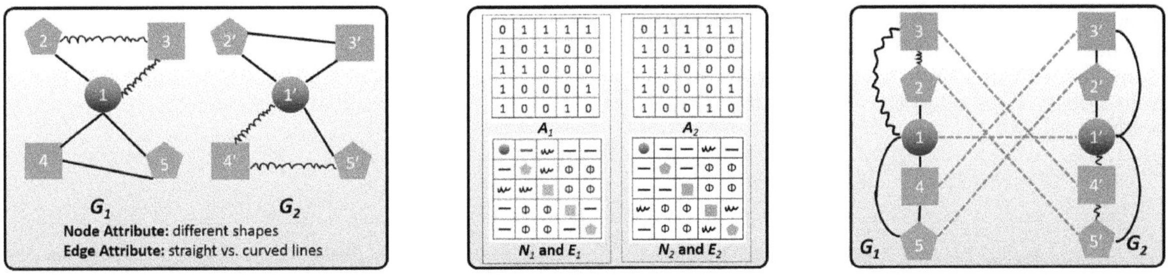

(a) Input Attributed Networks. (b) Matrix Representation. (c) Alignment Output.

Figure 1: An illustrative example of the attributed network alignment problem. (a): two input attributed networks. (b): the matrix representation for attributed networks, where the upper matrices represent the adjacency matrices, and the bottom matrices represent the node attribute (the diagonal positions) and the edge attribute (the off-diagonal entries) matrices. (c): the desired alignment output (denoted by the red dashed lines).

and $\mathcal{G}_2 = \{\mathbf{A}_2, \mathbf{N}_2, \mathbf{E}_2\}$ *with* n_1 *and* n_2 *nodes respectively, (2 - optional) a prior alignment preference* $\mathbf{H}$.

Output: *the* $n_2 \times n_1$ *alignment/similarity matrix* $\mathbf{S}$, *where* $\mathbf{S}(x, a)$ *represents the alignment/similarity between node-a in* $\mathcal{G}_1$ *and node-x in* $\mathcal{G}_2$.

In the above definition, we have an optional input, to encode the prior knowledge of pairwise alignment preference $\mathbf{H}$, which is an $n_2 \times n_1$ matrix. An entry in $\mathbf{H}$ reflects our prior knowledge of the likelihood to align two corresponding nodes across the two input networks. When such prior knowledge is absent, we set all entries of $\mathbf{H}$ equal, i.e., a uniform distribution. Without loss of generality, we assume that $\mathbf{A}_1$ and $\mathbf{A}_2$ share a comparable size, i.e., $O(n_1) = O(n_2) = O(n)$ and $O(m_1) = O(m_2) = O(m)$. This will also help simplify the complexity analysis in the next two sections.

Notice that the alignment matrix $\mathbf{S}$ in Problem 1 is essentially a *cross-network node similarity* matrix. In some applications, we might be interested in finding a small number of similar nodes in one network w.r.t a query node from the other network. For instance, we might want to find the top-10 most similar `LinkedIn` users for a given `Facebook` user. We could first solve Problem 1 and then return the corresponding row or column in the alignment matrix $\mathbf{S}$, which might be computationally too costly as well as unnecessary. Having this in mind, we further define the on-query attributed network alignment problem as follows:

PROBLEM 2. ON-QUERY ATTRIBUTED NETWORK ALIGNMENT.

Given: *(1) two attributed networks* $\mathcal{G}_1 = \{\mathbf{A}_1, \mathbf{N}_1, \mathbf{E}_1\}$ *and* $\mathcal{G}_2 = \{\mathbf{A}_2, \mathbf{N}_2, \mathbf{E}_2\}$, *(2 -optional) a prior alignment preference* $\mathbf{H}$, *(3) a query node-a in* $\mathcal{G}_1$.

Output: *an* $n_2 \times 1$ *vector* $\mathbf{s}_a$ *measuring similarities between the query node-a in* $\mathcal{G}_1$ *and all the nodes in* $\mathcal{G}_2$ *efficiently.*

3. TOPOLOGY MEETS ATTRIBUTES

In this section, we present our solutions for Problem 1. We start by formulating Problem 1 as a regularized optimization problem, and then propose effective algorithms to solve it, followed by some theoretic analysis.

3.1 FINAL: Optimization Formulation

The key idea behind our proposed formulation lies in the *alignment consistency* principle, which basically says that the alignments between two pairs of nodes across the two input networks should be consistent if these two pairs of nodes themselves are "similar/consistent" with each other. Let us elaborate this using the following example. In Figure 2, we are given two pairs of nodes: (1) node-a in $\mathcal{G}_1$ and node-x in $\mathcal{G}_2$; and (2) node-b in $\mathcal{G}_1$ and node-y in $\mathcal{G}_2$. By the *alignment consistency* principle, we require the alignment between a and x, and that between b and y to be consistent (i.e., small $\|\mathbf{S}(x, a) - \mathbf{S}(y, b)\|$), if all of the following conditions hold, including

- C1 *Topology Consistency.* a and b are close neighbors in $\mathcal{G}_1$ (i.e., large $\mathbf{A}_1(a, b)$), and x, y are also close neighbors in $\mathcal{G}_2$ (i.e., large $\mathbf{A}_2(x, y)$);
- C2 *Node Attribute Consistency.* a and x share the same node attribute value, and so do b and y;
- C3 *Edge Attribute Consistency.* Edge (a, b) and (x, y) share the same edge attribute value.

The intuition behind the *alignment consistency* principle is as follows. If we already know that node-a is aligned to node-x (i.e., large $\mathbf{S}(x, a)$), then their close neighbors (e.g., b and y) with same node attribute value should have a high chance to be aligned with each other (i.e., large $\mathbf{S}(y, b)$), where we say that b and y are close neighbors of a and y respectively if they are connected by the same edge attribute value, with large edge weights (i.e., large $\mathbf{A}_1(a, b)$ and $\mathbf{A}_2(x, y)$). This naturally leads to the following objective function which we wish to minimize in terms of the alignment matrix $\mathbf{S}$:

$$J_1(\mathbf{S}) = \sum_{a,b,x,y} \left[\frac{\mathbf{S}(x, a)}{\sqrt{f(x, a)}} - \frac{\mathbf{S}(y, b)}{\sqrt{f(y, b)}}\right]^2 \underbrace{\mathbf{A}_1(a, b)\mathbf{A}_2(x, y)}_{\text{C1: Topology Consistency}}$$
$$\times \underbrace{\mathbb{1}(\mathbf{N}_1(a, a) = \mathbf{N}_2(x, x))\mathbb{1}(\mathbf{N}_1(b, b) = \mathbf{N}_2(y, y))}_{\text{C2: Node Attribute Consistency}}$$
$$\times \underbrace{\mathbb{1}(\mathbf{E}_1(a, b) = \mathbf{E}_2(x, y))}_{\text{C3: Edge Attribute Consistency}} \quad (1)$$

where (1) $a, b = 1, ..., n_1$, and $x, y = 1, ..., n_2$; (2) $\mathbb{1}(\cdot)$ is the indicator function, which takes 1 if the condition inside the parenthesis is true and zero otherwise; and (3) $f(\cdot)$ is a node-pair normalization function that is defined as

$$f(x, a) = \begin{cases} \sum_{b,y} \mathbb{1}(\mathbf{E}_1(a, b) = \mathbf{E}_2(x, y))\mathbf{A}_1(a, b) & \text{if } \mathbf{N}_1(a, a) = \mathbf{N}_2(x, x) \\ \quad \times \mathbf{A}_2(x, y)\mathbb{1}(\mathbf{N}_1(b, b) = \mathbf{N}_2(y, y)) & \\ 1 & \text{otherwise} \end{cases} \quad (2)$$

The function $f(x, a)$ measures how many (weighted) neighbor-pairs a and x have that (1) share the same node attribute value between themselves (e.g., b and y), and (2) connect to a and x via the same edge attribute value, respectively.

Notice that the indicator function $\mathbb{1}(\cdot)$ reflects whether the two input nodes/edges share the same attribute value[2], we factorize it as follows

$$\mathbb{1}(\mathbf{N}_1(a,a) = \mathbf{N}_2(x,x)) = \sum_{k=1}^{K} \mathbf{N}_1^k(a,a)\mathbf{N}_2^k(x,x)$$
$$\mathbb{1}(\mathbf{E}_1(a,b) = \mathbf{E}_2(x,y)) = \sum_{l=1}^{L} \mathbf{E}_1^l(a,b)\mathbf{E}_2^l(x,y) \tag{3}$$

Substitute Eq. (3) into Eq. (1) and Eq. (2), we have

$$J_1(\mathbf{S}) = \sum_{a,b,x,y} [\frac{\mathbf{S}(x,a)}{\sqrt{f(x,a)}} - \frac{\mathbf{S}(y,b)}{\sqrt{f(y,b)}}]^2 \sum_{k,k'=1}^{K} \sum_{l=1}^{L} \mathbf{N}_1^k(a,a)\mathbf{N}_2^k(x,x)$$
$$\times \mathbf{A}_1(a,b)\mathbf{E}_1^l(a,b)\mathbf{A}_2(x,y)\mathbf{E}_2^l(x,y)\mathbf{N}_1^{k'}(b,b)\mathbf{N}_2^{k'}(y,y) \tag{4}$$

and for nodes with the same attribute value, i.e., $\mathbf{N}_1(a,a) = \mathbf{N}_2(x,x)$

$$f(x,a) = \sum_{b,y}\sum_{k=1}^{K}\sum_{l=1}^{L} \mathbf{N}_1^k(b,b)\mathbf{N}_2^k(y,y)\mathbf{E}_1^l(a,b)\mathbf{E}_2^l(x,y)$$
$$\times \mathbf{A}_1(a,b)\mathbf{A}_2(x,y) \tag{5}$$

Next, we present an equivalent matrix form of J_1, which is more convenient for the following algorithm description and the theoretic proof. By vectorizing the alignment matrix $\mathbf{S}$ (i.e., $\mathbf{s} = \text{vec}(\mathbf{S})$), and with the notation of element-wise product and Kronecker product, Eq. (1) can be re-written as

$$J_1(\mathbf{s}) = \sum_{v,w} [\frac{\mathbf{s}(v)}{\sqrt{\mathbf{D}(v,v)}} - \frac{\mathbf{s}(w)}{\sqrt{\mathbf{D}(w,w)}}]^2 \mathbf{W}(v,w)$$
$$= \mathbf{s}^T(\mathbf{I} - \widetilde{\mathbf{W}})\mathbf{s} \tag{6}$$

where $v = n_2(a-1)+x$, $w = n_2(b-1)+y$, $\mathbf{N} = \sum_{k=1}^{K} \mathbf{N}_1^k \otimes \mathbf{N}_2^k$, $\mathbf{E} = \sum_{l=1}^{L} \mathbf{E}_1^l \otimes \mathbf{E}_2^l$ and $\mathbf{W} = \mathbf{N}[\mathbf{E} \odot (\mathbf{A}_1 \otimes \mathbf{A}_2)]\mathbf{N}$. $\widetilde{\mathbf{W}} = \mathbf{D}^{-\frac{1}{2}}\mathbf{W}\mathbf{D}^{-\frac{1}{2}}$ is the symmetric normalized matrix of $\mathbf{W}$. The diagonal degree matrix $\mathbf{D}$ of $\mathbf{W}$ is defined as

$$\mathbf{D} = \text{diag}(\sum_{k,k'=1}^{K}\sum_{l=1}^{L}(\mathbf{N}_1^k(\mathbf{E}_1^l \odot \mathbf{A}_1)\mathbf{N}_1^{k'}\mathbf{1}) \otimes (\mathbf{N}_2^k(\mathbf{E}_2^l \odot \mathbf{A}_2)\mathbf{N}_2^{k'}\mathbf{1}))$$

Note that some diagonal elements in $\mathbf{D}$ could be zero (e.g., $\mathbf{D}(v,v) = 0$). For such elements, we define the corresponding $\mathbf{D}(v,v)^{-1/2} \triangleq 0$.

Putting everything together, our proposed optimization problem can be stated as follows.

$$\text{argmin}_{\mathbf{s}}\ J(\mathbf{s}) = \alpha\mathbf{s}^T(\mathbf{I} - \widetilde{\mathbf{W}})\mathbf{s} + (1-\alpha) \parallel \mathbf{s} - \mathbf{h} \parallel_F^2 \tag{7}$$

where $\|\cdot\|_F$ denotes the Frobenius norm, and α is the regularization parameter. Notice that compared with J_1, we have an additional regularization term $\|\mathbf{s} - \mathbf{h}\|_F^2$ to reflect the prior alignment preference, where $\mathbf{h} = \text{vec}(\mathbf{H})$. When no such prior information is given, we set $\mathbf{h}$ as a uniform column vector. From the optimization perspective, this additional regularization term would also help prevent a trivial solution of J_1 with a zero alignment matrix $\mathbf{S}$.

3.2 FINAL: Optimization Algorithms

The objective function in Eq. (7) is essentially a quadratic function w.r.t. $\mathbf{s}$. We seek to find its fixed-point solution by setting its derivative to be zero

$$\frac{\partial J(\mathbf{s})}{\partial \mathbf{s}} = 2(\mathbf{I} - \alpha\widetilde{\mathbf{W}})\mathbf{s} + 2(1-\alpha)\mathbf{h} = 0$$

[2]We remark that by replacing the indicator function $\mathbb{1}(\cdot)$ by an attribute value similarity function, the proposed formulation can be naturally generalized to handle the numerical attributes on nodes and/or edges.

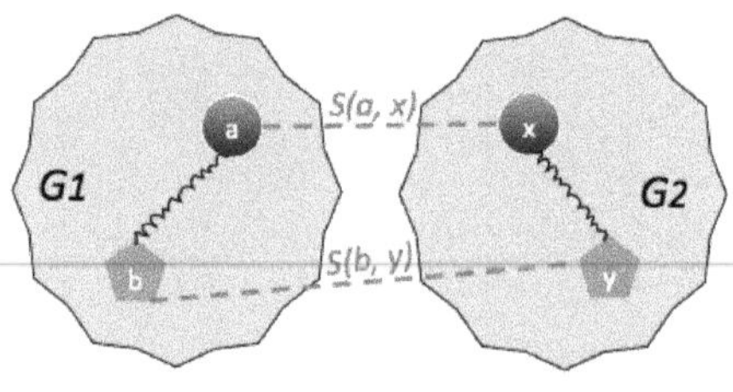

Figure 2: An illustration of alignment consistency.

which leads to the following equation

$$\mathbf{s} = \alpha\widetilde{\mathbf{W}}\mathbf{s} + (1-\alpha)\mathbf{h}$$
$$= \alpha\mathbf{D}^{-\frac{1}{2}}\mathbf{N}(\mathbf{E} \odot (\mathbf{A}_1 \otimes \mathbf{A}_2))\mathbf{N}\mathbf{D}^{-\frac{1}{2}}\mathbf{s} + (1-\alpha)\mathbf{h} \tag{8}$$

We could directly develop an iterative algorithm based on Eq. (8). However, such an iterative procedure involves the Kronecker product between $\mathbf{A}_1$ and $\mathbf{A}_2$ whose time complexity is $O(m^2)$.

In order to develop a more efficient algorithm, thanks to a key Kronecker product property (i.e., $\text{vec}(\mathbf{ABC}) = (\mathbf{C}^T \otimes \mathbf{A})\text{vec}(\mathbf{B})$), we re-write Eq. (8) as follows

$$\mathbf{s} = \alpha\mathbf{D}^{-\frac{1}{2}}\mathbf{N}\text{vec}(\sum_{l=1}^{L}(\mathbf{E}_2^l \odot \mathbf{A}_2)\mathbf{Q}(\mathbf{E}_1^l \odot \mathbf{A}_1)^T) + (1-\alpha)\mathbf{h} \tag{9}$$

where $\mathbf{Q}$ is an $n_2 \times n_1$ matrix reshaped by $\mathbf{q} = \mathbf{N}\mathbf{D}^{-\frac{1}{2}}\mathbf{s}$ in column order, i.e., $\mathbf{Q} = \text{mat}(\mathbf{q}, n_2, n_1)$. We can show that Eq. (8) and Eq. (9) are equivalent with each other (detailed proofs are omitted due to space). The advantage of Eq. (9) is that it avoids the expensive matrix Kronecker product, which leads to a more efficient iterative algorithm FINAL-NE (summarized in Algorithm 1).

Algorithm 1 FINAL-NE: Attributed Network Alignment.

Input: (1) $\mathcal{G}_1 = \{\mathbf{A}_1, \mathbf{N}_1, \mathbf{E}_1\}$ and $\mathcal{G}_2 = \{\mathbf{A}_2, \mathbf{N}_2, \mathbf{E}_2\}$, (2) optional prior alignment preference $\mathbf{H}$, (3) the regularization parameter α, and (4) the maximum iteration number $t_{\max}$.

Output: the alignment matrix $\mathbf{S}$ between $\mathcal{G}_1$ and $\mathcal{G}_2$.

1: Construct degree matrix $\mathbf{D}$ and node attribute matrix $\mathbf{N}$;
2: Initiate the alignment $\mathbf{s} = \mathbf{h} = \text{vec}(\mathbf{H})$, and $t = 1$;
3: **while** $t \le t_{\max}$ **do**
4: Compute vector $\mathbf{q} = \mathbf{N}\mathbf{D}^{-\frac{1}{2}}\mathbf{s}$;
5: Reshape $\mathbf{q}$ as $\mathbf{Q} = \text{mat}(\mathbf{q}, n_2, n_1)$;
6: Initiate an $n_2 \times n_1$ zero matrix $\mathbf{T}$;
7: **for** $l = 1 \to L$ **do**
8: Update $\mathbf{T} \leftarrow \mathbf{T} + (\mathbf{E}_2^l \odot \mathbf{A}_2)\mathbf{Q}(\mathbf{E}_1^l \odot \mathbf{A}_1)^T$;
9: **end for**
10: Update $\mathbf{s} \leftarrow \alpha\mathbf{D}^{-\frac{1}{2}}\mathbf{N}\text{vec}(\mathbf{T}) + (1-\alpha)\mathbf{h}$;
11: Set $t \leftarrow t + 1$;
12: **end while**
13: Reshape $\mathbf{s}$ to $\mathbf{S} = \text{mat}(\mathbf{s}, n_2, n_1)$.

Variants of FINAL-NE.

Our proposed FINAL-NE algorithm assumes that the input networks have both node and edge attributes. It is worth pointing out that it also works when the node and/or the edge attribute information is missing.

First, when only node attributes are available, we can set all entries in the edge attribute matrix $\mathbf{E}$ to 1 where an edge indeed exists. The intuition is that we treat all the edges in the networks to share a common edge attribute value. In this case, the fixed-point solution in Eq. (8) becomes

$$\mathbf{s} = \alpha\mathbf{D}_N^{-\frac{1}{2}}\mathbf{W}_N\mathbf{D}_N^{-\frac{1}{2}}\mathbf{s} + (1-\alpha)\mathbf{h}$$
$$= \alpha\mathbf{D}_N^{-\frac{1}{2}}\mathbf{N}(\mathbf{A}_1 \otimes \mathbf{A}_2)\mathbf{N}\mathbf{D}_N^{-\frac{1}{2}}\mathbf{s} + (1-\alpha)\mathbf{h} \tag{10}$$

where $\mathbf{D}_N = \text{diag}(\sum_{k,k'=1}^{K}(\mathbf{N}_1^k\mathbf{A}_1\mathbf{N}_1^{k'}\mathbf{1}) \otimes (\mathbf{N}_2^k\mathbf{A}_2\mathbf{N}_2^{k'}\mathbf{1}))$ denotes the degree matrix of $\mathbf{W}_N$. Similar to Eq. (9), we can use the vectorization operator to accelerate the computation. We refer to this variant as FINAL-N, and omit the detailed algorithm description due to space.

Second, when only the edge attributes are available, we treat all nodes to share one common node attribute value by setting $\mathbf{N}$ to be an identity matrix. In this case, the fixed-point solution in Eq. (8) becomes

$$\mathbf{s} = \alpha \mathbf{D}_E^{-\frac{1}{2}}(\mathbf{E} \odot (\mathbf{A}_1 \otimes \mathbf{A}_2))\mathbf{D}_E^{-\frac{1}{2}}\mathbf{s} + (1-\alpha)\mathbf{h} \quad (11)$$

where $\mathbf{D}_E = \text{diag}(\sum_{l=1}^{L}[(\mathbf{E}_1^l \odot \mathbf{A}_1)\mathbf{1}] \otimes [(\mathbf{E}_2^l \odot \mathbf{A}_2)\mathbf{1}])$. Again, we omit the detailed algorithm description due to space, and refer to this variant as FINAL-E.

Finally, if neither the node attributes nor the edge attributes are available, Eq. (8) degenerates to

$$\mathbf{s} = \alpha \mathbf{D}_U^{-\frac{1}{2}}(\mathbf{A}_1 \otimes \mathbf{A}_2)\mathbf{D}_U^{-\frac{1}{2}}\mathbf{s} + (1-\alpha)\mathbf{h} \quad (12)$$

where $\mathbf{D}_U = \mathbf{D}_1 \otimes \mathbf{D}_2$, $\mathbf{D}_1$ and $\mathbf{D}_2$ are the degree matrix of $\mathbf{A}_1$ and $\mathbf{A}_2$ respectively. This variant is referred to as FINAL-P.

3.3 Proofs and Analysis

In this subsection, we first analyze the *convergency*, the *optimality* and the *complexity* of our FINAL algorithms. Due to the space limit, we only present the results for the most general case (i.e., FINAL-NE). Then we analyze the relationships between FINAL and several classic graph mining problems.

We start with Theorem 1, which says the proposed FINAL-NE algorithm converges to the global optimal solution of Eq. (7).

THEOREM 1. ***Convergency and Optimality of* FINAL-NE.** *Algorithm 1 converges to the closed-form global minimal solution of $J(\mathbf{s})$: $\mathbf{s} = (1-\alpha)(\mathbf{I} - \alpha\widetilde{\mathbf{W}})^{-1}\mathbf{h}$.*

PROOF. To prove the convergency of Eq. (8), we first show the eigenvalues of $\alpha\widetilde{\mathbf{W}}$ are in $(-1, 1)$. Since $\widetilde{\mathbf{W}}$ is similar to the stochastic matrix $\mathbf{W}\mathbf{D}^{-1} = \mathbf{D}^{\frac{1}{2}}\widetilde{\mathbf{W}}\mathbf{D}^{-\frac{1}{2}}$, the eigenvalues of $\widetilde{\mathbf{W}}$ are within $[-1, 1]$. Since $0 < \alpha < 1$, the eigenvalues of $\alpha\widetilde{\mathbf{W}}$ are in $(-1, 1)$.

We denote the alignment vector $\mathbf{s}$ in the t-th iteration as $\mathbf{s}^{(t)}$. We have that

$$\mathbf{s}^{(t)} = \alpha^t \widetilde{\mathbf{W}}^t \mathbf{h} + (1-\alpha)\sum_{i=0}^{t-1} \alpha^i \widetilde{\mathbf{W}}^i \mathbf{h}$$

Since the eigenvalues of $\alpha\widetilde{\mathbf{W}}$ are in $(-1, 1)$, we have that $\lim_{t\to+\infty} \alpha^t \widetilde{\mathbf{W}}^t = 0$ and $\lim_{t\to+\infty} \sum_{i=0}^{t-1} \alpha^i \widetilde{W}^i = (\mathbf{I} - \alpha\widetilde{\mathbf{W}})^{-1}$. Putting these together, we have that

$$\mathbf{s} = \lim_{t\to+\infty} \mathbf{s}^{(t)} = (1-\alpha)(\mathbf{I} - \alpha\widetilde{\mathbf{W}})^{-1}\mathbf{h}$$

Next, we prove that the above result is indeed the global minimal solution of the objective function defined in Eq. (7). We prove this by showing that $J(\mathbf{s})$ in Eq. (7) is convex. To see this, we have that the Hessian matrix of Eq. (7) is $\nabla^2 J = 2(\mathbf{I} - \alpha\widetilde{\mathbf{W}})$. By the Weyl's inequality theorem [4], all eigenvalues of $2(\mathbf{I} - \alpha\widetilde{\mathbf{W}})$ are greater than 0. In other words, we have that $\nabla^2 J$ is positive definite. Therefore, the objective function defined in Eq. (7) is convex, and its fixed-point solution by Algorithm 1 corresponds to its global minimal solution, which completes the proof. □

The time and space complexity of Algorithm 1 are summarized in Lemma 1. Notice that such a complexity is comparable to the complexity of topology-alone network alignment methods, such as *IsoRank* [21]. In the next section, we will propose an even faster algorithm.

LEMMA 1. ***Complexity of* FINAL-NE.** *The time complexity of Algorithm 1 is $O(Lmnt_{max} + LK^2n^2)$, and its space complexity is $O(n^2)$. Here, n and m are the orders of the number of nodes and edges of the input networks, respectively; K, L denote the number of unique node and edge attributes respectively, and t_{max} is the maximum iteration number.*

PROOF. Omitted for space. □

Finally, we analyze the relationships between the proposed FINAL algorithms and several classic graph mining problems. Due to the space limit, we omit the detailed proofs and summarize the major findings as follows.

A - FINAL *vs. Node Proximity.*

An important (single) network mining task is the node proximity, i.e., to measure the proximity/similarity between two nodes on the *same* network. By ignoring the node/edge attributes and setting $\mathbf{A}_1 = \mathbf{A}_2$, our FINAL algorithms, up to a scaling operation $\mathbf{D}^{1/2}$, degenerate to *SimRank* [12] - a prevalent choice for node proximity. Our FINAL algorithms are also closely related to another popular node proximity method, *random walk with restart* [24]. That is, Eq. (8) can be viewed as random walk with restart on the *attributed Kronecker graph* with $\mathbf{h}$ being the starting vector. Note that neither the standard *SimRank* nor *random walk with restart* considers the node or edge attribute information.

B - FINAL *vs. Graph Kernel.*

The alignment result $\mathbf{s}$ by our FINAL algorithms is closely related to the random walk based graph kernel [25]. To be specific, if $k(\mathcal{G}_1, \mathcal{G}_2)$ is the random walk graph kernel between the two input graphs and $\mathbf{p}$ is the stopping vector, we can show that $k(\mathcal{G}_1, \mathcal{G}_2) = \mathbf{p}^T\mathbf{s}$. This intuitively makes sense, as we can view the graph kernel/similarity as the weighted aggregation (by the stopping vector $\mathbf{p}$) over the pairwise cross-network node similarities (encoded by the alignment vector $\mathbf{s}$). We also remark that in the original random walk graph kernel [25], it mainly focuses on the edge attribute information.

C - FINAL *vs. Existing Network Alignment Methods.*

If we ignore all the node and edge attribute information, our FINAL-P algorithm is equivalent to *IsoRank* [21] by scaling the alignment result and alignment preference by $\mathbf{D}^{1/2}$. We would like to point out that such a scaling operation is important to ensure the convergence of the iterative procedure. Recall that the key idea behind our optimization formulation is the *alignment consistency*. When the attribute information is absent, the *alignment consistency* principle is closely related to the concept of "squares" behind *NetAlign* algorithm [2]. Like most, if not all of the, existing network alignment algorithms, the node or the edge attribute information is ignored in *IsoRank* and *NetAlign*.

We remark that these findings are important in the following two aspects. First, they help establish a quantitative relationship between several, seemingly unrelated graph mining problems, which might in turn help better understand these existing graph mining problems. Second, these findings also have an important algorithmic implication. Take *SimRank* as an example, it was originally designed for plain graphs (i.e., without attributes), and was formulated from random walk perspective and it is not clear what the algorithm tries to optimize. By setting $\mathcal{G}_1 = \mathcal{G}_2$ and ignoring the attribute information, our objective function in Eq. (7)

provides a natural way to interpret *SimRank* from an optimization perspective. By setting $\mathcal{G}_1 = \mathcal{G}_2$ alone (i.e., keeping the attribute information), our FINAL algorithms can be directly used to measure node proximity on an *attributed* network. Finally, our upcoming FINAL ON-QUERY algorithm also naturally provides an efficient way (i.e., with a linear time complexity) for *on-query SimRank* with or without attribute information (i.e., finding the similarity between a given query node and all the remaining nodes in the same network).

4. SPEED-UP COMPUTATION

In this section, we address the computational issue. To be specific, we will focus on two scenarios. First, to solve Problem 1, our proposed FINAL algorithms in Section 3 have a time complexity of $O(mn)$, where we have dropped the lower order terms. We will propose an effective approximate algorithm that reduces the time complexity to $O(n^2)$. Second, for Problem 2, solving the full alignment problem not only still requires $O(n^2)$ time, but also is unnecessary, as we essentially only need a column or a row from the alignment matrix $\mathbf{S}$. To address this issue, we will propose an effective algorithm for Problem 2 with a *linear* time complexity. For presentation clarity, we restrict ourselves to the case where there is only node attribute information, although our proposed strategies can be naturally applied to the more general case where we have both node and edge attributes.

4.1 Speed-up FINAL-N

According to Theorem 1, the alignment vector $\mathbf{s}$ in FINAL-N converges to its closed-form solution as follows.

$$\begin{aligned}\mathbf{s} &= (1-\alpha)(\mathbf{I}-\alpha\widetilde{\mathbf{W}}_N)^{-1}\mathbf{h} \\ &= (1-\alpha)(\mathbf{I}-\alpha\mathbf{D}_N^{-\frac{1}{2}}\mathbf{N}(\mathbf{A}_1\otimes\mathbf{A}_2)\mathbf{N}\mathbf{D}_N^{-\frac{1}{2}})^{-1}\mathbf{h}\end{aligned} \tag{13}$$

The key idea to speed up FINAL-N is to efficiently approximate such a closed-form solution. To be specific, we first approximate the two adjacency matrices by top-r eigenvalue decomposition: $\mathbf{A}_1 = \mathbf{U}_1\mathbf{\Lambda}_1\mathbf{U}_1^T$ and $\mathbf{A}_2 = \mathbf{U}_2\mathbf{\Lambda}_2\mathbf{U}_2^T$. Then the rank-$r$ approximation of $\mathbf{W}_N$ can be defined as follows

$$\begin{aligned}\hat{\mathbf{W}}_N &= \mathbf{N}[(\mathbf{U}_1\mathbf{\Lambda}_1\mathbf{U}_1^T)\otimes(\mathbf{U}_2\mathbf{\Lambda}_2\mathbf{U}_2^T)]\mathbf{N} \\ &= \mathbf{N}(\mathbf{U}_1\otimes\mathbf{U}_2)(\mathbf{\Lambda}_1\otimes\mathbf{\Lambda}_2)(\mathbf{U}_1^T\otimes\mathbf{U}_2^T)\mathbf{N}\end{aligned} \tag{14}$$

Substitute Eq. (14) into Eq. (13), we can approximate the alignment vector $\mathbf{s}$ as

$$\begin{aligned}\mathbf{s} \approx& (1-\alpha)[\mathbf{I}-\alpha\mathbf{D}_N^{-\frac{1}{2}}\mathbf{N}\mathbf{U}(\mathbf{\Lambda}_1\otimes\mathbf{\Lambda}_2)\mathbf{U}^T\mathbf{N}\mathbf{D}_N^{-\frac{1}{2}}]^{-1}\mathbf{h} \\ =& (1-\alpha)(\mathbf{I}+\alpha\mathbf{D}_N^{-\frac{1}{2}}\mathbf{N}\mathbf{U}\mathbf{\Lambda}\mathbf{U}^T\mathbf{N}\mathbf{D}_N^{-\frac{1}{2}})\mathbf{h}\end{aligned} \tag{15}$$

where $\mathbf{U} = \mathbf{U}_1\otimes\mathbf{U}_2$, and $\mathbf{\Lambda}$ is an $r^2\times r^2$ matrix computed by Sherman-Morrison Lemma [18]: $\mathbf{\Lambda} = [(\mathbf{\Lambda}_1\otimes\mathbf{\Lambda}_2)^{-1} - \alpha(\mathbf{U}_1^T\otimes\mathbf{U}_2^T)\mathbf{N}\mathbf{D}_N^{-1}\mathbf{N}(\mathbf{U}_1\otimes\mathbf{U}_2)]^{-1}$.

Based on Eq. (15), our proposed FINAL-N+ algorithm is summarized in Algorithm 2. The time complexity of FINAL-N+ is summarized in Lemma 2. Notice that we often have $r \ll n$, $m \ll n^2$ and $K \ll n$. Therefore, compared with FINAL-N, FINAL-N+ is much more efficient in time complexity.

LEMMA 2. ***Time Complexity of* FINAL-N+.** FINAL-N+ *takes* $O(n^2r^4+Kn^2)$ *in time ,where* n *is the order of the number of nodes,* r *is the rank of eigenvalue decomposition and* K *is the number of node attributes.*

PROOF. Omitted for space. □

Algorithm 2 FINAL-N+: Low-Rank Approximation of FINAL-N.

Input: (1) $\mathcal{G}_1 = \{\mathbf{A}_1, \mathbf{N}_1\}$ and $\mathcal{G}_2 = \{\mathbf{A}_2, \mathbf{N}_2\}$, (2) optional prior alignment preference $\mathbf{H}$, (3) the regularization parameter α, and (4) the rank of eigenvalue decomposition r.
Output: approximate alignment matrix $\mathbf{S}$ between $\mathcal{G}_1$ and $\mathcal{G}_2$.

Construct degree matrix $\mathbf{D}_N$ and node attribute matrix $\mathbf{N}$;
Construct alignment preference vector $\mathbf{h} = \text{vec}(\mathbf{H})$;
Eigenvalue decomposition $\mathbf{U}_1\mathbf{\Lambda}_1\mathbf{U}_1^T \leftarrow \mathbf{A}_1$, $\mathbf{U}_2\mathbf{\Lambda}_2\mathbf{U}_2^T \leftarrow \mathbf{A}_2$
Compute $\mathbf{U} = \mathbf{U}_1\otimes\mathbf{U}_2$;
Compute $\mathbf{\Lambda} = [(\mathbf{\Lambda}_1\otimes\mathbf{\Lambda}_2)^{-1} - \alpha\mathbf{U}^T\mathbf{N}\mathbf{D}_N^{-1}\mathbf{N}\mathbf{U}]^{-1}$;
Compute $\mathbf{s}$ by Eq. (15);
Reshape vector $\mathbf{s}$ to $\mathbf{S} = \text{mat}(\mathbf{s}, n_2, n_1)$.

4.2 Proposed Solution for Problem 2

In Problem 2, we want to find an $n_2\times 1$ vector $\mathbf{s}_a$ which measures the similarities between the query node-a in $\mathcal{G}_1$ and all the n_2 nodes in $\mathcal{G}_2$ (i.e., cross-network similarity search). It is easy to see that $\mathbf{s}_a$ is essentially the a-th column of the alignment matrix $\mathbf{S}$, or equivalently a certain portion of the alignment vector $\mathbf{s}$, i.e.,

$$\mathbf{s}_a = \mathbf{S}(:,a) = \mathbf{s}(v:w)$$

where $v = (a-1)n_2+1$ and $w = an_2$.

However, if we call FINAL-N or FINAL-N+ to find $\mathbf{S}$ (or $\mathbf{s}$) and then return the ranking vector $\mathbf{s}_a$, it would take at least $O(n^2)$ time. Next, we propose an approximate algorithm (FINAL ON-QUERY) which directly finds the ranking vector $\mathbf{s}_a$ in *linear* time, without solving the full alignment matrix $\mathbf{S}$.

We first relax the degree matrix $\mathbf{D}_N$ to its upper-bound $\hat{\mathbf{D}}_N = \mathbf{D}_1\otimes\mathbf{D}_2$. There are two reasons for taking such a relaxation. First, it would take $O(n^2)$ time to compute the $\mathbf{D}_N$ matrix directly. On the other hand, $\hat{\mathbf{D}}_N$ can be indirectly expressed by the Kronecker product between $\mathbf{D}_1$ and $\mathbf{D}_2$, each of which only takes $O(m)$ time. Second, since $\hat{\mathbf{D}}_N$ is an upper-bound of the $\mathbf{D}_N$ matrix, such a relaxation will not affect the convergence of FINAL-N. By this relaxation, the fixed-point solution in Eq. (10) can be approximated as

$$\mathbf{s} = \alpha\mathbf{N}\hat{\mathbf{D}}_N^{-\frac{1}{2}}(\mathbf{A}_1\otimes\mathbf{A}_2)\hat{\mathbf{D}}_N^{-\frac{1}{2}}\mathbf{N}\mathbf{s} + (1-\alpha)\mathbf{h} \tag{16}$$

where $\hat{\mathbf{D}}_N = \mathbf{D}_1\otimes\mathbf{D}_2$.

By a similar procedure in FINAL-N+, the low-rank approximate solution for $\mathbf{s}$ is

$$\mathbf{s} \approx (1-\alpha)\mathbf{h} + \alpha(1-\alpha)\hat{\mathbf{D}}_N^{-\frac{1}{2}}\mathbf{N}\mathbf{U}\hat{\mathbf{\Lambda}}\mathbf{U}^T\mathbf{N}\hat{\mathbf{D}}_N^{-\frac{1}{2}}\mathbf{h} \tag{17}$$

where $\hat{\mathbf{\Lambda}} = [(\mathbf{\Lambda}_1\otimes\mathbf{\Lambda}_2)^{-1} - \alpha\mathbf{U}^T\mathbf{N}\hat{\mathbf{D}}_N^{-1}\mathbf{U}]^{-1}$.

Since both $\hat{\mathbf{D}}_N$ and $\mathbf{N}$ are diagonal matrices, the ranking vector for node-a is

$$\begin{aligned}\mathbf{s}_a =& (1-\alpha)[\mathbf{h}(v:w) + \alpha[\hat{\mathbf{D}}_N^{-\frac{1}{2}}\mathbf{N}\mathbf{U}\hat{\mathbf{\Lambda}}\mathbf{U}^T\mathbf{N}\hat{\mathbf{D}}_N^{-\frac{1}{2}}\mathbf{h}](v:w)] \\ =& (1-\alpha)[\mathbf{H}(:,a) + \alpha[(\mathbf{D}_1(a,a)\mathbf{D}_2)^{-\frac{1}{2}}(\sum_{k=1}^{K}\mathbf{N}_1^k(a,a)\mathbf{N}_2^k)] \\ &\times[\underbrace{(\mathbf{U}_1(a,:)\otimes\mathbf{U}_2)}_{O(nr^2)}\underbrace{\hat{\mathbf{\Lambda}}}_{O(n^2r^4+r^6)}\underbrace{\mathbf{U}^T\mathbf{N}\hat{\mathbf{D}}_N^{-\frac{1}{2}}\mathbf{h}]}_{O(n^2r^2)}\end{aligned} \tag{18}$$

Notice that Eq. (18) still needs $O(n^2)$ time due to the last two terms. We reduce the time cost for computing $\mathbf{g} = \mathbf{U}^T\mathbf{N}\hat{\mathbf{D}}_N^{-\frac{1}{2}}\mathbf{h}$ as follows. First, we take a rank-p singular value decomposition (SVD) on $\mathbf{H}$, i.e., $\mathbf{H} = \sum_{i=1}^{p}\sigma_i\mathbf{u}_i\mathbf{v}_i^T$. Then, by the vectorization operator, we have that

$$\mathbf{g} = \sum_{i=1}^{p}\sum_{k=1}^{K} \underbrace{\sigma_i(\overbrace{\mathbf{U}_1^T\mathbf{N}_1^k\mathbf{D}_1^{-\frac{1}{2}}\mathbf{v}_i}^{O(nr)}) \otimes (\overbrace{\mathbf{U}_2^T\mathbf{N}_2^k\mathbf{D}_2^{-\frac{1}{2}}\mathbf{u}_i}^{O(nr)})}_{O(nr+r^2)=O(nr)} \tag{19}$$

We can see that the time cost for Eq. (19) is reduced to $O(pKrn)$, which is linear w.r.t the number of nodes n.

We reduce the time cost for computing $\hat{\mathbf{\Lambda}}$ by reformulating as follows, whose time complexity is $O(Knr^2 + Kr^4 + r^6)$

$$\hat{\mathbf{\Lambda}} = [\underbrace{(\mathbf{\Lambda}_2 \otimes \mathbf{\Lambda}_1)^{-1}}_{O(r^2)} - \alpha \underbrace{\sum_{k=1}^{K} (\overbrace{\mathbf{U}_1^T\mathbf{N}_1^k\mathbf{D}_1^{-1}\mathbf{U}_1}^{O(nr^2)}) \otimes (\overbrace{\mathbf{U}_2^T\mathbf{N}_2^k\mathbf{D}_2^{-1}\mathbf{U}_2}^{O(nr^2)})}_{O(nr^2+r^4)}]^{-1} \tag{20}$$

Putting everything together, the ranking vector of node-a now becomes

$$\mathbf{s}_a = (1-\alpha)\mathbf{H}(:,a) + \alpha(1-\alpha)[\overbrace{(\mathbf{D}_1(a,a)\mathbf{D}_2)^{-\frac{1}{2}}}^{O(n)} \overbrace{\sum_{k=1}^{K}\mathbf{N}_1^k(a,a)\mathbf{N}_2^k}^{O(Kn)}]$$
$$\times [\underbrace{(\mathbf{U}_1(a,:) \otimes \mathbf{U}_2)}_{O(nr^2)} \underbrace{\hat{\mathbf{\Lambda}}}_{O(Knr^2+Kr^4+r^6)} \underbrace{\mathbf{g}}_{O(pKnr)}] \tag{21}$$

Based on Eq. (21), our proposed FINAL On-Query algorithm is summarized in Algorithm 3. The time complexity of FINAL On-Query is summarized in Lemma 3. Notice that we often have $r, p \ll n$, $m_H \ll m \ll n^2$ and $K \ll n$. FINAL On-Query has a *linear* time complexity w.r.t the size of the input network, which is much more scalable than both FINAL-N and FINAL-N+.

Algorithm 3 FINAL On-Query: Approximate On-Query Algorithm for Node Attributed Networks.

Input: (1) $\mathcal{G}_1 = \{\mathbf{A}_1, \mathbf{N}_1\}$ and $\mathcal{G}_2 = \{\mathbf{A}_2, \mathbf{N}_2\}$, (2) optional prior alignment preference $\mathbf{H}$, (3) the regularization parameter α, (4) the rank of eigenvalue decomposition r, and (5) the rank of SVD for $\mathbf{H}$ p.
Output: approximate ranking vector $\mathbf{s}_a$ between node-a in $\mathcal{G}_1$ and all nodes in $\mathcal{G}_2$.

Pre-Compute:
1: Compute degree matrices $\mathbf{D}_1$ and $\mathbf{D}_2$;
2: Compute $\mathbf{D}_a = \mathbf{D}_1(a,a)\mathbf{D}_2$, and $\mathbf{N}_a = \sum_{k=1}^{K}\mathbf{N}_1^k(a,a)\mathbf{N}_2^k$;
3: Rank r eigenvalue decomposition $\mathbf{U}_1\mathbf{\Lambda}_1\mathbf{U}_1^T \leftarrow \mathbf{A}_1$;
4: Rank r eigenvalue decomposition $\mathbf{U}_2\mathbf{\Lambda}_2\mathbf{U}_2^T \leftarrow \mathbf{A}_2$;
5: Rank p singular value decomposition $\sum_{i=1}^{p}\sigma_i\mathbf{u}_i\mathbf{v}_i^T \leftarrow \mathbf{H}$;
6: Compute $\mathbf{g}$ by Eq. (19);
7: Compute $\hat{\mathbf{\Lambda}}$ by Eq. (20);

Online-Query:
8: Compute $\mathbf{s}_a$ by Eq. (21).

Lemma 3. **Time complexity of FINAL On-Query.** *The time complexity of* FINAL On-Query *is* $O(r^6 + mr + nr^2 + m_H p + np^2 + Knr^2 + Kr^4 + pKnr)$*. where* n, m *are the orders of the number of nodes and edges respectively,* r, p *is the rank of eigenvalue decomposition and SVD, respectively,* K *is the number of node attributes and* m_H *is the number of non-zero elements in* $\mathbf{H}$.

Proof. Omitted for brevity. □

5. EXPERIMENTAL RESULTS

In this section, we present the experimental results and analysis of our proposed algorithms FINAL. The experiments are designed to evaluate the following aspects:

- *Effectiveness*: How accurate are our algorithms for aligning attributed networks?
- *Efficiency*: How fast are our proposed algorithms?

5.1 Experimental Setup

Datasets. We evaluate our proposed algorithms on six real-world attributed networks.

- *DBLP Co-Authorship Network:* This dataset contains 42,252 nodes and 210,320 edges [19]. Each author has a feature vector which represents the number of publications of the author in each of 29 major conferences.
- *Douban:* This Douban dataset was collected in 2010 and contains $50k$ users and $5M$ edges [31]. Each user has rich information, such as the location and offline event participation. Each edge has an attribute representing whether two users are contacts or friends.
- *Flickr:* This dataset was collected in 2014 and consists of 215,495 users and 9,114,557 friend relationships. Users have detailed profile information, such as gender, hometown and occupation, each of which can be treated as the node attributes [30].
- *Lastfm:* This dataset was collected in 2013 and contains 136,420 users and 1,685,524 following relationships [30]. A detailed profile of some users is also provided, including gender, age and location, etc.
- *Myspace:* This dataset contains 854,498 users and 6 ,489,736 relationships. The profile of users includes gender, hometown and religion, etc. [30].
- *ArnetMiner:* ArnetMiner dataset consists of the information up to year 2013. The whole dataset has 1,053,188 nodes and 3,916,907 undirected edges [30].

Based on these datasets, we construct the following five alignment scenarios for evaluations.

S1. DBLP vs. DBLP. We extract a subnetwork with 9,143 users/nodes from the original dataset, together with their publications in each conference. We randomly permute this subnetwork with noisy edge weights and treat it as the second network. We choose the most active conference of a given author as the node attribute, i.e., the conference with the most publications. We construct the prior alignment preference $\mathbf{H}$ based on the node degree similarity. For this scenario, the prior alignment matrix $\mathbf{H}$ alone leads to a very poor alignment result, with only 0.6% one-to-one alignment accuracy.

S2. Douban Online vs. Douban Offline. We construct an alignment scenario for *Douban* dataset in the same way as [31]. We construct the offline network according to users' co-occurrence in social gatherings. We treat people as (1) 'contacts' of each other if they participate in the same offline events more than ten times but less than twenty times, and (2) 'friends' if they co-participate in more than twenty social gatherings. The constructed offline network has 1,118 users and we extract a subnetwork with 3,906 nodes from the provided online network that contains all these offline users. We treat the location of a user as the node attribute, and 'contacts'/'friends' as the edge attribute. We use the degree similarity to construct the prior alignment preference $\mathbf{H}$. The prior alignment matrix $\mathbf{H}$ alone leads to 7.07% one-to-one alignment accuracy.

S3. Flickr vs. Lastfm. We have the partial ground-truth alignment for these two datasets [30]. We extract the subnetworks from them that contain the given ground-truth

nodes. The two subnetworks have 12,974 nodes and 15,436 nodes, respectively. We consider the gender of a user as node attribute. For those users with the missing information of gender, we treat them as 'unknown'. Same as [30], we sort nodes by their pagerank scores and label 1% highest nodes as 'opinion leaders', the next 10% nodes as 'middle class' and remaining nodes as 'ordinary users'. Edges are attributed by the level of people they connect to (e.g., leader with leader). We use the username similarity as the prior alignment preference by the Jaro-Winkler distance [6]. The username similarity alone can correctly align 61.50% users.
S4. Flickr-Myspace. Same as *S3*, we have the partial ground-truth alignment for these two datasets. We extract two subnetworks that contain these ground-truth nodes. The subnetwork of *Flickr* has 6,714 nodes and the subnetwork of *Myspace* has 10,733 nodes. We use the same way as *S3* for node attributes, edge attributes and the prior alignment preference. The username similarity alone can correctly align 61.80% users.
S5. ArnetMiner-ArnetMiner. We use the same method as *S1* to construct the alignment scenario as well as the prior alignment preference. This scenario contains the largest networks, and therefore is used for efficiency evaluations.
Comparison Methods. For the proposed FINAL algorithms, we test the following variants, including (1) FINAL-NE with both node and edge attributes; (2) FINAL-N with node attributes only; (3) FINAL-E with edge attributes only; (4) FINAL-N+, a low-rank based approximate algorithm of FINAL-N. We compare them with the following existing network alignment algorithms including (1) *IsoRank* [21], (2) *NetAlign* [2], (3) *UniAlign* [11] and (4) *Klau's Algorithm* [2, 9].
Machines and Repeatability. All experiments are performed on a Windows machine with four 3.6GHz Intel Cores and 32G RAM. The algorithms are programmed with MATLAB using a single thread. We intend to release the source code as well as all the non-proprietary datasets after the paper is published.

5.2 Effectiveness Analysis

We first evaluate the impact of the permutation noise on the alignment accuracy. We use a heuristic greedy matching algorithm [10] as a post-processing step on the similarity matrix to obtain the one-to-one alignments between the two input networks, and then compute the alignment accuracy with respect to the ground-truth. The results are summarized in Figure 3. We have the following observations. First, all of our proposed methods outperform the three existing alignment methods. Specifically, FINAL-NE achieves a 20%-30% improvement in terms of the alignment accuracy over the existing methods (i.e., *IsoRank*, *NetAlign* and *UniAlign*). Second, FINAL-N and FINAL-E both outperform the existing methods, yet are not as good as FINAL-NE, suggesting that node attributes and edge attributes might be complementary in terms of improving the alignment accuracy. Third, the alignment accuracy of FINAL-N+ is very close to its exact counterpart FINAL-N (i.e., with a 95% accuracy compared with FINAL-N). Fourth, by jointly considering the attributes and the topology of networks, our methods are more resilient to the permutation noise. Finally, for the two networks whose topologies are dramatically different from each other (e.g., Douban online-offline networks), the accuracy gap between FINAL-N+ and

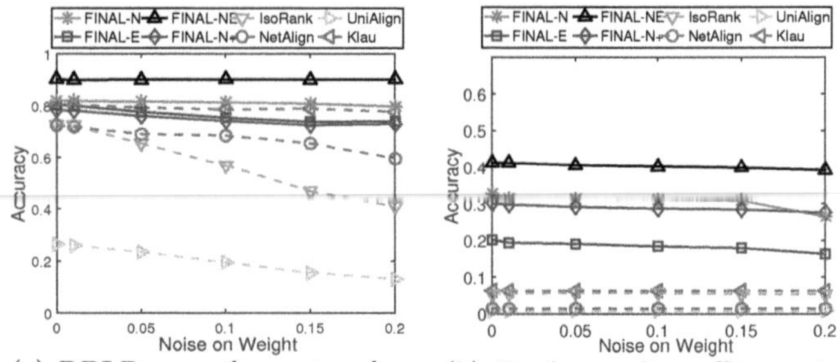

(a) DBLP co-author networks. ($\alpha = 0.8$). (b) Douban online-offline networks. ($\alpha = 0.6$).

Figure 3: (Higher is better.) Alignment accuracy vs. the noise level in networks. ($t_{\max} = 30$, $r = 5$).

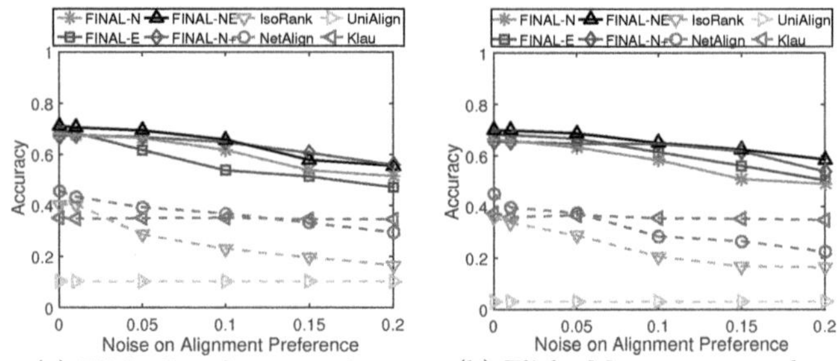

(a) Flickr-Lastfm networks. (b) Flickr-Myspace networks.

Figure 4: (Higher is better.) Alignment accuracy vs. the noise level in **H**. ($\alpha = 0.3$, $t_{\max} = 30$, $r = 5$).

the existing methods is even bigger (Figure 3(b)). This is because in this case, the topology information alone (*IsoRank*, *NetAlign* and *Klau*) could actually mislead the alignment process.

Second, we evaluate the impact of the noise in the prior alignment preference (i.e., **H**) on the alignment results, which is summarized in Figure 4. As expected, a higher noise in **H** has more negative impacts on the alignment accuracy for most of the methods. Nonetheless, our FINAL algorithms still consistently outperform all other four existing methods across different noise levels.

5.3 Efficiency Analysis

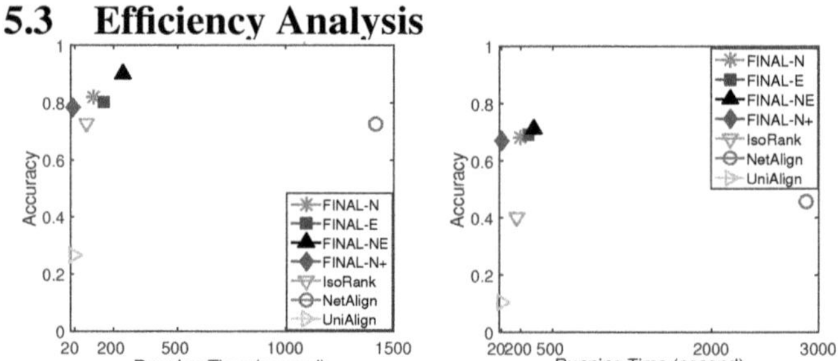

(a) DBLP co-author networks. $\alpha = 0.8$. (b) Flickr-Lastfm networks. $\alpha = 0.3$.

Figure 5: Balance between the accuracy and the speed. $t_{\max} = 30$, $r = 5$.

Quality-Speed Trade-off. We first evaluate how different methods balance the alignment accuracy and the running time for the full network alignment problem (i.e., Problem 1). The results are summarized in Figure 5. As we can see, the running time of our proposed exact methods (e.g., FINAL-N, FINAL-E) is only slightly higher than its topology-alone counterpart (i.e., *IsoRank*), and in the meanwhile, they all achieve a 10%-20% accuracy improvement. FINAL-N+ and *UniAlign* are the fastest, yet the proposed FINAL-N+ produces a much higher alignment

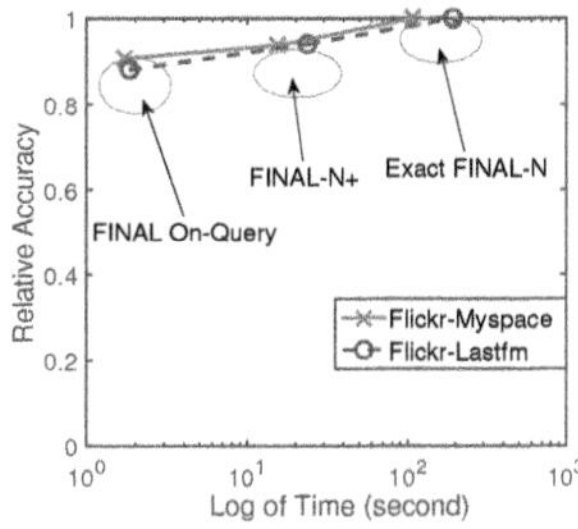

Figure 6: Alignment accuracy vs. running time for on-query alignment.

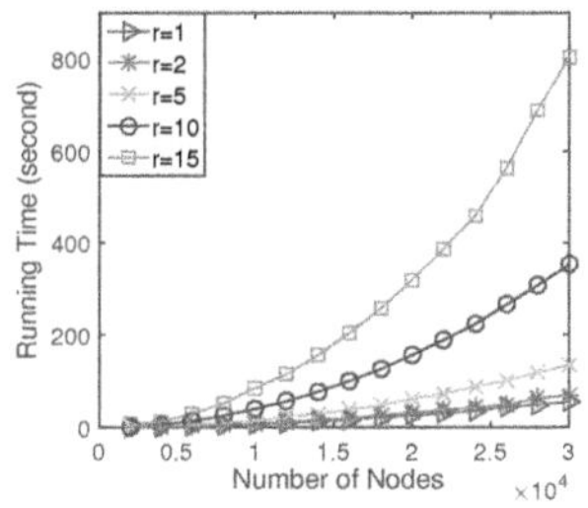

Figure 7: Scalability of FINAL-N+.

accuracy. *NetAlign* takes the longest running time as it involves a time-consuming, greedy/max-weight matching process during each iteration. We do not show the balance of *Klau's Algorithm* because the running time is usually several hours which is not comparable with other methods. Overall, FINAL-N+ achieves the best trade-off between the alignment accuracy and the running time.

Second, we evaluate the quality-speed trade-off for on-query alignment problem (i.e., Problem 2). Here, we treat the top-10 ranking results by FINAL-N as the ground-truth, and compare the average ranking accuracy of 500 random nodes with two proposed approximate algorithms (FINAL-N+ and FINAL ON-QUERY). The results are summarized in Figure 6. We can see, that (1) FINAL-N+ preserves a 95% ranking accuracy, with a more than 10× speedup over FINAL-N, (2) FINAL ON-QUERY preserves an about 90% ranking accuracy, and it is 100× faster than the exact FINAL-N.

Scalability. We first evaluate the scalability of FINAL-N+, which is summarized in Figure 7. We can see that the running time is quadratic w.r.t the number of nodes of the input networks, which is consistent with the time complexity results in Lemma 2. Second, we evaluate the scalability of FINAL ON-QUERY, for both its pre-compute phase and online-query phase. As we can see from Figure 8, the running time is *linear* w.r.t the number of nodes in both stages, which is consistent with Lemma 3. In addition, the actual online-query time on the entire ArnetMiner data set (with $r = 10$) is less than 1 second, suggesting that the proposed FINAL ON-QUERY method might be well suitable for the real-time query response.

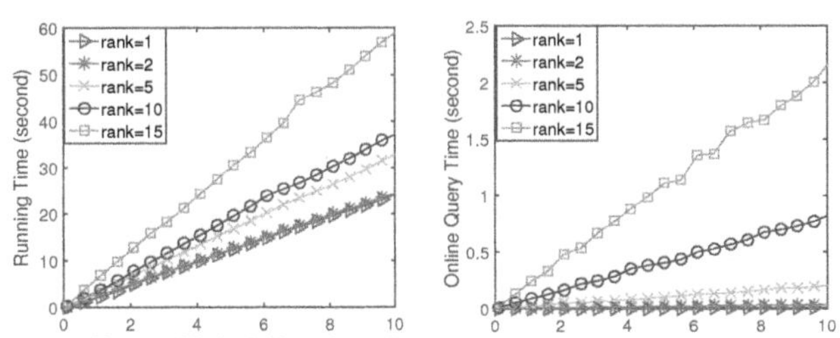

(a) Pre-compute phase. (b) Online-query phase.

Figure 8: Scalability of FINAL ON-QUERY.

6. RELATED WORK

The network alignment has attracted lots of research interests with extensive literatures. It appears in numerous domains, ranging from database schema matching [15], bioinformatics [21, 13, 8], chemistry [22], computer vision [7, 20], to data mining [11, 2].

A classic alignment approach can be attributed to *IsoRank* algorithm [21], which is in turn inspired by PageRank [17]. The original *IsoRank* algorithm propagates the pairwise node similarity in the Kronecker product graph. Several approximate algorithms have been proposed to speed up its computation. Kollias et al. [10] propose an efficient method based on uncoupling and decomposition. *SpaIsoRank* modifies *IsoRank* to maximize the number of "squares" for sparse networks [2]. In addition, *IsoRankN* [13] extends the original *IsoRank* algorithm and uses a similar approach as PageRank-Nibble [1] to align multiple networks.

Bayati et al. [3] propose a maximum weight matching algorithm for graph alignment using the max-product belief propagation [26]. Bradde et al. [5] propose another distributed message-passing algorithm based on belief propagation for protein-protein interaction network alignment. Recently, *NetAlign* [2] is proposed by formulating the network alignment problem as an integer quadratic programing problem to maximize the number of "squares". A near-optimal solution is obtained by finding the maximum a posteriori (MAP) assignment using message-passing approach. *BigAlign* formulates the bipartite network alignment problem and uses the alternating projected gradient descent to solve it [11]. Zhang et al. solve the multiple anonymized network alignment in two steps, i.e., unsupervised anchor link inference and transitive multi-network matching [28].

A related problem is to identify users from multiple social networks (i.e., the cross-site user identification problem). Zafarani et al. identify users by modeling user behavior patterns based on human limitations, exogenous and endogenous factors [27]. Tan et al. [23] propose a subspace learning method, which models user relationship by a hypergraph. Liu et al. propose a method to identify same users by behavior modeling, structure consistency modeling and learning by multi-objective optimization [14]. *COSNET* [30] considers both local the global consistency and uses an energy-based model to find connections among multiple heterogeneous networks.

7. CONCLUSION

In this paper, we study the attributed network alignment problem, including the full alignment version as well as its on-query variant. We propose an optimization-based formulation based on the alignment consistency principle. We propose a family of effective and efficient algorithms to solve the attributed network alignment problem. In detail, we first propose exact algorithms (FINAL) which are proved to converge to the global optima, with a comparable complexity with their topology-alone counterparts. We then propose (1) an approximate alignment algorithm (FINAL-N+) to further reduce the time complexity; and (2) an effective alignment algorithm (FINAL ON-QUERY) to solve the on-query network alignment problem with a *linear* time complexity. We conduct extensive empirical evaluations on real networks, which demonstrate that (1) by assimilating the attribute information during the alignment process, the proposed FINAL algorithms significantly improve the alignment accuracy by up to 30% over the existing methods; (2) the proposed approximate alignment algorithm (FINAL-N+) achieves a good balance between the running time and the alignment accuracy; and (3) the proposed on-query alignment algorithm (FINAL ON-QUERY) (a) preserves an around 90%+ ranking accuracy, (b) scales linearly w.r.t the size of the input networks, and (c) responds in near real time. Future work includes generalizing FINAL algorithms to handle dynamic networks.

8. ACKNOWLEDGEMENTS

This work is partially supported by the National Science Foundation under Grant No. IIS1017415, by DTRA under the grant number HDTRA1-16-0017, by Army Research Office under the contract number W911NF-16-1-0168, by National Institutes of Health under the grant number R01LM 011986, Region II University Transportation Center under the project number 49997-33 25 and a Baidu gift. We would like to sincerely thank Dr. Jie Tang and Dr. Yutao Zhang for their generosity to share the datasets, and anonymous reviewers for their insightful and constructive comments.

9. REFERENCES

[1] R. Andersen, F. Chung, and K. Lang. Local graph partitioning using pagerank vectors. IEEE, 2006.

[2] M. Bayati, M. Gerritsen, D. F. Gleich, A. Saberi, and Y. Wang. Algorithms for large, sparse network alignment problems. IEEE, 2009.

[3] M. Bayati, D. Shah, and M. Sharma. Maximum weight matching via max-product belief propagation. IEEE, 2005.

[4] R. Bhatia. Linear algebra to quantum cohomology: the story of alfred horn's inequalities. *The American Mathematical Monthly*, 108(4):289–318, 2001.

[5] S. Bradde, A. Braunstein, H. Mahmoudi, F. Tria, M. Weigt, and R. Zecchina. Aligning graphs and finding substructures by a cavity approach. *EPL (Europhysics Letters)*, 89(3):37009, 2010.

[6] W. Cohen, P. Ravikumar, and S. Fienberg. A comparison of string metrics for matching names and records. 2003.

[7] D. Conte, P. Foggia, C. Sansone, and M. Vento. Thirty years of graph matching in pattern recognition. *International journal of pattern recognition and artificial intelligence*, 18(03):265–298, 2004.

[8] S. Hashemifar and J. Xu. Hubalign: an accurate and efficient method for global alignment of protein–protein interaction networks. *Bioinformatics*, 30(17):i438–i444, 2014.

[9] G. W. Klau. A new graph-based method for pairwise global network alignment. *BMC bioinformatics*, 10(Suppl 1):S59, 2009.

[10] G. Kollias, S. Mohammadi, and A. Grama. Network similarity decomposition (nsd): A fast and scalable approach to network alignment. *Knowledge and Data Engineering, IEEE Transactions on*, 24(12):2232–2243, 2012.

[11] D. Koutra, H. Tong, and D. Lubensky. Big-align: Fast bipartite graph alignment. In *Data Mining (ICDM), 2013 IEEE 13th International Conference on*, pages 389–398. IEEE, 2013.

[12] C. Li, J. Han, G. He, X. Jin, Y. Sun, Y. Yu, and T. Wu. Fast computation of simrank for static and dynamic information networks. ACM, 2010.

[13] C.-S. Liao, K. Lu, M. Baym, R. Singh, and B. Berger. Isorankn: spectral methods for global alignment of multiple protein networks. *Bioinformatics*, 25(12):i253–i258, 2009.

[14] S. Liu, S. Wang, F. Zhu, J. Zhang, and R. Krishnan. Hydra: Large-scale social identity linkage via heterogeneous behavior modeling. ACM, 2014.

[15] S. Melnik, H. Garcia-Molina, and E. Rahm. Similarity flooding: A versatile graph matching algorithm and its application to schema matching. IEEE, 2002.

[16] J. Ni, H. Tong, W. Fan, and X. Zhang. Inside the atoms: ranking on a network of networks. In *Proceedings of the 20th ACM SIGKDD international conference on Knowledge discovery and data mining*, pages 1356–1365. ACM, 2014.

[17] L. Page, S. Brin, R. Motwani, and T. Winograd. The pagerank citation ranking: bringing order to the web. 1999.

[18] W. W. Piegorsch and G. Casella. Erratum: inverting a sum of matrices. *SIAM review*, 32(3):470, 1990.

[19] A. Prado, M. Plantevit, C. Robardet, and J.-F. Boulicaut. Mining graph topological patterns: Finding covariations among vertex descriptors. *Knowledge and Data Engineering, IEEE Transactions on*, 25(9):2090–2104, 2013.

[20] C. Schellewald and C. Schnörr. Probabilistic subgraph matching based on convex relaxation. Springer, 2005.

[21] R. Singh, J. Xu, and B. Berger. Global alignment of multiple protein interaction networks with application to functional orthology detection. *Proceedings of the National Academy of Sciences*, 105(35):12763–12768, 2008.

[22] A. Smalter, J. Huan, and G. Lushington. Gpm: A graph pattern matching kernel with diffusion for chemical compound classification. IEEE, 2008.

[23] S. Tan, Z. Guan, D. Cai, X. Qin, J. Bu, and C. Chen. Mapping users across networks by manifold alignment on hypergraph. 2014.

[24] H. Tong, C. Faloutsos, and J.-Y. Pan. Fast random walk with restart and its applications. 2006.

[25] S. V. N. Vishwanathan, N. N. Schraudolph, R. Kondor, and K. M. Borgwardt. Graph kernels. *The Journal of Machine Learning Research*, 11:1201–1242, 2010.

[26] J. S. Yedidia, W. T. Freeman, and Y. Weiss. Understanding belief propagation and its generalizations. *Exploring artificial intelligence in the new millennium*, 8:236–239, 2003.

[27] R. Zafarani and H. Liu. Connecting users across social media sites: a behavioral-modeling approach. In *Proceedings of the 19th ACM SIGKDD international conference on Knowledge discovery and data mining*, pages 41–49. ACM, 2013.

[28] J. Zhang and S. Y. Philip. Multiple anonymized social networks alignment. *Network*, 3(3):6, 2015.

[29] Y. Zhang. Browser-oriented universal cross-site recommendation and explanation based on user browsing logs. ACM, 2014.

[30] Y. Zhang, J. Tang, Z. Yang, J. Pei, and P. S. Yu. Cosnet: Connecting heterogeneous social networks with local and global consistency. ACM, 2015.

[31] E. Zhong, W. Fan, J. Wang, L. Xiao, and Y. Li. Comsoc: adaptive transfer of user behaviors over composite social network. ACM, 2012.

Come-and-Go Patterns of Group Evolution: A Dynamic Model

Tianyang Zhang[1], Peng Cui[1], Christos Faloutsos[2], Yunfei Lu[1],
Hao Ye[3], Wenwu Zhu[1], Shiqiang Yang[1]
[1]Tsinghua National Laboratory for Information Science and Technology,
Department of Computer Science and Technology, Tsinghua University, Beijing, China
[2]Computer Science Department, Carnegie Mellon University, PA, USA
[3]Tencent Corporation, Shenzhen, China
zhangty09@foxmail.com, cuip@tsinghua.edu.cn, christos@cs.cmu.edu
luyf12@mails.tsinghua.edu.cn, dariaye@tencent.com, wwzhu@tsinghua.edu.cn, yangshq@tsinghua.edu.cn

ABSTRACT

How do social groups, such as Facebook groups and Wechat groups, dynamically evolve over time? How do people join the social groups, uniformly or with burst? What is the pattern of people quitting from groups? Is there a simple universal model to depict the come-and-go patterns of various groups?

In this paper, we examine temporal evolution patterns of more than 100 thousands social groups with more than 10 million users. We surprisingly find that the evolution patterns of real social groups goes far beyond the classic dynamic models like SI and SIR. For example, we observe both diffusion and non-diffusion mechanism in the group joining process, and power-law decay in group quitting process, rather than exponential decay as expected in SIR model. Therefore we propose a new model COMENGO, a concise yet flexible dynamic model for group evolution. Our model has the following advantages: (a) unification power: it generalizes earlier theoretical models and different joining and quitting mechanisms we find from observation. (b) succinctness and interpretability: it contains only six parameters with clear physical meanings. (c) accuracy: it can capture various kinds of group evolution patterns preciously and the goodness of fit increase by 58% over baseline. (d) usefulness: it can be used in multiple application scenarios such as forecasting and pattern discovery.

CCS Concepts

•**Information systems** → **Data mining;**

Keywords

Group Evolution; Dynamic Model; Temporal Patterns

KDD '16, August 13-17, 2016, San Francisco, CA, USA

© 2016 ACM. ISBN 978-1-4503-4232-2/16/08...$15.00

DOI: http://dx.doi.org/10.1145/2939672.2939795

1. INTRODUCTION

Forming social groups is an inherent human nature and the evolution of social groups is an essential mechanism in society. Understanding how these groups take shape and evolve over time is one of the central building blocks of modeling and understanding various social phenomena such as information spreading [13, 4], social-tie formation [10, 25], and social cooperations and competitions [9, 3]. Furthermore, studying the dynamics of groups also has rich practical use in various application scenarios. For example, the evolution of certain industry association can provide insight into the development trend of the business; the activities of online communities can become the vane of the popularity of new topics; and the detection of abnormal group growth can even help to handle the threat of online terrorist recruitment or find the trace of terrorist organization.

In literature, group evolution is a theme that runs through large parts of social science research [5]. Recently, some computational studies on social groups provide an profound foundation of the mechanism of group growth and also find several features that have significant influence on the group growth process [2, 11]. However, previous works still have some limitations and leave some fundamental problems unsolved.

The first fundamental problem is **how to model the temporal patterns of group evolution.** A comprehensive understanding of group evolution should contain both spatial dimension and temporal dimension. The spatial dimension studies how groups evolve over the underlying network while the temporal dimension studies how groups evolve over time. Several studies have been done in spatial dimension and they have found serval structure features influencing the evolution of group and the mechanism of how groups attract new member through the network [2, 22, 25, 11]. However, such feature based models can not capture the temporal patterns and reveal the inherent mechanism in temporal dimension.

The second fundamental problem is **how to model the quit process of group.** Group evolution process is the resultant of both come and go: a group attracts new members through diffusion or non-diffusion mechanisms [11] and meanwhile, members in the group may also leave the group. Most studies mainly focus on the growth mechanism but ignore the fact that, in most situations, groups also have quit mechanism, for both online and offline groups. Although

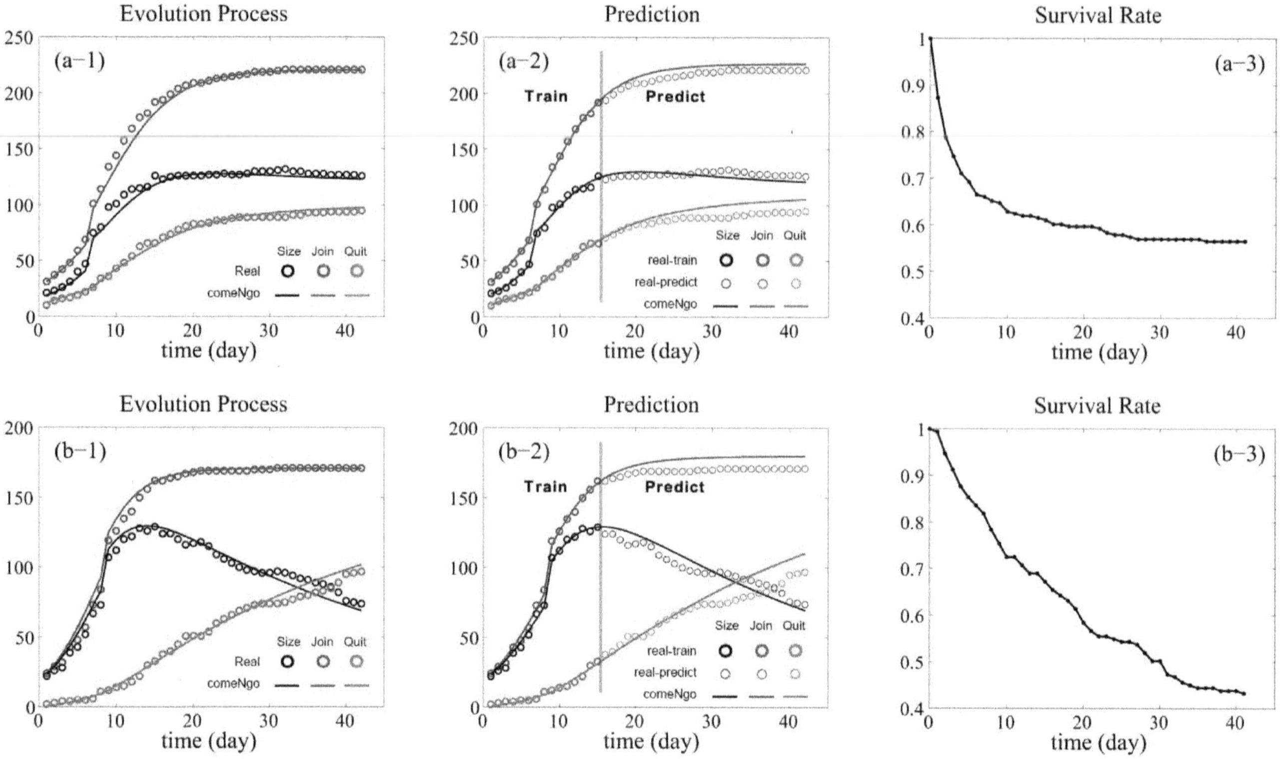

Figure 1: (a-1) and (b-1) The evolution process of two groups and in 42 days, the dots represent real data and the lines are the results of our model. (a-2) and (b-2) The prediction result of our model. We use the data of first 15 days to train the model. (a-3) and (b-3) Survival rate of holding time of these two groups.

some researches find the importance of member mobility in group evolution [7], there is no explicit model for the quit mechanism of groups. Compared to our understanding about how people join groups, how people quit groups remains quite unclear.

In order to solve the two fundamental problems, we analyze a large real dataset with 103,548 groups from Wechat, the largest social communication network in China. Note that this is the first-ever large-scale dataset providing detailed logs of users joining and quiting social groups.. We observe rich complexities in the temporal patterns of group evolution. In fig 1 we showcase the group evolution process of two online groups over a time period of 42 days. From Figure 1.1, we can see different growth patterns with respect to group size of the two groups: one group gradually grows and then stays relatively stable while the other group shows continuous decline after a quick growth. We further look into the joining and quitting processes respectively. In quitting process, we observe different patterns of quit rates in different groups, as shown in Figure 1.3. The resulted holding time (the time interval between join group and quit group) distributions for different groups follows exponential decay (as expected in SIR, only account for 15% of all groups), power-law decay or inbetween. However, there is no published model to deal with the latter two cases, which account for the majority of groups. Moreover, we observe both diffusion and non-diffusion mechanism in joining process, while non-diffusion mechanism is beyond the capability of traditional dynamic models such as SI and SIR. Based on the observations, we propose a unified dynamic model for the group evolution process with temporal data. Our proposed model has the following appealing advantages:

- **Unification power:** It is a general model that includes previous models as special case and also embodies new mechanisms.
- **Succinctness and interpretability:** It uses only six parameters and every parameter has a clear physical meaning.
- **Accuracy:** It can capture the temporal patterns of different groups precisely as shown in fig 1.1. We achieve an improvement of **58%** in goodness of fit in a real dataset with more than 100 thousands groups.
- **Usefulness:** It is useful in multiple application scenarios such as forecasting and pattern discovery. Fig 1.2 is a showcase. With the early stage information of the group evolution process, our model can predict the remained evolution process accurately.

The rest of the paper goes as follows: Section 2 presents the fundamental concepts about dynamic models and Section 3 the proposed model. Section 4 shows our experiment on a large-scale real dataset. We conclude in Section 5.

2. RELATED WORK

With the rapid growth of different kinds of online social network, we have more source and opportunity to study the structure and dynamics of social groups. In recent years, a lot of studies have been done on online group evolution patterns.

As one of the first empirical investigations on online groups, Backstrom, et al. study how structural features influence group formation and evolution in large social networks [2]. They reveal an important mechanism that group grows through the ties its members have to individuals outside the group. This mechanism is similar to the 'word-of-mouth' mechanism in diffusion process [21]. Several studies also focus on the influence of structural properties of groups in various underlying networks such as online games [8], mobile communication network [24, 25], co-authorship network [25, 14] and online social networks [22, 15]. Lin, et al. propose a probabilistic framework to analyze the evolution of community structures on a dynamic network [19]. Kairam, et al. conduct further research to reveal the more complex group evolve mechanism by making a conceptual difference between diffusion and non-diffusion growth in groups [11]. They find that non-diffusion mechanism also plays an important role in group evolution process.

As noted earlier, the previous works provide a profound explanation of how group grows through the network but do not answer the equally fundamental question that how group grows over time. Another limitation is that the do not reveal and model the mechanism of quitting the group. To both utilize the achievements and overcome the limitations of the previous works, we propose a dynamic model that captures the temporal patterns of both join and quit process.

3. PROPOSED METHOD

In this section we present our proposed method and analyze it.

First of all, our model should be a dynamic model that can present both temporal dimension and spatial dimension of group evolution. Besides, our model tries to capture the following behaviours, that we observed from our real data.

- P1: dependence mechanism: power-law holding time distribution in quit process.
- P2: non-diffusion mechanism: impulses in join process

To handle P1, we assume that the recoverability of a node may decay with the holding time exponentially, which is discussed in subsection 3.2. To handle P2, we import external shocks in our model, which is discussed in subsection 3.3.

We describe our model in steps, adding complexity, and we start with preliminaries..

3.1 Preliminaries

Dynamic models are widely used to describe the mechanism of temporal process such as epidemic spreading [1, 27], information diffusion [17, 20, 28], network evolving [16, 6]. In this subsection, we present the fundamental concepts about dynamic model. We start from one of the most basic dynamic models in spreading process: epidemiology models. We consider epidemic models as the baseline because they can capture the 'word-of-mouth' diffusion mechanism and can deal with the quit mechanism.

Susceptible-Infected model. The most basic epidemiology model is 'Susceptible-Infected'(SI) model. Each object/node is in one of two states - Susceptible(S) or Infected(I). Each infected node attempts to infect each of its neighbors independently at a constant rate β, which reflects the strength of the virus. Once infected, each node stays infected forever. The dynamic equation of the basic SI model is:

$$\frac{dI(t)}{dt} = \beta * (N - I(t))I(t) \quad (1)$$

where N is the total amount of obejcts/nodes and we assume that the underlying network is a clique of N, the time t is considered continuous, dI/dt is the derivative, and the initial condition I(0)>0 need to be given.

Susceptible-Infected-Recovered model. Another basic epidemiology model is an extension of SI model called 'Susceptible-Infected-Recovered'(SIR) model [12]. It allows Infected node to get recovered. Each object/node is in one of three states - Susceptible(S), Infected(I) or Recovered(R). The infect process is similar to SI model with a constant infect rate β while each infected node may get recovered at a constant rate γ. Once get recovered, the node will neither infect other nodes nor get infected by other nodes. The dynamic equation of the basic SIR model is:

$$\begin{aligned}\frac{dI(t)}{dt} &= \beta * (N - I(t) - R(t))I(t) - \gamma I(t) \\ \frac{dR(t)}{dt} &= \gamma I(t)\end{aligned} \quad (2)$$

where the initial condition R(0)=0.

In SIR model, the recover rate $\gamma(\tau)$ is a constant γ and we can derive the holding time follows an exponential distribution, that is,

THEOREM 1. *Let $f(\tau)$ be the probability density function of holding time τ in SIR model, then*

$$f(\tau) = \gamma e^{-\gamma\tau}$$

PROOF. By definition of $f(\tau)$,

$$f(\tau) = -\frac{dPr\{T > \tau\}}{d\tau} \quad (3)$$

By definition of $\gamma(\tau)$,

$$f(\tau) = Pr\{T > \tau\}\gamma(\tau) = \gamma Pr\{T > \tau\} \quad (4)$$

Take the derivative of Eq.5 with respect to τ and combine with Eq.4, we can derive that,

$$\frac{df(\tau)}{d\tau} = -\gamma f(\tau)$$

Solve this differential equation with initial condition $f(0) = \gamma$ and we can derive that,

$$f(\tau) = \gamma e^{-\gamma\tau}$$

□

This theorem demonstrate that the holding time distribution of SIR model follows an exponential distribution with an exponent of $-\gamma$. However, as is shown in Fig. 2, the holding time distribution of real data follows a power-law distribution, so the recover function $\gamma(\tau)$ should be a function decays verses holding time τ.

The above are the parameters of the base model and we will model the group evolve process as follows:

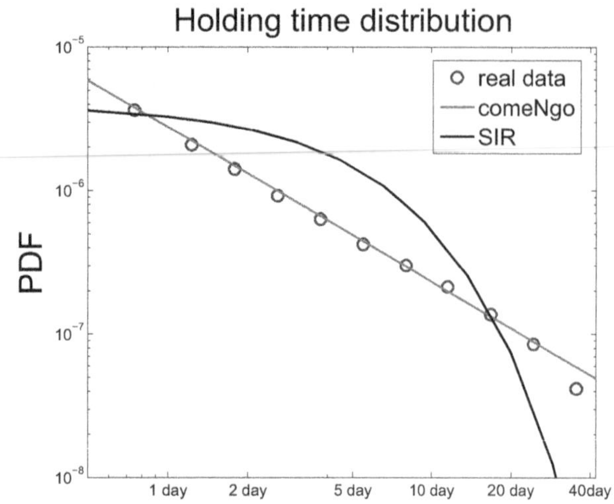

Figure 2: holding time distribution.

- n initial users found a group at birth time 0
- the group occasionally attracts other users in the population N
- users in the group may also quit the group

Note that the n initial users are also included in the population N and we assume that users who quit the group will not add it again, which is similar to SIR model.

Next we present our COMENGO model, which is a concise yet flexible dynamic model with several desirable properties.

3.2 Base model

3.2.1 *Dynamics equation*

A group evolve process can be seen as the interaction of two processes: join process and quit process. We also build our model on these two processes. Let $J(t)$ be the cumulative number of people who ever joined the group before time t, and $Q(t)$ be the cumulative number of people who quit the group before time t. Let $I(t)$ be the number of people in the group at time t, so the group evolve process $I(t)$ can be defined as follows,

$$I(t) = J(t) - Q(t) \tag{5}$$

So our task is to find the dynamics equation for $J(t)$ and $Q(t)$. For join process $J(t)$, we only consider the word-of-mouth mechanism in base model. We assume that each member in the group occasionally attracts other users to join the group and the possibility is determined by the attractiveness of the group β. So the dynamic equation of join process is as follows,

$$J'(t) = \frac{dJ}{dt} = \beta(N - J(t))I(t) \tag{6}$$

For quit process $Q(t)$, we need to consider the holding time distribution problem. As is proved in Theorem. 1, a constant recover function $\lambda(\tau)$ will lead to a exponential holding time distribution. In our model, we add an power-law decay with an exponent α to the recover function as follows,

$$\gamma(\tau) = \gamma_0 \tau^{-\alpha} \tag{7}$$

We will prove that the $\gamma(\tau)$ can generate both power-law and exponential holding time distribution depending on α. We first derive the probability density function $f(\tau)$ of holding time distribution as follows,

LEMMA 1. *Let $f(\tau)$ be the probability density function of holding time τ in COMENGO model, then*

$$f(\tau) = c\tau^{-\alpha} \exp(\frac{\gamma_0 \tau^{1-\alpha}}{\alpha - 1}) \tag{8}$$

PROOF. By definition of $f(\tau)$,

$$f(\tau) = -\frac{dPr\{T > \tau\}}{d\tau} \tag{9}$$

By definition of $\gamma(\tau)$

$$f(\tau) = Pr\{T > \tau\}\gamma(\tau) \tag{10}$$

this is,

$$Pr\{T > \tau\} = \frac{1}{\gamma_0}\tau^{\alpha} f(\tau) \tag{11}$$

Take the derivative of Eq.9 with respect to τ and combine with Eq.11, we can derive that,

$$-f(\tau) = \frac{\alpha}{\gamma_0}\tau^{\alpha-1} f(\tau) + \frac{1}{\gamma_0}\tau^{\alpha}\frac{df(\tau)}{d\tau}$$

Solve this differential equation, we can get that,

$$f(\tau) = c\tau^{-\alpha} \exp(\frac{\gamma_0 \tau^{1-\alpha}}{\alpha - 1})$$

where c is a constant decided by the initial condition. □

Now we prove that the holding time distribution can be both power-law tail and exponential tail depending on α.

THEOREM 2. *when $\alpha > 1$,*

$$\lim_{\tau \to \infty} f(\tau) \propto \tau^{-\alpha}$$

PROOF.

$$\lim_{\tau \to \infty} \frac{f(\tau)}{\tau^{-\alpha}} = \lim_{\tau \to \infty} c \cdot exp(\frac{\gamma_0 \tau^{1-\alpha}}{\alpha - 1})$$

$$\because \alpha > 1 \quad \therefore \lim_{\tau \to \infty} \tau^{1-\alpha} = 0, \quad \lim_{\tau \to \infty} \exp(\frac{\gamma_0 \tau^{1-\alpha}}{\alpha - 1}) = 1$$

$$\therefore \lim_{\tau \to \infty} \frac{f(\tau)}{\tau^{-\alpha}} = c, \quad \lim_{\tau \to \infty} f(\tau) \propto \tau^{-\alpha}$$

□

THEOREM 3. *when $\alpha < 1$,*

$$\lim_{\tau \to \infty} f(\tau) \propto e^{-\gamma \tau^{1-\alpha}}$$

PROOF.

$$\lim_{\tau \to \infty} \frac{\log f(\tau)}{\tau^{1-\alpha}} = \lim_{\tau \to \infty} \frac{\log c}{\tau^{1-\alpha}} - \alpha \frac{\log \tau}{\tau^{1-\alpha}} + \frac{\gamma_0}{\alpha - 1}$$

$$\because \alpha < 1 \quad \therefore \lim_{\tau \to \infty} \tau^{\alpha-1} = 0, \quad \lim_{\tau \to \infty} \tau^{\alpha-1} \log \tau = 0$$

$$\therefore \quad \lim_{\tau \to \infty} f(\tau) \propto e^{-\gamma \tau^{1-\alpha}}$$

□

As a result,the tail of the holding time distribution generated by our model mainly depends on the decay parameter α. When $\alpha > 1$, the holding time distribution will be power-law tailed while when $\alpha < 1$, it will have an exponential decay, and when $\alpha \to 0$, it will become an exact exponential distribution.

We also show the result of holding time distribution in Fig.2. The blue dot represents the holding time distribution of all groups and the red line is the result of our model. We can see from the figure that it can approximate the real data quit well. This evidence further demonstrates the correctness of our model.

With the appropriate recover function $\gamma(\tau) = \gamma_0\tau^{-\alpha}$, we can derive the dynamics equation for the quit process as follows,

$$Q'(t) = \frac{dQ}{dt} = \int_0^t J'(x)f(t-x)dx \tag{12}$$

where $f(\tau)$ is defined in Eq.8.

Now we have the dynamics equation for join process (Eq.7) and quit process (Eq.15), in the next section, we will propose our dynamic model in discrete time based on the equation.

3.2.2 COMENGO-BASE

Let $I(n)$ be the number of people in the group at time-tick n, let $\Delta J(n)$ be the number of people join the group at time-tick n, and let $\Delta Q(n)$ be the number of people quit the group at time-tick n. Our base model is governed by the equations

MODEL 1 (COMENGO-BASE). *Our base model is generated by the equations*

$$\begin{aligned} I(n+1) &= I(n) + \Delta J(n) - \Delta Q(n) \\ \Delta J(n+1) &= \beta(N - J(n))I(n)/N \\ \Delta Q(n+1) &= \sum_{t=0}^{n} \Delta J(n) \cdot f(n+1-t) \end{aligned} \tag{13}$$

where,

$$f(\tau) = \gamma_0\tau^{-\alpha}\exp(\frac{\gamma_0(\tau^{1-\alpha}-1)}{\alpha-1})$$

and initial conditions:

$$\Delta J(0) = J_0, \Delta Q(0) = 0$$

and also, by definition

$$J(n) = \sum_{t=0}^{n} \Delta J(t), \quad Q(n) = \sum_{t=0}^{n} \Delta Q(t)$$

Justification of the model. There are 4 parameters in our base model, $\{\beta, \gamma, \alpha, N\}$. An advantage of our dynamic model is that all the parameters have clear and explainable physical meaning, which means our model is more than fitting the data. Following is a brief explanation to each parameter:

- $\boldsymbol{\beta}$ indicates the attractiveness of the group. It determines how fast the group will attract new users and grow larger.
- $\boldsymbol{\gamma_0}$ indicates group members' short time satisfaction degree of the group. The higher the value is, the higher percentage of users will feel boring and quit the group soon.
- $\boldsymbol{\alpha}$ indicates group members' long time dependence on the group. If α is high, it means that the users who have been in the group for some time may become dependent on the group and are unlikely to quit anymore. In contrast, if α is low, group members are less likely to develop the long term interest in the group and the will gradually quit the group, sooner of later.
- $\boldsymbol{N}$ is the population of all potential members of the group. Although N may change over time, but it is relatively steady in most condition. So we set it to a constant in our model for brief.

We should also note that the initial condition in our model $\Delta J(0) = J_0$ needs to be given. It is the initial size of the group when found. Since group evolves mainly through diffusion mechanism, the initial size will greatly influence the growth speed at the beginning.

3.3 With Non-diffusion Growth

Although groups grow mainly through influence between nodes, non word-of-mouth mechanism may also plays an important part in group evolution process. Let's take the evolution of a new association in university for example. In the one hand, the founders and members may try to attract their friends into the association. This is 'word-of-mouth' mechanism and such mechanism will last all the time. In the other hand, they may also conduct membership recruitment meeting to attract new members. Such activity may attract a lot of new members in a short time, causing a burst like an external shock. Such non-diffusion mechanism may have great impact on the whole evolve process so we need to reflect it in our model.

We add the external shocks in the join process to model the non-diffusion growth. The dynamics equation of the join process is as follows,

$$J'(t) = \frac{dJ}{dt} = \beta(N - J(t))I(t) + \sum \lambda_i\delta(t - t_i) \tag{14}$$

where $\delta(t - t_i)$ is dirac delta function that indicates an impulse at time t_i, and λ_i is the strength of the shock.

So we propose our model as follows,

MODEL 2 (COMENGO).

$$\begin{aligned} I(n+1) &= I(n) + \Delta J(n) - \Delta Q(n) \\ \Delta J(n+1) &= \beta(N - J(n))I(n)/N + \sum_{i=1}^{k} \lambda_i \cdot \mathbf{1}_{\{t_i\}}(n) \\ \Delta Q(n+1) &= \sum_{t=0}^{n} \Delta J(n) \cdot f(n+1-t) \end{aligned} \tag{15}$$

where $\mathbf{1}_{\{t_i\}}(n)$ is an indicator function, by definition,

$$\mathbf{1}_A(x) := \begin{cases} 1 & \text{if } x \in A, \\ 0 & \text{if } x \notin A. \end{cases}$$

Justification of the model. The model is identical to COMENGO-BASE with the addition of the impulse term $\lambda_i\delta(t-t_i)$. This term captures the effect of non-diffusion mechanism in group evolution process. The impulse term indicates an external shock occurs at time t_i and attracts λ_i users to the group. Following is a brief explanation to the parameters of this term:

- $\boldsymbol{t_i}$ is the time when the external shock, such as a recruitment campaign, occurs. Such campaign can also last for some time but we regard it as an impulse because the duration is actually quite short compared with the duration of the word-of-mouth effect.
- $\boldsymbol{\lambda_i}$ is the effect strength of the impulse. λ_0 users will be recruited into the group and after that they can attract other users through word-of-mouth mechanism.

3.4 Parameter Learning

Our base model consists of four parameters: $\boldsymbol{\theta} = \{\beta,\gamma,\alpha,N\}$. Given two real time sequences X(n) and Y(n), X(n) is the cumulative number of people who ever joined the group before time-tick n and Y(n) is the cumulative number of people who ever quit the group before time-tick n, $(n = 1,...,n_d)$. Note that the initial condition J_0 means the initial size of the group, so we can directly get from the data. To learn the parameters of the base model, we use Levenberg-Marquardt (LM) [18] to minimize the sum of errors:

$$\min_{\theta} D(X,Y,\theta) = \sum_{n=1}^{n_d}(X(n)-J(n))^2+(Y(n)-Q(n))^2 \quad (16)$$

Our model with non-diffusion mechanism consists two more parameters in impulse term, location parameter t_i and strength parameter λ_i. We first determine the location parameter by detecting external shock larger than predefined threshold and then learn the strength parameter together with other parameters using Levenberg-Marquardt(LM) method [18].

4. EXPERIMENTS

To evaluate the effectiveness of COMENGO model, we conduct experiments on a real dataset. First we provide a brief data description in Section 4.1. In Section 4.2, we show how well we match the real data. In Section 4.3, we demonstrate the strong predicting power of our model. In section 4.4, we analyze the distribution of parameters and illustrate how to recognize different group evolving patterns.

4.1 Data Description

We conduct experiments on a real large-scale social network dataset - **Wechat**. Wechat is the most widely used social network and messaging service in China with more than 600 million monthly active users.

Group is one of the most important feature in Wechat. Every user can found groups to chat together. According to our statistics, more than one million groups are founded everyday. There are mainly two ways to add new members to the group. The usual way is by invitation. Every member in the group can invite their friends to the group, which is a typical diffusion (word-of-mouth) mechanism. The other way is by scanning the QR code. Users can generate a QR code for their group and promote the group by publishing the QR code in open places. For example, the group of an association can print the QR code on their posters and leaflets so that people who are interested in the association can scan it and join the group. This is a non-diffusion mechanism.

Name	Value
Group Number	103548
Time Duration	42 days
Total Join Records Number	10675984
Average Number of Join Records	103.10
Total Quit Records Number	5713719
Average Number of Quit Records	55.18

Table 1: Dataset Description

We use the logs of wechat group as our data. From the groups established in November 20th, 2015 which contain at least 40 join records before January 1st, 2016, we sampled 103,548 groups as our experiment data. For each group we have the following three kinds of records. Table 1 summarizes the statistics of the dataset used for this study.

- **Group Founding Records** $\mathcal{G}$: It consists of all the group foundation records (C,T) for each of the sampled groups. Each record means group C is founded at time T.
- **Group Joining Records** $\mathcal{J}$: It consists of all the group joining records (u,C,T) for each of the sampled groups. Each record means user u joined group C at time T.
- **Group Quitting Records** $\mathcal{Q}$: It consists of all the group quitting records (u,C,T) for each of the sampled groups. Each record means user u quitted group C at time T.

This is the first dataset for large scale social groups with detailed log of both joining and quitting behaviours. The dataset provides valuable opportunity to get insight about the temporal dynamics of group evolution mechanism. For privacy issues, the dataset is fully anonymized and all data are collected according to the terms and conditions of Wechat.

4.2 Discovering and Matching Group Evolution Patterns

In this section, we demonstrate how well our model matches the real data. First, we give the formulation of group evolving process for the real data. As is mentioned in section 3.1.1, a group evolving process can be regarded as the integral of join process and quit process. For each group C_i in $\mathcal{G}$ founded at timestamp T_i, we can generate the join process sequence $X_i(n)$ and quit process sequence $Y_i(n)$ with a daily time tick as follows,

$$\begin{aligned} X_i(n) &= \|\{(u,C,T) \in \mathcal{J}|C = C_i, T - T_i < n * \Delta T\}\| \\ Y_i(n) &= \|\{(u,C,T) \in \mathcal{Q}|C = C_i, T - T_i < n * \Delta T\}\| \end{aligned} \quad (17)$$

where ΔT is the length of each time tick, which is one day in our experiment. Then the group size sequence $G(n)$ can be derived by

$$G_i(n) = X_i(n) - Y_i(n) \quad (18)$$

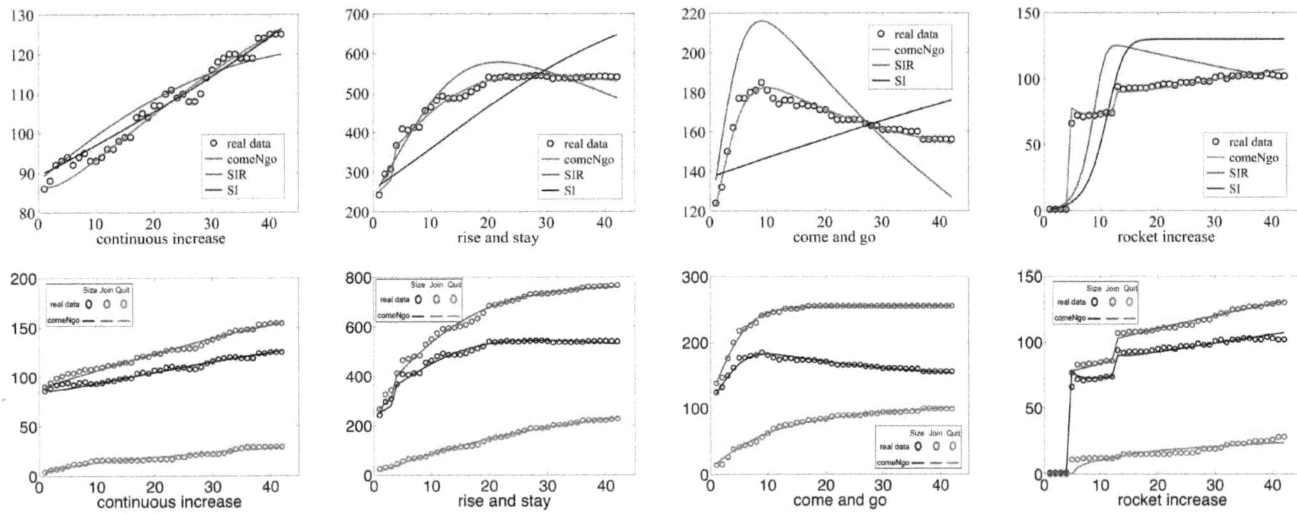

Figure 3: Fitting result of four kinds of patterns. Upper: Fitting result of group size. The dots present real data, the red line is the result of our model and blue for SIR model, black for SI model. Below: Fitting result of group size(black), join process(blue) and quit process(black).

Model	RMSE-I	RMSE-J	RMSE-Q
SI	18.17	-	-
SIR	11.07	5.36	9.12
COMENGO-BASE	6.01	4.80	4.41
COMENGO	**4.64**	**2.63**	**3.81**

Table 2: Fitting accuracy of different models. Our comeNgo model outperforms all the baselines in fitting group size, join number and quit number.

Figure 3 shows the results of model fitting on Wechat dataset. We select 4 typical groups which represent different group evolving patterns. We show the original sequences $G(n)$(black dots) and fitting result of COMENGO $I(n)$(red line). We compare our result with SI model(blue line) and SIR model(black line). The second line of Figure 3 shows the fitting results of joining and quitting process. We can see that although the groups have quite different temporal patterns, our model can fit all the patterns very well, including the groups with external shocks (as shown in the fourth column of Figure 3). It demonstrates that our model is not only accurate but also has strong unification power.

We further evaluate the fitting accuracy using the root mean square error(RMSE) between estimated values and real values: $RMSE = \sqrt{\frac{1}{n_d}\sum^{n_d}(G(n) - I(n))^2}$. Besides group size sequences I(n), we also compare the fitting goodness of group joining sequences J(n) and group quitting sequences Q(n). We can see from the Table 2 that our model outperforms all the baselines. The fitting accuracy of our model increases by **58.08%** than baselines in fitting group size, **50.9%** in fitting joining process and **58.22%** in fitting quitting process.

4.3 Group Evolution Prediction

As a dynamic model, COMENGO model can be used to predict the whole process of group evolution. Here we consider a more practical problem: given the group evolving process in early stage, can we forecast the future evolution of the group? To answer the question, we designed two tasks, trend prediction and size prediction, to measure the predicting power of our model.

4.3.1 *Trend Prediction*

An important aspect of group evolving process is the evolving trend: will the group grow larger or begin to decline? For each group, we use the data of the first 10 days to train our model and use the learned parameters to predict the trend in the next 5, 15 and 30 days to demonstrate the predicting power in both short term and long term. Here we define the trend prediction problem as a classification problem: if the group size increases more than 20%, we regard it as a 'positive example' and if it decreases more than 20%, we regard it as a 'negative example'. Note that the external shocks are unpredictable to all models without external information, so we ignore the groups that have external shocks in prediction period. Besides, the number of positive and negative examples are balanced in this experiment.

We use the parameters of our model as features, and the distribution for each feature were standardized to have a mean of 0 and standard deviation of 1. Then we conduct Logistics Regression for the classification problem. We use 5-fold cross validation, that is, we randomly select 80% of the data as training data and the remaining 20% as testing data. The experiments are repeated for 5 times and the average performances are reported in Figure 4. We can see that our model outperforms all the baselines in three prediction tasks. In short term prediction, our accuracy is 81.13%, **14.3%** higher than baseline. In long term prediction, our accuracy is 80.10%, **14.9%** higher than baseline.

Table.3 shows the regression coefficients of the parameters of our model and we can find some meaningful information from them.

Parameters β, N and $\Sigma\lambda$ influence the dynamics of joining process. β and λ determine the growth speed through

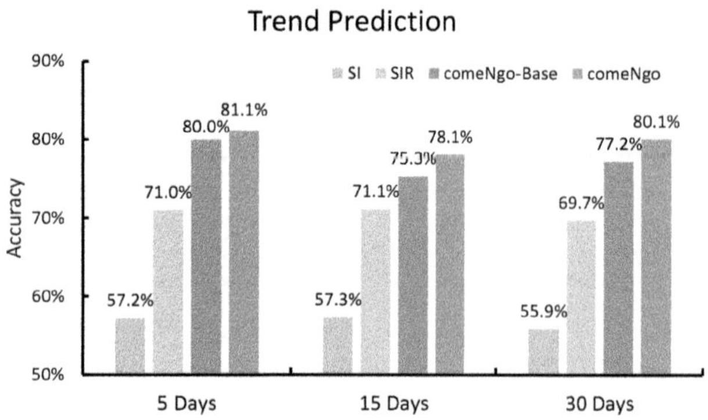

Figure 4: Prediction accuracy of the group growth trend in 5, 15 and 30 days. The accuracy of our model is 81.13%, 78.06% and 80.10% respectively.

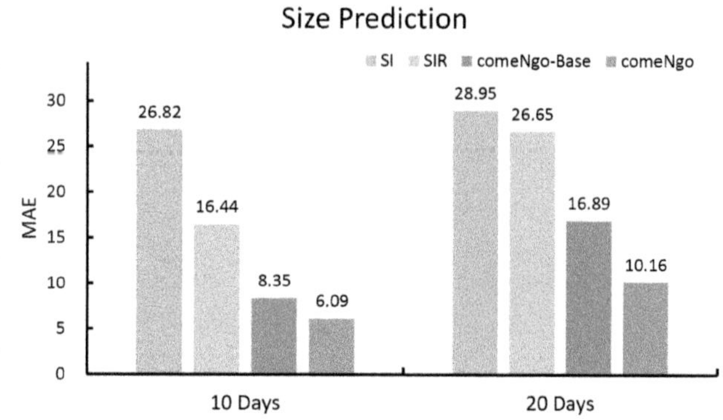

Figure 5: Prediction accuracy of the group size in 10 and 20 days. The average MAE of our model is 6.09 and 10.16 respectively.

Feature	5 Days	15 Days	30 Days
β	0.164**	—	-0.083*
γ	-1.52***	-1.13***	-1.05***
α	1.89***	1.95***	2.26***
N	0.318***	0.298***	0.295***
$\Sigma\lambda$	-0.598***	-0.652***	-0.731***
t_i	—	—	—

Table 3: Regression coefficients for comeNgo model predicting the trend in 5, 15 and 30 days after the 10th day(For this table, * p<0.01,** p<0.005, *** p<0.001). Coefficients with p>0.05 are not reported.

	10 Days		20 Days	
Model	MAE-J	MAE-Q	MAE-J	MAE-Q
SI	23.78	-	29.66	-
SIR	7.78	13.77	17.50	21.58
COMENGO-BASE	8.36	6.39	20.73	12.02
COMENGO	**5.51**	**5.39**	**11.53**	**9.10**

Table 4: Results of predicting the join process and quit process. MAE-J and MAE-Q represent the average MAE of predicting cumulative join number and cumulative quit number in 10 and 20 days.

diffusion mechanism and non-diffusion mechanism respectively, while N determines the population of the users who can be reached by these mechanisms. A counterintuitive but interesting finding is that infection rate β and the external shock strength λ have negative coefficients for the long term growth trend. Meanwhile, the total population N of potential members shows significant positive coefficient for both short term and long term trend prediction. This finding indicates that growing breadth is more important than growing speed to the long term growth.

Parameters γ and α influence the dynamics of quit process. γ embodies more short term effect while α has more long term effect. We can find that the regression coefficient of α becomes larger when the prediction period is longer, in consist with its physical meaning. Also, γ plays an important role when predicting short term trend but decreases obviously when predicting long term trend. Considering that γ and α have the largest coefficients among all parameters, we can draw a conclusion that quit process has great impacts on group evolution trend.

4.3.2 *Size Prediction*

A more challenging and practical task to evaluate the prediction power of a model is the size prediction problem: if we only have the sizes of a group at different time ticks in early stage, can we predict the group size in future?

To demonstrate the predicting power of our model, we use the temporal data in the first 20 days to train our model and use it to predict the group size in the next 10 days and 20 days. We also ignore the groups with external shocks in prediction period, and there are 93660 groups left for the prediction problem.

We evaluate our prediction accuracy using the mean absolute error(MAE) between estimated values and real values: $MAE = |G(n) - I(n)|$. We also use SI and SIR as baseline models to predict the group size. The results are shown in Fig.5. We can see from the figure that our model achieves a significant improvement than baselines in both short term and long term. When predicting the group size in 10 days, the average MAE of our model is 6.09, **63.0%** better than SIR and in 20 days, the MAE is 10.16, also **61.9%** better than SIR.

Table.4 shows the predicting accuracy of group joining and quitting processes, measured by average MAE. SI model can only capture the joining process so it performs worst. SIR and COMENGO-BASE model perform similar in predicting joining process, but our model performs much better in predicting quitting process. As is mentioned above, SIR model can only capture the non-dependence mechanism while our base model can capture both non-dependence and dependence mechanism. The improvement further demonstrates the importance of the dependence mechanism in quitting process.

4.4 Model Parameters Analysis

A specific advantage of our model is that all of the parameters have clear physical meanings. As a result, we can recognize different group evolving patterns through parameter analysis. In this subsection, we analyze the distribution

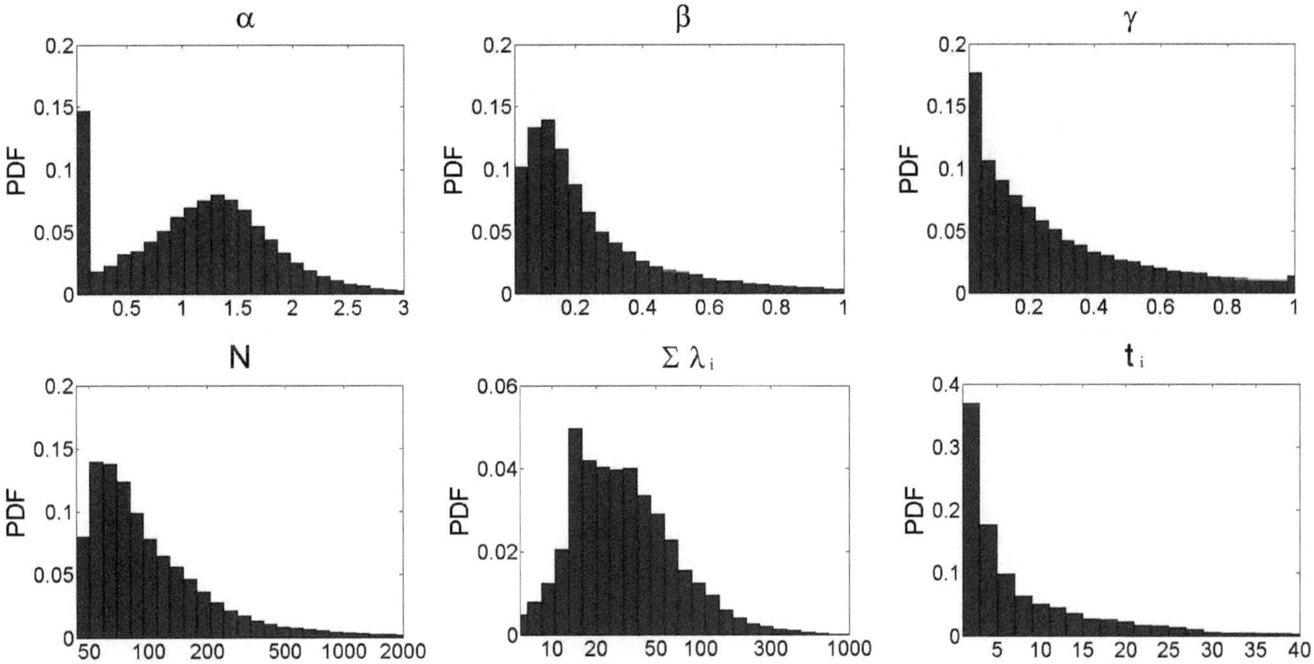

Figure 6: The distribution of six parameters in our model.

of the parameters and use them to recognize the temporal patterns in group evolution. Fig. 6 shows the distribution of six parameters in our model, and we get the following findings.

- **α :** The distribution of α is a typical bimodal distribution with one peak near 0 and the other near 1.4. As we proved in Theorem 2 and 3, the clustering near the first peak represents the groups with exponential holding time distribution. In such groups, most people will quit by the non-dependence mechanism, and thus the group will gradually dies out. Such groups usually have weak ties between members. The other peak represents a typical power-law holding time distribution with an exponent near 1.5, which is consistent with many study in human dynamics [23, 26]. Groups with α much larger than 1.5 represents the groups with stable and strong relations, and thus members become dependent on the group shortly, such as phenomena are often observed in the the group of associations or organizations.

- **β :** It follows an natural exponential distribution and most groups have an infection rate less than 0.5.

- **γ :** It also follows an exponential distribution but it has an obvious peak near 0. This peak indicates that these groups have strong stickness and members barely quit the group. These groups are usually established by strong ties, such as classmates groups or working groups.

- **N :** The distribution of N follows a power-law (note that the x axis of N is presented in log scale) and the cutoff near 50 is resulted from our sampling strategy. The power-law decay indicates that the potential population N can be quite large and as we analyzed in Section 4.3.1, such groups are more likely to grow continuously.

- **$\Sigma\lambda_i$:** We find that 57.46% of groups do not have any external shocks in the group evolution, which are omitted in the figure. For the groups with external shocks, the non-diffusion mechanism are usually not strong,indicated by the peak near 20 and an power-law decay. This means that the diffusion mechanism plays more important roles for the evolution of most groups.

- **t_i :** Most external shocks occur at the early stage of the group, which is consistent with our intuition. For example, a new association usually holds many publicity campaigns to attract new members right after its establishment.

5. CONCLUSIONS

In this paper, we study the come-and-go patterns in group evolution process. We analyze the temporal patterns of group joining and quitting behaviours and revealed the dynamic mechanism behind these patterns. We propose COMENGO, a general, accurate and succinct dynamic model that is able to accurately model and comprehensively explain the temporal patterns. Our proposed model has the following appealing advantages:

- **Unification power:** It is a general model that includes previous models as special case and also embodies new mechanisms.

- **Succinctness and interpretability:** It uses only six parameters, what's more, every parameter has a clear physical meaning.

- **Accuracy:** It can capture the temporal patterns of different groups precisely, with an improvement of **58%** than baseline in goodness of fit.

- **Usefulness:** We showed how to use our model to do trend prediction, size prediction and recognize the temporal patterns by parameters analysis.

6. ACKNOWLEDGMENTS

This work was supported by National Program on Key Basic Research Project, No. 2015CB352300; National Natural Science Foundation of China, No. 61370022, No. 61531006, No. 61472444 and No. 61210008. Thanks for the research fund of Tsinghua-Tencent Joint Laboratory for Internet Innovation Technology.

This material is based upon work supported by the National Science Foundation under Grant No. CNS-1314632 IIS-1408924 Any opinions, findings, and conclusions or recommendations expressed in this material are those of the author(s) and do not necessarily reflect the views of the National Science Foundation, or other funding parties.

7. REFERENCES

[1] R. M. Anderson, R. M. May, and B. Anderson. *Infectious diseases of humans: dynamics and control*, volume 28. Wiley Online Library, 1992.

[2] L. Backstrom, D. Huttenlocher, J. Kleinberg, and X. Lan. Group formation in large social networks: membership, growth, and evolution. In *Proceedings of the 12th ACM SIGKDD international conference on Knowledge discovery and data mining*, pages 44–54. ACM, 2006.

[3] R. S. Burt. The social structure of competition. *Explorations in economic sociology*, 65:103, 1993.

[4] D. Centola. The spread of behavior in an online social network experiment. *science*, 329(5996):1194–1197, 2010.

[5] J. S. Coleman and J. S. Coleman. *Foundations of social theory*. Harvard university press, 1994.

[6] R. Crane and D. Sornette. Robust dynamic classes revealed by measuring the response function of a social system. *Proceedings of the National Academy of Sciences*, 105(41):15649–15653, 2008.

[7] C. Danescu-Niculescu-Mizil, R. West, D. Jurafsky, J. Leskovec, and C. Potts. No country for old members: User lifecycle and linguistic change in online communities. In *Proceedings of the 22nd international conference on World Wide Web*, pages 307–318. International World Wide Web Conferences Steering Committee, 2013.

[8] N. Ducheneaut, N. Yee, E. Nickell, and R. J. Moore. The life and death of online gaming communities: a look at guilds in world of warcraft. In *Proceedings of the SIGCHI conference on Human factors in computing systems*, pages 839–848. ACM, 2007.

[9] R. I. Dunbar. Coevolution of neocortical size, group size and language in humans. *Behavioral and brain sciences*, 16(04):681–694, 1993.

[10] M. S. Granovetter. The strength of weak ties. *American journal of sociology*, pages 1360–1380, 1973.

[11] S. R. Kairam, D. J. Wang, and J. Leskovec. The life and death of online groups: Predicting group growth and longevity. In *Proceedings of the fifth ACM international conference on Web search and data mining*, pages 673–682. ACM, 2012.

[12] W. O. Kermack and A. G. McKendrick. A contribution to the mathematical theory of epidemics. In *Proceedings of the Royal Society of London A: mathematical, physical and engineering sciences*, volume 115, pages 700–721. The Royal Society, 1927.

[13] R. Kumar, J. Novak, P. Raghavan, and A. Tomkins. On the bursty evolution of blogspace. *World Wide Web*, 8(2):159–178, 2005.

[14] T. Lappas, E. Terzi, D. Gunopulos, and H. Mannila. Finding effectors in social networks. In *Proceedings of the 16th ACM SIGKDD international conference on Knowledge discovery and data mining*, pages 1059–1068. ACM, 2010.

[15] J. Leskovec, L. Backstrom, R. Kumar, and A. Tomkins. Microscopic evolution of social networks. In *Proceedings of the 14th ACM SIGKDD international conference on Knowledge discovery and data mining*, pages 462–470. ACM, 2008.

[16] J. Leskovec, J. Kleinberg, and C. Faloutsos. Graphs over time: densification laws, shrinking diameters and possible explanations. In *Proceedings of the eleventh ACM SIGKDD international conference on Knowledge discovery in data mining*, pages 177–187. ACM, 2005.

[17] J. Leskovec, M. McGlohon, C. Faloutsos, N. S. Glance, and M. Hurst. Patterns of cascading behavior in large blog graphs. *SDM*, 7:551–556, 2007.

[18] K. Levenberg. A method for the solution of certain non–linear problems in least squares. 1944.

[19] Y.-R. Lin, Y. Chi, S. Zhu, H. Sundaram, and B. L. Tseng. Analyzing communities and their evolutions in dynamic social networks. *ACM Transactions on Knowledge Discovery from Data (TKDD)*, 3(2):8, 2009.

[20] Y. Matsubara, Y. Sakurai, B. A. Prakash, L. Li, and C. Faloutsos. Rise and fall patterns of information diffusion: model and implications. In *Proceedings of the 18th ACM SIGKDD international conference on Knowledge discovery and data mining*, pages 6–14. ACM, 2012.

[21] S. Milgram. The small world problem. *Psychology today*, 2(1):60–67, 1967.

[22] A. Mislove, M. Marcon, K. P. Gummadi, P. Druschel, and B. Bhattacharjee. Measurement and analysis of online social networks. In *Proceedings of the 7th ACM SIGCOMM conference on Internet measurement*, pages 29–42. ACM, 2007.

[23] J. G. Oliveira and A.-L. Barabási. Human dynamics: Darwin and einstein correspondence patterns. *Nature*, 437(7063):1251–1251, 2005.

[24] J.-P. Onnela, J. Saramäki, J. Hyvönen, G. Szabó, D. Lazer, K. Kaski, J. Kertész, and A.-L. Barabási. Structure and tie strengths in mobile communication networks. *Proceedings of the National Academy of Sciences*, 104(18):7332–7336, 2007.

[25] G. Palla, A.-L. Barabási, and T. Vicsek. Quantifying social group evolution. *Nature*, 446(7136):664–667, 2007.

[26] A. Vázquez, J. G. Oliveira, Z. Dezsö, K.-I. Goh, I. Kondor, and A.-L. Barabási. Modeling bursts and heavy tails in human dynamics. *Physical Review E*, 73(3):036127, 2006.

[27] Y. Wang, D. Chakrabarti, C. Wang, and C. Faloutsos. Epidemic spreading in real networks: An eigenvalue viewpoint. In *Reliable Distributed Systems, 2003. Proceedings. 22nd International Symposium on*, pages 25–34. IEEE, 2003.

[28] L. Yu, P. Cui, F. Wang, C. Song, and S. Yang. From micro to macro: Uncovering and predicting information cascading process with behavioral dynamics. In *2015 IEEE International Conference on Data Mining, ICDM 2015*, pages 559–568, 2015.

NetCycle: Collective Evolution Inference in Heterogeneous Information Networks

Yizhou Zhang[1,2] Yun Xiong[1,2] Xiangnan Kong[3] Yangyong Zhu[1,2]
[1]Shanghai Key Laboratory of Data Science, Shanghai, China
[2]School of Computer Science, Fudan University, Shanghai, China
[3]Worcester Polytechnic Institute, Worcester, MA, USA
{yizhouzhang14, yunx, yyzhu}@fudan.edu.cn xkong@wpi.edu

ABSTRACT

Collective inference has attracted considerable attention in the last decade, where the response variables within a group of instances are correlated and should be inferred collectively, instead of independently. Previous works on collective inference mainly focus on exploiting the *autocorrelation* among instances in a *static* network during the inference process. There are also approaches on time series prediction, which mainly exploit the autocorrelation within an instance at different time points during the inference process. However, in many real-world applications, the response variables of related instances can co-evolve over time and their evolutions are not following a static correlation across time, but are following an internal *life cycle*. In this paper, we study the problem of *collective evolution inference*, where the goal is to predict the values of the response variables for a group of related instances at the end of their life cycles. This problem is extremely important for various applications, *e.g.*, predicting fund-raising results in crowd-funding and predicting gene-expression levels in bioinformatics. This problem is also highly challenging because different instances in the network can co-evolve over time and they can be at different stages of their life cycles and thus have different evolving patterns. Moreover, the instances in collective evolution inference problems are usually connected through *heterogeneous information networks*, which involve complex relationships among the instances interconnected by multiple types of links. We propose an approach, called *NetCycle*, by incorporating information from both the correlation among related instances and their life cycles. We compared our approach with existing methods of collective inference and time series analysis on two real-world networks. The results demonstrate that our proposed approach can improve the inference performance by considering the autocorrelation through networks and the life cycles of the instances.

KDD '16, August 13-17, 2016, San Francisco, CA, USA

DOI: http://dx.doi.org/10.1145/2939672.2939742

Categories and Subject Descriptors

H.2.8 [**Database Management**]: Database Applications-Data Mining

Keywords

Collective Inference, Evolution Inference, Heterogeneous Information Networks, Graph Mining, Data Mining

1. INTRODUCTION

Conventional supervised learning usually assumes that the instances are independent and identically distributed (i.i.d.), where the response variables of different instances are inferred independently. In many relational data, however, the response variables of different instances can be related. For example, in financial networks, the loan listings borrowed by the same individual are more likely to share similar default risks than those borrowed by different people. An effective model for these relational data should be able to capture the dependencies among different instances during the inference process. Motivated by this challenge, collective inference problem [17, 15] has attracted much attention in recent years, where the response variables within a group of instances are correlated and should be inferred collectively.

In the literature, collective inference for both classification and regression problems, has been extensively studied [17, 15, 1, 10]. Previous works on collective inference mainly focus on exploiting the *autocorrelation* among instances in a *static* network during the inference process, as shown in Figure 2(a). However, in many real-world applications, the response variables of the instances can evolve over time, and the network can involve multiple kinds of relationships among the instances. For example, in *P2P Lending networks*, such as *Prosper.com* and *Kickstarter.com*, the financial activities of different loan listings can evolve over their entire fund-raising periods. These loan listings are interacting with different borrowers and lenders [14], as shown in Figure 1(a). In *PPI networks*, the expression-level of different genes can also change over time, which is regulated by their complex chemical reactions with different molecules [18]. Besides, *transportation networks*, such as road traffic networks and public transit networks, can also involve multiple evolving attributes, representing the traffic volumes of different road segments or subway stations.

There are many approaches on time series prediction, which mainly exploit the autocorrelation within an instance at different time points during the inference process [5, 12, 9].

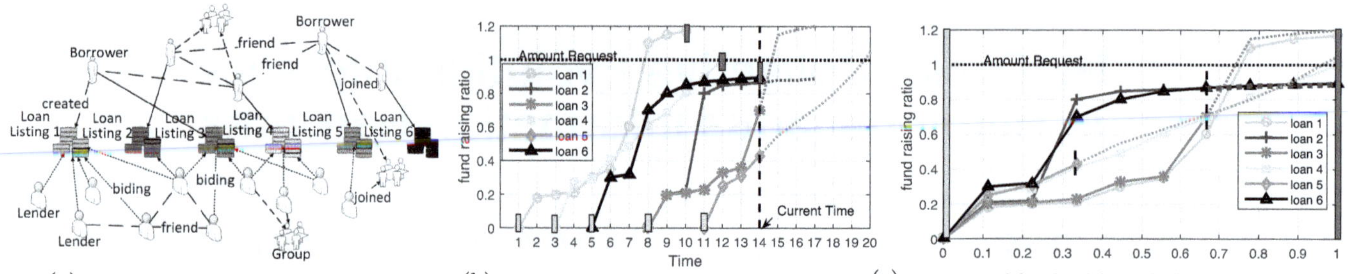

(a) Prosper P2P Lending Network (b) progress of fund-raising across time (c) progress of fund-raising within a life cycle

Figure 1: An example of collective evolution inference problem in P2P Lending networks. (a) an example of heterogeneous information network in P2P lending. (b) fund-raising progress of the loan listings across *time*. (c) fund-raising progress for the loan listings across fund-raising periods, *i.e.*, their *life cycles*.

However, in many real-world applications, the response variables of related instances can co-evolve over time and their evolutions are not following a static correlation across time, but are following an internal *life cycle*. For example, in the fund-raising networks, evolution of the fund-raising activities in a loan listing usually follows its fund-raising period (life cycle), which includes a predefined starting time and ending time. Activities of the loan listing may show different patterns at different stages of its life cycle, as shown in Figure 1(c). This problem can be called as *evolution inference*, where each instance can evolve within its life cycle, and the response variable is associated with a series of values. As shown in Figure 2(b), the goal of evolution inference is to estimate $y_i^{e_i}$.

In this paper, we study the problem of *collective evolution inference*, where the goal is to predict the values of the response variables for a group of related instances at the end of their life cycles. This problem is very important in various applications, *e.g.*, predicting fund-raising results in crowd-funding and predicting gene-expression levels in bioinformatics. Formally, *collective evolution inference* problem corresponds to predicting the response variables of a group of related instances at the end of their life cycles. This problem is highly challenging because different instances in the network can co-evolve over time and they can be at different stages of their life cycles and thus have different evolving patterns. We summarize the unique challenges of collective evolution inference as follows:

- **Collective Evolution with Life Cycles**: One major challenge of the collective evolution inference problem lies in the fact that the response variables values (response values for short) of the instances are evolving with a certain life cycle. Fortunately, the instances which have strong correlations are more likely to share similar evolution pattern during their life cycles. To better understand the collective evolution with life cycles, we give an example in Figures 1(b) and 1(c), which describes the evolution of the fund-raising ratio of the loan listings in P2P lending networks. As shown in Figure 1(b), the fund-raising ratio is evolving during fund-raising period. It is easy to think that the fund-raising ratio at time T depends on previous status at time $T-1$. However, the learning strategy of collective inference strictly follows the assumption that the response values of each instance will not change, which ignores the temporal information of the instances. Moreover, if we align the evolution of each loan listing by fund-raising period, as shown in Figure 1(c), the loan listings 1 and 3 which created by same borrower are more likely to obey similar fund-raising tendency during their life cycles. But collective inference problems usually focus on a "snapshot" of dynamic networks, while the snapshot captures the network at a certain time point. At a certain time point, the instances may be at different stages of their life cycles, which increased the difficulty of collective evolution inference.

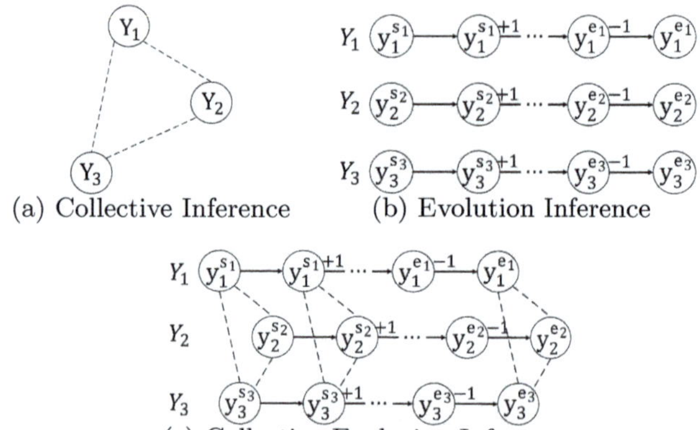

(a) Collective Inference (b) Evolution Inference

(c) Collective Evolution Inference

Figure 2: Comparison of different inference problems. Y_i denotes the response variable of the i-th instance. y_i^k denotes the value of response variable Y_i at time point k. Here s_i/e_i is the starting/ending time point of the life cycle in the i-th instance. The instances directly linked by a dotted line are related.

- **Heterogeneous Dependencies**: Another challenge of collective evolution inference is the complex correlations among instances in HINs. It turns out strongly connected instances are more likely to show up with similar growth/evolving patterns in the same stages of their life cycles. The fundamental problem is how to effectively use the information provided by these multiple types of nodes and links, as well as the evolving tendency of each node. Collective inference approaches usually focus on homogeneous networks[1, 16] with one type of links and nodes. It is necessary to study how to exploit the complex dependencies among nodes' evolution in their life cycles in HINs, in order to predict the related instances more effectively.

In this paper, we first present collective evolution inference problem, which extends collective inference problem into dynamic networks, with the concept of life cycle. Then, we design a novel algorithm to solve the collective evolution inference problem, called NetCycle, which collectively infer the final values of a collection of nodes in a dynamic heterogeneous network by modeling the evolution tendency of the response variable. Finally, the experiments on real-world networks indicate the effectiveness of our algorithm. To our

Table 1: Important Notations.

Symbol	Definition
$\mathcal{G} = (\mathcal{V}, \mathcal{E})$	A heterogeneous network.
$\mathcal{V} = \{\mathcal{V}_1, \cdots, \mathcal{V}_K\}$	The set of nodes, involving K types of nodes. The target node type is $\mathcal{V}_1$.
$\mathcal{D} = \{(\mathbf{x}_i, \mathbf{y}_i, s_i, e_i)\}_{i=1}^n$	The data set with n instances, $\mathcal{D} = \mathcal{V}_1$.
$\mathcal{X} = \{\mathbf{x}_1, \cdots, \mathbf{x}_n\}$	The set of inherent attributes for all instances in $\mathcal{D}$.
$\mathcal{Y} = \{\mathbf{y}_1, \cdots, \mathbf{y}_n\}$	The set of response variables for all instances in $\mathcal{D}$.
s_i and e_i	The starting time and ending time of life cycle of i-th instance in $\mathcal{D}$.
$\mathbf{y}_i = (y_i^{s_i}, y_i^{s_i+1}, \cdots, y_i^{e_i})$	A time series of values for the response variable Y_i of the i-th instance in $\mathcal{D}$.
T and t	T denotes current time, while t can indicates any time.
$\mathcal{L}$ and $\mathcal{U}$	The training set and testing set, where $\mathcal{L} \bigcup \mathcal{U} = \mathcal{D}$ and $\mathcal{L} \bigcap \mathcal{U} = \emptyset$.
$\mathcal{U} = \bigcup_{k=1}^M \mathcal{U}_k$	For $\forall i \in \mathcal{U}_k$, the evolution process of Y_i is only observed on the first k stages of its life cycle at time T, *i.e.*, $\mathbf{y}_i^k = \left(y_i^{s_i}, \cdots, y_i^{s_i+k-1}\right)$.
$\mathcal{N}_i$	The instances set which correlated with node v_{1i}. $\mathcal{N}_i \subseteq \mathcal{V}_1$.
$S = \{\mathcal{P}_1, \cdots, \mathcal{P}_{\|S\|}\}$	The set of meta paths type. Each $\mathcal{P}_l$ denotes a composite relationship between instances in $\mathcal{V}_1$.

best knowledge, this kind of problem has not been studied in the literature until recently.

2. PROBLEM DEFINITION

In this section, we first introduce some related concepts and notations, then define the problem.

2.1 Evolution Inference

Suppose we have a data set $\mathcal{D} = \{(\mathbf{x}_i, \mathbf{y}_i, s_i, e_i)\}_{i=1}^n$ with n instances. Here $\mathbf{x}_i \in \mathbb{R}^d$ corresponds to the feature vector of the i-th instance in the d-dimensional space. $\mathbf{y}_i = (y_i^{s_i}, y_i^{s_i+1}, \cdots, y_i^{e_i})$ corresponds to a time series of values for the response variable Y_i of the i-th instance. Y_i is evolving between time s_i (starting time) and e_i (ending time). $\forall t \in [s_i, e_i], y_i^t$ corresponds to the value of Y_i at time t. Here the response variable Y_i is only evolving during the period of time $[s_i, e_i]$, *i.e.*, the *life cycle* of the i-th instance. s_i is the starting time of the life cycle for Y_i, when the response variable Y_i starts to evolve. e_i is the ending time of the life cycle for Y_i, after which the response variable Y_i stops changing. Each instance in $\mathcal{D}$ can have a different life cycle, with different starting time and ending time. $\mathcal{X} = \{\mathbf{x}_1, \cdots, \mathbf{x}_n\}$ represents the set of features for all instances in $\mathcal{D}$. $\mathcal{Y} = \{\mathbf{y}_1, \cdots, \mathbf{y}_n\}$ represents the set of target values for all instances in $\mathcal{D}$.

The indices of the instances in $\mathcal{D}$ are then divided into a training set $\mathcal{L} \subset \{1, \cdots, n\}$ and a test set $\mathcal{U} \subset \{1, \cdots, n\}$, where $\mathcal{L} \cup \mathcal{U} = \{1, \cdots, n\}$ and $\mathcal{L} \cap \mathcal{U} = \emptyset$. $\forall i \in \mathcal{L}$, the evolution of the response variable Y_i, *i.e.* $\mathbf{y}_i$, is fully observed. While in the test set $\mathcal{U}$, $\forall i \in \mathcal{U}$, the evolution of the response variable Y_i is only partially observed with different fractions. Suppose the life cycle of each instance has M stages, based upon the fraction of the evolution process being observed, the test set $\mathcal{U}$ can be divided into M disjoint groups, *i.e.*, $\mathcal{U} = \bigcup_{k=1}^M \mathcal{U}_k$. For $\forall i \in \mathcal{U}_k$, the evolution process of Y_i is only observed on the first k stages of its life cycle, *i.e.*, $\mathbf{y}_i^k = \left(y_i^{s_i}, \cdots, y_i^{s_i+k-1}\right)$. $\forall 1 \leq k \leq M$ and $\forall i \in \mathcal{U}_k$, the task of **evolution inference** on the i-th instance is to predict the value of Y_i at the end of its life cycle, *i.e.*, $y_i^{e_i}$, based upon $\mathbf{x}_i$ and $\mathbf{y}_i^k$. We use $\mathcal{Y}_\mathcal{U}^e = \{y_i^{e_i} | \forall i \in \mathcal{U}\}$ to denote all the target values for prediction. We then use $\mathcal{Y}_\mathcal{U}^o = \{\mathbf{y}_i^k \mid \forall 1 \leq k \leq M, i \in \mathcal{U}_k\}$ to denote all the observed evolution process in the test set and $\mathcal{Y}_\mathcal{L} = \{\mathbf{y}_i \mid \forall i \in \mathcal{L}\}$ to denote all the evolution process in the training set. The overall goal of *evolution inference* is to estimate the probability distribute $\Pr(\mathcal{Y}_\mathcal{U}^e | \mathcal{X}, \mathcal{Y}_\mathcal{L}, \mathcal{Y}_\mathcal{U}^o)$.

In this work, we simplify the problem by assuming the lengths of all life cycles are equal, *i.e.*, each instance has the same length in its life cycle. This assumption can be easily extended to unequal-length cases by normalization.

2.2 Collective Evolution Inference

To estimate $\Pr(\mathcal{Y}_\mathcal{U}^e | \mathcal{X}, \mathcal{Y}_\mathcal{L}, \mathcal{Y}_\mathcal{U}^o)$, conventional inference approaches usually require i.i.d. assumptions, and ignore dependency between different instances. The inference for each instance is performed independently:

$$\Pr(\mathcal{Y}_\mathcal{U}^e | \mathcal{X}, \mathcal{Y}_\mathcal{L}, \mathcal{Y}_\mathcal{U}^o) \propto \prod_{i \in \mathcal{U}} \Pr(y_i^{e_i} | \mathbf{x}_i)$$

Link-based Dependency

Collective inference approaches assume that the instances which directly linked in the network are related [1]. Given a network $\mathcal{G} = (\mathcal{V}, \mathcal{E})$, $\mathcal{V}$ is the set of instances (nodes), $\mathcal{V} = \mathcal{D}$. $\mathcal{E} \subseteq \mathcal{V} \times \mathcal{V}$ is the set of links between instances. We use T to represent the current time. $\forall v_i \in \mathcal{V}$, collective inference methods can model $\Pr(y_i^{e_i} | \mathcal{Y}_{\mathcal{N}_i}^T, \mathbf{x}_i)$. Here $\mathcal{Y}_{\mathcal{N}_i}^T$ contains all variables $Y_j (\forall v_j \in \mathcal{N}_i)$ at time T, *i.e.*, $\mathcal{Y}_{\mathcal{N}_i}^T = \{y_j^T | v_j \in \mathcal{N}_i\}$, and $\mathcal{N}_i$ denotes the instances set which correlated with v_i, $\mathcal{N}_i \subseteq \mathcal{V}$. Hence, by considering the correlation between instances, we will have:

$$\Pr(\mathcal{Y}_\mathcal{U}^e | \mathcal{X}, \mathcal{Y}_\mathcal{L}, \mathcal{Y}_\mathcal{U}^o) \propto \prod_{v_i \in \mathcal{U}} \Pr(y_i^{e_i} | \mathcal{Y}_{\mathcal{N}_i}^T, \mathbf{x}_i) \qquad (1)$$

Collective Evolution with Life Cycles

Note that different instances may be at different stages of their life cycles at time T, so it is inappropriate to infer $y_i^{e_i}$ with $\mathcal{Y}_{\mathcal{N}_i}^T$, because the evolution tendency varies at different stages, which may mislead the inference result. Correlated instances share similar evolving pattern during their life cycles rather than during the absolute time. Suppose $v_i \in \mathcal{U}_k$, one better way is to replace $\mathcal{Y}_{\mathcal{N}_i}^T$ by using $\mathcal{Y}_{\mathcal{N}_i}^k$. Here $\mathcal{Y}_{\mathcal{N}_i}^k = \{y_j^{s_j+k} | v_j \in \mathcal{N}_i\}$, contains all response values $Y_j (\forall v_j \in \mathcal{N}_i)$ at k-th stage of their life cycles.

Moreover, with the assumption that the network is static, collective inference methods usually ignore the evolution information. In order to utilize this information, one way is to iteratively predict the target value $y_i^{s_i+k}$ based upon previous value $y_i^{s_i+k-1}$, until $s_i + k = e_i$, *e.g.*, autoregressive

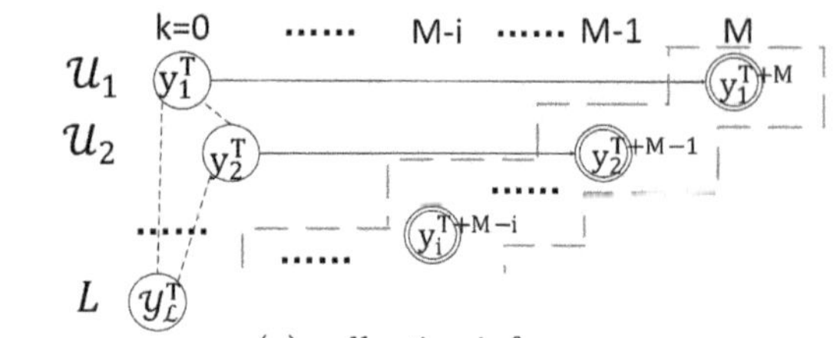

(a) collective inference

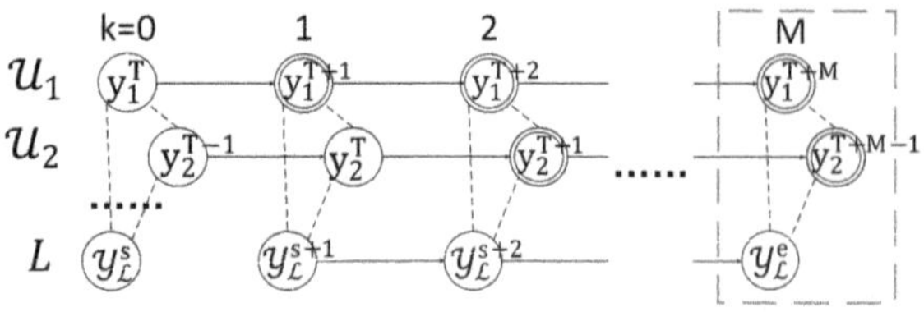

(b) collective evolution inference

Figure 3: The basic idea of collective inference and collective evolution inference. Here k represents the k-th stage of life cycle. $\mathcal{U}_k$ is the instances set which stay in k-th stage of life cycle at current time T. The single circle means observed values of the response variable, and the double circle means predict values of the response variable.

model of order one (AR(1) for short). These methods can model $\Pr(y_i^{s_i+k}|y_i^{s_i+k-1}, \mathbf{x}_i)$, but the results usually have large errors when the prediction horizon is long, because it only utilizes previous evolution process. Note that the instances with strong correlations may obey similar evolution tendency during their life cycles, as shown in Figure 1(c). By considering both link-based dependencies and evolution information of instances, the idea of *collective evolution inference* is to model $\Pr(y_i^{s_i+k}|y_i^{s_i+k-1}, \mathcal{Y}_{\mathcal{N}_i}^k, \mathbf{x}_i)$, which utilizes the correlations between instances during their life cycles to reduce prediction errors. The task of collective evolution inference is to estimate:

$$\Pr(\mathcal{Y}_{\mathcal{U}}^e|\mathcal{X}, \mathcal{Y}_{\mathcal{L}}, \mathcal{Y}_{\mathcal{U}}^o) \propto \prod_{v_i \in \mathcal{U}} \Pr(y_i^{e_i}|y_i^{e_i-1}, \mathcal{Y}_{\mathcal{N}_i}^{e_i}, \mathbf{x}_i) \quad (2)$$

$$y_i^{s_i+k} = \begin{cases} \mathcal{F}\left(y_i^{s_i+k-1}, \mathcal{Y}_{\mathcal{N}_i}^k, \mathbf{x}_i\right) & T < s_i + k \le e_i \\ y_i^{s_i+k} & s_i + k \le T \end{cases}$$

Here $\mathcal{F}$ denotes the models which estimate response variable Y_i at time $s_i + k$, *e.g.*, AR(1).

Compared with collective inference, collective evolution inference avoids inferring $\mathcal{Y}_{\mathcal{U}}^e$ simultaneously, by aligning the life cycle of each instance into the same position. And it also makes use of the evolution process during the life cycles of instances. We use time T to indicate s_i and e_i ($\forall v_i \in \mathcal{V}$), as shown in Figure 3, we describe the difference between collective inference and collective evolution inference based upon Eq. 1, 2. Note that $\forall v_i \in \mathcal{U}_k$, $T = s_i + k - 1$, and $\forall v_i \in \mathcal{L}$, $T \ge e_i$, *i.e.*, $y_i^T = y_i^{e_i}$.

Heterogeneous Dependencies

In many real-world applications, the networks include multiple types of nodes and links, which are called *heterogeneous information networks* [10].

Definition 1. Heterogeneous information network is a special kind of information network, which can be represented as a directed graph $\mathcal{G} = (\mathcal{V}, \mathcal{E})$. $\mathcal{V}$ denotes the set of nodes, including K types of instances: $\mathcal{V}_1 = \{v_{11}, \cdots, v_{1n_1}\}, \cdots, \mathcal{V}_K = \{v_{K1}, \cdots, v_{Kn_K}\}$, where v_{ji} represents the ith instance of type j. $\mathcal{E} \subseteq \mathcal{V} \times \mathcal{V}$ denotes the links between the instances in $\mathcal{V}$, which involves multiple types of links.

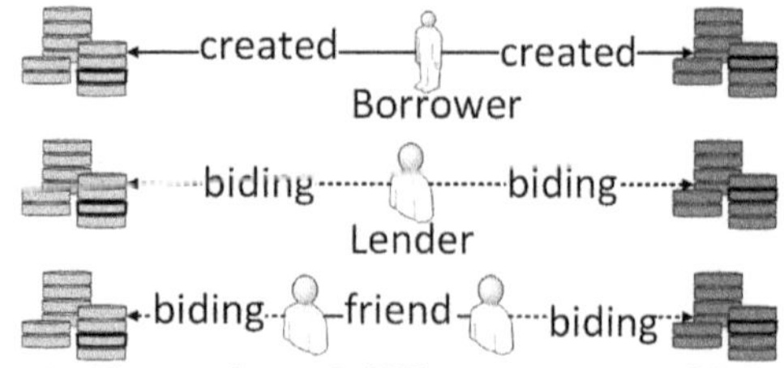

Figure 4: Examples of different types of Meta-path between two loan listings in P2P Lending Network.

For example, as shown in Figure 1(a), the P2P Lending network includes multiple types of nodes, *e.g.*, loan listing, borrower, lender, group, which are connected through multiple types of links, *e.g.*, created, bidding, friend, joined. In this paper, we focus on studying the collective evolution inference problem on one type of nodes, instead of on all of them in HINs. The reason is different type of nodes have different variables in HINs, so it's unreasonable to assume all types of nodes share the same set of response variables.

Without loss of generality, we define the first node type $\mathcal{V}_1$ as the target node type, *i.e.*, $\mathcal{V}_1 = \mathcal{D}$. By mining the linkage structure of HINs, multiple types of dependencies among instances can be extracted. In next section, we propose a method to solve the collective evolution inference in HINs. We summarized all notations in Table 1.

3. PROPOSED METHOD

In this section, we first introduce a concept named *meta path* [11] in section 3.1, which is often used to extract complex relationships among the instances in HINs. Then, we discuss how to solve the collective evolution inference problem in HINs based on meta path in section 3.2, and propose a simple and effective algorithm for meta path-based collective evolution inference in section 3.3. Finally, we discuss how to predict the node evolution process during the life cycle in section 3.4.

3.1 Meta Path

The *meta path* is defined as a sequence of relations in the network schema. The instances in HINs are inter-connected through multiple types of links. Each type of links from node type $\mathcal{V}_i$ to node type $\mathcal{V}_j$ corresponds to a binary relation R, where $R(v_{ip}, v_{jq})$ holds if the object v_{ip} and v_{jq} are linked in R. For example, in Figure 1(a), the link type "bidding" is a relation between *lender* nodes and *loan listing* nodes, where $R(v_{ip}, v_{jq})$ holds if the *lender* node v_{ip} has a link of type "bidding" to the *loan listing* node v_{jq} in the network. We can write the link type as "lender $\xrightarrow{bidding}$ loan listing".

A meta path $\mathcal{P}$ corresponds a type of path within the network, containing a certain sequence of link types. For instance, we give three types of meta path between *loan listings* in Figure 4, *e.g.*, a meta-path "loan listing $\xrightarrow{bidding^{-1}}$ lender $\xrightarrow{bidding}$ loan listing" denotes the composite relationship between *loan listing* nodes, where the semantic meaning of this meta-path is that the two *loan listing* nodes had been invested by same *lender* nodes. Here the link type "bidding^{-1}" represents the inverted relation of "bidding".

Input:

$\mathcal{G}$: a heterogeneous information network, M: number of stages in a life cycle, p_max: maximum meta-path length (default=4).
$\mathcal{X}$: attribute vectors for all instances, A: a base learner for local model, Max_{It}: maximum # of iteration (default=10)

Meta-path Construction:

- Construct the meta-path set $S = \{\mathcal{P}_1, \cdots, \mathcal{P}_{|S|}\}$:
  Breadth search on schema graph of $\mathcal{G}$, starting from V_1 by adding short meta-path $\mathcal{P}_l$ that ends with V_1 into S first:
  1. If the length of meta-path $\mathcal{P}_l$ is greater than p_max, exit the BFS;
  2. If current meta-path $\mathcal{P}_l$ cannot be reconstructed by the paths in $\mathcal{S}$, then add P_l into S; Otherwise, prune the current path from BFS.

Segment Training:

- For each stage $k = 1, \cdots, M$, learn the segment model f_k:
  1. Construct an extended training set $\mathcal{D}^k = \{(\mathbf{x}'^k_i, y_i^{s_i+k})\}$ by converting each instance $\mathbf{x}_i$ to $\mathbf{x}'^k_i$ as follows:
     $\mathbf{x}'^k_i = \left(\mathbf{x}_i, y_i^{s_i+k-1}, \text{PathRelFeature}(v_{1i}, \mathcal{Y}^k_{\mathcal{L}}, S)\right)$. Note that $y_i^{s_i-1} = [\,]$
  2. Let $f_k = A(\mathcal{D}^k)$ be the segment model trained on $\mathcal{D}^k$.

Collective Evolution Inference:

- For each stage $k = 1, \cdots, M$:
  Bootstrap: Estimate the response values sets in k-th stage, for each $v_{1i} \in \bigcup_{j=1}^k \mathcal{U}_j$, suppose $v_{1i} \in \mathcal{U}_j$, produce an estimated values y_i^{T-j+k} (*i.e.*, $y_i^{s_i+k}$) as: $y_i^{T-j+k} = f_k\left((\mathbf{x}_i, y_i^{T-j+k-1}, \mathbf{0})\right)$. Note that $y_i^{T-j} = [\,]$.
  Iterative Inference: Repeat until convergence or #iteration $> Max_{It}$
  1. Construct the associate features $\mathbf{x}'_i$ for each testing instance $v_{1i} \in \bigcup_{j=1}^k \mathcal{U}_j)$ as follows:
     $\mathbf{x}'^{T-j+k}_i = \left(\mathbf{x}_i, y_i^{T-j+k-1}, \text{PathRelFeature}(v_{1i}, \mathcal{Y}^k_{\mathcal{L}} \bigcup \{y_i^{T-j+k} | v_{1i} \in \bigcup_{j=1}^k \mathcal{U}_j\}, S)\right)$.
  2. Update y_i^{T-j+k} as $y_i^{T-j+k} = f_k(\mathbf{x}'^{T-j+k}_i)$ for each testing instance $v_{1i} \in \bigcup_{j=1}^k \mathcal{U}_j$ (Suppose $v_{1i} \in \mathcal{U}_j$).

Output: $\mathcal{Y}^e_{\mathcal{U}} = \left(y_1^{e_1}, \cdots, y_{|\mathcal{U}|}^{e_{|\mathcal{U}|}}\right)$: the response values sets of testing instances ($v_{1i} \in \mathcal{U}$).

Figure 7: The NetCycle algorithm

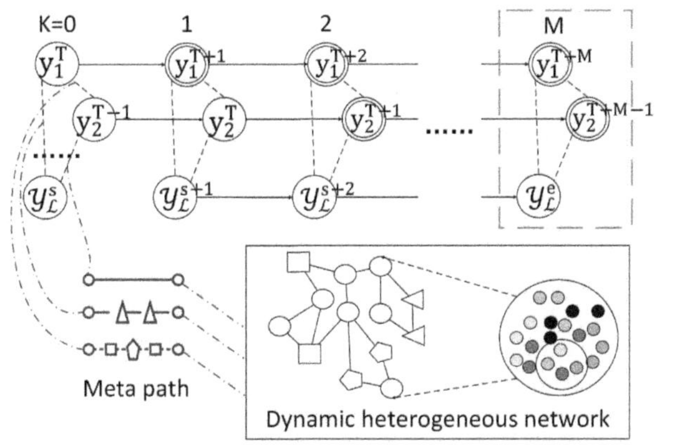

Figure 5: Meta path-based collective evolution inference in heterogeneous networks.

- $\mathcal{Y}^k_{\mathcal{N}_i} = \text{PathRelFeature}\left(v_{1i}, \mathcal{Y}^k, S = \{\mathcal{P}_1, \cdots, \mathcal{P}_{|S|}\}\right)$
  For each meta-path $\mathcal{P}_l \in S$:
  1. Get related instances for node v_{1i} through meta path $\mathcal{P}_l$, *i.e.*, the related index set $\mathcal{C} = \mathcal{P}_l(i)$
  2. $\mathcal{Y}^k_{\mathcal{P}_l(i)} = Aggregation\left(\{y_j | v_{1j} \in \mathcal{C}\}\right)$
  Return $[\mathcal{Y}^k_{\mathcal{P}_1(i)}, \cdots, \mathcal{Y}^k_{\mathcal{P}_{|S|}(i)}]^{\mathrm{T}}$

Figure 6: The function of constructing relational features(PathRelFeature).

3.2 Meta path-based Collective Evolution Inference

In HINs, there are complex dependencies not only among instances directly linked through links, but also among instances indirectly linked through different meta paths. In order to solve the collective evolution inference problem more effectively, we explicitly consider different types of meta path-based dependencies among instances.

Meta path-based dependencies refer to the dependencies among instances that are inter-connected through a meta path, *e.g.*, the co-borrower relation between loan listings can be represented as the meta-path "loan listing $\xrightarrow{created^{-1}}$ borrower $\xrightarrow{created}$ loan listing". Most relationships studied in network data can naturally be captured by different meta paths. Given a set of meta paths $S = \{\mathcal{P}_1, \cdots, \mathcal{P}_{|S|}\}$, $\mathcal{P}_l(i)$ denotes the nodes set where the nodes relate to node v_{1i} through the meta path $\mathcal{P}_l$, $\mathcal{P}_l(i) = \{v_{1j} | (v_{1i}, v_{1j}) \in \mathcal{P}_l\}$. The meta path-based dependencies can be used as follows:

$$\Pr\left(\mathcal{Y}^e_{\mathcal{U}} | \mathcal{X}, \mathcal{Y}_{\mathcal{L}}, \mathcal{Y}^o_{\mathcal{U}}\right) \propto \prod_{v_i \in \mathcal{U}} \Pr(y_i^{e_i} | y_i^{e_i-1}, \mathcal{Y}^{e_i}_{\mathcal{P}_1(i)}, \cdots, \mathcal{Y}^{e_i}_{\mathcal{P}_{|S|}(i)}, \mathbf{x}_i) \tag{3}$$

$$y_i^{s_i+k} = \begin{cases} \mathcal{F}\left(y_i^{s_i+k-1}, \mathcal{Y}^k_{\mathcal{P}_1(i)}, \cdots, \mathbf{x}_i\right) & T < s_i + k \le e_i \\ y_i^{s_i+k} & s_i + k \le T \end{cases}$$

Here $\mathcal{Y}^k_{\mathcal{P}_l(i)} = \{y_j^{s_j+k} | v_j \in P_l(i)\}$, denotes the response values set in k-th stage of life cycle, which the instances belong to $\mathcal{P}_l(i)$. The basic idea of meta path-based collective evolution inference as shown in Figure 5. An aggregation function (*e.g.*, mean, count, etc.) is often used to extract relational features from meta paths-based correlated variables set [11], as shown in Figure 6.

3.3 NetCycle Algorithm

In this section, we propose an algorithm, called NetCycle, to estimate Eq. 3. Inspired by the success of ICA framework [1] in collective inference, we designed a similar inference procedure for our NetCycle method as shown in Figure 7. The algorithm includes the following steps:

Meta-path Construction: Given a HIN, we first extract all non-redundant meta-paths for correlations of target instances type separately. A meta-path $\mathcal{P}_l$ in S is non-redundant if $\mathcal{P}_l$ cannot be reconstructed by combining any subset of the meta-paths in S. We only extract short meta-paths with a maximum path length p_max. It has been shown in [20] that long meta-paths are not quite useful in capturing the linkage structure of HINs.

Segmentation Training: We construct M extended training sets $\forall 1 \le k \le M, \mathcal{D}^k = \left\{(\mathbf{x}'^k_i, y_i^{s_i+k})\right\}$ by converting each instance $\mathbf{x}_i$ to $\mathbf{x}'^k_i$ using the functions in Figure 6, and combining with previous value $y_i^{s_i+k-1}$. Here $\mathcal{Y}^k = \{y_j^{s_j+k} | v_{1j} \in \mathcal{V}_1\}$, contains all response variables $Y_j (\forall v_{1j} \in \mathcal{V}_1)$ at k-th stage of their life cycles in Figure 6. We use base learner to train one segment model on each stage, by using the extended training sets.

Collective Evolution Inference: Overall, it is an ex-

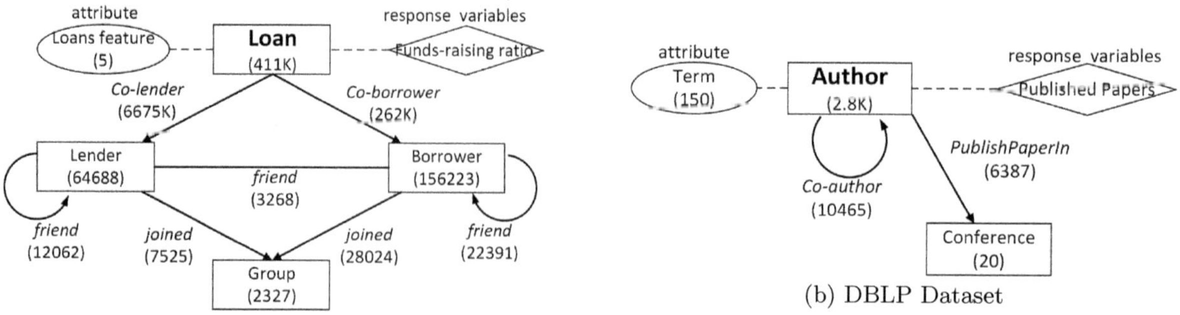

(b) DBLP Dataset

(a) Prosper Datasets

Figure 8: Schema of datasets. The numbers of each type are tagged under the corresponding type.

tension of iterative inference algorithm [1] for the inference step. During the inference, we iteratively update the response variables set predictions of the testing instances in k-th stage of life cycle, for each $v_{1i} \in \bigcup_{j=1}^{k} \mathcal{U}_j$. We use the predicted value y_i^{T-j+k} as one of input attribute in predict the response values set in $k+1$ stage, until $k = M$. In the end, we will get $\mathcal{Y}_{\mathcal{U}}^{e}$ for the testing instances.

Suppose the complexity of base learner A is C, the time complexity of learning the NetCycle model is $\mathcal{O}(p_{max} \cdot \mathcal{V}_1^3 + M \cdot C)$. While the time complexity of constructing meta paths is $\mathcal{O}(p_{max} \cdot \mathcal{V}_1^3)$, which usually constructed through matrix multiplication.

3.4 Extension: Node Evolution Process Prediction

During the collective evolution inference process, for each instance v_{1i} in test set $\mathcal{U}$, suppose $v_{1i} \in \mathcal{U}_k$, the NetCycle algorithm can not only infer the target value $y_i^{e_i}$, but also the whole time series values of response variable Y_i, *i.e.*, $\left(y_i^{s_i}, \cdots, y_i^{s_i+k}, y_i^{s_i+k+1}, \cdots, y_i^{e_i}\right)$. It can help to discover the evolution tendency over the instances' life cycle. Further, the weight of parameters learned by segment models f_k, can help to reflect the importance of each feature during life cycle (including inherent attributes, previous value and topology features). Greater weight means greater impact on evolution, so we can use it to find the major factor of node evolution in different stages. For example, in P2P lending network, previous studies [2] validated that the fund raising process is mainly influenced by the investment rate in early stage, and mostly affected by social interactions (*e.g.*, herding effect) in latter stage over fund-raising period.

4. EXPERIMENTS

4.1 Data Collection

In order to validate the collective evolution inference performances, we apply our methodology to three real-world HINs (Summarized in Table 2).

•**Prosper Dataset:** Our first two datasets studied in this paper were extracted from Prosper P2P Lending platform[1]. *Prosper.com* provides abundant lending information on website, including loan information, bidding, borrower and investor information, *etc.* The network schema of Prosper datasets is shown in Figure 8(a). In this network, there are four types of nodes: loan listing, borrower, lender and group, connected by four types of relations/links: *created*, *friend*, *bidding* and *joined* relationship. We treat loan listings as

[1]https://www.prosper.com/

Table 2: Summary of datasets.

Dataset	Node Type	Link Type	Feature	Instance
Prosper: 2006 ∼ 2007	4	4	5	30K+ 100K(Unobserved)
Prosper: 2008 ∼ 2009	4	4	5	30K+ 100K(Unobserved)
DBLP Dataset	3	2	150	2792

our target instances, with their funds-raising ratio as the response variables. Then the life cycle of the instances is the loan listing's fund-raising period. Each loan listing has five inherent attributes: maximum rate borrower willing to accept br, debt-to-income ratio dr, total amount requested ta, whether or not borrower is a home owner h, and loan description length dl [2]. We extract two subsets of loan listings in the network from 2006∼2011, and remove all isolated points (which did not receive any fund). The first dataset is extracted from Prosper: 2006∼2007, and the second from Prosper: 2008∼2009, each have $30K$ loan listings, we add $100K$ unobserved loan listings which randomly sampled from 2006∼2011 for each dataset. The fund-raising period of each loan is divided into M stages, here $M = 10$ for all experiments in these two datasets.

•**DBLP Dataset:** The third dataset, *i.e.*, DBLP four areas [8], is a bibliography information network extracted from DBLP[2], which involves three types of nodes: conference, paper and author, connected by two types of relations/links: conference-author links and co-author links. We treat authors as our target instances, with the number of published papers as the response variables. In this dataset, the life cycle is defined as the first five years since the author published his/her first paper. The inference task is to predict the numbers of papers published in the first five years of each author's academic life, which we call the authors' academic career problem, because most PhD degrees take five years, *i.e.*, $M = 5$. For each author, we extracted a bag-of-words representation of all the paper titles published by this author as inherent attributes, which include 150 words (terms) as node features. In this paper, we select the authors who published more than 2 papers, and the network schema of DBLP dataset is shown in Figure 8(b). For detailed description of the DBLP dataset, please refer to [8].

4.2 Algorithms for comparison

In order to demonstrate the effectiveness of our methodology, we compared with the following state-of-the-art algorithms (summarized in Table 3):

[2]http://dblp.uni-trier.de/db/

Table 3: Types of models, based on the kinds of features used.

Method	Self attr.	Neigh. labels	Time info	Publication
LIBLINEAR	✓			[4]
Herding Para[3]	✓		✓	[2]
GNetMine		✓		[8]
HCC	✓	✓		[11]
HCC(with kernel)[4]	✓	✓	✓	[11, 19]
NetCycle(w/o network)	✓		✓	This paper
NetCycle	✓	✓	✓	This paper

• LIBLINEAR [4]: This method is the base learner for following algorithms. It supposes that each instance is independent in the network.
• Herding Para [2]: This method is only applied to Prosper dataset. This method extracts the temporal features of bidding behavior to predict whether the loan will raise enough funds with logistic regression. However, it is a verifying experiment which can only be used after fund-raising period. We use a horizontal line to represent this method's performance in each stage.
• GNetMine [8]: This is a graph-based transductive classification approach based on information propagation model, which makes prediction on heterogeneous networks. It only uses static network structure, and assumes each node type shared by a group of similar labels.
• HCC [11]: This is a collective classification approach, which works on heterogeneous network by exploiting dependencies based on multiple meta paths in the network. The same as our method, it focuses on predicting one type of nodes in heterogeneous networks.
• HCC (with kernel) [19]: This framework can model both temporal and relational dependencies in dynamic networks, by giving different weight with *temporal-relational kernel* to links in the temporal dimension. But the paper focuses on link prediction instead of collective inference problem. In order to compare with the method, we combine the idea of modeling dynamic networks with kernels and HCC method, to solve the collective inference problem in dynamic networks.
• NetCycle (w/o network): This is a weak version of our method without network structure. It only uses the inherent attributes of nodes and the previous values of the nodes response variables, and does not consider the dependencies between related instances.
• NetCycle: This is our method proposed in Section 3.3, which tries to solve collective evolution inference in HINs.

For a fair comparison, all above algorithms use LIBLINEAR [4]. We use L2 regularized logistic regression as the base classifier and support vector regression as the base regression model. The weight of regularized item λ is set to be 0.001, and the maximum number of iterations Max_{iter} is set to be 10. The evaluation metric of classification is accuracy, and the evaluation metric of regression is root mean square error (RMSE). For all experiments, we use $k = 0/k = 1$ represents the start/end stage of nodes life cycles. 5-fold cross validations are used in all experiments.

[3]Prosper datasets only.

[4]Sharan et al. proposed an original way to model temporal network, however, they focus on the link prediction problem, we combined the idea with HCC as one of compared method.

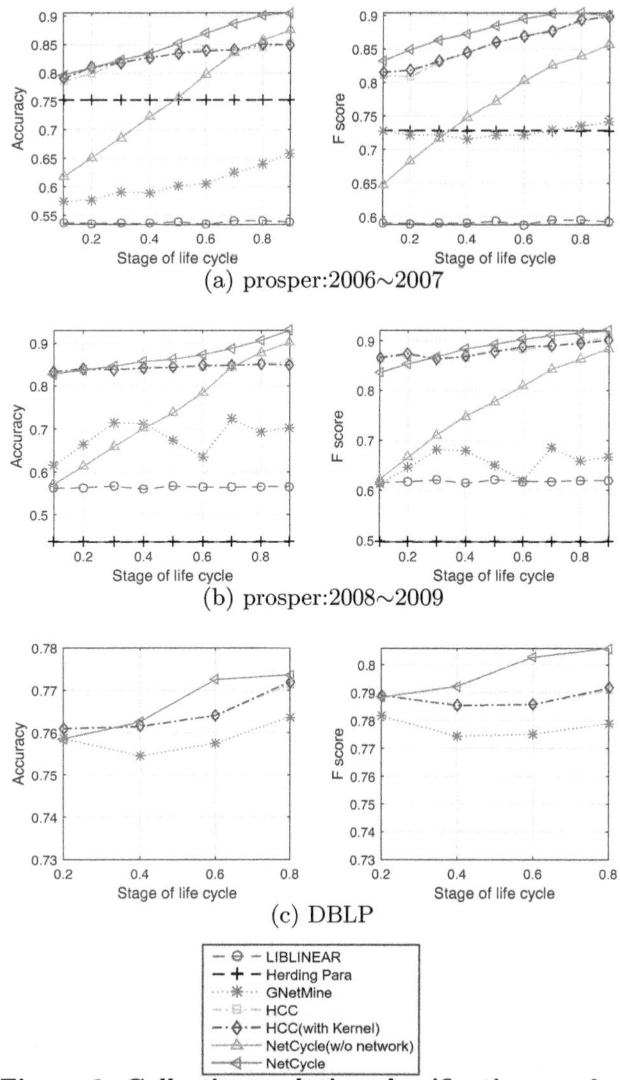

Figure 9: Collective evolution classification results.

4.3 Performances of Collective Evolution Classification

In our first experiment, we evaluate the effectiveness of the proposed NetCycle method on collective evolution classification problem. We apply our method on two problems: one is "biding detection" problem, which attempts to predict whether the loan listing will raise enough funds after fund-raising period. We binary the predicting result of fund-raising ratio to *Succeed* or *Failed* for comparison. Another is "academic career" problem, which tries to predict whether one author will engage in academic after graduation. The task can be represented as whether the author will publish his/her paper after five years. By hiding the response variables and links after stage k, we test all algorithms since different beginning stage k, and predict the final response values after their life cycles. Note that people pay more attention to positive instances, *e.g.*, investor only care about the loan listings which can receive enough funds in the end, and people care more about whether the author will continue to engage in academic career after PhD. We add F_β score as another classification evaluation metric, here we set $\beta = 0.5$. The results are reported in Figure 9. Due to the accuracy and F score are too small of logistic regression and

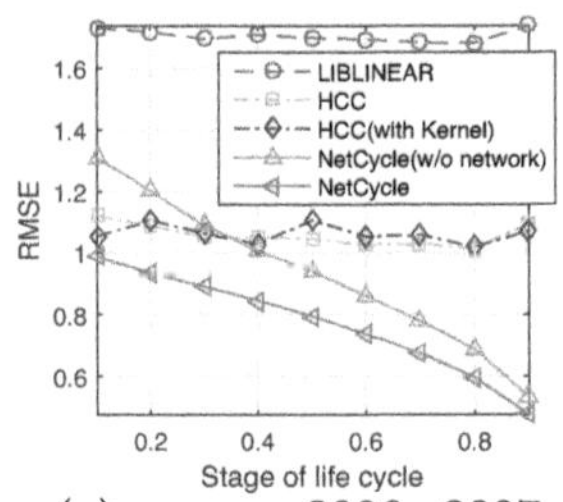

(a) prosper:2006~2007

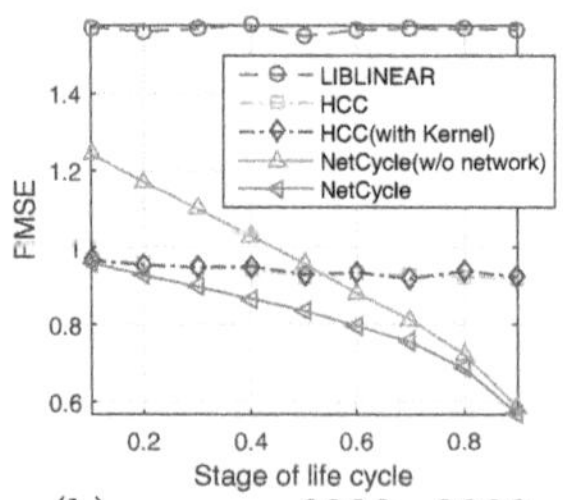

(b) prosper:2008~2009

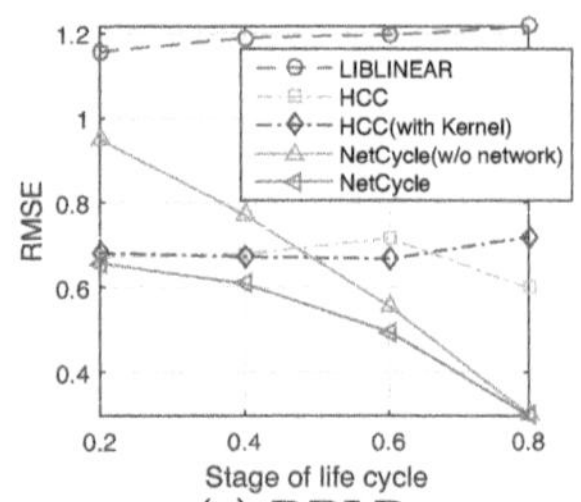

(c) DBLP

Figure 10: Collective evolution regression results.

NetCycle (w/o network) in DBLP dataset (less than 55%), so we did not shown the result in Figure 9(c).

The first observation in Figure 9 is: Most collective classification methods, *e.g.*, HCC and GNetMine, can achieve better accuracies than the baseline logistic regression. These results support that the heterogeneous dependencies among instances can improve classification performance. We also find that NetCycle (w/o network) and Herding Para are consistently and significantly outperforms than baseline, which support our claim that the evolution information of instances can also improve classification performance. Compared with all above algorithms, NetCycle always has best performance in each stage of life cycle, which explains that both heterogeneous dependencies among instances and the evolution information of node response variables can improve prediction performance in the classification task. Finally, we find that HCC method with kernel does not perform well, although it utilizes both heterogeneous dependencies among instances and the temporal information of instances. One possible reason is that it is hard to choose the suitable kernel to model the graph. Our algorithm almost achieves the best performance in all datasets.

4.4 Performances of Collective Evolution Regression

Compare with all above competing algorithms, NetCycle is not only able to solve the classification problem, but also able to solve the regression problem. In order to validate the effectiveness of NetCycle, we made slight modifications to the competing algorithms, by referring the works of [13] in collective regression. The competing algorithms include: LIBLINEAR, HCC, HCC (with Kernel) and NetCycle (w/o network). In this experiment, we apply NetCycle in collective evolution regression on two problems: predicting "how much fund of the loan will be raised after bidding period", and predicting "how many papers one author will publish during his/her PhD". The results are shown in Figure 10.

The first observation in Figure 10 we have is that most approaches have better performance than the baseline in each dataset, especially in latter stages of life cycle. We also find that although most algorithms' RMSEs have slightly decreasing tendency as time goes on, our methods (including w/o network) have more obviously decreasing tendency during life cycle, with the help of evolution information of the response variables during life cycles. Compared with NetCycle (w/o network), NetCycle have better performance in the early stage of life cycle, which demonstrates the heterogeneous dependencies among instances can improve performance in collective regression problem. In all datasets, NetCycle has outstanding performance in every stage.

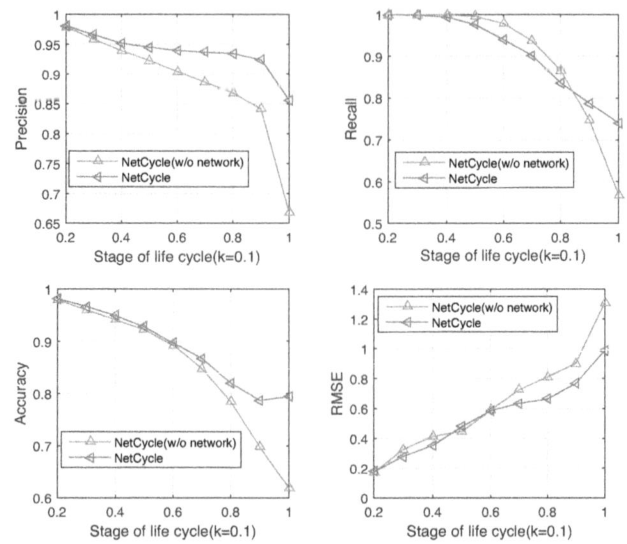

Figure 11: Node evolution during life cycle

4.5 Performances of Node Evolution Process Prediction

In our third experiment, we validate NetCycle (including w/o network) on predicting node evolution process in Prosper: 2006~2007 dataset. We record the evolution process of the nodes since stage $k = 0.1$, and use following metrics to evaluate the performance in each stage during their life cycles, including: *precision* of positive nodes, *recall* of positive nodes, *accuracy* and *RMSE*. The results are shown in Figure 11, where similar trend holds for the other two datasets which cannot be shown due to space limitation.

We can find that both NetCycle and NetCycle (w/o network) have high precision in early stage, and only have little descent as time goes on. The decreasing tendency of NetCycle is greater than NetCycle (w/o network). The recall of positive nodes is also very high in the early stage, but the decreasing tendency is more obvious than precision for both algorithms. The results show that the decreasing performance in dataset mostly due to the descent of recall. The last two figures are accuracy and RMSE, where the errors are monotone increasing for both algorithms, however, NetCycle has much slower increment speed of errors than NetCycle (w/o network), which demonstrates our claim that the instances are collective evolution with life cycles.

4.6 Influence of different Meta paths

In this experiment, we study the influence of different meta paths on the collective evolution inference performance of our NetCycle model. Different types of meta paths have different semantic meanings, which correspond to different types of dependencies among the instances in HINs. We summarize all metapaths in Table 4, which are extracted

Table 4: Summary of Meta Paths among Loan Nodes

Notation	Meta Path	Semantics of the Dependency
LBL	$Loan \xrightarrow{created^{-1}} Borrower \xrightarrow{created} Loan$	Co-borrower relation
$LLeL$	$Loan \xrightarrow{bidding^{-1}} Lender \xrightarrow{bidding} Loan$	Co-investor relation
$LBBL$	$Loan \xrightarrow{created^{-1}} Borrower \xrightarrow{friend} Borrower \xrightarrow{created} Loan$	Loan's borrower are friend
$LLeLeL$	$Loan \xrightarrow{bidding^{-1}} Lender \xrightarrow{friend} Lender \xrightarrow{bidding} Loan$	Loan's lender are friend
$LBLeL$	$Loan \xrightarrow{created^{-1}} Borrower \xrightarrow{friend} Lender \xrightarrow{bidding} Loan$	Loan's borrower and Loan's lender are friend
$LLeBL$	$Loan \xrightarrow{bidding^{-1}} Lender \xrightarrow{friend} Borrower \xrightarrow{created} Loan$	Loan's lender and Loan's borrower are friend
$LBGBL$	$Loan \xrightarrow{created^{-1}} Borrower \xrightarrow{joined} Group \xrightarrow{joined^{-1}} Borrower \xrightarrow{created} Loan$	Loan's borrower joined same group
$LLeGLeL$	$Loan \xrightarrow{bidding^{-1}} Lender \xrightarrow{joined} Group \xrightarrow{joined^{-1}} Lender \xrightarrow{bidding} Loan$	Loan's lender joined same group
$LBGLeL$	$Loan \xrightarrow{created^{-1}} Borrower \xrightarrow{joined} Group \xrightarrow{joined^{-1}} Lender \xrightarrow{bidding} Loan$	Loan's borrower and lenders joined same group
$LLeGBL$	$Loan \xrightarrow{bidding^{-1}} Lender \xrightarrow{joined} Group \xrightarrow{joined^{-1}} Borrower \xrightarrow{created} Loan$	Loan's lenders and borrower joined same group

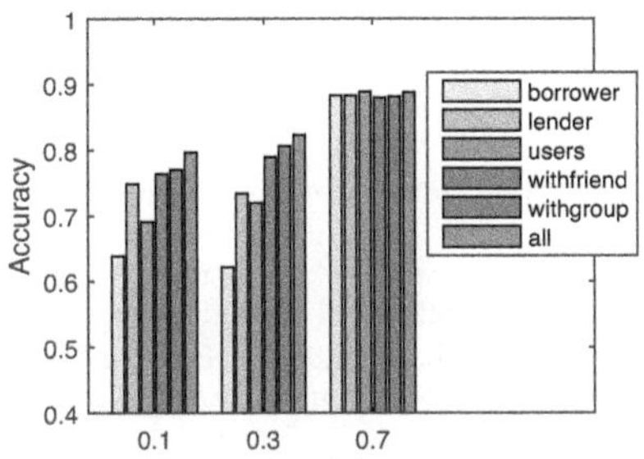

Figure 12: Influence of meta path on NetCycle.

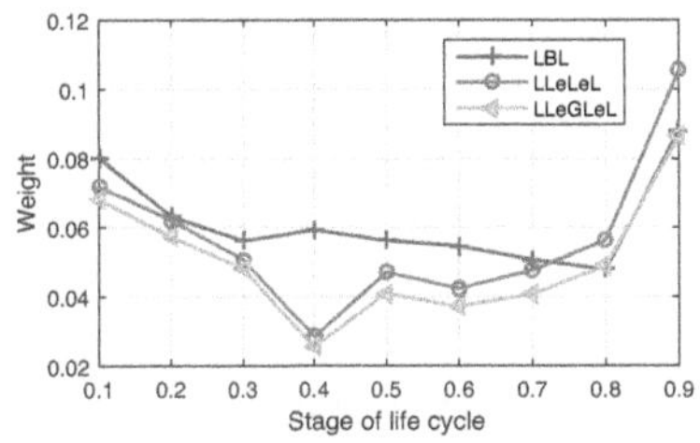

Figure 13: The weights of meta paths during life cycle.

from P2P lending network. In order to illustrate the influence of each path, we apply NetCycle with 6 groups of meta paths in the Prosper networks, including: *only borrowers*{LBL}, *only lenders*{LLeL}, *users*{LBL and LLeL}, *withfriend*{*users*, LBBL, LBLeL, LLeLeL and LLeBL}, *withgroup*{*users*, LBGBL, LBGLeL, LLeGLeL and LLeGBL} and *all*. We test each meta-path group in 3 stages of loan's life cycle in Prosper:2006~2007 dataset, the results as shown in Figure 12. We find that NetCycle can get better performance with the increase number of meta-path types. This support our intuition that meta path is very expressive and can represent indirect relationships that are very important for collective evolution inference tasks.

4.7 Case Studies

To better understand the output of our methods, we give a case study of the weights of meta paths in each stage of life cycle, to show the effectiveness of NetCycle in matching the node evolution pattern. The meta paths we used are from Prosper:2006~2007 dataset, including: *only borrowers* (LBL), *only lenders* (LLeLeL), and *with group* (LLeGLeL). In Figure 13, we display the weights of each meta path learned by segment models during the life cycle.

As shown in Figure 13, the first observation is that all meta paths have large weights in the early stages, and the weights of meta paths have a declining tendency in the early stages. This result proves a phenomenon: "investors prefer to invest new loan listings", which validated by Ceyhan [2]. The weights of meta paths *LLeLeL* and *LLeGLeL* have an similar increasing tendency in latter stage, it may be due to the following reason: as time goes on, the increased numbers of bids will attract more lenders to invest the loan, which also known as *herding effect* in financial domains. Ceyhan [2] also verified the herding effect in P2P Lending service. Compared with *LLeLeL* and *LLeGLeL*, we can find that the weights of *LBL* did not have obvious variation during loan's life cycle, because the relationship between borrower and loan will not change in the fund-raising period. There exists a sharp increasing tendency for all meta paths in the last stage, however, the weights of all features have a sharp variation in the last stage, because we need to normalize the results into discrete values in the last stage. These variation tendency of meta paths provides insightful knowledge for us to understand the node evolution process.

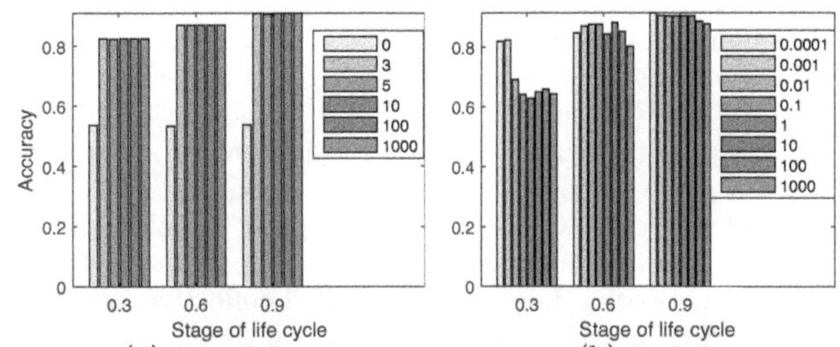

(a) Max_{iter} (b) λ

Figure 14: Influence of Parameters on NetCycle.

4.8 Model selection

There exist two essential parameters in NetCycle, Max_{iter} and λ. Max_{iter} is the maximum number of iterations # in the iterative inference part of NetCycle, and λ is the weight of LIBLINEAR's penalty item (L2 regularization). In previous experiments, we empirically set Max_{iter} as 10, and set λ as 0.001. To test the stability of the performances of NetCycle method, we test the accuracies of different values of Max_{iter} and λ in 3 stages of loan's life cycle on Prosper:2006~2007 dataset, the result as shown in Figure 14. Similar trend holds for the other two datasets which cannot be shown due to space limitation.

Figure 14 illustrates that NetCycle performs quite well and stably, and it is not sensitive to the values of Max_{iter}

and λ. In Figure 14(a), when the number of iterations is very small, *e.g.*, $Max_{iter}<3$, the results did not perform well, because the algorithm not reached convergence yet. However, with the increase of the number of iterations, the results do not change obviously. In Figure 14(b), we can find that smaller λ always has better performance at the early stage (k=0.3), and the results don't change obviously as time goes on (*e.g.*, k=0.6 or 0.9). There does not exist obvious differences at each stage.

5. RELATED WORK

Our work on collective evolution inference is related to both collective inference and dynamic networks analysis. We will introduce recent related works of them in this section.

Collective inference [6] of relational data, including collective classification [1] and collective regression [13], have been investigated by many researchers. Basic collective classification problems focus on classification in homogeneous network [17]. Ji [7] studied a specialized classification problem on heterogeneous networks, where different types of nodes share a same set of label concepts. Kong [11] proposed a method called HCC based on meta-path to solve the collective classification problem on one-type nodes in heterogeneous networks. Loglisci [13] studied collective regression for handling autocorrelation of network data. All of them only paid attention to static networks, instead of dynamic networks. In this work, we compare with the methods in [7, 11] as two competing algorithms.

On the other hand, in dynamic networks, Sharan [19] proposed a representational framework to model both temporal and relational dependencies in networks, but they only tested the model on the link prediction problem. Yu [21] used cascading process to predict the propagation of information. Cho [3] presented a point process to model the Spatial-Temporal Networks. However, none of them focused on collective inference problem. Moreover, the evolution inference problem are very similar with autoregressive process. They both try to infer a time series values of the instances response variables in the future. But autoregressive process commonly studied the evolution pattern from previous sequence, while the evolution inference studied from correlated instances with the restrictions of their life cycles.

In addition, there exist several works in P2P lending networks [2, 14]. Ceyhan [2] examined a simple model to validate the lenders' bidding behavior during fund-raising period on bidding detection problem, which we also used as one of competing algorithms.

6. CONCLUSION

In this paper, we first present the collective evolution problem in dynamic networks, where the response variables of the nodes are evolving with a certain period time. Then we extend the problem into HINs, where the network includes multiple types of nodes connected through multiple types of links. We propose an effective algorithm, called NetCycle, to solve the collective evolution inference problem in HINs. The NetCycle method can not only predict the values of node response variables for collective inference problems, but also can predict the evolution tendency of the node response variables during life cycles. Empirical studies on real-world tasks demonstrate the effectiveness of the proposed method.

7. ACKNOWLEDGMENTS

The work was supported in part by the National High Technology Research and Development Program of China No.2015AA020105, and the National Natural Science Foundation of China Projects No.61170096, No.71331005. The authors would like to thank Jinhong Mi and Lu Ruan for their comments.

8. REFERENCES

[1] M. Bilgic, T. Eliassi-Rad, P. Sen, G. Namata, L. Getoor, and B. Gallagher. Collective classification in network data. *AI Magazine*, 29(3):93–106, 2008.

[2] S. Ceyhan, X. Shi, and J. Leskovec. Dynamics of bidding in a P2P lending service: effects of herding and predicting loan success. In *WWW*, 2011.

[3] Y. S. Cho, A. Galstyan, J. Brantingham, and G. Tita. Latent point process models for spatial-temporal networks. *DCDS-B*, 2013.

[4] R. E. Fan, K. W. Chang, C. J. Hsieh, X. R. Wang, and C. J. Lin. LIBLINEAR: a library for large linear classification. *JMLR*, 9(12):1871–1874, 2008.

[5] J. Hamilton. *Time Series Analysis.* Princeton Univ. Press, 1994.

[6] D. Jensen, J. Neville, and B. Gallagher. Why collective inference improves relational classification. *KDD*, 2004.

[7] M. Ji, J. Han, and M. Danilevsky. Ranking-based classification of heterogeneous information networks. In *KDD*, 2011.

[8] M. Ji, Y. Sun, M. Danilevsky, J. Han, and J. Gao. Graph regularized transductive classification on heterogeneous information networks. In *ECML*, 2010.

[9] E. Keogh, K. Chakrabarti, S. Mehrotra, and M. J. Pazzani. Locally adaptive dimensionality reduction for indexing large time series databases. In *SIGMOD*, 2001.

[10] X. Kong, B. Cao, and P. S. Yu. Multi-label classification by mining label and instance correlations from heterogeneous information networks. In *KDD*, 2013.

[11] X. Kong, P. S. Yu, Y. Ding, and D. J. Wild. Meta path-based collective classification in heterogeneous information networks. In *CIKM*, 2012.

[12] L. Li, J. McCann, N. S. Pollard, and C. Faloutsos. Dynammo: mining and summarization of coevolving sequences with missing values. In *KDD*, 2009.

[13] C. Loglisci, A. Appice, and D. Malerba. Collective regression for handling autocorrelation of network data in a transductive setting. *JIIS*, 2015.

[14] C.-T. Lu, S. Xie, X. Kong, and P. S. Yu. Inferring the impacts of social media on crowdfunding. In *WSDM*, 2014.

[15] Q. Lu and L. Getoor. Link-based classification. In *ICML*, 2003.

[16] L. K. Mcdowell and D. W. Aha. Labels or attributes?: rethinking the neighbors for collective classification in sparsely-labeled networks. In *CIKM*, 2013.

[17] J. Neville and D. Jensen. Iterative classification in relational data. *In AAAI Workshop*, 2000.

[18] J. Ren, J. Wang, M. Li, H. Wang, and B. Liu. *Prediction of Essential Proteins by Integration of PPI Network Topology and Protein Complexes Information.* Springer Berlin Heidelberg, 2011.

[19] U. Sharan and J. Neville. Temporal-relational classifiers for prediction in evolving domains. In *ICDM*, 2008.

[20] Y. Sun, J. Han, X. Yan, P. Yu, and T. Wu. PathSim: Meta path-based top-k similarity search in heterogeneous information networks. In *VLDB*, 2011.

[21] L. Yu, P. Cui, F. Wang, C. Song, and S. Yang. From Micro to Macro: Uncovering and predicting information cascading process with behavioral dynamics. In *ICDM*, 2015.

Accelerating Online CP Decompositions for Higher Order Tensors

Shuo Zhou[1], Nguyen Xuan Vinh[1], James Bailey[1], Yunzhe Jia[1], Ian Davidson[2]
[1]Dept. of Computing and Information Systems, The University of Melbourne, Australia
[1]{zhous@student., vinh.nguyen@, baileyj@, yunzhej@student.}unimelb.edu.au
[2]Dept. of Computer Science, University of California, Davis, USA
[2]davidson@cs.ucdavis.edu

ABSTRACT

Tensors are a natural representation for multidimensional data. In recent years, CANDECOMP/PARAFAC (CP) decomposition, one of the most popular tools for analyzing multi-way data, has been extensively studied and widely applied. However, today's datasets are often dynamically changing over time. Tracking the CP decomposition for such dynamic tensors is a crucial but challenging task, due to the large scale of the tensor and the velocity of new data arriving. Traditional techniques, such as Alternating Least Squares (ALS), cannot be directly applied to this problem because of their poor scalability in terms of time and memory. Additionally, existing online approaches have only partially addressed this problem and can only be deployed on third-order tensors. To fill this gap, we propose an efficient online algorithm that can incrementally track the CP decompositions of dynamic tensors with an arbitrary number of dimensions. In terms of effectiveness, our algorithm demonstrates comparable results with the most accurate algorithm, ALS, whilst being computationally much more efficient. Specifically, on small and moderate datasets, our approach is tens to hundreds of times faster than ALS, while for large-scale datasets, the speedup can be more than 3,000 times. Compared to other state-of-the-art online approaches, our method shows not only significantly better decomposition quality, but also better performance in terms of stability, efficiency and scalability.

Keywords

Tensor Decomposition; CP Decomposition; Online Learning

1. INTRODUCTION

Numerous types of data are naturally represented as multidimensional structures. The *Tensor*, a multi-way generalization of the matrix, is useful for representing such data. Similar to matrix analysis tools, such as PCA and SVD, *tensor decomposition* (TD) is a popular approach for feature extraction, dimensionality reduction and knowledge discovery on multi-way data. It has been extensively studied and widely applied in various fields of science, including chemometrics [1], signal processing [7], computer vision [14, 29], graph and network analysis [10, 17] and time series analysis [5].

In the era of big data, data is often dynamically changing over time, and a large volume of new data can be generated at high velocity. In such dynamic environments, a data tensor may be expanded, shrunk or modified on any of its dimensions. For example, given a network monitoring tensor structured as $source \times destination \times port \times time$, a large number of network transactions are generated every second, which can be recorded by appending new slices to the tensor on its time mode. Additionally, new IP addresses may be added and invalid addresses may be removed from the data tensor. Overall, this data tensor is highly dynamic.

As TD is usually the first and necessary step for analyzing multi-way data, in this work, we aim to address the problem of how to adaptively track the decompositions for such time-evolving tensors. Specifically, we are particularly interested in dynamic tensors that are incrementally growing over time, while the other dimensions remain unchanged. These are the most common type of dynamic tensors that occur in practice. We refer to such tensors as *online tensors*, also known as *tensor streams* and *incremental tensors* [27, 28].

Finding the decompositions for large-scale online tensors is challenging. The difficulty mainly arises from two factors. First, as online tensors are growing with time, their overall size is potentially unbounded. Thus, TD techniques for such tensors need to be highly efficient and scalable, from both time and space perspectives. Second, a high data generation rate demands decomposition methods providing real-time or near real-time performance [6]. However, traditional TD techniques, such as *Tucker* and *CANDECOMP/PARAFAC* (CP) decompositions, cannot be directly applied to this scenario because: (i) they require the availability of the full data for the decomposition, thus having a large memory requirement; and (ii) their fitting algorithms, *Higher-Order SVD* (HOSVD) for Tucker [9], and *Alternating Least Squares* (ALS) or other variants for CP [8], are usually computationally too expensive for large-scale tensors.

A recipe for addressing the above challenges is to adapt existing approaches using online techniques. In recent years, several studies have been conducted on tracking the Tucker decomposition of online tensors by incorporating online techniques, such as incremental SVD [14, 18, 26], and incremental update of covariance matrices [27, 28]. However, there is a limited amount of work on tracking the CP decomposition of an online tensor. The only work in the literature, pro-

KDD '16, August 13-17, 2016, San Francisco, CA, USA

DOI: http://dx.doi.org/10.1145/2939672.2939763

posed by Nion and Sidiropoulos [20], specifically only deals with third-order tensors and there is no provision for higher-order tensors with more than 3 dimensions. To fill this gap, we propose an efficient algorithm to find the CP decomposition of large-scale high-order online tensors, with low space and time usage. We summarize our contributions as follows:

- We propose a scalable algorithm for efficiently tracking the CP decompositions of online tensors. Not limited to basic third-order tensors, our model can also handle higher-order tensors that have more than 3 dimensions.
- Through experimental evaluation on seven real world datasets, we show that our approach can provide more accurate results and better efficiency, compared with state-of-the-art approaches.
- Based on empirical analysis on synthetic datasets, our algorithm produces more stable decompositions than existing online approaches, as well as better scalability.

The rest of this paper is organized as follows. Section 2 gives a review of current techniques and Section 3 introduces background knowledge. Our proposal is discussed in Section 4. We start from third-order tensors and then extend this model to general tensors that have an arbitrary number of dimensions. After that, the performance of our approach is evaluated on both real world and synthetic datasets in Section 5. Lastly, Section 6 concludes and discusses future research directions.

2. RELATED WORK

The problem of decomposing online tensors was originally proposed by Sun *et al.* [27, 28], wherein they refer to this problem as *Incremental Tensor Analysis* (ITA). Three variants of ITA are discussed in their work: (1) dynamic tensor analysis (DTA) modifies the covariance matrices calculation step in typical HOSVD in an incremental fashion; (2) stream tensor analysis (STA) is an approximation of DTA by the SPIRIT algorithm [21]; and (3) window-based tensor analysis (WTA) uses a sliding window strategy to improve the efficiency of DTA. The main issue of these techniques is that they have not fully optimized the most time consuming step, i.e., diagonalizing the covariance matrix for each mode, which limits their efficiency. To overcome this issue, Liu *et al.* [17] propose an efficient algorithm that enforces the diagonalization on the core tensors only. Additionally, another trend for improving the efficiency of HOSVD on online tensors is to replace SVD with incremental SVD algorithms. Several applications of this idea can be found in computer vision [14, 18, 26] and anomaly dectection [25] fields.

The major difference between the aforementioned techniques and our approach is that they are online versions of Tucker decomposition. Although CP decomposition can be viewed as a special case of Tucker with super-diagonal core tensor, none of the above methods provides a way to enforce this constraint. As a result, these algorithms are not suitable for tracking the CP decompositions of online tensors.

Unlike the existing extensive studies on online Tucker decomposition, there is a limited research reported for online CP decomposition. The most related work to ours was proposed by Nion and Sidiropoulos [20], which introduced two adaptive algorithms that specifically focus on CP decomposition: Simultaneous Diagonalization Tracking (SDT) that incrementally tracks the SVD of the unfolded tensor; and Recursive Least Squares Tracking (RLST), which recursively updates the decomposition factors by minimizing the mean squared error. However, the major drawback of this work is that they work on third-order tensors only, while in contrast we propose a general approach that can incrementally track the CP decompositions of tensors with arbitrary dimensions.

In another related area, among the studies that focus on improving CP decomposition for handling large-scale tensors, GridTF, a grid-based tensor factorization algorithm [22] is particularly related to our problem. The main idea of GridTF is to partition the large tensor into a number of small grids. These grids are then factorized by a typical ALS algorithm in parallel. Finally, the resulting decompositions of these sub-tensors are combined together using an iterative approach. In fact, as stated by the authors, if such partitioning is enforced on the time mode only, then GridTF can be used for tracking the CP decomposition of tensor streams.

3. PRELIMINARIES

3.1 Notation and Basic Operations

Following the notation in [16], vectors are denoted by boldface lowercase letters, e.g., $\mathbf{a}$, matrices by boldface uppercase letters, e.g., $\mathbf{A}$, and tensors by boldface Euler script letters, e.g., $\mathcal{X}$. The *order* of a tensor, also known as the number of *ways* or *modes*, is its number of dimensions. For example, vectors and matrices are tensors of order 1 and 2. A tensor $\mathcal{X} \in \mathbb{R}^{I_1\times\cdots\times I_N}$ is an Nth-order one consisting of real numbers and the cardinality of its i-th order, $i \in [1, N]$ is I_i. We refer to tensors with more than 3 modes as *higher-order* ones. The elements of a tensor are retrieved by their indices, and a *slice* of an Nth-order tensor is an $(N-1)^{th}$-order tensor with the index of a particular mode fixed.

Let $\mathbf{A}^\top$, $\mathbf{A}^{-1}$, $\mathbf{A}^\dagger$ and $\|\mathbf{A}\|$ denote the transpose, inverse, Moore-Penrose pseudoinverse and Frobenius norm of $\mathbf{A}$. Let $\mathbf{A}^{(1)}, \mathbf{A}^{(2)}, \ldots, \mathbf{A}^{(N)}$ represent a sequence of N matrices. The *Khatri-Rao* and *Hadamard* products [16] and element-wise division are denoted by $\odot$, $\circledast$ and $\oslash$, respectively. Furthermore, the Khatri-Rao and Hadamard products of a sequence of N matrices $\mathbf{A}^{(N)}, \mathbf{A}^{(N-1)}, \ldots, \mathbf{A}^{(1)}$ are denoted by $\bigodot^N \mathbf{A}^{(i)}$ and $\circledast^N A^{(i)}$. Note that the superscripts in the sequence are inverted and the subscript $i \neq n$ is used when the n-th matrix is not included in above operations, as $\bigodot_{i\neq n}^N \mathbf{A}^{(i)}$ and $\circledast_{i\neq n}^N A^{(i)}$.

Tensor unfolding, or *matricization*, is a process to transform a tensor into a matrix [15]. Generally, given an Nth-order tensor $\mathcal{X} \in \mathbb{R}^{I_1\times I_2\times\cdots\times I_N}$, its mode-$n$ unfolding $\mathbf{X}_{(n)} \in \mathbb{R}^{I_n\times\prod_{i\neq n}^N I_i}$ can be obtained by permuting the dimensions of $\mathcal{X}$ as $[I_n, I_1, \ldots, I_{n-1}, I_{n+1}, \ldots, I_N]$ and then reshaping the permuted tensor into a matrix of size $I_n \times \prod_{i\neq n}^N I_i$.

3.2 CP Decomposition

CP decomposition is a widely used technique for exploring and extracting the underlying structure of the multi-way data. Basically, given an Nth-order tensor $\mathcal{X} \in \mathbb{R}^{I_1\times\cdots\times I_N}$, CP decomposition approximates this tensor by N *loading* matrices $\mathbf{A}^{(1)}, \ldots, \mathbf{A}^{(N)}$, such that

$$\begin{aligned}\mathbf{X}_{(n)} &\approx \mathbf{A}^{(n)}(\mathbf{A}^{(N)} \odot \cdots \mathbf{A}^{(n+1)} \odot \mathbf{A}^{(n-1)} \cdots \odot \mathbf{A}^{(1)})^\top \\ &= \mathbf{A}^{(n)}(\textstyle\bigodot_{i\neq n}^N \mathbf{A}^{(i)})^\top \\ &= [\![\mathbf{A}^{(1)}, \ldots, \mathbf{A}^{(N)}]\!]\end{aligned} \quad (1)$$

where $[\![\bullet]\!]$ is defined as the CP decomposition operator and each loading matrices $\mathbf{A}^{(i)}, i \in [1, N]$ is of size $I_i \times R$, where R is the tensor rank, indicating the number of latent factors.

To find the CP decomposition $[\![\mathbf{A}^{(1)}, \ldots, \mathbf{A}^{(N)}]\!]$ for an Nth-order tensor $\mathcal{X}$, the objective is to minimize the estimation error $\mathcal{L}$, which is defined as

$$\mathcal{L} = \frac{1}{2} \left\| \mathbf{X}_{(n)} - \mathbf{A}^{(n)} (\odot_{i \neq n}^{N} \mathbf{A}^{(i)})^{\top} \right\|^2$$

However, directly minimizing $\mathcal{L}$ over $\mathbf{A}^{(1)}, \ldots, \mathbf{A}^{(N)}$ is difficult, since $\mathcal{L}$ is not convex w.r.t. $\mathbf{A}^{(1)}, \ldots, \mathbf{A}^{(N)}$. As a result, a widely applied approach is ALS. The main idea is to divide the above optimization problem into N sub-problems and the n-th one, $n \in [1, N]$ fixes all variables but $\mathbf{A}^{(n)}$, and then minimizes the convex objective $\mathcal{L}$ w.r.t. $\mathbf{A}^{(n)}$, that is

$$\mathbf{A}^{(n)} \leftarrow \arg\min_{\mathbf{A}^{(n)}} \frac{1}{2} \left\| \mathbf{X}_{(n)} - \mathbf{A}^{(n)} (\odot_{i \neq n}^{N} \mathbf{A}^{(i)})^{\top} \right\|^2 \quad (2)$$

3.3 Online CP Decomposition

Here we briefly introduce the main idea of existing online CP decomposition algorithms. A third-order online tensor $\mathcal{X} \in \mathbb{R}^{I \times J \times (t_{old} + t_{new})}$ is used as a running example, where $\mathcal{X}$ is expanded from $\mathcal{X}_{old} \in \mathbb{R}^{I \times J \times t_{old}}$ by appending a new chunk of data $\mathcal{X}_{new} \in \mathbb{R}^{I \times J \times t_{new}}$ at its last mode. Considering that in most online systems, the size of the new incoming data is usually much smaller than that of all existing historical data, thus we assume $t_{new} \ll t_{old}$. The CP decomposition of $\mathcal{X}_{old}$ is written as $[\![\mathbf{A}_{old}, \mathbf{B}_{old}, \mathbf{C}_{old}]\!]$ and the aim is to find the CP decomposition $[\![\mathbf{A}, \mathbf{B}, \mathbf{C}]\!]$ of $\mathcal{X}$.

SDT and RLST [20]: Both SDT and RLST transform the online tensor decomposition problem into an incremental matrix factorization problem, by letting $\mathbf{D} = \mathbf{B} \odot \mathbf{A}$, so that equation (1) can be written as $\mathbf{X}_{(3)} = \mathbf{C}\mathbf{D}^{\top}$. Then the problem is how to estimate $\mathbf{C}$ and $\mathbf{D}$.

Different strategies are used in SDT and RLST for calculating $\mathbf{C}$ and $\mathbf{D}$. SDT chooses to do this by making use of the SVD of $\mathbf{X}_{old(3)}$, $\mathbf{U}_{old}\mathbf{\Sigma}_{old}\mathbf{V}_{old}^{\top}$. Specifically, there will always be a matrix $\mathbf{W}_{old}$ that $\mathbf{C}_{old} = \mathbf{U}_{old}\mathbf{W}_{old}^{-1}$ and $\mathbf{D}_{old} = \mathbf{V}_{old}\mathbf{\Sigma}_{old}\mathbf{W}_{old}^{\top}$. Similarly, a matrix $\mathbf{W}$ can be found to make $\mathbf{C} = \mathbf{U}\mathbf{W}^{-1}$ and $\mathbf{D} = \mathbf{V}\mathbf{\Sigma}\mathbf{W}^{\top}$, where $\mathbf{U}\mathbf{\Sigma}\mathbf{V}^{\top}$ is the SVD of $\mathbf{X}_{(3)}$, which can be efficiently calculated by incremental SVD algorithms. Furthermore, the authors assume that there is only a tiny difference between $\mathbf{D}$ and $\mathbf{D}_{old}$ so that the first t_{old} rows of $\mathbf{C}$ are approximately equal to $\mathbf{C}_{old}$. Under this assumption, $\mathbf{W}^{-1}$ can be calculated as $\tilde{\mathbf{U}}^{\dagger}\mathbf{U}_{old}\mathbf{W}_{old}^{-1}$, where $\tilde{\mathbf{U}}$ is the first t_{old} rows of $\mathbf{U}$. Consequently, $\mathbf{W}$, $\mathbf{C}$ and $\mathbf{D}$ can be obtained.

In contrast, RLST follows a more direct approach to get $\mathbf{C}$ and $\mathbf{D}$. Recall that $\mathbf{X}_{(3)} = \mathbf{C}\mathbf{D}^{\top}$, firstly, $\mathbf{C}_{new}$ is calculated as $\mathbf{X}_{new(3)}(\mathbf{D}_{old}^{\top})^{\dagger}$ and $\mathbf{C}$ is updated by appending $\mathbf{C}_{new}$ to $\mathbf{C}_{old}$. Then $\mathbf{D}$ is incrementally estimated with $\mathbf{X}_{new(3)}$ and $\mathbf{C}_{new}$ based on the matrix inversion and pseudo-inversion lemmas. Due to the page limit, we refer interested readers to the original papers [20] for more details.

After getting $\mathbf{C}$ and $\mathbf{D}$, the last step for both SDT and RLST is to estimate $\mathbf{A}$ and $\mathbf{B}$ from $\mathbf{D}$. This process is done by applying SVD on the matrix formed by each column of $\mathbf{D}$, and then putting the left and right principal singular vectors into $\mathbf{A}$ and $\mathbf{B}$, respectively.

Overall, SDT and RLST both deal with the online CP decomposition problem by flattening the non-temporal modes. However, this is the main limitation to their performance. Firstly, it is time consuming due to the cost of SVD. Although the authors replaced the traditional SVD with the Bi-SVD algorithm, the complexity of this is still $\mathcal{O}(R^2IJ)$, which limits their applications on large-scale tensors. Additionally, this flattening process makes SDT and RLST not easy to extend to higher-order tensors, since the flattened matrix will be much larger and it has to be recursively decomposed to loading matrices in the end, which is also costly.

GridTF [22]: As mentioned earlier, the basic idea of GridTF is to partition the whole tensor into smaller tensors and then combine their CP decompositions together. In regards to the example here, $\mathcal{X}$ is the online tensor, $\mathcal{X}_{old}$ and $\mathcal{X}_{new}$ are the two partitions. To obtain the CP decomposition of $\mathcal{X}$, the first step of GridTF is to decompose $\mathcal{X}_{new}$ by ALS as $[\![\mathbf{A}_{new}, \mathbf{B}_{new}, \mathbf{C}_{new}]\!]$, while the decomposition of $\mathcal{X}_{old}$ is already known from the last time step.

The combination step is a recursive update procedure such that in every iteration, each mode is updated with a modified ALS rule, until the whole estimation converges, or the maximum number of iterations has been reached. In our notation, the update rules are given as follows, of which further details can be found in [22].

1) For non-temporal modes $\mathbf{A}$ and $\mathbf{B}$

$$\mathbf{A} \leftarrow \frac{\mathbf{A}_{old}(\mathbf{P}_{old} \oslash (\mathbf{A}_{old}^{\top}\mathbf{A}))}{\mathbf{Q} \oslash (\mathbf{A}^{\top}\mathbf{A})} + \frac{\mathbf{A}_{new}(\mathbf{P}_{new} \oslash (\mathbf{A}_{new}^{\top}\mathbf{A}))}{\mathbf{Q} \oslash (\mathbf{A}^{\top}\mathbf{A})}$$

$$\mathbf{B} \leftarrow \frac{\mathbf{B}_{old}(\mathbf{P}_{old} \oslash (\mathbf{B}_{old}^{\top}\mathbf{B}))}{\mathbf{Q} \oslash (\mathbf{B}^{\top}\mathbf{B})} + \frac{\mathbf{B}_{new}(\mathbf{P}_{new} \oslash (\mathbf{B}_{new}^{\top}\mathbf{B}))}{\mathbf{Q} \oslash (\mathbf{B}^{\top}\mathbf{B})}$$

2) For temporal mode $\mathbf{C}$

$$\mathbf{C} \leftarrow \begin{bmatrix} \dfrac{\mathbf{C}_{old}(\mathbf{P}_{old} \oslash (\mathbf{C}_{old}^{\top}\mathbf{C}))}{\mathbf{Q} \oslash (\mathbf{C}^{\top}\mathbf{C})} \\ \dfrac{\mathbf{C}_{new}(\mathbf{P}_{new} \oslash (\mathbf{C}_{new}^{\top}\mathbf{C}))}{\mathbf{Q} \oslash (\mathbf{C}^{\top}\mathbf{C})} \end{bmatrix}$$

where $\mathbf{A}$, $\mathbf{B}$, $\mathbf{C}$ are randomly initialized at the beginning and $\mathbf{P}_{old} = (\mathbf{A}_{old}^{\top}\mathbf{A}) \circledast (\mathbf{B}_{old}^{\top}\mathbf{B}) \circledast (\mathbf{C}_{old}^{\top}\mathbf{C})$, $\mathbf{P}_{new} = (\mathbf{A}_{new}^{\top}\mathbf{A}) \circledast (\mathbf{B}_{new}^{\top}\mathbf{B}) \circledast (\mathbf{C}_{new}^{\top}\mathbf{C})$, and $\mathbf{Q} = (\mathbf{A}^{\top}\mathbf{A}) \circledast (\mathbf{B}^{\top}\mathbf{B}) \circledast (\mathbf{C}^{\top}\mathbf{C})$.

The main issue of applying GridTF to online CP decomposition is its efficiency. Firstly, even though only the new data need to be decomposed, this is still expensive, especially when the size of new data is large. Secondly, for estimating $\mathbf{C}$ and calculating $\mathbf{P}_{old}$ and $\mathbf{Q}$, $\mathbf{C}_{old}^{\top}\mathbf{C}$ needs to be calculated, costing $R^2 t_{old}$ operations. This means the time complexity of the update procedure is linear in the length of the existing data, t_{old}, which can be huge, thus significantly limiting its ability for processing online tensors.

4. OUR APPROACH

In this section, we introduce our proposal for tracking the CP decomposition of online multi-way data in an incremental setting. For presentation clarity, initially a third-order case will be discussed. Then, we further extend to more general situations, where our proposed algorithm is able to handle tensors that have arbitrary number of modes. Without loss of generality, we assume the last mode of a tensor is always the one growing over time, while the size of the other modes are kept unchanged with time.

4.1 Third-order Tensors

Following the same notation introduced in Section 3.3, similar to the classic ALS algorithm, our approach handles the problem in an alternating update fashion. That is, we first fix $\mathbf{A}$ and $\mathbf{B}$, to update $\mathbf{C}$, and then sequentially update $\mathbf{A}$ and $\mathbf{B}$, by fixing the other two.

4.1.1 Update Temporal Mode C

By fixing $\mathbf{A}$ and $\mathbf{B}$, from (2) we have

$$\begin{aligned}\mathbf{C} &\leftarrow \arg\min_{\mathbf{C}} \frac{1}{2} \left\| \mathbf{X}_{(3)} - \mathbf{C}(\mathbf{B} \odot \mathbf{A})^\top \right\|^2 \\ &= \arg\min_{\mathbf{C}} \frac{1}{2} \left\| \begin{bmatrix} \mathbf{X}_{old(3)} \\ \mathbf{X}_{new(3)} \end{bmatrix} - \begin{bmatrix} \mathbf{C}^{(1)} \\ \mathbf{C}^{(2)} \end{bmatrix} (\mathbf{B} \odot \mathbf{A})^\top \right\|^2 \\ &= \arg\min_{\mathbf{C}} \frac{1}{2} \left\| \begin{bmatrix} \mathbf{X}_{old(3)} - \mathbf{C}^{(1)}(\mathbf{B} \odot \mathbf{A})^\top \\ \mathbf{X}_{new(3)} - \mathbf{C}^{(2)}(\mathbf{B} \odot \mathbf{A})^\top \end{bmatrix} \right\|^2 \end{aligned} \tag{3}$$

It is clear that the norm of the first row is minimized with $\mathbf{C}_{old}$, since $\mathbf{A}$ and $\mathbf{B}$ are fixed as $\mathbf{A}_{old}$ and $\mathbf{B}_{old}$ from the last time step. The optimal solution to minimize the second row is $\mathbf{C}^{(2)} = \mathbf{X}_{new(3)}((\mathbf{B} \odot \mathbf{A})^\top)^\dagger$. As a result, $\mathbf{C}$ is updated by appending the projection $\mathbf{C}_{new}$ of $\mathbf{X}_{new(3)}$ via the loading matrices $\mathbf{A}$ and $\mathbf{B}$ of previous time step, to $\mathbf{C}_{old}$, i.e.,

$$\mathbf{C} = \begin{bmatrix} \mathbf{C}_{old} \\ \mathbf{C}_{new} \end{bmatrix} = \begin{bmatrix} \mathbf{C}_{old} \\ \mathbf{X}_{new(3)}((\mathbf{B} \odot \mathbf{A})^\top)^\dagger \end{bmatrix} \tag{4}$$

4.1.2 Update Non-temporal Modes A and B

First, we update $\mathbf{A}$. By fixing $\mathbf{B}$ and $\mathbf{C}$, the estimations error $\mathcal{L}$ can be written as $\frac{1}{2} \left\| \mathbf{X}_{(1)} - \mathbf{A}(\mathbf{C} \odot \mathbf{B})^\top \right\|^2$, and the derivative of $\mathcal{L}$ w.r.t. $\mathbf{A}$ is

$$\frac{\partial \mathcal{L}}{\partial \mathbf{A}} = \mathbf{X}_{(1)}(\mathbf{C} \odot \mathbf{B}) - \mathbf{A}(\mathbf{C} \odot \mathbf{B})^\top (\mathbf{C} \odot \mathbf{B})$$

By setting the derivative to zero and letting $\mathbf{P} = \mathbf{X}_{(1)}(\mathbf{C} \odot \mathbf{B})$ and $\mathbf{Q} = (\mathbf{C} \odot \mathbf{B})^\top (\mathbf{C} \odot \mathbf{B})$, we have

$$\mathbf{A} = \mathbf{P}\mathbf{Q}^{-1} \tag{5}$$

Directly calculating $\mathbf{P}$ and $\mathbf{Q}$ is costly. This is mainly because the output of $(\mathbf{C} \odot \mathbf{B})$ is a huge matrix of size $J(t_{old} + t_{new}) \times R$, where R is the tensor rank. It further results in $\mathcal{O}(RIJ(t_{old} + t_{new}))$ and $\mathcal{O}(R^2 J(t_{old} + t_{new}))$ operations to get $\mathbf{P}$ and $\mathbf{Q}$, respectively. Although for $\mathbf{Q}$, the Khatri-Rao product can be avoided by calculating it as $(\mathbf{C}^\top \mathbf{C}) \circledast (\mathbf{B}^\top \mathbf{B})$ [16], which has a complexity of $\mathcal{O}(R^2(J + t_{old} + t_{new}))$, this is still expensive since t_{old} is usually quite large. As a result, in order to improve the efficiency, we need a faster approach.

Firstly, let us look at $\mathbf{P}$. By representing $\mathbf{X}_{(1)}$ and $\mathbf{C}$ with the *old* and *new* components, we have

$$\begin{aligned}\mathbf{P} &= \mathbf{X}_{(1)}(\mathbf{C} \odot \mathbf{B}) \\ &= \left[\mathbf{X}_{old(1)}, \mathbf{X}_{new(1)}\right] \left(\begin{bmatrix} \mathbf{C}_{old} \\ \mathbf{C}_{new} \end{bmatrix} \odot \mathbf{B} \right) \\ &= \left[\mathbf{X}_{old(1)}, \mathbf{X}_{new(1)}\right] \begin{bmatrix} \mathbf{C}_{old} \odot \mathbf{B} \\ \mathbf{C}_{new} \odot \mathbf{B} \end{bmatrix} \\ &= \mathbf{X}_{old(1)}(\mathbf{C}_{old} \odot \mathbf{B}) + \mathbf{X}_{new(1)}(\mathbf{C}_{new} \odot \mathbf{B}) \end{aligned} \tag{6}$$

recall that $\mathbf{B}$ has been fixed as $\mathbf{B}_{old}$, so that the first part of the last line of equation (6) only contains components from the previous time step. Suppose we know this part already and denote it by $\mathbf{P}_{old}$, then (6) can be rewritten as

$$\mathbf{P} = \mathbf{P}_{old} + \mathbf{X}_{new(1)}(\mathbf{C}_{new} \odot \mathbf{B}) \tag{7}$$

This means that by keeping a record of the previous $\mathbf{P}$, the large computation can be avoided and it can be efficiently updated in an incremental way. Specifically, suppose $\mathbf{P}$ is initialized with a small partition $\mathcal{X}(\tau) \in \mathbb{R}^{I \times J \times \tau}$ that contains the first τ slices of the data, where $\tau \ll t_{old}$, we only need $\mathcal{O}(RIJ\tau)$ operations to construct $\mathbf{P}$. Afterwards, whenever new data comes, $\mathbf{P}$ can be efficiently updated at the cost of $\mathcal{O}(RIJt_{new})$, which is independent to t_{old}.

Likewise, $\mathbf{Q}$ can be estimated as

$$\begin{aligned}\mathbf{Q} &= \mathbf{Q}_{old} + (\mathbf{C}_{new} \odot \mathbf{B})^\top (\mathbf{C}_{new} \odot \mathbf{B}) \\ &= \mathbf{Q}_{old} + (\mathbf{C}_{new}^\top \mathbf{C}_{new}) \circledast (\mathbf{B}^\top \mathbf{B}) \end{aligned} \tag{8}$$

Thus, by storing the information of previous decomposition with *complementary* matrices $\mathbf{P}$ and $\mathbf{Q}$, we achieve the update rule for $\mathbf{A}$ as follows,

$$\begin{aligned}&\mathbf{P} \leftarrow \mathbf{P} + \mathbf{X}_{new(1)}(\mathbf{C}_{new} \odot \mathbf{B}) \\ &\mathbf{Q} \leftarrow \mathbf{Q} + (\mathbf{C}_{new}^\top \mathbf{C}_{new}) \circledast (\mathbf{B}^\top \mathbf{B}) \\ &\mathbf{A} \leftarrow \mathbf{P}\mathbf{Q}^{-1} \end{aligned} \tag{9}$$

The update rule for $\mathbf{B}$ can be derived in a similar way as

$$\begin{aligned}&\mathbf{U} \leftarrow \mathbf{U} + \mathbf{X}_{new(2)}(\mathbf{C}_{new} \odot \mathbf{A}) \\ &\mathbf{V} \leftarrow \mathbf{V} + (\mathbf{C}_{new}^\top \mathbf{C}_{new}) \circledast (\mathbf{A}^\top \mathbf{A}) \\ &\mathbf{B} \leftarrow \mathbf{U}\mathbf{V}^{-1} \end{aligned} \tag{10}$$

where $\mathbf{U} = \mathbf{X}_{(2)}(\mathbf{C} \odot \mathbf{A})$, $\mathbf{V} = (\mathbf{C} \odot \mathbf{A})^\top (\mathbf{C} \odot \mathbf{A})$ are the two complementary matrices of mode 2.

To sum up: For a third-order tensor that grows with time, we propose an efficient algorithm for tracking its CP decomposition on the fly. We name this algorithm as *OnlineCP*, comprising the following two stages:

1) Initialization stage: for non-temporal modes, complementary matrices $\mathbf{P}$, $\mathbf{Q}$, $\mathbf{U}$ and $\mathbf{V}$ are initialized with the initial tensor $\mathcal{X}_{init}$ and its CP decomposition $[\![\mathbf{A}, \mathbf{B}, \mathbf{C}]\!]$ as

$$\begin{aligned}&\mathbf{P} = \mathbf{X}_{init(1)}(\mathbf{C} \odot \mathbf{B}), \mathbf{Q} = (\mathbf{C}^\top \mathbf{C}) \circledast (\mathbf{B}^\top \mathbf{B}) \\ &\mathbf{U} = \mathbf{X}_{init(2)}(\mathbf{C} \odot \mathbf{A}), \mathbf{V} = (\mathbf{C}^\top \mathbf{C}) \circledast (\mathbf{A}^\top \mathbf{A}) \end{aligned}$$

2) Update stage: for each new incoming data chunk $\mathcal{X}_{new}$, it is processed as

a) for the temporal mode 3, $\mathbf{C}$ is updated with (4)

b) for non-temporal modes 1 and 2, $\mathbf{A}$ is updated with (9) and $\mathbf{B}$ is updated with (10), respectively.

4.2 Extending to Higher-Order Tensors

We now show how to extend our approach to higher-order cases. Let $\mathcal{X}_{old} \in \mathbb{R}^{I_1 \times \cdots \times I_{N-1} \times t_{old}}$ be an Nth-order tensor, $[\![\mathbf{A}_{old}^{(1)}, \ldots, \mathbf{A}_{old}^{(N-1)}, \mathbf{A}_{old}^{(N)}]\!]$ be its CP decomposition, the N-th mode be the time. A new tensor $\mathcal{X}_{new} \in \mathbb{R}^{I_1 \times \cdots \times I_{N-1} \times t_{new}}$ is added to $\mathcal{X}_{old}$ to form a tensor $\mathcal{X} \in \mathbb{R}^{I_1 \times \cdots \times I_{N-1} \times (t_{old} + t_{new})}$, where $t_{old} \gg t_{new}$. In addition, two sets of complementary matrices $\mathbf{P}^{(1)}, \ldots, \mathbf{P}^{(N-1)}$ and $\mathbf{Q}^{(1)}, \ldots, \mathbf{Q}^{(N-1)}$ are stored, where $\mathbf{P}^{(n)}$ and $\mathbf{Q}^{(n)}, n \in [1, N-1]$, are the complementary matrices for mode n. We are interested in finding the CP decomposition $[\![\mathbf{A}^{(1)}, \ldots, \mathbf{A}^{(N-1)}, \mathbf{A}^{(N)}]\!]$ of $\mathcal{X}$.

4.2.1 Update Temporal Mode

Similar to the third-order case, the loading matrix of the time mode, $\mathbf{A}^{(N)}$, is updated at first by fixing the other loading matrices and minimizing the estimation error $\mathcal{L}$

$$\mathbf{A}^{(N)} \leftarrow \arg\min_{\mathbf{A}^{(N)}} \frac{1}{2} \left\| \mathbf{X}_{(N)} - \mathbf{A}^{(N)}(\odot^{N-1} \mathbf{A}^{(i)})^\top \right\|^2$$

Basically, the above equation has the same structure as (3), so we have a similar update rule for $\mathbf{A}^{(N)}$

$$\mathbf{A}^{(N)} \leftarrow \begin{bmatrix} \mathbf{A}^{(N)}_{old} \\ \mathbf{A}^{(N)}_{new} \end{bmatrix} = \begin{bmatrix} \mathbf{A}^{(N)}_{old} \\ \mathbf{X}_{new(N)}((\bigodot^{N-1}\mathbf{A}^{(i)})^\top)^\dagger \end{bmatrix}$$

4.2.2 Update Non-temporal Modes

For each non-temporal mode $n \in [1, N-1]$, the estimation error $\mathcal{L}$ on mode n is $\frac{1}{2}\left\|\mathbf{X}_{(n)} - \mathbf{A}^{(n)}(\bigodot_{i\neq n}^{N}\mathbf{A}^{(i)})^\top\right\|^2$, and similar update rule as equation (9) can be applied, that is

$$\mathbf{P}^{(n)} \leftarrow \mathbf{P}^{(n)} + \mathbf{X}_{new(n)}\left(\mathbf{A}^{(N)}_{new} \odot \mathbf{K}^{(n)}\right)$$
$$\mathbf{Q}^{(n)} \leftarrow \mathbf{Q}^{(n)} + \left({\mathbf{A}^{(N)}_{new}}^\top \mathbf{A}^{(N)}_{new}\right) \circledast \mathbf{H}^{(n)}$$
$$\mathbf{A}^{(n)} \leftarrow \mathbf{P}^{(n)}(\mathbf{Q}^{(n)})^{-1}$$

where we denote the Khatri-Rao product of the first $N-1$ but the n-th loading matrices, $\bigodot_{i\neq n}^{N-1}\mathbf{A}^{(i)}$, as $\mathbf{K}^{(n)}$ and the Hadamard product, $\circledast_{i\neq n}^{N-1}{\mathbf{A}^{(i)}}^\top\mathbf{A}^{(i)}$, as $\mathbf{H}^{(n)}$.

4.2.3 Avoid Duplicated Computation

In fact, if we were to compute every $\mathbf{K}^{(n)}$ for each $n \in [1, N-1]$, there would be some redundant computation among them. Take a 5th-order tensor for example, where $\mathbf{K}^{(1)} = \mathbf{A}^{(4)} \odot \mathbf{A}^{(3)} \odot \mathbf{A}^{(2)}$, $\mathbf{K}^{(2)} = \mathbf{A}^{(4)} \odot \mathbf{A}^{(3)} \odot \mathbf{A}^{(1)}$, $\mathbf{K}^{(3)} = \mathbf{A}^{(4)} \odot \mathbf{A}^{(2)} \odot \mathbf{A}^{(1)}$, and $\mathbf{K}^{(4)} = \mathbf{A}^{(3)} \odot \mathbf{A}^{(2)} \odot \mathbf{A}^{(1)}$. It is clear that both $\mathbf{K}^{(1)}$ and $\mathbf{K}^{(2)}$ have computed $\mathbf{A}^{(4)} \odot \mathbf{A}^{(3)}$, and $\mathbf{K}^{(3)}$ and $\mathbf{K}^{(4)}$ share a common computation $\mathbf{A}^{(2)} \odot \mathbf{A}^{(1)}$. These redundant Khatri-Rao products are computationally expensive to calculate, and more importantly, the amount of redundancy will dramatically increase with the number of modes N, since more common components are shared.

To overcome this issue, we use a dynamic programming strategy to compute all the $\mathbf{K}^{(n)}$'s in one run, by making good use of the intermediate results and avoiding duplicated operations. This process is detailed in Algorithm 1 and an illustrating example of a 6th-order tensor is given in Figure 1. The main idea is to go through the loading matrix list $\mathbf{A}^{(N-1)}, \ldots, \mathbf{A}^{(2)}, \mathbf{A}^{(1)}$ from both ends, until the algorithm reaches the results of $\mathbf{K}^{(1)}$ and $\mathbf{K}^{(N-1)}$ (lines 3 to 8). After that, for the rest of $\mathbf{K}^{(i)}$ where $i \in [2, N-2]$, they are computed as the Khatri-Rao products of the intermediate results from the last loop (lines 11 to 15).

For the $\mathbf{H}^{(n)}$'s, it is obvious that calculating each individual $\mathbf{H}^{(n)}$ by itself is inefficient. Exploiting the fact that for $\forall i, j \in [1, N-1]$, $\mathbf{H}^{(i)} \circledast ({\mathbf{A}^{(i)}}^\top\mathbf{A}^{(i)}) = \mathbf{H}^{(j)} \circledast ({\mathbf{A}^{(j)}}^\top\mathbf{A}^{(j)}) = \mathbf{H}$, in each round of update, $\mathbf{H}$ is calculated first, then each $\mathbf{H}^{(n)}$ is obtained as $\mathbf{H} \oslash ({\mathbf{A}^{(n)}}^\top\mathbf{A}^{(n)})$, where $\oslash$ is the element-wise division.

Finally, by putting everything together, we obtain the general version of our OnlineCP algorithm[1], as presented in Algorithm 2 and 3.

4.3 Complexity Analysis

Following the same notation as Section 4.2, let R be the tensor rank, $S = \prod_{i=1}^{N-1} I_i$, and $J = \sum_{i=1}^{N-1} I_i$. To process a new chunk of data $\mathfrak{X}_{new}$, it takes up to $(N-1)S$ operations to get all the $\mathbf{K}^{(n)}, n \in [1, N-1]$, and $\mathbf{H}$ can be obtained in $R^2J + (N-2)R^2$ operations (lines 1 and 2 in Algorithm 3). To update the time mode, RS, St_{new}, and $RSt_{new} + R^2t_{new} + R^3$ operations are required to get $\mathbf{K}^{(N)}$, $\mathbf{X}_{new(N)}$, and $\mathbf{A}^{(N)}_{new}$, respectively (lines 3, 4). Note that the pseudoinverse $((\mathbf{K}^{(N)})^\top)^\dagger$ can be replaced by $\mathbf{K}^{(N)}\mathbf{H}^\dagger$ as $(\mathbf{A} \odot \mathbf{B})^\dagger = ((\mathbf{A}^\top\mathbf{A}) \circledast (\mathbf{B}^\top\mathbf{B}))^\dagger(\mathbf{A} \odot \mathbf{B})^\top$ [16]. For each non-temporal mode n (lines 7 to 10), St_{new}, RSt_{new}/I_n ($\approx St_{new}$, since R is usually smaller than I_n), RSt_{new} and RI_n operations are required for the unfolding, Khatri-Rao, multiplication and addition in the step to update $\mathbf{P}^{(n)}$; and $\mathbf{Q}^{(n)}$ takes $R^2I_n + R^2t_{new} + 3R^2$ operations to update; then the updated $\mathbf{A}^{(n)}$ can be calculated in $R^3 + R^2I_n$ operations. Thus, to update the loading matrix $\mathbf{A}^{(n)}$ of mode n, $(2R^2+R)I_n + (R+2)St_{new} + R^3 + (3+t_{new})R^2$ operations is required and the whole update procedure for non-temporal modes takes $(2R^2 + R)J + (N-1)(R+2)St_{new} + (N-1)(R^3 + (3 + t_{new})R^2)$ operations. Overall, as S is usually much larger than other factors, the time complexity of OnlineCP can be written as $\mathcal{O}(NRSt_{new})$, which is constant w.r.t. the length of processed data t_{old}.

In terms of space consumption, unlike ALS that needs to store all the data, OnlineCP is quite efficient since only the new data, previous loading matrices and complementary matrices need to be recorded. Hence, the total cost of space is $St_{new} + (2J + t_{old})R + (N-1)R^2$.

[1] We provide our Matlab implementation of `OnlineCP` at `http://shuo-zhou.info`.

Algorithm 1: Get a list of Khatri-Rao products

Input: A list of loading matrices $[\mathbf{A}^{(N-1)}, \ldots, \mathbf{A}^{(1)}]$
Output: A list of Khatri-Rao products $[\mathbf{K}^{(1)}, \ldots, \mathbf{K}^{(N-1)}]$

1 $left \leftarrow [\mathbf{A}^{(N-1)}]$
2 $right \leftarrow [\mathbf{A}^{(1)}]$
3 **if** $N > 3$ **then**
4   **for** $n \leftarrow 2$ **to** $N-2$ **do**
5         $left[n] \leftarrow left[n-1] \odot \mathbf{A}^{(N-n)}$
6         $right[n] \leftarrow \mathbf{A}^{(n)} \odot right[n-1]$
7   **end**
8 **end**
9 $\mathbf{K}^{(1)} \leftarrow left[N-2]$
10 $\mathbf{K}^{(N-1)} \leftarrow right[N-2]$
11 **if** $N > 3$ **then**
12   **for** $n \leftarrow 2$ **to** $N-2$ **do**
13         $\mathbf{K}^{(n)} \leftarrow left[N-n-1] \odot right[n-1]$
14   **end**
15 **end**

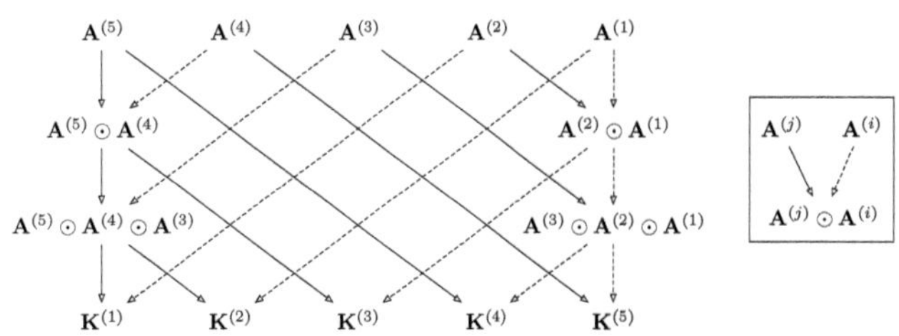

Figure 1: A 6th-order example to get all $\mathbf{K}^{(n)}$'s together. A Khatri-Rao product is represented by two arrows, of which the solid one linked to the first input. The two lists, *left* and *right*, are indicated by the two columns on the graph.

Table 1: Complexity comparison between OnlineCP and existing methods.

	Time	Space	Source
OnlineCP	$\mathcal{O}(NRSt_{new})$	$St_{new} + (2J + t_{old})R + (N-1)R^2$	
ALS	$\mathcal{O}(NRS(t_{old} + t_{new}))$	$S(t_{old} + t_{new})$	[4]
SDT	$\mathcal{O}(R^2(t_{old} + S))$	$St_{new} + (J + S + 2t_{old})R + 3R^2$	[20]
RLST	$\mathcal{O}(R^2 S)$	$St_{new} + (J + t_{old} + 2S)R + 2R^2$	[20]
GridTF	$\mathcal{O}(NRSt_{new} + R^2(J + t_{old} + t_{new}))$	$St_{new} + (J + t_{old})R$	[22]

Algorithm 2: Initialization stage of OnlineCP

Input: Initial tensor $\mathcal{X}_{init}$, loading matrices $\mathbf{A}^{(1)}, \ldots, \mathbf{A}^{(N)}$
Output: complementary matrices $\mathbf{P}^{(1)}, \ldots, \mathbf{P}^{(N-1)}$ and $\mathbf{Q}^{(1)}, \ldots, \mathbf{Q}^{(N-1)}$

Get $\mathbf{K}^{(1)}, \mathbf{K}^{(2)}, \ldots, \mathbf{K}^{(N-1)}$ by Algorithm 1
$\mathbf{H} \leftarrow \circledast^N \mathbf{A}^{(i)\top} \mathbf{A}^{(i)}$
for $n \leftarrow 1$ **to** $N-1$ **do**
  $\mathbf{P}^{(n)} \leftarrow \mathbf{X}_{init(n)}(\mathbf{A}^{(N)} \odot \mathbf{K}^{(n)})$
  $\mathbf{Q}^{(n)} \leftarrow \mathbf{H} \oslash (\mathbf{A}^{(n)\top} \mathbf{A}^{(n)})$
end

Algorithm 3: Update stage of OnlineCP

Input: Loading matrices $\mathbf{A}^{(1)}, \ldots, \mathbf{A}^{(N)}$, complementary matrices $\mathbf{P}^{(1)}, \ldots, \mathbf{P}^{(N-1)}$, $\mathbf{Q}^{(1)}, \ldots, \mathbf{Q}^{(N-1)}$, and new data tensor $\mathcal{X}_{new}$
Output: Updated loading matrices $\mathbf{A}^{(1)}, \ldots, \mathbf{A}^{(N)}$, and updated complementary matrices $\mathbf{P}^{(1)}, \ldots, \mathbf{P}^{(N-1)}$, $\mathbf{Q}^{(1)}, \ldots, \mathbf{Q}^{(N-1)}$

Get $\mathbf{K}^{(1)}, \mathbf{K}^{(2)}, \ldots, \mathbf{K}^{(N-1)}$ by Algorithm 1
$\mathbf{H} \leftarrow \circledast^{N-1} \mathbf{A}^{(i)\top} \mathbf{A}^{(i)}$
// update $\mathbf{A}^{(N)}$
$\mathbf{K}^{(N)} \leftarrow \mathbf{K}^{(1)} \odot \mathbf{A}^{(1)}$
$\mathbf{A}^{(N)}_{new} \leftarrow \mathbf{X}_{new(N)}((\mathbf{K}^{(N)})^\top)^\dagger$
$\mathbf{A}^{(N)} \leftarrow \begin{bmatrix} \mathbf{A}^{(N)}_{old} \\ \mathbf{A}^{(N)}_{new} \end{bmatrix}$
// update other modes
for $n \leftarrow 1$ **to** $N-1$ **do**
  $\mathbf{P}^{(n)} \leftarrow \mathbf{P}^{(n)} + \mathbf{X}_{new(n)}(\mathbf{A}^{(N)}_{new} \odot \mathbf{K}^{(n)})$
  $\mathbf{H}^{(n)} \leftarrow \mathbf{H} \oslash (\mathbf{A}^{(n)\top} \mathbf{A}^{(n)})$
  $\mathbf{Q}^{(n)} \leftarrow \mathbf{Q}^{(n)} + (\mathbf{A}^{(N)\top}_{new} \mathbf{A}^{(N)}_{new}) \circledast \mathbf{H}^{(n)}$
  $\mathbf{A}^{(n)} \leftarrow \mathbf{P}^{(n)}(\mathbf{Q}^{(n)})^{-1}$
end

We summarize the complexity of our approach in Table 1, along with other existing approaches. Note that the complexities of SDT and RLST are based on the exponential window [20], which considers all existing data while leverages their importance by a forgetting factor λ. In addition, as they only work on third-order tensors, when other methods are compared to them, N should be set to 3. Another remark is that the time complexities of ALS and GridTF are based on one iteration only, in reality they would take a few iterations until convergence.

5. EMPIRICAL ANALYSIS

In this section, we evaluate our OnlineCP algorithm, compared to existing techniques. We first examine their effectiveness and efficiency on seven real world datasets. After that, based on the investigation on synthetic tensors, we further analyze the critical factors that can affect the performance of our approach, along with other baselines.

5.1 Real World Datasets

5.1.1 Experimental Specifications

Datasets: The experiments are conducted on seven real world datasets of varying characteristics, all are naturally of multi-way structures. These are two image datasets: (i) Columbia Object Image Library (COIL); (ii) ORL Database of Faces (FACE); three human activity datasets: (iii) Daily and Sports Activities Data Set (DSA); (iv) University of Southern California Human Activity Dataset (HAD); (v) Daphnet Freezing of Gait Data Set (FOG); one chemical laboratory dataset: (vi) Gas sensor array under dynamic gas mixtures Data Set (GAS); and a (vii) road traffic dataset collected from loop detectors in Victoria, Australia (ROAD).

Each dataset is represented by a tensor with its most natural structure. For instance, FACE is represented by a $pixel \times pixel \times shot$ third-order tensor, while DSA is stored as an 4th-order tensor of $subject \times trail \times sensor \times time$. Furthermore, since some of our baselines can only work with third-order tensors, for tensors with higher-order, DSA, GAS, and HAD, we randomly extract third-order sub-tensors from them. Conversely, to enlarge the number of higher-order tensors, image datasets, COIL and FACE have been transformed into 4th-order tensors by treating each image as a collection of small *patches*, which forms the extra order. As a result, there are five datasets having two versions of representation: a third-order one, indicated by suffix *3D*, and a higher-order form with suffix *HD*. The details of these datasets can be found in Table 2.

Baselines: In this experiment, five baselines have been selected as the competitors to evaluate the performance.

(i) Batch Cold: an implementation of ALS algorithm in Tensor Toolbox [4] without special initialization.

(ii) Batch Hot: the same ALS algorithm as above but the CP decomposition of the last time step is used as the initialization for decomposing the current tensor.

(iii) SDT [20]: an adaptive algorithm based on incrementally tracking the SVD of the unfolded tensor.

(iv) RLST: another online approach proposed in [20]. Instead of tracking the SVD, recursive updates are performed to minimize the mean squared error on new data.

Table 2: Details of datasets

Datasets	Size	Slice Size $S=\prod_{i=1}^{N-1} I_i$	Source
COIL-3D	$128\times128\times240$	16,384	[19]
COIL-HD	$64\times64\times25\times240$	102,400	
DSA-3D	$8\times45\times750$	360	[2]
DSA-HD	$19\times8\times45\times750$	6,840	
FACE-3D	$112\times92\times400$	10,304	[23]
FACE-HD	$28\times23\times16\times400$	10,304	
FOG	$10\times9\times1000$	90	[3]
GAS-3D	$30\times8\times2970$	240	[12]
GAS-HD	$30\times6\times8\times2970$	1,440	
HAD-3D	$14\times6\times500$	64	[30]
HAD-HD	$14\times12\times5\times6\times500$	3,840	
ROAD	$4666\times96\times1826$	447,936	[24]

(v) GridTF [22]: an divide-and-conqure based algorithm. To find CP decompositions for online tensors, the partitioning is enforced on the time mode only.

Evaluation metrics: Two performance metrics are used in our evaluation. *Fitness* is the effectiveness measurement defined as

$$fitness \triangleq \left(1-\frac{\left\|\hat{\mathcal{X}}-\mathcal{X}\right\|}{\left\|\mathcal{X}\right\|}\right)\times 100\%$$

where $\mathcal{X}$ is the ground truth, $\hat{\mathcal{X}}$ is the estimation and $\|\bullet\|$ denotes the Frobenius norm. In addition, the *average running time* for processing one data slice, measured in seconds, is used to validate the time efficiency of an algorithm.

Experimental setup: The experiments are divided into two parts. The first part is to decompose the third-order tensors with all baselines. For the second part, only Batch Hot, GridTF and our approach are used. This is because both SDT and RLST work on third-order tensors only, and Batch Cold does not show better performance compared to Batch Hot, while taking a much longer time to run.

Apart from the difference in the number of competitors, the experimental protocol is the same for both third and higher order tests. Specifically, for a given dataset, the first 20% of the data is decomposed by ALS and its CP decomposition is used to initialize all algorithms. After that, the remaining 80% of the data is appended to the existing tensor by one slice at a time. At each time step, after processing the appended data slice, all methods calculate the fitness of their current decomposition with their updated loading matrices, as well as their processing time for this new slice. The same experiment is replicated 10 times for all datasets on a workstation with dual Intel Xeon processors, 64 GB RAM. The final results are averaged over these 10 runs.

There are some settings of parameters that need to be clarified. Firstly, since we only care about the relative performance comparison among different algorithms, it is not necessary to pursue the best rank decomposition for each dataset. As a result, the rank R is fixed to 5 for all datasets. Additionally, for the initial CP decomposition, the tolerance ε is set to $1e-8$ and the maximum number of iterations $maxiters$ is set to 100 to ensure a good start, as the performance of all online algorithms depends on the quality of the initial decomposition.

In terms of method-specific parameters, for the two batch algorithms, the default settings, $\varepsilon = 1e-4$ and $maxiters = 50$ are used. For GridTF, which contains an ALS procedure for the *new* data slice and a recursively update procedure for estimating the *whole* current tensor, the same default parameters are chosen for the ALS step; while $\varepsilon = 1e-2$ and $maxiters = 50$ are used for the update phase. Additionally, since batch algorithms do not provide a weighting strategy to differentiate the importance of data, in order to make a fair comparison, all the data slices are equally treated and there is no difference between older and newer ones in terms of their weights, which means the exponential window is used with $\lambda = 1$ in SDT and RLST.

5.1.2 Results

Given a particular dataset and a specific algorithm, its fitness and processing time are two time series (averaged over 10 runs). We take the mean values of them and report the results for third-order tensors in Table 3 and the higher-order tensors in Table 4. In addition, for the four online approaches, SDT, RLST, GridTF and OnlineCP, their relative performances compared to Batch Hot are also shown in the parenthesis. Finally, the best results among these four are indicated by boldface.

As can be seen from Table 3, for the two batch methods, there is no significant difference on their effectiveness. However, on all third-order datasets, the fitness of Batch Cold is slightly worse than that of Batch Hot. The main reason is that using the previous results as initialization can provide the ALS algorithm with a descent seeding point. In contrast, every time Batch Cold totally discards this useful information and starts to optimize from the beginning, which cannot guarantee a better or even same-quality estimation in the end. In fact, this also results in the longer running time of Batch Cold compared with Batch Hot, where the former is usually more than 10 times slower than the latter. On the other hand, even though Batch Hot improves the efficiency, its time cost is still considerably high, especially for large-scale datasets. For example, on average it takes more than 20 seconds to process one additional data slice on the ROAD dataset, while OnlineCP takes only 0.0068 seconds.

As the earliest studies of online CP decomposition, both SDT and RLST address this efficiency issue very well. Compared with Batch Hot, they shorten the mean running time by up to 400 times. RLST, in particular, was the most efficient online algorithm on 4 out of 7 third-order tensor datasets. In fact, the efficiency of SDT is quite close to RLST, except for the GAS dataset, whose length of time mode is significantly higher than other datasets. This shows that SDT is more sensitive to the growth of time. However, the main issue of SDT and RLST is their estimation accuracy. For some datasets, such as COIL and HAD, they work fine, while for some others like DSA, they exhibit fairly poor accuracy, achieving only nearly half of the fitness of batch methods. The same accuracy problem can be observed in GridTF as well. In terms of efficiency, there is no significant difference between GridTF and Batch Hot, at least on the small size datasets. In fact, we notice that a substantial amount of time of GridTF is consumed by decomposing the new data slice and this cost is particularly dominant when the tensor size is not large enough. This can be confirmed by observing its generally better efficiency on higher-order datasets, compared to the third-order ones.

Table 3: Experimental results of third-order datasets

(a) Mean fitness of third-order datasets over time (in %, the higher the values the better). For SDT, RLST, GridTF and OnlineCP, ratios of their fitness to the result of Batch Hot are shown in parenthesis. Boldface indicates the best result among these four online approaches.

Datasets	Batch Cold	Batch Hot	SDT	RLST	GridTF	OnlineCP
COIL-3D	58.31	58.76	51.31(0.87)	56.27(0.96)	54.13(0.92)	**57.43(0.98)**
DSA-3D	57.50	57.88	26.30(0.45)	27.44(0.47)	48.85(0.84)	**57.51(0.99)**
FACE-3D	75.35	75.69	70.64(0.93)	46.84(0.62)	71.91(0.95)	**75.31(0.99)**
FOG-3D	48.38	48.95	40.90(0.84)	41.28(0.84)	25.94(0.53)	**44.39(0.91)**
GAS-3D	86.56	87.06	43.93(0.50)	57.92(0.67)	48.64(0.56)	**84.94(0.98)**
HAD-3D	28.97	29.34	26.14(0.89)	28.33(0.97)	27.56(0.94)	**28.54(0.97)**
ROAD*	79.25	79.94	15.45(0.21)	61.23(0.77)	N/A	**79.72(1.00)**

(b) Mean running time of third-order datasets for processing one data slice (in seconds). For SDT, RLST, GridTF and OnlineCP, the ratios between the running time of Batch Hot and theirs are shown in parenthesis. Boldface indicates the best result among these four online approaches.

Datasets	Batch Cold	Batch Hot	SDT	RLST	GridTF	OnlineCP
COIL-3D	3.0255	0.1944	0.0037(52.06)	0.0041(47.79)	0.0446(4.36)	**0.0017(115.36)**
DSA-3D	0.3627	0.0246	0.0005(52.41)	**0.0003(72.45)**	0.0332(0.74)	0.0004(57.28)
FACE-3D	1.2616	0.1430	0.0034(42.06)	0.0037(38.47)	0.0439(3.26)	**0.0019(73.87)**
FOG-3D	0.2805	0.0198	0.0005(39.43)	**0.0003(72.01)**	0.0285(0.70)	0.0004(53.33)
GAS-3D	0.4095	0.0314	0.0015(20.82)	**0.0003(91.53)**	0.0265(1.18)	0.0005(64.91)
HAD-3D	0.1867	0.0154	0.0004(41.44)	**0.0003(60.94)**	0.0158(0.98)	0.0004(43.76)
ROAD*	309.5064	23.6683	0.0582(406.67)	0.0573(413.0593)	N/A	**0.0068(3480.63)**

* The result is based on only 1 run, due to the huge time consumption of batch methods. Figures of Batch Cold are estimated based on its average performance on other datasets, compared to Batch Hot. GridTF failed on this dataset because of the singular matrix problem, resulting from the large chunks of missing data in some sensors.

Table 4: Experimental results of higher-order datasets.

(a) Mean fitness of higher-order datasets over time (in %, the higher the values the better). For GridTF and OnlineCP, ratios of their fitness to the result of Batch Hot are also shown in parenthesis. Boldface indicates the best result between these two online approaches.

Datasets	Batch Hot	GridTF	OnlineCP
COIL-HD	57.43	42.69(0.74)	**56.83(0.99)**
DSA-HD	62.76	61.33(0.98)	**62.54(1.00)**
FACE-HD	74.78	67.47(0.90)	**74.45(1.00)**
GAS-HD	79.38	61.05(0.77)	**75.71(0.95)**
HAD-HD	67.36	65.57(0.97)	**67.28(1.00)**

(b) Mean running time of higher-order datasets for processing one data slice (in seconds). For GridTF and OnlineCP, the ratios between the running time of Batch Hot and theirs are shown in parenthesis. Boldface indicates the best result between these two online approaches.

Datasets	Batch Hot	GridTF	OnlineCP
COIL-HD	2.1264	0.1935(10.99)	**0.0076(280.44)**
DSA-HD	0.2217	0.0896(2.48)	**0.0029(75.43)**
FACE-HD	0.3795	0.1438(2.64)	**0.0040(94.15)**
GAS-HD	0.3154	0.1807(1.75)	**0.0016(203.47)**
HAD-HD	0.1750	0.0922(1.90)	**0.0041(42.23)**

Our proposed algorithm, OnlineCP, shows very promising results in both accuracy and speed. On every dataset, both third-order and higher-order ones, our method reaches the best fitness among all online algorithms. More importantly, the estimation performance of our approach is quite stable and very comparable to the results of batch techniques. In most of the cases, the fitness of OnlineCP is less than 3% lower than that of the most accurate algorithm, Batch Hot. However, the speed of OnlineCP is orders of magnitudes faster than Batch Hot. On small and moderate size datasets, OnlineCP can be tens to hundreds of times faster than Batch Hot; and on the largest dataset, ROAD, OnlineCP improves the efficiency of Batch Hot by more than 3,000 times. Additionally, compared with another fast approach, RLST, although OnlineCP is outperformed on four datasets, its speed on these datasets is quite close to the best. On the other hand, we notice that all these datasets have fairly small slice size. In contrast, on those datasets with larger slices, such as COIL and FACE, the time consumption of our method clearly grows slower than that of RLST, showing that OnlineCP is less sensitive to the size of the data, and thus, having better scalability.

5.2 Sensitivity to Initialization

Throughout our experiments, an interesting observation was made: for all adaptive algorithms that make use of the previous step results, namely Batch Hot, SDT, RLST, GridTF, and OnlineCP, their best results are usually linked to a good initial fitness, while poor-quality initializations often lead them to subsequent under-fitting. To explore the impact of initialization to each algorithm, the following ex-

Table 5: The final fitness averaged over 200 runs with different initial fitness. Results are displayed as *mean* ± *std*, where *mean* is the average final fitness and *std* is the standard deviation, both in % (the higher the values the better).

	Final Fitness
Batch Hot	82.57±10.1474
SDT	7.68±55.5205
RLST	33.15±36.9270
GridTF	57.43±15.2148
OnlineCP	67.67±12.9846

periment has been conducted. We generate a synthetic tensor $\mathcal{X} \in \mathbb{R}^{20\times 20\times 100}$ by constructing from random loading matrices and then downgrade it by a Gaussian noise with a Signal-to-Interference Rate (SIR) of 20 dB. The best fitness to $\mathcal{X}$ in 10 runs of ALS is 90.14%. This tensor is then repeatedly decomposed by the above five methods for 200 times. At the beginning of each run, half of the data is used for initialization by ALS with a random tolerance from $9e-1$ to $1e-4$, to produce different level of initial fitness. Then the rest of data is sequentially added and processed by each online algorithm. The averaged final fitness over all runs is used as the effectiveness indicator, as well as the standard deviation. Table 5 shows the experimental results with average initial fitness as 65.78% and standard deviation as 15.3704%.

As shown in Table 5, overall, the low quality initialization has a negative impact on all algorithms. Even the most powerful one, Batch Hot, cannot always reach the best fitness and shows a decline of 10%. For SDT and RLST, it turns out that both algorithms are significantly dependent on the initial fitness. When the initial fitness is lower than the best value, their performance can quickly drop to an unacceptable level. In addition, their results are also highly unstable, as demonstrated by a large variance. While both GridTF and OnlineCP exhibit much more stable performance, the final fitness of GridTF is considerably lower than our approach OnlineCP. This experimental evidence demonstrates that the proposed algorithm, OnlineCP, is less sensitive to the quality of the initialization, compared with exiting online methods. However, it can be seen that good initialization still plays an important role to our algorithm. Thus, for applying our method, we suggest to validate the goodness of the initialization at the beginning, in order to obtain the best subsequent effectiveness.

5.3 Scalability Evaluation

According to Section 4.3, the time complexity of each algorithm is mainly determined by the slice size and the length of processed data. To confirm our analysis and evaluate the scalability of our algorithm, firstly, a tensor $\mathcal{X} \in \mathbb{R}^{20\times 20\times 10^5}$ of small slice size but long time dimension is decomposed. After initializing with data of the first 100 timestamps, each method's running time for processing one data slice at each time step is measured and displayed in Figure 2. In addition, to examine the impact of slice size to efficiency, we fix the time mode to 100, and generate a group of tensors of different slice sizes, ranging from 100 to 9×10^6. For each tensor, its first 20% of data is used for initialization and the average running time for processing the rest data slices is shown in Figure 3. For better comparison, both Batch Hot and GridTF are forced to execute 1 iteration only in these two experiments. Note that the y-axis of Figures 2a and 3a is displayed in log scale and in Figure 2b, Batch Hot has been removed for better visibility.

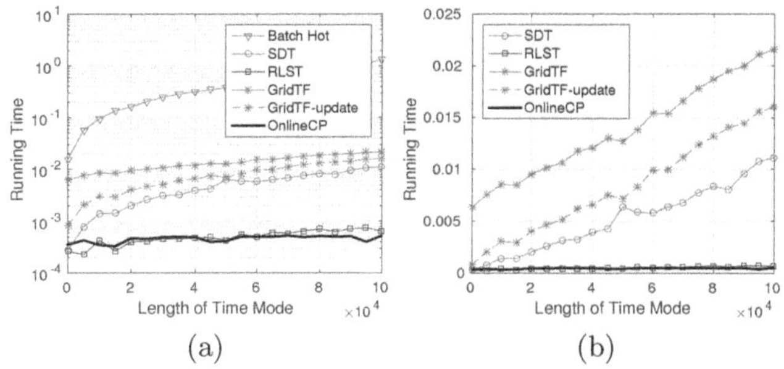

Figure 2: Running time (in seconds) for adding one slice to a $20\times 20\times (t-1)$ tensor at time t. Two figure represents the same information, differing only in the y-axis scale.

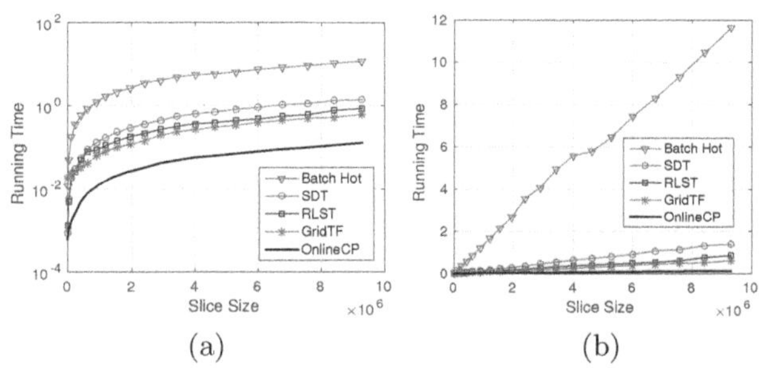

Figure 3: Running time (in seconds) for processing different size of tensors. Two figure represents the same information, differing only in the y-axis scale.

As can be seen from Figure 2, both RLST and OnlineCP show constant complexities and the increasing length of processed data has no impact on them. For the other approaches, a clear linear growth with time can be observed in Batch Hot and SDT, which makes them less feasible for online learning purposes. The change of time consumption in GridTF is less obvious compared with Batch Hot and SDT. However, after removing the time used by its inner ALS procedure, similar linear trend can be seen, marked as GridTF-update in the figure.

In terms of slice size, it turns out that the time consumption of all approaches are linearly increasing as the slice size grows. However, their slopes vary. Both Batch Hot and SDT show quicker growth compared to others. This is reasonable since the impact of slice size to them is also leveraged by the time mode. On the other hand, GridTF outperforms SDT and RLST when the slice gets larger. This is because the growth of slice size has impact only on its ALS procedure, which is scaled by R times, while the coefficients in the complexities of SDT and RLST w.r.t. slice size contain an R^2 term. Once again, our proposed algorithm illustrates the best performance in this experiment and even a large 3000×3000 data slice can be efficiently processed in 0.1 second.

6. CONCLUSIONS AND FUTURE WORK

To conclude, in this paper, we address the problem of tracking the CP decomposition of online tensors. An online algorithm, OnlineCP, is proposed, which can efficiently track the new decomposition by using complementary matrices to temporally store the useful information of the previous time step. Furthermore, our method is not only applicable to third-order tensors, but also suitable for higher-order tensors that have more than 3 modes. As evaluated on both real world and synthetic datasets, our algorithm demonstrates comparable effectiveness with the most accurate batch techniques, while significantly outperforms them in terms of efficiency. Additionally, compared with the state-of-art online techniques, the proposed algorithm shows advantages in many aspects, including effectiveness, efficiency, stability and scalability.

There is still room for improving our method. One direction is to further extend it for more general dynamic tensors that may be changed on any modes [11]. Another potential direction is to incorporate constraints, such as non-negativity [13], so that our method can be more suitable for applications such as computer vision.

Acknowledgments

This work is supported by the Australian Research Council via grant number DP140101969.

7. REFERENCES

[1] E. Acar, et al. Scalable tensor factorizations for incomplete data. *Chemometrics and Intelligent Laboratory Systems*, 106(1):41–56, March 2011.

[2] K. Altun, et al. Comparative study on classifying human activities with miniature inertial and magnetic sensors. *Pattern Recognition*, 43(10):3605–3620, 2010.

[3] M. Bächlin, et al. Wearable assistant for parkinson's disease patients with the freezing of gait symptom. *IEEE Trans. Inf. Tech. Biomed.*, 14(2):436–446, 2010.

[4] B. W. Bader, T. G. Kolda, et al. Matlab tensor toolbox version 2.6. Available online, February 2015.

[5] Y. Cai, et al. Facets: Fast comprehensive mining of coevolving high-order time series. In *SIGKDD*, 2015.

[6] A. Cichocki. Era of big data processing: a new approach via tensor networks and tensor decompositions. *arXiv preprint arXiv:1403.2048*, 2014.

[7] A. Cichocki, et al. Tensor decompositions for signal processing applications: From two-way to multiway component analysis. *Signal Processing Magazine, IEEE*, 32(2):145–163, 2015.

[8] P. Comon, X. Luciani, and A. L. De Almeida. Tensor decompositions, alternating least squares and other tales. *J. Chemometrics*, 23(7-8):393–405, 2009.

[9] L. De Lathauwer, et al. On the best rank-1 and rank-(r 1, r 2,..., rn) approximation of higher-order tensors. *SJMAEL*, 21(4):1324–1342, 2000.

[10] D. M. Dunlavy, T. G. Kolda, and E. Acar. Temporal link prediction using matrix and tensor factorizations. *TKDD*, 5(2):10, 2011.

[11] H. Fanaee-T and J. Gama. Multi-aspect-streaming tensor analysis. *Knowledge-Based Systems*, 89:332–345, 2015.

[12] J. Fonollosa, et al. Reservoir computing compensates slow response of chemosensor arrays exposed to fast varying gas concentrations in continuous monitoring. *Sens. Actuator B-Chem.*, 215:618–629, 2015.

[13] C. Hu, et al. Scalable bayesian non-negative tensor factorization for massive count data. In *ECML-PKDD*, 2015.

[14] W. Hu, et al. Incremental tensor subspace learning and its applications to foreground segmentation and tracking. *IJCV*, 91(3):303–327, 2011.

[15] T. G. Kolda. Multilinear operators for higher-order decompositions. Tech. Report SAND2006-2081, Sandia National Laboratories, April 2006.

[16] T. G. Kolda and B. W. Bader. Tensor decompositions and applications. *SIAM review*, 51(3):455–500, 2009.

[17] W. Liu, et al. Utilizing common substructures to speedup tensor factorization for mining dynamic graphs. In *CIKM*, 2012.

[18] X. Ma, et al. Dynamic updating and downdating matrix svd and tensor hosvd for adaptive indexing and retrieval of motion trajectories. In *ICASSP*, 2009.

[19] S. A. Nene, et al. Columbia Object Image Library (COIL-20). Tech. report, Feb 1996.

[20] D. Nion, et al. Adaptive algorithms to track the parafac decomposition of a third-order tensor. *IEEE Trans. Sig. Process.*, 57(6):2299–2310, 2009.

[21] S. Papadimitriou, et al. Streaming pattern discovery in multiple time-series. In *VLDB*, 2005.

[22] A. H. Phan, et al. Parafac algorithms for large-scale problems. *Neurocomputing*, 74(11):1970–1984, 2011.

[23] F. S. Samaria, et al. Parameterisation of a stochastic model for human face identification. In *WACV*, 1994.

[24] F. Schimbinschi, et al. Traffic forecasting in complex urban networks: Leveraging big data and machine learning. In *Big Data*, 2015.

[25] L. Shi, et al. Stensr: Spatio-temporal tensor streams for anomaly detection and pattern discovery. *KAIS*, 43(2):333–353, 2015.

[26] A. Sobral, et al. Incremental and multi-feature tensor subspace learning applied for background modeling and subtraction. In *ICIAR*, 2014.

[27] J. Sun, D. Tao, and C. Faloutsos. Beyond streams and graphs: dynamic tensor analysis. In *SIGKDD*, 2006.

[28] J. Sun, et al. Incremental tensor analysis: Theory and applications. *TKDD*, 2(3):11, 2008.

[29] M. A. O. Vasilescu, et al. Multilinear analysis of image ensembles: Tensorfaces. In *ECCV*, 2002.

[30] M. Zhang and A. A. Sawchuk. Usc-had: A daily activity dataset for ubiquitous activity recognition using wearable sensors. In *Ubicomp-SAGAware*, 2012.

Author Index

www.ingramcontent.com/pod-product-compliance
Ingram Content Group UK Ltd.
Pitfield, Milton Keynes, MK11 3LW, UK
UKHW051420290926
15471UKWH00009B/1698

9 781450 346238